sydney 200

19th edition

COMPACT STREET DIRECTORY

CAFÉS

RESTAURANTS

SHOPS

HOTELS

TRANSPORT

ACCOMMODATION

www.gregorys-online.com

Proudly Australian
Family Owned Company

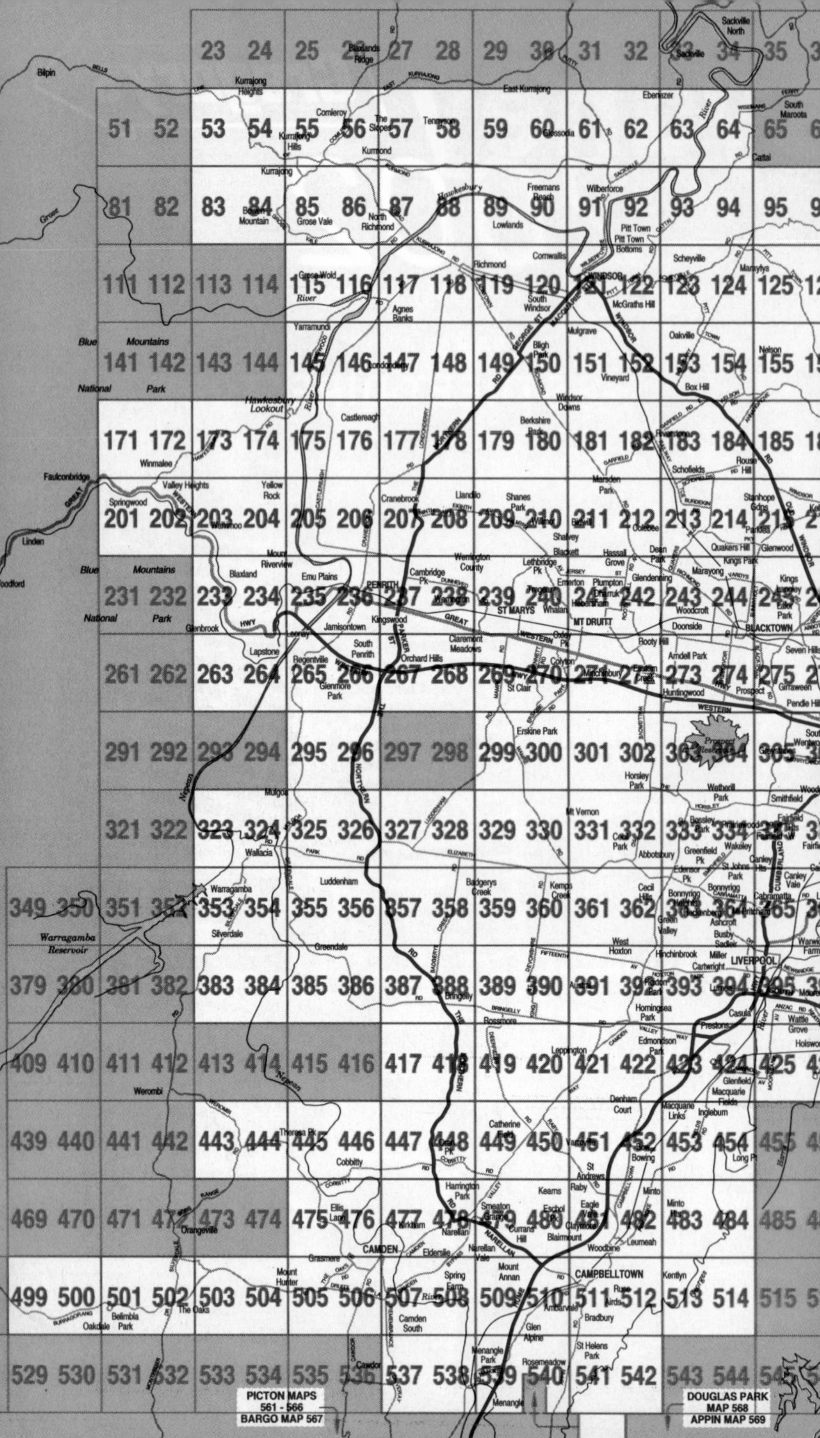

23 24 25 27 28 29 31 32 34 35
Blaxlands Ridge
Sackville North
Sackville
Bilpin
Kurrajong Heights
East Kurrajong
Ebenezer
South Maroota
51 52 53 54 55 56 57 58 59 60 61 62 63 64 65
Comleroy
The Slopes
Tennyson
Glossodia
Kurrajong Hills
Kurmond
Cattai
Kurrajong
81 82 83 84 85 86 87 88 89 90 91 92 93 94 95
Hawkesbury
Freemans Reach
Wilberforce
Bowen Mountain
Grose Vale
North Richmond
Lowlands
Pitt Town
Pitt Town Bottoms
Grose
Cornwallis
Scheyville
Maraylya
Richmond
111 112 113 114 115 116 117 118 119 120 122 124 125
Grose Wold
River
WINDSOR
McGraths Hill
Agnes Banks
South Windsor
Yarramundi
Mulgrave
Oakville
Nelson
Blue Mountains National Park
141 142 143 144 146 147 148 150 151 153 154 155
Bligh Park
Vineyard
Box Hill
Hawkesbury Lookout
Windsor Downs
Castlereagh
Berkshire Park
171 172 174 175 176 177 179 180 181 183 184 185
Riverstone
Rouse Hill
Winmalee
Schofields
Faulconbridge
Valley Heights
Yellow Rock
Marsden Park
Springwood
Cranebrook
Llandilo
Shanes Park
Stanhope Gdns
201 202 204 205 207 208 210 211 212 213 214
Linden
Willmot
Bidwill
Colebee
Parklea
Glenwood
Shalvey
Blackett
Hassall Grove
Dean Park
Quakers Hill
Kings Park
Mount Riverview
Werrington County
Lethbridge Pk
Woodford
Blaxland
Emu Plains
Cambridge Pk
Emerton
Plumpton
Glendenning
Marayong
Blue Mountains National Park
231 232 234 235 236 238 239 240 242 243 244
PENRITH
Werrington
Tregear
Hebersham
Whalan
ST MARYS
MT DRUITT
Woodcroft
Kingswood
Jamisontown
Doonside
BLACKTOWN
Glenbrook
Lapstone
South Penrith
Claremont Meadows
Oxley Pk
Booty Hill
Arndell Park
Seven Hills
Regentville
Orchard Hills
Colyton
Minchinbury
261 262 263 264 265 267 268 270 273 275
Glenmore Park
St Clair
Huntingwood
Prospect
Girraween
Pendle Hill
Erskine Park
291 292 294 295 297 298 300 301 302
Horsley Park
Wetherill Park
Smithfield
Mulgoa
321 322 323 324 325 326 327 328 329 330 331 332
Mt Vernon
Cecil Park
Abbotsbury
Greenfield Pk
Wakeley
Canley Hts
Wallacia
Luddenham
Badgerys Creek
Kemps Creek
Cecil Hills
Edensor Pk
St Johns Park
Canley Vale
Warragamba
Bonnyrigg
Cabramatta
349 351 353 354 355 356 358 359 360 361 362
Silverdale
Green Valley
Busby
Warragamba Reservoir
Greendale
West Hoxton
Hinchinbrook
Miller
Cartwright
LIVERPOOL
379 381 382 383 384 385 386 387 389 390
Bringelly
Hoxton Park
Horningsea Park
Casula
Rossmore
Prestons
Edmondson Park
Wattle Grove
409 410 411 413 415 416 417 419 420 421 422
Leppington
Glenfield
Macquarie Fields
Werombi
Denham Court
Macquarie Links
Ingleburn
439 440 441 443 444 446 447 450 453 454
Catherine Field
Theresa Pk
Cobbitty
Varroville
Long Pt
St Andrews
Harrington Park
Kearns
Raby
Minto
Bow Bowing
469 470 471 473 474 475 477 483
Orangeville
Ellis Lane
Kirkham
Smeaton Grange
Currans Hill
Eschol Pk
Eagle Vale
Claymore
Blairmount
Leumeah
Narellan
Elderslie
Narellan Vale
Woodbine
CAMDEN
Grasmere
Mount Hunter
Spring Farm
Mount Annan
CAMPBELLTOWN
Kentlyn
499 500 501 503 504 505 506 507 509 511 513 514 515
The Oaks
Ambarvale
Airds
Ruse
Oakdale
Belimbia Park
Camden South
Bradbury
Glen Alpine
Menangle Park
Rosemeadow
St Helens Park
529 530 531 533 534 535 537 538 540 542 543 544
Cawdor
Menangle
PICTON MAPS 561 - 566
BARGO MAP 567
DOUGLAS PARK MAP 568
APPIN MAP 569

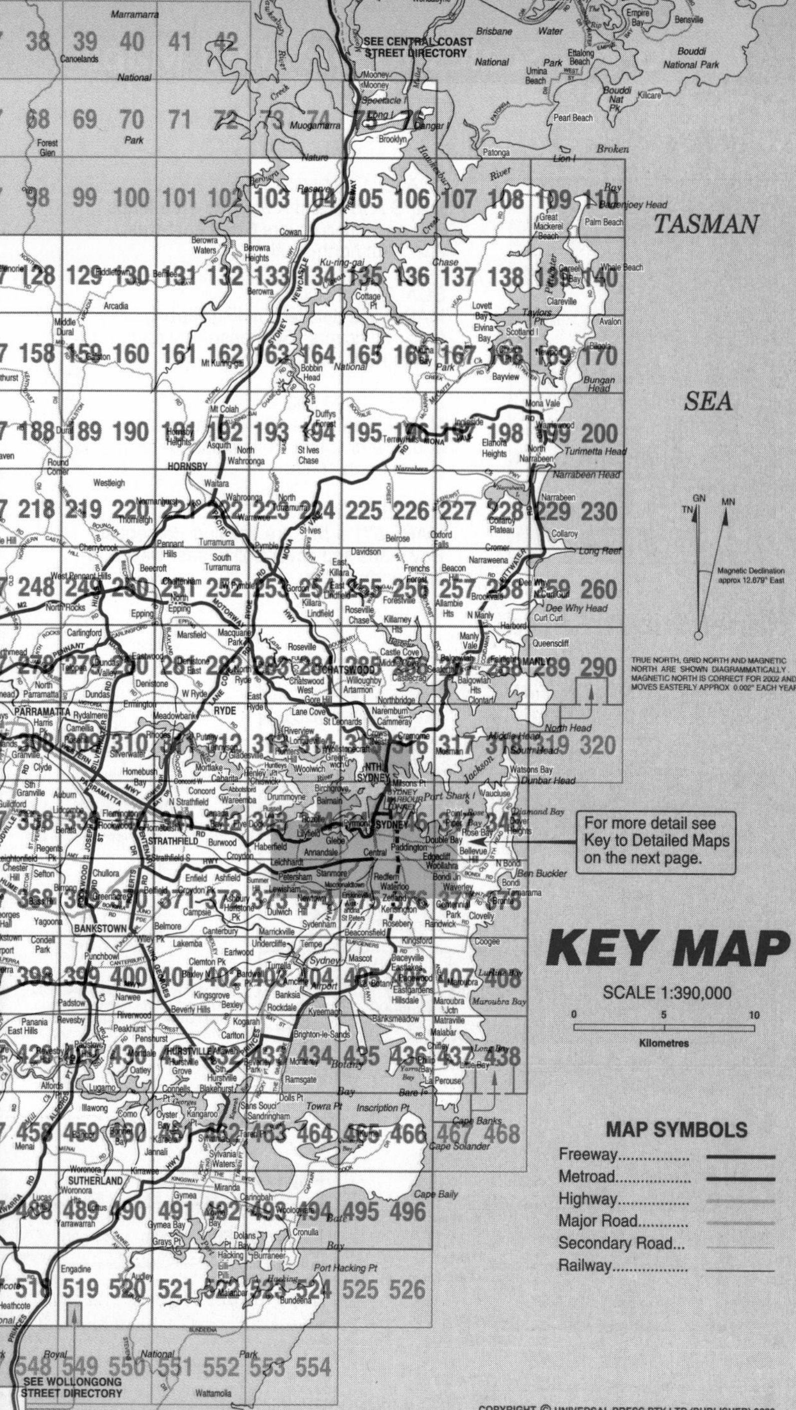
SEE CENTRAL COAST STREET DIRECTORY
TASMAN
SEA
GN
TN
MN
Magnetic Declination approx 12.679° East
TRUE NORTH, GRID NORTH AND MAGNETIC NORTH ARE SHOWN DIAGRAMMATICALLY. MAGNETIC NORTH IS CORRECT FOR 2002 AND MOVES EASTERLY APPROX 0.002° EACH YEAR.
For more detail see Key to Detailed Maps on the next page.
KEY MAP
SCALE 1:390,000
0
5
10
Kilometres
MAP SYMBOLS
Freeway................
Metroad.................
Highway..................
Major Road...........
Secondary Road...
Railway..................
SEE WOLLONGONG STREET DIRECTORY
COPYRIGHT © UNIVERSAL PRESS PTY LTD (PUBLISHER) 2002

Key & Scales to Detailed Maps

City Area

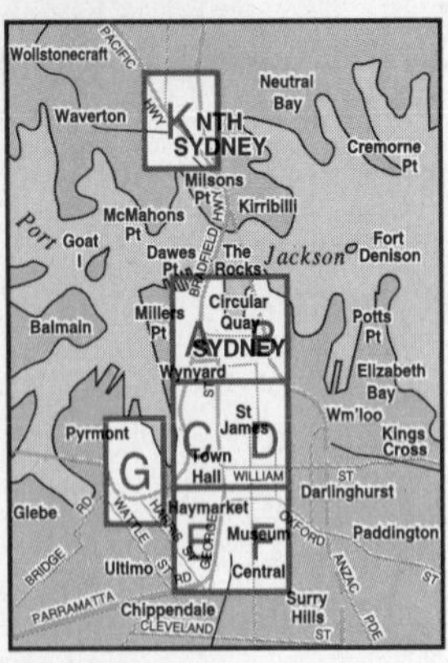

SCALE 1 : 6 250
MAPS A to G and K are City Area Maps and each map covers 625m east-west and 1 km north-south.

SCALE 1 : 7 500
MAP H is a detailed Darling Harbour map and covers 750m east-west and 1.2km north-south.

SCALE 1 : 20 800
MAP J is a detailed Parking map and covers 1.4km east-west and 3.4km north-south.

SCALE 1 : 20 250
MAPS 571 & 572 are detailed Homebush Bay maps and cover 3.2km east-west and 4km north-south.

Inner Suburb Area

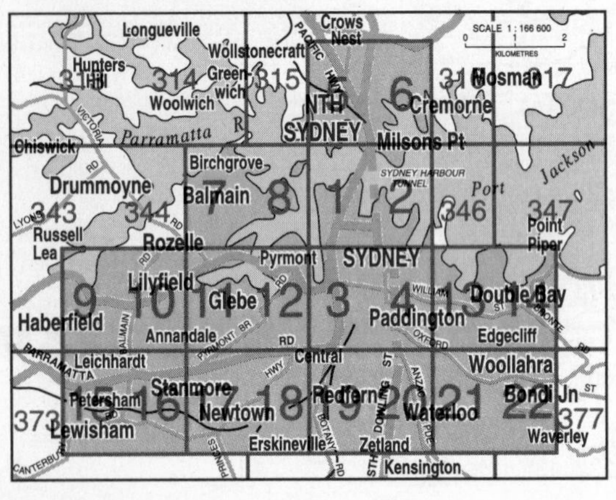

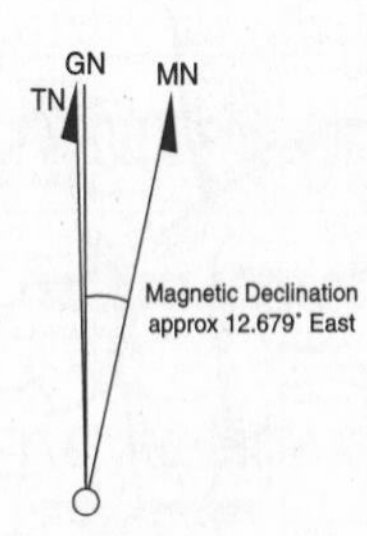

TRUE NORTH, GRID NORTH AND MAGNETIC NORTH ARE SHOWN DIAGRAMMATICALLY. MAGNETIC NORTH IS CORRECT FOR 2002 AND MOVES EASTERLY APPROX 0.002° EACH YEAR.

Map Scales

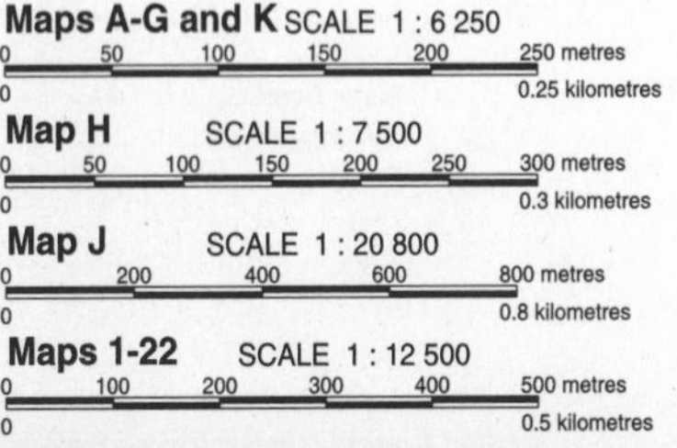

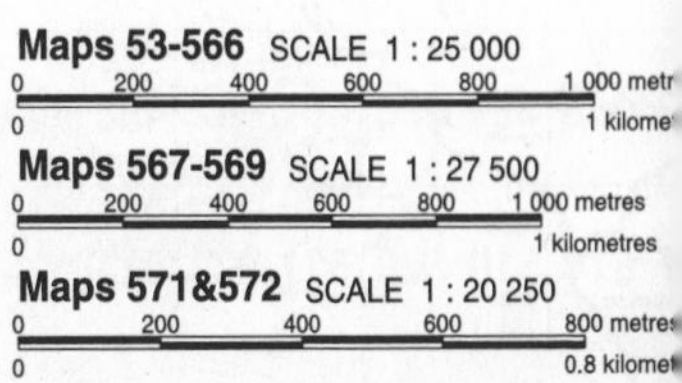

Explanation of Map Symbols

Symbol	Example
Freeway or Motorway	WARRINGAH FREEWAY
Highway or Main Traffic Route	PRINCES HIGHWAY
Trafficable Road	JONES AV
Un-trafficable / Proposed Road	THOMAS ST
Traffic Light, Level Crossing & Roundabout	
Road and Railway Bridges	
One-way Traffic Route	
National and State Route Numbers	1 33
Metroad and Tourist Route Numbers	5 14
Proposed Freeway	Proposed Freeway
Direction of Sydney City Centre	CITY
Distance by Road from GPO	22
Railway Line, Station (distance from Central)	Dulwich Hill 8
Suburb Name	EASTWOOD
Locality Name	Audley
Walking Tracks, Horse Tracks and Cycleways	
Park, Reserve or Golf Course	
School or Hospital	
Caravan Park, Cemetery, Shopping Centre,etc	
Mall, Plaza	

Symbol	Example	Symbol	Example
Car Park	P	Place of Worship	
Council Office	Cncl Off	Point of Interest	Museum
Fire Station	F	Police Station	★
Hospital	✚	Post Office	
Library		Rural Fire Service	RFS
Picnic Area		Shopping Centre	

STREET MAPS overlap on each page to help in re-locating position on an adjoining page.
ADJOINING MAP NUMBERS are shown in the borders and corners of the street maps.
REFERENCE NUMBERS AND LETTERS within the borders of the street maps are the reference co-ordinates given in the indexes.

Cityside Guide

Sydney is Australia's most vibrant city. The **Cityside Guide** covers Sydney's CBD and inner city areas and includes **sightseeing** and **shopping** suggestions; **restaurant** and café recommendations; listings of Sydney's best **entertainment** venues including theatres, pubs, bars, nightclubs, cinemas, galleries, and museums; a guide to **youth hostels** and backpacker accommodation in and around the city, as well as comprehensive **public transport** info.

around the harbour

Sydney Harbour and its surroundings makes the City of Sydney spectacular. Sydneysiders are fortunate to have this stunning all-year-round playground at their disposal. Here you can sail from Rushcutters Bay, windsurf at Balmoral Beach, swim in harbourside pools and beaches, picnic at waterfront parks or sightsee from a ferry. Circular Quay, Sydney's ferry terminal, is the departure point for scenic cruises and ferry rides around picturesque Sydney Harbour and between harbourside suburbs.

• **Circular Quay (Map B, Ref D6)**, at the northern edge of the **Central Business District (CBD)**, is a bustling interchange connecting rail and ferry services. This busy waterfront, surrounded by some of Sydney's most famous landmarks, is the perfect place to sit back and admire the views at one of many restaurants or as a starting point from which to begin exploring the city.

• **Sydney Opera House (Map B, Ref J1)** (9250 7111), at **Bennelong Point** is both an architectural marvel and a performing arts mecca. This unique white sail-like structure, set strikingly against the blue waters of Sydney Harbour, houses numerous restaurants and cafes, as well as frequent and diverse performance, ranging from the classical to the innovative, in its concert hall, theatres, and forecourt. The walkways provide some of the best views of Sydney Harbour.

• **Sydney Harbour Bridge (Map 1, Ref J5)** is one of Sydney's most well know landmarks, and the view from the top is truly breathtaking (to climb call **Bridge Climb** on 9252 0077). For the not so adventurous, the southeast **Pylon Lookout** (9247 3408) contains an exhibition illustrating the construction of the bridge, which was completed in 1932.

• **The Rocks (Map B, Ref A3)** is our link to Sydney's colonial heritage, and has some of the best shopping Sydney has to offer. The Rocks Markets, held every weekend is a must for those looking for something special. **Cadman's Cottage** (110 George Street, 9247 8861) is the oldest surviving building in the city, and **Campbell's Storehouses** (27 Circular Quay W), a former bond store completed in 1890, now houses galleries and waterfront restaurants. It's also a great place to relax, having some of the best pubs in the city, with friendly atmospheres and heritage charm. The cosy **Lord Nelson Brewery Hotel**,(Cnr Kent and Argyle Street. 9251 4044), was built in 1842 and serves beer that has been brewed-on-the-premises. After dark, The Rocks maintains its attraction, offering nightly sky viewings at the astronomy museum, **Sydney Observatory** (Watson Road, Observatory Hill, 9217 0485).

• **Fort Denison (Map 2, Ref K6)** (9247 5033) was constructed to defend Sydney during the 1850's on **Pinchgut Island**, so named because of the limited rations given to convicts once incarcerated on the island. Book a tour to explore the island's barracks, tower and gun battery or plan a picnic to watch holiday fireworks displays from one of the best vantage points in the harbour.

• **Taronga Zoological Park (Map 316, Ref K14)** (Bradley's Head Rd, Mosman, 9969 2777), with its magnificent harbour views, is a conservation leader. Once voted the world's best zoo, it utilises moats where possible, rather than bars and fences, to ensure its enclosures resemble the animals' natural habitat. Highlights include the nocturnal exhibit, native Australian animals and the Walk-through Rainforest.

• **Manly (Map 288, Ref H9)** (Manly Visitor Information Centre, Ocean Beach, North Steyne, (9977 1088) is a fantastic place to get a taste of Sydney's beach culture. Framed by the harbour on one side and the ocean on the other, it has a permanent holiday feel. One of Manly's main attractions is **Oceanworld** (West Esplanade 9949 2644), an aquarium exhibiting, sharks and the colourful coral and marine life of the Great Barrier Reef, as well as live shows. Enjoy free entertainment, shops and cafes at **Manly Wharf**, stroll from harbour to beach along downtown Manly's **Corso** or wander through the pretty backstreets to the surf beach and promenade. Explore **Fairy Bower** and secluded **Shelly Beach**, or visit the historic **Quarantine Station** (9977 5145) at North Head.

• **Watsons Bay (Map 318, Ref E13)** offers panoramic harbour and city views from **Wharf Beach**, and is a perfect place for a picnic or dine on fresh seafood at one of the high calibre restaurants spilling out onto the foreshore. Watch the activity on the harbour from this relaxed vantage point, or go for a swim at nearby **Camp Cove**. Explore **South Head**, the harbour's southern entrance, and climb **The Gap's** dramatic cliffs with views of the crashing waves below.

• **Darling Harbour (Map H)** (9286 0111) can be reached by foot, **monorail** (9552 2288) or **light rail** (8584 5288). It is the home to the **Sydney Aquarium** (9262 2300), which contains walk-through Perspex tunnels where sea life swim around you, providing a view from above, beside and below these amazing creatures. Wander across **Pyrmont Bridge**, the world's oldest electrically-operated swingspan bridge, to the shops and eateries at the **Harbourside Festival Marketplace**. Visit the adjacent **National Maritime Museum** for an exploration into Australia's sea faring past. For time out from the fast paced city environment, take a relaxing stroll amid the waterfalls, bridges and Cantonese pavilions of the tranquil **Chinese Gardens**, before catching a film on the 3D screen at the **IMAX Theatre** (9281 3300). **Chinatown**, the **Powerhouse Museum**, the **Sydney Fish Markets** and the **Star City Casino** are also close by, making it a great place to explore.

• **Milsons Point (Map 1, Ref K1)** is a great walking destination, as well as a place to meet people or unwind. Alight at the historic fun fair at **Milson's Point Wharf**, and walk across **Bradfield Park** to admire the massive **Sydney Harbour Bridge** above you. Enjoy the views at the **North Sydney Olympic Pool** (Alfred St, Milson's Point 9955 2309), then wander along Blues Point Road before venturing to nearby **McMahon's Point** for a return ferry to Circular Quay. This area is spectacular at night, with possibly the best views of the city lights.

• **Cockle Bay Wharf (Map H)** (9269 9800) at **Darling Park**, on the city side of **Darling Harbour**, is a newly redeveloped harbour side venue and is the best place to experience Sydney's nightlife. It is a lively collection of a eateries and bars. It houses one of Sydney's best nightclubs, and a Museum of Contemporary Art store. Restaurants such as **Chinta Ria...The Temple of Love** are exciting places to eat, **Home** nightclub boasts one of the most incredible nightclub experiences in Sydney, carrying this feel through to the **Home Bar**. The **Pontoon Bar** at the other end of Cockle Bay Wharf is extremely popular with a diverse crowd and beautiful surroundings.

city sights

Sydney city boasts a wide variety of attractions to interest both locals and tourists alike. From the charming sandstone architecture of The Rocks, to the majestic grandeur of the Queen Victoria Building; from the city's lively shopping malls to the peaceful Royal Botanic Gardens; from bustling Martin Place to elegant Macquarie Street, there are numerous sights worth seeing. The NSW Visitor Info Line (132 077) and Sydney Visitors Centre (Martin Place, 9235 2424) can also suggest places of interest.

• **AMP Tower (Map D, Ref A7)** (Centrepoint, 100 Market St, 9229 7430) is the tallest public building in the southern hemisphere. Its 360-degree views provide the best vantage point to familiarise yourself with Sydney and its surrounds. An observation level, coffee shop and two revolving restaurants offer magnificent views of the CBD, Blue Mountains to the west, Botany Bay to the south, Pittwater to the north and from across the harbour out to sea.

• **Hyde Park (Map D, Ref E10)**, on the eastern border of the CBD, is a popular lunch time venue for city workers to take a break and a picnic destination, allowing you to bask in the sun on the grass by the **Archibold Fountain** or sunken **Sandringham Garden**, or watch the chess players test their skills. Stroll along the tree-covered walkways (at night lit by millions of star-like fairy lights) to the pretty poplar lined **Pool of Remembrance** to admire the art deco **Anzac Memorial**, where a photographic and military exhibition can be viewed honouring those Australians killed in battle.

• **St Mary's Cathedral (Map D, Ref H9)** (Cathedral & College Sts, 9220 0400), an awesome Gothic Revival-style cathedral, was opened in 1882 and the twin southern spires originally proposed by the architect have recently been completed. Join a tour to admire the crypt's terrazzo mosaic floor, which took 15 years to complete.

• **Macquarie Street (Maps B & D)** extends from **Hyde Park** to **Bennelong Point** and by following this route many elegant examples of Georgian architecture can be seen, as can many attractions worth visiting. **Hyde Park Barracks** (9223 8922), originally designed to house convicts, is a now a museum featuring changing exhibitions on Australia's history and culture. It also contains it own café/restaurant (9223 1155) and Function Centre (9361 6288) with an ideal proximity to the city and public transport. The **Sydney Mint Museum** (9217 0311) contains exhibitions on Australia's currency, history and culture. Further down Macquarie Street, rub the snout of the brass boar **Il Porcellino** for good luck, found at the front of **Sydney Hospital**, then admire the art deco fountain in the inner courtyard. **Parliament House** (9230 2111), the seat of the New South Wales parliament, has daily tours as well as an educational display on the building's development and the State's legislative history. The **State Library** (9273 1414) is housed by two buildings, the modern Reference Library and the Majestic Mitchell library. Both provide free services, and are worth visiting to view the periodically changing exhibitions and the Mitchell Library's reading room's impressive skylight. Free tours of the library are held on Tuesdays from 11am to 12noon and on Thursdays from 2pm to 3pm.

• **The Domain (Map D, Ref K6)**, the grassy parkland behind Macquarie Street, is a lively venue, being a public rallying point, a site of numerous and varied concerts and a favourite exercise and lunch spot for city workers. From its eastern edge near the **Art Gallery of NSW** you can view historic **Woolloomooloo Finger Wharf**, **Garden Island** and **Potts Point**. The harbourside **Andrew "Boy" Charlton Pool** is on the way to **Mrs Macquarie's Chair**, an ideal place to sit and take in the harbour views and activity.

• **Royal Botanic Gardens (Map 2, Ref D15)** (9231 8111) extends over 30 lush hectares from **Mrs Macquarie's Chair** around **Farm Cove** to **Bennelong Point**. Explore Australia's first farm, Palm Grove, Sydney Tropical Centre, the National Herbarium of New South Wales and the Herb Garden, or relax in the Rose Garden's rotunda, the site of many weddings. Situated on the Macquarie Street side of the gardens, **Government House** (9931 5222), formerly the official residence of the Governor, houses collections of the 19th and early 20th century furnishings.

• **Martin Place (Map C, Ref K2)**, a plaza between George and Macquarie Streets, contains the 1929 art deco **Cenotaph** where annual Anzac Day war remembrance services are held; the recently refurbished renaissance-style **General Post Office** and other grand buildings such as the Commonwealth Bank. Concerts are also held in the amphitheatre.

• **Pitt Street Mall (Map C, Ref K6)**, between King and Market Streets, is Sydney's shopping heart, surrounded by numerous department stores and shopping malls. One of the most beautiful of these is the ornate **Strand Arcade** (9232 4199), a lovingly restored Victorian-era building houses some of Australia's premiere fashion designers and labels.

• **State Theatre (Map C, Ref J9)** (1902 262 588), nearby on Market Street, is a 1929 movie palace and is decorated in true Cinema Baroque style. It boasts a magnificent Wurlitzer organ and 20,000-piece chandelier. It is a premier venue for concerts, theatre and special events and is home to the annual Sydney Film Festival.

• **Queen Victoria Building (Map C, Ref H10)** (George St, York, Market and Park Sts, 9264 1864), is a majestic Romanesque shopping arcade. Built in 1898 it was originally a fresh produce market, but now houses many fashion and gift stores a, well as cafes and other shops. The restoration of the building retained many of its original features, including the giant domes and roof statues, combining these features with an up-market, modern feel. An underground promenade connects Town Hall railway station to Sydney Central Plaza and Grace Bros department store.

• **Sydney Town Hall (Map C, Ref G13)** (483 George St, 9265 9333), is an excellent example of high Victorian architecture. As Sydney's civic centre, it is the venue for concerts, balls and public meetings and continues the tradition of being Sydney's favourite city meeting place on the front steps, due to its proximity to Town Hall Station.

shopping & markets

Sydney offers world-class shopping, with vibrant retail streets, elegant arcades, modern malls, large department stores and colourful markets in the CBD and city fringe. They offer an impressive range of high quality, locally made and imported goods, including indigenous art, handmade crafts, funky clothes and innovative jewellery. Bargains can be found at weekend markets and factory and designer seconds outlets stores selling remarkably reduced items from labels such as Marcs and Diesel.

• The Rocks (Map B, Ref A4)
Sydney's historic heart has an extensive range of quality stalls, in one of Sydney's most unique markets. The **Rocks Market** (9240 8717) is open every Saturday and Sunday between 10am and 5pm, or until 6pm in summer, and is held at the northern end of George Street. With over 145 stalls selling arts, crafts, homeware, antiques and jewellery, as well as street performers adding to the carnival atmosphere and the overhead canopy promising fantastic shopping whatever the weather, it's the perfect place to explore on the weekend.
Aboriginal and Tribal Art Centre 117 George St, The Rocks, 9241 5998. Duty Free Indigenous paintings and artefacts.
Australian Craftworks 127 George St, The Rocks, 9247 7156 Ceramics, textiles, pottery and more.

• Pitt Street Mall & George Street (Map C, Ref K6)
A wide variety of specialty stores can be found on George Street, and in the many shopping centres on Pitt Street Mall, such as **Sky Garden, Strand Arcade, Mid City Centre, Centrepoint** and **Sydney Central Plaza.**
Gowings Cnr George & Market Sts, 9264 6321. Basic menswear, footwear, travel goods as well as unusual gifts and lifestyle products.
Dinosaur Designs Shop 77, Strand Arcade, 9223 2953. Fun and funky homeware and jewellery made from brightly coloured resin have become a modern classic.

• Castlereagh Street, CBD (Map D, Ref B6)
Exclusive international couture and Australian designer labels can be found at the **MLC Centre** and the Castlereagh Street stores of **Chanel, Louis Vuitton** and **Hermes.** and **Cartier Tiffany & Co.** are at **Chifley Plaza** and **Emporio Armani** is in Martin Place.
Chanel Boutique 70 Castlereagh St, 9233 4800. Pinnacle of classic French style.
David Jones Department Store Castlereagh & Elizabeth Sts, 9266 5544. Two building full of fashion, fragrances, furnishings and the fabulous **Food Hall.**

• Queen Victoria Building (QVB) (Map C, Ref H10)
This majestic shopping centre contains more than 200 stores selling quality souvenirs, homeware, knitwear, lingerie, cosmetics, shoes, jewellery and fashion, including chain stores **Country Road, Espirit, Lush** and **Guess.**
ABC Shop Shop 48, 1st floor, QVB, 9333 1635. Merchandise associated with Australia's national broadcaster, including books, videos, music, toys and clothing.
Red Earth Shop 22, Lower Level, QVB, 9264 4019. Natural beauty products.

• Darling Harbour (Map H)
The **Harbourside Festival Marketplace** is home to over 200 stores offering souvenirs, fashion, music, books, toys and other gifts, as well as a wide array of eateries.
Redline Sports Shop 225, 9281 9180 Motor racing merchandise.
Surf Dive 'N' Ski Shop 205-207, 9281 4040. Fashion and sports equipment reflecting Australia's beach culture.

• Chinatown (Map E, Ref D4)
This cosmopolitan part of town has everything from traditional herbalists to hip designer labels, as well as the best Chinese restaurants in Sydney.
Market City 9-13 Hay St, 9212 1388. A bargain hunters delight, featuring over 100 retail shops, including one whole level of factory outlets offering up to 80% off retail prices of some of the best names in fashion. Other features are an amazing food court, and entertainment at Galaxy World and Reading Cinemas.
Paddy's Market (below Market City), Thursday - Sunday, with over 800 stalls offering fresh food to fashion to electronic gadgets in Sydney's oldest, most traditional market.
Chinatown Centre Food Hall 25 Dixon St, 9281 7568. Exotic, varied and popular food outlet.

• Oxford Street, Darlinghurst (Map F, Ref G3)
Leather, gymwear, fashion, music, books and homewares are all to be found on the lower end of this popular street.
Fish 33 Oxford St, Darlinghurst, 9267 5142. Dance & alternative music.
Home 153 Oxford St, Darlinghurst, 9332 4840. Stylish essentials for city living.

• Crown Street, Darlinghurst (Map F, Ref K9)
Scattered along Crown Street are shops selling inner-city fashion and accessories, from retro groove to basic black, interspersed with bric-a-brac and interior design stores.
Route 66 257 Crown St, Darlinghurst, 9331 6686. Classic jeans, jackets and cowboy garb.

• Oxford Street, Paddington (Map 4, Ref H15)
Sydney's innovative fashion labels can be found at the upper end of Oxford Street, interspersed with interesting bookshops, gift and homeware stores. On Saturday check out **Paddington Bazaar** (9331 2923), the coolest markets in town, which has previously been the starting point of many of Australia's best designers.
Ariel Booksellers 42 Oxford St, Paddington, 9332 4581. Quality books: fiction, film, art and design; great novelty cards and slick gift-wrapping.
Mambo 17 Oxford St, Paddington, 9331 8034. Wild beach and street wear, reflecting our beach culture.

[Most shops open from 9.00 am – 5.30 pm weekdays, until 9.00 pm Thursday nights and 9.00 am – 4.00 pm Saturdays]

lifestyle mix

Begin with the freshest of foods and supermarket, add over 30 factory fashion outlets, mix with Sydney's largest Yum Cha restaurant and 15 specialty foodcourt, finish with Reading Cinemas superior 5 screen cinema complex and you'll discover Market City.

Open everyday 10am - 7pm (till 8pm Thursdays), explore Market City located above Sydney's Paddy's Markets in Haymarket.

Shopping with a Difference.

CORNER THOMAS AND HAY STREETS, HAYMARKET
115 Speciality Stores with over 30 Factory Outlets including:
Marcs ■ Oxford ■ Voi ■ Atelier ■ Nine West ■ Esprit Mens
Done Art & Design ■ Esprit ■ Cue ■ Events & more
FOR MORE INFORMATION CALL (02) 9212 1388

culture & entertainment

Sydney's diverse and exciting cultural scene is reflected in the remarkable range of galleries, museums, theatres and cinemas; and the orchestras, classical and modern dance, opera and theatre companies which make Sydney their home. Guides providing information on what's on include *Sydney Morning Herald's Friday Metro, Beat, Drum Media, 3D World, Revolver, On the Street* or alternatively check out citysearch.com.au. Tickets may be purchased through Ticketek (9266 4800) and HalfTix (9286 3310).

MUSEUMS

• **Australian Museum (Map D, Ref G14)** 6 College St, Sydney, 9320 6000. Natural history museum of Australia and the Pacific.

• **The Museum of Sydney (Map B, Ref E11)** Cnr Phillip and Bridge Sts, Sydney, 9251 5988. State-of-the-art museum imaginatively brings Sydney's past to life on the site of the first government house.

• **Powerhouse Museum (Map 3, Ref B11)** 500 Harris St, Ultimo, 9217 0111. An interactive museum with exhibitions focusing on innovation, technology and learning.

• **National Maritime Museum (Map 3, Ref A3)** Darling Harbour, 9298 3777. Charts Australia and the world's sea faring history and coastal lifestyle, providing tours of numerous seagoing craft.

GALLERIES

• **Art Gallery of New South Wales (Map 4, Ref D2)** Art Gallery Rd, The Domain, 9225 1744. Australia's foremost collection of Australian, Asian and European art.

• **Museum of Contemporary Art (Map B, Ref A5)** Circular Quay, The Rocks, 9252 4033. An adventurous and eclectic collection of modern art, Aboriginal painting and video art.

• **State Library of NSW (Map B, Ref G16)** Macquarie St, Sydney, 9273 1414. Exhibitions of art, photography, drawings and unusual treasures providing an insight into Australia's culture and past.

• **Artspace/The Gunnery (Map 4, Ref G3)** 43-51 Cowper Wharf Road, Woolloomooloo, 9368 1899 Installations and performances.

• **Australian Centre for Photography (Map 21, Ref B1)** 257 Oxford St, Paddington, 9332 1455 Contemporary photography displays and courses, as well as public photographic facilities.

• **Brett Whiteley Studio (Map 20, Ref C4)** 2 Raper St, Surry Hills, 9225 1881. This well-known artist's works and memorabilia are displayed in his former home.

• **Byron Mapp Gallery (Map 4, Ref K16)** 18 Argyle St, The Rocks, 9252 9800. This gallery, bookstore and café features local and international photography.

MUSIC AND PERFORMING ARTS

• **Sydney Opera House (Map B, Ref J1)** Bennelong Point, 9250 7777. Features performances by acclaimed organisations such as Opera Australia, Australian Ballet, Sydney Theatre Company, Sydney Dance Company and Sydney Symphony Orchestra.

• **The Performance Space (Map 19, Ref D5)** 199 Cleveland Street, Redfern, 9319 5091. Experimental dance, movement, mime and performance arts.

• **The Wharf Theatre (Map 1, Ref F7)** Pier 4, Hickson Rd, Millers Point, 9250 1700. Exciting theatre, dramatic water views and the Wharf Restaurant (9250 1761).

• **State Theatre (Map C, Ref J8)** 49 Market St, Sydney, 9373 6655 Its opulence steals the attention of audiences there to see theatre, musicals, concerts and the Sydney Film Festival in June.

• **Capitol Theatre (Map E, Ref H7)** 13-17 Campbell St, Haymarket, 9320 5000. Lavishly restored 1920's lyric theatre with a starry-sky ceiling.

• **Seymour Theatre Centre (Map 18, Ref G4)** Cnr Cleveland St & City Rd, Darlington, 9351 7944 (Box Office 9351 7940) A stimulating mix of theatre.

• **Belvoir Street Theatre (Map 19, Ref G4)** 25 Belvoir St, Surry Hills, 9699 3444. Experimental and daring productions.

• **The Stables Theatre (Map 4, Ref H10)** 10 Nimrod St, Darlinghurst, 9361 3817. A venue showcasing new Australian works.

CINEMAS

• **Hoyts/Village (Map C, Ref G16)** 9273 7373 & **Greater Union** 9267 8666, 505 George St, Sydney Blockbusters at this multiplex.

• **Hoyts Cinemas Fox Studios (Map 21, Ref B9)** Bent St, Moore Park 9332 1300. Mostly mainstream movies.

• **Palace Academy Twin (Map 4, Ref F14)** 3a Oxford St, Paddington, 9361 4453. Quality international arthouse.

• **Verona Cinema (Map 4, Ref G15)** 17 Oxford St, Paddington, 9360 6099. Many small theatres screen an eclectic range of films.

• **Chauvel Cinema (Map 21, Ref A1)** 149 Oxford St, Paddington, 9361 5398. Australian cinema, independent international and movie classics at the national cinematheque

• **Dendy Cinemas** MLC Centre **(Map D, Ref A2)**, 19 Martin Place, Sydney, 9233 8166, Opera Quays **(Map B, Ref G6)** 2 Circular Quay E, Sydney, 9247 3800 261 King St, Newtown **(Map 17, Ref G11)**, 9550 5699 Independent Australian and international cinema.

restaurants & cafes

Sydney's exciting eating scene offers an overwhelming choice of ethnically diverse restaurants and cafes, taking advantage of the fabulous fresh local produce. Sydney's top-end restaurants provide sublime dining experiences and often require reservations to be made weeks in advance. Your culinary memories will make them well worth both the trouble and expense.

per person Prices	(GST incl.)
$	under $10
$$	$10 - $20
$$$	$20 - $30
$$$$	$30 - $40
$$$$$	$40 & over

[2 courses, excluding drinks, corkage & tips.]

RESTAURANTS

- **Angkor Wat Cambodian Restaurant $$ (Map 4, Ref E13)** 227 Oxford St, Darlinghurst, 9360 5500. Authentic Cambodian cuisine featuring fresh and fragrant flavours in a warm and exotic environment.
- **Capitan Torres $$ (Map E, Ref F2)** 73 Liverpool St, Sydney, 9264 5574. Spanish sangria makes an excellent companion to the 20 plus types of tapas in this family-run rustic bar.
- **Chinta Ria...The Temple of Love $$ (Map C, Ref B9)** Level 2, The Roof Terrace, Cockle Bay Wharf, Darling Park, 9264 3211. Malaysian based menu favoured by a young crowd – one of the most beautiful restaurants in Sydney.
- **Edna's Table $$$$ (Map C, Ref F9)** 204 Clarence St, Sydney, 9267 3933. Showcases Australian bush foods, using indigenous ingredients with great effect.
- **Eleni's $$$ (Map 4, Ref E9)** 185a Bourke St, East Sydney, 9331 5306. Innovative Greek flavours, stylishly presented in an intimate, Aegean-inspired setting.
- **Fez $$ (Map 4, Ref H11)** 247 Victoria St, Darlinghurst, 9360 9581. Contemporary Middle Eastern in a bright, breezy Moroccan-style décor. Specialities include breakfasts and mezze plates.
- **Forty One $$$$$ (Map B, Ref D16)** Level 41, Chifley Tower, Chifley Square, Sydney, 9221 2500. Summit of modern Australian cuisine accompanied by magnificent views of Sydney.
- **Fu Manchu $$ (Map 4, Ref H11)** 249 Victoria St, Darlinghurst, 9360 9424. Buzzy atmosphere and funky décor at this popular Asian noodle bar.
- **Hard Rock Café $$$$ (Map 4, Ref D8)** 121-129 Crown St, Darlinghurst 9331 1116. Enjoy the American-style menu whilst surrounded by rock 'n' roll memorabilia.
- **Kam Fook $$$ (Map E, Ref D7)** Level 3, Market City, 9 Hay St, Haymarket 9211 8988. Wide array of delectable dishes at Sydney's largest Chinese restaurant.
- **Macleay Street Bistro $$$ (Map 4, Ref K3)** 73a Macleay St, Potts Point, 9358 4891. A wine buff's BYO, take your treasured reds for the steak and mash.
- **Mezzaluna $$$$$ (Map 4, Ref J5)** 123 Victoria St, Potts Point, 9357 1988. Excellent, contemporary Italian and a terrace with a spectacular city view.
- **Odeon $$$ (Map 4, Ref K4)** 32 Orwell St, Potts Point 9331 0172. Appealing menu to match the modern-deco dining room and suit the groovy crowd.
- **Pig and The Olive Pizzeria $$ (Map 4, Ref K3)** 71a Macleay St, Potts Point, 9357 3745. Gourmet pizzas to pig out on at this popular eatery.
- **Planet Hollywood $$$$ (Map E, H1)** Level 2, 600 George St, Sydney 9267 7827. Perfect place for dinner before a movie, or go after the movie for some of Sydney's most decadent desserts.
- **Rockpool $$$$$ (Map A, Ref K5)** 107 George St, The Rocks, 9252 1888. East imaginatively meets West in this striking combination of swanky design, swish service, innovative cuisine and the freshest seafood.
- **Star City $$-$$$$ (Map 12, Ref H2)** 80 Pyrmont Rd, Pyrmont 9777 9000. With a choice of over 5 restaurants, sure to satisfy every palate.
- **Tetsuya's $$$$$ (Map C, Ref F16)** 529 Kent St, Sydney, 9267 2900. Japanese-French cuisine served in this unmatched experience of Sydney dining.
- **Yipiyiyo $$$ (Map 4, Ref C13)** 290 Crown St, Darlinghurst, 9332 3114. Sydney's best Sante Fe Style cuisine.

CAFES & FAST EATS

- **BBQ King $$ (Map E, Ref F4)** 18 Goulburn St, Chinatown, 9267 2586. Traditional Chinese barbecued meats. Where the chefs go for a late night bite.
- **Cafe Hernandez $$ (Map 4, Ref J8)** 60 Kings Cross Rd, Rushcutters Bay, 9331 2343. Strong Spanish coffee, interesting crowd and open 'til late.
- **Harry's Cafe de Wheels $ (Map 4, Ref G3)** Cowper Wharf Rd, Woolloomooloo, 9357 3074. One of Sydney's late night institutions serving the city's best pie and peas.
- **Ippon Sushi $$ (Map E, Ref E6)** 404 Sussex St, Chinatown, 9212 7669. Choose fresh, cheap Japanese sushi from the conveyor belt.
- **Le Petit Crème $$ (Map 4, Ref G10)** 118 Darlinghurst Rd, Darlinghurst, 9361 4738. Arrive early for the Eggs Benedict weekend special and le bowl of coffee.
- **MCA Cafe $$ (Map B, Ref B6)** MCA, Circular Quay West, 9241 4253 Stylish contemporary Australian food, with spectacular harbour views.
- **QVB Jet $ (Map C, Ref H11)** Shop G55, Queen Victoria Building, York St, Town Hall end, 9283 5004. Sip strong lattes, while looking like or looking at the locals. Outdoor European style seating – great for watching the passers-by whilst recharging your shopping batteries.
- **Spring $ (Map 4, Ref K2)** Challis Ave, Potts Point, 9331 0190. Tiny café with a buzzy, sunny sidewalk scene and coffee with a kick.
- **Starbuck's Coffee $ (Map D, Ref C12)** Cnr Park & Elizabeth Sts, Sydney, 9268 0184. Perfect for a caffeine fix, with its own specially roasted coffee, known worldwide.
- **The Vinyl Lounge $$ (Map 13, Ref C5)** 1/17 Elizabeth Bay Rd, Elizabeth Bay, 9326 9224. Very Funky. Very French.
- **Wedge Cafe $ (Map 13, Ref B5)** 70 Elizabeth Bay Rd, Elizabeth Bay, 9326 9015. A mecca for great coffee, good food and genuine service.

bars, pubs & clubs

Like any great city, Sydney has a wide range of bars, pubs and nightclubs to suit all types and tastes. There are after work bars offering cheap drinks during 'happy hour'; sophisticated bars in international hotels; upmarket pubs providing complementary snacks; fun cocktail bars; noisy pubs with live music; restaurant bars where you drink and eat; large nightclubs offering pinball, pool and dancing; and dingy late-nighters where you go when there's nowhere else to go. Hours of operation do vary, with many nightclubs beginning late, around 10 pm or 11 pm, and staying open until sunrise.

CITY DRINKING

- **'The Bar' Sir Stamford (Map B, Ref G8)** 93 Macquarie St, Sydney, 9252 4600. Elegant decor, at Circular Quay.
- **'Hotel' CBD (Map C, Ref G4)** Cnr King and York St, Sydney, 9299 1700. Cool décor, good vibes and the best bar in the city centre.
- **Customs House Bar (Map B, Ref B11)** Sydney Renaissance Hotel, Macquarie Place, Sydney, 9259 7000. Perfect place to unwind at the end of the day with a drink under the trees.
- **Dendy Bar (Map C, Ref K2)** 19 Martin Place, Sydney, 9233 8166. At Dendy Cinema, perfect for a post-film drink and discussion.
- **Horizon's Bar (Map A, Ref G7)** L36, ANA Hotel, 176 Cumberland St, The Rocks, 9250 6000. Some of Sydney's best cocktails, accompanied by views from Darling Harbour to Circular Quay.
- **Pontoon Bar (Map C, Ref A11)** Cockle Bay Wharf, Darling Harbour, 9267 7099. the place to be seen.

PADDINGTON & DARLINGHURST BARS

- **Burdekin Hotel (Map 4, Ref E3)** 2 Oxford St, Darlinghurst, 9331 3066. Join the Dugout Bar's cigar set or boogie at the main bar.
- **Elephant Bar (Map 13, Ref C14)** The Royal Hotel, Five Ways, Paddington, 9331 2604. Sip on a drink and enjoy the sunset views over eastern Sydney.
- **Fringe Bar (Map 4, Ref H15)** 106 Oxford St, Paddington, 9360 3554. Popular bar with pool tables, booths and a warm and friendly atmosphere.
- **Gilligan's (Map 4, Ref D12)** Above Oxford Hotel, Taylor Square, Darlinghurst, 9331 3467. Open from 5pm, with the wildest cocktails in Sydney.
- **Grand Pacific Blue Room (Map 4, Ref F14)** Cnr Oxford & South Dowling Sts, Darlinghurst, 9331 7108. Classy and classic cocktails in this sophisticated setting.
- **Lizard Lounge (Map F, Ref H4)** Exchange Hotel, 34 Oxford St, Darlinghurst, 93311936. Meet all types while enjoying the complementary happy hour snacks.
- **L'otel (Map 4, Ref G10)** 114 Darlinghurst Rd, Darlinghurst, 9360 6868. A hip crowd squeezes into this small buzzy bar to sip vodkas see and be seen.

INNER CITY PUBS

- **Clock Hotel (Map 20, Ref C2)** 470 Crown St, Surry Hills, 9331 5333. This revamped pub now attracts an eclectic, young, inner city crowd.
- **Cricketer's Arms Hotel (Map 20, Ref E1)** 106 Fitzroy St, Surry Hills, 9331 3301. Funky music and cool beer garden.
- **Hopetoun Hotel (Map 20, Ref D1)** Cnr Bourke & Fitzroy Sts, Surry Hills, 9361 5257. Live music every night and small underground bar.
- **Lord Nelson Brewery Hotel (Map A, Ref C2)** Cnr Kent & Argyle Sts, 9251 4044. This cosy, historic, sandstone pub brews their own ales, keeping punters happy for more than 150 years.
- **O Bar, Clarendon Hotel (Map 19, Ref K3)** 156 Devonshire St, Surry Hills, 9319 6881. Stylish and sleek drinking and dining.
- **Paddington Inn (Map 21, Ref D2)** 338 Oxford St, Paddington, 9380 5277. A fun, local pub, popular after Saturday's markets.
- **Palace Hotel (Map 4, Ref E16)** 122 Flinders St, Darlinghurst, 9361 5170. Several levels, pool tables and great quality modern Aussie pub food.
- **The Spirit of Sydney Hotel (Map F, Ref K10)** Warm and inviting hotel with a refurbished cocktail bar upstairs.

NIGHTCLUBS

- **Gas Nightclub (Map E, Ref F13)** 477 Pitt St, Haymarket 9211 3088. One room on two levels featuring soul, funk and hip-hop.
- **Goodbar (Map 4, Ref F14)** 11 Oxford St, Paddington, 9360 6759. Fresh and funky sounds in this laid-back setting.
- **Home (Map C, Ref A11)** Cockle Bay Wharf, Darling Harbour, 9266 0600. The ultimate clubbing experience in Sydney.
- **Luna Lounge @ Jackson's on George (Map A, Ref J10)** 176 George St, Circular Quay, 9247 2727. Commercial dance, disco, house and hi NRG near the wharf and The Rocks.
- **Q Bar (Map F, Ref H4)** 44 Oxford St, Darlinghurst, 9360 1375. Pool tables, pinball, chill out corner, three bars and two funky dance spaces.
- **Retro (Map C, Ref C2)** Bristol Arms Hotel, 81 Sussex St, Sydney, 9262 5491. Five levels of '70's, '80's, '90's pop, disco, indie, Britpop and techno.
- **Slip Inn (Map C, Ref C4)** 111 Sussex St, Sydney 9299 1700. Favoured by a very cool & beautiful crowd.
- **Soho (Map 4, Ref H6)** 171 Victoria St, Kings Cross, 9358 4221. Different rooms, different moods, but always very sleek and sophisticated.
- **Sugareef (Map 4, Ref J8)** 20 Bayswater Rd, Potts Point, 9368 0763. Chill out to funky beats in this friendly atmosphere.
- **Tantra Bar (Map 4, Ref D12)** 169 Oxford St, Darlinghurst, 9331 7729. Popular with toned body and pierced navel set.
- **The Basement (Map B, Ref B9)** 29 Reiby Pl, Sydney 9251 2797. Well known throughout Sydney as the ultimate late night jazz and relaxed vibes spot.

city fringe

The fringes of Sydney's CBD house an array of interesting suburbs well worth exploring for their own distinct characters, whether it be the ethnic diversity of Newtown, the Italianness of Leichhardt, the bohemian nature of Surry Hills, the refined atmosphere of Woollahra or the leisurely mood of Bronte. Many suburbs, such as Glebe and Paddington, are within walking distance from the city centre, while other areas like Bondi Beach and Newtown can readily be reached by bus or train.

• **Newtown (Map 374, Ref H5)** is one of Sydney's most bohemian suburbs. A favoured spot of students attending the nearby **University of Sydney**, Newtown is jam-packed with cheap cafes, busy pubs, bookstores, galleries and second-hand clothes shops. Walk from the city, take a train, or catch a bus (L23, L28, 426) to bustling **King St.** The university campus warrants a visit to admire the original Victorian Gothic architecture of the Main Quadrangle with its intricate stonework and gargoyles, and relax on the lawns.

• **Glebe (Map 345, Ref C15)** is home to Sydney's café society. **Glebe Point Rd** is lined with many cafes and eateries. The colourful **Badde Manors Café** (37 Glebe Point Rd, 9660 3797) is a Glebe icon, while **Russel's Natural Food Market** (55 Glebe Point Rd, 9660 8144), as the name suggests, is a mega store for organic and macrobiotic food supplies. Bookstores are also a Glebe feature, drawing literary types to explore everything from pulp crime and collector comics to feminist writings and new age tracts. **Gleebooks** (49 Glebe Point Rd, 9660 2333) has a eclectic range, while their second-hand store a few blocks up (191 Glebe Point Rd, 9552 2526) specialises in children's books and offers many bargains. Wander the side streets, with their rows of workers cottages and historic stately mansions. Bargain-hunt for jewellery, music, second hand clothes or unique items on Saturdays at **Glebe Markets** (Glebe Public School, Glebe Point Rd); or head to the end of Glebe Point Road to **Jubilee Park**, for stunning city views and the striking outline of the **Anzac Bridge**. Catch a bus from the city (431, 433).

• **Balmain (Map 344, Ref J5)** should be visited on Saturday to explore the treasure trove of **Balmain Markets** at St Andrews churchyard, opposite **Gladstone Park**. Take a bus (442) from Town Hall, or ferry from Circular Quay to **Darling St Wharf**, and walk up to Balmain Village through the historic narrow streets with their quaint sandstone cottages and Victorian terraces. Browse in the bookstores and gift shops, lunch in a café or pub or buy picnic food from a delicatessen or patisserie to take to one of Balmain's many waterfront parks – **Birchgrove Park, Mortbay Park** and **Illuora Reserve** all have city skyline or Darling Harbour views.

• **Leichhardt (Map 343, Ref J14)** is Sydney's Little Italy. Scores of Italian restaurants, late-night cafes, delis, bakeries and shops line **Norton and Marion Streets**, giving the suburbs the distinct Italian flavour, exemplified by the Italian Forum, a villa-like centre containing shopping and restaurants. Take a bus (461, 480, 483) to Norton Street and embark on a culinary tour of the area. Enjoy a traditional home style Italian cuisine or contemporary variations in one of the many eateries such as **Portofino** (166 Norton St, 9550 0782), but save room for Sydney's best gelato at **Bar Italia** (169-171 Norton St 9560 9981).

• **Woollahra (Map 347, Ref A15)** is Sydney's premier antiques centre. Catch the bus (380, 382, 389) along **Oxford Street** and alight at **Queen Street**, the heart of this exclusive suburb. Hours can be spent in the fine antiques and interior design stores, galleries and shops. Explore the backstreets with their grand homes and terrace houses, or walk to nearby **Centennial Park** (9331 5056) where you can laze by the lake, feed the ducks or join a nature walk. If you're feeling more energetic, you can hire a bicycle or roller blades.

• **Double Bay (Map 347, Ref D15)** is home to Sydney's society set. Take the train to **Edgecliff** or bus (324, 325) to this prestigious harbour side suburb and take in its village-like atmosphere. Browse in the exclusive designer boutiques or dine at a sophisticated restaurant or coffee shop. Walk up to hilly **Darling Point** an admire **Lindesay** (9363 2401), an impressive house built in 1834 which opens for exhibitions and special events. Alternatively, explore the ritzy suburb of **Vaucluse** to the east where you can visit the Gothic mansion and museum **Vaucluse House** (9388 7922) and enjoy their famous Devonshire teas.

• **Bondi Beach (Map 378, Ref E4)** is synonymous with surf, sand and sun. It's now just as popular for its buzzy **Campbell Parade** café scene and **Sunday Bondi Markets**. Take a bus (380, 382, 389) or the Bondi and Bay Explorer (131 500) that stops around Sydney Harbour and its shores, continuing on to Bondi Beach. There is much to do along the lively promenade: roller blade, skateboard, jog, walk the dog, eat fresh seafood on the beach, attend a play, film, dance, band festival at **Bondi Pavilion**. To take an invigorating walk with breathtaking ocean views, head south from Notts Avenue past Bondi Icebergs' clubhouse and along the rocky headland path to tiny **Tamarama** and **Bronte** beaches.

• **Bronte (Map 378, Ref B8)** is a small, white-sand beach in a bay, is favoured by families who flock to its pretty wooded park and barbecue area on weekends. Bronte can be reached by bus (378) from the city or foot from Bondi Beach around the popular cliff's edge trail, with its spectacular open ocean views. Be sure to take food for the barbie as the fish and chips queue is always long. Perhaps try one of the excellent cafes across the road such as **Sejuiced** (9389 9538), which offers fresh fruit juices.

backpackers accommodation

There are many reasonably priced places for travellers on a limited budget to stay in Sydney. All types of people stay in youth and backpacker hostels, groups of young people, older people, singles or families. Some hostels attract younger and exuberant people while others have a quieter atmosphere. It is always a good idea to ring ahead so that you end up staying in the place most suitable for your needs. Listed are backpacker and youth hostels within the city, from Darlinghurst to Glebe.

AA Tremayne Backpackers (Map 6, Ref C15)
89 Carabella Street, Kirribilli
9955 4155

Backpackers Accommodation (Map E, Ref J6)
412 Pitt Street, Sydney
9571 9049

Backpackers Connection (Map 13, Ref A7)
2 Roslyn Street, Elizabeth Bay
9358 4844

Bee-Hive Hostel (Map 18, Ref K4)
103 Cleveland Street, Sydney
9699 5315

Bell City (Map 18, Ref H2)
42 City Road, Chippendale
9211 5197

CB Hotel (Map E, Ref J6)
417 Pitt Street, Haymarket
9211 5115

Crown Budget Inn (Map 4, Ref C10)
199-203 Crown Street, Darlinghurst
9360 9744

Dury House (Map 4, Ref J7)
34b Darlinghurst Road, Darlinghurst 9368 0188

Excelsior Hotel (Map 3, Ref K16)
64 Foveaux Street, Surry Hills
9211 4945

Fact Tree Youth Service Inc (Map 19, Ref G13)
703 Elizabeth Street, Waterloo
9319 2708

Funk House – Backpacker (Map 4, Ref K6)
23 Darlinghurst Road, Darlinghurst
9358 6455

George Street Private Hotel (Map E, Ref G7)
700a George Street, Sydney
9211 1800

Glebe Point YHA (Map 12, Ref B12)
262 Glebe Point Road, Glebe
9692 8418

Glebe Village (Map 12, Ref B12)
256-258 Glebe Point Road, Glebe
9660 8878

Globe Backpackers Hostel (Map 4, Ref J7)
40 Darlinghurst Road, Darlinghurst
9326 9675

Gracelands Budget Accommodation (Map 20, Ref D7)
461 Cleveland Street, Surry Hills
9699 1399

Harbour City Hotel (Map 4, Ref D5)
50 Sir John Young Crescent, Woolloomooloo 9380 2922

Jolly Swagman Backpackers (Map 4, Ref K5)
27 Orwell Street, Potts Point
9358 6400

Kangaroo Bak-Pak (Map 20, Ref D7)
665 South Dowling Street, Surry Hills
9319 5915

Kings Cross Holiday Apartments (Map 4, Ref F8)
169 William Street, Forbes Square, Darlinghurst 9361 0637

Nomads Captain Cook Hotel (Map 20, Ref F2)
162 Flinders Street, Darlinghurst
9331 6487

Nomads City Central Backpackers (Map E, Ref F9)
752 George Street, Sydney
9212 4833

Nomads Downtown City Backpackers (Map E, Ref G5)
611 George Street, Sydney
9211 8801

Nomads Forest Lodge (Map 12, Ref A16)
17 Arundel Street, Glebe 9660 1872

Original Backpackers Lodge (Map E, Ref J6)
162 Victoria Street, Potts Point
9356 3232

Pink House Travellers Hostel (Map 13, Ref A7)
6 Barncleuth Square, Darlinghurst
9358 1689

Plane Tree Lodge (Map E, Ref J6)
174 Victoria Street, Potts Point
9356 4551

Potts Point House (Map E, Ref J5)
154 Victoria Street, Potts Point
9368 0733

Redback Steve Sydney Australian Backpackers (Map F, Ref B7)
198 Elizabeth Street, Surry Hills
9211 4200

Royal Nomads (Map 18, Ref F8)
370 Abercrombie Street, Darlington
9698 8557

Sydney Backpackers (Map C, Ref H16)
7 Wilmont Street, Sydney 9267 7772

Sydney Central Backpackers (Map 4, Ref J5)
6 Orwell Street, Potts Point
9358 6600

Sydney Central YHA (Map E, Ref G11)
Cnr Pitt Street and Rawson Place, Sydney 9281 9111

Sydney City Centre (Map D, Ref D1)
7 Elizabeth Street, Sydney 9221 7528

The Virgin Backpackers (Map 4, Ref J5)
144 Victoria Street, Darlinghurst
9357 4733

Tokyo Joe's Budget Accommodation (Map 4, Ref E7)
132 Bourke Street, Woolloomooloo
9331 0822

Travellers Rest (Map 4, Ref J5)
156 Victoria Street, Darlinghurst
9358 4606

Wattle House Travellers Accommodation (Map 11, Ref K12)
44 Hereford Street, Glebe 9552 4997

YHA New South Wales (Map C, Ref E9)
422 Kent Street, Sydney 9261 1111

public transport

Sydney's extensive public transport system is both convenient and clean. As many of Sydney's sights are within easy walking distance, sightseeing is generally best done on foot. Driving into the city is not recommended; the network of buses, trains, ferries, light rail and taxis will assist you reach any destination. Ferries offer a scenic route between the city and harbourside suburbs — and they are even worth taking just for the ride.

• Getting to and around Sydney
For information on how to travel in Sydney by bus, train or ferry contact the Public Transport Info Line between 6am to 10pm daily (131 500). They provide details of routes, fares and timetables. Composite tickets are offered, which combine travel by bus, train and ferry at a cheaper price. These tickets can be purchased from State Transit Information Kiosks, Ticket Kiosks, newsagents, train stations and newspaper stands. Metro Light Rail/ Metro Monorail (8584 5288) can be contacted for details of their services.
To get to and from **Sydney's Airport (Map 404)** Domestic and International Flight terminals, taxis, buses and trains are the primary options. The airport is 9 kilometres from the city centre, and although there are many taxis, the queues during peak hour can be long. State Transit offers four buses: Airport Express 350 to Kings Cross, Airport Express 300 to Circular Quay, metro route bus 100 from Dee Why via the city and metro route bus 400, which travels from Bondi Junction to Burwood via the airport. There are also bus services to a number of city hotels offered by Kingsford Smith Sydney Airporter (9667 0663). The Airport Shuttle (9317 3311) takes passengers between the airport and Darling Harbour and city hotels. **Homebush Bay (Map 572)**, the home of the Sydney 2000 Olympic and Paralympic Games, is situated 16 kilometres from the city centre. To get there on weekdays, catch a Cityrail train to Strathfield or Lidcombe and connect with a Sydney Bus service to Homebush Bay. On weekends, rail services operate directly from Central Station to Olympic Park Station within close walking distance to the venues at Homebush Bay.

• Train Travel
Cityrail, www.cityrail.nsw.gov.au; Public Transport Info Line: 131 500. The Cityrail network offers convenient and regular train services, between 4:30am and midnight daily. Central Station in the city is the main urban and country terminus. To move around the city quickly, use the underground City Circle loop, which links all the stops in the CBD. Sydney's wider rail network has 6 major lines, extending to the Blue Mountains in the west, Berowra in the north, Bondi Junction in the east and Waterfall in Sydney's south. For a full listing of the suburban lines, please refer to the Cityrail Suburban Network map on the back cover of this directory. In the evening, be sure to stand in the designated 'Nightsafe' area and travel in carriages marked with a blue light, as they are near the train guard. After midnight, Cityrail provides the Nightride bus service, which replaces the train service — a handy tip is to arrange for a taxi to meet you once you reach your destination. Most tickets are either single or return, however weekly and monthly tickets are offered at a cheaper rate, contact the Public Transport Info Line (131 500) for details.
• The Rail Link to Sydney Airport (131 500), Mascot, is a fast rail from Central Train Station to the Domestic and International Air Terminals. It operates every 7 minutes and a one-way journey takes 10 minutes. Luggage space is available. Lifts operate at Central. The price is $10 one-way per person or $15 return per person.

• The Bus System
State Transit Authority, www.sydneybuses.nsw.gov.au; Public Transport Info Line: 131 500. **Sydney Buses** provide a reliable service that links up effectively with the train and ferry systems. The major city bus terminals are at Circular Quay, Wynyard, the western side of the Queen Victoria Building and Central Station. The route number and destination are displayed on the front, left side and back of all buses. Single journey tickets are purchased on the bus, but Travelten tickets, which allow you to make 10 bus trips, are more economical if you use buses frequently. Express buses are marked with an 'X' at the front, while Limited stop buses are marked with an 'L' in front of the route number. Additional buses are provided for special and sporting events. Contact State Transit Authority for details (9941 6814).
A number of **private bus companies** operate to and between Sydney's outlying suburbs, such as Westbus (9890 0000 or 131 500), State Transit (9941 6814); Shorelink (9457 8888) for the Sydney's northern suburbs; Harris Park Buses (9689 1066) for Sydney's western suburbs; Hopkins (9632 3344) for Sydney's western suburbs: and Forest Coast Lines (9450 2277) for the north shore suburbs.

• Ferry Travel
Sydney Ferries Information Office is opposite Wharf 4, Circular Quay, 9207 3166, Public Transport Info Line, 131 500. **Ferries** have taken passengers on scenic journeys across Sydney Harbour for more than a century. Circular Quay is the city departure point for ferries, which operate daily, travelling to the eastern suburbs, North Shore and up the Parramatta River to Parramatta. Many ferry stops are also key tourist destinations, such as Darling Harbour, Manly, Watsons Bay, Balmain and Taronga Zoo. The ferries are conveniently linked to the train and bus networks at Circular Quay. State Transit also offers a number of reasonably priced sightseeing cruises. Private harbour tour operators are Hegarty's Ferries (9206 1167), which offers a Circular Quay and Inner Harbour Loop tour, and Matilda Cruises – Rocket Ferry Services (9264 7377), running between Darling Harbour, the Star City Casino and Circular Quay.
A map of the Sydney Ferry Network is included in this directory on the inside back cover of this book.

• Light Rail & Monorail

Metro Light Rail, 8584 5288, operates 24 hours daily, Metro Light Rail runs trams every 8 to 15 minutes. Services run between Central and Wentworth Park, going to Capitol Square, Haymarket, Sydney Convention and Exhibition Centre, Pyrmont Bay, Star City, Sydney Fish Market, Glebe, Jubilee Park, Rozelle Bay and Lilyfield, 6 am – midnight. Tickets can be purchased on the tram.

Metro Monorail, 8584 5288

The Monorail runs from:

8am – 10pm, Sundays; 7 am – 10 pm, Monday to Wednesday;

7 am – midnight, Thursday to Saturday, every 3 to 5 minutes.

It connects key sightseeing spots such as the Powerhouse Museum, City Centre, Darling Park, as well as Harbourside stop - attractions including Star City and the National Maritime Museum. Purchase your ticket at the Monorail station. The Monorail Day Pass for $7 provides unlimited rides for an entire day.

• Travelling by Taxi

Efficiently organised, flexible and readily available, Sydney's taxi operators provide a fast service. To catch a cab, you can either hail one on the street – vacant cabs have an illuminated orange light on their roof; wait at a taxi rank in the queue; or telephone a company and order a cab to collect you from your location. Phone numbers for Sydney's many taxi companies are available by contacting Telstra (1223), or refer to the Info Guide at the back of this book. The flagfall starts from $2.45 once the meter has started. There is a cost of $1.38 per kilometre, which has a 20% surcharge between 10 pm – 6 am. A $1.15 surcharge is charged if you book by telephone. Passengers pay for all bridge and road tolls.

• Disabled Access

For information to assist people with a disability to readily travel around Sydney, contact NICAN (1800 806 769), IDEAS (1800 029 904) or Australian Quadriplegics Association's 'Ask AQA' help-line (1800 819 775). A number of taxis are specifically designed to enable passengers with wheelchairs to travel comfortably; they can be booked by phoning any of the major taxi companies.

• Purchasing Tickets

Sydney's public transport network offers a range of tickets including singles, returns, all-day, weekly and long term tickets. Some tickets allow you to catch a bus, train or ferry using the same ticket. In terms of train travel, for people who only travel occasionally, single or return tickets are usually the best option, and during the day off-peak tickets are available at a discounted price. For frequent travellers, Cityrail offers a 7 day rail pass; flexipasses offer substantial discounts and can be purchased for between 4 weeks and 1 year periods. For travelling by bus, single tickets can be purchased on the bus from the driver; while for frequent travellers there are Travelten tickets, which allow 10 journeys within the bus route sections covered by the ticket; a good option for sightseeing is the Bus Tripper ticket, a 1 day ticket which allows unlimited travel in the Sydney bus network, and is also valid on the Sydney and Bondi & Bay Explorers. For occasional ferry travellers, single and return tickets can be purchased from ticket booths at ferry terminals; for more regular travellers the FerryTen ticket allows for 10 rides on Sydney Ferry services. Sydney Light Rail offers weekly tickets and day passes, which provide unlimited travel on the day of purchase; or single and return tickets. Sydney Monorail offers a standard fare, all-day pass, family pass and free tickets for children under 5 years of age.

There are also a number of tickets that combine train, bus and ferry travel. The CityHopper provides unlimited train and bus travels within a limited area covering the CBD and some of the inner city. DayRover tickets provide unlimited all-day travel in Cityrail suburban trains, Sydney Buses and Sydney Ferries. DayPasses allow unlimited travel on Sydney Buses and Sydney Ferries for one day. TravelPasses are available for periods of a week, a quarter or a year, and are colour-coded depending on the boundaries they are valid to travel in, allowing unlimited train, bus and ferry travel within the specified boundaries during the time period of the ticket. The SydneyPass is a good option for visitors wishing to explore Sydney over a few days; it provides for unlimited travel for either 3, 5 or 7 day periods and can be used on trains, buses and ferries within a specified boundary. For more detailed information on any of these ticketing options contact the Public Transport Info Line (131 500).

• Special Events Arrangements

Sydney's range of special attractions and events can be enjoyed with the assistance of Sydney's extensive public transport system. Major sporting and entertainment events are accompanied by special transport arrangements for all major venues. The Moore Park precinct — including Sydney Cricket Ground (SCG), Sydney Football Stadium (SFS) and the Fox Studios Complex — all have State Transit shuttle buses arranged for special events held at their major venues, leaving from Chalmers St, near Central train station. A bus station opposite the SCG at Moore Park, provides speedy access to all major events held at this location. Additional bus and train services are provided for New Year's Eve celebrations to and from the CBD. Cityrail and Sydney Buses also provide additional services for the Australia Day public holiday. Also refer to the Info Guide at the back of this book.

Suburbs and Localities Index

Listed below are the suburbs and localities included in this directory, together with their postcodes and map references.

Suburbs and localities are differentiated in the index as follows:

Abbotsbury — Suburb
Anzac Village — Locality shown on maps
Avalon Heights — Local name
[Map reference indicates approximate location]

Note: Streets are indexed to suburbs only, not localities.

e	Postcode	Map	Ref
rendon	2756	120	C11
'eville	2107	169	E2
ymore	2559	481	D10
nton Park	2206	402	D5
ton Gardens	2088	317	F14
ntarf	2093	287	E13
velly	2031	377	H11
velly West	2031	377	F12
ourn	2144	309	A15
de	2142	308	H12
sters Retreat	2108	139	A4
bitty	2570	446	B10
katoo Island	2000	314	F16
ra Bay	2083	76	D1
ebee	2761	212	H12
laroy	2097	229	D12
laroy Beach	2097	229	B10
laroy Plateau	2097	228	H10
yton	2760	270	D3
nleroy	2758	56	B6
no	2226	460	G6
no West	2226	460	F6
cord	2137	341	J3
ncord East	2137	342	B5
ncord North	2138	311	E14
ncord South	2137	342	K9
ncord West	2138	341	E3
dell Park	2200	398	E4
nnells Point	2221	431	G14
ogee	2034	377	E14
ogee North	2034	377	J14
nwallis	2756	90	J15
tage Point	2084	135	F8
uridjah	2571	564	J15
wan	2081	104	B14
nebrook	2749	207	D10
morne	2090	316	E10
morne Junction	2090	316	F6
morne Point	2090	316	F14
mer	2099	228	A14
mer Heights	2099	227	G13
nulla	2230	493	H13
nulla South	2230	523	K1
ws Nest	2065	315	F5
ydon	2132	342	E12
ydon North	2132	342	H12
ydon Park	2133	372	C7
l Curl	2096	258	K13
rrans Hill	2567	479	K12
rawong Beach	2108	109	B16
ceyville	2032	406	G5
ngar Island	2083	76	G5
ling Harbour	2000	345	F12
rlinghurst	2010	346	C13
rling Point	2027	346	J10
rlington	2008	375	D4
vidson	2085	255	E3
wes Point	2000	345	H3
an Park	2761	242	J1
e Why	2099	258	G6
e Why Beach	2099	259	B6
e Why North	2099	83	J14

	Postcode	Map	Ref
Dee Why West	2099	83	D9
Denham Court	2565	422	D11
Denistone	2114	281	E12
Denistone East	2122	281	J11
Denistone West	2114	281	A13
Dharruk	2770	241	B6
Diamond Bay	2030	348	H5
Dobroyd Head	2093	288	C16
Dobroyd Point	2045	343	G11
Dolans Bay	2229	492	K16
Dolls Point	2219	463	G1
Doonside	2767	243	B11
Double Bay	2028	347	D15
Douglas Park	2569	568	C11
Dover Heights	2030	348	H11
Drummoyne	2047	343	H4
Duffys Forest	2084	195	C4
Dulwich Hill	2203	373	E8
Dundas	2117	279	G14
Dundas Valley	2117	280	B8
Dundas West	2117	279	A11
Dunheved	2760	239	F5
Dural	2158	189	D10
Eagle Vale	2558	481	G7
Earlwood	2206	402	G4
Earlwood West	2206	372	G16
Eastern Creek	2766	273	A11
Eastgardens	2036	406	F9
East Hills	2213	427	J2
East Killara	2071	254	H8
East Kurrajong	2758	56	K3
Eastlakes	2018	406	C6
East Lindfield	2070	254	K14
East Roseville	2069	285	C2
East Ryde	2113	283	C15
East Sydney	2010	4	C8
Eastwood	2122	281	E7
Ebenezer	2756	63	E10
Edensor Park	2176	363	G1
Edgecliff	2027	346	K15
Edmondson Park	2171	423	D4
Elanora Heights	2101	198	B14
Elderslie	2570	507	E4
Elizabeth Bay	2011	346	G9
Ellis Lane	2570	476	E6
Elvina Bay	2105	168	E3
Emerton	2770	240	K5
Emu Heights	2750	235	B1
Emu Plains	2750	235	G6
Enfield	2136	371	H5
Enfield South	2133	371	F6
Engadine	2233	518	G5
Engineer Barracks	2170	425	C2
Englorie Park	2560	510	H10
Enmore	2042	374	F8
Epping	2121	251	D14
Epping West	2121	250	F15
Ermington	2115	310	F5
Erskine Park	2759	270	J15
Erskineville	2043	375	A9
Erskineville South	2043	374	K9
Eschol Park	2558	481	A3

	Postcode	Map	Ref
Eveleigh	2015	375	D5
Fairfield	2165	336	G9
Fairfield East	2165	337	C12
Fairfield Heights	2165	336	B10
Fairfield West	2165	335	D10
Fairlight	2094	288	C6
Fairy Bower	2095	288	K11
Faulconbridge	2776	171	B14
Fiddletown	2159	129	G3
Five Dock	2046	343	B9
Flemington	2140	340	F9
Forest Lodge	2037	344	J15
Forestville	2087	255	F9
Forty Baskets Beach	2093	288	B12
Fox Valley	2076	221	G16
Freemans Reach	2756	90	D6
Frenchs Forest	2086	256	J1
Frenchs Forest East	2086	257	B5
Fullers Bridge	2067	283	K8
Gallows Hill	2000	345	J6
Galston	2159	159	E7
Garden Island	2000	346	G4
Georges Hall	2198	367	H13
Georges Heights	2088	317	J9
Gilead	2560	539	H7
Girraween	2145	276	B12
Gladesville	2111	312	J7
Glebe	2037	345	C15
Glebe Island	2039	344	K9
Glebe Point	2037	11	H6
Glen Alpine	2560	510	D12
Glenbrook	2773	234	D13
Glendenning	2761	242	F6
Glenfield	2167	424	D6
Glenhaven	2156	217	J2
Glenmore	2570	503	G5
Glenmore Park	2745	266	H9
Glenorie	2157	128	A5
Glenwood	2768	215	G14
Glossodia	2756	59	G7
Goat Island	2000	345	E2
Golden Grove	2008	18	E8
Goodyears	2142	309	D5
Gordon	2072	253	F8
Gore Hill	2065	315	B5
Grantham Heights	2147	275	E8
Granville	2142	308	F13
Granville North	2142	308	J8
Grasmere	2570	476	A12
Grays Point	2232	491	C14
Great Mackerel Beach	2108	109	C14
Greenacre	2190	370	G10
Greendale	2745	385	H7
Greenfield Park	2176	334	B15
Green Valley	2168	363	B11
Greenwich	2065	315	B7
Greenwich Point	2065	314	H14
Greystanes	2145	306	A7
Gronos Point	2756	93	E5
Grose Vale	2753	85	F12
Grose Wold	2753	116	B7
Guildford	2161	337	J6

	Postcode	Map	Ref
Guildford East	2161	338	D7
Guildford Heights	2161	337	H5
Guildford North	2160	338	A2
Guildford West	2161	336	H4
Gundamaian	2232	521	J1
Gunnamatta Bay	2230	493	G14
Gymea	2227	491	F5
Gymea Bay	2227	491	G9
Haberfield	2045	343	D13
Hammondville	2170	396	J15
Harbord	2096	288	D1
Harbord West	2096	258	E14
Hardies	2142	309	A5
Harrington Park	2567	478	J3
Harris Park	2150	308	G5
Hassall Grove	2761	212	A15
Hawkesbury Heights	2777	174	F2
Hawkesbury River		76	C11
Haymarket	2000	345	J14
Heathcote	2233	518	E12
Hebersham	2770	241	E3
Heckenberg	2168	364	B14
Henley	2111	313	A14
Hewitt	2759	270	H12
Hillsdale	2036	406	G15
Hillside	2157	127	B3
Hilltop		307	A8
Hinchinbrook	2168	363	C16
HMAS Penguin	2091	317	G7
Hobartville	2753	118	C7
Holroyd	2160	307	K11
Holsworthy	2173	426	D5
Holsworthy Barracks	2173	426	E9
Homebush	2140	341	B4
Homebush Bay	2127	340	J2
Homebush West	2140	340	H10
Hookhams Corner	2077	191	F11
Horningsea Park	2171	392	D12
Hornsby	2077	221	E3
Hornsby Heights	2077	191	E5
Horsley Park	2164	302	E12
Hoxton Park	2171	392	F9
Hunters Hill	2110	313	G10
Huntingwood	2148	273	E13
Huntleys Point	2111	313	E14
Hurlstone Park	2193	373	A12
Hurstville	2220	432	B4
Hurstville Grove	2220	431	H11
Illawong	2234	459	E6
Ingleburn	2565	453	E9
Ingleburn Military Camp	2174	423	C10
Ingleburn Village	2174	423	C8
Ingleside	2101	197	G5
Jamisontown	2750	265	J1
Jannali	2226	460	H11
Jannali West	2226	460	F13
Kangaroo Point	2224	461	J5
Kareela	2232	461	D10
Kearns	2558	451	B15

Name	Postcode	Map	Ref
Kellyville	2155	216	D6
Kemps Creek	2171	360	C8
Kensington	2033	376	B13
Kenthurst	2156	187	E5
Kentlyn	2560	513	E5
Killara	2071	254	C11
Killarney Heights	2087	255	J15
Kings Cross	2011	4	J8
Kingsford	2032	406	J5
Kingsgrove	2208	401	H9
Kings Langley	2147	245	F6
Kings Park	2148	244	G4
Kingsway	2208	401	G15
Kingswood	2747	237	F14
Kingswood Park	2750	237	B3
Kirkham	2570	477	H8
Kirrawee	2232	491	A3
Kirribilli	2061	316	C16
Kissing Point	2074	252	B9
Kogarah	2217	433	E4
Kogarah Bay	2217	432	K14
Kogarah South	2217	433	C8
Kogarah West	2207	432	K15
Ku-Ring-Gai Chase National Park		163	G1
Kurmond	2757	86	F5
Kurnell	2231	465	K8
Kurraba Point	2089	316	E16
Kurrajong	2758	85	G3
Kurrajong Heights	2758	53	G5
Kurrajong Hills	2758	54	F14
Kyeemagh	2216	404	A13
Kyle Bay	2221	431	K15
Lakemba	2195	401	C2
Lake Parramatta	2151	278	E7
Lakesland	2572	561	A7
Lalor Park	2147	245	F13
Lane Cove	2066	314	B2
Lane Cove North	2066	284	A14
Lane Cove West	2066	283	G15
Lansdowne	2163	367	C6
Lansvale	2166	366	H7
La Perouse	2036	436	H15
Lapstone	2773	264	G2
Lavender Bay	2060	315	J14
Leichhardt	2040	343	J14
Leightonfield	2163	367	G1
Lemon Grove	2750	237	C9
Leonay	2750	235	A14
Leppington	2171	421	D7
Lethbridge Park	2770	240	F2
Leumeah	2560	482	D15
Lewisham	2049	373	F6
Liberty Grove	2138	311	C13
Lidcombe	2141	339	F9
Lilli Pilli	2229	522	E2
Lilyfield	2040	344	D11
Lindfield	2070	284	B2
Linley Point	2066	313	H7
Linns Hill	2570	443	F1
Little Bay	2036	437	E12
Liverpool	2170	395	C6
Liverpool North	2170	365	A16
Liverpool South	2170	395	B8
Liverpool West	2170	394	H5
Llandilo	2747	208	D4
Loftus	2232	489	J9
Loftus Heights	2232	489	K11
Londonderry	2753	148	C12
Long Bay	2036	437	G4
Long Point	2564	454	E10
Long Reef	2097	259	D2
Longueville	2066	314	E9
Loquat Valley	2104	168	K13
Lovett Bay	2105	168	C2
Lucas Heights	2234	487	G8
Luddenham	2745	356	E1
Lugarno	2210	429	H11
Lugarno North	2210	430	A10
Lurline Bay	2035	407	J8
Lurnea	2170	394	F10
McCallums Hill	2195	401	D8
Macdonaldtown	2042	17	K11
McGraths Hill	2756	121	H10
McMahons Point	2060	315	F15
Macquarie Fields	2564	424	H15
Macquarie Links	2565	423	D14
Macquarie Park	2113	282	H2
Macquarie University	2109	252	B15
Maianbar	2230	523	C7
Malabar	2036	437	E7
Malabar Heights	2036	437	F8
Manahan	2200	399	B4
Manly	2095	288	J8
Manly East	2095	288	J11
Manly Vale	2093	287	J2
Manly West	2093	287	J2
Maraylya	2765	124	H5
Marayong	2148	243	J4
Marayong Heights	2148	244	B4
Marayong South	2148	244	C11
Maroubra	2035	407	D11
Maroubra Junction	2035	407	D9
Maroubra South	2035	407	D15
Marrickville	2204	373	J13
Marrickville South	2204	373	J16
Marrickville West	2204	373	E14
Marsden Park	2765	181	H12
Marsfield	2122	281	H2
Martin Place	2000	345	K9
Mascot	2020	405	C4
Matraville	2036	436	H6
Mays Hill	2145	307	H5
Meadowbank	2114	311	C3
Melrose Park	2114	310	J1
Melville	2759	269	J12
Menai	2234	458	G5
Menangle	2568	538	J14
Menangle Park	2563	538	J8
Merrylands	2160	307	F11
Merrylands West	2160	306	J12
Middle Cove	2068	286	C9
Middle Dural	2158	158	F7
Middle Harbour	2088	317	F1
Middle Head	2088	318	B7
Miller	2168	393	H4
Millers Point	2000	345	F5
Mill Hill	2022	377	B4
Milperra	2214	397	E8
Milperra Bridge	2170	397	E6
Milsons Point	2061	315	K16
Minchinbury	2770	271	D8
Minto	2566	482	D3
Minto Heights	2566	483	H5
Miranda	2228	492	B6
Miranda North	2228	492	E2
Mobbs Hill	2118	280	B3
Model Farms	2153	247	H16
Mona Vale	2103	199	D5
Monterey	2217	433	H7
Mooney Mooney	2083	75	F1
Moorebank	2170	395	F10
Moorebank Village	2170	395	F12
Moore Park	2021	376	C6
Morning Bay	2108	138	G15
Mortdale	2223	431	B5
Mortlake	2137	312	A12
Mosman	2088	316	K10
Mount Annan	2567	479	D12
Mount Colah	2079	192	B2
Mount Druitt	2770	241	F13
Mount Hunter	2570	504	H9
Mount Kuring-Gai	2080	162	K10
Mount Lewis	2190	369	K15
Mount Pritchard	2170	364	G10
Mount Riverview	2774	234	G3
Mount Vernon	2759	331	B11
Mowbray Park	2571	561	E6
Mulgoa	2745	295	F11
Mulgrave	2756	151	H3
Museum	2000	345	K13
Narellan	2567	478	H11
Narellan Vale	2567	478	K11
Naremburn	2065	315	E2
Narrabeen	2101	229	C6
Narrabeen Peninsula	2101	229	E1
Narraweena	2099	258	C3
Narwee	2209	400	H11
Nelson	2765	154	J9
Neutral Bay	2089	316	B10
Neutral Bay Junction	2089	316	D9
Newington	2127	310	C12
Newport	2106	169	F10
Newport Beach	2106	170	A9
Newtown	2042	374	H5
Newtown South	2042	374	G8
Normanhurst	2076	221	G11
Normanhurst West	2120	221	D9
North Balgowlah	2093	287	E5
North Bankstown	2199	369	F11
North Bondi	2026	348	E14
Northbridge	2063	286	B15
North Cremorne	2090	316	E6
North Cronulla	2230	494	D8
North Curl Curl	2099	258	J11
North Engadine	2233	488	G
North Epping	2121	251	F
North Head	2095	290	E
North Manly	2100	258	B
Northmead	2152	277	
North Narrabeen	2101	228	
North Parramatta	2151	278	
North Richmond	2754	87	F
North Rocks	2151	249	A
North Ryde	2113	282	F
North St Ives	2075	224	
North Steyne	2095	288	
North St Marys	2760	240	
North Strathfield	2137	341	
North Sydney	2060	315	J
North Turramurra	2074	223	
North Wahroonga	2076	222	
North Willoughby	2068	285	
Northwood	2066	314	
Oakdale	2570	500	C
Oakhurst	2761	242	
Oakville	2765	153	
Oatlands	2117	279	C
Oatley	2223	431	B
Oatley West	2223	430	G
Old Guildford	2161	337	F
Old Toongabbie	2146	277	
Olympic Park	2140	340	
Orange Grove	2040	344	B
Orangeville	2570	443	E
Oran Park	2570	448	
Orchard Hills	2748	267	
Osborne Park	2066	314	
Oxford Falls	2100	227	C
Oxley Park	2760	270	
Oyster Bay	2225	461	
Paddington	2021	346	F
Padstow	2211	399	E
Padstow Heights	2211	429	
Padstow North	2211	399	C
Pagewood	2035	406	
Palm Beach	2108	139	
Panania	2213	428	
Parklea	2768	215	A
Parramatta	2150	308	
Parramatta East	2150	278	K
Peakhurst	2210	430	
Peakhurst Heights	2210	430	
Peakhurst South	2210	430	
Peakhurst West	2210	430	
Pearces Corner	2076	222	
Pendle Hill	2145	276	F
Pennant Hills	2120	220	F
Penrith	2750	236	F
Penshurst	2222	431	
Petersham	2049	373	
Phillip Bay	2036	436	
Picnic Point	2213	428	
Picton	2571	563	
Pitt Town	2756	92	H
Pitt Town Bottoms	2756	92	B
Pleasure Point	2171	427	
Plumpton	2761	242	

me	Postcode	Map	Ref
int Piper	2027	347	D8
rt Botany	2036	436	C7
rt Hacking	2229	522	J3
tts Hill	2143	369	E4
tts Point	2011	346	E10
airiewood	2176	334	G9
estons	2170	393	E11
ospect	2148	275	C14
nchbowl	2196	400	C1
nchbowl South	2196	400	B7
tney	2112	312	B7
mble	2073	253	B3
rmont	2009	345	E9
akers Hill	2763	214	B10
eenscliff	2096	288	F2
eens Park	2022	377	C5
by	2566	451	E14
msgate	2217	433	E13
msgate Beach	2217	433	G11
ndwick	2031	377	C12
ndwick South	2031	407	B2
dfern	2016	375	H4
gents Park	2143	369	C1
gentville	2745	265	E3
vesby	2212	398	G11
vesby Heights	2212	428	K6
vesby North	2212	398	J12
odes	2138	311	D10
chmond	2753	118	C4
chmond East	2753	119	B5
hmond Lowlands	2753	88	E11
verstone	2765	182	G7
verview	2066	313	K6
verwood	2210	400	C11
ckdale	2216	403	F14
dd Point	2046	343	F8
gans Hill	2154	218	G14
okwood	2141	340	D10
oty Hill	2766	272	E2
se Bay	2029	348	A8
se Bay North	2030	348	H8
sebery	2018	375	H14
sehill	2142	308	J7
selands	2196	400	G8
selea	2118	250	A12
semeadow	2560	540	F5
seville	2069	284	J3
seville Chase	2069	285	F1
ssmore	2171	389	G8
und Corner	2158	188	F14
use Hill	2155	184	E9
yal National Park	2232	520	F6
zelle	2039	344	E7
se	2560	512	E4
shcutters Bay	2011	346	G12
ssell Lea	2046	343	D4
dalmere	2116	309	E2
de	2112	312	C2
dleir	2168	394	B2
Andrews	2566	481	J4
Clair	2759	270	C11
Helens Park	2560	541	E5

	Postcode	Map	Ref
St Ives	2075	224	F12
St Ives Chase	2075	223	H3
St James	2000	345	K10
St Johns Park	2176	364	F1
St Leonards	2065	315	C4
St Marys	2760	239	E9
St Peters	2044	374	H15
Sandown	2192	309	E5
Sandringham	2219	463	E4
Sandy Point	2171	428	B10
Sans Souci	2219	433	E15
Scheyville	2756	123	G5
Schofields	2762	183	F14
Scotland Island	2105	168	G1
Scotts Hill	2570	443	K5
Seaforth	2092	287	B9
Sefton	2162	368	F4
Seven Hills	2147	275	G5
Seven Hills North	2147	246	D11
Seven Hills West	2147	245	C16
Shalvey	2770	210	K15
Shanes Park	2760	209	G7
Sherwood Grange	2160	306	G13
Silverdale	2752	354	C10
Silverwater	2128	309	G13
Smeaton Grange	2567	479	F8
Smithfield	2164	335	H3
Smithfield West	2164	335	D3
Sorlie	2086	256	B3
South Coogee	2034	407	K5
South Curl Curl	2096	258	K15
South Engadine	2233	518	H7
South Granville	2142	338	F4
South Hurstville	2221	432	B9
South Maroota	2756	65	H7
South Penrith	2750	266	G3
South Steyne	2095	288	H10
South Turramurra	2074	251	J7
South Wentworthville	2145	307	B5
South Windsor	2756	120	J15
Spectacle Island	2000	344	C1
Spit Junction	2088	317	A4
Spring Farm	2570	507	H8
Springwood	2777	201	F2
Stanhope Gardens	2768	215	E7
Stanmore	2048	374	D6
Strathfield	2135	341	E13
Strathfield South	2136	371	B6
Strawberry Hills	2010	19	K3
Summer Hill	2130	373	B4
Surry Hills	2010	346	A15
Sutherland	2232	490	C2
Sydenham	2044	374	E15
Sydney	2000	345	G8
Sydney (GPO)	2001	345	J9
Sylvania	2224	461	J10
Sylvania Heights	2224	461	F11
Sylvania Waters	2224	462	E11
Tahmoor	2573	566	E12
Tamarama	2026	378	E7
Tarban	2111	313	D12
Taren Point	2229	462	K12

	Postcode	Map	Ref
Taronga Zoological Park	2088	317	A14
Taverners Hill	2040	373	H4
Taylors Point	2107	169	C2
Telopea	2117	279	F9
Tempe	2044	404	D2
Tennyson (Hawkesbury)	2754	57	J9
Tennyson	2111	312	E10
Terrey Hills	2084	196	B7
The Basin	2108	138	G3
The Cross Roads	2170	424	B3
The Oaks	2570	502	G11
Theresa Park	2570	444	H5
The Rocks	2000	345	K4
The Slopes	2754	56	H7
The Spit	2088	287	C13
The Trongate	2142	338	F2
Thirlmere	2572	565	E4
Thompsons Corner	2125	249	J5
Thornleigh	2120	220	J13
Tom Uglys Point	2221	462	F5
Toongabbie	2146	276	E8
Toongabbie West	2146	276	G7
Town Hall	2000	3	H6
Towra Point	2231	464	D4
Tregear	2770	240	D6
Turramurra	2074	222	G15
Turrella	2205	403	E4
Ultimo	2007	345	E14
Undercliffe	2206	403	F3
University of NSW	2052	376	G14
University of Sydney	2006	375	B1
Valley Heights	2777	202	H6
Varroville	2566	451	H5
Vaucluse	2030	348	C4
Vaucluse Heights	2030	348	D6
Villawood	2163	367	G3
Villawood East	2163	367	G4
Vineyard	2765	152	H11
Voyager Point	2171	427	E3
Wahroonga	2076	222	G6
Wahroonga South	2076	221	H16
Waitara	2077	221	J2
Waitara East	2077	222	B3
Wakehurst	2085	226	B16
Wakeley	2176	334	K13
Wallacia	2745	324	F13
Wallgrove	2164	272	G11
Wareemba	2046	343	A5
Warragamba	2752	353	E6
Warrawee	2074	222	G10
Warriewood	2102	199	A10
Warriewood Beach	2102	199	F10
Warrimoo	2774	203	F13
Warumbul	2229	521	K7
Warwick Farm	2170	365	K12
Waterfall	2233	519	C14
Waterloo	2017	375	G7
Watsons Bay	2030	318	G11
Wattle Grove	2173	396	A15

	Postcode	Map	Ref
Waverley	2024	377	G7
Waverley South	2024	377	H10
Waverton	2060	315	E13
Wedderburn	2560	540	C12
Wentworthville	2145	277	B14
Werombi	2570	443	F7
Werrington	2747	239	C12
Werrington County	2747	238	K7
Werrington Downs	2747	238	B4
West Gordon	2072	253	C10
West Hoxton	2171	392	B4
Westleigh	2120	220	F4
West Lindfield	2070	283	G2
Westmead	2145	307	E1
West Pennant Hills	2125	249	D4
West Pymble	2073	252	J11
West Ryde	2114	281	G14
Wetherill Park	2164	334	D2
Whalan	2770	241	B11
Whale Beach	2107	140	D6
Wheeler Heights	2097	228	F9
White Bay	2039	344	K7
Wilberforce	2756	92	B4
Wiley Park	2195	400	G1
Willmot	2770	210	D12
Willoughby	2068	285	H11
Wilton	2571	568	K14
Windsor	2756	121	C11
Windsor Downs	2756	180	J2
Wingala	2099	258	H11
Winji Jimmi	2103	169	D14
Winmalee	2777	173	F10
Winston Hills	2153	277	C2
Wollstonecraft	2065	315	D9
Wondabyne	2256	76	H1
Woodbine	2560	481	H13
Woodcroft	2767	243	G8
Woodpark	2164	306	G14
Woollahra	2025	377	B1
Woollahra Point	2028	347	G7
Woolloomooloo	2011	346	D11
Woolooware	2230	493	E11
Woolwich	2110	314	F13
Woronora	2232	460	A15
Woronora Heights	2233	489	F4
Wynyard	2000	1	E16
Yagoona	2199	369	C11
Yanderra	2574	567	D15
Yarra Junction	2036	436	K12
Yarramundi	2753	145	H7
Yarrawarrah	2233	489	F12
Yellow Rock	2777	204	D4
Yennora	2161	337	D10
Yowie Bay	2228	492	A12
Yowie Point	2228	492	A15
Zetland	2017	375	K11

[ABBREVIATIONS USED IN THE STREET INDEX]

ABBREVIATIONS FOR DESIGNATIONS

Alley	al
Approach	app
Arcade	arc
Avenue	av
Bend	bnd
Boulevard	bvd
Bowl	bl
Brace	br
Brae	br
Break	brk
Brook	brk
Broadway	bwy
Brow	brw
Bypass	bps
Centre	ctr
Chase	ch
Circle	cir
Circuit	cct
Circus	crc
Close	cl
Common	cmn
Concourse	cnc
Copse	cps
Corner	cnr
Corso	cso
Court	ct
Courtyard	cyd
Cove	cov
Crescent	cr
Crest	cst
Cross	cs
Crossing	csg
Curve	cve
Dale	dle
Down/s	dn
Drive	dr
Driveway	dwy
East	e
Edge	edg
Elbow	elb
End	end
Entrance	ent
Esplanade	esp
Expressway	exp
Fairway	fy
Freeway	fwy
Frontage	fr
Garden/s	gdn
Gate/s	gte
Gateway	gwy
Glade	gld
Glen	gln
Grange	gra
Green	grn
Grove	gr
Grovet	gr
Haven	hvn
Heights	hts
Highway	hwy
Hill	hill
Junction	jnc
Key	key
Lane	la
Link	lk
Loop	lp
Mall	ml
Mead	md
Meander	mdr
Mews	mw
Motorway	mwy
Nook	nk
North	n
Outlook	out
Parade	pde
Park	pk
Parkway	pky
Pass	ps
Pathway	pwy
Place	pl
Plaza	plz
Pocket	pkt
Point/Port	pt
Promenade	prm
Quadrant	qd
Quay/s	qy
Ramble	ra
Reach	rch
Reserve	res
Rest	rst
Retreat	rt
Return	rtn
Ridge	rdg
Rise	ri
Road	rd
Roadway	rdy
Route	rte
Row	row
Serviceway	swy
South	s
Square	sq
Strand	sd
Street	st
Tarn	tn
Terrace	tce
Tollway	twy
Top	top
Tor	tor
Track	tr
Trail	trl
Turn	trn
Underpass	ups
Vale	va
View	vw
Vista	vst
Walk	wk
Walkway	wky
Way	wy
West	w
Wynd	wyn

ABBREVIATIONS FOR SUBURB NAMES

Where it has been necessary to abbreviate the suburb names in the street index the following conventions have been used.
If any difficulty is experienced with the suburban manes refer to the SUBURBS and LOCALITIES index.

Airport	Aprt
Basin	Bsn
Bay	B
Beach	Bch
Bridge	Br
Central	Ctrl
Chase	Ch
Corner	Cnr
Creek	Ck
Crossing	Csg
Down/s	Dn
East	E
Field/s	Fd
Flat	Fl
Forest	Frst
Garden/s	Gdn
Grove	Gr
Gully	Gly
Harbor/our	Hbr
Head/s	Hd
Headland	Hd
Heights	Ht
Hill/s	Hl
Island	I
Junction	Jctn
Lagoon	Lgn
Lakes	L
Lodge	Ldg
Lookout	Lkt
Lower	Lr
Meadows/s	Mdw
Mount	Mt
Mountain/s	Mtn
North	N
Paradise	Pdse
Park	Pk
Plain/s	Pl
Plateau	Plat
Pocket	Pkt
Point/Port	Pt
Range	Rge
Reach	Rch
Reserve	Res
Ridge	Rdg
River	R
Rocks	Rks
Saint	St
South	S
Terminal	Term
University	Uni
Upper	Up
Valley	Vy
Vale	Va
Village	Vill
Waters	Wtr
West	W

NON-STANDARD ABBREVIATIONS FOR SUBURB NAMES

Banksmeadow	Bnksmeadw
Bankstown Airport	Bnkstn Aprt
Brighton-Le-Sands	Btn-Le-Sds
Cabramatta West	Cabramtta W
Cambridge Gardens	Cmbrdg Gdn
Cambridge Park	Cambrdg Pk
Campbelltown	Campbelltwn
Camperdown	Camperdwn
Centennial Park	Centnnial Pk
Chatswood West	Chatswd W
Chipping Norton	Chipping Ntn
Claremont Meadows	Clarmnt Ms
Edmondson Park	Edmndsn Pk
Faulconbridge	Faulconbdg
Freemans Reach	Freemns Rch
Great Mackerel Beach	Gt Mckrl Bch
Greenfield Park	Greenfld Pk
Hammondville	Hamondvle
Harrington Park	Harringtn Pk
Hawkesbury Heights	Hawkesbry Ht
Hinchinbrook	Hinchinbrk
Homebush West	Homebsh W
Horningsea Park	Horngsea Pk
Huntingwood	Huntingwd
Kings Langley	Kings Lngly
Ku-ring-gai Chase National Park	Krngai Ch N P
Lethbridge Park	Lethbrdg Pk
Macquarie Fields	Mcquarie Fd
Macquarie Links	Mcquarie Lk
Macquarie Park	Mcquarie Pk
Meadowbank	Meadowbnk
Merrylands West	Merrylnds W
Mooney Mooney	Mooney
Mount Ku-ring-gai	Mt Krngai
North Turramurra	N Turramrra
North Wahroonga	N Wahrnga
North Willoughby	N Willghby
Old Guildford	Old Guildfrd
Old Toongabbie	Old Tngabbie
Pitt Town Bottoms	Pitt Twn Bttms
Rosemeadow	Rsemeadow
Royal National Park	Royal N P
Rushcutters Bay	Rcuttrs Bay
Smeaton Grange	Smeaton Gra
South Wentworthville	S Wntwthvle
Stanhope Gardens	Stanhpe Gdn
Warwick Farm	Warwck Frm
Wentworthville	Wentwthvle
Werrington County	Wrrngtn Cty
Werrington Downs	Wrrngtn Dns
West Pennant Hills	W Pnnant Hl
Wollstonecraft	Wollstncraft
Woolloomooloo	Woolmloo

SPECIAL NOTE

The LANES shown in *italics* in the street index are not chartered on the street maps.
For reasons of clarity it is not practical to show them.

A

ON
Carlingford.........249 J16
Plumpton...........242 A11
Silverdale...........353 H12
Wahroonga........222 A8
DAL
Ingleburn...........453 H8
ROO
Ryde..................282 E16
E RECEVEUR
Little Bay............437 A12
ERTON
Jamisontown 266 C4
EVILLE
Prestons............392 K12
EY
Greenacre..........370 F11
Parramatta.........278 F15
Wrrngtn Dns, off
Abbey Row.........238 D5
Cherrybrook.......219 E14
Kemps Ck...........330 G7
Wrrngtn Dns......238 D5
Hunters Hill........313 A7
Randwick...........377 A12
Glenhaven..........218 B5
OTFORD
Kensington.........376 E9
Kensington.........376 F9
OTSBURY
Horsley Pk.........332 B5
OTSFORD
Abbotsford.........342 H1
Homebush.........341 B10
Picton...............563 C1
OTSFORD COVE
Abbotsford.........342 K2
OTT
Sefton................338 F15
Edensor Pk........333 H14
Cammeray, off
Abbott St............315 J4
Glenorie.............128 D10
Ingleburn...........452 J10
Artarmon...........284 K16
Heathcote..........518 D9
N Curl Curl.........258 E10
Seven Hills.........246 A14
Balgowlah Ht......287 G14
Cammeray.........315 J4
Coogee.............377 E14
Merrylands.........308 D16
BOTTS
Mt Hunter..........504 J1
Kemps Ck..........330 E7
DALE
Glenwood..........215 H13
ECKETT
Ashfield.............372 H4
Granville............308 G9
Granville............308 J9
EL
Petersham...........15 H10
Cronulla.............493 K11
Canley Ht...........335 C16
Greenacre..........370 F15
Jamisontown.....236 D15
ELIA
Cherrybrook.......219 K5
Tahmoor............566 A11
. Blacktown..........274 F12
ER
Mount Druitt......271 C2
ERCORN
Bexley................402 G13
ERCROMBIE
Seven Hills.........275 E10
Sydney...................A K12
Cabramatta W....365 B8
Chippendale.........19 A1
Darlington............18 E8
Leumeah............482 C16
Redfern................19 A5
ERDARE
Cartwright..........394 E4
ERDEEN
. Glenmore Pk......266 H8
Stanhpe Gdn......215 F9
Busby.................363 K16
St Andrews........452 B13

rd. Winston Hills......277 E3
st. Bossley Park......334 B12
st. Cmbrdg Pk.........237 K8
ABERFELDY
cr. St Andrews........482 A1
ABERFOYLE
pl. Grasmere.........475 K15
rd. Wedderburn.......540 C9
rd. Wedderburn.......541 J16
ABERGELDIE
st. Dulwich Hill........373 B8
ABERMAIN
pl. Cartwright..........394 D4
ABERNETHY
st. Seaforth............286 K9
ABHAY
pl. Glenwood..........215 B16
pl. Glenwood..........245 B1
ABICHT
cl. Kemps Ck..........360 G10
ABIGAIL
la. Newtown.............17 E11
st. Hunters Hill........313 D8
st. Seven Hills.........275 J4
ABINGDON
rd. Roseville............284 B5
st. Chipping Ntn......366 F16
st. N Balgowlah.......287 G5
ABINGTON
cr. Glen Alpine........510 A14
ABOUD
av. Kingsford...........406 C2
ABOUKIR
st. Dover Ht............348 G12
st. Rockdale............403 F16
ABRAHAM
cl. Menai................458 H11
st. Rooty Hill...........241 J12
ABRAHAMS
wy. Claymore...........481 E10
ABUKLEA
rd. Eastwood...........281 G3
rd. Epping...............281 D2
rd. Marsfield............281 G3
ACACIA
av. Glenmore Pk......265 G8
av. Greenacre..........370 D15
av. Oakdale.............500 B13
av. Prestons............394 A15
av. Punchbowl..........400 D2
av. Ruse..................512 F7
av. Ryde..................312 D6
av. St Marys............239 G14
cl. Turramurra..........252 D3
ct. Narellan Vale......478 K11
ct. Oatlands.............279 B8
gr. Stanhpe Gdn......215 E10
la. Belmore..............371 F16
la. Eastwood............281 H8
la. Roseville.............284 Z9
pl. Greystanes..........305 E11
pl. Newington, off
Watt Av...............310 B12
rd. Berowra.............133 D15
rd. Kirrawee.............490 H6
rd. Seaforth..............286 K6
rd. Sutherland..........490 H6
rd.n,Kirrawee...........490 H4
rd.n,Sutherland.........490 H4
st. Belmore..............371 F16
st. Cabramatta..........365 H8
st. Collaroy Plat.......228 H10
st. Eastwood............281 H8
st. Oatley.................431 A10
st. Rooty Hill.............272 D4
st. Rydalmere...........279 J16
tce. Bidwill................211 F14
ACACIA PARK
wy. Acacia Gdn.........214 J16
ACCLAIM
la. Luddenham.........356 F12
ACE
av. Fairfield..............336 F9
ACER
ct. Cherrybrook.........219 H8
gln. Castle Hill..........218 F16
ACHIEVEMENT
av. Glenbrook...........264 D3
ACHILLES
rd. Engadine.............488 E14
ACHILPA
cl. Bangor................459 H15

ACKLING
st. Baulkham Hl.......247 H8
ACLAND
st. Guildford............337 D5
ACOLA
ct. Wattle Grove......396 B15
ACORN
cl. Mt Colah............162 E13
gr. Elderslie............507 F2
st. Emu Plains.........235 A11
wy. Acacia Gdn.........214 J14
ACRES
la. Ingleburn............453 F8
pl. Bligh Park..........150 H7
rd. Kellyville.............216 D5
ACRI
st. Prestons............393 E15
ACRON
rd. St Ives...............224 G11
ACROPOLIS
av. Rooty Hill...........271 H3
ACTINOTUS
av. Caringbah..........492 J12
ACTION
st. Greenacre..........370 A9
ACTIVE
pl. Kellyville.............185 K14
ACTON
st. Croydon.............342 E13
st. Hurlstone Pk......372 J13
st. Sutherland.........490 F1
ACUBA
gr. Quakers Hill.......214 C11
ADA
av. Brookvale...........258 D12
av. Strathfield..........341 A16
av. Wahroonga.........222 C11
av.s,Wahroonga.......222 C13
la. Erskineville...........18 C14
la. Randwick............377 B14
pl. Carlingford..........249 J15
pl. Doonside............243 D8
pl. Pyrmont................12 H6
pl. Ultimo...................12 J9
st. Bexley..................402 C16
st. Canley Vale.........366 E3
st. Concord..............341 H9
st. Cremorne............316 F7
st. Erskineville............18 C14
st. Harris Park..........308 E5
st. Kingsgrove..........401 G6
st. North Ryde..........282 D9
st. Oatley.................431 D11
st. Padstow..............429 F3
st. Randwick.............377 C15
ADAH
st. Guildford............338 D4
ADAIR
pl. East Killara.........254 H8
ADALUMA
av. Bangor...............459 F15
ADAM
cl. Berowra..............133 H10
cl. S Windsor...........150 J3
pl. Glenhaven...........217 H2
pl. Lalor Park...........245 E10
pl. Mcquarie Fd........424 A14
st. Campsie.............372 C10
st. Fairfield..............336 E9
st. Guildford.............338 C3
st. Ryde...................282 C15
ADAMINABY
st. Heckenberg.........364 B12
ADAMS
av. Malabar..............437 F7
av. Turramurra.........223 E11
cr. St Marys.............269 K3
la. Baulkham Hl.......247 D11
la. Bondi Jctn............22 K9
la. Concord..............342 B1
rd. Luddenham.........356 J3
st. Curl Curl.............258 J13
st. Frenchs Frst........256 C3
ADAMSON
av. Dundas Vy..........280 B11
av. Thornleigh..........221 B8
st. Glenfield.............424 H12
ADARE
pl. Killarney Ht.........255 K15
pl. Tregear...............240 E7
ADCOCH
pl. Bidwill.................211 B16

ADDER
st. Beecroft..............250 G4
ADDERLEY
st.e, Lidcombe..........309 J16
st.w,Auburn..............309 D13
ADDERSTONE
av. N Sydney................6 C11
ADDERTON
rd. Carlingford..........279 H6
rd. Dundas...............279 H6
rd. Telopea...............279 H6
ADDINGTON
av. Ryde..................311 J2
ADDISCOMBE
rd. Manly Vale..........288 C4
ADDISON
av. Concord..............341 K7
av. Little Bay.............437 G13
av. Roseville.............285 A3
gr. Bidwill.................211 C16
rd. Ingleside.............197 F7
rd. Manly..................288 G14
rd. Marrickville...........15 J14
rd. Petersham............15 J14
st. Balmain..................7 C7
st. Kensington..........376 D12
st. Thirlmere............562 E8
st. Wetherill Pk........334 E6
wy. West Hoxton.......392 A13
ADDLESTONE
rd. Merrylands..........307 G14
ADDY
la. N Strathfield........341 F7
ADELAIDE
av. Campbelltwn.......512 B5
av. E Lindfield...........254 K14
gr. Bella Vista...........246 G2
la. Oxley Park, off
Adelaide St.........270 G2
pde. Woollahra............22 K3
pl. Cecil Hills............362 J4
pl. Surry Hills..............19 K3
pl. Sylvania...............461 K8
rd. Padstow..............429 F3
st. Balgowlah Ht.......287 G14
st. Belmore...............371 F14
st. Bondi Jctn.............22 K3
st. Meadowbnk.........311 B2
st. Melrose Pk..........311 B2
st. Oxley Park...........269 K1
st. Rooty Hill.............242 A14
st. St Marys..............269 K1
st. Surry Hills..............19 K2
st. West Ryde...........281 B16
st. Woollahra..............22 K3
ADELINE
st. Bass Hill..............367 K7
st. Rydalmere...........279 D15
ADELLA
av. Blacktown...........243 K15
ADELONG
cl. Emu Plains..........234 K7
cl. Wakeley...............334 H13
pl. Camden S............507 B13
pl. Wahroonga..........222 C13
st. Sutherland...........490 D3
ADELPHI
cr. Doonside.............243 D8
rd. Marsfield..............282 C5
st. Rouse Hill............184 J7
ADEN
st. Quakers Hill........214 E13
st. Seaforth..............287 B10
ADEPT
la. Bankstown...........399 F6
ADHARA
st. Erskine Park.......301 A1
ADINA
av. Phillip Bay...........436 K12
cl. Fairfield W...........335 F12
pl. Beverly Hills.........401 C12
pl. Bradbury..............511 D15
rd. Curl Curl...............258 K13
st. Miranda...............491 K5
st. Seven Hills...........245 K14
st. Telopea................279 G7
wy. La Perouse..........436 K13
ADLER
pde. Greystanes.........306 G7
pde. Greystanes.........306 G9
ADMIRALTY
wy. Minto..................482 H7

ADNA
st. Plumpton..............242 C6
ADNUM
la. Bankstown, off
Fetherstone St....369 E16
ADOLPHUS
cl. Hinchinbrk...........363 B14
st. Balmain....................8 B10
st. Canley Ht.............365 G4
st. Naremburn...........315 G2
ADOR
av. Rockdale..............403 G16
ADRIAN
av. Lurnea.................394 D8
ct. Carlingford...........279 D4
pl. Balgowlah Ht........287 H14
pl. Greystanes...........306 F6
st. Glenwood.............215 J14
st. Mcquarie Fd.........424 A14
ADRIENNE
st. Glendenning..........242 F5
ADVANCE
st. Schofields............183 C16
ADY
st. Hunters Hill..........313 J11
AEOLIA
la. Randwick, off
Aeolia St..............377 B16
st. Randwick.............377 B16
AEOLUS
av. Ryde...................282 A13
AERO
rd. Ingleburn.............453 C2
st. Btn-le-Sds............433 H1
AERODROME
rd. Cobbitty...............476 K10
AFTERNOON
ct. St Clair.................270 C14
AFTON
pl. Quakers Hill.........214 E12
AGAR
st. Marrickville............16 E16
AGATE
pl. Eagle Vale............481 D8
AGATHA
pl. Oakhurst..............241 K4
AGINCOURT
pl. Glenwood.............245 H2
rd. Marsfield..............281 J2
AGIUS
st. Winston Hills........277 C1
AGNES
st. Strathfield............341 E16
AGNEW
cl. Bossley Park........334 C11
AGONIS
cl. Banksia................403 G12
AGRA
pl. Riverstone...........183 A4
AGRAFE
pl. Minchinbury.........272 A10
AGRIPPA
st. Rsemeadow.........540 G2
AHEARN
av. S Coogee............407 H4
AHMET
ct. Oakhurst..............242 D2
AIKEN
rd. W Pnnant Hl.........249 A7
AILSA
av. Blacktown............275 B3
cl. E Lindfield............255 B10
pl. Riverstone...........182 K5
wy. Canley Vale.........366 G6
AIMEE
st. Quakers Hill.........214 C9
AINSBURY
rd. St Marys..............269 F6
AINSLEE
ct. Cranebrook..........206 J9
AINSLEY
av. Glendenning.........242 E2
AINSLIE
cl. St Ives Ch............224 A6
pde. Carlingford.........249 H14
pl. Condell Park.........398 G2
pl. Ruse....................512 G4
st. Fairfield W...........335 F8
st. Kingsford.............407 A4

AINSWORTH
cr. Wetherill Pk 334 H3
st. Leichhardt...........10 D11
st. Lilyfield...............10 D11
AINTREE
cl. Casula................424 E1
AIRD
st. Parramatta.........308 B4
AIRDS
rd. Leumeah............482 A12
rd. Minto.................482 C7
AIRDSLEY
la. Bradbury............511 D13
AIREDALE
av. Earlwood 402 F6
AIRLIE
cr. Cecil Hills...........362 G3
pl. Oatlands 278 J10
AIRPORT
av. Bnkstn Aprt........367 K16
dr. Mascot 404 D4
AIRSTRIP
rd. Pitt Town 93 B15
AITAPE
cr. Whalan 240 H10
pl. Holsworthy 426 C3
AITCHANDAR
rd. Ryde..................312 E1
AITKEN
av. Queenscliff.........288 F3
AJAX
pl. Blacktown...........245 D8
pl. Engadine............488 J14
AJUGA
ct. Voyager Pt 427 D5
AKMA
cl. Bonnyrigg...........363 K9
AKOONAH
cl. Westleigh...........220 F2
pl. Peakhurst 430 C9
AKORA
av. Baulkham Hl 247 C5
cl. Chipping Ntn......396 F6
st. Frenchs Frst.......256 F6
AKRON
pl. Toongabbie........275 F14
AKUNA
av. Bangor...............459 G14
av. Bangor...............459 G15
av. Bradbury............511 F15
av. Bradbury............511 G14
la. Mona Vale..........199 C4
ALABAMA
av. Bexley................432 F3
ALABASTER
pl. Eagle Vale 481 D8
ALADORE
av. Cabramatta 365 F8
ALAINE
pl. Cecil Park...........332 D10
ALAM
pl. Campbelltwn......511 K3
st. Blacktown..........244 B12
st. Colyton..............270 B6
ALAMAR
cr. Quakers Hill 214 F16
ALAMEDA
wy. Warriewood 198 K6
ALAMEIN
av. Carlingford.........250 A14
av. Liverpool............394 K3
av. Mt Annan...........479 A10
av. Narellan Vale......479 A10
av. Narraweena........258 C4
rd. Bossley Park.......334 A5
rd. Revesby Ht 428 J6
st. Engadine............489 A10
ALA MOANA
rd. E Kurrajong..........57 B2
ALAN
av. Hornsby.............191 E10
av. Ryde..................281 K11
av. Seaforth.............287 A11
rd. Berowra Ht.........133 B8
st. Box Hill...............154 B16
st. Cammeray 316 C4
st. Fairfield..............336 G12
st. Mount Druitt 271 B4
st. Rydalmere 309 B2
st. Yagoona 368 J11

ALANA
dr. W Pnnant Hl.......248 J6
pl. St Ives Ch 224 A3
ALANAS
av. Oatlands 278 K11
ALAN BOND
pl. Marsfield............282 B3
ALASKA
la. Parramatta, off Thomas St.........308 E1
ALBAN
st. Lidcombe............339 J1
ALBANY
cl. Wakeley 334 H15
cr. East Killara 254 K5
la. Colyton...............270 G8
la. Crows Nest 315 E5
la. St Leonards 315 E5
la. Stanmore..............16 G6
pl. Kareela 461 D14
pl. Kearns 451 C16
rd. Petersham 16 B8
rd. Stanmore..............16 B8
st. Busby 363 H15
st. Crows Nest 315 E6
st. Ermington............280 D12
st. St Leonards 315 E6
ALBATROSS
av. Hinchinbrk..........393 C2
cct. Woronora Ht......489 D5
ALBEMARLE
av. Rose Bay 348 B11
la. Rose Bay, off Albemarle Av..........348 C11
pl. Cecil Hills...........362 F1
st. Dundas...............279 G14
st. Narrabeen...........229 B3
ALBERMARLE
st. Marrickville 373 F13
st. Newtown 17 C11
ALBERT
av. Chatswood.........284 H11
av. Sylvania.............461 G13
av. Thirlmere 562 B16
cr. Burwood.............342 B14
cr. Croydon..............342 B14
dr. Killara 283 D2
la. Bronte.................377 K9
la. Forest Lodge.........11 F14
la. Hornsby..............191 H16
la. Hornsby..............221 H1
la. Chatswood, off Albert Av...........284 H10
la. Earlwood, off Banks Rd..........403 B4
pde. Ashfield 342 H16
pde. Rooty Hill...........272 E4
pl. Bligh Park 150 E6
pl. Leumeah.............482 G12
rd. Auburn 339 A11
rd. Avalon 140 D11
rd. Beecroft..............250 C4
rd. Croydon Pk.........372 C8
rd. Strathfield 341 A13
sq. Paddington 21 C1
st. Banksia...............403 F12
st. Belfield................371 F13
st. Belmore 371 F13
st. Berala 339 D9
st. Bexley.................432 E1
st. Botany 405 J12
st. Bronte.................377 K9
st. Cabramatta 366 A10
st. Campsie 371 F13
st. Drummoyne.........343 K2
st. Edgecliff................14 A13
st. Erskineville.............17 J13
st. Forest Lodge.........11 E13
st. Gladesville 312 J6
st. Granville 308 F9
st. Greenwich............314 K13
st. Guildford W 306 J16
st. Harbord 288 G1
st. Hornsby...............191 J16
st. Hurstville 431 K9
st. Ingleburn 453 A8
st. Leichhardt..............15 E5
st. Lurnea 394 E9
st. McGraths Hl.........122 A10
st. Mount Druitt 270 J2
st. Narrabeen 229 A4
st. Newtown 17 B10
st. N Parramatta........278 C14
st. Paddington 21 D1
st. Petersham 15 K14

st. Randwick............377 B13
st. Redfern.................19 D9
st. Revesby..............398 H14
st. Riverstone 153 A13
st. Rozelle..................10 J4
st. St Peters............374 J13
st. Sydney ....B F8
st. Sydney 2 A12
st. Warrimoo 203 B14
st. Werrington..........239 A11
st.e, N Parramatta......278 H15
st.s, Hornsby............221 H2
ALBERTA
av. Cowan 104 B13
st. Jannali 460 G12
st. Sydney ....F D5
ALBERTO
st. Lilyfield 10 F2
ALBI
pl. Randwick............377 C14
ALBILLO
pl. Eschol Park.........481 D3
ALBION
av. Merrylands..........307 J13
av. Paddington 4 F16
av. Pymble 252 K1
cl. Bossley Park 333 E9
la. Annandale.............16 E4
la. Mosman 317 B6
la. St Peters.............374 F14
la. Waverley.............377 G9
pl. Baulkham Hl 246 J2
pl. Engadine.............489 A8
pl. Sydney ....E G1
st. Annandale.............16 E3
st. Clovelly...............377 F10
st. Concord...............342 B2
st. Dundas................279 F13
st. Harris Park..........308 E6
st. Leichhardt..............16 E3
st. Marrickville 373 J13
st. Pennant Hills.......220 J16
st. Randwick.............377 F10
st. Roselands............401 A7
st. Rozelle.................344 D8
st. Surry Hills..............F B12
st. Surry Hills...............3 J14
st. Waverley..............377 F10
wy. Surry Hills..............F C13
ALBUERA
rd. Epping................281 C3
ALBURY
av. Campbelltwn.......512 C5
ct. Harringtn Pk.......478 G7
st. Yagoona 368 J9
ALBYN
la. Bexley.................402 K14
rd. Strathfield 341 C15
st. Bexley.................402 K14
ALCHIN
st. Dharruk 241 B7
ALCOCK
av. Casula.................424 D3
av. Casula.................424 F4
ALCOOMIE
st. Villawood 367 D3
ALDAN
pl. St Clair................269 J14
ALDEBARAN
st. Cranebrook 207 F6
ALDEN
gr. Oakhurst 241 K1
ALDER
av. Lane Cove W......283 H15
dr. St Ives 224 E5
gr. Menai 458 K14
st. Clontarf................287 H15
ALDERNEY
rd. Merrylands..........307 A10
st. Minto...................482 G7
ALDERSON
av. Liverpool.............394 H9
av. North Rocks.........248 F11
ALDERTON
av. Springwood 201 H1
ALDGATE
st. Prospect 275 B12
st. Sutherland 490 G5
ALDINGA
pl. Bradbury.............541 D1
pl. Clarmnt Ms.........268 H2
pl. Forestville 255 H10

ALDINGTON
rd. Kemps Ck 300 G13
ALDOUS
cl. Hornsby Ht 161 J8
ALE
st. Ingleburn 454 A10
ALEPPO
st. Quakers Hill 214 F13
ALERT
pl. Yagoona 368 E15
ALETA
cl. Wahroonga.........251 G2
wy. Seven Hills.........275 K6
ALEX
av. Schofields...........213 H5
pl. Baulkham Hl 217 A16
pl. Bligh Park 150 H9
rd. Yowie Bay..........492 B13
ALEXANDER
av. Mosman 317 D10
av. N Willghby 285 F9
av. Taren Point 462 J14
cr. Mcquarie Fd........423 J16
la. Surry Hills.............20 C2
la. Crows Nest, off Pacific Hwy..........315 G7
pde. Blacktown..........273 J8
pde. Carlingford.........250 B15
pde. Roseville 284 F6
rd. Avalon 140 E11
st. Alexandria.............18 G13
st. Auburn 339 A14
st. Balmain 8 B7
st. Bligh Park 150 B6
st. Collaroy 229 A12
st. Coogee 407 G2
st. Crows Nest 315 G7
st. Dundas Vy 280 A7
st. Eveleigh 18 G12
st. Manly 288 F6
st. Paddington 21 B2
st. Penshurst 431 G8
st. Smithfield 335 H7
st. Surry Hills.............20 C2
st. Sylvania..............461 K11
st. Tamarama 378 C6
st. Yagoona 368 K9
ALEXANDRA
av. Croydon.............342 E12
av. Westmead 277 E16
cct. Camperdwn 11 E16
cct. St Clair..............269 J8
cr. Bayview 169 A13
cr. Glenbrook............264 E1
la. Glebe 11 G8
la. St Clair, off Alexandra Cct.....269 J8
pde. Rockdale...........403 C16
pl. Carlingford..........249 E14
pl. Glendenning.........242 H5
rd. Glebe 11 G8
st. Ashfield 342 H14
st. Blacktown............274 E14
st. Concord..............341 H9
st. Drummoyne........343 K2
st. Hunters Hill..........313 J11
st. Turrella 403 E6
ALEXANDRIA
av. Eastwood.............281 E6
la. Surry Hills.............20 C6
pde. S Coogee 407 J5
pde. Wahroonga 221 J3
pde. Waitara 221 J3
pl. Busby.................363 J16
ALEXANDRINA
ct. Wattle Grove 396 B14
ALEXIS
pl. Rsemeadow.........540 H3
ALFA
pl. Ingleburn 453 F13
ALFORD
rd. Kellyville..............215 H1
st. Quakers Hill 243 D4
ALFORDS POINT
rd. Alfords Point......429 C15
rd. Illawong 459 B5
rd. Menai 458 G10
rd. Padstow Ht.........429 C15
ALFRED
av. Woolooware.......493 J8
la. Rozelle..................10 K3
la. Mascot, off Wentworth Av....405 F6
pl. Quakers Hill 213 K8

pl. S Turramrra.......252
rd. Brookvale...........258
rd. Chipping Ntn......396
rd. Forest Lodge........11
rd. Narraweena........258
st. Annandale............10
st. Bronte................377
st. Campsie 402
st. Cromer 228
st. Croydon.............342
st. Granville 308
st. Harris Park.........308
st. Hurstville 432
st. Leichhardt............10
st. Lewisham 15
st. Lilyfield 10
st. Marrickville 373
st. Mascot 405
st. Merrylands.........307
st. Narraweena........258
st. Parramatta.........308
st. Ramsgate Bch....433
st. Rhodes 311
st. Rhodes 311
st. Rosehill 308
st. Rozelle.................11
st. St Peters............374
st. Sans Souci.........433
st. Sydney ....B
st. Sydney 1
st. Westmead 277
st. Woolwich...........314
st.n, Neutral Bay 5
st.n, N Sydney 5
st.s, Milsons Point ....K
st.s, Milsons Point.........5
ALFREDA
st. Coogee 377
ALGERNON
st. Oatley 461
ALGIE
cr. Kingswood.........238
ALGONA
st. Bilgola 169
ALI
pde. Newington 310
pl. Glenwood 245
ALIBERTI
dr. Blacktown 273
ALICANTE
st. Minchinbury.......271
ALICE
av. Newtown 374
av. Russell Lea 343
cl. Collaroy Plat.......228
ct. Cherrybrook.......219
la. Newtown 374
la. Randwick, off Pine St..............377
pl. Cecil Hills...........362
st. Auburn 339
st. Caringbah 492
st. Harris Park.........308
st. Jannali 460
st. Mcquarie Fd.......424
st. Newtown 374
st. Padstow 399
st. Rooty Hill...........241
st. Rosehill 308
st. Rozelle.................10
st. Sans Souci.........433
st. Seven Hills.........275
st. Turramurra 222
st. Wiley Park.........400
st.n, Wiley Park.........400
ALICE HANCOX
cl. Castle Hill, off Vittoria Smith Av...218
ALICIA
la. Roselands..........401
pl. Kenthurst...........155
rd. Mt Krng-gai........162
ALICK
st. Cabramatta 365
ALINDA
cl. Middle Dural 157
ALINGA
pl. Doonside 243
st. Cabramatta W 365
ALINJARRA
rd. Tennyson.............58
ALINTA
cl. Thornleigh 221

SON
Coogee 377 G14
Centnnial Pk 16 K16
Coogee 377 E14
Cromer 228 H15
Kensington 376 E8
Randwick 376 E8
Ashbury 372 D7
Croydon Pk 372 D7
Eastwood 281 J7
Roseville 284 C7
Russell Lea 343 E7
Seven Hills 245 D16
KARINGA
Miranda 491 H8
KIRA
Narraweena 257 J3
Caringbah 493 C16
Carlingford 249 F14
St Ives 224 B15
KOO
Little Bay 437 B10
KOOMIE
Forestville 255 J9
S Penrith 266 H2
Pymble 252 K8
Beverly Hills 401 B10
LAMBEE
Beverly Hills 401 B11
LAMBI
Colyton 270 G6
LAMBIE
Caringbah 492 G15
E Lindfield 255 A13
Northmead 277 G7
Allambie Ht 257 B9
Castle Cove 285 K5
Edensor Pk 333 F14
Frenchs Frst 257 A7
LAN
Belmore 371 C14
Clovelly 377 K12
Ryde 311 J1
Turramurra 222 G14
Mowbray Pk 561 J7
Roseville Ch 285 D1
Mulgoa 325 B1
Bexley 402 F13
Kangaroo Pt 461 J4
Lidcombe 339 F11
Roseville Ch 285 D1
LANDALE
Baulkham Hl 246 H5
LANS
Petersham 15 E13
LARA
N Turramrra 223 F6
Castle Hill 218 K6
LARD
Roseville Ch 285 G1
Hassall Gr 211 K16
Ingleburn 453 G10
Penrith 237 D2
LLARS
Denistone W 280 J12
LLAWAH
Carss Park 432 G15
Elanora Ht 198 E16
Sefton 368 E5
Bangor 459 J15
Mt Colah 162 B15
Erskine Park 300 D2
Carss Park, off Allawah Av 432 F14
Greenwich 315 A7
Pymble 253 A3
Blacktown 274 D2
LLAY
Blacktown 243 K10
LLDER
Yagoona 369 A8
LLEGRA
v. Belmore 401 E4
Belmore, off Allegra Av 401 E3
LLEN
v. Alexandria 18 E14
v. Bilgola 170 B5
v. Ingleburn 422 H12
Alexandria 18 H13
Glebe 11 H8
Menai 458 H14
Minto 452 J16

pl. Penrith 236 J10
pl. Wetherill Pk 334 D2
rd. Blacktown 245 A9
st. Arncliffe 403 H7
st. Blaxland 233 K7
st. Canterbury 372 C15
st. Glebe 11 H8
st. Harris Park 308 E7
st. Homebush 341 D7
st. Leichhardt 9 D13
st. N Strathfield 341 D7
st. Pyrmont 12 J7
st. S Hurstville 432 B10
st. S Wntwthvle 307 A5
st. Waterloo 19 D16
wy. Dural 188 H13
ALLENA
cl. Georges Hall 367 K11
ALLENBY
cr. Strathfield 341 B14
la. Clontarf 287 F15
rd. Rossmore 389 F16
st. Canley Ht 365 D2
st. Clontarf 287 F14
st. Doonside 273 F1
ALLENBY PARK
pde. Allambie Ht 257 G11
ALLENDALE
st. Marayong 244 C6
ALLENGROVE
cr. North Ryde 282 H7
ALLENS
pde. Bondi Jctn 22 J9
ALLERTON
rd. Beecroft 250 D9
ALLEYNE
av. N Narrabeen 198 J16
st. Chatswood 285 E6
ALLIANCE
av. Revesby 398 E11
ALLIBONE
st. Ashbury 372 H6
ALLIEDALE
cl. Hornsby 221 G5
ALLIES
rd. Barden Rdg 488 G5
ALLIGATOR
pl. Kearns 451 B16
ALLINGHAM
st. Condell Park 398 B1
ALLINGTON
cr. Elanora Ht 198 E13
ALLIOTT
st. Bradbury 511 H11
ALLIRA
pl. Hassall Gr 211 K13
ALLISON
av. Condell Park 398 E1
av. Lane Cove 314 G2
cr. Menai 458 H12
dr. Glenmore Pk 265 J7
pde. Croydon 372 D2
rd. Cronulla 493 J15
rd. Guildford 337 D6
ALLISTER
st. Cremorne 316 F9
ALLMAN
av. Summer Hill 373 B4
st. Campbelltwn 511 E6
ALLOWRIE
rd. Villawood 367 B3
ALLPORT
wy. Claymore, off Colquhoun Wy 481 C11
ALL SAINTS
cl. Cherrybrook 219 F14
ALLSOPP
av. Baulkham Hl 248 C8
dr. Cmbrdg Gdn 237 G3
ALLUM
pl. Glebe 12 C11
st. Bankstown 369 B16
st. Haberfield 343 A13
st. Yagoona 369 B16
ALLUNGA
cl. Mona Vale 169 E16
ALLWOOD
cr. Lugarno 429 H12
ALLWORTH
dr. Davidson 255 C2
ALMA
av. Campsie 371 G13
av. Enmore 16 H15
cr. Emu Heights 205 B16
pl. Rooty Hill 242 A16
pl. Thirlmere 565 D2
rd. Leppington 419 J9
rd. Mcquarie Pk 282 G1
rd. Maroubra 407 B9
rd. Padstow 429 B4
st. Ashfield 372 G5
st. Clontarf 287 G15
st. Granville 308 A7
st. Hurstville 431 K7
st. Paddington 13 D12
st. Parramatta 308 A7
st. Pymble 253 D2
st. Rydalmere 309 J2
st. Vineyard 151 K9
ALMADA
st. Engadine 489 C9
ALMANDINE
pl. Eagle Vale 481 G5
ALMERIA
av. Baulkham Hl 246 H13
ALMETA
st. Schofields 213 J6
ALMONA
st. Glenwood 215 H11
ALMOND
st. Wentwthvle 277 A8
st. Wilton 568 K14
ALMORA
la. Mosman, off Upper Almora St 317 C6
ALOE
st. Quakers Hill 243 F3
ALOHA
st. Mascot 405 D3
ALONSO
cl. Rsemeadow 540 J6
ALPEN
la. Mount Druitt 241 B16
ALPHA
av. Roselands 400 K8
rd. Camden 507 B1
rd. Greystanes 305 E11
rd. Lane Cove 314 E4
rd. Northbridge 285 G15
rd. Willoughby 285 G15
st. Blacktown 244 F16
st. Chester Hill 337 H10
ALPHILL
av. Cabramatta 366 C6
ALPHIN
st. Lidcombe 339 H11
ALPHONSUS
wy. Auburn 338 K2
ALPIN
gr. Oakhurst 242 A4
ALPINE
cct. St Clair 269 G9
la. St Clair, off Alpine Cct 269 F9
pl. Engadine 488 C12
pl. Mcquarie Fd 454 D3
wy. Glenwood 245 G1
ALPITA
st. Kareela 461 C14
ALROY
cr. Hassall Gr 212 B16
ALSACE
av. Bardwell Vy 402 K10
la. Peakhurst 430 C13
ALSON
st. Mount Druitt 271 D2
ALSOP
pl. Bligh Park 150 C7
ALSTON
dr. Berowra Ht 132 J3
st. Bexley North 402 C13
st. Glenmore Pk 266 E8
st. Kingsgrove 402 C13
wy. Roseville 284 E5
ALT
cl. West Hoxton 392 B12
cr. Davidson 225 C16
la. Queens Park 22 F12
pl. Doonside 273 E3
st. Ashfield 342 H16
st. Haberfield 343 C13
st. Queens Park 22 E12
st. Smithfield 336 C6

ALTAIR
pl. Hinchinbrk 393 D5
pl. Jamisontown 266 E2
ALTHORPE
dr. Green Valley 362 K8
ALTO
av. Seaforth 287 A4
pl. Artarmon 314 G1
st. S Wntwthvle 307 B6
ALTON
av. Concord 341 G7
la. Newtown 17 F12
st. Merrylands 307 J15
st. Woollahra 22 A2
ALTONA
av. Forestville 256 A7
pl. Blacktown 274 C3
pl. Greenacre 370 B11
pl. North Rocks 248 J16
st. Abbotsford 342 J1
st. Hornsby Ht 161 H16
ALUA
cl. North Manly 258 A13
ALVA
pl. Riverstone 183 C9
ALVERNA
st. Rooty Hill 272 D7
ALVERSTONE
st. Riverwood 400 B11
ALVIS
pl. Ingleburn 453 J10
pl. Plumpton 241 G10
ALVISTON
st. Strathfield 341 E14
ALVONA
av. St Ives 254 A1
ALWYN
av. Wallacia 324 J12
cr. Glenwood 215 H13
ALYAN
pl. St Helens Park 541 A7
ALYSSE
cl. Baulkham Hl 247 C1
AMADIO
pl. Mt Pritchard 364 J9
AMALFI
pl. Longueville 314 C10
st. Lurnea 394 G11
AMANDA
cl. Berowra Ht 133 A6
cl. Dean Park 213 A16
pl. Annangrove 155 D4
pl. Ingleburn 453 D12
AMARAL
st. Narraweena 258 B5
AMARANTHUS
pl. Mcquarie Fd 454 B5
AMARINA
av. Bass Hill 367 K5
av. Greenacre 370 G9
AMARNA
pde. Roseville 284 K1
AMAROO
av. Blaxland 234 E7
av. Castle Cove 285 J4
av. Elanora Ht 198 B16
av. Georges Hall 367 F12
av. Mt Colah 191 K2
av. Strathfield 371 B4
av. Wahroonga 222 C11
cr. Mosman 317 E9
cr. Mosman 317 F9
st. Bonnyrigg 364 B9
st. Kingswood 237 K12
st. Sylvania 461 G15
AMAROO PARK
dr. Annangrove 155 E11
AMARYLLIS
wy. Bidwill 211 D13
AMAX
av. Girraween 275 H15
AMAZON
la. St Clair, off Amazon Pl 269 K16
pl. Kearns 481 D1
pl. St Clair 269 J16
rd. Seven Hills 275 E9
AMBER
cl. Bossley Park 334 A7
cl. Thornleigh 220 K12
la. Woolooware 493 F7
pl. Bass Hill 367 F8
pl. Eagle Vale 481 A7
AMBERDALE
av. Picnic Point 428 D9
AMBERLEA
ct. Castle Hill 218 J6
st. Glenwood 245 G3
AMBERWOOD
pl. Castle Hill 218 H16
pl. Menai 458 H13
wy. Castle Hill 218 G15
AMBLECOTE
pl. Tahmoor 565 J8
AMBLER
cl. Emu Heights 235 C5
pl. Narellan Vale 478 K16
AMBLESIDE
dr. Castle Hill 247 K5
st. Collaroy Plat 228 D12
AMBON
av. Holsworthy 426 F8
cl. Bossley Park 334 A5
rd. Holsworthy 396 C15
AMBROSE
la. Condell Park 398 J4
st. Condell Park 398 H4
st. Glendenning 242 H5
st. Hunters Hill 313 K11
AMBROSIA
st. Mcquarie Fd 454 D6
AMBRYM
av. Frenchs Frst 255 J2
AMBULANCE
av. Haymarket E E14
av. Haymarket 3 E15
AMBYNE
st. Woolooware 493 E8
AMEDE
pl. Illawong 459 K3
AMELIA
cl. Cecil Hills 362 F5
cr. Canley Ht 335 B14
gr. Pitt Town 92 H11
pl. N Narrabeen 198 G14
st. North Ryde 282 G8
st. Waterloo 20 B16
wy. Bidwill 211 H13
AMELIA GODBEE
av. Glenhaven 218 B1
AMERICAN
ml. Rooty Hill 272 F5
AMESBURY
av. St Ives 224 B16
av. Sefton 368 F1
AMETHYST
pl. Eagle Vale 481 C7
AMHERST
st. Cammeray 315 J5
st. Guildford 337 E2
AMIENS
av. Engadine 488 F16
av. Milperra 397 E11
av. Mosman 317 A3
cl. Bossley Park 334 A6
rd. Clontarf 287 F14
rd. Moorebank 395 D12
st. Gladesville 312 G12
wy. Matraville 407 B15
AMILCAR
st. Ingleburn 453 G12
AMINTA
cr. Hassall Gr 211 K14
AMINYA
cr. Bradbury 541 D1
pl. Baulkham Hl 248 B10
pl. Riverview 313 K5
pl. St Ives 224 B14
AMITAF
av. Caringbah 492 E10
AMOR
st. Asquith 191 H9
st. Hornsby 191 H9
AMOS
la. Elizabeth Bay 13 A6
pl. Marayong 244 C6
pl. Sylvania 461 K12
pl. Westmead 307 J3
rd. West Hoxton 391 J7
st. Parramatta 307 F4
st. Westmead 307 F4
AMOUR
av. Maroubra 407 F9
st. Milperra 398 A8

st. Revesby 398 A8
AMOURIN
st. North Manly 258 C13
AMPHITHEATRE
cct. Baulkham Hl 246 G9
AMRON
pl. Acacia Gdn 214 H16
AMSTERDAM
st. Oakhurst 242 C3
AMUET
pl. Glenwood 215 B15
AMUNDSEN
st. Leumeah 482 H13
st. Tregear 240 F7
AMUR
pl. Kearns 451 B15
AMY
cl. Glendenning 242 E2
la. Campsie 372 A13
la. Erskineville, off Macdonald St 374 K9
pl. Hornsby Ht 161 J11
pl. Narellan Vale 478 H15
rd. Riverwood 429 J1
st. Blakehurst 432 A15
st. Campsie 371 J14
st. Erskineville 374 K10
st. Marrickville 374 A9
st. Regents Pk 369 B1
st. Turrella 403 D5
AMY HAWKINS
cct. Kellyville 217 B1
ANAKAI
dr. Jamisontown 236 A16
ANANA
rd. Elanora Ht 198 F15
rd. N Narrabeen 198 F15
ANASTASIO
rd. Liverpool 364 J15
ANATOL
pl. Pymble 253 G4
ANCHORAGE
la. St Clair, off Anchorage St 270 J13
st. St Clair 270 J13
ANCILIA
cl. Quakers Hill 213 F7
ANCONA
av. Toongabbie 276 D7
rd. Turramurra 223 A7
ANCRUM
st. N Sydney 5 B9
ANCURA
ct. Wattle Grove 396 B16
ANDAMAN
st. Kings Park 244 F2
ANDAMOOKA
pl. Cartwright 394 B4
ANDERSON
av. Blackett 241 A3
av. Dundas 279 B15
av. Hobartville 118 D9
av. Liverpool 394 J3
av. Mt Pritchard 364 E10
av. Panania 398 B16
av. Ryde 311 J2
av. S Turramrra 252 A9
cl. Appin 569 E7
la. Belmore 401 G2
la. Penrith 237 B11
la. Ryde 311 H2
la. Concord, off Archer St 342 A2
la. Sefton, off Torrington Av 368 G3
pl. Cottage Pt 135 F9
pl. S Windsor 120 H15
rd. Badgerys Ck 359 B6
rd. Concord 342 A2
rd. Kings Lngly 246 C10
rd. Mortdale 430 G6
rd. Northmead 278 A4
rd. Smeaton Gra 479 C5
st. Alexandria 18 J14
st. Bnksmeadw 406 A12
st. Belmore 401 G1
st. Bexley 432 F4
st. Chatswood 284 J8
st. Double Bay 14 D11
st. Kingsford 406 H3
st. Neutral Bay 6 F6
st. Panania 428 B2
st. Parramatta 308 D6
st. St Helens Park 541 B6
st. Westmead 307 G4
ANDERTON
st. Marrickville 373 H11
ANDORA
pl. Glen Alpine 510 G11
ANDORRA
cl. Glendenning 242 J4
ANDOVE
st. Belrose 226 B14
ANDOVER
cr. Hebersham 241 F6
la. Allawah 432 G8
st. Carlton 432 G7
ANDRE
pl. Blacktown 274 E10
ANDREA
cl. Bonnyrigg 364 F5
ANDREAS
st. Petersham 15 F6
ANDREW
av. Canley Ht 365 C1
av. West Pymble 253 A12
cl. Mt Colah 192 C5
la. Melrose Pk 310 J2
pl. Birrong 368 K4
pl. Earlwood 403 F4
pl. Girraween 276 D12
pl. North Rocks 248 G15
rd. Kellyville 186 D7
st. Belrose 225 D15
st. Bronte 378 A8
st. Brooklyn 75 K11
st. Clovelly 377 K12
st. Melrose Pk 310 J3
st. Richmond 119 D4
st. West Ryde 310 J3
ANDREW LLOYD
dr. Doonside 273 E5
ANDREW NASH
la. Parramatta, off George St 308 D2
ANDREWS
av. Ashbury 372 G9
av. Bondi 378 B5
av. Toongabbie 276 F10
cct. Horngsea Pk 392 F12
la. N Sydney K A3
la. N Sydney 5 E6
pl. St Helens Park 541 A8
pl. Yellow Rock 173 G14
rd. Cranebrook 237 B1
ANDREW THOMPSON
dr. McGraths Hl 121 J12
pl. Colyton 270 H9
ANDREW TOWN
pl. Richmond 118 C5
ANDRO
pl. Werrington 238 G10
ANDROMEDA
cr. Engadine 488 D11
dr. Cranebrook 207 F5
ANDY
st. Guildford W 336 J3
ANDYS
ct. St Clair 269 G11
ANEBO
st. Liverpool 394 K4
ANELLA
av. Castle Hill 217 C12
ANEMBO
av. Georges Hall 367 J11
cr. Killara 283 F1
pl. Eastwood 281 F2
rd. Berowra 133 D15
rd. Duffys Frst 194 J7
st. Bradbury 511 G15
ANEMONE
pl. Kirrawee 461 A14
ANEURA
ct. Wattle Grove 396 C15
ANGARA
cct. Glenwood 245 J2
cl. Kearns 451 C16
ANGAS
cl. Barden Rdg 488 J3
st. Meadowbnk 311 F4
st. Wrrngtn Cty 238 H7
ANGEL
cl. Cherrybrook 219 F15
ct. Glenwood 245 D2
la. Newtown 17 H13
pl. Cherrybrook 219 F15
pl. Forestville 256 B8
pl. Sydney C J1
pl. Sydney 3 G1
rd. Strathfield 341 G16
st. Newtown 17 G16
st. Wrrngtn Cty 238 G6
ANGELA
st. Cecil Hills 362 F4
ANGELINA
cr. Cabramatta 365 E10
ct. Green Valley 362 K9
ANGELINI
av. Rozelle 10 H1
ANGELO
av. Liverpool 394 H10
st. Burwood 371 J2
st. N Sydney K B1
st. N Sydney 5 E5
st. Woolwich 314 G12
ANGLE
rd. Grays Point 491 A14
rd. Leumeah 482 B14
rd.s, Leumeah 512 C1
st. Balgowlah 287 J8
ANGLEDOOL
av. Hinchinbrk 392 H3
ANGLESEA
st. Bondi 377 H4
ANGLE VALE
rd. Edensor Pk 363 D1
ANGLO
la. Greenwich 315 B7
rd. Campsie 371 J14
rd. Greenwich 315 B7
sq. Carlton 432 J8
st. Chatswd W 284 F9
ANGOPHORA
av. Kingswood 267 G2
cct. Mt Annan 509 F3
cr. Forestville 255 E8
ct. Voyager Pt 427 B5
gr. Greenacre 370 F5
pl. Alfords Point 459 B3
pl. Castle Hill 248 E3
pl. Pennant Hills 250 J4
pl. Valley Ht 202 G9
ANGORRA
rd. Terrey Hills 196 C6
ANGOURIE
ct. Dural 219 B3
pl. Bow Bowing 452 C14
ANGUS
av. Auburn 339 B9
av. Epping 280 E1
av. Lane Cove 314 G2
av. Peakhurst 430 G3
av. Rooty Hill 271 H6
cr. Yagoona 368 H10
pl. Busby 363 K16
pl. St Andrews 482 A3
rd. Kenthurst 188 D8
rd. Schofields 212 H4
rd. Smeaton Gra 479 F5
st. Earlwood 402 D6
ANICH
pl. Prestons 423 A1
ANIMBO
st. Miranda 491 K6
ANISEED
st. Prestons 393 H14
ANITA
st. Glenwood 215 E12
ANITRA
av. Kareela 461 D12
pl. Shalvey 210 H15
ANJOU
cct. Cecil Hills 362 C4
ANJUDY
cl. Casula 394 F16
ANKA
av. Old Tngabbie 276 J10
ANKALI
pl. North Manly 258 A14
ANN
cr. Mt Pritchard 364 H13
pl. Bligh Park 150 F8
pl. Narellan Vale 508 J2
st. Arncliffe 403 H7
st. Balmain 8 A10
st. Bondi Jctn 22 J8
st. Earlwood 372 G16
st. Enfield 371 H4
st. Fairfield Ht 335 J10
st. Faulconbdg 172 B5
st. Frenchs Frst 256 D6
st. Lidcombe 339 H7
st. Longueville 314 D8
st. Marrickville 373 J13
st. N Willghby 285 G10
st. Surry Hills F E12
st. Surry Hills 3 K14
st. Willoughby 285 G10
ANNABELLA
rd. Camden 506 K5
ANNABELLE
cr. Kellyville 216 F5
pl. Mt Colah 162 E16
pl. Pymble 253 A9
ANNAM
rd. Bayview 168 J15
ANNAN
pl. Baulkham Hl 246 G11
ANNANDALE
st. Annandale 16 G4
st. Darling Point 13 H6
ANNANGROVE
rd. Annangrove 187 B7
rd. Kenthurst 187 B7
rd. Rouse Hill 184 H5
ANNE
av. Seven Hills 245 A16
cr. Blaxland 234 C5
pl. Cecil Hills 363 A3
pl. Cherrybrook 219 K4
pl. Wahroonga 223 B5
pl. Wilberforce 92 C2
st. Blacktown 274 C4
st. Oatlands 278 K11
st. Revesby 399 A12
st. St Marys 239 F8
wy. Mcquarie Fd 424 F15
ANNELIESE
pl. Castle Hill 218 C10
ANNE MARIE
cl. St Ives 223 K16
pl. Belfield 371 F10
pl. Carlingford 249 E14
ANNESLEY
st. Leichhardt 10 C12
ANNETT
st. Emu Plains 235 F12
ANNETTE
av. Ingleburn 453 B6
av. Kogarah 433 E5
pl. Baulkham Hl 248 C7
pl. Belrose 226 B16
pl. Castle Hill 216 K9
pl. Hobartville 118 G7
st. Cabramatta W 365 B6
st. Oatley 431 C16
ANNE WILLIAM
dr. W Pnnant Hl 249 F7
ANNFIELD
st. Kellyville 215 A2
ANNIE
la. West Ryde 281 B16
st. Hurstville 401 J16
ANNIE SPENCE
cl. Emu Heights 235 B3
ANNIVERSARY
st. Botany 405 H16
ANNUAL
la. St Clair 270 C14
ANSCHAU
cr. Windsor 121 D8
ANSELM
st. Strathfield S 371 A4
ANSON
pl. Castle Hill 247 F1
ANTARES
av. Hinchinbrk 393 D4
pl. Cranebrook 207 F5
ANTHEA
pl. Dean Park 212 K16
ANTHONY
av. Mt Riverview 234 C1
av. Padstow 429 C3
cl. Beacon Hill 257 H5
cl. St Ives 254 A1
cr. Kingswood 238 A14
dr. Rsemeadow 540 G3
la. Matraville 406 J15
la. West Ryde, off Anthony Rd 281 D15
rd. Bargo 567
rd. Castle Hill 217
rd. Catherine Fd 419
rd. Denistone 281
rd. Leppington 419
rd. West Ryde 281
st. Blacktown 245
st. Carlingford 250
st. Chatswood 285
st. Croydon 342
st. Epping 250
st. Fairfield 336
st. Matraville 406
st. Yagoona 369
ANTILL
cl. Camden S 507
cr. Baulkham Hl 247
pl. Blackett 241
pl. Mt Pritchard 364
rd. Mt Pritchard 364
st. Blaxland 234
st. Picton 563
st. Thirlmere 565
st. Yennora 337
wy. Airds 511
ANTIQUE
cr. Woodcroft 243
ANTOINE
st. Rydalmere 309
ANTOINETTE
av. Narellan Vale 508
cl. Warrawee 222
ANTON
pl. Bonnyrigg 363
rd. Luddenham 357
ANTONIA
cr. Cranebrook 207
ANTONIETTA
st. Cabramatta 365
ANTONIO
cl. Rsemeadow 540
st. St Johns Pk 364
ANTRIM
st. Hebersham 241
ANTWERP
st. Auburn 338
st. Bankstown 399
ANULLA
pl. Wahroonga 222
ANVIL
pl. Jamisontown 236
rd. Seven Hills 276
ANZAC
av. Cammeray 315
av. Collaroy 229
av. Collaroy Plat 228
av. Denistone 281
av. Engadine 518
av. Fairfield 336
av. Ryde 281
av. Smeaton Gra 479
av. West Ryde 281
la. Campbelltwn 511
la. West Ryde, off Wattle St 281
mw. Holsworthy 396
pde. Chifley 437
pde. Kensington 376
pde. Kingsford 406
pde. La Perouse 436
pde. La Perouse 436
pde. Little Bay 437
pde. Malabar 437
pde. Maroubra 407
pde. Matraville 407
pde. Moore Park 20
pde. Phillip Bay 436
rd. Bangor 459
rd. Holsworthy 396
rd. Moorebank 395
rd. Wattle Grove 395
sq. Campsie 371
st. Canterbury 372
st. Chullora 369
st. Greenacre 369
st. Miranda 492
st. N St Marys 239
ANZIO
av. Allambie Ht 257
AOMA
st. Scotland I 168
APACHE
gr. Stanhpe Gdn 215
rd. Bossley Park 333

NIE
Westleigh...220 E8
AP
Castle Hill...217 C6
ARA
Forestville...255 F10
ERTA
Beacon Hill...257 K7
EX
Picnic Point...428 F7
Blacktown...274 D7
Liverpool...365 B15
Naremburn...315 F1
A
Lethbrdg Pk...240 F2
Guildford...337 E5
LIN
St Ives Ch...223 J6
Bonnyrigg Ht...363 E8
OLLO
Baulkham Hl...246 K14
West Pymble...252 G12
St Clair...269 F11
Eastwood...280 E7
Lane Cove W...283 F15
Port Hacking...522 K3
Greenfld Pk...334 C13
Warriewood...198 H5
PALOOSA
Blairmount...481 A14
PIAN
Baulkham Hl...246 G10
Burwood...371 K2
PIN
Engadine...489 D10
St Marys...239 F4
Ambarvale...511 B15
Appin...569 F9
Bradbury...511 B15
Campbelltwn...511 B15
Gilead...540 H15
Rsemeadow...540 H15
St Helens Park...540 H15
PLAUSE
Riverwood...400 C10
PLE
Mcquarie Fd...454 A4
Wentwthvle...277 B8
PLEBEE
St Peters...374 J12
PLEBOX
Glenwood...215 H16
PLEBY
Agnes Banks...117 E16
Plumpton...242 B8
PLECROSS
Castle Hill...218 A7
PLEGUM
Mt Riverview...234 E3
Prestons...393 K14
PLETON
Lurnea...394 D11
PLETREE
Cherrybrook...219 J7
Oakhurst...211 H16
Menai...458 H13
PS
N Turramrra...223 D8
Narellan Vale...508 K1
PSLEY
Kingsford...406 H4
Cranebrook...206 J9
Kingsford...406 H4
Campbelltwn...511 J8
Taren Point...462 G13
Guildford...337 E1
Penshurst...431 F5
QUA
Marayong...244 B5
QUAMARINE
Eagle Vale...481 E8
Quakers Hill...214 H13
QUARIUS
Erskine Park...300 K1
Erskine Park, off Aquarius Cr...300 K1
QUATIC
Frenchs Frst...257 A7
QUILA
Erskine Park, off Pegasus St...301 A2
Erskine Park...301 A2

AQUILINA
dr. Plumpton...242 D11
ARA
cr. Narraweena...258 A1
pl. Hinchinbrk...393 E3
ARAB
rd. Padstow...399 C15
ARABANOO
st. Seaforth...287 C7
ARABELLA
pl. Bella Vista...246 G5
st. Longueville...314 D9
st. Northwood...314 D9
ARAFURA
av. Cranebrook...207 C10
ARAGON
st. Cecil Hills...362 D4
ARAKOON
av. Penrith...237 D7
ARALUEN
av. Moorebank...396 G6
av. St Marys...239 G14
pl. Bayview...168 F11
pl. Camden S...507 D12
pl. Glenhaven...217 H2
pl. Sutherland...460 H15
rd. Lansvale...366 C10
st. Kingsford...407 A4
ARAMON
cl. Edensor Pk...363 E2
ARANA
cl. Bangor...459 J15
cl. Banksia...403 G12
cl. Georges Hall...368 A15
pl. Cabramatta W...365 C7
st. Manly Vale...287 G3
ARANDA
dr. Davidson...255 E2
dr. Frenchs Frst...255 E2
ARANDA PATH
Winmalee...173 B10
ARARAT
cl. Bossley Park...333 E9
ARBITRATION
st. Sydney...B C9
ARBOR
gln. Castle Hill...217 E2
ARBOUR
gr. Quakers Hill...213 G9
ARBROATH
pl. St Andrews...482 A3
ARBUTUS
st. Canley Ht...365 E3
st. Canley Vale...365 E3
st. Mosman...317 C6
ARCADIA
av. Drummoyne...344 B3
av. Gymea Bay...491 C11
av. Woolooware...493 F7
cr. Berowra...133 C11
la. Coogee...377 H14
la. Glebe...11 G10
la. Colyton, off Arcadia Pl...270 B8
pl. Colyton...270 B8
rd. Arcadia...129 E16
rd. Chester Hill...368 D1
rd. Galston...159 D2
rd. Glebe...11 G10
st. Coogee...377 G14
st. Merrylands W...307 A12
st. Penshurst...431 C1
ARCADIAN
cct. Carlingford...279 B4
ARCHBALD
av. Btn-le-Sds...403 K15
ARCHBOLD
av. Rouse Hill...185 D1
rd. Eastern Ck...271 E12
rd. E Lindfield...254 H15
rd. Lindfield...254 H15
rd. Minchinbury...271 E12
rd. Roseville...284 J1
ARCHDALE
wky. Wahroonga...222 D7
ARCHDALL
gr. Bella Vista...246 F4
ARCHER
cl. Bossley Park...333 K8
cr. Bankstown...399 D6
ct. St Clair...270 E11
la. Windsor Dn...180 H1
pl. Maroubra...407 C8
pl. Minto...483 A3
row. Menai...458 K15
st. Blacktown...274 B6
st. Burwood...342 B12
st. Chatswood...284 J6
st. Concord...341 K2
st. Mosman...317 A8
st. Mount Druitt...271 B4
st. Roseville...284 J6
wy. West Hoxton...392 D10
ARCHIBALD
cr. Rsemeadow...540 G8
st. Belmore...401 H5
st. Granville...308 G14
st. Padstow...399 B13
ARCHITECTS
pl. St Clair...270 B10
ARCTURUS
cl. Cranebrook...207 F6
ARDATH
av. Panania...428 B5
ARDEN
la. Clovelly, off Arden St...377 H12
pl. Frenchs Frst...256 G3
rd. Pymble...253 A2
st. Clovelly...377 H12
st. Coogee...377 H16
st. S Coogee...407 G3
st. Waverley...377 H12
ARDGRYFFE
st. Burwood Ht...372 A4
ARDILL
la. Warrimoo...203 B15
ARDING
st. Lane Cove W...284 B15
ARDISIA
pl. Loftus...489 K12
ARDITTOS
la. Strathfield...341 E12
ARDNO
st. Busby...363 G14
ARDRISHAIG
pl. Glenhaven...218 F6
ARDROSSAN
cr. St Andrews...451 K14
rd. Engadine...488 J11
ARDSLEY
av. Frenchs Frst...256 D3
ARDUA
pl. Engadine...488 D15
ARELEY
ct. Jamisontown...266 E5
ARGO
pl. Miranda...461 J16
wy. Airds...512 C11
ARGONNE
st. N Strathfield...341 C3
ARGOWAN
rd. Schofields...183 B16
ARGUIMBAU
st. Annandale...10 J13
ARGUS
la. Parramatta...308 F3
ARGYLE
av. Ryde...312 B2
cr. S Coogee...407 E6
la. Millers Pt...A B3
pl. Bonnyrigg Ht...363 B6
pl. Emu Plains...235 B9
pl. Kareela...461 B14
pl. Mcquarie Fd...423 J16
pl. Millers Pt...A C2
pl. Millers Pt...1 D9
pl. W Pnnant Hl...249 A6
st. Arncliffe...403 H7
st. Auburn...309 D15
st. Bilgola...169 F8
st. Camden...477 B15
st. Carlton...432 J6
st. Dawes Point...A D2
st. Dawes Point...1 E9
st. Millers Pt...A D2
st. Millers Pt...1 E9
st. Parramatta...308 B4
st. Penshurst...431 B2
st. Picton...563 D13
st. Picton...563 E11
st. Riverstone...182 F13
st. S Windsor...120 J12
st. The Rocks...A J3
st. The Rocks...1 G10
st. Wilton...568 K14
ARGYLE REACH
rd. Freemns Rch...91 E12
rd. Wilberforce...91 G8
ARGYLE STAIRS
The Rocks...A J3
ARGYLL
pl. Cheltenham...250 J6
rd. Winmalee...173 C12
rd. Winmalee...173 D12
ARIANA
pl. Acacia Gdn...214 J16
ARIANNA
av. Normanhurst...221 J11
ARIEL
cr. Cranebrook...207 C16
pl. Rsemeadow...540 K6
ARIELLA
pl. Edensor Pk...333 E14
ARIES
pl. Erskine Park...270 G15
ARIETTA
cct. Harringtn Pk...478 F7
ARIKA
cl. Bangor...459 G15
ARILLA
av. Riverwood...400 F11
pl. Bangor...459 J15
rd. Pymble...253 A3
ARINA
rd. Bargo...567 K12
ARINYA
st. Kingsgrove...401 K7
ARISAIG
pl. St Andrews...451 K16
ARISTOTLE
la. Winmalee...173 J8
ARIZONA
pl. North Rocks...278 H2
pl. Riverwood...400 A12
pl. Stanhpe Gdn...215 C11
ARJEZ
pl. Marayong...244 B5
ARK
pl. Riverstone...183 A4
ARKANA
pl. Engadine...489 A8
st. Telopea...279 D7
ARKANSAS
pl. Kearns...451 C16
ARKELL
dr. Bligh Park...150 H5
ARKENA
av. Epping...250 C14
ARKLAND
st. Cammeray...316 B4
ARKLEY
st. Bankstown...399 F6
ARLENE
pl. Plumpton...241 G10
ARLEWIS
st. Chester Hill...338 B14
ARLEY
pl. North Rocks...248 K13
ARLINGTON
av. Castle Hill...217 G10
av. Riverstone...183 G9
dr. Fairlight...288 C10
st. Dulwich Hill...373 B8
st. Five Dock...342 J12
st. Rockdale...403 B13
ARMATA
ct. Wattle Grove...426 B1
ARMEN
wy. Hornsby Ht...161 G16
ARMENTIERES
av. Milperra...397 G11
wy. Matraville...407 B15
ARMIDALE
av. Hoxton Park...392 G6
pl. Engadine...488 G12
ARMINE
wy. Kellyville...185 J14
ARMITAGE
dr. Glendenning...242 E3
la. Mosman, off Rosherville Rd...317 D2
ARMITREE
st. Kingsgrove...401 E7
st. Kingsgrove...401 F8

ARMOUR
av. Camden S...507 B14
av. Kellyville...215 A2
av. Kellyville...215 C2
ARMSTEIN
cr. Werrington...238 F11
la. Werrington, off Armstein Cr...238 G11
ARMSTRONG
ct. Bnkstn Aprt...367 J16
la. Lidcombe...339 H10
pl. Castle Hill...218 C10
pl. Dean Park...242 H1
st. Ashcroft...394 D1
st. Ashfield...372 J7
st. Cammeray...315 H4
st. Raby...451 D12
st. Seaforth...286 K4
st. Willoughby...285 E15
st.e, Willoughby...285 F16
ARMYTAGE
pl. Glen Alpine...510 E13
ARNCLIFFE
rd. Earlwood...403 C4
st. Arncliffe...403 H7
ARNDELL
st. Camden S...507 B10
st. Windsor...121 E7
wy. Minto...482 H6
ARNDILL
av. Baulkham Hl...247 E3
ARNETT
st. Pendle Hill...306 F2
ARNHEM
pl. Leumeah...482 F9
pl. Willmot...210 C12
rd. Allambie Ht...257 B8
ARNO
tce. Glenwood...245 K4
ARNOLD
av. Camden S...507 C16
av. Green Valley...363 A11
av. Kellyville...215 J8
av. St Marys...270 A4
av. Yagoona...369 C10
la. Darlinghurst...F K8
la. Panania...428 D2
pl. Darlinghurst...F J6
pl. Glenwood...215 K16
pl. Glenwood...245 K1
pl. Menai...458 H11
st. Killara...254 B12
st. Leumeah...512 C2
st. N Richmond...87 C14
st. Peakhurst...430 B3
st. Queens Park...22 H13
st. Ryde...312 D5
st. Wetherill Pk...334 E6
ARNOLD JANSSEN
dr. Kellyville...185 K16
dr. Kellyville...215 K1
ARNOTT
cr. Warriewood...199 D11
pl. Wetherill Pk...304 E13
rd. Marayong...244 A4
ARNOTTS
pl. Huntingwd...273 E12
AROA
pl. Glenfield...424 D13
ARONIA
av. St Ives...224 G9
AROONA
rd. Oxford Falls...227 A13
ARRABRI
pl. Warriewood...199 B8
ARRAGONG
st. Bangor...459 J15
ARRAN
pl. St Andrews...481 J3
ARRAS
pde. Ryde...312 C3
ARRAWATTA
cl. Edensor Pk...333 D14
ARRIONGA
pl. Hornsby...191 D12
ARRIVAL
ct. Mascot...404 D8
ARROW
la. Old Tngabbie...277 F10
pl. Raby...481 F1
ARROWFIELD
av. Burwood...371 H1

dr. Wattle Grove......396 A16
ARROWHEAD
rd. Greenfld Pk........333 K12
ARROWSMITH
st. Glenwood..........215 E15
ARRUNGA
av. Roseville............284 G1
rd. Arcadia..............129 C15
st. Dundas...............279 F14
ARTARMON
rd. Artarmon...........285 A14
rd. Willoughby.........285 D16
ARTEGALL
st. Bankstown.........399 A8
ART GALLERY
rd. Campbelltwn......511 C7
rd. Sydney.................D J6
rd. Sydney.................4 C3
ARTHUR
av. Blacktown..........244 A11
av. Cronulla.............494 A15
la. Fairlight..............288 D7
la. Lavender Bay.........K H14
la. Lavender Bay.........5 H12
la. Randwick.............377 A14
la. Surry Hills.............20 C3
pl. Bonnet Bay..........460 B7
st. Ashfield..............372 G4
st. Auburn................338 J5
st. Balmain..................7 C8
st. Bankstown...........399 B7
st. Baulkham Hl.......247 H12
st. Bellevue Hill..........14 H14
st. Bexley..................402 H13
st. Bonnet Bay..........460 C7
st. Burwood Ht..........372 B4
st. Cabramatta..........365 J7
st. Carlton.................432 H9
st. Chipping Ntn.......397 A4
st. Concord...............341 H5
st. Croydon...............372 B4
st. Croydon Pk..........372 B4
st. Dee Why..............258 F4
st. Dover Ht..............348 F14
st. Edgecliff.................13 J12
st. Fairlight.................288 E7
st. Five Dock.............343 D8
st. Forest Lodge...........11 F13
st. Forestville.............255 D8
st. Granville..............308 H10
st. Granville..............308 H8
st. Hornsby...............191 J13
st. Killara..................254 A8
st. Lavender Bay..........K H15
st. Lavender Bay..........5 H11
st. Leichhardt..............10 A14
st. Marrickville...........373 H13
st. Marsden Pk...........182 B14
st. Mascot.................405 H4
st. Merrylands W.......307 A12
st. Parramatta............308 J6
st. Punchbowl............400 C4
st. Randwick..............376 K14
st. Redfern...................19 J6
st. Rodd Point............343 D8
st. Rookwood.............340 E10
st. Rosehill.................308 H8
st. Rosehill.................308 J6
st. Ryde.....................282 C12
st. Strathfield.............340 J11
st. Surry Hills...............20 B2
st. Surry Hills...............20 C3
st. Warrimoo..............203 B14
st.n, N Sydney...............K H10
st.n, N Sydney...............5 H9
ARTHUR PHILLIP
dr. N Richmond.............86 K13
ARTHURS
cir. Mt Colah...............162 D9
ARTHURSLEIGH
st. Burwood................342 B11
ARTHUR TAYLOR
av. Matraville..............436 G9
ARTIE
st. Carramar...............366 G1
ARTILLERY
cr. Holsworthy............426 F3
cr. Seven Hills.............245 H16
dr. Manly.....................289 B13
rd. Holsworthy.............425 D11
rd. Holsworthy.............426 G12
ARTISAN
rd. Seven Hills.............276 F2
ARTLETT
st. Edgecliff..................13 F11
ARTORNISH
pl. Rooty Hill, off Barker St...........272 C1
ARU
pl. Kings Park..............244 J2
ARUM
pl. Mcquarie Fd...........454 D6
wy. Cherrybrook...........219 G14
ARUMA
av. Kellyville................216 H8
cl. Chipping Ntn..........396 D5
pl. Dharruk..................241 C9
ARUNDEL
rd. Horsley Pk..............302 D14
st. Engadine................489 A11
st. Forest Lodge.............11 K16
st. Glebe........................18 C1
st. Longueville.............314 D9
st. West Pymble...........252 G10
wy. Cherrybrook............219 C14
ARUNDELL
st. Dharruk..................241 A7
ARUNDEL PARK
dr. St Clair...................270 F14
ARUNDLE
rd. Bass Hill.................367 J8
ARUNTA
av. Green Valley...........363 G11
cl. Bangor....................459 F15
cr. Leumeah..................482 G11
ARWON
av. Casula....................394 E16
ASAPH
cl. Hornsby Ht.............161 E15
ASCHE
st. Doonside.................243 B9
ASCOT
av. Wahroonga.............222 C2
av. Zetland...................376 A11
dr. Chipping Ntn...........366 F15
dr. Chipping Ntn...........366 G13
pl. Miranda...................492 B3
pl. S Penrith..................266 H1
pl. Wilberforce................92 A2
rd. Kenthurst.................157 H9
st. Bexley.....................402 H13
st. Canley Ht................365 E4
st. Kensington..............376 F11
st. Randwick.................376 F11
ASEKI
av. Glenfield.................424 C14
ASH
av. Caringbah...............492 F13
cl. Bossley Park............333 H11
la. Haberfield................343 A13
pl. Bradbury..................511 D9
pl. Lugarno...................429 H16
pl. Narellan Vale...........478 J14
pl. S Coogee.................407 E6
rd. Prestons..................393 G13
rd. Prestons..................393 J8
st. Blacktown................243 K15
st. Cherrybrook.............219 G12
st. Georges Hall............367 F11
st. Greystanes...............306 E4
st. N St Marys................239 K10
st. Sydney........................C J1
st. Sydney........................3 G1
ASHBURN
la. Gladesville...............312 H11
pl. Baulkham Hl............216 E15
pl. Bella Vista...............216 D15
pl. Gladesville...............312 G12
ASHBURNER
st. Manly......................288 H11
ASHBURTON
av. S Turramrra.............252 B10
ct. Kellyville.................186 H16
ASHBY
av. Yagoona..................369 C10
cl. Bargo.......................567 A3
la. Randwick.................377 D9
st. Guildford..................338 A7
st. Kingsgrove...............401 G13
st. Prospect...................274 F12
ASHCOTT
st. Kings Lngly..............245 D7
ASHCROFT
av. Casula.....................394 K14
st. Ermington.................280 B13
st. Georges Hall............367 E14
ASHDOWN
pl. Frenchs Frst............256 F3
ASHER
pl. Campbelltwn...........511 E6
st. Coogee.....................407 G2
ASHERS
la. Artarmon..................314 J2
ASHFIELD
pl. Glen Alpine..............540 C2
ASHFORD
av. Castle Hill................217 F13
av. Milperra...................397 J11
cct. Currans Hill............479 H7
cl. Hinchinbrk...............392 H5
gr. St Clair....................270 G14
la. St Clair, off Ashford Gr.........270 G14
rd. Cherrybrook.............219 C14
rd. Vineyard..................152 F12
st. Ashfield...................372 J8
ASHFORDBY
st. Chipping Ntn............396 F1
ASHGATE
av. Vaucluse..................348 C6
ASHGROVE
cr. Blacktown................274 F9
st. St Johns Pk..............364 E1
ASHLAR
st. St Ives.....................224 D6
ASHLEIGH MADISON
wy. Mt Colah..................191 K4
ASHLEY
av. W Pnnant Hl............249 G8
cl. St Johns Pk..............364 E1
gr. Gordon.....................253 H5
la. Hornsby....................221 F1
la. Westmead.................277 G16
pde. Fairlight..................288 B10
st. Chatswood................284 J7
st. Hornsby....................221 E1
st. Roseville...................285 A6
st. Tamarama..................378 A7
ASHMEAD
av. Castle Hill................217 H9
av. Revesby...................428 H2
rd. Minto........................483 B1
rd. Minto........................483 C1
ASHMONT
pl. Prestons...................393 B15
ASHMORE
av. Pymble....................252 J2
st. Erskineville...............375 A8
ASHTON
av. Chester Hill..............338 A15
av. Earlwood..................372 J16
av. Ermington.................310 B3
av. Forestville.................255 K9
av. Seaforth....................287 A12
cl. Eagle Vale.................480 K9
gdn. Bellevue Hill............347 F11
la. Paddington...................21 E1
pl. Doonside...................273 F2
pl. Mt Pritchard..............364 J12
st. Queens Park................22 C11
st. Rockdale...................433 D2
ASHTONS
rd. Grose Wold...............116 A9
ASHUR
cr. Greenfld Pk..............334 A15
ASHWELL
rd. Blacktown.................274 F2
ASHWICK
cct. St Clair...................270 G10
ASHWOOD
cl. Menai........................458 H14
rd. Kenthurst..................187 C3
st. Parklea.....................215 B13
ASHWORTH
av. Belrose.....................225 E14
ASPEN
cl. Prestons....................393 J13
st. Bossley Park..............333 H9
st. S Penrith....................267 D5
wy. Acacia Gdn...............215 A14
ASPINALL
av. Minchinbury..............272 B8
pl. Mulgrave....................121 H16
pl. Woolwich...................314 G11
ASPLIN
pl. Kurrajong Hl...............55 F7
ASQUITH
av. Rosebery...................375 J16
av. Winston Hills.............247 J15
st. Oatley.......................431 E12
st. Silverwater................309 E12
ASSETS
st. Campsie....................371 K12
ASSISI
pl. Rooty Hill..................272 D7
ASSUNTA
st. Rooty Hill..................272 D7
ASTELIA
st. Mcquarie Fd..............454 C4
ASTER
av. Asquith.....................191 K9
av. Miranda.....................492 D2
av. Punchbowl.................399 G4
cl. Glenmore Pk..............265 F10
pl. Quakers Hill...............243 F3
st. Eastwood...................281 D7
st. Greystanes.................305 J12
ASTLEY
av. Padstow.....................429 E1
pl. Edensor Pk.................363 G4
wy. Casula......................424 G4
ASTOLAT
st. Randwick...................377 C11
ASTON
av. Lucas Ht....................487 F12
av. S Penrith....................267 B1
cl. Hoxton Park...............392 K6
la. S Penrith, off Aston Av...........267 B1
pl. Leumeah....................482 B14
rd. Kenthurst..................187 E8
st. Hunters Hill...............313 A7
ASTOR
st. Moorebank................396 E7
ASTORIA
cct. Maroubra..................407 B12
ASTORIA PARK
rd. Baulkham Hl..............246 F10
ASTRAL
dr. Doonside...................243 G15
ASTRID
av. Baulkham Hl..............247 E7
cl. Cabramatta................365 E11
ASTROLABE
rd. Daceyville..................406 E3
ASTRON
cr. Bexley North..............402 D9
ASTWIN
st. Croydon.....................342 G14
ASTWOOD
st. Colyton......................270 D8
ATAMI
pl. Picnic Point................428 A7
ATCHISON
la. Crows Nest................315 E5
la. St Leonards...............315 E5
rd. Mcquarie Fd..............453 K1
st. Crows Nest................315 E5
st. St Leonards...............315 E5
st. St Marys....................269 F5
ATHABASKA
av. Seven Hills.................275 H8
ATHEL
st. Georges Hall..............367 F11
st. N St Marys.................240 C13
ATHELLA
pl. Dural..........................219 C7
ATHELSTANE
av. Arncliffe.....................403 D9
ATHEL TREE
cr. Bradbury.....................511 F14
ATHENA
av. St Ives........................224 G7
ct. St Clair........................269 G11
ATHENE
pl. Collaroy Plat..............228 K13
ATHENS
av. Hassall Gr..................212 A16
ATHERDEN
st. The Rocks......................A K1
ATHERTON
cr. Auburn.......................339 B12
rd. Engadine....................489 A10
st. Fairfield W.................335 E10
ATHLONE
cr. Killarney Ht................256 D15
st. Blacktown...................273 K1
st. Cecil Hills...................362 H9
ATHOL
pl. Carlingford.................279
st. Frenchs Frst...............255
st. Leichhardt.......................9
st. S Coogee....................407
ATHOL WHARF
rd. Mosman.....................317
ATKA
st. Tregear......................240
ATKINS
av. Carramar....................336
av. Russell Lea.................343
cr. Hobartville..................118
ct. Baulkham Hl...............247
pl. Barden Rdg.................488
rd. Ermington....................280
rd. Ermington....................310
ATKINSON
av. Padstow.....................399
cl. Glenmore Pk...............265
rd. Taren Point.................463
st. Arncliffe......................403
st. Liverpool.....................395
ATLANTA
pl. Casula........................395
ATLANTIC
pl. Kellyville.....................185
ATLAS
pl. Winston Hills...............277
wy. Kellyville.....................185
wy. Narellan Vale..............508
ATNATU
wy. Doonside....................243
ATOLL
pl. Quakers Hill................213
ATTAR
st. Guildford.....................337
ATTARD
av. Marayong....................244
ATTILIO
pl. Edensor Pk..................363
ATTLEE
pl. Winston Hills...............277
ATTOW
st. Winston Hills...............277
ATTUNGA
av. Earlwood....................402
av. Moorebank..................396
av. W Pnnant Hl...............249
pl. Bradbury.....................511
pwy. Moorebank, off Attunga Av..........396
rd. Blaxland......................233
rd. Miranda.......................492
rd. Newport.......................169
rd. Roseville Ch................255
rd. Yowie Bay...................492
st. Baulkham Hl...............247
st. Seven Hills..................275
st. Woollahra......................22
AUBER
gln. St Clair......................300
la. St Clair, off Auber Gln..........300
AUBERT
st. Narellan.......................478 G
AUBIN
st. Neutral Bay.....................6
AUBREEN
st. Collaroy Plat................228
AUBREY
cl. Castle Hill.....................248
pl. Berowra........................133
rd. Northbridge..................286
st. Ingleburn......................453
st. S Granville...................338
st. Stanmore........................16 C
AUBURN
rd. Auburn........................339 C
rd. Auburn........................339
rd. Berala..........................339 C
rd. Birrong.........................368
rd. Regents Pk...................369
rd. Yagoona.......................368 K
st. Hunters Hill..................313
st. Parramatta....................307
st. Sutherland....................490
st.s, Sutherland..................490
AUCKLAND
st. Bonnyrigg Ht...............363
st. Engadine......................518

INE
Epping ... 280 E3
LEY
Petersham ... 15 H11
Royal N P ... 520 E2
Petersham ... 15 H11
REY
Condell Park ... 398 J5
Quakers Hill ... 213 G8
Balgowlah ... 287 F9
Thirlmere ... 565 D2
USTA
Rouse Hill ... 185 B9
Allawah ... 432 F9
Manly ... 288 F8
St Clair ... 270 J11
Fairlight ... 288 E7
Manly ... 288 E7
Allawah ... 432 G9
Bankstown ... 399 A4
Blacktown ... 274 F14
Casula ... 395 A13
Concord ... 341 K1
Condell Park ... 398 H4
Five Dock ... 343 C10
Punchbowl ... 400 C9
Strathfield ... 371 A2
USTINE
Hunters Hill ... 313 B9
USTUS
Enmore ... 17 A12
Enmore ... 17 A12
Ambarvale ... 510 K15
KANE
Green Valley ... 362 K11
LD
Eastwood ... 280 J7
Milperra ... 397 B7
Eagle Vale ... 481 B9
Schofields ... 183 E15
LT
Illawong ... 459 K6
LUBA
S Turramrra ... 252 B6
MUNA
Terrey Hills ... 195 K9
RELIA
Toongabbie ... 276 B8
RORA
Tregear ... 240 E7
Whalan ... 240 F8
Eveleigh ... 18 E12
STEN
Wetherill Pk ... 334 G6
Kellyville ... 215 F3
STIN
Beverly Hills ... 430 K1
Campbelltwn ... 511 H9
Croydon ... 372 B3
Homebush W ... 340 H7
N Curl Curl ... 259 A10
. Picnic Point ... 428 E7
Belfield ... 371 E11
Lane Cove ... 314 D2
Wentwthvle ... 277 D9
Zetland ... 375 K9
Surry Hills ... 20 C4
Orchard Hills ... 268 D8
Fairlight ... 288 B8
Illawong ... 459 H6
Lane Cove ... 314 D3
STIN WOODBURY
Toongabbie ... 276 H6
STRAL
Beecroft ... 250 C8
Lindfield ... 284 B5
North Manly ... 258 B15
Westmead ... 307 E1
e. Fairfield ... 336 D15
St Helens Park ... 541 A6
Kogarah ... 433 D8
Malabar ... 437 D4
Mount Druitt ... 241 C13
Penshurst ... 431 D5
STRALIA
Homebush B ... 340 J1
Matraville ... 436 F3
Camperdwn ... 17 D6
Camperdwn ... 17 D8
Woollahra ... 22 H4
Barden Rdg ... 488 G2
Bass Hill ... 368 D10
Camperdwn ... 17 C4
Croydon ... 342 H13

st. Hurstville ... 432 A9
st. Merrylands ... 308 A13
st. Newtown ... 17 E8
st. St Marys ... 269 K1
AUSTRALIS
av. Wattle Grove ... 396 B16
cl. Cranebrook ... 207 H6
AUSTRALORP
av. Seven Hills ... 275 E5
AUTUMN
gr. Glendenning ... 242 H4
pl. Guildford ... 337 C2
AUTUMN LEAF
gr. Cherrybrook ... 219 J15
pde. St Clair ... 270 C13
AVALON
av. Lane Cove W ... 283 H16
cl. Bossley Park ... 333 F9
pde. Avalon ... 169 K1
pl. Woodbine ... 481 J9
st. Birrong ... 369 A5
st. Turramurra ... 223 D12
AVELINE
pl. Hassall Gr ... 211 K13
AVELING
st. Blakehurst ... 432 C16
AVENAL
la. Arncliffe ... 403 H9
st. Arncliffe ... 403 G10
st. Guildford ... 337 D2
AVENEL
rd. Gymea Bay ... 491 C8
st. Canley Vale ... 365 J1
AVENUE
la. Glebe ... 11 H8
rd. Glebe ... 11 H8
rd. Hunters Hill ... 313 E10
rd. Mosman ... 316 H10
AVENUE OF AFRICA
Newington ... 310 C10
AVENUE OF ASIA
Newington ... 310 C11
AVENUE OF EUROPE
Newington ... 310 B11
AVENUE OF OCEANIA
Homebush B ... 310 C11
Newington ... 310 C11
AVENUE OF THE AMERICAS
Newington ... 310 B11
AVERIL
pl. Lindfield ... 284 C2
AVERILL
st. Rhodes ... 311 E7
AVERY
av. Kirrawee ... 491 B4
st. Normanhurst ... 221 E7
wy. Narellan Vale ... 508 K1
AVIA
cl. Raby ... 451 B13
AVIAN
cr. Lane Cove W ... 283 G12
AVIATION
pl. Bnkstn Aprt ... 397 J1
AVISFORD
st. Fairfield ... 336 B14
AVOCA
av. Belfield ... 371 E9
av. Emu Plains ... 236 B7
cl. West Hoxton ... 392 E6
la. Randwick ... 407 B1
la. Bondi, off Avoca St ... 378 A5
la. Canley Ht, off Birchgrove Av ... 364 K3
pl. Woodbine ... 481 K10
rd. Canley Ht ... 365 A3
rd. Grose Wold ... 115 F7
rd. Silverdale ... 383 A11
rd. Silverdale ... 413 A1
rd. Turramurra ... 222 H16
rd. Wakeley ... 335 A16
st. Bondi ... 377 K5
st. Glenbrook ... 264 C1
st. Kingsford ... 407 A5
st. Randwick ... 377 B16
st. Yagoona ... 369 D10
AVOCET
pl. Hinchinbrk ... 393 C2
AVON
cl. Asquith ... 192 D10
cl. Pymble ... 252 K4
grn. W Pnnant Hl ... 249 C5
la. Glebe ... 12 A9
la. St Clair, off Avon Pl ... 269 J13
pl. Kirrawee ... 491 A10
pl. Leumeah ... 482 D12
pl. St Clair ... 269 J13
pl. Toongabbie ... 276 G7
pl. Windsor Dn ... 151 B12
rd. Bringelly ... 387 F5
rd. Dee Why ... 258 J6
rd. North Ryde ... 282 H9
rd. Pymble ... 253 B2
st. Bankstown ... 369 D12
st. Cammeray ... 316 B5
st. Canley Ht ... 365 A3
st. Glebe ... 12 A9
AVONA
av. Glebe ... 11 K8
cr. Seaforth ... 287 C11
AVONDALE
pl. Cartwright ... 394 E4
pl. West Pymble ... 252 H7
rd. Pitt Town ... 93 H16
rd. Scheyville ... 123 D1
AVON DAM
rd. Bargo ... 567 G8
AVONLEA
cr. Bass Hill ... 368 C8
dr. Carlingford ... 250 C13
st. Canley Ht ... 335 E15
AVONLEIGH
ct. Glenwood ... 245 G2
wy. W Pnnant Hl ... 249 C3
AVRIL
ct. Glenwood ... 215 C16
ct. Glenwood ... 245 C1
ct. Kellyville ... 216 G3
AVRO
pl. Raby ... 451 G15
rd. Lane Cove W ... 283 G12
st. Bnkstn Aprt ... 367 H16
st. Mascot ... 404 K4
AWABA
la. Mosman, off Killarney St ... 317 B4
pl. Warriewood ... 199 C9
st. Mosman ... 316 H3
st. Mosman ... 317 A4
AWATEA
pl. Engadine ... 518 F5
pl. Lethbrdg Pk ... 240 E2
rd. St Ives Ch ... 223 K2
AXAM
wy. Narellan Vale ... 509 A1
AXFORD
pl. Fairfield W ... 335 A9
AXINITE
pl. Eagle Vale ... 481 G9
AXON
pl. Bonnyrigg ... 364 B6
AYCLIFFE
av. Hebersham ... 241 F8
AYLES
rd. Winston Hills ... 246 G16
AYLESBURY
cr. Chipping Ntn ... 396 G2
st. Botany ... 405 H12
st. Newtown ... 17 K7
AYLETT
st. N St Marys ... 239 J8
AYLSHAM
cl. Chipping Ntn ... 366 G13
AYLWARD
av. Quakers Hill ... 214 B10
AYR
pl. Riverstone ... 183 C8
st. Ashbury ... 372 E8
st. Banksia ... 403 J13
AYRES
cr. Georges Hall ... 367 J15
cr. Leumeah ... 482 G10
gr. Mount Druitt ... 241 F15
rd. St Ives ... 224 D7
rd.w, St Ives ... 224 B7
AYRSHIRE
pl. Narellan Vale ... 508 J2
st. Bossley Park ... 334 B11
st. Busby ... 363 K16
AYRTON
st. Blacktown ... 273 J7
AYSHFORD
st. Casula ... 424 B3
AZALEA
ct. Glenmore Pk ... 265 G8
gdn. Wahroonga ... 223 C6
gr. Castle Hill ... 217 F16
gr. Pennant Hills ... 250 G2
pl. Loftus ... 489 K9
pl. Mcquarie Fd ... 453 K6
pl. Panania ... 428 E5
st. Blacktown ... 274 E12
st. Greystanes ... 305 H11
AZILE
ct. Carlingford ... 279 F6
AZTEC
cl. Greenfld Pk ... 333 K14
AZZOPARDI
av. Glendenning ... 242 E5

B

BAANYA
pl. Cranebrook ... 207 D15
BAARTZ
tce. Glenwood ... 215 H16
BABBAGE
rd. Roseville ... 285 D3
rd. Roseville Ch ... 255 E16
BABBIN
av. Caringbah ... 492 F9
BACH
av. Emerton ... 240 H6
cl. Cranebrook ... 207 D15
pl. Bonnyrigg Ht ... 363 D7
pl. Engadine ... 518 E5
BACHELL
av. Lidcombe ... 340 C6
BACK
cl. Kearns ... 451 C16
BACKS
pl. Narellan Vale ... 478 H15
BADAJOZ
rd. North Ryde ... 282 G15
rd. Ryde ... 282 G15
BADANA
pl. Cromer ... 228 D15
BADARENE
pl. E Lindfield ... 255 A11
BADCOE
rd. Cromer ... 227 K13
BADDELEY
st. Padstow ... 399 B16
BADEN
av. Bass Hill ... 368 A6
pl. Blaxland ... 233 D3
rd. Neutral Bay ... 6 J14
st. Coogee ... 377 H15
st. Greystanes ... 306 E10
BADENOCH
av. Glenhaven ... 218 B6
BADEN POWELL
av. Kingswood ... 237 G15
pl. Lakemba ... 401 C4
pl. North Rocks ... 249 A13
pl. Winston Hills ... 277 F6
st. Brooklyn ... 75 K11
BADGALLY
rd. Blairmount ... 480 K11
rd. Campbelltwn ... 511 E1
rd. Claymore ... 480 K11
rd. Eagle Vale ... 480 K11
rd. The Oaks ... 502 D13
rd. Woodbine ... 481 C15
BADGER
av. Sefton ... 368 F5
pl. Green Valley ... 363 A8
BADGERY
av. Homebush ... 340 J11
wy. Bonnyrigg ... 364 C4
BADGERYS CREEK
rd. Badgerys Ck ... 328 G16
rd. Bringelly ... 388 B7
BADHAM
av. Mosman ... 316 H12
st. Merrylands ... 308 C16
st. Woolmloo, off Crown St ... 4 D6
BADMINTON
rd. Croydon ... 372 B3
BADTO
av. Gymea ... 491 C4
BAECKEA
pl. Oxford Falls ... 226 H15
BAGALA
st. Glenwood ... 215 J16
BAGDAD
st. Regents Pk ... 369 B2
BAGGOT
pl. Baulkham Hl ... 247 C2
BAGLIN
st. Bronte ... 377 H10
BAGO
st. Pendle Hill ... 276 G12
BAGUETTE
cl. Casula ... 394 G16
BAHRI
pl. Glenwood ... 245 K4
BAIL
wy. Glenwood ... 215 F13
BAILEY
av. Lane Cove W ... 284 A12
av. West Hoxton ... 391 G8
cr. N Epping ... 251 E8
pde. Peakhurst ... 430 F1
pl. Blacktown ... 243 K9
st. Newtown ... 17 E13
st. Westmead ... 307 G1
BAILEYANA
ct. Wattle Grove ... 426 B1
BAILEYS
la. Kurrajong Hl ... 54 J16
BAILLEY
st. Leumeah ... 512 D1
BAIN
gr. Quakers Hill ... 214 E15
pl. Barden Rdg ... 488 H2
pl. Dundas Vy ... 280 C9
st. Glenbrook ... 264 A2
BAINBRIDGE
av. Chipping Ntn ... 396 B5
av. Ingleburn ... 453 A12
cr. Rooty Hill ... 271 H4
BAINES
cl. Mulgoa ... 324 C5
BAINTON
pl. Doonside ... 243 E16
rd. Mt Pritchard ... 364 K9
BAIRD
av. Matraville ... 406 H16
av. Ryde ... 312 E2
ct. W Pnnant Hl ... 249 F7
la. Sefton ... 368 E6
la. Matraville, off Baird Av ... 406 H16
st. Bass Hill ... 368 E8
st. Sefton ... 368 E8
BAKEHOUSE
pl. The Rocks ... A K5
BAKER
av. Newington ... 310 A15
cl. Bossley Park ... 333 H11
cr. Baulkham Hl ... 248 A9
la. Bundeena ... 524 B10
pl. Lindfield ... 284 A1
pl. Minto ... 453 D15
pl. Penshurst ... 431 E2
st. Bnksmeadw ... 406 B12
st. Blacktown ... 245 A15
st. Bundeena ... 524 A9
st. Carlingford ... 279 F5
st. Enfield ... 371 J4
st. Galston ... 159 E9
st. Kensington ... 376 B11
st. Merrylands ... 307 J16
st. Oatley ... 430 H13
st. Springwood ... 202 D10
st. Windsor ... 121 D7
BAKERI
ct. Voyager Pt ... 427 B4
BAKERS
la. Forest Lodge ... 17 J1
la. Kemps Ck ... 300 B12
la. Strathfield, off Cooper St ... 341 F10
la. Earlwood, off Homer St ... 403 A3
la. St Peters, off Mary St ... 374 G14
rd. Church Point ... 168 G9
BALA
pl. Marayong ... 243 K6

BALACLAVA
- la. Alexandria 19 A16
- rd. Berowra 133 E10
- rd. Eastwood 281 D6
- rd. Emu Heights 235 A2
- rd. Mcquarie Pk 281 J3
- rd. Marsfield 281 J3

BALAKA
- dr. Carlingford 249 C16

BALALA
- ct. Wattle Grove 396 A16

BALANADA
- av. Chipping Ntn 396 G6

BALANAMING
- la. Petersham 15 G11

BALANDRA
- pl. Kareela 461 E10

BALARANG
- pl. Bangor 459 D10

BALBEEK
- av. Blacktown 243 K11

BALBOA
- pl. Willmot 210 C13
- st. Kurnell 465 G8

BALDER
- st. Doonside 243 F15

BALDI
- av. Panania 398 C14

BALDINI
- pl. Hinchinbrk 393 A3

BALDO
- st. Edensor Pk 333 H12

BALDRY
- st. Chatswood 285 A8

BALDWIN
- av. Asquith 192 B10
- av. Glenfield 424 E10
- av. Winston Hills 247 H16
- st. Erskineville 17 K13
- st. Gordon 253 K5
- st. Padstow 429 B1
- wy. Currans Hill 479 F12

BALEMO
- pl. Bangor 459 B12

BALFOUR
- av. Caringbah 492 G3
- dr. Kellyville 186 B15
- la. Bellevue Hill 347 H14
- la. Kensington 376 D10
- la. Lindfield 254 C16
- la. Wollstncraft 315 D8
- rd. Bellevue Hill 347 H11
- rd. Kensington 376 D12
- rd. Narwee 400 J15
- rd. Rose Bay 347 H11
- st. Allawah 432 G8
- st. Chippendale 19 B4
- st. Dulwich Hill 373 D13
- st. Greenwich 314 J6
- st. Lindfield 254 C16
- st. Northmead 277 K12
- st. Wollstncraft 315 D8

BALGA
- cl. Berowra Ht 132 H10

BALGANG
- av. Kirrawee 491 B4

BALGOWLAH
- rd. Balgowlah 287 H6
- rd. Fairlight 288 A7
- rd. Manly 288 D6

BALI
- dr. Quakers Hill 213 H9

BALIGA
- av. Caringbah 492 E10

BALIMBA
- pl. Whalan 240 K9

BALIMO
- pl. Glenfield 424 G11

BALIN
- pl. Blacktown 274 K7

BALINTORE
- dr. Castle Hill 218 C7
- dr. Castle Hill 218 D8

BALKE
- st. Minto 452 J13

BALL
- av. Eastwood 281 C6
- *la. Colyton, off Ball St 270 C3*
- pl. Willmot 210 D13
- st. Colyton 270 C3

BALLAH
- ct. S Penrith 266 H6
- *la. S Penrith, off Ballah Ct 266 H6*

BALLA MACHREE
- wy. Gymea Bay 491 E9

BALLANDA
- av. Lugarno 430 B15
- pl. Bangor 459 D12
- pl. Dural 158 E13
- st. Frenchs Frst 256 D8

BALLANDELLA
- rd. Pendle Hill 276 E12
- rd. Toongabbie 276 E12

BALLANTRAE
- dr. St Andrews 451 K15

BALLANTYNE
- rd. Mortdale 430 G9
- st. Mosman 316 K9

BALLAR
- av. Gymea Bay 491 H9

BALLARAT
- av. St Clair 270 B10
- pl. Cartwright 394 B5
- pl. St Johns Pk 364 H1

BALLARD
- pl. Doonside 273 E3

BALLAST POINT
- rd. Birchgrove 7 J3

BALLATER
- wy. Kellyville 217 B2

BALLENY
- pl. Tregear 240 F5

BALLERDO PATH
- Winmalee 173 C9

BALLINA
- av. Killarney Ht 286 B1
- cl. Hoxton Park 392 K7
- pl. Bangor 459 B11
- pl. Bossley Park 333 F10
- st. Georges Hall 367 J13
- st. Greystanes 305 H4

BALLS HEAD
- dr. Waverton 315 D15
- rd. Waverton 315 D14

BALLYBUNNION
- tce. Glenmore Pk 266 F8

BALLYLEANEY
- pl. Erskine Park 300 F2

BALLYMENA
- st. Hebersham 241 F4
- wy. Kellyville 217 C2

BALLYSHANNON
- rd. Killarney Ht 255 J13

BALMAIN
- pl. Doonside 273 E2
- rd. Leichhardt 10 B14
- rd. Leichhardt 16 B1
- rd. Lilyfield 10 B6
- rd. Lilyfield 10 C5
- rd. McGraths Hl 121 K13
- st. Cartwright 394 D5
- wy. Minto 483 A2

BALMARINGA
- av. S Turramrra 252 B5

BALMORAL
- av. Croydon Pk 371 K9
- av. Mosman 317 C7
- cct. Cecil Hills 362 F4
- cr. Georges Hall 367 H14
- dr. Cmbrdg Pk 237 J9
- pl. Carlingford 279 C5
- rd. Ingleburn 453 K15
- rd. Kellyville 215 J12
- rd. Mortdale 430 G8
- rd. Northmead 277 H11
- st. Blacktown 274 E2
- st. Hornsby 192 A16
- st. Waitara 222 A4

BALOG
- st. St Marys 270 A7

BALOOK
- cr. Bradbury 511 B16

BALOWRIE
- st. Yowie Bay 492 C11

BALSON
- cl. Abbotsbury 333 A15

BALTHASAR
- cl. Rsemeadow 540 H4

BALTIC
- la. Newtown 17 D11
- st. Fairlight 288 D7
- st. Newtown 17 C11

BALTIMORE
- rd. Mortdale 430 H9
- st. Belfield 371 E11

BALYATA
- av. Caringbah 493 B12

BAMBARA
- av. Bradbury 541 D1
- cr. Beecroft 250 C11
- pl. Baulkham Hl 248 C10
- rd. Frenchs Frst 256 B1
- st. Dharruk 241 C9

BAMBI
- cl. Cranebrook 207 B10
- st. Ryde 282 D15

BAMBIL
- pl. Blaxland 234 E8
- rd. Berowra 133 D16
- st. Georges Hall 367 G13
- st. Greystanes 305 J10

BAMBOO
- av. Earlwood 403 H3
- wy. Stanhpe Gdn 215 D9

BAMBRA
- av. Roselands 400 J6

BAMBRIDGE
- *la. Riverstone, off Pitt St 182 J8*
- st. Chester Hill 368 B5

BAMENT
- pl. Minchinbury 271 F8

BAMFIELD
- av. Yagoona 368 F12

BAMFORD
- pl. Lalor Park 245 G10

BAMPI
- pl. Castle Cove 286 D5

BAMPTON
- av. Illawong 459 A7

BANARO
- av. Whalan 240 K10

BANBAL
- rd. Engadine 488 H14

BANBURY
- cr. Chipping Ntn 396 E3

BANCKS
- av. Thornleigh 221 B10

BANCROFT
- av. Roseville 284 H4
- av. W Pnnant Hl 220 B15
- *la. Roseville, off Bancroft Av 284 H4*
- rd. Abbotsbury 333 B15
- st. Oakhurst 241 H1

BANDA
- pl. Fairfield W 335 F9

BANDAIN
- av. Kareela 461 C14

BANDALONG
- av. West Pymble 253 B13
- cr. Bangor 459 D11

BANDERRA
- rd. S Penrith 237 B15

BANDO
- rd. Cronulla 494 A9
- rd. Girraween 276 C12

BANDON
- rd. Vineyard 152 F10

BANFF
- pl. Winston Hills 277 E3

BANGALAY
- pl. Leonay 234 K14
- pl. Mcquarie Fd 454 G3
- st. Georges Hall 367 G11

BANGALEE
- pl. Bangor 459 D11

BANGALLA
- av. Bradbury 511 F15
- av. Chipping Ntn 396 F4
- pl. Forestville 255 H11
- rd. Concord W 311 D15
- rd. Rose Bay 348 E12
- st. Turramurra 222 G9
- st. Warrawee 222 G9

BANGALLEY
- *wy. Avalon, off Barrenjoey Rd 140 D13*

BANGALOW
- av. Beecroft 250 C5
- av. Chipping Ntn 396 G4
- av. Mona Vale 199 D1
- pl. Baulkham Hl 247 A7
- pl. Stanhpe Gdn 215 B10

BANGAR
- cl. Killarney Ht 256 A16

BANGAROO
- st. Bangor 459 D12
- st. N Balgowlah 287 D6

BANGOR
- rd. Middle Dural 128 E16
- st. Auburn 338 J1
- st. Guildford 337 D4

BANGU
- pl. Glenmore Pk 266 B11

BANJO
- cr. Emu Plains 235 A8
- ct. Castle Hill 217 D9
- pl. Springwood 202 J1
- st. Heathcote 518 C15

BANJO PATERSON
- cl. Glenmore Pk 265 K5
- pl. Padstow Ht 429 D7

BANK
- la. Kogarah 433 C4
- la. McMahons Pt 5 B10
- la. N Sydney 5 B10
- st. Lidcombe 339 G10
- st. McMahons Pt 5 B10
- st. Meadowbnk 311 E4
- st. N Sydney 5 B10
- st. Pyrmont 12 C3
- st. West Ryde 311 E4

BANKS
- av. Berrilee 131 D9
- av. Daceyville 406 F8
- av. Eastgardens 406 E11
- av. N Turramrra 223 E3
- av. Pagewood 406 E11
- dr. St Clair 269 G9
- la. Earlwood 403 A4
- pl. Camden S 507 A11
- rd. Busby 363 F16
- rd. Castle Hill 218 E9
- rd. Earlwood 403 A4
- rd. Miller 393 E5
- st. Ashfield 342 G16
- st. Campbelltwn 511 K6
- st. Maroubra 407 J9
- st. Mays Hill 307 H6
- st. Monterey 433 H6
- st. Padstow 399 E15
- st. Parramatta 307 H6

BANKSHILL
- cr. Carlingford 280 B5

BANKSIA
- av. Banksia 403 E12
- av. Engadine 488 G16
- cl. Kings Lngly 245 J10
- cr. Fairfield E 336 J12
- dr. Valley Ht 202 E5
- pl. Arcadia 129 G7
- pl. Canada Bay 342 E8
- pl. Greystanes 305 F11
- pl. Ingleburn 453 D8
- pl. Kenthurst 156 J15
- pl. Lugarno 429 H14
- pl. Newington 310 B13
- pl. Oakdale 500 C13
- pl. Wattle Grove 396 B16
- rd. Bellevue Hill 377 J1
- rd. Caringbah 492 J6
- rd. Caringbah 493 A7
- rd. Greenacre 369 H11
- rd. Mt Annan 509 D3
- st. Botany 405 F11
- st. Couridjah 564 F16
- st. Dee Why 259 A8
- st. Eastwood 281 H8
- st. Normanhurst 221 D12
- st. N St Marys 240 A10
- st. Pagewood 405 K10
- st. S Granville 338 G2
- st. Stanhpe Gdn 215 D10

BANKSIDE
- av. Earlwood 403 F2

BANN
- *wy. Wentwthvle, off Portadown Rd 277 D11*

BANNER
- rd. Kingsgrove 402 A13

BANNERMAN
- cr. Rosebery 375 K16
- rd. Glenhaven 187 B12
- rd. Kenthurst 187 B12
- st. Cremorne 6 J6
- st. Ermington 310
- st. Mortdale 430

BANNISTER
- pl. Mt Pritchard 364
- wy. Wrrngtn Cty 238

BANNOCKBURN
- av. St Andrews 481
- la. N Turramrra 223
- rd. Pymble 223
- rd. Turramurra 223

BANOOL
- av. St Ives 223
- av. S Penrith 266
- *la. S Penrith, off Banool Av 266*
- st. Chester Hill 338
- st. Kareela 461

BANQUO
- pl. Rsemeadow 540

BANTRY BAY
- rd. Frenchs Frst 256

BANYEENA
- pl. Belrose 226

BANYULA
- pl. Killara 253
- pl. Mt Colah 162

BANYULE
- ct. Wattle Grove 425

BANZ
- pl. Glenfield 424

BAPAUME
- pde. Matraville 407
- pl. Milperra 397
- rd. Moorebank 395
- rd. Mosman 317

BAPTIST
- la. Redfern 19
- st. Redfern 20

BARA
- pl. Quakers Hill 243

BARABA
- cl. Glenmore Pk 266

BARADINE
- pl. Yarrawarrah 489
- wy. Hoxton Park 392

BARAGIL
- mw. Mt Annan 479

BARAGOOLA
- av. Phillip Bay 436
- st. Fairfield W 335

BARALGA
- cr. Riverwood 400

BARAMBAH
- la. Roseville 285
- rd. Roseville 285

BARANA
- pde. Roseville Ch 255
- pl. Kareela 461

BARANBALI
- av. Seaforth 287
- st. Beverly Hills 401
- st. Doonside 243

BARANGAROO
- rd. Toongabbie 276

BARARA
- pl. Fairfield W 335

BARASI
- pl. Kenthurst 157

BARB
- pl. Blairmount 480

BARBARA
- bvd. Seven Hills 245
- cr. Merrylands 307
- ct. Mona Vale 198
- pl. Lugarno 429
- st. Fairfield 336

BARBARO
- la. Horsley Pk 332

BARBER
- av. Eastlakes 405
- av. Kingswood 237
- av. Penrith 237
- la. Panania 398
- pl. Glenwood 215

BARBERS
- rd. Chester Hill 337
- rd. Guildford 337

BARBOUR
- rd. Thirlmere 565

BARCELONA
- dr. Prestons 393

Prestons 393 K15
RCHAM
W Pnnant Hl 249 A9
RCLAY
Pymble 252 K4
North Rocks 249 A14
Marrickville 374 C14
Quakers Hill 213 F15
Waverley 377 H10
RCOM
Darlinghurst 4 G13
Darlinghurst 4 J12
Paddington 4 G13
Merrylands W 307 B14
RCOO
Leumeah 482 B15
Erskine Park 270 G15
St Clair, off
Barcoo Cl 270 G15
St Ives 254 D4
Peakhurst 430 D8
Roseville 285 C4
RCOO ISLAND
Sylvania Wtr 462 F12
RCOOLA
Bayview 168 C11
RCOTE
Castle Hill 219 A8
RD
St Clair 270 C16
RDEN
Randwick 377 A11
Barden Rdg 458 G16
Arncliffe 403 F8
Northmead 277 J12
Tempe 404 C3
RDIA
Mt Annan 479 D11
e. Holsworthy 396 D16
Bossley Park 334 B5
E Lindfield 254 K10
Carlingford 249 K13
RDO
Newport 169 E11
Glenmore Pk 266 D7
RDOLPH
Rsemeadow 540 G8
RDON
St Johns Pk 334 F16
RDOO
N Balgowlah 287 C4
RDSLEY
Rouse Hill 184 J6
n. N Sydney 315 J7
RDWELL
Earlwood 402 G5
Mosman, off
Holt Av 316 J9
Bardwell Pk 402 J7
Bardwell Vy 403 A7
Mosman 316 J8
y. Bardwell Pk, off
Crewe St 402 J6
RE
Lurnea 394 D7
Bnksmeadw 436 C1
REE
Warriewood 199 B8
REENA
Wahroonga 222 D4
Balgowlah Ht 287 H14
Hamondvle 396 E14
Marsfield 251 J14
Avalon 140 E13
Cabramatta 366 B5
Canley Vale 366 B5
Lilli Pilli 522 E4
Strathfield 340 K16
k. Wahroonga 222 E5
RELLAN
Carlingford 280 C2
Turramurra 252 F1
Merrylands 306 J10
RFF
Camperdwn 18 E2
Ingleburn 453 A10
RFIL
S Wntwthvle 306 J4
RGAROO
Glenmore Pk 266 G15
RGO
Prestons 392 K16

rd. Bargo 567 F7
rd. Bargo 567 K6
st. Maianbar 523 B7
BARGO RIVER
rd. Couridjah 564 E16
rd. Couridjah 565 A16
rd. Couridjah 565 E16
rd. Tahmoor 565 E16
BARHAM
st. Heckenberg 364 A12
st. Maianbar 523 B7
st. Parramatta 278 J15
BARILLA
pl. Bonnyrigg Ht 362 K6
st. Bonnyrigg Ht 363 A5
BARINA
cr. Emu Plains 234 K8
pl. Blaxland 234 D5
rd. Riverview 314 C5
BARINA DOWNS
rd. Baulkham Hl 246 G1
rd. Bella Vista 246 G1
BARINGA
av. Seaforth 287 B6
cl. Belrose 225 K11
cl. Green Valley 363 H11
rd. Earlwood 402 D4
rd. Engadine 488 H16
rd. Mortdale 430 G9
rd. Northbridge 285 J16
st. Berowra Ht 133 B10
st. Blaxland 233 F5
st. North Ryde 282 E8
BARISTON
av. Cremorne 316 G5
BARITE
pl. Eagle Vale 481 F6
BARJADDA
av. Sylvania 462 B11
BARK
pl. Kings Lngly 245 E8
BARKALA
pl. Westleigh 220 G4
BARKDUK
av. Miranda 491 J5
BARKER
av. Silverwater 309 J15
cl. Camden S 506 K10
dr. Castle Hill 218 J13
la. Lewisham 15 C8
la. Kingsford, off
Houston Rd 376 F16
pl. Leumeah 482 D16
rd. Strathfield 341 A14
st. Bossley Park 334 C11
st. Cmbrdg Pk 237 F7
st. Kensington 376 E16
st. Kingsford 376 E16
st. Lewisham 15 B8
st. Randwick 376 E16
st. Rooty Hill 272 D2
st. St Marys 269 E5
BARKERS LODGE
rd. Mowbray Pk 562 D1
rd. Oakdale 500 C16
rd. Picton 563 A2
BARKL
av. Padstow 429 C1
BARKLEY
cl. Cherrybrook 219 C14
st. Carramar 366 J1
BARKLY
cl. Bonnyrigg Ht 363 G5
dr. Windsor Dn 180 G1
BARLEY
gln. Wrrngtn Dns 238 B5
BARLOW
cr. Canley Ht 364 K3
pl. Georges Hall 367 J12
pl. Horngsea Pk 392 C15
st. Cmbrdg Pk 237 J6
st. Haymarket E F10
st. Haymarket 3 F13
BARNABY
pl. Ambarvale 510 K15
BARNARD
cr. Oakhurst 241 H4
pl. St Helens Park 541 A8
BARNARDO
cl. Wahroonga 221 K10
BARNARDS
av. Hurstville 401 J16

BARNCLEUTH
la. Potts Point 4 K6
sq. Elizabeth Bay 13 A6
sq. Potts Point 13 A6
BARNES
av. Earlwood 372 F16
cr. Menai 458 D10
la. Blacktown 274 D6
pl. Rouse Hill 184 K7
rd. Frenchs Frst 257 B3
rd. Llandilo 179 G15
st. Girraween 276 B10
st. Lidcombe 339 J11
st. Minto 453 C16
BARNET
av. Rookwood 340 A12
pl. Doonside 273 H2
st. Glenbrook 234 C15
BARNETT
la. Bondi Jctn 377 H2
la. Darlinghurst 4 D8
la. S Penrith, off
Barnett St 266 F3
pl. Cabramatta W 365 C6
st. Ashcroft 394 F2
st. S Penrith 266 F3
BARNETTS
rd. Berowra Ht 133 A10
rd. Winston Hills 277 C4
BARNEY
pl. Davidson 225 C15
st. Drummoyne 343 F5
st. N Parramatta 278 B11
BARNFIELD
pl. Dean Park 212 K16
BARNIER
dr. Quakers Hill 214 B8
BARNSBURY
gr. Bardwell Pk 402 H8
gr. Bexley North 402 F10
gr. Dulwich Hill 373 F10
BARNSLEY
pl. Menai 458 J14
BARNSTAPLE
la. Five Dock 343 A8
rd. Five Dock 343 A9
rd. Rodd Point 343 A9
rd. Russell Lea 343 A9
BARNWELL
pl. Cecil Hills 362 G3
BARODA
la. Elizabeth Bay 13 A5
st. Elizabeth Bay 13 A5
BAROMBAH
rd. Epping 250 J12
BARON
cl. Kings Lngly 245 D6
BARONBALI
st. Dundas 279 H13
BARONESA
la. S Penrith, off
Baronesa Rd 237 C16
rd. S Penrith 237 B16
BARONGA
av. Queens Park 22 E14
BARONS
av. Carlingford 279 D5
cr. Hunters Hill 313 D4
BARONTA
st. Blacktown 275 A2
BAROO
st. Thirlmere 565 C5
BAROOGA
av. Bradbury 511 F16
BAROOK
pl. Mt Pritchard 364 D9
BAROONA
pl. Seven Hills 246 B13
rd. Northbridge 315 J1
st. Church Point 168 F8
st. Dangar I 76 J7
BAROSSA
cl. St Clair 270 D12
ct. Baulkham Hl 246 H4
dr. Minchinbury 271 J9
pl. Edensor Pk 333 D16
pl. Mona Vale 199 B5
BARR
st. Balmain 7 C9
st. Camperdwn 17 G1
st. Colyton 270 F8
st. Mortdale 430 J8

st. North Ryde 282 H7
BARRABA
pl. Bella Vista 246 F8
BARRABOOKA
st. Clontarf 287 H16
BARRA-BRUI
cr. St Ives 254 C3
BARRACE
rd. Mosman, off
Middle Head Rd 317 F10
BARRACK
cct. Mcquarie Lk 423 E14
la. Parramatta 308 D3
la. Sydney C G2
st. Sydney C F2
st. Sydney 3 G1
BARRACKS
st. Emu Plains 235 C10
BARRACLOUGH
wy. Bonnyrigg 364 B4
BARRACLUFF
av. Bondi Beach 378 A2
BARRAKEE
pl. Westleigh 220 G3
BARRALLIER
wy. St Clair 270 E11
BARRARAN
st. Gymea Bay 491 E11
BARRATT
av. Camden S 507 B13
st. Hurstville 432 A5
wy. Minto 482 K1
BARRATTA
pl. Bangor 459 C11
BARRAWARN
pl. Castle Hill 218 B12
BARRAWINGA
st. Telopea 279 G8
BARRE
st. Hurlstone Pk 373 A11
BARREMMA
rd. Lakemba 371 B14
BARREN
cl. Green Valley 363 A12
BARRENJOEY
cl. Woodbine 481 H11
rd. Avalon 140 C10
rd. Bilgola 170 A5
rd. Mona Vale 199 E4
rd. Newport 169 H16
rd. Palm Beach 139 H2
BARRETT
av. Thornleigh 220 J11
pl. Cranebrook 207 F8
pl. Randwick 377 E10
st. Guildford 337 G3
BARRIE
pl. Davidson 255 D1
pl. Leumeah 512 C3
st. East Killara 255 A8
BARRIER
cl. Casula 424 C1
pl. Illawong 459 H3
BARRIGON
gr. Menai 458 J14
BARRINGTON
ct. Holsworthy 426 E5
dr. Dural 219 C4
pl. Carlingford 279 E2
rd. Silverdale 384 A4
st. Bossley Park 334 C9
st. Ruse 512 F5
BARRON
pl. Bossley Park 333 G5
BARRON FIELD
dr. Glenmore Pk 265 H5
BARROW
cl. Green Valley 363 B12
pl. Silverdale 353 H16
st. Revesby 399 A15
BARRY
av. Catherine Fd 419 C2
av. Mortdale 430 G6
av. Rossmore 419 C2
cr. Padstow Ht 429 G7
la. Neutral Bay 6 G3
pl. Bidwill 211 C16
pl. Cherrybrook 219 F16
pl. Wentwthvle 307 C3
rd. Chipping Ntn 366 J16
rd. Kellyville 185 J7
rd. Menai 458 G13

st. Cmbrdg Pk 237 G9
st. Clovelly 377 G12
st. Neutral Bay 6 F4
BARRY COE
pl. Cranebrook 207 G10
BARSBY
av. Allawah 432 F7
BARSDEN
st. Camden 506 K1
BARSEDEN
st. Bonnyrigg 364 D4
BARTIL
cl. Epping 251 E14
BARTLETT
la. Paddington 20 G1
st. Ermington 280 B14
st. S Wntwthvle 307 B7
st. Summer Hill 373 C6
BARTLEY
la. Chippendale 19 B3
st. Cabramatta 365 H5
st. Canley Vale 365 H5
st. Chippendale 19 B4
BARTOK
gr. St Clair 300 B1
pl. Bonnyrigg Ht 363 D5
BARTON
av. Haberfield 343 E14
av. Hurlstone Pk 373 A11
av. W Pnnant Hl 249 A8
cr. N Wahrnga 222 G1
rd. Artarmon 285 A16
st. Concord 342 A1
st. Ermington 310 E1
st. Kogarah 433 D8
st. Marsden Pk 181 K13
st. Monterey 433 D8
st. N Parramatta 278 K14
st. Smithfield 336 A8
st. Strathfield S 371 C5
BARUDA
pl. Erskine Park 270 F16
BARUNGA
st. Concord W 311 F15
BARWELL
av. Castle Hill 218 B15
BARWING
pl. Woronora Ht 489 F4
BARWON
av. S Turramrra 251 K5
cr. Matraville 436 K2
ct. Wattle Grove 395 J12
pl. Campbelltwn 512 A7
pl. Sylvania Wtr 462 E10
rd. Lane Cove W 313 J1
rd. Mortdale 430 H9
st. Greystanes 306 C5
BARWON PARK
rd. Alexandria 374 J12
rd. St Peters 374 J12
BARWOOD
cl. Westleigh 220 G2
BASIL
rd. Bexley 432 C1
st. Riverwood 399 J16
BASILDON
pl. Hebersham 241 F6
rd. Canley Ht 365 B4
BASILISK
pl. Whalan 240 J9
BASINGSTOKE
pl. Hebersham 241 F5
BASS
av. East Hills 427 G3
cl. Hinchinbrk 363 B16
dr. Baulkham Hl 247 B11
pl. Camden S 506 J13
pl. Mt Colah 162 C11
pl. Ruse 512 F3
pl. St Ives 224 A8
pl. Willmot 210 B12
rd. Earlwood 403 B1
rd. Ingleburn 423 A10
rd. Lansvale 367 B10
st. Colyton 270 E8
st. Ermington 280 C15
st. Kingsford 406 K4
st. Port Hacking 522 J2
st. Putney 312 D7
BASSELL
la. Seven Hills 245 G16
BASSETT
pl. Castle Hill 218 J11

pl. Menai 458 H13
st. Hurstville 431 E1
st. Mona Vale 199 D1
BASSIA
pl. Alfords Point 428 K13
BASTABLE
st. Croydon 372 F1
BASTILLE
cl. Padstow Ht 429 H7
BATAAN
cl. Illawong 459 J4
pl. Kings Park 244 K3
pl. Lethbrdg Pk 210 K16
BATAVIA
pl. Baulkham Hl 246 G6
pl. Illawong 459 F5
pl. Willmot 210 E14
BATCHELOR
av. Panania 398 A16
cl. Menai 458 H15
BATE
av. Allambie Ht 257 G16
BATE BAY
rd. Cronulla 494 B6
BATEHAVEN
cl. Prestons 392 K13
BATEMAN
cr. Bass Hill 367 F8
pl. Bligh Park 150 C6
BATEMANS
rd. Gladesville 312 K11
BATES
av. Blaxland 233 F9
av. Paddington 13 B13
av. S Wntwthvle 306 H7
cl. Elderslie 507 J4
dr. Kareela 461 B11
dr. Kareela 461 C14
dr. Kirrawee 461 D14
pl. Doonside 273 H1
pl. Edensor Pk 333 J14
st. Birchgrove 7 J3
st. Homebush 340 K9
st. Strathfield 340 K9
wy. Ambarvale 540 K1
BATH
la. Avalon 170 C2
rd. Kareela 461 B14
rd. Kirrawee 491 B3
rd.s, Kirrawee 491 A6
st. Monterey 433 H7
BATHO
st. Harbord 258 J15
BATHURST
la. Woollahra 22 H3
st. Berala 339 E13
st. Greystanes 305 J3
st. Gymea 461 G16
st. Leumeah 512 C3
st. Liverpool 395 C4
st. Liverpool 395 D1
st. Pitt Town 92 H15
st. Sydney C D14
st. Sydney 3 E7
st. Wakeley 334 H13
st. Warwck Frm 365 D16
st. Woollahra 22 H3
BATLOW
pl. Bossley Park 333 E13
st. Heckenberg 364 A13
BATMAN
cr. Springwood 202 C11
la. Surry Hills F E11
pl. St Johns Pk 364 G1
rd. Ingleburn 422 J14
wk. Parramatta, off Macquarie St 308 D3
BATT
st. Jamisontown 266 D1
st. Penrith 266 D1
st. Sefton 368 E5
BATTEN
av. Melrose Pk 310 J1
cct. S Windsor 150 F1
cr. Ermington 280 A15
pl. Doonside 273 H1
BATTENBERG
cl. Cecil Hills 362 D5
BATTERSEA
st. Abbotsford 312 H16
BATTERY
rd. Mosman 317 K6
st. Clovelly 377 J13
BATTLE
bvd. Seaforth 287 B11
BATTLEMENT
cr. Castle Hill 217 F3
BATTUNGA
pl. Engadine 489 D10
BATTY
st. Rozelle 7 F14
BATTYE
av. Beverley Pk 433 B8
BAUDIN
cl. Illawong 459 C4
cr. Fairfield W 335 D11
pl. Willmot 210 A11
BAUER
ct. Mt Annan 509 G3
rd. Cabramatta W 365 B9
BAULKHAM HILLS
rd. Baulkham Hl 247 A12
BAUMANS
rd. Peakhurst 430 G1
rd. Riverwood 400 F15
BAUXITE
pl. Eagle Vale 481 D8
BAVIN
av. Ryde 282 B16
BAX
gln. St Clair 300 B2
BAXTER
av. Kogarah 433 D3
av. Springwood 202 C1
cr. Glendenning 242 H6
dr. Old Tngabbie 277 A5
la. Kogarah 433 D3
rd. Bass Hill 367 F6
rd. Mascot 405 B5
st. S Penrith 237 A15
BAXTERS
la. Picton 563 H5
BAY
la. Cronulla 523 H1
la. Ultimo 12 H14
pde. Malabar 437 F4
pl. Quakers Hill 243 K1
rd. Arcadia 130 F9
rd. Berowra Wtr 132 A6
rd. Berrilee 131 A11
rd. N Sydney K A1
rd. N Sydney 5 A6
rd. Oatley 430 G11
rd. Russell Lea 343 D3
rd. Taren Point 462 J15
rd. Waverton 5 A6
st. Birchgrove 7 H4
st. Birchgrove 7 H5
st. Botany 405 F11
st. Btn-le-Sds 433 G1
st. Coogee 407 F2
st. Croydon 342 F12
st. Double Bay 14 C10
st. Glebe 12 H13
st. Greenwich 314 J10
st. Mosman 316 K3
st. North Bondi 378 G3
st. Pagewood 405 J10
st. Rockdale 403 D15
st. Ryde 312 D3
st. Tempe 404 A3
st. Ultimo 12 H13
vst. Lilli Pilli 522 G1
BAYAN
pl. Bargo 567 E13
BAYARD
la. Concord, off Bayard St 312 A15
st. Concord 312 A15
st. Mortlake 312 A15
BAYBERRY
wy. Castle Hill 218 G16
BAYDON
st. Castle Hill 219 A8
BAYFIELD
rd. Arcadia 159 H2
rd. Galston 159 H2
rd. Galston 159 H7
rd. Greystanes 306 B11
BAYHAVEN
pl. Gymea Bay 491 H12
BAYLDON
pl. Glenmore Pk 266 A6
BAYLEY
rd. S Penrith 267 A6
st. Marrickville 373 E13
BAYLIS
pl. N Richmond 86 K13
BAYLY
ct. Hobartville 118 H7
st. Minchinbury 272 G9
BAYNES
st. Mount Druitt 271 A2
BAYNTON
pl. St Helens Park 540 K6
pl. St Helens Park 541 A6
BAYSIDE
dr. Lugarno 430 B14
pl. Caringbah 492 E10
st. Lilyfield 9 G6
BAYSWATER
av. Hurstville Gr 431 G11
rd. Darlinghurst 13 B9
rd. Lindfield 284 D4
rd. Potts Point 4 J8
rd. Rcuttrs Bay 13 B9
st. Drummoyne 343 H1
st. St Johns Pk 364 C3
BAYTON
st. Oxley Park 270 D2
BAY VIEW
st. Lavender Bay 5 F14
BAYVIEW
av. Earlwood 403 C2
av. Mosman 317 D8
cr. Annandale 11 B6
cr. Henley 313 C14
la. Annandale 11 B6
la. Earlwood, off Bayview St 403 E2
pl. Bayview 169 B14
pl. Frenchs Frst 256 J5
rd. Canada Bay 342 E10
rd. Peakhurst 430 D11
rd. Woolooware 493 D13
st. Arncliffe 403 D10
st. Bexley 402 J11
st. Bronte 378 A8
st. Concord 342 B3
st. Glebe 12 C10
st. Kogarah Bay 432 K12
st. Mt Krng-gai 163 B10
st. Northwood 314 G7
st. Pyrmont 8 G15
st. Scotland I 168 H4
st. Tennyson 312 D9
BAYVIEW HILL
la. Rose Bay 348 A7
rd. Rose Bay 348 B7
BAYVILLE
st. Balmain 344 E5
BAYWATER
dr. Homebush B 310 J8
BAZENTIN
st. Belfield 371 B11
BEACH
av. Vaucluse 318 G16
la. Coogee 377 H14
la. Emu Plains, off Beach St 235 F13
la. Mosman, off Military Rd 317 B6
rd. Bondi Beach 378 C1
rd. Collaroy 229 D14
rd. Dulwich Hill 373 E10
rd. Newport 169 H15
rd. North Bondi 348 B16
rd. Palm Beach 109 K14
st. Blakehurst 462 F1
st. Bundeena 524 A9
st. Clovelly 377 H15
st. Coogee 377 H15
st. Coogee 407 H2
st. Cronulla 524 A2
st. Curl Curl 258 J15
st. Double Bay 14 D7
st. Emu Plains 235 F13
st. Kogarah 433 D2
st. Tennyson 312 D10
BEACHCOMBER
av. Bundeena 524 A11
pl. Chipping Ntn 366 K15
BEACH PARK
av. Cronulla 493 K13
BEACHVIEW
pl. Brookvale 257 H10
BEACON
av. Beacon Hill 257 J8
av. Glenhaven 217 J3
av. Ryde 311 K5
BEACON HILL
rd. Beacon Hill 257 J7
rd. Brookvale 257 J7
BEACONIA
cl. Mona Vale 169 D16
BEACONSFIELD
av. Concord 342 A6
av. Kingsgrove 402 B7
la. Concord, off Beaconsfield Av 342 A6
la. Alexandria, off Beaconsfield St 375 F14
la. Beaconsfield, off Beaconsfield St 375 G13
pde. Lindfield 284 C1
rd. Chatswd W 284 A11
rd. Chatswd W 284 C12
rd. Lane Cove W 284 A11
rd. Lane Cove W 284 C12
rd. Mortdale 430 H9
rd. Mosman 317 E9
rd. Rooty Hill 272 C5
rd. Rooty Hill 272 C7
st. Alexandria 375 F13
st. Beaconsfield 375 F13
st. Bexley 403 A16
st. Milperra 398 B12
st. Newport 169 F13
st. Revesby 398 B12
st. Silverwater 309 F13
BEACONVIEW
st. Balgowlah Ht 287 K14
BEACROFT
pl. Cranebrook 207 D13
BEAGLE
pl. Willmot 210 B12
BEAHAN
pl. Cherrybrook 219 K13
BEAL
pl. Glenmore Pk 266 A6
BEALE
cr. Fairfield W 335 C13
cr. Peakhurst 430 E6
st. Georges Hall 367 D15
st. Liverpool 395 B4
BEAMES
av. Mount Druitt 241 C16
av. Rooty Hill 272 B1
st. Lilyfield 10 C9
BEAMISH
la. Campsie 372 A13
rd. Northmead 277 J11
st. Campsie 372 A11
st. Padstow 399 D12
BEAN
pl. Bonnyrigg 364 C6
BEARD
pl. Glenorie 128 C14
BEARING
rd. Seven Hills 276 E1
BEASLEY
pl. S Windsor 150 K2
BEATHAM
pl. Milperra 397 G10
BEATRICE
cl. Berowra Ht 133 A7
st. Ashfield 372 F2
st. Auburn 339 C4
st. Balgowlah Ht 287 F14
st. Bass Hill 367 K7
st. Cecil Hills 362 K3
st. Clontarf 287 F14
st. Hurstville 431 H1
st. Lane Cove W 313 G2
st. Lidcombe 339 G12
st. North Ryde 282 H8
st. Rooty Hill 242 A13
BEATSON
la. Kingswood 237 D16
BEATTIE
av. Denistone E 281 J12
la. Surry Hills 19 H1
st. Balmain 7 F10
st. Rozelle 7 A12
BEATTY
la. Maroubra 407 C11
pde. Georges Hall 367 D13
st. Balgowlah Ht 288 A12
st. Maroubra 407 C11
st. Mortdale 430 H8
st. St Marys 270 A6
BEAU
ct. Quakers Hill 213 H7
BEAUCHAMP
av. Chatswood 284
la. Surry Hills F
rd. Bnksmeadw 436
rd. Hillsdale 406
rd. Maroubra 407
rd. Matraville 406
st. Marrickville 373
st. Wiley Park 400
BEAUFIGHTER
st. Raby 451
BEAUFORD
av. Caringbah 492
BEAUFORT
pl. Chullora 370
rd. Blacktown 275
st. Croydon Pk 372
st. Guildford 337
st. Northmead 277
BEAUMARIS
av. Castle Hill 217
cr. Mortdale 430
dr. Menai 458
st. Enfield 371
BEAUMETZ
wy. Matraville 407
BEAUMOND
av. Maroubra 407
BEAUMONT
av. Denistone 281
av. Glenwood 215
av. N Richmond 87
cr. Bayview 169
dr. Kellyville 185
pl. Castle Hill 248
rd. Killara 253
rd. Mt Krng-gai 162
st. Auburn 338
st. Campsie 371
st. Kingsgrove 402
st. Rose Bay 348
st. Smithfield 335
st. Waterloo 19
BEAUMOUNT
st. Chippendale 18
BEAUREPAIRE
av. Newington 310
BEAUTY
dr. Whale Beach 140
BEAUTY POINT
cr. Leonay 264
rd. Mosman 287
BEAVORS
rd. Prairiewood 334
BEAZLEY
pl. Baulkham Hl 246
st. Ryde 312
BEBE
av. Revesby 428
la. Revesby 428
BECHARRY
rd. Blacktown 243
BECK
pl. Kellyville 215
rd. Old Tngabbie 276
st. N Epping 251
BECKE
ct. Glenmore Pk 265
BECKENHAM
st. Canley Vale 366
BECKET
ct. S Penrith 266
BECKHAUS
st. St Johns Pk 364
BECKMAN
pde. Frenchs Frst 255
pl. Tennyson 58
BECKTON
pl. Lilli Pilli 522
BECKY
av. North Rocks 279
BECQUEREL
pl. Lucas Ht 487
BEDDEK
st. McGraths Hl 121
BEDDINGTON
ct. Wattle Grove 426
BEDE
st. Lidcombe 339
st. Strathfield S 371
BEDERVALE
ct. Wattle Grove 426

DFORD
N Turramrra 223 F8
Collaroy 229 B16
Dulwich Hill 373 E13
Newtown 17 B10
Rockdale 403 H15
S Coogee 407 H6
Sylvania 462 A11
Blacktown 244 K11
Homebush W 340 K6
N Epping 251 H11
Earlwood 402 G2
Emu Plains 234 K11
Newtown 17 B11
N Willg.by 285 F8
Surry Hills 19 G3
DIVERE
Blacktown 274 K7
DLEY
Cranebrook 207 E14
DNAL
Springwood 201 G2
DWIN
Marrickville 374 G12
St Peters 374 G12
ECH
Lugarno 429 J14
Mcquarie Fd 454 G1
Casula 423 J3
Prestons 393 J15
Quakers Hill 243 F5
ECHCRAFT
Raby 451 F15
ECHWOOD
. Greystanes 306 F11
e. Cherrybrook 219 G8
Bass Hill 367 J8
ECHWORTH
Mt Colah 162 F14
Pymble 253 A2
ECROFT
Beecroft 250 D3
Cheltenham 251 A12
Epping 251 A12
Pennant Hills 250 D3
Wilberforce 62 A14
E FARM
Springwood 201 G9
EF CATTLE
. Richmond 118 J13
. Richmond 119 A14
EHAG
. Arncliffe 403 E11
. Kyeemagh 404 B13
ELAR
Canley Ht 365 B1
ELONG
Dharruk 241 A6
EMERA
Fairfield Ht 335 H10
EMRA
Auburn 309 C15
ERSHEBA
e. Holsworthy 426 D11
ESON
Leichhardt 15 B4
ETHOVEN
. Cranebrook 207 H9
. Engadine 518 D5
. Seven Hills 246 D12
GA
. Little Bay 437 B11
. Prestons 393 A13
. Bossley Park 333 G9
. Georges Hall 367 J11
. Jannali 460 H10
. Northbridge 286 B15
Marayong 243 J7
Pendle Hill 276 C16
St Marys 269 K5
GG
Paddington 13 B15
GGS
Eastern Ck 272 G6
Roselands 400 K10
GONIA
. Cabramatta 365 G11
Glenmore Pk 265 H8
Mcquarie Fd 454 A7
Woolooware 493 D9
Normanhurst 221 D13
Pagewood 405 K10

BEGOVICH
cr. Abbotsbury 333 A15
BEIHLER
la. Ryde 282 A14
BELAH
av. Vaucluse 348 H1
gdn. Vaucluse 318 H16
pl. Mcquarie Fd 424 E16
BEL-AIR
rd. Penrith 237 B7
BELAIR
av. Caringbah 493 B10
cl. Hornsby 191 K15
pl. Bayview 169 A15
pl. Mt Krng-gai 163 B10
pl. Prairiewood 334 F7
st. Bow Bowing 452 D14
st. Punchbowl 400 A7
BELAR
av. Villawood 367 C4
av. Villawood 367 E5
rd. Camden 507 A8
st. St Marys 239 G14
BELARADA
cl. Bangor 459 B11
BELBOWRIE
cl. Bangor 459 C10
cl. Galston 159 G13
gln. St Clair 270 B16
BELCOTE
rd. Longueville 314 C10
BELEMBA
av. Roselands 401 B5
BELFAST
pl. Killarney Ht 286 B1
BELFIELD
la. Belfield 371 D9
rd. Bossley Park 333 F13
rd. Edensor Pk 333 G13
BELFORD
pl. Greenacre 369 K10
st. Ingleburn 453 A9
BELGENNY
av. Camden 507 B6
BELGIAN
st. Westmead 307 J3
BELGICA
st. Tregear 240 D5
BELGIUM
av. Roseville 284 G2
st. Auburn 338 J10
st. Lidcombe 340 B5
st. Riverwood 400 B11
BELGRAVE
esp. Sylvania 462 E8
esp. Sylvania Wtr 462 C11
la. Bronte 377 J7
la. Cremorne, off Ben Boyd La 316 D8
la. Neutral Bay, off Ben Boyd La 316 D8
st. Bronte 377 J6
st. Burwood 341 H16
st. Cremorne 316 D8
st. Kogarah 433 B5
st. Manly 288 G10
st. Petersham 15 J13
BELIMLA
st. Auburn 309 C16
BELINDA
cr. Glenwood 245 E2
cr. N Epping 251 B9
ct. Castle Hill 217 C10
pl. Mays Hill 307 F6
pl. Newport 169 G9
rd. Alfords Point 459 C2
st. Bass Hill 367 H8
BELL
av. Beverly Hills 400 H16
av. Hobartville 118 B8
av. Kogarah Bay 432 J12
av. Lindfield 283 H2
av. West Ryde 280 G13
cr. Fairfield 336 H11
cr. Leumeah 512 E1
la. Glebe 11 J10
la. Randwick 377 A13
pl. Burraneer 523 E3
pl. Moorebank 396 E10
pl. Mt Pritchard 364 J11
rd. Londonderry 148 F9
st. Concord 341 H8
st. Glebe 11 H11

st. Gordon 254 B7
st. Hornsby 191 J11
st. Maroubra 407 E9
st. Panania 428 D4
st. Riverwood 400 A10
st. S Windsor 120 J12
st. Thirlmere 565 A5
st. Toongabbie 276 H5
st. Vaucluse 318 G16
BELLA
pl. Barden Rdg 488 H1
st. Randwick 377 E9
BELLAMBI
pl. Cartwright 394 E4
st. Northbridge 285 K15
BELLAMY
av. Eastwood 281 F4
la. Eastwood, off Bellamy Av 281 F4
st. Pennant Hills 220 D16
BELLAMY FARM
rd. W Pnnant Hl 249 E7
BELLARA
av. N Narrabeen 198 G15
BELLATA
ct. Glenbrook 264 D2
pl. Hinchinbrk 392 J4
BELLATRIX
la. Cranebrook, off Bellatrix St 207 D5
st. Cranebrook 207 E5
BELLA VISTA
ct. Warriewood 198 K7
dr. Bella Vista 246 E3
st. Heathcote 518 D11
BELLBIRD
av. Kurrajong Ht 54 B14
cl. Canada Bay 342 E8
cr. Blaxland 234 B7
cr. Bowen Mtn 83 K9
cr. Forestville 255 K12
ct. Quakers Hill 213 J10
dr. W Pnnant Hl 249 D7
pl. Cartwright 394 D4
pl. Kareela 461 C13
rd. Wedderburn 540 A11
st. Canterbury 402 D2
BELLBROOK
av. Emu Plains 235 G9
av. Hornsby 191 J16
BELLE ANGELA
dr. Theresa Park 444 H8
BELLEDALE
cl. St Clair 270 E14
BELLE MARIE
dr. Castle Hill 216 K9
dr. Castle Hill 217 Z9
BELLENDEN
ct. Glenwood 215 B15
pl. Dural 219 B2
BELLEREEVE
av. Mt Riverview 234 B4
BELLEREVE
pl. Leonay 234 J13
BELLERIVE
cl. West Hoxton 392 F5
BELLETTE
cl. Abbotsbury 333 A13
BELLEVALE
ct. Stanhpe Gdn 215 G9
BELLEVARDE
pde. Mona Vale 199 F1
BELLEVERDE
av. Strathfield 371 B4
BELLEVISTA
st. Blacktown 274 B3
BELLEVUE
av. Avalon 170 A3
av. Denistone 281 A11
av. Georges Hall 367 K13
av. Greenwich 315 A6
av. Lakemba 400 K1
av. Paddington 13 A16
av. West Ryde 281 B14
cl. Rossmore 389 G5
ct. Arncliffe 403 H10
dr. Carlingford 249 D14
gdn. Bellevue Hill, off Kendall St 377 G2
la. Arncliffe 403 H11
la. Glebe 12 E10
la. Hurstville 432 C7
la. Surry Hills F E15

la. West Ryde, off Dickson Av 281 C15
pde. Allawah 432 C7
pde. Caringbah 493 A6
pde. Carlton 432 E9
pde. Hurstville 432 C7
pde. N Curl Curl 258 J9
pl. N Curl Curl 258 K9
rd. Bellevue Hill 14 F10
rd. Regentville 235 E16
st. Arncliffe 403 H11
st. Blacktown 274 B4
st. Cammeray 315 K5
st. Chatswd W 284 B10
st. Fairlight 288 C9
st. Glebe 12 E10
st. Kogarah 433 A6
st. Maroubra 407 H10
st. N Parramatta 278 D12
st. Riverstone 183 C6
st. St Peters 374 E16
st. Surry Hills F E16
st. Surry Hills 3 K16
st. Tempe 404 E1
st. Thornleigh 221 A14
BELLEVUE PARK
rd. Bellevue Hill 377 H1
BELLFIELD
av. Rossmore 389 D11
BELLINGARA
rd. Miranda 461 K16
rd. Sylvania 462 B13
BELLINGEN
wy. Hoxton Park 392 H8
BELLINGER
cl. Narellan Vale 478 G15
pl. Sylvania Wtr 462 F15
rd. Ruse 512 C8
BELLINGHAM
av. Glendenning 242 F3
st. Narellan 478 D8
BELLINI
la. St Clair, off Bellini Pl 300 A2
pl. St Clair 300 B2
BELLOC
cl. Wetherill Pk 334 E5
pl. Winston Hills 247 G16
BELLOMBI
st. Campsie 372 D12
BELLONA
av. Homebush 341 A5
av. Regents Pk 368 H1
st. Winston Hills 277 A2
BELLOTTI
av. Winston Hills 277 F1
BELLS
av. Cammeray 316 A6
la. Kurmond 86 F2
la. Strathfield, off Morwick St 341 G13
rd. Grose Vale 85 B13
rd. Oatlands 279 C13
rd. Schofields 212 E4
BELLS LINE OF
rd. Kurmond 56 A16
rd. Kurrajong 55 B15
rd. Kurrajong Ht 54 A4
rd. Kurrajong Hl 54 D12
rd. N Richmond 87 C10
BELLTREE
cr. Castle Hill 218 K5
BELLTREES
cl. Glen Alpine 510 C11
BELLWOOD
cl. Werrington 239 B11
pl. Castle Hill 219 B9
BELMONT
av. Penshurst 431 H6
av. Sans Souci 433 F16
av. Wollstncraft 315 D9
la. Alexandria 18 G16
la. Mosman 317 A8
la. Wollstncraft, off Shirley Rd 315 D9
pde. Mt Colah 192 B5
rd. Glenfield 424 D10
rd. Mosman 316 H7
st. Alexandria 18 G16
st. Merrylands 307 E16
st. Sutherland 490 F4
st.s, Sutherland 490 F6
BELMORE
av. Belmore 371 D15

av. Mount Druitt 241 B15
la. Cromer 227 J13
la. Enmore 17 B13
la. Ryde 311 K2
la. Surry Hills F B14
la. Sydenham 374 D16
la. Surry Hills, off Belmore St 3 K16
pl. Paddington 13 C16
rd. Bringelly 418 C1
rd. Eastern Ck 272 H8
rd. Peakhurst 430 A7
rd. Punchbowl 400 B14
rd. Randwick 377 A13
rd. Riverwood 400 B14
rd. Riverwood 400 B16
st. Arncliffe 403 G8
st. Burwood 341 K15
st. Enmore 17 B13
st. N Parramatta 278 E13
st. Penrith 236 J9
st. Rozelle 344 E8
st. Ryde 311 H4
st. Surry Hills F D15
st. Surry Hills 3 K16
st. Tempe 374 D16
st. Villawood 337 B16
st.e, N Parramatta 278 H12
st.e, Oatlands 279 A12
wk. Arncliffe, off Station St 403 G7
BELROSE
ct. Bankstown 368 H15
pl. Prospect 275 D12
BELTANA
av. Bonnyrigg 363 K8
av. Terrey Hills 196 F6
cl. Bangor 459 B12
ct. Wattle Grove 425 K2
pl. Glen Alpine 510 D16
pl. Leonay 234 K13
pl. Wahroonga 251 G1
st. Denistone 281 H13
BELUS
wy. Doonside 243 E15
BELVEDERE
arc. Cabramatta, off John St 365 H7
av. Castle Hill 217 H12
st. Mt Pritchard 364 B11
BELVOIR
rd. Moorebank 425 B4
st. Surry Hills 19 G4
BEMBRIDGE
st. Carlton 432 H7
BEN
pl. Kellyville 185 J13
pl. Kings Lngly 245 K6
st. Marsden Pk 182 A12
BENAARA
gdn. Castle Hill 218 A16
BENA BENA
pl. Holsworthy 426 C2
BENALLA
av. Ashfield 372 G1
av. Kellyville 216 G7
cr. Marayong 243 K4
BENALONG
st. St Marys 239 F14
BENARES
cr. Acacia Gdn 214 G16
BENAROON
av. St Ives 223 J10
rd. Belmore 371 A12
rd. Lakemba 371 A12
BENAUD
cl. Menai 458 F9
ct. St Clair 269 K16
la. St Clair, off Benaud Ct 269 K16
pl. Telopea 279 H10
st. Blacktown 274 F4
st. Greystanes 306 A9
BENBOW
cl. Stanhpe Gdn 215 B10
BEN BOYD
la. Cremorne 316 C8
la. Neutral Bay 316 C8
rd. Cremorne 316 C10
rd. Neutral Bay 6 E4
BEN BULLEN
rd. Glenorie 128 K1
BENBURY
st. Quakers Hill 214 B8

BENCOOLEN
av. Denistone 281 C14
av. West Ryde 281 C14
BENCUBBIN
st. Sadleir 394 A1
BENDA
st. Belmore..............371 C14
BENDIGO
cl. Wakeley...........334 H13
pl. Cartwright..........394 A5
BENDTREE
wy. Castle Hill...........248 G4
BEN EDEN
st. Bondi Jctn...........377 G3
BENEDICT
cl. Cecil Hills...........362 D5
ct. Holroyd..............308 A10
BENEDICTINE
pl. Cherrybrook.......219 E14
BENELONG
av. Smithfield 335 D7
cr. Bellevue Hill 347 J16
la. Cremorne............316 E6
rd. Cremorne............316 E6
st. Seaforth.............287 C7
BENFIELD
pde. Panania..............398 C14
BENGHAZI
rd. Carlingford.........249 K13
st. Bossley Park......334 A6
BENHAM
rd. Minto.................452 K16
st. Dulwich Hill........373 D6
BENINE
dr. Cmbrdg Pk.........238 C8
BENJAMIN
la. Glenbrook...........233 J14
pl. Currans Hill.........479 K14
rd. Mt Pritchard.......364 H9
st. Bexley North 402 G9
st. Greystanes..........306 F8
BENJI
pl. Dean Park...........242 J2
BEN LOMOND
rd. Minto..................482 C2
rd. Minto Ht 483 A6
st. Bossley Park......333 D11
BENNABRA
pl. Frenchs Frst.......255 J3
BENNALONG
st. Granville 308 A13
st. Merrylands..........308 A13
BENNELONG
pl. E Kurrajong..........60 H2
pl. Narellan 478 E15
rd. Homebush B......310 K13
rd. Homebush B......340 K1
st. Ruse..................512 H5
BENNET
pl. Maroubra...........407 D15
BENNETT
av. Carramar 366 K4
av. Darling Point........13 J3
av. Five Dock...........343 B8
av. Roselands...........401 B7
av. Strathfield S.......371 E5
gr. Bidwill................211 C15
la. Kurrajong Ht 54 A7
la. Mortlake 312 A15
la. Riverwood 400 A15
pl. Castle Hill...........218 F11
pl. Surry Hills............20 D2
rd. Colyton...............270 C9
rd. Londonderry 149 F10
rd. Riverwood 400 A15
rd. St Clair...............270 D11
rd. S Granville 338 G4
st. Bass Hill.............367 K4
st. Bondi..................377 J5
st. Burwood.............342 C11
st. Chester Hill 367 K4
st. Cremorne 6 H4
st. Curl Curl 258 F13
st. Dee Why............258 F4
st. Glenbrook...........233 H16
st. Kingsgrove.........402 B13
st. Minto..................482 K10
st. Mortlake 312 A14
st. Neutral Bay 6 H4
st. Newtown 18 C9
st. Surry Hills............20 D2
st. Wentwthvle.........307 A2
st. West Ryde 281 A15

BENNETTS
rd.e, Dundas.............280 B13
rd.w, Dundas 279 H14
BENNETTS GROVE
av. Paddington 13 C16
BEN NEVIS
rd. Cranebrook........207 D14
BENNING
av. S Turramrra 252 A9
BENNISON
rd. Hinchinbrk 392 K1
BENNY
la. Yagoona 369 B13
pl. St Helens Park....541 B8
BENOWIE
cl. Berowra Ht.........132 J5
BENOWRA
pl. Belrose 225 E15
BENSBACH
rd. Glenfield 424 D13
BENSLEY
rd. Ingleburn 453 F16
rd. Mcquarie Fd.......453 K10
rd. Minto..................453 F16
BENSON
cl. Wahroonga 222 C5
la. West Ryde 281 J13
rd. Ingleburn 452 J3
st. Carramar 366 H1
st. S Wntwthvle 307 D5
st. West Ryde 281 J13
BENSONS
la. Richmond Lwld ..118 J4
BENT
la. Greenwich...........314 K9
la. Neutral Bay 6 C1
pl. Ruse..................512 G1
st. Carlton...............432 J5
st. Chester Hill 338 B16
st. Chipping Ntn.......366 F14
st. Concord.............342 A4
st. Greenwich...........314 K9
st. Lindfield.............254 C16
st. Moore Park..........21 A9
st. Moore Park..........21 B7
st. Neutral Bay 6 B3
st. Paddington 21 C4
st. Petersham 16 B10
st. St Marys............239 F8
st. Sydney ....B C12
st. Sydney 1 J14
st. Villawood...........367 B4
BENTINCK
dr. Green Valley.......363 B10
BENTLEY
av. Forestville 256 B8
av. Kellyville............185 E9
gr. Menai 458 J15
la. Pendle Hill...........276 E14
rd. Colyton...............270 E6
st. Balgowlah..........287 K9
st. Rooty Hill............271 H2
st. Wetherill Pk 333 J2
BENTON
av. Artarmon 284 J15
BENTS BASIN
rd. Wallacia.............324 G14
rd. Wallacia.............354 F10
rd. Wallacia.............384 G1
BENVENUE
st. Kingsford...........407 A6
BENWERRIN
av. Baulkham Hl 247 B5
av. Carss Park 432 F14
cl. East Killara.........254 H5
cr. Grasmere............505 H4
la. Carss Park 432 F13
BERALA
st. Berala 339 E12
BERALLIER
dr. Camden S...........507 A12
BEREN
la. Cranebrook 207 D14
pl. Cranebrook 207 D15
BERENBEL
pl. Westleigh...........220 E9
BERENICE
st. Roselands..........401 A9
BERENICES
wy. Chatswd W 284 F10
BERES
rd. Greendale 384 K8

BERESFORD
av. Bankstown..........369 G11
av. Baulkham Hl 248 A8
av. Beverly Hills 401 D15
av. Chatswd W 284 F12
av. Croydon Pk.........372 C5
av. Greenacre 369 G10
cr. Bellevue Hill 347 G12
pde. Kingsgrove..........402 B7
rd. Bellevue Hill 347 G11
rd. Caringbah 492 G3
rd. Greystanes.........305 K5
rd. Rose Bay 347 G11
rd. Strathfield 341 B12
rd. Strathfield 341 D11
rd. Thornleigh 221 C6
st. Mascot 405 E7
st. St Marys 270 A5
BERG
st. Blacktown 274 J8
BERGALIA
cl. Prestons 393 A12
BERGER
rd. S Windsor...........150 J3
BERGIN
pl. Minchinbury.......271 J10
st. Denistone W 280 J11
BERGONIA
st. Mona Vale..........198 K3
BERILDA
av. Warrawee 222 D14
BERITH
rd. Greystanes.........306 F4
st. Auburn 339 B8
st. Collaroy Plat.......228 F11
st. Kingsgrove..........402 B10
BERKELEY
cl. Berowra Ht.........133 A10
st. Peakhurst 430 C8
st. S Wntwthvle 307 B6
st. Yanderra............567 B16
BERKLEY
rd. Padstow Ht 429 G9
wy. Rsemeadow.......540 J2
BERKSHIRE
rd. Riverstone 182 G10
BERLIET
pl. Ingleburn 453 K7
BERMILL
st. Rockdale............433 G2
BERMUDA
pl. Burraneer...........493 F13
pl. Kings Park 244 F3
rd. Tahmoor.............566 G10
BERNA
la. Canterbury 372 F15
st. Canterbury 372 F14
BERNACCI
st. Tregear..............240 C4
BERNADETTE
pl. Baulkham Hl 247 B3
pl. Fairfield..............336 E6
BERNADOTTE
st. Riverwood 400 E15
BERNARD
av. Bardwell Pk.........402 G8
av. Gladesville 312 H13
la. Crows Nest, off Emmett St..........315 H8
pl. Castle Hill...........248 C4
pl. Cherrybrook.......219 D13
pl. Mount Druitt 271 A4
rd. Padstow Ht 429 F9
st. Lidcombe............339 H10
st. Westmead 307 F5
BERNARDO
st. Rsemeadow........540 J8
BERNARRA
pl. Cranebrook 207 D15
BERNE
st. St Peters............374 G15
BERNERA
rd. Prestons 393 C15
BERNICE
st. Seven Hills 246 B11
BERNIE
av. Forestville 255 K12
st. Bundeena............524 A10
st. Greystanes.........306 E11
BERNIER
st. Minchinbury.......272 B8
wy. Green Valley.......363 A9

BERNOTH
pl. Edensor Pk 363 D3
BERONGA
av. Hurstville 402 B16
st. N Strathfield.......341 E5
BEROWRA
pde. Berowra.............133 G13
rd. Mt Colah 192 C5
BEROWRA WATERS
rd. Berowra..............133 D11
rd. Berowra Ht..........132 H4
rd. Berowra Ht..........133 A9
rd. Berowra Wtr 132 G4
BERRARA
cl. Prestons 393 C13
BERRICO
pl. Bangor...............459 C10
pl. Bargo.................567 D7
BERRIDALE
av. S Penrith............266 F5
la. S Penrith, off Berridale Av 266 F5
pl. Heckenberg........364 A12
BERRIGAN
cl. St Clair...............270 B16
cr. Mcquarie Fd........454 D1
pl. Bossley Park 333 F9
st. Northmead.........277 K3
BERRIL
pl. Glenmore Pk......266 D10
BERRILLE
rd. Narwee 400 K14
BERRILLEE
la. Turramurra 223 B14
st. Turramurra 223 B13
BERRIMA
av. Padstow 429 F5
pl. Doonside 243 C11
st. Heathcote 518 E9
BERRIMILLA
wy. Kellyville.............185 J15
BERRINDA
pl. Frenchs Frst.......255 K3
BERRING
av. Roselands..........400 K8
BERRIPA
cl. North Ryde 282 G14
BERRY
av. Fairlight..............288 D9
av. Naremburn 315 D3
av. N Narrabeen.......199 B14
cl. Grasmere............475 J15
gr. Menai 459 A12
la. St Leonards 315 C7
pl. Wrrngtn Cty 238 F9
rd. St Leonards 315 C7
st. Cronulla..............494 B6
st. Granville 308 H12
st. Mount Druitt 271 B2
st. N Sydney..............K A4
st. N Sydney..............K C3
st. N Sydney...............5 D6
st. Prairiewood 334 K8
st. Prestons 392 H14
st. Regents Pk 369 C2
st. Rosebery 405 H2
BERRYMAN
st. North Ryde 282 K10
BERRY PARK
wy. Mt Colah 192 D5
BERT
cl. Warriewood 198 F6
la. N Parramatta......278 G14
BERTANA
cr. Warriewood 199 A6
BERT BAILEY
st. Moore Park..........21 B6
BERTHA
rd. Cremorne 6 J5
st. Fairfield..............336 G13
st. Merrylands.........307 J16
BERTRAM
cr. Beverley Pk.........433 B8
la. Mortlake 312 A15
pl. Narellan Vale......479 C11
st. Chatswood.........285 A9
st. Concord.............312 A15
st. Eastwood............281 C5
st. Mortlake 312 A15
st. Yagoona 368 E13
BERTRAND
cl. Marsfield............282 B4

rd. N Turramrra.......223
BERWICK
la. Darlinghurst...........4
pl. Menai 458
pwy. Winston Hills 277
st. Coogee 407
st. Guildford.............337
BERWIN
pl. Baulkham Hl 247
BERYL
av. Mt Colah 162
cl. Claymore 481
pl. Greenacre 370
pl. Rooty Hill............242
st. Westmead 307
BESANT
pl. Rooty Hill............272
BESBOROUGH
av. Bexley................402
BESFORD
wy. Minto.................482
BESLEY
st. Cmbrdg Pk.........237
BESSBROOK
wy. Wentwthvle, off Tanderagee St....277
BESSEMER
st. Blacktown 244
BEST
cr. Kirrawee 490
pl. Prairiewood 335
rd. Middle Dural 158
rd. Seven Hills.........275
st. Lane Cove..........313
st. Woolmloo.............4
BESTIC
st. Kyeemagh..........404
st. Rockdale............403
BESWICK
av. North Ryde 282
BESZANT
st. Merrylands.........308
BETA
pl. Engadine............518
pl. Quakers Hill 214
rd. Lane Cove..........314
BETH
wy. Glenwood 215
BETHAM
pl. Kirrawee 490
BETHANY
ct. Baulkham Hl 216
pl. Glenwood 245
BETHEL
cl. Rooty Hill...........271
la. Paddington 4
st. Toongabbie.........276
BETHEL STEPS
The Rocks ....B
BETOLA
st. Ryde..................282
BETSEY
wy. Ambarvale..........510
BETTINA
ct. Greenacre 370
pl. Dural 188
st. Merrylands W 307
BETTINGTON
rd. Carlingford.........279
rd. Oatlands 279
rd. Telopea..............279
st. Millers Pt..............A
st. Millers Pt 1
BETTONG
cr. Bossley Park 333
pl. St Helens Park....541
BETTOWYND
rd. Pymble 223
BETTS
av. Blakehurst..........432
av. Five Dock...........343
pl. W Pnnant Hl.......249
rd. Merrylands W 306
rd. Smithfield 306
rd. Woodpark...........306
st. Kellyville.............215
st. Parramatta 278
st. West Ryde 281
BETTY
av. Winston Hills......277
pl. Thirlmere 562
pl. Thirlmere 565

Blacktown...274 G8
Roseville...285 B4
TY CUTHBERT
Ermington...310 B2
TY HENDRY
North Ryde...282 J9
JLA
Loftus...489 J11
LAH
Engadine...518 E3
Kingsford...406 J5
Kirribilli...2 D3
AN
Carlingford...279 J1
Northmead...277 J11
ANS
Galston...160 B8
ERLEY
Chester Hill...337 H10
Marsfield...282 B7
Penshurst...431 H6
Roselands...401 B9
Darling Point...13 K1
Cherrybrook...219 E6
Curl Curl...258 J14
Wrrngtn Cty...238 D8
Campbelltwn...511 H2
ERLY
Beverly Hills...401 A16
Plumpton...242 C11
IN
Five Dock...342 G9
LEY
Bexley...402 H12
Bexley North...402 E10
Campsie...402 B1
Earlwood...402 C5
Kingsgrove...402 C5
Mt Pritchard...364 C11
ER
Currans Hill...479 H11
MI
Bangor...459 C12
NCA
Acacia Gdn...244 J1
Rsemeadow...540 H5
RA
Campsie...402 B3
Marsfield...282 B3
Turramurra...223 C8
Bargo...567 C5
Chester Hill...338 A15
RGAR
Miranda...491 J5
B
West Hoxton...391 J12
BALONG
Blacktown...273 H3
BENLUKE
Duffys Frst...194 G7
BY
Carlton...432 G11
Chiswick...343 C2
BYS
Bonnyrigg...364 B3
St Johns Pk...364 B2
URY
Chipping Ntn...396 D4
ANE
Edensor Pk...363 D2
HENO
West Hoxton...392 C6
KELL
Mosman...317 A2
KERTON
Green Valley...362 K13
KLEIGH
Abbotsford...342 K4
Wareemba...342 K4
KLEY
S Penrith...267 A7
DY
Ambarvale...510 G14
GEE
Ryde...282 E16
URA
Glen Alpine...510 F10
URGAL
Kirrawee...491 C4
WILL
Bidwill...211 E16

BIFFINS
la. Cawdor...505 D16
la. Mt Hunter...505 D16
BIGGE
st. Liverpool...395 E4
st. Warwck Frm...365 F16
wy. Minto...482 K6
BIG HILL
rd. The Oaks...503 B2
BIGLAND
av. Denistone...281 B13
av. West Ryde...281 B13
BIGNELL
la. Annandale...17 D3
st. Illawong...460 F1
BIJA
dr. Glenmore Pk...266 B9
BIJIJI
st. Pendle Hill...276 G12
BIJOU
la. Haymarket...E C13
BIKILA
st. Newington...310 B13
BILAMBEE
av. Bilgola...169 G4
la. Bilgola...169 H4
BILBERRY
av. Bilgola...169 H4
BILBETTE
pl. Frenchs Frst...257 B3
BILBOA
pl. Edensor Pk...363 C1
BILBY
pl. Quakers Hill...214 E12
BILDERA
pl. Grays Point...491 E15
BILGA
av. Bilgola...169 H4
cr. Malabar...437 D8
st. Kirrawee...490 K6
BILGOLA
av. Bilgola...170 A5
st. Campbelltwn...511 J6
tce. Bilgola...170 A5
BILKURRA
av. Bilgola...169 H4
BILLA
rd. Bangor...459 C12
BILLABONG
av. Turramurra...223 A10
gln. Wrrngtn Dns...238 E4
pl. Rouse Hill...185 D7
st. Pendle Hill...276 E14
BILLAGAL
pl. Blaxland...234 A6
BILLARA
av. Gymea Bay...491 D8
BILLARGA
rd. Westleigh...220 F5
BILLARONG
av. Dee Why...258 J2
BILL BARNACLE
av. Faulconbdg...171 G12
BILLEROY
av. Baulkham Hl...246 J7
BILLETT
st. Silverdale...353 J13
BILLIKIN
wy. Ambarvale...511 A16
wy. Ambarvale...541 B1
BILLING
la. Greenacre, off Glover St...370 F3
BILLINGTON
pl. Emu Plains...236 A7
BILLONG
av. Vaucluse...348 E5
st. Neutral Bay...6 H9
BILLYARD
av. Elizabeth Bay...13 A3
av. Wahroonga...222 F7
gr. Turramurra...222 K7
la. Wahroonga, off Illoura Av...222 E7
pl. Carlingford...279 F4
wk. Wahroonga, off Cleveland St...222 E7
BILMARK
pl. Btn-le-Sds...403 K14
BILOELA
pl. Gymea Bay...491 H10

st. Villawood...367 E3
st. Villawood...367 F3
BILOOLO
rd. Green Valley...363 J10
BILPIN
cl. Bangor...459 C12
pl. Bossley Park...333 D10
st. Greystanes...305 F9
BILSTON
st. Berowra...133 E9
BILWARA
av. Bilgola...169 G4
cr. S Penrith...266 J7
BILYANA
pl. Rouse Hill...185 C5
BIMAN
pl. Whalan...240 K10
BIMBADEEN
av. Bradbury...511 F16
av. Lugarno...430 A13
av. Miranda...492 D4
cr. Frenchs Frst...256 J5
st. Epping...280 G5
BIMBAI
cl. Bangor...459 D12
BIMBERI
st. Horngsea Pk...392 D15
BIMBI
pl. Bonnyrigg...363 J9
BIMBIL
av. Mt Colah...192 A4
pl. Castle Hill...218 A12
pl. Killara...283 E3
st. Blacktown...244 A14
BIMBIMBIE
pl. Bayview...168 K15
BIMBURRA
av. St Ives...223 H9
BINALONG
av. Allambie Ht...257 F14
av. Caringbah...492 F6
av. Georges Hall...367 H11
rd. Belimbla Pk...501 D14
rd. Kenthurst...156 H7
rd. Mt Colah...162 B16
rd. Old Tngabbie...276 H14
rd. Pendle Hill...276 H14
rd. Toongabbie...276 H14
rd. Wentwthvle...276 H14
rd. Yellow Rock...174 K14
st. West Pymble...252 J10
BINARA
cl. Hamondvle...396 G14
BINAVILLE
av. Burraneer...523 E2
BINBA
pl. Brookvale...258 C8
BINBURRA
av. Avalon...140 D13
BINDA
cr. Little Bay...437 B10
pl. Baulkham Hl...246 K9
rd. Yowie Bay...492 A11
st. Merrylands W...307 B12
BINDAREE
pl. Kellyville...216 F2
st. Hebersham...241 F9
st. Lansvale...367 B10
BINDEA
st. Como...460 F8
st. Jannali...460 F8
st. Mt Pritchard...364 C10
BINDEE
cl. Glenmore Pk...266 A7
BINDER
st. Hurstville...431 H1
BINDI
pl. Beacon Hill...257 F5
BINDON
pl. Kellyville...216 F2
BINDOOK
cr. Terrey Hills...196 D7
BINDOWAN
pl. Erskine Park...300 D2
BINET
wy. Glenhaven...218 D5
BINGARA
cr. Bella Vista...246 E7
dr. Sandy Point...427 K10
rd. Beecroft...250 C11
rd. Mcquarie Fd...453 J2
st. West Pymble...253 A13

BINGARRA
pl. Bargo...567 D7
BINGHAM
pl. Edensor Pk...333 J15
BINHAM
pl. Chipping Ntn...366 G13
BINNA BURRA
st. Villawood...367 D2
BINNARI
rd. Hornsby Ht...191 G5
BINNAWAY
av. Hoxton Park...392 G8
BINNEY
rd. Kings Park...244 F4
st. Caringbah...492 H15
BINNING
la. Erskineville...18 B16
st. Erskineville...18 C16
BINNIT
pl. Glenmore Pk...266 B12
BINNOWEE
av. St Ives...223 K9
pl. Bayview...169 A15
BINOMEA
pl. Pennant Hills...250 G2
BINYA
cl. Hornsby Ht...162 A7
pl. Como...460 H6
st. Blaxland...234 E6
st. Pendle Hill...276 G12
BINYON
cl. Wetherill Pk...334 H4
BIRALEE
cr. Beacon Hill...257 K6
BIRCH
av. Casula...394 G14
gr. Baulkham Hl...248 B12
pl. Bidwill...211 D14
pl. Kirrawee...490 K1
pl. Mcquarie Fd...424 F16
st. Bnkstn Aprt...368 B16
st. Condell Park...368 B16
st. East Ryde...283 A14
st. N St Marys...240 A11
BIRCHGROVE
av. Canley Ht...364 K3
rd. Balmain...7 D6
rd. Birchgrove...7 D6
BIRD
av. Guildford...337 K4
av. Lurnea...394 G9
la. St Clair, off Banks Dr...269 H11
pl. St Clair...269 H11
pl. St Helens Park...541 C3
pl. West Hoxton...392 A10
st. Ryde...282 H16
BIRDS
la. Bondi Jctn...22 J9
la. Maraylya...125 A14
BIRDSALL
av. Condell Park...398 H4
BIRDSVILLE
cr. Leumeah...482 G10
BIRDWOOD
av. Belfield...371 F9
av. Cabramatta W...364 G7
av. Collaroy...229 C13
av. Daceyville...406 G6
av. Doonside...243 E16
av. East Killara...254 D8
av. Holsworthy...396 A13
av. Killara...254 D8
av. Lane Cove...314 D1
av. Pagewood...406 G6
av. Winmalee...172 H13
cl. Narrabeen...228 G7
la. Lane Cove...314 D1
la. Georges Hall, off Georges Cr...367 F14
rd. Bnkstn Aprt...367 G14
rd. Georges Hall...367 G14
st. Denistone E...281 J11
st. Sylvania...461 J8
BIRGITTE
cr. Cecil Hills...362 G7
BIRINTA
st. Narraweena...258 A2
BIRK
pl. Bligh Park...150 G6
BIRKDALE
cct. Glenmore Pk...266 F10

cr. Liverpool...395 C9
BIRKLEY
la. Fairlight...288 E8
la. Manly...288 E8
rd. Manly...288 E8
BIRMINGHAM
av. Villawood...337 G16
rd. S Penrith...266 F4
st. Alexandria...375 E16
st. Merrylands...307 H10
BIRNAM
av. Blacktown...243 J15
gr. Strathfield...341 C16
BIRNIE
av. Homebush B...340 E4
av. Lidcombe...340 C6
BIROK
av. Engadine...518 K1
BIRRAMAL
rd. Duffys Frst...194 H7
BIRR CROSS
rd. Moorebank...425 C4
BIRRELL
la. Queens Park...22 D11
st. Bondi...377 H6
st. Bondi Jctn...22 D9
st. Tamarama...377 H6
st. Waverley...377 H6
BIRRELLEA
av. Earlwood...402 E5
BIRRIGA
av. Chester Hill...368 B2
rd. Bellevue Hill...377 J1
rd. Croydon...342 G13
BIRRIMA
st. N Balgowlah...287 H5
BIRRIWA
av. Belfield...371 B8
pl. Baulkham Hl...246 H6
pl. Northwood...314 G8
st. Greystanes...305 G9
BIRRONG
av. Belrose...225 H15
av. Birrong...368 K6
BIRRU
pl. Belrose...225 K14
BIRTLES
av. Pendle Hill...276 G11
BIRTLEY
pl. Elizabeth Bay...13 A6
BIRUBI
av. Gymea...491 E1
av. Pymble...223 C14
cr. Bilgola...169 E8
BIRUNNA
av. Gymea...491 G1
BISCAYNE
av. S Wntwthvle...306 K9
BISCOE
pl. Tregear...240 F8
BISDEE
pl. Engadine...489 C13
BISHOP
av. W Pnnant Hl...249 K2
av. Matraville, off Cemetery Av...436 G8
cl. Green Valley...363 B12
cl. S Windsor...150 F2
cr. Bonnyrigg...364 E5
rd. Menai...458 G15
st. Cabarita...342 D1
st. Newport...169 G11
st. Petersham...15 F15
st. Revesby...399 A11
st. St Peters...374 J14
BISHOPGATE
av. Castle Hill...217 G4
la. Camperdwn...17 D9
st. Camperdwn...17 D9
st. Newtown...17 D9
BISHOPS
av. Randwick...377 F12
BISHOPSCOURT
pl. Glen Alpine...510 B12
BISMARCK
st. McGraths Hl...122 B14
BISMARK
rd. Northmead...278 B5
BISMIRE
st. Panania...398 A15
BITTERN
cl. Erskine Park...270 H14

cl. Hinchinbrk 393 D2
gr. Glenwood 215 F14
BIWA
cl. St Clair..............269 G15
la. St Clair, off
Rotarua Rd 269 F16
BIX
rd. Dee Why 258 F3
BIZET
pl. Bonnyrigg Ht......363 D7
BLACK
cl. Illawong.............459 F5
st. Marrickville 374 E10
st. Vaucluse............348 D6
BLACKALL
st. Revesby.............399 B14
BLACKASH
pl. Hornsby Ht 162 A5
BLACKBIRD
gln. Erskine Park.......271 A14
la. St Clair, off
Blackbird Gln......271 A14
BLACKBURN
av. North Rocks.......249 A16
av. West Hoxton.......392 A10
pl. Gymea Bay.........491 D7
rd. Wedderburn.......540 A16
st. St Ives 224 F7
st. Surry Hills.............F B9
BLACKBUTT
av. Bradbury............511 F11
av. Lugarno..............429 J11
av. Pennant Hills......250 K4
cir. Mt Riverview......204 E15
cr. Greystanes.........306 E12
pl. Engadine.............488 H16
pl. Leonay...............235 A16
pl. The Oaks.............502 E12
st. Bossley Park......333 G9
st. Parklea 215 A13
BLACKBUTTS
rd. Frenchs Frst.......255 F2
BLACKET
pl. West Hoxton 392 B10
st. Heathcote 518 H10
BLACKETT
dr. Castle Hill...........247 F3
pl. Cabramatta W 365 B4
st. Kings Park 244 D2
BLACKFORD
cr. S Penrith............266 G4
st. Fairfield E...........337 D14
BLACKFRIAR
pl. Wetherill Pk 335 A1
BLACKFRIARS
la. Chippendale.........19 A2
pl. Chippendale.........19 A1
st. Chippendale.........19 A1
BLACK LION
pl. Kensington.........376 C9
BLACKMAN
cr. Horngsea Pk 392 G15
cr. S Windsor...........120 K16
ct. Wrrngtn Cty.........238 E5
la. Bass Hill.............368 E10
la. Yagoona 368 E10
BLACKMORE
la. Redfern................19 K11
pl. Wetherill Pk 334 F6
rd. Smeaton Gra......479 B8
BLACKROCK
mw. Baulkham Hl 216 E14
BLACKS
rd. Arcadia 159 D2
rd. W Pnnant Hl.......248 H7
BLACKSHAW
av. Mortdale 430 H7
BLACKSMITH
cl. Stanhpe Gdn......215 F9
ct. Bella Vista 246 F3
st. Greenfld Pk........334 D13
BLACKSTONE
st. Wetherill Pk 305 C16
BLACK SWAN
pl. Yarramundi........145 E6
BLACKTHORN
cct. Menai 458 K12
BLACKTOWN
rd. Blacktown..........275 A2
rd. Freemns Rch........90 G3
rd. Londonderry......149 F1
rd. Prospect 275 C11
rd. Richmond..........118 K8
rd. S Windsor..........149 F1
BLACKWALL POINT
rd. Abbotsford.........342 K2
rd. Chiswick 343 A2
BLACK WATTLE
gr. Narellan Vale......479 A14
pl. Sydney 3 D6
st. Peakhurst 430 E4
BLACKWATTLE
cct. Old Tngabbie......277 D6
la. Ultimo 12 J14
pl. Alfords Point 459 A1
pl. Cherrybrook........219 J8
pl. Sydney ....C B12
BLACKWELL
av. St Clair..............270 A16
av. St Clair..............300 A2
BLACKWOOD
av. Ashfield 372 F5
av. Casula...............394 J15
av. Clovelly 378 A12
av. Dulwich Hill........373 E11
av. Minto.................452 J15
av. Mt Krng-gai........162 J14
cl. Beecroft 250 D3
cl. Bossley Park 333 E9
cr. Mcquarie Fd.......454 E1
la. Dulwich Hill, off
Blackwood Av 373 E11
pl. Oatlands 278 G10
rd. Merrylands.........307 C9
rd. N Curl Curl 258 K10
rd. Vineyard 152 D7
st. Belfield...............371 D10
st. Miranda 491 K7
BLADES
pl. Douglas Park 568 H1
pl. Mt Annan 479 F15
BLAIKIE
rd. Jamisontown 235 J15
BLAIN
st. Toongabbie........276 F9
BLAIR
av. Croydon.............342 E13
av. East Hills............427 J4
av. St Marys 239 H15
la. St Marys, off
Blair Av...............239 H15
pl. Cabramatta 366 A10
pl. Minto..................453 C16
pl. St Ives 253 K2
st. Bondi Beach.......378 C1
st. Gladesville 312 H10
st. North Bondi 378 C1
BLAIR ATHOL
dr. Blair Athol 511 A3
BLAIRGOWIE
pl. Oatlands 278 J11
BLAIRGOWRIE
cct. St Andrews 452 B16
la. Dulwich Hill, off
Windsor Rd........373 D6
st. Dulwich Hill........373 D6
BLAKE
av. Blakehurst.........462 F3
av. Hunters Hill........314 B13
cl. Wetherill Pk 334 J6
pl. Eagle Vale 481 B9
rd. Mt Annan 479 D15
st. Balmain 8 C10
st. Dover Ht 348 D10
st. Kogarah 433 A6
st. Quakers Hill 213 K8
st. Rose Bay 348 D10
BLAKEFORD
av. Ermington..........280 E15
BLAKESLEY
rd. Allawah..............432 F10
rd. Carlton...............432 F10
rd. S Hurstville 432 C11
st. Chatswood..........285 A8
BLAMEY
av. Caringbah 492 G15
pl. Doonside 273 F1
pl. Narellan Vale 479 C10
pl. Revesby.............398 J16
pl. St Ives 224 F16
rd. Holsworthy 396 A13
st. Allambie Ht 257 H16
st. Colyton 270 B5
st. North Ryde 282 J11
st. Revesby.............398 H16
wy. Cherrybrook, off
Tennyson Cl........219 E10
BLAMIRE
la. Marrickville 373 J14
BLANC
av. East Hills...........428 A4
BLANCHE
av. Padstow 429 E2
st. Belfield...............371 B9
st. Minto..................482 F2
st. Oatley 431 E11
BLAND
rd. Oakville 124 E7
rd. Springwood 202 A2
st. Ashfield 372 J2
st. Bradbury............511 E8
st. Carramar 336 H16
st. Haberfield 343 A15
st. Woolmloo 4 F3
BLANDFORD
av. Bronte...............377 H7
st. Collaroy Plat.......228 J12
BLANE
st. Granville 308 C10
st. Minto..................482 J4
BLANTYRE
cl. Thornleigh 221 C12
BLARNEY
av. Killarney Ht 286 B1
BLATTMAN
av. Oakdale.............500 C12
cl. Blacktown 273 H5
st. Colyton 270 C7
BLAXCELL
pl. Harringtn Pk.......478 F6
st. Granville 308 F16
st. Guildford............338 D9
st. S Granville 338 E3
BLAXLAND
av. Luddenham........356 H2
av. Newington 310 D11
av. Newington 310 D12
av. Penrith...............237 B9
dr. Illawong 459 E6
la. Penrith, off
Blaxland Av........237 B9
la. Ryde, off
Devlin St............311 K1
pl. Glenhaven..........218 B3
pl. Milperra 397 J7
rd. Bellevue Hill 347 J16
rd. Camden S 506 K12
rd. Campbelltwn......511 B4
rd. Denistone 281 F10
rd. Denistone E........281 F10
rd. Eastwood...........281 F10
rd. Epping...............281 C1
rd. Ingleburn 423 A9
rd. Killara 253 D15
rd. Orchard Hills 298 C10
rd. Rhodes..............311 D9
rd. Ryde..................312 A2
st. Frenchs Frst........256 E2
st. Hunters Hill.........313 B6
st. Lalor Park 245 D13
st. Matraville............437 A2
st. Silverwater.........309 K8
st. Yennora 337 B10
BLAXLANDS CORNER
Lane Cove..........314 F5
BLEND
pl. Woodcroft..........243 G7
BLENHEIM
av. Rooty Hill...........241 J13
la. Queens Park 22 J13
pl. Glenfield 424 F9
pl. St Clair...............270 F14
rd. Carlingford 279 F5
rd. Lindfield..............254 D14
rd. North Ryde 283 A11
rd. Schofields 182 H15
st. Croydon Pk 371 F7
st. Queens Park 22 K11
st. Randwick............376 K14
BLENMAN
av. Punchbowl.........400 A7
BLETCHLEY
pl. Hebersham 241 F5
BLICK
pde. Canterbury 372 H13
BLIGH
av. Camden S 506 J10
av. Lurnea 394 B12
cl. Georges Hall 368 C15
cr. Seaforth.............286 J9
ct. St Clair...............270 A11
la. Eastwood...........281 F5
pl. Kellyville.............215 G4
pl. Randwick...........377 D11
st. Burwood Ht.........371 K3
st. Chifley 437 C3
st. East Killara 254 F7
st. Eastwood...........281 F5
st. Guildford............338 C8
st. Kirrawee 490 J7
st. Kirribilli....................6 A15
st. Milsons Point.........6 A15
st. Northbridge 286 A16
st. Riverstone 183 C11
st. Silverwater.........309 H14
st. Sydney ....B C15
st. Sydney 1 J16
st. Villawood 337 B15
BLIGHS
rd. Cromer 227 J12
BLIND
rd. Nelson 155 A8
BLOMFIELD
rd. Denham Ct.........422 G15
BLOODWOOD
pl. Bradbury............511 E9
rd. Fiddletown 130 A3
rd. Ingleside 197 F3
BLOOMFIELD
la. Surry Hills.............4 D14
st. S Coogee 407 H5
st. Surry Hills.............4 D14
BLOOMSBURY
av. Pymble 253 E4
BLOSSOM
pl. Quakers Hill 213 K12
BLOXSOME
la. Mosman 316 G9
BLUCHER
st. Sans Souci.........463 C6
BLUE
pl. Wetherill Pk 334 D5
st. N Sydney...............K C11
st. N Sydney 5 F10
BLUE ANCHOR
la. Sydney ....A K8
BLUE BELL
pl. Heathcote 518 E9
rd. Heathcote 518 E9
BLUEBELL
cl. Glenmore Pk......265 H8
BLUEBERRY
ct. Narellan Vale......478 H14
dr. Colyton 270 H6
gr. Glenwood 245 C2
pl. Alfords Point......429 C16
pl. Alfords Point......459 C1
BLUEBIRD
rd. Cranebrook.........207 B11
BLUEBUSH
cl. Bossley Park 333 J9
BLUE CRANE
cl. W Pnnant Hl.......248 F8
BLUE CREST
pl. Kingswood.........267 H3
BLUEFISH
dr. Manly 289 A13
BLUE GUM
av. Chatswd W 284 F8
av. Gymea Bay.........491 E8
av. Ingleburn 453 F5
av. Roseville 284 F8
cr. Blaxland.............234 C9
cr. Stanhpe Gdn 215 B11
dr. East Ryde...........283 A15
rd. Annangrove 156 A14
rd. Kenthurst 156 A14
rd. Wentwthvle 277 A9
st. Newington, off
Newington Bvd...310 B14
BLUEGUM
av. Prestons 394 C14
av. S Penrith............267 B1
cct. Old Tngabbie......277 F7
cr. Frenchs Frst 256 F4
cr. Picnic Point.........428 H7
cr. Stanhpe Gdn 215 B11
gr. Glenwood 245 J2
pl. Roseville 284 C6
st. Normanhurst 221 E13
wy. Menai 458 J10
BLUE GUMS
wy. Castle Hill...........218 J13
BLUE HILLS
cr. Blacktown 244
dr. Glenmore Pk......266
BLUE JAY
ct. W Pnnant Hl.......249
BLUE RIDGE
cr. Berowra Ht.........132
ct. Glenhaven..........218
BLUES POINT
rd. McMahons Pt........K
rd. McMahons Pt 5
rd. N Sydney...............K
rd. N Sydney 5
BLUETT
av. East Ryde...........282
cr. Doonside 243
st. Marayong 244
BLUE WREN
pl. Oakdale..............500
BLUEWREN
cl. Glenmore Pk......265
BLUFF
st. Green Valley.......363
BLUNDELL
cct. Kellyville.............216
st. Marsfield............282
BLUNT
pl. Rsemeadow.......540
BLYTHE
av. Glenwood 215
BLYTHESWOOD
av. Turramurra 222
av. Warrawee 222
BOAB
pl. Casula................423
BOADA
pl. Winston Hills......277
BOAKE
cl. Glenmore Pk......265
BOALA
pl. Engadine............489
BOAMBILLEE
av. Vaucluse............348
BOANBONG
rd. Palm Beach........140
BOARD
st. Lidcombe...........339
st. N Parramatta......278
BOARDMAN
st. Dundas Vy 280
st. Yagoona 369
BOATWRIGHT
av. Lugarno 430
BOB
rd. Moorebank 425
BOBADAH
st. Kingsgrove.........402
BOBART
st. Parramatta.........308
BOBBIN
pl. Bangor...............459
BOBBIN HEAD
rd. Krngai Ch NP 163
rd. N Turramrra.......223
rd. Pymble 223
rd. Turramurra 223
BOBIN
rd. Sadleir 364
BOBS
pl. Matraville 406
BOBS RANGE
rd. Orangeville.........443
BOBUCK
pl. St Helens Park....541
BOCKING
av. Bradbury............511
BOCKS
rd. Oakville 152
BODALLA
cr. Bangor...............459
ct. Wattle Grove 426
st. Fairfield Ht 335
BODE
pl. Barden Rdg........458
BODEN
av. Strathfield 340
pl. Castle Hill...........217
rd. Seven Hills.........276
BOEING
cr. Raby..................451

3tn-le-Sds.........433 J1
St Clair.........270 D16
Mascot.........404 J4
FIN
ambarvale.........510 F16
ALARA
Old Tngabbie.........276 J11
AN
Baulkham Hl.........247 G4
Sylvania Wtr.........462 E10
Ruse.........512 E7
Seven Hills.........275 F10
Wahroonga.........222 A15
Greystanes.........306 A4
Summer Hill.........373 E3
IE
Allawah.........432 C7
Hurstville.........432 C7
ONG
Prairiewood.........334 F7
OTA
Neutral Bay.........6 J7
AN
Minto.........482 H6
EMIA
Malabar.........437 F6
R
Lucas Ht.........487 H11
ER
Blacktown.........274 C14
ANA
North Rocks.........248 J16
HARA
Greystanes.........306 C5
AND
Springwood.........201 J2
Marrickville.........373 K10
Springwood.........201 K2
ARO
Greystanes.........305 G10
Gymea.........491 F2
D
Burwood.........371 J1
Cabramatta W.........364 J7
Granville.........308 F10
DERO
Glenmore Pk.........266 H13
DREWOOD
Casula.........424 F2
Cherrybrook.........219 C8
Blackett.........241 B3
GER
Campbelltwn.........510 K7
INDA
Busby.........363 G12
INGBROKE
Fairlight.........288 B10
IVIA
Cabramatta.........365 G8
LARD
Picton.........563 C13
TA
Cromer.........258 A1
TON
Mt Colah.........192 C5
Mt Pritchard.........364 F9
Pymble.........253 J2
Guildford.........337 G7
Prospect.........275 D12
St Peters.........374 E14
Sydenham.........374 E14
TONS
Horngsea Pk.........392 D15
WARRA
West Pymble.........253 C14
Castle Hill.........248 G2
N Narrabeen.........198 G13
MADERRY
Prestons.........393 D16
MBALA
Quakers Hill.........243 K3
Pendle Hill.........276 C16
MBARDIERE
Baulkham Hl.........248 B7
MBAY
Lidcombe.........339 K6
MBELL
Engadine.........518 F3
MBO
Prestons.........393 A16
Bangor.........459 C13

BOMBORA
av. Bundeena.........524 B11
BON
st. Chipping Ntn.........396 C5
BONA
cr. Morning Bay.........138 E13
BON ACCORD
av. Bondi Jctn.........377 G3
la. Bondi Jctn, off Bon Accord Av.........377 G2
BONALBO
st. Kingsgrove.........402 B9
BONANZA
la. Sans Souci.........433 C16
pde. Sans Souci.........433 C16
BONAPARTE
st. Riverwood.........400 D14
BONAR
st. Arncliffe.........403 G7
st. Telopea.........279 F8
BONA VISTA
av. Maroubra.........407 H10
BOND
av. Toongabbie.........276 F7
cr. Wetherill Pk.........333 G4
la. Mosman.........316 K4
la. Mosman, off Bond St.........316 J4
pl. Ellis Lane.........476 D6
pl. Illawong.........459 F7
st. Hurstville.........431 K4
st. Maroubra.........407 H10
st. Mosman.........316 K5
st. North Ryde.........282 D11
st. Sydney.........A J13
st. Sydney.........1 G15
BONDELL
av. Gymea.........491 G2
BONDI
pl. Woodbine.........481 F13
rd. Bondi.........377 F3
rd. Bondi Jctn.........377 F3
st. Bundeena.........523 J11
BONDS
rd. Peakhurst.........430 E1
rd. Punchbowl.........400 E7
rd. Riverwood.........400 E13
rd. Riverwood.........400 E16
rd. Roselands.........400 E7
rd. Thirlmere.........564 A3
st. Austral.........390 F8
BONEDA
cl. Annangrove.........155 K16
BONGALONG
st. Naremburn.........315 E3
BONHAM
st. Canley Vale.........366 E2
BON MART
Winston Hills.........277 G2
BONNEFIN
pl. Castle Hill.........218 E16
rd. Hunters Hill.........313 D8
BONNER
av. Manly.........288 H5
rd. Agnes Banks.........117 D13
BONNET
av. Como.........460 D6
BONNEY
cl. St Ives Ch.........224 A6
pl. Doonside.........273 E4
pl. St Helens Park.........541 C5
st. Sans Souci.........433 A16
BONNIE DOON
pl. Burraneer.........523 E3
BONNIE FIELD
cl. Catherine Fd.........449 D3
BONNIE VIEW
st. Gymea.........491 D6
BONNIEVIEW
st. Woolooware.........493 D12
BONNYRIGG
av. Bonnyrigg.........363 K5
BONTON
rd. Springwood.........202 C7
BONTOU
rd. Pymble.........223 K16
rd. St Ives.........223 K16
BONUS
st. North Bondi.........348 C15
BONZER
pl. Glendenning.........242 E5

BOOBOOK
pl. Ingleburn.........453 F10
BOOKER
rd. Hawksbry Ht.........174 G3
BOOKS
cr. McGraths Hl.........121 K12
st. Dean Park.........212 H15
BOOLA
av. Yennora.........337 B8
pl. Cromer.........228 E13
pl. Westleigh.........220 G9
BOOLARONG
av. Chipping Ntn.........396 G5
rd. Pymble.........223 F14
BOOLEROO
pl. Westleigh.........220 G6
BOOLIGAL
rd. Terrey Hills.........195 H3
BOOMERANG
av. Earlwood.........402 G5
av. Lilli Pilli.........522 G1
cr. Raby.........451 E12
dr. Glossodia.........59 G4
pl. Cmbrdg Gdn.........237 F4
pl. Seven Hills.........275 H2
pl. Woolmloo.........D J13
rd. Collaroy Plat.........228 H13
rd. Edensor Pk.........363 H3
rd. Springwood.........201 G3
st. Granville.........308 B11
st. Haberfield.........343 E12
st. Maroubra.........407 G9
st. Turramurra.........223 A12
BOOMI
pl. Woronora.........459 K16
BOON
rd. Londonderry.........148 F16
BOONA
rd. Terrey Hills.........195 H7
BOONAH
av. Eastgardens.........406 F12
la. Eastgardens.........406 G12
st. Wentwthvle.........276 K11
BOONAL
st. Baulkham Hl.........247 A6
BOONARA
av. Bondi.........378 A5
la. Bondi, off Boonara Av.........378 A5
BOONDAH
pl. Kareela.........461 B12
pl. Warrawee.........222 H10
rd. Warriewood.........199 A11
BOONGARY
st. St Helens Park.........541 J1
BOONGIL
st. West Pymble.........252 J8
BOONOKE
cr. Miller.........393 H2
pl. Airds.........512 C12
wy. Airds.........512 C13
BOORABA
av. Lindfield.........283 H6
BOORAGUL
st. Beverly Hills.........401 B10
BOORALEE
st. Botany.........405 C12
BOORALIE
rd. Duffys Frst.........195 A2
rd. Terrey Hills.........196 A5
BOORALLA
rd. Edensor Pk.........333 K16
BOORARA
av. Oatley.........430 K16
av. Oatley.........431 A15
BOOREA
av. Lakemba.........371 A14
st. Blaxland.........233 H6
st. Lidcombe.........339 G3
BOOREE
ct. Wattle Grove.........426 A2
BOOREEA
st. Blacktown.........274 E2
BOORIMA
pl. Cronulla.........494 A14
BOORROO
st. Kangaroo Pt.........461 J4
BOOTES
av. Hinchinbrk.........393 E4
BOOTH
cl. Fairfield W.........335 A12

la. Annandale.........11 B14
pl. Cherrybrook.........219 K10
pl. Minchinbury.........271 F9
st. Annandale.........11 A14
st. Arncliffe.........403 H6
st. Balmain.........7 H11
st. Camperdwn.........17 D1
st. Marsfield.........282 C4
st. Westmead.........307 H4
BOOTIE
pl. Kings Lngly.........246 D10
BOOTLE
pl. Cranebrook.........207 G12
BOOTLES
la. Pitt Town.........92 H12
BOOTS
la. Ingleburn.........453 D5
BOOYONG
av. Caringbah.........492 J4
av. Lugarno.........430 A13
st. Cabramatta.........365 H10
BORA
pl. Toongabbie.........276 H10
pl. Wilberforce.........92 C1
BORAMBIL
pl. Longueville.........314 E6
pl. Oyster Bay.........461 D4
st. Warrawee.........222 F10
BORDEAUX
cr. Castle Hill.........216 K9
cr. Castle Hill.........217 A9
pl. Orchard Hills.........268 H14
BORDER
cl. Elderslie.........507 K1
cl. Hinchinbrk.........363 A14
la. Mosman.........317 D4
rd. Horsley Pk.........332 H8
BORDLEY
pl. Oakhurst.........242 B5
BOREC
rd. Penrith.........236 F3
BOREE
pl. Bangor.........459 C12
pl. Mcquarie Fd.........454 F4
pl. Wrrngtn Dns.........238 B3
pl. Westleigh.........220 E7
rd. Forestville.........255 D8
st. Marsfield.........282 A4
BORELLA
rd. Milperra.........397 D9
BORG
pl. Prairiewood.........334 E12
BORGAH
st. Carss Park.........432 F14
BORGNIS
st. Belrose.........225 E16
st. Davidson.........225 E16
BORLAISE
st. Willoughby.........285 E14
BORNEO
ct. Bossley Park.........334 B5
BORO
pl. Prestons.........393 B13
BORODIN
cl. Cranebrook.........207 F9
BORODINO
pl. Narellan Vale.........479 A16
BOROJEVIC
st. Bonnyrigg Ht.........363 A5
BOROMI
wy. Cromer.........227 K11
BORONGA
av. West Pymble.........252 H13
cl. Bangor.........459 B11
pl. Berowra Ht.........133 B10
BORONIA
av. Beecroft.........250 F9
av. Burwood.........342 C13
av. Cheltenham.........250 F9
av. Croydon.........372 C3
av. Engadine.........518 H2
av. Epping.........280 G1
av. Hunters Hill.........313 C7
av. Mt Annan.........509 C3
av. Russell Lea.........343 D5
av. Turramurra.........252 E1
cr. Stanhpe Gdn.........215 E10
cr. Winmalee.........173 K6
dr. Voyager Pt.........427 B5
gr. Heathcote.........518 H12
la. Denistone E.........281 G9
la. Redfern.........20 B8

la. Seaforth.........286 K7
la. Mosman, off Brady St.........317 A5
pde. Lugarno.........430 B15
pde.w, Lugarno.........430 A14
pl. Cheltenham.........250 J11
rd. Bellevue Hill.........347 J14
rd. Bossley Park.........333 F10
rd. Glenorie.........127 G8
rd. Greenacre.........369 J11
rd. Ingleside.........198 A4
rd. Kentlyn.........483 F12
rd. N St Marys.........239 J7
rd. N St Marys.........240 B9
st. Belfield.........371 B11
st. Concord W.........311 E14
st. Cronulla.........523 K2
st. Dee Why.........259 A7
st. Ermington.........310 D4
st. Kensington.........376 E11
st. Kyle Bay.........431 J15
st. Lalor Park.........245 B11
st. N Balgowlah.........287 F6
st. Redfern.........19 K8
st. S Granville.........338 G2
st. S Wntwthvle.........306 K5
st. Wollstncraft.........315 D8
BORRODALE
rd. Kingsford.........406 D2
BORROWDALE
cl. Lurnea.........394 C12
cl. Narellan.........478 E14
pl. Beacon Hill.........257 F4
pl. Bligh Park.........150 C5
wy. Cranebrook.........207 D11
wy. Kellyville.........185 K15
BORTFIELD
dr. Chiswick.........343 D1
BORTHWICK
st. Minto.........482 G7
BORU
pl. Killarney Ht.........286 D2
BOSAVI
st. Glenfield.........424 G14
BOSCI
rd. Ingleburn.........452 K5
BOSCO
pl. Schofields.........213 J6
BOSCOBEL
rd. Londonderry.........177 G4
BOSLEY
av. Liverpool.........364 K15
BOSNJAK
av. Edensor Pk.........333 G15
BOSSLEY
rd. Bossley Park.........333 F7
tce. Woolmloo.........4 E5
BOSTOCK
st. Richmond.........120 A5
BOSTON
cl. Hinchinbrk.........392 K1
pl. St Clair.........270 G13
pl. Toongabbie.........275 F14
wy. Kellyville.........216 A1
BOSWORTH
st. Richmond.........118 F5
BOTANIC
rd. Mosman.........317 D8
BOTANICAL
dr. Kellyville.........216 A4
BOTANY
bvd. Kings Lngly.........246 A10
bvd. Seven Hills.........246 A10
cir. Matraville.........436 G8
la. Alexandria.........19 B13
la. Kingsford.........406 J1
la. Mascot.........405 E6
la. St Clair, off Bennett Rd.........270 C12
pl. Bondi Jctn.........377 F5
pl. Ruse.........512 G8
pl. Yagoona.........368 H11
rd. Alexandria.........19 B12
rd. Bnksmeadw.........435 J1
rd. Bnksmeadw.........436 C3
rd. Beaconsfield.........375 F16
rd. Botany.........405 E9
rd. Mascot.........405 E5
rd. Matraville.........436 C3
rd. Port Botany.........436 C3
rd. Rosebery.........405 E5
rd. Waterloo.........19 B12
rd. Zetland.........375 F16
st. Allawah.........432 E4

st. Bondi Jctn..........377 F5
st. Kensington.........376 K16
st. Kingsford...........406 H5
st. Randwick...........406 J3

BO TREE
pl. Prestons 393 J15

BOTTLE BRUSH
dr. Faulconbdg........171 D12
pl. Colyton...............270 H6
rd. Westleigh...........220 H8

BOTTLEBRUSH
av. Bradbury............511 F10
av. Lugarno..............430 A9
cl. Picton.................561 C4
dr. Cranebrook.........237 E1
gr. Acacia Gdn.........214 J15
la. Cranebrook, off
Greygums Rd.....207 E16
pl. Alfords Point......429 B15

BOTTLE FOREST
rd. Heathcote...........518 J11

BOTTLES
rd. Plumpton............241 K7

BOUCHET
cr. Minchinbury.......271 K8

BOUDDI
st. Bow Bowing.......452 C15

BOUGAINVILLE
av. Bossley Park......333 K6
ct. Maroubra...........407 C14
rd. Blackett.............241 A1
rd. Glenfield............424 E12
rd. Lethbrdg Pk.......240 G2

BOUGHTON
st. Richmond...........118 J7

BOULT
cl. Bligh Park..........150 D5

BOULTON
av. Baulkham Hl......247 E4
st. Putney................311 K6

BOUNDARY
la. Cabramatta........365 J8
la. Cabramatta........365 K8
la. Darlington...........18 E8
la. Paddington............4 J12
la. Paddington............4 K12
rd. Box Hill..............153 D13
rd. Carlingford.........279 J3
rd. Cherrybrook.......219 G13
rd. Chester Hill........338 E13
rd. Cranebrook........206 K8
rd. Faulconbdg........201 D1
rd. Glossodia..............60 C8
rd. Heathcote...........518 D14
rd. Liverpool............394 G9
rd. Lurnea................394 G9
rd. Maraylya.............124 A15
rd. Mortdale.............430 G3
rd. N Epping.............251 E8
rd. Northmead..........277 K11
rd. Oakville..............153 D13
rd. Oatley.................431 A8
rd. Peakhurst...........430 G3
rd. Pennant Hills......250 E1
rd. Pennant Hills......250 F1
rd. Schofields...........183 G11
rd. Sefton.................338 E13
rd. Springwood.........201 D1
rd. Vineyard.............153 D13
rd. Wahroonga..........222 F2
st. Alexandria.............19 A10
st. Berowra...............133 E12
st. Castle Cove..........285 E3
st. Clovelly...............377 J11
st. Clovelly...............378 A12
st. Croydon...............342 D15
st. Darlinghurst............4 H13
st. Darlington..............18 H5
st. Granville..............308 A8
st. Paddington..............4 H13
st. Parramatta...........308 A8
st. Redfern..................18 K10
st. Roseville..............284 J5
st. Roseville Ch.........285 E3
st. Thirlmere.............564 J10
st. Thirlmere.............565 A10
st. Warriewood..........198 E6

BOUNTY
av. Castle Hill............217 H10
av. Kirrawee..............491 A9
cr. Bligh Park............150 H9
pl. Old Tngabbie........277 C7

BOURKE
la. Paddington..............4 K16
la. Queens Park...........22 H12
la. Redfern..................20 B11
la. Pymble, off
Bannockburn Rd...223 C13
pl. Abbotsford...........343 A4
pl. Blairmount...........480 K13
pl. Botany.................405 F11
pl. Camden S.............506 K12
rd. Alexandria............375 B15
rd. Mascot.................405 B3
rd. Pendle Hill............276 G13
st. Blaxland...............233 D5
st. Darlinghurst.............4 E12
st. Liverpool..............395 C5
st. Mascot.................405 B2
st. N Parramatta........278 B10
st. Pymble.................223 C13
st. Queens Park...........22 H13
st. Redfern..................20 B11
st. Richmond..............118 J8
st. Riverstone............182 H5
st. Smithfield.............335 E7
st. Surry Hills.................4 D16
st. Waterloo...............375 H9
st. Woolmloo..................4 E7
st. Zetland.................375 H9

BOURMAC
av. Northbridge.........286 F15

BOURNE
st. Marrickville..........374 E11
st. Wentwthvle..........277 A15

BOURNEMOUTH
st. Bundeena.............524 A11

BOUSSOLE
rd. Daceyville.............406 E3

BOUVARDIA
ct. Acacia Gdn...........214 J14
st. Asquith.................191 K10
st. Caringbah.............492 H16
st. Punchbowl............400 D1
st. Russell Lea...........343 C4

BOVIS
pl. Rooty Hill..............272 C6

BOW
la. Kingsford..............406 H2
pl. Glen Alpine...........510 B14

BOWAGA
av. Blaxland...............234 E7

BOWATER
cl. N Wahrnga............222 K1

BOW BOWING
cr. Bradbury...............511 H12

BOWDEN
bvd. Yagoona..............369 C9
cl. Green Valley.........363 B11
cr. Connells Pt...........461 G1
la. Woollahra................22 A5
pl. Belfield.................371 E12
st. Alexandria............375 E9
st. Cabramatta...........365 D11
st. Guildford..............337 A1
st. Harris Park...........308 F8
st. Meadowbnk...........311 E5
st. Merrylands W.......307 B16
st. N Parramatta........278 J15
st. Ryde....................311 G2
st. Woollahra................21 K5

BOWEN
av. S Turramrra..........252 A10
cl. Cherrybrook...........219 C10
pl. Maroubra...............407 D16
pl. Seven Hills............275 D6
st. Chatswd W............284 H13

BOWENIA
ct. Stanhpe Gdn.........215 E10

BOWEN MOUNTAIN
rd. Bowen Mtn..............84 A12
rd. Grose Vale..............84 D11

BOWER
la. Manly...................288 K11
st. Bankstown.............369 B14
st. Manly...................288 K11
st. Plumpton...............242 B10
st. Roselands.............401 D6

BOWER BIRD
ct. Kenthurst..............158 A15

BOWER-BIRD
st. Hinchinbrk............393 B4

BOWERBIRD
av. Ingleburn..............453 F9
cr. St Clair..................269 J10

BOWERMAN
pl. Cherrybrook...........219 F15

BOWERS
pl. Leumeah...............482 K11

BOWES
av. Edgecliff..................13 H13
av. Killara...................253 F15
av. S Penrith...............266 H2
cl. Cecil Hills..............362 J9
pl. Doonside...............273 E2

BOWIE
pl. Wetherill Pk...........334 D5

BOWLER
av. Fairfield.................336 D9

BOWLERS
av. Bexley...................403 A14

BOWLING GREEN
la. Avalon...................170 A1

BOWMAN
av. Camden S.............507 B13
av. Castle Hill..............247 J4
av. Frenchs Frst..........256 D2
rd. Londonderry..........148 G13
st. Drummoyne...........343 G4
st. Mortdale...............430 H8
st. Pyrmont...................12 C2
st. Richmond..............119 B5
wy. Minto....................482 K1

BOWMANS
rd. Kings Park.............244 E5

BOWMER
st. Banksia.................403 D12

BOWNESS
ct. Kellyville................186 K15
st. Collaroy Plat..........228 D9

BOWNS
rd. Kogarah................433 A6

BOWOOD
av. Bexley..................402 H14
la. St Marys, off
Bowood Pl.........270 A6
pl. St Marys...............270 A6
rd. Mt Vernon.............331 B7

BOWRA
cl. Bangor..................459 C12

BOWRAL
cl. Hornsby Ht............161 J7
la. Kensington, off
Doncaster Av.....376 F11
rd. Blacktown.............274 F2
st. Greystanes............305 H4
st. Kensington............376 E11
st. North Rocks...........279 A2

BOWREY
pl. Shalvey.................211 C12

BOWTELL
av. St Johns Pk...........364 J2

BOX
av. Wilberforce..............62 G12
la. Jannali...................460 H12
pl. Mcquarie Fd...........454 H3
pl. Box Hill..................184 E1
rd. Caringbah..............462 G15
rd. Casula...................424 B2
rd. Jannali...................460 H12
rd. Kareela..................461 B13
rd. Prestons................394 B16
rd. Rouse Hill..............184 E1
rd. Sylvania.................461 J14
rd. Sylvania Wtr..........462 G15
rd. Wakeley................334 F13

BOXER
pl. Rooty Hill..............272 D5

BOXLEY
cr. Bankstown.............399 G6

BOXSELL
cl. Menai....................458 K11

BOXWOOD
pl. Cherrybrook...........219 E10

BOYCE
av. Strathfield..............341 A11
la. Glebe........................11 H12
la. Maroubra...............407 E10
pl. Ruse.....................512 H7
rd. Maroubra...............406 H8
rd. Maroubra...............407 A9
st. Glebe........................11 H12
st. Ryde.....................282 E14
wy. Clarmnt Ms...........268 G3

BOYD
av. Lugarno................429 K10
av. W Pnnant Hl..........249 K3
ct. Harringtn Pk..........478 E7
la. Gladesville.............313 A3
la. Glenbrook..............234 A14
la. Neutral Bay...............6 D8
la. Berala, off
Sixth Av............339 D16
pl. Barden Rdg............458 G16
pl. Wrrngtn Cty...........238 E5
st. Austral..................390 E11
st. Blacktown..............244 K16
st. Cabramatta W........364 K7
st. Claymore...............481 C8
st. Eagle Vale.............481 C8
st. Turramurra.............222 H14

BOYER
pl. Minto....................453 A16
rd. Beacon Hill............257 E4

BOYLE
la. Sutherland.............490 E3
pl. Shalvey.................211 B15
st. Balgowlah..............287 K9
st. Cremorne...............316 F11
st. Croydon Pk............372 A6
st. Ermington..............310 D4
st. Mosman................316 F11
st. Sutherland.............490 E3

BOYLES
la. Valley Ht................203 E7

BOYLSON
pl. Cromer..................227 H13

BOYNE
av. Pendle Hill.............306 E1
pl. Baulkham Hl..........246 J4
pl. Killarney Ht............256 B15
pl. Wahroonga.............222 B14

BOYNTON
st. Blaxland................233 D6

BOYS
av. Blacktown..............244 H15

BOYTHORN
av. Ambarvale..............510 J14

BOZ
pl. Ambarvale..............511 A14

BRABHAM
dr. Eastern Ck.............273 C13

BRABYN
st. Denistone E...........281 F9
st. Fairfield W.............335 C8
st. N Parramatta.........278 H15
st. Parramatta.............278 H15
st. Windsor.................120 K11

BRACHER
st. East Hills................427 J2

BRACK
cl. Abbotsbury.............333 C12

BRACKEN
cl. Berowra..................163 C1
cl. Engadine................488 K15

BRACKEN FELL
cl. Castle Hill...............217 G10

BRACKNELL
av. Hebersham............241 F5
rd. Canley Ht...............365 A3

BRAD
pl. Kings Lngly.............245 F8

BRADBURY
av. Bradbury................511 E6
av. Campbelltwn..........511 E6
st. Tahmoor.................565 K10

BRADDOCK
pl. Winston Hills..........247 K15

BRADDON
la. Oxley Park, off
Braddon St.........240 F16
pl. Edensor Pk.............363 G3
st. Blacktown..............273 K4
st. Concord.................312 A16
st. Oxley Park.............240 D15

BRADEY
av. Hamondvle.............396 E15

BRADFIELD
cr. Bonnyrigg...............364 A5
hwy. Dawes Point...........A G4
hwy. Dawes Point...........1 G8
hwy. Millers Pt................A G4
hwy. Millers Pt................1 G8
hwy. Milsons Point..........5 K13
pl. Doonside...............273 G4
rd. Lindfield.................283 F4
st. Leumeah...............482 D16

BRADFORD
la. Balmain......................7 J11
st. Alexandria.............375 E16
st. Balmain......................7 J11
st. Pymble..................223 E14

BRADLEY
av. Bellevue Hill.........34
av. Berala...................33
cr. Wiley Park.............40
ct. W Pnnant Hl..........248
dr. Carlingford............249
la. Elizabeth Bay.........13
la. Randwick, off
Bradley St..........376
pl. Illawong.................460
pl. Liberty Gr..............311
pl. Ruse.....................512
rd. N Richmond..............87
rd. S Windsor..............150
st. Drummoyne............343
st. Ingleburn...............453
st. Mulgoa..................296
st. Randwick...............376

BRADLEYS HEAD
rd. Mosman................317

BRADLY
av. Milsons Point.............6

BRADMAN
av. St Clair.................270
rd. Menai...................458
rd. Shalvey.................211
st. Greystanes............305
st. Greystanes............306
st. Merrylands.............308
st. Narwee..................400

BRADSHAW
av. Moorebank............395
pl. Prairiewood...........334

BRADY
pl. Glenmore Pk..........266
pl. Kellyville................216
pl. Prairiewood...........334
st. Croydon.................342
st. Merrylands.............308
st. Mosman................317
wy. Bonnyrigg.............364

BRADYN
pl. Glenmore Pk..........265

BRAE
st. Bronte...................377
st. Prospect................274

BRAEFIELD
pl. Castle Hill..............218

BRAEKELL
pl. Kellyville................186

BRAEMAR
av. Auburn..................309
av. Kellyville................217
av. St Andrews............451
dr. S Penrith...............267
pl. Roseville...............255
st. Smithfield..............336

BRAEMORE
ct. Castle Hill..............218

BRAESIDE
av. Penshurst..............431
av. Smithfield..............335
cr. Earlwood...............402
cr. Glen Alpine............510
pl. Engadine...............488
rd. Greystanes............306
st. Wahroonga............222

BRAESMERE
rd. Panania.................427

BRAHMA
cl. Bossley Park..........334
rd. N Richmond..............87

BRAHMS
st. Seven Hills............246
wy. Clarmnt Ms...........268

BRAIDWOOD
av. N Epping...............251
dr. Prestons...............392
dr. Prestons...............392
dr. Prestons...............393
dr. Prestons...............422
st. Strathfield S..........370

BRAIKFIELD
av. Kemps Ck..............359

BRAIN
av. Lurnea..................394

BRALLAS
av. St Ives Ch.............223

BRALLOS
av. Holsworthy............396

BRAMBLE
pl. Mcquarie Fd...........454
pl. Whalan..................240

MHALL
Punchbowl 399 J7
MLEY
Newport 169 J11
Fairfield W 335 B8
MPTON
Hinchinbrk 363 B16
Kellyville 185 J13
Kellyville 186 A14
Kellyville 216 A1
Greystanes 305 J1
MSTON
Earlwood 402 F2
MWELL
Illawong 460 A3
NCOURT
Bankstown 369 C13
Bankstown 369 C16
Yagoona 369 C13
ND
Artarmon 284 K14
Croydon 342 D15
Dundas Vy 279 J6
NDE
Belmore 371 C15
NDERS
N Richmond 87 C6
NDLING
Alexandria 18 F13
Alexandria 18 F13
NDON
Bankstown 399 C1
Bankstown, off
Brandon Av 399 D2
St Ives 224 F7
Clovelly 377 H11
NDOWN
Austral 361 G15
NDS
Warriewood 198 K8
NKSOME
Glenmore Pk 266 F15
NSBY
Mt Annan 479 G13
NSFIELD
Tregear 240 F6
NSGROVE
Panania 397 J13
Revesby 398 A13
Wentwthvle 307 B3
ANTWOOD
Sans Souci 463 B5
ASSIE
North Bondi 348 C16
ATSELL
Moorebank 396 C11
AUNBECK
Bankstown 369 B15
AY
Earlwood 402 G6
North Rocks 249 B16
Menai 458 K15
Neutral Bay 6 A8
N Sydney 6 A8
Erskineville, off
Bray St 374 J10
Ambarvale 510 F15
Drummoyne 343 G3
Dundas 280 A12
Erskineville 374 K10
Fairfield 336 E7
Mosman 316 H4
N Sydney 5 K8
AYE
Padstow Ht 429 F7
AYS
Breakfast Pt 341 K1
Concord 341 K1
AYTON
Prestons 392 H15
AZIER
Guildford 338 B7
EAKFAST
Marayong 243 K7
EAKWELL
Mortdale 431 A4
Mortdale 430 K5
EAM
Como 460 E6
Coogee 377 E15

BREASLEY
av. Yagoona 368 J12
pl. Yagoona 369 A11
BRECHIN
cl. Emu Plains 235 E14
rd. St Andrews 451 K15
BRECON
ct. Castle Hill 218 C11
BREDBO
st. Prestons 393 B13
BREDON
av. W Pnnant Hl 218 K16
pl. Jamisontown 266 C4
BREELLEN
cl. Tahmoor 565 F12
BREEZA
pl. Bangor 459 B13
BREILLAT
la. Annandale 11 A8
st. Annandale 11 A8
BRELL
pl. Kingswood 237 F9
BRELOGAIL
st. Northmead 277 J11
BREMER
pl. Hinchinbrk 392 K1
BREN
cl. St Clair 269 K12
BRENAN
st. Fairfield 335 J6
st. Lilyfield 10 G8
st. Smithfield 335 J6
BRENDA
av. Lidcombe 340 B7
ct. North Rocks 248 J15
rd. Kemps Ck 360 B11
st. Ingleburn 453 A9
wy. Epping 251 C15
BRENDAN
pl. Quakers Hill 213 K9
BRENDON
pl. Carlingford 279 J1
st. North Ryde 282 C9
BRENNAN
cl. Asquith 192 A14
la. Newtown 17 G12
pl. Blackett 241 B1
pl. Minto 482 J1
st. Alexandria 19 A15
st. Yagoona 368 F10
BRENNANS
la. Russell Lea 343 D4
rd. Arncliffe 403 J10
BRENNANS DAM
rd. Vineyard 152 C3
BRENT
st. Rozelle 7 B15
st. Russell Lea 343 E6
BRENTFORD
rd. Wahroonga 222 B6
BRENTIN
pl. Hebersham 241 E10
BRENTWOOD
av. Hobartville 118 G7
av. Turramurra 222 G11
av. Warrawee 222 G11
gr. Wrrngtn Dns 237 J4
pl. Frenchs Frst 257 A2
st. Fairfield W 335 B8
wy. Castle Hill 248 H3
BRERETON
av. Marrickville 373 J9
la. Marrickville, off
Brereton Av 373 K10
st. Gladesville 312 G7
BRETON
pl. Emu Heights 235 B2
BRETT
av. Balmain East 8 G7
av. Hornsby Ht 191 E2
av. Wentwthvle 277 A10
pl. Ingleburn 453 E11
pl. W Pnnant Hl 249 H4
st. Kings Lngly 245 G9
st. Revesby 428 H1
st. Tennyson 312 E10
BREUC
pl. Box Hill 154 E13
BREUST
pl. Punchbowl 400 C3
BREWER
av. Liberty Gr 311 B10
cr. S Wntwthvle 307 D5
pl. Lugarno 430 A12
st. Concord 342 A4
st. Marsden Pk 182 A10
BREWERS
la. Freemns Rch 91 B2
BREWON
cl. Bossley Park 333 F9
BREWONGLE
av. Penrith 237 E4
BREWSTER
pl. Leumeah 482 F12
BREYLEY
st. Cmbrdg Pk 237 J8
BRIAL
pl. Minto 482 H8
BRIALY
pl. Picton 561 D4
BRIAN
st. Merrylands W 306 H12
st. Ryde 282 A9
BRIAR
la. St Peters, off
Henry St 374 F14
pl. Georges Hall 367 H11
rd. Airds 511 J13
rd. Bradbury 511 J13
st. St Ives 224 D11
BRIARWOOD
av. Glenmore Pk 266 H12
BRIBIE
cl. Green Valley 363 A12
BRICE
cl. Illawong 459 K5
wy. St Helens Park 540 K7
BRICKENDON
ct. Wattle Grove 395 K16
BRICKETWOOD
dr. Woodcroft 243 G7
BRICKFIELD
pl. Blacktown 275 A4
pl. Sydney E J2
rd. Windsor 121 B13
st. N Parramatta 278 E16
st. Parramatta 278 E16
st. Ruse 512 H3
BRICKPIT
lk. Homebush B 310 K13
BRICKWORKS
dr. Holroyd 307 K11
BRIDDON
cl. Pennant Hills 220 D14
BRIDGE
la. Drummoyne 313 G15
la. Glebe 12 D10
la. Sydney A J12
la. Belmore, off
Gladstone St 371 D16
rd. Belmore 371 D16
rd. Blaxland 233 C5
rd. Forest Lodge 11 H15
rd. Glebe 12 C11
rd. Homebush 341 A10
rd. Hornsby 191 G14
rd. Hornsby 191 H14
rd. Manly 288 H4
rd. Marsfield 282 A8
rd. North Ryde 282 A8
rd. Parramatta 277 K13
rd. Queenscliff 288 H3
rd. Ryde 282 A8
rd. Stanmore 17 A6
rd. Ultimo 12 D9
rd. Westmead 307 D3
st. Balmain 344 E4
st. Bexley 402 C16
st. Brooklyn 76 C11
st. Cabramatta 365 K8
st. Epping 251 A16
st. Erskineville 18 A16
st. Erskineville 18 B14
st. Granville 308 F10
st. Hurstville 431 F5
st. Lane Cove 314 A3
st. Lidcombe 339 H8
st. Padstow 399 G15
st. Parramatta 279 A16
st. Penshurst 431 F5
st. Picton 563 A14
st. Picton 565 D1
st. Pymble 253 E5
st. Rydalmere 309 C1
st. Schofields 183 B14
st. Sydney A K11
st. Sydney 1 H14
st. Tempe 374 C15
st. Thirlmere 565 D1
st. Werrington 239 C16
st. Windsor 121 D7
st. Artarmon, off
Cameron Av 284 K15
st.w, Lidcombe, off
Samuel St 339 G8
BRIDGE END
Wollstncraft 315 D10
BRIDGE QUARRY
pl. Glenbrook 234 D11
BRIDGES
av. Croydon 342 F13
av. Holsworthy 396 B13
rd. Moorebank 395 H5
st. Kurnell 465 H9
st. Maroubra 407 F13
BRIDGE STAIRS
The Rocks A G3
BRIDGET
pl. Kellyville 215 G5
BRIDGE VIEW
st. Blacktown 274 F8
BRIDGEVIEW
av. Cammeray 315 J4
cr. Forestville 255 F11
cr. Mt Riverview 204 G16
cr. Thornleigh 221 B13
rd. Beverly Hills 430 J2
rd. Engadine 489 D14
BRIDLE
av. Currans Hill 479 K9
av. Oakdale 500 G11
BRIDPORT
cl. West Hoxton 392 D7
BRIENS
rd. Northmead 277 G11
rd. Wentwthvle 277 D13
BRIER
cr. Quakers Hill 243 G4
pl. Mt Pritchard 364 E9
BRIERLEY
cr. Plumpton 241 H11
pl. Eagle Vale 480 K9
BRIERLY
st. Mosman 316 G9
BRIERWOOD
pl. Frenchs Frst 255 J1
BRIERY
pl. Cranebrook 207 E12
BRIGADOON
av. Glenmore Pk 266 F12
ct. Epping 281 C3
BRIGALOW
av. Camden S 507 B11
av. Casula 394 E14
pl. Engadine 489 F9
pl. Westleigh 220 E9
st. Cabramatta 365 G9
BRIGANTINE
st. Chipping Ntn 366 K15
BRIGG
rd. Epping 281 C2
BRIGGS
pl. Doonside 273 F4
pl. St Helens Park 541 A11
st. Camperdwn 17 F4
BRIGHT
cl. Edensor Pk 333 J14
st. Guildford 338 A5
st. Marrickville 16 B15
st. Ryde 312 E3
BRIGHTMAN
cr. Bidwill 241 G1
BRIGHTMORE
la. Cremorne, off
Illiliwa St 316 E7
st. Cremorne 316 E6
BRIGHTON
av. Btn-le-Sds 433 K5
av. Campsie 372 A10
av. Croydon Pk 372 B8
av. Panania 398 C16
bvd. Bondi Beach 378 E1
bvd. North Bondi 378 E1
dr. Bella Vista 216 C13
la. Croydon Pk 372 C5
la. Petersham 15 K9
la. Riverstone 183 B11
pde. Btn-le-Sds 433 K1
rd. Coogee 377 E15
rd. Peakhurst 400 F16
st. Balgowlah 287 G7
st. Botany 405 K13
st. Bundeena 523 K11
st. Croydon 372 C3
st. Croydon Pk 372 C5
st. Curl Curl 258 E13
st. Greystanes 305 K8
st. Harbord 258 E13
st. Kogarah Bay 432 J11
st. Petersham 15 F9
st. Riverstone 183 A12
BRIGID
pl. Quakers Hill 214 F15
BRINAWA
st. Mona Vale 199 A5
BRINDABELLA
dr. Horngsea Pk 392 F16
la. Narellan 478 B10
pl. W Pnnant Hl 248 J5
st. Ruse 512 H7
BRINDISI
pl. Avalon 139 H14
BRINGELLY
av. Pendle Hill 276 G14
la. Kingswood, off
Bringelly Rd 237 H13
pl. Bonnyrigg Ht 363 B5
rd. Austral 391 A16
rd. Bringelly 388 E13
rd. Horngsea Pk 392 A16
rd. Kingswood 237 G16
rd. Leppington 421 A1
rd. Rossmore 389 B14
rd. West Hoxton 421 H1
BRIONY
pl. Mona Vale 198 K3
BRISBANE
av. E Lindfield 254 J14
av. Lurnea 394 D13
av. Mt Krng-gai 162 J13
av. Rodd Point 9 B1
la. Waterloo 19 G13
pl. Cromer 227 J13
rd. Campbelltwn 512 B6
rd. Castle Hill 218 E14
rd. Riverstone 182 H1
rd. St Johns Pk 334 D16
rd. Vineyard 152 G14
st. Bondi Jctn 22 H9
st. Chifley 437 A5
st. Fairlight 288 C8
st. Harris Park 308 F7
st. Illawong 459 H4
st. Oxley Park 240 E16
st. St Marys 239 K15
st. Surry Hills F E7
st. Surry Hills 3 K12
BRISCOE
cr. Kings Lngly 245 C5
BRISSENDEN
av. Collaroy 229 C13
BRISTOL
av. Pymble 253 J1
av. Raby 451 G15
av. Wahroonga 221 J11
cct. Blacktown 274 B7
la. N Narrabeen 228 J2
rd. Hurstville 432 A3
st. Merrylands W 306 K15
st. N Parramatta 278 C9
BRISTOW
la. Peakhurst 430 F2
BRITANNIA
av. Burwood 341 K11
av. Merrylands 307 K13
la. Woollahra 21 J3
rd. Castle Hill 217 J12
st. Pennant Hills 250 J2
BRITTAIN
cr. Hillsdale 406 G14
BRITTANIA
pl. Bligh Park 150 E7
BRITTANY
pl. Peakhurst 430 C13
BRITTEN
cl. Cranebrook 207 H9
pl. Bossley Park 333 J12
BRITTON
cl. Elderslie 507 G2
st. Smithfield 336 B1

BRIXHAM
pl. Chipping Ntn 366 G16
BRIXTON
rd. Berala 339 E13
rd. Lidcombe 339 E13
BROAD
st. Bass Hill 368 D7
st. Cabramatta 365 D8
st. Croydon Pk 371 K8
st. Prospect 275 B11
BROAD ARROW
rd. Beverly Hills 401 A13
rd. Narwee 400 K14
rd. Riverwood 400 D15
BROADBENT
st. Kingsford 406 K5
BROADFORD
st. Bexley 402 J11
st. St Andrews 452 A12
BROADHURST
pl. Baulkham Hl 246 K12
rd. Ingleburn 453 A7
BROADLEAF
cr. Kellyville 215 K1
BROADLEYS
la. Marrickville, off Malakoff St 373 K12
BROADMEADOWS
st. St Johns Pk 364 F3
BROADOAK
pl. Castle Hill 218 J7
BROADSIDE
st. Balmain East 8 D9
BROADSWORD
pl. Castle Hill 217 G5
BROADWAY
Chippendale 18 G1
Punchbowl 400 E5
Ultimo 3 C16
BROCAS
pl. Quakers Hill 214 E13
BROCK
av. St Marys 239 H16
la. St Marys, off Brock Av 239 H16
st. Mount Druitt 271 F3
BROCKAMIN
dr. S Penrith 267 C5
BROCKLEHURST
la. Kingsgrove 402 A11
BROCKLEY
st. Lilyfield 10 H3
st. Rozelle 10 H3
BROCKMAN
av. Revesby Ht 429 A7
st. Wakeley 334 J12
BROCKS
la. Newtown 18 A9
BROCKWELL
pl. Blakehurst 432 F16
BRODERICK
st. Balmain 344 E4
st. Camperdwn 17 F3
BRODIE
av. Little Bay 437 G14
cir. Baulkham Hl 248 A11
st. Baulkham Hl 248 A10
st. Paddington 4 K16
st. Rydalmere 309 B2
st. Yagoona 368 G9
BROE
av. Arncliffe 403 F7
av. East Hills 427 H5
BROGO
pl. Prestons 393 C13
BROKENWOOD
pl. Baulkham Hl 246 J2
pl. Cherrybrook 219 E12
BROLEN
wy. Cecil Park 331 J12
BROLGA
cr. Green Valley 363 F14
gln. St Clair 270 E12
pl. Belrose 225 F14
pl. Gymea Bay 491 G9
pl. Ingleburn 453 D8
wy. Westleigh 220 H9
wy. W Pnnant Hl 249 E7
BROMBOROUGH
rd. Roseville 284 E5
BROMFIELD
av. Prospect 275 C11
av. Toongabbie 276 E9
BROMLEY
av. Greenacre 370 B13
av. Pymble 253 G3
av. Cremorne, off Kareela Rd 316 G12
gr. Parklea 214 K13
rd. Emu Heights 235 A6
st. Canley Vale 366 G5
wy. Glenhaven 218 D5
BROMPTON
rd. Kensington 376 C10
st. Marrickville 374 D10
BROMUS
pl. Mcquarie Fd 454 G5
BROMWICH
pl. Menai 458 H7
st. Greystanes 306 A10
BRON
cl. W Pnnant Hl 248 H5
BRONHILL
av. East Ryde 283 B16
BRONSDON
st. Smithfield 335 B4
BRONSGROVE
cl. S Penrith 267 B7
BRONTE
av. Glenwood 215 H14
cl. West Hoxton 392 E6
cl. Wetherill Pk 334 H6
pl. Winston Hills 277 F2
pl. Woodbine 481 D14
rd. Bondi Jctn 22 J7
rd. Bondi Jctn 22 J9
rd. Bronte 377 J8
rd. Waverley 377 E6
wy. Glenmore Pk 266 F12
BRONTE MARINE
dr. Bronte 378 B8
BRONTI
st. Mascot 405 E7
BRONZEWING
st. Ingleburn 453 F6
st. Tahmoor 565 C11
st. Tahmoor 565 J13
st. Thirlmere 565 B9
tce. Bella Vista 216 D14
BROOK
la. Fairfield Ht 335 K9
la. Crows Nest, off Brook St 315 G5
rd. Currans Hill 479 G6
rd. Glenbrook 264 C4
rd. Seaforth 287 D8
st. Coogee 377 G16
st. Crows Nest 315 G5
st. Marayong 243 G5
st. Naremburn 315 G4
BROOKDALE
tce. Glenbrook 234 D16
BROOKE
av. Castle Hill 217 C10
pl. Silverdale 353 K13
st. Bass Hill 367 G8
st. Engadine 489 A16
BROOKER
av. Beacon Hill 257 E4
av. Oatlands 279 A13
st. Colyton 270 C3
BROOKES
la. Newtown 17 E9
st. Hunters Hill 314 B12
st. Thornleigh 221 D7
BROOKFIELD
av. Wrrngtn Dns 238 B5
pl. St Ives 223 H8
rd. Minto 482 H4
BROOKHOLLOW
av. Baulkham Hl 216 H15
BROOKLANDS
rd. Glenbrook 264 D2
BROOKLYN
la. Double Bay 14 B10
la. Tempe, off Brooklyn St 404 C2
rd. Brooklyn 75 C11
st. Burwood 342 B15
st. Strathfield S 371 B5
st. Tempe 404 B1
BROOKPINE
pl. W Pnnant Hl 248 K3
BROOKS
la. Agnes Banks 146 K1
rd. Denham Ct 452 F1
rd. Denham Ct 452 J1
rd. Ingleburn 452 J1
st. Guildford 337 D6
st. Linley Point 313 H7
st. Mcquarie Fd 454 B3
BROOKSBANK
rd. Gilead 539 F11
BROOKS BEND
Mt Annan 479 B16
BROOKS POINT
rd. Appin 569 A12
BROOKVALE
av. Brookvale 257 K10
BROOKVIEW
st. Currans Hill 479 J10
BROOM
pl. Loftus 489 J10
pl. St Andrews 452 A14
BROOMAN
st. Prestons 422 K1
BROOME
av. Centnnial Pk 22 B6
pl. Bligh Park 150 C5
st. Maroubra 407 D15
BROOMFIELD
st. Cabramatta 365 J10
st. Canley Vale 365 K6
BROOS
rd. Oakville 152 F3
BROTCHIE
av. Matraville 436 G8
BROTHERS
av. Cammeray 316 C3
av. Northbridge 316 C3
pl. Narellan Vale 479 A16
st. Dundas Vy 280 A11
BROTHERSON
av. Matraville 436 G4
BROTHERTON
st. S Wntwthvle 307 B7
BROUGHAM
la. Glebe 12 C11
la. Potts Point 4 G7
la. Woolmloo 4 G7
la. Emu Plains, off Brougham St 235 B12
pl. Raby 451 E12
st. Emu Plains 235 B12
st. Potts Point 4 H7
st. Woolmloo 4 H7
BROUGHTON
av. Castle Hill 218 J14
cr. Appin 569 G9
ct. Kellyville 217 A3
la. Drummoyne 343 H4
la. Glebe 12 E13
pl. Barden Rdg 488 F3
pl. Davidson 225 B16
rd. Artarmon 284 H16
rd. Strathfield 341 B11
st. Ashfield 342 H15
st. Camden 507 A3
st. Campbelltwn 511 G3
st. Canterbury 372 F12
st. Concord 341 K10
st. Drummoyne 343 H5
st. Glebe 12 D11
st. Hinchinbrk 362 K16
st. Kirribilli 6 A13
st. Milsons Point 6 A13
st. Mortdale 431 A7
st. Old Guildford 337 E9
st. Paddington 13 D15
st. Parramatta 308 H2
st. Sans Souci 463 A1
st. Wilton 568 K15
st. Woolmloo 4 D6
BROULA
av. Baulkham Hl 246 H8
cl. Caringbah 492 F6
rd. Wahroonga 223 C4
BROULEE
pl. Carlingford 280 C5
pl. Engadine 518 G1
BROWALLIA
cr. Loftus 489 K10
BROWLEE
pl. Mt Pritchard 364 K10
BROWN
av. Botany 405 J11
cl. Menai 458 G15
la. Newtown 17 J11
la. Paddington 4 K13
pl. Mt Annan 509 G3
pl. Shalvey 211 B14
rd. Bonnyrigg 363 K8
rd. Bonnyrigg Ht 363 G6
rd. Maroubra 407 F15
st. Alexandria 18 G15
st. Ashfield 372 H2
st. Bronte 377 H8
st. Camperdwn 17 J7
st. Chatswood 284 H10
st. Chester Hill 337 H12
st. Forestville 255 K7
st. Lewisham 15 A9
st. Lewisham 15 B7
st. Newtown 17 J10
st. N Parramatta 278 D10
st. Paddington 4 K14
st. Penrith 236 G13
st. Riverstone 182 D11
st. St Peters 374 G13
st. Smithfield 335 C6
BROWNE
pde. Warwck Frm 365 F16
pl. Baulkham Hl 247 D1
st. Campbelltwn 511 F3
BROWNING
av. Campbelltwn 512 B3
av. Lakemba 401 A1
cl. Mount Druitt 241 F11
cl. Wetherill Pk 334 H6
la. Hurlstone Pk 372 K11
pl. Lalor Park 245 J13
rd. N Turramrra 223 F7
st. Campsie 372 A11
st. East Hills 427 K5
BROWNLOW
ct. Wattle Grove 425 K1
pl. Ambarvale 510 G13
BROWNLOW HILL LOOP
rd. Brownlow Hl 475 C8
BROWNS
av. Austral 391 E14
av. Austral 421 E1
av. Enmore 16 F14
la. N Sydney K A2
la. N Sydney 5 E5
la. Hunters Hill, off Ady St 313 K10
rd. Blaxland 233 G6
rd. Blaxlands Rdg 56 C1
rd. Gordon 253 F10
rd. The Oaks 502 G8
rd. Wahroonga 221 E15
rd. Wilberforce 62 A11
wy. Terrey Hills 196 D6
BROWSE
pl. Green Valley 363 A9
BROXBOURNE
st. Westmead 307 G4
BRUBRI
st. Busby 363 H13
BRUCE
av. Belfield 371 E12
av. Caringbah 492 E15
av. Clovelly 378 A13
av. Killara 253 J10
av. Manly 288 G13
av. Panania 428 E4
la. Kingsford 406 F2
la. Newtown 17 K11
la. N Curl Curl 259 B10
la.e, Stanmore 16 D9
la.w, Stanmore 16 C9
pl. Kellyville 185 K5
rd. Glenbrook 264 A5
rd. Vineyard 152 D7
st. Ashfield 373 A2
st. Bexley 432 H3
st. Blacktown 244 K15
st. Btn-le-Sds 433 K1
st. Crows Nest 315 F8
st. Kingsford 406 F2
st. Kogarah Bay 432 H13
st. Lansvale 366 F9
st. Marrickville 373 E16
st. Merrylands W 306 G13
st. Mona Vale 199 D10
st. Rozelle 7 A12
st. Ryde 282 D13
st. Springwood 202 C10
st. Stanmore 16 C9
st. Waterloo 20 B15
st. Wollstncraft 31
BRUCE BENNETTS
pl. Maroubra 406
BRUCEDALE
av. Epping 281
dr. Baulkham Hl 247
BRUCE NEALE
dr. Penrith 236
BRUCHHAUSER
cr. Elderslie 507
BRUCKNER
pl. Clarmnt Ms 268
BRUDENELL
av. Leumeah 481
BRUMBY
cr. Emu Heights 235
la. Emu Heights, off Brumby Cr 235
st. Surry Hills 19
BRUNDAH
rd. Tahmoor 565
rd. Tahmoor 565
rd. Thirlmere 565
BRUNDY
cl. W Pnnant Hl 249
BRUNE
st. Doonside 243
BRUNEI
cr. Holsworthy 426
BRUNEL
cl. Cherrybrook 219
BRUNETTE
dr. Castle Hill 248
BRUNKER
rd. Chullora 369
rd. Greenacre 369
rd. Potts Hill 369
rd. Yagoona 369
BRUNSWICK
av. Liberty Gr 311
av. Strathfield 341
cl. Colyton 270
cr. St Johns Pk 334
pde. Ashfield 372
st. Granville 308
st. Merrylands 308
st. Waterloo 19
BRUNSWICK HEADS
cr. Hoxton Park 392
BRUNTON
pl. Marsfield 251
st. Panania 428
BRUSH
cl. Green Valley 363
rd. Eastwood 280
rd. West Ryde 280
wy. Airds 512
BRUSHBOX
pl. Bradbury 511
pl. Cherrybrook 219
pl. Newington, off Clarke St 310
BRUSHFORD
av. Castle Hill 248
BRUSHWOOD
dr. Alfords Point 428
dr. Alfords Point 429
dr. Alfords Point 459
dr. Rouse Hill 185
pl. Hornsby 221
BRUSSELS
cr. Rooty Hill 271
st. Mascot 405
st. N Strathfield 341
st. S Granville 338
BRUTON
wy. Canley Vale 366
BRUTUS
wy. Rsemeadow 540
BRUXNER
pl. Doonside 273
BRUZZANO
pl. Cromer 258
BRYAN
av. Normanhurst 221
BRYANT
la. Rockdale 403
pl. Fairfield W 335
st. Narwee 400
st. Padstow 399
st. Rockdale 403
wy. Claymore 481

CE
St Ives 254 E1
SON
Toongabbie 276 G8
Chatswood 284 H13
Toongabbie 276 G8
NGI
Gymea Bay 491 E11
HAN
Edmndsn Pk 422 H5
Kings Lngly 245 G6
Wetherill Pk 334 F6
HANAN
Bonnet Bay 460 B10
Windsor Dn 180 K4
Balmain 7 G14
Carlton 432 K6
KARA
Erskine Park 300 D2
KERIDGE
Kellyville 216 G5
KETT
Kurrajong 85 C2
KHURST
Point Piper 14 J4
KINBAH
Lilli Pilli 522 F2
KINGHAM
Normanhurst 221 F9
Chipping Ntn 366 H15
Killara 253 J13
Baulkham Hl 247 D5
Killara 253 J14
Canley Ht 365 G2
Canley Vale 365 G2
Kellyville 215 A3
Pitt Town 92 H14
Stanhpe Gdn 215 A3
Surry Hills 19 G4
KLAND
Carlingford 279 H1
Alexandria 18 J14
Newtown 17 J10
Casula 394 K15
Casula 395 A13
St Clair 269 J8
Springwood 202 C1
Alexandria 19 A13
Chippendale 18 K3
Greenacre 370 E8
CKLE
Engadine 488 D15
CKLEY
Revesby 398 K15
Fairfield W 335 A9
Marrickville 374 D14
Marrickville 374 C14
CKLEYS
Winston Hills 276 H2
CKNELL
Newtown 17 K9
Newtown 17 K9
CKRA
Turramurra 223 D11
CKRIDGE
Pitt Town 92 J16
CKWALL
Greenacre 370 B14
CKWELL
Hassall Gr 211 K15
DAPEST
Rooty Hill 271 J4
DBURY
Harringtn Pk 478 F6
DD
Little Bay 437 B12
Drummoyne 343 F4
DDS
Stanmore 16 B8
DERIM
Kareela 461 B12
DGE
Glenmore Pk 265 F7
Glenmore Pk, off Budge Cl 265 G7
DGEREE
Toongabbie 276 D9
DGERIGAR
Green Valley 363 F11
DINS
Kenthurst 187 D6

BUDYAN
rd. Grays Point 491 B15
BUENA VISTA
av. Denistone 281 B11
av. Mona Vale 198 J5
av. Mosman 317 C13
rd. Winmalee 173 A14
wy. St Ives 224 F6
BUFFALO
pl. Toongabbie 275 G13
rd. Gladesville 312 G3
rd. Ryde 282 B15
wy. Airds 511 J16
wy. Kellyville 186 A15
BUGATTI
dr. Ingleburn 453 H9
BUGDEN
av. Milperra 397 E11
pl. Campbelltwn 511 A7
BUGONG
st. Prestons 392 H13
BUICK
pl. Ingleburn 453 G10
rd. Cromer 258 E1
BUIN
pl. Glenfield 424 C13
BUIST
st. Bass Hill 368 B8
st. Sefton 368 D8
st. Yagoona 368 D8
BUJAN
st. Glenmore Pk 266 C12
BUJARA
pl. Bangor 459 D12
BUJWA BAY
rd. Cowan 104 B12
BUKA
pl. Glenfield 424 G9
BUKARI
wy. Glenmore Pk 266 D8
BULA
av. Campsie 401 K3
BULAH
cl. Berowra Ht 132 J10
wy. Seven Hills 275 K6
BULARA
st. Duffys Frst 165 A15
BULBA
rd. Engadine 489 F9
BULBERRY
pl. Engadine 489 F9
BULBI
av. Winmalee 173 A10
pl. Glenmore Pk 266 B12
BULBINE
st. Engadine 518 E2
BULBUL
av. Green Valley 363 F13
BULGA
cl. Hornsby Ht 161 J12
pl. Hoxton Park 392 H7
rd. Dover Ht 348 G8
BULGALLA
pl. Caringbah 492 H12
BULIMBA
av. Kareela 461 B12
BULKARA
rd. Bellevue Hill 14 H9
BULKIRA
rd. Epping 281 C3
BULL
pl. Harringtn Pk 478 C1
st. Warwck Frm 365 J16
BULLARA
cr. Narraweena 258 A3
BULLAWAI
pl. Beecroft 250 E10
BULLDOG
rd. Moorebank 425 A3
BULLECOURT
av. Engadine 518 F1
av. Milperra 397 G9
av.n, Mosman 317 A1
av.s, Mosman 317 A3
la. Milperra 397 H9
la. Ultimo 3 A10
wy. Matraville 407 B15
BULLER
la. Lane Cove 314 F1
rd. Artarmon 284 J15
st. Bellevue Hill 377 H1

st. Jannali 460 H13
st. N Parramatta 278 F16
st. Parramatta 278 F16
st. S Turramrra 252 C6
BULLETIN
pl. Sydney B B9
BULLI
cl. Prestons 392 J14
rd. Old Tngabbie 276 F9
rd. Toongabbie 276 F8
rd. Wentwthvle 277 A9
st. Badgerys Ck 358 G8
BULLI APPIN
rd. Appin 569 H13
BULLIVANT
la. N Sydney K F3
BULLOCK
av. Chester Hill 337 J12
BULLS
av.w, Burraneer 523 E1
rd. Burraneer 523 E1
rd. Wakeley 334 H15
BULMANN
av. Horngsea Pk 392 F16
BULOLO
dr. Whalan 240 J10
pl. Glenfield 424 G9
BULU
dr. Glenmore Pk 265 K10
BULUMIN
st. Como 460 G5
BULWARA
rd. Pyrmont 12 G4
rd. Pyrmont 12 H6
rd. Ultimo 3 A12
BULWARRA
av. Sefton 368 E5
pl. Berowra Ht 133 D8
st. Caringbah 492 H9
BUMBERA
st. Prestons 392 H15
BUMBORAH POINT
rd. Matraville 436 F7
rd. Port Botany 436 F7
BUNA
cl. Glenmore Pk 266 D12
cl. Mt Annan 479 C12
cl. N Turramrra 223 D1
ct. Ryde 282 E14
pl. Allambie Ht 257 D10
pl. Glenfield 424 H12
rd. Holsworthy 426 G9
st. Holsworthy 426 D3
BUNARBA
rd. Gymea Bay 491 F8
BUNBIE
la. West Ryde 311 F1
BUNBINLA
av. Mt Riverview 234 D1
BUNBURY
av. Sutherland 460 C14
rd. Mcquarie Fd 453 J2
BUNCE
pl. Wrrngtn Cty 238 G5
rd. Liverpool 394 H2
BUNDA
pl. Glenmore Pk 266 D11
BUNDABAH
av. St Ives 224 B9
BUNDAH
st. Winmalee 173 A10
BUNDALEER
st. Belrose 225 K4
BUNDANOON
pl. Hornsby Ht 191 H5
rd. Engadine 489 A6
rd. Prestons 392 K16
rd. Woronora Ht 489 A6
BUNDARA
cl. Mona Vale 169 E16
st. Beverly Hills 401 E13
wy. Baulkham Hl 246 E11
BUNDARRA
av.n, Wahroonga 222 C5
av.s, Wahroonga 222 B7
ct. Wattle Grove 395 K12
rd. Bellevue Hill 347 H15
rd. Campbelltwn 511 K6
rd. Regentville 235 E16
st. Lansvale 366 G8
st. Waterfall 519 D13

BUNDEENA
dr. Bundeena 523 H9
dr. Royal N P 523 B14
rd. Woodbine 481 F12
BUNDELL
st. Harringtn Pk 478 E2
BUNDELUK
cr. Glenmore Pk 266 C12
BUNDEMAR
st. Miller 393 H2
wy. Airds 512 E10
BUNDILLA
av. Winston Hills 277 F6
pl. Dee Why 258 E4
BUNDOCK
la. Randwick 407 B3
la. S Coogee 407 B3
st. Kingsford 407 B3
st. Randwick 407 B3
st. S Coogee 407 B3
BUNDOON
la. Manly 288 F7
BUNDY
cl. Mcquarie Fd 454 H5
BUNGAL
st. Engadine 488 G14
BUNGALOE
av. Balgowlah 287 H12
av. Balgowlah Ht 287 H12
BUNGALOW
av. Pymble 253 C1
cr. Bankstown 369 D16
pde. Wrrngtn Dns 238 B6
rd. Peakhurst 400 E16
rd. Plumpton 241 J10
rd. Roselands 401 A9
BUNGAN
la. Mona Vale 199 C4
pl. Woodbine 481 K8
st. Mona Vale 199 B4
BUNGAN HEAD
rd. Newport 169 H13
BUNGAREE
la. Mosman, off Beaconsfield Rd. 317 E8
pl. Miller 393 H3
rd. Pendle Hill 276 F13
rd. Toongabbie 276 F13
rd. Yellow Rock 174 J14
BUNGARN
pl. Caringbah 493 A12
BUNGARRA
cr. Chipping Ntn 396 G4
BUNGARRIBEE
rd. Blacktown 274 B2
rd. Doonside 273 F2
BUNGAY
st. Leichhardt 10 F14
BUNGENDORE
st. Ingleside 197 E5
BUNGONIA
ct. Wattle Grove 395 J12
rd. Leumeah 482 D14
st. Prestons 392 H15
BUNGOONA
av. Elanora Ht 198 A16
BUNGOWEN
av. Thornleigh 221 A7
BUNGULLA
st. Sadleir 364 A16
BUNKER
pde. Bonnyrigg 364 C5
st. Minchinbury 271 H9
st. Minto 452 H14
BUNN
la. Pyrmont 12 J5
st. Pyrmont 12 J5
BUNNAL
av. Winmalee 173 B11
BUNNERONG
rd. Chifley 436 K6
rd. Daceyville 406 G4
rd. Eastgardens 406 G12
rd. Hillsdale 406 G12
rd. Kingsford 406 G4
rd. Maroubra 406 G12
rd. Matraville 436 H1
rd. Pagewood 406 G4
rd. Pagewood 406 G8
BUNNING
pl. Doonside 273 G2

BUNROY
cr. Horngsea Pk 392 F15
BUNSEN
av. Emerton 240 J4
BUNT
av. Greenacre 370 B10
BUNTING
st. Emerton 241 A6
BUNYA
cl. Baulkham Hl 246 K2
cr. Bowen Mtn 83 K10
pde. S Coogee 407 J6
pl. Glenmore Pk 265 H11
pl. Mcquarie Fd 454 G4
pl. Spring Farm 508 E1
pl. Wakeley 334 H12
rd. Bidwill 241 F1
wy. Horngsea Pk 392 F14
BUNYALA
la. Carss Park 432 F15
st. Blakehurst 432 E15
st. Carss Park 432 E14
BUNYAN
pl. Bangor 459 B12
rd. Glenbrook 234 A12
rd. Leonay 235 C14
st. Wetherill Pk 334 E6
BUNYANA
av. Wahroonga 223 B5
BUNYARRA
dr. Emu Plains 235 A9
BUNYIP BLUE GUM
rd. Faulconbdg 171 F12
BUNYULA
rd. Bellevue Hill 347 J15
BURAN
cl. Mount Druitt 241 E15
BURANDA
cr. St Johns Pk 334 C16
BURBANG
cr. Rydalmere 309 G2
BURBANK
av. East Hills 427 J6
av. Picnic Point 427 K7
pl. Baulkham Hl 216 F15
BURBONG
st. Kingsford 406 K4
BURCH
la. Mascot 405 E2
BURCHMORE
rd. Manly Vale 288 B4
BURDEKIN
cr. St Ives 254 D4
ct. Wattle Grove 396 A13
la. Surry Hills 20 E4
pl. Engadine 488 J9
rd. Quakers Hill 213 F6
rd. Wilberforce 92 H1
BURDETT
cr. Blacktown 244 A16
st. Canley Ht 365 H4
st. Hornsby 221 H1
st. Wahroonga 222 A1
BURFITT
pde. Glenbrook 263 K1
rd. Riverstone 182 F15
st. Leichhardt 9 D14
BURFORD
st. Colyton 270 F6
st. Merrylands 307 F14
st. Minto 452 J13
BURGAN
cl. Menai 458 H13
BURGE
st. Vaucluse 348 F5
BURGESS
rd. Freemns Rch 90 D5
rd. Freemns Rch 90 F4
rd. S Penrith 267 C2
st. Beverley Pk 433 C10
st. Richmond 118 J5
BURGOYNE
la. Gordon 253 H6
la. Mt Lewis, off Frank St. 369 K16
st. Gordon 253 H6
BURGUNDY
cl. Cecil Hills 362 E1
ct. Eschol Park 481 C5
pl. Minchinbury 271 K9
BURILLA
av. N Curl Curl 258 F10

BURING
av. Leonay 235 B16
cr. Minchinbury 271 H9
BURKE
av. Berala 339 D12
av. Wrrngtn Cty 238 H8
cr. Oatley 430 H13
pl. Mt Colah 162 B11
pl. St Johns Pk 364 H1
rd. Cronulla 493 K9
rd. Ingleburn 422 K9
rd. Lalor Park 245 F13
sq. Lansdowne 367 C5
st. Appin 569 G12
st. Blacktown 274 B6
st. Chifley 437 A4
st. Como 460 F7
st. Concord W 341 E1
st. Newport 169 K7
st. Oatley 430 H13
st. Ruse 512 F3
st. Ryde 282 F15
st. Telopea 279 G11
BURLEIGH
av. Caringbah 493 A4
st. Burwood 342 A14
st. Lindfield 284 E3
BURLEY
cl. Illawong 459 K3
rd. Horsley Pk 302 D11
rd. Padstow 429 E1
st. Lane Cove W 284 F16
BURLEY GRIFFIN
cl. St Clair 270 B11
BURLINGTON
av. Earlwood 372 G16
la. Crows Nest 315 G7
rd. Homebush 341 B9
st. Crows Nest 315 G7
st. Monterey 433 G8
st. Northmead 277 K11
BURLISON
st. Warwck Frm 365 G13
BURMAH
rd. Denistone 281 B12
BURNE
av. Dee Why 258 F6
BURNELL
pl. Darlinghurst 4 C9
st. Drummoyne 343 F7
st. Russell Lea 343 F7
BURNETT
av. Mt Annan 509 H1
pl. Sylvania Wtr 462 C12
st. Hurlstone Pk 373 A14
st. Mays Hill 307 H6
st. Merrylands 307 C11
st. Parramatta 307 H6
st. Redfern 19 F7
wk. Denistone 281 C12
BURNHAM
av. Glenwood 215 D14
pl. N Parramatta 278 C9
st. Belfield 371 E12
BURNIE
la. Clovelly, off Winchester Rd 377 J11
st. Blacktown 275 B2
st. Clovelly 377 J12
BURNLEIGH
cr. Cmbrdg Gdn 237 J1
BURNLEY
av. N Turramrra 223 G7
BURNS
av. Mcquarie Fd 454 A3
cl. Rooty Hill 271 K6
cr. Chiswick 343 C2
la. Caringbah 492 H7
la. Petersham 15 K8
la. Picnic Point 428 F8
pl. Springwood 201 K12
rd. Campbelltwn 512 A2
rd. Heathcote 518 C16
rd. Kellyville 215 H9
rd. Leumeah 512 A2
rd. Picnic Point 428 D8
rd. Riverstone 184 A1
rd. St Ives 223 A6
rd. Springwood 202 A11
rd. Thirlmere 561 J12
rd. Turramurra 223 A6
rd. Wahroonga 222 D5
rd. Wakeley 334 H16
rd. Winston Hills 276 H1
rd.n, Beecroft 250 B6
rd.s, Beecroft 250 B7
st. Campsie 372 B10
st. Croydon 342 H12
st. Marsfield 282 C7
st. Petersham 15 K8
BURNS BAY
rd. Lane Cove 313 F8
rd. Lane Cove 313 J2
rd. Lane Cove W 313 F8
rd. Linley Point 313 F8
BURNSIDE
gr. Windsor Dn 180 K3
st. N Parramatta 278 F11
BURNT
st. Seaforth 286 K3
BURNT BRIDGE CREEK DEVIATION
Balgowlah 287 E8
Manly Vale 287 E8
N Balgowlah 287 E8
Seaforth 287 E8
BURR
cl. Bossley Park 334 C10
BURRA
cl. Glenmore Pk 266 B9
cl. Mt Colah 162 D16
pl. Greystanes 305 F10
rd. Artarmon 285 A15
st. Busby 363 H14
st. Pendle Hill 276 G12
BURRABIRRA
av. Vaucluse 348 D3
BURRABOGEE
rd. Old Tngabbie 276 E11
rd. Pendle Hill 276 E11
rd. Toongabbie 276 E11
BURRADDAR
av. Engadine 488 G14
BURRADOO
cl. North Rocks 279 A2
rd. Beverly Hills 401 A11
rd. Lansvale 366 D9
st. Caringbah 492 G12
st. Padstow 429 G3
BURRAGA
av. Terrey Hills 196 C5
pl. Glenmore Pk 266 B8
pl. Lindfield 284 A2
BURRAGATE
cr. Prestons 393 C15
BURRAGORANG
av. Woodcroft 243 F11
rd. Belimbla Pk 501 B10
rd. Bickley Vale 505 B7
rd. Brownlow Hl 505 B7
rd. Camden 506 H8
rd. Camden S 506 H8
rd. Cawdor 506 H8
rd. Glenmore 503 C4
rd. Grasmere 505 J7
rd. Mt Hunter 505 B7
rd. Oakdale 500 B13
rd. Ruse 512 F8
rd. The Oaks 502 J9
st. Oakdale 500 G11
st. The Oaks 502 E11
BURRAHPORE
la. Woolmloo 4 F7
BURRALOO
st. Frenchs Frst 256 G1
BURRALOW
rd. Kurrajong Ht 53 H13
BURRAMY
cl. Bossley Park 333 G7
BURRAN
av. Mosman 317 E3
BURRANDONG
cr. Baulkham Hl 246 J10
BURRANEER
av. St Ives 254 D3
cl. Allawah 432 C8
cr. Greenacre 369 K11
st. Leumeah 482 C15
BURRANEER BAY
rd. Caringbah 492 E10
rd. Cronulla 493 A11
rd. Woolooware 493 A11
BURRAWAL
pl. Cromer 227 K11
BURRAWALLA
rd. Caringbah 493 B6
BURRAWANG
dr. Nelson 155 D8
pl. Alfords Point 429 A13
st. Cherrybrook 219 K5
BURRAWONG
av. Mosman 317 D13
cr. Elderslie 477 F16
rd. Avalon 140 D11
BURRELL
cr. Baulkham Hl 247 E11
pde. Blacktown 273 H4
rd. Kenthurst 156 C9
st. Beverly Hills 401 F14
BURREN
st. Erskineville 18 A11
st. Eveleigh 18 A11
st. Newtown 18 A11
BURRENDONG
pl. Avalon 139 K15
rd. Leumeah 482 D12
BURRIA
pl. Winmalee 173 B10
BURRILL
pl. Leumeah 482 F14
BURRIMUL
st. Kingsgrove 401 F6
BURRINGBAR
st. N Balgowlah 287 C5
BURRINJUCK
dr. Woodcroft 243 G10
pl. Miranda 491 H7
st. Leumeah 482 E13
BURROGY
la. Mosman, off Cardinal St 316 J5
BURROWAY
rd. Homebush 311 A6
st. Neutral Bay 6 H5
BURROWES
gr. Dean Park 212 F16
BURROWS
av. Chester Hill 338 B13
av. Sydenham 374 D14
la. Minto, off Erica La 482 F2
rd. Alexandria 375 A15
rd. St Peters 375 A15
rd.s, St Peters 374 H16
st. Arncliffe 403 H8
BURRSWOOD
cl. Belrose 225 K12
BURRUNDULLA
cr. Airds 511 K14
BURSARIA
cr. Glenmore Pk 265 F10
rd. Mt Annan 509 D4
BURSILL
st. Guildford 337 H3
BURT
st. Rozelle 10 K3
BURTENSHAW
st. Panania 398 D14
BURTON
av. Chester Hill 338 D15
av. Moorebank 396 D11
av. Northmead 278 B2
la. Glebe 12 C9
la. Milsons Point, off Alfred St 5 K15
la. Randwick, off Prince St 376 K11
st. Balgowlah 287 K9
st. Concord 341 K10
st. Darlinghurst 4 D11
st. Glebe 12 B10
st. Linley Point 313 G7
st. Milsons Point 5 K15
st. Mosman 316 J2
st. Randwick 376 K11
st. Werrington 238 E8
st. Wrrngtn Cty 238 E8
BURU
pl. Kings Park 244 J2
BURUNDA
st. Como 460 E6
BURUWAN
la. Annandale 11 B6
BURWOOD
pl. St Johns Pk 364 G4
rd. Belfield 371 D10
rd. Belmore 371 D13
rd. Burwood 341 K15
rd. Burwood Ht 371 J8
rd. Concord 342 B8
rd. Croydon Pk 371 J8
rd. Enfield 371 J8
BURY
rd. Guildford 337 J4
BUSACO
rd. Marsfield 252 C12
BUSBY
av. Edensor Pk 363 E1
la. Woolmloo D K13
la. Woolmloo 4 C6
la. Bronte, off Busby Pde 377 K10
pde. Bronte 377 J11
pl. Frenchs Frst 255 H4
rd. Busby 393 J1
BUSH
pl. Glenbrook 264 B4
rd. Kenthurst 125 E4
tr. Belrose 226 D6
BUSHELLS
la. Freemns Rch 90 G12
pl. Wetherill Pk 304 B16
BUSHEY
pl. Dee Why 258 J8
BUSHLAND
av. Forestville 255 K10
cr. Carlingford 249 F16
dr. Padstow Ht 429 D8
pl. Erskine Park 270 F16
pl. Kenthurst 188 D4
BUSHLANDS
av. Gordon 253 F10
av. Hornsby Ht 191 G8
pl. Hornsby Ht 191 F8
BUSHLARK
pl. Clarmnt Ms 268 J4
BUSHLEY
pl. Jamisontown 266 C2
BUSHRANGERS
hill, Newport 169 H13
BUSHVIEW
dr. Kellyville 186 K15
pl. Berowra Ht 133 A5
BUSHY
gln. Glenhaven 217 K5
BUTCHERBIRD
pl. Glenmore Pk 265 K12
BUTE
pl. St Andrews 481 K5
BUTIA
wy. Stanhpe Gdn 215 E10
BUTLER
av. Bossley Park 334 B7
av. Campsie 371 J13
cl. Menai 459 A10
cr. Bnkstn Aprt 397 K1
cr. S Penrith 237 B15
la. Hurstville 432 A6
la. S Penrith, off Butler Cr 237 C15
pl. Lalor Park 245 G14
rd. Hurstville 432 A6
wy. S Windsor 150 F1
BUTLERS
cl. West Hoxton 392 D7
BUTLIN
av. Darlington 18 E5
BUTT
st. Surry Hills 19 H3
BUTTERCUP
pl. Mt Annan 509 E4
st. Mcquarie Fd 454 C5
BUTTERFIELD
pl. Mt Annan 509 C1
st. Blacktown 244 G11
st. Thornleigh 221 C13
BUTTIGIEG
pl. Plumpton 242 C8
BUTTSWORTH
la. Wilberforce 91 K7
BUVELOT
wy. Claymore 481 D13
BUXLFOLIA
ct. Voyager Pt 427 A4
BUXTON
pl. N Turramrra 223 G7
pl. Prestons 392 J14
BUYU
rd. Glenmore Pk 266 D10
BUYUMA
pl. Avalon 139
st. Carlingford 280
BY
st. N Parramatta 278
BYAMEE
st. East Killara 254
BYANBI
pl. Castle Hill 248
BYDOWN
st. Neutral Bay 6
BYER
st. Enfield 371
BYFIELD
st. Mcquarie Pk 282
BYGRAVE
st. Ryde 282
BYKOOL
av. Kingsgrove 401
BYLONG
pl. Ruse 512
BYLOSS
st. Chester Hill 338
BYNA
st. Malabar 437
BYNG
la. Maroubra 407
st. Maroubra 407
BYNYA
rd. Palm Beach 140
BYORA
cr. Northbridge 286
BYRD
av. Kingsford 406
pl. Tregear 240
st. Canley Ht 365
BYRNE
av. Drummoyne 343
av. Russell Lea 343
av. S Coogee 407
bvd. Marayong 243
cr. Maroubra 407
pl. Camden 506
pl. Prairiewood 334
st. Ashcroft 364
st. Auburn 309
st. Lapstone 264
st. Wentwthvle 277
wy. Bradbury 511
wy. Glenmore Pk 265
BYRNES
av. Neutral Bay 316
st. Bexley 432
st. Botany 405
st. Marrickville 373
st. N Parramatta 278
st. Rozelle 344
st. S Granville 338
BYRON
av. Campbelltwn 512
av. Ryde 282
av. St Ives 224
av. Wallacia 324
la. Mount Druitt 241
pl. Illawong 459
pl. Northmead 278
rd. Guildford 337
rd. Leppington 421
rd. Tahmoor 565
rd. Tahmoor 565
rd. Yennora 337
st. Campsie 372
st. Coogee 377
st. Croydon 342
st. Peakhurst 430
BYRON BAY
cl. Hoxton Park 392
BY THE SEA
rd. Mona Vale 199
BYWONG
pl. Bonnyrigg 364
pl. Sylvania 461

C

CABARITA
pl. Caringbah 492
rd. Avalon 139
rd. Cabarita 342
rd. Concord 342

BBAGE TREE
Bayview 169 A16
Grose Vale 85 A16
Grose Vale 115 A3
Grose Vale 115 A4
Ingleside 168 C16
BBAN
Mosman 317 A11
BER
Dural 219 B8
BERNET
Eschol Park 481 C2
. Orchard Hills 268 F15
BLE
Eastern Ck 272 G7
Wollstncraft 315 C11
BLES
Waverley 377 F8
BRAMATTA
Miller 393 F5
Cremorne 316 H8
Mosman 316 H8
Woolooware 493 E11
e,Cabramatta 366 A7
w,Bonnyrigg 364 D7
w,Cabramatta 365 B9
w,Cabramatta W 364 D7
w,Mt Pritchard 364 D7
BRAMURRA
Heckenberg 364 A14
CIA
Seven Hills 245 J14
DAC
Schofields 213 K6
DBURY
Quakers Hill 213 G14
DDENS
Clarmnt Ms 268 D4
Kingswood 267 F3
DDO
Greenfld Pk 333 K14
DELL
. St Clair 270 D10
St Clair, off
Cadell Gln 270 C10
DENCE
Kareela 461 D12
DIA
Kogarah 433 B2
DIGAL
. Pyrmont 12 E1
DILLAC
Ingleburn 453 H9
DMAN
Castle Hill 217 H14
Woodcroft 243 F6
DOGAN
Marrickville 374 D12
. Mcquarie Fd 454 C4
. Marrickville 374 D12
DOW
. Frenchs Frst 256 E1
. Pymble 253 B9
DWELLS
. Kenthurst 126 H15
. Kenthurst 156 H1
ERLEON
. Randwick 377 D11
ERNARVON
. Kirkham 477 C9
ESAR
. Prairiewood 334 D12
St Clair, off
Caesar Wy 270 C16
y. St Clair 270 C16
AHILL
xp. Sydney A K7
xp. Sydney 1 H12
xp. The Rocks A K7
xp. The Rocks 1 H12
. Annandale 17 B3
. Greenacre 370 B6
. Marrickville 373 F16
. Annandale 17 B3
. Beverly Hills 401 D14
. Smithfield 335 F6
AHIR
Marrickville 373 K12
AHORS
. Padstow 399 C14
AIN
. Plumpton 242 B10

CAINES
cr. St Marys 269 J7
la. *St Marys, off*
Caines Cr. 269 J7
CAINS
pl. Waterloo 19 E12
CAIRA
pl. Quakers Hill 244 A1
CAIRD
cl. Edensor Pk 363 C2
pl. Seven Hills 245 K15
st. Wentwthvle 277 C9
CAIRDS
av. Bankstown 369 D15
CAIRNES
la. Glenorie 128 D2
rd. Glenorie 128 D4
CAIRNGORM
av. Glenhaven 218 A6
CAIRNS
av. Rodd Point 343 D8
pl. Wakeley 334 H15
st. Riverwood 400 B16
CAIRO
av. Padstow 399 B15
av. Revesby 399 B15
st. Cammeray 316 A4
st. Rockdale 403 E16
st. S Coogee 407 H4
CAITHNESS
cr. Winston Hills 277 D2
st. Killara 253 K13
CALABASH
rd. Arcadia 130 F7
CALABRESE
st. Blairmount 481 A15
CALABRIA
pl. Erskine Park 300 F2
st. Prestons 393 E13
CALABRO
av. Liverpool 394 H7
av. Lurnea 394 H7
CALABY
st. Toongabbie 276 H8
CALADENIA
cl. Elanora Ht 197 H13
cl. Ingleside 197 H13
st. Rooty Hill 272 C3
CALAIS
pl. Erskine Park 270 H15
CALALA
st. Mount Druitt 241 C13
CALANDRA
av. Quakers Hill 214 A7
CALARIA
cl. Edensor Pk 363 D1
CALBINA
rd. Earlwood 402 C3
rd. Northbridge 315 J1
CALCA
cr. Forestville 255 K14
CALCITE
pl. Eagle Vale 481 C8
CALDARRA
av. Engadine 518 J2
pl. Westleigh 220 G2
CALDER
cl. Rydalmere 279 H15
la. Darlington 18 H5
pl. St Ives 224 B6
rd. Darlington 18 H6
rd. Rydalmere 279 D14
st. N Curl Curl 258 F10
CALDERON
la. Padstow 429 C3
CALDERWOOD
rd. Galston 160 D13
CALDWELL
la. Bexley North 402 D10
pde. Yagoona 369 B11
pl. Blacktown 274 J3
pl. Edensor Pk 333 G13
st. Darlinghurst 4 J10
st. S Windsor 150 J3
CALDY
pl. Glenhaven 217 K4
CALEDONIA
cr. Peakhurst 430 B5
la. Paddington 21 G2
st. Paddington 21 G2

CALEDONIAN
av. Winston Hills 277 D3
rd. Rose Bay 348 B9
st. Bexley 403 A15
CALEEN
st. Glenwood 245 F1
CALEY
cr. Lapstone 264 H4
dr. Mt Annan 509 D9
pl. Barden Rdg 488 G1
pl. Horngsea Pk 392 F15
rd. Bradbury 511 G13
st. Chifley 437 A4
CALEYI
wy. Belrose 226 B10
CALF FARM
rd. Mt Hunter 504 D16
CALGA
av. Bronte 378 B10
av. Malabar 437 E8
av. Normanhurst 221 D12
pl. Bronte 378 B10
pl. Old Tngabbie 276 K8
pl. Sylvania 461 G14
st. Roseville Ch 285 F2
CALGAROO
cr. Kingswood 237 H16
CALIBAN
pl. Rsemeadow 540 K6
CALIDA
cr. Hassall Gr 212 A15
CALIDORE
st. Bankstown 399 A7
CALLA
gr. Pendle Hill 276 G13
CALLABONNA
pl. Woodcroft 243 F12
CALLAGHAN
la. *Ryde, off*
Badajoz Rd 282 G15
st. Ryde 282 H15
CALLAGHER
st. Mount Druitt 271 D1
CALLAN
st. Rozelle 344 C7
wy. Wentwthvle 277 D10
CALLICOMA
rd. Seaforth 286 K7
CALLIOPE
la. *Mosman, off*
Calliope St 316 G10
pl. Busby 363 J13
rd. Miranda 492 C7
st. Guildford 337 D4
st. Mosman 316 G10
CALLISTEMON
cl. Alfords Point 429 C15
cl. Baulkham Hl 247 C15
cl. N Epping 251 C11
gr. Greenacre 370 F6
st. Mt Annan 509 C2
CALLISTO
dr. Cranebrook 207 D11
CALLOW
la. Kingswood 237 J15
pl. Woodcroft 243 E10
CALMAR
cl. Glen Alpine 510 C14
CALMSLEY
pl. Horsley Pk 332 C5
CALOOL
cr. Belrose 225 H12
rd. Beecroft 250 D12
st. Lidcombe 339 J4
CALOOLA
av. Penrith 237 E6
cr. Beverly Hills 401 E11
cr. Penshurst 431 H7
pl. Baulkham Hl 246 J10
rd. Wentwthvle 277 A11
st. Condell Park 398 E1
CALPAC
pl. Old Tngabbie 276 H11
CALPURNIA
wy. Rsemeadow 540 H2
CALVADOS
st. Glenfield 424 E13
CALVER
av. Mt Riverview 204 C16
CALVERT
av. Killara 253 G12
la. *Marrickville, off*
Fernbank St 374 A13
pde. Newport 169 K11
st. Marrickville 373 K13
CALVERTS
rd. Orchard Hills 268 D13
CALYPSO
av. Mosman 316 K10
pl. Miranda 491 K10
rd. Cranebrook 207 C15
CALYPTA
gr. Quakers Hill 214 F11
CAM
la. North Ryde 282 J8
st. Cmbrdg Pk 237 G9
st. North Ryde 282 J7
st. Wahroonga 222 A6
CAMBAGE
ct. Frenchs Frst 255 E4
CAMBALAN
st. Bargo 567 D4
CAMBERWELL
rd. Vineyard 152 F12
CAMBEWARRA
av. Castle Hill 248 B3
cr. Berowra Ht 132 K7
rd. Fairfield W 335 E10
st. Ruse 512 G7
CAMBOURNE
av. St Ives 224 H7
CAMBRAI
av. Engadine 518 H1
pl. Milperra 397 D12
CAMBRIAN
av. Voyager Pt 427 E4
CAMBRIDGE
av. Bankstown 399 A2
av. Glenfield 424 G8
av. Moorebank 425 A9
av. Narraweena 258 D2
av. North Rocks 278 H2
av. Vaucluse 348 F1
av. Windsor 120 J11
la. Chatswood 284 J9
la. Enmore 17 A13
la. Paddington 13 E13
la. *Cmbrdg Pk, off*
Cambridge St 237 F9
pl. Narellan 478 G11
rd. Artarmon 284 K13
rd. Drummoyne 313 H15
st. Berala 339 D10
st. Blacktown 244 K11
st. Cmbrdg Pk 237 G9
st. Cammeray 315 J4
st. Canley Ht 365 D3
st. Enmore 17 A13
st. Epping 251 B15
st. Fairfield W 335 D16
st. Fairfield W 335 E13
st. Gladesville 312 J7
st. Harris Park 308 E7
st. Ingleburn 453 E5
st. Lidcombe 339 D10
st. Merrylands 307 F13
st. Mount Druitt 241 C11
st. N Willghby 285 F8
st. Paddington 13 E13
st. Penshurst 431 D1
st. Rozelle 344 D8
st. S Turramrra 252 B8
st. Stanmore 16 F10
st. The Rocks A J4
st. Valley Ht 202 H10
CAMDEN
bps. Camden 507 A9
bps. Camden S 507 A9
bps. Elderslie 507 J4
bps. Narellan 478 F16
bps. Narellan Vale 478 F16
bps. Spring Farm 507 J4
gdn. N Turramrra 223 F2
la. Newtown 17 F16
la. Pyrmont 12 J7
rd. Campbelltwn 511 C6
rd. Douglas Park 568 F7
rd. Douglas Park 568 G1
st. Enmore 374 G9
st. Fairfield Ht 335 K10
st. Newtown 17 F16
st. Penrith 236 G1
st. Sylvania 462 B13
st. Wilton 568 K15
wy. Bidwill 211 F16

CAMDEN VALLEY
wy. Casula 423 G3
wy. Catherine Fd 449 E15
wy. Currans Hill 479 A6
wy. Edmndsn Pk 392 D16
wy. Edmndsn Pk 422 F1
wy. Elderslie 477 F15
wy. Harringtn Pk 478 D10
wy. Horngsea Pk 392 D16
wy. Kirkham 477 F15
wy. Leppington 421 H5
wy. Narellan 478 D10
wy. Oran Park 449 E15
wy. Prestons 423 B2
wy. Smeaton Gra 479 A6
CAMDEN VIEW
dr. Narellan 478 C10
CAMELLIA
av. Glenmore Pk 265 F10
ct. Cherrybrook 219 G7
gr. Gymea Bay 491 C8
pl. Lalor Park 245 B10
st. Greystanes 306 A12
CAMELOT
cl. Kirkham 477 E8
cl. Mt Colah 162 G14
ct. Carlingford 279 A4
dr. Cranebrook 207 A12
pl. St Ives 254 A2
CAMEO
cr. St Clair 269 H13
pl. Eagle Vale 481 B7
CAMERA
st. Manly 288 F9
CAMERON
av. Artarmon 285 A15
av. Bass Hill 368 D13
av. Baulkham Hl 247 G5
av. Earlwood 402 H3
av. Manly 288 G4
av. W Pnnant Hl 249 G1
cr. Ryde 282 D16
ct. Merrylands W 306 J14
pl. Alfords Point 429 C13
pl. Parramatta 278 J15
pl. St Helens Park 541 B8
rd. Pymble 253 J3
st. Balmain 7 G4
st. Banksia 403 F13
st. Bexley 432 H4
st. Birchgrove 7 G4
st. Doonside 243 B11
st. Edgecliff 13 H12
st. Hobartville 118 G8
st. Jamisontown 266 B2
st. Lidcombe 339 F9
st. Rockdale 403 F16
st. Strathfield 371 E2
CAMILLA
wy. Ambarvale 510 K15
CAMILLE
pl. Glenhaven 187 K15
st. Sans Souci 433 C16
CAMILLERI
av. Quakers Hill 213 G7
CAMILLO
st. Pendle Hill 306 D1
st. Seven Hills 245 G14
CAMIRA
cl. Belrose 225 J14
pl. Bonnyrigg 363 J9
st. Maroubra 407 E12
st. St Marys 239 G13
st. Villawood 367 G5
st. West Pymble 252 K14
CAMIRI
st. Hornsby Ht 191 G1
CAMMARAY
rd. Castle Cove 286 D6
CAMMARLIE
st. Panania 427 J1
CAMMERAY
av. Cammeray 315 K6
rd. Cammeray 316 B5
CAMORTA
cl. Kings Park 244 H3
CAMP
la. Bondi Jctn 22 E5
st. Watsons Bay 318 E13
CAMPASPE
av. Wiley Park 400 G4
CAMPBELL
av. Cromer 228 H16

av. Dee Why 258 H1
av. Lane Cove 314 G5
av. Lilyfield 9 J5
av. Normanhurst 221 E10
av. Paddington 4 J13
cl. Minto 482 K9
cr. Glenorie 128 G1
dr. Wahroonga 222 A14
la. Glebe 12 C14
la. Narellan 478 E9
la. Newtown 17 D11
la. St Peters 374 K14
la. Clovelly, off Park La 378 A12
pde. Bondi Beach 378 D3
pde. Manly Vale 287 H2
pl. Merrylands 307 H16
rd. Alexandria 374 K14
rd. Kenthurst 156 F15
rd. St Peters 374 K14
st. Abbotsford 342 K4
st. Artarmon 314 K3
st. Auburn 309 C15
st. Balmain 7 K9
st. Berala 339 C13
st. Bexley 432 H1
st. Blacktown 244 H16
st. Clovelly 378 A12
st. Darlinghurst 4 A13
st. Eastwood 280 J10
st. Fairfield E 336 K14
st. Glebe 12 D13
st. Gymea 461 G16
st. Haymarket E G7
st. Haymarket 3 G12
st. Hunters Hill 313 K10
st. Liverpool 395 B1
st. Liverpool 395 C1
st. Luddenham 356 G3
st. Narellan 478 E8
st. Newtown 17 J8
st. Northmead 277 K8
st. N Richmond 87 B13
st. Parramatta 308 B5
st. Picton 563 G8
st. Punchbowl 400 C5
st. Ramsgate 433 D15
st. Riverstone 183 B5
st. St Peters 374 H12
st. Sans Souci 433 D15
st. S Windsor 120 H13
st. Surry Hills F B8
st. Surry Hills 4 A13
st. Thirlmere 564 K5
st. Villawood 336 K14
st. Waverley 377 G7

CAMPBELLFIELD
av. Bradbury 511 D13

CAMPBELL HILL
rd. Chester Hill 338 B15
rd. Guildford 338 B15

CAMPBELLS
rd. Cobbitty 415 B7

CAMPBELLTOWN
rd. Bow Bowing 452 C14
rd. Denham Ct 422 F15
rd. Glenfield 423 J6
rd. Ingleburn 452 C14
rd. Leumeah 481 J15
rd. Minto 482 A3
rd. St Andrews 452 C14

CAMPFIRE
ct. Wrrngtn Dns 238 E4

CAMPHORLAUREL
ct. Doonside 243 G16

CAMPI
ct. Prestons 422 K1

CAMPION
st. Wetherill Pk 334 K4

CAMPSIE
la. Canterbury, off Wonga St 372 D12
st. Campsie 371 G14
st. Campsie 371 H13
st. Wilton 568 K15

CAMPTON
av. Cmbrdg Pk 238 A10
ct. Carlingford 250 C13

CAMPUS
dr. Richmond 119 A11

CANADA
cl. Minto 482 G5

CANADIAN
pl. Kearns 450 J16

CANAL
rd. Greystanes 306 E12
rd. Greystanes 306 E13
rd. Leichhardt 9 D9
rd. Lilyfield 9 E7
rd. St Peters 374 G15

CANARA
av. Phillip Bay 436 J11
pl. Frenchs Frst 255 F2
pl. Palm Beach 139 J2
pl. Smithfield 335 E4

CANARY
cl. St Clair 269 H10

CANARYS
rd. Roselands 400 K7

CANBERRA
av. Casula 394 J15
av. Richmond 119 K4
av. St Leonards 315 D7
av. Turramurra 223 C10
cr. Campbelltwn 512 B6
cr. E Lindfield 255 B15
la. Randwick 407 B2
pwy. Casula, off Canberra Av 394 K15
rd. Sylvania 462 C9
st. Epping 251 A13
st. Hurlstone Pk 372 H13
st. Lane Cove W 284 B15
st. Oxley Park 240 A16
st. Randwick 407 C3
st. St Johns Pk 364 F1
st. St Marys 240 A16

CANDICE
cr. Stanhpe Gdn 215 B10

CANDLEBARK
cct. Glenmore Pk 265 H11

CANDLEBUSH
cr. Castle Hill 248 F5

CANDLENUT
gr. Parklea 215 B13

CANDLEWOOD
st. Bossley Park 333 G9

CANDOWIE
cr. Baulkham Hl 248 C8

CANEA
cr. Allambie Ht 257 D10

CANHAM
cl. Castle Hill 247 H1

CANIDIUS
st. Rsemeadow 540 E3

CANISIUS
cl. Pymble 223 F15

CANLEY VALE
rd. Canley Ht 365 A2
rd. Canley Vale 365 J3
rd. St Johns Pk 334 F15
rd. Wakeley 334 F15
rd. Wetherill Pk 334 C3

CANN
st. Bass Hill 368 B6
st. Bass Hill 368 B9
st. Guildford 337 D7

CANNA
pl. Quakers Hill 243 E3
pl. St Andrews 482 A1

CANNAN
cl. Cherrybrook 219 C11

CANNERY
rd. Plumpton 241 K7

CANNES
dr. Avalon 139 J13

CANNING
pl. Pitt Town 93 F8

CANNON
la. Stanmore 16 E5
st. Prospect 275 B11
st. Stanmore 16 E5

CANNONS
pde. Forestville 255 K11

CANOBOLAS
pl. Yarrawarrah 489 D13
st. Fairfield W 335 E11

CANONBURY
gr. Bexley North 402 E12
gr. Bexley North 402 G10
gr. Dulwich Hill 373 E12

CANOON
rd. S Turramrra 251 K5

CANOONA
av. Windsor Dn 150 E14

CANOPUS
cl. Engadine 488 D13
cl. Erskine Park 300 H1

CANOWIE
pl. Busby 363 G14

CANROBERT
st. Mosman 316 K9

CANSDALE
pl. Castle Hill 217 J7
st. Blacktown 273 H4

CANTELLO
av. Hamondvle 396 H15

CANTERBURY
rd. Bankstown 399 A9
rd. Belmore 401 B4
rd. Campsie 372 B16
rd. Canterbury 372 G13
rd. Glenfield 424 E14
rd. Hurlstone Pk 372 G13
rd. Lakemba 401 B4
rd. Punchbowl 399 A9
rd. Revesby 399 A9
rd. Roselands 400 H6
rd. St Johns Pk 364 H3
rd. Wiley Park 400 H6

CANTERTON
st. Hurlstone Pk 372 J12

CANTON
st. Canterbury 372 E15
st. Kings Park 244 E2

CANTOR
cr. Croydon 342 F15
la. Croydon, off Cantor St 342 F15
st. Croydon 342 F15

CANTRELL
st. Bankstown 368 G15
st. Yagoona 368 G15

CANTRILL
av. Maroubra 407 E8

CANTWELL
st. Glenwood 215 C14

CANUNGRA
pl. Elanora Ht 198 C15

CANVA
st. Canley Vale 366 D5

CANYON
dr. Stanhpe Gdn 215 B12
pl. Engadine 488 C13
rd. Baulkham Hl 248 A13

CAPE
pl. Cherrybrook 219 J6

CAPE BARRON
av. Green Valley 363 A14

CAPELLA
pl. Normanhurst 221 E12
rd. Hinchinbrk 393 E3
st. Erskine Park 270 H16

CAPER
pl. Quakers Hill 243 E3

CAPERTEE
st. Ruse 512 F7

CAPE SOLANDER
dr. Kurnell 466 F5

CAPITAL
pl. Sylvania 462 D9

CAPITOL HILL
dr. Mt Vernon 331 A8

CAPPARIS
cct. Bidwill 211 D13

CAPPER
st. Lindfield 254 G16

CAPRERA
rd. Northmead 278 A6

CAPRI
cl. Avalon 139 J12
cl. Heathcote 518 E7
pl. Erskine Park 300 E1

CAPRICORN
av. Cranebrook 207 F15
rd. Kings Lngly 245 D7

CAPTAIN COOK
dr. Caringbah 492 H2
dr. Cronulla 493 E6
dr. Kurnell 465 A15
dr. Willmot 210 B11
dr. Woolooware 493 E6

CAPTAIN HUNTER
rd. Bayview 168 E8

CAPTAIN JACKA
cr. Daceyville 406 F3

CAPTAIN PIPERS
rd. Vaucluse 348 D5

CAPTAINS
rd. Penrith 236 A10

CAPTAIN STROM
pl. Dundas Vy 279 J6

CAPUA
pl. Avalon 139 J14

CAPULET
pl. Rsemeadow 540 H4

CARA
ct. S Penrith 266 K7

CARABEELY
pl. Harringtn Pk 478 F5

CARABEEN
st. Cabramatta 365 G9

CARABELLA
rd. Caringbah 493 A5
st. Kirribilli 6 B14
st. Milsons Point 6 B14

CARAHERS
la. The Rocks A H6

CARAMAR
st. Dharruk 241 B8

CARANDINI
st. St Helens Park 541 B7

CARANYA
pl. Cabramatta W 365 C6

CARATEL
cr. Marayong 243 J5

CARAVAN HEAD
rd. Oyster Bay 461 A6

CARAWA
rd. Cromer 228 B16

CARAWATHA
st. Beecroft 250 E11
st. Villawood 367 C4

CARBASSE
cr. St Helens Park 540 K10

CARBEEN
av. St Ives 223 J10
rd. Westleigh 220 D8

CARBERRY
ct. Kellyville 217 A1
la. Campbelltwn 511 E5

CARBETHON
cr. Beverly Hills 401 D9

CARBINE
cl. Casula 424 E1

CARBONI
st. Liverpool 395 A2

CARBOONA
av. Earlwood 403 G3

CARCLEW
pl. Glen Alpine 510 D11

CARCOAR
cl. Erskine Park 300 C3

CARCOOLA
av. Chipping Ntn 396 H4
cr. Normanhurst 221 F7
rd. Cromer 228 B15
rd. St Ives 224 D12
st. Campbelltwn 511 K7
st. Canley Vale 366 B4
st. Castle Hill 218 C11

CARDEN
av. Wahroonga 222 A5

CARDEW
wy. Bradbury 511 J11

CARDIFF
st. Blacktown 244 K14
st. Engadine 489 C15
wy. Castle Hill 248 A3

CARDIGAN
la. Camperdwn 17 A9
la. Camperdwn 17 B6
pl. Camperdwn 17 B4
rd. Greenacre 370 A7
rd. Roseville Ch 255 E14
st. Auburn 339 A1
st. Camperdwn 17 A6
st. Glebe 12 D10
st. Guildford 337 E3
st. Stanmore 17 A9

CARDILLO
st. Wentwthvle 277 E13

CARDINAL
av. Beecroft 250 A5
av. W Pnnant Hl 249 K2
st. Mosman 316 J6

CARDINAL CLANCY
av. Glendenning 242

CARDWELL
st. Balmain 7
st. Canley Vale 365

CAREDEN
av. Beacon Hill 257

CAREEBONG
rd. Frenchs Frst 256

CAREEL BAY
cr. Avalon 139

CAREEL HEAD
rd. Avalon 140

CAREFREE
rd. N Narrabeen 228

CAREW
la. Marrickville 373
st. Dee Why 258
st. Mount Druitt 241
st. Padstow 429

CAREX
cl. Glenmore Pk 265

CAREY
la. Glenbrook 234
la. Randwick, off Carey St 377
st. Bass Hill 367
st. Liverpool 395
st. Manly 288
st. Randwick 377

CARGELLIGO
pl. Woodcroft 243 H

CARHULLEN
st. Merrylands 308

CARIBBEAN
pl. Mt Colah 162

CARIBOU
cl. St Clair 270 D
pl. Raby 451 G

CARIEVILLE
la. Balmain 7
st. Balmain 7

CARILLA
st. Burwood 341

CARILLON
av. Camperdwn 17
av. Newtown 17

CARINA
av. Hinchinbrk 393
la. Oyster Bay, off Drummond Rd 461
pl. Castle Hill 218
pl. Cranebrook 207
pl. St Johns Pk 364
rd. Oyster Bay 461
rd. Turramurra 252

CARINDA
dr. Glenhaven 187 G
dr. S Penrith 266
la. S Penrith, off Carinda Dr 266
st. Ingleburn 453

CARINGAL
pl. St Ives 223 G
st. Chipping Ntn 396

CARINGBAH
rd. Caringbah 492
rd. Woolooware 493

CARINGTON
st. Riverstone 182 E

CARINYA
av. Beverly Hills 431
av. Btn-le-Sds 403 K
av. Mascot 405
av. St Marys 239 G
cl. Allambie Ht 257 G
pl. Carss Park 432 G
pl. Kirrawee 490
pl. Moorebank 396
rd. Girraween 276 C
rd. Mt Colah 191
rd. Picnic Point 428 B
rd. Pymble 223 G
st. Blacktown 244 E

CARINYAH
cr. Castle Hill 218 A

CARIOCA
ct. W Pnnant Hl 249
wy. W Pnnant Hl 249

CARISBROOK
st. Linley Point 313

RISSA
St Ives 224 F8
Alfords Point 458 K3
RITTA
Parklea 214 K13
RL
Eastern Ck 273 K15
Kings Lngly 246 B11
RLEEN
Werrington 238 E10
RLENE
Padstow 429 G5
RLINGFORD
Carlingford 280 A2
Epping 251 A15
Regents Pk 369 A2
Sefton 368 G2
RLISLE
Bidwill 211 E16
Blackett 241 D8
Colyton 270 K7
Dharruk 241 D8
Hebersham 241 D8
Minchinbury 271 B6
Mount Druitt 241 C16
Hinchinbrk 393 B1
Mcquarie Pk 252 J16
Beecroft 249 K6
Kellyville 186 J16
Yanderra 567 B14
Ashfield 372 G4
Collaroy Plat 228 E11
Ingleburn 453 B7
Leichhardt 9 G15
Rose Bay 348 C10
Tamarama 378 B6
RLON
Harringtn Pk 478 G6
RLOS
Artarmon 285 A14
RLOTTA
Gordon 253 G6
Greenwich, off Ffrench St 314 K9
Double Bay 14 F11
Artarmon 314 K3
Greenwich 315 A9
RLOW
Killarney Ht 256 C15
N Sydney 5 F1
RLOWRIE
East Hills 428 A4
RLTON
:. Sydney 3 J2
Carss Park 432 H14
Kogarah Bay 432 H14
Summer Hill 373 B3
Kensington 376 F10
e. Allawah 432 F7
le. Carlton 432 F7
le. Punchbowl 399 J8
Cecil Hills 362 E7
North Rocks 248 H12
Thirlmere 562 A16
Thirlmere 565 A2
Arncliffe 403 B11
Chippendale 19 B2
Granville 308 E11
Harbord 258 H16
Kensington 376 F10
Manly 288 G7
Riverstone 182 J9
Waverley 377 H10
y. Minto 482 K2
RLY
Quakers Hill 214 C13
RLYLE
Cmbrdg Gdn 237 G4
Wollstncraft 315 D8
Cmbrdg Gdn, off Carlyle Cr 237 G4
E Lindfield 255 B14
Bossley Park 334 C8
Enfield 371 H3
Wollstncraft 315 E8
RMAN
Schofields 183 C15
RMARTHEN
Menai 458 J9
RMEL
Baulkham Hl 247 C1
Winston Hills 276 H1
Glenbrook 233 K14

CARMELITA
cct. Rouse Hill 185 B6
CARMEN
cr. Cherrybrook 219 J3
dr. Carlingford 249 E11
pl. Caringbah 493 A14
pl. Freemns Rch 90 A4
st. Bankstown 369 C14
st. Guildford W 336 J2
st. Marsfield 282 B7
st. St Ives 224 E13
CARMICHAEL
dr. West Hoxton 392 B5
dr. West Hoxton 392 B9
dr. West Hoxton 392 E7
CARMINYA
st. Kensington 376 B10
CARNARVON
av. Glenhaven 218 C5
dr. Frenchs Frst 256 G2
rd. Bow Bowing 452 E14
rd. Riverstone 182 E11
rd. Roseville 254 K16
rd. Schofields 212 H1
st. Carlton 432 H7
st. Silverwater 309 E12
st. Wakeley 334 K11
st. Yarrawarrah 489 G13
CARNATION
av. Bankstown 399 H1
av. Casula 394 G12
av. Clarmnt Ms 238 H16
av. Old Guildford 337 F8
st. Greystanes 306 A11
CARNAVON
cr. Georges Hall 367 J13
CARNE
cl. Austral 391 D8
pl. Oxley Park 240 D15
wy. Bidwill 211 H14
CARNEGIE
cct. Chifley 436 K5
pl. Blacktown 244 F9
pl. Castle Hill 247 J1
rd. Chester Hill 368 C3
st. Auburn 338 K6
CARNEY
la. Mosman, off Avenue Rd 317 B8
st. Casula 394 C16
CARNIVAL
wy. Kellyville 186 C16
CARNOUSTIE
pl. Glenmore Pk 266 F11
st. Rouse Hill 185 A10
CAROB
pl. Cherrybrook 219 E7
CAROL
av. Jannali 460 F14
cr. Roselands 400 F8
CAROLE
av. Baulkham Hl 247 K10
st. Seven Hills 246 B11
CAROLES
rd. Orangeville 443 C14
CAROLINE
cr. Georges Hall 367 F10
la. Balmain 8 B8
la. Redfern 18 K6
st. Balmain 8 B8
st. Earlwood 372 G16
st. Guildford 338 C6
st. Kingsgrove 402 A10
st. Oyster Bay 461 A6
st. Redfern 18 K6
st. Westmead 277 H15
wy. Minto 482 J2
CAROLINE CHISHOLM
dr. Camden S 507 B10
dr. Winston Hills 277 A1
la. Lane Cove 313 H4
CAROLYN
av. Beacon Hill 257 J5
av. Carlingford 249 G12
ch. Orchard Hills 267 B13
cl. Castle Hill 217 J9
st. Greystanes 306 F4
st. Silverwater 309 J10
CAROMA
av. Kyeemagh 404 B14
CARONIA
av.e, Cronulla 493 J11
av.w, Cronulla 493 F10
av.w, Woolooware 493 F10
CAROONA
wy. Glenwood 215 F16
CAROTANA
st. Padstow 399 A13
CAROUSEL
cl. Cromer 258 G2
CARPENTER
av. Rookwood 340 B12
cr. Warriewood 199 D11
la. Ashcroft, off Sutton Rd 364 E16
pl. Minchinbury 271 G7
st. Colyton 269 J3
st. St Marys 269 J3
CARR
la. Coogee 407 E1
pl. Bradbury 511 J11
rd. Bringelly 387 F8
st. Chatswd W 284 E11
st. Coogee 407 E1
st. Waverton 5 A6
CARRA
av. Douglas Park 568 J12
CARRABAI
pl. Baulkham Hl 248 A11
CARRAMAR
av. Carramar 366 H2
av. North Ryde 283 B13
cr. Miranda 492 E5
cr. Winmalee 173 F12
gr. Terrey Hills 196 D6
pl. Peakhurst 430 C9
rd. Lindfield 283 F4
st. Berowra 133 F11
CARRAMARR
rd. Castle Hill 218 B13
CARRANYA
rd. Riverview 314 B6
CARRARA
pl. Plumpton 241 H11
rd. Vaucluse 348 B4
CARRBRIDGE
dr. Castle Hill 218 C7
CARRE
av. Canley Ht 335 E16
CARRICK
cl. West Hoxton 392 D7
CARRINGTON
av. Bellevue Hill 347 F13
av. Caringbah 492 F4
av. Cromer 228 B13
av. Hurstville 431 G1
av. Mortdale 431 D8
av. Mosman 316 K2
av. Strathfield 341 F13
cct. Leumeah 482 D16
dr. Centnnial Pk 21 G6
la. Coogee 377 E14
la. Petersham 15 J9
la. Bellevue Hill, off Carrington Av 347 F13
la. N Strathfield, off Carrington St 341 F8
pde. Curl Curl 258 K16
pde. Harbord 258 K16
rd. Bringelly 418 H2
rd. Castle Hill 217 D13
rd. Coogee 377 D15
rd. Guildford 337 D6
rd. Hornsby 191 F11
rd. Londonderry 148 C10
rd. Marrickville 373 K16
rd. Randwick 377 D15
rd. Wahroonga 222 E2
rd. Waverley 377 F10
sq. Campsie 371 J13
st. Auburn 339 A3
st. Balmain 7 C11
st. Bexley 402 H16
st. Campsie 371 J13
st. Granville 308 E13
st. Lewisham 15 C7
st. Lilyfield 10 D4
st. N Strathfield 341 F8
st. Parramatta 307 K7
st. Penshurst 431 G5
st. Revesby 398 C10
st. St Marys 269 J6
st. Seven Hills 275 K4
st. Summer Hill 373 D6
st. Sydney A G16
st. Sydney 1 F16
st. Wahroonga 222 D2

CARRISBROOK
av. Bexley North 402 F10
av. Punchbowl 400 A1
CARROL
ct. Menai 458 J14
CARROLL
cr. Plumpton 242 B11
la. Woollahra 22 K5
la. Mosman, off Ourimbah Rd 317 A5
pl. Westleigh 220 E8
st. Beverley Pk 433 C10
st. Lidcombe 339 G10
st. Warwck Frm 365 E13
st. Wetherill Pk 334 F5
CARROWBROOK
av. Glenwood 245 F1
CARRS
rd. Galston 159 F4
rd. Wilberforce 61 G5
CARRUTHERS
dr. Dolls Point 463 H2
dr. Horngsea Pk 392 F16
dr. Sans Souci 433 H16
st. Penshurst 431 C4
CARSHALTON
st. Croydon 372 E5
st. Croydon Pk 372 E5
CARSON
cr. Bexley North 402 C10
st. Dundas Vy 280 E10
st. Panania 398 E15
st. Pymble 253 E1
CARSONS
la. St Marys 239 G16
CARSTAIRS
pl. St Andrews 482 B2
CARSTONE
wy. Ambarvale 510 K16
CARTELA
cr. Smithfield 335 E4
CARTER
cr. Gymea Bay 491 E9
cr. Padstow Ht 429 E8
la. Marrickville 373 F14
la. Randwick, off Castle La 377 B10
pl. Claymore 481 B10
rd. Brookvale 258 D10
rd. Menai 458 H13
st. Belfield 371 D12
st. Bronte 377 H8
st. Cammeray 316 A5
st. Gordon 254 A7
st. Greystanes 305 H9
st. Homebush B 340 C2
st. Randwick 377 B9
st. Seven Hills 276 A4
CARTERET
av. Willmot 210 D13
CARTERS
rd. Dural 189 E3
rd. Grose Vale 84 G11
CARTHONA
av. Darling Point 14 A1
CARTIER
cr. Green Valley 363 B9
st. Bonnyrigg 363 H8
CARTLEDGE
av. Miranda 491 J6
CARTMORE
la. Surry Hills 20 B6
CARTREF
la. Mosman, off Rangers Av 316 G9
CARTWRIGHT
av. Busby 393 H1
av. Cartwright 393 H1
av. Homebush 341 B6
av. Merrylands 307 B11
av. Miller 393 H1
av. Sadleir 393 H1
cl. Glenmore Pk 265 F7
cr. Lalor Park 245 G11
st. Bonnyrigg Ht 363 G6
st. S Windsor 150 H2
CARVER
cr. Baulkham Hl 247 G6
pl. Dundas Vy 280 C8
CARVERS
rd. Oyster Bay 461 A8

CARVOSSA
pl. Bligh Park 150 J6
CARWAR
av. Carss Park 432 G13
la. Carss Park 432 G12
CARY
gr. Minto 482 C2
la. Bondi Jctn 22 K8
st. Baulkham Hl 248 B9
st. Drummoyne 344 B4
st. Emu Plains 235 E11
st. Leichhardt 15 G2
st. Marrickville 373 H16
CARYSFIELD
rd. Bass Hill 368 C12
rd. Georges Hall 368 C12
CARYSFORT
st. Hurstville 432 A8
CASABLANCA
av. Kellyville 186 B16
CASANDA
av. Smithfield 335 C4
CASBEN
cl. Carlingford 250 D12
CASBY
pl. Ambarvale 510 G13
CASCADE
la. Paddington 13 E13
rd. Cranebrook 207 A12
st. Paddington 13 E16
st. Seven Hills 275 C10
CASCADES
cl. West Hoxton 392 D5
CASERTA
pl. Allambie Ht 257 D8
CASEY
pl. Blackett 241 D3
CASH
pl. Prairiewood 334 E11
CASHEL
cr. Killarney Ht 255 H12
ct. Kellyville 215 A1
CASHMAN
dr. Kurrajong 55 E11
pl. Edensor Pk 333 J14
rd. Btn-le-Sds 404 A15
st. Rozelle 10 K4
CASHMANS
la. Five Dock, off Ramsay Rd 342 K10
CASHMERE
av. Rouse Hill 185 E2
dr. Elderslie 507 J1
CASINO
pl. Hoxton Park 393 B7
rd. Greystanes 305 G3
st. Bossley Park 333 D13
st. Eastlakes 406 A4
st. Glenwood 245 G1
CASPIAN
pl. Plumpton 242 C8
pl. Woronora Ht 489 F5
CASS
ct. Currans Hill 479 J14
pl. Cranebrook 207 E13
CASSAM
pl. Valley Ht 202 D4
CASSANDRA
av. St Ives 224 D14
cr. Heathcote 518 F9
pl. Carlingford 279 K2
CASSAR
cr. Cranebrook 207 G6
CASSIA
cl. Bossley Park 333 E8
cl. St Clair 269 H9
gr. Beecroft 250 F3
la. Dee Why 258 K9
pl. Bass Hill 368 A10
pl. Eastwood 281 C5
pl. Loftus 489 J11
pl. Mcquarie Fd 454 E1
st. Dee Why 258 K9
CASSIDY
st. Denham Ct 422 C4
CASSILIS
st. Monterey 433 G8
CASSINA
pl. Baulkham Hl 246 G9
CASSINIA
ct. Wattle Grove 426 A2
pl. Mt Annan 509 F4

CASSINO
cl. Allambie Ht 257 D9
CASSINS
av. N Sydney 5 F1
la. N Sydney 5 F1
CASSIUS
wy. Rsemeadow 540 H3
CASSOLA
pl. Penrith 236 E2
CASTELNAU
st. Caringbah 492 G11
CASTLE
cct. Seaforth 286 K6
cct. Westleigh 220 F8
cr. Belrose 225 J14
la. Randwick, off Carter St 377 B9
pl. Castle Hill 218 B14
pl. Padstow Ht 429 H5
pl. Sylvania 461 J14
rd. Orchard Hills 267 E5
rd. Richmond 118 G11
st. Blacktown 274 C5
st. Blakehurst 462 C4
st. Castle Hill 217 K12
st. Castle Hill 218 A13
st. Castlereagh 176 A5
st. N Parramatta 278 C11
st. Randwick 377 B9
CASTLE CIRCUIT
cl. Seaforth 286 J5
CASTLECOVE
dr. Castle Cove 285 F4
CASTLEFERN
ct. Kellyville 186 K15
CASTLEFIELD
la. Bondi, off Castlefield St 378 A4
st. Bondi 378 A4
CASTLE HILL
rd. Castle Hill 218 H14
rd. Cherrybrook 249 D1
rd. W Pnnant Hl 249 D1
CASTLE HOWARD
rd. Beecroft 250 F9
rd. Cheltenham 250 F9
CASTLE LEA
ct. Castle Hill 219 A12
CASTLEREAGH
cr. Sylvania Wtr 462 D11
la. Redfern 19 G7
la. Penrith, off Castlereagh Rd 236 F7
rd. Agnes Banks 117 A14
rd. Castlereagh 205 G11
rd. Penrith 236 F7
rd. Richmond 117 H8
rd. Wilberforce 91 K1
st. Bossley Park 333 F5
st. Concord 341 H6
st. Haymarket F A8
st. Haymarket F B7
st. Haymarket 3 H11
st. Liverpool 395 C4
st. Penrith 236 H13
st. Riverstone 182 K8
st. Sydney D A16
st. Sydney 3 H11
st. Tahmoor 565 H12
st. Tahmoor 565 J10
CASTLE ROCK
cr. Clontarf 287 G15
ct. Wattle Grove 395 K14
CASTLEROCK
av. Glenmore Pk 266 H8
CASTLESTEAD
st. Concord W 311 D14
CASTLEWOOD
av. Woolooware 493 E10
dr. Castle Hill 248 H1
CASTRA
pl. Double Bay 14 F7
CASUARINA
av. Glenorie 128 C5
cct. Kingswood 267 H2
cl. The Oaks 502 E14
ct. Wattle Grove 396 C16
dr. Cherrybrook 219 G13
pl. Mcquarie Fd 454 B5
rd. Alfords Point 429 C14
rd. Gymea Bay 491 F12
CASULA
pl. Forestville 255 H9
rd. Casula 394 H15
CASURINA
pl. Narellan Vale 478 J14
CAT
pl. Seven Hills 275 B5
CATALINA
cr. Avalon 140 D14
pl. Kellyville 186 F16
pl. Raby 481 H1
st. Mascot 404 K4
st. N St Marys 239 J10
CATALPA
av. Avalon 139 J15
av. Blaxland 233 G6
cr. Turramurra 222 H16
gr. Menai 458 K13
wy. Blacktown 274 E12
CATANIA
pl. Quakers Hill 214 D9
CATARACT
pl. Leumeah 482 E13
rd. Appin 569 E14
rd. Box Hill 154 A1
CATCHMENT
cl. Mulgoa 323 E4
CATCHPOLE
av. Hobartville 118 D6
st. St Helens Park 541 C3
CATERSON
dr. Castle Hill 217 E9
CATES
pl. St Ives 224 D8
CATHAN
st. Quakers Hill 214 E11
CATHCART
st. Fairfield 336 A16
CATHEDRAL
st. Sydney D J10
st. Sydney 4 B5
st. Woolmloo D J10
st. Woolmloo 4 B5
st. Woolmloo 4 E6
CATHERINE
av. Lurnea 394 D10
cr. Blaxland 234 C7
cr. Rooty Hill 272 C2
la. Belmore 401 H1
st. Glebe 12 B16
st. Kurrajong 85 F3
st. Leichhardt 16 D3
st. Lilyfield 10 F8
st. Punchbowl 370 B16
st. Rockdale 433 C1
st. Rozelle 10 J2
st. St Ives 224 D13
st. Werrington 238 H9
st. Windsor 121 B9
CATHERINE FIELD
rd. Catherine Fd 449 D1
CATHY
st. Blaxland 233 J11
wy. Seven Hills 275 K5
CATKIN
wy. Mcquarie Fd 454 G4
CATLETT
av. North Rocks 248 K16
CATO
cl. Edensor Pk 363 F3
pl. Blackett 241 D3
pl. Illawong 459 D5
wy. Casula 424 F3
CATON
pl. Quakers Hill 213 H16
CATRIONA
cl. Berowra Ht 133 A6
CATTAI
ct. Holsworthy 426 E5
pl. Kenthurst 188 D6
rd. Cattai 94 C4
rd. Pitt Town 93 A13
CATTAI CREEK
dr. Kellyville 187 A16
dr. Kellyville 216 K1
dr. Kellyville 217 C1
CATTAI RIDGE
rd. Glenorie 128 D12
rd. Maraylya 95 B13
CATTON
pl. Menai 458 J14
CAULFIELD
cr. St Johns Pk 364 E2
CAVALLARO
ct. Mount Druitt 241 D11
CAVALLI
wy. Clarmnt Ms 268 F4
CAVALRY
gr. Glenwood 245 K3
CAVAN
pl. Airds 512 B13
rd. Killarney Ht 255 K13
CAVE
av. North Ryde 282 C9
cl. Green Valley 363 B11
rd. Strathfield 370 J2
CAVELL
av. Rhodes 311 E7
CAVENDISH
av. Blacktown 275 A7
la. Stanmore 16 F12
st. Concord W 341 D1
st. Enmore 16 E11
st. Pennant Hills 220 K16
st. Stanmore 16 E11
CAVERS
st. Currans Hill 479 H8
CAVERSHAM
ct. Cherrybrook 219 F9
CAVES
la. Dulwich Hill 373 E9
CAVEY
st. Marrickville 373 K14
CAVILL
av. Ashfield 372 G2
st. Harbord 288 F2
st. Hebersham 241 F10
st. Queenscliff 288 F2
CAWARRA
pl. Fairfield 336 F7
pl. Gordon 253 E9
rd. Caringbah 492 J6
st. Eastern Ck 272 F7
CAWARRAH
rd. Middle Cove 285 J8
CAWDOR
pl. Acacia Gdn 214 H16
pl. Rsemeadow 540 D3
rd. Camden 506 H4
rd. Cawdor 506 C16
rd. Cawdor 537 A10
CAWDOR FARMS
rd. Grasmere 475 H16
CAWTHORNE
st. Hornsby Ht 191 G7
CAYLEY
av. Punchbowl 400 B6
pl. Cabramatta W 364 F6
CECIL
av. Castle Hill 217 K14
av. Castle Hill 218 B16
av. Pennant Hills 250 J1
la. Paddington 13 G14
pl. Greenfld Pk 334 C16
rd. Cecil Park 331 G8
rd. Hornsby 192 C14
rd. Newport 169 G16
rd. Rose Bay 348 D8
st. Ashfield 373 A1
st. Caringbah 492 K16
st. Denistone E 281 H10
st. Dolans Bay 492 K16
st. Fairlight 288 E8
st. Gordon 253 G11
st. Guildford 337 G2
st. Hurstville Gr 431 H9
st. Merrylands 307 G16
st. Monterey 433 H6
st. Paddington 13 G14
st. Scotland I 168 H4
st. Wareemba 342 K6
CECILIA
st. Belmore 371 E13
st. Marrickville 373 K11
st. Toongabbie 276 B7
CECIL MUNRO
av. Cronulla, off Ozone St 494 A12
CECILY
st. Belfield 371 B10
st. Lilyfield 10 G2
CEDAR
av. Bradbury 511 E14
cl. Bossley Park 333 H9
cr. N St Marys 240 A11
gr. Castle Hill 217 D10
gr. Frenchs Frst 256 F2
la. N St Marys, off Cedar Cr 240 A12
pl. Blacktown 274 B7
pl. Ermington 280 D13
pl. Kirrawee 490 K5
pl. Newington 310 B14
pl. S Coogee 407 E6
pl. The Oaks 502 F13
rd. Casula 423 K3
rd. Prestons 394 A15
st. Greystanes 306 E4
st. Lugarno 429 G16
st. Normanhurst 221 D12
CEDAR CREEK
rd. Thirlmere 561 H11
rd. Thirlmere 561 H12
CEDAR WATTLE
pl. Narellan Vale 478 K14
CEDARWOOD
cl. Greystanes 306 F12
dr. Cherrybrook 219 H15
gr. Dean Park 212 F16
pl. Carlingford 249 D15
pl. Cranebrook 207 F15
CEDRIC
la. Mosman, off Mulbring St 317 D9
st. Mcquarie Fd 423 K15
CELEBES
st. Kings Park 244 K2
CELEBRATION
dr. Bella Vista 216 A15
rd. Sadleir 364 B16
CELESTE
av. Castle Hill 217 C7
ct. Rooty Hill 272 A5
CELESTIAL
pl. Cranebrook 207 G5
CELIA
pl. Kings Lngly 245 G8
rd. Kellyville 185 F1
st. Granville 308 F15
CELOSIA
pl. Loftus 489 H13
CELTIS
pl. Mcquarie Fd 454 F2
CEMETERY
av. Matraville 436 G8
rd. Riverstone 182 E10
CENTAUR
st. Padstow 429 A2
st. Revesby 429 A5
st. Revesby Ht 429 A5
CENTAURI
cct. Cranebrook 207 E5
CENTAURUS
dr. Hinchinbrk 393 D4
CENTENARY
av. Hunters Hill 313 D11
av. Matraville 436 J8
av. Moorebank 395 K11
av. Old Tngabbie 277 E7
av. Old Tngabbie 277 E8
dr. Homebush W 340 F12
dr. Mosman 316 H11
dr. Strathfield 340 F12
rd. Merrylands 306 K5
rd. S Wntwthvle 307 A5
CENTENNIAL
av. Chatswd W 284 E11
av. Lane Cove 284 B16
av. Lane Cove W 313 J1
av. Randwick 377 C9
ct. Mt Vernon 331 E3
la. Centnnial Pk 21 C10
la. Ellis Lane 476 C13
sq. Centnnial Pk 21 G4
sq. Paddington 21 G4
st. Marrickville 373 K10
CENTENNIAL PARK
ct. Wattle Grove 426 A3
CENTRAL
av. Chipping Ntn 366 F16
av. Chipping Ntn 366 H15
av. Como 460 F4
av. Eastwood 280 K5
av. Eveleigh 18 H11
av. Lane Cove 314 E2
av. Lilyfield 10 C2
av. Mcquarie Pk 282 C1
av. Manly 288 H9
av. Marrickville 373 K13
av. Mosman 317
av. Thornleigh 221
av. Westmead 277
la. Chipping Ntn 366
la. Marrickville, off Victoria Rd 374
pl. Baulkham Hl 247
rd. Avalon 139
rd. Beverly Hills 430
rd. Miranda 492
st. Belfield 371
st. Naremburn 315
st. Sydney E
st. Sydney 3
CENTRAL PARK
dr. Bow Bowing 452
CENTRE
av. Roselands 400
cr. Blaxland 234
la. Kingsford, off Kennedy St 406
pl. Wetherill Pk 334
rd. Mascot 404
st. Blakehurst 462
st. Leichhardt 16
st. Penshurst 431
st. Redfern 19
CENTURY
cct. Baulkham Hl 216
CEPHEUS
la. Erskine Park, off Cepheus Pl 300
pl. Erskine Park 300
CERAMIC
la. Manly 288
wy. Woodcroft 243
CEREMONIAL
dr. Richmond 118
dr. Richmond 119
CERES
pl. Rsemeadow 540
st. Penrith 237
CESSNA
pl. Raby 481
CESTRUM
av. Mcquarie Fd 454
CETUS
pl. Erskine Park 301
CEVU
av. Willoughby 285
CHABLIS
pl. Eschol Park 481
pl. Minchinbury 272
pl. Orchard Hills 268
CHAD
pl. St Clair 299
CHADD
st. Galston 160
CHADDERTON
st. Cabramatta 366
st. Canley Vale 366
CHADLEY
ct. Cherrybrook 219
pl. West Hoxton 392
CHADWICK
av. Marrickville 373
av. Regents Pk 339
cr. Fairfield W 335
st. Lucas Ht 487
st. Putney 312
CHADWORTH
pl. Baulkham Hl 248
CHAFFEY
pl. Bonnyrigg Ht 363
CHAINMAIL
cr. Castle Hill 217
CHAIN-O-PONDS
cct. Mt Annan 479
rd. Mulgoa 295
CHAKOLA
av. Hornsby Ht 191
pl. Kirrawee 461
CHALCEDONY
st. Eagle Vale 481
CHALDER
av. Marrickville 374
la. Marrickville, off Chalder St 374
st. Marrickville 374
st. Newtown 17
CHALET
pl. Minchinbury 272

Kellyville 216 E5
LEYER
N Willghby 285 F7
Rose Bay 348 C13
LFORD
Canterbury 402 E1
LIS
Randwick, off
Castle St 377 B9
LLENGER
Belrose 225 H6
Cranebrook, off
Pensax Rd 207 G14
Birchgrove 7 K4
Voyager Pt 427 D4
Cranebrook 207 G14
LLIS
Dulwich Hill 373 F12
Potts Point 4 J2
Turramurra 222 K10
Randwick 377 B9
LLONER
Chipping Ntn 396 E4
LMER
St Johns Pk 364 E1
LMERS
Beacon Hill 257 H7
Emu Plains 235 J10
Mascot 405 A3
Old Tngabbie 276 J11
Surry Hills 19 G3
Strathfield 341 B16
Belmore 401 C3
Haymarket 19 G4
Lakemba 401 C3
Redfern 19 F10
Surry Hills 19 G4
MBERLAIN
Caringbah 492 G4
Rose Bay 348 C8
Smithfield 335 B6
Bexley 402 H12
Guildford 337 J7
Padstow 429 D5
Padstow Ht 429 D6
Campbelltwn 511 H2
Narwee 400 J14
MBERS
Bondi Beach 378 B3
Epping 251 B16
Wrrngtn Cty 238 F9
MELEON
Erskine Park 300 D3
Erskine Park, off
Chameleon Dr 300 F1
MPION
Glenorie 128 G13
Tennyson 312 E11
Glenfield 424 H10
MPNESS
St Marys 239 J15
St Marys, off
Champness Cr 239 K15
NCERY
Canley Vale 366 E5
NDLER
Chippendale 18 H1
Cowan 104 C14
Chippendale, off
City Rd 18 H2
Rockdale 433 D2
Rooty Hill 271 J6
NDOS
Crows Nest, off
Alexander St 315 F5
Horsley Pk 303 A12
Yanderra 567 C15
Ashfield 343 A16
Canley Vale 365 J2
Crows Nest 315 E5
Haberfield 343 B16
Manly Vale 287 J5
Naremburn 315 E5
St Leonards 315 E5
ANEL
Toongabbie 276 G4
ANG
Kearns 481 B1
ANNEL
Mt Annan 479 G15
Dulwich Hill 373 D7
ANNEY
Bossley Park 333 H7

CHANSA
pl. Blacktown 273 K5
CHANT
av. Pagewood 406 G7
CHANTER
rd. Thirlmere 564 G9
CHAPALA
cl. St Ives 224 E8
CHAPEL
cct. Prospect 274 K13
cl. Cherrybrook 219 E14
la. Alexandria 18 K10
la. Alexandria 19 A10
la. Baulkham Hl 246 G8
la. Baulkham Hl 247 B4
la. Belmore 401 F3
la. Marrickville 374 B10
la. Rockdale 403 D16
la. St Marys, off
Champness Cr 239 J15
la. Crows Nest, off
Holterman St 315 F6
rd. Bankstown 369 E16
rd. Vaucluse 348 D2
rd.s, Bankstown 399 C7
st. Belmore 401 D2
st. Darlinghurst 4 D9
st. Kingsgrove 401 D2
st. Kogarah 433 C6
st. Lakemba 401 D2
st. Lilyfield 9 H4
st. Marrickville 374 C10
st. Randwick 377 C11
st. Richmond 118 E3
st. Rockdale 403 E16
st. Roselands 401 D2
st. St Marys 239 H16
CHAPERON
cr. Minto 453 B15
CHAPLAIN
pl. Bligh Park 150 J7
CHAPLIN
cr. Quakers Hill 243 H1
dr. Lane Cove W 283 F16
CHAPMAN
av. Beecroft 250 B5
av. Castle Hill 217 H13
av. Chatswood 284 J11
av. Maroubra 407 G11
av. Penrith 236 H13
cct. Currans Hill 479 H9
la. Annandale 10 J15
la. Surry Hills 20 E3
la. Lindfield, off
Tyron Rd 254 D16
pde. Faulconbdg 171 D13
pl. Wakeley 334 G14
rd. Annandale 11 D6
rd. Vineyard 152 H9
st. Gladesville 312 E7
st. Green Valley 363 B13
st. Gymea 491 E3
st. Gymea 491 E6
st. Strathfield 341 F10
st. Summer Hill 373 E4
st. Surry Hills 20 E3
st. Tahmoor 565 H10
st. Werrington 238 K12
st. West Hoxton 392 B11
st. West Hoxton 392 C11
CHAPPEL
av. Green Valley 363 A9
ct. Mt Annan 479 C12
CHARADE
st. Riverwood 400 C10
CHARD
rd. Brookvale 258 B10
CHARDONNAY
av. Eschol Park 481 A4
rd. St Clair 270 G11
CHARKER
cl. Harringtn Pk 478 C3
CHARKERS
st. S Penrith 266 H6
CHARLBURY
st. Chipping Ntn 396 F2
CHARLECOT
st. Dulwich Hill 373 G10
CHARLEMONT
wy. Wentwthvle 277 E11
CHARLEROI
rd. Belrose 226 A9

CHARLES
ct. North Rocks 278 F3
la. Burwood 342 B15
la. Forest Lodge 11 G15
la. Mosman, off
Muston St 317 C9
pl. Cherrybrook 219 H5
pl. Jannali 460 H11
pl. Mt Annan 509 F2
st. Arncliffe 403 H9
st. Balmain 8 C10
st. Baulkham Hl 247 G13
st. Blacktown 245 A8
st. Burwood 342 C15
st. Canterbury 372 E13
st. Carlingford 279 G6
st. Castlecrag 286 A11
st. Eastlakes 405 J6
st. Enmore 17 A12
st. Erskineville 18 A13
st. Fairlight 288 D8
st. Five Dock 343 A7
st. Forest Lodge 11 G15
st. Granville 308 F15
st. Guildford W 336 H3
st. Harbord 288 H2
st. Killara 283 E2
st. Leichhardt 9 G10
st. Lilyfield 9 G7
st. Lindfield 283 E2
st. Liverpool 395 B8
st. McGraths Hl 121 J11
st. Marrickville 374 B9
st. Marsden Pk 182 A12
st. N Richmond 87 D13
st. N Sydney K B5
st. N Sydney 5 E7
st. Oatlands 279 A10
st. Oatley 431 B15
st. Parramatta 308 E4
st. Petersham 16 C5
st. Putney 311 K8
st. Redfern 20 C8
st. Riverwood 400 E16
st. Ryde 312 B5
st. St Marys 239 E5
st. Smithfield 335 B6
st. Springwood 201 F3
st. Woolmloo 4 F5
CHARLES BABBAGE
av. Currans Hill 479 G12
CHARLESCOTTE
av. Punchbowl 400 D7
CHARLES HACKETT
dr. St Marys 239 F16
CHARLES HAYMAN
la. Collaroy 229 B14
CHARLES STURT
dr. Wrrngtn Cty 238 F9
CHARLES TODD
cr. Wrrngtn Cty 238 E7
la. Wrrngtn Cty, off
Charles Todd Cr 238 E7
CHARLESTON
av. Earlwood 402 E6
CHARLESWORTH
cl. Catherine Fd 449 G8
CHARLIE YANKOS
st. Glenwood 215 K16
CHARLISH
la. Lane Cove 313 K1
CHARLOTTE
av. Marrickville 373 K15
cl. Lurnea 394 B12
cr. Canley Vale 366 F4
gr. Bella Vista 246 G3
la. Darlinghurst F G2
la. Pennant Hills 250 J1
pl. Beacon Hill 257 F2
pl. Bligh Park 150 D4
pl. Illawong 459 G3
rd. Pennant Hills 250 J1
rd. Port Botany 436 B9
rd. Rooty Hill 271 J3
st. Ashfield 372 J1
st. Campsie 401 K1
st. Dundas Vy 280 B7
st. Lilyfield 10 C10
st. Marsden Pk 181 J12
st. Merrylands 307 C16
st. Rozelle 10 K1
wy. Minto 482 H7
CHARLTON
av. Chipping Ntn 366 E15

av. Turramurra 223 E12
av. Newington, off
Spitz Av 309 K15
dr. Castle Hill 219 A13
dr. Liberty Gr 311 C15
la. Brookvale 258 B11
pl. Menai 458 E13
pl. St Clair 270 C9
pwy. Chipping Ntn, off
Charlton Av 366 E14
rd. Lalor Park 245 E10
st. Abbotsford 342 J2
st. Yagoona 369 C9
wy. Glebe 11 K8
CHARLTONS CREEK
rd. Berrilee 131 D11
CHARM
pl. Peakhurst 429 K6
CHARMAINE
av. Greenacre 370 C7
CHARMAN
av. Maroubra 406 H7
CHARMER
cr. Minchinbury 271 G8
CHARMIAN
pl. Rsemeadow 540 H3
CHARNWOOD
ct. Glen Alpine 510 E9
CHARTER
st. Sadleir 394 B2
CHASE
av. Roseville Ch 255 E14
dr. Acacia Gdn 214 J14
dr. Acacia Gdn 214 J16
CHASELING
av. Springwood 201 G1
pl. The Oaks 502 E10
st. Greenacre 370 D13
CHASSELAS
av. Eschol Park 481 A4
CHATEAU
cl. Kellyville 185 E7
cr. St Clair 270 B9
tce. Quakers Hill 213 G9
CHATFIELD
av. Belfield 371 C8
st. Ryde 312 D1
CHATHAM
av. Moorebank 425 A3
cl. Belrose 226 A13
ct. Cherrybrook, off
Glamorgan Wy 219 E9
pl. Abbotsford 342 K2
pl. N Turramrra 223 E6
rd. Denistone 281 B12
rd. Eastwood 281 B11
rd. West Ryde 281 B12
st. Botany 405 G12
st. Canley Ht 365 G4
st. Pitt Town 92 H15
st. Randwick 377 D15
CHATRES
st. St Clair 270 F11
CHATSWOOD
av. Chatswood 285 B8
CHATSWORTH
rd. St Clair 270 D10
st. Fairfield 336 B14
CHAUCER
cr. Leumeah 512 B2
pl. Winmalee 173 J9
rd. Riverstone 182 C10
st. Wetherill Pk 334 G6
CHAUSSON
pl. Cranebrook 207 G8
CHAUVEL
av. Holsworthy 396 B13
av. Milperra 397 E12
cl. Wahroonga 223 B5
st. North Ryde 282 J11
CHAVIN
pl. Greenfld Pk 333 K13
CHEAL
la. Neutral Bay 6 F1
CHEATLE
st. East Hills 427 H2
CHECKLEY
ct. Ermington 280 B15
st. Abbotsford 342 H1
CHEDDAR
st. Blakehurst 432 D12

CHEDLEY
pl. Marayong 244 D8
CHEERS
st. West Ryde 280 J13
CHEERYBLE
pl. Ambarvale 510 K14
CHEESMANS
rd. Cattai 64 J4
CHEGWYN
av. Matraville 436 H8
la. Botany, off
Chegwyn St 405 E12
st. Botany 405 E11
CHELLASTON
st. Camden 507 B3
CHELMSFORD
av. Artarmon 285 D16
av. Artarmon 315 C1
av. Bankstown 399 B2
av. Belmore 401 H2
av. Botany 405 F15
av. Cronulla 523 K3
av. Croydon 372 C1
av. E Lindfield 254 G16
av. Epping 280 H3
av. Haberfield 343 D12
av. Lindfield 284 E2
av. Maroubra 407 C15
av. Willoughby 285 D16
rd. Asquith 192 D10
rd. S Wntwthvle 306 J5
st. Camperdwn 17 D10
st. Newtown 17 D10
CHELSEA
av. Baulkham Hl 247 H8
dr. Canley Ht 335 C16
pl. Colyton 270 E6
pl. Glenfield 424 C11
rd. W Pnnant Hl 219 K16
st. Merrylands 307 B10
st. Redfern 20 C8
tce. Glenwood 215 H14
CHELSEA GARDEN
ct. Wattle Grove 426 B5
CHELTENHAM
av. Cmbrdg Pk 237 K8
cl. Castle Hill 218 E12
rd. Burwood 342 C14
rd. Cheltenham 250 H10
rd. Croydon 342 C14
st. Chipping Ntn 366 F15
st. Rozelle 10 J3
CHEPSTOW
st. Randwick 377 B10
CHERANA
cr. Forestville 255 E9
pl. Kareela 461 E12
CHERIE
pl. Bass Hill 367 F7
CHERITON
av. Castle Hill 218 A15
CHEROKEE
av. Greenfld Pk 333 K14
pl. Raby 451 H16
CHERRY
av. Carlingford 249 E16
ct. Marsfield 282 A4
pl. Castle Cove 286 D7
pl. Mcquarie Fd 454 C5
pl. Prestons 393 H14
st. Marsden Pk 182 A13
st. Mt Pritchard 364 E9
st. Warrawee 222 G13
CHERRYBROOK
ch. Londonderry 178 C1
rd. Lansvale 366 C10
rd. W Pnnant Hl 219 J15
CHERRY HAVEN
wy. Cherrybrook 218 Z9
wy. Cherrybrook 219 C15
CHERRYWOOD
av. Mt Riverview 234 D3
av. Wahroonga 223 B4
cl. Cranebrook 207 E7
gr. Menai 458 K13
st. Glenwood 245 C2
CHERTSEY
av. Bankstown 399 B3
CHERYL
cr. Newport 169 E9
pl. Castle Hill 217 C10
pl. Plumpton 242 D11

CHERYLE
av. Chester Hill 337 J10
CHESHAM
pde. Glenfield 424 E9
pl. Chipping Ntn......366 G14
pl. Plumpton..........241 H8
st. St Marys..........239 J14
CHESNUT
cr. Prestons 393 K15
CHESSELL
la. Ashfield, off Brown St...........372 H2
CHESTER
av. Baulkham Hl 247 B13
av. Cmbrdg Pk.........237 H10
av. Maroubra............407 C12
la. Woollahra............22 E4
la. Zetland, off Joynton Av.........375 H12
pl. Ermington..........280 D14
pl. Narraweena........258 C2
rd. Ingleburn............453 B7
rd. Turramurra 223 D9
st. Annandale............17 B1
st. Annandale............17 C1
st. Blacktown 244 B15
st. Epping 251 B14
st. Merrylands..........307 F8
st. Mount Druitt 241 C14
st. Petersham 15 H12
st. Schofields...........183 E12
st. Sylvania 461 J13
st. Woollahra............22 E3
CHESTERFIELD
la. Bronte.................377 J10
pde. Bronte...............377 J10
rd. Epping 280 J3
rd. S Penrith.............266 K3
CHESTER HILL
rd. Bass Hill.............368 A8
rd. Chester Hill 368 B4
CHESTERMAN
cr. Davidson 255 B1
CHESTERTON
ct. Cmbrdg Gdn 237 H5
CHESTNUT
av. Telopea..............279 G12
cr. Bidwill................211 D13
dr. Banksia..............403 F12
dr. Glossodia.............59 C6
rd. Auburn 339 A6
rd. Mt Colah 162 E13
st. Loftus 489 J12
CHETWYN
pl. Wentwthvle.........277 C12
CHETWYND
rd. Guildford.............337 D3
rd. Merrylands.........307 E16
CHEVALIER
cr. Hunters Hill........314 A14
wy. Claymore 481 B12
CHEVIOT
dr. Cobbitty 416 F6
pl. Airds...................512 A12
st. Ashbury..............372 D8
st. Mount Druitt 241 C13
CHEVROLET
pl. Ingleburn 453 K7
CHEVRON
pl. Rouse Hill 185 F4
CHEYENNE
rd. Greenfld Pk........333 K14
CHEYNE
rd. Terrey Hills.........196 F5
wk. Castlecrag.........286 F12
wk. W Pnnant Hl.......219 J16
CHIANTI
ct. Glenwood 246 A3
CHICAGO
av. Blacktown..........244 G12
av. Maroubra...........407 C14
CHICHESTER
st. Maroubra............406 K10
CHICK
st. Roselands...........400 H10
CHICKASAW
cr. Greenfld Pk........334 A16
CHIENTI
pl. Prestons 393 H15
CHIFLEY
av. Sefton................338 F16
cl. N Wahrnga........192 G16

pl. Bligh Park..........150 G8
sq. Sydney ....B D16
sq. Sydney 1 K16
st. Smithfield 335 C2
st. Wetherill Pk 335 C2
wy. Penrith..............237 B7
CHILAW
av. St Marys 269 G6
CHILCOTT
rd. Berrilee 131 D8
CHILDERS
st. Bonnyrigg Ht......363 F6
CHILDREY
pl. Castle Hill...........219 A9
CHILDS
pl. Mt Annan 479 G15
pwy. Chipping Ntn, off Childs Rd............396 G1
rd. Chipping Ntn.......396 F2
st. East Hills............427 J1
st. Lidcombe............339 H7
st. Panania..............427 J1
CHILE
pl. Seven Hills.........275 H4
CHILTERN
cr. Castle Hill..........217 H10
rd. Guildford............337 H8
rd. Ingleside 197 J4
rd. Willoughby..........285 F14
CHILTON
av. Oakhurst 242 D3
pde. Warrawee 222 G8
CHILVERS
la. S Maroota.............65 K5
rd. Thornleigh 221 A10
CHILWORTH
cl. Beecroft 250 D7
CHINDOO
cl. Kingswood...........267 F3
la. Kingswood, off Chindoo Cl..........267 F3
CHIOS
pl. Rooty Hill...........272 A3
CHIPALEE
ct. Erskine Park.......300 E2
CHIPILLY
av. Engadine............518 G1
CHIPMAN
st. Eastlakes............405 J5
CHIPP
ct. Bella Vista 246 E3
CHIPPEN
la. Chippendale 19 C4
st. Chippendale 19 B4
CHIPPENHAM
pl. Chipping Ntn......366 G13
st. Chipping Ntn......366 G14
CHIPPING
pl. S Penrith............266 F4
CHIPS RAFFERTY
av. Moore Park..........21 B6
CHIRCAN
st. Old Tngabbie......277 A6
CHISHOLM
av. Avalon 139 H15
av. Belmore..............401 J4
av. Wrrngtn Cty 238 F9
cr. Blaxland..............233 E9
cr. Bradbury.............511 E9
pl. Windsor..............121 D16
rd. Auburn 338 J6
rd. Catherine Fd........449 F3
rd. Sefton.................368 H1
st. Belfield...............371 B8
st. Darlinghurst............4 E14
st. Greenwich............315 A10
st. North Ryde 282 J8
st. Quakers Hill 213 H14
st. Smithfield 336 C5
st. S Turramrra 252 A5
CHISOLM
rd. Kurnell...............465 J12
CHISWICK
la. Woollahra 22 B1
pl. Cherrybrook.........219 C10
rd. Auburn 338 K7
rd. Greenacre 369 K10
rd. S Granville 338 E6
st. Chiswick 343 D1
st. Strathfield S 371 E7
CHITTICK
la. Cobbitty 446 J13

CHIVE
pl. Quakers Hill 243 G4
CHIVERS
av. Lugarno..............429 K10
pl. Tahmoor.............566 D8
CHOBE
wy. Glenwood 215 A16
CHOMA
wy. Leppington.........420 A10
CHOPIN
cl. Bonnyrigg Ht......363 E5
cr. Clarmnt Ms.........268 G3
st. Seven Hills.........246 D13
CHORLEY
av. Cheltenham........250 K7
CHOWDER BAY
rd. Mosman 317 G11
CHOWNE
pl. N Willghby 285 G6
pl. Yennora 336 K11
CHRIS
pl. Dean Park 212 J16
st. Lansvale 367 B10
st. Windsor 121 K6
CHRISALEX
pl. St Clair...............269 J8
CHRISAN
cl. Werrington..........238 K10
CHRIS BANG
cr. Vaucluse 348 F6
CHRISTABEL
pl. Cecil Hills...........362 F3
CHRISTEL
av. Carlingford 249 D13
CHRISTENSEN
cct. Oatley 430 D14
CHRISTIAN
rd. Punchbowl...........400 D8
CHRISTIE
la. Glebe....................12 G13
la. Surry Hills.............20 A5
la. St Leonards, off Christie St..........315 D6
rd. Mcquarie Pk.......252 E15
st. Liverpool............395 A8
st. Minto..................452 H16
st. Prairiewood 334 E10
st. St Leonards 315 D5
st. St Marys 239 C8
st. S Penrith............236 J15
st. Werrington..........239 C8
st. Windsor..............121 B9
st. Wollstncraft 315 D5
CHRISTIES
la. Zetland, off Merton St..........375 H10
CHRISTINA
pl. Kareela 461 E12
rd. Villawood 337 E16
st. Longueville 314 E7
st. Rydalmere 309 H1
CHRISTINE
av. Ryde..................282 C10
cr. Lalor Park 245 H12
ct. Kellyville.............217 C3
st. Northmead...........277 F10
st. S Penrith.............267 C3
CHRISTMAS
pl. Green Valley.......363 B10
CHRISTOPHER
av. Camden 507 B6
av. Georges Hall 367 F9
pl. Beacon Hill.........257 E3
pl. N Richmond.........87 B16
pl. Woolooware........493 E13
st. Baulkham Hl 247 H7
CHRYSANTHEMUM
av. Lurnea 394 F12
CHUBB
pl. Rooty Hill...........241 K14
CHUDLEIGH
st. Rydalmere 279 F15
CHULLORA
cr. Engadine............488 D14
CHUNOOMA
rd. N Wahrnga.........222 G1
CHURCH
av. Mascot 405 A1
av. Westmead 307 E2
la. Allawah..............432 D8
la. Castlereagh 176 B14
la. Cranebrook.........206 G1

la. Glebe...................11 K10
la. N Sydney 5 E3
la. Pitt Town 92 G14
la. Randwick...........377 A11
la. Ryde..................311 K2
la. Surry Hills...............4 D14
pl. Paddington 21 F4
rd. Denham Ct..........422 E15
rd. Moorebank 395 F9
rd. Mulgoa 325 D2
rd. Wilberforce 92 B1
rd. Yagoona 369 A11
st. Appin.................569 F12
st. Appin.................569 H13
st. Ashfield 342 H14
st. Balmain 7 G8
st. Birchgrove 7 G8
st. Blakehurst..........462 E2
st. Burwood.............342 A16
st. Cabramatta 365 J10
st. Camperdwn 17 F4
st. Canterbury 372 H13
st. Castle Hill............248 B1
st. Castlereagh.........176 G16
st. Chatswood..........285 C9
st. Cranebrook 176 G16
st. Croydon.............342 F13
st. Drummoyne.......343 K3
st. Eastern Ck..........272 G5
st. Elderslie..............507 F1
st. Granville 308 C6
st. Greenwich..........314 J12
st. Harris Park.........308 C6
st. Hunters Hill........313 F11
st. Hurlstone Pk......372 H13
st. Lidcombe............339 H8
st. Lidcombe............340 B8
st. Lilyfield 9 G5
st. Mcquarie Fd 453 J2
st. Marrickville 373 H14
st. Mt Krng-gai.........163 A12
st. Newtown 17 G7
st. N Parramatta.......278 B10
st. N Sydney 5 E3
st. N Willghby 285 C9
st. Old Guildford......337 G10
st. Paddington 4 F16
st. Parramatta 308 C1
st. Parramatta 308 C4
st. Peakhurst 430 B3
st. Petersham 16 A11
st. Pitt Town 92 G15
st. Pymble 253 E2
st. Randwick...........376 K12
st. Riverstone 182 J6
st. Rossmore 389 F14
st. Ryde..................311 H5
st. Ryde..................311 K3
st. St Peters............374 H13
st. S Windsor...........120 G14
st. Waverley.............377 F6
st. W Pnnant Hl.......249 J4
st. Windsor..............120 G14
st. Woolooware.......493 E10
CHURCH HILL
la. Gordon 253 H8
CHURCHILL
av. Kirrawee 491 A5
av. Riverwood 400 F14
av. Strathfield 341 E12
av. Wahroonga 222 C4
cr. Allambie Ht 257 D12
cr. Cammeray 316 D5
cr. Concord..............341 H5
ct. Narellan Vale......479 A11
dr. Northmead.........277 H2
dr. Winston Hills......277 H2
pl. Springwood 201 D2
rd. East Killara 254 E8
rd. Padstow Ht 429 F8
rd. Rose Bay 348 C8
st. Bardwell Pk.........402 G9
st. Fairfield..............336 A12
st. Fairfield Ht 336 A12
st. Guildford.............338 D7
st. Silverwater..........309 H13
st. Springwood 201 D1
CHURCH STREET
ml. Parramatta, off Church St..........308 C3
CHUSAN
pl. Plumpton............242 C5
CHUTER
av. Monterey 433 G9
av. Ramsgate Bch.....433 F13
av. Sans Souci.........433 F16

st. McMahons Pt 5
CICADA GLEN
rd. Ingleside 197
CICERO
wy. Rsemeadow.......540
CIGOLINI
pl. Kellyville.............216
CILENTO
cr. East Ryde...........282
CINDY
pl. Colyton 270
CINI
pl. Quakers Hill 213
CINNABAR
st. Eagle Vale 481
CIPOLIN
cl. Eagle Vale 481
CIRCULAR
qy. Sydney ....B
qy. Sydney 1
CIRCULAR QUAY
e. Sydney ....B
e. Sydney 2
w. The Rocks ....B
w. The Rocks 1
CIRELLA
cl. North Manly.......258
CIRRUS
pl. Bnkstn Aprt........397
CISTICOLA
st. Hinchinbrk 363
CITADEL
cr. Castle Hill...........217
pl. Glenwood 246
CITRINE
cl. Bossley Park......333
CITRINUS
pl. Narellan Vale......478
CITROEN
pl. Ingleburn 453
CITRON
pl. Oakhurst............241
CITRONELLE
ct. Cranebrook........207
CITRUS
av. Hornsby.............191
gr. Carlingford.........279
st. Quakers Hill 214
CITY
rd. Camperdwn 18
rd. Chippendale 18
rd. Darlington............18
rd. Newtown 18
CITY VIEW
rd. Pennant Hills.......250
CITY WEST LINK
rd. Leichhardt............10
rd. Lilyfield 9
rd. Lilyfield 10
rd. Lilyfield 343
rd. Rozelle.................10
CIVIC
arc. Chatswood, off Victoria Av 284
av. Kogarah 433
av. Pendle Hill...........276
dr. Bankstown..........369
dr. Dee Why.............258
la. Frenchs Frst 256
la. Blacktown, off Campbell St 244
la. Mosman, off Clifford St 317
pl. Parramatta 308
rd. Auburn 339
CLACK
rd. Chester Hill 337
CLACKMANNAN
rd. Winston Hills......277
CLADDEN
cl. Pennant Hills.......250
CLAFTON
av. Northbridge 286
CLAIR
cr. Padstow Ht 429
CLAIRE
pl. Baulkham Hl 247
st. Naremburn 315
CLAIRVAUX
rd. Vaucluse 348

NALPINE
Eastwood 281 A9
Mosman 317 A11
NCY
Seven Hills 275 G2
Padstow Ht 429 E6
Padstow Ht 429 G6
Smithfield 335 K6
NVILLE
Roseville 284 F3
NWILLIAM
Chatswood 285 C10
Eastwood 280 J11
N Willghby 285 C10
PHAM
Regents Pk 368 G1
Sefton 368 G1
PTON
Darlinghurst 4 F9
RA
Erskineville 18 C13
Newtown 374 G9
Randwick 377 A14
RE
Oakville 122 E13
Russell Lea 343 C6
Killarney Ht 286 C1
Blacktown 274 D11
Blacktown 274 E11
Cabramatta W 364 G5
Gladesville 312 G12
Glebe 11 K13
Rozelle 7 B12
Surry Hills 4 E15
Sylvania 462 D7
REMONT
Canley Ht 335 E16
Greenacre 369 G9
Glen Alpine 510 D16
Hinchinbrk 363 B14
Windsor 120 J9
Wattle Grove 425 K4
Bargo 567 B2
W Pnnant Hl 249 C4
S Penrith 266 F4
Burwood Ht 372 A3
Balmain 7 A9
Campsie 371 J15
Merrylands 307 J15
Penshurst 431 F9
Richmond 119 A6
REMOUNT
Cherrybrook 219 D12
RENCE
Dee Why 258 J5
Killara 254 C13
Sylvania Wtr 462 D11
Sydney A D13
St Clair, off
Clarence Rd 300 B1
Double Bay 14 G14
Cattai 94 G2
Rockdale 403 A12
St Clair 300 B1
Balgowlah 287 J11
Belfield 371 E10
Blacktown 243 J13
Burwood 342 A15
Canley Ht 335 F16
Condell Park 399 A4
Glenbrook 234 A14
Lidcombe 339 G7
Mcquarie Fd 423 J16
Matraville 436 K2
Merrylands 307 E11
North Ryde 283 B11
Penshurst 431 E3
Smithfield 335 H2
Strathfield 341 F9
Sydney C E2
Sydney 3 E1
Wentwthvle 277 C12
RENDON
Wattle Grove 425 J3
Stanhpe Gdn 215 G9
Stanmore 16 G7
,Stanmore 16 F7
Airds 511 K15
Burwood 341 K14
Riverwood 429 K2
Stanmore 16 E7
Artarmon 314 J2
Richmond 119 D4
Vaucluse 348 E6
Waterloo 19 H11

CLARET
pl. Eschol Park 481 E3
st. Bossley Park 333 H9
CLARET ASH
gr. Menai 458 K14
CLAREVALE
st. Edensor Pk 333 D16
CLAREVILLE
av. Sandringham 463 D5
av. Sans Souci 463 E1
cl. Belfield 371 D8
cl. Woodbine 481 H11
CLARGO
st. Dulwich Hill 373 B10
CLARIBEL
st. Bankstown 399 A8
CLARICE
cr. Campbelltwn 511 J5
CLARIDGE
cl. Cherrybrook 219 D15
CLARINDA
st. Hornsby 191 E10
CLARISSA
pl. Ambarvale 511 B13
pl. Castle Hill 248 C6
CLARK
pl. Minto 482 J8
rd. Londonderry 149 B5
rd. Milsons Point 6 A12
rd. Neutral Bay 6 B8
rd. N Sydney 6 A12
CLARKE
av. Hobartville 118 C8
cl. Hinchinbrk 393 A1
cl. Prairiewood 334 J7
dr. Castle Hill 218 H13
la. Bass Hill 368 D11
la. Earlwood 402 H4
la. Panania 428 F2
la. Crows Nest, off
Oxley St 315 E6
la. St Leonards, off
Oxley St 315 E6
pl. Castle Hill 218 E12
pl. Killara 254 F11
pl. Menai 458 E12
pl. Mt Annan 479 G16
pl. Punchbowl, off
Turner St 400 C4
rd. Hornsby 221 E5
rd. Pennant Hills 250 J4
rd. Waitara 221 H5
rd. Woolwich 314 E13
st. Annandale 16 F3
st. Bass Hill 368 D13
st. Berala 339 B12
st. Chatswd W 284 E9
st. Crows Nest 315 F6
st. Earlwood 402 H4
st. Granville 308 C12
st. Guildford 337 C7
st. Narrabeen 229 A8
st. Newington 310 B12
st. Riverstone 183 F5
st. Rydalmere 279 G16
st. Sydney F C4
st. Sydney 3 J10
st. Vaucluse 348 G4
st. West Ryde 281 H15
st.n, Peakhurst 429 K3
st.s, Peakhurst 429 K5
st.w, Narrabeen 228 J8
wy. Kenthurst 126 A16
CLARKES
rd. Ramsgate 433 D12
CLAROS
cl. Hornsby Ht 161 H13
CLASSEN
st. Sylvania 462 A13
CLASSERS
pl. Currans Hill 480 A10
CLAUD
pl. S Windsor 150 G3
CLAUDARE
st. Collaroy Plat 228 H12
CLAUDE
av. Cremorne 6 K6
st. Chatswood 284 K10
CLAUDE JAMES
cr. Regents Pk 369 E1
CLAUDIA
rd. Toongabbie 275 G11

CLAUDIUS
pl. Rsemeadow 540 D2
CLAVERDON
av. Picnic Point 428 G9
CLAVERING
rd. Seaforth 286 J7
CLAXTON
cct. Rouse Hill 184 J8
CLAY
pl. Eagle Vale 481 E7
st. Balmain 7 D12
CLAYPOLE
st. Ambarvale 540 E1
CLAYTON
la. Camperdwn 17 D7
pl. Girraween 276 A16
pl. W Pnnant Hl 249 A8
st. Balmain 7 J8
st. Blacktown 244 A12
st. Peakhurst 430 B2
st. Prairiewood 335 A9
st. Ryde 312 D2
wy. Clarmnt Ms 268 F4
CLEAL
st. Ermington 280 C15
CLEARVIEW
pl. Brookvale 257 H10
CLEARY
av. Belmore 371 D15
av. Forestville 256 B7
cl. Edensor Pk 363 F2
la. St Clair, off
Cleary Pl 270 B12
la. Belmore, off
Dean Av 371 E15
pl. Blackett 241 D2
pl. Casula 424 D4
pl. St Clair 270 A12
CLEAVER
pl. Ambarvale 510 K15
CLEEVE
cl. Mount Druitt 241 E16
pl. Cmbrdg Gdn 237 F3
CLEG
st. Artarmon 315 B2
CLEGG
pl. Glenhaven 217 K4
pl. Prairiewood 334 J9
CLELAND
rd. Artarmon 285 B16
st. Mascot 405 H5
CLEM
pl. Shalvey 211 B14
CLEMATIS
cl. Cherrybrook 220 A7
pl. Mcquarie Fd 454 D2
pl. Mt Annan 509 E4
CLEMENT
cl. Pennant Hills 250 G3
la. Rcuttrs Bay 13 B8
pl. Ingleburn 453 H8
pl. Rcuttrs Bay 13 C8
st. Guildford 337 D6
st. Rooty Hill 242 B16
st. Rcuttrs Bay 13 B8
st. Strathfield S 371 E6
CLEMENTINA
cct. Cecil Hills 362 D4
CLEMENTS
av. Bankstown 399 E7
pde. Kirrawee 491 B4
st. Drummoyne 343 F6
st. Russell Lea 343 F6
CLEMENTSON
dr. Rossmore 359 G16
CLEMSON
st. Kingswood 237 F15
CLEMTON
av. Earlwood 402 C5
pl. Earlwood, off
Clemton Av 402 D5
CLENNAM
av. Ambarvale 510 G12
CLENT
st. Jamisontown 266 C5
CLEONE
st. Guildford 338 A4
CLEOPATRA
dr. Rsemeadow 540 E2
CLERGY
rd. Wilberforce 91 K1

CLERKE
pl. Kings Lngly 246 C11
CLERKENWELL
st. Ambarvale 510 G15
CLERMISTON
av. Roseville 285 A4
CLERMONT
av. Concord 341 F5
av. N Strathfield 341 F5
av. Ryde 282 A12
la. Concord, off
Wellbank St 341 F5
la. N Strathfield, off
Wellbank St 341 F5
CLEVEDON
rd. Hurstville 431 K2
st. Botany 405 H13
CLEVELAND
av. Cromer 228 A14
av. Surry Hills 20 A6
la. Chippendale 18 H3
pl. Bonnet Bay 460 B9
rd. Riverstone 182 C10
st. Chippendale 18 H4
st. Darlington 18 H4
st. Ermington 280 E11
st. Moore Park 20 D7
st. Redfern 19 J6
st. Strathfield S 370 K6
st. Surry Hills 19 J6
st. Wahroonga 222 E7
CLEVELEY
av. Kings Lngly 245 A5
CLEY
pl. Prospect 274 K11
CLIFF
av. Northbridge 315 K2
av. N Wahrnga 222 J2
av. Peakhurst 430 B12
av. Winston Hills 277 F6
pl. Cranebrook 207 B11
rd. Collaroy 229 C14
rd. Epping 250 H15
rd. Freemns Rch 89 F6
rd. Northwood 314 H8
st. Manly 288 J11
st. Milsons Point K J16
st. Milsons Point 5 J13
st. Watsons Bay 318 F12
tce. Forest Lodge 11 F13
CLIFFBROOK
cr. Leonay 235 A16
pde. Clovelly 377 K14
CLIFFE
st. Picton 563 F2
st. Regents Pk 369 G2
CLIFF HAVEN
pl. Miranda 491 K9
CLIFFORD
av. Canley Vale 365 K4
av. Fairlight 288 C10
av. Thornleigh 221 C15
cr. Ingleburn 453 D12
la. Canley Vale, off
Clifford Av 366 A4
rd. Miranda 492 A7
st. Coogee 407 F2
st. Gordon 254 B7
st. Mosman 317 B6
st. Panania 428 B5
st. Rockdale 403 B14
CLIFF POINT
pl. Frenchs Frst 257 A2
CLIFFVIEW
rd. Berowra Ht 133 D5
CLIFT
cl. Edensor Pk 363 G2
CLIFTON
av. Burwood 342 B16
av. Glenbrook 264 C1
av. Kemps Ck 360 D1
la. Bronte, off
Busby Pde 377 K11
pl. Cartwright 394 C5
pl. Cherrybrook 219 B14
rd. Clovelly 377 J12
rd. Marsden Pk 182 A16
rd. Riverstone 182 A15
res. Surry Hills F K13
res. Surry Hills 4 C15
st. Balmain East 8 F7
st. Blacktown 244 J15
st. Mosman 317 D12
st. Oatley 461 C1

st. Waverton 5 A8
st. West Ryde 280 J14
CLIMUS
st. Hassall Gr 212 B15
CLINGAN
av. Lurnea 394 D9
CLINIC
cct. Narrabeen, off
Snake Gulley Cl 228 E8
CLINKER
gr. Woodcroft 243 F6
CLINTON
cl. Berowra Ht 132 J9
dr. Narellan 478 J11
st. Quakers Hill 214 B8
CLIO
la. Maroubra 407 C10
st. Sutherland 490 F1
st. Wiley Park 400 K4
CLIPPER
cl. Chipping Ntn 366 K15
CLIPSHAM
la. Gordon, off
St Johns Av 253 H8
CLISBY
wy. Matraville 437 C1
CLISDELL
av. Canterbury 402 D1
st. Surry Hills 19 J4
CLISSOLD
la. Campsie 372 A12
pde. Campsie 372 A12
rd. Wahroonga 223 C6
st. Ashfield 372 J6
st. Cmbrdg Pk 238 A7
CLIVE
cr. Bayview 168 H12
rd. Eastwood 281 A7
rd. Riverstone 182 F8
st. Fairfield 336 F15
st. Revesby 428 H5
st. Roseville 285 D3
st. Roseville Ch 285 D3
CLIVEDEN
ct. Wattle Grove 426 B3
CLONCURRY
pl. Wakeley 334 G14
CLONMORE
st. Kellyville 185 C16
st. Kellyville 215 C1
CLONTARF
cl. Woodbine 481 J10
st. Seaforth 287 A5
st. Seaforth 287 A7
CLOPTON
dr. Killara 254 C8
CLORINDA
st. Rooty Hill 272 C5
CLOSE
pl. Hebersham 241 F1
st. Canterbury 372 G14
st. S Coogee 407 J6
st. Thirlmere 564 J4
st. Thirlmere 565 A5
CLOTHIER
rd. Menai 459 A11
CLOUGH
av. Illawong 459 K2
CLOUTA
pl. Emu Plains 234 J9
CLOVE
la. Randwick, off
Darley La 377 B9
CLOVELLY
cct. Kellyville 215 F4
pl. Woodbine 481 F14
rd. Clovelly 377 F12
rd. Coogee 377 F12
rd. Hornsby 221 D3
rd. Randwick 377 B9
st. Clovelly 377 K13
st. Watsons Bay 318 G14
CLOVER
cl. Carlingford 279 J5
pl. Mcquarie Fd 454 E6
CLOVERDALE
cct. Glenmore Pk 266 F14
CLOVERTOP
pl. Wrrngtn Dns 238 B5
CLOWER
av. Rouse Hill 185 A8

CLUB
la. Ermington, off River Rd ...310 B3
CLUBB
cr. Miranda ...492 B3
st. Rozelle ...344 C7
CLUCAS
rd. Dharruk ...241 C10
rd. Regents Pk ...369 E1
CLUDEN
cl. Toongabbie ...276 H6
CLUMP
pl. Green Valley ...362 K10
CLUNE
cl. Casula ...424 E4
pl. Blackett ...241 D2
CLUNES
la. Canterbury ...372 D14
CLUNIES
pl. Bonnyrigg Ht ...363 F7
CLUNIES ROSS
st. Greystanes ...275 E16
st. Prospect ...275 E16
CLUSTER
pl. Cranebrook ...207 F11
CLWYDON
cl. Belrose ...226 B12
pl. Wahroonga ...222 E6
CLYBURN
av. Jamisontown ...266 B3
CLYDE
av. Cronulla ...493 K15
av. Moorebank ...396 E13
av. St Clair ...269 H14
la. Kurrajong Ht ...54 C14
pl. Campbelltwn ...511 K9
pl. Mt Hunter ...504 K7
pl. Wahroonga ...222 A14
rd. Dee Why ...258 K6
st. Croydon Pk ...372 A7
st. Granville ...308 G16
st. Guildford ...337 E4
st. North Bondi ...348 D14
st. Randwick ...377 C14
st. Rydalmere ...309 D2
st. Silverwater ...309 K8
st. S Granville ...338 F8
st. Vineyard ...152 F14
CLYDEBANK
cr. Glen Alpine ...510 A13
CLYDESDALE
dr. Blairmount ...480 K14
la. Richmond ...118 G13
pl. Pymble ...253 B2
CLYFFORD
pl. Panania ...428 E6
COACH HOUSE
pl. Bella Vista ...246 E2
pl. Kurrajong Ht ...53 K3
rd. Kurrajong Ht ...53 K3
COACHLINE
pl. Belrose ...226 A11
COACHMAN
cr. Kellyville ...215 B2
COACHWOOD
cl. Rouse Hill ...185 B7
cr. Alfords Point ...459 A2
cr. Bradbury ...511 F12
cr. Picton ...563 E13
COAL
st. Silverwater ...309 J10
COALLEE
pl. S Penrith ...267 A3
COAST
av. Cronulla ...494 A16
COAST HOSPITAL
rd. Little Bay ...437 G14
COASTVIEW
pl. Harbord ...258 K16
COATES
pl. Wetherill Pk ...303 J15
st. Mount Druitt ...271 D4
wy. Claymore ...481 A11
COATES PARK
rd. Cobbitty ...416 B14
COBAC
av. Eastwood ...280 J5
COBAH
rd. Arcadia ...129 E12
rd. Arcadia ...129 J7
rd. Fiddletown ...129 J7
COBAIN
pl. Acacia Gdn ...214 G15
COBAR
cl. Wakeley ...334 H13
pl. Cartwright ...394 A4
pl. Erskine Park ...270 K16
st. Dulwich Hill ...373 A9
st. Greystanes ...305 H3
st. Willoughby ...285 C14
wy. Mcquarie Pk ...282 E4
COBARGO
rd. Gymea Bay ...491 C10
COBB
av. Jamisontown ...266 C1
la. Blacktown, off Campbell St ...244 H16
pl. Ambarvale ...511 B14
st. Frenchs Frst ...256 E4
COBBADAH
av. Pennant Hills ...250 J4
pl. Harbord ...258 D15
COBBETT
st. Wetherill Pk ...334 D4
st. Wetherill Pk ...334 F3
COBBITTEE
la. Mosman, off Cobbittee St ...317 G9
st. Mosman ...317 G9
COBBITTY
av. Croydon Pk ...371 K6
rd. Brownlow Hl ...475 H2
rd. Cobbitty ...447 C14
rd. Harringtn Pk ...447 J13
rd. Harringtn Pk ...448 D13
rd. Oran Park ...448 D13
COBBITY
av. Wrrngtn Dns ...237 K3
st. Seven Hills ...246 C14
COBBLE
cct. West Hoxton ...391 K10
COBBLER
cr. Minchinbury ...271 F9
COBBLERS
cl. Kellyville ...186 H16
COBBLERS BEACH
rd. Mosman ...317 J6
COBBLESTONE
ct. Glenhaven ...218 B4
gr. Woodcroft ...243 F9
pl. Wrrngtn Dns ...238 C5
COBBY
pl. Bidwill ...211 C14
COBCROFT
rd. Wilberforce ...61 K13
COBDEN
av. Lane Cove ...314 G2
la. Enfield ...371 H2
la. Belmore, off Rydge St ...401 G1
st. Belmore ...401 H1
st. Enfield ...371 H3
COBHAM
av. Melrose Pk ...280 H15
la. Melrose Pk ...280 H15
st. Horsley Pk ...332 D2
st. Ingleburn ...453 B6
st. Kings Park ...244 E5
st. Maroubra ...406 G10
st. Yanderra ...567 B16
COBOURG
pl. Bow Bowing ...452 D13
COBRA
pl. Raby ...451 B14
st. Cranebrook ...207 B9
COBRAN
rd. Cheltenham ...251 B9
COBURG
pl. St Johns Pk ...364 G1
rd. Wilberforce ...61 K15
rd. Wilberforce ...92 C1
COCHRAN
pl. Abbotsbury ...333 B14
COCHRANE
st. Minto ...482 J10
COCKATIEL
cct. Green Valley ...363 F10
COCKATOO
cl. Hinchinbrk ...363 A14
la. St Clair, off Cockatoo Rd ...270 J14
rd. Erskine Park ...270 J14
COCKBURN
cr. Fairfield E ...336 J12
COCKLE
pl. N Turramrra ...193 D15
COCKROFT
pl. Lucas Ht ...487 J11
COCKTHORPE
rd. Auburn ...339 F7
COCO
dr. Glenmore Pk ...266 A7
COCOS
av. Eastwood ...281 A4
cl. Green Valley ...363 C10
pl. Quakers Hill ...213 F13
COCUPARA
av. Lindfield ...283 K3
CODLIN
st. Ambarvale ...510 J12
CODRINGTON
st. Darlington ...18 F7
st. Fairfield ...336 B15
CODY
pl. Oakhurst ...242 A4
COE
pl. Riverstone ...183 C8
COEN
cl. Bossley Park ...333 F11
COFFEY
st. Ermington ...310 B4
wy. Claymore, off Colquhoun Wy ...481 C11
COFFS HARBOUR
av. Hoxton Park ...392 K9
COFTON
ct. Wrrngtn Cty ...238 F6
COGAN
pl. Lane Cove ...314 H5
COGGINS
pl. Mascot ...404 K2
COGHILL
st. Narellan ...478 E10
COGHLAN
cr. Doonside ...243 A14
COHEN
av. Rookwood ...339 K11
st. Fairlight ...288 C8
st. Merrylands ...308 C15
COILA
pl. Woodpark ...306 G14
st. Turramurra ...223 A10
COLAC
pl. Marayong ...243 J7
COLAH
rd. Mt Colah ...192 C4
COLANE
st. Concord W ...311 E15
COLBARRA
pl. W Pnnant Hl ...249 B6
COLBECK
st. Tregear ...240 E5
COLBOURNE
av. Glebe ...12 D12
COLBRAN
av. Kenthurst ...187 A9
COLDEN
st. Picton ...563 G4
COLDENHAM
dr. Picton ...561 F3
wy. Airds ...512 A13
COLDSTREAM
st. S Coogee ...407 G5
COLE
av. Baulkham Hl ...246 F12
cr. Liberty Gr ...311 B10
la. Bankstown ...369 D16
la. Hurstville ...432 B7
pl. St Marys ...269 E2
st. Brooklyn ...75 G12
st. S Hurstville ...432 B8
COLEBEE
cr. Hassall Gr ...212 A13
pl. Narellan ...478 E15
COLEBORNE
av. Mortdale ...431 C8
COLECHIN
st. Yagoona ...368 G13
COLEMAN
av. Bankstown ...369 C15
av. Carlingford ...279 J5
av. Homebush ...341 A6
av. Regents Pk ...369 D1
pl. Blacktown ...244 F9
rd. Minto Ht ...483 D9
rd. Wedderburn ...540 B10
st. Mascot ...405 A5
st. Merrylands ...307 D7
st. S Wntwthvle ...307 D7
COLENSO
cr. Daceyville ...406 F3
COLERAINE
av. Killarney Ht ...256 B15
st. Fairfield ...336 B14
COLERIDGE
rd. Wetherill Pk ...334 H5
st. Leichhardt ...10 D15
st. Pymble ...223 D16
st. Riverwood ...399 K14
COLES
pde. Newport ...169 J9
rd. Harbord ...258 D15
st. Concord ...341 J9
COLETTA
pl. Prestons ...393 C14
COLETTE
pl. East Killara ...254 G8
COLEVILE
pl. Rsemeadow ...540 H8
COLEY
pl. Bligh Park ...150 H8
COLGATE
av. Balmain ...8 B9
COLIN
av. Riverwood ...400 A16
pl. Carlingford ...249 G13
pl. Westleigh ...220 H4
st. Cammeray ...316 A4
st. Lakemba ...370 H15
COLINDIA
av. Neutral Bay ...6 C7
COLING
pl. Quakers Hill ...214 D13
COLL
pl. St Andrews ...482 A3
COLLARENEBRI
rd. Hinchinbrk ...392 H4
COLLAROY
av. Peakhurst ...430 G1
rd. Woodbine ...481 K10
st. Collaroy ...229 A12
COLLEEN
av. Picnic Point ...428 B6
cl. Cherrybrook ...219 K5
COLLEGE
cr. Hornsby ...221 G4
cr. St Ives ...224 C12
dr. Richmond ...118 G10
la. Darlinghurst ...F G1
la. Petersham ...16 C13
la. Rose Bay ...347 G12
la. Bellevue Hill, off Cranbrook Rd ...347 F12
rd. Campbelltwn ...511 J9
rd.n, Lane Cove ...314 A3
rd.s, Riverview ...313 K5
st. Balmain ...7 G8
st. Cmbrdg Pk ...237 H10
st. Croydon ...342 E16
st. Darlinghurst ...D G16
st. Darlinghurst ...4 A8
st. Drummoyne ...343 J3
st. Gladesville ...312 G5
st. Liverpool ...395 F3
st. Manly ...288 K12
st. Newtown ...17 E15
st. Richmond ...118 H8
st. Sydney ...D G16
st. Sydney ...4 A8
COLLEN
pl. Cranebrook ...207 D13
COLLESS
st. Penrith ...237 B14
COLLETT
cr. Kings Lngly ...246 C9
pde. N Parramatta ...278 K15
COLLEY
pl. Hebersham ...241 G3
COLLICOTT
pl. Barden Rdg ...488 G2
COLLIE
ct. Wattle Grove ...395 H12
pl. Bonnyrigg ...364 A8
COLLIER
av. Beverly Hills ...401
cl. St Helens Park ...541
pl. Maroubra ...407
COLLIMORE
av. Liverpool ...395
COLLING
av. Wrrngtn Cty ...238
COLLINGS
st. Wahroonga ...222
COLLINGWOOD
av. Cabarita ...342
av. Earlwood ...402
st. Bronte ...378
st. Drummoyne ...343
st. Manly ...288
st. Woolwich ...314
COLLINS
av. Lurnea ...394
av. Rose Bay ...348
cl. Edensor Pk ...363
cr. Lapstone ...264
cr. Yagoona ...368
ct. Rouse Hill ...184
gr. Mt Annan ...479
la. Annandale ...10
la. Surry Hills ...20
la. Beaconsfield, off Collins St ...375
pl. Engadine ...488
prm. Ingleburn ...453
prm. Minto ...453
rd. St Ives ...223
rd. St Ives Ch ...223
st. Alexandria ...375
st. Annandale ...17
st. Beaconsfield ...375
st. Belmore ...401
st. N Narrabeen ...199
st. North Ryde ...282
st. Pagewood ...406
st. Pendle Hill ...276
st. Rozelle ...7
st. St Marys ...269
st. Seven Hills ...245
st. Surry Hills ...20
st. Tempe ...404
COLLINS BEACH
rd. Manly ...288
COLLINSVILLE
pl. Miller ...393
COLLIS
pl. Minto ...452
COLLITH
av. S Windsor ...150
COLLITT
cr. Cranebrook ...207
la. Cranebrook, off Sherringham La ...207
COLLY
pl. Busby ...363
COLO
ct. Wattle Grove ...395
la. Blacktown ...274
pl. Campbelltwn ...512
pl. Greystanes ...306
st. Couridjah ...564
COLONEL BRAUND
cr. Daceyville ...406
COLONEL PYE
dr. Cobbitty ...416
COLONEL WOODS
dr. Narrabeen ...228
COLONG
cl. Hoxton Park ...392
cr. Leumeah ...482
COLONIAL
ct. Winston Hills ...277
dr. Bligh Park ...150
pl. Casula ...395
st. Campbelltwn ...511
COLOOLI
lp. Narrabeen, off Stack St ...228
rd. Narrabeen ...228
COLORADO
dr. St Clair ...270
st. Kearns ...450
COLOSSEUM
cr. Baulkham Hl ...246
COLQUHOUN
st. Rosehill ...309
wy. Claymore ...481

LSON
Monterey 433 G6
Wrrngtn Cty 238 F5
LSTON
Ryde 281 K16
LT
Cranebrook 237 F1
LUMBA
St Clair, off
Columba Pl 270 G16
Erskine Park 300 G1
LUMBIA
Baulkham Hl 216 K14
Homebush 341 E9
Seven Hills 275 C10
Kearns 450 J16
. Baulkham Hl 216 J14
LUMBINE
Bankstown 399 H4
Punchbowl 399 H4
Loftus 489 J7
LUMBUS
St Clair 270 H11
LVILLE
Bonnyrigg Ht 363 C7
Yellow Rock 204 H1
Kings Lngly 246 A7
LVIN
Carlton 432 H10
Kingsgrove 401 K11
Denistone E 281 H9
Frenchs Frst 256 A1
LWELL
Chatswd W 284 C12
Kingsgrove 401 F13
LYTON
Minchinbury 271 E6
MANCHE
Bossley Park 333 K12
MANECI
Newington 310 B12
MBARA
Caringbah 492 K9
Castle Hill 247 F1
MBE
West Pymble 252 F12
MBER
Pendle Hill 276 F13
Paddington 4 H14
MBERFORD
Prairiewood 334 D10
MBET
Minchinbury 271 H9
MBINGS
Currans Hill 480 A10
MBLES
e. Matraville 407 A16
MBOYNE
Hoxton Park 392 H9
St Clair 270 B16
MER
Burwood 341 K12
MEROY
Frenchs Frst 256 F1
MET
. Kellyville 185 K13
. St Clair 270 E15
Raby 481 G3
Springwood 172 G15
Ashfield 342 J16
METROWE
Drummoyne 343 G2
MIN
Abbotsbury 333 C10
MLEROY
Blaxlands Rdg 56 D4
Comleroy 56 A12
Kurrajong 55 J14
MMERCE
Glenbrook 264 A1
Balgowlah Ht, off
Dobroyd Rd 287 J14
MMERCIAL
Regents Pk 338 K16
Merrylands, off
Bertha St 308 A16
Kellyville 185 B11
Kingsgrove 401 J10
Lalor Park 245 E12
Lilyfield 9 H6
Rouse Hill 185 B11
Vineyard 152 E3

COMMISSIONERS
rd. Denistone 281 G13
COMMODORE
cr. McMahons Pt 5 A10
st. McMahons Pt 5 B10
st. Newtown 374 H10
COMMONS
st. Hurlstone Pk 373 A13
COMMONWEALTH
av. Mosman 317 G11
cr. N St Marys 239 H8
la. Surry Hills F D14
pde. Manly 288 E10
rd. Lindfield 254 A15
st. Surry Hills F C15
st. Surry Hills 3 J15
st. Sydney F D9
st. Sydney 3 K12
COMMUNITY
pl. Greenacre 370 C12
COMO
cl. St Clair 269 G14
ct. Wattle Grove 395 K14
la. Cremorne 316 C7
la. St Clair, off
Como Cl 269 G14
pde. Como 460 H5
pde. Como 460 H6
pl. St Johns Pk 364 H3
rd. Greenacre 370 D5
rd. Oyster Bay 461 C7
st. Blakehurst 462 C2
st. Merrylands W 307 C13
COMPER
st. Bnkstn Aprt 397 K1
COMPTON
av. Lurnea 394 E9
grn. W Pnnant Hl 249 C6
st. Bass Hill 368 B6
CONCETTINA
dr. Prestons 392 H14
CONCISE
st. Balgowlah Ht 287 K13
CONCORD
av. Concord W 311 C16
la. Erskineville, off
Concord St 374 K10
la. N Strathfield, off
Nelson Rd 341 F7
pl. Gladesville 312 J8
pl. St Johns Pk 364 H4
rd. Concord 341 E1
rd. Concord W 341 E1
rd. N Strathfield 341 E1
rd. Rhodes 311 D9
st. Erskineville 374 K10
CONCORDE
pl. Raby 451 H16
pl. St Clair 270 F14
CONDAMINE
st. Allambie Ht 257 K14
st. Balgowlah 287 K8
st. Campbelltwn 511 G6
st. Manly Vale 287 K4
st. North Manly 257 K14
st.s, Balgowlah 287 J12
st.s, Balgowlah Ht 287 J12
CONDELLO
cr. Edensor Pk 333 H14
CONDER
av. Mt Pritchard 364 J12
st. Burwood 341 J16
wy. Claymore 481 B12
CONDON
av. Panania 428 F3
st. Caringbah 492 H9
CONDOR
cr. Blakehurst 432 A13
pl. Abbotsbury 333 B12
pl. Glenmore Pk 266 A13
st. Quakers Hill 214 F13
CONDOVER
st. N Balgowlah 287 G5
CONEILL
pl. Forest Lodge 11 E12
CONEY
rd. Earlwood 402 J3
CONFERTA
ct. Wattle Grove 396 B16
CONGEWOI
la. Mosman 316 H4
rd. Mosman 316 J4

CONGHAM
rd. West Pymble 252 H12
CONGO
pl. Kearns 451 A14
CONGRESSIONAL
dr. Liverpool 395 B9
CONIE
av. Baulkham Hl 247 G12
CONIFER
cl. Stanhpe Gdn 215 D11
ct. Greystanes 306 F10
pl. Engadine 518 F3
CONISTON
pl. Castle Hill 247 K5
st. Collaroy Plat 228 D11
CONJOLA
cr. Leumeah 482 F15
pl. Gymea Bay 491 C10
pl. Hamondvle 396 F14
pl. Woodcroft 243 F11
CONLAN
st. Bligh Park 150 K7
CONNAUGHT
st. Brookvale 258 B8
st. Narraweena 258 B8
CONNECTICUT
av. Five Dock 343 B11
CONNELL
cl. Baulkham Hl 246 K4
rd. Oyster Bay 461 F6
CONNELLAN
cr. Picton 563 E9
CONNELLS POINT
rd. Connells Pt 431 K14
rd. S Hurstville 431 K14
CONNELLY
st. Penshurst 431 F5
CONNELS
rd. Cronulla 493 G11
rd. Woolooware 493 G11
CONNEMARA
av. Killarney Ht 286 C2
CONNEMARRA
st. Bexley 432 J2
CONNER
cl. Liberty Gr 311 B10
CONNOLLY
av. Padstow Ht 429 D6
la. Beaconsfield, off
Reserve St 375 F12
CONNOR
pl. Illawong 459 D7
pl. Rouse Hill 185 C7
pl. Tahmoor 565 J9
CONRAD
rd. Kellyville 215 A6
st. North Ryde 283 B13
st. Richmond 118 J7
st. Wetherill Pk 334 D6
CONROY
la. Revesby 398 H15
rd. Wattle Grove 426 B3
CONSERVATORIUM
rd. Sydney B H10
rd. Sydney 2 B13
CONSETT
av. Bondi Beach 378 C3
st. Concord W 341 D2
st. Dulwich Hill 373 D10
CONSOLO
av. Glenwood 215 G10
CONSTANCE
av. Oxley Park 240 E15
cl. Epping 251 C12
st. Guildford 338 A3
st. Revesby 398 K13
CONSTELLATION
rd. Mascot 404 K4
CONSTITUTION
ct. Carlingford 279 D4
la. Dulwich Hill, off
Union St 373 C8
rd. Dulwich Hill 373 C8
rd. Meadowbnk 311 E3
rd. Ryde 311 E3
rd. Wentwthvle 277 B9
rd.w, Meadowbnk 311 B2
rd.w, West Ryde 311 B2
CONSUL
rd. Brookvale 258 A9
rd.n, Narraweena 258 A7

CONTAPLAS
st. Arndell Park 273 F7
CONTINUA
ct. Wattle Grove 396 C15
CONVAIR
pl. Raby 451 E12
CONVENT
la. Marrickville 373 K12
la. Woollahra 22 K5
CONVICT
pl. Castle Hill 218 F13
CONWAY
av. Cmbrdg Pk 237 H10
av. Concord W 341 C3
av. N Strathfield 341 C3
av. Randwick 377 F11
av. Rose Bay 348 C9
av. St Ives 224 K2
ct. Baulkham Hl 247 A3
pl. Kings Lngly 245 F6
pl. Oatlands 279 C13
pl. St Peters 374 G13
rd. Bankstown 369 F14
st. Menai 458 K9
COOBA
pl. Mcquarie Fd 454 E2
st. Lidcombe 339 J6
COODE
pl. Bonnyrigg 364 B5
COOEEYANA
pde. Mt Lewis 370 B15
COOGAN
pl. Campbelltwn 511 E4
pl. Dean Park 212 H16
COOGARAH
st. Blakehurst 462 D2
COOGEE
pl. Woodbine 481 D15
st. Randwick 377 C14
COOGEE BAY
rd. Coogee 377 C15
rd. Randwick 377 C15
COOGHANS
la. Five Dock, off
Lyons Rd W 342 K8
COOINDA
cl. Marsfield 281 J1
pl. Baulkham Hl 248 B7
pl. Bilgola 169 F5
pl. Doonside 243 A14
pl. Northmead 278 A2
st. Colyton 270 G6
st. Engadine 489 D14
st. Seven Hills 246 A14
COOK
av. Canada Bay 342 D8
av. Canley Vale 366 G3
av. Daceyville 406 F4
cr. East Hills 427 F5
la. Bondi Jctn 22 K6
la. St Clair, off
Cook Pde 269 J14
la. Mortdale, off
Cook St 431 C7
la. St Marys, off
Cook St 269 H3
la. Zetland, off
Joynton Av 375 J10
pde. St Clair 269 J16
pl. Lalor Park 245 C13
pl. West Hoxton 392 B11
rd. Centnnial Pk 21 C11
rd. Killara 253 K15
rd. Marrickville 374 D10
rd. Moore Park 21 C11
rd. Oakhurst 241 J1
rd. Oyster Bay 461 D4
rd. Ruse 512 G2
st. Baulkham Hl 247 K13
st. Caringbah 492 J14
st. Croydon Pk 371 K7
st. Forestville 256 B10
st. Glebe 11 J8
st. Kurnell 466 B10
st. Lewisham 15 B7
st. Lidcombe 339 G9
st. Mortdale 431 C7
st. North Ryde 282 C8
st. Randwick 377 A12
st. Rozelle 10 H1
st. St Marys 269 H3
st. Sutherland 490 F4
st. Telopea 279 J9
st. Tempe 404 A3

st. Turrella 403 D6
st. Woolooware 493 H7
tce. Mona Vale 199 D9
COOKE
wy. Epping 250 G14
COOKNEY
pl. West Hoxton 392 C10
COOKS
av. Canterbury 372 D15
la. Canterbury, off
Cooks Av 372 D15
COOKSEY
av. Harbord 258 H14
COOKSON
pl. Glenwood 215 C13
COOKS RIVER
av. Mascot 404 C7
COOLABAH
av. Greenwich 315 A8
av. Turramurra 223 C11
cl. Thornleigh 221 B7
cr. Forestville 256 C9
cr. Glenmore Pk 266 F12
la. Greenwich 315 A8
pl. Blacktown 273 K6
pl. Caringbah 492 J3
pl. Mcquarie Fd 454 G1
pl. Turramurra 223 C11
rd. Valley Ht 202 F9
st. Beverly Hills 401 C9
COOLAH
av. Campbelltwn 511 K7
pl. Lansvale 366 G8
wy. Hoxton Park 392 G8
COOLALIE
av. Camden S 507 B11
pl. Allambie Ht 257 F16
pl. Kenthurst 157 B9
st. Villawood 367 E4
COOLAMON
cl. Arcadia 130 J9
rd. Agnes Banks 146 A3
COOLANGATTA
av. Burraneer 493 E15
av. Elanora Ht 198 D16
COOLARN
st. Chipping Ntn 396 H4
COOLAROO
cr. Lurnea 394 G7
rd. Lane Cove W 284 C13
COOLATAI
cr. Bossley Park 333 G12
COOLAWIN
rd. Avalon 169 K2
rd. Northbridge 286 F16
COOLEEN
la. Blakehurst 432 B13
st. Blakehurst 432 C13
COOLEENA
rd. Elanora Ht 198 F13
COOLGARDIE
pl. Sutherland 460 D14
COOLGUN
la. Eastwood 281 A8
COOLIBAH
la. S Penrith, off
Coolibah Pl 266 H6
pl. S Penrith 266 G6
st. Castle Hill 218 B11
st. Merrylands W 306 K12
COOLIBAR
st. Canley Ht 365 A1
COOLIDGE
cr. Bonnet Bay 460 A8
COOLINGA
st. Mcquarie Pk 282 H5
COOLOCK
cr. Baulkham Hl 247 C2
COOLONG
cr. St Clair 269 H8
rd. Vaucluse 348 B1
st. Castle Hill 217 G16
COOLOONGATTA
rd. Beverly Hills 401 B10
COOLOWIE
rd. Terrey Hills 195 K9
COOLUM
pl. Yowie Bay 492 C10
COOMA
ct. Wattle Grove 396 B16
rd. Greystanes 305 G3
st. Carramar 366 H1

st. Dharruk 241 C8

COOMALIE
av. Castle Hill 248 F2

COOMASSIE
av. Faulconbdg 201 C1

COOMBAH
pl. Engadine 518 G7

COOMBES
dr. Penrith 237 A6

COONABARABRAN
cr. Hoxton Park 392 J7
pl. Caringbah 493 C14

COONAH
pde. Riverview 313 H6

COONAMBLE
st. Hoxton Park 392 G7

COONANBARRA
rd. N Wahrnga 222 E3
rd. Wahroonga 222 D7

COONANGA
rd. Avalon 140 E15

COONARA
av. W Pnnant Hl 249 A4

COONARDOO
cl. Canada Bay 342 F9
pl. Castle Hill 218 A12

COONAWARRA
dr. St Clair 270 E13
rd. Terrey Hills 195 H8
st. Edensor Pk 333 D16

COONEY
rd. Artarmon 285 B15
st. North Ryde 282 G9

COONGRA
st. Busby 363 G12

COONONG
rd. Concord W 311 D15
rd. Gymea Bay 491 D12
st. Busby 363 H15
wy. Airds 512 E10

COOPER
av. Moorebank 395 F8
av. Newington, off Jordan Av 310 B15
cl. Beacon Hill 257 K5
cr. Smithfield 336 C5
cr. Wahroonga 222 B15
ct. Castle Hill 218 C10
la. Maroubra 407 C11
la. Paddington 13 A14
la. Surry Hills 19 K1
la. Cremorne, off Belgrave St 316 D8
la. Neutral Bay, off Belgrave St 316 D8
la. Yagoona, off Cooper Rd 369 B12
la. Penrith, off Cooper St 237 E3
la. Strathfield, off Cooper St 341 G11
pl. Currans Hill 479 H9
pl. Zetland 376 A10
rd. Birrong 369 B7
rd. Yagoona 369 B10
st. Balmain 8 C9
st. Blacktown 274 D3
st. Double Bay 14 A9
st. Engadine 518 H5
st. Kingsford 407 C7
st. Maroubra 407 C9
st. Marsfield 282 A5
st. Paddington 13 A13
st. Penrith 237 C3
st. Penrith 237 E3
st. Redfern 19 H7
st. Smithfield 305 H15
st. Strathfield 341 G11
st. Surry Hills 19 J1
st. Waterloo 19 C12

COOPERNOOK
av. E Lindfield 255 B11
av. Gymea Bay 491 G13

COOPER PARK
rd. Bellevue Hill 347 F16

COOPWORTH
rd. Elderslie 507 K2

COORA
av. Belrose 225 J15
pl. Connells Pt 431 G15
rd. Westleigh 220 G3
rd. Yowie Bay 492 B12
st. Sans Souci 433 F16

COORABAN
rd. Milperra 398 B6

COORABIN
pl. Riverwood 400 C12
rd. Northbridge 286 C14

COORADILLA
pl. Bradbury 541 E1

COORI
pl. Bonnyrigg 364 A9

COORIENGAH HEIGHTS
rd. Engadine 488 F13

COORILLA
av. Croydon Pk 372 D9

COOROY
cr. Yellow Rock 204 K1

COORUMBENE
ct. Bella Vista 246 H1

COOT
pl. Erskine Park 270 K14
pl. Hinchinbrk 363 E16

COOTAMUNDRA
dr. Allambie Ht 257 E13
rd. Hornsby Ht 161 J7

COOTHA
cl. Bossley Park 334 C5

COOWARRA
dr. St Clair 270 B16
la. St Clair, off Coowarra Dr 300 B1

COOYAL
pl. Glenwood 215 F16

COOYONG
cr. Toongabbie 276 D7
rd. Terrey Hills 196 A8

COPAIN
pl. S Penrith 266 H4

COPE
pl. Bass Hill 368 C12
st. Lane Cove 313 G4
st. Lane Cove W 313 G4
st. Redfern 19 B10
st. Waterloo 19 C12

COPELAND
av. Newtown 18 A12
la. Alexandria 18 E15
rd. Beecroft 249 K8
rd. Emerton 240 G2
rd. Engadine 518 G6
rd. Heathcote 518 G9
rd. Lethbrdg Pk 240 G2
rd. Wilberforce 61 K16
rd.e, Beecroft 250 F6
st. Alexandria 18 E15
st. Erskineville 18 E15
st. Liverpool 395 C3
st. Penrith 237 D10
st. Richmond 119 A5

COPPABELLA
cr. Bradbury 511 G15
rd. Middle Dural 158 J9

COPPERFIELD
dr. Ambarvale 510 K16
dr. Rsemeadow 540 J5

COPPERLEAF
pl. Castle Hill 248 H3
pl. Cherrybrook 219 H7
wy. Castle Hill 248 G4

COPPIN
pl. Doonside 243 C5
pl. Shalvey 211 B13

COPPINS
cl. St Ives 254 B1
pl. Castle Hill 248 A5

COPPLESTONE
pl. Castle Hill 218 J7

COPPSLEIGH
cl. Westleigh 220 G6

COQUET
wy. Green Valley 363 A11

CORAKI
av. Campbelltwn 512 A6
cl. Bonnyrigg 363 K8
pl. Westleigh 220 D8
rd. Bass Hill 367 K5

CORAL
av. Kentlyn 513 A3
av. Padstow 399 B16
cl. Avalon 140 E10
cr. Kellyville 216 G6
ct. Cherrybrook 220 A7
la. Cmbrdg Pk, off Coral Pl 238 C7
pl. Cmbrdg Pk 238 C7
pl. Canley Vale 366 C2
pl. N Richmond 87 B15
pl. Quakers Hill 213 F14
rd. Woolooware 493 C11
st. Balgowlah 287 E9
st. Marsfield 281 J1

CORALGUM
pl. Blacktown 275 A4

CORAL HEATH
av. Westleigh 220 G8

CORALIE
st. Wareemba 343 A4

CORAL PEA
ct. Colyton 270 H6

CORAL TREE
dr. Carlingford 249 G11
dr. Carlingford 249 H11

CORAMANDEL
av. Winmalee 173 J7

CORAMBA
st. N Balgowlah 287 C5

CORANG
rd. Westleigh 220 G6
st. Ruse 512 C8

CORANTO
st. Wareemba 343 A5

CORBEN
av. Moorebank 396 C11
st. Surry Hills F F16
st. Surry Hills 4 A16

CORBETT
pl. Barden Rdg 488 G5
st. Bankstown 369 F12

CORBIERE
gr. Stanhpe Gdn 215 A5

CORBIN
av. Quakers Hill 214 E8
av. S Penrith 266 K5
st. Ingleburn 453 E13

CORBY
av. Concord 342 C7
pl. Chipping Ntn 366 G16

CORCORAN
st. Riverstone 182 D13

CORD
pl. Ingleburn 453 K8

CORDEAUX
cr. Sylvania Wtr 462 E14
st. Campbelltwn 511 F4
st. Leppington 420 B6

CORDELIA
cr. Green Valley 363 B11
cr. Rooty Hill 271 J3
st. Rsemeadow 540 J6

CORDEN
av. Five Dock 342 H8

CORDNERS
la. Cornwallis 90 K15

COREA
st. Miranda 461 K14
st. Sylvania 461 K12

COREE
pl. St Ives 224 B15
rd. Artarmon 284 K13

COREEN
av. Cecil Park 331 F10
av. Loftus 489 K6
av. Peakhurst 430 H3
av. Penrith 237 A7
av. Terrey Hills 196 D4
cl. Berowra Ht 132 K3
pl. Banksia 403 H12
pl. Blaxland 234 E9

CORELLA
cr. Glenmore Pk 266 C13
ct. W Pnnant Hl 249 D6
rd. Green Valley 363 F10
rd. Kirrawee 491 B6
rd. Lalor Park 245 J11
st. Harbord 258 H14
wy. Westleigh 220 J9

CORELLI
cr. Clarmnt Ms 268 G4

CORE PARK
rd. Warragamba 353 E3

CORFIELD
rd. Prestons 422 K1

CORFU
st. Woolmloo 4 F7

CORIN
wy. Bonnyrigg 364 A5

CORINDA
st. St Johns Pk 364 D1

CORINDI
cl. Hoxton Park 392 J8

CORINGLE
cl. Woodcroft 243 F11

CORINNE
st. Acacia Gdn 214 G15

CORINTH
rd. Heathcote 518 E7

CORIO
dr. St Clair 299 K2
la. St Clair, off Corio Dr 299 K2
rd. Prairiewood 334 J8

CORISH
cir. Bnksmeadw 406 E12
cir. Eastgardens 406 E12

CORK
pl. Bidwill 211 D16

CORKERY
cr. Allambie Ht 257 G13

CORLETTE
wy. Bonnyrigg 364 B3

CORLISS
st. Regents Pk 369 A2

CORMACK
pl. Glendenning 242 E3
rd. Beacon Hill 257 J4
st. Balgowlah 287 K7

CORMISTON
av. Concord 341 K5

CORMO
cl. Elderslie 507 J3

CORMORANT
av. Hinchinbrk 393 E1
cr. Glenmore Pk 265 J13
st. Grays Point 491 D15

CORNDEW
cr. Wrrngtn Dns 238 A5
la. Wrrngtn Dns, off Corndew Cr 238 A5

CORNELIA
rd. Middle Dural 158 C5
rd. Toongabbie 276 A7
st. Wiley Park 400 F1

CORNELIAN
av. Eagle Vale 481 G5

CORNELIUS
la. Regentville, off Cornelius Pl 265 J4
pl. Regentville 265 H4

CORNELL
st. Blacktown 275 C2
st. Leonay 235 C15

CORNHILL
pl. Cherrybrook 219 F8

CORNICHE
rd. Church Point 168 G10

CORNISH
av. Beacon Hill 257 H6

CORNOCK
av. Toongabbie 276 G10

CORNUTA
cl. Narellan Vale 478 K15

CORNWALL
av. Turramurra 222 F16
pl. Bella Vista 246 H4
rd. Auburn 339 A11
rd. Ingleburn 453 A6
st. Agnes Banks 117 E15
st. N Epping 251 H11

CORNWALLIS
la. Redfern 19 A9
rd. Cornwallis 120 J7
st. Eveleigh 18 K9
st. Redfern 19 A9

CORNWELL
av. Hobartville 118 C8
rd. Allambie Ht 287 J1

CORNWELLS
la. Richmond Lwld 88 H14

COROMANDEL
cl. Baulkham Hl 246 H5
rd. Ebenezer 63 G7
wy. Minto 482 H6

CORONA
av. Roseville 284 G6
rd. Fairfield W 335 C13

CORONATA
wy. Mcquarie Fd 424 D16

CORONATION
av. Cronulla 493
av. Eastwood 280
av. Five Dock 343
av. Kings Park 244
av. Mosman 317
av. Peakhurst 430
av. Petersham 15
dr. Green Valley 363
gr. Cmbrdg Gdn 237
la. Cmbrdg Gdn, off Coronation Gr 237
pde. Enfield 371
pde. Strathfield S 371
rd. Baulkham Hl 247
st. Mona Vale 199
st. Hornsby, off Jersey St 191

CORONET
ct. North Rocks 278

CORONGA
cr. Killara 253

CORR
la. Werrington 238

CORREA
ct. Voyager Pt 427
pl. Mcquarie Fd 454

CORREY
pl. Carlingford 279

CORREYS
av. Concord 341
av. N Strathfield 341

CORRIE
rd. North Manly 258

CORRIEDALE
cl. Elderslie 507
st. Miller 393
st. Wakeley 364

CORRIN
ct. Wattle Grove 396

CORRY
ct. N Parramatta 278
st. Bonnyrigg 363

CORRYONG
st. Fairfield W 335

CORRYTON
ct. Wattle Grove 425
pl. Glen Alpine 510

CORSAIR
cr. Cranebrook 207
st. Raby 481

CORUNDUM
cl. Eagle Vale 481

CORUNNA
av. Leumeah 482
av. North Rocks 279
la. Stanmore 16
rd. Eastwood 281
rd. Petersham 16
rd. Stanmore 16

CORVUS
cl. Glenmore Pk 265
rd. Hinchinbrk 393

CORY
av. Padstow 399
pl. Prospect 274

CORYMBIA
cct. Oxford Falls 226

CORYULE
pl. Warriewood 199

COSFORD
cl. Chipping Ntn 396

COSGROVE
cr. Kingswood 238
rd. Belfield 371
rd. Strathfield S 370

COSIMO
st. Ryde 282
st. Toongabbie 276

COSMOS
pl. Mcquarie Fd 454

COSSINGTON
wy. Claymore 481

COSTAIN
pl. Seven Hills 275

COSTATA
ct. Voyager Pt 427
pl. Mcquarie Fd 454

COSTELLO
pl. Seven Hills 246

COSTENS POINT
rd. Royal N P 522

CRESS
pl. Mcquarie Fd 454 F6
pl. Quakers Hill 243 E4
CRESSBROOK
dr. Wattle Grove 425 K3
CRESSFIELD
av. Carlingford 279 F4
CRESSY
av. Kellyville 215 H3
rd. East Ryde 282 J15
rd. Mt Vernon 331 A14
rd. North Ryde 282 J15
rd. North Ryde 283 A13
rd. Ryde 312 E4
rd. Ryde 312 H1
st. Canterbury 372 D16
st. Rosebery 375 H13
CREST
pl. Engadine 488 C15
pl. Jamisontown 266 C4
pl. Kellyville 215 D2
pl. Stanhpe Gdn 215 D2
rd. Warragamba 353 B4
CRESTA
cl. St Ives 224 A13
CRESTANI
pl. Edensor Pk 333 J16
CRESTBROOK
st. Seven Hills 245 C15
CRESTREEF
dr. Acacia Gdn 214 G15
CRESTVIEW
av. Kellyville 216 G1
dr. Glenwood 246 B5
pl. Cherrybrook 219 D13
pl. Cranebrook 207 A12
CRESTWOOD
av. Thornleigh 221 B5
dr. Baulkham Hl 246 J3
wk. Baulkham Hl 247 B7
CRESWELL
st. Revesby 398 E14
CRESWICK
pl. Dharruk 241 D8
CRETE
pl. E Lindfield 254 K11
pl. Lugarno 429 K8
st. Narraweena 258 D6
CRETNEY
pl. Peakhurst 430 D7
CREWE
pl. Rosebery 375 J14
st. Bardwell Pk 402 J7
CREWS
rd. Seven Hills 246 B11
CRICHTON
st. Rooty Hill 272 G1
CRICK
av. Elizabeth Bay 13 A4
st. Chatswood 285 B7
CRICKETERS ARMS
rd. Prospect 274 F16
CRIEFF
st. Ashbury 372 D9
CRIMEA
rd. Marsfield 251 H14
st. Parramatta 307 H7
CRIMSON
la. Ashbury 372 H6
st. Ashbury 372 H6
CRINAN
ct. Castle Hill 218 D7
la. Hurlstone Pk 372 K11
st. Hurlstone Pk 372 K11
CRINUM
pl. Mcquarie Fd 454 F5
CRIPPLE
rd. Blaxland 233 G4
CRIPPS
av. Kingsgrove 401 G6
CRISPIN
pl. Quakers Hill 214 B12
CRISPSPARKLE
dr. Ambarvale 540 F1
CRITCHETT
rd. Chatswd W 284 G12
CRITERION
cr. Doonside 243 C6
CROATIA
av. Edmndsn Pk 423 B4
pl. Quakers Hill 214 A10

CROCKET
wy. Minto 482 K5
CROCODILE
dr. Green Valley 363 B9
CROCUS
pl. Quakers Hill 243 F3
CROFT
av. Merrylands 307 B11
pl. Bradbury 511 J13
pl. Glenwood 246 B5
CROFTS
av. Hurstville 432 A5
la. Rockdale 403 D15
CROISSY
av. Hunters Hill 313 J12
CROKER
cr. Colyton 270 D5
la. Colyton, off Croker Cr 270 D5
pl. Green Valley 362 J12
pl. Guildford W 336 J1
CROMARTY
cr. Winston Hills 277 C3
pl. St Andrews 481 K5
CROMDALE
st. Mortdale 430 J8
CROMER
pl. St Johns Pk 364 E2
rd. Cromer 227 J11
CROMERTY
pl. Glenhaven 218 D5
CROMER VALLEY
rd. Belrose 227 B7
rd. Cromer 227 B7
rd. Oxford Falls 227 B7
CROMMELIN
cr. St Helens Park 541 A6
CROMPTON
pl. W Pnnant Hl 249 B3
CROMWELL
pl. Malabar 437 D2
st. Croydon 372 E5
st. Croydon Pk 372 E5
st. Leichhardt 9 H14
CRONDALL
st. Bonnyrigg Ht 363 A7
CRONIN
av. Penshurst 431 H7
pl. Bonnyrigg 364 D4
st. Penrith 237 B14
CRONULLA
cr. Woodbine 481 D15
la. Allawah 432 E4
st. Allawah 432 E5
st. Cronulla 493 K13
CROOKED
la. N Richmond 87 D10
CROOKS
la. Newtown 17 H10
CROOKSTON
dr. Camden S 507 A13
CROOKWELL
av. Miranda 491 J7
CROOT
st. Hurstville 401 H15
CROPLEY
dr. Baulkham Hl 247 C13
la. Rhodes 311 F8
st. Rhodes 311 E8
CROQUET
la. Mosman 317 D10
CROSBY
av. Hurstville 432 D3
av. Kellyville 215 H1
cr. Fairfield 336 E7
st. Denistone W 280 K12
st. Greystanes 306 E3
st. Greystanes 306 F3
CROSIO
pl. Bonnyrigg 364 F6
CROSS
la. Double Bay 14 E9
la. Enmore 17 A15
la. Kogarah 433 D4
la. Mortdale 431 C7
la. Woolmloo 4 F6
pl. Bligh Park 150 K7
pl. Mt Annan 479 G16
rd. Longueville 314 B9
rd. Orchard Hills 267 C11
rd. Regentville 235 E16
rd. Woolooware 493 F13

st. Balgowlah 287 J6
st. Bankstown 399 G2
st. Baulkham Hl 248 B9
st. Bronte 378 A7
st. Brookvale 257 J11
st. Campsie 402 B1
st. Concord 341 G6
st. Croydon 342 D14
st. Doonside 243 A13
st. Double Bay 14 B8
st. Five Dock 342 J10
st. Forest Lodge 11 G15
st. Glebe 11 G15
st. Glenbrook 264 A1
st. Guildford 337 F6
st. Hurstville 432 A5
st. Kemps Ck 360 B3
st. Kogarah 433 E4
st. Kyle Bay 431 J16
st. Lidcombe 339 K6
st. Merrylands 307 A9
st. Miranda 492 D7
st. Mortdale 431 C6
st. Mosman 317 C11
st. Pymble 253 B7
st. Pyrmont 12 F1
st. Rozelle 7 A14
st. Ryde 312 E6
st. Strathfield 371 D4
st. Tahmoor 566 D11
st. Warrimoo 203 F11
CROSSANDRA
cl. Cranebrook 207 F15
CROSSING
la. Concord, off Ada St 341 G9
CROSSLAND
st. Merrylands 338 C1
CROSSLANDS
rd. Galston 160 B10
CROSSLEY
av. McGraths Hl 122 A13
st. Ingleburn 453 F13
CROSTON
rd. Engadine 489 E8
CROSWELL
pl. N Parramatta 278 E10
CROTON
pl. Mcquarie Fd 454 C4
CROTOYE
pl. Marsfield 281 K6
CROW
pl. Bossley Park 333 K11
CROWBILL
pl. Erskine Park 270 J13
CROWEA
pl. Oxford Falls 226 H15
CROWGEY
st. Rydalmere 279 C16
CROWLE
rd. S Penrith 267 A4
CROWLEY
cr. Melrose Pk 310 K4
rd. Berowra 133 D13
CROWLEYS
la. Agnes Banks 117 C8
CROWN
cl. Henley 313 B13
la. Darlinghurst 4 C8
mw. Bella Vista 246 E4
pl. Tahmoor 565 F7
rd. Pymble 223 C13
rd. Queenscliff 288 F2
st. Darlinghurst F K9
st. Darlinghurst 4 C12
st. Epping 250 J16
st. Fairfield E 337 A11
st. Glebe 12 G14
st. Granville 307 K8
st. Harris Park 308 F7
st. Henley 313 B14
st. Riverstone 182 H4
st. St Peters 374 J13
st. Surry Hills F J16
st. Surry Hills F K9
st. Surry Hills 4 B16
st. Surry Hills 20 B5
st. Woolmloo 4 C12
tce. Bella Vista 246 E4
CROWS NEST
rd. Waverton 5 A5
rd. Wollstncraft 5 A5

CROWTHER
av. Greenwich 314 J5
CROXON
cr. Lalor Park 245 G11
CROYDON
av. Croydon 372 D5
av. Croydon Pk 372 C9
la. Petersham 15 K7
la. Cronulla, off Cronulla St 493 K13
la. Lakemba, off Croydon St N 400 K1
rd. Bexley 402 A15
rd. Croydon 342 F16
rd. Hurstville 402 A15
st. Cronulla 493 K12
st. Lakemba 401 A2
st. Petersham 15 J7
st.n, Lakemba 400 K1
CROZET
st. Kings Park 244 F3
CROZIER
rd. Belrose 225 K5
st. Eagle Vale 481 B9
CRUCIE
av. Bass Hill 367 G6
CRUCIS
la. Erskine Park, off Crucis Pl 300 J3
pl. Erskine Park 300 J2
CRUDGE
rd. Marayong 244 A7
CRUIKSHANK
av. Elderslie 507 G1
st. Stanmore 17 A5
CRUMMOCK
st. Collaroy Plat 228 D12
CRUMP
st. Mortdale 431 A6
CRUSADE
av. Padstow 399 C16
pl. Woolooware 493 C10
CRUSADER
rd. Galston 160 E13
CRUX
la. Mosman 316 J11
st. Mosman 316 J10
CRYSTAL
la.w, Petersham 16 A9
pl. Doonside 243 E8
pl. Kellyville 216 A3
st. Greystanes 306 A2
st. Newport 169 D10
st. Petersham 16 A9
st. Rozelle 344 D7
st. Sylvania 461 H12
wy. Mt Annan 479 C15
wy. Mt Annan 479 C16
CUBBY
cl. Castle Hill 217 B10
CUBITT
cr. Quakers Hill 214 D12
dr. Denham Ct 422 C7
CUDAL
cl. Terrey Hills 196 E5
pl. Carlingford 249 D13
pl. Kirrawee 490 J6
CUDDLEPIE
pl. Faulconbdg 171 D15
CUDGEE
cl. Baulkham Hl 246 H9
la. Penrith, off Cudgee Rd 237 E4
pl. Dharruk 241 D9
pl. Greystanes 305 K10
rd. Gymea Bay 491 G8
rd. Penrith 237 E4
st. Turramurra 223 A9
CUDGEGONG
rd. Rouse Hill 184 C8
rd. Ruse 512 B8
CULBARA
pl. Allambie Ht 257 G15
CULBURRA
rd. Miranda 492 B1
st. Prestons 393 C14
CULDEES
rd. Burwood Ht 372 A3
CULGOA
av. Eastwood 281 J5
ct. Wattle Grove 395 K13
pl. Sylvania Wtr 462 E9

st. Chatswd W 284
CULL
rd. Harringtn Pk 478
CULLAMINE
rd. Duffys Frst 164
CULLEN
av. Mosman 317
av. Richmond 119
la. Maianbar 523
pl. Dharruk 241
pl. Minto 482
pl. Smithfield 306
st. Forestville 255
st. Lane Cove W 313
st. Maianbar 523
CULLENS
av. Liverpool 394
la. Hunters Hill 313
pl. Liverpool 394
rd. Punchbowl 400
CULLENYA
cl. Berowra 133
CULLIS
pl. Woodpark 306
CULLODEN
rd. Mcquarie Pk 252
rd. Marsfield 281
CULLUM
st. Bossley Park 333
CULMARA
pl. Engadine 489
CULMONE
cl. Edensor Pk 363
CULTOWA
rd. Pymble 253
CULVER
st. Monterey 433
st. S Wntwthvle 307
CULVERSTON
av. Denham Ct 422
rd. Minto 482
CULWORTH
av. Killara 254
CULWULLA
st. S Hurstville 432
CULYA
st. Marayong 243
CUMBEE
la. Caringbah 493
CUMBERLAND
av. Castle Hill 217
av. Collaroy 259
av. Dee Why 258
av. Georges Hall 368
av. Lane Cove W 283
hwy. Beecroft 249
hwy. Cabramatta 365
hwy. Cabramatta W 365
hwy. Canley Ht 365
hwy. Carlingford 279
hwy. Fairfield W 335
hwy. Greystanes 306
hwy. Liverpool 365
hwy. Merrylands W 306
hwy. Normanhurst 221
hwy. Northmead 277
hwy. N Parramatta 278
hwy. Oatlands 278
hwy. Pennant Hills 250
hwy. Smithfield 335
hwy. S Wntwthvle 306
hwy. Thornleigh 221
hwy. Wahroonga 221
hwy. Warwck Frm 365
hwy. Wentwthvle 277
hwy. W Pnnant Hl 249
hwy. Woodpark 306
pl. Colyton 270
pl. The Rocks A
rd. Auburn 339
rd. Greystanes 306
rd. Ingleburn 453
rd. Minto 453
sq. Newington, off Monterey St 310
st. Blacktown 274
st. Cabramatta 366
st. Carlton 432
st. Epping 280
st. The Rocks A
st. The Rocks 1
CUMBERNAULD
cr. Dharruk 241

MBORA
Berowra 133 B13
MBRAE
Erskine Park 300 F2
Oatlands 278 H10
MBRIAN
Northmead 278 C5
MMING
Concord 341 F3
Concord W 341 F3
Quakers Hill 213 H14
MMINGS
Lansvale 366 H8
MMINS
Menangle Pk 539 B6
NLIFFE
East Killara 254 G7
NNEEN
Mulgrave 121 H15
NNINGHAM
St Clair 270 D10
Blacktown 245 B12
Ingleburn 423 B11
Mt Annan 509 J5
Camden S 506 K11
S Windsor 150 H1
.Moorebank, off Cunningham St 395 J8
Ingleburn 423 A9
Haymarket E H6
Matraville 437 B2
Moorebank 395 J9
N Sydney 5 F2
Telopea 279 G11
NNINGHAME
Fairfield 336 D10
PANIA
Bidwill 211 E13
PAR
St Andrews 451 K16
PITTS
Richmond 120 B3
RAC
Casula 424 C3
RAGUL
N Turramrra 193 E14
RBAN
Balgowlah Ht 287 J13
RIE
Little Bay 437 G14
Lucas Ht 487 H12
RL CURL
Curl Curl 258 H13
Woodbine 481 J9
RLEW
Newington 310 E11
Woronora Ht 489 B3
Glenwood 215 E14
RLEW CAMP
Mosman 316 J12
RLEWIS
Ashcroft 364 F15
Bondi Beach 378 B1
RRA
Frenchs Frst 255 K2
Greystanes 305 K10
RRAGHBEENA
Mosman 316 J13
RRAGUNDI
Belrose 226 B10
RRAH
Como 460 G5
RRAN
Mcquarie Fd 453 J2
Marayong 244 A8
Prairiewood 335 A7
RRANA
Beverly Hills 401 C9
RRANS HILL
Currans Hill 479 G11
RRAWANG
Como 460 H6
Cammeray 316 B4
Carss Park 432 F13
Concord W 311 E13
RRAWEELA
Forestville 255 K7
RRAWONG
Lane Cove W 313 H1
Normanhurst 221 F12
Palm Beach 140 B9

av. Valley Ht 202 E5
cr. Bowen Mtn 84 A8
cr. Leonay 234 K13
pl. Blaxland 234 E5
rd. Berowra Ht 132 J8
rd. Glenorie 127 K9
st. Glenwood 215 C16
st. Green Valley 363 E9
st. Ingleburn 453 G7
CURRENCY
ct. Winston Hills 277 A3
rd. Freemns Rch 60 J10
CURRENT
st. Padstow 429 H2
CURREY
pl. Fairfield W 335 A11
CURRIE
av. Annangrove 186 E4
rd. Forestville 256 C9
rd. Oakville 122 H12
CURRINGA
rd. Villawood 367 A3
CURRONG
cct. Terrey Hills 196 D8
pl. S Turramrra 252 B9
st. S Wntwthvle 306 J7
CURRY
la. Artarmon 314 K2
pl. Seven Hills 275 G8
st. Eastern Ck 272 G2
st. Rooty Hill 272 G2
CURT
pl. Quakers Hill 214 A10
st. Ashfield 343 A16
CURTALE
ct. Green Valley 363 C10
CURTIN
av. Abbotsford 343 A4
av. N Wahrnga 192 E15
cr. Maroubra 407 E14
gr. Penrith 237 C6
la. Canterbury 372 F15
pl. Concord 341 H5
pl. Condell Park 398 G1
pl. Narellan Vale 479 B11
pl. Sydney A J14
pl. Sydney 1 G15
pl. Westmead 307 E3
st. Cabramatta 366 A5
st. Canley Vale 366 A5
CURTIS
av. Taren Point 462 G13
cl. Cherrybrook 249 E1
cr. Moorebank 396 D9
ct. Carlingford 279 F7
la. Catherine Fd 449 D6
pl. Kings Park 244 F2
rd. Balmain 7 F6
rd. Chester Hill 338 A14
rd. Kellyville 186 A13
rd. Mulgrave 121 H15
st. Banksia 403 D12
st. Caringbah 492 G7
st. Ryde 312 E6
CURTISS
pl. Raby 481 E1
CURVERS
dr. Mt Riverview 234 C1
CURZON
rd. Padstow Ht 429 B5
st. Ryde 282 A16
wy. Ambarvale 511 A16
CUSACK
av. Casula 424 G3
cl. St Helens Park 541 C3
pl. Blackett 241 D3
rd. Oakville 124 C8
st. Denistone W 280 J12
st. Merrylands W 307 A16
CUSAK
cl. Edensor Pk 333 H16
CUSCUS
pl. St Helens Park 541 H2
CUSHER
wy. Wentwthvle, off Portadown Rd 277 D11
CUSTOM HOUSE
la. Sydney B D9
CUSTOMS OFFICERS STAIRS
The Rocks 1 J8
CUTBUSH
av. Belfield 371 C9

CUTCLIFFE
av. Regents Pk 369 F2
CUTHBERT
av. Kellyville 215 H5
cr. Edensor Pk 363 D2
cr. Revesby 428 H2
pl. Menai 458 F12
st. Queens Park 22 E11
st. Sydney C A3
CUTHEL
pl. Campbelltwn 511 K2
st. Badgerys Ck 359 C4
CUT HILL
rd. Cobbitty 446 D9
CUTHILL
st. Randwick 377 B15
CUTLER
av. St Marys 270 A1
cct. Narrabeen 228 F6
cl. Westleigh 220 H8
la. St Marys, off Cutler Av 270 A2
pde. North Ryde 282 K11
pl. Cromer 227 K11
rd. Clontarf 287 G15
rd. Engadine 518 E4
rd. Lansvale 366 E8
st. Bondi 378 B4
CUTLER FOOTWAY
Paddington 4 J13
CUTLER HALL
wy. Narrabeen, off Cutler Cct 228 F7
CUVEE
pl. Minchinbury 271 K10
CUZCO
st. S Coogee 407 H6
CYCAS
pl. Stanhpe Gdn 215 D10
CYCLAMEN
pl. Mcquarie Fd 454 E5
CYGNET
av. Green Valley 363 D14
pl. Illawong 459 C5
pl. Willmot 210 F12
CYGNUS
cl. Doonside 243 E13
pl. Cranebrook 207 G7
CYNTHEA
rd. Palm Beach 140 A4
CYNTHIA
av. Castle Hill 248 A5
st. Pymble 252 K7
wk. Pymble 252 K7
CYPERUS
pl. Glenmore Pk 265 H14
CYPRESS
cl. Alfords Point 458 K3
ct. Baulkham Hl 248 B11
dr. Lugarno 429 K8
la. Blacktown, off Kildare Rd 243 K15
pl. Liverpool 395 B9
rd. N St Marys 240 C12
st. Normanhurst 221 D13
CYPRIAN
st. Mosman 317 C1
CYPRUS
st. Mcquarie Fd 453 K4
CYRIL
pl. Baulkham Hl 247 E11
st. Greystanes 306 G4
CYRUS
av. Wahroonga 222 A12

D

DABAGE
pl. Kurrajong Ht 54 A5
DACEY
av. Moore Park 20 D15
pl. Doonside 273 F3
DACRE
la. Malabar 437 E3
st. Malabar 437 E3
DADLEY
st. Alexandria 18 H13
DADSWELL
pl. Mt Pritchard 364 K11

DAFFODIL
pl. Glenmore Pk 265 G7
st. Eastwood 281 D7
st. Greystanes 306 C12
st. Marayong 244 B6
DAGMAR
cr. Blacktown 274 C3
DAHLIA
pl. Clarmnt Ms 238 H16
pl. Prestons 393 J14
st. Greystanes 305 G11
st. Quakers Hill 243 E2
DAIHATSU
dr. Riverwood, off Applause St 400 C10
DAIMLER
pl. Ingleburn 453 H12
DAINES
pde. Beacon Hill 257 F6
DAINTON
av. St Ives 224 D11
DAINTREE
dr. Wattle Grove 426 A4
gln. St Clair 270 D11
la. St Clair, off Daintree Gln 270 D11
pl. Dural 219 A3
pl. Kellyville 216 G2
wy. Menai 458 H10
DAINTREY
cr. Randwick 377 C16
st. Fairlight 288 D8
DAIRY
ct. Glenwood 215 E13
rd. Belimbla Pk 501 D8
DAISY
av. Penshurst 431 G6
la. Bargo 567 A5
pl. Clarmnt Ms 238 H16
pl. Lalor Park 245 C11
pl. Mcquarie Fd 454 D5
st. Chatswood 284 J8
st. Croydon Pk 372 A5
st. Dee Why 259 A8
st. Greystanes 305 H7
st. N Balgowlah 287 F6
st. Revesby 398 F10
st. Roselands 400 F8
DAKARA
cl. Pymble 252 J4
dr. Frenchs Frst 256 A2
pl. Frenchs Frst 256 B2
DAKING
st. N Parramatta 278 B10
DAKOTA
ct. Stanhpe Gdn 215 C12
dr. Bossley Park 333 K11
pl. Raby 451 B13
pl. St Clair 269 F13
DALBERTIS
st. Abbotsbury 333 A13
DALBY
pl. Chipping Ntn 366 H16
pl. Eastlakes 405 K2
DALCASSIA
st. Hurstville 431 K4
DALE
av. Chippendale 19 B4
av. Liverpool 394 F5
cl. Thornleigh 220 H12
cr. Narwee 400 G15
gr. Hebersham 241 F10
la. Mcquarie Fd 453 K2
pde. Bankstown 399 D1
pl. Cranebrook 237 D1
pl. North Rocks 248 J12
pl. Winston Hills 277 H3
st. Brookvale 258 A11
st. Fairfield 336 F13
st. Seven Hills 245 D15
DALES
cl. Blairmount 481 A14
rd. Silverdale 353 K12
DALEY
cl. Belimbla Pk 501 G16
pl. Fairfield W 335 B12
rd. Yagoona 369 B10
st. Pendle Hill 276 D16
DALGETY
rd. Millers Pt A A1
rd. Millers Pt 1 C8
tce. Millers Pt 1 C8

DALHOUSIE
st. Haberfield 343 C16
DALKEITH
la. Sans Souci 433 C13
pl. St Helens Park 511 J16
rd. Cherrybrook 219 B14
st. Busby 363 G16
st. Northbridge 285 K15
st. Ramsgate 433 C13
st. Sans Souci 433 C13
DALLAS
av. S Penrith 266 K4
pl. St Ives 224 G9
pl. Toongabbie 275 H11
DALLEY
av. Pagewood 406 B9
av. Vaucluse 348 C6
la. Redfern 20 B8
la. Pagewood, off Holloway St 406 B10
la. Bondi Jctn, off Waverley Cr 377 F3
rd. Heathcote 518 G9
st. Bondi Jctn 377 G4
st. Harris Park 308 E8
st. Jamisontown 265 J2
st. Kogarah 432 K4
st. Lidcombe 340 B7
st. Queenscliff 288 E2
st. Sydney A K11
st. Sydney 1 H13
st. Bondi Jctn, off Waverley St 377 G4
DALLEYS
rd. Naremburn 315 D3
DALLWOOD
av. Epping 250 E16
DALMAN
pl. Baulkham Hl 246 H6
pl. Sylvania 462 B10
DALMAR
pl. Carlingford 280 D5
st. Croydon 342 G12
DALMATIA
av. Edmndsn Pk 423 A4
st. Carramar 336 J15
DALMENY
av. Rosebery 375 K14
av. Rosebery 405 J1
av. Russell Lea 343 D7
dr. Prestons 393 D16
dr. Prestons 393 E14
dr. Prestons 423 E2
rd. Northbridge 286 E15
DALPRA
cr. Bossley Park 333 E12
DALPURA
pl. Bangor 459 A15
st. Cromer 228 D14
DALRAY
st. Lalor Park 245 E9
DALRYMPLE
av. Chatswd W 284 D14
av. Chatswd W 284 F13
av. Lane Cove W 284 D14
cr. Pymble 223 J16
pl. Barden Rdg 488 G2
DALSTRAITH
pl. Glen Alpine 510 D14
DALTON
av. Condell Park 398 E1
av. Eastwood 281 E9
av. Homebush 341 A7
av. Lucas Ht 487 K12
cl. Rouse Hill 185 D4
la. Mosman, off Awaba St 317 A4
pl. Fairfield W 335 A11
pl. Prestons 393 C13
rd. Mosman 317 A4
rd. St Ives Ch 223 K4
st. Colyton 270 G5
DALWOOD
av. Seaforth 287 A8
pl. Carlingford 249 E13
pl. Eschol Park 481 F3
pl. Mt Annan 509 J1
DALY
av. Concord 341 H9
av. N Wahrnga 222 K2
ct. Wrrngtn Cty 238 F7
la. Wrrngtn Cty, off Daly Ct 238 F7

rd. Faulconbdg 171 C10
st. Bilgola 169 G6
DALZIEL
av. Panania 428 C3
st. Engadine 489 D13
st. Fairfield W 335 A12
DAMASCUS
rd. Holsworthy 426 D11
DAMEELI
av. Kirrawee 491 A4
DAME MARY GILMORE
rd. Oatley 430 G11
DAMIEN
av. Greystanes 306 G5
av. S Penrith 266 K5
DAMON
av. Epping 250 E15
cl. Glendenning 242 H4
DAMOUR
av. E Lindfield 254 J12
st. Holsworthy 396 D16
DAMPIER
av. Wrrngtn Cty 238 F5
cr. Fairfield W 335 C9
pl. Leumeah 482 F11
pl. Prestons 393 H7
pl. Whalan 240 J9
st. Chifley 437 A5
st. Kurnell 465 J9
DAMSEL
ct. Castle Hill 217 G4
DAN
av. Blacktown 244 B13
av. Maroubra 407 F14
cr. Castle Hill 218 F15
cr. Colyton 270 B5
cr. Lansvale 366 E9
st. Campbelltwn 511 J3
st. Marsfield 282 A7
st. Merrylands 307 C10
DANA
cl. Castle Hill 247 F2
pde. Regents Pk 369 A3
DANALAM
st. Liverpool 394 K8
DANBURITE
pl. Eagle Vale 481 H4
DANBURY
cl. Marsfield 282 A6
DANBY
st. Prospect 275 A11
DANDAR
pl. Bradbury 511 C15
DANDARBONG
av. Bangor 459 B14
av. Carlingford 280 D7
DANDENONG
cl. Bossley Park 334 B6
cr. Ruse 512 H6
rd. Terrey Hills 196 E6
DANELLA
st. The Oaks 502 F9
DANGAR
cl. Hinchinbrk 363 B13
pl. Chippendale 19 A3
pl. Davidson 255 C2
rd. Brooklyn 76 D11
st. Chippendale 19 A4
st. Lindfield 254 F14
st. Randwick 377 A10
wy. Airds 512 A14
DANGIN
cl. Bonnyrigg 364 C9
DANIEL
av. Baulkham Hl 246 J12
cl. Cherrybrook 220 A6
la. St Clair, off Daniel Pde 269 J9
pde. St Clair 269 J9
pl. Green Valley 362 K10
st. Botany 405 G10
st. Granville 308 C11
st. Greystanes 306 D8
st. Leichhardt 9 C15
st. Wetherill Pk 334 E3
DANIELA
pl. Blacktown 273 G5
DANIELS
rd. Bidwill 211 H16
rd. Bidwill 241 G3
rd. Hassall Gr 211 H16
rd. Hebersham 241 G3
rd. Oakhurst 241 G3
st. Chippendale 18 J2
DANIEL WILLIAMS
pl. Glenbrook 234 D11
DANKS
st. Waterloo 19 J12
DANNY
rd. Lalor Park 245 D11
st. Werrington 238 H11
DANS
av. Coogee 377 G12
DANTIC
pl. Cherrybrook 219 B12
DANUBE
cr. Kearns 451 A14
pl. St Clair 270 B8
DAPHINE
la. Kingswood, off Daphine Cl 238 A14
DAPHNE
av. Bankstown 399 G3
av. Castle Hill 247 J4
cl. Cherrybrook 220 A6
cl. Kingswood 238 A14
la. Botany 405 E10
pl. Blacktown 244 K10
pl. Mcquarie Fd 454 F7
st. Botany 405 E10
st. Caringbah 492 H16
st. Merrylands 307 C10
st. West Ryde 280 H13
DAPLYN
wy. Claymore 481 A12
DAPTO
cl. Prestons 393 A14
pl. Bangor 459 A14
DARA
cr. Glenmore Pk 266 C7
D'ARAM
st. Hunters Hill 313 H10
DARANGAN
cl. Waterfall 519 D11
DARAYA
rd. Marayong 244 A8
st. Colyton 270 B6
DARCEY
rd. Castle Hill 248 E4
st. Prestons 393 B10
D'ARCY
av. Lidcombe 339 H11
wy. Minto 482 K1
wy. Minto 483 A1
DARCY
av. Appin 569 E9
pl. E Kurrajong 56 G4
rd. Wentwthvle 276 H13
rd. Wentwthvle 277 A14
rd. Westmead 277 A14
st. Casula 423 H2
st. Granville 308 K11
st. Marsfield 282 A5
st. Parramatta 308 C4
D'ARCY IRVINE
dr. Castle Hill 218 K12
DARDANELLES
rd. Chatswd W 284 F11
st. Mortdale 431 D8
DARE
st. Glenwood 215 C13
DAREEN
st. Beacon Hill 257 B5
st. Frenchs Frst 257 B5
DARGAN
st. Naremburn 315 E2
st. S Windsor 150 K1
st. Yagoona 368 F14
DARGHAN
la. Glebe 12 E10
st. Glebe 12 E10
DARGIE
pl. Eagle Vale 481 A9
st. Mt Pritchard 364 J10
DARICE
pl. Plumpton 242 D12
DARIUS
av. N Narrabeen 199 B15
DARK
cl. Edensor Pk 363 F3
DARKON
pl. Oakhurst 241 H2
DARLEY
ct. Rouse Hill 185 F3
la. Newtown 374 J10
la. Randwick 22 D16
pl. Darlinghurst 4 F11
rd. Bardwell Pk 402 J7
rd. Centnnial Pk 22 B16
rd. Leichhardt 9 C13
rd. Manly 288 H10
rd. Randwick 376 H10
st. Darlinghurst 4 F11
st. Forestville 255 K13
st. Killarney Ht 255 K13
st. Marrickville 373 F11
st. Mona Vale 199 C2
st. Neutral Bay 5 K6
st. Newtown 374 H11
st. Sans Souci 433 B15
st. Thirlmere 562 D16
st. Thirlmere 565 D1
st.e, Mona Vale 199 E4
st.w, Mona Vale 199 B1
DARLING
av. Kentlyn 512 J7
av. Lurnea 394 D13
av. Ruse 512 H1
av. Ruse 512 J7
dr. Haymarket E A8
dr. Haymarket 3 A9
dr. Sydney 3 A4
la. Glebe 12 D10
la. Kensington, off Darling St 376 E12
pl. Sylvania Wtr 462 E10
st. Abbotsbury 333 A13
st. Balmain 7 F8
st. Balmain East 8 C9
st. Bronte 378 A7
st. Chatswood 284 K5
st. Glebe 12 D10
st. Greystanes 306 A5
st. Kensington 376 E12
st. Penrith 237 A14
st. Roseville 284 K5
st. Rozelle 344 D8
st. St Ives 224 F9
DARLINGHURST
rd. Darlinghurst 4 F13
rd. Potts Point 4 J7
DARLING ISLAND
rd. Pyrmont 8 H16
DARLING POINT
rd. Darling Point 13 H9
DARLINGTON
dr. Cherrybrook 219 C11
la. Darlington 18 D7
rd. Darlington 18 D7
rd. Newtown 18 D7
DARLY
pl. Dharruk 241 C8
st. Miranda 492 C6
DARMENIA
av. Greystanes 306 E11
DARMOUR
av. Allambie Ht 257 C10
DARNAY
pl. Ambarvale 540 E1
DARNLEY
st. Gordon 253 K4
DAROOK PARK
rd. Cronulla 523 H1
DARRA
pl. St Johns Pk 364 D1
DARRAGH
la. Haberfield 9 A15
DARRAMBAL
av. Baulkham Hl 248 C10
DARRELL
pl. Oakhurst 241 K4
DARREN
ct. Glenwood 215 K16
DARRI
av. N Wahrnga 222 F3
av. S Penrith 266 F2
DARRYL
pl. Gymea Bay 491 F8
DART
rd. Bringelly 388 A9
DARTBROOK
rd. Auburn 339 F2
DARTFORD
rd. Thornleigh 221 D6
st. Mt Pritchard 364 B11
DARTLE
wy. Ambarvale 511 A15
DARTMOOR
cct. Emu Heights 235 A5
la. Emu Heights, off Dartmoor Cct 235 B6
DART THRU
la. Croydon Pk 372 B6
DARU
pl. Glenfield 424 F10
wy. Whalan 241 B10
DARVALL
rd. Denistone W 280 J12
rd. Eastwood 280 G8
rd. West Ryde 280 J12
st. Balmain 7 J11
st. Centnnial Pk 21 D9
st. St Leonards 315 E4
DARVELL
st. Bonnyrigg Ht 363 G5
DARVILL
rd. Orchard Hills 268 B13
DARWIN
av. Little Bay 437 G14
cl. Wakeley 334 K13
dr. Lapstone 264 H2
pl. Barden Rdg 458 G16
rd. Campbelltwn 512 B6
st. Carlingford 280 A1
st. West Ryde 281 A16
DARYL
st. Merrylands W 306 H12
wy. Claymore 481 D12
DASEA
st. Chullora 369 G5
DASHMERE
st. Bossley Park 333 K9
DASSAULT
cl. Raby 451 F12
DATCHETT
st. Balmain 8 F9
st. Balmain East 8 F9
DATE
gr. Glenwood 215 J16
DAUNT
av. Matraville 406 J16
DAVENEY
wy. W Pnnant Hl 248 K2
DAVENPORT
dr. Wallacia 324 K15
DAVESTA
rd. Springwood 172 C16
DAVEY
ct. Emu Heights 235 A6
rd. Dural 188 G7
st. Jannali 460 K12
st. Lidcombe 339 K9
DAVID
av. Caringbah 492 H14
av. Casula 394 G13
av. North Ryde 282 F6
cl. St Ives Ch 224 A5
la. Blacktown 244 G16
la. Forest Lodge 11 J16
la. Crows Nest, off Emmett St 315 G8
pl. Mt Annan 479 H15
pl. Peakhurst 430 A3
pl. Seaforth 286 J12
rd. Barden Rdg 488 G3
rd. Castle Hill 219 A14
rd. Cherrybrook 219 A14
rd. Collaroy Plat 228 J14
rd. Emu Plains 235 F7
rd. Springwood 202 A4
rd.e, Springwood 202 B5
st. Concord 342 A8
st. Crows Nest 315 G8
st. Croydon 372 C2
st. Dundas Vy 280 A9
st. Earlwood 403 D3
st. Forest Lodge 11 H16
st. Glenbrook 234 A14
st. Greenacre 370 E7
st. Marrickville 373 H12
st. Mascot 405 H4
st. Mosman 317 D12
st. Mt Pritchard 364 G10
st. S Wntwthvle 306 J9
st. Wilberforce 91 K4
DAVIDSON
av. Concord 341 F5
av. Forestville 255 H9
av. North Rocks 278 J3
av. N Strathfield 341 F5
av. Warrawee 222
cl. St Clair 270
cr. Maroubra 407
la. Concord 341
la. Lakemba 401
la. St Clair, off Davidson Cl 269
pde. Cremorne 316
pl. Airds 512
rd. Guildford 338
rd. Menai 458
st. Balmain 7
st. Greenacre 370
DAVIES
av. Springwood 201
av. Vaucluse 348
ct. Baulkham Hl 247
la. Surry Hills 20
pl. Picton 563
rd. Padstow 399
rd. Seven Hills 275
st. Chatswd W 284
st. Leichhardt 15
st. Marsden Pk 182
st. Merrylands 307
st. Mount Druitt 240
st. Newington 310
st. N Parramatta 278
st. Surry Hills 20
wy. Claymore 481
DAVIESIA
pl. Glenmore Pk 265
DAVINA
cr. Cecil Hills 362
DAVIS
av. Baulkham Hl 248
av. Epping 281
la. Bankstown 369
la. Pitt Twn Bttms 122
la. Woollahra 22
la. Yagoona 369
pl. Bligh Park 150
pl. Glenhaven 217
pl. Menai 458
pl. Rooty Hill 272
pl. Thirlmere 565
rd. Marayong 244
rd. Marayong 244
rd. Wetherill Pk 304
st. Dulwich Hill 373
st. Richmond 120
swy. Liverpool, off Northumberland St 395
DAVISON
la. Picton 563
st. Cromer 228
st. Merrylands 307
DAVOREN
la. Surry Hills 20
DAVY
pl. St Helens Park 541
st. Warwck Frm 365
DAVY ROBINSON
dr. Chipping Ntn 397
DAWES
av. Castle Hill 217
av. Regents Pk 369
cr. Eastwood 281
pl. Barden Rdg 488
pl. Bligh Park 150
pl. Cherrybrook 219
pl. Lapstone 264
pl. Ruse 512
rd. Belrose 226
st. Little Bay 437
st. Mt Pritchard 364
st. Wentwthvle 306
DAWKINS
pl. Ambarvale 510
DAWN
av. Chester Hill 368
av. Mt Pritchard 364
cl. Lurnea 394
cr. Mt Riverview 234
cr. Regents Pk 339
dr. Seven Hills 245
st. Greystanes 305
st. Peakhurst 430
DAWN FRASER
av. Homebush B 340
DAWSON
av. Camden S 506
av. Earlwood 402

Thornleigh 221 C14
Bass Hill 368 D10
Woollahra 22 H5
Mount Druitt 241 E16
Bass Hill 367 H7
Menai 458 K11
Ruse 512 E5
Turramurra 252 D3
Mt Hunter 505 B8
Croydon 342 F12
Epping 250 F12
Fairfield Ht 335 G12
Naremburn 315 J2
Rookwood 340 C12
Surry Hills 19 H3
AX
Prospect 274 H10
AY
Hobartville 118 E9
Kensington 376 C15
Kensington 376 E16
Kingsford 406 E2
Minto 482 K9
Prospect 274 J10
Cheltenham 251 A8
Ashcroft 394 E1
Avalon 140 A14
Chatswood 284 H9
Colyton 270 C4
Drummoyne 344 A3
Lansvale 366 J7
Leichhardt 15 G1
Marrickville 373 G16
Sydney C C13
Sydney E D1
Windsor 121 B10
n, Silverwater 310 A14
s, Lidcombe 339 J1
AYDREAM
Hinchinbrk 393 A1
Warriewood 198 G4
AYMAN
Marsfield 251 J15
AYMAR
Avalon 139 J12
Castle Cove 286 B5
AYRELL
Mosman 317 G9
AYS
Hurstville 431 K9
EADMAN
Moorebank 395 J8
EAKIN
Glenwood 215 H13
Haberfield 343 D15
Penrith 237 C7
Springwood 202 E11
Bonnyrigg 364 C3
East Killara 254 H6
Kirrawee 490 J5
W Pnnant Hl 249 A8
Concord 311 K15
Ermington 280 E16
Forestville 256 A7
Silverwater 309 E13
West Ryde 311 A1
Wahroonga 222 D3
AL
Green Valley 363 B10
AN
Belmore 371 E15
Oakdale 500 D11
Ermington 280 G15
Baulkham Hl 247 B14
Crows Nest, off Willoughby La 315 F7
Acacia Gdn 214 J16
Penrith 236 K5
Caringbah 492 F14
Granville 308 E11
Greystanes 306 E7
Strathfield S 371 B6
W Pnnant Hl 249 K2
ANE
Bligh Park 150 G7
Burwood 342 A14
Glenbrook 263 J1
ANS
Airds 512 B11
BBIE
Mount Druitt 241 H12
BBY
Toongabbie 276 A6

DEBENHAM
av. Leumeah 482 H12
DEBORAH
av. Lidcombe 340 A7
cl. Fairfield 336 E6
cl. Mt Colah 192 A4
cr. Cmbrdg Pk 237 J7
pl. Eastwood 281 F4
pl. Punchbowl 400 E7
pl. Riverstone 183 B7
rd. Annangrove 186 D3
st. Greystanes 305 H6
DEBRINCAT
av. N St Marys 239 K11
av. Tregear 240 D9
av. Whalan 240 D9
DE BURGH
rd. Killara 253 E15
DEBUSSY
pl. Cranebrook 207 J9
DE CASTELLA
dr. Blacktown 273 G6
DECCAN
wy. Bidwill 211 G13
DE CHAIR
av. Springwood 202 B5
rd. Narraweena 258 C7
DECKER
pl. Huntingwd 273 J12
DEE
cl. Prestons 423 F2
pl. Prospect 274 K13
DEEBAN
wk. Cronulla 493 J12
DEEBLE
st. Tennyson 312 E11
DEED
pl. Northmead 277 H7
DEEPFIELDS
rd. Catherine Fd 449 H2
DEEP POOL
wy. Mt Annan 479 D14
DEEPWATER
rd. Castle Cove 285 F4
DEERWOOD
av. Liverpool 395 B10
DEESIDE
av. Baulkham Hl 246 K12
cl. S Penrith 266 K2
la. S Penrith, off Deeside Cl 266 K2
DEE WHY
la. N Curl Curl, off Headland Rd 259 C9
pde. Dee Why 258 J5
pl. Woodbine 481 H9
DEFARGE
wy. Ambarvale 541 A1
DEFOE
la. Wiley Park 400 F2
pl. Wetherill Pk 334 G5
pl. Winston Hills 247 F16
st. Wiley Park 400 F2
DEFRIES
av. Zetland 376 A10
pl. Doonside 273 F4
DEHAVILLAND
cr. Raby 451 H15
DEHLSEN
av. W Pnnant Hl 249 H6
DEIRDRE
dr. Riverstone 183 C7
DELA
cl. Dee Why 258 E5
cl. St Ives Ch 224 A5
DELAGE
pl. Ingleburn 453 K7
DELAGOA
pl. Caringbah 492 K7
DELAIGH
av. Baulkham Hl 247 C7
av. N Curl Curl 258 H10
DELAMERE
st. Canley Vale 335 J16
DELANEY
av. Silverdale 353 J15
dr. Baulkham Hl 247 B1
dr. Doonside 243 C5
la. Revesby Ht 428 J5
DE LANGE
pl. Oakhurst 242 C1

DELANGE
rd. Putney 312 A8
DELARUE
st. Richmond 119 K5
DE LA SALLE
pl. Castle Hill 218 K10
DELAUNAY
st. Ingleburn 453 F13
DE LAURET
av. Newport 169 E7
DELAVOR
pl. Glenhaven 217 J3
DELAWARE
av. St Ives 224 C8
rd. Ermington 280 C13
rd. Horsley Pk 301 K16
st. Epping 250 H15
DELECTA
av. Clareville 169 F1
av. Mosman 286 K15
DELEWARE
rd. Riverstone 182 E9
DELFIN
dr. Wattle Grove 395 H13
DELGARNO
rd. Bonnyrigg Ht 363 E8
DELGAUN
pl. Baulkham Hl 246 J11
DELHI
rd. Chatswd W 283 B9
rd. Mcquarie Pk 283 B9
rd. North Ryde 283 B9
st. Lidcombe 340 A6
DELIA
av. Revesby 398 J15
pde. Engadine 518 F4
DELIVERY
dr. Randwick, off Hospital Rd 377 A15
DELL
pl. Georges Hall 367 H9
st. Belrose 225 K5
st. Blacktown 274 A3
st. Woodpark 306 G16
DELLA
pl. Glendenning 242 G3
DELLER
av. Cabramatta W 365 A8
pl. Blakehurst 432 D13
DELLIT
pl. Doonside 273 G3
DELLS
la. Richmond Lwld 88 H11
DELLVIEW
la. Tamarama, off Silva St 378 B6
st. Glenbrook 264 B2
st. Tamarama 378 C6
DELLWOOD
av. Earlwood 372 J16
st. Bankstown 399 D4
st. Chatswd W 284 E12
st. S Granville 338 E4
DELMAR
pde. Dee Why 258 G7
pde. Gladesville 312 F12
DELOITTE
av. Birchgrove 7 H1
DELORAINE
cl. Hinchinbrk 363 A16
dr. Leonay 234 J14
DELPHINIUM
pl. Kellyville 216 D3
wy. Kellyville, off Delphinium Pl 216 D3
DELRAY
av. Wahroonga 223 B4
DELTA
cl. Raby 451 D11
pl. Blacktown 245 D8
pl. Lane Cove 314 F5
pl. Sutherland 490 B1
rd. Lane Cove 314 F4
row. Wrrngtn Dns 238 E4
DELVES
st. Mortdale 430 J5
DELWOOD
cl. Mona Vale 199 E1
DEMAINE
av. Bexley North 402 D9

DE MESTRE
pl. Sydney A J15
DEMETRIUS
rd. Rsemeadow 540 D3
DE MEYRICK
av. Casula 394 E12
av. Lurnea 394 E12
DE MILHAU
rd. Hunters Hill 313 D11
DEMPSEY
pl. Drummoyne 343 H2
st. Emu Heights 235 A5
st. North Ryde 282 E11
DEMPSTER
cr. Regents Pk 339 B16
DENAWEN
av. Castle Cove 285 K5
DENBERN
st. Bossley Park 334 A8
st. Dean Park 242 H2
DENBIGH
pl. Harringtn Pk 478 E5
pl. Menai 458 H9
DENBY
st. Marrickville 374 D9
DENDROBIUM
cr. Elanora Ht 197 J15
DENEB
pl. Hinchinbrk 393 D5
DENFIELD
cct. St Helens Park 541 A5
la. Tahmoor 565 J13
DENGATE
av. Ashfield 372 J2
st. Epping 250 F16
DENHAM
la. Surry Hills 4 D14
la. Bondi, off Edward St 378 B4
pl. Dundas 279 E13
rd. Kenthurst 187 K9
st. Bondi 378 B5
st. Bondi Beach 378 B5
st. Rhodes 311 E8
st. Surry Hills 4 C14
DENHAM COURT
rd. Denham Ct 422 A13
DENIEHY
st. Granville 309 A11
DENING
cl. Chipping Ntn 366 E16
st. Drummoyne 343 F2
DENINTEND
pl. S Penrith 266 F3
DENISE
av. Glenbrook 263 J2
cr. Peakhurst 430 C4
pl. Hornsby 221 E6
DENISON
av. Lurnea 394 E13
la. Camperdwn 17 D8
la. Newtown 17 D8
pl. Appin 569 E8
pl. Cromer 227 H13
pl. Windsor Dn 180 K3
rd. Dulwich Hill 373 D9
rd. Lewisham 15 A13
st. Arncliffe 403 E6
st. Bnksmeadw 406 E13
st. Bondi Jctn 22 E11
st. Camperdwn 17 C4
st. Carramar 366 K3
st. Concord 342 B2
st. Eastgardens 406 E13
st. Granville 308 A7
st. Hillsdale 406 E13
st. Hornsby 191 J14
st. Manly 288 H8
st. Newtown 17 D8
st. N Sydney K F7
st. N Sydney 5 G7
st. Parramatta 308 A7
st. Penshurst 431 H7
st. Queens Park 22 E11
st. Rozelle 10 H1
st. Ruse 512 H3
st. Villawood 367 A3
DENISTONE
rd. Denistone 281 D9
rd. Eastwood 281 D9
rd. N Parramatta 278 G8
DENIS WINSTON
dr. Doonside 273 F2

DENLEY
la. St Ives 223 K12
DENMAN
av. Caringbah 492 J7
av. Haberfield 343 B14
av. Wiley Park 400 H4
av. Woolooware 493 D8
ct. Glenwood 245 G1
la. Glebe 12 E12
pde. Normanhurst 221 F9
rd. Georges Hall 367 F11
st. Eastwood 280 H10
st. Hurstville 431 J8
st. Turramurra 222 F14
DENMARK
rd. Riverstone 182 H10
st. Merrylands 307 G15
DENMEAD
st. Thirlmere 565 C10
DENNING
st. Petersham 16 B13
st. S Coogee 407 H4
DENNIS
av. Wahroonga 222 B12
av. West Hoxton 362 B15
pl. Beverly Hills 401 B15
st. Campbelltwn 512 A5
st. Colyton 270 J9
st. Ermington 310 A1
st. Greystanes 306 E7
st. Lakemba 371 B16
st. Lakemba 401 B1
st. Lalor Park 245 E12
st. Thirlmere 565 C7
DENNISON
cl. Rouse Hill 185 D6
DENNISTOUN
av. Guildford 337 A5
av. Guildford W 336 H5
av. Yennora 336 H5
DENNY
rd. Picnic Point 428 B7
DENOS
la. Cremorne 316 D5
DENT
cl. Hinchinbrk 363 B14
pl. Shalvey 210 K14
st. Bnksmeadw 435 J1
st. Epping 250 C16
st. Jamisontown 236 E14
DENTON
gr. Quakers Hill 214 A9
la. Cabramatta, off Arthur St 365 J7
pl. Wallacia 324 K15
DENTS
pl. Gymea Bay 491 C9
DENVER
pl. Toongabbie 275 H12
rd. St Clair 270 G11
DENYA
cl. Glenmore Pk 266 E8
DENZIL
av. St Clair 270 A9
la. St Clair, off Denzil Av 269 K10
DEODAR
wy. Blacktown 274 E12
DEODARA
gdn. N Turramrra 223 D2
DEPARTURE
plz. Mascot 404 D6
DEPOT
la. Marrickville, off Malakoff St 373 K12
pl. Bankstown 369 D16
rd. Mortdale 430 F7
st. Rooty Hill 272 D1
DEPTFORD
av. Kings Lngly 245 G5
DERBY
cr. Chipping Ntn 396 H1
la. Camperdwn 17 D6
la. Surry Hills F J14
pl. Camperdwn 17 C5
pl. Glebe 12 F16
pl. Glossodia 59 B9
pl. Yarrawarrah 489 E13
pwy. Chipping Ntn, off Derby Cr 366 H16
pwy. Chipping Ntn, off Derby Cr 396 H1
rd. Hornsby 222 C1

st. Blacktown 244 C15
st. Camperdwn 17 C6
st. Canley Ht 365 D4
st. Epping 251 B12
st. Kingswood 237 E13
st. Kogarah 433 B5
st. Merrylands 308 B16
st. Minto 452 H16
st. Minto Ht 483 F1
st. Penrith 237 A12
st. Rooty Hill 242 C15
st. St Ives 224 C15
st. Silverwater 309 F11
st. Vaucluse 318 G16

DERBYSHIRE
av. Toongabbie 276 F9
rd. Leichhardt 10 A10
rd. Lilyfield 10 A8

DEREK
pl. Hassall Gr 212 C15

DERMONT
st. Hassall Gr 211 J14

DERNA
av. Holsworthy 426 E8
cr. Allambie Ht 257 F11
rd. Holsworthy 396 C16

DERNANCOURT
av. Engadine 518 J1
pde. Milperra 397 H11

DEROWIE
av. Homebush 341 A7

DERRIA
st. Canley Ht 365 D3

DERRIBONG
cr. Bangor 459 C13
pl. Thornleigh 221 B6
st. Villawood 367 D4

DERRIG
rd. Tennyson 58 B11

DERRILIN
cl. Bangor 459 B14

DERRING
la. Kurrajong 55 C12

DERRIWONG
la. Dural 189 B11
rd. Dural 188 G8
rd. Dural 189 A13

DERRY
wy. Bonnyrigg 364 B3

DERWENT
av. N Wahrnga 222 K2
ct. Wattle Grove 395 H12
la. Glebe 12 C14
pde. Blacktown 274 A4
pl. Bligh Park 150 G7
pl. Bossley Park 333 F5
pl. Castle Hill 247 K5
pl. Kearns 481 C1
pl. St Clair 300 C1
rd. Bringelly 387 K5
st. Collaroy Plat 228 D11
st. Glebe 12 C14
st. Mount Druitt 241 C12
st. S Hurstville 432 B10

DE SAXE
cl. Thornleigh 220 G11

DESBOROUGH
rd. Colyton 269 J5
rd. St Marys 269 J5

DESDEMONA
st. Rsemeadow 540 F6

DESLEY
cr. Prospect 274 H13

DESLIE
av. Werrington 238 F11

DESMOND
st. Eastwood 281 H3
st. Ingleburn 453 C10
st. Merrylands 307 B13
st. Merrylands W 307 B13

DESOUTTER
av. Bnkstn Aprt 367 J16

DESPOINTES
st. Marrickville 373 K12

DETTMANN
av. Longueville 314 C8

DETZNER
pl. Whalan 240 K9

DEVANEY
av. Glenmore Pk 265 J8
st. Blackett 241 D2

DEVENISH
st. Greenfld Pk 334 B12

DEVERE
av. Belrose 226 A13

DEVERON
pl. St Andrews 481 K1

DE VILLIERS
av. Chatswd W 284 E11

DE VILNITS
pde. Penrith 236 F10

DEVINE
st. Erskineville 374 K10

DEVITT
av. Newington 310 B15
cr. The Oaks 502 F14
pl. Hillsdale 406 H15
st. Blacktown 244 J16
st. Narrabeen 229 A7

DEVLIN
pl. Menai 458 J6
pl. Quakers Hill 214 B12
rd. Castlereagh 145 H14
rd. Londonderry 177 A1
rd. N Epping 251 C10
st. Ashcroft 364 F15
st. Ryde 311 K2
wy. Bonnyrigg 364 C6

DEVON
cl. Bossley Park 334 B12
pl. Busby 363 K15
pl. Collaroy 229 A15
pl. Galston 159 E10
pl. Narellan Vale 508 J2
pl. North Rocks 278 J2
rd. Bardwell Pk 402 J7
rd. Cmbrdg Pk 237 K9
rd. Ingleburn 452 K6
st. N Epping 251 E11
st. Rooty Hill 272 D3
st. Rosehill 309 C8
st. Wahroonga 223 C4

DEVONPORT
st. Wakeley 334 G16

DEVONSHIRE
rd. Kemps Ck 360 C16
rd. Rossmore 390 B7
st. Chatswood 284 K11
st. Crows Nest 315 G6
st. Croydon 372 B2
st. Surry Hills 19 H2

DEWAR
pl. Riverstone 183 C8
pl. St Andrews 451 J14
st. Campsie 371 K13

DEWBERRY
cl. Menai 458 J13
wy. Castle Hill 248 H3

DEWDNEY
rd. Emu Plains 235 H11

DEWDROP
pl. Acacia Gdn 214 H14
pl. Wrrngtn Dns 238 C4

DEWEY
ct. Maroubra 407 E14
pl. St Helens Park 540 K11

DEWHURST
av. Castle Hill 218 B10

DE WITT
la. Bankstown 399 D4
pl. Fairfield W 335 C10
pl. Willmot 210 E13
st. Bankstown 399 D5

DEWRANG
av. Bradbury 511 D15
av. Elanora Ht 198 E16
st. Carss Park 432 F13
st. Lidcombe 339 J4

DEWSBURY
st. Botany 405 E14
swy. Liverpool 395 E3

DEXTER
la. Rockdale 403 B15
pl. Plumpton 242 C10
st. St Helens Park 541 A6

DHARUG
cl. Mulgoa 324 A5

DIAMANTINA
av. Windsor Dn 151 A16
cl. St Clair 270 G12

DIAMOND
av. Glenwood 215 E14
av. Granville 308 F12
cr. Bonnyrigg 363 G8
pl. Eagle Vale 481 C7

DIAMOND BAY
rd. Vaucluse 348 E6

DIAMOND HILL
dr. Kurrajong Hl 55 C8

DIAMONTINA
av. Kearns 451 C16

DIANA
av. Kellyville 216 D3
av. Roselands 400 J7
av. West Pymble 252 G12
ct. Cecil Hills 363 A4
pl. S Penrith 267 B7
st. Pendle Hill 306 E2

DIANE
cl. Greenacre 370 C6
dr. Lalor Park 245 H12
st. Marsfield 281 K4

DIANELLA
pl. Kingswood 267 H2
pl. Mt Annan 509 E4
st. Caringbah 492 J5
wy. Mt Colah 162 E12

DIANNE
pl. Berowra Ht 132 J9
pl. Hawksbry Ht 174 J4

DIANTHUS
pl. Jannali 460 J10

DIBBLE
av. Marrickville 373 D14

DIBBLER
pl. St Helens Park 541 G2

DIBBS
la. Alexandria 18 F15
st. Alexandria 18 F15
st. Canterbury 372 E14
st. Centnnial Pk 20 K14

DICK
st. Balmain 7 G11
st. Chippendale 19 A2
st. Harbord 258 K16
st. Henley 313 B14
st. Randwick 377 E12

DICKENS
dr. Centnnial Pk 21 F11
rd. Ambarvale 511 A14
rd. Ambarvale 541 A1
rd. Wetherill Pk 334 H6
st. Winston Hills 247 F16

DICKENSON
st. Panania 398 D14

DICKIN
av. Sandringham 463 D2

DICKINSON
av. Croydon 372 D2

DICKSON
av. Artarmon 314 J3
av. W Pnnant Hl 249 D10
av. West Ryde 281 B14
la. Bronte 377 J6
la. S Windsor 120 G15
la. West Ryde 281 C15
la. Newtown, off King La 374 J10
rd. Denham Ct 422 F16
rd. Leppington 420 G6
st. Bronte 377 J7
st. Haberfield 343 D15
st. Newtown 374 H10
st. Strathfield 341 A12

DIDRIKSEN
av. Newington, off Henricks Av 309 K15

DIEFFENBACH
tce. Bidwill 211 E16

DIENELT
pl. Glenwood 215 B15

DIETZ
la. Oakdale 500 F4

DIFFEY
la. Yagoona 368 H11
st. Yagoona 368 H11

DIGBY
pl. Chipping Ntn 366 G16

DIGGER
cr. Gt Mckrl Bch 109 A13

DIGGERS
av. Gladesville 312 J4
la. Canley Vale, off Freeman Av 366 A3

DIGGINS
st. Kellyville 186 A14

DIGHT
st. Richmond 119 B4
st. Windsor 121 B10

DILGA
cl. Bangor 459 C14
cr. Erskine Park 270 G15
st. Kings Lngly 245 G7

DILKARA
ct. Menai 459 A16

DILKE
rd. Padstow 429 F6
rd. Padstow Ht 429 F8

DILKERA
cl. Hornsby 191 C13
rd. Glenorie 127 K4

DILLON
cl. Barden Rdg 488 H2
la. Paddington 13 A12
pl. Oakhurst 242 C2
st. Paddington 4 K12
st. Ramsgate 433 D13

DILLWYNIA
dr. Glenmore Pk 265 H13

DILLWYNNIA
gr. Heathcote 518 H12

DILSTON
cl. West Hoxton 392 E6

DI MASCIO
pl. Oakhurst 211 H16

DIMBY
pl. Busby 363 G15

DIMENT
wy. Hurstville 432 A6

DINA BETH
av. Blacktown 273 J1

DIND
st. Milsons Point 5 J16

DINDIMA
pl. Bangor 459 B14
pl. Belrose 226 B14

DINE
la. Randwick 407 B1
pl. Camden S 506 K13
st. Randwick 377 B16

DINGLE
st. Riverstone 183 A5

DINJERRA
cl. Bangor 459 A15
cr. Oatley 461 A1

DINMORE
pl. Castle Hill 219 A9

DINO
cl. Rooty Hill 271 J3

DINORA
st. Belmore 371 C14

DINTON
st. Prospect 274 K10

D'INZEO
pl. Hinchinbrk 393 A4

DION
pl. Plumpton 241 H8

DIONE
ct. St Clair 269 G11

DIOSMA
pl. Engadine 488 E14

DIPROSE
st. Fairfield 336 J15

DIRE STRAITS
wy. Berala 339 C15

DIRK
cl. Green Valley 363 B10

DISALVO
cl. Cabramatta W 365 C5

DISCOVERY
av. Willmot 210 C12
pl. Oyster Bay 461 D3

DISPENSARY
la. Campsie 371 K12

DISRAELI
rd. Winston Hills 277 J1

DISTILLERS
pl. Huntingwd 273 G12

DIVE
st. Matraville 406 J15

DIVISION
la. Coogee, off Brook St 377 G13
st. Coogee 377 G13

DIXMUDE
st. S Granville 338

DIXON
av. Frenchs Frst 257
cl. Illawong 459
la. Revesby, off Blamey Pl 398
rd. Blaxland 234
st. Abbotsbury 333
st. Haymarket E
st. Haymarket 3
st. Mount Druitt 271
st. Parramatta 308
st. Sydney
st. Sydney 3

DIXSON
av. Dulwich Hill 373

DOAK
av. Llandilo 178

DOBBIE
pl. Glenorie 128

DOBELL
cct. St Clair 270
la. St Clair, off Dobell Cct 270
pl. Kenthurst 158
pl. St Ives 224
rd. Claymore 481
rd. Eagle Vale 480
rd. Engadine 489
st. Mt Pritchard 364

DOBROYD
av. Camden 507
la. Haberfield 9
pde. Haberfield 9
pde. Haberfield 342
pde. Haberfield 343
pde. Haberfield 343
pde. Haberfield 343
pde. Haberfield 343
rd. Balgowlah Ht 287

DOBROYD SCENIC
dr. Balgowlah Ht 287

DOBSON
cl. Edensor Pk 363
cr. Baulkham Hl 247
cr. Dundas Vy 280
cr. Ryde 282
pl. Emu Heights 234
st. Thornleigh 220

DOBSON DORKING
pl. Faulconbdg 171

DOBU
pl. Glenfield 424

DOCHARTY
rd. Bradbury 511

DOCK
rd. Birchgrove 7

DOCKER
la. Chippendale 18

DOCOS
cr. Bexley 432

DOCTOR LAWSON
pl. Rooty Hill 272

DODD
pl. Cranebrook 207

DODDS
st. Naremburn 315

DODFORD
rd. Llandilo 178

DODS
pl. Doonside 273

DODSON
av. Cronulla 493
cr. Winston Hills 277

DOHENY
cl. Baulkham Hl 247

DOHERTY
av. Glenhaven 218
st. Quakers Hill 214

DOIG
av. Denistone E 281
st. Wentwthvle 277

DOLAN
la. Woollahra 22
st. Ryde 312

DOLANS
rd.s, Woolooware 493

DOLE
pl. Kenthurst 156

DOLGE
pl. Ambarvale 510

LIN
Colyton ... 270 C7
OMITE
Eagle Vale ... 481 E5
Cranebrook ... 207 D14
PHIN
Clarmnt Ms ... 238 J16
Green Valley ... 363 A12
Avalon ... 140 D10
Coogee ... 377 E15
Coogee ... 377 E15
Randwick ... 377 C15
MAIN
Bella Vista ... 246 J4
MBEY
Ambarvale ... 510 J13
MINIC
Woolooware ... 493 C12
MINION
Mosman ... 317 F10
MINISH
Camden S ... 506 K15
N
St Clair ... 269 K16
Kearns ... 451 B15
Kurrajong Ht ... 53 K7
Newtown ... 17 D14
IAHUE
Prairiewood ... 334 E9
IALBAIN
Rsemeadow ... 540 C4
IALD
Epping ... 281 E3
Bondi Jctn ... 22 J10
Carlingford ... 279 J2
Hurstville ... 431 H1
North Ryde ... 283 A10
Old Guildford ... 337 E11
Picnic Point ... 428 B7
Yennora ... 337 E11
IALDSON
Bradbury ... 511 G10
Pagewood ... 406 D8
IATO
Smithfield ... 336 A5
ICASTER
Casula ... 394 G16
Cawdor ... 506 D16
Kensington ... 376 E15
Kingsford ... 406 E2
Narellan ... 478 H10
West Pymble ... 252 G9
IE
Arncliffe ... 403 G7
IEGAL
Smithfield ... 335 E2
Rouse Hill ... 185 D8
Killarney Ht ... 286 B2
IELLY
Frenchs Frst ... 255 G1
IGOLA
Schofields ... 213 J5
IINGTON
Georges Hall ... 368 C14
I JUAN
Randwick ... 377 B15
ILEA
Mt Colah ... 162 E15
I MILLS
Hebersham ... 241 F4
INA
Acacia Gdn ... 214 G14
Miranda ... 491 J1
INAN
Bexley ... 402 G15
INELLAN
Clovelly ... 377 K13
Blacktown, off Campbell St ... 244 H16
Blacktown, off Campbell St ... 274 H1
INELLY
Liberty Gr ... 311 B10
Balmain ... 7 J12
Crows Nest ... 315 F4
Guildford ... 337 B2
Naremburn ... 315 F4
Putney ... 312 C7
IOHOES
Mulgoa ... 323 K3
IOHUE
Kings Park ... 244 D1

DONOVAN
av. Maroubra ... 406 G12
pl. Bonnyrigg ... 364 D5
st. Eastwood ... 281 J8
st. Revesby Ht ... 428 K6
DONS
rd. Dural ... 189 E15
DOODSON
av. Lidcombe ... 339 J7
DOODY
st. Alexandria ... 375 D14
st. Gladesville ... 312 G11
DOOHAT
av. N Sydney ... K A2
av. N Sydney ... 5 E5
la. N Sydney ... K A3
DOOLAN
la. Balmain ... 7 A8
st. Dean Park ... 212 F16
DOOLEY
av. Bass Hill ... 368 C13
DOOMBEN
av. Eastwood ... 281 B6
cl. Casula ... 394 D15
DOON
dr. Sans Souci ... 462 K5
pl. St Andrews ... 482 A1
st. Marayong ... 243 G6
DOONKUNA
st. Beverly Hills ... 401 D8
DOONMORE
st. Penrith ... 237 A14
DOONSIDE
cr. Blacktown ... 243 J13
cr. Blacktown ... 244 B14
cr. Doonside ... 243 C13
cr. Woodcroft ... 243 C13
rd. Arndell Park ... 273 D9
rd. Doonside ... 243 C15
rd. Doonside ... 243 D16
DORA
cr. Dundas ... 279 G14
st. Blacktown ... 274 E6
st. Hurstville ... 431 G1
st. Marsfield ... 282 C4
DORADILLO
pl. Eschol Park ... 481 B4
DORADO
pl. Hinchinbrk ... 393 D3
st. Erskine Park ... 270 F16
DORAHY
st. Dundas ... 279 K12
DORAL
pl. Liverpool ... 395 A10
DORAN
av. Lurnea ... 394 E7
dr. Castle Hill ... 217 F12
st. Kingsford ... 406 E2
DORCAS
pl. Rsemeadow ... 540 J10
DORE
pl. Mt Annan ... 479 H15
DOREEN
cr. Baulkham Hl ... 247 C10
DORHAUER
la. Woollahra ... 21 K4
pl. Woollahra ... 21 J4
DORIS
av. Earlwood ... 402 G3
av. Miranda ... 461 J16
la. N Sydney ... 6 A9
pl. Emerton ... 240 K5
st. Greystanes ... 305 G5
st. N Sydney ... 6 A9
st. Picnic Point ... 428 B8
st. Ashfield, off Heighway Av ... 372 G2
DORIS HIRST
pl. W Pnnant Hl ... 218 K15
DORKING
rd. Cabarita ... 342 E1
DORLTON
st. Kings Lngly ... 245 E7
DORMAN
cr. Lindfield ... 283 H2
DORMER
cl. Elderslie ... 507 K2
gr. Quakers Hill ... 214 D14
DORMITORY HILL
rd. Scheyville ... 124 A6

DORNOCH
ct. Castle Hill ... 218 E7
st. Winston Hills ... 277 D3
DOROTHY
cr. Colyton ... 270 E5
ct. Baulkham Hl ... 247 D3
st. Cromer ... 228 C15
st. Freemns Rch ... 90 D2
st. Hebersham ... 241 F10
st. Merrylands ... 307 C7
st. Mt Pritchard ... 364 G11
st. Rydalmere ... 309 J3
st. Ryde ... 282 A10
st. Sefton ... 338 E13
st. Wentwthvle ... 276 J13
DOROTHY ALISON
st. Moore Park ... 21 C6
DORRE
pl. Green Valley ... 363 B10
DORRIE
pl. Quakers Hill ... 214 C13
DORRIGO
av. Hoxton Park ... 392 K6
av. N Balgowlah ... 287 B4
cl. Bangor ... 459 C14
cr. Bow Bowing ... 452 D15
la. Sans Souci ... 463 A5
DORRINGTON
cr. S Windsor ... 151 B8
pl. Glenmore Pk ... 266 A5
DORRIT
wy. Ambarvale ... 511 B15
DORRITT
st. Lane Cove ... 314 E3
DORSET
av. Northmead ... 278 C4
cl. Belrose ... 225 K11
cl. Elderslie ... 507 K1
cl. Wakeley ... 364 J1
dr. St Ives ... 223 K16
dr. St Ives ... 224 A14
pl. Miller ... 393 H3
rd. Heathcote ... 518 D10
rd. Northbridge ... 316 F1
st. Blacktown ... 274 G6
st. Cmbrdg Pk ... 237 J8
st. Epping ... 251 D13
DOT
la. Leichhardt ... 16 A4
st. Marrickville ... 373 G12
DOTTEREL
pl. Ingleburn ... 453 H6
pl. Woronora Ht ... 489 E5
st. Hinchinbrk ... 393 D1
DOUGAN
st. Ashfield ... 372 F6
DOUGHERTY
la. N Willghby ... 285 D10
st. Rosebery ... 405 H3
DOUGLAS
av. Chatswood ... 285 D6
av. N Epping ... 251 F8
av. Wahroonga ... 222 D3
cl. Green Valley ... 363 C11
la. Randwick ... 377 F11
la. Stanmore ... 16 D9
pde. Dover Ht ... 348 G14
pl. Miranda ... 461 J16
rd. Blacktown ... 273 E4
rd. Doonside ... 273 E4
rd. Kurrajong Ht ... 54 B8
rd. Quakers Hill ... 213 G13
st. Bardwell Vy ... 402 J9
st. Clovelly ... 377 F10
st. Earlwood ... 402 D7
st. Fairfield ... 336 F9
st. Faulconbdg ... 171 C15
st. Hobartville ... 118 D6
st. Merrylands ... 307 A9
st. N Richmond ... 87 E10
st. Panania ... 428 D5
st. Putney ... 311 K8
st. Randwick ... 377 F10
st. Redfern ... 19 E10
st. St Ives ... 224 B10
st. Springwood ... 201 D1
st. Stanmore ... 16 B9
st. Waterloo ... 19 E10
DOUGLAS FARM
rd. Kurrajong Hl ... 54 J7
DOUGLAS HAIG
st. Oatley ... 430 H12
DOUGLAS McMASTER
pl. Llandilo ... 209 G2

DOUGLAS PARK
dr. Douglas Park ... 568 E11
dr. Douglas Park ... 568 E13
dr. Douglas Park ... 568 G7
DOUGLASS
av. Carlingford ... 249 J15
la. Sydney ... E F2
pl. Cromer ... 228 A16
st. Sydney ... E E2
DOULTON
av. Beacon Hill ... 257 G8
dr. Cherrybrook ... 219 C13
DOUNE
ct. Castle Hill ... 218 E7
DOURO
pl. Airds ... 511 K15
st. Marayong ... 243 J7
DOUST
pl. Grasmere ... 475 J16
pl. Shalvey ... 211 C13
st. Bass Hill ... 368 C7
st. Chester Hill ... 368 C7
DOVE
cl. Woronora Ht ... 489 E2
la. Randwick ... 377 F10
pl. Hinchinbrk ... 363 C16
pl. Ingleburn ... 453 H7
pl. St Clair ... 269 H11
st. Revesby ... 399 A12
DOVECOTE
gln. Wrrngtn Dns ... 237 K4
DOVELEY
rd. Como ... 460 E6
DOVER
ct. Castle Hill ... 219 A11
la. Rose Bay, off Dover Rd ... 348 C11
pl. Engadine ... 489 C16
pl. West Hoxton ... 392 C8
rd. Dover Ht ... 348 D11
rd. Rose Bay ... 348 B10
st. Botany ... 405 F12
st. Marsfield ... 281 K4
st. Summer Hill ... 373 E4
DOW
pl. Marayong ... 244 A4
DOWD
la. East Ryde ... 282 K16
DOWDING
cl. Cecil Hills ... 362 J8
st. Panania ... 398 B14
DOWE
pl. Bligh Park ... 150 D6
DOWEL
st. Chatswood ... 285 A6
DOWLAND
st. Bonnyrigg Ht ... 363 D7
DOWLE
pl. Camden S ... 507 B16
st. Douglas Park ... 568 G4
DOWLES
la. Bickley Vale ... 505 J12
DOWLING
la. Kensington, off Ingram St ... 376 A12
pl. S Windsor ... 120 K15
st. Arncliffe ... 403 D7
st. Bardwell Vy ... 403 D7
st. Kensington ... 376 A12
st. Leumeah ... 482 D15
st. Queenscliff ... 288 F2
st. West Hoxton ... 391 J12
st. Woolmloo ... 4 G7
st. Zetland ... 376 A12
DOWNES
cl. Illawong ... 459 K4
cr. Currans Hill ... 479 G10
st. Belfield ... 371 D9
st. Colyton ... 270 D7
st. N Epping ... 251 J9
DOWNEY
la. Fairfield, off Harris St ... 336 E12
st. Bexley ... 402 F16
DOWNING
av. Cmbrdg Gdn ... 237 G1
av. Regents Pk ... 369 E1
pl. Gladesville ... 313 A11
st. Epping ... 250 F14
st. Picton ... 563 G2
DOWNPATRICK
rd. Killarney Ht ... 255 K15

DOWNSHIRE
pde. Chester Hill ... 368 C4
pl. Dawes Point ... 1 F8
st. Dawes Point ... 1 F8
DOWRENA
pl. Berowra ... 133 D10
DOWSETT
rd. Kingsgrove ... 402 A12
DOYLE
cl. Wetherill Pk ... 334 D4
pl. Baulkham Hl ... 246 J15
pl. Gordon ... 253 D12
pl. Marayong ... 244 C3
rd. Padstow ... 429 D1
rd. Revesby ... 399 A13
DRACIC
st. S Wntwthvle ... 306 J9
DRAGO
rd. Hinchinbrk ... 393 D4
DRAKE
av. Caringbah ... 492 K4
la. Jamisontown, off Drake St ... 266 D5
pl. Blacktown ... 275 A7
pl. Shalvey ... 211 B13
st. Artarmon ... 284 J14
st. Concord ... 342 A1
st. Jamisontown ... 266 D5
st. Panania ... 398 D16
DRAKES
la. Ashfield ... 372 J3
DRANSFIELD
av. Mascot ... 405 F7
rd. Edensor Pk ... 363 F4
DRAPER
av. Roselands ... 400 F7
st. Glenwood ... 215 D14
DRAVA
pl. Kearns ... 451 B16
DRAVET
st. Padstow ... 399 B11
DRAWBRIDGE
pl. Castle Hill ... 217 E4
DRAYTON
av. Castle Hill ... 248 A5
pl. Edensor Pk ... 333 F14
DREADNOUGHT
rd. Oxford Falls ... 227 A16
st. Roselands ... 401 B5
DREAM HOUSE
la. Mosman, off Spit Rd ... 287 B16
DREDGE
av. Douglas Park ... 568 J14
av. Moorebank ... 396 D7
pwy. Moorebank, off Dredge Av ... 396 E7
DREMEDAY
st. Northmead ... 248 B15
DRESDEN
av. Beacon Hill ... 257 F7
av. Castle Hill ... 247 F1
DRESS CIRCLE
rd. Avalon ... 170 A4
DRESSLER
ct. Holroyd ... 307 K11
DREW
pl. Belrose ... 256 A1
st. Greenacre ... 370 G11
st. Westmead ... 307 H3
DRIFT
rd. Richmond ... 117 H7
DRISCOLL
av. Rooty Hill ... 272 B5
pl. Barden Rdg ... 488 F4
st. Abbotsbury ... 333 B15
DRIVER
av. Moore Park ... 20 H3
av. Wallacia ... 324 K13
pl. Bonnyrigg ... 364 C4
st. Denistone W ... 280 K13
DROMANA
rd. Marsden Pk ... 181 K14
DRONE
st. Greenacre ... 370 H10
DROOD
pl. Ambarvale ... 510 J14
DROVER
rd. Bnkstn Aprt ... 367 H16
DROVERS
wy. Lindfield ... 284 C2

DRUERY
la. Hurstville 431 K8
DRUITT
la. Sydney C E13
pl. Sydney C E11
pl. Wrrngtn Cty 238 E9
st. Mount Druitt 241 C11
st. Sydney C E12
st. Sydney 3 E6
DRUMALBYN
rd. Bellevue Hill 347 G13
st. Ingleburn 453 C9
DRUMARD
av. Leumeah 482 C14
DRUMCLIFF
av. Killarney Ht 255 K15
DRUMMOND
la. Belmore 401 F2
la. Warwck Frm 365 G16
rd. Kurrajong 85 E3
rd. Oyster Bay 461 A7
st. Belmore 401 F1
st. S Windsor 120 G15
st. Warwck Frm 365 G16
DRUMMOYNE
av. Drummoyne 313 G15
cr. St Johns Pk 364 G4
DRURY
la. Mosman, off Gordon St 317 D8
pl. Hebersham 241 G1
DRYAD
pl. Leonay 264 J2
DRYBERRY
av. St Clair 269 G16
DRY DEN
pl. Wetherill Pk 334 J6
DRYDEN
av. Carlingford 249 E13
av. Oakhurst 242 A5
rd. N Turramrra 223 E7
st. Campsie 372 B11
DRY LAKES
rd. Thirlmere 564 A4
DRYNAN
st. Summer Hill 373 B5
DRYSDALE
av. Picnic Point 428 E8
cr. Plumpton 242 C7
pl. Casula 424 F2
pl. Kareela 461 D13
rd. Elderslie 507 J2
rd. Mt Pritchard 364 J11
st. Claymore 481 A10
st. Eagle Vale 481 A9
DUARDO
st. Edensor Pk 333 H15
DUBARDA
st. Engadine 488 F16
DUBBO
pl. Bangor 459 C14
st. Quakers Hill 244 A2
DUBLIN
av. Killarney Ht 256 C16
st. Glendenning 242 J3
st. Smithfield 335 D6
DUCHESS
av. Rodd Point 343 E8
st. Kellyville 215 B3
st. Stanhpe Gdn 215 B3
wy. Minto 482 J7
DUCK
pl. Hinchinbrk 393 D1
st. Auburn 309 B13
DUCKER
av. Hobartville 118 E9
DUCKMALLOIS
av. Blacktown 274 G5
DUCROS
st. Petersham 15 F13
DUDLEY
av. Bankstown 399 C4
av. Blacktown 244 B15
av. Caringbah 492 J11
av. Roseville 284 J2
la. Woollahra 22 G5
pl. Tahmoor 565 F12
rd. Guildford 338 D10
rd. Rose Bay 348 D8
st. Asquith 192 B9
st. Auburn 339 B3
st. Balgowlah 287 F8
st. Berala 339 D10
st. Bondi 378 C5
st. Coogee 407 D1
st. Haberfield 343 E13
st. Hurstville 431 F1
st. Kirrawee 491 C1
st. Lidcombe 339 D10
st. Marrickville 373 E13
st. Mount Druitt 241 C14
st. Paddington 21 E1
st. Pagewood 405 K10
st. Penshurst 431 H7
st. Punchbowl 400 D3
st. Punchbowl 400 E4
st. Randwick 377 D16
st. Rydalmere 279 C16
DUER
pl. Cherrybrook 219 J11
DU FAUR
st. N Turramrra 193 F12
DUFEK
pl. Tregear 240 B5
DUFF
pl. Castle Hill 218 B9
rd. Cecil Park 331 E13
st. Arncliffe 403 D7
st. Burwood 341 K16
st. Turramurra 222 F15
DUFFY
av. Grose Vale 85 D15
av. Kingsgrove 401 K6
av. Thornleigh 221 A10
av. Westleigh 220 E9
st. Merrylands W 306 J14
DUGALD
rd. Mosman 317 D8
st. Riverstone 183 D8
DUGGAN
cr. Connells Pt 431 J13
pl. Lalor Park 245 E14
st. Douglas Park 568 G5
DUGUID
st. Mascot 405 A5
DUIGNAN
cl. Epping 281 D3
DUKE
av. Concord 342 D5
av. Rodd Point 343 E8
cl. Green Valley 362 K11
pl. Balmain East 8 E8
rd. Wilberforce 92 A1
st. Balmain East 8 E7
st. Btn-le-Sds 433 K3
st. Campsie 372 B13
st. Canley Ht 365 G1
st. East Hills 427 K4
st. Forestville 255 F10
st. Granville 308 E9
st. Kensington 376 D11
st. Merrylands 307 A9
st. Rooty Hill 241 H13
st. Strathfield 341 E11
DUKE OF EDINBURGH
pde. Clontarf 287 F15
DUKES
pl. Emu Plains 235 C11
DUKIC
st. Bonnyrigg Ht 363 A7
DULCIE
st. Seven Hills 245 B16
DULHUNTY
ct. Cranebrook 207 D9
DULIN
cl. Bangor 459 B15
DULWA
rd. Menai 459 A4
DULWICH
rd. Chatswd W 284 F7
rd. Roseville 284 F7
rd. Vineyard 152 F11
st. Dulwich Hill 373 E9
DUMARESQ
rd. Rose Bay 348 B8
st. Campbelltwn 511 E5
st. Gordon 253 F8
DUMAS
pl. Winston Hills 247 E16
DU MAURIER
pl. Wetherill Pk 335 A6
DUMBARTON
pl. Engadine 489 A8
st. McMahons Pt 5 B12
DUMBLE
st. Seven Hills 275 D3
DUMFRIES
rd. St Andrews 451 K16
st. Winston Hills 277 E5
DUMIC
pl. Cromer 228 E15
DUMPU
st. Holsworthy 426 G7
DUNALLEY
st. West Hoxton 392 D5
DUNARA
gdn. Point Piper 14 K2
DUNBAR
av. Regents Pk 369 C2
av. Wrrngtn Cty 238 E8
cl. Normanhurst 221 F11
pl. Illawong 459 D1
pl. Kellyville 217 A2
pl. Mt Annan 479 E16
st. Ryde 281 K16
st. St Andrews 452 A13
st. Silverdale 353 H16
st. Watsons Bay 318 G15
DUNBARS
rd. Werombi 443 D6
DUNBIER
av. Lurnea 394 F7
DUNBIL
ct. Bangor 459 B15
DUNBLANE
st. Camperdwn 17 F4
DUNCAN
cl. Glenmore Pk 265 F9
cr. Collaroy Plat 228 K13
la. Maroubra 407 E11
pl. Epping 280 J1
st. Arncliffe 403 J8
st. Balmain 8 A9
st. Drummoyne 343 J5
st. Maroubra 407 E11
st. Minto Ht 483 J2
st. Punchbowl 400 D5
st. Richmond 120 B5
DUNCANS
rd. Greendale 355 A14
DUNCANSBY
cr. St Andrews 452 B15
DUNCRAIG
dr. Kellyville 186 K15
DUNDAS
pl. Wakeley 334 G13
st. Coogee 407 H3
DUNDEE
pl. St Andrews 481 J3
st. Cmbrdg Pk 237 H9
st. Engadine 488 J10
st. Sadleir 364 C16
DUNDILLA
rd. Frenchs Frst 256 D2
DUNDRA
cl. Bangor 459 B14
DUNDRUM
gr. Kellyville 185 C16
gr. Kellyville 215 C1
DUNEBA
av. Kirrawee 491 A8
av. West Pymble 253 B12
dr. Westleigh 220 E9
pl. Frenchs Frst 255 K2
DUNGARA
cr. Glenmore Pk 266 C11
cr. Stanhpe Gdn 215 D8
pl. Winmalee 173 A10
DUNGARTH
la. Emu Heights, off Dungarth Pl 234 K6
pl. Emu Heights 234 K6
DUNGATE
la. Sydney F A2
DUNGOG
pl. Bangor 459 C13
DUNGOWAN
la. Manly, off Ashburner St 288 H10
DUNHEVED
cct. St Marys 239 F6
rd. Cmbrdg Gdn 237 G5
rd. Cmbrdg Pk 238 A6
rd. Wrrngtn Cty 238 G7
rd. Wrrngtn Dns 238 A6
DUNK
cl. Green Valley 363 A13
pl. Kings Lngly 245 E6
DUNKELD
av. Baulkham Hl 246 J10
av. Hurlstone Pk 372 J12
cl. Burraneer 493 E15
la. Hurlstone Pk 372 J12
pl. Dural 219 G4
pl. St Andrews 452 C12
DUNKIRK
av. Kingsgrove 402 B5
DUNKLEY
ct. Rooty Hill 272 C5
pl. Werrington 238 K10
st. Smithfield 335 B7
DUNLEA
rd. Engadine 518 F3
DUNLEAVY
st. Prairiewood 334 D11
DUNLEY
pl. Castle Hill 219 A8
DUNLOP
la. Roselands 400 H6
pl. Picton 563 E10
st. Epping 280 E3
st. N Parramatta 278 B12
st. Roselands 400 J6
st. Strathfield S 371 B6
wy. Minto 482 J8
DUNMORE
av. Carlingford 279 F5
cr. Casula 394 K15
pl. Barden Rdg 488 H4
pl. Wrrngtn Cty 238 F4
rd. Epping 250 K12
rd. West Ryde 281 C16
st. Croydon Pk 372 B7
st. Pendle Hill 276 E15
st. Wentwthvle 277 A16
st.n, Bexley 402 K15
st.s, Bexley 433 A1
DUNN
pl. Cranebrook 207 E13
pl. Prairiewood 334 E10
rd. Smeaton Gra 479 D5
DUNNA
la. Glenmore Pk, off Dunna Pl 266 C11
pl. Glenmore Pk 266 C11
DUNNING
av. Rosebery 375 G16
av. Zetland 375 G16
DUNNS
la. Burwood 341 K13
rd. Maraylya 124 E3
DUNOIS
st. Longueville 314 D8
DUNOON
av. West Pymble 253 B12
pl. Bangor 459 B13
st. Berowra Ht 132 J11
DUNRAVEN
wy. Cherrybrook 219 B14
DUNROSSIL
av. Carlingford 250 A16
av. Casula 394 J12
av. Fairfield E 336 J12
DUNSHEA
pl. Guildford 337 B3
st. Denistone W 280 K12
DUNSMORE
st. Rooty Hill 272 E2
DUNSTABLE
rd. Blacktown 244 K10
DUNSTAFFENAGE
st. Hurlstone Pk 372 K12
DUNSTAFFNAGE
pl. Erskine Park 300 F3
DUNSTAN
av. Milperra 397 D10
pl. Bligh Park 150 K6
pl. Engadine 518 E4
st. Croydon Pk 372 D9
st. Fairfield W 334 J10
DUNTROON
av. Epping 250 F16
av. Roseville 285 B3
av. Roseville Ch 285 D2
av. St Leonards 315 D7
la. Hurlstone Pk, off Duntroon St 373 B10
st. Hurlstone Pk 373
st. Hurlstone Pk 373
DUNWELL
av. Loftus 490
DUPAS
st. Smithfield 305
DURABA
pl. Caringbah 492
pl. S Penrith 266
DURACK
cl. Edensor Pk 363
pl. Casula 424
pl. St Helens Park 541
pl. St Ives 224
DURAL
cr. Engadine 489
la. Hornsby 221
pl. Dharruk 241
rd. Maraylya 94
st. Dural 158
st. Hornsby 221
st. Kenthurst 188
DURAL DOWNS
wy. Dural 158
DURALI
av. Winmalee 173
rd. Glenmore Pk 266
DURANT
la. Yagoona 369
pl. Cherrybrook 219
DURBAN
wy. Minto 482
DURBAR
av. Kirrawee 491
DURDANS
av. Rosebery 375
DURDEN
pl. Ambarvale 540
DURHAM
av. St Ives, off Denley La 223
cl. Bonnyrigg Ht 363
cl. Dural 188
cl. Mcquarie Pk 252
gr. Windsor Dn 151
la. Springwood 201
la. Stanmore 16
la. Dulwich Hill, off Durham St 373
pl. Sylvania 461
rd. Schofields 212
st. Allawah 432
st. Carlton 432
st. Concord 342
st. Douglas Park 568
st. Dulwich Hill 373
st. Hunters Hill 313
st. Hurstville 432
st. Minto 452
st. Mount Druitt 271
st. N Epping 251
st. Oxley Park 240
st. Rosehill 309
st. Stanmore 16
DURI
cl. Bangor 459
pl. Bonnyrigg 364
st. Malabar 437
DURKIN
pl. Peakhurst 430
DURNESS
pl. St Andrews 452
DURRAS
cl. Woodcroft 243
pl. Leumeah 482
st. Prestons 422
DURROW
av. Killarney Ht 256
DURSLEY
rd. Yennora 336
DURUMBIL
rd. Duffys Frst 195
D'URVILLE
av. Tregear 240
DURWARD
st. Dean Park 212
DUTBA
la. Glenmore Pk, off Dutba Pl 266
pl. Glenmore Pk 266
DUTCH
la. St Clair, off Dutch Pl 269

)akhurst............242 C3
St Clair...............269 G11
ERREAU
Claymore...........481 E11
RUC
Randwick...........377 C13
TON
Cabramatta........365 J7
Glenmore Pk......266 A7
Kellyville.............185 J16
Bankstown.........369 A14
Yagoona............369 A14
AL
Hebersham........241 G2
FORD
Paddington, off
Broughton St........13 D15
Paddington..........13 C15
GHT
Greystanes.........306 D7
ER
Blakehurst..........432 E12
Little Bay............437 A12
Fairfield W..........335 A13
Seven Hills.........245 D15
Blakehurst..........432 F12
Woollahra............21 J4
St Helens Park....541 A7
S Penrith............236 K16
Bringelly............387 A6
Leppington.........450 C1
Chippendale...........E A16
Chippendale...........3 C16
Gymea...............491 G2
Ryde..................282 G15
E
St Andrews........481 K1
AL
Mona Vale..........199 B3
DA
Miranda.............492 A1
AN
V Pnnant Hl.......248 H7
OND
Bargo..................567 F5
PNA
Cromer..............228 F13
ON
Woollahra............22 J4
Fairfield W..........335 B12
Glenmore Pk......265 K8
Putney...............312 A9
Hackett..............241 B2
Claymore...........481 B12

E

AM
Fairfield W..........335 G8
AR
Sydney...................E E3
Sydney...................E F3
LE
St Johns Pk.......334 C16
Theresa Park......414 D12
Ryde..................311 K3
Wallacia.............324 J13
Glenwood..........215 G14
E CREEK
Verombi.............443 D6
EHAWK
V Pnnant Hl.......248 E8
Heckenberg........363 K14
EMONT
Campbelltwn......511 H4
E VALE
Eagle Vale..........481 B6
Eschol Park........481 B6
EVIEW
Ingleburn...........453 C16
Minto.................483 A4
NG
Quakers Hill.......214 D9

Riverstone.........181 K8
ES
Baulkham Hl......247 C10

Randwick, off
Stephen St.........377 B9
Cecil Hills...........362 K5

pl. Potts Point.............4 J6
st. Beacon Hill.........257 E6
st. Canley Ht...........365 G2
st. Canley Vale........365 G2
st. Hunters Hill........313 B6
st. Merrylands.........338 B1
st. Mosman............316 J5
st. Mount Druitt......241 E13
st. Potts Point.............4 J6
st. Randwick...........377 B9
st. Roseville...........285 A2
st. Wilberforce..........91 J5
EARLE
av. Ashfield.............342 K14
st. Arncliffe............403 C10
st. Cremorne...........316 C6
st. Doonside...........243 B12
st. Harringtn Pk......478 F8
st. Narellan.............478 F8
wy. Claymore...........481 B11
EARLS
av. Riverwood.........400 E12
ct. Cherrybrook.......219 E12
ct. Roseville Ch.......255 F15
EARLWOOD
av. Earlwood...........402 J3
cr. Bardwell Pk........402 H8
EARLY
st. Parramatta.........308 B6
EARN
pl. St Andrews.......482 A2
EARNGLEY
la. Edgecliff...............13 F10
EARNSHAW
st. Gladesville.........312 K9
EAST
av. Cammeray.........316 B3
cr. Hurstville Gr.......431 H11
dr. Bexley North......402 C9
esp. Manly..............288 G11
la. Randwick...........407 B2
la. St Marys............239 H16
pde. Campsie..........372 D12
pde. Canley Vale......366 C2
pde. Couridjah.........564 D16
pde. Denistone........281 B8
pde. Eastwood.........281 B8
pde. Fairfield...........336 D16
pde. Sutherland.......490 D4
rd. Riverstone.........182 F9
st. Bardwell Vy........403 B8
st. Blakehurst..........462 D2
st. Couridjah...........564 H16
st. Five Dock...........342 K9
st. Granville............308 G11
st. Greenwich...........314 K13
st. Kurrajong Ht........54 D8
st. Kurrajong Hl.........54 F8
st. Lidcombe............339 J12
st. Marrickville..........16 D16
st. Parramatta..........279 B16
st. Redfern.................19 E9
tce. Bankstown.........399 G1
EAST BANK
st. Collaroy.............229 B13
EASTBANK
av. Lansvale............366 E9
EASTBOURNE
av. Avalon..............140 C15
av. Clovelly.............378 A13
av. Wahroonga.........222 A9
rd. Darling Point........13 K6
rd. Homebush W.......340 F10
wy. Bella Vista.........246 E5
EASTCOTE
rd. N Epping............251 G10
EAST CRESCENT
st. McMahons Pt........5 E16
EASTER
st. Leichhardt............15 E5
EASTERBROOK
pl. S Penrith...........266 J5
EASTERN
av. Camperdwn..........18 E3
av. Dover Ht............348 F8
av. Kensington.........376 D16
av. Kingsford...........376 D16
av. Panania.............428 G3
av. Revesby.............428 G3
cct. Parramatta........278 A12
rd. Doonside............243 A15
rd. Mcquarie Pk........282 D1
rd. Matraville...........406 K16
rd. Quakers Hill.......213 G13

rd. Rooty Hill...........272 F3
rd. Turramurra........222 J13
rd. Wahroonga........222 K5
EASTERN ARTERIAL
rd. East Killara........254 E10
rd. E Lindfield..........254 E10
rd. Gordon..............254 D7
rd. Killara................254 E10
rd. Lindfield.............254 E10
rd. St Ives..............254 C2
EASTERN DISTRIBUTOR
Darlinghurst.......346 C13
Moore Park..........20 D13
Moore Park.........376 B7
Redfern..............376 B7
Surry Hills..........376 B7
Woolmloo...............4 D11
EASTERN VALLEY
wy. Castle Cove.......285 E4
wy. Castlecrag.........285 J15
wy. Chatswood.........285 E4
wy. Middle Cove.......285 E4
wy. Northbridge........285 J15
wy. N Willghby..........285 E4
wy. Roseville............285 E4
wy. Willoughby..........285 J15
EASTGATE
av. East Killara........254 G9
EAST KURRAJONG
rd. Comleroy..............56 F5
rd. E Kurrajong...........56 F5
EASTLEA
av. Springwood.......171 F16
gdn. Springwood.......171 F16
EASTLEWOOD
st. Narellan.............478 H10
EAST MARKET
st. Hobartville..........118 G8
st. Richmond...........118 G8
EASTMORE
pl. Maroubra............406 H7
EASTON
av. Sylvania.............461 K9
rd. Berowra Ht.........133 A11
st. Rozelle.................10 J3
EASTVIEW
av. North Ryde.........282 D8
dr. Orangeville.........443 A15
dr. Orangeville.........473 B1
rd. Church Point.......168 F7
st. Greenwich...........315 C8
EAST WILCHARD
rd. Castlereagh........176 D12
rd. Cranebrook.........176 H15
EASTWOOD
av. Eastwood............281 A4
av. Epping...............280 J4
rd. Leppington..........420 A9
EASY
st. Randwick............377 A16
st. Randwick............407 A1
EATHER
av. North Rocks.......248 F12
rd. Ingleburn...........422 H13
EATON
av. Normanhurst.......221 G8
pl. Chiswick.............343 D1
rd. Luddenham.........356 K4
rd. W Pnnant Hl.......249 C10
rd. W Pnnant Hl.......249 G9
sq. Allambie Ht........257 B8
st. Agnes Banks......117 D12
st. Balmain.................7 K10
st. Neutral Bay............6 A5
st. Rooty Hill...........271 K5
st. Willoughby..........285 F12
EBAL
pl. Seven Hills.........275 D11
EBB
st. Quakers Hill.......214 C11
EBB TIDE
st. Chipping Ntn......366 J15
EBDEN
st. Quakers Hill.......214 A9
EBENEZER WHARF
rd. Ebenezer..............63 A10
EBER
pl. Minchinbury........271 G10
EBLEY
st. Bondi Jctn...........22 F8

EBON
la. Erskineville...........17 J16
EBONY
av. Carlingford.........249 C15
av. North Rocks.......249 C15
cl. Casula................394 F14
cr. Quakers Hill.......243 D2
pl. Mcquarie Fd.......454 H3
pwy. Casula, off
Ebony Cl...........394 F14
row. Menai..............458 K14
EBOR
pl. Hoxton Park.......392 H6
rd. Palm Beach........140 A4
EBRO
pl. Kearns...............481 A2
st. Seven Hills.........275 F9
EBSWORTH
rd. Rose Bay...........348 D9
ECCLES
av. Ashfield.............372 G1
pl. Prairiewood........334 F7
st. Ermington...........280 B16
ECHIDNA
pl. Blaxland.............233 D12
ECHO
cl. Penrith...............237 C2
pl. Winston Hills......277 A1
st. Cammeray..........316 A5
st. Roseville............285 C1
ECHUCA
cl. Bonnyrigg..........363 K10
ECHUNGA
rd. Duffys Frst.........195 F3
ECOLE
av. Winmalee...........173 F5
la. Carlton...............432 K8
st. Carlton...............432 K8
ECONO
pl. Silverdale...........353 J8
EDDIE
av. Panania..............428 B3
rd. Minchinbury.......271 B6
EDDY
av. Haymarket.............E H12
av. Haymarket.............3 G14
rd. Chatswd W.........284 E12
st. Merrylands W.....306 G12
st. Thornleigh.........220 J12
EDDYSTONE
rd. Bexley...............402 G13
rd. Bexley...............402 J12
EDEL
pl. Fairfield W..........335 C9
EDEN
av. Croydon Pk.........371 J7
av. Punchbowl.........400 B8
av. S Turramrra........252 C9
dr. Asquith..............192 D9
gln. St Clair..............269 J14
la. N Sydney...............5 D2
la. S Turramrra........252 D10
pl. Bossley Park.......333 F10
pl. Caringbah..........492 E14
pl. Prestons............392 J16
pl. Winston Hills......247 H16
st. Arncliffe.............403 G9
st. Chatswood..........285 D7
st. Marayong...........244 B8
st. N Sydney...............5 E1
st. Ryde..................282 D11
EDENBOROUGH
rd. Lindfield.............284 B4
EDENHOLME
rd. Russell Lea........343 C4
rd. Wareemba..........343 A4
rd. West Pymble......252 F11
EDENLEE
st. Epping..............280 H3
EDEN PARK
dr. Mcquarie Pk.......282 K5
EDENSOR
rd. Bonnyrigg..........364 E4
rd. Cabramatta W....364 E4
rd. Edensor Pk.........333 D16
rd. Greenfld Pk........363 K1
rd. St Johns Pk........364 E4
st. Epping...............251 A13
EDGAR
cr. Belfield...............371 E10
la. Tempe, off
Edgar St...........404 A1
pl. Kings Lngly........245 H7

st. Auburn..............339 A5
st. Bankstown.........368 H15
st. Baulkham Hl......247 G13
st. Chatswd W.........284 F10
st. Condell Park.......398 G6
st. Condell Park.......398 G8
st. Eastwood...........281 D7
st. Harbord.............288 K1
st. Kingsford...........407 C7
st. Mcquarie Fd.......424 A16
st. Revesby.............398 G8
st. St Marys............269 G3
st. Strathfield..........340 J13
st. Tempe...............404 A1
st. Yagoona............368 H15
EDGAR BUGGY
st. Merrylands.........337 H1
EDGBASTON
rd. Beverly Hills.......401 A16
EDGE
st. Lakemba.............400 J4
st. Wiley Park..........400 J4
EDGECLIFF
pl. Engadine............488 D16
pl. Peakhurst...........430 B11
rd. Edgecliff................14 B12
rd. Glenhaven..........187 H13
rd. Woollahra.............22 C1
rd. Woolwich............314 E14
sq. Edgecliff...............13 K12
EDGECLIFFE
av. S Coogee...........407 H7
bvd. Collaroy Plat.....228 H9
esp. Seaforth............287 A11
EDGECOMBE
av. Moorebank.........396 B7
av. Wahroonga.........221 K12
rd. St Ives..............224 B6
EDGECUMBE
av. Coogee.............407 F2
EDGEHILL
av. Botany..............405 F15
st. Carlton..............432 J5
EDGELY
st. Surry Hills............20 C5
EDGEWARE
la. Enmore................17 A15
rd. Enmore................17 A15
rd. Newtown............374 G10
rd. Prospect............275 B12
EDGEWATER
dr. Baulkham Hl......216 E16
dr. Bella Vista..........216 A14
dr. Bella Vista..........216 E16
pde. Parramatta.........308 D1
EDGEWOOD
pl. St Ives...............224 A16
EDGEWORTH
pl. Cartwright...........394 A6
EDGEWORTH DAVID
av. Hornsby.............221 H2
av. Wahroonga.........222 B3
av. Waitara..............221 H2
EDINA
av. Waverley............377 F6
EDINBURGH
av. Carlingford.........279 D4
cct. Cecil Hills.........362 J4
cl. Woolooware.......493 G7
cr. St Andrews.........452 A13
cr. Woolooware.......493 F7
dr. Revesby.............428 J5
dr. Revesby Ht........428 J5
pl. Winston Hills......277 F4
rd. Castlecrag.........285 H12
rd. Forestville..........255 G9
rd. Marrickville.........374 E10
rd. Willoughby..........285 H12
st. Tahmoor.............566 A16
EDISON
la. Belmore.............371 G16
pde. Winston Hills......277 B5
pl. Leumeah.............482 E16
st. Belmore.............371 G16
EDITH
av. Concord.............342 C6
av. Liverpool............364 K16
av. Mcquarie Fd.......454 A2
la. Leichhardt............15 F2
la. St Peters, off
Edith St...........374 H14
pl. Northmead.........278 C5
pwy. Liverpool, off
Edith Av...........364 J15

st. Bardwell Pk...403 B6
st. Castlecrag...286 A12
st. Girraween...276 C13
st. Hurstville...401 J16
st. Kingswood...237 J16
st. Lansdowne...367 B5
st. Leichhardt...15 F1
st. Lidcombe...339 K4
st. Marsfield...282 B8
st. Mount Druitt...271 B2
st. St Peters...374 G13

EDMONDSON
av. Austral...391 C7
av. St Marys...270 A1
cr. Carramar...366 K4
dr. Narrabeen...228 G8
st. North Ryde...282 K9

EDMUND
pl. Cecil Hills...362 E2
pl. Rsemeadow...540 J7
st. Beverly Hills...401 E16
st. Chatswood...284 K7
st. Lindfield...283 F3
st. Queens Park...377 F8
st. Riverstone...153 A13
st. Riverstone...183 C1

EDMUND BLACKET
cl. St Clair...270 C11

EDMUND HOCK
av. Avalon...170 B2

EDMUNDS
st. Carramar...366 J2

EDMUNDSON
cl. Thornleigh...220 H11

EDNA
av. Merrylands W...307 B14
av. Mt Pritchard...364 F12
av. Penshurst...431 G6
av. Springwood...202 A11
av. Toongabbie...276 C4
la. Kingswood, off Edna St...237 J15
pl. Dee Why...258 G3
pl. Ermington...280 C13
pl. Ingleburn...453 C10
pl. Kings Lngly...245 K6
st. Bass Hill...368 D11
st. Kingswood...237 J15
st. Lilyfield...10 G11
st. N Willghby...285 H10
st. Sans Souci...463 C4
st. Warrimoo...203 E13
st. Wiley Park...400 F1

EDROM
cl. Prestons...393 B16
cl. Prestons...423 B1

EDSEL
pl. Hassall Gr...211 J14

EDUCATION
la. Cremorne, off Murdoch St...316 F9

EDWARD
av. Kensington...376 E16
av. Kingsford...406 E1
av. Miranda...492 E1
av. Mulgoa...265 C3
cl. Werrington...238 K10
la. Bondi...378 A3
la. Darlington...18 K6
la. Dulwich Hill...373 E6
la. Glebe...11 G7
la. Pyrmont...12 J5
la. Concord, off Edward St...341 G9
pl. Canley Ht...335 B16
rd. Marayong...244 A7
st. Balmain East...8 J10
st. Bankstown...399 B6
st. Baulkham Hl...247 J5
st. Bexley North...402 B11
st. Bondi...377 K3
st. Bondi Beach...377 K3
st. Botany...405 F11
st. Camden...477 B14
st. Carlton...432 H9
st. Concord...341 G9
st. Cranebrook...207 B9
st. Darlington...18 K5
st. Glebe...11 H7
st. Gordon...253 K7
st. Guildford W...336 H2
st. Kingsgrove...402 B11
st. Kingswood...237 J16
st. Kurrajong Ht...54 B7
st. Lilyfield...10 C7
st. Lurnea...394 G11
st. Mcquarie Fd...423 K14
st. Marrickville...374 B11
st. Narraweena...258 A6
st. Northmead...277 F10
st. N Sydney...5 D5
st. Oatley...431 D10
st. Pyrmont...12 J4
st. Riverstone...182 G2
st. Ryde...312 A2
st. Strathfield S...371 D6
st. Summer Hill...373 E5
st. Sylvania...461 F12
st. The Oaks...502 F13
st. Turrella...403 F6
st. Waverton...5 D5
st. Willoughby...285 E15
st. Woollahra...22 H2

EDWARD BENNETT
dr. Cherrybrook...249 E1

EDWARD EDGAR
st. Minto...482 H5

EDWARD HOWE
pl. Narellan Vale...509 A1

EDWARDS
av. Beecroft...250 A10
la. Killara...254 C10
pl. Penrith...236 K10
rd. Barden Rdg...488 G8
rd. Box Hill...154 J15
rd. Lakemba...370 H14
rd. Middle Dural...158 J4
rd. Nelson...155 A15
rd. Richmond Lwld...88 F8
rd. Rouse Hill...155 A15
rd. Wahroonga...221 H7

EDWARDS BAY
rd. Mosman...317 D4

EDWIN
av. Avalon...140 A14
la. Cammeray, off Edwin St...315 J6
pl. Glenwood...245 H3
pl. Liverpool...394 J8
st. Cammeray...315 J6
st. Colyton...270 G5
st. Drummoyne...343 J3
st. Fairlight...288 D8
st. Greenwich...315 A10
st. Mortlake...312 A14
st. Oatlands...279 A13
st. Regents Pk...369 B2
st. Tempe...404 A2
st.n, Croydon...342 F16
st.s, Croydon...372 E2

EDWINA
pl. Plumpton...241 J10

EDWIN FLACK
av. Homebush B...340 D1

EDWIN WARD
pl. Mona Vale...169 E16

EERAWY
rd. Allambie Ht...257 H15

EFFINGHAM
st. Mosman...317 C10

EGAN
la. Newtown...17 D14
pl. Beacon Hill...257 H4
pl. Woolmloo...4 E7
st. Bankstown...399 C1
st. Newtown...17 J8

EGANS
rd. Oakdale...500 E11

EGERSZEGI
av. Newington, off Newington Bvd...310 B14

EGERTON
st. Silverwater...309 J11

EGGLETON
st. Blacktown...245 B6
st. Campbelltwn...510 J7

EGLINGTON
st. Lidcombe...339 H12

EGLINTON
la. Glebe...11 G7
rd. Glebe...11 G7

EGRET
cl. Bella Vista...246 F1
cr. Yarramundi...145 C5
pl. Clarmnt Ms...268 H5
pl. Hinchinbrk...363 D16
pl. Ingleburn...453 H7
pl. Quakers Hill...214 E11
pl. Woronora Ht...489 E5
wy. Mt Annan...509 B1

EGYPT
st. Holsworthy...426 E10

EIDELWEISS
pl. Lugarno...430 A14

EIGER
pl. Cranebrook...207 F14
st. Seven Hills...275 C9

EIGHTEENTH
av. Austral...361 G15
st. Warragamba...353 E5

EIGHTH
av. Austral...391 A11
av. Campsie...371 H12
av. Jannali...461 A12
av. Llandilo...208 C6
av. Loftus...489 J7
av. Seven Hills...275 J4
av. Shanes Park...209 A8

EILDON
ct. Wattle Grove...396 B15
st. Wentwthvle...277 A10

EILEEN
av. Beverly Hills...401 A12
la. Campsie...372 B14
st. N Balgowlah...287 C6
st. Picnic Point...428 C8
st. Ryde...282 C14

EINSTEIN
av. Lucas Ht...487 G13
st. Winston Hills...277 C5

EISENHOWER
pl. Bonnet Bay...460 A9

ELABANA
cr. Castle Hill...219 B9

EL ADEM
rd. Holsworthy...426 D8

ELAINE
av. Avalon...140 C15
ct. Werrington...238 J11
pl. Hornsby...192 D16
pl. Middle Dural...128 C16
st. Regents Pk...368 K2

ELAMANG
av. Kirribilli...6 C14

ELANORA
av. Blacktown...274 E3
cl. Baulkham Hl...247 F14
pl. Cecil Hills...362 D4
rd. Elanora Ht...198 D14
st. Rose Bay...347 J11

ELAROO
av. La Perouse...436 J12
av. Phillip Bay...436 J12

ELATA
ct. Wattle Grove...396 B16
pl. Kingswood...267 J2
wy. Bidwill...211 E13

ELAYNE
pl. Guildford...338 B8

ELBA
wy. Glenwood...246 A3

ELBE
pl. Kearns...451 A15
st. Seven Hills...275 H8

ELBERTA
av. Castle Hill...247 G2

ELBON
av. Epping...280 D1

ELBRUS
st. Seven Hills...275 C9

ELCAR
pl. Chullora...369 J5

ELCEDO
la. Greenwich...315 A6

ELCHO
cl. Green Valley...362 K13

ELDER
av. Baulkham Hl...247 D5
la. Wrrngtn Cty, off Elder Pl...238 G4
pl. Alfords Point...459 B1
pl. Mcquarie Fd...454 G2
pl. Wrrngtn Cty...238 G4
rd. Dundas...279 F14
wy. Mt Annan...509 F1

ELDERBERRY
pl. Cherrybrook...219 K13

ELDERSHAW
rd. Edensor Pk...333 G16

ELDERSLIE
ct. Wattle Grove...425 K2

ELDON
av. Georges Hall...368 B15
grn. W Pnnant Hl...249 D5
la. Beecroft...250 B7
st. Pitt Town...92 H15
st. Riverwood...400 B16

ELDRED
st. Silverdale...353 G13

ELDRIDGE
rd. Bankstown...399 A7
rd. Condell Park...398 F6
rd. Greystanes...306 C11
st. Cherrybrook...219 K5

ELEANOR
av. Belmore...401 F5
cr. Rooty Hill...241 K15
st. Rosehill...308 G8

ELEBANA
st. Colyton...270 G6

ELECTRA
pl. Raby...451 G13
st. Heathcote...518 F9

ELEGANS
av. St Ives...224 E15

ELEHAM
rd. Lindfield...254 C15

ELENA
la. Belmore...401 H1

ELEVATED
rd. The Rocks...B B2
rd. The Rocks...1 J9

ELEVATION
av. Balgowlah Ht...287 K14

ELEVENTH
av. Austral...391 B7
st. Mascot...405 B7
st. Warragamba...353 F5

ELEY HAWKINS
dr. Warrimoo...203 B12

ELFORD
cr. Merrylands W...306 J12

ELFRED
st. Paddington...4 K15

ELFRIDA
st. Mosman...317 A11

ELFRIEDA
st. Old Tngabbie...277 B6

ELGA
pl. Cherrybrook...219 F16

ELGAR
cl. Bonnyrigg Ht...363 E6
pl. Narellan Vale...478 G15
pl. Seven Hills...246 E11

ELGATA
cl. Avalon...139 J12
cr. Bradbury...511 E16

ELGATTA
pl. Epping...250 F13

ELGER
st. Glebe...12 G13

ELGIN
av. St Andrews...451 K15
pl. Winston Hills...277 E3
st. Gordon...253 K4
st. Schofields...183 B16
st. Woolwich...314 E13
wy. Kellyville...217 B2

ELIAS
wy. Kellyville...186 A14

ELIM
pl. Chippendale...18 H1

ELIMATTA
rd. Mona Vale...199 A6
st. Lidcombe...339 J3

ELIZA
av. Liberty Gr...311 B10
pl. Glenmore Pk...265 F9
st. Fairfield Ht...335 J13
st. Newtown...17 F11
wy. Leumeah...482 C13

ELIZABETH
av. Dulwich Hill...373 A9
av. Kurmond...86 E1
av. Mascot...405 D5
cl. Appin...569 F10
cr. Kingswood...237 F16
cr. Northmead...278 A4
cr. Yagoona...368 H12
dr. Abbotsbury...363 D3
dr. Ashcroft...364 C8
dr. Badgerys Ck...328
dr. Bonnyrigg...364
dr. Bonnyrigg Ht...363
dr. Cecil Hills...362
dr. Cecil Park...361
dr. Edensor Pk...363
dr. Kemps Ck...361
dr. Liverpool...395
dr. Luddenham...327
dr. Mt Pritchard...364
la. Campsie...372
la. Redfern...19
la. Seven Hills...275
la. Randwick, off Elizabeth St...377
la. Parramatta, off Thomas St...308
pde. Lane Cove W...284
pl. Brookvale...258
pl. Cronulla...494
pl. Darling Point...13
pl. Galston...159
pl. Paddington...21
plz. N Sydney...K
rd. Mt Riverview...234
st. Allawah...432
st. Artarmon...284
st. Ashfield...372
st. Avalon...139
st. Berala...339
st. Berowra Ht...133
st. Burwood...342
st. Camden...477
st. Campsie...401
st. Croydon...342
st. Five Dock...342
st. Granville...308
st. Guildford...337
st. Haymarket...F
st. Haymarket...3
st. Hurstville...431
st. Kingsgrove...402
st. Liverpool...395
st. Newtown...18
st. N Richmond...87
st. Paddington...21
st. Paddington...21
st. Parramatta...308
st. Picton...563
st. Randwick...377
st. Redfern...19
st. Riverstone...182
st. Rooty Hill...242
st. Rozelle...10
st. Ryde...282
st. Surry Hills...F
st. Surry Hills...19
st. Sydney...D
st. Sydney...3
st. Wahroonga...221
st. Waterloo...19
st. Wetherill Pk...334
st. Windsor...121
st. Zetland...375
wy. Airds...512

ELIZABETHAN
pl. St Ives Ch...224

ELIZABETH BAY
cr. Elizabeth Bay...13
rd. Elizabeth Bay...13
rd. Elizabeth Bay...13
rd. Rcuttrs Bay...13

ELIZABETH HAKE
cl. Castle Hill, off Vittoria Smith Av...21

ELIZABETH HENRIET
cct. Mcquarie Lk...423

ELIZABETH MACART
av. Camden S...507
dr. Bella Vista...246

ELK
pl. Cranebrook...237
pl. Seven Hills...275
st. Marsfield...281

ELKE
cr. Chester Hill...368
wy. Toongabbie...276

ELKHORN
pl. Alfords Point...429

ELLA
st. Artarmon...315
st. Rydalmere...309
st. St Leonards...315

ELLALONG
pl. Doonside...24

Cremorne, off
Ellalong Rd........316 F5
Cremorne..........316 F5
N Turramrra.......223 F8
AM
Seven Hills.........275 D7
AMATTA
Mosman...........317 C10
EN
Ingleburn...........453 D10
Curl Curl...........258 J15
Panania.............428 E3
Randwick...........407 D2
Randwick...........407 D3
Rozelle....................7 A16
Ryde..................281 K9
ENDALE
Kenthurst...........157 G14
ENGOWAN
Whalan.............240 J9
EN SUBWAY
Mortdale...........431 C8
ERMAN
Kenthurst...........188 D4
ERSLIE
W Pnnant Hl.......249 A6
Bexley................402 F12
Bexley North......402 F12
ERSTON
Wattle Grove......396 A16
ERY
St Ives Ch..........224 B1
Seaforth.............287 A9
Caringbah..........493 A15
Bossley Park......334 B8
ESMERE
Hunters Hill........313 J11
Schofields..........183 A15
Wattle Grove......395 K14
Gymea Bay.........491 G12
Panania..............398 D13
IM
Cranebrook........207 D8
IMATTA
Rydalmere.........279 J16
Cherrybrook, off
Tennyson Cl.......219 D10
IOT
Hillsdale............406 G14
Beacon Hill.........257 H8
IOTDALE
Elderslie............507 K3
IOTT
East Ryde...........282 K15
Erskineville...........18 C16
Baulkham Hl.......246 J3
Cherrybrook.......219 J10
St Helens Park....541 A9
Menai.................458 F12
Balmain.............344 E4
Belfield..............371 D7
Kings Park.........244 D4
Kingswood.........237 E16
Lalor Park..........245 C9
North Bondi.......348 C14
N Strathfield......341 D7
N Sydney..............5 H3
Picnic Point.......428 A7
IS
Alexandria..........375 D16
Ingleburn...........453 E7
Miller.................363 G16
Ellis Lane...........476 B11
Yennora.............337 A10
Kings Lngly.........245 K6
Beacon Hill.........257 E5
Botany...............405 J10
Chatswood.........284 H11
Concord.............342 A3
Condell Park.......398 F5
Merrylands.........307 C9
Oatlands............279 A9
St Marys............269 E2
Sylvania............462 E8
IS BENT
Greendale..........385 A9
ISON
Greenwich..........314 K10
Emu Plains.........235 G9
Pymble...............253 C7
Castlereagh........176 D13
Springwood.......172 G14

ELLISTON
pl. Barden Rdg........488 G5
st. Chester Hill........338 C14
ELLSMORE
av. Killara...............253 K15
ELLSWORTH
dr. Tregear..............240 B4
st. Leumeah.............482 K11
ELM
av. Belrose..............225 H11
ct. Cherrybrook........219 G13
pl. Narellan Vale......479 A12
pl. North Rocks........278 E2
pl. Rydalmere..........309 H1
pl. Wentwthvle.........277 A8
pl. Woolooware........493 C11
rd. Auburn..............339 A7
st. Acacia Gdn.........214 K14
st. Burwood Ht.........371 K3
st. Greystanes.........306 F9
st. Lugarno.............429 H16
st. N St Marys..........239 H11
st. Villawood............366 K2
st. Villawood............367 A2
st. Villawood............367 Z9
ELMBRIDGE
rd. Jamisontown.....266 C2
ELMSLEA
pl. Airds.................512 C10
ELONERA
st. Rydalmere..........309 G2
ELOORA
st. Lane Cove W......313 H2
ELOUERA
cr. Moorebank.........396 G7
cr. Woodbine...........481 D14
ct. Clarmnt Ms.........268 H1
la. Blacktown...........275 B2
rd. Avalon...............169 K1
rd. Cronulla.............494 A10
rd. Westleigh...........220 E8
st. Beverly Hills.......401 C11
ELOURA
pl. Bonnyrigg..........364 A7
st. Dharruk.............241 B7
ELPHICK
av. Mascot..............405 D2
ELPHIN
st. Tahmoor............565 H9
ELPHINSTONE
pl. Davidson...........225 B16
rd. S Coogee...........407 F4
st. Cabarita.............342 D1
ELRINGTON
pl. Cartwright..........394 C5
ELSE
pl. Springwood.......201 K2
ELSEY
pl. Leumeah............482 G11
ELSHAM
rd. Auburn..............339 E7
ELSIE
st. Burwood............341 K13
st. Earlwood............372 G16
st. Scotland I..........168 J4
wy. Parklea.............214 J14
ELSINORE
st. Merrylands.........307 G15
ELSMERE
st. Kensington.........376 F10
ELSMORE
pl. Carlingford.........280 C3
ELSOM
st. Kings Lngly........244 K5
ELSTON
av. Denistone..........281 E11
av. Narwee..............400 G14
la. Narwee, off
Elston Av.........400 G13
ELSWICK
la. Leichhardt............15 F4
st. Leichhardt............15 G1
st. Petersham............15 K5
st.n, Leichhardt............9 F10
ELTHAM
pl. Cecil Hills...........362 D6
pl. Heathcote...........519 A11
st. Beacon Hill.........257 K4
st. Blacktown...........275 A9
st. Dulwich Hill...........15 A13
st. Dulwich Hill.........373 E7
st. Gladesville..........312 H6

st. Lewisham...............15 A13
st. Lewisham.............373 E7
ELTON
pl. Plumpton.............241 H7
ELTONS
rd. Silverdale............383 D6
ELVA
av. Killara.................253 K10
st. Cabramatta W....365 B6
st. Strathfield...........341 F11
st. Toongabbie..........276 G8
ELVINA
av. Avalon................140 A15
av. Newport..............169 D7
st. Dover Ht..............348 E8
st. Greystanes...........305 J6
ELVSTROM
av. Newington...........310 B15
ELVY
pl. Newtown................18 D8
st. Bargo..................567 A2
ELWIN
st. Peakhurst............429 J3
st. Strathfield...........341 C14
ELWOOD
cr. Quakers Hill.........213 E15
pl. St Johns Pk.........364 H2
ELWYN
cl. Mona Vale............199 A4
ELY
pl. Marayong............243 J6
st. Revesby...............398 G13
ELYARD
cr. West Hoxton........392 A12
st. Narellan..............478 F11
EMANUEL
la. Rosebery, off
Queen St............375 G13
EMERALD
dr. Eagle Vale...........481 B7
pl. Cartwright...........393 J5
pl. Emu Plains...........235 E13
pl. Grays Point..........491 C15
rd. Seven Hills...........275 C7
st. Emu Plains...........235 D13
st. Narrabeen............229 B1
st. W Pnnant Hl.........248 J6
EMERSON
pl. Menai..................458 H7
st. Leumeah..............512 B2
st. Shalvey................211 A13
st. Wetherill Pk.........334 J5
EMERSTAN
dr. Castle Cove..........286 E6
EMERT
pde. Emerton..............240 H7
st. Greystanes...........306 H4
st. S Wntwthvle..........306 H4
st. Wentwthvle...........306 J1
EMERY
av. Yagoona..............369 E10
rd. Kellyville..............185 J16
rd. Kellyville..............215 J1
st. Rooty Hill.............271 K3
EMEX
pl. Mcquarie Fd.........454 D4
EMILIA
cl. Rsemeadow...........540 G6
pl. Prestons..............393 F13
EMILY
av. Emu Plains...........235 H10
pl. Cherrybrook..........219 G16
st. Breakfast Pt.........312 B16
st. Hurstville..............401 J15
st. Leichhardt...............16 D2
st. Mortlake...............312 B16
st. Mount Druitt.........271 C4
st. Rozelle....................10 J2
EMLYN
pl. Kellyville..............186 B16
EMMA
cl. Bonnyrigg.............364 C5
cr. Wentwthvle...........277 B9
gr. Glenwood.............215 D13
pde. Winmalee............172 K13
pl. Ambarvale.............510 G14
pl. Berowra................133 G9
st. Lakemba...............370 J16
st. Leichhardt...............10 F15
st. Mona Vale.............198 J4
EMMALINE
st. Ramsgate Bch....433 G11

EMMANUEL
tce. Glenwood...........215 J12
EMMAUS
rd. Ingleside.............197 E3
EMMERICK
st. Lilyfield....................9 K6
EMMETT
cl. Picton..................563 H4
la. Crows Nest..........315 G8
pl. Killarney Ht.........256 C16
st. Crows Nest..........315 G8
st. Tahmoor..............565 J12
EMMETTS FARM
rd. Rossmore.............389 F5
EMPEROR
pl. Forestville............256 C8
pl. Kenthurst.............157 E14
EMPIRE
av. Blakehurst...........432 C16
av. Concord...............342 B5
ct. Carlingford...........279 D4
la. Sydney....................A K15
la. Marrickville, off
Victoria Rd.........374 F10
pl. Illawong...............459 E4
st. Haberfield............343 C14
EMPRESS
av. Rouse Hill............185 E3
la. Hurstville.............432 A7
st. Hurstville.............432 B7
EMPYREAN
gr. Doonside.............243 F15
EMU
av. Hinchinbrk...........363 C16
cl. Bossley Park.........334 C10
la. Canterbury...........372 D14
pl. Hornsby Ht...........161 J8
rd. Glenbrook............264 D5
st. Canterbury...........372 D14
st. Collaroy Plat.........228 H13
st. Strathfield............371 G1
st. West Ryde.............280 G11
EMU PLAINS
rd. Mt Riverview.........204 F15
ENDEAVOUR
av. La Perouse...........436 J14
av. St Clair.................270 A12
cl. Castle Hill..............217 J9
dr. Beacon Hill............257 G4
dr. Narrabeen.............228 F8
dr. Winmalee..............173 H7
la. Sans Souci............463 A3
la. St Clair, off
Endeavour Av.....270 A12
pl. Riverwood.............400 E14
rd. Caringbah.............493 B3
rd. Daceyville.............406 F3
rd. Georges Hall.........367 D15
st. Chatswood............284 J9
st. Ruse.....................512 G3
st. Sans Souci............463 A2
st. Seven Hills............275 D2
st. Sylvania...............462 D9
st. Wahroonga............223 A5
st. West Ryde............281 C15
ENDERBY
cl. Hinchinbrk...........362 K14
pl. Barden Rdg..........458 J16
st. Tregear................240 F8
ENDGATE
gln. Wrrngtn Dns.......237 K3
ENFIELD
av. N Richmond............87 C15
cl. St Johns Pk...........364 H4
st. Jamisontown.........266 C5
st. Marrickville...........373 H10
ENGADINE
av. Engadine..............518 G4
pl. Engadine..............518 J3
ENGEL
av. Marsfield..............281 H3
ENGESTA
av. Camden................506 K7
ENGLAND
av. Marrickville.............16 E16
rd. Ingleburn..............422 J14
st. Btn-le-Sds.............433 H2
wk. Lalor Park............245 D11
ENGLART
pl. Baulkham Hl.........247 F7
ENGLEWOOD
wy. Glenmore Pk.........266 E10

ENGLISH
av. Camden S.............507 B15
av. Castle Hill.............248 A4
la. Kogarah................433 B7
st. Camperdwn..............17 G6
st. Carlton..................432 K6
st. Glenfield...............424 E10
st. Kogarah.................433 A7
st. Revesby.................398 K14
st. Woolooware...........493 D10
ENGLORIE PARK
dr. Ambarvale.............510 F16
dr. Englorie Park.........510 F16
dr. Glen Alpine...........510 F16
dr. Rsemeadow............540 C2
ENID
av. Granville...............308 F12
av. Roselands..............401 B8
pl. Ingleburn...............453 E10
st. Denistone...............281 G12
st. Greystanes.............305 J8
ENID BENNETT
st. Moore Park...............21 C7
ENMORE
la. Enmore....................17 A14
rd. Enmore....................17 A14
rd. Marrickville..............16 K16
rd. Marrickville............374 E10
rd. Newtown..................17 A14
ENNERDALE
cr. Collaroy Plat..........228 E9
ENNIS
av. Killarney Ht............286 B1
la. Balmain......................7 E12
pl. Lalor Park...............245 F13
rd. Milsons Point.............5 K12
st. Balmain......................7 E11
ENOCH
pl. Winston Hills...........277 B4
ENOGGERA
rd. Beverly Hills...........401 A10
ENRIGHT
st. East Hills................427 H2
ENSIGN
pl. Castle Hill...............218 A11
ENTERPRISE
av. Padstow.................399 E12
dr. Glendenning...........242 F6
pl. Wetherill Pk...........333 K4
rd. Cranebrook.............207 A9
ENTRANCE
rd. Parramatta.............278 B13
EOS
pl. Schofields...............213 B1
EPACRIS
av. Caringbah..............492 J13
av. Forestville..............256 A8
EPHRAIM HOWE
pl. Narellan Vale..........508 K2
EPIC
pl. Villawood...............337 J15
EPIDOTE
cl. Eagle Vale..............481 F9
EPO
pl. Glenfield.................424 F9
EPPING
av. Eastwood................280 J5
av. Epping...................280 K4
cl. Cmbrdg Pk..............237 J10
dr. Frenchs Frst............256 F3
rd. Double Bay................14 E12
rd. Epping...................251 C16
rd. Lane Cove W...........283 H14
rd. Mcquarie Pk............282 D4
rd. Marsfield................251 C16
rd. North Ryde.............282 D4
EPPING FOREST
dr. Eschol Park............481 A1
dr. Kearns...................481 A1
EPPLESTON
pl. West Pymble..........252 J10
wk. West Pymble, off
Eppleston Pl.......252 J11
EPSOM
pwy. Chipping Ntn, off
Epsom Rd..........396 E2
rd. Chipping Ntn..........396 B6
rd. Rosebery................375 H12
rd. Zetland..................375 H12
EPWORTH
pl. N Narrabeen...........198 F11

EQUESTRIAN
dr. Picton...............563 B1
st. Glenwood 245 J3
EQUITY
la. Erskineville...........18 B14
pl. Canley Vale 365 J4
ERANG
av. Kirrawee 491 A6
st. Carss Park 432 G13
ERAWAR
cl. Westleigh...........190 J16
ERBY
pl. Parramatta.........308 C2
ERCILDOUNE
av. Beverley Pk........433 C9
av. Kogarah............433 C9
EREBUS
cr. Tregear..............240 F8
ERIC
av. Bass Hill.............368 C13
av. Merrylands..........307 D16
cl. Emu Plains..........234 K7
cr. Lidcombe............340 A8
la. Mosman, off Earl St...............316 J5
rd. Artarmon 284 H15
st. Bundeena.............524 B12
st. Eastwood.............280 G9
st. Harbord 258 G16
st. Lilyfield.................10 B7
st. Wahroonga..........223 B6
ERICA
cl. Westleigh............220 E8
cr. Georges Hall 367 H15
la. Minto..................482 F2
pl. Minto..................482 F2
pl. Rooty Hill.............272 C4
st. Kurmond 86 E1
ERIC COOPER
dr. Castle Hill...........217 B8
ERIC FELTON
st. Castle Hill, off Old Castle Hill Rd...................218 C13
ERIC GREEN
dr. Mona Vale..........169 C15
ERIE
la. Petersham 16 B8
pl. St Clair................269 H16
pl. Seven Hills...........275 E6
st. S Granville 338 G8
ERIN
pl. Casula................423 H3
st. Quakers Hill 214 G12
ERINA
av. Five Dock...........343 B8
cl. Bossley Park......333 H8
pl. S Windsor...........150 D2
st. Eastwood.............281 F4
ERINLEIGH
ct. Kellyville.............216 D1
ERITH
st. Blacktown...........275 A9
st. Botany 405 D12
st. Mosman 316 H6
ERLESTOKE
pl. Castle Hill...........219 A10
ERMINGTON
la. Ermington...........310 C2
la. Ermington...........310 D1
la. Ermington...........310 E2
st. Botany 405 J14
ERNA
av. Lansvale 366 K8
pl. Quakers Hill 214 D12
ERNEST
av. Chipping Ntn......366 H15
la. Crows Nest 315 H6
pl. Crows Nest 315 F6
st. Balgowlah Ht......287 G13
st. Cammeray 315 H7
st. Cremorne.............315 H7
st. Crows Nest 315 H7
st. Glenwood 215 D13
st. Guildford.............337 E6
st. Hunters Hill.........313 J10
st. Lakemba..............401 A4
st. Lugarno 430 A9
st. Neutral Bay 315 H7
st. Sefton..................368 H3
st.n, Lakemba............400 J1
ERNST
pl. Edensor Pk 333 H12

ERNSTINE HILL
cl. Glenmore Pk.......265 K7
EROLA
cir. Lindfield.............283 K3
EROS
pl. Rsemeadow.......540 F2
pl. Winston Hills......277 F3
ERRICA
st. Greenfld Pk.........334 C13
ERRIGAL
pl. Killarney Ht 286 D1
ERRINGHI
pl. McGraths Hl.......122 A13
ERROL
pl. Quakers Hill 214 F13
ERROL FLYNN
bvd. Moore Park..........21 A9
ERSKINE
rd. Caringbah 462 H16
st. Chatswood..........284 K11
st. Riverwood 400 C16
st. Sydney ....C A1
st. Sydney ....C D1
st. Sydney 3 E1
wy. Minto..................483 A1
ERSKINE PARK
rd. Erskine Park.......299 K5
rd. St Clair...............270 E16
ERSKINEVILLE
la. Erskineville...........18 A15
la. Newtown 17 J13
rd. Erskineville...........17 H12
rd. Newtown 17 H12
ERVINE
st. Winston Hills......277 E1
ERYNE
pl. Dural 219 B7
ESCHOL PARK
dr. Eschol Park........481 C3
dr. Kearns 481 C3
ESDAILE
pl. Arncliffe 403 E9
ESHELBY
st. Green Valley.......363 C11
ESHER
la. Burwood, off Burwood Rd.......342 A10
mw. Wattle Grove 425 K4
st. Burwood..............342 A11
ESK
av. Green Valley.......362 J11
la. Marrickville, off Grove St 373 J15
st. Marrickville 373 J15
st. N Wahrnga..........223 B1
ESKDALE
cl. Narellan Vale 508 F2
st. Minchinbury.......272 C8
ESME
av. Chester Hill 338 C15
ESMOND
pl. Wakeley 334 G13
ESPALIER
pl. Minchinbury.......272 B10
ESPERANCE
cr. Wakeley 334 K11
pl. Yarrawarrah 489 H13
ESPLANADE
Elizabeth Bay.........13 C4
ESPLIN
av. Strathfield 341 H15
ESSENDON
st. St Johns Pk 364 F3
ESSEX
av. Castle Hill...........217 K11
st. Blacktown 244 B13
st. Epping 281 D1
st. Guildford.............337 C4
st. Killara 253 G11
st. Marrickville 16 A16
st. Minto..................452 E16
st. The Rocks ....A G8
st. The Rocks 1 F12
ESSEY
pl. Merrylands.........307 E8
ESSILIA
st. Collaroy Plat.......228 H12
ESSINGTON
cr. Sylvania 461 K13
st. Wentwthvle.........307 B3
wy. Glenwood, off Kosmina St........215 J16

ESSON
pl. Glenmore Pk......265 J6
ESTELLA
pl. Ambarvale..........510 H15
ESTELLE
pl. Frenchs Frst.......256 A3
ESTHER
la. Surry Hills.............20 B4
la. Mosman, off Esther Rd...........317 D6
rd. Mosman 317 D6
st. Greystanes..........305 K8
st. Surry Hills.............20 C4
st. Winston Hills......277 A4
ESTONIAN
rd. Thirlmere 561 A16
rd. Thirlmere 564 A1
ESTRAMINA
wy. Minto..................482 J7
ETA
st. Blacktown 274 C4
ETCHELL
la. Cranebrook, off Etchell Pl............207 A10
pl. Cranebrook 207 A10
ETELA
st. Belmore 371 E15
ETHAM
av. Darling Point........13 K4
ETHEL
av. Brookvale...........258 D12
la. Allawah 432 E5
la. Eastwood.............281 C7
st. Balgowlah 287 E10
st. Burwood..............342 A16
st. Carlton................432 E4
st. Condell Park........398 E6
st. Eastwood.............281 C7
st. Erskineville............18 C14
st. Hornsby..............191 F9
st. Merrylands..........307 K16
st. Randwick.............407 C2
st. Seaforth..............287 E10
st. Vaucluse.............348 F7
ETHELL
rd. Kirrawee 461 C15
ETHERDEN
rd. Bligh Park 150 J6
ETHIE
rd. Beacon Hill..........257 D8
ETHNE
av. Randwick............377 C10
ETIVAL
st. Palm Beach.........140 B10
ETNA
cl. Cranebrook 207 E14
pl. Bossley Park 334 B10
ETON
ct. Cmbrdg Pk..........238 A8
la. Camperdwn 17 D7
la. Sutherland 490 E4
rd. Cmbrdg Pk...........237 F6
rd. Lindfield..............284 B5
st. Bexley.................402 H14
st. Camperdwn 17 D7
st. Fairfield 336 D7
st. Smithfield 335 K5
st.n, Sutherland 490 E5
st.s, Sutherland 490 E6
ETONVILLE
pde. Croydon............342 G16
ETRUSCAN
ct. Glenwood 245 K4
ETTALONG
pl. Woodbine 481 K11
rd. Greystanes..........306 D4
st. Auburn 339 A8
st. Collaroy Plat.......228 F11
ETTLESDALE
rd. Spring Farm.......507 H6
ETTRICK
st. Ashbury..............372 F8
EUCALYPT
rd. Springwood 202 B2
EUCALYPTS
wk. Newington 310 C13
EUCALYPTUS
cl. St Ives 253 K1
ct. Baulkham Hl 247 E14
ct. Picnic Point.........428 E8
ct. Stanhpe Gdn.......215 B11
dr. Cranebrook 237 E1

dr. Mcquarie Fd.......424 E16
dr. Westleigh...........220 F8
st. Alfords Point......459 B3
st. Peakhurst 430 E4
st. St Ives 254 A1
st. Wentwthvle.........277 A9
EUCHORA
la. Springwood 202 B1
EUCLA
cr. Malabar 437 F8
pl. Sutherland 460 C14
EUCLASE
pl. Eagle Vale 481 F8
EUCLID
st. Winston Hills......277 D5
EUCRA
st. Schofields..........213 K6
EUCUMBENE
cr. Heckenberg........363 K12
dr. Woodcroft..........243 H8
la. St Clair, off Eucumbene Pl....269 J16
pl. St Clair...............269 J16
EUDON
st. Doonside 243 C4
EUGENES
gln. Kellyville............185 J14
EUGENIA
st. Loftus 489 K9
wy. Bidwill................211 G13
EULABAH
av. Earlwood 402 C5
EULALIA
st. West Ryde 280 H14
EULALIE
av. Randwick...........377 C12
EULBERTIE
av. Warrawee 222 F12
EULDA
st. Belmore 371 B14
EULO
pde. Ryde.................282 A13
EUMINA
st. Beverly Hills 401 D10
EUMUNG
ct. Wattle Grove 426 A2
EUNGAI
pl. N Narrabeen.......198 F15
EUPHRATES
pl. Kearns 451 B14
EURABALONG
rd. Burraneer...........523 E4
EURABBA
rd. Duffys Frst 195 A1
EURABBIE
gln. St Clair..............270 A15
pl. Mcquarie Fd........454 E4
st. Cabramatta 365 H10
EURALLA
st. Westmead 307 F3
EUREKA
cr. Sadleir 394 C3
gr. Glenwood 215 C15
EURELLA
av. N Balgowlah.......287 D4
st. Burwood.............342 B13
EURIMBLA
av. Randwick...........376 K15
EUROA
pl. Engadine............489 D9
EUROBIN
av. Manly 288 F4
EUROKA
la. N Sydney 5 B8
rd. Glenbrook...........264 A1
rd. Mulgoa 294 D14
rd. Westleigh............220 F9
st. Ingleburn 453 B10
st. Northbridge 286 A15
st. N Sydney 5 B8
st. Waverton................5 B8
EURONG
st. Wahroonga..........251 G1
EURYALUS
st. Mosman 286 K16
EUSTACE
pde. Killara 253 D16
st. Fairfield...............335 K13
st. Fairfield Ht 335 K13
st. Manly 288 F9

EUSTON
la. Alexandria...........375
rd. Alexandria...........375
rd. Auburn 338
rd. Hurlstone Pk 372
st. Rydalmere 309
EUTHELLA
av. Hunters Hill........313
EVA
av. Green Valley.......362
la. Northwood...........314
pl. Glenfield 424
pl. Northmead..........277
st. Condell Park........398
st. Greystanes..........305
st. Northwood...........314
st. Riverwood 400
st. Roselands...........400
EVALINE
st. Campsie 371
st. Canterbury..........372
EVAN
la. Waterloo...............19
pl. Kings Lngly.........245
st. Gladesville 312
st. Penrith................237
st. S Penrith.............266
st. S Penrith.............266
EVANDA
st. Berowra 133
EVANDALE
ct. Wattle Grove 425
EVANS
av. Eastlakes............405
av. Eastlakes............406
av. Moorebank 396
av. Newington 309
cr. Richmond............119
la. Eastlakes............405
la. Redfern.................19
la. St Leonards 315
la. Mosman, off Muston St...........317
pde. Lapstone............264
pl. Mt Pritchard.......364
rd. Carlingford..........280
rd. Dundas Vy 280
rd. Glenhaven...........217
rd. Hornsby Ht 191
rd. Rooty Hill...........272
rd. Rcuttrs Bay...........13
rd. Telopea 279
rd. Wilberforce 61
st. Balmain 7
st. Bronte.................377
st. Como 460
st. Fairfield Ht 335
st. Harbord 258
st. Newington 310
st. Peakhurst 429
st. Randwick.............377
st. Rozelle....................7
st. Sans Souci...........463
st. West Pymble.......252
wy. Minto..................482
EVE
ct. Cabramatta 365
pl. Berowra Ht...........133
pl. Winston Hills.......276
st. Arncliffe 403
st. Banksia 403
st. Erskineville...........375
st. Guildford.............338
st. Strathfield 371
EVELEIGH
st. Redfern..................19
EVELYN
av. Concord...............342
av. Turramurra 223
cl. Wetherill Pk 334
cr. Berowra Ht...........133
pl. Belrose 226
pl. Glendenning.........242
st. Baulkham Hl 247
st. Greenwich...........314
st. Mcquarie Fd.........454
st. S Coogee 407
st. Sylvania 462
st. Sylvania Wtr.........462
st.n, Sylvania 462
EVELYN GRACE
wy. Cherrybrook........219
EVENING
row. St Clair...............270

NSTAR
St Clair 270 D14
RARD
Hunters Hill 313 A7
REST
Seven Hills 275 B9
RETT
Annangrove 155 D6
Maroubra 406 K8
Wahroonga 222 C7
RGOLD
Eagle Vale 481 B8
RGREEN
Bradbury 511 D11
Kellyville 185 E6
RITT
Minchinbury 272 C10
Strathfield S 371 E6
RLEY
Auburn 338 H12
Sefton 338 F11
RS
Edensor Pk 363 F3
RTON
Belrose 226 A15
Faulconbdg 171 A16
Strathfield 341 G11
Pymble 253 D3
RVIEW
Mosman 316 K4
SHAM
Baulkham Hl 216 H16
Chipping Ntn 366 G13
SSON
Woollahra 22 K4
E
Doonside 243 A10
AN
Mascot 405 A5
ART
Dulwich Hill 373 D13
Dulwich Hill 373 C12
Claymore, off
Colquhoun Wy 481 C11
ELL
Bondi 377 J6
Balmain 7 B12
Bondi 377 J5
EN
Roselands 400 H6
ENTON
Balmain 8 C11
Balmain 8 C11
NG
Little Bay 437 G14
Bligh Park 150 K7
OS
Cronulla 493 K16
URY
Wattle Grove 426 B5
ALIBUR
Castle Hill 217 G5
Mt Colah 162 E11
ELLER
Bankstown 399 F7
ELSIOR
Belfield 371 C7
Castle Hill 247 F2
Castle Hill 248 A4
Marrickville 373 H16
Cronulla 493 H12
Mt Colah 162 E11
Concord 342 B7
Guildford 338 B4
Guildford 338 B7
Leichhardt 15 H3
Merrylands 308 C16
Castle Hill 247 F2
HANGE
Smeaton Gra 479 A9
LL
Bnksmeadw 436 A2
TER
Kings Lngly 245 G4
Bidwill 241 E1
North Rocks 278 J2
Homebush W 340 G9
Kemps Ck 360 B6
Wahroonga 222 A11
Camden 477 A14
ORD
Wattle Grove 425 J2

EXHIBITION
pde. Mt Pritchard 364 F13
pl. Haymarket E A3
pl. Haymarket 3 C9
EXILE
la. Concord 342 E5
EXLEY
pl. S Penrith 266 K6
rd. Wedderburn 540 A15
EXMOOR
pl. Blairmount 481 B14
EXMOUTH
pl. Yarrawarrah 489 G13
EXPERIMENT
st. Pyrmont 12 J5
EXPLORER
st. Eveleigh 18 D12
EXPLORERS
rd. Glenbrook 264 C1
rd. Glenbrook 264 C3
rd. Lapstone 264 C3
wy. St Clair 270 D11
EXTON
wy. Rsemeadow 540 J2
EYLES
av. Epping 250 C16
st. Telopea 279 H10
EYNHAM
rd. Milperra 397 F11
EYRE
av. Ingleburn 423 B10
pl. Camden S 507 B10
pl. Kirrawee 460 J16
pl. Mt Colah 162 C11
st. Chifley 437 A6
st. Lalor Park 245 B14
st. Smithfield 335 D1
st. Wrrngtn Cty 238 G8
EZZY
la. Chester Hill 337 F13

F

F3
Asquith 192 D16
Berowra 163 A9
Brooklyn 75 A13
Cowan 104 E13
Krngai Ch NP 192 D16
Mooney Mooney 75 A13
Mt Colah 162 F16
Mt Krng-gai 163 A9
N Wahrnga 222 B6
Wahroonga 222 B6
F6
Waterfall 519 D16
FABIAN
pl. Mona Vale 199 A5
pl. Rsemeadow 540 G6
FABOS
pl. Croydon Pk 372 D6
pl. Smithfield 335 J7
FABRY
st. Botany 405 G13
FACER
ct. Castle Hill 217 F15
FACEY
cr. Lurnea 394 B8
FACTORY
ct. Padstow 399 G12
rd. Regentville 265 E1
st. Granville 308 H15
st. Haymarket E C5
st. N Parramatta 278 C13
FADDEN
pl. N Wahrnga 192 F14
rd. Springwood 202 D12
FAGAN
pl. Bonnyrigg 363 J10
FAGANS
rd. Arcadia 129 G11
FAHEY
la. Marrickville, off
Philpott St 374 D9
FAHY
pl. Loftus 490 B6
FAIR
rd. Glenorie 96 E4
FAIRBAIRN
av. Clontarf 287 E12
av. East Killara 254 F8
FAIRBURN
av. W Pnnant Hl 249 J3
cr. Minchinbury 272 C8
rd. Wedderburn 540 E13
FAIREY
rd. S Windsor 121 B16
rd. Windsor 121 A12
FAIRFAX
rd. Bellevue Hill 14 G9
rd. Mosman 317 C2
FAIRFIELD
av. Windsor 120 J10
pl. Jamisontown 266 B1
rd. Guildford W 336 H2
rd. Woodpark 306 H16
rd. Yennora 336 F7
st. Fairfield 336 G12
st. Fairfield E 336 J11
st. Old Guildford 337 A11
st. Yennora 337 A11
FAIRFORD
rd. Padstow 399 F11
FAIRFOWL
la. Dulwich Hill, off
Fairfowl St 373 F10
st. Dulwich Hill 373 F10
FAIRGREEN
pl. Castle Hill 217 J7
FAIRHOLM
st. Strathfield 371 D1
FAIRLAND
av. Greenacre 370 C10
FAIRLAWN
av. Turramurra 223 B11
cl. Lansvale 366 D10
FAIRLIGHT
av. East Killara 254 F10
av. Fairfield 336 E14
cr. Fairlight 288 B10
pl. Woodbine 481 J9
rd. Mulgoa 295 A16
st. Fairlight 288 B9
st. Five Dock 342 K11
st. Lilyfield 9 G8
st. Manly 288 C9
FAIRMONT
av. Baulkham Hl 216 J16
FAIRMOUNT
cct. Glenwood 246 A5
st. Dulwich Hill 373 D6
st. Lakemba 370 H15
st. Merrylands 307 A8
FAIRPORT
st. N Curl Curl 258 G10
FAIRS
av. Woolooware 493 E10
FAIRVIEW
av. Engadine 518 D4
av. Roselands 400 H6
av. St Ives Ch 223 K4
pl. Mt Krng-gai 162 J10
rd. Cabramatta 366 C7
rd. Canley Vale 366 C7
st. Arncliffe 403 B10
st. Concord 341 J6
st. Guildford 337 B2
FAIRWATER
dr. Harringtn Pk 478 D5
FAIRWAY
av. Kogarah 433 E6
av. Mortdale 430 G8
av. Pymble 223 H14
av. Springwood 172 D13
cl. Manly Vale 288 C5
dr. Kellyville 216 E10
pl. Narellan 478 C9
FAIRWAYS
av. Leonay 235 B15
cr. Springwood 172 B13
FAIRWEATHER
pl. Eagle Vale 481 E9
st. Bellevue Hill 347 F15
FAIRY BOWER
rd. Manly 288 J12
FAIRY DELL
cl. Westleigh 220 G9
FAIRYLAND
av. Chatswd W 283 J10
FAIRYWREN
cl. Glenmore Pk 265 J12

FAITH
ct. Georges Hall 367 G10
FAITHFULL
pl. Airds 512 D10
st. Elderslie 477 G16
st. Richmond 119 B4
wy. Airds 512 D10
FALCON
cct. Green Valley 363 D12
cl. Greenfld Pk 334 C12
cr. Clarmnt Ms 268 J4
la. Clarmnt Ms, off
Falcon Cr 268 J4
la. Crows Nest, off
Sophia St 315 G7
pl. Ingleburn 453 G6
st. Crows Nest 315 G7
st. Neutral Bay 315 G7
st. Newington 310 C11
st. N Sydney 315 G7
wy. Glenwood 215 F14
FALCONER
st. West Ryde 281 G16
FALKINER
wy. Airds 512 C12
FALKIRK
dr. Kellyville 217 B2
pl. Dharruk 241 D6
pl. St Andrews 481 J1
FALKLAND
cl. Winmalee 173 B12
pl. St Andrews 481 K2
FALKLANDS
av. Bossley Park 334 A8
FALL
st. Cammeray 316 C5
st. Cremorne 316 C5
st. Revesby 398 K13
FALLEN LEAF
ct. W Pnnant Hl 248 J3
FALLON
dr. Dural 219 D5
st. Quakers Hill 214 E16
st. Rydalmere 310 A5
FALLONS
rd. Orangeville 443 G12
FALLOWFIELD
ct. Wrrngtn Dns 237 K5
la. Wrrngtn Dns, off
Fallowfield Ct 237 K5
FALLOWS
wy. Cherrybrook 219 E15
FALLS
st. Leichhardt 9 E10
FALMAR
pl. Woronora Ht 489 D3
FALMER
st. Abbotsbury 333 A14
FALMOUTH
rd. Quakers Hill 243 G5
FALSTAFF
pl. Rsemeadow 540 G7
FAMILY HILL
rd. Oran Park 448 B10
FAN
wy. Stanhpe Gdn 215 D10
FANE
pl. Doonside 243 B8
FANNICH
pl. St Andrews 452 B14
FANNIN
pl. Kings Lngly 245 A2
FANNING
st. Tempe 404 C3
FANNY
pl. Surry Hills 20 D2
FANTAIL
cr. Erskine Park 270 K15
la. St Clair, off
Fantail Cr 271 A15
pl. Green Valley 363 D10
pl. Ingleburn 453 G10
FANTOME
st. Voyager Pt 427 D4
FARADAY
av. Rose Bay 348 B12
la. Meadowbnk 311 E3
rd. Leumeah 482 E16
rd. Padstow 429 D2
FARAH
pl. Yagoona 368 H11

FARHALL
pl. Glenhaven 218 A4
FARIOLA
st. Silverwater 309 J11
FARLEIGH
st. Ashfield 372 J6
FARLEY
pl. Londonderry 148 C10
rd. Cecil Park 332 G9
FARLOW
pl. Kingswood 237 E9
FARM
rd. Kenthurst 155 J3
rd. Mulgoa 295 E14
rd. Riverstone 181 K7
rd. Springwood 202 B9
st. Gladesville 312 G6
FARMAN
pl. Raby 451 C12
FARMER
cct. Kellyville 186 A13
cl. Glenwood 215 F12
pl. St Clair 270 A10
rd. Clontarf 287 E11
FARMHOUSE
pl. Currans Hill 479 K11
FARMING
av. Richmond Lwld 88 J14
FARMINGDALE
dr. Blacktown 274 D10
FARMRIDGE
wy. Glenhaven 218 C3
FARMVIEW
dr. Cranebrook 207 C15
FARNBOROUGH
ct. Wattle Grove 426 B4
rd. Dural 189 H4
FARNELL
av. Carlingford 249 E15
av. Royal N P 490 B14
rd. Yagoona 369 A10
st. Curl Curl 258 K13
st. Granville 308 B15
st. Hunters Hill 313 C6
st. Merrylands 308 B15
st. West Ryde 280 F12
st. Surry Hills, off
Sandwell St 20 D1
FARNHAM
av. Randwick 377 D14
av. Roselands 400 F7
rd. Quakers Hill 214 F13
FARNINGHAM
st. Mt Pritchard 364 B11
FARNSWORTH
av. Campbelltwn 511 G9
av. Warragamba 353 E9
FARNWORTH
la. Point Piper, off
Wyuna Rd 347 F8
FARR
st. Banksia 403 F16
st. Marrickville 374 B11
st. Rockdale 403 F16
FARRAN
la. Woollahra 22 E4
st. Lane Cove W 283 K13
FARRANT
pl. Carlingford 249 H15
FARRAR
av. Krngai Ch NP 163 J15
av. Rookwood 340 A12
pl. Bonnyrigg Ht 363 F7
pl. Jamisontown 266 B3
pl. Lalor Park 245 B12
st. Arncliffe 403 D9
st. Balgowlah Ht 287 J12
FARRELL
av. Darlinghurst 4 G8
pl. Fairfield W 334 K10
rd. Bass Hill 367 F7
rd. Kingsgrove 402 A13
st. Hebersham 241 F4
FARRELLS
la. Castlereagh 206 G8
la. Cranebrook 206 G8
FARRELLYS
av. Tamarama 378 A5
FARRENDON
pl. Mt Annan 509 E1
FARRER
av. W Pnnant Hl 248 K9

pl. Frenchs Frst 255 H5
pl. Oyster Bay 461 C5
pl. Sydney B D12
FARRIER
pl. Castle Hill 217 F5
wy. Kellyville 215 D2
wy. Stanhpe Gdn 215 D2
FARRINGTON
pde. North Ryde 282 H10
st. Minchinbury 272 C10
FARROW
la. Tempe 404 B2
rd. Campbelltwn 511 E3
FARTHING
pl. Maroubra 407 D15
FARVIEW
rd. Bilgola 169 H6
FASSIFERN
pl. Cartwright 394 B4
FAUCETT
la. Woolmloo 4 D6
FAULDS
rd. Guildford W 337 A4
FAULKLAND
cr. Kings Park 244 F3
FAULKNER
st. Old Tngabbie 277 B7
FAUNA
pl. Kirrawee 490 J4
rd. Erskine Park 270 E16
st. Earlwood 402 J5
FAUNCE
st. Burwood Ht 371 K4
FAUST
gln. St Clair 270 D15
FAUX
st. Wiley Park 400 F4
FAVA
pl. Rooty Hill 271 K3
FAVELL
av. Rouse Hill 184 J8
st. Toongabbie 276 G9
FAVERSHAM
cr. Chipping Ntn 366 G15
la. Marrickville, off Hans Pl 374 C12
st. Marrickville 374 C12
FAWCETT
st. Balmain 7 K10
st. Glenfield 424 C12
st. Ryde 282 A11
FAWKENER
pl. Wrrngtn Cty 238 G6
FAWKNER
pl. Barden Rdg 488 H5
FAY
pl. Marsfield 281 K6
st. N Curl Curl 258 F10
FAYE
av. Blakehurst 432 D13
av. Earlwood 372 H16
st. Seven Hills 245 B16
FEARN
st. Toongabbie 276 H8
FEATHER
la. St Clair, off Feather St 269 G14
st. St Clair 269 G14
FEATHERWOOD
av. Cherrybrook 219 J5
wy. Castle Hill 248 F5
FEATON
pl. Mortdale 430 H8
FEDERAL
av. Ashfield 373 A3
pde. Brookvale 258 B8
pde.w, Brookvale 258 A8
rd. Glebe 11 G6
rd. Seven Hills 275 D2
rd. West Ryde 311 C2
FEDERATION
pl. Frenchs Frst 256 G1
pl. Sadleir 394 C2
rd. Newtown 17 F9
FEDOTOW
pl. Rooty Hill 271 H3
FEHON
rd. Chatswd W 284 H12
FEILBERG
pl. Abbotsford 343 B3

FELD
av. Elderslie 507 F3
FELDSPAR
rd. Eagle Vale 481 F5
FELICIA
pl. Blacktown 244 K10
FELL
pl. Schofields 212 H1
FELLOWS
rd. Bonnyrigg Ht 363 G5
FELS
av. Springwood 202 B5
FELTON
av. Lane Cove W 284 B14
rd. Carlingford 279 B5
rd. Carlingford 279 F4
st. Horsley Pk 302 F16
st. Telopea 279 D7
FELUGA
pl. Acacia Gdn 214 G15
FENCHURCH
st. Prospect 275 C12
FENDER
pl. Chifley 437 B5
FENECH
pl. Quakers Hill 213 H7
FENNELL
st. Parramatta 278 B15
FENTON
av. Caringbah 493 B4
av. Maroubra 407 G12
cr. Minto 483 A2
st. Panania 427 K1
FENWICK
av. Roselands 400 J7
cl. Kellyville 217 A2
pl. Westmead 307 F2
st. Bankstown 368 J15
st. Yagoona 368 J15
FEODORE
dr. Cecil Hills 362 E5
FERAMIN
av. Whalan 240 J8
FERDINAND
pl. Rsemeadow 540 K5
st. Birchgrove 7 F3
st. Hunters Hill 313 H10
FERGERSON
av. Fairfield 336 E9
FERGUSON
av. Castle Hill 248 C6
av. Thornleigh 221 C15
av. Wiley Park 400 H4
cl. Menai 458 F12
cr. Ingleburn 423 B13
la. Chatswood 284 J9
la. Grasmere 506 E1
la. Chatswood, off Archer St 284 K9
rd. Springwood 201 G4
st. Forestville 255 F7
st. Forestville 255 K8
st. Maroubra 407 A10
FERGUSSON
st. Glenfield 424 G8
FERMI
st. Lucas Ht 487 G12
FERMO
rd. Engadine 489 C9
FERMOY
av. Bayview 169 A13
rd. Marsden Pk 182 C14
FERN
av. Bradbury 511 C11
av. Wahroonga 222 B4
cct.e, Menai 458 K14
cct.w, Menai 458 J14
pl. Blacktown 244 K9
pl. Leonay 234 J15
pl. Woollahra 377 F3
rd. Hunters Hill 314 A14
st. Clovelly 377 F10
st. Pymble 253 F4
st. Randwick 377 G12
FERNBANK
la. Marrickville, off Fernbank St 374 A13
pl. Cherrybrook 219 B13
st. Marrickville 374 A13
FERNBROOK
pl. Castle Hill 218 K6

FERNCLIFFE
rd. Glenhaven 218 A3
FERNCOURT
av. Chatswood 285 A5
av. Roseville 285 A5
FERN CREEK
rd. Warriewood 198 G8
FERNCREEK
ct. Kellyville 186 K14
FERNDALE
av. Blaxland 233 K8
av. Carlingford 279 C3
cl. Wentwthvle 277 D10
la. Newtown, off Camden St 374 H9
rd. Badgerys Ck 357 K3
rd. Beecroft 250 E9
rd. Normanhurst 221 H12
rd. Revesby 428 G4
st. Chatswd W 284 D12
st. Ingleburn 454 A10
st. Newtown 17 D16
FERNDELL
st. Sefton 338 E12
st. S Granville 338 E12
FERNGREEN
wy. Castle Hill 248 J2
FERNGROVE
pl. Chester Hill 338 D12
rd. Canley Ht 335 D16
FERNHILL
av. Epping 250 J13
pl. Glen Alpine 510 F10
pl. Grays Point 491 D14
pl. Wrrngtn Dns 237 J5
st. Hurlstone Pk 373 A11
FERNHURST
av. Cremorne 316 G4
FERNLEA
pl. Canley Ht 335 D16
FERNLEAF
cr. Kellyville 185 K16
ct. Wattle Grove 396 B16
FERNLEIGH
av. Rose Bay 348 C9
cl. Cherrybrook 219 D15
cl. Ryde 312 B4
gdn. Rose Bay 348 C9
pl. Glen Alpine 510 B16
rd. Caringbah 493 B15
FERNS
la. Five Dock, off Lyons Rd W 342 K8
FERN TREE
cl. Hornsby 191 F13
FERNTREE
cl. Glenmore Pk 265 H11
rd. Engadine 488 E16
FERNVALE
av. West Ryde 281 C14
FERNVIEW
pl. Cranebrook 207 B11
pl. Glenwood 246 A5
FEROX
ct. S Penrith 266 G3
FEROZA
st. Riverwood 400 C10
FERRABETTA
av. Eastwood 281 J7
FERRARI
pl. Ingleburn 453 J7
FERRARO
cl. Edensor Pk 363 E2
cr. West Hoxton 391 K13
FERRERS
rd. Eastern Ck 273 A16
rd. Horsley Pk 303 D16
FERRIER
cr. Minchinbury 271 F6
dr. Menai 458 H5
pde. Campsie 402 B3
rd. Birrong 368 G7
rd. Sefton 368 G7
rd. Yagoona 368 G7
st. Rockdale 403 B14
FERRINGTON
cr. Liverpool 394 H4
FERRIS
st. Annandale 16 F3
st. Ermington 310 E2
st. N Parramatta 278 B11

FERRY
av. Beverley Pk 433 A11
la. Drummoyne 343 K2
la. Glebe 12 A9
rd. Glebe 12 A10
rd. Lansvale 366 K9
st. Hunters Hill 313 J12
st. Kogarah 433 A5
FESQ
pwy. Winmalee 172 K14
FESTIVAL
st. Sadleir 394 C1
FETHERSTONE
st. Bankstown 369 E16
FEWINGS
st. Clovelly 377 H12
FEWTRELL
av. Revesby Ht 428 K8
FFRENCH
st. Greenwich 314 K8
FIASCHI
pl. S Windsor 150 E3
FIAT
pl. Ingleburn 453 K7
FICUS
pl. Mcquarie Fd 454 B4
pl. Narellan Vale 478 J13
FIDDENS WHARF
rd. Killara 253 G16
FIDDICK
pl. Menai 458 G14
FIDDLEWOOD
gr. Menai 458 J15
FIELD
av. Rookwood 340 D13
cl. Moorebank 395 J7
la. Mosman, off Clifford St 317 B6
pl. Blackett 241 A1
pl. Cranebrook 207 G10
pl. Currans Hill 479 K11
pl. Illawong 459 H5
pl. Telopea 279 G9
pl. Wahroonga 222 E11
FIELDERS
st. Seven Hills 245 F16
FIELDING
cl. Wetherill Pk 334 J6
st. Collaroy 229 B12
FIELD OF MARS
av. S Turramrra 251 K5
FIELDS
rd. Ingleburn 453 J6
rd. Mcquarie Fd 453 J6
FIFE
pl. Cecil Hills 362 H9
st. Blacktown 275 A10
FIFTEENTH
av. Austral 391 A2
av. Kemps Ck 390 A1
av. Rossmore 390 D1
av. West Hoxton 392 A4
st. Warragamba 353 E7
FIFTH
av. Austral 391 A15
av. Berala 339 D14
av. Blacktown 244 H13
av. Campsie 371 J10
av. Canley Vale 366 C3
av. Condell Park 398 E5
av. Cremorne 316 G5
av. Denistone 281 D10
av. Jannali 460 K10
av. Llandilo 207 K1
av. Loftus 489 K7
av. Mcquarie Fd 454 F5
av. Seven Hills 275 J3
rd. Berkshire Pk 179 H5
st. Ashbury 372 G8
st. Granville 308 F14
st. Mascot 404 K6
st. Warragamba 353 G7
FIG
la. Ultimo 12 J9
la. Pymble, off Peace Av 253 H1
pl. Eastwood 281 D7
pl. Mt Pritchard 364 D8
st. Pyrmont 12 H9
tce. Glenwood 215 C14
FIG TREE
av. Abbotsford 342 K2
av. Telopea 279 H9

la. N Sydney 5
la. Woollahra, off Fletcher St 377
st. Lane Cove 313
FIGTREE
av. Randwick 377
cr. Glen Alpine 510
dr. Homebush B 340
rd. Hunters Hill 313
FIJI
av. Lethbrdg Pk 240
FILANTE
st. Stanhpe Gdn 215
FILEY
st. Blacktown 274
FILLMORE
rd. Bonnet Bay 460
FINCH
av. Concord 342
av. East Ryde 282
av. Rydalmere 309
ct. Revesby 398
pl. Davidson 225
pl. Glenwood 215
pl. Greystanes 306
pl. Hinchinbrk 393
pl. Ingleburn 453
pl. Lugarno 429
pl. St Clair 269
pl. Woronora Ht 489
FINCHLEY
pl. Glenhaven 218
pl. Turramurra 223
FINDLAY
av. Roseville 284
la. Dulwich Hill 373
FINDLEY
rd. Bringelly 387
FINEGAN
la. Yagoona, off Brodie St 368
FINGAL
av. Glenhaven 217
FINGLETON
cl. Rouse Hill 184
cl. Rouse Hill 185
FINIAN
av. Killarney Ht 255
FINISTERRE
av. Whalan 240
FINLAY
av. Beecroft 250
av. Mt Pritchard 364
rd. Turramurra 222
rd. Warrawee 222
st. Blacktown 274
FINLAYS
av. Earlwood 403
la. Earlwood, off Finlays Av 403
FINLAYSON
st. Lane Cove 314
st. S Wntwthvle 307
FINLEY
pl. Glenhaven 187
FINN
cl. Cranebrook 206
pl. Marayong 244
FINNAN
pl. Bligh Park 150
FINNEY
la. Hurstville 432
st. Hurstville 432
st. Old Tngabbie 276
FINNIE
av. Matraville 436
FINNS
la. Merrylands, off Merrylands Rd 307
rd. Menangle 537
FINSCHHAFEN
st. Holsworthy 426
FINTRY
ct. Kellyville 217
FINUCANE
cr. Matraville 437
FIONA
av. Castle Hill 247
av. Wahroonga 223
cl. Padstow Ht 429
pl. Ingleburn 453
rd. Beecroft 250

Belrose 226 A10
Mt Pritchard 364 C10
Woodpark 306 H16
Toongabbie 276 A5
Lugarno 429 J16
BALL
Cranebrook 207 B10
Cranebrook, off
Fireball Av 207 B9
NZE
Glenwood 245 K4
STONE
Glenmore Pk 266 E11
TAIL
Plumpton 242 B8
TRAIL
Castlereagh 176 H8
Londonderry 147 A14
Londonderry 176 J5
ISTONE
Arncliffe 403 J10
ST
Allawah 432 C8
Belfield 371 G10
Berala 339 F15
Blacktown 244 H15
Campsie 371 G10
Canley Vale 366 A4
Eastwood 281 C8
Epping 280 G3
Five Dock 343 A10
Gymea Bay 491 C10
Hoxton Park 393 A6
Hurstville 432 C8
Jannali 460 J11
Lane Cove 314 G3
Lindfield 254 E12
Loftus 490 B5
Mcquarie Fd 424 A16
Maroubra 407 G9
Narrabeen 228 G9
North Ryde 282 H12
N Willghby 285 G10
Rodd Point 343 D9
Seven Hills 275 H2
Toongabbie 276 F8
Willoughby 285 G10
Kingswood, off
First St 237 H16
Berkshire Pk 180 D1
Ashbury 372 G9
Granville 308 H13
Kingswood 237 H16
Parramatta 279 A15
Warragamba 353 G7
Chester Hill 337 J13
ST FARM
Castle Hill 218 E11
ST FLEET
W Pnnant Hl 249 B2
ST ORCHARD
Bella Vista 246 E7
TH
Green Valley 363 G11
Strathfield 341 A16
Arncliffe 403 G9
Waverley 377 H10
TREE
West Ryde 280 H14
CHER
Kingsford 406 K5
Kingsford 406 K5
HBOURNE
Allambie Ht 257 J15
HBURN
Lurnea 394 C12
Castle Hill 217 G13
Beacon Hill 257 G3
Bligh Park 150 C5
Narellan 478 F14
Galston 160 C10
Port Botany 436 A11
HER
N Wahrnga 192 F15
Pennant Hills 250 F1
Ryde 282 F12
S Penrith 237 B15
Vaucluse 348 B4
Pendle Hill 276 D15
Narwee 400 H14
Campbelltwn 511 H8
Narwee 400 J14
Camperdwn 18 D3

rd. Dee Why 258 G6
rd. Lalor Park 245 G10
rd. Maraylya 94 G12
rd.n, Cromer 258 F1
st. Balgowlah Ht 288 A14
st. Cabramatta 365 K6
st. Petersham 15 J11
st. Silverwater 309 F12
st. Yagoona 368 K8
FISHERMANS
rd. Malabar 437 F3
FISHERS
res. Petersham 15 J8
FISK
cl. Bonnyrigg Ht 363 E7
FITCH
av. Penrith 236 B10
FITTON
pl. St Helens Park 540 K8
st. Doonside 243 B8
FITZELL
pl. Brookvale 257 J10
FITZGERALD
av. Beverley Pk 433 C9
av. Edensor Pk 363 J2
av. Hamondvle 396 G14
av. Kogarah 433 C9
av. Maroubra 406 H12
cr. Blackett 241 D1
cr. Strathfield 370 K3
la. Maroubra 407 F13
la. Queens Park 22 H11
pl. Glenmore Pk 265 K6
rd. Ermington 280 F14
st. Newtown 17 G7
st. Queens Park 22 H11
st. Windsor 121 C8
wy. Bella Vista 246 H4
FITZGIBBON
la. Rsemeadow 540 K4
FITZPATRICK
av. Scotland I 168 G3
av.e, Frenchs Frst 256 E6
av.w, Frenchs Frst 256 C6
cr. Casula 394 G13
la. Bankstown, off
Stanley St 399 F2
pl. Bligh Park 150 H9
rd. Mt Annan 479 F14
st. Marsfield 282 B6
st. Menangle Pk 539 B2
st. Revesby 398 D10
FITZROY
av. Balmain 7 C6
av. Pymble 223 D13
cl. Hinchinbrk 363 A15
cl. St Johns Pk 364 G2
cr. Leumeah 481 K16
la. Newtown 17 C11
la. Newtown 18 A8
la. Pymble 223 D13
la. Surry Hills 20 E1
la. Windsor Dn 180 G2
la. Emu Plains, off
Fitzroy St 235 H10
pl. Kellyville 215 F4
pl. Surry Hills F K16
pl. Sylvania Wtr 462 C14
rd. Cromer 227 K14
st. Abbotsford 312 J16
st. Burwood 342 B16
st. Campsie 371 J16
st. Croydon 372 C1
st. Emu Plains 235 G9
st. Killara 253 G12
st. Kirribilli 5 K16
st. Marrickville 374 C12
st. Milsons Point 5 K16
st. Newtown 18 B9
st. Surry Hills F G15
st. Surry Hills 4 A16
st. Surry Hills 20 D1
st. Wilton 568 K15
wy. Bidwill 211 E16
FITZSIMMONS
av. Lane Cove W 283 G13
FITZSIMONS
la. Gordon 253 E6
FITZWATER
wy. Rsemeadow 540 J3
FITZWILLIAM
rd. Old Tngabbie 276 F6
rd. Toongabbie 276 F6
rd. Vaucluse 348 D1

st. Parramatta 308 C4
FIVEASH
st. St Helens Park 540 K7
FIVE WAYS
Killara 254 C12
Paddington 13 B14
FIZELL
pl. Minchinbury 271 F7
FLACK
av. Hillsdale 406 G16
cl. Edensor Pk 363 D3
FLAGSTAFF
st. Engadine 489 C8
st. Gladesville 312 J9
st. Stanhpe Gdn 215 C12
FLAGSTONE
gr. Bella Vista 246 E3
FLAHERTY
bvd. S Granville 338 G4
FLAME
cr. Mcquarie Fd 454 E3
pl. Blacktown 274 C7
FLAME TREE
pl. Cherrybrook 219 H14
FLAMINGO
ct. Bella Vista 246 H2
gr. Plumpton 242 A10
pl. Pendle Hill 276 B16
FLANAGAN
av. Moorebank 396 C7
FLANDERS
av. Matraville 437 A1
av. Milperra 397 G12
av. Mt Krng-gai 162 J14
FLAT
cl. Green Valley 363 C8
st. Leichhardt 9 E10
FLAT ROCK
dr. Naremburn 315 G1
dr. Northbridge 315 G1
rd. Gymea Bay 491 G12
rd. Kingsgrove 402 C8
FLAUMONT
av. Riverview 314 B6
FLAVEL
st. S Penrith 267 D6
FLAVELLE
st. Concord 341 H4
FLAX
pl. Mcquarie Fd 454 F6
pl. Quakers Hill 213 K10
FLEECE
cl. St Clair 270 F12
FLEET
av. Earlwood 402 E4
la. Chatswood, off
Albert Av 284 H10
la. Mosman, off
Orlando Av 316 G11
pl. Beacon Hill 257 G3
pl. Bligh Park 150 G6
st. Carlton 432 F5
st. N Parramatta 278 B14
st. Parramatta 278 B14
st. Summer Hill 373 D4
FLEET STEPS
Sydney 2 G12
FLEETWOOD
st. Shalvey 211 A15
FLEMING
st. Beverly Hills 401 F14
st. Carlingford 250 A16
st. Little Bay 437 G14
st. St Marys 269 K2
st.e, Northwood 314 G7
FLEMINGS
la. Darlinghurst 4 E16
FLEMINGTON
cl. Casula 394 E16
rd. Homebush W 340 J6
st. St Johns Pk 364 G4
FLEMMING
cl. Merrylands W 306 K12
gr. Doonside 273 E5
FLERS
av. Earlwood 402 J1
st. Allambie Ht 257 D11
wy. Matraville 407 B16
FLETCHER
av. Blakehurst 462 C4
av. Miranda 492 A6
cl. Elderslie 507 J4

cl. Old Tngabbie 277 E10
la. Woollahra, off
Fletcher St 377 F2
pl. Davidson 225 C15
rd. Heathcote 518 B15
st. Auburn 338 K3
st. Bondi 378 B5
st. Burwood 341 H13
st. Campsie 371 K16
st. Glenbrook 233 H15
st. Marrickville 373 J13
st. Minto 452 K16
st. Northmead 277 K6
st. Revesby 398 F11
st. S Penrith 267 B3
st. Tamarama 378 B5
st. Vineyard 153 B9
st. Woollahra 22 J3
FLEUR
cl. W Pnnant Hl 249 H4
FLEURBAIX
av. Milperra 397 F14
av. Milperra 397 G10
av. Panania 397 F14
FLEURS
rd. Mt Vernon 331 A13
st. Minchinbury 272 B9
FLIDE
st. Caringbah 492 G6
FLINDERS
av. Baulkham Hl 247 B11
av. Camden S 506 K12
av. Orchard Hills 269 A9
av. St Ives 224 D11
cr. Ermington 280 D16
cr. Hinchinbrk 363 A15
cr. Ingleburn 423 B10
pl. Davidson 225 B14
pl. Mt Colah 162 C13
pl. N Richmond 87 E15
rd. Earlwood 373 B16
rd. Georges Hall 367 F12
rd. North Ryde 282 C9
rd. Woolooware 493 G8
st. Darlinghurst 4 E14
st. Ermington 280 D15
st. Fairfield W 335 E11
st. Matraville 437 A2
st. Moore Park 20 F1
st. Mount Druitt 240 J16
st. Paddington 20 F1
st. Ruse 512 E3
st. Surry Hills 4 E14
FLINT
av. Penrith 236 H14
pl. Illawong 460 A4
pl. Kellyville 216 D5
st. Eastgardens 406 G13
st. Hillsdale 406 G13
st. Ingleburn 453 E5
st. Kings Lngly 245 A2
FLINTLOCK
dr. St Clair 269 K12
la. St Clair, off
Banks Dr 269 J12
FLITCROFT
pl. Glenmore Pk 265 G6
FLITTON VALLEY
cl. Frenchs Frst 256 A2
FLOOD
av. Revesby 398 J15
la. Bondi Jctn, off
Bondi Rd 377 H4
st. Bondi 377 H4
st. Clovelly 377 J13
st. Leichhardt 15 E5
FLOODS
pl. Surry Hills 4 D16
FLORA
av. Mt Colah 192 C1
av. S Penrith 266 G2
cl. Merrylands W 306 J14
ct. Baulkham Hl 217 A16
ct. Baulkham Hl 247 A1
st. Arncliffe 403 J7
st. Erskineville 374 K10
st. Kirrawee 491 A4
st. Mascot 405 E4
st. Narwee 400 G15
st. Oyster Bay 461 A6
st. Plumpton 242 C6
st. Roselands 401 C5
st. Sutherland 490 F3

FLORABELLA
st. Warrimoo 203 B16
FLOREAT
pl. Seven Hills 275 E5
FLORENCE
av. Collaroy 229 D14
av. Denistone 281 E11
av. Eastlakes 406 A4
av. Kurrajong 55 C16
av. Kurrajong 85 C1
av. Minto Ht 483 J6
cl. Bargo 567 C2
ct. N Balgowlah 287 E6
la. Cremorne, off
Murdoch St 316 F10
pl. Epping 250 E13
st. Cremorne 316 F10
st. Glendenning 242 D3
st. Hornsby 221 J1
st. Hurlstone Pk 372 J11
st. Mt Pritchard 364 H14
st. Oakhurst 242 D3
st. Prospect 274 G16
st. Ramsgate Bch 433 G12
st. St Peters 374 G13
st. S Wntwthvle 306 K4
st. Strathfield 341 C14
tce. Scotland I 168 J2
tce. Scotland I 168 J4
FLOREY
av. Pymble 223 E15
cr. Mt Pritchard 364 H11
cr. Springwood 202 E11
pl. Abbotsford 343 A3
pl. Barden Rdg 488 H6
FLORIAN
gr. Oakhurst 242 A2
FLORIBUNDA
av. Glenmore Pk 265 H7
rd. Kemps Ck 360 E8
FLORIDA
av. Ermington 280 E11
cr. Riverwood 400 A14
pl. Seven Hills 275 D5
rd. Palm Beach 139 K1
st. Sylvania 462 C8
FLORRIE
st. Granville 308 C12
FLOSS
st. Hurlstone Pk 372 J12
st. Hurlstone Pk 373 B12
FLOWER
la. Maroubra 407 D11
st. Maroubra 407 D10
FLOWERDALE
rd. Liverpool 394 J4
FLOYD
pl. Mt Pritchard 364 H10
FLOYDS
rd. S Maroota 66 A2
FLUORITE
pl. Eagle Vale 481 D6
FLUSHCOMBE
rd. Blacktown 274 G7
FLYNN
cr. Leumeah 482 F11
pl. Bonnyrigg Ht 363 F7
FOAL
wy. Glenwood 245 J3
FOAM
st. Harbord 258 H15
FOAMCREST
av. Newport 169 J10
FOCH
av. Gymea 491 C2
FOGG
pl. Yellow Rock 204 A5
FOGGITS
wk. Hunters Hill 313 B11
FOLEY
la. Georges Hall 367 J13
pl. Castle Hill 218 K10
st. Darlinghurst F K5
st. Darlinghurst 4 C11
st. Georges Hall 367 J14
st. Mona Vale 198 J5
FOLINI
av. Northmead 278 A2
FOLKARD
st. North Ryde 282 G8
FOLKESTONE
pde. Botany 405 E14

pl. Dural 219 B5
FOLLY
rd. Silverdale 354 E11
FONDA
pl. Glendenning 242 F3
FONTAINE
st. Chatswood 285 B6
FONTAINEBLEAU
st. Sans Souci 463 A5
FONTANA
cl. St Clair 300 C2
FONTENOY
rd. Mcquarie Pk 282 J1
FONTHILL
pl. Airds 512 C10
FONTI
st. Eastwood 281 G6
FOORD
av. Hurlstone Pk 372 K14
FOOTMAN
cr. Kellyville 215 C2
FOOTS
pl. Maroubra 407 G8
FOOTSCRAY
st. St Johns Pk 364 E3
FORAY
st. Guildford W 336 F5
st. Yennora 336 F5
FORBES
av. Belmore 401 H2
cl. Abbotsbury 333 C16
cr. Engadine 488 F13
la. Newtown 18 D8
la. Turramurra 222 H14
la. Warwck Frm 365 G16
pl. Allambie Ht 257 F13
pl. Leumeah 481 J16
pl. Newtown 18 C8
rd. Marayong 244 D7
st. Croydon Pk 372 D7
st. Darlinghurst 4 E12
st. Emu Plains 235 A11
st. Hornsby 221 F2
st. Liverpool 395 G1
st. Newtown 18 C8
st. Paddington 13 J16
st. Warwck Frm 365 G16
st. Windsor 121 B11
st. Woolmloo 4 F5
st. Woolmloo 4 F7
wy. Mcquarie Lk 423 G14
FORCETT
cl. West Hoxton 392 E8
FORD
la. Burwood, off Railway Pde 342 A14
pl. Erskine Park 270 G15
pl. Ingleburn 453 K7
rd. Maroubra 407 F14
st. Balmain 7 H9
st. Greenacre 370 G7
st. Greenwich 314 J10
st. Huntingwd 273 G13
st. North Ryde 282 D8
st. Old Tngabbie 276 H10
FORDE
pl. Currans Hill 479 J11
pl. N Wahrnga 192 F15
FORE
st. Canterbury 372 E14
FOREMAN
la. Tempe 404 C1
pl. Barden Rdg 488 J1
st. Glenfield 424 E8
st. Tempe 404 C1
FORESHORE
rd. Bnksmeadw 435 H1
rd. Botany 405 C13
FOREST
cl. Cherrybrook 219 A14
cr. Kellyville 185 K16
gln. Cherrybrook 219 E9
gr. Epping 281 C1
gr. Lansvale 366 D9
pl. Galston 159 F10
rd. Arncliffe 403 A11
rd. Baulkham Hl 248 A13
rd. Bexley 402 G16
rd. Double Bay 14 E12
rd. Gymea 491 D7
rd. Gymea Bay 491 D7
rd. Heathcote 518 K10
rd. Hurstville 431 K5
rd. Hurstville 432 C6
rd. Kirrawee 490 E5
rd. Kirrawee 490 H6
rd. Lugarno 429 K12
rd. Miranda 491 J8
rd. Mortdale 431 A3
rd. Peakhurst 430 E3
rd. Penshurst 431 F4
rd. Sutherland 490 E5
rd. Warriewood 198 F6
st. Forest Lodge 11 K16
st. Glebe 11 K16
wy. Belrose 226 A2
wy. Frenchs Frst 256 C1
wy. Terrey Hills 195 K16
wy. Wrrngtn Cty 238 F5
FORESTER
cr. Cherrybrook 219 H4
pl. Bossley Park 333 E10
FOREST GLEN
cr. Belrose 226 B15
dr. Cranebrook 207 B8
wy. Menai 458 H14
FORESTGROVE
dr. Menai 458 K13
FOREST GUM
pl. Greystanes 306 C3
FOREST HILL
rd. Werombi 413 H13
FOREST KNOLL
Castle Hill 218 J16
av. Bondi Beach 378 B3
FORESTVILLE
av. Forestville 255 J10
FORESTWOOD
cr. W Pnnant Hl 249 G4
FORGE
pl. Narellan 478 C8
st. Blacktown 244 H9
FORK
la. Kurmond 86 D4
FORMAN
av. Glenwood 215 E15
FORMER HUME
hwy. Camden 507 A15
hwy. Camden S 507 A15
FORMOSA
st. Drummoyne 343 J3
st. Sylvania 461 K12
st. Sylvania 462 A9
FORNASIER
la. Canley Vale, off Canley Vale Rd 366 A3
FORREST
av. Earlwood 402 E7
av. N Wahrnga 222 F1
cr. Camden 507 B2
rd. East Hills 427 G3
rd. Lalor Park 245 C13
rd. Ryde 312 E1
st. Chifley 437 A6
st. Ermington 280 E16
st. Haberfield 343 E14
FORRESTER
pl. Maraylya 94 K13
rd. Lethbrdg Pk 240 A4
rd. N St Marys 240 A4
rd. St Marys 239 H12
rd. Tregear 240 A4
st. Kingsgrove 401 J9
FORRESTERS
cl. Woodbine 481 H11
FORRESTWOOD
pl. Prospect 274 H12
FORSHAW
av. Chester Hill 338 D16
av. Peakhurst 430 H2
FORSTER
la. West Ryde 281 F14
pl. Dundas Vy 280 D9
pl. Penrith 237 B7
st. Blakehurst 432 E13
st. Concord 341 K10
st. Mascot 405 D3
st. West Ryde 281 F14
FORSYTH
cl. Wetherill Pk 334 A3
la. Glebe 12 B8
pl. Oatlands 279 A14
st. Belmore 401 G6
st. Glebe 11 K9
st. Killara 253 K9
st. Kingsford 406 G1
st. Kingsgrove 401 G6
st. N Willghby 285 D10
st. West Ryde 311 G1
FORT
pl. Quakers Hill 214 E16
st. Petersham 15 H6
FORTESCUE
st. Bexley North 402 D10
st. Chiswick 343 C1
FORTH
st. Woollahra 22 B2
FORTHORN
pl. N St Marys 239 K12
FORTINBRAS
cl. Rsemeadow 540 J8
FORTRIL
av. Bankstown 399 F7
FORTUNATO
gr. Prestons 392 K14
st. Prestons 392 J14
FORTUNE
gr. Kellyville 186 G16
FORUM
cr. Baulkham Hl 246 G11
dr. Heathcote 518 E7
FORWOOD
av. Turramurra 252 D4
FOSS
st. Blacktown 274 K9
st. Forest Lodge 11 G16
st. Glebe 11 G16
st. Hunters Hill 313 J11
FOSTER
av. Bellevue Hill 347 G15
cl. West Hoxton 391 K4
la. Leichhardt 15 D2
la. Surry Hills F B10
pl. Quakers Hill 213 K16
st. Leichhardt 15 C1
st. Surry Hills F B9
st. Surry Hills 3 J13
st. Valley Ht 202 F6
FOSTERS
la. Bickley Vale 505 E11
la. Mt Hunter 505 E11
FOTEA
cl. Edensor Pk 333 F15
FOTHERINGHAM
la. Marrickville, off Cowper St 374 E9
st. Enmore 16 J16
FOUCART
st. Rozelle 10 H2
FOUNDRY
rd. Seven Hills 246 E15
FOUNTAIN
av. Croydon Pk 371 G8
mw. Bella Vista 216 C13
st. Alexandria 18 H15
FOURTEENTH
av. Austral 390 H3
st. Warragamba 353 F7
FOURTH
av. Austral 390 K16
av. Berala 339 D15
av. Blacktown 244 G13
av. Campsie 371 J10
av. Canley Vale 366 C3
av. Condell Park 398 D5
av. Eastwood 281 D9
av. Jannali 460 K10
av. Lane Cove 314 G4
av. Lindfield 254 F13
av. Llandilo 178 C16
av. Loftus 489 K6
av. Mcquarie Fd 454 C3
av. N Willghby 285 H9
av. Seven Hills 275 J3
av. Willoughby 285 H9
rd. Berkshire Pk 179 K4
st. Ashbury 372 G8
st. Granville 308 G14
st. Parramatta 279 A16
st. Warragamba 353 F7
FOUVEAUX
cct. Harringtn Pk 478 C2
FOVEAUX
av. Lurnea 394 D13
pl. Airds 511 K15
pl. Barden Rdg 488 G3
pl. Cromer 227 H12
st. Surry Hills F A15
st. Surry Hills 20 A1
tce. Bella Vista 246 G3
FOWKES
wy. West Hoxton 392 B13
FOWLER
av. Bexley North 402 F10
cr. Maroubra 407 G8
cr. S Coogee 407 G8
la. Camperdwn 17 E6
rd. Guildford 337 A4
rd. Guildford W 337 A4
rd. Illawong 459 D4
rd. Merrylands 307 B16
rd. Merrylands W 307 B16
st. Camperdwn 17 E6
st. Leichhardt 10 C15
st. Seven Hills 275 D5
st.n, Woolooware 493 G9
st.s, Woolooware 493 G9
FOX
av. Erskineville 18 E16
cr. Padstow 429 B1
pl. Penrith 237 D3
rd. East Ryde 282 K14
st. Holroyd 308 A10
st. Lane Cove 314 B3
st. Malabar 437 F4
st. Narellan 478 E9
st. Riverview 314 B3
wy. Claymore 481 D11
FOXALL
rd. Kellyville 186 D8
st. Elanora Ht 198 D11
FOXGLOVE
rd. Mt Colah 162 F13
FOX GROVE
av. Casula 423 J2
FOX HILLS
cr. Prospect 275 E14
FOXLOW
pl. Airds 512 D11
st. Canley Ht 335 B15
FOXS
la. Ashfield, off Brown St 372 H3
FOXTON
st. Quakers Hill 214 D11
FOX VALLEY
rd. Denham Ct 421 J9
rd. Wahroonga 221 H16
rd. Wahroonga 222 B12
FOXWOOD
av. Quakers Hill 213 H11
cl. Silverdale 383 J3
wy. Cherrybrook 219 D13
FOY
la. Sydney F B6
st. Balmain 7 F12
FOYLE
av. Birrong 369 A6
FRAGAR
rd. S Penrith 267 B6
FRAM
pl. Tregear 240 G7
FRAMPTON
av. Marrickville 374 B13
av. St Clair 270 F15
la. Marrickville 374 B13
st. Lidcombe 339 J3
FRANCE
st. Canterbury 372 F16
FRANCES
av. Strathfield S 371 D5
la. Randwick, off Frances St 377 A12
pl. Miranda 492 E2
rd. Putney 312 B7
st. Lidcombe 339 K5
st. Lindfield 284 B2
st. Merrylands 307 C8
st. Narellan 478 H10
st. Northmead 277 J9
st. Randwick 376 K12
st. S Wntwthvle 307 C8
FRANCESCO
cr. Bella Vista 246 D8
FRANCINE
st. Seven Hills 245 H14
FRANCIS
av. Btn-le-Sds 403 J16
av. Emu Plains 235 J9
la. Darlinghurst F H1
la. Emu Plains, off Francis Av 235 J9
la. Manly, off Raglan St 288
pl. Currans Hill 479
rd. Artarmon 284
rd. Faulconbdg 171
rd. Rooty Hill 272
st. Artarmon 315
st. Bondi 377
st. Bondi Beach 378
st. Bringelly 387
st. Cmbrdg Pk 238
st. Campsie 372
st. Carlton 432
st. Castle Hill 248
st. Colyton 270
st. Darlinghurst F
st. Darlinghurst 4
st. Dee Why 258
st. Earlwood 402
st. Enmore 17
st. Epping 280
st. Fairfield 336
st. Fairlight 288
st. Glebe 12
st. Homebush 340
st. Hunters Hill 314
st. Leichhardt 9
st. Leichhardt 9
st. Lilyfield 9
st. Longueville 314
st. Manly 288
st. Marrickville 373
st. Mascot 405
st. Minto 452
st. Mount Druitt 240
st. Naremburn 315
st. Naremburn 315
st. Richmond 118
st. Strathfield 340
FRANCISCO
cr. Rsemeadow 540
FRANCIS GREENWAY
av. St Clair 270
dr. Cherrybrook 219
FRANCIS MARTIN
dr. Randwick, off Hospital Rd 377
FRANCIS OAKES
wy. W Pnnant Hl 249
FRANGIPANE
av. Liverpool 394
FRANGIPANI
ct. Erskine Park 300
pl. Caringbah 492
FRANK
st. Gladesville 312
st. Guildford 337
st. Guildford 337
st. Mount Druitt 271
st. Mt Lewis 369
st. Wetherill Pk 304
FRANK BEAMES
la. Harris Park 308
FRANKI
av. Woolwich 314
la. Prospect 275
FRANKIE
la. Concord 342
FRANKISH
pl. W Pnnant Hl 248
FRANKLIN
cr. Blackett 241
pl. Bossley Park 333
pl. Carlingford 249
pl. Colyton 270
rd. Cherrybrook 219
rd. Chipping Ntn 396
rd. Woolooware 493
st. Chifley 437
st. Leumeah 482
st. Malabar 437
st. Matraville 436
st. Mays Hill 307
st. Parramatta 307
FRANKLYN
st. Concord 341
st. Glebe 12
FRANK OLIVERI
dr. Chipping Ntn 366
FRANKSON
pl. Mona Vale 199
FRANKUM
dr. Orangeville 473

NLEE
Dural 188 G14
SCATTI
Mosman 317 E9
SER
Eastgardens 406 F12
Kellyville 215 H5
Mt Annan 509 G3
Shalvey 210 K13
Canley Vale 366 D4
Cowan 104 B14
Normanhurst 221 G9
Springwood 172 B16
Auburn 338 K10
Homebush 340 J11
Homebush W 340 J11
Lane Cove W 283 K15
Mcquarie Fd 424 A14
Randwick 377 D10
Rockdale 433 G2
Strathfield 340 J12
Tahmoor 565 G12
Wentwthvle 277 A9
Westmead 307 F5
TERS
Sans Souci 463 A6
ZER
Lurnea 394 E12
Birrong 368 J7
Collaroy 229 B11
Dulwich Hill 15 C16
Lakemba 371 A13
Lilyfield 9 G5
Marrickville 15 C16
ZIER
Liberty Gr 311 B10
AME
Wentwthvle 276 K16
D
Lilyfield 10 G1
Rozelle 10 G1
Lewisham 373 E6
Lilyfield 10 G2
DA
Hamondvle 396 C13
Panania 428 A6
D ALLEN
Rooty Hill 272 B2
DBEN
Cammeray 315 J5
Cammeray, off Fredben Av 315 J5
DBERT
Lilyfield 10 A5
DE
Marrickville 373 J15
DERICK
Beverly Hills 401 C14
S Granville 338 E3
Oatley 431 C12
Rockdale 403 C15
Kurrajong Ht 53 K7
Cecil Hills 362 G8
Taren Point 462 J10
Artarmon 315 B3
Ashfield 372 F2
Bankstown 369 G12
Blacktown 245 A8
Campsie 372 B12
Canterbury 372 G11
Concord 342 B2
Fairfield 336 C14
Hornsby 221 D2
Killara 283 E1
Lalor Park 245 E9
Lidcombe 339 K8
Miranda 492 E6
North Bondi 348 F16
Oatley 431 C12
Pendle Hill 306 E2
Petersham 16 A11
Randwick 407 D2
Rockdale 403 A13
Ryde 312 C5
St Leonards 315 B3
St Peters 374 E14
Sydenham 374 E14
DRIKA
Carlingford 249 E13
EBODY
S Windsor 150 K1
EEDOM
Cabramatta, off Arthur St 365 J7

FREEMAN
av. Canley Vale 365 K2
av. Castle Hill 247 J2
av. Oatley 430 H14
cct. Ingleburn 452 J10
pl. Carlingford 280 E4
pl. Chester Hill 338 E16
pl. Concord 342 B5
rd. Agnes Banks 117 D11
rd. Chatswd W 284 G11
rd. Heathcote 518 D11
st. Colyton 270 C5
st. Lalor Park 245 F12
st. Warwck Frm 365 H14
FREEMANS
la. Middle Dural 128 J16
FREEMANS REACH
rd. Freemns Rch 121 C3
FREEMANTLE
pl. Wakeley 334 H15
FREEMASONS ARMS
la. Parramatta, off George St 308 C2
FREESIA
pl. Glenmore Pk 265 H7
FREESTONE
av. Carlingford 249 C15
FREITAS
la. Lidcombe, off Olympic Dr 339 G9
FREMANTLE
pl. Yarrawarrah 489 G13
FREMLIN
st. Botany 405 J16
FREMONT
av. Ermington 280 C13
st. Concord W 311 E12
FRENCH
av. Bankstown 369 E14
av. Toongabbie 276 C5
la. Kogarah 433 D3
la. Maroubra 407 E10
pl. Currans Hill 479 K14
pl. Hinchinbrk 362 K16
st. Artarmon 284 H16
st. Kingswood 238 C13
st. Kogarah 433 D3
st. McMahons Pt 5 D14
st. Maroubra 407 E11
FRENCHMANS
rd. Randwick 377 C11
FRENCHS
la. Summer Hill 15 A6
pl. Belrose 225 E14
rd. Willoughby 285 F14
FRENCHS FOREST
rd. Seaforth 287 B7
rd.e, Frenchs Frst 256 J5
rd.w, Frenchs Frst 256 F4
FRENSHAM
pl. Dural 188 G13
FRERE
pl. Cherrybrook 220 B13
FRERES
rd. Kentlyn 483 G14
FRESHWATER
cl. Woodbine 481 H10
FREYA
cr. Shalvey 210 H13
st. Kareela 461 D12
FREYCINET
cl. Dural 219 B3
FRIAR
pl. Ingleburn 453 H7
FRIARBIRD
cr. Glenmore Pk 265 H12
FRICOURT
av. Earlwood 402 J2
FRIEDLANDER
pl. St Leonards, off Nicholson St 315 E6
FRIEDMANN
pl. S Penrith 267 A5
FRIEND
av. Five Dock 342 G8
pl. Blacktown 274 D10
st. Merrylands 307 C6
wy. Mt Pritchard 364 J11
FRIENDSHIP
av. Kellyville 216 C2
pl. Beacon Hill 257 H4
pl. Bligh Park 150 C5
pl. Illawong 459 G7
rd. Port Botany 436 B10
st. Dundas Vy 280 B6
wy. Minto 482 J7
FRIESIAN
st. Busby 363 K16
FRIGATE-BIRD
av. Hinchinbrk 393 B3
FRIPP
cr. Beverly Hills 401 A15
la. Springwood 171 F16
st. Arncliffe 403 C9
FRITH
av. Normanhurst 221 J8
st. Doonside 243 D6
FROBISHER
av. Caringbah 492 K4
FROGGATT
cr. Croydon 342 E15
FROGMORE
la. Mascot 405 F6
rd. Orchard Hills 267 D7
st. Mascot 405 F6
FROME
pl. Castle Hill 217 H10
st. Fairfield W 335 G9
FROMELLES
av. Milperra 397 G10
av. Seaforth 287 A6
wy. Matraville 407 A15
FRONTIGNAN
st. Eschol Park 481 A5
FROST
av. Matraville 436 H8
av. Narellan 478 G14
cl. St Clair 299 K2
ct. Wetherill Pk 334 H6
la. Chester Hill 368 C1
rd. Campbelltwn 511 C1
st. Earlwood 402 D7
FRUTICOSA
wy. Mcquarie Fd 454 G3
FRY
pl. Quakers Hill 213 G15
st. Chatswood 285 C11
FRYAR
row. Tarban 313 B13
FRYER
av. Wentwthvle 276 K14
st. Mt Annan 479 D16
FUCHSIA
cr. Mcquarie Fd 454 A3
cr. Quakers Hill 243 E3
ct. Baulkham Hl 247 F14
pl. Bossley Park 333 F8
FUGGLES
rd. Kenthurst 156 K9
rd. Kenthurst 157 A10
FULBOURNE
av. Pennant Hills 220 H14
FULHAM
st. Busby 363 J12
st. Newtown 17 D16
FULLAGAR
rd. Wentwthvle 307 A3
FULLAM
rd. Blacktown 274 G6
FULLARTON
st. Telopea 279 J8
FULLER
av. Earlwood 402 F1
av. Hornsby 221 G3
pl. St Clair 270 H10
st. Badgerys Ck 358 F8
st. Chester Hill 337 H11
st. Collaroy Plat 228 G11
st. Mount Druitt 271 D2
st. Narrabeen 228 G11
st. Seven Hills 275 K5
FULLERS
rd. Chatswd W 284 A9
rd. Chatswd W 284 D10
rd. Glenhaven 218 C3
FULLERTON
cct. St Helens Park 541 D4
cr. Bligh Park 150 C6
cr. Riverwood 400 F14
pl. Glenmore Pk 265 K7
st. Woollahra 14 B16
st. Woollahra 22 B1
FULLFORD
st. Dundas Vy 280 B10

FULLWOOD
pl. Claymore 481 F11
FULTON
av. Wentwthvle 277 B12
la. Penrith 237 A11
pl. Kellyville 186 E9
pl. N Richmond 86 K14
rd. Marsden Pk 211 H6
st. Penrith 237 A11
FUNDA
cr. Lalor Park 245 F14
pl. Brookvale 257 K10
FUR
pl. Rooty Hill 241 K12
FURBER
la. Centnnial Pk 21 D7
la. Moore Park 21 D7
pl. Davidson 225 B14
rd. Centnnial Pk 21 D6
FURCI
av. Edensor Pk 333 H15
FURLONG
av. Casula 424 C1
pwy. Casula, off Furlong Av 394 C16
FURNER
av. Camden S 506 K14
FURSORB
st. Marayong 244 B7
FURY
st. Kingswood 237 H15
FUTUNA
st. Hunters Hill 314 A12
FUTURA
pl. Toongabbie 276 F5
FYALL
av. Wentwthvle 276 J14
st. Ermington 280 B13
FYFE
pl. Glenfield 424 F13
pl. N Sydney 5 F3
rd. Kellyville 214 J6
FYNE
cl. St Andrews 451 K12
FYSH
pl. Bidwill 211 C16

G

GABEE
pl. Malabar 437 E8
GABO
cr. Sadleir 364 A16
cr. Sadleir 394 A1
cr. Sadleir 394 B2
ct. Baulkham Hl 247 D1
pl. Gymea 491 F2
GABRIELLA
av. Cecil Hills 362 G7
GABRIELLE
av. Baulkham Hl 247 B8
cl. Mt Colah 162 F14
GABRIELS
la. St Marys 239 F16
GADARA
dr. S Penrith 266 F6
GADDS
la. Kurmond 57 C14
GADSHILL
pl. Rsemeadow 540 C3
GAERLOCH
av. Tamarama 378 C7
GAGA
rd. Illawong 459 F4
GAGGIN
st. Parramatta 278 H16
GAGOOR
cl. Clarmnt Ms 268 H2
la. Clarmnt Ms, off Gagoor Cl 268 H2
GAHNIA
wy. Winmalee 172 H13
GAIETY
pl. Doonside 243 B8
GAIL
pl. Bankstown 369 B16
GAILES
st. Sutherland 460 G16

GAINFORD
av. Matraville 407 A14
GAINSFORD
dr. Kellyville 215 H5
GAIWOOD
pl. Castle Hill 248 H1
GAL
cr. Moorebank 396 B9
GALA
av. Croydon 372 C4
GALAH
cl. St Clair 269 J10
GALAHAD
cl. Mt Colah 162 E11
cr. Castle Hill 217 G7
GALASHIELS
av. St Andrews 481 J2
GALATEA
st. Plumpton 241 G8
GALAXY
pl. Raby 451 H14
rd. Luddenham 326 D8
GALBA
cl. Prestons 392 K16
GALE
pl. Oakhurst 211 J16
rd. Maroubra 406 H8
st. Concord 342 B1
st. Ryde 311 G4
st. Woolwich 314 E13
GALEA
dr. Glenwood 245 D2
GALEN
st. Hornsby 221 F3
GALENA
pl. Eagle Vale 481 G4
GALGA
st. Sutherland 460 D16
GALILEE
cl. Bossley Park 333 K8
GALLAGHER
st. St Helens Park 541 B9
GALLARD
st. Denistone E 281 H10
GALLEON
cl. Chipping Ntn 366 J15
GALLIMORE
av. Balmain East 8 G7
GALLIPOLI
cl. Narrabeen, off Endeavour Dr 228 F8
la. Concord, off Gallipoli St 342 A5
st. Bankstown 398 K7
st. Bossley Park 333 J6
st. Concord 342 A5
st. Condell Park 398 K7
st. Hurstville 432 A8
st. Lidcombe 340 C5
st. St Marys 269 F6
GALLOP
gr. Lalor Park 245 G11
st. Warwck Frm 365 G14
GALLOWAY
cr. St Andrews 482 A1
st. Bossley Park 334 C12
st. Busby 393 K1
st. N Parramatta 278 C13
GALLUS
pl. Rsemeadow 540 E2
GALSTON
rd. Dural 189 B6
rd. Galston 159 G11
rd. Hornsby 191 E1
rd. Hornsby Ht 191 E1
GALTON
st. Smithfield 335 C2
st. Wetherill Pk 335 C2
GALVIN
rd. Llandilo 179 C14
st. Elderslie 507 G1
st. Maroubra 407 C10
GALWAY
av. Killarney Ht 286 B1
ct. St Clair 269 K10
pl. Smithfield 335 F2
GAMA
rd. Cranebrook 207 E10
GAMACK
ct. Rouse Hill 185 A9

GAMAY
pl. Minchinbury.......272 B7
GAMBIA
pl. Cranebrook........207 E10
st. Kearns...............481 C1
GAMBIER
av. Sandy Point.......427 K10
st. Bossley Park......334 B9
GAMBOOLA
wy. Airds.................512 B14
GAME
st. Bonnyrigg..........363 K7
GAMENYA
av. S Penrith...........267 A1
pl. Engadine............489 F8
GAMMA
rd. Lane Cove..........314 F3
GAMMELL
st. Rydalmere.........309 K3
GAMMIE
av. Matraville..........436 G8
GAMUT
rd. Engadine............489 F8
GANDANGARA
st. Douglas Park.....568 B8
st. Douglas Park.....568 C6
GANDELL
cr. S Penrith...........266 G5
la. S Penrith, off Gandell Cr..........266 G5
GANDER
pl. Hinchinbrk.........363 E15
GANDY
la. Greenacre..........370 G2
GANGES
wy. Kellyville............185 K14
GANGURLIN
st. Heckenberg........364 B13
GANMAIN
cr. Milperra.............397 F11
rd. Pymble..............223 F15
GANNET
pl. Acacia Gdn.........214 J16
pl. Hinchinbrk.........393 C2
pl. Woronora Ht......489 C5
st. Gladesville.........313 A5
st. Raby..................481 G3
GANNON
av. Dolls Point.........463 G1
cl. Bradbury............511 J10
la. Tempe...............404 B3
st. Kurnell..............466 C7
st. Tempe...............404 A2
GANNONS
av. Hurstville...........432 B1
rd. Caringbah..........493 C7
rd.s, Caringbah..........493 B15
GANORA
st. Gladesville..........313 A4
GAP
rd. Watsons Bay......318 G14
GARAH
cl. Westleigh...........220 E7
GARBALA
rd. Gymea..............491 F1
GARBETT
pl. Doonside...........273 E4
GARBUTT
pl. Oakdale.............500 E11
GARDA
st. Seven Hills.........275 H7
GARDEN
cl. Hinchinbrk.........362 K15
ct. W Pnnant Hl.......248 J9
gr. Beverly Hills.......400 K16
la. Belmore..............401 F3
la. Maroubra............407 B10
la. Eastlakes, off Maloney La........405 J4
pl. Bonnyrigg..........364 E6
pl. Picnic Point.........428 D7
sq. Faulconbdg.........201 C1
sq. Gordon..............253 J6
st. Alexandria............18 K11
st. Belmore.............401 F4
st. Blacktown..........245 B8
st. Eastlakes............405 J4
st. Eveleigh...............18 K11
st. Kingsford............407 B10
st. Kogarah..............433 A7
st. Maroubra............407 B10
st. Marrickville........374 E13
st. Mt Pritchard.......364 J13
st. N Narrabeen.......198 J13
st. Telopea..............279 F9
st. Warriewood.......198 H10
wy. Lilyfield................10 B4
GARDENER
av. Ryde..................282 D16
GARDENERS
la. Kingsford...........406 F2
la. West Ryde.........281 A15
rd. Alexandria.........375 B16
rd. Daceyville..........406 B2
rd. Eastlakes............406 B2
rd. Kensington.........406 B2
rd. Kingsford...........406 B2
rd. Mascot..............375 B16
rd. Rosebery...........405 C1
GARDEN HILL
rd. Mulgoa..............325 K2
GARDENIA
av. Bankstown.........399 H2
av. Emu Plains.........235 F9
av. Lane Cove W......313 K1
gr. Lalor Park..........245 D11
pde. Greystanes.........305 K12
pl. Castle Hill...........248 H2
pl. Mcquarie Fd.......454 E5
st. Asquith...............191 K9
st. Cronulla.............524 A2
GARDENSET
gr. Blacktown..........274 D10
GARDENVALE
rd. Oatlands............279 C12
GARDERE
av. Curl Curl............258 H14
av. Harbord.............258 H14
st. Caringbah..........492 G6
GARDINER
av. Banksia.............403 C12
cr. Fairfield W..........335 E11
rd. Badgerys Ck.......358 H2
rd. Galston..............159 G10
st. Bondi Jctn...........22 H9
st. Minto.................482 K4
GARDINIA
st. Narwee..............400 G15
GARDNER
st. Rooty Hill...........272 A6
GARDYNE
st. Bronte...............377 J8
GAREMA
cct. Kingsgrove.........401 G8
GAREMYN
rd. Middle Dural......158 D3
GARETH
cl. Mt Colah............162 F11
st. Blacktown..........274 H8
GARFIELD
av. Bonnet Bay........460 C9
la. Carlton, off Shaftsbury St.....432 H7
rd. Horsley Pk.........331 G5
rd.e, Riverstone.........182 J8
rd.w, Marsden Pk.......181 J16
rd.w, Riverstone.........182 D12
st. Carlton...............432 H7
st. Five Dock...........342 H10
st. McGraths Hl.......122 B12
st. Oakville..............122 B12
st. Wentwthvle........306 J3
st. Wentwthvle........306 K2
GARGERY
st. Ambarvale..........510 F14
GARIE
cl. Woodbine..........481 F12
pl. Frenchs Frst.......256 J4
pl. S Coogee...........407 H5
GARIGAL
pl. Mona Vale..........199 B2
rd. Belrose..............195 K16
rd. Belrose..............225 K1
GARING
st. Richmond..........120 B6
GARLAND
av. Epping...............280 K2
cr. Bonnyrigg Ht......363 B3
rd. Naremburn.........315 F1
wy. Ambarvale..........511 A15
GARLICKS RANGE
rd. Orangeville.........473 A10
GARLING
av. West Hoxton......391 J11
pl. Barden Rdg........488 G5
pl. Currans Hill........479 J10
rd. Kings Park..........244 H5
st. Lane Cove W......283 K16
wy. Claymore...........481 C10
GARMENT
st. Fairfield W..........335 B8
st. Prairiewood.......335 B8
GARNER
av. Frenchs Frst.......256 G7
st. St Marys............269 G2
GARNERS
av. Marrickville........374 A12
la. Marrickville........374 A12
GARNET
av. Lilyfield................10 E7
cr. Killara...............254 D12
la. Dulwich Hill.........373 C11
pl. Cartwright..........393 K5
pl. Kellyville............185 E9
rd. Gymea..............461 G15
rd. Kareela..............461 B14
rd. Kirrawee............461 B14
rd. Miranda.............461 G15
st. Bossley Park......334 B9
st. Dulwich Hill.........373 B11
st. Eagle Vale..........481 F5
st. Hurlstone Pk......373 B11
st. Killara...............254 D12
st. Rockdale.............433 F1
st. S Coogee...........407 H4
GARNETT
st. Guildford............338 C4
st. Merrylands.........338 C4
GARNSEY
av. Panania.............428 F5
GARONNE
st. Kearns...............451 D16
st. Seven Hills.........275 G7
GARRALLAN
pl. Airds.................512 C10
GARRAN
la. Glebe...................12 A7
st. Fairfield W..........335 F11
GARRARD
la. Balmain East..........8 D9
st. Granville............308 D13
GARRAWEEN
av. N Balgowlah.......287 C4
GARREFFA
cl. Edensor Pk........333 J13
GARRETT
av. Glenhaven..........218 D3
av. S Turramrra........252 B8
av. Terrey Hills........196 F5
pl. Shalvey..............211 A15
rd. Beecroft.............250 F5
st. Kingsford...........407 B8
st. Maroubra...........407 B8
wy. Glenwood...........246 B5
GARRICK
av. Hunters Hill........313 K12
la. St Clair, off St Clair Av.........269 H8
pl. Doonside............243 B7
rd. St Clair...............269 G8
rd. St Ives...............224 B10
GARRISON
rd. Bossley Park......333 H8
wy. Glenwood..........246 B5
GARRONG
rd. Lakemba...........371 A15
GARRY
ct. Georges Hall.....367 K15
GARSWOOD
rd. Glenmore Pk......266 F9
GARTFERN
av. Five Dock...........343 A6
GARTHONS
la. Hurstville.............431 J5
GARTHOWEN
av. Lane Cove..........313 K2
cr. Castle Hill...........218 E13
GARTMORE
av. Bankstown.........399 F5
GARTUNG
rd. Galston..............159 C4
GARTY
la. Greenacre...........370 G2
GARVAN
rd. Heathcote..........518 C15
GARY
gr. Marayong...........244 D6
st. Castle Hill...........248 B3
st. Merrylands W....306 J13
GAS
la. Millers Pt.............A C9
la. N Sydney..............K D10
GASCOGNE
st. Prestons............393 H15
GASCOIGNE
rd. Birrong..............368 H7
rd. Yagoona............368 H8
st. Penrith...............237 D9
GASCOYNE
pl. Illawong.............460 B3
GASMATA
cr. Whalan..............240 H10
GASPARD
pl. Ambarvale..........510 H13
GAS WORKS
rd. Wollstncraft.......315 D11
GATACRE
av. Lane Cove..........314 F1
GATE
rd. Blacktown..........244 G9
GATEHOUSE
cct. Wrrngtn Dns......238 A3
GATENBY
pl. Barden Rdg........458 H16
GATES
rd. Luddenham........326 F1
GATHREY
cr. Kings Lngly........245 D5
GATLEY
ct. Wattle Grove......426 A5
GATTO
pl. West Hoxton......392 C7
GAUSS
pl. Tregear.............240 E5
GAUTHORPE
st. Rhodes..............311 D8
GAVIN
pl. Cherrybrook.......219 J9
pl. Kings Lngly........245 K6
GAWAIN
ct. Glenhaven..........217 J5
GAWLER
pl. Bossley Park......333 E10
pl. N Turramrra........223 D1
GAY
st. Castle Hill...........218 D12
st. Lane Cove W......284 D15
GAYLINE
dr. Narellan Vale......479 B13
GAYMARK
la. Penrith...............236 J10
GAZA
av. Hunters Hill........313 E5
la. West Ryde, off Gaza Rd............281 D15
rd. Naremburn.........315 F1
rd. West Ryde.........281 D16
st. Holsworthy........426 D10
GAZALA
rd. Holsworthy........426 E7
GAZANIA
rd. Faulconbdg........171 E14
GAZELLE
pl. Werrington.........238 E11
st. Glenfield............424 F9
GAZI
cl. Bossley Park......334 A6
GAZZARD
st. Birrong..............368 K6
GEAKES
rd. Freemns Rch........61 A14
rd. Glossodia.............61 A8
rd. Wilberforce...........61 A8
GEARS
av. Drummoyne.........343 F4
GEARY
st. Campbelltwn......510 H7
GEDDES
pl. Cabramatta W.....365 C8
st. Balgowlah Ht......288 A13
st. Botany...............405 J16
GEE
wy. Minto.................482 K2
GEEBUNG
cl. Arcadia...............129 J10
ct. Voyager Pt.........427 C4
GEEHI
pl. Heckenberg........364
GEELANS
rd. Arcadia..............130
GEELONG
cr. St Johns Pk........364
rd. Cromer...............228
rd. Engadine............489
GEER
av. Sans Souci.........463
GEES
av. Strathfield..........371
GEEVES
av. Rockdale............403
la. Pennant Hills......220
la. Pennant Hills......250
GEEWAN
av. Kellyville............216
pl. Clarmnt Ms.........268
GEHRIG
la. Annandale............17
GELDING
st. Dulwich Hill........373
GELLING
av. Strathfield..........341
GEM
pl. Greystanes.........306
GEMALLA
st. Bonnyrigg..........363
GEMALONG
pl. Glenmore Pk......266
GEMAS
pl. St Ives Ch..........223
st. Holsworthy........426
GEMEREN
gr. W Pnnant Hl.......248
GEMINI
cl. S Penrith............267
GEMOORE
st. Smithfield..........335
GEMSTONE
wy. Oakhurst, off Dillon Pl............242
GENDERS
av. Burwood............371
la. Burwood, off Genders Av.........371
GENERAL BRIDGES
cr. Daceyville..........406
GENERAL HOLMES
dr. Botany...............405
dr. Btn-le-Sds..........404
dr. Kyeemagh..........404
dr. Mascot..............404
GENEVA
cr. Seven Hills.........275
pl. Engadine............489
rd. Cranebrook.........207
st. Berowra.............133
GENISTA
st. Loftus................490
GENNER
st. Denistone W......281
GENOA
st. Como................460
GENTIAN
av. Mcquarie Fd.......454
pl. Lugarno.............430
GENTLE
cl. Casula...............424
st. Lane Cove..........314
st.w, Lane Cove W......314
GENTY
st. Campbelltwn......511
GEOFFREY
cr. Loftus...............490
st. S Turramrra.......252
st. Wentwthvle........277
GEORGANN
st. Turramurra........223
GEORGE
la. Paddington..........21
la. Eastlakes, off George St.........405
pde. Baulkham Hl......247
pl. Artarmon...........284
rd. Leppington.........420
rd. Wilberforce..........91
st. Appin................569
st. Appin................569
st. Avalon...............139

Balmain 7 C13
Bankstown 369 D11
Bardwell Vy 402 J10
Bexley 402 J10
Blacktown 244 H15
Box Hill 154 D9
Brooklyn 76 D12
Burwood 341 J13
Burwood Ht 371 K4
Campbelltwn 511 G8
Canley Ht 365 G1
Concord W 341 C1
Dover Ht 348 E8
Eastlakes 405 J4
Epping 280 G1
Erskineville 18 A16
Gladesville 312 G10
Granville 308 H11
Greenwich 314 J13
Guildford 337 C3
Haymarket ..... E E12
Haymarket ..... E F6
Haymarket 3 D16
Hornsby 221 G1
Hunters Hill 313 D11
Kingswood 238 B13
Leichhardt 15 D5
Lidcombe 339 G9
Liverpool 395 E4
Manly 288 E9
Marrickville 373 H10
Miranda 492 B7
Mortdale 431 B9
Mount Druitt 271 F5
N Strathfield 341 D4
Paddington 21 F3
Parramatta 308 C2
Pennant Hills 250 J1
Penshurst 431 C3
Randwick 377 C13
Redfern 19 C9
Riverstone 182 H4
Rockdale 403 E15
St Marys 269 D2
Schofields 182 H15
Seven Hills 275 G3
S Hurstville 432 C8
S Windsor 120 E16
Springwood 202 A2
Sydenham 374 E14
Sydney ..... C H16
Sydney 1 G16
Sydney 3 G6
Tahmoor 565 J12
Tahmoor 565 K10
The Rocks ..... A J10
The Rocks 1 H8
Ultimo ..... E C15
Ultimo 3 D16
Warwck Frm 365 E16
Waterloo 19 D12
Waterloo 19 E16
Windsor 120 H13
Windsor 121 B9
Yagoona 369 D11
RGE BRANSBY
Harringtn Pk 478 C2
RGE CALEY
Mt Annan 509 H2
RGE HUNTER
Narellan 478 H8
RGE JULIUS
Zetland 375 K11
RGE MOBBS
Castle Hill 248 B5
RGE MUIR
Baulkham Hl 248 D10
RGE PING
Thirlmere 564 J6
RGES
Berala 339 G12
Lidcombe 339 G12
Georges Hall 367 F13
Roselands 400 K9
Glenfield 424 K12
Vaucluse 348 G2
Liverpool 395 D4
RGES RIVER
Oyster Bay 461 C4
Airds 512 A9
Campbelltwn 512 A9
Croydon Pk 371 G7
Jannali 460 J12
Kentlyn 513 A7
Lansvale 366 G8

rd. Oyster Bay 461 A10
rd. Ruse 512 A9
GEORGE WALLACE
st. Moore Park 21 C6
GEORGIA
st. Quakers Hill 214 G11
tce. Kellyville 187 A16
GEORGIA LEE
pl. Clareville 169 E2
GEORGIAN
av. Carlingford 249 G15
GEORGIANA
cr. Ambarvale 511 B11
GEORGINA
av. Elanora Ht 198 F15
cl. Wahroonga 221 K14
la. Newtown 18 B9
rd. Mt Vernon 331 D12
st. Bass Hill 368 D14
st. Bonnyrigg Ht 363 B7
st. Newtown 18 A9
GERALD
av. Roseville 284 H2
cr. Doonside 243 E5
rd. Illawong 459 A6
st. Cecil Hills 362 J7
st. Greystanes 306 F6
st. Marrickville 374 B14
GERALDINE
av. Baulkham Hl 247 D8
GERALDTON
pl. Yarrawarrah 489 F12
GERANIUM
av. Mcquarie Fd 454 F6
cl. Glenmore Pk 265 G13
GERARD
av. Condell Park 368 F16
la. Cremorne 316 E7
la. Gladesville, off Gerard St 312 H8
pl. Glenmore Pk 266 H15
st. Alexandria 18 K12
st. Cremorne 316 F7
st. Gladesville 312 H8
GERBULIN
st. Glendenning 242 F3
GERLEE
pl. Quakers Hill 214 F9
GERMAINE
av. Mt Riverview 234 B3
GERONIMO
cl. Greenfld Pk 334 A14
GERRALE
st. Cronulla 493 K13
GERRING
st. Colyton 270 B6
GERRISH
st. Gladesville 312 K7
GERROA
av. Bayview 169 B14
pl. Prestons 393 A14
GERSHAM
gr. Oakhurst 242 A4
GERSHWIN
cr. Clarmnt Ms 268 G3
GERTRUDE
av. Newport 169 J13
rd. Ingleburn 453 D12
st. Arncliffe 403 K6
st. Balgowlah Ht 287 G12
st. Beacon Hill 257 E7
GETYUNGA
rd. Oyster Bay 461 C4
GEUM
pl. Mcquarie Fd 454 F6
GHURKA
st. Sadleir 394 B2
GIBB
av. Casula 394 J11
cl. N Parramatta 278 G12
pl. Springwood 201 D1
st. North Ryde 282 E8
GIBBENS
la. Camperdwn 17 E6
st. Camperdwn 17 E6
GIBBER
pl. Annangrove 186 H4
GIBBES
la. Newtown 17 H14
st. Banksia 403 F16
st. Chatswood 285 E5
st. Newtown 17 G14

st. Regentville 265 G4
st. Rockdale 403 F16
GIBBINS
cl. Hornsby 191 G9
GIBBON
rd. Winston Hills 246 G15
GIBBONS
la. Arncliffe 403 B10
pl. Marayong 244 C8
st. Auburn 339 D1
st. Eveleigh 19 A9
st. Oatlands 279 D6
st. Redfern 19 A9
st. Telopea 279 D6
wy. Claymore 481 C12
GIBBS
la. Manly Vale 287 H2
la. Newtown 17 D10
st. Auburn 338 K5
st. Croydon 342 E15
st. Manly Vale 287 H3
st. Miranda 492 A5
GIBLETT
av. Thornleigh 220 H11
GIBRAN
pl. St Ives 224 E16
GIBSON
av. Casula 394 J12
av. Chatswood 284 J7
av. Padstow 399 C9
av. Werrington 238 K11
la. Horsley Pk 302 E16
pl. Blacktown 274 C5
pl. Chifley 437 B6
pwy. Casula, off Gibson Av 394 K12
rd. Denham Ct 452 G3
rd. Mosman 317 C8
st. Bronte 377 H8
st. Hobartville 118 G7
st. Pagewood 405 K10
st. Richmond 118 G7
st. Silverdale 353 G14
st. Waterloo 19 F13
st. Waverley 377 H8
st. Yarrawarrah 489 F11
GIDDINGS
av. Cronulla 493 K14
GIDEON
st. Winston Hills 276 H2
GIDGEE
st. Cabramatta 365 G9
GIDJI
rd. Miranda 491 K5
GIDLEY
cr. Claymore 481 A11
st. St Marys 239 H16
GIDYA
st. Frenchs Frst 256 F4
GIFFARD
st. Silverwater 309 J10
GIFFNOCK
av. Mcquarie Pk 282 G4
GILAI
pl. Allambie Ht 257 G15
GILBA
rd. Girraween 275 J11
rd. Pendle Hill 276 A12
GILBERT
cr. Kings Lngly 245 A5
pl. Frenchs Frst 256 G8
rd. Castle Hill 217 F10
rd. Glenhaven 217 J6
st. Cabramatta 365 D7
st. Colyton 270 B7
st. Dover Ht 348 E11
st. Manly 288 G10
st. N Parramatta 278 D11
st. Sylvania 462 A12
wy. Minto 482 K1
GILBULLA
av. Camden 507 A3
GILCHRIST
dr. Campbelltwn 510 K9
dr. Englorie Park 510 J10
pl. Balmain East 8 E8
GILDA
av. S Penrith 266 F2
av. Wahroonga 222 D10
st. North Ryde 283 C11
wy. Toongabbie 276 B5
GILDEA
av. Five Dock 343 A7

GILDERTHORPE
av. Randwick 377 D10
GILES
cl. Glenmore Pk 265 K6
cr. Ruse 512 F3
pl. Bligh Park 150 J7
pl. Cabramatta 365 E10
pl. Plumpton 241 G9
st. Chifley 437 A6
st. Yarrawarrah 489 F11
GILGANDRA
av. Thornleigh 221 A8
rd. North Bondi 348 C15
st. West Hoxton 392 G7
GILHAM
st. Castle Hill 218 B11
st. Chatswood 284 J13
GILI
pl. Glenmore Pk 266 A7
GILJA
gln. Kingswood 267 J2
GILL
av. Liverpool 394 K9
la. Strathfield S 370 J3
pl. Ruse 512 G1
pl. Schofields 183 D15
GILLEN
cl. Bonnyrigg Ht 363 F7
ct. Wrrngtn Cty 238 H4
GILLES
cr. Beacon Hill 257 J5
GILLESPIE
av. Alexandria 375 E16
pl. Windsor 121 A10
st. Liverpool 395 B6
GILLHAM
av. Caringbah 492 G14
GILLIAN
cr. Hassall Gr 211 H15
pde. West Pymble 252 J13
pl. Punchbowl 399 J3
GILLIANA
pl. Frenchs Frst 255 H3
GILLIES
av. Haberfield 343 C15
la. Lakemba 401 B1
st. Annandale 10 J12
st. Lakemba 401 B2
st. Wollstncraft 5 A1
GILLIGANS
rd. Dural 189 F2
GILLIVER
av. Vaucluse 348 C5
cr. Greenacre 370 C8
GILLIVERS
pl. Lidcombe 339 K7
GILLOOLY
av. Matraville 436 K9
GILLOTT
wy. St Ives 224 B12
GILLWINGA
av. Caringbah 492 F12
GILMORE
av. Collaroy Plat 228 G13
av. Kirrawee 490 J2
av. Leumeah 512 C2
cl. Glenmore Pk 265 K7
rd. Casula 424 F5
rd. Lalor Park 245 E10
st. Cabramatta 365 J5
GILMOUR
cl. Glenhaven 218 C1
la. Colyton, off Gilmour St 270 H8
pl. Penshurst 431 D2
st. Colyton 270 H8
GILPIN
la. Camperdwn 17 B9
pl. Plumpton 242 D10
st. Camperdwn 17 B9
st. Newtown 17 B9
GILROY
la. Turramurra, off Gilroy Rd 222 J14
rd. Turramurra 222 J13
GILWINGA
dr. Bayview 168 C12
GIMLET
cl. Kingswood 237 H16
cl. Kingswood 267 H1
pl. Mcquarie Fd 454 E3

GINAHGULLA
rd. Bellevue Hill 14 J7
GINAHGULLAH
av. Grose Vale 85 H9
GINDURRA
av. Castle Hill 217 C8
cl. Hamondvle 396 G14
GIOVANNA
ct. Castle Hill 217 C7
GIPPS
av. Little Bay 437 A12
cl. Turramurra 252 B3
pl. Cromer 227 G12
rd. Greystanes 305 D11
rd. Smithfield 305 D13
st. Arncliffe 403 C8
st. Bardwell Vy 403 C8
st. Birchgrove 7 F6
st. Bradbury 511 G14
st. Bronte 377 H8
st. Clarmnt Ms 239 A16
st. Clarmnt Ms 268 J4
st. Concord 341 H8
st. Drummoyne 343 F4
st. Paddington 4 J15
st. Pyrmont 12 H5
st. Smithfield 335 C7
st. Werrington 239 A15
GIPSY
st. Bnkstn Aprt 397 K1
GIRA
pl. Dharruk 241 D8
GIRARD
st. Harbord 288 D2
GIRD
pl. Marayong 243 K6
GIRILANG
av. Vaucluse 348 E6
GIRRA
av. S Penrith 266 J1
rd. Blacktown 243 H16
st. Fairfield W 335 G10
GIRRALONG
av. Baulkham Hl 248 A7
GIRRAWEEN
av. Como 460 F6
av. Lane Cove W 284 A14
rd. Girraween 275 K16
st. Kingsgrove 402 A9
GIRRILANG
rd. Cronulla 494 A8
GIRROMA
st. Carss Park 432 G13
GISSING
st. Wetherill Pk 334 F4
GIUFFRE
pl. W Pnnant Hl 249 H7
GLADE
pl. Engadine 488 K15
pl. Engadine 489 Z9
pl. W Pnnant Hl 249 C2
st. Balgowlah Ht 287 J13
GLADES
av. Gladesville 312 G10
GLADESVILLE
rd. Hunters Hill 313 B10
GLADIATOR
st. Raby 451 C13
GLADSTONE
av. Hunters Hill 314 C13
av. Mosman 317 B8
av. Ryde 312 A4
av. Warrawee 222 H11
la. Marrickville 374 A13
la. Newtown 17 C13
la. Kogarah, off Gladstone St 433 C3
pde. Lindfield 284 C3
pde. Riverstone 183 A10
pl. West Hoxton 392 D8
rd. Castle Hill 217 B15
st. Balmain 7 K10
st. Belmore 401 D1
st. Bexley 402 J16
st. Burwood 341 J12
st. Cabramatta 365 F7
st. Canley Ht 365 F4
st. Concord 342 B7
st. Enmore 17 A11
st. Kogarah 433 C3
st. Lilyfield 10 H10
st. Marrickville 374 A13
st. Merrylands 307 J12

st. Newport 169 E12
st. Newtown 17 A11
st. N Parramatta 278 E13
st. Stanmore 17 A11
st. Surry Hills 19 J2
st. Vaucluse 318 F16

GLADSWOOD
av. S Penrith 267 B2
gdn. Double Bay 14 F6

GLADYS
av. Frenchs Frst 256 G4
av. Wahroonga 223 A4
cr. Seven Hills 245 C16
st. Kingswood 237 D16
st. Rydalmere 309 J3

GLAISHER
pde. Cronulla 523 K4

GLAMIS
st. Kingsgrove 401 F8

GLAMORGAN
st. Blacktown 274 H7
wy. Cherrybrook 219 F9

GLANARA
ct. Wattle Grove 426 A1

GLANCE
rd. The Slopes 56 K11

GLANDORE
st. Woolooware 493 G6

GLANFIELD
st. Maroubra 406 H9

GLANMIRE
rd. Baulkham Hl 247 A9

GLANVILLE
av. Pagewood 406 G6

GLASGOW
av. Bondi Beach 378 D1
st. Holsworthy 396 B14
st. St Andrews 452 B14
st. Winston Hills 277 D4

GLASSOP
la. Yagoona 368 F13
st. Balmain 7 A8
st. Bankstown 368 J13
st. Caringbah 492 K6
st. Yagoona 368 F13

GLEAM
pl. Cranebrook 206 H8

GLEBE
cl. Appin 569 F14
la. Glebe 12 D13
pl. Penrith 237 D9
pl. St Johns Pk 364 F5
rd. Pitt Town 122 K1
st. Edgecliff 13 J13
st. Glebe 12 D13
st. Parramatta 307 K6
st. Randwick 377 E12

GLEBE POINT
rd. Glebe 12 C14

GLEDITSIA
cl. Narellan Vale 479 A11

GLEDSWOOD
pl. Glen Alpine 510 G12

GLEESON
av. Baulkham Hl 247 E10
av. Condell Park 398 K6
av. Sydenham 374 D14
pl. Abbotsbury 333 C12

GLEN
av. Randwick 377 D13
la. Bondi 378 B5
la. Glebe 11 G11
la. Glenbrook 264 A1
la. Randwick 377 E12
pl. Currans Hill 479 K11
pl. Pendle Hill 276 C16
rd. Castle Hill 218 H14
rd. Emu Heights 234 K6
rd. Oatley 430 J10
rd. Roseville 284 D6
st. Belrose 225 J16
st. Blaxland 233 D5
st. Bondi 378 B5
st. Eastwood 281 A8
st. Galston 159 F9
st. Glenbrook 264 A1
st. Granville 308 E13
st. Harbord 258 G16
st. Marrickville 373 F15
st. Milsons Point 5 J15
st. Mosman 316 K3
st. Paddington 13 B13

GLEN ABBEY
st. Rouse Hill 185 A9

GLENAEON
av. Belrose 226 B8

GLEN ALLAN
rd. Rossmore 390 A15

GLEN ALPINE
dr. Glen Alpine 510 E10

GLENALVON
pl. West Hoxton 392 B11

GLENANNE
pl. Tahmoor 565 F7

GLENARM
cr. Killarney Ht 256 B15

GLENARVON
st. Strathfield 371 A1

GLEN AVON
av. Narwee 400 H15

GLENAVON
pl. Glen Alpine 510 E13

GLENAVY
st. Wentwthvle 276 K15

GLEN-AYR
av. Yowie Bay 492 C10

GLENAYR
av. Bondi Beach 378 C2
av. Denistone W 280 K13
av. North Bondi 348 D16
av. West Ryde 280 K13
gr. W Pnnant Hl 249 B1
la. Bondi Beach, off Blair St 378 C1

GLENBAWN
pl. Leumeah 482 D13
pl. Woodcroft 243 J11

GLENBROOK
cr. Georges Hall 367 J10
pl. The Oaks 502 E13
rd. Blaxland 233 J14
rd. Glenbrook 233 J14
st. Jamisontown 266 B2

GLENCARRON
av. Mosman 317 C4

GLENCOE
av. Chatswd W 284 F8
av. Oatlands 278 H10
av. Wrrngtn Cty 238 D9
cl. Berowra 133 G10
rd. Woollahra 22 E1
st. Sutherland 490 G4
st.s, Sutherland 490 F6

GLENCORSE
av. Milperra 397 G12

GLENCROFT
rd. Roseville 284 J4

GLENDA
pl. Mt Krng-gai 162 J11
pl. North Rocks 248 J13
pl. Plumpton 241 J8

GLENDALE
av. Mt Pritchard 364 H14
av. Narwee 400 J13
av. Padstow 429 D3
dr. Lilyfield 10 C5
gr. W Pnnant Hl 249 A3
pl. Jannali 460 J13
rd. Cowan 133 K2
rd. Turramurra 223 A8

GLEN DAVIS
av. Bossley Park 333 E11

GLENDENNING
rd. Glendenning 242 F11

GLENDEVIE
st. West Hoxton 392 D6

GLENDIVER
rd. Glenmore 503 A12
rd. The Oaks 502 F12

GLENDON
rd. Double Bay 14 F12

GLENDOWER
av. Eastwood 281 H5
st. Gilead 540 F7
st. Rsemeadow 540 F7

GLENEAGLES
av. Killara 253 F15
cr. Hornsby 192 D15
pl. St Andrews 481 K4
wy. Glenmore Pk 266 E9

GLENELG
ct. Wattle Grove 395 H13
pl. Beecroft 250 G7
pl. St Ives Ch 223 K3
st. Sutherland 460 F16

GLEN ELGIN
cr. Edensor Pk 333 D15

GLENELGIN
rd. Winmalee 173 D12

GLENELL
st. Blaxland 233 J10

GLENELLA
av. Beverly Hills 400 J16
wy. Minto 482 G9

GLENESS
pl. Glenorie 127 J13

GLENFARNE
st. Bexley 432 G2

GLENFERN
cl. W Pnnant Hl 248 G8
cr. Bossley Park 334 A9
pl. Gymea Bay 491 E8
rd. Epping 250 J16

GLENFERRIE
av. Cremorne, off Iredale Av 316 F11

GLENFIELD
dr. Currans Hill 479 K13
rd. Casula 424 A5
rd. Glenfield 424 A5
rd. Glenfield 424 E7

GLENGARIFF
av. Killarney Ht 256 A16

GLENGARRIE
rd. Marsden Pk 211 D5

GLENGARRY
av. N Turramrra 223 E2
dr. Glenmore Pk 266 G12
dr. Glenmore Pk 266 G14
la. Carlingford 280 A2
la. Mosman, off Effingham St 317 C10

GLENGYLE
ct. Wattle Grove 425 K2

GLENHARE
la. Glenbrook, off Moore St 233 K15

GLENHAVEN
pl. Oyster Bay 461 C5
rd. Glenhaven 218 C1
rd. Kellyville 186 J15

GLEN HELEN
gr. Dural 219 B3

GLENHOPE
rd. W Pnnant Hl 249 B3

GLENIDOL
rd. Oakville 152 H4

GLEN INNES
rd. Hinchinbrk 392 H6
rd. Hoxton Park 392 H6

GLENISIA
av. Georges Hall 367 J11

GLENLEA
ct. Glenwood 215 B15
st. Canley Ht 335 D15

GLENLEE
cl. Mt Krng-gai 162 K13
ct. Narellan Vale 508 F2
rd. Gilead 509 E14
rd. Glen Alpine 509 E14
rd. Menangle Pk 509 E14
rd. Spring Farm 508 E7

GLENLEIGH
av. Mulgoa 324 C6

GLEN LOGAN
rd. Bossley Park 333 E10

GLEN MARGARET
av. Lurnea 394 E12

GLENMORE
la. S Penrith, off Glenmore Pl 266 F4
pky. Glenmore Pk 265 G5
pky. Glenmore Pk 265 H9
pky. Glenmore Pk 266 A12
pky. Glenmore Pk 266 F11
pl. S Penrith 266 F3
rd. Edgecliff 13 F12
rd. Paddington 4 J15
rd. Paddington 13 F12
st. Naremburn 315 F3

GLENN
av. Northmead 277 H9
pl. N Richmond 87 C13
pl. Yagoona 368 K8
st. Dean Park 242 G1

GLENNIE
st. Colyton 270 D8

GLENOAK
wy. Cherrybrook 219 C9

GLENORA
rd. Yarrawarrah 489 E14

GLENORE
rd. Canterbury 402 D1

GLEN ORMOND
av. Abbotsford 342 J3

GLEN OSMOND
cr. Bossley Park 333 E10

GLENRIDGE
av. W Pnnant Hl 249 B2

GLENROBEN
pl. Mount Druitt 241 F12

GLENROCK
av. Edgecliff 13 J11
av. Wahroonga 223 C5
ct. Wattle Grove 426 A1
pl. Glen Alpine 510 E13

GLENROE
av. W Pnnant Hl 249 B3

GLENROSE
pl. Belrose 225 H16

GLENROTHES
pl. Dharruk 241 D7

GLENROWAN
av. Kellyville 216 G6
dr. Harringtn Pk 478 C2
wy. St Clair 270 D12

GLENROY
av. Middle Cove 285 J7
cr. St Johns Pk 364 F1
pl. Glenwood 245 H3
pl. Middle Dural 158 C9

GLENSHEE
pl. Glenhaven 218 E6
pl. St Andrews 481 J6

GLENSIDE
st. Balgowlah Ht 287 K13

GLENTON
st. Abbotsbury 333 B13

GLENTREES
av. Forestville 256 A12
pl. Cherrybrook 219 H10

GLENUGIE
st. Maroubra 407 E12

GLENVALE
cl. W Pnnant Hl 249 H6

GLEN VIEW
cr. Hunters Hill 314 A13

GLENVIEW
av. Earlwood 402 F4
av. Revesby 398 F15
cl. Bella Vista 216 D16
gr. Glendenning 242 H4
la. Paddington 4 K12
la. Earlwood, off Glenview Av 402 F4
la. St Marys, off Glenview St 269 K4
pl. Engadine 488 J14
rd. Hunters Hill 314 B13
rd. Mt Krng-gai 162 J11
st. Gordon 253 K5
st. Greenwich 315 A9
st. Kogarah Bay 432 K12
st. Paddington 4 K12
st. St Marys 269 J5

GLENWALL
st. Kingsgrove 401 G14

GLENWARI
st. Sadleir 394 A1

GLENWOOD
av. Coogee 377 F16
st. Beecroft 250 A10
wy. Castle Hill 218 G16

GLENWOOD PARK
dr. Glenwood 215 D16
dr. Glenwood 245 D1
dr. Glenwood 245 H1

GLENWORTH
pl. Theresa Park 445 B3

GLOBE
st. The Rocks A J6

GLORIA
cl. Mt Colah 162 F12
pl. S Penrith 267 C5
st. Merrylands W 306 J13

GLORY
wy. Kellyville 185

GLOSSOP
st. N St Marys 239

GLOUCESTER
av. Burwood 341
av. Merrylands 307
av. N Parramatta 278
av. Padstow 429
av. West Pymble 252
pl. Kensington 376
rd. Beverly Hills 401
rd. Epping 251
rd. Hoxton Park 392
rd. Hurstville 431
st. Bexley 432
st. Bonnyrigg Ht 363
st. Concord 341
st. Mcquarie Fd 423
st. N Balgowlah 287
st. Rockdale 403
st. The Rocks A
st. The Rocks A
st. The Rocks 1
st. The Rocks 1
wk. The Rocks A

GLOVER
av. Quakers Hill 214
la. Mosman, off Glover St 316
pl. West Hoxton 392
st. Greenacre 370
st. Lilyfield 9
st. Mosman 316
st. N Willghby 285

GLYN
av. Picnic Point 428
st. Wiley Park 400

GLYNN
cl. Cranebrook 207

GNARBO
av. Carss Park 432
la. Carss Park, off Allawah Av 432

GOBURRA
pl. Engadine 518

GODALLA
rd. Freemns Rch 60

GODDARD
cr. Quakers Hill 214
st. Erskineville 375
st. Newtown 17
st. Turrella 403

GODERICH
la. Potts Point 4

GODFREY
av. Turramurra 222
av. West Hoxton 391
rd. Artarmon 285
st. Banksia 403
st. Hurstville Gr 431
st. Penshurst 431

GODWIN
st. Bexley 402

GODWIT
cl. Hinchinbrk 363

GOGOL
pl. Wetherill Pk 335

GOLD
st. Blakehurst 462

GOLDEN
gr. Beacon Hill 257
gr. Bligh Park 150
gr. Cherrybrook 219
gr. Freemns Rch 89
gr. Stanhpe Gdn 215
gr. Westleigh 220
wy. Silverdale 353

GOLDEN GROVE
av. Kellyville 216
st. Darlington 18
st. Newtown 18

GOLDEN STAVE
wy. Berala 339

GOLDEN VALLEY
dr. Glossodia 59

GOLDERS GREEN
wy. Glenhaven 218

GOLDFINCH
pl. Bella Vista 246
pl. Grays Point 491
st. Moorebank 396

DIE
Bondi Jctn..........377 G5
Colyton..............270 G4
DING
Glendenning.......242 G4
DMAN
Double Bay..........14 C10
Double Bay, off
Knox St...............14 D9
DMARK
Cranebrook........207 G10
Cranebrook........207 G9
Cranebrook, off
Goldmark Cr.......207 J9
DSBOROUGH
Yennora.............337 C11
DSMITH
Campbelltwn......510 H6
Killarney Ht........286 D1
Winston Hills......277 G1
Wetherill Pk.......334 J6
F
Mona Vale..........199 E4
Manly..................288 F5
F COURSE
Glen Alpine........510 E12
FERS
Roseville............255 A16
Pymble...............253 A6
F LINKS
Killara................253 G14
FVIEW
Wallacia.............324 K13
IATH
Winston Hills......276 H3
LAN
Oatlands............278 J9
SPIE
Prestons............392 H15
A
Narraweena........258 C6
Glenfield............424 G12
Holsworthy........426 E2
DOLA
N Narrabeen.......228 H1
BARAH
Burraneer...........523 D2
D
Granville............308 F10
Harris Park.........308 G8
Parramatta.........307 J4
Rosehill.............308 G8
Westmead.........307 H2
DACRE
Fairfield W..........335 B14
Miranda.............492 C1
Winston Hills......277 G3
DALL
Pendle Hill..........276 F14
DCHAP
Chatswd W........284 G12
Surry Hills.............F G10
Surry Hills.............4 A13
DE
Currans Hill........479 H9
DEN
Baulkham Hl......247 A12
DENIA
Voyager Pt.........427 D5
Mt Annan...........509 C3
DENOUGH
Glenfield............424 H8
DHALL
Baulkham Hl......246 J15
DHOPE
Paddington..........13 C14
Paddington..........13 C14
DIA
Bidwill................211 G13
DIER
Kenthurst...........156 J11
DIN
Winston Hills......247 K15
DLANDS
Thornleigh.........220 J12
DLET
Lane Cove W, off
Walkers Dr.........283 F12
Surry Hills............19 J5
Ashbury.............372 E7
Merrylands.........307 F11

st. Surry Hills............19 J5
st. Thirlmere...........565 A3
GOODMAN
pl. Cherrybrook.......219 J6
wy. Bonnyrigg..........364 B4
GOODMANS
tce. Surry Hills...........19 J2
GOODOOGA
cl. Hinchinbrk.........392 G4
GOODRICH
av. Kingsford...........376 C15
rd. Cecil Park...........331 K11
GOODS
rd. Oakville..............152 H2
GOODSELL
st. Minto.................482 K9
st. St Peters............374 J11
GOODSIR
cl. Rossmore..........389 J6
st. Rozelle..................7 C13
GOODSTATE
pl. Chester Hill........368 A2
GOODWIN
av. Ashfield.............372 J8
av. Mt Lewis............370 B15
cr. Minto.................482 H5
rd. Newport.............169 G9
st. Denistone...........281 G13
st. Narrabeen..........229 A7
st. West Ryde..........281 G13
st. Woolooware.......493 G8
GOODWOOD
st. Kensington.........376 F10
GOODWYN
rd. Berowra.............133 D14
GOOLAGONG
av. Toongabbie........276 F5
ct. Milperra.............397 F11
pl. La Perouse.........436 J13
pl. Menai................458 H6
GOOLD
st. Chippendale.........19 D1
GOOLGUNG
av. Baulkham Hl......248 A10
GOOLMA
pl. Hornsby.............192 D13
GOOLWA
cr. Cranebrook........207 F9
GOOMERAH
cr. Darling Point.........13 J4
GOONAROI
st. Villawood...........367 J4
st. Villawood...........367 J5
GOONDA
av. La Perouse.........436 K12
GOONDAH
rd. Engadine............489 C10
st. Villawood...........367 E4
GOONDARI
rd. Allambie Ht........257 G14
GOONGOORA
cl. Jamisontown.....266 A4
GOORA
st. Little Bay............437 B11
GOORARI
av. Bella Vista..........246 F6
GOORAWAHL
av. La Perouse.........436 J14
GOORAWAY
dr. Castle Hill...........217 J7
pl. Berowra Ht.........132 K5
GOOREEN
st. Lidcombe............339 K3
GOORGOOL
rd. Bangor...............459 H14
GOORIWA
pl. Engadine............488 E13
GOOROA
st. Carss Park.........432 G13
GOOSE
cl. Hinchinbrk.........363 D15
GOOSEBERRY
la. Mosman............317 G8
pl. Glenwood...........215 E14
GORADA
av. Kirrawee............491 C6
GORDON
av. Castle Hill...........218 B11
av. Chatswood.........284 H12
av. Coogee..............377 J14
av. Ingleburn...........453 F3

av. S Granville.........338 F5
cr. Denistone...........281 D11
cr. Lane Cove W......284 B14
cr. Stanmore.............16 B10
la. Paddington...........21 D3
la. Petersham............15 G11
pl. Bronte.................377 J10
pl. Narellan Vale.......478 G16
pl. Windsor Dn.........180 K4
rd. Auburn...............339 A8
rd. Schofields...........183 J14
sq. Marrickville..........16 B16
st. Annandale.............17 C2
st. Bankstown..........369 D15
st. Blacktown...........244 J15
st. Btn-le-Sds...........433 K1
st. Burwood.............341 J13
st. Campsie.............372 C10
st. Caringbah...........492 J6
st. Carramar............336 J15
st. Clontarf..............287 F13
st. Eastwood............281 D6
st. Fairfield...............336 J15
st. Hurstville.............431 K4
st. Manly Vale..........287 K2
st. Marrickville.........374 D9
st. Mosman.............317 D9
st. Paddington...........21 C3
st. Penrith...............236 G1
st. Petersham............15 F11
st. Randwick.............377 B11
st. Rosebery.............405 H3
st. Rozelle..................11 B2
st. Rydalmere...........310 A2
st. St Marys.............269 K2
st. Thirlmere............565 B1
GORDON BRAY
cct. Lidcombe...........339 J13
GORDONIA
gr. Baulkham Hl.......247 E16
GORDON McKINNON
la. Harris Park.........308 E6
GORDON PARKER
st. Revesby.............398 E10
GORDONS
la. Concord, off
Finch Av..............342 B8
GORE
av. Kirrawee............490 J8
cr. Bella Vista..........246 G5
la. Kirrawee.............490 H8
pl. Willmot...............210 D12
st. Arncliffe..............403 E10
st. Greenwich...........315 A8
st. Harbord..............288 H2
st. Parramatta..........278 H16
GORE HILL
fwy. Artarmon...........315 A1
fwy. Lane Cove..........314 J1
fwy. Naremburn.........315 A1
GORINSKI
rd. Toongabbie........276 G4
GORMAN
av. Panania..............428 E4
pl. Cranebrook.........207 D10
st. Marrickville.........374 B11
st. Willoughby..........285 E15
GORMLEY
st. Freemns Rch.........89 F6
st. Lidcombe...........339 J11
GORNALL
av. Earlwood............372 G15
GOROKA
pl. Beacon Hill.........257 E8
st. Glenfield.............424 F10
st. Whalan..............240 H10
GORRICKS
la. Freemns Rch.........90 G5
GORSE
cl. Loftus.................489 K10
st. Prospect.............274 G10
GORT
rd. Engadine............488 K12
GORTON
cl. Penrith...............237 B7
GOSBELL
la. Paddington...........13 B11
st. Paddington...........13 A11
GOSBY
av. Miranda.............491 J5
GOSHA
cl. Rooty Hill...........271 H6

GOSHAWK
cr. Woronora Ht......489 D2
pl. Green Valley.......363 C12
GOSLING
av. Green Valley.......363 C14
st. Emu Heights.......234 J6
st. Greenacre..........370 E14
GOSPER
st. Windsor.............120 J10
GOSPORT
st. Cronulla.............493 J10
GOSSAMER
pl. Mcquarie Fd.......454 E4
GOSSE
ct. St Clair...............270 D10
la. St Clair, off
Gosse Ct............270 D10
pl. Bonnyrigg Ht......363 F8
GOSSELL
gr. Carlingford.........249 C13
GOTHER
av. Greenwich..........314 K13
GOTTENHAM
la. Glebe...................12 C12
st. Glebe...................12 C11
GOTTWALD
pl. W Pnnant Hl.......249 H6
GOUDA
cl. Abbotsbury.........333 B14
GOUGH
av. Chester Hill........337 K12
dr. Castle Hill...........218 K13
st. Emu Plains..........235 C12
st. Holroyd...............307 K10
GOULBURN
la. Surry Hills.............F E7
st. Darlinghurst...........F C5
st. Haymarket.............E D4
st. Haymarket.............3 E10
st. Kings Park..........244 E6
st. Liverpool.............395 F2
st. Ruse..................512 C9
st. St Ives...............223 K15
st. Surry Hills..............F C5
st. Surry Hills..............3 J11
st. Sydney..................E D4
st. Sydney..................3 E10
st. Warwck Frm........365 F16
swy. Liverpool............395 F1
GOULBURN PENINSULA
Sylvania Wtr.......462 D14
GOULD
av. Kellyville.............215 J5
av. Lewisham.............15 C15
av. Narraweena.........258 D1
av. St Ives Ch...........224 A1
la. Lewisham..............15 C13
la. West Hoxton, off
Harraden Dr........391 K11
pl. Menai.................458 E15
pl. Parramatta..........308 J1
rd. Claymore............481 E10
rd. Eagle Vale...........481 E10
st. Bankstown..........368 H14
st. Bondi Beach.......378 D3
st. Campsie.............372 C13
st. Canterbury..........372 C13
st. Strathfield S........370 J4
st. West Hoxton........391 J11
st.n. North Bondi.......348 E16
GOULDING
rd. Ryde..................282 D13
GOULDSBURY
st. Mosman.............317 A7
GOURLAY
av. Balgowlah..........287 K11
GOVE
av. Green Valley.......363 J11
GOVER
st. Peakhurst...........430 C2
GOVERNMENT
rd. Bargo.................567 J2
rd. Beacon Hill.........257 E7
rd. Berkshire Pk.......179 H13
rd. Brooklyn...............76 B11
rd. Cromer...............227 K13
rd. Hinchinbrk.........392 G4
rd. Hornsby.............221 G2
rd. Mona Vale..........198 K2
rd. Mosman.............287 A16
GOVERNMENT HOUSE
dr. Emu Plains.........235 D9

GOVERNOR
pl. Winston Hills, off
Mangalore Dr.....277 A3
GOVERNOR MACQUARIE
dr. Chipping Ntn......396 H1
dr. Warwck Frm......365 K15
GOVERNOR PHILLIP
pl. W Pnnant Hl.......248 H8
GOVERNORS
dr. Concord.............342 F6
dr. Lapstone............264 H3
rd. Mosman.............317 K6
wy. Mcquarie Lk.......423 E15
wy. Oatlands............279 A7
GOVETT
la. Randwick, off
Govett St............376 K10
pl. Davidson............225 A15
st. Mt Pritchard.......364 C10
st. Randwick...........376 K9
GOW
av. Port Hacking......522 K3
la. Cornwallis...........120 G1
st. Abbotsford..........342 J2
st. Balmain..................7 C5
st. Padstow............399 C9
GOWAN
ct. Carlingford.........279 B5
pl. Denham Ct.........452 G4
GOWAN BRAE
av. Oatlands............278 K10
GOWER
cl. Wetherill Pk.......334 J5
st. Ashfield.............373 C2
st. Hurlstone Pk.......372 K12
st. Summer Hill.......373 C2
GOWLLAND
pde. Panania.............398 D13
GOWRIE
av. Bondi Jctn..........377 G3
av. Punchbowl..........399 K5
cl. St Ives...............224 F6
cr. Westmead...........307 E2
dr. Castle Hill...........218 K13
la. Newtown..............17 H15
pl. Cabramatta.........365 C11
pl. Cromer...............227 H13
st. Bondi Jctn............22 D6
st. Cronulla.............523 K4
st. Newtown..............17 H16
st. Ryde..................312 A3
GOYA
pl. Old Tngabbie......276 K6
GOYEN
av. Bexley...............403 A15
pl. Padstow.............429 E5
GOZO
rd. Greystanes.........305 H8
GRACE
av. Beecroft.............249 K5
av. Cabramatta.........365 F9
av. Condell Park.......398 D1
av. Forestville...........256 C7
av. Frenchs Frst.......256 C3
av. Lakemba............401 C3
av. Lidcombe...........340 A2
av. Riverstone..........183 A4
cr. Merrylands..........307 E15
st. Carlingford..........279 F7
st. Kingswood..........237 F16
st. Lane Cove..........314 A2
st. Liverpool.............394 H3
st. Telopea..............279 F7
GRACE CAMPBELL
cr. Hillsdale.............406 F15
GRACELANDS
dr. Quakers Hill.......213 H7
GRACEMAR
av. Panania..............428 A5
GRACEMERE
ct. Wattle Grove......425 K1
pl. Glen Alpine........510 F11
st. Concord W.........341 E5
GRACILIS
wy. Bidwill...............211 D16
GRADY
gdn. Smithfield..........335 D4
st. Quakers Hill.......214 B13
GRAEME
pl. Freemns Rch.........90 E2
GRAF
av. Potts Hill............369 E8
av. West Ryde.........281 D15

av. Yagoona 369 E8
GRAFTON
av. Naremburn 315 H3
cr. Dee Why 258 H3
la. Balmain 8 D11
la. Chippendale 18 J1
la. Bondi Jctn, off Adelaide St 377 F3
pl. Jamisontown 266 C2
st. Balmain 8 C11
st. Blacktown 274 J1
st. Bondi Jctn 22 E5
st. Cammeray 316 C6
st. Chippendale 18 J1
st. Cremorne 316 C6
st. Eastlakes 406 A4
st. Greystanes 305 H4
st. Sutherland 490 E6
GRAHAM
av. Casula 394 D11
av. Eastwood 281 F6
av. Harbord 258 H16
av. Lurnea 394 D11
av. Marrickville 373 J11
av. Miranda 461 J16
av. Pymble 253 D1
av. Rookwood 340 E10
av. Wentwthvle 276 J14
cl. Berowra Ht 133 F8
cl. Cranebrook 207 A13
cr. Baulkham Hl 247 J13
pl. Earlwood 402 F6
pl. Picnic Point 428 H7
rd. Leppington 419 J6
rd. Narwee 400 G12
rd. Rossmore 419 J6
st. Auburn 339 C11
st. Berala 339 C11
st. Bundeena 524 A10
st. Doonside 243 B12
st. Greystanes 306 D5
st. Lane Cove 314 B1
st. Rozelle 11 C1
st. Silverdale 353 H14
GRAHAME
av. Glenfield 424 F8
st. Blaxland 233 H11
GRAHAM HILL
rd. Narellan 478 D8
GRAINGER
av. Ashfield 372 J2
av. Mt Pritchard 364 H9
av. N Curl Curl 258 J10
pl. N Richmond 86 K14
st. Marsden Pk 181 K13
GRANARY
ct. Wrrngtn Dns 238 B4
la. Wrrngtn Dns, off Granary Ct 238 B4
GRAND
av. Camellia 309 B5
av. Rosehill 309 B5
av. Westmead 307 E1
av. West Ryde 311 B2
av.n,Camellia 308 K4
dr. Centnnial Pk 21 D11
pde. Glossodia 59 D7
GRAND FLANEUR
av. Richmond 118 B5
GRAND HAVEN
rd. E Kurrajong 57 D1
GRANDIS
pl. Kingswood 267 J2
GRANDOAKS
pl. Castle Hill 218 H16
wy. Castle Hill 218 H16
GRANDSTAND
pde. Zetland 375 K10
GRAND VIEW
ct. Bella Vista 246 D8
dr. Mt Riverview 204 G14
GRANDVIEW
av. Seven Hills 275 F10
cr. Lugarno 429 K10
dr. Bilgola 169 G7
dr. Campbelltwn 511 F9
dr. Newport 169 G7
gr. Seaforth 287 B9
la. Bowen Mtn 84 C12
la. Pymble 253 D3
pde. Caringbah 493 C13
pde. Epping 250 H16
pde. Mona Vale 199 G1
st. Naremburn 315 D1

st. Parramatta 278 J16
st. Pymble 253 D3
st. S Penrith 266 J2
GRANGE
av. Marsden Pk 211 J3
av. Schofields 183 A16
cr. Cmbrdg Gdn 237 G3
la. Cmbrdg Gdn, off Grange Cr 237 G4
rd. Glenhaven 218 B2
rd. Leumeah 482 A11
GRANGEWOOD
pl. W Pnnant Hl 248 G6
GRANITE
pl. Eagle Vale 481 E7
pl. Hinchinbrk 362 K15
GRANT
av. Cabramatta 365 C9
cl. Epping 250 G15
cl. Kemps Ck 360 G10
cr. Merrylands 306 J10
gld. Bella Vista 246 G2
pl. Bonnet Bay 460 C9
pl. St Ives 224 A16
st. Blacktown 243 J10
wy. Minto 482 K7
GRANTHAM
cr. Dangar I 76 H7
la. Potts Point 4 J1
pl. Chipping Ntn 366 F13
rd. Seven Hills 275 F4
st. Burwood 341 J11
st. Carlton 432 J5
st. Potts Point 4 K1
st. Riverstone 153 B14
GRANTOWN
ct. Castle Hill 218 D7
GRANVILLE
st. Fairfield 336 C7
st. Fairfield Ht 336 B9
GRAPHITE
pl. Eagle Vale 481 E6
GRASMERE
av. Northmead 278 C5
cr. Collaroy Plat 228 E10
la. Cremorne 316 C7
rd. Cremorne 316 C6
GRASSMERE
av. S Penrith 266 F2
gr. Grasmere 475 K16
rd. Killara 254 A16
st. Guildford 337 K5
GRASSY
cl. Hinchinbrk 363 A14
GRATTAN
cr. Frenchs Frst 256 F10
GRAWIN
cl. Hinchinbrk 392 H4
GRAY
av. Kogarah 433 C7
cr. Eastlakes 405 K2
cr. Yagoona 368 J10
la. Kogarah 433 C7
la. Sutherland, off President Av 490 D4
pl. Bradbury 511 G11
pl. Kings Lngly 246 A9
pl. Wetherill Pk 335 A3
st. Annandale 10 K9
st. Bondi Jctn 22 J8
st. Granville 308 G9
st. Henley 313 B14
st. Kogarah 433 B5
st. Kogarah 433 C7
st. Mt Colah 192 D4
st. Randwick 377 C15
st. Sutherland 490 E4
GRAYLIND
av. W Pnnant Hl 249 G1
cl. Collaroy 229 A11
pl. Vaucluse 348 C5
GRAYLING
rd. West Pymble 252 K9
GRAYS
la. Cranebrook 207 C8
la. Waterloo 19 C11
GRAYS FOLLY
pl. Theresa Park 444 G7
GRAYSON
rd. N Epping 251 D10
st. Glendenning 242 G3
GRAY SPENCE
cr. W Pnnant Hl 249 B8

GRAYS POINT
rd. Grays Point 491 A14
GRAZIER
cr. Wrrngtn Dns 238 D6
pl. Minchinbury 271 F9
GREAT BUCKINGHAM
st. Redfern 19 G7
GREAT NORTH
rd. Abbotsford 342 J2
rd. Five Dock 342 J11
rd. Wareemba 343 A7
GREATREX
av. Regents Pk 369 D1
GREAT SOUTHERN
rd. Bargo 567 E1
GREAT THORNE
st. Edgecliff 13 J13
GREAT WESTERN
hwy. Annandale 16 D4
hwy. Arndell Park 273 A9
hwy. Ashfield 342 G11
hwy. Auburn 309 E14
hwy. Blacktown 274 A12
hwy. Blaxland 233 D4
hwy. Burwood 342 G11
hwy. Camperdwn 17 H2
hwy. Canada Bay 342 G11
hwy. Colyton 270 A2
hwy. Concord 342 G11
hwy. Croydon 342 G11
hwy. Doonside 273 A9
hwy. Eastern Ck 273 A9
hwy. Emu Plains 234 J10
hwy. Faulconbdg 201 C1
hwy. Five Dock 342 G11
hwy. Forest Lodge 17 H2
hwy. Girraween 275 B14
hwy. Glebe 17 H2
hwy. Glenbrook 233 D4
hwy. Granville 308 D9
hwy. Greystanes 305 J1
hwy. Haberfield 373 D2
hwy. Homebush 342 G11
hwy. Homebush W 340 A2
hwy. Huntingwd 273 A9
hwy. Kingswood 237 E12
hwy. Lapstone 264 F1
hwy. Leichhardt 15 E6
hwy. Lewisham 15 E6
hwy. Lidcombe 340 A2
hwy. Mays Hill 307 A4
hwy. Minchinbury 271 B4
hwy. Mount Druitt 271 B4
hwy. Oxley Park 270 A2
hwy. Parramatta 307 A4
hwy. Pendle Hill 305 J1
hwy. Penrith 236 G10
hwy. Petersham 15 E6
hwy. Prospect 275 B14
hwy. Rooty Hill 272 B7
hwy. St Marys 269 C1
hwy. S Wntwthvle 307 A4
hwy. Springwood 201 C1
hwy. Stanmore 16 D4
hwy. Summer Hill 373 D2
hwy. Valley Ht 202 D4
hwy. Warrimoo 203 A13
hwy. Wentwthvle 307 A4
hwy. Werrington 238 D14
hwy. Westmead 307 A4
GREBE
pl. Hinchinbrk 393 E1
st. Erskine Park 270 F16
st. Ingleburn 453 G8
GRECH
st. Glenwood 245 F2
GRECIA
la. Mosman 317 C1
GRECO
pl. Rsemeadow 540 D4
GREEK
st. Glebe 12 G15
GREEN
av. Smithfield 335 K6
la. Bradbury 511 E13
la. Kogarah 433 D4
pde. Valley Ht 202 G7
pl. Oyster Bay 461 B5
pl. Peakhurst 430 B6
rd. Kellyville 216 K1
sq. Alexandria, off Botany Rd 375 G10
st. Bnksmeadw 406 B11
st. Blacktown 274 J8

st. Brookvale 257 K11
st. Cremorne Pt 316 G13
st. Glenbrook 234 B16
st. Kogarah 433 D4
st. Maroubra 407 B9
st. Pleasure Pt 427 H7
st. Revesby 398 B10
st. Tempe 404 A3
st. Wallacia 324 K13
st. Woolooware 493 H10
GREENACRE
dr. Tahmoor 566 C13
rd. Bankstown 369 H13
rd. Connells Pt 431 K13
rd. Greenacre 369 J13
rd. S Hurstville 431 K13
GREENAWAY
av. Camden S 507 B9
GREENBANK
dr. Glenhaven 217 J4
dr. Wrrngtn Dns 238 D5
st. Hurstville 431 K7
st. Marrickville 373 H14
GREENDALE
av. Frenchs Frst 256 D2
av. Pymble 223 F14
cct. Quakers Hill 243 J2
cr. Chester Hill 338 C15
rd. Bringelly 387 A13
rd. Greendale 355 B13
rd. Wallacia 324 J13
st. Greenwich 315 B8
GREENE
av. Ryde 282 C16
GREENFIELD
av. Middle Cove 285 J7
pde. Bankstown 399 E1
pl. Forestville 256 C9
pl. Maraylya 94 A11
rd. Greenfld Pk 334 B13
rd. Prairiewood 334 B13
st. Bnksmeadw 435 K1
GREENFIELDS
pl. Theresa Park 445 A3
GREENFINCH
st. Green Valley 363 F12
GREENGATE
la. Killara 253 J10
rd. Airds 511 J16
rd. Killara 253 J11
rd. St Helens Park 511 J16
GREENHALG
rd. Cranebrook 207 D14
GREENHALGH
la. Padstow 429 E1
GREENHAVEN
dr. Emu Heights 234 K4
dr. Pennant Hills 250 G3
pl. Silverdale 354 A14
rd. Grays Point 491 A13
GREENHILL
av. Normanhurst 221 D12
cl. Castle Hill 218 B10
cr. St Ives Ch 223 J4
dr. Glenwood 245 K3
GREEN HILLS
dr. Rouse Hill 185 A9
dr. Silverdale 383 J2
GREENHILLS
av. Moorebank 395 G13
av. Moorebank 395 H10
av. S Penrith 236 H16
rd. Holsworthy 425 F10
st. Croydon 372 D5
st. Croydon Pk 372 D5
GREENKNOWE
av. Elizabeth Bay 13 A5
GREENLANDS
av. Peakhurst 430 G1
rd. Lane Cove W 284 C14
GREENLEAF
st. Wentwthvle 277 A7
GREENLEE
st. Berala 339 C15
GREENLEES
av. Concord 342 B5
GREENMEADOWS
cr. Toongabbie 276 E6
GREENMOUNT
wy. Mt Colah 192 D5
GREENOAKS
av. Bradbury 511 D13
av. Cherrybrook 219 H15

av. Darling Point 13
GREEN POINT
rd. Oyster Bay 461
GREENS
av. Oatlands 279
dr. Cammeray 316
rd. Paddington 4
rd. Warrimoo 202
GREENSBOROUGH
av. Rouse Hill 185
GREENSLOPE
st. S Wntwthvle 306
GREENSPAN
cct. Lidcombe 339
GREENSTEAD
la. Randwick 377
GREENTREE
pl. Wilberforce 92
GREENVALE
gr. Hornsby 221
pl. Castle Hill 248
st. Fairfield W 335
GREEN VALLEY
rd. Busby 363
rd. Green Valley 363
GREENVALLEY
av. St Ives 224
GREENVIEW
pde. Berowra 163
GREENWAY
av. Shalvey 211
cr. Windsor 120
dr. Milsons Point 5
dr. Pymble 252
dr. S Penrith 267
dr. West Hoxton 392
dr. West Pymble 252
la. Springwood 202
la. The Rocks A
pde. Revesby 398
pl. Horsley Pk 331
st. Gymea 491
st. Ruse 512
GREENWELL
rd. Prestons 392
GREENWICH
cl. St Johns Pk 364
pl. Kellyville 216
rd. Greenwich 315
GREENWOOD
Blacktown 274
av. Bankstown 399
av. Narraweena 258
av. S Coogee 407
cl. Hamondvle 396
gr. Blacktown 244
la. Enfield 371
pl. Harbord 258
pl. St Helens Park 541
rd. Kellyville 216
GREER
st. Bonnyrigg Ht 363
st. Merrylands 307
GREG
pl. Dean Park 212
GREGGS
rd. Kurrajong 85
GREGORACE
pl. Bonnyrigg 363
GREGORY
av. Baulkham Hl 247
av. Croydon 342
av. N Epping 251
av. Oxley Park 270
cr. Beverly Hills 401
la. Earlwood 402
pl. Harris Park 308
rd. Leppington 419
st. Ermington 310
st. Fairfield W 335
st. Glendenning 242
st. Granville 308
st. Greystanes 306
st. Maroubra 407
st. N Richmond 87
st. Rsemeadow 540
st. Roseville 284
st. Ryde 312
st. S Coogee 407
st. Strathfield S 371
st. Yagoona 368
tce. Lapstone 264

GSON
Quakers Hill ...214 E8
G TAYLOR
Matraville ...436 K8
IG
Engadine ...518 D4
Seven Hills ...246 E13
NACHE
Eschol Park ...481 A5
NADA
Fairfield W ...335 B11
NFELL
N Narrabeen ...228 J2
Blakehurst ...432 C15
NVILLE
Cabarita ...342 E1
Caringbah ...493 A4
Pitt Town ...92 G14
SHAM
W Pnnant Hl ...249 G8
Cowan ...104 B13
Sydney ...B B12
Sydney ...1 J14
TA
Cartwright ...394 D4
Hebersham ...241 G3
TCHEN
Earlwood ...402 E5
TEL
Greenfld Pk ...334 D15
TNA
West Hoxton ...392 E6
St Andrews ...482 A2
TTA
Kellyville ...186 J16
VILLE
Chatswd W ...284 C13
Chatswd W ...284 D9
Clovelly ...377 G11
Randwick ...377 G11
VILLEA
St Ives ...224 D14
Bossley Park ...333 E8
Greystanes ...305 E11
Hornsby Ht ...191 G5
Mcquarie Fd ...454 G4
Prestons ...394 A14
Stanhpe Gdn ...215 D11
St Clair ...270 A15
Baulkham Hl ...247 D16
Heathcote ...518 J11
Narellan Vale ...478 K14
St Clair, off
Grevillea Dr ...270 A15
Kenthurst ...156 K15
S Coogee ...407 E6
Valley Ht ...202 E5
Chester Hill ...368 C1
Collaroy Plat ...228 H11
EX
Minchinbury ...271 D7
EY
Carlton ...432 F4
Emu Plains ...235 A11
Glenbrook ...264 C2
Silverwater ...309 J14
EYCAIRN
Woollahra ...22 E3
EYCLIFFE
Pennant Hills ...220 F16
Vaucluse ...348 B2
Queenscliff ...288 G4
EY GUM
Narellan Vale ...478 H14
Mt Colah ...191 K2
Newington, off
Lewis Wy ...310 C13
EYGUM
Rouse Hill ...184 K7
Gymea Bay ...491 F11
Old Tngabbie ...277 E6
EYGUMS
Cranebrook ...207 B13
EYSTANES
Greystanes ...305 G8
EYSTOKE
Collaroy Plat ...228 D9
EYSTONES
Killarney Ht ...255 K14
EYWOOD
Cherrybrook ...219 C11

GRIBBENMOUNT
rd. Galston ...159 H8
GRIBBLE
pl. Blacktown ...244 E15
GRIDE
pl. Ambarvale ...511 B14
GRIEVE
cr. Milperra ...397 E11
GRIFFIN
av. Bexley ...432 J3
pde. Illawong ...459 K3
pl. Doonside ...273 F3
pl. Kenthurst ...157 K5
rd. Dee Why ...259 A12
rd. N Curl Curl ...259 A12
st. Manly ...288 E9
st. Surry Hills ...20 B1
GRIFFINS
rd. Tennyson ...58 A5
GRIFFITH
av. North Bondi ...348 C16
av. Roseville Ch ...285 F2
cl. Galston ...159 G10
st. Ashfield ...372 J10
st. Hurlstone Pk ...372 J10
GRIFFITHS
av. Bankstown ...399 H1
av. Camden S ...507 B16
av. McGraths Hl ...121 K12
av. Punchbowl ...399 H1
av. West Ryde ...311 G1
la. West Ryde ...281 G16
pl. Eagle Vale ...480 K11
st. Balgowlah ...287 J7
st. Blacktown ...274 K1
st. Ermington ...310 C2
st. Fairlight ...288 A7
st. N St Marys ...239 J9
st. Oatley ...431 A9
st. Sans Souci ...463 B2
st. Tempe ...404 A2
st. Wentwthvle ...307 B3
st. Woolmloo ...4 F4
GRIGG
av. N Epping ...251 D11
cl. Ellis Lane ...476 C11
st. Oatley ...431 D10
GRIGOR
pl. Allambie Ht ...257 D12
GRIMES
la. Carlingford ...280 D5
la. Epping ...280 D5
pl. Bonnyrigg ...364 B8
pl. Davidson ...225 B15
GRIMLEY
cl. Penrith ...237 F2
la. Penrith, off
Grimley Cr ...237 F2
GRIMMET
av. Rouse Hill ...184 K7
GRIMMETT
ct. St Clair ...269 K16
la. St Clair, off
Grimmett Ct ...269 K16
st. Greystanes ...305 H8
GRIMSON
cr. Liverpool ...365 B16
la. Liverpool, off
Grimson Cr ...365 B16
GRIMWIG
cr. Ambarvale ...510 H12
GRIMWOOD
st. Granville ...308 B11
GROGAN
st. Croydon ...342 E11
GRONO
pl. McGraths Hl ...121 K13
GRONO FARM
rd. Wilberforce ...62 H15
GROOTE
av. Hinchinbrk ...363 A15
GROSE
av. Lurnea ...394 B13
av. N St Marys ...239 J8
la. Bowen Mtn ...84 E15
la. Grose Vale ...84 E15
pl. Camden S ...507 B9
pl. Ruse ...512 G8
pl. Seven Hills ...275 F10
rd. Faulconbdg ...171 B16
st. Camperdwn ...17 G5
st. Glebe ...12 G16
st. Little Bay ...437 A13
st. Parramatta ...278 C15
st. Richmond ...118 G6
GROSE RIVER
rd. Grose Wold ...116 E8
GROSE VALE
rd. Grose Vale ...84 J9
rd. Kurrajong ...85 A6
rd. N Richmond ...87 A16
GROSE VALE COMMUNITY CENTRE
rd. Grose Vale ...85 A15
GROSE VALLEY
ct. Faulconbdg ...171 D11
GROSE WOLD
rd. Grose Vale ...85 C15
rd. Grose Wold ...115 H5
GROSVENOR
cr. Cronulla ...493 G13
cr. Summer Hill ...373 C3
la. Cremorne ...6 H1
la. Neutral Bay ...6 H1
la. Lindfield, off
Grosvenor Rd ...284 D3
pl. Brookvale ...258 B12
pl. W Pnnant Hl ...249 D2
rd. Lindfield ...283 J5
rd. S Hurstville ...432 C11
st. Bondi Jctn ...22 J5
st. Cremorne ...316 D8
st. Croydon ...342 D16
st. Kensington ...376 D13
st. Neutral Bay ...316 C8
st. N Wahrnga ...192 F16
st. Sydney ...A G11
st. Sydney ...1 F14
st. Wahroonga ...222 F5
st. Woollahra ...22 J5
GROSVERNOR
la. Bondi Jctn ...22 H6
GROUNDSEL
av. Mcquarie Fd ...454 E5
GROUT
pl. Menai ...458 E11
pl. Rouse Hill ...184 K5
GROVE
av. Hurstville Gr ...431 E7
av. Narwee ...400 G11
av. Penshurst ...431 E7
la. Eastwood ...281 G7
la. Lilyfield ...10 F5
pl. Prospect ...275 A10
st. Birchgrove ...7 G4
st. Bondi ...377 K5
st. Casula ...394 H11
st. Dulwich Hill ...373 D9
st. Earlwood ...402 H2
st. Eastwood ...281 G8
st. Guildford ...337 F3
st. Lilyfield ...10 E5
st. Marrickville ...373 J15
st. St Peters ...374 F14
GROVER
av. Cromer ...227 K15
cr. Mulgoa ...296 D11
st. Lapstone ...264 G4
GROVES
av. Mulgrave ...151 H2
rd. Minto Ht ...483 G2
GROVEWOOD
pl. Castle Hill ...218 J6
GRUMMAN
la. St Clair, off
Grumman Pl ...270 E15
pl. Raby ...451 D15
pl. St Clair ...270 E15
GRUNER
pl. Mt Pritchard ...364 J11
wy. Claymore ...481 D11
GUAM
pl. Kings Park ...244 F2
GUARDIAN
av. Kellyville ...185 H11
cr. Bligh Park ...150 E8
pde. Beacon Hill ...257 F3
GUELPH
st. Regents Pk ...368 J2
GUERIE
st. Marayong ...244 C3
GUERIN
la. Bass Hill ...367 K4
st. Doonside ...243 C6
GUERNSEY
av. Minto ...452 K16
st. Busby ...363 J16
st. Guildford ...337 D7
wy. Stanhpe Gdn ...215 F10
GUESS
av. Arncliffe ...403 H5
GUEUDECOURT
av. Earlwood ...402 J1
GUIHEN
st. Annandale ...17 C1
GUILDFORD
la. Cmbrdg Pk, off
Guildford Rd ...237 J10
pl. Leumeah ...482 C16
rd. Cmbrdg Pk ...237 J11
rd. Guildford ...337 G5
rd.w, Guildford ...337 A3
rd.w, Guildford W ...337 A3
GUILFOYLE
av. Double Bay ...14 B8
st. Berala ...339 C12
GUINEA
st. Kogarah ...433 A4
GUINEVIERE
ct. Castle Hill ...217 G4
GUIREN
pl. Toongabbie ...276 G6
GUISE
av. Casula ...394 C15
pwy. Casula, off
Guise Av ...394 D16
rd. Bradbury ...511 F10
GULIA
st. Mona Vale ...198 G1
GULL
pl. Erskine Park ...270 H14
pl. Hinchinbrk ...363 E16
pl. Lugarno ...429 H12
pl. Prospect ...274 J11
st. Little Bay ...437 G14
GULLALIE
cir. Blaxland ...233 K6
GULLIVER
st. Brookvale ...258 A9
GULLY
rd. Valley Ht ...202 G3
GULLY GULLY
rd. Mooney Mooney ..75 D2
GUM
st. Greystanes ...306 E4
st. Riverstone ...182 K3
GUMBLETON
pl. Narellan Vale ...508 H1
GUM BLOSSOM
dr. Westleigh ...220 H9
GUMBOOYA
st. Allambie Ht ...257 H14
GUMBUYA
av. Baulkham Hl ...246 H7
GUMDALE
av. St Johns Pk ...364 C1
GUM GROVE
pl. W Pnnant Hl ...249 H9
GUM LEAF
cl. Hornsby Ht ...162 A9
GUMLEAF
pl. W Pnnant Hl ...249 G3
row. Wrrngtn Dns ...238 D6
wy. Kellyville ...215 K1
GUM NUT
cl. Kellyville ...186 C15
GUMNUT
cl. Blaxland ...233 F4
pl. Cherrybrook ...219 F12
pl. Mcquarie Fd ...454 E1
rd. Cherrybrook ...219 F11
GUMNUT BABY
wk. Faulconbdg ...171 D14
GUMTREE
la. Double Bay ...14 C10
wy. Smithfield ...335 G7
GUNARA
tce. Glenmore Pk ...265 K10
GUNBALANYA
av. Beecroft ...250 C4
GUNBOWER
rd. Bowen Mtn ...84 B10
GUNDAGAI
cr. Wakeley ...334 F14
GUNDAH
rd. Mt Krng-gai ...162 J5
GUNDAIN
la. Kirrawee, off
Gundain Rd ...461 D16
rd. Kirrawee ...461 D16
GUNDAMAIAN ROAD SERVICE
trl. Royal N P ...521 H4
GUNDAROO
st. Villawood ...367 E4
GUNDARY
cl. Prestons ...422 J1
GUNDAWARRA
pl. Kenthurst ...157 G9
st. Lilli Pilli ...522 G1
GUNDIBRI
st. Busby ...363 H14
GUNDIMAINE
av. Neutral Bay ...6 J9
GUNDOWRINGA
pl. Airds ...512 A10
GUNDY
pl. Westleigh ...220 F10
GUNELL
pl. Cranebrook ...207 F13
GUNGAH BAY
rd. Oatley ...430 J12
GUNGARLIN
dr. Horngsea Pk ...392 F14
GUNGAROO
pl. Beverly Hills ...401 B10
GUNGARTEN
cl. Kellyville ...216 C1
GUNGURRU
st. Kingswood ...267 H2
GUNJULLA
pl. Avalon ...139 J16
GUNN
pl. St Helens Park ...540 K9
rd. Lalor Park ...245 F10
GUNNAMATTA
rd. Cronulla ...493 G13
rd. Woolooware ...493 G13
GUNNEDAH
rd. Hoxton Park ...392 H7
GUNNERS
mw. Holsworthy ...426 F4
GUNNING
cl. Prestons ...393 D16
GUNSYND
av. Casula ...394 G15
st. Stanhpe Gdn ...215 A5
GUNTAWONG
rd. Rouse Hill ...183 K9
GUNYA
pl. Hebersham ...241 E10
st. Regents Pk ...369 A2
GUNYAH
cr. Roselands ...401 D6
pl. Avalon ...140 A13
pl. Glen Alpine ...510 D13
st. Cronulla ...523 J2
st. Marsfield ...281 G2
st. Northbridge ...286 A16
GUNYAH PATH
Winmalee ...173 A9
GURGAR
pl. Harringtn Pk ...478 G2
GURIN
av. Killara ...253 E14
GURLEY
pl. Bonnyrigg ...363 J10
GURNER
av. Austral ...361 A15
av. Kemps Ck ...360 E13
la. Paddington ...13 D14
pl. Kellyville ...216 G5
st. Paddington ...13 D14
GURNEY
cr. Fairfield W ...335 A12
cr. Seaforth ...286 J8
rd. Chester Hill ...337 G12
GURRAWILLIE
st. Villawood ...367 J3
GURRIER
av. Miranda ...492 C4
GURRIGAL
st. Mosman ...316 K6
GURU
pl. Glenmore Pk ...266 C6

GUTHEGA
cl. Woodcroft.........243 H9
cr. Heckenberg........364 A12
pl. Bossley Park......334 C8
GUTHRIE
av. Cremorne 6 J6
GUY
pl. Emu Heights 205 A15
pl. Rooty Hill...........271 K5
GUYONG
st. Lindfield.............283 H6
GUYRA
cl. Bossley Park......333 F11
rd. Hinchinbrk 392 G5
GUYS
pl. St Johns Pk 364 G1
GWANDALAN
cr. Berowra.............133 A16
pl. Emu Plains.........235 E12
rd. Edensor Pk 363 F2
rd. Padstow 399 C12
st. Emu Plains.........235 E11
GWAWLEY
pde. Miranda 462 E16
GWEA
av. Daceyville...........406 F4
GWEN
cr. Warrimoo 203 C11
pl. Padstow Ht 429 B6
pl. W Pnant Hl.......249 E10
GWENDALE
cr. Eastwood...........281 D5
GWYDIR
av. Matraville...........436 K1
av. N Turramrra.......193 D14
av. Quakers Hill 213 K7
pl. Campbelltwn......512 A8
st. Engadine.............488 E12
st. Greystanes..........306 A4
wy. Glenhaven..........218 D6
GWYN
cl. St Ives 224 G10
st. Doonside 243 D9
GWYNELLEN
pl. Cherrybrook.......219 D8
GWYNN
cl. Emu Plains.........235 A10
GWYNNE
st. Ashcroft.............364 D16
GWYNN HUGHES
rd. Bargo.................567 A6
GYMEA
pl. Jamisontown 266 D5
GYMEA BAY
rd. Gymea...............491 E3
rd.s, Gymea.............491 D8
rd.s, Gymea Bay.........491 E9
GYMKHANA
pl. Glenwood 245 J3
GYMNASIUM
rd. Mcquarie Pk.......252 B15
GYMPIE
pl. Wakeley.............334 H13
GYPSUM
pl. Eagle Vale 481 H6
GYRA
pl. Dharruk 241 B6

H

HABERFIELD
rd. Haberfield 373 D1
HACKETT
pl. North Rocks.......248 F15
rd. Abbotsbury........363 A2
st. Ultimo 3 A11
HACKING
av. Wrrngtn Cty 238 F6
dr. Narellan Vale......478 F16
HACKNEY
st. Greystanes........306 B4
HADDENHAM
st. Chipping Ntn......366 H15
HADDIN
cl. Turramurra 222 H13
pl. Kirkham.............477 C8
HADDON
cl. Bonnyrigg Ht......363 H5
cl. Glenwood 215 C16
cr. Revesby.............398 K14
pl. Picton 563 F12
HADDON RIG
pl. Airds..................512 D12
pl. Miller 393 G2
HADENFELD
av. Mcquarie Pk.......282 A1
HADLEIGH
av. Collaroy 259 B1
HADLEY
pl. Jamisontown 266 D5
HADLOW
cl. Kellyville.............185 K15
HADRIAN
av. Blacktown..........275 A8
HAERSE
av. Chipping Ntn......396 B5
HAFEY
rd. Kenthurst...........157 J6
HAFLINGER
cl. Emu Heights 235 C3
HAGEN
pl. Glenfield 424 G13
pl. Whalan 241 A8
HAGUE
gr. Oakhurst............242 C2
HAHN
st. Lucas Ht 487 H12
HAIG
av. Daceyville..........406 F4
av. Denistone E........281 J11
av. Georges Hall 367 D15
av. Summer Hill.........15 A7
la. Maroubra...........407 B10
la. Woolmloo..............4 C6
st. Bexley................432 D1
st. Chatswood.........285 D7
st. Maroubra...........407 B10
st. Mt Pritchard......364 G8
st. Roseville............285 C1
st. Wentwthvle........307 C2
HAIGH
av. Belrose 225 H15
av. Roselands..........400 J7
pl. Castle Hill..........218 F15
HAINES
av. Carlingford.........249 C13
gr. Mt Annan...........509 H1
pl. Menangle...........538 G16
HAINING
st. Cmbrdg Pk.........237 K7
HAINSWORTH
st. Westmead 277 J13
HAIR
cl. Greenfld Pk........334 C12
HAITE
cl. West Pymble......252 F9
HAKEA
av. Belrose 225 F16
av. Frenchs Frst.......255 F1
cl. Casula...............394 F13
cr. Galston 159 D10
ct. St Clair..............269 G8
pl. Baulkham Hl 247 C15
pl. Epping...............280 E4
pl. Mcquarie Fd.......454 G4
st. Engadine............489 C13
st. Mt Annan............509 F3
st. Stanhpe Gdn 215 C10
HALCROWS
rd. Cattai...................95 F1
HALCYON
av. Padstow 399 D12
av. Wahroonga.........222 H8
av. Winmalee...........172 K11
ct. Harringtn Pk.......478 G5
pl. Kellyville.............216 A3
st. Gladesville 312 K6
HALDANE
cr. Lane Cove...........314 G2
la. Lane Cove...........314 G2
st. Asquith 192 A10
HALDIS
pl. Plumpton............241 H7
HALDON
la. Lakemba............401 B4
st. Lakemba............401 A1
st.n, Lakemba..........401 A1
HALE
cr. S Windsor..........150 K2
pl. Fairfield Ht 336 B11
rd. Mosman 316 H6
st. Botany 405 C12
HALELUKA
cr. Plumpton...........242 D10
HALES
pl. Blackett.............241 A4
HALESMITH
rd. Mona Vale..........169 D14
HAL HAMMOND
pl. Belrose 226 B13
HALIFAX
av. Roselands..........400 G10
ct. St Clair..............270 E15
la. St Clair, off
Halifax Ct..........270 E16
st. Raby..................451 D15
HALINDA
st. Whalan 240 K7
HALL
av. Collaroy Plat.......228 G12
av. Thornleigh 221 A11
cr. Padstow 429 F5
cr. Padstow Ht 429 F5
dr. Menai 458 E15
pde. Lakemba............401 B3
pl. Eagle Vale 481 A10
pl. Fairfield W..........334 K10
pl. Guildford W 336 K1
pl. Minto.................452 J13
rd. Hornsby.............221 E4
st. Auburn 339 E1
st. Belmore..............371 G14
st. Bondi Beach.......378 A1
st. Chifley 437 B8
st. Pitt Town..............92 H8
st. St Marys.............269 E5
st. S Turramrra 252 A6
st. West Ryde 281 B14
HALLAM
av. Lane Cove W......283 H16
wy. Cherrybrook, off
Tennyson Cl.......219 D9
HALLEN
pl. West Hoxton 392 B13
rd. Cherrybrook.......219 J12
HALLEY
av. Bexley...............402 G15
st. Five Dock...........343 A6
HALLORAN
av. Davidson 225 C16
st. Lilyfield...............10 F6
HALLS
la. Woollahra 21 H3
rd. Arcadia 159 B2
rd. Cattai 64 J2
rd. Galston 159 B2
HALLSTROM
cl. Northbridge 286 G16
pl. Mona Vale..........199 C2
pl. Wetherill Pk 333 J2
HALMAHERA
cr. Lethbrdg Pk.......240 J1
HALSALL
st. Granville 308 D10
HALSLEY
st. Hassall Gr 211 K15
HALSTEAD
st. S Hurstville 431 K10
HAM
st. S Windsor...........120 F15
st. S Windsor...........120 H16
HAMBIDGE
pl. Bow Bowing.......452 D14
HAMBLEDON
av. Baulkham Hl 247 E3
av. Castle Hill...........247 E3
rd. Quakers Hill 213 J12
rd. Schofields 214 A5
wy. West Hoxton 392 B12
HAMBLY
st. Botany 405 J12
st. Fairfield W..........335 D13
HAMBRIDGE
rd. Bargo.................567 B4
rd. Bargo.................567 D3
HAMBRO
av. Glenwood 215 E13
HAMEL
cl. Milperra..............397 H11
cr. Earlwood 402 K1
rd. Matraville............407 A16
rd. Mt Pritchard.......364 B10
HAMELIN
pl. Illawong.............459 D6
HAMER
st. Epping 250 E13
st. Kogarah Bay 432 H12
HAMERSLEY
pl. Bow Bowing.......452 C14
st. Fairfield W..........335 F10
HAMILTON
av. Earlwood 402 H3
av. Holsworthy 396 B13
av. Naremburn 315 H4
av. Matraville, off
Cemetery Av......436 H8
cr. Ryde..................311 G5
cr.w, Ryde 311 G4
dr. Centnnial Pk.........21 G8
la. Naremburn 315 H4
pde. Pymble..............253 B8
pl. Narellan 478 G12
rd. Fairfield..............335 H13
rd. Fairfield Ht 335 H13
rd. Fairfield W..........335 A11
rd. Kentlyn 513 C4
st. Allawah...............432 G7
st. Arncliffe..............403 A10
st. Coogee 377 G14
st. Granville.............308 J10
st. Lidcombe............339 G9
st. N Strathfield.......341 D6
st. Riverstone 183 A4
st. Riverview............314 A4
st. Rose Bay 348 C10
st. S Wntwthvle 307 B5
st. Sydney ....A K14
st. Vineyard 152 F12
st. Rozelle, off
Merton St...........344 E7
st.e, N Strathfield.......341 D6
wy. Kellyville.............185 J14
HAMISH
ct. Kellyville.............186 B16
HAMLET
cl. St Clair..............300 C1
cr. Rsemeadow.......540 J7
la. Mosman, off
Raglan St...........317 B9
HAMLEY
rd. Mt Krng-gai........162 K6
HAMLIN
st. Quakers Hill 214 J13
HAMMAL
wy. Minto.................482 J5
HAMMENT
pl. Glenbrook, off
Great Western
Hwy...................234 B16
HAMMERLI
wy. Shalvey.............210 J12
HAMMERS
rd. Northmead..........277 H8
rd. Old Tngabbie......277 E8
HAMMERSLEY
rd. Grays Point 491 A13
HAMMERSMITH
rd. Homebush W.....340 H6
HAMMON
av. Doonside 243 G16
HAMMOND
av. Croydon.............342 G12
av. Normanhurst 221 F8
ct. Baulkham Hl 247 C14
pl. Campbelltwn......511 F8
pl. Mascot 405 C9
pl. Narwee 400 H10
HAMPDEN
av. Cremorne 6 K1
av. Darling Point........13 J3
av. Marrickville 373 G16
av. Wahroonga.........223 B6
pl. Raby...................451 H13
rd. Abbotsford..........343 A4
rd. Artarmon 284 J14
rd. Lakemba.............370 J14
rd. Pennant Hills......250 H2
rd. Russell Lea 343 A4
rd. S Wntwthvle 306 J5
rd. Wareemba 343 A4
st. Ashfield 372 F4
st. Belrose 226 B12
st. Beverly Hills 401 C15
st. Hurlstone Pk......373 B12
st. Mosman 317 B3
st. North Rocks........278 H1
st. N Sydney ....K J2
st. N Sydney 5 J5
st. Paddington 13
HAMPSHIRE
av. W Pnant Hl.......249
av. West Pymble......252
ct. Cherrybrook, off
Glamorgan Wy...219
la. Camperdwn 17
pl. Seven Hills 275
pl. Wakeley 334
st. Camperdwn 17
st. Cronulla 493
HAMPSON
av. Maroubra............407
HAMPSTEAD
rd. Auburn 309
rd. Dulwich Hill........373
rd. Homebush W.....340
HAMPTON
cl. Castle Hill...........248
cr. Prospect 274
ct. Wattle Grove 426
rd. Sylvania Wtr.......462
st. Balmain 7
st. Canley Vale 366
st. Croydon Pk.........372
st. Fairfield..............336
st. Fairfield..............336
st. Hurstville Gr.......431
HAMPTON COURT
rd. Carlton...............432
HAM RUN
cct. Rooty Hill...........271
HANBURY
cl. S Penrith............267
st. Greystanes.........306
HANCEY
av. North Rocks.......248
HANCKEL
rd. Oakville..............153
HANCOCK
dr. Cherrybrook.......219
pl. Edensor Pk 333
st. Bexley................402
st. Rozelle, off
Belmore St.........344
HANCOTT
st. Ryde..................282
HAND
av. Penrith...............236
HANDCOCK
la. Greenwich, off
Greenwich Rd 315
HANDEL
av. Emerton..............240
st. Bonnyrigg Ht......363
HANDLE
st. Bass Hill.............367
HANDLEY
av. Bexley North 402
av. Thornleigh 221
av. Turramurra 223
pl. Raby...................451
st. Auburn 338
st. Marrickville 374
HANDOUB
pde. Dee Why 259
pde. N Curl Curl 259
HANDS
la. Surry Hills.............F
HANGER
pl. Narellan 478
HANIGAN
st. Penshurst 431
HANKINS
ct. Greenacre 370
HANKS
st. Ashbury 372
st. Ashfield 372
HANLAN
st. Cranebrook 207
HANLON
cl. Minto.................453
HANLY
st. Lansdowne 367
HANNA
av. Lurnea 394
pl. Oakhurst.............241
st. Botany 405
HANNABUS
pl. Mulgrave 151
HANNAFORD
st. Campbelltwn......511

NAH
- Kellyville 217 C1
- Mt Annan 479 D16
- Beecroft 249 K6
- Westmead 307 G4

NAH BELLAMY
- W Pnnant Hl 249 E5

NAM
- Englorie Park 510 J10
- Bardwell Vy 403 C6
- Darlinghurst 4 E15
- Turrella 403 C6

NAN
- Maroubra 406 J9

NANS
- Narwee 400 C13
- Riverwood 400 C13

NON
- Botany 405 G14

NONS
- Peakhurst 430 E4

OVER
- N Epping 251 G8
- Cecil Hills 362 D6
- Rozelle 7 B14
- Wilberforce 91 J2

S
- Casula 424 H1
- Marrickville 374 C12

SARD
- Zetland 375 H12

SEN
- Earlwood 402 F2
- Galston 159 D9

SENS
- Minto Ht 482 J13

NSFORD
- Bilgola 169 E4

NSLOW
- Surry Hills F K16

NSON
- Fairfield 337 A13
- Fairfield E 337 A13

NWELL
- /.Liverpool 395 E3

NWOOD
- Edensor Pk 363 C1

PP
- Auburn 339 B3

RAH
- Bonnyrigg 363 K9

RAN
- Mascot 405 C2

RBER
- Alexandria 375 A14
- St Peters 374 K14

RBORD
- Brookvale 258 E12
- Dee Why 258 E12
- Harbord 258 E14
- N Curl Curl 258 E12
- North Manly 258 E14
- Woodbine 481 J11
- Granville 308 K11

RBOUR
- Middle Cove 285 K8
- Clontarf 287 G16
- Cronulla 523 K3
- Haymarket E C2
- Haymarket 3 D8
- Mosman 316 K7
- Sydney E C2
- Sydney 3 D8

RBOURNE
- *Kingsford, off Harbourne Rd 376 G16*
- Kingsford 406 G1

RBOUR VIEW
- Lavender Bay K H16
- Lavender Bay 5 H12
- Clontarf 287 F11

RBOURVIEW
- Abbotsford 343 A2
- Woollahra 22 H4

RCOURT
- Campsie 371 H13
- East Hills 427 J4
- Castle Hill 218 K7
- Glenwood 245 G3
- . Rosebery 375 G16
- Eagle Vale 481 A8
- East Killara 254 E7

HARCUS
- st. Merrylands 307 D13

HARDEN
- av. Northbridge 285 J15
- cr. Georges Hall 367 H12
- rd. Artarmon 285 B15
- st. Canley Ht 335 A16

HARDIE
- av. Summer Hill 373 C4
- la. Mascot 405 E6
- st. Darlinghurst 4 G11
- st. Mascot 405 E6
- st. Neutral Bay 6 D2

HARDIMAN
- av. Randwick 377 C16

HARDING
- la. Bexley 402 H12
- pl. Bonnet Bay 460 B9
- pl. Minto 482 G5

HARDWICKE
- st. Riverwood 430 C1
- st. The Oaks 502 G14

HARDY
- av. Riverwood 400 C13
- la. Riverwood 400 B13
- pl. Casula 424 F4
- st. Ashbury 372 H10
- st. Ashfield 372 H10
- st. Blackett 241 A3
- st. Dover Ht 348 E14
- st. Eschol Park 481 B6
- st. Fairfield 336 C11
- st. Hurlstone Pk 372 H10
- st. North Bondi 348 E14

HARE
- st. Glenbrook 233 K15

HAREBELL
- cl. Carlingford 280 D5

HAREDALE
- st. Ambarvale 540 D2

HAREFIELD
- cl. N Epping 251 H10

HAREWOOD
- pl. Cecil Hills 362 J8
- pl. Warriewood 199 D11

HARFORD
- av. East Hills 427 K3
- st. Jamisontown 236 E15
- st. North Ryde 282 K13

HARGRAVE
- la. Darlinghurst F H2
- la. Darlinghurst F J2
- la. Paddington 13 F14
- rd. Auburn 339 D7
- rd. Lalor Park 245 B12
- st. Darlinghurst F H2
- st. Darlinghurst 4 B9
- st. Kingswood 237 F13
- st. Leumeah 512 D1
- st. Paddington 13 F15

HARGRAVES
- av. Punchbowl 400 E8
- pl. Maroubra 407 D15
- pl. Wetherill Pk 304 D16
- st. Allambie Ht 257 J15

HARGREAVES
- st. Condell Park 398 D2

HARKEITH
- st. Mona Vale 199 D3

HARKNESS
- av. Glenorie 128 C5
- rd. Oakville 153 D9
- st. Woollahra 22 G4

HARLAND
- st. Ashfield 372 K8
- st. Fairlight 288 B7

HARLECH
- cl. Menai 458 K8
- ct. Castle Hill 218 K11

HARLEY
- cr. Condell Park 398 B3
- cr. Eastwood 280 K4
- pl. Kellyville 216 D4
- rd. Avalon 140 E16
- st. Alexandria 375 D9
- st. Sylvania 461 H11
- st. Yanderra 567 B16

HARLOW
- av. Hebersham 241 F8

HARLOWE
- pl. Bronte 378 A7

HARMAN
- st. Ingleburn 453 A11

HARMER
- st. Greenacre 370 G10
- st. Woolmloo 4 F5

HARMONY
- st. Ashbury 372 D9

HARMSTON
- av. Frenchs Frst 257 A5

HARNESS
- pl. Wrrngtn Dns 238 A4

HARNETT
- av. Marrickville 373 G14
- av. Mosman 316 H11
- pl. Chatswd W 284 C11
- st. N Sydney K G2
- st. N Sydney 5 H5
- st. Woolmloo 4 H3

HARNEY
- st. Marrickville 373 G11

HARNLEIGH
- av. Woolooware 493 D8
- av.s,Woolooware 493 D9

HAROLD
- av. Hobartville 118 E8
- av. Pennant Hills 250 J1
- av. Scotland I 168 J5
- pl. Dee Why 258 F2
- st. Blacktown 244 K14
- st. Campsie 372 A13
- st. Fairfield 336 C14
- st. Guildford 337 J2
- st. Ingleburn 453 H8
- st. Mcquarie Fd 424 D16
- st. Matraville 436 G2
- st. Mt Lewis 369 K15
- st. Newtown 17 H15
- st. Parramatta 278 C14

HARP
- st. Belmore 401 G4
- st. Campsie 401 G4

HARPER
- cl. Tahmoor 565 K13
- gr. Mt Annan 479 J15
- pl. Frenchs Frst 255 F4
- pl. Kellyville 216 F4
- st. Merrylands 307 J15
- st. N Epping 251 F11
- wy. Ingleburn 453 A10
- *wy. Menai, off Forest Glen Wy 458 J14*

HARPUR
- cl. Glenmore Pk 265 J6
- cr. S Windsor 150 E2
- pl. Casula 424 E4
- pl. Lalor Park 245 E11
- st. Fairfield W 335 B13

HARRABROOK
- av. Five Dock 342 K12

HARRADANCE
- pl. Liverpool 394 J9

HARRADEN
- dr. West Hoxton 391 K11
- dr. West Hoxton 391 K12

HARRADINE
- cr. Bligh Park 150 E5

HARRICKS
- pl. Bonnyrigg 364 B5

HARRIER
- av. Green Valley 363 C12
- av. Raby 481 F2
- pl. Clarmnt Ms 268 J5
- pl. Woronora Ht 489 E2

HARRIES
- wky.Revesby 428 H2

HARRIET
- av. Castle Hill 247 G1
- pl. Currans Hill 480 A12
- st. Marrickville 374 A15

HARRIETT
- cl. Glenmore Pk 265 F11
- *la. Glenmore Pk, off Harriett Cl 265 F10*

HARRIETTE
- la. Neutral Bay 6 H8
- st. Neutral Bay 6 F7

HARRINGTON
- av. Warrawee 222 H10
- la. Enmore 16 G14
- *la. The Rocks, off Globe St 1 H11*
- pky. Harringtn Pk 478 F3
- st. Cabramatta W 364 J7
- st. Elderslie 477 F16
- st. Enmore 16 G13
- st. The Rocks A H10
- st. The Rocks A J6
- st. The Rocks 1 G13

HARRIOTT
- la. Waverton 5 A6
- st. Waverton 5 A5

HARRIS
- ct. Five Dock 342 G10
- *la. Fairfield, off Hamilton Rd 336 E13*
- *la. Jamisontown, off Harris St 236 C15*
- pl. Baulkham Hl 247 F5
- pl. West Hoxton 392 C11
- rd. Dural 189 D15
- rd. Five Dock 342 G11
- rd. Normanhurst 221 E9
- rd. Wentwthvle 277 D11
- st. Balmain 7 A11
- st. Condell Park 398 G7
- st. Fairfield 336 C13
- st. Guildford 337 C3
- st. Harris Park 308 F7
- st. Ingleburn 453 E7
- st. Jamisontown 236 B15
- st. Merrylands 307 C16
- st. N St Marys 239 H13
- st. Paddington 13 H15
- st. Parramatta 308 F7
- st. Pyrmont 12 F1
- st. Rosebery 405 G3
- st. Sans Souci 462 J5
- st. Thirlmere 562 D7
- st. Ultimo E A13
- st. Ultimo 3 A10
- st. Warriewood 198 J5
- st. Willoughby 285 F14
- st. Windsor 121 C14
- st. Woolooware 493 F12

HARRISON
- av. Bonnet Bay 460 B10
- av. Concord W 311 D12
- av. Eastwood 280 H8
- av. Maroubra 407 G8
- la. Cremorne 6 K3
- pl. Minto 482 H4
- rd. Kentlyn 513 C8
- rd. Kentlyn 513 D5
- st. Ashcroft 394 E2
- st. Cremorne 6 H3
- st. Greenwich 314 J13
- st. Marrickville 373 H11
- st. Old Tngabbie 277 F9
- st. Revesby 398 F15

HARRISONS
- la. Glenorie 128 F5

HARROD
- st. Prospect 275 A12

HARROW
- av. Lansvale 366 D9
- la. Stanmore 16 J10
- rd. Auburn 339 B11
- rd. Auburn 339 C7
- rd. Berala 339 B11
- rd. Bexley 403 A14
- rd. Cmbrdg Pk 238 B9
- rd. Glenfield 424 G13
- rd. Kogarah 433 C1
- rd. Stanmore 16 H10
- rd.n,Glenfield 424 G9
- rd.s,Glenfield 424 D13
- st. Marayong 243 H6
- st. Sylvania 462 C7

HARROWER
- pl. Glenmore Pk 265 K6

HARRY
- av. Lidcombe 339 K5
- pl. Bella Vista 246 D7
- st. Eastlakes 405 J5

HARRY KNOX
- pl. Harbord 258 F13

HARRY LAWLER
- rd. Cranebrook 207 C15

HARSLETT
- cr. Beverley Pk 433 A10

HARST
- pl. Belrose 226 A10

HARSTON
- av. Mosman 316 K3

HART
- dr. Wentwthvle 277 A15
- pl. Kellyville 216 G8
- pl. St Clair 270 C9
- rd. S Windsor 150 G2
- st. Balmain East 8 C9
- st. Dundas Vy 280 A8
- st. Lane Cove W 283 K13
- st. Redfern 19 B5
- st. Smithfield 335 E3
- st. Surry Hills 19 J2
- st. Tempe 404 B3
- st. Warwck Frm 365 H16

HARTAM
- st. Kings Lngly 245 F5

HARTFORD
- av. Glen Alpine 510 D15

HARTHOUSE
- rd. Ambarvale 510 G16

HARTIGAN
- av. Emu Plains 235 F9
- wy. Bradbury 511 J12

HARTILL-LAW
- av. Earlwood 402 J5

HARTINGTON
- st. Granville 308 E13
- st. Rooty Hill 242 C14

HARTLAND
- st. Northmead 277 K5

HARTLEY
- cl. Bligh Park 150 K7
- cl. N Turramrra 223 E1
- pl. Ruse 512 F8
- pl. Wrrngtn Cty 238 H8
- rd. Currans Hill 479 F12
- rd. Seven Hills 275 G1
- rd. Smeaton Gra 479 B7
- st. Rozelle 7 B16

HARTNETT
- pl. Doonside 273 E1

HARTOG
- av. Fairfield W 335 D11
- av. Willmot 210 C12
- dr. Wrrngtn Cty 238 H4
- *la. Wrrngtn Cty, off Henry Lawson Av 238 H5*
- pl. Illawong 459 F5

HARTREE
- pl. Cherrybrook 220 A10

HARTZELL
- pl. Bnkstn Aprt 367 K16

HARVARD
- cct. Rouse Hill 185 D4
- la. Sutherland 490 D1
- st. Gladesville 312 J8

HARVEST
- dr. Wrrngtn Cty 238 D4
- dr. Wrrngtn Dns 238 D4

HARVEY
- av. Moorebank 396 E7
- av. Padstow 429 D5
- cct. St Clair 270 B13
- *la. St Clair, off Harvey Cct 270 B13*
- pl. Cherrybrook 219 G16
- pl. Menai 458 E10
- pl. Toongabbie 276 B9
- *pwy.Moorebank, off Harvey Av 396 D7*
- rd. Ingleside 197 C6
- rd. Kings Park 244 C2
- st. Little Bay 437 G14
- st. Mcquarie Fd 424 B16
- st. Parramatta 308 G2
- st. Pyrmont 12 F1
- st.e, Seaforth 287 A9
- st.w,Seaforth 287 A9

HARWOOD
- av. Chatswood 285 D7
- av. Mt Krng-gai 163 B11
- cct. Glenmore Pk 265 J4
- la. Pyrmont 12 K4
- pl. St Helens Park 541 A10
- st. Pyrmont 12 J4
- st. Seven Hills 275 J6

HASCOMBE
- *la. St Clair, off Hascombe Wy 270 F13*
- wy. St Clair 270 F13

HASLEM
- dr. Rookwood 340 A14

HASLEWOOD
- pl. Hinchinbrk 363 B16

HASLUCK
- pl. Glenmore Pk 265 J6

rd. Bonnyrigg..........363 H7
HASSALL
st. Camellia..........308 H4
st. Elderslie..........477 G14
st. Harris Park..........308 E4
st. Harris Park..........308 H4
st. Parramatta..........308 E4
st. Smithfield..........335 C3
st. Westmead..........307 G2
st. Wetherill Pk..........335 C3
HASSELBURGH
rd. Tregear..........240 F8
HASSELL
st. St Ives..........224 D6
HASSELT
rd. Shanes Park..........209 F4
HASSETT
cl. Menai..........458 G9
la. St Clair, off Hassett Pl..........269 K16
pl. Rouse Hill..........184 J8
pl. St Clair..........269 K16
HASTINGS
av. Chifley..........437 A7
cr. Greystanes..........306 A3
la. Surry Hills..........20 B6
la. Marrickville, off Livingstone Rd..........373 J11
pde. Bondi Beach..........378 E1
pde. North Bondi..........378 E1
pl. Campbelltwn..........511 K9
pl. Sylvania Wtr..........462 D10
rd. Beverley Pk..........433 C12
rd. Castle Hill..........218 H7
rd. Glenhaven..........218 H7
rd. Warrawee..........222 G10
st. Botany..........405 F12
st. Lidcombe..........339 K2
st. Marrickville..........373 J11
HATCHINSON
cr. Jamisontown..........265 K2
HATFIELD
pl. Hebersham..........241 F6
rd. Canley Ht..........365 C4
st. Blakehurst..........462 C1
st. Lane Cove W..........283 K13
st. Mascot..........405 D5
HATHAWAY
rd. Lalor Park..........245 G10
HATHERN
st. Leichhardt..........15 B5
HATHERTON
rd. Lethbrdg Pk..........240 C3
rd. Tregear..........240 C3
HATHOR
st. Doonside..........243 F15
HATTAH
wy. Bow Bowing..........452 E12
HATTERSLEY
st. Arncliffe..........403 E11
st. Banksia..........403 E12
HATTON
la. Ryde, off Gladstone Av..........312 A3
pl. Barden Rdg..........488 H3
st. Ryde..........312 B3
HAUGHTON
ct. Wattle Grove..........426 B4
st. Carramar..........336 H16
st. Linley Point..........313 G8
HAULTAIN
st. Minto..........452 K13
HAVANNAH
pl. Illawong..........459 E5
HAVARD
pl. Ashcroft..........394 E1
HAVELOCK
av. Coogee..........407 F1
av. Engadine..........488 D14
st. McGraths Hl..........122 B12
st. S Turramrra..........252 C5
HAVEN
ct. Cherrybrook..........219 B12
pl. Dural..........188 C13
st. Merrylands..........307 B10
st. Plumpton..........242 A10
HAVENDALE
av. Penshurst..........431 H6
HAVEN VALLEY
wy. Lansvale..........366 C10
HAVENWOOD
pl. Blacktown..........274 A8
HAVERHILL
av. Hebersham..........241 E8
HAVILAH
av. Wahroonga..........221 K10
ct. Wattle Grove..........426 A1
la. Lindfield..........254 D15
pl. Carlingford..........279 J1
rd. Lindfield..........254 D15
st. Chatswood..........285 A8
HAVISHAM
wy. Ambarvale..........511 A15
HAWAII
av. Lethbrdg Pk..........240 F2
HAWDON
av. Wrrngtn Cty..........238 E8
cl. Elderslie..........507 H3
HAWEA
pl. Belrose..........226 A16
HAWICK
ct. Kellyville..........187 A16
HAWK
cl. Green Valley..........363 D12
pl. Erskine Park..........270 E16
st. Penshurst..........431 B3
HAWKE
la. Kings Lngly..........245 K9
pl. Kings Lngly..........245 J9
HAWKEN
st. Newtown..........374 G10
HAWKER
pl. Raby..........451 D16
pl. West Hoxton..........392 C12
st. Kings Park..........244 C2
HAWKES
av. Newington, off Newington Bvd..........310 A15
HAWKESBURY
av. Dee Why..........258 J4
cr. Brooklyn..........75 G12
esp. Sylvania Wtr..........462 F13
rd. Hawksbry Ht..........175 A4
rd. Springwood..........202 B2
rd. Westmead..........307 E4
rd. Winmalee..........173 H7
st. Fairfield W..........335 C14
st. Pitt Town..........92 H9
HAWKESWORTH
pde. Kings Lngly..........245 A5
pl. Cherrybrook..........219 K7
HAWKEY
cr. Camden..........507 B5
HAWKHURST
st. Marrickville..........373 J10
HAWKINS
av. Luddenham..........356 H1
pde. Blaxland..........233 E10
pl. Wilberforce..........92 A3
rd. Tahmoor..........565 J16
st. Artarmon..........284 J14
st. Blacktown..........275 A6
HAWKRIDGE
pl. Dural..........219 B5
HAWKSLEY
st. Waterloo, off Bourke St..........375 J9
HAWKSVIEW
st. Guildford..........337 C1
st. Merrylands..........307 C16
HAWLEY
ct. St Ives..........224 C8
HAWTHORN
pl. Cherrybrook..........219 K6
rd. Penrith..........237 C8
st. Loftus..........489 H11
st. St Johns Pk..........364 G2
HAWTHORNE
av. Chatswd W..........284 B10
av. Rookwood..........340 C14
pde. Haberfield..........15 A2
pl. Mcquarie Fd..........454 F2
rd. Bargo..........567 F3
rd. Bargo..........567 F7
st. Leichhardt..........15 C1
st. Ramsgate Bch..........433 F12
HAY
av. Caringbah..........492 J7
cl. St Clair..........269 J14
la. Caringbah, off Hay Av..........492 J7
la. Randwick, off Hay St..........376 K16
pl. Quakers Hill..........244 A4
pl. Wakeley..........334 K12
st. Ashbury..........372 D9
st. Collaroy..........229 C14
st. Croydon Pk..........372 D7
st. Haymarket..........E D7
st. Haymarket..........E J8
st. Haymarket..........3 E12
st. Leichhardt..........16 B4
st. Liverpool..........395 C6
st. Randwick..........376 K16
st. Vaucluse..........348 D7
st. West Ryde..........281 A15
HAYBERRY
la. Crows Nest, off Bernard La..........315 H8
st. Crows Nest..........315 G8
HAYBURN
av. Rockdale..........403 D16
HAYDEN
la. Darlinghurst..........4 G10
pl. Botany..........405 G16
pl. Darlinghurst..........4 G11
pl. Engadine..........518 E5
HAYDN
pl. Bonnyrigg Ht..........363 E6
st. Seven Hills..........246 E13
HAYDOCK
la. Revesby..........398 J15
HAYES
av. Kellyville..........216 K3
av. Northmead..........277 H9
av. S Wntwthvle..........307 D5
ct. Harringtn Pk..........478 F7
pl. Bonnet Bay..........460 C10
pl. Minto..........452 K13
rd. Rosebery..........375 G15
rd. Seven Hills..........275 C4
rd. Wilberforce..........61 A4
st. Balgowlah..........287 K5
st. Lidcombe..........339 G12
st. Neutral Bay..........6 E10
HAYLE
st. St Ives..........224 H8
HAYLEN
pl. Blackett..........241 B2
pl. Edensor Pk..........363 G1
HAYLEY
gr. Blacktown..........273 G6
pl. Cherrybrook..........219 J5
HAYMAN
av. Hinchinbrk..........393 A1
st. N Richmond..........87 C14
HAYMET
st. Blaxland..........233 H11
st. Kirrawee..........490 J6
HAYNES
av. Seven Hills..........245 C15
st. Penrith..........237 B10
HAYTER
pde. Camden S..........506 J15
HAYWARD
st. Kingsford..........406 H4
HAYWOOD
cl. Wetherill Pk..........335 A3
pl. Greystanes..........305 J1
st. Epping..........250 D16
HAZEL
av. Lurnea..........394 C10
cl. Cranebrook..........207 B13
pl. Burraneer..........493 F15
pl. Ingleburn..........453 E11
st. Bass Hill..........367 E10
st. Georges Hall..........367 E10
st. Girraween..........276 A16
st. Lansdowne..........367 E10
HAZELBANK
pl. N Sydney..........5 E2
rd. N Sydney..........5 A3
rd. Wollstncraft..........5 A3
HAZELDEAN
av. Hebersham..........241 F10
pl. Kenthurst..........157 D2
wy. Airds..........512 F10
HAZELGLEN
av. Panania..........398 C15
HAZELMEAD
rd. Asquith..........192 B9
HAZLEWOOD
pl. Epping..........250 J15
HEADLAND
rd. Castle Cove..........285 H4
rd. N Curl Curl..........258 F9
HEALD
rd. Ingleburn..........452 K7
HEALEY
cct. Huntingwd..........273 F13
wy. Killarney Ht..........255 G15
HEALY
av. Newington..........310 A16
HEANEY
cl. Mt Colah..........162 E14
HEAPY
st. Blacktown..........274 F9
HEARD
av. Tregear..........240 G7
st. Denistone E..........281 H10
HEARN
st. Leichhardt..........16 D3
HEARNE
cl. Eastlakes..........405 K2
st. Bligh Park..........150 H5
st. Mortdale..........430 H5
HEARNSHAW
st. North Ryde..........282 K9
HEART
pl. Blacktown..........244 C15
HEATH
cl. East Killara..........254 G6
la. Heathcote..........518 G12
la. Hunters Hill..........313 F11
la. Ryde..........281 K12
pl. Heathcote..........518 K10
rd. Blakehurst..........432 D13
rd. Kellyville..........186 D7
rd. Leppington..........420 E6
st. Asquith..........191 K12
st. Auburn..........338 K6
st. Bankstown..........369 F13
st. Bexley North..........402 E12
st. Concord..........311 K16
st. Five Dock..........343 C9
st. Granville..........338 G1
st. Kingswood..........238 B12
st. Merrylands..........307 G8
st. Mona Vale..........199 F3
st. Prospect..........274 G10
st. Punchbowl..........400 A6
st. Randwick..........377 C15
st. Ryde..........281 K12
st. Turrella..........403 C6
HEATHCLIFF
cr. Balgowlah Ht..........287 K14
HEATHCOTE
rd. Engadine..........518 C1
rd. Hamondvle..........426 F1
rd. Heathcote..........518 C1
rd. Holsworthy..........427 H11
rd. Lucas Ht..........487 A12
rd. Moorebank..........395 H7
rd. Pleasure Pt..........427 B6
rd. Sandy Point..........427 H11
rd. Voyager Pt..........427 B6
st. Picton..........563 F9
st. Rockdale..........403 B13
HEATHER
cl. Baulkham Hl..........247 E6
pl. Acacia Gdn..........214 G15
pl. Hornsby Ht..........161 G11
pl. Wilberforce..........92 A2
rd. Winmalee..........173 E8
st. Caringbah..........492 J15
st. Collaroy Plat..........228 E12
st. Girraween..........276 A16
st. Leonay..........234 J15
st. Loftus..........489 J10
st. Yagoona..........368 E13
HEATHERBRAE
pl. Castle Hill..........218 E12
HEATHERFIELD
cl. Catherine Fd..........449 E1
HEATHER GLEN
rd. Yellow Rock..........173 F15
HEATHERWOOD
cl. Winmalee..........173 B12
HEATHFIELD
pl. Airds..........512 A11
HEATLEY
cl. Abbotsbury..........333 D14
HEATON
av. Clontarf..........287 E11
HEAVEY
st. Werrington..........238 F10
HEBBLEWHITE
pl. Bonnyrigg..........364 A6
HEBBURN
pl. Cartwright..........394
HEBE
pl. Kellyville..........186
st. Greenacre..........370
HEBER
pl. Prospect..........274
st. Hurstville..........431
HEBRIDES
av. Mcquarie Lk..........423
pl. St Andrews..........482
HECKENBERG
av. Busby..........393
av. Heckenberg..........364
av. Sadleir..........364
rd. Glenorie..........128
HECTOR
rd. Willoughby..........285
st. Bass Hill..........368
st. Chester Hill..........368
st. Greystanes..........306
st. Illawong..........459
st. Sefton..........338
HEDDA
st. Oakhurst..........241
HEDGER
av. Ashfield..........342
HEDGES
av. Strathfield..........370
st. Fairfield..........336
HEDLEY
st. Greystanes..........306
st. Marayong..........244
st. Riverwood..........430
HEDLUND
st. Revesby..........428
HEELEY
la. Paddington..........13
st. Paddington..........13
HEFFERMAN
la. Cranebrook, off Hefferman Rd..........207
rd. Cranebrook..........207
HEFFERNAN
cr. Richmond..........119
HEFFRON
rd. Eastgardens..........406
rd. Lalor Park..........245
rd. Pagewood..........406
HEGARTY
la. Bondi Jctn..........22
st. Glebe..........11
HEGEL
av. Emerton..........240
HEGERTY
st. Rockdale..........403
HEGGIE
la. Punchbowl..........400
HEIDELBERG
av. Newington..........310
HEIDI
pl. W Pnnant Hl..........249
HEIGHTS
cr. Middle Cove..........285
pl. Hornsby Ht..........161
HEIGHWAY
av. Ashfield..........372
av. Croydon..........372
HEINDRICH
av. Padstow..........399
HEINE
av. Emerton..........240
HEINZE
av. Mt Pritchard..........364
HELDER
st. Ingleburn..........454
HELEN
ct. Castle Hill..........248
pl. Rooty Hill..........241
st. Epping..........280
st. Lane Cove W..........284
st. Sefton..........368
st. Sefton..........368
st. Smithfield..........335
st. Westmead..........277
st.n, Sefton..........338
HELENA
av. Emerton..........240
rd. Cecil Hills..........362
rd. Minto Ht..........483
st. Auburn..........339
st. Guildford W..........336

Kirrawee 490 H7
Lilyfield 10 C6
Randwick 407 B2
ELGA
Padstow 429 E4
Hassall Gr 212 A13
ELICIA
Mcquarie Fd 454 G7
ELIODOR
Eagle Vale 481 G8
ELIOS
Doonside 243 E14
ELIOTROPE
Blacktown 274 E12
ELIPORT
Mascot 405 D9
ELLES
Moorebank 395 D10
ELMAN
Ingleburn 452 J11
ELM COTTAGE
Blair Athol 511 A3
ELP
Chatswood 284 H9
ELVETIA
Berowra 163 D2
Earlwood 402 J3
ELY
Wrrngtn Cty 238 F5
EMERS
Dural 189 H15
EMINGWAY
Fairfield 336 D6
EMMINGS
Penrith 237 B9
EMPHILL
Mt Pritchard 364 F10
EMSBY
Doonside 243 E5
EMSWORTH
Northmead 277 H9
ENDERSON
Panania 428 B4
Jamisontown 266 D3
Alexandria 18 E13
Alexandria 18 E13
Bexley 402 F14
Eveleigh 18 E13
Ingleburn 453 D1
Mcquarie Fd 453 H4
Bondi 377 K4
Denistone E 281 F9
Merrylands 307 J9
Turrella 403 D5
ENDLE
Baulkham Hl 246 J5
ENDON
rn. W Pnnant Hl 249 C4
ENDRA
St Johns Pk 364 E1
Warwck Frm 395 K1
ENDREN
Colyton 270 G6
ENDRENS
Ebenezer 63 F10
ENDY
Collaroy 229 A14
Coogee 407 D3
v. Panania 428 F1
v. S Coogee 407 D3
ENLEY
Belrose 225 K13
Castle Hill 248 F3
Hornsby Ht 191 F9
St Clair 270 G10
Homebush W 340 G10
Drummoyne 343 H5
Lane Cove W 283 J16
Rosebery 405 F2
ENLEY MARINE
r. Drummoyne 343 J6
r. Five Dock 343 B12
r. Rodd Point 343 E9
r. Russell Lea 343 E9
ENNESSY
Croydon 342 E16
ENNESY
r. Shalvey 211 A13
ENNING
v. Kingsford 407 D7
v. Maroubra 407 D7

av. S Coogee 407 D7
HENNINGS
la. Newtown 17 K11
HENRICKS
av. Drummoyne 313 G16
av. Newington 309 K15
pl. Beacon Hill 257 J8
HENRIETTA
cl. Cecil Hills 362 D3
dr. Narellan Vale 508 F2
la. Double Bay 14 B10
la. Manly, off Raglan St 288 H9
st. Chippendale 19 B3
st. Double Bay 14 B10
st. Waverley 377 G8
HENRY
av. Sylvania 461 H13
av. Ultimo 12 J9
la. Lewisham 15 B10
la. St Leonards 315 E5
la. Sydenham, off Reilly La 374 E15
la.n, Lewisham 15 B10
pl. Narellan Vale 508 K2
pl. Plumpton 241 G10
rd. Riverwood 399 J15
rd. Vineyard 152 B2
st. Ashfield 342 J13
st. Balmain 7 C13
st. Baulkham Hl 247 K8
st. Carlton 432 J5
st. Cecil Hills 362 H7
st. Dee Why 259 A9
st. Five Dock 342 H9
st. Gordon 253 J8
st. Guildford 337 H7
st. Leichhardt 9 K9
st. Lewisham 15 B10
st. Lidcombe 339 J10
st. Lilyfield 9 K8
st. Old Guildford 337 E7
st. Parramatta 308 F1
st. Penrith 237 A10
st. Picton 563 C15
st. Punchbowl 370 C16
st. Queens Park 22 K15
st. Randwick 407 D2
st. Ryde 312 C5
st. St Peters 374 E15
st. Strathfield 371 G1
st. Sydenham 374 E15
st. Tempe 374 D16
st. Turrella 403 E5
HENRY COX
dr. Mulgoa 324 C1
HENRY KENDALL
av. Padstow Ht 429 C6
cl. Heathcote 518 C15
cr. Mascot 405 D2
HENRY LAWSON
av. Abbotsford 342 J3
av. McMahons Pt 5 E16
av. Wrrngtn Cty 238 E6
dr. Bnkstn Aprt 397 C1
dr. East Hills 427 F5
dr. Georges Hall 367 C16
dr. Lansdowne 367 B6
dr. Milperra 397 C1
dr. Padstow 429 F6
dr. Padstow Ht 429 A9
dr. Panania 428 B9
dr. Peakhurst 430 A3
dr. Picnic Point 428 B9
dr. Revesby Ht 429 A9
rd. Peakhurst 430 D4
HENSHAW
cl. Bonnyrigg 364 F6
HENSON
la. Ultimo 12 K12
st. Btn-le-Sds 403 K16
st. Marrickville 373 F15
st. Merrylands 307 D12
st. Summer Hill 373 B7
st. Toongabbie 276 H8
HENSTOCK
rd. Arcadia 129 C12
HENTIC
ct. Wrrngtn Cty 238 H5
HENTY
pl. Bonnyrigg 363 H7
pl. Quakers Hill 214 B9
rd. Ingleburn 422 K13
st. Yagoona 368 G9

HENVILLE
pl. Bass Hill 367 G7
HENZE
cr. Clarmnt Ms 268 G4
HEPBURN
av. Carlingford 280 C2
av. Gladesville 312 H8
rd. North Rocks 248 H12
HERA
pl. St Clair 269 G11
pl. Winston Hills 277 D1
HERAKLES
pl. Doonside 243 F16
HERALD
pl. Kellyville 185 K14
sq. Sydney A K8
HERB ELLIOTT
av. Homebush B 340 G1
HERBER
pl. Wahroonga 222 C11
HERBERT
av. Newport 169 C7
av. Wahroonga 222 B2
la. Newtown 17 J12
la. West Ryde, off Herbert St 281 F16
pl. Narellan 478 G15
pl. Smithfield 336 C2
rd. Edgecliff, off New McLean St 13 J12
st. Artarmon 315 B2
st. Bankstown 399 C7
st. Cmbrdg Pk 238 A10
st. Dulwich Hill 373 F9
st. Kemps Ck 359 K11
st. Malabar 437 D4
st. Manly 288 E6
st. Marsden Pk 182 A12
st. Merrylands 308 B13
st. Mortlake 312 B16
st. Newtown 17 J12
st. Oatley 431 C16
st. Pyrmont 8 F15
st. Regentville 265 F4
st. Rockdale 403 A12
st. St Leonards 315 B2
st. Summer Hill 373 B6
st. West Ryde 281 F15
HERBERTO
la. Glebe 11 K10
HERBERTON
av. Hunters Hill 313 F11
HERBORN
pl. Minto 452 K14
HERCULES
av. Padstow 429 C2
cl. Cranebrook 207 E6
cl. Raby 451 H14
la. Dulwich Hill 373 D11
pl. Bligh Park 150 E7
rd. Btn-le-Sds 433 K4
st. Ashfield 372 J3
st. Chatswood 285 B9
st. Dulwich Hill 373 D11
st. Fairfield E 337 A15
st. Surry Hills 19 J1
st. Villawood 337 A15
HEREFORD
pl. Minto Ht 482 J13
pl. S Wntwthvle 306 H6
pl. West Pymble 252 H14
st. Busby 393 J1
st. Forest Lodge 11 F15
st. Glebe 11 J13
st. Hobartville 118 E6
HEREWARD
hwy. Blacktown 274 H3
st. Maroubra 407 G11
HERFORD
st. Botany 405 J16
HERING
av. Emerton 240 K6
HERITAGE
ct. Castle Hill 248 E4
ct. Dural 219 B6
dr. Illawong 459 E4
pl. Glenwood 245 F3
wy. Glen Alpine 510 C13
HERLEY
av. Rossmore 390 E4
HERMAN
cr. Hornsby Ht 161 F15

HERMES
pl. Emu Plains 235 F8
HERMIES
av. Milperra 397 G11
HERMINGTON
st. Epping 280 E1
HERMIT
av. Vaucluse 348 B6
HERMITAGE
av. Kellyville 185 F9
cr. Cartwright 394 C4
ct. Orchard Hills 268 E5
la. West Ryde, off Hermitage Rd 281 F16
pl. Eschol Park 481 A4
pl. Minchinbury 271 K9
rd. Kurrajong Hl 54 H12
rd. West Ryde 281 F16
HERMOSA
ct. Castle Hill 217 D9
HERMOYNE
st. West Ryde 280 G13
HERON
av. Georges Hall 367 K13
cr. St Clair 270 B14
ct. Castle Hill 218 D8
pl. Dee Why 258 H2
pl. Grays Point 491 F14
pl. Hinchinbrk 393 C1
pl. Ingleburn 453 F7
pl. Yarramundi 145 D4
HERRICK
cl. West Hoxton 392 E5
st. Blacktown 275 A8
st. Wetherill Pk 334 D4
HERRING
rd. Mcquarie Pk 282 D3
rd. Marsfield 282 A6
HERRON
wk. Mosman, off Raglan St 316 H14
HERSEY
st. Blaxland 233 H11
HERSHON
st. St Marys 269 K6
HERSTON
rd. St Johns Pk 364 C2
HERTZ
pl. Emerton 240 J4
HERVEY
st. Georges Hall 367 E13
HESELTINE
pl. Rooty Hill 272 B4
HESPERUS
st. Pymble 252 K7
HESSEL
pl. Emu Heights 234 J7
HESSION
rd. Nelson 155 A14
rd. Oakville 124 A12
HESTEN
la. Rockdale, off Gloucester St 403 C14
la. Rockdale, off Walz St 403 C15
HESTER
st. Castlereagh 146 D15
wy. Kellyville 186 A15
HESWELL
av. Morning Bay 138 G14
HEVINGTON
rd. Auburn 339 E7
HEVRELL
ct. Glenwood 215 D14
HEWETT
la. Penrith, off Warwick St 236 J13
HEWIN
cl. Liberty Gr 311 B10
HEWISON
av. Green Valley 363 C11
wy. Minto 482 H8
HEWIT
av. Glebe 12 A14
HEWITT
av. Greystanes 306 F11
av. Wahroonga 221 K11
pl. Minto 482 J9
st. Colyton 270 G9
st. Greenacre 370 F9

HEWLETT
st. Bronte 377 K7
st. Granville 308 C11
HEWS
ct. Belrose 226 C13
pde. Belrose 226 A13
HEXHAM
pl. Wetherill Pk 304 A15
HEXTOL
st. Croydon Pk 371 H9
HEYDE
av. Strathfield 341 B13
HEYDON
av. Warrawee 222 F11
st. Enfield 371 J3
st. Mosman 317 A5
HEYSEN
av. Ermington 310 B5
cl. Pymble 253 F1
pl. Casula 424 H2
st. Abbotsbury 333 B11
HEYSON
wy. Claymore 481 F11
HEYWARD
cl. Jamisontown 266 C2
HEYWOOD
cl. Hinchinbrk 362 K16
ct. Bella Vista 246 H3
HEZLET
st. Chiswick 343 E1
HEZLETT
rd. Kellyville 186 C11
HIBBERTIA
pl. Westleigh 220 G8
HIBBERTS
la. Freemns Rch 90 D3
HIBBLE
st. West Ryde 311 A2
HIBERNIA
pl. Harringtn Pk 478 G5
HIBERTIA
pl. Mt Annan 509 E2
HIBISCUS
av. Carlingford 249 C16
cl. Acacia Gdn 214 J14
cl. Alfords Point 429 B13
cr. Mcquarie Fd 454 D2
ct. St Clair 270 B15
pl. Cherrybrook 219 F11
st. Greystanes 305 G11
HICKETTS
av. Glebe 11 K7
HICKEY
cl. Abbotsbury 333 C11
la. Darlinghurst 13 A9
pl. Mt Annan 479 F15
HICKEYS
la. Penrith 237 A5
HICKLER
gr. Bidwill 211 C14
HICKORY
cl. Alfords Point 459 C2
mw. Wattle Grove 396 C16
pl. Acacia Gdn 214 J14
pl. Dural 219 B6
pl. Mcquarie Fd 424 G16
pl. St Clair 270 G11
st. Greystanes 306 D4
HICKS
av. Mascot 405 G6
av. S Turramrra 252 A4
pl. Kings Lngly 245 J8
HICKSON
rd. Dawes Point 1 D8
rd. Millers Pt A B4
rd. Millers Pt 1 D10
rd. Millers Pt 1 D8
rd. Sydney A B4
rd. Sydney 1 D10
rd. The Rocks B A1
rd. The Rocks 1 H8
st. Botany 405 E10
HICKSON STEPS
Dawes Point 1 G6
HIDES
st. Glenfield 424 H11
HIGGERSON
av. Engadine 518 F5
HIGGINBOTHAM
rd. Gladesville 312 G3
rd. Ryde 312 G3

HIGGINS
la. Penrith 236 K11
pl. Westleigh 220 J2
st. Condell Park 398 D1
st. Penrith 237 A11
HIGGS
la. Turramurra, off William St 222 H14
pl. Cranebrook 207 C10
st. Coogee 407 D2
st. Randwick 407 D2
HIGH
la. Millers Pt A B3
la. Moorebank 395 G7
la. Waverley, off High St 377 G8
st. Balmain 7 A10
st. Bankstown 399 B5
st. Berowra 133 E11
st. Cabramatta W 365 A8
st. Campbelltwn 511 F8
st. Canterbury 372 E16
st. Caringbah 492 G8
st. Carlton 432 F4
st. Chatswood 285 D6
st. Concord 341 J5
st. Dee Why 258 E4
st. Edgecliff 13 K13
st. Epping 281 B1
st. Gladesville 313 A3
st. Glenbrook 234 B13
st. Granville 308 D7
st. Gymea 491 D6
st. Harris Park 308 D7
st. Hornsby 221 G1
st. Hunters Hill 313 C5
st. Kensington 376 F14
st. Kogarah 433 A7
st. McGraths Hl 121 J11
st. Manly 288 J12
st. Marrickville 373 K15
st. Mascot 405 B5
st. Millers Pt A B3
st. Millers Pt 1 D10
st. Milsons Point 6 A11
st. Mt Krng-gai 163 B11
st. N Sydney 6 A11
st. N Willghby 285 F10
st. Penrith 236 D7
st. Penrith 236 H10
st. Penrith 237 A11
st. Randwick 377 A15
st. Strathfield 371 B3
st. Waverley 377 G8
st. Willoughby 285 F10
st. Willoughby 285 G15
st. Woolooware 493 H8
HIGHBRIDGE
rd. Killara 253 F13
HIGHBROOK
pl. Castle Hill 218 K7
HIGHBURY
st. Croydon 372 E2
HIGHCLAIRE
pl. Glenwood 245 H3
HIGHCLERE
av. Banksia 403 H13
av. Burwood 371 H1
av. Punchbowl 370 D16
cr. North Rocks 279 A2
pl. Castle Hill 218 H8
HIGHCLIFF
la. Earlwood 403 E3
rd. Earlwood 403 E3
HIGHERDALE
av. Miranda 492 C4
HIGHETT
pl. Glenhaven 218 A2
HIGHFIELD
cr. Strathfield 371 E4
la. Lindfield 254 A16
pl. Kellyville 186 B15
rd. Guildford 338 D9
rd. Lindfield 283 H1
rd. Quakers Hill 214 A14
HIGHGATE
cct. Kellyville 185 E6
pl. Cherrybrook 219 D13
pl. Glenwood 246 B4
rd. Lindfield 254 D15
st. Auburn 309 B14
st. Bexley 402 F13
st. Strathfield 371 D1
HIGHGROVE
ct. Cecil Hills 362 G3
HIGH HOLBORN
st. Surry Hills 20 A6
HIGHLAND
av. Bankstown 369 A15
av. Roselands 400 F7
av. Toongabbie 276 C5
av. Yagoona 369 A15
cr. Earlwood 403 C3
rd. Peakhurst 430 G1
rdg. Middle Cove 285 K8
st. Guildford 337 K2
HIGHLANDS
av. Gordon 253 G5
av. Wahroonga 222 B4
cr. Blacktown 274 B2
wy. Rouse Hill 185 E3
HIGHPOINT
dr. Blacktown 274 B8
pl. Como 460 E5
HIGHS
rd. W Pnnant Hl 219 A15
HIGH SCHOOL
dr. Winmalee 173 H7
HIGHVIEW
av. Faulconbdg 171 E14
av. Greenacre 369 J13
av. Manly Vale 287 K4
av. Neutral Bay 6 D4
av. Penrith 237 B6
av. Queenscliff 288 G2
cl. N Epping 251 C10
cr. Oyster Bay 461 B6
la. Neutral Bay 6 D4
st. Blacktown 274 C7
HIGHWORTH
av. Bexley 402 H14
HILAND
cr. Smithfield 336 A6
HILAR
av. Carlingford 279 E4
HILARY
cr. Dundas 279 K13
st. Winston Hills 276 G1
HILDA
av. Casula 394 H12
av. Scotland I 168 G4
rd. Baulkham Hl 247 A11
st. Bass Hill 367 K6
st. Blaxland 234 B5
st. Prospect 274 K12
HILDEGARD
pl. Baulkham Hl 247 B2
HILDER
rd. Balgowlah Ht 287 H12
rd. Ermington 310 B4
st. Elderslie 477 J14
wy. Claymore 481 D12
HILDERLEIGH
cl. Faulconbdg 171 B13
HILES
la. Alexandria 19 B16
st. Alexandria 19 B16
HILL
av. Hobartville 118 C9
la. Campsie 372 B14
la. Carlton 432 K5
rd. Birrong 368 J6
rd. Homebush B 340 B2
rd. Lidcombe 340 B2
rd. Lurnea 394 C10
rd. W Pnnant Hl 249 B5
st. Arncliffe 403 D7
st. Balgowlah 288 A9
st. Baulkham Hl 247 J9
st. Berowra 133 E13
st. Cabramatta 365 H7
st. Camden 477 B16
st. Campsie 372 A14
st. Carlton 432 J5
st. Coogee 377 G15
st. Dulwich Hill 373 D8
st. Fairlight 288 A9
st. Five Dock 342 K6
st. Glenbrook 234 B15
st. Hurstville 432 C6
st. Leichhardt 10 B13
st. Marrickville 373 F15
st. N Sydney K F9
st. N Sydney 5 G9
st. Picton 563 D11
st. Queenscliff 288 G2
st. Roseville 284 G4
st. Strathfield S 371 E5
st. Surry Hills 4 D15
st. Wareemba 342 K6
st. Warriewood 199 C9
st. Wentwthvle 277 A15
st. Woolooware 493 F11
HILLARD
st. Wiley Park 370 G16
HILLARY
cl. Eastlakes 406 A3
pde. Matraville 437 C2
st. Greystanes 306 D9
st. West Pymble 252 F11
HILLAS
av. Kellyville 216 G4
HILLBAR
la. Glenbrook 234 B15
HILL CLIMB
dr. Annangrove 155 H11
HILLCOT
st. Hurlstone Pk 372 J10
HILLCREST
av. Ashfield 372 J7
av. Bardwell Vy 402 H10
av. Epping 250 H14
av. Gladesville 312 K11
av. Greenacre 369 K14
av. Hurstville 431 H8
av. Hurstville Gr 431 E10
av. Mona Vale 199 H1
av. Moorebank 396 C11
av. Mt Lewis 369 J16
av. Oatley 431 E10
av. Penrith 237 B6
av. Penshurst 431 E10
av. Strathfield S 371 E6
av. Villawood 367 B3
av. Winston Hills 277 D2
dr. St Ives 224 D8
la. Tempe 374 B16
la. Emu Heights, off Hillcrest Rd 235 A2
pl. North Manly 288 C1
rd. Berowra 133 D10
rd. Emu Heights 235 A2
rd. Pennant Hills 220 G16
rd. Quakers Hill 214 A15
rd. Wedderburn 541 F15
rd. Yarramundi 145 A8
st. Homebush 341 B7
st. Punchbowl 400 D5
st. Tempe 374 C16
st. Wahroonga 222 J6
st. Wiley Park 400 D5
HILLCROSS
st. Lugarno 429 K14
HILL END
rd. Doonside 243 C13
HILLEND
pl. Wakeley 334 G14
HILLGATE
av. Castle Hill 219 B11
HILLIARD
dr. Castle Hill 218 J12
HILLIER
rd. Liverpool 395 A3
st. Concord W 341 E4
st. Edensor Pk 363 C2
st. Merrylands 307 E9
HILLIGER
rd. S Penrith 267 C2
HILLINA
wy. Mcquarie Fd 454 H4
HILLMAN
av. Rydalmere 309 J1
HILLMONT
av. Thornleigh 221 B13
HILLOAK
ct. Castle Hill 218 K6
wy. Menai 458 H13
HILLPINE
av. Kogarah 433 C9
pl. Terrey Hills 196 D4
HILLS
av. Epping 250 E16
st. Bnksmeadw 435 K1
HILLSBOROUGH
ct. Cherrybrook 219 D12
wy. Baulkham Hl 216 K16
HILLSIDE
av. Belmore 401 K4
av. St Ives Ch 224 A5
av. Vaucluse 348 C7
cct. Cranebrook 207 D8
cr. Epping 281 A3
cr. Glenbrook 234 E16
dr. Harringtn Pk 478 C3
la. Blacktown 275 B2
la. Carlingford 249 G11
pde. Mt Colah 162 B16
pl. Glen Alpine 510 G10
pl. W Pnnant Hl 249 J9
rd. Blacktown 274 B4
rd. Newport 169 J7
st. Chatswd W 284 F8
st. Roseville 284 F8
HILLSLOPE
rd. Newport 169 H7
HILL TOP
rd. Tennyson 57 G12
HILLTOP
av. Blacktown 274 A3
av. Currans Hill 480 A9
av. Marrickville 403 E1
av. Mt Pritchard 364 F13
av. Padstow Ht 429 G7
cr. Campbelltwn 511 F9
cr. Fairlight 288 A9
cr. Fairlight 288 C9
ct. Castle Hill 217 B10
rd. Avalon 139 G16
rd. Merrylands 307 C8
rd. Penrith 237 C6
st. Kingsgrove 402 A5
HILLVIEW
av. Bankstown 369 J15
av. S Penrith 266 J1
cr. Warriewood 198 F6
la. Eastwood 281 A8
la. Sans Souci 433 C14
pde. Lurnea 394 B11
pl. Glendenning 242 H4
pl. Narellan 478 H13
rd. Eastwood 281 A7
rd. Kellyville 185 F5
st. Auburn 339 A10
st. Hornsby Ht 161 H12
st. Narellan 478 H13
st. Roselands 401 D4
st. Sans Souci 433 B14
HILLY
st. Mortlake 312 A13
HILMA
st. Collaroy Plat 228 K14
HILMER
st. Frenchs Frst 256 G6
HILSDEN
st. Rooty Hill 272 B5
HILTON
av. Roselands 400 J9
av. Sydenham 374 E16
cr. Casula 394 G16
cr. Casula 424 G1
pl. Kenthurst 157 G8
rd. Cmbrdg Gdn 237 H4
rd. Springwood 202 C6
st. Greystanes 306 E9
HILTON PARK
rd. Tahmoor 565 H6
rd. Tahmoor 565 J7
HILTS
rd. Strathfield 341 F10
HILVERSUM
cr. Belrose 226 B4
HILWA
st. Villawood 367 C2
HIMALAYA
cr. Seven Hills 275 B8
HINCHEN
st. Guildford 338 A6
HINCHINBROOK
dr. Hinchinbrk 363 A15
HINCKS
st. Kingsford 406 J4
HIND
pl. Chipping Ntn 396 C4
HINDEMITH
av. Emerton 240 J6
HINDER
cl. Abbotsbury 333 B11
HINDLE
tce. Bella Vista 246 F4
HINDMARSH
rd. Liverpool 365 A15
st. Cranebrook 207 D8
HINDSON
pl. Belrose 226
HINEMOA
av. Normanhurst 221
st. Panania 428
HINES
pl. Mt Annan 509
HINGERTY
pl. S Penrith 266
HINKLER
av. Caringbah 492
av. Condell Park 398
av. Ryde 281
av. S Turramrra 251
av. Warwck Frm 365
cr. Lane Cove W 283
ct. Drummoyne 343
pl. Doonside 273
pwy. Warwck Frm, off Hinkler Av 365
st. Btn-le-Sds 433
st. Ermington 280
st. Greenwich 314
st. Maroubra 406
st. Smithfield 335
HINTON
cl. St Johns Pk 364
gln. N St Marys 239
la. N St Marys, off Hinton Gln 239
pl. Chipping Ntn 366
HINXMAN
rd. Castlereagh 176
HIPWOOD
st. Milsons Point 6
st. N Sydney 6
HIRST
pl. Fairfield W 335
st. Arncliffe 403
st. Bardwell Vy 403
HISHION
pl. Georges Hall 367
HISPANO
pl. Ingleburn 453
HITTER
av. Bass Hill 368
av. Casula 394
av. Mt Pritchard 364
HIXSON
st. Bankstown 399
HOAD
pl. Greystanes 306
pl. Menai 458
pl. Shalvey 211
HOADLEY
pl. Arndell Park 273
HOBART
av. Campbelltwn 512
av. E Lindfield 254
pl. Illawong 459
pl. Wakeley 334
st. Oxley Park 240
st. Richmond 119
st. Riverstone 153
st. Riverstone 182
st. St Marys 240
HOBBITS
gln. Wrrngtn Dns 237
HOBBS
st. Bligh Park 150
st. Kingsgrove 401
st. Lewisham 15
HOBBY
cl. S Penrith 266
la. S Penrith, off Hobby Cl 266
HOBLER
av. West Hoxton 392
HOBSON
pl. Plumpton 242
HOCKING
av. Earlwood 403
la. Earlwood, off Hocking Av 403
pl. Erskine Park 300
HOCKLEY
rd. Eastwood 280
HODDLE
av. Bradbury 511
av. Campbelltwn 511
cr. Davidson 255
pl. West Hoxton 392

Paddington 13 C13
DGE
Hurstville 431 J1
DGES
Currans Hill 479 G11
Kings Lngly 245 A3
DGKINSON
Panania 428 E1
DGSON
Cremorne 316 F12
Cremorne Pt 316 F12
Wedderburn 540 C10
Baulkham Hl 247 D13
Glenbrook 264 C4
Randwick 377 B11
DKIN
Ingleburn 453 A11
FF
Mt Pritchard 364 K11
FFMAN
Newtown 17 E12
Oakhurst 242 C4
FFMANN
y.Springwood 201 D1
FFMANS
Balmain 7 J9
GAN
Bass Hill 367 F7
Green Valley 362 K8
Sydenham 374 E14
Panania 428 D2
Kingswood 267 E2
Mt Annan 479 E15
Quakers Hill 214 C12
Balgowlah Ht 287 K12
GANS
Bargo 567 B3
Bargo 567 D1
GARTH
Dee Why 258 F5
GBEN
Kogarah 433 C5
GUE
Mt Annan 509 D1
LBEACH
Tempe 404 B4
LBECHE
Arndell Park 273 E8
LBORN
Dee Why 258 G3
Ambarvale 510 G12
LBOROW
Croydon 372 D5
Croydon Pk 372 D5
LBORROW
Hobartville 118 B7
LBROOK
Kirribilli 2 F1
Stanhpe Gdn 215 D12
Bossley Park 333 G10
LBURN
Kings Lngly 245 G8
LCROFT
Cherrybrook 219 K7
LDEN
Epping 250 G13
Ashbury 372 H10
Ashfield 372 J6
Canterbury 372 H10
Chester Hill 337 K11
Maroubra 406 H11
Northwood 314 G7
Redfern 19 B6
Toongabbie 276 G8
LDIN
Bonnyrigg 364 A7
LDSWORTH
Rcuttrs Bay 13 C6
St Leonards 315 C7
Mt Annan 479 A12
Narellan Vale 479 A12
Newtown 18 C10
Paddington 4 G14
Neutral Bay 6 C6
Merrylands 307 C14
Neutral Bay 6 B6
Newtown 18 C10
Woollahra 21 K1
LFORD
Gordon 253 D8
Cabramatta W 365 B6

HOLKER
st. Homebush B 309 K9
st. Silverwater 309 K9
HOLKER BUSWAY
Homebush B 310 F12
HOLKHAM
av. Randwick 376 K11
HOLLAND
av. Rockdale 403 B12
cr. Casula 394 J14
cr. Frenchs Frst 256 E5
ct. Glenmore Pk 266 F15
pl. Lakemba 370 J14
pl. Telopea 279 J11
rd. Bellevue Hill 14 J16
rd. Glenhaven 187 H13
st. Birrong 369 B5
st. Chatswood 285 B11
st. Cronulla 493 H12
st. N Epping 251 E10
st. St Peters 374 K14
st. Springwood 202 A2
HOLLANDS
av. Marrickville 373 G12
HOLLEY
la. Beverly Hills 430 J3
rd. Beverly Hills 430 J2
HOLLIDAY
av. Berowra 133 C11
av. Berowra Ht 133 C11
la. Auburn 339 E2
HOLLIER
pl. Baulkham Hl 247 D10
rd. Picton 561 C4
st. Cmbrdg Pk 238 A6
HOLLINGS
cr. Heathcote 518 G9
pl. Plumpton 241 G9
HOLLINGSHED
la. Mascot, off Johnson St 405 E6
st. Mascot 405 E6
HOLLINSWORTH
rd. Marsden Pk 211 J11
HOLLIS
av. Denistone E 281 E8
la. Newtown 18 B9
st. Wentwthvle 277 B9
st. Wentwthvle 277 C9
HOLLISTER
pl. Carlingford 249 G14
HOLLOWAY
la. Pagewood, off Holloway St 406 B10
pl. Curl Curl 258 F12
st. Pagewood 405 K10
HOLLOWFORTH
av. Neutral Bay 6 H10
HOLLOWS
pl. Bonnyrigg 363 H8
HOLLY
av. Chipping Ntn 396 D5
av. Ryde 312 G3
rd. Cherrybrook 219 H12
st. Caringbah 493 A11
st. Castle Cove 285 F3
HOLLYDALE
pl. Prospect 275 B10
HOLLYDENE
cr. Edensor Pk 333 D16
HOLLYLEA
rd. Leumeah 481 K13
HOLLYWOOD
av. Bondi Jctn 22 K8
cr. Willoughby 285 F11
dr. Lansvale 366 G8
rd. Newport 169 J12
st. Merrylands 307 A8
st. Monterey 433 G10
st. S Wntwthvle 307 A8
HOLMAN
pl. St Helens Park 541 B3
st. Canley Ht 335 A16
HOLMEGATE
cr. Cranebrook 207 G11
HOLMES
av. Ashbury 372 E8
av. Clontarf 287 E14
av. Oatlands 279 D12
av. Sefton 338 F15
cr. Richmond 119 K5
rd. Minto 482 C2

st. Colyton 270 D6
st. Kingsford 407 A6
st. Lalor Park 245 G13
st. Turramurra 222 F15
HOLMESDALE
st. Marrickville 374 A10
HOLMLEA
pl. Engadine 488 F11
HOLMWOOD
av. Strathfield S 371 C5
la. Newtown, off King La 374 J10
st. Newtown 374 H9
HOLROYD
rd. Merrylands 307 B11
HOLST
cl. Bonnyrigg Ht 363 E7
HOLSTEIN
cl. Emu Heights 235 B3
HOLSTON
st. Casula 395 A12
HOLT
av. Cremorne 316 G8
av. Mosman 316 G8
av. N Wahrnga 192 G16
cr. Marrickville 403 H1
ct. Penrith 237 C6
pl. Dundas Vy 280 B11
rd. Sylvania 461 J11
rd. Sylvania 462 A11
rd. Taren Point 462 G12
st. Ashcroft 364 F16
st. Doonside 243 C8
st. Double Bay 13 K10
st. McMahons Pt 5 D11
st. Newtown 17 E15
st. Newtown 17 F15
st. North Ryde 282 F6
st. Stanmore 16 E11
st. Surry Hills F B16
st. Surry Hills 19 J1
HOLTERMAN
pl. Cartwright 393 J6
HOLTERMANN
st. Crows Nest 315 G6
HOLTS POINT
pl. Sylvania Wtr 462 F10
HOLWAY
st. Eastwood 280 H7
HOLWOOD
av. Ashfield 372 K8
HOLYWOOD
wy. Glenmore Pk 266 H8
HOMANN
av. Leumeah 512 A1
HOMEBUSH
rd. Homebush 341 D13
rd. Strathfield 341 D16
rd. Strathfield S 371 C5
st. St Johns Pk 364 H4
HOMEBUSH BAY
dr. Concord W 311 C16
dr. Homebush 341 A3
dr. Homebush B 340 J5
dr. Rhodes 311 C16
HOMEDALE
av. Bexley North 402 E12
av. Concord 341 G6
cr. Connells Pt 431 J12
rd. Bankstown 399 G7
st. Springwood 201 H4
HOMELANDS
av. Carlingford 279 G7
HOMELEA
av. Panania 397 K15
HOMEPRIDE
av. Warwck Frm 365 D14
HOMER
la. Earlwood 402 J3
pl. Caringbah 493 B16
pl. Wetherill Pk 335 A5
st. Earlwood 402 H4
st. Kingsgrove 401 K7
st. Winston Hills 277 E1
HOMESTEAD
av. Chipping Ntn 366 G12
av. Collaroy 229 B13
cct. Mcquarie Lk 423 G14
ct. Bella Vista 246 G2
rd. Bonnyrigg Ht 363 H5
rd. Orchard Hills 267 B9

HOMEWOOD
av. Hornsby 221 E6
HONDA
rd. Neutral Bay 6 J7
HONEMAN
cl. Huntingwd 274 B12
HONEYCUP
cl. Westleigh 220 G8
HONEYEATER
cr. Blaxland 233 E11
la. St Clair, off Honeyeater Pl 270 K13
pl. Erskine Park 270 K13
pl. Hinchinbrk 363 E15
pl. Ingleburn 453 F9
pl. Woronora Ht 489 F2
tce. Glenwood 215 F14
HONEYSUCKLE
av. Glenmore Pk 265 G9
pl. Kellyville 216 E1
pl. Leonay 234 K14
st. Jannali 460 J9
HONEYTREE
pl. Baulkham Hl 246 J3
HONITON
av.e, Carlingford 279 K6
av.w, Carlingford 279 J6
HONOR
st. Ermington 310 D4
HONOUR
av. Fairfield 336 G14
HOOD
av. Earlwood 402 E4
av. Rodd Point 9 A1
cl. Wetherill Pk 334 H6
la. Old Tngabbie 277 F8
st. Miranda 491 K7
st. Old Tngabbie 277 F8
st. Yagoona 368 E10
HOOK
cl. Hinchinbrk 363 A16
pl. Wakeley 334 H12
HOOP
pl. Spring Farm 508 E1
HOOPER
la. Randwick 377 E10
st. Clovelly 377 E9
st. Randwick 377 E9
HOOVER
pl. Bonnet Bay 460 E11
pl. Cromer 228 D14
HOP-BUSH
pl. Mt Annan 509 F3
HOPE
av. North Manly 258 A15
cr. Bossley Park 334 C6
pl. McGraths Hl 122 A12
st. Blaxland 233 F7
st. Ermington 310 F3
st. Harringtn Pk 478 F6
st. Penrith 237 B12
st. Pymble 253 E1
st. Regents Pk 369 B3
st. Rosehill 308 J6
st. Seaforth 287 E9
st. Seven Hills 245 F15
st. Strathfield S 371 A8
st. Warwck Frm 365 K16
HOPE FARM
rd. Cattai 63 K12
HOPETOUN
av. Chatswood 284 J12
av. Denistone E 281 F10
av. Mosman 317 D2
av. Vaucluse 348 E4
av. Watsons Bay 318 F16
la. Camperdwn 17 E7
la. Paddington 13 E16
mw. Vaucluse 348 D3
st. Camperdwn 17 E7
st. Hurlstone Pk 373 A13
st. Paddington 13 E16
st. Petersham 16 B10
HOPEWELL
la. Paddington 4 H15
st. Paddington 4 H15
HOPKINS
pl. Austral 391 C8
pl. Forestville 255 G9
pl. N Turramrra 193 E14
st. Wentwthvle 277 C12
st. Wetherill Pk 334 G4

HOPMAN
av. Menai 458 G7
cr. Shalvey 210 J14
st. Greystanes 306 A10
HOPPING
rd. Ingleburn 453 A11
HOPPYS
la. Kingsgrove 401 H11
HOPSON
av. Camden S 507 C13
st. Douglas Park 568 G5
HORACE
st. St Ives 254 B1
st. Waverton 315 D12
HORAN
rd. Glenorie 126 H3
HORANS
la. Grose Vale 84 F6
HORATIO
pl. Plumpton 241 H9
st. Rsemeadow 540 J6
HORBLING
av. Georges Hall 368 C15
HORBURY
la. Newtown 17 D12
st. Sans Souci 433 E16
HORDERN
av. Petersham 16 A7
av. Putney 311 K7
la. Mosman 317 B5
pde. Croydon 372 F1
pl. Camperdwn 17 B5
pl. Mosman 317 A5
st. Newtown 17 H8
HORDERNS
la. Bundeena 523 H9
pl. Potts Point 4 H4
HORIZON
pl. Cranebrook 206 J8
HORIZONS
pl. Kellyville 216 B3
HORLER
av. Vaucluse 348 E2
HORN
cl. Abbotsbury 333 B14
HORNBY
av. Sutherland 460 E15
st. Wilton 568 K15
HORNE
cl. Bargo 567 A4
pl. Blackett 241 B2
HORNER
av. Mascot 405 G5
HORNET
pl. Raby 451 H16
st. Greenfld Pk 334 B15
HORNING
pde. Manly Vale 287 J4
st. Kurnell 465 H10
HORNINGSEA PARK
dr. Horngsea Pk 392 E14
dr. Horngsea Pk 392 F16
HORNS
av. Gymea Bay 491 D12
HORNSBY
st. Hornsby 221 H3
HORNSEY
cl. Bonnyrigg Ht 363 B6
rd. Homebush W 340 G10
st. Burwood 341 J14
st. Rozelle 11 B2
HORNSEYWOOD
av. Penrith 236 K14
HORSELL
av. Arncliffe 403 D8
HORSESHOE
cct. St Clair 299 H2
HORSFALL
st. Ermington 280 B16
HORSHAM
pl. Chipping Ntn 366 H15
HORSLEY
av. N Willghby 285 E10
rd. Horsley Pk 302 E16
rd. Milperra 398 A11
rd. Panania 398 A11
rd. Panania 398 A15
rd. Revesby 398 A15
HORSNELL
la. Mosman, off Civic La 317 A6

HORST
pl. Mona Vale..........199 A2
HORTICULTURE
dr. Richmond..........118 F11
HORTON
la. Bass Hill..........368 D13
la. Yagoona..........368 D13
st. Bass Hill..........368 E13
st. Marrickville..........374 A9
st. Mt Pritchard..........364 A11
st. Yagoona..........368 E13
HORWOOD
av. Baulkham Hl..........247 J14
av. Killara..........283 D2
pl. Kings Lngly..........245 B3
pl. Parramatta..........308 C3
HOSIER
pl. Bligh Park..........150 C6
HOSKING
av. West Hoxton..........392 C8
cr. Glenfield..........424 D10
pl. Sydney..........D B1
st. Balmain East..........8 G10
st. Cranebrook..........207 C11
wy. Bonnyrigg..........364 C5
HOSKINS
av. Bankstown..........399 D6
HOSPITAL
la. Marrickville, off Stanley St..........373 J11
la. Crows Nest, off Willoughby La..........315 F6
rd. Concord W..........311 E13
rd. Randwick..........377 A15
rd. Sydney..........D H5
HOTHAM
pde. Artarmon..........314 H2
rd. Gymea..........491 C5
rd. Kirrawee..........461 D16
st. Chatswd W..........284 H7
HOTSON
av. Matraville..........436 J8
HOTSPUR
cl. Rsemeadow..........540 H8
HOUGH
st. Bondi Jctn..........22 D9
st. Colyton..........270 J9
HOUISON
pl. Parramatta, off Horwood Pl..........308 C3
st. Westmead..........307 G2
HOURGLASS
gln. St Clair..........270 D14
HOURIGAN
la. Potts Point..........4 H6
HOUSMAN
av. Kellyville..........215 J5
st. Wetherill Pk..........334 E6
HOUSTON
la. Kensington..........376 F16
la. Kingsford..........406 F1
pl. Mt Pritchard..........364 E8
rd. Kensington..........376 F16
rd. Kingsford..........406 F1
rd. Yagoona..........369 A8
st. Gymea..........491 G5
HOUTMAN
av. Willmot..........210 D12
HOVEA
ct. Voyager Pt..........427 C5
pl. Glenmore Pk..........265 J9
pl. Kirrawee..........491 A10
pl. Mcquarie Fd..........454 D4
wy. Mt Annan..........509 E3
HOVELL
rd. Ingleburn..........422 J14
rd. Smithfield..........305 F13
st. Narellan..........478 F12
HOVEY
av. St Ives..........254 D1
HOWARD
av. Dee Why..........258 H6
av. Northmead..........277 K10
cl. Green Valley..........363 A8
la. Lindfield..........254 G16
la. Randwick, off Howard St..........407 B1
pl. Castle Hill..........248 D4
pl. Hebersham..........241 F7
pl. Hunters Hill..........313 E11
pl. N Epping..........251 G11
pl. Randwick..........407 D1
rd. Minto Ht..........483 K6
rd. Padstow..........399 C16
st. Canterbury..........372 D15
st. Greystanes..........306 E5
st. Lansvale..........366 K11
st. Lindfield..........254 G16
st. Randwick..........407 B1
st. Strathfield..........340 J13
st. Telopea..........279 J7
st. Ultimo..........12 K16
HOWARTH
rd. Lane Cove W..........284 G16
HOWE
av. Horngsea Pk..........392 F16
pl. Canley Ht..........365 A4
pl. Kings Lngly..........245 H6
st. Campbelltwn..........511 F4
st. Malabar..........437 F5
st. Westmead..........307 G4
HOWELL
av. Lane Cove..........313 K3
av. Matraville..........406 K16
cl. Newport..........169 J8
cr. S Windsor..........150 J1
pl. Lane Cove..........314 A2
rd. Londonderry..........149 B13
HOWES
cl. Westleigh..........220 J1
rd. E Kurrajong..........57 F3
st. Richmond..........118 F6
HOWIE
av. Woolooware..........493 J10
HOWITT
pl. Bonnyrigg..........364 B8
HOWLETT
cl. Chipping Ntn..........396 D4
HOWLEY
st. Five Dock..........343 C9
HOWSE
cr. Cromer..........227 J14
HOWSON
av. Turramurra..........252 A2
HOXTON PARK
rd. Cartwright..........393 G6
rd. Hinchinbrk..........393 A6
rd. Hoxton Park..........393 A6
rd. Liverpool..........395 A6
rd. Lurnea..........394 F5
HOYA
pl. Cherrybrook..........220 A7
HOYLE
av. Castle Hill..........217 D14
dr. Dean Park..........242 G1
pl. Greenfld Pk..........334 A14
pl. S Penrith..........267 A6
HOYS
rd. Lansvale..........366 E9
HUBER
av. Cabramatta..........365 G6
HUBERT
st. Condell Park..........398 H6
st. Fairfield..........335 K14
st. Harbord..........258 E14
st. Leichhardt..........9 G10
st. Lilyfield..........9 G7
HUCKSTEPP
swy. Liverpool..........395 D4
swy. Liverpool, off Northumberland St..........395 D3
HUDDART
av. Normanhurst..........221 F10
la. Randwick..........376 K9
HUDDLESTON
st. Colyton..........270 G7
HUDSON
av. Castle Hill..........217 A14
av. Willoughby..........285 F13
cl. S Turramrra..........252 D5
pde. Avalon..........139 G16
pde. Birrong..........369 A6
pde. Clareville..........169 D2
pl. Ingleburn..........453 J8
pl. Mulgrave..........151 H1
rd. Frenchs Frst..........257 B6
st. Annandale..........10 J10
st. Homebush..........341 A8
st. Hurstville..........432 A3
st. Lewisham..........15 A10
st. Redfern..........19 A5
st. Seven Hills..........275 J6
st. S Granville..........338 F1
st. Tempe..........374 C16
st. Wentwthvle..........307 C2
wy. Currans Hill..........479 G11
HUEN
pl. Tahmoor..........565 G9
HUETT
pl. Berowra..........133 G10
HUGH
av. Dulwich Hill..........373 A9
av. Peakhurst..........430 E2
pl. Greystanes..........306 E9
pl. Kings Lngly..........245 F8
st. Ashfield..........372 H4
st. Belmore..........371 A12
HUGHES
av. Castle Hill..........217 G14
av. Ermington..........310 F1
av. Hobartville..........118 B7
av. Maroubra..........407 D16
av. Mascot..........405 D2
av. Penrith..........237 C7
la. Potts Point..........4 J5
pl. Chester Hill..........368 A2
pl. E Lindfield..........255 A12
pl. Potts Point..........4 J5
rd. Glenorie..........129 B2
st. Cabramatta..........365 E6
st. Earlwood..........402 H6
st. Kings Lngly..........246 B10
st. Leumeah..........481 J15
st. Londonderry..........148 B9
st. Petersham..........16 C5
st. Potts Point..........4 J5
st. West Ryde..........311 D1
st. Woolooware..........493 E9
HUGHES STEPS
Mosman..........286 K15
Mosman..........287 A15
HUGO
pl. Quakers Hill..........214 F13
st. Redfern..........19 A6
HUIE
st. Cabramatta..........365 E10
HULL
av. Lurnea..........394 E9
pl. Moorebank..........395 H4
pl. Seven Hills..........275 C5
rd. Beecroft..........250 B1
rd. W Pnnant Hl..........220 A15
HULLICK
la. East Hills..........427 G5
HULLS
rd. Leppington..........450 E1
HUMBER
pl. Ingleburn..........453 J8
HUMBERSTONE
av. Gymea..........491 G1
HUME
av. Castle Hill..........218 A16
av. Ermington..........280 B16
av. St Ives..........224 E10
cr. Wrrngtn Cty..........238 G7
dr. West Hoxton..........392 A12
hwy. Ashfield..........372 E2
hwy. Bankstown..........369 C12
hwy. Bargo..........567 G16
hwy. Bass Hill..........368 B9
hwy. Blairmount..........481 B14
hwy. Burwood Ht..........371 C5
hwy. Cabramatta..........366 B10
hwy. Campbelltwn..........481 B15
hwy. Canley Vale..........366 B10
hwy. Carramar..........366 B10
hwy. Casula..........424 B3
hwy. Claymore..........481 B15
hwy. Croydon..........372 E2
hwy. Denham Ct..........422 K16
hwy. Douglas Park..........568 B15
hwy. Eagle Vale..........481 B15
hwy. Enfield..........371 D5
hwy. Gilead..........509 H16
hwy. Glen Alpine..........510 A8
hwy. Glenfield..........423 B15
hwy. Greenacre..........369 C12
hwy. Greenacre..........370 B6
hwy. Ingleburn..........423 B15
hwy. Lansdowne..........367 D5
hwy. Lansvale..........366 B10
hwy. Liverpool..........395 A9
hwy. Menangle..........539 B16
hwy. Menangle Pk..........509 H16
hwy. Mt Annan..........510 A8
hwy. Raby..........481 B15
hwy. St Andrews..........481 B15
hwy. Strathfield S..........371 D5
hwy. Summer Hill..........373 A3
hwy. Varroville..........451 J15
hwy. Villawood..........367 E5
hwy. Warwck Frm..........365 F16
hwy. Woodbine..........481 B15
hwy. Yagoona..........369 C12
hwy. Yanderra..........567 G16
la. Crows Nest..........315 F6
pl. Appin..........569 F9
pl. Frenchs Frst..........256 C1
pl. Mt Colah..........162 D12
rd. Cronulla..........493 K7
rd. Ingleburn..........422 J14
rd. Lapstone..........264 H3
rd. Smithfield..........305 F13
st. Campbelltwn..........511 J7
st. Chifley..........437 B3
st. Crows Nest..........315 F6
st. Narellan..........478 F11
st. Wollstncraft..........315 E7
HUMPHREY
pl. Milsons Point..........6 A15
st. Lidcombe..........339 F10
st. Rosebery..........405 H3
HUMPHREYS
av. Casula..........394 H12
wy. Claymore..........481 E12
HUMPHRIES
la. Hurstville, off Crofts Av..........432 A6
la. Blacktown, off Sunnyholt Rd..........244 H15
rd. Bonnyrigg..........364 E6
rd. Mt Pritchard..........364 D9
rd. St Johns Pk..........364 H3
rd. Wakeley..........335 A15
HUNGERFORD
dr. Glenwood..........245 F1
HUNT
av. Dural..........189 E10
la. Lakemba..........401 D3
pl. Wrrngtn Cty..........238 G8
st. Croydon..........342 G15
st. Enfield..........371 J4
st. Glenbrook..........263 K1
st. Guildford W..........336 H4
st. N Parramatta..........278 B10
st. Schofields..........183 C15
st. Surry Hills..........F D7
st. Surry Hills..........3 K12
HUNTER
av. Lurnea..........394 B13
av. Matraville..........436 J2
av. St Ives..........254 C1
cr. N Sydney..........K B12
cr. N Sydney..........5 E10
la. Greenacre..........370 E6
la. Hornsby..........191 H16
la. Hornsby..........221 H1
la. Penshurst..........431 D6
la. Woolwich, off Gale St..........314 F13
la. Mosman, off Hunter Rd..........317 D5
pl. Castle Hill..........218 C10
rd. Mosman..........317 D6
st. Abbotsford..........342 H1
st. Auburn..........309 E15
st. Blacktown..........273 H5
st. Camden S..........507 B9
st. Campbelltwn..........511 K9
st. Condell Park..........398 J4
st. Dover Ht..........348 G9
st. Emu Plains..........235 G12
st. Fairfield..........336 C12
st. Heathcote..........518 G10
st. Hornsby..........221 H1
st. Kirrawee..........491 A8
st. Lewisham..........15 D10
st. McGraths Hl..........121 K14
st. N Balgowlah..........287 D6
st. Parramatta..........308 A3
st. Penshurst..........431 D6
st. Riverstone..........182 K9
st. Riverwood..........400 A14
st. St Clair..........269 K9
st. Strathfield..........371 D2
st. Sydney..........A J15
st. Sydney..........1 H16
st. Tahmoor..........565 H11
st. Warriewood..........199 D10
st. Waterloo..........19 H15
st. Woolwich..........314 F13
st.n. Mona Vale..........199 D10
st.s. Warriewood..........199 D11
wy. Faulconbdg..........171 E14
HUNTERFORD
cr. Oatlands..........279
HUNTINGDALE
av. Lansvale..........366
av. Miranda..........461
av. Narwee..........400
cir. Castle Hill..........218
dr. Denham Ct..........422
dr. Glenmore Pk..........266
wy. Thornleigh..........220
HUNTINGDON
pde. Cmbrdg Gdn..........237
pl. Berowra..........133
HUNTINGTON
st. Crows Nest..........315
HUNTINGWOOD
dr. Huntingwd..........273
HUNTLEY
dr. Blacktown..........274
pl. Cartwright..........394
st. Alexandria..........375
HUNTLEY GRANGE
rd. Springwood..........172
HUNTLEYS POINT
rd. Huntleys Pt..........313
HUNTS
av. Eastwood..........281
la. Epping, off Bridge St..........251
HUNTSMORE
rd. Minto..........482
HUON
cr. Holsworthy..........426
pl. Bella Vista..........246
pl. Glenfield..........424
pl. Illawong..........459
st. Cabramatta..........365
st. N Wahrnga..........223
HURDIS
av. Frenchs Frst..........256
HURKETT
pl. Bossley Park..........333
HURLEY
cr. Matraville..........437
st. Campbelltwn..........511
st. Toongabbie..........276
HURLSTONE
av. Glenfield..........424
av. Hurlstone Pk..........372
av. Summer Hill..........373
HURNDELL
la. Panania..........428
HURON
pl. Jamisontown..........266
pl. Seven Hills..........275
HURRICANE
dr. Raby..........481
HURST
pl. Glenorie..........127
HURSTVILLE
bvd. Hurstville..........431
rd. Hurstville..........431
rd. Hurstville Gr..........431
rd. Oatley..........431
st. St Johns Pk..........364
HUSKISSON
st. Gymea Bay..........491
st. Prestons..........393
HUSKY
la. East Hills..........427
HUSSELBEE
st. Blaxland..........233
HUSTON
pde. N Curl Curl..........259
HUTCH
wy. Minto..........482
HUTCHENS
av. Mt Pritchard..........364
HUTCHESON
st. Rozelle..........10
HUTCHINS
cr. Kings Lngly..........246
HUTCHINSON
pl. Surry Hills..........20
st. Annandale..........11
st. Auburn..........309
st. Bardwell Pk..........402
st. Granville..........308
st. St Peters..........374
st. Surry Hills..........4
wk. Zetland..........376

JTHNANCE
. Camden S 506 K15
JTTON
. Canterbury 372 H14
. Hurlstone Pk 372 H14
JXLEY
. Winston Hills 277 G4
. Colyton 270 E6
. Wetherill Pk 334 F5
. West Ryde 311 A1
JXTABLE
. Lane Cove W 284 G14
YACINTH
. Mcquarie Fd 454 E5
. Asquith 191 J10
. Greystanes 305 K12
YALIN
. Eagle Vale 481 F7
YAM
. Balmain 7 G13
YATT
. Rouse Hill 185 E4
YATTS
. Oakhurst 241 K4
. Plumpton 241 J10
YDE
. Glenhaven 217 K1
. Killarney Ht 286 D2
. Illawong 459 F3
YDE BRAE
. Strathfield 341 A12
YDE PARK
. Wattle Grove 426 A3
. Berala 339 D13
YDRA
. Erskine Park 300 G1
YDRAE
. Revesby 428 K4
YDRANGEA
. Acacia Gdn 214 J15
. Mcquarie Fd 454 B5
YDRUS
. Cranebrook 207 E4
YLAND
. W Pnnant Hl 249 G8
. Minchinbury 271 H8
. Greystanes 305 B12
YMEN
. Peakhurst 429 J3
YNDES
. Belrose 225 E16
YNDMAN
de. Woolooware 493 E11
YNDS
. Box Hill 154 C14
YNES
. Elderslie 507 F3
. Lansdowne 367 B8
YTHE
. Glen Alpine 510 B13
. Drummoyne 313 H16
. Mount Druitt 241 D13
YTON
. Cranebrook 207 F13

I

GO
. Rsemeadow 540 G6
N
. Canley Vale 366 B5
. N Curl Curl 259 C10
. Chester Hill 337 K11
. *N Curl Curl, off Ian Av 259 C10*
Rose Bay, off Ian St 348 B9
de. Concord 342 B4
. Casula 424 D3
. Glossodia 59 G5
. Greystanes 306 E9
. Kingsford 407 A6
. Lalor Park 245 F14
. North Ryde 283 B11
. Rose Bay 348 B10
NDO
y. Currans Hill 479 H11
NDRA
. Concord W 311 E15

IAN SMITH
dr. Milperra 397 J10
IBBOTSON
st. Tahmoor 565 G10
IBERIA
st. Padstow 399 E15
IBEX
st. Earlwood 402 H5
IBIS
pl. Bella Vista 246 F1
pl. Grays Point 491 F15
pl. Hinchinbrk 393 B1
pl. Ingleburn 453 H7
pl. St Clair 270 E13
rd. Lalor Park 245 J10
wy. Mt Annan 479 C14
IBSEN
pl. Wetherill Pk 335 A4
ICARUS
pl. Quakers Hill 214 D16
ICASIA
la. Woollahra 377 F3
ICE
st. Darlinghurst 4 H13
ICETON
st. Burwood 341 J16
IDA
av. Lurnea 394 E10
av. Mosman 287 A16
cl. Edensor Pk 333 F16
pl. Blacktown 244 C15
pl. Cecil Hills 362 G5
st. Hornsby 191 G9
st. Hurlstone Pk 372 J11
st. Putney 312 C7
st. Sandringham 463 B3
st. Sans Souci 463 B3
IDAHO
pl. Riverwood 399 K12
IDALINE
st. Collaroy Plat 228 K12
IDRIESS
cr. Blackett 241 D4
pl. Casula 424 D3
pl. Edensor Pk 363 K2
IGNATIUS
av. N Richmond 87 C14
rd. Lindfield 283 K2
IKARA
av. Kellyville 216 H8
cr. Moorebank 396 F8
pl. Peakhurst 430 E1
pl. St Ives 224 B14
IKIN
st. Jamisontown 266 C4
ILFORD
av. Ashfield 342 K15
pl. Abbotsbury 333 A15
rd. Frenchs Frst 256 K3
ILFRACOMBE
av. Burwood 341 J12
ILIFFE
st. Bexley 432 C1
ILIKAI
pl. Dee Why 258 G2
ILKA
st. Lilyfield 10 F11
ILKINIA
pl. Engadine 489 A12
ILLABO
st. Quakers Hill 244 A1
ILLALONG
av. N Balgowlah 287 D4
st. Granville 308 B12
ILLARANGI
st. Carlingford 280 C7
ILLAROO
pl. Mona Vale 199 B3
rd. Hoxton Park 393 C7
rd. Prestons 393 C9
st. Bangor 459 H12
ILLAWARRA
cl. Woodcroft 243 E11
dr. St Clair 300 C1
la. Allawah 432 F9
la. Marrickville, off Illawarra St 373 K13
pde. Beverly Hills 401 E14
rd. Earlwood 403 E2
rd. Holsworthy 426 G11
rd. Holsworthy 426 H6
rd. Leumeah 482 F14

rd. Marrickville 374 A12
st. Allawah 432 E8
st. Appin 569 H14
st. Mosman 316 J12
ILLAWONG
av. Caringbah 492 G14
av. Penrith 237 C5
av. Riverview 314 B5
av. Tamarama 378 A6
cr. Greenacre 370 C9
dr. N Parramatta 278 E9
rd. Leumeah 482 B14
st. Lugarno 430 A15
ILLEROY
av. Killara 254 B8
ILLILIWA
la. Cremorne 316 F6
st. Cremorne 316 E6
ILLINGA
pl. Lugarno 430 B16
ILLINGWORTH
rd. Yellow Rock 204 H2
ILLINOIS
rd. Five Dock 343 B12
ILLOCA
pl. Toongabbie 276 G9
ILLOURA
av. Wahroonga 222 E7
la. Wahroonga 222 E7
pl. Doonside 243 B14
pl. Nelson 155 F8
ILLUTA
pl. Engadine 488 C13
ILLYARIE
pl. Castle Hill 218 G15
ILMA
av. Kangaroo Pt 461 H4
cl. McGraths Hl 121 K10
st. Condell Park 398 G7
st. Marsfield 281 H1
ILSA
pl. Hebersham 241 F10
ILUKA
av. Elanora Ht 198 C15
av. Manly 288 F4
cl. Wakeley 334 H16
pl. Cronulla 523 K3
pl. Hebersham 241 F10
pl. St Ives 224 E16
pl. S Coogee 407 F4
rd. Mosman 317 D13
rd. Palm Beach 139 H2
st. Revesby 398 E15
st. Riverwood 400 E13
st. Rose Bay 347 J11
ILUMBA
pl. Bangor 459 H13
ILYA
av. Bayview 168 G11
IMBARA
pl. Newport 169 E10
IMBER
pl. Kings Lngly 245 K7
IMHOFF
pl. Kenthurst 156 H9
IMITA
cl. Mt Annan 479 C11
IMLAY
av. Carlingford 249 D14
pl. Barden Rdg 488 G2
IMMARNA
av. Lilli Pilli 522 F3
pl. Oatlands 279 C8
pl. Penshurst 431 D3
pl.w, Penshurst 431 C3
IMPALA
av. Werrington 238 E11
IMPERIAL
arc. Sydney 3 H3
av. Bondi 378 A5
av. Emu Plains 235 H10
av. Gladesville 313 B3
la. Emu Plains, off Imperial Av 235 J9
pl. Mosman 317 G11
IMPLEXA
ct. Wattle Grove 426 B2
IMUNGA
pl. Bradbury 511 G15
INALA
av. Kyle Bay 432 A15
pl. Carlingford 280 E7

pl. N Narrabeen 198 G12
INALLS
la. Richmond 117 H3
INCA
cl. Greenfld Pk 333 K15
INCH
pl. Minto 452 K16
INDAAL
pl. St Andrews 481 K6
INDERI
pl. Grays Point 491 E15
INDI
st. Heckenberg 363 K13
INDIANA
av. Belfield 371 E11
pl. Belfield 371 E11
INDIGO
ct. Voyager Pt 427 D5
wy. Blacktown 274 F11
INDRA
pl. Baulkham Hl 248 B9
INDURA
rd. N Narrabeen 198 G12
INDUS
pl. Kearns 481 B1
st. Erskine Park 301 B2
INDUSTRY
rd. Mulgrave 151 K1
rd. Vineyard 152 B3
st. Regents Pk 339 A16
INDY
pl. Cranebrook 207 F8
INELGAH
rd. Como 460 G6
INFANTRY
pde. Holsworthy 426 E3
INGA
pl. Quakers Hill 214 E9
INGAL
wy. Cabramatta, off John St 365 J7
INGALARA
av. Cronulla 494 A15
av. Wahroonga 222 C4
INGARA
av. Miranda 492 E1
ct. Erskine Park 300 D2
INGHAM
av. Five Dock 343 B10
dr. Casula 394 D16
INGLEBAR
av. Allambie Ht 257 C11
cl. Bangor 459 H13
st. Villawood 367 H5
INGLEBURN
rd. Ingleburn 453 A8
rd. Leppington 421 A6
INGLEBY
st. Oatlands 279 B7
INGLESIDE
rd. Ingleside 198 B6
INGLETHORPE
av. Kensington 376 D14
INGLEWOOD
pl. Baulkham Hl 216 E16
rd. Grays Point 491 C15
INGLIS
av. St Marys 269 H4
ct. Harringtn Pk 478 F8
la. St Marys, off Inglis Av 269 H4
rd. Ingleburn 452 G9
INGOLDS
la. Clarendon 120 A4
INGOOLA
cl. Moorebank 396 F7
INGRAM
av. Milperra 397 E9
la. Crows Nest, off Chandos St 315 F5
rd. Wahroonga 222 A6
rd. Wahroonga 222 A7
st. Kensington 376 B12
INGRID
pl. Hassall Gr 211 K13
rd. Kareela 461 E11
INKERMAN
la. Emu Heights, off Inkerman Rd 235 A1
rd. Denistone 281 G11
rd. Emu Heights 235 A1

st. Granville 308 B7
st. Mosman 316 J3
st. Parramatta 308 B7
INLET
rd. Brooklyn 76 A10
INMAN
rd. Cromer 228 G15
st. Maroubra 407 J9
INNES
av. Hornsby 221 F4
cr. Mount Druitt 241 A16
pl. Werrington 238 G11
rd. Greenwich 314 J5
rd. Manly Vale 288 A3
st. Campbelltwn 511 H5
st. Five Dock 342 K8
st. Thirlmere 562 F16
st. Thirlmere 565 F1
INNESDALE
rd. Arncliffe 403 K7
INNIS
pl. Kurrajong Hl 55 E5
INNISFAIL
rd. Wakeley 334 J13
INNOVATION
rd. Mcquarie Pk 282 E1
INSIGNIA
st. Sadleir 394 B1
INSPIRATION
pl. Berrilee 131 E13
INSTITUTE
dr. Little Bay 437 G14
rd. Westmead 277 F14
INTER-TERMINAL ACCESS
rd. Bnksmeadw 436 C4
rd. Port Botany 436 C4
INTREPID
pl. Greenfld Pk 334 E14
INVERALLAN
av. West Pymble 253 A9
INVERARY
dr. Kurmond 86 J3
st. Concord 341 H8
INVERELL
av. Hinchinbrk 392 H4
INVERGOWRIE
av. Glen Alpine 510 D15
cl. W Pnnant Hl 249 A3
INVERNESS
av. Frenchs Frst 257 A5
av. Penshurst 431 C2
cct. Cecil Hills 362 E5
cr. Glenhaven 218 C5
pl. Kareela 461 B14
pl. St Andrews 452 A16
rd. Riverstone 183 C8
rd. S Penrith 266 K2
st. Bronte 377 J10
INVESTIGATOR
av. Yagoona 368 E15
INWOOD
cl. Castle Hill 218 K13
IOLANTHE
st. Campbelltwn 511 G2
IONA
av. North Rocks 278 G2
av. West Pymble 252 K9
ct. Yennora 337 A8
la. Paddington 4 G15
pl. Bass Hill 368 A10
pl. St Andrews 452 A16
st. Blacktown 273 K1
IOWA
cl. St Clair 269 G13
IPEL
cl. St Clair 269 G16
IPOH
st. Holsworthy 426 F11
IPSWICH
av. Glenwood 215 G12
IRAGA
av. Peakhurst 430 H2
pl. Forestville 256 C7
IRAKING
av. Moorebank 396 A7
IRALBA
av. Emu Plains 235 A9
IRAMIR
pl. Warriewood 198 K6

IRAS
pl. Rsemeadow 540 E2
IRBY
pl. Quakers Hill 243 K2
IREDALE
av. Cremorne 316 F11
la. Cremorne, off Hodgson Av 316 F12
st. Newtown 374 J9
IRELAND
st. Burwood 371 J1
st. St Clair 269 H10
IRELANDS
rd. Blacktown 243 J13
IRENE
cr. Eastwood 281 H4
cr. Hurstville 401 K15
la. Panania 428 A6
pl. Ingleburn 453 E11
st. Kogarah 433 D9
st. Panania 428 A6
st. S Penrith 267 C3
st. Wareemba 342 K5
IRETON
st. Malabar 437 D4
IRIS
av. Riverwood 399 K10
ct. Glenmore Pk 265 G7
pl. Blacktown 245 C8
st. Beacon Hill 257 A4
st. Frenchs Frst 257 A4
st. Guildford W 336 G2
st. North Ryde 282 D8
st. Paddington 20 G1
st. Sefton 368 G4
IRMA
pl. Oakhurst 241 H4
IRON
st. N Parramatta 278 C10
IRON BARK
gr. Bella Vista 246 H3
wy. Colyton 270 H6
IRONBARK
av. Camden 507 A8
av. Casula 394 E14
cl. Alfords Point 429 C16
cr. Blacktown 273 K7
cr. Mcquarie Fd 454 F1
dr. Cranebrook 207 F16
dr. Wilberforce 62 G13
gr. Greenacre 370 G5
pl. Westleigh 220 F7
rd. Bargo 567 F3
IRONMONGER
av. Rouse Hill, off Grimmet Av 184 K7
IRONSIDE
av. St Helens Park 541 C2
st. St Johns Pk 364 D1
IRONWOOD
pl. Newington 310 C14
IRRABELLA
pl. Erskine Park 300 D2
IRRARA
st. Croydon 342 E14
IRRAWONG
rd. N Narrabeen 198 F11
IRRIBIN
st. Marayong 243 H6
IRRIGATION
rd. Merrylands 306 J9
rd. S Wntwthvle 306 J9
IRRUBEL
rd. Caringbah 493 B6
rd. Newport 169 E10
IRRUKA
pl. Cranebrook 207 H11
IRVINE
cr. Ryde 312 D3
pl. Bella Vista 246 B1
pl. Ruse 512 H6
st. Bankstown 399 B6
st. Elderslie 477 K16
st. Kingsford 406 J6
IRVING
st. Parramatta 308 K1
wy. Doonside 273 E3
IRWIN
cr. Bexley North 402 F9
ct. Narellan Vale 478 K16
pl. Wentwthvle 307 B3
st. N Parramatta 278 C10
st. Werrington 238 J9
IRWINE
rd. Caringbah 493 B16
ISA
cl. Bossley Park 334 B10
pl. Cartwright 393 K5
ISAAC
pl. Quakers Hill 213 J8
pl. Ruse 512 D4
st. Peakhurst 430 B6
ISAAC SMITH
pde. Kings Lngly 245 B4
rd. Castlereagh 176 B7
st. Daceyville 406 E3
ISABEL
av. Vaucluse 348 E6
cl. Cherrybrook 219 D8
st. Belmore 371 F15
st. Cecil Hills 362 E1
st. Ryde 282 B16
ISABELLA
cl. Bella Vista 246 G2
la. Queens Park 22 J12
st. Balmain 7 C9
st. Camperdwn 17 E2
st. N Parramatta 278 E14
st. Queens Park 22 J11
st. Revesby 398 K16
st. Werrington 238 H10
ISABELLE
st. Seven Hills 275 J6
ISAR
st. Seven Hills 275 G8
ISCA
pl. Glenmore Pk 266 G12
ISCHIA
st. Cronulla 524 A4
ISIS
la. Kingsford 406 J4
pl. Quakers Hill 243 G5
st. Fairfield W 335 D8
st. Wahroonga 222 B7
ISLA
pl. Belrose 225 K11
ISLAND
pl. Kurrajong Ht 54 B6
ISLAY
st. Winston Hills 277 B3
ISLER
st. Gladesville 313 A11
ISLES
pl. Plumpton 241 H11
ISLINGTON
cr. Greenacre 369 J10
st. Cranebrook 207 C10
ISMAY
av. Homebush 341 C6
ISMONA
av. Newport 169 J8
ISOBEL
cl. Mona Vale 199 A3
ISOBELL
av. W Pnnant Hl 249 D8
ITHACA
cl. St Johns Pk 334 E16
rd. Elizabeth Bay 13 C4
st. Emu Plains 235 C9
ITHIER
la. Quakers Hill 213 H13
IVAN
cl. Illawong 460 F1
st. Greystanes 306 C6
st. Minchinbury 271 G7
IVANHOE
pl. Mcquarie Pk 282 D4
pl. Oatlands 278 H11
rd. Croydon 342 F14
st. Ingleburn 453 B10
st. Marrickville 373 J15
st. St Johns Pk 364 H1
IVERS
pl. Minto 483 A2
IVERYS
la. Newtown 18 C10
IVES
av. Liverpool 394 H9
ct. St Clair 300 C2
la. Crows Nest, off Willoughby La 315 F5
IVEY
st. Lindfield 284 A3
IVOR
st. Lidcombe 340 A4
IVORY
la. Leichhardt 15 F2
pl. Jamisontown 266 B4
pl. Richmond 117 J6
IVY
av. McGraths Hl 122 A10
la. Darlington 18 J5
la. Randwick, off Ivy St 407 C1
pl. Cherrybrook 219 H11
pl. Kenthurst 187 J1
rd. Mosman 317 D13
st. Botany 405 F10
st. Canterbury 372 E15
st. Chatswd W 284 F13
st. Darlington 18 H5
st. Greenacre 370 E7
st. Liverpool 395 B7
st. Randwick 407 C1
st. Ryde 282 F15
st. Toongabbie 276 B5
st. Wollstncraft 315 E10
IWAN
pl. Kellyville 216 B1
IWUNDA
rd. Guildford 338 D9
rd. Lalor Park 245 E12
IXION
la. Cammeray, off Amherst St 315 K5
st. Winston Hills 277 C1

J

JABEZ
st. Marrickville 374 C9
JABIRU
cl. Mona Vale 169 E16
pl. Blacktown 274 B9
pl. Ingleburn 453 F10
pl. Woronora Ht 489 F2
st. Green Valley 363 D14
JACANA
cl. Wahroonga 223 C3
gr. Heathcote 519 A10
pl. Ingleburn 453 F6
pl. W Pnnant Hl 248 F8
wy. Glenmore Pk 265 K13
wy. Plumpton, off Sanctuary Park Dr 242 A9
JACARANDA
av. Baulkham Hl 247 K10
av. Blaxland 233 G5
av. Bradbury 511 E13
av. Lugarno 430 B14
cr. Casula 394 F13
ct. Villawood 337 A15
dr. Cabarita 342 E3
dr. Georges Hall 367 F11
dr. Parramatta 278 A12
pl. Beecroft 250 F3
pl. Doonside 243 G16
pl. Manly Vale 287 J5
pl. S Coogee 407 F5
rd. Caringbah 492 K10
st. Cabarita 342 E3
JACEVA
pl. Cattai 94 D4
JACINTA
av. Beecroft 250 D4
pl. Picton 561 F4
JACKA
st. St Marys 270 A2
JACKAMAN
st. Bondi 377 K6
JACKARANDA
rd. N St Marys 240 A9
JACK McLURE
pl. Northbridge 285 K14
JACK McNAMEE
pl. Kellyville 217 D1
JACK O'SULLIVAN
rd. Moorebank 396 B7
JACK RUSSELL
rd. Berrilee 131 H10
JACKS
ct. Currans Hill 479 G13
JACKSON
av. Miranda 492 B5
cl. Menai 458 F13
cr. Chester Hill 338 D16
cr. Denistone E 281 G10
cr. Pennant Hills 220 F12
pl. Cabramatta W 365 B8
pl. Earlwood 403 E4
pl. Kellyville 215 K5
rd. Lalor Park 245 C10
rd. Luddenham 357 F2
st. Balgowlah 287 J9
st. Ermington 310 B3
st. Marsden Pk 182 A14
JACKSONS
rd. Warriewood 199 A13
JACLYN
st. Ingleburn 453 C9
JACOB KING
pl. Emu Plains 235 G9
JACOBS
av. Asquith 192 B11
cl. Menai 458 G15
cl. N Epping 251 F9
pl. Bligh Park 150 D6
st. Bankstown 369 F15
JACOBSON
av. Kyeemagh 404 B14
JACQUELENE
cl. Bayview 168 E8
JACQUELINE
cr. Greenacre 370 C10
pl. Kurmond 86 E1
pl. Moorebank 396 F13
JACQUES
av. Peakhurst 430 B2
la. Balmain 7 D8
pl. Minchinbury 271 H7
st. Balmain 7 D8
st. Chatswood 285 C9
st. Kingsford 406 H3
JACQUIE
st. Cabramatta 365 E9
JACQUINOT
ct. Moorebank 425 B4
pl. Glenfield 424 E12
rd. Moorebank 425 B4
JADCHALM
st. W Pnnant Hl 249 J3
JADE
ct. Georges Hall 367 J11
pl. Eagle Vale 481 C8
pl. St Clair 269 J13
pl. Seven Hills 275 C7
pl. W Pnnant Hl 249 H5
JAEGER
pl. Woronora Ht 489 B4
JAF
pl. Blairmount 481 B14
JAFFA
rd. Dural 188 J13
st. Fairfield W 335 F13
JAGELMAN
rd. Badgerys Ck 358 D9
JAGGERS
pl. Ambarvale 511 A11
JAGO
pl. Toongabbie 276 G5
st. Greenwich 314 K11
JAGUNGAL
pl. Heckenberg 364 C14
JAKARI
cr. Whalan 240 H12
JAMAICA PARK
rd. Ellis Lane 476 B8
JAMBEROO
av. Baulkham Hl 246 K8
av. Terrey Hills 196 D6
la. Double Bay 14 E9
pl. Bangor 459 J12
JAMES
av. Lurnea 394 C11
cl. Menai 459 A12
la. Balmain East 8 H8
la. Paddington 13 D13
la. Sydney C D15
la. Waitara 221 H3
la. Woollahra 21 H4
pl. Castle Hill 217 G15
pl. Darlinghurst 4 D12
pl. Hillsdale 406 G14
pl. N Sydney 5 F3
rd. Brooklyn 76 A11
st. Allambie Ht 257 K16
st. Balmain 7 F11
st. Baulkham Hl 247
st. Blakehurst 432
st. Bondi Jctn 377
st. Canterbury 372
st. Carlingford 279
st. Chatswd W 284
st. Enmore 374
st. Fairfield E 337
st. Five Dock 342
st. Glossodia 59
st. Guildford W 336
st. Hornsby 221
st. Hunters Hill 313
st. Ingleburn 453
st. Leichhardt 9
st. Lidcombe 339
st. Lilyfield 9
st. Manly 288
st. Melrose Pk 311
st. Mosman 317
st. Northwood 314
st. Petersham 15
st. Punchbowl 399
st. Redfern 19
st. Redfern 19
st. Riverstone 183
st. Seven Hills 275
st. S Windsor 120
st. Strathfield S 371
st. Summer Hill 373
st. Sydney C
st. Wallacia 325
st. Waterloo 19
st. Woollahra 21
wy. Mt Annan 479
JAMES BAILEY
dr. Harringtn Pk 478
JAMES BARNETT
gln. St Clair 270
la. St Clair, off James Barnett Gln 270
JAMES BELLAMY
pl. W Pnnant Hl 249
JAMES BERES BRIDGE
Silverdale 384
JAMES COOK
dr. Castle Hill 218
dr. Kings Lngly 245
JAMES COOK ISLAND
Sylvania Wtr 462
JAMES CRAIG
rd. Rozelle 11
JAMES FLYNN
av. Harringtn Pk 478
JAMES HENTY
dr. Dural 219
JAMES KING
la. Mosman, off Union St 317
JAMES MACARTHUR
ct. N Parramatta 278
JAMES MEEHAN
st. Windsor 121
wy. Mcquarie Lk 423
JAMES MILEHAM
dr. Kellyville 186
dr. Kellyville 216
JAMESON
la. Sans Souci 463
JAMES RANDALL
pl. Glenbrook 234
JAMES RUSE
cl. Windsor 121
dr. Camellia 308
dr. Granville 308
dr. N Parramatta 278
dr. Oatlands 278
dr. Oatlands 279
dr. Parramatta 308
dr. Rosehill 308
JAMES WHEELER
pl. Collaroy Plat 228
JAMIESON
av. Baulkham Hl 247
av. Fairlight 288
av. N Curl Curl 258
cl. Horsley Pk 332
la. Fairfield E 337
la. Greenacre 370
pde. Collaroy 229
sq. Forestville 256
st. Emu Plains 235
st. Granville 308

Revesby 428 K1
Silverwater 310 D10
Thornleigh 220 K10
MISON
Barden Rdg 488 H1
Jamisontown 235 J13
Kingswood 237 D15
S Penrith 237 A14
Blaxland 234 A5
Luddenham 356 H2
Ruse 512 F8
Sydney A E13
Sydney 1 F15
N
Lurnea 394 C9
Greystanes 305 J7
Quakers Hill 213 K8
Picton 561 E3
NACEK
Bonnyrigg Ht 363 D4
NALI
Bonnyrigg 364 A10
NAMBA
Kellyville 216 F4
NDIGA
Winmalee 173 A11
NE
Narellan Vale 508 H2
Narellan Vale 508 J2
Cecil Hills 363 B3
Dural 188 H7
Heathcote 518 H9
Balmain 7 K10
Blacktown 274 K1
Penrith 236 F8
Randwick 406 K1
Smithfield 335 B5
NELL
Carlingford 279 K4
NET
Thornleigh 220 J13
Bass Hill 368 A11
Drummoyne 343 F5
Merrylands 307 C7
Mount Druitt 271 D5
Russell Lea 343 F5
NETTE
Oakdale 500 E12
NICE
Padstow 429 G5
Smithfield 335 H5
Tahmoor 566 A11
Cherrybrook 219 C12
Narraweena 258 C3
Seven Hills 245 B16
NITA
Mt Colah 162 D14
Bossley Park 333 H11
NNALI
Jannali 460 F16
Sutherland 490 F1
Jannali 460 K10
NNARN
Seven Hills 246 A13
NPIETER
Box Hill 154 G3
Maraylya 125 A14
NSSEN
Kellyville 215 K1
NSZ
Fairfield W 335 C11
PONICA
Loftus 490 A10
Epping 250 E13
PURA
Kearns 450 K15
QUES
Bondi Beach 378 C3
QUETTA
Cecil Hills 362 E2
RANDA
Berowra 133 F10
RDIN
/. Mount Druitt 241 E11
RDINE
Edmndsn Pk 422 G3
RI
St Clair 269 F15
RLEY
Ambarvale 510 G15
RNDYCE
Ambarvale 511 A13

JAROCIN
av. Glebe 11 K14
JARRA
cr. Glenmore Pk 266 A9
JARRAH
av. Bradbury 511 F13
av. Prestons 394 C15
cl. Alfords Point 459 C1
pl. Bossley Park 333 F8
pl. Castle Hill 248 F1
pl. Doonside 243 G16
pl. Faulconbdg 171 E13
pl. Frenchs Frst 255 G1
JARRETT
la. Leichhardt, off Jarrett St 373 J3
st. Campsie 402 A3
st. Leichhardt 15 H4
JARVIE
av. Petersham 15 E15
la. Marrickville, off Northcote St 373 K11
JARVIS
pl. Hebersham 241 G3
st. Thirlmere 565 B6
JARVISFIELD
rd. Picton 561 D4
rd. Picton 563 K1
JASMINE
av. Padstow Ht 429 D7
av. Quakers Hill 243 E2
cl. Arcadia 130 H3
cl. Glenmore Pk 265 G9
cr. Cabramatta 365 G10
ct. Cherrybrook 219 K12
pl. Castle Hill 248 G1
pl. Greystanes 305 G11
pl. Sylvania 462 B13
rd. Normanhurst 221 J9
st. Botany 405 G10
tce. Bidwill 211 E15
wy. Castle Hill 248 G1
JASNAR
st. Greenfld Pk 334 C15
JASON
av. S Penrith 266 J6
la. S Penrith, off Jason Av 266 J5
pl. North Rocks 248 J16
st. Greystanes 306 C6
st. Miranda 461 J16
JASPER
ct. Prestons 392 H14
pl. Ambarvale 540 F2
rd. Baulkham Hl 247 A8
rd. Baulkham Hl 247 D9
st. Greystanes 306 D9
st. Seaforth 286 K9
JAUNCEY
pl. Hillsdale 406 H14
JAVA
pl. Kellyville 185 J13
pl. Quakers Hill 214 B11
JAVELIN
la. St Clair, off Javelin Row 270 F15
pl. Raby 451 G15
row. St Clair 270 F15
JAY
av. Belfield 371 D10
pl. Oxley Park 240 F16
pl. Rooty Hill 271 K4
st. Lidcombe 339 F10
JAYELEM
cr. Padstow 399 G14
JAYNE
st. West Ryde 280 G11
JEAN
av. Miranda 461 J16
st. Greenacre 370 F3
st. Kingswood 237 D15
st. North Rocks 278 B8
st. Rydalmere 309 H4
st. Seven Hills 245 D16
st. Villawood 337 A16
JEANETTE
av. Mona Vale 198 H3
st. East Ryde 283 B15
st. Padstow 399 E15
st. Regentville 265 J4
st. Seven Hills 245 E16
JEANNERET
av. Hunters Hill 314 A13

JED
pl. Marayong 244 A8
JEDDA
pl. Mona Vale 199 E1
rd. Lurnea 394 B9
rd. Prestons 393 E8
JEENGA
pl. Sylvania 461 G15
JEFFERIES
pl. Prairiewood 334 J8
JEFFERSON
av. St Ives 224 C7
cr. Bonnet Bay 460 D11
gr. Kenthurst 157 C14
JEFFERY
av. N Parramatta 278 D10
JEFFREY
av. Greystanes 306 D6
av. St Clair 299 K2
st. Canterbury 372 G13
st. Kirribilli 6 B16
st. Kurnell 466 E8
JELENA
cl. Bossley Park 333 G12
JELLICOE
av. Kingsford 407 A4
st. Balgowlah Ht 288 A14
st. Caringbah 492 G11
st. Concord 342 A5
st. Condell Park 398 J7
st. Hurstville Gr 431 G10
st. Lidcombe 340 B5
JELLIE
pl. Oakhurst 242 C4
JELLINGAL
rd. Engadine 489 B12
JEM
pl. Blacktown 275 A9
JENDI
av. Bayview 168 J12
JENKINS
av. Penrith 237 D10
la. Crows Nest, off Brook St 315 G5
la. S Wntwthvle, off Hereford Pl 306 H6
rd. Carlingford 279 H4
st. Berala 339 B14
st. Cammeray 315 H5
st. Chatswd W 284 G10
st. Collaroy 229 A11
st. Douglas Park 568 C7
st. Dundas 280 B13
st. Millers Pt A C10
st. Mona Vale 199 C7
st. Regents Pk 339 B14
JENKYN
pl. Bligh Park 150 E5
JENNA
cl. Allambie Ht 287 G1
cl. Rooty Hill 271 K2
JENNER
rd. Dural 219 B7
st. Baulkham Hl 247 J10
st. Little Bay 437 G14
st. Minto 482 J4
st. Seaforth 287 A9
wy. Minto 482 H7
JENNIE
pl. Carlingford 249 C14
JENNIFER
av. Allambie Ht 257 F14
av. Blacktown 273 K2
pl. Baulkham Hl 247 A14
pl. Cherrybrook 219 K4
pl. Smithfield 335 G8
st. Little Bay 437 B13
st. Ryde 282 A13
JENNINGS
av. Bass Hill 367 G7
rd. Faulconbdg 171 D6
rd. Heathcote 518 D14
st. Alexandria 18 F14
st. Matraville 406 G16
JENNY
pl. Oakville 122 E12
pl. Rooty Hill 272 C2
JENOLA
la. Woolooware 493 C9
JENOLAN
cl. Hornsby Ht 161 J9
ct. Wattle Grove 395 H13
st. Leumeah 482 D14

JENSEN
av. Vaucluse 348 G4
pl. Engadine 518 F4
pl. S Coogee 407 H7
st. Colyton 270 H8
st. Condell Park 398 E2
st. Fairfield W 335 A11
JEREMY
wy. Cecil Hills 362 H9
JERILDERIE
av. Kellyville 216 G7
JEROME
av. Winston Hills 247 E16
JERRARA
st. Engadine 488 J13
JERRAWA
pl. Glenhaven 187 J14
JERSEY
av. Mortdale 431 B4
gln. St Clair 270 A13
la. Hornsby 191 G15
la. S Wntwthvle 306 H6
la. Five Dock, off Barnstaple Rd 343 A8
pde. Minto 482 H9
pl. Cromer 227 H14
rd. Artarmon 284 J16
rd. Blackett 241 A5
rd. Bringelly 388 K14
rd. Dharruk 241 A5
rd. Emerton 240 J4
rd. Greystanes 306 H9
rd. Hebersham 241 A5
rd. Maroubra 406 J15
rd. Matraville 406 J15
rd. Merrylands 306 H10
rd. Oakhurst 241 H5
rd. Plumpton 241 H5
rd. Schofields 212 J7
rd. S Wntwthvle 306 H9
rd. Strathfield 341 G15
rd. Woollahra 21 G3
st. Busby 393 J1
st. Hornsby 191 G15
st. Marrickville 373 H13
st. Mt Colah 192 A5
st. Richmond 119 A5
st. Turramurra 222 J15
st.n. Asquith 191 H13
st.n. Hornsby 191 H13
JERSEYWOLD
av. Springwood 201 H3
JERVIS
dr. Illawong 459 A7
st. Ermington 310 F2
st. Fairfield 336 F8
st. Prestons 392 K16
JERVOIS
av. Centnnial Pk 21 E9
JESMOND
av. Dulwich Hill 373 B10
av. Vaucluse 318 G16
cr. Beecroft 250 A4
st. Surry Hills F K14
st. Surry Hills 4 C15
JESSICA
gdn. St Ives 224 G5
pl. Mt Colah 162 D15
pl. Plumpton 241 J7
pl. Rsemeadow 540 K4
JESSIE
st. Smithfield 335 G8
st. Westmead 277 J14
JESSON
la. Surry Hills 20 B4
st. Surry Hills 20 B3
JESSOP
pl. Westmead 307 E3
JESSUP
pl. Glenmore Pk 265 E9
JET
pl. Eagle Vale 481 E9
JETTY
rd. Putney 312 C9
JEWEL
st. Quakers Hill 214 H13
JEWELL
cl. Hamondvle 426 G1
JEWELSFORD
rd. Wentwthvle 306 G2
JIBBON
pl. Woodbine 481 G12
st. Cronulla 524 A3

JILL
st. Marayong 244 A9
JILLAK
cl. Glenmore Pk 266 A11
JILLIAN
pl. Mcquarie Fd 424 F15
JILLIBY
pl. Belrose 225 K15
JILLONG
st. Rydalmere 279 J14
JIMADA
av. Frenchs Frst 257 A4
JIMBI
pl. Glenmore Pk 266 B8
JIMBOUR
ct. Wattle Grove 425 J4
JIMBUCK
cl. Glenmore Pk 266 B11
JIM RING
la. Birrong, off Rodd St 369 A5
JIM SIMPSON
la. Blacktown, off Main St 244 G15
JINATONG
st. Miranda 491 J2
JINCHILLA
rd. Terrey Hills 196 C6
JINDABYNE
av. Baulkham Hl 248 A8
cct. Woodcroft 243 G12
cr. Peakhurst 430 C9
st. Bossley Park 333 E11
st. Frenchs Frst 256 E1
st. Heckenberg 363 K13
JINDALEE
pl. East Killara 254 J6
pl. Riverwood 400 D11
JINDALLA
cr. Hebersham 241 D9
JINGARA
pl. Sylvania 461 G14
JINIWIN
pl. Ambarvale 510 K11
JINKINS
pl. Ambarvale 510 H14
JINNA
rd. Peakhurst 430 D10
JIPP
st. Penrith 237 A14
JIRANG
pl. Glenmore Pk 266 A8
JIRI
pl. Engadine 518 G4
JIRRAMBA
ct. Glenmore Pk 266 B7
JIRRANG
cl. Mount Druitt 241 E16
JOADJA
cr. Glendenning 242 G5
rd. Prestons 393 F8
JOALAH
av. Blaxland 234 E9
cl. St Ives 224 D16
cr. Berowra Ht 133 B10
rd. Duffys Frst 194 H3
JOAN
la. Belmore 401 G3
pl. Baulkham Hl 247 K9
pl. Currans Hill 479 K13
pl. Greystanes 305 J6
pl. Mount Druitt 271 A3
st. Chester Hill 368 C5
st. Hurstville 431 H1
JOANIE
pl. Glendenning 242 F2
JOANNA
st. S Penrith 266 K5
JOANNE
cl. Cherrybrook 219 E6
ct. Sefton 368 H3
pl. Bilgola 169 E7
JOB
st. Harbord 258 C14
JOCARM
av. Condell Park 398 F1
JOCELYN
av. Marrickville 373 F11
bvd. Quakers Hill 213 J7
bvd. Quakers Hill 214 A7
la. N Curl Curl 258 G9

st. Chester Hill 368 B4
st. N Curl Curl 258 G9

JOCELYN HOWARTH
st. Moore Park..........21 B5

JOCKBETT
st. Agnes Banks......117 F16
st. Agnes Banks......147 F2
st. Londonderry......147 F2

JOCKEY
cl. Casula...............394 F16

JODIE
pl. Quakers Hill 244 A2

JODY
pl. St Clair...............299 K2

JOEL
pl. Kings Lngly........246 C10

JOFFRE
cr. Daceyville...........406 G4
st. Gymea Bay.........491 D7
st. S Hurstville 432 B10

JOHANNA
pl. Schofields..........213 H5

JOHN
av. Mcquarie Fd.......454 A3
la. Glebe...................11 K14
la. Randwick, off John St..............376 J10
pl. Cecil Hills............362 E2
rd. Cherrybrook.......219 C13
st. Ashfield 342 G15
st. Avalon 140 C12
st. Bardwell Vy........403 B7
st. Baulkham Hl 247 H13
st. Beecroft.............250 B10
st. Bexley................402 F15
st. Blacktown...........274 C5
st. Burwood............341 K13
st. Cabramatta 365 D6
st. Cabramatta W 365 A6
st. Camden 477 A14
st. Canterbury 372 F12
st. Concord.............341 J8
st. Cronulla.............523 K2
st. Croydon.............342 G15
st. Erskineville...........18 A13
st. Glebe...................11 K13
st. Granville 308 B13
st. Hunters Hill........313 B9
st. Hurstville 431 J2
st. Kogarah Bay 432 J11
st. Leichhardt............10 F15
st. Lidcombe............339 J4
st. McMahons Pt 5 B11
st. Marsden Pk........181 K11
st. Mascot 405 B2
st. Merrylands.........308 B13
st. Newtown 374 H11
st. Petersham 16 A14
st. Punchbowl.........399 H7
st. Pyrmont 12 E2
st. Queens Park 377 E8
st. Randwick............376 J10
st. Rooty Hill...........271 J5
st. Rydalmere 309 H3
st. St Marys.............269 E3
st. Schofields...........182 H14
st. Strathfield S 371 A5
st. Tempe 374 C16
st. The Oaks............502 F12
st. Waterloo...............19 C14
st. West Ryde 280 G11
st. Woollahra 21 J5

JOHN ALBERT
cl. Kellyville.............216 H7

JOHN BATMAN
av. Wrrngtn Cty 238 G5

JOHN BOY
pl. Blacktown 273 J7

JOHN DAVEY
av. Cronulla 494 B7

JOHN DWYER
rd. Lalor Park..........245 F12

JOHN DYKES
av. Vaucluse............348 G1

JOHN EWART
st. Moore Park..........21 C6

JOHN FORREST
av. Sutherland 460 C14

JOHN HARGREAVES
av. Moore Park..........20 K8
av. Moore Park..........21 Z9

JOHN HINES
av. Minchinbury.......270 K5
av. Minchinbury.......271 A5

JOHN HUGHES
pl. Wahroonga 222 B6

JOHN HUNTER
gr. Mt Annan...........479 H16

JOHN KIDD
dr. Blair Athol 511 C2

JOHN McLENNON
cct. Harringtn Pk.......478 D2

JOHN MELLION
st. Moore Park..........21 B7

JOHN MILLER
st. Ryde..................282 H16

JOHN NORTHCOTT
pl. Surry Hills............19 K4

JOHN OXLEY
av. Werrington..........238 G7
av. Wrrngtn Cty 238 G7
dr. Davidson 255 E4
dr. Frenchs Frst 255 E4

JOHN RADLEY
av. Dural 219 B8

JOHNS
av. Normanhurst 221 G7

JOHN SAVAGE
cr. W Pnnant Hl.......219 J16

JOHNSON
av. Camden S 506 K10
av. Dulwich Hill........373 A9
av. Kenthurst...........156 A7
av. Melrose Pk.........280 J16
av. Seven Hills.........245 K14
cl. Bonnet Bay 460 A9
la. Mascot 405 E6
pl. Ruse..................512 H4
pl. Springwood 172 G16
rd. Campbelltwn.......481 B16
rd. Campbelltwn.......511 B1
rd. Galston 159 D10
st. Alexandria..........375 G11
st. Beaconsfield 375 G11
st. Chatswood.........285 A11
st. Harbord 258 E15
st. Hunters Hill........313 B10
st. Lindfield.............283 F3
st. Mascot 405 E6

JOHNSTON
av. Cammeray 316 D4
av. Kirrawee 490 K7
av. Kogarah Bay 432 H12
av. Lurnea 394 C13
cr. Lane Cove W.......283 K15
la. Annandale............11 A16
la. Lane Cove W.......313 H3
la. Marrickville 373 J16
pde. Maroubra...........407 D7
pde. Maroubra...........407 E7
pde. S Coogee 407 E7
rd. Bargo.................567 G8
rd. Bass Hill.............367 F7
rd. Eastwood...........280 F6
st. Annandale............16 H3
st. Balmain East..........8 G9
st. Earlwood 402 E8
st. Pitt Town 92 H9
st. Windsor..............121 C8

JOHNSTONE
st. Guildford W 336 K5
st. Peakhurst 429 K4

JOHN SULMAN
la. St Clair, off John Sulman Pl..270 B11
pl. St Clair...............270 B11

JOHN TEBBUT
pl. Richmond...........118 E4

JOHN TIPPING
gr. Penrith...............236 F10

JOHN WALL
la. Yagoona 369 E11

JOHN WARREN
av. Glenwood 215 J16

JOHORE
pl. E Lindfield..........254 J12
rd. Holsworthy 426 F10

JOINER
pl. Bonnyrigg...........364 D6

JOKIC
st. Bonnyrigg Ht......362 K7

JOLLY
st. Castlereagh 176 E8

JOLY
pde. Hunters Hill........313 C11

JONATHAN
pl. Miranda 491 J1
st. Greystanes.........306 C7

JONATHON
pl. Cherrybrook.......219 J7
pl. Frenchs Frst 256 B4

JONES
av. Kingsgrove.........402 C8
av. Monterey 433 H9
ct. Currans Hill........479 G13
la. Pyrmont 12 H8
la. Redfern.................19 D8
la. Rosebery, off Hayes Rd 375 G15
la. Kingswood, off Jones St 237 H16
pl. Mt Pritchard.......364 D11
rd. Castlereagh.........175 G6
rd. Eastwood...........280 G6
rd. Kenthurst............187 G1
st. Beacon Hill.........257 C5
st. Blacktown 274 J5
st. Concord.............342 A6
st. Croydon.............342 G14
st. Engadine............518 F1
st. Kingswood.........237 H16
st. Pyrmont 12 E2
st. Pyrmont 12 H9
st. Ryde..................282 D15
st. Ultimo 12 K12
st. Wentwthvle.........306 F2

JONES BAY
rd. Pyrmont 12 H1

JONQUIL
pde. Kellyville.............216 H6
pl. Alfords Point......459 A3
pl. Glenmore Pk......265 G10

JOPLING
cr. Lalor Park 245 B11
st. North Ryde 283 A12

JORDAN
av. Beverly Hills 401 A12
av. Glossodia.............59 K11
av. Newington 310 B15
cl. Mt Colah 162 E16
la. Valley Ht 202 H10
pl. Kearns 451 A15
rd. Moorebank 425 B1
rd. Wahroonga.........221 K16
st. Fairfield W..........335 C9
st. Gladesville 312 H9
st. Rosehill 308 H8
st. Seven Hills..........245 F15
st. Wentwthvle.........307 C1
st. West Hoxton 392 D4

JORDANA
pl. Castle Hill...........248 E4

JORDANS
la. Matraville 436 J4

JORDON
st. Cmbrdg Pk..........238 A7

JORGENSEN
av. St Clair..............270 D10

JORJA
pl. Kellyville.............216 D1

JOSEPH
cl. Liberty Gr...........311 B10
cr. Sefton.................368 F6
la. Yagoona 369 E10
rd. Leppington..........420 B9
st. Ashfield 372 J5
st. Avalon 140 A13
st. Berala 339 G16
st. Blacktown 274 E6
st. Blakehurst...........432 C15
st. Cabramatta 365 C8
st. Cabramatta W 365 C8
st. Chipping Ntn 396 C5
st. Kingswood..........237 H11
st. Lane Cove 314 G3
st. Lidcombe............339 G16
st. Lidcombe............339 H10
st. Lilyfield 10 D6
st. Regents Pk 369 G2
st. Richmond 118 K7
st. Rozelle....................7 B16
st. Rydalmere 279 E15

JOSEPH BANKS
ct. Mt Annan.............509 G4
dr. Kings Lngly.........245 H7

JOSEPHINE
cr. Cherrybrook.......219 J4
cr. Georges Hall 367 F10
cr. Moorebank 396 C11
st. Merrylands W 306 H13
st. Riverwood 400 C14
wy. Glendenning, off Tony Pl 242 F1

JOSEPHSON
st. Paddington 20 F2

JOSHUA
rd. Freemns Rch........61 A11
wy. Cranebrook 207 E13
wy. Dean Park, off Medea Pl.............212 F15

JOSHUA MOORE
dr. Horngsea Pk 392 C14

JOSQUIN
wy. Clarmnt Ms 268 F4

JOSSELYN
pl. Concord..............342 B3

JOUBERT
st.n, Hunters Hill........313 F9
st.s, Hunters Hill........313 E11

JOWARRA
pl. Bow Bowing.......452 E13
wy. Merrylands W 306 K11

JOWETT
pl. Ingleburn 453 J8

JOWYN
pl. Kirrawee 491 C3

JOY
av. Earlwood 402 J4
la. Earlwood, off Joy Av 402 J4
pl. Maroubra...........407 C15
st. Gladesville 313 A4
st. Mt Pritchard.......364 G10

JOYCE
av. Picnic Point........428 D8
dr. Mascot 405 B6
pl. Dural 219 C7
st. Fairfield..............336 A13
st. Glenwood 245 D2
st. Pendle Hill..........276 E14
st. Punchbowl..........399 J9

JOYCELYN
cl. Hornsby Ht 161 J12

JOYLYN
rd. Annangrove 155 E12

JOYNER
av. Newington 309 K16
st. Westmead 307 J4

JOYNT
av. Milperra 397 F10

JOYNTON
av. Zetland 375 J11

JUBA
cl. St Clair...............269 J16

JUBILEE
av. Beverley Pk........433 A8
av. Carlton...............432 J7
av. Pymble 252 K1
av. Warriewood 198 F5
la. Parramatta..........308 D6
la. Lewisham, off Jubilee St.............15 B10
pl. Balmain 8 D10
pl. Balmain East..........8 D10
st. Lewisham 15 B9
st. Wahroonga 222 C2

JUDD
av. Hamondvle 396 H16
st. Banksia..............403 C12
st. Berkshire Pk.......179 H11
st. Cronulla..............493 K9
st. Mortdale 431 D9
st. Oatley 431 D10
st. Penshurst 431 D9

JUDE
av. Kogarah Bay 432 H11

JUDGE
la. Woolmloo.............4 F7
la. Randwick, off Coogee Bay Rd...377 C15
pl. Woolmloo..............4 G6
pl. Randwick, off Judge St 377 C15
st. Randwick...........377 C15
st. Woolmloo..............4 G7

JUDGES
la. Waverley, off Bronte Rd 377 F8

JUDITH
av. Cabramatta 365 C10
av. Mt Colah 192 B3
av. Mt Riverview......234 D2
av. Seven Hills.........275
cl. Werrington..........238
pl. Cromer 228
st. Baulkham Hl 247
st. Berala 339
st. Chester Hill 368
st. Pendle Hill..........306
st. Seaforth..............286

JUDITH ANDERSON
dr. Doonside 243

JUDSON
rd. Thornleigh 221

JUGIONG
st. West Pymble......252

JUKES
cl. Barden Rdg........488

JULAR
pl. Jamisontown 266

JULIA
cl. Cherrybrook.......220
cl. West Hoxton 391
gr. Castle Hill..........217
st. Ashfield 342

JULIAN
pl. Arcadia 130
pl. Glenwood 245
pl. Sefton................368
st. Mosman 316
st. Willoughby..........285
wy. Claymore 481

JULIANA
cr. Baulkham Hl 246
pl. Bligh Park 150
wy. Cherrybrook.......219

JULIANNE
pl. Canley Ht 365

JULIE
av. Campsie 402
cr. St Clair...............269
ct. Kellyville..............216
st. Blacktown 274
st. Marsfield.............282

JULIET
cl. Rsemeadow.......540

JULIETT
la. Marrickville 16
la. Marrickville 374
st. Enmore................16
st. Marrickville 16
st. Marrickville 374

JULIETTE
av. Punchbowl.........370

JULIUS
av. North Ryde 283
rd. Rsemeadow........540
st. Fairfield W...........335

JULL
pl. St Helens Park....541

JUMAL
pl. Smithfield 306

JUMBUNNA
pl. Terrey Hills.........196

JUNCTION
la. N Sydney..............K
la. Wahroonga 223
la. Woolmloo.............4
rd. Baulkham Hl 247
rd. Beverly Hills 400
rd. Heathcote 518
rd. Leumeah............482
rd. Moorebank 396
rd. Peakhurst 430
rd. Riverstone 153
rd. Ruse..................512
rd. Schofields...........183
rd. Summer Hill.......373
rd. Wahroonga.........222
rd. Winston Hills......247
st. Auburn 309
st. Cabramatta 365
st. Forest Lodge.........11
st. Gladesville 312
st. Granville 308
st. Marrickville 373
st. Miranda 492
st. Mortdale 431
st. Old Guildford......337
st. Ryde...................311
st. Silverwater..........309
st. Strathfield S 371
st. Woollahra 22
st. Woolmloo..............4
st. Yennora 337

NE
Glenhaven..........218 B1
Gymea Bay..........491 C9
Bankstown..........399 C4
Blacktown..........274 H8
Seven Hills..........245 C15
NEE
Bossley Park......333 G9
Kingsgrove..........402 B6
Minto..........482 F9
Marayong..........243 K8
NIA
Toongabbie..........276 B8
NIOR
Leichhardt..........15 H3
NIPER
Baulkham Hl......248 B11
Prestons..........393 K15
Sylvania..........462 A9
Blacktown..........274 E12
Mcquarie Fd.......454 H4
NO
. Greenacre..........370 E11
PITER
Cranebrook..........207 F15
Cranebrook, off
Pensax Rd..........207 F14
Kellyville..........216 C2
Kellyville..........216 C3
Gladesville..........312 K9
Lansvale..........366 J8
Winston Hills......277 C1
P
Eastwood..........281 E4
RA
Cranebrook..........207 E15
Winmalee..........173 E12
St Andrews..........481 J1
Seven Hills..........275 C8
RDS
Ryde..........281 K9
RY
Minto..........482 J7
STIN
Quakers Hill.......214 F12
Lilyfield..........10 F4
Smithfield..........335 J5
STINE
Baulkham Hl......247 C8
Bargo..........567 B4
STUS
North Bondi.......348 C15
VENIS
Oyster Bay..........461 C3

K

BAN
Doonside..........243 D14
BARLI
Lalor Park..........245 E13
BLE
Bradbury..........511 G13
Windsor..........121 C7
BUL
St Clair..........269 K16
St Clair, off
Kabul Cl..........269 K16
DER
Bargo..........567 A5
Bargo..........567 D6
DIERA
Wallacia..........325 A15
DIGAL
Beacon Hill..........257 D6
DINA
Quakers Hill.......214 B16
FIR
Cherrybrook..........219 E7
GA
Marsfield..........281 K5
GA PATH
Blaxland..........233 G13
HIBAH
Mosman..........317 F10
Mosman..........317 F9
N
Matraville..........437 C1
Bonnyrigg..........364 C6

KAIRAWA
st. S Hurstville..........432 C10
KALA
cct. St Clair..........269 H14
la. St Clair, off
Kala Cct..........269 H14
KALAMBO
pl. St Clair..........270 H11
KALANA
cl. Moorebank..........396 H7
KALANG
av. Killara..........254 C9
av. St Marys..........239 F15
la. Yowie Bay..........492 C10
rd. Edensor Pk..........333 D16
rd. Edensor Pk..........363 D2
rd. Elanora Ht..........198 D14
rd. Greystanes..........306 B6
rd. Kenthurst..........187 F6
rd. Mt Colah..........191 K5
rd. Seven Hills..........275 G4
KALAUI
st. N Balgowlah..........287 E4
KALBARRI
cr. Bow Bowing..........452 C13
KALESKI
st. Moorebank..........395 G9
KALGAL
st. Frenchs Frst..........255 J1
KALGOORLIE
pl. Cartwright..........393 K5
pl. Sutherland..........460 D14
st. Leichhardt..........9 F13
st. Willoughby..........285 D13
KALIANNA
cr. Beacon Hill..........257 H8
KALIMNA
dr. Baulkham Hl..........247 A7
st. Moorebank..........396 F7
KALINDI
pl. St Clair..........270 H11
KALINYA
st. Newport..........169 E12
KALKADA
av. Gymea Bay..........491 E11
KALLANG
pde. Wahroonga..........221 J16
KALLAROO
rd. Riverview..........314 C7
rd. Terrey Hills..........195 K7
st. Mosman..........316 K11
KALLAWATTA
gr. McGraths Hl..........122 B10
KALLISTA
av. St Ives..........254 E1
KALMIA
pl. Miranda..........491 K5
KALOE
pl. Marayong..........244 B3
KALOONA
pl. Kirrawee..........460 J16
KALORA
av. Dee Why..........258 J1
av. Fairfield W..........335 G14
KALUA
pl. Glenmore Pk..........266 B6
KALUGA
st. Busby..........363 H13
KALUMNA
cl. Cherrybrook..........219 F12
KALUNA
av. Smithfield..........336 B5
st. Putney..........312 A8
KALUNGA
la. Rooty Hill..........242 D16
la. Rooty Hill..........272 C1
KALYAN
av. Bradbury..........511 F16
KAMAROOKA
cr. W Pnnant Hl..........249 G5
KAMBAH
pl. W Pnnant Hl..........249 A8
KAMBALA
cr. Fairfield W..........335 F14
pl. Bellevue Hill..........347 F15
rd. Bellevue Hill..........14 J9
KAMBALDA
pl. Yarrawarrah..........489 E13
KAMBER
rd. Terrey Hills..........196 C12

KAMBORA
av. Davidson..........255 D1
av. Frenchs Frst..........255 D1
KAMERUKA
rd. Northbridge..........285 K14
KAMILAROI
rd. Bayview..........169 A14
KAMILAROY
rd. West Pymble..........253 A12
KAMIRA
av. Villawood..........367 C1
ct. Villawood..........367 C1
rd. Lilli Pilli..........522 F3
KAMIRI
st. Seaforth..........287 B5
KAN
cl. St Clair..........269 H15
KANA
cl. Cranebrook..........207 E6
KANADAH
av. Baulkham Hl..........246 J8
KANANDAH
rd. Engadine..........488 C13
KANANGRA
av. Baulkham Hl..........247 B4
cr. Balgowlah..........287 E11
cr. Cherrybrook..........219 J7
cr. Clontarf..........287 E11
cr. Elderslie..........477 H16
cr. Ruse..........512 F5
ct. Wattle Grove..........426 B4
rd. Terrey Hills..........196 F7
KANANGUR
av. Gymea..........491 H1
KANANOOK
av. Bayview..........168 H10
KANDARA
cl. Middle Dural..........157 H1
KANDOS
st. Glenwood..........245 F1
KANDRA
rd. Beacon Hill..........257 H8
KANDY
av. Epping..........251 A12
KANE
pl. Casula..........424 D3
pl. Glendenning..........242 E4
st. Guildford..........337 F4
KANERUKA
pl. Baulkham Hl..........246 K8
KANGAROO
cl. Green Valley..........363 A12
la. Manly, off
Carlton St..........288 G7
pl. Emu Plains..........235 A11
rd. Collaroy Plat..........228 J13
rd. Tahmoor..........565 B13
st. Manly..........288 F7
KANGAROO POINT
rd. Kangaroo Pt..........461 J7
KANILI
av. Baulkham Hl..........247 B15
KANIMBLA
cr. Bilgola..........169 H7
st. Ruse..........512 F8
KANINA
pl. Cranebrook..........207 B13
KANINI
cl. Cromer..........227 K16
KANNAN
pl. Kirrawee..........461 D15
KANNING
av. Gymea Bay..........491 E8
KANO
cl. Bonnyrigg..........364 C8
KANOONA
av. Homebush..........341 A7
av. St Ives..........223 J11
st. Caringbah..........492 F8
KANOWAR
av. East Killara..........254 J6
KANSAS
pl. Toongabbie..........275 H12
KANUKA
st. Bossley Park..........333 F8
KANYA
st. Frenchs Frst..........256 F8
KAPALA
av. Bradbury..........511 E16

KAPITI
st. St Ives Ch..........223 J2
KAPOVIC
st. Edensor Pk..........363 F1
KAPUNDA
pl. Belrose..........226 A14
KAPUTAR
ct. Holsworthy..........426 C5
pl. Prairiewood..........334 F7
KAPYONG
st. Belrose..........226 A15
KARA
cr. Bayview..........168 K13
la. Peakhurst..........430 B10
la. Randwick, off
Howard St..........407 B1
st. Lane Cove W..........284 E16
st. Randwick..........407 B1
st. Sefton..........368 E3
KARABAH
pl. Frenchs Frst..........257 C4
tce. Warrimoo..........203 C15
KARABAR
st. Fairfield Ht..........335 H9
KARABI
cl. Glenmore Pk..........266 C10
KARABIL
cr. Baulkham Hl..........248 C8
KARA KAROOK
st. Maianbar..........523 B8
KARALEE
cl. Marsfield..........281 K1
rd. Galston..........160 J7
KARALTA
cr. Belrose..........225 G14
KARAMARRA
rd. Engadine..........488 J13
KARANA
pl. Chatswd W..........284 C10
KARANGI
pl. Illawong..........460 B4
rd. Whalan..........241 A9
KARANI
av. Guildford W..........336 G3
KARDA
pl. Gymea..........491 F1
KARDELLA
av. Killara..........254 D11
cr. Narwee..........400 K13
ct. Condell Park..........368 H16
la. Killara..........254 E11
KARDINIA
rd. Mosman..........317 D13
KAREELA
av. Penrith..........237 E6
cr. Greenacre..........370 B13
la. Cremorne Pt..........316 F12
la. Penrith, off
Kareela Av..........237 E5
rd. Baulkham Hl..........247 F7
rd. Chatswd W..........284 E8
rd. Cremorne Pt..........316 F12
rd. Cremorne, off
Hodgson Av..........316 F12
st. Doonside..........243 B15
KAREELAH
rd. Hunters Hill..........313 G12
KAREEMA
st. Balgowlah..........287 F10
KAREENA
rd.n, Miranda..........492 E5
rd.s, Miranda..........492 E7
KARELLA
av. Villawood..........367 B2
KAREN
av. Picnic Point..........428 D8
ct. Baulkham Hl..........247 A10
ct. Cranebrook..........206 J8
pl. Faulconbdg..........171 D15
pl. Ingleburn..........453 D12
pl. Mount Druitt..........270 K1
pl. Silverdale..........354 B11
rd. Rossmore..........419 E3
rd. St Ives..........224 F9
KAREN MORAS
dr. Ryde..........312 E5
KARIBOO
cl. Mona Vale..........199 E1
KARILLA
av. Lane Cove W..........284 C15

KARIMBLA
rd. Miranda..........491 J4
KARINA
cr. Belrose..........226 D15
KARINGAL
av. Carlingford..........279 E3
cr. Frenchs Frst..........256 E6
ct. Marsfield..........281 K1
pl. Greenacre..........370 B14
rd. Riverview..........314 C7
st. Kingsgrove..........401 J9
st. Seaforth..........287 B7
KARINI
cl. Green Valley..........363 H11
KARINYA
pl. Kellyville..........216 C2
pl. Wahroonga..........221 H6
KARIOLA
st. Lane Cove W..........284 C15
KARIUS
st. Glenfield..........424 H9
KARIWARA
st. Dundas..........279 G13
KARLOO
cl. Moorebank..........396 H6
pde. Newport..........169 H15
st. Turramurra..........223 B10
KARLOON
rd. W Pnnant Hl..........249 H9
KARNAK
st. Denistone E..........281 F9
KARNE
st. Narwee..........400 G13
st. Riverwood..........400 G13
st. Roselands..........400 G13
KARNU
pl. Kareela..........461 D14
KARONGA
cl. Epping..........250 D15
KAROO
av. E Lindfield..........255 A13
cr. Hornsby Ht..........161 F15
pl. Malabar..........437 D8
KAROOL
av. Earlwood..........372 H16
KAROOLA
cr. Caringbah..........492 F4
st. Brooklyn..........76 D11
st. Busby..........363 J14
st. Narraweena..........258 C2
KAROOM
av. St Ives..........223 H9
KAROON
av. Canley Ht..........335 B15
KARRABA
st. Sefton..........368 G6
KARRABAH
rd. Auburn..........309 C16
KARRABEE
av. Tarban..........313 B13
st. Dee Why..........258 E7
KARRABUL
pl. Bossley Park..........333 F6
rd. Airds..........511 H16
rd. St Helens Park..........541 G3
KARRANGA
av. Killara..........254 B11
KARREE
pl. Heathcote..........518 E10
KARRI
pl. Alfords Point..........429 A14
pl. Bradbury..........511 E10
KARRIL
av. Beecroft..........249 K12
KARRONG
st. Clarmnt Ms..........268 G2
KARUAH
pl. Engadine..........488 K8
rd. Penrith..........237 C5
rd. Turramurra..........222 J11
st. Campbelltwn..........511 K7
st. Doonside..........243 B7
st. Greenacre..........370 E11
st. Greystanes..........306 C7
st. Strathfield..........340 H13
KARUK
st. Glenmore Pk..........266 D11
KARWARRA
pl. Peakhurst..........430 C9
KASCH
cl. Tahmoor..........565 D12

KASHMIR
av. Quakers Hill 214 D7
KASIE
la. St Clair, off Kasie Pl.............299 J3
pl. St Clair..............299 K3
KASTELAN
st. Blacktown..........273 J3
KATANDRA
cl. Avalon 139 J16
KATANNA
rd. Wedderburn.......540 D14
KATAVICH
cr. Bonnyrigg Ht......363 C4
KATE
pl. Cherrybrook.......219 J4
pl. Quakers Hill 213 K7
st. Turramurra 252 E2
KATELLA
pl. Airds..................512 B14
KATER
pl. Croydon Pk........372 A5
KATH
pl. Kings Lngly........245 C4
KATHERIN
rd. Baulkham Hl 247 E11
KATHERINE
cl. Cranebrook.........207 D4
cl. Galston 160 F11
pl. Castle Hill...........248 C1
st. Cecil Hills...........362 J3
st. Leumeah............482 F12
st. Chatswood, off Victoria Av 284 H10
KATHLEEN
av. Castle Hill...........217 F11
av. Lurnea 394 D10
la. Emu Plains, off Kathleen St 235 B9
pde. Picnic Point........428 D7
pl. Thirlmere 565 C6
st. Emu Plains..........235 A9
st. North Ryde 282 H8
st. Wiley Park..........400 J2
KATHRYN
pl. Gymea Bay.........491 F8
pl. Lalor Park 245 C13
KATHY
cl. Pymble 223 B14
wy. Dean Park..........212 F15
KATIA
st. N Parramatta......278 F12
KATINA
st. Turramurra 223 A11
KATINKA
st. Bonnyrigg 364 D7
KATNOOK
pl. W Pnnant Hl.......249 A2
KATO
av. Newington 310 A15
KATOA
cl. N Narrabeen.......198 J13
pl. Marsfield............282 A3
KATRINA
av. Mona Vale..........198 J2
cl. Hobartville 118 E7
cr. Cabramatta W 364 H6
ct. Normanhurst 221 J11
pl. Baulkham Hl 247 G13
pl. Ermington..........280 D14
pl. Roselands..........401 E4
rd. Bringelly 418 J3
st. Seven Hills.........245 K12
KATTA
cl. Hornsby.............191 J7
KAUAI
pl. Kings Park 244 H3
KAURI
av. Berowra.............163 D1
pl. Blaxland............234 B8
st. Blacktown..........244 A15
st. Cabramatta 365 G10
KAVENAGH
cl. Prairiewood 335 A8
KAVIENG
av. Whalan 241 A8
KAWANA
cl. Epping...............250 H13
ct. Bella Vista..........246 E7
pl. Bangor...............459 J14
pl. Erskine Park.......270 G16
st. Bass Hill.............367 K6
st. Frenchs Frst.......255 G3
KAY
cl. Cherrybrook.......220 A11
cl. Jamisontown 266 B2
cl. Mona Vale..........198 H3
la. Jamisontown, off Kay Cl 266 B2
st. Blacktown..........274 H7
st. Carlingford.........280 C4
st. Granville 308 K10
st. Old Guildford......337 F7
KAYLEY
pl. Glenhaven..........218 D3
KAYLYN
pl. Mount Druitt 241 G12
KAYS
av.e, Marrickville 373 F13
av.w, Dulwich Hill.......373 E12
KAZANIS
ct. Werrington.........239 A12
KEA
cl. Acacia Gdn.........214 G15
KEADY
wy. Wentwthvle........277 E11
KEARNEY
ct. Baulkham Hl 247 A2
pl. Bonnyrigg 363 J8
rd. S Maroota............66 E1
KEARNS
av. Kearns 451 C16
la. Yagoona 369 D11
pl. Horngsea Pk 392 C14
KEARY
st. Willoughby.........285 F12
KEATES
av. Padstow Ht 429 E6
KEATING
pl. Denham Ct.........422 G16
st. Lidcombe...........339 J7
st. Maroubra...........407 C7
wy. Narellan Vale 508 G1
KEATO
av. Hamondvle 396 F16
KEATS
av. Riverwood 400 C13
av. Rockdale............403 C16
av. Ryde..................282 D12
cl. Wetherill Pk 334 H5
pl. Heathcote 518 C16
pl. Ingleburn 453 C12
pl. Winston Hills.......277 G1
rd. N Turramrra 223 E7
st. Carlingford.........250 B16
KEDA
cct. N Richmond.........87 D16
KEDDIE
pl. Riverstone 183 C9
KEDRON
av. Beecroft.............250 C8
pl. St Johns Pk 334 E15
rd. Ingleside............197 A8
st. Glenbrook 233 K13
KEDUMBA
cr. N Turramrra.......223 F2
KEECH
rd. Castlereagh........176 E12
KEEDEN
pl. Bonnyrigg 364 A7
KEEGAN
av. Glebe...................12 B11
pl. Forestville 256 A12
rd. Bass Hill.............367 G8
KEELE
st. Como 460 E5
st. Vaucluse............318 F15
KEELENDI
rd. W Pnnant Hl.......250 A1
KEELER
st. Carlingford.........280 A2
KEELO
st. Quakers Hill 243 D4
KEENAN
la. Chester Hill 368 C2
st. Mona Vale..........199 B3
KEENE
st. Baulkham Hl 247 F10
KEERA
st. Quakers Hill 243 F5
KEESING
cr. Blackett.............241 D4
st. Edensor Pk 363 G3
KEEVIN
st. Roselands..........401 A7
KEEYUGA
rd. Huntleys Pt 313 F13
KEGWORTH
st. Leichhardt............15 B3
KEIGHRAN
pl. Cherrybrook.......219 E6
pl. Minto.................482 H8
KEILEY
st. Marsfield............281 K5
KEINO
av. Newington 310 A15
KEIR
av. Hurlstone Pk 372 K14
KEIRA
av. Greenacre 370 F4
cl. Terrey Hills.........196 D5
pl. Beecroft.............249 K12
pl. Ruse..................512 F4
KEIRAN
la. Bondi Jctn 22 F9
st. Bondi Jctn 22 F9
KEIRLE
rd. Kellyville.............215 A4
st. North Manly 258 B14
KEITH
ct. Cherrybrook.......219 F6
la. Dulwich Hill........373 D12
pl. Baulkham Hl 247 E11
st. Clovelly..............377 K12
st. Dulwich Hill........373 D12
st. Earlwood 373 A16
st. Lindfield.............284 G1
st. Peakhurst 430 E1
st. S Penrith.............266 J2
wy. Mosman 317 A12
KEITH SMITH
av. Mascot 404 J6
KELBRAE
cl. Castle Hill...........247 J1
KELBURN
pl. Airds..................512 B13
rd. Roseville............284 F2
KELD
pl. Blacktown..........244 D15
KELDIE
st. Forestville 255 K6
KELHAM
st. Glendenning.......242 G7
KELLAWAY
pl. Wetherill Pk 304 G15
st. Doonside 243 B7
st. East Ryde...........282 J16
KELLER
pl. Casula...............395 A12
KELLERMAN
dr. St Helens Park....540 K9
KELLETT
pl. Rcuttrs Bay............4 K7
st. Potts Point.............4 J7
wy. Potts Point.............4 K7
KELLICAR
rd. Campbelltwn......510 H8
KELLICK
st. Waterloo..............19 F13
KELLOGG
rd. Rooty Hill...........242 E13
KELLOWAY
av. Camden 507 A7
KELLS
la. Darlinghurst...........4 D11
rd. Ryde..................312 D1
KELLY
cl. Baulkham Hl 247 A2
cl. Mount Druitt 241 E15
la. Brooklyn...............75 F12
la. Matraville...........436 G2
la. Padstow, off Watson Rd.........399 D14
pl. Mt Pritchard.......364 H14
rd. Ingleburn 422 G10
st. Austral 390 F15
st. Henley 313 B14
st. Matraville...........436 G1
st. Punchbowl..........400 B3
st. Sylvania.............461 K13
st. Ultimo 12 H14
KELLYS
esp. Northwood.........314 F7
KELMSCOTT
la. St Clair, off Kelmscott Wy.....270 G14
wy. St Clair..............270 F14
KELPA
pl. Allambie Ht, off Roosevelt Av......257 D12
KELRAY
pl. Asquith 192 A13
KELSALL
pl. Barden Rdg........488 G5
st. Doonside 273 E4
KELSEY
st. Arncliffe 403 F7
KELSO
cl. Bonnyrigg Ht......363 C6
cr. Moorebank 395 K7
la. Blacktown 274 H1
la. Randwick............377 A12
pl. St Andrews 452 A15
st. Burwood Ht........372 A3
st. Engadine............489 A8
KELTON
pl. Engadine............488 K8
KELVEDON
la. Marsden Pk........182 B11
KELVIN
ct. Oatlands 279 A10
gr. Winston Hills......277 F6
pde. Picnic Point........428 B7
pl. Busby.................363 H16
rd. St Ives 224 D16
st. Ashbury..............372 F8
KELVIN PARK
dr. Bringelly 388 G12
KEMBLA
av. Chester Hill 368 D1
cr. Ruse..................512 F4
st. Arncliffe..............403 D8
st. Croydon Pk.........371 F7
st. Dharruk 241 C8
st. Wakeley.............334 H14
KEMBLE
la. Mosman............317 A8
pl. Bilgola 169 F8
KEMERTON
la. St Clair, off Kemerton St......269 J11
st. St Clair..............269 J10
KEMIRA
pl. Cartwright..........394 D5
KEMMEL
cl. Bossley Park 334 B10
KEMMIS
st. Randwick...........377 D11
KEMP
av. Kirrawee 490 K8
av. Matraville...........436 J2
pl. Bonnyrigg 364 D5
pl. Glenorie 126 E4
pl. Minto..................482 G9
pl. Tregear 240 E7
st. Granville 308 G10
st. Mortdale 431 A6
st. Tennyson...........312 E9
KEMPBRIDGE
av. Seaforth............287 E9
KEMPE
pde. Kings Lngly.......246 B10
KEMPSEY
cl. Dee Why............258 H3
la. Jamisontown, off Kempsey St.........266 D5
pl. Bossley Park 333 D13
st. Blacktown 274 J2
st. Jamisontown 266 D5
wy. Hoxton Park......392 G9
KEMPT
st. Bonnyrigg..........363 K6
KENARF
cl. Kingswood.........238 A14
KENBURN
av. Cherrybrook.......219 G10
KENDAL
cr. Collaroy Plat.......228 E11
KENDALL
dr. Casula...............394 H16
dr. Casula...............424 C3
dr. Casula...............424 F2
la. Surry Hills............20 D3
la. The Rocks ....A K3
pl. Kareela 461 C13
pl. Kellyville.............186 G12
rd. Castle Cove 285 F3
st. Cabarita 342 D1
st. Campbelltwn......512
st. Ermington...........310
st. Fairfield W...........335
st. Granville 308
st. Harris Park.........308
st. Mortdale 430
st. Penrith...............237
st. Pymble 253
st. Riverstone 182
st. Rydalmere 310
st. Sans Souci.........463
st. Surry Hills............20
st. Thirlmere 562
st. West Pymble.......252
st. Woollahra 377
KENDALL INLET
Cabarita 312
KENDEE
st. Sadleir 364
KENEALLY
cr. Edensor Pk 333
wy. Casula...............424
KENELDA
av. Guildford...........338
KENGE
pl. Ambarvale..........510
KEN HALL
pl. Agnes Banks 117
KENIBEA
pl. Dee Why 258
KENILWORTH
cr. Cranebrook.........207
la. Bondi Jctn, off Flood La............377
rd. Dundas Vy 280
rd. Lindfield.............254
st. Bondi Jctn..........377
st. Croydon.............342
st. Miller..................393
KENJI
pl. Blacktown 273
KENLEY
rd. Normanhurst 221
KENMARE
rd. Londonderry 148
KENNA
pl. Cromer 227
pl. Gymea...............491
KENNEDIA
pl. Mt Annan 509
KENNEDY
av. Belmore.............371
cr. Bonnet Bay 460
dr. S Penrith.............236
gr. Appin.................569
la. Gladesville 313
la. Kingsford 376
pde. Lalor Park 245
pl. Bayview 168
pl. St Ives 224
st. Appin..................569
st. Appin..................569
st. Gladesville 313
st. Guildford............338
st. Kingsford 376
st. Liverpool............394
st. Panania..............428
st. Picnic Point........428
st. Revesby.............428
st. Ruse..................512
st. Woolmloo...............4
wy. Bonnyrigg..........364
KENNELLY
st. Colyton 270
KENNETH
av. Baulkham Hl 247
av. Kirrawee 490
av. Panania..............428
cr. Dean Park 242
la. Kingsford, off Kennedy St 376
pl. Dural 219
rd. Balgowlah 288
rd. Fairlight..............288
rd. Manly 288
rd. Manly Vale 287
rd. Manly Vale 288
st. Longueville 314
st. Mcquarie Fd 424
st. Ryde..................312
st. Tamarama 378
KENNETH SLESSOR
dr. Glenmore Pk......265

NNETT
Glenfield 424 D10
NNIFF
Rozelle 10 K1
NNINGTON
Quakers Hill 214 C12
NNINGTON OVAL
Auburn 339 A12
NNY
Casula 394 G13
Chifley 437 B8
St Marys 240 A14
St Helens Park 541 C3
Marayong 244 D6
Dundas Vy 279 H5
Fairfield W 334 K10
Pagewood 406 F9
NNY HILL
Currans Hill 510 C1
NOMA
Arndell Park 273 H9
NS
Frenchs Frst 255 H2
Yarramundi 145 B1
NSINGTON
Harringtn Pk 478 C1
Waterloo 19 G14
Kogarah, off
Kensington St 433 B5
v. Waterloo 19 H14
Cecil Hills 362 D7
Kensington 376 D13
Summer Hill 373 D2
Chippendale 19 C1
Kogarah 433 B5
Punchbowl 400 B9
Waterloo 19 H14
NSINGTON PARK
Schofields 183 B13
NT
Croydon Pk 371 K6
Roselands 400 J7
Newtown 17 D11
Newtown 17 E16
Turramurra 223 E10
Beverly Hills 430 J1
Bossley Park 333 H11
Colyton 270 E4
Heathcote 518 D11
Clarmnt Ms 268 J9
Marsfield 282 B6
Mascot 404 K3
Mascot 405 A1
Narellan Vale 478 H16
North Ryde 282 B6
Orchard Hills 268 J9
Rose Bay 347 K11
Tahmoor 566 F7
Turramurra 223 E9
Baulkham Hl 247 C7
Belmore 401 E1
Blacktown 244 D13
Collaroy 229 A14
Epping 250 H12
Glenbrook 234 B14
Hamondvle 396 G14
Millers Pt A C1
Millers Pt 1 D10
Minto 482 G3
Newtown 17 D16
Regents Pk 339 B16
Rockdale 403 E14
Sydney C D2
Sydney 3 E2
Waverley 377 H10
Winmalee 172 H14
NTHURST
Chester Hill 368 B5
Dural 188 E11
Kenthurst 188 B1
Kenthurst 188 E11
St Ives 224 A10
NTIA
Stanhpe Gdn 215 C9
. Cherrybrook 219 F7
Alfords Point 429 B13
NTUCKY
Glossodia 58 K8
Riverwood 400 A12
NTVILLE
Annandale 11 B7
Annandale 11 B7
NTWELL
Castle Hill 218 A14

av. Concord 341 H7
av. Thornleigh 220 J10
dr. S Windsor 151 A7
rd. Allambie Ht 257 G16
rd. North Manly 258 A16
st. Baulkham Hl 247 E12
KENTWOOD
pl. Narellan 478 G11
KENWARD
av. Chester Hill 338 A14
KENWICK
la. Beecroft 250 D7
KENWOOD
rd. Wedderburn 540 B11
KENWORTHY
st. Rydalmere 279 E14
KENWYN
cl. St Ives 224 J8
st. Bonnyrigg Ht 362 K7
st. Hurstville 432 D4
KENYON
cr. Doonside 243 D6
la. Fairfield 336 E12
rd. Bexley 432 D2
st. Fairfield 336 D12
KENYONS
rd. Merrylands W 307 A13
KEON
pl. Quakers Hill 214 F11
KEPOS
la. Redfern 20 A11
st. Redfern 20 A11
KEPPEL
av. Concord 341 H8
av. Riverwood 400 A16
cct. Hinchinbrk 362 K14
rd. Ryde 282 E12
st. Kings Lngly 245 E6
KERELA
av. Wahroonga 221 H16
KEREMA
pl. Glenfield 424 C13
KERILEE
ct. Bella Vista 246 H1
KERIN
av. Five Dock 342 K7
KERLE
cr. Castle Hill 218 J14
KERR
av. Bundeena 523 G8
cl. Narraweena 258 D3
cr. Pagewood 406 G7
pde. Auburn 339 E3
rd. Ingleburn 453 D3
st. Appin 569 E10
st. Hornsby 191 E11
KERRABEE
ct. Engadine 488 K10
KERRAN
cl. Cmbrdg Pk 238 A11
la. Cmbrdg Pk, off
Kerran Cl 238 A11
KERRAWAH
av. St Ives 223 K7
KERRIBEE
pl. Carlingford 249 H10
KERRIDGE
pl. Forest Lodge 18 A1
KERRIE
av. Regents Pk 369 A3
cr. Panania 397 K16
cr. Peakhurst 430 B4
pl. Hornsby 191 J9
rd. Oatlands 278 J12
st. Woodpark 306 H16
KERRINEA
rd. Sefton 368 F3
KERRS
rd. Berala 339 F10
rd. Castle Hill 247 J1
rd. Lidcombe 339 F10
rd. Mt Vernon 330 G12
KERRUISH
av. Homebush W 340 G8
KERRY
av. Epping 250 F11
av. Springwood 202 A5
cl. Beacon Hill 257 H5
cr. Roselands 401 C8
pl. Oakdale 500 D13
rd. Blacktown 243 J16
rd. Schofields 212 K4

KERSLAKE
av. Regents Pk 369 C3
gr. Menai 458 H15
KERSTIN
st. Quakers Hill 213 H9
KERULORI
cl. Hornsby Ht 161 H12
KERWICK
ct. Baulkham Hl 247 B3
KERWIN
cir. Hebersham 241 F1
KERYN
pl. Cabramatta 365 E10
KESAWAI
pl. Holsworthy 426 D2
KESSELL
av. Homebush W 340 H10
KESTER
cr. Oakhurst 241 K3
KESTON
av. Mosman 317 A8
la. Mosman, off
Keston Av 317 A8
KESTREL
av. Hinchinbrk 393 B3
cr. Erskine Park 270 K13
la. St Clair, off
Kestrel Cr 270 K13
pl. Bnkstn Aprt 397 J1
pl. Bella Vista 216 D14
pl. Ingleburn 453 G5
pl. Woronora Ht 489 C5
wy. Yarramundi 145 C6
KESWICK
av. Castle Hill 247 K5
st. Dee Why 259 A8
st. Georges Hall 367 H14
KETHEL
rd. Cheltenham 250 J7
KETTLE
la. Ultimo 12 H15
st. Redfern 19 H9
KETURAH
st. Glenwood 245 E2
KEVIN
av. Avalon 140 A14
av. Scotland I 168 J3
pl. Thirlmere 565 A2
st. Wentwthvle 277 D10
KEVIN COOMBS
av. Homebush B 310 E14
KEW
cl. Belrose 225 K13
pl. Dharruk 241 B7
pl. St Johns Pk 364 G3
wy. Airds 511 H16
KEW GARDENS
ct. Wattle Grove 426 A3
KEWIN
av. Mt Pritchard 364 D8
KEWOL
pl. Port Hacking 522 J2
KEY
ct. Baulkham Hl 246 J12
KEYNE
st. Prospect 275 A12
KEYPORT
cr. Glendenning 242 G4
KEYS
cl. Westleigh 220 J1
pde. Milperra 397 B9
pl. Liverpool 394 K4
KEYSOR
pl. Milperra 397 G9
rd. Pagewood 406 G7
KEYWORTH
dr. Blacktown 275 A7
KHANCOBAN
st. Heckenberg 363 K13
KHARTOUM
av. Gordon 253 J7
la. Gordon 253 J8
rd. Mcquarie Pk 282 G3
KIA
pl. Ambarvale 511 B13
KIAH
cl. Bayview 168 J16
cl. Hornsby Ht 191 G4
pl. Baulkham Hl 247 A5
pl. Bonnyrigg 364 B9
pl. Greystanes 306 B7

pl. Miranda 491 H5
KIAKA
cr. Jamisontown 266 D6
KIALBA
rd. Campbelltwn 481 H16
KIAMA
cl. Terrey Hills 196 E6
pl. Emu Plains 234 K9
st. Greystanes 305 J2
st. Miranda 462 B15
st. Padstow 429 F3
st. Prestons 392 K14
KIAMALA
cr. Killara 254 C14
KIANDRA
cl. Terrey Hills 196 E5
pl. Heckenberg 364 A15
pl. Wakeley 334 F14
KIANGA
cl. Prestons 422 J1
KIAORA
la. Double Bay 14 D10
rd. Double Bay 14 E10
KIARA
cl. Bangor 459 H14
cl. N Sydney 6 C11
st. Marayong 244 C2
KIATA
cr. Doonside 243 H14
KIBAH
st. Busby 363 J13
KIBBLE
pl. Narellan 478 C8
KIBER
dr. Glenmore Pk 266 C12
dr. Glenmore Pk 266 E11
KIBO
rd. Regents Pk 339 C16
KIDD
cl. Bidwill 211 G16
ct. Currans Hill 479 H13
pl. Minto 453 B14
st. Richmond 119 K5
KIDMAN
la. Paddington 4 H15
st. Blaxland 233 H13
st. Coogee 377 F16
st. Glenwood 215 H15
KIDMANS
tce. Woolmloo, off
Junction La 4 E5
KIDNER
cl. Castle Hill 218 J13
KIERANS
pl. Duffys Frst 194 G7
KIEREN
dr. Blacktown 273 G5
KIERNAN
rd. Abbotsbury 363 B2
KIEV
st. Merrylands 307 C11
KIEWA
cl. Bayview 168 J16
pl. Kirrawee 460 K15
rd. St Marys 239 H3
KIEWARRA
st. Kingsgrove 401 F7
KIHILLA
rd. Auburn 309 C16
st. Fairfield Ht 335 H9
KIKORI
cr. Whalan 241 A9
pl. Glenfield 424 F10
KILBENNY
rd. Kellyville 185 D16
KILBORN
pl. Menai 458 G12
KILBRIDE
av. Dharruk 241 C5
st. Hurlstone Pk 372 H13
KILBURN
cl. Beacon Hill 257 K9
KILBY
pl. Illawong 459 J6
st. Kellyville 185 B15
KILCARN
pl. Wakeley 334 G14
KILDARE
gr. Killarney Ht 286 D2
la. Coogee, off
Beach St 377 J14

rd. Blacktown 244 B16
rd. Doonside 243 D14
KILGOUR
ct. Glen Alpine 510 F9
KILIAN
st. Winston Hills 246 J16
KILKEE
av. Kingsgrove 402 B6
KILKENNY
av. Killarney Ht 256 B14
av. Smithfield 335 E2
rd. S Penrith 266 K2
KILLALA
av. Killarney Ht 255 J13
KILLALOE
av. Pennant Hills 250 C1
KILLANOOLA
st. Villawood 367 G4
KILLARA
av. Killara 254 A14
av. Kingsgrove 402 B6
av. Panania 398 A15
av. Riverwood 400 A14
cr. Winmalee 173 F4
pl. Dharruk 241 C7
KILLARNEY
av. Blacktown 274 A1
av. Glenmore Pk 266 H8
cl. Castle Hill 248 E2
ct. McGraths Hl 121 J11
dr. Killarney Ht 256 A15
la. Mosman, off
Killarney St 317 B4
st. Mosman 317 A3
KILLAWARRA
pl. Wahroonga 222 E2
rd. Duffys Frst 195 A6
KILLEATON
st. St Ives 223 H10
KILLEEN
st. Auburn 338 H8
st. Balmain 8 D9
st. Balmain East 8 D9
st. Wentwthvle 307 B2
KILLINGER
av. Liverpool 394 J1
KILLOOLA
st. Concord W 311 D13
st. Concord W 311 E12
KILLURAN
av. Emu Heights 234 K5
KILLYLEA
wy. Wentwthvle 277 E11
KILMARNOCK
rd. Engadine 488 J10
KILMINSTER
la. Woollahra 22 B2
KILMORE
st. Kellyville 185 C16
KILMOREY
st. Busby 363 G15
KILMORY
pl. Mt Krng-gai 162 K14
KILN
pl. Woodcroft 243 F9
KILNER
la. Camperdwn 17 B4
KILPA
pl. St Ives 254 A3
KILTO
cr. Rooty Hill 242 F11
KIM
av. Regents Pk 369 A3
cl. Cabramatta 365 E11
cl. Thirlmere 564 J4
pl. Ingleburn 453 E12
pl. Quakers Hill 214 E16
pl. Toongabbie 276 G9
st. Gladesville 312 K3
KIMBA
cl. Westleigh 220 G6
KIMBAR
pl. Yarrawarrah 489 E14
KIMBARRA
av. Baulkham Hl 248 A8
av. Camden 507 A4
cl. Berowra Ht 133 D6
rd. Pymble 252 K2
KIMBER
la. Forest Lodge 11 H16
la. Haymarket E D5

KIMBERLEY
av. Lane Cove 314 F1
cr. Fairfield W 335 F9
ct. Bella Vista 246 E8
gr. Rosebery 375 K14
la. Hurstville 431 K3
la. Windsor Dn 181 A1
pl. Gymea Bay 491 J9
rd. Carlingford 250 B13
rd. Hurstville 432 A2
st. East Killara 254 H5
st. Guildford 338 B2
st. Leumeah 482 E10
st. Merrylands 338 B2
st. Rooty Hill 241 K15
st. Vaucluse 348 F7
KIMBRIKI
rd. Ingleside 196 H11
KIMO
pl. Marayong 244 B3
st. N Balgowlah 287 F5
st. Roseville 284 B5
KIMPTON
st. Banksia 403 C12
KIMS
av. Lugarno 429 K16
KINALDY
cr. Kellyville 186 K16
KINARRA
av. Kellyville 216 F4
KINCHEGA
cr. Glenwood 215 E15
ct. Holsworthy 426 C5
ct. Wattle Grove 426 C5
pl. Bow Bowing 452 D14
KINCRAIG
ct. Castle Hill 218 D7
KINCUMBER
pl. Engadine 489 B10
rd. Bonnyrigg 363 J9
KINDEE
av. Bonnyrigg 363 K9
KINDELAN
rd. Winston Hills 246 H16
KINDER
st. Lalor Park 245 F10
KINDILAN
pl. Miranda 492 E5
KINDILEN
cl. Rouse Hill 185 D6
KING
av. Balgowlah 287 K9
la. Balmain 7 D7
la. Moorebank 395 G8
la. Newtown 374 J9
la. Randwick 377 A11
la. Rockdale 403 E14
la. Waverton 5 A4
la. Wollstncraft 5 A4
la. Penrith, off King St 237 C9
la. Rockdale, off King St 403 D15
la. Marrickville, off Renwick St 373 J16
la. Mascot, off Sutherland St 405 F5
pl. Kings Lngly 245 C3
rd. Camden S 506 K11
rd. Fairfield W 335 A13
rd. Hornsby 192 A15
rd. Hornsby 192 C15
rd. Ingleside 197 J7
rd. Prairiewood 335 A8
rd. Wahroonga 222 D1
rd. Wilberforce 91 K4
sq. Bidwill 211 G15
st. Alexandria 374 H8
st. Appin 569 F11
st. Ashbury 372 F9
st. Ashfield 372 G4
st. Auburn 309 D14
st. Balmain 7 D7
st. Berowra 133 E12
st. Bondi 377 J5
st. Campbelltwn 511 G3
st. Canterbury 372 F10
st. Concord W 311 C16
st. Croydon 342 D15
st. Dundas Vy 280 C9
st. Eastlakes 405 J5
st. Enfield 371 F4
st. Glenbrook 233 J14
st. Guildford W 336 H1
st. Heathcote 518 F10
st. Hunters Hill 313 E11
st. Kogarah 433 A4
st. Maianbar 522 K9
st. Manly Vale 287 G3
st. Marrickville 374 B10
st. Mascot 405 A4
st. Mt Krng-gai 163 A13
st. Naremburn 315 G2
st. Narrabeen 229 A5
st. Newport 169 F10
st. Newtown 17 G12
st. Newtown 374 H8
st. Parramatta 307 K5
st. Penrith 237 C10
st. Randwick 376 J10
st. Riverstone 182 H6
st. Rockdale 403 D15
st. Rossmore 390 C15
st. St Marys 269 H1
st. St Peters 374 H8
st. S Hurstville 432 C10
st. Sydney C A4
st. Sydney C D4
st. Sydney 3 E2
st. Tahmoor 565 G11
st. Turramurra 222 H12
st. Waverton 315 D11
st. Wilberforce 91 J4
st. Wollstncraft 5 A4
st. Wollstncraft 315 D11
st.w, Appin 569 E11
KINGARTH
st. Busby 363 G13
KINGDOM
pl. Kellyville 215 H4
KINGDON
pde. Long Point 454 E13
KING EDWARD
av. Bayview 169 B13
st. Croydon 342 D11
st. Pymble 253 E3
st. Rockdale 403 B15
st. Roseville 285 B5
KINGFISHER
av. Bossley Park 333 F7
av. Hinchinbrk 363 C15
cr. Grays Point 491 F14
dr. Duffys Frst 195 C1
pl. Glendenning 242 H5
pl. W Pnnant Hl 249 D6
st. Ingleburn 453 H8
wy. St Clair 270 F13
KING GEORGE
st. Lavender Bay 5 E13
st. McMahons Pt 5 E13
KING GEORGES
rd. Beverly Hills 401 A10
rd. Blakehurst 432 A9
rd. Hurstville 431 F3
rd. Penshurst 431 F3
rd. Roselands 400 K7
rd. S Hurstville 432 A9
rd. Wiley Park 400 G1
KINGHORNE
rd. Bonnyrigg Ht 363 H6
KING MAX
st. Mosman 317 C10
KINGMORE
la. Glenbrook 233 K15
KINGS
av. Roseville 284 F6
la. Btn-le-Sds 433 K4
la. Darlinghurst F K4
la. Darlinghurst 4 C10
pl. Beverly Hills 401 F15
pl. Carlingford 279 B6
pl. Kingsgrove 401 F15
rd. Btn-le-Sds 433 H3
rd. Castle Hill 217 C8
rd. Denistone E 281 G10
rd. Five Dock 342 G10
rd. Ingleburn 453 G4
rd. Vaucluse 348 G3
KINGS BAY
av. Five Dock 342 G9
KINGSBURY
la. Kingswood, off Kingsbury Pl 238 C12
pl. Jannali 460 K13
pl. Kingswood 238 C13
st. Croydon Pk 371 G6
KINGSCLARE
st. Leumeah 481 K15
st. Leumeah 482 B16
KINGSCLEAR
la. Alexandria 18 G13
rd. Alexandria 18 G13
KINGSCOTE
pl. Kingswood 267 H3
KINGSCOTT
pl. Castle Hill 218 J8
KINGS CROSS
rd. Darlinghurst 4 H8
rd. Potts Point 4 H8
rd. Rcuttrs Bay 13 A9
KINGSDALE
rd. Prestons 392 K16
KINGSFIELD
av. Glenmore Pk 266 F14
KINGSFORD
av. Eastwood 281 J6
av. Five Dock 343 A11
av. S Turramrra 251 K7
st. Blacktown 245 C7
st. Ermington 280 A14
st. Maroubra 406 G10
st. Smithfield 335 F3
KINGSGROVE
av. Bexley North 402 A9
av. Kingsgrove 402 A9
rd. Belmore 401 H3
rd. Kingsgrove 401 K9
KINGSHILL
rd. Mulgoa 295 F13
KINGSLAND
rd. Berala 339 C16
rd. Regents Pk 369 C2
rd. Strathfield 371 E1
rd.n, Bexley North 402 F9
rd.s, Bexley 402 H12
KINGSLANGLEY
rd. Greenwich 314 J6
KINGSLEA
pl. Canley Ht 335 E15
KINGSLEY
cl. S Windsor 120 H15
cl. Wahroonga 222 A9
gr. Kingswood 238 B12
la. Kingswood, off Kingsley Gr 238 C12
st. Blackett 241 B4
KINGS LYNN
ct. W Pnnant Hl 249 G5
KINGSMERE
dr. Glenwood 245 H3
KINGS PARK
cct. Five Dock 342 G9
rd. Five Dock 342 G9
KINGSTON
av. Concord 312 A15
av. Panania 428 F3
cl. W Pnnant Hl 249 A8
la. Camperdwn 17 B10
la. Newtown 17 B10
pl. Abbotsbury 363 C1
pl. Airds 511 J14
rd. Camperdwn 17 A9
rd. Mt Annan 479 G14
rd. Newtown 17 A10
st. Botany 405 E13
st. Haberfield 343 D15
KINGSVIEW
wy. Glenwood, off Citadel Pl 246 C7
KINGSWAY
Beverly Hills 401 G14
Caringbah 492 H5
Cronulla 493 J11
Dee Why 258 H4
Gymea 491 D3
Kingsgrove 401 G14
Miranda 492 C4
Woolooware 493 E9
KINGSWOOD
rd. Engadine 489 A12
rd. Orchard Hills 267 H12
KINGTON
la. Cranebrook, off Pendock Rd 207 F14
pl. Cranebrook 207 F14
st. Minchinbury 272 E8
KINGUSSIE
av. Castle Hill 218 B7
KING WILLIAM
st. Greenwich 314 K9
KINKA
rd. Duffys Frst 195 C7
rd. Terrey Hills 195 C7
KINKUNA
st. Busby 363 G13
KINLEY
pl. Baulkham Hl 247 H10
KINMONT
rd. S Penrith 267 C6
KINNANE
cr. Acacia Gdn 214 H14
KINNARD
wy. Kellyville 217 A1
KINNEAR
st. Harringtn Pk 478 D2
st. Harringtn Pk 478 F2
KINROSS
ct. Wattle Grove 426 A5
pl. Engadine 518 F4
pl. Revesby 428 G5
pl. St Andrews 452 A15
st. Riverstone 183 C9
KINROSS PATH
Winmalee 173 E12
KINSDALE
cl. Killarney Ht 255 H12
KINSEL
av. Kingsgrove 401 H14
gr. Bexley 402 J15
KINSELA
st. Illawong 460 B4
KINSELLA
ct. Kellyville 186 K16
KINSELLAS
dr. Lane Cove W, off Whitfield Av 283 F12
KINSON
cr. Denistone 281 C11
KINTORE
st. Dulwich Hill 373 D10
st. Wahroonga 222 G4
KINTYRE
pl. St Andrews 481 K4
st. Cecil Hills 362 D3
KIOGLE
st. Wahroonga 221 H16
KIOLA
pl. Castle Hill 218 A11
rd. Northbridge 285 K15
st. Smithfield 336 A4
KIOLOA
wy. Merrylands W 306 J11
KIORA
av. Mosman 317 C2
cr. Yennora 337 A9
ct. Prestons 392 H13
la. Miranda 492 A4
rd.n, Miranda 492 A4
rd.s, Miranda 491 K9
rd.s, Yowie Bay 491 K9
st. Canley Ht 365 E3
st. Canley Vale 365 E3
st. Panania 398 C16
KIOWA
pl. Bossley Park 333 K10
KIPARA
cr. Warragamba 353 G3
KIPARRA
cr. S Penrith 266 G6
st. Engadine 488 F12
st. Pymble 253 C9
KIPLING
dr. Colyton 270 J8
rd. Wetherill Pk 334 J6
KIPPARA
pl. Bradbury 511 E14
rd. Dover Ht 348 E14
KIPPAX
la. St Clair, off Kippax Pl 269 K15
pl. Menai 458 F8
pl. St Clair 269 K15
pl. Shalvey 211 A15
st. Greystanes 305 J9
st. Surry Hills F A16
st. Surry Hills 3 H16
KIPPIST
av. Minchinbury 271 B6
KIRA
av. Northmead 248 B16
KIRAWA
cl. Turramurra 222
KIRBY
pl. St Ives 224
st. Dundas 279
st. Rydalmere 309
wk. Zetland 375
KIRIWINA
pl. Glenfield 424
KIRK
av. Guildford 338
cr. Kirrawee 491
pl. Carlingford 249
st. Chatswood 284
st. Ultimo 12
KIRKBRIDE
wy. Lilyfield 10
KIRKBY
pl. Miranda 492
KIRKCALDY
ct. Kellyville 217
KIRKETON
rd. Darlinghurst 4
KIRKHAM
la. Elderslie 477
la. Kirkham 477
mw. Wattle Grove 425
rd. Auburn 338
st. Beecroft 250
st. Narellan 478
KIRKMAN
la. Chester Hill 337
rd. Blacktown 274
KIRKOSWALD
av. Mosman 317
KIRK PATRICK
la. Petersham 15
KIRKPATRICK
av. West Hoxton 391
st. N Turramrra 193
wy. Berowra Wtr 132
KIRKSTONE
rd. Collaroy Plat 228
KIRKTON
pl. Edensor Pk 333
KIRKWOOD
av. N Epping 251
ct. Castle Hill 248
rd. Cronulla 494
st. Seaforth 286
KIRRA
pl. Wilberforce 91
rd. Allambie Ht 257
KIRRANG
av. Villawood 367
st. Beverly Hills 401
st. Cromer 227
st. Wareemba 343
KIRRAWEE
av. Kirrawee 490
KIRRIBILLI
av. Kirribilli 2
KIRRIFORD
wy. Carlingford 249
KIRRILY
pl. Bass Hill 367
wy. Castle Hill 248
KIRSTY
cr. Hassall Gr 212
KISDON
cr. Prospect 274
KISHANLAL
cl. Glenwood 215
KISSING POINT
rd. Dundas 279
rd. Dundas 280
rd. Dundas Vy 279
rd. Ermington 280
rd. N Parramatta 279
rd. Oatlands 279
rd. S Turramrra 252
rd. Turramurra 222
KISTA DAN
av. Tregear 240
KIT
pl. Rooty Hill 272
KITA
rd. Berowra Ht 133
KITAVA
pl. Glenfield 424

'CHEN
West Hoxton......392 D11
'CHENER
Concord......342 C2
Earlwood......402 J2
Regents Pk......369 B2
Holsworthy......426 G3
Cherrybrook......220 B13
. Bankstown......369 E15
Artarmon......284 H15
Cherrybrook......220 B14
Balgowlah......287 G6
Caringbah......492 K6
Kogarah......433 A4
Maroubra......407 B11
Oatley......431 E13
St Ives......224 D5
CHING
Currans Hill......479 H13
E
Green Valley......363 D12
Ingleburn......453 H8
Emu Plains......235 C8
SON
Minto......453 A16
Casula......424 E3
TANI
Killara......253 E14
Kirrawee......491 B6
TY
Bligh Park......150 E7
TYHAWK
Raby......481 F2
TYS
Mcquarie Pk......282 H5
VI
St Clair......269 G16
Lethbrdg Pk......240 F1
VONG
Yowie Bay......492 A10
EINS
Northmead......277 H7
EIST
Emerton......240 J4
EMM
Bnkstn Aprt......367 J16
APSACK
Jamisontown......266 D3
Glenbrook......234 F16
APTON
St Johns Pk......364 D3
EALE
Edensor Pk......333 G14
IGHT
Kings Lngly......245 C3
Panania......398 A15
Kingswood......238 B13
Newtown......17 D11
Erskineville, off
Knight St......374 J9
Bligh Park......150 G8
Castlecrag......286 E11
Castle Hill......248 D4
Minto......453 B15
Arncliffe......403 C10
Erskineville......374 K9
Homebush......341 D9
Lansvale......366 K6
Castle Hill......248 D3
IGHTON
S Penrith......267 B7
IGHTS
Galston......159 J8
IGHTSBRIDGE
Belrose......226 A12
Glenwood......245 G3
Castle Hill......217 F6
OCK
Beverly Hills......430 J2
OCK FARRELL
Glenorie......128 F7
OCKLAYDE
Ashfield......342 J14
OLL
Turrella......403 G6
OLTON
Oakhurst......241 H3
OT
Hinchinbrk......393 D2
OTWOOD
Mcquarie Fd......454 F7

KNOWLES
av. Matraville......437 A1
av. North Bondi......348 E16
pl. Bossley Park......334 C9
KNOWLMAN
av. Pymble......253 G3
KNOX
av. Epping......281 D2
la. Double Bay......14 C9
pl. Normanhurst......221 F9
pl. Rouse Hill......185 C6
rd. Doonside......243 A9
st. Ashfield......372 H3
st. Belmore......371 B13
st. Chippendale......18 H1
st. Clovelly......377 G12
st. Double Bay......14 C9
st. Glenmore Pk......265 K5
st. Lindfield......283 E3
st. Pendle Hill......276 G11
st. St Marys......269 K3
KOALA
av. Ingleburn......453 F5
cl. St Ives......253 K2
gln. Cranebrook......237 C1
pl. Avalon......170 A2
pl. Hornsby Ht......191 F1
rd. Blaxland......233 E4
rd. Greenacre......370 G15
rd. Lilli Pilli......522 E4
rd. Punchbowl......370 F16
wy. Horsley Pk......332 B8
KOBADA
pl. Sylvania......461 G14
rd. Dover Ht......348 E8
KOBINA
av. Glenmore Pk......266 A6
av. Glenmore Pk......266 A7
KOCHIA
la. Lindfield......254 E16
KODALA
la. Glenbrook......233 K13
wy. Bangor......459 H14
KOEL
pl. Ingleburn......453 H6
pl. Woronora Ht......489 D3
st. Hinchinbrk......393 C4
KOKERA
st. Hunters Hill......314 A11
KOKODA
av. Wahroonga......223 C6
cct. Mt Annan......479 D11
cr. Beacon Hill......257 F8
pl. Bossley Park......333 K6
pl. Glenfield......424 H10
st. Abbotsford......343 A3
st. North Ryde......282 K11
KOLODONG
dr. Quakers Hill......244 A1
KOLONGA
pl. Frenchs Frst......256 G7
KOLOONA
dr. Emu Plains......234 K8
st. Berowra......133 F10
st. Berowra Ht......133 F8
KOLORA
rd. Ebenezer......63 B5
KOMIATUM
st. Holsworthy......426 E3
KOMIRRA
rd. Cranebrook......207 D5
KOMMER
pl. St Marys......239 D4
KONA
cl. Berowra......133 F10
KONDA
cl. Bayview......168 J15
pl. Bangor......459 J14
pl. Turramurra......252 E4
KONRAD
av. Greenacre......369 J14
KONRADS
av. Newington......310 B15
pl. Menai......458 E14
KONTISTA
rd. Leppington......419 J11
KOOBA
av. Chatswd W......284 E8
st. Merrylands......306 H10
KOOBILYA
st. Seaforth......287 C7

KOOEMBA
rd. Beverly Hills......401 D11
KOOKABURRA
cl. Bayview......168 H12
cr. Glenmore Pk......266 D13
gr. Glenwood......215 D16
la. Kingsgrove......402 B10
la. St Clair, off
Kookaburra Pl......270 K14
pl. Blaxland......234 D5
pl. Erskine Park......270 K14
pl. Grays Point......491 F15
pl. W Pnnant Hl......248 J6
rd. Hornsby Ht......191 E1
rd. Prestons......392 K15
rd.n,Prestons......392 K12
rd.n,Prestons......393 A12
st. Greystanes......306 C3
st. Ingleburn......453 F7
KOOLA
av. East Killara......254 E8
KOOLOONA
cr. Bradbury......511 F14
cr. West Pymble......253 A14
KOOLOORA
av. Harbord......288 H1
KOOMBALAH
av. S Turramrra......252 C9
KOOMOOLOO
cr. Shalvey......210 G14
KOONAWARRA
av. Lindfield......283 J3
st. Villawood......367 J4
KOONGARA
rd. Roseville Ch......285 F1
KOONOONA
av. Villawood......367 A2
KOONYA
av. Bankstown......399 B3
cct. Caringbah......492 H1
KOORA
av. Wahroonga......222 B10
KOORABAN
st. Waterfall......519 D13
KOORABAR
rd. Bangor......459 H15
KOORABEL
av. Gymea......491 D5
la. Gymea, off
Koorabel Av......491 E5
pl. Baulkham Hl......247 A13
rd. Lalor Park......245 D12
st. Lugarno......430 A13
KOORALA
st. Manly Vale......288 A4
KOORANA
cl. Baulkham Hl......247 D5
rd. Tahmoor......566 F7
KOORANGA
pl. Normanhurst......221 H8
KOORANGI
av. Elanora Ht......198 B16
KOORAWATHA
st. Hornsby Ht......161 E15
KOOREELA
st. Kingsgrove......402 A9
KOORINDA
av. Kensington......376 E14
av. Villawood......367 B2
KOORINE
av. Emu Plains......235 A8
KOORINGA
rd. Chatswood......285 C8
KOORINGAI
av. Phillip Bay......436 H11
KOORINGAL
av. Thornleigh......221 A6
dr. Agnes Banks......146 B4
KOORONG
pl. Bangor......459 H14
st. Berowra......133 E9
st. Marsfield......282 A3
KOOROOL
av. Lalor Park......245 J12
KOOROOMA
pl. Sylvania......462 D7
KOOTINGAL
st. Greystanes......306 B7
KOOWONG
av. Mosman......317 A1

KOOYONG
av. Mt Colah......192 D3
rd. Riverview......313 J5
st. Pymble......253 C9
st. St Johns Pk......364 G2
wy. Shalvey......210 J14
KORANGI
rd. Pymble......223 F14
KORBEL
pl. Georges Hall......367 H10
KORIMUL
cr. S Penrith......266 H7
la. S Penrith, off
Korimul Cr......266 H7
KORINYA
pl. Castle Cove......286 D6
KOROKAN
rd. Lilli Pilli......522 G3
KORTUM
pl. Auburn......339 A4
KOSCIUSKO
pl. Bow Bowing......452 D13
pl. Heckenberg......363 K11
st. Bossley Park......334 B7
KOSMALA
cl. Newington......310 C12
KOSMINA
st. Glenwood......215 J16
KOTA BAHRU
rd. Holsworthy......426 F11
KOTARA
pl. Miranda......492 E2
KOVACS
st. Rooty Hill......271 K5
KOWAN
rd. Mooney Mooney..75 D2
KOWARI
st. St Helens Park....511 H16
KRAHE
rd. Wilberforce......61 F13
KRECKLER
cr. Lalor Park......245 G11
KRESSER
gr. Canterbury......372 E15
KRISTA
pl. Tahmoor......566 A9
KRISTEN
pl. W Pnnant Hl......249 B6
KRISTINE
av. Baulkham Hl......247 K9
pl. Cherrybrook......219 E6
pl. Mona Vale......198 H1
st. Winmalee......173 E7
KRISTY
pl. Berowra......133 C13
KROOMBIT
st. Dulwich Hill......373 B10
KRUGER
la. Erskine Park, off
Kruger Pl......300 K1
la. Erskine Park, off
Kruger Pl......301 A1
pl. Erskine Park......300 K1
KRUI
st. Fairlight......288 B9
KUALA
cl. Dean Park......242 G1
KUBOR
cr. Whalan......241 A13
st. Glenfield......424 G13
KUDILLA
st. Engadine......488 G12
KUHN
st. Blair Athol......511 B2
KUKUNDI
dr. Glenmore Pk......266 C6
KULA
ct. Baulkham Hl......246 J7
pl. Bangor......459 H14
KULALYE
pl. Belrose......226 A10
KULAMAN
cr. Glenmore Pk......266 A12
KULGOA
av. Ryde......282 A14
cr. Terrey Hills......195 E6
la. Bellevue Hill......14 G10
rd. Bellevue Hill......14 H11
rd. Pymble......253 H4
st. Lalor Park......245 H10
st. Leumeah......481 J15

KULGUN
av. Auburn......339 B11
KULINIA
st. Engadine......488 H11
KULLAH
pde. Lane Cove W......283 K14
KULLAROO
av. Bradbury......511 H14
av. Castle Hill......217 K7
KULLEROO
cr. Clarmnt Ms......268 H1
KULLI
pl. Engadine......489 C10
KUMA
pl. Glenmore Pk......266 E12
KUMALI
cl. Allambie Ht......257 H14
KUMARNA
st. Duffys Frst......194 J1
KUMBARA
cl. Glenmore Pk......266 D10
KUMBARDANG
av. Miranda......492 B2
KUMQUAT
wy. Glenwood......215 E13
KUMULLA
rd. Miranda......492 F1
KUNARI
pl. Mona Vale......199 A1
KUNDABUNG
st. Belimbla Pk......501 B16
KUNDI
st. Blaxland......234 D7
KUNDIBAH
rd. Elanora Ht......198 F15
KUNDUL
pl. Engadine......488 K9
KUNGALA
rd. Beecroft......250 A11
st. St Marys......239 F15
st. Villawood......367 F4
KUNGAR
rd. Caringbah......492 F13
KUNIPIPI
st. St Clair......269 G8
KUNYAL
pl. Greystanes......306 B6
KUPPA
rd. Ryde......282 B13
KURA
pl. Seven Hills......275 H8
KURAGI
cl. Glenmore Pk......266 D7
KURAMA
cr. Whalan......241 A9
KURANDA
av. Padstow......399 F14
cr. St Marys......269 C4
KURARA
cl. Terrey Hills......196 C6
KU-RING-GAI
av. Turramurra......222 K14
pl. Bow Bowing......452 C14
KU-RING-GAI CHASE
rd. Krngai Ch NP......163 E16
rd. Mt Colah......192 C6
KURMOND
rd. Freemns Rch......90 B3
rd. Kurmond......56 F16
rd. N Richmond......87 K1
rd. Wilberforce......61 B15
st. Jamisontown......266 D4
KURNELL
rd. Cronulla......493 J10
rd. Woolooware......493 J10
st. Botany......405 J13
st. Btn-le-Sds......433 H3
KUROKI
st. Penshurst......431 F7
KURPUN
pl. Glenmore Pk......266 A11
KURRABA
rd. Neutral Bay......5 K7
rd. N Sydney......5 K7
KURRABI
rd. Allambie Ht......257 C8
KURRAGHEIN
av. Rcuttrs Bay......13 B8
KURRAGLEN
pl. Comleroy......56 A9

KURRAJONG
av. Georges Hall 367 J10
av. Mount Druitt 241 A14
cct. Mt Annan 509 E5
cr. Blacktown 274 E8
rd. Casula 394 E14
rd. Frenchs Frst 256 F1
rd. Greystanes 305 E12
rd. Horngsea Pk 392 F10
rd. Hoxton Park 392 E10
rd. Kurrajong 85 E1
rd. Lurnea 394 E14
rd. N St Marys 240 A13
rd. Prestons 393 G13
rd. Richmond 117 K1
st. Cabramatta 365 G8
st. Cheltenham 251 A5
st. Pennant Hills 250 K4
st. Sutherland 460 E16
KURRAMATTA
pl. Cronulla 493 G12
KURRARA
st. Lansvale 366 F8
KURRAWA
av. Coogee 407 H1
KURRAWONG
la. Mosman, off Warringah La 317 C3
KURREWA
pl. Kareela 461 C10
KURRI
st. Lane Cove W 284 D15
st. Loftus 489 K11
KURU
st. N Narrabeen 198 J14
KURUK
pl. Turramurra 252 E5
KURWIN
st. Engadine 488 H10
KUTA
pl. Quakers Hill 213 H9
KUTMUT
st. Glenmore Pk 266 D9
KUTS
av. Newington 310 B13
KUTTABUL
pl. Elanora Ht 198 F12
KUYORA
pl. N Narrabeen 198 G12
KWANI
pl. Narraweena 258 B2
KYALITE
st. Glenwood 245 F1
KYANITE
pl. Eagle Vale 481 G5
KYARRA
tce. Glenmore Pk 266 H12
KYD
pl. Wetherill Pk 334 G3
KYDRA
cl. Prestons 393 B16
cl. Prestons 423 B1
KYEEMA
pde. Belrose 225 H15
pl. Bow Bowing 452 C16
pl. Doonside 243 H16
st. Picton 561 D2
KYEEMAGH
av. Mascot 404 E12
KYLE
av. Glenhaven 218 D2
pde. Connells Pt 431 J14
pde. Kyle Bay 431 J15
st. Arncliffe 403 H8
KYLEANNE
pl. Dean Park 242 H1
KYLIE
av. Killara 254 B9
cr. W Pnnant Hl 249 B11
pde. Punchbowl 399 K9
pl. Camden S 507 B13
pl. Frenchs Frst 256 F8
pl. Ingleburn 453 D10
wy. Casula 424 F2
KYLIE TENNANT
cl. Glenmore Pk 265 J7
KYMEA
pl. Hebersham 241 E9
KYNASTON
av. Randwick 376 K12
KYNGDON
st. Cammeray 315 H4
KYOGLE
pl. Frenchs Frst 256 F8
pl. Grays Point 491 B14
pl. Hoxton Park 393 A6
rd. Bass Hill 367 K5
rd. Northbridge 285 K14
st. Eastlakes 405 K5
st. Maroubra 407 E12
KYONG
st. Lane Cove W 284 C16
KYRA
pl. Rooty Hill 241 J14
KYRE
cr. Emu Plains 234 K8
KYWONG
av. Castle Hill 218 B11
av. Pymble 253 F2
rd. Berowra 133 B16
rd. Elanora Ht 198 D13
st. Telopea 279 F7

L

LA BOHEME
av. Caringbah 492 D11
LABRADOR
st. Rooty Hill 272 C5
LABUAN
rd. Wattle Grove 396 B15
LACEBARK
wy. Castle Hill 248 G2
LACEY
pl. Blacktown 275 A3
st. Kogarah Bay 432 J11
st. Surry Hills 20 A2
LACHAL
av. Kogarah 433 D6
LACHLAN
av. Harringtn Pk 478 D6
av. Mcquarie Pk 282 E3
av. Sylvania Wtr 462 F10
av. West Pymble 252 H9
dr. Winston Hills 277 A2
gr. Carlingford 279 J7
pl. Berowra 133 B15
pl. Campbelltwn 511 G9
pl. Silverdale 354 B10
st. Bossley Park 333 G6
st. Liverpool 365 D16
st. Liverpool 365 F16
st. Revesby 399 A9
st. St Marys 269 C1
st. Warwck Frm 365 D16
st. Warwck Frm 365 F16
st. Waterloo 20 A14
LACK
pl. Werrington 238 F10
LACKENWOOD
cr. Galston 159 E9
LACKEY
pl. Currans Hill 479 J11
st. Fairfield 336 D14
st. Merrylands 338 B1
st. N Parramatta 278 D9
st. St Peters 374 H12
st. S Granville 338 E1
st. Summer Hill 373 C4
LACKS
pl. Blair Athol 511 A3
LACOCKE
wy. Airds 511 J15
LACROZIA
la. Darlinghurst 4 H13
LACY
pl. Mt Annan 479 H16
LADBROKE
st. Milperra 398 A8
LADBURY
av. Penrith 236 B10
LADY
ct. Stanhpe Gdn 215 D9
st. Mt Colah 191 K5
LADY ANNE
wy. Narellan Vale 478 H15
LADY CARRINGTON
dr. Royal N P 520 D8
LADY CUTLER
av. Bankstown 369 G15
LADY DAVIDSON
cct. Forestville 255 K6
LADY GAME
dr. Chatswd W 283 J6
dr. Killara 253 B15
dr. Lindfield 283 G1
dr. West Pymble 253 B15
LADY JAMISON
dr. Glenmore Pk 265 F8
LADY PENRHYN
cl. Lurnea 394 B12
dr. Beacon Hill 257 G2
dr. Bligh Park 150 C4
LADY WOODWARD
pl. Miller 393 J3
LAE
pl. Allambie Ht 257 C8
pl. Glenfield 424 H10
pl. Narellan Vale 478 K10
pl. Narellan Vale 479 A10
pl. Whalan 240 K8
rd. Holsworthy 426 C3
LAGANA
pl. Wetherill Pk 334 A4
LAGGAN
av. Balmain 344 E4
LAGO
pl. St Clair 269 G15
LAGONDA
av. Killara 254 A9
dr. Ingleburn 453 H12
LAGOON
dr. Blaxland 233 H13
dr. Glenbrook 233 H13
st. Narrabeen 229 A4
LAGOON FLATS
pl. Cawdor 506 D16
LAGOON VIEW
rd. Cromer 258 D1
LAGUNA
dr. Glenmore Pk 266 E10
pl. Glen Alpine 510 A14
rd. Bilgola 169 J5
rd. Northbridge 286 F16
st. Caringbah 492 F8
st. Vaucluse 348 E5
LAING
av. Killara 254 A9
pl. West Hoxton 392 A10
LAITOKI
rd. Terrey Hills 196 B7
LAKE
st. Collaroy Plat 228 D11
st. N Parramatta 278 F10
wy. Narellan 478 B9
LAKELAND
cct. Harringtn Pk 478 E3
rd. Cattai 94 A6
LAKEMBA
st. Belmore 371 C15
st. Lakemba 371 A16
st. Wiley Park 400 G2
LAKE PARK
rd. N Narrabeen 199 B15
LAKER
st. Blacktown 274 H6
LAKES
st. Penrith 206 G16
st. Thirlmere 564 E3
LAKESIDE
av. Monterey 433 F9
cr. North Manly 288 D3
dr. Mt Hunter 504 C16
rd. Eastwood 281 A6
rd. Narrabeen 228 K7
st. Currans Hill 479 J9
LAKESLAND
rd. Lakesland 561 A6
LAKEVIEW
cl. Baulkham Hl 216 J16
ct. Harringtn Pk 478 E4
pde. Warriewood 199 C10
pl. Glen Alpine 540 D1
LAKEWOOD
cr. Casula 395 B11
dr. Woodcroft 243 F10
LALANDA
cl. Cranebrook 207 F5
LALCHERE
st. Curl Curl 258 K12
LALICH
av. Bonnyrigg 364 A9
LALOKI
st. Seven Hills 275 H7
LALOR
cr. Engadine 488 K12
dr. Springwood 202 D11
rd. Quakers Hill 213 K13
st. Cabramatta 365 E11
st. Glenfield 424 F9
LALS
pde. Villawood 337 A16
LA MASCOTTE
av. Concord 342 C6
LAMATTINA
pl. Green Valley 362 J8
LAMB
av. Campsie 371 H10
cl. Wetherill Pk 334 F6
cr. Merrylands 337 K1
pl. Elderslie 507 H1
st. Bellevue Hill 347 F15
st. Glendenning 242 F5
st. Lilyfield 10 F4
st. Marsden Pk 182 A11
st. Oakhurst 242 C5
st. Plumpton 242 C5
LAMBE
pl. Cherrybrook 219 H13
st. West Hoxton 392 A13
LAMBERT
av. Ermington 310 B3
av. Plumpton 242 D8
cr. Baulkham Hl 246 K16
pl. Leumeah 482 C16
pl. Mt Pritchard 364 H11
rd. Bardwell Pk 402 K7
st. Cammeray 316 C5
st. Camperdwn 17 E2
st. Cremorne 316 C5
st. Erskineville 18 A15
st. West Ryde 280 G12
st. Yagoona 369 E8
LAMBETH
pl. Illawong 459 G6
rd. Schofields 183 C13
st. Panania 428 B4
st. Picnic Point 428 B8
LAMBIE
pl. Ruse 512 G8
LAMBS
rd. Artarmon 315 C1
LAMERTON
st. Oakhurst 242 A3
LAMETTE
st. Chatswood 285 B7
LAMINGTON
pl. Bow Bowing 452 C13
LAMMING
pl. St Marys 269 K7
LAMOND
dr. Turramurra 222 G13
LAMONERIE
st. Toongabbie 276 E10
LAMONT
cl. Kellyville 216 B3
pl. Cartwright 393 K5
pl. S Windsor 150 E2
st. Parramatta 308 D1
st. Wollstncraft 315 E7
LAMORNA
av. Beecroft 249 K10
LAMROCK
av. Bondi Beach 378 A2
av. Glossodia 60 G4
av. Russell Lea 343 D7
pl. Bondi Beach, off Lamrock Av 378 C4
st. Emu Plains 236 A7
LAMSON
pl. Greenacre 370 C6
LANA
cl. Kings Park 244 G2
LANAI
pl. Beacon Hill 257 H5
LANARK
av. Earlwood 402 H3
ct. Castle Hill 218 D8
pl. St Andrews 451 J16
LANCASHIRE
pl. Gymea 491 F3
LANCASTER
av. Beecroft 250 A3
av. Cecil Hills 362 F2
av. Melrose Pk 310
av. Punchbowl 399
av. Punchbowl 399
av. St Ives 224
cr. Collaroy 259
cr. Kingsford 406
dr. Marsfield 281
la. Seaforth 286
rd. Dover Ht 348
st. Blacktown 274
st. Ingleburn 453
wy. W Pnnant Hl 248
LANCASTRIAN
rd. Mascot 404
LANCE
av. Blakehurst 432
cr. Greystanes 306
la. Millers Pt A
LANCELEY
av. Carlingford 249
pl. Abbotsbury 333
pl. Artarmon 315
LANCELOT
ct. Castle Hill 217
st. Allawah 432
st. Bankstown 399
st. Blacktown 274
st. Concord 341
st. Condell Park 398
st. Five Dock 342
st. Mt Colah 162
st. Punchbowl 400
LANCEWOOD
rd. Dural 188
LANCIA
dr. Ingleburn 453
LANDAIS
la. Emu Heights, off Landais Pl 235
pl. Emu Heights 235
LANDENBURG
pl. Greenwich 314
LANDER
av. Blacktown 244
la. Darlington 18
st. Darlington 18
st. Leumeah 481
LANDERS
rd. Lane Cove W 284
st. Werrington 239
LANDON
st. Fairfield E 336
LANDOR
rd. Barden Rdg 488
LANDRA
av. Mt Colah 192
LANDS
la. Newtown 17
LANDSCAPE
av. Forestville 256
st. Baulkham Hl 247
LANDSDOWNE
cl. Hornsby Ht 161
rd. Lansdowne 367
LANDY
av. Penrith 237
cl. Edensor Pk 363
cl. Menai 458
pl. Beacon Hill 257
pl. Kellyville 215
rd. Lalor Park 245
st. Matraville 437
LANE
av. Newington 310
gr. Schofields 213
pl. Minto 453
st. Wentwthvle 307
LANE COVE
rd. Ingleside 197
rd. Mcquarie Pk 282
rd. North Ryde 282
rd. Ryde 282
LANFORD
av. Killarney Ht 255
LANG
av. Pagewood 406
cr. Blackett 241
pl. Glenmore Pk 265
rd. Casula 394
rd. Centnnial Pk 21
rd. Earlwood 373
rd. Kenthurst 155
rd. Moore Park 20

S Windsor 150 G2
Croydon 342 F13
Mosman 316 J5
Padstow 429 B5
Smithfield 336 B7
Sydney A G12
Sydney 1 F14

GDALE
Revesby 399 A13
Collaroy Plat 228 E10

GDON
Campbelltwn 511 G2
Baulkham Hl 246 J16
Winston Hills 276 J1

GER
Caringbah 492 J16
Dolans Bay 492 J16
Banksia 403 E13

GFORD
Dural 188 G4

GFORD SMITH
Kellyville 216 K2

GHAM
Belrose 225 E15

GHOLM
Kellyville 217 B3

GLAND
Wetherill Pk 334 F6

GLANDS
Annangrove 155 J16

GLEE
Waverley 377 H6
Bronte, off Brown St 377 H7

GLEY
Cremorne 316 G7
Glenmore Pk 265 J8
Glenmore Pk, off Langley Av 265 J8
Blackett 241 D2
Richmond 117 J7
Darlinghurst 4 D11
Rsemeadow 540 J2

GMEAD
Silverdale 354 C12

GSHAW
Connells Pt 431 J13

GSTON
Epping 251 B16

GSWORTH
Five Dock 342 K11

GTRY
Auburn 339 B4

HAMS
Wedderburn 541 F15
Winston Hills 277 B2

SBURY
Edensor Pk 363 F3

SDOWNE
Oatley 430 J14
Surry Hills 20 A4
Oatley 430 H14
Brownlow Hl 475 E10
Canley Vale 366 C4
Orchard Hills 268 F9
Arncliffe 403 A10
Concord 342 A9
Eastwood 281 D6
Greenwich 314 K6
Merrylands 337 J1
Parramatta 307 H6
Parramatta 308 B6
Penshurst 431 E7
Surry Hills 20 A5

TANA
Collaroy Plat 228 F9
Faulconbdg 171 E13
Engadine 488 H14
Mcquarie Fd 454 D4

YON
Wattle Grove 426 A2
Newport 169 D10

PEROUSE
Fairlight 288 B8

IS
Bardwell Vy 403 A9

ISH
Ashfield 372 G3

STONE
Blaxland 233 G12
Leonay 265 A3

LAPWING
wy. Plumpton, off Sanctuary Park Dr 242 A10

LARA
cl. Illawong 459 H4
pl. Frenchs Frst 256 E1

LARAPINTA
cr. St Helens Park 541 H1
cr. St Helens Park 541 H3
pl. Glenhaven 187 D14

LARBERT
av. Wahroonga 222 J8
pl. Prestons 392 J13

LARCHMONT
av. East Killara 254 F9
pl. W Pnnant Hl 249 H9

LARCOM
rd. Kellyville 215 J1

LARCOMBE
st. Regents Pk 369 D1

LARIEN
cr. Birrong 369 A7
cr. Yagoona 369 A7

LARISSA
av. W Pnnant Hl 249 G3
rd. Allambie Ht 257 C9

LARK
pl. Green Valley 363 E11
pl. Greystanes 306 C3
pl. Ingleburn 453 H8
pl. Wallacia 324 K13
st. Belmore 371 G15

LARKARD
st. North Ryde 282 H7

LARKEN
av. Baulkham Hl 247 A14

LARKHALL
av. Earlwood 402 H3
la. Earlwood, off Larkhall Av 402 H3

LARKHILL
av. Riverwood 400 D16

LARKIN
la. Roseville 284 G5
pl. Camden 477 B15
st. Camperdwn 17 H1
st. Riverwood 400 E11
st. Roseville 284 G5
st. Tahmoor 565 J12
st. Waverton 315 E13

LARKSPUR
pl. Heathcote 518 E9

LARKVIEW
av. Chester Hill 337 K14

LARMAR
pl. West Hoxton 391 K12

LARMER
pl. Narraweena 258 D2

LARNACH
pl. Elderslie 477 G15

LARNE
pl. Killarney Ht 255 K14
st. Prestons 423 E2

LARNOCK
av. Pymble 253 J2

LARNOOK
cl. Oatlands 279 B14

LAROOL
av. Lindfield 284 B4
av. Oatley 431 B13
cr. Castle Hill 218 B13
cr. Thornleigh 221 A8
pl. Engadine 489 A12
rd. Terrey Hills 196 A9

LAROSE
av. Matraville 437 A2

LAROW
pl. Bonnyrigg 364 A10

LARRA
cr. North Rocks 248 F12
ct. Wattle Grove 425 J2
pl. Dundas Vy 279 J8
pl. Glen Alpine 510 C16
st. Yennora 337 B9

LARRY
pl. Annangrove 155 F2

LASA
st. Cabramatta 366 C8

LASBURN
cr. Carlingford 279 G2

LASCELLES
av. Greenacre 370 E14
la. Greenacre 370 E14
rd.n, Narraweena 258 A4
rd.s, Narraweena 258 A6
st. Cecil Hills 362 G8

LASSETER
av. Chifley 437 A7

LASSETTER
pl. Ruse 512 F2

LASSWADE
st. Ashbury 372 E8

LATAN
wy. Stanhpe Gdn 215 B10

LATHAM
pl. Canley Vale 366 D6
tce. Newington 310 C11

LATIMER
rd. Bellevue Hill 347 J14

LATINA
cct. Prestons 393 F13

LATONA
av. Vineyard 152 E6
la. Pymble 252 K7
st. Pymble 252 K8
st. Winston Hills 277 B1

LA TROBE
cl. Barden Rdg 488 H1

LATROBE
rd. West Hoxton 392 E8

LATTY
st. Fairfield 336 F15

LATVIA
av. Greenacre 370 D8

LATYNINA
wk. Newington, off Newington Bvd 310 C11

LAUDER
st. Doonside 243 E6

LAUDERDALE
av. Fairlight 288 A9
st. West Hoxton 392 F6

LAUMA
av. Greenacre 370 A9

LAUNCELOT
av. Croydon Pk 371 J7

LAUNDESS
av. Panania 398 B14

LAURA
cl. Bargo 567 C5
pl. St Clair 270 J12
st. Gladesville 313 B3
st. Merrylands 307 E7
st. Mount Druitt 241 C10
st. Newtown 374 G10
st. Seaforth 287 A12

LAURANTUS
swy. Liverpool 395 D3

LAUREL
av. Turramurra 222 H12
ch. Forestville 255 G10
cl. Hornsby 191 H10
cr. Revesby 399 A11
gr. Menai 458 K13
pl. Lalor Park 245 B10
pl. Liverpool 394 J9
pl. Mcquarie Fd 454 G1
rd.e, Ingleside 198 C6
rd.w, Ingleside 198 B4
st. Carramar 366 J3
st. N Willghby 285 D11
st. Willoughby 285 D11

LAUREN
av. Castle Hill 248 C2
pl. Cherrybrook 220 A3
pl. Plumpton 241 G9

LAURENCE
av. Bundeena 523 H9
av. Turramurra 222 K10
rd. Londonderry 149 C13
st. Greystanes 306 D7
st. Hobartville 118 D9
st. Manly 288 D10
st. Pennant Hills 220 D14
st. Sans Souci 433 D15

LAURIE
rd. Dural 189 J8
rd. Manly Vale 288 B5

LAURIETON
rd. Hoxton Park 392 H10

LAURINA
av. Earlwood 372 H16
av. Engadine 489 B16
av. Villawood 337 A15

LAURISTON
pl. Glen Alpine 510 F10
pl. St Clair 270 G14

LAVARACK
st. Ryde 282 C12

LAVENDER
av. Bexley 402 D16
av. Kellyville 216 J7
av. Punchbowl 399 H4
cl. Casula 423 J2
cl. Glenmore Pk 265 H9
cr. Lavender Bay K C15
cr. Lavender Bay 5 F12
pl. Alfords Point 459 A1
pl. Blacktown 245 B9
pl. Fairfield W 335 B10
pl. St Helens Park 541 A8
st. Five Dock 342 H11
st. Lavender Bay K C14
st. Lavender Bay 5 F11
st. McMahons Pt K C14
st. McMahons Pt 5 F11
st. Milsons Point K C14
st. Milsons Point 5 F11
st. Narellan 478 F13

LAVER
av. Menai 458 G7
pl. Greystanes 305 K11
st. Shalvey 210 K13

LAVERACK
cr. S Granville 338 G4

LAVIN
cr. Wrrngtn Cty 238 E7

LAVINGTON
av. Chipping Ntn 366 E15
pwy. Chipping Ntn, off Lavington Pwy 366 E14
st. Yagoona 368 J8

LAVINIA
pl. Ambarvale 511 B13
st. Merrylands 338 C2
st. Riverstone 183 B10
st. Seven Hills 275 H9
st. S Granville 338 C2

LA'VISTA
gr. Castle Hill 217 C6

LAVONI
st. Mosman 317 D5

LAW
cr. Tregear 240 C3
st. North Rocks 279 A3

LAWFORD
st. Fairfield W 335 F11
st. Greenacre 370 F4

LAWLER
st. Panania 428 B6

LAWLEY
cr. Pymble 252 J3
st. Bossley Park 334 C7

LAWN
av. Bradbury 511 D9
av. Campsie 402 B3
av. Lane Cove W 313 K1

LAWNDALE
av. North Rocks 249 A15

LAWRENCE
cr. Lucas Ht 487 H12
la. Alexandria 18 H16
rd. Kenthurst 157 D3
st. Alexandria 18 H16
st. Chatswood 285 C8
st. Fairfield 336 D7
st. Harbord 288 F1
st. Peakhurst 430 C2
st. Seven Hills 275 G8
st. West Ryde 280 G11

LAWRENCE HARGRAVE
rd. Warwck Frm 365 E14

LAWRY
pl. Shalvey 211 B14
st. Greystanes 306 A9

LAWS
la. Strathfield S 371 C6

LAWSON
av. Camden S 506 K13
av. Marrickville 15 F16
la. Bondi Jctn 22 E9
la. Naremburn 315 E4
la. Paddington 13 D12
pde. St Ives 224 D12
pl. Barden Rdg 488 G1
pl. Castle Hill 218 A9
pl. Cherrybrook 220 B12
pl. Manly 288 F8
rd. Badgerys Ck 329 C16
rd. Ingleburn 423 A9
rd. Springwood 202 C2
sq. Redfern 19 B7
st. Balmain 7 B9
st. Bondi Jctn 22 F9
st. Campbelltwn 512 A5
st. Eastwood 280 F9
st. Emu Plains 235 F10
st. Ermington 310 B2
st. Eveleigh 19 A7
st. Fairfield 336 E14
st. Lalor Park 245 B11
st. Matraville 437 B1
st. Paddington 13 B12
st. Panania 398 A13
st. Penrith 236 K10
st. Redfern 19 A7
st. Sans Souci 463 A4

LAWTON
pl. Oakhurst 242 A4

LAYBUTT
rd. Lalor Park 245 F10

LAYCOCK
av. Cronulla 493 K13
pl. Bonnyrigg 364 C6
rd. Hurstville Gr 431 F6
rd. Penshurst 431 F6
st. Bexley North 402 C11
st. Cranebrook 207 A13
st. Mascot 405 B2
st. Neutral Bay 6 D1

LAYDEN
av. Engadine 518 H4

LAYTON
av. Blaxland 233 H7
ct. Harringtn Pk 478 E1
st. Camperdwn 17 E2
st. Wentwthvle 276 H16
wy. Kellyville 185 K15

LEA
av. N Willghby 285 D11
av. Russell Lea 343 B7
rd. Bringelly 388 B9
st. Croydon 372 C1
st. Quakers Hill 244 A3

LEABONS
la. Seven Hills 275 B4

LEACH
rd. Guildford W 336 H4

LEACOCKS
la. Casula 424 F4

LEADENHAM
pl. Chipping Ntn 366 H16

LEADER
st. Padstow 429 B3

LEAGAY
cr. Frenchs Frst 257 B4

LEAH
av. Picnic Point 428 E6
cl. Smithfield 335 F8

LEAL
ct. Pymble 253 J3

LEAMINGTON
av. Newtown 18 B11
la. Newtown 18 B11
rd. Dundas 279 F12

LEANE
pl. Cranebrook 207 G10

LEANNE
pl. Quakers Hill 214 B15

LEAR
cl. St Clair 270 D15
pl. Rsemeadow 540 J7

LEARMONTH
av. Balgowlah 287 K8
st. Haberfield 9 A7
st. Rooty Hill 272 D3

LEAT
pl. Blacktown 244 D15

LEATHERWOOD
ct. Baulkham Hl 247 C16

LEAVESDEN
pl. Sylvania 461 K7

LEAWARRA
st. Engadine 488 G11

LEAWILL
pl. Gladesville 312 J4

LE COS
la. Marrickville 374 A12
LEDBURY
pl. Chipping Ntn 396 H2
LEDGER
cl. Casula 394 G15
pwy. Casula, off Ledger Cl 394 G15
rd. Merrylands 307 J8
LEE
av. Beverly Hills 401 D14
av. Ryde 311 K1
cl. Edensor Pk 333 H13
la. Sydenham, off Yelverton St 374 F15
pl. Illawong 458 K7
pl. Killarney Ht 256 D15
pl. St Ives Ch 224 B1
rd. Beacon Hill 257 H6
rd. Cherrybrook 220 B15
rd. Winmalee 173 C11
st. Chippendale E C16
st. Chippendale 3 D16
st. Condell Park 398 F3
st. Emu Plains 235 J6
st. Haymarket E C16
st. Haymarket 3 D16
st. Randwick 407 C1
st. Seven Hills 245 G14
LEE AND CLARK
rd. Kemps Ck 360 B15
LEEDER
av. Penshurst 431 G6
LEEDHAM
pl. Riverwood 400 A10
LEEDS
pl. Turramurra 222 F16
st. Merrylands 307 F10
st. Rhodes 311 E7
LEE HOLM
rd. St Marys 239 E7
LEEMING
st. Mt Krng-gai 163 A12
LEEMON
st. Condell Park 398 E3
LEES
av. Croydon Pk 371 G8
cr. Blacktown 274 J5
ct. Sydney D A4
pl. Kellyville 186 A15
rd. Kingsgrove 401 D8
LEESWOOD
ct. Wattle Grove 425 K4
LEETON
av. Coogee 377 F14
cr. Panania 398 E16
st. Merrylands 306 J10
LEGANA
st. West Hoxton 392 F6
LEGGE
st. Roselands 401 D4
LEGGO
st. Badgerys Ck 358 F6
LE HANE
plz. Caringbah 492 K14
LEHMANN
av. Glenmore Pk 265 K4
av. Liverpool 394 H1
LEHN
rd. East Hills 427 H4
LEICESTER
av. Strathfield 341 F10
pl. Miller 393 G3
sq. Blacktown 274 A3
st. Bexley 432 E1
st. Chester Hill 368 C1
st. Epping 250 E14
st. Leumeah 482 E11
st. Marrickville 374 E10
st. Narellan 478 H11
st. Wakeley 364 J1
wy. St Clair 270 F13
LEICHHARDT
av. Fairfield W 335 C9
av. Glebe 11 J7
av. Wrrngtn Cty 238 G4
cr. Sylvania 462 A12
la. Waverley, off Leichhardt St 377 G9
rd. Ingleburn 422 J14
st. Bronte 377 H9
st. Chifley 436 K6
st. Darlinghurst 4 H12
st. Glebe 11 J7
st. Horngsea Pk 392 D14
st. Lalor Park 245 D14
st. Leichhardt 10 B16
st. Ruse 512 E4
st. Waverley 377 H9
LEIDICH
la. Kurrajong Ht 54 F8
la. Kurrajong Hl 54 F8
LEIGH
av. Concord 341 J8
av. Roselands 400 G10
cr. Claymore 481 D9
pl. Ashcroft 364 E15
pl. Kings Lngly 246 B9
pl. Riverwood 400 F10
pl. S Windsor 150 J2
pl. W Pnnant Hl 249 D9
st. Merrylands 307 C16
LEIGHDON
st. Bass Hill 368 D14
LEIGHTON
pl. Hornsby 192 B14
st. Rooty Hill 272 E4
LEIHA
pl. Tahmoor 565 H8
LEILA
st. Berala 339 G13
LEILANI
cl. Casula 394 F15
st. Stanhpe Gdn 215 A5
LEINSTER
av. Killarney Ht 256 D16
st. Paddington 21 B3
LEIST
wy. Claymore, off Duterreau Wy 481 E11
LEISURE
cl. Mcquarie Pk 282 J1
LEITCH
av. Londonderry 149 A14
LEITH
pl. St Andrews 482 A2
rd. Pennant Hills 220 E16
st. Ashbury 372 D7
st. Croydon Pk 372 D7
LEITZ
st. Liverpool 395 A1
LELAND
st. Penrith 236 F1
LELIA
av. Freemns Rch 90 D2
LE MAIRE
av. Lethbrdg Pk 240 D3
LEMAIRES
la. Glenbrook 233 G15
LE MERTON
pl. Rooty Hill 271 J2
LEMKO
pl. Penrith 236 G3
LEMM
st. Birchgrove 8 A4
LEMNOS
av. Milperra 397 D12
st. N Strathfield 341 D7
LEMON
cl. Prairiewood 334 H7
gr. Glenwood 215 E13
LEMONGRASS
pl. Cherrybrook 219 E10
LEMON GROVE
rd. Penrith 237 A9
LEMONGROVE
av. Carlingford 249 F16
LEMONGUM
pl. Alfords Point 459 C2
pl. Quakers Hill 214 A7
LEMON TREE
cl. Frenchs Frst 256 H1
cr. Minto 482 J4
LEMONWOOD
pl. Castle Hill 248 F4
LEN
cl. Plumpton 242 A11
LENA
av. Allambie Ht 257 C9
pl. Kearns 451 B16
pl. Merrylands 307 E9
pl. Tregear 240 D4
st. Granville 308 D12
st. Mt Pritchard 364 E8
st. Sandringham 463 E5
LENNA
pl. Jannali 460 H14
LENNARTZ
st. Croydon Pk 371 G7
LENNOX
pl. Barden Rdg 488 G1
pl. St Andrews 481 K1
pl. West Hoxton 392 A12
pl. Wetherill Pk 305 C16
st. Banksia 403 G14
st. Bellevue Hill 347 G16
st. Colyton 270 F6
st. Glenbrook 233 J16
st. Gordon 253 K5
st. Mosman 317 A12
st. Newtown 17 E11
st. Normanhurst 221 D8
st. Northmead 277 K5
st. Old Tngabbie 276 H11
st. Parramatta 308 B6
st. Richmond 118 H6
st. Rockdale 403 G14
LENNOX BRIDGE
Glenbrook 234 E11
LENORDS
la. Kurrajong 85 F1
LENORE
la. Erskine Park 300 C4
pl. Lidcombe 340 B6
st. Russell Lea 343 E6
LENTARA
ct. Georges Hall 367 F13
rd. Bayview 168 G12
LENTHALL
st. Kensington 376 B13
LENTHEN
la. Botany 405 H15
LENTON
av. Fairfield W 335 C12
cr. Oakhurst 241 K4
pde. Waterloo 19 F12
pl. North Rocks 248 E16
LEO
av. Lurnea 394 C9
cr. Greystanes 306 D6
pl. Erskine Park 300 G2
pl. Hebersham 241 E8
pl. Telopea 279 F7
rd. Pennant Hills 220 D16
st. Hunters Hill 313 A7
st. Mt Pritchard 364 E8
LEOFRENE
av. Marrickville 373 K14
LEON
av. Georges Hall 367 G10
av. Roselands 400 G8
pl. Ingleburn 453 J9
st. Wilberforce 91 K5
LEONARD
av. Greystanes 306 G6
av. Kingsford 406 D2
cr. Earlwood 403 B1
la. Colyton, off Leonard Pl 270 D6
pl. Bonnyrigg 363 K8
pl. Colyton 270 D5
pl. Marsfield 282 B5
st. Bankstown 399 F3
st. Blacktown 244 A12
st. Colyton 270 C5
st. Hornsby 221 H3
st. Thirlmere 565 A7
st. Waitara 221 H3
LEONARDS
wy. Kellyville 185 K16
LEONAY
pde. Leonay 235 A16
st. Sutherland 460 C16
LEONE
av. Baulkham Hl 247 B1
LEONELLO
pl. Edensor Pk 333 H14
LEONG
pl. Baulkham Hl 247 E8
LEONIE
cr. Berala 339 B14
pl. Hassall Gr 212 B15
LEONORA
av. Kingsford 406 J6
av. St Ives 224 C7
cl. Hornsby Ht 161 K12
st. Earlwood 402 F5
LEONTES
cl. Rsemeadow 540 J8
LEOPARDWOOD
pl. Mcquarie Fd 454 F1
LEOPOLD
pl. Cecil Hills 362 G5
st. Ashbury 372 E7
st. Croydon Pk 372 E7
st. Merrylands 307 J9
st. Rooty Hill 241 J14
LERIDA
av. Camden 507 B3
LERWICK
pl. St Andrews 452 A14
LES BURNETT
la. Harris Park 308 E7
LESLEY
av. Carlingford 279 D2
av. Revesby 428 H2
cl. Elanora Ht 198 F13
cr. Mortdale 430 K4
LESLIE
ct. Wrrngtn Cty 238 F6
la. Wrrngtn Cty, off Leslie Ct 238 F6
rd. Bexley 432 C1
rd. Glenbrook 234 C16
st. Bass Hill 368 B11
st. Blacktown 274 A5
st. North Ryde 282 D6
st. Roselands 401 C6
st. Tempe 374 C16
st. Winmalee 173 F6
wk. Narrabeen 228 G8
LESNIE
av. Matraville 436 K8
LES SHORE
pl. Castle Hill 218 C13
LESSING
st. Emerton 240 H7
st. Hornsby 191 K13
LESTER
pl. Abbotsford 342 K3
rd. Greystanes 306 D8
rd. Revesby 399 A13
st. Lurnea 394 F6
LESWELL
la. Woollahra 22 E4
st. Bondi Jctn 22 E5
LETHBRIDGE
av. Werrington 238 J11
st. Penrith 237 A12
st. St Marys 239 J15
LETI
pl. Marayong 244 B4
LETITIA
st. Oatley 431 B15
st. Oatley 431 C12
LETTER BOX
la. Illawong 460 C2
LEUMEAH
av. Baulkham Hl 246 J6
cl. W Pnnant Hl 220 A16
rd. Leumeah 482 D13
st. Cronulla 493 H16
LEUNA
av. Wahroonga 251 H3
LEURA
cl. Bossley Park 333 E13
cr. N Turramrra 193 F11
pl. Prospect 275 C11
rd. Auburn 338 K8
rd. Double Bay 14 E10
LEVEL CROSSING
rd. Vineyard 151 J9
LEVEN
pl. Northmead 278 C5
pl. St Andrews 481 K1
LEVENDALE
st. West Hoxton 392 D7
LEVER
st. Rosebery 405 F2
LEVERTON
cl. St Ives 224 E14
LE VESINET
dr. Hunters Hill 314 A14
LEVETT
av. Beverly Hills 401 A14
LEVEY
st. Arncliffe 403 K7
st. Chippendale 19 A3
LEVICK
rd. Greystanes 306
st. Cremorne 316
LEVUKA
st. Cabramatta 366
LEVY
av. Matraville 436
cl. Hamondvle 426
st. Glenbrook 233
st. Pendle Hill 306
st. Putney 312
wk. Zetland 376
LEWERS
cl. Abbotsbury 333
LEWIN
cr. Bradbury 511
cr. Chipping Ntn 396
st. Blaxland 234
st. Springwood 201
LEWINS
la. Earlwood, off Clarke St 402
st. Earlwood 402
LEWIS
cl. Warriewood 198
ct. Castle Hill 248
la. N Strathfield 341
la. Tahmoor 565
la. Cmbrdg Gdn, off Lewis Rd 237
pl. Bonnyrigg Ht 363
pl. Panania 428
rd. Cmbrdg Gdn 237
rd. Liverpool 395
st. Appin 569
st. Avalon 140
st. Balgowlah Ht 287
st. Bexley 402
st. Bradbury 511
st. Cronulla 493
st. Dee Why 258
st. Epping 280
st. Lapstone 264
st. Merrylands 307
st. Regents Pk 369
st. Schofields 183
st. Silverdale 353
st. S Wntwthvle 307
wy. Newington 310
LEWISHAM
st. Dulwich Hill 373
LEXCEN
pl. Marsfield 282
LEXIA
cl. Mona Vale 199
LEXINGTON
av. Eastwood 280
av. St Clair 270
dr. Bella Vista 216
dr. Bella Vista 246
la. St Clair, off Lexington Av 270
pl. Maroubra 407
LEYLAND
gr. Zetland 375
pl. Ingleburn 453
LEYLANDS
pde. Belmore 401
pde. Lakemba 401
LEYS
av. Lilyfield 10
LEYSDOWN
av. North Rocks 249
LEYTE
av. Lethbrdg Pk 240
LIBERA
av. Padstow 399
LIBERATOR
st. Raby 451
wy. St Clair 270
LIBERATOR GENERAL SAN MARTIN
dr. Krngai Ch NP 167
LIBERTY
rd. Huntingwd 273
st. Belmore 401
st. Enmore 16
st. Enmore 17
wy. Kellyville 185
wy. Old Tngabbie 277
LIBRA
pl. Erskine Park 300

YA
Allambie Ht 257 F11
Marsfield 252 B13
HEN
Westmead 307 J3
BURY
Berala 339 B12
CO
Arndell Park 273 F9
DLE
N St Marys 239 J8
ELL
Bonnyrigg Ht 363 B7
O
N Narrabeen 228 J1
WINA
Cromer 228 A16
GE
Russell Lea 343 E5
UTENANT BOWEN
Bowen Mtn 83 K13
Bowen Mtn 83 K10
FEY
Woronora 460 B15
AR
Fairfield Ht 335 H11
ATO
Liverpool 364 J16
HT BODY
Narellan Vale 508 G1
HTCLIFF
Lindfield 254 F15
HT HORSE
Holsworthy 426 E4
HTNING
Raby 481 G3
HTNING RIDGE
Hinchinbrk 392 H3
HTWOOD
Ambarvale 510 G15
Kellyville 185 K16
NITE
Eagle Vale 481 E9
UORI
Pennant Hills 250 H2
URIA
Maroubra 407 H7
S Coogee 407 H7
ION
Lane Cove W 313 G3
AC
Eastwood 281 G7
Jamisontown 266 B4
Quakers Hill 213 K10
Loftus 490 A12
Punchbowl 400 D1
IAN
Campsie 371 H14
Campbelltwn 511 H5
Campsie 371 J13
IAN FOWLER
Marrickville 374 D12
LA
Quakers Hill 214 D12
Pennant Hills 250 E2
LAS
Minto 482 J1
LE
Milperra 397 H11
LEY
St Clair 269 G14
LIAN
Revesby 398 H14
Annangrove 155 C1
Riverwood 399 J15
Berala 339 F13
LIE
N Curl Curl 258 H11
LIHINA
Cromer 258 B1
LI PILLI
Beverley Pk 433 B8
Peakhurst 430 E4
Epping 250 G15
LI PILLI POINT
Lilli Pilli 522 E4
LIS
Cammeray 315 K7
LY PILLY
Kellyville, off Lilly Pilly Pl 185 J14
pl. Kellyville 185 J14
LILLYVICKS
cr. Ambarvale 510 J13
LILY
av. Riverwood 399 K10
ct. Glenmore Pk 265 H9
ct. Narellan Vale 479 A15
la. Allawah 432 D5
pl. Lalor Park 245 H13
st. Auburn 339 B4
st. Burwood Ht 371 K4
st. Croydon Pk 371 K4
st. Hurstville 432 D5
st. North Ryde 282 D8
st. Wetherill Pk 334 G6
LILYDALE
av. Peakhurst 430 E5
st. Marrickville 373 J11
LILYFIELD
cl. Catherine Fd 449 F2
rd. Lilyfield 9 F6
rd. Rozelle 11 A3
LIMA
cl. Clarmnt Ms 268 J1
la. Clarmnt Ms, off Lima Cl. 268 J2
pl. Erskine Park 270 H15
st. Greenacre 370 G14
LIME
gr. Carlingford 279 F1
st. Cabramatta W 364 J7
st. Quakers Hill 243 E3
st. Sydney C A2
LIME KILN
rd. Lugarno 430 A15
LIMONITE
pl. Eagle Vale 481 D7
LIMPOPO
cr. Seven Hills 275 F9
LINARA
cct. Glenmore Pk 265 J11
LINCLUDEN
pl. Airds 512 C10
pl. Oatlands 278 J10
LINCOLN
av. Collaroy 229 A16
av. Middle Cove 285 K10
av. Riverstone 183 C10
cl. Asquith 191 K7
cr. Bonnet Bay 460 F9
cr. Sydney 4 F1
cr. Woolmloo 4 F1
dr. Cmbrdg Pk 237 J9
la. Stanmore 16 K9
la. Cmbrdg Pk, off Lincoln Dr 238 A9
pl. Castle Hill 218 B16
pl. Edgecliff 14 A13
rd. Cecil Park 331 H7
rd. Georges Hall 368 C15
rd. Horsley Pk 331 K6
rd. St Ives 224 A10
st. Belfield 371 G12
st. Campsie 371 G13
st. Dulwich Hill 373 G10
st. Eastwood 281 G3
st. Lane Cove W 313 F1
st. Miller 393 F4
st. Minto 482 E2
st. Stanmore 16 J9
tce. Marsden Pk 182 B14
LIND
av. Oatlands 279 A9
st. Minto 482 J4
LINDA
av. Bass Hill 367 E6
av. Oatley 430 K8
pl. Merrylands 308 A15
st. Belfield 371 C10
st. Fairfield Ht 335 G12
st. Hornsby 191 H16
st. Seven Hills 246 A13
LINDE
rd. Glendenning 242 H4
LINDEL
pl. Lindfield 284 B1
LINDEMAN
cr. Green Valley 363 A13
LINDEN
av. Belrose 225 K5
av. Punchbowl 400 A5
av. Pymble 252 K2
av. Woollahra 22 F1
cl. Pymble 253 A3
cr. Cranebrook 207 D7
cr. Lugarno 429 J12
dr. Freemns Rch 89 H4
gr. Ermington 310 F1
la. Surry Hills 4 D14
pl. Seven Hills 245 H14
st. Mascot 405 G4
st. Mount Druitt 241 B15
st. Sutherland 460 D15
st. Sutherland 490 D4
st. Toongabbie 276 C8
wy. Bella Vista 246 E1
wy. Castlecrag 286 F11
LINDESAY
st. Campbelltwn 511 E6
st. Leumeah 511 K3
LINDFIELD
av. Concord 342 C6
av. Killara 254 C14
av. Lindfield 254 C14
av. Winmalee 173 E4
pl. Dean Park 212 F16
LINDISFARNE
cr. Carlingford 279 G1
LINDLEY
av. Mcquarie Fd 424 B15
av. Narrabeen 228 J8
sq. Bidwill 211 E15
LINDRIDGE
pl. Colyton 270 A7
st. S Penrith 267 A7
LINDSAY
av. Darling Point 14 A1
av. Ermington 310 B5
av. Smithfield 335 E5
av. Summer Hill 373 B5
cl. Pymble 223 E15
cr. S Penrith 267 A5
la. Darlinghurst 4 K11
la. Mosman 316 H8
pl. Doonside 243 D11
pl. Glossodia 59 C6
pl. Mt Pritchard 364 J11
pl. Richmond 118 B5
rd. Faulconbdg 171 J11
st. Baulkham Hl 247 F11
st. Burwood 371 H2
st. Campsie 372 C10
st. Caringbah 492 F12
st. Neutral Bay 6 D3
st. Panania 398 C14
st. Phillip Bay 436 K11
st. Rockdale 433 F2
st. Wentwthvle 277 A14
LINDSAY GORDON
pl. Heathcote 518 D15
LINDSELL
pl. Tahmoor 565 G12
LINDSEY
pl. Elderslie 507 J1
LINDUM
pl. St Johns Pk 334 F16
rd. Kurnell 465 B16
LINDWALL
cl. Menai 458 F9
ct. St Clair 269 K15
la. St Clair, off Lindwall Ct 269 K15
pl. Rouse Hill 184 K7
pl. Shalvey 211 A15
LINEATA
pl. Glenmore Pk 265 H13
LINEY
av. Campsie 401 K4
LINFORD
pl. Kellyville 216 A2
LINGARD
st. Randwick 377 B13
LINGAYEN
av. Lethbrdg Pk 240 E2
LINGELLEN
st. Berowra Ht 133 A7
LINIFOLIA
mw. Wattle Grove 396 B16
LINIGEN
pl. St Ives 224 G6
LINK
cct. Menai 459 A10
rd. Bnkstn Aprt 367 F15
rd. Hornsby 191 G9
rd. Mascot 404 D5
rd. Mt Annan 479 E14
rd. St Ives 224 B11
rd. Zetland 376 A12
st. Manly Vale 287 J4
LINKMEAD
av. Clontarf 287 E11
LINKS
av. Cabramatta 365 C10
av. Concord 341 G4
av. Cronulla 494 B7
av. Milperra 397 C10
av. Roseville 285 C1
la. Concord 341 G4
rd. St Marys 239 E2
wy. Narellan 478 B10
LINKSLEY
av. Glenhaven 217 J5
LINKSVIEW
av. Leonay 235 B15
pl. Comleroy 56 B8
rd. Springwood 172 C12
LINLEE
st. Girraween 276 B15
LINLEY
cl. Carlingford 279 B4
la. Linley Point, off Burns Bay Rd 313 G6
pl. Cecil Hills 362 G9
pl. Linley Point 313 G8
wy. Ryde 312 A4
LINNE
pl. Hinchinbrk 392 K1
LINNET
pl. Quakers Hill 214 D12
st. Winmalee 173 J6
LINSLEY
st. Gladesville 312 H10
LINTHORN
av. Croydon Pk 371 G8
LINTHORNE
st. Guildford 338 A3
LINTHORPE
la. Newtown 17 H12
st. Newtown 17 J12
LINTINA
av. Tahmoor 565 K13
LINTON
av. Revesby 398 J14
av. West Ryde 281 G16
la. West Ryde 281 G16
rd. Currans Hill 479 H8
st. Baulkham Hl 248 B13
LINUM
pl. Mt Annan 509 F3
st. Mcquarie Fd 454 E6
LINWOOD
av. Bexley 403 A14
st. Guildford W 336 J4
LION
la. Randwick, off Oberon St 407 B2
st. Croydon 372 E3
st. Randwick 407 B2
LIONEL
av. North Ryde 283 A12
st. Georges Hall 367 D14
st. Ingleburn 453 D7
LIONS
av. Lurnea 394 E7
LIPARI
pl. Acacia Gdn 214 H15
LIPSIA
pl. Carlingford 279 E2
LIPSOM
av. Bondi Jctn, off James St 377 G5
LIQUIDAMBER
dr. Narellan Vale 478 K12
LISA
cl. Narellan 478 H12
cl. Westleigh 220 E7
cr. Castle Hill 217 G10
pl. Bilgola 169 F3
pl. Leonay 234 K14
st. Quakers Hill 214 C16
LISA VALLEY
cl. Wahroonga 221 F15
LISBON
ct. Castle Hill 247 H3
rd. Kenthurst 157 H14
st. Fairfield E 337 B12
st. Mount Druitt 241 C12
st. Sylvania 461 J10
LISGAR
av. Baulkham Hl 247 C6
la. Hornsby 221 D1
rd. Hornsby 221 D1
st. Merrylands 338 C1
st. S Granville 338 C1
LISLE
ct. W Pnnant Hl 249 G9
st. Narrabeen 229 B1
LISMORE
av. Dee Why 258 H3
cl. Bossley Park 333 D13
st. Blacktown 274 J2
st. Eastlakes 406 A4
st. Hoxton Park 392 K7
st. Pendle Hill 276 D13
LISSON
pl. Minto 452 K14
LISTER
av. Cabramatta W 365 B7
av. Ermington 310 A3
av. Little Bay 437 G15
av. Rockdale 403 D16
av. Seaforth 287 A5
pl. Rooty Hill 241 J14
st. N Wahrnga 222 H2
st. Winston Hills 277 E5
LISZT
pl. Cranebrook 207 G8
LITCHFIELD
pl. St Helens Park 541 D4
LITERATURE
pl. Blackett 241 C2
LITHGOW
av. Yagoona 369 E9
st. Campbelltwn 511 F5
st. Russell Lea 343 E6
st. St Leonards 315 D6
st. Wollstncraft 315 D6
LITORIA
pl. Glenmore Pk 265 H13
LITTIMER
wy. Ambarvale 510 K16
LITTLE
la. Lane Cove 314 E2
pl. Whale Beach 140 C9
rd. Bankstown 369 A16
rd. Yagoona 369 A16
st. Austral 390 F11
st. Balmain 7 F10
st. Cmbrdg Pk 238 B7
st. Camden 506 K3
st. Dee Why 258 E6
st. Dulwich Hill 373 E7
st. Granville 308 C11
st. Lane Cove 314 E2
st. Marayong 244 A9
st. Maroubra 407 F11
st. Mosman 317 C5
st. Parramatta 308 E4
st. Smithfield 335 K3
st. Yellow Rock 174 H16
LITTLE ADA
st. Canley Vale 366 E4
LITTLE ALBION
st. Surry Hills F E13
LITTLE ALFRED
st. N Sydney 5 K10
LITTLE ARTHUR
st. Balmain 7 C8
LITTLE BAY
rd. Chifley 437 A9
rd. Little Bay 437 A9
LITTLE BEATTIE
st. Balmain 7 D10
LITTLE BLOOMFIELD
st. Surry Hills 4 C14
LITTLE BOURKE
st. Surry Hills 4 D14
LITTLEBOY
st. Kings Lngly 245 A5
LITTLE BRIGHTON
st. Petersham 15 G9
LITTLE BUCKINGHAM
st. Surry Hills 19 H4
LITTLE BURTON
st. Darlinghurst F K5
LITTLE BYRNE
st. Camden 506 K3
LITTLE CHAPEL
st. St Marys 239 H15

LITTLE CHURCH
st. Ryde 311 K3
st. Windsor 121 B9
LITTLE CLEVELAND
st. Redfern 20 C7
LITTLE COLLINS
st. Surry Hills 20 A2
LITTLE COMBER
st. Paddington 4 G14
LITTLE COMMODORE
st. Newtown, off Pearl St 374 H10
LITTLE CORMISTON
av. Concord 341 K5
LITTLE DARLING
st. Balmain 7 E8
LITTLE DOWLING
st. Paddington 4 F16
LITTLE EDWARD
st. Balmain East 8 H10
st. Pyrmont 12 J4
LITTLE EVELEIGH
st. Eveleigh 18 K7
st. Eveleigh 19 A7
st. Redfern 19 A7
LITTLEFIELDS
rd. Luddenham 325 J1
rd. Mulgoa 295 D16
LITTLE FOREST
rd. Lucas Ht 487 D9
LITTLE HAY
st. Haymarket E D6
st. Haymarket 3 E11
LITTLE HUNTER
st. Sydney A J14
LITTLE JANE
st. Penrith 236 H9
LITTLE LLEWELLYN
st. Balmain 7 E9
LITTLE MONTAGUE
st. Balmain 7 E10
LITTLE MORT
st. Randwick 376 K10
LITTLE MOUNT
st. Pyrmont 12 G4
LITTLE NAPIER
st. Paddington 4 F15
LITTLE NICHOLSON
st. Balmain East 8 F9
LITTLE NORTON
la. Surry Hills F H16
st. Surry Hills F H16
st. Surry Hills 4 B16
LITTLE OXFORD
st. Darlinghurst 4 C12
LITTLE PIER
st. Haymarket E A4
LITTLE QUEEN
st. Chippendale 19 A3
st. Newtown 18 B7
LITTLE QUEENS
la. Vaucluse 348 B5
LITTLE REGENT
st. Chippendale E C16
st. Chippendale 3 D16
LITTLE RILEY
st. Surry Hills F G13
st. Surry Hills F G16
st. Surry Hills 4 A14
st. Surry Hills 20 A3
LITTLE SELWYN
st. Paddington 4 F16
LITTLE SMITH
st. Surry Hills F F11
LITTLE SPRING
st. N Sydney K F6
st. N Sydney 5 G7
st. Sydney B A12
LITTLE STEPHEN
st. Balmain 7 H10
LITTLE STEWART
st. Paddington 21 B2
LITTLE SURREY
st. Darlinghurst 4 H10
LITTLE TARONGA
wy. Faulconbdg 171 B13
LITTLE THEODORE
st. Balmain 7 D9
LITTLETON
st. Riverwood 400 C15
LITTLE TURRIELL BAY
rd. Lilli Pilli 522 H2
rd. Port Hacking 522 H2
LITTLE WALKER
st. N Sydney K H10
st. N Sydney 5 H9
LITTLE WEST
st. Darlinghurst 4 J10
LITTLE WILLANDRA
rd. Cromer 228 A16
LITTLE WONGA
rd. Cremorne 316 F5
LITTLE WYNDHAM
st. Alexandria 19 A11
LITTLE YOUNG
st. Cremorne 316 E5
st. Redfern 19 J7
LITTON
st. Emu Heights 235 A4
LIVERPOOL
la. Darlinghurst F K3
la. Darlinghurst 4 C10
rd. Ashfield 372 C2
rd. Burwood Ht 372 C2
rd. Cabramatta 366 E8
rd. Canley Vale 366 E8
rd. Croydon 372 C2
rd. Enfield 371 A3
rd. Strathfield 371 A4
rd. Strathfield S 371 A3
rd. Summer Hill 373 B3
st. Bundeena 523 H10
st. Cabramatta 365 K10
st. Darlinghurst F C3
st. Darlinghurst 4 C10
st. Dover Ht 348 C12
st. Ingleburn 453 A6
st. Liverpool 394 G10
st. Lurnea 394 G10
st. Paddington 4 J13
st. Pitt Town 92 H14
st. Rose Bay 348 C12
st. Sydney E D1
st. Sydney 3 F9
LIVINGSTON
av. Dharruk 241 C6
LIVINGSTONE
av. Baulkham Hl 247 J14
av. Botany 405 G15
av. Ingleburn 453 C12
av. Pymble 253 A8
ct. Shanes Park 179 K16
la. Botany, off Livingstone Av 405 G15
la. Burwood, off Livingstone St 341 K15
pl. Mt Colah 162 D12
pl. Newport 169 G12
rd. Lidcombe 339 F8
rd. Marrickville 15 H16
rd. Marrickville 373 G13
rd. Petersham 15 H16
st. Burwood 341 K15
wy. Thornleigh 220 K10
LIVISTONA
la. Palm Beach 139 K1
LIVORNO
gr. Glenwood 246 A4
LIZ
pl. Ashfield 372 G2
LIZARD
cl. Green Valley 363 A12
LIZZIE WEBBER
pl. Birchgrove 7 K4
LLANBERIS
dr. Menai 459 A8
LLANDAFF
st. Bondi Jctn 377 F4
LLANDILO
av. Strathfield 341 E16
rd. Berkshire Pk 179 H5
rd. Llandilo 179 A16
LLANFOYST
st. Randwick 377 B14
LLANGOLLAN
av. Enfield 371 J5
LLANKELLY
pl. Potts Point 4 K6
LLEWELLYN
av. Villawood 367 E1
la. Marrickville 374 F9
la. Lindfield, off Llewellyn St 284 E2
st. Balmain 7 D9
st. Lindfield 284 D2
st. Marrickville 374 F9
st. Oatley 431 A15
st. Rhodes 311 E8
LLOYD
av. Cremorne 316 F4
av. Hunters Hill 313 K11
av. Yagoona 369 E9
pl. Casula 424 C4
st. Bexley 402 H11
st. Blacktown 273 J3
st. Greystanes 306 D6
st. Oatley 430 G12
st. Sans Souci 433 B13
LLOYD GEORGE
av. Concord 341 H9
av. Winston Hills 247 J16
LLOYD REES
dr. Lane Cove W 313 F1
LLOYDS
av. Carlingford 279 J4
wy. Bargo 567 A4
LOADER
av. Beverly Hills 401 A16
LOBB
cr. Beverley Pk 433 A9
LOBELIA
cr. Quakers Hill 243 F4
pl. Gymea 491 C6
st. Chatswd W 283 J11
st. Mcquarie Fd 454 B6
LOBLAY
cr. Bilgola 169 F4
LOCH
av. Centnnial Pk 21 J12
av. Penshurst 431 C2
la. Campsie 371 J14
st. Campsie 371 H13
st. Harbord 258 J15
LOCHALSH
st. St Andrews 451 K12
LOCH AWE
cr. Carlingford 250 A15
LOCHEE
av. Minto 452 G16
LOCH ETIVE
pl. Narraweena 258 A4
LOCHIEL
pl. Georges Hall 367 H14
rd. Engadine 488 H12
LOCHINVAR
pde. Carlingford 249 H14
rd. Revesby 428 G4
st. Winmalee 173 C12
LOCHINVER
pl. St Andrews 452 B15
LOCH LOMOND
cr. Burraneer 523 D4
LOCH MAREE
av. Thornleigh 221 B12
cr. Connells Pt 431 H16
pde. Concord W 311 E11
pl. Vaucluse 348 C2
st. Kingsford 407 B8
st. Maroubra 407 B8
LOCH NESS
pl. Hornsby 221 A1
LOCHNESS
pl. Engadine 488 J12
LOCHVILLE
st. Wahroonga 222 C4
st. Wahroonga 222 E4
LOCK
av. Padstow 399 F16
la. Forest Lodge 11 H16
rd. Wilberforce 61 C16
st. Blacktown 274 J6
st. Girraween 276 B15
st. Ryde 282 J15
LOCKE
st. Wetherill Pk 334 F4
LOCKER
av. Lurnea 394 C9
LOCKERBIE
rd. Thornleigh 221 C8
LOCKHART
av. Castle Hill 217 K10
av. Balmain, off Elliott St 344 E4
ct. Harringtn Pk 478 E4
pl. Belrose 226 A9
LOCKHEED
cct. St Clair 270 E16
st. Raby 481 G3
LOCKINVAR
pl. Hornsby 191 C16
LOCKLEY
pde. Roseville Ch 285 G1
LOCKSLEY
av. Merrylands 307 J14
cl. Wahroonga 221 K11
rd. Bexley 432 D2
st. Killara 254 B12
st. Woolooware 493 H7
LOCKUNDY
la. Hurstville 431 G1
LOCKWOOD
av. Frenchs Frst 255 H1
av. Greenacre 370 C5
gr. Bidwill 211 B16
st. Asquith 191 K12
st. Merrylands 307 F11
LOCKYER
av. Wrrngtn Cty 238 F6
cl. Dural 219 A3
LOCOMOTIVE
st. Eveleigh 18 G11
LODDON
cl. Bossley Park 333 G5
cr. Campbelltwn 511 J8
LODER
cr. S Windsor 150 F2
la. Punchbowl 400 A4
pl. Glen Alpine 510 B15
LODESTONE
pl. Eagle Vale 481 H6
LODGE
av. Old Tngabbie 277 C7
la. Harbord 258 J16
la. Mosman, off Rangers Av 316 G9
pl. Chester Hill 368 A4
pl. Wetherill Pk 335 A5
rd. Cremorne 316 G3
st. Balgowlah 287 J6
st. Forest Lodge 12 A15
st. Glebe 12 A15
st. Hornsby 191 J10
LODGES
rd. Elderslie 478 A16
rd. Narellan 478 D15
LODI
cl. West Hoxton 392 D5
LODORE
pl. Northmead 278 B6
LOFBERG
rd. West Pymble 253 A10
LOFT
pl. Kellyville 215 D2
pl. Stanhpe Gdn 215 D2
LOFTS
av. Roselands 401 D5
LOFTUS
av. Loftus 489 J13
av. Sutherland 490 B8
cr. Homebush 341 A8
la. Homebush 341 B8
la. Sydney B D10
rd. Bringelly 388 C14
rd. Darling Point 13 G7
rd. Pennant Hills 250 C1
rd. Yennora 337 A8
st. Ashfield 373 A1
st. Bundeena 524 A9
st. Campsie 371 H13
st. Campsie 371 H14
st. Concord 342 B10
st. Dulwich Hill 373 E10
st. Fairfield E 337 A14
st. Leichhardt 9 B15
st. Marsden Pk 181 J13
st. Merrylands 308 A13
st. Narrabeen 229 B2
st. Regentville 265 F4
st. Riverstone 182 H2
st. Sydney B C11
st. Sydney 1 J13
st. Turrella 403 E5
LOFTY
cr. Bossley Park 334 B9
pl. Cranebrook 207 F9
pl. Ruse 512 F6
LOGAN
av. Haberfield 373 D1
st. Loftus 490
LOGANS
pl. Quakers Hill 214
LOGIE
rd. Kenthurst 186
LOIRE
pl. Kearns 451
LOIS
ct. Jamisontown 266
la. Minto 452
la. Pennant Hills 220
pl. Merrylands 307
st. Northmead 278
LOLA
pl. Miranda 461
rd. Dover Ht 348
LOLITA
av. Forestville 255
LOLOMA
pl. Rooty Hill 241
st. Cabramatta 366
LOMANDRA
cct. Castle Hill 217
cr. Mt Annan 509
pl. Alfords Point 429
pl. S Coogee 407
LOMANI
st. Busby 363
LOMATIA
la. Springwood 201
LOMAX
st. Epping 280
LOMBARD
la. Glebe 12
pl. Bella Vista 246
pl. Prospect 275
st. Balgowlah 287
st. Fairfield 335
st. Fairfield W 335
st. Glebe 12
st. Northmead 277
LOMBARDO
st. Prestons 393
LOMOND
cr. Winston Hills 277
ct. Wattle Grove 395
pl. Castle Hill 218
st. Guildford W 336
st. Wakeley 334
LONACH
cl. Baulkham Hl 247
LONARD
av. Wiley Park 400
LONDON
ct. Cecil Hills 362
la. Campsie, off London St 371
pl. Grose Wold 116
rd. Berala 339
rd. Lidcombe 339
st. Blacktown 243
st. Campsie 371
st. Enmore 17
LONDONDERRY
dr. Killarney Ht 256
rd. Londonderry 177
rd. Richmond 118
LONE PINE
av. Chatswd W 284
av. Milperra 397
pde. Matraville 407
pl. N Balgowlah 287
LONG
av. East Ryde 283
cl. Green Valley 363
cl. Menai 458
dr. Mcquarie Pk 282
st. Hobartville 118
st. Smithfield 305
st. Strathfield 371
LONG ANGLE
rd. Yellow Rock 173
LONGBOW
cl. Old Tngabbie 277
LONGDON
cl. S Penrith 267
la. S Penrith, off Longdon Cl 267
LONGDOWN
st. Newtown 17
LONGFELLOW
st. Wetherill Pk 335

GFIELD
Cabramatta ...366 A6
GFORD
Roseville ...284 C6
G HAI
Moorebank ...395 C16
GHURST
Minto ...453 A14
Minto ...482 J4
GLEAT
Kurmond ...86 A2
Kurmond ...56 D16
GLEY
Castle Hill ...217 D6
S Windsor ...150 F2
GLEYS
Badgerys Ck ...358 B4
Luddenham ...357 G4
GPORT
Lewisham ...15 A9
GREACH
Bella Vista ...246 G1
G REEF
Woodbine ...481 H9
GS
The Rocks ...A H6
GSTAFF
Chipping Ntn ...396 C5
Chipping Ntn ...396 E5
Claymore ...481 E11
G TAN
Scheyville ...123 D8
GUEVILLE
Lane Cove ...314 E1
GVIEW
Mulgoa ...295 J14
Balmain ...344 E5
Eastwood ...281 H5
Five Dock ...342 J11
GWORTH
Eastlakes ...405 K3
Point Piper ...347 F8
Castle Hill ...219 A10
Point Piper, off Longworth Av ...347 F8
NICERA
Cherrybrook ...219 K14
NSDALE
Berowra Ht ...133 B6
Pymble ...252 K4
W Pnnant Hl ...249 H5
Lilyfield ...10 E9
St Marys ...269 G4
OKES
Balmain East ...8 G8
OKOUT
Blaxland ...234 C8
Dee Why ...259 B9
Mt Pritchard ...364 F14
OMBAH
E Lindfield ...254 J13
S Penrith ...266 G1
Dover Ht ...348 F14
Bilgola ...169 E6
OP
Mt Annan ...479 E14
ORANA
Leumeah ...482 B15
Roseville Ch ...285 E2
PEZ
Bankstown ...399 F1
QUAT VALLEY
Bayview ...168 J13
RAINE
Caringbah ...492 G14
RANDO
Sefton ...338 F16
RANTHUS
Bidwill ...211 F13
RD
Dundas Vy ...279 K9
Barden Rdg ...488 F3
Orchard Hills ...267 D9
Belrose ...226 D15
Botany ...405 E9
Cabramatta W ...364 K7
Haberfield ...373 E2
Mt Colah ...192 C6
Narellan ...478 F11
Newtown ...374 H11
N Sydney ...5 D8
Rockdale ...403 E15

st. Roseville ...284 H4
wy. Glenwood ...215 J16
LORD CASTLEREAGH
cct. Mcquarie Lk ...423 E14
LORD ELDON
dr. Harringtn Pk ...478 D2
LORD HOWE
dr. Green Valley ...363 A11
dr. Hinchinbrk ...363 A13
dr.n,Green Valley ...363 A8
st. Dover Ht ...348 F13
LORDS
av. Asquith ...192 A9
rd. Leichhardt ...15 B3
LORENZO
cr. Rsemeadow ...540 K4
LORETTA
av. Como ...460 H5
pl. Belrose ...225 K14
pl. Glendenning ...242 J3
LORIKEET
av. Ingleburn ...453 F10
cl. Woronora Ht ...489 C4
cr. Green Valley ...363 D9
pl. St Clair ...270 G13
st. Glenwood ...215 D15
wy. W Pnnant Hl ...249 D7
LORING
pl. Quakers Hill ...214 B11
LORKING
st. Canterbury ...372 E16
LORNA
av. Blakehurst ...432 C15
av. North Ryde ...282 H7
la. Stanmore ...16 C8
LORNE
av. Kensington ...376 E13
av. Killara ...253 K12
av. S Penrith ...266 H2
pl. Bossley Park ...333 D11
st. Girraween ...276 A15
st. Prospect ...274 K10
st. Summer Hill ...373 C5
LOROY
cr. Frenchs Frst ...255 G1
LORRAINE
av. Arncliffe ...403 A10
av. Bardwell Vy ...403 A10
av. Padstow Ht ...429 H7
pl. Merrylands W ...307 B15
pl. Oatlands ...278 J12
st. N Strathfield ...341 C5
st. Peakhurst ...430 E6
st. Seven Hills ...245 J15
LORRINA
cl. W Pnnant Hl ...249 K1
LOSCOE
st. Fairfield ...336 E8
LOSTOCK
pl. Leumeah ...482 E13
LOT
la. Hunters Hill ...313 H10
LOTHIAN
st. Winston Hills ...277 F4
LOTOS
la. Petersham ...15 G8
st. Petersham ...15 G8
LOTTIE LYELL
av. Moore Park ...21 A6
LOTUS
cl. Baulkham Hl ...246 J4
pl. Mcquarie Fd ...454 D6
LOUDEN
av. Illawong ...460 C3
st. Canada Bay ...342 D10
LOUDON
av. Haberfield ...343 D12
LOUGH
av. Guildford ...337 K7
la. Guildford ...337 K7
LOUGHLIN
st. Rozelle ...7 C16
LOUIE
la. Revesby, off Louie St ...399 C11
st. Padstow ...399 B11
LOUIS
av. Newington, off Newington Bvd ...310 B12
st. Granville ...308 B14
st. Merrylands ...308 B14
st. Redfern ...19 A6

tce. Hurstville ...431 K1
LOUISA
rd. Birchgrove ...7 F3
st. Auburn ...339 E5
st. Earlwood ...402 G2
st. Oatley ...431 E11
st. Summer Hill ...373 B4
LOUISE
av. Baulkham Hl ...247 B9
av. Chatswd W ...284 A9
av. Ingleburn ...453 C4
pl. Bonnyrigg ...364 B5
pl. Cecil Hills ...362 J4
st. Dean Park ...242 H1
st. Jannali ...460 G13
wy. Cherrybrook ...219 C15
LOUISE LOVELY
la. Moore Park ...21 B6
LOUISIANA
pl. Riverwood ...400 B13
LOURDES
av. Lindfield ...254 E13
LOUTH
pl. Hoxton Park ...392 F7
LOVAT
av. Earlwood ...372 K16
st. West Pymble ...252 H11
LOVE
av. Emu Plains ...235 H11
la. Guildford ...337 G5
pl. Picton ...563 G1
st. Blacktown ...244 A10
LOVEGROVE
dr. Quakers Hill ...213 H14
LOVELL
rd. Denistone E ...281 E8
rd. Eastwood ...281 E8
LOVERIDGE
st. Alexandria ...19 A16
LOVERING
pl. Newport ...169 K12
LOVES
av. Oyster Bay ...461 B9
LOVETT
st. Manly Vale ...288 A3
st. Thornleigh ...220 J13
LOVILLE
av. Peakhurst ...430 D10
av. Seven Hills ...245 C15
LOVONI
st. Cabramatta ...366 B10
LOW
st. Hurstville ...401 H16
st. Mt Krng-gai ...163 A12
st. Smithfield ...336 A4
LOWAN
pl. Kellyville ...216 K1
pl. Woronora Ht ...489 D5
LOWANA
av. Kirrawee ...491 B5
av. Merrylands ...307 E10
av. Roseville ...284 G2
cr. Seven Hills ...246 C12
pl. Beverly Hills ...401 B13
st. Villawood ...367 G5
LOWANNA
av. Baulkham Hl ...247 B4
dr. S Penrith ...266 G7
pl. Hornsby ...221 C1
st. Belrose ...225 K16
st. Scotland I ...168 J4
LOWE
cr. Elderslie ...477 H15
rd. Bexley North ...402 F9
rd. Hornsby ...192 B16
st. Clovelly ...378 A14
st. Merrylands ...307 K15
LOWER ALMORA
st. Mosman ...317 D6
LOWER AVON
st. Glebe ...12 B10
LOWER BEACH
st. Balgowlah ...287 H10
LOWER BLIGH
st. Northbridge ...286 A14
LOWER BOYLE
st. Mosman ...316 G11
LOWER CAMPBELL
st. Surry Hills ...F J8
LOWER CLIFF
av. Northbridge ...316 A2

LOWER FORT
st. Dawes Point ...A F2
st. Dawes Point ...1 F9
st. Millers Pt ...A F2
st. Millers Pt ...1 F9
LOWER MOUNT
st. Wentwthvle ...277 A13
LOWER PLATEAU
rd. Bilgola ...169 E5
LOWER PUNCH
st. Mosman ...317 C5
LOWER ST GEORGES
cr. Drummoyne ...313 K16
LOWER SERPENTINE
rd. Greenwich ...314 J14
LOWER SPOFFORTH
wk. Cremorne, off Lower Boyle St ...316 F11
LOWER WASHINGTON
dr. Bonnet Bay ...460 B8
dr. Bonnet Bay ...460 E10
LOWER WYCOMBE
rd. Neutral Bay ...6 F10
LOWERY
cl. Emu Plains ...234 K10
LOWES
dr. Cobbitty ...416 H6
LOWING
cl. Forestville ...255 K8
LOWRY
av. West Hoxton ...391 G7
cr. St Ives ...253 K2
pl. Prairiewood ...334 K9
pl. Woronora Ht ...489 B5
rd. Lalor Park ...245 J10
st. Mt Lewis ...370 A16
LOWTHER PARK
av. Warrawee ...222 G12
LOXTON
pl. Bossley Park ...333 E11
pl. Forestville ...256 B6
LOXWOOD
av. Cmbrdg Pk ...238 C8
LOY
pl. Quakers Hill ...243 K3
LOYALTY
rd. North Rocks ...278 F2
sq. Balmain ...7 H9
LOZANO
pl. Bossley Park ...333 K10
LUCAN
pl. Minchinbury ...271 K8
LUCAS
av. Malabar ...437 F6
av. Moorebank ...396 E8
av. Russell Lea ...343 C5
cct. Kellyville ...215 G4
la. Camperdwn ...17 F5
rd. Burwood ...342 C14
rd. East Hills ...427 K5
rd. Lalor Park ...245 F15
rd. Seven Hills ...245 F15
st. Camperdwn ...17 G5
st. Cronulla ...524 A2
st. Emu Plains ...235 C12
st. Guildford ...337 B3
wy. Ingleburn ...453 A10
LUCASVILLE
rd. Glenbrook ...234 B16
LUCE
pl. St Andrews ...481 K6
LUCENA
cr. Lethbrdg Pk ...240 D2
LUCERNE
av. S Wntwthvle ...306 K9
st. Belmore ...371 B13
LUCETTE
pl. Castle Hill ...216 K9
pl. Castle Hill ...217 A9
LUCIA
av. Baulkham Hl ...247 E9
av. St Ives ...224 F11
LUCIDUS
pl. Glenmore Pk ...265 H14
LUCILLE
cr. Casula ...394 H12
LUCINDA
av. Bass Hill ...367 E7
av. Georges Hall ...367 E7
av. Springwood ...201 F1
av. Wahroonga ...222 A11

av.s,Wahroonga ...222 A13
gr. Winston Hills ...277 A2
pl. Mona Vale ...169 D15
rd. Greystanes ...306 G8
rd. Marsfield ...282 A7
LUCIUS
pl. Rsemeadow ...540 C3
st. Bondi Beach ...378 B4
LUCKNOW
st. Willoughby ...285 D15
LUCRETIA
av. Longueville ...314 E9
rd. Seven Hills ...275 E7
rd. Toongabbie ...275 H10
LUCULIA
av. Baulkham Hl ...247 D14
LUCY
av. Lansvale ...366 K8
cl. Hornsby ...191 J10
ct. Ashfield ...342 H14
st. Ashfield ...342 H14
st. Kingswood ...237 D16
st. Merrylands W ...306 J13
LUDDENHAM
rd. Luddenham ...327 H12
rd. Orchard Hills ...269 E16
rd. Orchard Hills ...299 C5
LUDGATE
st. Concord ...341 J5
st. Fairfield ...336 D5
st. Roselands ...401 A5
LUDLOW
rd. Castle Hill ...218 D16
LUDMILA
cl. Carlingford ...279 F3
LUDOVIC
cl. Beecroft ...250 D4
LUDWIG
sq. Bidwill ...211 G14
LUE
pl. Airds ...512 B10
LUELLA
pl. Rooty Hill ...241 J13
LUFF
pl. Ingleburn ...453 A11
st. Botany ...405 G14
LUGANO
av. Burraneer ...523 E2
av. Springwood ...201 F3
ct. Springwood ...201 F2
LUGAR
st. Bronte ...377 H9
LUGAR BRAE
av. Bronte ...377 H9
LUGARD
st. Penrith ...236 G2
LUGARNO
av. Leumeah ...482 C15
pde. Lugarno ...429 J15
pl. The Oaks ...502 A12
LUKAS
av. Kenthurst ...158 B16
LUKE
av. Burwood ...342 C11
pl. Rooty Hill ...272 B1
rd. Londonderry ...178 C7
st. Hunters Hill ...313 D10
LUKER
st. Elderslie ...507 F2
LUKES
la. Baulkham Hl ...247 D5
LUKIS
av. Richmond ...119 B6
st. Richmond ...119 K5
LULAND
st. Botany ...405 D12
LUMEA
pl. Dharruk ...241 C9
LUMEAH
av. Elanora Ht ...198 D16
av. Punchbowl ...400 D8
rd. Lindfield ...284 C3
st. Merrylands ...308 A15
LUMLEY
st. Granville ...308 E12
LUMSDAINE
av. East Ryde ...313 B1
dr. Harbord ...288 K2
st. Picton ...563 F6
LUMSDEN
st. Cammeray ...316 A5

LUNA
st. Milsons Point 5 K11
LUNAR
av. Heathcote 518 E14
LUND
st. Denistone 281 G13
LUNDY
av. Kingsgrove 402 B7
LUNN
ct. Cabramatta 365 H10
LUONGO
cl. Prestons 393 B13
LUPIN
av. Riverwood 399 K10
av. Villawood 337 B16
pl. Greystanes 306 A11
LUPTON
pl. Horngsea Pk 392 F14
pwy. Warrimoo 203 C15
LURGAN
st. Wentwthvle 277 D10
LURLINE
st. Maroubra 407 J9
LURNEA
av. Georges Hall 367 G13
cr. Forestville 255 H9
LURR
pl. Bonnyrigg 364 A7
LUSKIN
pl. Bossley Park 333 K9
LUSS
ct. Glenhaven 218 E6
LUSTY
pl. Moorebank 396 F6
st. Arncliffe 403 H5
st. Arncliffe 403 J5
LUTANA
pl. Baulkham Hl 248 B8
LUTANDA
cl. Pennant Hills 220 C15
LUTHER
rd. Winmalee 172 K12
LUTON
pl. Colyton 270 E5
pl. St Ives 224 A9
rd. Blacktown 244 K10
LUTTRELL
st. Glenmore Pk 265 J10
st. Glenmore Pk 265 K7
st. Hobartville 118 D10
wy. Minto 482 K5
LUXFORD
rd. Bidwill 211 A14
rd. Emerton 240 G6
rd. Hassall Gr 241 K1
rd. Lethbrdg Pk 240 F2
rd. Londonderry 148 K5
rd. Mount Druitt 241 E14
rd. Oakhurst 241 K1
rd. Shalvey 211 A14
rd. Tregear 240 G6
rd. Whalan 240 G6
LUXOR
pde. Roseville 284 K1
LUYTEN
cl. Cranebrook 207 E6
LUZON
av. Lethbrdg Pk 240 D2
LYALL
av. Dean Park 212 K16
st. Leichhardt 9 D12
LYCETT
av. Kellyville 215 F3
av. West Hoxton 391 J12
LYDBROOK
st. Wentwthvle 277 D15
LYDHAM
av. Rockdale 403 A12
pl. Castle Hill 219 A10
LYDIA
pl. Hassall Gr 211 J14
LYELL
pl. Bow Bowing 452 C15
pl. Cartwright 394 A5
st. Bossley Park 334 C7
LYGON
pl. Castle Hill 217 J11
wy. Cranebrook 207 G13
LYLA
st. Narwee 400 G14

LYLE
av. Lindfield 283 K5
st. Girraween 276 A15
st. Hurstville 401 H15
st. Ryde 281 K9
LYLY
rd. Allambie Ht 257 H13
LYMERSTON
st. Tempe 404 C1
LYMINGE
rd. Croydon Pk 371 K8
LYMINGTON
st. Bexley 402 H16
LYMM
st. Belrose 225 J13
LYMOORE
av. Thornleigh 221 C9
LYN
cct. Jamisontown 266 B2
la. Jamisontown, off Lyn Cct 266 C3
pde. Prestons 394 A8
pl. Wentwthvle 277 C9
LYNBARA
av. St Ives 254 A1
LYNBRAE
av. Beecroft 250 C10
LYNCH
av. Caringbah 492 G13
av. Enmore 374 F9
av. Queens Park 22 D12
cl. Carlingford 279 G3
la. Marrickville 374 F9
rd. Faulconbdg 171 D10
rd. Glenbrook 264 B2
LYNDEL
cl. Quakers Hill 213 J9
pl. Castle Hill 218 D15
LYNDELLE
pl. Carlingford 250 C14
LYNDEN
av. Carlingford 249 H14
LYNDHURST
cr. Hunters Hill 313 H11
ct. Wattle Grove 425 J5
ct. W Pnnant Hl 249 C2
pl. Glen Alpine 510 C13
st. Gladesville 312 H4
st. Glebe 12 D11
st. Riverstone 182 D12
wy. Belrose 226 C10
wy. Cherrybrook, off Purchase Rd 219 D10
LYNDIA
st. Ingleburn 453 C10
LYNDLEY
st. Busby 363 G15
LYNDON
st. Fairfield 336 E15
wy. Beecroft 250 A4
LYNE
la. Alexandria 18 G13
rd. Cheltenham 250 K11
st. Alexandria 18 G13
LYNEHAM
pl. W Pnnant Hl 249 A8
LYNESTA
av. Bexley North 402 D10
av. Fairfield W 335 B12
LYNETTE
av. Carlingford 249 H13
cl. Hornsby Ht 191 H1
cr. S Wntwthvle 307 E5
pl. Belrose 226 A13
LYNNE
pl. Hornsby 221 F6
LYNN RIDGE
av. Gordon 253 E10
LYNROB
pl. Thornleigh 220 G11
LYNSTOCK
av. Castle Hill 218 D12
LYNTON
grn. W Pnnant Hl 249 D5
LYNVALE
cl. Lane Cove W 284 G14
LYNWEN
cr. Banksia 403 H12
LYNWOOD
av. Cromer 258 E2
av. Dee Why 258 E2

av. Doonside 243 J14
av. Killara 254 A11
av. Narraweena 258 E2
cl. Pennant Hills 220 F14
la. Blakehurst 432 C13
pl. Castle Hill 217 J9
rd. St Helens Park 541 H3
st. Blakehurst 432 C14
LYNX
pl. Cranebrook 207 G5
pl. Quakers Hill 214 C9
LYON
av. Punchbowl 399 K7
av. S Turramrra 252 A5
cl. Killara 253 J12
pl. Cecil Hills 362 G3
st. Mascot 405 F4
LYONPARK
rd. Mcquarie Pk 282 F4
LYONS
av. Cabramatta 365 D10
la. Sydney F E4
pl. Cherrybrook 219 D9
pl. Drummoyne 343 K1
pl. St Clair 270 B10
rd. Camperdwn 17 F1
rd. Drummoyne 343 E5
rd. Five Dock 343 A8
rd. Russell Lea 343 E5
rd.w, Canada Bay 342 E7
rd.w, Five Dock 342 G8
st. Dover Ht 348 E12
st. Strathfield 341 G13
wy. Minto 482 K2
wy. Minto 483 A2
LYPTUS
wy. Plumpton 241 G9
LYRA
la. Seven Hills 246 C14
pl. Hinchinbrk 393 D4
LYREBIRD
cr. Green Valley 363 D10
cr. St Clair 269 H11
ct. Kenthurst 158 A16
la. St Clair, off Banks Dr 269 H12
pl. Ingleburn 453 F9
pl. St Ives Ch 223 K1
LYSAGHT
rd. Wedderburn 540 B16
LYSANDER
av. Rsemeadow 540 H9
LYTE
pl. Prospect 275 A12
LYTHAM
ct. Glenmore Pk 266 G8
LYTON
st. Blacktown 244 B14
LYTTON
la. Riverstone 182 D8
pl. Campbelltwn 511 K2
rd. Riverstone 182 F9
st. Cammeray 315 K7
st. Wentwthvle 307 B3

M

M2
mwy. Baulkham Hl 246 J15
mwy. Beecroft 250 A9
mwy. Carlingford 249 A13
mwy. Cheltenham 251 F12
mwy. Epping 250 A10
mwy. Mcquarie Pk 283 A5
mwy. Marsfield 251 F12
mwy. N Epping 251 F12
mwy. North Rocks 248 B14
mwy. North Ryde 283 A5
M4
Auburn 309 C12
Blacktown 273 C14
Clarmnt Ms 269 B7
Eastern Ck 272 C11
Emu Plains 235 A12
Glenbrook 234 H15
Granville 308 C8
Greystanes 306 E3
Harris Park 308 C8
Homebush 341 A7
Homebush B 340 A1
Homebush W 340 A1
Huntingwd 273 C14
Jamisontown 265 G1

Lapstone 234 H15
Leonay 234 H15
Lidcombe 340 A1
Mays Hill 307 B4
Merrylands 307 B4
Minchinbury 271 C10
N Strathfield 341 A7
Orchard Hills 267 D8
Parramatta 308 C8
Prospect 275 B16
St Clair 270 A8
Silverwater 309 C12
S Penrith 266 D6
S Wntwthvle 307 B4
M5
Beverly Hills 400 A11
Casula 423 G5
Hamondvle 396 C12
Liverpool 393 K16
Lurnea 393 K16
Milperra 397 B14
Moorebank 396 C12
Narwee 400 A11
Padstow 399 B11
Panania 398 B12
Prestons 423 G5
Revesby 398 B12
Riverwood 400 A11
MAAS
st. Cromer 258 C1
MABEL
st. Hurstville 431 K7
st. Kingsgrove 402 B12
st. Willoughby 285 D12
McADAM
pl. Lalor Park 245 H11
MACADAMIA
st. Prestons 393 K15
McALEER
st. Leichhardt 15 D6
McALISTER
av. Cronulla 494 A13
av. Engadine 518 G3
la. Chippendale 19 A3
rd. Galston 160 D4
McANALLY
la. Randwick, off Carrington Rd 377 D16
McANDREW
cl. Lurnea 394 F12
McARDLE
st. Ermington 280 B14
MACARTHUR
av. Crows Nest 315 J7
av. Pagewood 406 C8
av. Revesby 398 J16
av. Strathfield 371 C3
cr. Westmead 307 E3
dr. Holsworthy 426 F7
dr. St Clair 270 A10
pde. Dulwich Hill 373 E11
pl. Ruse 512 G1
rd. Elderslie 477 F16
rd. Kellyville 217 D5
rd. Spring Farm 507 G5
st. Douglas Park 568 C3
st. Ermington 310 E1
st. Parramatta 308 F3
st. St Ives 254 D1
st. Sylvania 462 A14
st. Ultimo 12 J13
st. Villawood 337 C15
wy. Bidwill 211 F15
McARTHUR
st. Guildford 337 J2
MACARTNEY
av. Chatswd W 284 E9
cr. Hebersham 241 E1
st. Ermington 310 D3
st. Miranda 461 K16
MACAULAY
la. Stanmore 16 G5
la.w, Stanmore 16 F5
rd. Stanmore 16 F6
st. Wetherill Pk 334 E4
MACAULEY
av. Bankstown 399 D3
st. Leichhardt 9 G14
McAULEY
cl. Heathcote 518 C15
cr. Emu Plains 235 F8
pl. Waitara 221 K5
McAULIFFE
pl. Silverdale 353 J13

MACBETH
gr. St Clair 270
wy. Rsemeadow 540
McBRIAN
pl. Wakeley 334
McBRIDE
av. Hunters Hill 313
McBRIEN
pl. Frenchs Frst 255
McBURNEY
av. Mascot 405
la. Kirribilli 6
la. Mascot 405
rd. Cabramatta 365
st. Naremburn 315
McCABE
cl. Prairiewood 334
cl. St Clair 269
la. St Clair, off McCabe Cl 269
pl. Chatswood 285
pl. Menai 458
pl. Rouse Hill 184
st. Greystanes 305
McCAHONS
av. Georges Hall 367
McCALL
av. Camden S 507
av. Croydon Pk 371
McCALLUM
av. East Ryde 313
st. Roselands 401
McCALLUMS
av. Berrilee 131
McCANN
pl. Hassall Gr 212
rd. Leppington 420
rd. Rossmore 419
rd. Rossmore 420
rd. Yellow Rock 204
wy. Minto 482
McCARRS CREEK
rd. Church Point 168
rd. Krngai Ch NP 166
rd. Krngai Ch NP 166
rd. Terrey Hills 196
McCARTHY
la. Annandale 17
la. Concord 341
la. Woolmloo D
pl. Woolmloo 4
st. Fairfield W 334
st. Richmond 119
McCARTHYS
la. Castlereagh 206
McCARTNEY
cr. St Clair 270
la. St Clair, off McCartney Cr 270
pwy. Warwck Frm, off McCartney St 365
st. Warwck Frm 365
McCAULEY
cr. Glenbrook 234
la. Alexandria 19
st. Alexandria 19
st. Matraville 436
McCLEAN
st. Blacktown 243
st. Georges Hall 367
McCLEER
st. Rozelle 344
McCLELLAND
st. Chester Hill 368
st. N Willghby 285
McCLYMONTS
rd. Kenthurst 125
rd. Maraylya 125
McCONVILLE
la. Beaconsfield, off Connolly La 375
McCORMACK
la. Revesby 398
pl. Denham Ct 452
st. Arndell Park 273
McCOURT
st. Wiley Park 370
McCOWEN
rd. Ingleside 197
McCOY
la. Btn-le-Sds 433
st. Toongabbie 276

Toongabbie........276 B4
RAE
Camden S..........506 K12
Blackett..............241 C3
REA
Edensor Pk 363 G4
READY
Berowra.............133 H11
REDIE
Horngsea Pk 392 F13
Guildford W 336 H3
Smithfield 336 E3
ROSSIN
Birrong 368 J7
UBBENS
Sutherland, off
Old Princes Hwy.490 E3
UBBIN
Casula..............424 E2
Mt Pritchard......364 J12
Plumpton..........242 C7
Claymore 481 F10
ULLOCH
Blacktown..........243 J13
Riverstone 183 C6
Russell Lea 343 E7
USKER
Cherrybrook.......219 D11
DONALD
Lalor Park 245 G11
Lurnea 394 E7
Bexley North 402 E11
Paddington 4 K13
Ingleburn 423 A14
Erskineville..........375 A9
Lakemba............370 J15
Paddington 4 K13
Ramsgate 433 D14
Sans Souci.........433 D14
Vaucluse............348 G5
ONALD
Auburn 339 B10
Winston Hills......277 J1
Strathfield 341 G16
Bankstown..........399 E2
N Sydney..............K F11
Potts Point............4 K2
McGraths Hl.......122 A14
Rooty Hill...........241 K12
Balmain 7 J9
Berala 339 E12
Cronulla 494 A11
Harbord 258 D16
Illawong............459 K4
Leichhardt...........16 A1
Mortlake 312 A15
North Rocks.......249 B16
Potts Point............4 K2
Greenacre 370 G5
DONNELL
Fairfield W..........335 F11
ONNELL
Raby.................451 C12
OUGALL
Baulkham Hl 247 F4
Castle Hill...........218 C15
Kensington..........376 B11
Milsons Point.........6 A12
DUFF
Rsemeadow.......540 K2
EDON
Warriewood 199 C10
Bossley Park 334 B10
LHONE
Surry Hills............20 E2
Woolmloo.............4 G7
Woolmloo.............4 H4
LIVER
Minto.................482 J5
NCROE
Strathfield S 371 A4
ERI
Edensor Pk 333 J15
VOY
Hamondvle 396 F14
Padstow 399 F14
Alexandria...........19 A16
Waterloo.............19 A16
WAN
Winston Hills......277 G3
Mt Annan..........479 F15
FADYEN
Botany..............405 E13

McFALL
pl. Rooty Hill...........271 K3
st. Botany 405 D12
MACFARLANE
pde. Sylvania............461 H13
st. Davidson 225 A16
McFARLANE
dr. Minchinbury.......271 F8
st. Merrylands.........307 G12
McGANN
pl. Cranebrook 207 E14
McGARVIE
st. Paddington 21 F2
McGEE
pl. Baulkham Hl 248 C10
pl. Fairfield W..........334 K10
McGETTIGAN
la. Panania.............398 E15
McGILL
pl. Menai 458 E14
st. Lewisham............15 A10
McGILVRAY
pl. Rouse Hill 184 K6
McGIRR
pde. Warwck Frm 365 F15
pl. Abbotsford.........343 A3
st. Padstow 399 B16
McGOVERN
cr. Merrylands W 307 A13
McGOVETT
pl. Menai 458 K12
McGOWAN
av. Marrickville 403 H1
st. Putney 312 C10
McGOWEN
av. Malabar 437 E5
cr. Liverpool............395 C8
McGRATH
av. Earlwood 402 F1
av. Five Dock............342 K8
pl. Currans Hill.........479 H12
rd. McGraths Hl.......121 K14
McGRATHS
la. Kensington, off
Doncaster Av......376 F12
MACGREGOR
st. Croydon.............342 E14
McGREGOR
st. Kingsgrove.........401 H13
st. North Ryde 282 G6
McGUIRK
wy. Rouse Hill 185 A8
McHALE
la. Sefton................338 E15
wy. Nelson 154 J13
McHATTON
pl. Hassall Gr 211 J15
st. N Sydney 5 C4
st. Waverton...............5 C4
McHENRY
rd. Cranebrook........207 C14
McILVENIE
st. Canley Ht 365 C3
McILWAINS
st. Ashcroft.............364 E15
McILWRAITH
st. Wetherill Pk 334 A3
MACINA
pl. St Clair...............269 H13
McINNES
pl. Ingleburn 453 B11
MACINTOSH
st. Mascot 405 D4
st. Melrose Pk.........310 K3
McINTOSH
av. Padstow Ht 429 G6
la. Kurrajong.............55 H11
la. Neutral Bay 6 B1
la. Newtown 17 E12
rd. Beacon Hill..........257 J4
rd. Dee Why.............258 E5
rd. Narraweena.........257 J4
st. Chatswood..........284 H9
st. Fairfield..............336 G15
st. Gordon 253 K8
st. Kings Park 244 D2
st. The Oaks.............502 D12
MACINTYRE
cr. Ruse..................512 C8
cr. Sylvania Wtr.......462 D13

McINTYRE
av. Btn-le-Sds..........403 K15
av. St Clair..............269 G16
la. Gordon 253 G7
la. St Clair, off
McIntyre Av.........269 G16
pl. Castle Hill............217 K7
st. Gordon 253 F7
st. Oatley 430 J12
McIVER
av. West Hoxton 362 B16
pl. Maroubra............407 D14
MACK
st. Wentwthvle........306 H2
MACKANESS
cl. Five Dock............342 G8
MACKAY
pl. Leumeah.............482 H12
rd. S Granville 338 G4
st. Ashfield 342 G16
st. Caringbah 492 J7
st. Emu Plains..........235 C11
wy. Rouse Hill 184 J6
McKAY
av. Moorebank 396 D7
dr. Silverdale...........353 H15
pl. Minchinbury.......271 K7
rd. Hornsby Ht 161 E15
rd. Palm Beach.........139 K4
st. Dundas Vy 280 B9
st. Toongabbie.........276 G5
McKEARNS
pl. Arncliffe 403 H9
McKECHNIE
st. Epping 250 C16
McKEE
rd. Theresa Park......444 D7
st. Ultimo 12 K13
McKELL
av. Casula................394 K12
cl. Bonnyrigg 363 K6
st. Birchgrove..............7 J6
MACKELLAR
cir. Springwood 202 H1
pl. Campbelltwn......512 B4
rd. Hebersham 241 E2
st. Casula................424 G3
st. Emu Plains..........235 K7
McKELLAR
cr. S Windsor...........150 H2
MACKEN
cl. Edensor Pk 363 E3
cr. Oatley 430 J13
st. Liverpool............365 B16
st. Oatley 430 J13
McKENDRICK
pl. Warrimoo 202 J13
McKENNY
wy. Narellan Vale......508 H1
McKENSIE
pl. McGraths Hl.......121 K12
MACKENZIE
av. Glenmore Pk.......265 G6
bvd. Seven Hills.........275 F8
pl. Kearns 481 B2
st. Bondi Jctn 22 H9
st. Canley Vale 366 B4
st. Concord W..........341 E2
st. Homebush 341 A11
st. Lavender Bay.........K D13
st. Lavender Bay 5 F11
st. Leichhardt.............10 C14
st. Lilyfield................10 C14
st. Lindfield..............254 E14
st. Revesby..............399 A13
st. Rozelle...................7 B16
st. Strathfield 341 A11
McKENZIE
av. Chifley 437 C10
cr. Wilberforce 62 C16
la. Earlwood 402 G3
pl. Menai 458 E9
st. Campsie 371 J16
wk. Cmbrdg Pk, off
Cambridge St.....237 J9
McKEON
st. Maroubra............407 G11
McKEOWN
st. Prairiewood 334 H7
McKERN
st. Campsie 371 J16
st. Wentwthvle.........307 A1

McKEVITTE
av. East Hills............427 J2
MACKEY
st. Surry Hills..............F F11
st. Surry Hills..............F H12
MACKEYS
st. Horngsea Pk 392 E14
McKIBBIN
st. Canley Ht 365 A2
MACKIE
la. Mosman 316 H5
MACKILLOP
cr. St Helens Park....540 K10
dr. Baulkham Hl 247 A3
pl. Erskine Park.......270 E16
McKILLOP
pl. Dundas Vy 279 J7
rd. Beacon Hill.........257 K6
MACKIN
cl. Barden Rdg.........488 F7
McKINLEY
av. Bonnet Bay 460 C11
pl. Cherrybrook.......219 J9
MACKINNON
av. Padstow 399 B12
st. St Helens Park....541 A9
McKINNON
av. Five Dock...........343 A7
McKINNONS
rd. Wilberforce 61 C11
MACKLIN
st. Pendle Hill..........276 D15
MACKS
gln. Kellyville.............185 K16
MACKSVILLE
st. Hoxton Park 392 K8
McKYE
st. Waverton 315 E11
McLACHLAN
av. Artarmon 314 J1
av. Darlinghurst.........13 B11
wy. Darlinghurst.........13 A11
McLAREN
gr. St Clair...............270 E13
pl. Ingleburn 453 J7
st. Blackett...............241 B4
st. Carramar 366 K1
st. N Sydney...............K G1
st. N Sydney...............5 E4
McLAUGHLAN
pl. Paddington 4 K15
McLAUGHLIN
av. Rcuttrs Bay..........13 B11
cct. Bradbury............511 J9
MACLAURIN
av. East Hills............427 G4
pde. Roseville 284 G5
st. Penshurst 431 H8
MACLEAN
st. Woolmloo...............4 G3
McLEAN
av. Chatswd W 284 E9
cr. Mosman 317 C1
rd. Campbelltwn......511 K4
st. Auburn 339 A3
st. Emu Plains..........235 E12
st. Ingleside.............198 A8
st. Liverpool.............394 H1
MACLEAY
av. Wahroonga 223 C4
cr. St Marys 269 J5
ct. Harringtn Pk.......478 F6
pl. Earlwood 402 F3
pl. Sylvania Wtr.......462 C11
st. Bradbury.............511 F13
st. Elizabeth Bay..........4 K6
st. Greystanes.........306 A3
st. North Bondi 348 E14
st. Potts Point..............4 K6
st. Ryde..................282 E13
st. S Coogee 407 G6
McLENNAN
av. Randwick............377 C11
MACLEOD
rd. Grose Wold........115 D9
McLEOD
av. Lindfield.............284 H1
av. Roseville 284 H1
rd. Middle Dural 158 C1
st. Hurstville 432 B3
st. Mosman 316 H13

MAC MAHON
pl. Menai 458 H11
MACMAHON
st. Hurstville 432 A5
st. N Willghby 285 E8
McMAHON
av. Liverpool.............365 A15
cl. Penrith................237 D7
gr. Glenwood 215 C14
rd. Yagoona 368 J11
McMAHONS
rd. Lane Cove...........314 F6
rd. Longueville 314 F6
rd. Wilberforce 62 B1
McMAHONS PARK
rd. Kurrajong..............85 C1
McMANUS
pl. Lugarno 430 A14
st. McMahons Pt 5 D15
MACMILLAN
st. Seaforth 287 A8
McMILLAN
av. Sandringham 463 E2
av. Winston Hills.......277 K1
rd. Artarmon 284 K16
st. Heckenberg.........364 B12
st. Yagoona 369 D9
McMINN
pl. Narellan Vale......478 G16
McMULLEN
av. Carlingford..........250 A13
av. Castle Hill...........218 D14
McMURDO
av. Tregear 240 F6
McNAIR
av. Kingsford 406 K3
MACNAMARA
av. Concord..............341 H6
pl. Appin..................569 F14
McNAMARA
av. Richmond 120 A6
rd. Cromer 227 J13
McNAUGHTON
st. Jamisontown 236 B15
McPHEE
pl. Bligh Park 150 B5
st. Chester Hill 338 D15
MACPHERSON
rd. Londonderry 149 A8
st. Bronte................377 J10
st. Cremorne.............316 G5
st. Hurstville 401 H15
st. Mosman 316 G5
st. Warriewood 198 G7
st. Waverley.............377 G9
McPHERSON
av. Punchbowl...........399 K5
la. Carlton................432 G9
la. Zetland, off
Joynton Av.........375 J9
la. Meadowbnk, off
McPherson St 311 F2
pl. Illawong..............459 J3
pl. Ruse...................512 H6
rd. Smeaton Gra......479 F11
st. Bnksmeadw 435 K1
st. Bnksmeadw 436 D1
st. Carlton................432 G8
st. Revesby..............398 K15
st. Wakeley..............334 H12
st. West Ryde 311 F2
McQUADE
av. S Windsor..........120 G12
MACQUARIE
av. Camden 507 A5
av. Campbelltwn 511 J6
av. Kellyville.............215 G4
av. Leumeah.............512 C3
av. Penrith................237 A9
cct. Holsworthy 426 C9
dr. Cherrybrook........219 H9
dr. Mcquarie Pk.......282 C1
la. Parramatta 308 D3
pl. Denistone E.........281 J10
pl. Glossodia..............59 F8
pl. Mortdale 431 B8
pl. Sydney..................B B11
pl. Tahmoor.............565 F10
rd. Auburn 339 D1
rd. Earlwood 403 B2
rd. Greystanes..........305 G11
rd. Ingleburn 453 E4
rd. Mcquarie Fd.......453 D4

rd. Pymble 253 H2
rd. Rouse Hill 184 C11
rd. Springwood 201 D3
rd. Vaucluse 348 G2
rd. Wilberforce 91 K2
st. Annandale 16 D4
st. Chatswood 285 A5
st. Chifley 437 A6
st. Cromer 227 H12
st. Fairfield 336 A12
st. Greenacre 370 D13
st. Gymea 461 H16
st. Leichhardt 16 D4
st. Liverpool 395 C6
st. Liverpool 395 D4
st. Liverpool 395 E1
st. Parramatta 308 A3
st. Rosebery 405 J2
st. Roseville 285 A5
st. S Windsor 120 G15
st. Sydney D F5
st. Sydney 4 A3
st. Warwck Frm 365 E16
st. Windsor 121 A11
tce. Balmain 7 E6

MACQUARIEDALE
rd. Appin 569 A7
rd. Appin 569 C10

MACQUARIE GROVE
rd. Camden 477 A11
rd. Cobbitty 447 F15
rd. Harringtn Pk 447 F15
rd. Kirkham 477 A9

MACQUARIE LINKS
dr. Glenfield 423 G12
dr. Mcquarie Lk 423 D16

MACQUEEN
pl. Mt Riverview 234 D4

McRAE
pl. N Turramrra 223 D7
rd. Sans Souci 433 G16
st. Petersham 15 H15

McRAES
av. Penshurst 431 E7

McROBERTS
st. N Parramatta 278 G10

McTAGGART
rd. N Turramrra 193 E12

MACTIER
av. Milperra 397 F12
st. Narrabeen 228 H7
st. Narrabeen 229 A8

MACULATA
cr. Mcquarie Fd 454 D2
pl. Kingswood 267 J1

McVEY
pl. Rooty Hill 241 K12

McVICARS
la. Lidcombe 339 H10

McVICKER
st. Moorebank 396 D10

McWILLIAM
dr. Douglas Park 568 D5

MADAGASCAR
dr. Kings Park 244 F2

MADANG
av. Whalan 240 J12
pl. Glenfield 424 G14
rd. Belrose 226 B3
st. Holsworthy 426 D4
wy. Matraville 407 C16

MADDECKS
av. Moorebank 396 C8

MADDEN
la. Blacktown 245 D8

MADDENS
rd. N Richmond 87 D6

MADDISON
la. Redfern 20 C9
st. Redfern 20 C10

MADDOCK
st. Dulwich Hill 373 C7

MADDOX
st. Alexandria 375 C10

MADDY
wy. Stanhpe Gdn 215 C9

MADEIRA
av. Kings Lngly 245 D7
pl. Surry Hills 19 J2
st. Sylvania 462 B7
wy. Minto 482 K2

MADELEINE
ct. Mt Colah 162 F14
pl. Kingsford 407 C4

MADELINE
av. Northmead 278 A5
st. Belfield 371 B8
st. Fairfield 335 G14
st. Fairfield W 335 G14
st. Hunters Hill 313 H10
st. Strathfield S 371 A7

MADIGAN
dr. Wrrngtn Cty 238 F6
gr. Thirlmere 565 C4

MADISON
cct. St Clair 269 F13
la. St Clair, off Madison Cct 269 G12
pl. Bonnet Bay 460 D11
pl. Kellyville 216 C2
pl. Schofields 213 H5

MADOLINE
pl. Springwood 201 J2

MADONNA
st. Winston Hills 246 G15

MADRERS
av. Kogarah 433 D9

MADRID
pl. Glendenning 242 G3

MADSON
pl. Bonnyrigg 364 B6

MAE
cr. Panania 398 B13

MAEVE
av. Kellyville 216 J3

MAFEKING
av. Lane Cove 314 F1

MAGARRA
pl. Seaforth 287 D10

MAGDALA
rd. North Ryde 283 B12

MAGDALENE
st. St Marys 269 J1

MAGDELLA
st. Birrong 369 A5

MAGEE
la. Glenfield 424 D10
pl. Killarney Ht 256 D15
st. Ashcroft 364 F16

MAGELLAN
av. Lethbrdg Pk 240 G5
st. Fairfield W 335 D9

MAGENTA
la. Paddington 4 F15

MAGGA DAN
av. Tregear 240 C5

MAGGIOTTO
pl. Mt Pritchard 364 K10

MAGIC
gr. Mosman 317 A11

MAGIC PUDDING
pl. Faulconbdg 171 F11

MAGILL
st. Randwick 376 K16

MAGNA
wy. Oakhurst, off Alpin Gr 242 A4

MAGNETIC
av. Hinchinbrk 393 A1

MAGNEY
av. Regents Pk 369 A3
la. Woollahra 377 F2
pl. Bella Vista 246 F4
st. Woollahra 22 G4

MAGNOLIA
av. Baulkham Hl 247 F14
av. Epping 250 E12
cl. Casula 423 K2
cl. Frenchs Frst 256 H1
dr. Picton 561 B3
gr. Schofields 214 A6
pde. Villawood 337 A16
pl. Mcquarie Fd 453 K6
st. Greystanes 306 C13
st. Kirrawee 460 J15
st. N St Marys 240 B9

MAGNUM
pl. Minto 482 E9

MAGOWAR
rd. Girraween 275 J13
rd. Pendle Hill 276 A14

MAGPIE
ct. Glenwood 215 E14
pl. Glenmore Pk 265 J12
pl. Ingleburn 453 H5
rd. Green Valley 363 D8

MAGRA
pl. Kings Lngly 245 C5

MAGRATH
pl. Emu Plains 235 E8

MAGREE
cr. Chipping Ntn 396 E5

MAGUIRES
rd. Maraylya 124 E10

MAGYAR
pl. Oakhurst 242 D2

MAHAN
wy. Minto 483 A1

MAHBUHAY
gr. Mount Druitt 241 D12

MAHER
cl. Beecroft 249 K11
la. Hurstville 432 A7
st. Hurstville 431 J8

MAHNKEN
av. Revesby 399 A13

MAHOGANY
cl. Alfords Point 429 C14
cl. Cranebrook 237 F1
cl. Glenwood 215 J16
ct. Castle Hill 218 K7
pl. Mcquarie Fd 454 E2
st. Prestons 393 H14
wy. Greenacre 370 F5

MAHON
ct. Ingleburn 453 A12
st. West Ryde 281 H14

MAHONEY
la. Edgecliff 13 E9

MAHONGA
st. Tahmoor 565 K10

MAHONS CREEK
rd. Yarramundi 145 A3

MAHONY
rd. Riverstone 182 K5
rd. Wentwthvle 277 B11

MAHRATTA
av. Wahroonga 222 B11

MAI
pl. Hebersham 241 D10

MAIANBAR
rd. Royal N P 522 B15

MAIDA
rd. Epping 281 C2
st. Five Dock 342 G8
st. Lilyfield 10 E4

MAIDEN
la. Surry Hills 4 D14
st. Greenacre 370 E11

MAIDOS
pl. Quakers Hill 214 D11

MAIDSTONE
pl. Glenmore Pk 266 E12
st. Picton 563 F11

MAILEY
cct. Rouse Hill 184 J5
pl. Shalvey 211 B15

MAIN
la. Merrylands 307 H12
st. Blacktown 244 H16
st. Earlwood 402 D4
st. Horngsea Pk 392 E11
st. Mt Annan 479 D13

MAINERD
av. Bexley North 402 F11

MAINO
cl. Green Valley 363 H11

MAINSBRIDGE
av. Liverpool 394 H4

MAIN SOUTHERN
rd. Camden 506 E10
rd. Cawdor 506 E10

MAINTENANCE
la. Richmond 118 F13

MAISMONDE
pl. Carlingford 280 E6

MAITLAND
av. Kingsford 406 C2
pl. Baulkham Hl 216 H14
pl. Kirrawee 491 B7
st. Davidson 255 D3
st. Killara 253 H12

wy. Airds 511 H15

MAJESTIC
dr. Stanhpe Gdn 215 D10

MAJOR
rd. Merrylands 307 E11
st. Coogee 377 J15
st. Mosman 317 A12
st. Punchbowl 400 C8

MAJORS
la. Concord, off Brewer St 341 K4

MAJORS BAY
rd. Concord 341 J1

MAJURA
cl. St Ives Ch 194 B16

MAKIM
st. N Curl Curl 258 F9

MAKINSON
st. Gladesville 312 K9

MALA
cr. Blacktown 244 B12
st. Smithfield 335 B3

MALABAR
rd. Dural 188 E15
rd. Maroubra 407 C16
rd. S Coogee 407 F4
st. Canley Vale 366 B1
st. Fairfield 335 K15

MALABINE
la. S Penrith, off Malabine Pl 266 H7
pl. S Penrith 266 H7

MALACHITE
rd. Eagle Vale 481 A8

MALACOOTA
rd. Northbridge 286 B16

MALAHIDE
rd. Pennant Hills 220 E16

MALAKOFF
st. Marrickville 373 K12

MALAKUA
st. Whalan 240 K11

MALANDA
pl. St Marys 269 C4

MALAWA
pl. Bradbury 511 C15

MALBARA
cr. Frenchs Frst 255 K2

MALBEC
pl. Eschol Park 481 C3

MALCOLM
av. Mt Pritchard 364 F9
av. Werrington 238 H10
la. Erskineville 18 B16
st. Blacktown 274 J5
st. Erskineville 18 B16
st. Mascot 405 H4
st. Narrabeen 229 C1
wy. Rsemeadow 540 K2

MALDON
st. S Penrith 266 F5

MALEY
gr. Glenwood 215 K15
st. Guildford 337 C5

MALGA
av. Roseville Ch 255 E16

MALIBU
st. Bundeena 524 B11

MALING
av. Ermington 310 C3

MALINYA
cr. Moorebank 396 F11
rd. Allambie Ht 257 H14

MALLACOOTA
cl. Prestons 393 B16
cl. Prestons 423 A1
pl. Woodcroft 243 F10
st. Wakeley 334 H12

MALLAM
rd. Picton 561 C3

MALLARD
dr. Oatley 430 E12
st. Woronora Ht 489 B3

MALLAWA
rd. Duffys Frst 194 J1

MALLEE
cl. Narellan Vale 478 H16
ct. Holsworthy 426 D5
pl. Mcquarie Fd 454 E2
st. Cabramatta 365 J9
st. N St Marys 240 B12

st. Quakers Hill 243

MALLENY
st. Ashbury 372

MALLET
cl. Kingswood 267

MALLETT
la. Camperdwn 17
st. Annandale 17
st. Camperdwn 17

MALLEY
av. Earlwood 402

MALLORY
st. Dean Park 242

MALLOW
pl. Cabramatta W 365

MALO
rd. Whale Beach 140

MALONE
cr. Dean Park 242

MALONEY
la. Eastlakes 405
st. Blacktown 273
st. Mascot 405
st. Mascot 405
st. Rosebery 405

MALONGA
av. Kellyville 216

MALORY
av. West Pymble 252
cl. Wetherill Pk 334

MALOUF
pl. Blacktown 243
st. Canley Ht 365
st. Colyton 270
st. Guildford W 336

MALSBURY
rd. Hornsby 221
rd. Normanhurst 221

MALTA
pl. Rooty Hill 271
st. Fairfield E 337
st. Fairfield E 337
st. N Strathfield 341

MALTI
wy. Parklea 214

MALTON
grn. W Pnnant Hl 249
rd. Beecroft 250
rd. Cheltenham 251
rd. N Epping 251

MALUA
st. Dolls Point 463

MALUKA
pl. Kingsgrove 401

MALVERN
av. Baulkham Hl 247
av. Chatswood 284
av. Croydon 372
av. Manly 288
av. Merrylands 307
av. Roseville 285
av. Roseville Ch 285
cl. St Johns Pk 364
cr. Strathfield 341
rd. Glenwood 215
rd. Miranda 492
st. Panania 428

MALVINA
st. Ryde 312

MALVOLIO
st. Rsemeadow 540

MAMBLE
pl. S Penrith 267

MAME
pl. Kearns 451

MAMIE
av. Seven Hills 245

MAMMONE
cl. Edensor Pk 333

MAMRE
cr. Airds 512
la. St Clair, off Mamre Rd 269
rd. Kemps Ck 330
rd. Orchard Hills 269
rd. St Clair 269
rd. St Marys 269

MANAHAN
st. Condell Park 398

MANAM
pl. Glenfield 424

AR
Prestons 392 J16
ARA
Seven Hills 275 F5
CHESTER
Auburn 338 K1
Gymea 491 F4
Gymea 491 F6
Dulwich Hill 373 C7
Merrylands 307 G10
Currans Hill 479 G11
IDA
Rooty Hill 272 A6
DALONG
Glenmore Pk 266 F12
DARIN
Fairfield E 337 C15
Villawood 337 C15
Glenwood 215 F11
DEMAR
Homebush W 340 F7
DIBLE
Alexandria 375 F10
DINA
Bringelly 389 A5
DOLONG
Mosman 317 D6
Mosman 317 B6
Bonnyrigg Ht 363 A6
DOO
Doonside 243 E15
DOON
Girraween 275 J14
DUR
Caringbah 492 H12
EROO
Allambie Ht 257 F13
ETTE
Ambarvale 510 J11
EY
Rozelle 11 B1
GALOO
Berowra Ht 133 A8
GALORE
Winston Hills 277 B3
GARIVA
Emerton 240 G6
Lethbrdg Pk 240 G6
GIRI
Beecroft 250 C3
GROVE
Taren Point 463 A14
Brooklyn 75 E12
IFOLD
Blackett 241 C1
ILA
Lethbrdg Pk 240 G5
ILDRA
Carlingford 279 D2
Earlwood 402 F6
Prestons 393 E15
ILLA
Woronora 459 K16
Hoxton Park 392 H6
INS
Kingsgrove 401 K7
ION
Rose Bay 347 J12
LY
Fairlight, off
Birkley Rd 288 E8
Manly, off
Birkley Rd 288 E8
Kings Lngly 245 D5
Woodbine 481 H9
Balgowlah 287 C11
Clontarf 287 C11
Mulgoa 293 J11
Seaforth 287 C11
IN
St Helens Park 541 A6
Chatswood 285 E6
Glenbrook 233 K16
INA
Mt Riverview 204 E15
Bossley Park 333 G9
Kingswood 237 H16
Silverdale 353 K16
INA GUM
Narellan Vale 479 A14

MANNERIM
pl. Castle Cove 286 B6
MANNIKIN
dr. Woronora Ht 489 B4
pl. Mount Druitt 241 E12
MANNING
av. Strathfield S 371 D5
cl. McGraths Hl 121 K12
dr. Carlingford 280 E5
pde. Dundas Vy 279 K10
pl. Currans Hill 479 F12
pl. Seven Hills 275 F10
rd. Camperdwn 18 B2
rd. Double Bay 14 C11
rd. Gladesville 313 A12
rd. Hunters Hill 313 A12
rd. Killara 253 D16
rd. North Ryde 282 H11
rd. Woollahra 22 F1
st. Campbelltwn 511 K9
st. Kingswood 237 J16
st. N Balgowlah 287 B3
st. Oyster Bay 461 A7
st. Potts Point 4 K4
st. Prospect 274 F16
st. Queens Park 22 G13
st. Rozelle 344 C7
st. Warwck Frm 365 J16
MANNIX
ct. Harringtn Pk 478 D1
pde. Warwck Frm 365 G15
pl. Quakers Hill 214 B9
st. Bonnyrigg Ht 363 F8
st. Warwck Frm 365 G15
MANNOW
av. West Hoxton 392 B6
MANNS
av. Greenwich 314 K12
av. Neutral Bay 6 E9
pl. Greenwich, off
O'Connell St 314 K14
rd. Wilberforce 93 F5
MANOOKA
cr. Bradbury 511 C15
pl. Kareela 461 D14
pl. Warriewood 199 A7
rd. Currans Hill 480 A9
MANOR
gln. Wrrngtn Dns 238 D5
pl. Baulkham Hl 247 F7
rd. Hornsby 191 C13
rd. Ingleside 197 J5
st. Kellyville 215 D1
MANOR HILL
rd. Miranda 461 J14
MANORHOUSE
bvd. Quakers Hill 213 F9
MANSFIELD
av. Caringbah 492 K8
la. Glebe 11 J10
rd. Galston 159 J4
st. Girraween 276 B16
st. Glebe 11 J10
st. Rozelle 7 B15
st. Wetherill Pk 334 J5
MANSION
ct. Quakers Hill 213 G9
la. Potts Point 4 K7
rd. Bellevue Hill 347 F14
st. Marrickville 403 H1
MANSION POINT
rd. Grays Point 491 E16
MANSON
pl. Clovelly 377 G11
rd. Strathfield 341 G10
st. S Wntwthvle 307 C5
st. Telopea 279 G11
MANTAKA
st. Blacktown 275 A2
MANTALINI
st. Ambarvale 510 H14
MANTILLUS
gr. Baulkham Hl 246 H4
MANTON
av. Newington 310 D11
MANTURA
ct. Winston Hills 276 H1
MANUELA
pl. Curl Curl 258 E12
MANUKA
av. Baulkham Hl 247 D15
cir. Cherrybrook 219 G11
cr. Bass Hill 368 A10

st. Wentwthvle 277 C12
MANUS
pl. Glenfield 424 G9
MANWARING
av. Maroubra 407 D16
MAPITI
pl. Acacia Gdn 214 G16
MAPLE
av. Pennant Hills 220 F15
cl. Canada Bay 342 F9
cr. Ermington 280 D13
ct. Greenacre 370 B14
gr. Kellyville 215 B1
gr. Narellan 478 C10
la. N St Marys, off
Maple Rd 240 B11
pl. Belrose 225 J14
pl. Mcquarie Fd 424 E16
pl. Wentwthvle 277 A9
rd. Casula 423 J2
rd. N St Marys 239 J8
st. Bowen Mtn 83 K7
st. Cabramatta 365 G8
st. Caringbah 492 J15
st. Dural 188 H12
st. Greystanes 306 E4
st. Lugarno 429 H15
MAPLELEAF
dr. Padstow 429 G2
MAPLES
av. Killara 254 A11
MARA
cl. Bonnyrigg 363 J10
cr. Mooney Mooney 75 E1
MARAGA
pl. Doonside 243 F16
MARAKET
av. Blaxland 234 D9
MARALINGA
av. Elanora Ht 198 B16
pl. W Pnnant Hl 249 G6
MARAMBA
cl. Kingsgrove 401 F7
MARAMPO
st. Marayong 243 H5
MARANA
rd. Earlwood 402 C3
rd. Northbridge 315 K1
st. Blacktown 274 F5
MARANATHA
cl. W Pnnant Hl 248 G7
st. Rooty Hill 271 K6
MARANIE
av. St Marys 269 K5
MARANOA
pl. Wahroonga 223 C4
st. Auburn 338 J11
MARANTA
st. Hornsby 191 F11
MARANUI
av. Dee Why 258 F4
MARATHON
av. Darling Point 13 K7
av. Newington 310 B13
la. Darling Point 13 K7
mw. Double Bay 14 B7
rd. Darling Point 13 K6
MARAU
pl. Yellow Rock 204 G1
MARBLE
cl. Bossley Park 334 A8
MARCEAU
dr. Concord 342 D6
MARCEL
av. Coogee 377 F12
av. Randwick 377 F12
cr. Blacktown 274 K2
pl. Baulkham Hl 247 K7
MARCELLA
st. Bankstown 399 G4
st. Bankstown 399 G5
st. Kingsgrove 401 K5
st. N Epping 251 D9
MARCELLUS
pl. Rsemeadow 540 H6
MARCH
pl. Earlwood 403 B5
st. Bellevue Hill 347 F15
st. Richmond 118 F4
MARCHMONT
pl. Airds 512 B10

MARCIA
la. Hurlstone Pk, off
Duntroon St 373 A12
st. Hurlstone Pk 373 A12
st. Toongabbie 276 A6
MARCIANO
cl. Edensor Pk 363 G4
MARCO
av. Panania 397 J16
av. Revesby 398 D16
MARCOALA
pl. St Ives 224 D10
MARCONI
pl. Little Bay 437 B13
rd. Bossley Park 333 H10
rd. Bossley Park 333 H7
st. Winston Hills 277 C5
MARCUS
pl. Frenchs Frst 255 K3
st. Asquith 191 K7
st. Kings Park 244 E3
MARCUS CLARK
wy. Hornsby 191 E12
MARCUS CLARKE
cr. Glenmore Pk 265 J8
MARDEN
st. Artarmon 314 H1
st. Georges Hall 367 G12
MARDI
ct. Kellyville 217 D2
st. Girraween 276 A14
MARE
cl. Harringtn Pk 478 F1
MAREE
av. Cabramatta W 365 C4
pl. Blacktown 243 K9
pl. Condell Park 398 F1
MARELLA
av. Kellyville 216 H2
MARETIMO
st. Balgowlah 287 F10
MARGA
rd. Gymea Bay 491 H9
MARGARET
av. Hornsby Ht 191 E2
cr. Lugarno 429 K16
ct. Shalvey 210 K13
la. Newtown 17 D16
la. Stanmore 16 D5
la. Sydney A G13
pl. Lane Cove W 283 G13
pl. Paddington 4 K16
st. Abbotsford 343 C3
st. Ashfield 342 H16
st. Beacon Hill 257 E7
st. Belfield 371 E9
st. Dulwich Hill 373 E11
st. Fairfield 335 G14
st. Fairfield W 335 G14
st. Fairlight 288 D10
st. Granville 308 D10
st. Greenacre 370 G3
st. Kingsgrove 401 J12
st. Kogarah 433 D9
st. Mays Hill 307 G7
st. Minto 482 G2
st. Newtown 17 D16
st. Northmead 278 A4
st. N Sydney 6 A10
st. Petersham 16 B5
st. Picton 563 G3
st. Redfern 19 A9
st. Riverstone 183 G8
st. Roseville 285 B3
st. Rozelle 344 D6
st. Russell Lea 343 C3
st. Ryde 312 E5
st. St Marys 269 G5
st. Seven Hills 275 F4
st. Stanmore 16 B5
st. Strathfield 341 F13
st. Sydney A F14
st. Sydney 1 F15
st. Woolwich 314 D13
tce. Silverdale 354 B16
wy. Cecil Hills 362 H4
MARGARETA
cl. Guildford 337 D3
MARGATE
st. Botany 405 G14
st. Ramsgate 433 D12
st. Sans Souci 433 E14

MARGO
pl. Schofields 213 J5
MARGOT
pl. Castle Hill 217 H16
MARGUERETTE
st. Ermington 310 D3
MARGUERITE
av. Mt Riverview 234 D2
cr. W Pnnant Hl 220 A15
MARI
cl. Glenmore Pk 266 D9
MARIA
la. Newtown, off
Darley St 374 J10
pl. Blacktown 274 E5
pl. Oakdale 500 D12
st. Petersham 15 G13
st. Strathfield S 371 D7
MARIALA
ct. Holsworthy 426 D5
MARIA LOCK
gr. Oakhurst 242 D4
MARIAM
cl. Cherrybrook 219 B15
MARIAN
ct. Baulkham Hl 247 B1
la. Enmore 17 B14
st. Enmore 17 B14
st. Eveleigh 19 A8
st. Guildford 337 H4
st. Killara 254 A13
st. Redfern 19 A8
st. S Coogee 407 F3
MARIANA
cl. St Ives 224 D14
cr. Lethbrdg Pk 240 G3
MARIANI
cl. Bossley Park 333 G11
MARIE
av. Glenwood 245 F3
cl. Bligh Park 150 H6
cr. Mona Vale 198 J3
la. Belmore 371 E16
st. Belmore 401 D1
st. Castle Hill 247 J2
st. Lurnea 394 E10
st. Wentwthvle 277 A10
MARIEANNE
pl. Minchinbury 271 D7
MARIEBA
rd. Kenthurst 157 A6
MARIE DODD
cr. Blakehurst 462 D3
MARIE PITT
pl. Glenmore Pk 265 H5
MARIGOLD
av. Marayong 244 B7
cl. Glenmore Pk 265 G10
la. Glenmore Pk, off
Marigold Cl 265 F10
pl. Revesby 398 B11
st. Revesby 398 B11
MARIKO
pl. Blacktown 273 J7
MARILLIAN
av. Waitara 221 H5
MARILYN
st. North Ryde 282 G8
MARIN
pl. Glendenning 242 F5
pl. Merrylands 307 C11
pl. Prestons 393 A16
MARINA
cl. Bossley Park 333 K9
cl. Mt Krng-gai 162 K6
cr. Cecil Hills 362 K3
cr. Greenacre 369 H12
cr. Gymea Bay 491 E13
pl. Belrose 225 J15
rd. Baulkham Hl 246 J12
st. Kingsgrove 401 J12
MARINE
cr. Hornsby Ht 191 D8
dr. Oatley 430 G15
esp. Cronulla 494 C7
pde. Avalon 140 E16
pde. Double Bay 14 B6
pde. Homebush B 310 K9
pde. Manly 288 K10
pde. Maroubra 407 G12
pde. Watsons Bay 318 F15
rd. Avalon 140 F14

MARINEA
st. Arncliffe 403 F11
st. Arncliffe 403 G10
MARINELLA
st. Manly Vale 287 H5
MARINER
cr. Abbotsbury 333 C15
rd. Illawong 459 C3
MARINNA
rd. Elanora Ht 198 E14
MARION
cr. Lapstone 264 H5
st. Auburn 339 E5
st. Bankstown 369 A16
st. Bnkstn Aprt 367 H15
st. Blacktown 274 H2
st. Cecil Hills 362 G5
st. Condell Park 368 C16
st. Georges Hall 367 H15
st. Gymea 491 G3
st. Haberfield 373 E1
st. Harris Park 308 E6
st. Leichhardt 15 G1
st. Parramatta 308 D6
st. Seven Hills 245 D16
st. Strathfield 340 J14
st. Thirlmere 565 D3
MARIPOSA
rd. Bilgola 169 H6
MARIST
pl. Parramatta 278 C16
MARJORIE
cl. Casula 423 H2
cr. Maroubra 406 H7
st. Roseville 284 G1
st. Sefton 368 H1
MARJORIE JACKSON
pky. Homebush B 310 H13
MARJORY
pl. Baulkham Hl 248 A10
MARJORY THOMAS
pl. Balgowlah 288 A7
MARK
la. Roselands 401 C7
la. Sydney C D5
pl. Bilgola 169 F4
pl. Cherrybrook 219 F8
pl. Penrith 236 E3
rd. Nelson 154 H9
rd. Rossmore 419 K4
st. Canley Ht 365 A2
st. Dundas Vy 280 D10
st. Hunters Hill 313 B9
st. Lidcombe 339 J9
st. Merrylands 306 K10
st. Mount Druitt 271 C3
st. St Marys 270 A5
MARKELL
pl. Liverpool 394 J5
MARKET
la. Manly 288 G10
la. Merrylands, off Baker St 307 J16
row. Sydney C G10
st. Appin 569 G10
st. Clarmnt Ms 269 B1
st. Condell Park 398 K4
st. Drummoyne 343 H6
st. Moorebank 395 G9
st. Naremburn 315 G2
st. Parramatta 308 C1
st. Randwick 377 C10
st. Randwick 377 D9
st. Riverstone 182 J7
st. Rockdale 403 D15
st. Smithfield 335 G5
st. Sydney C D8
st. Sydney 3 E4
st. Tahmoor 565 G12
st. West Ryde 281 D15
st.e. Naremburn 315 H2
MARKETOWN
la. Riverstone, off Garfield Rd E 182 J8
MARKET PLACE
st. Horngsea Pk 392 E11
MARKEY
st. Guildford 338 D5
MARKHAM
av. Ashfield 372 H2
av. Penrith 237 D11
cl. Mosman 317 E10
ct. Acacia Gdn 214 H16
pl. Ashfield 372 H2
st. Holsworthy 426 C4
MARKOVINA
st. Edensor Pk 333 F16
MARKS
av. Seven Hills 245 H14
la. Bass Hill 368 A5
la. Chester Hill 368 A5
la. Tamarama 378 D6
st. Bass Hill 368 A5
st. Chester Hill 368 A5
st. Chester Hill 368 B5
st. Naremburn 315 H3
MARKWELL
pl. Agnes Banks 117 E11
MARL
pl. Eagle Vale 481 F7
MARLBOROUGH
av. Harbord 258 C15
la. Glebe 12 B11
pl. St Ives 223 J7
rd. Homebush W 340 G8
rd. Willoughby 285 G15
st. Drummoyne 343 H1
st. Fairfield Ht 336 B9
st. Glebe 12 B12
st. Leichhardt 9 G16
st. Smithfield 336 B9
st. Surry Hills 20 A5
MARLE
av. The Oaks 502 F9
MARLEE
rd. Engadine 489 E9
st. Hornsby 191 H8
st. N Balgowlah 287 G5
MARLENE
cr. Greenacre 370 F1
pl. Belmore 401 F6
st. Freemns Rch 90 A3
MARLEY
cr. Bonnyrigg Ht 363 B3
st. Ambarvale 511 A14
MARLIS
av. Revesby 398 E11
MARLO
rd. Cronulla 494 A9
MARLOCK
pl. Alfords Point 429 C13
pl. Mcquarie Fd 454 D4
st. Kingswood 267 H1
MARLOO
pl. St Helens Park 541 H3
MARLOW
av. Denistone 281 F13
la. Denistone 281 F12
pl. Campbelltwn 511 H9
rd. Artarmon 285 C13
MARLOWE
st. Campsie 372 A15
st. Wetherill Pk 334 K4
MARMADUKE
st. Burwood 342 A14
MARMION
la. Abbotsford 312 K16
la. Camperdwn 17 B8
rd. Abbotsford 312 K16
st. Birrong 369 B5
st. Camperdwn 17 B8
wy. Kellyville 185 J14
MARMORA
st. Harbord 258 G16
MARNE
la. St Clair, off Marne Pl 269 G16
pl. St Clair 269 G15
st. Vaucluse 348 G5
MARNIE
gr. Kings Lngly 245 K8
MARNOO
pl. Belrose 226 C15
MARNPAR
rd. Seven Hills 246 A13
MAROA
cr. Allambie Ht 287 G1
MARONG
st. Panania 398 D16
MARONI
pl. St Clair 269 F14
MAROOBA
pl. Engadine 488 G11
rd. Northbridge 285 K15
MAROOK
st. Carlingford 280 E6
MAROOPNA
rd. Yowie Bay 492 A10
MAROUBRA
cr. Woodbine 481 F13
la. Maroubra 407 B10
rd. Maroubra 406 H9
rd. Maroubra 407 G10
MARPLE
av. Villawood 367 F1
MARQUESA
cr. Lethbrdg Pk 240 F3
MARQUET
st. Rhodes 311 C9
MARRA
pl. Sylvania 462 E8
MARRAKESH
pl. Arcadia 129 B12
MARRETT
wy. Cranebrook 207 F9
MARRICKVILLE
av. Marrickville 373 G12
la. Marrickville 374 A13
rd. Dulwich Hill 373 F10
rd. Marrickville 373 F10
MARRIOTT
gr. Castle Hill 217 D10
rd. Bonnyrigg 363 F9
rd. Bonnyrigg Ht 363 F9
st. Redfern 19 K11
st. Redfern 20 A7
MARRON
pl. Beecroft 250 A12
MARROO
st. Bronte 377 J11
MARS
la. Gladesville 313 A3
pl. Lansvale 366 H8
rd. Lane Cove W 283 E16
st. Epping 280 D2
st. Gladesville 312 K10
st. Padstow 429 B3
st. Revesby 428 J3
MARSALA
st. Mosman 287 A15
MARSANNE
pl. Eschol Park 481 C2
MARSCAY
st. Stanhpe Gdn 215 A5
MARSDEN
av. Elderslie 507 H1
av. Kellyville 215 G4
cl. Bossley Park 334 D11
cr. Bligh Park 150 E5
cr. Peakhurst 430 E1
la. Riverstone 182 C9
rd. Barden Rdg 458 G16
rd. Carlingford 280 B4
rd. Dundas Vy 280 B4
rd. Liverpool 395 A1
rd. Riverstone 182 E9
rd. St Marys 270 A7
rd. West Ryde 280 F11
st. Camperdwn 17 F3
st. Granville 308 B7
st. Lidcombe 339 J9
st. Parramatta 308 B5
st. Ruse 512 G2
MARSH
av. Woolooware 493 J8
pde. Casula 394 K14
pl. Cranebrook 207 D10
pl. Lane Cove 314 G3
pl. The Oaks 502 F14
rd. Silverdale 353 F15
st. Arncliffe 403 J8
st. Condell Park 398 F2
st. Granville 308 H11
st. Wakeley 364 K1
MARSHALL
av. Bargo 567 F10
av. Moorebank 396 E12
av. Newington 310 A16
av. St Leonards 315 C6
av. Warrawee 222 D13
cl. Hornsby Ht 161 J10
cr. Beacon Hill 257 H9
la. Panania 398 B16
la. Petersham 16 C13
la. St Leonards, off Berry Rd 315 C6
rd. Dundas Vy 279 H9
rd. Kirrawee 461 C16
rd. Mt Riverview 234 B4
rd. Telopea 279 H9
st. Balmain 7 K8
st. Bankstown 399 E6
st. Bnkstn Aprt 368 B16
st. Kogarah 433 D7
st. Manly 288 H13
st. Paddington 4 F14
st. Petersham 16 B13
st. Surry Hills 20 D2
MARTEN
cl. Prestons 392 J16
MARTENS
cct. Kellyville 215 G3
la. Mosman, off Raglan St 317 C9
la. Cremorne, off Waters La 316 D8
la. Neutral Bay, off Waters La 316 D8
pl. Abbotsbury 333 B11
wy. Claymore 481 B10
MARTHA
av. Northmead 277 K6
cr. Cranebrook 207 D11
la. Cranebrook, off Martha Cr 207 D10
st. Granville 308 K11
st. Hunters Hill 313 K11
st. Yagoona 369 A10
wy. Ambarvale 510 K15
MARTI
pl. Hebersham 241 E10
MARTIN
av. Arncliffe 403 G6
av. Pagewood 406 C8
bvd. Plumpton 241 K11
cr. Milperra 397 C10
cr. Woodpark 306 H14
gr. Colyton 270 G9
la. Roseville 284 H3
pl. Dural 188 G12
pl. Dural 188 H13
pl. Mortdale 431 A8
pl. Mt Annan 479 H14
pl. Sydney C K2
pl. Sydney 3 G1
rd. Badgerys Ck 329 D16
rd. Centnnial Pk 21 A14
rd. Galston 159 H9
rd. Moore Park 20 J14
rd. Oakville 124 E6
st. Blakehurst 432 A14
st. Emu Plains 235 C10
st. Haberfield 343 B12
st. Harbord 288 D1
st. Heathcote 518 F11
st. Hunters Hill 313 E9
st. Lidcombe 340 A8
st. Mulgoa 265 D4
st. Paddington 21 B3
st. Regentville 265 D4
st. Roselands 400 F9
st. Ryde 282 D14
st. St Leonards 315 F4
MARTINA
st. Plumpton 241 J11
MARTINDALE
av. Baulkham Hl 247 F5
ct. Wattle Grove 395 K16
MARTINE
av. Camden S 507 B11
MARTIN LUTHER
la. Allambie Ht 257 A10
pl. Allambie Ht 257 B10
MARTINO
cl. Prestons 422 H1
MARTINS
av. Bondi 377 J2
la. Carlingford 279 G6
la. Freemns Rch 90 J2
MARTLEY
la. Cranebrook, off Martley Wy 207 F14
wy. Cranebrook 207 F14
MARTON
cr. Kings Lngly 245 G8
MARULAN
wy. Prestons 392 H15
MARUM
st. Ashcroft 364 F14
MARVELL
rd. Wetherill Pk 334 E6
MARVILLE
av. Kingsford 406 H6
MARWOOD
dr. Beecroft 250
MARX
av. Beverley Pk 433
pl. Quakers Hill 243
MARY
av. Cranebrook 206
cr. Liverpool 394
la. Bundeena 523
la. Surry Hills F
pde. Rydalmere 309
pl. Bligh Park 150
pl. Paddington 4
pl. Surry Hills 4
st. Auburn 339
st. Beacon Hill 257
st. Beecroft 250
st. Blacktown 244
st. Bundeena 524
st. Burwood 342
st. Drummoyne 343
st. Ermington 310
st. Glebe 11
st. Granville 308
st. Hunters Hill 313
st. Jannali 460
st. Lidcombe 339
st. Lilyfield 9
st. Lilyfield 9
st. Longueville 314
st. Mcquarie Fd 424
st. Merrylands 337
st. Newtown 17
st. Northmead 278
st. N Parramatta 278
st. Regents Pk 368
st. Rhodes 311
st. Riverwood 399
st. Rooty Hill 241
st. Rozelle 10
st. St Peters 374
st. Schofields 182
st. Surry Hills F
st. Surry Hills 3
st. The Oaks 502
st. Turrella 403
st. Wetherill Pk 334
st. Wiley Park 400
MARY ANN
st. Ultimo 12
MARY ANNE
cl. Mt Annan 509
MARY BROWN
pl. Blair Athol 511
MARYFIELDS
dr. Blair Athol 510
MARY GILMORE
pl. Heathcote 518
MARY-HELEN
ct. Baulkham Hl 247
MARY HOWE
pl. Narellan Vale 508
MARY IRENE
pl. Castle Hill 248
MARYL
av. Roselands 401
MARY MARGARET
la. Mosman 317
MARY ROSE
st. Green Valley 362
MARYVALE
av. Liverpool 394
MARY WALL
cr. Berowra 133
MARY WOLLSTONECRAFT
la. Milsons Point 5
MASCOT
dr. Eastlakes 405
MASEFIELD
pl. Woolooware 493
MASER
st. Cranebrook 207
MASERATI
dr. Ingleburn 453
MASHMAN
av. Kingsgrove 401
av. Wentwthvle 306
MASIKU
pl. Glendenning 242
MASLIN
cr. Quakers Hill 214

ON
;heltenham ... 250 H9
lobartville ... 118 D6
3ondi, off
lackaman St ... 377 K6
3arden Rdg ... 488 F7
3onnyrigg ... 364 D6
3ox Hill ... 154 C13
;amperdwn ... 17 E2
)enistone E ... 281 G10
Aaroubra ... 406 H8
Aerrylands ... 307 D13
Aount Druitt ... 240 H16
'arramatta ... 278 H16
hirlmere ... 564 J4
hirlmere ... 565 A4
ONS
I Parramatta ... 278 H8
I Parramatta ... 278 H7
SA
Clarmnt Ms, off
Massa Pl ... 268 J3
Clarmnt Ms ... 268 J3
SEY
Gladesville ... 312 J9
St Ives Ch ... 223 K6
Cammeray ... 315 H4
Carlton ... 432 G11
Gladesville ... 312 J9
Glenmore Pk ... 265 H5
SIE
Ermington ... 310 F3
TERFIELD
Rossmore ... 389 C16
TERS
Girraween ... 276 B14
Penrith ... 236 J10
AHIL
Harringtn Pk ... 478 H7
ARO
Edensor Pk ... 333 C16
Eschol Park ... 481 E3
HERS
Menai ... 458 G15
HESON
Chatswood ... 285 C11
Mt Pritchard ... 364 F11
N Richmond ... 87 D15
Hassall Gr ... 211 J15
HEW
Belmore ... 371 A12
West Hoxton ... 392 D10
HEWS
Menai ... 458 F12
Davidson ... 225 A15
HEWSON
Eastgardens ... 406 G13
HIESON
Annandale ... 17 B3
HINNA
West Hoxton ... 392 D6
HIS
Ingleburn ... 453 J6
IKA
Lethbrdg Pk ... 210 G15
ILDA
Kellyville ... 185 K15
Rozelle ... 10 G1
Glenwood ... 245 K5
INGARA
Wallacia ... 354 K2
LOCK
Glenwood ... 215 B16
ONG
Gymea Bay ... 491 G10
Gordon ... 254 A7
ORA
Cremorne ... 316 D5
RA
Raby ... 451 H13
RUM
Holsworthy ... 426 E6
SON
Miranda ... 492 C7
TERSON
Redfern ... 20 B7
THES
Yennora ... 337 B11
THEW
Heckenberg ... 363 K13
Galston ... 160 J10
Mt Annan ... 509 D1

cl. St Ives ... 224 F10
cr. Blacktown ... 274 D4
la. Crows Nest, off Atchison St ... 315 H5
pde. Blaxland ... 233 J9
pl. Bella Vista ... 246 F2
pl. Richmond ... 119 C3
rd. Lidcombe ... 339 F10
st. Beverley Pk ... 433 A12
st. Crows Nest ... 315 G5
st. Hunters Hill ... 313 D10
st. Merrylands ... 307 C15
wy. W Pnnant Hl ... 219 A16
MATTHEW FLINDERS
pl. Burraneer ... 523 D3
MATTHEWS
av. East Hills ... 427 K4
av. Lane Cove ... 313 K2
la. Picton ... 563 H10
sq. Ingleburn ... 453 E8
st. Carramar ... 336 J16
st. Emu Heights ... 235 A5
st. Greenacre ... 370 G11
st. Punchbowl ... 400 D4
MATTS
av. Panania ... 398 C14
la. Revesby ... 398 H15
MAUBEUGE
st. S Granville ... 338 G6
MAUD
cl. Cecil Hills ... 362 G7
la. Marrickville ... 374 B14
st. Blacktown ... 274 H8
st. Fairfield Ht ... 335 G12
st. Fairfield W ... 335 G14
st. Granville ... 308 E12
st. Lidcombe ... 339 K6
st. Randwick ... 376 K16
MAUDE
st. Regents Pk ... 369 B3
MAUGHAM
cr. Wetherill Pk ... 334 G3
MAUGHAN
st. Lalor Park ... 245 E13
MAUNDER
av. Girraween ... 276 B14
av. St Ives ... 224 C8
pl. Warragamba ... 353 E8
st. Regents Pk ... 369 D2
MAUREEN
pl. Blacktown ... 274 B3
MAURICE
la. St Clair, off Maurice St ... 270 A9
st. Marsden Pk ... 182 B14
st. St Clair ... 270 A9
MAURIE FIELDS
st. Moore Park ... 21 C7
MAURITIUS
av. Georges Hall ... 368 C15
MAVICK
cr. Leumeah ... 511 K1
MAVIS
av. Peakhurst ... 430 H4
st. Greystanes ... 305 G7
st. North Ryde ... 282 D9
st. Revesby ... 398 J9
st. Rooty Hill ... 272 D1
MAVOR
cr. Frenchs Frst ... 256 C8
MAWARRA
av. Miranda ... 491 J5
cl. Forestville ... 255 G8
cr. Kellyville ... 216 E3
cr. Marsfield ... 251 H15
MAWBANNA
pl. West Hoxton ... 392 E5
MAWSON
av. Beecroft ... 250 D10
cr. Ermington ... 310 C1
ct. Wrrngtn Cty ... 238 F8
dr. Cartwright ... 393 J5
la. Chifley, off Mawson Pde ... 437 B7
pde. Chifley ... 437 B7
pl. Pitt Town ... 92 J15
rd. Tregear ... 240 C5
st. Bardwell Vy ... 403 C7
st. Leumeah ... 482 J10
st. Punchbowl ... 399 J4
st. St Ives ... 224 C7
MAX
st. Kurrajong Ht ... 54 A7

MAX ALLEN
dr. Lindfield ... 283 G8
MAXIM
la. West Ryde, off Maxim St ... 281 D16
pl. St Marys ... 239 G10
st. West Ryde ... 281 D16
MAXINE
rd. Greystanes ... 306 G9
MAXWELL
av. Maroubra ... 407 G11
av. Milperra ... 397 E14
cl. Illawong ... 459 D1
la. Glebe ... 11 G10
la. Pagewood, off Maxwell Rd ... 406 G9
pde. Frenchs Frst ... 256 C9
pl. Blaxland ... 233 F6
pl. Narellan ... 478 J8
pl. W Pnnant Hl ... 249 C9
rd. Glebe ... 11 F9
rd. Pagewood ... 406 G9
st. Blacktown ... 274 D3
st. Mcquarie Fd ... 424 A14
st. Mona Vale ... 198 J3
st. S Penrith ... 266 F2
st. S Turramrra ... 252 C8
MAXWELLS
av. Ashcroft ... 364 F16
av. Sadleir ... 394 B3
MAXWELTON
pl. Narraweena ... 258 C5
MAY
av. Rossmore ... 389 C12
la. Eastwood ... 281 C7
la. Neutral Bay ... 6 G1
la. St Peters ... 374 J11
la. Dulwich Hill, off Union St ... 373 C10
pl. Illawong ... 459 H6
pl. St Andrews ... 482 A3
rd. Dee Why ... 258 D7
rd. Narraweena ... 258 D7
st. Bardwell Pk ... 403 A7
st. Dulwich Hill ... 373 B10
st. Eastwood ... 281 B7
st. Fairfield ... 336 J14
st. Glenbrook ... 234 D16
st. Hornsby ... 191 J16
st. Lilyfield ... 10 C5
st. Merrylands ... 308 D15
st. St Peters ... 374 H12
st. Turramurra ... 252 D2
st. Wentwthvle ... 277 A10
wk. Lalor Park ... 245 H11
MAYA
cl. Bossley Park ... 333 K12
MAYBANKE
ct. Mona Vale ... 169 D15
MAYBERRY
cr. Liverpool ... 395 A2
MAYBROOK
av. Cromer ... 227 G13
MAYBUSH
ct. Schofields ... 213 H5
pl. Cherrybrook ... 219 J14
wy. Castle Hill ... 248 F1
MAYCOCK
st. Denistone E ... 281 H10
MAYDA
pl. Kellyville ... 186 A15
MAYES
st. Annandale ... 16 G1
MAYFAIR
av. Kellyville ... 185 E8
cr. Beverly Hills ... 401 A13
pl. E Lindfield ... 255 D12
rd. Mulgoa ... 295 A7
st. Auburn ... 338 K14
MAYFARM
rd. Brownlow Hl ... 505 D3
rd. Mt Hunter ... 505 E4
MAYFIELD
av. Pymble ... 253 A2
av. Woolwich ... 314 F13
st. Wentwthvle ... 277 C13
MAYGAR
cl. Milperra ... 397 D13
MAY GIBBS
pl. Frenchs Frst ... 256 G3
wy. Frenchs Frst ... 256 H3
MAYLIE
cl. Ambarvale ... 510 H13

MAYMAN
row. Menai ... 458 J12
MAYNE
la. Abbotsford ... 342 J3
st. Wilberforce ... 91 K3
MAYO
pl. Killarney Ht ... 256 D16
rd. Llandilo ... 179 B16
st. Little Bay ... 437 G15
MAYOR
st. Kogarah Bay ... 432 H13
MAYTONE
av. Killara ... 254 C8
MAYVIC
st. Greenacre ... 370 G7
MAZARI
gr. Stanhpe Gdn ... 215 A10
MAZARIN
st. Riverwood ... 400 D14
MAZE
av. Ryde ... 312 C2
cr. Darlington ... 18 E5
la. Chippendale ... 18 H3
MAZEPA
av. S Penrith ... 267 D1
pl. Lidcombe ... 340 B7
MEACHER
st. Mount Druitt ... 241 D12
MEAD
dr. Chipping Ntn ... 366 J14
pl. Chipping Ntn ... 366 K14
st. Banksia ... 403 F13
MEADE
st. Allawah ... 432 E9
MEADOW
cl. Beecroft ... 250 F10
cr. Meadowbnk ... 311 D4
la. Wollstncraft, off Rocklands Rd ... 315 E10
pl. Kellyville ... 216 E1
pl. Miranda ... 461 J15
rd. Schofields ... 212 G8
st. Concord ... 341 J7
MEADOWBANK
la. West Ryde ... 311 A1
MEADOWLAND
rd. Peakhurst ... 400 F16
MEADOWLANDS
Blacktown ... 274 D12
MEADOWS
rd. Cabramatta W ... 364 F8
rd. Mt Pritchard ... 364 D12
rd. N Richmond ... 58 E15
st. Merrylands ... 308 B15
wy. Minto ... 482 J4
MEADOWVIEW
wy. Wrrngtn Dns ... 237 J5
MEADWAY
cl. Pymble ... 253 J4
MEAGER
av. Padstow ... 399 G16
MEAGHER
av. Maroubra ... 407 E14
st. Chippendale ... 19 B3
MEAKEM
st. Hurstville ... 431 J5
MEAKIN
cr. Chester Hill ... 338 D16
st. Merrylands ... 307 F15
MEALIA
la. Edgecliff ... 13 F11
MEANDER
cl. West Hoxton ... 392 D6
MEARES
rd. McGraths Hl ... 121 K13
MEARS
av. Randwick ... 377 B15
MEATH
pl. Blacktown ... 243 J15
pl. Killarney Ht ... 256 E16
MEATWORKS
av. Oxford Falls ... 227 B14
MECHANIC
st. Newtown ... 17 H10
MECKIFF
av. North Rocks ... 278 J3
cl. Menai ... 458 E9
MEDCALFE
pl. Edensor Pk ... 363 E3
MEDEA
pl. Dean Park ... 212 F15

MEDHURST
rd. Gilead ... 539 F10
MEDIATI
av. Kellyville ... 216 G7
MEDICH
pl. Bringelly ... 388 E10
MEDICI
pl. Glenwood ... 246 A4
MEDIKA
pl. Kirrawee ... 461 D15
MEDLEY
av. Liverpool ... 365 A14
MEDLOW
dr. Quakers Hill ... 243 H1
MEDORA
la. Cabarita ... 312 E15
st. Cabarita ... 312 D16
MEDUSA
st. Mosman ... 287 A16
MEDWAY
rd. Bringelly ... 387 K11
rd. Bringelly ... 388 A12
st. Bexley ... 402 H14
MEDWIN
pl. Quakers Hill ... 214 C11
MEEGAN
pl. Colyton ... 270 F8
MEEHAM
st. West Hoxton ... 392 A12
MEEHAN
av. Hamondvle ... 396 D13
av. Wrrngtn Cty ... 238 J5
la. Georges Hall ... 367 H9
la. Matraville ... 437 D3
la. Wrrngtn Cty, off Meehan Av ... 238 H5
pl. Baulkham Hl ... 247 F3
pl. Campbelltwn ... 511 E8
pl. Harringtn Pk ... 478 E5
pl. Kirrawee ... 490 H7
rd. Cromer ... 228 C15
st. Granville ... 308 A8
st. Matraville ... 437 C1
tce. Harringtn Pk ... 478 F5
MEEKATHARRA
pl. Yarrawarrah ... 489 H12
MEEKS
cr. Faulconbdg ... 171 A15
la. Kingsford ... 406 G1
la. Marrickville, off Meeks Rd ... 374 A14
la. Marrickville, off Meeks Rd ... 374 B13
rd. Marrickville ... 374 A14
st. Kingsford ... 406 G1
MEELA
st. Blacktown ... 273 K3
MEGALONG
av. N Willghby ... 285 H8
cr. Campbelltwn ... 512 A7
MEGAN
av. Bankstown ... 399 F4
av. Smithfield ... 335 F2
rd. Galston ... 160 F10
st. Telopea ... 279 D6
MEIG
pl. Marayong ... 244 D9
MEITNER
pl. Lucas Ht ... 487 J12
MEKEO
pl. Glenfield ... 424 G13
MEKONG
pl. Kearns ... 481 B1
MELALEUCA
av. Villawood ... 337 B16
cl. Castle Hill ... 248 G4
cr. Carlingford ... 280 E8
dr. Mcquarie Fd ... 454 F3
dr. St Ives ... 224 D15
gr. Greenacre ... 370 F6
la. Mosman, off Mandolong Rd ... 317 B6
la. Kingswood, off Melaleuca Pl ... 267 F2
pl. Alfords Point ... 429 B15
pl. Kingswood ... 267 G2
pl. Prestons ... 393 J16
rd. Narellan Vale ... 478 H14
st. Newport ... 169 K13
MELALUCA
st. Stanhpe Gdn ... 215 D10

MELANESIA
av. Lethbrdg Pk...240 G3
MELANIE
pl. Bella Vista...246 F6
st. Bankstown...369 C13
st. Hassall Gr...211 K15
st. Yagoona...369 C13
MELBA
av. Chifley...437 B7
dr. East Ryde...282 K15
pl. Casula...424 G1
pl. St Helens Park...541 D3
rd. Lalor Park...245 C10
MELBOURNE
av. Mona Vale...199 D9
rd. E Lindfield...254 K13
rd. Riverstone...182 G1
rd. St Johns Pk...364 D3
rd. Winston Hills...247 J16
st. Concord...341 J9
st. Fairlight...288 B8
st. Oxley Park...270 G1
MELDON
pl. Stanhpe Gdn...215 G9
MELDRUM
av. Miranda...492 C1
av. Mt Pritchard...364 J11
st. Ryde...282 G15
wy. Claymore...481 D12
MELFORD
st. Hurlstone Pk...372 J13
MELHAM
av. Panania...398 D14
MELIA
ct. Castle Hill...218 J14
pl. Mcquarie Fd...424 F16
MELINDA
cl. Kellyville...185 J15
MELINGA
pl. Revesby...428 G4
MELINZ
pl. Quakers Hill...214 F12
MELISSA
pl. Cherrybrook...219 F7
pl. Kings Park...244 G6
pl. W Pnnant Hl...248 K7
st. Auburn...338 G14
MELITA
rd. Cmbrdg Pk...237 H8
MELKARTH
pl. Doonside...243 E16
MELKIN
end, Gordon...253 J6
MELLA
pl. West Hoxton...392 C5
MELLFELL
rd. Cranebrook...207 F10
MELLICK
st. Fairfield W...335 F13
MELLIODORA
wy. Mcquarie Fd...454 F3
MELLOR
pl. Bonnyrigg Ht...363 A7
pl. Hebersham...241 F9
st. West Ryde...311 F1
MELNOTTE
av. Roseville...284 J5
MELODY
la. Collaroy...229 A15
la. Coogee...377 E15
st. Coogee...377 E16
st. Toongabbie...276 B5
MELROSE
av. Lakemba...400 K3
av. Quakers Hill...243 G2
av. Sylvania...461 K9
av. Wiley Park...400 K3
la. Woollahra...21 F4
pde. Clovelly...377 K13
pl. Bossley Park...333 E12
rd. Abbotsford...343 A2
rd. Chiswick...343 A2
st. Brooklyn...75 F11
st. Chester Hill...338 C16
st. Croydon Pk...372 A7
st. Epping...280 J2
st. Homebush...341 D11
st. Lane Cove W...284 A12
st. Mosman...316 J6
MELTON
rd. Glenorie...127 H9
st.n, Silverwater...309 G14
st.s, Auburn...309 G15
MELUCA
cr. Hornsby Ht...191 D1
MELVILLE
av. Cabramatta...366 A6
av. Strathfield...340 H15
cl. Berowra...133 C16
cl. Hinchinbrk...393 A1
la. Newtown...17 E12
pl. Barden Rdg...488 F2
rd. Rooty Hill...272 A4
rd. St Clair...269 J12
st. Ashbury...372 F8
st. Parramatta...308 H1
st. Ryde...281 J15
st. West Ryde...281 H15
MELVIN
st.n, Beverly Hills...401 A14
st.s, Beverly Hills...401 B15
MELWOOD
av. Forestville...255 J12
av. Killarney Ht...255 K14
MEMA
pl. Quakers Hill...243 H3
MEMBREY
st. Granville...308 F16
MEMMANG
pl. Kirrawee...461 D15
MEMORIAL
av. Ingleburn...453 B4
av. Kellyville...216 E8
av. Liverpool...395 A4
av. Merrylands...307 H14
av. Penrith...236 D8
av. Rookwood...340 C15
av. St Ives...224 A11
dr. Granville...308 G12
dr. Padstow...399 E15
dr. Richmond...120 A6
MEMPHIS
cr. Toongabbie...275 H11
st. Minto...452 G13
st. Minto...452 J13
st. Mount Druitt...241 A16
MEMTEC
pky. S Windsor...121 A15
MENA
av. Lansvale...367 A8
st. Belfield...371 C11
st. N Strathfield...341 C4
wy. Bidwill...211 F13
MENAI
rd. Bangor...459 A13
rd. Bangor...459 H13
rd. Menai...458 H12
rd. Woronora...459 K14
MENANGLE
rd. Camden...507 A3
rd. Campbelltwn...511 A6
rd. Douglas Park...568 C2
rd. Gilead...509 K16
rd. Glen Alpine...510 C10
rd. Menangle...538 H16
rd. Menangle Pk...538 J11
st. Picton...563 G4
st.w, Picton...563 F3
MENDANA
st. Lethbrdg Pk...240 F4
MENDELEEF
av. Lucas Ht...487 F12
MENDELSSOHN
av. Emerton...240 H5
MENDI
pl. Glenfield...424 B13
pl. Whalan...240 H12
MENDOS
pl. Engadine...489 F7
MENIN
pl. Milperra...397 G12
rd. Matraville...407 A16
rd. Oakville...153 B7
MENINDEE
av. Leumeah...482 F13
wy. Woodcroft...243 H10
MENSA
pl. Castle Hill...218 K9
pl. Jamisontown...266 D6
MENTHA
pl. Mcquarie Fd...454 B4
MENTMORE
av. Rosebery...375 G16
MENTONE
av. Cronulla...494 A13
MENUS
pl. Rsemeadow...540 H2
MENZIES
arc. Sydney...1 F16
cct. St Clair...270 A12
la. Marsfield...281 G2
la. St Clair, off Menzies Cct...270 A13
pl. Edensor Pk...333 H13
rd. Marsfield...281 G1
MEPUNGA
st. Concord W...341 F2
MERA
st. Guildford...337 C4
MERAUKE
st. Whalan...240 J11
MERCATOR
cr. Willmot...210 E14
MERCEDES
pl. Kareela...461 D11
rd. Ingleburn...453 H13
MERCER
cr. Beverly Hills...400 K16
st. Castle Hill...218 D15
st. Castle Hill...218 E15
MERCHANT
st. Mascot...405 E7
st. Stanmore...16 G12
MERCURY
pl. Kings Lngly...246 B8
st. Beverly Hills...400 J14
st. Narwee...400 J14
MERCUTIO
pl. Gilead...540 F7
MERCY
av. Chester Hill...337 K12
MERDLE
pl. Ambarvale...540 F1
MEREDITH
av. Hornsby Ht...191 D8
av. Kellyville...216 G5
cl. Fairfield...336 E6
cr. St Helens Park...541 B8
pl. Frenchs Frst...256 F7
rch. Westleigh...220 H7
st. Bankstown...369 D15
st. Blaxland...233 E9
st. Epping...280 F4
st. Homebush...341 B11
st. Strathfield...341 B11
wy. Cecil Hills...362 E1
MEREIL
st. Campbelltwn...511 K3
MERELYN
rd. Belrose...226 B16
MERELYNNE
av. W Pnnant Hl...248 K8
MEREVALE
pl. Oakhurst...241 J4
MERIDIAN
pl. Bella Vista...216 A15
pl. Doonside...243 H16
st. Eastlakes...405 J6
MERIEL
st. Sans Souci...463 A5
MERINDA
av. Baulkham Hl...248 B8
av. Epping...250 F11
pl. Bonnyrigg...364 B8
st. Lane Cove W...283 J14
st. St Marys...239 F14
MERINDAH
rd. Baulkham Hl...247 A7
wy. Kurrajong...55 J10
MERINO
cct. St Clair...270 D12
cr. Airds...511 H15
dr. Elderslie...507 H1
pl. Sylvania...462 B13
st. Miller...393 G2
MERION
ct. Glenmore Pk...266 G9
MERITON
st. Gladesville...312 G12
MERLE
st. Bass Hill...368 D7
st. N Epping...251 C8
st. Sefton...338 F13
MERLEN
cr. Yagoona...369 B9
MERLEY
rd. Strathfield...341 A13
MERLIN
cl. Mt Colah...162 D8
ct. Castle Hill...217 H4
pl. Emu Heights...235 C3
st. Blacktown...274 G8
st. Neutral Bay...6 B1
st. Neutral Bay...316 A8
st. Roseville...284 K1
st. The Oaks...502 F13
st. The Oaks...502 G10
MERLOT
pl. Edensor Pk...333 C16
MERMAID
av. Maroubra...407 H8
MERNAGH
st. Ashcroft...364 E15
MEROO
cl. Wakeley...334 J13
st. Auburn...338 J11
st. Blacktown...244 D16
MERRANG
ct. Wattle Grove...425 J6
MERREDIN
cl. Yarrawarrah...489 F13
MERRENBURN
av. Naremburn...315 G3
MERRETT
cr. Greenacre...370 C9
MERRI
av. Peakhurst...430 D9
pl. St Johns Pk...364 F2
MERRIC
ct. Oakhurst...242 A4
MERRICK
av. Lakemba...371 A14
pl. N Richmond...87 A12
wy. Glenhaven...217 K6
MERRIDONG
rd. Elanora Ht...198 F13
MERRILEE
cr. Frenchs Frst...255 K3
MERRILONG
av. Mt Krng-gai...163 B10
st. Castle Hill...247 G3
MERRIMAN
cl. Elderslie...507 H2
pl. Airds...512 B11
st. Kyle Bay...432 A15
st. Millers Pt...A A1
st. Millers Pt...1 C9
MERRIN
cl. St Helens Park...541 E2
MERRINA
st. Hebersham...241 E9
MERRINDAL
cl. Cranebrook...207 E7
MERRINGTON
pl. Woolwich...314 F14
MERRIS
pl. Milperra...397 H10
st. Kingsgrove...401 H6
MERRIT
pl. Mcquarie Fd...454 G4
MERRIVALE
la. Turramurra...223 F12
rd. Pymble...223 D16
rd. St Ives...223 D16
MERRIVILLE
rd. Kellyville...215 B2
MERRIWA
av. Hoxton Park...392 G7
pl. Cherrybrook...219 D10
pl. Yarrawarrah...489 E14
st. Gordon...253 E7
MERROO
rd. Kurrajong...55 D9
MERRYL
av. Old Tngabbie...276 J8
MERRYLANDS
rd. Greystanes...306 F10
rd. Merrylands...307 B11
rd. Merrylands W...307 B11
MERRYN
cl. Cobbitty...448 A13
cl. Harringtn Pk...448 A13
MERRYVALE
rd. Minto...482 C2
MERRYVILLE
ct. Wattle Grove...425 K2
MERRYWEATHER
cl. Minto...483
MERSEY
cl. Bossley Park...333
rd. Bringelly...387
st. Woronora...460
MERTON
av. Cmbrdg Gdn...237
la. Stanmore...16
st. Dean Park...242
st. Kogarah Bay...432
st. Petersham...16
st. Rozelle...7
st. Stanmore...16
st. Zetland...375
st.n, Sutherland...490
st.s, Sutherland...490
MERTZ
pl. Leumeah...482
MERU
pl. St Clair...269
MERVILLE
st. Concord W...311
MERYLA
st. Burwood...342
MERYLL
av. Baulkham Hl...247
MESA
wy. Stanhpe Gdn...215
MESSIMA
pl. Prestons...393
MESSINA
cr. Bonnyrigg Ht...362
st. Parklea...214
MESSINES
av. Milperra...397
pl. Matraville...407
MESSITER
st. Campsie...372
META
st. Caringbah...492
st. Croydon...342
st. Ryde...282
METCALF
av. Carlingford...249
METCALFE
av. Moorebank...396
la. Lidcombe...339
st. Cammeray...315
st. Maroubra...407
METELLA
cr. Belfield...371
rd. Toongabbie...275
METEOR
pl. Raby...451
METEREN
cl. Milperra...397
METHIL
pl. St Andrews...452
METHUEN
av. Mosman...317
pde. Riverwood...400
METHVEN
st. Mount Druitt...241
METROPOLITAN
rd. Enmore...17
METTERS
pl. Wetherill Pk...334
METZ
pl. Plumpton...241
METZLER
pl. Gordon...253
MEURANTS
la. Glenwood...245
la. Ramsgate...433
MEWS
la. Marrickville...373
MEWTON
rd. Maraylya...94
MEY
cl. Cecil Hills...362
MEYERS
av. Hunters Hill...313
la. Sefton...368
MEYMOTT
st. Coogee...407
st. Randwick...407
MEZEN
pl. St Clair...299
MIA
pl. Clareville...169

Marayong ... 244 C3
MBA
Carlingford ... 279 D1
MI
Greenfld Pk ... 333 K13
Cranebrook ... 207 H11
Frenchs Frst ... 256 G7
Glenwood ... 215 H12
MIA
Girraween ... 276 D12
NGA
Engadine ... 518 J2
X
Dharruk ... 241 B8
A
Eagle Vale ... 481 A8
AWBER
Ambarvale ... 511 A14
HAEL
Belfield ... 371 F12
Luddenham ... 356 H2
Cranebrook ... 207 B14
Ingleburn ... 453 C10
N Richmond ... 87 B14
North Ryde ... 282 D7
HAELS
Punchbowl ... 399 H5
HELAGO
Prestons ... 393 B13
HELE
Cmbrdg Pk ... 237 H7
Regents Pk ... 339 B16
Kingsgrove, off
Bykool Av ... 401 E8
Camden S ... 507 C11
Turramurra ... 222 K7
Cromer ... 228 H16
HELL
Thirlmere ... 564 E6
HELLE
Wentwthvle ... 277 C10
Blaxland ... 234 F8
Dural ... 188 G13
Marayong ... 244 A6
HIGAN
Asquith ... 192 B11
Riverwood ... 399 K12
Seven Hills ... 275 E6
DLE
Kingsford ... 406 G1
Oxford Falls ... 227 A12
Kingsford ... 406 G1
McMahons Pt ... 5 E16
Marrickville ... 16 C15
Randwick ... 406 G1
DLEBROOK
Bella Vista ... 216 D16
DLE HARBOUR
Belrose ... 225 F14
E Lindfield ... 254 F16
Lindfield ... 284 E1
DLE HEAD
Mosman ... 317 C9
DLEHOPE
Bonnyrigg ... 363 A6
DLEMISS
Lavender Bay ... K G13
Lavender Bay ... 5 H11
Mascot ... 405 F4
Rosebery ... 405 F4
DLETON
Castle Hill ... 217 G13
Cranebrook ... 207 E9
Richmond ... 119 J4
Richmond ... 119 J6
Bidwill ... 211 B15
Picton ... 561 C4
Chester Hill ... 337 G12
Cromer ... 228 E14
Leumeah ... 512 B2
Petersham ... 16 C13
-DURAL
Galston ... 159 A7
Middle Dural ... 158 J7
ELTON
Bexley North ... 402 F10
North Bondi ... 348 E15
IN
Glenmore Pk ... 266 C9
Mount Druitt ... 241 F15
LOTHIAN
Beverly Hills ... 401 A12

rd. St Andrews ... 452 A12
MIDSON
rd. Eastwood ... 280 H1
rd. Epping ... 280 H1
rd. Oakville ... 123 K13
MIDWAY
dr. Maroubra ... 407 C13
pl. Lethbrdg Pk ... 240 F3
MIDWINTER
row. St Clair ... 270 D14
MIFSUD
cr. Oakhurst ... 241 H3
st. Girraween ... 276 A10
MIGGS
pl. Ambarvale ... 511 A10
MIKADO
wy. Doonside ... 243 F16
MIKARIE
pl. Kirrawee ... 461 D15
MIKKELSEN
av. Tregear ... 240 F7
MILA
pl. Marayong ... 243 J6
MILAK
pl. Whalan ... 240 H12
MILAN
st. Prestons ... 393 F16
MILANO
pl. Edensor Pk ... 363 F1
MILBA
rd. Caringbah ... 493 C6
MILBURN
pl. St Ives Ch ... 194 B16
rd. Gymea ... 491 E2
st. Quakers Hill ... 214 C12
MILDARA
pl. Edensor Pk ... 333 D15
pl. W Pnnant Hl ... 249 A2
MILDRED
av. Hornsby ... 191 H13
av. Manly Vale ... 287 H4
st. Warrawee ... 222 D14
st. Wentwthvle ... 306 J1
MILDURA
pl. Prestons ... 393 E14
st. Killara ... 253 G14
MILE END
rd. Rouse Hill ... 184 J9
rd. Rouse Hill ... 185 B6
MILEHAM
av. Baulkham Hl ... 247 H5
av. Castle Hill ... 247 H5
st. S Windsor ... 120 G16
st. Windsor ... 121 A11
wy. Minto ... 482 H6
MILENA
av. Glenwood ... 245 G3
MILES
st. Bnkstn Aprt ... 367 K16
st. Brookvale ... 258 D12
st. Chester Hill ... 338 C16
st. Mascot ... 405 D1
st. Surry Hills ... 20 B4
MILES FRANKLIN
cl. Glenmore Pk ... 265 K6
MILFORD
av. Panania ... 428 A5
dr. Rouse Hill ... 185 C7
dr. Rouse Hill ... 185 D3
gr. Cherrybrook ... 219 A13
pl. Turramurra ... 252 F5
rd. Ellis Lane ... 476 A9
rd. Londonderry ... 148 F10
rd. Miranda ... 492 D3
rd. Peakhurst ... 400 F16
st. Randwick ... 377 B14
wy. Wentwthvle ... 277 E11
MILGA
rd. Avalon ... 140 E13
MILGATE
la. Campbelltwn ... 511 E4
MILGUY
av. Castle Hill ... 247 F1
MILHAM
av. Eastwood ... 281 F5
cr. Forestville ... 255 D8
st. St Marys ... 269 J4
MILI
pl. Kings Park ... 244 J2
MILITARY
dr. Lilyfield ... 10 A1
la. Cremorne ... 6 H2

rd. Cremorne ... 316 C9
rd. Dover Ht ... 348 F8
rd. Guildford ... 337 G4
rd. Matraville ... 436 G8
rd. Merrylands ... 307 J16
rd. Mosman ... 316 H6
rd. Neutral Bay ... 6 F1
rd. North Bondi ... 378 G1
rd. Vaucluse ... 348 F7
rd. Watsons Bay ... 318 G14
MILK
av. Vaucluse ... 348 E2
MILL
dr. North Rocks ... 248 F12
la. Hurlstone Pk ... 373 A12
la. The Rocks ... B A2
pl. St Clair ... 270 E10
rd. Campbelltwn ... 481 H14
rd. Kurrajong ... 55 F12
rd. Kurrajong Hl ... 54 J12
rd. Liverpool ... 395 C6
st. Bnksmeadw ... 406 D12
st. Carlton ... 432 G4
st. Currans Hill ... 479 J10
st. Hurlstone Pk ... 373 A12
st. Riverstone ... 182 J6
MILLAR
cr. Dural ... 188 H12
st. Drummoyne ... 343 G5
MILLARD
cr. Plumpton ... 241 G9
MILLBROOK
pl. Cherrybrook ... 219 E12
MILLEN
st. Kingswood ... 238 A13
MILLENNIUM
ct. Matraville ... 436 H7
ct. Silverwater ... 309 G11
MILLER
av. Ashfield ... 372 G3
av. Bexley North ... 402 F11
av. Dundas Vy ... 280 E10
av. Hornsby ... 191 H14
la. Cammeray ... 315 K5
la. Petersham ... 15 F16
la. Pyrmont ... 12 G4
pl. Menai ... 458 F10
pl. Mt Pritchard ... 364 J10
pl. Tahmoor ... 565 G9
rd. Bass Hill ... 367 J6
rd. Chester Hill ... 337 J11
rd. Chester Hill ... 367 J6
rd. Glenorie ... 126 D3
rd. Miller ... 393 G4
rd. Villawood ... 367 J6
st. Bondi ... 378 A4
st. Cammeray ... 315 J6
st. Crows Nest ... 315 J6
st. Haberfield ... 343 C13
st. Kingsgrove ... 402 B5
st. Kingsgrove ... 402 C6
st. Lavender Bay ... K C14
st. Lavender Bay ... 5 F11
st. McMahons Pt ... 5 F11
st. Merrylands ... 307 H13
st. Mount Druitt ... 271 C3
st. N Sydney ... K C14
st. N Sydney ... K D10
st. N Sydney ... K D6
st. N Sydney ... 5 F11
st. N Sydney ... 5 F7
st. Petersham ... 15 G15
st. Pyrmont ... 12 F4
st. S Granville ... 338 E7
st. S Penrith ... 236 H15
wy. Claymore ... 481 D11
wy. Stanhpe Gdn ... 215 E2
MILLERS
rd. Cattai ... 94 B7
wy. W Pnnant Hl ... 248 H7
MILLET
row. Wrrngtn Dns ... 238 E5
MILLETT
rd. Mosman ... 316 J10
st. Hurstville ... 431 F1
MILLEWA
av. Wahroonga ... 222 C6
av. Warrawee ... 222 C6
la. Wahroonga, off
Millewa Av ... 222 D6
MILL HILL
rd. Bondi Jctn ... 22 D8
MILLICENT
st. Greystanes ... 305 J1

MILLIE
st. Guildford ... 337 E6
MILLIGAN
la. Cranebrook, off
Milligan Rd ... 207 C13
rd. Cranebrook ... 207 C13
MILLING
st. Hunters Hill ... 313 A8
MILL POND
rd. Botany ... 405 D8
MILLS
av. Asquith ... 191 K7
av. North Rocks ... 249 A16
cr. Burwood ... 342 C12
la. Chatswood ... 284 K9
la. Winmalee ... 173 J7
pl. Beacon Hill ... 257 D7
rd. Glenhaven ... 187 F16
rd. Londonderry ... 148 G15
st. Croydon ... 372 D3
st. Lidcombe ... 339 J7
st. Merrylands ... 307 A10
MILLSTREAM
gr. Dural ... 219 A3
rd. Wrrngtn Dns ... 237 K5
MILLWOOD
av. Chatswd W ... 284 A8
av. Narellan ... 478 C9
MIL MIL
st. McMahons Pt ... 5 D14
MILNE
av. Kingswood ... 237 G15
av. Matraville ... 406 H16
cl. Wetherill Pk ... 335 A7
la. Tempe, off
Lymerston St ... 404 D1
la. Merrylands, off
Terminal Pl ... 307 J13
pl. Narellan Vale ... 478 K10
st. Ryde ... 282 G16
st. Tahmoor ... 565 F12
MILNER
av. Hornsby ... 221 C4
av. Kirrawee ... 490 H6
cr. Wollstncraft ... 315 C9
la. Mosman, off
Milner St ... 317 A10
rd. Artarmon ... 284 J16
rd. Guildford ... 337 H7
rd. Peakhurst ... 400 F16
st. Mosman ... 317 A9
MILPARINKA
av. Glenwood ... 245 F1
cl. Hoxton Park ... 392 F7
MILPERA
pl. Cromer ... 228 B16
MILPERRA
rd. Bnkstn Aprt ... 397 G6
rd. Milperra ... 397 G6
rd. Revesby ... 397 G6
MILRAY
av. Wollstncraft ... 315 B11
st. Lindfield ... 254 D15
MILROY
av. Kensington ... 376 B10
st. North Ryde ... 282 E8
MILSON
pde. Normanhurst ... 221 D9
pde. Thornleigh ... 221 D9
rd. Cremorne Pt ... 316 F13
rd. Doonside ... 243 E12
rd. Woodcroft ... 243 E12
MILSOP
pl. Mortdale ... 431 B4
st. Bexley ... 432 H4
MILSTED
rd. Terrey Hills ... 196 E5
MILTON
av. Eastwood ... 280 G7
av. Mosman ... 317 B11
av. Woollahra ... 22 F2
cl. Wetherill Pk ... 334 K5
cr. Leumeah ... 512 B2
cr. Prestons ... 392 H13
la. Burwood, off
Neich Pde ... 342 A11
la. Ashfield, off
Norton St ... 372 F3
pl. Frenchs Frst ... 256 D8
pl. Greystanes ... 306 C11
rd. N Turramrra ... 223 F3
rd. Riverstone ... 182 D10
st. Ashbury ... 372 F5

st. Ashfield ... 372 F4
st. Ashfield ... 372 F5
st. Bankstown ... 369 G14
st. Burwood ... 342 A11
st. Carlingford ... 280 A1
st. Chatswood ... 285 B7
st. Colyton ... 270 H7
st. Granville ... 308 C10
st. Leichhardt ... 10 D14
st. Lidcombe ... 339 F7
st. Riverstone ... 182 F13
st. Rydalmere ... 309 J4
st. Thirlmere ... 562 C15
st.n, Ashfield ... 372 F2
wy. Shalvey ... 210 J14
MILVAY
pl. Ambarvale ... 511 B15
MIMA
st. Sefton ... 368 G2
MI MI
st. Oatley ... 431 A12
MIMIKA
av. Whalan ... 240 J12
MIMOS
st. Denistone W ... 281 A13
MIMOSA
av. Toongabbie ... 276 C5
cl. St Clair ... 270 B15
gr. Glenwood ... 245 G2
rd. Bossley Park ... 334 A10
rd. Greenacre ... 369 J12
rd. Greenfld Pk ... 334 A12
rd. Turramurra ... 252 E3
st. Bargo ... 567 D5
st. Bexley ... 402 E14
st. Frenchs Frst ... 255 F3
st. Granville ... 308 G16
st. Heathcote ... 519 A10
st. Oatley ... 431 A14
st. S Hurstville ... 432 A11
st. Westmead ... 307 H3
MIMULUS
la. Regents Pk ... 369 B2
pl. Caringbah ... 492 E13
pl. Mcquarie Fd ... 454 G4
MINA
rd. Menai ... 458 G9
rd. Menai ... 458 H10
MINAGO
pl. Castle Hill ... 218 A7
MINAHAN
pl. Plumpton ... 241 G9
MINA ROSA
st. Enfield ... 371 G4
MINARTO
la. N Narrabeen ... 228 K2
MINCHIN
av. Hobartville ... 118 D9
dr. Minchinbury ... 271 J7
MINCHINBURY
st. Eastern Ck ... 272 D7
tce. Eschol Park ... 481 A6
MINDA
pl. Whalan ... 240 H11
MINDANAO
av. Lethbrdg Pk ... 240 F3
MINDAR
st. Como ... 460 H7
MINDARIBBA
av. Rouse Hill ... 185 D7
MINDARIE
st. Lane Cove W ... 283 J14
MINDONA
wy. Woodcroft ... 243 J11
MINDORO
pl. Lethbrdg Pk ... 240 G5
MINELL
ct. Harringtn Pk ... 478 E1
MINER
gln. Erskine Park ... 271 A11
pl. Ingleburn ... 453 F7
MINERAL SPRINGS
rd. Picton ... 563 G11
MINERVA
cr. Kellyville ... 186 A14
pl. Prestons ... 392 K13
rd. Wedderburn ... 540 B11
st. Kirrawee ... 490 H5
MINGA
st. Ryde ... 282 F15
MINIMBAH
rd. Northbridge ... 286 D14

MINJ
pl. Glenfield 424 J9
MINKARA
rd. Bayview 168 E15
MINKI
wy. Glenwood 215 C15
MINMAI
rd. Chester Hill 337 F13
rd. Mona Vale 198 G2
MINNA
cl. Belrose 225 H1
st. Burwood 371 H1
MINNAMORRA
av. Earlwood 403 A5
MINNAMURRA
av. Miranda 492 F3
av. Pymble 253 C8
cct. Prestons 393 B16
cct. Prestons 423 A1
gr. Dural 219 A3
pl. Pymble 253 C9
rd. Northbridge 286 D15
MINNEAPOLIS
cr. Maroubra 407 C13
MINNEK
cl. Glenmore Pk 266 C11
MINNESOTA
av. Five Dock 343 B11
av. Riverwood 400 A13
MINNIE
st. Belmore 371 A12
MINNS
rd. Gordon 253 J6
MINOGUE
cr. Forest Lodge 11 E13
cr. Forest Lodge 11 E14
MINORCA
wy. Minto 482 H7
MINSTREL
pl. Rouse Hill 185 C6
MINT
cl. St Clair 269 G11
la. St Clair, off Mint Cl 269 G11
pl. Quakers Hill 243 F4
MINTARO
av. Strathfield 371 C2
MINTER
st. Canterbury 372 G13
MINTO
av. Haberfield 343 E12
cl. Bonnyrigg Ht 363 C4
pl. Erskine Park 270 J15
rd. Minto 453 A14
st. Hebersham 241 D9
wk. Minto 482 H4
MINTOFF
pl. Dean Park, off Raupach St 212 F16
MINTON
av. Dolls Point 463 E1
MINUET
ct. Glenwood 245 C1
MINYA
av. Kingsford 406 D2
MIOWERA
av. Carss Park 432 E15
rd. Chester Hill 337 F14
rd. Northbridge 286 F15
rd. N Turramrra 223 G6
MIRAGE
av. Raby 481 E1
MIRAMBENA
cl. Cherrybrook 220 A13
MIRAMONT
av. Riverview 314 A6
MIRANDA
cl. Cherrybrook 219 J3
pl. Rsemeadow 540 K6
rd. Miranda 492 C2
rd. Miranda 492 C5
st. S Penrith 267 C5
MIRANG
pl. Engadine 488 J9
MIRBELIA
ct. Voyager Pt 427 C5
pde. Elanora Ht 197 J12
pde. Ingleside 197 J12
pl. Caringbah 493 B6
MIRCA
pl. Appin 569 C7

MIRETTA
pl. Castle Hill 247 J3
MIRI
cr. Holsworthy 426 D2
ct. St Ives 223 K16
MIRIAM
cl. Smithfield 336 B7
ct. Baulkham Hl 247 C2
rd. Denistone 281 D12
rd. West Ryde 281 D12
st. Bass Hill 368 C10
st. Wilton 568 K16
MIRIMAR
av. Bronte 378 B7
MIROOL
st. Denistone W 280 K13
st. West Ryde 280 K13
MIRRA
pl. Cromer 228 D14
MIRRABOOK
pl. Heathcote 518 F10
MIRRABOOKA
av. Strathfield 341 B11
cr. Little Bay 437 A11
ct. Emu Heights 234 K5
st. Bilgola 169 E5
MIRRADONG
pl. Kirribilli 2 E3
MIRRAL
rd. Caringbah 492 G15
rd. Lilli Pilli 522 G1
MIRRI
pl. Glenmore Pk 266 B10
MIRROOL
st. N Narrabeen 198 G16
st. N Narrabeen 228 G2
st. N Wahrnga 192 E15
MISIMA
pl. Glenfield 424 J10
MISSENDEN
rd. Camperdwn 17 G3
rd. Newtown 17 J6
MISSISSIPPI
cr. Kearns 451 A15
rd. Seven Hills 275 D9
MISSOURI
pl. Riverwood 400 A13
st. Kearns 451 A14
MISTLETOE
av. Clarmnt Ms 238 J16
av. Mcquarie Fd 454 B6
st. Loftus 489 K11
MISTRAL
av. Mosman 316 K11
pl. Shalvey 210 J13
st. Greenfld Pk 334 C13
MISTY
gln. Wrrngtn Dns 238 B4
MITALA
st. Newport 169 D10
MITCHAM
rd. Bankstown 369 B15
st. Punchbowl 400 A7
MITCHELL
av. Jannali 460 F12
cl. Tahmoor 565 K13
cr. Turramurra 222 C16
cr. Warrawee 222 C16
dr. Glossodia 59 G9
dr. West Hoxton 392 B12
la. Alexandria 18 G15
la. Mosman, off Mitchell Rd 317 B3
la.e, Glebe 12 F13
la.w, Glebe 12 E13
pl. Douglas Park 568 F12
pl. Kenthurst 188 E7
rd. Alexandria 18 G16
rd. Alexandria 375 B10
rd. Brookvale 258 C12
rd. Cronulla 494 A10
rd. Darling Point 13 K4
rd. Dural 190 A9
rd. Erskineville 375 B10
rd. Moorebank 395 J9
rd. Mosman 317 B3
rd. Palm Beach 140 A3
rd. Pitt Town 93 B11
rd. Rose Bay 348 D8
rd. Strathfield 340 G12
st. Arncliffe 403 E8
st. Bondi Beach 378 D1
st. Camden 477 A15

st. Campbelltwn 511 J7
st. Carramar 336 H16
st. Centnnial Pk 21 E7
st. Chifley 437 A3
st. Condell Park 398 F3
st. Croydon Pk 371 G5
st. Enfield 371 G5
st. Ermington 280 D16
st. Five Dock 343 B7
st. Glebe 12 D16
st. Greenwich 314 J13
st. Lalor Park 245 C13
st. McMahons Pt 5 C13
st. Marrickville 374 C11
st. Naremburn 315 E5
st. North Bondi 378 D1
st. Putney 312 B8
st. St Leonards 315 E5
st. St Marys 269 H3
st. S Penrith 236 H14
st. Villawood 337 A16
wy. Eveleigh 18 K10
MITCHELL PARK
rd. Cattai 94 F3
MITCHELLS
ps. Blaxland 233 K9
ps. Glenbrook 234 F10
MITTABAH
rd. Asquith 191 J8
rd. Hornsby 191 J8
MITTIAMO
st. Canley Ht 365 B1
MITUMBA
rd. Seven Hills 275 C10
MIVO
st. Holsworthy 426 D1
MIYAL
pl. Engadine 518 H2
MOALA
st. Concord W 311 E15
MOANI
av. Gymea 491 D4
MOAT
st. Kellyville 215 B3
st. Stanhpe Gdn 215 B3
MOATE
av. Btn-le-Sds 433 K2
MOBBS
la. Carlingford 280 E6
la. Epping 280 E6
MOCATTA
av. Pymble 253 E3
MOCKRIDGE
av. Newington 310 C12
MODEL FARMS
rd. Northmead 277 H1
rd. Winston Hills 247 H16
MODERN
av. Canterbury 402 E1
MOFFAT
pl. Minto 482 H9
MOFFATT
dr. Lalor Park 245 H10
wy. Kellyville 185 J14
MOFFATTS
dr. Dundas Vy 279 J10
MOFFITT
cr. Edensor Pk 333 G15
MOFFITTS
la. Ellis Lane 476 C6
MOGILA
st. Seven Hills 275 E4
MOGO
ct. Prestons 392 J13
pl. Glenmore Pk 266 B11
MOHAVE
pl. Bossley Park 334 A12
MOHAWK
cr. Greenfld Pk 334 A16
pl. Erskine Park 271 A16
MOIR
av. Northmead 277 J6
pl. Bidwill 211 B16
st. Smithfield 335 E3
MOIRA
av. Denistone W 281 A14
av. West Ryde 281 A14
cr. Coogee 377 F13
cr. Randwick 377 F13
cr. St Marys 269 J4
la. St Marys, off Moira Cr 269 K3

pl. Frenchs Frst 256 F10
st. Sutherland 460 H16
MOJO
pl. Greenfld Pk 333 K13
MOKARI
st. N Richmond 87 C14
MOKERA
av. Kirrawee 461 A15
MOLES
rd. Wilberforce 61 B1
MOLESWORTH
la. Longueville 314 E7
MOLISE
av. Kellyville 186 H16
MOLLE
pl. Narellan Vale 478 G16
MOLLER
av. Birrong 369 A6
MOLLISON
cr. Ermington 280 A16
MOLLOY
av. S Coogee 407 G7
ct. Mortdale 430 F6
pl. Minchinbury 272 C9
MOLLS
la. Mowbray Pk 561 J8
MOLLUSO
cl. Wakeley 334 G15
MOLLYMOOK
st. Prestons 393 B13
MOLONG
rd. Gymea Bay 491 E12
st. N Curl Curl 259 B11
st. Quakers Hill 243 K1
wy. Bidwill 211 E13
MOLONGLO
rd. Seven Hills 275 E10
MOLYNEAUX
av. Kings Lngly 245 J7
MOMBRI
st. Merrylands 307 K12
MONA
la. Darling Point 13 F8
rd. Darling Point 13 G9
rd. Menai 458 K11
rd. Riverwood 400 E15
st. Allawah 432 E7
st. Auburn 339 A2
st. Bankstown 399 E1
st. Mona Vale 199 C1
st. S Granville 338 G1
st. Wahroonga 222 J7
MONACO
av. Kellyville 185 F8
pl. Prestons 393 C15
pl. Quakers Hill 214 E13
MONAGHAN
st. Minto 482 H2
MONAHAN
av. Banksia 403 E13
MONARCH
cct. Glenmore Pk 266 C13
cl. Rouse Hill 185 E5
pl. Quakers Hill 213 K8
MONARO
av. Kingsgrove 401 H12
cl. Bossley Park 333 K9
pl. Beacon Hill 258 A5
pl. Emu Plains 234 K7
pl. Heckenberg 364 A15
st. Seven Hills 246 C13
MONASH
av. East Hills 427 H4
av. East Killara 254 G10
av. Gt Mckrl Bch 109 A13
av. Holsworthy 396 B13
cr. Clontarf 287 E14
gdn. Pagewood 406 F7
pde. Croydon 342 E12
pde. Dee Why 259 B9
pl. Bonnyrigg 364 A6
rd. Blacktown 273 J1
rd. Doonside 273 G1
rd. Gladesville 312 H5
rd. Menai 458 J6
st. Wentwthvle 306 J3
MONASTERY
pl. Cherrybrook 219 F15
MONA VALE
pl. Woodbine 481 J10
rd. Ingleside 197 B9
rd. Krngai Ch NP 224 F4

rd. Mona Vale 198
rd. Pymble 253
rd. St Ives 224
rd. Terrey Hills 195
rd. Warriewood 198
MONCKTON
pl. Glenfield 424
MONCRIEFF
cl. St Helens Park 541
dr. East Ryde 282
pl. Milperra 397
rd. Lalor Park 245
MONCUR
av. Belmore 401
la. Woollahra 21
st. Marrickville 373
st. Woollahra 21
MONDIAL
pl. West Ryde 281
MONDOVI
cl. Prestons 393
MONDS
la. Picton 561
la. Picton 563
MONET
ct. Kellyville 216
MONFARVILLE
st. St Marys 269
MONFORD
pl. Cremorne 316
MONGA
pl. Prestons 392
MONGON
pl. St Helens Park 541
MONI
wy. Doonside 243
MONICA
av. Hassall Gr 211
cl. Lurnea 394
pl. Jamisontown 265
pl. Tahmoor 565
MONIE
av. East Hills 427
MONIER
sq. Villawood 367
MONITOR
rd. Merrylands 307
MONK
av. Arncliffe 403
MONKEY
rd. The Oaks 502
MONKS
la. Alexandria 18
la. Erskineville 18
la. Mt Hunter 504
MONMOUTH
av. East Killara 254
st. Randwick 377
MONOMEETH
pl. Miranda 462
st. Bexley 402
MONRO
av. Kirrawee 491
MONROE
st. Blacktown 274
st. Ermington 280
MONS
av. Maroubra 407
av. West Ryde 311
rd. N Balgowlah 287
rd. Wentwthvle 277
rd. Westmead 277
st. Canterbury 372
st. Condell Park 398
st. Lidcombe 340
st. Revesby 398
st. Russell Lea 343
st. S Granville 338
st. Vaucluse 348
MONSERRA
rd. Allambie Ht 257
MONT
pl. St Clair 269
MONTAGUE
cl. Green Valley 363
pl. Rsemeadow 540
rd. Cremorne 316
st. Balmain 7
st. Fairfield Ht 335
st. Greystanes 306
st. Illawong 459
st. North Manly 258

NTAH
Killara 254 C9
NTANA
North Rocks 278 G2
Riverwood 399 K12
Stanhpe Gdn 215 B11
Mcquarie Fd 454 H4
NTAUBAN
Seaforth 287 A7
NT CLAIR
Darlinghurst 4 F11
NTEBELLO
Green Valley 362 K14
NTECLAIR
Liverpool 395 A10
NTEITH
Turramurra 222 D15
Warrawee 222 D15
Baulkham Hl 247 D6
Turramurra 222 D15
Warrawee 222 D15
NTELIMAR
Wallacia 325 A13
NTELLA
Prestons 393 F14
NTERAY
Glenmore Pk 266 G14
NTEREY
. Ermington 280 E11
Cherrybrook 219 D11
Bilgola 169 H6
Monterey 433 F9
Newington 310 D12
St Ives 224 D6
S Wntwthvle 307 A7
NTERRA
Peakhurst 430 D8
NTGOMERY
Revesby 398 K16
S Granville 338 E6
Bonnyrigg 363 J9
Carlingford 250 B15
Kogarah 433 C4
Miranda 492 C3
Narellan Vale 479 A10
NTI
N Richmond 87 C13
NTORE
Minto 482 C4
NTPELIER
The Oaks 502 D16
Neutral Bay 6 B5
NTREAL
Killara 283 E1
NTROSE
Fairfield E 337 B14
Merrylands 307 K14
St Andrews 451 K12
Abbotsford 342 K1
Winmalee 173 B12
Quakers Hill 213 K14
Turramurra 222 E16
NTVIEW
. Hornsby Ht 191 E1
Glenwood, off
Crestview Dr 246 B6
OCULTA
Russell Lea 343 B6
ODIE
Cammeray 316 A8
Cammeray 315 K8
Rozelle 344 D8
ODY
Rooty Hill 272 C4
OKARA
Port Hacking 522 H1
OKI
Miranda 492 C6
OLA
. Chatswd W 284 D13
. Lane Cove W 284 D13
OLAH
Terrey Hills 196 C6
OLANA
. S Penrith 266 G7
Bnksmeadw 405 K15
OLANDA
W Pnnant Hl 249 C10
OMBARA
Peakhurst 430 H3
Port Hacking 522 J3

MOOMIN
pl. Busby 363 J15
st. Lalor Park 245 H10
MOONA
av. Baulkham Hl 246 K7
av. Matraville 436 H4
pde. Wahroonga 221 H16
rd. Kirrawee 460 J15
st. Hornsby 191 H8
MOONAH
cl. St Ives Ch 194 B15
cl. West Hoxton 392 E6
gr. St Clair 270 B15
pl. Mcquarie Fd 454 D4
rd. Alfords Point 428 K13
rd. Alfords Point 429 A13
MOONARIE
pl. Cromer 228 A15
MOONBEAM
cl. St Clair 270 D13
MOONBI
cl. Greenfld Pk 334 C15
cr. Frenchs Frst 256 E2
pl. Kareela 461 E10
rd. Penrith 237 D3
MOONBIE
st. Summer Hill 373 C6
MOONBRIA
pl. Airds 512 C12
st. Naremburn 315 E3
MOONDANI
la. Beverly Hills, off
Moondani Rd 401 A10
rd. Beverly Hills 401 A10
MOONDO
st. Greenacre 370 F11
MOONEY
av. Blakehurst 432 A14
av. Earlwood 402 F2
pl. Ruse 512 C8
st. Lane Cove W 284 A12
st. Strathfield S 371 B5
MOONLIGHT
rd. Prairiewood 334 E10
MOON POINT
rd. Illawong 459 D4
MOONS
av. Lugarno 429 F14
MOONSHINE
av. Cabramatta W 364 G6
MOONSTONE
pl. Eagle Vale 481 E6
MOONYEAN
pl. Cromer 228 C16
MOORA
st. Chester Hill 338 A15
MOORAL
av. Punchbowl 400 A9
MOORAMBA
av. Riverview 314 A5
rd. Dee Why 258 F7
MOORAMIE
av. Kensington 376 E15
MOORANYAH
cl. Woodcroft 243 H12
MOORE
av. Lindfield 283 F1
cr. Faulconbdg 171 C15
cr. Faulconbdg 171 D14
la. Campsie 372 B10
la. East Hills 427 J4
la. Harbord 288 G1
la. Leichhardt 10 F12
la. Rozelle 7 D16
pl. Bligh Park 150 E5
pl. Currans Hill 479 J12
pl. Doonside 243 D5
rd. Harbord 288 G1
rd. Oakdale 500 D11
rd. Springwood 202 B1
st. Bnksmeadw 406 C11
st. Bardwell Pk 402 J8
st. Bexley 402 A16
st. Blaxland 234 B6
st. Bondi 377 K4
st. Cabarita 342 D1
st. Campbelltwn 511 F5
st. Campbelltwn 511 G4
st. Campsie 372 B10
st. Canley Vale 366 F4
st. Clontarf 287 G15
st. Coogee 377 J14
st. Drummoyne 343 F3
st. Glenbrook 233 J15
st. Hurstville 402 A16
st. Lane Cove W 283 H15
st. Lansdowne 367 B4
st. Leichhardt 10 C12
st. Leumeah 481 J16
st. Liverpool 395 A3
st. Roseville 285 B2
st. Rozelle 7 C14
st. St Clair 269 K11
st. Strathfield 341 J10
st. Sutherland 490 D3
st. Vaucluse 318 G15
st.w,Leichhardt 10 A11
MOOREBANK
av. Moorebank 395 E10
MOORECOURT
av. Springwood 201 G3
MOOREFIELD
av. Hunters Hill 313 G11
av. Kogarah 433 E6
la. Kogarah 433 C4
MOOREFIELDS
la. Beverly Hills, off
Moorefields Rd 401 A10
rd. Beverly Hills 401 B9
rd. Kingsgrove 401 B9
rd. Roselands 401 B9
MOOREHEAD
av. Silverdale 353 H15
MOOREHOUSE
cr. Edensor Pk 363 H1
MOORE-OXLEY
bps. Campbelltwn 511 D6
bps. Leumeah 511 H4
st. Bradbury 511 D6
MOORE PARK
rd. Moore Park 20 G2
rd. Paddington 20 G2
MOORES
la. Alexandria 19 B15
rd. Glenorie 128 J3
wy. Glenmore 503 E4
wy. The Oaks 503 E4
MOORESFIELD
la. Ellis Lane 476 D8
MOORES STEPS
Sydney B G5
MOORFOOT
rd. St Andrews 451 J15
MOORGATE
la. Chippendale 18 J1
st. Chippendale 18 K1
st. Toongabbie 276 H7
MOORHEN
st. Ingleburn 453 G5
MOORHOUSE
av. St Ives 254 D4
MOORILLA
av. Carlingford 249 G11
st. Dee Why 258 E8
MOORINA
av. Matraville 436 H4
cl. Greenfld Pk 334 D14
rd. Pymble 223 G14
MOORLAND
rd. Tahmoor 566 B10
rd. Tahmoor 566 C9
MOORLANDS
rd. Ingleburn 452 J8
MORAGO
wy. Airds 512 E10
MORAN
cl. Bonnyrigg Ht 363 E8
pl. Currans Hill 479 J13
st. Mosman 316 K12
wy. Minto 482 H8
MORANDOO
rd. Elanora Ht 198 F14
MORANT
st. Edensor Pk 363 H2
MORAR
pl. St Andrews 452 C12
MORAY
pl. Sylvania 461 G10
st. Richmond 118 J8
st. Winmalee 173 F13
MORDEN
st. Cammeray 315 K6
MOREE
av. Westmead 307 E1
pl. Bossley Park 333 E10
st. Gordon 253 F8
MOREHEAD
av. Mount Druitt 241 G11
st. Redfern 19 H14
st. Waterloo 19 H14
MORELLA
av. Sefton 368 E6
pl. Castle Cove 286 C6
rd. Mosman 317 D12
rd. Whale Beach 140 B6
MOREN
st. Blacktown 274 F7
MORESBY
av. Glenfield 424 C13
cr. Whalan 240 H12
pl. Allambie Ht 257 E11
MORESTONE
pl. Windsor Dn 180 K1
MORETON
av. Kingsgrove 401 J12
cl. Hinchinbrk 363 B15
rd. Illawong 459 C5
rd. Minto Ht 483 G6
st. Concord 342 B9
st. Douglas Park 568 G6
st. Douglas Park 568 G7
st. Lakemba 401 C1
MORETON BAY
av. Spring Farm 508 E1
sq. Bidwill 241 F1
MORETON PARK
rd. Douglas Park 568 H7
rd. Menangle 538 K16
MOREY
pl. Kings Lngly 245 C3
MORGAN
av. Matraville 436 G8
cl. Prairiewood 334 E12
la. Bankstown, off
West Tce 399 F1
pl. Bligh Park 150 H8
pl. Glendenning 242 J4
pl. Strathfield 370 K2
rd. Belrose 226 B8
rd. Mt Annan 479 D15
st. Beverly Hills 401 C14
st. Botany 405 J11
st. Earlwood 402 G5
st. Ingleburn 453 E13
st. Kingsgrove 401 G12
st. Merrylands 307 F7
st. Miller 393 G4
st. Petersham 15 E14
st. Thornleigh 220 G12
MORIAC
st. Warriewood 198 K6
MORIAL
la. Pymble, off
Peace Av 253 H1
MORIARTY
rd. Chatswd W 284 H13
MORIL
av. Mt Riverview 204 E16
MORINDA
st. Mt Annan 509 C3
MORISON
dr. Lurnea 394 B11
la. Panania 428 B6
MORLEY
av. Hamondvle 396 G15
av. Kingswood 237 K12
av. Rosebery 375 G14
ct. Baulkham Hl 246 H4
la. Kingswood, off
Kingsley Gr 238 B12
st. Sutherland 490 E5
MORNA
pl. Kareela 461 E11
pl. Quakers Hill 214 D11
pl. Turramurra 252 F5
st. Greenfld Pk 334 E13
MORNINGBIRD
cl. St Clair 270 D13
la. St Clair, off
Morningbird Cl 270 D13
MORNINGTON
av. Castle Hill 247 H1
pl. Hinchinbrk 393 B2
MORO
av. Padstow 399 D13
MOROBE
st. Whalan 240 H12

MORONA
av. Wahroonga 251 G2
MORONEY
av. Castle Hill 217 B7
cl. Blacktown 273 G5
MOROTAI
av. Riverwood 400 A15
cr. Castlecrag 285 K13
rd. Revesby Ht 428 J6
st. Whalan 240 J11
MORPHETT
st. Kingswood 238 B14
MORREL
pl. Kingswood 267 H1
MORRELL
cr. Quakers Hill 213 H8
st. Woollahra 21 K2
MORRICE
st. Lane Cove 314 C4
MORRIS
av. Croydon Pk 372 C8
av. Kingsgrove 401 J13
av. Thornleigh 220 H11
av. Wahroonga 223 A3
cl. Menai 458 D10
gr. Zetland 375 K10
la. Burwood 341 J16
la. St Marys, off
Morris St 270 A3
pl. Ingleburn 453 G11
pl. Maroubra 407 D13
st. Dundas Vy 280 E8
st. Merrylands 307 D14
st. Regents Pk 369 A3
st. St Marys 269 J2
st. Seven Hills 245 H15
st. Smithfield 335 K6
st. Summer Hill 373 C5
MORRISEY
wy. Rouse Hill 185 E2
wy. Rouse Hill 185 F3
MORRISON
av. Chester Hill 368 D4
av. Engadine 488 J16
pl. Pennant Hills 220 C13
rd. Gladesville 312 E8
rd. Putney 312 A6
rd. Ryde 311 J3
rd. Tennyson 312 E8
st. Glenmore Pk 265 J9
MORRISSEY
rd. Erskineville 17 K16
MORSE
pl. Blaxland 233 G6
st. Villawood 337 A16
MORSHEAD
av. Carlingford 250 B13
cr. S Granville 338 G4
dr. Connells Pt 431 G13
dr. Hurstville Gr 431 F13
dr. Hurstville Gr 431 G13
dr. S Hurstville 431 J13
rd. Narellan Vale 479 B12
st. Colyton 270 C5
st. North Ryde 282 K8
MORT
cl. Barden Rdg 488 G3
la. Randwick 377 A10
la. Surry Hills 20 D6
pl. Glenmore Pk 265 E10
st. Balmain 7 H8
st. Blacktown 245 A14
st. Granville 308 D9
st. Randwick 376 K9
st. Surry Hills 20 C6
MORTAIN
av. Allambie Ht 257 C9
MORTIMER
cl. Cecil Hills 362 F2
la. Emu Plains, off
Mortimer St 235 H9
st. Emu Plains 235 G9
st. Minto 482 K2
st. Yanderra 567 B16
MORTIMER LEWIS
dr. Tarban 313 C13
gr. St Clair 270 B11
la. St Clair, off
Mortimer Lewis
Cr 270 B11
MORTLAKE
la. Concord, off
Archer St 342 B2
st. Concord 342 B1

MORTLEY
av. Haberfield 343 E11
MORTON
av. Carlingford.........249 D12
av. Dulwich Hill..........15 B15
cl. Wakeley..............334 H12
ct. Wattle Grove......426 B3
la. Woollahra............21 K4
la. Wollstncraft, off Sinclair St...........315 F8
rd. Lalor Park..........245 E13
st. Lilyfield...................9 G4
st. N Richmond.........87 B12
st. Parramatta.........308 H2
st. Wollstncraft...........5 A1
tce. Harringtn Pk......478 E5
MORTS
rd. Mortdale............431 A5
MORUBEN
rd. Mosman............317 B5
MORUYA
av. Sylvania Wtr.......462 G12
cl. Prestons............392 K15
cr. Greystanes.........305 H5
MORVAN
st. Denistone W......281 A13
st. West Ryde.........281 A13
MORVEN
ct. Castle Hill..........218 C7
st. Old Guildford......337 F9
MORVEN GARDENS
la. Greenwich..........314 K5
MORWICK
st. Strathfield..........341 G13
MOSELEY
st. Carlingford.........279 H2
MOSELLE
pl. Eschol Park........481 C5
MOSELY
av. S Penrith............266 F3
st. Strathfield..........341 G11
MOSES
st. Windsor.............120 K9
MOSMAN
pl. Barden Rdg........488 H6
sq. Mosman, off Military Rd..........317 A6
st. Mosman............316 H12
MOSS
gln. Cranebrook.......207 B12
la. Mosman............287 A16
pl. Galston..............159 E8
pl. St Helens Park....540 K10
pl. Westmead..........307 J3
st. Chester Hill.........337 K11
st. Northmead..........277 H7
st. Sans Souci.........463 B5
st. West Ryde..........281 A16
MOSSBERRY
st. Blair Athol..........511 A3
MOSSGIEL
st. Fairlight.............288 E7
MOSSGLEN
st. Minto.................482 J3
MOTH
cl. Cranebrook........207 B10
pl. Raby..................481 G1
MOTORKHANA
rd. Leppington.........451 A1
MOTTLE
gr. Woodcroft..........243 F7
MOTU
pl. Glenfield............424 F13
MOULAMEIN
tce. Glenwood..........215 E15
MOULTON
av. Newington.........310 D11
MOUNT
av. Roselands..........400 G6
cl. Cranebrook........207 B12
la. Coogee, off Dolphin St..........377 F15
st. Arncliffe.............403 D10
st. Bonnyrigg Ht......363 B4
st. Coogee..............377 F14
st. Coogee..............377 F16
st. Georges Hall.......368 B13
st. Glenbrook..........234 E16
st. Hunters Hill.........313 G11
st. Hurlstone Pk.......372 J10
st. Mt Colah............192 A5
st. Mount Druitt......241 F16
st. N Sydney..............K A7
st. N Sydney..............K F8
st. N Sydney...............5 E8
st. N Sydney...............5 G8
st. Pyrmont...............12 F2
st. Redfern................20 D8
st. Strathfield..........371 F2
st. Wentwthvle.........277 A11
st. West Ryde.........281 J14
MT ADELAIDE
st. Darling Point........13 K6
MOUNTAIN
av. Yarramundi.........115 F15
cr. Mt Pritchard.......364 G10
la. Ultimo.................12 J14
st. Engadine............488 D13
st. Epping...............250 F14
st. Ultimo.................12 J15
MOUNTAIN VIEW
av. Glen Alpine.........510 E15
cl. Kurrajong Hl.........55 E5
cl. Vineyard............152 F4
cr. W Pnnant Hl........249 F8
pl. Narellan.............478 B9
rd. Berowra.............133 C16
MOUNTAINVIEW
cr. Penrith...............237 A9
MT ANNAN
dr. Mt Annan...........479 J16
dr. Mt Annan...........509 C2
dr. Mt Annan...........509 E5
MT AUBURN
rd. Auburn..............339 C10
rd. Berala...............339 C10
MOUNTBATTEN
st. Oatley................431 E10
MT CARMEL
pl. Engadine............488 E12
MT DRUITT
pl. Mount Druitt......241 B16
rd. Mount Druitt......271 A3
MOUNTFORD
av. Greystanes.........305 K1
av. Guildford...........337 H4
MOUNTFORT
st. Lalor Park..........245 B13
MT HUON
cct. Glen Alpine.........510 F9
MT IDA
st. Gordon...............254 B5
MT LEWIS
av. Mt Lewis............370 B16
av. Punchbowl.........370 B16
MT MORRIS
la. Woolwich, off Mt Morris St......314 G12
st. Woolwich...........314 H12
MT PLEASANT
av. Burwood............341 J12
av. Frenchs Frst.......256 B2
av. Mona Vale...........199 E2
av. Normanhurst......221 G13
MOUNTSIDE
av. Mt Colah............192 D3
MT SION
pl. Glenbrook..........234 A11
MT STREET
wk. Pyrmont.................8 E16
wk. Pyrmont...............12 E1
MT SUGARLOAF
dr. Glen Alpine.........510 B15
dr. Glen Alpine.........540 B1
MT VERNON
la. Glebe...................12 B15
pde. Blakehurst..........462 D1
rd. Mt Vernon...........331 A16
st. Glebe...................12 A15
MOUNTVIEW
av. Beverly Hills......400 H14
av. Chester Hill........337 K11
av. Doonside...........243 D14
av. Narwee.............400 H14
pl. Bilgola...............169 E8
MT WILLIAM
st. Gordon...............253 G6
MOURNE
cl. Killarney Ht........256 A16
MOUTRIE
pl. Castle Hill...........218 E13
MOVERLY
rd. Kingsford...........407 B7
rd. Maroubra...........407 B7
rd. S Coogee...........407 F7
MOWATT
st. Narellan.............478 G13
MOWBRAY
cl. Castle Hill...........218 J6
pl. Willoughby..........285 H13
rd. Artarmon...........284 J13
rd. Chatswood..........284 J13
rd. Willoughby..........285 F13
rd.w,Chatswd W.........284 D14
rd.w,Lane Cove W......283 F12
st. Prestons.............393 A13
st. Sylvania..............462 D8
wy. Rsemeadow.......540 J3
MOWBRAY PARK
rd. Mowbray Pk.......561 B7
MOWER
pl. S Windsor...........150 J1
MOWLA
av. Jamisontown......266 A3
MOWLE
st. Westmead..........307 G2
MOXHAM
la. Cranebrook, off Moxham St.........207 D9
st. Cranebrook........207 D9
st. N Parramatta.......278 C10
MOXHAMS
rd. Northmead..........277 H6
rd. Winston Hills......277 G5
MOXON
rd. Punchbowl.........399 H7
MOY
cl. Prestons............423 E2
MOYA
cr. Kingsgrove..........401 K11
MOYARTA
st. Hurstville............431 H2
MOYES
st. Marrickville.........373 H14
MOYRAN
pde. Grays Point........491 A16
MOZART
pl. Bonnyrigg Ht......363 E7
pl. Cranebrook........207 G8
st. Seven Hills.........246 D13
MRS MACQUARIE
dr. Frenchs Frst.......256 H2
MRS MACQUARIES
rd. Sydney...................2 F15
MUBO
cr. Holsworthy.........426 C3
MUCCILLO
st. Quakers Hill.......214 F14
MUDGEE
pl. St Clair...............270 E14
MUDIE
pl. Blackett.............241 C4
MUDIES
rd. St Ives...............223 H8
MUELLER
pl. Tregear..............240 F5
wy. Mt Annan...........509 G3
MUIR
pl. St Andrews.........452 A13
pl. Wetherill Pk........304 F13
rd. Chullora.............369 G5
rd. Yagoona............369 G5
MUIRBANK
av. Hunters Hill........313 J12
MUIRFIELD
cr. Glenmore Pk......266 F8
MUJAR
pl. Winmalee...........173 C9
MULAWA
pl. Frenchs Frst.......255 H2
MULBERRY
st. Loftus................489 J10
MULBRING
st. Mosman............317 D9
MULGA
pl. Kirrawee............460 K14
pl. Mcquarie Fd.......454 D1
rd. Oatley...............431 A12
st. N St Marys.........240 C11
st. Punchbowl.........399 K4
MULGARA
pl. Bossley Park.......333 F7
pl. St Helens Park....511 H16
MULGI
st. Blacktown..........274 G8
MULGOA
rd. Glenmore Pk......265 F4
rd. Jamisontown.....236 C15
rd. Mulgoa..............265 B9
rd. Mulgoa..............295 C6
rd. Penrith..............236 C15
rd. Regentville.........265 F4
rd. Wallacia............324 J12
MULGOWRIE
cr. Balgowlah Ht......287 J15
MULGRAVE
rd. Mulgrave............121 G16
MULGRAY
av. Baulkham Hl......247 E10
av. Maroubra...........407 E10
MULHERON
av. Baulkham Hl......247 A12
MULHOLLANDS
rd. Mowbray Pk.......561 D7
rd. Mowbray Pk.......562 A7
rd. Thirlmere...........561 D7
rd. Thirlmere...........562 A7
MULL
pl. St Andrews........481 J2
MULLA
rd. Yagoona............369 C13
MULLANE
av. Baulkham Hl......247 B12
MULLENDERREE
st. Prestons............392 H16
st. Prestons............422 J1
MULLENS
rd. N Richmond.........87 A1
st. Balmain.................7 E12
st. Rozelle..................7 D14
MULLER
av. West Hoxton......392 D5
MULLET
pl. Warriewood.......199 C10
MULLEY
pl. Belrose..............225 H12
MULLIGAN
cl. St Clair..............270 D10
la. St Clair, off Mulligan Cl.........270 C10
st. Bossley Park......334 B9
MULLINGER
la. S Windsor..........120 G14
MULLINS
st. Sydney..................C G10
MULLION
cl. Hornsby Ht........191 H4
MULLOO
la. Cranebrook, off Mulloo Pl..........207 J10
pl. Cranebrook........207 J10
MULLUMBIMBY
av. Hoxton Park.......392 H6
MULQUEENEY
la. Newtown.............17 E12
MULVIHILL
st. West Ryde.........311 F1
MULWARREE
av. Randwick...........376 K11
MULYAN
av. Carlingford.........280 D6
st. Como................460 G8
MUMFORD
rd. Cabramatta W....365 B9
MUNCASTER
pl. Cranebrook........207 F12
MUNDAKAL
av. Kirrawee............490 J6
MUNDAMATTA
st. Villawood...........367 H6
MUNDARA
pl. Narraweena........258 C5
MUNDARDA
pl. St Helens Park....541 G3
MUNDARRAH
st. Clovelly.............377 J13
MUNDAY
pl. Currans Hill........479 H13
st. Warwck Frm......365 J15
MUNDERAH
st. Wahroonga........222 D9
MUNDIN
st. Doonside...........243 C9
MUNDON
pl. W Pnnant Hl.......249 G10
MUNDOWI
rd. Mt Krng-gai........162
MUNDOWIE
pl. Clarmnt Ms........268
MUNDOWY
pl. Bradbury............511
MUNDURRA
pl. Kellyville.............216
MUNDY
st. Emu Plains.........235
MUNEELA
pl. Yowie Bay..........492
MUNGADAL
wy. Airds..................512
MUNGARRA
av. St Ives...............223
pl. W Pnnant Hl.......248
MUNGERIE
rd. Kellyville.............185
MUNMORA
pl. Oxley Park..........240
MUNMORAH
cct. Woodcroft..........243
st. Leumeah............482
MUNMURRA
rd. Riverwood.........400
MUNN
pl. Toongabbie........276
st. Millers Pt...............A
MUNNI
st. Newtown.............17
st. Woolooware.......493
MUNNUMBA
av. Belrose..............226
MUNOORA
st. Seaforth.............287
MUNRO
st. Baulkham Hl......248
st. Canley Vale........366
st. Eastwood...........281
st. Greystanes.........305
st. Lane Cove W......284
st. McMahons Pt.........5
st. Sefton.................338
MUNROE
pl. Hamondvle.........396
MUNROS
la. Glenorie.............128
MUNYANG
st. Heckenberg........364
MURA
la. Baulkham Hl......247
MURABAN
pl. Belrose..............226
rd. Dural.................189
MURCH
pl. Eagle Vale..........481
MURCHISON
st. St Ives...............224
st. Sylvania.............461
MURDOCH
cr. Connells Pt........431
ct. Harringtn Pk.......478
rd. Orangeville.........443
st. Blackett..............241
st. Cremorne...........316
st. Ermington...........310
st. Rozelle...................7
st. Turramurra.........223
MURDOCK
cr. Lugarno.............429
la. Guildford............337
st. Cronulla.............494
st. Guildford............337
MURIEL
av. Epping...............281
av. Rydalmere.........309
la. Hornsby.............191
la. Hornsby.............221
st. Faulconbdg.........171
st. Hornsby.............221
wy. Glenwood..........215
MURNDAL
ct. Wattle Grove......425
MURONGA
pl. Kirrawee............461
MURPHY
av. Liverpool............394
pl. Blackett..............241
st. Blaxland.............233
st. Merrylands W....307

Revesby....398 K16
Minto....482 K1
Minto....483 A1
RPHYS
Croydon, off
Young St....342 E14
RRABIN
Matraville....436 G3
RRALAH
Lane Cove....313 J3
RRALIN
Sylvania....462 B8
RRALONG
Five Dock....342 K11
Mt Colah....162 A15
RRAMI
Caringbah....493 B5
RRANDAH
Camden....507 A4
RRAY
Springwood....201 F1
Wattle Grove....395 J12
Lane Cove W....284 E15
Marrickville....373 E13
Blacktown....274 H5
Beecroft....250 G9
Harbord....288 H1
Pagewood....406 G8
Bronte....377 J8
Camden....477 A16
Campbelltwn....511 K8
Croydon....372 C1
Greenacre....370 E3
Lane Cove W....284 E15
Lidcombe....339 F11
Maroubra....407 B14
Marrickville....374 F11
Merrylands....307 G9
Northmead....277 K7
N Parramatta....278 J14
Pyrmont....12 K6
Russell Lea....343 D5
St Marys....269 K6
Smithfield....335 K8
Sydney....12 K6
Waterloo....20 B15
West Ryde....281 A14
RRAY FARM
Beecroft....249 K11
Carlingford....249 E12
RRAY ISLAND
Sylvania Wtr....462 E11
RRAY JONES
Bnkstn Aprt....397 J6
RRAY PARK
Kenthurst....187 A2
RRAY ROSE
Homebush B....340 G1
RRAYS
Tennyson....57 J7
RRELL
Dural....219 A5
Ashfield....372 K3
RRILLS
Winston Hills....247 K15
RRIVERIE
North Bondi....348 C15
RRONG
La Perouse....436 J12
RROOBAH
Wallacia....324 K14
RRUA
N Turramrra....193 E13
RRUMBA
Castle Hill....217 K8
East Killara....254 K6
RRUMBIDGEE
Sylvania Wtr....462 F13
Bossley Park....333 H6
Heckenberg....364 A15
RRUMBURRAH
Wakeley....334 H14
RTHA
Arndell Park....273 J10
RU
Winmalee....173 A11
Glenmore Pk....266 B11
Glenmore Pk, off
Muru Dr....266 C11
RUBA
Carlingford....279 E3

MURULLA
pl. Airds....511 J15
MURWILLUMBAH
av. Hoxton Park....393 A6
MUSCAT
gr. Glenwood....215 D14
pl. Eschol Park....481 C2
pl. Orchard Hills....268 D9
rd. Warwck Frm....365 K13
MUSCATEL
wy. Orchard Hills....268 F12
MUSCHARRY
rd. Londonderry....148 C10
MUSCIO
st. Colyton....270 C4
MUSCIOS
rd. Glenorie....128 J12
MUSGRAVE
av. Centnnial Pk....22 B16
av. Queens Park....22 B16
cr. Fairfield W....335 E9
pl. Ruse....512 F6
st. Mosman....316 H13
st. Turramurra....223 E12
MUSGROVE
cr. Doonside....243 E8
MUSSELBURGH
cl. Glenmore Pk....266 E10
MUSSON
la. Richmond....118 G4
MUSTANG
av. St Clair....270 F11
dr. Raby....451 D16
MUSTON
la. Sutherland, off
Flora St....490 E3
pl. Glenhaven....187 K16
st. Mosman....317 C7
MUSWELLBROOK
rd. Hoxton Park....392 G9
st. Glenwood....245 G1
MUTCH
av. Kyeemagh....404 A14
MUTTAMA
av. Kirrawee....491 B6
rd. Artarmon....284 K13
st. Wahroonga....251 J1
MUTUAL
dr. Old Tngabbie....277 C7
rd. Mortdale....431 A5
MYAHGAH
mw. Mosman, off
Vista St....317 A6
rd. Mosman....317 A7
MYALL
av. Vaucluse....348 H1
av. Wahroonga....222 E11
cr. Strathfield....340 H12
pl. Leumeah....482 F14
rd. Casula....424 C1
rd. Mt Colah....192 D5
st. Auburn....338 K11
st. Belmore....371 F16
st. Cabramatta....365 H8
st. Concord W....311 F16
st. Doonside....243 D15
st. Merrylands....307 E16
st. Oatley....430 K13
st. Punchbowl....400 A3
MYALLIE
av. Baulkham Hl....247 C16
MYALORA
st. Russell Lea....343 C6
MYAMBA
rd. Collaroy....229 A16
MYCUMBENE
av. E Lindfield....255 A15
MYDDLETON
av. Fairfield....336 C8
MYDELL
st. Kingsgrove....401 F9
MYEE
av. Strathfield....340 J15
cr. Baulkham Hl....246 F11
cr. Lane Cove W....313 F3
rd. Mcquarie Fd....453 H2
st. Lakemba....401 A3
st. Merrylands....307 H15
MYERLA
cr. Connells Pt....431 H16
MYERS
st. Roselands....401 D5

st. Sans Souci....463 A1
MYLER
st. Five Dock....342 G9
MYLES
pl. Minto....452 K15
MYNAH
cl. St Clair....270 E12
MYOLA
rd. Newport....169 J12
MYOORA
rd. Terrey Hills....195 J14
st. Pymble....253 A2
st. Seven Hills....245 K13
MYORA
cl. Green Valley....363 H10
MYPOLONGA
av. Gymea Bay....491 H10
MYRA
av. Ryde....282 B15
la. Dulwich Hill....373 C11
pl. Ingleburn....453 C10
pl. Oatley....431 B15
rd. Dulwich Hill....373 C11
st. Frenchs Frst....257 B4
st. Plumpton....242 C7
st. Wahroonga....222 A4
MYRNA
rd. Strathfield....341 A15
MYRTLE
ct. Voyager Pt....427 C4
gr. Bella Vista....246 G6
la. Chippendale....18 H2
la. Stanmore....16 G8
la.w,Stanmore....16 E7
pl. St Ives....224 B10
rd. Bankstown....369 G14
rd. Clarmnt Ms....268 J3
rd. Greenfld Pk....334 E13
rd. Prairiewood....334 E13
st. Botany....405 H9
st. Chippendale....18 H2
st. Chippendale....19 A3
st. Crows Nest....5 D1
st. Granville....308 G16
st. Kensington....376 B12
st. Leichhardt....15 E3
st. Loftus....489 J13
st. Marrickville....374 A15
st. Minto Ht....483 F7
st. Normanhurst....221 E13
st. N Balgowlah....287 F6
st. N Sydney....5 D1
st. Oatley....430 K12
st. Oatley....431 A13
st. Pagewood....405 H9
st. Prestons....393 K14
st. Prospect....274 G11
st. Rydalmere....309 G1
st. Stanmore....16 E8
MYRTLE CREEK
av. Tahmoor....566 B8
MYRTUS
cr. Bidwill....211 F13
MYSON
dr. Cherrybrook....219 E13
MYUNA
cl. Westleigh....220 E7
cr. Seven Hills....275 C7
pl. Camden S....507 C10
pl. Port Hacking....522 H2
rd. Dover Ht....348 F10

N

NAALONG
pl. Cranebrook....207 H11
NABIAC
av. Belrose....225 H12
av. Gymea Bay....491 G8
pl. Westleigh....220 G10
NABILLA
rd. Palm Beach....139 G2
NADA
st. Old Tngabbie....276 K7
NADENE
pl. Pymble....253 C7
NADER
pl. Horngsea Pk....392 E16
NADIA
pl. Guildford....338 B7

NADIE
pl. Kings Lngly....245 K7
NADINE
cl. Cherrybrook....219 J4
NADZAB
rd. Holsworthy....426 F9
NAGLE
av. Springwood....172 E12
cl. Menai....458 H6
pl. N Turramrra....193 F12
st. Liverpool....395 C7
st. Maroubra....406 K11
wy. Quakers Hill....214 B12
NAILON
pl. Mona Vale....199 C1
NAIRANA
dr. Marayong....244 B4
NAIRN
st. Kingsgrove....402 B9
NAIROBI
pl. Toongabbie....275 E13
NALAURA
cl. Beecroft....250 B6
NALLADA
pl. Beecroft....250 B12
rd. Alfords Point....429 C14
NALONG
st. St Clair....270 F10
NALYA
av. Baulkham Hl....246 K7
la. Berowra Ht....132 J5
rd. Berowra Ht....132 J6
rd. Narraweena....258 B1
NAMAN
cl. Bossley Park....334 B5
NAMARA
pl. Engadine....518 G6
NAMATJIRA
av. Londonderry....148 C9
cl. Eagle Vale....481 A10
pl. Chifley....437 B9
pwy.Winmalee....172 K10
NAMBA
rd. Duffys Frst....194 H4
NAMBOUR
pl. Engadine....489 E9
NAMBRUK
cl. Cranebrook....207 E7
NAMBUCCA
pl. Clarmnt Ms....268 K1
pl. Padstow Ht....429 G8
rd. Terrey Hills....196 C5
st. Ruse....512 E6
st. Turramurra....223 C8
NAMBUCCA HEADS
cr. Hoxton Park....392 H9
NAMBUNG
pl. Bow Bowing....452 D13
NAME
la. Dulwich Hill....373 E7
NAMOI
ct. Wattle Grove....395 H13
la. Georges Hall, off
Surrey Av....368 B16
pl. E Lindfield....255 B14
pl. Ruse....512 B9
pl. Sylvania Wtr....462 D10
pl. Toongabbie....275 F10
rd. Matraville....436 K1
rd. Northbridge....316 B1
st. Greystanes....305 K4
st. N Epping....251 E10
NAMONA
st. N Narrabeen....199 A14
NAMUR
st. S Granville....338 G5
NANBAREE
rd. Ryde....282 E16
NANCARROW
av. Ryde....311 F4
la. Ryde....311 F4
NANCE
av. Cabramatta....365 D9
la. Croydon Pk....372 B6
NANCY
pl. Ambarvale....510 F15
pl. Galston....159 H8
st. North Bondi....348 D15
st. Pendle Hill....306 C1
st. St Marys....269 J3

NANCYE
st. Randwick....377 C16
NANDEWAR
pl. Airds....512 A10
NANDI
av. Frenchs Frst....256 J4
NANDINA
tce. Avalon....139 K15
NANETTE
pl. Castle Hill....217 H11
NANGANA
rd. Bayview....168 J14
NANGAR
pl. Emu Plains....235 A8
st. Fairfield W....335 E12
NANNA GLEN
rd. Hoxton Park....392 J9
NANOWIE
av. Wahroonga....221 J12
st. Narwee....400 H13
NANT
st. Bnksmeadw....436 C1
NAOI
pl. Glenmore Pk....266 A11
NAOLI
la. St Clair, off
Naoli Pl....269 G14
pl. St Clair....269 G13
NAOMI
ct. Cherrybrook....219 K4
st.n, Winston Hills....248 A16
st.s, Northmead....278 A1
NAPIER
av. Emu Plains....235 K8
av. Lurnea....394 C13
cr. North Ryde....282 G7
la. Emu Plains, off
Napier St....235 K8
pl. Bossley Park....334 C8
pl. Ingleburn....453 F13
st. Canterbury....372 E16
st. Dover Ht....348 F11
st. Drummoyne....343 K1
st. Engadine....518 G6
st. Lindfield....284 B3
st. Malabar....437 E6
st. Mays Hill....307 J5
st. N Strathfield....341 F7
st. N Sydney....K B4
st. N Sydney....5 E6
st. Paddington....4 F15
st. Parramatta....307 J5
st. Petersham....15 G15
st. Rooty Hill....242 C14
NAPOLEON
rd. Greenacre....370 D15
st. Mascot....405 F4
st. Riverwood....400 D14
st. Rosebery....405 F4
st. Rozelle....7 A14
st. Sans Souci....463 C5
st. Sydney....A C13
st. Sydney....1 D15
NAPOLI
rd. Minto Ht....484 B7
st. Padstow....399 A9
st. Revesby....399 A9
NAPPER
av. Riverwood....400 C16
st. S Coogee....407 H5
NAPULYA
st. Duffys Frst....165 A14
NAPUNYAH
wy. St Clair....270 A16
NARA
pl. St Ives....224 D7
NARABANG
wy. Belrose....225 H1
NARAMBI
cl. Berowra Ht....132 J10
NARANG
pl. St Marys....239 G10
NARANGA
av. Engadine....518 G5
NARANGANAH
av. Gymea Bay....491 F12
NARANGHI
av. Telopea....279 E9
st. Busby....363 G13
NARANI
cr. Earlwood....402 D2
cr. Northbridge....286 C16

NARCISSUS
av. Quakers Hill 243 D3
NARDANGO
rd. Bradbury............511 C16
NARDOO
rd. Willoughby.........285 D13
st. Ingleburn...........453 B7
st. Ingleburn...........453 C6
wy. Mt Annan...........479 C14
NARDU
la. S Penrith, off Nardu Pl 266 H7
pl. S Penrith............266 H7
NAREE
av. Glenwood 245 E2
rd. Frenchs Frst.......256 D4
NAREEN
pde. N Narrabeen.......228 K1
NARELLAN
cr. Bonnyrigg Ht......363 C7
rd. Blairmount.........510 C1
rd. Campbelltwn.......510 C1
rd. Currans Hill........479 B10
rd. Mt Annan...........479 B10
rd. Narellan.............478 J9
rd. Narellan Vale......478 J9
rd. Smeaton Gra......479 B10
NARELLE
av. Castle Hill...........248 C2
av. Pymble..............253 G4
av.e, Castle Hill.........248 C3
cr. Greenacre..........370 C8
pl. Silverdale...........354 A11
st. Mount Druitt.......271 A3
st. North Bondi.......348 D14
st. N Epping............251 D10
NARENA
cl. Beecroft.............250 F3
NARETHA
la. Green Valley.......363 F10
NARGONG
rd. Allambie Ht........257 G13
NARIEL
pl. Peakhurst...........430 D9
st. St Marys............239 G13
NARLA
rd. Bayview.............168 F12
NAROO
rd. Terrey Hills.........196 G5
NAROOMA
av. S Penrith............266 F6
cl. Panania..............428 G3
dr. Prestons.............393 C16
pl. Gymea Bay.........491 C9
rd. Northbridge.......286 C15
NARRABEEN
rd. Leumeah............482 F12
st. Narrabeen...........229 A5
NARRABEEN PARK
pde. Mona Vale..........199 D9
pde. N Narrabeen.......199 D14
pde. Warriewood.......199 D14
NARRABRI
st. Quakers Hill.......243 K3
NARRABURRA
cl. Mt Colah............191 K6
NARRAGA
pl. Gymea Bay.........491 D8
NARRAMORE
st. Kingsgrove.........402 A14
NARRAN
ct. Woodcroft..........243 H10
pl. Glenmore Pk......266 C6
NARROMINE
pl. Bonnyrigg Ht......363 C5
wy. Mcquarie Pk.......282 E4
NARROW
la. Paddington, off Broughton St.......13 D15
NARROY
rd. N Narrabeen.......228 J1
NARRUN
cr. Dundas..............279 F11
NARRYNA
pl. Glen Alpine........510 B16
NARTEE
pl. Wilberforce..........92 B1
NARVA
pl. Seven Hills.........275 G6
NARWEE
av. Narwee.............400 H14
NASH
la. Carramar...........366 H3
pl. Blacktown...........244 B12
pl. Currans Hill.........479 G13
pl. North Ryde.........283 B12
st. S Penrith............267 A4
NASHS
la. Concord.............312 A15
NASSAU
cl. Bossley Park......333 K6
NATAL
pl. Seven Hills.........275 H4
NATALIE
cl. Casula................423 K2
cl. Hornsby Ht.........191 G3
cr. Fairfield W..........335 E12
ct. Glenhaven..........218 D2
pl. Oakhurst............242 D2
NATASHA
pl. Picton................561 G3
NATCHEZ
cr. Greenfld Pk.........333 K15
NATHAN
cr. Dean Park..........212 H15
la. Willoughby..........285 F15
la. Mosman, off Harbour St..........316 K6
la. Mosman, off Vista St..............316 K6
pl. Engadine............518 E3
st. Coogee..............377 E15
st. Mulgoa...............296 F1
NATHANIEL
pde. Kings Lngly........245 E7
NATHIA
st. Glenwood...........215 B16
NATIONAL
av. Loftus.................490 A12
la. Rozelle..................7 A14
st. Cabramatta..........365 K10
st. Leichhardt.............15 F4
st. Rozelle....................7 A14
st. Warwck Frm 365 J16
NATIONAL PARK
rd. Holsworthy.........426 H6
NATTAI
cl. Thornleigh..........221 B6
pl. Banksia...............403 H12
st. Couridjah............564 G13
st. Couridjah............565 A14
st. Loftus.................490 B10
st. Ruse...................512 B9
st. Seven Hills.........246 C13
NATUNA
pl. Lethbrdg Pk........240 K1
st. N Narrabeen.......198 J13
NAUGHTON
av. Lansdowne.........367 D7
st. Greenacre..........370 G7
NAURU
cr. Lethbrdg Pk........240 J1
NAVAHO
st. Bossley Park......334 A10
NAVAJO
cl. Stanhpe Gdn......215 D11
NAVINS
la. Zetland, off Elizabeth St.........375 H10
NAYLA
cl. Bardwell Vy........403 C7
NAYLOR
pl. Ingleburn...........453 A11
NEA
cl. Glenmore Pk......266 C8
st. Chatswood.........284 J12
NEAGLE
la. Colyton, off Neagle St...........270 E7
st. Colyton..............270 E7
NEAL
pl. Appin..................569 F13
pl. Minto..................482 H8
NEALE
av. Cherrybrook.......219 E15
av. Forestville..........256 A11
st. Belmore..............371 C13
st. St Marys.............269 E1
wy. Berrilee..............131 E12
NEALES
la. Penrith................237 A10
NEBO
pl. Cartwright..........394 C5
NEBULA
gln. N St Marys.........239 K7
NECROPOLIS
cct. Rookwood.........340 A11
dr. Rookwood..........339 K10
dr. Rookwood..........340 B11
dr. Rookwood..........340 C11
NEEDLEBRUSH
cl. Alfords Point......459 B1
NEEDLEWOOD
cl. Rouse Hill...........185 A7
gr. Padstow Ht........429 D8
NEENAN
pl. Erskine Park.......270 H16
NEERIM
cl. Berowra.............133 E9
rd. Castle Cove........285 J3
NEERINI
av. Smithfield..........336 A8
NEETA
av. Cmbrdg Pk.........238 C8
NEEWORRA
rd. Northbridge.......286 D15
NEICH
pde. Burwood............342 A11
rd. Glenorie.............126 J1
rd. Maraylya............124 G1
NEICHS
la. Concord.............342 B10
NEIL
pl. Canley Ht...........365 D1
st. Bundeena............524 B8
st. Epping................280 F2
st. Holroyd..............307 H11
st. Hornsby..............221 E6
st. Merrylands..........307 H11
st. North Ryde.........283 A12
NEILD
av. Darlinghurst..........13 B12
av. Paddington...........13 B12
NEILSON
av. Peakhurst...........430 G2
cl. Glenmore Pk.......265 J6
cr. Bligh Park..........150 G8
st. Granville............308 G16
wy. Blackett.............241 B2
NEIRBO
av. Hurstville...........431 J6
NEIWAND
av. Kellyville.............215 H6
NELL
pl. Ambarvale..........511 A14
NELLA
st. Padstow.............429 F4
NELLA DAN
av. Tregear..............240 C5
NELLELLA
st. Blakehurst..........432 B14
NELLIE
st. Lalor Park...........245 D9
NELLIE STEWART
dr. Doonside............243 D5
NELLIGEN
cl. Prestons.............393 C14
NELLO
pl. Wetherill Pk........334 C4
NELSON
av. Belmore..............401 G3
av. Bronte................378 A9
av. Padstow.............399 C9
la. Annandale.............11 C14
la. Waterloo...............19 E11
la. Woollahra..............22 C3
pde. Hunters Hill........314 C14
pl. Petersham.............15 G11
rd. Box Hill..............184 D2
rd. Cattai....................94 G3
rd. Earlwood.............403 B2
rd. Ingleburn.............423 A12
rd. Killara.................254 D13
rd. Lindfield..............254 E15
rd. Nelson.................154 F16
rd. N Strathfield........341 F7
rd. Yennora..............337 A9
st. Annandale..............17 A3
st. Bondi Jctn.............22 D5
st. Chatswood..........284 H13
st. Dulwich Hill.........373 E7
st. Engadine.............488 J14
st. Fairfield...............336 C11
st. Fairfield Ht..........336 A11
st. Gladesville..........312 H4
st. Gordon...............253 K7
st. Kenthurst............158 B15
st. Minto..................452 G15
st. Minto..................452 J14
st. Mount Druitt........271 B4
st. Penshurst...........431 D5
st. Randwick.............407 C1
st. Riverstone..........182 G13
st. Rozelle.....................7 A13
st. Sans Souci...........462 J4
st. Thornleigh...........221 C11
st. Turrella...............403 F5
st. Woollahra..............22 C3
NEMBA
st. Hunters Hill.........313 F10
NEMESIA
av. Caringbah...........493 A12
st. Greystanes..........305 K11
NENAGH
st. North Manly.......258 C16
NENTOURA
pl. Forestville...........255 G10
pl. N Turramrra........193 D15
NEOSHO
wy. Maroubra............407 D13
NEOTSFIELD
av. Dangar I...............76 J7
NEPEAN
av. Camden..............507 B7
av. Normanhurst.......221 F12
av. Penrith................236 A10
pl. Sylvania Wtr........462 E10
st. Campbelltwn.......512 A8
st. Cranebrook.........206 J12
st. Douglas Park......568 C8
st. Emu Plains..........235 E14
st. Fairfield W...........335 C14
st.s, Leonay...............235 C16
wy. Yarramundi.........145 F9
NEPEAN GARDENS
pl. Glenbrook...........264 G1
NEPEAN GORGE
dr. Mulgoa...............323 K1
NEPEAN TOWERS
av. Glen Alpine.........510 B16
NEPTUNE
cr. Bligh Park...........150 E6
cr. Green Valley........363 A12
pl. W Pnnant Hl........249 B8
rd. Newport..............169 J8
st. Coogee...............407 H3
st. Dundas Vy..........280 A8
st. Padstow.............429 A5
st. Padstow.............429 B5
st. Raby...................451 F16
st. Revesby..............428 J5
NERADA
st. Blacktown...........274 C2
NERANG
av. Terrey Hills.........196 D5
cct. S Penrith............266 H6
cl. W Pnnant Hl.........249 J1
la. Cronulla, off Nerang Rd 494 A10
rd. Cronulla..............494 A10
st. Ryde...................282 G14
st. Wahroonga.........222 B16
tce. Yellow Rock........204 K2
NEREID
rd. Cranebrook.........207 E10
NERI
pl. Jamisontown.......266 A4
NERIBA
cr. Whalan...............240 H8
NERIDA
pl. Shalvey...............210 H13
rd. Kareela...............461 E10
NERIDAH
av. Belrose...............226 B10
av. Mt Colah.............192 D3
st. Chatswood..........285 A10
NERINE
wy. Bidwill.................211 D13
NERINGAH
av.n, Wahroonga........222 D6
av.s, Wahroonga........222 C7
NERLI
st. Abbotsbury.........333 C11
wy. Claymore............481 B11
NERRIGA
ct. Prestons.............392 K13
NESBITT
pl. Prairiewood........335 A7
st. Woolmloo..............4
NESS
av. Dulwich Hill........373
pl. Winston Hills......277
NESTOR
la. Lewisham.............15
st. Winston Hills......277
NET
rd. Avalon................140
NETHERBY
st. Wahroonga.........221
NETHERBYES
wy. Narellan Vale......508
NETHERCOTE
cl. Prestons.............393
cl. Prestons.............423
NETHERTON
av. St Clair...............269
NETTLETON
av. Riverwood..........400
NETTLE TREE
pl. Casula.................423
NEUTRAL
av. Birrong...............369
rd. Hornsby..............221
st. N Sydney................5
NEVADA
av. Colyton..............270
cr. Punchbowl..........399
NEVELL
la. Cranebrook, off Nevell Pl............207
pl. Cranebrook.........207
NEVERFAIL
pl. Oatley.................461
NEVERTIRE
pl. Kenthurst............156
NEVIL
wy. Casula................424
NEVILLE
ct. Castle Hill............248
la. Marrickville...........16
la. Bankstown, off Greenfield Pde....399
rd. Riverstone...........182
st. Bass Hill..............368
st. Colyton...............270
st. Lidcombe............339
st. Marayong............244
st. Marrickville............16
st. Marrickville..........373
st. N Willghby...........285
st. Oatley.................431
st. Ryde...................282
st. Smithfield............335
st. Yagoona..............368
NEVIN
cl. Menai.................459
NEVIS
cr. Seven Hills..........275
pl. Castle Hill............218
NEVORIE
cr. Maroubra............406
NEW
la. Mosman..............317
pl. Narellan Vale......508
rd. Ingleburn............422
st. Ashfield..............372
st. Auburn...............339
st. Balgowlah............287
st. Balgowlah Ht.......287
st. Bondi..................377
st. Burwood..............342
st. Longueville..........314
st. N Parramatta.......278
st. Windsor..............121
st.e, Lidcombe...........339
st.w, Balgowlah.........287
st.w, Balgowlah Ht......287
st.w, Clontarf.............287
st.w, Lidcombe...........339
NEWARK
cr. Lindfield..............284
pl. St Clair...............270
NEW BEACH
rd. Darling Point.........13
NEWBERY
la. Panania, off Tower St...........428
NEWBIGIN
cl. North Ryde.........283

BOLT
Wetherill Pk 334 F5
BRIDGE
Glenbrook 264 G1
Chipping Ntn 396 B6
Liverpool 395 E5
Moorebank 396 B6
BURY
Eagle Vale 480 K10
BY
Collaroy Plat 228 F12
Oakhurst 242 A4
CAMBRIDGE
Fairfield W 335 D12
CANTERBURY
Dulwich Hill 373 A10
Hurlstone Pk 373 A10
Lewisham 15 A15
Petersham 15 A15
CASTLE
Five Dock 342 J8
Rose Bay 348 B11
Wakeley 334 H15
COMBE
Lurnea 394 D11
Toongabbie 276 G5
Maianbar 522 K9
Paddington 21 D3
Sans Souci 433 B16
EENA
Avalon 140 D10
ELL
Frenchs Frst 256 J4
ENGLAND
Kingsgrove 401 G14
Castle Hill 217 H7
EY
Padstow 399 D13
Padstow, off Newey Av 399 D13
FARM
W Pnnant Hl 219 J16
HAM
Cmbrdg Gdn 237 G2
Chipping Ntn 366 G13
HAVEN
Blacktown 274 G5
St Ives 224 B12
ILLAWARRA
Barden Rdg 487 D12
Bexley North 402 E10
Lucas Ht 487 D12
INGTON
Newington 310 B14
Marrickville 16 A13
Petersham 16 A13
Silverwater 310 B9
JERSEY
Five Dock 343 B11
JERUSALEM
Oakdale 500 J3
LAND
Milperra 397 D10
Queens Park 22 G12
Engadine 489 D13
Bondi Jctn 377 C6
Queens Park 22 F12
Woollahra 377 C6
LANDS
Wollstncraft 5 A1
Baulkham Hl 247 G4
Wollstncraft 315 E9
LEAF
Wrrngtn Dns 237 J4
LINE
Castle Hill 218 K4
Cherrybrook 219 A6
Dural 189 A16
Glenhaven 218 K4
W Pnnant Hl 249 H1
LYN
St Ives 224 H10
McLEAN
Edgecliff 13 H11
MAN
Newtown 17 G14
Glenorie 95 G9
Minto Ht 483 D9
Bass Hill 368 C6
Blacktown 274 C2
Merrylands 307 F13
Mortdale 431 B7

st. Newtown 17 F13
NEWMARCH
pl. Bligh Park 150 C6
NEWMEN
cl. Wetherill Pk 334 E4
NEWMOON
pl. St Clair 270 C13
NEWNES
cl. Glenwood 245 F1
NEWNHAM
st. Dean Park 212 F15
NEW NORTH ROCKS
rd. North Rocks 249 A16
NEW ORLEANS
cr. Maroubra 407 D14
NEWPORT
cl. Woodbine 481 H11
pl. Oatlands 279 B13
rd. Yellow Rock 204 C1
st. Cmbrdg Pk 237 J8
NEWRY
pl. Hinchinbrk 392 K2
pl. Quakers Hill 244 A3
wy. Wentwthvle, off Ferndale Cl 277 D11
NEWS
rd. Werombi 443 A12
NEWSOME
la. Merrylands 307 D7
NEW SOUTH HEAD
rd. Bellevue Hill 347 E10
rd. Double Bay 14 B11
rd. Edgecliff 13 F9
rd. Point Piper 14 B11
rd. Rose Bay 348 A10
rd. Vaucluse 348 D5
NEWSTAN
pl. Cartwright 394 C4
NEWTIMBER
cct. St Clair 270 D9
NEWTON
av. Richmond 119 K6
cl. Liberty Gr 311 B11
la. Alexandria 18 F13
la. Sydney C D4
la. Mosman, off Medusa St 287 A16
pde. Forestville 256 A8
rd. Blacktown 274 B1
rd. Strathfield 341 A15
rd. Wetherill Pk 333 G3
st. Alexandria 18 E13
st. Guildford W 306 J16
st. Little Bay 437 G15
st. N Epping 251 G10
st.n, Silverwater 309 D12
st.s, Auburn 309 D13
wy. Winmalee 173 H8
NEWTOWN
rd. Glenfield 424 C13
NEW YORK
st. Granville 308 F14
NEW ZEALAND
st. Parramatta 308 G2
NEY
st. Mascot 405 H6
st. Sans Souci 463 C4
NIANBILLA
pl. Frenchs Frst 255 H2
NIANGALA
cl. Belrose 195 J16
pl. Frenchs Frst 256 F1
NIANGLA
pl. Carlingford 279 F4
NIARA
st. Ryde 282 F16
NIAS
pl. Schofields 183 A16
NIBLICK
av. Roseville 285 C1
cr. Oatlands 279 B11
st. Arncliffe 403 J10
st. North Bondi 348 C16
NIBLO
st. Doonside 243 D9
NICE
pl. Seven Hills 275 H5
NICHOL
pde. Strathfield 341 F14
NICHOLAS
av. Campsie 372 A16
av. Concord 342 B6

av. Forestville 256 B10
cl. Bella Vista 246 F7
cl. Bonnyrigg 364 B7
cr. Cecil Hills 362 K5
cr. Normanhurst 221 J12
st. Blacktown 274 E4
st. Lidcombe 340 A5
st. N Sydney 6 A8
NICHOLI
pl. Alfords Point 459 A3
pl. Cherrybrook 219 D7
st. Kellyville 215 B1
NICHOLII
pl. Kenthurst 156 G16
pl. Mcquarie Fd 454 D3
NICHOLLS
av. Haberfield 373 D1
pde. Enmore 16 F13
st. Warwck Frm 365 G14
wy. Minto 482 H5
NICHOLS
av. Beverly Hills 401 A15
av. Revesby 398 F13
pde. Mt Riverview 234 E2
pl. Kingswood 237 F10
st. Surry Hills 4 D16
NICHOLSON
av. Leumeah 482 A16
av. St Ives 254 D4
av. Thornleigh 220 H10
cr. Kings Lngly 245 H7
la. Wollstncraft, off Nicholson St 315 F7
pde. Cronulla 493 J15
pl. Windsor Dn 180 H4
pl. St Leonards, off Cristie St 315 D5
pl. Crows Nest, off Hume St 315 F7
pl. Wollstncraft, off Hume St 315 F7
st. Balmain East 8 F7
st. Burwood 341 G16
st. Chatswood 284 K8
st. North Manly 258 B13
st. Penshurst 431 B1
st. St Leonards 315 E6
st. Strathfield 341 G16
st. Tempe 404 A3
st. Wollstncraft 315 E6
st. Woolmloo 4 G3
NICKLEBY
wy. Ambarvale 510 K16
NICKSON
la. Surry Hills 20 C5
st. Surry Hills 20 B6
NICOBAR
st. Kings Park 244 K3
NICOL
av. Maroubra 407 F10
la. Berala 339 C12
la. Maroubra 407 F10
la. Northbridge 286 A14
pl. Hinchinbrk 362 J15
pl. Minchinbury 272 C10
NICOLAIDIS
cr. Rooty Hill 272 A3
NICOLE
pl. Winmalee 173 D5
NICOLL
av. Earlwood 402 G3
av. Ryde 311 K1
la. Burwood 342 A11
la. Ryde, off Lee Av 311 K1
st. Roselands 400 K5
NICOLSON
cct. Menai 458 G14
NIELA
gr. Baulkham Hl 246 F12
NIELD
av. Balgowlah 287 H10
av. Greenwich 315 A5
av. Rodd Point 343 E8
NIELSEN
av. Carlton 432 J8
NIEMUR
rd. St Marys 239 H2
NIEUPORT
av. Milperra 397 E12
NIGEL
pl. Mcquarie Fd 424 A15
pl. Padstow 399 F15

pl. Rooty Hill 271 K4
NIGEL LOVE
cr. Mascot 405 A10
NIGER
pl. Kearns 481 C1
NIGHTINGALE
dr. Blaxland 233 G9
sq. Glossodia 59 G4
NIGHTMIST
gr. St Clair 270 D15
la. St Clair, off Nightmist Gr 270 E15
NILAND
cr. Blackett 241 B2
pl. Edensor Pk 363 J3
wy. Casula 424 G2
NILE
av. Seven Hills 275 F7
cl. Marsfield 251 K13
pl. Kearns 481 A1
pl. St Clair 270 B9
st. Fairfield Ht 335 H10
NILLERA
av. Terrey Hills 196 C6
NILSON
av. Hillsdale 406 F15
NILSSON
la. Botany 405 F11
NIMBEY
av. Narraweena 258 B6
NIMBIN
av. Hoxton Park 393 B7
pl. Yarrawarrah 489 E14
st. N Balgowlah 287 C4
NIMBRIN
st. Turramurra 252 D4
NIMOOLA
rd. Engadine 489 D9
NIMROD
pl. Tregear 240 E4
st. Darlinghurst 4 H10
NINA
pl. Kurrajong Ht 53 K7
pl. Oakhurst 241 H1
st. Revesby 398 K12
NINDI
cr. Glenmore Pk 266 C6
NINETEENTH
av. Hoxton Park 392 G7
st. Warragamba 353 E9
NINEVEH
cr. Greenfld Pk 334 A15
NINNIS
st. Leumeah 482 H11
NINTH
av. Austral 391 A10
av. Belfield 371 H13
av. Campsie 371 H13
av. Jannali 461 A12
av. Llandilo 207 K8
av.n, Loftus 490 A8
av.s, Loftus 489 H11
rd. Berkshire Pk 180 C10
st. Mascot 405 A7
st. Warragamba 353 F5
NIOBE
la. Turramurra 252 E1
NIOKA
pl. Bankstown 369 H13
pl. Caringbah 492 F6
pl. St Ives Ch 223 K4
rd. Narrabeen 228 H7
rd. Penrith 237 C3
st. Gladesville 312 F8
NIPIGON
rd. Seven Hills 275 G6
NIRIMBA
av. Narwee 400 G13
av. N Epping 251 E9
cr. Heathcote 518 J9
dr. Quakers Hill 213 H12
dr. Schofields 213 H12
NIRRANDA
st. Concord W 341 F1
NIRVANA
st. Pendle Hill 276 E12
NITH
pl. St Andrews 451 J14
NITHDALE
st. Pymble 223 D15
NITHSDALE
la. Sydney F B5

la. Sydney F D4
st. Sydney F C5
st. Sydney 3 J11
NIX
av. Malabar 437 F7
NIXON
av. Ashfield 372 H2
la. Strathfield 341 J11
pl. Bonnet Bay 460 B8
pl. Cherrybrook 219 G6
rd. Thirlmere 562 B14
st. Emu Plains 235 E9
st. Glenwood 215 J14
NOAKES
pde. Lalor Park 245 F13
NOBBS
la. Surry Hills 20 D5
rd. Yagoona 369 A9
st. S Granville 338 F2
st. Surry Hills 20 D4
NOBEL
pl. Castle Hill 217 K13
pl. Winston Hills 277 D5
NOBLE
av. Greenacre 370 B10
av. Mt Lewis 370 A16
av. Punchbowl 370 A16
av. Strathfield 371 C4
cl. Kings Lngly 245 D7
cl. Menai 458 G8
la. St Clair, off Noble Pl 269 K15
pl. St Clair 269 K15
pl. Telopea 279 F9
st. Allawah 432 D7
st. Canley Vale 366 F2
st. Concord 342 A2
st. Five Dock 343 C8
st. Hornsby 221 E4
st. Mosman 316 K8
st. Rodd Point 343 C8
wy. Rouse Hill 184 J7
NOCK
la. Mosman, off Avenue Rd 317 A9
NOCKOLDS
av. Punchbowl 370 A16
NODDY
pl. Hinchinbrk 363 F16
NOEL
st. Georges Hall 367 H14
st. Marayong 244 D11
NOELA
pl. Oxley Park 270 D2
NOELENE
st. Fairfield W 335 G11
NOELINE
av. Mcquarie Fd 454 B2
st. Hurstville 401 G16
NOFFS
pl. Bonnyrigg Ht 363 F6
NOLA
la. Roseville, off Nola Rd 284 G6
pl. Baulkham Hl 247 D1
rd. Roseville 284 G5
st. Marsfield 282 C4
NOLAN
av. Clovelly 377 G11
av. Engadine 518 K1
cr. Naremburn 315 D2
cr. Westmead 307 F2
pl. Balgowlah Ht 287 J14
pl. Mt Pritchard 364 K10
pl. Seven Hills 245 K14
st. Casula 424 E4
NOLLAND
pl. Kenthurst 156 K8
NOLLANDS
rd. Fiddletown 129 J4
NOLLER
pde. Parramatta 308 G4
NOMAD
gr. St Clair 270 E15
pl. Raby 481 H2
NOOAL
st. Newport 169 E10
NOOK
av. Neutral Bay 6 A5
la. Neutral Bay 6 A5
la. West Ryde 281 F16
pl. Leonay 235 A16

NOOLA
av. Kellyville 216 J8
NOOLINGA
rd. Bayview 168 J10
NOONAN
rd. Ingleburn 453 B1
NOONBINNA
cl. Northbridge 286 A14
cr. Northbridge 286 B14
NOONGAH
pl. Canada Bay 342 E8
st. Bargo 567 C7
NOORA
av. Little Bay 437 A10
pl. Marayong 244 C2
st. Lidcombe 339 H5
NOORAL
st. Bargo 567 E8
NOORONG
av. Frenchs Frst 256 G1
cl. Baulkham Hl 247 C5
NORA
ct. Rouse Hill 184 K9
ct. Rouse Hill 185 A9
NORBAR
la. Kingsford 376 J16
NORE
pl. Minto 482 K4
NOREE
pl. Wrrngtn Dns 238 A3
NORFOLK
av. Beverly Hills 401 D15
av. Collaroy 229 A16
av. Fairfield W 335 B10
la. Paddington 13 E15
la. Matraville, off Franklin St. 436 J2
pde. Matraville 436 J2
pl. Carlingford 279 B3
pl. Miranda 492 D6
pl. N Richmond 87 H13
rd. Cmbrdg Pk 237 H10
rd. Epping 251 D14
rd. Greenacre 370 E6
rd. Longueville 314 B9
rd. N Epping 251 D10
st. Blacktown 244 C13
st. Ingleburn 453 C6
st. Killara 253 G11
st. Liverpool 395 C5
st. Mount Druitt 240 K16
st. Newtown 17 G14
st. Paddington 13 E15
swy. Liverpool 395 C5
wy. North Ryde 282 J13
NORIKA
pl. Toongabbie 276 E10
NORMA
av. Belmore 401 F5
av. Eastwood 281 G7
cl. Bargo 567 A2
cr. Cheltenham 250 K7
pl. Merrylands 307 E15
rd. Palm Beach 140 C4
NORMAC
rd. Girraween 276 A11
st. Roseville Ch 285 G1
NORMAN
av. Auburn 339 A12
av. Dolls Point 463 F1
av. Hamondvle 396 F15
av. Thornleigh 221 A4
cr. Claymore 481 C12
pl. Bligh Park 150 K7
st. Allawah 432 F9
st. Berala 339 D10
st. Concord 341 H1
st. Condell Park 398 H2
st. Darlinghurst F J4
st. Darlinghurst 4 B10
st. Five Dock 343 C10
st. Merrylands 307 B8
st. Peakhurst 430 F5
st. Prospect 274 G13
st. Punchbowl 400 B6
st. Rozelle 344 E6
swy. Hamondvle 396 F15
NORMANBY
rd. Auburn 339 B1
st. Fairfield E 337 A14
st. Villawood 337 A14
NORMAN DUNLOP
cr. Minto 482 J4
NORMANDY
rd. Allambie Ht 257 C10
tce. Leumeah 482 F11
NORMANHURST
rd. Normanhurst 221 G10
st. Elvina Bay 168 C4
NORMAN LINDSAY
cr. Faulconbdg 171 H11
NORMAN MAY
dr. Lidcombe 339 J13
NORMANS
rd. Silverdale 354 C15
NORMIC
av. Blaxland 234 A8
la. Blaxland 234 A8
NORMURRA
av. N Turramrra 223 F5
NORN
cl. Greenfld Pk 334 D14
NORRIE
pl. Oakhurst 242 A2
st. Yennora 337 A8
NORRIS
pl. Narellan Vale 478 K16
wy. Wentwthvle, off Portadown Rd 277 D11
NORSEMAN
cl. Green Valley 363 J11
pl. Yarrawarrah 489 F13
NORTH
av. Cammeray 315 K3
av. Leichhardt 16 E1
av. Rossmore 389 J14
av. Westmead 277 E15
cir. Blaxland 233 H6
cr. Lilyfield 10 E1
pde. Auburn 339 E3
pde. Campsie 372 A12
pde. Guildford 337 G7
pde. Hunters Hill 313 H10
pde. Mount Druitt 241 C16
pde. Rooty Hill 272 A1
rd. Denistone E 281 K10
rd. Eastwood 281 G5
rd. N Curl Curl 258 K10
rd. Ryde 281 K11
st. Auburn 339 A6
st. Balmain 7 E7
st. Fairfield 336 E15
st. Gymea 491 E4
st. Leichhardt 9 G11
st. Marrickville 16 C14
st. Mt Colah 162 B16
st. Penrith 237 A9
st. Schofields 182 H15
st. Thirlmere 565 A1
st. Thirlmere 565 B2
st. Windsor 121 F7
tce. Bankstown 369 F16
NORTHAM
av. Bankstown 399 A8
av. Newington, off Spitz Av 309 K14
dr. North Rocks 279 A3
st. Belrose 225 K15
NORTHAMPTON DALE
rd. Appin 569 A14
NORTH ARM
rd. Middle Cove 285 K7
NORTH AVALON
rd. Avalon 140 D14
NORTHBROOK
pl. Illawong 459 D5
st. Bexley 432 H1
NORTHBURY
ct. Glen Alpine 510 C11
NORTHCLIFF
st. Milsons Point 5 J16
NORTHCLIFFE
av. Narraweena 258 A7
NORTHCOTE
av. Caringbah 492 J12
av. Fairlight 288 A9
av. Killara 254 A10
la. Glebe 11 G6
rd. Glebe 11 G6
rd. Greenacre 370 A8
rd. Hornsby 192 A16
rd. Lindfield 254 E14
st. Auburn 339 A2
st. Canterbury 372 C16
st. Earlwood 402 C2
st. Haberfield 343 A13
st. Marrickville 373 K11
st. Mortlake 312 A14
st. Naremburn 315 D4
st. Rose Bay 348 E9
st. St Leonards 315 D4
st. Sans Souci 433 B15
NORTHCOTT
av. Kingsgrove 401 J11
la. Parramatta 278 B15
rd. Blacktown 245 C10
rd. Cromer 227 G12
rd. Lalor Park 245 C10
st. North Ryde 282 D10
st. S Wntwthvle 306 J8
wy. Cherrybrook, off Tennyson Cl 219 E10
NORTH COURT
rd. Russell Lea 343 D5
NORTH EAST
cr. Lilli Pilli 522 G3
NORTHEND
av. S Penrith 266 G3
NORTH FORT
rd. Manly 290 B13
NORTH HARBOUR
st. Balgowlah 287 J11
NORTH HEAD SCENIC
dr. Manly 289 A16
NORTHLAND
rd. Bellevue Hill 14 H16
NORTH LIVERPOOL
rd. Bonnyrigg 363 K11
rd. Bonnyrigg Ht 363 A8
rd. Green Valley 363 A8
rd. Heckenberg 363 K11
rd. Mt Pritchard 363 K11
NORTHMEAD
av. Northmead 277 J9
NORTHRIDGE
av. Bella Vista 216 C15
av. Bella Vista 246 D1
NORTH ROCKS
rd. Carlingford 249 H13
rd. N Parramatta 278 B9
rd. North Rocks 249 A16
rd. North Rocks 278 B9
NORTHROP
st. Raby 451 C13
NORTH STEYNE
Manly 288 H5
rd. Woodbine 481 D15
NORTHUMBERLAND
av. Mt Colah 192 C1
av. Stanmore 16 H5
la. Clovelly, off Warner Av 378 B12
la.e, Stanmore 16 J5
la.w, Stanmore 16 H5
rd. Auburn 309 E16
st. Blacktown 274 H6
st. Bonnyrigg Ht 363 A7
st. Clovelly 378 B12
st. Liverpool 395 D4
st. Woolwich 314 D12
swy. Liverpool 395 D4
NORTH VANDERVILLE
st. The Oaks 502 F9
NORTHVIEW
pl. Mt Colah 192 A3
rd. Palm Beach 109 K15
NORTH WEST ARM
rd. Grays Point 491 B11
rd. Gymea 491 B9
rd. Gymea Bay 491 B9
NORTHWOOD
cl. Mona Vale 199 A2
la. Camperdwn 17 F7
pl. Dundas Vy 280 D8
rd. Lane Cove 314 F6
rd. Longueville 314 F6
rd. Northwood 314 F6
st. Camperdwn 17 F7
wy. Cherrybrook 219 E11
NORTON
av. Chipping Ntn 366 F13
av. Dover Ht 348 E8
av. Springwood 171 K16
ct. Berowra Ht 133 A7
la. Lane Cove W 284 G15
la. Kingsford, off Barker St 376 J16
pl. Glenmore Pk 265 E10
pl. Minto 483 A1
rd. North Ryde 282 G13
st. Ashfield 372 F3
st. Croydon 372 D3
st. Glebe 12 D14
st. Kingsford 376 J16
st. Leichhardt 9 J8
st. Lilyfield 9 J8
st. Surry Hills 20 B1
NORTONS BASIN
rd. Wallacia 323 K12
NORVAL
pl. Illawong 459 G5
st. Auburn 339 C6
NORVEGIA
av. Tregear 240 C4
NORVIC
pl. Seven Hills 275 D9
NORWEST
bvd. Baulkham Hl 216 G16
bvd. Bella Vista 246 B2
NORWICH
la. Rose Bay 348 B11
pl. Cherrybrook 219 A13
rd. Ingleburn 453 B5
rd. Rose Bay 348 A11
NORWIN
pl. Stanhpe Gdn 215 G9
NORWOOD
av. Beecroft 250 B12
av. Carlingford 250 B12
av. Lindfield 284 C3
la. Marrickville 15 K16
pl. Baulkham Hl 246 K3
rd. Vineyard 152 F13
st. Burwood 341 H15
st. Sandringham 463 D4
NOTE
st. Hunters Hill 313 B6
NOTLEY
st. Mount Druitt 241 E12
NOTT
la. Longueville 314 E8
pl. Mt Annan 479 F14
NOTTING
la. Cottage Pt 135 F10
NOTTINGHAM
av. Castle Hill 217 K10
cr. Chipping Ntn 366 F13
pl. Ryde 312 B4
pl. Yowie Bay 492 B12
pwy. Chipping Ntn, off Nottingham Cr 366 H13
st. Old Tngabbie 277 E9
NOTTINGHILL
rd. Berala 339 F13
rd. Lidcombe 339 F13
rd. Regents Pk 369 F1
NOTTLE
st. Ashfield 373 A4
NOTTS
av. Bondi Beach 378 D5
NOUMEA
av. Bankstown 399 E5
st. Lethbrdg Pk 240 K1
st. Shalvey 210 K16
NOVA
pl. Mount Druitt 241 H12
pl. S Penrith 267 D4
NOVAR
st. St Johns Pk 364 H1
NOVARA
cr. Como 460 H10
cr. Jannali 460 H10
NOWILL
st. Condell Park 398 H6
st. Rydalmere 309 J5
NOWLAND
pl. Abbotsbury 333 B14
st. Seven Hills 246 B14
wy. Bradbury 511 J12
NOWRA
cl. Prestons 423 B2
la. Campsie 372 D12
pl. Gymea Bay 491 C11
st. Campsie 372 D12
st. Greystanes 305 H2
st. Marayong 244 B3
st. Merrylands 308 D15
NOWRANIE
pl. Windsor Dn 151 A15
st. Summer Hill 373 D5
NOYANA
av. Grays Point 491
NUGENT
pl. Prairiewood 334
NULANG
rd. Forestville 255
st. Old Tngabbie 276
NULGARRA
av. Gymea Bay 491
pl. Bradbury 511
st. Frenchs Frst 256
st. Northbridge 285
NULLA
st. Vaucluse 348
NULLABOR
pl. Yarrawarrah 489
NULLABURRA
rd. Newport 169
rd.n, Caringbah 493
rd.s, Caringbah 493
NULLAGA
wy. Clarmnt Ms 268
NULLA NULLA
st. Turramurra 222
NULLAWARRA
av. Concord 341
av. Concord W 311
NUMA
rd. North Ryde 282
st. Birchgrove 314
NUMANTIA
rd. Engadine 518
NUNANA
pl. Frenchs Frst 255
NUNATAK
la. Tregear 240
NUNDA
cl. Pennant Hills 220
NUNDAH
pl. Woronora 460
st. Lane Cove W 284
st. St Johns Pk 334
NUNDLE
st. Smithfield 335
NUNGA
pl. Baulkham Hl 246
pl. Marayong 243
NUNGEROO
av. Jamisontown 266
NUNKERE
cr. Rouse Hill 185
NURLA
av. Little Bay 437
NURMI
av. Newington 310
NURRAGI
pl. Belrose 225
st. Villawood 367
NURRAN
rd. Vaucluse 348
NURSEL
pl. Tregear 240
NURSERY
pl. Belrose 226
st. Hornsby 221
NURSES
dr. Randwick 377
wk. The Rocks A
NUTMANS
la. Grose Wold 116
rd. Grose Wold 116
NUTMEG
cl. Casula 424
NUTT
rd. Londonderry 177
NUTWOOD
la. Windsor Dn 151
NUWARRA
rd. Chipping Ntn 396
rd. Moorebank 396
NYALLA
pl. Castle Hill 247
NYAN
st. Chifley 437
NYARA
rd. Mt Krng-gai 162
NYARDO
pl. Jannali 460
NYARI
rd. Kenthurst 157

Narraweena........258 B3
)EGGAR
Glenwood..........215 D14
NYA
Gymea..............491 G4
.ETA
Doonside...........243 D13
MAGEE
Glenwood..........215 E16
MBOIDA
Hoxton Park.......392 J8
Ruse...............512 D6
Sylvania Wtr......462 D13
Greystanes........306 A2
S Coogee..........407 G6
IGAN
Miranda...........462 D16
Hoxton Park.......392 H7
Quakers Hill......244 A2
Mcquarie Pk.......282 E4
ORA
Smithfield........336 B8
Chester Hill......368 C3
Killara...........254 C10
ORIE
Frenchs Frst.......256 B2
RANG
Kirrawee...........490 J5
Allambie Ht........257 F16
Lidcombe..........339 H4

O

OBY
Chipping Ntn......396 G1
G
Kingswood.........267 E2
K
Georges Hall......367 F11
N Sydney..............K A6
N Sydney..............5 E7
Potts Point............4 K1
N St Marys, off
Oak St..........240 A10
Banksia.............403 F12
Bradbury...........511 G13
Mt Pritchard.......364 D10
Kirrawee...........490 K6
n,Kirrawee...........460 K16
Ashfield.............372 K2
Clovelly..............377 K13
Greystanes.........306 F9
Lugarno.............429 J16
Normanhurst.....221 D12
N Narrabeen.......199 A14
N St Marys........240 A10
N Sydney.............K A5
N Sydney..............5 D7
Parramatta.........308 H5
Prestons............394 A14
Rosehill.............308 H5
Schofields..........183 K12
KBORNE
Liverpool...........395 B9
KDALE
Kogarah.............433 E6
Baulkham Hl......246 J4
Cartwright..........394 E5
KES
Eastwood...........281 F6
North Bondi.......348 F15
Carlingford.........249 F9
Old Tngabbie......277 A6
W Pnnant Hl......249 F9
Winston Hills......277 A6
Westmead.........307 H2
KHAM
Sylvania............461 J13
KHILL
St Ives..............224 F11
Castle Hill..........218 J8
KLAND
Baulkham Hl......248 A13
Wrrngtn Dns, off
Oakland Pde.......237 K5
e.Wrrngtn Dns......237 K5
KLANDS
Beecroft............250 F9
Summer Hill.......373 B3
KLEA
Canley Ht..........335 C15
. Castle Hill..........218 J6

OAKLEAF
st. Glenwood..........245 C1
OAKLEIGH
av. Banksia..........403 J13
av. Milperra..........397 F11
av. S Granville..........338 E6
av. Thornleigh..........220 J11
OAKLEY
rd. Long Point..........454 B7
rd. Mcquarie Fd..........454 B7
rd. North Bondi..........348 D16
OAKMONT
av. Glenmore Pk..........266 G9
wy. Rouse Hill..........185 C9
OAKRIDGE
pl. Kenthurst..........156 H2
OAKS
av. Cremorne..........316 C7
av. Dee Why..........258 H6
rd. Mowbray Pk..........561 B7
rd. Thirlmere..........561 B7
rd. Thirlmere..........561 F16
rd. Thirlmere..........564 F1
st. Cronulla..........523 K2
st. Thirlmere..........564 J3
st. Thirlmere..........565 A3
OAKTREE
gr. Prospect..........274 H11
pl. Penshurst..........431 D1
OAKURA
st. Rockdale..........403 C14
OAKVILLE
rd. Oakville..........122 G15
rd. Willoughby..........285 F12
OAKWOOD
pl. Busby..........363 H16
pl. Hornsby Ht..........162 A8
rd. Toongabbie..........275 F14
st. Sutherland..........490 C1
wy. Menai..........458 H10
OAKY
rd. Luddenham..........326 B7
OATES
av. Gladesville..........312 J5
pl. Belrose..........226 B9
pl. Leumeah..........482 J11
rd. Mortdale..........430 J7
OATLANDS
cr. Oatlands..........279 A8
ct. Wattle Grove..........426 B3
st. Wentwthvle..........276 G16
OATLEY
av. Oatley..........431 B14
av. Oatley..........431 C11
pde. Oatley..........431 B14
pl. Padstow Ht..........429 C6
rd. Paddington..........21 A3
st. Kingsgrove..........401 H6
OATLEY PARK
av. Oatley..........430 G12
OATS
pl. Rooty Hill..........242 F13
OATWAY
pde. North Manly..........258 C15
OBA
pl. Toongabbie..........275 E12
OBADIAH
pl. S Penrith..........266 H4
OBAN
cl. Windsor Dn..........180 H3
pl. St Andrews..........481 K2
st. Schofields..........183 B16
OBELISK
av. Mosman..........317 K7
OBERON
cr. Gordon..........253 G9
cr. S Penrith..........267 C4
la. Randwick, off
Oberon St..........407 B2
rd. Ruse..........512 F6
st. Blakehurst..........462 C1
st. Coogee..........407 F3
st. Georges Hall..........367 J10
st. Randwick..........407 C2
O'BRIEN
la. Windsor..........121 C9
pde. Liverpool..........365 A14
pl. Barden Rdg..........488 G3
rd. Londonderry..........148 C10
rd. Mt Annan..........479 F14
st. Bondi Beach..........378 A2
st. Chatswood..........284 H8
st. Mount Druitt..........241 E11

O'BRIENS
la. Darlinghurst..........4 D9
rd. Cattai..........64 G1
rd. Hurstville..........431 J6
OCCUPATION
rd. Kyeemagh..........404 A14
OCEAN
av. Double Bay..........13 K11
av. Newport..........169 J9
gr. Collaroy..........229 B15
la. Manly..........288 F8
la. Mortdale..........431 B4
la. Pagewood..........405 K10
la. Bondi, off
Bennett St..........377 J4
la. Clovelly, off
Warner Av..........378 B12
pl. Illawong..........459 H4
pl. Palm Beach..........139 K1
pl. Woodbine..........481 K9
rd. Manly..........288 F8
rd. Palm Beach..........109 K16
st. Bnksmeadw..........405 K10
st. Beverley Pk..........433 C7
st. Bondi..........377 J5
st. Clovelly..........378 B13
st. Cronulla..........493 K8
st. Edgecliff..........13 K12
st. Kogarah..........433 A6
st. Kogarah..........433 C7
st. Narrabeen..........229 A6
st. Pagewood..........405 K10
st. Penshurst..........431 C5
st. Woollahra..........22 A1
st.n, Bondi..........377 J4
OCEANA
st. Narraweena..........258 C5
st.e, Dee Why..........258 D7
OCEAN GROVE
av. Cronulla..........493 K12
OCEANIA
cr. Newport..........169 K13
OCEAN VIEW
rd. Harbord..........258 H16
st. Woolooware..........493 E11
wy. Belrose..........226 C10
OCEANVIEW
av. Dover Ht..........348 F7
av. Vaucluse..........348 F7
O'CONNELL
av. Killarney Ht..........286 C1
av. Matraville..........407 A15
cl. Lurnea..........394 D14
st. Clarmnt Ms..........268 C1
st. Greenwich..........314 K14
st. Kingswood..........268 C1
st. Monterey..........433 G6
st. Newtown..........17 J8
st. N Parramatta..........278 B12
st. Parramatta..........308 A4
st. Smithfield..........335 H5
st. Sydney..........B B14
st. Sydney..........1 J15
st. Vineyard..........152 G11
O'CONNOR
la. Marrickville, off
Llewellyn St..........374 F10
la. Beaconsfield, off
Queen St..........375 G11
st. Chippendale..........19 A2
st. Eastlakes..........405 K5
st. Guildford..........337 C1
st. Haberfield..........343 D16
O'CONNORS
rd. Beacon Hill..........257 F7
OCTAGON
rd. Darling Point..........13 J8
OCTAVIA
av. Rsemeadow..........540 F3
st. Narrabeen..........229 B2
st. Toongabbie..........276 A8
O'DEA
av. Kyeemagh..........404 D13
av. Waterloo..........375 J9
av. Zetland..........375 J9
pl. N Richmond..........87 A12
rd. Mt Annan..........479 D16
ODELIA
cr. Plumpton..........241 G10
O'DELL
st. Vineyard..........153 A9
ODELL
ct. Kellyville..........185 C15

ODEON
pl. Heathcote..........518 G8
ODETTE
rd. Dural..........189 F12
ODNEY
pl. Castle Hill..........219 A10
O'DONNELL
av. Greenacre..........369 H11
st. North Bondi..........348 D16
st. North Bondi..........348 F16
O'DOWD
cl. Edensor Pk..........333 H16
st. Waverley..........377 G7
OERTER
av. Newington..........309 K15
O'FARRELL
la. Penrith..........236 K11
OFFENBACH
av. Emerton..........240 H5
OFFERTON
wy. Cranebrook..........207 F13
OFT
pl. Blacktown..........274 G9
OGDEN
cl. Abbotsbury..........333 B14
cl. St Clair..........270 H13
la. Redfern..........19 K9
la. St Clair, off
Ogden Cl..........270 H13
rd. Oakville..........122 K12
OGILVIE
pl. Blackett..........241 C4
st. East Hills..........427 H2
OGILVY
rd. Clontarf..........287 H16
st.n, Peakhurst..........430 A3
st.s, Peakhurst..........430 A6
OGMORE
ct. Bankstown..........399 B4
O'GRADY
pl. Kellyville..........216 D2
O'HAGON
st. Chester Hill..........368 A3
O'HARA
st. Marrickville..........373 K14
O'HARAS CREEK
rd. Middle Dural..........158 B3
O'HARES
rd. Wedderburn..........540 A9
rd. Wedderburn..........541 E16
OHIO
pl. Erskine Park..........271 A16
pl. Kearns..........451 A15
pl. Quakers Hill..........214 D9
OHLFSEN
rd. Minto..........453 A15
O'KEEFE
cr. Eastwood..........281 G6
rd. Annangrove..........156 B11
O'KEEFES
la. Kogarah, off
Kensington St..........433 B5
pl. Horngsea Pk..........392 C14
OKLAHOMA
av. Toongabbie..........275 H12
OKRA
pl. Quakers Hill..........243 E4
OLA
pl. Oakhurst..........241 J3
OLBURY
pl. Airds..........512 B13
OLD
la. Cremorne, off
Waters La..........316 D8
st. Tempe..........404 B4
OLDAKER
st. Doonside..........243 C5
OLD BARRENJOEY
rd. Avalon..........170 A3
OLD BATHURST
rd. Blaxland..........233 J7
rd. Emu Heights..........235 A6
rd. Emu Plains..........235 A6
OLD BEECROFT
rd. Cheltenham..........251 A11
OLD BELLS LINE OF
rd. Kurrajong..........55 H16
OLD BEROWRA
rd. Hornsby..........191 G9

OLD BRIDGE
st. Windsor..........121 D7
OLDBURY
ct. Wattle Grove..........426 A2
pl. West Hoxton..........392 B12
OLD BUSH
rd. Engadine..........489 D14
OLD CANTERBURY
rd. Ashfield..........373 A8
rd. Dulwich Hill..........373 A8
rd. Lewisham..........15 A10
rd. Summer Hill..........373 A8
OLD CASTLE HILL
rd. Castle Hill..........218 D14
OLD CHURCH
la. Prospect..........275 B11
OLD EAST KURRAJONG
rd. E Kurrajong..........60 C9
rd. Glossodia..........60 C9
OLD FERRY
rd. Illawong..........459 F4
OLDFIELD
ct. St Clair..........269 K14
la. St Clair, off
Oldfield Ct..........269 K14
pl. Menai..........458 G8
rd. Seven Hills..........275 D3
st. Greystanes..........305 G9
OLD FOREST
rd. Lugarno..........429 K14
OLD FORT
rd. Mosman..........317 K6
OLD GLENFIELD
rd. Casula..........424 A4
rd. Glenfield..........424 A4
OLD GLENHAVEN
rd. Glenhaven..........187 J14
OLD GRAND
dr. Moore Park..........20 J10
OLDHAM
av. Wrrngtn Cty..........238 H4
cr. Dolls Point..........433 E16
OLD HAWKESBURY
rd. McGraths Hl..........122 A12
rd. Vineyard..........152 C1
rd. Vineyard..........152 E6
OLD HILL ROAD
lk. Homebush B..........310 C16
OLD HUME
hwy. Camden..........507 A5
OLD ILLAWARRA
rd. Barden Rdg..........488 F2
rd. Barden Rdg..........488 F4
rd. Holsworthy..........426 E16
rd. Illawong..........458 G8
rd. Illawong..........459 A6
rd. Lucas Ht..........487 G11
rd. Menai..........458 G8
OLD JERUSALEM
rd. Oakdale..........500 H10
OLD KENT
rd. Greenacre..........369 J14
rd. Greenacre..........370 D15
rd. Kentlyn..........512 F5
rd. Mt Lewis..........369 J14
rd. Ruse..........512 F5
OLD KURRAJONG
rd. Casula..........394 G14
rd. Richmond..........118 C1
OLD LEUMEAH
rd. Leumeah..........482 A13
OLD LIVERPOOL
rd. Lansvale..........366 B10
OLD LLANDILO
rd. Llandilo..........179 B16
OLD MENANGLE
rd. Campbelltwn..........511 C7
OLD NORTHERN
rd. Baulkham Hl..........247 H9
rd. Castle Hill..........218 C15
rd. Dural..........188 G16
rd. Dural..........189 A14
rd. Glenhaven..........218 E3
rd. Glenorie..........128 B2
rd. Middle Dural..........158 H1
OLD PEATS FERRY
rd. Cowan..........104 C14
OLD PITT TOWN
rd. Box Hill..........153 K4
rd. Nelson..........154 F8
rd. Oakville..........153 H2
rd. Pitt Town..........92 K15

rd. Pitt Town 93 A15
OLD PITTWATER
rd. Brookvale 257 J10
OLD POST OFFICE
rd. Cattai 64 K14
OLD PRINCES
hwy. Engadine 518 G5
hwy. Sutherland 490 E3
OLD PROSPECT
rd. Greystanes 306 D5
rd. S Wntwthvle 306 D5
rd. S Wntwthvle 307 A4
OLD RACECOURSE
cl. Picton 561 E2
OLD RAZORBACK
rd. Cawdor 506 D16
OLD SACKVILLE
rd. Wilberforce 61 K16
OLD SAMUEL
st. Mona Vale 198 G1
OLDSMOBILE
pl. Ingleburn 453 K8
OLD SOUTH HEAD
rd. Bellevue Hill 377 F3
rd. Bondi 377 F3
rd. Bondi Beach 348 B16
rd. Bondi Jctn 377 F3
rd. Dover Ht 348 B16
rd. North Bondi 348 B16
rd. Rose Bay 348 B16
rd. Vaucluse 348 E5
rd. Watsons Bay 318 G15
rd. Woollahra 377 F3
OLD STOCK ROUTE
rd. Oakville 122 F15
rd. Pitt Town 93 F13
OLD SYDNEY
rd. Seaforth 287 C10
OLD TAREN POINT
rd. Taren Point 462 J11
OLD WALLGROVE
rd. Eastern Ck 302 B3
rd. Horsley Pk 301 G9
OLD WINDSOR
rd. Bella Vista 246 A1
rd. Glenwood 215 E3
rd. Kellyville 215 E3
rd. Kings Lngly 246 D8
rd. Old Tngabbie 277 B7
rd. Seven Hills 246 F14
rd. Stanhpe Gdn 215 E3
rd. Toongabbie 276 G2
rd. Winston Hills 246 F14
OLEA
pl. Mcquarie Fd 454 C4
OLEANDER
av. Baulkham Hl 246 K14
av. Lidcombe 339 F11
cr. Riverstone 182 K4
ct. Peakhurst 430 E1
la. N St Marys, off Oleander Rd 240 A12
pde. Caringbah 493 B10
rd. N St Marys 239 J10
rd. Wahroonga 222 B4
st. Greenacre 370 G9
st. Greystanes 306 A11
OLGA
cl. Bossley Park 334 C5
pl. Belrose 225 E14
pl. Cecil Hills 362 H7
pl. Leumeah 482 G12
st. Blacktown 243 K10
st. Chatswood 285 B9
st. Greystanes 306 G8
OLIN
cl. Cranebrook 207 B13
OLINDA
cr. Carlingford 279 D1
pl. St Ives 254 C1
OLIPHANT
st. Mt Pritchard 364 H11
OLIVE
cr. Peakhurst 430 E1
la. Neutral Bay 6 F1
la. Turramurra 222 H13
pl. Mcquarie Fd 454 G1
st. Artarmon 285 A16
st. Asquith 191 K12
st. Baulkham Hl 247 H11
st. Condell Park 398 J6
st. Fairfield 336 C16
st. Kingsgrove 402 B5
st. Liverpool 395 D6
st. Minto Ht 483 F8
st. Paddington 13 B15
st. Ryde 281 K10
st. Seven Hills 275 G3
st. Wentwthvle 276 J13
OLIVE LEE
st. Quakers Hill 213 J7
OLIVER
av. Rookwood 339 K12
la. Roseville, off Oliver Rd 284 G4
rd. Chatswd W 284 G11
rd. Roseville 284 G3
st. Bexley North 402 C10
st. Curl Curl 258 F16
st. Harbord 288 E2
st. Heathcote 518 D10
st. Mascot 405 D3
st. Queenscliff 288 E2
st. Riverstone 183 A6
wy. Mona Vale 199 A4
OLIVERI
cl. Edensor Pk 363 H1
cr. Green Valley 363 G10
pl. Schofields 213 K6
OLIVET
st. Glenbrook 233 K12
OLIVIA
cl. Rsemeadow 540 F6
la. Surry Hills 20 C5
OLIVIERI
pl. Ryde 282 C12
OLLIER
cr. Prospect 274 F12
OLLIVER
cr. St Clair 270 B9
OLOLA
av. Castle Hill 218 D16
av. Vaucluse 348 B3
O'LOUGHLIN
st. Surry Hills 19 H1
OLPHERT
av. Vaucluse 348 F3
OLSEN
st. Guildford 338 D9
OLSSON
cl. Hornsby Ht 161 J11
OLWEN
pl. Quakers Hill 214 C8
OLWYN
pl. Earlwood 403 G2
OLYMPIA
rd. Naremburn 315 D1
OLYMPIC
bvd. Homebush B 310 E15
ct. Bradbury 511 D8
ct. Carlingford 279 D2
dr. Lidcombe 339 H5
dr. Milsons Point 1 K1
pde. Bankstown 399 D1
pde. Mt Riverview 204 C16
pl. Doonside 243 E7
OLYMPUS
dr. St Clair 269 G11
st. Winston Hills 276 K1
OMAGH
pl. Killarney Ht 256 B14
OMAHA
st. Belfield 371 E12
O'MALLEY
pl. Glenfield 424 E13
OMAR
cl. Illawong 459 F3
la. Greenwich 314 J6
pl. Winston Hills 277 F2
OMAROO
av. Doonside 243 B14
OMARU
av. Miranda 491 H2
cr. Bradbury 511 F16
st. Beverly Hills 400 H16
OMATI
st. Whalan 240 J8
OMDURMAN
st. Harbord 288 D1
O'MEALLY
st. Prairiewood 334 E11
O'MEARA
st. Carlton 432 K9
OMEGA
av. Lapstone 264 H5
cl. Prestons 392 K14
la. St Clair, off Omega Pl 270 E16
pl. Greenacre 370 A12
pl. St Clair 270 E16
OMEO
st. St Clair 269 K9
OMNIBUS
la. Ultimo 3 C13
rd. Kingsgrove 401 J8
ONA
cl. Bossley Park 333 K11
ONDIEKI
ct. Blacktown 273 H6
ONDINE
pl. Kareela 461 E10
ONEATA
la. Lakemba 401 A1
st. Lakemba 401 A2
O'NEIL
wk. Mosman 317 D7
O'NEILE
cr. Lurnea 394 D6
O'NEILL
av. Newington 310 B14
la. Btn-le-Sds 433 H4
la. Lilyfield 10 E4
rd. Menai 458 F8
st. Btn-le-Sds 433 H5
st. Granville 308 E16
st. Guildford 337 F2
st. Guildford 337 F4
st. Lalor Park 245 G13
st. Lilyfield 10 E4
ONSLOW
av. Camden 507 B6
av. Elizabeth Bay 13 A3
la. Gordon 254 B5
la. Canterbury, off Onslow St 372 D15
pl. Elizabeth Bay 13 A3
pl. Leumeah 482 B14
pl. Rose Bay 348 E13
pl. Sylvania 462 A14
st. Canterbury 372 D15
st. Granville 308 H10
st. Rose Bay 348 C12
st. St Clair 269 K10
st. Seven Hills 275 K4
ONTARIO
av. Roseville 284 E4
av. St Clair 269 H15
cl. Illawong 459 D5
cl. Seven Hills 275 E6
ONUS
av. Hobartville 118 F8
la. Richmond Lwld 118 F2
ONYX
cl. Bossley Park 333 K8
pl. Eagle Vale 481 A7
rd. Artarmon 285 B14
OORANA
av. Phillip Bay 436 J12
OORIN
rd. Hornsby Ht 191 H4
OPAL
cl. S Penrith 267 B1
la. Northmead 278 A5
pl. Bossley Park 333 K8
pl. Cartwright 393 H6
pl. Eagle Vale 481 H7
pl. Greystanes 306 B2
pl. Gymea 461 F16
pl. Northmead 278 A5
pl. Padstow Ht 429 F8
pl. Rooty Hill 242 A12
OPALA
st. Belrose 225 J15
OPEL
pl. Ingleburn 453 J10
OPHELIA
pl. Oakhurst 241 K1
st. Rsemeadow 540 J6
OPHIR
gr. Mount Druitt 271 A4
pl. Illawong 459 E4
OPREY
cl. Minto 452 J14
OPUS
pl. Cranebrook 207 E16
ORALLO
av. Blacktown 244 F14
ORAMZI
rd. Girraween 275 K11
ORAN
pl. Fairfield W 335 E12
ORANA
av. Hornsby 191 J9
av. Kirrawee 490 J2
av. Penrith 237 D6
av. Pymble 253 F2
av. Seven Hills 275 C3
cr. Blakehurst 432 D16
cr. Peakhurst 430 D7
la. Merrylands 307 H14
pl. Greenacre 369 J11
pl. Liverpool 394 J3
pl. Telopea 279 E8
rd. Kenthurst 156 F5
rd. Mona Vale 199 G2
st. North Ryde 282 F8
ORANGE
av. Clarmnt Ms 238 G16
gr. Castle Hill 218 C16
gr. Frenchs Frst 255 J2
la. Hurstville 432 C5
la. Randwick, off Clovelly Rd 377 C9
pl. Seven Hills 275 G7
st. Eastwood 281 F8
st. Greystanes 305 H5
st. Greystanes 305 J5
st. Hurstville 432 C3
ORANGE GROVE
rd. Cabramatta 365 B12
rd. Liverpool 365 B12
rd. Warwck Frm 365 B12
ORANGERY
pl. Bella Vista 246 G4
ORANGEVILLE
st. Marsden Pk 181 K11
ORARA
ct. Wattle Grove 395 J13
pl. Plumpton 242 C10
rd. Allambie Ht 257 J15
st. Chatswood 285 D6
st. Waitara 221 J3
ORATAVA
av. W Pnnant Hl 249 D7
ORBELL
st. Kingsgrove 401 G12
ORCAM
la. Rooty Hill 272 E5
ORCHARD
av. Winston Hills 277 G1
cr. Ashfield 372 J3
gr. Oakhurst 242 A2
pl. Glenwood 215 E12
pl. Ingleburn 453 D8
rd. Bass Hill 368 A7
rd. Beecroft 250 B10
rd. Brookvale 258 B11
rd. Busby 363 G13
rd. Chatswood 284 J12
rd. Chatswood 284 J9
rd. Chester Hill 368 A4
rd. Colyton 270 A8
rd. Fairfield 336 F16
st. Balgowlah 287 K9
st. Baulkham Hl 247 K12
st. Croydon 342 E14
st. Epping 280 D2
st. Pennant Hills 221 A15
st. Pymble 223 D15
st. Thornleigh 221 A15
st. Warriewood 198 F9
st. West Ryde 281 F14
ORCHARDLEIGH
st. Old Guildford 337 C10
st. Yennora 337 C10
ORCHID
cl. Colyton 270 H6
ct. Quakers Hill 214 A10
pl. Mcquarie Fd 454 C5
pl. W Pnnant Hl 248 G8
rd. Old Guildford 337 E8
st. Loftus 489 K12
ORD
cl. Bossley Park 333 G5
cr. Sylvania Wtr 462 E14
pl. Leumeah 482 G11
ORDAK
av. Gymea Bay 491 D8
ORDE
pl. Prospect 274 H13
ORDER
pl. Redfern 19
ORE
la. Erskine Park 300
pl. Eagle Vale 481
OREADES
wy. Bidwill 211
O'REGAN
dr. Ryde 312
OREGON
st. Blacktown 243
O'REILLY
cl. Menai 458
st. Parramatta 307
wy. Rouse Hill 184
ORELIA
wy. Minto 482
ORFORD
pl. Illawong 459
ORIANA
dr. Illawong 459
ORIELTON
rd. Smeaton Gra 479
st. Narellan 478
ORIENT
av. Cronulla 524
rd. Greendale 385
rd. Padstow 429
st. Gladesville 312
ORIENTAL
st. Bexley 402
ORINOCO
cl. Seven Hills 275
st. Pymble 253
ORIOLE
pl. Green Valley 363
pl. Ingleburn 453
st. Glenmore Pk 265
st. Woronora Ht 489
ORION
cl. Castle Hill 218
pl. Leonay 234
rd. Lane Cove W 283
st. Bardwell Vy 403
st. Engadine 488
st. Rooty Hill 272
O'RIORDAN
st. Alexandria 375
st. Beaconsfield 375
st. Mascot 405
ORISON
st. Georges Hall 367
ORISSA
la. Cammeray 316
st. Campsie 371
wy. Doonside 243
ORKNEY
pl. Prestons 423
ORLANDER
av. Glenmore Pk 266
ORLANDO
av. Mosman 316
cr. Seven Hills 275
cr. Voyager Pt 427
pl. Edensor Pk 333
rd. Cromer 228
ORLEANS
cct. Cecil Hills 362
cr. Toongabbie 275
ORLETON
la. Wrrngtn Cty, off Orleton Pl 238
pl. Wrrngtn Cty 238
ORLICK
st. Ambarvale 510
ORMISTON
av. Gordon 253
av. N Sydney 5
av. West Hoxton 392
ORMOND
gdn. Coogee 377
st. Ashfield 373
st. Bondi Beach 378
st. Paddington 13
ORMONDE
av. Epping 251
cl. Glenmore Pk 266
pde. Hurstville 432
rd. E Lindfield 255
rd. Roseville Ch 255
ORMSBY
pl. Wetherill Pk 333

RNELLA
Glendenning 242 F4
RO
Glenfield 424 G14
RONGA
Baulkham Hl 248 B8
RONTES
Burwood 341 J16
ROURKE
Eastlakes 405 J2
ROYA
de. Roseville 285 A2
RPHAN
Horsley Pk 332 E3
RPHEUS
Green Valley 363 B12
RPINGTON
Ashfield 373 A2
Bexley 402 G12
Bexley North 402 G11
RR
Davidson 255 D3
Bondi 377 H2
Gladesville 312 H10
RRS
Strathfield 341 G12
RSINO
Rsemeadow 540 G5
RTH
Kingswood 237 F13
RTON
Concord 311 K15
Currans Hill 479 J12
Barden Rdg 488 G6
Kings Lngly 245 E4
RTONA
de. Como 460 J6
Lindfield 284 D4
RWELL
Potts Point 4 K5
Blacktown 274 E10
Potts Point 4 J5
SBERT
Acacia Gdn 214 H16
SBORN
Normanhurst 221 G12
SBORNE
Dundas Vy 279 K9
Ryde 311 H6
Woollahra 22 B1
Lane Cove 314 G5
Greenwich 314 G5
Lane Cove 314 G5
Manly 288 H12
Marayong 244 A8
Chipping Ntn 396 F5
SBURN
St Helens Park 541 B6
SCAR
Acacia Gdn 214 H14
Chatswood 285 A9
Greenwich 315 A8
SGATHORPE
Gladesville 312 G7
SGOOD
Marrickville 373 E14
Guildford 338 A2
SHANNASSY
Mt Pritchard 364 F10
SHEA
Edensor Pk 363 F1
SHEAS
Surry Hills 4 C16
Surry Hills 20 C1
SLO
Marsfield 281 J1
SMOND
Warwck Frm 365 D14
Hassall Gr 212 A15
SMUND
Bondi Jctn 22 D5
SPREY
Glenmore Pk 266 D13
Green Valley 363 D12
Maroubra 407 D14
Illawong 459 F6
Clarmnt Ms 268 H4
Bella Vista 216 D16
SROY
Earlwood 403 D3

OSSARY
st. Mascot 404 K1
OSTEND
st. Bankstown 399 A5
st. Condell Park 398 K5
st. Lidcombe 340 C5
st. S Granville 338 F6
O'SULLIVAN
av. Maroubra 406 J11
la. Queens Park 22 E12
pl. Kellyville 216 D2
rd. Bellevue Hill 347 H11
rd. Leumeah 482 A15
rd. Rose Bay 347 H11
OSWALD
cl. Warrawee 222 E13
cr. Rsemeadow 540 J7
la. Darlinghurst 13 A10
la. Darling Point 13 F9
la. *Campsie, off Redman St 372 C13*
la. *Canterbury, off Redman St 372 C13*
st. Campsie 372 C13
st. Edgecliff 13 F9
st. Guildford 337 C6
st. Mosman 316 H10
st. Randwick 377 D14
OSWALD PARK
pl. Kurrajong 55 H12
OSWELL
st. Rockdale 403 A12
OSWIN
la. Rockdale 403 C13
OTAGO
cl. Glenorie 128 C1
pde. Miranda 492 A8
pl. Northmead 248 C15
st. Vineyard 152 H12
OTAKI
pl. St Ives Ch 223 J3
OTHELLO
av. Rsemeadow 540 H6
pl. St Clair 270 D15
st. Blakehurst 432 B15
OTTAWA
cl. Cranebrook 207 H10
st. Kearns 481 Z9
st. Toongabbie 275 E12
OTTER
la. *Erskine Park, off Otter Pl 301 A1*
pl. Erskine Park 301 A1
OTTEY
av. Newington 310 A14
OTTLEY
st. Quakers Hill 244 A3
OTTO
st. Merrylands W 307 A16
OTTWAY
cl. St Ives 224 D9
OTWAY
cl. Wetherill Pk 334 J5
pl. Illawong 459 C5
OULTON
av. Concord W 311 C12
av. Rhodes 311 C12
st. Prospect 274 G10
OURIMBAH
rd. Mosman 316 H4
OUSE
cl. West Hoxton 392 C6
OUSLEY
pl. Milperra 397 E9
OUTLOOK
av. Emu Heights 235 A6
av. Mt Riverview 204 G15
cct. Menai 458 G9
st. Blacktown 274 E11
OUTRAM
pl. Currans Hill 479 J14
st. Chippendale 19 D2
OVAL
la. Glenbrook 234 A15
la. Kingsford 376 J15
st. Old Tngabbie 276 K8
OVENS
cl. Horngsea Pk 392 F15
dr. Wrrngtn Cty 238 G6
pl. St Ives Ch 224 A3
OVER
pl. Shalvey 210 K15

OVERETT
av. Kemps Ck 359 G1
OVERTON
av. Chipping Ntn 366 F14
cl. Berowra 133 C16
rd. Comleroy 56 A5
OWEN
av. Baulkham Hl 247 G12
av. Kyeemagh 404 C13
la. Ultimo 12 K16
pl. Illawong 459 D7
pl. S Windsor 150 F3
rd. Georges Hall 367 J15
st. E Lindfield 254 G15
st. Gladesville 312 H5
st. Glendenning 242 H8
st. Lindfield 254 G15
st. North Bondi 348 C14
st. N Willghby 285 E10
st. Punchbowl 400 C5
st. Thirlmere 562 D14
st. Ultimo 12 K16
st. Wentwthvle 277 B13
OWEN JONES
row. Menai 458 G15
OWENS
av. Newington 309 K16
pl. Cranebrook 207 F10
OWEN STANLEY
av. Allambie Ht 257 E10
av. Beacon Hill 257 D9
rd. Glenfield 424 F13
st. Mt Annan 479 C11
OWL
cl. Green Valley 363 D11
pl. Ingleburn 453 D9
pl. St Clair 269 H11
OXFORD
av. Bankstown 399 B4
av. Castle Hill 217 K10
cl. Belrose 226 C13
la. Cmbrdg Pk 237 H8
la. Mount Druitt 241 C15
la. Newtown 17 D10
pl. St Ives 224 A7
rd. Ingleburn 453 D6
rd. Strathfield 341 C13
sq. Darlinghurst 4 B11
sq. Surry Hills 4 B11
st. Belmore 371 D15
st. Berala 339 E10
st. Blacktown 244 J16
st. Bondi Jctn 22 E6
st. Burwood 341 H15
st. Cmbrdg Pk 237 G7
st. Centnnial Pk 21 C1
st. Chipping Ntn 366 G16
st. Darlinghurst F G3
st. Darlinghurst 4 A10
st. Epping 251 B15
st. Gladesville 312 J7
st. Guildford 337 J2
st. Lidcombe 339 E10
st. Merrylands 307 E14
st. Mortdale 431 A8
st. Newtown 17 C10
st. Paddington 4 F13
st. Petersham 15 H13
st. Riverstone 182 K8
st. Rozelle 344 D8
st. St Marys 269 J6
st. Smithfield 335 J8
st. Surry Hills F G3
st. Surry Hills 4 A10
st. Sutherland 490 D2
st. Woollahra 21 K6
OXFORD FALLS
rd. Beacon Hill 257 C1
rd. Oxford Falls 257 C1
rd.w, Oxford Falls 226 H12
OXFORD STREET
ml. Bondi Jctn 22 H6
OXLEY
av. Castle Hill 247 H4
av. Jannali 460 G11
av. Panania 428 E2
av. St Ives 224 E10
dr. Mt Colah 162 B10
gr. Tahmoor 566 A11
la. Centnnial Pk 21 A14
pl. Frenchs Frst 256 D1
rd. Ingleburn 423 A10
st. Bradbury 511 C7
st. Camden 477 A15
st. Campbelltwn 511 C7
st. Crows Nest 315 E5
st. Ermington 280 C16
st. Fairfield 336 B14
st. Glebe 11 K6
st. Lalor Park 245 C14
st. Matraville 437 C1
st. St Leonards 315 D7
OYAMA
av. Manly 288 F13
OYSTER BAY
rd. Como 460 K8
rd. Oyster Bay 461 A8
OZARK
pl. Cranebrook 207 D9
st. Seven Hills 275 B9
OZONE
pde. Dee Why 259 B9
st. Cronulla 494 A12
st. Harbord 258 C15

P

PACEY
av. North Ryde 282 K12
PACHA
pl. Shalvey 210 G14
PACIFIC
av. Penshurst 431 F6
av. Tamarama 378 B7
cr. Maianbar 523 B7
hwy. Artarmon 284 H15
hwy. Asquith 192 A9
hwy. Berowra 133 E14
hwy. Brooklyn 75 A13
hwy. Chatswood 284 H6
hwy. Chatswd W 284 H6
hwy. Cowan 104 D13
hwy. Crows Nest 5 D3
hwy. Gordon 253 J10
hwy. Greenwich 315 A5
hwy. Hornsby 221 G2
hwy. Killara 253 J10
hwy. Lane Cove 314 G1
hwy. Lane Cove W 284 H15
hwy. Lindfield 284 D1
hwy. Mooney Mooney 75 A13
hwy. Mt Colah 162 F16
hwy. Mt Krng-gai 162 F16
hwy. N Sydney K B2
hwy. N Sydney 315 G8
hwy. Pymble 253 B1
hwy. Roseville 284 D1
hwy. St Leonards 315 A5
hwy. Turramurra 222 H13
hwy. Wahroonga 222 C8
hwy. Waitara 221 G2
hwy. Warrawee 222 C8
hwy. Waverton 5 D3
hwy. Wollstncraft 5 D3
la. Manly 288 G6
la. Penshurst 431 F6
la. *Crows Nest, off Clarke St 315 F6*
la. *St Clair, off Pacific Rd 270 H15*
pde. Dee Why 258 G6
pde. Manly 288 F6
pl. Palm Beach 140 B2
rd. Erskine Park 270 H15
rd. Palm Beach 139 J1
rd. Quakers Hill 213 F14
st. Blakehurst 462 C2
st. Bronte 378 A9
st. Caringbah 492 F9
st. Clovelly 377 J11
st. Greystanes 306 E7
st. Kingsgrove 401 K7
st. Manly 288 G5
st. Watsons Bay 318 E13
PACIFIC PALMS
cct. Hoxton Park 392 G6
PACKARD
av. Castle Hill 217 E16
cl. Ingleburn 453 G11
pl. Horngsea Pk 392 C13
PACKENHAM
pl. Mt Annan 509 F1
PACKSADDLE
st. Glenwood 215 F16
PADBURY
st. Chipping Ntn 396 G2
PADDINGTON
la. Paddington 21 G1
st. Paddington 21 F1
PADDISON
av. Gymea 491 G4
PADDOCK
cl. Casula 394 B16
PADDY MILLER
av. Currans Hill 479 H13
PADEMELON
av. St Helens Park 541 F3
PADSTOW
pde. Padstow 399 E16
st. Rozelle 10 G1
PADUA
cl. Prestons 393 D13
pl. Hebersham 241 G4
PADULLA
pl. Castle Cove 286 C5
PAGANINI
cr. Clarmnt Ms 268 G3
PAGE
av. Ashfield 342 J13
av. Illawong 459 D3
av. N Wahrnga 192 F14
cl. Minto 452 J14
ct. Carlingford 249 G15
la. Canterbury 402 C2
pl. Cabramatta W 364 H5
pl. Moorebank 396 D9
rd. East Ryde 283 C14
rd. North Ryde 283 C14
st. Canterbury 402 C2
st. Pagewood 405 K11
st. Wentwthvle 277 A12
PAGES
rd. St Marys 269 D3
PAGET
ct. Winmalee 173 G12
st. Richmond 118 H7
PAGODA
cr. Quakers Hill 214 B9
PAILS
pl. Shalvey 210 K12
PAINE
av. Moorebank 396 D11
pl. Bligh Park 150 J8
st. Kogarah 433 A4
st. Maroubra 406 H10
PAINS
pl. Currans Hill 479 H10
rd. Hunters Hill 313 C3
PAINTERS
pde. Dee Why 258 E7
PAINTS
la. Chippendale 18 H2
PAISLEY
cl. St Andrews 482 A2
pl. Carlingford 249 J16
rd. Burwood 342 B14
rd. Croydon 342 B14
rd. Croydon 372 E1
PALACE
la. Mortlake 312 A13
la. Petersham 15 J8
rd. Baulkham Hl 247 D8
st. Ashfield 372 G6
st. Petersham 15 H9
st. Stanhpe Gdn 215 A4
PALAMARA
pl. Chester Hill 337 H10
PALANA
cl. West Hoxton 392 F5
PALARA
pl. Dee Why 258 J1
PALAU
cr. Lethbrdg Pk 240 G1
PALAWAN
av. Kings Park 244 J2
PALENA
cr. St Clair 269 F15
la. *St Clair, off Rotarua Rd 269 F14*
PALERMO
pl. Allambie Ht 257 C9
PALFREY
pl. Emu Heights 235 C3
PALING
pl. Beacon Hill 257 K4
st. Cremorne 316 F7
st. Lilyfield 10 F11
st. Thornleigh 220 K14
PALINGS
la. Sydney C J1

PALISADE
cr. Bonnyrigg 364 D6
PALISANDER
pl. Castle Hill 218 G12
PALLAMANA
pde. Beverly Hills 401 B12
PALLISTER
st. Kings Lngly 246 B10
PALM
av. North Manly 288 D2
cl. Green Valley 362 J13
ct. Narellan Vale 479 A13
ct. Woodbine 481 J11
gr. Beverly Hills 400 K15
gr. Normanhurst 221 D13
pl. Bidwill 211 C14
rd. Newport 169 J11
st. Girraween 275 K12
st. St Ives 224 D5
tce. N Narrabeen 228 H3
PALM BEACH
rd. Palm Beach 109 J16
PALMER
av. Strathfield 371 A2
cl. Illawong 459 E2
cr. Bexley 403 A14
la. Darlinghurst 4 D10
la. Parramatta, off Palmer St 278 D16
pl. Blacktown 274 J3
pl. Emu Plains 235 C13
st. Artarmon 284 J14
st. Balmain 7 G10
st. Belmore 371 H16
st. Cammeray 315 J4
st. Campsie 371 H16
st. Darlinghurst 4 D12
st. Guildford W 336 K3
st. Ingleburn 453 C8
st. Parramatta 308 D1
st. Sefton 368 E6
st. S Coogee 407 J6
st. Windsor 121 F7
st. Woolmloo 4 E6
wy. Bonnyrigg 364 D5
PALMERSTON
av. Bronte 377 H7
av. Glebe 12 B11
av. Winston Hills 247 H15
pl. Seaforth 287 B11
rd. Fairfield W 335 D12
rd. Hornsby 192 B16
rd. Mount Druitt 241 A16
rd. Waitara 222 B2
st. Canley Ht 365 H3
st. Canley Vale 365 H3
st. Kogarah 433 C2
st. Vaucluse 318 F16
PALMETTO
cl. Stanhpe Gdn 215 E9
PALMGROVE
rd. Avalon 169 K3
PALMYRA
av. Lethbrdg Pk 240 F1
av. St Marys 210 B12
av. Shanes Park 209 G10
av. Willmot 210 B12
PALOMAR
pde. Harbord 288 E1
pde. Yagoona 369 C11
PALOMINO
cl. Eschol Park 481 B4
rd. Emu Heights 235 B4
PALONA
cr. Engadine 488 F15
st. Marayong 244 A4
PALYA
pl. Narraweena 258 E3
PAMBULA
av. Prestons 393 D16
av. Revesby 398 G16
cr. Woodpark 306 G14
pl. Forestville 255 J7
rd. Engadine 489 A12
PAMELA
av. Peakhurst 430 D10
cr. Bayview 168 J12
cr. Berala 339 B13
cr. Bowen Mtn 83 K12
la. Leonay, off Pamela Pde 235 B14
pde. Leonay 235 B14
pde. Leonay 235 C14
pde. Marayong 244 D6
pl. Concord 342 A3
pl. Girraween 276 A12
pl. Kenthurst 157 E9
st. North Ryde 282 H9
PAM GREEN
pl. Doonside 273 G1
PAMPAS
cl. Clarmnt Ms 238 H15
PAMSHAW
pl. Bidwill 211 C15
PAN
cr. Greystanes 306 E7
PANAMA
cl. Illawong 459 G5
PANANIA
av. Panania 398 A15
PANAVIEW
cr. North Rocks 279 C1
PANDALA
pl. Woolooware 493 C9
PANDANUS
ct. Stanhpe Gdn 215 D10
PANDORA
cr. Greystanes 306 E7
pl. Tahmoor 566 A12
st. Greenacre 370 D11
PANETH
st. Lucas Ht 487 H13
PANETTA
av. Liverpool 394 J8
PANGARI
cr. Dharruk 241 B5
rd. Glenorie 127 J3
PANGEE
st. Kingsgrove 402 A7
PANICUM
pl. Glenmore Pk 265 G12
PANIMA
pl. Newport 169 F14
PANK
pde. Blacktown 243 J12
PANKLE
st. S Penrith 266 H5
PANMURE
st. Rouse Hill 184 K9
PANORA
av. North Rocks 248 H16
PANORAMA
av. Cabramatta 365 C11
av. Leonay 264 K1
av. Woolooware 493 F9
cr. Freemns Rch 90 A3
cr. Frenchs Frst 256 E7
cr. Mt Riverview 234 C4
la. Seaforth 287 B11
pde. Blacktown 274 K3
pde. Panania 428 D1
pde. Seaforth 287 C10
rd. Kingsgrove 401 K5
rd. Lane Cove 314 H4
rd. Penrith 237 B6
st. Bargo 567 D6
st. Penshurst 431 E9
PANTHER
pl. Penrith 236 D12
PANTON
cl. Glenmore Pk 266 F9
PAPEETE
av. Lethbrdg Pk 240 G1
PAPER BARK
pl. Mcquarie Fd 454 E1
PAPERBARK
cct. Casula 423 J3
cl. Glenmore Pk 265 H10
cr. Kellyville 186 A16
cr. Kellyville 216 A1
pl. Alfords Point 429 B16
pl. Narellan Vale 478 J13
wy. Westleigh 220 J9
PAPPAY
st. Glenwood 245 A1
wy. Glenwood 215 A16
PAR
cl. Pymble 252 J7
la. Randwick 377 F10
PARADISE
av. Avalon 139 H12
av. Roseville 284 K5
cl. Cherrybrook 219 E13
cl. Plumpton 242 B10
pl. St Clair 269 H9
PARAGON
dr. North Rocks 249 B16
la. Belmore, off Collins St 371 E16
rd. Dural 189 C16
PARAKA
cl. Bangor 459 E14
pl. Bradbury 511 C15
PARAKEET
pl. W Pnnant Hl 248 E9
PARAMOUNT
cr. Kellyville 185 E8
PARANA
av. Revesby 428 G1
PARAPET
pl. Glenhaven 217 K6
st. Fairfield 336 D6
PARBURY
la. Dawes Point 1 G7
la. Ultimo 12 K12
PARDALOTE
pl. Glenmore Pk 265 H12
st. Glenwood 215 C15
st. Ingleburn 453 F7
wy. W Pnnant Hl 249 D7
PARDEY
st. Kingsford 406 J6
PARE
av. Loftus 490 A11
PARER
av. Condell Park 398 C2
st. Kings Park 244 E1
st. Maroubra 406 G11
st. Melrose Pk 310 J2
st. Springwood 202 D12
PARINGA
pl. Bangor 459 F14
PARIS
av. Earlwood 403 A2
pl. Miranda 461 K15
pl. Toongabbie 276 C4
st. Balgowlah 287 G7
st. Carlton 432 G11
PARK
av. Ashfield 372 F5
av. Avalon 140 A14
av. Beecroft 250 F4
av. Bexley 403 A16
av. Blaxland 233 J6
av. Burwood 341 K12
av. Cammeray 316 B7
av. Chatswd W 284 E10
av. Concord 341 K9
av. Cremorne 316 B7
av. Denistone 281 C13
av. Drummoyne 344 A4
av. Glebe 11 H9
av. Gordon 253 H7
av. Hurstville Gr 431 F10
av. Kingswood 237 H12
av. Manly 288 F9
av. Mosman 316 H10
av. Neutral Bay 316 B8
av. Oatley 430 G11
av. Penshurst 431 E9
av. Punchbowl 370 F16
av. Randwick 377 D10
av. Roseville 285 A2
av. Springwood 201 K1
av. Tahmoor 566 C8
av. Waitara 221 K4
av. Westmead 277 H16
av. West Ryde 281 C13
cr. Pymble 253 D2
dr. Bondi Beach 378 E2
dr. Lilyfield 10 E1
la. Ashfield 372 F5
la. Caringbah 492 H7
la. Erskineville 18 D14
la. Glebe 12 F12
la. Gordon 253 H7
la. Greenwich 315 B7
la. Newtown 18 A10
la. Sydenham 374 D15
la. Waitara 221 K3
la. Waterloo 19 F12
la. Mosman, off Lower Almora St 317 D6
la. Clovelly, off Park St 378 A12
pde. Bondi 377 H5
pde. Pagewood 406 F8
pde. Parramatta 307 J1
pl. Caringbah 492 H7
rd. Alexandria 18 J14
rd. Auburn 339 B8
rd. Baulkham Hl 248 B11
rd. Berala 339 A15
rd. Burwood 341 J13
rd. Cabramatta 365 J6
rd. Carlton 432 G9
rd. Cowan 104 B14
rd. Dundas 279 G13
rd. East Hills 427 G4
rd. Five Dock 343 A10
rd. Homebush 341 A7
rd. Homebush W 340 K6
rd. Hunters Hill 313 C6
rd. Hurstville 431 K3
rd. Kenthurst 157 K6
rd. Kogarah Bay 432 J11
rd. Leppington 420 J12
rd. Liverpool 395 A2
rd. Luddenham 325 C13
rd. Maianbar 522 K9
rd. Marrickville 15 K16
rd. Marrickville 373 K9
rd. Marsden Pk 181 J13
rd. Naremburn 315 D2
rd. Panania 427 G4
rd. Regents Pk 339 A15
rd. Riverstone 181 J9
rd. Rydalmere 309 G3
rd. St Leonards 315 B7
rd. Sans Souci 433 D14
rd. Seven Hills 246 A16
rd. Springwood 202 D8
rd. Sydenham 374 D15
rd. Vineyard 152 A4
rd. Wallacia 325 B13
rd.n, Moore Park 21 A8
rd.s, Moore Park 21 A9
rd.s, Mulgrave 151 J5
row. Bradbury 511 E13
st. Arncliffe 403 E7
st. Bexley North 402 C12
st. Camden 507 A1
st. Campsie 372 B13
st. Carlton 432 K7
st. Clovelly 378 A12
st. Collaroy 229 A10
st. Croydon Pk 371 K9
st. Curl Curl 258 H13
st. Emu Plains 235 F9
st. Epping 280 F2
st. Erskineville 18 D13
st. Glenbrook 234 A16
st. Homebush B 310 H16
st. Ingleburn 453 C8
st. Kingsgrove 402 C12
st. Kogarah 433 A7
st. Merrylands 308 B16
st. Mona Vale 199 A2
st. Mortdale 431 D8
st. Mulgoa 325 C3
st. Narrabeen 229 A10
st. Northmead 277 G10
st. Peakhurst 430 B4
st. Petersham 15 E6
st. Riverstone 182 J7
st. Rossmore 390 C5
st. Rozelle 344 D8
st. Sutherland 490 D4
st. Sydney C J12
st. Sydney 3 G6
st. Tahmoor 565 G9
st. Woronora 489 J1
PARKCREST
pl. Kenthurst 156 H2
PARKER
av. Earlwood 402 C5
av. West Pymble 252 F9
cl. Beecroft 250 F9
la. Haymarket E F10
la. Padstow 399 F16
rd. Kentlyn 513 D8
rd. Londonderry 149 E14
st. Canley Vale 335 J15
st. Fairfield 335 J15
st. Granville 308 J9
st. Guildford 337 D5
st. Haymarket E G10
st. Haymarket 3 F13
st. Kings Lngly 246 A10
st. Kingswood 237 D15
st. McMahons Pt 5 D15
st. Northbridge 286 B14
st. Rockdale 403 C14
PARKERS
la. Erskineville, off Victoria St 17 K16
PARKES
av. Werrington 239
cr. Blackett 241
dr. Centnnial Pk 21
rd. Artarmon 315
rd. Collaroy 228
rd. Collaroy Plat 228
rd. Cromer 228
st. Ermington 310
st. Guildford W 337
st. Harris Park 308
st. Heathcote 518
st. Kirribilli 6
st. Manly Vale 288
st. Naremburn 315
st. Parramatta 308
st. Ryde 281
st. Thornleigh 221
st. West Ryde 281
PARKFIELDS
pl. Kingsgrove 401
PARKHAM
la. Surry Hills 20
pl. Surry Hills 20
rd. Oatlands 279
st. Chester Hill 337
st. Surry Hills 20
PARK HILL
rd. Minchinbury 271
PARKHILL
av. Leumeah 482
cr. Cherrybrook 220
st. Croydon Pk 371
PARKHOLME
cct. Englorie Park 510
PARKHURST
av. Panania 428
PARKIN
rd. Colyton 270
PARKINSON
av. S Turramrra 252
gr. Minchinbury 272
st. Kings Lngly 245
PARKLAND
av. Mcquarie Fd 424
av. Pendle Hill 276
av. Punchbowl 400
av. Rydalmere 279
pl. Thornleigh 220
rd. Carlingford 249
rd. Mona Vale 198
st. Blacktown, off Outlook St 274
wy. Warriewood 198
PARKLANDS
av. Heathcote 519
av. Lane Cove W 284
av. Leonay 265
rd. Glenbrook 264
rd. Mt Colah 192
rd. North Ryde 282
PARKLAWN
la. N St Marys, off Parklawn Pl 239
pl. N St Marys 239
PARKLEA
cl. Dural 190
dr. Parklea 214
pde. Canley Ht 335
pl. Carlingford 279
PARKRIVER
cl. Mulgoa 323
PARKSIDE
av. Miranda 491
av. Wrrngtn Dns 238
ct. Currans Hill 479
dr. Kogarah Bay 432
dr. Lalor Park 245
dr. Sandringham 463
dr. S Hurstville 432
la. Chatswood 284
la. Westmead 307
pl. Mt Pritchard 364
PARKTREE
pl. Narellan 478
PARK VIEW
gr. Blakehurst 432
PARKVIEW
av. Belfield 371
av. Glenorie 128
av. Picnic Point 428
av. S Penrith 236
dr. Homebush B 310

Fairlight, off
Parkview Rd 288 E9
Manly, off
Parkview Rd 288 E9
Westleigh 220 H8
Abbotsford 343 C3
Chiswick 343 C3
Fairlight 288 E8
Russell Lea 343 C3
Miranda 492 D7
RKWOOD
Castle Hill 218 K8
Menai 459 A12
Emu Heights 234 K3
West Pymble 253 A13
North Rocks 279 B2
RLAND
Illawong 459 D1
RLIAMENT
Mcquarie Fd 454 A2
e. Bexley 402 J11
RMA
St Helens Park 541 F3
Carlingford 249 F14
RMAL
Padstow 399 F16
RNELL
Quakers Hill 214 D16
Minto 483 A2
East Killara 254 J7
Strathfield 341 G12
RNI
Frenchs Frst 256 D7
RNOO
Castle Cove 285 J4
ROO
Sylvania Wtr 462 F14
Wattle Grove 395 J13
Hornsby Ht 191 H4
Seven Hills 275 G8
S Turramrra 252 B7
Greystanes 306 B5
Ruse 512 D6
RR
N Curl Curl 258 H9
Bossley Park 333 G9
e. Beacon Hill 257 J3
e. Faulconbdg 171 D14
e. Narraweena 258 B3
Marayong 243 H5
RRAMATTA
Annandale 16 C4
Ashfield 343 A15
Auburn 309 B13
Burwood 341 H10
Camperdwn 17 C3
Canada Bay 342 E11
Concord 341 H10
Croydon 342 E11
Five Dock 342 E11
Forest Lodge 17 C3
Glebe 18 D1
Granville 308 G10
Haberfield 373 C1
Homebush 341 B8
Homebush W 339 J1
Leichhardt 15 C6
Lewisham 15 C6
Lidcombe 339 J1
N Strathfield 341 B8
Petersham 15 C6
Silverwater 309 B13
Stanmore 16 C4
Strathfield 341 B8
Summer Hill 15 C6
Cronulla 493 K15
RRAWEEN
Cremorne 316 F8
RRAWEENA
Baulkham Hl 248 B7
Caringbah 462 J16
Miranda 462 C16
RRELLA
Glendenning 242 F3
RRISH
Mt Colah 162 C15
RRIWI
Mosman 317 B2
RROO
St Clair 299 J2
RROT
Green Valley 363 F11

PARRY
av. Narwee 400 K12
cl. Bonnyrigg 364 B8
st. Pendle Hill 276 C14
st. Putney 312 B6
wy. Glenmore Pk 265 J6
PARSLEY
rd. Vaucluse 348 E2
PARSON
pl. Harringtn Pk 478 F6
PARSONAGE
rd. Castle Hill 247 F1
st. Ryde 311 G5
PARSONS
av. S Penrith 266 F2
av. Strathfield 341 E15
pl. Barden Rdg 488 H2
st. Ashcroft 364 D15
st. Rozelle 7 D16
PARTANNA
av. Matraville 436 G4
PARTHENIA
st. Caringbah 493 A16
st. Dolans Bay 492 K16
PARTRIDGE
av. Castle Hill 217 F13
av. Hinchinbrk 393 C1
av. Miranda 492 B6
av. Yennora 336 K10
PARUKALA
pl. N Narrabeen 199 B15
PARUNA
pl. Cromer 228 A15
PARYS
cl. Menai 458 K10
PASADENA
pl. St Clair 270 J12
st. Monterey 433 G10
PASCHA
pl. Kareela 461 F9
PASHLEY
st. Balmain 7 F10
PASKIN
st. Kingswood 237 H14
PASLEY
rd. Georges Hall 368 B15
PASSEFIELD
st. Liverpool 395 A7
PASSEY
av. Belmore 371 D13
PASSIONFRUIT
wy. Glenwood 215 E13
PASSY
av. Hunters Hill 313 K12
PASTUREGATE
av. Cmbrdg Gdn 237 J4
av. Wrrngtn Dns 237 J4
PATAK
rd. Ingleside 167 K16
PATANGA
rd. Frenchs Frst 257 A5
PATCHING
cl. Minto 482 K4
PAT DEVLIN
cl. Chipping Ntn 396 K5
PATE
av. East Ryde 313 B1
PATEN
st. Revesby 398 E14
PATENT
sq. Holroyd 308 A10
sq. Holroyd, off
Refractory Ct 307 K10
PATER
st. Bnksmeadw 406 A13
PATERNOSTER
row. Pyrmont 12 H4
PATERSON
av. Kingsgrove 401 K11
av. Lurnea 394 C13
cr. Fairfield W 335 B12
pl. Colyton 270 H8
rd. Springwood 172 F15
st. Camden S 507 B9
st. Campbelltwn 512 A6
st. Carlingford 250 B16
st. Matraville 436 J1
PATEY
st. Dee Why 258 H7
PATHERTON
pl. Narellan Vale 478 H15

PATIENCE
av. Yagoona 369 E8
PATON
pl. Balgowlah 288 A5
st. Kingsford 406 K4
st. Merrylands W 306 H12
st. Merrylands W 307 A12
st. Rookwood 340 B11
PATONGA
cl. Woodbine 481 J8
pl. Engadine 489 A11
st. Kingsgrove 401 G10
PATONS
la. Orchard Hills 299 A6
PATRICIA
av. Mt Pritchard 364 D12
ct. Castle Hill 248 B3
pl. Cherrybrook 220 A4
st. Belfield 371 B10
st. Blacktown 274 F10
st. Cecil Hills 362 H6
st. Chester Hill 368 B2
st. Colyton 270 F5
st. Marsfield 282 A7
st. Mays Hill 307 G6
st. Rydalmere 309 J3
PATRICK
av. Castle Hill 217 J12
pl. Berowra Ht 133 B5
pl. Currans Hill 479 G10
st. Avalon 139 K11
st. Beacon Hill 257 E8
st. Blacktown 274 F2
st. Campbelltwn 511 E4
st. Casula 424 F3
st. Greystanes 306 C8
st. Hurstville 431 H1
st. N Willghby 285 E8
st. Punchbowl 400 E8
PATRICK O'POSSUM
pl. Faulconbdg 171 G13
PATRINE
pl. Bella Vista 246 E6
PATRIOT
pl. Rouse Hill 185 D8
PATSY
pl. Kings Park 244 E2
PATTEN
av. Merrylands 307 J15
pl. Kings Lngly 245 D4
PATTERN
pl. Woodcroft 243 G7
PATTERSON
av. Kellyville 216 H7
av. West Pymble 252 H12
cl. Padstow 429 H5
la. Concord 341 J7
la. Surry Hills 4 D14
la. Avalon, off
Central Rd 170 C1
rd. Heathcote 518 C16
rd. Lalor Park 245 D11
st. Concord 341 G8
st. Double Bay 14 D11
st. Ermington 310 B1
st. North Bondi 348 C15
st. Rydalmere 309 K1
st. Tahmoor 565 H10
PATTERSONS
la. Grose Vale 85 A8
PATTISON
av. Hornsby 221 H3
av. Waitara 221 H3
PATTON
la. Willoughby 285 D13
PATTYS
pl. Jamisontown 265 K1
PATU
pl. Cherrybrook 219 D12
PATYA
cl. Epping 250 J14
cl. Kellyville 186 F16
pl. N Richmond 87 D16
PAUL
av. St Ives 224 F14
cl. Camden 507 B2
cl. Cranebrook 207 C15
cl. Hornsby Ht 161 J13
cl. Mona Vale 199 E2
cr. Canley Ht 335 F16
cr. S Wntwthvle 306 H8
ct. Baulkham Hl 247 G15
la. Coogee 407 G2

la. Bondi Jctn, off
Paul St 377 G4
pl. Carlingford 279 J2
st. Auburn 339 A3
st. Balmain East 8 G9
st. Blacktown 274 B1
st. Bondi Jctn 377 G4
st. Dundas 279 J14
st. Hunters Hill 313 B8
st. Milsons Point 5 K16
st. North Ryde 282 G6
st. Panania 428 E5
st. Pitt Town 93 B5
st.n, Mcquarie Pk 282 F5
PAULA
st. Marayong 244 A9
PAULA PEARCE
pl. Bella Vista 246 E8
PAULINE
pl. Baulkham Hl 247 D3
PAULING
av. Coogee 377 E13
PAULL
st. Mount Druitt 271 C3
PAULWOOD
av. Winmalee 172 J11
PAVASOVIC
pl. Bonnyrigg Ht 363 D5
PAVER
pl. Woodcroft 243 F8
PAVESI
st. Guildford 336 F1
st. Guildford W 336 F1
st. Smithfield 336 F1
PAVEY
pl. Cranebrook 207 E12
PAVIA
rd. Como 460 H9
rd. Jannali 460 H9
PAVILION
dr. Little Bay 437 G15
st. Queenscliff 288 H3
PAVO
cl. Hinchinbrk 393 D4
PAVONIA
wy. Blacktown 274 F12
PAWLEY
st. Surry Hills 20 C5
PAWSON
pl. S Windsor 150 K2
PAXTON
av. Belmore 371 D13
cr. Cherrybrook 219 E16
la. Belmore, off
Paxton Av 371 E13
pl. Castle Hill 217 G16
st. Frenchs Frst 257 A4
PAYNE
st. Oakhurst 211 J16
st. S Penrith 237 C16
PAYTEN
av. Roselands 400 F8
st. Kogarah Bay 432 H11
st. Menangle Pk 539 A6
st. Putney 312 A6
PAYTON
ct. Narellan Vale 509 A2
st. Canley Vale 366 B5
PEACE
av. Peakhurst 430 D7
av. Pymble 253 H1
av. St Clair 299 H1
PEACH
ct. Carlingford 249 G16
gdn. Glenwood 215 D13
PEACH TREE
la. Kirrawee 490 J2
rd. Mcquarie Pk 282 E3
PEACHTREE
av. Wentwthvle 277 B8
la. Penrith, off
Peachtree Rd 236 E7
rd. Penrith 236 E7
wy. Menai 458 H10
PEACOCK
cl. Green Valley 363 F11
pde. Frenchs Frst 255 G1
st. Bardwell Pk 402 K7
st. Seaforth 287 A8
wy. Claymore 481 A11
wy. Currans Hill 479 G11

PEAK
st. Engadine 488 D12
st. Glenwood 215 G16
PEAKE
pde. Peakhurst 430 E3
PEAKER
la. Woollahra 21 K3
PEAL
pl. Warriewood 199 E14
PEAR
cl. Casula 424 C2
PEARCE
av. Newington 310 C13
av. Peakhurst 430 E2
la. Hurlstone Pk, off
Fernhill St 373 A10
pl. Emu Plains 235 E11
pl. Narellan Vale 508 F1
rd. Quakers Hill 213 J13
st. Baulkham Hl 247 K6
st. Double Bay 14 E7
st. Ermington 280 A16
st. Liverpool 395 A6
st. S Coogee 407 H5
wk. Rockdale 403 F15
PEARL
av. Belmore 371 E13
av. Chatswd W 284 G12
av. Epping 281 C4
cl. Erskine Park 270 H16
ct. Woodbine 481 K10
la. Newtown 374 H10
pl. Seven Hills 275 B7
st. Hurstville 431 H4
st. Newtown 374 H10
st. West Ryde 311 B1
PEARL BAY
av. Mosman 287 A15
PEARRA
wy. Clarmnt Ms 268 H1
PEARSON
av. Gordon 253 G6
cr. Harringtn Pk 478 G7
la. Gladesville 312 J10
pl. Baulkham Hl 247 B15
st. Balmain East 8 H9
st. Bligh Park 150 H5
st. Gladesville 312 J11
st. Kingswood 237 K14
st. S Wntwthvle 307 C6
PEAT
cl. Eagle Vale 481 D7
pl. Camden S 507 D12
st. Brooklyn 75 F12
PEBBLEWOOD
ct. W Pnnant Hl 248 K1
PEBBLY HILL
rd. Cattai 94 E8
rd. Maraylya 94 E11
PEBWORTH
pl. S Penrith 267 A8
PECAN
cl. Cherrybrook 220 A9
cl. St Clair 269 G16
PECK
la. Bardwell Pk 402 J6
PECKHAM
av. Chatswd W 284 G7
PECKS
rd. Kurrajong Ht 54 A6
rd. N Richmond 87 A12
PECOS
cl. St Clair 299 J2
pl. Seven Hills 275 D7
PEDDER
cl. Woodcroft 243 G10
ct. Wattle Grove 396 A14
st. Glenbrook 264 C5
PEDIT
pl. Cherrybrook 219 C12
PEDRICK
pl. Dundas Vy 280 B11
PEDVIN
pl. Annangrove 155 K9
PEEBLES
av. Kirrawee 461 A15
rd. Fiddletown 129 H1
st. Winston Hills 277 E4
PEEK
pl. Chester Hill 338 A14
PEEL
pde. Comleroy 56 A8

pl. Sylvania Wtr 462 F12
pl. Winston Hills 277 J2
rd. Baulkham Hl 246 G8
st. Belmore 371 C15
st. Belmore 371 C16
st. Canley Ht 365 E4
st. Dover Ht 348 F9
st. Glenbrook 233 J16
st. Holroyd 308 A10
st. Kirribilli 2 D1
st. Quakers Hill 214 D11
st. Ruse 512 D8
st. Wilton 568 K16

PEELER
pl. Milperra 397 D10

PEERLESS
cl. Ingleburn 453 G11

PEFFER
st. Panania 428 C1

PEGAR
pl. Marayong 243 H5

PEGASUS
av. Hinchinbrk 393 D5
la. Erskine Park, off Weaver St 301 A3
st. Erskine Park 301 A2

PEGGOTTY
av. Ambarvale 511 A15

PEGGY
st. Mays Hill 307 G6

PEGLER
av. S Granville 338 E5
la. S Granville 338 E4
wy. Ambarvale 511 A16

PEITA
cr. Mona Vale 198 J2

PEKE
pl. Rooty Hill 272 D5

PELARGONIUM
cr. Mcquarie Fd 454 G6

PELICAN
la. St Clair, off Swamphen St 271 A13
pl. Hinchinbrk 393 C1
pl. Woronora Ht 489 D5
rd. Schofields 213 E3
st. Erskine Park 271 A13
st. Gladesville 312 K6
st. Surry Hills F H6
st. Surry Hills 4 B11

PELLATT
pl. Emu Plains 235 F9

PELLEAS
st. Blacktown 275 A9

PELLION
st. Blaxland 233 E9

PELLISIER
pl. Putney 312 A9
rd. Putney 312 B9

PELLITT
la. Dural 188 G11

PELMAN
av. Belmore 371 E14
av. Greenacre 370 F14

PELORUS
av. Voyager Pt 427 D5

PELSART
av. Penrith 237 D2
av. Willmot 210 D12

PEMBERTON
la. Parramatta 308 J1
st. Botany 405 H15
st. Parramatta 308 J2
st. Strathfield 340 H14

PEMBREW
cr. Earlwood 403 C3

PEMBROKE
av. Earlwood 402 F3
av. Summer Hill 373 B3
av. Turramurra 252 F5
pl. Belrose 226 A13
rd. Leumeah 482 B14
rd. Marsfield 251 G15
rd. Minto 452 H16
st. Ashfield 373 A2
st. Blacktown 273 J5
st. Bronte 377 K10
st. Cmbrdg Pk 237 F8
st. Epping 251 C15
st. Epping 251 E15
st. Surry Hills 19 G4
st. Sylvania 462 C9

PEMBURY
av. North Rocks 249 B15
cl. Denham Ct 422 C9
rd. Minto 482 B6

PEMELL
la. Newtown 17 C14
st. Newtown 17 C15

PENDANT
av. Blacktown 274 J8

PENDERGAST
av. Minto 482 J7

PENDERLEA
dr. W Pnnant Hl 248 K6

PENDEY
st. Northbridge 285 G16
st. Willoughby 285 G16

PENDLE
wy. Pendle Hill 306 D1

PENDLEBURY
pl. Abbotsbury 333 D11

PENDLEY
cr. Quakers Hill 214 C12

PENDOCK
la. Cranebrook, off Pendock Rd 207 F14
rd. Cranebrook 207 E14

PENDRILL
st. Glebe 11 H7

PENELOPE
cr. Arndell Park 273 D9
la. Cranebrook, off Milligan Rd 207 C13
pl. Cranebrook 207 C13

PENELOPE LUCAS
la. Rosehill 308 J8

PENFOLD
pl. Edensor Pk 333 E15
pl. Sydney D A1
st. Eastern Ck 272 E7

PENGILLY
st. Riverview 314 A5

PENGUIN
pde. Hinchinbrk 393 C1
pl. Tregear 240 B4
pl. Woronora Ht 489 C6

PENINSULA
rd. Valley Ht 202 F4

PENINSULAR
rd. Grays Point 491 E15

PENKIVIL
st. Bondi 377 J4
st. Willoughby 285 D13

PENMON
cl. Menai 458 H9

PENN
cr. Quakers Hill 213 G15

PENNA
pl. Bonnyrigg Ht 363 C4

PENNANT
av. Denistone 281 G11
av. Gordon 253 G10
pde. Carlingford 250 C13
pde. Epping 280 C1
st. Castle Hill 218 B14
st. N Parramatta 278 J15
st. Parramatta 278 J15
wy. Castle Hill 218 C13

PENNANT HILLS
rd. Beecroft 249 J9
rd. Carlingford 279 A7
rd. Normanhurst 221 A13
rd. N Parramatta 278 D13
rd. Oatlands 279 A7
rd. Pennant Hills 220 H16
rd. Thornleigh 221 A13
rd. Wahroonga 221 A13
rd. W Pnnant Hl 249 J7

PENNICOOK
la. Pennant Hills, off Hillcrest Rd 220 G16

PENNINGTON
av. Georges Hall 367 K14

PENNSYLVANIA
rd. Riverwood 400 A13

PENNY
la. Thirlmere 565 B3
pl. Arndell Park 274 B11

PENNYBRIGHT
pl. Kellyville 216 C2

PENNYS
la. Potts Point 4 J8

PENOLA
ct. Baulkham Hl 247 A2

PENPRASE
la. Miranda 491 K3
st. Riverstone 182 D11

PENRHYN
av. Beecroft 249 K7
av. Pymble 253 C6
pl. Castle Hill 217 K7
rd. Bnksmeadw 435 K4

PENRITH
av. Collaroy Plat 228 D13
pl. St Ives 224 F4
st. Jamisontown 236 D16

PENROSE
av. Belmore 401 G5
av. Cherrybrook 219 J10
av. East Hills 428 A5
cl. Prestons 392 K14
cr. S Penrith 237 A15
pl. Frenchs Frst 256 G9
pl. Menai 458 H6
st. Lane Cove 313 G3
st. Lane Cove W 313 G3
st. Minto 483 A2

PENRUDDOCK
st. S Windsor 150 K2

PENSACOLA
pl. Casula 395 A11

PENSAX
la. Cranebrook, off Pensax Rd 207 G14
rd. Cranebrook 207 F14

PENSHURST
av. Neutral Bay 6 H8
av. Penshurst 431 G6
la. Penshurst 431 E5
rd. Narwee 400 J13
rd. Roselands 400 J13
st. Beverly Hills 401 A15
st. Chatswood 285 C5
st. N Willghby 285 D9
st. Penshurst 431 C1
st. Roseville 285 C5
st. Willoughby 285 D9

PENTECOST
av. Pymble 223 G13
av. St Ives 223 C12
av. Turramurra 223 C12
st. Hinchinbrk 392 K2

PENTLAND
av. Roselands 400 G6
ct. Quakers Hill 213 K14

PENTLANDS
dr. Winmalee 173 E11

PENZA
pl. Quakers Hill 214 C10

PEONY
pl. Quakers Hill 243 F3

PEPLER
rd. Cabramatta W 365 B7

PEPLOW
pl. Doonside 273 E3

PEPPER
la. Clovelly, off Thorpe St 377 K14

PEPPERCORN
av. Mt Hunter 505 B8
av. Narellan 478 G14
av. Villawood 337 A15
dr. Frenchs Frst 256 H1
pl. Cranebrook 207 B8
pl. Glenwood 245 H2
pl. Horngsea Pk 392 F13
pl. Kirrawee 460 K16
pl. Mt Hunter 504 B16

PEPPERIDGE
av. Oakhurst 242 D1

PEPPERINA
pl. Carlingford 249 H11

PEPPERMINT
cl. Prestons 394 C14
cr. Kingswood 267 G1
cr. Mcquarie Fd 454 G3
gr. Engadine 518 D2
gr. Panania 428 E5

PEPPERMINT GUM
pl. Westleigh 220 F7

PEPPERTREE
dr. Erskine Park 270 G15
gr. Quakers Hill 214 C14
la. St Clair, off Swallow Dr 270 K16

PEPPIN
cl. St Clair 270 B13
cr. Airds 512 D9
la. St Clair, off Peppin Cl 270 B13
pl. Elderslie 507 H1

PERA
pl. Fairfield W 335 C9

PERABO
cl. Bossley Park 333 F9

PERAK
st. Mona Vale 199 E2

PERCEVAL
cl. Abbotsbury 333 A11

PERCHERON
st. Blairmount 480 K14

PERCIVAL
av. Appin 569 E9
la.e, Stanmore 16 G5
la.w, Stanmore 16 F5
rd. Caringbah 492 J16
rd. Smithfield 336 C1
rd. Stanmore 16 F5
st. Bexley 432 H3
st. Carlton 432 H3
st. Clarendon 120 B4
st. Lilyfield 10 G9
st. Maroubra 406 J7
st. Penshurst 431 E3

PERCY
st. Auburn 339 G2
st. Bankstown 399 F3
st. Fairfield Ht 335 H10
st. Gladesville 312 J7
st. Greystanes 306 D9
st. Haberfield 373 E1
st. Ingleburn 453 D10
st. Marayong 244 C10
st. Rozelle 10 J1

PEREGRINE
cl. Green Valley 363 E11

PEREIRA
st. Newington, off Newington Bvd 310 A15

PERENTIE
rd. Belrose 226 D13

PERFECTION
av. Kellyville 215 C2
av. Stanhpe Gdn 215 C8

PERI
cl. Woodcroft 243 J11
ct. Wattle Grove 395 K15

PERIDOT
cl. Eagle Vale 481 E5

PERIGEE
cl. Doonside 243 F14

PERIMETER
rd. Mascot 404 C12
rd. Mascot 404 E4
rd. Mascot 404 K11

PERINA
cl. Bangor 459 E14
cl. Casula 424 C3

PERISHER
rd. Kellyville 185 H15
rd. Kellyville 215 H1
st. Horngsea Pk 392 C15

PERKINS
av. Newington 310 A14
dr. Kellyville 215 J5
pl. Bonnyrigg Ht 363 E8
st. Bligh Park 150 K7
st. Denistone W 280 K12
st. Rooty Hill 272 B1
wy. Maroubra 407 C12

PERMANENT
av. Earlwood 372 H15

PERMIAN
dr. Cartwright 394 D4

PERON
pl. Willmot 210 D14

PERONNE
av. Clontarf 287 E11
cl. Milperra 397 D12
pde. Allambie Ht 257 J16
wy. Matraville 407 A15

PEROUSE
rd. Randwick 377 B15

PERRETT
st. Rozelle 7 D14

PERREY
st. Collaroy Plat 228 H13

PERRI
la. Haberfield 343

PERRIN
av. Plumpton 241

PERRITT
pl. S Penrith 236

PERRUMBA
pl. Bradbury 511

PERRY
av. Springwood 201
cr. Engadine 518
ct. Harringtn Pk 478
la. Campsie 372
la. Lilyfield 9
la. Lilyfield 9
la. Paddington 13
rd. Arcadia 129
st. Bossley Park 334
st. Campsie 372
st. Dundas Vy 280
st. Kings Lngly 245
st. Lilyfield 9
st. Lilyfield 9
st. Marrickville 16
st. Marrickville 374
st. Matraville 436
st. North Rocks 248
st. Surry Hills 19
st. Wentwthvle 307
wy. Auburn 338

PERRYMAN
pl. Cronulla 494

PERRYS
av. Bexley 432

PERSEUS
cct. Kellyville 186

PERSHORE
la. Cranebrook, off Pendock Rd 207
rd. Cranebrook 207

PERSIC
st. Belfield 371

PERSIMMON
wy. Glenwood 215

PERTAKA
pl. Narraweena 258

PERTARINGA
wy. Glenorie 128

PERTH
av. Campbelltwn 512
av. E Lindfield 254
cl. West Hoxton 392
st. Kirrawee 461
st. Oxley Park 270
st. Riverstone 152
st. Vineyard 152

PERU
pl. Illawong 459

PESSOTTO
pl. Wakeley 334

PETER
av. Camden 507
cl. Hornsby Ht 161
cr. Greenacre 370
ct. Jamisontown 266
pde. Old Tngabble 277
pl. Bligh Park 150
pl. Gymea Bay 491
st. Baulkham Hl 247
st. Blacktown 244
st. Glossodia 59

PETER BROCK
dr. Oran Park 448

PETER FINCH
av. Moore Park 20

PETERLEE
pl. Hebersham 241
rd. Canley Ht 365

PETER MEADOWS
rd. Kentlyn 483
rd. Leumeah 482

PETER PAN
av. Wallacia 324
gln. St Clair 270
la. St Clair, off Peter Pan Gln 270

PETERS
pl. Maroubra 407
pl. Ruse 512

PETERS CORNER
Randwick 377

TERSEN
Tregear 240 C4
TERSHAM
Petersham 16 A5
Marrickville 373 K13
Bonnyrigg Ht 363 C7
Petersham 16 A5
TERSON
North Rocks 248 K14
TER WILSON
Glenwood 245 J1
TITE
Springwood 201 K3
TITH
Hurstville 401 H16
TRARCH
Vaucluse 348 E5
TREL
Hinchinbrk 393 C1
Tregear 240 B4
Woronora Ht 489 E4
TRIE
Bidwill 211 D15
Georges Hall 368 C15
TRIKAS
Tennyson 58 D4
TRINA
Baulkham Hl 248 B13
TRIZZI
Baulkham Hl 247 E8
TTIT
Lakemba 371 A13
TTY
Yagoona 368 K11
TUNIA
Bankstown 399 G3
Mcquarie Fd 454 E4
Marayong 244 A6
UGEOT
Ingleburn 453 J9
VENSEY
Canley Vale 365 J4
AR LAP
Casula 394 E16
St Clair, off Phar Lap Pl 270 E12
St Clair 270 E11
ARLAP
Bossley Park 333 J8
EASANT
Canterbury 402 E2
EASANTS
Wedderburn 540 D9
ELPS
Bradbury 511 E7
Surry Hills 20 D3
Canley Vale 365 K4
Surry Hills 20 C3
ILBY
Bonnyrigg 363 H8
ILIP
West Pymble 252 J10
West Pymble 252 J10
Carlingford 249 F13
Cherrybrook 220 B4
Leppington 420 D7
Mona Vale 169 G16
Blacktown 244 B11
Bondi 377 K5
Strathfield 341 H11
Woolooware 493 J9
ILIPPA
Cecil Hills 362 E2
ILLIP
Cabramatta 365 F9
Seaforth 287 B7
Btn-le-Sds 403 K15
Newtown 17 C12
Penshurst 431 B3
Sydney B F13
St Marys, off Champness Cr 239 K15
Parramatta, off Phillip St 308 C2
. Eastern Ck 272 H4
. Rooty Hill 242 D14
. Rooty Hill 272 E1
McGraths Hl 121 J12
Putney 311 K6
Ryde 311 K6
St Ives Ch 194 B16
Balmain 7 F8
st. Birchgrove 7 F8
st. Blakehurst 432 C15
st. Campbelltwn 511 J6
st. Glebe 12 E12
st. Guildford W 336 J4
st. Kingswood 237 F11
st. Liverpool 394 H2
st. Newtown 17 B12
st. Oatlands 278 K10
st. Oyster Bay 461 B8
st. Panania 428 B5
st. Parramatta 308 C2
st. Petersham 16 C4
st. Redfern 19 C10
st. Riverwood 400 C15
st. Roselands 401 C5
st. St Marys 239 H14
st. Seven Hills 245 E16
st. S Coogee 407 G6
st. Stanmore 16 C4
st. Sydney B D15
st. Sydney D D4
st. Sydney 1 K16
st. Sydney 3 K2
st. Waterloo 19 C10
PHILLIPA
ct. Kellyville 217 C1
pl. Bargo 567 B5
PHILLIPS
av. Canterbury 372 D13
av. Regents Pk 339 C16
la. Marrickville 373 F15
la. Neutral Bay 6 C6
rd. Kogarah 433 D10
st. Alexandria 18 J13
st. Auburn 339 A4
st. Cabarita 342 E2
st. Neutral Bay 6 D7
st. Rookwood 340 C12
PHILLIPSON
la. Springwood 172 A15
PHILO
cl. Rsemeadow 540 E2
PHILOS
st. Minchinbury 272 B8
PHILPOTT
la. Marrickville, off Philpott St 374 D9
st. Marrickville 16 H16
st. Marrickville 374 D9
PHINEY
rd. Ingleburn 453 E1
PHIPPS
rd. Maraylya 94 C10
st. Oatley 461 D1
PHLOX
cl. Lalor Park 245 C10
PHOEBE
st. Balmain 7 A7
PHOENIX
av. Ingleburn 453 A9
av. Kellyville 215 J3
av. Rhodes 311 D11
av. Stanhpe Gdn 215 A11
cl. Castle Hill 218 K9
cr. Casula 395 A11
cr. Erskine Park 270 H15
la. St Clair, off Phoenix Cr 270 J15
pl. Illawong 459 G3
pl. Narellan Vale 479 B14
st. Lane Cove 314 E1
PHYLLIS
av. Picnic Point 428 G5
av. Thornleigh 221 B12
cr. Guildford 337 D3
la. N Curl Curl, off Phyllis St 259 C10
st. Minto 482 G2
st. Mt Pritchard 364 G12
st. N Curl Curl 259 C10
PHYSICS
rd. Camperdwn 18 B4
PIAF
cl. Bonnyrigg Ht 363 C4
PIANOSA
pl. Glenwood 245 K3
PIBRAC
av. Warrawee 222 G10
PICASSO
cr. Old Tngabbie 276 K6
la. Emu Plains, off Picasso Pl 236 A7
pl. Emu Plains 236 A7
PICCADILLY
pl. Maroubra 407 A9
st. Riverstone 183 A6
st. Riverstone 183 B8
PICCOLO
wy. Shalvey 210 H14
PICHOLA
pl. Castle Hill 218 E15
PICKEN
la. Blacktown 244 F13
st. Silverwater 309 K8
PICKERING
la. Woollahra 22 B2
PICKERING PATH
Winmalee 173 A14
PICKERSGILL
st. Kings Lngly 245 H7
PICKETT
av. Minto 453 A15
PICKFORD
av. Eastwood 281 F7
PICKWICK
wy. Ambarvale 540 K1
wy. Ambarvale 541 A1
PICKWORTH
av. Balgowlah 287 G8
pl. Menai 458 J6
PICNIC
gln. Springwood 201 H6
gr. Ingleburn 454 A8
pl. Clarmnt Ms 238 K16
PICNIC POINT
rd. Panania 428 D5
rd. Picnic Point 428 C8
PICOT
pl. Blackett 241 C1
PICTON
av. Picton 563 F5
rd. Picton 563 H11
rd. Wilton 568 K16
st. Mascot 405 H6
st. Quakers Hill 244 A1
PICTOR
st. Erskine Park 300 K3
PIDCOCK
st. Camperdwn 17 D4
PIDDING
rd. Ryde 312 G1
PIER
st. Haymarket E A4
st. Haymarket 3 B10
st. Prospect 274 H11
st. Sydney E A4
st. Sydney 3 B10
PIERCE
pl. Bonnet Bay 460 D10
st. Mount Druitt 241 F13
st. Newtown 17 A10
st. Prairiewood 334 H7
PIERRE
cl. Mt Colah 192 C3
PIERSON
la. Canterbury 372 G13
PIESLEY
st. Prairiewood 334 K9
PIGEON
cl. Hinchinbrk 393 C4
PIGGERY
la. Richmond 118 K12
PIGGOTT
wy. Ingleburn 452 K10
PIGOTT
la. Marrickville 373 E15
st. Dulwich Hill 373 D8
PIKE
rd. Hornsby Ht 191 F2
st. Rydalmere 309 E4
PIKES
la. Eastern Ck 272 J11
la. Newtown 17 E11
PILBARA
pl. Grays Point 491 A14
PILBARRA
pl. Cartwright 394 A4
PILCHER
av. Castle Hill 218 J12
st. Strathfield S 370 K7
PILCHERS
la. Burwood, off Belmore St 342 A15
PILDRA
av. St Ives 223 J14
pl. Frenchs Frst 256 E8
PILE
pl. N Sydney 6 A10
st. Dulwich Hill 373 G9
st. Gladesville 312 G13
st. Marrickville 373 H9
st.n, Bardwell Pk 402 K8
st.s, Bardwell Vy 403 A9
PILGRIM
av. Marrickville 373 D14
av. Strathfield 341 F11
PILLARS
pl. Matraville 436 J1
PILLIGA
cr. Bossley Park 333 G12
ct. Wattle Grove 426 C3
pl. Bangor 459 E14
PIMA
cl. Greenfld Pk 334 B16
PIMELEA
pl. Rooty Hill 272 B3
PIMELIA
ct. Voyager Pt 427 C5
st. Tahmoor 565 H8
PINANG
pl. Whalan 240 K7
PINAROO
cr. Bradbury 511 C16
pl. Gymea Bay 491 H8
pl. Lane Cove W 283 J14
PINCOMBE
cr. Harringtn Pk 478 F8
PINDARI
av. Camden 506 K4
av. Carlingford 279 F3
av. Castle Cove 285 H3
av. Loftus 490 B10
av. Mosman 287 A16
av. St Ives 254 A2
cr. S Wntwthvle 306 H7
dr. S Penrith 266 J7
pl. Bardwell Vy 403 C7
pl. Bayview 168 K13
rd. Dover Ht 348 F14
rd. Peakhurst 430 C9
st. Hornsby Ht 191 G2
st. North Ryde 282 F8
st. Winmalee 173 A9
PINDARUS
wy. Rsemeadow 540 H3
PINDOS
pl. Emu Heights 235 B5
PINDRIE
pl. Belrose 225 H16
st. Miranda 492 C9
PINDURO
pl. Cromer 227 H13
PINE
av. Bradbury 511 C13
av. Brookvale 258 C9
av. Earlwood 403 H2
av. Five Dock 343 B7
av. Narraweena 258 C7
av. Russell Lea 343 B7
av. Wareemba 343 B7
cr. Bella Vista 246 E5
cr. Bidwill 211 G13
la. Chippendale 18 H3
la. Manly 288 G6
la. Newtown 18 A11
la. Rydalmere 309 H1
la. Bondi Jctn, off Hollywood Av 377 F3
la. Engadine, off Mianga Av 518 J2
pl. Chippendale 18 J3
pl. Grose Vale 84 J13
pl. Narraweena 258 C7
pl. Riverstone 182 K4
rd. Auburn 339 A6
rd. Casula 423 J1
rd. Casula 423 K1
rd. Casula 424 D2
rd. Fairfield 336 H7
rd. Yennora 336 H7
sq. Leichhardt 16 B1
st. Cammeray 316 A3
st. Chippendale 18 J3
st. Lugarno 429 J15
st. Manly 288 E6
st. Manly 288 F6
st. Marrickville 373 F11
st. Newtown 18 B10
st. Normanhurst 221 D13
st. North Ryde 282 F7
st. Randwick 377 D9
st. Rozelle 7 D14
st. Rydalmere 309 G1
st.e, Cammeray 316 B4
PINE CREEK
cct. St Clair 299 H1
PINECREST
st. Winmalee 173 E5
PINEDALE
pl. Kurrajong Ht 53 K4
PINEGROVE
tce. Minchinbury 272 D8
PINE HILL
av. Double Bay 14 D12
PINEHURST
av. Glenmore Pk 266 G10
av. Rouse Hill 185 B9
PINELEIGH
rd. Lalor Park 245 K13
PINERA
cl. Hornsby 221 B2
PINERIDGE
cr. Silverdale 383 A11
cr. Silverdale 413 A4
PINES
av. Little Bay 437 G15
pde. Gymea 491 G7
PINETREE
av. Cranebrook 237 E1
dr. Carlingford 249 H13
PINE VALLEY
rd. Galston 160 D13
PINEVIEW
av. Manly Vale 287 H3
av. Roselands 400 G8
pl. Dural 219 B7
PINNACLE
st. Miranda 491 H4
st. Sadleir 394 B1
wy. Glenwood 215 G16
PINNER
cl. N Epping 251 G11
PIN OAK
gr. Menai 458 J15
pl. Narellan Vale 479 A12
PINOT
pl. Minchinbury 271 G7
st. Eschol Park 481 D2
PINTA
pl. Cromer 228 B15
PINTO
la. St Clair, off Pinto Pl 270 E12
pl. St Clair 270 E11
PINUS
av. Glenorie 128 F12
PIO
wy. Acacia Gdn 214 J16
PIONEER
av. Thornleigh 221 B11
dr. Menai 459 A12
gr. Wrrngtn Dns 238 C5
la. Wrrngtn Dns, off Pioneer Gr 238 D5
pl. Castle Hill 218 F13
rd. Cronulla 493 J16
st. Seven Hills 245 E15
st. Wentwthvle 276 H13
PIPER
cl. Kingswood 267 E3
cl. Milperra 397 C10
la. Annandale 11 A12
la. Kingswood, off Piper Cl 267 F2
pl. Minchinbury 271 H8
st. Annandale 10 J11
st. Lilyfield 10 D9
st. West Hoxton 392 C9
st.n, Annandale 11 B12
st.s, Annandale 11 A12
wy. Minto 482 K2
wy. Narellan 478 G13
PIPERITA
cl. Mt Colah 191 K3
pl. Winmalee 173 E8
PIPERS
la. Silverdale 384 A4
PIPET
pl. Hinchinbrk 393 C3

PIPINO
pl. Dee Why 258 H1
PIPIT
pl. Ingleburn 453 H8
PIPON
cl. Green Valley 362 K11
PIPPA
st. Seven Hills 246 A11
PIPPEN
pl. Rooty Hill 242 A12
st. Harringtn Pk 478 F6
PIPPITA
pl. Bangor 459 F14
st. Lidcombe 340 D6
PIPPITTA
st. Marayong 244 B2
PIQUET
pl. Toongabbie 276 D5
PIRA
pl. Forestville 255 F8
PIRIE
cl. Wakeley 334 J14
st. Liverpool 395 D5
PIRIWAL
cl. Bangor 459 D14
PIROL
pl. Dean Park 242 K1
PIRON
pl. Woronora Ht 489 C6
PIRRAMA
rd. Pyrmont 8 F16
PISA
pl. Plumpton 241 G8
PISCES
la. Erskine Park, off Pisces Pl 300 H1
pl. Erskine Park 300 H1
PITAPUNGA
cl. Woodcroft 243 G11
PITCAIRN
av. Lethbrdg Pk 210 F16
PITLOCHRY
rd. St Andrews 452 A15
PITMAN
av. Hornsby Ht 161 F15
PITT
la. N Richmond 87 F14
la. Rockdale 403 E15
la. Parramatta, off Steele St 307 K5
rd. N Curl Curl 258 G10
st. Badgerys Ck 358 G4
st. Balgowlah 287 J6
st. Canley Ht 335 G16
st. Concord 341 H7
st. Granville 307 K8
st. Haymarket E F13
st. Haymarket 3 F15
st. Holroyd 307 J12
st. Hunters Hill 313 E11
st. Kirribilli 6 A16
st. Loftus 490 C9
st. Manly Vale 287 J5
st. Mays Hill 307 K8
st. Merrylands 307 J12
st. Mortdale 431 B9
st. Parramatta 308 A4
st. Randwick 377 C14
st. Redfern 19 E10
st. Richmond 119 B5
st. Riverstone 182 J7
st. Rockdale 403 E15
st. Springwood 201 E4
st. Sydney C K16
st. Sydney 1 H16
st. Sydney 3 H6
st. Tahmoor 565 H13
st. Waterloo 19 E11
st. Waterloo 19 F15
st. Windsor 121 F7
PITTMAN STEPS
pl. Blair Athol 511 B4
PITT-OWEN
av. Arncliffe 403 F9
PITT TOWN
rd. Kenthurst 157 A13
rd. McGraths Hl 121 J12
rd. Maraylya 125 B2
rd. Pitt Town 122 F7
PITT TOWN BOTTOMS
rd. Pitt Town 92 A8
rd. Pitt Twn Bttms 122 A3
PITT TOWN DURAL
rd. Maraylya 94 A14
rd. Pitt Town 93 E12
PITT TOWN FERRY
rd. Wilberforce 92 D2
PITT VIEW
st. Scotland I 168 J2
PITTWATER
rd. Bayview 168 J10
rd. Brookvale 258 A12
rd. Church Point 168 F7
rd. Collaroy 229 A6
rd. Dee Why 258 F7
rd. East Ryde 283 B11
rd. Gladesville 312 J9
rd. Hunters Hill 313 A7
rd. Mcquarie Pk 283 A6
rd. Manly 288 G8
rd. Mona Vale 199 C6
rd. Narrabeen 229 A6
rd. North Manly 258 A13
rd. N Narrabeen 229 A2
rd. North Ryde 283 B11
rd. Queenscliff 288 D2
rd. Warriewood 199 A16
PITURI
pl. Alfords Point 429 A14
wy. Kellyville 215 A1
PIUS
la. Marsden Pk 211 J2
PIVETTA
st. Revesby 399 A14
PLAINS VIEW
cr. Mt Riverview 204 H14
PLANA
cr. Springwood 202 B2
PLANE
pl. Prestons 393 J14
PLANE TREE
dr. Narellan Vale 479 A13
dr. Stanhpe Gdn 215 D10
PLANT
la. Mortlake, off Herbert St 312 B16
st. Balgowlah 287 E10
st. Carlton 432 H11
PLANTE
wk. Lalor Park 245 G12
PLANTHURST
rd. Carlton 432 F10
PLASSER
cr. N St Marys 240 A13
PLASSEY
rd. Mcquarie Pk 283 D7
PLASTO
st. Greenacre 370 F15
PLATEAU
cl. Hornsby Ht 161 H15
pde. Blaxland 233 C6
rd. Avalon 169 K4
rd. Bilgola 169 F6
rd. Collaroy Plat 228 J15
rd. Springwood 201 D1
PLATFORM
st. Lidcombe 340 A6
PLATO
pl. Wetherill Pk 335 A6
PLATTS
av. Belmore 401 H3
PLAYER
st. St Marys 269 D3
PLAYFAIR
av. Moore Park 21 B10
rd. Mt Colah 192 D1
rd. N Curl Curl 258 H11
st. The Rocks A K2
PLAYFORD
rd. Padstow Ht 429 E8
PLEASANT
av. E Lindfield 255 A13
av. Erskineville 374 K9
ct. Carlingford 279 G5
pl. Leonay 234 K16
pl. Yarramundi 145 F8
st. Bossley Park 334 B10
wy. Blakehurst 462 B1
PLEASURE POINT
rd. Pleasure Pt 427 G9
PLIMSOLL
la. Belmore, off Plimsoll St 401 H1
st. Belmore 401 H1
st. McGraths Hl 122 A11
st. Sans Souci 462 J4
PLOUGH INN
rd. Leumeah 481 K13
PLOUGHMAN
cr. Wrrngtn Dns 238 A4
cr. Wrrngtn Dns 238 A5
PLOVER
cl. St Clair 270 B14
gln. Bella Vista 246 F1
la. St Clair, off Plover Cl 270 B14
pl. Ingleburn 453 G10
st. Grays Point 491 F15
st. Newington 310 D12
st. Plumpton 241 K9
PLOWMAN
rd. Currans Hill 479 K8
rd. Minto 453 C15
st. North Bondi 348 D16
PLUKAVEC
cct. Prestons 393 C13
PLUM
cl. Casula 424 B2
gdn. Glenwood 215 D13
PLUME
cl. Mcquarie Fd 454 A3
PLUMER
rd. Rose Bay 347 G12
PLUMPTON
rd. Glendenning 242 C7
rd. Plumpton 242 C7
PLUMTREE
ct. W Pnnant Hl 248 K4
PLUNKETT
cr. Kingswood 267 F1
cr. Mount Druitt 241 G11
la. Drummoyne 343 H4
pl. Gladesville 312 K12
rd. Mosman 317 E8
st. Drummoyne 343 G5
st. Kirribilli 2 F2
st. Marsfield 281 K2
st. St Leonards 315 D5
st. Woolmloo 4 F4
PLYMOUTH
av. Chester Hill 338 C14
av. North Rocks 278 H3
cl. Wahroonga 222 G7
cr. Kings Lngly 246 C8
st. Enfield 371 G3
PLYMPTON
rd. Carlingford 250 C12
rd. Epping 250 C12
wy. Glenhaven 218 E5
POA
pl. Glenmore Pk 265 H12
POATE
la. Centnnial Pk 21 D5
pl. Davidson 225 B15
rd. Centnnial Pk 21 C6
rd. Moore Park 21 C6
POBJE
av. Birrong 368 K6
POBJOY
pl. Bnkstn Aprt 397 K1
POCKET
cl. Ambarvale 540 G1
POCKLEY
av. Roseville 284 F5
PODARGUS
pl. Ingleburn 453 G8
PODMORE
pl. Hillsdale 406 G14
POETS
gln. Wrrngtn Dns 238 E6
la. Wrrngtn Dns, off Poets Gln 238 E6
POGSON
dr. Cherrybrook 219 K9
POIDEVIN
la. Wilberforce 91 J1
POINCIANA
cl. Greystanes 306 E12
cl. Mt Colah 192 B2
row. Menai 458 J15
POINSETTIA
av. North Rocks 279 B1
POINT
la. Northwood 314 H9
rd. Mooney Mooney 75 D1
rd. Northwood 314 H9
rd. Lilyfield, off Central Av 344 A7
st. Lilyfield 10 B6
st. Pyrmont 8 F15
POINT PIPER
la. Paddington 21 H2
POKOLBIN
pl. Edensor Pk 363 E2
POLAR
st. Tregear 240 E7
POLARIS
pl. Rooty Hill 272 B2
POLDING
la. Drummoyne 343 H4
pl. Telopea 279 G10
rd. Lindfield 283 J2
st. Bossley Park 334 C6
st. Drummoyne 343 G4
st. Fairfield Ht 335 G8
st. Fairfield W 335 G8
st. Smithfield 335 G8
st. Wetherill Pk 334 C6
st.n, Fairfield 336 F9
POLE
la. Crows Nest, off Hume St 315 F6
la. St Leonards, off Oxley St 315 E6
POLITO
ct. Kellyville 217 A2
POLK
pl. Bonnet Bay 460 C10
POLLACK
st. Blacktown 274 B5
POLLARD
pl. Sutherland 490 G6
POLLOCK
st. Georges Hall 367 H12
POLLUX
cl. Erskine Park 301 A1
POLLY
pl. Plumpton 241 H10
POLO
av. Mona Vale 199 E3
cr. Girraween 276 A11
pl. Jamisontown 236 A16
pl. Prestons 392 J16
rd. Rossmore 419 H4
st. Kurnell 466 D7
st. Revesby 398 G15
POLONIA
av. Plumpton 242 D12
POLONIUS
st. Rsemeadow 540 J5
POLWARTH
pl. Bradbury 511 D13
st. Miller 393 F3
POLWORTH
cl. Elderslie 507 J2
POLYBLANK
pde. North Bondi 348 C14
pde. Rose Bay 348 C14
POLYGON
cr. Earlwood 372 K16
POMARA
gr. Narellan Vale 508 G2
POMEGRANATE
pl. Glenwood 215 F13
POMEROY
st. Homebush 341 C6
st. N Strathfield 341 C6
POMO
cl. Greenfld Pk 334 A16
POMONA
st. Greenacre 370 H12
st. Pennant Hills 220 K15
POMROY
av. Earlwood 373 B16
PONDAGE
lk. Homebush B 310 D15
PONDEROSA
pde. Warriewood 198 G5
pl. Lugarno 430 A12
PONDS
rd. Prospect 275 A15
rd. Wilberforce 62 A6
wy. Airds 511 J16
PONSFORD
av. Rouse Hill 184 K5
PONSONBY
pde. Seaforth 287 A10
PONTIAC
pl. Ingleburn 453
PONTO
pl. Kings Lngly 245
PONYARA
rd. Beverly Hills 401
PONYTAIL
dr. Stanhpe Gdn 215
POOL
la. Glenbrook 233
pl. Fairfield W 335
st. Maroubra 407
POOLE
rd. Kellyville 215
rd. Kellyville 216
rd. West Hoxton 392
st. Kingsgrove 402
st. Longueville 314
st. Wrrngtn Cty 238
POOLEY
st. Ryde 282
POOLMAN
st. Abbotsford 342
POPE
pl. Campbelltwn 512
pl. Fairfield W 334
rd. Londonderry 147
rd. Mount Druitt 241
st. Matraville 436
st. Ryde 312
POPIO
wy. Woodcroft 243
POPLAR
av. Sans Souci 463
cr. Bradbury 511
ct. Castle Hill 218
la. Narraweena 258
pl. Kirrawee 490
pl. Lugarno 429
pl. Picton 561
pl. Westleigh 220
st. N St Marys 240
st. Surry Hills F
st. Surry Hills 4
POPONDETTA
pl. Glenfield 424
rd. Bidwill 211
rd. Blackett 211
rd. Dharruk 241
rd. Emerton 240
rd. Whalan 240
POPOV
av. Newington 310
POPPERWELL
dr. Menai 458
POPPLE
cl. Casula 394
POPPLEWELL
pl. S Coogee 407
POPPY
cl. Clarmnt Ms 238
pl. Greystanes 306
pl. Mcquarie Fd 454
PORLOCK
wy. Canley Vale 366
PORPOISE
cr. Bligh Park 150
pl. Willmot 210
PORRENDE
st. Narellan 478
PORST
pl. Guildford 338
PORT
pl. Kings Lngly 245
st. Tempe 404
PORTADOWN
rd. Wentwthvle 277
PORTAL
rd. Glenbrook, off Great Western Hwy 234
PORTEOUS
st. Edensor Pk 363
PORTER
av. Marrickville 373
pl. Blackett 241
rd. Engadine 489
st. Bondi Jctn 377
st. Minto 453
st. Ryde 311
PORT ERRINGHI
rd. Ebenezer 63

RTERS
St Ives...224 A13
Kenthurst...158 A10
RT HACKING
Miranda...492 C1
Sylvania...462 B10
s,Caringbah...492 H16
s,Dolans Bay...522 H1
s,Port Hacking...522 H1
RTIA
Rsemeadow...541 A4
Toongabbie...275 K8
RTICO
e.Toongabbie...276 B5
RTLAND
Illawong...459 F6
Maroubra...407 D14
Stanhpe Gdn...215 A6
Croydon Pk...371 G7
Dover Ht...348 F11
Enfield...371 G7
Waterloo...19 H12
RT MACQUARIE
Hoxton Park...392 H9
RTMADOC
Menai...459 A10
RTMAN
Zetland, off Merton St...375 H10
Zetland...375 H10
RTSEA
Castle Hill...217 J7
RTSMOUTH
Cronulla...493 J16
RTVIEW
Burraneer...523 E3
Greenwich...315 B7
ST OFFICE
Kogarah...433 B5
Merrylands...307 H13
Pymble...253 C2
Croydon, off Paisley Rd...372 D1
Mosman, off Upper Almora St...317 B7
Chatswood, off Victor St...284 J10
Castlereagh...176 A4
Ebenezer...63 C8
Glenorie...128 B8
Carlingford...279 H3
Pymble...253 C2
TOROO
St Helens Park...511 H16
TTER
Earlwood...372 F16
Wetherill Pk...303 H16
Old Tngabbie...276 J9
Quakers Hill...214 F12
Russell Lea...343 D7
TTERY
Woodcroft...243 E9
Richmond...119 A5
TTINGER
Dawes Point...1 F8
TTS
Beverly Hills...401 E9
Hobartville...118 D9
Homebush...340 K7
Kingsgrove...401 E9
Ryde...312 E5
ULET
Matraville...406 J16
ULTER
Engadine...488 G13
ULTON
Beverley Pk...432 K10
Frenchs Frst...257 A2
ULTRY
Richmond...118 H13
UND
Frenchs Frst...255 F2
Hamondvle...396 G16
Ashfield, off Frederick St...372 G1
Hornsby...221 G2
WDER WORKS
Elanora Ht...198 D12
Ingleside...197 J7
N Narrabeen...198 H14
WDRILL
Prestons...394 B9

POWELL
cl. Edensor Pk...333 H15
cl. Liberty Gr...311 B11
la. Coogee, off Melody St...377 E16
pl. Cherrybrook...219 F13
rd. Rose Bay...347 G11
rt. Westleigh...220 G7
st. Blaxland...233 G12
st. Coogee...377 E16
st. Glenbrook...233 G12
st. Hobartville...118 E6
st. Homebush...341 C8
st. Killara...253 K11
st. Neutral Bay...6 H6
st. Waterloo...19 G16
st. Yagoona...369 E9
POWELLS
la. Brookvale...258 B11
la. Richmond Lwld...88 F9
rd. Brookvale...258 B12
POWER
av. Alexandria...19 A15
cl. Eagle Vale...481 A10
pl. Kings Lngly...245 G6
pl. Menai...458 F12
st. Doonside...243 A9
st. Glendenning...242 G9
st. Plumpton...242 C8
st. Prairiewood...334 H7
st. St Marys...239 G10
POWERS
pl. Bass Hill...368 C13
rd. Seven Hills...276 E2
POWHATAN
st. Greenfld Pk...334 A13
POWIE
cl. Clarmnt Ms...268 J3
POWYS
av. Bardwell Pk...402 K6
cct. Castle Hill...217 C9
cl. S Penrith...267 C7
POZIERES
av. Matraville...407 A16
av. Milperra...397 D11
pde. Allambie Ht...257 J14
st. Woolooware...493 J7
PRAHRAN
av. Davidson...255 D2
av. Frenchs Frst...255 G4
rd. Engadine...518 G8
PRAIRIE
gln. Clarmnt Ms...268 G1
PRAIRIE VALE
rd. Bankstown...369 H15
rd. Bossley Park...333 E12
rd. Mt Lewis...369 H15
rd. Prairiewood...334 B11
PRAIRIEVALE
rd. S Hurstville...432 B12
PRATIA
pl. Glenmore Pk...265 G12
PRATO
ct. Glenwood...245 K5
PRATTEN
av. Ryde...282 C16
la. Punchbowl...399 J5
st. Kemps Ck...360 H6
PREDDYS
rd. Bexley...402 E13
rd. Bexley North...402 E13
PRELI
pl. Quakers Hill...214 C11
PRELL
pl. Airds...512 B10
PREMIER
la. Darlinghurst...4 F8
la. Rooty Hill...272 C1
st. Canley Vale...366 D3
st. Gymea...491 E7
st. Gymea...491 F3
st. Kogarah...433 C4
st. Marrickville...373 H16
st. Neutral Bay...6 D4
st. Toongabbie...276 C5
PRENTICE
la. Strathfield...371 A3
la. Willoughby...285 F15
st. Bnkstn Aprt...398 A1
PRENTIS
la. Ebenezer...63 F2
PRESCOT
pde. Milperra...397 D12

PRESCOTT
av. Cromer...258 E3
av. Dee Why...258 E3
av. Narraweena...258 E3
cct. Quakers Hill...214 D13
PRESIDENT
av. Caringbah...492 D7
av. Gymea...491 B5
av. Kirrawee...491 B5
av. Kogarah...433 D4
av. Miranda...491 H6
av. Monterey...433 D4
av. Rockdale...433 D4
av. Sutherland...490 F4
rd. Kellyville...216 G6
st. Croydon Pk...371 K7
PRESLAND
av. Revesby...398 F13
PRESTIGE
av. Bella Vista...246 E6
av. Roselands...401 C4
PRESTON
av. Bellevue Hill...14 G7
av. Double Bay...14 G7
av. Engadine...518 H3
av. Five Dock...342 J7
pl. Roseville...284 G1
rd. Old Tngabbie...276 J10
st. Jamisontown...236 D14
wy. Claymore...481 F10
PRESTWICK
tce. Glenmore Pk...266 G8
PRETORIA
av. Mosman...317 F9
pde. Hornsby...221 A1
rd. Seven Hills...275 H5
st. Lilyfield...10 D9
PRIAM
st. Chester Hill...338 C16
PRICE
av. Belmore...401 G5
la. Agnes Banks...117 B12
la. Bankstown...369 F12
la. Riverwood...400 B15
st. Merrylands...307 C13
st. Ryde...282 A15
st. S Penrith...266 F5
st. Wetherill Pk...334 G6
PRICES
cct. Woronora...459 K16
rd. Douglas Park...568 H7
PRIDDIS
av. Carlingford...279 D1
PRIDDLE
st. Warwck Frm...365 J16
st. Westmead...307 G1
wy. Bonnyrigg...364 B4
PRIEST
pl. Barden Rdg...458 K16
PRIESTLEY
cl. St Ives...224 B14
PRIMA
pl. Arndell Park...273 E7
PRIME
dr. Seven Hills...276 D1
PRIMROSE
av. Frenchs Frst...256 G6
av. Rosebery...375 H16
av. Rydalmere...309 K5
av. Ryde...311 J2
av. Sandringham...463 E3
cct. Clarmnt Ms...268 G1
pl. Loftus...490 B7
pl. Windsor...121 A8
PRIMULA
st. Lindfield...283 J2
PRINCE
la. Mosman, off Macpherson St...316 G7
la. Randwick, off Prince St...376 K10
la. Mosman, off Union St...317 B11
rd. Killara...253 J15
st. Blacktown...244 H15
st. Canley Ht...365 G1
st. Canley Vale...365 G1
st. Cronulla...494 B10
st. Glenbrook...233 G15
st. Granville...308 F9
st. Mosman...316 H6
st. Mosman...316 H7
st. Newtown...374 G9

st. N Parramatta...278 D11
st. Oatlands...279 A12
st. Picnic Point...428 G7
st. Picton...563 F8
st. Randwick...376 K12
st. Rozelle...11 A1
st. Springwood...202 A1
st. Wrrngtn Cty...238 H9
PRINCE ALBERT
rd. Sydney...D G6
rd. Sydney...4 A4
st. Mosman...317 B12
PRINCE ALFRED
pde. Newport...169 C7
PRINCE CHARLES
pde. Kurnell...465 E7
rd. Belrose...226 C16
rd. Frenchs Frst...256 B4
PRINCE EDWARD
av. Earlwood...372 J16
av. Earlwood...373 A16
cir. Daceyville...406 F6
cir. Pagewood...406 F6
pde. Hunters Hill...314 C13
rd. Seaforth...287 A5
st. Carlton...432 J8
st. Gladesville...313 A12
st. Malabar...437 D3
PRINCE EDWARD PARK
rd. Woronora...460 A16
PRINCE GEORGE
pde. Hunters Hill...314 C13
PRINCE HENRY
av. Little Bay...437 G15
PRINCE OF WALES
dr. Matraville...436 B13
dr. Phillip Bay...436 B13
dr. Port Botany...436 B13
dr. West Pymble...253 A11
PRINCES
av. Vaucluse...348 G2
hwy. Arncliffe...403 K5
hwy. Banksia...403 D14
hwy. Beverley Pk...433 A8
hwy. Blakehurst...432 E15
hwy. Carlton...432 H11
hwy. Carss Park...432 E15
hwy. Engadine...489 C16
hwy. Engadine...518 D15
hwy. Gymea...491 B3
hwy. Heathcote...518 D15
hwy. Kirrawee...490 J3
hwy. Kirrawee...491 B3
hwy. Kogarah...433 C6
hwy. Kogarah Bay...432 H11
hwy. Rockdale...403 D14
hwy. Rockdale...403 D16
hwy. St Peters...374 E16
hwy. Sutherland...490 C9
hwy. Sydenham...374 E16
hwy. Sylvania...461 F16
hwy. Tempe...374 E1
hwy. Waterfall...519 D11
hwy. Yarrawarrah...489 C16
la. Kogarah...433 B6
la. Newport...169 E11
pl. McMahons Pt...5 D13
prm. Seaforth...286 K11
rd. Schofields...183 B14
rd.e, Auburn...339 A14
rd.e, Regents Pk...339 A14
rd.w, Auburn...338 G14
st. Bexley...402 K10
st. Burwood...342 C12
st. Guildford W...336 J3
st. Hunters Hill...313 B5
st. McMahons Pt...5 D13
st. Marrickville...373 E15
st. Mortdale...431 D9
st. Newport...169 E11
st. Penshurst...431 F8
st. Putney...311 J6
st. Riverstone...153 A14
st. Ryde...312 A4
st. Turramurra...223 D11
PRINCESS
av. N Strathfield...341 F8
av. Rodd Point...343 E8
av. Rosebery...375 G13
la. N Strathfield, off Queens La...341 F8
st. Ashbury...372 G10
st. Btn-le-Sds...433 K2
st. Canterbury...372 G10
st. Hurlstone Pk...372 G10

st. Lidcombe...340 B6
st. Rose Bay...348 E10
st. Werrington...238 J10
PRINCESS MARY
st. Beacon Hill...257 K5
st. St Marys...269 F1
PRINCETON
av. Oatlands...279 B8
PRINCE WILLIAM
dr. Seven Hills...276 F3
PRINDLE
st. Oatlands...279 A10
PRING
st. Woolmloo...4 H4
PRINGLE
av. Bankstown...399 A4
av. Belrose...225 K13
av. Frenchs Frst...256 A2
la. Woollahra, off Kendall St...377 G2
pl. Woollahra, off Old South Head Rd...377 G2
rd. Hebersham...241 G10
rd. Plumpton...241 G10
PRION
pl. Hinchinbrk...393 C2
PRIOR
av. Cremorne...6 K7
cl. Illawong...459 F4
rd. Prestons...394 A8
st. Winston Hills...246 G16
PRIORY
cl. Cherrybrook...219 F14
cl. St Ives Ch...224 B2
ct. Baulkham Hl...247 A12
pde. Cmbrdg Gdn...237 J2
rd. Waverton...5 C5
PRISCILLA
pl. Baulkham Hl...247 D3
pl. Quakers Hill...213 J7
PRITCHARD
av. Hamondvle...396 E15
la. Annandale...10 K8
pl. Glenmore Pk...265 K9
pl. Peakhurst...430 F4
rd. Mcquarie Fd...453 K3
st. Annandale...10 K8
st. Auburn...339 B3
st. Marrickville...16 H16
st. Mt Pritchard...364 G8
st. Thornleigh...220 H13
st.e, Wentwthvle...277 A16
st.w, Wentwthvle...276 K16
PRIVATE
rd. Northwood...314 H8
PRIVET
wy. Blacktown...274 E12
PROBATE
st. Naremburn...315 G2
PROBERT
la. Camperdwn...17 C8
st. Camperdwn...17 D8
st. Newtown...17 D8
PROCTER
cl. Abbotsbury...333 A14
PROCTOR
av. Kingsgrove...402 A5
pde. Chester Hill...368 B3
pde. Sefton...368 E3
pl. Berowra...163 D2
wy. Claymore...481 D11
PROCYON
pl. Cranebrook...207 G5
PRODUCTION
av. Kogarah...433 D11
av. St Marys...239 D8
av. Warragamba...353 F10
la. Kogarah...433 E11
pl. Jamisontown...266 D1
rd. Taren Point...462 K14
PROGRESS
av. Eastwood...281 A8
la. Cranebrook, off Pendock La...207 F14
rd. Eveleigh...18 E12
st. Tahmoor...566 A12
wy. Cranebrook...207 F14
PROSPECT
av. Cremorne...316 G6
cr. Canley Vale...366 D2
hwy. Prospect...275 A13
hwy. Seven Hills...275 G2

la. Carlton 432 K5
pl. Como 460 F4
rd. Canley Vale 366 D3
rd. Peakhurst 430 G2
rd. Summer Hill 373 A4
st. Blacktown 274 C4
st. Carlton 432 K5
st. Erskineville 17 K16
st. Greenwich 314 K14
st. Leichhardt 16 B1
st. Newtown 17 H9
st. Paddington 4 J15
st. Rosehill 308 G7
st. Surry Hills 20 D2
st. Waverley 377 G8

PROSPER
la. Rozelle 7 A15
st. Condell Park 398 F6
st. Rozelle 7 A15

PROSPERITY
pde. Warriewood 198 H6

PROSPERO
cl. Rsemeadow 540 K5

PROSS
ct. Ambarvale 540 G1

PROSSER
av. Padstow 429 F2

PROTEA
pl. Cherrybrook 219 E7

PROTEUS
pl. Kellyville 216 G3

PROTHERO
pl. Pagewood 406 D8

PROUT
la. West Hoxton, off Harraden Dr 391 J11
pl. Quakers Hill 214 E11
st. Cabramatta 366 B9
st. West Hoxton 391 K10
wy. Claymore 481 A11

PROVIDENCE
dr. Bella Vista 246 F6
la. Darlinghurst F K7
pl. Darlinghurst F K7
rd. Ryde 312 D3

PROVINCE
st. Abbotsbury 333 A14

PROVINCIAL
rd. Lindfield 254 A16
st. Auburn 339 B5

PROVINS
la. Cranebrook, off Milligan Rd 207 C14
wy. Cranebrook 207 C13

PROVOST
mw. Holsworthy 426 F3

PROYART
av. Milperra 397 G12

PRUNE
st. Wentwthvle 277 B8

PRUNELLA
pl. Faulconbdg 171 E15

PRUNUS
cl. Glenmore Pk 265 G11

PRYCE
ct. Kellyville 186 K16
pl. Rooty Hill 272 C6

PRYOR
st. Rydalmere 279 D15
st. Springwood 202 D3

PUEBLO
st. Greenfld Pk 333 K13

PUKARA
pl. Cromer 258 C1

PULBROOK
pde. Hornsby 192 A15

PULHAM
pl. Chipping Ntn 366 F14

PULLMAN
pl. Emu Plains 235 C7

PULPIT
la. Mosman 286 J16

PUNCH
la. Mosman 317 B5
pl. Glenbrook 264 E1
st. Artarmon 315 B1
st. Balmain 7 C5
st. Mosman 317 B5

PUNCHBOWL
rd. Belfield 371 B10
rd. Belmore 371 B11
rd. Lakemba 370 H15
rd. Minto 482 C4
rd. Punchbowl 400 C3
rd. Wiley Park 400 C3

PUNCTATA
ct. Voyager Pt 427 B5

PUNICEA
wy. Mcquarie Fd 454 H4

PUNKA
pl. Glenmore Pk 266 D7

PUNT
rd. Emu Plains 236 B7
rd. Gladesville 312 J13
rd. Pitt Town 92 G8

PURCELL
cr. Lalor Park 245 E13
rd. Londonderry 148 H12
st. Elderslie 477 F16

PURCHASE
rd. Cherrybrook 219 D9
st. Parramatta 308 G4

PURDIE
la. Pendle Hill 276 E14

PURDY
st. Minchinbury 271 C5

PURKIS
st. Camperdwn 17 E2

PURLEY
cl. Bonnyrigg Ht 363 A7
pl. Cronulla 493 K12

PURRI
av. Baulkham Hl 246 E10

PURSELL
av. Mosman 287 B16

PURSER
av. Castle Hill 217 K15

PURVES
st. Glebe 12 A14

PURVINES
rd. Yellow Rock 204 A3

PUSAN
pl. Belrose 226 A15

PUTARRI
av. St Ives 223 J14

PUTLAND
cl. Kirrawee 490 K8
pl. Vineyard 153 A8
st. Clarmnt Ms 269 A1
st. St Marys 269 E1

PUTNEY
pde. Putney 312 C10

PUTTY
rd. Wilberforce 91 J2

PYALLA
st. Northbridge 285 H16

PYE
av. Northmead 278 C6
rd. Acacia Gdn 214 F15
rd. Bringelly 386 K10
rd. Quakers Hill 214 A15
st. Westmead 307 G2

PYES
rd. Dural 219 F2

PYKETT
pl. Dural 219 A5

PYLARA
pl. Busby 363 H15

PYMBLE
av. Pymble 253 A5
av. Winmalee 173 F5
st. Dharruk 241 C7

PYRAMID
av. Padstow 399 C14
st. Emu Plains 235 B9

PYRAMUS
cct. Rsemeadow 540 H9
pl. St Clair 270 D16

PYREE
st. Bangor 459 D14

PYRENEES
wy. Kellyville 185 J13

PYRITE
pl. Eagle Vale 481 H5

PYRL
rd. Artarmon 285 B15

PYRMONT
st. Ashfield 372 J5
st. Pyrmont 12 G2
st. Sydney 3 A8
st. Ultimo 3 A8

PYRMONT BRIDGE
rd. Annandale 17 C3
rd. Camperdwn 17 C3
rd. Pyrmont 12 F7

Q

QANTAS
dr. Mascot 405 A4

QUAAMA
cl. Prestons 393 B16

QUADRANT
cl. Pymble 252 J4
la. Sadleir 364 B16

QUAIL
pl. Grays Point 491 F16
pl. Hinchinbrk 393 C2
pl. Ingleburn 453 D8
pl. Woronora Ht 489 C6
rd. Blacktown 274 B9
st. Coogee 377 H13
st. Cranebrook 207 C16

QUAKERS
rd. Marayong 243 G1
rd. Marayong 243 K4
rd. Mosman 316 K1
rd. Mosman 317 A1
rd. Quakers Hill 243 G1

QUAKERS HILL
pky. Acacia Gdn 214 F14
pky. Quakers Hill 213 H12
pky. Quakers Hill 243 C3

QUALLEE
pl. Engadine 488 G16

QUAMBI
pl. Edgecliff 14 B13

QUAMBY
ct. Wattle Grove 425 J6

QUANDONG
av. Burwood 371 J2
pl. Concord W 341 G1
st. Concord W 341 F1

QUARRION
pl. Woronora Ht 489 D4

QUARRY
cl. Yagoona 369 B8
la. Dural 189 F14
la. Ultimo 12 J10
la. Glebe, off Quarry St 12 B9
pl. Pymble 253 C5
rd. Bossley Park 333 F6
rd. Dundas Vy 280 A10
rd. Dural 189 C14
rd. Greystanes 275 F16
rd. Hornsby 191 E16
rd. Prospect 275 F16
rd. Ryde 281 K10
rd. The Oaks 501 K11
st. Glebe 12 B9
st. Naremburn 315 J3
st. Paddington 13 K16
st. Tempe 404 A3
st. Ultimo 12 H10
st. Woollahra 13 J16

QUARRY MASTER
dr. Pyrmont 12 D3

QUARTER MASTER
row. Ingleburn 423 F13

QUARTERS
pl. Currans Hill 480 A11

QUARTER SESSIONS
rd. Church Point 168 E7
rd. Glenfield 423 G9
rd. Westleigh 220 G10

QUARTZ
pl. Eagle Vale 481 G8

QUAY
st. Haymarket E B8
st. Haymarket 3 D13

QUEANBEYAN
av. Miranda 462 A15

QUEBEC
av. Killara 283 E1
rd. Chatswd W 283 J9
st. Toongabbie 275 F12

QUEEN
la. St Marys, off Queen St 239 H15
rd. Paddington 21 E1
st. Arncliffe 403 G8
st. Ashfield 372 J10
st. Auburn 339 C2
st. Auburn 339 E4
st. Beaconsfield 375 F13
st. Botany 405 J12
st. Burwood 342 D13
st. Campbelltwn 511 E4
st. Campbelltwn 511 F3
st. Canley Ht 365 G1
st. Canley Vale 365 G1
st. Chippendale 19 B3
st. Concord W 341 D1
st. Croydon 342 D13
st. Croydon Pk 371 F6
st. Glebe 12 G14
st. Granville 308 E12
st. Guildford W 336 H3
st. Hurlstone Pk 372 J10
st. Kurrajong Ht 54 B9
st. Marrickville 374 A14
st. Mosman 317 B10
st. Narellan 478 F10
st. Newtown 18 C8
st. N Strathfield 341 E6
st. Petersham 15 J5
st. Randwick 377 D15
st. Revesby 398 F14
st. Riverstone 182 D13
st. Rosebery 375 G14
st. St Marys 239 G16
st. Woollahra 21 G4

QUEEN ELIZABETH
dr. Bondi Beach 378 D3

QUEENS
av. Avalon 140 A13
av. Kogarah 433 B6
av. McMahons Pt 5 C13
av. Parramatta 308 E2
av. Rcuttrs Bay 13 C8
av. Vaucluse 348 B5
la. Mortdale 431 D7
la. N Strathfield, off Princess Av 341 F8
la. Beaconsfield, off William St 375 F13
pde. Newport 169 E12
pde.e, Newport 169 H12
pl. Balmain 7 K9
rd. Asquith 192 B8
rd. Btn-le-Sds 433 J3
rd. Canada Bay 342 E10
rd. Connells Pt 431 F16
rd. Five Dock 342 E10
rd. Hurstville 432 A4
rd. Westmead 277 H15
sq. Sydney 3 K3
st. Sydney A K10

QUEENSBOROUGH
rd. Croydon Pk 372 C7

QUEENSBURY
rd. Padstow Ht 429 H7
rd. Penshurst 431 A2

QUEENSCLIFF
dr. Woodbine 481 H10
rd. Queenscliff 288 E3

QUEENSHILL
dr. Luddenham 326 C7

QUEENS PARK
rd. Queens Park 22 E13

QUEENSWAY
Blacktown 274 H4

QUEEN VICTORIA
st. Bexley 402 J16
st. Drummoyne 344 A2
st. Kogarah 433 A2

QUENDA
pl. St Helens Park 541 G1

QUENTIN
pl. Oatlands 279 B9
st. Bass Hill 368 B11

QUEST
av. Carramar 366 J4
av. Miranda 491 K8

QUIAMONG
st. Naremburn 315 F2

QUIBEREE
st. Miranda 462 B16

QUIG
pl. Narellan Vale 508 G1

QUIGG
la. Lakemba 401 C4
pl. Orchard Hills 267 F3
st. Lakemba 371 A16
st. Lakemba 401 B1

QUILP
pl. Ambarvale 510 K11

QUILPIE
st. North Manly 258

QUINDALUP
pl. Bella Vista 246

QUINE
la. Punchbowl 400

QUINION
pl. Ambarvale 510

QUINLAN
pde. Manly Vale 287

QUINN
av. Seven Hills 245
pl. Prairiewood 334
st. Castlereagh 176
st. S Wntwthvle 306

QUINTANA
av. Baulkham Hl 246

QUINTON
la. Manly, off Birkley Rd 288
rd. Manly 288

QUIRK
rd. Balgowlah 288
rd. Manly Vale 288
st. Dee Why 258
st. Rozelle 11

QUIROS
av. Fairfield W 335

QUIST
av. Lurnea 394
pl. Greystanes 306
pl. Menai 458
pl. Shalvey 211

QUOKKA
pl. St Helens Park 541

QUOTA
av. Chipping Ntn 396
pl. Edensor Pk 333

R

RABAT
cl. Cranebrook 207

RABAUL
av. Whalan 240
cl. Bossley Park 333
rd. Bnkstn Aprt 367
rd. Georges Hall 367
rd. N Curl Curl 258
wy. Matraville 407

RABBETT
st. Frenchs Frst 256

RABETT
cr. Horngsea Pk 392

RABY
la. Randwick 377
rd. Catherine Fd 450
rd. Leppington 450
rd. Raby 481
rd. St Andrews 481
rd. Varroville 450

RACECOURSE
av. Menangle Pk 538
av. Menangle Pk 539
pl. Eastlakes 406
pl. S Penrith 236
rd. Clarendon 119
rd. S Penrith 236

RACEMOSA
cl. Kemps Ck 360

RACHAEL
cl. Silverwater 310
pl. Glenwood 215
pl. Glenwood 245

RACHEL
av. W Pnnant Hl 249
cr. Mt Pritchard 364
ct. Minto 482
la. Belmore, off Dean Av 371
st. Greystanes 305

RACO
cl. Edensor Pk 333

RADALJ
cl. Rooty Hill 271

RADBURN
rd. Hebersham 241

RADCLIFFE
st. Ingleburn 453

RADFORD
av. Bondi Jctn 377

Castle Hill 218 C10
Gordon 253 G7
Oakhurst 242 B2
IATA
Baulkham Hl 247 F14
IO
Balgowlah Ht 287 H13
ISSON
Kellyville 185 E8
LEY
Cherrybrook 219 E16
Seven Hills 245 B16
NOR
Campbelltwn 511 H9
Smithfield 335 D1
S Turramrra 252 C8
Bargo 567 D4
Galston 160 E5

Moorebank 396 D12
Randwick 377 C12
Currans Hill 479 J11
Woolmloo 4 H6
Randwick 377 C13
Seven Hills 245 D15
BURN
Castlecrag 285 K11
MOT
Baulkham Hl 247 J11
FO
Harbord 258 E15
TER
Abbotsbury 363 A1
TREE
Padstow Ht 429 J7
LAN
Ingleburn 453 A9
Waterloo 19 F12
Auburn 339 A13
Miranda 491 H7
Darlington 18 F6
Drummoyne 313 J16
Malabar 437 E5
Manly 288 E8
Mosman 316 J13
Mosman 317 C8
Turramurra 223 D12
Waterloo 19 C11
T
Doonside 273 H3
DELL
N Epping 251 F10
-
Chipping Ntn 396 C6
SIDE
Bargo 567 E4
WAY
Eastwood 281 B6
Lavender Bay K E16
Seven Hills 276 A3
Stanmore 16 G9
Strathfield 341 H12
Wahroonga 222 D7
Burwood 341 J13
Jannali 460 G11
Newtown 17 G13
N Strathfield 341 E8
Sydenham 374 E15
Kogarah, off
Railway Pde 433 B2
Allawah 432 F7
Annandale 10 K7
Belmore 371 C16
Blacktown 244 B14
Blaxland 233 E2
Burwood 341 J13
Cabramatta 365 J10
Cabramatta 365 K6
Canley Vale 366 B3
Carlton 432 F7
Condell Park 398 E3
Douglas Park 568 F6
Eastwood 281 B7
Engadine 518 H7
Erskineville 18 B14
Eveleigh 18 B14
Fairfield 336 D16
Glenfield 424 A12
Granville 308 D10
Hornsby 191 H14
Hurstville 432 B6
Kogarah 433 A6
Lakemba 400 J2
Lidcombe 339 G6

pde. Mcquarie Fd 423 H16
pde. Mcquarie Fd 423 K14
pde. Marrickville 374 D14
pde. Mortdale 431 D7
pde. Penshurst 431 D7
pde. Springwood 202 C4
pde. Thornleigh 220 K13
pde. Warrimoo 203 D13
pde. Waverton 5 A8
pde. Westmead 277 G16
pde. Marrickville, off
Edinburgh Rd 374 G11
pde.n,Kogarah 433 B3
pwy.Warwck Frm, off
Station St 365 H15
rd. Como 460 J7
rd. Marayong 244 D4
rd. Meadowbnk 311 E3
rd. Quakers Hill 213 J13
rd. Sydenham 374 D15
rd.n,Mulgrave 151 H1
rd.s,Mulgrave 151 H1
rd.s,Vineyard 151 H1
row.Emu Plains 235 K7
sq. Haymarket 3 F15
st. Banksia 403 C15
st. Baulkham Hl 247 J11
st. Campbelltwn 511 E3
st. Carlton 433 A5
st. Chatswood 284 H9
st. Croydon 372 F1
st. Emu Plains 235 J6
st. Glebe 12 C10
st. Glenbrook 233 J14
st. Granville 308 A9
st. Hurlstone Pk 373 A13
st. Kogarah 433 A5
st. Lidcombe 339 J9
st. Liverpool 395 E4
st. Mount Druitt 241 H14
st. N Strathfield 341 E8
st. Old Guildford 337 A10
st. Parramatta 307 H7
st. Pennant Hills 250 G1
st. Petersham 15 K8
st. Rockdale 403 C15
st. Rookwood 340 A9
st. Rooty Hill 241 H14
st. Wentwthvle 277 B15
st. Werrington 239 A12
st. Yennora 337 A10
tce. Granville 308 A11
tce. Guildford 337 F5
tce. Lewisham 15 C9
tce. Merrylands 307 J16
tce. Petersham 373 G5
tce. Riverstone 182 J9
tce. Schofields 183 A12
RAILWAY VIEW
pde. Rooty Hill 242 B15
RAIMONDE
rd. Carlingford 280 E7
rd. Eastwood 280 E7
RAINBOW
cl. Glenmore Pk 265 H9
cr. Kingsgrove 402 C6
la. Randwick 407 A2
la. St Clair, off
Dobell Cct 270 C14
pde. Peakhurst 430 C12
pl. Kareela 461 E11
pl. St Clair 270 C14
st. Coogee 407 F3
st. Kingsford 406 H2
st. Randwick 406 H2
st. Randwick 407 C3
st. S Coogee 407 F3
st. S Wntwthvle 307 D6
wy. Agnes Banks 117 E16
RAINE
av. Liverpool 394 H8
av. North Rocks 248 G11
pl. Barden Rdg 458 H16
rd. Padstow 399 A15
rd. Revesby 399 A15
st. Woollahra 377 G2
RAINFORD
st. Surry Hills 20 B3
RAINHAM
cct. West Hoxton 391 K11
RAIN RIDGE
rd. Kurrajong Ht 53 J7
RAJ
pl. Mount Druitt 241 H13

RAJOLA
pl. North Rocks 248 F13
RALEIGH
av. Caringbah 493 A3
cl. St Clair 270 J12
cr. St Ives Ch 224 A7
pl. Bonnyrigg Ht 363 A6
rd. Milperra 397 D12
st. Artarmon 284 J13
st. Blakehurst 462 E2
st. Cammeray 315 K5
st. Coogee 377 E13
st. Dover Ht 348 F13
st. Guildford 337 C3
RALFE
st. Tahmoor 565 K14
RALPH
pl. Mount Druitt 241 F15
st. Alexandria 375 F16
st. Cabramatta 366 D7
st. Westmead 307 G3
RALSTON
av. Belrose 225 H11
rd. Palm Beach 139 J1
rd. Palm Beach 139 K3
st. Lane Cove W 284 F15
RAMATA
pl. Wetherill Pk 334 A2
RAMBLER
pl. Ingleburn 453 K9
RAMEAU
wy. Clarmnt Ms 268 G4
RAMILLIES
wy. Kellyville 185 K15
RAMLEH
st. Hunters Hill 313 D5
RAMONA
st. Quakers Hill 213 J13
RAMOSUS
wy. Bidwill 211 F13
RAMSAY
av. West Pymble 252 F7
cl. Narellan Vale 479 C10
rd. Five Dock 342 K10
rd. Kemps Ck 359 E16
rd. Panania 428 D7
rd. Pennant Hills 220 F15
rd. Picnic Point 428 D7
rd. Rossmore 389 E8
st. Canley Vale 366 G3
st. Collaroy 229 A10
st. Haberfield 343 B13
st. Picton 563 G1
wy. Claymore 481 E12
RAMSEY
st. Kings Lngly 245 H7
RAMSGATE
av. Bondi Beach 378 E1
av. North Bondi 378 G3
rd. Beverley Pk 433 A13
rd. Kogarah Bay 433 A13
rd. Ramsgate 433 D13
rd. Ramsgate Bch 433 D13
rd. Sans Souci 433 A13
st. Botany 405 G12
RAMU
cl. Sylvania Wtr 462 D15
pl. Whalan 240 J10
RANCE
rd. Werrington 239 B13
RANCH
av. Glenbrook 264 B5
RANCOM
st. Botany 405 H15
RAND
av. Pymble 253 C5
RANDAL
cr. North Rocks 248 F14
RANDALL
av. Minto 453 B16
ct. Collaroy Plat 228 H15
st. Agnes Banks 117 D12
st. Marrickville 373 G13
RANDELL
av. Lilli Pilli 522 F2
RANDLE
la. Newtown 18 B11
la. Surry Hills E K16
la. Surry Hills 19 H1
st. Granville 308 B11
st. Newtown 18 B10
st. Surry Hills 19 G1

RANDOLPH
la. Wahroonga, off
Billyard Av 222 H7
st. Campbelltwn 511 K5
st. Guildford 338 D7
st. Rosebery 405 J3
st. S Granville 338 F7
st. Wahroonga 222 H7
RANDWICK
cl. Casula 394 D15
st. Randwick 377 B11
RANELAGH
cr. Chatswood 285 C10
RANFURLEY
rd. Bellevue Hill 14 J16
RANGE
pl. Engadine 488 C14
rd. W Pnnant Hl 249 B9
st. Chatswd W 284 D9
RANGER
rd. Croydon 342 G14
RANGERS
av. Mosman 316 G9
la. Cremorne 6 H2
rd. Cremorne 6 J2
rd. St Helens Park 541 H4
rd. Yagoona 368 G8
RANGERS RETREAT
rd. Frenchs Frst 256 F8
RANGIHOU
cr. Parramatta 308 G3
RANI
pl. Kareela 461 D9
RANIERI
pl. Hoxton Park 392 K8
RANKIN
pl. Doonside 273 F1
RANMORE
rd. St Marys 269 K4
RANNOCH
pl. Thornleigh 221 C12
st. St Andrews 451 K14
RANSLEY
st. Penrith 236 E12
RAPER
st. Newtown 17 H8
st. Surry Hills 20 C4
RAPHAEL
dr. Hornsby Ht 191 F3
pl. Old Tngabbie 277 A7
st. Greenfld Pk 364 B1
st. Lidcombe 339 K9
RAPLEYS LOOP
rd. Werombi 443 D1
rd. Werombi 443 H3
RASCHKE
st. Cmbrdg Pk 237 G10
RASP
cl. West Hoxton 392 B13
RASPA
pl. Quakers Hill 213 K10
RATA
pl. Sutherland 460 C16
RATCLIFFE
st. Ryde 312 D2
RATHANE
rd. Royal N P 521 J7
RATHMORE
cct. Glendenning 242 J3
ct. Kellyville 216 D2
RATHOWEN
pde. Killarney Ht 256 B14
RAU
pl. Bonnyrigg Ht 363 B5
RAUPACH
st. Dean Park 212 F16
RAUSCH
st. Toongabbie 276 G6
RAVEL
st. Seven Hills 246 D12
RAVEN
gr. Bidwill 211 D13
pl. Ingleburn 453 H6
pl. S Windsor 150 D3
st. Gladesville 312 G9
RAVENGLASS
pl. Cranebrook 207 F12
RAVENHILL
rd. Turramurra 252 E6
st. Kings Lngly 245 B4

RAVENNA
st. Strathfield 371 A1
RAVENSBOURNE
cct. Dural 219 B4
wy. Dural 219 B4
RAVENSWOOD
av. Gordon 253 J9
av. Randwick 377 E11
st. Canley Vale 366 G4
RAVENSWORTH
pl. Airds 512 B10
RAVENUE
la. Stanmore 16 H9
RAVINE
av. Blaxland 233 J6
cl. Cranebrook 207 B11
RAW
av. Bankstown 369 E14
sq. Strathfield 341 F12
RAWDON
pl. Airds 512 A15
RAWHITI
st. Roseville 284 F3
RAWSON
av. Bexley 432 G3
av. Drummoyne 343 J4
av. Loftus 490 C8
av. Penrith 236 H14
av. Queens Park 22 D11
av. Sutherland 490 C8
cr. Horngsea Pk 392 F15
cr. Pymble 223 D13
la. Haymarket E F11
la. Newtown 17 D15
la. Queens Park 22 D11
la. Sans Souci 433 B16
la. Mascot, off
Rawson St 405 E3
la. Mosman, off
Rawson St 317 C4
pde. Caringbah 493 A13
pl. Cromer 227 J14
pl. Haymarket E F11
pl. Haymarket 3 F14
rd. Berowra 133 C14
rd. Fairfield W 335 F11
rd. Greenacre 369 K9
rd. Guildford 337 K8
rd. Rose Bay 348 C8
rd. S Wntwthvle 306 J4
st. Auburn 309 B15
st. Croydon Pk 371 H7
st. Epping 251 A15
st. Haberfield 343 D14
st. Lidcombe 340 A7
st. Mascot 405 E3
st. Mosman 317 B4
st. Neutral Bay 6 A7
st. Newtown 17 E15
st. Rockdale 403 B16
st. Sans Souci 433 B16
st. Wiley Park 400 F4
RAWTON
av. Northmead 277 H8
RAY
av. Vaucluse 348 C5
la. Erskineville 18 A13
pl. Kings Lngly 245 C5
pl. Minto 453 B15
pl. Penrith 237 C3
pl. Woodpark 306 G14
rd. Epping 251 A13
st. Blakehurst 462 B4
st. Turramurra 222 H13
st. Vaucluse 348 G7
RAYBEN
st. Glendenning 242 H8
RAYFORD
cl. Bossley Park 333 J8
RAYM
rd. Kenthurst 187 C7
RAYMENT
av. Kingsgrove 401 J14
RAYMOND
av. Campbelltwn 511 K5
av. Drummoyne 313 F16
av. Matraville 436 E2
av. Northmead 277 J9
av. Roselands 400 J10
av. Warrawee 222 H9
la. Springwood 201 K3
pl. Engadine 518 F5
pl. Epping 251 F15
rd. Bilgola 169 E8

rd. Kurrajong 85 J5
rd. Neutral Bay 6 E4
rd. Neutral Bay 6 F6
rd. Springwood 201 K6
st. Bankstown 399 F1
st. Blacktown 245 A7
st. Eastwood 281 G3
st. Freemns Rch 90 E2
st. Glenbrook 264 A1
st. Granville 308 D7
st. Harris Park 308 D7
st. Oatley 430 H14
st.e, Lidcombe 339 H10
st.w, Lidcombe 339 G10

RAYNER
av. Narraweena 258 D2
pl. Bonnyrigg 364 A8
rd. Whale Beach 140 E9
st. Lilyfield 10 A7

RAYNOR
av. Abbotsford 342 K3
pl. Baulkham Hl 247 D6
st. Mount Druitt 241 C13

REA
st. Greenacre 370 E9

REACH
cl. Abbotsbury 333 B15

READ
la. Bronte 377 J7
pl. Seven Hills 276 E1
pl. W Pnnant Hl 249 F7
st. Blakehurst 462 C1
st. Bronte 377 J7
st. Eastwood 280 H11
wy. Claymore 481 B11

READFORD
pl. Ryde 282 B13

READING
av. East Killara 254 F7
av. Kings Lngly 246 B9
rd. Btn-le-Sds 404 A16
st. Glenbrook 233 G15

REAGHS FARM
rd. Minto 482 E7

REALM
st. Arncliffe 403 D7

REARDEN
av. Kings Lngly 245 K9

REARWIN
pl. Bnkstn Aprt 397 K1

REBECCA
ct. Rouse Hill 184 K8
pde. Winston Hills 276 J3
pl. Cherrybrook 219 H4
pl. Ingleburn 453 D10
rd. Greenacre 370 F4
st. Colyton 270 D8

RECREATION
av. Penrith 236 C8
av. Roseville 284 J4
dr. Waverton 315 D11
dr. Wollstncraft 315 D11
pl. Busby 363 H12

RECTORY
av. Ashfield 342 K15

RED
pl. Westleigh 220 J8

REDAN
la. Mosman 317 C7
st. Mosman 317 C7

REDBANK
pl. Northmead 277 G9
pl. Picton 563 B14
rd. Killara 253 K16
rd. Kurrajong 86 A7
rd. Northmead 277 G9
rd. Northmead 277 H11
rd. N Richmond 86 A7

REDBUSH
cl. Rouse Hill 185 C8
gr. Menai 458 K15

RED CEDAR
dr. Mt Colah 162 E14

RED-CROWNED
ct. Winmalee 173 G6

REDDALL
st. Campbelltwn 511 G5
st. Manly 288 J11

REDDAN
av. Penrith 237 C13

REDDEN
dr. Kellyville 216 B3
dr. Kellyville 216 D3

REDDINGTON
av. St Clair 270 E12

REDDISH
cl. Lane Cove W, off Whitfield Av 283 F12

REDDITCH
cr. Hebersham 241 E7
wy. Cranebrook 207 G13

REDDY
la. Edgecliff 13 E10
st. Edgecliff 13 F10

REDFERN
gln. St Clair 270 D10
la. Redfern 19 G8
pde. Dee Why 258 F5
pl. Gymea 461 H16
pl. Pitt Town 93 A12
rd. Minto 482 F3
st. Blaxland 234 B7
st. Granville 338 F1
st. Ingleburn 453 E3
st. Redfern 19 C8
st. Wetherill Pk 335 A1

REDFIELD
rd. East Killara 254 H7

RED GABLES
rd. Box Hill 124 C14

REDGRAVE
pl. W Pnnant Hl 248 K9
rd. Normanhurst 221 H12

REDGROVE
av. Beecroft 250 E10

RED GUM
cr. Bowen Mtn 83 K7

REDGUM
av. Cronulla 523 J3
av. Killara 254 D11
av. Pennant Hills 220 D13
cct. Glendenning 242 J5
cl. Kellyville 186 A16
dr. Lugarno 429 K9
dr. Padstow 429 G2
pl. Frenchs Frst 256 B2

REDHEAP
rd. Faulconbdg 172 A5

RED HOUSE
cr. McGraths Hl 121 J13

REDIN
pl. Connells Pt 431 H14

REDLEAF
av. Wahroonga 222 D8
cl. Galston 159 F9
la. Wahroonga, off Redleaf Av 222 D8

RED LION
st. Rozelle 344 E8

REDMAN
av. Illawong 459 J7
la. Belmore 371 E14
pde. Belmore 371 F15
pl. W Pnnant Hl 248 K2
rd. Dee Why 258 E6
st. Campsie 372 B14
st. Canterbury 372 B14
st. Seaforth 287 B8

REDMAYNE
rd. Horsley Pk 302 G13

REDMILL
cl. Cheltenham 250 J10

REDMOND
av. Baulkham Hl 246 K15
st. Leichhardt 16 C3

REDMYRE
rd. Strathfield 341 C14
rd. Strathfield 341 G12

REDNAL
st. Mona Vale 169 D14

REDSHAW
st. Ryde 312 E1

REDSTONE
pl. St Clair 299 H1

REDWOOD
av. Berowra 133 C16
cl. Castle Hill 218 D8
pl. Clarmnt Ms 238 G16
pl. Forestville 256 B7
pl. Mcquarie Fd 424 E15
pl. Padstow Ht 429 E7
rd. Engadine 488 G15
st. Blacktown 244 K7

REE
pl. Bidwill 211 C16

pl. St Clair 299 K2

REED
la. Cremorne, off Florence La 316 F10
pl. Fairfield W 335 C9
pl. Shalvey 211 B13
st. Cremorne 316 F11
st. Croydon 342 D16

REEDE
st. Turrella 403 D5

REEDY
rd. Cattai 94 G6
rd. Horsley Pk 302 F10
rd. Maraylya 94 G6

REEF
st. Bundeena 524 A11
st. Manly Vale 287 H5
st. Quakers Hill 213 G14

REELY
st. Pymble 223 C12

REEN
rd. Prospect 274 A16

REES
av. Belmore 401 H4
cl. Eagle Vale 480 K10
st. Mays Hill 307 G6

REEVE
cr. Doonside 243 D9
pl. Barden Rdg 488 G7
pl. Camden S 507 A13
st. Waterloo 19 E13

REEVES
av. Epping 251 D16
cr. Bonnyrigg 364 C4

REFALO
pl. Quakers Hill 213 H7

REFINERY
dr. Pyrmont 8 D16
dr. Pyrmont 12 D1

REFRACTORY
ct. Holroyd 307 K10
ct. Holroyd, off Brickworks Dr 308 A10

REGAL
av. Kings Lngly 245 D6
ct. North Rocks 278 J3
st. Regents Pk 338 J15

REGAN
cl. Jamisontown 266 B4
pl. Rooty Hill 272 A4
st. Hurstville 401 G15
st. Rsemeadow 540 J5

REGATTA
av. Caringbah 492 H16
la. Leonay, off Regatta Pl 264 K2
pl. Leonay 265 A2
rd. Canada Bay 342 E10
rd. Five Dock 342 E11

REGENCY
ct. Oatlands 279 A8
gr. Woodcroft 243 F8

REGENT
cr. Moorebank 396 A9
la. Kogarah 433 D3
la. Newtown 17 E12
la. Paddington 21 C3
la. Ryde 311 J5
pl. Castle Hill 217 C8
pl. Illawong 459 G3
pl. Redfern 19 B7
st. Berala 339 B16
st. Bexley 432 E1
st. Chippendale E B16
st. Chippendale 19 C4
st. Dee Why 258 G4
st. Kogarah 433 B3
st. Leichhardt 9 E15
st. Paddington 21 C4
st. Petersham 15 J11
st. Redfern 19 B9
st. Regents Pk 339 B16
st. Riverstone 182 K10
st. Rozelle 10 G1
st. Ryde 311 J6
st. Summer Hill 373 C5

REGENTVILLE
rd. Glenmore Pk 265 F5
rd. Jamisontown 236 C16
rd. Mulgoa 265 B5

REGIMENT
gr. Winston Hills 277 A3

REGIMENTAL
sq. Sydney C G2

REGINA
av. Brookvale 258 C9
st. Guildford W 306 K16

REGINALD
av. Belmore 401 F2
pl. Merrylands W 307 B15
st. Bexley 402 J12
st. Chatswd W 284 E10
st. Mosman 316 G10
st. Wareemba 342 K5

REGREME
rd. Picton 561 B3
rd. Picton 563 G1

REGULUS
la. Erskine Park, off Regulus St 300 H2
st. Erskine Park 300 F2

REIBA
cr. Revesby 399 A10

REIBY
dr. Baulkham Hl 247 G5
la. Newtown 17 D14
pl. Bradbury 511 H11
pl. McGraths Hl 122 A12
pl. Sydney B B8
rd. Hunters Hill 313 F9
st. Newtown 17 D14

REID
av. Campsie 402 A3
av. Castle Hill 247 K5
av. Greenacre 370 D7
av. Matraville 436 K8
av. Narraweena 258 C6
av. N Curl Curl 258 J10
av. Wentwthvle 277 C16
av. Woolmloo 4 G6
cir. Winmalee 173 D10
dr. Chatswd W 283 K9
pl. Chipping Ntn 396 C6
pl. Illawong 459 A7
rd. Winmalee 173 C11
st. Ermington 310 C1
st. Lindfield 254 C15
st. Merrylands 308 D16
st. Seaforth 287 C9
st. Werrington 238 K9

REILLEYS
rd. Winston Hills 277 F6

REILLY
la. Sydenham 374 E15
st. Liverpool 395 A9
st. Lurnea 394 C8

REIMS
st. Russell Lea 343 E5

REIN
rd. Greystanes 306 G8

REINA
st. North Bondi 348 D15

REINDEER
la. Werrington, off Reindeer Pl 238 G11
pl. Werrington 238 F11

RELIANCE
av. Yagoona 368 E16
cr. Willmot 210 C13
pl. Illawong 459 G5
wy. Airds 511 J16

REMBRANDT
dr. Baulkham Hl 247 G10
dr. Middle Cove 285 K8
st. Carlingford 280 A1

REMEMBRANCE
av. Warwck Frm 365 H15
dwy. Bargo 567 D1
dwy. Bargo 567 G9
dwy. Camden S 537 A3
dwy. Cawdor 537 A3
dwy. Menangle 537 A3
dwy. Picton 561 D4
dwy. Picton 563 F
dwy. Picton 563 K1
dwy. Tahmoor 565 G16
dwy. Yanderra 567 E16

REMI
st. Bankstown 369 G12

REMLY
st. Roselands 401 B5

REMUERA
st. Willoughby 285 H13

REMUS
pl. Winston Hills 276 K1

RENA
st. S Hurstville 432

RENARD
cl. Illawong 460

RENATA
pl. Hassall Gr 211

RENAULT
pl. Ingleburn 453

RENE
pl. Cecil Hills 362
pl. Doonside 243
st. East Ryde 313

RENEE
cl. Glenhaven 218

RENFORD
cl. Menai 458

RENFREW
st. Guildford W 337
st. St Andrews 452

RENMARK
pl. Engadine 518
st. Engadine 518

RENN
st. Kogarah Bay 432

RENNELL
av. Green Valley 362
st. Kings Park 244

RENNIE
rd. Woodbine 481
st. Redfern 20
st. Wetherill Pk 333

RENNY
la. Paddington 21
st. Paddington 21

RENOIR
st. Old Tngabbie 276

RENOWN
av. Miranda 492
av. Oatley 431
av. Wiley Park 400
rd. Baulkham Hl 248
st. Canada Bay 342

RENSHAW
av. Auburn 339
st. Warwck Frm 365

RENTON
av. Moorebank 396

RENTOUL
st. Glenfield 424

RENWAY
av. Lugarno 429

RENWICK
cl. Blaxland 234
la. Alexandria 18
la. Leichhardt, off Norton St 15
st. Alexandria 18
st. Drummoyne 343
st. Leichhardt 15
st. Marrickville 373
st. Redfern 19

REPON
pl. Belfield 371

REPPAN
av. Baulkham Hl 248

RESEARCH PARK
dr. Mcquarie Pk 282

RESERVE
av. Blaxland 233
la. Annandale 16
la. Chatswd W 284
la. Mona Vale 198
la. Randwick 407
rd. Artarmon 315
rd. Casula 394
rd. Clarmnt Ms 239
rd. Freemns Rch 60
rd. Kurnell 466
rd. St Leonards 315
rd. St Leonards 315
st. Abbotsford 312
st. Alexandria 375
st. Annandale 16
st. Beaconsfield 375
st. Denistone 281
st. Hunters Hill 313
st. Neutral Bay 6
st. Penrith 236
st. Rydalmere 279
st. Seaforth 287
st. Smithfield 335
st. West Ryde 281

RVOIR
reenacre...369 G10
yde...281 J13
urry Hills...F J12
argo...567 J11
lacktown...274 D9
t Pritchard...364 F13
rospect...274 C15
rospect...275 B16
ymble...253 B1
ittle Bay...437 A12
urry Hills...F B10
urry Hills...3 J13
DENTIAL
t Annan...479 E15
LUTE
t Mckrl Bch...109 A14
LUTION
Villmot...210 G13
aringbah...493 B3
URCES
ichmond...118 G12
HAVEN
ankstown...369 J15
Hurstville...432 A12
IO
oyager Pt...427 B5
ON
ebersham...241 F4
ella Vista...246 G1
ORMEL
Voolooware...493 G6
WELL
ossley Park...333 F9
ossley Park...333 J9
rairiewood...334 C8
ankstown...399 E3
ORD
ornsby Ht...161 J14
MO
t Ives Ch...224 A4
EAT
enrith...236 E11
lexandria...19 C16
EN
Vinston Hills...276 K3
S
irchgrove...7 F4
lebe...12 A14
eichhardt...15 G3
SBY
evesby...398 J16
NGSTONE
rairiewood...334 J7

ooty Hill...241 K14
eorges Hall...367 E14
Vest Ryde...311 B1
AM
hipping Ntn...366 F15
OTH
untingwd...273 E11
ROFT
uakers Hill...213 F7
S
Merrylands, off
Merrylands Rd...307 H13
ALDO
semeadow...540 J8
ELL
astern Ck...272 E7
ELLA
densor Pk...363 E1
OLDS
ankstown...369 D15
obartville...118 F8
ozelle...7 F13
eacon Hill...257 E4
alston...160 H9
ondonderry...148 D3
almain...7 C12
remorne...316 F7
d Tngabbie...276 J6
ymble...223 E14
oongabbie...276 J6
E
earns...481 B2
Clair...270 B10
ENS
illers Pt...A A1
ES
uildford...337 H6

av. Naremburn...315 G3
pl. Harringtn Pk...478 E1
pl. Kellyville...216 F6
st. Hillsdale...406 G16
st. West Ryde...311 F1
RHONDA
av. Frenchs Frst...256 D9
av. Narwee...400 G11
cl. Wahroonga...222 D10
pl. Concord...342 B6
pl. Plumpton...241 H6
st. Pendle Hill...306 D1
st. Revesby...399 A15
RHONDDA
st. Smithfield...335 F1
RHYL
st. Auburn...338 H1
RHYS
pl. Edensor Pk...363 H1
RIALTO
av. Cremorne Pt...316 G14
la. Manly...288 H10
pl. Heathcote...518 F7
RIBBLE
rd. Bringelly...357 G14
RIBBON GUM
cl. Alfords Point...459 C3
pl. Picton...561 B3
RICE
pl. Oxley Park...270 E2
pl. Shalvey...211 C13
RICH
cl. Bligh Park...150 A6
pl. Jamisontown...266 E3
st. Marrickville...374 C10
RICHARD
av. Campbelltwn...512 A4
av. Earlwood...402 H5
cl. North Rocks...278 D1
cr. Bardwell Pk...402 H8
cr. Cecil Hills...362 E3
la. Bardwell Pk...402 H8
rd. Emu Plains...235 F7
rd. St Ives...224 B13
rd. Scotland I...168 G3
st. Colyton...270 D7
st. Greenwich...314 J13
st. Panania...428 F4
st. Richmond...118 J6
RICHARD ARTHUR
wk. Mosman, off
Ballantyne St...316 K9
RICHARD JOHNSON
cr. Ryde...311 F3
sq. Sydney...B B15
sq. Sydney...1 J16
RICHARD PORTER
wy. Pymble...253 B1
RICHARDS
av. Drummoyne...343 G5
av. Eastwood...280 J8
av. Marrickville...403 H1
av. Peakhurst...430 B2
av. Riverstone...182 G6
av. Surry Hills...20 C2
cl. Berowra...133 G10
la. Surry Hills...20 C2
pl. Concord...342 B6
rd. Riverstone...181 K6
rd. Wakeley...334 G12
st. Blaxland...233 J10
RICHARDSON
av. Padstow Ht...429 C6
av. Regents Pk...339 C16
cr. Hebersham...241 E2
pl. Bella Vista...246 H3
pl. Glenmore Pk...265 J6
pl. North Ryde...283 E10
rd. Narellan...478 E10
rd. Narellan Vale...478 F16
rd. Spring Farm...508 D6
st. Fairfield...335 K14
st. Merrylands...307 D9
st. Thirlmere...562 C14
st.e, Lane Cove...314 G15
st.w, Lane Cove...314 E5
wk. Hillsdale...406 H15
RICHARDSONS
cr. Marrickville...403 K1
RICHLAND
st. Kingsgrove...401 J8
RICHLANDS
pl. Prestons...392 K12

RICHMOND
av. Ashfield...342 J15
av. Auburn...338 J8
av. Cremorne...316 G5
av. Dee Why...258 J5
av. Padstow Ht...429 G6
av. St Ives...224 E4
av. Sylvania Wtr...462 C10
av. Willoughby...285 D16
cl. St Johns Pk...364 D3
cr. Campbelltwn...511 K7
cr. Cecil Hills...362 E7
cr. Hunters Hill...313 B11
ct. Castle Hill...219 A11
la. Cmbrdg Pk, off
Richmond Rd...237 F8
rd. Berkshire Pk...180 F1
rd. Blacktown...244 C11
rd. Cmbrdg Pk...237 F8
rd. Clarendon...120 C9
rd. Colebee...212 C10
rd. Dean Park...242 F1
rd. Doonside...243 G7
rd. Glendenning...242 F1
rd. Hassall Gr...212 C10
rd. Homebush W...340 F9
rd. Kingswood...237 F8
rd. Marayong...243 G7
rd. Marsden Pk...211 J2
rd. Penrith...237 E6
rd. Plumpton...212 C10
rd. Quakers Hill...243 A3
rd. Rose Bay...348 B10
rd. Seaforth...286 J12
rd. Windsor...120 C9
rd. Windsor Dn...180 F1
rd. Woodcroft...243 G7
st. Banksia...403 G14
st. Croydon...342 F13
st. Denistone E...281 H10
st. Earlwood...402 G2
st. Merrylands...307 A8
st. Rockdale...403 G14
st. S Wntwthvle...307 A8
RICHMOUNT
st. Cronulla...493 J15
RICHTER
cr. Davidson...255 D3
RICKABY
st. Clarendon...119 K13
st. S Windsor...150 C1
RICKARD
av. Bondi Beach...378 A3
av. Mosman...317 A13
rd. Bankstown...369 E15
rd. Berowra...133 D14
rd. Bossley Park...334 B9
rd. Chipping Ntn...397 D4
rd. Leppington...421 B1
rd. N Narrabeen...228 G1
rd. Oyster Bay...461 E5
rd. Quakers Hill...213 K16
rd. S Hurstville...431 K11
rd. Strathfield...371 B3
rd. Warrimoo...203 E12
st. Auburn...339 A6
st. Balgowlah...287 H8
st. Carlingford...280 B3
st. Concord...342 A1
st. Denistone E...281 J12
st. Five Dock...343 C10
st. Guildford...337 J5
st. Merrylands...307 H9
st. Punchbowl...400 D3
st. Ryde...281 J12
st. Turrella...403 C6
RICKARDS
rd. Agnes Banks...146 C11
rd. Castlereagh...146 A13
rd. Castlereagh...146 C11
RICKETTY
st. Mascot...404 J1
RICKMAN
st. Kings Lngly...245 E4
RIDDELL
cl. Glenmore Pk...265 K8
cr. Blackett...241 B4
la. Bellevue Hill, off
Riddell St...377 H1
st. Bellevue Hill...347 G16
st. West Hoxton...392 C8
RIDDLES
la. Pymble...253 H1
RIDER
pl. Minto...453 B14

RIDGE
la. N Sydney...5 F2
la. Surry Hills...20 C7
pl. Richmond...118 H7
pl. Surry Hills...20 C7
rd. Arcadia...129 H9
rd. Engadine...488 D12
sq. Leppington...420 H10
st. Chester Hill...368 A4
st. Epping...250 D14
st. Glenwood...215 G16
st. Gordon...253 D8
st. Merrylands...307 A11
st. N Sydney...5 E2
st. S Penrith...266 G1
st. Surry Hills...20 C6
RIDGECROP
dr. Castle Hill...217 F2
RIDGEHAVEN
pl. Baulkham Hl...216 G16
pl. Baulkham Hl...246 G1
pl. Bella Vista...246 G1
rd. Silverdale...353 J14
RIDGELAND
av. Killara...253 F12
RIDGEMONT
cl. Cherrybrook...219 D15
cl. W Pnnant Hl...248 K10
pl. Kings Park...244 G2
RIDGES
la. Richmond...88 B15
la. Richmond Lwld...88 B15
RIDGETOP
dr. Glenmore Pk...266 B13
dr. Glenmore Pk...266 F15
pl. Dural...219 F4
RIDGE VIEW
cl. Winmalee...173 D4
pl. Narellan...478 C9
RIDGEVIEW
cr. Erskine Park...300 E2
pl. Oakhurst...242 D3
wy. Cherrybrook...219 E11
RIDGEWAY
cr. Quakers Hill...213 H15
cr. Valley Ht...203 A5
RIDGEWELL
st. Roselands...401 A6
RIDGEWOOD
pl. Dural...219 C5
RIDLEY
pl. Blacktown...275 A6
RIESLING
pl. Eschol Park...481 B3
RIFLE RANGE
rd. Bligh Park...150 H6
rd. Northmead...278 B1
rd. S Windsor...150 D3
RIGA
av. Greenacre...370 A8
RIGEL
pl. Glendenning...242 F5
RIGELSFORD
st. Mt Annan...479 E16
RIGG
pl. Bonnyrigg...364 B7
RIGNEY
av. Kingsford...406 K3
la. Kingsford, off
Rigney Av...407 A3
la. Cranebrook, off
Rigney Pl...207 D10
pl. Cranebrook...207 C9
pl. Harringtn Pk...478 F6
RIGNOLD
st. Doonside...243 C9
st. Seaforth...286 K7
RIGO
pl. Glenfield...424 D13
RIKARA
pl. Frenchs Frst...256 A2
RILEY
av. W Pnnant Hl...249 E8
la. Burwood...342 A11
pl. Quakers Hill...213 E16
rd. Leppington...420 D14
st. Darlinghurst...F K4
st. Darlinghurst...4 C10
st. N Sydney...5 C7
st. Oatley...430 H11
st. Penrith...236 H9
st. Surry Hills...F G16

st. Surry Hills...F H10
st. Surry Hills...19 K5
st. Surry Hills...20 A3
st. Woolmloo...4 C7
RIMA
pl. Hassall Gr...211 K16
RIMFIRE
cl. Bossley Park...334 A8
RIMMINGTON
st. Artarmon...284 H16
RIMU
st. Cherrybrook...219 J6
RING
st. Belmore...371 D14
st. Sefton...368 G1
RINGAROOMA
cct. West Hoxton...392 D6
RINGROSE
av. Greystanes...306 F6
RINGTAIL
cr. Bossley Park...333 H7
RIO
wk. Seven Hills...275 J4
RIO GRANDE
dr. Kearns...480 K1
dr. Kearns...481 Z9
RIPLEY
gld. Bella Vista...246 F3
pl. Hassall Gr...212 A16
RIPON
rd. Moorebank...425 B2
wy. Rosebery...375 K15
RIPPLE
cl. Greenfld Pk...334 C13
st. Kareela...461 E10
RIPPON
av. Dundas...279 C15
RISBEY
pl. Bligh Park...150 J9
RISCA
pl. Quakers Hill...214 B9
RISDONI
wy. Mcquarie Fd...424 D16
RISORTA
av. St Ives...254 E1
RITA
av. Faulconbdg...171 K8
pl. Oakhurst...241 J5
st. Merrylands...307 E6
st. Narwee...400 H15
st. Thirlmere...565 C3
RITCHARD
av. Coogee...377 E12
RITCHIE
la. Mosman, off
Upper Almora St.317 B6
rd. Silverdale...354 B13
rd. Yagoona...369 A11
st. Rosehill...308 G8
st. Sans Souci...433 C15
RIVAL
pl. Shalvey...210 H12
st. Kareela...461 C11
RIVATTS
dr. Yarramundi...145 F6
RIVENDELL
cr. Wrrngtn Dns...237 J5
wy. Glenhaven...217 K4
RIVENOAK
av. Padstow...429 E3
RIVER
av. Carramar...366 H2
av. Chatswd W...283 J9
av. Villawood...367 A1
cl. Freemns Rch...89 H5
la. Drummoyne...313 G16
la. Wollstncraft...315 E7
la. Chatswd W, off
River Av...283 J8
la. Emu Plains, off
River Rd...235 H12
rd. Elderslie...507 E3
rd. Emu Plains...235 D16
rd. Ermington...310 A5
rd. Greenwich...314 G6
rd. Lane Cove...314 G6
rd. Leonay...235 D16
rd. Northwood...314 G6
rd. Oatley...431 B12
rd. Osborne Park...314 G6
rd. Parramatta...278 A13
rd. St Leonards...315 D7

rd. Sutherland 460 C14
rd. Tahmoor 566 D7
rd. Tahmoor 566 D9
rd. Wollstncraft 315 D7
rd. Woronora 489 H1
rd. Yarramundi 115 K16
rd.w, Camellia 308 J4
rd.w, Lane Cove 314 B3
rd.w, Longueville 314 B3
rd.w, Parramatta 308 J4
rd.w, Riverview 314 B3
st. Birchgrove 7 E4
st. Blakehurst 462 C2
st. Earlwood 402 G2
st. Silverwater 309 J9
st. Strathfield S 371 A4

RIVERDALE
av. Marrickville 373 K14

RIVERGLEN
pl. Illawong 459 K6

RIVERGUM
wy. Rouse Hill 185 A6

RIVERHAVEN
pl. Oyster Bay 461 B6

RIVER HEIGHTS
rd. Pleasure Pt 427 J8

RIVERHILL
av. Forestville 255 J10

RIVERINE
ct. Warriewood 198 J7

RIVER OAK
wy. Westleigh 220 J8

RIVERPARK
dr. Liverpool 395 E7

RIVERPLAINS
la. Mt Riverview 204 H14

RIVERS
st. Bellevue Hill 347 G16

RIVERSDALE
av. Connells Pt 431 G15
pl. Glen Alpine 510 B13
pl. Mt Annan 479 J15

RIVERSFORD
cl. Menangle 538 J16

RIVERSIDE
av. Picnic Point 427 K7
av. Ryde 311 H5
cr. Dulwich Hill 373 D13
cr. Marrickville 373 D14
dr. Airds 512 A11
dr. Lugarno 429 H14
dr. Mcquarie Pk 283 B2
dr. North Ryde 283 F9
dr. Sandringham 463 B6
dr. Sans Souci 463 B6
dr. Yarramundi 145 F10
rd. Chipping Ntn 397 A1
rd. Croydon Pk 371 K9
rd. Emu Heights 205 A15
rd. Lansvale 366 K8
rd. Royal N P 520 E5

RIVERSTONE
pde. Riverstone 182 G2
pde. Vineyard 152 E12
rd. Riverstone 183 A11

RIVERTOP
cl. Normanhurst 221 F12

RIVER VIEW
rd. Pleasure Pt 427 J7

RIVERVIEW
av. Connells Pt 431 K14
av. Dangar I 76 G8
av. Kyle Bay 431 K16
av. Woolooware 493 H8
cr. Mt Riverview 204 H14
pde. Leonay 264 K1
pde. North Manly 288 C2
pl. Oatlands 278 K8
rd. Avalon 139 H13
rd. Earlwood 373 C15
rd. Fairfield 336 F16
rd. Kentlyn 513 C2
rd. Oyster Bay 460 K6
rd. Padstow Ht 429 H5
rd. Pleasure Pt 427 H7
st. Chiswick 343 C1
st. Concord 342 C2
st. N Richmond 87 E14
st. Riverview 313 J5
st. West Ryde 281 B15

RIVETT
pl. Doonside 273 H1
rd. North Ryde 283 C10

RIVIERA
av. Avalon 139 J13
av. North Rocks 249 A15
pl. Glenmore Pk 266 E9

RIX
av. Hamondvle 396 D14
pl. Camden S 507 D13

RIXON
rd. Appin 569 F8
st. Bass Hill 368 B8

ROA
pl. Blacktown 274 J9

ROACH
av. Thornleigh 220 J10
st. Arncliffe 403 E10
st. Marrickville 373 H15

ROAD 4
Kurnell 466 D12

ROAD 6
Kurnell 466 C12

ROAD 9
Kurnell 466 B11

ROAD 12
Kurnell 466 A10

ROAD 13
Kurnell 466 A10

ROAD J
Kurnell 466 A10

ROAD L
Kurnell 466 A10

ROAD N
Kurnell 466 B12

ROATH
pl. Prospect 274 G12

ROB
pl. Vineyard 152 A3

ROBARDS
pl. Stanhpe Gdn 215 G10

ROBB
av. Bexley 432 K1
st. Revesby 398 G15

ROBBIE
cr. Carlingford 249 F16

ROBBINS
rd. Box Hill 154 F16
st. Fairfield W 335 C14

ROBBS
pl. Dundas Vy 279 K7

ROBECQ
av. Cheltenham 251 A7

ROBENS
cr. Catherine Fd 419 B6

ROBERT
av. North Manly 258 A13
av. Russell Lea 343 D7
la. Arncliffe 403 K7
la. Marrickville 373 H12
la. St Peters, off Mary St 374 G14
rd. Cherrybrook 219 C15
st. Artarmon 284 J15
st. Ashfield 372 J5
st. Ashfield 372 K5
st. Belmore 401 H4
st. Canterbury 372 F13
st. Gordon 253 J8
st. Greenwich 314 J12
st. Harbord 258 E14
st. Holroyd 307 K9
st. Kingsgrove 401 H4
st. Marrickville 373 H12
st. Marsden Pk 182 A12
st. N Richmond 87 B15
st. N Willghby 285 G11
st. Penrith 237 A8
st. Petersham 16 B6
st. Riverstone 182 A12
st. Rozelle 7 D16
st. Ryde 311 G3
st. Sans Souci 433 C15
st. Smithfield 336 A3
st. Telopea 279 D9
st. Telopea 279 E9
st. Willoughby 285 G11

ROBERTA
st. Greystanes 305 J8

ROBERTS
av. Mortdale 430 F7
av. Mt Pritchard 364 K12
av. Randwick 377 E11
av. Wahroonga 222 B6
cl. Liberty Gr 311 B11
la. Camperdwn 17 F7
la. Hurstville 432 D5
la. Lane Cove W, off Whitfield Av 283 F12
pde. Hawksbry Ht 174 H3
pl. McGraths Hl 121 K11
rd. Casula 424 H2
rd. Greenacre 370 F16
rd. Greenacre 370 F9
rd. Strathfield S 370 F9
rd. Werombi 443 A11
st. Cabarita 342 D1
st. Camperdwn 17 F7
st. Jannali 460 H13
st. Rose Bay 348 D10
st. St Peters 374 G14
st. Strathfield 341 H11
wy. Claymore 481 E10

ROBERTSON
av. Seven Hills 245 J15
cl. Holsworthy, off Chauvel Av 396 B13
cr. Mt Lewis 370 B16
la. Kirribilli 6 B16
la. Sutherland, off Adelong St 490 D2
pl. Bella Vista 246 G3
pl. Jamisontown 266 D1
pl. Watsons Bay 318 G14
rd. Bass Hill 368 C9
rd. Centnnial Pk 21 A13
rd. Chester Hill 368 C6
rd. Moore Park 21 A13
rd. Newport 169 H9
rd. N Curl Curl 259 B10
rd. Scotland I 168 G3
st. Campsie 372 B16
st. Greenwich 314 J10
st. Guildford 338 C9
st. Guildford 338 D4
st. Guildford W 337 A2
st. Kogarah 433 A4
st. Kurrajong 85 E4
st. Merrylands 338 D4
st. Narrabeen 229 A6
st. Parramatta 308 E2
st. Sutherland 490 D2

ROBERTSWOOD
av. Blaxland 234 B5

ROBERT TUDAWALI
pl. Moore Park 21 C6

ROBEY
st. Maroubra 407 A10
st. Mascot 405 A5
st. Matraville 407 A10

ROBILLIARD
st. Mays Hill 307 H6

ROBIN
av. S Turramrra 252 D8
cr. S Hurstville 432 A10
pl. Caringbah 492 J9
pl. Glenmore Pk 265 J13
pl. Ingleburn 453 G8
pl. Roselands 400 H9
st. Carlingford 250 A15
st. Hinchinbrk 363 D16

ROBINA
st. Blacktown 274 H3
st. St Ives Ch 223 K2

ROBINIA
av. Villawood 337 A15
pl. Alfords Point 429 C14

ROBINSON
cl. Hornsby Ht 191 G3
cl. Lurnea 394 D14
dr. Centnnial Pk 22 B10
la. Woollahra 22 F4
la. Eastlakes, off Robinson St 405 K4
pl. Baulkham Hl 247 C12
pl. S Turramrra 252 A8
rd. Bringelly 388 F15
rd. Cranebrook 207 E11
st. Belfield 371 B9
st. Campbelltwn 510 J7
st. Chatswood 285 B9
st. Croydon 342 F15
st. Eastlakes 405 J4
st. E Lindfield 254 J12
st. Greenacre 370 E3
st. Minchinbury 271 F7
st. Monterey 433 H7
st. Riverstone 182 K10
st. Ryde 312 F2
st. Wiley Park 400 E2
st. Wiley Park 400 F4
st. Woolmloo 4 D7
st. Woolooware 493 J8

ROBIN VALE
pl. Baulkham Hl 247 G11

ROBSHAW
rd. Marayong 244 C4

ROBSON
cr. St Helens Park 541 B2
rd. Kenthurst 187 A11

ROBVIC
av. Kangaroo Pt 461 H7

ROBYN
av. Belfield 371 E11
av. Frenchs Frst 256 K3
av. S Penrith 266 J2
cr. Mt Pritchard 364 H14
la. Panania 428 B1
pl. Northmead 277 H8
pl. Tahmoor 565 F10
rd. Winmalee 173 J6
st. Blacktown 243 K12
st. Peakhurst 430 C10
st. Revesby 398 K14
st. Woodpark 306 G16

ROBYNE
pl. W Pnnant Hl 249 D10

ROCCA
st. Ryde 281 K10

ROCCO
pl. Green Valley 362 J10

ROCHE
gr. Shalvey 211 C13
la. Northbridge 316 B1
pl. Merrylands W 306 K11

ROCHER
av. Hunters Hill 313 C11

ROCHES
av. Bayview 169 B13

ROCHESTER
gr. Castle Hill 217 B10
st. Botany 405 F13
st. Camperdwn 17 H6
st. Strathfield 341 C11

ROCHFORD
st. Erskineville 17 J16
st. Erskineville 374 K9
st. St Clair 269 H9
wy. Cherrybrook 219 B15

ROCK
la. Balgowlah 288 A6
la. Glebe 11 G12
st. Yagoona 368 G10

ROCK BATH
rd. Palm Beach 140 B3

ROCKDALE
st. Banksia 403 D13
st. Rockdale 403 D13

ROCKDALE PLAZA
dr. Rockdale 433 C1

ROCK FARM
av. Dundas 279 E11

ROCKFORD
rd. Tahmoor 565 J14

ROCKLANDS
la. Wollstncraft 5 A1
rd. Crows Nest 5 A2
rd. Wollstncraft 5 A2

ROCKLEA
cr. Sylvania 461 F12

ROCKLEIGH
st. Croydon 342 E13
wy. Epping 251 C14

ROCKLEY
av. Baulkham Hl 247 A9
st. Bondi 378 A4
st. Castlecrag 286 C13

ROCKLILY
av. Westleigh 220 G8

ROCKTON
pl. Prestons 393 C15

ROCKWALL
cr. Potts Point 4 K3
la. Potts Point 4 K3
pl. Potts Point 4 K3
pl. W Pnnant Hl 249 B6

ROCK WALLABY
wy. Blaxland 233 D12

ROCKY
cl. East Killara 254 F6

ROCKY HALL
pl. Wilberforce 61 G1

ROCKY MAIN
dr. Holsworthy 42

ROCKY POINT
rd. Beverley Pk 43
rd. Kogarah 43
rd. Ramsgate 43
rd. Sans Souci 46

ROD
st. Belmore 40

RODBOROUGH
av. Crows Nest 31
rd. Frenchs Frst 25

RODD
la. Five Dock 34
rd. Five Dock 34
st. Birrong 36
st. Sefton 36

RODENS
la. Millers Pt

RODEO
dr. Green Valley 36

RODERIGO
cl. Rsemeadow 54

RODGERS
av. Kingsgrove 40
av. Panania 42
st. Kingswood 23

ROD LAVER
dr. Homebush B 34
dr. Homebush B 34

RODLEY
av. Penrith 23
la. Penrith, off Rodley Av 23

RODMAN
av. Maroubra 40

RODNEY
av. Beecroft 25
cr. Beverly Hills 40
pl. Ingleburn 45
pl. W Pnnant Hl 24
st. Dover Ht 34
st. East Ryde 28

RODWELL
pl. Kellyville 21

ROE
pl. Wetherill Pk 30
st. North Bondi 34

ROEBOURNE
st. Yarrawarrah 48

ROEBUCK
cr. Willmot 21
pl. Illawong 45
rd. Werrington 23
st. Cabramatta 36

ROENTGEN
st. Lucas Ht 48

ROFE
cr. Hornsby Ht 19
pl. Grasmere 50
st. Leichhardt 1

ROGAL
pl. Mcquarie Pk 28

ROGAN
cr. Wakeley 33

ROGER
av. Castle Hill 24
cr. Mt Riverview 23
pl. Blacktown 27
st. Brookvale 25

ROGER BOWMAN
la. Chester Hill 33

ROGERS
av. Haberfield 34
av. Liverpool 36
pl. Campbelltwn 51
st. Kingsgrove 40
st. Merrylands 30
st. Roselands 40
st. Wentwthvle 27
wy. Mt Annan 47

ROHAN
pl. N Richmond 8
st. Naremburn 31

ROHINI
st. Turramurra 22

ROKEBY
rd. Abbotsford 34

ROKER
st. Cronulla 49

ROKEVA
st. Eastwood 28

LAND
Liverpool 394 G5
Northmead 248 B15
Wahroonga 222 C15
Warrawee 222 C15
Wilberforce 61 D10
Bossley Park 334 B5
Greystanes 306 D11
Mulgoa 265 C3
LESTONE
Kingsgrove 401 H7
LF
St Peters 374 F14
LFE
Manly 288 F5
Rosebery 405 E2
LLA
Kellyville 185 K14
LTON
Newington, off
Henricks Av 309 K15
MA
Blacktown 244 F14
Kensington 376 D13
Mt Pritchard 364 F11
Padstow Ht 429 E7
Wallacia 324 K14
W Pnnant Hl 248 J8
Blacktown 244 F12
Ingleburn 453 C10
Sylvania 462 A12
St Ives 224 F7
N Epping 251 E10
MAINE
Wrrngtn Cty 238 D8
MANA
Prestons 393 F15
MANI
Hurstville 432 C2
Riverview 314 B7
Matraville 437 B1
N Parramatta 278 F12
Matraville 407 B16
MANO
Edensor Pk 333 H15
ME
Shalvey 211 A14
Canterbury 372 F15
MEO
Rsemeadow 540 H4
Dural 219 A6
MFORD
Epping 250 J12
Frenchs Frst 256 K4
Kings Park 244 K6
MILLY
Ambarvale 540 D2
Riverwood 400 D15
MINA
Winmalee 173 G10
MLEY
Oakhurst 242 C1
MNEY
Miller 393 H3
Wakeley 334 K16
St Ives Ch 224 A6
Airds 512 A13
MSEY
Waitara 221 J4
MSLEY
Jamisontown 266 C2
MULUS
Winston Hills 277 A1
N
Plumpton 241 H10
NA
Berowra Ht 132 K10
Peakhurst 430 D6
NALD
Dundas 279 K14
Earlwood 372 H15
Greenwich 314 J4
Harbord 258 J16
Lane Cove 314 H3
Narraweena 258 A4
Ryde 281 K9
Guildford 337 D1
Birchgrove 8 C4
Blacktown 243 K12
Campbelltwn 511 K3
Carramar 366 J2
Hornsby 221 F6

st. Padstow 399 B12
RONDELAY
dr. Castle Hill 247 H3
RON FILBEE
pl. Maroubra 407 H8
RON SCOTT
cct. Greenacre 370 F5
ROOKE
ct. Kellyville 186 H15
la. Hunters Hill 313 K11
st. Hunters Hill 314 A12
ROOKIN
pl. Minchinbury 271 J10
ROOKWOOD
rd. Bankstown 369 F10
rd. Potts Hill 369 F10
rd. Yagoona 369 F10
ROONY
av. Abbotsbury 333 A12
ROOSEVELT
av. Allambie Ht 257 D12
av. Riverwood 400 A12
av. Sefton 338 F15
la. Allambie Ht, off
Roosevelt Av 257 D12
pl. Bonnet Bay 460 A10
ROOTS
av. Luddenham 356 G3
ROOTY HILL
rd.n, Oakhurst 242 B11
rd.n, Plumpton 242 B11
rd.n, Rooty Hill 242 B14
rd.s, Eastern Ck 272 F4
rd.s, Rooty Hill 272 D2
ROPE
st. Dundas Vy 280 B10
ROPER
av. S Coogee 407 G5
cr. Sylvania Wtr 462 E14
la. Hornsby 191 G13
pl. East Killara 254 H10
rd. Colyton 270 H5
ROPES CREEK
rd. Mount Druitt 271 A2
RORKE
st. Beecroft 250 B6
ROSA
cr. Castle Hill 218 D14
pl. West Hoxton 392 C8
st. Acacia Gdn 214 H14
st. Croydon 342 D16
st. Oatley 431 D12
ROSAKI
cl. Edensor Pk 333 E16
ROSALIE
av. Camden 507 A6
cr. Greenacre 370 C7
ROSALIND
cr. Campbelltwn 511 K4
rd. Marayong 244 B7
st. Cammeray 315 J6
st. Crows Nest 315 J6
st. Greystanes 305 J7
ROSAMOND
st. Hornsby 191 F11
ROSANNAH
wy. Cranebrook 207 E13
ROSCOE
st. Bondi Beach 378 B1
ROSCOMMON
cr. Killarney Ht 286 B2
rd. Arcadia 129 F14
ROSCREA
av. Randwick 377 D10
ROSE
av. Bexley 402 C16
av. Collaroy Plat 228 D9
av. Concord 341 K6
av. Connells Pt 431 F16
av. Mt Pritchard 364 D9
av. Neutral Bay 6 A2
cir. Winmalee 173 E9
cr. Glossodia 58 K9
cr. Mosman 316 H12
cr. N Parramatta 278 E10
cr. Regents Pk 369 A1
dr. Mt Annan 479 F16
la. Annandale 11 C10
la. Cmbrdg Gdn, off
Rose Pl 237 G2
pl. Cmbrdg Gdn 237 G2
pl. Lalor Park 245 C12

st. Annandale 11 A9
st. Ashfield 372 H5
st. Auburn 309 D16
st. Baulkham Hl 247 G13
st. Birchgrove 7 G2
st. Botany 405 F10
st. Bronte 377 J9
st. Campbelltwn 481 G16
st. Chatswood 284 K7
st. Chippendale 18 H3
st. Cronulla 524 A3
st. Croydon Pk 371 K6
st. Darlington 18 E7
st. Epping 281 C2
st. Hurstville 432 B6
st. Liverpool 395 A8
st. Newtown 17 J9
st. Pendle Hill 306 F1
st. Petersham 15 K15
st. Punchbowl 400 A5
st. Sefton 368 G8
st. Smithfield 335 C7
st. Wilberforce 91 K6
st. Winmalee 173 D9
st. Yagoona 368 F10
tce. Paddington 4 F14
ROSEA
pl. Glenmore Pk 265 H12
ROSEANNE
av. Roselands 400 H10
ROSEBANK
av. Dural 188 G12
av. Epping 250 K14
av. Kingsgrove 401 E8
cr. Hurstville 431 J6
st. Darlinghurst 4 G9
st. Glebe 12 B12
st. Panania 398 D13
ROSE BAY
av. Bellevue Hill 347 E11
ROSEBERRY
pl. Balmain 7 H12
st. Balgowlah 287 K6
st. Balmain 7 C11
st. Manly Vale 287 K6
st. Merrylands 337 F1
st. Riverstone 153 C14
ROSEBERY
av. Rosebery 375 J15
la. Mosman 316 K4
rd. Guildford 337 H7
rd. Kellyville 217 B4
rd. Killara 254 D8
st. Heathcote 518 F12
st. Mosman 316 J5
st. Penshurst 431 B2
ROSEBRIDGE
av. Castle Cove 285 F3
ROSEBUD
la. Paddington 4 G15
ROSEBY
st. Drummoyne 344 B4
st. Leichhardt 15 H3
st. Marrickville 403 G1
ROSEDALE
av. Bankstown 369 G10
av. Fairlight 288 A9
av. Greenacre 369 G10
av. Penrith 237 C14
cr. Croydon Pk 371 K8
pl. W Pnnant Hl 248 K3
rd. Gordon 253 J6
rd. Pymble 223 K16
rd. St Ives 223 K16
st. Canley Ht 335 B15
st. Dulwich Hill 373 C7
ROSEGREEN
ct. Glendenning 242 H3
ROSEGUM
pl. Alfords Point 429 B15
pl. Silverdale 384 B2
st. Quakers Hill 213 K7
ROSEHILL
cl. Casula 394 D15
st. Parramatta 308 A7
st. Redfern 19 A8
ROSELAND
av. Roselands 400 J8
ROSELANDS
av. Frenchs Frst 255 H3
dr. Roselands 400 J8
ROS[illegible]EA
wy. Beecroft 249 J13

ROSELLA
cl. Blaxland 234 E5
gr. Bidwill 211 D13
la. Darlinghurst 4 D8
pl. Cranebrook 207 C15
st. Dural 190 A7
st. Prestons 423 A1
wy. W Pnnant Hl 249 E7
ROSEMARY
cr. Glenmore Pk 265 G10
pl. Blacktown 244 K9
pl. Cherrybrook 219 F10
pl. Mcquarie Fd 454 D2
row. Menai 458 K14
ROSEMEAD
rd. Hornsby 221 B1
ROSEMEADOW
dr. Cabarita 342 F2
ROSEMEATH
av. Kingsgrove 402 A5
ROSEMONT
av. Emu Plains 235 H9
av. Mortdale 431 D7
av. Smithfield 335 H7
av. Woollahra 14 B15
pl. Gymea Bay 491 G13
st. Punchbowl 400 E3
st. Punchbowl 400 E4
st. Wiley Park 400 E4
ROSEMOUNT
av. Pennant Hills 220 G15
av. Summer Hill 373 B7
ROSEN
st. Epping 250 J14
ROSENEATH
pl. Baulkham Hl 247 G6
pl. Engadine 518 F6
ROSENTHAL
av. Lane Cove 314 D1
la. Valley Ht 203 B7
la. Lane Cove, off
Rosenthal Av 314 D1
st. Doonside 273 E2
ROSE PAYTEN
dr. Leumeah 482 A11
dr. Minto 482 A11
ROSES RUN
Westleigh 220 G7
ROSETTA
av. Killara 254 E11
cl. Cranebrook 207 D11
cl. N Richmond 87 G13
la. Cranebrook, off
Rosetta Cl 207 D11
la. Beverly Hills, off
Rosetta St 401 A12
st. Beverly Hills 401 A12
st. Warwck Frm 366 D16
ROSEVALE
pl. Narellan 478 H12
ROSEVEAR
st. Stanmore 16 H8
ROSEVIEW
av. Roselands 400 H9
ROSEVILLE
av. Roseville 284 H4
la. Roseville, off
Roseville Av 284 G4
tce. Glenmore Pk 266 G12
ROSEWALL
dr. Menai 458 G6
pl. Shalvey 210 J13
st. Greystanes 306 B10
st. N Willghby 285 E10
st. Willoughby 285 E10
ROSEWOOD
av. Carlingford 249 E16
av. Prestons 393 J14
av. Prestons 393 K14
dr. Greystanes 306 F11
dr. Mcquarie Fd 454 E1
pl. Cherrybrook 219 K13
row. Menai 458 K12
st. Parklea 215 A12
wy. Werrington 239 B11
ROSFORD
av. Petersham 15 G13
st. Smithfield 335 D1
ROSHERVILLE
rd. Mosman 317 D2
ROSIEVILLE
la. Balmain 7 A8

ROSINA
cr. Kings Lngly 245 G4
st. Fairfield 335 G13
st. Fairfield W 335 G13
ROSITANO
pl. Rooty Hill 271 H4
ROSLEEN
pl. Baulkham Hl 247 E10
ROSLYN
av. Btn-le-Sds 433 J5
av. Northmead 277 H9
av. Panania 428 E1
av. Roseville 284 F2
gdn. Elizabeth Bay 13 A8
gdn. Rcuttrs Bay 13 A8
la. Elizabeth Bay 13 A7
pl. Cherrybrook 219 C13
st. Ashbury 372 D8
st. Elizabeth Bay 13 A7
st. Lane Cove W 284 D15
st. Liverpool 394 J1
st. Potts Point 4 K7
st. Rcuttrs Bay 13 A7
ROSLYNDALE
av. Woollahra 14 D15
ROSS
av. Kingsgrove 401 G6
cr. Blaxland 233 D7
pl. Kellyville 185 F1
pl. Minto 452 K13
pl. N Wahrnga 222 K1
pl. St Marys 239 H14
pl. Wetherill Pk 303 H15
st. Bankstown 399 E3
st. Blacktown 274 J4
st. Brooklyn 75 H11
st. Camperdwn 17 C6
st. Chipping Ntn 396 C5
st. Currans Hill 479 J8
st. Dulwich Hill 373 A10
st. Epping 280 B1
st. Forest Lodge 11 H13
st. Gladesville 312 G10
st. Glenbrook 264 A1
st. Naremburn 315 E4
st. Newport 169 J10
st. N Curl Curl 258 J10
st. Parramatta 278 C16
st. Seaforth 287 C10
st. Seven Hills 275 K6
st. Waverton 315 D12
st. Windsor 121 D8
ROSSELL
pl. Glenfield 424 E13
ROSSER
la. Rozelle 7 E14
st. Balmain 7 E13
st. Rozelle 7 E13
wy. Ryde, off
O'Regan Dr 312 C4
ROSSETTI
st. Wetherill Pk 334 H4
ROSSFORD
av. Jannali 460 J13
ROSSI
st. S Hurstville 432 B10
ROSSIAN
pl. Cherrybrook 219 H10
ROSSINI
dr. Hinchinbrk 393 A4
ROSSITER
av. Maroubra 407 F11
la. Maroubra, off
Rossiter Av 407 F11
st. Granville 308 G15
st. Smithfield 335 K7
ROSSIVILLE
pl. Glen Alpine 510 F12
ROSSKELLY
la. Quakers Hill 243 B2
ROSSLYN
st. Bellevue Hill 347 G16
st. Berowra 133 E10
ROSSMORE
av. Punchbowl 400 C5
av.e, Rossmore 389 J14
av.w, Rossmore 389 C13
cr. Rossmore 419 E3
ROSSMOYNE
la. Ellis Lane 476 C8
ROSS PHILLIPS
la. Padstow, off
Alice St 399 D15

ROSS SMITH
- av. Mascot 405 B6
- av. Meadowbnk 311 D3
- pde. Gt Mckrl Bch 109 A14
- pde. Lane Cove 313 K2
- st. Kings Park 244 C1
- st. Quakers Hill 244 C1

ROSTHERNE
- av. Croydon 342 D12

ROSTREVOR
- st. Cronulla 524 A2

ROSTROV
- st. Penshurst 431 D4

ROTA
- pl. Kings Park 244 K2

ROTARUA
- *rd. St Clair, off Rotarua Rd 269 F14*

ROTARY
- st. Liverpool 365 B15

ROTHBURY
- pl. Cherrybrook 219 C13
- st. Edensor Pk 333 F16

ROTHERWOOD
- av. Asquith 192 A7
- pl. Turramurra 222 H16

ROTHERY
- st. Gordon 254 A4

ROTHESAY
- av. Ryde 311 F5
- st. Winston Hills 277 C3

ROTHSCHILD
- av. Rosebery 375 H16

ROTHWELL
- av. Concord W 341 C3
- av. N Strathfield 341 C3
- cct. Glenwood 215 G10
- cr. Lane Cove 314 E3
- la. Schofields 183 C15
- rd. Turramurra 222 C15
- rd. Warrawee 222 C15
- st. Eastwood 280 K4

ROTORUA
- pl. St Ives Ch 223 J2
- rd. St Clair 269 F14
- st. Lethbrdg Pk 240 E1

ROTTNEST
- av. Hinchinbrk 362 J14

ROTUMA
- st. Oakhurst 211 J16

ROUGHLEY
- rd. Kenthurst 157 K5

ROUNCE
- av. Forestville 256 A6

ROUND TABLE
- cl. Mt Colah 162 E9

ROUSE
- la. N Richmond 87 G7
- pl. Illawong 459 H5
- rd. Rouse Hill 184 F11

ROWALLAN
- av. Castle Hill 217 K13

ROWAN
- st. Mona Vale 199 B6

ROWANBRAE
- cr. Baulkham Hl 216 D15
- cr. Bella Vista 216 D15

ROWANY
- cl. Bonnyrigg 363 H9

ROWE
- av. Lurnea 394 E7
- cl. Wetherill Pk 334 F6
- la. Bondi Jctn 22 G6
- la. Eastwood 281 B8
- la. Paddington 4 J14
- *la. Sydenham, off Park Rd 374 D15*
- pl. Baulkham Hl 247 E5
- pl. Doonside 273 H3
- pl. Greystanes 305 J9
- st. Eastwood 280 H9
- st. Eastwood 281 B8
- st. Five Dock 342 F9
- st. Harbord 288 E2
- st. Manly 288 F10
- st. Roseville Ch 285 D1
- st. S Hurstville 432 A12
- st. Sydney D A3
- st. Woollahra 22 H5

ROWELL
- st. Granville 308 G10
- st. North Ryde 282 J10
- st. Revesby Ht 428 K7

ROWENA
- pl. Cherrybrook 219 C9
- pl. Potts Point 4 H5
- rd. Narraweena 258 D2
- st. Greystanes 305 J7

ROWLAND
- av. Bondi 378 C6
- av. Kurmond 56 E16
- st. Revesby 428 H3

ROWLEY
- la. Camperdwn 17 B8
- la. Eveleigh 18 F11
- la. Eveleigh 375 C6
- pl. Airds 511 J15
- rd. Guildford 338 A7
- rd. Russell Lea 343 C5
- st. Btn-le-Sds 404 A15
- st. Burwood 341 J11
- st. Camperdwn 17 A9
- st. Eveleigh 18 F12
- st. Eveleigh 375 C6
- st. Pendle Hill 276 E16
- st. Seven Hills 245 F16
- st. Smithfield 335 F4

ROWLEYS POINT
- rd. Lansvale 366 J11

ROWLISON
- pde. Cammeray 316 B3

ROWNTREE
- st. Balmain 7 F7
- st. Birchgrove 7 F7
- st. Quakers Hill 213 G16

ROWOOD
- rd. Prospect 275 B14

ROXANA
- rd. Kurrajong 55 H15

ROXBOROUGH PARK
- rd. Baulkham Hl 247 F6
- rd. Castle Hill 247 F6

ROXBURGH
- pl. Bella Vista 246 H3

ROXBY
- gr. Quakers Hill 214 D8
- pl. Hinchinbrk 362 J14

ROY
- pl. Marayong 244 C8
- st. Kingsgrove 401 J5

ROYAL
- arc. Sydney 3 G5
- av. Baulkham Hl 247 G8
- av. Birrong 368 J3
- av. Plumpton 242 C5
- pl. Bardwell Pk 402 K8
- pl. Blair Athol 511 A3
- pl. Greystanes 306 H10
- pl. St Clair 270 E10
- row. Menai 459 A14
- st. Chatswood 285 C7
- st. Maroubra 406 J9

ROYALA
- cl. Prestons 393 D16

ROYAL GEORGE
- dr. Harringtn Pk 478 C3

ROYALIST
- rd. Mosman 316 G11

ROYAL OAK
- dr. Alfords Point 459 A3
- pl. W Pnnant Hl 248 J4

ROYCE
- av. Croydon 342 D12
- st. Greystanes 306 C10

ROYCROFT
- av. Newington 309 K15
- pl. Edensor Pk 363 C2

ROYENA
- wy. Blacktown 274 E12

ROYLSTON
- la. Paddington 13 F13
- st. Fairfield W 335 D13
- st. Paddington 13 F14

ROYSTON
- cl. Pymble 223 D16
- pde. Asquith 192 A10
- pde. Mt Colah 192 A10
- st. Darlinghurst 4 J9

ROY WATTS
- rd. Glenfield 423 J7

RUBIDA
- wy. Mcquarie Fd 424 D16

RUBIE
- *la. Malabar, off Nix Av 437 F7*

RUBINA
- st. Merrylands W 307 B12

RUBY
- ct. Kellyville 185 F7
- pl. Seven Hills 275 D8
- rd. Gymea 461 F16
- st. Carramar 366 G1
- st. Guildford 337 J2
- st. Hurstville 431 G3
- st. Marrickville 373 K15
- st. Mosman 317 B12
- st. Yagoona 368 G11
- wy. Claymore 481 C12

RUCKLE
- pl. Doonside 273 E5

RUDD
- cl. Casula 424 G3
- cl. Edensor Pk 363 F3
- pde. Campsie 371 K14
- pl. Blackett 241 C4
- pl. Doonside 243 B8
- rd. Leumeah 481 J16
- st. East Ryde 283 A16
- st. Narellan 478 F12

RUDDERS
- la. Eastern Ck 273 B12

RUDELLE
- cr. Yagoona 369 B9

RUDGE
- pl. Ambarvale 511 A15

RUDHAM
- pl. Chipping Ntn 366 H15

RUDOLF
- rd. Seven Hills 275 F7

RUDYARD
- st. Winston Hills 247 G16

RUFUS
- av. Glenwood 215 E15

RUGBY
- cr. Chipping Ntn 396 F1
- pl. Sydney A K8
- *pwy. Chipping Ntn, off Rugby Cr 396 G1*
- rd. Marsfield 281 G2
- st. Cmbrdg Pk 238 B7
- st. Wrrngtn Cty 238 B7

RULANA
- st. Acacia Gdn 214 H16

RULE
- st. Cmbrdg Pk 237 H9

RULES
- pl. Horngsea Pk 392 F16

RULWALLA
- pl. Gymea 491 C7

RUM CORP
- la. Windsor 120 J9

RUMKER
- st. Picton 563 D10
- st. Picton 563 D12

RUMSAY
- la. Rozelle 7 F13
- st. Rozelle 7 F14

RUMSEY
- cr. Dundas Vy 279 K11

RUNCORN
- av. Hebersham 241 E8
- st. St Johns Pk 334 F16

RUNDLE
- pl. Gladesville 312 K5
- rd. Busby 363 F14
- rd. Green Valley 363 F14
- st. S Granville 338 F3

RUNIC
- la. Maroubra 406 K7

RUNNYMEDE
- wy. Carlingford 249 H11

RUNYON
- av. Greystanes 306 G5

RUPARI
- pl. Belrose 225 F15

RUPERT
- st. Bass Hill 368 A11
- st. Ingleburn 453 B10
- st. Merrylands W 307 B14
- st. Mt Colah 192 A6

RUPERTSWOOD
- av. Bellevue Hill 14 K9
- rd. Rooty Hill 271 H5

RUSDEN
- ml. Mt Riverview 234 C1
- rd. Blaxland 234 A7
- rd. Mt Riverview 234 A7

RUSE
- pl. Campbelltwn 511 H9
- pl. Illawong 459 E4
- st. Harris Park 308 F5
- st. North Ryde 282 C7

RUSH
- pl. Quakers Hill 243 E4
- st. Woollahra 21 H3

RUSHALL
- st. Pymble 223 C14

RUSHES
- pl. Minto 453 B14

RUSKIN
- cl. Wetherill Pk 334 F6

RUSKIN ROWE
- Avalon 169 H2

RUSSELL
- av. Dolls Point 463 C1
- av. Frenchs Frst 256 D4
- av. Lindfield 284 E1
- av. Sans Souci 463 C1
- av. Valley Ht 202 H11
- av. Wahroonga 221 J7
- av. Winston Hills 277 J1
- cl. Green Valley 363 B13
- cr. Westleigh 220 H2
- ct. Maroubra 407 E13
- la. Allawah 432 D9
- la. Lindfield 254 F16
- la. Oakdale 500 C16
- la. Sans Souci 463 C1
- la. Strathfield 341 G14
- rd. N Parramatta 279 A7
- st. Blacktown 274 G4
- st. Campbelltwn 511 J5
- st. Clontarf 287 F11
- st. Denistone E 281 F8
- st. Emu Heights 235 C7
- st. Emu Plains 235 B12
- st. Granville 308 F11
- st. Greenacre 370 E7
- st. Lilyfield 10 E9
- st. Mt Pritchard 364 H11
- st. Northmead 248 B14
- st. Oatley 431 D14
- st. Riverwood 400 B10
- st. Russell Lea 343 C6
- st. Strathfield 341 G13
- st. The Oaks 502 E10
- st. Vaucluse 318 G16
- st. Wollstncraft 315 C8
- st. Woollahra 22 G3

RUSTIC
- pl. Woodcroft 243 G7

RUTAR
- pl. Abbotsbury 333 B10

RUTH
- pl. Cherrybrook 219 J4
- pl. Minto 482 G2
- pl. Panania 398 D15
- st. Canley Ht 365 A2
- st. Marsfield 281 K5
- st. Merrylands W 307 C12
- st. Naremburn 315 E1
- st. Winston Hills 277 A4

RUTHERFORD
- av. Burraneer 523 E4
- av. Lucas Ht 487 G12
- st. Blacktown 274 A3

RUTHERGLEN
- av. Hobartville 118 D8
- av. Northmead 278 C1
- dr. St Andrews 481 K2
- pl. Minchinbury 271 J10

RUTHVEN
- av. Milperra 397 D9
- la. Bondi Jctn 22 D6
- st. Bondi Jctn 22 D8

RUTLAND
- av. Baulkham Hl 247 F4
- av. Castlecrag 285 K11
- pl. N Wahrnga 222 J2
- st. Allawah 432 F8
- st. Blacktown 274 J7
- st. Surry Hills 19 G2

RUTLEDGE
- cr. Quakers Hill 214 C8
- st. Eastwood 280 H10
- st. West Ryde 280 F10

RUZAC
- st. Campbelltwn 511 J5

RYAN
- av. Beverly Hills 401 B16
- av. Cabramatta 365 D9
- av. Hornsby Ht 191
- av. Maroubra 407
- av. Mosman 317
- cl. St Andrews 452
- cr. Riverstone 183
- la. Forest Lodge 11
- la. St Leonards 315
- la. Yagoona 369
- *la. East Hills, off Park Rd 427*
- pl. Beacon Hill 257
- pl. Emu Plains 235
- pl. Illawong 459
- pl. Mount Druitt 270
- rd. Padstow 399
- st. Bnkstn Aprt 367
- st. Dundas Vy 280
- st. Lilyfield 10
- st. St Marys 269
- st. Thirlmere 564
- st. Thirlmere 564

RYDAL
- av. Castle Hill 247
- pl. Collaroy Plat 228
- pl. Cranebrook 207
- st. Prospect 274

RYDE
- pl. St Johns Pk 364
- rd. Gladesville 312
- rd. Gordon 253
- rd. Hunters Hill 313
- rd. Pymble 253
- rd. West Pymble 253
- st. Epping 280

RYDER
- ct. Rouse Hill 184
- rd. Greenfld Pk 334
- st. Darlinghurst 4
- st. Glenwood 215

RYDGE
- *la. Belmore, off Rydge St 371*
- *la. Belmore, off Rydge St 401*
- st. Belmore 401

RYE
- av. Bexley 402

RYEDALE
- *la. West Ryde, off Wattle St 281*
- rd. Denistone 281
- rd. Eastwood 281
- rd. West Ryde 281

RYELAND
- cl. Elderslie 507
- pl. Airds 512
- st. Miller 393

RYLAND
- cl. Wakeley 334

RYMILL
- pl. Bundeena 523
- pl. Leumeah 482
- rd. Tregear 240

RYNAN
- av. Edmndsn Pk 422

RYRIE
- av. Cromer 228
- av. Forestville 255
- rd. Earlwood 402
- rd. N Parramatta 278
- st. Mosman 317
- st. North Ryde 282

RYRIES
- pde. Cremorne 316

S

SABA
- st. Fairfield W 335

SABER
- st. Woollahra 22

SABINA
- pl. St Ives 224
- st. Mosman 317

SABINE
- cl. Glenwood 245

SABRE
- cr. Holsworthy 426
- pl. Raby 451

SABRINA
- gr. Plumpton 241

BUGAL
Engadine...488 D13
CKVILLE
Ebenezer...63 A9
Wilberforce...62 G16
Bardwell Vy...402 K10
Bexley...402 K10
Blacktown...245 A13
Canley Ht...365 H4
Canley Vale...365 H4
Fairfield...336 A15
Hurstville...401 G16
Ingleburn...453 A10
Lalor Park...245 A13
Maroubra...407 J10
COYA
Bella Vista...246 G6
DDINGTON
St Marys...269 E2
S Turramrra...252 A8
DDLE
v. Holsworthy...426 E4
DDLEBACK
Hinchinbrk...363 B16
DDLER
. Glenmore Pk...266 G13
DLEIR
Ashcroft...394 D1
Heckenberg...364 C14
Sadleir...394 D1
DLIER
Milperra...397 D9
Fairfield W...335 A10
Petersham...15 G11
Mosman, off
Awaba St...317 A4
FORD
Forestville...256 A5
GARS
Dural...188 A11
GE
Oyster Bay...461 C8
Mount Druitt...270 K3
St Ives...253 K2
GER
East Ryde...282 K16
GGART FIELD
Minto...482 C1
GGAS
Springwood...171 D16
ALA
East Killara...254 G7
D
Quakers Hill...214 H14
DOR
Whalan...241 A13
L
Illawong...459 B7
LORS BAY
Northbridge...285 H15
NSBURY
St Marys...269 G1
AGNES
Rooty Hill...272 F6
Blair Athol...511 C2
AIDANS
Oatlands...279 A11
Oatlands...279 A12
ALBANS
Kingsgrove...401 H7
Schofields...183 C14
Abbotsford...342 J1
ANDREWS
Casula...395 A11
Glenmore Pk...266 F11
Pymble...252 J4
Elanora Ht...198 D12
Cronulla...493 J11
Leppington...420 J15
Raby...451 G8
St Andrews...451 K13
Varroville...451 C3
Balmain...8 B9
Rydalmere...279 E14
Rouse Hill...185 B8
ANN
Merrylands...307 F14
ANNE
Blair Athol...510 K2
ANNES
Belrose...226 B12
Strathfield S...371 A5

st. Ryde...312 A3
ST ANTHONY
cl. Kings Park...244 E5
ST AUBINS
pl. Glen Alpine...510 F12
ST BARBARAS
av. Manly...289 A16
ST BARNABAS
st. Ultimo...12 J16
ST BARTHOLOMEWS
pl. Prospect...275 B15
ST CATHERINE
cl. Blair Athol...510 K2
st. Mortdale...431 B6
ST CLAIR
av. St Clair...269 H9
st. Belmore...371 E14
ST DAVID
av. Dee Why...258 G5
ST DAVIDS
rd. Haberfield...343 C16
rd. Varroville...451 G3
ST ELMO
pde. Kingsgrove...401 H12
st. Mosman...317 C13
ST ERMES
ct. Wahroonga, off
Isis St...222 A7
ST GEORGE
cr. Sandy Point...428 A14
ST GEORGES
cr. Cecil Hills...362 E7
cr. Drummoyne...344 A2
pde. Allawah...432 C7
pde. Earlwood...402 K4
pde. Hurstville...432 C7
rd. Bexley...402 D14
rd. Penshurst...431 D4
ST GILES
av. Greenwich...315 B8
ST HELENA
la. Eastlakes...405 K4
pde. Eastlakes...405 K5
ST HELENS
av. Mt Krng-gai...162 J14
cl. West Hoxton...392 E8
ST HELENS PARK
dr. St Helens Park...541 B3
ST HILLIERS
rd. Auburn...339 G1
ST IVES
av. Hunters Hill...314 A12
ST JAMES
arc. Sydney...3 J3
av. Baulkham Hl...247 E7
av. Earlwood...402 J4
av. Glebe...11 K13
av. Menangle...538 G16
la. Glebe...12 A13
la. Turramurra...222 H12
pl. Appin...569 E13
pl. Narellan...478 H12
pl. Seven Hills...276 D1
rd. Bondi Jctn...22 C8
rd. Sydney...D D6
rd. Sydney...3 K3
rd. Varroville...451 D4
rd. Vineyard...152 D10
ST JOHN
st. Balmain...8 B9
st. Lewisham...15 B7
st. Newtown...17 G16
ST JOHNS
av. Auburn...339 A12
av. Gordon...253 F9
cl. Brookvale...258 A8
la. Gordon, off
St Johns Av...253 H8
pl. Narellan...478 B10
rd. Auburn...339 A12
rd. Blaxland...233 F10
rd. Bradbury...511 C14
rd. Busby...363 K14
rd. Busby...363 K15
rd. Cabramatta...365 E4
rd. Cabramatta W...365 A4
rd. Campbelltwn...511 H12
rd. Canley Ht...365 A4
rd. Forest Lodge...11 J16
rd. Glebe...11 J16
rd. Heckenberg...363 K14
rd. Heckenberg...363 K15
rd. Maraylya...95 C12

rd. Maraylya...95 D8
rd. St Johns Pk...364 H3
wk. Gordon...253 F9
ST JUDE
cr. Belmore...401 H3
rd. Varroville...451 G3
ST KILDA
la. Woolmloo, off
Bourke St...4 E6
st. Bexley North...402 C10
st. Kingsgrove...402 C10
st. St Johns Pk...364 F3
ST LAWRENCE
av. Kearns...451 A16
st. Greenwich...314 J13
ST LUKE
st. Randwick...377 D15
ST MALO
av. Hunters Hill...314 A14
ST MARKS
av. Castle Hill...217 K9
la. Randwick...377 C10
rd. Darling Point...13 J8
rd. Randwick...377 D13
ST MARTINS
cr. Blacktown...274 K5
ST MARYS
av. Bondi Jctn...377 G5
la. Camperdwn...17 C10
la. Newtown...17 C10
rd. Berkshire Pk...180 A13
rd. Sydney...D H7
rd. Sydney...4 B4
st. Balmain East...8 H10
st. Camperdwn...17 C10
st. Newtown...17 C10
st. West Hoxton...392 D9
ST MATTHEWS
la. Baulkham Hl, off
Rose St...247 G13
ST MERVYNS
av. Point Piper...14 J4
ST MICHAELS
pl. Baulkham Hl...247 D4
pl. Vaucluse...348 B5
ST NEOT
av. Potts Point...4 K1
ST PAULS
cl. Burwood...341 K16
cr. Emu Plains...235 D9
cr. Liverpool...394 G5
la. Cobbitty...446 J11
pl. Chester Hill...337 H12
pl. Chippendale...19 C5
rd. N Balgowlah...287 C6
st. Randwick...377 B16
wy. Blacktown...274 A6
ST PETER
cl. Hinchinbrk...392 K2
ST PETERS
la. Darlinghurst...4 E8
la. Redfern...19 D10
st. Darlinghurst...4 E8
st. St Peters...374 H13
ST THOMAS
rd. Mulgoa...295 D11
st. Bronte...377 K11
st. Clovelly...377 K11
ST VINCENT
rd. Bexley...432 D1
ST VINCENTS
rd. Greenwich...314 K8
rd. Greenwich...315 A7
SAIPAN
av. Lethbrdg Pk...240 H1
SALADILLO
gr. Wallacia...325 A16
SALADINE
av. Punchbowl...399 H4
SALAMANDER
gr. Baulkham Hl...246 K2
pl. Mt Lewis...370 A15
pl. Raby...451 E12
st. St Clair...269 F15
SALAMAUA
cr. Holsworthy...426 D3
pl. Glenfield...424 G12
rd. Whalan...241 A13
SALECICH
pl. Bonnyrigg...364 E6
SALEM
cl. St Clair...269 G13

SALERNO
cl. Emu Heights...235 B5
la. Emu Heights, off
Salerno Cl...235 B4
pl. St Ives Ch...223 J5
st. Forestville...256 A6
SALERWONG
pl. Ryde...282 E12
SALES
av. Silverdale...353 J15
SALFORD
st. Ingleburn...453 E5
st. St Clair...270 G10
SALIGNA
wy. Mcquarie Fd...424 E16
SALIGNUS
pl. Narellan Vale...478 J14
SALINA
av. W Pnnant Hl...249 H7
SALISBURY
av. Bexley...402 H14
av. Glenfield...424 C11
av. Kemps Ck...360 E1
ct. West Hoxton...392 B11
la. Camperdwn...17 A7
la. Stanmore...17 A7
la. Rosebery, off
Queen St...375 G13
pl. Gymea Bay...491 C7
pl. Watsons Bay...318 F15
rd. Asquith...192 A12
rd. Bellevue Hill...347 G11
rd. Camperdwn...17 E7
rd. Camperdwn...17 G6
rd. Castle Hill...217 A13
rd. East Killara...254 H11
rd. Guildford...337 H7
rd. Hornsby...192 A12
rd. Kensington...376 D10
rd. Rose Bay...347 G11
rd. Stanmore...16 F9
rd. Willoughby...285 F15
sq. Seaforth...287 A10
st. Botany...405 G14
st. Canley Ht...365 F4
st. Concord...342 A8
st. Mount Druitt...241 B14
st. Penshurst...431 C3
st. Riverwood...400 F14
st. Silverwater...309 H13
st. S Hurstville...432 A9
st. Watsons Bay...318 F15
st. Waverley...377 G6
SALISBURY DOWNS
dr. W Pnnant Hl...249 A2
SALIX
pl. Engadine...488 H16
SALLAWAY
pl. W Pnnant Hl...249 B1
rd. Galston...159 B8
rd. Galston...159 C9
rd. Middle Dural...159 B8
SALLEE
gln. Kingswood...267 F2
la. Kingswood, off
Sallee Gln...267 F2
SALLY
pl. Glendenning...242 E4
pl. Kellyville...217 C2
SALMON
cl. Asquith...192 C8
rd. S Windsor...150 F2
SALT
rd. Church Point...168 F9
st. Concord...342 D4
SALTASH
st. Yagoona...368 F15
SALTBUSH
pl. Bossley Park...333 J9
SALTER
av. Minto...452 K14
cr. Denistone E...281 H9
ct. Harringtn Pk...478 E6
rd. Bossley Park...333 K9
st. Gladesville...313 A12
SALTERS
rd. Wilberforce...62 D12
SALT PAN
rd. Riverwood...429 J1
SALTPETRE
cl. Eagle Vale...481 H5
SALVANA
wy. Claymore...481 C11

SALVESTRO
pl. Bella Vista...246 G6
SALVIA
av. Bankstown...399 H2
cl. Cherrybrook...219 F10
SAMANTHA
cr. Glendenning...242 J4
pl. Smeaton Gra...479 E9
SAMANTHA RILEY
dr. Kellyville...215 H5
SAMARAI
pl. Beacon Hill...257 H4
rd. Whalan...241 A12
SAMES
cl. Mona Vale...198 K3
SAM JOHNSON
wy. Lane Cove W...283 G15
SAMMUT
cr. Chipping Ntn...396 D4
st. Smithfield...305 F14
SAMOA
av. Picnic Point...428 D8
pl. Lethbrdg Pk...240 H1
SAMORA
av. Cremorne...316 F4
SAMPSON
cr. Acacia Gdn...214 F16
cr. Quakers Hill...214 F16
pl. Rsemeadow...540 J4
SAMUEL
la. Tempe, off
Samuel St...374 C16
pl. Airds...512 B14
pl. Quakers Hill...214 A8
pl. St Clair...269 K11
st. Bligh Park...150 J8
st. Lidcombe...339 G8
st. Mona Vale...198 H3
st. Peakhurst...430 B5
st. Ryde...281 K15
st. Surry Hills...F F10
st. Surry Hills...4 A13
st. Tempe...374 C16
st. Wiley Park...400 J3
SAMUEL FOSTER
dr. S Penrith...267 A4
SAMUEL MARSDEN
rd. Orchard Hills...269 A10
SAMUELS
av. Jannali...461 A9
SANANANDA
av. Allambie Ht...257 D11
rd. Holsworthy...396 D16
SANBROOK
la. Newtown...17 A10
SAN CRISTOBAL
dr. Green Valley...363 A8
SANCTUARY
av. Avalon...140 A15
cl. Cherrybrook...219 F14
dr. Kellyville...185 H16
dr. Kellyville...215 H1
dr. Windsor Dn...180 F1
pl. Chipping Ntn...366 K14
SANCTUARY PARK
dr. Plumpton...242 A9
SANCTUARY POINT
rd. W Pnnant Hl...248 F8
SAND
pl. Illawong...459 C3
SANDAKAN
cr. Lethbrdg Pk...210 H16
rd. Revesby Ht...428 J7
SANDAL
cr. Carramar...366 G2
SANDALWOOD
av. St Clair...270 G11
cl. Casula...423 K2
SANDBAR
pl. Port Hacking...522 K3
SANDEFORD
wy. Minto...482 K1
wy. Minto...483 A1
SANDELL
pl. Dean Park...242 K2
SANDERLING
st. Hinchinbrk...393 E1
SANDERS
cr. Kings Lngly...245 H6
la. Avalon...170 B2
pde. Concord...342 D4

rd. Baulkham Hl.....247 B10
SANDERSON
st. Carramar.....366 J1
st. Cronulla.....494 C6
SANDFORD
rd. Turramurra.....223 D10
SANDGATE
st. Botany.....405 F14
SANDHURST
cr. Glenhaven.....218 C4
SAN DIEGO
st. Clarmnt Ms.....268 J2
SANDILANDS
rd. Bonnyrigg.....364 E5
SANDLER
av. North Rocks.....279 A2
SANDLEWOOD
cl. Rouse Hill.....185 B8
SANDO
cr. Roselands.....401 C7
SANDON
st. Seven Hills.....275 J8
SANDOVER
ct. Wattle Grove.....395 K13
SANDOWN
cl. Casula.....394 D15
cl. St Johns Pk.....364 F5
SANDPIPER
av. Hinchinbrk.....363 D15
cr. Clarmnt Ms.....268 H4
cr. Newington.....310 D12
pl. Kenthurst.....188 A1
pl. Woronora Ht.....489 C6
tce. Plumpton.....241 K10
SANDPLOVER
pl. Hinchinbrk.....363 D15
SAND POINT
la. Palm Beach, off Iluka Rd.....139 H3
SANDRA
av. Panania.....398 A15
cr. Roselands.....401 A8
pl. Ingleburn.....453 D11
pl. Miranda.....491 J1
pl. Mount Druitt.....241 D14
pl. Seaforth.....286 K6
pl. S Penrith.....267 A1
st. Ryde.....312 D7
st. Woodpark.....306 G16
SANDRIDGE
st. Bondi.....378 C5
SANDRINGHAM
av. Cmbrdg Pk.....237 J10
dr. Carlingford.....279 D5
dr. Cecil Hills.....362 G4
st. Dolls Point.....463 H1
st. St Johns Pk.....364 D4
st. Sans Souci.....433 C16
SANDS
st. Sydney.....C D14
SANDSTOCK
pl. Woodcroft.....243 F7
SANDWELL
st. Surry Hills.....20 D1
SANDY
gln. Wrrngtn Dns.....238 B3
la. Thirlmere.....561 G11
rd. Burraneer.....493 E15
SANDY BAY
rd. Clontarf.....287 E12
SANFORD
st. Glendenning.....242 F3
SANGRADO
st. Seaforth.....287 A10
SAN MARINO
dr. Prestons.....393 E14
SAN MICHEL
cr. Ryde, off O'Regan Dr.....312 B4
SAN MICHELLE
av. Baulkham Hl.....247 G14
SANONI
av. Sandringham.....463 E2
SAN REMO
av. Gymea.....491 E2
pl. Dural.....189 C5
pl. Guildford.....337 D2
SAN STEFANO
pl. Ryde, off O'Regan Dr.....312 B4

SANTA
pl. Bossley Park.....334 C11
SANTA FE
pl. Dural.....189 D6
SANTA MARINA
av. Waverley.....377 F8
SANTANGELO
cl. Edensor Pk.....363 G3
SANTA ROSA
av. Ryde.....282 B11
SANTIAGO
pl. Seven Hills.....275 H4
SANTLEY
cr. Kingswood.....237 H13
SANTON
pl. Cranebrook.....207 F12
SANTOS
pl. Toongabbie.....275 F11
SAPIUM
wy. Mcquarie Fd.....454 F3
SAPPHIRE
cct. Parklea.....214 G12
cct. Quakers Hill.....214 G12
pl. Eagle Vale.....481 C7
st. Greystanes.....306 A1
SAPPHO
rd. Warwck Frm.....365 K13
st. Canley Ht.....365 B1
SARACEN
rd. Beecroft.....250 E10
SARAH
cr. Baulkham Hl.....247 F7
pl. Appin.....569 E10
pl. Bossley Park.....334 C9
pl. Cecil Hills.....362 J4
pl. Illawong.....459 D8
pl. Minchinbury.....271 G8
st. Enmore.....17 B16
st. Mascot.....405 A5
wy. Minto.....482 J3
SARAH DURACK
av. Homebush B.....340 G4
SARAH HOLLANDS
dr. Horngsea Pk.....392 D14
SARAH JANE
av. Kellyville.....185 K12
SARAHS
wk. Mosman.....317 E13
SARAH WEST
pl. Mt Annan.....509 G1
SARDAM
av. Cranebrook.....206 H8
SARDAN
cr. Fairfield.....336 F8
SARDINIA
av. Glenwood.....245 J3
pl. Birchgrove.....7 G4
SARDONYX
av. Hobartville.....118 E9
SARDYGA
st. Plumpton.....242 A7
SARGENTS
rd. Ebenezer.....62 H7
rd. Minchinbury.....271 B7
rd. Wilberforce.....61 K11
SARIC
av. Georges Hall.....368 C16
SARISSA
wy. Mcquarie Fd.....454 H4
SARK
gr. Minto.....482 F8
SARNER
rd. Greenwich.....315 A7
SARNIA
cr. Killara.....253 G11
SARRE
pl. Prospect.....274 G12
SARSFIELD
cct. Bexley North.....402 E9
st. Blacktown.....244 K14
SARTOR
cr. Bossley Park.....333 G11
SASSAFRAS
cl. Bradbury.....511 G12
la. Cabramatta.....365 H8
la. Vaucluse.....318 E16
SASSAFRAS GULLY
rd. Springwood.....201 G5
SATARA
av. Cabramatta W.....365 B6

SATELBERG
st. Holsworthy.....426 D4
SATINASH
st. Parklea.....215 A13
SATINWOOD
cl. Alfords Point.....429 B14
SATTERLEY
av. Turramurra.....252 D4
SATURN
pl. Doonside.....243 D15
SAUNDERS
av. Liverpool.....365 B16
la. Pyrmont.....12 E2
la. Quakers Hill.....243 C2
la. Yagoona.....368 K11
pl. Menai.....458 H14
pl. Raby.....451 D12
rd. Ermington.....310 E4
rd. Oakville.....122 G8
st. N Parramatta.....278 E12
st. Pyrmont.....12 E3
SAUNDERS BAY
rd. Caringbah.....492 K12
SAURINE
st. Bankstown.....368 H15
SAUTERNE
cr. Minchinbury.....272 A8
SAUTERNES
pl. Eschol Park.....481 D5
SAUVAGE
pl. Doonside.....273 F5
pl. Newington.....310 A16
SAUVIGNON
cl. Eschol Park.....481 B4
SAVA
pl. Bonnyrigg.....364 A10
SAVANNAH
la. St Clair, off Fantail Cr.....271 A15
pl. Erskine Park.....271 A15
SAVERY
cr. Blacktown.....274 C8
pl. Fairfield W.....335 C12
SAVIC
pl. Bonnyrigg Ht.....363 C7
SAVOY
av. East Killara.....254 H6
cr. Chester Hill.....368 B3
ct. W Pnnant Hl.....249 H9
SAWELL
st. Bossley Park.....333 G11
SAWMILL
ct. Castle Hill.....248 E5
SAWTELL
cl. Hoxton Park.....392 K9
SAWYER
cr. Lane Cove W, off Whitfield Av.....283 F12
la. Artarmon.....314 H2
SAXBY
st. Girraween.....276 C14
wy. Blacktown.....273 G5
SAXON
pl. Cecil Hills.....362 E8
pl. Wentwthvle.....277 C9
st. Belfield.....371 D9
wy. Airds.....512 A13
SAXONVALE
cr. Edensor Pk.....333 E14
rd. Baulkham Hl.....246 H3
rd. Bella Vista.....246 H3
SAXONY
rd. Horsley Pk.....332 G6
SAYERS
st. N Balgowlah.....287 E4
SAYONARA
pl. Greenfld Pk.....334 E14
SAYWELL
la. Btn-le-Sds.....433 K2
rd. Mcquarie Fd.....453 J1
rd. Mcquarie Fd.....454 A2
st. Chatswood.....284 K12
st. Marrickville.....374 D12
SCADDAN
st. Quakers Hill.....214 E9
SCAHILL
st. Campsie.....372 B16
SCAIFE
st. Padstow.....429 B4
SCALES
pde. Balgowlah Ht.....287 H12

SCANLEN
wy. Ingleburn.....452 K10
SCAPOLITE
pl. Eagle Vale.....481 E7
SCARAB
st. Bnkstn Aprt.....397 K1
SCARBOROUGH
cl. Lurnea.....394 C12
cl. Narellan.....478 E16
cl. W Pnnant Hl.....249 A1
cr. North Bondi.....378 G3
la. Kogarah.....433 E8
pl. Beacon Hill.....257 G2
st. Bundeena.....523 J10
st. Monterey.....433 G9
wy. Cherrybrook.....219 A14
SCARCELLA
pl. Edensor Pk.....333 J15
SCARFE
st. Fairfield W.....335 F13
SCARSBOROUGH
cr. Bligh Park.....150 C5
SCARUS
pl. Rsemeadow.....540 F3
SCARVELL
av. McGraths Hl.....121 J13
SCENIC
cct. Cranebrook.....237 C1
cir. Blaxland.....234 A5
cr. Mt Riverview.....204 G15
cr. S Hurstville.....432 A13
gr. Glenwood.....246 A5
SCHAEFER
tce. Glenwood.....215 K16
SCHERELL
pl. Shalvey.....211 A14
st. Dharruk.....241 B7
SCHEYVILLE
rd. Maraylya.....124 B5
rd. Oakville.....122 K8
rd. Scheyville.....123 B8
SCHILLER
pl. Emerton.....240 K6
SCHLEICHER
st. St Marys.....269 D3
SCHOEFFEL
gr. Horngsea Pk.....392 F13
SCHOFIELD
av. Earlwood.....402 F4
av. Rockdale.....433 D2
pde. Pennant Hills.....220 D12
pl. Menai.....458 J11
rd. Pitt Town.....122 K3
rd. Scheyville.....123 A4
st. Riverwood.....400 A10
SCHOFIELDS
rd. Rouse Hill.....185 A13
rd. Schofields.....183 G16
SCHOFIELDS FARM
rd. Schofields.....183 F13
SCHOOL
av. Villawood.....337 G16
la. Five Dock.....342 J10
la. Earlwood, off William St.....402 H4
pde. Doonside.....243 C13
pde. Marrickville.....373 F13
pde. Padstow.....429 C2
pde. Westmead.....307 E4
rd. Galston.....159 D8
st. Balmain East.....8 G7
SCHOOL HOUSE
la. Glenbrook, off Mann St.....233 K16
rd. Regentville.....265 H4
SCHUBERT
pl. Bonnyrigg Ht.....363 E5
wy. Clarmnt Ms.....268 G4
SCHULTZ
st. Balmain.....7 A9
st. St Marys.....269 K4
SCHUMACK
st. North Ryde.....282 J11
SCHWEBEL
la. Glenorie.....127 G3
st. Marrickville.....373 J14
SCIARRA
cr. Acacia Gdn.....244 J1
SCIENCE
rd. Camperdwn.....18 B2
rd. Richmond.....118 G12

SCINTILLA
gr. Doonside.....243
SCIPIO
st. Yagoona.....368
SCOBIE
pl. Mt Annan.....479
st. Doonside.....273
SCONE
pl. Doonside.....243
SCORPIUS
pl. Cranebrook.....207
SCOT
st. Bargo.....567
SCOTCHEY
st. Prairiewood.....334
SCOTLAND
rd. Ingleburn.....423
SCOTNEY
pl. Collaroy Plat.....228
pl. Quakers Hill.....213
SCOTT
cl. Rossmore.....389
cr. Roseville.....285
ct. Cherrybrook.....249
la. Kogarah.....433
la. Maroubra.....407
pl. Baulkham Hl.....247
pl. Kirrawee.....460
pl. St Ives.....224
rd. Colyton.....270
st. Bankstown.....400
st. Belfield.....371
st. Bronte.....377
st. Campbelltwn.....512
st. Croydon.....342
st. Fairfield E.....337
st. Five Dock.....342
st. Kogarah.....433
st. Liverpool.....395
st. Maroubra.....407
st. Marsfield.....282
st. Mortdale.....430
st. Narellan.....478
st. Punchbowl.....399
st. Pyrmont.....12
st. Springwood.....202
st. Toongabbie.....276
st. Willoughby.....285
SCOTTS-DALE
cct. West Hoxton.....392
cct. West Hoxton.....392
SCOTTSDALE
st. Stanhpe Gdn.....215
SCOTTS FARM
rd. Grose Wold.....115
SCOULLER
la. Marrickville.....374
st. Marrickville.....374
SCOUT
pl. Sydney.....B
SCOUTS
la. Paddington.....21
SCRIBBLY
pl. Mcquarie Fd.....454
SCRIBBLY GUM
cl. Hornsby Ht.....161
ct. Voyager Pt.....427
pl. Alfords Point.....459
SCRIBBLYGUM
cct. Rouse Hill.....184
cct. Rouse Hill.....185
SCRIVENER
la. Springwood.....202
st. Warwck Frm.....395
SCRIVIN
st. Leumeah.....482
SCROGGIES
rd. Thirlmere.....561
SCRUBWREN
pl. Glenmore Pk.....265
SCULLIN
pl. N Wahrnga.....192
pl. Penrith.....237
SCULLY
pl. Mt Annan.....479
SCYLLA
rd. Oyster Bay.....461
SEA
st. Hunters Hill.....313
SEABEACH
av. Mona Vale.....199

ABORG
Lucas Ht 487 J12
ABROOK
Grays Point 491 B11
Russell Lea 343 E7
Doonside 273 G3
AEAGLE
Green Valley 363 C11
AFORTH
Oatley 430 J10
Woolooware 493 F11
Seaforth 287 A10
Bexley 402 K16
AL
Tregear 240 C3
ALE
Beecroft 250 G5
Leumeah 512 A1
Darlinghurst F J2
Burwood 371 J2
Darlinghurst F J2
Leichhardt 15 F3
. Oakhurst 242 D3
ALY
Mt Lewis 369 K16
AMAN
Villawood 337 C16
Greenwich 314 J9
AMANS
Horngsea Pk 392 D14
AMER
Forest Lodge 12 B16
ARL
Cronulla 493 H11
Petersham 15 G9
ARLE
Randwick 377 E11
Canterbury 372 G11
Ryde 312 F6
ARS
Prairiewood 334 K8
ASIDE
e. S Coogee 407 J7
A SPRAY
Chipping Ntn 366 K15
ATON
Wahroonga 222 A10
Cranebrook 207 G13
ATTLE
St Clair 270 J11
AVIEW
Harbord 258 J14
Newport 169 H10
e. Collaroy 229 D15
Ashfield 372 J7
Balgowlah 287 G10
Clovelly 377 G11
Cronulla 493 K9
Dulwich Hill 373 F9
Mt Krng-gai 163 B10
Summer Hill 373 A7
Waverley 377 H7
BASTIAN
Rsemeadow 540 F6
Dural 219 A2
BASTOPOL
Emu Heights 235 A1
Enmore 16 G14
CANT
Liverpool 395 D1
COND
Berala 339 E15
Blacktown 244 H14
Campsie 371 G10
Canley Vale 366 B3
Condell Park 398 D4
Eastwood 281 C9
Epping 280 G3
Five Dock 343 A9
Gymea Bay 491 D10
Jannali 460 J11
Kingswood 237 H14
Lane Cove 314 G4
Lindfield 254 F13
Llandilo 208 K9
Loftus 490 A5
Mcquarie Fd 454 A1
Mcquarie Pk 283 C7
Maroubra 407 G9
Narrabeen 228 G9
North Ryde 282 H13
Seven Hills 275 H2
Toongabbie 276 F8

av. West Hoxton 362 D16
av. West Hoxton 392 C6
av. Willoughby 285 H11
rd. Berkshire Pk 180 B2
st. Ashbury 372 G9
st. Granville 308 G13
st. Parramatta 279 A15
st. Warragamba 353 G6
wk. Chester Hill 337 J13
SEDDON
pl. Campbelltwn 511 K3
st. Bankstown 399 F6
SEDDON HILL
rd. Harbord 258 J16
SEDGEMAN
av. Menai 458 G7
SEDGER
rd. Kenthurst 187 G4
SEDGMAN
cr. Shalvey 210 J14
st. Greystanes 306 A10
SEDGWICK
st. Leumeah 482 A16
st. Leumeah 512 B1
st. Smeaton Gra 479 E10
SEE
la. Kingsford 406 E1
st. Kingsford 406 E1
st. Meadowbnk 311 F3
SEEANA
pl. Belrose 225 K10
SEEBREES
st. Manly Vale 287 J3
SEELAND
pl. Padstow Ht 429 B6
SEFTON
rd. Thornleigh 220 J8
rd. Westleigh 220 J8
SEGEFIELD
pl. Casula 395 B12
SEGENHOE
pl. Richmond 118 C5
st. Arncliffe 403 G11
SEGERS
av. Padstow 399 D16
SEIDEL
av. Picnic Point 428 G7
pl. Abbotsbury 333 C13
SEINE
pl. Kearns 451 C16
pl. Miranda 461 K15
SELBORNE
st. Burwood 342 C12
SELBY
av. Dee Why 258 E6
pl. Blacktown 274 D5
pl. Minto 482 K10
pl. St Johns Pk 364 G3
SELDON
st. Quakers Hill 213 F7
SELEMS
pde. Revesby 398 H15
SELF
pl. Shalvey 211 B13
SELINA
pl. Cherrybrook 219 D7
pl. Glenwood 245 E2
SELKIRK
av. Cecil Park 331 E12
pl. Bligh Park 150 B7
pl. Camden S 507 B12
st. St Andrews 452 B13
st. Winston Hills 277 D4
SELLERS
la. Greenacre 370 D12
SELLWOOD
st. Btn-le-Sds 434 A1
SELMA
pl. Oakhurst 242 A2
SELMON
st. Sans Souci 433 D14
SELMS
pl. Minto 452 J16
SELWA
pl. Kareela 461 C12
SELWAY
av. Moorebank 396 D10
SELWYN
av. Cmbrdg Gdn 237 G2
cl. Pennant Hills 220 D14
pl. Cartwright 393 K6

pl. Fairfield W 335 E10
pl. Quakers Hill 243 J3
st. Artarmon 285 B13
st. Paddington 20 F1
st. Pymble 223 B15
st. Wollstncraft 315 D9
SEMAAN
st. Werrington 238 H10
SEMANA
pl. Winmalee 173 G12
st. Whalan 241 B13
SEMILLON
cr. Eschol Park 481 D2
SEMPLE
st. Ryde 282 C15
SENIOR
st. Canley Vale 366 C3
SENNAR
la. Erskine Park, off Sennar Rd 271 A16
rd. Erskine Park 271 A16
SENTA
rd. Londonderry 177 J12
SENTINEL
av. Glenwood 215 C16
av. Kellyville 216 H3
cl. Horngsea Pk 392 F16
SENTRY
dr. Glenwood 215 A13
dr. Parklea 214 K13
dr. Stanhpe Gdn 215 A10
SEPIK
pl. Kearns 451 C16
st. Holsworthy 426 G7
SEPPELT
pl. Edensor Pk 333 D15
st. Eastern Ck 272 F8
SEPTIMUS
av. Punchbowl 399 K7
st. Chatswood 285 B9
st. Erskineville 17 K13
SEQUOIA
cl. West Pymble 252 H11
gr. Menai, off Fern Cct W 458 J14
SERA
st. Lane Cove 314 C2
SERAM
pl. Kings Park 244 D2
SERCIAL
pl. Eschol Park 481 C3
SERGEANT LARKIN
cr. Daceyville 406 G3
SERGEANTS
la. St Leonards, off Chandos St 315 D5
SERI
pl. Bossley Park 333 K10
SERINA
av. Castle Hill 248 C3
SERMELFI
dr. Glenorie 127 K1
SERPENTINE
cr. N Balgowlah 287 E7
la. Bowen Mtn 84 D11
pde. Vaucluse 348 E4
pl. Eagle Vale 481 B7
rd. Hunters Hill 314 C12
rd. Kirrawee 491 A9
st. Bossley Park 333 G5
st. Merrylands W 306 J11
SERVICE
av. Ashfield 372 K9
la. Five Dock 343 A8
SESQUICENTENARY
sq. Sydney C G2
SESTO
pl. Bossley Park 333 G8
SETA
cl. St Clair 299 H2
SETON
rd. Moorebank 395 K8
SETTLERS
bvd. Liberty Gr 311 C14
cl. Castle Hill 218 F11
cr. Bligh Park 150 H7
gld. Wrrngtn Dns 238 B4
wy. Westleigh 220 G7
SEVEN HILLS
rd. Baulkham Hl 247 A11
rd. Bella Vista 246 E9
rd. Seven Hills 246 A14

rd.s, Seven Hills 275 D6
wy. Baulkham Hl 246 F9
SEVENOAKS
cr. Bass Hill 367 G7
pl. Jannali 461 A13
SEVENTEENTH
av. Austral 361 F16
av.e, West Hoxton 391 K1
SEVENTH
av. Austral 391 A12
av. Berala 339 D14
av. Campsie 371 H11
av. Jannali 460 K12
av. Llandilo 207 J4
av. Loftus 490 A7
av. Seven Hills 275 K3
st. Granville 308 G15
st. Mascot 405 A7
st. Warragamba 353 G4
SEVEN WAYS
Bondi Beach 348 C16
North Bondi 348 C16
SEVERN
pl. Kearns 450 K16
rd. Bringelly 387 G3
rd. Woronora 489 H1
st. Maroubra 407 H11
st. St Marys 239 G6
SEVILLE
pl. Glenwood 215 F12
pl. Kenthurst 157 J11
st. Fairfield E 337 A13
st. Lane Cove 314 B3
st. N Parramatta 278 B10
SEWELL
av. Padstow Ht 429 E7
av. Seven Hills 246 A13
st. Ryde 311 H1
SEXTANS
pl. Cranebrook 207 H6
SEXTON
av. Castle Hill 217 G13
SEYMOUR
cl. Wahroonga 221 H16
la. Marrickville, off Frampton Av 374 A13
pde. Belfield 371 C10
pl. Bossley Park 333 E11
pl. Paddington 20 F1
st. Croydon Pk 372 B6
st. Drummoyne 343 J1
st. Dundas Vy 280 A7
st. Hurstville Gr 431 G11
wy. Kellyville 216 K3
SEYTON
pl. Rsemeadow 540 C3
SHAARON
ct. Banksia 403 F12
la. Banksia, off Shaaron Ct 403 F12
SHACKEL
av. Brookvale 258 C8
av. Clovelly 378 A13
av. Concord 341 J6
av. Gladesville 312 G12
av. Kingsgrove 401 K5
av. Old Guildford 337 E7
rd. Bangor 459 D14
SHACKLETON
av. Birrong 368 J5
av. Tregear 240 F4
SHADDOCK
av. Pymble 253 B10
av. Villawood 367 F2
SHADE
pl. Lugarno 429 K9
SHADFORTH
pl. Paddington 4 K16
st. Mosman 316 J11
st. Paddington 4 K15
st. Wiley Park 400 G1
SHADFORTH BRIDGE
Silverdale 384 G1
SHADLOW
cr. St Clair 269 H10
SHADWELL
cr. Kings Lngly 246 A7
SHAFT
st. Silverwater 309 K10
st. Silverwater 309 K9
SHAFTESBURY
rd. Burwood 342 B15
st. Carlton 432 H7

SHAFTSBURY
rd. Denistone W 281 A10
rd. Eastwood 280 K7
rd. West Ryde 281 A11
SHAKESPEARE
dr. St Clair 270 C15
dr. Winmalee 173 J8
pl. Sydney B G15
st. Campbelltwn 512 A3
st. Campsie 372 A11
st. Wetherill Pk 334 G5
SHALOM
cl. Old Guildford 337 F8
SHAMROCK
cl. Winmalee 173 D10
ct. St Clair 269 K10
pde. Killarney Ht 286 D1
pl. Glendenning 242 H3
st. Smithfield 335 F2
SHAND
cl. Illawong 459 G4
cr. Turramurra 252 G2
SHANDLIN
pl. S Penrith 267 A7
SHANE
pl. Bella Vista 246 E5
pl. Kurrajong Ht 53 K6
st. Colyton 270 E4
SHANE PARK
rd. Shanes Park 209 H9
SHANKE
cr. Kings Lngly 245 C3
SHANNON
av. Killarney Ht 256 C15
av. Merrylands 307 E10
gln. St Clair 270 A12
la. St Clair, off Menzies Cct 270 A13
pl. Kearns 481 A2
rd. Bringelly 387 J1
rd. Mt Colah 162 B16
st. Greenacre 370 F7
st. Lalor Park 245 G9
st. St Ives 224 E11
SHANUK
st. Frenchs Frst 255 G1
SHARAN
pl. Forestville 255 G8
SHARI
av. Picnic Point 428 G5
av. Picnic Point 428 G6
SHARK
av. Vaucluse 348 B5
rd. Kurnell 495 B1
SHARLAND
av. Chatswd W 284 F14
pl. Smithfield 335 C3
SHARMAN
cl. Harringtn Pk 478 H8
SHARN
st. Kurnell 466 E8
SHARON
cl. Bossley Park 333 J11
cl. Hornsby 192 A16
pl. Engadine 488 E15
pl. N Richmond 86 K15
pl. Rooty Hill 271 J6
st. Holsworthy 426 D12
SHARP
cl. Castle Hill 218 A9
st. Belmore 401 G1
st. Matraville 406 K15
SHARPE
pl. Camden S 507 B15
SHARREE
wy. Acacia Gdn, off Elm St 214 K14
SHARRET
wy. Acacia Gdn, off Snowgum St 215 A14
SHARROCK
av. Glenwood 215 J13
SHARWEN
pl. Blaxland 234 B5
SHAUGHNESSY
st. Oakhurst 242 C4
SHAULA
cr. Erskine Park 300 H2
la. Erskine Park, off Shaula Cr 300 H2
SHAUN
st. Glenwood 215 J15

SHAW
av. Earlwood 402 E6
av. Kingsford 376 C16
cl. Barden Rdg 488 G1
la. Sefton 368 F2
pl. Fairfield W 335 D13
pl. Prospect 274 G12
pl. Rooty Hill 242 A12
rd. Ingleburn 452 K7
st. Beverly Hills 401 B15
st. Bexley North 402 A10
st. Cmbrdg Pk 238 B11
st. East Ryde 283 A14
st. Kingsgrove 402 A10
st. Kogarah 433 C8
st. North Bondi 348 B14
st. Petersham 15 J14

SHAWNEE
st. Greenfld Pk 334 A13

SHAWS
pl. Yarramundi 145 B7

SHAYNE
ct. Oakdale 500 D13

SHEAFFE
pl. Davidson 225 A16

SHEAHAN
av. Guildford 338 D7
pwy. Warwck Frm, off Sheahan St 365 H15
st. Warwck Frm 365 H15

SHEARER
la. Padstow 399 C15
la. St Clair, off Shearer St 270 F12
pl. Elderslie 477 H16
st. St Clair 270 F12

SHEARING
pl. Bonnyrigg 364 C5

SHEARS
wy. Minto 482 J5

SHEARWATER
av. Woronora Ht 489 D4
cr. Yarramundi 145 E6
dr. Glenmore Pk 266 A13
rd. Hinchinbrk 393 E2

SHEAS
st. Mascot 405 A4

SHEATHER
av. St Ives 254 D1
pl. Campbelltwn 511 H8

SHEATHERS
la. Camden 506 E2
la. Cawdor 506 E2
la. Grasmere 506 E2

SHEBA
cr. S Penrith 267 C1

SHEDWORTH
st. Marayong 244 B5

SHEEHAN
st. Eastwood 281 H7
st. Wentwthvle 276 H14

SHEEHY
st. Glebe 12 A7

SHEENS
la. Penrith 205 F16

SHEFFIELD
st. Auburn 339 A1
st. Kingsgrove 401 J9
st. Merrylands 307 G11

SHEILA
pl. Kellyville 216 F6

SHELBY
rd. St Ives Ch 223 K5

SHELDON
pl. Bellevue Hill 14 J8

SHELL
rd. Burraneer 493 E15

SHELLBANK
av. Mosman 316 H2
pde. Cremorne 316 G3

SHELLCOTE
rd. Greenacre 370 C6

SHELLCOVE
rd. Neutral Bay 6 H5

SHELLEY
cr. Blacktown 273 G6
pl. Wetherill Pk 334 K6
rd. N Turramrra 223 E8
rd. Wallacia 324 J13
st. Campbelltwn 512 B3
st. Campsie 372 A10
st. Enfield 371 H3
st. Sydney A A16
st. Sydney C B1
st. Winston Hills 277 F2

SHELLEYS
la. Thirlmere 561 G15
la. Marrickville, off Llewellyn St 374 F10

SHELLY
cr. Kellyville 185 J16

SHELSLEY
pl. S Penrith 267 A7

SHELTON
av. Winmalee 173 E6
la. Richmond 119 A5

SHENSTONE
rd. Riverwood 429 J1

SHENTON
av. Bankstown 399 B4

SHE-OAK
gr. Narellan Vale 478 J14

SHEOAK
cl. Cherrybrook 219 G11
pl. Alfords Point 459 A2
pl. Bossley Park 333 G8
pl. Colyton 270 J6
pl. Glenmore Pk 265 H11

SHEPHARD
st. Marayong 244 D7

SHEPHERD
av. Padstow Ht 429 G7
la. Ashfield 372 G5
la. Baulkham Hl 248 A7
la. Chippendale 18 J2
la. Darlington 18 J5
pde. Bardwell Vy 403 B8
rd. Artarmon 285 A13
st. Ashfield 372 G5
st. Chippendale 18 J3
st. Colyton 270 E8
st. Darlington 18 H6
st. Kurnell 466 B9
st. Lalor Park 245 D10
st. Liverpool 395 D8
st. Maroubra 406 K8
st. Marrickville 374 B10
st. Ryde 311 H2
st. St Marys 269 K7

SHEPHERDS
dr. Cherrybrook 219 E10
rd. Freemns Rch 60 B15
rd. Freemns Rch 90 B2

SHEPPARD
la. Emu Plains, off Sheppard Rd 235 J9
rd. Emu Plains 235 H11
rd. Narraweena 258 D4

SHER
pl. Prospect 275 A11

SHERACK
pl. Minto 453 A14

SHERARS
av. Strathfield 341 H16

SHERBORNE
pl. Glendenning 242 G2

SHERBROOK
rd. Asquith 192 A12
rd. Hornsby 221 K1

SHERBROOKE
av. Double Bay 14 F7
rd. West Ryde 311 D2
st. Darlinghurst 4 D11
st. Rooty Hill 242 A16

SHEREDAN
rd. Castlereagh 176 D11

SHERIDAN
cl. Milperra 398 A7
pl. Manly 288 F7
st. Granville 308 F16
wy. Mt Annan 479 E16

SHERIFF
st. Ashcroft 394 D1

SHERLOCK
av. Panania 428 A1

SHERMAN
st. Greenacre 370 B5

SHERRIDON
cr. Quakers Hill 214 C16

SHERRINGHAM
la. Cranebrook, off Sherringham Rd 207 E13
la. Cranebrook, off Sherringham Rd 207 F13
rd. Cranebrook 207 D12

SHERRITT
pl. Prairiewood 334 H8

SHERRY
pl. Minchinbury 271 G7
st. Mona Vale 199 B5

SHERWIN
av. Castle Hill 217 K14
st. Henley 313 B15
wy. Minto 482 J6

SHERWOOD
av. Springwood 201 F2
av. Yowie Bay 492 B11
cct. Penrith 237 D10
cl. Pennant Hills 250 E2
cr. Narraweena 258 C2
ct. Carlingford 249 E13
la. Penrith, off Sherwood Cct 237 D10
pl. North Ryde 282 J14
pl. St Ives 254 A2
rd. Merrylands W 306 K14
st. Kensington 376 C12
st. Kurrajong 85 D3
st. Old Tngabbie 277 D9
st. Revesby 398 G13

SHETLAND
rd. Blairmount 481 A13

SHIEL
pl. St Andrews 452 B13

SHIELDS
la. Pennant Hills 220 H15
rd. Colyton 270 F7
st. Marayong 244 C3

SHIELS
ct. Glenmore Pk 265 E10

SHIERS
av. Mascot 404 J6

SHINFIELD
av. St Ives 223 J13

SHINNICK
dr. Oakhurst 241 H4

SHIPHAM
st. Concord 342 A3

SHIPLEY
av. N Strathfield 341 F6

SHIPROCK
rd. Port Hacking 523 A3

SHIPTON
pl. Dean Park 242 F1

SHIPWAY
st. Marsfield 251 J14

SHIPWRIGHT
pl. Oyster Bay 461 A6

SHIRAZ
cl. Edensor Pk 363 E1
pl. Eschol Park 481 D2
pl. Minchinbury 271 K7

SHIRLEY
av. Roselands 400 J10
cl. Narraweena 258 E3
cr. Matraville 436 J4
la. Wollstncraft 315 D9
la. Campsie, off Canterbury Rd 372 A16
la. Matraville, off Jordons La 436 J3
rd. Crows Nest 315 E8
rd. Miranda 462 G16
rd. Roseville 284 C7
rd. Wollstncraft 315 B11
rd. Wollstncraft 315 E8
st. Alexandria 375 F15
st. Bexley 432 G1
st. Blacktown 245 A15
st. Carlingford 279 K3
st. Epping 250 D16
st. Padstow 429 A1
st. Rosehill 309 B9

SHIRLEY STRICKLAND
av. Homebush B 340 H4

SHIRLOW
st. Marrickville 374 D13

SHOAL
pl. Illawong 459 C5

SHOALHAVEN
rd. Sylvania Wtr 462 C11
rd. Sylvania Wtr 462 C13
st. Ruse 512 D6
st. Wakeley 334 K12

SHOEMAKER
pl. Bonnyrigg 364 C6

SHOEMARK
pl. Narellan 478 F15

SHOPLANDS
rd. Annangrove 155 F4

SHORE
br. Avalon 139 H10
cl. Illawong 459 C3
st. Warwck Frm 366 A16

SHOREHAM
cr. Chipping Ntn 366 G15

SHORLAND
av. Jannali 460 K13

SHORT
av. Bundeena 523 G9
la. Neutral Bay, off Byrnes Av 316 B8
la. Woollahra, off Fletcher St 377 G2
la. Rose Bay, off Hamilton St 348 C11
la. Emu Plains, off Short St 235 E9
la. S Hurstville, off Short St 432 B11
pl. Surry Hills 4 D15
rd. Riverwood 400 A16
st. Auburn 309 B13
st. Balmain 7 F7
st. Banksia 403 F12
st. Bankstown 399 G8
st. Birchgrove 7 F7
st. Blaxland 233 G8
st. Brookvale 258 B13
st. Campbelltwn 511 E3
st. Canterbury 372 D16
st. Carlton 432 H5
st. Chatswood 285 D5
st. Croydon 342 F11
st. Double Bay 14 C9
st. Drummoyne 343 F3
st. Dulwich Hill 373 E7
st. Emu Plains 235 E9
st. Enfield 371 H4
st. Enmore 16 J16
st. Enmore 374 F9
st. Forest Lodge 17 J1
st. Gladesville 313 A5
st. Heathcote 518 E13
st. Hunters Hill 313 D10
st. Hurlstone Pk 373 A11
st. Kogarah 433 C6
st. Leichhardt 9 K15
st. Lidcombe 339 J6
st. Lindfield 254 F16
st. Liverpool 395 C5
st. Manly 288 H9
st. Mosman 316 K6
st. North Manly 258 B13
st. N St Marys 239 J8
st. N Sydney 5 D8
st. Oatley 430 H11
st. Oyster Bay 461 B9
st. Paddington 4 F16
st. Parramatta 278 F15
st. Randwick 377 B14
st. Redfern 19 D6
st. Rooty Hill 242 C15
st. Rosehill 308 J8
st. St Peters 374 J12
st. S Hurstville 432 B11
st. Springwood 201 G4
st. Summer Hill 373 B4
st. Surry Hills 4 D14
st. Tahmoor 565 G12
st. Thornleigh 221 A15
st. Waterloo 19 F16
st. Watsons Bay 318 F13
st. Waverley 377 F7
st. Wentwthvle 277 B15
st. Woolooware 493 E8
st.e, Homebush 341 C7
st.w, Homebush 341 B8

SHORTER
av. Beverly Hills 400 G10
av. Narwee 400 G10
la. Darlinghurst 4 E10
la. Narwee 400 H10
la. Roselands 400 H10

SHORTLAND
av. Lurnea 394 B12
av. Strathfield 341 A12
cl. N Richmond 87 F15
pl. Doonside 273 E2
pl. Ruse 512 H5
st. Canley Vale 366 E4
st. Lidcombe 339
st. Telopea 279
st. Wrrngtn Cty 238

SHOULTS
la. Padstow 399

SHOWFREIGHT
wy. Berala 339

SHOWGROUND
rd. Castle Hill 217
rd. Homebush B 340

SHRIKE
gln. Erskine Park 270
pl. Ingleburn 453

SHROPSHIRE
cl. Wakeley 334
st. Miller 393

SHUTE
wy. Casula 424

SHUTTLEWORTH
av. Raby 451

SIANDRA
av. Fairfield 336
av. Shalvey 210
dr. Kareela 461

SIBBICK
st. Chiswick 343
st. Russell Lea 343

SIBELIUS
cl. Seven Hills 246

SIBLEY
cl. Abbotsbury 333

SICILIA
st. Prestons 393

SICKLES
dr. Grasmere 475

SIDDELEY
pl. Raby 451

SIDDINS
av. Pagewood 406

SIDNEY
cl. Quakers Hill 213
pl. Casula 424

SIDON
pl. Mt Pritchard 364

SIDWELL
av. Shalvey 210

SIEBEL
st. Blacktown 243

SIEMENS
cr. Emerton 240

SIENA
cl. Prestons 393

SIENNA
gr. Woodcroft 243

SIERRA
pl. Baulkham Hl 246
pl. Seven Hills 275
rd. Engadine 488

SIGLINGEN
st. Emerton 240

SIKES
pl. Ambarvale 510

SILAS
wy. Ambarvale 511

SILDOR
ct. Kenthurst 188

SILEX
rd. Mosman 317

SILICA
cr. Eagle Vale 481
rd. Bargo 567
rd. Yanderra 567

SILK
pl. Prestons 393

SILKS
la. N Richmond 87
rd. Kurmond 56

SILKWOOD
gr. Quakers Hill 214

SILKY
cl. Bossley Park 333

SILKY OAK
pl. Castle Hill 248

SILKY-OAK
gr. Elderslie 507

SILKYOAK
gr. Greenacre 370
pl. Glenwood 245

SILLOT
pl. Narellan Vale 508

LWOOD
West Hoxton 392 A12
VA
Springwood 202 A2
Tamarama 378 B6
VEN PARK
Silverdale 353 K12
VER
Westleigh 220 G3
St Peters 374 H14
Marrickville, off
Calvert St 373 K13
Marrickville 374 A12
Randwick 376 K13
St Peters 374 G13
Silverwater 309 K9
VER BEACH
Kurnell 466 A8
VERBURN
Richmond 118 A6
VERDALE
Orangeville 473 A6
Silverdale 353 F16
The Oaks 502 G7
Wallacia 324 A15
Silverdale 353 K10
Wallacia 354 A1
Werombi 413 A15
VEREYE
Glenmore Pk 265 H13
Woronora Ht 489 C4
Hinchinbrk 363 F15
VERFERN
W Pnnant Hl 248 K2
VERLEAF
Menai 458 J15
VER MIST
Castle Hill, off
Barker Dr 218 J13
VERTON
Glenwood 215 F16
VERTOP
Glenwood 245 H1
Westleigh 220 F7
VERWATER
Lansvale 366 E10
Miranda 462 B16
Auburn 309 H16
Dundas 280 A15
Ermington 280 A15
Rydalmere 309 K10
Silverwater 309 K10
VERWOOD
Luddenham 356 A6
Brownlow Hl 475 E11
VIA
Hornsby 191 G13
IBLIST
Port Botany 436 B11
IEON
Liberty Gr 311 B11
Orchard Hills 267 D8
Clovelly 377 G10
IEON PEARCE
Randwick, off
Easy St 377 A16
ILA
Denistone 281 B12
Lidcombe 340 B4
IMAT
Condell Park 398 F6
IMONDS
Avalon 170 B2
W Pnnant Hl 249 A6
Kings Lngly 246 A9
IMONS
Kingsgrove 401 J13
Balmain East 8 F7
Enmore 17 C14
Enmore 17 C16
Newtown 17 C14
Revesby 398 J15
Warwck Frm 365 F13
IMS
Glendenning 242 D2
Oakhurst 242 C2
Oakhurst 242 D2
ION
Bonnyrigg 364 A8
Illawong 459 D7
Hornsby Ht 191 E8
Winston Hills 246 G15

wk. Pagewood 406 A11
SIMONE
cr. Casula 394 G14
cr. Strathfield 341 A11
pl. Peakhurst 430 C4
SIMPSON
av. Baulkham Hl 247 C13
av. Burwood 342 B13
av. Casula 394 G13
cl. Narrabeen 228 G8
la. Lidcombe 339 F9
pl. Kings Lngly 245 D4
pl. Leumeah 482 H11
rd. Bonnyrigg Ht 363 E5
rd. Bundeena 523 G9
st. Artarmon 315 A1
st. Auburn 339 F1
st. Bondi 377 K2
st. Bondi Beach 377 K2
st. Dundas Vy 279 J10
st. Greystanes 306 B9
st. Mosman 317 A13
st. Northmead 278 A1
st. Ryde 311 J4
SIMPSON HILL
rd. Mount Druitt 270 J3
SIMS
gr. Maroubra 407 D13
la. Maroubra 407 D13
pl. St Johns Pk 364 J2
st. Darlinghurst 4 F14
SINAI
av. Milperra 397 H10
SINCLAIR
av. Blacktown 274 K4
av. Thornleigh 220 K11
rd. Ashcroft 394 E1
st. Wollstncraft 5 B1
SINDEL
cl. Bonnyrigg 363 K7
st. West Ryde 280 J13
SINDONE
pl. Caringbah 492 J3
SINFIELD
st. Ermington 280 B15
SINGER
pl. Ingleburn 453 J8
SINGH
la. Chester Hill 368 C2
SINGLE
la. S Penrith, off
Single Rd 267 B4
rd. S Penrith 267 A4
SINGLE RIDGE
rd. The Slopes 56 E8
SINGLES RIDGE
rd. Winmalee 173 A12
rd. Yellow Rock 203 G1
SINGLETON
av. East Hills 428 A3
av. Stanhpe Gdn 215 B5
av. Wrrngtn Cty 238 E5
pl. Kirrawee 491 B7
rd. Wilberforce 91 J3
st. Earlwood 402 F5
st. Horngsea Pk 392 D14
SINNOTT
st. Villawood 336 K16
SIOBHAN
pl. Mona Vale 198 J2
SIOUX
cl. Greenfld Pk 334 A15
SIOVI
rd. Londonderry 177 J12
SIR BERTRAM STEVENS
dr. Royal N P 520 E7
SIR HENRYS
pde. Faulconbdg 201 A1
pde. Springwood 201 A1
SIRIUS
av. Mosman 316 K12
cct. Narellan 478 E15
pde. Beacon Hill 257 G3
pl. Berkshire Pk 179 H14
pl. Engadine 488 D12
pl. Kellyville 215 H4
pl. Riverwood 400 C13
rd. Bligh Park 150 D5
rd. Lane Cove W 283 F16
rd. Voyager Pt 427 B4
rd. Voyager Pt 427 C4
st. Cremorne Pt 316 F13
st. Dundas Vy 280 C8

st. Fairfield W 335 B10
st. Ruse 512 H4
SIRIUS COVE
rd. Mosman 317 A12
SIR JOHN JAMISON
cct. Glenmore Pk 265 D9
SIR JOHN YOUNG
cr. Sydney 4 D5
cr. Woolmloo 4 D5
SIR JOSEPH BANKS
dr. Kurnell 465 J12
st. Bankstown 369 G14
st. Botany 405 G15
SIROIS
st. Toongabbie 276 J5
SIR REGINALD ANSETT
dr. Mascot 405 A7
SIR THOMAS MITCHELL
dr. Davidson 255 B1
rd. Bondi Beach 378 B3
rd. Chester Hill 367 K3
rd. Villawood 367 K3
SISKIN
st. Quakers Hill 214 E11
SISTERS
cr. Drummoyne 343 K4
la. Edgecliff 14 A13
SITAR
pl. Plumpton 241 H9
SITELLA
pl. Ingleburn 453 D9
SITTELLA
pl. Glenmore Pk 265 J12
SIWA
st. Holsworthy 426 F7
SIWARD
pl. Rsemeadow 540 D4
SIXTEENTH
av. Austral 391 F2
av.e,West Hoxton 391 K2
SIXTH
av. Austral 391 A14
av. Berala 339 D15
av. Campsie 371 K10
av. Condell Park 398 E5
av. Denistone 281 D11
av. Jannali 460 K9
av. Llandilo 208 C3
av. Loftus 489 K7
av. Seven Hills 275 J3
av. West Hoxton 391 F14
rd. Berkshire Pk 179 H6
st. Granville 308 G15
st. Mascot 404 K7
st. Warragamba 353 G5
SIXTH MILE
la. Roseville 284 G4
SKAIN
pl. Horngsea Pk 392 C13
SKARRATT
av. Glenbrook 233 J13
st.n, Silverwater 309 E12
st.s, Auburn 309 D14
SKATE
st. Cranebrook 207 A10
SKELTON
st. Leichhardt 16 C1
SKENE
pl. Belrose 225 K9
SKENES
av. Eastwood 280 G6
SKERRETT
la. Doonside 243 C13
SKILLCORN
av. Jannali 460 G9
SKINNER
av. Riverwood 400 F10
pde. Roseville 284 J1
SKINNERS
av. Dolls Point 463 H1
SKIPTON
la. Prestons 393 H15
SKONE
st. Condell Park 398 J6
SKYE
cl. Merrylands W 306 K13
ct. Kellyville 216 K1
pl. Engadine 488 J12
pl. Prospect 274 G10
pl. St Andrews 481 K2
pl. Winston Hills 277 B3

SKYFARMER
pl. Raby 481 F2
SKYHAWK
av. Raby 481 F1
SKYLARK
cct. Bella Vista 246 F1
cr. Erskine Park 270 H14
SKYLINE
pl. Frenchs Frst 256 J5
st. Greenacre 370 H13
SKYROS
la. Emu Heights, off
Skyros Pl 235 B4
pl. Emu Heights 235 B5
SLADDEN
rd. Engadine 489 B15
SLADE
av. Castle Hill 218 J13
av. Lindfield 254 F14
la. Bardwell Pk 402 H7
pl. Prospect 274 G12
rd. Bardwell Pk 402 F8
rd. Bexley North 402 F8
rd. Ingleside 196 G11
st. Narellan 478 H9
st. Naremburn 315 G3
st. Rozelle 7 A12
SLADES
rd. Couridjah 564 E10
SLAPP
st. Merrylands 307 E8
SLATER
rd. Ingleburn 452 J8
SLATTERY
pl. Eastlakes 406 B2
wy. Eastlakes 406 C3
SLAVIN
st. S Penrith 267 D6
SLEIGH
pl. Wetherill Pk 303 H15
SLENDER
av. Smithfield 335 J8
SLESSOR
pl. Blackett 241 C3
pl. Heathcote 518 D14
rd. Casula 424 F5
SLIGAR
av. Hamondvle 396 E16
SLIGO
cl. Killarney Ht 255 J14
SLIM
pl. Cabramatta 365 D11
pl. Wentwthvle 277 A12
SLIP
st. Sydney C C3
st. Sydney 3 D2
SLOANE
cr. Allambie Ht 287 J1
cr. Manly Vale 287 J1
la. Marrickville 374 D13
st. Haberfield 373 D3
st. Marrickville 374 D13
st. Newtown 17 D15
st. Summer Hill 373 D3
SLOOP
st. Seven Hills 275 B5
SLOPER
av. Hobartville 118 F8
SLOPES
rd. Comleroy 56 F7
rd. Kurmond 56 K12
rd. Kurmond 57 A12
rd. N Richmond 87 C6
rd. The Slopes 56 F7
SLOUGH
av. Silverwater 309 K11
SLUMAN
st. Denistone W 281 A11
SMAIL
la. Ultimo 12 J15
st. Ultimo 12 J15
SMALL
cr. Glenmore Pk 265 F7
la. Petersham 15 G11
la. Woollahra, off
Fletcher St 377 F2
rd. Illawong 459 D4
st. Marayong 244 D4
st. Northbridge 285 F16
st. Ryde 311 J4
st. Willoughby 285 F16
st. Woollahra 377 F2

SMALLS
pl. Kellyville 185 H7
rd. Arcadia 129 J16
rd. Brownlow Hl 475 G15
rd. Grasmere 475 G15
rd. Ryde 282 B11
SMALLWOOD
av. Homebush 341 A8
rd. Glenorie 96 E3
rd. McGraths Hl 121 K13
SMART
av. Camden S 507 B15
cl. Minto 482 K4
st. Fairfield 336 E10
st. Fairfield Ht 336 B9
SMARTS
cr. Burraneer 493 F14
SMEATON GRANGE
rd. Smeaton Gra 479 A8
SMEE
av. Roselands 400 F8
SMEETON
rd. Londonderry 177 A9
SMERDON
pl. Kenthurst 126 G15
SMIDMORE
st. Marrickville 374 F11
SMIKE
pl. Ambarvale 510 H16
SMITH
av. Allambie Ht 257 J14
av. Hobartville 118 E10
av. Hurlstone Pk 373 A14
cr. Liverpool 394 J5
gr. Shalvey 211 C13
la. Newtown 17 F14
la. Five Dock, off
Ramsay Rd 342 K11
pl. Mt Annan 509 D1
rd. Artarmon 285 B14
rd. Castlereagh 175 G6
rd. Oakville 122 J14
st. Annandale 10 J11
st. Balmain 7 E13
st. Bexley 402 J13
st. Chatswood 285 E5
st. Eastgardens 406 F13
st. Emu Plains 235 J6
st. Epping 251 C16
st. Granville 308 D10
st. Hillsdale 406 F13
st. Kentlyn 513 B6
st. Kingsford 406 K6
st. Kingswood 267 E1
st. Lindfield 254 E15
st. Manly 288 G6
st. Marrickville 374 D10
st. Parramatta 308 D4
st. Pendle Hill 306 E1
st. Regents Pk 369 E2
st. Rozelle 7 E13
st. Ryde 282 B16
st. St Marys 269 D3
st. S Penrith 237 A16
st. Summer Hill 373 B4
st. Surry Hills F F11
st. Surry Hills 4 A14
st. Taren Point 462 J12
st. Tempe 404 C2
st. Wentwthvle 306 E1
st. Woollahra 21 H4
st. Yagoona 368 E10
SMITHERS
st. Chippendale 19 A2
SMITHFIELD
av. Coogee 377 G15
rd. Edensor Pk 363 J4
rd. Fairfield W 335 A9
rd. Greenfld Pk 334 C15
rd. Prairiewood 335 A9
rd. Smithfield 335 F7
rd. Wakeley 334 C15
SMITHS
av. Cabramatta 365 C10
av. Hurstville 401 J15
la. Freemns Rch 90 J3
la. Glenorie 127 E14
la. Erskineville, off
Victoria St 374 K9
SMITHYS
pl. Richmond 118 F12
SMOOTHY
pl. Arndell Park 273 H10

SMYTHE
st. Merrylands 307 K13
SMYTHES
st. Concord 342 A3
SNAILHAM
cr. S Windsor 150 J1
SNAKE GULLEY
cl. Narrabeen 228 E8
SNAPE
st. Kingsford 406 H6
st. Maroubra 406 H6
SNAPPER
cl. Green Valley 362 K12
SNAPPERMAN
la. Palm Beach, off Iluka Rd 139 J3
SNELL
pl. West Hoxton 392 B12
SNIPE
cl. Hinchinbrk 363 E15
pl. Ingleburn 453 H7
wy. Mt Annan 479 B15
SNOWBIRD
la. Erskine Park, off Snowbird Pl 300 K1
la. Erskine Park, off Snowbird Pl 301 A1
pl. Erskine Park 301 A1
SNOWDEN
av. Sylvania 461 K10
cl. Cecil Hills 362 F3
pl. St Ives Ch 224 C1
st. Jamisontown 266 B1
SNOWDON
av. Carlingford 279 B4
cr. Smithfield 335 D1
SNOWDRIFT
ct. St Clair 270 D13
SNOW GUM
pl. Alfords Point 429 C12
SNOWGUM
st. Acacia Gdn 214 K14
st. Acacia Gdn 215 A14
SNOWSILL
av. Revesby 399 B9
SNOWY
cl. St Clair 269 H15
pl. Heckenberg 364 A12
pl. Sylvania Wtr 462 D10
st. Seven Hills 275 E10
SNOWY BAKER
st. Moore Park 21 B5
SNUG
pl. West Hoxton 392 E8
SNUGGLEPOT
dr. Faulconbdg 171 D15
SOBRAON
rd. Marsfield 282 A4
SODBURY
st. Chipping Ntn 396 F2
SOFA
st. Marayong 244 B6
SOFALA
av. Riverview 314 A4
st. Riverwood 400 B11
SOFTWOOD
av. Kellyville 216 A1
SOL
pl. Rooty Hill 272 A2
SOLANDER
av. West Hoxton 392 B13
cl. Turramurra 252 D4
dr. St Clair 269 F13
la. Daceyville, off Cook Av 406 F3
pl. Mt Annan 509 G3
rd. Daceyville 406 F3
rd. Kings Lngly 245 K9
st. Kurnell 466 A9
st. Matraville 436 G1
st. Monterey 433 H6
st. Ruse 512 H3
SOLAR
av. Baulkham Hl 246 F9
SOLARIS
dr. Doonside 243 H16
SOLDIERS
av. Harbord 258 D16
pl. Woodbine 481 K10
rd. Jannali 460 F9
SOLENT
cct. Baulkham Hl 216 F14
cct. Baulkham Hl 216 F16
SOLERO
pl. Eschol Park 481 B4
SOLING
cr. Cranebrook 207 A9
SOLITAIRE
ct. Stanhpe Gdn 215 B10
SOLITARY
pl. Ruse 512 H7
SOLO
cr. Fairfield 336 D5
pl. Shalvey 210 J12
st. Kareela 461 D11
SOLOMON
av. Kings Park 244 F2
ct. Greenacre 370 D6
SOLVEIG
cr. Kareela 461 D12
SOLWAY
rd. Bringelly 388 A10
SOMERCOTES
cl. Glen Alpine 510 F9
ct. Wattle Grove 425 H5
SOMERS
st. Bonnyrigg 363 J6
SOMERSET
av. Narellan 478 G9
av. N Turramrra 223 G4
ct. Wattle Grove 426 A4
dr. North Rocks 278 J2
st. Epping 251 C12
st. Hurstville 432 B1
st. Kingswood 237 E14
st. Marsfield 251 E12
st. Minto 482 E2
st. Mosman 316 J10
st. Pitt Town 92 J15
wy. Castle Hill 248 B3
SOMERVILLE
av. Ashfield 372 F4
pl. Manly Vale, off Sunshine St 287 K4
rd. Hornsby Ht 191 F2
st. Arncliffe 403 F10
SOMME
cr. Milperra 397 H12
wy. Matraville 407 B15
SOMMERVILLE
rd. Rozelle 11 J2
SOMOV
pl. Tregear 240 C4
SONDER
pl. Leumeah 482 H10
SONIA
pl. Hassall Gr 212 B14
SONIVER
rd. N Curl Curl 259 B11
SONJA
cl. Cabramatta 365 F9
pl. Picton 561 F4
SONTER
st. Quakers Hill 213 H8
SONYA
cl. Jamisontown 266 B2
SOPER
pl. Penrith 236 K9
SOPHIA
cr. North Rocks 248 E14
la. Surry Hills 20 A1
la. Croydon, off Croydon Rd 342 H12
pl. Blair Athol 511 C2
st. Crows Nest 315 G6
st. Surry Hills F B16
SOPHIE
pl. Cecil Hills 363 A3
st. Glenwood 245 B1
st. Telopea 279 J9
SOPWITH
av. Raby 481 G1
pl. Bnkstn Aprt 397 K1
SORBELLO
pl. Kenthurst 157 J14
SORELL
pl. Barden Rdg 488 H2
SORENSEN
cr. Blackett 241 B2
SORENSON
cr. Glenmore Pk 266 A6
SORLIE
av. Northmead 248 B16
pl. Doonside 243 E8
pl. Frenchs Frst 256 D5
rd. Frenchs Frst 256 A3
SORRELL
la. N Parramatta 278 D13
st. N Parramatta 278 D16
st. Parramatta 278 D16
SORRENTO
ct. Kellyville 186 H15
dr. Glenwood 215 C14
pl. Burraneer 523 D3
pl. Erskine Park 300 E2
SORRIE
st. Balmain 7 G10
SORTIE
pt. Castlecrag 286 B12
SOUDAN
la. Newtown 18 A9
la. Paddington 13 G14
la. Randwick, off Soudan St 377 B15
st. Bexley North 402 D13
st. Merrylands 308 A13
st. Randwick 377 B16
SOULT
st. Sans Souci 463 C5
SOUTER
pl. Hebersham 241 E2
st. Kogarah Bay 432 J13
SOUTH
av. Double Bay 14 A9
av. Leichhardt 16 E1
av. Petersham 15 H9
av. Westmead 277 D15
cr. Lilyfield 10 D2
la. Double Bay 14 A9
pde. Auburn 339 C1
pde. Campsie 372 A13
pde. Canterbury 372 A13
pde. Old Guildford 337 G8
rd. Windsor 121 B13
st. Drummoyne 343 H3
st. Edgecliff 13 F10
st. Ermington 309 J3
st. Glenmore Pk 266 J9
st. Granville 308 F12
st. Gymea 491 F4
st. Kogarah 433 C5
st. Marrickville 373 G12
st. Marsden Pk 211 D9
st. Rydalmere 309 D3
st. Schofields 212 E3
st. Strathfield 341 A16
st. Tempe 404 C4
st. Thirlmere 565 B2
tce. Bankstown 399 G1
tce. Bankstown 399 J1
tce. Punchbowl 399 J1
SOUTHBOURNE
wy. Mona Vale 199 A2
SOUTH CREEK
rd. Collaroy Plat 228 C11
rd. Cromer 228 E14
rd. Dee Why 258 H1
rd. Shanes Park 209 F5
SOUTH DOWLING
st. Darlinghurst 4 F16
st. Moore Park 20 C16
st. Paddington 4 F16
st. Redfern 20 C16
st. Surry Hills 20 E7
st. Waterloo 20 C16
SOUTHDOWN
pl. Airds 512 A13
rd. Elderslie 507 H3
rd. Horsley Pk 332 H6
st. Miller 393 F3
SOUTHEE
cct. Oakhurst 241 H2
rd. Hobartville 118 B7
SOUTHERN
fwy. Waterfall 519 D16
st. Oatley 460 K1
SOUTHERN CROSS
dr. Eastlakes 406 A6
dr. Kensington 376 A15
dr. Mascot 405 G8
dr. Rosebery 376 A15
wy. Allambie Ht 257 F14
SOUTHLEIGH
av. Castle Hill 217 H16
SOUTH LIVERPOOL
rd. Busby 363 C14
rd. Green Valley 363 C14
rd. Heckenberg 364 A14
rd. Hinchinbrk 363 C14
SOUTH PACIFIC
av. Mt Pritchard 364 F14
SOUTH STEYNE
Manly 288 H10
SOUTHSTONE
cl. S Penrith 266 K6
SOUTH VANDERVILLE
st. The Oaks 502 E11
SOUTHWAITE
cr. Glenwood 215 E12
SOUTH WESTERN
mwy. Beverly Hills 400 A11
mwy. Casula 423 G5
mwy. Hamondvle 396 C12
mwy. Liverpool 393 K16
mwy. Lurnea 393 K16
mwy. Milperra 397 B14
mwy. Moorebank 396 C12
mwy. Narwee 400 A11
mwy. Padstow 399 B11
mwy. Panania 398 B12
mwy. Prestons 423 G5
mwy. Revesby 398 B12
mwy. Riverwood 400 A11
SOUTHWOOD
pl. W Pnnant Hl 248 G6
SOVEREIGN
av. Carlingford 279 B3
pl. S Windsor 121 A14
SPA
pl. Prospect 274 H12
SPAGNOLO
pl. Prestons 423 A1
SPAINS WHARF
rd. Neutral Bay 6 H10
SPALDING
cr. Hurstville Gr 431 G12
SPARK
st. Earlwood 402 G2
SPARKES
av. Mortdale 430 J5
la. Camperdwn 17 H1
rd. Jamisontown 266 B3
st. Camperdwn 17 H1
SPARKLE
av. Blacktown 274 A5
SPARKS
la. Greenacre 370 F8
st. Eastlakes 405 G6
st. Mascot 405 G6
SPARMAN
cr. Kings Lngly 245 H9
SPARROW
la. Green Valley 363 F12
SPARTA
cl. Bossley Park 333 J8
SPEARMAN
st. Chatswood 284 K5
st. Roseville 284 K5
SPEDDING
rd. Hornsby Ht 191 E9
SPEED
av. Russell Lea 343 E7
st. Liverpool 395 D7
SPEEDWELL
pl. S Windsor 151 B1
SPEERS
cr. Oakhurst 241 J3
rd. North Rocks 278 B6
SPEETS
rd. Oakville 123 E16
SPEKE
pl. Bligh Park 150 E7
SPELLING
st. Picton 563 C8
SPENCE
pl. Belrose 225 F14
pl. St Helens Park 540 K9
rd. Berkshire Pk 179 D10
st. Revesby 428 J1
SPENCER
ct. Baulkham Hl 248 A9
la. Alexandria 19 A11
la. Rose Bay, off Hamilton St 348 C10
la. Fairfield, off Nelson St 336
pl. Illawong 459
pl. Lane Cove W 284
rd. Cecil Hills 362
rd. Cremorne 316
rd. Killara 253
rd. Londonderry 147
rd. Mosman 316
st. Berala 339
st. Eastwood 280
st. Fairfield 336
st. Five Dock 342
st. Gladesville 312
st. Regentville 265
st. Rooty Hill 241
st. Rose Bay 348
st. Sefton 368
st. Summer Hill 373
wy. Minto 482
SPERRING
av. Oakhurst 242
SPEY
pl. St Andrews 451
st. Winston Hills 277
SPHINX
av. Padstow 398
av. Revesby 398
SPICA
la. Erskine Park, off Spica Pl 300
pl. Erskine Park 300
pl. Quakers Hill 214
st. Sadleir 393
SPICER
av. Hamondvle 396
la. Woollahra 21
rd. Silverdale 354
rd.n, Oxford Falls 227
rd.s, Oxford Falls 226
st. Woollahra 21
SPILSTEAD
pl. Beacon Hill 257
rd. Horsley Pk 301
SPINEBILL
pl. Ingleburn 453
SPINEL
st. Eagle Vale 481
SPINKS
rd. Freemns Rch 58
rd. Glossodia 58
rd. Llandilo 178
rd. N Richmond 58
SPINOSA
pl. Glenmore Pk 265
SPIRE
wy. Narellan 478
SPIRETON
pl. Pendle Hill 276
SPIT
rd. Mosman 317
SPITFIRE
dr. Raby 481
SPITZ
av. Newington 309
SPLITTERS
av. Mt Hunter 505
SPOFFORTH
av. Rouse Hill 184
la. Cremorne, off Florence La 316
st. Cremorne 316
st. Ermington 310
st. Mosman 316
SPOONBILL
av. Blacktown 274
av. Woronora Ht 489
la. St Clair, off Spoonbill St 270
st. Erskine Park 270
st. Hinchinbrk 393
wy. Mt Annan 479
SPOONER
av. Cabramatta W 365
SPORING
av. Kings Lngly 245
SPORTSGROUND
pde. Appin 569
SPOTTED GUM
pl. Greystanes 306
rd. Westleigh 220
SPOTTEDGUM
pl. Rouse Hill 184

RIGG
Mt Colah 162 D16
RIGGS
Fairlight 288 B7
RING
Chatswood 284 K9
Kellyville 216 E5
N Curl Curl 258 K11
Abbotsford 342 H1
Arncliffe 403 F11
Beecroft 250 C3
Birchgrove 7 G5
Bondi Jctn 22 F7
Chatswood 284 K10
Concord 342 A4
Double Bay 14 B6
Dural 188 J13
Eastwood 281 G8
Fairfield E 337 C14
Kurrajong Ht 54 B9
N Sydney ....K F7
N Sydney 5 G8
Paddington 4 J15
Padstow 429 B1
Pagewood 405 K11
Springwood 202 A8
Sydney ....B A13
Sydney 1 H15
RING CREEK
Glenmore 503 H16
Mt Hunter 504 F15
RINGDALE
Bella Vista 216 D14
East Killara 254 F10
Killara 254 C12
Wentwthvle 276 H16
RINGFERN
Valley Ht 202 E5
RINGFIELD
Blacktown 244 F13
Potts Point 4 J6
Roselands 400 F7
Bella Vista 246 F7
Springwood 172 C16
Wattle Grove 425 J4
Potts Point, off Springfield Av 4 J5
Penrith, off Springfield Pl 237 E9
Airds 512 D10
Penrith 237 D9
Catherine Fd 449 D6
Hornsby Ht 191 E8
Padstow 429 C3
Old Guildford 337 G8
RING GARDEN
Granville, off Milton St 308 C10
Granville 308 D10
RING GULLY
N Wahrnga 192 D16
Wahroonga 222 D1
RING HILL
Currans Hill 479 K9
RINGMEAD
Denham Ct 422 A10
RING MILL
Rouse Hill 185 B9
RINGROVE
Kurrajong Hl 54 H15
RINGS
Spring Farm 507 H6
RINGSIDE
Rozelle 344 C7
RINGVALE
Frenchs Frst 256 A3
RINGWOOD
Springwood 201 J4
Springwood 201 J4
Agnes Banks 117 A12
Yarramundi 116 E13
RITE
Ingleburn 453 F14
ROULE
Illawong 459 K6
Lakemba 401 A3
RUCE
Menai 458 K14
Blacktown 274 B7
RUSON
Camperdwn 17 G6
Neutral Bay 6 C4

SPUMANTE
cl. Eschol Park 481 C5
SPUR
cr. Loftus 489 J11
st. Warrimoo 203 F9
SPURGIN
st. Wahroonga 222 C2
SPURWAY
dr. Baulkham Hl 216 H13
st. Dundas 280 A12
st. Ermington 310 B1
SPURWOOD
cl. Dural 188 D10
cl. Kenthurst 188 D10
rd. Turramurra 223 D8
rd. Warrimoo 203 E15
SQUEERS
pl. Ambarvale 510 J15
SQUILL
pl. Arndell Park 273 F10
SQUIRE
pl. Castle Hill 217 G6
st. Ryde 311 G2
SQUIRES
rd. Springwood 202 E10
SRAID NA'H ALBAINN
Mosman, off Cross St 317 D11
STABLE SQUARE
pl. Richmond 118 F12
STABLE VIEW
pl. Narellan 478 B9
STACEY
rd. Castlereagh 176 F12
st. Bankstown 369 G10
st. Cronulla 523 J3
st. Fairfield W 335 G11
st. Greenacre 369 G10
st.s, Bankstown 399 G5
st.s, Punchbowl 399 G5
STACK
st. Balmain East 8 E8
st. Narrabeen 228 G8
STADDON
cl. St Ives 224 C6
STAFF
av. Glenwood 215 D14
STAFFORD
la. Paddington 13 C15
la. Stanmore 16 K9
pl. N Turramrra 223 G4
rd. Artarmon 285 A12
st. Cabramatta 365 C11
st. Double Bay 14 E7
st. Kingswood 237 E14
st. Minto 482 F2
st. Paddington 13 C15
st. Penrith 237 A13
st. S Granville 338 E8
st. Stanmore 16 K9
wy. Kellyville 216 A1
STAGG
pl. Ambarvale 510 F16
STAHLS
rd. Oakville 153 A2
STAINSBY
av. Kings Lngly 246 A9
cl. Turramurra 252 A2
STALEY
ct. W Pnnant Hl 249 C1
STALLION
gln. Glenwood 245 J4
STALWART
st. Prairiewood 334 J7
STAMFORD
av. Cabarita 342 D1
av. Ermington 280 D12
STAN
st. N Willghby 285 G10
STANBROOK
st. Fairfield Ht 335 K9
STANBURY
pl. Quakers Hill 214 A12
st. Gladesville 312 F8
STANDARD
wy. Minto 482 H7
STANDISH
av. Oakhurst 241 H3
STANFORD
cct. Rouse Hill 185 D4
wy. Airds 511 H15

STANHOPE
pky. Parklea 215 B8
pky. Stanhpe Gdn 215 B8
pwy. Quakers Hill 214 B7
pwy. Schofields 214 B7
rd. Killara 254 A14
row. Bella Vista 246 G3
st. Auburn 338 J3
STANIER
cl. Cherrybrook 219 K7
STANLEA
pde. Wiley Park 400 G2
STANLEY
av. Kurrajong Ht 54 B12
av. Mosman 317 C5
av. W Pnnant Hl 249 G5
cl. St Ives 224 A12
la. Darlinghurst ....D K16
la. Darlinghurst 4 C8
la. Ermington 310 B2
la. Queens Park 22 H11
la. St Ives 224 A12
la. Stanmore 16 B9
la. Kogarah, off Regent St 433 C3
la. Arncliffe, off Stanley St 403 F9
pl. Illawong 459 H5
rd. Epping 251 E15
rd. Hunters Hill 313 H11
rd. Ingleburn 453 B7
rd. Lidcombe 339 F7
st. Arncliffe 403 F9
st. Bankstown 399 F2
st. Blacktown 274 G7
st. Burwood 341 J15
st. Campsie 372 A15
st. Chatswood 285 C11
st. Concord 342 A8
st. Croydon Pk 371 J7
st. Darlinghurst ....D G16
st. Darlinghurst 4 B8
st. Fairfield Ht 335 H12
st. Kogarah 433 C2
st. Leichhardt 10 B15
st. Marrickville 373 J11
st. Merrylands 307 C10
st. Mona Vale 199 G3
st. Newport 169 K12
st. Peakhurst 430 F4
st. Putney 312 B9
st. Queens Park 22 G11
st. Randwick 377 B10
st. Redfern 20 C9
st. St Ives 224 A12
st. St Marys 269 H5
st. Shanes Park 209 K1
st. Silverwater 309 J13
st. Stanmore 16 B9
st. Tempe 404 B2
st. Woollahra 22 E3
STANMORE
la. Stanmore 16 G8
rd. Enmore 16 B12
rd. Petersham 16 B12
rd. Stanmore 16 B12
STANNARDS
pl. N Sydney 6 D13
STANNIX PARK
rd. Ebenezer 62 D3
rd. Wilberforce 61 F4
STANNUM
cl. Hinchinbrk 392 H5
STANSBURY
st. Emu Plains 235 E11
STANSELL
av. Jannali 460 J10
st. Gladesville 312 J8
STANTON
dr. W Pnnant Hl 249 C9
la. Mosman, off Spit Rd 317 B3
pl. Emu Plains 236 B6
rd. Haberfield 373 D1
rd. Mosman 317 B3
rd. Mosman 317 E3
rd. Seven Hills 246 B15
st. Liverpool 394 H3
STANWAY
av. Springwood 201 E4
STANWELL
cr. Ashcroft 394 E2
STAPLES
pl. Glenmore Pk 265 F8

st. Kingsgrove 402 B10
STAPLETON
av. Sutherland 490 F2
la. St Marys, off Stapleton Pde 239 J16
pde. St Marys 269 J1
pl. Pymble 223 G16
st. Pendle Hill 276 E14
st. Wentwthvle 276 E14
STAPLEY
st. Kingswood 237 E16
STAPYLTON
st. Winmalee 173 D5
STAR
cr. Pennant Hills 220 B15
cr. W Pnnant Hl 220 B15
ct. Cmbrdg Gdn 237 F4
la. Rooty Hill 272 B2
st. Eastwood 281 H6
st. Picton 563 C9
STARFIGHTER
av. Raby 481 F1
STARK
st. Coogee 377 D16
STARKEY
dr. Bnkstn Aprt 397 F5
st. Forestville 256 A13
st. Hurlstone Pk 373 B13
st. Killarney Ht 256 A14
STARLEAF
wy. Mcquarie Fd 454 H3
STARLIGHT
pl. Kellyville 186 B16
pl. Richmond 118 D5
pl. St Clair 270 C13
STARLING
st. Green Valley 363 F12
st. Lilyfield 10 G10
st. Rozelle 7 C15
STARR
av. Padstow 429 E5
cl. Camden 507 A9
pl. Blacktown 274 A5
STARTOP
pl. Ambarvale 510 J14
STATHAM
av. Faulconbdg 171 C16
av. North Rocks 278 K2
st. Belfield 371 G11
STATION
av. Concord W 341 C1
la. Hurstville 432 E7
la. Narwee 400 J13
la. Newtown 17 E14
la. Penrith 236 G11
la. Wahroonga, off Coonabarra Rd 222 D7
la. Penshurst, off The Strand 431 F6
pl. Eveleigh 18 E12
rd. Auburn 309 F16
rd. Belmore 371 C16
rd. Menangle Pk 539 A5
rd. Seven Hills 245 K15
rd. Toongabbie 276 A2
st. Arncliffe 403 E9
st. Ashfield 372 J2
st. Blaxland 233 F7
st. Camden 477 B15
st. Concord 341 G6
st. Couridjah 564 E15
st. Douglas Park 568 F6
st. Dundas 279 D14
st. Engadine 518 J2
st. Fairfield 335 K10
st. Fairfield Ht 335 K10
st. Glenbrook 263 K2
st. Guildford 337 G6
st. Homebush 341 D9
st. Hornsby 221 G1
st. Kogarah 433 B4
st. Marrickville 373 J14
st. Menangle 538 H16
st. Mortdale 431 A7
st. Naremburn 315 C1
st. Newtown 17 D12
st. Newtown 17 F15
st. Penrith 236 H10
st. Petersham 15 E6
st. Picton 563 G8
st. Pymble 253 E2
st. Regents Pk 368 K1
st. Rooty Hill 242 D16
st. St Marys 239 H14

st. Schofields 183 C15
st. S Wntwthvle 307 A3
st. Thirlmere 564 H9
st. Thirlmere 565 A6
st. Thornleigh 221 A14
st. Warwck Frm 365 H14
st. Wentwthvle 307 A3
st. West Ryde 281 C16
st. Springwood, off Jerseywold Av 201 J3
st.e, Harris Park 308 D4
st.e, Parramatta 308 D4
st.e, Tempe 404 B3
st.s, Emu Plains 235 K7
st.w, Harris Park 308 D7
st.w, Tempe 404 A3
STAUNER
pl. Quakers Hill 213 H13
STAVE
pl. Stanhpe Gdn 215 D2
STEAD
cl. Edensor Pk 363 H2
pl. Casula 424 F5
STEAMER
pl. Currans Hill 480 A12
STEDHAM
gr. Oakhurst 241 J4
STEEL
la. Surry Hills 19 K3
st. Blacktown 244 H10
st. S Granville 338 E7
st. Surry Hills 19 K3
STEELE
av. Revesby Ht 428 K8
pl. Bligh Park 150 F5
pl. Bonnyrigg 364 A6
st. Mays Hill 307 K6
st. Parramatta 307 K6
STEEPLE
wy. Narellan 478 B10
STEERFORTH
wy. Ambarvale 510 K16
wy. Ambarvale 511 Z9
STEFAN
la. Doonside 243 C12
STEFANIE
pl. Bonnyrigg 364 A11
STEFIE
pl. Kings Lngly 245 G8
STEIN
pl. Cecil Hills 362 K5
pl. Glenmore Pk 265 F8
STEINTON
st. Manly 288 H8
STELLA
cl. East Killara 254 E6
dr. Green Valley 362 K9
pl. Blacktown 274 F8
st. Collaroy Plat 228 J12
st. Fairfield Ht 335 H12
STENHOUSE
dr. Mt Annan 509 F2
STENNETT
rd. Ingleburn 452 E9
STEPHANIE
la. Belmore 371 G16
la. Belmore 401 G1
pl. Bella Vista 246 F5
pl. N Turramrra 223 G5
st. Padstow 399 E15
STEPHANO
pl. Rsemeadow 540 C3
STEPHEN
av. Matraville 436 G9
av. Ryde 281 K11
cl. Castle Hill 218 F16
la. Paddington 13 C12
la. Randwick 377 B10
pl. Roselands 401 B9
rd. Botany 405 K12
rd. Engadine 518 G6
st. Balmain 8 A10
st. Beacon Hill 257 E7
st. Blacktown 245 A10
st. Bondi 377 J5
st. Chatswood 285 C12
st. Hornsby 191 J13
st. Newtown 17 K9
st. N Richmond 87 B14
st. Paddington 13 B13
st. Penshurst 431 A2
st. Randwick 377 B10
st. Woolmloo 4 G5

STEPHENS
- la. Padstow 399 E16

STEPHENSON
- pl. Currans Hill 479 J14
- st. Birrong 368 J4
- st. Leumeah 512 D1
- st. Roselands 400 J6
- st. Winston Hills 277 E5

STERLAND
- av. North Manly 258 A14

STERLING
- rd. Minchinbury 271 C6

STERLINI
- pl. Blacktown 274 D10

STERN
- pl. Roselands 400 K7

STEVEN
- pl. Vineyard 152 A2

STEVENAGE
- rd. Canley Ht 365 B3
- rd. Hebersham 241 E5

STEVENS
- av. Miranda 491 K1
- cr. Smithfield 336 C5
- *la. Marrickville, off Philpott St 374 D9*
- rd. Glenorie 128 G2
- rd. Ingleburn 422 J11
- st. East Hills 428 A2
- st. Ermington 310 C1
- st. Panania 428 A2
- st. Pennant Hills 220 G14
- st.e. Pennant Hills 220 J15

STEVENSON
- *av. Newington, off Heidelberg Av 310 B14*
- st. Lane Cove 314 F6
- st. S Penrith 266 K1
- st. S Penrith 267 A1
- st. Wetherill Pk 334 G4

STEVEYS FOREST
- rd. Oakdale 499 H7
- rd. Oakdale 500 A12

STEWARD
- st. Lilyfield 9 K7

STEWART
- av. Blacktown 244 E12
- av. Curl Curl 258 H12
- av. Hamondvle 396 F15
- av. Hornsby 191 E11
- av. Mcquarie Pk 283 B7
- av. Matraville 406 J16
- av. Peakhurst 430 B3
- cl. Cheltenham 251 A11
- dr. Castle Hill 248 C2
- la. Bankstown 399 E1
- *la. Sydenham, off Park Rd 374 E16*
- pl. Balmain 7 E10
- pl. Glenmore Pk 265 J7
- pl. Paddington 21 D4
- pl. Strathfield 341 E12
- *pwy. Hamondvle, off Stewart Av 396 G16*
- st. Arncliffe 403 D9
- st. Artarmon 285 A13
- st. Balmain 7 E11
- st. Campbelltwn 511 G7
- st. Eastwood 280 K10
- st. Ermington 280 C11
- st. Glebe 11 J7
- st. Harringtn Pk 478 G8
- st. North Bondi 348 D14
- st. Paddington 21 B2
- st. Paddington 21 D3
- st. Parramatta 308 F2
- st. Randwick 407 C1
- st. S Windsor 150 H3

STEWARTS
- la. Wilberforce 61 D10

STILES
- av. Padstow 399 B9
- st. Croydon Pk 371 H6

STILL
- cl. Arcadia 129 J10

STILLER
- pl. Greenacre 369 J12

STILT
- av. Cranebrook 207 H10
- cl. Hinchinbrk 363 D16

STILTON
- la. Picton 563 C16

STIMPSON
- cr. Grasmere 505 J3

STIMSON
- st. Guildford 337 D3
- st. Smithfield 336 A6

STINGRAY
- cl. Raby 451 C13
- st. Cranebrook 207 B10

STINSON
- cr. Bnkstn Aprt 367 J16
- *la. Marrickville, off Warren Rd 373 J15*
- pl. Forestville 256 A7

STIPA
- pl. Mt Annan 509 D4

STIRGESS
- av. Curl Curl 258 G12

STIRLING
- av. Kirrawee 461 A15
- av. North Rocks 248 J16
- ct. Castle Hill 219 A11
- dr. Camperdwn 17 Z9
- la. Chatswood 285 D8
- la. Glebe 12 G13
- pl. Belrose 225 K12
- pl. Glenfield 424 E10
- rd. Camperdwn 11 D16
- st. Cmbrdg Pk 237 K9
- st. Cecil Hills 362 D7
- st. Glebe 12 G13
- st. Redfern 19 D6

STOCK
- av. Kingswood 237 H15
- pl. Winston Hills 276 H1

STOCKADE
- *la. Emu Plains, off Stockade St 235 D10*
- pl. Woodcroft 243 E8
- st. Emu Plains 235 D10

STOCKALLS
- pl. Minto 452 K16

STOCKDALE
- cr. Abbotsbury 333 C12
- rd. Orchard Hills 298 C11

STOCK FARM
- av. Bella Vista 246 F2

STOCKHOLM
- av. Hassall Gr 211 H13

STOCKMAN
- pl. Wrrngtn Dns 238 D5
- rd. Currans Hill 479 K9

STOCKTON
- av. Moorebank 396 C7

STOCKWOOD
- st. S Penrith 266 G4

STODDART
- pl. Dee Why 258 F3
- rd. Prospect 275 A13
- st. Roselands 400 K6

STOKE
- av. Marrickville 373 H9
- cr. S Penrith 266 G5

STOKES
- av. Alexandria 375 E9
- av. Asquith 192 B11
- pl. Lindfield 254 B16
- pwy. Springwood 201 H1
- rd. Tahmoor 565 D15
- st. Lane Cove W 284 F15

STOKOE
- st. Warwck Frm 365 F14

STOLLE
- cl. Menai 458 J7
- st. Shalvey 210 K14

STONE
- pde. Davidson 225 C14
- pl. Wrrngtn Dns 238 C3
- st. Earlwood 402 G2
- st. Glendenning 242 F2
- st. Lidcombe 339 E10
- st. Meadowbnk 311 F2
- tce. Kurrajong Hl 54 E13

STONE BRIDGE
- dr. Glenbrook 234 B12

STONEBRIDGE
- pl. Gymea Bay 491 C7

STONECROP
- rd. N Turramrra 193 E15

STONEHAVEN
- pde. Cabramatta 365 D11
- pl. Castle Hill 218 A7
- rd. Mt Colah 162 D14

STONELEA
- ct. Dural 188 G13

STONE PINE
- wy. Bella Vista 246 G4

STONEQUARRY
- pl. Picton 563 F9

STONES
- rd. Ebenezer 63 K1

STONEX
- la. Turramurra 222 H14

STONEY CREEK
- rd. Beverly Hills 401 C16
- rd. Bexley 402 A14
- rd. Kingsgrove 401 C16
- rd. Narwee 430 J2

STONNY BATTER
- rd. Minto 482 E7

STONY CREEK
- rd. Shanes Park 209 K9

STOREY
- av. West Hoxton 391 G13
- st. Maroubra 406 J7
- st. Ryde 311 J5

STORNOWAY
- av. St Andrews 451 J15

STORY
- pl. Quakers Hill 213 H15

STOTT
- cl. Bonnyrigg 363 G8

STOTTS
- av. Bardwell Pk 402 G8

STOULTON
- wy. Cranebrook 207 G13

STOUT
- rd. Mount Druitt 241 A15

STOW
- cl. Edensor Pk 363 K2
- pl. Illawong 459 G3

STOWE
- ct. Wattle Grove 426 A5

STRABANE
- av. Killarney Ht 256 C15

STRACHAN
- ct. Kellyville 217 A2
- *la. Kingsford, off Houston Rd 406 F1*
- st. Kingsford 406 F1

STRADBROKE
- av. Green Valley 363 A13

STRAITS
- av. Guildford 338 E10

STRAND
- arc. Sydney 3 G3
- la. Penshurst 431 F6

STRANG
- pl. Bligh Park 150 F6
- pwy. Castle Hill 218 E14

STRANRAER
- dr. St Andrews 481 K3

STRAPPER
- cl. Casula 394 F16

STRASSMANN
- cr. Lucas Ht 487 G12

STRATFORD
- av. Denistone 281 E12
- cl. Asquith 192 E10
- dr. Belrose 225 K10
- pl. St Ives 254 A3
- rd. North Rocks 278 J2
- rd. Tahmoor 565 H16
- st. Cammeray 316 C4

STRATH
- pl. Kenthurst 157 F5

STRATHALBYN
- dr. Oatlands 278 H11

STRATHALLEN
- av. Northbridge 315 K1

STRATHAM
- pl. Belrose 225 K12

STRATHCARRON
- av. Castle Hill 218 B7

STRATHDARR
- st. Miller 393 F1

STRATHDON
- cr. Blaxland 233 F12
- *la. Emu Heights, off Strathdon Rd 205 B15*
- rd. Emu Heights 205 A15

STRATHEDEN
- av. Kellyville 185 J14

STRATHFIELD
- av. Strathfield 341 F14
- cl. St Johns Pk 364 G5
- sq. Strathfield 341 G12

STRATHFILLAN
- wy. Kellyville 186 K16

STRATHLORA
- st. Strathfield 341 A16

STRATHMORE
- la. Glebe 11 K7
- pde. Chatswood 284 K6
- pl. Glen Alpine 510 F13

STRATHWOOD
- ct. Pymble 253 G2

STRATTON
- cr. Milperra 397 D11
- pl. N Turramrra 193 F11

STRAUSS
- cl. Bonnyrigg Ht 363 F5
- pl. Seven Hills 246 E12
- rd. St Clair 300 A2

STRAWBERRY
- rd. Casula 424 E1
- wy. Glenwood 215 F12

STREAM
- st. Darlinghurst D K15

STREAMDALE
- gr. Warriewood 198 J6

STREATFIELD
- rd. Bellevue Hill 347 E16

STREBER
- pl. Hornsby 191 D12

STREETON
- av. Mt Pritchard 364 J12
- pl. Plumpton 242 C7

STRETHAM
- av. Picnic Point 428 G6

STRETTON
- la. Illawong 460 A7
- wy. Claymore 481 F11

STRIATA
- wy. Mcquarie Fd 454 G4

STRICKLAND
- av. Cromer 227 H13
- av. Lindfield 284 E2
- av. Maroubra 407 C15
- cr. Ashcroft 364 D15
- *la. Lindfield, off Strickland Av 284 E3*
- *la. St Clair, off Strickland Pl 270 G16*
- pl. Edensor Pk 363 C2
- pl. Erskine Park 270 F16
- pl. Wentwthvle 276 K14
- rd. Guildford 338 C9
- st. Bass Hill 368 B8
- st. Heathcote 518 G11
- st. Rose Bay 348 D11

STRICTA
- pl. Oxford Falls 226 G16

STRINGER
- pl. Oatlands 279 E12
- rd. Kellyville 185 G2

STRINGYBARK
- av. Cranebrook 237 E1
- cl. Westleigh 220 F7
- pl. Alfords Point 429 C12
- pl. Bradbury 511 E10
- pl. Castle Hill 248 G3

STROKER
- st. Canley Ht 365 C1

STROMBOLI
- pl. Bilgola 169 F3

STROMEFERRY
- cr. St Andrews 481 J5

STROMLO
- pl. Ruse 512 F4
- st. Bossley Park 334 D9

STRONE
- av. Wahroonga 221 K13

STRONG
- pl. Richmond 119 A4

STROUD
- pl. Belrose 226 B12
- st. North Ryde 282 G13
- st. Warwck Frm 365 K16
- wy. Bonnyrigg 364 D5

STROUTHION
- ct. Green Valley 363 F14

STRUAN
- st. Tahmoor 566 A9

STRUEN MARIE
- st. Kareela 461

STRUTHERS
- st. Cronulla 524

STRZELECKI
- cl. Wakeley 334

STRZLECKI
- dr. Horngsea Pk 392

STUART
- av. Normanhurst 221
- av. Springwood 201
- cl. Illawong 460
- cr. Blakehurst 462
- cr. Drummoyne 343
- la. Blakehurst 432
- *la. Wahroonga, off Illoura Av 222*
- pl. Tahmoor 565
- rd. Dharruk 241
- st. Blakehurst 432
- st. Burwood 342
- st. Canley Vale 366
- st. Collaroy 229
- st. Concord W 341
- st. Granville 308
- st. Jamisontown 236
- st. Kogarah 433
- st. Longueville 314
- st. Manly 288
- st. Newport 169
- st. Padstow 399
- st. Ryde 282
- st. Wahroonga 222
- *wk. Mosman, off Bloxsome La 316*

STUART MOULD
- cr. Lalor Park 245

STUBBS
- pl. Bonnyrigg 364
- pl. Ingleburn 453
- st. Auburn 309
- st. Beverley Pk 432
- st. Silverwater 309

STUCKEY
- pl. Narellan Vale 478

STUDDY
- cl. Bligh Park 150

STUDENTS
- la. Mt Riverview 204

STUDLEY
- ct. Narellan 478
- st. Carramar 366
- st. Londonderry 148

STUKA
- cl. Raby 451

STURDEE
- la. Lovett Bay 168
- pde. Dee Why 258
- st. North Ryde 282
- st. Wentwthvle 306

STURGESS
- pl. Eagle Vale 481

STURT
- av. Georges Hall 368
- la. Kingsford 406
- pl. Camden S 507
- pl. Castle Hill 218
- pl. Mt Colah 162
- pl. St Ives 224
- pl. Windsor Dn 151
- rd. Ingleburn 423
- rd. Woolooware 493
- st. Campbelltwn 511
- st. Darlinghurst 4
- st. Frenchs Frst 256
- st. Kingsford 406
- st. Lalor Park 245
- st. Smithfield 336
- st. Telopea 279

STUTT
- pl. S Windsor 150
- st. Kings Park 244

STUTZ
- pl. Ingleburn 453

STYLES
- cr. Minto 482
- pl. Merrylands 307
- st. Leichhardt 10

STYPANDRA
- pl. Springwood 201

SUAKIN
- dr. Mosman 317
- st. Pymble 253

BIACO
Carlingford 280 D4
BWAY
Homebush 341 C9
Banksia 403 D11
Rockdale 403 C16
CCESS
Kellyville 216 H1
Greenfld Pk 334 D13
DBURY
Belmore 371 E14
E
Mt Colah 162 G13
EZ CANAL
The Rocks A K4
FFOLK
Collaroy 229 A15
St Ives 224 D9
Paddington 13 D15
Colyton 270 E5
Elderslie 507 J1
Tahmoor 566 E8
Blacktown 244 C13
Ingleburn 453 B7
Miller 393 G2
Paddington 13 D15
Windsor 121 C9
GAR HOUSE
Canterbury, off Hutton St 372 H14
GARLOAF
Middle Cove 285 K10
Ingleside 198 C4
GARWOOD
Greenacre 370 F6
LLIVAN
Lurnea 394 C7
Douglas Park 568 G1
Blacktown 273 K5
Fairfield W 335 A12
LLY
Randwick 407 D1
LMAN
Doonside 273 F3
Menangle 538 G16
Cabramatta W 365 B5
LTANA
Glenwood 215 D15
LU
Glenfield 424 E11
MBRAY
Kemps Ck 359 J3
MMER
Faulconbdg 171 B13
MMERCROP
Wrrngtn Dns 237 K4
MMERFIELD
Quakers Hill 214 B15
Quakers Hill 214 E15
Cmbrdg Gdn 237 H2
MMERHAZE
Hornsby Ht 161 H15
MMER HILL
St Clair, off Summer Hill Pl 270 C10
St Clair 270 C10
Lewisham 15 A11
MMERS
Hornsby 191 F13
Bradbury 511 J12
Dundas Vy 279 K11
MMERSTONE
Ambarvale 510 J16
MMERVILLE
N Willghby 285 E9
MMERWOOD
Beecroft 250 J7
MMIT
Dee Why 259 B9
Marsfield 281 J4
Glenwood 215 G16
Cranebrook 207 B11
Cranebrook, off Summit Gln 207 B11
Baulkham Hl 246 F11
Strathfield 341 C16
Earlwood 402 E5
Mt Riverview 204 G14
MNER
Hassall Gr 212 B15
Sutherland 460 F15

SUNART
pl. St Andrews 481 J5
SUNBEAM
av. Burwood 371 J2
av. Croydon 342 H13
av. Kogarah 433 D10
la. Campsie 401 K2
pl. Ingleburn 453 K7
SUNBIRD
cl. Hinchinbrk 393 B4
tce. Glenmore Pk 266 A12
SUNBLEST
cr. Mount Druitt 240 K15
SUNBURY
st. Sutherland 460 D15
SUNCREST
av. Newport 169 G15
pl. Doonside 243 H15
SUNCROFT
av. Georges Hall 368 D15
SUNDA
av. Whalan 241 B13
SUNDALE
pl. Chester Hill 368 C2
SUNDERLAND
av. Rose Bay, off New South Head Rd 347 K10
cr. Bligh Park 150 J6
dr. Raby 451 F15
SUNFLOWER
dr. Clarmnt Ms 268 H1
SUNHAVEN
st. Beecroft 250 A11
SUNHILL
pl. North Ryde 282 F7
SUNLAND
cr. Mt Riverview 204 G16
SUNLEA
av. Mortdale 430 J5
cr. Belfield 371 C8
pl. Allambie Ht 257 B8
SUNNDAL
cl. St Clair 269 H15
SUNNING
pl. Summer Hill 373 C3
SUNNINGDALE
Blacktown 274 D11
dr. Glenmore Pk 266 E9
dr. Glenmore Pk 266 F10
SUNNY
cr. Punchbowl 399 J6
pl. St Johns Pk 334 E15
SUNNYDALE
pl. Narellan, off Links Wy 478 B10
SUNNYHOLT
rd. Acacia Gdn 215 A16
rd. Blacktown 244 J15
rd. Glenwood 215 A16
rd. Kings Lngly 244 K8
rd. Kings Park 244 K8
rd. Parklea 215 A16
rd. Stanhpe Gdn 215 D12
SUNNYMEADE
cl. Asquith 192 C10
rd. Berkshire Pk 179 E9
SUNNY RIDGE
rd. Winmalee 172 K12
SUNNYRIDGE
pl. Bayview 168 J11
rd. Arcadia 129 E8
SUNNYSIDE
av. Caringbah 492 J6
av. Lilyfield 10 G3
cr. Castlecrag 285 K11
cr. N Richmond 87 E15
dr. Ellis Lane 476 D5
pl. Blakehurst 462 C2
st. Gladesville 312 K11
SUNNYVALE
rd. Middle Dural 158 K10
SUNRAY
cr. St Clair 270 D14
SUNRIDGE
pl. W Pnnant Hl 248 K3
SUNRISE
pl. Horngsea Pk 392 C14
pl. Kellyville 216 H3
rd. Palm Beach 109 J16

SUNSET
av. Bankstown 399 B5
av. Cabramatta W 365 C5
av. Cronulla 523 J2
av. Elderslie 507 F2
av. Hornsby Ht 161 G12
av. Lurnea 394 C7
av. S Penrith 266 F1
bvd. Winmalee 173 E5
la. Seaforth 286 K11
pl. Earlwood 402 H5
pl. Frenchs Frst 256 K4
pl. North Rocks 278 G3
SUNSHINE
av. Penrith 237 A7
pde. Peakhurst 430 C11
st. Manly Vale 287 J3
SUNTER
wy. Castle Hill 217 K6
SUNTOP
pl. Glenmore Pk 266 H14
SUN VALLEY
pl. Carlingford 279 F2
rd. Valley Ht 203 A6
SUNVILLE
ct. Blacktown 274 B8
SUPERBA
av. Cronulla 494 C6
la. Mosman, off Superba Pde 317 C6
pde. Mosman 317 C6
SUPERIOR
av. Seven Hills 275 F7
SUPPLY
av. Beacon Hill 257 G2
av. Lurnea 394 C12
cl. Narellan 478 E16
ct. Kellyville 216 H1
pl. Bligh Park 150 E4
rd. Lilyfield 10 A2
st. Dundas Vy 280 B7
st. Ruse 512 H3
SURADA
av. Riverview 314 B7
SURF
la. Cronulla 493 K12
rd. Cronulla 493 K12
rd. N Curl Curl 259 A11
rd. Palm Beach 140 B7
rd. Whale Beach 140 B7
rd. Whale Beach 140 C6
SURFERS
pde. Harbord 258 E16
SURFSIDE
av. Avalon 170 C2
av. Clovelly 377 K12
SURFVIEW
rd. Mona Vale 199 G4
SURGEONS
ct. The Rocks A K5
SURPRISE
cr. Bligh Park 150 C7
SURREY
av. Castle Hill 217 K9
av. Collaroy 258 K1
av. Georges Hall 368 B15
la. Darlinghurst 4 J9
la. Waterloo 19 F11
pl. Kareela 461 B13
rd. Turramurra 223 D9
st. Blacktown 274 G6
st. Darlinghurst 4 H10
st. Epping 251 B13
st. Guildford 337 G3
st. Marrickville 374 A9
st. Minto 452 G16
st. Stanmore 16 G9
st. Waterloo 19 F11
SURVEY
pl. St Ives 224 B16
SURVEYOR
av. Heathcote 518 D13
SURVEYOR ABBOT
dr. Glenbrook 234 C11
SURVEYORS CREEK
rd. Glenmore Pk 266 E9
SUSAN
av. Padstow Ht 429 D6
la. Annandale 11 B16
la. Clovelly, off Fern St 377 G12
pde. Castle Hill 217 K16
pl. Eastwood 281 G6

pl. Gymea Bay 491 F9
pl. Minto 482 G3
st. Annandale 17 B2
st. Auburn 339 D5
st. Camperdwn 17 J6
st. Newtown 17 J7
st. S Wntwthvle 306 H8
SUSANNE
la. Cmbrdg Pk, off Susanne Pl 238 C7
pl. Cmbrdg Pk 238 C7
SUSELLA
cr. N Richmond 87 A12
SUSSEX
la. Sydney A C15
pl. Narellan 478 H12
pl. Seven Hills 275 E5
rd. Kellyville 216 B4
rd. St Ives 254 A2
st. Cabramatta 365 G10
st. Epping 251 C12
st. Haymarket E E3
st. Haymarket 3 E7
st. Minto 482 E1
st. Sydney A C13
st. Sydney E E3
st. Sydney 1 D15
SUSSMAN
av. Bass Hill 368 C13
cr. Smithfield 336 C5
SUTCLIFFE
pl. Barden Rdg 488 G4
st. Kingsgrove 401 H12
SUTHERLAND
av. Kings Lngly 245 D6
av. Paddington 13 F14
av. Ryde 311 H3
av. Wahroonga 222 F8
cr. Darling Point 14 B4
la. Merrylands 307 J13
la. Sutherland 490 D2
la. Cremorne, off Ben Boyd La 316 D7
la. Chippendale, off O'Connor St 19 A2
rd. Beecroft 250 F5
rd. Chatswd W 284 G12
rd. Cheltenham 251 A9
rd. Jannali 460 F14
rd. Londonderry 148 J16
rd. N Parramatta 278 E11
st. Canley Ht 365 B3
st. Cremorne 316 C7
st. Granville 308 H12
st. Lane Cove 314 B1
st. Mascot 405 F6
st. Paddington 13 F14
st. Rosebery 405 F6
st. St Peters 374 F14
st. Sutherland 490 D3
st. Yagoona 369 D8
SUTTIE
rd. Bellevue Hill 14 H16
rd. Double Bay 22 G1
rd. Woollahra 22 G1
SUTTON
av. Earlwood 402 K5
grn. W Pnnant Hl 249 C4
la. Darlinghurst, off Bourke St 4 E9
la. Balmain, off Sutton St 7 F11
la. Darlinghurst, off Wisdom La 4 E9
pl. Minto 453 C15
pl. St Ives 224 B16
rd. Ashcroft 364 D16
rd. Cmbrdg Pk 238 B8
st. Balmain 7 F10
st. Blacktown 274 H4
st. Five Dock 343 A9
st. Hornsby 191 F9
SUTTOR
av. Moore Park 21 B9
av. Ryde 311 J4
pl. Baulkham Hl 247 E4
rd. N Parramatta 278 K6
st. Alexandria 18 F15
st. Silverwater 309 G12
st. Woolmloo 4 C7
SUVA
cr. Greenacre 369 K14
pl. Lethbrdg Pk 240 G1
SUWARROW
st. Fairlight 288 D7

SUZANNE
cl. Berowra Ht 133 A6
rd. Mona Vale 198 J2
st. Seven Hills 275 J6
SVENSDEN
pl. Ingleburn 453 B12
SVERGE
st. Mosman 316 K12
SWAFFHAM
rd. Minto 482 A6
SWAGER
pl. Canley Ht 335 E16
SWAGMAN
la. Wrrngtn Dns, off Swagman Pl 238 D4
pl. Wrrngtn Dns 238 D4
SWAIN
st. Moorebank 395 H9
st. Sydenham 374 D14
SWAINE
dr. Wilton 568 K16
SWALES
pl. Colyton 270 J9
SWALLOW
dr. Erskine Park 270 G16
dr. Erskine Park 270 J14
la. Ebenezer 63 G2
la. St Clair, off Swallow Dr 270 J14
pl. Hinchinbrk 363 D15
pl. Ingleburn 453 G9
st. Jamisontown 236 B16
SWALLOW ROCK
dr. Grays Point 491 C15
SWAMP
rd. Tempe 404 D3
SWAMPHEN
la. St Clair, off Swamphen St 271 A14
st. Erskine Park 271 A13
SWAN
av. Strathfield 341 G10
cct. Green Valley 363 C14
ct. Harringtn Pk 478 D4
la. Granville 308 H12
pl. Ingleburn 453 D9
pl. Jamisontown 266 D4
pl. Lalor Park 245 J11
pl. Pennant Hills 220 D16
rd. Edensor Pk 333 G16
st. Gladesville 312 K5
st. Lilli Pilli 522 E3
st. Revesby 398 H15
st. Rydalmere 279 F16
st. Woolooware 493 G9
SWANE
st. Ermington 310 F2
SWANLEY
st. Mt Pritchard 364 C11
SWANN
pl. Kellyville 215 F4
SWANNELL
av. Chiswick 343 D2
SWANNS
la. Allawah 432 G9
SWANSEA
ct. Glenwood 215 J14
pl. West Hoxton 392 E5
SWANSON
la. Erskineville 18 C15
st. Erskineville 18 B14
st. Eveleigh 18 A14
wy. Claymore 481 B11
SWANSTON
st. St Marys 269 H2
SWEENEY
av. Plumpton 241 G10
SWEETHAVEN
rd. Bossley Park 333 J10
rd. Edensor Pk 333 J13
rd. Greenfld Pk 333 J13
st. Bankstown 399 E1
SWEETWATER
gr. Orchard Hills 268 H12
SWETE
st. Lidcombe 339 K8
SWETTENHAM
rd. Minto 482 B3
SWIFT
gln. Erskine Park 270 K11
pl. Hinchinbrk 393 C3
pl. Ingleburn 453 F6

pl. Wetherill Pk.......334 K6
st. Guildford............337 F5

SWINBORNE
cr. Wetherill Pk.......335 A4

SWINBOURNE
st. Bnksmeadw.......405 J13
st. Botany..............405 J13

SWINDON
cl. Turramurra........222 J16
pl. Chipping Ntn......366 E16

SWINSON
rd. Blacktown..........274 G3

SWIVELLER
cl. Ambarvale..........540 F1

SWORDFISH
av. Raby...................481 G2

SWORDS
pl. Mount Druitt......271 A1

SYBIL
la. Btn-le-Sds..........433 H4
st. Beverley Pk........432 K10
st. Eastwood............280 G8
st. Guildford W.......306 J16
st. Newport.............169 H7

SYCAMORE
av. Casula................394 F14
cr. Quakers Hill.......243 D3
gr. Menai.................458 J13
st. N St Marys.........240 B9

SYD EINFELD
dr. Bondi Jctn...........22 E5
dr. Woollahra............22 E5

SYDENHAM
la. Marrickville, off Shirlow St..........374 D13
rd. Brookvale...........258 B11
rd. Marrickville.......373 K9

SYDNEY
arc. Sydney..................3 G3
gte. Waterloo..............19 K15
la. Erskineville............18 B14
la. Marrickville........374 B14
pl. Ruse..................512 G1
pl. Woolmloo.................4 H5
rd. Balgowlah..........287 F9
rd. E Lindfield..........254 J14
rd. Fairlight.............288 B8
rd. Hornsby Ht........191 E4
rd. Manly..................288 B8
rd. Seaforth.............287 D10
rd. Warriewood.........199 E13
rd. Warwck Frm........365 D16
st. Artarmon............285 C14
st. Blacktown...........245 A15
st. Chatswood..........285 C12
st. Concord..............341 H8
st. Erskineville...........18 C14
st. Marrickville........374 C13
st. N Willghby..........285 C12
st. Panania..............398 B15
st. Randwick.............377 A11
st. Riverstone..........182 H4
st. St Marys.............270 B2
st. Willoughby..........285 C14

SYDNEY HARBOUR TUNNEL
Milsons Point.........2 A4
Sydney....................B H1
Sydney....................2 A4

SYDNEY JOSEPH
dr. Seven Hills.........246 B13

SYDNEY LUKER
rd. Cabramatta W....365 C6

SYDNEY-NEWCASTLE
fwy. Asquith..............192 D16
fwy. Berowra.............163 A9
fwy. Brooklyn..............75 A13
fwy. Cowan...............104 E13
fwy. Krngai Ch NP.....192 D16
fwy. Mooney Mooney..75 A13
fwy. Mt Colah............162 F16
fwy. Mt Krng-gai........162 F16
fwy. N Wahrnga.........222 B6
fwy. Wahroonga.........222 B6

SYDNEY PARK
rd. Alexandria..........375 A11
rd. Erskineville.........374 K11

SYDNEY STEEL
rd. Marrickville........374 E12

SYKES
pl. Colyton..............270 E4
pl. Mount Druitt......271 A1

SYLVA
av. Miranda.............491 J4

SYLVAN
av. E Lindfield..........255 B12
gr. Glenhaven...........187 K16
gr. Picnic Point.........428 C12
pl. Leonay................264 K2
st. Galston...............159 E10
st. Sylvania..............461 J10

SYLVANIA
av. Springwood.........201 G3
av. Thornleigh..........221 C10
rd.n, Miranda............491 H4
rd.n, Sylvania............461 H16
rd.s, Gymea Bay.........491 G8
rd.s, Miranda.............491 G7

SYLVAN RIDGE
dr. Illawong..............459 C1

SYLVANUS
st. Greenacre..........370 H11

SYLVESTER
av. Roselands...........400 J8

SYLVIA
av. Carlingford.........249 F12
pl. Frenchs Frst.......256 F4
pl. Greystanes..........305 H8
st. Blacktown...........273 H1
st. Chatswd W.........284 D10
st. Rydalmere...........309 K5

SYLVIA CHASE
sq. Sydney....................4 C5
sq. Woolmloo................4 C5

SYM
av. Burwood.............341 K15
la. Burwood, off Livingstone St....341 K15

SYMONDS
av. Parramatta.........278 J15
rd. Colebee..............213 A16
rd. Dean Park...........242 K2
rd. Londonderry.......148 F7
wky. Denistone..........281 D11

SYMONS
pl. West Hoxton......392 B11
st. Fairfield.............336 D16

SYNCARPIA
wy. Winmalee...........173 E8

SYRUS
pl. Quakers Hill.......213 H8

SYSTRUM
st. Ultimo......................3 B12

T

TABALI
st. Whalan...............241 A11

TABALUM
rd. Balgowlah Ht......287 J16

TABARD
pl. Illawong.............459 D5

TABELL
cl. Hornsby Ht.........191 F8

TABER
pl. Bradbury............511 G11
st. Menangle Pk.......539 A3

TABERS
rd. Orangeville.........473 E10

TABITHA
pl. Plumpton............241 H6

TABLETOP
cct. Horngsea Pk......392 C15

TABOOBA
st. Wentwthvle.........277 A9

TABOR
st. Glenbrook...........233 K14

TABORA
st. Forestville...........255 K13

TABOURIE
st. Leumeah.............482 F15

TABRETT
st. Banksia...............403 E12

TADMORE
rd. Cranebrook.........206 K1

TAFFS
av. Lugarno..............430 A10

TAFT
pl. Bonnet Bay.........460 F11

TAGGARTS
la. Darlinghurst............4 C13

TAGU
pl. Kings Park..........244 K3

TAGUDI
pl. Bangor................459 E12

TAGULA
pl. Glenfield.............424 H10

TAHITI
av. Lethbrdg Pk.......240 H2
pl. Kings Lngly.........245 C6

TAHLEE
cl. Castle Hill............218 J8
cr. Leumeah.............482 A15
st. Burwood..............342 B16

TAHMOOR
rd. Tahmoor.............566 A10

TAHOE
pl. Erskine Park.......271 A15

TAIN
pl. Schofields...........183 B16

TAIO
pl. Kings Lngly.........245 E8

TAIRORA
st. Whalan...............241 A10

TAIT
la. Russell Lea.........343 E5
st. Russell Lea.........343 E5
st. Smithfield...........336 A1

TAIWAN
pl. Sylvania..............462 A12

TAIYUL
rd. N Narrabeen.......198 H14

TALARA
av. Glenmore Pk.......266 A8
rd.n, Gymea...............491 D3
rd.s, Gymea...............491 D6

TALASEA
st. Whalan...............241 A11

TALAVERA
rd. Mcquarie Pk.......282 F1
rd. Marsfield.............252 C13

TALBINGO
pl. Heckenberg........364 D13
pl. Ruse...................512 H6
pl. Woodcroft...........243 H9

TALBOT
cl. Menai.................458 E15
ct. Wattle Grove.......395 K16
pl. Ingleburn............453 G13
pl. Woolmloo................4 F7
rd. Guildford............337 H4
rd. Yagoona..............368 K8
st. Riverwood...........400 D16
st. St Peters............374 E16

TALBRAGAR
st. Ruse...................512 D7

TALC
pl. Eagle Vale...........481 B7

TALEEBAN
rd. Riverview...........314 B5

TALFOURD
la. Glebe....................12 B12
st. Glebe....................12 C12

TALGAI
av. Wahroonga.........251 H1

TALGARA
pl. Beacon Hill.........257 J8

TALIA
cl. Kingswood...........267 J3

TALINGA
av. Georges Hall.......368 A15
pl. Cherrybrook........219 B12
pl. Lilli Pilli..............522 G2
st. Carlingford..........280 B3

TALISMAN
av. Castle Hill...........247 H3

TALKOOK
pl. Baulkham Hl.......246 K6

TALLAGANDRA
dr. Quakers Hill........243 D3

TALLARA
pl. Busby.................363 J15
pl. Terrey Hills.........196 F5

TALLAROOK
cl. Mona Vale...........199 D1
pl. Bangor................459 F12

TALLAWALLA
st. Beverly Hills.......401 C12

TALLAWARRA
av. Padstow.............429 G2
pl. Narrabeen...........229 A5
rd. Leumeah.............482 A15

TALLAWONG
av. Blacktown...........273 H4
rd. Rouse Hill...........184 A9

TALLAWUNG
pl. Kenthurst............156 E11

TALLGUMS
av. W Pnnant Hl.......249 J2

TALLINN
gr. Rooty Hill............271 K5

TALLONG
pl. Caringbah...........492 F13
pl. Turramurra.........223 D11
st. Prestons.............393 B13

TALLOW
pl. Glenwood...........245 J2
pl. S Coogee............407 E5

TALLOWOOD
av. Casula................394 F14
cr. Bossley Park.......333 E8
ct. Plumpton............242 C8
gdn. Blaxland............234 B8
gr. Kellyville.............186 A16
pl. Cranebrook.........207 B8
wy. Frenchs Frst.......256 F1

TALLOW WOOD
cl. Wilberforce...........93 F4

TALLOW-WOOD
av. Narellan Vale......479 A13

TALLOWWOOD
av. Cherrybrook........219 F11
av. Lugarno..............429 K9
cl. Alfords Point......429 C15
cr. Bradbury.............511 F12

TALL SHIPS
av. W Pnnant Hl.......249 A1

TALL TIMBERS
rd. Winmalee............173 E12

TALL TREES
av. Castle Hill, off Barker Dr...........218 J13

TALLWOOD
av. Eastwood............281 K8
dr. North Rocks........278 G3
pl. St Clair...............270 D9

TALMIRO
st. Whalan...............241 A11

TALOFA
pl. Castle Hill...........218 C8

TALOMA
av. Lurnea................394 E6
la. S Penrith.............237 A16
st. Picnic Point.........428 G6
st. S Penrith.............237 A15

TALOOMBI
st. Cronulla..............493 H16

TALPA
cl. Thornleigh...........221 A5

TALUS
st. Naremburn..........315 D3

TALWONG
st. Hornsby Ht.........161 K11

TAMAR
ct. Glenhaven...........218 D5
pl. Fairfield W..........335 B10
pl. N Wahrnga..........223 A1
st. Marrickville........373 F13
st. Sutherland..........490 C1

TAMARA
cl. Oakdale...............500 D12
pl. Kellyville.............186 C16
rd. Faulconbdg.........171 E13

TAMARAMA
st. Tamarama...........378 A6

TAMARAMA MARINE
dr. Tamarama...........378 B7

TAMARIND
dr. Acacia Gdn.........214 J15
pl. Alfords Point......429 B16

TAMARISK
cr. Cherrybrook........219 H6

TAMARIX
cr. Banksia...............403 G12
st. Greystanes..........305 E11

TAMARO
av. Whalan...............241 A10

TAMBA
pl. Port Hacking.......522 H2

TAMBAROORA
cr. Marayong............243 H6
pl. W Pnnant Hl.......248 G7

TAMBOON
av. Turramurra.........252

TAMBOURA
av. Baulkham Hl......247

TAMBOURINE BAY
rd. Lane Cove...........314
rd. Riverview............314

TAMBOY
av. Carlingford..........279

TAMBU
st. St Ives................224

TAMINA
pl. S Penrith.............267

TAMINGA
rd. Green Valley........363
st. Bayview..............168

TAMMAR
pl. St Helens Park....541

TAMPLIN
rd. Guildford.............337

TAMWORTH
cr. Hoxton Park........392
pl. Allambie Ht.........257
pl. Engadine.............488

TANA
pl. Kings Park..........244

TANAMI
cl. Belrose...............225
cl. Wakeley, off Mallacoota St.....334
pl. Bow Bowing........452

TANBARK
cct. Wrrngtn Dns......238
pl. Dural..................219

TANCRED
av. Kyeemagh...........404

TANDARA
av. Bradbury.............511

TANDERAGEE
st. Wentwthvle.........277

TANDERRA
av. Carlingford.........279
pl. Curl Curl.............258
st. Colyton...............270
st. Wahroonga.........222

TANGALOA
cr. Lethbrdg Pk........240

TANGARA
st. Eveleigh................18

TANGARRA
st. Croydon Pk.........371
st.e, Croydon Pk........371

TANGERINE
dr. Quakers Hill........214
st. Fairfield E...........337

TANGLEWOOD
cl. Glenmore Pk.......266
pl. W Pnnant Hl.......248
wy. Hornsby Ht.........161

TANGO
av. Dee Why............258

TANIA
av. S Penrith.............267
cl. Hornsby Ht.........161
st. Greystanes..........305

TANJA
cl. Prestons.............393

TANK STREAM
wy. Sydney..................B

TANN-DARBY
ct. Glenwood...........215

TANNER
av. Allawah..............432
av. Carlton...............432
la. Carlton...............432
pl. Minchinbury........271

TANNERS
wy. Kellyville............216

TANTALLON
av. Arncliffe.............403
la. Arncliffe.............403
rd. Lane Cove W.......284

TANTANGARA
pl. Woodcroft...........243
st. Heckenberg.........363

TANTANI
av. Green Valley........363

TANYA
pl. Tahmoor.............566

TAO
cl. St Clair...............269

I
St Clair....300 A3
IOLA
Hebersham....241 E4
LAN
Como....460 F7
LEY
Ambarvale....511 B15
LIN
Camden S....506 K15
P
Bidwill....211 B15
PEINER
Baulkham Hl....217 A16
RA
Yennora....336 K11
Lugarno....430 A13
Blacktown....273 J1
Kangaroo Pt....461 H7
Merrylands....308 D15
Sylvania....461 H7
Woollahra....21 K1
RAGO
E Lindfield....255 B11
Prestons....392 J15
RAKAN
Northbridge....285 J14
Narraweena....257 K4
Moorebank....425 A4
Holsworthy....396 D16
RALGA
Old Guildford....337 G9
Prestons....392 H14
RANA
Casula....394 C16
Baulkham Hl....246 J9
Dharruk....241 B7
RANAKI
Lethbrdg Pk....240 H2
Northmead....248 B16
RANTO
Marsfield....252 B13
RAWA
Lethbrdg Pk....240 H3
RBAN
Gladesville....313 B11
RBERT
St Andrews....481 J3
RCOOLA
Ellis Lane....476 C6
Engadine....488 D13
REE
N Balgowlah....287 B5
Greystanes....305 J5
Dharruk....241 B8
Hoxton Park....392 J9
RELLA
Cammeray, off
Amherst St....315 J5
REN
s, Caringbah....492 E11
REN POINT
Caringbah....492 G5
Taren Point....462 H15
RGO
Beverley Pk....433 B13
Girraween....276 B16
Toongabbie....276 C8
RI
. Glenfield....424 E11
RINGA
Kellyville....216 A3
Ashfield....342 J15
RINGHA
Blaxland....233 D6
RLINGTON
e. Bonnyrigg....364 A5
Prospect....275 C15
Smithfield....305 D12
RO
Quakers Hill....243 F4
Blakehurst....462 D1
RONGA
e. Caringbah....492 K5
Mona Vale....199 D3
Blacktown....274 E8
Como....460 F6
Hurstville....401 K15
. Faulconbdg....171 A13
ROO
Forestville....255 G11

TAROOK
av. S Turramrra....252 A5
TAROONA
st. St Marys....239 G14
TARPAN
pl. Emu Heights....235 B2
TARPEIAN
wy. Sydney....B H5
TARPLEE
av. Hamondvle....396 F15
TARRA
cr. Dee Why....258 J2
TARRABUNDI
dr. Glenmore Pk....266 C7
TARRAGEN
av. Hobartville....118 C7
TARRAGUNDI
rd. Epping....250 J12
TARRANT
av. Bellevue Hill....14 G10
cl. Picton....563 F12
pl. Doonside....243 E16
TARRANTS
av. Eastwood....280 J9
TARRILLI
pl. Kellyville....216 E4
st. Beverly Hills....401 B12
TARRO
av. Revesby....428 G1
cl. Hornsby....191 H7
TARUN
pl. Dharruk....241 B6
TARWIN
av. Glenwood....215 H12
TASKER
av. Campsie....402 A3
av. Peakhurst....430 A4
TASMA
pl. Airds....512 C11
TASMAN
av. Lethbrdg Pk....240 H2
cr. Killara....254 C10
ct. Castle Hill....218 D10
la. Bundeena....524 B11
pde. Fairfield W....335 C11
pl. Mcquarie Pk....282 J1
pl. S Windsor....150 E3
rd. Avalon....140 D16
rd. Mulgoa....325 G4
st. Bondi....377 K6
st. Cmbrdg Pk....237 H6
st. Dee Why....259 A9
st. Hinchinbrk....363 B15
st. Kurnell....465 G9
st. Phillip Bay....436 J12
TATE
cr. Horngsea Pk....392 F16
pl. Lugarno....429 J16
st. Panania....428 C4
TATES
la. Kurrajong....85 B5
TATHIRA
cr. Merrylands W....306 J11
TATHRA
av. Prestons....393 D16
ct. Dural....219 B3
pl. Bow Bowing....452 D12
pl. Castle Hill....218 D16
pl. Forestville....255 G8
pl. Gymea Bay....491 C8
TATIARA
cr. N Narrabeen....198 G14
TATLER
pl. Woronora Ht....489 B4
TATTERSALL
pl. Emu Plains....235 D14
rd. Kings Park....244 H6
TATTLER
pl. Hinchinbrk....363 E16
TAUBMAN
dr. Horngsea Pk....392 E14
TAUNTON
la. Pymble, off
Taunton St....253 D2
rd. Hurstville....432 A1
st. Blakehurst....432 D12
st. Pymble....253 D2
TAUPO
rd. Glenorie....128 C1
TAURUS
pl. Gilead....540 F8

st. Erskine Park....300 K2
TAVISTOCK
rd. Homebush W....340 F10
rd. Kemps Ck....360 B7
rd. S Hurstville....432 A12
st. Auburn....338 J4
st. Croydon Pk....371 G7
st. Drummoyne....343 H2
TAWA
st. Ashfield....342 J15
TAWARRI
cr. Kyle Bay....431 J16
TAWMII
pl. Castle Hill....218 H9
TAWNY
cl. Glenwood....215 E15
TAWORRI
st. Doonside....243 C15
TAY
la. Kensington....376 E9
pl. St Andrews....481 K6
pl. Winston Hills....277 E4
pl. Woronora....489 G2
st. Kensington....20 K16
TAYLEE
pl. Rouse Hill....185 D6
TAYLER
rd. Valley Ht....202 E4
TAYLOR
av. Banksia....403 E12
av. Lugarno....430 A15
av. Melrose Pk....310 H1
av. Turramurra....252 E3
cl. Miranda....492 B5
ct. Springwood....202 D11
la. Artarmon....315 A2
la. Glebe....12 B9
la. N Strathfield, off
Carrington St....341 G8
pl. Ermington....280 A14
pl. Kings Lngly....245 H8
pl. Pennant Hills....220 F12
pl. Theresa Park....445 A11
rd. Cranebrook....177 D15
sq. Darlinghurst....4 D13
st. Annandale....17 C1
st. Condell Park....398 H3
st. Darlinghurst....4 E14
st. Fairfield....336 E16
st. Five Dock....342 D10
st. Glebe....12 B8
st. Gordon....254 A6
st. Greystanes....305 K10
st. Kogarah....433 A4
st. Lakemba....371 B16
st. Lakemba....401 C1
st. Lidcombe....339 J9
st. Maroubra....406 H11
st. N Curl Curl....259 B10
st. Paddington....21 H1
st. Queens Park....377 F7
st. Waterloo....20 C16
st. W Pnnant Hl....248 K5
wy. Claymore....481 B10
TAYLORS
dr. Lane Cove W....283 F13
la. Lane Cove W....284 F16
rd. Badgerys Ck....328 E16
rd. Badgerys Ck....358 E4
rd. Dural....189 G3
rd. Silverdale....353 G16
TAYLORS POINT
rd. Clareville....169 D2
TAYNISH
av. Camden S....507 B14
TAYWOOD
av. Winston Hills....277 G4
st. Woolooware....493 F8
TEAGAN
pl. Blacktown....274 B6
TEA GARDENS
av. Kirrawee....491 C1
TEAGUE
st. Girraween....276 A10
st. Toongabbie....276 A10
TEAK
cl. Bossley Park....333 F8
pl. Cherrybrook....219 H7
pl. Miranda....462 C16
st. St Clair....269 G10
wy. Acacia Gdn....214 K14
wy. Prestons....393 K14

TEAKLE
st. Summer Hill....373 B5
TEAL
pl. Blacktown....273 K7
pl. Hinchinbrk....363 C15
pl. Ingleburn....453 H9
pl. Woronora Ht....489 C5
TEALE
pl. Parramatta....278 G15
TEA TEA
wk. Newington, off
Newington Bvd....310 B13
TEA TREE
cr. Mcquarie Fd....424 F16
gln. Jamisontown....266 A3
pl. Bossley Park....333 H9
pl. Kellyville....216 A1
pl. Kirrawee....460 K15
wy. Colyton....270 H7
TEA-TREE
pl. Mt Annan....509 E5
TEAWA
cr. Glenwood....215 G13
TEBBUTT
st. Leichhardt....15 C5
st. Windsor....121 A9
TECHNOLOGY
dr. Appin....569 D15
TECOMA
dr. Glenorie....128 C2
st. Heathcote....518 K12
TEDDICK
pl. Cherrybrook....219 G6
TEDDLES
rt. Moorebank....396 F13
TEDMAN
pde. Sylvania....461 H12
TEDWIN
av. Kensington....376 C14
st. Mt Pritchard....364 C11
TEELE
rd. Harringtn Pk....478 F2
TEEMER
st. Tennyson....312 E9
TEESWATER
pl. Airds....512 A13
TEGGS
la. Chippendale....19 B3
TEKAPO
rd. Glenorie....128 C3
TEKLA
st. W Pnnant Hl....249 K2
TELAK
cl. N Willghby....285 H7
TELEGRAPH
rd. Eastern Ck....272 J5
rd. Pymble....253 C1
TELFER
pl. Westmead....307 H4
rd. Castle Hill....218 G14
wy. Castle Hill....218 G15
TELFORD
la. Willoughby....285 J11
pl. N St Marys....239 J11
pl. Prairiewood....335 B8
st. Leumeah....512 C1
TELL
cl. Abbotsbury....333 B16
TELLICHERRY
cct. Kellyville....185 J13
TELOPEA
av. Caringbah....492 F12
av. Homebush W....340 G6
av. Strathfield....371 D4
cl. Glenmore Pk....265 J9
la. Redfern....20 A9
pl. Mcquarie Fd....454 G3
st. Collaroy Plat....228 G12
st. Mt Colah....192 D3
st. Punchbowl....370 D16
st. Redfern....19 K9
st. Telopea....279 G9
st. Wollstncraft....315 B10
TELOPIA
st. Mt Annan....509 B2
TELOWIE
ct. Dural....219 C4
TEME
pl. Jamisontown....266 A3
TEMI
pl. Marayong....243 G6

TEMORA
rd. Glenhaven....187 G16
st. Prestons....393 E14
TEMPE
st. Earlwood....403 H3
st. Greenacre....370 D11
TEMPI
pl. Dharruk....241 C7
TEMPLAR
st. Blacktown....274 K7
TEMPLE
la. Stanmore....16 E8
st. Stanmore....16 C8
TEMPLEMAN
cr. Hillsdale....406 G13
TEMPLETON
cr. Baulkham Hl....247 E5
cr. Moorebank....396 C9
rd. Elderslie....507 H1
wy. Airds....512 C13
TENBY
st. Blacktown....274 H9
TENCH
av. Jamisontown....235 G14
pl. Glenmore Pk....265 F5
wy. West Hoxton....392 A11
TENELLA
st. Canley Ht....335 A16
TENGAH
cr. Mona Vale....199 E2
TENILBA
rd. Northbridge....285 J14
TENISON
av. Cmbrdg Gdn....237 H5
ct. Baulkham Hl....247 B2
TENNANT
pl. Blackett....241 A3
pl. Edensor Pk....363 J3
pl. Illawong....459 C7
rd. Werrington....239 B15
st. Casula....424 F3
TENNENT
pde. Dulwich Hill....373 A14
pde. Hurlstone Pk....373 A14
TENNESSEE
pl. Riverwood....400 A13
TENNIS COURT
la. Mosman, off
Countess St....316 J4
TENNYSON
av. Turramurra....222 K8
dr. Cherrybrook....219 D9
pde. Guildford W....306 K15
pl. Sylvania....462 C14
rd. Breakfast Pt....312 A13
rd. Concord....312 B16
rd. Cromer....258 E1
rd. E Kurrajong....59 A2
rd. Gladesville....312 F8
rd. Greenacre....370 B7
rd. Mortlake....312 A13
rd. Ryde....312 F8
rd. Tennyson....87 H1
rd. Tennyson....312 E11
st. Campsie....372 A10
st. Dulwich Hill....373 C13
st. Enfield....371 H3
st. Granville....309 B11
st. Parramatta....308 J1
st. Wetherill Pk....334 J7
st. Winston Hills....277 G1
TENT
st. Kingswood....267 E1
TENTERDEN
rd. Botany....405 G11
TENTERFIELD
av. Hinchinbrk....392 J5
st. N Strathfield....341 E5
TENTH
av. Austral....391 B9
av. Loftus....490 B9
av. Oyster Bay....461 B11
rd. Berkshire Pk....180 C11
st. Warragamba....353 F5
TEPKO
rd. Terrey Hills....196 C6
TERALBA
rd. Btn-le-Sds....433 J4
rd. Leumeah....482 A15
TERAMA
st. Bilgola....169 F8

TERANGLE
cl. Prestons...........393 A13
TERAWEYNA
cl. Woodcroft..........243 G11
TERESA
pl. Cromer.............228 A16
st. Birrong.............369 B5
TERGUR
cr. Caringbah..........492 F3
TERMEIL
st. Prestons...........392 K16
TERMINAL
ct. Bnkstn Aprt........397 J2
pl. Merrylands.........307 J12
TERMINUS
la. Petersham, off Terminus St.........15 K9
rd. Seven Hills.........275 G1
rd. Seven Hills.........275 H1
st. Castle Hill..........218 C15
st. Liverpool............395 D5
st. Petersham...........15 J9
TERN
pl. Erskine Park.......300 F1
pl. Hinchinbrk.........393 C2
pl. Tregear.............240 C4
pl. Woronora Ht......489 B3
pl. Yarramundi........145 C4
TERNEN
st. Balmain East..........8 E9
TERONE
pl. Bossley Park......333 G8
TERPENTINE
pl. Yagoona............369 C9
TERRA
ct. Glenmore Pk......266 E7
st. Thornleigh.........221 C10
TERRACE
av. Sylvania............461 K10
dr. Cranebrook.........207 E15
la. Dulwich Hill........373 C11
rd. Dulwich Hill........373 C11
rd. Freemns Rch.........89 A5
rd. Killara...............253 C16
rd. N Richmond.........87 F12
TERRACOTTA
cl. Woodcroft..........243 E9
TERRAL
pl. Kings Lngly.......246 A8
TERRANORA
pl. Bangor..............459 F10
wy. Woodcroft..........243 G11
TERRA NOVA
pl. Tregear.............240 D6
TERRELL
av. Wahroonga........221 K16
TERRENE
st. Regents Pk........369 B1
TERRIE
pl. Kellyville............216 G4
TERRIGAL
av. Turramurra........222 K15
pl. Engadine............489 B13
pl. Woodbine...........481 K8
rd. Terrey Hills.........196 C7
st. Marayong...........243 H5
TERROL
cr. Mona Vale..........199 F4
TERRY
av. Seven Hills.........245 B15
la. Arncliffe.............403 G11
rd. Box Hill..............154 B15
rd. Denistone...........281 F11
rd. Dulwich Hill.........373 C8
rd. Eastwood...........280 G8
rd. Rouse Hill..........184 H10
rd. Theresa Park......444 K9
rd. West Ryde..........281 F13
st. Arncliffe.............403 G11
st. Balmain..............344 E6
st. Blakehurst...........432 A14
st. Connells Pt.........431 G16
st. Greenacre..........370 F4
st. Greystanes.........306 C9
st. Kyle Bay.............431 G16
st. Rozelle...............344 D6
st. Surry Hills...............F A16
st. Tempe...............374 D16
TERRYBROOK
rd. Llandilo.............208 A7
TERRYMONT
rd. Warrimoo..........203 C12
TESSA
st. Chatswd W........284 G8
TETBURY
cl. Cmbrdg Pk.........238 C9
TEUMA
pl. Glendenning.......242 F5
TEVIOT
av. Abbotsford.........312 K15
pl. St Andrews........452 A15
st. Richmond...........118 H7
TEWINGA
rd. Birrong..............369 A4
TEWKESBURY
av. Darlinghurst..........4 G10
st. Chipping Ntn......396 F3
THACKER
cl. Gymea...............491 G5
st. Gymea...............491 G4
THACKERAY
cl. Wetherill Pk.......335 A6
st. Camellia.............309 G5
st. Winston Hills......277 E1
THALIA
st. Hassall Gr..........211 K14
THALLON
st. Carlingford.........279 J3
THAMES
pl. Kearns...............481 B2
pl. Seven Hills.........275 D7
rd. Bringelly............388 C11
st. Balmain.................7 J8
st. Merrylands W....306 H11
st. Woronora...........460 B15
THANE
cl. Rsemeadow.......540 D3
st. Pendle Hill..........276 H12
st. Wentwthvle........276 H13
THARAWAL
rd. Thirlmere...........564 G8
THARKINNA
cl. Cranebrook........207 J10
THEA
pl. Rooty Hill...........272 B5
THEA DARE
dr. Castle Hill..........219 A13
THE APPIAN
wy. Avalon...............139 H14
wy. Bankstown.........369 F16
wy. Mt Vernon..........331 D5
wy. S Hurstville........432 A12
THE ARCADE
Arncliffe..............403 G8
THE AVENUE
Annandale...............16 K3
Ashfield.................372 G2
Balmain East..........8 D8
Bankstown.............368 H12
Bundeena..............524 A9
Canley Vale...........366 B1
Collaroy.................229 A12
Condell Park..........368 G16
Eastwood...............281 A8
Gladesville.............312 H6
Glenmore Pk.........265 F6
Granville................308 D14
Heathcote..............518 J9
Hunters Hill............313 F10
Hurlstone Pk..........372 K10
Hurstville...............432 A3
Kingsgrove.............402 A11
Leichhardt...............16 D1
Linley Point............313 F8
Mount Druitt..........271 B1
Newport.................169 F14
N Sydney..................6 B10
Petersham...............15 G8
Randwick...............377 B12
Riverstone.............182 D10
Rose Bay...............348 C13
Valley Ht...............202 D4
Voyager Pt.............427 C6
Waitara.................221 H4
Warrimoo..............203 B13
Yagoona................368 H12
THE BARBETTE
Castlecrag.............286 C13
THE BARBICAN
Castlecrag.............286 C12
THE BARRICADE
Castlecrag.............286 D12
THE BARTIZAN
Castlecrag.............286 C11
THE BASTION
Castlecrag.............286 B12
Hornsby.................221 B4
THE BATTLEMENT
Castlecrag.............286 B12
THE BOOMERANG
Freemns Rch...........90 B5
THE BOULEVARD
Harringtn Pk.........478 E2
THE BOULEVARDE
Btn-le-Sds.............433 K3
Cammeray.............316 A3
Camperdwn..............17 E1
Canley Vale...........335 J15
Caringbah.............492 B1
Cheltenham...........250 K9
Dulwich Hill.............15 A14
Epping..................280 J2
Fairfield.................335 J15
Fairfield Ht............335 J10
Fairfield W............335 J15
Gymea..................491 F1
Kirrawee...............460 G15
Kirrawee...............461 A16
Lakemba...............400 K1
Lewisham................15 A14
Lidcombe...............339 G11
Lilyfield...................10 D5
Malabar.................437 E5
Miranda.................492 B1
Newport.................169 J11
Petersham...............15 A14
Punchbowl.............400 E4
Sans Souci.............462 K3
Smithfield..............335 J10
Strathfield.............341 F16
Sutherland.............460 G15
Warrimoo..............203 C14
Wiley Park.............400 E4
Yagoona................369 E11
THE BROADWAY
Enfield..................371 E3
Penrith..................236 H11
Strathfield.............371 E3
Strathfield S..........371 E3
Wahroonga............221 H16
THE BULWARK
Castlecrag.............286 C12
THE CARRIAGEWAY
Glenmore Pk.........265 E10
North Rocks...........278 D6
THE CASCADES
Mt Annan..............479 C14
Oatlands...............278 K8
THE CAUSEWAY
Beverley Pk...........433 A13
Maroubra...............407 G10
Strathfield S..........371 D6
THE CENTRE
Forestville.............256 A10
THE CHASE
Orchard Hills.........267 E14
Valley Ht...............202 G4
rd. Turramurra.........223 A9
THE CIRCLE
Bilgola..................169 J3
Jannali..................461 A10
Narraweena............258 C6
Oatlands...............279 A8
THE CITADEL
Castlecrag.............286 C11
THE CLEARWATER
Mt Annan..............479 B14
THE CLOISTERS
Cherrybrook...........219 E15
St Ives..................224 E8
THE CLOSE
Hunters Hill...........313 G11
Strathfield.............340 J12
THE COAL
rd. Bickley Vale.......506 E8
rd. Camden.............506 E8
rd. Camden S..........506 E8
rd. Cawdor.............506 E8
rd. Grasmere..........506 E8
THE COMENARRA
pky. S Turramrra.......251 K2
pky. Thornleigh.........221 B13
pky. Turramurra........252 D5
pky. Wahroonga........221 B13
pky. West Pymble......252 D5
THE CORSO
Manly...................288 G10
Maroubra...............407 J9
THE COTTELL
wy. Baulkham Hl......247 G9
THE CREEL
Lansvale...............366 E10
THE CRESCENT
Annandale...............11 B5
Auburn..................339 B1
Avalon..................170 B3
Beecroft................250 G8
Berala...................339 D11
Chatswd W............284 F9
Cheltenham...........250 G8
Dee Why...............258 J7
Fairfield.................336 F13
Forest Lodge...........11 C8
Homebush.............341 A9
Homebush W.........340 G9
Hurstville Gr..........431 F12
Kingsgrove.............401 F11
Linley Point............313 G8
Manly...................288 D10
Marayong..............244 C5
Mosman................317 A6
Narrabeen..............228 F7
N Narrabeen...........198 J15
Pennant Hills..........250 H1
Penrith..................237 A9
Rozelle....................11 C4
Russell Lea............343 D7
Toongabbie............275 F11
Vaucluse................348 E1
Woronora..............489 G3
Yagoona................369 A12
Zetland.................375 K10
THE CRESENT
North Ryde............282 H12
THE CREST
Frenchs Frst..........256 D1
Hornsby Ht............161 E14
Killara...................254 E11
THE CROFT
wy. W Pnnant Hl.......249 H6
THE DRIFTWAY
Agnes Banks..........117 F13
Londonderry..........149 B3
S Windsor..............149 B3
THE DRIVE
Concord W.............311 E16
Harbord.................258 K16
North Ryde............282 G11
THE ENTRANCE
Earlwood...............402 F1
THE ESPLANADE
Ashfield.................372 H2
Botany..................405 E15
Cronulla................524 A4
Drummoyne............343 E3
Drummoyne............343 G1
Frenchs Frst..........256 C1
Guildford...............337 E4
Mona Vale..............169 D14
Mosman................317 D4
Narrabeen..............228 H7
S Hurstville............432 B12
Sylvania................461 E12
Thornleigh.............220 K13
THE FAIRWAY
Chatswd W............283 K9
Elanora Ht.............198 D14
THE FRESHWATER
Mt Annan..............479 B16
THE GLADE
Belrose.................226 D16
Galston.................159 F10
Kirkham.................477 G4
Wahroonga............222 B9
W Pnnant Hl..........249 C4
wk. Wahroonga........222 C9
THE GLEN
Beecroft................250 B4
cr. Springwood.........201 J4
rd. Bardwell Vy.........403 A8
THE GRAND
pde. Btn-le-Sds.........404 B16
pde. Btn-le-Sds.........433 J9
pde. Monterey...........433 J9
pde. Ramsgate Bch....433 G16
pde. Sans Souci.........433 G16
pde. Sutherland.........490 B1
pde. Sutherland.........490 D1
THE GRANDSTAND
St Clair..................270 A15
THE GRANGE
Cherrybrook...........219
Kirkham.................477
Mona Vale..............198
Mowbray Pk...........561
Mowbray Pk...........561
THE GREENWAY
Duffys Frst............195
Elanora Ht.............198
THE GROVE
Belrose.................226
Fairfield.................336
Mosman................317
Padstow Ht............429
Penrith..................237
Roseville................284
Woollahra.................22
Oatlands, off Hunterford Cr.....279
wy. Normanhurst.......221
THE GULLY
rd. Berowra.............133
THE HAVEN
Orchard Hills.........267
THE HERMITAGE
W Pnnant Hl..........248
THE HIGH
rd. Blaxland.............234
THE HIGH TOR
Castlecrag.............286
THE HIGHWATER
Mt Annan..............479
THE HILLS
cr. Seven Hills.........275
THE HORSLEY
dr. Carramar...........366
dr. Fairfield.............336
dr. Horsley Pk.........302
dr. Smithfield..........336
dr. Villawood...........367
dr. Wetherill Pk.......334
THEILE
av. Newington..........309
THE IRONBARKS
Mowbray Pk...........561
THE KINGSWAY
Roseville Ch..........255
St Marys................239
Wentwthvle............277
Werrington.............239
THE KNOLL
Avalon..................169
Blakehurst.............462
Galston.................159
Lansvale...............366
Miranda.................461
THE KRAAL
dr. Blair Athol.........510
dr. Blair Athol.........511
THE LAKES
dr. Glenmore Pk......266
THE LAMBETH
wk. Bundeena...........524
THE LEE
Middle Cove...........285
THELMA
av. Panania.............398
st. Greystanes.........305
st. Lurnea..............394
st. Marsfield............281
THE McKELL
av. Waterfall............519
THE MAIN
av. Mcquarie Pk.......283
THE MALL
Bankstown.............369
Punchbowl.............400
S Hurstville............432
Turramurra............223
Warrimoo..............203
Wiley Park.............400
THE MEADOWS
Kirkham.................477
THE MEADOWS FIRE
trl. Royal N P...........521
THE MEWS
Kirkham.................477
THE NINE WAYS
Kingsford...............406
THE NOOK
West Ryde.............281

E NORTHERN
Bringelly 388 B8
Cobbitty 448 B6
Cranebrook 207 G16
Glenmore Pk......266 J16
Harringtn Pk.......448 A10
Llandilo.............207 H7
Londonderry 149 D15
Luddenham........356 G2
Mulgoa 296 D14
Narellan 478 B2
Oran Park...........448 A10
Orchard Hills 267 A9
S Penrith............267 A9
EO
Liverpool............365 B15
E OAKS FIRE
Blue Mtn N P......263 B15
EODORE
Balmain 7 D9
E OLD OAKS
Brownlow Hl 505 H6
Grasmere...........505 H6
E OUTLOOK
Bilgola 169 H5
Harringtn Pk.......477 F4
Hornsby Ht 191 D4
Kirkham..............477 F4
E OUTPOST
Castlecrag..........286 A14
Northbridge 286 A14
E PALISADE
Castlecrag..........286 A13
E PALMS
Blacktown..........274 D12
E PARADE
Drummoyne........343 E4
Dulwich Hill........373 C12
Enfield 371 H3
Russell Lea 343 E4
Telopea..............279 H9
E PARAPET
Castlecrag..........286 A12
E PARKWAY
Bradbury............511 D14
Bradbury............511 D8
Kellyville.............185 H13
E PINNACLE
Bilgola 169 J3
E PLATEAU
Lansvale 366 F9
E PLAZA
Rose Bay 348 D13
E POINT
S Wntwthvle 306 H7
Woolwich............314 F12
E PONDS
Mt Annan...........479 B15
Mt Annan...........479 C15
E PORTICO
Toongabbie........276 C7
E POSTERN
Castlecrag..........285 K12
E PROMENADE
Cheltenham........250 J9
Old Guildford......337 D9
Sans Souci.........433 A16
Sylvania.............461 G10
Yennora.............337 D9
E QUARTERDECK
Middle Cove 286 A7
Mt Annan............479 B15
E RAMPART
Castlecrag..........286 A13
Hornsby.............221 C3
E RAPIDS
Mt Annan...........479 C15
E REDOUBT
Castlecrag..........286 B13
ERESA
Blacktown..........274 E5
Greystanes.........306 F6
Smithfield 336 B8
ERESA VIEW
Theresa Park......444 A5
ERESE
Baulkham Hl 247 C3
E RETREAT
Bringelly 388 G5
E RIDGE
Frenchs Frst.......256 D1
Lansvale 366 D10

THE RIVER
rd. Picnic Point........428 J7
rd. Revesby.............428 J5
rd. Revesby Ht 428 J7
THE RIVULET
Mt Annan...........509 C1
THE ROAD
Penrith..............237 B7
THE ROCKS
sq. The Rocks ....A K2
THERRY
rd. Ambarvale..........511 A10
rd. Campbelltwn......510 K10
rd. Englorie Park......510 K10
st. Avalon 139 K13
st. Bligh Park 150 K7
st. Drummoyne.........343 H5
st.e, Strathfield S 371 B5
st.w, Strathfield S 371 A5
THE SANCTUARY
Westleigh...........220 H9
dr. Leonay...............264 J1
THE SCARP
Castlecrag..........286 D11
THE SERPENTINE
Bilgola 170 A6
Kensington.........376 C10
THESEUS
cct. Rsemeadow.......540 J10
THE SEVEN WAYS
Rockdale............403 C16
THESIGER
rd. Bonnyrigg..........363 J7
THE SPRINGS
Mt Annan...........479 B16
Mt Annan...........509 B1
THE STABLES
la. Darlinghurst...........F H2
THE STONE COTTAGE
pl. Blair Athol 511 A2
THE STRAIGHT
rd. Mulgoa 325 B2
THE STRAND
Croydon.............372 E1
Dee Why.............259 A7
Gladesville 313 A4
Mortdale.............431 A6
Penshurst 431 F6
Rockdale.............403 E16
Whale Beach 140 C7
THE TAR
Mosman, off
Wolseley Rd.......317 D9
THE TERRACE
Abbotsford..........312 J15
Birchgrove..............7 G3
Warrimoo 203 B12
Windsor..............121 A9
Windsor..............121 C7
Oatlands, off
Governors Wy 279 A8
THE TOR
wk. Castlecrag..........286 F10
THE TRONGATE
Granville 308 F16
S Granville 338 F2
THE UPPER SANCTUARY
dr. Leonay...............234 J16
THE VALE
Belrose 225 K13
THE VALLEY
rd. Valley Ht 202 G5
THE VILLAGE
pl. Dural 188 J13
THE VINES
Mowbray Pk.......561 J5
THE VINTAGE
Mowbray Pk.......561 J3
THEW
pde. Cromer 228 F14
THE WALK
Clontarf.............287 G12
Earlwood 403 B5
THE WATER
la. Box Hill..............184 G1
la. Rouse Hill 184 G1
THE WATERMARK
Mt Annan...........479 B15
THE WATERS
Mt Annan...........479 C16

THE W E MIDDLETON MEMORIAL
dr. Couridjah 564 B16
THE WHITE WATER
Mt Annan...........479 C16
THE WOODS
cct. Menai 458 J14
THIELE
rd. Kenthurst...........156 J12
THIRD
av. Berala 339 E15
av. Blacktown 244 F14
av. Campsie 371 H10
av. Canley Vale 366 B4
av. Condell Park.......398 D5
av. Eastwood............281 C9
av. Epping 280 E3
av. Gymea Bay..........491 D11
av. Jannali................460 J10
av. Lane Cove...........314 G5
av. Lindfield.............254 F13
av. Llandilo...............208 E8
av. Loftus.................490 A6
av. Mcquarie Fd.........454 A2
av. North Ryde 282 H13
av. N Willghby 285 H11
av. Seven Hills...........275 H3
av. Willoughby...........285 H11
rd. Berkshire Pk........180 A3
st. Ashbury..............372 G8
st. Granville 308 G14
st. Parramatta...........279 A16
st. Warragamba 353 F7
THIRLMERE
av. Northmead..........278 D5
pl. Leumeah.............482 F12
wy. Picton 562 C16
wy. Picton 563 B11
wy. Tahmoor..............565 C9
wy. Thirlmere............562 C16
wy. Thirlmere............565 B8
wy. Thirlmere............565 C3
THIRROUL
cct. Prestons.............393 C13
THIRTEENTH
av. Austral................391 B5
st. Warragamba 353 F5
THIRTIETH
av. West Hoxton 391 F14
THIRTYFIRST
av. West Hoxton 391 F14
THIRTYSECOND
av. West Hoxton 391 G7
THIRTYTHIRD
av. West Hoxton 391 G9
THISBE
pl. Rsemeadow..........540 H9
THISTLE
cct. Green Valley.......363 A8
st. Ryde....................311 H3
wy. Blacktown...........274 E12
THOAR
pl. Clarmnt Ms 268 J3
THOM
av. West Hoxton 391 J6
THOMAS
av. Hamondvle 396 H16
av. Lurnea 394 C10
av. Roseville..............284 D5
la. Darlington.............18 K5
la. Haymarket.............E C10
la. Crows Nest, off
Huntingdon St....315 H6
la. St Marys, off
Thomas St..........269 J6
pl. Bligh Park 150 F6
rd. Freemns Rch.........60 J10
rd. Galston 159 C6
rd. Londonderry 178 A9
st. Appin 569 E11
st. Ashfield 372 E1
st. Birchgrove................7 E5
st. Campbelltwn 511 J2
st. Chatswood...........284 H10
st. Coogee 407 E2
st. Croydon...............372 E1
st. Darlington..............18 J5
st. Fairfield................336 C13
st. Granville 308 E15
st. Haymarket.............E B11
st. Haymarket..............3 D14
st. Hornsby...............221 J2
st. Hurstville 401 E16
st. Kingsgrove...........401 K6

st. Lewisham 15 C8
st. McMahons Pt 5 C12
st. Merrylands.........307 J9
st. Merrylands.........308 E15
st. Newtown 17 G13
st. North Manly 258 C13
st. Northmead..........277 J7
st. Parramatta 308 F1
st. Picnic Point.........428 G8
st. St Marys.............269 H6
st. Seven Hills..........246 B11
st. Strathfield 371 E2
st. Ultimo 3 A15
st. Woolooware.........493 J10
wy. Currans Hill.........479 H10
THOMAS BELL
av. Wrrngtn Cty 238 H6
THOMAS CLARKE
st. Westmead 307 H3
THOMAS FRANCIS
wy. Rouse Hill 184 K8
THOMAS HOLT
dr. Mcquarie Pk.........282 J6
THOMAS KELLY
cr. Lalor Park 245 G12
THOMAS LAYCOCK
pl. Bringelly 388 J9
THOMAS MITCHELL
dr. Barden Rdg..........488 F7
THOMAS NELSON
pl. Glenbrook.............234 B11
THOMAS ROSE
dr. Rsemeadow 540 K3
THOMAS TELFORD
pl. Glenbrook 234 B11
THOMAS WILKINSON
av. Dural 219 A5
THOMOND
st. Hurstville 401 G16
THOMPSON
av. Hobartville 118 D6
av. Illawong..............459 J3
av. Maroubra.............407 E15
av. Moorebank 396 B8
av. Newington 309 K15
av. St Marys 240 A15
cl. W Pnnant Hl........250 B1
cr. Glenwood 215 E12
dr. Terrey Hills..........196 C11
la. Belmore...............401 F2
la. Bondi Jctn 22 C9
la. East Hills...............427 G5
la. Five Dock 342 K10
pl. Baulkham Hl 247 D7
pl. Camden S 507 A15
pl. Darlinghurst.............4 E10
pl. Minto...................482 H8
sq. Windsor...............121 D7
st. Arncliffe 403 H5
st. Bundeena.............523 H9
st. Drummoyne...........343 G3
st. Earlwood 372 H16
st. Gladesville 312 K4
st. Marrickville 374 B11
st. Mosman 317 B12
st. Scotland I 168 G3
st. Scotland I 168 G4
st. Tamarama 378 B7
st. Turrella 403 G5
st. Wetherill Pk 334 G4
THOMPSONS
la. Yagoona 369 B12
rd. Bringelly 387 H8
THOMSON
av. Artarmon 285 A16
av. Beverly Hills.........430 J1
av. Lucas Ht 487 J11
av. Springwood 172 C12
la. Darlinghurst.............4 E10
st. Darlinghurst.............4 E11
THOR
pl. Hebersham 241 G4
THORA
st. Greystanes............305 H6
THORBY
av. Leichhardt.............10 E16
THORLEY
st. S Windsor.............150 A6
THORN
pl. Mt Pritchard.........364 D9
pl. North Rocks..........248 F14
st. Hunters Hill...........313 E5
st. Liverpool...............395 A8

st. Pennant Hills......220 E12
st. Revesby.............398 J13
st. Ryde..................311 G3
wy. Penrith...............237 D2
THORNBILL
cr. Glenmore Pk.......265 J13
wy. W Pnnant Hl.......249 D8
wy. Yarramundi........145 C6
THORNBURY
pl. Bella Vista 246 H3
pl. Minto..................483 A2
THORNCRAFT
pde. Campsie 371 J16
THORNCROFT
pl. Bargo..................567 B3
THORNE
av. Pendle Hill...........276 G14
st. Edgecliff................13 K14
st. Ingleburn 453 B12
THORNEY
rd. Fairfield W..........335 B13
THORNFLAT
rd. Cranebrook........207 F12
THORNHILL
cr. Wrrngtn Dns 238 B6
pl. Cherrybrook.......219 C14
THORNLEIGH
av. Concord.............341 G8
st. Thornleigh 221 A14
THORNLEY
la. Drummoyne, off
Roseby St 344 B4
rd. Prospect 305 A1
st. Drummoyne.......344 A4
st. Leichhardt............15 J2
st. Marrickville 403 G1
THORNTON
av. Bass Hill.............368 C13
av. Carlingford.........279 E2
av. Glenmore Pk......266 E14
pl. Kangaroo Pt.......461 H7
st. Canada Bay........342 D9
st. Darling Point.........13 J2
st. Fairlight..............288 D8
st. Rozelle...................7 A10
THORP
rd. Woronora 489 J3
THORPE
av. Cherrybrook.......219 J11
av. Liberty Gr..........311 B11
pl. Abbotsbury 363 B1
rd. Kingsgrove.........401 J14
st. Clovelly..............377 K13
st. Colyton 270 G7
THORSBY
pl. Emu Plains.........235 E9
THOW
pl. Currans Hill........479 G12
THREDBO
st. Heckenberg........364 C13
THRELFALL
st. Eastwood...........281 G5
THRELKELD
dr. Cattai....................94 A5
THRIFT
cl. W Pnnant Hl........249 A7
st. Colyton 270 B7
THROSBY
dr. Narellan Vale......508 G1
st. Casula................394 C16
st. Fairfield Ht 335 H11
wy. Ambarvale..........511 B12
THRUPP
st. Neutral Bay 6 F8
THUDDUNGRA
rd. Duffys Frst.........194 K4
THUNDERBOLT
dr. Raby..................451 C13
THURBON
av. Peakhurst 430 H1
THURLGONA
rd. Engadine............488 F13
THURLOW
la. Redfern.................20 C9
st. Redfern.................20 C9
st. Riverwood 400 C15
THURN
pl. Elderslie.............507 F4
THURNBY
la. Newtown 17 C13
st. Chipping Ntn......396 G1

THUROONG
pl. Cranebrook 207 D5
THURSDAY
pl. Green Valley 362 K8
THURSO
pl. St Andrews 452 A12
THURSTON
st. Penrith 237 B8
THURWOOD
av. Jamisontown 266 D2
THYME
st. Quakers Hill 243 F5
THYRA
rd. Palm Beach 140 A6
TIA
pl. Hoxton Park 392 J10
pl. Ruse 512 D9
TIANIE
pl. Rouse Hill 185 D7
TIARA
pl. Granville 307 K8
TIARRI
av. Terrey Hills 196 B7
TIBBETT
pl. Kellyville 216 E5
TIBER
pl. Heathcote 518 E7
pl. Kearns 451 B16
st. Seven Hills 275 D8
TIBOOBURRA
rd. Hoxton Park 392 G7
st. Engadine 489 B12
TICH
pl. Doonside 243 C5
TICHBORNE
dr. Quakers Hill 213 J14
TICKLE
dr. Tahmoor 565 G5
TICKNER
st. Castlereagh 146 B14
TIDESWELL
st. Ashfield 373 C2
TIDSWELL
st. Mount Druitt 271 E2
st. St Marys 270 A3
TIERNAN
av. North Rocks 248 J14
TIERNEY
av. Eastgardens 406 G13
rd. Kurmond 56 H15
rd. The Slopes 56 H15
TIFFANY
pl. Rooty Hill 271 K2
TIGG
pl. Ambarvale 511 A10
TIGRIS
st. Kearns 450 K16
TILBA
av. Balmain 7 A6
pl. Woodpark 306 G14
pl. Yarrawarrah 489 F14
rd. Mulgoa 295 H15
st. Berala 339 D11
TILDEN
st. Plumpton 242 C11
TILEY
la. Cammeray, off Tiley St 316 B4
st. Cammeray 316 B4
TILFORD
st. Zetland 375 J10
TILLEARD
dr. Winston Hills 277 C3
TILLETT
pde. Lansdowne 367 C5
TILLEY
st. Dundas Vy 279 J10
TILLFORD
gr. Rooty Hill 272 C6
rd. Kenthurst 187 F6
rd. Royal N P 522 D9
TILLOCK
st. Haberfield 9 B10
st. Pennant Hills 220 G13
st. Thornleigh 220 H13
TILPA
pl. Hoxton Park 392 F7
TIMARU
gr. S Penrith 266 J7
pl. Kirrawee 491 B8
rd. Terrey Hills 196 E4
st. Glenorie 128 B2
st. Turramurra 222 K16
TIMBARA
ct. Wattle Grove 395 K12
TIMBARAM
wy. Woodcroft 243 E10
TIMBARRA
pl. Sutherland 460 C16
rd. St Ives Ch 194 A15
rd. Westleigh 220 G10
TIMBER
gr. Glenhaven 217 K5
gr. Wrrngtn Dns 238 D4
la. Wrrngtn Dns, off Timber Gr 238 D4
TIMBERLEA
cl. Bradbury 511 E14
TIMBERLINE
av. W Pnnant Hl 249 F6
av. W Pnnant Hl 249 G7
TIMBERTOP
av. Carlingford 249 H11
wy. Beecroft 250 J5
TIMBILLICA
pl. Prestons 393 C15
TIMBRELL
dr. Five Dock 343 D10
TIMESWEEP
dr. St Clair 270 C13
TIMGALEN
av. S Penrith 237 A16
TIMMS
cl. Edensor Pk 363 F4
st. Hebersham 241 E2
TIMMS HILL
rd. Kurrajong 85 F2
TIMOR
cl. Kirrawee 490 K8
pl. Kings Park 244 F1
TIMOTHY
av. Castle Hill 248 E1
cl. Cherrybrook 219 D7
la. Belmore 401 G3
pl. Edensor Pk 363 G2
rd. Londonderry 178 B8
st. Hurstville 431 J3
TIMOTHY LACEY
la. The Oaks 502 F9
TIMS
cr. Guildford W 336 H1
TIM WHIFFLER
pl. Richmond 118 A6
TINA
av. Lethbrdg Pk 210 G15
TINAKILL
av. Engadine 488 K11
TINAM
av. Whalan 240 K11
TINANA
pl. Bidwill 211 F16
st. Haberfield 343 B16
TINARRA
cr. Erskine Park 300 C2
cr. Erskine Park 300 D2
TINCOMBE
st. Canterbury 372 G13
TINDAL
wy. Mt Annan 479 H16
TINDALE
la. Woollahra 377 F2
rd. Artarmon 284 K14
st. Penrith 236 J11
TINDALL
av. Liverpool 395 F1
st. Campbelltwn 511 A6
TINDELL
st. Bligh Park 150 H5
TINGARA
av. Vaucluse 348 B4
la. Cabarita 342 E1
TINGCOMBE
pl. Camden 507 B2
TINGHA
av. S Penrith 266 E6
cl. Hinchinbrk 392 G4
st. Chatswood 284 K11
st. Engadine 488 F12
TINGIRA
pl. Forestville 255 K12
TINTAGEL
pl. Glenhaven 217 J6
pl. Turramurra 222 G15
TINTERN
av. Carlingford 279 E9
av. Telopea 279 E9
rd. Ashfield 373 A5
TINTO
pl. Acacia Gdn 244 K1
TIPANI
pl. Erskine Park 300 E2
TIPPER
av. Bronte 378 A10
TIPPERARY
av. Killarney Ht 256 D14
TIPPET
pl. Quakers Hill 214 C8
TIPPING
pl. Ambarvale 510 H15
TIPTREE
av. Strathfield 341 E16
TIPTREES
av. Carlingford 279 H5
la. Carlingford 279 J5
TIRAGE
pl. Minchinbury 272 B10
TIRANNA
pl. Oyster Bay 461 C4
TIREE
av. Hunters Hill 314 B13
TIRRABEENA
pl. Bangor 459 E12
TIRTO
st. Barden Rdg 488 F8
TISANE
av. Frenchs Frst 256 G2
TISHER
pl. Ambarvale 511 A14
TITANIA
la. Randwick, off Lion St 407 B2
la. Randwick, off Rainbow La 407 A1
la. Cranebrook, off Titania Pl 207 E10
pl. Cranebrook 207 F10
pl. Rsemeadow 540 J10
st. Randwick 407 B2
TI TREE
cr. Berowra 163 C1
pl. Wilberforce 62 G12
TITUS
pl. Acacia Gdn 244 K1
TIVERTON
wy. Airds 512 E9
TIVOLI
av. Rose Bay 348 B7
ct. Wattle Grove 426 C3
esp. Como 460 J6
pl. Doonside 243 B9
st. Mosman 317 C3
st. Paddington 21 F3
TIVY
pl. Marayong 243 H6
TIZZANA
rd. Ebenezer 63 E6
TOBERMORY
av. St Andrews 481 J2
TOBIAS
pl. Kings Lngly 245 A4
TOBIN
pl. Marayong 243 H6
TOBRUK
av. Allambie Ht 257 F11
av. Balmain 7 E12
av. Belmore 371 F16
av. Carlingford 250 A13
av. Cremorne 316 F4
av. Engadine 488 J16
av. Liverpool 394 J4
av. St Ives Ch 223 J4
pl. Bossley Park 334 A6
rd. Narellan Vale 479 A11
st. North Ryde 282 K11
st. N St Marys 239 J10
TOBY
cr. Panania 398 A13
mw. Bella Vista 246 G3
pl. Kings Lngly 246 B10
TOBYS
bvd. Mt Pritchard 364 G13
TOCAL
ct. Wattle Grove 426 A1
TOD
pl. Minchinbury 271 G9
TODD
cir. Old Tngabbie 277 B6
cr. Peakhurst 400 H16
ct. Wattle Grove 395 H12
la. St Clair, off Banks Dr 269 K13
pl. Bossley Park 333 J6
pl. Cherrybrook 219 J11
pl. Illawong 459 J5
pl. Leumeah 482 G11
pl. Mt Annan 509 F1
row. St Clair 269 J12
st. Kingsgrove 402 A12
st. Merrylands W 307 A12
TODMAN
av. Kensington 376 B9
av. Kensington 376 D12
av. West Pymble 252 H9
la. St Clair, off Todman Pl 270 E12
pl. St Clair 270 E11
pl. Strathfield 341 B14
rd. Warwck Frm 365 J14
TOELLE
st. Rozelle 344 C7
TOGGERAI
st. Appin 569 F13
TOGIL
st. Canley Vale 366 E2
TOKANUE
pl. St Ives Ch 223 J3
TOKARA
st. Allambie Ht 257 G15
TOKAY
ct. Edensor Pk 363 D1
pl. Eschol Park 481 E2
TOLEDO
pl. Baulkham Hl 246 J13
TOLL
st. N Parramatta 278 A10
TOLLAND
st. Prestons 393 B15
TOLLEY
pl. Edensor Pk 333 F14
TOLLGATE
cr. Windsor 121 C9
TOLL HOUSE
wy. Windsor 121 C9
TOLMER
st. Bossley Park 334 C5
TOLOL
av. Miranda 491 H2
TOM
st. Ermington 310 F3
st. Sylvania 462 A8
wy. Casula 424 H2
TOMAGO
ct. Wattle Grove 425 K3
TOMAH
pl. Bossley Park 334 B10
pl. Ruse 512 G5
pl. Sylvania 461 K8
pl. Westleigh 220 G9
st. Carlingford 280 C4
st. Kurrajong Ht 54 B7
st. St Ives Ch 224 B1
TOM HAYDON
st. Moore Park 21 D8
TOMINTOUL
wy. Glenhaven 218 A6
TOMKI
st. Carramar 366 J1
TOMKINS
st. Bexley North 402 E11
TOMKO
gr. Parklea 214 J13
TOMPSON
rd. Panania 428 E3
rd. Revesby 428 E3
TOM SCANLON
cl. Kellyville 216 E1
TONBRIDGE
st. Ramsgate 433 F14
st. Sans Souci 433 F14
TONGA
cl. Greenacre 370 C14
cl. St Clair 270 B16
cr. Smithfield 336
pl. Lethbrdg Pk 240
TONGARIRO
tce. Bidwill 211
TONGARRA
cl. Bangor 459
pl. Westleigh 220
TONI
cr. Ryde 282
pl. Baulkham Hl 247
TONITTO
av. Peakhurst 430
TONKIES
pl. Menai 459
TONKIN
cr. Schofields 213
st. Cronulla 493
TONY
cr. Padstow 399
pl. Glendenning 242
st. Collaroy 229
TOOCOOYA
la. Hunters Hill 313
rd. Hunters Hill 313
TOOGOOD
la. Erskineville 17
TOOHEY
av. Westmead 307
cr. Bexley 402
rd. Wetherill Pk 333
TOOHEYS
la. Lidcombe 339
TOOLANG
rd. St Ives 223
TOOLE
st. Doonside 243
TOOLONG
st. Horngsea Pk 392
TOOMA
pl. Heckenberg 364
TOOMEVARA
st. Kogarah 433
TOOMEY
cr. Quakers Hill 213
TOOMUNG
cct. Clarmnt Ms 268
TOONA
pl. Bossley Park 333
TOONGABBIE
rd. Girraween 275
rd. Toongabbie 275
rd. Toongabbie 276
TOONGARAH
rd. Roseville 284
rd. Waverton 5
TOORADIN
pl. W Pnnant Hl 250
TOORAH
rd. Londonderry 149
TOORAK
av. Beverly Hills 401
av. Taren Point 462
cl. St Johns Pk 364
cr. Emu Plains 234
ct. Cherrybrook 219
pl. Avalon 140
TOORONGA
rd. Terrey Hills 195
tce. Beverly Hills 401
TOOTH
av. Newington 309
la. Camperdwn 17
TOOTHILL
la. Lewisham, off Old Canterbury Rd 15
st. Lewisham 15
TOOTHS
pl. Camperdwn 17
TOPAROA
cl. Casula 394
TOPAZ
cr. Seven Hills 275
pl. Bankstown 399
pl. Bossley Park 334
pl. Eagle Vale 481
TOPE
pl. Ambarvale 510
TOPEKA
gln. St Clair 270
la. St Clair, off Topeka Gln 270

HAM
Smeaton Gra 479 B6
IN
Moorebank 396 C12
LICA
Canley Ht 365 B4
NOT
Hinchinbrk 393 C4
PER
Englorie Park 510 J10
PING
Panania 398 A16

Dee Why 258 F3
A
Dharruk 241 A6
Forestville 255 K12
BERT
Quakers Hill 214 F10
CH
Voyager Pt 427 C4
ICELLI
Whalan 241 A11
KINGTON
Londonderry 147 D7
NADO
Cranebrook 207 B10
Cranebrook, off
Tornado Cr 207 B10
Raby 451 E16
NAROS
Penrith 237 A13
OKINA
St Ives 224 C15
ONTO
Cromer 227 J12
Jannali 460 F16
Sutherland 490 F1
QUAY
Glenmore Pk 266 G14
QUIL
Carlingford 250 A15
RANCE
Quakers Hill 214 C12
RENS
Wattle Grove 396 A14
Cherrybrook 219 F12
Cromer 228 C16
Kearns 481 A2
Blakehurst 432 F16
Canley Ht 365 E3
Canley Vale 365 E3
Matraville 437 B3
Merrylands W 306 K13
Punchbowl 400 B8
St Ives 254 F1
RES
Emu Plains 234 K11
Whalan 241 A10
Whalan 241 A11
Kings Lngly 245 D3
St Ives 224 A8
Kurnell 465 H8
RRINGTON
Sefton 368 G3
Marsfield 281 H3
Maroubra 407 H9
Strathfield 341 F14
RRS
Baulkham Hl 247 J14
RTON
Penrith 236 J13
RULOSA
Winmalee 173 F8
RUMBA
Bayview 168 E11
Bangor 459 E11
RVER
Collaroy Plat 228 D10
RWOOD
St Johns Pk 334 E16
Sans Souci 433 B14
Warrimoo 203 A10
SCANA
Prestons 393 E13
SCANO
Erskine Park 300 F2
SH
Zetland, off
Dunning Av 375 H11

TOSICH
pl. Bonnyrigg Ht 363 F5
TOTALA
pl. Elanora Ht 198 F12
TOTEM
la. Balgowlah 287 J8
TOTTENHAM
pl. Blakehurst 462 F2
st. Granville 308 D8
st. N Balgowlah 287 F5
TOUCAN
cr. Plumpton 241 H7
TOULOUSE
st. Cecil Hills 362 C4
TOURMALINE
st. Eagle Vale 481 F8
st. Narrabeen 229 B1
TOURNAY
st. Peakhurst 430 H2
TOUT
rd. Bidwill 211 F12
rd. Marsden Pk 211 F12
TOWARRI
pl. Belrose 226 C16
TOWER
ct. Castle Hill 217 B9
pl. Berowra 133 E12
rd. Bnkstn Aprt 397 E5
res. Castlecrag, off
Edinburgh Rd 286 C11
st. Coogee 377 K13
st. Glenwood 215 C15
st. Manly 288 F9
st. Panania 428 A2
st. Revesby 428 E2
st. Vaucluse 348 G5
TOWERS
pl. Arncliffe 403 E9
st. Arncliffe 403 E9
st. Cabramatta 365 C9
TOWN
st. Hobartville 118 E7
tce. Glenmore Pk 265 J10
TOWNER
av. Milperra 397 D10
gdn. Pagewood 406 F7
st. Galston 160 H6
TOWN HALL
la. Auburn, off
Queen St 339 D3
TOWNS
pl. Millers Pt 1 D8
rd. Vaucluse 348 C7
st. Gladesville 312 G8
TOWNSEND
av. Frenchs Frst 255 H4
rd. N Richmond 86 J14
st. Condell Park 398 E3
st. Guildford 337 J3
TOWNSON
av. Leumeah 482 F11
av. Minto 482 G8
rd. Marsden Pk 212 D9
rd. Schofields 212 D9
st. Blakehurst 462 D2
TOWNSVILLE
rd. Wakeley 334 K14
TOWNVIEW
rd. Mt Pritchard 364 J9
TOWRADGI
pl. Bangor 459 G10
st. Narraweena 257 K3
TOWRA POINT
rd. Kurnell 463 K12
TOWRI
cl. St Ives 224 C15
pl. Marsfield 251 H16
TOWSON
la. Bexley 402 C16
TOXANA
st. Richmond 118 J4
TOXTETH
la. Glebe 11 H11
rd. Glebe 11 G11
TOYER
av. Sans Souci 463 B3
st. Tempe 374 B16
TRABB
pl. Ambarvale 510 J16
TRACEY
av. Carlingford 249 F13
cl. Normanhurst 221 H7
la. Chippendale 18 H3
pl. Orchard Hills 268 E8
st. Revesby 398 D11
TRACY
st. Rooty Hill 242 A15
TRADE
la. Newtown 17 B10
st. Newtown 17 B10
TRADEWINDS
pl. Kareela 461 E10
TRAFALGAR
av. Lindfield 284 F1
av. Roseville 284 F1
la. Annandale 11 B14
la. Concord, off
Trafalgar Pde 341 K4
pde. Concord 341 J4
pl. Marsfield 252 A13
pl. Northmead 278 C6
rd. Emu Heights 235 A2
st. Annandale 16 K3
st. Belmore 401 F4
st. Btn-le-Sds 433 K3
st. Bronte 378 A10
st. Crows Nest 315 J6
st. Engadine 488 J14
st. Enmore 17 A11
st. Glenfield 424 E10
st. Peakhurst 430 C2
st. Petersham 15 H10
st. Riverstone 182 F13
st. Stanmore 16 C10
TRAHLEE
rd. Bellevue Hill 14 H9
rd. Londonderry 148 B10
rd. Londonderry 148 D10
TRAILL
cl. Mt Annan 479 J16
TRAINER
av. Casula 394 F16
TRALEE
av. Killarney Ht 256 A16
TRAM
la. Randwick, off
Church St 376 K12
TRAMINER
gr. Orchard Hills 268 G13
pl. Eschol Park 481 E3
pl. Minchinbury 272 B8
TRAMORE
pl. Killarney Ht 256 B16
TRAMWAY
arc. Rockdale, off
Frederick St 403 B15
arc. Rockdale, off
Princes Hwy 403 C15
av. Camellia 308 J4
av. Parramatta 308 J4
dr. Currans Hill 479 J12
la. Randwick 377 A10
la. Rosebery 405 F1
la. Concord, off
Frederick St 342 B2
st. Denistone W 280 J13
st. Rosebery 405 F1
st. Tempe 404 A2
st. West Ryde 280 J13
TRANMERE
st. Drummoyne 343 J3
TRANQUILITY
ct. Bella Vista 246 F6
TRANSVAAL
av. Double Bay 14 D9
TRAPPERS
wy. Avalon 139 H10
TRAVERS
rd. Curl Curl 258 J13
TRAVIS
pl. Menai 458 K6
TRAWALLA
st. Hebersham 241 E9
TRAYNOR
av. Kogarah 433 E6
TREACY
st. Hurstville 432 B6
TREADGOLD
st. Leichhardt 15 D4
st. Milperra 397 F10
TREATT
av. Padstow 429 A1
TREATTS
rd. Lindfield 254 B15

TREBARTHA
st. Bass Hill 368 C9
TREBBIANO
pl. Eschol Park 481 B4
TREBLE
cl. Hamondvle 396 D13
TREBOR
rd. Pennant Hills 250 F1
TREBORTH
pl. Menai 459 B9
TREELANDS
av. Ingleburn 453 C8
cl. Galston 160 J4
TREES
wy. Rooty Hill 271 K6
TREE TOPS
av. S Penrith 267 A1
pl. Valley Ht 202 E6
TREETOPS
rd. Cherrybrook 219 A13
TREEVIEW
pl. Epping 251 A12
pl. North Rocks 248 K15
TREGENNA
cl. St Ives 224 E11
TREHARNE
cl. Marsfield 282 B4
TRELAWNEY
st. Croydon Pk 371 H9
st. Eastwood 280 K11
st. Eastwood 281 A9
st. Thornleigh 221 C11
st. Woollahra 14 A15
TRELOAR
av. Mortdale 430 J5
cr. Chester Hill 338 A13
pl. Edensor Pk 363 C2
pl. Menai 458 D12
TREMA
pl. Mt Annan 509 D3
TREMAIN
av. Kellyville 216 E4
TREMERE
st. Concord 342 D6
TREMLOW
cr. Ambarvale 511 B11
TRENT
pl. Ambarvale 511 B14
pl. Hassall Gr 211 J14
pl. N Richmond 87 C12
rd. North Rocks 278 F1
st. S Penrith 266 J4
TRENTBRIDGE
rd. Belrose 225 J12
TRENTHAM
av. Douglas Park 568 J12
TRENTHAM PARK
ct. Wattle Grove 425 K5
TRENTINO
rd. Turramurra 222 K7
TRENTON
rd. Guildford 337 D5
TRENTWOOD
pk. Avalon 139 J16
TRESALAM
st. Mt Pritchard 364 H15
TRESCO
st. St Marys 239 G7
TRESIDDER
av. Kingsford 406 C1
TRESS
st. Blacktown 274 K5
TRESSIDER
av. Haberfield 9 A16
av. Haberfield 343 E16
TREUER
la. Yagoona, off
The Crescent 369 A12
pde. Yagoona 368 F14
TREVALGAN
pl. St Ives 224 F5
TREVALSA
pl. Burraneer 523 D3
TREVANION
st. Five Dock 343 A8
TREVANNA
st. Busby 363 H13
TREVELLYAN
st. Cronulla 523 J1

TREVELYAN
st. Botany 405 J13
TREVENA
la. Enfield 371 J3
TREVENAR
st. Ashbury 372 F7
TREVES
st. Merrylands 307 G12
TREVILYAN
av. Rosebery 375 K16
TREVITHICK
st. Riverstone 182 J10
TREVITT
rd. North Ryde 282 D6
TREVLYN
wy. Acacia Gdn 244 K1
TREVONE
st. Padstow 399 G16
TREVOR
pl. Castle Hill 217 G15
rd. Newport 169 H12
st. Lilyfield 10 D6
TREVORS
la. Cherrybrook 220 A3
TREVOR TOMS
dr. Acacia Gdn 214 K16
TREWILGA
av. Earlwood 372 J16
TREZISE
pl. Quakers Hill 213 K16
TRIABUNNA
av. West Hoxton 392 E5
TRIAL
pl. Illawong 459 D5
TRIANGLE
la. Richmond 88 C16
la. Richmond Lwld 88 C16
TRICKETT
rd. Woolooware 493 G11
TRIDA
pl. Emu Plains 235 G11
TRIDENT
cl. Raby 481 H1
TRIGALANA
pl. Frenchs Frst 256 E1
TRIGG
av. Carlingford 279 J1
TRIGGS
st. St Marys 239 E2
TRIGON
rd. Abbotsbury 362 G1
TRILLER
pl. Ingleburn 453 F10
st. Green Valley 363 D10
TRINA
cr. Canterbury 402 E1
pl. Hassall Gr 211 K16
TRINDER
av. Kingswood 237 F15
TRINERVIS
wy. Mcquarie Fd 454 H4
TRINEURA
ct. Wattle Grove 396 B15
TRINITY
av. Dawes Point A G2
av. Dawes Point 1 F9
dr. Cmbrdg Gdn 237 G2
la. Cmbrdg Gdn, off
Trinity Dr 237 G5
pl. Cherrybrook 219 F14
pl. Kings Lngly 245 H5
TRIPOD
st. Concord 342 C5
TRIPOLI
av. Carlingford 249 K14
pl. Eagle Vale 481 H4
rd. Fairfield W 335 F13
TRIPP
pwy. Warwck Frm, off
Tripp St 365 E14
st. Warwck Frm 365 E14
TRIS
pl. Kings Lngly 246 B9
TRISH
pl. Castle Hill 248 F3
TRISTAN
cl. Oakhurst 242 D2
ct. Castle Hill 217 G4
TRISTANIA
ct. Baulkham Hl 247 C15

gr. Greenacre 370 F5
gr. Menai 459 A14
pl. West Pymble 252 G11
st. Mt Annan 509 C3
wy. Beecroft 250 F3
wy. Winmalee 173 F7
TRISTRAM
rd. Beacon Hill 257 F5
st. Ermington 310 B4
TRITEN
av. Greenfld Pk 334 D15
TRITON
pl. S Penrith 267 C4
TRITTONS
la. Lakemba 370 H15
TRIUMPH
pl. Ingleburn 453 G11
TRIVET
st. Horsley Pk 303 G13
TRIVETTS
la. Balmain 7 H8
TROBRIAND
cr. Glenfield 424 H11
TROON
ct. Glenmore Pk 266 E11
pl. Pymble 252 J4
pl. St Andrews 481 K5
TROOPERS
mw. Holsworthy 426 F4
TROPIC-BIRD
cr. Hinchinbrk 393 C3
TROTT
st. Parramatta 278 C15
TROTWOOD
av. Ambarvale 510 H15
TROUT
pl. St Clair 269 H16
TROUTON
st. Balmain 7 K6
TROUVE
st. Lane Cove 314 B3
TROY
la. Campsie 401 K2
pl. Winston Hills 277 D1
rd. Heathcote 518 F7
st. Campsie 401 K1
st. Emu Plains 235 D13
TRUDY
pl. Hassall Gr 211 J14
TRUEMAN
pl. North Rocks 278 J3
TRUK
pl. Kings Park 244 J3
TRUMAN
av. Bonnet Bay 460 C8
av. Cromer 227 J13
av. Riverwood 400 B14
pl. Bonnet Bay 460 C8
rd. Horsley Pk 331 H4
st. Hurstville 431 K9
st. S Hurstville 431 K9
TRUMBLE
av. Ermington 310 C3
pl. Rouse Hill 184 K8
TRUMFIELD
la. Mosman 316 H13
TRUMPER
pl. Menai 458 F9
st. Ermington 310 E2
wy. Rouse Hill 184 J6
TRURAN
cl. Hornsby 221 E4
TRURO
pde. Padstow 429 G1
pl. Dural 188 A12
TRUSCOTT
av. Matraville 407 C16
la. Panania 427 K1
pl. Bidwill 211 C15
pl. East Killara 254 G9
st. North Ryde 282 J10
st. Panania 427 K1
TRYAL
pl. Willmot 210 C11
TRYON
av. Wollstncraft 315 C12
la. Lindfield 254 E16
la. Chatswood, off Orchard Rd 284 J12
pl. Lindfield, off Pacific Hwy 284 D1
rd. E Lindfield 254 G15
rd. Lindfield 254 E16
st. Chatswood 284 J12
TSAR
cl. Cecil Hills 362 J5
TUAM
pl. Killarney Ht 255 H11
st. Concord 342 D6
TUART
cir. Narellan Vale 478 J15
pl. Narellan Vale 478 J15
TUART PARK
la. Narellan Vale 478 J15
TUCABIA
av. Georges Hall 367 H10
st. S Coogee 407 G7
TUCANA
st. Erskine Park 300 G2
TUCKER
la. Bass Hill, off Tucker St 368 D11
pl. Edensor Pk 363 G2
rd. Casula 424 D4
st. Bass Hill 368 D11
st. N Sydney 5 G1
st. Ryde 312 A1
st. Wiley Park 400 H4
TUCKS
rd. Seven Hills 276 E2
rd. Toongabbie 276 F6
TUCKWELL
pl. Mcquarie Pk 283 A2
rd. Castle Hill 217 G10
TUCSON
gr. Stanhpe Gdn 215 B11
TUDAR
rd. Bonnet Bay 460 D10
rd. Sutherland 460 D10
TUDOR
av. Blacktown 275 A6
av. Cherrybrook 219 K9
cl. Belrose 226 C12
cr. Cecil Hills 362 E7
pl. Carlingford 279 B5
pl. Glenfield 424 C11
pl. St Ives Ch 224 B6
pl. Surry Hills 20 B3
st. Belmore 401 J1
st. Campsie 401 J1
st. Surry Hills 20 A3
TUFFY
av. Sans Souci 463 B6
TUGA
pl. Glenmore Pk 266 A11
TUGGERAH
cl. St Clair 300 C1
pl. Woodcroft 243 H11
st. Leumeah 482 E14
TUGLOW
pl. Leumeah 482 C14
TUGRA
cl. Glenmore Pk 266 C10
TUKARA
rd. S Penrith 267 A6
TUKIDALE
cl. Elderslie 507 J2
TULA
pl. Tregear 240 F6
TULICH
av. Dee Why 258 H2
av. Prestons 393 A15
TULIP
cl. Alfords Point 459 A2
gr. Fairfield W 335 B9
pl. Quakers Hill 243 D3
pl. St Clair 269 G10
st. Chatswood 284 J8
st. Greystanes 306 A12
st. North Ryde 282 C8
TULIPWOOD
dr. Colyton 270 H7
TULLAMORE
av. Killarney Ht 256 A14
TULLAROAN
st. Kellyville 185 C16
st. Kellyville 215 C1
TULLIMBAR
rd. Cronulla 494 A8
st. Croydon Pk 371 F7
TULLOCH
av. Concord W 311 E12
av. Rhodes 311 D11
cl. Casula 394 G15
la. St Clair, off Tulloch Pl 270 D11
pl. Baulkham Hl 246 J3
pl. Edensor Pk 333 E15
pl. St Clair 270 E11
st. Blacktown 243 K10
TULLOH
st. Willoughby 285 F15
TULLOONA
st. Mount Druitt 241 C12
TULLY
av. Liverpool 394 H10
pl. Quakers Hill 214 D14
TULONG
av. Oatlands 279 B13
pl. Kirrawee 491 A9
TULSA
ct. Quakers Hill 214 F11
TULUKERA
pl. Bangor 459 G10
TUMBARUMBA
cr. Heckenberg 364 C13
TUMBRIDGE
cr. Cmbrdg Pk 238 C8
TUMBURRA
st. Ingleside 197 D6
TUMMUL
pl. St Andrews 452 B15
TUMUT
cl. Bankstown 399 B5
la. St Clair, off Tumut Pl 269 J15
pl. Bossley Park 333 J5
pl. Heckenberg 363 K15
pl. St Clair 269 J16
pl. Seven Hills 275 E10
pl. Sylvania Wtr 462 D11
st. Ruse 512 G8
TUNA
pl. St Clair 269 H16
TUNBRIDGE
pl. Cherrybrook 219 H5
pl. Jannali 461 A13
st. Busby 363 G14
st. Mascot 405 E4
TUNCOEE
rd. Villawood 367 A4
TUNCURRY
st. Bossley Park 333 E12
TUNGARRA
rd. Girraween 276 B10
TUNGOO
pl. St Helens Park 511 J16
TUNIS
pl. Quakers Hill 214 C9
TUNKS
av. Cammeray 316 A3
pl. Barden Rdg 488 G3
rd. Dural 190 C4
st. Northbridge 286 B16
st. Ryde 282 B14
st. Waverton 315 D11
TUNLEY
pl. Kings Lngly 245 B3
TUNNACK
cl. West Hoxton 392 E7
TUNNEL
pl. Horsley Pk 333 B9
TUNSTALL
av. Kensington 376 C16
av. Kingsford 376 C16
TUNUNDA
pl. Eschol Park 481 A3
TUOHY
la. Marrickville 373 K13
TUPELO
gr. Menai 458 J12
wy. Acacia Gdn, off Hydrangea Ct 214 J15
TUPIA
pl. Kings Lngly 245 H6
st. Botany 405 G16
TUPPEL
wy. Airds 512 C12
TUPPER
st. Enmore 16 H15
TURBO
rd. Kings Park 244 F5
TURELLA
cl. Belrose 225 K14
st. Glenbrook 264 D2
TURF
pl. Quakers Hill 214 G16
TURI
cl. Bangor 459 F12
TURIMETTA
av. Leumeah 482 B16
st. Mona Vale 199 B6
TURLINJAH
cl. Prestons 393 A13
TURNBERRY
cr. Glenmore Pk 266 F11
wy. Rouse Hill 185 B8
TURNBULL
av. Kemps Ck 359 J5
av. Wilberforce 92 C1
st. Winmalee 173 J6
TURNER
av. Baulkham Hl 247 D13
av. Concord 342 A1
av. Haberfield 9 A11
av. Haberfield 343 E13
av. Ryde 312 C2
cl. Bligh Park 150 G5
la. Punchbowl 400 B4
la. Woolmloo 4 D6
pl. Casula 424 D4
rd. Berowra Ht 133 A7
rd. Currans Hill 479 D3
rd. Smeaton Gra 479 D3
st. Balmain 7 D7
st. Blacktown 244 K8
st. Bronte 378 A7
st. Colyton 270 J8
st. Dee Why 258 H1
st. Ermington 310 D2
st. Guildford 337 E6
st. Punchbowl 400 B5
st. Redfern 19 C8
st. Riverwood 399 K16
st. Ryde 311 K2
st. Thirlmere 565 C3
TURON
av. Baulkham Hl 247 B8
av. Kingsgrove 401 J11
pl. Ruse 512 C9
TUROSS
av. Five Dock 343 C7
av. Sylvania Wtr 462 F12
cl. Prestons 393 D16
pl. Leumeah 482 G14
st. Seven Hills 275 E10
TURPENTINE
av. Peakhurst 430 E4
cl. Alfords Point 429 C16
TURQUOISE
cr. Bossley Park 333 K7
pl. Eagle Vale 481 A7
st. Quakers Hill 214 G13
TURRA
st. S Turramrra 252 C5
TURRAMURRA
av. Turramurra 222 J13
TURRELLA
rd. Yarrawarrah 489 E13
st. Turrella 403 E5
TURRET
pl. Castle Hill 217 F4
pl. Glenmore Pk 266 D6
TURRIELL BAY
rd. Caringbah 492 G16
rd. Lilli Pilli 492 F16
TURRIELL POINT
rd. Port Hacking 522 H2
TURTLE
cct. Green Valley 363 B9
la. Erskineville 17 K16
la. Newtown 17 D10
rd. Caringbah 492 D11
TURTON
av. Belmore 401 J5
la. Belmore, off Turton Av 401 J5
pl. Castle Hill 217 H15
TURUGA
pl. Bangor 459 F11
st. Turramurra 223 A14
TURUNEN
av. Silverdale 353 H12
TURVEY
rd. Blacktown 274 F3
st. Padstow 399 A10
st. Revesby 398 K10
TUSCAN
av. Kellyville 186
av. Kellyville 186
pl. Beacon Hill 257
pl. Casula 395
wy. Cherrybrook 220
wy. Glenwood 245
TUSCANY
gr. S Penrith 267
TUSCULUM
ct. Wattle Grove 425
la. Potts Point 4
rd. Valley Ht 202
st. Potts Point 4
TUSMORE
st. Punchbowl 400
TUTOR
cl. Winmalee 173
TUTT
cr. Chiswick 343
TUTUS
st. Balgowlah Ht 288
TWAIN
st. Winston Hills 277
TWEED
ct. Wattle Grove 395
pl. Ruse 512
pl. St Clair 270
pl. Sylvania Wtr 462
TWEEDMOUTH
av. Rosebery 405
TWELFTH
av. Austral 391
av. Rossmore 390
av. West Hoxton 392
st. Warragamba 353
TWENTIETH
av. Hoxton Park 393
st. Warragamba 353
TWENTYEIGHTH
av. Austral 391
TWENTYFIFTH
av. West Hoxton 391
TWENTY FOURTH
st. Warragamba 353
TWENTYFOURTH
av. West Hoxton 391
TWENTYNINTH
av. Austral 391
TWENTYSECOND
av. West Hoxton 391
TWENTYSEVENTH
av. West Hoxton 391
TWENTYSIXTH
av. West Hoxton 391
TWENTY THIRD
st. Warragamba 353
TWENTYTHIRD
av. West Hoxton 391
TWICKENHAM
av. Cmbrdg Pk 238
cl. Normanhurst 221
TWIN
rd. North Ryde 282
TWINGLETON
av. Ambarvale 510
TWYFORD
av. Earlwood 403
TWYNAM
pl. Horngsea Pk 392
rd. Davidson 255
TYAGARAH
la. Cromer 228
pl. Cromer 228
st. Ryde 312
TYALGUM
av. Panania 428
TYALLA
av. Frenchs Frst 256
cl. Casula 394
TYARAN
pl. Bangor 459
TYCANNAH
pl. Bangor 459
rd. Northbridge 286
TYGH
st. Lapstone 264
TYLER
cr. Abbotsford 343
pl. Bonnet Bay 460
st. Campbelltwn 511

ERS
Bargo ... 567 A10
Bargo ... 567 E9
E
Baulkham Hl ... 246 J5
N Richmond ... 87 A13
St Clair ... 299 K1
Prospect ... 274 G13
ESIDE
N Willghby ... 285 G7
HOON
Raby ... 451 E16
ELL
Fairfield W ... 335 G9
Gladesville ... 312 G9
INGHAM
Hoxton Park ... 392 J8
ONE
Forestville ... 256 B11
Blacktown ... 275 A8
RELL
Rockdale ... 403 A13
WHITT
Maroubra ... 407 F14
ON
Emu Plains ... 235 D14
North Rocks ... 278 J3
Bringelly ... 387 G11
Wilton ... 568 K16

U

ALL
Five Dock ... 342 J8
RIG
Homebush B ... 340 D2
RS
Rhodes ... 311 E7

Picnic Point ... 428 G5

Baulkham Hl ... 247 K11
NDI
Northmead ... 277 J4
NGA
Engadine ... 488 G14
ADULLA
Prestons ... 393 B14
Kareela ... 461 B13
ATHORNE
Drummoyne ... 343 H5
M
S Turramrra ... 251 K6
Doonside ... 273 F4
Orchard Hills ... 268 C6
Ermington ... 280 A14
Lane Cove W ... 283 J13
Maroubra ... 406 G11
MARRA
Camden S ... 507 B10
E Lindfield ... 255 D11
OLO
Hornsby Ht ... 191 D1
ONGA
Greenwich ... 314 K5
Toongabbie ... 276 E9
OOLA
Gymea Bay ... 491 E11
PHA
Cranebrook ... 207 E12
RIC
Northbridge ... 316 B2
STER
Cecil Hills ... 362 E6
Paddington ... 21 E4
Peakhurst ... 430 A7
TIMO
Haymarket ... E A11
Haymarket ... E E9
Haymarket ... 3 C14
Ultimo ... E A11
Ultimo ... 3 C14
Caringbah ... 492 G10
UNDRI
Castle Hill ... 218 A9
VERSTONE
Fairfield ... 336 F14
BRIA
Prestons ... 393 E15

UMINA
pl. Woodbine ... 481 J10
UNA
la. Campsie, off Una St ... 372 B15
pl. Toongabbie ... 276 G10
st. Campsie ... 372 C15
st. Harris Park ... 308 F5
st. Wentwthvle ... 306 H2
st. Redfern, off Regent Pl ... 19 B7
UNARA
la. Campsie ... 372 A14
st. Campsie ... 372 A15
UNCLE WATTLEBERRY
cr. Faulconbdg ... 171 F11
UNDERCLIFF
rd. Harbord ... 288 G2
st. Neutral Bay ... 6 E5
UNDERCLIFFE
la. Earlwood ... 403 G3
rd. Earlwood ... 403 F2
st. Dee Why ... 259 A8
UNDERDALE
la. Meadowbnk, off Railway Rd ... 311 E4
UNDERWOOD
av. Botany ... 405 E11
la. Paddington ... 21 E1
la. Sydney ... A J10
la. Sydney ... 1 G13
pl. Barden Rdg ... 488 H4
rd. Homebush ... 341 A4
rd. Prairiewood ... 334 K8
rd. St Clair ... 270 E9
st. Minto ... 482 G7
st. Paddington ... 13 B16
st. Paddington ... 21 D1
st. Sydney ... A K10
UNDINE
st. Maroubra ... 407 K9
st. Russell Lea ... 343 F6
UNDULA
pl. Belrose ... 225 J13
UNGARRA
st. Rydalmere ... 279 J14
UNICOMBE
cr. Oakhurst ... 242 A2
UNION
ct. Bella Vista ... 246 B1
la. Carlton ... 432 K5
la. Dulwich Hill ... 373 C9
la. Newtown ... 17 J15
la. Paddington ... 13 D16
la. Penrith ... 236 G10
la. Pyrmont ... 12 K4
la. Windsor ... 121 C8
la. Erskineville, off Union St ... 374 K9
la. Fairlight, off William St ... 288 D8
rd. Auburn ... 339 A5
rd. Penrith ... 236 F10
st. Arncliffe ... 403 F8
st. Balmain East ... 8 F9
st. Dulwich Hill ... 373 C9
st. Eastwood ... 280 G7
st. Erskineville ... 17 J16
st. Erskineville ... 374 J9
st. Granville ... 308 B10
st. Kogarah ... 432 K4
st. Lidcombe ... 340 A8
st. McMahons Pt ... 5 B10
st. Mosman ... 317 B11
st. Newtown ... 17 J16
st. N Sydney ... 5 B10
st. Paddington ... 13 D16
st. Parramatta ... 308 E3
st. Pyrmont ... 12 H3
st. Riverstone ... 152 J12
st. Riverwood ... 399 K14
st. Tempe ... 404 B1
st. Toongabbie ... 276 B5
st. Vineyard ... 152 J12
st. Waterloo ... 19 F11
st. Waverton ... 5 B10
st. West Ryde ... 311 D2
UNITED
la. Parramatta ... 308 C3
UNIVERSAL
av. Georges Hall ... 367 G12
la. Eastlakes, off Universal St ... 405 K3
st. Eastlakes ... 405 J3

st. Mortdale ... 431 A7
UNIVERSITY
av. Mcquarie Pk ... 282 C1
pl. Camperdwn ... 18 E2
rd. Miranda ... 491 J4
UNSTED
cr. Hillsdale ... 406 G14
UNSWORTH
st. Abbotsbury ... 333 A16
UNWIN
la. Earlwood, off Unwin St ... 403 H3
rd. Cabramatta W ... 365 B7
rd. Wahroonga ... 221 H7
rd. Waitara ... 221 H7
st. Bexley ... 402 C16
st. Canterbury ... 372 G12
st. Earlwood ... 403 H3
st. Rosehill ... 309 A8
UNWINS
la. Hunters Hill ... 313 B5
UNWINS BRIDGE
rd. St Peters ... 374 E14
rd. Sydenham ... 374 E14
rd. Tempe ... 374 B16
UPFIELD
la. Catherine Fd ... 449 D5
st. Edensor Pk ... 363 H2
UPPER
rd. Forest Lodge ... 11 E14
UPPER ALMORA
st. Mosman ... 317 B7
UPPER AVENUE
rd. Mosman ... 316 J11
UPPER BEACH
st. Balgowlah ... 287 G10
UPPER CARRIAGE
la. Haymarket ... E E14
UPPER CLIFF
av. Northbridge ... 316 A1
rd. Northwood ... 314 H7
UPPER CLIFFORD
av. Fairlight ... 288 B9
UPPER CLONTARF
st. Seaforth ... 287 A3
UPPER FAIRFAX
rd. Mosman ... 317 B2
UPPER FORT
st. Millers Pt ... A E5
st. Millers Pt ... 1 E11
UPPER GILBERT
st. Manly ... 288 F9
UPPER GREYCLIFF
st. Queenscliff, off Greycliff St ... 288 H3
UPPER MINIMBAH
rd. Northbridge ... 286 E14
UPPER PITT
st. Kirribilli ... 2 C1
st. Kirribilli ... 6 B16
UPPER RAILWAY
pde. Condell Park ... 398 G4
UPPER SERPENTINE
rd. Greenwich ... 314 J13
UPPER SPIT
rd. Mosman ... 287 B16
UPPER WASHINGTON
dr. Bonnet Bay ... 460 B9
dr. Bonnet Bay ... 460 D10
UPTON
pl. Bonnyrigg ... 364 A5
st. S Penrith ... 236 K16
UPWARD
st. Leichhardt ... 15 C5
UPWEY
cl. Mt Krng-gai ... 162 H7
pl. St Johns Pk ... 364 E2
st. Prospect ... 274 G10
URALBA
av. Caringbah ... 492 F10
pl. N Wahrnga ... 192 E16
pl. Oatlands ... 279 B14
URALLA
av. Padstow ... 429 D3
pl. S Coogee ... 407 E4
rd. Dural ... 189 D4
rd. E Kurrajong ... 56 H4
st. Hebersham ... 241 E9
URAMBI
pl. Engadine ... 488 G14

URANA
pl. Leumeah ... 482 F15
rd. Yarrawarrah ... 489 D12
st. Villawood ... 367 D2
URANUS
rd. Padstow ... 429 A1
rd. Revesby ... 428 K1
URARA
rd. Avalon ... 140 E14
URBANE
st. Leonay ... 235 D15
URDALA
pl. Sutherland ... 490 C1
UREN
pl. Bligh Park ... 150 E6
pl. Merrylands ... 308 A16
st. S Penrith ... 237 C16
URIAH
pl. Ambarvale ... 510 H14
URQUHART
st. Riverwood ... 400 D15
URSULA
pl. Cecil Hills ... 362 E2
st. Winston Hills ... 276 G1
URUNGA
cl. Hoxton Park ... 392 K9
pde. Miranda ... 492 B4
pde. Punchbowl ... 400 D3
pde. Wiley Park ... 400 D3
pl. Bossley Park ... 333 F10
st. N Balgowlah ... 287 B4
USHER
cl. Abbotsbury ... 333 A13
cr. Sefton ... 368 E5
UTAH
pl. Erskine Park ... 270 K15
pl. Toongabbie ... 275 H12
UTE
pl. Bossley Park ... 333 K10
UTHER
av. Bradbury ... 511 G12
st. Surry Hills ... 19 K1
UTINGU
pl. Bayview ... 168 K15
UTYANA
pl. Frenchs Frst ... 256 G11
UTZON
ct. St Clair ... 270 A10
rd. Cabramatta W ... 365 B5

V

VAIRYS
cr. Merrylands ... 337 J1
VALDA
av. Arncliffe ... 403 J8
pl. Baulkham Hl ... 247 C2
pl. Ingleburn ... 453 D10
pl. Marsfield ... 281 K5
st. Bexley ... 402 G12
st. Blacktown ... 274 F6
st. Merrylands W ... 306 H13
st. W Pnnant Hl ... 249 H1
VALDER
av. Hobartville ... 118 C8
VALE
av. Dee Why ... 258 F4
cct. Narellan Vale ... 478 K10
cct. Narellan Vale ... 479 A10
ct. Canley Vale ... 366 A4
la. Peakhurst ... 430 B10
rd. Thornleigh ... 221 A4
st. Cabramatta ... 366 C7
st. Cammeray ... 315 J4
st. Canley Vale ... 366 C7
st. Clovelly ... 377 H11
st. Gordon ... 253 E7
st. Woodpark ... 306 F15
VALEDICTION
rd. Kings Park ... 244 J5
VALENCIA
cr. Toongabbie ... 275 F11
st. Dural ... 188 J12
st. Greenacre ... 370 E10
VALENTIA
av. Lugarno ... 429 H11
st. Woolwich ... 314 G12
VALENTINE
av. Parramatta ... 308 D5
cl. Winston Hills ... 277 C2
pl. Rsemeadow ... 540 G6

st. Blacktown ... 274 F6
st. Haymarket ... E D12
st. Haymarket ... 3 E14
st. Horngsea Pk ... 392 E16
st. Yagoona ... 368 F11
VALERIA
st. Toongabbie ... 276 B6
VALERIE
av. Baulkham Hl ... 246 F12
av. Chatswd W ... 284 A9
st. Mt Pritchard ... 364 G12
st. Pendle Hill ... 306 E1
VALES
la. Auburn ... 339 D2
VALETTA
ct. Blacktown ... 274 G6
VALEWOOD
cr. Marsfield ... 281 K4
VALINDA
cr. Campbelltwn ... 512 A5
VALIS
rd. Glenwood ... 215 B16
rd. Glenwood ... 245 B1
VALLANCE
st. St Marys ... 239 F5
VALLEN
pl. Quakers Hill ... 214 D13
VALLEY
cl. Bayview ... 168 J12
gln. W Pnnant Hl ... 249 A5
la. Lindfield ... 254 F16
pl. Warriewood ... 198 G6
rd. Balgowlah Ht ... 287 J12
rd. Campbelltwn ... 512 A6
rd. Eastwood ... 280 G5
rd. Epping ... 280 G5
rd. Forestville ... 255 G11
rd. Hornsby ... 221 A1
rd. Lindfield ... 254 F16
rd. Padstow Ht ... 429 F8
rd. Springwood ... 201 G5
rd. Valley Ht ... 202 D4
st. Balmain ... 7 G10
wy. Glossodia ... 59 A5
wy. Gymea Bay ... 491 G9
wy. Tennyson ... 59 A5
VALLEYFIELD
ct. Wattle Grove ... 395 K15
VALLEY PARK
cr. N Turramrra ... 223 E5
VALLEY VIEW
cct. Warriewood ... 198 J7
cl. Roseville ... 284 B6
cr. Engadine ... 489 A14
cr. N Epping ... 251 C10
dr. Narellan ... 478 B9
rd. Frenchs Frst ... 257 A3
VALLEYVIEW
cr. Greenwich ... 314 J6
cr. Wrmgtn Dns ... 237 K5
pl. Kellyville ... 186 K15
VALLINGBY
av. Hebersham ... 241 E4
VALMA
pl. Colyton ... 270 G4
VALMAY
av. Picnic Point ... 428 E9
VALPARAISO
av. Toongabbie ... 275 F12
VALS
ct. St Ives ... 224 B15
VALVE HOUSE
rd. Warragamba ... 353 C5
VAL WHEELER
dr. Kurrajong Ht ... 53 F3
VAN BENTUM
pl. Blacktown ... 273 H6
VAN BUREN
cct. Bonnet Bay ... 460 D9
VANCE
st. Dean Park ... 212 H16
VANCOUVER
av. Toongabbie ... 275 E12
pl. Fairfield W ... 335 C10
VAN DIEMAN
cr. Fairfield W ... 335 C10
pl. Caringbah ... 492 F7
rd. St Clair ... 299 J3
VAN DIEMEN
av. Willmot ... 210 B11
VAN DYKE
pl. Punchbowl ... 400 D4

CENT
Emu Plains....235 J9
Liverpool....365 A15
Mulgoa....325 C3
Canley Vale....366 F1
Davidson....225 B14
Cranebrook....206 J3
Kurrajong....85 G2
Balmain....8 A11
Baulkham Hl....247 H14
Blacktown....274 C3
Canterbury....372 H11
Marrickville....374 C13
Merrylands....307 D8
Mount Druitt....271 C2
St Marys....269 D3
CENTIA
Marsfield....281 K3
CENTS
Arncliffe....403 F11
E
Darlington....18 J4
Condell Park....398 G3
Darlington....18 K4
Ashfield....342 G15
Darlington....18 J4
Fairfield....336 G14
Hurstville....432 C3
Redfern....19 A5
, Schofields....182 E16
,Marsden Pk....211 K1
EGAR HILL
Kellyville....185 B16
ES
Forestville....256 A6
Minto....482 K5
Richmond....118 E11
EY
N St Marys....239 J9
EYARD
Smithfield....336 B5
Mulgoa....296 C16
Mona Vale....199 A5
Rydalmere....279 D15
EYS
Dural....189 C12
Dural....189 C12
TAGE
Minchinbury....272 A8
LA
Glenmore Pk....265 H8
Greystanes....305 J12
Heathcote....518 K9
Lalor Park....245 C10
Rsemeadow....540 F6
Punchbowl....399 K6
Punchbowl....400 A6
Mt Annan....509 F3
LET
Forestville....256 A11
Liverpool....365 A15
Wilberforce....92 A5
Quakers Hill....214 A10
Greystanes....306 G5
Balgowlah....287 F9
Bronte....377 J9
Chatswood....284 J7
Croydon Pk....371 K5
Miranda....461 J16
Revesby....398 E10
Roselands....400 G8
Surry Hills....20 C4
. Liverpool, off
Violet Av....365 A15
ET
Hunters Hill....314 A11
GIL
Chester Hill....338 A16
Sefton....368 E1
Bronte....377 K9
Greystanes....306 D7
GINIA
Bardwell Vy....403 A9
Baulkham Hl....247 B9
Forestville....256 A7
Riverwood....400 B13
W Pnnant Hl....249 B11
Blacktown....244 A11
Guildford W....306 J15
Kensington....376 B12
Rosehill....308 G7
GINIUS
Padstow....429 B4

VIRGO
pl. Erskine Park....300 G2
VIRIA
ct. Glenhaven....218 C3
VIRTUE
st. Condell Park....398 H5
VISCOUNT
cl. Raby....451 F13
pl. Warwck Frm....365 C13
VISCOUNT VAMPIRE
pl. Richmond, off
Davis St....120 B5
VISION VALLEY
rd. Arcadia....130 A13
VISTA
av. Balgowlah Ht....287 H15
av. Bayview....169 A14
av. Peakhurst....430 C11
cl. Hornsby....191 H9
cl. Kings Park....244 G2
cr. Chester Hill....338 C13
la. Bellevue Hill....347 J14
la. Greenwich, off
Edwin St....315 A10
la. Penrith, off
Vista St....236 F10
pde. Mt Riverview....204 J13
pl. Kurrajong Ht....53 K4
pl. Narellan....478 C10
st. Caringbah....492 G8
st. Greenwich....315 A10
st. Mosman....316 K7
st. Oatlands....278 J9
st. Penrith....236 F10
st. Pymble....223 H16
st. Sans Souci....462 J3
VISTA HEIGHTS
rd. Miranda....461 K16
VITTORIA SMITH
av. Castle Hill....218 J14
VIVALDI
cr. Clarmnt Ms....268 G4
pl. Kellyville....216 C1
VIVIAN
cr. Berala....339 E11
st. Bellevue Hill....347 G15
st. Bexley....432 G1
st. Manly....288 J12
st. Scotland I....168 G4
VIVIEN
pl. Castle Hill....218 C12
VIVIENNE
av. Lakemba....371 A13
st. Kingsgrove....401 J12
st. Woodpark....306 G15
VIVYAN
cl. Denistone....281 H12
VLATKO
dr. West Hoxton....392 C11
VOGAN
st. Mt Riverview....234 E3
VOLANS
la. Erskine Park, off
Volans Pl....300 J1
pl. Erskine Park....300 J2
VOLLERS
la. Freemns Rch....90 K1
VOLMER
rd. Scheyville....123 E1
st. Oatlands....279 C7
VOLTA
pl. Winston Hills....277 B5
VOLTAIRE
rd. Winston Hills....277 F2
VOLUNTEER
rd. Kenthurst....188 A4
VONN
av. Smithfield....335 B3
VONNE
pl. Condell Park....398 H8
VON NIDA
pl. Menai....458 J5
VORE
st. Silverwater....309 H13
VOYSEY
cl. Quakers Hill....213 D15
VUKAS
pl. Bonnyrigg Ht....363 C7
VUKO
pl. Warriewood....199 C11

VULCAN
pl. Raby....451 H15
st. Guildford....337 C3
wy. Currans Hill....479 G10

W

WABASH
av. Cromer....228 A13
WABBA
st. Marayong....243 J6
WACKETT
st. Bnkstn Aprt....398 B2
st. Maroubra....406 H11
WADDELL
cr. Hornsby Ht....161 J9
WADDS
av. Cabramatta....366 D8
WADE
cl. Illawong....459 J5
la. Gordon....253 H7
la. Ryde....311 J6
pl. Kings Lngly....246 B9
pl. Surry Hills....F F13
rd. Leumeah....481 J13
rd. N Parramatta....278 K6
st. Campsie....401 K1
st. Maroubra....407 A13
st. Ryde....311 J6
st. Telopea....279 G10
st. Toongabbie....276 E5
WADSLEY
cr. Connells Pt....431 H16
WAGGA WAGGA
st. Prestons....393 B15
WAGNER
pl. Cranebrook....207 G9
pl. Seven Hills....246 D12
WAGSTAFF
st. Edensor Pk....363 D2
WAGTAIL
cr. Ingleburn....453 E9
pl. Erskine Park....270 K13
WAHROONGA
av. Wahroonga....222 G5
pl. W Pnnant Hl....248 G6
rd. Winmalee....173 F4
WAIKANDA
cr. Whalan....240 H9
WAIMEA
av. Woollahra....22 B3
rd. Lindfield....284 E2
st. Burwood....342 B14
st. N Balgowlah....287 D4
WAINE
la. Cabarita....312 E16
st. Cabarita....342 E1
st. Harbord....288 D1
st. Surry Hills....F H6
st. Surry Hills....4 B11
WAINES
cr. Rockdale....403 D14
WAINEWRIGHT
av. West Hoxton....391 K11
WAINWRIGHT
av. Padstow....429 G5
la. Kingswood....237 G12
mw. Bella Vista....246 F2
rd. Mount Druitt....241 A14
rd. Whalan....241 A14
st. Guildford....337 D1
WAIPORI
st. St Ives Ch....223 J3
WAIROA
av. Bondi Beach....378 E2
av. North Bondi....378 E2
la. Canterbury....372 D12
st. Campsie....372 D12
st. Canterbury....372 D12
WAITAKI
st. Lethbrdg Pk....240 F1
WAITANGI
pl. Glenorie....128 C2
WAITARA
av. Waitara....221 K3
pde. Hurstville Gr....431 H10
pl. Dharruk....241 D8
WAITE
av. Balmain....8 B10
WAITOVU
st. Mosman....317 D5

WAIWERA
av. North Manly....258 C16
st. Lavender Bay....K B16
st. Lavender Bay....5 E13
WAKE
pl. Kings Park....244 J3
WAKEFIELD
st. North Manly....258 B16
WAKEFORD
pl. Blaxland....233 F12
rd. Strathfield....371 E1
WAKEHURST
pky. Belrose....227 E6
pky. Elanora Ht....228 B3
pky. Frenchs Frst....256 H6
pky. N Narrabeen....228 B3
pky. Oxford Falls....227 B15
pky. Seaforth....286 J3
WAKELIN
av. Mt Pritchard....364 J11
wy. Claymore....481 D12
WAKELY
av. Quakers Hill....214 D7
pl. Forestville....256 A5
WAKOOKA
av. Elanora Ht....198 C16
WALANA
cr. Warriewood....198 F3
WALAR
cr. East Killara....254 K6
WALBURGA
cl. Bradbury....511 J10
WALCHA
ct. Mt Krng-gai....162 G3
la. S Penrith, off
Walcha Pl....266 H6
pl. S Penrith....266 G6
wy. Hoxton Park....392 G5
WALDEN
rd. N Parramatta....278 F10
WALDER
rd. Hamondvle....396 E15
WALDO
cr. Peakhurst....430 C3
WALDON
rd. Belrose....225 K5
WALDRON
la. Sandringham, off
Norwood St....463 D4
pl. Cmbrdg Pk....238 A6
rd. Chester Hill....368 A1
rd. Sefton....368 E2
st. Sandringham....463 D5
WALENORE
av. Kingsford....406 H5
av. Newtown....374 H9
WALER
pl. Blairmount....481 A13
WALES
cl. Illawong....459 E5
la. Greenacre....370 G14
pl. Kings Lngly....245 B3
st. Greenacre....370 G15
WALGETT
cl. Hinchinbrk....392 H4
WALKER
av. Edgecliff....13 F11
av. Gymea....491 F7
av. Haberfield....343 A14
av. Mascot....405 E4
av. Narrabeen....228 J8
av. Peakhurst....430 H3
av. St Ives....224 E6
cl. Silverdale....353 H15
la. Lavender Bay....K G13
la. Lavender Bay....5 H11
la. Paddington....4 K15
pde. Riverstone....181 K10
pl. Church Point....168 C9
pl. N Epping....251 F9
pl. Wetherill Pk....334 A1
rd. Port Hacking....522 J2
st. Belmore....371 C12
st. Canada Bay....342 D10
st. Clovelly....378 A13
st. Five Dock....342 D10
st. Lavender Bay....K F14
st. Lavender Bay....5 G11
st. Merrylands....307 G16
st. N Sydney....K G10
st. N Sydney....5 H9
st. Putney....312 C8
st. Quakers Hill....213 G7

st. Quakers Hill....213 K10
st. Redfern....19 H10
st. Rhodes....311 D9
st. S Windsor....120 J16
st. Springwood....202 H1
st. Turrella....403 F5
st. Waterloo....19 H12
st. Werrington....239 A13
wy. Minto....482 H5
WALKERS
cr. Emu Plains....234 K10
dr. Lane Cove W....283 F12
la. St Clair....300 A1
WALKOM
av. Forestville....256 B9
WALL
av. Asquith....192 A7
av. Panania....398 C13
pl. Bonnyrigg....364 C5
WALLABA
pl. Greystanes....305 H10
WALLABY
cl. Blacktown....273 J5
cl. Bossley Park....333 F7
gr. Winmalee....173 K5
WALLACE
av. Hunters Hill....313 A8
av. Hurlstone Pk....373 A11
cl. Hornsby Ht....161 J10
la. Balmain....8 C10
la. Hurlstone Pk....372 K11
la. Kingsford, off
Wallace St....406 J2
pde. Lindfield....254 B16
pl. Mt Pritchard....364 J9
rd. Vineyard....152 C7
st. Ashfield....373 A2
st. Balmain....8 C10
st. Bexley....432 G3
st. Blacktown....244 J15
st. Burwood....342 C16
st. Concord....342 B6
st. Eastwood....280 H8
st. Granville....308 C10
st. Greenwich....314 J13
st. Kingsford....406 H2
st. Marrickville....373 F16
st. Sefton....368 G5
st. Waverley....377 G10
st. Willoughby....285 D12
WALLAGA
av. Leumeah....482 G16
wy. Woodcroft....243 G10
WALLALONG
cr. West Pymble....252 G11
WALLAMI
st. Caringbah....492 G16
WALLAN
av. Glenmore Pk....266 B6
WALLANGRA
rd. Dover Ht....348 E13
WALLARINGA
av. Neutral Bay....6 G10
cl. Mt Colah....162 B15
WALLAROO
cl. Killara....253 K11
WALLAROY
cr. Woollahra....14 D13
rd. Woollahra....14 E14
rd. Woollahra....22 D2
st. Concord W....311 D14
WALLAWA
av. Engadine....488 H15
WALLCLIFFE
ct. Wattle Grove....425 H6
WALLENDBEEN
av. Port Hacking....523 A2
pl. Bardwell Vy....403 C7
WALLGROVE
rd. Cecil Park....332 E13
rd. Eastern Ck....302 G2
rd. Horsley Pk....302 H15
WALLINA
av. Belrose....225 H14
WALLINGA
pl. Airds....512 A14
WALLINGTON
rd. Mosman....317 D2
WALLIS
av. Matraville....436 K8
av. Strathfield....371 B3
cr. Cecil Hills....362 J6
gln. Cranebrook....207 E9

la. Woollahra 22 D4
pde. North Bondi 378 F1
pl. St Ives 224 B15
pl. Willmot 210 B11
st. Leumeah 482 G14
st. Maianbar 522 K9
st. Woollahra 21 J5
st. Woollahra 22 C4
WALL PARK
av. Blacktown 275 C2
av. Seven Hills 275 C2
WALLUMATTA
rd. Newport 169 D8
rd.n, Caringbah 493 B8
rd.s, Caringbah 493 B8
WALMAN
av. Lurnea 394 B10
WALMER
st. Ramsgate 433 E14
st. Sans Souci 433 E14
WALMSLEY
cl. Prairiewood 334 K9
WALNUT
gr. Cherrybrook 219 H7
st. Greystanes 306 E5
WALPA
pl. Quakers Hill 213 G7
WALPOLE
cl. Wetherill Pk 334 J3
pl. Wahroonga 222 D11
st. Holroyd 307 K10
st. Merrylands 307 F9
WALRUS
pl. Raby 451 D15
WALSH
av. Castle Hill 248 E2
av. Croydon Pk 371 F8
av. Glebe 11 J12
av. Maroubra 406 H11
cl. Edensor Pk 333 H13
cl. Illawong 459 E7
la. Greenacre 369 J10
pl. Kingswood 267 F1
st. Eastwood 281 H7
st. N Narrabeen 199 B13
WALSHE
gr. Bidwill 211 B15
WALTER
cl. Bligh Park 150 D5
pl. Greystanes 306 E12
pl. Northmead 278 D4
rd. Ingleside 198 C2
st. Balmain 7 C8
st. Bondi Jctn 22 G9
st. Croydon 372 E1
st. Granville 308 D11
st. Kingswood 237 K12
st. Leichhardt 9 B16
st. Mortdale 431 A5
st. Paddington 21 B2
st. Roselands 401 B5
st. Sans Souci 433 E15
st. Wetherill Pk 334 H1
st. Willoughby 285 E16
WALTERS
av. Glenbrook 234 E16
rd. Arndell Park 274 A10
rd. Berala 339 D14
rd. Blacktown 274 B4
st. Arncliffe 403 E8
st. Auburn 339 A2
wy. Castle Hill, off Kerle Cr 218 J14
WALTHAM
st. Artarmon 315 A2
st. Coogee 407 G1
wy. Glenwood 215 C13
WALTHER
av. Bass Hill 367 E7
WALTON
cl. Pymble 253 F5
cr. Abbotsford 342 K1
la. Abbotsford 312 K15
la. Picton 563 F3
pl. Emu Plains 235 B12
pl. Minchinbury 271 F6
st. Blakehurst 432 C14
WALUMETTA
dr. Wollstncraft 315 D10
WALWORTH
av. Newport 169 H13
ct. Newport 169 H12
rd. Horsley Pk 302 E11
WALZ
la. Rockdale, off Walz St 403 C15
st. Rockdale 403 C15
WAMBIRI
pl. Cromer 227 K14
WAMBOOL
pl. Brooklyn 76 C11
st. Turramurra 222 J16
WAMINDA
av. Campbelltwn 511 J8
WANAARING
tce. Glenwood 215 E16
WANAKA
pl. Belrose 226 A16
pl. Glenorie 128 C3
WANARI
rd. Terrey Hills 196 E7
WANAWONG
dr. Thornleigh 220 J12
rd. Avalon 139 K12
WANDA
cr. Berowra Ht 133 C7
pl. Woodbine 481 D15
st. Merrylands W 307 B14
st. Strathfield S 371 E7
WANDANA
av. Baulkham Hl 247 C4
WANDARRA
cr. Bradbury 511 D15
WANDARRI
rd. Kenthurst 157 E10
WANDEARAH
av. Avalon 139 J12
WANDEEN
av. Beecroft 250 F5
pl. St Ives Ch 223 K3
rd. Clareville 169 D2
WANDELLA
av. Hunters Hill 313 F12
av. Northmead 278 C2
av. Roseville 284 K4
pl. Glen Alpine 510 E14
rd. Allambie Ht 257 G16
rd.n, Miranda 491 K4
rd.s, Miranda 491 K5
WANDOBAH
st. Engadine 489 E8
WANDOO
av. Ryde 311 K4
gln. Kingswood 237 H16
pl. Bradbury 511 E10
WANDSWORTH
st. Parramatta 308 G1
WANGAL
pl. Five Dock 342 K12
WANGALLA
rd. Riverview 314 C5
WANGANELLA
cl. Mt Colah 162 B15
rd. St Ives Ch 223 K3
st. Balgowlah 287 G10
st. Balgowlah 287 G8
st. Miller 393 F4
wy. Airds 512 E10
WANGANUI
rd. Kirrawee 491 B8
WANGARA
st. Doonside 243 B15
st. Mona Vale 199 A3
WANGAROA
cr. Lethbrdg Pk 240 E1
WANGEE
rd. Greenacre 370 E12
rd. Lakemba 370 K14
WANGI
av. Cronulla 523 J4
WANGOOLA
wy. Minto 482 K3
WANILL
pl. Berowra 133 E10
WANINGA
rd. Hornsby Ht 161 J8
WANJINA
pl. North Rocks 278 H2
WANNITI
rd. Belrose 225 H14
WANNYL
rd. Kirrawee 490 J5
WANSEY
rd. Randwick 376 J14
WANSTEAD
av. Earlwood 403 G2
WANT
st. Caringbah 492 K14
st. Mosman 317 B9
st. Rosebery 405 H2
WARABIN
st. Waterfall 519 D12
WARAGAL
av. Rozelle 344 E6
WARANA
rd. Cecil Park 331 E14
WARANDOO
st. Gordon 254 C6
st. Hornsby 221 G6
WARATAH
av. Casula 394 J11
av. Randwick 377 A14
cr. Mcquarie Fd 453 G1
ct. Narellan Vale 478 K12
la. Canterbury 372 C14
la. Sutherland 490 E4
pde. Narraweena 258 B6
pl. Glenorie 127 K10
rd. Berowra 133 D14
rd. Botany 405 H16
rd. Engadine 518 E3
rd. Ingleside 197 H6
rd. Ingleside 198 A6
rd. Kentlyn 483 C13
rd. Palm Beach 109 J14
rd. Turramurra 252 E3
rd. Warrimoo 202 K11
st. Arncliffe 403 D10
st. Balgowlah 288 A8
st. Bexley 432 D2
st. Blakehurst 432 B15
st. Bowen Mtn 83 K13
st. Burwood Ht 372 A6
st. Canterbury 372 D14
st. Chatswood 284 J6
st. Cronulla 493 K14
st. Croydon Pk 372 A6
st. Eastwood 281 H8
st. Ermington 310 H3
st. Granville 308 B10
st. Haberfield 9 A10
st. Haberfield 343 D12
st. Harbord 258 F14
st. Kirrawee 490 G1
st. Kyle Bay 432 B15
st. Leichhardt 10 B14
st. Mona Vale 199 A2
st. North Bondi 348 F15
st. N Strathfield 341 E6
st. Oatley 431 A12
st. Oatley 431 A14
st. Old Guildford 337 E9
st. Punchbowl 400 C2
st. Rooty Hill 272 E4
st. Rcuttrs Bay 13 C8
st. St Marys 239 F14
st. Stanhpe Gdn 215 D10
st. Sutherland 490 G1
WARAYAMA
pl. Rozelle 344 C6
WARBLER
av. Ingleburn 453 F10
cl. Hinchinbrk 363 E15
la. St Clair, off Warbler St 271 A12
st. Erskine Park 270 K14
WARBRICK
st. Concord 342 A5
WARBROON
ct. Bella Vista 246 H2
WARBURTON
cr. Wrrngtn Cty 238 E4
la. Earlwood 402 D4
pde. Earlwood 402 E3
st. Chifley 437 A5
st. Condell Park 398 F1
st. Gymea 491 E3
st. Marrickville 373 J14
WARBY
st. Campbelltwn 511 G2
WARCOO
av. Gymea Bay 491 G12
WARD
av. Canterbury 372 D14
av. Darlinghurst 4 K9
av. Elizabeth Bay 13 A7
av. Potts Point 4 K9
cl. Prairiewood 334 J7
cr. Oyster Bay 461 F5
la. Concord 342 D6
pl. Dural 188 H13
pl. Hinchinbrk 362 J16
pl. Northmead 277 H8
st. Bass Hill 368 E9
st. Concord 342 D6
st. Eastwood 280 J6
st. Epping 250 G16
st. Kurnell 465 F8
st. N Sydney K F3
st. N Sydney 5 G6
st. Pymble 253 A7
st. Willoughby 285 E12
st. Yagoona 368 E9
wy. Minto 482 K1
WARDANG
rd. Hinchinbrk 362 J16
WARDELL
cl. Earlwood 403 B1
dr. Barden Rdg 488 H2
dr. S Penrith 267 C4
la. Blaxland 233 E10
la. Dulwich Hill, off Keith St 373 E12
pl. Agnes Banks 117 C12
rd. Dulwich Hill 15 E16
rd. Dulwich Hill 373 G9
rd. Earlwood 403 A3
rd. Lewisham 373 G9
rd. Marrickville 373 D13
rd. Petersham 373 G9
st. Arncliffe 403 G10
wy. Minto 482 J6
WARDIA
st. Glenwood 245 E1
WARDINGTON
ri. Bella Vista 246 H2
WARDLE
cl. Currans Hill 479 F12
WARDROP
st. Greenwich 315 A9
WARE
st. Fairfield 336 E12
st. Fairfield Ht 336 B10
WAREEMBA
av. Thornleigh 221 A4
pl. Lilli Pilli 492 F16
st. Wareemba 343 A5
WAREHAM
cr. Frenchs Frst 256 D3
WAREJEE
st. Kingsgrove 402 A8
WAREKILA
cl. Berowra Ht 133 D8
rd. Beacon Hill 257 H8
WARESLEY
la. Cranebrook, off Waresley Wy 207 G14
wy. Cranebrook 207 F14
WARFIELD
pl. Cecil Hills 362 J9
WARGON
cr. Glenmore Pk 266 A10
WARHAM
la. Marrickville 374 A11
WARI
av. Glenmore Pk 266 D10
WARIALDA
st. Kogarah 433 A3
st. Merrylands W 307 B13
wy. Hinchinbrk 392 H5
WARILDA
av. Engadine 489 B10
la. Beverly Hills 401 C13
st. Villawood 367 F4
WARILI
rd. Frenchs Frst 255 K2
WARILLA
pl. Riverview 314 A6
WARIN
pl. Glenmore Pk 266 C12
WARING
av. Caringbah 492 D15
cr. Plumpton 242 C11
st. Marsfield 282 B2
WARINGA
cr. Glenmore Pk 266 A6
WARK
av. Pagewood 406 G6
WARKS HILL
rd. Kurrajong Ht 53 J3
WARLENCOURT
av. Milperra 397
WARMAN
st. Dundas Vy 280
st. Pendle Hill 276
WARNDON
la. Cranebrook, off Warndon Rd 207
rd. Cranebrook 207
WARNE
cr. Beverly Hills 400
pl. Marrickville 373
st. Pennant Hills 220
WARNER
av. Clovelly 378
av. S Turramrra 252
pl. Greystanes 306
st. Gladesville 312
WARNERS
av. Bondi Beach 378
av. North Bondi 348
av. Willoughby 285
WARNING
pl. Ruse 512
WARNOCK
rd. Agnes Banks 117
st. Guildford W 336
WAROOGA
av. Baulkham Hl 246
WAROON
rd. Cromer 228
WARRA
st. Wentwthvle 276
WARRABA
rd. N Narrabeen 198
st. Como 460
st. Hurstville 402
WARRABINA
av. St Ives 224
WARRABRI
pl. West Pymble 252
WARRADALE
rd. Silverdale 353
WARRAGAL
rd. Turramurra 222
WARRAGAMBA
cr. Bossley Park 333
cr. Jamisontown 266
cr. Leumeah 482
WARRAH
pl. Greystanes 305
rd. Miranda 492
rd. Yowie Bay 492
st. Chatswood 285
WARRAMUNGA
st. St Marys 239
WARRAN
pl. Castle Hill 218
WARRANA
st. Botany 405
WARRANE
pl. Castle Cove 285
rd. Chatswood 285
rd. N Willghby 285
rd. Roseville Ch 285
WARRANGARREE
dr. Woronora Ht 489
WARRANGI
st. Turramurra 223
WARRAROON
rd. Riverview 314
WARRAROONG
st. Beverly Hills 401
WARRATTA
pl. Oatlands 279
WARRAWEE
av. Castle Cove 285
av. Warrawee 222
pl. Beverly Hills 401
WARRAWIDGEE
rd. Chester Hill 337
WARRAWONG
st. Eastwood 280
st. Glenmore Pk 266
WARREGO
av. Sylvania Wtr 462
ct. Wattle Grove 395
pl. East Killara 254
pl. Greystanes 306
rd. Berowra Ht 133
st. N St Marys 239

RRELL
Rooty Hill 272 B4
RREN
Bankstown 399 F7
Bankstown 399 G7
Grays Point 491 A15
Kogarah 433 E5
Marrickville, off Church St 373 H14
Punchbowl 400 E5
Silverdale 353 J9
Wakeley 334 H12
Bellevue Hill 14 J15
Marrickville 373 G14
Smithfield 336 B2
Woodpark 306 E16
Woodpark 306 F16
Quakers Hill 244 B2
Ryde 282 B10
Liverpool 395 E3
RREN BALL
Newtown 18 A9
RRENTON
St Clair 270 J11
RRI
Narraweena 258 A6
RRICK
Blacktown 244 H15
RRIEWOOD
Warriewood 199 A8
Woodbine 481 G11
RRIGAL
Westleigh 220 H5
Wrrngtn Dns 238 E5
Canterbury, off Warrigal St 372 D13
Frenchs Frst 256 G2
Blacktown 244 A10
Canterbury 372 D13
Jannali 460 G9
RRIGO
Sadleir 364 B15
RRIMOO
St Ives 223 G9
St Ives Ch 223 K4
Quakers Hill 243 J1
RRINA
Baulkham Hl 246 K6
Parramatta 278 A13
Glendenning 242 G5
Greystanes 305 H10
Londonderry 148 B11
Bradbury 511 C16
Caringbah 492 G12
Berowra Ht 133 D9
RRING
Emu Plains 235 H10
RRINGA
Cammeray 316 A6
Bass Hill 368 E14
Yagoona 368 E14
RRINGAH
Cammeray 315 G4
Crows Nest 315 G4
Naremburn 315 G4
N Sydney K K6
N Sydney 5 J6
Mosman 317 C3
Beacon Hill 257 B5
Dee Why 258 A6
Forestville 255 F16
Frenchs Frst 256 C8
Mosman 317 C3
Narraweena 258 A6
N Balgowlah 287 D3
RRINGTON
Caringbah 493 A6
East Killara 254 F7
Epping 281 A2
RRIOR
St Marys 239 F9
RROWA
West Pymble 252 J7
RRUGA
Berowra Ht 133 C8
N Narrabeen 198 H13
Riverview 313 J6
RRUMBUNGLE
Bow Bowing 452 D12
Fairfield W 335 E11
RRUNG
St Helens Park 541 E2

WARSAW
st. N Strathfield 341 C5
WARSOP
st. Kurnell 464 C16
WARUDA
av. Kirribilli 2 D2
st. Bankstown 368 E14
st. Kirribilli 2 C2
st. Yagoona 368 E14
WARUMBUI
av. Baulkham Hl 246 H8
av. Miranda 492 A1
WARUMBUL
rd. Royal N P 520 K10
WARUNDA
pl. Tarban 313 D12
WARUNG
av. Frenchs Frst 255 F2
st. Georges Hall 368 D15
st. McMahons Pt 5 E16
st. Yagoona 368 D15
WARWICK
av. Cabramatta 365 C10
av. Cammeray 316 B5
cl. Berowra 133 E9
cl. Blaxland 234 A9
cr. Canterbury 402 E1
la. Hurstville 401 F16
la. Stanmore 16 H9
pde. Castle Hill 217 J15
pl. Wahroonga 221 K15
rd. Dundas Vy 280 A6
rd. Merrylands 307 F12
st. Hurstville 401 E16
st. Killara 253 H11
st. Minto 482 F1
st. North Ryde 283 B11
st. Penrith 236 J13
st. Punchbowl 399 J5
st. St Marys 269 F3
st. Stanmore 16 H9
st. Sylvania 461 K13
st. Warwck Frm 365 J15
WARWILLA
av. Wahroonga 222 C6
wk. Wahroonga, off Warwilla Av 222 D7
WARWILLAH
rd. Russell Lea 343 C5
WASCOE
st. Glenbrook 233 H14
WASDALE
st. Collaroy Plat 228 E12
WASHINGTON
av. Cromer 228 A13
av. Riverwood 400 B13
dr. Bonnet Bay 460 A10
dr. Bonnet Bay 460 E11
pl. Castle Hill 247 E1
st. Bexley 432 K2
st. Bexley 433 A1
wy. Cecil Park 332 A12
WASSALL
la. Alexandria 18 J13
WASSELL
st. Chifley 437 A4
st. Dundas 279 K12
st. Matraville 437 A4
WATCH HOUSE
rd. Prospect 304 K1
WATER
la. Carlton 432 K5
la. Mosman 317 A12
la. Emu Plains, off Water St 235 D10
st. Annandale 17 B2
st. Auburn 339 D7
st. Bardwell Pk 402 K6
st. Belfield 371 C8
st. Birchgrove 7 E4
st. Blakehurst 432 E16
st. Cabramatta W 365 A8
st. Caringbah 493 B13
st. Emu Plains 235 C10
st. Hornsby 191 J15
st. Lidcombe 339 D7
st. Sans Souci 462 K5
st. Strathfield S 371 C7
st. Wahroonga 222 F6
st. Wallacia 324 J11
st. Wentwthvle 277 B15
st. Werrington 238 K15
st. Werrington 239 A15

WATERFALL
av. Forestville 256 A13
cr. Bella Vista 216 D16
cr. Bella Vista 246 D1
cr. Cranebrook 207 B12
pl. Duffys Frst 195 C7
rd. Heathcote 518 F10
rd. Oatley 430 H10
rd. Oatley 430 J11
WATERFORD
pl. Killarney Ht 255 J14
st. Kellyville 185 C15
WATERFRONT
dr. Lilyfield, off Military Dr 10 A1
wy. Harringtn Pk 478 D5
WATERGUM
cl. Rouse Hill 185 C8
cr. Silverdale 384 A2
pl. Alfords Point 459 C1
wy. Greenacre 370 F5
WATERHOUSE
av. St Ives 254 D1
dr. Silverdale 353 K10
pl. Airds 511 J14
pl. Camden S 507 C10
st. Abbotsbury 333 C12
WATER LILY
tce. Bidwill 211 E14
WATERLOO
av. Castle Hill 217 K11
pl. Glenfield 424 E9
rd. Greenacre 370 C15
rd. Mcquarie Pk 251 J13
rd. Mcquarie Pk 282 F2
rd. Mcquarie Pk 283 A6
rd. Marsfield 251 J13
rd. Mt Lewis 370 C15
rd. N Epping 251 G11
st. Narrabeen 229 B4
st. Rozelle 344 D8
st. Surry Hills F F16
st. Surry Hills 19 K2
WATER RESERVE
rd. N Balgowlah 287 F5
WATERS
la. Cremorne 316 E8
la. Neutral Bay 316 E8
la. Richmond Lwld 88 E9
rd. Cremorne 6 J1
rd. Cremorne 316 E8
rd. Glenbrook 264 B2
rd. Naremburn 315 D3
rd. Naremburn 315 E2
rd. Neutral Bay 6 J1
WATERSIDE
av. Maroubra 407 J8
cr. Carramar 366 H4
cr. Earlwood 372 J15
gr. Warriewood 198 J7
gr. Woodcroft 243 G9
pde. Peakhurst 430 D11
WATERSLEIGH
la. Cremorne 316 E7
WATERTON
av. Matraville 436 J2
WATERVIEW
av. Caringbah 492 E12
cr. Blaxland 233 H12
st. Balmain 8 A9
st. Carlton 432 F11
st. Five Dock 342 K10
st. Mona Vale 199 E1
st. Oyster Bay 461 C7
st. Putney 311 J6
st. Ryde 311 J6
st. Seaforth 286 K3
WATERWORTH
dr. Mt Annan 479 A15
dr. Narellan Vale 478 G16
dr. Narellan Vale 508 F1
WATFORD
cl. N Epping 251 G9
WATKIN
av. Earlwood 403 A3
la. Newtown 17 K10
la. Concord, off Watkin St 312 A16
st. Bexley 403 A16
st. Concord 342 A1
st. Hurlstone Pk 372 J11
st. Newtown 17 K10
st. Rockdale 403 A16

WATKINS
cr. Currans Hill 479 H13
rd. Avalon 140 F14
rd. Baulkham Hl 247 E15
st. Bondi 377 H3
WATKIN WOMBAT
wy. Faulconbdg 171 H12
WATKISS
st. Glenwood 215 H16
WATLING
av. West Hoxton 392 A14
wy. Claymore 481 B11
WATSFORD
rd. Campbelltwn 511 F2
WATSON
av. Ashbury 372 E6
av. Hornsby 191 F12
av. N Wahrnga 192 F16
dr. Penrith 237 C7
la. Balmain 7 H9
la. Narwee, off Arrow Rd 400 F15
pl. Doonside 243 B5
pl. Minto 453 A13
pl. Northmead 278 C4
rd. Lapstone 264 F2
rd. Millers Pt A E3
rd. Millers Pt 1 E10
rd. Mt Annan 479 G14
rd. Padstow 399 D14
st. Bondi 377 K5
st. Ermington 310 D1
st. Glenbrook 264 A4
st. Hamondvle 396 E14
st. Neutral Bay 6 E1
st. Paddington 21 E3
st. Pennant Hills 220 D14
st. Putney 311 J7
st. Rosehill 308 H8
WATSONIA
st. Emu Plains 235 H8
WATT
av. Newington 310 B12
av. Ryde 282 B16
pde. Lansdowne 367 C6
pl. Emu Plains 235 E9
st. Leumeah 512 C1
st. Rooty Hill 272 B2
WATTING
st. Abbotsbury 333 B11
WATTLE
av. Carramar 366 H2
av. Fairlight 288 C7
av. Mcquarie Fd 453 K4
av. N St Marys 239 K11
av. Villawood 367 A1
cr. Glossodia 59 C5
cr. Pyrmont 12 G7
la. N St Marys 239 K11
la. Ultimo 12 K13
la. West Ryde 281 G15
la. Asquith, off Amor St 191 K10
la. Hurlstone Pk, off New Canterbury Rd 372 K10
pl. Carlingford 249 F15
pl. Rooty Hill 272 D3
pl. Turramurra 252 D2
pl. Ultimo 3 A16
pl. Ultimo 12 K16
rd. Brookvale 258 C12
rd. Casula 423 H2
rd. Ingleside 197 K8
rd. Jannali 460 H14
rd. Jannali 460 J9
rd. North Manly 258 C12
rd. Ruse 512 E8
rd. Sutherland 460 H15
st. Asquith 191 K10
st. Bankstown 369 J16
st. Bargo 567 G4
st. Blacktown 243 J14
st. Bowen Mtn 84 A10
st. Enfield 371 G5
st. Greystanes 306 E4
st. Haberfield 343 A13
st. Killara 254 B10
st. Peakhurst 430 H4
st. Punchbowl 370 B16
st. Rydalmere 309 G1
st. Springwood 202 E8
st. Ultimo 3 A15
st. Ultimo 12 G9
st. West Ryde 281 F14

wk. Newington, off Newington Bvd 310 B13
WATTLEBIRD
cr. Glenmore Pk 266 A13
pl. Glenwood 245 B1
WATTLE CREEK
dr. Theresa Park 445 A10
WATTLE GREEN
pl. Narellan Vale 478 J13
WATTLE GROVE
dr. Wattle Grove 396 A16
WATTON
rd. Carlingford 249 F12
st. Quakers Hill 214 F16
WATTS
gr. Blacktown 273 H5
pl. Cherrybrook 220 A11
pl. Prairiewood 335 B8
pl. West Hoxton 392 C10
rd. Kemps Ck 359 G13
rd. Ryde 281 K9
st. Canada Bay 342 E9
st. North Rocks 249 A16
WAU
pl. Glenfield 424 J10
pl. Holsworthy 426 C3
pl. Whalan 240 K8
WAUCHOPE
rd. Hoxton Park 392 H10
WAUGH
av. N Parramatta 278 G13
cr. Blacktown 273 H3
WAUGOOLA
la. Gordon 254 B5
st. Gordon 254 A5
WAUHOPE
cr. S Coogee 407 F4
WAVEHILL
av. Windsor Dn 180 J1
WAVELL
av. Carlingford 250 A15
pde. Earlwood 403 D4
WAVERLEY
cr. Bondi Jctn 377 F3
la. Belmore, off Plimsoll St 401 H1
st. Belmore 401 H1
st. Bondi Jctn 22 K7
st. Bondi Jctn 377 F4
st. Fairfield W 335 D8
st. Randwick 377 B11
WAVERLY
pl. Illawong 459 K5
WAVERTON
av. Waverton 5 B6
la. Waverton 5 B6
WAY
cl. Carlingford 250 B13
st. Kingsgrove 402 B11
st. Tempe 374 B16
WAYCOTT
av. Kingsgrove 402 B13
WAYELLA
st. West Ryde 280 J12
WAYFIELD
rd. Dural 218 F2
rd. Glenhaven 218 F2
WAYGARA
av. Green Valley 363 H11
WAYGROVE
av. Earlwood 402 F3
WAYLAND
av. Lidcombe 339 H13
WAYMAN
pl. Merrylands 307 G13
WAYNE
av. Lugarno 430 A11
cr. Condell Park 398 F5
cr. Greystanes 306 F13
st. Dean Park 242 J2
WAYS
tce. Pyrmont 8 G16
WAZIR
st. Bardwell Vy 403 C8
WEALTHEASY
st. Riverstone 182 B9
WEARDEN
rd. Belrose 226 C15
rd. Frenchs Frst 226 C15
rd. Frenchs Frst 257 B1

WEARNE
av. Pennant Hills 220 E14
rd. Bonnyrigg 363 K10
st. Canterbury 402 C1
WEATHERBY
av. Cmbrdg Pk 238 A10
WEAVER
la. Erskine Park, off Weaver St 301 B2
pl. Minchinbury 271 G7
pl. Woronora Ht 489 C5
st. Erskine Park 300 K2
st. Erskine Park 301 A1
st. Ryde 312 F6
WEBB
av. Hornsby 221 F2
av. Liberty Gr 311 B11
cl. Edensor Pk 333 H16
cl. Illawong 459 J5
pl. Blackett 241 D1
pl. Bligh Park 150 J7
pl. W Pnnant Hl 249 G3
st. Croydon 342 D15
st. McMahons Pt 5 C12
st. Merrylands 307 E7
st. N Parramatta 278 H15
st. Parramatta 278 H15
st. Riverwood 399 J16
st. Werrington 238 K12
tce. Westleigh 220 G7
WEBBER
pl. Kings Lngly 245 A2
pl. Prairiewood 335 A8
st. Greenacre 370 G11
st. Sylvania 461 K12
WEBBS
av. Ashfield 372 J1
av. Auburn 338 J5
la. Burwood 342 A11
st. Ashfield 342 H16
WEBER
cr. Emerton 240 H6
WEBSTER
av. Peakhurst 430 B6
rd. Lurnea 394 E10
st. Milperra 397 D16
st. Pendle Hill 276 B16
st. Picton 563 G7
WEDDELL
av. Tregear 240 E4
WEDDERBURN
rd. St Helens Park 541 F4
rd. Wedderburn 540 B9
rd. Wedderburn 541 F11
WEDDIN
pl. Ruse 512 F7
WEDDLE
av. Abbotsford 343 B3
av. Chiswick 343 B3
WEDGE
pl. Lurnea 394 C7
WEDGEWOOD
cr. Beacon Hill 257 G8
rd. The Oaks 502 J1
WEDMORE
la. Emu Heights, off Wedmore Rd 235 A5
rd. Emu Heights 235 A5
wy. Canley Vale 366 D5
WEEDON
av. Paddington 13 A16
rd. Artarmon 285 A14
WEEKES
av. Rookwood 340 B12
la. Newtown 17 F11
rd. Clontarf 287 H15
WEEKS
pl. Narellan Vale 508 J1
WEELSBY PARK
dr. Cawdor 505 E16
WEEMALA
av. Doonside 243 B14
av. Kirrawee 490 J2
av. Riverwood 399 K16
cr. Bradbury 511 H14
rd. Duffys Frst 195 A3
rd. Northbridge 286 F16
rd. Pennant Hills 220 F16
rd. Terrey Hills 195 A3
st. Chester Hill 338 B16
st. Northmead 277 K3
WEEM FARM
rd. Grose Vale 84 G16
WEENA
rd. Kurrajong Hl 55 A15
WEENAMANA
pl. Padstow 429 G2
WEENEY
st. Beverley Pk 433 C11
st. Kurnell 464 C16
WEERONA
pl. Caringbah 492 D14
WEEROONA
av. Elanora Ht 228 F1
av. Woollahra 22 D1
pl. Dundas 279 H15
pl. Rouse Hill 185 C5
rd. Edensor Pk 363 G1
rd. Lidcombe 369 H2
rd. Rookwood 340 E16
rd. Rookwood 340 F14
rd. Strathfield 340 F14
WEETA
st. Picton 561 D3
WEETALIBAH
rd. Northbridge 286 E15
WEETAWA
rd. Northbridge 286 D15
WEETAWAA
rd. Bilgola 169 J3
WEE WAA
cl. Hoxton Park 392 J7
WEGG
pl. Ambarvale 511 A14
WEHLOW
st. Mount Druitt 271 D1
WEIGAND
av. Bankstown 369 C15
WEIL
av. Croydon Pk 371 H8
WEIPA
cl. Green Valley 363 J11
WEIR
cr. Lurnea 394 F10
pl. Kings Lngly 246 A10
rd. Warragamba 353 F8
WEISEL
pl. Willmot 210 D12
WEJA
cl. Prestons 422 J1
WELBY
st. Eastwood 281 E8
tce. Acacia Gdn 214 G14
WELCH
av. Greenacre 370 A10
pl. Minto 452 K15
st. North Manly 258 B14
WELCOME
st. Wakeley 334 H13
WELD
pl. Prestons 393 G8
WELDER
rd. Seven Hills 246 F15
WELDON
la. Woollahra 21 K2
st. Burwood 372 A2
WELFARE
av. Beverly Hills 400 K12
av. Narwee 400 K12
st. Homebush W 340 J6
WELHAM
st. Beecroft 250 E8
WELL
st. Ryde 311 G5
WELLAND
cl. Jamisontown 236 B15
WELLARD
pl. Bonnyrigg 364 A7
WELLBANK
st. Concord 341 J5
st. N Strathfield 341 E6
WELLE
cl. St Clair 299 H1
WELLER
pl. Rydalmere 279 F16
WELLERS
rd. Bargo 567 B1
WELLESLEY
cr. Kings Park 244 K3
pl. Green Valley 363 A10
rd. Pymble 253 E3
st. Pitt Town 92 J15
st. Summer Hill 373 D5
WELLGATE
av. Kellyville 185 F9
WELLING
dr. Mt Annan 479 F13
dr. Narellan Vale 508 F1
pl. Mt Pritchard 364 C10
WELLINGTON
av. Ingleburn 453 A8
la. Lavender Bay 5 E13
la. McMahons Pt 5 E13
la. Waterloo 19 G12
la. E Lindfield, off Wellington Rd 255 A12
pl. Bondi 377 J4
rd. Auburn 338 G8
rd. Auburn 339 C9
rd. Birrong 368 J3
rd. Chester Hill 368 B2
rd. Earlwood 403 B3
rd. E Lindfield 255 A12
rd. Hurstville 432 A1
rd. Ryde 312 H2
rd. Sefton 368 E2
rd. S Granville 338 G8
st. Bondi 377 K3
st. Bondi Beach 378 A2
st. Chippendale 19 C2
st. Croydon 342 E13
st. Mascot 405 F4
st. Narrabeen 229 A3
st. Riverstone 153 A16
st. Riverstone 182 H3
st. Rosebery 405 F4
st. Rozelle 344 E7
st. Sans Souci 462 J4
st. Wakeley 334 H13
st. Waterloo 19 C13
st. Woollahra 22 B1
WELLMAN
rd. Forestville 256 B6
WELLS
av. Tempe 404 A1
ct. Baulkham Hl 247 E5
st. Annandale 11 A16
st. Balmain 8 A8
st. Chifley 437 B5
st. Jamisontown 266 C5
st. Newtown 374 G11
st. Pitt Town 92 J9
st. Redfern 19 C7
st. S Granville 338 F2
st. Thornleigh 220 H13
WELLUMBA
st. Horngsea Pk 392 D15
WELLWOOD
av. Moorebank 396 B11
WELSFORD
st. Merrylands 307 C8
WELSH
pl. Narellan Vale 479 A16
WELSTED
st. S Windsor 150 H3
WELWYN
rd. Canley Ht 365 A3
rd. Hebersham 241 E8
WEMBLEY
av. Cmbrdg Pk 238 B7
WEMBURY
rd. St Ives 224 C6
WEMYSS
la. Surry Hills F E5
st. Enmore 16 F16
st. Marrickville 16 F16
WENBAN
la. Mosman, off Dugald Rd 317 D9
pl. Wetherill Pk 304 F14
rd. Glossodia 60 K4
rd. Glossodia 61 A4
WENDEN
av. Kellyville 215 H6
av. West Hoxton 392 A7
av. Newington, off Newington Bvd 310 C13
st. Fairfield 335 K14
WENDLEBURY
rd. Chipping Ntn 396 G3
WENDOUREE
st. Busby 363 G14
WENDOVER
st. Doonside 243 B10
WENDRON
cl. St Ives 224 G9
WENDY
av. Georges Hall 367 F10
av. Normanhurst 221 F11
cl. Cabramatta 365 E9
pl. Glenwood 215 D13
pl. Toongabbie 276 G8
WENKE
cr. Yagoona 368 H10
WENONA
la. N Sydney K J1
la. N Sydney 5 J5
WENTON
av. Liberty Gr 311 B11
WENTWORTH
av. Bnksmeadw 406 A8
av. Blakehurst 432 B15
av. Eastgardens 406 A8
av. East Killara 254 F8
av. Eastlakes 405 E7
av. Glenfield 424 C11
av. Hillsdale 406 A8
av. Mascot 405 E7
av. North Rocks 278 F3
av. Pagewood 406 A8
av. Pendle Hill 276 G14
av. Surry Hills F C7
av. Surry Hills 3 J12
av. Sydney F C7
av. Sydney 3 J12
av. Toongabbie 276 D9
av. Waitara 222 A2
av. Wentwthvle 276 G14
av. Wentwthvle 277 B16
dr. Camden S 507 A13
dr. Liberty Gr 311 C13
pde. Yennora 337 B10
pl. Belrose 226 C16
pl. Point Piper 14 K1
pl. Point Piper 347 E8
rd. Burwood 341 H16
rd. Eastwood 280 J9
rd. Ingleburn 423 B9
rd. Orchard Hills 266 K12
rd. Orchard Hills 267 A12
rd. Strathfield 371 H1
rd. Vaucluse 348 B3
rd. Vaucluse 348 C3
rd.n, Homebush 341 A5
rd.s, Homebush 341 A6
st. Auburn 309 C16
st. Bardwell Vy 403 C7
st. Birrong 368 J4
st. Caringbah 492 J14
st. Croydon Pk 372 A7
st. Dolans Bay 492 J14
st. Dover Ht 348 G15
st. Ermington 310 C1
st. Glebe 12 F12
st. Granville 308 K11
st. Greenacre 370 H7
st. Greenacre 370 J12
st. Manly 288 H10
st. Paddington 21 F3
st. Parramatta 308 D5
st. Petersham 15 F8
st. Point Piper 14 K2
st. Point Piper 347 E8
st. Randwick 22 C16
st. Randwick 377 A11
st. Tempe 404 B3
WENTWORTH PARK
rd. Glebe 12 E9
WEONGA
rd. Dover Ht 348 F10
WERAMBIE
st. Woolwich 314 H11
WERINGA
av. Cammeray 316 B4
WERNA
pl. Hornsby 221 F4
WERNICKE
cl. Prairiewood 335 A9
WEROMBI
rd. Brownlow Hl 475 G9
rd. Ellis Lane 476 B11
rd. Grasmere 506 C1
rd. Orangeville 444 A10
rd. Theresa Park 445 A12
rd. Werombi 443 D2
WEROMBIE
rd. Mt Colah 192 B4
WERONA
av. Abbotsford 342 J3
av. Clarmnt Ms 268 J1
av. Gordon 253
av. Killara 253
av. Padstow 429
av. Punchbowl 400
pl. Dharruk 241
rd. Riverview 314
st. Pennant Hills 220
WERRIBEE PARK
pl. Glen Alpine 510
WERRINGTON
rd. Werrington 239
WESCOE
pl. Cranebrook 207
WESLEY
pl. Cherrybrook 220
pl. Greystanes 306
pl. Horngsea Pk 392
st. Elanora Ht 198
st. Greenacre 370
st. Oatlands 279
st. Telopea 279
WESSEL
cl. Hinchinbrk 363
WESSEX
la. Wentwthvle 277
pl. Raby 451
WESSON
rd. W Pnnant Hl 249
WEST
av. Darlinghurst 4
cir. Blaxland 233
cl. Illawong 459
cr. Hurstville Gr 431
ct. Carlingford 279
dr. Bexley North 402
esp. Manly 288
la. Carlton 432
la. Darlinghurst 4
la. Randwick 407
la. St Marys 239
lk. Eveleigh 18
pde. Chatswd W 284
pde. Couridjah 564
pde. Denistone 281
pde. Eastwood 281
pde. Riverstone 182
pde. Roseville 284
pde. Thirlmere 564
pde. West Ryde 281
pl. Camden S 506
prm. Manly 288
st. Auburn 338
st. Balgowlah 287
st. Balgowlah 287
st. Blacktown 274
st. Blakehurst 432
st. Brookvale 258
st. Cammeray 315
st. Canley Vale 366
st. Carlton 432
st. Crows Nest 315
st. Croydon 342
st. Darlinghurst 4
st. Darlinghurst 4
st. Five Dock 342
st. Glenbrook 233
st. Guildford 337
st. Hurstville 432
st. Kingswood 237
st. Lewisham 15
st. Lurnea 394
st. Naremburn 315
st. N Sydney 5
st. Paddington 4
st. Parramatta 279
st. Petersham 15
st. Petersham 15
st. Pymble 253
st. S Hurstville 432
st. Strathfield 371
st. Waterloo 19
tce. Bankstown 399
WESTACOTT
la. Canley Vale, off Railway Pde 366
WESTALL
cl. Abbotsbury 333
WESTBANK
av. Emu Plains 235
WEST BOTANY
st. Arncliffe 403
st. Kogarah 433
st. Rockdale 403

STBOURNE
Thirlmere 565 B3
Petersham 16 B7
Stanmore 16 B7
Lindfield 284 D4
Artarmon 315 A5
Bexley 432 E3
Carlton 432 J9
Drummoyne 343 H1
Petersham 16 B7
St Leonards 315 A5
Stanmore 16 B7
STBROOK
Wahroonga 223 A5
Bickley Vale 505 F13
Cawdor 505 F13
Mt Hunter 504 K8
Beverly Hills 401 F13
STBURY
Grose Vale 84 H10
Chipping Ntn 396 E3
STCHESTER
Casula 395 A12
STCOMBE
Rooty Hill 272 B2
STCOTT
Oakhurst 241 J1
Eastlakes 405 J5
ST CRESCENT
McMahons Pt 5 D15
STELLA
Roselands 401 B7
ST END
Ultimo 12 H15
STERLY
Glenmore Pk 266 F13
STERN
Blaxland 234 A5
Camperdwn 18 B5
North Manly 258 C16
Blacktown 274 D5
Gladesville 312 G10
Gladesville 312 H8
Westleigh 220 H1
y.Auburn 309 C12
y.Blacktown 273 C14
y.Clarmnt Ms 269 B7
y.Eastern Ck 272 C11
y.Emu Plains 235 A12
y.Glenbrook 234 H15
y.Granville 308 C8
y.Greystanes 306 E3
y.Harris Park 308 C8
y.Homebush 341 A7
y.Homebush B 340 A1
y.Homebush W 340 A1
y.Huntingwd 273 C14
y.Jamisontown 265 G1
y.Lapstone 234 H15
y.Leonay 234 H15
y.Lidcombe 340 A1
y.Mays Hill 307 B4
y.Merrylands 307 B4
y.Minchinbury 271 C10
y.N Strathfield 341 A7
y.Orchard Hills 267 D8
y.Parramatta 308 C8
y.Prospect 275 B16
y.St Clair 270 A8
y.Silverwater 309 C12
y.S Penrith 266 D6
y.S Wntwthvle 307 B4
Castle Hill 218 H13
Kemps Ck 359 K13
Mcquarie Pk 282 C1
Chatswd W 284 G10
STERN DISTRIBUTOR
Pyrmont 12 E5
Sydney A C16
Sydney 1 D16
STFIELD
Eastgardens 406 F11
Blacktown, off Flushcombe Rd 244 G16
Earlwood 402 E3
THALL
Claymore 481 B10
T HEAD
Krngai Ch NP 167 E13
Terrey Hills 196 G4
T HILL
Green Valley 362 J11
McGraths Hl 121 K11

WESTLAKE
pl. Balgowlah 287 G7
WESTLAND
cl. Raby 451 G13
WESTLEIGH
dr. Westleigh 220 D6
la. Neutral Bay 6 F4
st. Neutral Bay 6 F5
WEST MARKET
st. Richmond 118 F5
WESTMEATH
av. Killarney Ht 286 D1
WESTMINSTER
av. Carlingford 279 D5
av. Dee Why 258 H4
dr. Castle Hill 219 A12
rd. Gladesville 312 J6
st. Bexley 402 J11
st. Rooty Hill 242 A16
st. Schofields 183 C13
wy. Rsemeadow 540 J2
WESTMONT
dr. S Penrith 267 B1
WESTMOOR
gr. Wrrngtn Dns 238 A5
WESTMORE
dr. W Pnnant Hl 249 C11
WESTMORELAND
av. Collaroy 259 A1
la. Glebe 12 B14
rd. Leumeah 482 F9
rd. Minto 482 F9
st. Glebe 12 B15
WESTON
av. Narwee 400 H11
la. Rooty Hill 242 C16
pl. West Hoxton 392 A10
rd. Hurstville 431 K1
st. Balmain East 8 H9
st. Dulwich Hill 373 D7
st. Fairfield 336 G13
st. Harris Park 308 F6
st. Panania 428 C1
st. Revesby 428 E1
st. Rosehill 308 F6
WESTRINGIA
pl. Gymea Bay 491 J10
pl. Mcquarie Fd 454 D3
WESTVILLE
pl. Westmead 307 E2
WESTWARD
av. Shalvey 210 J12
st. Kareela 461 C11
WEST WILCHARD
rd. Castlereagh 176 A7
WESTWOOD
av. Belmore 401 H2
pl. Theresa Park 445 B8
st. Bossley Park 334 D10
st. Pennant Hills 220 G13
st. Prairiewood 334 D10
wy. Bella Vista 246 D2
WETHERILL
cr. Bligh Park 150 B5
st. Croydon 372 E2
st. Croydon 372 E3
st. Leichhardt 10 A16
st. Narrabeen 229 A9
st. Smithfield 335 A6
st. Wetherill Pk 335 A6
st.n, Silverwater 309 J15
st.s, Lidcombe 309 J16
WETSTONE
wy. Dural 219 C6
WEWAK
pl. Allambie Ht 257 F13
pl. Bossley Park 333 K5
rd. Holsworthy 396 C16
WEXFORD
gr. Kellyville 185 C16
pl. Killarney Ht 255 K13
WEYLAND
st. Punchbowl 399 J7
WEYMOUTH
av. Auburn 338 J9
WEYNTON
la. Annandale 11 A7
mw. Bella Vista 246 G5
st. Annandale 11 B8
WHADDON
av. Dee Why 258 E6

WHALAN
pl. Gymea 491 G1
pl. Whalan 240 K10
WHALANS
rd. Greystanes 305 G8
WHALE
pl. Woodbine 481 K9
WHALE BEACH
rd. Avalon 140 D12
rd. Palm Beach 140 B2
rd. Whale Beach 140 B7
WHALING
rd. N Sydney 5 K9
WHARF
rd. Birchgrove 7 K2
rd. Ermington 280 H15
rd. Gladesville 312 H13
rd. Kogarah Bay 432 J14
rd. Lansvale 367 A10
rd. Lilyfield 10 B4
rd. Longueville 314 B9
rd. Melrose Pk 280 H15
rd. Vaucluse 318 F16
rd. Cremorne Pt, off Cremorne Rd 316 G15
st. Brooklyn 75 F11
st. Marrickville 403 E1
WHARF HOUSE STEPS
The Rocks B B1
WHATELEY
la. Newtown 17 H11
st. Newtown 17 J11
WHATMORE
la. Waverton, off Bay Rd 315 E12
st. Waverton 315 D12
WHEAT
pl. Horngsea Pk 392 E15
rd. Sydney C A11
WHEATLEIGH
st. Crows Nest 315 G4
st. Naremburn 315 G4
WHEATLEY
pl. Harringtn Pk 478 G7
rd. Hawksbry Ht 174 E7
rd. Yarrawarrah 489 E15
st. St Johns Pk 364 J2
WHEEDON
st. Glenwood 215 H14
WHEELER
av. Camden S 507 C16
av. Lurnea 394 C10
la. N Sydney K A6
la. Surry Hills, off Brumby St 19 H3
pde. Dee Why 258 K8
pl. Minto 453 B16
st. Carlton 432 K8
st. Lalor Park 245 C13
st. Narrabeen 228 F9
WHEENEY
rd. Kurrajong 84 J5
WHEENY
st. Cattai 65 B6
WHELAN
av. Chipping Ntn 396 A5
av. Rookwood 340 E14
la. Paddington 21 G3
WHELLER
st. Bossley Park 334 D8
WHERRITT
cl. Picton 563 F10
WHIBLEY
av. Glenwood 215 J13
WHIDDON
cl. Denham Ct 422 C8
WHIMBREL
av. Hinchinbrk 393 D1
pl. Woronora Ht 489 E4
wy. Glenmore Pk 266 B13
WHIPBIRD
av. Ingleburn 453 G9
la. St Clair, off Whipbird Pl 270 J14
pl. Castle Hill 219 B10
pl. Erskine Park 270 J14
pl. Green Valley 363 E9
WHISSON
cl. Abbotsbury 333 D12
WHISTLER
av. Ingleburn 453 F10
cr. Erskine Park 270 K14
la. St Clair, off Whistler Cr 271 A14
st. Green Valley 363 E9
st. Manly 288 G9
WHITAKER
rd. Rossmore 389 F7
st. Old Guildford 337 C9
st. Yennora 337 C9
WHITBAR
wy. Cherrybrook 219 B12
WHITBECK
la. Cranebrook, off Whitbeck Pl 207 G11
pl. Cranebrook 207 F11
WHITBREAD
pl. North Rocks 278 C7
WHITBY
rd. Kings Lngly 245 F7
WHITCROFT
pl. Oxley Park 270 D2
pl. Thornleigh 220 K10
WHITE
av. Bankstown 399 C4
av. Maroubra 407 D15
la. Paddington 13 C15
pde. St Marys 270 A3
pl. Bossley Park 334 C5
pl. Castle Hill 217 J13
pl. Rooty Hill 272 D3
pl. S Windsor 120 K16
rd. Pagewood 406 G6
st. Artarmon 284 H16
st. Artarmon 284 J16
st. Balgowlah 287 G9
st. Balmain 7 A6
st. Brookvale 257 K12
st. Jannali 460 H12
st. Lilyfield 10 G12
st. Randwick 377 A9
st. Strathfield 341 J11
wy. Casula 424 F3
WHITE CEDAR
dr. Castle Hill 217 F16
WHITECHAPEL
cl. Ambarvale 510 K16
WHITE CLIFFS
av. Hoxton Park 392 F8
WHITE CROSS
rd. Winmalee 173 E4
WHITEFRIARS
wy. Winston Hills 276 H1
WHITEGATES
av. Peakhurst 430 C8
rd. Londonderry 178 B4
WHITE GUM
pl. Greystanes 306 C4
pl. Kellyville 185 H8
WHITEHALL
rd. Kenthurst 187 A5
st. Kellyville 215 B2
st. Stanhpe Gdn 215 B2
WHITEHAVEN
av. Quakers Hill 213 H9
pl. Castle Hill 217 H16
rd. Northmead 277 H6
st. St Ives 224 F7
WHITEHEAD
ct. Glendenning 242 F8
WHITEHORSE
st. Newtown 17 F15
WHITELEY
cl. Casula 424 C4
WHITEMAN
av. Bella Vista 246 H2
la. Ellis Lane 476 C11
WHITEMORE
av. Georges Hall 367 H11
WHITES
av. Caringbah 492 G15
la. Darlinghurst 4 G11
rd. Glenorie 128 C8
rd. Shanes Park 209 F5
WHITES CREEK
la. Annandale 16 E3
WHITESIDE
st. North Ryde 282 E5
WHITES RIDGE
rd. Annangrove 156 B14
WHITEWOOD
pl. Caringbah 492 K10
WHITFIELD
av. Ashbury 372 F7
av. Beverly Hills 400 K16
av. Lane Cove W 283 F12
pde. Hurstville Gr 431 H12
pl. Picton 563 E6
WHITFORD
rd. Green Valley 363 E12
rd. Hinchinbrk 393 C5
WHITING
st. Artarmon 314 J2
st. Leichhardt 9 E12
st. Regents Pk 369 E1
WHITING BEACH
rd. Mosman 317 A13
WHITLAM
av. Edensor Pk 333 H13
sq. Darlinghurst 4 A9
sq. Surry Hills 4 A9
sq. Sydney F F3
WHITLEY
pl. Abbotsbury 332 K14
WHITLING
av. Castle Hill 217 K15
WHITMONT
cr. St Ives Ch 224 B1
WHITMORE
rd. Maraylya 94 A12
rd. Maraylya 94 A13
WHITNEY
st. East Killara 254 K8
st. Mona Vale 198 H2
WHITSUNDAY
cct. Green Valley 362 J11
WHITTAKER
st. Mortlake 312 A13
WHITTALL
st. Russell Lea 343 E7
WHITTELL
st. Surry Hills 20 C4
WHITTIER
st. Quakers Hill 213 G16
WHITTLE
av. Balgowlah 287 E10
av. Milperra 397 F9
WHITTON
pl. Bligh Park 150 H5
pl. Doonside 273 E3
rd. Chatswd W 284 G11
st. Heathcote 518 F12
WHITWORTH
pl. Raby 451 F16
st. Westmead 307 F5
WHORLONG
st. St Helens Park 541 A7
WHYALLA
cl. Wakeley 334 J13
pl. Prestons 393 H8
WIAK
rd. Jannali 460 H10
WIANAMATTA
dr. Cartwright 394 A5
WIBLEN
st. Silverwater 309 J12
WICK
pl. St Andrews 481 K5
WICKFIELD
cct. Ambarvale 511 A12
WICKHAM
la. Avalon 170 B2
st. Arncliffe 403 H9
WICKLOW
pl. Killarney Ht 255 K14
pl. Rouse Hill 185 B6
st. Bidwill 211 C16
WICKS
av. Marrickville 373 E14
la. Kogarah, off South St 433 B4
rd. Mcquarie Pk 282 F11
rd. North Ryde 282 F11
WIDE BAY
cct. Bidwill 211 F14
WIDEMERE
rd. Wetherill Pk 304 K14
WIDEVIEW
rd. Berowra Ht 133 C7
WIDGIEWA
rd. Northbridge 286 D14
WIGAN
rd. Dee Why 258 E3
WIGENS
av. Como 460 D5

Narwee 400 F15
Newtown 17 G12
Newtown 17 H11
North Ryde 282 D7
Panania 398 B16
St Marys 269 D4
Strathfield 340 J16
Woolmloo 4 F4
Blaxland 233 E4
Blaxland 233 H7
SONS
Arncliffe 403 B9
SONS RD LOWER
Bardwell Vy 403 A8
SONS ROAD UPPER
Bardwell Vy 403 B9
TON
Castle Hill 217 K16
Gordon 253 G4
Georges Hall 367 G9
Appin 569 B16
Doonside 243 B9
Wilton 568 K16
Narellan 478 F12
Surry Hills 19 J5
Wilton 568 K16
Bonnyrigg 363 K5
TONA
Girraween 275 K10
TSHIRE
Liberty Gr 311 B11
Cherrybrook, off
Glamorgan Wy 219 E9
Turramurra 222 J8
The Slopes 56 K6
Miller 393 H3
Minto 482 E3
IBLEDON
N Narrabeen 228 J3
Wattle Grove 426 B5
IBOW
S Windsor 150 E3
IANI
Belrose 225 J13
IBOURNE
Airds 511 K15
Brookvale 258 B10
Mulgoa 295 C16
West Ryde 280 F11
West Ryde 280 G13
West Ryde 280 G11
IBURN
Kingsford 376 D15
IBURNDALE
Wakeley 334 F14
ICHCOMBE
Haberfield 343 C15
Castle Hill 218 E13
ICHESTER
Lindfield 283 J5
Clovelly, off
Winchester Rd 377 J11
Clovelly 377 J12
Carlton 432 J7
ICHMORE
Merrylands 307 G16
IDAM
Westleigh 220 D8
IDAMERE
Woodcroft 243 F10
IDARRA
Wahroonga 221 K7
Castle Hill 217 D6
Cromer 258 B1
Narwee 400 H12
IDERMERE
Cmbrdg Pk 237 J10
Miranda 492 C3
Northmead 278 B3
Panania 398 D14
Collaroy Plat 228 D10
Epping 250 J12
IDERS
Revesby 398 H15
IDEYER
Gladesville 313 A10
N Parramatta 279 A6
Thirlmere 565 C2
Woolmloo 4 H5
DHOVER
Bella Vista 246 E6
DLE
Hoxton Park 392 J7

pl. Menai 458 E15
WINDMILL
cl. Seven Hills 275 C6
pl. Wrrngtn Dns 237 K3
st. Dawes Point .... A C1
st. Dawes Point 1 E9
st. Millers Pt .... A B1
st. Millers Pt .... A C1
st. Millers Pt 1 D9
WINDMILL STEPS
Millers Pt .... A C1
WINDORRA
av. Glenmore Pk 266 G13
WINDRUSH
av. Belrose 225 J11
cct. St Clair 269 J15
la. St Clair, off
Windrush Cct 269 K14
WINDSOR
av. Carlingford 279 B6
av. Croydon Pk 371 J8
ct. Castle Hill 219 A11
dr. Mcquarie Pk 282 D2
la. Paddington 13 F15
la. Dulwich Hill, off
Weston St 373 E6
pde. N Narrabeen 228 K2
pl. Bargo 567 C4
pl. St Ives Ch 223 J5
rd. Baulkham Hl 247 G10
rd. Box Hill 184 C1
rd. Castle Hill 247 E1
rd. Cecil Hills 362 K3
rd. Cronulla 493 J16
rd. Dulwich Hill 373 C8
rd. Kellyville 215 E1
rd. Kellyville 217 A14
rd. McGraths Hl 121 G10
rd. Merrylands 307 G12
rd. Northmead 277 K7
rd. Padstow 429 D2
rd. Richmond 119 E7
rd. Riverstone 184 C1
rd. Rouse Hill 184 C1
rd. Vineyard 152 A1
rd. Willoughby 285 J13
rd. Windsor 121 G10
st. Mcquarie Fd 423 K16
st. Matraville 436 K1
st. Paddington 13 F16
st. Paddington 21 G1
st. Richmond 118 J5
wy. West Pymble 253 A12
WINDWARD
av. Mosman 317 F9
WINES
st. Emu Plains 235 G9
WINESHOP
rd. Oakdale 500 J12
WINFORD
dr. Mulgrave 121 K15
WING
pde. Homebush B 310 A15
pde. Newington 310 A15
WINGADAL
pl. Point Piper 14 H1
WINGADEE
pl. Windsor Dn 150 F16
st. Lane Cove W 284 B16
WINGARA
gr. Belrose 225 H15
st. Chester Hill 338 A15
WINGARIE
pl. Berowra Ht 133 C7
WINGATE
av. Eastwood 281 A6
av. West Hoxton 391 J11
pl. Guildford W 336 H1
rd. Mulgrave 121 J14
WINGELLO
rd. Miranda 492 B1
st. Guildford 337 F6
WINGHAM
rd. Hoxton Park 392 H10
WINGROVE
av. Epping 250 G12
WINIFRED
av. Caringbah 492 F6
av. Epping 281 E3
cr. Blacktown 245 A16
st. Condell Park 398 H5
WINIFRED FALLS FIRE
trl. Royal N P 521 A11

WINJEEL
av. Richmond 119 K3
WINKIN
av. Gymea Bay 491 E11
WINKURRA
st. Kensington 376 B10
WINNA
pl. Glenmore Pk 266 B7
WINNALEAH
st. West Hoxton 392 C7
WINNALL
pl. Ashcroft 364 E14
WINNICOOPA
rd. Blaxland 233 F4
WINNIE
st. Cremorne 316 E7
WINNIFRED
rd. McGraths Hl 121 K10
WINNIPEG
st. Seven Hills 275 G6
WINNOW DOWN
la. Cobbitty 446 A16
WINNUNGA
rd. Dural 158 D10
rd. Lilli Pilli 522 G3
rd. Middle Dural 158 D10
WINPARA
cl. Tahmoor 565 H8
WINSFORD
av. Hebersham 241 E5
WINSLEA
av. Frenchs Frst 257 B4
WINSLOW
av. Castle Hill 217 C6
av. Stanhpe Gdn 215 D11
la. Milsons Point 6 B13
st. Milsons Point 6 A13
WINSOME
av. N Balgowlah 287 E6
av. Plumpton 241 J9
WINSPEAR
av. Bankstown 369 C16
WINSTANLEY
pl. Mt Pritchard 364 K9
WINSTON
av. Bass Hill 368 C6
av. Cammeray 316 D4
av. Earlwood 372 G15
av. Guildford W 336 H1
cl. Badgerys Ck 358 D3
ct. Baulkham Hl 248 A8
pl. Narellan Vale 479 B11
pl. Sylvania 462 A10
st. Asquith 192 A11
st. Marsfield 282 B5
st. Penrith 236 H14
WINTAROO
cr. St Helens Park 541 G1
WINTEN
dr. Glendenning 242 G3
WINTER
av. Kellyville 216 A4
av. Neutral Bay 6 A3
pl. Blacktown 274 J9
pl. Oatley 431 B14
rd. Springwood 203 B2
st. Telopea 279 F11
WINTERCORN
row. Wrrngtn Dns 237 J4
WINTERGREEN
pl. W Pnnant Hl 248 J3
WINTHINGTON
pky. Denistone 281 C11
WINTON
av. Edensor Pk 333 J14
av. Northmead 248 C15
cl. Wedderburn 540 E12
st. Appin 569 F9
st. Warrawee 222 G12
WIRANDA
ct. Windsor Dn 151 A14
WIRE
la. Camden S 507 A16
la. Cawdor 506 E14
la. Freemns Rch 88 K5
la. N Richmond 88 K5
WIREGA
av. Kingsgrove 401 G7
WIRILDA
wy. Blacktown 274 E11

WIRRA
cl. Edensor Pk 333 F16
cl. St Ives 224 D16
pl. Glenorie 128 C4
WIRRABARA
rd. Dural 188 H11
WIRRALEE
st. S Wntwthvle 306 K7
WIRRALIE
av. Baulkham Hl 247 A7
WIRRAWAY
pl. Doonside 273 F4
st. Raby 451 D13
WIRREANDA
cl. Warrawee 222 E13
rd. Ingleside 197 B8
rd.n, Ingleside 197 C6
WIRRILDA
wy. Forestville 256 A12
WIRRINA
pl. N Narrabeen 198 H13
WIRRINDA
rd. Mt Krng-gai 162 H6
WIRRINGULLA
av. Elvina Bay 168 C3
WIRRINYA
pl. Grasmere 505 H4
WIRRUNA
st. Blacktown 244 A10
WIRUNA
cr. Narwee 400 K14
cr. Newport 169 G14
WISBEACH
la. Balmain 7 B11
st. Balmain 7 A10
WISDOM
la. Darlinghurst 4 E8
rd. Greenwich 314 K5
st. Annandale 10 J12
st. Connells Pt 431 H15
st. Currans Hill 479 J12
st. Guildford W 336 K3
st. S Coogee 407 J5
wy. Connells Pt 431 H15
WISE
st. Maroubra 407 A11
st. Rozelle 7 A12
WISEMAN
rd. Castle Hill 247 G1
WISEMANS FERRY
rd. Cattai 64 F16
rd. Cattai 64 G7
rd. S Maroota 65 C5
WISHART
rd. Kemps Ck 359 E15
st. Eastwood 281 F7
WISTARIA
pl. Baulkham Hl 247 F15
pl. Blacktown 245 A9
st. Dolans Bay 492 J16
WISTERIA
cl. Glenmore Pk 265 G10
cr. Cherrybrook 219 K6
cr. Stanhpe Gdn 215 C11
pl. Villawood 337 A15
WISTON
gdn. Double Bay 14 B6
WITCOM
st. Cranebrook 207 C11
WITHAM
pl. Chipping Ntn 366 H14
WITHECOMBE
st. Rozelle, off
Belmore St 344 E8
WITHERS
la. Kurrajong Ht 54 B7
la. Surry Hills 20 A2
pl. Abbotsbury 333 B11
pl. Surry Hills 20 B2
rd. Kellyville 185 K11
rd. Rouse Hill 184 J4
st. Arncliffe 403 D11
st. Chiswick 343 D1
wy. Claymore 481 D12
WITHNELL
cr. St Helens Park 541 B9
WITHYBROOK
pl. Sylvania 462 A12
WITLEY
cl. St Marys 269 K7

WITNEY
st. Prospect 274 G9
WITONGA
cr. Baulkham Hl 248 C10
WITT
cl. Edensor Pk 333 J12
WITTAMA
dr. Glenmore Pk 266 C7
WITTENOOM
pl. Yarrawarrah 489 H13
WOBURN
pl. Glenmore Pk 266 F10
WOBURN ABBEY
ct. Wattle Grove 425 K5
WODROW
pl. Rooty Hill 241 K13
WOIDS
av. Allawah 432 D7
av. Carlton 432 D7
av. Hurstville 432 D7
WOKARI
st. Engadine 489 C10
WOLARA
av. Glenmore Pk 266 D8
WOLAROI
cr. Revesby 399 B10
cr. Tamarama 378 B7
WOLBAH
pl. Cromer 228 A11
WOLDHUIS
st. Quakers Hill 214 E15
WOLF
cl. St Clair 269 H15
WOLFE
rd. East Ryde 283 B14
WOLGER
la. Mosman 316 J8
rd. Mosman 316 K8
rd. Ryde 282 A14
st. Como 460 F8
WOLI
pl. Malabar 437 F8
WOLLABI
cr. Glenmore Pk 266 A11
WOLLATON
gr. Oakhurst 241 H2
WOLLEMI
ct. Wattle Grove 426 B3
gr. Kellyville 215 B1
pl. Dural 219 A4
pl. Kurrajong Ht 53 E3
WOLLI
av. Earlwood 402 D8
av. Earlwood 402 E7
pl. Greenacre 370 F9
st. Kingsgrove 402 B10
WOLLI CREEK
rd. Arncliffe 403 A10
rd. Banksia 403 A10
WOLLOMBI
rd. Bilgola 169 J5
rd. Northbridge 286 F16
WOLLOMOMBI
wy. Hoxton Park 392 H6
WOLLONDILLY
pl. Sylvania Wtr 462 G14
WOLLONGBAR
av. Panania 428 F2
WOLLONGONG
rd. Arncliffe 403 B10
WOLLSTONECRAFT
av. Avalon 140 B15
WOLLUN
st. Como 460 G8
WOLLYBUTT
rd. Engadine 488 H12
WOLSELEY
cr. Point Piper 347 E7
gr. Zetland 375 K9
pl. Ingleburn 453 H12
rd. Coogee 407 H3
rd. Lindfield 254 B15
rd. McGraths Hl 122 C11
rd. Mosman 317 D9
rd. Oakville 122 C11
rd. Point Piper 14 J1
rd. S Coogee 407 H4
st. Bexley 433 A3
st. Drummoyne 313 J16
st. Fairfield 335 K15
st. Fairfield 336 B15

st. Guildford 338 D4
st. Haberfield 342 K13
st. Jamisontown 265 K2
st. Merrylands 338 D3
st. Rooty Hill 242 A13
WOLSLEY
av. Riverstone 183 B12
WOLSTEN
av. Turramurra 223 A10
WOLSTENHOLME
av. Greendale 385 H6
av. Gymea 491 F2
WOLUMBA
st. Chester Hill 338 B13
WOLVERTON
av. Chipping Ntn 366 E15
pl. Bringelly 388 H8
pwy. Chipping Ntn, off Wolverton Av 366 E14
WOMBERRA
pl. S Penrith 266 H3
WOMBEYAN
ct. Wattle Grove 395 H12
pl. Leumeah 482 D14
st. Forestville 255 K7
WOMBIDGEE
av. St Clair 269 H8
WOMBOYNE
av. Kellyville 216 F3
WOMERAH
av. Darlinghurst 4 J11
la. Darlinghurst 4 K10
st. Turramurra 222 K15
WOMRA
cr. Glenmore Pk 266 A11
la. Glenmore Pk 266 B10
WONAWONG
st. Belimbla Pk 501 F14
WONDABAH
pl. Carlingford 249 H13
WONDAKIAH
dr. Wollstncraft 315 D11
WONDERLAND
av. Tamarama 378 B6
WONGA
la. Canterbury 372 C12
pl. Ingleburn 453 F7
rd. Cremorne 316 E4
rd. Lalor Park 245 J11
rd. Lurnea 394 B13
rd. Lurnea 394 F8
rd. Miranda 491 K9
rd. Mt Colah 192 D2
rd. Picton 563 F15
rd. Yowie Bay 491 K9
st. Canterbury 372 D13
st. N Balgowlah 287 C4
st. Strathfield 371 G1
WONGAJONG
cl. Castle Hill 218 F10
WONGALA
av. Elanora Ht 198 C16
cr. Beecroft 250 F5
cr. Pennant Hills 250 F2
WONGALARA
pl. Woodcroft 243 H12
WONGALEE
av. Wahroonga 251 H1
WONGAWILLI
st. Couridjah 564 G16
WONGA WONGA
st. Turramurra 222 K12
WONIORA
av. Wahroonga 222 D6
rd. Blakehurst 432 C9
rd. Hurstville 431 J5
rd. S Hurstville 432 C9
WONNAI
pl. Clarmnt Ms 268 G1
WONOONA
pde.e, Oatley 431 C11
pde.w, Oatley 431 A11
WONSON
st. Wilton 568 K16
WOOD
cl. Green Valley 362 J8
ct. Mt Annan 479 G14
la. Cronulla 493 K15
la. Randwick 377 C12
pl. Emu Plains 235 F13
st. Ashfield 372 J2
st. Bexley 432 G2
st. Chatswd W 284 D9
st. Eastwood 281 F3
st. Fairfield 336 C8
st. Forest Lodge 11 F15
st. Lane Cove W 313 G2
st. Manly 288 H12
st. Picton 563 E13
st. Randwick 377 C12
st. Richmond 119 K3
st. Tempe 404 C2
st. Thornleigh 221 A14
st. Waverton 315 E13
WOODBERRY
rd. Winston Hills 277 B3
WOODBINE
av. Normanhurst 221 G7
cr. Ryde 282 C15
st. N Balgowlah 287 D4
st. Yagoona 369 C10
WOODBRIDGE
rd. Menangle 538 B16
WOODBROOK
rd. Casula 395 B11
WOODBURN
av. Panania 428 D1
ct. Glenbrook 234 B15
pl. Glenhaven 187 H15
rd. Berala 339 D12
rd. Kurrajong 85 E2
rd. Lidcombe 339 E10
st. Redfern 19 B5
WOODBURY
rd. St Ives 224 C8
st. Marrickville 373 H11
st. North Rocks 248 H16
WOODCHESTER
cl. Castle Hill 217 H8
WOODCLIFF
pde. Lugarno 430 B14
WOODCOCK
pl. Lane Cove W 283 F16
WOODCOURT
rd. Berowra Ht 133 B6
st. Ambarvale 540 F2
st. Marrickville 373 G11
WOODCREST
av. Ingleburn 453 G9
pl. Cherrybrook 219 J14
WOODCROFT
dr. Woodcroft 243 F8
WOODD
rd. Denham Ct 452 G2
WOODFIELD
av. Bundeena 523 F10
bvd. Caringbah 492 K2
pl. Castle Hill 248 H2
pl. Lalor Park 245 E12
WOODFORD
cl. Jamisontown 266 C5
cr. Heathcote 519 A12
la. Lindfield 284 C1
rd. Rockdale 403 C12
st. Longueville 314 F7
st. Northwood 314 F7
WOODFULL
ct. Rouse Hill 185 A9
WOODGATE
cr. Cranebrook 207 E12
WOODGLEN
pl. Cherrybrook 219 C8
WOODGROVE
av. Castle Hill 219 B11
av. Cherrybrook 219 B11
WOODHILL
st. Castle Hill 248 B2
WOODHOUSE
dr. Ambarvale 511 A12
WOODI
cl. Glenmore Pk 266 B9
WOODLAKE
ct. Wattle Grove 395 K16
WOODLAND
av. Oxley Park 270 E2
cr. Narellan 478 J9
pl. Newington, off Newington Bvd 310 C12
rd. Annangrove 186 B1
rd. Bradbury 541 C1
rd. Chester Hill 337 K12
rd. St Helens Park 541 C1
st. Coogee 377 G13
st. Marrickville 374 B10
st. Riverstone 153 C14
st.n, Balgowlah 287 J8
st.s, Balgowlah 287 H11
st.s, Balgowlah Ht 287 H13
WOODLANDS
av. Blakehurst 462 C4
av. Bossley Park 333 K11
av. Lugarno 430 A16
av. Narwee 400 K11
av. Pymble 253 G2
dr. Glenmore Pk 265 J12
la. Glenmore Pk, off Woodlands Dr 265 J13
rd. Ashbury 372 G6
rd. E Lindfield 254 J16
rd. Forestville 255 J9
rd. Liverpool 364 K16
rd. Taren Point 462 J12
rd. Wilberforce 62 F11
st. Winston Hills 248 A15
WOODLARK
pl. Castle Hill 219 B11
pl. Glenfield 424 F14
st. Rozelle 10 H1
WOODLAWN
av. Earlwood 402 E7
dr. Toongabbie 276 D5
WOODLEAF
cl. W Pnnant Hl 249 B1
WOODLEY
cr. Glendenning 242 E4
st. St Peters 374 K14
WOODMAN
pl. Abbotsbury 333 B16
WOODPARK
rd. Guildford W 306 E14
rd. Smithfield 305 G13
rd. Smithfield 306 E14
rd. Woodpark 306 E14
WOOD RIDGE
pl. Baulkham Hl 247 B10
WOODRIDGE
av. N Epping 251 H9
WOODRIFF
st. Penrith 236 G13
st.n, Penrith 236 J10
WOODRUSH
ct. Dural 219 C6
WOODS
av. Cabramatta 365 D9
av. Woollahra 22 C4
cl. Huntingwd 273 K12
la. Darlinghurst 4 D9
pde. Earlwood 373 B15
pde. Fairlight 288 D10
rd. Birrong 368 H6
rd. Sefton 368 H6
rd. S Windsor 150 E1
rd. Yagoona 368 G8
st. N Epping 251 G8
st. Riverstone 183 B7
WOODSIDE
av. Blacktown 243 J15
av. Hurlstone Pk 373 A10
av. Lindfield 254 D15
av. West Hoxton 392 B9
av. West Hoxton 392 D9
av.e, Burwood 341 J16
av.w, Strathfield 341 G15
gln. Cranebrook 207 B6
gr. Forestville 256 B8
WOODS RESERVE
rd. Grose Wold 115 A11
WOODSTOCK
av. Dharruk 241 A7
av. Glendenning 242 B12
av. Hebersham 241 E11
av. Mount Druitt 241 E11
av. Plumpton 241 E11
av. Rooty Hill 242 B12
av. Whalan 241 A7
la. Bondi Jctn, off Paul St 377 G3
rd. Carlingford 249 H15
st. Bondi Jctn 377 G3
st. Botany 405 G13
st. Guildford 337 J3
st. St Johns Pk 364 F4
WOODVALE
av. N Epping 251 G12
cl. Plumpton 241 K11
cl. St Ives 254 B2
pl. Castle Hill 218 D11
WOODVIEW
la. Oxley Park, off Woodview Rd 270 F2
rd. Oxley Park 270 F2
WOODVILLE
av. Wahroonga 222 E8
la. Hurstville, off Barratt St 432 A5
rd. Chester Hill 337 E15
rd. Fairfield E 337 E15
rd. Granville 308 A15
rd. Guildford 337 K6
rd. Merrylands 308 A15
rd. Old Guildford 337 E15
rd. Villawood 367 C3
st. Glenbrook 233 J16
st. Hurstville 432 A5
WOODWARD
av. Caringbah 492 K11
av. Strathfield 341 E14
cr. Miller 393 J2
pl. St Ives 254 F1
rd. Hunters Hill 313 H11
st. Cromer 227 J12
st. Ermington 280 B16
tce. Bella Vista 246 G3
WOODY
av. Morning Bay 138 E16
WOOL
pl. Miller 393 F4
WOOLCOTT
av. Wahroonga 221 K6
st. Earlwood 372 G16
st. Newport 169 G11
st. Waverton 5 A9
st. Waverton 315 E12
WOOLEY
la. Marrickville 373 H14
WOOLGEN PARK
rd. Leppington 420 G13
WOOLGOOLGA
av. Hoxton Park 392 J9
st. N Balgowlah 287 B4
WOOLISIA
pl. Baulkham Hl 247 G15
WOOLLEY
ct. Agnes Banks 117 F16
la. Glebe 11 K13
st. Glebe 12 A13
WOOLLSIA
ct. Voyager Pt 427 C6
WOOLLYBUTT
pl. Mcquarie Fd 454 E2
WOOLMERS
ct. Wattle Grove 425 H5
pl. Glen Alpine 510 D14
WOOLNOUGH
pl. Cartwright 394 B5
WOOLOOWARE
rd.n, Woolooware 493 F8
rd.s, Burraneer 493 E16
rd.s, Woolooware 493 E12
WOOLPACK
st. Elderslie 477 G16
WOOLRYCH
cr. Davidson 255 C1
WOOLSHED
pl. Currans Hill 480 A10
WOOLWASH
rd. Airds 512 A15
WOOLWICH
rd. Hunters Hill 313 K12
WOOLWONGA
pl. Bow Bowing 452 D14
WOOLYBUTT
pl. Mt Riverview 204 E15
WOOMBA
cl. Hornsby Ht 161 H12
WOOMBYE
cl. Berowra Ht 132 K6
WOOMERA
rd. Little Bay 437 A10
WOOMERA PATH
Winmalee 173 B9
WOONAH
st. Little Bay 437 B10
st. Miranda 492 C6
WOONGARA
wy. Glenhaven 218 D3
WOONGARRA
av. Chipping Ntn 396 B5
WOONONA
av. Wahroonga 222
av.n, Wahroonga 222
av.s, Wahroonga 222
rd. Northbridge 286
WOORAIL
av. Kingsgrove 402
WOORAK
cr. Miranda 491
rd. Palm Beach 139
WOORANG
st. Eastwood 281
st. Milperra 398
WOORARRA
av. Elanora Ht 228
av. N Narrabeen 228
WOOTTEN
rd. Ingleburn 422
st. Colyton 270
WORBOYS
pl. N St Marys 239
WORCESTER
pl. Turramurra 222
rd. Cmbrdg Pk 237
rd. Rouse Hill 184
st. Collaroy 229
WORDIE
pl. Padstow 399
WORDOO
st. St Marys 239
WORDSWORTH
av. Concord 341
av. Leumeah 512
pl. Sylvania 462
st. Wetherill Pk 334
WORKMAN
pl. Leonay 235
WORKS
pl. Greenacre 370
pl. Milperra 397
WORLAND
st. Yagoona 368
WORONORA
av. Leumeah 482
cr. Como 460
cr. Como 460
pde. Oatley 431
pl. St Clair 270
rd. Engadine 518
WORROBIL
st. N Balgowlah 287
WORSLEY
st. East Hills 427
WORTH
la. Blaxland 233
st. Chullora 369
st. Penrith 236
WORTHING
av. Castle Hill 218
pl. Cherrybrook 219
WORTLEY
av. Belmore 371
st. Balmain 7
WOYLIE
pl. St Helens Park 541
WRAY
st. Fairfield Ht 336
WRAYSBURY
pl. Oakhurst 241
WREN
ct. Castle Hill 219
ct. Woronora Ht 489
pl. Clarmnt Ms 268
pl. Greystanes 306
pl. Lugarno 429
pl. Thirlmere 565
pl. Woolooware 493
st. Condell Park 398
tce. Plumpton 242
WRENCH
pl. Kenthurst 157
st. Cmbrdg Pk 238
WRENTMORE
st. Fairfield 336
WRIDE
st. Maroubra 407
WRIGHT
cl. Georges Hall 367
cl. Heathcote 518
la. Surry Hills F
pl. Bligh Park 150
pl. Narellan Vale 479

rd. Thornleigh.........220 H15
rd. West Pymble......252 J10

YARRA VISTA
ct. Yarrawarrah.......489 G14

YARRAWA
st. Prestons...........393 B9

YARRAWIN
wy. Airds................512 D10

YARRAWONGA
cl. Pymble.............253 H3
st. S Windsor..........120 E16

YARREN
av. Btn-le-Sds.........403 K16

YARRENNAN
av. West Pymble......253 A10

YARROWEE
rd. Strathfield..........370 K1

YARRUNGA
st. Prestons...........393 A10

YARWOOD
la. Woollahra, off Fletcher St..........377 G2
rd. Bligh Park..........150 H5
st. Marsfield............281 K1

YASMAR
av. Haberfield..........343 C15

YASS
cl. Bossley Park......333 E11
cl. Frenchs Frst.......255 K4
pl. Prestons...........392 K16
pl. Quakers Hill.......244 B2

YATALA
rd. Mt Krng-gai........162 J6

YATAMA
st. Seaforth............287 C7

YATAY
cl. Plumpton...........242 D5

YATE
av. Mt Riverview......204 E14
cl. Kingswood.........267 J1
pl. Mcquarie Fd.......454 E3
pl. Marayong..........243 J6
pl. Narellan Vale......478 K15

YATES
av. Dundas Vy.........280 A9
cr. Padstow............429 F4
rd. Bangor..............459 H13

YATHONG
rd.n,Caringbah........493 A7
rd.s,Caringbah.........493 A10

YATTENDEN
cr. Baulkham Hl......247 H12

YAWL
pl. Seven Hills.........275 B5

YAWUNG
av. Baulkham Hl......246 H8
st. Dundas.............279 G13

YEATS
av. Killarney Ht........256 D16
st. Wetherill Pk.......334 K4

YEELANNA
pl. Kingswood.........267 G2

YEEND
st. Birchgrove............8 A4
st. Merrylands.........307 G9

YELL
pl. St Andrews........481 J5

YELLAMBIE
st. Yowie Bay..........492 A13

YELLOW
pl. Clarmnt Ms........238 G15

YELLOW GUM
cl. Glenmore Pk.......265 F11

YELLOWGUM
av. Rouse Hill..........185 A6
gr. Glenwood..........215 H16

YELLOW ROCK
rd. Yellow Rock.......204 G2

YELVERTON
st. Sydenham.........374 E15

YENA
st. Kurnell...............466 C9

YENDA
av. Queens Park........22 J13

YENGO
ct. Holsworthy........426 E5

YENNA
pl. Glenmore Pk.......266 B7

YENNORA
av. Yennora............337 A9
st. Campbelltwn......511 K6

YEO
av. Ashfield.............372 K7
la. Bexley...............402 H13
la. Neutral Bay...........6 F1
pl. Menai...............459 A12
st. Cremorne.............6 D1
st. Neutral Bay...........6 D1
st. Yagoona............368 J9

YEOMANS
rd. N Richmond.........86 H7

YERAMBA
av. Caringbah..........493 A15
cr. Berowra.............133 C14
pl. Rydalmere.........279 E15
st. Turramurra.........252 D3

YERAN
st. Sylvania.............462 C9

YERANDA
pl. Kenthurst...........187 K8

YEREVAN
pl. Belrose..............226 A12

YERONA
st. Prestons............423 B1

YERONG
pl. Castle Hill...........218 B8
st. Ryde..................311 H3

YERONGA
cl. St Johns Pk.......364 F1

YERRAWAR
pl. Springwood.......201 H4

YERRICK
rd. Lakemba............371 A13
rd. Lakemba............371 A14

YERRIEBAH
pl. Castle Hill..........218 A8

YERRINBOOL
cl. Prestons............392 K12

YERROULBIN
st. Birchgrove.........314 K16

YERTON
av. Hunters Hill........313 J12

YETHOLME
av. Baulkham Hl.......246 K9

YETHONGA
av. Lane Cove W......313 J1

YEW
pl. Casula...............424 A2
pl. Quakers Hill.......214 E13

YILKI
cl. Cranebrook........207 E8

YILLOWRA
st. Auburn..............309 C15

YIMBALA
st. Rydalmere.........279 J15

YINDELA
st. Davidson...........255 F3

YINDI
pl. Doonside...........243 G14

YINNELL
pl. Castle Hill..........218 C8

YIRAK
la. Como................460 G4

YIREMBA
pl. Forestville..........255 F10

YIRGELLA
av. East Killara.........254 G10

YIRRA
rd. Mt Colah............192 A5

YODALLA
av. Emu Plains.........235 G11
la. Emu Plains, off Yodalla Av.........235 G11

YONDELL
av. Springwood.......201 G9

YOOGALI
st. Merrylands.........306 J10
tce. Blaxland...........234 D7

YOORAMI
rd. Beverly Hills.......401 D12

YOORANA
pl. Castle Hill..........219 A8

YORK
av. Five Dock..........342 J11
cl. Yowie Bay..........492 B12
cr. Petersham..........16 A9
la. Glebe..................11 J13
la. Queens Park........22 C10
la. Sydney.................A F15
pl. Bondi Jctn...........22 C7
pl. Kensington.........376 C11
pl. Rozelle..............344 E6
rd. Bondi Jctn...........22 C8
rd. Ingleburn...........453 A4
rd. Jamisontown.....236 F16
rd. Kellyville............216 G2
rd. Queens Park........22 C10
rd. Riverstone.........182 D10
rd. S Penrith............266 E4
st. Beecroft.............250 D6
st. Belmore.............401 D2
st. Berala...............339 B13
st. Casula...............424 A3
st. Condell Park.......398 K1
st. Emu Plains.........235 K9
st. Epping...............251 E12
st. Fairfield.............336 D14
st. Gladesville.........312 G11
st. Glebe..................11 J14
st. Glenbrook...........234 B14
st. Kingsgrove.........401 K9
st. Marrickville.........374 C9
st. Merrylands.........307 H15
st. Oatlands............279 B9
st. Rockdale............403 E14
st. Sydney.................A F12
st. Sydney.................1 F15
st. Tahmoor.............565 J13
tce. Bilgola..............169 G8

YORKSHIRE
cl. Catherine Fd.......449 G1
st. Rosehill.............309 B9

YORKTOWN
pde. Maroubra..........407 C12

YORLIN
pl. Rouse Hill..........185 C5

YORREL
cl. Alfords Point......429 A15

YOSEFA
av. Warrawee..........222 F11

YOUL
pl. Bligh Park..........150 E5

YOUNG
cr. Frenchs Frst.......256 B3
la. Annandale............16 G3
la. Cremorne...........316 D8
la. Neutral Bay.........316 D8
la. Redfern................19 K7
la. Redfern................19 K9
pde. Eastwood.........281 C9
pl. Eagle Vale.........481 A10
pl. S Hurstville........431 K11
rd. Carlingford.........279 K1
st. Annandale............16 F4
st. Balmain.................7 B7
st. Chatswood.........284 J12
st. Colyton..............270 J8
st. Cremorne...........316 D6
st. Cremorne...........316 D8
st. Croydon.............342 E15
st. Kings Lngly.........245 E8
st. Mt Krng-gai........163 C11
st. Mt Pritchard.......364 E9
st. Neutral Bay...........6 G1
st. Neutral Bay.........316 D8
st. N Strathfield.......341 G9
st. Paddington..........13 A16
st. Parramatta.........307 J8
st. Penshurst...........431 C1
st. Randwick............406 K1
st. Redfern................19 J10
st. Sydney.................B D12
st. Sydney.................1 K14
st. Sylvania.............461 H10
st. Tempe...............404 B3
st. Vaucluse............348 F5
st. Wahroonga.........222 H9
st. Warrawee..........222 H9
st. Waterloo..............19 H15
st. N Strathfield, off Parramatta Rd....341 F9

YOUNGER
av. Earlwood...........372 K15

YOUTH
la. Burwood, off Deane St.........342 A14

YOWAN
cl. Bangor..............459 G13

YOWIE
av. Caringbah..........492 F12

YPRES
rd. Moorebank.........395 E12

YUGILBAR
av. Villawood...........367 D3

YUKKA
rd. Regents Pk........369 D3

YUKON
cl. Kearns..............481 A2
pl. Quakers Hill.......214 C9

YULAN
gr. Acacia Gdn........214 K15
rd. Narellan Vale.....479 A13

YULE
pl. Glenfield............424 G9
st. Dulwich Hill..........15 B16

YULONG
av. Terrey Hills........196 E7

YULUMA
cl. Bangor..............459 F13

YULUNGA
pl. Bradbury............511 C14

YUMA
pl. Bossley Park......333 K12

YUNGA
rd. Glenmore Pk......266 C9

YUNGABURRA
st. Villawood...........367 E5

YUNGANA
pl. Bangor..............459 F13

YUROKA
st. Glenmore Pk......266 D7
st. Glenmore Pk......266 D8

YURONG
la. Darlinghurst..........D K14
la. Darlinghurst..........4 C7
pky. Woolmloo............D K12
pky. Woolmloo............4 C6
st. Darlinghurst..........D J16
st. Darlinghurst..........F J2
st. Darlinghurst..........4 B10

YURREEL
cl. Bangor..............459 H13

YURUGA
av. Caringbah..........492 H12
av. Doonside...........243 B15
pl. Allambie Ht........257 D13
pl. Lindfield............283 J3
rd. Dural................188 D12
st. Beverly Hills.......400 G16

YURUNGA
st. Telopea.............279 E8

YVES
pl. Minchinbury.......272 B10

YVETTE
st. Baulkham Hl......247 K12

YVONNE
av. Hawksbry Ht......174 H2
cl. Cobbitty............448 A13
cr. Bass Hill............367 G8
cr. Georges Hall......367 G8
pl. Castle Hill..........248 C2
pl. N Richmond.........87 B14
st. Cabramatta W....364 H6
st. Greystanes.........306 G4
st. Seven Hills.........246 A11

Z

ZADRO
av. Bossley Park......333 H8

ZAHEL
la. Mosman............316 H4

ZAHRA
pl. Quakers Hill.......214 D13

ZAMBESI
rd. Seven Hills.........275 F9

ZAMBEZI
pl. Kearns..............450 K16
pl. Kearns..............451 A16

ZAMIA
st. Redfern................19 K10

ZAMMIT
av. Quakers Hill.......213 K10

ZANCO
rd. Marsfield............282 A2

ZANE
cl. Bella Vista..........246 E6

ZANITH
wy. Kellyville............186 K15

ZAPPIA
pl. Edensor Pk........363 J1

ZARA
cl. Cecil Hills...........362
rd. Willoughby.........285

ZARITA
av. Waverley...........377

ZARLEE
st. Fairfield W..........335

ZATOPEK
av. Newington, off Newington Bvd...310

ZEALANDER
st. Sandringham.....463

ZEBRA
pl. Quakers Hill.......214

ZELA
st. Mortdale............430

ZELDA
av. Wahroonga........222

ZELENY
rd. Minchinbury.......271

ZENITH
cl. Wakeley.............334
ct. Glenwood..........245

ZEOLITE
pl. Eagle Vale..........481

ZEPPELIN
st. Raby..................451

ZERAFA
pl. Quakers Hill.......214

ZERMATT
av. Seven Hills.........275

ZETA
cl. Oakdale..............500
rd. Lane Cove..........314

ZEYA
cl. St Clair...............269

ZIERIA
pl. Belrose..............225

ZIG ZAG
la. Crows Nest, off Albany St...........315

ZILLAH
st. Guildford............338
st. Merrylands.........338

ZINNIA
wy. Blacktown..........274

ZIONS
av. Malabar.............437

ZIRCON
pl. Bossley Park......334
pl. Eagle Vale..........481

ZODIAC
pl. Erskine Park.......270

ZOE
cl. Yennora.............336
pl. Mount Druitt......241

ZOELLER
st. Concord.............342

ZOLA
av. Ryde..................282

ZOLYOMI
la. Blacktown, off First Av...........244

ZONNEBEKE
cr. Milperra.............397

ZORIC
cl. Prestons............423

ZOUCH
rd. Denham Ct.........422

ZULFI
pl. Cherrybrook.......219

ZULLO
ct. Castle Hill..........217

ZUNI
cl. Bossley Park......333

ZUTTION
av. Beverly Hills.......401
la. Tempe, off Union St...........404

AIRPORTS / AIRFIELDS

BAYS, EACHES, ETC

s Creek 185 G8
s Creek 311 C3
leys Point............288 F14
s Creek 135 B13
s Creek 512 B8
Bay 7 K1
Creek 226 C7
er Island............344 D2
erman Beach......139 G2
ottom Point 429 E14
rs Point 139 C2
nerville Point........344 D3
Beach 169 D4
Creek............121 F8
Creek............238 J4
Creek............257 F4
Creek............299 E12
Creek............419 B10
Head 318 F9
West Arm 522 A10
West Arm Creek...521 A14
& Pigs Reef..........318 C10
acle Island............75 H3
acle Island 344 B1
rs Gully 503 E4
g Cove............288 H15
g Creek............503 G16
g Gully Creek 222 D4
n Beach 109 J13
Point............347 K1
reek 130 H16
reek 459 A8
s Point 139 G8
quarry Creek 563 G5
Creek 253 J5
Beach............288 H15
gers Creek 216 B6
gers Creek 282 J16
ybark Creek 283 G14
co Creek............309 D1
bag Creek 284 B7
loaf Bay 286 E8
loaf Creek 286 A11
loaf Point............286 G9
rland Point..........466 D4
es Creek............284 A11
ow Rock Reach......64 A6
y Cove............B E2
gai Gap 466 H15
s Creek 473 B15
rama Bay 378 C7
ourine Bay............314 B8
n Creek 313 E12
Point............462 K8
's Bay 317 D14
's Point 169 C1
ry Creek 220 D11
tation Creek.........490 H15
Creek 281 E3
asin 138 G4
asin 484 E11
asin 522 K12
g Gully 444 B12
g Gully 473 G4
obblers 524 E15
ap 318 G14
ong Swamp............125 K4
erries Reef............495 G7
ld Mans Hat 318 K4
onds Creek............279 H13
oit 287 C13
oolwash 132 E6
pson Creek 481 J5
psons Bay............460 E3
psons Creek............388 A13
Brothers Rocks...313 B15
s Weir 507 G10
glys Point 462 F5
abbie Creek............246 D16
rs Bay............138 G13
Beach 464 E5
Point............464 D4
Spit Beach............464 A6
ern Gully Creek ...194 F14
wa Rill............519 F10
Creek 513 K16
Creek 190 G7
Gully 264 F1

Turimetta Beach............199 F14
Turimetta Head 199 H12
Uhrs Point............311 G7
Vaucluse Bay............318 B16
Vaucluse Point............318 B15
Village Point 318 D15
Vineyard Creek............309 B2
Voodoo Point 496 A7
Waddells Gully............190 G1
Waitara Creek 191 A16
Walker Point............107 J2
Walls Gully 191 J3
Wallumatta Bay............313 D14
Walsh Bay............1 C6
Wanda Beach 494 E7
Wants Beach 520 F4
Wants Point............522 A1
Waratah Gully 133 H15
Warragamba Dam............353 B5
Warragamba River 353 D3
Warriewood Beach.......199 E10
Washaway Beach.........317 J1
Waterfall Gully 195 A9
Watsons Bay 318 E14
Wattle Creek 445 B10
Wattle Creek............473 C11
Wearne Bay 460 A2
Wedding Cake Island....408 A2
Weeney Bay 464 D12
Wentworth Point............311 C5
Werrington Creek.........238 C10
Werrington Lake 238 D10
West Head............109 E9
Whale Beach 140 C7
Wheeler Creek............227 G14
Wheeny Lagoon 65 B8
White Bay 7 K14
White Horse Point.......344 E3
Whites Creek............10 H12
Whitewater Channel 206 C12
Whiting Beach 316 K15
Wilberforce Reach 91 J13
Wildlife Island............366 K9
Wildlife Lagoon............93 K1
Willarong Point............492 C16
Williams Creek............427 A4
Willoughby Bay............316 E4
Willow Pond............22 A14
Windsor Reach 121 G5
Winson Bay............163 K5
Winson Gully 163 F5
Wirreanda Creek 197 B6
Wolli Creek............401 G11
Wollstonecraft Bay.......315 C12
Woodford Bay 314 F9
Woody Point 138 H14
Woollahra Point 347 G7
Woolloomooloo Bay 2 H15
Woolooware Bay..........463 F14
Woronora River 460 A16
Wrights Point 313 J14
Wudyong Point 6 G15
Wyargine Point............317 E2
Yacht Bay............314 C11
Yaralla Bay 311 G13
Yarra Bay 436 F10
Yarramundi Lagoon 116 K13
Yarra Point 436 G12
Yatala Creek 134 C5
Yena Gap 466 J10
Yennabilli Point............522 J7
Yeoland Point............286 G4
Yeomans Bay 136 B6
Yeramba Lagoon 428 E11
York Reach 92 B7
Yowie Bay 492 C14
Yowie Point............492 A15
Yurulbin Point............315 A16

CARAVAN, TOURIST & MOBILE HOME PARKS

BARGO
Avon Caravan Village
Avon Dam Rd 567 J10
BASS HILL
Bass Hill Tourist Park
713 Hume Hwy............368 A9
BEROWRA
La Mancha Cara-Park
9 Pacific Hwy............163 C3
BUNDEENA
Bonnie Vale
Camping Ground
Bundeena Dr............523 D9
Bundeena Caravan Park
Scarborough St.........523 J10
CANLEY VALE
Lansdowne
61 Hume Hwy............366 H6
CARINGBAH
Cronulla Carapark
cnr Kingsway &
Gannons Rd S 493 C9
DURAL
Dural Village Park
269 New Line Rd 189 A15
EBENEZER
Kallawatta Park
Coromandel Rd 63 K6
ELDERSLIE
Poplars Park
Macarthur Rd 477 E16
EMU PLAINS
Nepean River
Mackellar St............236 B6
FAIRFIELD WEST
320 Polding St............335 C7
HEATHCOTE
Heathcote Tourist Park
Princes Hwy 518 F13
INGLEBURN
Denham Court
505 Campbelltown
Rd 422 F14
KURNELL
Silver Beach Resort
288 Prince Charles
Parade 465 F8
LEPPINGTON
Casa Paloma
105 Camden Valley
Wy............421 G5
Four Lanterns
1481 Camden Valley
Wy 421 E6
MACQUARIE PARK
Lane Cove River
Plassey Rd 283 E7
MARSDEN PARK
Town & Country
25 Hollinsworth Rd 211 H11
MIRANDA
Harts
215 Port Hacking Rd ..462 B16
NORTH NARRABEEN
Lakeside
Lake Park Rd 199 C15
OAKDALE
Burragorang Rd 500 F11
PARKLEA
Meriton Mobile Village
512 Sunnyholt Rd........215 A12
Parklea Garden Village
30 Majestic Dr 215 C11
PITT TOWN
Percy Place
Hall St............93 B5
PITT TOWN BOTTOMS
Powers Ski Gardens
Pitt Town Bottoms Rd ..92 B8
ROCKDALE
Sheralee
88 Bryant St 403 J15
ROUSE HILL
OK Caravan Corral
51 Terry Rd 184 J12
SANS SOUCI
Grand Pines
Tourist ParkThe
289 The Grand Pde
Ramsgate Beach 433 G14
TERREY HILLS
319 Mona Vale Rd......196 A13
VINEYARD
A-Vina
217 Commercial Rd ...153 A7
WALLACIA
cnr Silverdale Rd &
Alwyn Av............324 H12
WILBERFORCE
Windsor Riverside
Putty Rd............91 J7
WORONORA
1 Menai Rd............460 A14

CLUBS

18 FOOT SAILING
76 McDougall St
Milsons Point 6 C13
ABRUZZI SPORTS
Elizabeth St
Wetherill Park 334 D3
AMERICAN
131 Macquarie St
Sydney ....B F12
ARNCLIFFE RSL
Wollongong Rd..........403 E8
ARNCLIFFE SCOTS
SPORTS & SOCIAL
29 Burrows St 403 G8
ASHFIELD CATHOLIC
7 Charlotte St............372 J2
ASHFIELD RSL
374 Liverpool Rd 372 F3
ASQUITH RUGBY LEAGUE
11 Alexandria Pde
Waitara 221 K3
AUBURN RSL
33 Northumberland
Rd 339 E1
AUSTRALASIAN PIONEERS
61 York St
Sydney ....C F2
AUSTRALIAN
165 Macquarie St
Sydney ....B F15
AUSTRALIAN JOCKEY
Alison Rd
Randwick 376 F9
AUSTRALIAN OPERA FRIENDS
480 Elizabeth St
Surry Hills 19 H4
AVALON BEACH RSL
1 Bowling Green La
Avalon............170 B1
BALMAIN LEAGUES
138 Victoria Rd
Rozelle 344 E7
BANKSTOWN
DISTRICT SPORTS
8 Greenfield Pde.........399 E1
BANKSTOWN RSL
Kitchener Pde 369 E15
BANKSTOWN
TROTTING RECREATIONAL
178 Eldridge Rd 398 E7
BARGO SPORTS CLUB
Bargo............567 H10
BASS HILL RSL
330 Hector St 368 C9
BAULKHAM HILLS SPORTING
6 Renown Rd............248 C12
BELFIELD RSL
cnr Persic &
Bazentin Sts............371 C11
BELMORE RSL
427 Burwood Rd
Belmore 401 F1
BERALA-CARRAMAR
TENNIS & RECREATION
181 Chisholm Rd
Auburn............338 J7
BEROWRA RSL & CITIZENS
997 Pacific Hwy 133 F13
BLACKTOWN CITY RUGBY
LEAGUE & SPORTS CLUB
122-128 Rooty Hill Rd N
Rooty Hill 242 B14
BLACKTOWN CITY SOCCER
106 Prospect Hwy
Seven Hills 245 J15
BLACKTOWN RSL
Second Av............244 G14
BLACKTOWN WORKERS
Campbell St............274 G1
BLACKTOWN
WORKERS CLUB SPORTS
Reservoir Rd 274 C10
BONDI DIGGERS
Campbell Pde
Bondi Beach 378 E2
BONDI ICEBERGS
Notts Av
Bondi Beach 378 D5
BONDI JUNCTION-
WAVERLEY RSL
Gray St
Bondi Junction 22 J8
BOTANY BAY YACHT
Endeavour St
Sans Souci 462 J2
BOTANY RSL
1421 Botany Rd.........405 F11
BOWLERS CLUB OF NSW
95 York St
Sydney ....C G7
BRIGHTON-LE-SANDS
AMATEUR FISHING
Bestic St
Kyeemagh............403 K14
BRIGHTON-LE-SANDS RSL
351 Bay St............433 K3
BRONTE RSL
113 Macpherson St
Waverley 377 K10
BUNDEENA RSL
71 Loftus St............524 A9
BURWOOD RSL
36 Shaftesbury Rd 342 B15
CABRAMATTA LEAGUES
Sussex St............365 J10
CABRA VALE EX-ACTIVE
SERVICEMENS
1 Bartley St
Canley Vale............365 K4
CAMPBELLTOWN CATHOLIC
20 Camden Rd...........511 C6
CAMPBELLTOWN RSL
6 Lithgow St............511 F5
CAMPBELLTOWN TENNIS
4 Leumeah Rd
Leumeah............482 B12
CAMPSIE RSL
25 Anglo Rd 371 K13
CANLEY HEIGHTS RSL
26 Humphries Rd
Wakeley 334 K16
CANTERBURY-BANKSTOWN
LEAGUES
26 Bridge Rd
Belmore 371 E16
CANTERBURY-
HURLSTONE PARK RSL
20 Canterbury Rd
Hurlstone Park...........372 K11
CARINGBAH RSL
cnr Mackay St &
Banksia Rd 492 J7
CASTELLORIZIAN
448 Anzac Pde
Kingsford 406 G1
CASTLE HILL RSL
Castle St............217 K12

CASTLE PINES COUNTRY
Spurway Dr
Baulkham Hills....216 K13
CATHOLIC
199 Castlereagh St
Sydney....D A13
CHATSWOOD RSL
1 Thomas St....284 H10
CHESTER HILL-
CARRAMAR RSL
cnr Proctor Pde &
Chester Hill Rd....368 B2
CITY OF SYDNEY RSL
565 George St
Sydney....E G2
CITY TATTERSALLS
198 Pitt St
Sydney....D A9
CLOVELLY RSL &
AIR FORCE
Clovelly Rd....377 G12
COMBINED SERVICES RSL
5 Barrack St
Sydney....C F3
COMMERCIAL TRAVELLERS
ASSOCIATION
MLC Centre,
Martin Pl
Sydney....D B3
CONCORD RSL
Nirranda St....311 H16
COOGEE LEGION
266a Coogee Bay Rd..377 G16
COOGEE RANDWICK
RETURNED SERVICEMENS
Carr St
Coogee....407 E1
CROATIAN (JADRAN HAJDUK)
130 Edensor Rd
Bonnyrigg....364 C3
CRONULLA
Elouera Rd
Cronulla....494 A7
CRONULLA RSL
38 Gerrale St....494 A13
CRUISING YACHT
New Beach Rd
Darling Point....13 G7
CYPRUS COMMUNITY
CENTRE OF NSW
Stanmore Rd
Enmore....16 J14
CYPRUS HELLENE
150 Elizabeth St
Sydney....F C4
DEEPWATER MOTOR BOAT
Webster St
Milperra....397 C16
DEE WHY RSL
932 Pittwater Rd....258 H4
DIGGERS ON THE PARK
Ivanhoe Park Raglan St
Manly....288 F8
DOBROYD AQUATIC
Rodd Park
Rodd Point....343 G8
DOUBLE BAY SAILING
79 Bay St....347 B11
DRUMMOYNE ROWING
Henley Marine Dr....344 A5
DRUMMOYNE RSL
162 Victoria Rd....343 K2
DRUMMOYNE SAILING
2 St Georges Cr....344 B3
DUNDAS VALLEY
RUGBY UNION FOOTBALL
35 Quarry Rd....280 A10
EARLWOOD-
BARDWELL PARK RSL
Hartill-Law Av....402 J6
EARLWOOD EX-SERVICEMENS
32 Fricourt Av....402 K2
EASTERN SUBURBS LEAGUES
93 Spring St
Bondi Junction....22 H7
EASTERN SUBURBS LEGION
213 Bronte Rd
Waverley....377 F8

ENFIELD RSL
236 Liverpool Rd....371 H2
ENGADINE RSL
1029 Old Princes
Hwy....518 J1
EPPING RSL
Rawson St....251 A16
FAIRFIELD RSL
12 Dale St....336 G13
FIVE DOCK RSL
66 Great North Rd....342 K11
FOGOLAR FURLAN VENETO
CLUB
Wharf Rd
Lansvale....366 K10
FORESTVILLE RSL
Melwood Av....255 J10
FRANCE PETANQUE CLUB
North Narrabeen....228 H3
GALLIPOLI MEMORIAL
12 Loftus St
Sydney....B D10
GEORGES RIVER SAILING
Sanoni Av
Sandringham....463 F2
GERMAN CONCORDIA
231 Stanmore Rd
Stanmore....16 E11
GLADESVILLE
BOWLING & SPORTS
cnr Ryde Rd &
Halcyon St....312 K6
GLADESVILLE RSL
Linsley St....312 J10
GLENORIE RSL
Post Office Rd....128 B4
GRANVILLE RSL
Memorial Dr....308 G12
GREEK COMMUNITY
206 Lakemba St
Lakemba....400 K1
GREEK MACEDONIAN CLUB
ALEXANDER THE GREAT
160 Livingstone Rd
Marrickville....373 J11
GREYHOUND SOCIAL
140 Rookwood Rd
Yagoona....369 F7
GUILDFORD RUGBY LEAGUE
Tamplin Rd....337 B4
HAKOAH
61 Hall St
Bondi Beach....378 C2
HARBORD
DIGGERS MEMORIAL
Evans St....288 K1
HAWKESBURY SPORTING
Beaumont Av
North Richmond....87 G13
HILLS DISTRICT MEMORIAL
21 Arcadia Rd
Galston....159 G10
HORNSBY RSL
4 High St....221 G1
HUBERTUS COUNTRY
Adams Rd
Luddenham....327 F16
HUBERTUS LIVERPOOL RIFLE
cnr Badgerys Creek Rd &
Elizabeth Dr
Badgerys Creek....328 H15
HUNTERS HILL RSL
cnr Ady &
Alexandra Sts....313 K11
HURSTVILLE RSL
1 Ormonde Pde....432 A6
HURSTVILLE UNITED SPORTS
311a Forest Rd....431 J5
INGLEBURN RSL
cnr Chester Rd &
Warbler Av....453 E10
JOHN EDMONDSON VC
MEMORIAL
185 George St
Liverpool....395 E3
JOURNALISTS
36 Chalmers St
Surry Hills....19 G1

KELLYVILLE COUNTRY
Mungerie Rd
Kellyville....185 H13
KENSINGTON WAR MEMORIAL
2 Goodwood St....376 F11
KIEV SPORTS
32 Broomfield St
Cabramatta....366 A5
KINGSGROVE RSL
The Avenue....401 K11
KING TOMISLAV CROATIAN
455 Edensor Rd
Edensor Park....333 E15
KOGARAH BAY SAILING
Princes Hwy
Blakehurst....462 G2
KOGARAH RSL
254 Railway Pde....432 K6
KURING-GAI MOTOR YACHT
1 Cottage Point Rd
Cottage Point....135 G9
KURNELL COMMUNITY
SPORTS & RECREATION
Captain Cook Dr....466 A10
KYEEMAGH RSL
Tancred Av....404 B13
LAKEMBA RETURNED
SOLDIERS
60 Quigg St....401 B2
LEICHHARDT-LILYFIELD
SOLDIERS SAILORS AIRMENS
38 Short St....10 A15
LEMNOS
44 Albert St
Belmore....371 F14
LE MONTAGE
38 Frazer St
Lilyfield....343 J11
LIDCOMBE
CATHOLIC WORKMENS
24 John St....339 H8
LIDCOMBE RSL
Joseph St....339 J9
LIVERPOOL CATHOLIC
Hoxton Park Rd
Cartwright....393 F7
MALABAR RSL
Ireton St....437 E3
MANDARIN
396 Pitt St
Haymarket....E K5
MANLY FISHING &
SPORTING ASSOCIATION
270 Pittwater Rd....288 F4
MANLY-WARRINGAH
MASTER BUILDERS
18 Fisher Rd
Dee Why....258 F6
MANLY WARRINGAH
RUGBY LEAGUE
563 Pittwater Rd
Brookvale....258 D9
MARCONI
Marconi Rd
Bossley Park....333 H10
MAROUBRA RSL
Haig St....407 B11
MAROUBRA SEALS
212 Marine Pde....407 G12
MARRICKVILLE RSL
359 Illawarra Rd....373 J14
MASCOT RSL
1271 Botany Rd....405 D6
MATRAVILLE RSL
Norfolk Pde....436 J2
MERRYLANDS RSL
14 Military Rd....307 H13
MIDDLE HARBOUR
YACHT CLUB
The Spit Lower Parriwi Rd
Mosman....287 D14
MIRANDA RSL
615 Kingsway....491 K3
MOONEY MOONEY WORKERS
SPORTS & RECREATION
Kowan Rd....75 D2

MOOREBANK SPORTS
Heathcote Rd
Hammondville....426 G2
MORTDALE RSL
Macquarie Pl....431 B8
MOSMAN RETURNED
SERVICEMENS
719 Military Rd....317 B7
MT DRUITT WORKERS
247 Woodstock Av
Dharruk....241 B9
MT PRITCHARD &
DISTRICT COMMUNITY
(MOUNTIES)
101 Meadows Rd....364 E8
NEPEAN MOTORSPORTS CLUB
Rickards Rd
Castlereagh....146 D11
NEPEAN ROWING
Bruce Neale Dr
Penrith....236 D7
NEWTOWN RSL
52 Enmore Rd....17 E13
NINEVEH CLUB
673 Smithfield Rd
Edensor Park....364 A2
NORTH BONDI RSL
120 Ramsgate Av....378 G3
NORTHBRIDGE SAILING
Clive Park....286 G13
NORTH RYDE RSL
cnr Magdala &
Pittwater Rds....283 C13
NORTH SYDNEY
88 Berry St....K J3
NSW CRICKETERS
11 Barrack St
Sydney....C G3
NSW GUN
Booralie Rd
Duffys Forest....195 B3
NSW LEAGUES
165 Phillip St
Sydney....D D4
NSW MASONIC
169 Castlereagh St
Sydney....D A11
NSW SPORTS
10 Hunter St
Sydney....A J14
OAKDALE WORKERS
Burragorang Rd....500 A12
OATLEY RSL
23 Letitia St....431 C13
PADDINGTON-
WOOLLAHRA RSL
226 Oxford St....13 A16
PADSTOW RSL
Howard Rd....399 D16
PALM BEACH RSL
1087 Barrenjoey Rd...139 H2
PANANIA EAST HILLS RSL
28 Childs St
Panania....427 H1
PANTHERS WORLD OF
ENTERTAINMENT
Mulgoa Rd
Penrith....236 D12
PARRAMATTA LEAGUES
15 O'Connell St....278 B15
PARRAMATTA MASONIC
163 George St....308 G4
PARRAMATTA RETURNED
EX-SERVICEMENS
Macquarie St....308 A3
PENRITH RSL
cnr Castlereagh &
Lethbridge Sts....236 J11
PITT TOWN DISTRICT SPORTS
30 Old Pitt Town Rd...123 D2
PITTWATER AQUATIC
Esplanade
Mona Vale....169 D14
PITTWATER RSL
cnr Mona Vale Rd &
Foley St
Mona Vale....198 J4

POLONIA SPORTS CLUB
Bungalow Rd
Plumpton....24
PORT HACKING OPEN SA
224 Attunga Rd
Yowie Bay....49
PUNCHBOWL & DISTRICT
RETURNED EX-SERVICEM
1 Broadway....40
QUEENS
cnr Elizabeth & Market St
Sydney....
RAMSGATE RSL
Chuter Av....43
RANDWICK LABOUR
135 Alison Rd....37
RANDWICK RUGBY
104 Brook St
Coogee....37
REDFERN RSL
Redfern St....1
REVESBY HEIGHTS
EX-SERVICEMENS
Donovan St....42
REVESBY WORKERS
26 Brett St....39
RICHMOND
6 East Market St
Richmond....11
RIVERSTONE SCOFIELDS
Market St
Riverstone....18
RIVERWOOD LEGION
32 Littleton St....40
ROCKDALE RSL
Bay St....40
ROOTY HILL RSL
cnr Sherbrooke Rd &
Railway St....24
ROSE BAY RSL
New South Head Rd...34
ROSEVILLE RETURNED
SERVICEMENS MEMORIA
64 Pacific Hwy....28
ROSNAY GOLF CLUB
5 Weymouth Av
Auburn....33
ROYAL AUTOMOBILE
89 Macquarie St
Sydney....
ROYAL MOTOR YACHT
Broken Bay
46 Prince Alfred Pde
Newport....16
New South Wales
21 Wunulla Rd
Point Piper....34
Port Hacking
228 Woolooware Rd
Burraneer....49
ROYAL PRINCE ALFRED
Mitala St
Newport....16
ROYAL SYDNEY
YACHT SQUADRON
Peel St
Kirribilli....
RUGBY
Rugby Pl
Sydney....
RUSSIAN CLUB THE
7 Albert Rd
Strathfield....34
RYDE EASTWOOD LEAG
117 Ryedale Rd
West Ryde....28
RYDE EX-SERVICES
724 Victoria Rd....31
ST GEORGE
BUDAPEST SOCCER
84 Victoria Av
Mortdale....43
ST GEORGE LEAGUES
124 Princes Hwy
Beverley Park....43
ST GEORGE MASONIC
86 Roberts Av
Mortdale....43

GEORGE MOTOR BOAT
Wellington St
ans Souci 462 J4
GEORGE ROWING
Levey St
ncliffe 404 A6
GEORGE SAILING
verside Dr
ans Souci 463 B7
MARYS BAND
1 Great Western
wy 239 G16
MARYS RSL
SERVICEMENS
amre Rd 269 G5
MARYS RUGBY LEAGUE
ronia Rd 239 J7
RBIAN CENTRE
mpson Rd
onnyrigg Heights 363 E4
VEN HILLS-
ONGABBIE RSL
est Rd 275 H3
ARKS INTERNATIONAL
aptain Cook Dr
oolooware 493 F5
VERWATER
r Silverwater Rd &
yde St 309 K8
VENIAN
Elizabeth St
etherill Park 334 E3
THFIELD RSL
nithfield Rd 335 J5
JTHERN DISTRICT RUGBY
3 Belgrave Esp
lvania Waters 462 D15
JTH HURSTVILLE RSL
Connells Point Rd ..432 B11
JTH SYDNEY
SINESSMENS
2 Coward St
ascot 405 D2
JTH SYDNEY JUNIOR
GBY LEAGUE
8a Anzac Pde
ngsford 406 H3
NISH
Liverpool St
dney ....E G2
HERLAND
TRICT TRADE UNION
Manchester Rd
mea 491 F3
HERLAND SHIRE
LING CLUB
rnell 465 E8
HERLAND
TED SERVICES
East Pde 490 E2
NEY
Rowe St ....D A4
NEY AMATEUR SAILING
eela Rd
emorne Point 316 G13
NEY AUSTRALIAN
TBALL
ver Av
ore Park 20 K3
NEY FLYING SQUADRON
Foot Sailing Club,
McDougall St
sons Point 6 C13
NEY LABOUR
Bourke St
ry Hills 20 D2
NEY MARKET INDUSTRIES
ramatta Rd
mebush West 340 J7
NEY OLYMPIC SPORTING
Tennent Pde
lstone Park 373 B14
NEY PISTOL
e Banks
Perouse 437 F16
ERSALLS
Elizabeth St
ney ....D B10

THE NEUTRAL BAY
Barry St 6 F5
THE PARRAMATTA
37 Hunter St
Parramatta 308 B3
UKRAINIAN
11 Church St
Lidcombe 339 H8
UNION
24 Bent St
Sydney ....B E14
UNIVERSITY & SCHOOLS
60 Phillip St
Sydney ....B F12
UPPER HAWKESBURY
POWER BOAT
George St
Windsor 121 G5
URUGUAYAN
31 Whitford Rd
Hinchinbrook 393 C3
UTS HABERFIELD ROWING
Dobroyd Pde
Haberfield 343 G10
VAUCLUSE AMATEUR
12 FOOT SAILING
Wharf Rd 318 E15
VAUCLUSE YACHT
Marine Pde
Watsons Bay 318 F14
WARRAGAMBA WORKERS &
SPORTING
Eighteenth St
Warragamba 353 F6
WENTWORTHVILLE LEAGUES
Smith St 306 H2
WENTWORTHVILLE
MEMORIAL RSL
Dunmore St 276 K16
WESTERN SUBURBS
AUSTRALIAN FOOTBALL
40 Hampton St
Croydon Park 372 A8
WESTERN SUBURBS
LEAGUES
115 Liverpool Rd
Ashfield 372 K3
Leumeah Rd
Leumeah 482 B13
WESTERN SUBURBS SOCCER
4 William St
Five Dock 342 G9
WEST PENNANT HILLS
SPORTS
103 New Line Rd
West Pennant Hills 219 G15
WILLOUGHBY LEGION
EX-SERVICES
26 Crabbes Av 285 E9
WINDSOR LEAGUES
Rifle Range Rd
Bligh Park 150 D4
WINDSOR RSL
Argyle St
South Windsor 120 K13
WOOLLAHRA SAILING
Vickery Av
Rose Bay 347 K10
WORONORA RIVER RSL &
CITIZENS
Prince Edward Park Rd
Woronora 489 J2
YARRA BAY SAILING
Yarra Rd
Phillip Bay 436 H11
YMCA (HEAD OFFICE)
154 Elizabeth St
Sydney ....F C5
YMCA (HEADQUARTERS)
5 Wentworth Av
Sydney ....F E3

COACH TERMINALS

Sydney ....E H12

GOLF COURSES & DRIVING RANGES

Antill Park 561 H4
Ashlar 244 F11
Asquith 192 C6
Auburn 338 H9
Avalon 170 C3
Avondale 252 K5
Balgowlah 287 F8
Bankstown 397 H8
Bardwell Valley 402 J10
Barnwell Park 342 F8
Barton Park
Driving Range 403 K11
Bayview 199 B1
Beverley Park 433 B10
Bexley Municipal 402 B14
Bondi 378 H1
Bonnie Doon 406 F6
Botany 435 K2
Cabramatta 365 B9
Camden 478 D14
Camden Lakeside 450 F7
Camden Valley
Golf Resort 449 K12
Campbelltown 510 E12
Canterbury 401 C9
Captain Cook 462 C16
Carnarvon 339 F15
Castlecove Country 285 J5
Castle Hill Country 216 H13
Casula Powerhouse 395 A15
Chatswood 284 B12
Colonial 239 C10
Concord 341 J3
Cromer 228 B11
Cronulla 494 A7
Cronulla Driving Range ..494 C4
Cullen Dan
Driving Range 437 C13
Cumberland Country 306 A5
Cumberland Grove
Country Club 365 B13
Dunheved 239 C6
Dural Golf
Driving Range 189 B16
Eastlake 406 D3
Elanora Country 198 B13
Fairfield City Council 334 J10
Fox Hills 275 F15
Glenmore 265 C14
Golf Paradise
Driving Range 195 J13
Gordon 253 E10
Grose River 116 A12
Hawkesbury Waters 63 K1
Hudson Park 340 G12
Hurstville 430 E8
Kareela 461 E14
Kellyville Country Club ..185 H13
Killara 253 K14
Killarney Golf
Practice Fairway 153 D13
Kogarah 404 B7
Kurrajong Hills
Country Club Estate 55 K8
Lane Cove Country 314 G6
Leonay 235 A14
Liverpool 367 A11
Llandilo Golf
Driving Range 207 K7
Long Reef 229 E15
Longshot
Driving Range 215 E3
Macquarie Links 423 H14
Macquarie University
Driving Range 252 A16
Manly 288 C6
Marrickville 403 D1
Marsden Park
Driving Range 181 D13
Massey Park 342 B3
Milperra Sports Centre
Driving Range 397 C9
Monash Country 197 H9
Mona Vale 199 E5
Moore Park 20 G11
Mt Steele
Driving Range 20 F11
Muirfield 248 G13
Narrabeen
Driving Range 199 C12
New Brighton 396 F13
New South Wales 437 B16
Northbridge 286 D16
North Ryde
Golf Course 282 E11
North Turramurra 193 F16
Oatlands 279 B10
Palm Beach 109 K14
Parramatta 307 J2
Pennant Hills 250 B7
Penrith 266 K11
Pymble 223 J13
RAAF Kingswood 296 H7
Randwick 437 G5
Richmond 118 K7
Riverlands 397 C13
Riverside Oaks 64 E5
Riverwood Golf Course &
Driving Range 397 D1
Roseville 285 C1
Royal Australian
Engineers 425 C4
Royal Sydney 347 K11
Rum Corps Barracks 120 G8
Ryde-Parramatta 280 J15
St Michaels 437 D13
Sefton 368 F8
Sharks
Golf Driving Range 333 B1
Sports Centre
Golf Driving Range 340 J3
Strathfield 370 H1
Terrey Hills
Golf & Country Club ...195 D1
Terrey Hills Par 3 ....195 H14
The Australian 376 A15
The Baulkham Hills
Day Night
Driving Range 246 G14
The Coast 437 F12
The Lakes 406 A6
Tree Valley 423 F3
University
Driving Golf Range 510 F6
Wakehurst 287 B2
Wallacia 324 K12
Windsor Country 120 H11
Woodville 337 K9
Woollahra 347 J14
Woolooware 493 D8

HOSPITALS

ALLOWAH
CHILDRENS PRIVATE
8 Perry St
Dundas Valley 280 E8
ALWYN REHABILITATION
1 Emu St
Strathfield 341 G16
ASHBURN HOUSE
30 Ashburn Pl
Gladesville 312 J12
AUBURN HOSPITAL &
COMMUNITY HEALTH
SERVICES
Norval St 339 D7
BALMAIN
29 Booth St 7 H11
BANKSTOWN-LIDCOMBE
Eldridge Rd
Bankstown 398 K7
BANKSTOWN PRIVATE
74 Chiswick Rd
Greenacre 370 A10
BELLEVUE
1a Edward St
Bondi 378 B4
BEXLEY
34 Harrow Rd 403 A14
BLACKTOWN
Blacktown Rd 274 K2
BRADLEYS HEAD
66 Bradleys Head Rd
Mosman 317 C11
BRAESIDE
Prairie Vale Rd
Prairiewood 334 F8
BUENA VISTA
132 Victoria Rd
Bellevue Hill 347 H16
CALVARY
91 Rocky Point Rd
Beverley Park 433 C9
CAMDEN
Menangle Rd 507 A3
CAMPBELLTOWN
Therry Rds 511 B10
CANTERBURY
Canterbury Rd
Campsie 401 J1
CARRINGTON CENTENNIAL
90 Werombi Rd
Grasmere 476 B15
CASTLECRAG PRIVATE
150 Edinburgh Rd 286 B12
CHARLES WENTWORTH
PRIVATE
21 Lytton St
Wentworthville 307 B1
CONCORD REPATRIATION
GENERAL
Hospital Rd
Concord West 311 F12
CUMBERLAND
1 Hainsworth St
Westmead 277 K13
DALCROSS PRIVATE
28 Stanhope Rd
Killara 254 B13
DALWOOD CHILDRENS HOME
21 Dalwood Av
Seaforth 286 K7
DAME EADITH WALKER
DIALYSIS TRAINING CENTRE
Nullawarra Av
Concord West 311 J13
DELMAR PRIVATE
58 Quirk St
Dee Why 258 H8
EASTERN SUBURBS SRVS
FOR DEVELOPMENTALLY
DISABLED
York St
Queens Park 22 D13
EVESHAM CLINIC
3 Harrison St
Cremorne 6 H3
FAIRFIELD
cnr Polding St &
Prairie Vale Rd
Prairiewood 334 F8
GLADESVILLE MACQUARIE
Wicks Rd
North Ryde 282 H11
GOVERNOR PHILLIP SPECIAL
Glebe Pl
Penrith 237 D9
HAWKESBURY DISTRICT
Day St
Windsor 121 C10
HIRONDELLE
10 Wyvern Av
Chatswood West 284 H7
HMAS PENGUIN
Naval Depot
Mosman 317 G7

INFORMATION

HOLROYD PRIVATE 123 Chetwynd Rd Guildford 337 D1

HORNSBY & KU-RING-GAI COMMUNITY HEALTH SERVICES Palmerston Rd....192 B16

HUNTERS HILL PRIVATE 9 Mount St....313 G11

HURSTVILLE COMMUNITY CO- OPERATIVE PRIVATE 37 Gloucester Rd....431 H4

JEAN COLVIN PRIVATE 9 Loftus Rd Darling Point....13 H7

KAREENA PRIVATE 86 Kareena Rd N Miranda....492 F4

KARITANE MOTHERCRAFT 171 Avoca St Randwick....377 B14

KENSINGTON PRIVATE 17 Alison Rd....376 F9

KING GEORGE V MEMORIAL Missenden Rd Camperdown....17 J5

KOGARAH 18 Garden St....433 B7

KURRAJONG COMMUNITY Old Bells Line of Rd Kurrajong....85 D2

LADY DAVIDSON REHABILITATION Bobbin Head Rd Turramurra....193 G11

LANGTON CENTRE cnr Dowling & Nobbs Sts Surry Hills....20 E5

LIVERPOOL cnr Goulburn & Elizabeth Sts....395 F2

LONGUEVILLE PRIVATE 47 Kenneth St....314 E7

LOTTIE STEWART 40 Stewart St Ermington....280 D11

LYNTON PRIVATE 40 Fullers Rd Chatswood West....284 F10

MACARTHUR PRIVATE 92 Dumaresq St Campbelltown....511 F6

MANDALAY PRIVATE HOSPITAL 2 Addison Rd Manly....288 F14

MANLY DISTRICT HOSPITAL & COMMUNITY HEALTH SERVICES Darley Rd....288 K13

MANLY WATERS PRIVATE 17 Cove Av Manly....288 G13

MATER MISERICORDIAE PRIVATE Rocklands Rd Crows Nest....5 C2

METROPOLITAN REHABILITATION 275 Addison Rd Petersham....373 K7

MINCHINBURY COMMUNITY cnr Great Western Hwy & Angus Av Rooty Hill....271 H5

MONA VALE HOSPITAL & COMMUNITY HEALTH SERVICES Coronation St....199 D8

MOSMAN PRIVATE 1 Ellamatta Av....317 C10

MOUNT DRUITT Railway St....241 H14

MT WILGA PRIVATE 2 Manor Rd Hornsby....191 E12

NEPEAN DISTRICT Parker St Kingswood....237 D13

NEPEAN PRIVATE Barber Av Kingswood....237 E12

NERINGAH 12 Neringah Av S Wahroonga....222 C7

NORTHCOTT CENTRE 2 Gross St Parramatta....278 B15

NSW PRIVATE HOSPITAL Victoria St Ashfield....372 K5

PACIFIC 171 Bay St Brighton-le-sands....433 G1

PARRAMATTA HEALTH SERVICE Marsden St....308 B2

PENINSULAR PRIVATE 12 McDonald St Harbord....258 D15

POPLARS PRIVATE 66 Norfolk Rd Epping....251 D12

PRESIDENT PRIVATE cnr President Av & Hotham Rd Kirrawee....491 C5

PRINCE HENRY THE Anzac Pde Little Bay....437 E11

PRINCE OF WALES PRIVATE THE Barker St Randwick....377 A16

PRINCE OF WALES THE Avoca St Randwick....377 A15

QUEEN VICTORIA MEMORIAL Thirlmere Wy Picton....562 H12

RACHEL FORSTER 150 Pitt St Redfern....19 D9

ROMA PRIVATE 9 William St Randwick....376 J10

ROSE BAY 84 Newcastle St....348 B12

ROYAL ALEXANDRA CHILDRENS (NEW CHILDRENS) Hawkesbury Rd Westmead....277 J13

ROYAL FAR WEST CHILDRENS HEALTH SCHEME 18 Wentworth St Manly....288 H10

ROYAL HOSPITAL FOR WOMEN Barker St Randwick....377 A16

ROYAL PRINCE ALFRED Missenden Rd Camperdown....17 J5

ROYAL REHABILITATION CENTRE, SYDNEY Coorabel 227 Morrison Rd Ryde....312 B6; Moorong 600 Victoria Rd Ryde....312 C3; Weemala 259 Morrison Rd Ryde....312 A5

ROYAL SOUTH SYDNEY COMMUNITY HEALTH COMPLEX Joynton Av Zetland....375 J11

ROZELLE cnr Church & Glover Sts Lilyfield....343 K10

RYDE HOSPITAL & COMMUNITY HEALTH SERVICES Denistone Rd Denistone....281 E10

SACRED HEART HOSPICE 279 Victoria St Darlinghurst....4 F13

ST CATHERINES AGED CARE SERVICES 162 Balaclava Rd Marsfield....281 K2

ST DAVIDS PRIVATE 7 Rowe St Eastwood....281 C8

ST EDMUNDS PRIVATE 13 Clanalpine St Eastwood....281 A9

ST GEORGE Gray St Kogarah....433 B6

ST GEORGE PRIVATE & MEDICAL CENTRE South St Kogarah....433 C5

ST JOHN OF GOD 177 Grose Vale Rd North Richmond....116 J4

ST JOHN OF GOD PRIVATE 13 Grantham St Burwood....341 J11

ST JOSEPHS Normanby Rd Auburn....339 C2

ST LUKES PRIVATE 18 Roslyn St Potts Point....13 A7

ST VINCENTS 406 Victoria St Darlinghurst....4 G12

ST VINCENTS CARITAS CENTRE 299 Forbes St Darlinghurst....4 E12

SCOTTISH THE 2 Cooper St Paddington....13 A13

SOUTH PACIFIC PRIVATE 18 Beach St Curl Curl....258 J16

STRATHFIELD 3 Everton Rd....341 H12

SUTHERLAND HOSPITAL & COMMUNITY HEALTH SERVICES cnr Kingsway & Kareena Rd N Caringbah....492 F5

SYDNEY Macquarie St....D G3

SYDNEY ADVENTIST PRIVATE 185 Fox Valley Rd Wahroonga....221 G14

SYDNEY CHILDRENS High St Randwick....377 A15

SYDNEY EYE Macquarie St....D G4

SYDNEY HOME NURSING SERVICE 36 Boyce St Glebe....11 J11

SYDNEY SOUTHWEST PRIVATE 40 Bigge St Liverpool....395 F1

SYDNEY UROLOGY & SURGERY CENTRE 5 Croydon St Petersham....16 A7

THE EASTERN SUBURBS PRIVATE 8 Chapel St Randwick....377 C12

THE HILLS PRIVATE 499 Windsor Rd Baulkham Hills....247 E4

TRESILLIAN Petersham cnr Addison Rd & Shaw St....373 K7; Second Av, Willoughby....285 H12

UNITED DENTAL 2 Chalmers St Surry Hills....E K16

UNITED GARDENS 11a Moonbie St Summer Hill....373 C5

WANDENE PRIVATE 7 Blake St Kogarah....433 A6

WAR MEMORIAL Birrell St Waverley....377 F6

WESLEY 84 Arthur St Ashfield....372 E5

WESTMEAD cnr Darcy & Hawkesbury Rds....277 G14

WESTSIDE PRIVATE 55 Burwood Rd Concord....342 B9

WOLPER JEWISH PRIVATE 8 Trelawney St Woollahra....347 B16

HOTELS & MOTELS

Aarons Hotel Haymarket....E C10

Abcot International Motor Inn Sylvania....461 G15

Airport Sydney International Motor Inn Arncliffe....403 K7

Alice Motel Bondi Beach....378 B6

A Line Hotel Glebe....12 H6

All Seasons Darling Harbour Hotel Sydney Haymarket....E B4

All Seasons Hotel Rosehill....308 J7

All Seasons On Crown Darlinghurst....4 D13

All Seasons Premier Menzies Hotel Sydney....A H15

ANA Hotel Sydney The Rocks....A G7

Angel Motel Narellan....478 F9

Apia Hotel Camperdown....17 G2

Appin Hotel Appin....569 F10

Artarmon Motor Inn Artarmon....284 H15

Ascot Motor Inn Wahroonga....222 A7

Ashfields Philip Lodge Motel Ashfield....373 B1

Astoria Hotel Potts Point....4 K6

Avillon Hotel Sydney....E J3

Banksia Motel Bass Hill....367 J7

Barclay Hotel Potts Point....4 J8

Barker Lodge Motor Inn Kingsford....376 G16

Bass Hill Tourist Park & Motel Bass Hill....368 A9

Bayside The Edgecliff....13 F9

Beach Road Hotel Bondi Beach....378 C1

Bellbird Motel Kurmond....56

Berowra Heights Hotel Motel Berowra Heights....133

Blacket Hotel Sydney....C

Burwood Motel Burwood....371

Cambridge Park Inn International Surry Hills....F

Camden Country Club Camden....507

Camden Valley Golf Resort Camden....449

Camden Valley Inn Bickley Vale....507

Camelot Inn Motel Darlinghurst....4

Camperdown Travelodge Camperdown....17

Capitol Square Hotel Haymarket....E

Carlton Crest Hotel Sydney Haymarket....E

Castlereagh Inn Sydney....D

C.B. Hotel Haymarket....E

Centra Camperdown Camperdown....17

Central Railway Motel Redfern....19

Chateau Sydney Hotel Elizabeth Bay....13

Checkers Resort Terrey Hills....195

Chifley On City View, The Pennant Hills....250

City Beach Motel Bondi Beach....378

City Crown Lodge Internatior Surry Hills....F

Colyton Hotel Motel Colyton....270

Coogee Bay Boutique Hotel Coogee....407

Coogee Bay Hotel Coogee....377

Coogee Sands Motor Inn Coogee....377

Cosy Private Hotel Haymarket....E

Country Comfort Blakehurst....432; Lane Cove....314; Rooty Hill....241

Country Comfort Sydney Central Haymarket....E

Courtyard By Marriott Parramatta....308

Cranbrook International Rose Bay....347

Crescent On Bayswater Potts Point....4

Crest Hotel Potts Point....4

Cronulla Motor Inn Woolooware....493

Devere Hotel Elizabeth Bay....13

Dural Hotel & Motel Dural....189

El Toro Motor Inn Warwick Farm....365

Engadine Motor Inn Engadine....518

Ermington Hotel Motel Ermington....310

Establishment Hotel Sydney....A

Fountainebleau Inn Casula....394

Four Points Hotel Sydney Sydney....C

Furama Central Hotel Surry Hills....F

rama Hotel Darling Harbour
aymarket..........E C5
rdenia Motor Inn
ass Hill..........368 B10
zebo Hotel
izabeth Bay..........13 A6
arramatta..........308 D1
mini Hotel
andwick..........377 A13
adesville Motel
ladesville..........312 J11
nsynd Motor Inn
ensington..........376 F9
lf View Hotel Motel
uildford..........337 K8
ace Hotel
ydney..........C F5
and Mercure Apartments
yrmont..........12 K5
ey Gums Hotel Motel
amisontown..........266 A1
eystanes Inn Hotel Motel
reystanes..........306 D10
mpton Court Hotel
otts Point..........4 J8
rbour Rocks Hotel
he Rocks..........A K4
ven Inn
lebe..........12 A10
wkesbury Campus
onference Centre & Motel
ichmond..........118 F11
ls Lodge Boutique Hotel
astle Hill..........217 A14
liday Inn
otts Point..........4 H7
liday Inn Coogee Beach
oogee..........407 G1
tel 10
reenacre..........369 K8
tel Bakpak Westend
aymarket..........E J6
tel Ibis Sydney Airport
lascot..........405 B4
tel Ibis World Square
ydney..........E K4
tel Inter-Continental Sydney
ydney..........B F10
ghenden Hotel
Voollahra..........21 G4
nts Motel
asula..........424 A3
de Park Plaza Hotel
arlinghurst..........F G2
mes Ruse Hotel Motel
ellyville..........215 D1
ly Knight Motel
asula..........394 H16
ara Inn
illara..........254 A15
ngsview
otts Point..........4 K6
ribilli Hotel
lilsons Point..........6 A14
ndmark Parkroyal
ydney Hotel
otts Point..........4 K4
nsdowne Motor Inn
ansvale..........366 F7
Meridien Sydney
ydney..........A G13
erty Plains Motor Inn
dcombe..........339 H6
combe Motor Inn
dcombe..........339 J9
chinvar Motel
ellyville..........215 D1
g Cabin Motor Inn
enrith..........236 C8
clin Lodge Motel
ampbelltown..........511 H1
disons Central City Hotel
izabeth Bay..........13 A7
nhattan Hotel
izabeth Bay..........13 B5
nly Pacific Parkroyal
lanly..........288 H8

Manly Seaview Motel
Manly..........288 G5
Marco Polo Motor Inn
Summer Hill..........373 E3
Markets Hotel Motel
Homebush West..........340 J7
Mecure Hotel Parramatta
Rosehill..........308 J4
Merchant Court Hotel
Sydney..........C K8
Mercure Hotel Lawson
City West
Ultimo..........3 A13
Mercure Hotel Sydney
Ultimo..........E C16
Metro Motor Inn
Chippendale..........19 A3
Double Bay..........13 K11
Haberfield..........343 B16
Miranda..........492 B4
Ryde..........311 G2
Millennium Hotel
Potts Point..........4 H8
Milperra Palms
Milperra..........398 B12
Mona Vale Motel
Mona Vale..........199 C7
Motel Formula One
Campbelltown..........481 J12
Wentworthville..........306 J3
Motel Voyager
Minchinbury..........272 D8
Mt Kuring-gai Motel
Mt Kuring-gai..........162 H13
Nepean Shores Riverside
Resort & Conference
Centre
Emu Plains..........235 J14
New Inn Motel
Richmond..........118 F4
Newport Mirage
Newport..........169 E12
North Sydney Harbourview
Hotel
North Sydney..........K G12
Norwest International Hotel
Baulkham Hills..........216 K14
Novotel Brighton Beach
Brighton-le-sands..........434 A2
Novotel Hotel Ibis
Homebush Bay..........340 G1
Novotel Sydney On
Darling Harbour
Pyrmont..........12 K6
Occidental Hotel
Sydney..........C F1
Old Sydney Parkroyal
The Rocks..........B A2
Overlander Hotel Motel
Cambridge Park..........237 F5
Oxford Koala Hotel &
Apartments
Surry Hills..........F H6
Pacific International Hotel
Parramatta..........308 D5
Pacific International Inn
Haymarket..........E E10
Palm Court Motor Inn
Haberfield..........373 E2
Palms Hotel Motel, The
Greenacre..........370 A7
Panthers World of
Entertainment
Penrith..........236 D12
Park Hyatt Sydney
The Rocks..........1 H7
Park Regis Hotel
Sydney..........D A12
Parkroyal At Darling Harbour
Sydney..........C C13
Parkroyal Sydney Airport
Mascot..........405 B3
Parkway Hotel Motel
Frenchs Forest..........256 K5
Parramatta City Motel
Parramatta..........308 B5
Parramatta Parkroyal
Parramatta..........308 C2

Penrith Hotel Motel
Penrith..........237 A10
Penrith Valley Inn
Penrith..........236 D8
Pentura On Pitt
Sydney..........C K15
Philip Lodge Motel
Ashfield..........372 K4
Pier Hotel
Botany..........436 A2
Pier One Parkroyal
Dawes Point..........1 H5
Plumpton Motor Inn
Glendenning..........242 K3
Pop-In Motel
Casula..........424 A3
Prospect Hotel Motel
Prospect..........275 E15
Quay West
The Rocks..........A H8
Radisson Hotel
Sydney..........E E1
Radisson Kestrel Hotel
On Manly Beach
Manly..........288 J10
Radisson Plaza Hotel
Sydney..........B A14
Renaissance Sydney
Sydney..........B B10
Rex Hotel
Potts Point..........4 K5
Richmond
Richmond..........118 F4
Ritz-Carlton Hotel
Double Bay..........347 B12
Rooftop Motel
Glebe..........12 B12
Roslyn Gardens Motor Inn
Elizabeth Bay..........13 C6
Royal Garden International
Sydney..........E J7
Rushcutters Harbourside
Sydney
Rushcutters Bay..........13 D9
Ryde Hotel
Ryde..........312 A2
Ryde Motor Inn
West Ryde..........280 J15
Rydges
Cronulla..........494 A11
North Sydney..........5 H4
Rydges Bankstown
Bass Hill..........368 B9
St George Tavern Hotel &
Accomadation
Rockdale..........403 D16
Sands Hotel Motel
Maroubra..........407 E14
Sans Souci Motor Inn
Sans Souci..........433 C15
Saville 2
Bond St Apartment Hotel
Sydney..........A J13
Sebel of Sydney
Elizabeth Bay..........13 B6
Sheraton On The Park
Sydney..........D C9
Sheraton Sydney Airport Hotel
Mascot..........405 A5
Sheridan Hotel Motel
Guildford West..........336 G3
Sir Stamford At Circular Quay
Sydney..........B F9
Sir Stamford Hotel
Double Bay..........347 B13
Sleep-Inn Express Motel
Greenacre..........370 D5
Southern Cross
Sydney..........F B6
Southern Cross On Harbour
Sydney..........E D4
Spanish Inn Motor Lodge
Strathfield..........371 C4
Stamford Plaza Sydney
Millers Point..........A C10
Star City
Pyrmont..........12 H2

Sullivans Hotel
Paddington..........4 G15
Sunnybrook Hotel
Warwick Farm..........366 A10
Sutherland Inn Motel
Sutherland..........490 H5
Swiss Grand Bondi
Beach all suite Hotel
Bondi Beach..........378 D2
Sydney Airport Hilton
Arncliffe..........404 A7
Sydney Boulevard Hotel
Woolloomooloo..........4 D7
Sydney Central YHA
Haymarket..........E F11
Sydney Hilton Hotel
Sydney..........C J10
Sydney Huntley Inn
Gladesville..........312 H7
Sydney Marriott
Sydney..........F G1
Sydney Park Lodge Hotel
Moore Park..........20 D9
Sydney Vista Hotel
Sydney..........A F14
The Blue Cattle Dog Tavern
St Clair..........269 G9
The Clovelly
Clovelly..........377 K13
The Falls Resort
Oxford Falls..........257 C2
The Goldsborough
Sydney..........12 K7
The Observatory Hotel
Millers Point..........A C6
The Regent Sydney Hotel
The Rocks..........A J8
The Russell Hotel
The Rocks..........A K6
The Stafford
The Rocks..........A J4
The Wahroonga Spanish Motel
Wahroonga..........222 A6
The Wentworth Sydney
(A Rydges Hotel)
Sydney..........B D14
Top of The Town Hotel
Potts Point..........4 H9
Town & Country Motel
Strathfield South..........371 E4
Tradewinds Hotel
Maroubra..........407 B10
Travelodge
Bankstown..........399 E1
Blacktown..........274 C10
Sydney..........D D4
Travelodge Macquarie
North Ryde
Macquarie Park..........252 E16
Travelodge Manly
Warringah
Manly..........258 D9
Unilodge Sydney Motel
Ultimo..........12 J16
University Motor Inn Broadway
Glebe..........12 D16
Waldorf Apartment Hotel, The
Sydney..........E F2
Warwick Farm Grandstand Motel
Warwick Farm..........366 A13
Wesley Lodge Motel
Westmead..........277 H15
Westin Sydney Hotel
Sydney..........C K3
Wild Orchid Private Hotel, The
Haymarket..........E J6
Windsor Motel
Windsor..........121 E7
Windsor Terrace Motel
Windsor..........121 E7
Winston Hotel Motel
Winston Hills..........277 A1
Woolloomooloo Bay Hotel
Woolloomooloo..........4 F3
Y on the Park Hotel
Sydney..........F F3

MOTOR REGISTRIES

BANKSTOWN
Shop 4a,
Bankstown Square
Shopping Centre..........369 F16
BEVERLY HILLS
cnr Cambridge St &
Stoney Creek Rd..........401 C16
BLACKTOWN
85 Flushcombe Rd..........274 G1
BONDI JUNCTION
88 Ebley St..........22 J8
BOTANY
5 Lord St..........405 F9
CAMDEN
167 Argyle St..........477 A16
CAMPBELLTOWN
cnr Tindall St &
Menagle Rd..........511 A6
CAMPSIE
Shop 43,
Campsie Centre..........372 A14
CASTLE HILL
18 Anella Av..........217 D12
CHATSWOOD
313 Victoria Av..........285 A9
ENGADINE
Shop 3,
101 Caldarra Av..........518 J2
FAIRFIELD
32 Harris St..........336 E13
FAIRFIELD HEIGHTS
Shop 4,
144 Polding St..........335 K8
FIVE DOCK
cnr Ramsay Rd &
Henley Marine Dr..........343 A12
FRENCHS FOREST
Shop 12, Forest Way
Shopping Centre..........256 D5
GLADESVILLE
230 Victoria Rd..........312 J9
HORNSBY
324 Pacific Hwy..........191 G14
HURSTVILLE
8 Woodville St..........432 A5
INGLEBURN
Shop 9,
Centennial House,
cnr Oxford &
Ingleburn Rds..........453 C6
JAMISONTOWN
Penrith South
81 York Rd..........266 E1
KOGARAH
60a Gray St..........433 C7
LIDCOMBE
cnr Swete & Mills Sts..339 K7
LIVERPOOL
357 Hume Hwy..........395 B8
MACQUARIE PARK
North Ryde
Shop 2,
Macquarie Centre..........282 F2
MANLY
239 Pittwater Rd..........288 F5
MAROUBRA
Maroubra Junction
832 Anzac Pde..........407 A9
MARRICKVILLE
Shop 9,
Marrickville Metro
Shopping Centre..........374 F10
MIRANDA
Shop 5, Kiora Mall..........492 A3
MOUNT DRUITT
23 Luxford Rd..........241 F14
NORTH SYDNEY
154 Pacific Hwy..........K B3
PARRAMATTA
cnr Macquarie &
Charles Sts..........308 E4
RICHMOND
173 Windsor St..........118 H4

ROSEBERY
52 Rothschild Av 375 H13
RYDE
cnr Blaxland & North Rds 281 K13
ST CLAIR
Shop 20, St Clair Shopping Centre 270 C12
SILVERWATER
1 River St 309 J9
SURRY HILLS
City South Centennial Plaza, 260 Elizabeth St F B12
SYDNEY
161 Clarence St C E3
THORNLEIGH
1 Central Av 221 A13
WARRIEWOOD
Shop 4, Warriewood Square Shopping Centre 198 K12
WETHERILL PARK
Unit 1, Greenway Plaza, 1183 The Horsley Dr 334 D4

PARKS, RESERVES, OVALS, ETC

Abbotsford Cove Foreshore Park
Abbotsford 343 A1
Abbott Park
Chester Hill 367 K1
Abel Reserve
Revesby 398 H16
Acacia Park
Dundas Valley 279 K9
Eastwood 281 J8
Ace Reserve
Fairfield 336 G8
Acron Oval
St Ives 224 G11
Adams Park
Canley Vale 365 K3
Adam St Ground
Curl Curl 258 K12
Ador Av Reserve
Rockdale 403 G16
Adventure Park
Ryde 282 A14
A E Watson Reserve
Bexley 402 J15
Agnes Banks Nature Reserve
Agnes Banks 146 F8
Airey Park
Homebush 340 J10
Airport Reserve
Bankstown Airport 397 F6
Aitken Reserve
Queenscliff 288 F3
Akuna Av Oval
Bangor 459 G14
Alamein Park
Liverpool 394 K3
Albert Brown Park
Ermington 280 E11
Albert Park
Earlwood 403 B4
Alcheringa Reserve
Miranda 491 J8
Alderson Park
Merrylands 307 C7
Alexandria Park 19 A14
Alfred Henry Whaling Memorial Reserve
Baulkham Hills 247 G4
Algie Park
Haberfield 343 C14
Alice Park
Bankstown 369 C13
Alison Park
Randwick 377 A12
Alison Playground
Dulwich Hill 373 C11
Allambie Heights Oval 257 C11
Allambie Rd Reserve
Edensor Park 333 G13
Allan Border Oval
Mosman 317 A7
Allan Small Park
East Killara 254 J6
Allder Park
Sefton 368 E4
Allenby Park
Allambie Heights 257 E9
Allen Robertson Reserve
Kings Langley 245 A5
Allison Park
Chiswick 343 B2
Allman Park
Ashfield 373 A4
Allsopp Oval
Cambridge Park 237 H7
Allum Park
Greenacre 370 E11
Alma Reserve
Padstow 429 G5
Alpha Park
Blacktown 244 F16
Alpha Rd Park
Greystanes 305 F12
Alroy Park
Plumpton 242 B6
Alston Reserve
Macquarie Park 282 K1
Amalfi Park
Lurnea 394 F9
Amaroo Reserve
Georges Hall 367 F13
Amour Park
Revesby 398 F16
Amundsen Reserve
Leumeah 482 J10
Amway Park
Castle Hill 217 E14
Anana Reserve
Elanora Heights 198 E16
Anderson Park
Neutral Bay 6 B9
Andrew Thompson Park
Erskine Park 270 G16
Andrew Town Park
Richmond 118 D5
Andromeda Fields
Cranebrook 207 G6
Anembo Reserve
Duffys Forest 194 J8
Angle Park
Chipping Norton 366 E12
Angophora Park
Forestville 255 F9
Angophora Reserve
Avalon 169 G3
Bilgola 169 G3
Angus Park
Rooty Hill 272 C2
Annangrove Park 186 E2
Ann Cashman Reserve
Balmain 7 C10
Annie Prior Reserve
Glenhaven 187 G16
Annie Wyatt Park
Palm Beach 140 B3
Ann Thorn Park
Ryde 311 G3
Ansell Park (Private)
Clarendon 120 F8
Anzac Oval
Engadine 488 F15
Anzac Park
West Ryde 281 F15
A P Austin Field
Arncliffe 403 K11
Apex Community Park
Ingleburn 453 J5
Apex Park
Bankstown 369 G11
Bradbury 511 D8
Liverpool 395 C2
Mona Vale 199 G4
Riverview 314 B4
Appin Park 569 G10
Applegum Reserve
Glenmore Park 265 G7
Aquatic Park
Longueville 314 D11
Aquatic Reserve
Frenchs Forest 256 J8
Aquilina Reserve
Rooty Hill 242 J15
Ararat Reserve
Frenchs Forest 256 G10
Arcadia Park 130 A10
Arcadia St Park
Merrylands West 307 A12
Ardill Park
Warrimoo 203 C12
Argyle Bailey Memorial Park
Ebenezer 63 H9
Argyle Place Park
Millers Point A E2
A R Hurst Reserve
Sylvania 461 F10
Arlington Recreation Reserve
Dulwich Hill 373 C9
Armitage Reserve
Chiswick 313 D16
Arncliffe Park 403 E7
Arnett Park
Guildford 337 B1
Arrowsmith Park 431 H6
Arrunga Gardens
Wentworthville 277 C12
Artarmon Oval 285 C16
Artarmon Reserve 285 B16
Arthur Byrne Reserve
Maroubra 407 G13
Arthur McElhone Reserve
Elizabeth Bay 13 A3
Arthur Park
Kings Cross 13 A9
Punchbowl 399 H5
Arthur Phillip Reserve
Northmead 277 G10
Ashcroft Reserve
Georges Hall 367 E14
Ashfield Park 373 B1
Ashford Reserve
Milperra 397 G6
Ashley Brown Park
Lalor Park 245 J13
Ashton Av Foreshore Reserve
Picnic Point 428 B13
Ashton Park
Mosman 317 C15
Asquith Park 192 A7
A S Tanner Reserve
Monterey 433 G7
Astrolabe Park
Pagewood 406 E4
Atchison Reserve
Macquarie Fields 423 K14
Atkinson Reserve
Gladesville 312 K5
Atlas Reserve
Narellan Vale 508 H2
Attunga Reserve
Bilgola 169 K6
Newport 169 K6
Auburn
Botanic Gardens 338 H6
Auburn Community
Picnic Area 338 G7
Auburn Park 309 D16
Auluba Reserve
South Turramurra 252 B6
Austin Park
Homebush West 340 G7
Austral Bringelly Lions Park
West Hoxton 392 F4
Australis Park
Wattle Grove 425 K3
Avenel Park
Canley Vale 365 J1
Avery Park
Fairfield West 335 E13
Baden Powell Reserve
Bradbury 511 H11
Badgally Reserve
Claymore 481 B12
Badgerys Creek Park 358 F1
Bain Playground
Stanmore 16 J7
Baird Reserve
Matraville 436 H1
Baker Park
Coogee 407 E1
Bald Face Point Reserve
Blakehurst 462 A5
Bales Park
Chatswood 285 C10
Balgowlah Oval
Balgowlah 287 F8
Balls Head Reserve
Waverton 315 D16
Balmaringa Reserve
South Turramurra 252 B5
Balmoral Park
Mosman 317 F8
Bancroft Rd Reserve
Abbotsbury 333 B15
Band Hall Reserve
Birrong 368 K7
Bangalow Reserve
Mona Vale 199 D1
Bangor Park
Coogee 407 D3
Banjo Paterson Park
Gladesville 312 J13
Banksia Field
Arncliffe 403 J11
Banksmeadow Park
Banksmeadow 435 J1
Botany 435 J1
Banks Reserve
Camden South 506 K12
Kings Langley 245 J9
Bankstown Memorial Park
Bankstown 399 E2
Bannockburn Park
Pymble 223 C15
Banool Reserve
North Ryde 283 D12
Bantry Reserve
Seaforth 287 A2
Barayly Park
Dundas Valley 280 B7
Barbara Long Park
Liverpool 395 A3
Bardia Park
Holsworthy 426 C1
Bardon Park
Coogee 377 F15
Bardwell Creek Reserve
Bexley 402 E13
Bareena Park
Balgowlah Heights 287 H14
Canley Vale 366 D5
Bargo Community Park
Bargo 567 D4
Barker Reserve
Camden South 507 A10
Bark Huts Reserve
Belfield 371 C8
Barnetts Rd Reserve
Berowra Heights 132 G10
Barney & Bligh Reserve
The Rocks B A3
Baronesa Park
South Penrith 237 B16
Barra Brui Oval
St Ives 254 C2
Barracluff Park
North Bondi 348 B16
Barralier Park
The Oaks 502 F12
Barratt Reserve
Camden South 507 C14
Bartlett Park
Ermington 280 G16
Barton Park
Banksia 403 K12
North Parramatta 278 J13
Barwell Park
Bexley 432 G3
Bass Reserve
Macquarie Fields 454 E3
Bates Dr Oval
Kirrawee 461
Bates Reserve
Elderslie 507
Bathurst Park
Greystanes 305
Batten Creek Reserve
Lane Cove West 284
Battersea Park
Abbotsford 312
Baythorn Reserve
Ambarvale 510
Bayview Park
Bayview 169
Concord 342
Greenwich 314
Beach Reserve
Mona Vale 199
Beacon Hill Reserve 257
Beale Reserve
Peakhurst 430
Beaman Park
Earlwood 373
Beare Park
Elizabeth Bay 13
Beatty Reserve
Georges Hall 367
Beatty St Reserve
Mortdale 430
Beauchamp Park
Chatswood 285
Beauford Avenue Reserve 492
Beaumont Park
Kingsgrove 402
Beauty Point Reserve
Padstow Heights 429
Bedlam Bay Regional Park
Henley 312
Beeby Park
Mona Vale 199
Beecroft Park 250
Begnell Park
Belfield 371
Belgenny Oval
Camden 507
Belgenny Reserve
Camden 507
Bellamy Creek Reserve
West Pennant Hills 249
Bellamy Farm Reserve
West Pennant Hills 249
Bella Vista Oval
Bella Vista 246
Bellbird Hill Reserve
Kurrajong Heights 54
Bellevue Park
Bellevue Hill 377
Leumeah 482
Bellevue Reserve
Georges Hall 368
Bell Park
Hurstville 431
West Ryde 280
Bell St Reserve
Thirlmere 565
Belmore Park
North Parramatta 278
Sydney E
Belrose Oval 256
Bendall Reserve
Ruse 512
Ben Lomond Reserve
Minto 482
Bennelong Park
Putney 311
Bennett Park
Riverwood 400
St Marys 239
Ben Prior Park
Casula 394
Bensley Reserve
Macquarie Fields 454
Bents Basin
State Recreation Area
Greendale 384
Silverdale 384

errin Reserve
mere 505 H2
r Road Reserve
h Windsor 150 J2
hire Park 179 J7
ra Oval 133 E13
ra Park 133 F12
ra Valley Regional Park
wra 132 J12
wra Heights 132 G6
lee 132 C9
rybrook 220 D2
al 190 E5
ton 161 C2
sby 191 A12
sby Heights 191 B3
sby Heights 191 H6
olah 191 H2
uring-gai 162 E2
nant Hills 220 D2
leigh 220 D2
o Playground
o 567 C7
erri Reserve
field 251 H12
ex Reserve
hinbury 271 K10
Island Reserve
stonecraft 315 B12
nan Reserve
vick Farm 365 H15
Park
olah 192 D5
Reserve
abeen 228 K4
aunders Reserve
nside 243 G14
Rd Park
n Hills 275 J3
ck Park
pool 394 G4
Park
leys Point 313 E13
idge Park
ping Norton 397 C6
ey Job Park
aweena 258 D5
y Grove Park
sgrove 401 F10
y Hills Park 401 F12
Park 402 G14
enary Reserve
burn 452 K11
ennial Park
ndale 11 D7
e 11 F6
ebush Bay 311 A15
kdale 433 G3
ennial Reserve
den 506 H1
ughby 285 F16
al Reserve
i Beach 378 F3
l Reserve 211 F15
Park
pool 395 F3
ng Reserve
n Narrabeen 228 F2
d Oval
gor 459 C10
yce Reserve
ebush 341 B7
tchell Park
yson 312 F9
orrison Park
rebank 395 G5
ters Reserve
eld 372 G2
atson Reserve
n Rocks 278 F2
ughes Park
h Wahroonga 192 F15
Reserve
stone 281 G13
ng Park
Toongabbie 276 J8
ittalang Garden
ey 402 H12

Bingara Reserve
Macquarie Fields 453 H2
Birchgrove Park 7 H2
Birdwood Park
Narrabeen 199 D16
Birdwood Reserve
Georges Hall 367 G15
Birriwa Reserve
Mount Annan 479 E14
Birrong Park
Balmain 7 K12
Blackburn Gardens
Double Bay 347 D11
Blackbutt Park
Pymble 223 G15
Blackbutt Reserve
Killara 253 D14
Blackman Park
Lane Cove West 313 F2
Blackmore Park
Leichhardt 343 H13
Black Muscat Park
Chipping Norton 366 J13
Blacktown
Showground 244 D14
Blackwall Point Reserve
Chiswick 313 D16
Blackwattle Bay Park
Glebe 11 K5
Blain Reserve
Raby 481 H1
Blair Oval
St Marys 239 D13
Blair Park
Croydon 342 E13
Blamfield Oval
Ashcroft 364 H16
Bland Oval
Riverwood 400 E12
Blankers-Koen Park
Newington 310 A15
Blaxland Dr Reserve
Illawong 459 A6
Blaxland Oval 233 F10
Blaxland Park 233 E4
Blaxlands Crossing Reserve
Wallacia 324 J11
Blenheim Park
Coogee 407 G3
North Ryde 283 A10
Blick Oval
Canterbury 372 G10
Blinman Park
Glenfield 424 G10
Blue Gum Park
Roseville 284 F7
Blue Hills Oval
Glenmore Park 266 F13
Blue Mountains National Park
Bowen Mountain 83 A10
Glenbrook 263 B3
Mulgoa 323 A1
Blues Point Reserve
McMahons Point 1 D2
Bluff Reserve
Glenbrook 264 C6
Bob Smith Reserve
Drummoyne 313 G16
Boden Reserve
Strathfield 340 H13
Boggabilla Reserve
Bass Hill 367 E6
Bon Andrews Oval
North Sydney 5 J1
Bona Park
Sans Souci 433 D16
Bondi Park
Bondi Beach 378 E2
Bonna Point Reserve
Kurnell 465 D7
Bonnet Bay Reserve 460 C11
Bonnyrigg Park
Bonnyrigg Heights 363 D6
Boobajool Reserve
North Ryde 283 C14
Boomerang Reserve
Revesby Heights 429 A9

Boondah Reserve
Warriewood 199 A12
Booralee Park
Botany 405 G10
Booral Reserve
North Ryde 282 D11
Booth Park
Beecroft 250 F7
Booth Reserve
Marsfield 282 D5
Boothtown Reserve
Greystanes 305 F10
Borgnis Reserve
Belrose 225 D15
Boronia Park
Epping 250 K16
Hunters Hill 313 D6
St Marys 240 D11
Bosnjak Park
Edensor Park 333 J16
Bossley Bush
Recreation Reserve
Prairiewood 334 G9
Botany Bay National Park
Kurnell 466 F8
La Perouse 436 J15
Little Bay 437 A13
Boundary Rd Reserve
Glossodia 60 D1
Boundi Reserve
Bondi Beach 378 C5
Bounty Reserve
Bligh Park 150 B6
Bow Bowing Park
Bow Bowing 452 D16
Bow Bowing Reserve
Bradbury 511 H12
Bowen Reserve
Bowen Mountain 83 K10
Bowman Reserve
Camden South 507 B14
Boyd St Reserve
Blacktown 275 A1
Boyla Reserve
Gladesville 312 H11
Bradbury Park 511 D7
Bradfield Park
Milsons Point 1 K1
Bradley Av Reserve
Bellevue Hill 347 H16
Bradley Bushland Reserve
Mosman 317 E10
Bradley Reserve
Wahroonga 251 J2
Bradshaw Park
Busby 393 H1
Miller 393 H2
Brady Park
Claymore 481 C9
Braemar Park
Eastwood 280 J7
Braeside Reserve
Glen Alpine 510 E14
Brallos Park
Holsworthy 396 D15
Brays Bay Reserve
Rhodes 311 E10
Breen Park
Caringbah 492 H8
Bremner Park
Gladesville 312 E7
Brenan Park
Smithfield 335 F7
Brennan Park
Waverton 315 E10
Brereton Park
East Ryde 283 C16
Bressington Park
Homebush 341 B3
Brett Park
Drummoyne 344 A4
Brewongle Walkway
Blacktown 274 D6
Brick Pit Reserve
Frenchs Forest 256 H6
Brigade Park
Ryde 282 D16

Brightmore Reserve
Mosman 316 E5
Brighton Street Park
Petersham 373 K4
Bright Park
Guildford 338 C5
Brimbecom Park
Balgowlah 287 H11
Brindley Park
Airds 512 B13
Bringelly
Recreation Reserve 388 B11
Brinsley Park
Pitt Town 92 K15
Brisbane Field
Holsworthy 426 D8
Brisbane Water National Park
Wondabyne 76 K1
Broadarrow Reserve
Maroubra 407 F12
Broadford Street Reserve
Bexley 402 J11
Broken Bay National
Fitness Camp 107 G1
Bromley Reserve
Greenacre 370 B12
Bronte Park 378 A8
Brooklyn Park 75 J11
Brookvale Park 258 B9
Brownlee Reserve
Birchgrove 8 B3
Browns Field
Wahroonga 222 A15
Browns Forest
St Ives 223 H15
Browns Rd Reserve
The Oaks 502 G9
Browns Reserve
Croydon Park 371 H9
Bruce Reserve
Panania 428 E4
Brunswick Park
Liberty Grove 311 C14
Brush Farm Park
Eastwood 280 G9
Brushwood Dr Reserve
Rouse Hill 185 B7
Bryce Oval
St Ives 254 F1
Buchanan Oval,
Newington College
Stanmore 16 E14
Buckle Reserve
Menai 458 E10
Buckley Park
Winston Hills 276 H1
Buffalo Creek Reserve
Hunters Hill 313 C3
Bullock Reserve
Chester Hill 337 J12
Bunbury Curran Park
Glenfield 424 D14
Macquarie Fields 424 D14
Bundara Reserve
North Ryde 283 B9
Bundeena Oval 523 H10
Bundeena Reserve
Bundeena 523 K9
Woodbine 481 F13
Bundock Park
Clovelly 378 B13
Bungan Head Reserve
Newport 170 A13
Burke Reserve
Matraville 437 B4
Burnie Park
Clovelly 377 J12
Burns Bay Reserve
Riverview 313 J5
Burraneer Park
Woolooware 493 C12
Burrows Park
Clovelly 378 B13
Ryde 312 D2
Buruwang Park
Newington 310 B13
Burwood Park 341 K12

Bushells Place
The Rocks ....B A1
Butler Park
South Penrith 237 B15
Byrne Reserve
St Andrews 451 J16
Byron Park
Ryde 282 D12
Cabarita Park 312 F15
Caber Park
Winston Hills 277 E4
Cabra-Vale Park
Cabramatta 365 J5
Caddies Creek Park
Kellyville 185 E7
Caffyn Park
Dover Heights 348 E11
Cahill Park
Arncliffe 403 K6
Calanagara Park
Carlingford 279 G7
Caldew Reserve
Macquarie Park 252 J16
Caley Park
Macquarie Fields 454 F2
Calga Reserve
Waverley 378 B10
Calgaroo Native Garden
West Pennant Hills 249 F2
Calga St Reserve
Roseville Chase 285 F1
Callan Park
Lilyfield 344 A8
Cambridge Park 237 H7
Camden Apex Park 506 K2
Camden Rugby Park
Camden South 506 H14
Camden Showground 476 K16
Camdenville Park
St Peters 374 H11
Cameron Park
Holsworthy 426 C2
Turramurra 222 J13
Wattle Grove 426 C2
Campbell Hill Pioneer Reserve
Guildford 338 C11
Campbell Oval
Canterbury 372 G10
Campbell Park
Chatswood West 284 F13
Chiswick 343 C3
West Pennant Hills 219 K16
Campbell Reserve
Blacktown 244 C12
Campbelltown
Showground 511 G3
Camperdown
Memorial Rest Park 17 F10
Camperdown Park 17 D5
Canally Reserve
Airds 512 G9
Canal Rd Park
Greystanes 306 E13
Canberra Rd Reserve
Sylvania 462 C9
Cann Park
La Perouse 436 K14
Canterbury Park 372 G10
Captain Cook Oval
Woolooware 493 D6
Captain Cook Reserve
Blacktown 274 J2
Carara Reserve
West Ryde 281 H14
Caravan Head
Bushland Reserve
Oyster Bay 461 D4
C A Redmond Field
Rockdale 403 J16
Careel Bay Ovals
Palm Beach 140 B10
Careel Headland Reserve
Avalon 140 G12
Carina Bay Reserve
Como 460 K6
Caringbah Oval 492 H8
Carlingford
Memorial Park 280 A4

Carmen Park
Cherrybrook 219 J3
Caroline Chisholm Park
Winston Hills..........276 K1
Carolyn St Park
Greystanes 306 G4
Carpenter Cr Reserve
Warriewood..........199 E11
Carrawood Park
Carramar..........366 J4
Carrington Park
Wahroonga 222 E2
Carroll Park
Casula..........395 A14
Carrs Bush
Galston 159 H4
Carss Bush Park
Carss Park..........432 G15
Carters Island Nature Reserve
Kurnell 463 J9
Carysfield Park
Bass Hill..........368 B10
Casement Reserve
Castlecrag 286 B13
Castle Cove Park..........285 G3
Castle Glen Reserve
Castle Hill 217 H5
Castle Haven Reserve
Castlecrag 286 C12
Castle Hill Heritage Park
Castle Hill 218 F8
Castle Hill Lions Park
Castle Hill 217 J6
Castle Hill Park..........218 D14
Castle Hill Showground...217 E11
Castlereagh Nature Reserve
Berkshire Park 178 G10
Castle Rock Reserve
Clontarf..........287 H16
Castlewood Village Green
Castle Hill 248 H1
Casuarina Rd Oval
Alfords Point..........429 B13
Casuarina Reserve
Forestville..........255 K11
Catherine Field Reserve...449 F3
Catherine Park
Scotland Island..........168 H2
Cattai Farm
Picnic Ground..........93 J1
Cattai National Park
Cattai..........64 A13
Maraylya..........95 B4
Cattle Duffers Flat
Picnic Point..........428 E12
Cavanagh Reserve
Lalor Park..........245 C11
Cawarra Reserve
Eastern Creek..........272 F7
C D Hensley Field
Hillsdale 406 E12
Cedars Park
Claremont Meadows ..238 G16
Centenary Park
Campbelltown..........511 J5
Croydon 342 F13
Centenary Place
Parramatta 308 C3
Centennial Parklands
Centennial Park..........21 H10
Central Gardens
Merrylands West..........306 H11
Central Park
Concord 341 H5
Longueville 314 E6
Maroubra..........407 C8
Central Tree Reserve
Glenmore Park..........266 A10
C F Williams Reserve
Lugarno 429 H12
Chadwick Reserve
Lidcombe..........339 H6
Chain of Ponds Reserve
Ebenezer 62 E6
Strathfield..........371 A2
Chambers Park
Chiswick..........343 E1

Chaplin Oval
Lane Cove West..........283 G16
Chapman Gardens
Kingswood..........237 J14
Charles Heath Reserve
Five Dock 342 F10
Charles Herbert Reserve
Northmead 277 J5
Charles Moore Reserve
Mount Annan..........509 F4
Charles Park
Smithfield..........335 C6
Charlotte Breen
Memorial Park
Kurnell 464 E15
Charlton Park
Liberty Grove..........311 C15
Chatswood Park..........284 J11
Chattan Park
North Narrabeen 228 K3
Chauvel Park
Chipping Norton..........396 D3
Cheltenham Oval..........250 G10
Cherrybrook Park
Cabramatta..........366 D11
Cherrywood Reserve
Wahroonga 223 B4
Chester Park
Blacktown 244 B15
Childs Park
Chipping Norton..........366 H13
Childs Reserve
Glenfield..........424 G12
Chilworth Recreation Reserve
Beecroft 250 D8
Chisholm Park
Canley Heights..........364 J3
Chiswick Park
Woollahra..........22 A1
Choma Park
Bossley Park..........334 C9
Chopin Park
Plumpton 242 A11
Chopin Reserve
Seven Hills 246 D13
Christie Park
Macquarie Park..........252 E14
Christison Park
Vaucluse 348 G3
Churchill Reserve
Narellan Vale..........479 A10
Padstow Heights..........429 D8
Church Point Reserve..........168 F6
Church St Native Flora Reserve
Blakehurst..........432 E16
Cintra Park
Concord 342 D9
Civic Park
Auburn..........339 D7
Pendle Hill 276 D13
Clareville Beach Reserve
Clareville..........169 D1
Clareville Reserve
Sandringham..........463 D4
Clarke Park
Oakville 123 C14
Clarke Reserve
Bella Vista..........246 F6
Padstow 429 F1
Vaucluse..........348 G4
Clarkes Point Reserve
Woolwich 314 F14
Clark Oval
Kearns 451 C15
Clark Park
Milsons Point ....K G16
Claude Cameron Grove
Wahroonga 223 A4
Claydon Reserve
Kogarah Bay..........433 B13
Claymore Park..........481 B13
Clementson Park
Bondi Junction 22 F8
Clemton Park
Kingsgrove..........401 G7
Cleopatra Reserve
Ambarvale..........540 F2

Clerkenwell Reserve
Ambarvale..........510 G16
Cliff Reserve
North Wahroonga 222 K1
Clifton Gardens Reserve
Mosman..........317 D12
Clinchs Pond Reserve
Moorebank..........395 H8
Clissold Reserve
Emu Heights..........234 K3
Clive Park
Northbridge..........286 G14
Clontarf Reserve 287 E14
Clyde Park
Moorebank..........396 E13
Clyne Reserve
Millers Point 1 C8
Cobbitty Walk
Cobbitty 446 H16
Cockayne Reserve
Castle Hill 217 F14
Col Barratt Reserve
Narellan..........478 B9
Colbee Park
Oakville 122 C14
Coleman Park
Bankstown Airport 367 D16
Berala..........339 G12
Cole Park
Moorebank..........396 F7
Collimore Park
Liverpool..........395 B2
Colquhoun Park
South Granville 338 E2
Col Sutton Park
Baulkham Hills..........246 H12
Colvin Park
Denistone East..........281 J9
Comenarra Playing Field
Turramurra..........252 D5
Commercial Rd
(Netball) Reserve
Kellyville..........185 G9
Commercial Rd Reserve
Kellyville..........185 E10
Community Hall Park
Mt Riverview 204 D16
Community Park
Pyrmont..........8 J16
Como
Pleasure Grounds 460 J4
Concord Oval..........342 C10
Condor Cr Reserve
Connells Point..........432 A13
Connells Point Reserve..431 G16
Coogee Oval 377 G16
Cooinoo Reserve
Enfield..........371 F5
Cooke Park
Belfield 371 B8
Cook Park
Cabramatta West 364 G7
Kyeemagh 404 C14
St Marys..........269 E3
Sandringham 463 E5
Sans Souci 433 G16
Sans Souci 463 B6
Sydney..........D H12
Cook Reserve
Ruse..........512 G3
Cooks Paddock
Paddington..........21 D1
Coolaroo Park
Lane Cove West..........284 D13
Cooleena Reserve
Elanora Heights..........198 F13
Coolibah Reserve
Bardwell Valley..........403 B7
Coolong Reserve
Castle Hill 217 G16
Coonong Creek Bushland
Gymea Bay..........491 F9
Cooper Park
Bellevue Hill..........22 H2
Woollahra..........22 H2
Cooper St Reserve
Engadine 518 H5

Copercornia Reserve
Glenwood..........215 C14
Copperfield Reserve
Ambarvale..........510 H13
Coralie Reserve
Wareemba..........343 A5
Coral Sea Park
Maroubra 407 C12
Corbin Reserve
Quakers Hill 214 D15
Corea Oval
Miranda..........461 K14
Coronation Park
Minto 482 F3
Coronation Playground
Surry Hills 19 E4
Corryton Park
Wattle Grove..........425 J2
Corteille Reserve
Castlecrag 286 A12
Corunna Reserve
Leumeah 482 G15
Costa Park
Busby 393 H1
Cowan Park
Chipping Norton..........396 G5
Cowan..........104 B12
Cowells La Reserve
Ermington 280 E15
Cox Park
Carlingford 279 K5
Craig St Reserve
Punchbowl 399 J9
Craik Park
Austral 391 B7
Crammond Park
Stanmore..........16 D10
Cranebrook Park..........206 H9
Crane Rd Reserve
Castle Hill 248 G1
Cremorne Reserve
Cremorne Point..........316 H16
Crest Park
Georges Hall..........368 A12
Crestwood Reserve
Baulkham Hills..........246 K6
Crete Reserve
Rosebery..........375 J16
Cripple Creek Reserve
Blaxland 234 A2
Mt Riverview..........234 A2
Croatia Park
Werrington 239 A14
Croft Playground
Marrickville..........373 D14
Croker Park
Five Dock 342 K12
Cromer Park
Cromer..........228 F16
Cromwell Park
Malabar..........437 F2
Cronulla Park..........494 A13
Crookston Reserve
Camden South..........506 K14
Croot Park
Hurstville..........432 B2
Crosslands Reserve
Hornsby Heights..........131 K16
Crossman Reserve
Wallacia 325 A13
Crown of Newport Reserve
Newport..........169 G6
Crown Reserve
Picton 563 C11
Croydon Park 372 C8
Cudal Reserve
Ryde 312 C6
Cumberland Park
Newington..........310 D11
Cumberland State Forest
Dural..........219 B1
West Pennant Hills..........249 E2
Cunninghams Reach Park
Linley Point 313 F7
Curagul Field
North Turramurra..........193 E14
Curraghbeena Park
Mosman..........316 J13

Currans Hill Park..........47
Curry Reserve
Elderslie 47
Curtis Oval
Dundas Valley..........28
Cut Hill Reserve
Cobbitty 44
C V Kelly Park
Girraween..........27
Cynthea Reserve
Palm Beach 14
Daisy St Park
Greystanes 30
Dalrymple Hay Nature Res
St Ives..........22
Dalton Reserve
Condell Park..........39
Dangar Oval
Rose Bay..........34
Daniel St Park
Greystanes 30
Dan Mahoney Reserve
Dundas 27
Dan Parklet
Lansvale..........36
Darcy Smith Oval
Emu Plains 23
Dardabong Falls Reserve
Terrey Hills 19
Dark Gully Park
Palm Beach 14
Darks Common
Lapstone 26
Darling Mills State Forest
West Pennant Hills.....24
Darling St Park
Greystanes 30
Darnley Oval
Gordon..........25
Darook Park
Cronulla 52
Darri Reserve
Gladesville 31
Daruk Park
Casula..........39
Darvall Park
Denistone..........28
Davey Sq Reserve
Strathfield..........34
David Frater Reserve
Parramatta 30
David Joel Reserve
Bellevue Hill..........34
David Scott Reserve
Epping 28
David Thomas Reserve
Manly Vale..........28
Davies Reserve
Padstow..........42
Davison Reserve
Parklea..........21
Davis Park
Claymore..........48
Dawes Point Park ....
Dawes Point Reserve
The Rocks..........
Day St Reserve
Drummoyne 34
Deakin Park
Silverwater 30
Dearin Park
Newport..........16
Deborah Wicks Walkway
Blacktown 27
Deep Creek Reserve
Elanora Heights..........22
Deepwater Park
Milperra 39
Deerbush Park
Prairiewood..........33
Deer Park
Royal National Park....52
Deerubbun Park
Cornwallis 12
Deerubbun Reserve
Mooney Mooney..........7
Dee Why Park..........25

Why West
creation Reserve 227 F9
otardi Park
Ives 254 B3
Lardes Reserve
wong 459 J2
ce Park
ping 251 E16
istone Park 281 F11
zil Joyce Oval
orth Curl Curl 258 F11
Creagh Reserve
alon 140 D16
erall Park
ndell Park 398 D5
ils Hole Creek Reserve
wen Mountain 83 G3
on Park
ambridge Park 237 K9
amilton Reserve
stwood 280 J7
mond Bay Reserve
aucluse 348 F6
kson Park
ondi 377 K3
ger Black Reserve
gleburn 453 F12
on St Reserve
addington 13 B12
eny Park
aymore 481 C12
gley Dell
Ives 224 D13
covery Park
ngs Langley 245 D4
bell Rd Reserve
gadine 489 A15
j Kennel Reserve
intingwood 273 J11
phin Park
valon 140 C9
miney Reserve
exley 432 H2
n Moon Memorial Park
amden 507 A4
n Moore Reserve
orth Rocks 248 K14
nnans Reserve
exley 402 J13
nnelly Park
onnells Point 431 J16
utney 312 C7
novan Park
astwood 281 J8
n Stewart Park
pping 280 D4
n't Worry Oval
indsor 120 K10
ris Fitton Park
orth Sydney K J5
rothy Park
ankstown 399 J2
rothy Radford Reserve
Clair 269 H12
uglas Park Sportsground
ouglas Park 568 G8
uglas Smith
emorial Park
lenbrook 263 K2
ver Heights Reserve 348 G8
ver Park
akehurst 462 F2
wnes Park
allacia 324 K14
yle Gardens
urstville 401 E16
yle Ground
orth Parramatta 278 H6
arramatta 278 G15
Charles McKay Reserve
ount Druitt 271 H2
H J Foley Rest Park
lebe 12 B13
vers Triangle
oore Park 20 F2
ummoyne Park 343 G2
ysdale Reserve
derslie 507 H3

Dudley Page Reserve
Dover Heights 348 F10
Dudley Park 339 D8
Duff Reserve
Point Piper 347 E7
Dukes Oval
Emu Plains 235 F10
Dumaresq Reserve
Rose Bay 348 B8
Dunbar Park
Avalon 170 B1
Marsfield 282 A3
Dunbar St Reserve
Silverdale 353 H16
Dunbier Park
Liverpool 395 C7
Duncan Park
Epping 280 J1
Seven Hills 275 G5
Dundas Park
Dundas Valley 280 A10
Dunholm Reserve
Macquarie Park 252 H16
Dunningham Park
Cronulla 494 A11
Dunningham Reserve
Coogee 377 J15
Dunrossil Reserve
Carlingford 250 B15
Dural Park 189 H16
Duri Reserve
Malabar 437 G8
Durrant Oval
Warwick Farm 365 G12
Dwyer Oval
Warwick Farm 365 E13
Eagle Creek Reserve
Eschol Park 481 B5
Eagle Farm Reserve
Eagle Vale 481 F6
Eagleview Reserve
Minto 483 B4
Earl Reserve
Beacon Hill 257 G7
Earlwood Park 402 G3
East Gordon Park
Gordon 254 C5
East Hills Park 427 F6
Eastlake Reserve
Lidcombe 339 J13
Eastlakes Reserve 405 K3
East Lindfield Park 255 C11
Easton Park
Rozelle 10 K3
Eastwood Park 281 A7
Ebenezer Park 63 D5
Eccles Reserve
Belfield 371 D12
Echo Point Park
Roseville Chase 285 H1
Edenborough Park
Lindfield 284 A4
Edgecombe Park
Moorebank 396 C7
Edinburgh Rd Reserve
Castlecrag 286 D10
Edna Hunt Sanctuary
Epping 281 B4
Edna Reserve
Ingleburn 453 C11
Edward Bennett Oval
Cherrybrook 219 G15
Edwards Park
Concord 342 A4
Edwin Wheeler Oval
Sadleir 394 B3
E G Waterhouse
National Camellia Gardens
Caringbah 492 E7
Elder Reserve
Mount Annan 509 F1
Eldridge Reserve
Condell Park 398 J6
Elizabeth Chaffey Reserve
Castle Hill 217 D7
Elizabeth Jonsson Reserve
Mount Druitt 241 F11

Elizabeth Macarthur Park
Telopea 279 F9
Elizabeth Macarthur Reserve
Camden South 507 C10
Elizabeth Park
Narellan Vale 478 H16
Northbridge 286 G16
Scotland Island 168 H3
Eliza Park
Liberty Grove 311 C16
Elkington Park
Balmain 7 B6
Ellerman Park
Dural 188 G11
Ellis Park
Miller 363 G16
Ellis Reserve
Ellis Lane 476 H1
Elms Reserve
Woollahra 22 B3
Elouera Reserve
Macquarie Park 282 E2
Eloura Nature Reserve
Liverpool 394 D3
E L S Hall Park
Marsfield 282 C6
Elvina Park
Elvina Bay 168 B3
Elyard Reserve
Narellan 478 G10
Embarkation Park
Potts Point 4 J2
Embrasure Reserve
Castlecrag 286 B12
Emerson St Reserve
Wetherill Park 334 J4
Emily McCarthy Park
South Coogee 407 G4
Empress Reserve
Hurstville 432 C8
Emu Park
Emu Plains 235 F10
Endeavour Park
Kings Langley 245 F5
Engadine Park 488 F15
Engesta Reserve
Camden 506 K6
Enmore Park
Marrickville 374 E9
Epping Oval 251 D11
Epworth Park
Elanora Heights 198 E11
Eric Green Reserve
Newport 170 A7
Eric Mobbs Memorial Park
Carlingford 280 A4
Eric Primrose Reserve
Rydalmere 309 K6
Eric Wood Reserve
Kenthurst 158 B16
Ernie Smith Recreation Area
Moorebank 396 B9
Erskineville Oval
Erskineville 18 E16
Erskineville Park 18 D15
Eskdale Reserve
Mount Annan 479 E12
E S Marks Memorial Field
Moore Park 376 E6
Esperance Reserve
Wakeley 334 K12
Esplanade Park
Fairlight 288 A10
Etchell Reserve
Minto 482 G8
Ethel Pyers Reserve
Greenacre 370 G12
Ettiesdale Reserve
Spring Farm 507 H6
Eugenie Byrne Park
Warragamba 353 G13
Eureka Cr Reserve
Sadleir 394 B3
Euroka Clearing
Blue Mountains
National Park 263 K15
Euston Park
Hurlstone Park 372 K12

Evatt Park
Bexley 432 D1
Everett Park
Liverpool 394 J8
Everley Park
Sefton 338 F12
Eve Sharp Reserve
Stanmore 16 K13
Eve St Wetlands
Arncliffe 403 J11
Ewen Park
Hurlstone Park 373 A14
Ewenton Park
Balmain 8 D10
Excelsior Reserve
Baulkham Hills 248 A12
Baulkham Hills 248 D8
Castle Hill 248 D8
Northmead 248 D14
North Rocks 248 D14
West Pennant Hills 248 D8
Explosives Reserve
Castle Cove 286 F5
Fagan Park
Galston 159 G6
Fairfield Heights Park 336 A10
Fairfield Oval 336 G14
Fairfield Park 336 G15
Fairfield Rd Park
Yennora 336 F6
Fairfield Showground
Prairiewood 334 G10
Faulkland Cr Reserve
Kings Park 244 G2
Fay St Ground
North Curl Curl 258 F11
Fearnley Park
Beecroft 250 B6
Federal Park
Annandale 11 D8
Ferdinand St Reserve
Hunters Hill 313 J9
Ferndale Park
Chatswood West 284 D12
Fern Rd Reserve
Hunters Hill 314 A14
Fiddens Wharf Oval
Lindfield 283 E4
Fieldhouse Park
Ambarvale 511 A13
Field of Mars Wildlife Refuge
Ryde 312 K1
Field Park
Chipping Norton 396 G6
Fifth Av Reserve
Macquarie Fields 454 G5
Fig La Park
Ultimo 12 J9
Fig Tree Park
Eschol Park 481 F3
Findlay Park
Mt Pritchard 364 E13
Fingleton Reserve
Bondi Junction 377 F3
First Fleet Park
The Rocks B A6
Firth Park
Ashcroft 394 F2
Fishers Ghost Reserve
Bradbury 511 D9
Fitzgerald Park
Homebush 341 C11
Fitzpatrick Park
Picnic Point 428 C13
Fitzroy Gardens
Potts Point 4 K6
Fiveash Reserve
St Helens Park 541 A7
Five Dock Park 343 B9
Flagstaff Reserve
Rosemeadow 540 G8
Fleming Playground
Newtown 17 E11
Flinders Field
Macquarie Fields 454 F1
Flinders Reserve
Camden South 506 K11

Flinders Slopes
Lansdowne 367 C10
Flockhart Park
Croydon Park 371 J9
Flood Reserve
Revesby 399 A9
Flora & Fauna Reserve
Hawkesbury Heights 174 H5
Flora Reserve
Curl Curl 259 A12
Florence Cotton Park
Hornsby 221 C2
Florence Park
Newport 169 D7
Flushcombe Turrets Reserve
Blacktown 274 G8
Flynn Reserve
St Helens Park 541 F1
Flynns Reserve
Bexley 402 C16
Foley Reserve
Georges Hall 367 J14
Fontenoy Park
Macquarie Park 282 J1
Forbes Creek Reserve
Engadine 488 J11
Ford Park
Strathfield South 371 C7
Foreshore Reserve
Greenwich 314 K11
Forest Park
Epping 281 C1
Forest Park Reserve
Harrington Park 478 E1
Forest Redgum Reserve
Glenmore Park 265 F6
Forestville Park 256 E9
Forestville War Memorial
Playing Fields 255 J11
Formica Park
Busby 363 J15
Forrester Park
Epping 281 D4
Forrester Reserve
Kingsgrove 401 J9
Forshaw Field
Sylvania Waters 462 D15
Forsyth Park
Neutral Bay 6 B3
Foundation Park
The Rocks A K2
Foveaux Gardens
Harrington Park 478 C2
Fowler Rd Park
Merrylands West 307 B16
Fowler Reserve
Wallacia 324 H13
Foxglove Oval
Mt Colah 162 F13
Fox Park
Collaroy 229 D14
Francis Park
Blacktown 244 E14
Francis St Park
Enmore 17 A16
Frappell Reserve
Narwee 400 G13
Fraser Park
Marrickville 374 C14
North Wahroonga 222 H1
Freame Park
Mays Hill 307 G6
Freda Park
Hammondville 396 B12
Fred Caterson Reserve
Castle Hill 217 D8
Fred Hollows Reserve
Randwick 377 D12
Fred Spurway Reserve
Eastwood 280 F5
Fred Vassel Fields
Kings Langley 245 C6
Freeman Oval
Warwick Farm 365 F12
Freemans Reach Park 90 G3

Frenchs Forest
Showground 226 A16
Freres Crossing Reserve
Kentlyn 483 G16
Freshwater Park
Strathfield 340 H16
Freshwater Reserve
Harbord 288 J2
Freya St Reserve
Kareela 461 D9
Friars Field
Pymble 223 F15
F Robertson Park
Dundas 279 C13
Frog Hollow
Centennial Park 21 E11
Frost Reserve
Narellan 478 G14
Frys Reserve
Kogarah 433 B2
F S Garside Park
Granville 308 H10
Fuchs Reserve
Elderslie 507 K1
Fullers Park
Chatswood West 284 A8
Fullers Rd Reserve
Chatswood West 284 E10
Fullwood Reserve
Claymore 481 F10
Eagle Vale 481 F10
Furber Park
Berowra Waters 132 E3
Gabo Park
Sadleir 394 A1
Gaden Park
Woollahra 22 D3
Gaiarine Gardens
Pagewood 405 J10
Galaringi Reserve
Carlingford 280 A5
Gallard Reserve
Greystanes 306 G7
Galston Park 159 D14
Gandangara Park
Casula 394 E16
Gannan Park
Ryde 282 F14
Gannons Park
Peakhurst 430 B8
Gap Park
Watsons Bay 318 H15
Gardenia Pde Park
Greystanes 306 B13
Gardiner Park
Banksia 403 C11
Gard Park
Ashcroft 364 F16
Garigal National Park
Belrose 226 D2
Davidson 224 H11
East Killara 254 J9
Forestville 256 E12
Frenchs Forest 255 G6
Ingleside 196 E14
Killarney Heights 255 H13
St Ives 224 K6
Seaforth 286 H1
Terrey Hills 196 E14
Garnet Jackson Reserve
Botany 405 K12
Gayline Reserve
Mount Annan 479 C13
Gazzard Park
Yagoona 369 A11
George Caley Reserve
Mount Annan 509 G2
George Christie Playing Field
Wahroonga 251 F2
George Harley Reserve
Eastwood 280 K4
George Kendall
Riverside Park
Ermington 310 D5
Georges Heights Oval
Mosman 317 F10

Georges River National Park
Alfords Point 428 J14
Illawong 459 E1
Lugarno 429 F15
Padstow Heights 429 C10
Picnic Point 428 F10
Georges River Nature Reserve
Airds 512 G9
Glenfield 424 J12
Ingleburn 454 A9
Kentlyn 484 A9
Georges River
Parkway Reserve
Airds 512 B14
Georges River Softball Complex
Panania 397 G15
George W I Brown Reserve
Quakers Hill 213 G13
Gibbs Park
Sadleir 364 C16
Gifford Park
Penshurst 431 C1
Gilbert Barry Reserve
Marrickville 373 F11
Gilchrist Oval
Campbelltown 511 A6
Gilgandra Reserve
North Bondi 348 C15
Gillespie Field
Warrawee 222 G9
Gilles Reserve
Beacon Hill 257 J5
Gillman Reserve
Yagoona 368 F12
Ginger Meggs Park
Hornsby 191 A16
Gipps Park
Smithfield 335 C5
Gipps Rd Oval
Greystanes 305 D14
Giriwa Picnic Ground
Oatley 430 H10
Girrahween Park
Earlwood 402 K5
Girraween Park
Toongabbie 276 A9
Glades Bay Park
Gladesville 312 G11
Gladesville Reserve
Henley 313 C13
Gladstone Park
Balmain 7 J10
Glenbrook
Native Plant Reserve 234 B15
Glenbrook Oval 234 A15
Glenbrook Park 234 B16
Glendenning Reserve 242 H3
Glenfield Park 424 D11
Glenhaven Reserve 188 A16
Glenlee Reserve
Narellan Vale 508 F1
Glenorie Park 128 B3
Glenrock Reserve
Picton 563 G12
Glenroy Park
Claymore 481 C13
Glossodia Park
Freemans Reach 60 C13
Goanna Park
Greystanes 305 D14
Goddard Park
Concord 341 K9
Golden Grove Park
Kings Langley 245 B4
Golden Jubilee Field
North Wahroonga 223 B1
Gollan Park
Doonside 243 C14
South Coogee 407 G6
Goodacre Reserve
Fairfield West 335 B14
Gooden Reserve
Baulkham Hills 247 A16
Gordon Park 254 A6
Gordon Parker Reserve
Milperra 397 C7
Goroka Park
Beacon Hill 257 D8

Gosling Park
Greenacre 369 K10
Gough Whitlam Park
Earlwood 403 H2
Governor Phillip Park
Palm Beach 109 K14
Windsor 121 F6
Governor Phillip Reserve
Gordon 254 D6
Gowlland Reserve
Panania 398 D13
Gow Park
Mulgoa 295 F15
Graf Park
Yagoona 369 D10
Grange Av Reserve
Schofields 212 F2
Granny Smith Memorial Park
Eastwood 281 J6
Grantham Reserve
Seven Hills 275 E8
Grant Park
Enfield 371 H4
Grant Reserve
Coogee 407 H2
Granville Park
Merrylands 308 A14
Grasmere Reserve
Cremorne 316 E6
Gravestone Park
Rouse Hill 185 C8
Grays Point Oval 491 A14
Greenacre Heights Reserve
Greenacre 369 J14
Greenbank Dr Reserve
Glenhaven 217 K3
Green Ban Park
Erskineville 17 J13
Greendale Reserve
Greenwich 315 B9
Greenhalgh Reserve
Quakers Hill 213 F14
Greenlees Park
Concord 342 A5
Green Park
Darlinghurst 4 G12
Green Point Reserve
Oyster Bay 460 K5
Watsons Bay 318 D13
Greenup Park
Castle Hill 248 D1
Greenway
Kellyville 215 J1
Greenway Park
Cherrybrook 219 G8
Greenway Reserve
Camden South 507 B9
Revesby 398 E11
Greenwich Park 314 H13
Greenwich Pt Reserve
Greenwich 314 H13
Greenwood Park
North Ryde 282 D7
Greygums Oval
Cranebrook 207 B15
Griffith Park
Collaroy 229 D16
Longueville 314 F10
Griffiths Reserve
Camden South 507 B16
Grotto Pt Reserve
Balgowlah Heights 317 J2
Grove Park
Hurstville Grove 431 H9
Guildford Park 337 H2
Guilfoyle Park
Regents Park 369 B1
Gundungarra Reserve
Mount Annan 509 D2
Gundungurra Park
Belimbla Park 501 D14
Gundungurra Reserve
Narellan Vale 508 G2
Gunnamatta Park
Cronulla 493 J15
Gwandalan Reserve
North Ryde 283 C13

Gwarra Reserve
Forestville 255 H8
Gwawley Park
Sylvania Waters 462 H14
Gwendale Park
Eastwood 281 D5
Gymea Baths Reserve
Gymea Bay 491 G11
Gymea Bay Oval 491 D9
Hagan Reserve
Airds 511 K16
Haigh Park
Moorebank 395 J4
Hall Drive Bushland Reserve
Menai 458 F11
Halliday Park
Five Dock 342 K7
Hallstrom Park
Willoughby 285 F16
Ham Common
Bicentenary Park
Richmond 119 D7
Hamilton Park
Turramurra 252 F1
Hammond Park
Ashfield 342 J14
Hammondville Park 426 H2
Hampshire Reserve
Wakeley 334 J16
Hanna Laycock Reserve
Bexley North 402 C13
Hannan Reserve
Oakhurst 241 K2
Hanna Park
North Richmond 87 H14
Harbord Park 258 F14
Harbour View Park
Woollahra 22 G3
Harcourt Reserve
Campsie 371 H11
Harden Reserve
Georges Hall 367 H12
Haredale Reserve
Ambarvale 540 D2
Hargrave Park
Warwick Farm 365 F14
Harley Park
Mt Riverview 204 G14
Harnett Park
Mosman 316 G12
Harold Bull Reserve
Lakemba 401 D3
Harold Corr Oval
Cambridge Park 238 C10
Harold Fraser Reserve
Kogarah Bay 432 G12
Harold Moon Reserve
Auburn 338 J2
Harold Noakes Reserve
The Oaks 502 F13
Harold Read Park
Girraween 275 K15
Harold Reid Reserve
Middle Cove 286 B8
Harold Reserve
Scotland Island 168 J5
Harold West Reserve
Carlingford 279 K1
Harrington Green
Elderslie 477 H14
Harrington Park 478 D4
Harris Creek Oval
Hammondville 426 J4
Harry Dennison Park
Rooty Hill 242 C14
Harry Gapes Reserve
Merrylands 338 D2
Harry Lawler Park
Penrith 237 C11
Hartley Oval
Canley Vale 366 D4
Hart Park
Warwick Farm 365 H16
Harvey Brown Reserve
Blair Athol 511 A3
Harvey Dixon Reserve
Peakhurst 429 J4

Harvey Park
Marayong 243
Hassell Park
St Ives 224
Hastings Park
Castle Hill 218
Haviland Park
Warragamba 353
Hawkesbury Park
North Richmond 87
Hawkesbury Reserve
Sylvania Waters 462
Hawkesbury Showground
Richmond 119
Hawthorne Canal Reserve
Leichhardt 343
Hayes Reserve
Ryde 311
Hayter Reserve
Camden South 506
Hazlett Oval
Macquarie Fields 454
H C Press Park
Castle Cove 286
H D Robb Reserve
Castle Cove 285
Headen Park
Thornleigh 220
Heathcote
National Park 518
Heathcote Oval 518
Heather King Park
Cabramatta 366
Heathfield Reserve
Raby 481
Heber Park
Hebersham 241
Heffron Park
Maroubra 406
Helen St Reserve
Lane Cove West 284
Helles Park
Moorebank 395
Henley Park
Concord 341
Enfield 371
Henri Dunant Reserve
Ryde 282
Henry Lawson Park
Abbotsford 342
Henson Park
Marrickville 374
Henty Park
Yagoona 368
Herbert Crabtree Reserve
Bass Hill 368
Herbert Rumsey Reserve
Dundas Valley 279
Hercules St Reserve
Dulwich Hill 373
Heritage Dr Reserve
Illawong 459
Heritage Park
Moore Park 21
Hermitage Foreshore Reserve
Rose Bay 348
Heron Park
Chipping Norton 367
Hewitt Park
Bilgola 169
Hews Reserve
Belrose 226
Heydon Park
Hunters Hill 313
Rosemeadow 540
Heynes Reserve
Earlwood 372
Hickeys Park
Penrith 237
Hickson Rd Reserve
The Rocks 1
Highfield Park
Claymore 481
High St Reserve
Mascot 405
Hilder Reserve
Elderslie 477

Kinnear Park
Harrington Park 478 E2
Kinta Park
Fairfield 336 A12
Kirkham Park
Elderslie 477 J13
Kirrawee Oval 490 H6
Kissing Point Oval
South Turramurra 252 C6
Kissing Point Park
Putney 311 J9
Kissing Point Village Green
South Turramurra 252 B7
Kitchener Park
Mona Vale 199 C5
Knapsack Park
Glenbrook 234 D14
Knight Park
Yennora 337 D11
Knights Field
Castle Hill 217 F7
Knox Park
Miller 393 F1
Knudsen Reserve
Riverstone 182 E10
Koala Reserve
Greenacre..................370 J13
Koala Walk Reserve
Ingleburn...................453 G6
Kobada Park
Chatswood 283 J9
Kogarah Jubilee Oval
Carlton 433 A8
Kogarah Park
Carlton 433 A8
Kokoda Fields
Holsworthy 426 G4
Kookaburra Reserve
Kingsgrove 402 A10
Koolangarra Reserve
Bonnet Bay 460 D8
Koola Park
East Killara 254 D7
Kooringa Reserve
Raby 451 J13
Korpie Reserve
Melrose Park 310 K4
Koshigaya Park
Campbelltown 511 C6
Kotara Park
Marsfield 281 K6
Kotori Field
Londonderry 148 D3
Kruse Park
Tregear 240 E8
Kulgoa Reserve
Ryde 282 B13
Kundibah Park
Elanora Heights..........198 F14
Ku-ring-gai Bicentennial Park
West Pymble 252 K11
Ku-ring-gai Chase
National Park 192 G3
Ku-ring-gai
Wildflower Garden 224 D1
Kurraba Pt Reserve
Neutral Bay...................6 H13
Kyeemagh Boat
Ramp Reserve
Kyeemagh 404 C12
Kyeemagh Reserve 404 A13
Kyle Williams
Recreation Reserve
Blakehurst 462 B1
Kyngmount Park
Minto 482 J8
Kywung Reserve
Macquarie Park..........283 B6
Lachlan Macquarie Park
Dundas Valley............280 C11
Lachlan Reserve
Centennial Park............21 G13
Lady Penhryn Park
Kings Langley.............245 F4
Lagoon Park
Manly.........................288 F4
Lake Burrendah Reserve
Raby 451 G12

Lake Malabar
Maroubra 407 D16
Lake Parramatta Reserve
North Parramatta 278 E7
Lakeside Park
North Narrabeen 199 A15
Wattle Grove..............396 A16
Lakewood City Reserve
Bonnet Bay.................460 A8
Lalich Av Reserve
Bonnyrigg 364 B10
Lalor Reserve
Glenfield.....................424 F9
Lambert Park
Leichhardt 373 F1
West Ryde..................280 G11
Lambert Reserve
Peakhurst...................430 D8
Lambeth Park
Picnic Point 428 A9
Lambeth St Reserve
Picnic Point 428 B9
Lance Hutchinson Oval
Riverwood..................400 D12
Lance Stoddert Reserve
Kyeemagh 403 K14
Landa Park
Ashcroft 394 G1
Sadleir........................394 B3
Lane Cove Bushland Park
Lane Cove 314 H5
Lane Cove National Park
Killara.........................283 A1
Lindfield 283 E5
Macquarie Park.........283 A1
Marsfield 252 A11
North Ryde 283 F10
Wahroonga.................221 F16
West Pymble 252 G15
Langlands Oval
Annangrove...............186 E4
Lang Park
St Marys 239 G16
Sydney...........................A F11
Lansdowne Park
Villawood 367 E8
Lansvale Reserve.........366 K5
Lapstone Oval.............264 G2
Larchmont Pl Reserve
West Pennant Hills.....249 H9
Larkins Reserve
Rodd Point 343 E8
Larool Playground
Thornleigh..................221 A8
Latham Park
South Coogee............407 E7
Laurel Park
Ryde 312 E2
Lauriston Park
Rosebery....................405 F3
Lawrence Hargrave Park
Elizabeth Bay 13 B6
Lawry Plunket Reserve
Mosman.....................317 D8
Lawson Park
Merrylands 307 D13
Lawson Reserve
Camden South...........506 K13
Leacock Regional Park
Casula 424 J2
Leahvera Reserve
Scotland Island 168 F3
Leemon Reserve
Greenwich 314 J12
Lee Park
Greenacre...................370 F8
Winmalee 173 F12
Lees Park
Ashbury 372 D10
Leeton St Park
Merrylands 306 K10
Le Gay Brereton Park
Mosman.....................316 H2
Lehmanns Oval
Liverpool 394 G1
Leichhardt Oval
Lilyfield 343 J10

Leichhardt Park
Lilyfield 343 J9
Lennox Park
Blaxland 233 J10
Lennox Reserve
Lansvale.....................366 J5
Leonard Reserve
Roselands 401 E5
Leon Lachal Reserve
Eastlakes....................405 J3
Leo Reserve
Greenacre..................369 K11
Leo Smith Reserve
Ramsgate...................433 F11
Leppington Oval..........421 A10
Lessing Park
Hornsby 191 K13
Les Tegel Oval
Catherine Field 449 G4
L'Estrange Park
Mascot.......................405 G5
Leumeah Park 482 E11
Lewis Hoad Reserve
Forest Lodge 11 E13
Lidcombe Oval............339 G5
Lieutenant Cantello Reserve
Hammondville 397 A15
Lighthorse Park
Liverpool 395 E5
Lighthouse Reserve
Vaucluse 348 H2
Lilli Pilli Point Park
Lilli Pilli......................522 G4
Lilli Pilli Reserve
Caringbah...................492 H16
Lime Kiln Bay
Bushland Sanctuary
Oatley.........................430 G10
Lincoln Park
Cambridge Park 237 K8
Linden Reserve
Castlecrag 286 F11
Lindfield Oval
East Lindfield 254 H14
Lindsay Reserve
Forestville...................256 A7
Lin Gordon Reserve
Thirlmere....................564 J1
Links Creek Reserve
Killara.........................253 F13
Lionel Watts Park
Frenchs Forest 255 J1
Lion Park
Lurnea 394 F6
Lions Park
West Ryde..................281 A14
Lions Park & Gardens
Tahmoor 566 A11
Liquidamber Reserve
Narellan Vale..............478 K11
Lisa Cr Reserve
Castle Hill 217 H9
Lisgar Gardens
Hornsby 221 D2
Little Digger Park 284 K2
Little Reserve
Camden 506 K4
Padstow 399 D15
Little Salt Pan Reserve
Padstow Heights........429 A5
Little Tasker Park
Campsie.....................372 E12
Liverpool Showground
Prestons.....................393 J11
Lloyd Rees Park
Northwood 314 H9
L M Graham Reserve
Manly.........................288 D6
Lockwood Park
Greenacre..................370 D5
Lofberg Oval
West Pymble 252 K11
Loftus Oval..................490 C12
Loftus Park
Liberty Grove.............311 C16
Londonderry Park........148 C10
Long Island Nature Reserve
Brooklyn 75 G9

Long Reef
Aquatic Reserve.........229 G14
Long St Park
Smithfield...................335 J2
Longueville Park 314 E11
Looking Glass Bay Park
Gladesville 312 J12
Lorraine Cibilic Reserve
Woodbine...................481 J11
Lough Playing Field
Double Bay...................22 G1
Louisa Lawson Reserve
Marrickville................373 H15
Louisa Reserve
Bass Hill 368 C11
Lovedale Place
Rhodes 311 F11
Lovetts Reserve
Lane Cove West.........313 F3
Lowe Cr Reserve
Elderslie 477 H16
Low Reserve
Smithfield...................336 B3
Loyal Henry Park
Roseville 284 D5
Lucas Heights Oval
Barden Ridge.............488 E6
Lucas Reserve
Cronulla 494 C6
Lucknow Park
Marsfield....................251 G14
Lucy Cobcroft Park
Oxley Park 270 G2
Luddenham
Showground...............326 F16
Ludovic Blackwood
Memorial Sanctuary
Beecroft 250 C2
Ludowici Reserve
Lane Cove 313 J3
Lukes Lane Reserve
St Clair 269 K13
Lumeah Reserve
Elanora Heights..........228 C1
Lynch Creek Reserve
Yarramundi 145 F13
Lynelle Park
Eastwood 281 H3
Lyne Park
Rose Bay....................347 K10
Lynn Park
Denistone West..........280 J11
Lynwood Park
Blacktown 245 A9
St Helens Park 541 J3
Lysaght Park
Chiswick.....................343 D3
Lytton St Park
Wentworthville...........307 B1
Macarthur Park
Camden 507 A2
McBurney Reserve
Baulkham Hills...........248 B9
McCarrs Creek Reserve
Ingleside 168 A11
McCarthy Park
Lurnea 394 D9
McCarthy Reserve
Rockdale....................403 G16
McCauley Park
Ryde 282 F14
McCoy Park
Toongabbie 276 C3
McCredie Park
Guildford....................337 B5
McGirr Park
Cartwright 394 A4
McIlwaine Park
Rhodes 311 E9
McKay Reserve
Palm Beach 139 K3
McKell Park
Brooklyn 76 E11
Darling Point..............347 A8
McKell Playground
Alexandria 18 K14
Mackey Park
Marrickville................403 K1

McKillop Park
Harbord.....................28
Macks Place
Lindfield 25
McLaughlin Oval
Riverwood..................39
McLean Reserve
Bass Hill 36
Macleay Reserve
Bradbury 51
McLeod Reserve
Bankstown 36
McMahons Park
Kurrajong ....
McMillan Park
Chipping Norton.........39
McNielly Park
Marrickville................37
McQuade Park
Windsor 12
Macquarie Fields Park ..45
Macquarie Park
Freemans Reach 12
Macquarie Place Park
Sydney ....
Macquarie Rd Reserve
Macquarie Fields........45
McRaes Reserve
Penshurst...................43
Maddison Reserve
Pymble.......................22
Magdala Park
North Ryde.................28
Magura Reserve
Mt Riverview 23
Maianbar Reserve
Maianbar....................52
Maitland Reserve
Davidson....................25
Major Mitchell Reserve
Blaxland 23
Majors Bay Reserve
Concord 31
Maley Park
Guildford West...........33
Mallee Reserve
Gladesville 31
Malta Park
Fairfield East 33
Maluga Passive Park
Birrong.......................36
Manaleuka Park
Raby 45
Manly Dam Reserve
Allambie Heights........28
Manly District Park
North Manly 25
Manly Oval 28
Manly-Warringah
War Memorial Park
Allambie Heights........25
Manly West Park
Balgowlah 28
Manna Gum Reserve
Narellan Vale.............47
Mannix Park
Heckenberg 36
Manns Point Park
Greenwich 31
Manooka Reserve
Bradbury 51
Manuka Reserve
Bass Hill 36
Maraylya Park.............12
Marayong Oval 24
Marconi Oval
Bossley Park..............33
Marconi Park
Bossley Park..............33
Marden Reserve
Georges Hall..............36
Marine Park
Avalon........................17
Bilgola 17
Marion Reserve
Yagoona.....................36
Marjorie Park
Eastwood 28

Park
rama.....378 D6
e Reserve
acre.....370 G1
ville Park.....373 J9
ayground
sham.....16 A12
en Park
belltown.....511 B7
eld Park.....251 K15
Knight Reserve
ille.....216 F3
Reserve
Ryde.....283 B13
Park
ll.....466 A9
owe Reserve
an Vale.....508 H2
ackillop Park
rys.....269 F2
Vade Reserve
bine.....481 G11
Memorial Park...405 D3
t Oval.....405 C3
t Park.....405 C3
ati Reserve
burn.....453 G10
ic School Oval
ham Hills.....247 E13
Park
ebush.....341 B5
Windsor.....120 G13
Gardens
s Nest.....5 C1
son Park
jong.....55 H14
ville Park
ubra.....406 J15
ws Park
acre.....370 G8
ogan Reserve
own.....374 H9
rell Park
sham.....16 B11
e Hughes Reserve
e Hill.....218 B12
e O'Connell Reserve
ford.....337 J7
na Cr Reserve
ville.....216 E3
on Park
belltown.....511 F4
uddock Reserve
ton Hills.....277 B1
ell Reserve
stown.....368 J15
owpe Reserve
y Hill.....271 J4
Hill Reserve.....307 J5
Park
Ryde.....280 J14
wbank
orial Park.....311 D4
wbank Park.....311 B4
Park
ea.....394 C13
uca Reserve
lan Vale.....478 J14
y Gardens
n Hills.....246 D12
se Park
ers Hill.....243 G2
e Reserve
ebush.....340 H11
rial Av Reserve
es.....224 A9
rial Oval
burn.....453 C3
rial Park
jong.....85 E2
aville.....407 B15
ylands.....307 G12
rial Playing Fields
ton-le-sands.....433 H4
ry Park
man.....316 K9
Park.....458 J12

Menangle River Reserve
Menangle Park.....538 J11
Mercer St Reserve
Castle Hill.....218 D15
Mereil Reserve
Campbelltown.....511 K3
Merino Reserve
Airds.....511 K15
Elderslie.....507 G2
Merrett Playground
Waverton.....315 E13
Merryland Remembrance Park
Merrylands West.....307 A11
Merrylands Park.....307 D11
Metcalfe Park
Moorebank.....396 D9
Metella Reserve
Toongabbie.....275 E13
Meyer Reserve
Oatley.....430 J13
Michael Simpson Reserve
Baulkham Hills.....246 K11
Middle Creek Reserve
Narrabeen.....228 A6
Middle Head Oval
Mosman.....317 J6
Middleton Park
Yagoona.....368 F10
Midgee Reserve
Marsfield.....251 J13
Midlothian Reserve
St Andrews.....452 B12
Mihajlovic Park
Green Valley.....363 D9
Mihkelson Reserve
Quakers Hill.....214 B10
Mildura Reserve
Campsie.....372 B9
Milkmaids Reserve
North Turramurra.....223 F7
Millennium Parklands
Homebush Bay.....310 F8
Miller Park.....393 G5
Miller Reserve
Ermington.....310 E2
Millers Reserve
Manly Vale.....287 K1
Mill Park
Liverpool.....395 C9
Mills Park
Asquith.....192 D11
Mill St Reserve
Riverstone.....182 H6
Millwood Park
Lindfield.....284 E3
Milperra Reserve.....397 J10
Milray Reserve
Wollstonecraft.....315 B10
Milson Park
Milsons Point.....6 B12
Wentworthville.....277 D13
Milton Park
Macquarie Fields.....453 G3
Mimosa Rd Oval
Turramurra.....252 F4
Minchinbury Reserve...271 J7
Minga Reserve
Ryde.....282 F15
Minkara Reserve
Bayview.....168 F12
Minnamurra Av Reserve
Pymble.....253 C8
Mirambeena Regional Park
Lansdowne.....367 A6
Miranda Park.....491 J2
Mission Fields
Centennial Park.....21 F14
Mitchell Cr Oval
Turramurra.....222 C16
Mitchell Park
Cattai.....95 B6
Mitchell Reserve
Blacktown.....275 A5
M J Bennett Reserve
Westmead.....307 E2
M Kenzie Field
Kingsford.....407 B5

Mobbs La Reserve
Epping.....280 F4
Model Farms Reserve
Northmead.....277 J2
Model Farms Siding Reserve
Northmead.....278 A3
Molly Moore Park
Chipping Norton.....396 G4
Mona Park
Auburn.....338 J2
Monarch Field
Macquarie Fields.....453 K5
Monash Park
Gladesville.....312 J6
Monash Reserve
East Hills.....427 J5
Mona Vale
Headland Reserve.....199 H3
Moncur Reserve
Woollahra.....21 J2
Monfarville Reserve
St Marys.....269 G6
Monro Park
Cronulla.....493 K13
Montague Gardens
Stanmore.....16 G11
Monteith Reserve
Baulkham Hills.....247 D6
Montgomery Reserve
Padstow.....428 K1
Montrose Reserve
Abbotsford.....343 A1
Montview Park And Oval
Hornsby Heights.....161 E16
Monty Bennett Oval
Wentworthville.....306 H3
Moore Park
Beverley Park.....433 A9
Busby.....363 H14
Eastwood.....281 D5
Merrylands.....307 D15
Moore Park.....20 F4
Moore Reserve
Oatley.....431 F11
West Pennant Hills.....249 C5
Moorfield Hills Reserve
Dural.....219 A3
Morella Park
Palm Beach.....140 B5
Morgan Park
Miller.....393 G4
Morgan Power Reserve
Kings Langley.....245 B6
Mornington Reserve
Hunters Hill.....314 B12
Morreau Reserve
Rooty Hill.....272 G4
Morrison Bay Park
Putney.....312 C8
Mort Bay Park
Birchgrove.....7 K5
Morton Park
Lewisham.....373 G7
Morts Reserve
Woolwich.....314 E14
Morunga Park
North Richmond.....87 D16
Mount Annan
Botanic Garden.....509 G7
Mountbatten Park
West Pymble.....253 B13
Mount Druitt Park
Bonnyrigg.....270 K3
Mount Druitt Town
Centre Reserve.....241 G15
Mt Kuring-gai Oval.....162 J14
Mt Lewis Park.....370 A16
Mt Pritchard Oval.....364 E7
Mt Royal Reserve
Strathfield.....341 A14
Mt Sion Park
Glenbrook.....234 A11
Mt Wilberforce
Lookout Reserve
West Pennant Hills.....249 J4
Mowbray Park
Lane Cove West.....283 J12

Moxham Park
Northmead.....277 J4
Mubo Park
Holsworthy.....426 D3
Mulgoa Nature Reserve
Glenmore Park.....265 D7
Mulgoa Park.....295 C15
Muller Reserve
Hillsdale.....406 G13
Mundurama Reserve
Ambarvale.....540 E2
Munn St Reserve
Millers Point.....A A2
Munro Park
Lurnea.....394 E11
Munro St Park
Greystanes.....305 D10
Murragan Reserve
Hinchinbrook.....363 D15
Murray Farm Reserve
Carlingford.....249 E12
Muston Park
Chatswood.....285 D6
Mutch Park
Pagewood.....406 D9
Myles Dunphy
Bushlands Reserve
Oatley.....431 B13
Myrtle St Fields
Claremont Meadows..268 H2
Nagle Park
Maroubra.....406 J10
Nanbaree Reserve
Balgowlah Heights.....287 J12
Nareen Reserve
North Narrabeen.....198 J16
Narellan Park.....478 B7
Narnia Park
Alfords Point.....459 A2
Narroy Park
North Narrabeen.....198 H16
Navua Reserve
Grose Wold.....116 F10
Navy Oval
Kingsford.....407 E5
Neal Park
Hornsby.....191 K16
Neat Reserve
Campsie.....371 H14
Nemesia St Park
Greystanes.....305 K12
Neptune Park
Revesby.....428 K5
Nerang Park
Ryde.....282 G14
Ness Park
Marrickville.....373 G12
Neville Reserve
Bass Hill.....368 D12
Newington Old Boys Oval
Stanmore.....16 F13
Newington Reserve
Silverwater.....310 A10
Newington Road Playground
Enmore.....16 G15
Newland Reserve
Milperra.....397 E10
Newlands La Reserve
Wollstonecraft.....315 E9
Newport Heights Reserve
Bilgola.....169 E5
Newport Park.....169 H11
Nicholls Reserve
Lane Cove.....314 A1
Nield Park
Rodd Point.....343 E8
Nielsen Park
Vaucluse.....348 A1
Nineveh Soccer Field
Edensor Park.....364 A2
Noel Seiffert Reserve
Sans Souci.....463 D1
Nolan Reserve
North Manly.....258 B16
Noorumba Reserve
Gilead.....540 F10
Nore Reserve
Minto.....482 K5

Norfolk Reserve
Greenacre.....370 E6
Norford Park
Sefton.....338 G14
Norman Griffiths Oval
West Pymble.....253 A11
Normanhurst Park.....221 E7
Norman May Reserve
Lidcombe.....339 J14
Norman Park
Auburn.....339 B9
Norman Peek Park
Penrith.....237 B8
North Arm Reserve
Castle Cove.....285 J6
North Caringbah Oval
Caringbah.....492 J4
Northcote Park
Greenacre.....370 D9
North Epping Oval.....251 J9
Northern Oval
Macquarie Park.....252 D11
Northern Winter Sportfield
Macquarie Park.....252 E12
North Harbour
Aquatic Reserve.....288 D15
North Harbour Reserve
Balgowlah.....287 J10
Northmead Reserve.....278 B4
North Narrabeen Reserve
Warriewood.....199 D12
North Pymble Park
Pymble.....223 D14
North Richmond Park....87 G12
North Rocks Park
Carlingford.....249 F15
North Ryde Park.....283 B12
North Sydney Oval.....5 H2
North Turramurra Oval...223 E4
Norton Russell Reserve
Newtown.....17 B11
Nott Oval
Narellan.....478 F11
Nuffield Park
Zetland.....376 A11
Nugent Park
Chester Hill.....368 B2
Nundah Reserve
North Ryde.....283 C12
Nunook Reserve
Marsfield.....281 H3
Nurragingy Reserve
Doonside.....242 J11
Nurra Reserve
Ambarvale.....510 K14
Oakdene Park
Fairfield.....336 H16
Oakes Reserve
Old Toongabbie.....277 A4
Oakleigh Park
Thornleigh.....220 G11
Oak Park
Cronulla.....524 A3
Oakville Reserve.....122 G15
Oatley Heights Park
Mortdale.....430 G10
Oatley Park.....430 F11
Oatley
Pleasure Grounds.....431 D14
Oatley Point Reserve
Oatley.....461 D1
Oatley Reserve
Paddington.....21 A2
O'Brien Park
Condell Park.....398 J2
Observatory Park
Millers Point.....A D3
Pennant Hills.....250 D2
Ocean View Reserve
Maroubra.....407 D15
O'Connor Reserve
Rozelle.....7 A16
O'Dea Reserve
Camperdown.....17 B6
O H Reid Memorial Park
Chatswood West.....284 A10
Old Boys Union Fields
North Parramatta.....278 G6

INFORMATION

Old Bush Rd Oval
Engadine 489 D14
Old Castle Hill Rd Reserve
Castle Hill 218 E10
Old Kings Oval
Parramatta 278 A16
Old Saleyards Reserve
North Parramatta 278 H13
Old School Park
Gymea Bay 491 F10
Olds Park
Mortdale 430 K3
Old Wharf Reserve
Clareville 139 G14
Ollie Webb Reserve
Parramatta 308 A6
Olola Av Reserve
Castle Hill 218 D16
Olson Reserve
Oakhurst 241 J5
Olympic Park
Ryde 312 E5
O'Neill Park
Yagoona 369 A9
One Tree Hill Reserve
Winston Hills 276 J3
Only Park
Moorebank 396 E11
Onslow Park
Camden 476 J15
Opala Reserve
Belrose 225 K15
Oppy Reserve
Quakers Hill 213 G10
Orana Park
Seven Hills 275 B3
Orara Park
Wattle Grove 395 J12
Orchard Park
Mt Colah 163 J13
Orchid St Oval
Loftus 489 K11
O'Regan Reserve
Baulkham Hills 248 A10
Origlass Park
Balmain 8 F8
Osborne Park
Lane Cove 314 G6
Oswald Reserve
Rosemeadow 540 J8
Oswald Scholes Reserve
Bexley North 402 E13
Otto Losco Reserve
Northmead 277 G6
Oxford Falls
Peace Park 227 B16
Oxley Reserve
Mt Colah 162 C12
Oyster Bay Oval 461 D7
Oyster Cove Reserve
Waverton 315 D12
Paciullo Park
Liverpool 394 H6
Paddy Grey Park
Glebe 11 J13
Padstow Park 399 G15
Paine Park
Moorebank 396 J7
Paine Reserve
Randwick 406 K2
Palestine Park
Winston Hills 276 J4
Palmgrove Park
Avalon 169 K3
Pannerong Reserve
Rose Bay 348 B10
Panorama Reserve
Cabramatta 365 B11
Paperbark Grove
Centennial Park 21 F8
Parabianga Reserve
Wentworthville 277 C13
Paringa Reserve
Balmain 344 E4
Parker St Reserve
Penrith 237 D8

Parkes Avenue
Sporting Complex
Werrington 239 B10
Parkes Reserve
Canley Vale 366 F2
Parkhill Reserve
Leumeah 482 F12
Parklands Oval
Mt Colah 162 A16
Parkside Dr Reserve
Kogarah Bay 432 H13
Parkside Gardens
Wattle Grove 426 B4
Parramatta Park 277 K16
Parriwi Park
Mosman 287 C15
Parry Park
Lakemba 370 G15
Ryde 312 C6
Parsley Bay Reserve
Vaucluse 348 E2
Paruna Reserve
Como 460 E4
Passfield Park
Minto 453 B16
Passmore Reserve
Manly Vale 288 B2
Paterson Oval
Cambridge Park 237 H6
Paterson Reserve
Quakers Hill 214 F10
Pathilda Reserve
Scotland Island 168 J3
Pat Kontista Reserve
Leppington 421 A10
Pat O'Connor Reserve
Canterbury 372 E16
Pat Zikan Reserve
Blacktown 274 G9
Paul Keating Park
Bankstown 369 F15
Pavich Reserve
Mona Vale 199 E2
Payten Reserve
Woodbine 481 J11
Peace Park
Ashbury 372 H7
Peakhurst Park 430 D2
Pearce Park
Liverpool 394 K6
Pearce Reserve
Kings Langley 245 K8
Peckys Playground
Prospect 304 J4
Peel Park
Gladesville 312 G8
Lakemba 371 C15
Pemberton Reserve
Sans Souci 433 F14
Pembroke Park
Marsfield 251 F15
Minto 482 E8
Pendle Hill Park
Girraween 276 A16
Pennant Hills Park 250 K2
Penrith
Football Stadium 236 E13
Penrith Showground 236 F11
Penrose Park
South Penrith 237 A15
Penshurst Park 431 F3
Peppercorn Park
Frenchs Forest 256 H2
Mt Hunter 505 A8
Peppercorn Reserve
Drummoyne 344 B3
Peppermint Reserve
Kingswood 267 G1
Peppertree Reserve
Erskine Park 270 J16
Peppin Park
Airds 512 F9
Percival Park
Rose Bay 348 A9
Perentie Park
Belrose 226 F13
Perry Park
Alexandria 375 E11

Peter Cotter Rest Area
Camperdown 17 D7
Peter Depena Reserve
Sandringham 463 F2
Peter Hislop Park
Auburn 338 G12
Peter Lowe Reserve
Kingsgrove 401 H13
Peter Pan Park
Hammondville 426 K1
Petersham Park 373 H4
Peterson Park
Chipping Norton 397 D5
Peter Van Hasselt Park
Shalvey 210 G13
Phillip Park
Sydney D H12
Phillips Park
Lidcombe 340 B6
Lurnea 394 E8
P H Jeffrey Reserve
North Parramatta 278 K14
Picken Oval
Croydon Park 372 B8
Pickering Park
Peakhurst 430 D7
Pidding Park
Ryde 312 G1
Piggott Reserve
Minto 483 B2
Pilgrim Reserve
Strathfield 340 K11
Pindari Reserve
Bayview 168 J13
Camden 507 A6
Pine Grove
Centennial Park 21 K11
Pine Tree Park
Carlingford 249 H13
Pioneer Memorial Park
Liverpool 365 E16
Pioneer Park
Marsfield 281 K1
Pioneers Memorial Park
Leichhardt 10 A11
Pioneers Park
Malabar 437 E1
Pittwater Rugby Park
Warriewood 199 D13
Plateau Park
Bilgola 169 G4
Collaroy Plateau 228 J11
Playford Park
Padstow 399 C13
Pleasure Point Reserve 427 J6
Plumb Reserve
Woollahra 377 F2
Plumpton Park 241 K8
Point Gilchrist Park
Bexley North 402 C10
Pope Paul VI Reserve
Glebe 11 G5
Poplar Park
St Marys 240 B12
Popondetta Park
Emerton 240 J2
Popplewell Park
South Coogee 407 H6
Portal Waterhole
Blue Mountains
National Park 264 B11
Porter Reserve
Newport 169 K8
Portius Park
North Ryde 283 A15
Potter Field
Colyton 270 C8
Pottery Green
Lane Cove 314 E2
Potts Park
Yagoona 369 F6
Poulton Park
Hurstville Grove 431 J11
Powell Park
Cartwright 393 G6
Kurrajong Heights 54 B12
Powells Creek Reserve
Concord West 341 C2

Powhatan Reserve
Greenfield Park 334 A13
Pratten Park
Ashfield 372 H5
Preston Park
Engadine 518 J4
Price Fields
North Parramatta 278 H7
Primrose Park
Cremorne 316 D5
Primula Oval
Lindfield 283 J2
Prince Alfred Park
Parramatta 278 C16
Surry Hills 19 F3
Prince Edward Park
Cabarita 342 F3
Sutherland 489 K3
Princes Park
Auburn 338 G13
Lindfield 283 J2
Prior Av Reserve
Cremorne 6 K7
Progress Park
Auburn 338 H8
Narwee 400 H14
North Narrabeen 198 K13
Progress St Reserve
Tahmoor 566 A12
Prospect Park 275 C12
Prospect View Park
Smithfield 335 H8
Prout Park
Mt Pritchard 364 G12
Pryor Park
East Ryde 283 A14
Pughs Lagoon Reserve
Richmond 118 C2
Pullen Reserve
Yagoona 369 B13
Pulpit Point Reserve
Hunters Hill 314 B15
Punchbowl Park 399 K6
Punch Park
Balmain 7 F12
Punt Park
Mortlake 312 A12
Purcell Park
Matraville 436 F3
Putney Park 312 B10
Pye Av Reserve
Northmead 278 D3
Pye Hill Reserve
Cecil Hills 362 H5
Pyrmont Bay Park
Pyrmont 12 J2
Pyrmont Point Park
Pyrmont 8 F14
Quakers Hill Park 213 J11
Quandong Reserve
Macquarie Park 282 E3
Quarantine Reserve
Abbotsford 342 G1
Quarry Reserve
Hurstville 431 J9
Maroubra 407 E8
Queen Elizabeth Park
Concord 341 K7
Queen Elizabeth Reserve
Lindfield 283 F2
Queens Park 22 H14
Queen St Reserve
Narellan 478 H13
Queens Wharf Park
Parramatta 308 G3
Quinn Playground
Petersham 16 A5
Quirk Reserve
Bradbury 511 E14
Quota Park
Chipping Norton 396 A4
RAAF Memorial Park
Mount Druitt 241 C10
Rainbow Farm Reserve
Carlingford 249 H11
Rance Oval
Werrington 239 A11

Rasdall Park
Narwee 40
Rawson Park
Mosman 31
Ray Marshall Reserve
South Granville 33
Ray O'Keefe
Bondi Beach 37
Ray Park
Epping 25
Rea Reserve
Drummoyne 31
Reconciliation Park
Redfern 1
Redbank Creek Reserve
North Richmond 8
Red Bank Reserve
Picton 56
Reddy Park
Hornsby 22
Redfern Oval 1
Redfern Park
Minto 48
Redfern 1
Red Hill Park
Oxford Falls 25
Redin Place Reserve
Connells Point 43
Reeve Reserve
Camden South 50
Refinery Square
Pyrmont 1
Regan Park
Moorebank 39
Regatta Park
Emu Plains 23
Reg Coady Reserve
Haberfield 34
Regimental Park
Killara 25
Reid Murray Reserve
St Andrews 45
Reid Park
Mosman 31
Reliance Reserve
Yagoona 36
Remount Park
Holsworthy 42
Renown Park
Oatley 43
Renton Park
Moorebank 39
Resolution Reserve
Kings Langley 24
Rest Park
Brooklyn 7
Reub Hudson Oval
North Curl Curl 25
Rex Reserve
Georges Hall 36
Reynolds Park
Toongabbie 27
Rhodes Park
Concord West 31
Rho-Ker Reserve
Duffys Forest 19
Richard Healey Reserve
Frenchs Forest 25
Richard Murden Reserve
Haberfield 34
Richard Podmore Reserve
Narwee 40
Richards Cl Reserve
Berowra 13
Richard Webb Reserve
West Pennant Hills 24
Richard Webb Reserve
(Deakin Pl)
West Pennant Hills 24
Richie Benaud Oval
North Parramatta 27
Richie Roberts Reserve
Curl Curl 25
Richmond Park
Gordon 25
Richmond 11
Rickaby Park
South Windsor 15

e Park
ey Park 270 E2
eview Park
erstone 182 K4
Range Park
orebank 395 C11
Park
ds 512 C11
rose Park
ntworthville 306 H2
glade Reserve
desville 313 B12
ine Park
cliffe 403 K10
Reserve
erslie 507 D3
Road Reserve
u Plains 236 A9
vesby Heights 428 J9
rstone Park 182 H9
wood Park 399 J14
Park
oty Hill 241 J12
semeadow 540 H3
Campbell Reserve
nkstown 369 G14
erta Street Park
eystanes 305 J6
ert Gardner Reserve
wee 400 G12
ertson Park
tsons Bay 318 F14
erts Park
eenacre 370 D14
erts Reserve
e Dock 343 D8
ertswood Park
xland 234 C5
in Place Reserve
ingbah 492 K10
inson Park
nisontown 266 C3
in Thomas Reserve
ramatta 308 F4
son Park
berfield 343 E11
kdale Park 403 G15
k Farm Reserve
ndas 279 E12
d Park
dd Point 343 G8
ney Reserve
ver Heights 348 G11
e Park
nsby Heights 191 G7
ramurra 252 G3
er Sheeran Oval
cquarie Park 252 D12
Darcey Oval
ler 393 J4
Dine Reserve
mden South 506 J11
Gosling Reserve
rdwell Park 403 A6
Hill Park
ongabbie 276 E6
Routley Oval
ncord 311 J16
y Hill Central Park 272 D2
e Bay Park 347 F10
edale Park
rwick Farm 365 K16
edale Reserve
oydon Park 372 A9
elea Park
ecroft 249 J12
ella Park
rris Park 308 E7
emeadow Reserve 541 A2
e Park
ton 368 G6
evale Reserve
ellan 478 J12
eville Chase Oval 255 D15
eville Park 254 H16
ewood Oval
itara 221 H5

Rosford Street Reserve
Smithfield 305 D16
Rosherville Reserve
Mosman 317 C2
Rosslyn Blay Park
Parramatta 278 E16
Rossmore Park 389 F15
Ross Reserve
Bangor 459 E14
Rotary Park
Condell Park 398 C2
Eastwood 281 G5
Kenthurst 158 B15
Ramsgate 433 F13
Riverwood 400 C11
Warwick Farm 365 G16
Rothwell Park
Concord 342 A6
Rouse Hill Regional Park
Riverstone 184 B3
Rouse Hill 184 G7
Rowland Park
Daceyville 406 G5
Rowland Reserve
Bayview 169 C14
Rowley Park
Lansvale 367 A10
Roxborough Park
Rose Garden
Castle Hill 247 H4
Royal Botanic Gardens
Sydney 2 D14
Royal National Park 520 A3
Rozelle Common
Rozelle 10 H2
RSL Memorial Park
Picton 563 G2
Rubie Reserve
Malabar 437 F7
Ruddock Park
Westleigh 220 G7
Rudd Park
Belfield 371 F10
Ruse Park
Bankstown 399 F4
Rushcutters Bay Park
Darling Point 13 D8
Rushcutters Bay 13 D8
Russell Park
Drummoyne 343 E3
Rutherford Reserve
Burraneer 523 D5
R Whack Allen Field
Ingleburn 453 B4
Ryan Park
Chester Hill 337 J12
Ryan Playground
Enmore 16 G13
Rydalmere Park 309 F2
Ryde Park 312 B2
Sadleir Park 394 C1
Saggart Reserve
St Andrews 481 K2
Saiala Oval
East Killara 254 J6
Sailors Bay Park
Castlecrag 286 D13
St Aloysius Oval
North Willoughby 285 H8
St Andrews Oval
University of Sydney 18 A6
St Andrews Park 452 B16
St Crispens Green
Killara 283 D2
St Helens Park 541 B4
St Helens Park
Playing Fields 541 C7
St Ives Showground 224 J1
St Ives Village Green 223 K11
St James Park
Glebe 11 K13
St Johns Oval
University of Sydney 17 J3
St Johns Park
Parramatta 308 C3
St Johns Park 364 C2
St Leonards Park
North Sydney 5 J1

St Lukes Park
Concord 342 C9
St Matthews
Farm Reserve
Cromer 228 D14
St Pauls Cobbitty Reserve
Cobbitty 446 G15
St Pauls Oval
University of Sydney 18 C5
St Peters Park
North Sydney K C12
St Pius X College
Playing Fields
Oxford Falls 227 A16
Salamaua Park
Holsworthy 426 D3
Sales Park
Luddenham 356 G3
Salmon Playground
Newtown 17 F15
Salmon Reserve
Punchbowl 399 K4
Salton Reserve
Drummoyne 344 B3
Salt Pan Reserve
Padstow 399 H13
Samuel King Park
North Turramurra 223 E4
Samuel Marsden Reserve
Orchard Hills 269 B8
Samuel Park
Vaucluse 348 E4
Sananada Park
Holsworthy 396 D16
Sandakan Park
North Turramurra 193 F12
Sando Reserve
Croydon Park 371 J9
Sandringham Gardens
Sydney D F11
Sandstone Ridge
Centennial Park 21 K8
Sandy Brennan Reserve
Penrith 236 D7
Sangrado Reserve
Seaforth 286 K10
Sanity Reserve
Warrawee 222 H8
Sans Souci Park 462 K6
Santa Rosa Park
Ryde 282 B10
Sarah Rose Reserve
Mount Annan 509 H1
Satelberg Park
Holsworthy 426 E4
Saunders Park
St Clair 270 A13
Sawmillers Reserve
McMahons Point 5 B14
Scarborough Park
Monterey 433 E10
Scattergood Reserve
St Helens Park 541 J1
SCEGS War Memorial
Playing Fields
Northbridge 285 H14
Schell Park
Liverpool 365 A15
Scheyville
National Park 123 D2
Schofields Park 183 D14
Scott Park
Sans Souci 463 C5
Scott Reserve
Roselands 400 E7
Scriven Reserve
Leumeah 482 A16
Scylla Bay Reserve
Como 460 J4
Seaforth Oval 286 J3
Seaforth Park
Bexley 403 A16
Searle Park
Telopea 279 G8
Seddon Park
Glenfield 424 B12
Sedgwick Reserve
Currans Hill 479 G11

Selkirk Park
Killara 254 A13
Sensory Garden
Lilyfield 343 H9
Septimus Reserve
Camden 507 A7
Settlers Park
Ryde 311 H6
Seven Little
Australians Park
Lindfield 254 G13
Seville Reserve
North Rocks 278 H3
Seymour Reserve
Hurstville Grove 431 F11
Seymour Shaw Park
Miranda 492 A2
Shane Park Reserve 209 F5
Shannon Reserve
Surry Hills 20 B2
Shaw Park
Cambridge Park 238 B10
Shaw Playground
Riverview 314 E7
Sheldon Forest
Pymble 222 K16
Shell Park
Greenwich 314 K12
Shelly Beach Park
Manly 289 B10
Shelly Park
Cronulla 494 A16
Shepherd Street Park
Colyton 270 C8
Sherwin Park
Canley Vale 366 E1
North Parramatta 278 F13
Sherwood Reserve
Quakers Hill 213 J12
Shields Playground
Leichhardt 343 G15
Shiel Reserve
Ambarvale 511 A14
Shiprock Aquatic Reserve
Port Hacking 523 B3
Shipwrights Bay Reserve
Blakehurst 462 D4
Shortland Brush
Lansdowne 367 A5
Sickles Creek Reserve
Grasmere 475 J13
Sidney Smith Park
Westmead 307 G3
Sid Sharpe Oval
Oakdale 500 A13
Sid Teale Memorial Grove
North Parramatta 278 G14
Sierra Pl Reserve
Baulkham Hills 246 G14
Signal Hill Reserve
Vaucluse 318 H16
Silverwater Park 309 K7
Simmons Point Reserve
Balmain East 8 G6
Simmos Beach
Recreation Reserve
Macquarie Fields 454 J5
Simpson Hill Rd Reserve
Mount Druitt 270 K3
Simpson Park
St Peters 374 H12
Simpson Reserve
Canterbury 372 F14
Sir David Martin Reserve
South Turramurra 252 B6
Sirius Cct Reserve
Narellan 478 F15
Sirius Cove Reserve
Mosman 316 K12
Sir Joseph Banks Park
Botany 405 D13
Sir Robert Menzies Park
Wahroonga 221 J16
Sir Thomas Mitchell Reserve
Dundas Valley 280 A8
S J Harrison Reserve
Earlwood 402 G6

Skarratt Park
Lapstone 234 H15
Skate Park
Engadine 518 H6
Skenes Reserve
Eastwood 280 H6
Skillinger Park
Busby 363 J16
Slade Rd Reserve
Bardwell Park 402 H7
Smalls Reserve
Grasmere 475 H16
Smart Av Reserve
Camden South 507 B16
Smithfield Park 336 B5
Smith Park
Castlereagh 176 A5
East Hills 427 J2
Richmond 118 E2
Smith Reserve
Kingsgrove 401 J11
Smiths Creek Reserve
Campbelltown 512 E1
Leumeah 512 E1
Ruse 512 E1
Smoothey Park
Wollstonecraft 315 B9
Snape Park
Maroubra 406 J7
Snapperman Beach Reserve
Palm Beach 139 H1
Snowy Park
Heckenberg 364 A15
Snowy Reserve
Seven Hills 275 E10
Solander Playing Fields
Woolooware 493 D4
Soldiers Memorial Park
East Killara 254 H12
Somerset Park
Marsfield 251 H13
Somerville Park
Eastwood 281 C4
Sophia Doyle Reserve
Baulkham Hills 247 A10
Soudan St Playground
Paddington 13 H14
South Creek Park
St Marys 239 E13
South Down Reserve
Elderslie 507 H2
Southlands Oval
South Penrith 266 J4
South Park
Chipping Norton 366 D14
South Sydney Rotary Park
Eveleigh 18 D13
South Windsor
Netball Complex
Mileham St
South Windsor 120 G16
Spain Reserve
Castle Hill 218 D9
Spectacle Island Nature Reserve
Mooney Mooney 75 G4
Spencer St Reserve
Berala 339 C15
Springfield Gardens
Potts Point 4 J5
Springfield Park
Old Guildford 337 E8
Spring Reserve
Spring Farm 508 A6
Spring St Reserve
Dural 188 K13
Stafford Walk
Earlwood 403 C1
Stanhope Reserve
Stanhope Gardens 215 E8
Stanmore Reserve
Stanmore 16 F9
Stan Moses Reserve
Sans Souci 463 D5
Stan Thomson Reserve
St Andrews 452 B13
Stanwell Oval
Ashcroft 394 F3

PLACES OF INTEREST

INFORMATION

Bobbin Head....163 H12
Bondi Pavilion
Bondi Beach....378 E3
Botanical Gardens
Regreme Rd
Picton....563 F1
Bushrangers Cave
Silverdale....384 D12
Butterfly Farm
Wilberforce Rd
Wilberforce....91 J7
Cable Water Ski Park
Panther Pl
Penrith....236 B13
Cadmans Cottage
110 George St....B A3
Camden Park Homestead
Camden South....508 A16
Campbelltown
City Bicentennial Art Gallery
Art Gallery Rd....511 C7
Campbelltown
Steam Museum
Gilead....509 H16
Canterbury Sugar Works
Sugar House Rd....372 H14
Captain Cooks Landing Place
Kurnell....466 C5
Carss Cottage
Carss Park....432 H16
Casula
Powerhouse Arts Centre
1 Casula Rd
Casula....395 A15
Cenotaph
Martin Pl
Sydney....C J2
Centennial Parklands
Centennial Park....21 H10
Central Gardens
Merrylands West....306 H11
Chinatown
Dixon St....E D5
Chinese
Garden of Friendship
Darling Harbour....E B3
Circular Quay....B D6
Cockle Bay Wharf
Sydney....C A11
Commodore Heights....108 J7
Cook Obelisk
Kurnell....466 D6
Crusader Union Centre
Crusader Rd
Galston....160 G14
CSIRO Research Station
Badgerys Creek....328 F8
Cumberland State Forest
Castle Hill Road
West Pennant Hills....249 E2
Darling Harbour....3 B8
Darling Harbour Passenger
Terminal
13 Sussex St
Sydney....1 C14
Darlinghurst Court &
Old Gaol
Oxford St....4 E13
Dee Why Lagoon
Wildlife Refuge....258 K3
Dobroyd Head Scenic Area
Balgowlah Heights....288 B14
Domain....4 D3
Dr H J Foley Memorial
Glebe....12 B13
Dunmore House
Dunmore St
Pendle Hill....276 F15
E G Waterhouse
National Camellia Gardens
President Av
Caringbah....492 E7
El Caballo Blanco
Camden Valley Wy
Catherine Field....450 B11
Elizabeth Bay House
7 Onslow Av....13 A3

Elizabeth Farmhouse
Alice St
Rosehill....308 H6
Elizabeth Macarthur
Agricultural Institute
Menangle....537 H9
Endeavour Light
La Perouse....438 A15
Entertainment Centre....E B5
Eryldene House & Garden
17 McIntosh St
Gordon....253 K9
Exchange Centre
20 Bond St....A K13
Experimental Farm Cottage
Ruse St
Harris Park....308 F5
Fairfield City Farm
Abbotsbury....332 J13
Fairfield
Regional Heritage Centre
632 The Horsley Dr
Smithfield....335 K5
Farm Cove
Sydney....2 E12
Featherdale Wildlife Park
217 Kildare Rd
Doonside....243 H14
Federation Pavilion
Centennial Park....22 A10
Ferry Wharves
(Sydney Harbour)
Sydney....B D5
Fish Markets
Gipps St
Pyrmont....12 F6
Fitzroy Bridge
Windsor....121 E8
Fleurs Radio Observatory
Field Station
Kemps Creek....330 A12
Fort Denison (Pinchgut)
Sydney Harbour....346 F3
Fox Studios Australia
cnr Lang Rd & Driver Av
Moore Park....21 C5
Fragrance Garden
Sydney....D J12
Galston Gorge....160 J16
Gardens of Many Nations
Fagan Park
Galston....159 F6
Garrison Church
Argyle Place....A F2
Gilroy House
Manly....288 J13
Gladesville Bridge....313 G14
Gledswood Homestead
Camden Valley Wy
Catherine Field....450 D9
Government House
Sydney Cove....B K4
Governors Bathhouse
Parramatta....307 K2
Governors Dairy
Parramatta....277 K15
GPO
1 Martin Pl
Sydney....C J2
Green Point Astronomical
Observatory
Oyster Bay....460 K5
Greycliffe House
Vaucluse....348 A2
Hambledon Cottage
Hassall St
Harris Park....308 G5
Harbourside....3 A5
Harrington
Park Homestead....478 H2
Hawkesbury Heritage Farm
Buttsworth La
Wilberforce....91 K6
Hawkesbury River
Railway Bridge....76 D5
Hills Centre,The
Carrington Rd
Castle Hill....217 F12

Hordern Pavilion
Driver Av
Moore Park....20 K9
Hornby Lighthouse
Watsons Bay....318 F9
Horseworld Stadium
Maraylya....125 B14
Hurstville Historical Museum
319 Forest Rd....431 H5
Hyde Park
Sydney....D E10
Hyde Park Barracks
Macquarie St....D G6
Information Centre
Great Western Hwy
Glenbrook....234 B16
Ingleburn
Military Camp....423 C12
Jackeroo Ranch
Kenthurst....125 F10
Jacksons Falls....235 F2
James Beres Bridge
Silverdale....384 C3
Japanese Gardens
cnr Chisholm &
Chiswick Sts
Auburn....338 J6
Jellybean Pool....263 K7
Joan Sutherland
Performing Arts Centre
Henry St
Penrith....236 F9
Justice & Police Museum
Phillip St
Sydney....B F8
Kalkari Visitors Centre..163 F16
Kidseum
cnr Pitt & Walpole Sts
Holroyd....307 J10
Kings Cross....4 J8
Kirinari
Box Rd
Sylvania....461 F13
Kirkham
Stables Homestead....477 F7
Kirribilli House....2 F3
Knapsack Viaduct....234 G13
Koala Park
Pennant Hills....249 H2
Lancer Barracks
Parramatta....308 D4
Lansdowne Bridge....366 K4
La Perouse Monument...436 H14
La Perouse Museum
Anzac Pde....436 J14
Lapstone Hill....234 H10
Lapstone Zig Zag....234 G15
Lavender Bay Gallery
Walker St
North Sydney....K F13
Law Courts....D E5
Lennox Bridge
Lapstone....234 E11
Lime Kiln Bay
Bushland Sanctuary
Oatley....430 G10
Linwood Horse Museum
Byron Rd
Guildford....337 C5
Liverpool Regional Museum
cnr Hume Hwy &
Congressional St....395 B8
Long Bay
Correctional Centre
Anzac Pde
Malabar....437 C6
Macarthur Bridge....507 D6
Macarthurs Homestead
Elizabeth Macarthur Av
Camden South....507 E13
Macquarie House
Ferguson La
Grasmere....476 F15
Macquarie Lighthouse
Vaucluse....348 H2
Macquarie Place....B B11

Mamre Homestead Tea Rooms
Mamre Rd
Orchard Hills....269 E10
Manly Art Gallery &
Museum....288 F10
Manly Dam....287 F2
Manly Oceanworld....288 F10
Man O'War Jetty....2 D9
Martin Place....C K2
Mary Mackillop Place
(Museum)
7 Mount St
North Sydney....5 E8
MLC Centre
19 Martin Pl
Sydney....D B4
Model Park
(open last Sunday each month)
Luddenham Rd
Luddenham....327 H11
Model Steam Trains
Darvall Park
West Ryde....281 D14
Monorail....C K9
Motor World Sydney
Harris St
Ultimo....12 J7
Mount Annan
Botanic Garden....509 G7
Mount Portal....264 F7
Mrs Macquaries Chair....2 H10
Museum
Camden Aerodrome
Cobbitty....476 J11
Gannon St
Tempe....404 A2
Museum of Applied Arts &
Sciences
Powerhouse Museum
500 Harris St
Ultimo....3 A11
Museum of Contemporary Art
Maritime Services Building,
George St....B A5
Museum of Fire
Castlereagh Rd
Penrith....236 G8
Museum of Sydney
37 Phillip St....B E11
National Maritime Museum
Shipyard
Balls Head Dr
Waverton....315 E15
National Park Office
Glenbrook....264 A6
National Parks &
Wildlife Service
Information Centre
110 George St
The Rocks....B A3
National Trust of Australia
Observatory Hill
Millers Point....A D7
Native Gardens
Picnic Point....428 C12
Notre Dame
Mulgoa Rd
Mulgoa....294 H4
NSWFB Operational &
Support Complex
Amarina Av
Greenacre....370 G8
NSW Govt Archives
Claremont Meadows
O'Connell St....268 F3
NSW Hall of Champions
State Sports Centre,
Olympic Bvd
Homebush Bay....340 H4
Nutcote
The Home of May Gibbs
Wallaringa Av
Neutral Bay....6 G10
Observatory
Flagstaff Hill
Millers Point....A D4
Old Government House
Parramatta....308 A2

Old Post Office
Community Art Centre
Great Western Hwy
St Marys....269
Old Quarantine Station
(organised tours)
Manly....318
Over The Road
70 Mulhollands Rd
Mowbray Park....562
Oxford Square
East Sydney....F
Parliament House
Macquarie St....D
Parramatta Museum
Church St....308
Peats Ferry Bridge....75
Pier One
Hickson Rd
Millers Point....1
Pitt Street Mall
Sydney....C
Police H Q
College St
Sydney....D
Pool of Reflection
Hyde Park
Sydney....D
Powerhouse Museum
Mary Ann St
Ultimo....3
Prospect Reservoir....304
Queens Square
Sydney....D
Queen Victoria Building
Sydney....C
Railway Square
Haymarket....E
Richmond Bridge....87
Rouse Hill Estate
Guntawong Rd
Rouse Hill....184
Royal Blind Society of NSW
Enfield....371
Royal Botanic Gardens....2
RSPCA Animals Shelter
Rookwood Rd
Chullora....369
St Andrews Cathedral
George St....C
St Andrews Home for Boys
St Andrews Rd
Leppington....450
St Benedicts Monastery
121 Arcadia Rd
Arcadia....129
St Johns Church
Menangle Rd
Camden....507
St Marys Cathedral
St Marys Rd....D
St Michaels Cave
Avalon....140
St Stephens Church
Macquarie St....D
Sandringham Gardens....D
Scots Church
Jamison St....A
Searles Monument
Henley....313
Shadforth Bridge
Silverdale....384
S H Ervin Gallery
National Trust Centre,
Observatory Hill
Millers Point....A
Silvicultural
Demonstration Area
Berkshire Park....178
Sir Joseph Banks Memorial
Kurnell....466
Solander Monument
Kurnell....466
South Head Signal Station
Vaucluse....348
Sphinx War Memorial...193

City Casino
rmont St
rmont...12 H2
e Archives
e Rocks
ilobe St...A K5
e Library of NSW
icquarie St...B H16
ny Range Flora Reserve
e Why...258 F8
nd Arcade
2 George St
dney...C J5
kland House
ucluse...348 A3
reme Court
eens Sq
dney...D E5
nerland
tertainment Centre
Eton St N
therland...490 F2
ney Aquarium
dney...C A6
ney
ntral Railway Station...E H13
ney
nservatorium of Music
nservatorium Rd
dney...B J11
ney Convention Centre
rling Dr
dney...3 A6
ney Cove...B E2
ney Cove Terminal...B C2
ney Customs House
red St...B D9
ney
tertainment Centre...E B5
ney Exhibition Centre..3 A8
ney Fish Markets
ops St...12 F6
ney Harbour Bridge...1 H4
ney Jewish Museum
3 Darlinghurst Rd
rlinghurst...4 G11
ney Olympic Park
mebush Bay...340 F2
ney Opera House
nnelong Point...B J1
ney Ports Corporation
rbour Control Centre
rriman St
lers Point...1 C8
ney Showground
howground Rd
mebush Bay...310 G15
ney Square...C G13
ney Town Hall
orge St...C G12
ney Tropical Centre
yal Botanic Gardens...B K15
ney Visitors Cemtre
6 George St
e Rocks...B A2
nga Zoological Park
sman...317 A14
outts Observatory
mer St
ndsor...121 G8
Ranch Holiday Camp
bbitty Rd
bbitty...446 J15
Gap
tsons Bay...318 G14
Mint (Historic House)
Macquarie St
dney...D G4
Rocks...1 K7
Sydney Art Gallery
Quarry St & Harris St
mo...12 K9
mere Railway Museum
bour Rd...565 A4
erary Falls
nters Hill...313 E6

Tramway Museum
(open Sun, Wed & Pub Hols)
Pitt St
Loftus...490 C9
Tudor Gatehouse The
Parramatta...308 B2
University of Sydney...18 B5
Vaucluse House
Wentworth Rd...348 C3
Victoria Barracks
Oxford St
Paddington...4 H16
Vision Valley Recreation Centre
Vision Valley Rd
Arcadia...130 C13
Waratah Park
Namba Rd
Terrey Hills...194 G4
Warragamba Dam...353 B5
Wascoe Siding Miniature
Railway...233 G10
Watsons Bay Naval Depot &
Memorial Chapel...318 F11
Watsons Bay School
Historical Site
Old South Head Rd...318 G15
Westpac Museum
6 Playfair St
The Rocks...A K1
Willandra Historical Home
Ryde...311 J3
Windsor Bridge...121 D7
Wollondilly Heritage Centre
43 Edward St
The Oaks...502 G13
Wonderland Sydney
Wallgrove Rd
Eastern Creek...272 E14
World War One Monument
Werombi Rd
Theresa Park...445 C13
World War Two Monument
Aerodrome Rd
Cobbitty...476 K9
Yarra Bay House
La Perouse...436 H12
YMCA Yarramundi
Youth Camp...116 B14

SHOPPING COMPLEXES - MAJOR

Ashfield Shopping Mall..372 H3
Auburn
Home Mega Mart...309 C13
Bankstown Square...369 G16
Bass Hill Plaza...367 K8
Birkenhead Point...344 B4
Bonnyrigg Plaza...364 A3
Bridgepoint...317 A5
Broadway
Shopping Centre...12 H16
Burwood Plaza...341 K14
Campbelltown Mall...511 D5
Campsie Centre...372 A14
Carlingford Court...280 A2
Carlingford Village...280 A3
Carnes Hill Marketplace...392 F10
Castle Mall...218 C15
Castle Towers...218 C14
Casula Mall...394 F15
Centrepoint...D A7
Chatswood Chase...284 K9
Cherrybrook...219 G9
Chifley Plaza...B E15
Christies
Homemaker Centre...399 D7
Christies
Homemaker Centres...217 C14
Chullora Marketplace...370 E5
Clocktower Square...A J3
Cosmopolitan...347 B13
Cronulla Plaza...493 K11
Doncaster...376 E13

Eagle Vale Marketplace...481 F5
Eastgate...22 H8
Eastlakes...406 A2
Eastwood Centre...281 B8
Edgecliff...13 H11
Emerton Village...240 K5
Engadine Court...518 J2
Fairfield Forum...336 E11
Forestway...256 D5
Galeries Victoria...C J11
Glasshouse...D A5
Glenquarie
Town Centre...424 C16
Glenrose...225 J16
Gordon Centre...253 G7
Greenfield
Shopping Village...334 A13
Greenway...308 C3
Harbourside...3 A5
Homebase...275 A13
Hunter Connection...A K16
Hurstville Super Centre...432 B6
Illawong Village...459 J4
Ingleburn Fair...453 D5
Kien Hay Centre...E E7
Kingsgate...4 H8
Leichhardt
Market Place...373 G1
Lemon Grove...284 J9
Lennox...235 E10
Liverpool Mega Centre...365 C13
Luxford Court...241 G15
Macarthur Square...510 K8
Macquarie...282 F1
Mandarin...284 J10
Market City...E C8
Marrickville Metro...374 F10
Menai Marketplace...458 J11
Mid City Centre...C K6
Miller...393 J2
Minchinbury
Hometown...271 D5
Minto Mall...482 H4
MLC Centre...D B4
Narellan Town Centre...478 G10
Neeta City...336 F11
Nepean Square...236 G12
Neutral Bay Village...6 J1
Northbridge Plaza...285 J15
North Sydney
Shoppingworld...K F5
Norwest Marketown...216 G15
Paddys Markets
Flemington...340 J7
Haymarket...E C8
Parkway Plaza...221 A13
Penrith Plaza...236 G9
Piccadilly...D A9
Plumpton Marketplace...241 K5
Quakers Court...243 H3
Queen Victoria Building...C H9
Richmond Marketplace...118 H6
Riverwood Plaza...400 B16
Rockdale Plaza...433 E1
Roselands...400 H8
Royal Randwick...377 A14
St Clair...270 C12
St Ives Village...223 K12
Skygarden...D A6
Southgate...462 B9
Southpoint...406 H14
South Terrace Plaza...369 G16
Station Street Plaza...239 H14
Stockland
City (Imperial Arcade)...D A6
Stockland Mall
Baulkham Hills...247 H10
Stockland Mall
Maroubra...407 A9
Stockland Mall
Merrylands...307 H12
Stockland
Wetherill Park...334 D7
Strand Arcade...C J5
Strathfield Plaza...341 G12
Supa Centa...20 D16

Surry Hills
Shopping Village...20 A7
Sussex Arcade...E F6
Sydney Central Plaza...C K7
Sydney Markets...340 J7
Sylvania Waters...462 F13
The Hills...275 F2
The Interchange...284 H10
The Valley Plaza...363 D13
Top Ryde
Shopping Square...312 A1
Totem...287 J8
Trash And Treasure
Markets...392 G15
Triple Cee...243 F7
Village...239 F16
Warriewood Square...198 K12
Warringah Mall...257 J12
Wentworthville
Shopping Plaza...307 A4
Westfield
Hornsby/Northgate...221 H1
Westfield Bondi Junction...22 J6
Westfield Burwood...342 A13
Westfield Chatswood...284 J10
Westfield Eastgardens..406 F11
Westfield Hurstville...432 B5
Westfield Liverpool...395 E2
Westfield Miranda...491 K4
Westfield Mount Druitt.241 D15
Westfield North Rocks..249 B14
Westfield Parramatta...308 B4
Westpac Plaza...A H13
Westpoint...244 F16
Winston Hills Mall...246 K16
Wintergarden Plaza...B B13

SPORTING VENUES

Alexandria
Basketball Stadium...375 E11
Ambarvale
Sports Complex...510 K12
Andrews Rd
Baseball Complex
Penrith...237 C1
Anzac Rifle Range
Malabar...437 H2
Australian Tennis Academy
Frenchs Forest...257 C2
Bankstown
Basketball Stadium
Condell Park...398 C4
Bankstown City
Sports Complex...399 A5
Bankstown
Football Centre...399 F5
Bankstown Oval...399 D3
Bargo Sportsground
Bargo...567 E8
Baulkham Hills Netball Assn
Kellyville...185 G9
Bellingara Netball Courts
Miranda...461 K15
Belmore Sportsground...371 G16
Bensons Lane
Sporting Complex
Richmond Lowlands..118 J3
Bernie Mullane
Sports Complex
Kellyville...216 J2
Blacktown Equestrian Centre
Marsden Park...212 B5
Blake Rimmer Diamond
Chipping Norton...397 B3
Botany Athletic Centre
Hillsdale...406 E12
Broken Bay Sports &
Recreation Centre...107 E1
Cabramatta
Sportsground...365 G12
Calabria Community Club
Prairiewood...334 D8

Campbelltown Sportsground
Minto...482 B12
Camperdown Velodrome..17 B6
Canterbury Velodrome
Earlwood...403 J3
Caringbah Oval...492 H8
Centennial Parklands
Equestrian Centre
Moore Park...21 B10
Chatswood Oval...284 J11
Chatswood War Memorial
Athletic Field
Lane Cove West...283 F11
Chopin Park
Plumpton...241 K11
Clive Rogers
Equestrian Ground
Warriewood...199 C13
Concord Oval...342 C10
Coogee Oval...377 G16
Cromer Park...228 F16
Dangar-Cranbrook
Sportsground
Rose Bay...347 K12
David Phillips Sports Field
Daceyville...406 E5
Drummoyne Oval...343 G2
Dudley Chesham
Sportsground
The Oaks...502 C13
Eastern Creek Dragway
Eastern Creek...303 C2
Eastern Creek Raceway...273 C15
E G Whitlam Leisure Centre
Liverpool...395 A5
Endeavour Sports Reserve
Fairfield...335 G15
Eschol Park
Sports Complex...481 D4
Fairfield Showground
Prairiewood...334 G10
Forshaw Field
Sylvania Waters...462 D15
Frank Downing
Sports Ground
Putney...312 D8
Gabbie Stadium
Seven Hills...245 J14
Gipps Rd
Sporting Complex
Greystanes...305 A13
Greystanes
Sportsground...305 J10
Guildford West
Sportsground...336 F4
Harold Laybutt
Sporting Complex
Arndell Park...274 C11
Hawkesbury
Indoor Stadium
South Windsor...150 G1
Hills Basketball Stadium
Castle Hill...217 D10
Hockey Centre
Homebush Bay...340 G4
Holroyd Sportsground..308 B9
Howell Oval
Penrith...236 E13
Hurstville Oval...431 K3
Jacqui Osmond Softball Centre
Warwick Farm...365 J12
Jim Campbell Sportfield
Macquarie Park...252 C12
Joshua Allen Diamond
Chipping Norton...397 B2
Kevin Betts Stadium
Mount Druitt...241 H15
King Tomislav Croatian Oval
Edensor Park...333 E15
Kogarah Jubilee Oval
Carlton...433 A8
Lambert Park
Leichhardt...373 F1
Leichhardt Oval...343 J10
Lidcombe Velodrome...339 G5
Little Bay Sports Field...437 C9
Liverpool City Hockey Centre
Moorebank...396 A10

INFORMATION

McKay Sportground.......21 C14
Makepeace
Athletic Field.............336 H14
Marcellin Sports Fields...407 A12
Marconi Oval
Bossley Park..............333 H9
Mark Leece Sporting Complex
St Clair......................270 C10
Melita Stadium
South Granville..........338 G11
Merrylands Park..........307 D11
Merrylands Velodrome.307 D11
National Equestrian
Sports Centre
Menangle Park...........509 C13
Nepean Raceway
Castlereagh...............146 D10
Nepean Rugby Union Oval
Penrith........................237 B2
North Sydney Oval..........5 H2
NSW Academy of Sport
Narrabeen.................227 G7
NSW Catholic
Lawn Tennis Assn
Haberfield..................343 F15
NSW Lawn Tennis
Assn Court (White City)
Paddington..................13 E12
NSW Netball Assn
Lidcombe...................339 F5
Old Kings Oval
Parramatta................278 A16
Oran Park Motorsport..448 E11
Oriole Stadium
Auburn.......................338 H3
Parramatta
City Raceway............309 A10
Parramatta Granville
Sportsground............309 A10
Parramatta Stadium.....278 B16
Penrith City Archers
Werrington.................239 C11
Penrith Park................236 E12
Penrith Sports Stadium
Cambridge Park.........238 C10
Penrith Whitewater Stadium
Castlereagh...............206 D11
Peter Kearns Memorial Oval
St Clair......................269 J9
Petersham Oval...........373 H4
Pittwater Rugby Park
Warriewood...............199 D13
Pratten Park
Ashfield.....................372 H5
Princess Anne
Equestrian Area
St Ives.......................194 J16
Raby Sports Complex...451 C14
Redfern Oval.................19 F10
Reg Bartley Oval The
Rushcutters Bay..........13 C7
Rockdale Womens
Sports Fields.............403 H15
Roper Rd Soccer Field
Colyton.....................270 H5
Ross Gwilliam Sportfield
Macquarie Park..........252 D12
St George Soccer Stadium
Banksia......................403 K12
St Josephs College
Sportsground............313 B7
Serbian Centre
Bonnyrigg Heights.....363 E4
Seymour Shaw Park
Miranda.....................492 A2
Soldiers Hockey Field...460 F12
Somerville Park
Eastwood...................281 C4
Sportsground
Appin.........................569 D9
Stadium Australia
Homebush Bay..........340 E1
State Sports Centre
Homebush Bay..........340 H4
Sydney Athletic Field......20 H16
Sydney Cricket Ground
Moore Park..................21 A6
Sydney Football Stadium
Moore Park..................21 A4
Sydney
International Aquatic Centre
Homebush Bay..........340 G2
Sydney
International Archery Park
Homebush Bay..........310 J11
Sydney
International Athletic Centre
Homebush Bay..........340 F2
Sydney
International Equestrian Centre
Horsley Park.............332 K2
Sydney
International Regatta Centre
Castlereagh...............205 J13
Sydney International
Shooting Centre
Cecil Park..................361 D5
Sydney University Ovals...18 A4
Tennis Centre
Homebush Bay..........340 H4
T G Millner Sportsground
Marsfield...................281 H1
Thirlmere
Sportsground............564 K3
Toyota Park
Woolooware..............493 E5
Trumper Oval
Paddington..................13 G12
University of NSW
Oval..........................376 G15
Warragamba
Sportsground............353 F9
Warwick Farm
Polo Field..................366 C14
Waverley Oval.............377 H4
Weigall Sportsground....13 D10
Wests Athletics Club
Lidcombe...................339 F4
Windsor Sporting Complex
South Windsor...........150 C3
Womens Athletic Field
Chifley.......................437 A8
Woodlands Baseball Complex
St Helens Park...........541 G2
Wran Leisure Centre
Villawood..................367 E4

TENPIN BOWLING

Balgowlah..................287 J8
Bankstown.................399 F1
Blacktown..................244 H15
Campbelltown.............511 H1
Campbelltown,
Macarthur Bowl.........510 J8
Castle Hill
(Wondabowl).............217 A14
Enfield.......................371 B4
Hornsby.....................191 H15
Mount Druitt...............241 G15
Parramatta Super Bowl..308 D6
Penrith.......................236 G12
Randwick Bowl...........377 A14
Rosebery....................405 E1
Ryde..........................312 A1
Sylvania.....................462 B9

TERTIARY & OTHER INSTITUTIONS

ACTORS COLLEGE OF
THEATRE & TELEVISION
505 Pitt St
Sydney..........................E F12
AQUINAS ACADEMY
152 Gloucester St
Sydney..........................A G10
AUSTRALIAN
CATHOLIC UNIVERSITY
Castle Hill Campus
521 Old Northern Rd...218 H9
Mackillop Campus
40 Edward St
North Sydney...............5 D7
Main Campus (Mt St Mary)
179 Albert Rd
Strathfield..................341 A13
AUSTRALIAN COLLEGE OF
APPLIED PSYCHOLOGY
414 Elizabeth St
Surry Hills...................19 H2
AUSTRALIAN FILM,
TELEVISION &
RADIO SCHOOL
cnr Epping & Balaclava Rds
Macquarie Park..........282 A1
AUSTRALIAN
INSTITUTE OF POLICE
Management
Collins Beach Rd
Manly.........................288 J15
AUSTRALIAN
PACIFIC COLLEGE
ADC Building,
189 Kent St
Sydney..........................A C11
BLACKTOWN DISTRICT
COMMUNITY COLLEGE
cnr Kildare Rd &
Lancaster St..............244 B16
CANISIUS
102 Mona Vale Rd
Pymble.......................223 G15
CATHOLIC THEOLOGICAL
Albert Rd
Strathfield..................341 C12
CHRISTIAN CITY CHURCH
Ministry Training College
Wakehurst Pky
Oxford Falls...............227 A16
CHURCH OF CHRIST
THEOLOGICAL COLLEGE
216 Pennant Hills Rd
Oatlands....................279 C6
COLUMBAN
MISSION INSTITUTE
420 Bobbin Head Rd
North Turramurra.......193 F13
DEAF EDUCATION NETWORK
Level 8,
Strathfield Plaza,
11 The Boulevard
Strathfield..................341 G12
DOROTHY WATTS
VOCATIONAL
TRAINING CENTRE
49 Blackbutts Rd
Frenchs Forest...........256 A2
EMMAUS BIBLE COLLEGE
25 Ray Rd
Epping.......................251 A14
GEORGES RIVER COLLEGE
Oatley Campus
cnr Hurstville Rd &
Oatley Av
Oatley........................431 C11
HILLS DISTRICT
COMMUNITY COLLEGE
129 Showground Rd
Castle Hill..................217 G12
INTERNATIONAL COLLEGE OF
TOURISM & HOTEL
MANAGEMENT
151 Darley St
Manly.........................288 K12
KVB INSTITUTE OF
TECHNOLOGY
99 Mount St
North Sydney...............K G8
MACQUARIE UNIVERSITY
Balaclava Rd
Macquarie Park..........282 D1
MACQUARIE COMMUNITY
COLLEGE
263b Marsen Rd
Carlingford................280 B3
MARTIN COLLEGE
161 Macquarie St
Parramatta................308 D3
METROPOLITAN
BUSINESS COLLEGE
Level 5,
28 Margaret St
Sydney..........................A E14
MORLING COLLEGE
(BAPTIST)
120 Herring Rd
Macquarie Park..........282 D3
NEW TRIBES MISSION
Plumpton...................242 D9
NORTHERN SYDNEY
INSTITUTE OF TAFE
Bradfield Campus
192 Pacific Hwy
Crows Nest....................5 C1
Brookvale Campus
154 Old Pittwater Rd...257 J13
Hornsby Campus
205 Pacific Hwy........191 F15
Meadowbank Campus
cnr See St &
Constitution Rd.........311 F2
Ryde Campus
250 Blaxland Rd........281 J15
Seaforth Campus
cnr Sydney &
Frenchs Forest Rds...287 D9
NSW BUSINESS &
ENGLISH COLLEGES
Wembley House,
841 George St
Ultimo..........................E C14
OPEN TRAINING &
EDUCATION NETWORK
EXTERNAL STUDIES
Strathfield
Wentworth Rd...........341 H12
PATRICIAN BROTHERS
TRAINING COLLEGE
134 Eastern Rd
Wahroonga................222 J6
REGENT COLLEGE
55 Regent St
Chippendale................19 D2
ROYAL AUSTRALASIAN
COLLEGE OF PHYSICIANS, THE
145 Macquarie St
Sydney..........................B F13
ST GEORGE & SUTHERLAND
COMMUNITY COLLEGE
131 Sutherland Rd
Jannali.......................460 F13
ST IVES INTENSIVE
ENGLISH CENTRE
Warrimoo Av..............224 B2
ST PAULS SEMINARY
1 Roma Av
Kensington................376 D14
SALVATION ARMY COLLEGE
OF FURTHER EDUCATION
School for Biblical &
General Studies
32a Barnsbury Gr
Bexley North.............402 G9
School for Officer Training
120 Kingsland Rd N
Bexley North.............402 G10
SEMINARY OF THE
GOOD SHEPHERD
50 Abbotsford Rd
Homebush.................341 B10
SOUTHERN SYDNEY
INSTITUTE OF TAFE
Bankstown Campus
500 Chapel Rd...........369 E13
Bankstown College,
Chullora Annex
Chullora.....................369 K5
Gymea Campus
cnr Kingsway &
Hotham Rd.................491 D3
Lidcombe Campus
East St.......................339
Loftus Campus
Rawson Av.................490
Padstow College
Raine Rd....................399
St George Campus
cnr Princes Hwy &
President Av
Kogarah.....................433
SOUTH WESTERN SYDNEY
INSTITUTE OF TAFE
Campbelltown Campus
Narellan Rd................510
Granville College
136 William St...........308
Liverpool Campus
College St..................395
Macquarie Fields Campus
Victoria Rd.................424
Miller Campus
cnr Hoxton Park &
Banks Rds.................393
Wetherill Park Campus
The Horsley Dr...........334
SYDNEY BIBLE
BAPTIST COLLEGE
214 Pennant Hills Rd
Oatlands....................279
SYDNEY
COMMUNITY COLLEGE
cnr Victoria Rd & Gordon St
Rozelle.........................11
SYDNEY INSTITUTE OF
TECHNOLOGY
Broadway Campus
George St.....................E
Design Centre
110 Edgeware Rd
Enmore......................374
East Sydney Campus
Forbes St
Darlinghurst..................4
Eora Centre
333 Abercrombie St....18
Petersham Campus
27 Crystal St...............16
Petersham West Campus
West St
Petersham.................373
Randwick Campus
cnr Darley Rd &
King St......................376
Ultimo Campus
Mary Ann St.................3
THE COLLEGE OF
SOMATIC STUDIES
20 Hudson Av
Castle Hill...................217
UNITED THEOLOGICAL
16 Masons Dr
North Parramatta.......278
UNIVERSITY OF NSW
College of Fine Arts
Selwyn St
Paddington....................4
Coogee Campus
Battery St
Clovelly.....................377
Kensington Campus
Anzac Pde
Kensington................376
Little Bay Campus
Prince Henry
Hospital.....................437
Randwick Campus
King St......................376
UNIVERSITY OF SYDNEY
Burren St Campus
(Australian Graduate School
of Management)
144 Burren St
Newtown.....................18
Camperdown Campus
Paramatta Rd
Camperdown..............18

berland Campus
th Sciences & Nursing)
St
mbe 339 K16
ngton Campus
Rd
ngton 18 F5
tt St Campus
ulty of Nursing)
Mallett St
perdown 17 F5
imes Campus
School)
Phillip St
ey....................D D5
y Hills Campus
ulty of Dentistry)
almers St
y Hills ....E K16
ey College of The Arts
ain Rd
eld....................10 D2
ey Conservatorium of
c
servatorium Rd.......B J11
ERSITY OF SYDNEY
MEAD HOSPITAL
AL CLINICAL SCHOOL
ty of dentist)
mead....................277 F14
ERSITY OF
NOLOGY, SYDNEY
Blackfriars Campus
kfriars St
pendale 18 K1
Campus, Broadway
oadway
no....................3 B15
Campus,
Quay St & Ultimo Rd
market....................E A8
ng-gai Campus
Rd
field 284 A6
ERSITY OF WESTERN
EY
kstown Campus
ecourt Av
erra 397 J10
pbelltown Campus
pbelltown...........510 F5
kesbury
ktown Campus,
ern Rd
ofields....................213 E12
kesbury Campus
rke St
mond....................118 G11
ean
ond Av
gswood 238 A15
ean,
amatta Campus
Victoria Rd &
es Ruse Dr 309 A1
rith Campus
at Western Hwy
rington 238 H13
stmead Precinct
stmead 277 G15
EY INSTITUTE FOR
STRY-THE ARTS
y St
nmoyne....................343 G5
TERN SYDNEY
TUTE OF TAFE
kham Hills Campus
Old Northern Rd &
ard St....................247 H5
ktown Campus
Main St &
ton Rd 274 J1
ding Industry Skills Centre
Showground &
oria Rds
le Hill 217 A11
unt Druitt Campus
Mount St &
th Pde....................241 F16

Nirimba Campus
Eastern Rd
Schofields....................213 C11
Penrith Campus
117 Henry St....................236 J9
Penrith Campus
cnr Second Av &
O'Connell St
Kingswood 238 D15
Richmond Campus
Ceremonial Dr...........118 J10
WESTPAC COLLEGE
30 Ingleside Rd
Ingleside 198 C8
WHITEHOUSE SCHOOL OF
FASHION & INTERIOR
DECORATION
Level 3,
53 Liverpool St
Sydney....................E E2
WIVENHOE VOCATION
229 Macquarie Grove Rd
Cobbitty 477 B2

THEATRES, CINEMAS & DRIVE-IN THEATRES

AVALON
Avalon Cinema Centre
(United Cinemas)
39 Old Barrenjoey Rd...170 B2
BANKSTOWN
Hoyts Cinemas
Bankstown
cnr Jacobs St &
The Mall 369 F15
BASS HILL
Greater Union Drive-in
Johnston Rd.............367 J9
BEVERLY HILLS
Beverly Hills Cinemas
(United Cinemas)
449 King Georges Rd...401 C15
BLACKTOWN
Greater Union Cinemas
Blacktown Twin Drive In
Cricketers Arms Rd....274 F16
Hoyts Cinemas
Westpoint
Marketown 244 F16
BONDI JUNCTION
Bondi Plaza Cinema
500 Oxford St.............22 J6
BROOKVALE
Hoyts Cinemas
Warringam Mall
cnr Old Pittwater Rd &
Condamine St...........257 J12
BURWOOD
Greater Union Cinemas
Burwood
Westfield,
100 Burwood Rd........342 A13
CAMPBELLTOWN
Greater Union Cinemas
Campbelltown
Macarthur Square,
Kellicar Rd....................510 J8
CASTLE HILL
Greater Union Cinemas
Castle Hill Megaplex 16
Castle Towers,
Old Northern Rd.........218 C14
Hills Centre
Carrington Rd 217 F12
Pavilion Theatre
Doran Dr....................217 E11
CHATSWOOD
Hoyts Cinema
Chatswood Mandarin
cnr Victor St and
Albert Av 284 J10

Hoyts Cinemas
Chatswood Westfield
cnr Albert Av and
Anderson St.............284 J10
COLLAROY
Collaroy Cinemas
(United Cinemas)
1097 Pittwater Rd 229 B13
CRONULLA
Cronulla Cinemas Centre
(United Cinemas)
2 Cronulla St.............493 K11
DARLINGTON
Seymour Theatre Centre
cnr Cleveland St &
City Rd....................18 G4
DAWES POINT
Australian Theatre for
Young People
Pier 4, Hickson Rd 1 F7
Wharf Theatre
Pier 4, Hickson Rd 1 F7
DOUBLE BAY
Village Cinemas
Double Bay
377 New South Head
Rd 347 B13
EASTGARDENS
Hoyts Cinemas
Easgardens
Westfield Shoppingtown
cnr Wentworth Av &
Bunnerong Rd 406 F11
ENMORE
Enmore Theatre
130 Enmore Rd 17 C14
ERSKINEVILLE
Edge Theatre, The
cnr King & Bray Sts....374 J10
FAIRFIELD
Fairfield Forum Cinema
cnr Station &
Nelson Sts................336 E11
GLEBE
Footbridge Theatre
Sydney University,
Parramatta Rd 18 C1
Hoyts Cinemas
Broadway
Broadway Shopping Centre,
Bay St....................12 H15
Valhalla Cinema Glebe
166d Glebe Point Rd...12 A12
GLENBROOK
Glenbrook Theatre
Great Western Hwy 234 A16
HAYMARKET
Capitol Theatre
13 Campbell St.............E H7
Reading Cinemas
Market City
Level 3, Market
City Shopping Centre,
9 Hay St ....E C8
Sydney Entertainment Centre
Harbour St....................E B5
HOMEBUSH BAY
Sydney Superdome
cnr Olympic Bvd &
Edwin Flac Av 310 E16
HORNSBY
Hornsby Odeon Cinema
155 Pacific Hwy 191 G16
HURSTVILLE
Greater Union Cinemas
Hurstville
Westfield Shopping Centre,
cnr Cross & Park Rds ..432 B5
KILLARA
Marian Street Theatre
2 Marian St................254 A13
KOGARAH
Mecca Movie City
28 Station St..............433 B3
LEICHHARDT
Palace Cinemas
Norton St Cinemas
99 Norton St................16 A1

LIDCOMBE
Reading Cinemas
Reading Cinemas At
Red Yard (Auburn)
100 Parramatta Rd.....339 J1
LIVERPOOL
Greater Union Cinemas
Liverpool
Westfield Shoppingtown
Northumberland St.....395 D2
MACQUARIE PARK
Greater Union Cinemas
Macquarie Centre.......282 F1
Lighthouse Theatre ...252 C15
MERRYLANDS
Hoyts Cinemas
Merrylands Shopping Centre,
McFarlane St 307 H12
MILSONS POINT
Ensemble Theatre
78 McDougall St............6 C13
MIRANDA
Greater Union Cinemas
Miranda
Westfield Shoppingtown,
Kiora Rd....................492 B4
MOORE PARK
Hoyts Cinemas
Cinema Paris At Fox Studios
Fox Studios,
Bent St....................21 A9
Hoyts Cinemas
Fox Studios, Australia
Fox Studios, Bent St....21 B9
MOSMAN
Greater Union Cinemas
9 Spit Rd....................317 B5
MOUNT DRUITT
Hoyts Cinemas
Mount Druitt
Westfield, Carlisle Av..241 D15
NEWTOWN
Dendy Cinemas
Newtown
261 King St 17 H11
New Theatre
542 King St...............374 J9
NORTH SYDNEY
Walker Cinema The
121 Walker St ....K G7
PADDINGTON
Palace Cinemas
Verona Cinemas
17 Oxford St..................4 G15
PARRAMATTA
Parramatta Riverside Theatres
cnr Church &
Market Sts................308 C1
Village Cinemas
Parramatta 8
Westfield Shoppingtown,
Church St 308 C4
Village Cinemas
Roxy Parramatta
69 George St.............308 D3
PENRITH
Hoyts Cinemas
Penrith Plaza
Cnr Jane & Riley Sts...236 G9
Joan Sutherland
Performing Art Centre
597 High St 236 F9
PRAIRIEWOOD
Hoyts Cinemas
Wetherill Park
Stockland Town Centre,
Polding St 334 E7
PYRMONT
Lyric Theatre
Star City 12 J3
RANDWICK
Ritz Theatre
43 St Pauls St...........377 C16
RICHMOND
Regent Twin Cinema
149 Windsor St..........118 H4

ROCKDALE
Guild Theatre
cnr Railway &
Waltz Sts....................403 C15
SURRY HILLS
Tom Mann Theatre
136 Chalmers St..........19 G3
SYDNEY
Australia Cinema
59 Goulburn St..............E H5
City Recital Hall Angel Place
Angel Pl ....C K1
Dendy Cinemas
Martin Place
MLC Centre,
19 Martin Pl ....D B3
Dendy Cinemas
Opera Quays
2 Circular Quay E..........B G4
Genesian Theatre Company
420 Kent St ....C F10
Greater Union Cinemas
George St (City)
525 George St ....C G16
Harbour City Cinema
6 Harbour St....................E D2
Hoyts Cinemas
Village Hoyts Centre
(George St)
505 George St ....C G16
IMAX Theatre At
Darling Harbour
Southern Prm,
Cockle Bay....................3 C7
Metro Theatre
624 George St ....E H1
Pilgrim Theatre
262 Pitt St....................C K13
State Theatre, The
49 Market St................C J8
Sydney
Conservatorium of Music
Conservatorium Rd.......B J11
Sydney Opera House
Bennelong Point...........B J1
Theatre Royal
MLC Centre, King St .....D A4
WARRIEWOOD
Warriewood Cinemas
(United Cinemas)
4 Vuko Pl....................199 C11

WINERIES

Camden Estate.............507 G6
Cobbitty 475 H2
Excelsior 268 C4
Gledswood....................450 D9
Kirkham Estate.............477 D15
Richmond Estate 57 D11
Vicarys....................357 A10

PUBLISHING DATES

1st Edition....................1967
2nd Edition....................1968
3rd Edition 1975
4th Edition 1977
5th Edition 1978
6th Edition....................1985
7th Edition....................1989
8th Edition....................1990
9th Edition 1991
10th Edition....................1992
11th Edition....................1993
12th Edition....................1994
13th Edition....................1995
14th Edition....................1996
15th Edition....................1998
16th Edition....................1999
17th Edition....................2000
18th Edition....................2001
19th Edition....................2002

MAP A

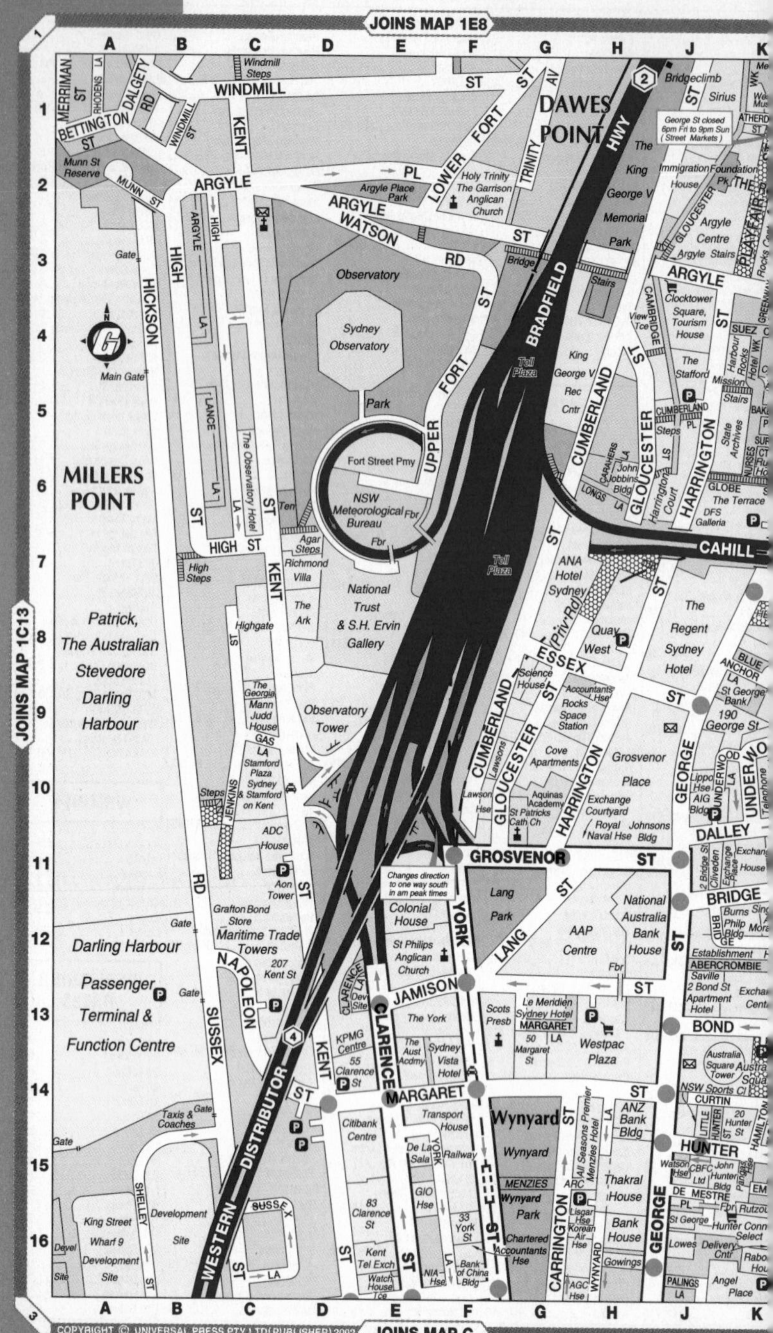

JOINS MAP 1E8
JOINS MAP 1C13
JOINS MAP C
COPYRIGHT © UNIVERSAL PRESS PTY LTD (PUBLISHER) 2002
DAWES POINT
MILLERS POINT
Sydney Observatory
Observatory
National Trust & S.H. Ervin Gallery
Fort Street Pmy
NSW Meteorological Bureau
Patrick, The Australian Stevedore Darling Harbour
Darling Harbour Passenger Terminal & Function Centre
King Street Wharf 9 Development Site
Development Site
WESTERN DISTRIBUTOR
BRADFIELD HWY
CAHILL
The King George V Memorial Park
Argyle Centre
Clocktower Square, Tourism House
ANA Hotel Sydney
The Regent Sydney Hotel
Grosvenor Place
Lang Park
AAP Centre
National Australia Bank House
Westpac Plaza
Wynyard Park
Observatory Tower
Maritime Trade Towers
Colonial House
St Philips Anglican Church
George St closed 6pm Fri to 9pm Sun (Street Markets)
Changes direction to one way south in am peak times

MAP B

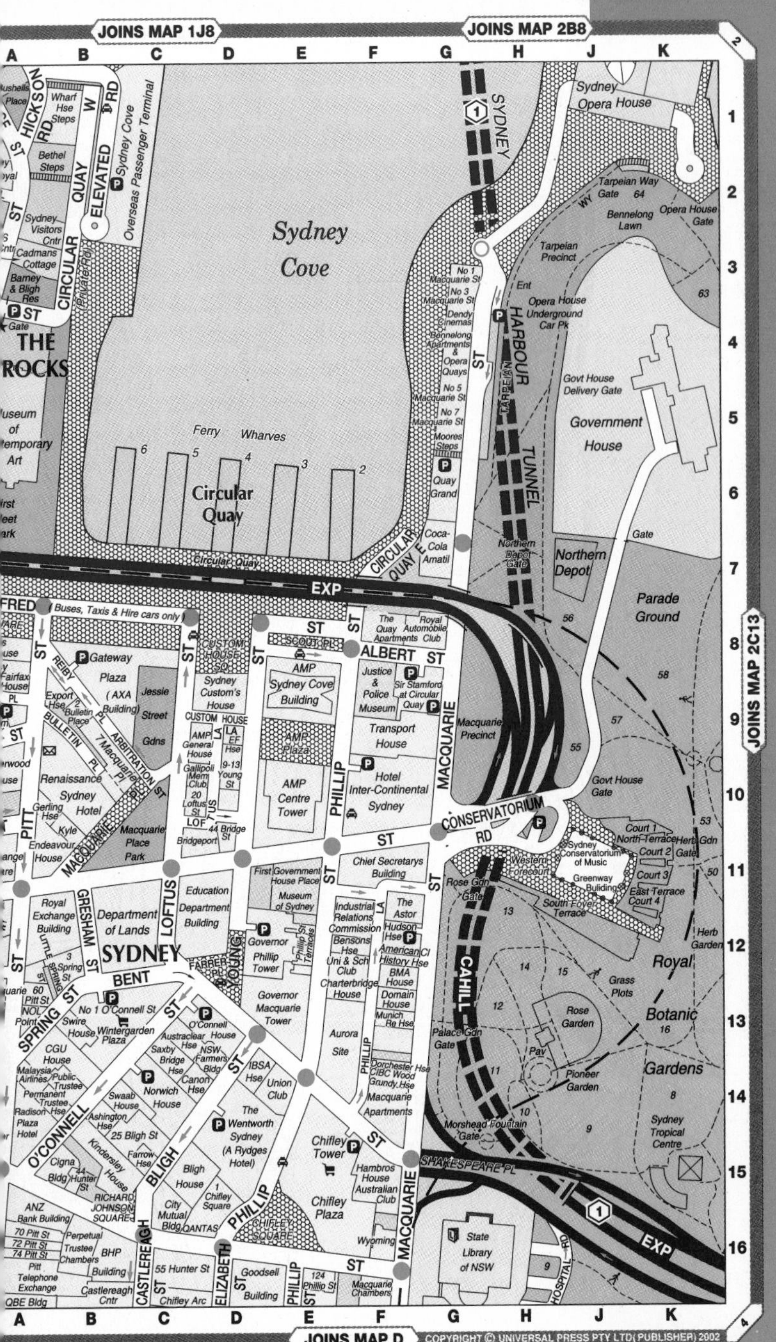
JOINS MAP 1J8
JOINS MAP 2B8
JOINS MAP 2C13
JOINS MAP D
Sydney Cove
Circular Quay
Ferry Wharves
THE ROCKS
Sydney Opera House
Government House
Parade Ground
Royal Botanic Gardens
Northern Depot
Macquarie Precinct
Sydney Conservatorium of Music
Rose Garden
Pioneer Garden
Sydney Tropical Centre
State Library of NSW
SYDNEY
SYDNEY HARBOUR TUNNEL
CAHILL EXP
CIRCULAR QUAY
CONSERVATORIUM RD
MACQUARIE ST
PHILLIP ST
ALBERT ST
BENT ST
BLIGH ST
O'CONNELL ST
HUNTER ST
LOFTUS ST
PITT ST
CASTLEREAGH ST
ELIZABETH ST
HOSPITAL RD
SHAKESPEARE PL
Overseas Passenger Terminal
Justice & Police Museum
Transport House
Hotel Inter-Continental Sydney
Chief Secretarys Building
Museum of Sydney
Governor Phillip Tower
Governor Macquarie Tower
Chifley Tower
Chifley Plaza
Education Department Building
Department of Lands
Sydney Custom's House
AMP Centre Tower
Renaissance Sydney Hotel
Royal Exchange Building
The Wentworth Sydney (A Rydges Hotel)
Sydney Visitors Cntr
Cadmans Cottage
Museum of Contemporary Art
COPYRIGHT © UNIVERSAL PRESS PTY LTD (PUBLISHER) 2002

MAP C

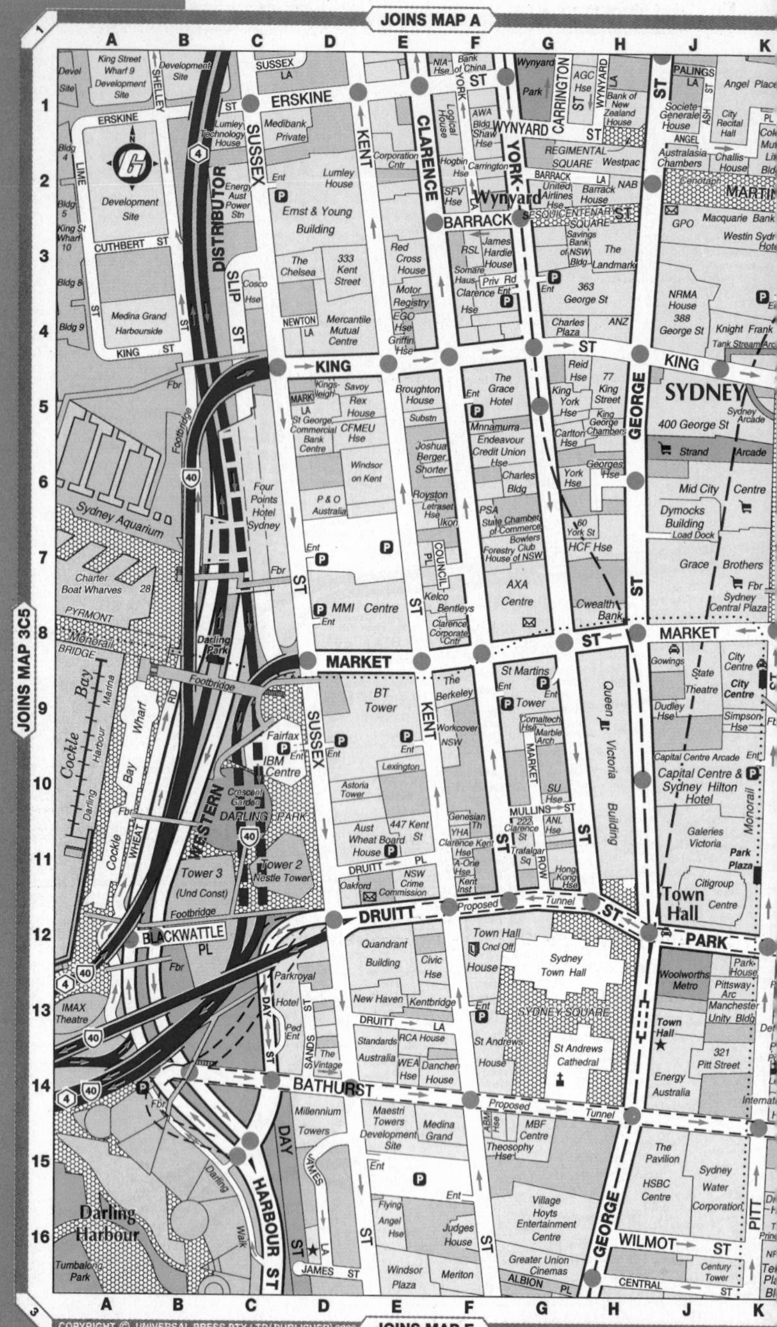

JOINS MAP A
JOINS MAP E
JOINS MAP 3C5
ERSKINE ST
KING ST
MARKET ST
DRUITT ST
BATHURST ST
PARK ST
SUSSEX ST
KENT ST
CLARENCE ST
YORK ST
GEORGE ST
DISTRIBUTOR
WESTERN DISTRIBUTOR
HARBOUR ST
DAY ST
PITT ST
WYNYARD ST
BARRACK ST
CARRINGTON ST
WILMOT ST
CENTRAL ST
SYDNEY
Wynyard
Sydney Aquarium
Cockle Bay
Darling Harbour
DARLING PARK
Sydney Town Hall
SYDNEY SQUARE
St Andrews Cathedral
Queen Victoria Building
Town Hall
Grace Brothers
BT Tower
MMI Centre
Four Points Hotel Sydney
Development Site
Medina Grand Harbourside
IMAX Theatre
Tumbalong Park
Charter Boat Wharves
PYRMONT BRIDGE
Monorail
Footbridge
Ernst & Young Building
Lumley House
Medibank Private
The Landmark
GPO
Macquarie Bank
Westin Sydney Hotel
Angel Place
Sydney Arcade
Strand Arcade
Mid City Centre
Dymocks Building
State Theatre
Capital Centre & Sydney Hilton Hotel
Galeries Victoria
Park Plaza
Citigroup Centre
Woolworths Metro
Pittsway Arc
Manchester Unity Bldg
321 Pitt Street
Energy Australia
The Pavilion
HSBC Centre
Sydney Water Corporation
Century Tower
Village Hoyts Entertainment Centre
Greater Union Cinemas
Judges House
Meriton
Windsor Plaza
Millennium Towers
Maestri Towers Development Site
Medina Grand
Quadrant Building
Civic Hse
New Haven
Kentbridge
Standards Australia
RCA House
Danchen House
St Andrews House
AXA Centre
Cwealth Bank
HCF Hse
St Martins Tower
The Grace Hotel
Broughton House
Fairfax IBM Centre
Tower 2 Nestle Tower
Tower 3 (Und Const)
Crescent Garden
BLACKWATTLE PL
Proposed Tunnel
COPYRIGHT © UNIVERSAL PRESS PTY LTD (PUBLISHER) 2002

MAP D

JOINS MAP B

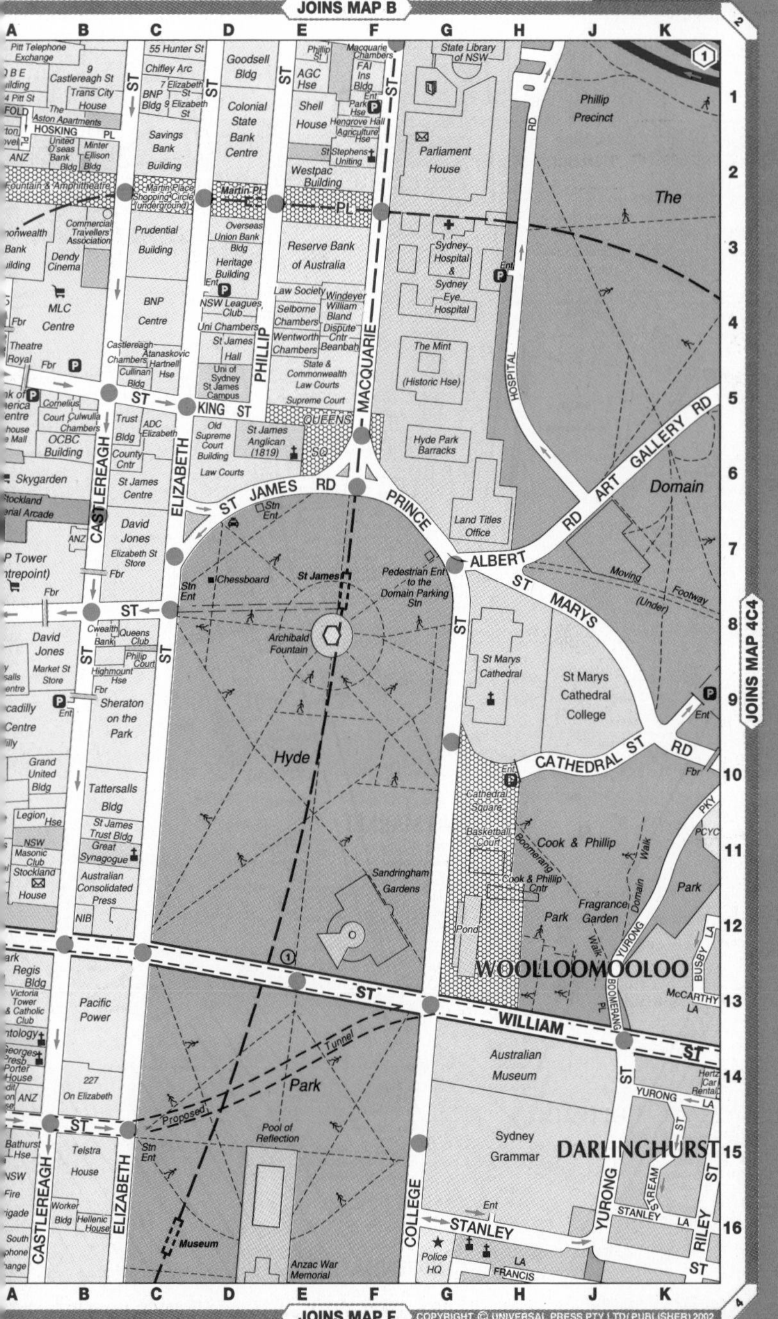

JOINS MAP 4C4

JOINS MAP F

MAP E

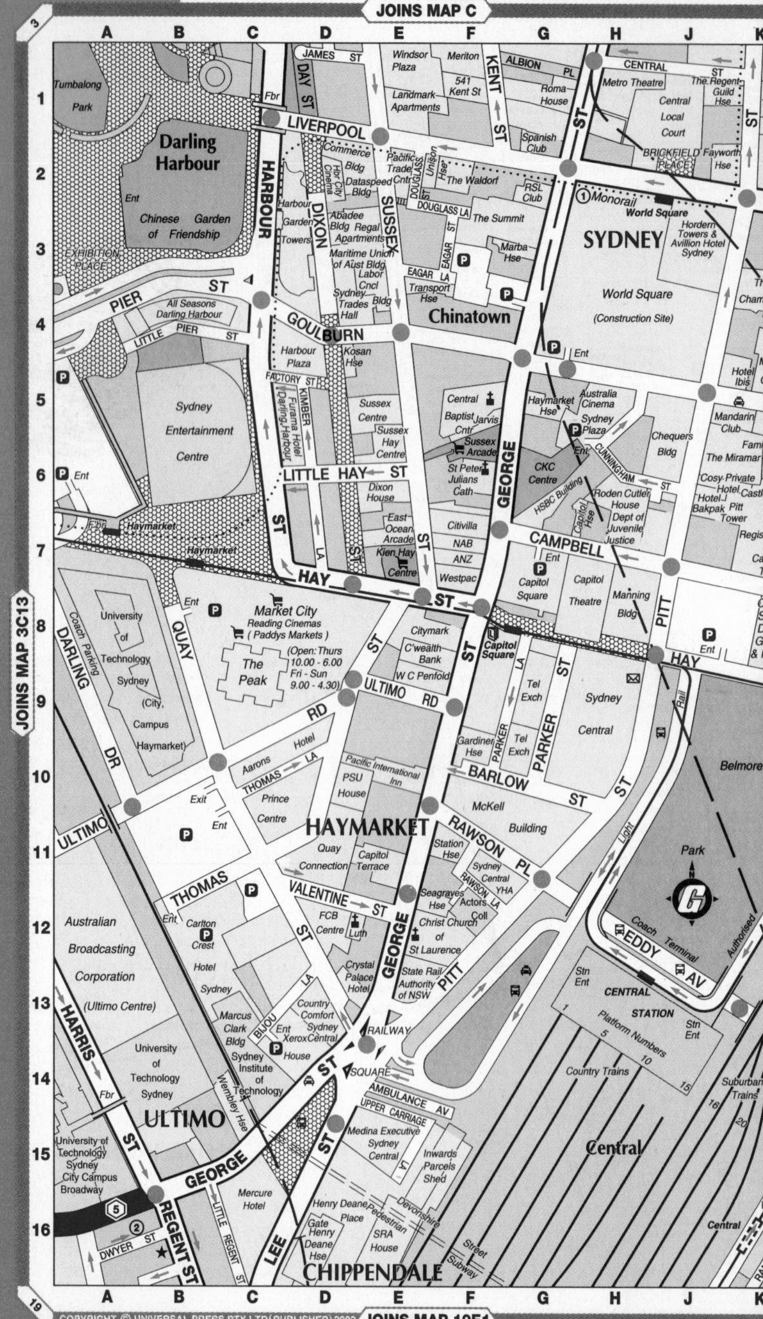

JOINS MAP C
JOINS MAP 3C13
JOINS MAP 19E1
Darling Harbour
Tumbalong Park
Chinese Garden of Friendship
EXHIBITION PLACE
Sydney Entertainment Centre
Chinatown
SYDNEY
World Square (Construction Site)
Market City
Reading Cinemas
(Paddys Markets)
The Peak
(Open: Thurs 10.00 - 6.00 Fri - Sun 9.00 - 4.30)
University of Technology Sydney (City Campus Haymarket)
HAYMARKET
Australian Broadcasting Corporation (Ultimo Centre)
ULTIMO
CHIPPENDALE
Central
CENTRAL STATION
Belmore Park
Sydney Central
Capitol Theatre
Capitol Square
Central Local Court
Metro Theatre
Monorail
World Square
Haymarket
LIVERPOOL ST
GOULBURN ST
HAY ST
CAMPBELL ST
GEORGE ST
PITT ST
SUSSEX ST
HARBOUR ST
DIXON ST
PIER ST
ULTIMO RD
QUAY ST
DARLING DR
THOMAS ST
HARRIS ST
REGENT ST
LEE ST
EDDY AV
RAILWAY SQUARE
ELIZABETH ST

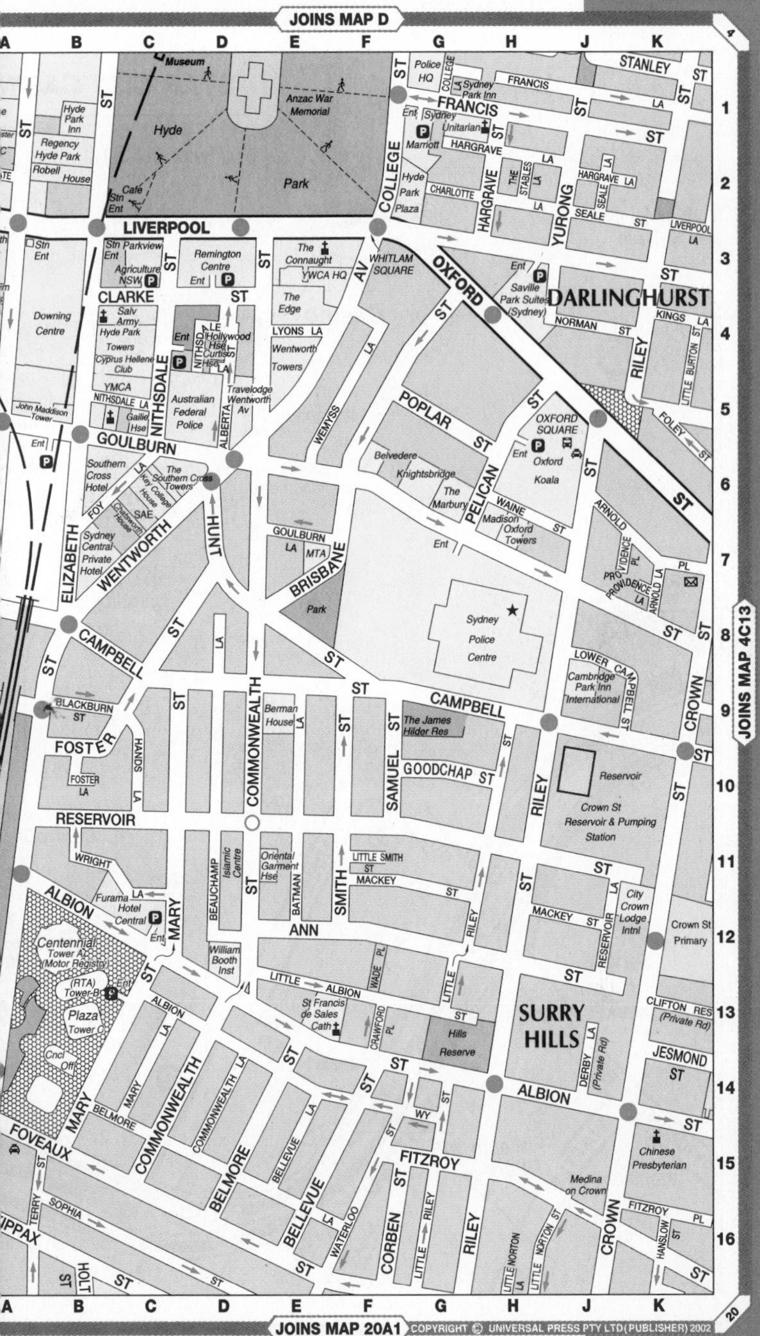
JOINS MAP D
JOINS MAP 20A1
JOINS MAP 4C13
Hyde Park
Anzac War Memorial
Museum
LIVERPOOL
OXFORD ST
DARLINGHURST
SURRY HILLS
Sydney Police Centre
COLLEGE ST
WHITLAM SQUARE
OXFORD SQUARE
CAMPBELL ST
GOULBURN ST
ELIZABETH ST
WENTWORTH AV
COMMONWEALTH ST
RILEY ST
CROWN ST
ALBION ST
FOVEAUX ST
RESERVOIR ST
BRISBANE ST
Crown St Reservoir & Pumping Station
Centennial Plaza
Downing Centre
Australian Federal Police

MAP G

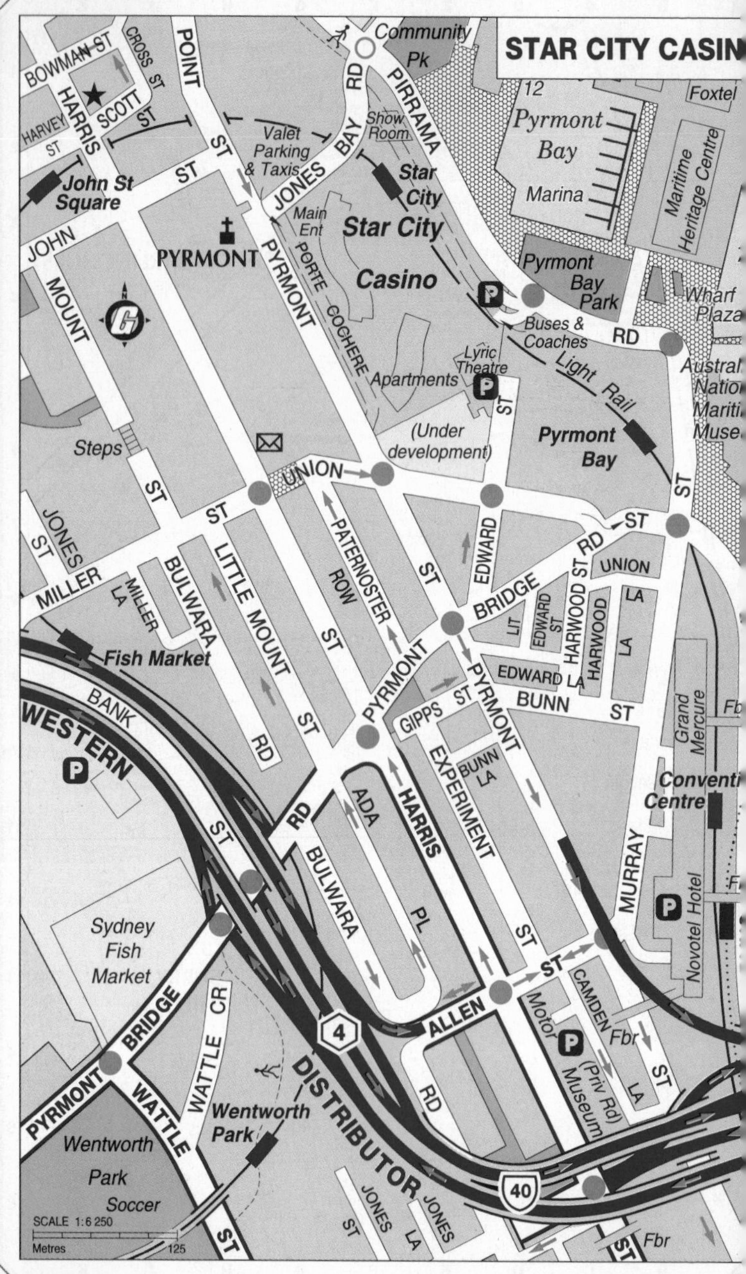

STAR CITY CASIN
Community
Pk
Pyrmont
Bay
Marina
Foxtel
Maritime Heritage Centre
Star City
Casino
Valet Parking & Taxis
Show Room
Main Ent
John St Square
PYRMONT
Pyrmont Bay Park
Wharf Plaza
Buses & Coaches
Light Rail
Lyric Theatre
Apartments
(Under development)
Pyrmont Bay
Steps
Fish Market
WESTERN
DISTRIBUTOR
Sydney Fish Market
Wentworth Park
Wentworth Park Soccer
Grand Mercure
Convent Centre
Novotel Hotel
Motor Museum
(Priv Rd)
SCALE 1:6 250
Metres
125

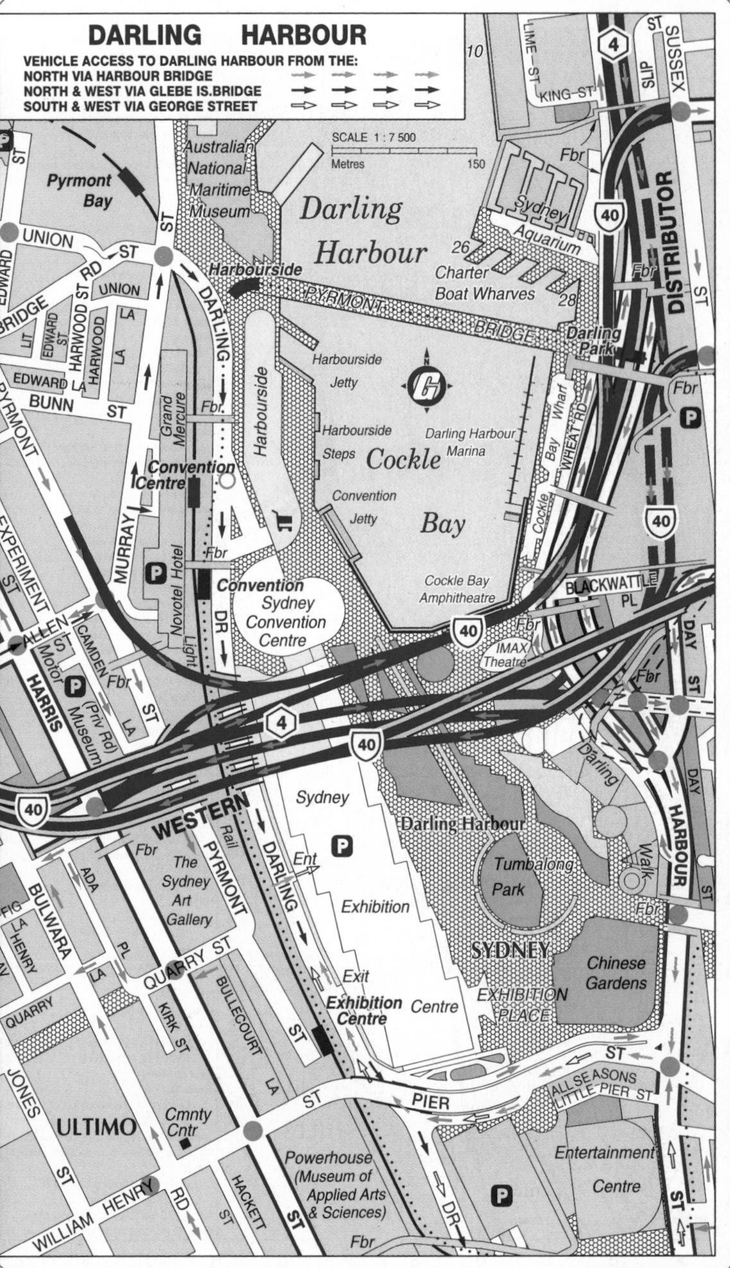

DARLING HARBOUR
VEHICLE ACCESS TO DARLING HARBOUR FROM THE:
NORTH VIA HARBOUR BRIDGE
NORTH & WEST VIA GLEBE IS.BRIDGE
SOUTH & WEST VIA GEORGE STREET
SCALE 1 : 7 500
Metres
150
Australian National Maritime Museum
Darling Harbour
Pyrmont Bay
Sydney Aquarium
Charter Boat Wharves
Harbourside
PYRMONT BRIDGE
Darling Park
Harbourside Jetty
Harbourside Steps
Cockle Bay
Darling Harbour Marina
Convention Jetty
Cockle Bay Amphitheatre
Convention Centre
Sydney Convention Centre
Grand Mercure
Novotel Hotel
IMAX Theatre
BLACKWATTLE PL
DISTRIBUTOR
SUSSEX ST
KING ST
LIME ST
SLIP ST
WHEAT RD
Cockle Bay Wharf
DARLING DR
UNION ST
BRIDGE RD
HARWOOD ST
EDWARD LA
BUNN ST
PYRMONT ST
MURRAY ST
EXPERIMENT ST
ALLEN ST
CAMDEN ST
HARRIS ST
Motor Museum (Priv Rd)
WESTERN
Light Rail
Sydney Exhibition Centre
Exhibition Centre
Darling Harbour
Tumbalong Park
SYDNEY
Chinese Gardens
EXHIBITION PLACE
DAY ST
HARBOUR ST
Darling Walk
The Sydney Art Gallery
PYRMONT ST
BULWARA RD
ADA PL
QUARRY ST
KIRK ST
BULLECOURT LA
ULTIMO
Cmnty Cntr
PIER ST
ALL SEASONS
LITTLE PIER ST
Entertainment Centre
Powerhouse (Museum of Applied Arts & Sciences)
JONES ST
WILLIAM HENRY ST
HACKETT ST
Fbr

MAP J

SCALE 1 : 20 800

Metres 200 400 600

CITY PARKING STATIONS

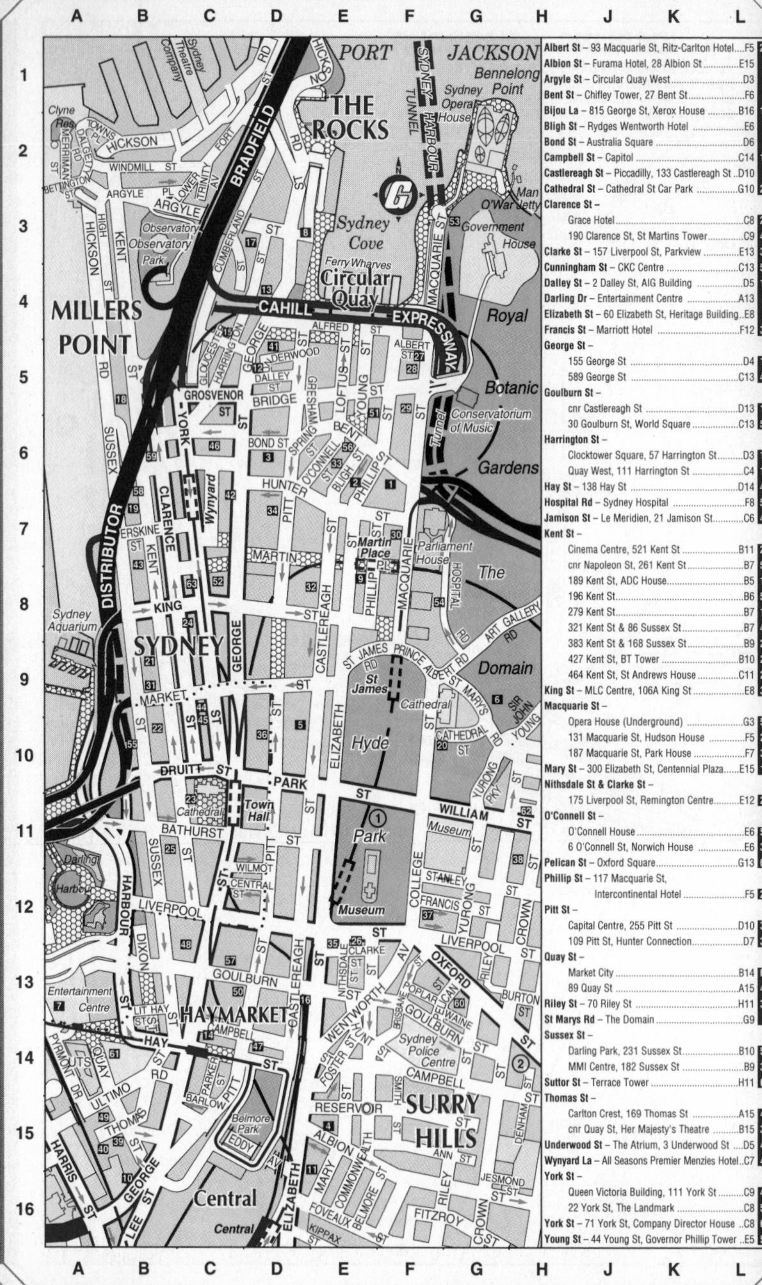

MAP K

MAP 1 FOLLOWS

JOINS MAP 5G4

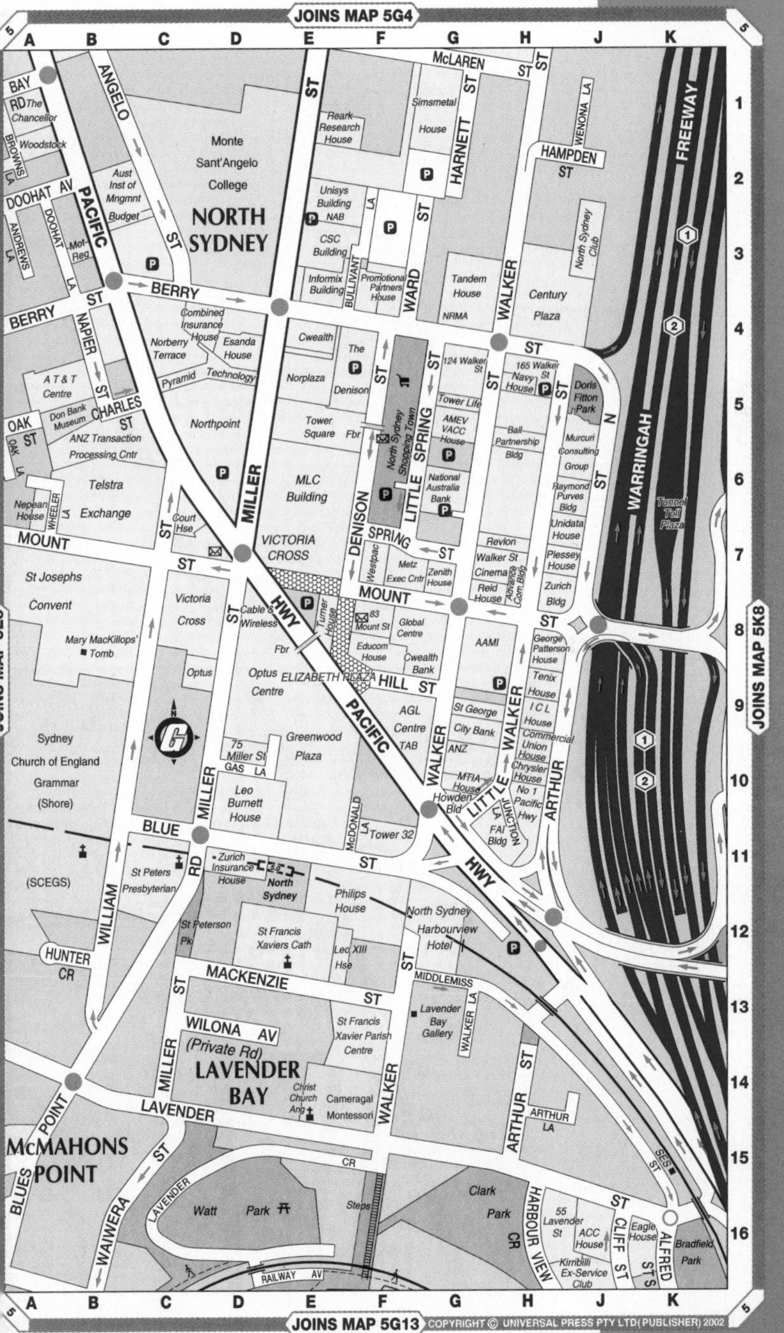

JOINS MAP 5K8

JOINS MAP 5G13

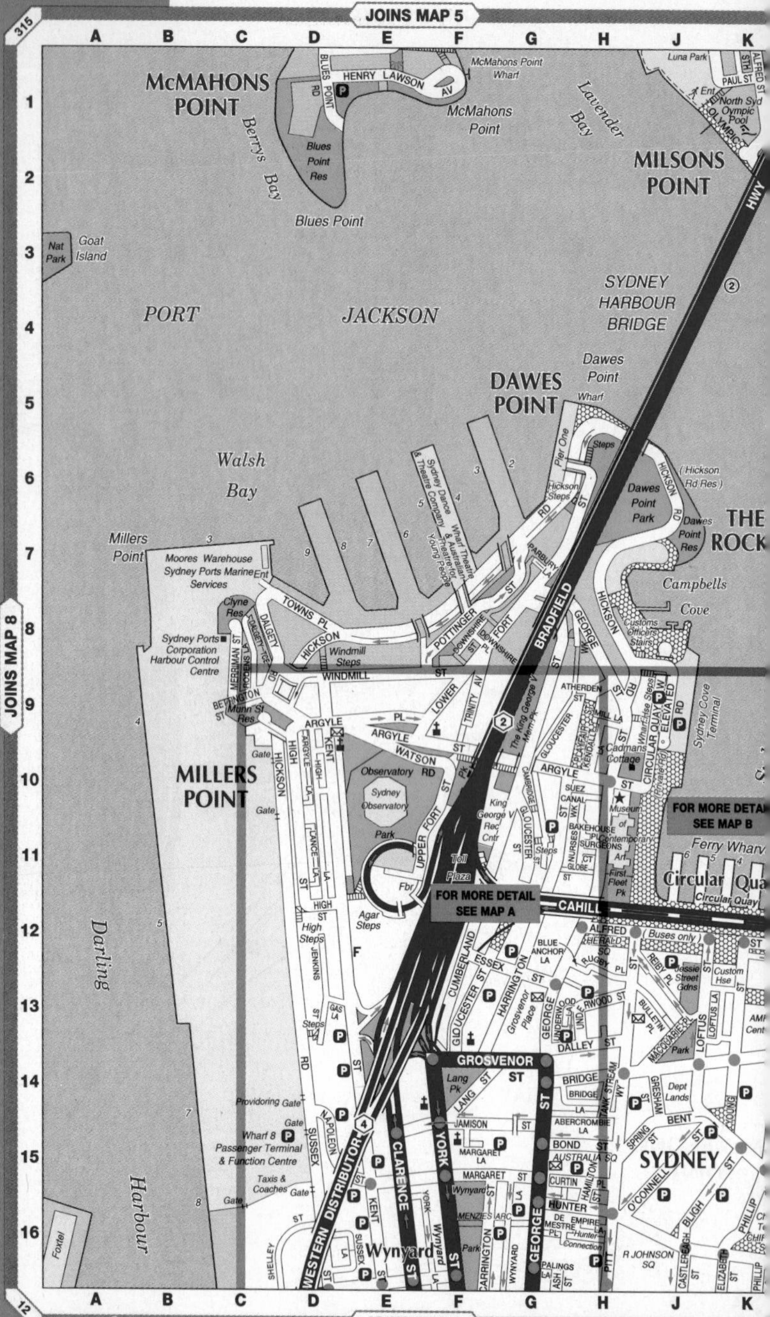

MAP 1

PREVIOUS MAP K

315

JOINS MAP 5

A B C D E F G H J K

1 2 3 4 5 6 7 8 9 10 11 12 13 14 15 16

McMAHONS POINT

BLUES POINT RD

HENRY LAWSON AV

McMahons Point Wharf

McMahons Point

Berrys Bay

Blues Point Res

Blues Point

Lavender Bay

Luna Park

STH

ALFRED ST

PAUL ST

Ent

North Syd Olympic Pool

OLYMPIC

MILSONS POINT

HWY

Nat Park

Goat Island

PORT JACKSON

SYDNEY HARBOUR BRIDGE

Dawes Point

Wharf

DAWES POINT

Walsh Bay

Pier One

Steps

Hickson Steps

HICKSON RD

(Hickson Rd Res)

Dawes Point Park

Dawes Point Res

THE ROCKS

Sydney Dance & Theatre Company

Wharf Theatre & Australian Theatre for Young People

9 8 7 6 5 4 3 2

Millers Point

Moores Warehouse

Sydney Ports Marine Services

Ent

Clyne Res

TOWNS PL

HICKSON RD

Windmill Steps

DALGETY RD

DALGETY TCE

PARBURY LA

BRADFIELD

POTTINGER ST

DOWNSHIRE ST

FORT ST

GEORGE ST

Campbells Cove

Customs Officers Stairs

Sydney Ports Corporation Harbour Control Centre

MERRIMAN ST

RODENS LA

WINDMILL ST

LOWER FORT ST

TRINITY AV

The King George V Mem Pk

ATHERDEN ST

MILL LA

GLOUCESTER WK

PLAYFAIR ST

KENDALL LA

CADMANS COTTAGE

WHARF HSE STEPS

CIRCULAR QUAY W

ELEVATED RD

Sydney Cove Terminal

BETTINGTON ST

Munn St Res

ARGYLE ST

ARGYLE PL

WATSON RD

Gate

MILLERS POINT

HICKSON RD

HIGH ST

KENT ST

ARGYLE LA

HIGH LA

LANCE LA

Observatory Park

Sydney Observatory

UPPER FORT ST

King George V Rec Cntr

CAMBRIDGE ST

GLOUCESTER ST

ARGYLE ST

SUEZ CANAL

NURSES WK

BAKEHOUSE PL

SURGEONS CT

GLOBE ST

Steps

Museum of Contemporary Art

First Fleet Pk

Toll Plaza

Fbr

Agar Steps

FOR MORE DETAIL SEE MAP A

FOR MORE DETAIL SEE MAP B

Ferry Wharf 6 5 4

Circular Quay

CAHILL

ALFRED ST

HERALD SQ

(Buses only)

Custom Hse

High Steps

JENKINS ST

Steps

GAS LA

CUMBERLAND ST

ESSEX ST

HARRINGTON ST

GLOUCESTER ST

Grosvenor Place

BLUE ANCHOR LA

RUGBY PL

UNDERWOOD ST

GEORGE ST

DALLEY ST

REIBY PL

Jessie Street Gdns

BULLETIN PL

MACQUARIE PL

Park

LOFTUS ST

LOFTUS LA

AMP Cent

Darling Harbour

4 5 7 8

GROSVENOR ST

Lang Pk

LANG ST

BRIDGE ST

BRIDGE LA

TANK STREAM WY

GRESHAM ST

Dept Lands

YOUNG ST

Providoring Gate

Gate

Wharf 8 Passenger Terminal & Function Centre

Taxis & Coaches

NAPOLEON ST

SUSSEX ST

WESTERN DISTRIBUTOR

CLARENCE ST

YORK ST

JAMISON ST

MARGARET LA

ABERCROMBIE LA

BOND ST

AUSTRALIA SQ

BENT ST

SPRING ST

SYDNEY

MARGARET ST

Wynyard

CURTIN PL

HAMILTON ST

HUNTER ST

O'CONNELL ST

BLIGH ST

PHILLIP ST

MENZIES ARC

DE MESTRE PL

EMPIRE LA

Hunter Connection

Foxtel

SHELLEY ST

KENT ST

SUSSEX ST

CARRINGTON ST

WYNYARD ST

GEORGE ST

PALINGS LA

ASH ST

PITT ST

R JOHNSON SQ

CASTLEREAGH ST

ELIZABETH ST

PHILLIP ST

Wynyard LA

JOINS MAP 8

12

JOINS MAP 3

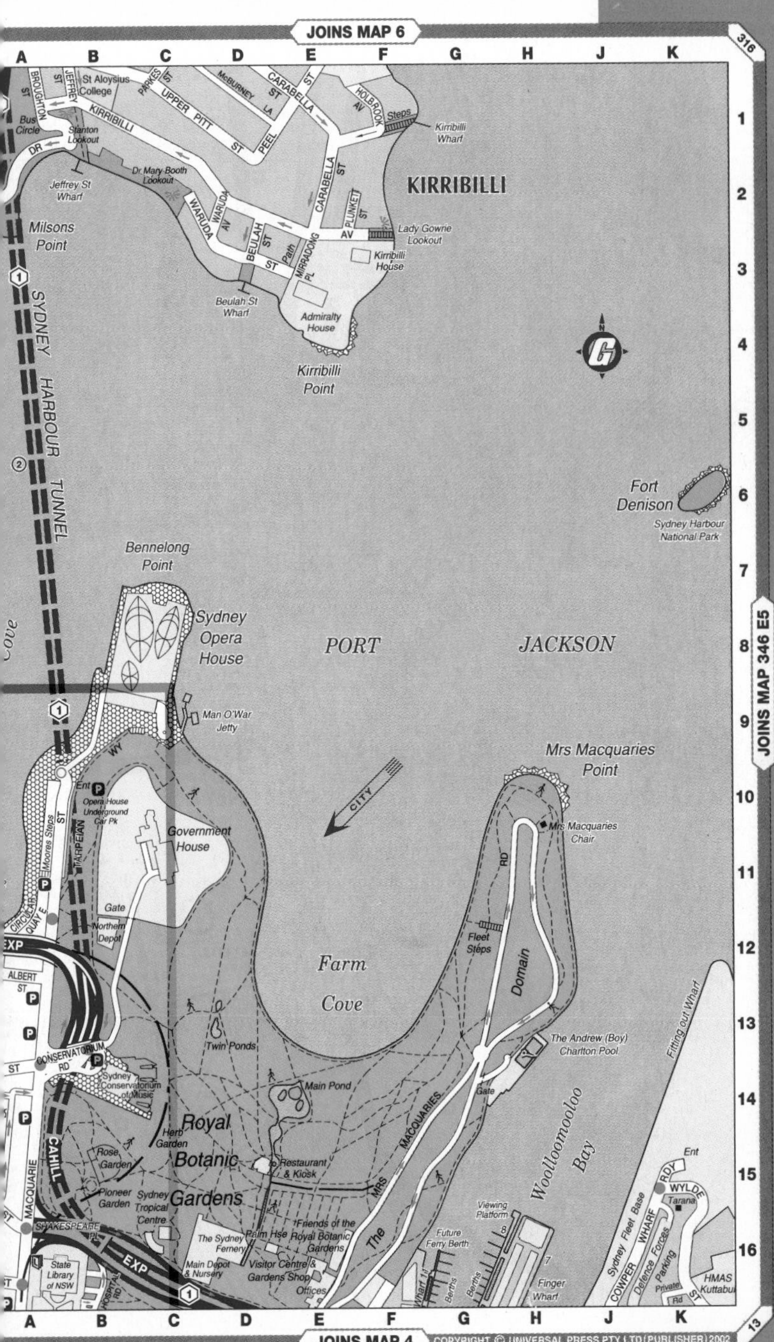
JOINS MAP 6
316
A B C D E F G H J K
1 2 3 4 5 6 7 8 9 10 11 12 13 14 15 16
KIRRIBILLI
St Aloysius College
Stanton Lookout
Bus Circle
Jeffrey St Wharf
Dr Mary Booth Lookout
Milsons Point
Kirribilli Wharf
Lady Gowrie Lookout
Kirribilli House
Admiralty House
Beulah St Wharf
Kirribilli Point
SYDNEY HARBOUR TUNNEL
Fort Denison
Sydney Harbour National Park
Bennelong Point
Sydney Opera House
PORT
JACKSON
Man O'War Jetty
Mrs Macquaries Point
Mrs Macquaries Chair
Opera House Underground Car Pk
Government House
Gate
Northern Depot
Moores Steps
CITY
Farm Cove
Fleet Steps
Domain
Twin Ponds
Main Pond
The Andrew (Boy) Charlton Pool
Woolloomooloo Bay
Fitting out Wharf
Sydney Conservatorium of Music
Royal Botanic Gardens
Herb Garden
Rose Garden
Pioneer Garden
Sydney Tropical Centre
Restaurant & Kiosk
The Sydney Fernery
Palm Hse
Friends of the Royal Botanic Gardens
Main Depot & Nursery
Visitor Centre & Gardens Shop
Offices
Future Ferry Berth
Viewing Platform
Finger Wharf
Berths
Sydney Fleet Base
Defence Forces Parking
Private
HMAS Kuttabul
Tarana
Ent
State Library of NSW
JOINS MAP 346 E5
JOINS MAP 4
13

MAP 3

JOINS MAP 1
JOINS MAP 12
JOINS MAP 19
8
18
A B C D E F G H J K
1 2 3 4 5 6 7 8 9 10 11 12 13 14 15 16
Darling Harbour
Cockle Bay
Wharf 7 Plaza
Australian National Maritime Museum
Harbourside
Sydney Aquarium
Charter Boat Wharves
Darling Park
Darling Harbour Marina
FOR MORE DETAIL SEE MAP H
FOR MORE DETAIL SEE MAP C
FOR MORE DETAIL SEE MAP E
Convention
Sydney Convention Centre
Cockle Bay Amphitheatre
IMAX Th
Darling Walk
Tumbalong Park
Chinese Gardens
Sydney Ent Exhibition Centre
Exhibition Centre
The Sydney Art Gallery
Powerhouse Museum (Museum of Applied Arts & Sciences)
Entertainment Centre
Haymarket
HAYMARKET
Uni of Technology Sydney
Market City The Peak
ULTIMO
Sydney Institute of Technology Ultimo
Australian Broadcasting Corporation
University of Technology Sydney
Broadway
CHIPPENDALE
Chinatown
SYDNEY
World Square
Capitol Square
Sydney Central
Belmore Park
Coach Terminal
CENTRAL STATION
Central
Country Trains
Suburban Trains
Devonshire Street Pedestrian Subway
RAILWAY SQ
Wynyard
GPO
Cmwlth Bank
MLC Centre
Sydney Arcade
Strand Arc
Glasshouse Skygarden
Imperial Arc
Mid City Cntr
(Centrepoint) AMP Tower
St James Arc
City Centre Royal Arcade
Piccadilly Centre
Town Hall
Park Plaza
Queen Victoria Building
Sydney Sq
St Andrews Cathedral
Town Hall Energy Australia
Sydney Water
Police Court
Hyde Park
Archibald Fountain
Pool of Reflection
Museum
Anzac War Memorial
Centennial Plaza (RTA)
Islamic Cntr
SURRY HILLS
DISTRIBUTOR
WESTERN
HARBOUR ST
GEORGE ST
YORK ST
CLARENCE ST
KENT ST
SUSSEX ST
PITT ST
CASTLEREAGH ST
ELIZABETH ST
KING ST
MARKET ST
DRUITT ST
PARK ST
BATHURST ST
LIVERPOOL ST
GOULBURN ST
HAY ST
CAMPBELL ST
BROADWAY
HARRIS ST
PIER ST
WATTLE ST
MARTIN PL
ERSKINE ST
BARRACK ST
DIXON ST
QUAY ST
RAWSON PL
ELIZABETH ST
FOVEAUX ST
COMMONWEALTH ST
ALBION ST

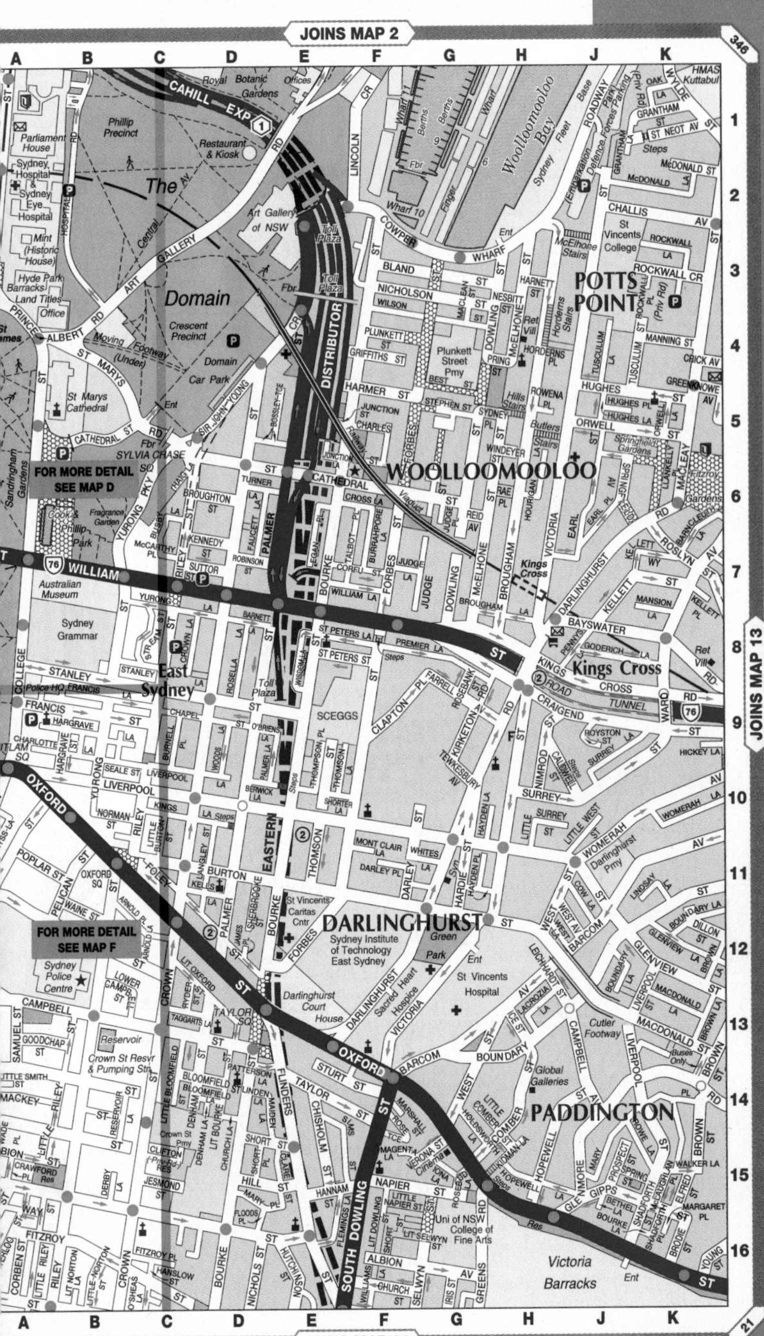
JOINS MAP 2
JOINS MAP 13
JOINS MAP 20
346
21
A B C D E F G H J K
1 2 3 4 5 6 7 8 9 10 11 12 13 14 15 16
CAHILL EXP
Royal Botanic Gardens
Offices
Phillip Precinct
Restaurant & Kiosk
Parliament House
Sydney Hospital & Sydney Eye Hospital
Mint (Historic House)
Hyde Park Barracks
Land Titles Office
The Domain
Crescent Precinct
Domain Car Park
Art Gallery of NSW
Toll Plaza
DISTRIBUTOR
Woolloomooloo Bay
Wharf 10
Finger Wharf
Sydney Fleet Base
St Vincents College
POTTS POINT
St Marys Cathedral
FOR MORE DETAIL SEE MAP D
Sandringham Gardens
Cook & Phillip Park
Fragrance Garden
WOOLLOOMOOLOO
Plunkett Street Pmy
Kings Cross
WILLIAM ST
Australian Museum
Sydney Grammar
East Sydney
Police HQ
Springfield Gardens
Fitzroy Gardens
KINGS CROSS RD
CROSS TUNNEL
SCEGGS
OXFORD ST
Darlinghurst Pmy
FOR MORE DETAIL SEE MAP F
Sydney Police Centre
DARLINGHURST
St Vincents Caritas Cntr
Sydney Institute of Technology East Sydney
Green Park
St Vincents Hospital
Darlinghurst Court House
Sacred Heart Hospice
Cutler Footway
Reservoir
Crown St Resvr & Pumping Stn
Global Galleries
PADDINGTON
Uni of NSW College of Fine Arts
Victoria Barracks
SOUTH DOWLING
COPYRIGHT © UNIVERSAL PRESS PTY LTD (PUBLISHER) 2002

MAP 5

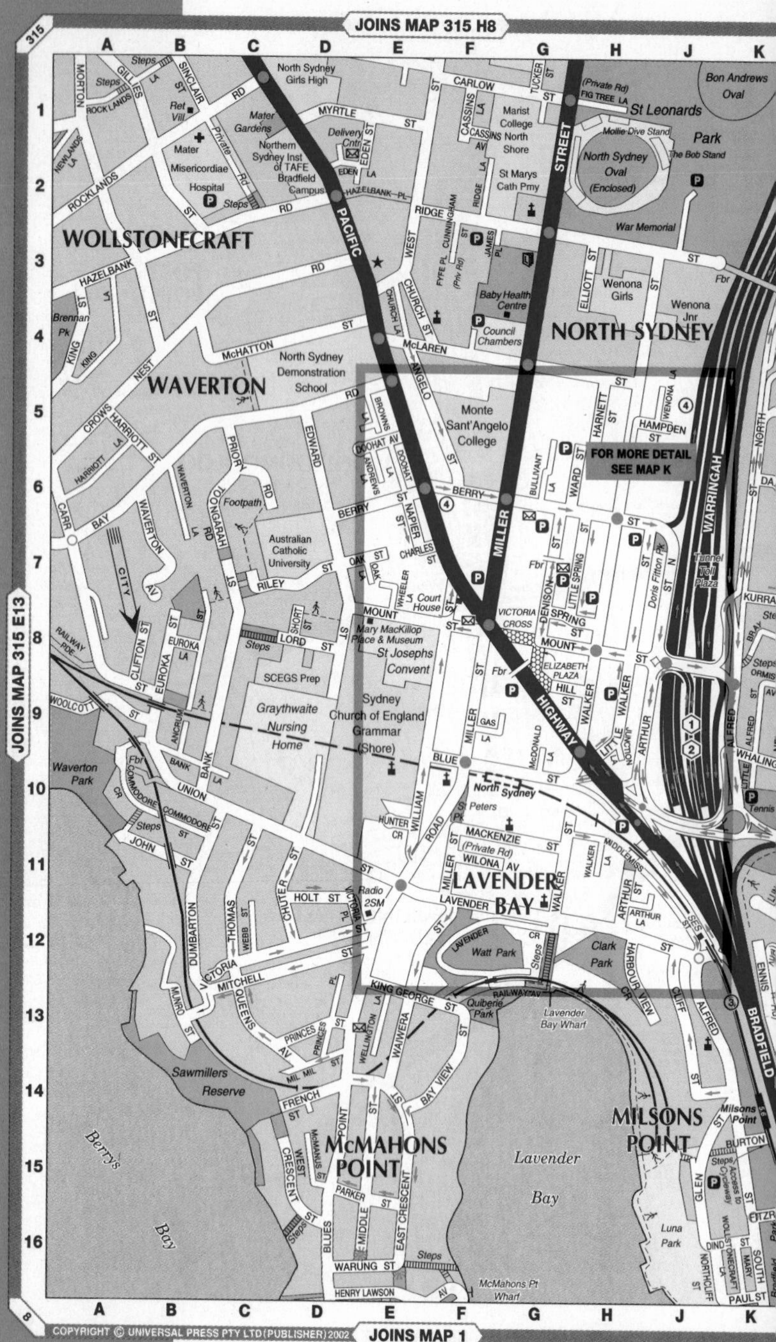

JOINS MAP 315 H8
JOINS MAP 315 E13
JOINS MAP 1
FOR MORE DETAIL SEE MAP K
WOLLSTONECRAFT
WAVERTON
NORTH SYDNEY
LAVENDER BAY
McMAHONS POINT
MILSONS POINT
St Leonards Park
North Sydney Oval (Enclosed)
Lavender Bay
Berrys Bay
Sawmillers Reserve
Waverton Park
Sydney Church of England Grammar (Shore)
Monte Sant'Angelo College
Mater Misericordiae Hospital
North Sydney Demonstration School
Australian Catholic University
Graythwaite Nursing Home
SCEGS Prep
St Josephs Convent
Wenona Girls
Luna Park
Clark Park
Watt Park
PACIFIC HIGHWAY
MILLER STREET
WARRINGAH
BRADFIELD

JOINS MAP 316 C8

JOINS MAP 316 F13

JOINS MAP 2

MAP 7

JOINS MAP 314 H16

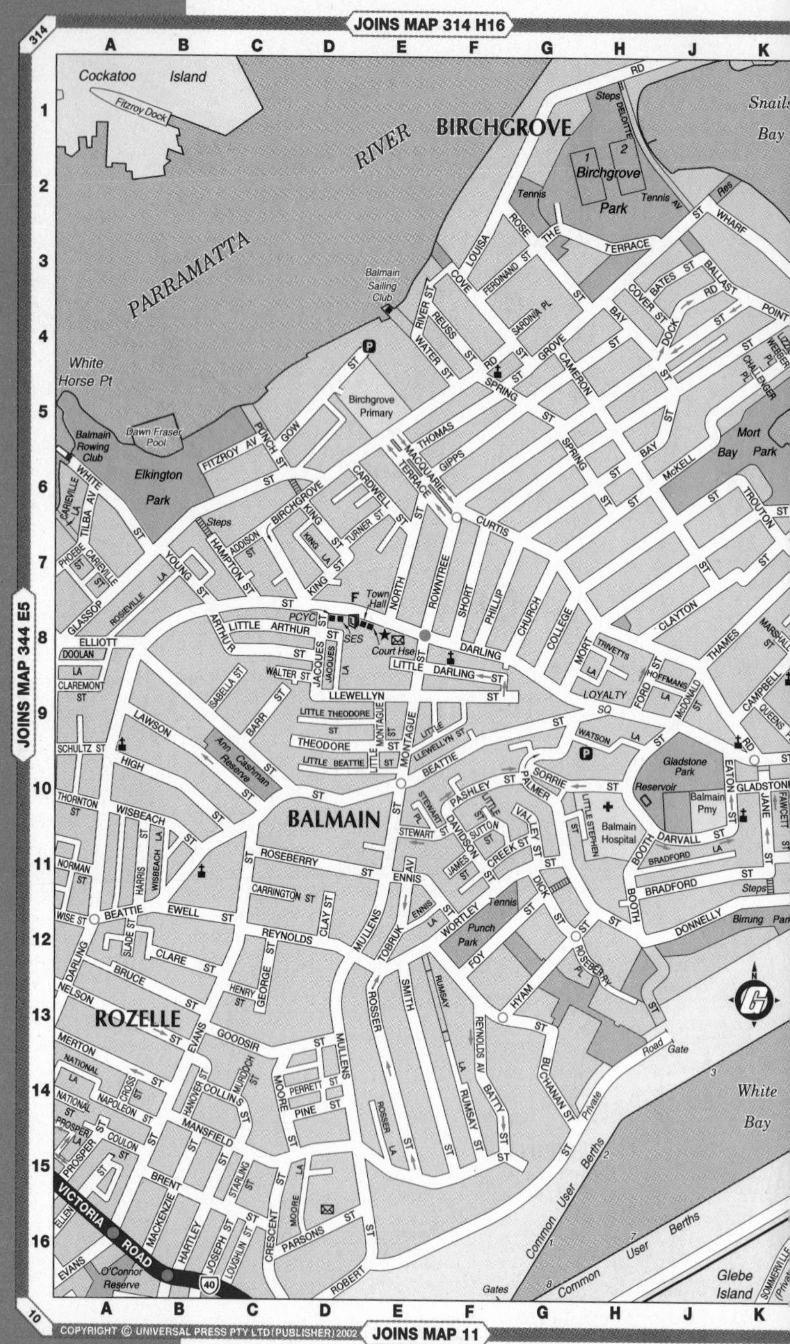

JOINS MAP 344 E5

JOINS MAP 11

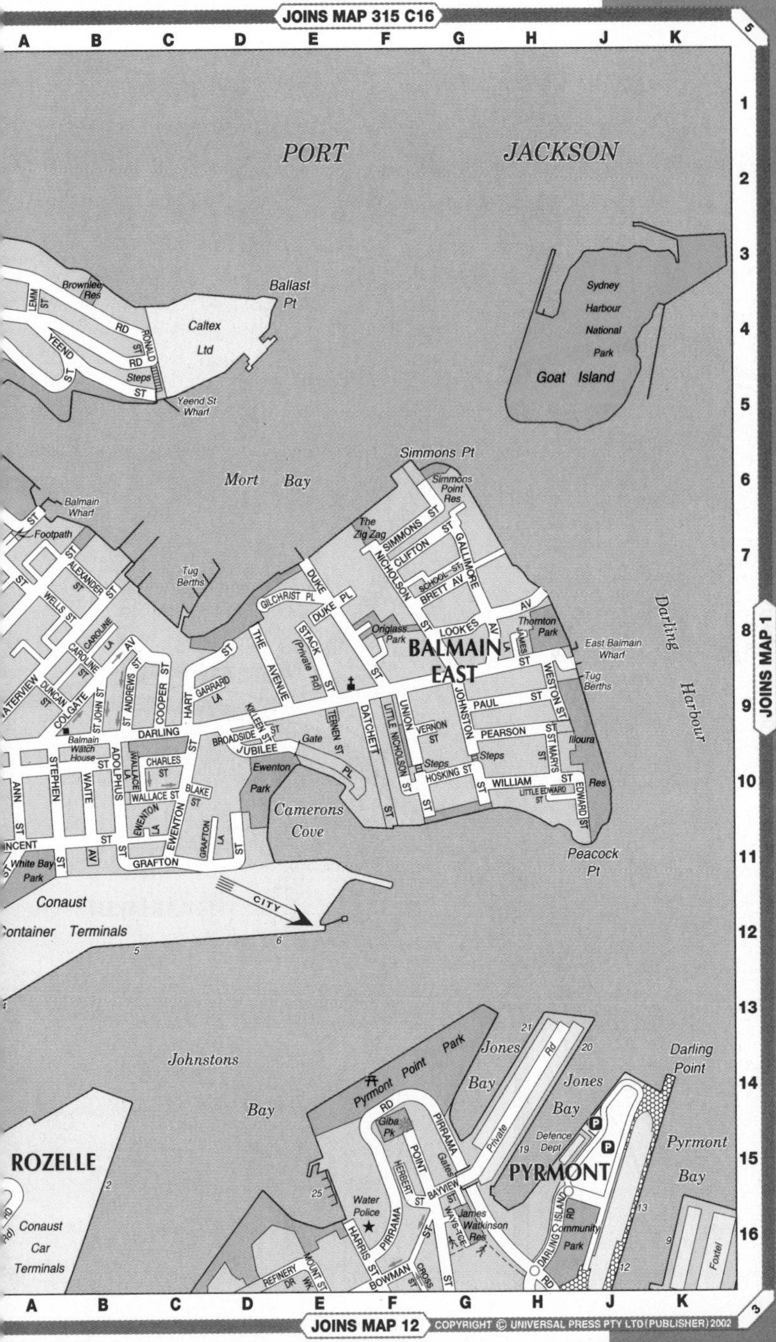
JOINS MAP 315 C16
JOINS MAP 1
JOINS MAP 12
PORT JACKSON
Ballast Pt
Caltex Ltd
Brownlee Res
Yeend St Wharf
Sydney Harbour National Park
Goat Island
Simmons Pt
Simmons Point Res
Mort Bay
Balmain Wharf
Footpath
Tug Berths
The Zig Zag
Origlass Park
BALMAIN EAST
Thornton Park
East Balmain Wharf
Darling Harbour
Illoura Res
Balmain Watch House
Ewenton Park
Camerons Cove
Peacock Pt
White Bay Park
Conaust Container Terminals
CITY
Johnstons Bay
Pyrmont Point Park
Giba Pk
Jones Bay
Darling Point
Defence Dept
Pymont Bay
PYRMONT
Water Police
James Watkinson Res
Community Park
Foxtel
ROZELLE
Conaust Car Terminals

JOINS MAP 343 H8

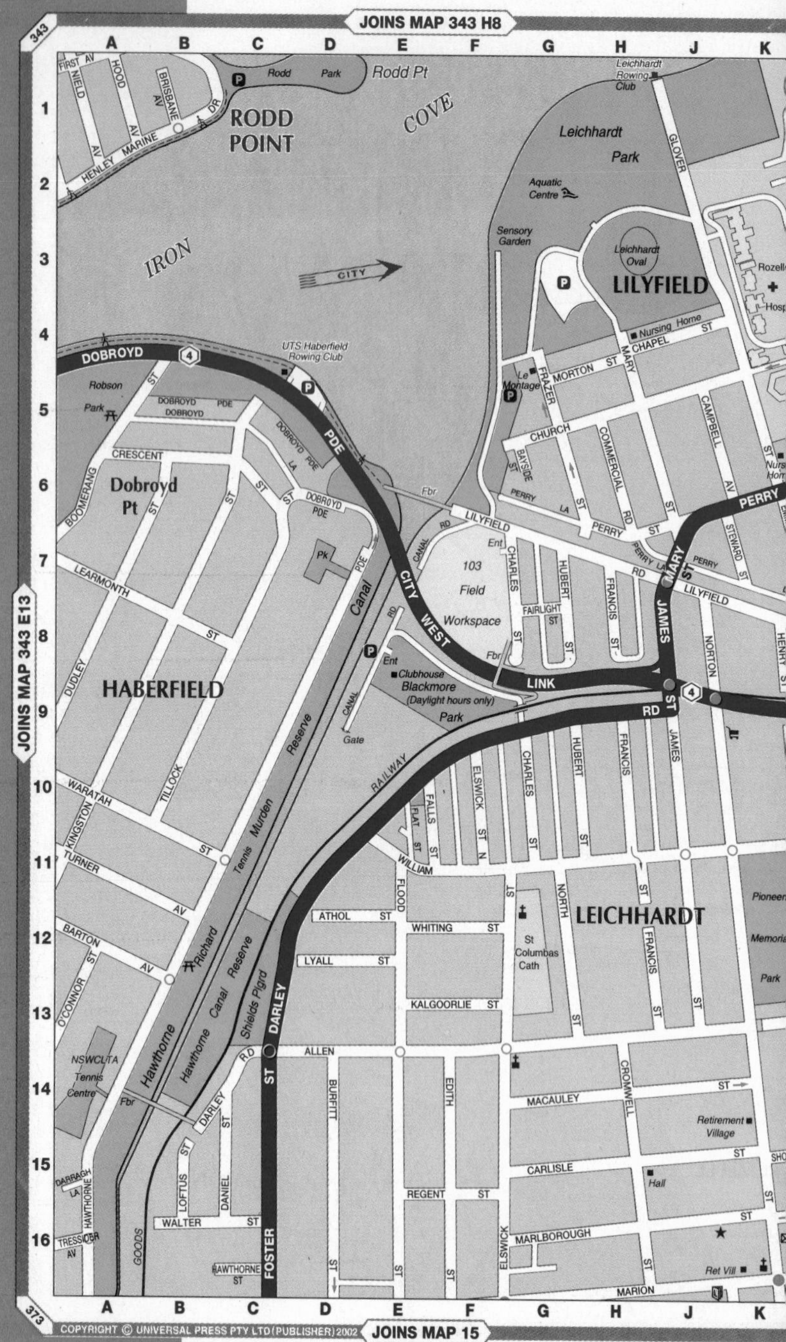

JOINS MAP 343 E13

JOINS MAP 15

JOINS MAP 344 C8

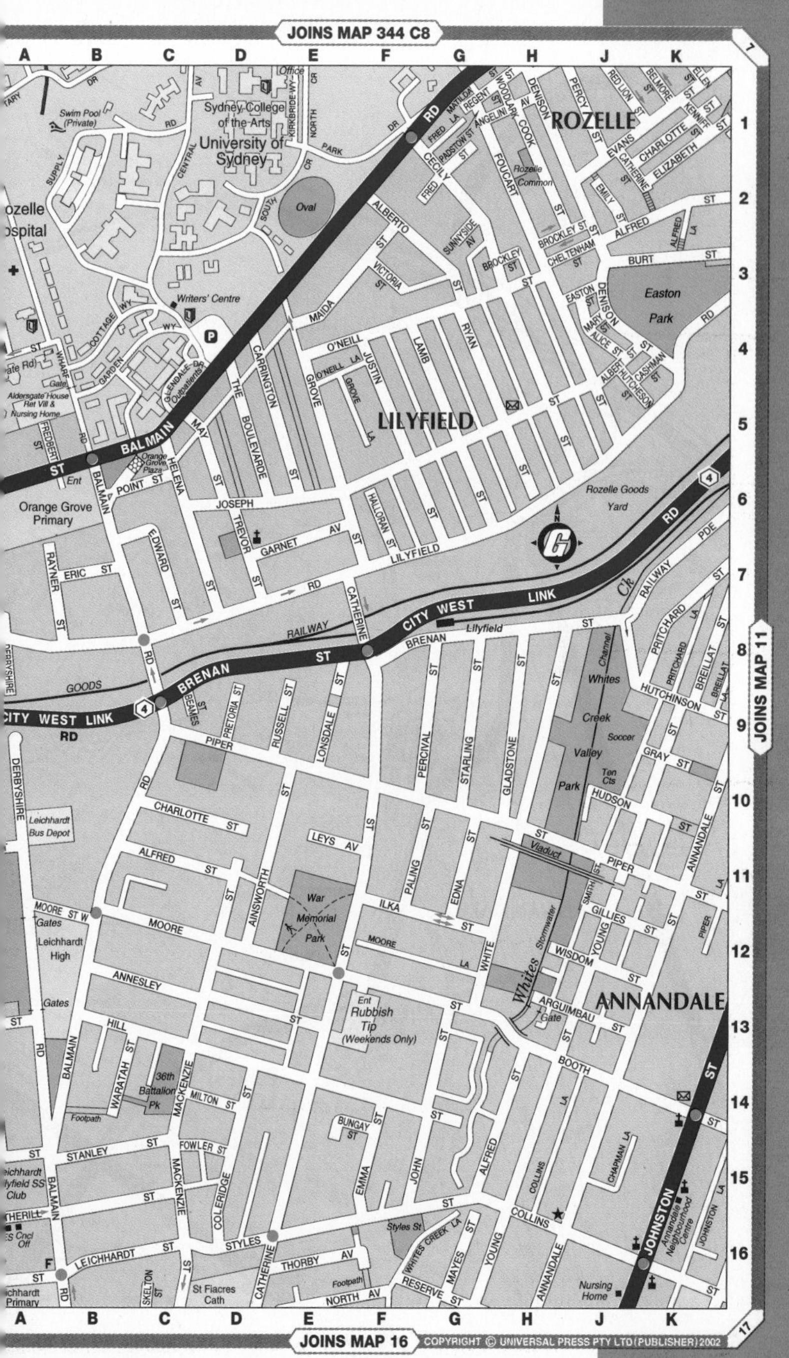

JOINS MAP 16

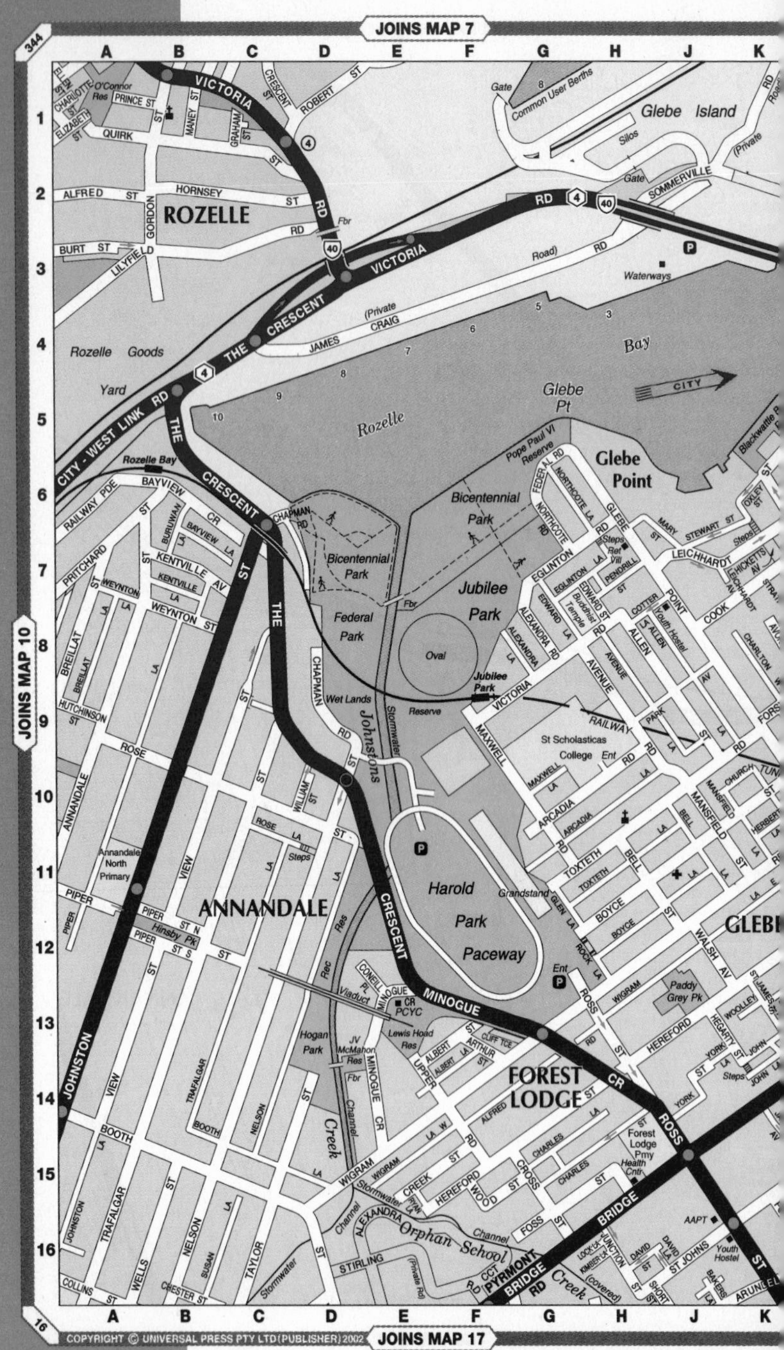
JOINS MAP 7
344
JOINS MAP 10
ROZELLE
Rozelle Goods Yard
Glebe Island
Rozelle Bay
Glebe Pt
Glebe Point
Bicentennial Park
Jubilee Park
Federal Park
ANNANDALE
Harold Park Paceway
FOREST LODGE
GLEBE
Johnstons Creek
Orphan School Creek
CITY
16
JOINS MAP 17

JOINS MAP 8

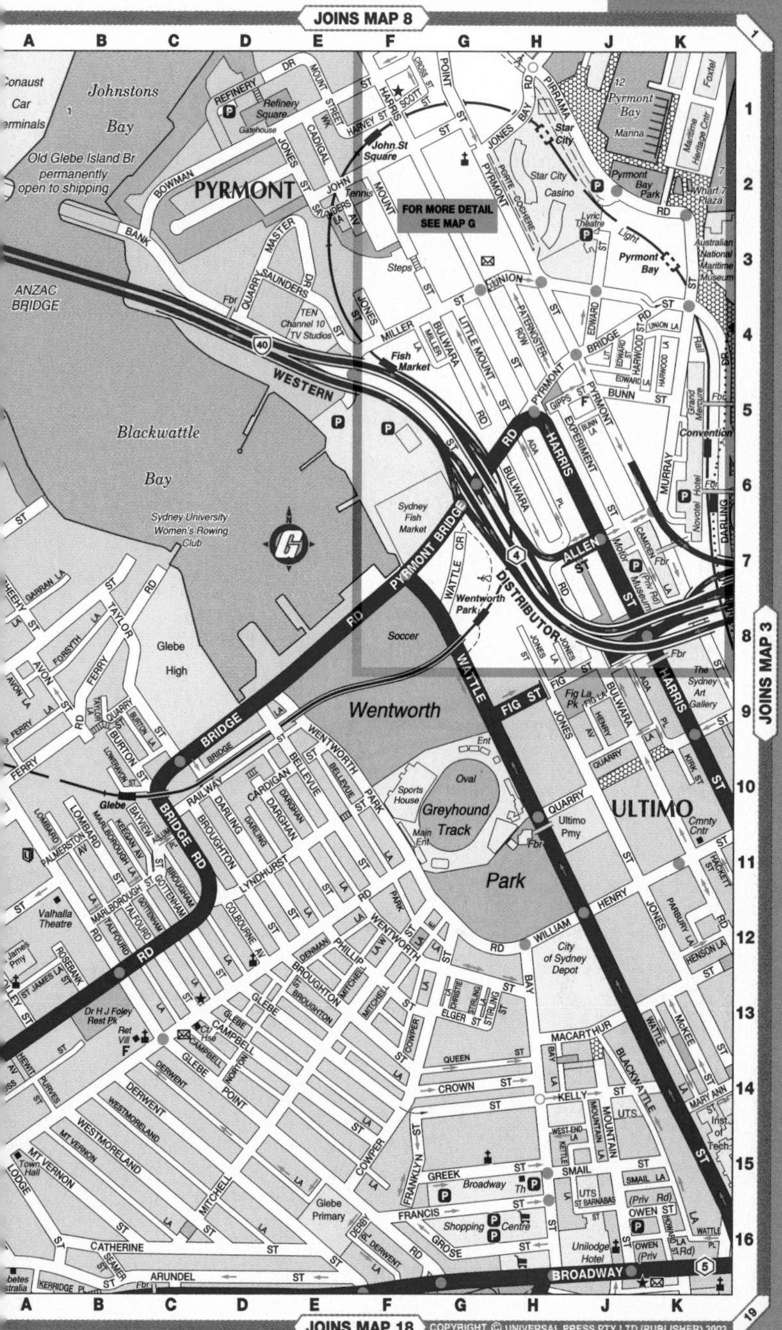

JOINS MAP 3

JOINS MAP 18

MAP 13

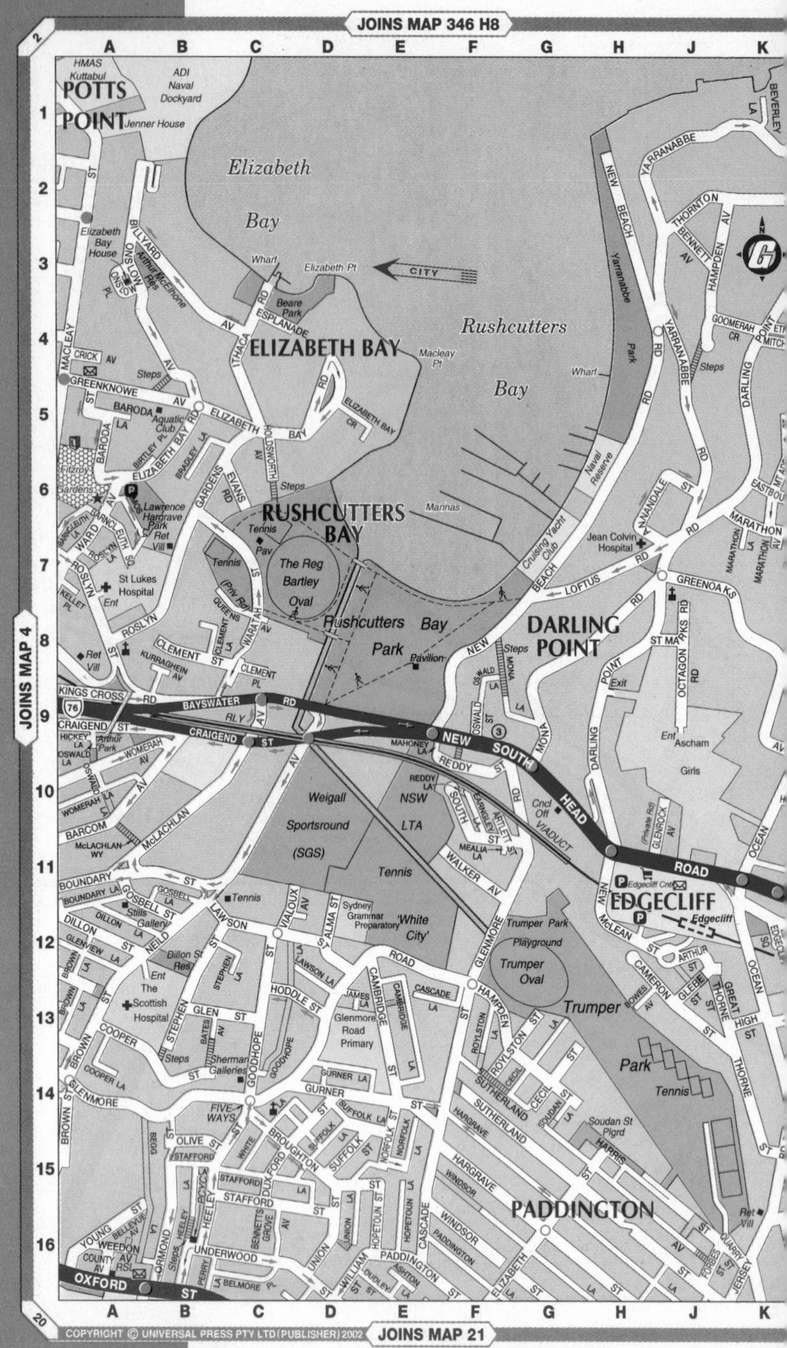

JOINS MAP 346 H8
JOINS MAP 4
JOINS MAP 21
A B C D E F G H J K
1 2 3 4 5 6 7 8 9 10 11 12 13 14 15 16
POTTS POINT
HMAS Kuttabul
ADI Naval Dockyard
Jenner House
Elizabeth Bay
Elizabeth Bay House
Wharf
Elizabeth Pt
CITY
Beare Park
ELIZABETH BAY
Rushcutters Bay
Macleay Pt
Arthur McElhone Res
Steps
Aquatic Club
Fitzroy Gardens
Lawrence Hargrave Park
Ret Vill
St Lukes Hospital
Ent
RUSHCUTTERS BAY
Marinas
Tennis
Pav
The Reg Bartley Oval
Rushcutters Bay Park
Pavilion
Cruising Yacht Club
Naval Reserve
Yarranabbe Park
Jean Colvin Hospital
DARLING POINT
Exit
Ascham Girls
KINGS CROSS RD
BAYSWATER RD
CRAIGEND ST
NEW SOUTH HEAD ROAD
VIADUCT
Arthur Park
Weigall Sportsground (SGS)
NSW LTA Tennis
Cncl Off
EDGECLIFF
Edgecliff Cntr
Edgecliff
Stills Gallery
Dillon St Res
Sydney Grammar Preparatory
'White City'
Trumper Park Playground
Trumper Oval
Trumper Park
Tennis
The Scottish Hospital
Glenmore Road Primary
Sherman Galleries
FIVE WAYS
Soudan St Plgrd
PADDINGTON
Ret Vill
OXFORD ST
MACLEAY ST
ELIZABETH BAY RD
BILLYARD AV
GREENKNOWE AV
BARODA ST
WARATAH ST
NEW BEACH RD
YARRANABBE RD
DARLING POINT RD
OCEAN ST
GLENMORE RD
BOUNDARY ST
McLACHLAN AV
LAWSON ST
HODDLE ST
GURNER ST
CASCADE ST
HAMPDEN ST
WALKER AV
GOODHOPE ST
BROUGHTON ST
UNDERWOOD ST
PADDINGTON ST
HARGRAVE ST
WINDSOR ST
SUTHERLAND ST
COPYRIGHT © UNIVERSAL PRESS PTY LTD (PUBLISHER) 2002

JOINS MAP 347 C8

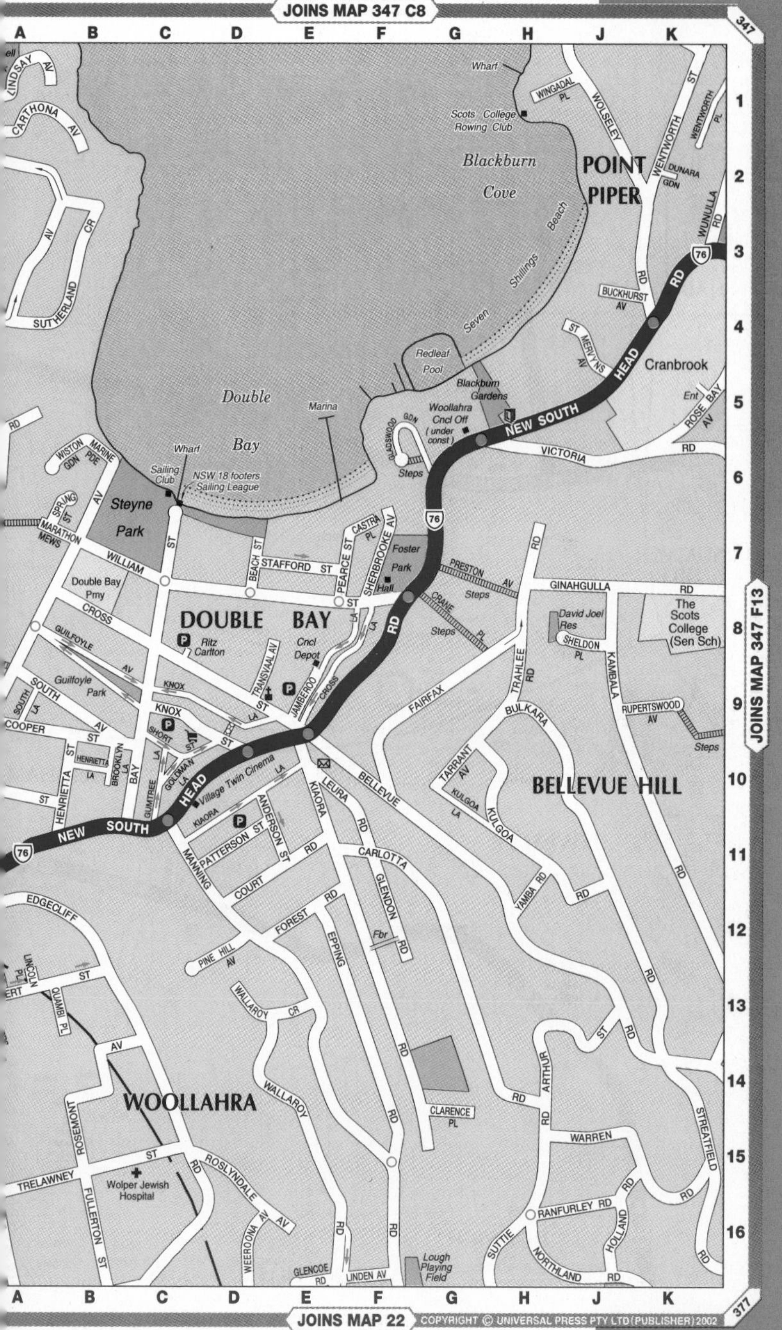

JOINS MAP 347 F13

JOINS MAP 22

MAP 15

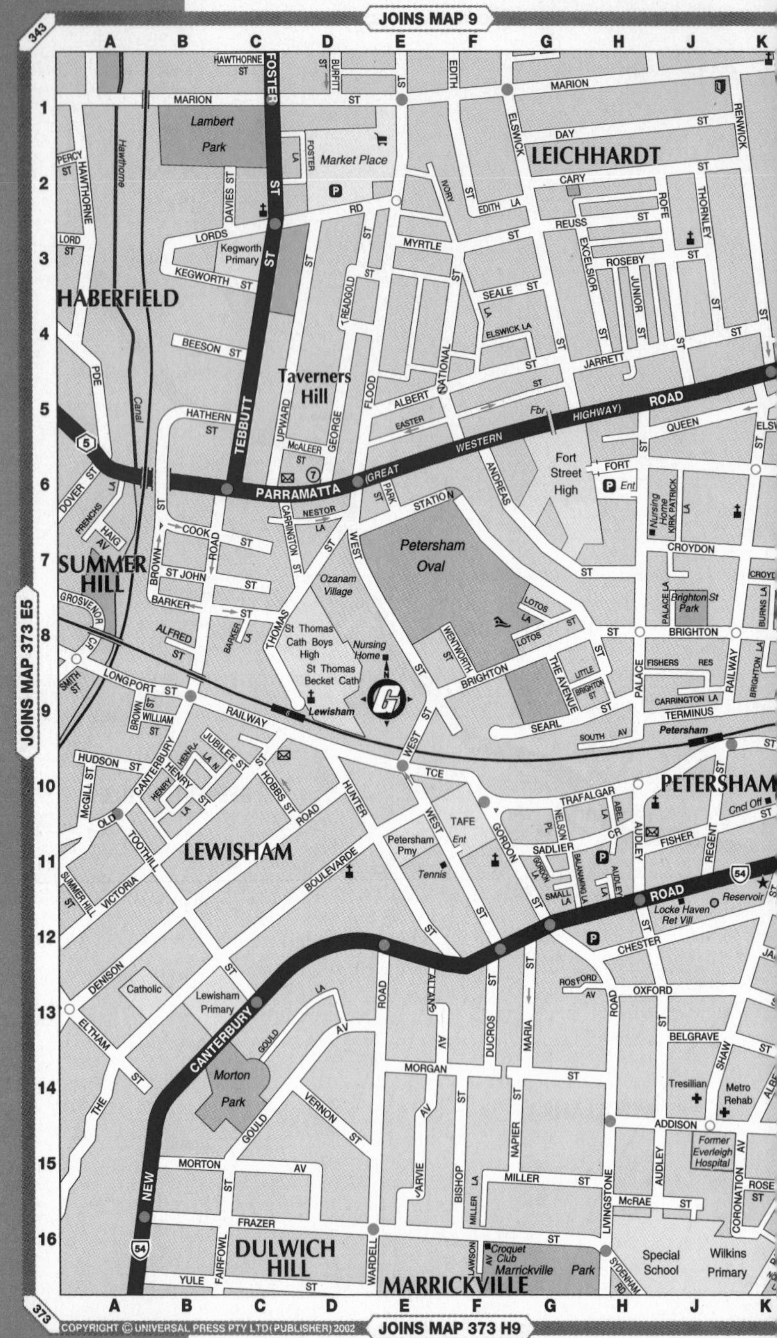
JOINS MAP 9
343
A B C D E F G H J K
1 2 3 4 5 6 7 8 9 10 11 12 13 14 15 16
HAWTHORNE ST
FOSTER ST
BURFITT ST
EDITH ST
MARION ST
Lambert Park
Market Place
FOSTER LA
RENWICK ST
DAY ST
LEICHHARDT
ELSWICK ST
CARY ST
PERCY ST
HAWTHORNE
Hawthorne Canal
DAVIES ST
LORDS RD
IVORY
EDITH LA
REUSS ST
ROFE ST
THORNLEY ST
LORD ST
Kegworth Primary
KEGWORTH ST
MYRTLE ST
EXCELSIOR ST
ROSEBY ST
JUNIOR ST
TREADGOLD ST
SEALE ST
SEALE LA
ELSWICK LA
HABERFIELD
BEESON ST
PDE
Taverners Hill
JARRETT ST
NATIONAL ST
ALBERT ST
FLOOD ST
HATHERN ST
TEBBUTT ST
UPWARD ST
GEORGE ST
EASTER ST
Fbr
HIGHWAY)
ROAD
QUEEN ST
McALEER ST
WESTERN
Fort Street High
FORT ST
Ent
(GREAT
PARRAMATTA
PARK ST
STATION ST
ANDREAS ST
DOVER ST
FRENCHS LA
HAIG AV
COOK ST
NESTOR LA
CARRINGTON ST
WEST ST
Petersham Oval
Nursing Home
KIRK PATRICK LA
CROYDON ST
SUMMER HILL
BROWN ST
ST JOHN ST
ROAD
Ozanam Village
GROSVENOR CR
BARKER ST
BARKER LA
ALFRED ST
THOMAS ST
St Thomas Cath Boys High
St Thomas Becket Cath
Nursing Home
LOTOS LA
WENTWORTH ST
BRIGHTON ST
PALACE LA
Brighton St Park
BURNS LA
FISHERS RES
RAILWAY ST
BRIGHTON LA
CARRINGTON LA
TERMINUS ST
SMITH ST
LONGPORT ST
Lewisham
THE AVENUE
LITTLE
BRIGHTON ST
PALACE ST
SEARL ST
SOUTH AV
Petersham
BROWN ST
WILLIAM ST
RAILWAY
JUBILEE LA
HENRY LA
HUDSON ST
CANTERBURY
HENRY ST
HOBBS ST
TCE
TRAFALGAR ST
ABEL
PETERSHAM
Cncl Off
McGILL ST
OLD
ROAD
HUNTER ST
WEST ST
TAFE
Ent
GORDON ST
NELSON PL
FISHER ST
REGENT ST
TOOTHILL ST
LEWISHAM
BOULEVARDE
Petersham Pmy
Tennis
SADLIER CR
BALANNING LA
AUDLEY ST
SUMMER HILL ST
VICTORIA
SMALL LA
ROAD
Locke Haven Ret Vill
Reservoir
CHESTER ST
DENISON
Catholic
Lewisham Primary
ALLANS AV
DUCROS ST
MARIA ST
ROSFORD AV
OXFORD
ELTHAM
CANTERBURY
GOULD
LA
AV
ROAD
BELGRAVE ST
SHAW
MORGAN ST
Morton Park
Tresillian
Metro Rehab
THE
VERNON ST
ADDISON
GOULD
Former Everleigh Hospital
CORONATION AV
MORTON AV
JARVIE AV
BISHOP ST
NAPIER ST
MILLER ST
AUDLEY ST
ROSE ST
NEW
MILLER LA
McRAE ST
LIVINGSTONE RD
FRAZER
ST
DULWICH HILL
FAIRFOWL ST
WARDELL RD
LAWSON AV
Croquet Club
Marrickville Park
SYDENHAM RD
Special School
Wilkins Primary
YULE ST
MARRICKVILLE
JOINS MAP 373 E5
373
JOINS MAP 373 H9

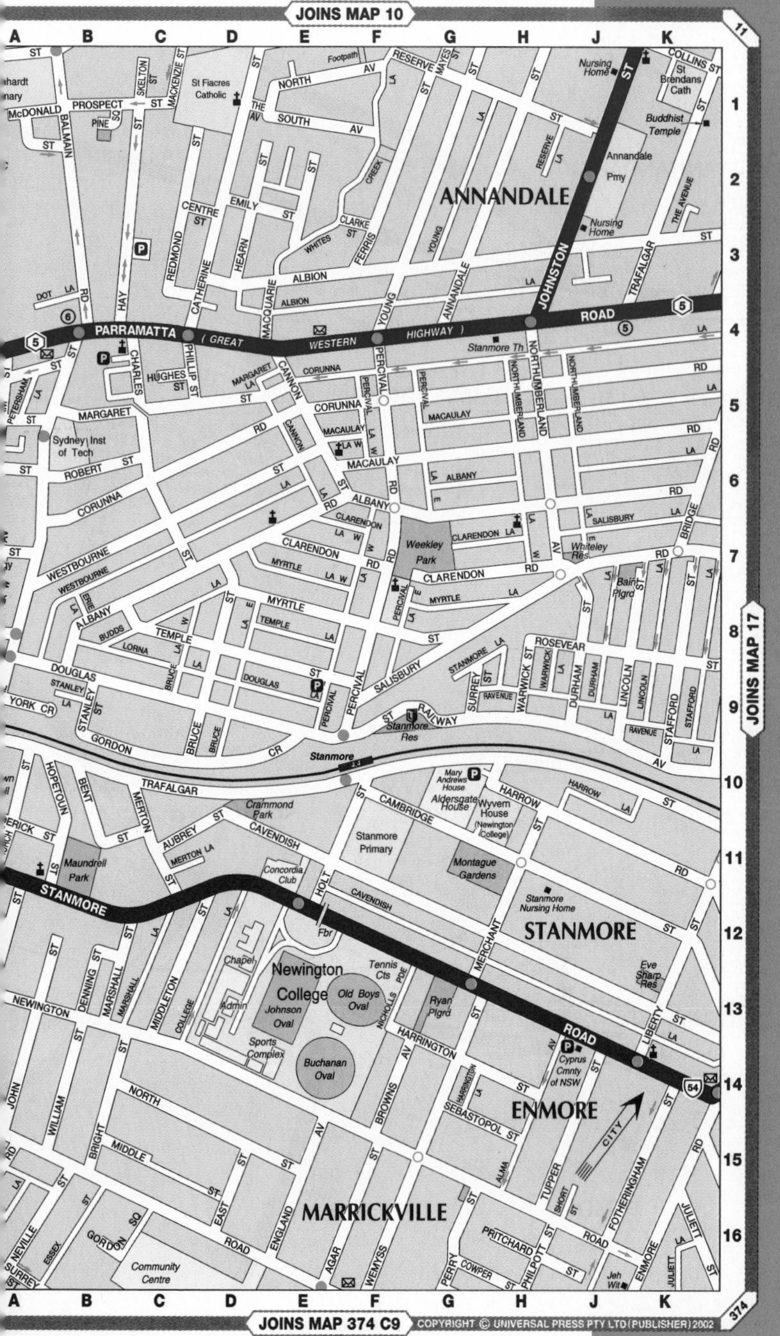
JOINS MAP 10
JOINS MAP 17
JOINS MAP 374 C9
ANNANDALE
STANMORE
ENMORE
MARRICKVILLE
PARRAMATTA (GREAT WESTERN HIGHWAY) ROAD
JOHNSTON ST
STANMORE ROAD
Newington College
Weekley Park
Stanmore
Annandale Pmy
Stanmore Primary
Montague Gardens
Crammond Park
Maundrell Park
Sydney Inst of Tech
St Fiacres Catholic
St Brendans Cath
Buddhist Temple
Stanmore Nursing Home
Old Boys Oval
Buchanan Oval
Johnson Oval
Community Centre
Cyprus Cmnty of NSW
CITY

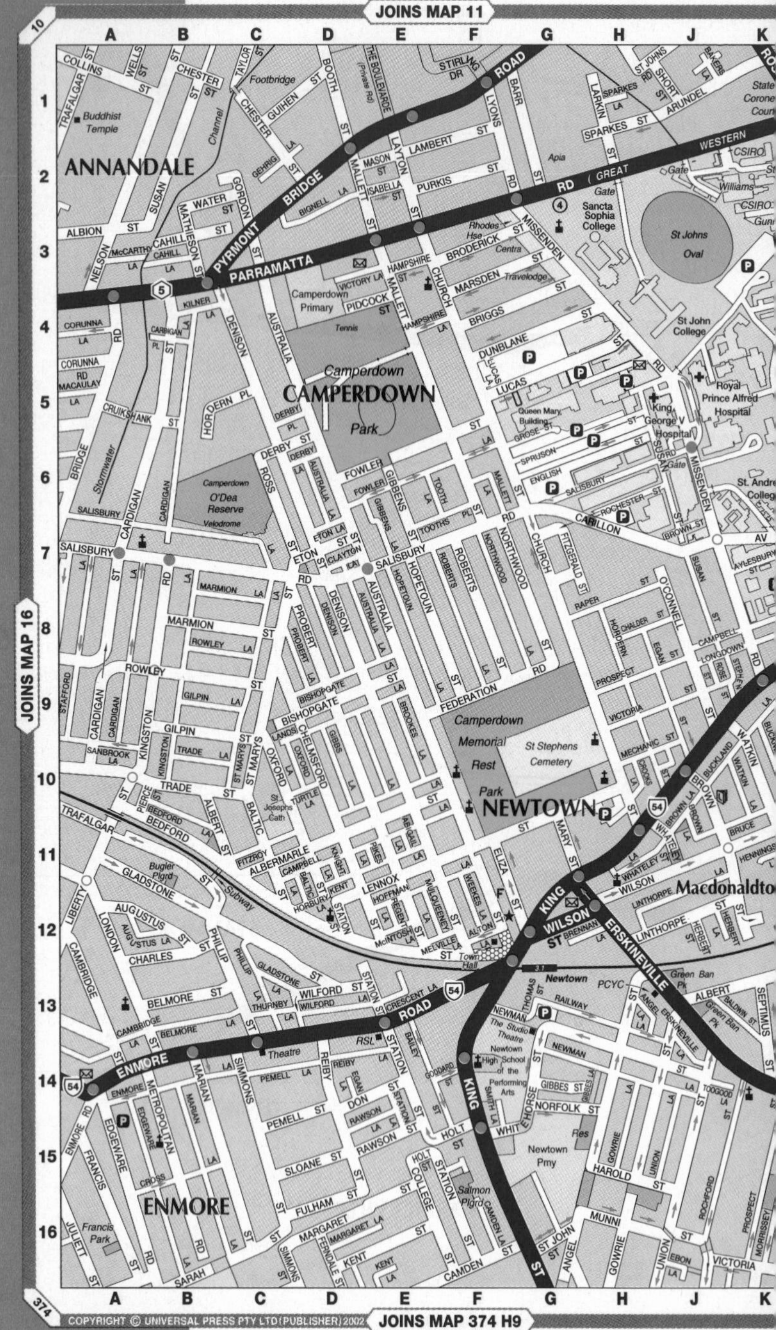
JOINS MAP 11
JOINS MAP 16
JOINS MAP 374 H9
10
374
A B C D E F G H J K
1 2 3 4 5 6 7 8 9 10 11 12 13 14 15 16
ANNANDALE
CAMPERDOWN
NEWTOWN
ENMORE
Macdonaldto
PARRAMATTA RD
GREAT WESTERN
PYRMONT BRIDGE ROAD
KING ST
ENMORE ROAD
ERSKINEVILLE
WILSON ST
MISSENDEN RD
CARILLON AV
SALISBURY RD
CHURCH ST
AUSTRALIA ST
DENISON ST
Buddhist Temple
Camperdown Primary
Camperdown Park
Camperdown O'Dea Reserve
Velodrome
Camperdown Memorial Rest Park
St Stephens Cemetery
Sancta Sophia College
St Johns Oval
St John College
Royal Prince Alfred Hospital
King George V Hospital
Queen Mary Building
Rhodes Hse
Travelodge
Apia
Newtown PCYC
Newtown High School of the Performing Arts
The Studio Theatre
Newtown Pmy
Salmon Plgrd
Francis Park
Bugler Plgrd
St Josephs Cath
Town Hall
Theatre
RSL
Green Ban Pk
Stormwater Channel
Subway
COPYRIGHT © UNIVERSAL PRESS PTY LTD (PUBLISHER) 2002

JOINS MAP 12

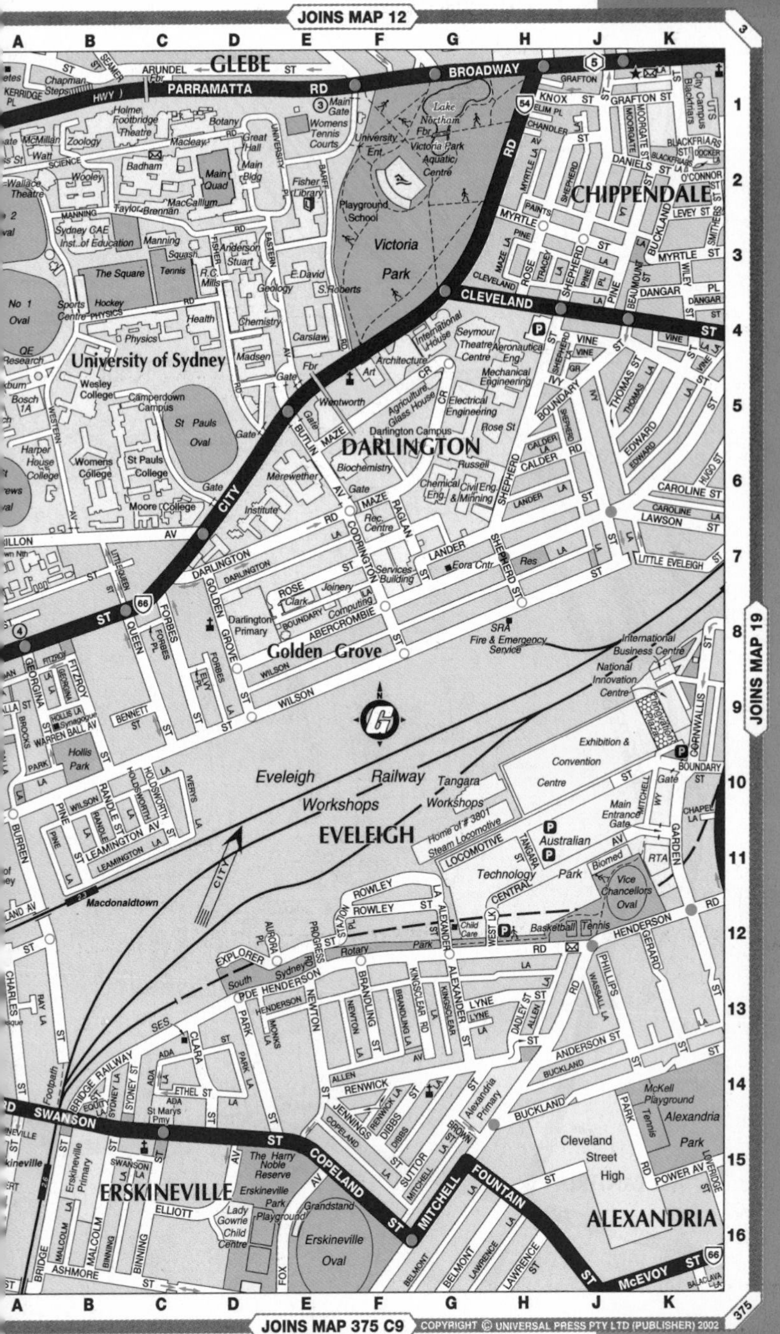

JOINS MAP 375 C9

MAP 19

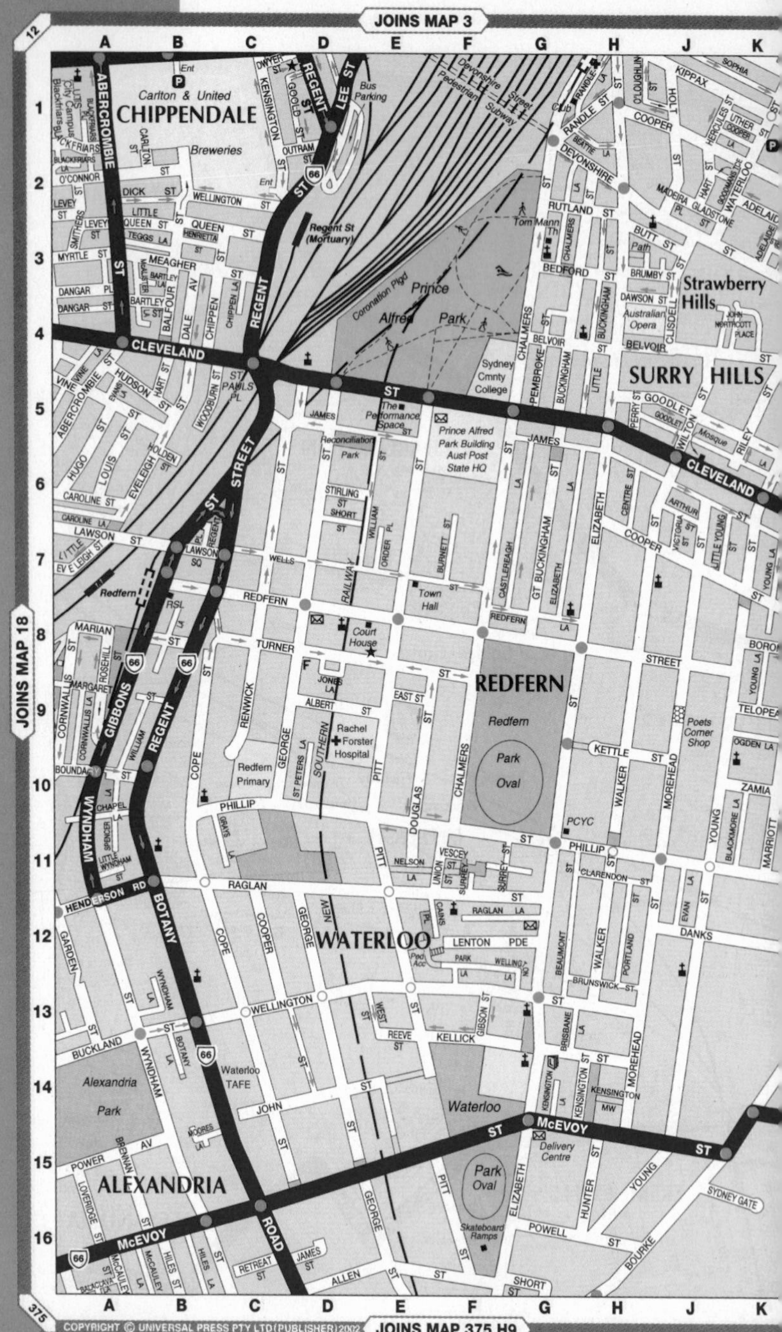

JOINS MAP 3
JOINS MAP 18
JOINS MAP 375 H9
12
375
A
B
C
D
E
F
G
H
J
K
1
2
3
4
5
6
7
8
9
10
11
12
13
14
15
16
CHIPPENDALE
Carlton & United Breweries
SURRY HILLS
Strawberry Hills
REDFERN
WATERLOO
ALEXANDRIA
Prince Alfred Park
Coronation Plgd
Devonshire Street Pedestrian Subway
Regent St (Mortuary)
Bus Parking
Tom Mann Th
Australian Opera
Sydney Cmnty College
The Performance Space
Prince Alfred Park Building Aust Post State HQ
Reconciliation Park
Town Hall
Court House
Rachel Forster Hospital
Redfern Primary
Redfern Park Oval
PCYC
Poets Corner Shop
Mosque
Waterloo TAFE
Alexandria Park
Waterloo Park Oval
Skateboard Ramps
Delivery Centre
Redfern
RSL
UTS City Campus Blackfriars
Ped Acc
CLEVELAND ST
REGENT ST
ABERCROMBIE ST
LEE ST
BOTANY ROAD
McEVOY ST
GIBBONS ST
WYNDHAM ST
HENDERSON RD
RAGLAN ST
PHILLIP ST
REDFERN ST
TURNER ST
WELLINGTON ST
ELIZABETH ST
CHALMERS ST
PITT ST
GEORGE ST
COPE ST
COOPER ST
BOURKE ST
YOUNG ST
MOREHEAD ST
WALKER ST
KETTLE ST
DEVONSHIRE ST
RANDLE ST
BUCKINGHAM ST
PEMBROKE ST
CASTLEREAGH ST
WILTON ST
RILEY ST
LAWSON ST
WELLS ST
JAMES ST
BEDFORD ST
BELVOIR ST
RUTLAND ST
KELLICK ST
JOHN ST
POWELL ST
SHORT ST
ALLEN ST
DANKS ST
SYDNEY GATE

JOINS MAP 4

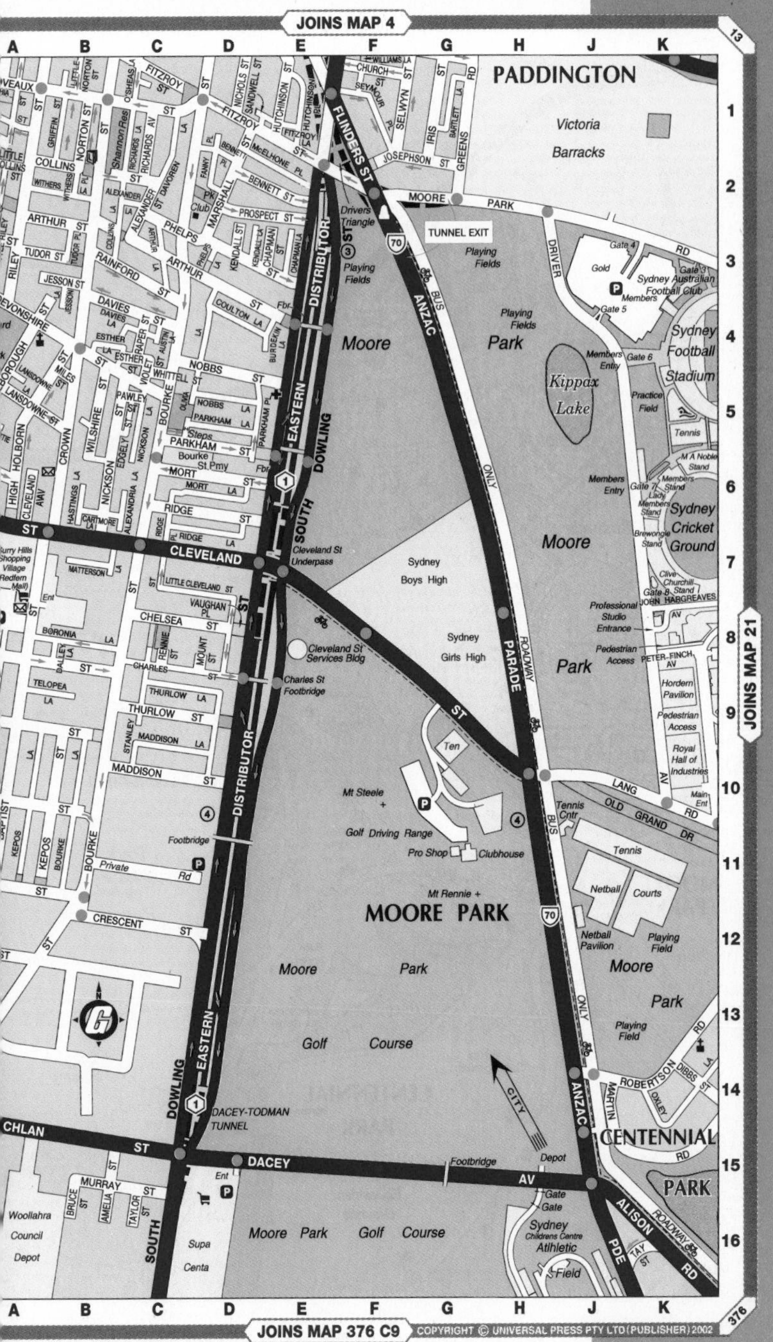

JOINS MAP 376 C9

JOINS MAP 13

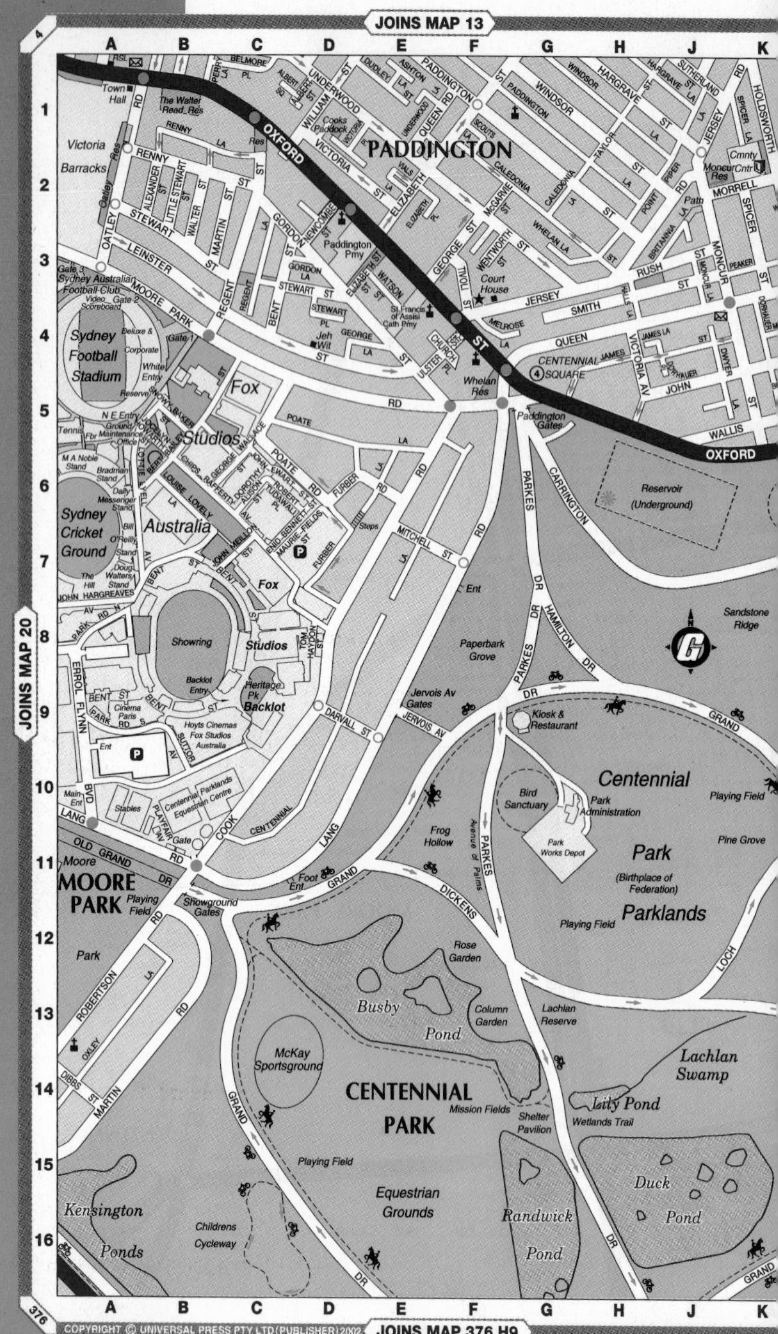

JOINS MAP 20

JOINS MAP 376 H9

JOINS MAP 14

JOINS MAP 377 C9

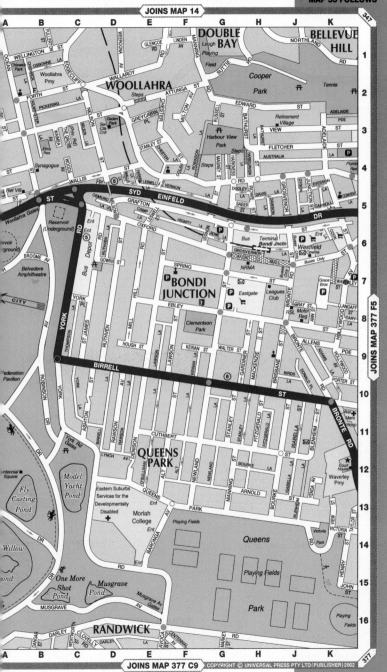

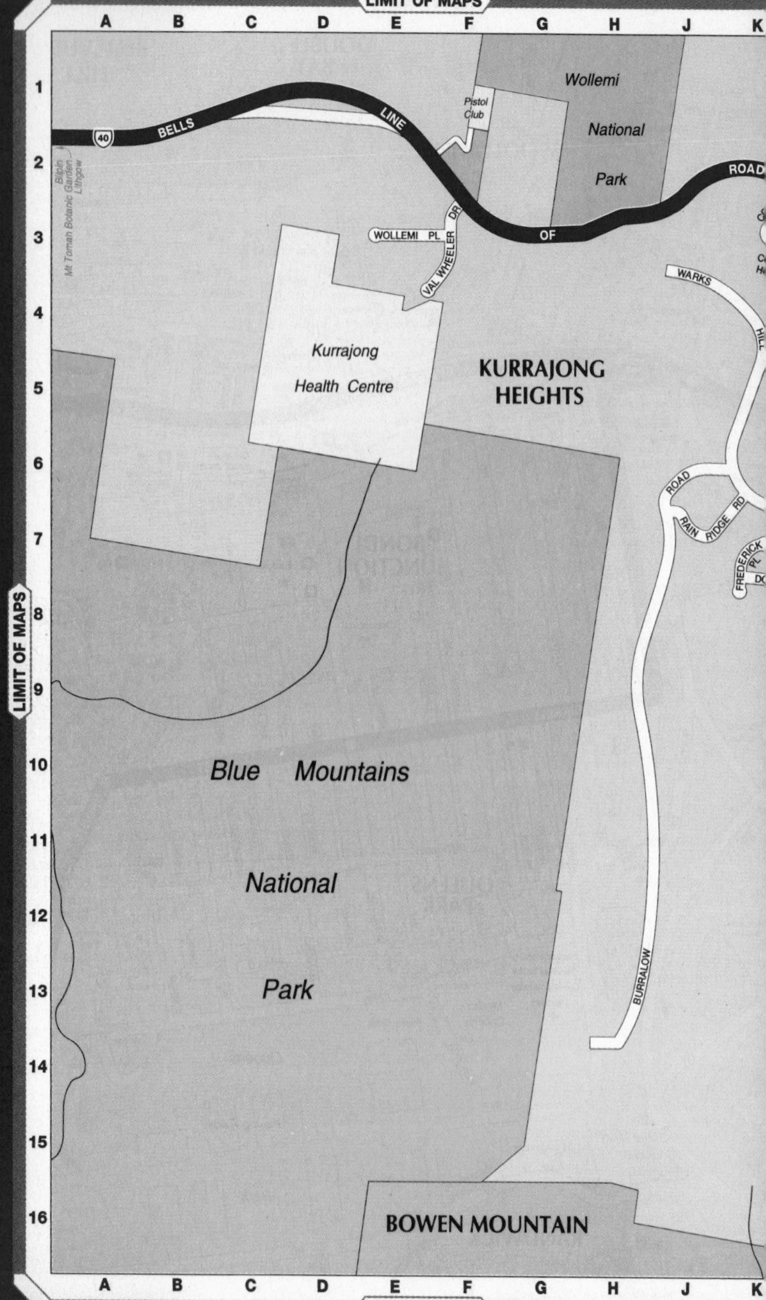
LIMIT OF MAPS
A B C D E F G H J K
1 2 3 4 5 6 7 8 9 10 11 12 13 14 15 16
Wollemi
National
Park
Pistol
Club
40
BELLS
LINE
OF
ROAD
Bilpin
Mt Tomah Botanic Garden
Lithgow
WOLLEMI PL
VAL WHEELER DR
WARKS
HILL
Kurrajong
Health Centre
KURRAJONG
HEIGHTS
ROAD
RAIN RIDGE RD
FREDERICK PL
LIMIT OF MAPS
Blue Mountains
National
Park
BURRALOW
BOWEN MOUNTAIN

JOINS MAP 83

LIMIT OF MAPS

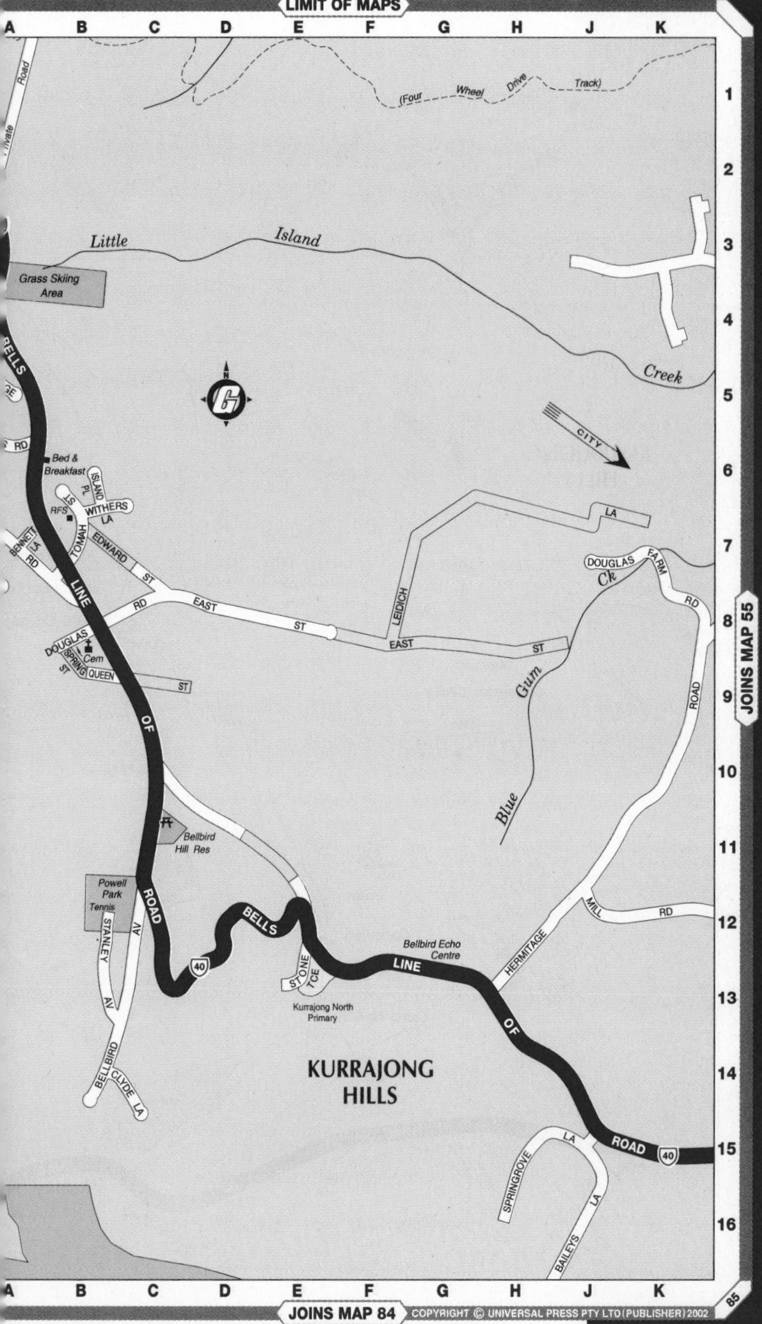

JOINS MAP 55

JOINS MAP 84

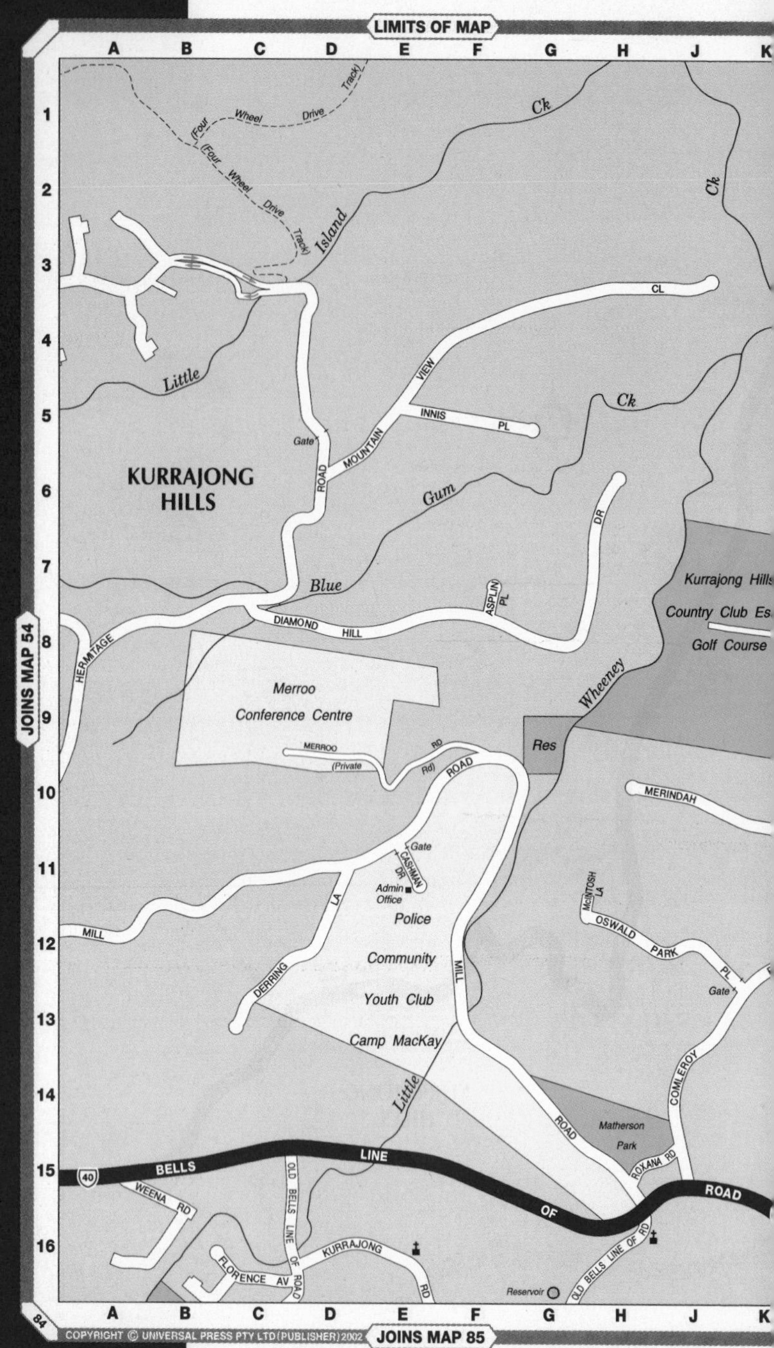
LIMITS OF MAP
A B C D E F G H J K
1 2 3 4 5 6 7 8 9 10 11 12 13 14 15 16
(Four Wheel Drive Track)
(Four Wheel Drive Track)
Island
Ck
Ck
Little
Ck
CL
VIEW
INNIS PL
MOUNTAIN
ROAD
Gate
KURRAJONG HILLS
Gum
DR
Blue
ASPLIN PL
DIAMOND HILL
Kurrajong Hills Country Club Es Golf Course
HERMITAGE
JOINS MAP 54
Merroo Conference Centre
Wheeney
Res
MERROO (Private Rd)
RD
ROAD
MERINDAH
Gate
CASHMAN DR
Admin Office
Police Community Youth Club Camp MacKay
McINTOSH LA
OSWALD PARK PL
MILL
LA
DERRING
MILL
Gate
COMLEROY
Little
ROAD
Matherson Park
ROXANA RD
40
BELLS LINE OF ROAD
WEENA RD
OLD BELLS LINE OF ROAD
KURRAJONG RD
FLORENCE AV
OLD BELLS LINE OF RD
Reservoir

LIMIT OF MAPS

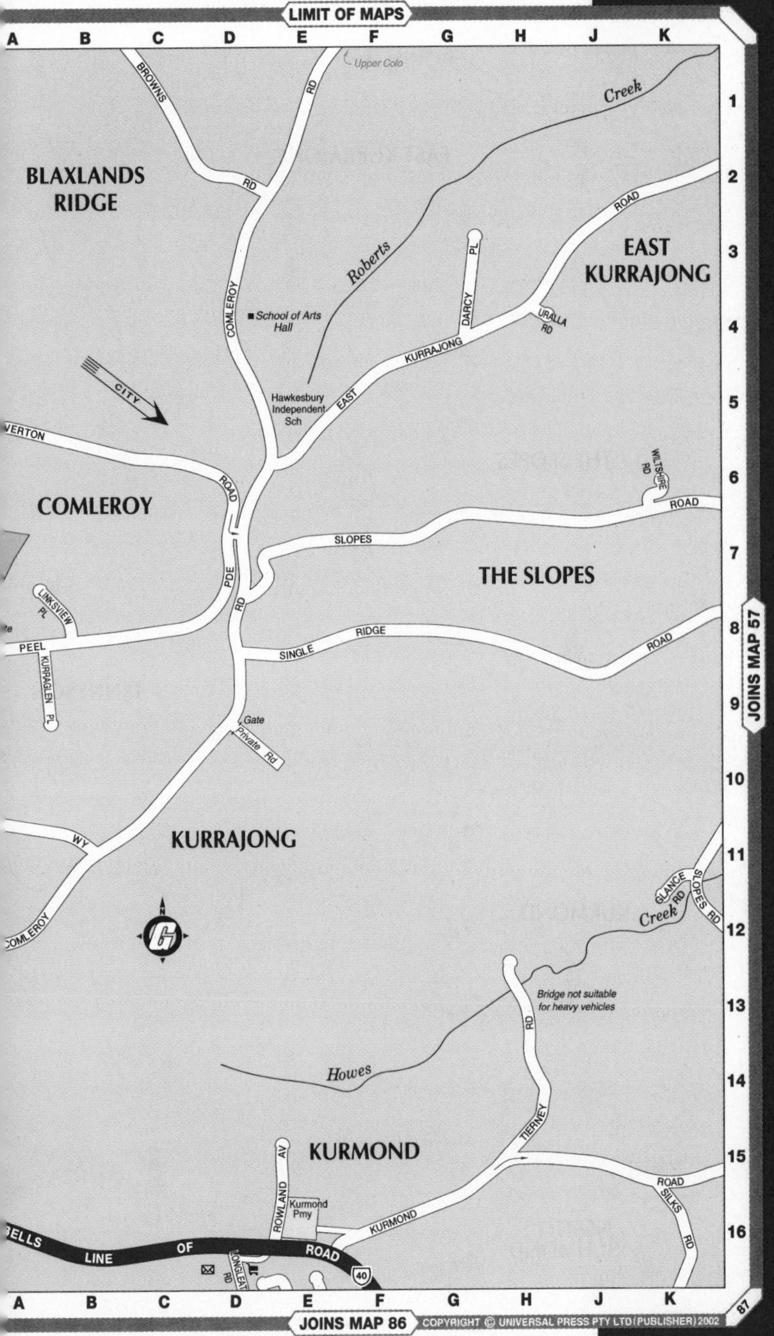

JOINS MAP 57

JOINS MAP 86

87

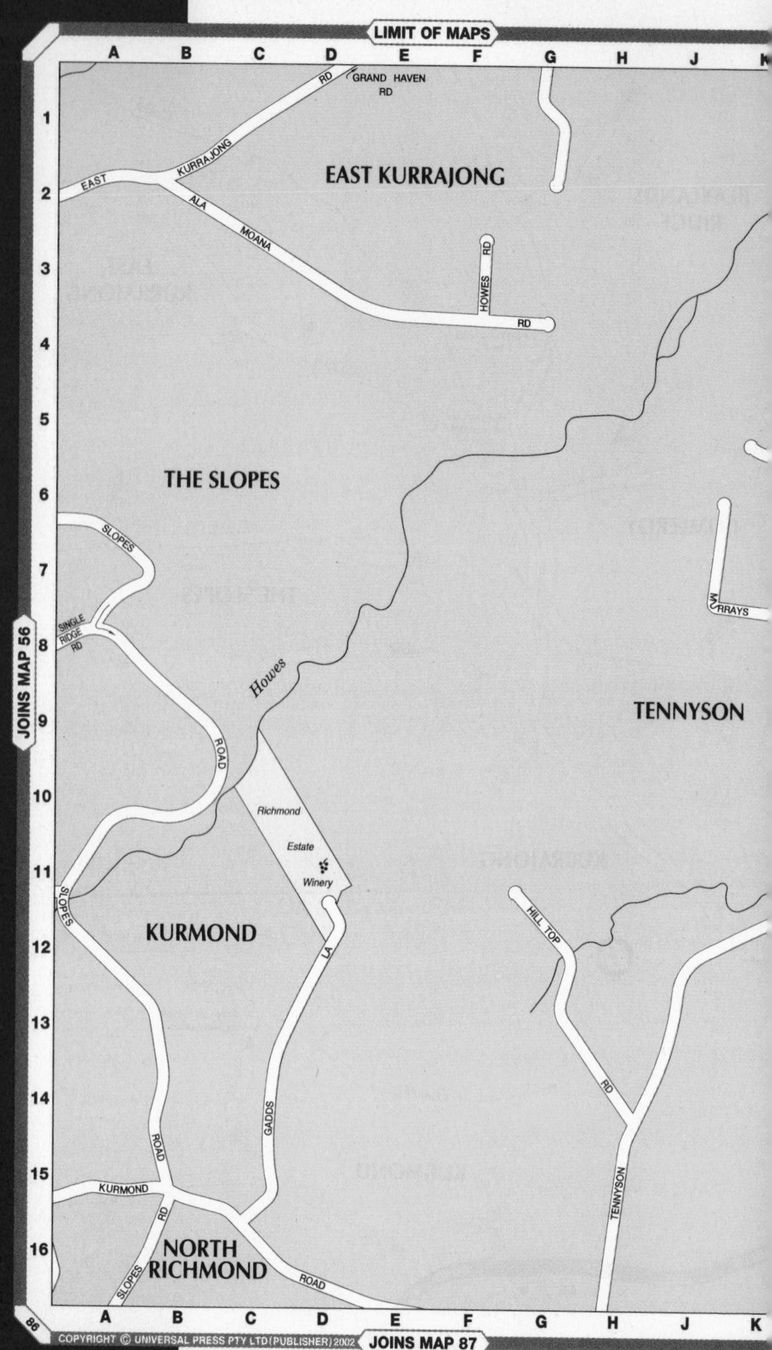
LIMIT OF MAPS
A
B
C
D
E
F
G
H
J
K
1
2
3
4
5
6
7
8
9
10
11
12
13
14
15
16
GRAND HAVEN RD
RD
KURRAJONG
EAST
EAST KURRAJONG
ALA
MOANA
HOWES RD
RD
THE SLOPES
SLOPES
SINGLE RIDGE RD
JOINS MAP 56
Howes
ROAD
Richmond
Estate
Winery
SLOPES
KURMOND
LA
HILL TOP
TENNYSON
RRAYS
GADDS
RD
ROAD
KURMOND
RD
TENNYSON
NORTH RICHMOND
SLOPES
ROAD
86
JOINS MAP 87

LIMIT OF MAPS

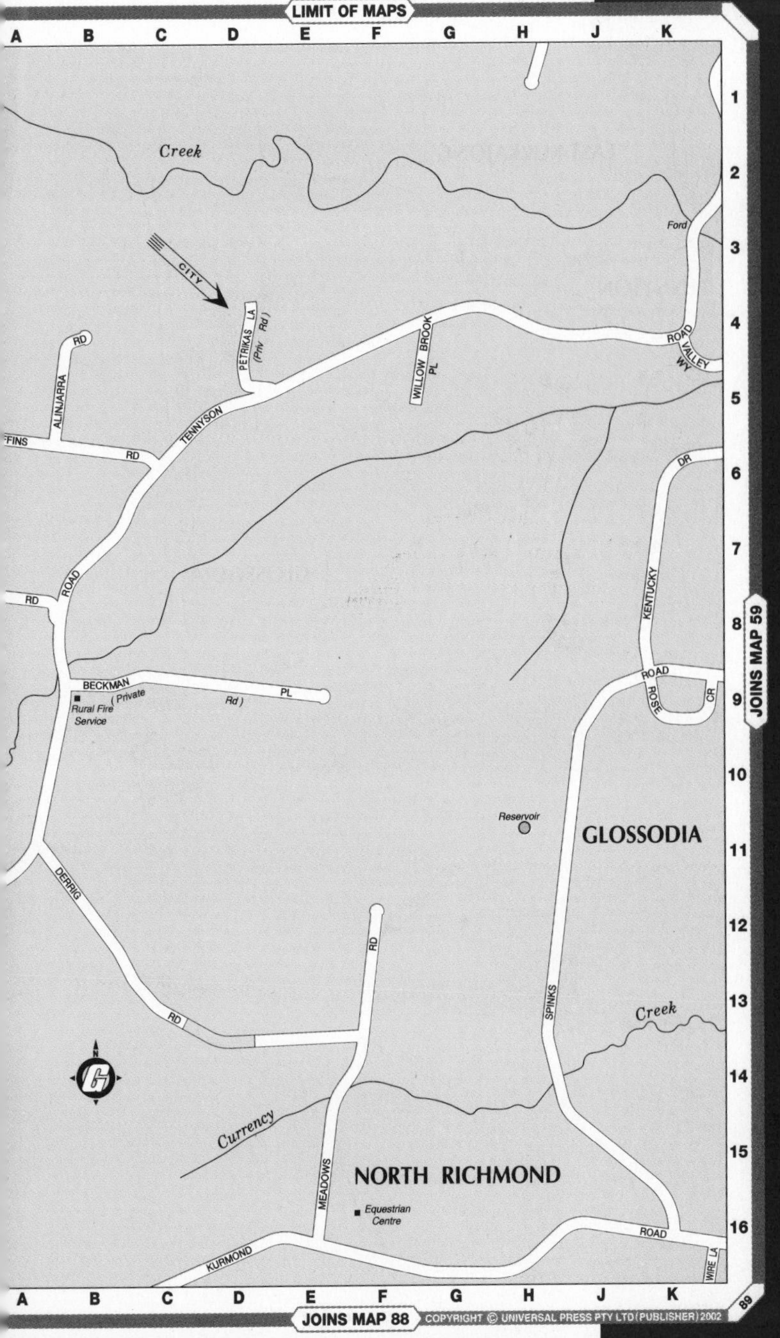

JOINS MAP 59

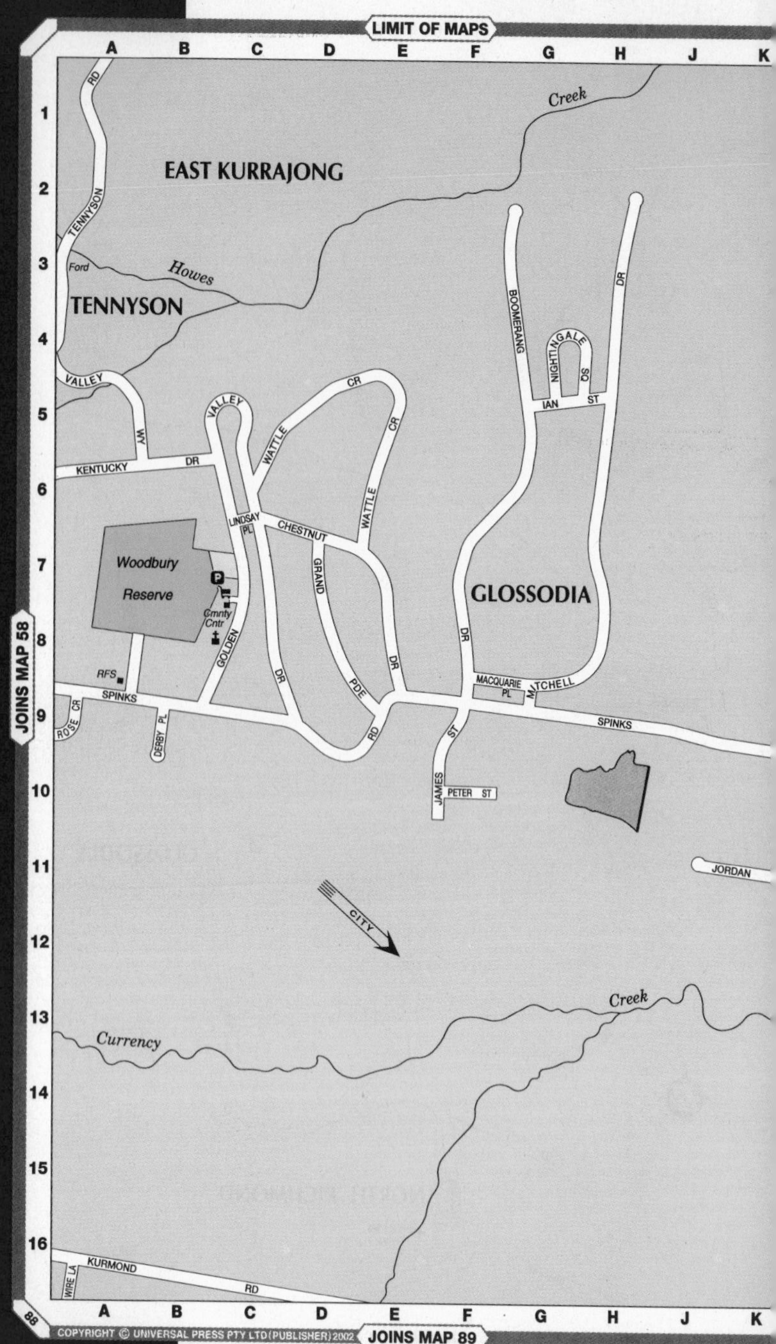
LIMIT OF MAPS
EAST KURRAJONG
TENNYSON
GLOSSODIA
Creek
Howes
Ford
TENNYSON RD
VALLEY
KENTUCKY DR
WY
WATTLE CR
LINDSAY PL
CHESTNUT
GRAND PDE
WATTLE DR
BOOMERANG DR
NIGHTINGALE SQ
IAN ST
Woodbury Reserve
Cmnty Cntr
GOLDEN
RFS
SPINKS
ROSE CR
DERBY PL
MACQUARIE PL
MITCHELL
JAMES ST
PETER ST
JORDAN
CITY
Currency
Creek
KURMOND RD
WIRE LA
JOINS MAP 58

JOINS MAP 89

LIMIT OF MAPS

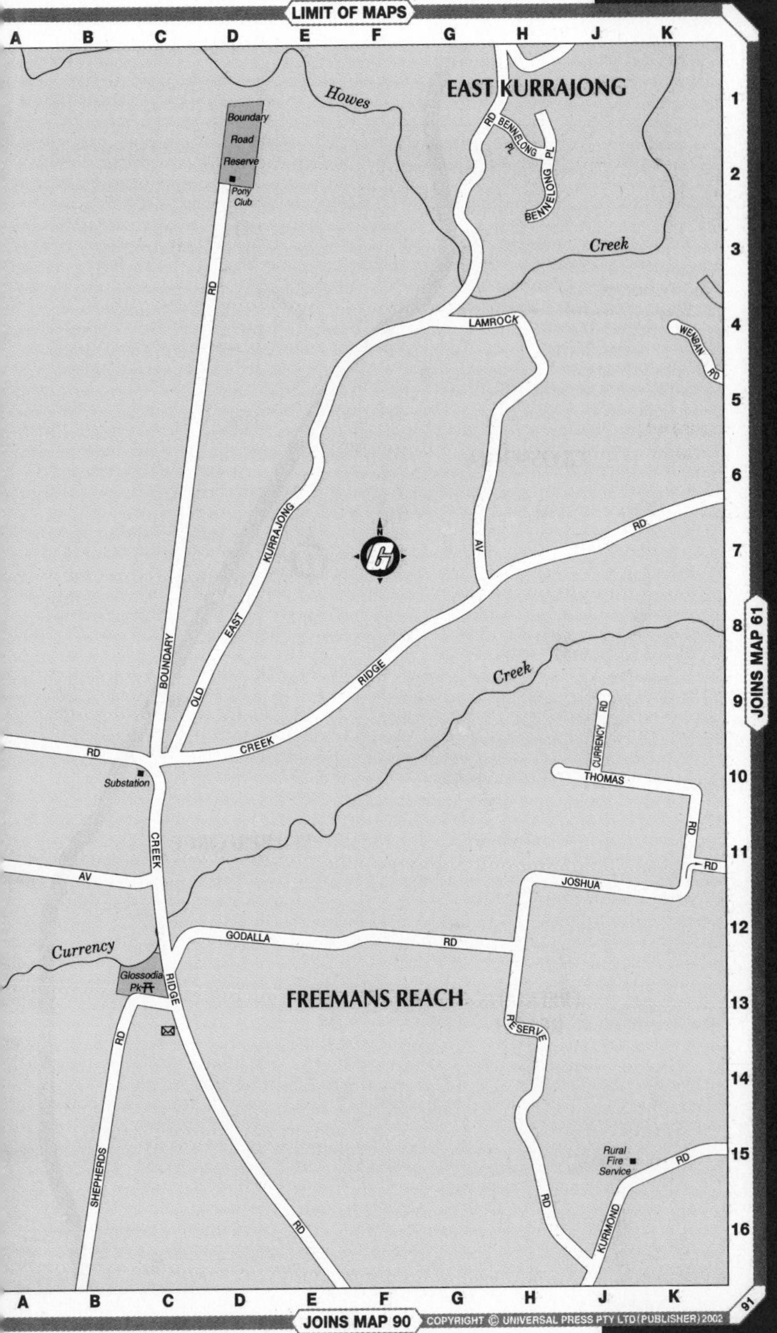

JOINS MAP 61

JOINS MAP 90

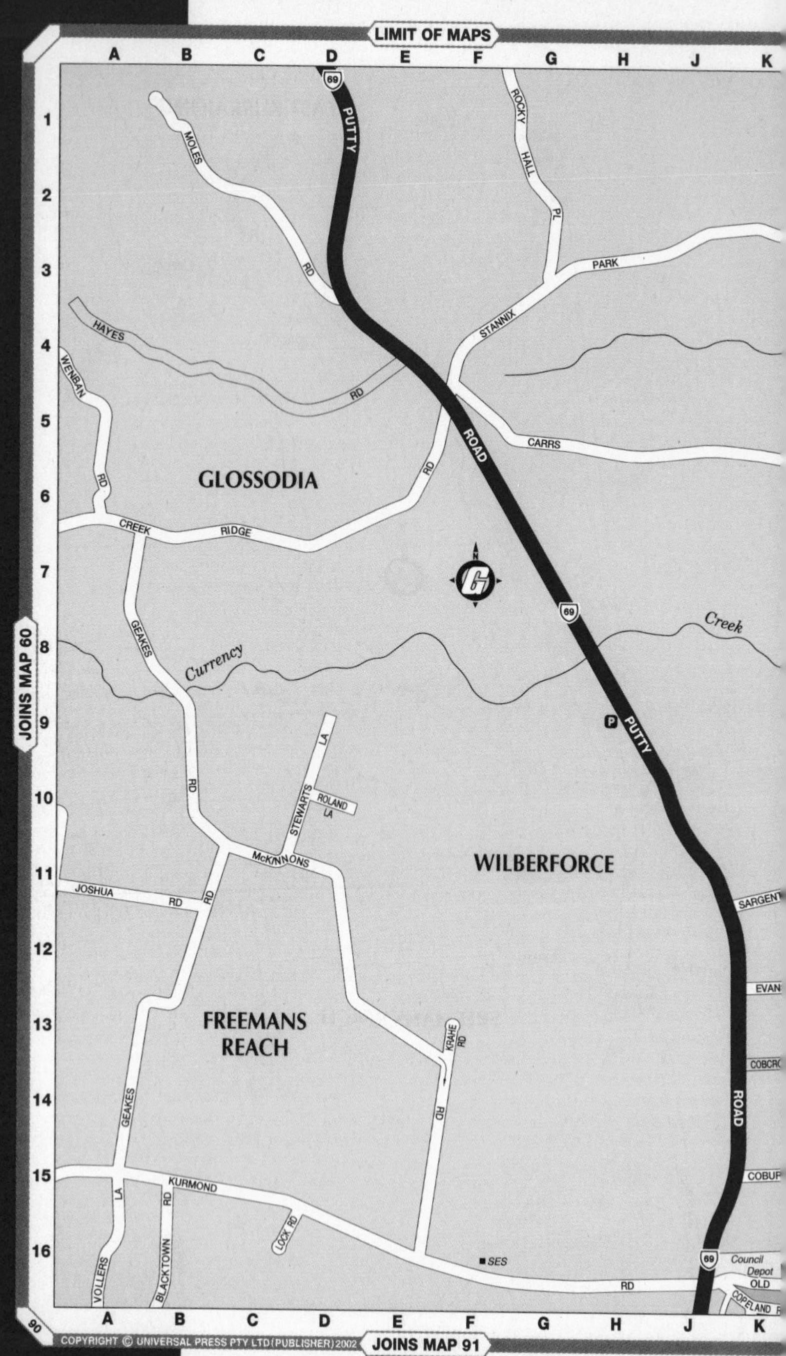
LIMIT OF MAPS
A B C D E F G H J K
1 2 3 4 5 6 7 8 9 10 11 12 13 14 15 16
69
PUTTY
ROAD
MOLES
RD
ROCKY
HALL
PL
PARK
STANNIX
HAYES
RD
WENBAN
RD
CARRS
RD
GLOSSODIA
CREEK
RIDGE
69
Creek
Currency
GEAKES
RD
P
PUTTY
LA
STEWARTS
ROLAND
LA
McKINNONS
WILBERFORCE
JOSHUA
RD
RD
SARGENT
EVANS
FREEMANS
REACH
KRAHE
RD
COBCRO
RD
GEAKES
ROAD
COBUR
KURMOND
LA
RD
LOCK RD
VOLLERS
BLACKTOWN
SES
69
Council
Depot
RD
OLD
COPELAND
JOINS MAP 60
JOINS MAP 91
90

LIMIT OF MAPS

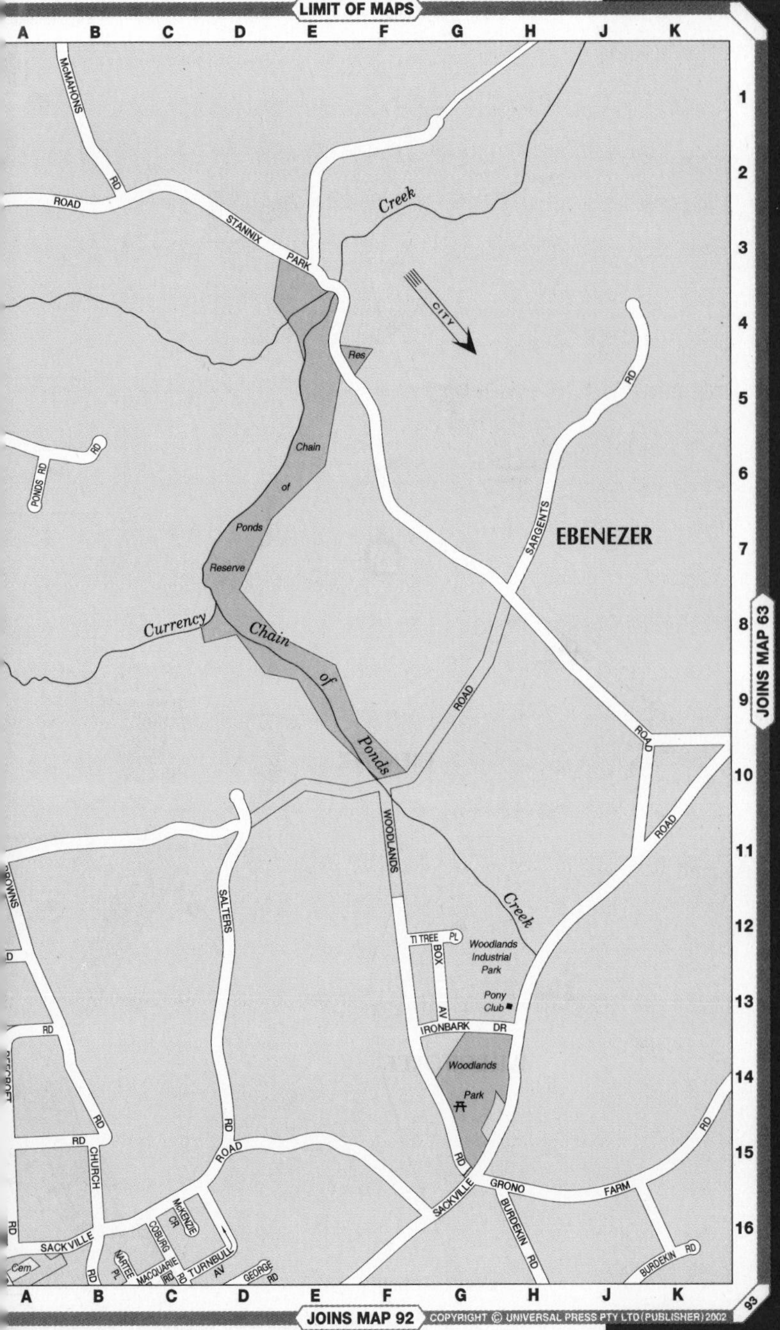

JOINS MAP 63

JOINS MAP 92

93

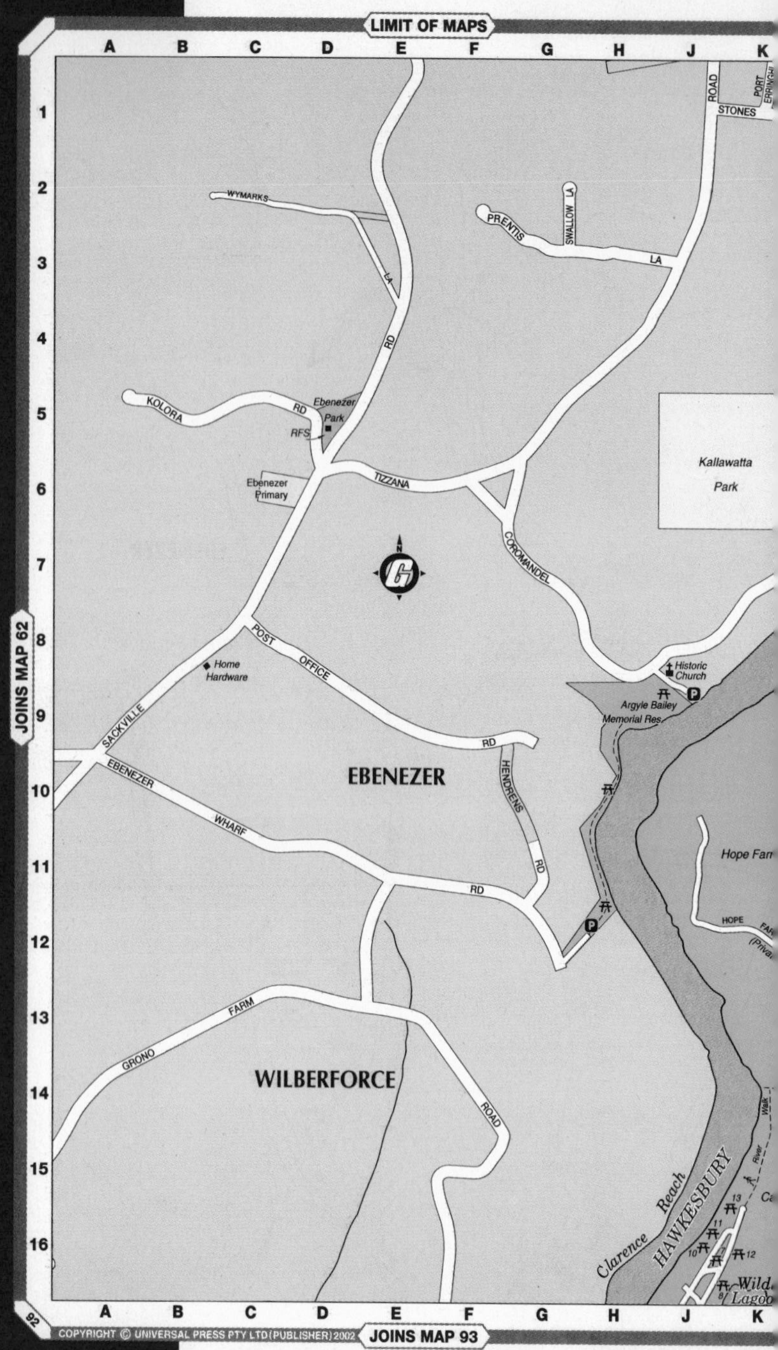
LIMIT OF MAPS
A B C D E F G H J K
1 2 3 4 5 6 7 8 9 10 11 12 13 14 15 16
JOINS MAP 62
JOINS MAP 93
ROAD
STONES
PORT
WYMARKS
LA
PRENTIS
SWALLOW LA
LA
RD
KOLORA
RD
Ebenezer
Park
RFS
Ebenezer
Primary
TIZZANA
Kallawatta
Park
COROMANDEL
POST
OFFICE
RD
Home
Hardware
SACKVILLE
Historic
Church
Argyle Bailey
Memorial Res.
EBENEZER
WHARF
RD
HENDRENS
RD
EBENEZER
Hope Far
HOPE
GRONO
FARM
WILBERFORCE
ROAD
Clarence
Reach
HAWKESBURY
River
Walk
13
11
10
12
Wild
Lago

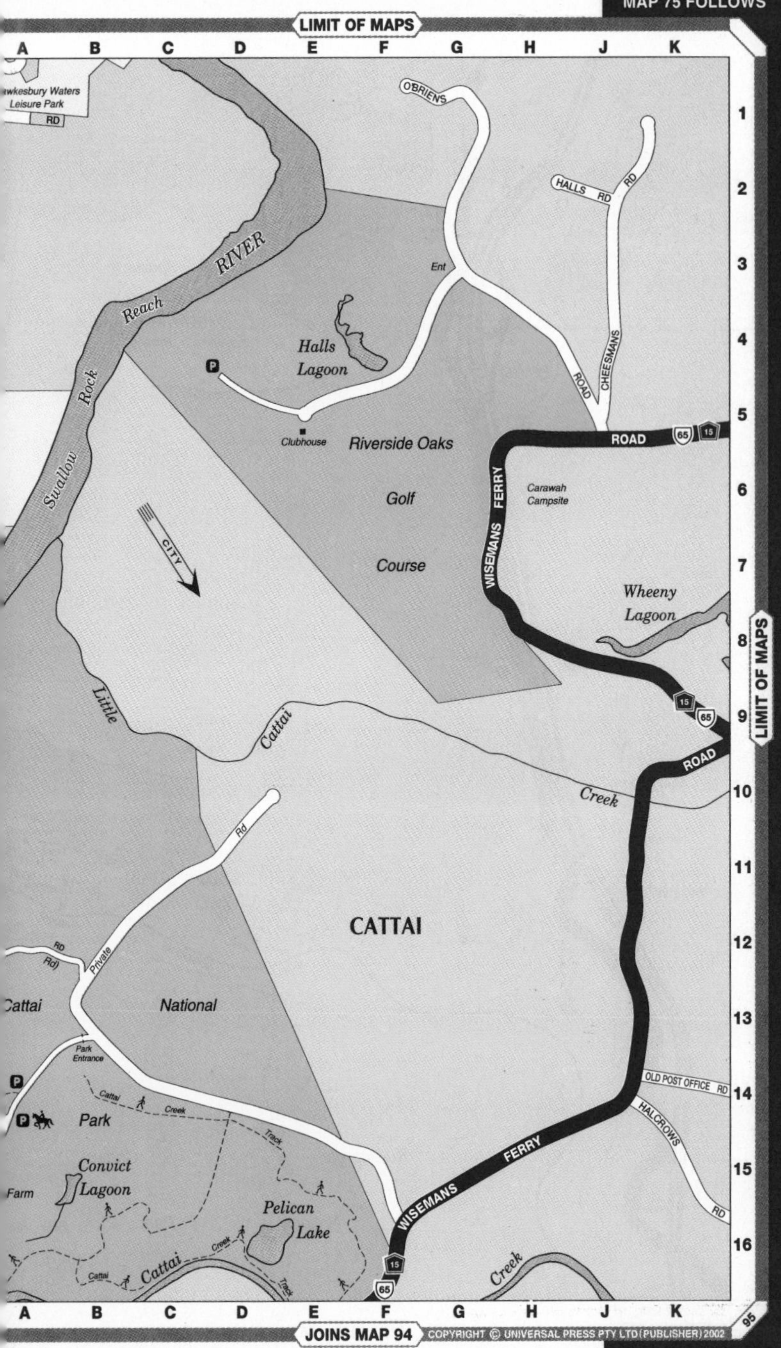
LIMIT OF MAPS
A B C D E F G H J K
1 2 3 4 5 6 7 8 9 10 11 12 13 14 15 16
awkesbury Waters
Leisure Park
RD
O'BRIENS
HALLS RD
RD
Swallow Rock Reach RIVER
Ent
Halls
Lagoon
CHEESMANS
ROAD
Clubhouse
Riverside Oaks
Golf
Course
ROAD
WISEMANS FERRY
Carawah
Campsite
CITY
Wheeny
Lagoon
Little
Cattai
Creek
ROAD
Rd
CATTAI
RD
Rd)
Private
Cattai
National
Park Entrance
OLD POST OFFICE RD
HALCROWS RD
Cattai Creek
Park
Track
WISEMANS FERRY
Convict
Lagoon
Farm
Pelican
Lake
Creek
Cattai
Cattai
Track
Creek
15
65
LIMIT OF MAPS

JOINS MAP 94

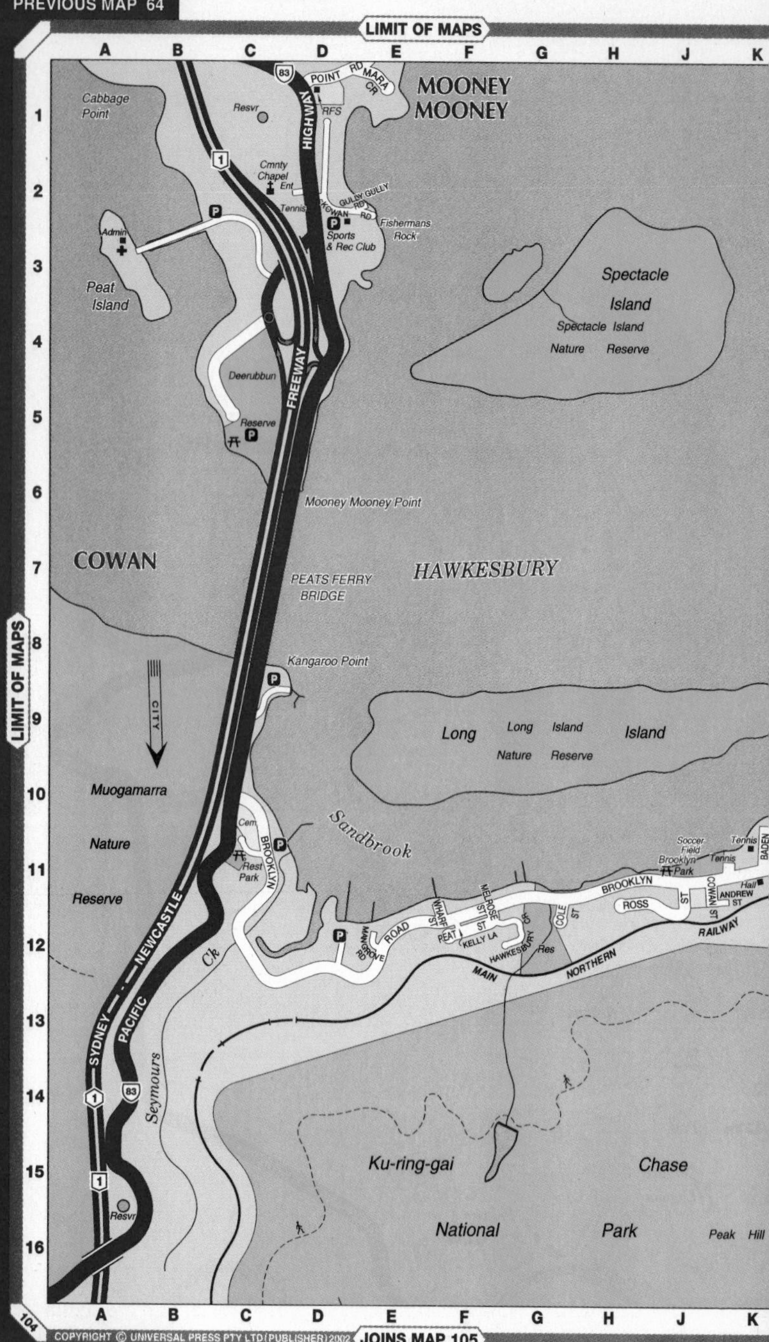
LIMIT OF MAPS
MOONEY MOONEY
Cabbage Point
Resvr
RFS
POINT RD
MARA CR
HIGHWAY
Cmnty Chapel
Ent
Tennis
GULLY RD
GULLY
KOWAN RD
Sports & Rec Club
Fishermans Rock
Admin
Peat Island
Spectacle Island
Spectacle Island Nature Reserve
Deerubbun Reserve
FREEWAY
Mooney Mooney Point
COWAN
HAWKESBURY
PEATS FERRY BRIDGE
Kangaroo Point
CITY
Long Island
Long Island Nature Reserve
Muogamarra Nature Reserve
Sandbrook
Cem
BROOKLYN
Rest Park
Soccer Field
Tennis
Brooklyn Park
BADEN
Hall
BROOKLYN
ROSS
ST
COWAN ST
ANDREW ST
NEWCASTLE
Ck
MANGROVE RD
ROAD
WHARF ST
PEAT ST
KELLY LA
MELROSE ST
HAWKESBURY CR
COLE ST
Res
RAILWAY
MAIN NORTHERN
SYDNEY
PACIFIC
Seymours
Ku-ring-gai Chase National Park
Peak Hill
Resvr
LIMIT OF MAPS

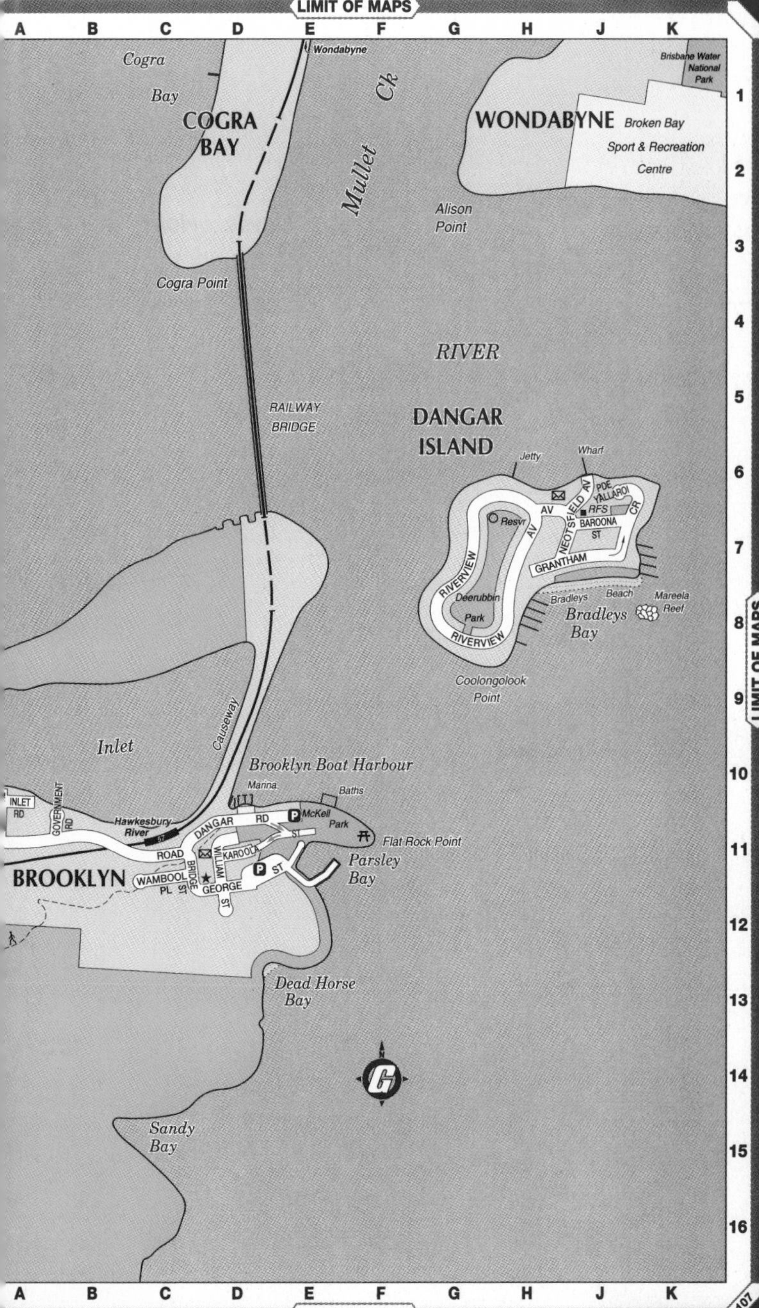
LIMIT OF MAPS
A B C D E F G H J K
1 2 3 4 5 6 7 8 9 10 11 12 13 14 15 16
Wondabyne
Cogra Bay
COGRA BAY
Mullet Ck
Brisbane Water National Park
WONDABYNE
Broken Bay Sport & Recreation Centre
Alison Point
Cogra Point
RIVER
RAILWAY BRIDGE
DANGAR ISLAND
Jetty
Wharf
PDE
YALLAROI
AV
NEOTSFIELD AV
RFS
CR
Resvr
AV
BAROONA ST
GRANTHAM
RIVERVIEW
Deerubbin Park
RIVERVIEW
Bradleys Beach
Mareela Reef
Bradleys Bay
Coolongolook Point
LIMIT OF MAPS
Inlet
Causeway
Brooklyn Boat Harbour
Marina
Baths
INLET RD
GOVERNMENT RD
Hawkesbury River
ST
DANGAR RD
McKell Park
ST
Flat Rock Point
ROAD
KAROOLA
WILLIAM
BRIDGE ST
ST
Parsley Bay
BROOKLYN
WAMBOOL PL
GEORGE ST
Dead Horse Bay
Sandy Bay

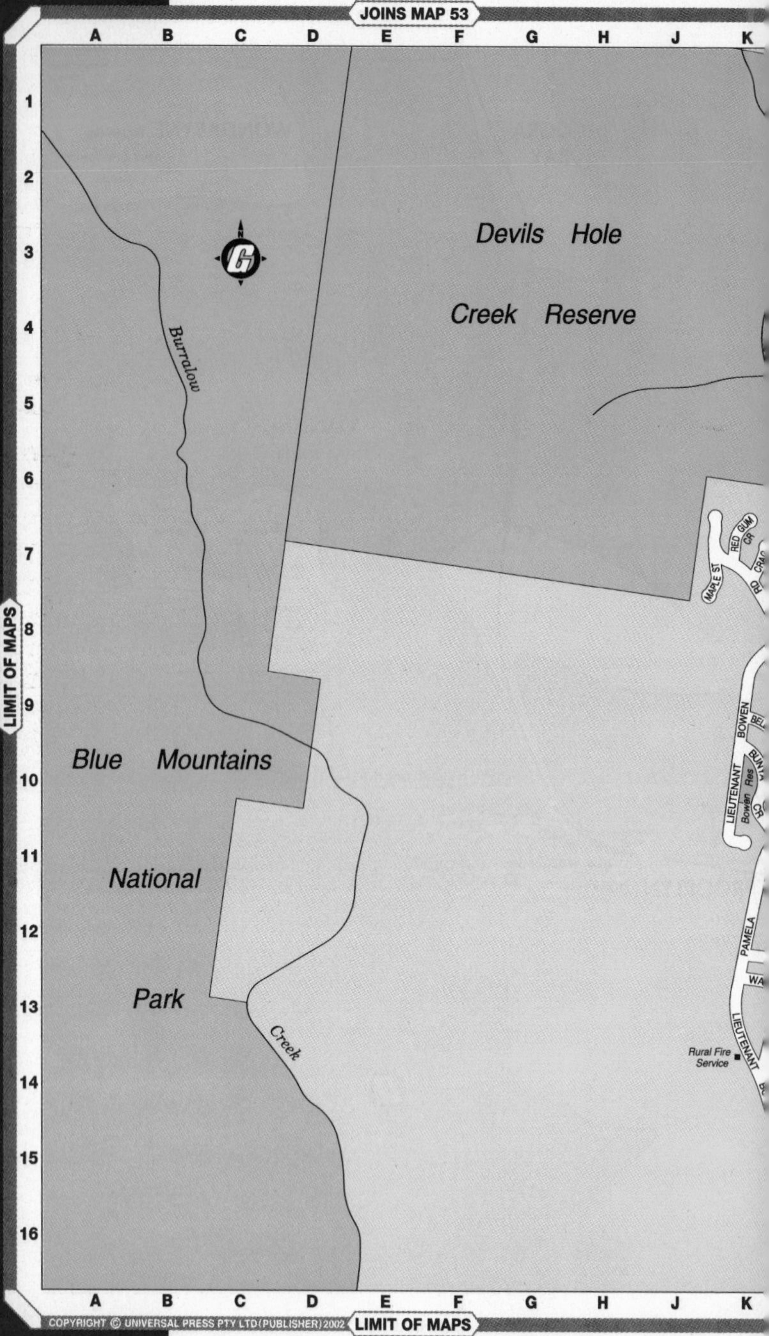
JOINS MAP 53
LIMIT OF MAPS
Devils Hole Creek Reserve
Blue Mountains National Park
Burralow Creek
RED GUM CR
MAPLE ST
RD
BOWEN
LIEUTENANT
Bowen Res
CR
PAMELA
LIEUTENANT
Rural Fire Service
LIMIT OF MAPS

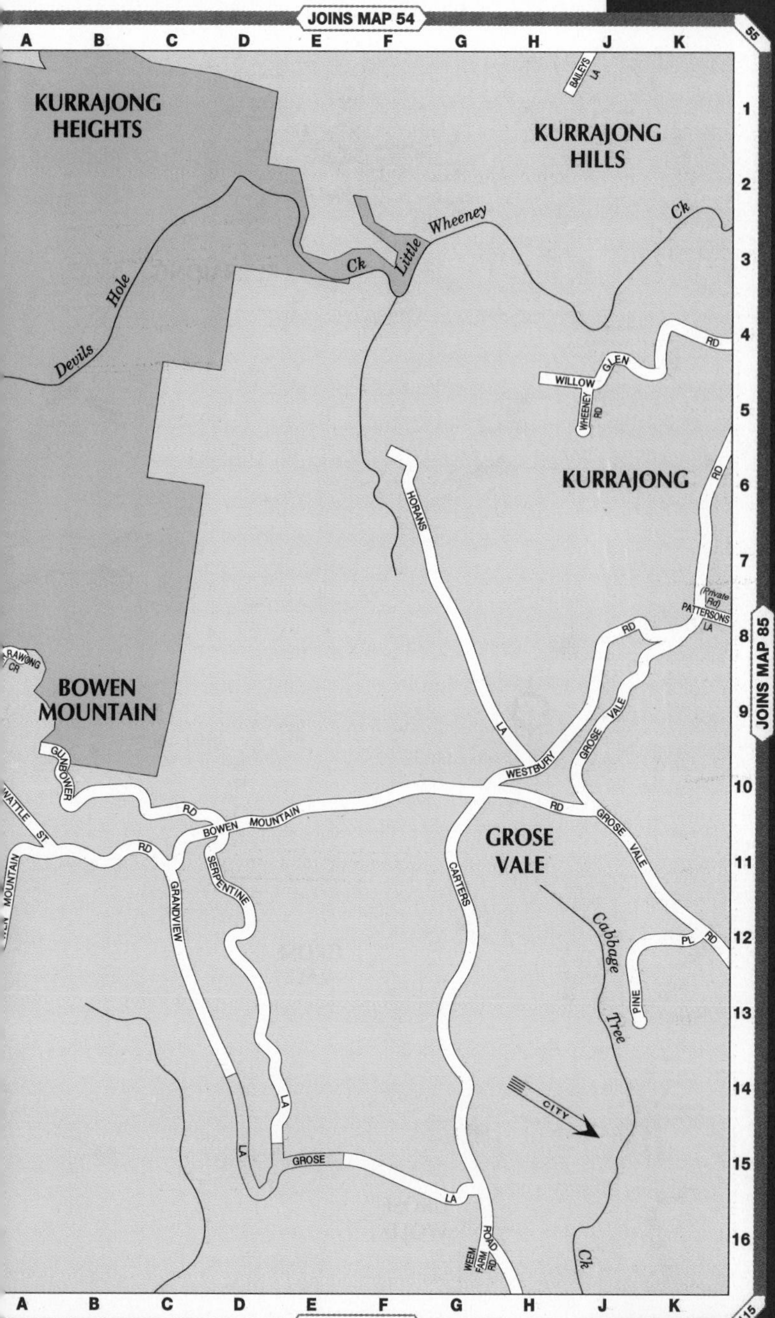
JOINS MAP 54
A
B
C
D
E
F
G
H
J
K
55
KURRAJONG HEIGHTS
KURRAJONG HILLS
BAILEYS LA
Little Wheeney Ck
Devils Hole
Ck
RD
WILLOW GLEN
WHEENEY RD
KURRAJONG
HORANS LA
RD
(Private Rd)
PATTERSONS LA
RD
BOWEN MOUNTAIN
GROSE VALE
WESTBURY RD
GUNBOWER
WATTLE ST
RD
BOWEN MOUNTAIN RD
MOUNTAIN
GROSE VALE
GRANDVIEW
SERPENTINE
CARTERS
Cabbage Tree Ck
PL
RD
PINE
CITY
LA
LA
GROSE LA
ROAD
WEEM FARM RD
1
2
3
4
5
6
7
8
9
10
11
12
13
14
15
16
JOINS MAP 85
LIMIT OF MAPS
115

JOINS MAP 55

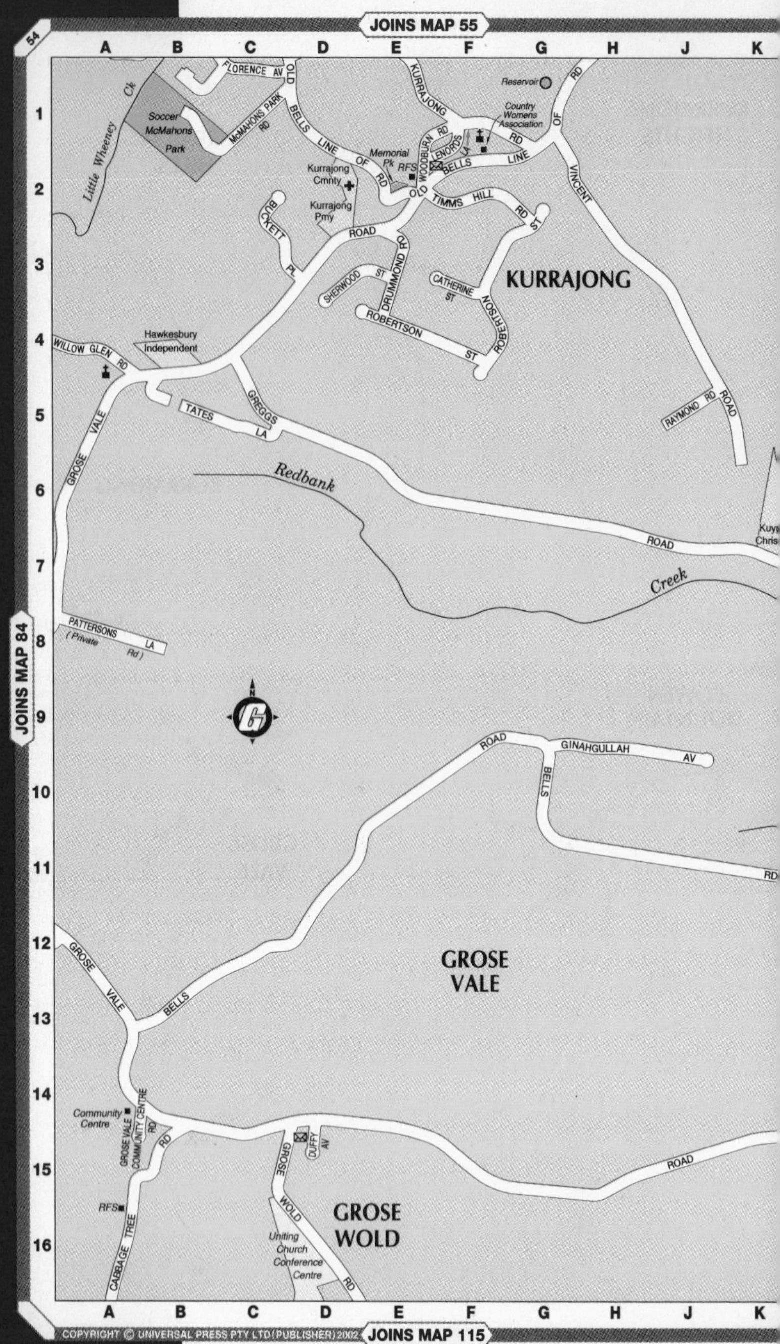

JOINS MAP 84

JOINS MAP 115

JOINS MAP 56

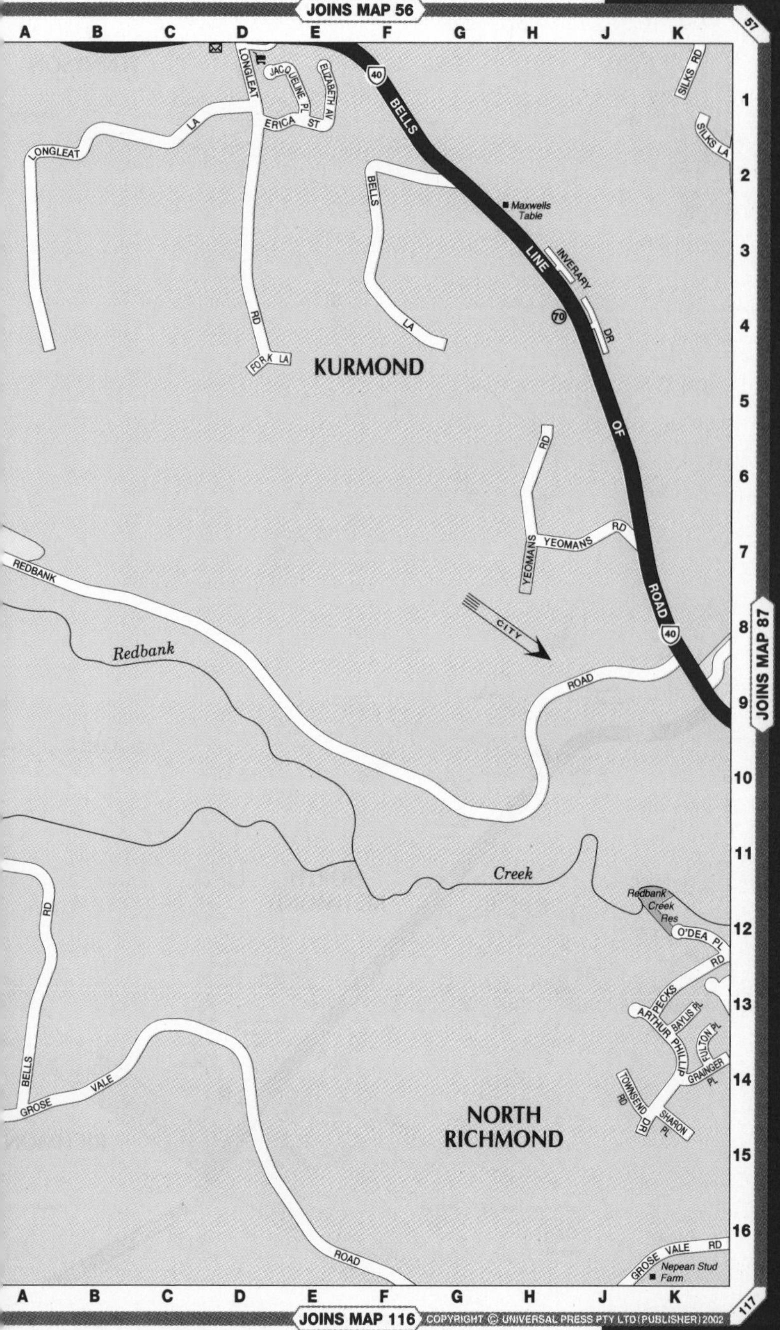

JOINS MAP 116

JOINS MAP 57

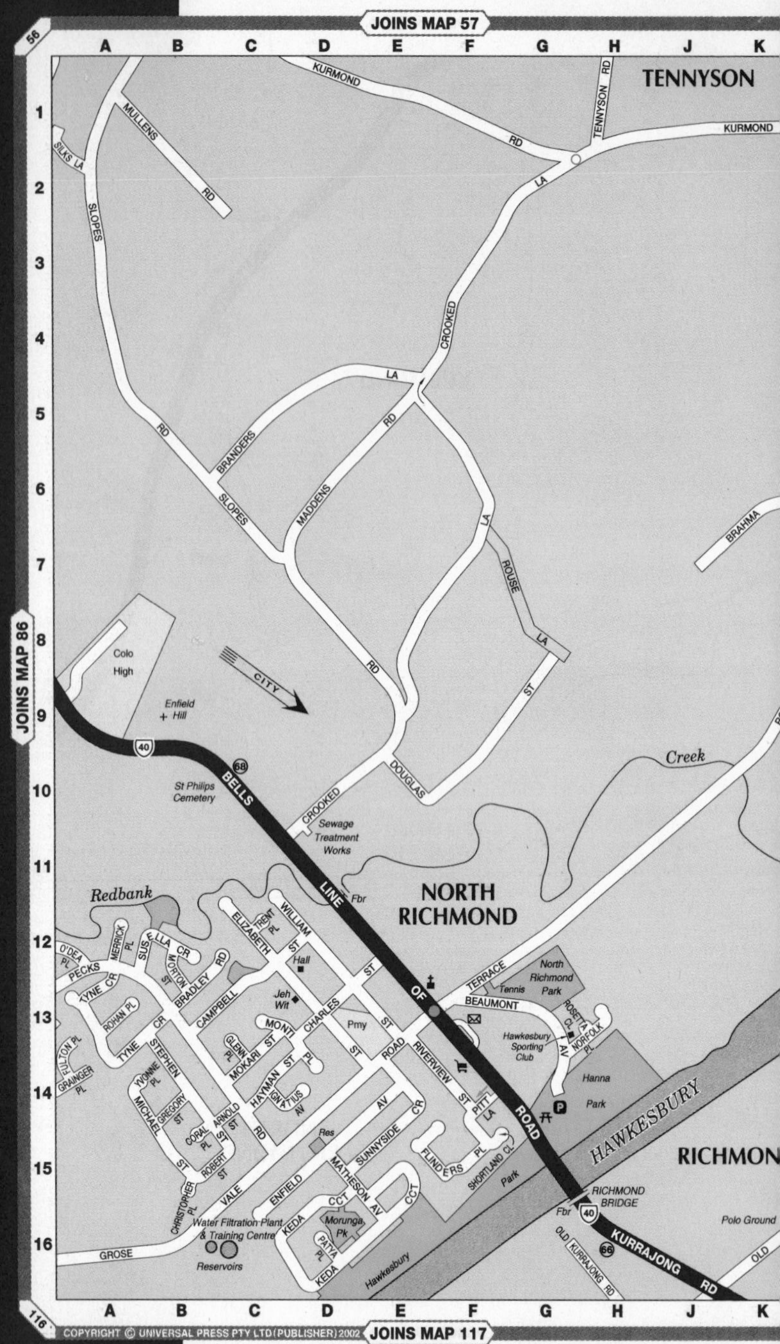

JOINS MAP 86

JOINS MAP 117

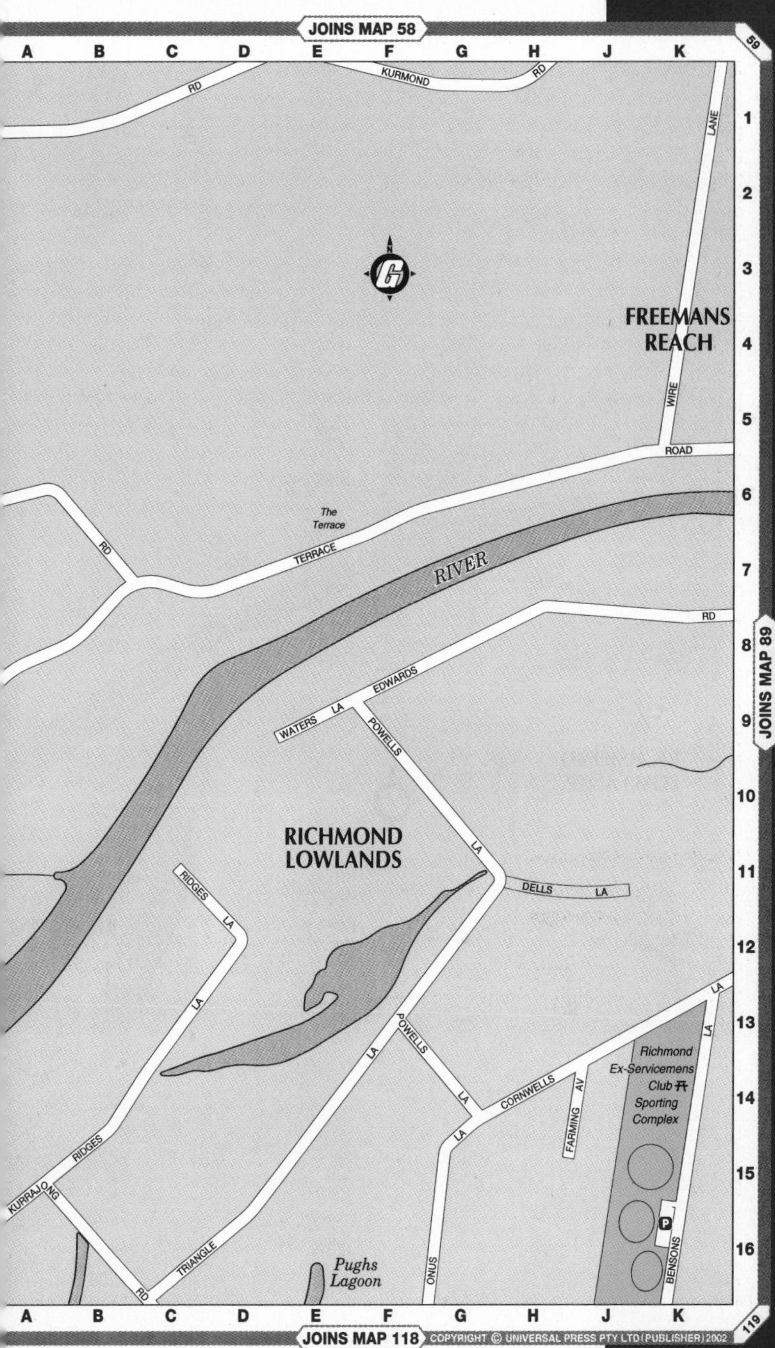
JOINS MAP 58
A B C D E F G H J K
59
1 2 3 4 5 6 7 8 9 10 11 12 13 14 15 16
RD
KURMOND
RD
LANE
FREEMANS
REACH
WIRE
ROAD
The
Terrace
RD
TERRACE
RIVER
RD
EDWARDS
WATERS
LA
POWELLS
JOINS MAP 89
RICHMOND
LOWLANDS
LA
DELLS
LA
RIDGES
LA
LA
LA
POWELLS
LA
LA
CORNWELLS
LA
LA
LA
Richmond
Ex-Servicemens
Club
Sporting
Complex
FARMING
AV
RIDGES
KURRAJONG
TRIANGLE
RD
Pughs
Lagoon
ONUS
BENSONS
P
A B C D E F G H J K
JOINS MAP 118
119

JOINS MAP 59

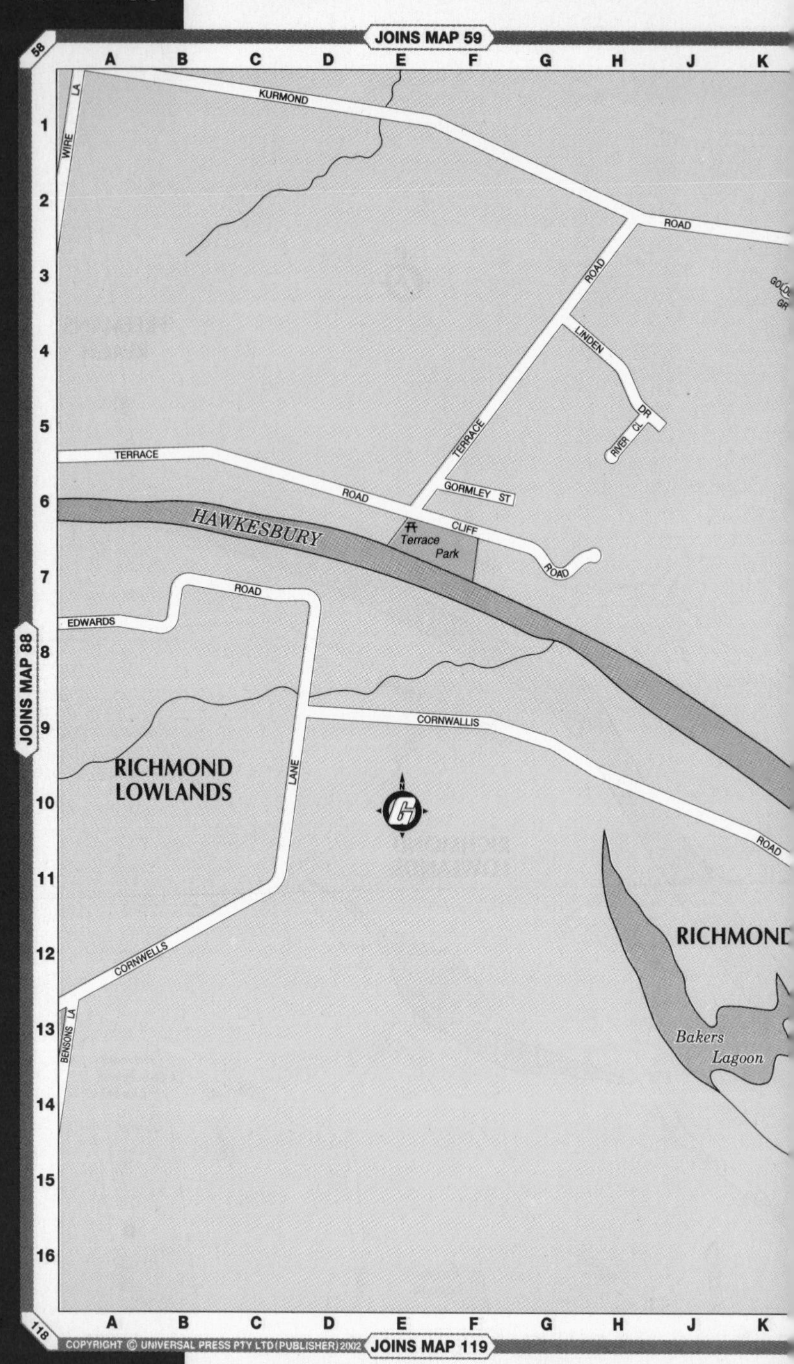

JOINS MAP 88

JOINS MAP 119

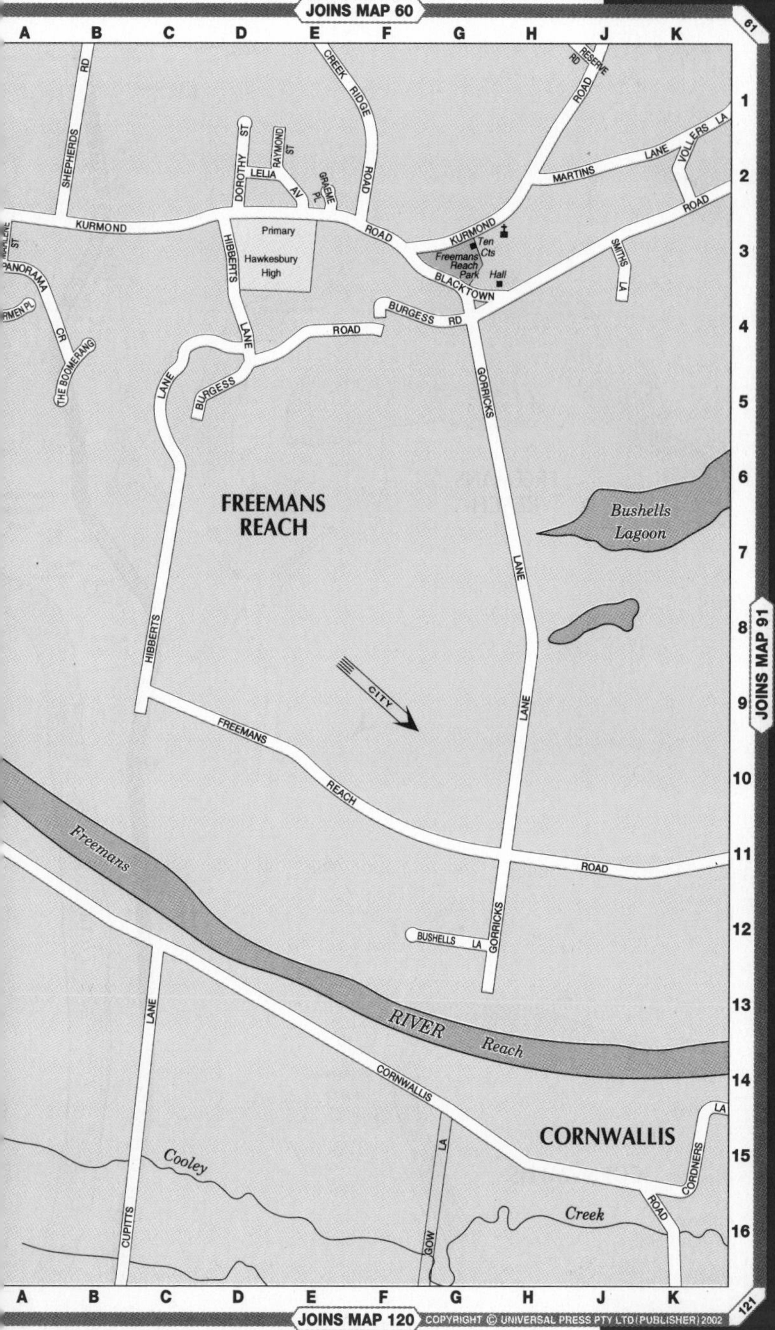
JOINS MAP 60
61
A B C D E F G H J K
1 2 3 4 5 6 7 8 9 10 11 12 13 14 15 16
SHEPHERDS RD
CREEK RIDGE ROAD
RESERVE RD
ROAD
DOROTHY ST
RAYMOND ST
LELIA AV
GRAEME PL
MARTINS LANE
VOLLERS LA
ROAD
KURMOND
KURMOND ROAD
KURMOND
Primary
Hawkesbury High
HIBBERTS
Ten Cts
Freemans Reach Park
Hall
BLACKTOWN
SMITHS LA
PANORAMA CR
CARMEN PL
THE BOOMERANG
BURGESS RD
ROAD
LANE
LANE
BURGESS
GORRICKS
FREEMANS REACH
Bushells Lagoon
LANE
HIBBERTS
CITY
LANE
JOINS MAP 91
FREEMANS
REACH
ROAD
Freemans
BUSHELLS LA
GORRICKS
RIVER
Reach
LANE
CORNWALLIS
LA
CORNWALLIS
CORDNERS
Cooley
ROAD
Creek
CUPITTS
GOW
JOINS MAP 120
121

JOINS MAP 61

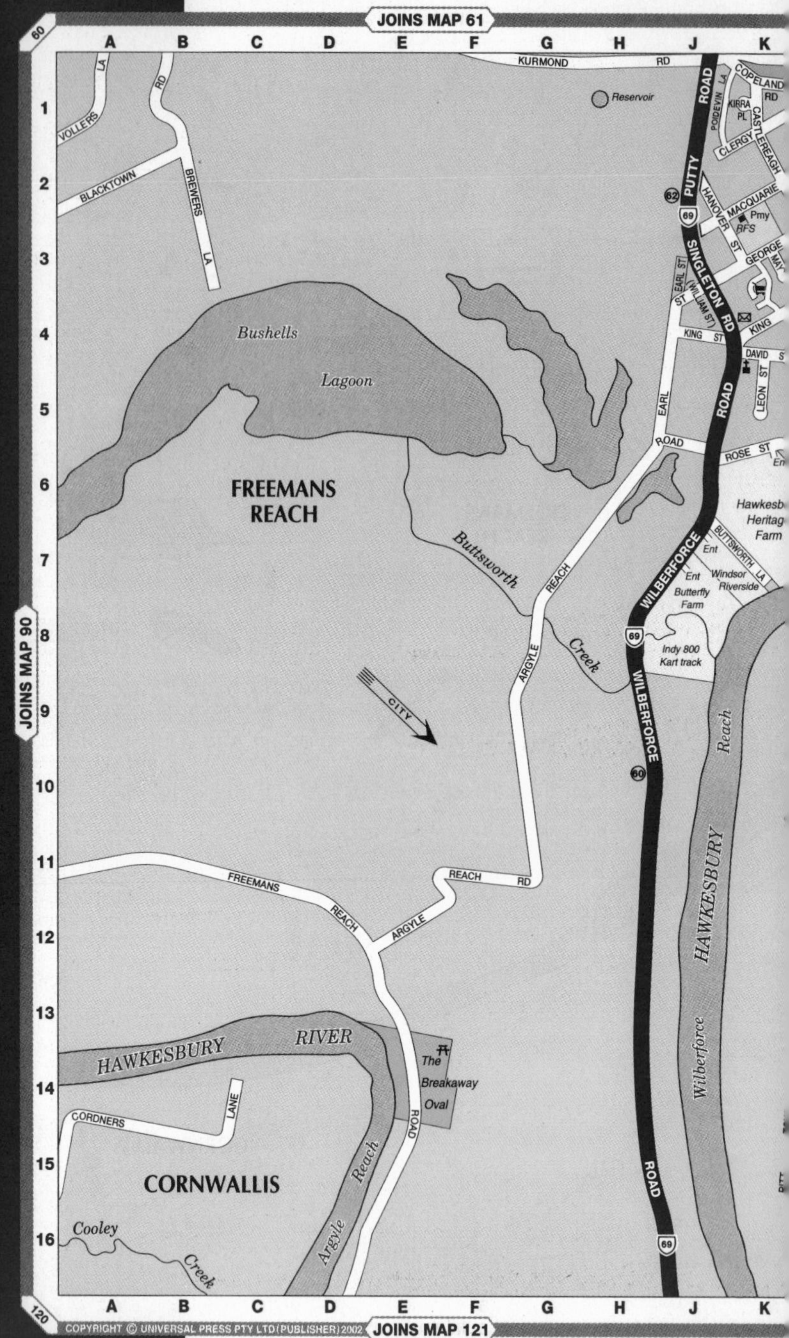

JOINS MAP 90

JOINS MAP 121

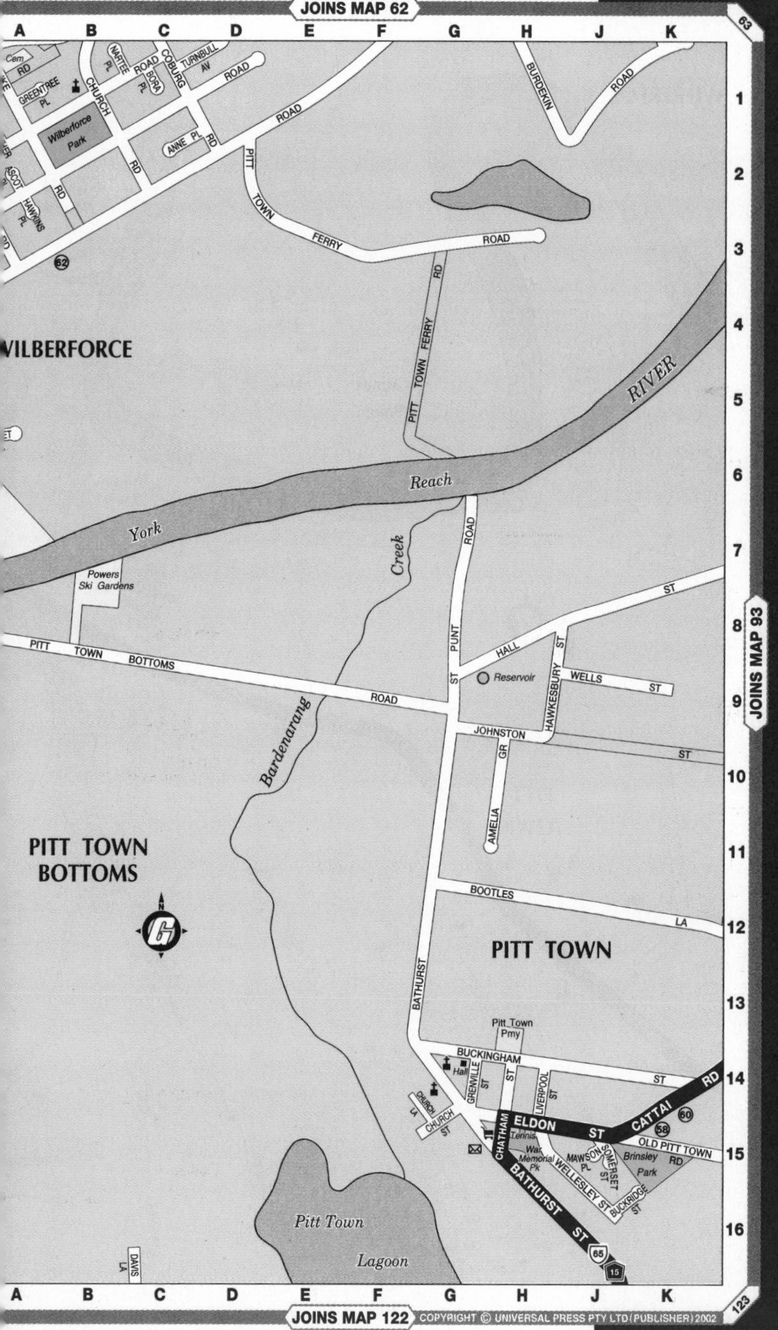
JOINS MAP 62
A
B
C
D
E
F
G
H
J
K
1
2
3
4
5
6
7
8
9
10
11
12
13
14
15
16
WILBERFORCE
PITT TOWN BOTTOMS
PITT TOWN
Wilberforce Park
CHURCH
GREENTREE PL
NARTEE PL
BORA PL
COBURG ROAD
TURNBULL AV
ROAD
ANNE PL
RD
ASCOT
HAWKINS PL
PITT TOWN FERRY ROAD
PITT TOWN FERRY RD
BURDEKIN
ROAD
RIVER
York
Reach
Creek
Powers Ski Gardens
PITT TOWN BOTTOMS ROAD
PUNT ROAD
PUNT ST
HALL ST
HAWKESBURY ST
WELLS ST
Reservoir
JOHNSTON ST
AMELIA GR
Bardenarang
BOOTLES LA
BATHURST
Pitt Town Pmy
BUCKINGHAM ST
Hall
GRENVILLE ST
LIVERPOOL ST
CHURCH LA
CHURCH ST
ELDON ST
CATTAI RD
CHATHAM
OLD PITT TOWN RD
Tennis
War Memorial Pk
MAWSON PL
SOMERSET ST
WELLESLEY ST
Brinsley Park
BUCKRIDGE ST
BATHURST ST
Pitt Town Lagoon
DAVIS LA
JOINS MAP 93
JOINS MAP 122
63
123
62
58
60
65
15

JOINS MAP 63

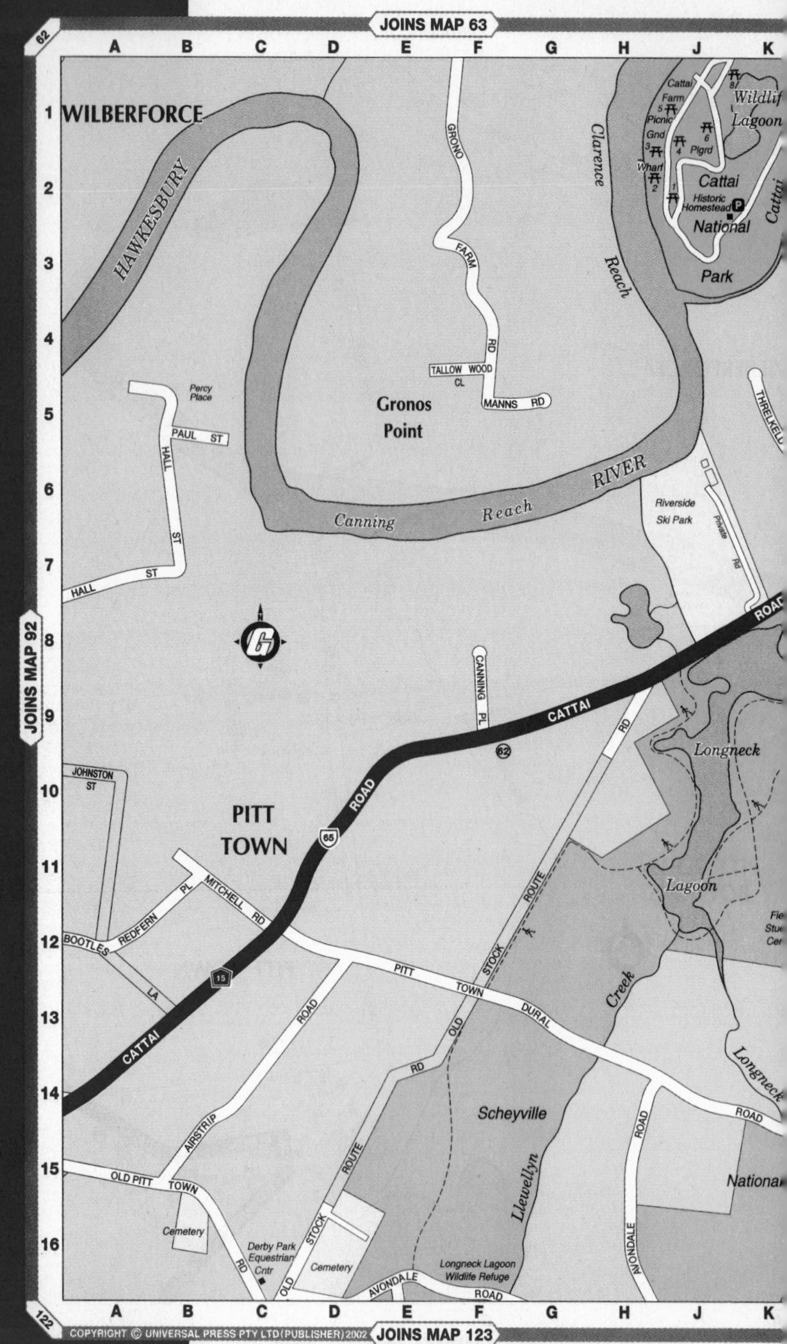

JOINS MAP 123

JOINS MAP 64

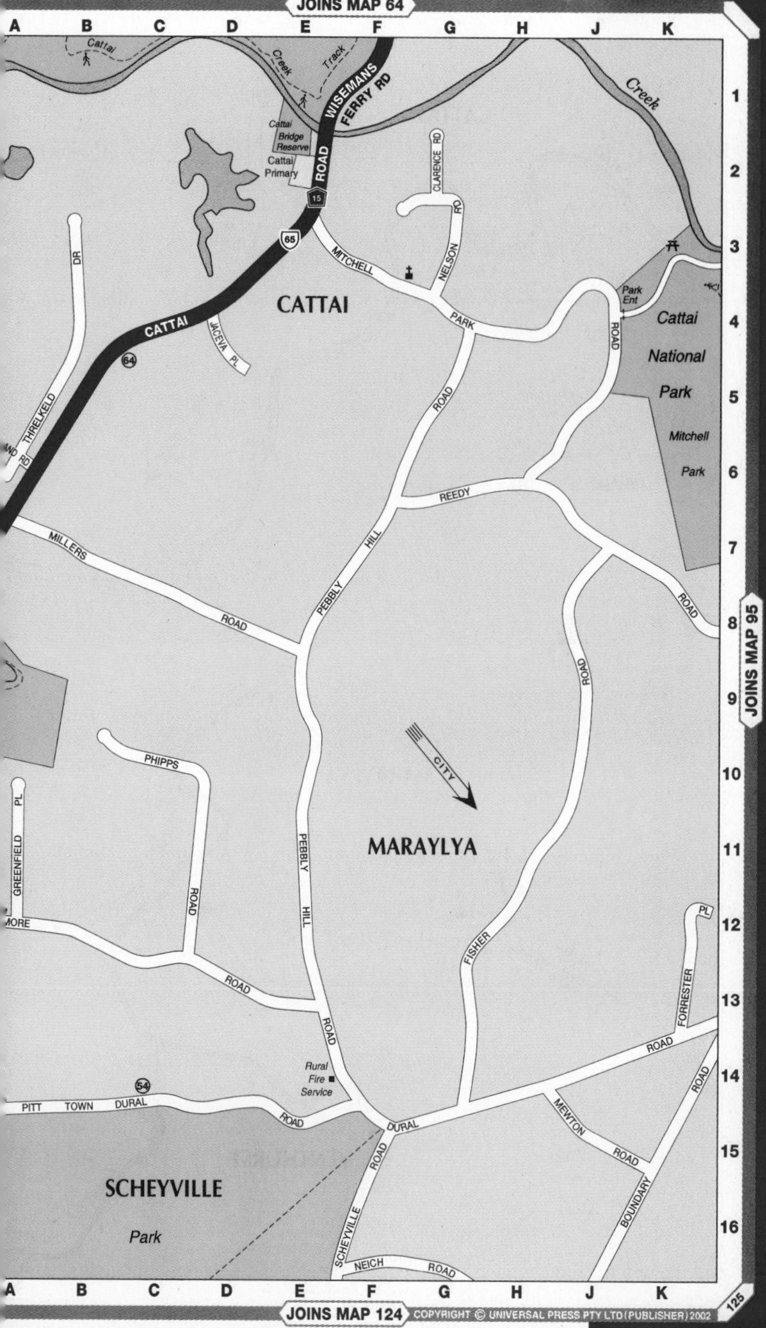

JOINS MAP 95

JOINS MAP 124

125

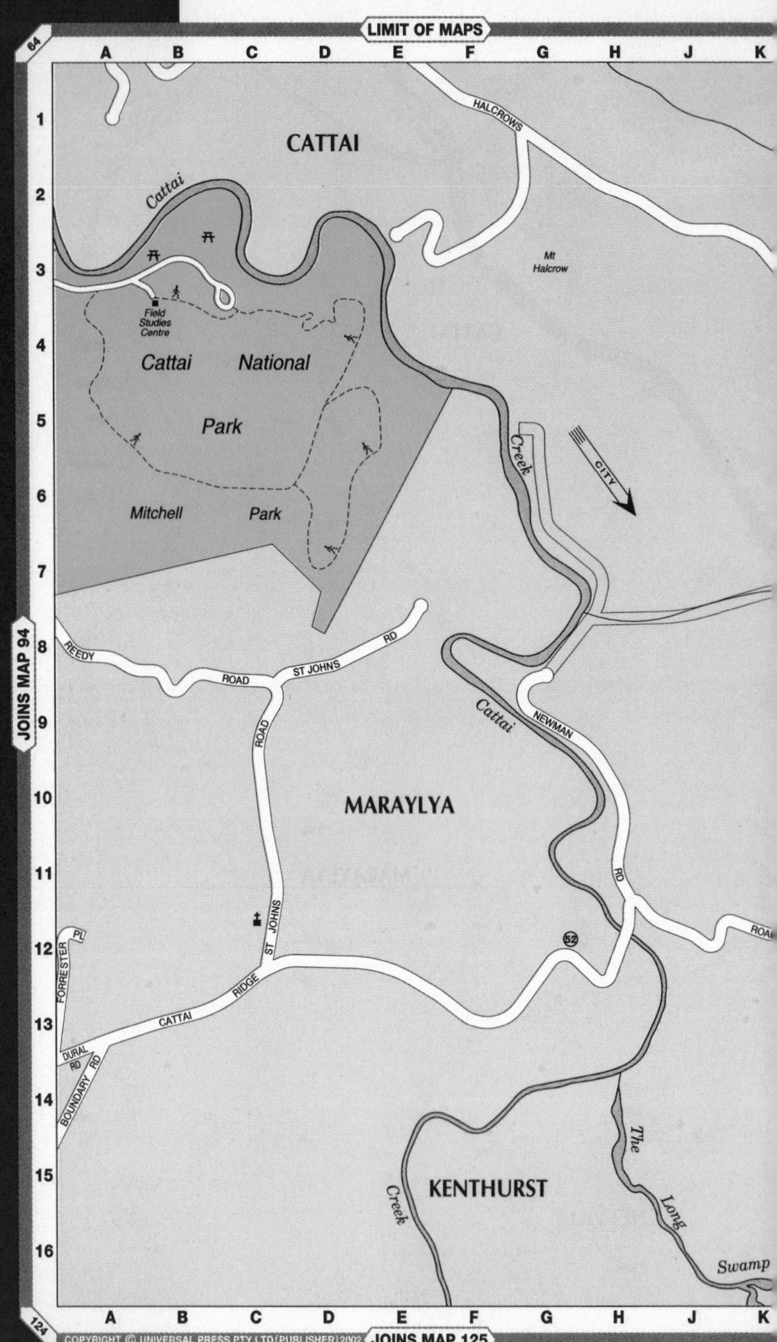
LIMIT OF MAPS
64
A B C D E F G H J K
1 2 3 4 5 6 7 8 9 10 11 12 13 14 15 16
CATTAI
HALCROWS
Cattai
Mt
Halcrow
Field
Studies
Centre
Cattai National
Park
Mitchell Park
Creek
CITY
REEDY
ROAD
ST JOHNS
RD
ROAD
Cattai
NEWMAN
RD
MARAYLYA
ST JOHNS
RD
ROA
52
FORRESTER
PL
CATTAI
RIDGE
DURAL
RD
BOUNDARY RD
The
Long
Swamp
Creek
KENTHURST
JOINS MAP 94
124
JOINS MAP 125

LIMIT OF MAPS

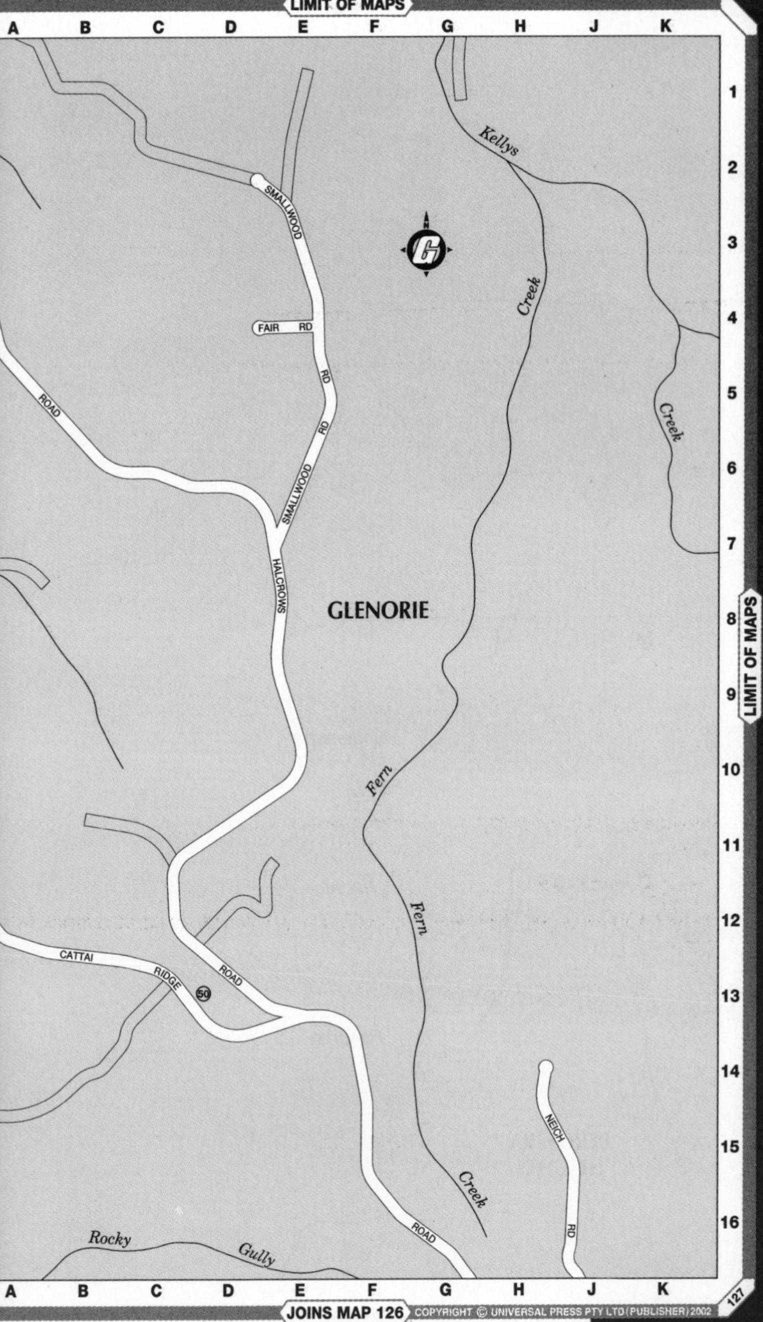

JOINS MAP 126

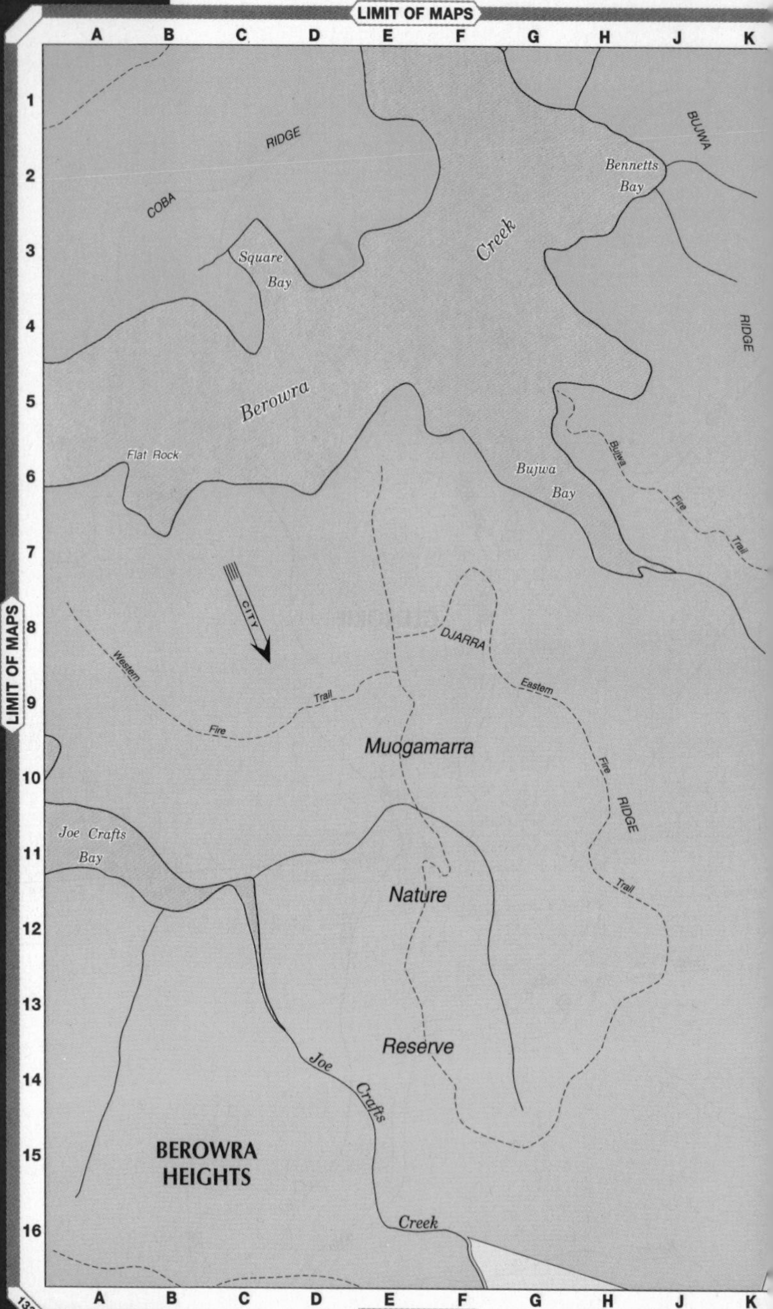

MAP 103
PREVIOUS MAP 96

JOINS MAP 133

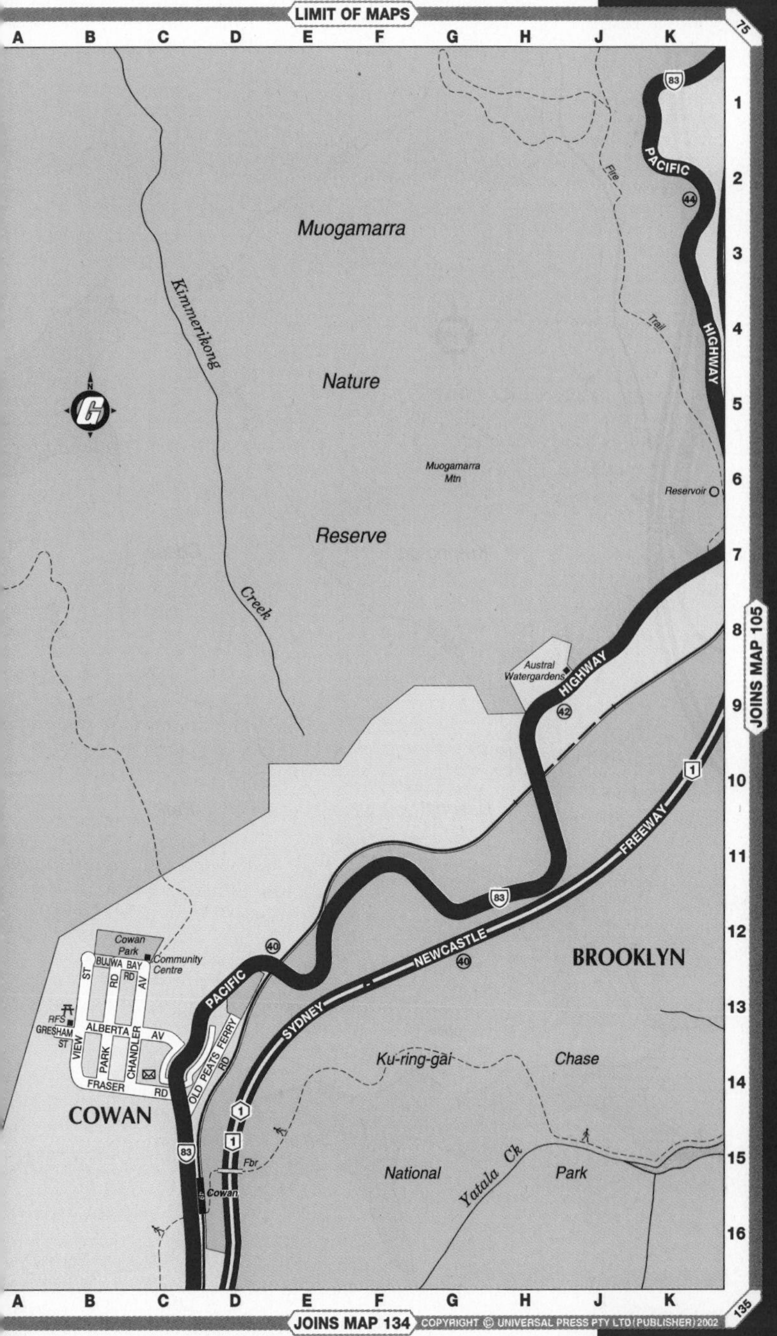

JOINS MAP 134

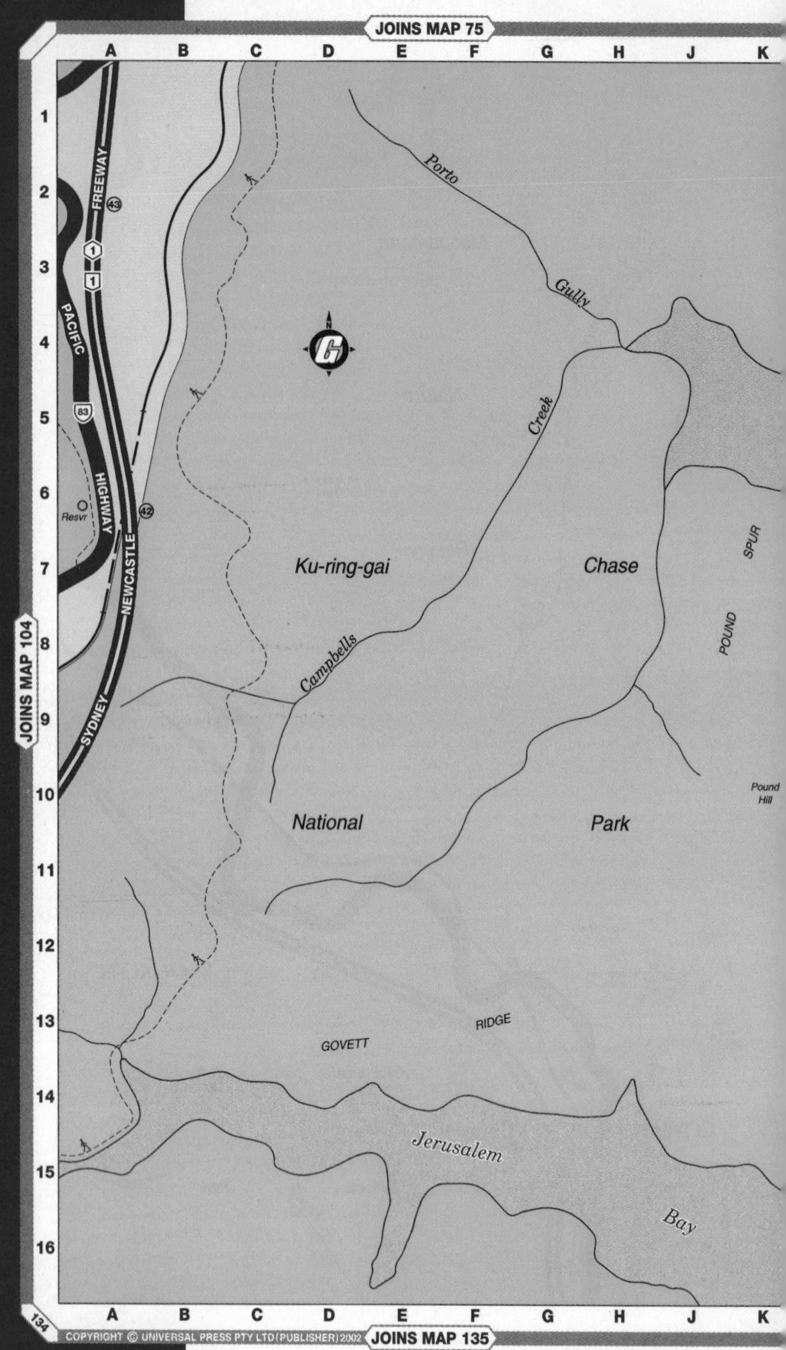
JOINS MAP 75
A B C D E F G H J K
1 2 3 4 5 6 7 8 9 10 11 12 13 14 15 16
JOINS MAP 104
FREEWAY
43
1
1
PACIFIC
83
HIGHWAY
Resvr
42
NEWCASTLE
SYDNEY
Porto
Gully
Creek
Ku-ring-gai
Chase
SPUR
POUND
Campbells
National
Park
Pound Hill
GOVETT
RIDGE
Jerusalem
Bay
JOINS MAP 135

JOINS MAP 76

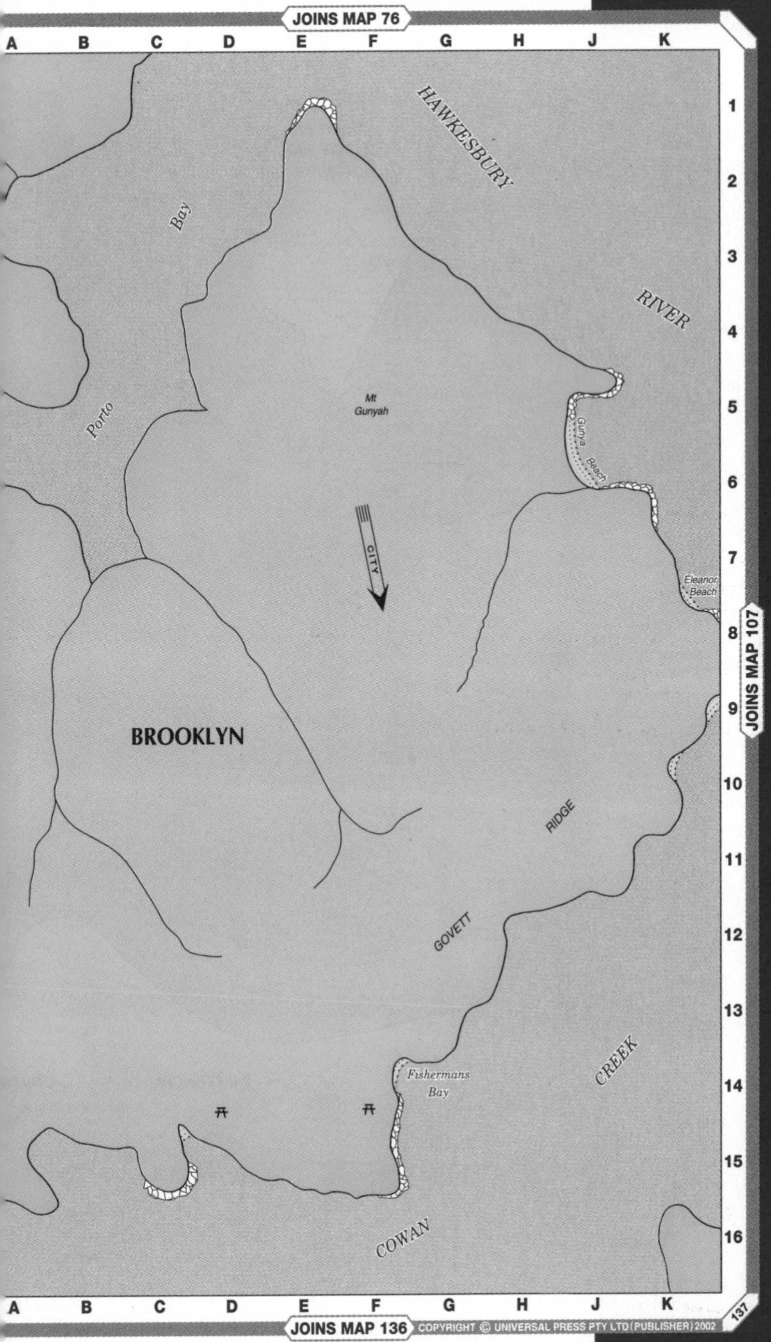

JOINS MAP 107

JOINS MAP 136

MAP 107

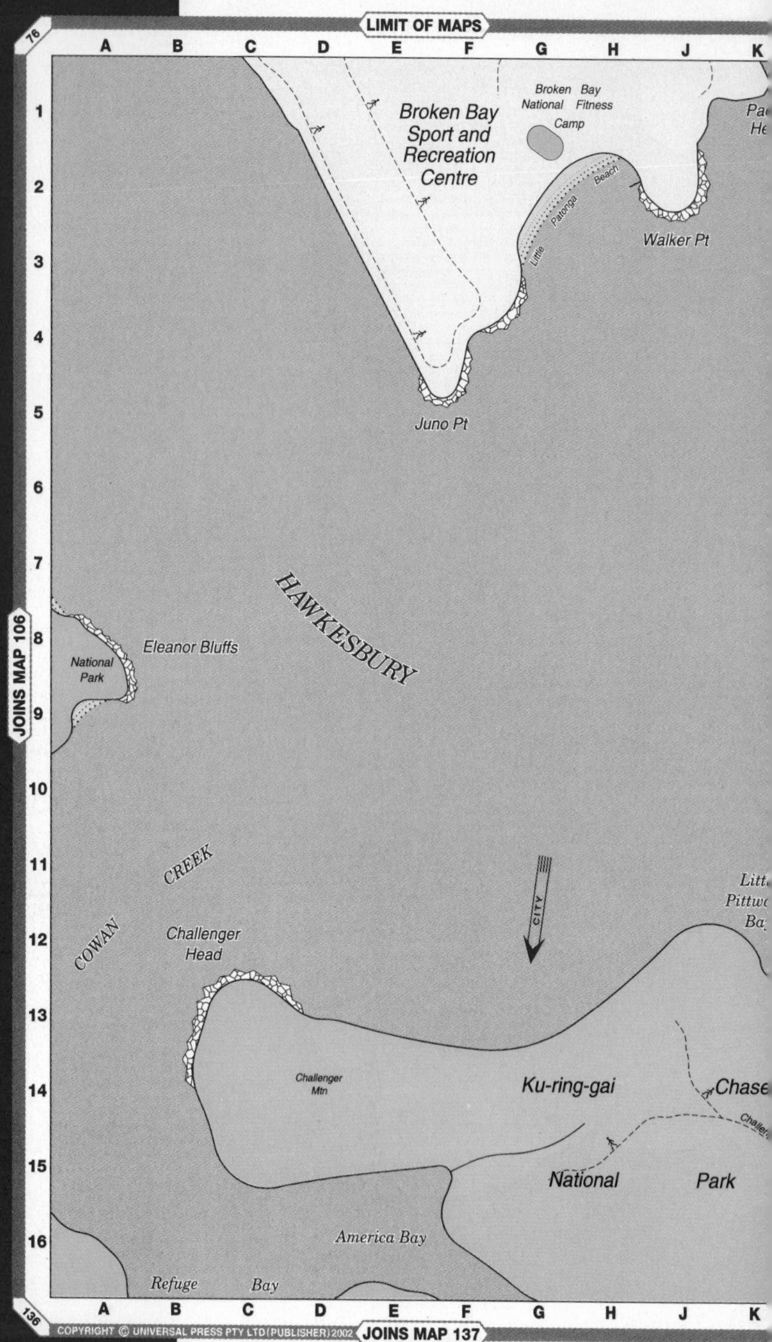

LIMIT OF MAPS
76
A B C D E F G H J K
1 2 3 4 5 6 7 8 9 10 11 12 13 14 15 16
Broken Bay Sport and Recreation Centre
Broken Bay National Fitness Camp
Little Patonga Beach
Walker Pt
Juno Pt
HAWKESBURY
Eleanor Bluffs
National Park
JOINS MAP 106
CREEK
COWAN
Challenger Head
CITY
Challenger Mtn
Ku-ring-gai
Chase
National
Park
America Bay
Refuge
Bay
136
JOINS MAP 137

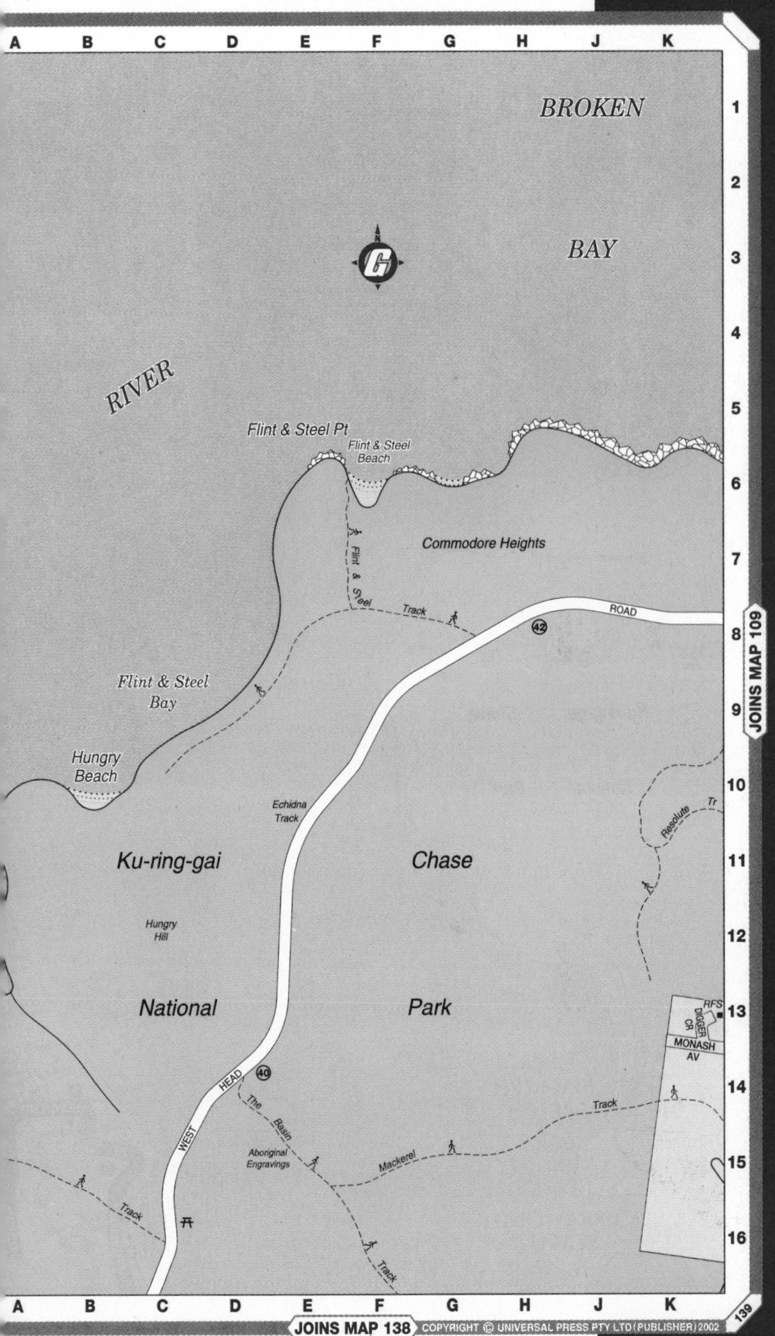
A
B
C
D
E
F
G
H
J
K
1
2
3
4
5
6
7
8
9
10
11
12
13
14
15
16
BROKEN
BAY
RIVER
Flint & Steel Pt
Flint & Steel
Beach
Commodore Heights
Flint & Steel Track
ROAD
42
Flint & Steel
Bay
Hungry
Beach
Echidna
Track
Resolute Tr
Ku-ring-gai
Chase
Hungry
Hill
National
Park
RFS
DIGGER
CR
MONASH
AV
WEST HEAD
40
The Basin
Track
Aboriginal
Engravings
Mackerel
Track
Track
JOINS MAP 109

JOINS MAP 138

139

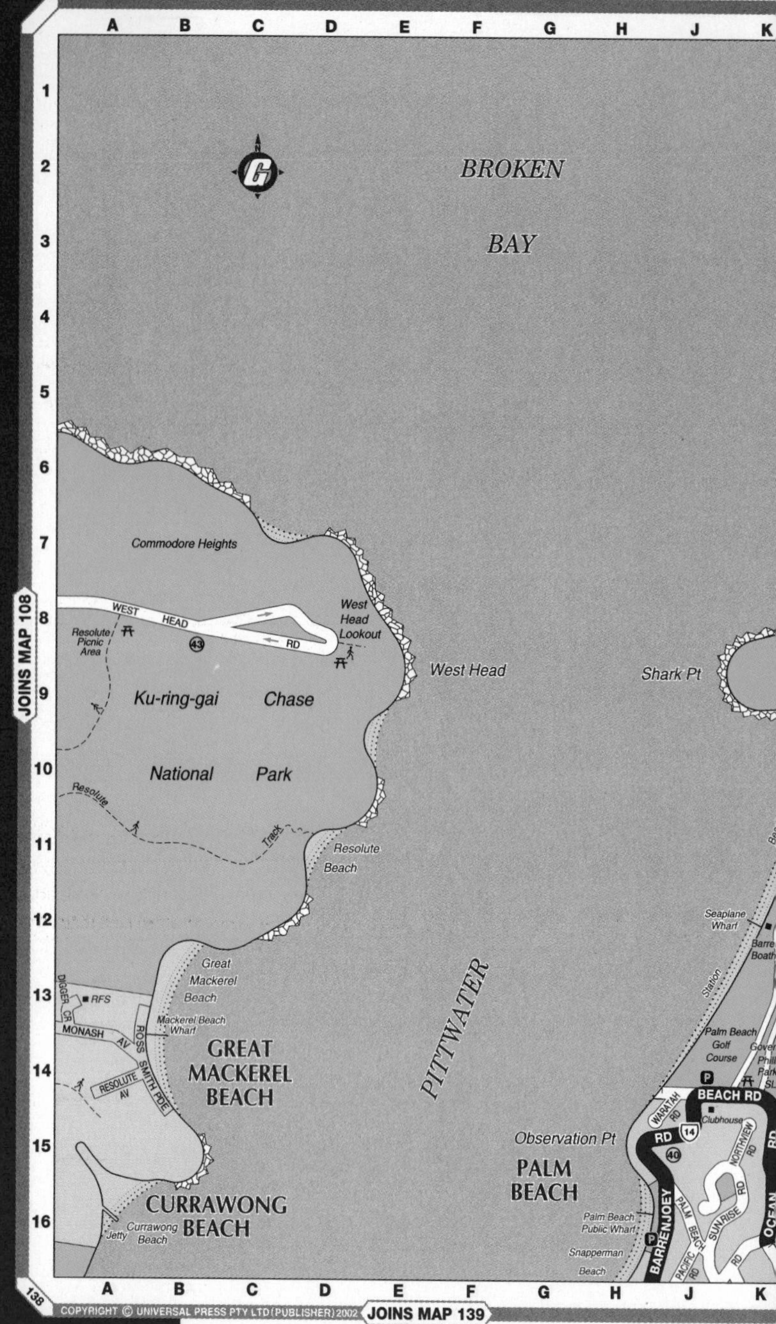
A B C D E F G H J K
1 2 3 4 5 6 7 8 9 10 11 12 13 14 15 16
BROKEN
BAY
Commodore Heights
WEST
HEAD
RD
43
West
Head
Lookout
Resolute
Picnic
Area
West Head
Shark Pt
Ku-ring-gai
Chase
National
Park
Resolute
Track
Resolute
Beach
Seaplane
Wharf
Station
Great
Mackerel
Beach
DIGGER CR
RFS
MONASH
AV
ROSS
SMITH PDE
Mackerel Beach
Wharf
RESOLUTE
AV
GREAT
MACKEREL
BEACH
PITTWATER
Palm Beach
Golf
Course
BEACH RD
WARATAH
RD
Clubhouse
14
RD
40
NORTHVIEW
RD
Observation Pt
PALM
BEACH
CURRAWONG
BEACH
Currawong
Beach
Jetty
Palm Beach
Public Wharf
Snapperman
Beach
BARRENJOEY
PALM
BEACH
PACIFIC
RD
SUNRISE
RD
OCEAN
JOINS MAP 108

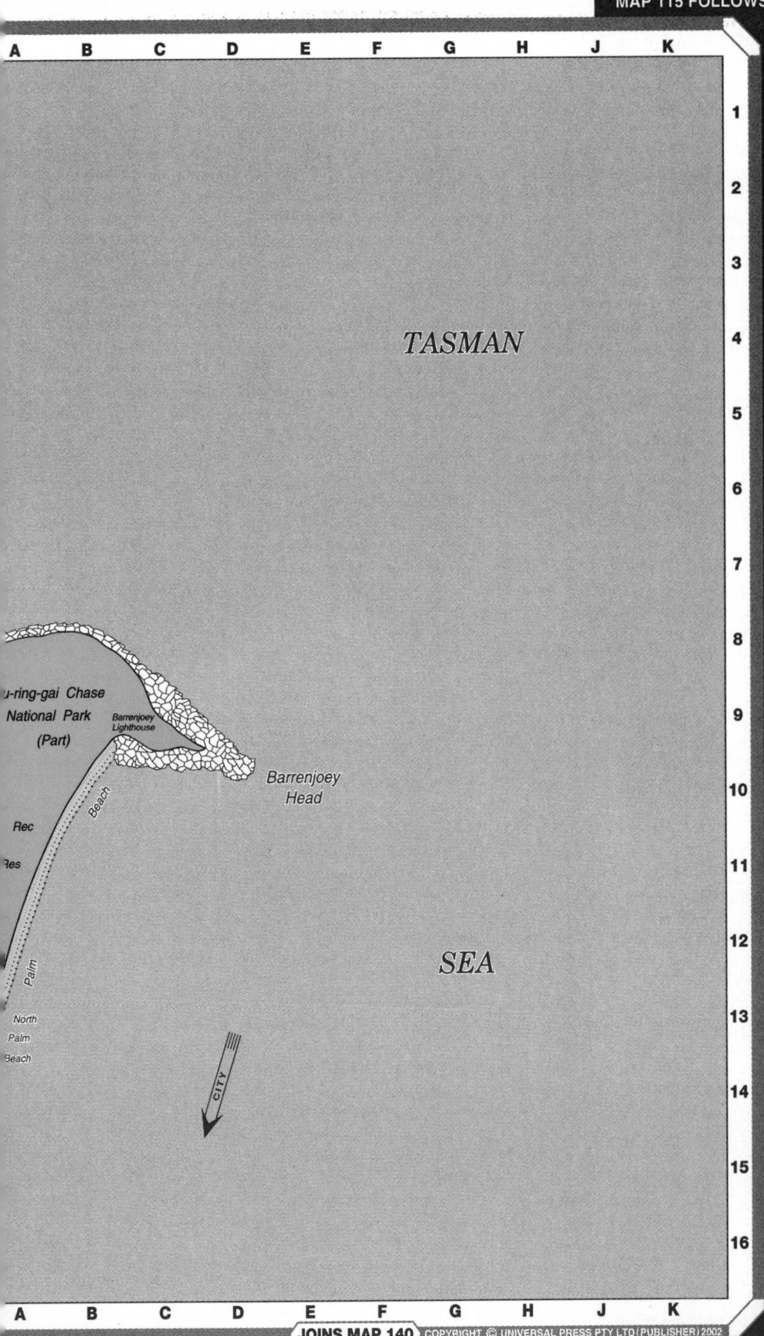

JOINS MAP 140

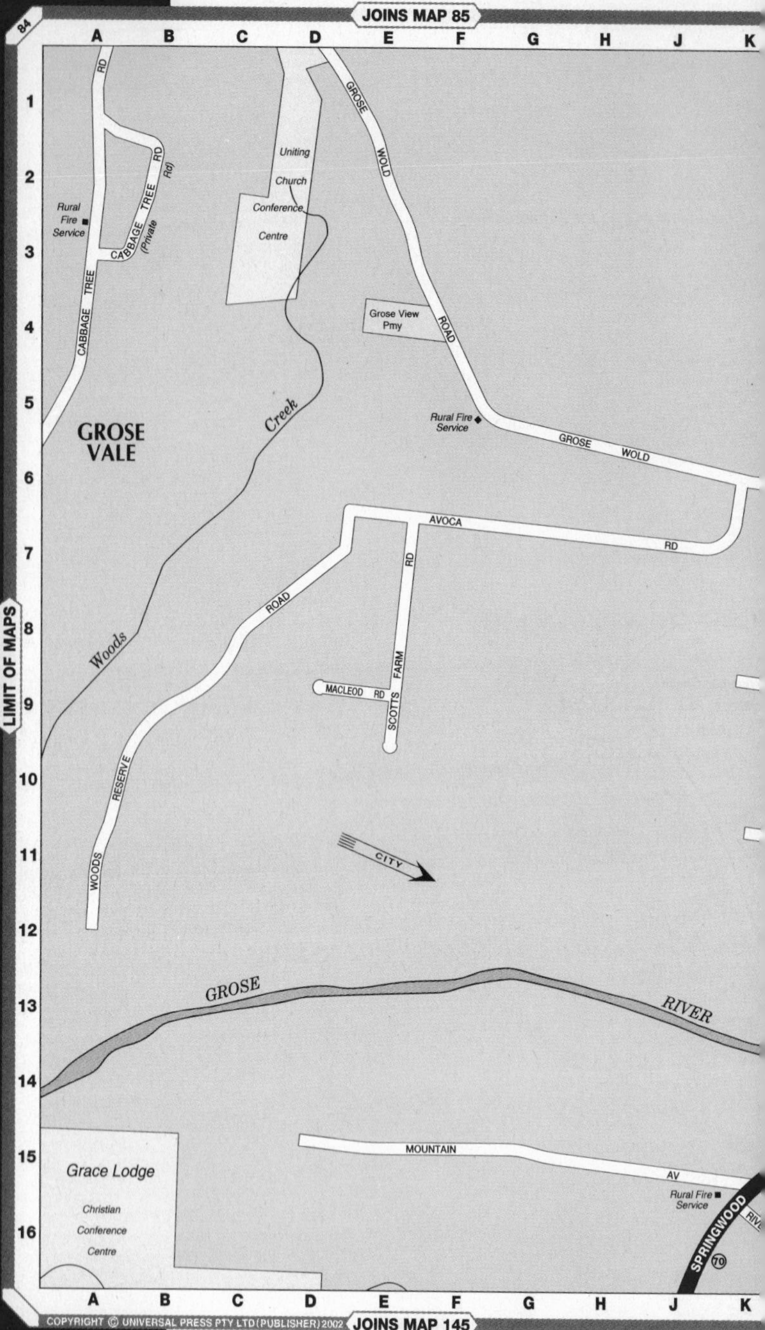

JOINS MAP 85

JOINS MAP 145

JOINS MAP 86
87
A B C D E F G H J K
1 2 3 4 5 6 7 8 9 10 11 12 13 14 15 16
GROSE VALE
GROSE VALE ROAD
RD
Nepean Stud Farm
NORTH RICHMOND
Private Rd
Belmont Park
"Belmont Park" St John of God Hospital
Clarks Island
PL
LONDON
ROAD
GROSE WOLD
GROSE RIVER
YARRAMAN RD
Macquarie Vale Pre School
ASHTONS RD
GROSE RIVER RD
Gate Close at 8pm
Navua Reserve
HAWKESBURY RIVER
JOINS MAP 117
MANS LA
NUTMANS RD
Grose River Course Course
RIVER
ROAD
68
YARRAMUNDI BRIDGE
RIVER
SPRINGWOOD ROAD
GROSE
Yarramundi YMCA Youth Camp
Ent
AGNES BANKS
Yarramundi Lagoon
YARRAMUNDI
73
CASTLEREAGH RD
NEPEAN
RD
147
JOINS MAP 146

JOINS MAP 87

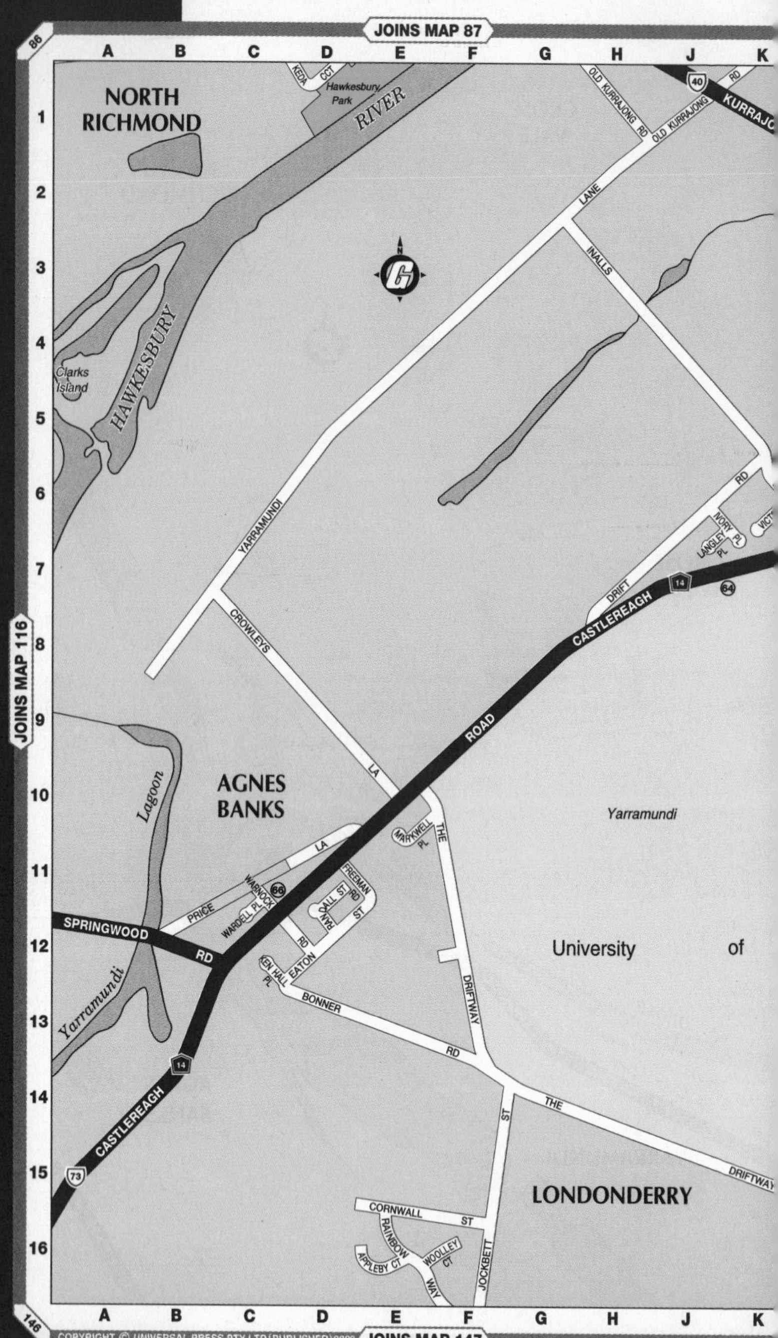

JOINS MAP 116

JOINS MAP 147

JOINS MAP 88

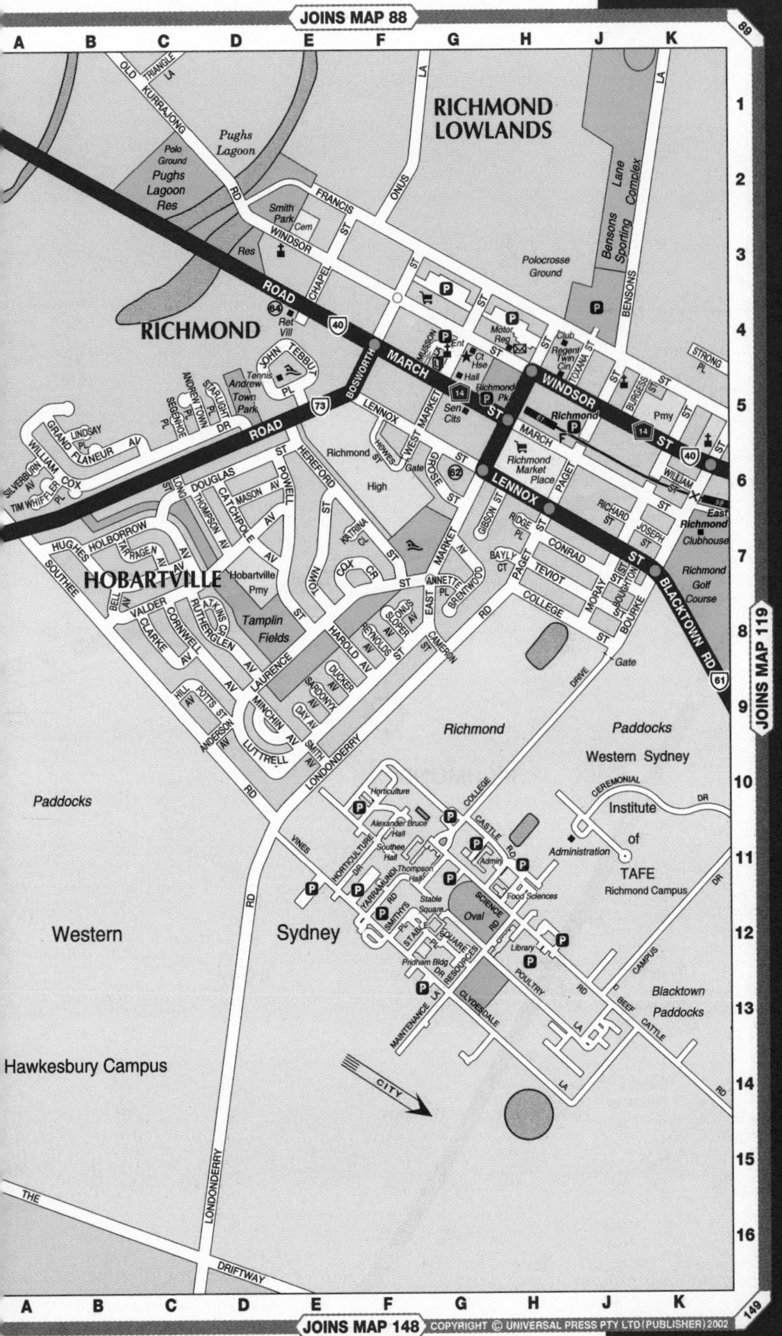

JOINS MAP 119

JOINS MAP 148

JOINS MAP 89

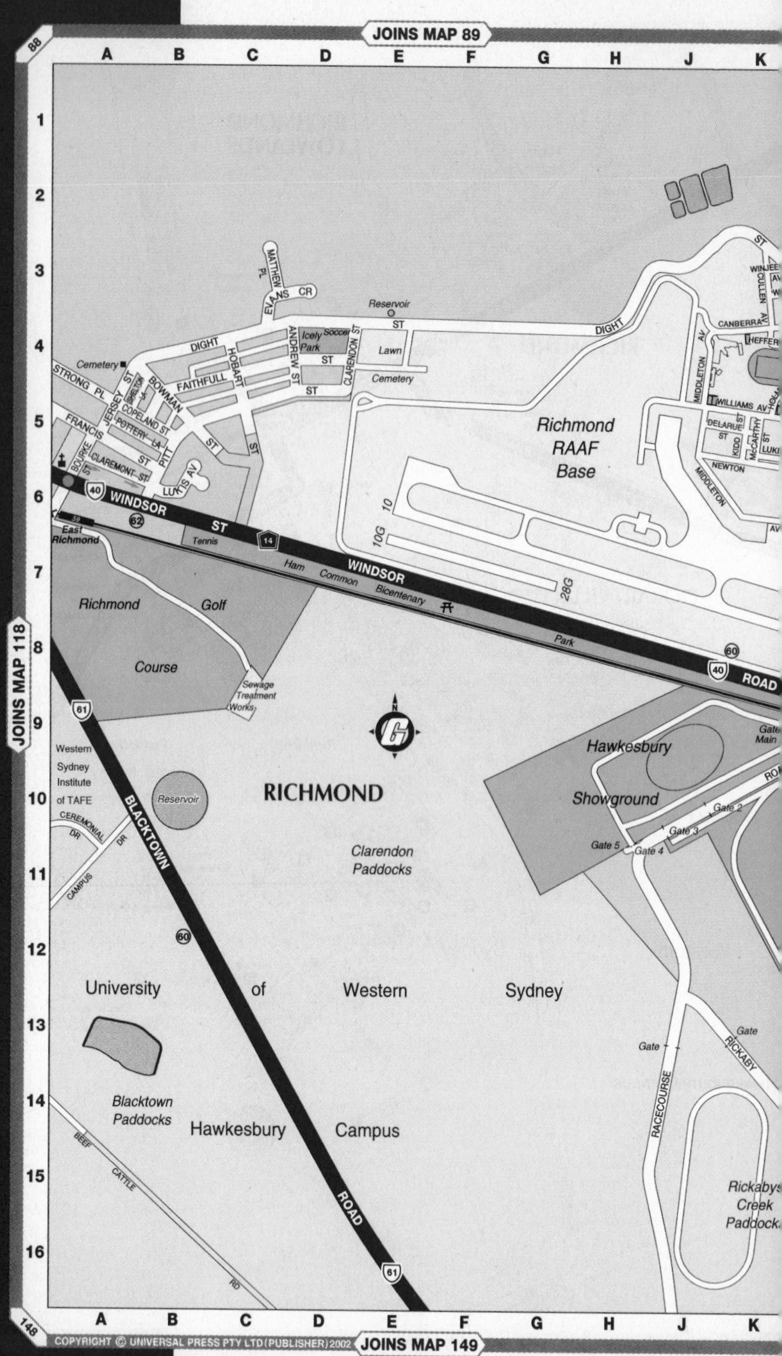

JOINS MAP 149

JOINS MAP 90

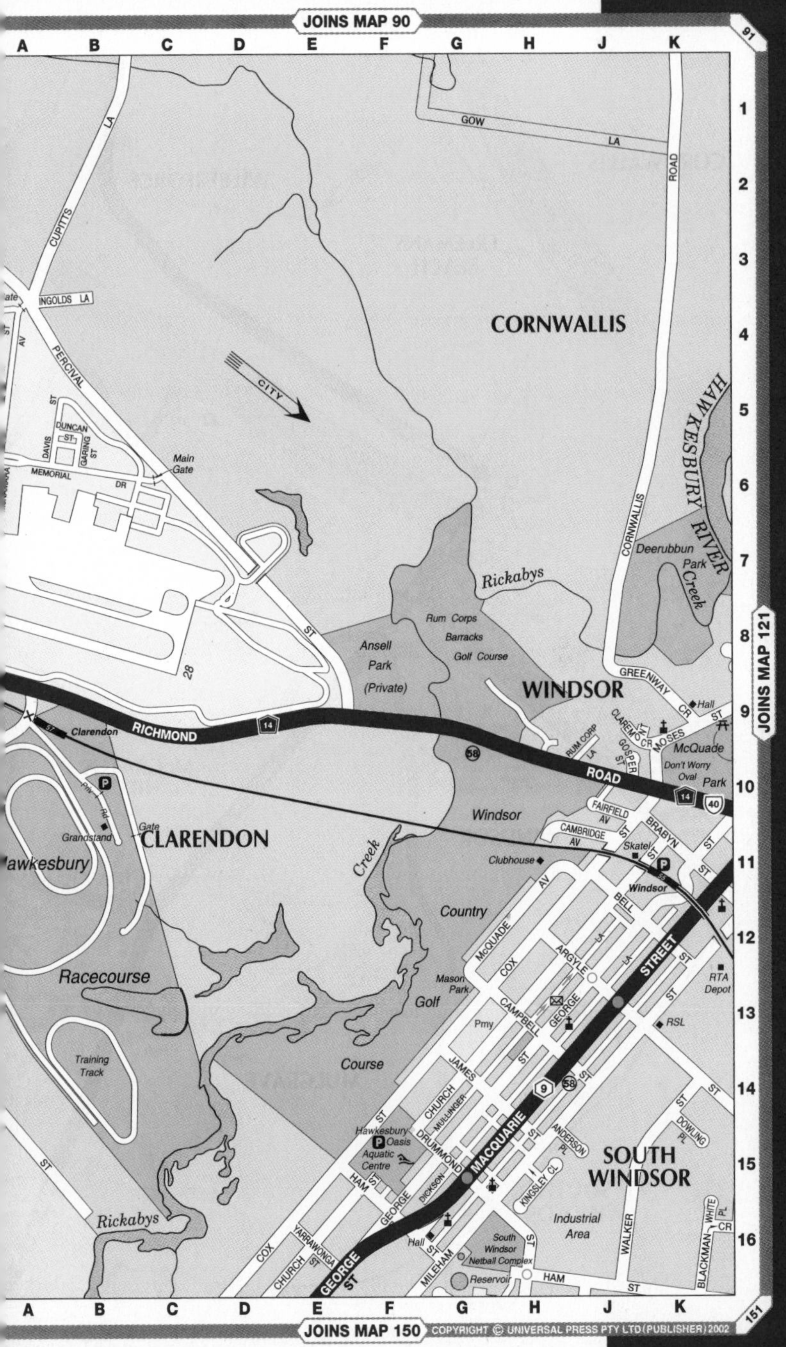

JOINS MAP 121

JOINS MAP 150

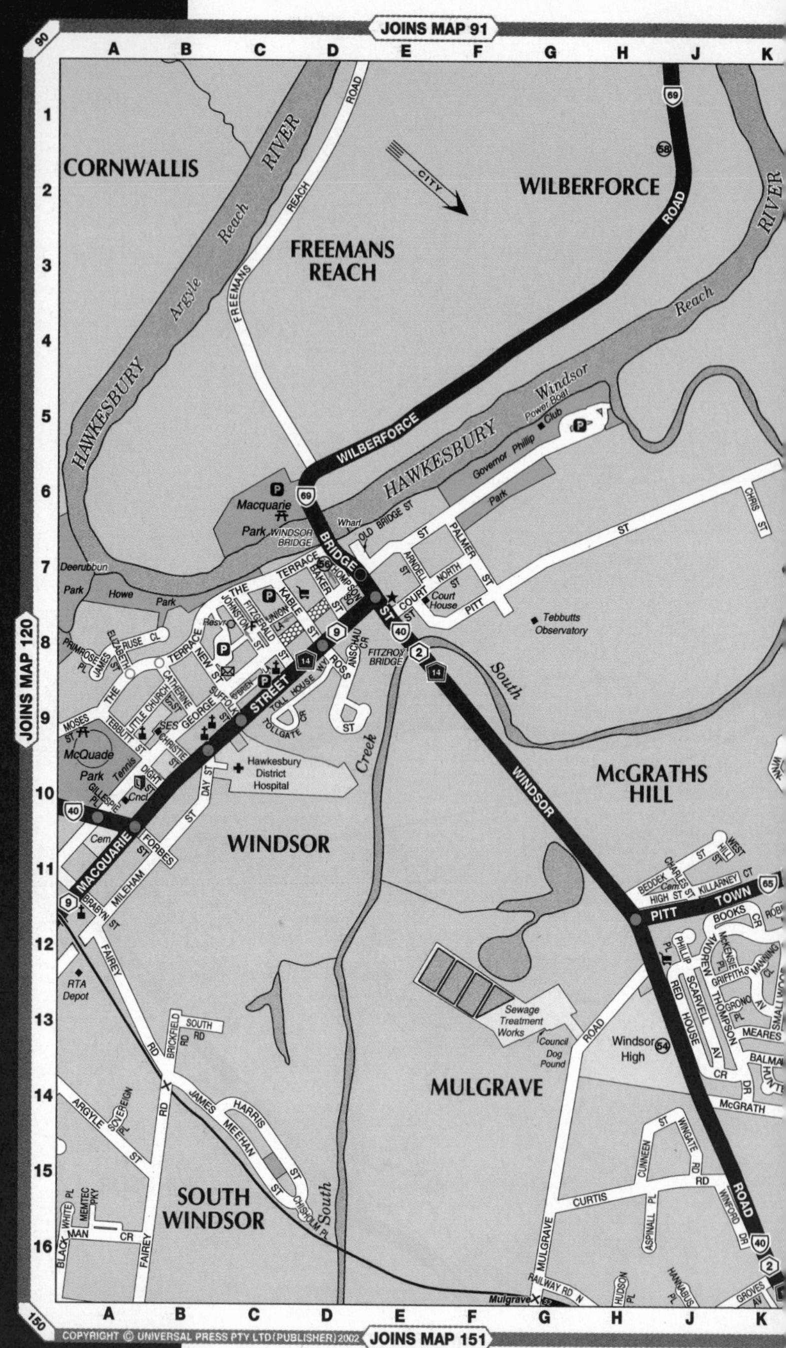
JOINS MAP 91
JOINS MAP 120
JOINS MAP 151
90
150
CORNWALLIS
WILBERFORCE
FREEMANS REACH
McGRATHS HILL
WINDSOR
MULGRAVE
SOUTH WINDSOR
HAWKESBURY
RIVER
Argyle Reach
Windsor Reach
CITY
Macquarie Park
WINDSOR BRIDGE
Deerubbun Park
Howe Park
McQuade Park
Governor Phillip Park
Windsor Power Boat Club
Tebbutts Observatory
Court House
Hawkesbury District Hospital
Sewage Treatment Works
Council Dog Pound
Windsor High
RTA Depot
South Creek
FITZROY BRIDGE
Mulgrave

JOINS MAP 92

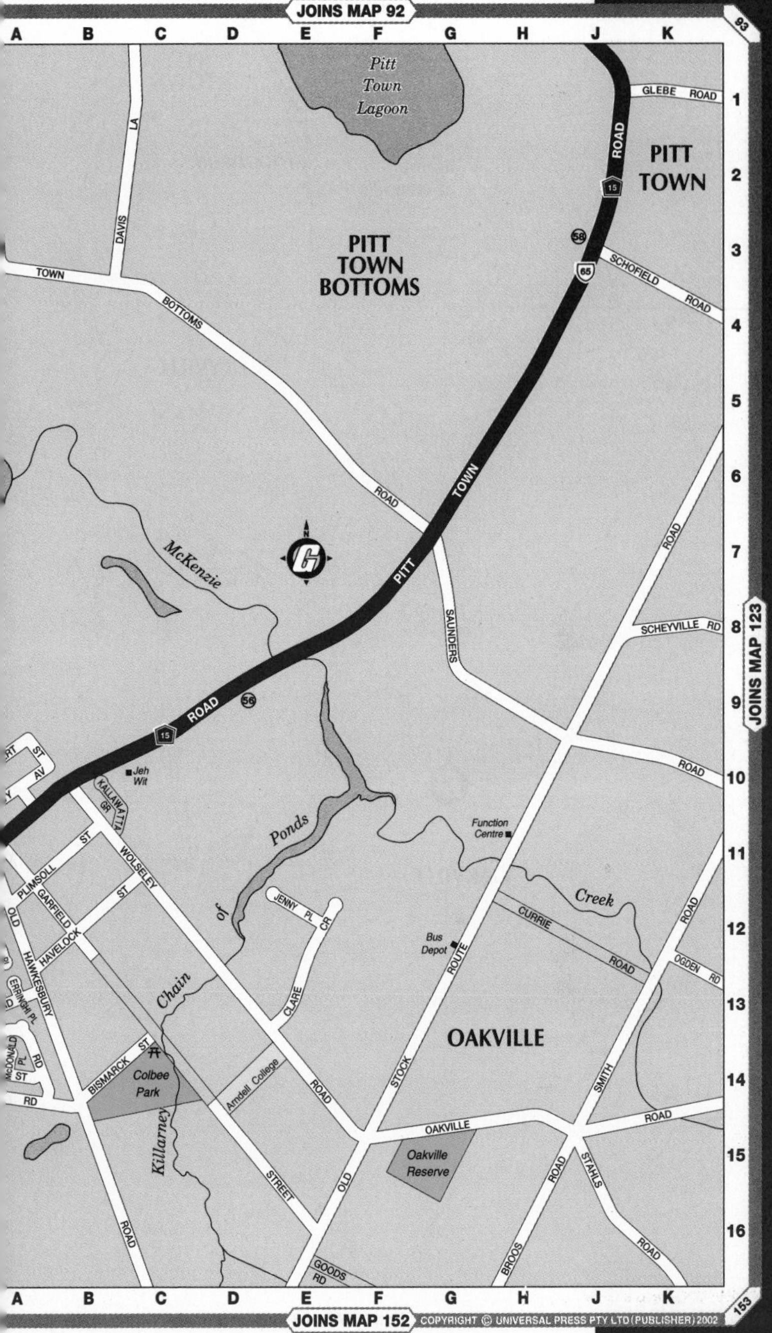

JOINS MAP 123

JOINS MAP 152

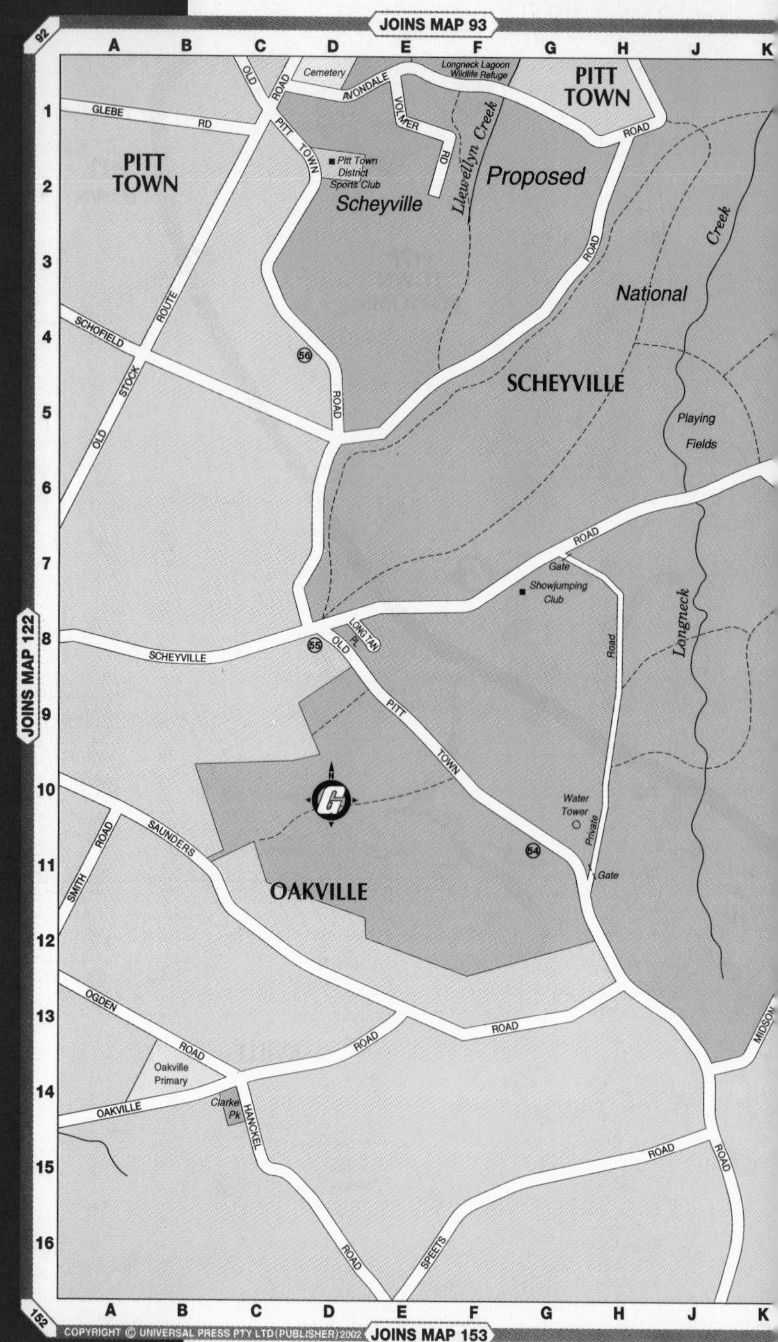
JOINS MAP 93
92
A B C D E F G H J K
1 2 3 4 5 6 7 8 9 10 11 12 13 14 15 16
Cemetery
Longneck Lagoon Wildlife Refuge
PITT TOWN
GLEBE RD
OLD ROAD
AVONDALE
VOLMER RD
ROAD
PITT TOWN
Pitt Town District Sports Club
Proposed
Llewellyn Creek
Scheyville
ROAD
Creek
National
SCHOFIELD
ROUTE
STOCK
OLD
56
ROAD
SCHEYVILLE
Playing Fields
ROAD
Gate
Showjumping Club
Road
Longneck
SCHEYVILLE
55
OLD
LONG TAN PL
PITT
TOWN
Water Tower
Private
54
Gate
ROAD
SAUNDERS
SMITH
OAKVILLE
OGDEN
ROAD
ROAD
ROAD
Oakville Primary
OAKVILLE
Clarke Pk
HANCKEL
ROAD
ROAD
MIDSON
ROAD
SPEETS
152
JOINS MAP 122
JOINS MAP 153

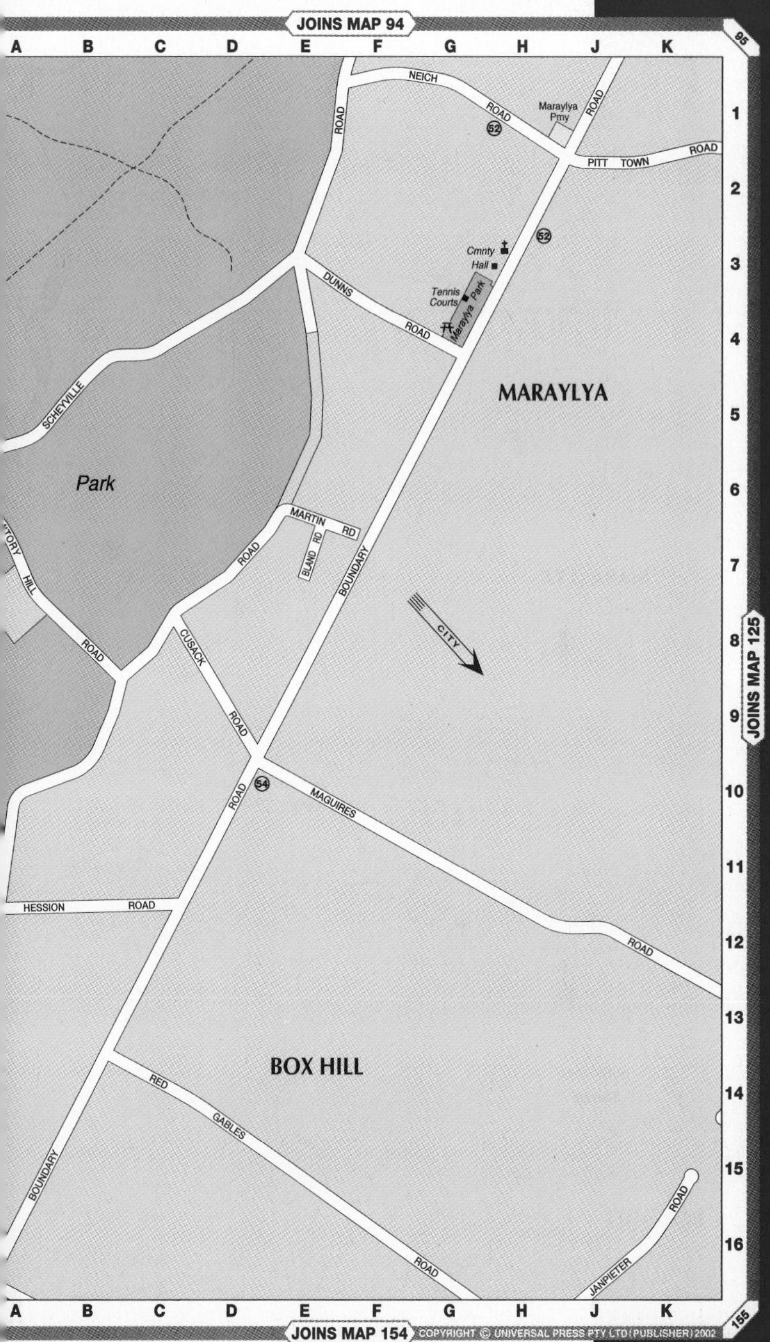
JOINS MAP 94
95
A B C D E F G H J K
1 2 3 4 5 6 7 8 9 10 11 12 13 14 15 16
NEICH ROAD
ROAD
52
Maraylya Pmy
ROAD
PITT TOWN ROAD
52
Cmnty
Hall
Tennis Courts
Maraylya Park
DUNNS ROAD
MARAYLYA
SCHEYVILLE
Park
MARTIN RD
BLAND RD
ROAD
BOUNDARY
TORY HILL ROAD
CITY
CUSACK ROAD
JOINS MAP 125
54
ROAD
MAGUIRES ROAD
HESSION ROAD
BOX HILL
RED GABLES ROAD
BOUNDARY
ROAD
JANPIETER
155
JOINS MAP 154

JOINS MAP 95

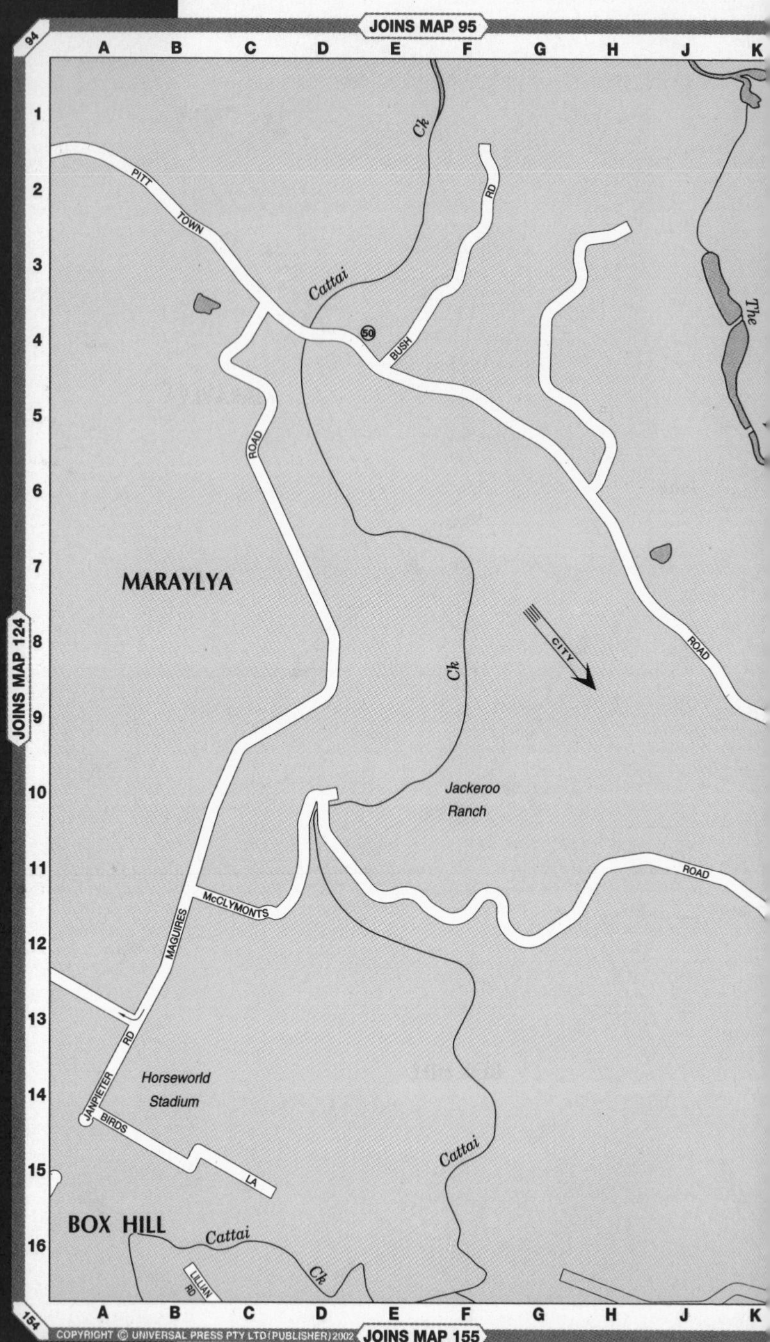

JOINS MAP 124

JOINS MAP 155

JOINS MAP 96

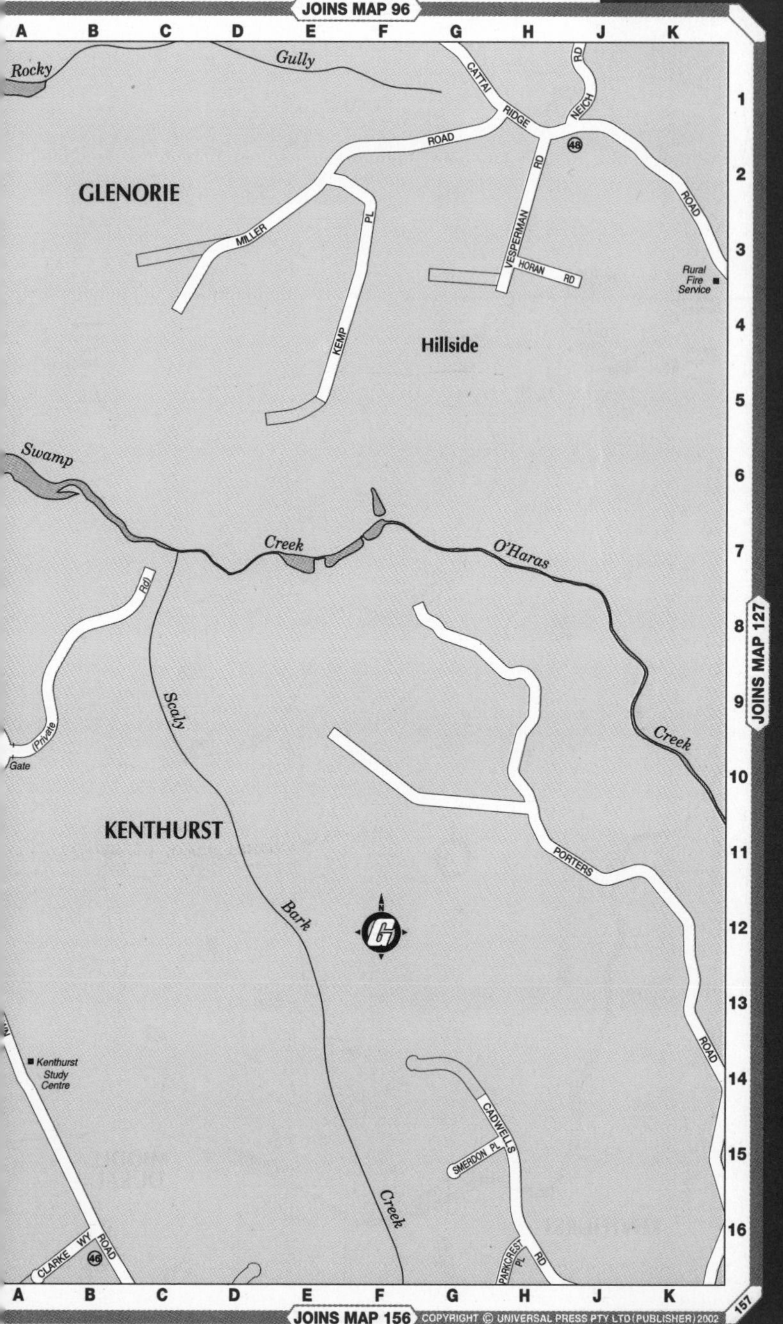

JOINS MAP 127

JOINS MAP 156

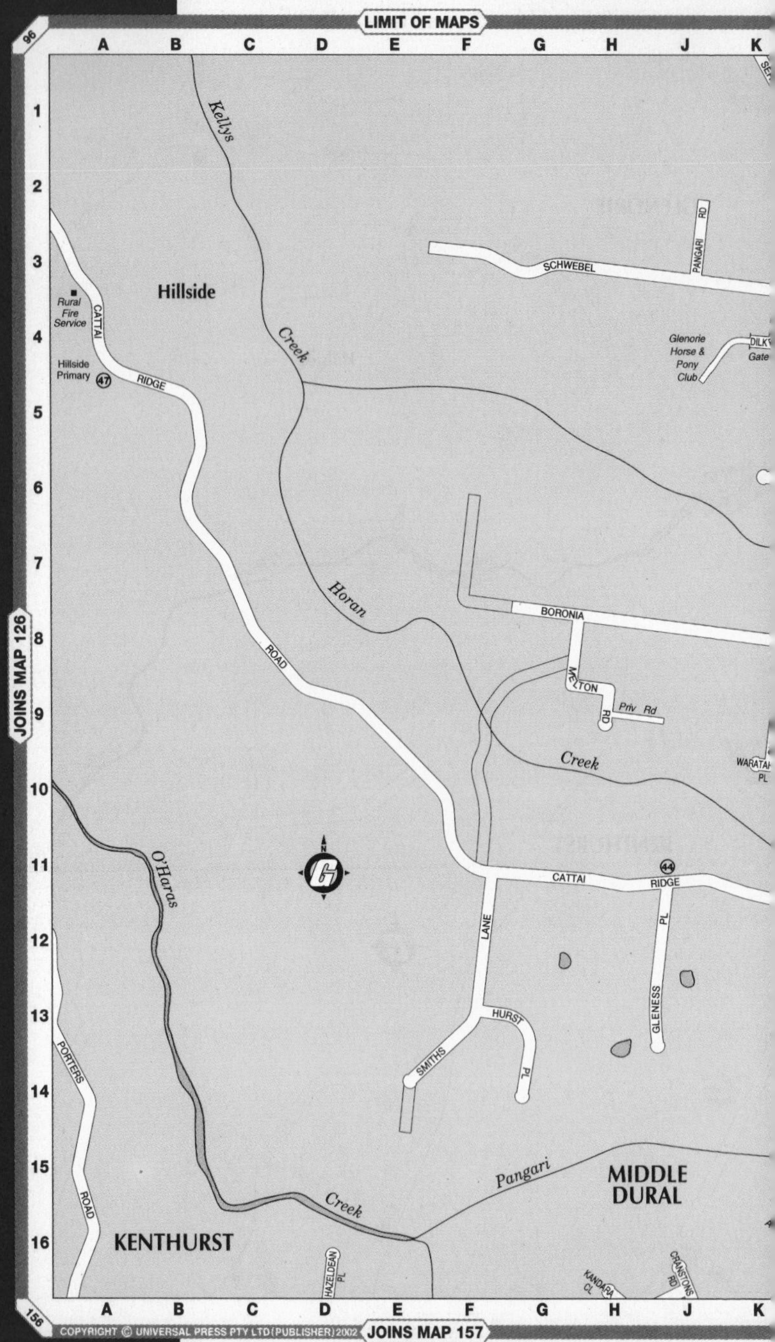
LIMIT OF MAPS
96
JOINS MAP 126
156
JOINS MAP 157
A B C D E F G H J K
1 2 3 4 5 6 7 8 9 10 11 12 13 14 15 16
Kellys Creek
Hillside
Rural Fire Service
Hillside Primary
47
CATTAI RIDGE ROAD
SCHWEBEL
PANGARI RD
Glenorie Horse & Pony Club
DILKY
Gate
Horan Creek
BORONIA
MELTON RD
Priv Rd
WARATAH PL
O'Haras Creek
CATTAI RIDGE
44
LANE
PL
HURST PL
SMITHS
GLENESS
PORTERS ROAD
Pangari
MIDDLE DURAL
KENTHURST
HAZELDEAN PL
KANDARA CL
CRANSTONS RD

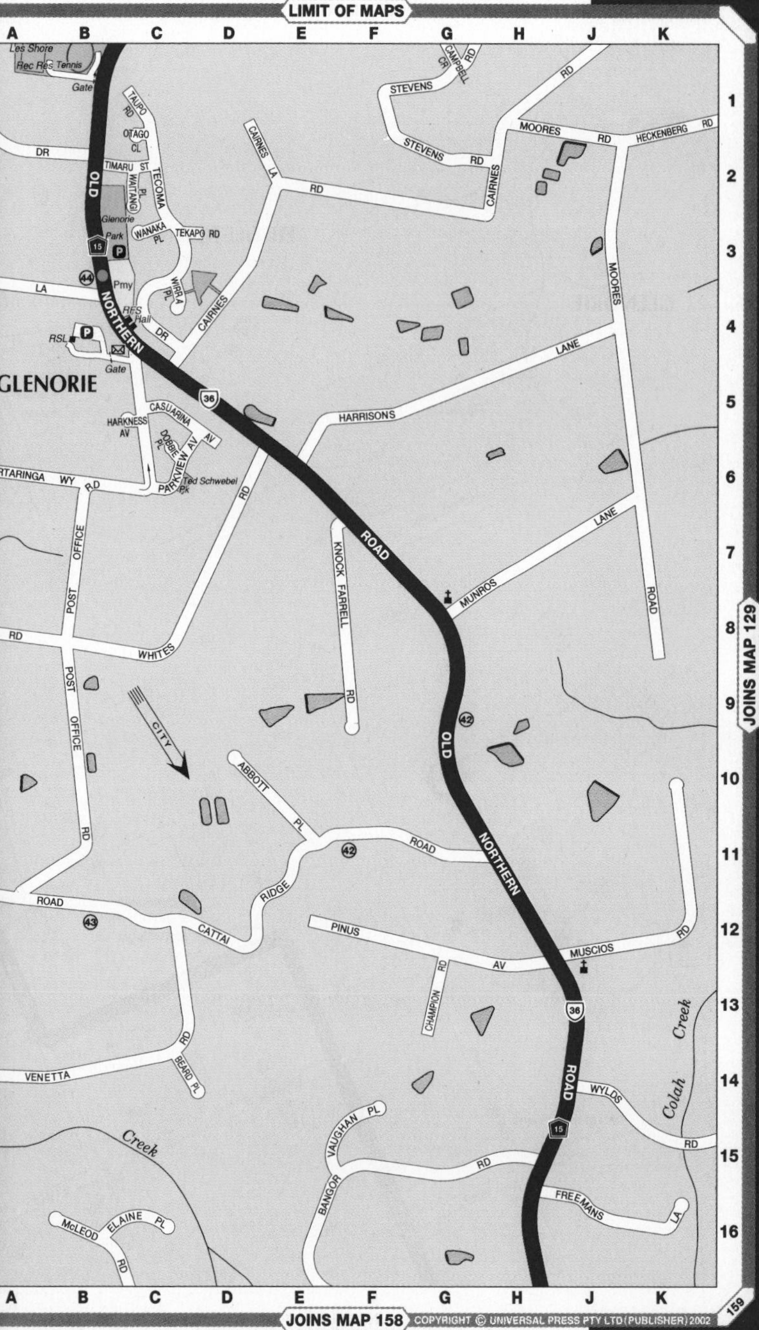
LIMIT OF MAPS
A B C D E F G H J K
1 2 3 4 5 6 7 8 9 10 11 12 13 14 15 16
GLENORIE
Les Shore Rec Res
Tennis
Gate
TAUPO RD
OTAGO CL
TIMARU ST
WAITANGI PL
TECOMA DR
Glenorie Park
WANAKA PL
TEKAPO RD
WIRRA PL
Pmy
RFS Hall
RSL
OLD NORTHERN ROAD
CAIRNES LA
CAIRNES RD
CAMPBELL CR
STEVENS RD
MOORES RD
HECKENBERG RD
MOORES ROAD
HARRISONS LANE
CASUARINA AV
HARKNESS AV
DOBBIE PL
PARKVIEW AV
Ted Schwebel Pk
TARINGA WY
POST OFFICE RD
WHITES RD
KNOCK FARRELL RD
MUNROS LANE
CITY
ABBOTT PL
RIDGE ROAD
CATTAI ROAD
PINUS AV
CHAMPION RD
MUSCIOS RD
VENETTA RD
BEARD PL
Creek
Colah Creek
WYLDS RD
VAUGHAN PL
BANGOR RD
FREEMANS LA
McLEOD RD
ELAINE PL
15 44 36 42 43
JOINS MAP 129
JOINS MAP 158

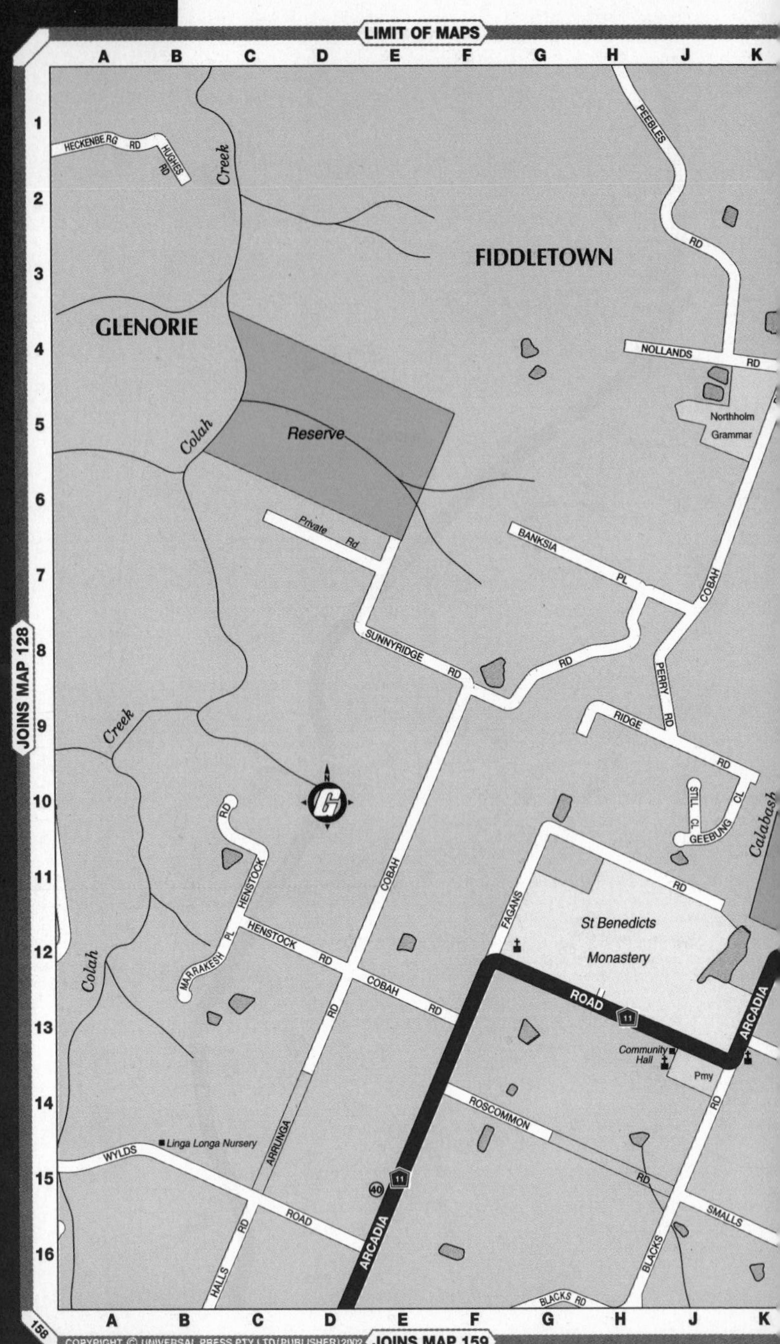
LIMIT OF MAPS
A B C D E F G H J K
1 2 3 4 5 6 7 8 9 10 11 12 13 14 15 16
JOINS MAP 128
FIDDLETOWN
GLENORIE
HECKENBERG RD
HUGHES RD
PEEBLES RD
Creek
Colah
Reserve
NOLLANDS RD
Northholm Grammar
Private Rd
BANKSIA PL
COBAH
SUNNYRIDGE RD
PERRY RD
RIDGE RD
Creek
STILL CL
GEEBUNG CL
Calabash
HENSTOCK RD
HENSTOCK PL
MARRAKESH PL
COBAH RD
FAGANS RD
St Benedicts Monastery
ROAD
ARCADIA
Colah
Community Hall
Pmy
ROSCOMMON RD
SMALLS
Linga Longa Nursery
WYLDS ROAD
ARRUNGA
HALLS RD
ARCADIA
BLACKS RD
BLACKS
11
40

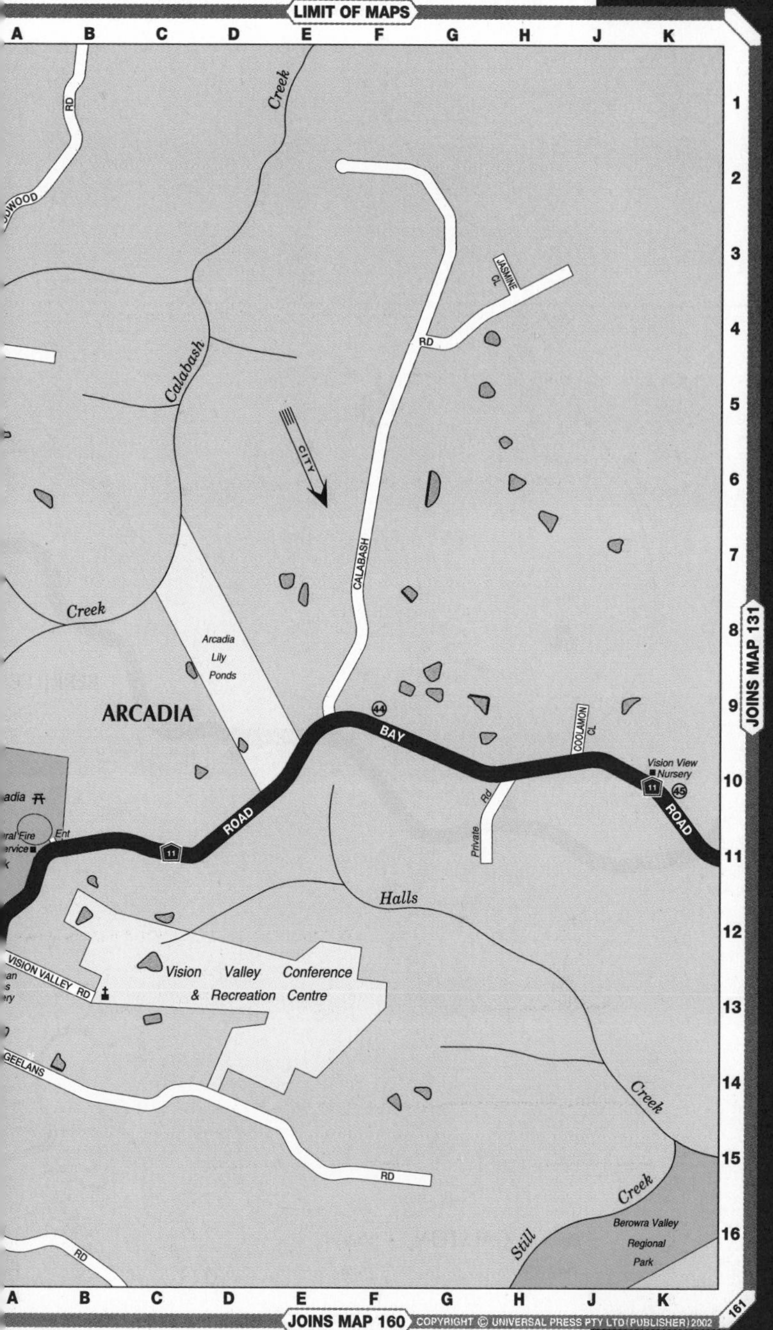
LIMIT OF MAPS
A B C D E F G H J K
1 2 3 4 5 6 7 8 9 10 11 12 13 14 15 16
RD
Creek
Calabash
Creek
CITY
CALABASH
RD
JASMINE CL
Arcadia
Lily
Ponds
ARCADIA
44
BAY
ROAD
11
COOLAMON CL
Private Rd
Vision View
Nursery
45
ROAD
Ent
Halls
Vision Valley Conference
& Recreation Centre
VISION VALLEY RD
GEELANS
RD
Creek
Creek
Still
Berowra Valley
Regional
Park
RD
JOINS MAP 131
JOINS MAP 160

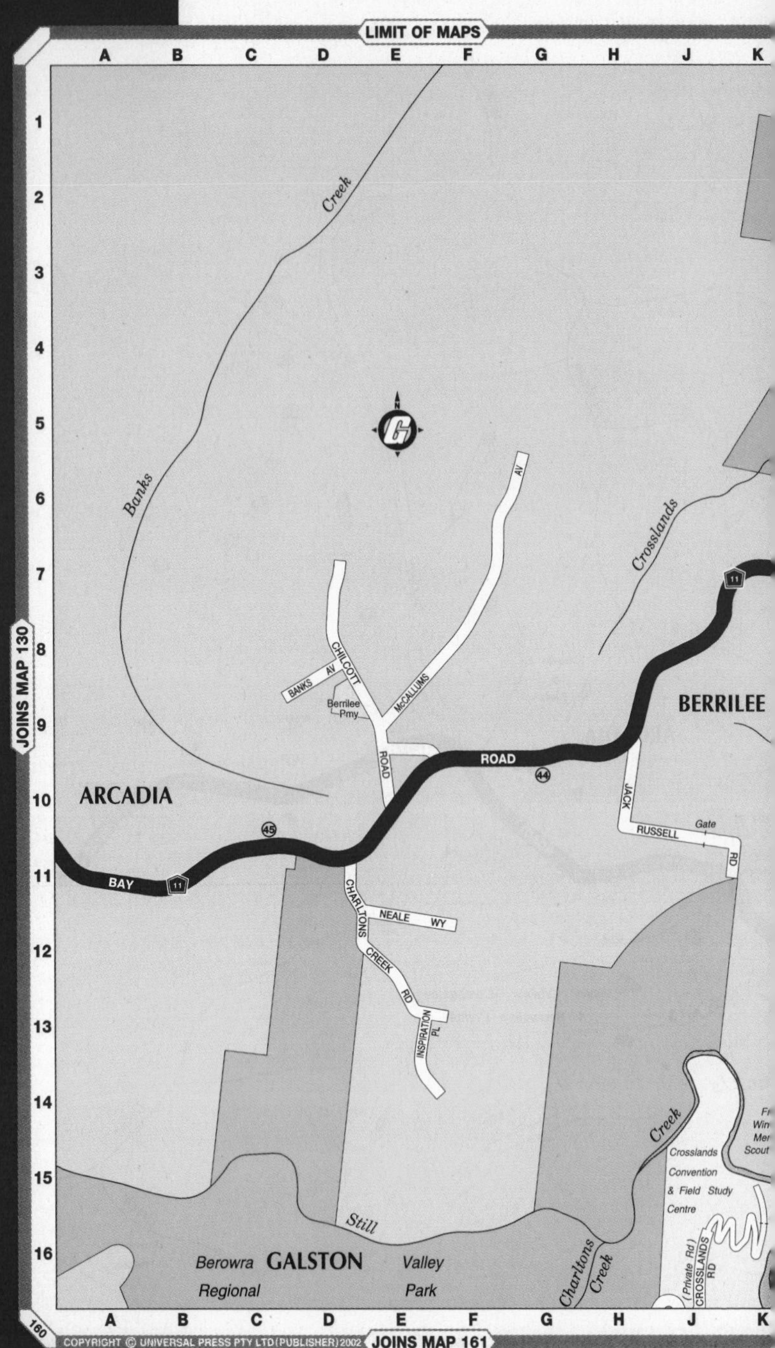

JOINS MAP 161

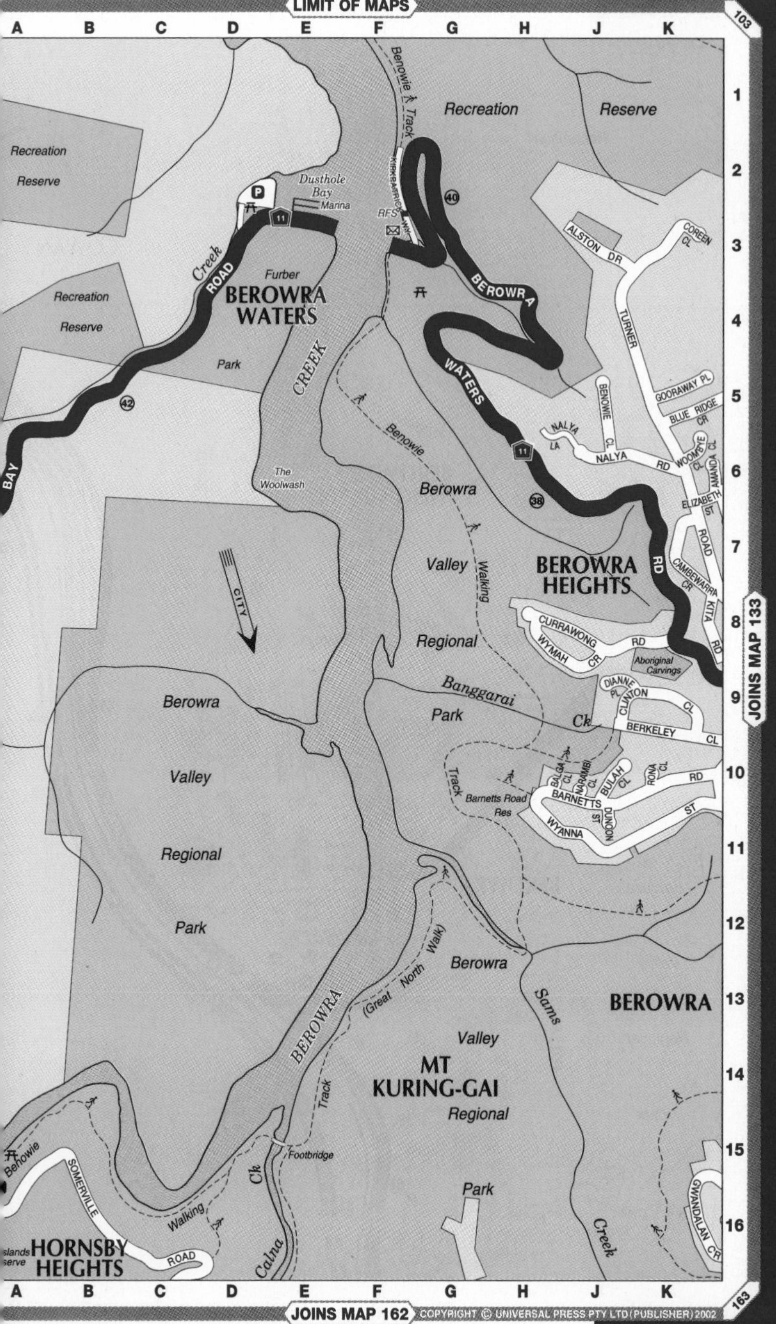
LIMIT OF MAPS
103
Recreation
Reserve
Benowie Track
Recreation Reserve
Dusthole Bay
Marina
KIRKPATRICK WY
RFS
ALSTON DR
COREEN CL
Creek
ROAD
Furber
BEROWRA WATERS
BEROWRA
Recreation Reserve
Park
CREEK
WATERS
TURNER
GOORAWAY PL
BLUE RIDGE CR
BENOWIE CL
NALYA LA
NALYA RD
WOOMBYE CL
AMANDA CL
BAY
Benowie
The Woolwash
Berowra
ELIZABETH ST
ROAD
RD
Valley
Walking
BEROWRA HEIGHTS
CAMBEWARRA CR
KITA RD
CITY
CURRAWONG RD
WYMAH CR
Regional
Aboriginal Carvings
Banggarai
DIANNE PL
CLINTON CL
Berowra
Park
Ck
BERKELEY CL
Valley
Track
BALGA CL
NARAMBI CL
BULAH CL
RONA CL
RD
BARNETTS
Barnetts Road Res
DUNOON ST
WYANNA ST
Regional
Park
(Great North Walk)
Berowra
Sams
BEROWRA
BEROWRA
Valley
MT KURING-GAI
Track
Regional
Benowie
Footbridge
SOMERVILLE
Ck
Park
Walking
GWANDALAN CR
Creek
Calna
HORNSBY HEIGHTS
ROAD
JOINS MAP 133
JOINS MAP 162
163

JOINS MAP 103

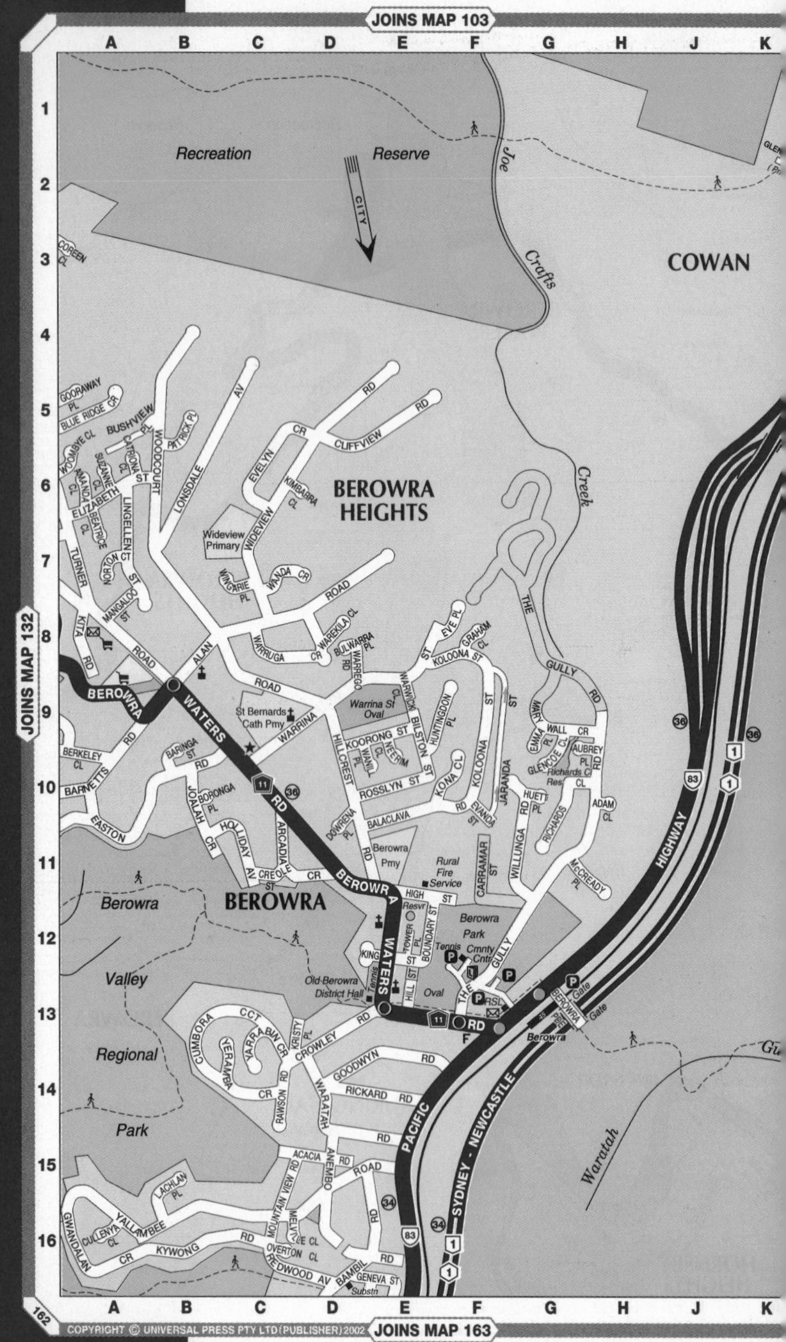

JOINS MAP 132

JOINS MAP 163

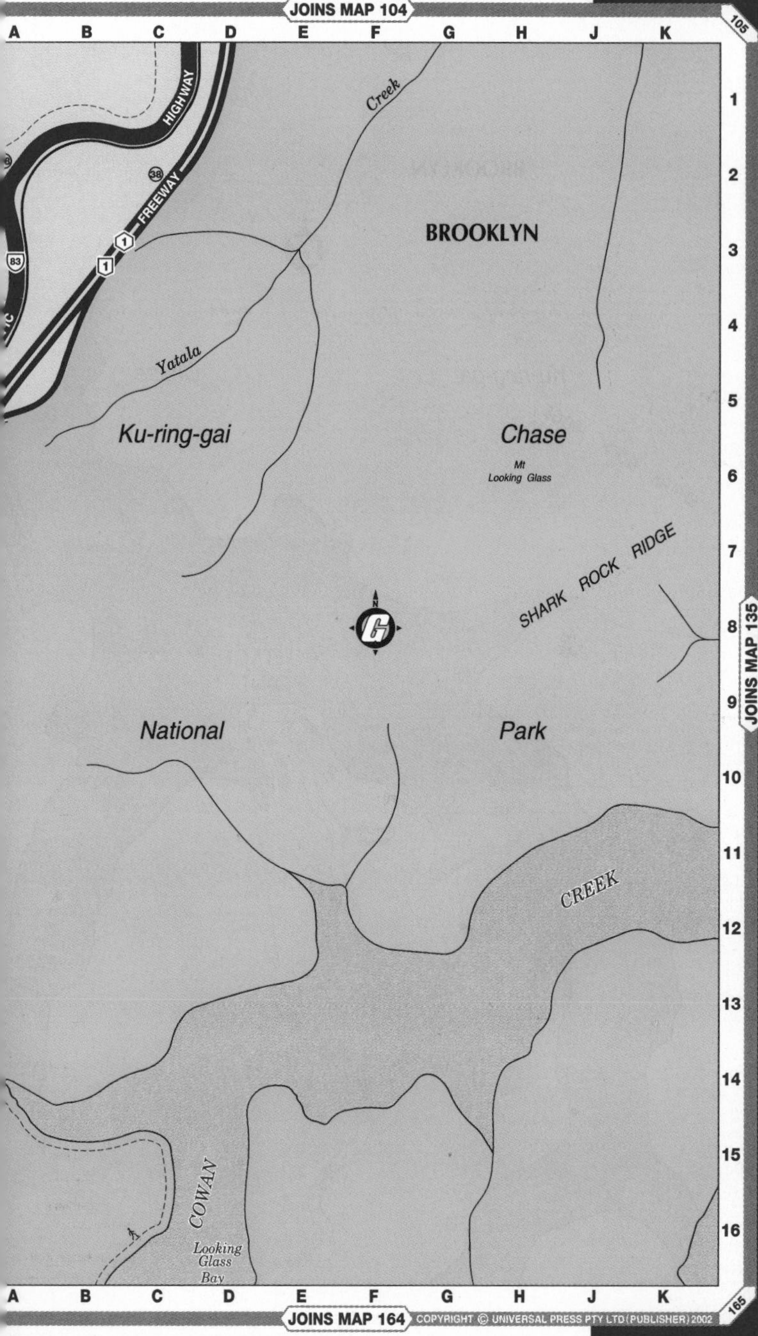

JOINS MAP 104
105
A B C D E F G H J K
1 2 3 4 5 6 7 8 9 10 11 12 13 14 15 16
HIGHWAY
FREEWAY
38
1
83
Creek
BROOKLYN
Yatala
Ku-ring-gai
Chase
Mt
Looking Glass
SHARK ROCK RIDGE
JOINS MAP 135
National
Park
CREEK
COWAN
Looking
Glass
Bay
JOINS MAP 164
165

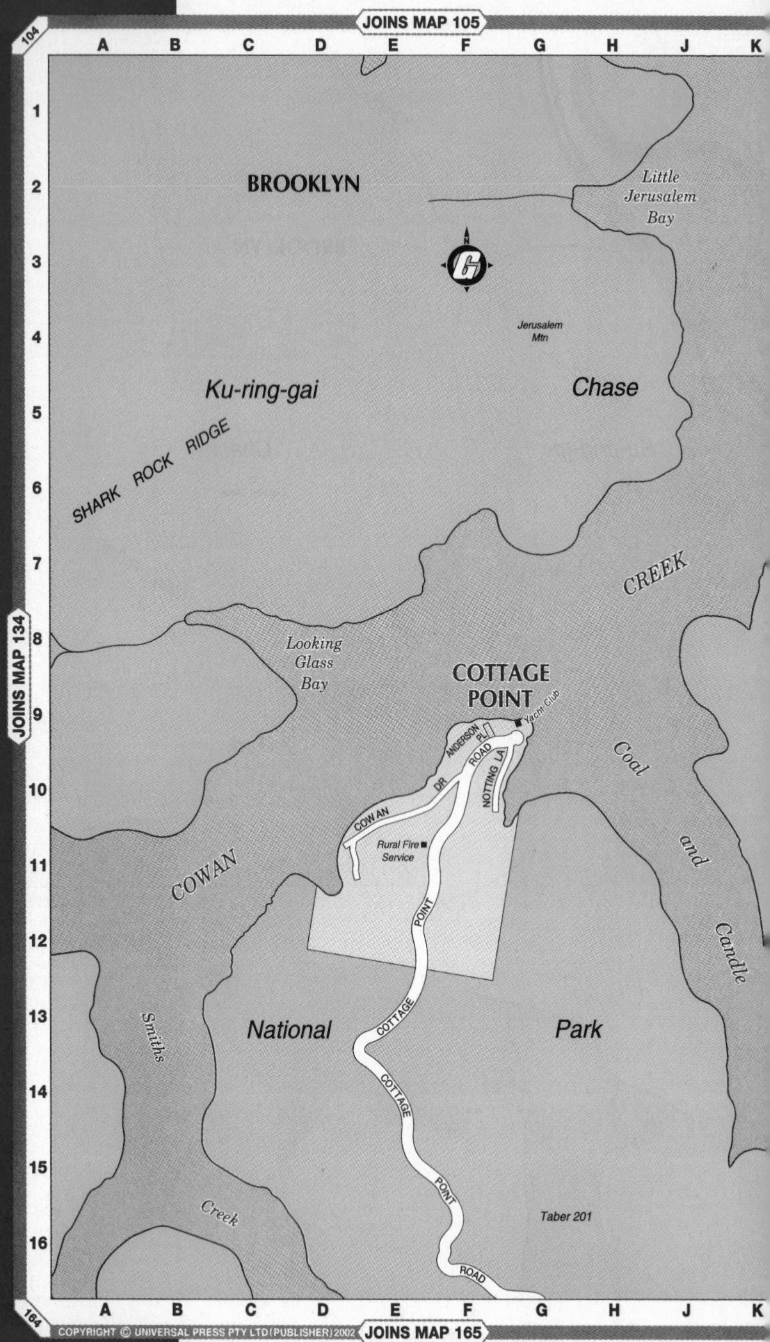
JOINS MAP 105
104
A B C D E F G H J K
1 2 3 4 5 6 7 8 9 10 11 12 13 14 15 16
BROOKLYN
Little Jerusalem Bay
Jerusalem Mtn
Ku-ring-gai
Chase
SHARK ROCK RIDGE
CREEK
JOINS MAP 134
Looking Glass Bay
COTTAGE POINT
Yacht Club
ANDERSON PL
ROAD
NOTTING LA
DR
COWAN
Coal
and
Candle
Rural Fire Service
COWAN
POINT
COTTAGE
National
Park
Smiths
COTTAGE
POINT
Creek
Taber 201
ROAD
164
JOINS MAP 165

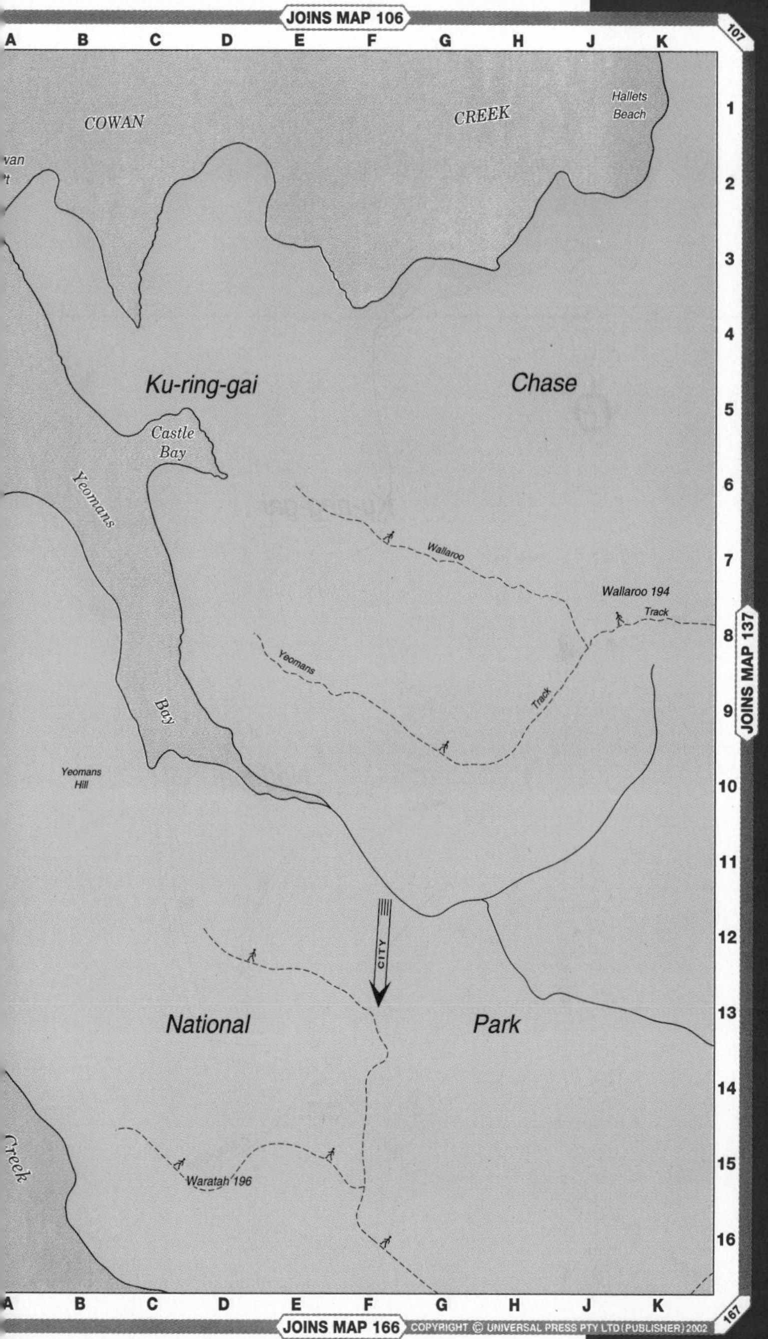
JOINS MAP 106
107
A
B
C
D
E
F
G
H
J
K
1
2
3
4
5
6
7
8
9
10
11
12
13
14
15
16
COWAN
CREEK
Hallets
Beach
Ku-ring-gai
Chase
Castle
Bay
Yeomans
Bay
Yeomans
Hill
Wallaroo
Wallaroo 194
Track
Yeomans
Track
CITY
National
Park
Creek
Waratah 196
JOINS MAP 137
JOINS MAP 166
167

MAP 137

JOINS MAP 107

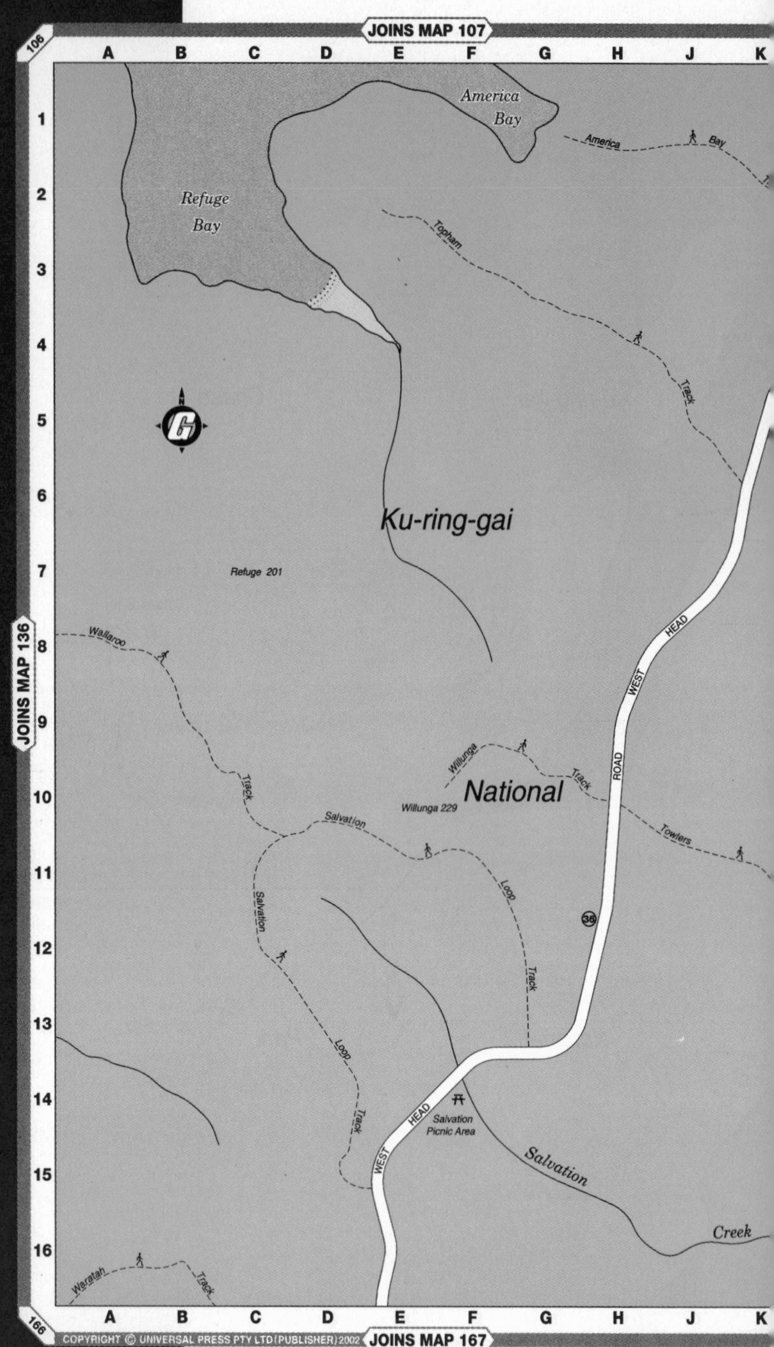

JOINS MAP 136

JOINS MAP 167

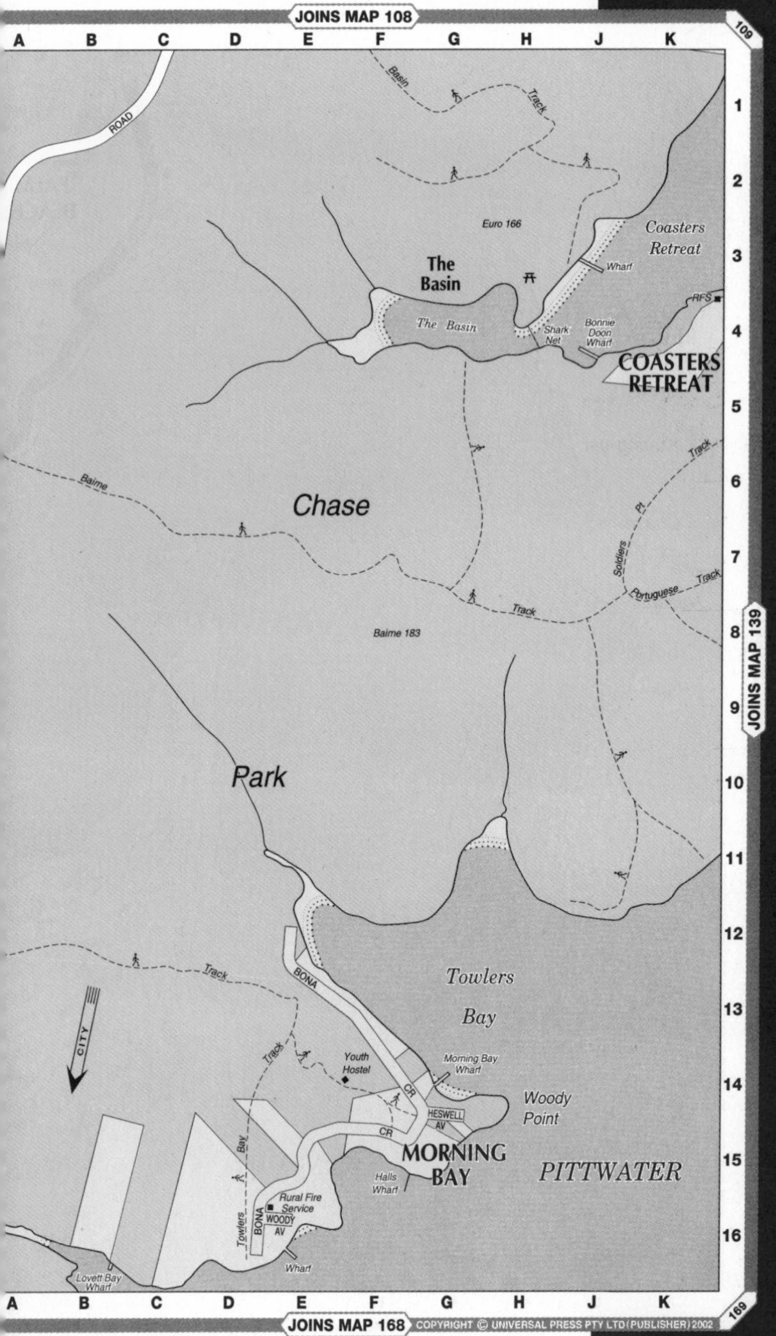
JOINS MAP 108
109
ROAD
Basin
Track
Euro 166
Coasters Retreat
The Basin
Wharf
RFS
The Basin
Shark Net
Bonnie Doon Wharf
COASTERS RETREAT
Track
Baime
Chase
Soldiers Pt
Portuguese
Track
Track
Baime 183
JOINS MAP 139
Park
Track
BONA
Towlers Bay
CITY
Track
Youth Hostel
Morning Bay Wharf
CR
Woody Point
HESWELL AV
CR
Bay
MORNING BAY
PITTWATER
Halls Wharf
Rural Fire Service
BONA
WOODY AV
Towlers
Wharf
Lovett Bay Wharf
JOINS MAP 168
169

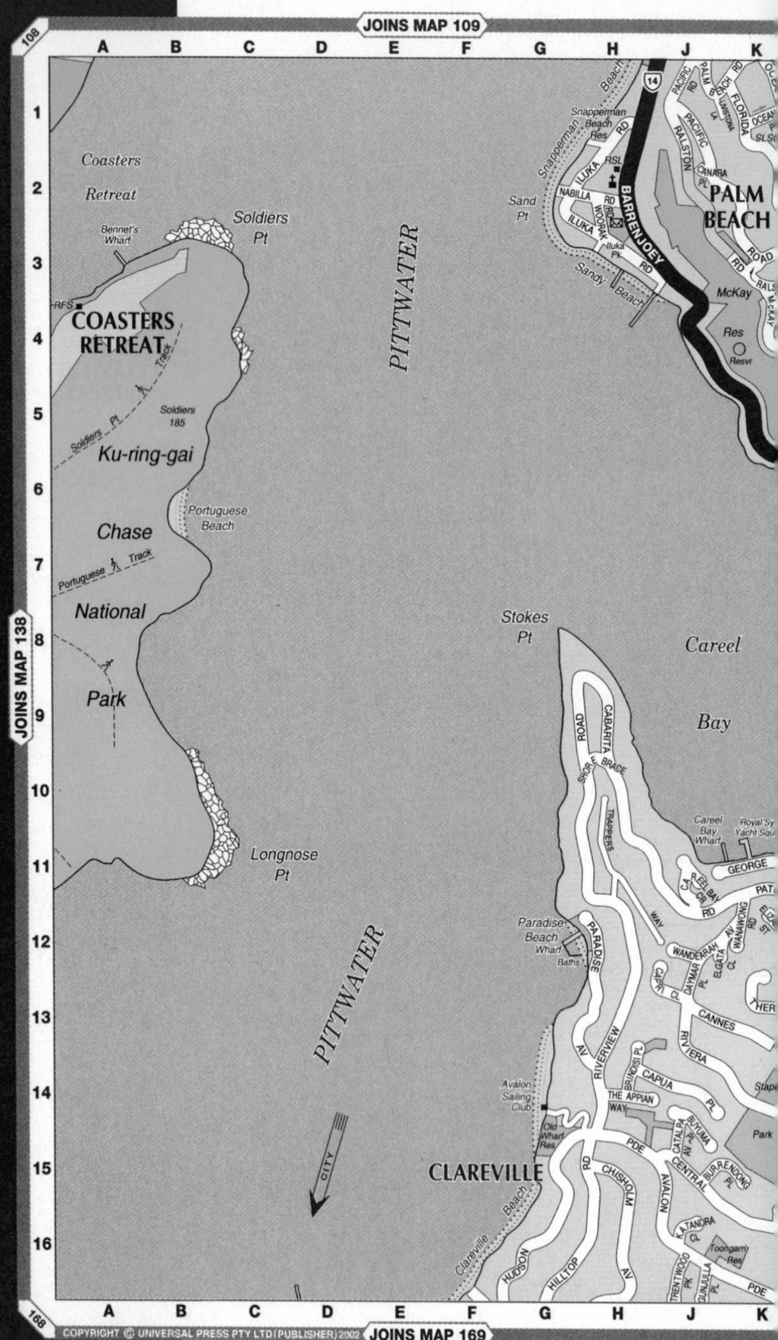
JOINS MAP 109
JOINS MAP 138
JOINS MAP 169
108
168
Coasters Retreat
Bennet's Wharf
Soldiers Pt
COASTERS RETREAT
RFS
Track
Soldiers Pt Track
Soldiers 185
Ku-ring-gai
Chase
National
Park
Portuguese Beach
Portuguese Track
Longnose Pt
PITTWATER
PITTWATER
CITY
Snapperman Beach
Snapperman Beach Res
Sand Pt
Sandy Beach
Iluka Pk
RSL
ILUKA RD
NABILLA RD
WOORAK RD
BARRENJOEY RD
PALM BEACH
PACIFIC RD
PALM BEACH RD
FLORIDA
OCEAN
RALSTON
CANARA PL
McKay Res
Resvr
Stokes Pt
Careel Bay
CABARITA ROAD
SHORE BRACE
TRAPPERS WAY
Careel Bay Wharf
Royal Sy Yacht Squ
GEORGE
CAREEL BAY CR
CAREEL BAY RD
Paradise Beach Wharf
Baths
PARADISE AV
WANDEARAH AV
WANAWONG RD
ELGATA CL
DAYMAR PL
CAPRI CL
CANNES
RIVIERA
RIVERVIEW
BRINDISI PL
CAPUA PL
THE APPIAN WAY
Avalon Sailing Club
Old Wharf Res
CLAREVILLE
Clareville Beach
PDE
CATALPA AV
BUYUMA PL
CENTRAL
BURRENDONG PL
CHISHOLM RD
AVALON
KATANDRA CL
Toongari Res
TRENTWOOD PK
GUNJULLA PL
HUDSON
HILLTOP
AV
Park
PDE

JOINS MAP 110

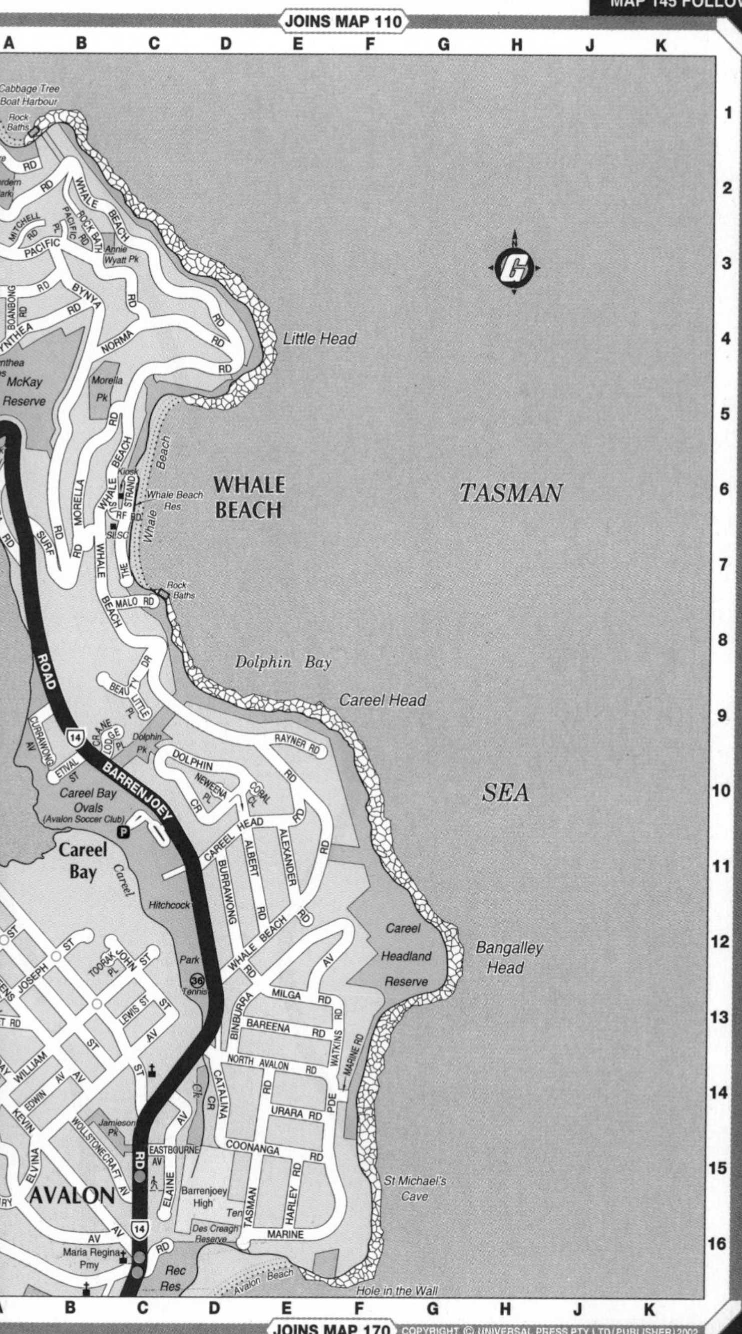

JOINS MAP 170

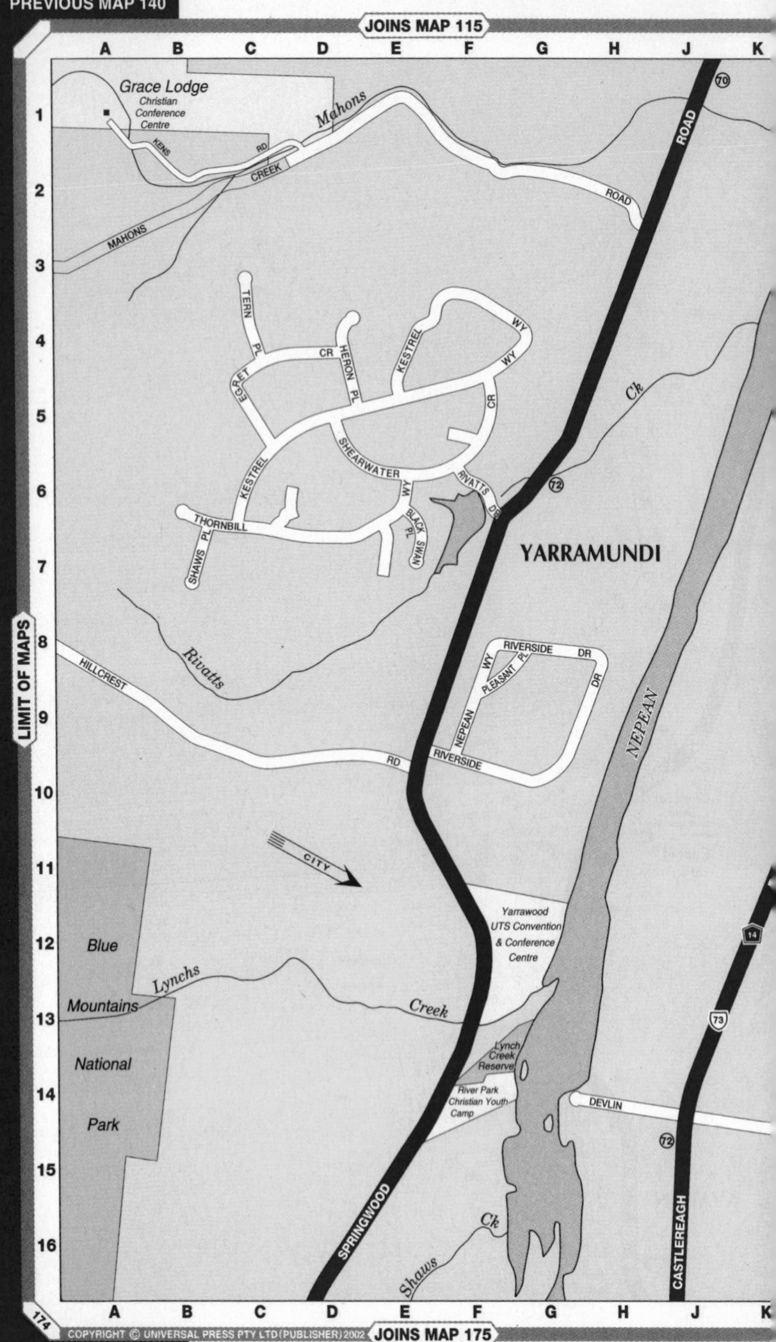
JOINS MAP 115
A B C D E F G H J K
1 2 3 4 5 6 7 8 9 10 11 12 13 14 15 16
LIMIT OF MAPS
Grace Lodge
Christian
Conference
Centre
KENS
RD
Mahons
CREEK
ROAD
MAHONS
ROAD
70
TERN
PL
CR
HERON
PL
EGRET
KESTREL
WY
WY
CR
SHEARWATER
KESTREL
WY
RIVATTS
DR
72
THORNBILL
SHAWS
PL
BLACK
SWAN
PL
Ck
YARRAMUNDI
Rivatts
HILLCREST
RIVERSIDE
DR
WY
PLEASANT
PL
DR
NEPEAN
RD
RIVERSIDE
NEPEAN
CITY
Yarrawood
UTS Convention
& Conference
Centre
Blue
Mountains
National
Park
Lynchs
Creek
14
73
Lynch
Creek
Reserve
River Park
Christian Youth
Camp
DEVLIN
72
SPRINGWOOD
Ck
Shaws
CASTLEREAGH
JOINS MAP 175

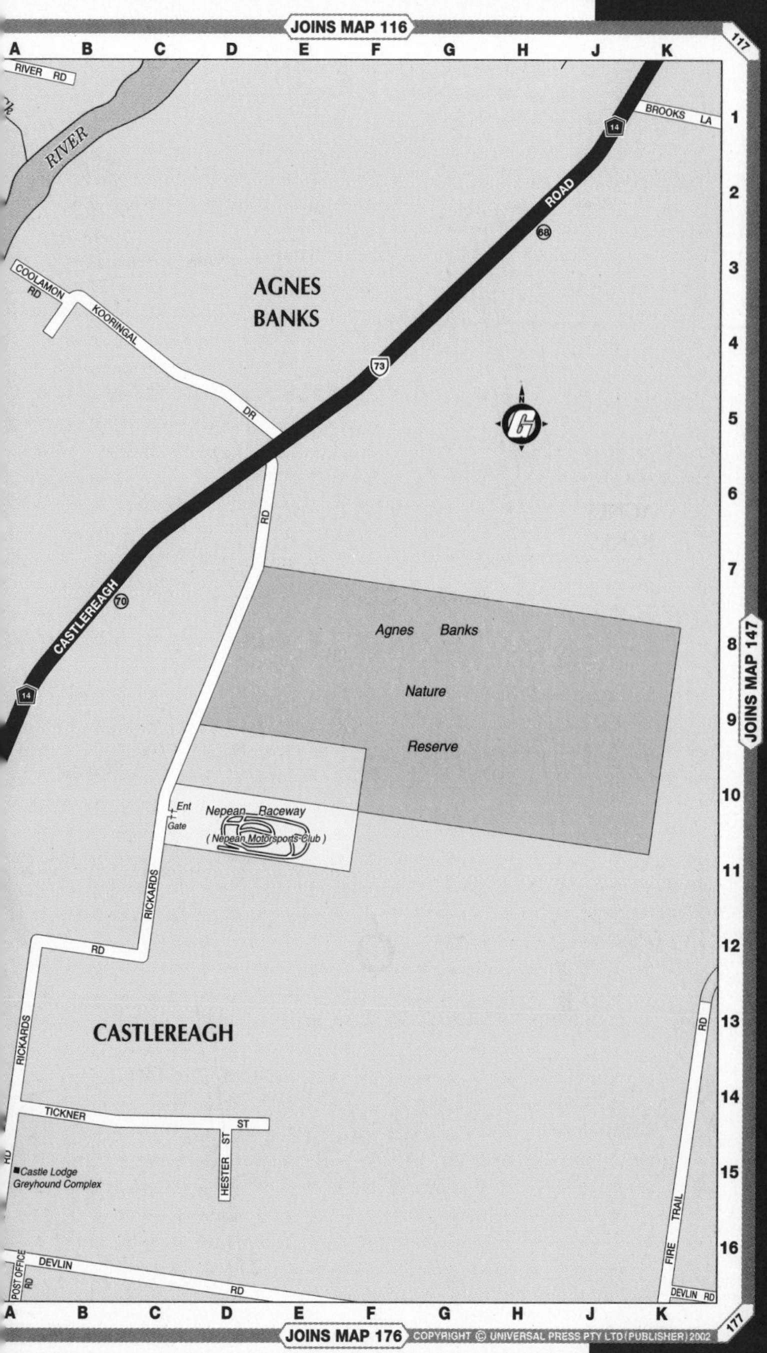

JOINS MAP 176

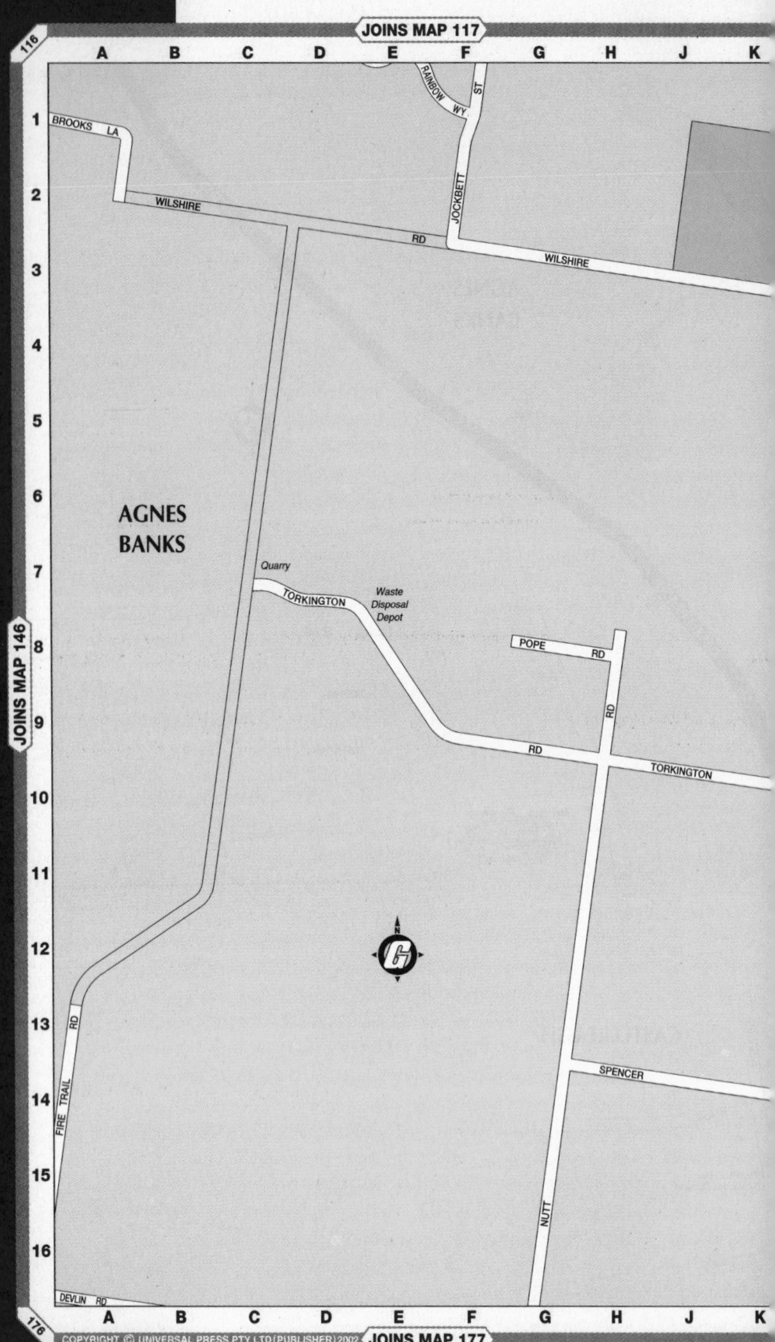
JOINS MAP 117
116
A
B
C
D
E
F
G
H
J
K
1
2
3
4
5
6
7
8
9
10
11
12
13
14
15
16
RAINBOW WY
ST
BROOKS LA
JOCKBETT
WILSHIRE
RD
WILSHIRE
AGNES
BANKS
Quarry
TORKINGTON
Waste
Disposal
Depot
POPE
RD
RD
RD
TORKINGTON
SPENCER
FIRE TRAIL
RD
NUTT
DEVLIN RD
JOINS MAP 146
176
JOINS MAP 177

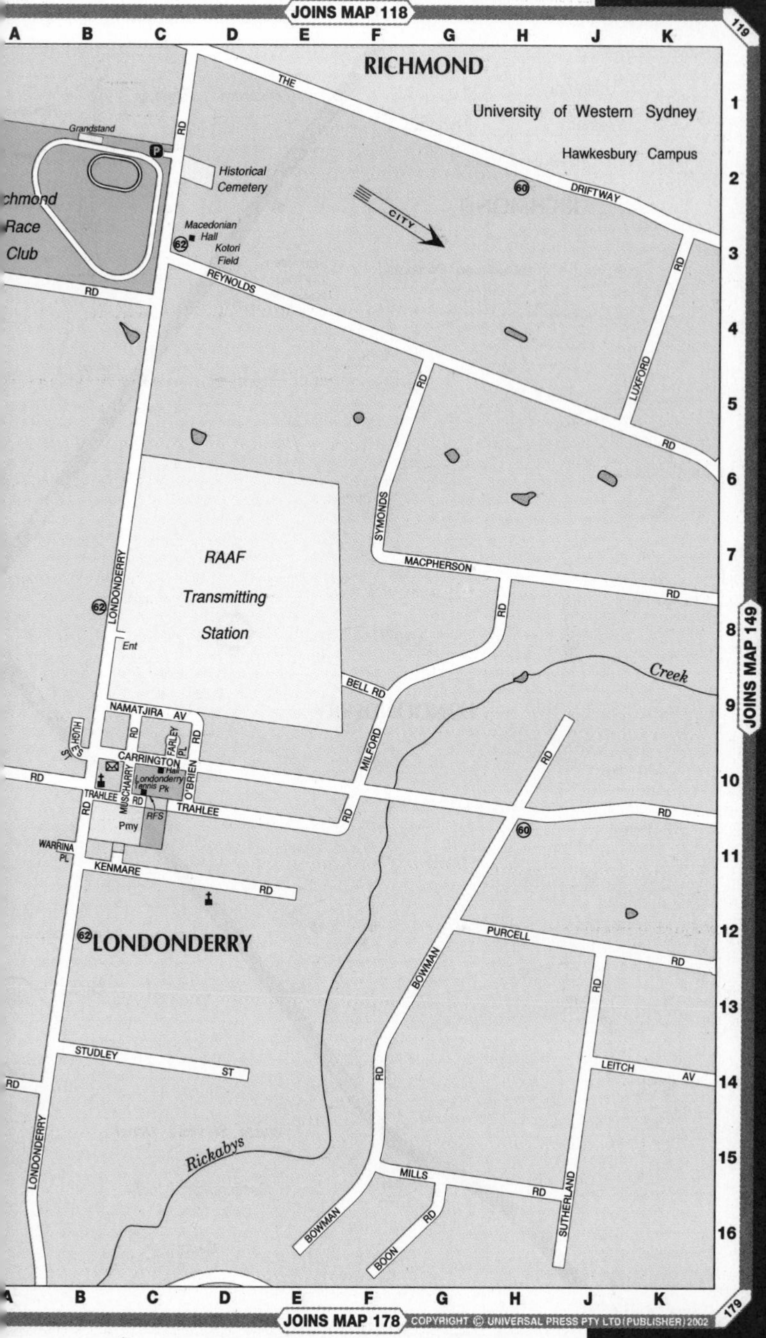
JOINS MAP 118
A B C D E F G H J K
119
RICHMOND
THE
University of Western Sydney
Hawkesbury Campus
DRIFTWAY
Grandstand
Historical
Cemetery
chmond
Race
Club
Macedonian
Hall
Kotori
Field
CITY
REYNOLDS
RD
LUXFORD
SYMONDS
MACPHERSON
RAAF
Transmitting
Station
Ent
LONDONDERRY
BELL RD
Creek
JOINS MAP 149
NAMATJIRA AV
HUGHES ST
FARLEY PL
CARRINGTON
Hall
Londonderry
Tennis Pk
MUSCHARRY
O'BRIEN
TRAHLEE
RFS
Pmy
MILFORD
WARRINA PL
KENMARE
LONDONDERRY
PURCELL
BOWMAN
STUDLEY ST
LEITCH AV
Rickabys
MILLS
SUTHERLAND
BOON
1 2 3 4 5 6 7 8 9 10 11 12 13 14 15 16
JOINS MAP 178
179

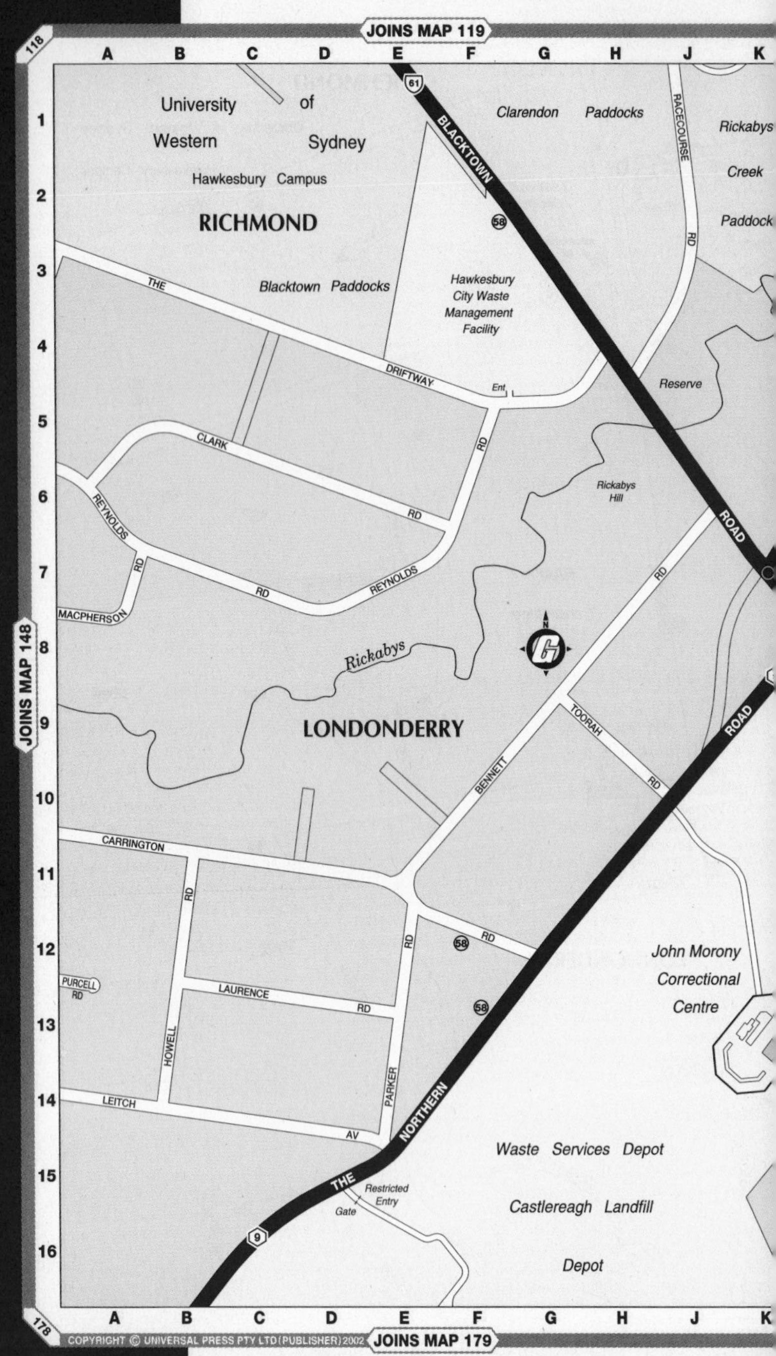
JOINS MAP 119
118
A
B
C
D
E
F
G
H
J
K
1
2
3
4
5
6
7
8
9
10
11
12
13
14
15
16
University of Western Sydney
Hawkesbury Campus
RICHMOND
Clarendon Paddocks
Rickabys Creek Paddock
RACECOURSE RD
BLACKTOWN ROAD
61
58
THE DRIFTWAY
Blacktown Paddocks
Hawkesbury City Waste Management Facility
Ent
Reserve
CLARK RD
RD
Rickabys Hill
REYNOLDS RD
REYNOLDS
RD
MACPHERSON
Rickabys
LONDONDERRY
TOORAH RD
BENNETT RD
ROAD
CARRINGTON RD
RD
PURCELL RD
LAURENCE RD
HOWELL
PARKER RD
LEITCH AV
THE NORTHERN ROAD
John Morony Correctional Centre
Waste Services Depot
Castlereagh Landfill Depot
Restricted Entry
Gate
9
JOINS MAP 148
178
JOINS MAP 179

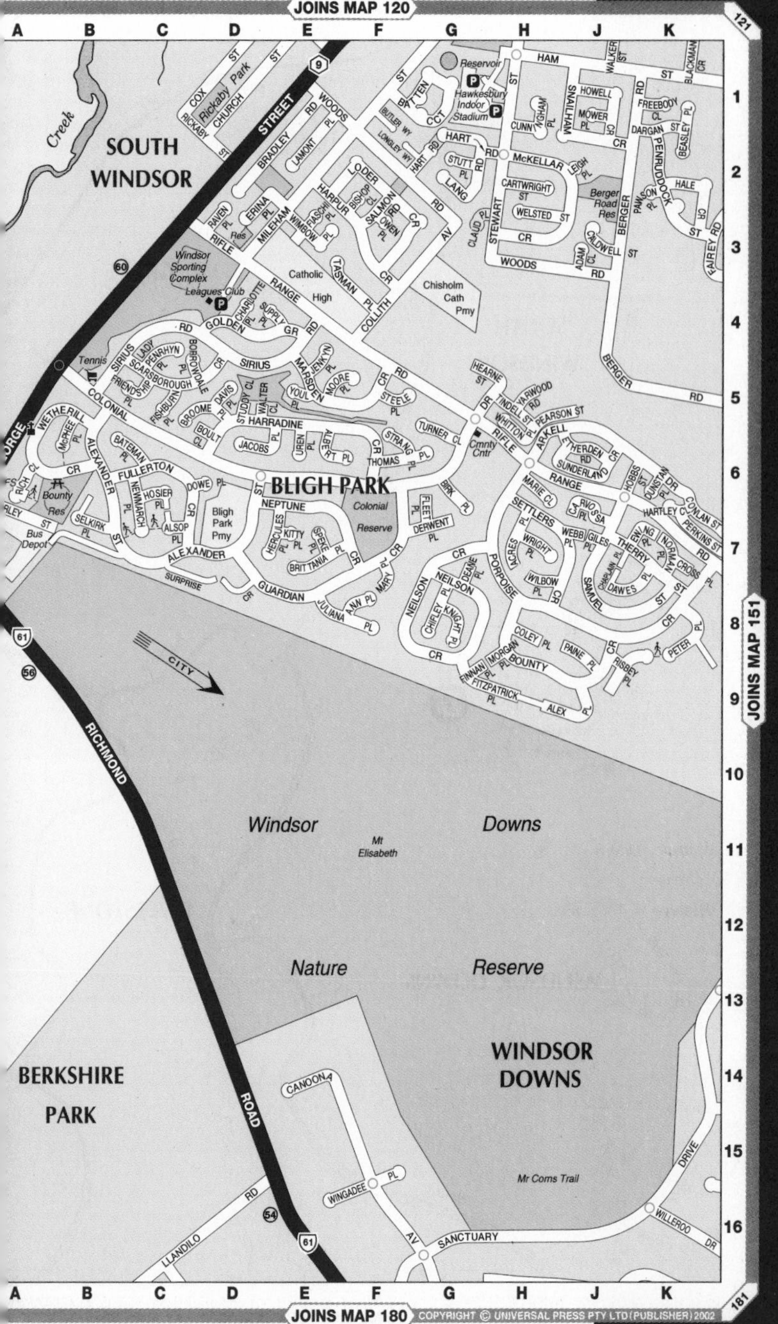

JOINS MAP 120
JOINS MAP 151
JOINS MAP 180
SOUTH WINDSOR
BLIGH PARK
Windsor Downs
Nature Reserve
WINDSOR DOWNS
BERKSHIRE PARK
Mt Elisabeth
Windsor Sporting Complex
Leagues Club
Catholic High
Chisholm Cath Pmy
Bligh Park Pmy
Colonial Reserve
Hawkesbury Indoor Stadium
Reservoir
Berger Road Res
Bounty Res
Bus Depot
Tennis
Cmnty Cntr
Mr Corns Trail
Creek
CITY
RICHMOND ROAD
STREET
RIFLE RANGE RD
COLONIAL DR
SANCTUARY
WILLEROO DR
LLANDILO RD
CANOONA AV
WINGADEE PL

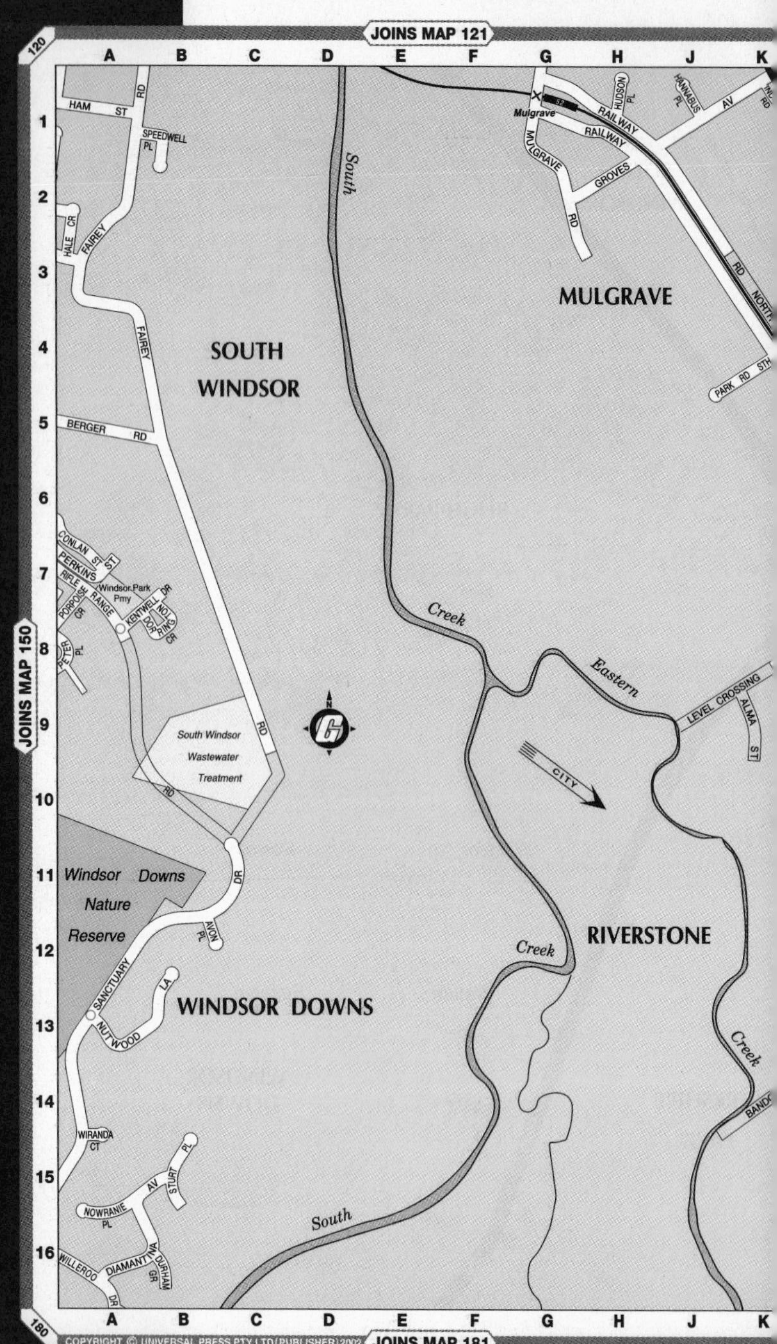
JOINS MAP 121
JOINS MAP 150
JOINS MAP 181
120
180
A B C D E F G H J K
1 2 3 4 5 6 7 8 9 10 11 12 13 14 15 16
SOUTH WINDSOR
MULGRAVE
RIVERSTONE
WINDSOR DOWNS
Windsor Downs Nature Reserve
South Windsor Wastewater Treatment
Windsor Park Pmy
Mulgrave
South Creek
Eastern Creek
Creek
South
CITY
HAM ST
RD
SPEEDWELL PL
HALE CR
FAIREY RD
BERGER RD
CONLAN ST
ST
PERKINS
RIFLE RANGE RD
PORPOISE CR
KENTWELL DR
DOPPING CR
NION
PETER PL
DR
AVON PL
SANCTUARY DR
LA
NUTWOOD
WIRANDA CT
STURT PL
AV
NOWRANIE PL
WILLEROO DR
DIAMANTINA
GR
DURHAM
RAILWAY
RAILWAY
MULGRAVE RD
GROVES
HUDSON PL
HANNABUS PL
AV
RD NORTH
PARK RD STH
LEVEL CROSSING
ALMA ST
BAND

JOINS MAP 122

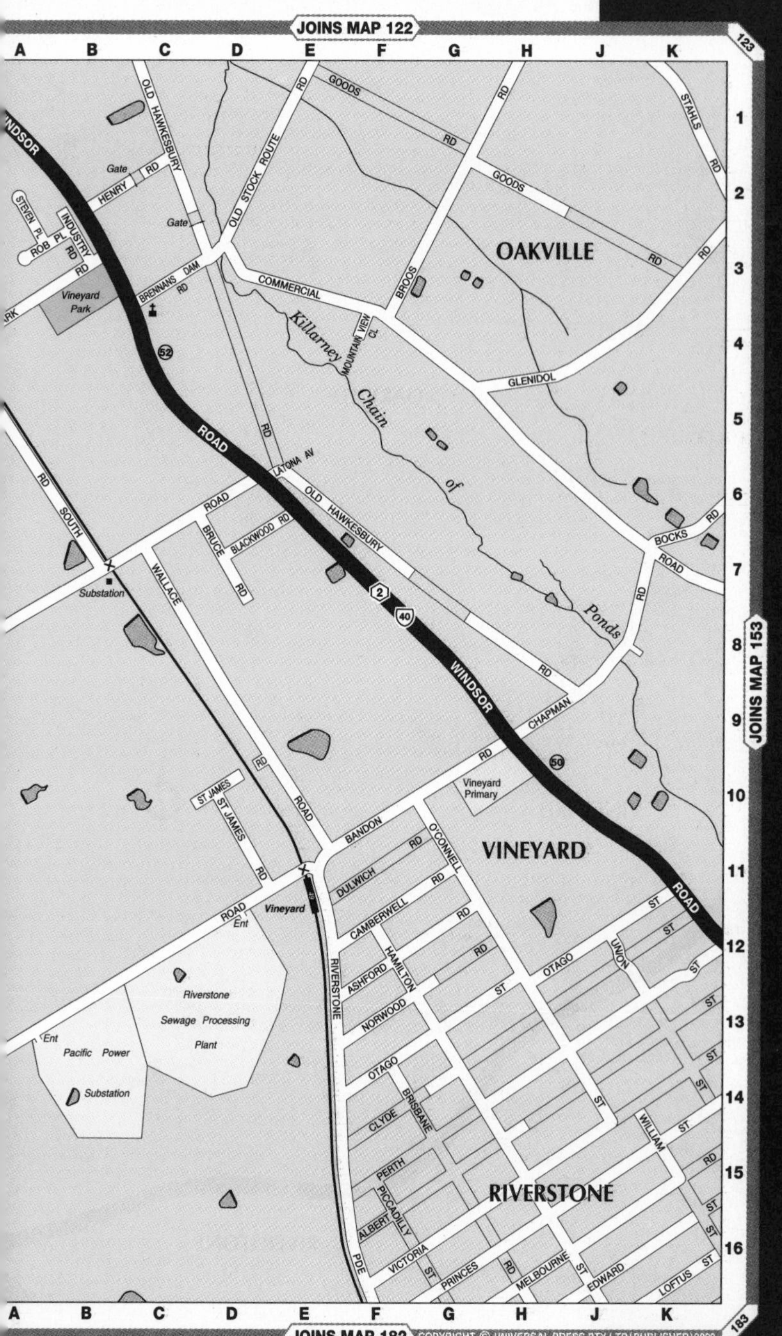

JOINS MAP 153

JOINS MAP 182

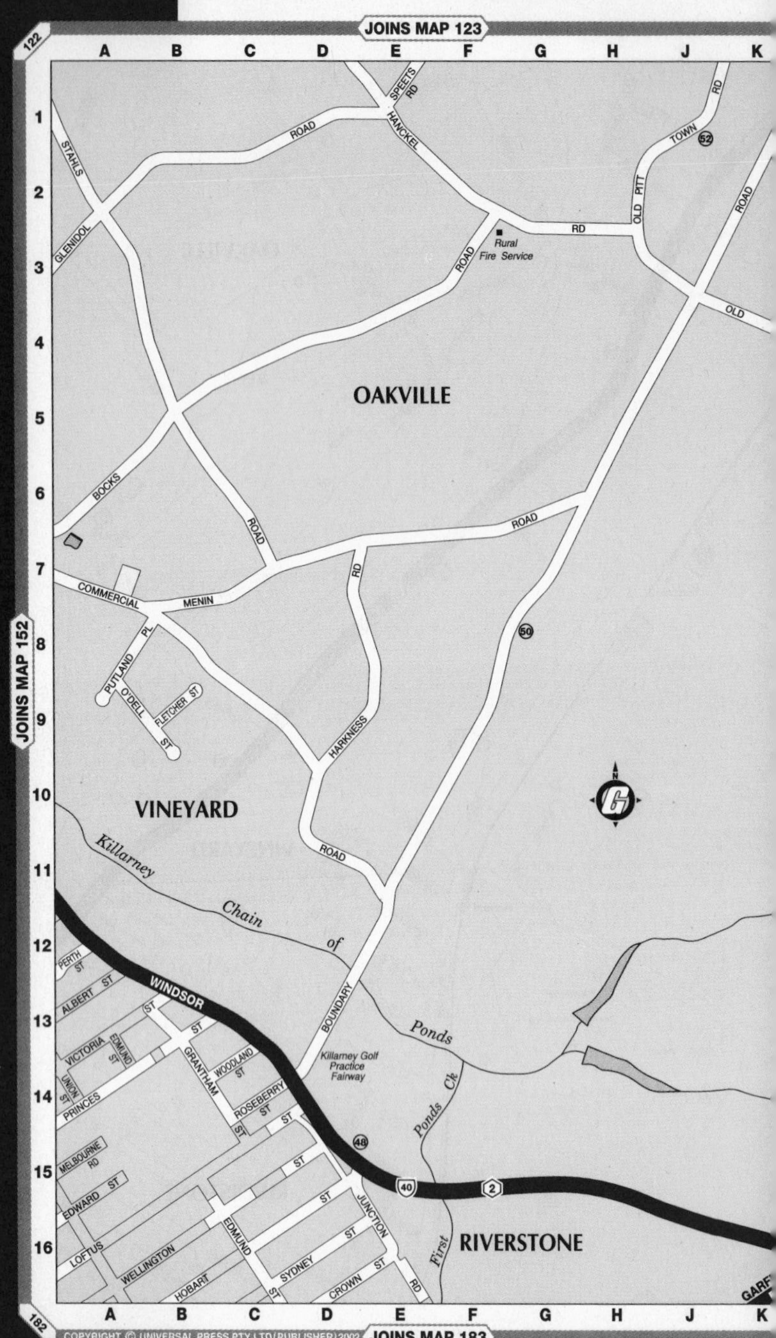
JOINS MAP 123
122
A B C D E F G H J K
1 2 3 4 5 6 7 8 9 10 11 12 13 14 15 16
SPEETS RD
HANCKEL
ROAD
STAHLS
GLENIDOL
RD
Rural
Fire Service
ROAD
OLD PITT
TOWN
RD
52
ROAD
OLD
OAKVILLE
BOCKS
ROAD
ROAD
RD
COMMERCIAL
MENIN
PL
PUTLAND
O'DELL
FLETCHER ST
ST
50
HARKNESS
VINEYARD
Killarney
ROAD
Chain
of
Ponds
BOUNDARY
Killarney Golf
Practice
Fairway
Ponds Ck
WINDSOR
PERTH ST
ALBERT ST
ST
ST
VICTORIA
EDMUND ST
UNION ST
GRANTHAM
WOODLAND ST
PRINCES
ROSEBERRY ST
ST
ST
48
MELBOURNE RD
ST
EDWARD ST
40
2
ST
JUNCTION
EDMUND
LOFTUS
WELLINGTON
ST
SYDNEY
First
RIVERSTONE
HOBART
ST
CROWN ST
RD
GARF
JOINS MAP 152
182
JOINS MAP 183

JOINS MAP 124

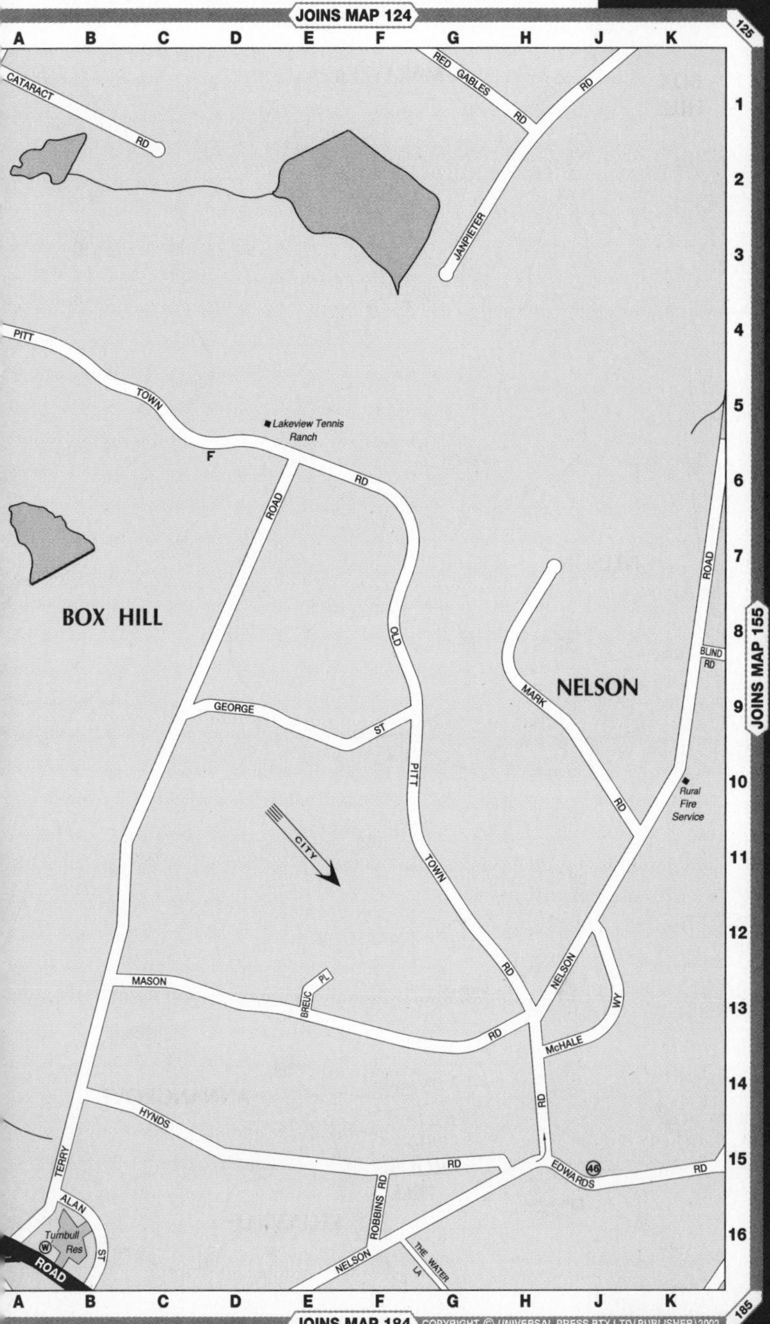

JOINS MAP 155

JOINS MAP 184

JOINS MAP 125

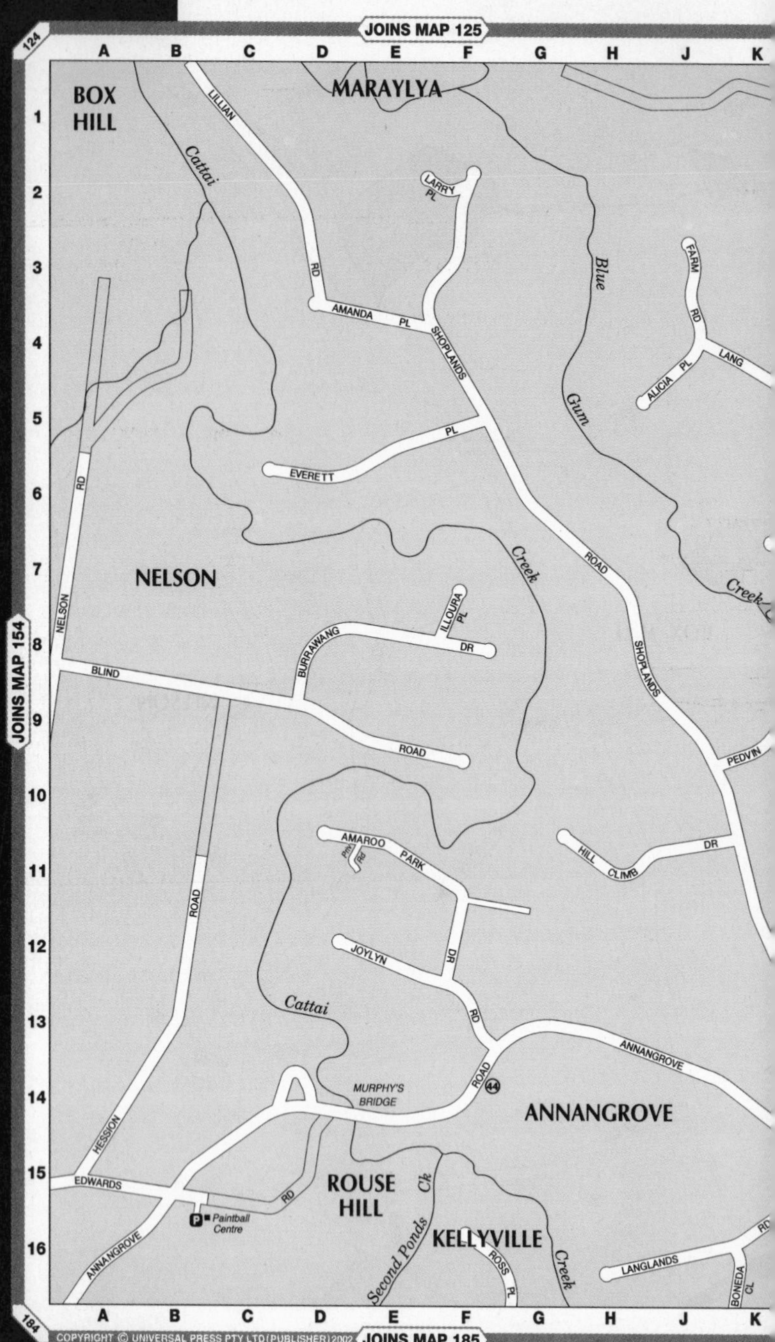

JOINS MAP 154

JOINS MAP 185

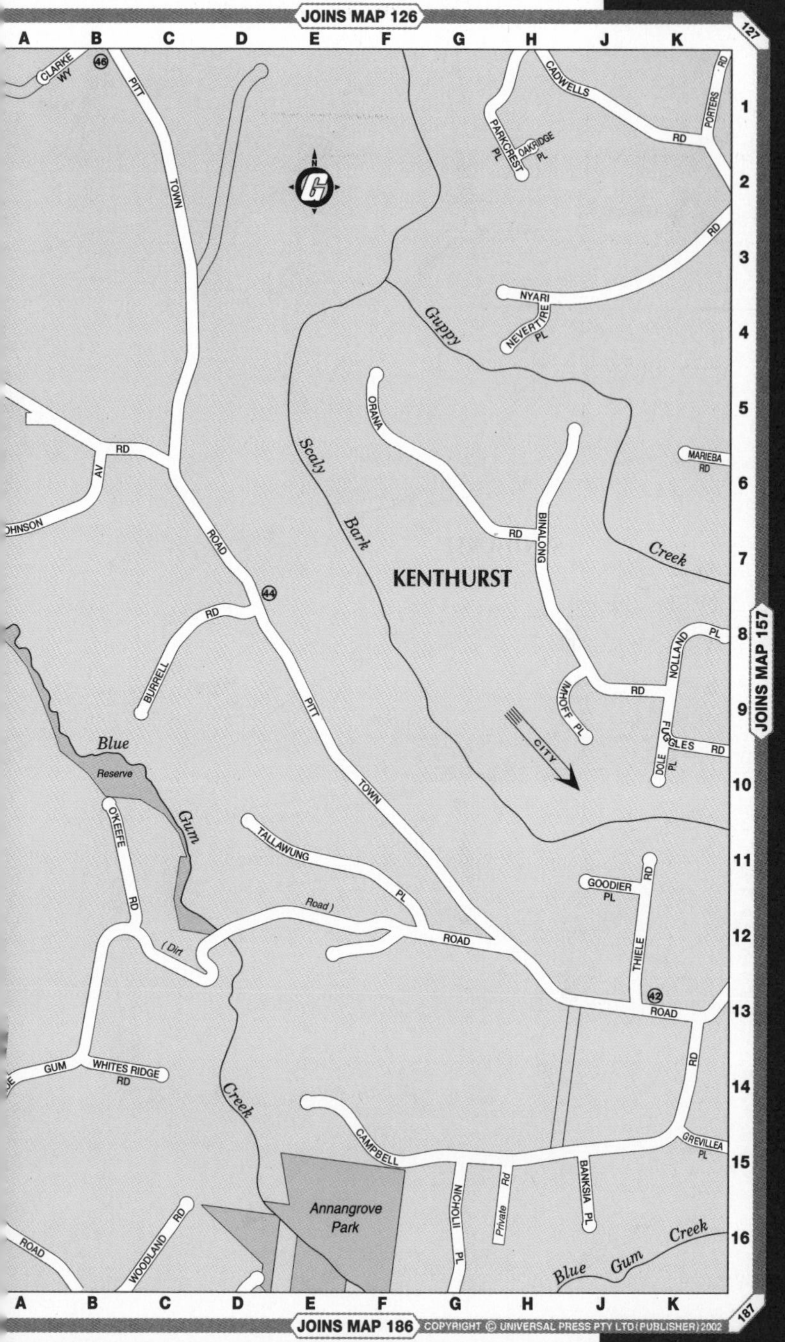
JOINS MAP 126
A B C D E F G H J K
127
1 2 3 4 5 6 7 8 9 10 11 12 13 14 15 16
CLARKE WY
PITT TOWN ROAD
CADWELLS RD
PORTERS RD
PARKCREST PL
OAKRIDGE PL
NYARI RD
NEVERTIRE PL
Guppy
ORANA RD
Scaly Bark
BINALONG RD
MARIEBA RD
AV
JOHNSON RD
Creek
KENTHURST
BURRELL RD
NOLLAND PL
IMHOFF PL
CITY
FUGGLES RD
DOLE PL
Blue Gum
Reserve
O'KEEFE RD
TALLAWUNG PL
(Dirt Road)
ROAD
GOODIER PL
THIELE RD
ROAD
RD
GUM
WHITES RIDGE RD
Creek
CAMPBELL
GREVILLEA PL
NICHOLII PL
Private Rd
BANKSIA PL
Annangrove Park
WOODLAND RD
ROAD
Blue Gum Creek
JOINS MAP 157
JOINS MAP 186
187

JOINS MAP 127

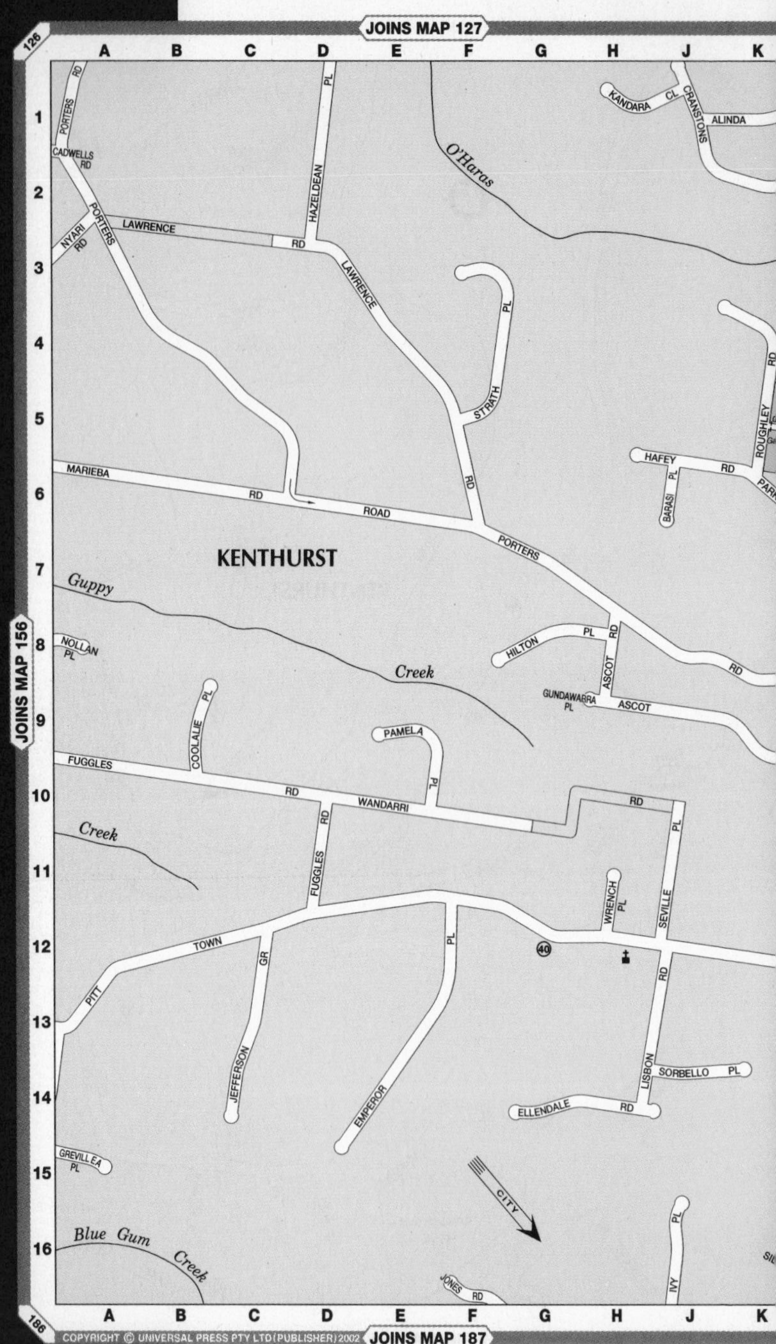

JOINS MAP 156

JOINS MAP 187

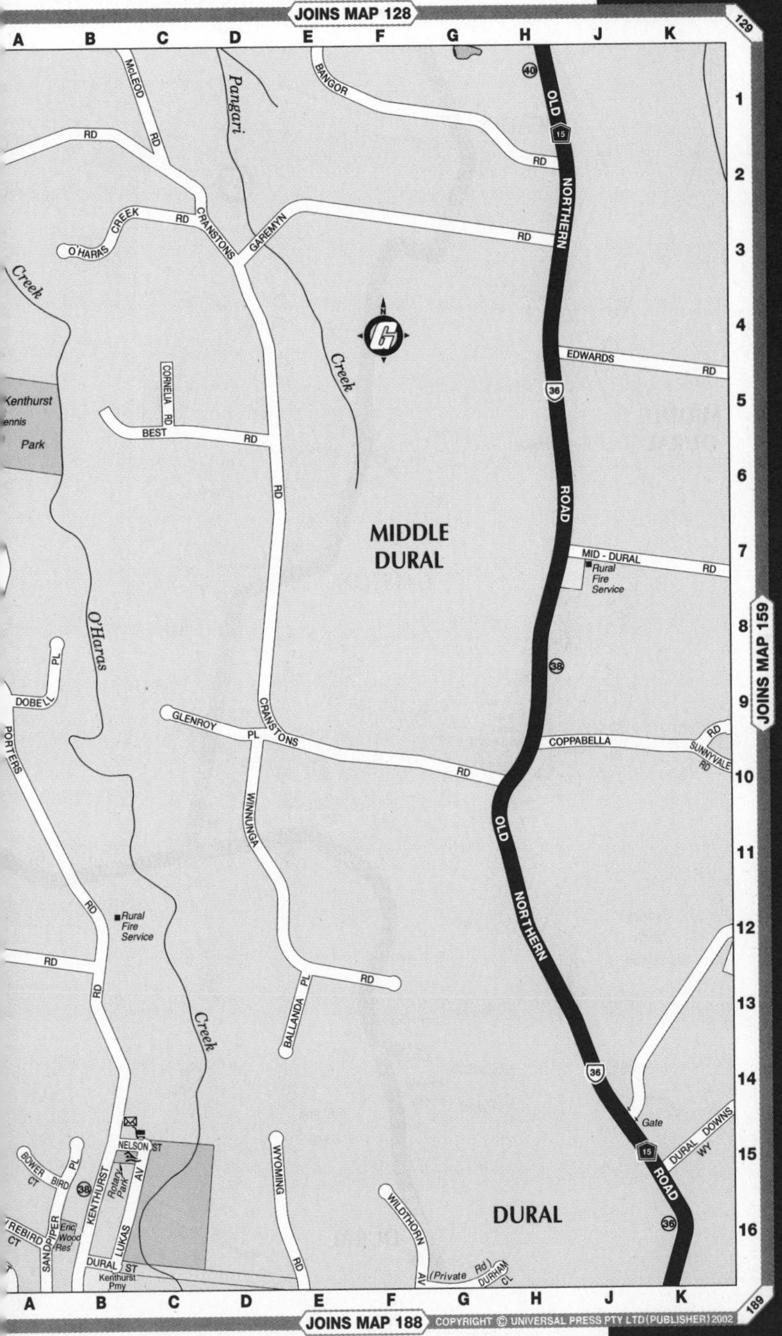
JOINS MAP 128
129
A B C D E F G H J K
1 2 3 4 5 6 7 8 9 10 11 12 13 14 15 16
McLEOD RD
Pangari
BANGOR RD
OLD NORTHERN ROAD
RD
O'HARAS CREEK RD
CRANSTONS
GAREMYN RD
Creek
Creek
EDWARDS RD
CORNELIA RD
Kenthurst
ennis
Park
BEST RD
RD
MIDDLE
DURAL
MID - DURAL RD
Rural
Fire
Service
O'Haras
DOBELL PL
GLENROY PL
CRANSTONS RD
COPPABELLA
RD
SUNNYVALE RD
PORTERS RD
WINNUNGA
OLD NORTHERN
Rural
Fire
Service
RD
RD
BALLANDA PL
Creek
Gate
DURAL DOWNS WY
ROAD
BOWER CT
BIRD PL
NELSON ST
Rotary
Park
KENTHURST
LUKAS AV
WYOMING RD
WILDTHORN AV
DURAL
REBIRD CT
SANDPIPER
Eric
Wood
Res
DURAL ST
Kenthurst
Pmy
(Private Rd)
DURHAM CL
JOINS MAP 159
189

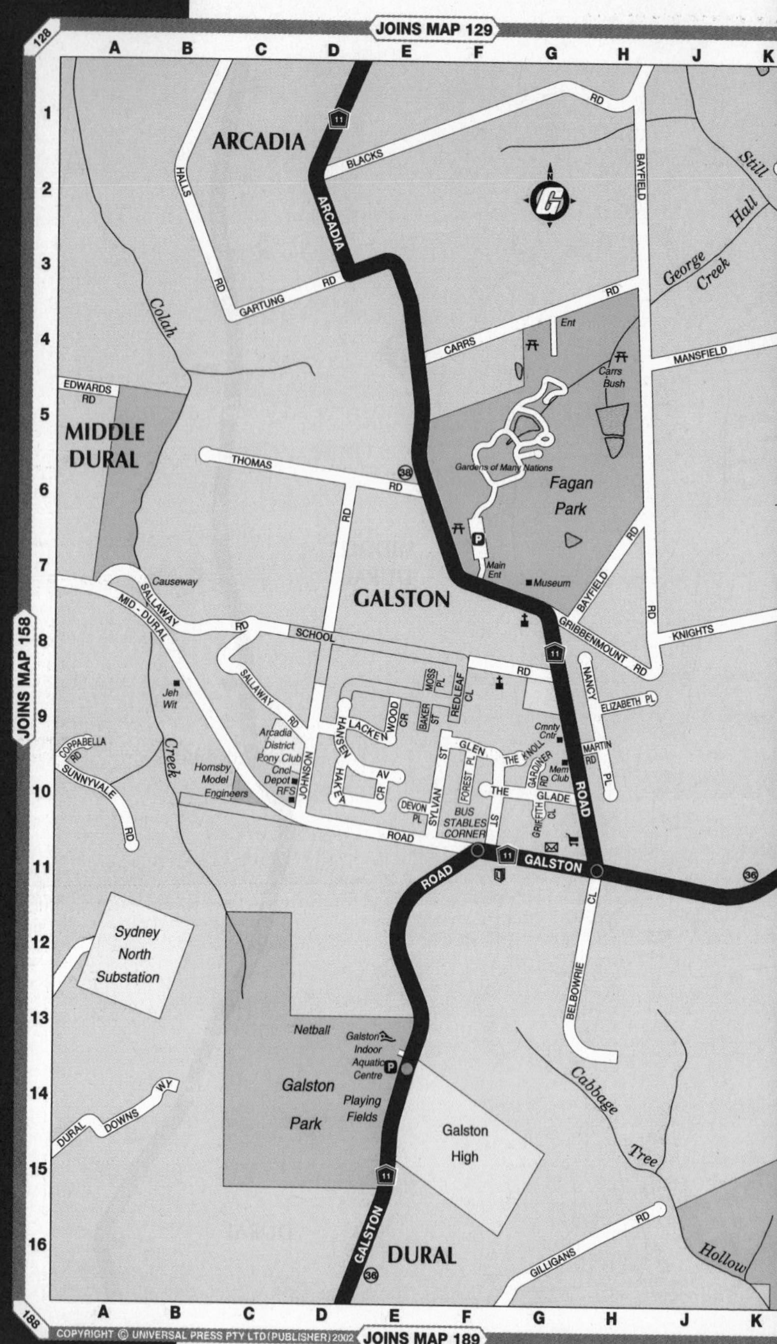
JOINS MAP 129
JOINS MAP 158
JOINS MAP 189
128
188
ARCADIA
MIDDLE DURAL
GALSTON
DURAL
BLACKS RD
HALLS RD
GARTUNG RD
ARCADIA
CARRS RD
BAYFIELD RD
MANSFIELD
Still
Hall
George Creek
Colah
EDWARDS RD
THOMAS RD
Gardens of Many Nations
Fagan Park
Carrs Bush
Ent
Main Ent
Museum
Causeway
SALLAWAY RD
MID - DURAL
SCHOOL RD
GRIBBENMOUNT RD
KNIGHTS
NANCY
ELIZABETH PL
MOSS PL
REDLEAF CL
BAKER ST
LACKEN
WOOD CR
HANSEN
HAKEA CR
AV
Jeh Wit
Arcadia District Pony Club
Cncl Depot
RFS
JOHNSON
Hornsby Model Engineers
COPPABELLA RD
SUNNYVALE RD
Creek
GLEN ST
SYLVAN
FOREST PL
DEVON PL
BUS STABLES CORNER
THE KNOLL
GARDINER RD
Cmnty Cntr
Mem Club
MARTIN RD
PL
THE GLADE
GRIFFITH CL
ROAD
GALSTON ROAD
BELBOWRIE CL
Sydney North Substation
Netball
Galston Indoor Aquatic Centre
Galston Park
Playing Fields
Galston High
Cabbage Tree
Hollow
DURAL DOWNS WY
GILLIGANS RD
GALSTON
11
36
38
A B C D E F G H J K
1 2 3 4 5 6 7 8 9 10 11 12 13 14 15 16

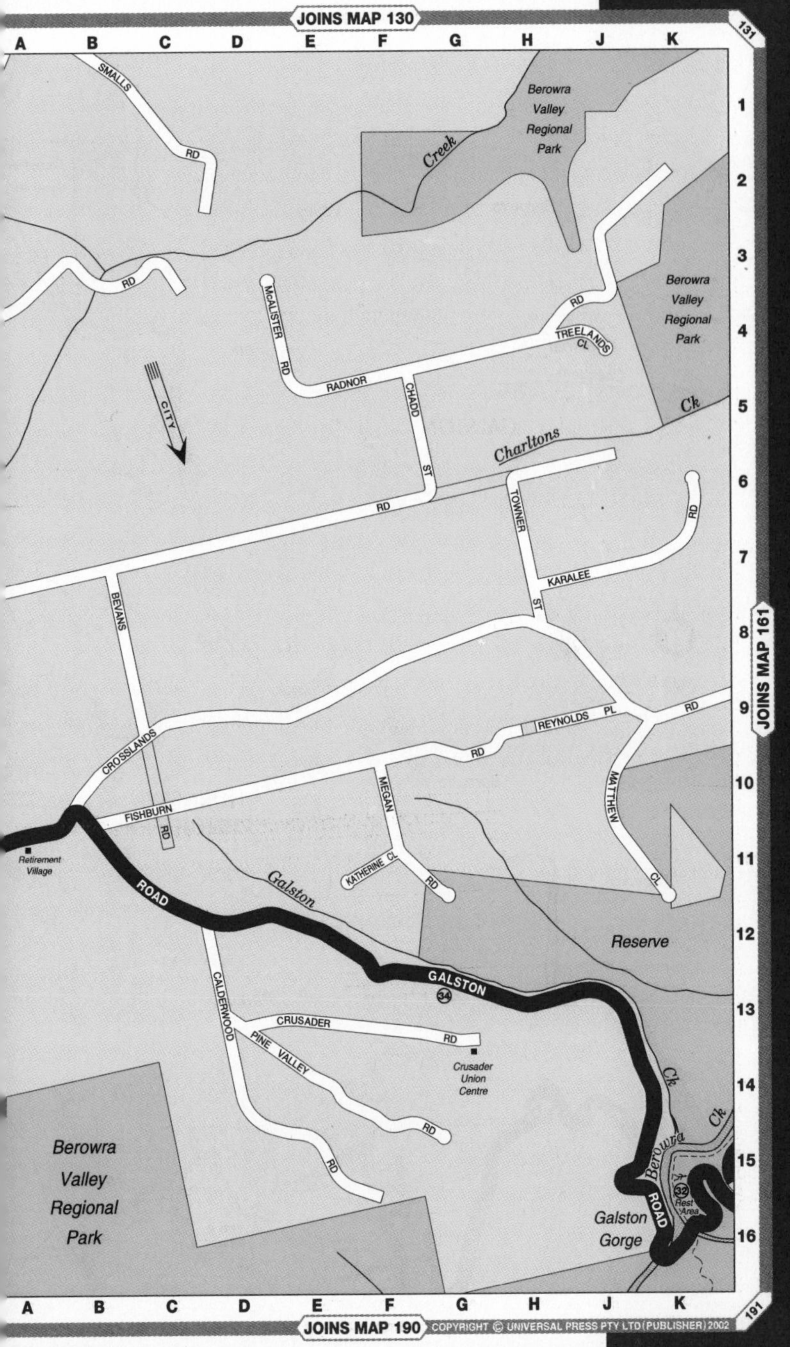
JOINS MAP 130
A B C D E F G H J K
131
1 2 3 4 5 6 7 8 9 10 11 12 13 14 15 16
SMALLS RD
Creek
Berowra Valley Regional Park
RD
McALISTER RD
RADNOR
CHADD ST
TREELANDS CL
Berowra Valley Regional Park
Ck
CITY
Charltons
RD
TOWNER ST
RD
KARALEE
BEVANS RD
JOINS MAP 161
REYNOLDS PL
RD
CROSSLANDS
RD
MEGAN
MATTHEW CL
FISHBURN
Retirement Village
KATHERINE CL
RD
Galston
ROAD
Reserve
GALSTON
34
CALDERWOOD
CRUSADER RD
PINE VALLEY RD
Crusader Union Centre
Ck
Ck
Berowra
RD
Berowra Valley Regional Park
ROAD
32
Rest Area
Galston Gorge
A B C D E F G H J K
191
JOINS MAP 190

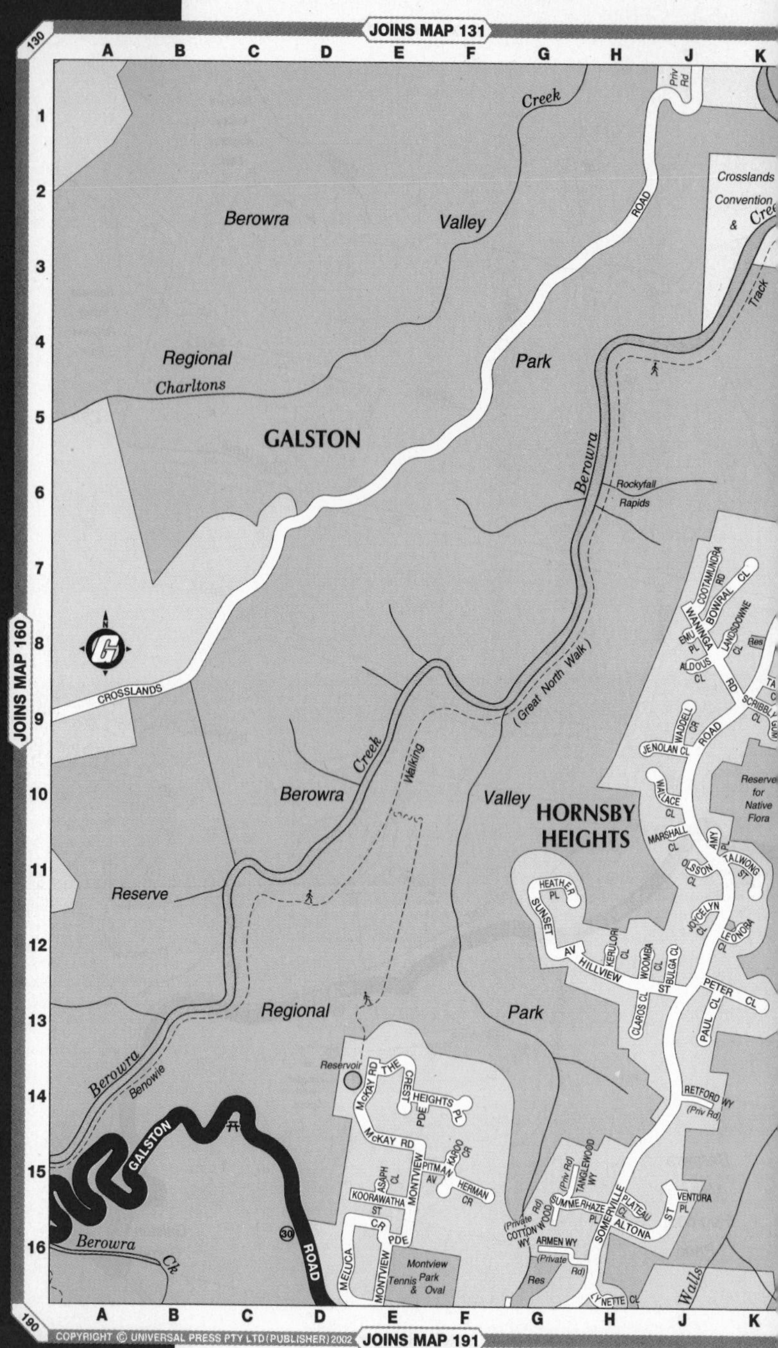
JOINS MAP 131
JOINS MAP 160
JOINS MAP 191
130
190
A B C D E F G H J K
1 2 3 4 5 6 7 8 9 10 11 12 13 14 15 16
Berowra
Valley
Regional
Park
Charltons
Creek
GALSTON
CROSSLANDS
ROAD
Crosslands
Convention
&
Track
Berowra
Rockyfall
Rapids
(Great North Walk)
Creek
Walking
Berowra
Valley
Reserve
Regional
Park
HORNSBY
HEIGHTS
Berowra
Benowie
GALSTON
ROAD
30
Berowra
Ck
Reservoir
McKAY RD
THE CREST
HEIGHTS PL
PDE
McKAY RD
MONTVIEW
PITMAN AV
KAROO CR
HERMAN CR
ASAPH CL
KOORAWATHA ST
CR
PDE
MELUCA
MONTVIEW
Montview
Tennis Park
& Oval
COOTAMUNDRA RD
BOWRAL CL
WANINGA
LANSDOWNE CL
EMU PL
ALDOUS CL
Res
RD
SCRIBBLY GUM CL
WADDELL CR
ROAD
JENOLAN CL
WALLACE CL
MARSHALL CL
AMY PL
Reserve
for
Native
Flora
OLSSON CL
TALWONG ST
HEATHER PL
SUNSET AV
KERULORI CL
WOOMBA CL
BULGA CL
JOYCELYN CL
LEONORA CL
HILLVIEW ST
CLAROS CL
PETER CL
PAUL CL
RETFORD WY
(Priv Rd)
TANGLEWOOD WY
(Priv Rd)
SUMMERHAZE PL
COTTONWOOD WY
(Private Rd)
SOMERVILLE
PLATEAU ST
ALTONA ST
VENTURA PL
ARMEN WY
(Private Rd)
Res
LYNETTE CL
Walls
Priv Rd

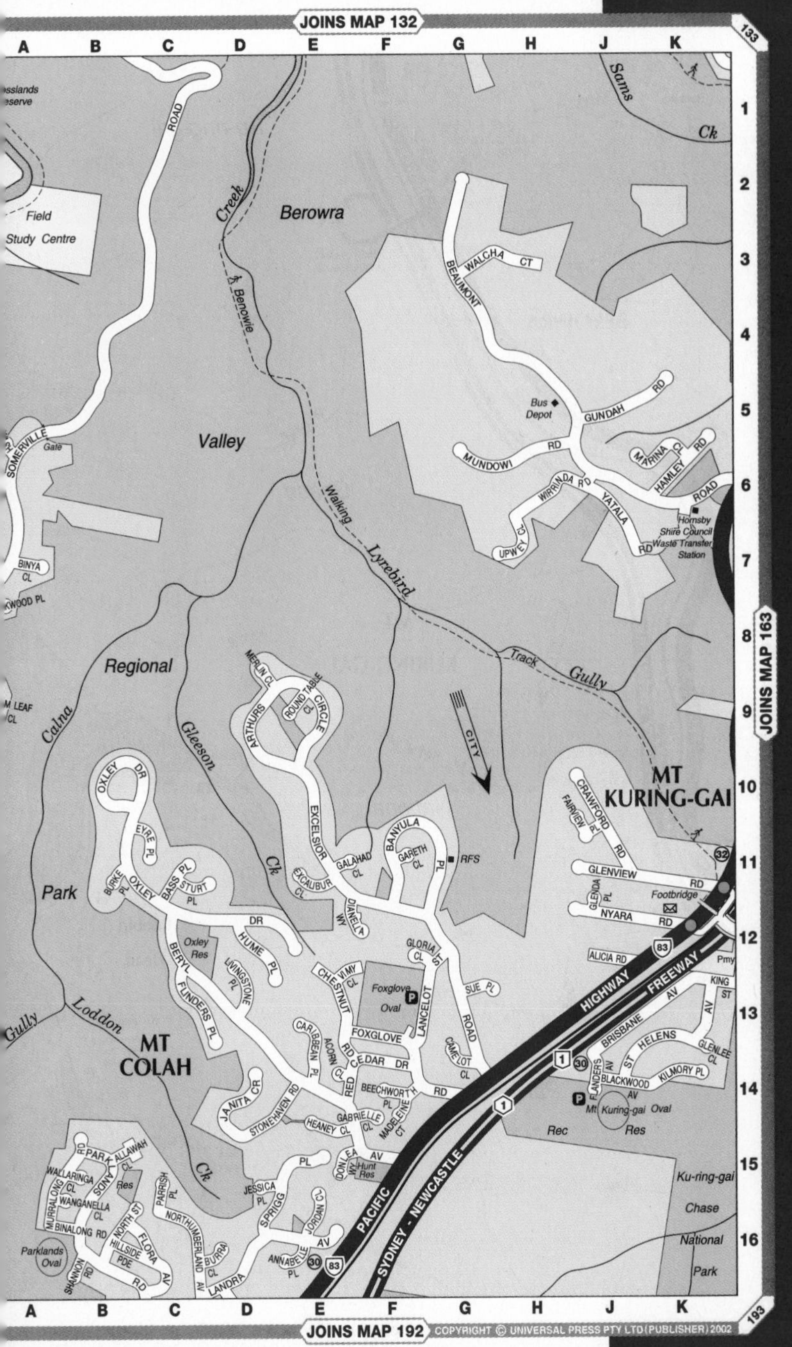
JOINS MAP 132
JOINS MAP 163
JOINS MAP 192
133
193
Field Study Centre
Berowra
Valley
Regional
Park
Benowie
Walking
Lyrebird
Track
Gully
Creek
Sams Ck
Calna
Gleeson
Ck
Loddon
Gully
MT COLAH
MT KURING-GAI
CITY
Bus Depot
Hornsby Shire Council Waste Transfer Station
RFS
Footbridge
Foxglove Oval
Oxley Res
Hunt Res
Mt Kuring-gai Oval
Rec Res
Parklands Oval
Ku-ring-gai Chase National Park
PACIFIC HIGHWAY
SYDNEY - NEWCASTLE FREEWAY
SOMERVILLE
Gate
BINYA CL
BEAUMONT
WALCHA CT
GUNDAH RD
MUNDOWI RD
WIRRINDA RD
YATALA RD
UPWEY CL
MARINA CL
HAMLEY RD
ROAD
CRAWFORD RD
FAIRVIEW PL
GLENVIEW RD
GLENDA PL
NYARA RD
ALICIA RD
KING ST
BRISBANE AV
ST HELENS
GLENLEE CL
KILMORY PL
BLACKWOOD AV
FLANDERS AV
MERLIN CL
ROUND TABLE CL
CIRCLE
ARTHURS
EXCELSIOR
GALAHAD CL
EXCALIBUR CL
DIANELLA WY
BANYULA PL
GARETH CL
OXLEY DR
EYRE PL
BURKE PL
BASS PL
STURT PL
HUME PL
BERYL
LIVINGSTONE PL
FLINDERS PL
CHESTNUT
VIMY
GLORIA CL
LANCELOT ST
SUE PL
ROAD
FOXGLOVE
CARIBBEAN PL
ACORN CL
RED CEDAR DR
BEECHWORTH RD
CAMELOT CL
MADELEINE CT
GABRIELLE
HEANEY CL
JANITA CR
STONEHAVEN RD
DONLEA WY
AV
PL
JESSICA PL
SPRIGG
JORDAN CL
ANNABELLE PL
PARKLANDS
ALLAWAH
WALLARINGA
MURRALONG CL
WANGANELLA CL
BINALONG RD
NORTH ST
HILLSIDE PDE
FLORA AV
SHANNON RD
PARRISH PL
NORTHUMBERLAND AV
BURRA CL
LANDRA
LEAF CL
WOOD PL
Pmy
1
30
32
83

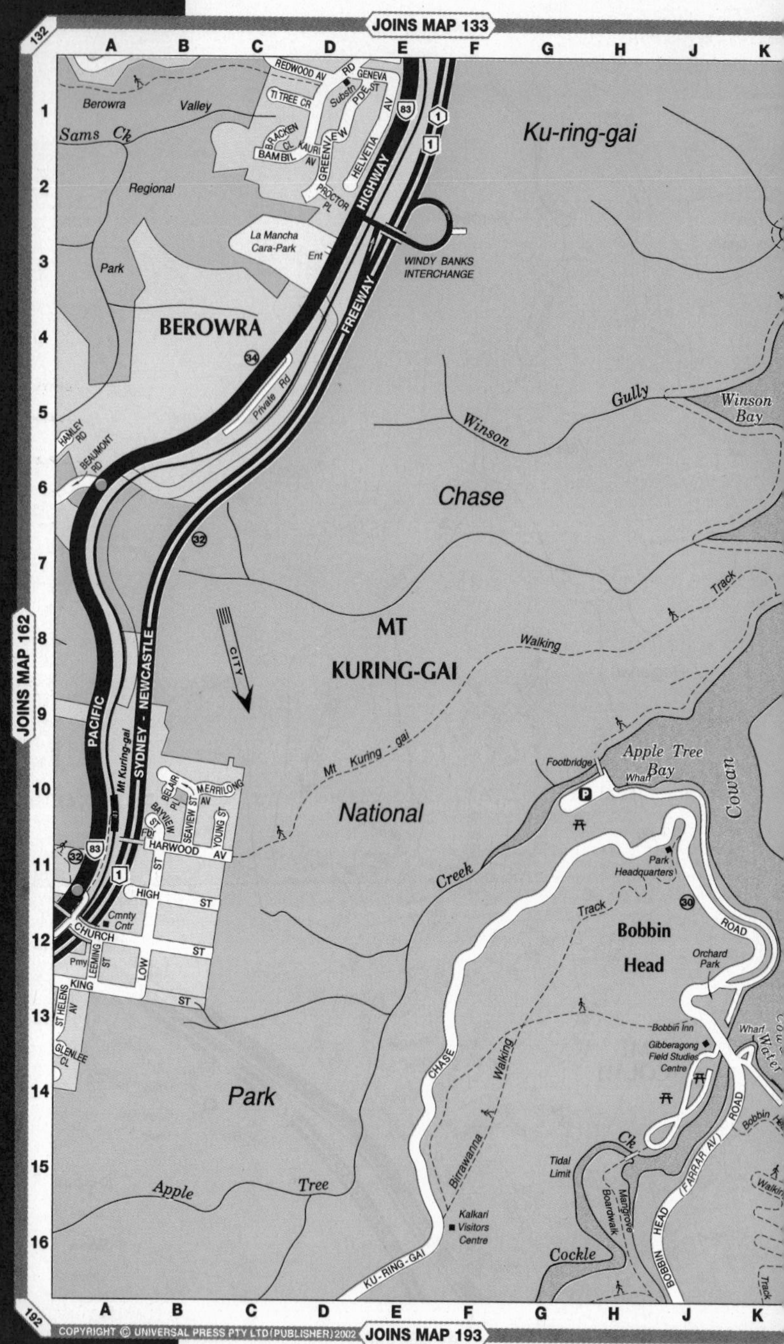
JOINS MAP 133
132
A B C D E F G H J K
1 2 3 4 5 6 7 8 9 10 11 12 13 14 15 16
Berowra Valley Regional Park
Sams Ck
REDWOOD AV
RD
GENEVA
PDE ST
TI TREE CR
Subsn
BRACKEN CL
KAURI
BAMBIL AV
GREENVIEW
HELVETIA AV
PROCTOR PL
La Mancha Cara-Park
Ent
HIGHWAY
FREEWAY
WINDY BANKS INTERCHANGE
83
1
Ku-ring-gai
BEROWRA
34
Private Rd
Winson Gully
Winson Bay
HAMLEY RD
BEAUMONT RD
Chase
32
Track
Walking
MT KURING-GAI
CITY
PACIFIC
SYDNEY - NEWCASTLE
Mt Kuring-gai
JOINS MAP 162
Mt Kuring - gai
Footbridge
Apple Tree Bay
Wharf
Cowan
BELAIR PL
MERRILONG AV
BAYVIEW ST
SEAVIEW ST
YOUNG ST
National
HARWOOD AV
Creek
Park Headquarters
30
HIGH ST
Cmnty Cntr
Track
Bobbin Head
ROAD
CHURCH ST
Orchard Park
LEEMING ST
LOW
KING ST
ST HELENS AV
Bobbin Inn
Wharf
Water
Gibberagong Field Studies Centre
GLENLEE CL
CHASE
Walking
Park
Birrawanna
Ck
ROAD
(FARRAR AV)
Tidal Limit
Boardwalk
Mangrove
Apple Tree
Kalkari Visitors Centre
HEAD
BOBBIN
Cockle
KU-RING-GAI
Track
192
JOINS MAP 193

JOINS MAP 134

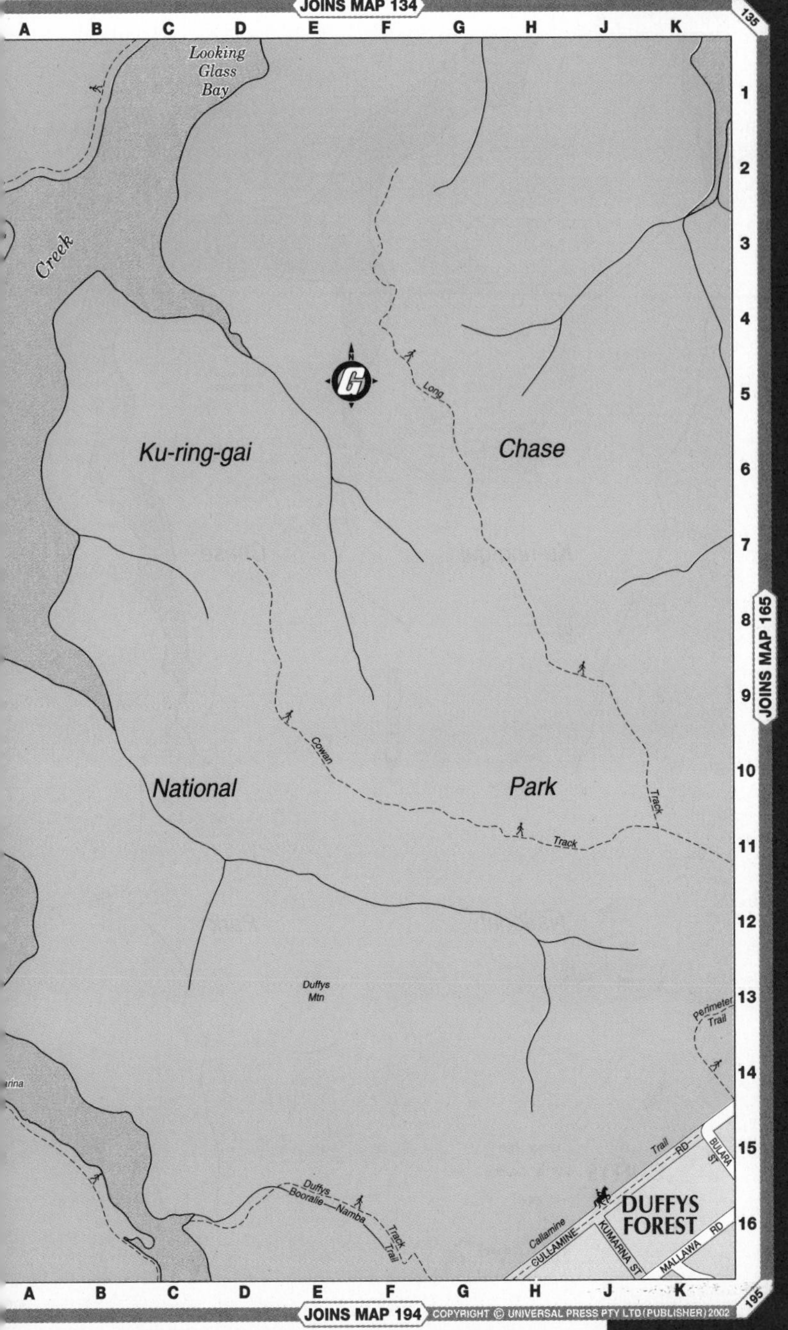

JOINS MAP 165

JOINS MAP 194

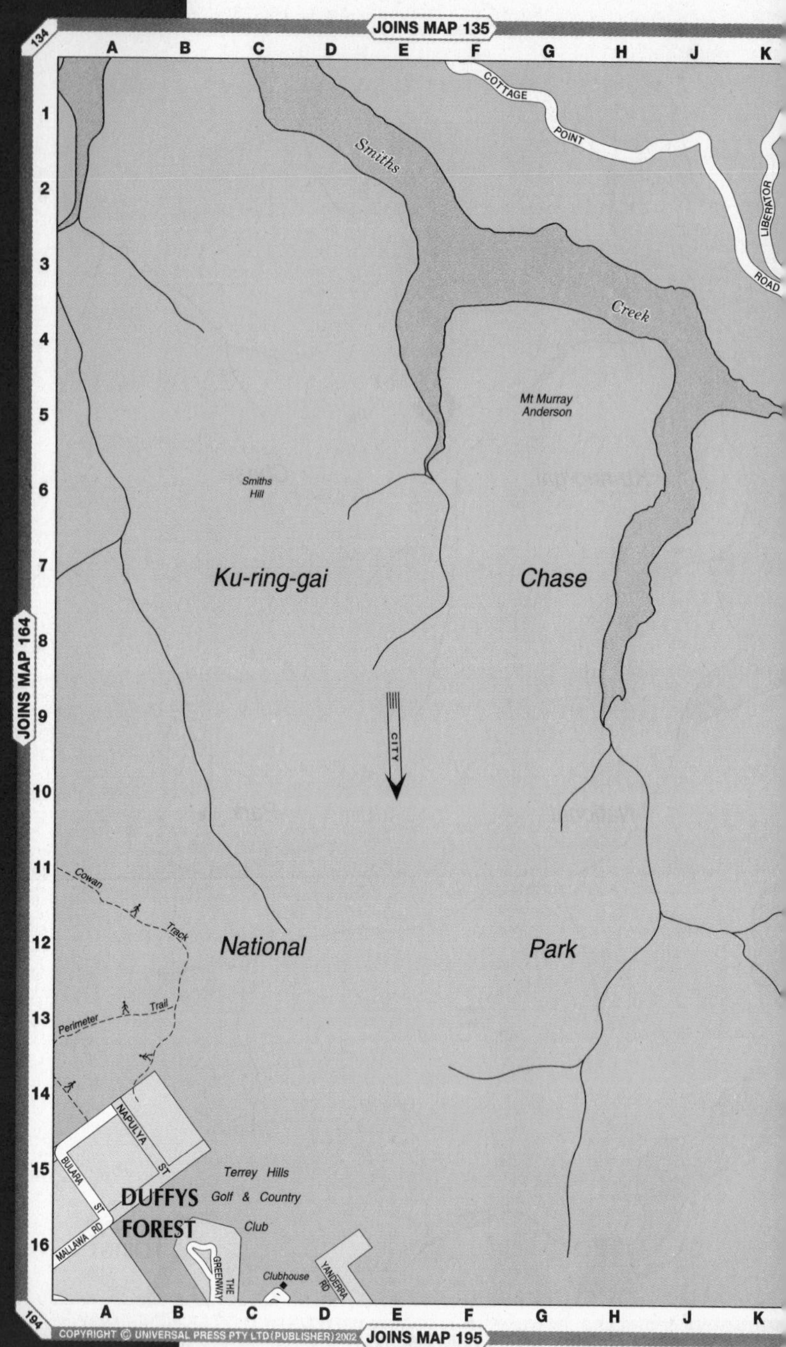

JOINS MAP 135
134
A
B
C
D
E
F
G
H
J
K
1
2
3
4
5
6
7
8
9
10
11
12
13
14
15
16
JOINS MAP 164
COTTAGE
POINT
ROAD
LIBERATOR
Smiths
Creek
Mt Murray
Anderson
Smiths
Hill
Ku-ring-gai
Chase
National
Park
CITY
Cowan
Track
Perimeter
Trail
NAPULYA
ST
BULARA
ST
MALLAWA RD
DUFFYS
FOREST
Terrey Hills
Golf & Country
Club
THE
GREENWAY
Clubhouse
YANDERRA
RD
194
JOINS MAP 195

JOINS MAP 136

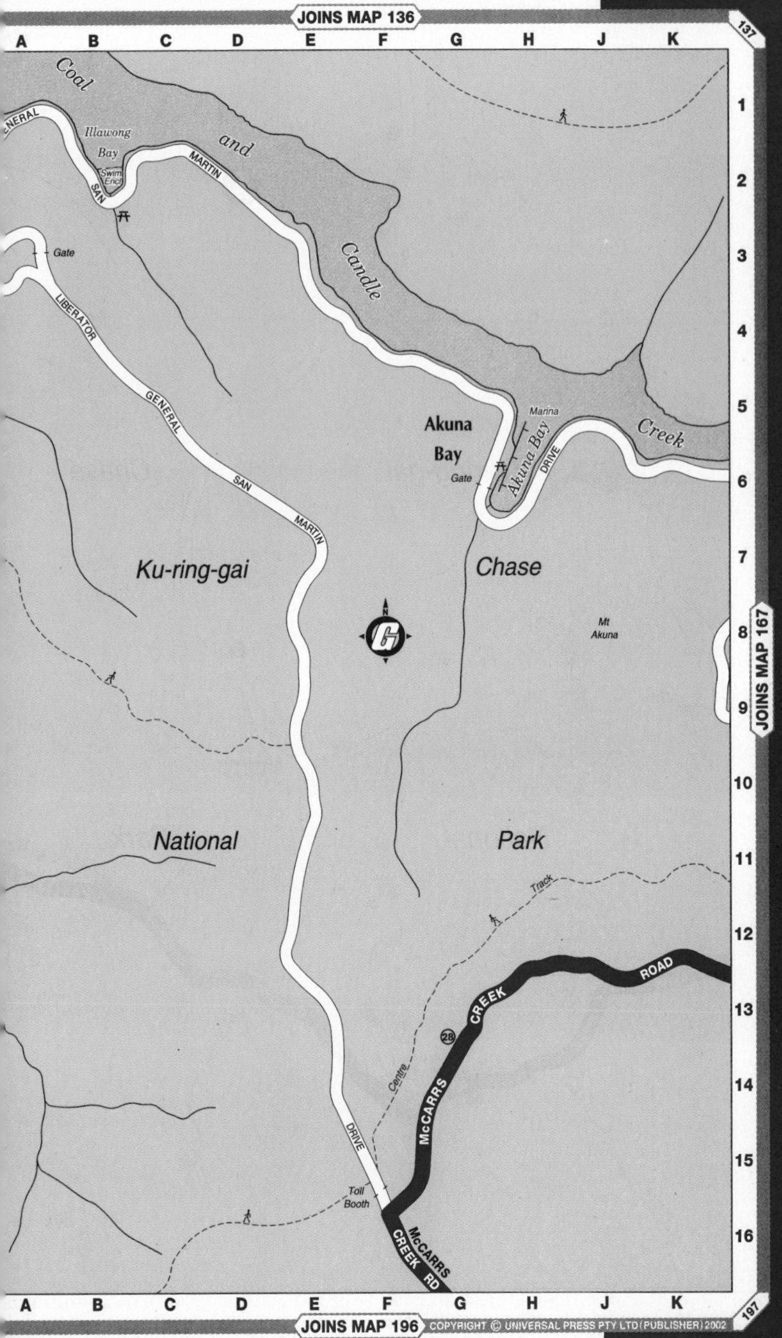

JOINS MAP 167

JOINS MAP 196

JOINS MAP 137

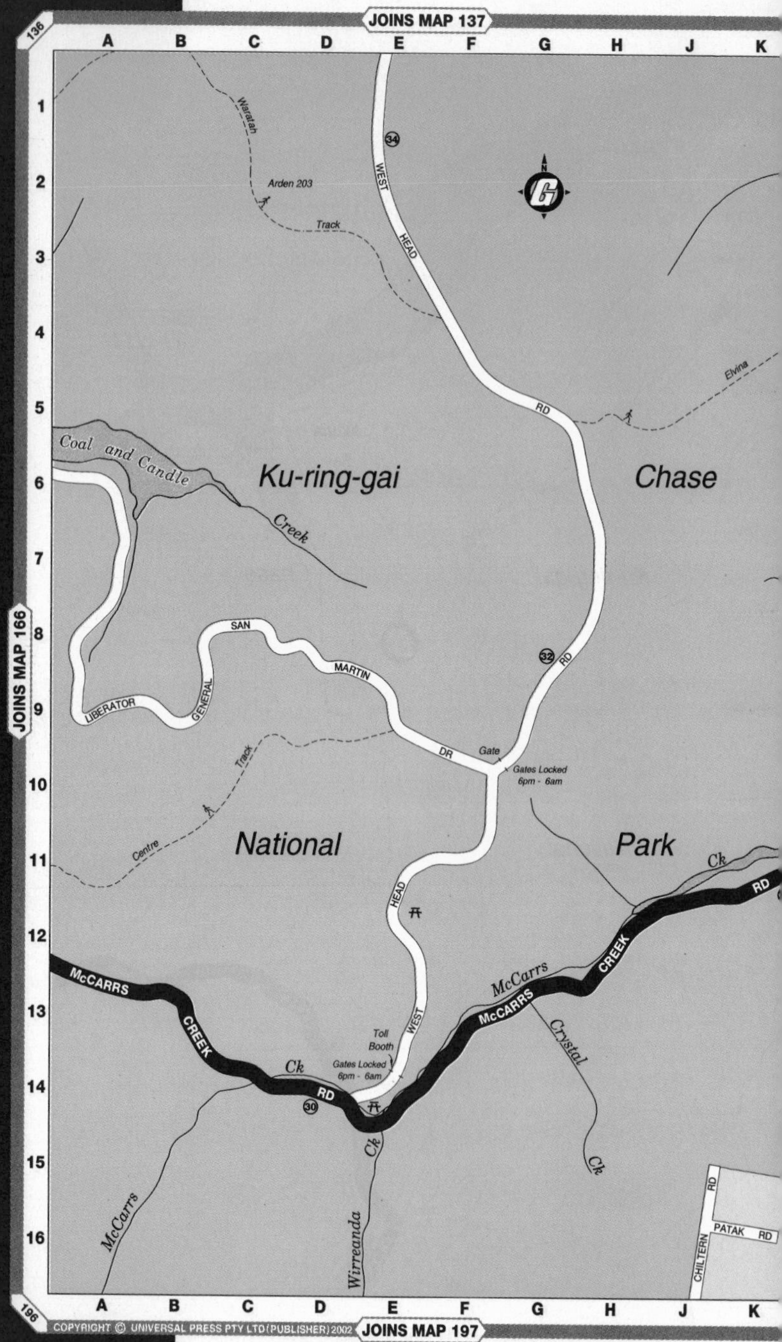

JOINS MAP 166

JOINS MAP 197

JOINS MAP 138

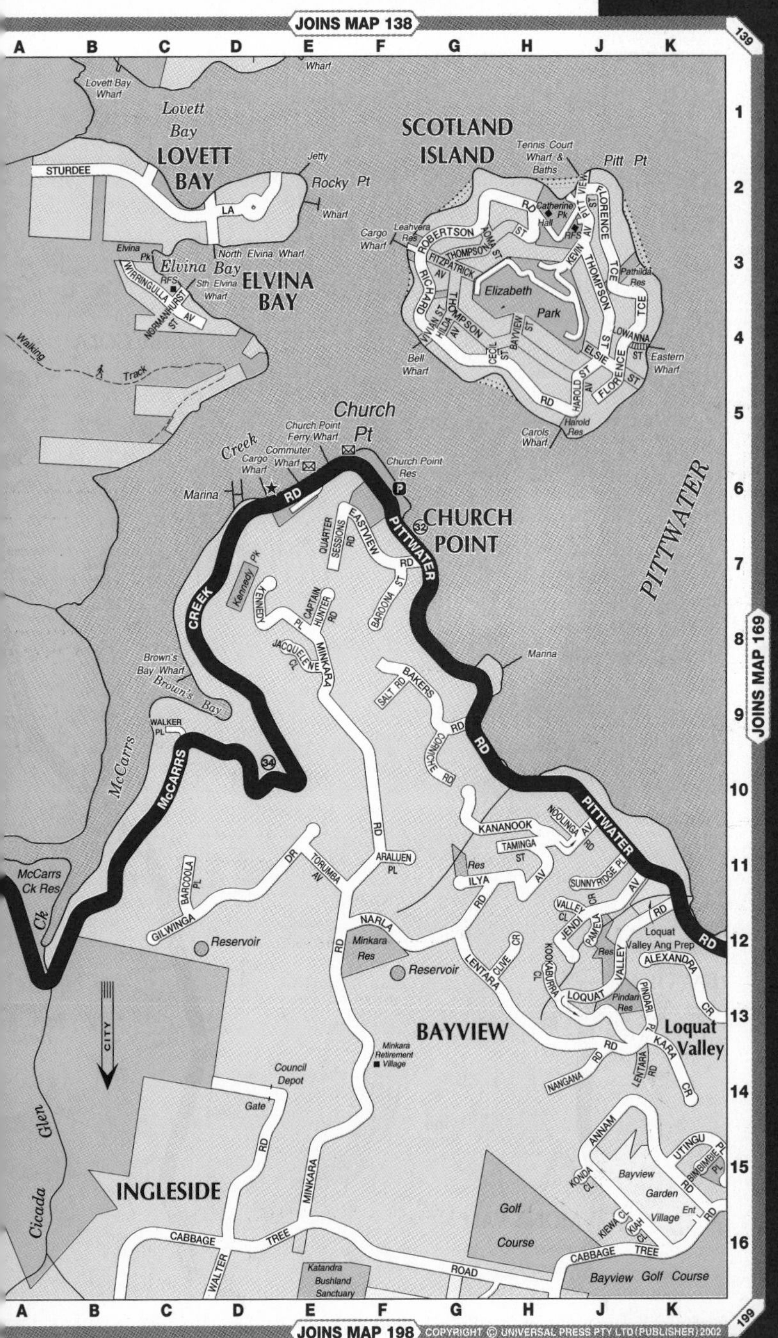

139

JOINS MAP 169

JOINS MAP 198

199

JOINS MAP 139

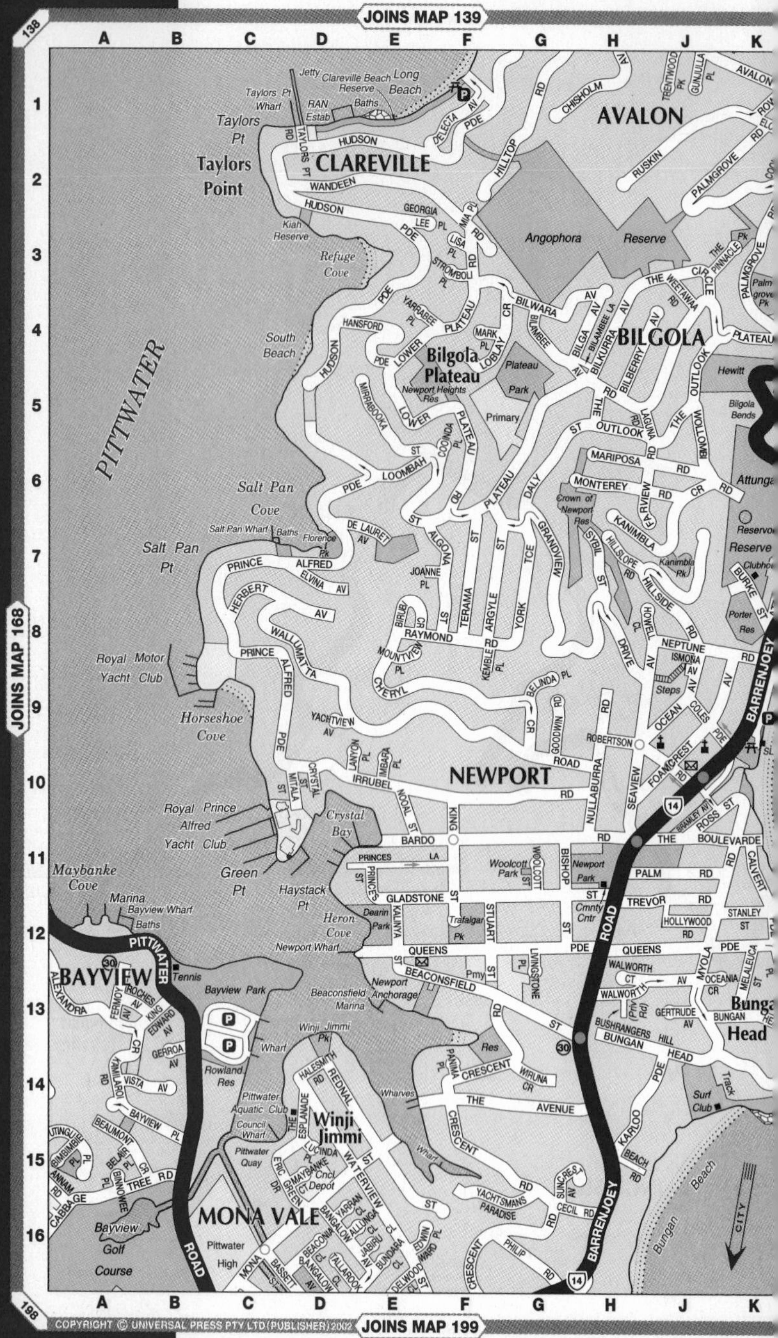

JOINS MAP 168

JOINS MAP 199

JOINS MAP 140

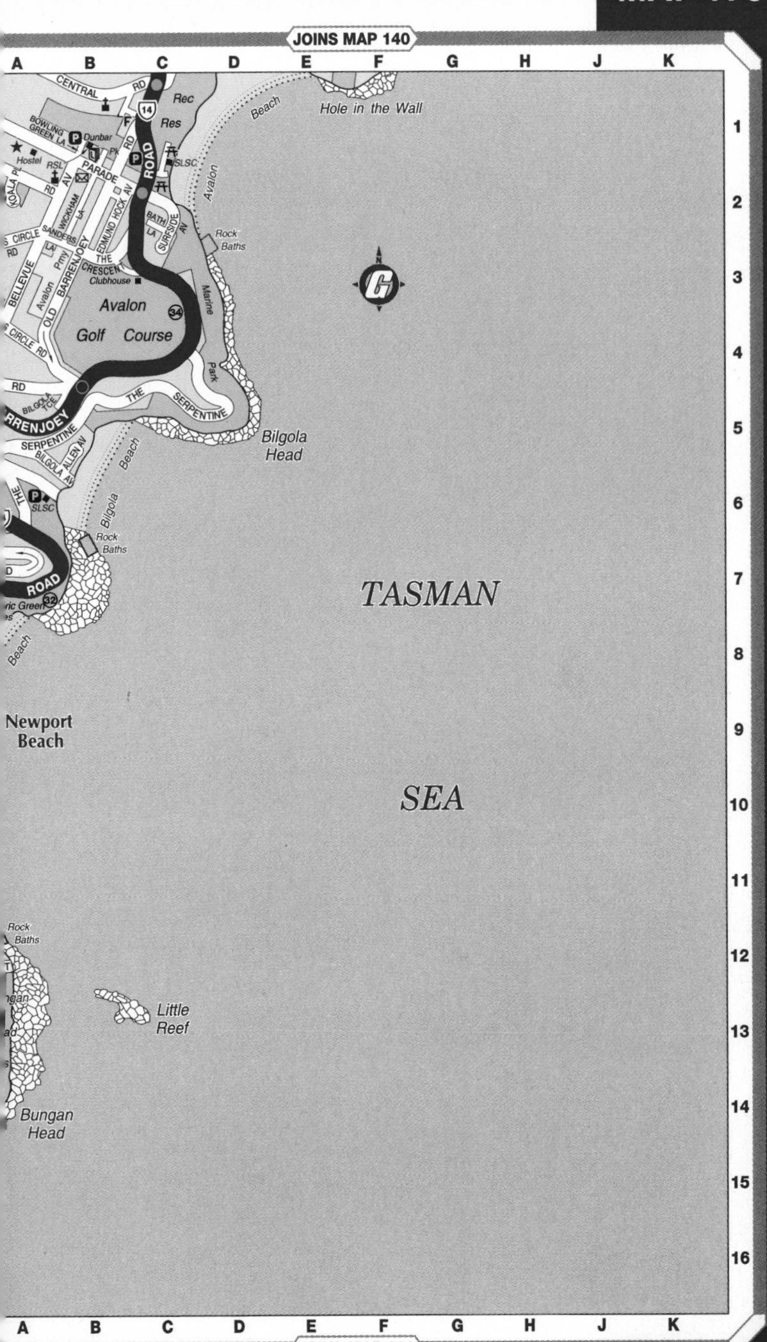

JOINS MAP 200

JOINS MAP 201

LIMIT OF MAPS

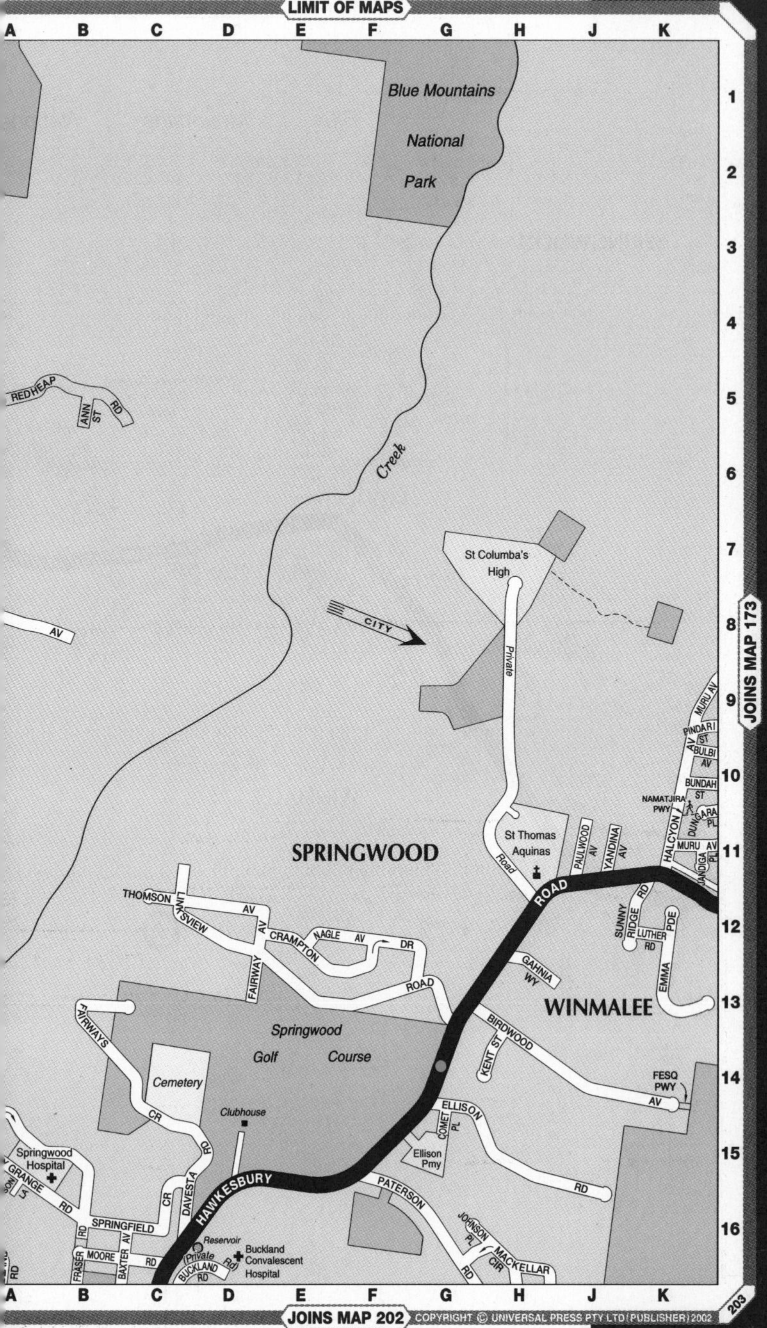

JOINS MAP 173

JOINS MAP 202

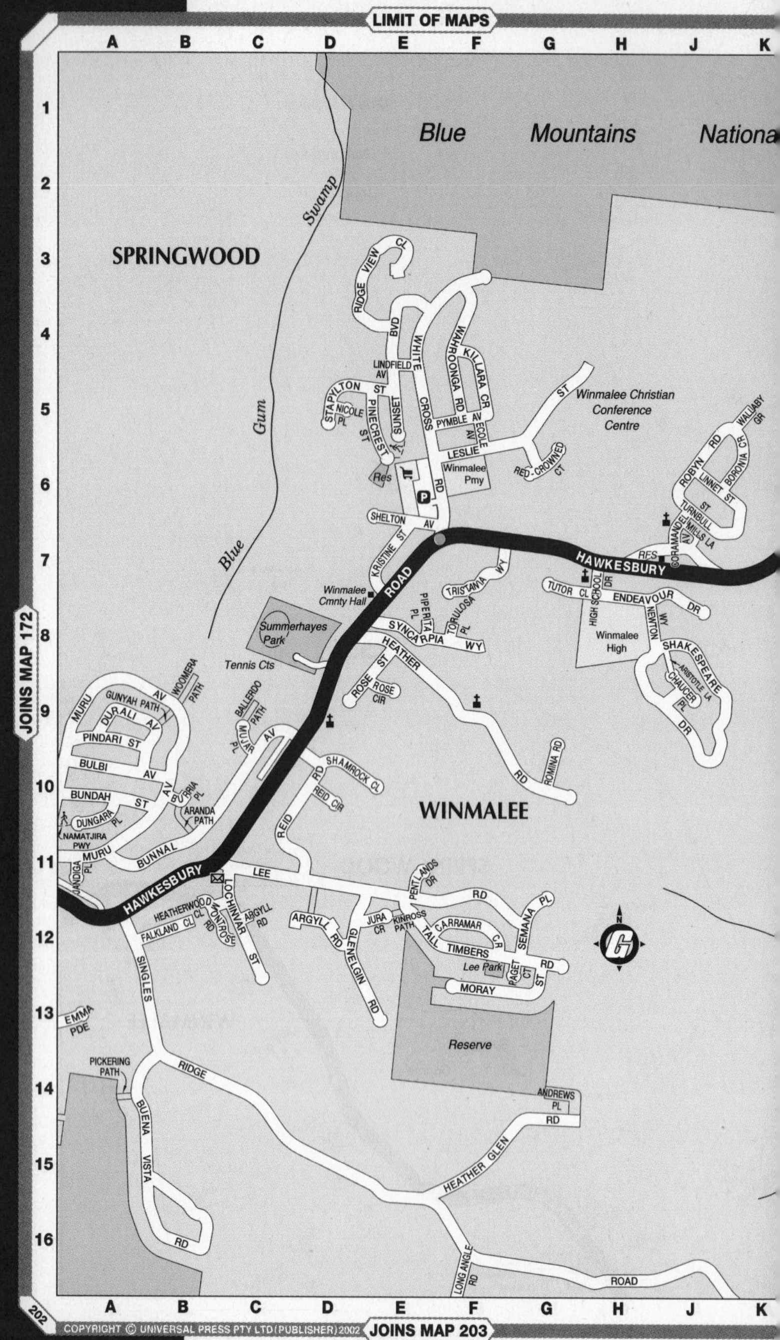

JOINS MAP 203

LIMIT OF MAPS

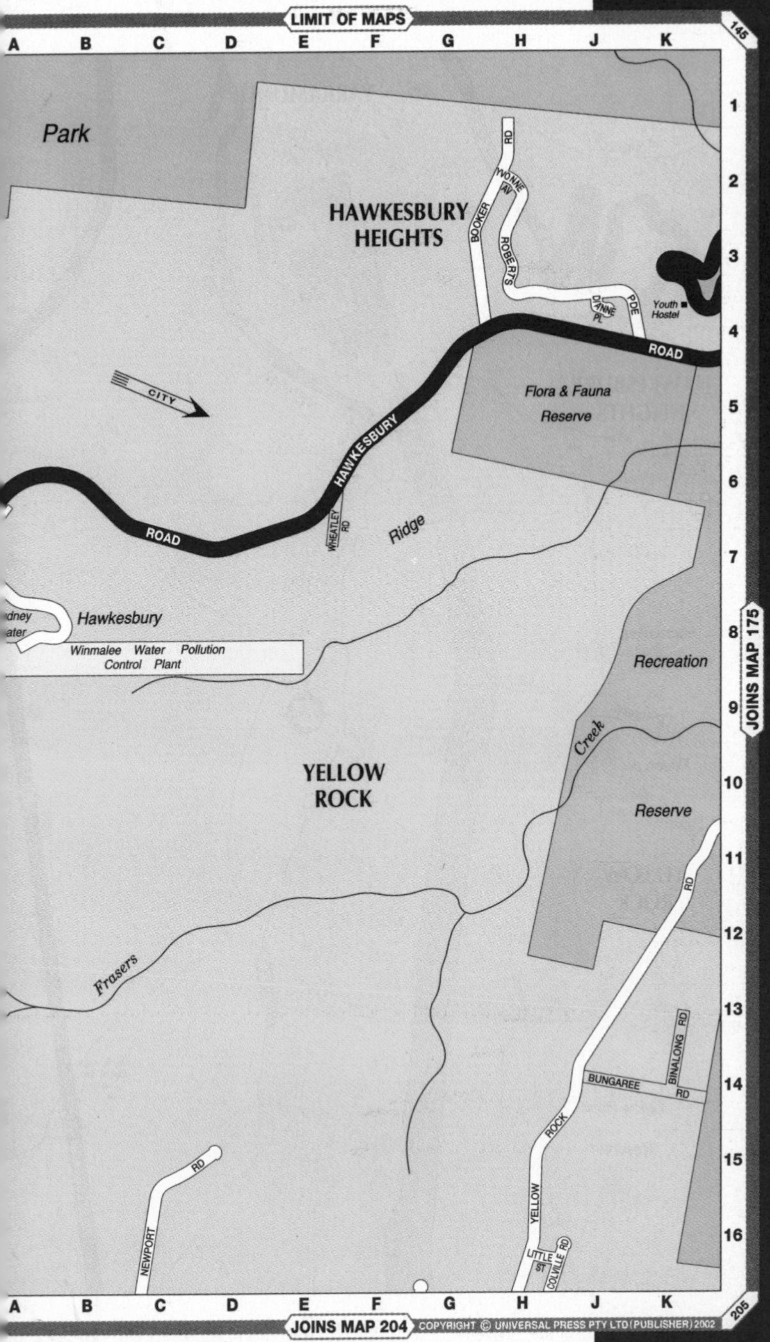

JOINS MAP 175

JOINS MAP 204

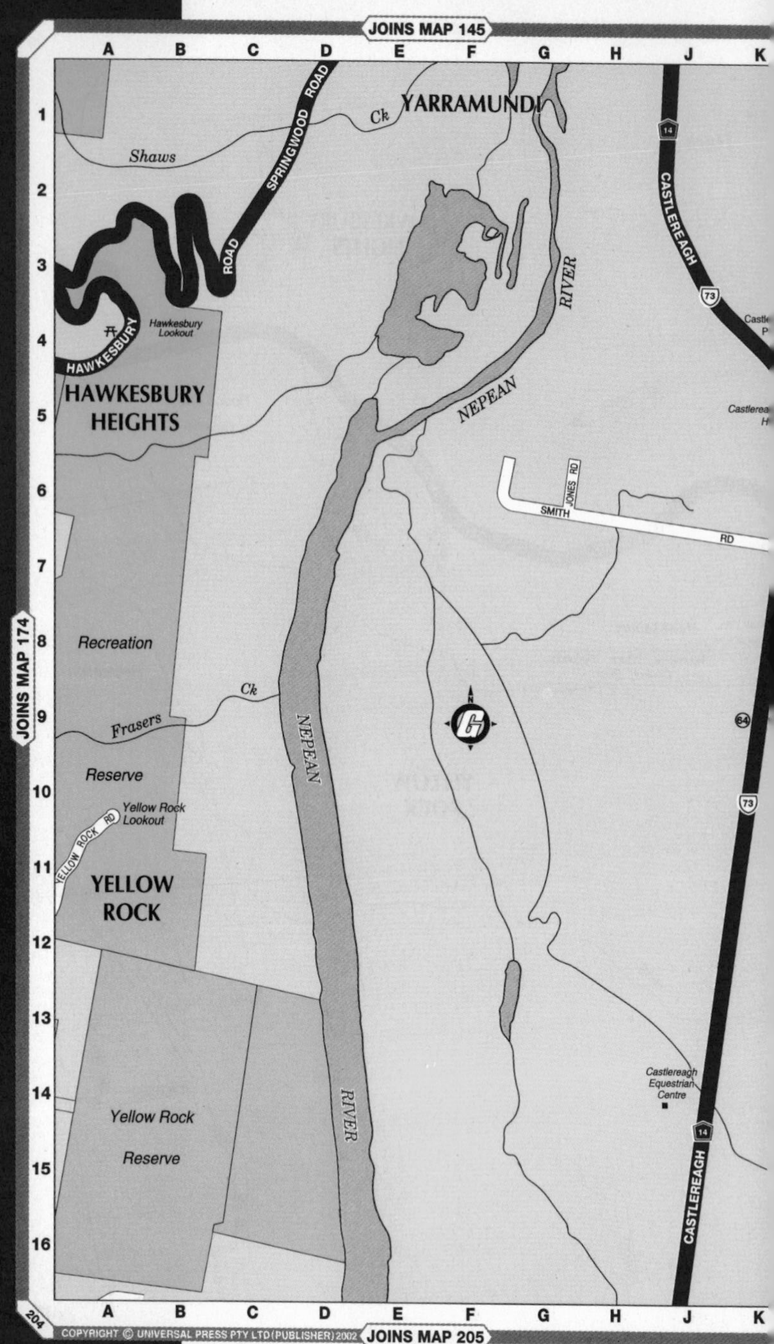
JOINS MAP 145
A B C D E F G H J K
1 2 3 4 5 6 7 8 9 10 11 12 13 14 15 16
YARRAMUNDI
Ck
Shaws
SPRINGWOOD ROAD
ROAD
HAWKESBURY
Hawkesbury Lookout
HAWKESBURY HEIGHTS
RIVER
NEPEAN
CASTLEREAGH
14
73
JONES RD
SMITH
RD
Recreation
Ck
Frasers
Reserve
NEPEAN
Yellow Rock Lookout
YELLOW ROCK RD
YELLOW ROCK
64
Yellow Rock
Reserve
RIVER
Castlereagh Equestrian Centre
CASTLEREAGH
JOINS MAP 174
JOINS MAP 205
204

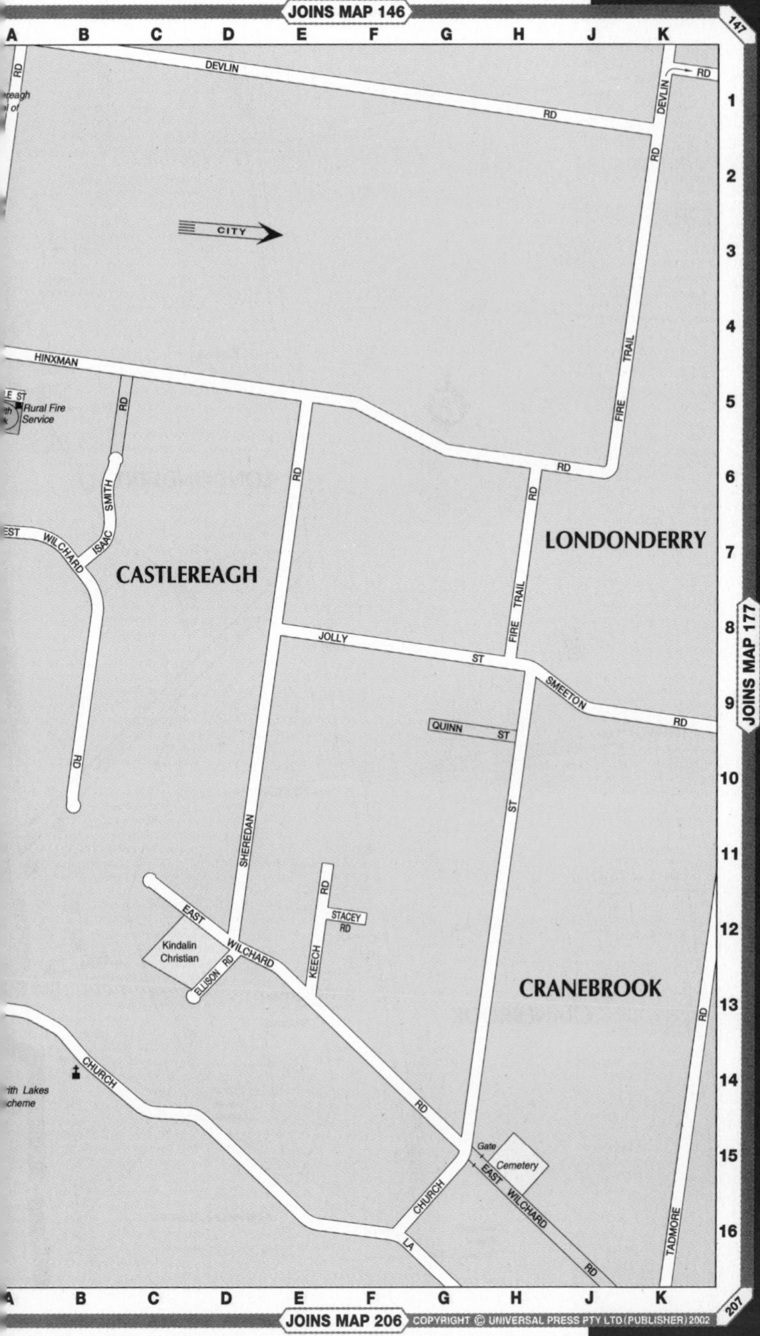
JOINS MAP 146
A
B
C
D
E
F
G
H
J
K
147
1
2
3
4
5
6
7
8
9
10
11
12
13
14
15
16
DEVLIN
RD
DEVLIN
RD
RD
CITY
HINXMAN
RD
FIRE
TRAIL
RD
Rural Fire
Service
RD
SMITH
ISAAC
WILCHARD
RD
CASTLEREAGH
LONDONDERRY
RD
FIRE
TRAIL
JOLLY
ST
SMEETON
RD
QUINN
ST
JOINS MAP 177
RD
SHEREDAN
ST
RD
STACEY
RD
KEECH
EAST
WILCHARD
RD
Kindalin
Christian
ELLISON
RD
CRANEBROOK
RD
CHURCH
RD
Gate
Cemetery
EAST
WILCHARD
RD
CHURCH
LA
TADMORE
207
JOINS MAP 206

MAP 177

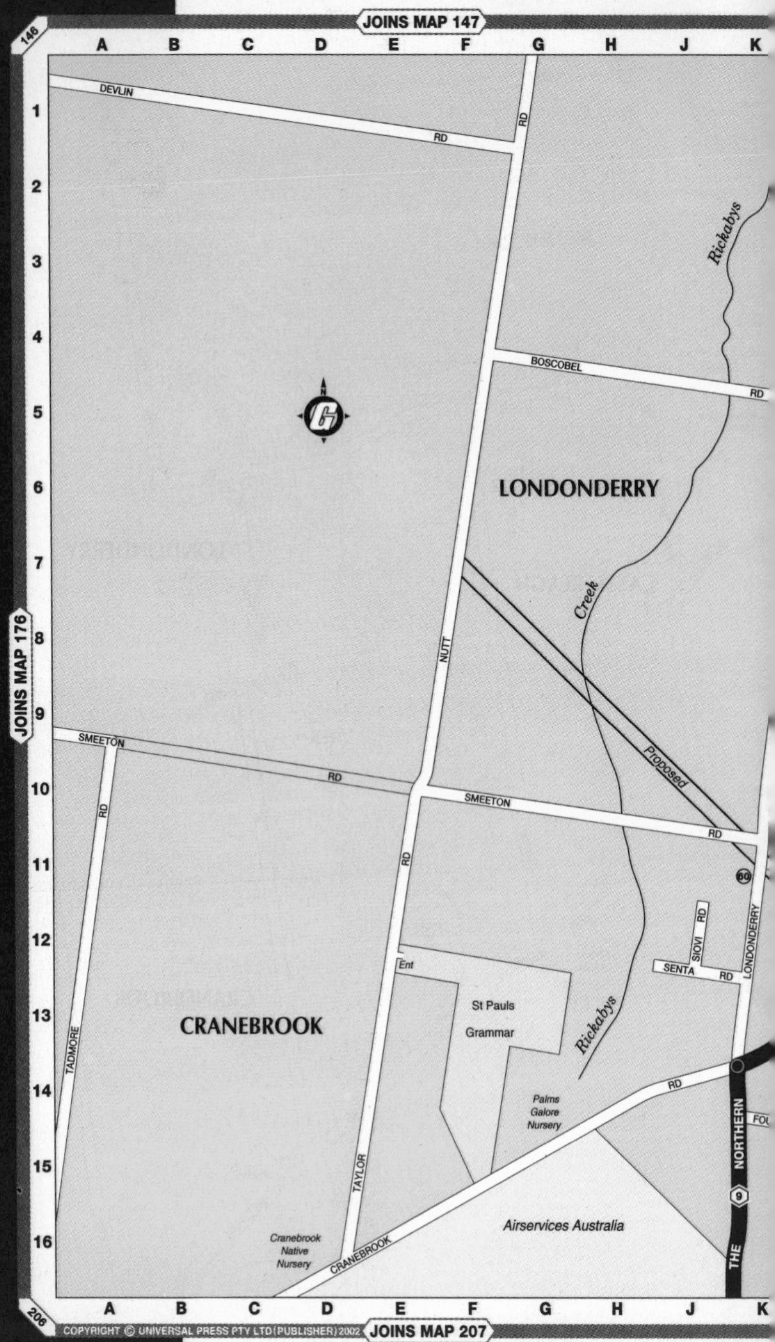

JOINS MAP 147
146
A B C D E F G H J K
1 2 3 4 5 6 7 8 9 10 11 12 13 14 15 16
JOINS MAP 176
DEVLIN
RD
RD
Rickabys
BOSCOBEL
RD
LONDONDERRY
Creek
NUTT
Proposed
SMEETON
RD
SMEETON
RD
RD
RD
60
RD
SIOVI
SENTA
RD
LONDONDERRY
Ent
St Pauls
Grammar
Rickabys
CRANEBROOK
TADMORE
RD
Palms
Galore
Nursery
NORTHERN
9
TAYLOR
Airservices Australia
Cranebrook
Native
Nursery
CRANEBROOK
THE
206
JOINS MAP 207

JOINS MAP 148

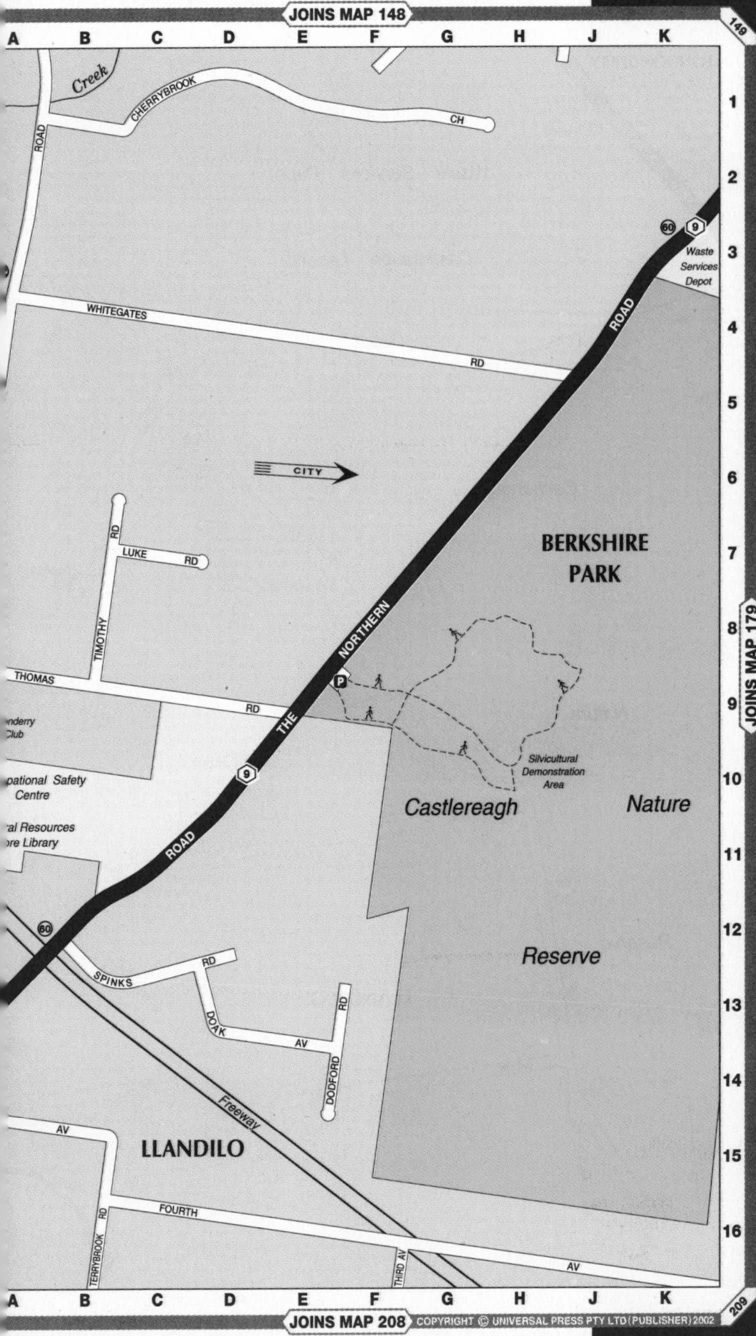

JOINS MAP 208

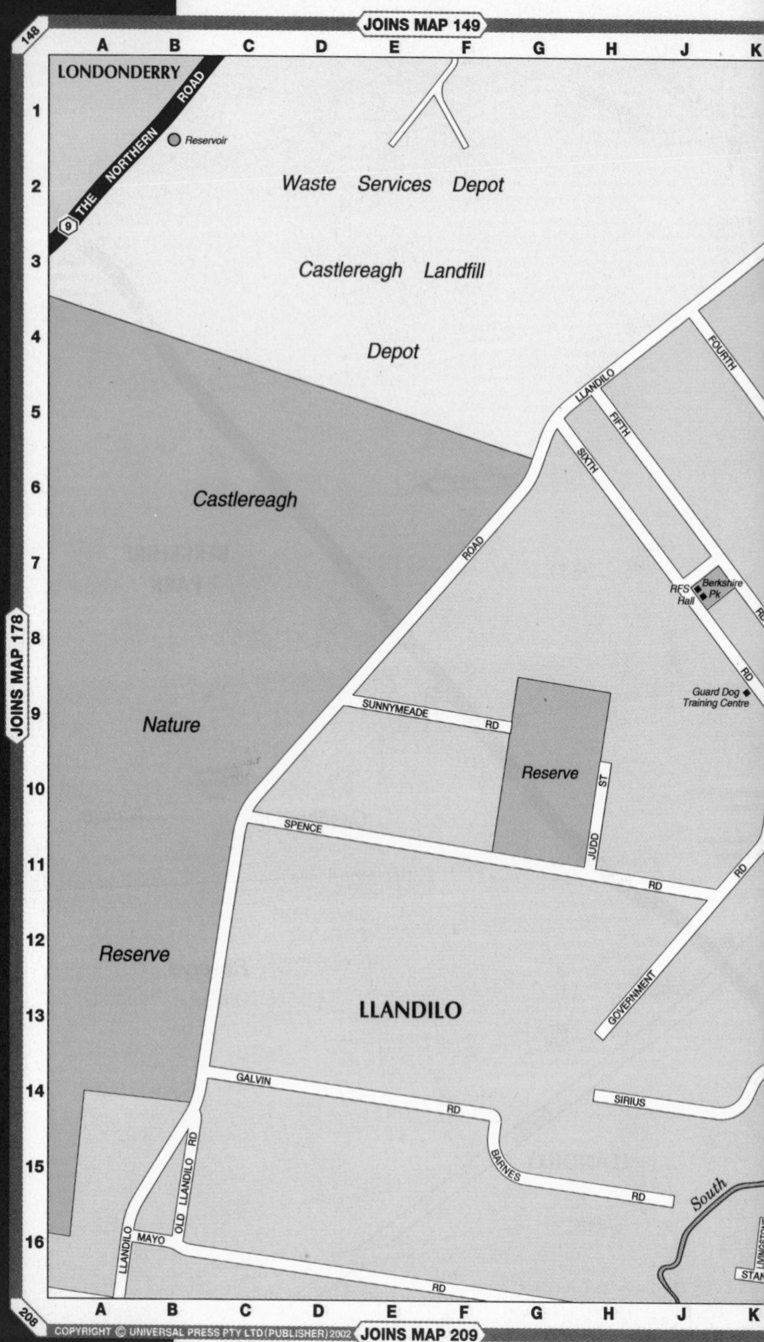
148
JOINS MAP 149
A
B
C
D
E
F
G
H
J
K
LONDONDERRY
THE NORTHERN ROAD
9
Reservoir
Waste Services Depot
Castlereagh Landfill
Depot
LLANDILO
FOURTH
FIFTH
SIXTH
ROAD
Castlereagh
RFS Hall
Berkshire Pk
RD
Guard Dog Training Centre
SUNNYMEADE
RD
Nature
Reserve
ST
JUDD
SPENCE
RD
RD
GOVERNMENT
Reserve
LLANDILO
GALVIN
RD
SIRIUS
BARNES
RD
South
OLD LLANDILO RD
LLANDILO
MAYO
RD
JOINS MAP 178
1
2
3
4
5
6
7
8
9
10
11
12
13
14
15
16
208
JOINS MAP 209

JOINS MAP 150

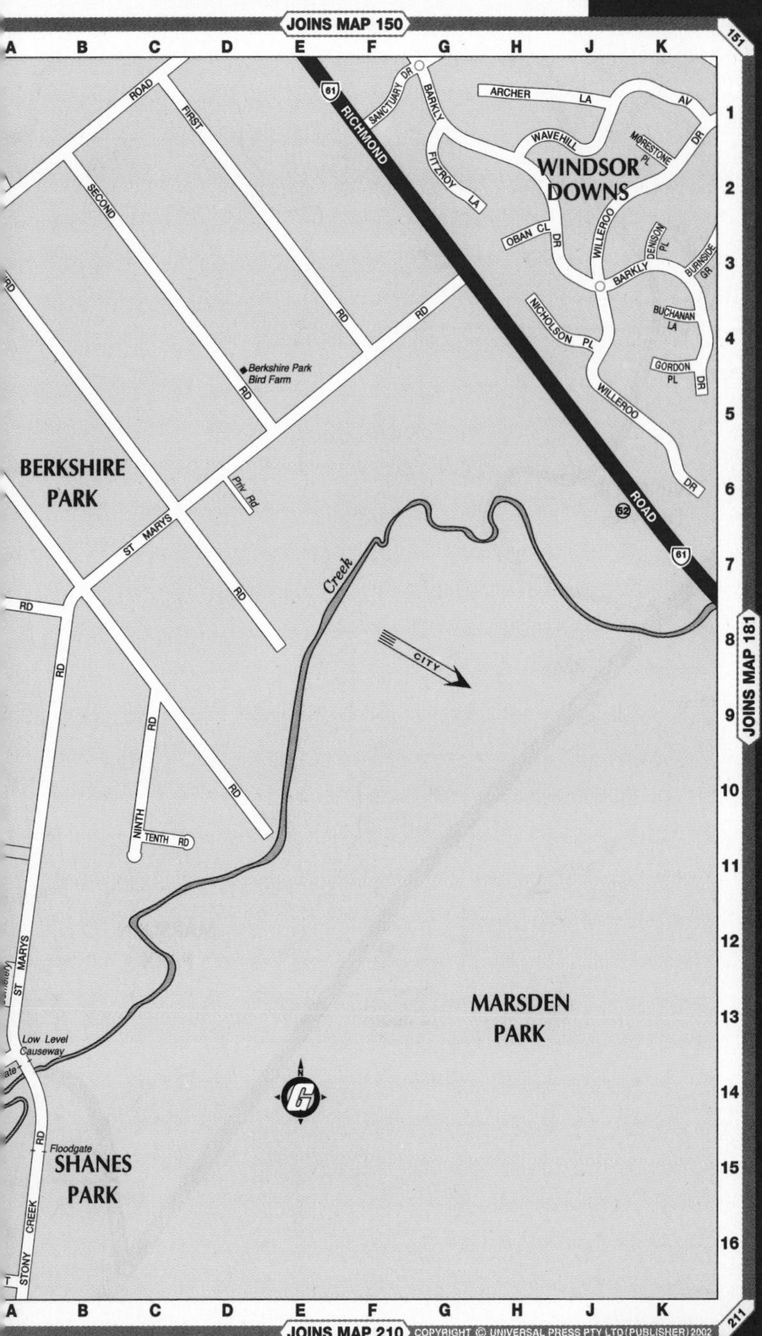

JOINS MAP 181

JOINS MAP 210

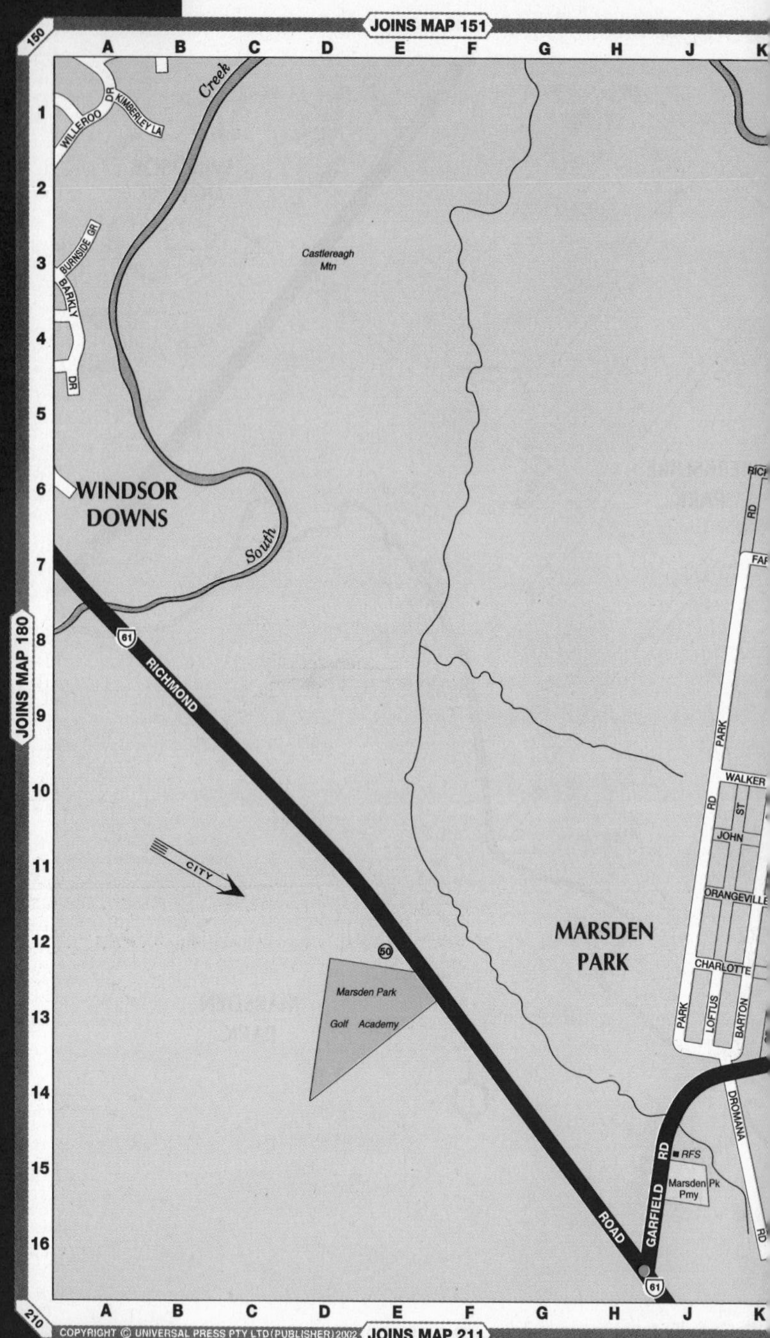
JOINS MAP 151
150
A B C D E F G H J K
1 2 3 4 5 6 7 8 9 10 11 12 13 14 15 16
WILLEROO DR
KIMBERLEY LA
Creek
BURNSIDE GR
BARKLY DR
Castlereagh Mtn
WINDSOR DOWNS
South
61
RICHMOND ROAD
JOINS MAP 180
CITY
50
Marsden Park Golf Academy
MARSDEN PARK
RICH RD
FAR
PARK RD
WALKER
ST
JOHN
ORANGEVILLE
CHARLOTTE
PARK
LOFTUS
BARTON
DROMANA RD
GARFIELD RD
RFS
Marsden Pk Pmy
210
JOINS MAP 211

JOINS MAP 152

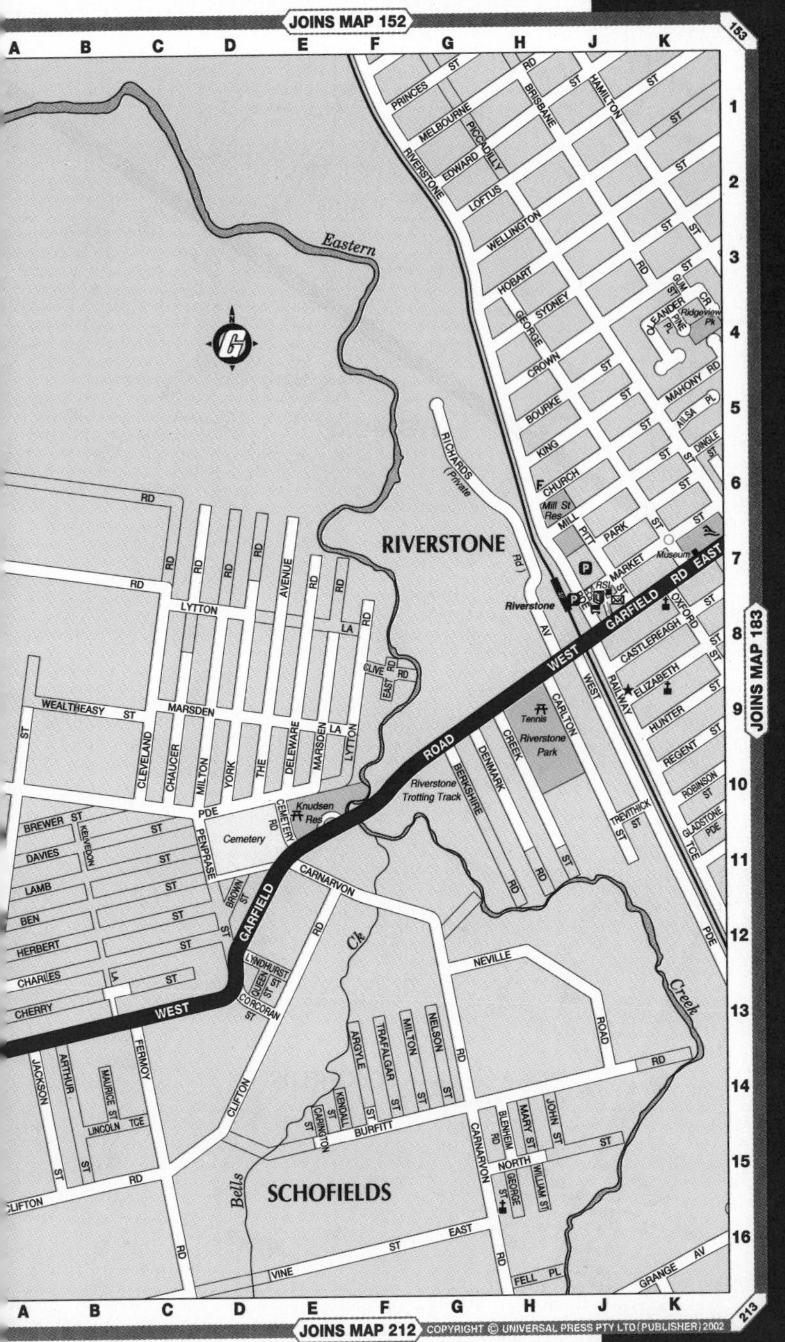

153
JOINS MAP 183
213
JOINS MAP 212

MAP 183

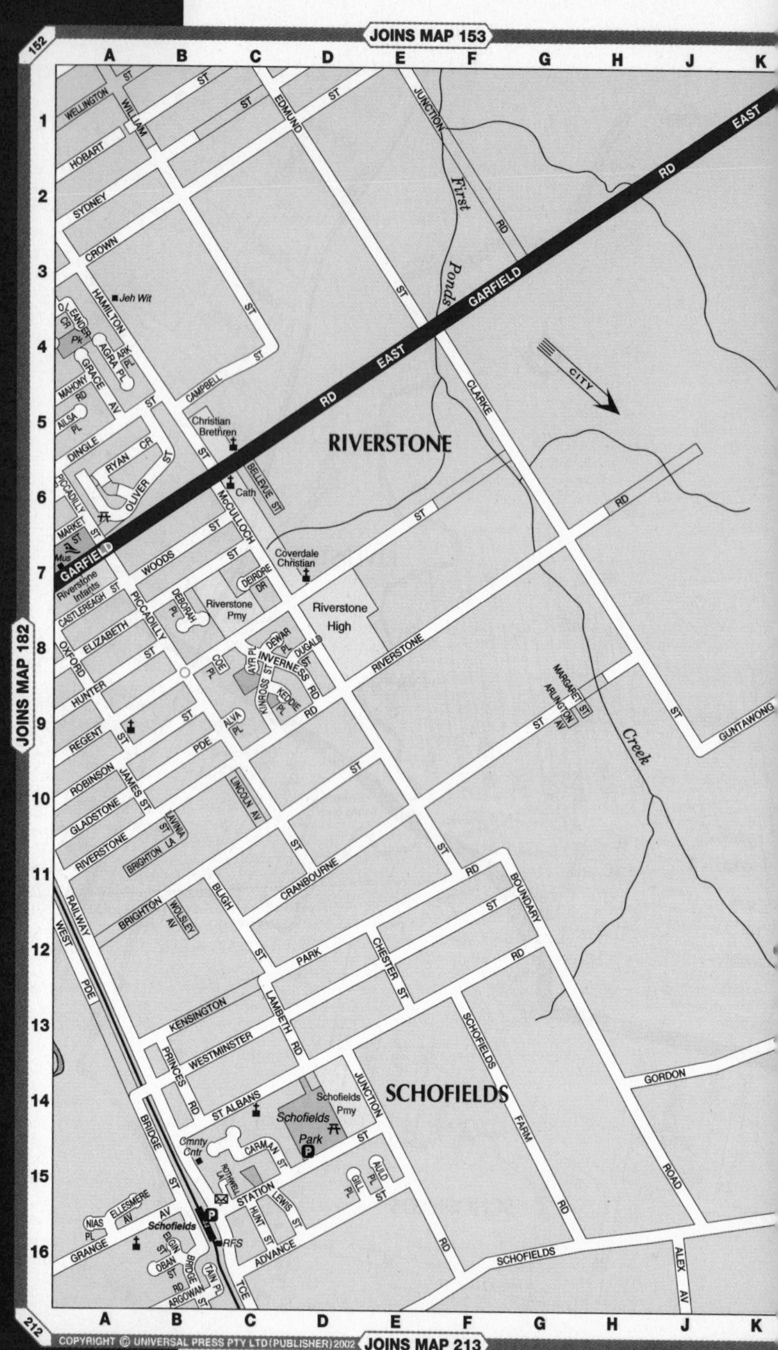

JOINS MAP 153
JOINS MAP 182
JOINS MAP 213
152
212
RIVERSTONE
SCHOFIELDS
GARFIELD RD EAST
JUNCTION
EDMUND
First Ponds Creek
CLARKE ST
CITY
WELLINGTON
WILLIAM
HOBART
SYDNEY
CROWN
HAMILTON
Jeh Wit
CAMPBELL ST
LEANDER CR
AGRA PL
ARK PL
GRACE AV
MAHONY RD
AILSA PL
DINGLE
RYAN CR
OLIVER ST
PICCADILLY
MARKET ST
Mus
Christian Brethren
Cath
BELLEVUE ST
McCULLOCH
WOODS
Coverdale Christian
DEIRDRE DR
Riverstone Infants
CASTLEREAGH ST
ELIZABETH
DEBORAH PL
Riverstone Pmy
Riverstone High
RIVERSTONE
DEWAR PL
DUGALD ST
INVERNESS RD
AYR PL
COE PL
KINROSS ST
KEDDIE PL
OXFORD
HUNTER
REGENT
ALVA PL
PDE
ROBINSON
JAMES ST
GLADSTONE
LINCOLN AV
LAVINIA ST
BRIGHTON LA
MARGARET ST
ARLINGTON AV
GUNTAWONG
CRANBOURNE
BLIGH
BRIGHTON
WOLSLEY AV
BOUNDARY
RAILWAY
WEST PDE
PARK
CHESTER ST
KENSINGTON
LAMBETH
WESTMINSTER
PRINCES
ST ALBANS
Schofields Pmy
Schofields Park
Cmnty Cntr
CARMAN ST
ROTHWELL LA
STATION
LEWIS ST
HUNT ST
GILL PL
AULD PL
BRIDGE ST
ELLESMERE AV
NIAS PL
GRANGE
Schofields
RFS
ELGIN ST
OBAN ST
ARGOWAN RD
TAIN PL
TCE
ADVANCE
SCHOFIELDS FARM RD
GORDON
ROAD
SCHOFIELDS
ALEX AV

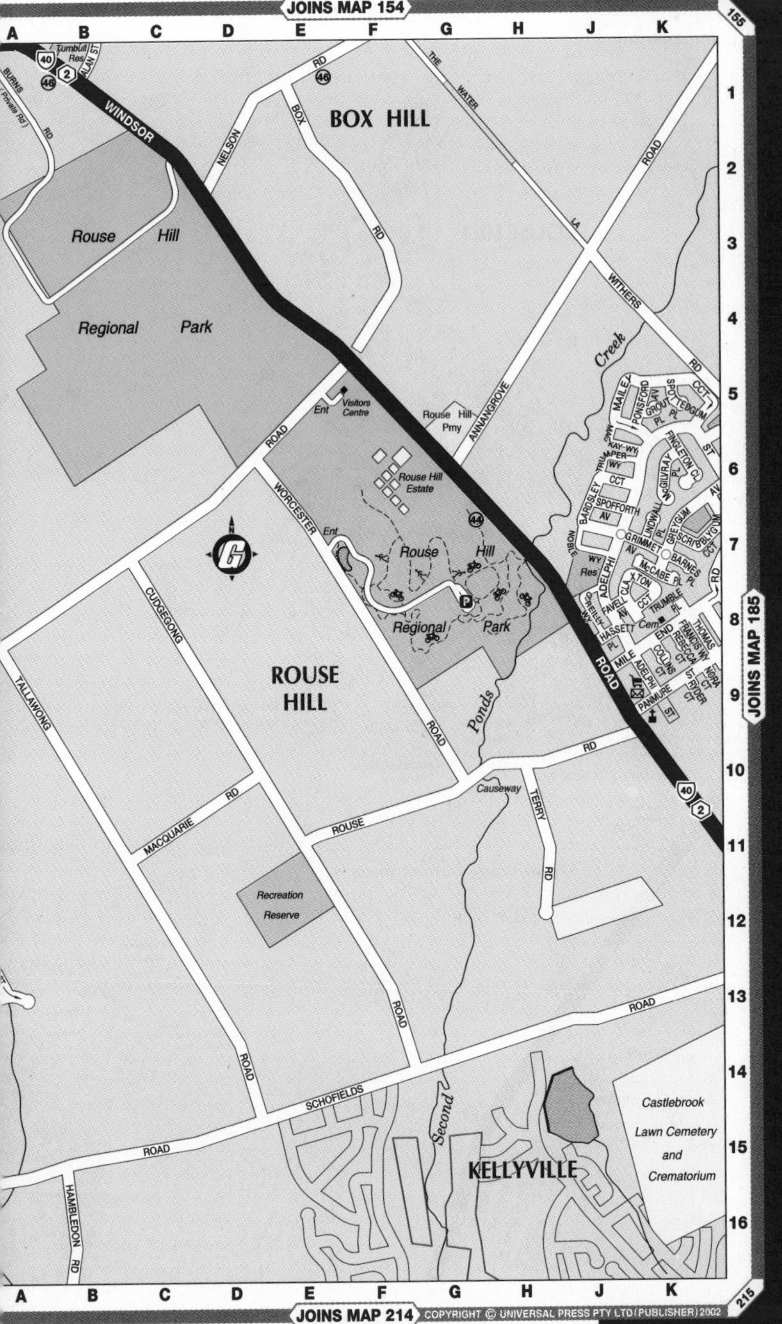
JOINS MAP 154
BOX HILL
ROUSE HILL
KELLYVILLE
Rouse Hill Regional Park
WINDSOR ROAD
NELSON ROAD
BOX RD
THE WATER LA
WITHERS RD
ANNANGROVE ROAD
Creek
Visitors Centre
Ent
Rouse Hill Pmy
Rouse Hill Estate
WORCESTER ROAD
CUDGEGONG ROAD
TALLAWONG
MACQUARIE RD
ROUSE RD
Causeway
TERRY RD
Ponds
Recreation Reserve
SCHOFIELDS ROAD
HAMBLEDON RD
Second
Castlebrook Lawn Cemetery and Crematorium
Turnbull Res
ALAN ST
BURNS RD
(Private Rd)
MAILEY
PONSFORD
GROUT PL
SPOT PL
TEDGUM
FINGLETON CL
McGILVRAY PL
TRUMPER WY
KAY-WY
SPOFFORTH AV
BARDSLEY
LINDWALL PL
GRIMMET AV
GREYGUM
SCRIBBLYGUM CCT
BARNES PL
McCABE PL
NOBLE
WY Res
ADELPHI
FAVELL AV
CLAXTON CCT
TRUMBLE PL
O'REILLY WY
HASSETT PL
Cem
MILE END
COLLINS CT
REBECCA CT
FRANCIS WY
THOMAS
NORA CT
ST RYDER CT
PANMURE ST
JOINS MAP 185
JOINS MAP 214
155
215

JOINS MAP 155

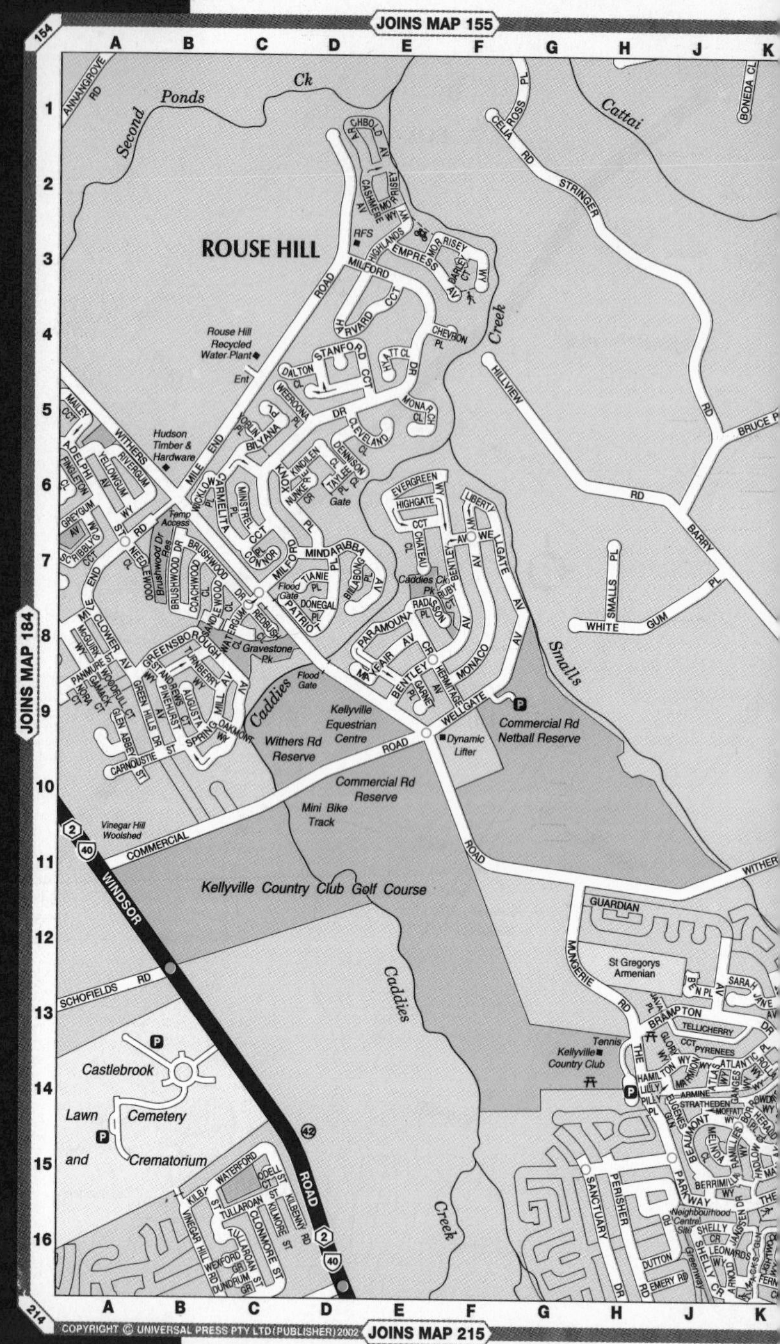

JOINS MAP 184

JOINS MAP 215

JOINS MAP 156

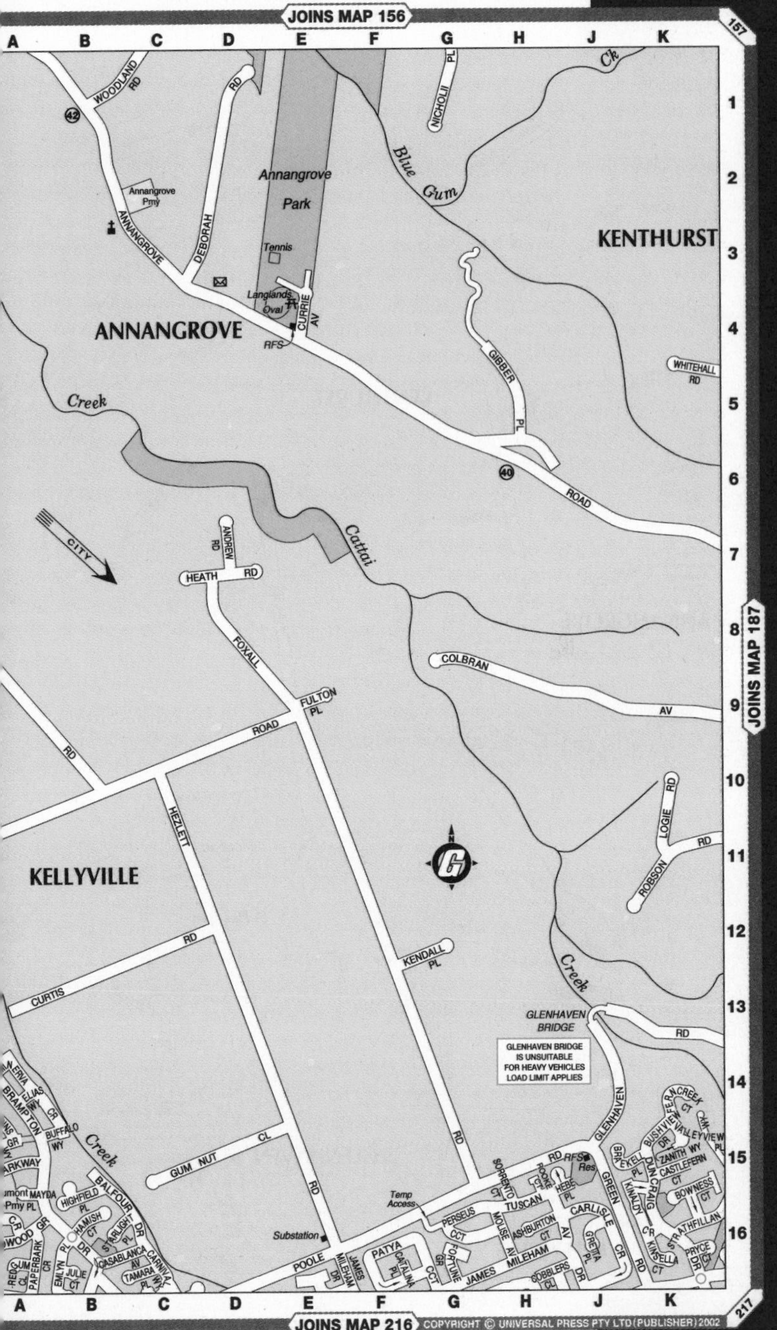

A B C D E F G H J K

1 2 3 4 5 6 7 8 9 10 11 12 13 14 15 16

157

JOINS MAP 187

JOINS MAP 216

217

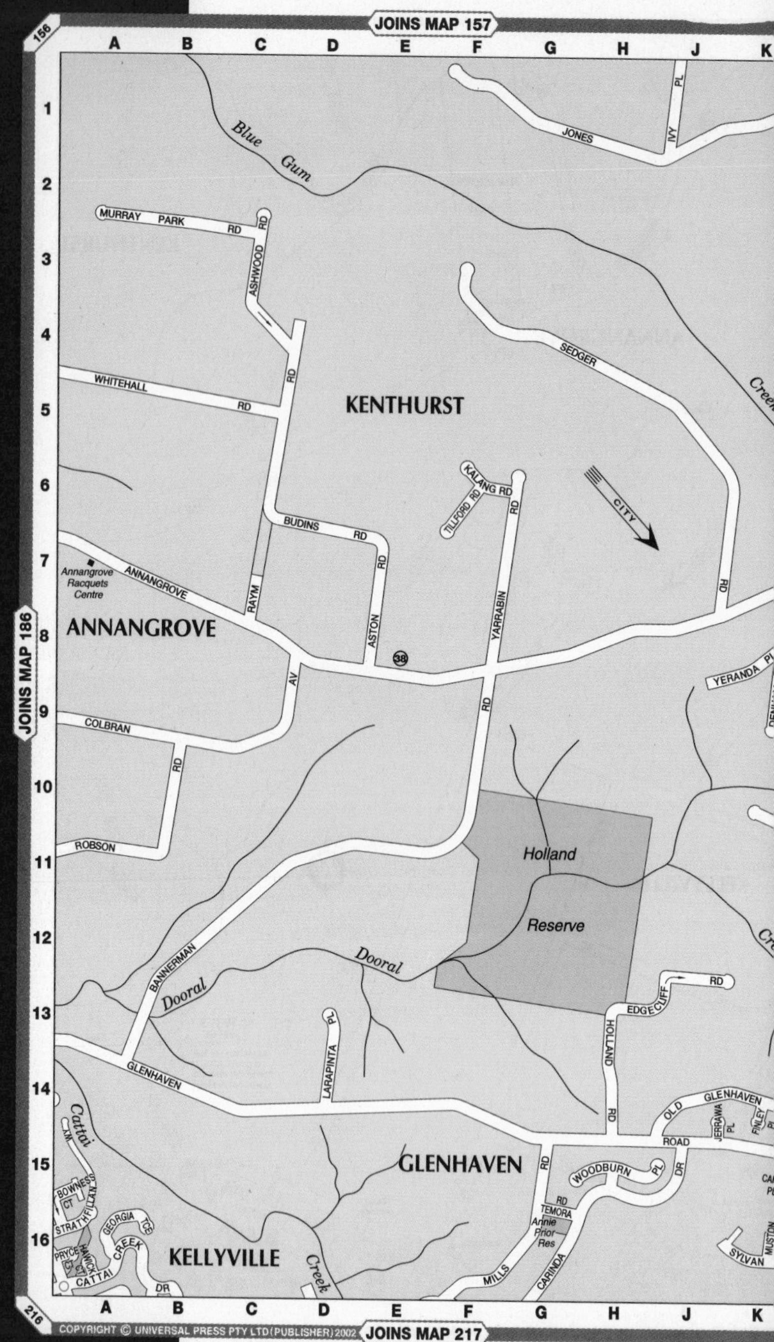
JOINS MAP 157
156
A
B
C
D
E
F
G
H
J
K
1
2
3
4
5
6
7
8
9
10
11
12
13
14
15
16
JONES
IVY
PL
Blue
Gum
MURRAY
PARK
RD
ASHWOOD
RD
SEDGER
RD
WHITEHALL
RD
KENTHURST
Creek
KALANG RD
TILLFORD RD
YARRABIN
RD
CITY
BUDINS
RD
ASTON
RD
RAYM
Annangrove Racquets Centre
ANNANGROVE
ANNANGROVE
AV
38
YERANDA PL
COLBRAN
RD
RD
ROBSON
Holland
Reserve
BANNERMAN
Dooral
Dooral
EDGECLIFF
RD
HOLLAND
RD
LARAPINTA
PL
GLENHAVEN
OLD
GLENHAVEN
JERRAWA
PL
FINLEY
PL
ROAD
Cattai
KM
BOWNESS
CT
STRATHFILLAN
GEORGIA
TCE
PRYCE
CT
HAWICK
CT
CATTAI
CREEK
DR
KELLYVILLE
Creek
GLENHAVEN
RD
WOODBURN
PL
DR
RD
TEMORA
Annie
Prior
Res
MILLS
CARINDA
SYLVAN
MUSTON
JOINS MAP 186
216
JOINS MAP 217

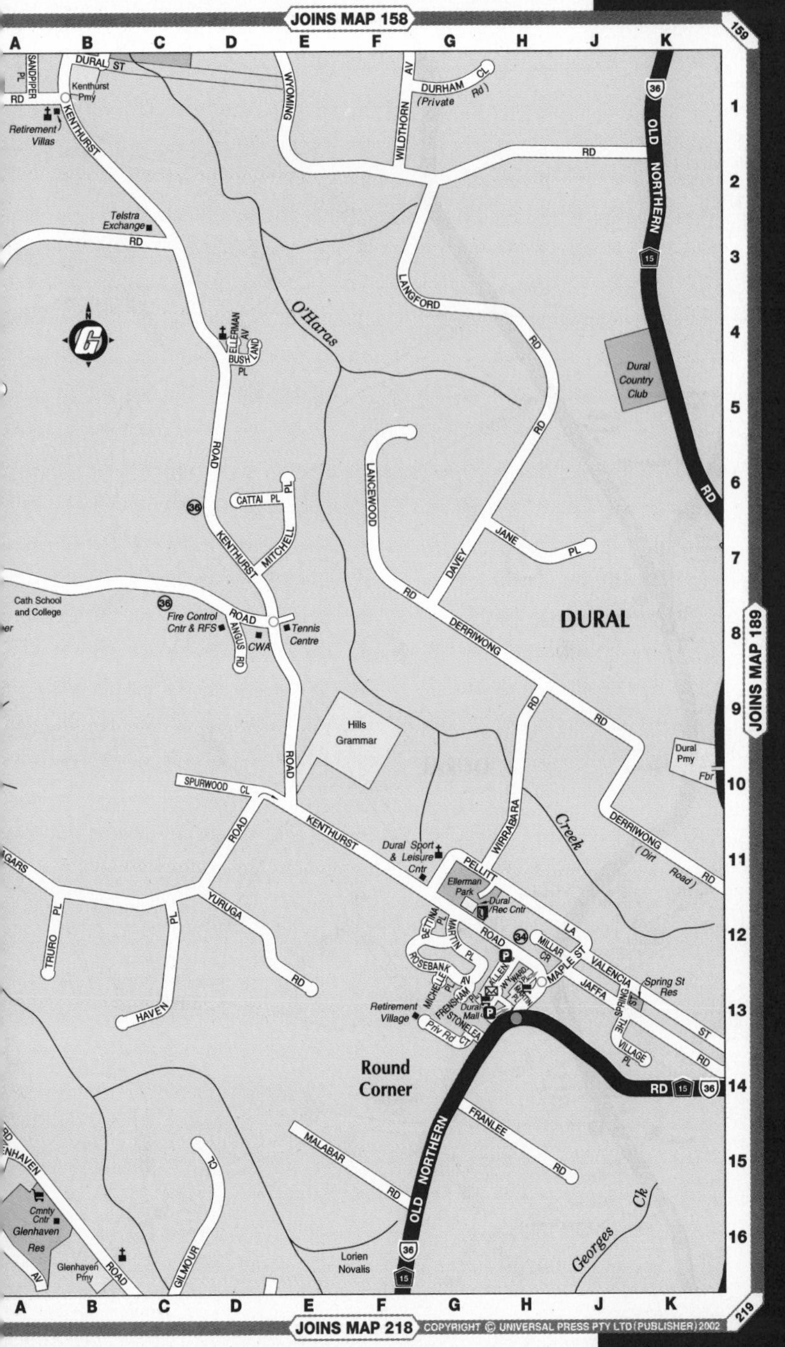

JOINS MAP 218

JOINS MAP 159

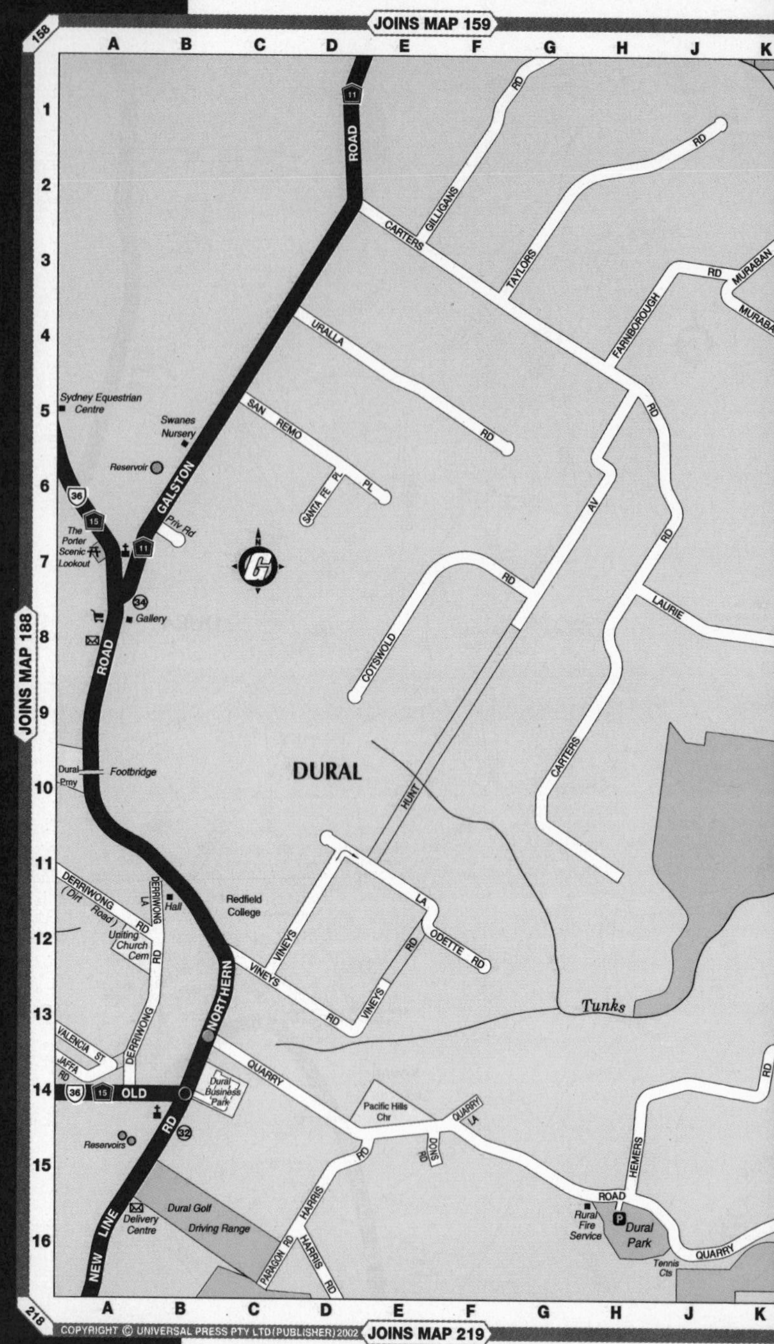

JOINS MAP 219

JOINS MAP 160

JOINS MAP 191

JOINS MAP 220

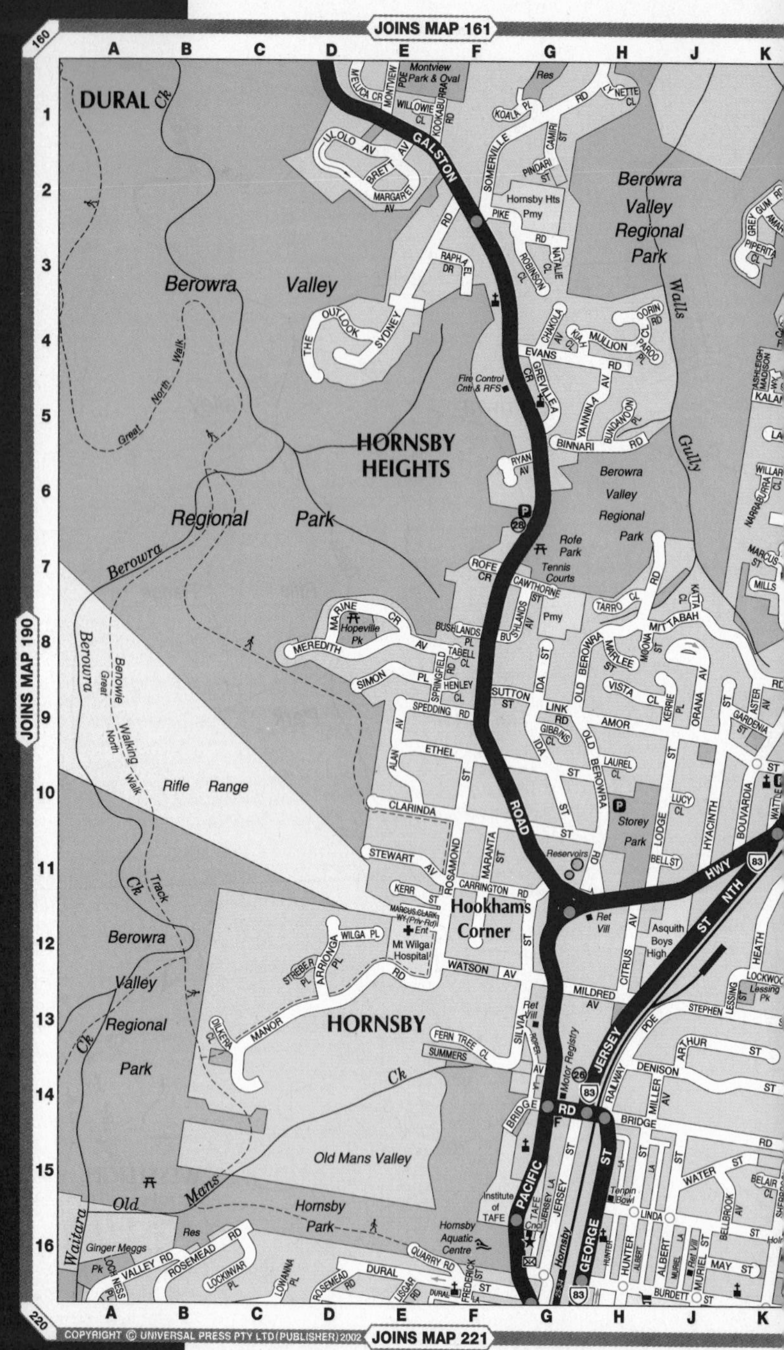
JOINS MAP 161
JOINS MAP 190
JOINS MAP 221
160
220
A B C D E F G H J K
1 2 3 4 5 6 7 8 9 10 11 12 13 14 15 16
DURAL Ck
Berowra Valley
Regional Park
HORNSBY HEIGHTS
Berowra Valley Regional Park
Walls Gully
Montview Park & Oval
MELUCA CR
MONTVIEW PDE
WILLOWIE CL
KOOKABURRA RD
ULOLO AV
BRETT AV
MARGARET AV
GALSTON ROAD
SOMERVILLE RD
KOALA PL
LYNETTE CL
CAMIRI ST
PINDARI ST
Hornsby Hts Pmy
PIKE RD
ROBINSON CL
NATALIE CL
RAPHAEL DR
SYDNEY RD
THE OUTLOOK
CHAKOLA AV
KIAH CL
MULLION CL
OORIN RD
PARDO PL
EVANS RD
GREVILLEA CR
YANNINA AV
BUNDANOON PL
BINNARI RD
Fire Control Cntr & RFS
RYAN AV
Rofe Park
Tennis Courts
ROFE CR
CAWTHORNE ST
BUSHLANDS AV
BUSHLANDS PL
Pmy
TARRO CL
KATTA CL
MITTABAH RD
MARINE CR
Hopeville Pk
MEREDITH AV
TABELL CL
SIMON PL
SPRINGFIELD RD
HENLEY CL
SPEDDING RD
SUTTON ST
IDA ST
OLD BEROWRA RD
MARLEE ST
MOONA ST
VISTA CL
KERRIE PL
ORANA AV
LINK RD
AMOR ST
GIBBINS CL
ALAN AV
ETHEL ST
LAUREL CL
CLARINDA ST
Storey Park
LUCY CL
LODGE ST
HYACINTH ST
BOUVARDIA ST
STEWART AV
ROSAMOND ST
MARANTA ST
Reservoirs
BELL ST
KERR ST
CARRINGTON RD
Hookhams Corner
MARCUS CLARK WY (Priv Rd)
Mt Wilga Hospital
WILGA PL
ARRIONGA PL
STREBER PL
WATSON AV
Ret Vill
CITRUS AV
Asquith Boys High
HWY
NTH ST
83
MILDRED AV
HEATH
LOCKWOOD
Lessing Pk
LESSING
STEPHEN
HORNSBY
DILKERA CL
MANOR RD
FERN TREE CL
SUMMERS
SILVIA ST
ROPER
Motor Registry
JERSEY RD
PDE
ARTHUR ST
DENISON ST
RAILWAY
MILLER AV
BRIDGE RD
Ck
Old Mans Valley
PACIFIC
JERSEY LA
GEORGE ST
Tenpin Bowl
LINDA
WATER ST
BELAIR CL
BELLBROOK AV
Institute of TAFE
TAFE Cnd
Hornsby Park
Hornsby Aquatic Centre
QUARRY RD
HUNTER
ALBERT
MURIEL ST
MAY ST
BURDETT ST
Rifle Range
Great North Walk
Benowie Walking Track
Berowra Ck
Old Mans Ck
Waitara
Ginger Meggs Pk
LOCH NESS PL
VALLEY RD
ROSEMEAD RD
LOCKINVAR PL
LOWANNA PL
DURAL ST
LISGAR RD
FREDERICK ST
Res
28
26
NARRABURRA CL
WILLARRA
MARCUS ST
MILLS
GARDENIA ST
ASTER AV
PIPERITA CL
GREY GUM

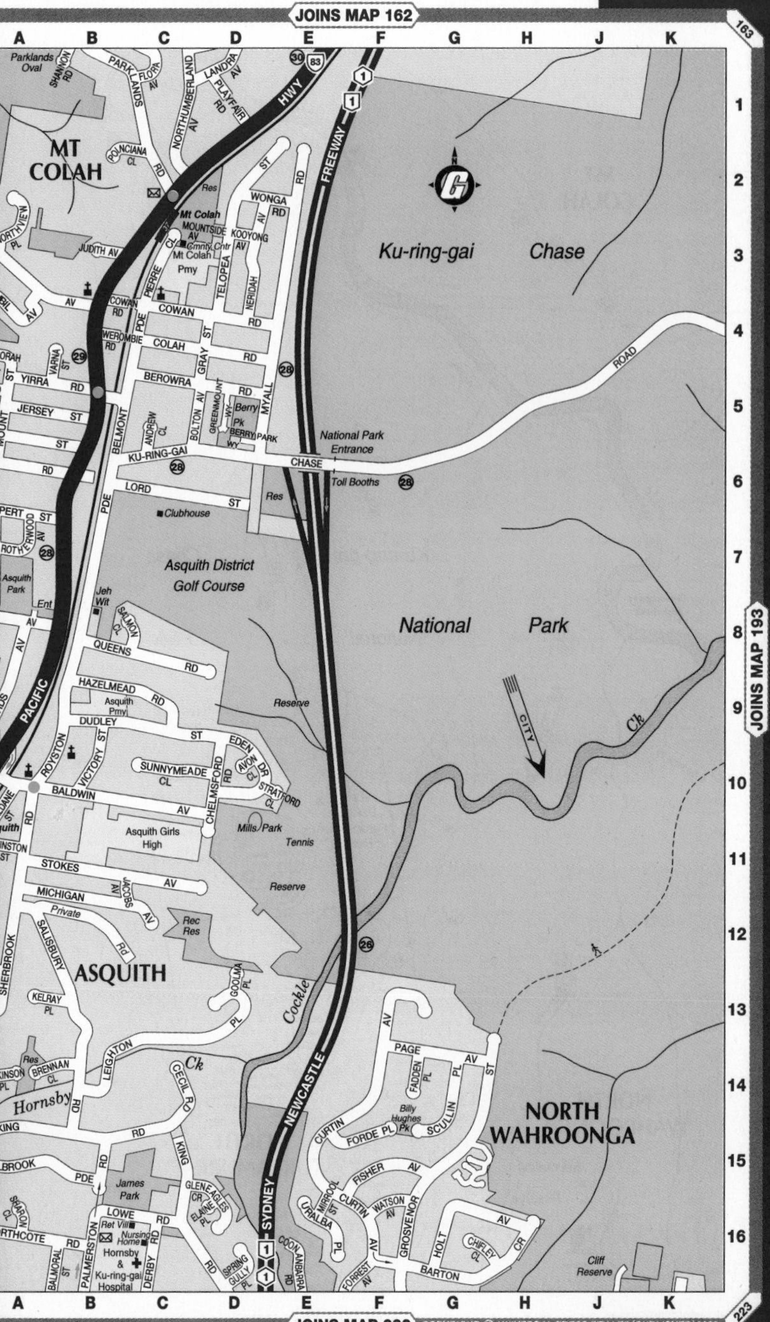
JOINS MAP 162
163
A B C D E F G H J K
1 2 3 4 5 6 7 8 9 10 11 12 13 14 15 16
MT COLAH
ASQUITH
NORTH WAHROONGA
Ku-ring-gai Chase National Park
Parklands Oval
PACIFIC HWY
FREEWAY
SYDNEY NEWCASTLE
National Park Entrance
Toll Booths
Asquith District Golf Course
Clubhouse
Asquith Park
Asquith Pmy
Asquith Girls High
Mills Park
Tennis
Reserve
Rec Res
Mt Colah Pmy
Cmnty Cntr
Berry Pk
Billy Hughes Pk
James Park
Hornsby & Ku-ring-gai Hospital
Nursing Home
Ret Vill
Cliff Reserve
Cockle Ck
Hornsby Ck
CITY
KU-RING-GAI CHASE ROAD
JOINS MAP 193
JOINS MAP 222
223

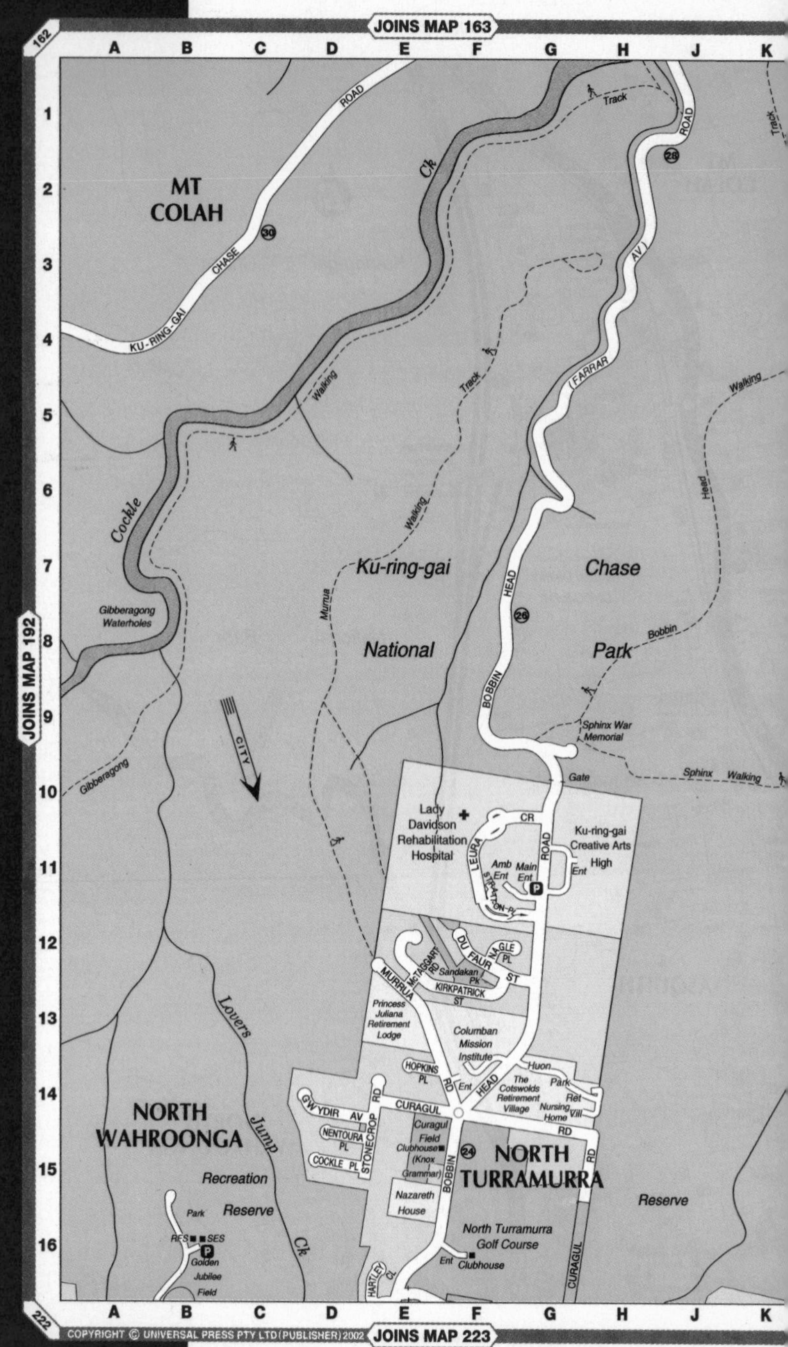
JOINS MAP 163
162
A B C D E F G H J K
1 2 3 4 5 6 7 8 9 10 11 12 13 14 15 16
MT COLAH
KU-RING-GAI CHASE ROAD
30
Cockle Ck
Walking Track
Track
FARRAR AV
ROAD
26
Ku-ring-gai National
Chase Park
BOBBIN HEAD
Gibberagong Waterholes
Gibberagong
Murrua
CITY
Bobbin
Head
Sphinx War Memorial
Gate
Sphinx Walking
Lady Davidson Rehabilitation Hospital
LEURA CR
Amb Ent
Main Ent
STRATTON PL
Ku-ring-gai Creative Arts High
Ent
DU FAUR ST
NAGLE PL
McTAGGART RD
Sandakan Pk
KIRKPATRICK ST
MURRUA
Princess Juliana Retirement Lodge
Columban Mission Institute
Huon Park
HOPKINS PL
RD
Ent
The Cotswolds Retirement Village
Nursing Home
Ret Vill
GWYDIR AV
CURAGUL RD
NENTOURA PL
COCKLE PL
STONECROP RD
Curagul Field
Clubhouse (Knox Grammar)
Nazareth House
24
NORTH TURRAMURRA
NORTH WAHROONGA
Lovers Jump Ck
Recreation Reserve
Park
RFS SES
Golden Jubilee Field
North Turramurra Golf Course
Ent Clubhouse
HARTLEY CL
CURAGUL
Reserve
JOINS MAP 192
222

JOINS MAP 164

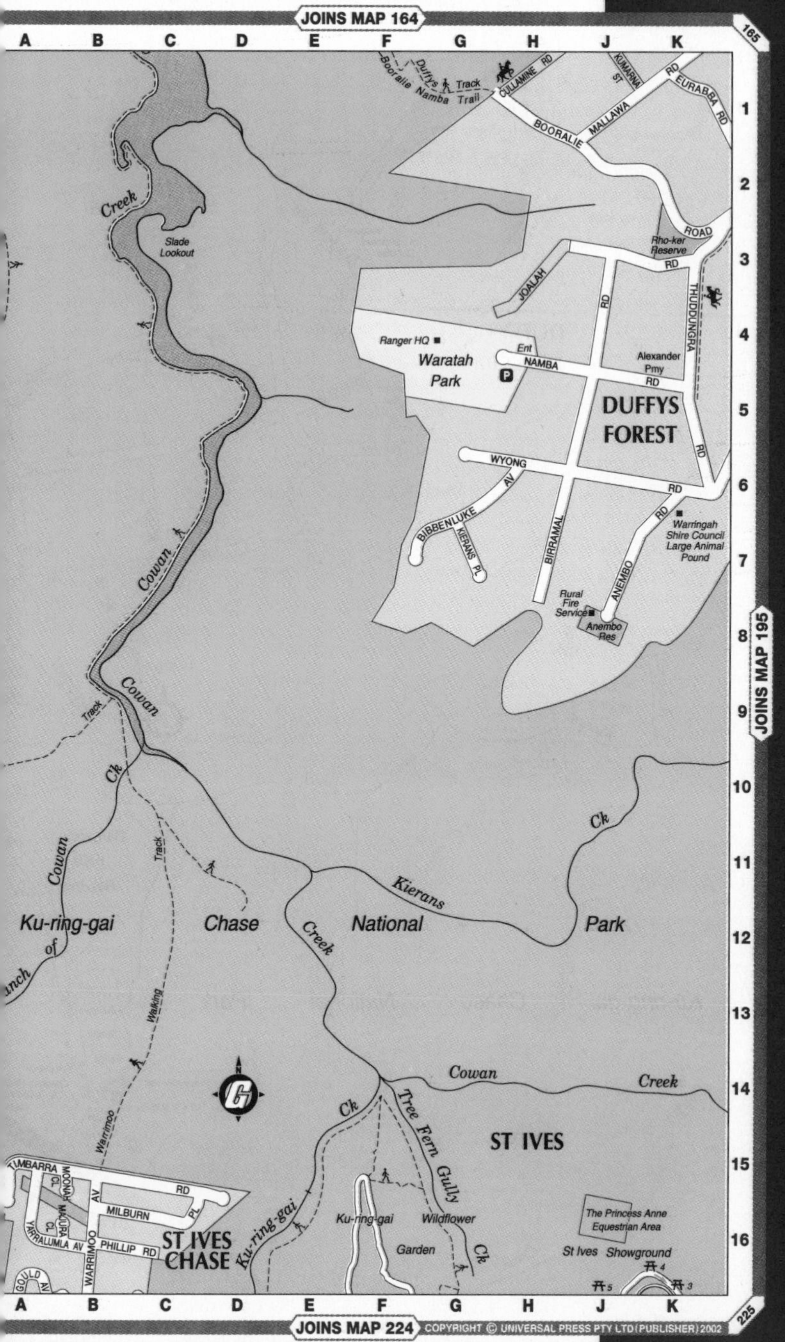

JOINS MAP 195

JOINS MAP 224

JOINS MAP 165

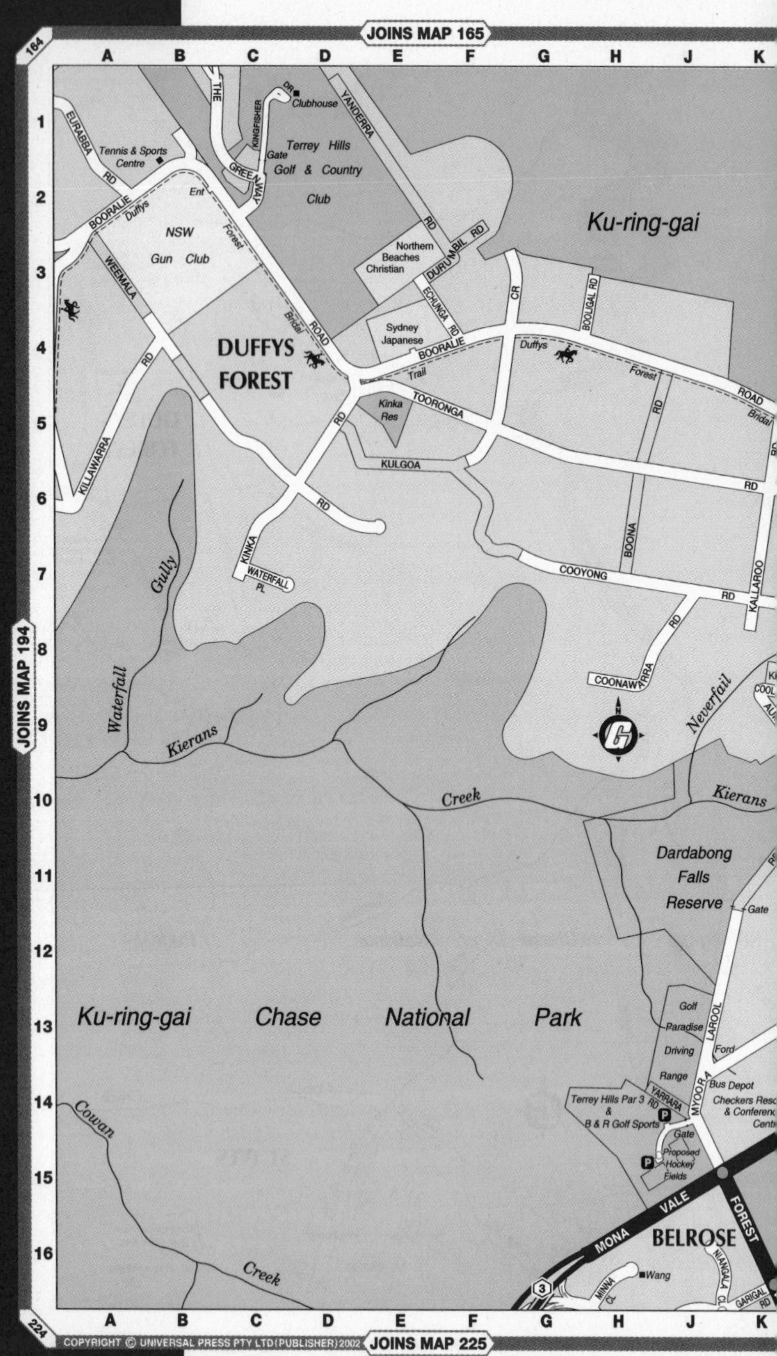

JOINS MAP 194

JOINS MAP 225

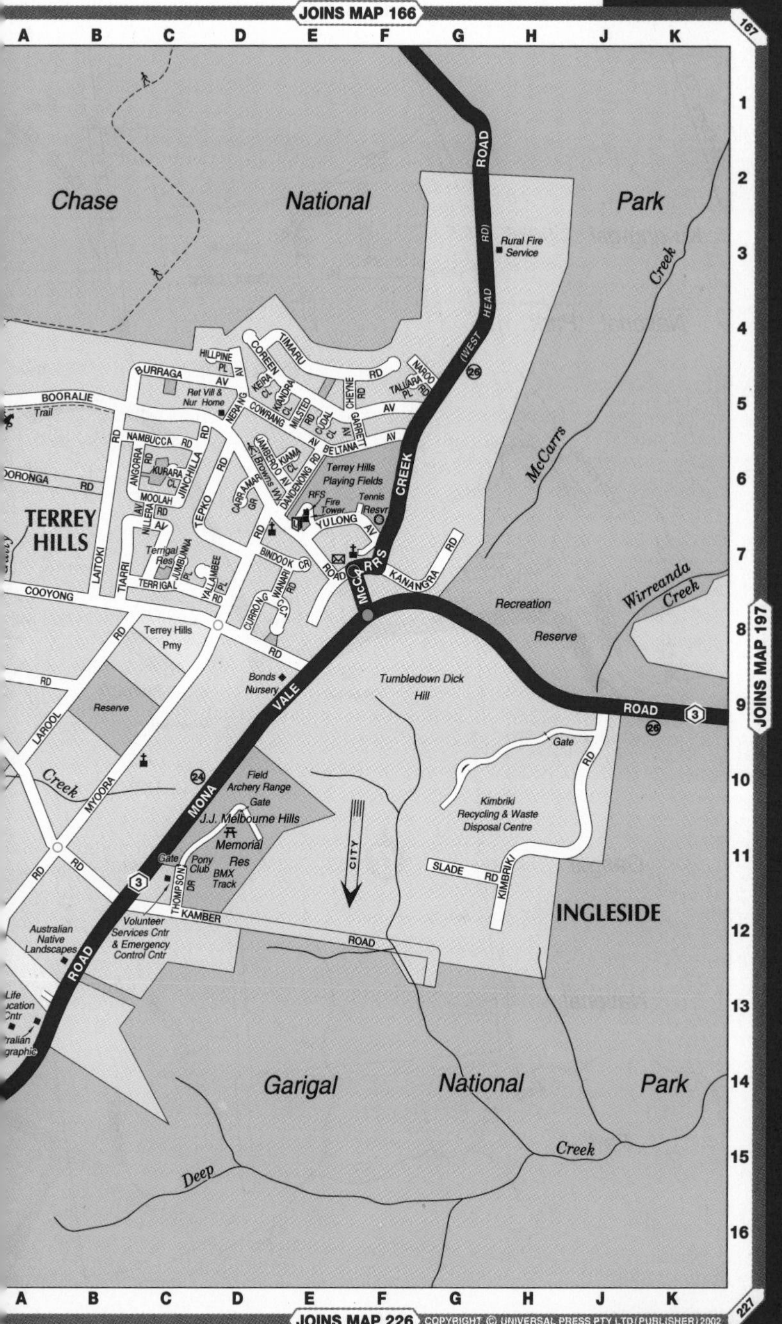
JOINS MAP 166
A B C D E F G H J K
1 2 3 4 5 6 7 8 9 10 11 12 13 14 15 16
Chase
National
Park
ROAD
(WEST HEAD RD)
Rural Fire Service
Creek
TIMARU
COREEN
HILLPINE PL
BURRAGA AV
Ret Vill & Nur Home
BOORALIE
Trail
NERANG
KEIRA CL
KIANDRA CL
MILSTED RD
CIDAL CL
CHEYNE RD
GARRETT AV
RD
TALLARA PL
NAROO RD
COWRANG
AV
BELTANA
AV
NAMBUCCA RD
RD
RD
ANGORRA RD
KURARA CL
JINCHILLA
DORONGA RD
TEPKO RD
JAMBEROO AV
KIAMA CL
Browns Wy
DANDENONG RD
Terrey Hills Playing Fields
CREEK
McCarrs
MOOLAH
NILLERA AV
RD
CARRAMAR GR
RFS Fire Tower
Tennis Resvr
YULONG
AV
TERREY HILLS
LAITOKI
TIARRI
Terrigal Res
JUMBUNNA PL
YALLAMBEE PL
TERRIGAL
RD
BINDOOK CR
ROAD
McCARRS
KANANGRA
RD
COOYONG
CURRONG
WANARI RD
CCT
Recreation Reserve
Wirreanda Creek
Terrey Hills Pmy
RD
RD
Bonds Nursery
VALE
Tumbledown Dick Hill
ROAD
JOINS MAP 197
RD
Reserve
LAROOL
Gate
RD
Creek
MYOORA
Field Archery Range
Gate
MONA
J.J. Melbourne Hills Memorial Res
Kimbriki Recycling & Waste Disposal Centre
CITY
Gate
Pony Club
Res
BMX Track
RD
RD
THOMPSON DR
SLADE RD
KIMBRIKI
KAMBER
ROAD
INGLESIDE
Volunteer Services Cntr & Emergency Control Cntr
Australian Native Landscapes
ROAD
Garigal
National
Park
Creek
Deep
JOINS MAP 226

JOINS MAP 167

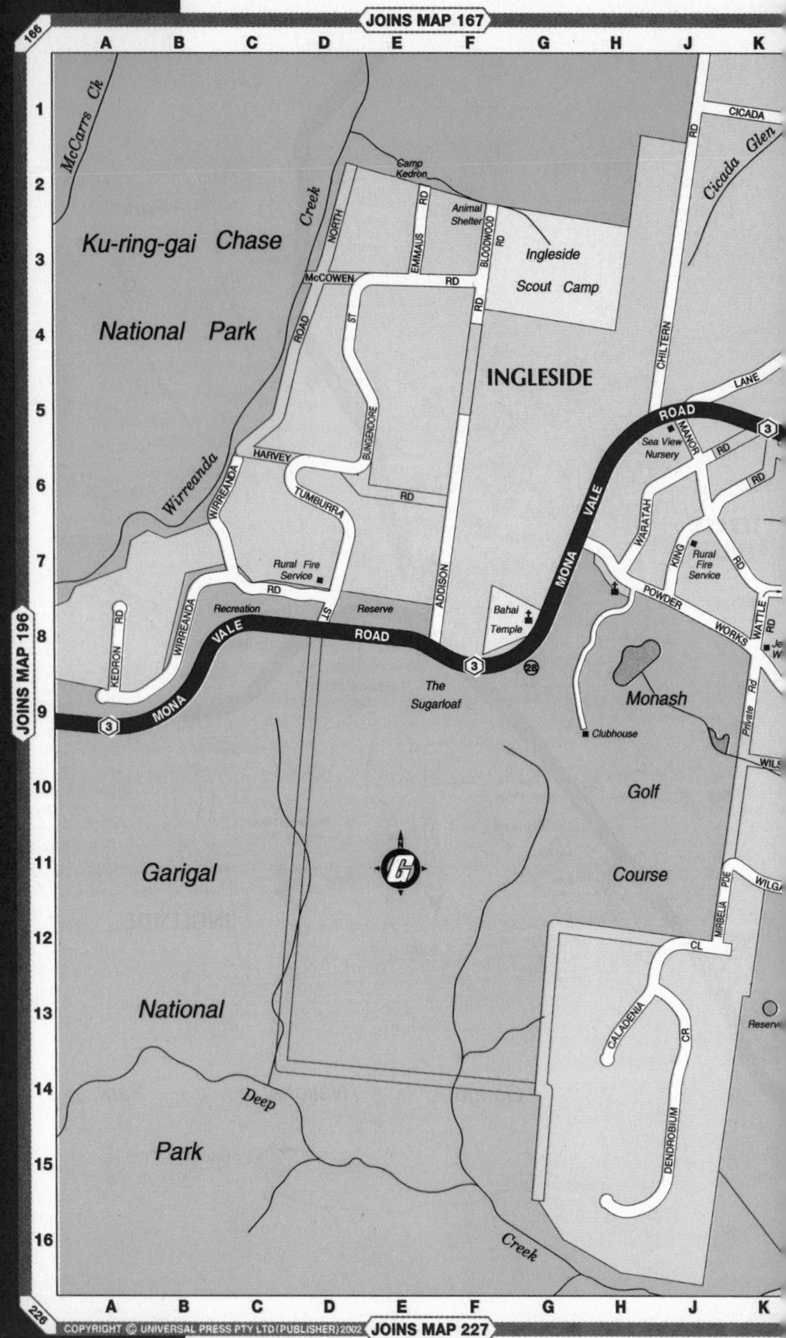

JOINS MAP 196

JOINS MAP 227

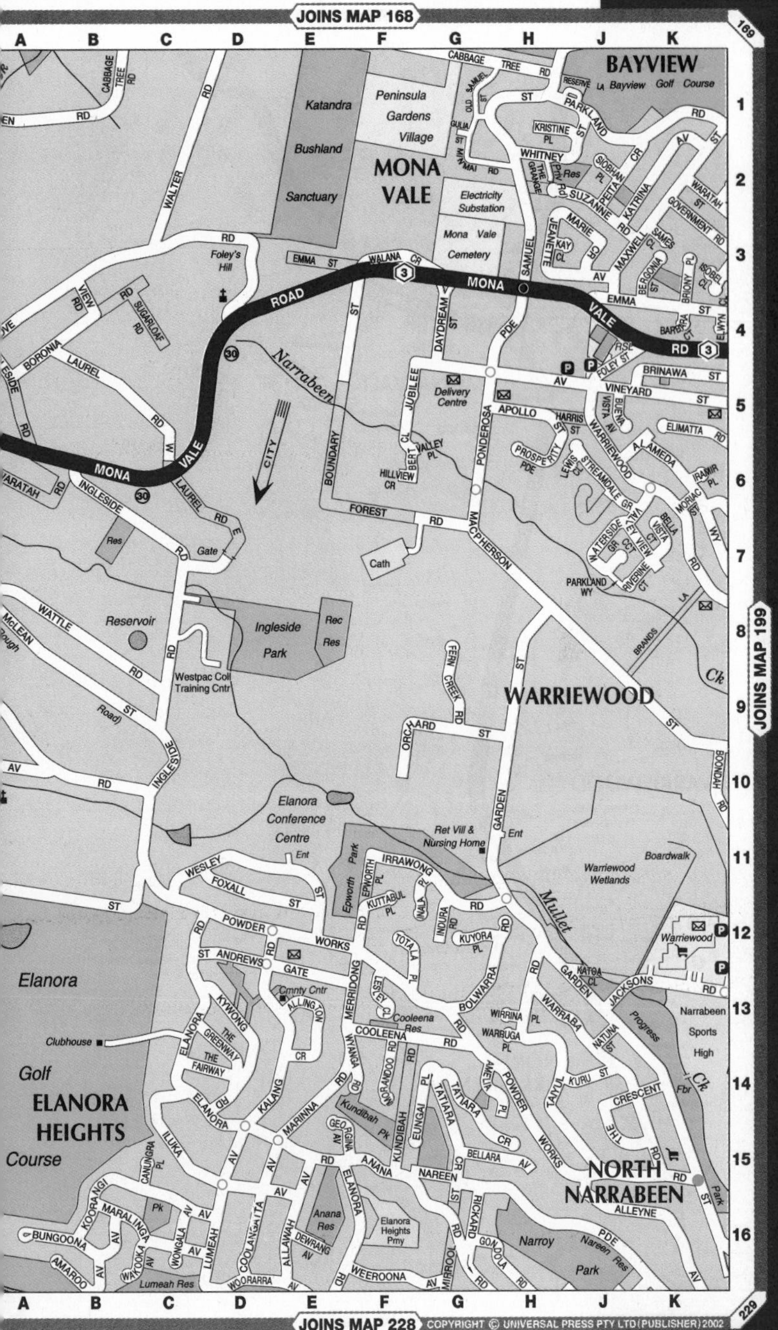
JOINS MAP 168
JOINS MAP 199
JOINS MAP 228
169
229
A B C D E F G H J K
1 2 3 4 5 6 7 8 9 10 11 12 13 14 15 16
BAYVIEW
Bayview Golf Course
MONA VALE
Katandra Bushland Sanctuary
Peninsula Gardens Village
Electricity Substation
Mona Vale Cemetery
Foley's Hill
MONA VALE ROAD
Narrabeen
CITY
Delivery Centre
Cath
Reservoir
Ingleside Park
Rec Res
Westpac Coll Training Cntr
WARRIEWOOD
Elanora Conference Centre
Ret Vill & Nursing Home
Warriewood Wetlands
Boardwalk
Mullet
Warriewood
Progress
Narrabeen Sports High
Elanora
Clubhouse
Golf
ELANORA HEIGHTS
Course
Cmnty Cntr
Cooleena Res
Kundibah Pk
Anana Res
Elanora Heights Pmy
Lumeah Res
NORTH NARRABEEN
Narroy Park
Nareen Res
Epworth Park
CABBAGE TREE RD
WALTER RD
SAMUEL ST
PARKLAND RD
EMMA ST
PONDEROSA PDE
DAYDREAM ST
JUBILEE AV
BOUNDARY ST
FOREST RD
MACPHERSON ST
VINEYARD ST
APOLLO ST
WARRIEWOOD RD
INGLESIDE RD
LAUREL RD
WATTLE ST
McLEAN ST
FERN CREEK RD
ORCHARD ST
GARDEN ST
IRRAWONG RD
WORKS RD
POWDER WORKS RD
JACKSONS RD
BOLWARRA RD
COOLEENA RD
ANANA RD
NAREEN PDE
ALLEYNE AV
BOONDAH RD
ELANORA RD
THE CRESCENT

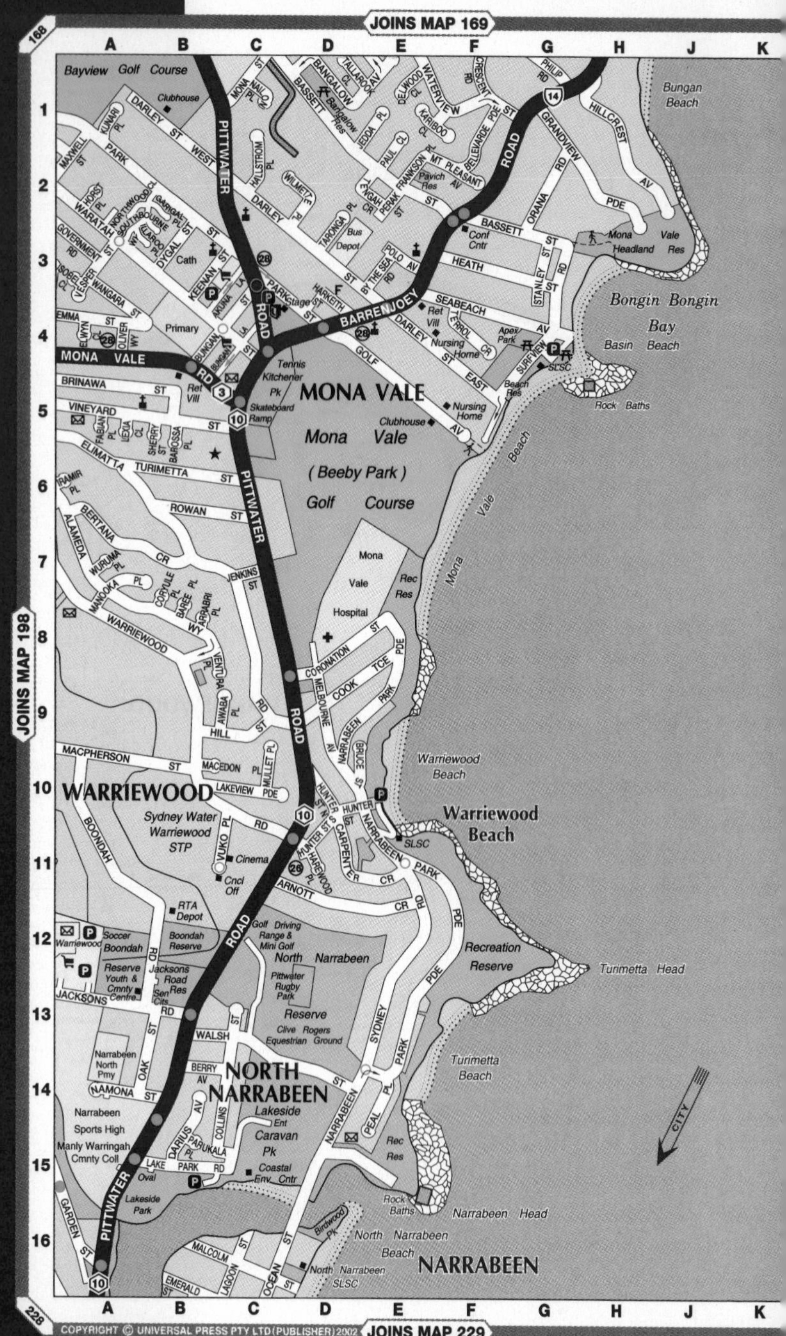

JOINS MAP 169
168
JOINS MAP 198
228
JOINS MAP 229
A B C D E F G H J K
1 2 3 4 5 6 7 8 9 10 11 12 13 14 15 16
Bayview Golf Course
Clubhouse
DARLEY ST WEST
PITTWATER ROAD
MONA VALE
Bungan Beach
HILLCREST AV
GRANDVIEW PDE
BASSETT ST
Bangalow Res
Pavich Res
MT PLEASANT AV
Conf Cntr
Mona Headland
Vale Res
Bongin Bongin Bay
Basin Beach
Rock Baths
HEATH ST
SEABEACH AV
BARRENJOEY ROAD
Bus Depot
Stage St
Cath
Primary
MONA VALE RD
Tennis
Kitchener Pk
Skateboard Ramp
Ret Vill
Nursing Home
Apex Park
SLSC
Beach Res
GOLF AV
Clubhouse
Mona Vale (Beeby Park) Golf Course
Mona Vale Beach
BRINAWA ST
VINEYARD ST
ELIMATTA
TURIMETTA ST
ROWAN ST
Mona Vale Hospital
Rec Res
WARRIEWOOD RD
CORONATION ST
COOK TCE
NARRABEEN PARK PDE
HILL ST
MACPHERSON ST
WARRIEWOOD
LAKEVIEW PDE
Sydney Water Warriewood STP
Cinema
Cncl Off
Warriewood Beach
ARNOTT CR
RTA Depot
Boondah Reserve
Soccer Boondah
Reserve Youth & Cmnty Centre
Jacksons Road Res
Sen Cits
JACKSONS RD
Golf Driving Range & Mini Golf
North Narrabeen
Pittwater Rugby Park
Reserve
Clive Rogers Equestrian Ground
Recreation Reserve
Turimetta Head
Turimetta Beach
SYDNEY PDE
Narrabeen North Pmy
NORTH NARRABEEN
WALSH ST
BERRY AV
NAMONA ST
Narrabeen Sports High
Manly Warringah Cmnty Coll
Lakeside Ent
Caravan Pk
Coastal Env Cntr
LAKE PARK RD
Oval
Lakeside Park
Rec Res
Rock Baths
Narrabeen Head
Birdwood Pk
North Narrabeen Beach
NARRABEEN
North Narrabeen SLSC
CITY

JOINS MAP 170

A B C D E F G H J K

1 2 3 4 5 6 7 8 9 10 11 12 13 14 15 16

TASMAN

SEA

A B C D E F G H J K

JOINS MAP 230

JOINS MAP 171

LIMIT OF MAPS

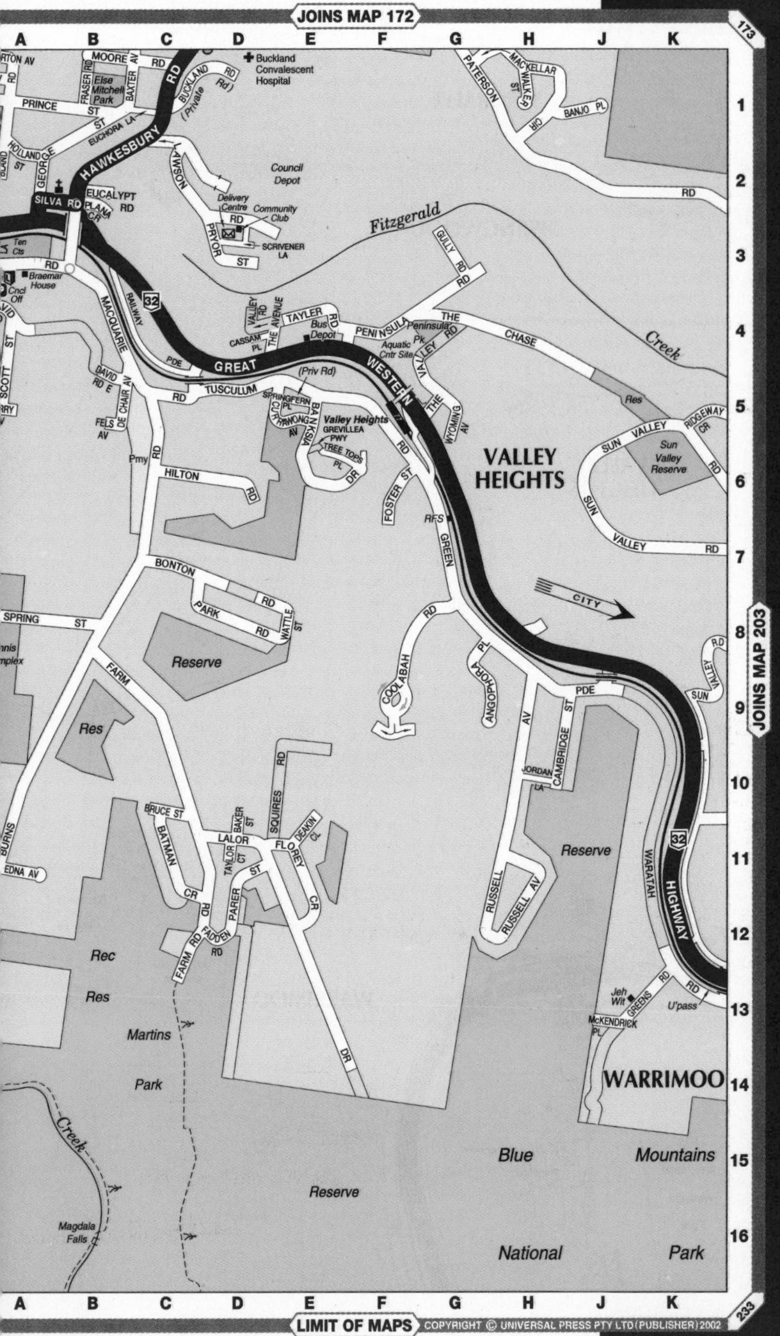
JOINS MAP 172
173
JOINS MAP 203
LIMIT OF MAPS
233
A B C D E F G H J K
1 2 3 4 5 6 7 8 9 10 11 12 13 14 15 16
VALLEY HEIGHTS
WARRIMOO
Blue Mountains National Park
Reserve
Martins Park
Rec Res
Magdala Falls
Creek
Fitzgerald Creek
Council Depot
Buckland Convalescent Hospital
Delivery Centre
Community Club
Braemar House
Cncl Off
Ten Cts
Eise Mitchell Park
Bus Depot
Aquatic Cntr Site
Peninsula Pk
Valley Heights
RFS
Sun Valley Reserve
Res
Jeh Wit
U'pass
Pmy
CITY
GREAT WESTERN HIGHWAY
HAWKESBURY RD
PRINCE ST
MOORE AV
FRASER RD
BAXTER AV
EUCHORA LA
HOLLAND ST
GEORGE ST
SILVA RD
EUCALYPT RD
PLANA CR
BUCKLAND RD (Private Rd)
LAWSON
PRYOR ST
SCRIVENER LA
MACQUARIE RD
RAILWAY PDE
DAVID RD E
DE CHAIR AV
FELS AV
TUSCULUM RD
HILTON RD
BONTON PARK RD
WATTLE ST
SPRING ST
FARM RD
BRUCE ST
BATMAN CR
LALOR
BAKER ST
TAYLOR CT
SQUIRES RD
FLOREY CR
DEAKIN CL
PARER ST
FADDEN RD
EDNA AV
BURNS
SCOTT ST
VALLEY RD
CASSAM PL
THE AVENUE
TAYLER RD
PENINSULA
THE CHASE
GULLY RD
THE VALLEY RD
WYOMING AV
SPRINGFERN PL
CURRAWONG AV
BANKSIA
GREVILLEA PWY
TREE TOPS PL
DR
(Priv Rd)
FOSTER ST
GREEN
COOLABAH RD
ANGOPHORA PL
PDE
CAMBRIDGE ST
JORDAN LA
AV
RUSSELL AV
WARATAH
GREENS RD
McKENDRICK PL
PATERSON
MACKELLAR
WALKER ST
CIR
BANJO PL
RD
SUN VALLEY RD
RIDGEWAY CR
32

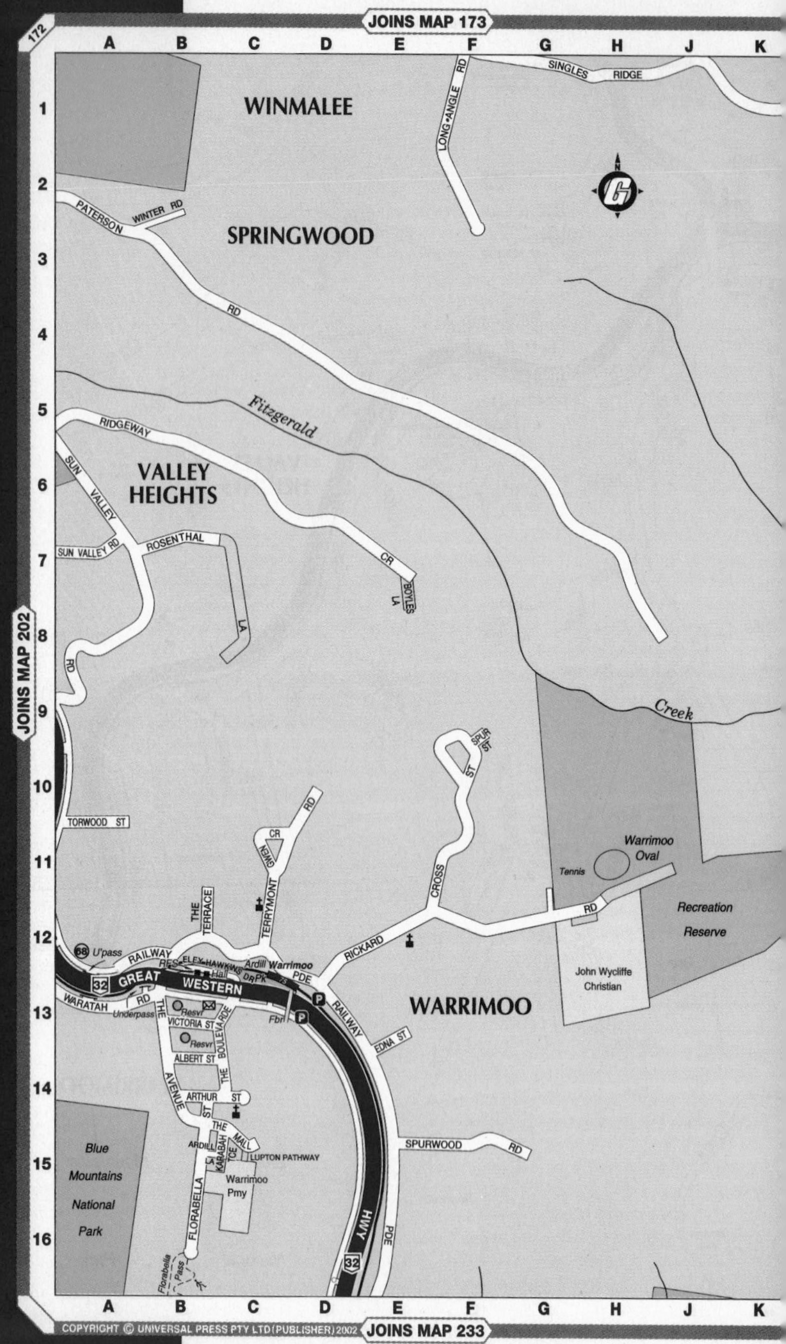
JOINS MAP 173
172
A
B
C
D
E
F
G
H
J
K
1
2
3
4
5
6
7
8
9
10
11
12
13
14
15
16
WINMALEE
SPRINGWOOD
VALLEY HEIGHTS
WARRIMOO
LONG ANGLE RD
SINGLES RIDGE
PATERSON RD
WINTER RD
RIDGEWAY CR
BOYLES LA
SUN VALLEY RD
ROSENTHAL LA
Fitzgerald Creek
TORWOOD ST
SPUR ST
CROSS ST
GWEN CR
TERRYMONT RD
THE TERRACE
RICKARD RD
Warrimoo Oval
Tennis
Recreation Reserve
John Wycliffe Christian
68 U'pass
RAILWAY PDE
RES
ELEY-HAWKINS DR
Hall
PK
Ardill
Warrimoo
32
GREAT WESTERN HWY
WARATAH RD
Underpass
THE AVENUE
Resvr
VICTORIA ST
THE BOULEVARDE
ALBERT ST
ARTHUR ST
Fbr
EDNA ST
RAILWAY PDE
SPURWOOD RD
THE MALL
ARDILL LA
KARABAH TCE
LUPTON PATHWAY
Warrimoo Pmy
FLORABELLA ST
Florabella Pass
Blue Mountains National Park
JOINS MAP 202
JOINS MAP 233

JOINS MAP 174

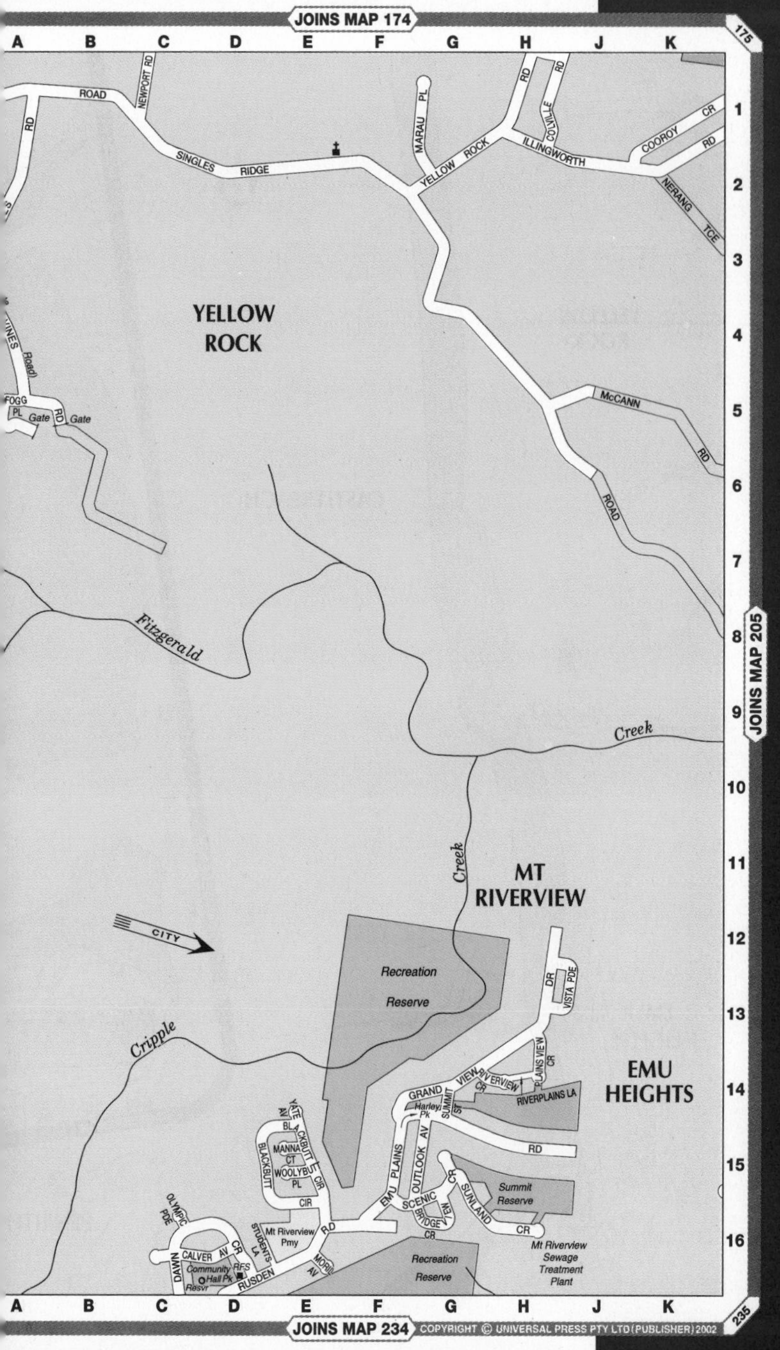

JOINS MAP 234

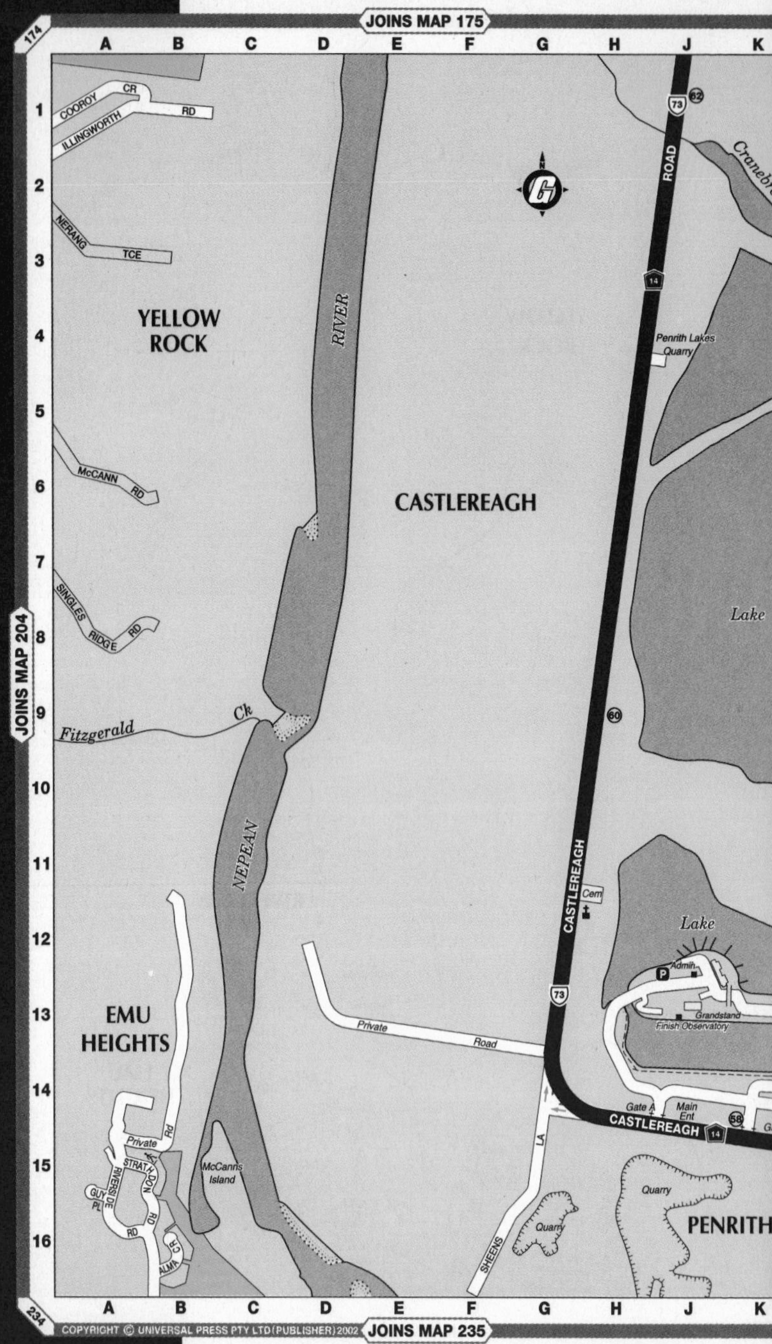
JOINS MAP 175
174
A B C D E F G H J K
1 2 3 4 5 6 7 8 9 10 11 12 13 14 15 16
COOROY CR
ILLINGWORTH RD
NERANG TCE
YELLOW ROCK
RIVER
ROAD
73
62
14
Cranebr
Penrith Lakes Quarry
CASTLEREAGH
McCANN RD
SINGLES RIDGE RD
Lake
JOINS MAP 204
Fitzgerald Ck
60
NEPEAN
CASTLEREAGH
Cem
Lake
Admin
Grandstand
Finish Observatory
Private Road
EMU HEIGHTS
Gate A
Main Ent
58
CASTLEREAGH
Private Rd
STRATH DON RD
RIVERSIDE DE
GUY PL
ALMA CR
McCanns Island
LA
Quarry
SHEENS
Quarry
PENRITH
234
JOINS MAP 235

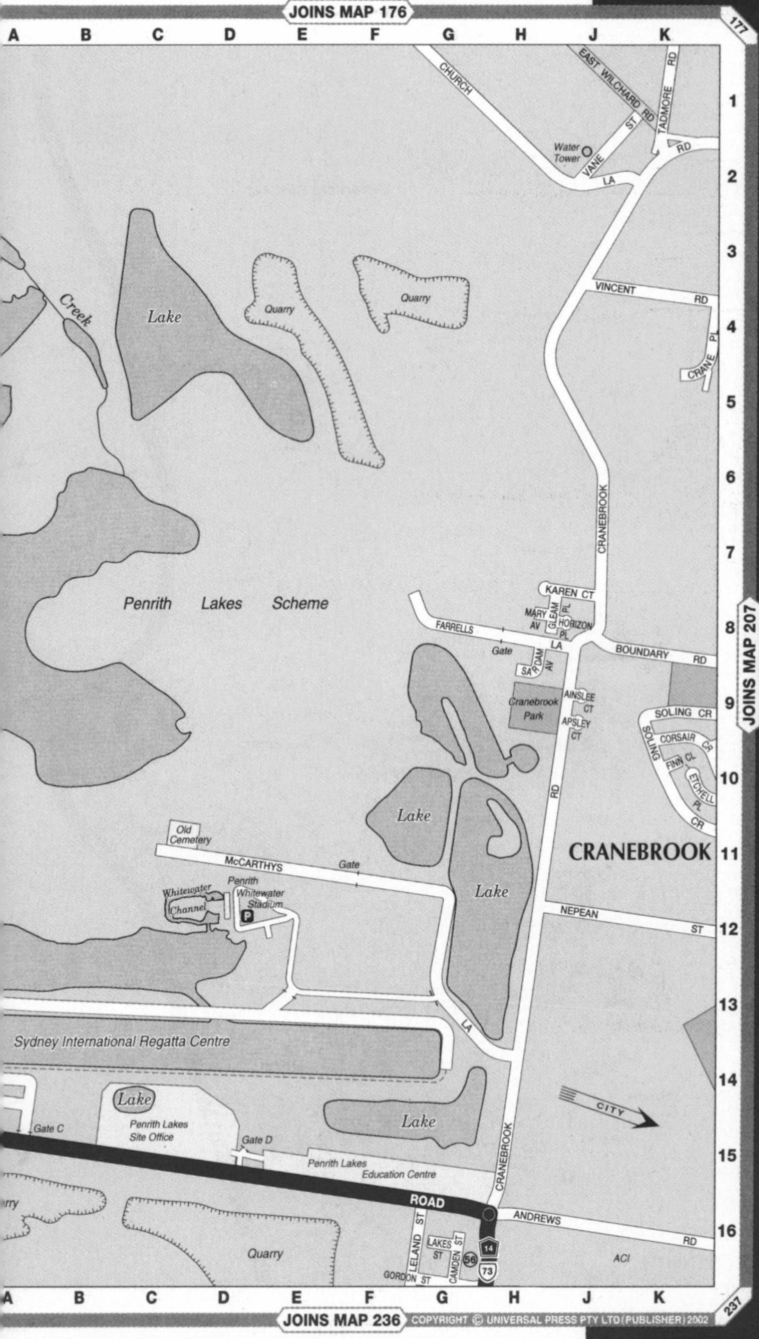

JOINS MAP 176
177
A
B
C
D
E
F
G
H
J
K
1
2
3
4
5
6
7
8
9
10
11
12
13
14
15
16
CHURCH
EAST WILCHARD RD
TADMORE RD
RD
ST
VANE
LA
Water Tower
Creek
Lake
Quarry
Quarry
VINCENT
RD
CRANE PL
CRANEBROOK
Penrith Lakes Scheme
KAREN CT
MARY AV
GLEAM PL
HORIZON PL
FARRELLS
LA
BOUNDARY RD
Gate
SA
ADAM AV
Cranebrook Park
AINSLEE CT
APSLEY CT
SOLING CR
SOLING
CORSAIR CR
FINN CL
ETCHELL PL
CR
RD
Lake
Old Cemetery
McCARTHYS
Gate
CRANEBROOK
Whitewater Channel
Penrith Whitewater Stadium
P
Lake
NEPEAN ST
LA
Sydney International Regatta Centre
Lake
Penrith Lakes Site Office
Gate C
Lake
CITY
Gate D
Penrith Lakes Education Centre
CRANEBROOK
ROAD
ANDREWS RD
LELAND ST
LAKES ST
CAMDEN ST
GORDON ST
56
14
73
Quarry
ACI
JOINS MAP 207
JOINS MAP 236
237

JOINS MAP 177

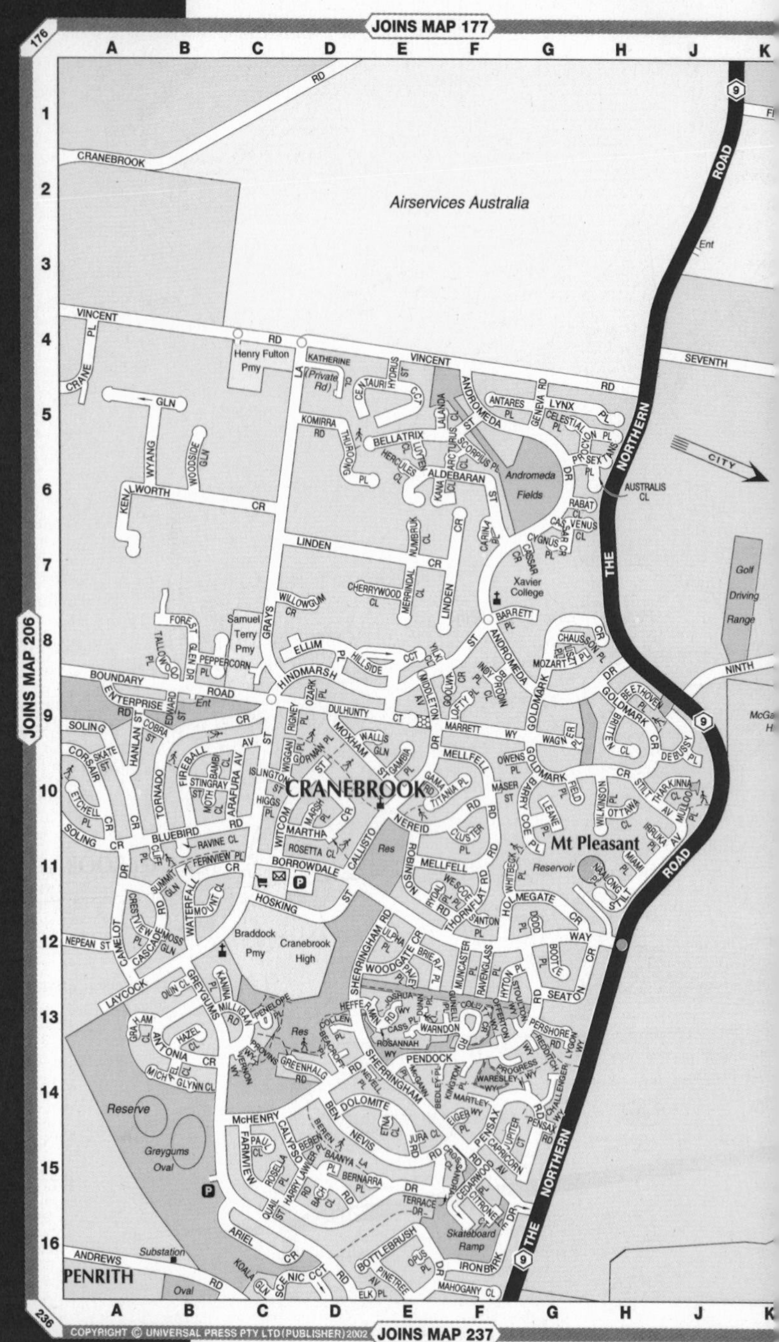

JOINS MAP 206

JOINS MAP 237

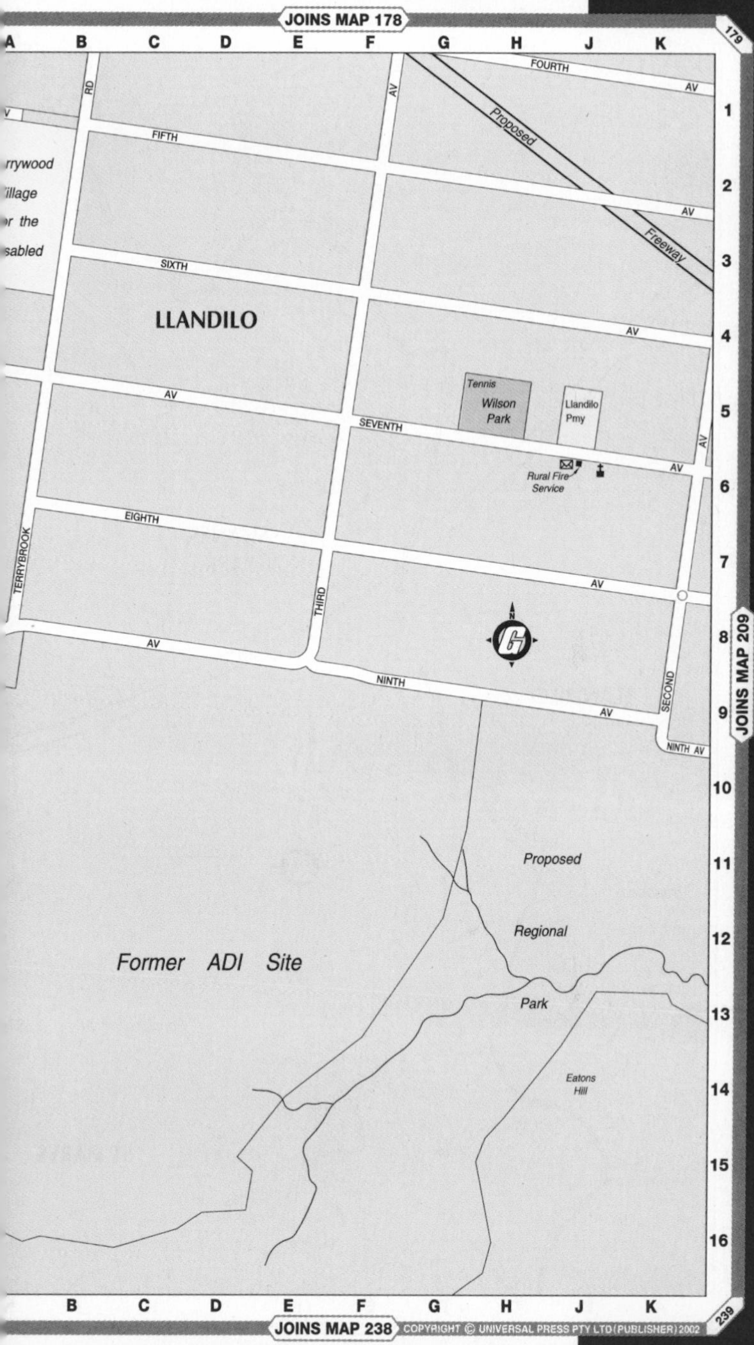
JOINS MAP 178
179
A B C D E F G H J K
1 2 3 4 5 6 7 8 9 10 11 12 13 14 15 16
FOURTH AV
Proposed
Freeway
FIFTH AV
SIXTH AV
SEVENTH AV
EIGHTH AV
NINTH AV
NINTH AV
RD
TERRYBROOK
THIRD
SECOND
AV
rrywood
'illage
r the
sabled
LLANDILO
Tennis
Wilson
Park
Llandilo
Pmy
Rural Fire
Service
N
Proposed
Regional
Park
Former ADI Site
Eatons
Hill
JOINS MAP 209
JOINS MAP 238
239

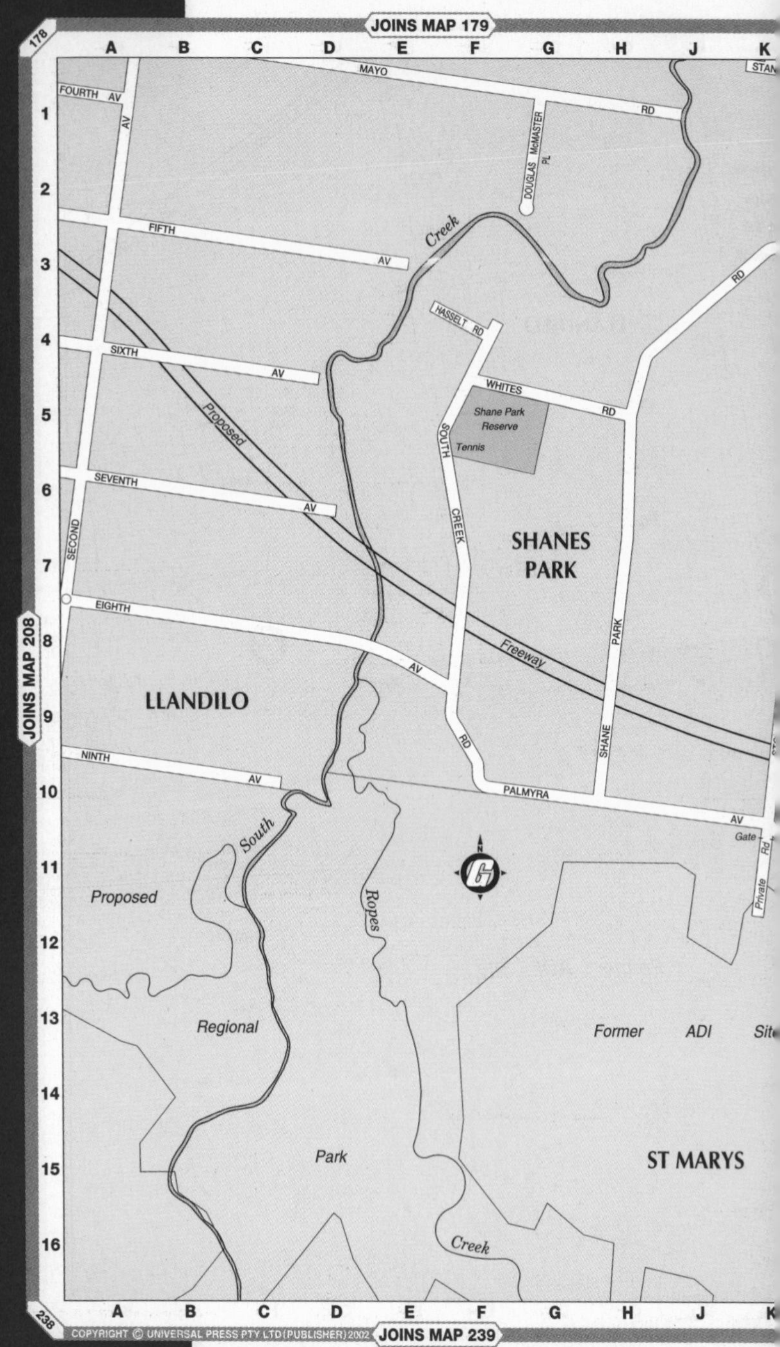

JOINS MAP 239

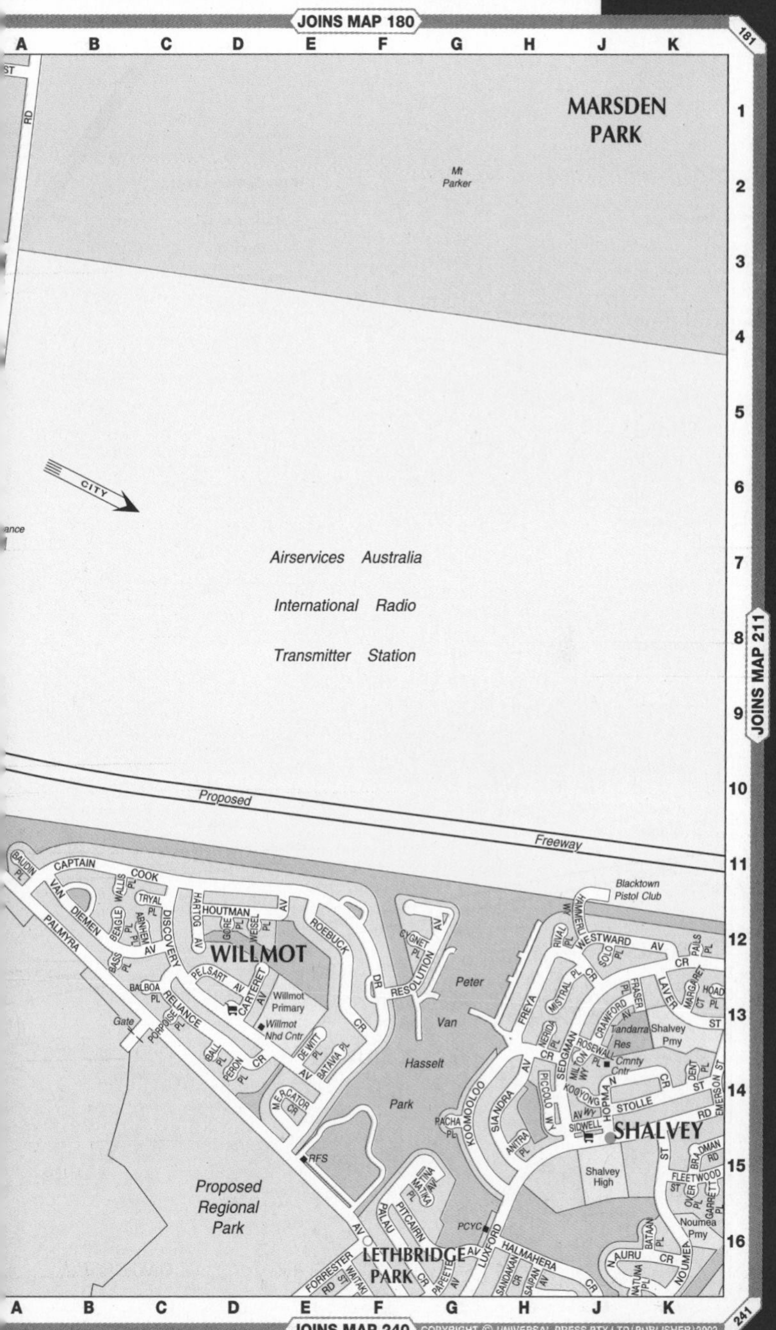
JOINS MAP 180
MARSDEN PARK
Mt Parker
CITY
Airservices Australia
International Radio
Transmitter Station
JOINS MAP 211
Proposed Freeway
WILLMOT
Willmot Primary
Willmot Nhd Cntr
Blacktown Pistol Club
Peter Van Hasselt Park
Tandarra Res
Shalvey Pmy
Cmnty Cntr
SHALVEY
Shalvey High
Noumea Pmy
RFS
PCYC
Proposed Regional Park
LETHBRIDGE PARK
Gate
CAPTAIN COOK
VAN DIEMEN AV
PALMYRA AV
DISCOVERY
HOUTMAN AV
HARTOG AV
ROEBUCK CR
RESOLUTION DR
CYGNET AV
RELIANCE CR
PELSART AV
CARTERET AV
BALBOA PL
PORPOISE PL
MERCATOR CR
BATAVIA PL
DE WITT PL
WESTWARD AV
FREYA CR
KOOMOOLOO CR
SIANDRA AV
PICCOLO WY
SEDGMAN CR
STOLLE RD
HOPMAN ST
EMERSON ST
FLEETWOOD ST
HALMAHERA CR
LUXFORD RD
FORRESTER RD
PITCAIRN AV
PALAU CR
PAPEETE AV
NOUMEA ST
AURU CR
JOINS MAP 240

JOINS MAP 181

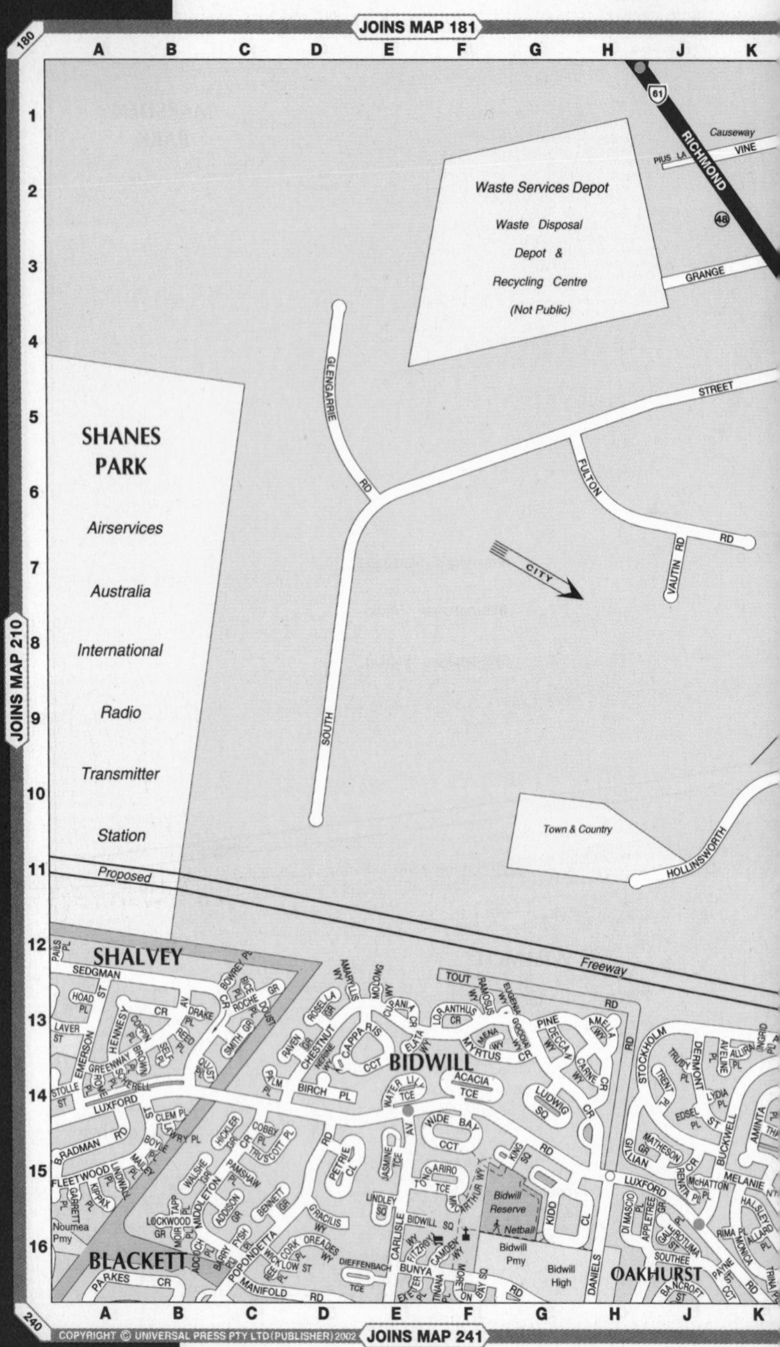

JOINS MAP 241

JOINS MAP 210

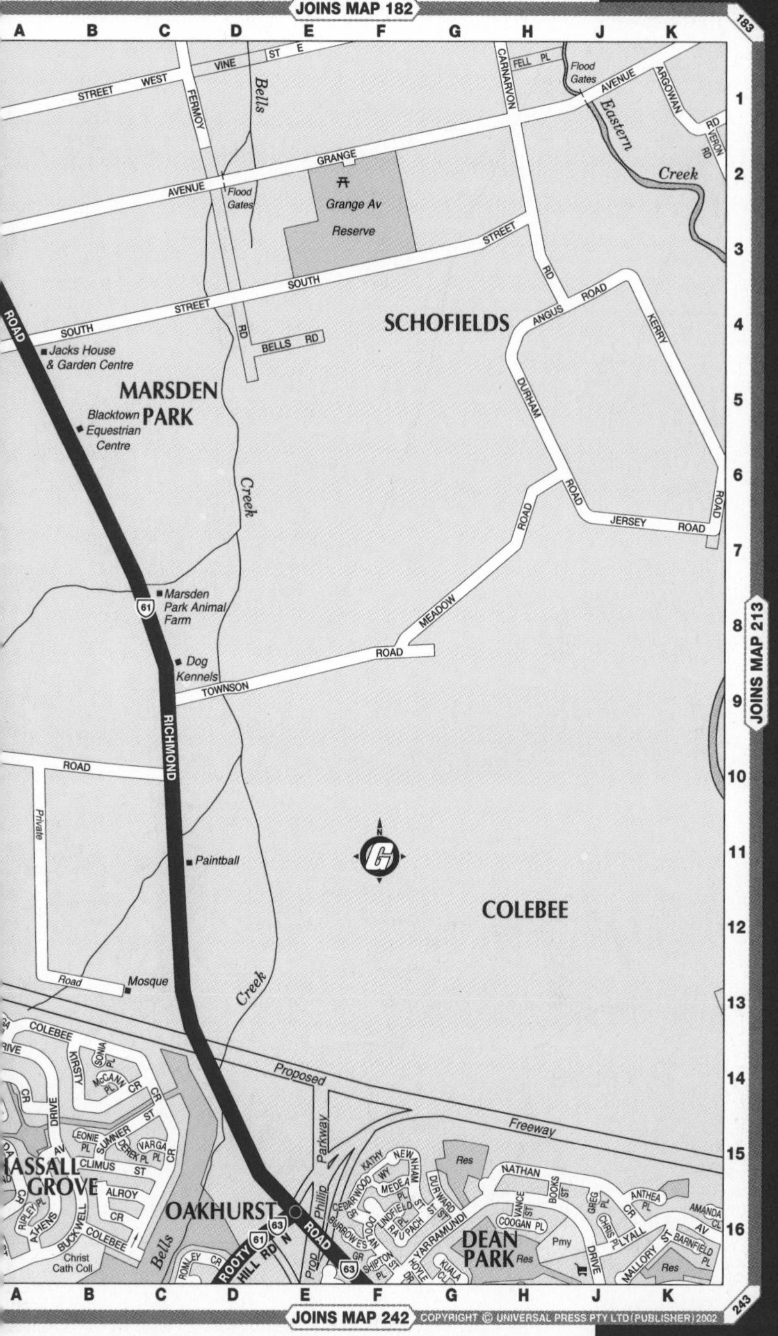
JOINS MAP 182
JOINS MAP 213
JOINS MAP 242
183
243
SCHOFIELDS
MARSDEN PARK
COLEBEE
OAKHURST
HASSALL GROVE
DEAN PARK
Grange Av Reserve
Jacks House & Garden Centre
Blacktown Equestrian Centre
Marsden Park Animal Farm
Dog Kennels
Paintball
Mosque
Christ Cath Coll
Flood Gates
Bells Creek
Eastern Creek
RICHMOND ROAD
SOUTH STREET
GRANGE AVENUE
WEST STREET
VINE ST E
FERMOY
CARNARVON
FELL PL
ARGOWAN
VERON RD
ANGUS ROAD
KERRY
DURHAM ROAD
JERSEY ROAD
MEADOW ROAD
TOWNSON ROAD
BELLS RD
Private Road
Proposed Freeway
Phillip Parkway
ROOTY HILL RD N
YARRAMUNDI
NATHAN
BOOKS ST
DRIVE
LYALL
MALLORY ST
BARNFIELD PL
AMANDA CL
ANTHEA PL
COLEBEE CR
ALROY CR
CLIMUS ST
SUMNER ST
VARGA PL
KIRSTY
SONIA PL
McCANN PL
ATHENS
BUCKWELL
RIPLEY PL
LEONIE PL
DEREK PL
ROMLEY CR
Res
Pmy

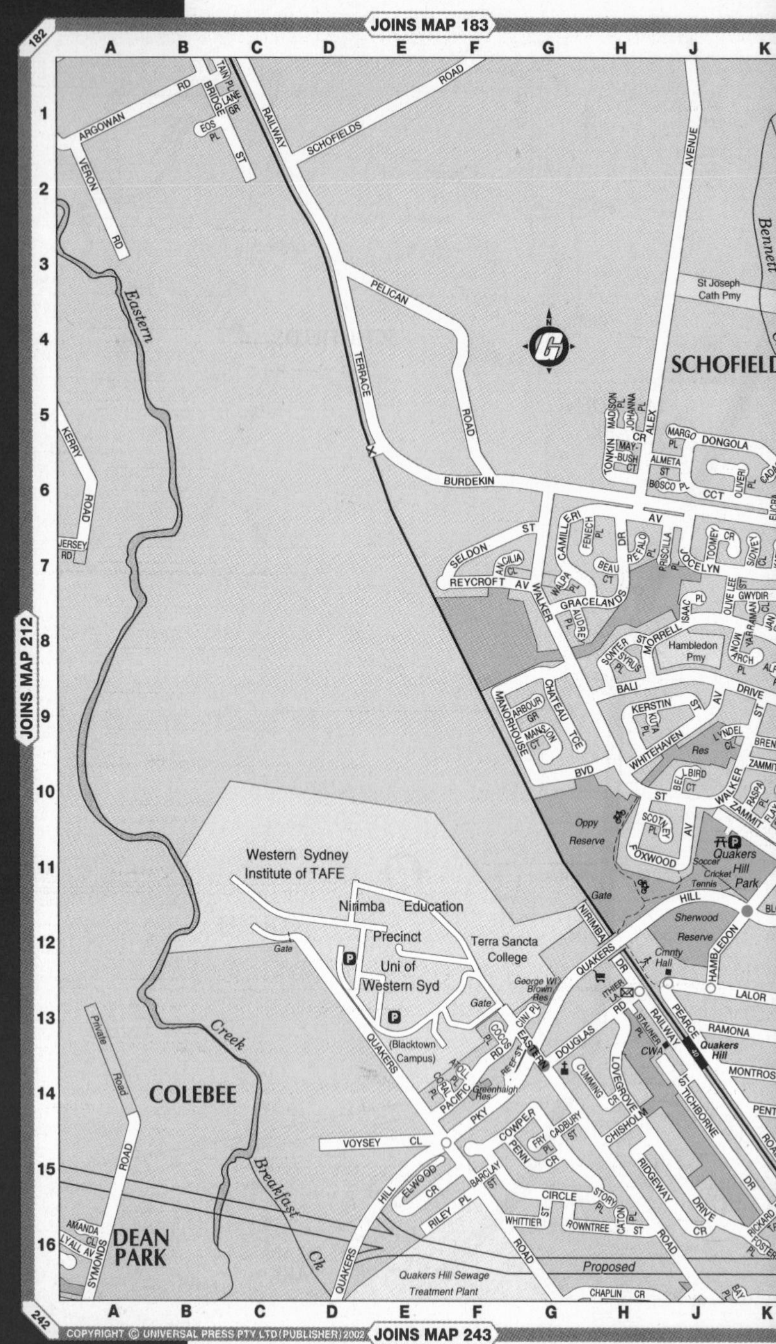
JOINS MAP 183
182
A B C D E F G H J K
1 2 3 4 5 6 7 8 9 10 11 12 13 14 15 16
JOINS MAP 212
ARGOWAN RD
VERON RD
BRIDGE ST
TAIN PL
LANE GR
EOS PL
RAILWAY TERRACE
SCHOFIELDS ROAD
PELICAN ROAD
AVENUE
Bennett
St Joseph Cath Pmy
SCHOFIELD
Eastern Creek
KERRY ROAD
JERSEY RD
MADISON PL
JOHANNA PL
ALEX CR
TONKIN PL
MAY-BUSH CT
MARGO PL
DONGOLA
ALMETA ST
BOSCO PL
CCT
OLIVERI PL
BURDEKIN AV
SELDON ST
ANCILIA CL
REYCROFT AV
CAMILLERI DR
FENECH PL
BEAU CT
REFALO PL
PRISCILLA PL
JOCELYN
TOOMEY CR
SIDNEY CL
WALKER
WALPA PL
GRACELANDS
AUDREY PL
ISAAC PL
OLIVE LEE ST
GWYDIR
YARRAMAN
JAN CL
MORRELL ST
SONTER
SYRUS PL
Hambledon Pmy
NOW ARCH PL
BALI DRIVE
CHATEAU TCE
MANORHOUSE BVD
ARBOUR GR
MANSION CT
KERSTIN ST
KUTA PL
AV
WHITEHAVEN
LYNDEL CL
Res
BRENT
ZAMMIT
LBIRD CT
BEL
ST
WALKER
ZAMMIT
RASPA PL
SCOTNEY PL
FOXWOOD AV
Oppy Reserve
Quakers Hill Park
Soccer
Cricket
Tennis
Gate
HILL
NIRIMBA
Sherwood Reserve
HAMBLEDON
Cmnty Hall
LALOR
RAMONA
Quakers Hill
MONTROSE
Western Sydney Institute of TAFE
Nirimba Education Precinct
Uni of Western Syd
(Blacktown Campus)
Terra Sancta College
Gate
George WI Brown Res
QUAKERS
DR
ITHIER LA
RAILWAY
STAUNER PL
CWA
PEARCE
TICHBORNE
DOUGLAS
RD
EASTERN
CINI PL
COCOS RD
REEF ST
ATOLL PL
CORAL PL
PACIFIC PKY
Greenhalgh Res
CUMMING CR
LOVEGROVE
CHISHOLM
QUAKERS HILL
Private Road
COLEBEE
VOYSEY CL
COWPER
PENN CR
FRY PL
CADBURY ST
RIDGEWAY
DRIVE
CR
ELWOOD CR
BARCLAY ST
RILEY PL
CIRCLE
STORY PL
WHITTIER ST
ROWNTREE ST
CATON PL
ROAD
Breakfast Ck
ROAD
AMANDA CL
LYALL AV
SYMONDS
DEAN PARK
QUAKERS
Quakers Hill Sewage Treatment Plant
Proposed
CHAPLIN CR
BAY PL
RICKARD
FOSTER PL
242
JOINS MAP 243

JOINS MAP 184

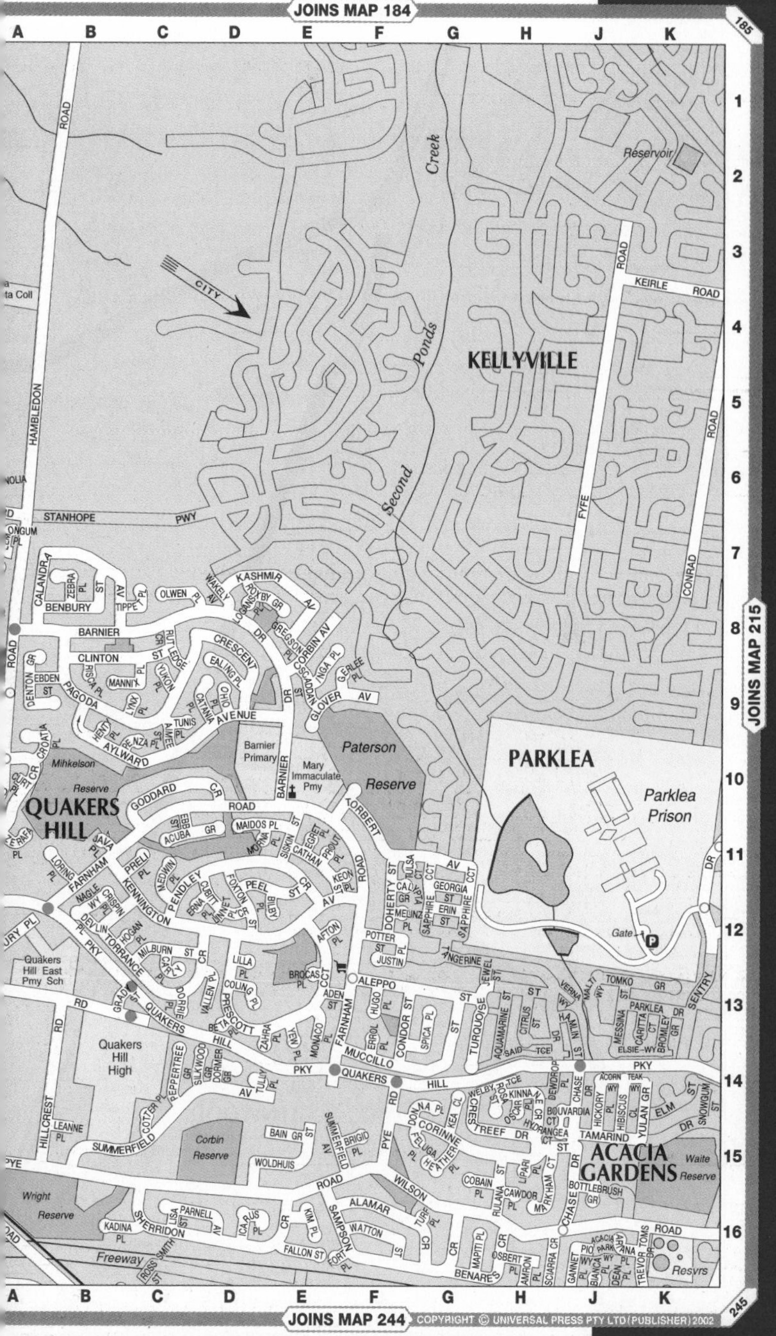

JOINS MAP 215

JOINS MAP 244

MAP 215

JOINS MAP 185
JOINS MAP 214
JOINS MAP 245
184
244
A B C D E F G H J K
1 2 3 4 5 6 7 8 9 10 11 12 13 14 15 16
STANHOPE GARDENS
PARKLEA
GLENWOOD
WINDSOR RD
OLD WINDSOR RD
WINDSOR RD
BURNS RD
SUNNYHOLT RD
Caddies Ck
Macarthur
Creek
Elizabeth
Macarthur Park
WHITEHEART BRIDGE
Golf Range
Display Village
Proposed Pond
Stanhope Reserve
Tennis
Softball
Parklea Leisure Centre
Parklea Markets
Meriton Mobile Village
Davison Reserve
Integral Energy
Tennis Coaching Centre
Kellyville Christmas Tree Farm
Detention Basin
High School Site
Waite Res
Copercornia Reserve
Cmnty Cntr
Reserve
Parklea Garden Village
Pmy Sch Site
Parklea Pmy
Reservoir
CONRAD RD
MERRIVILLE RD
PERFECTION AV
STANHOPE PKY
PHOENIX DR
SENTRY DR
QUAKERS HILL PKY
MALVERN RD
FORMAN AV
GLENWOOD PARK DR
BALMORAL
ARNOLD AV

JOINS MAP 186

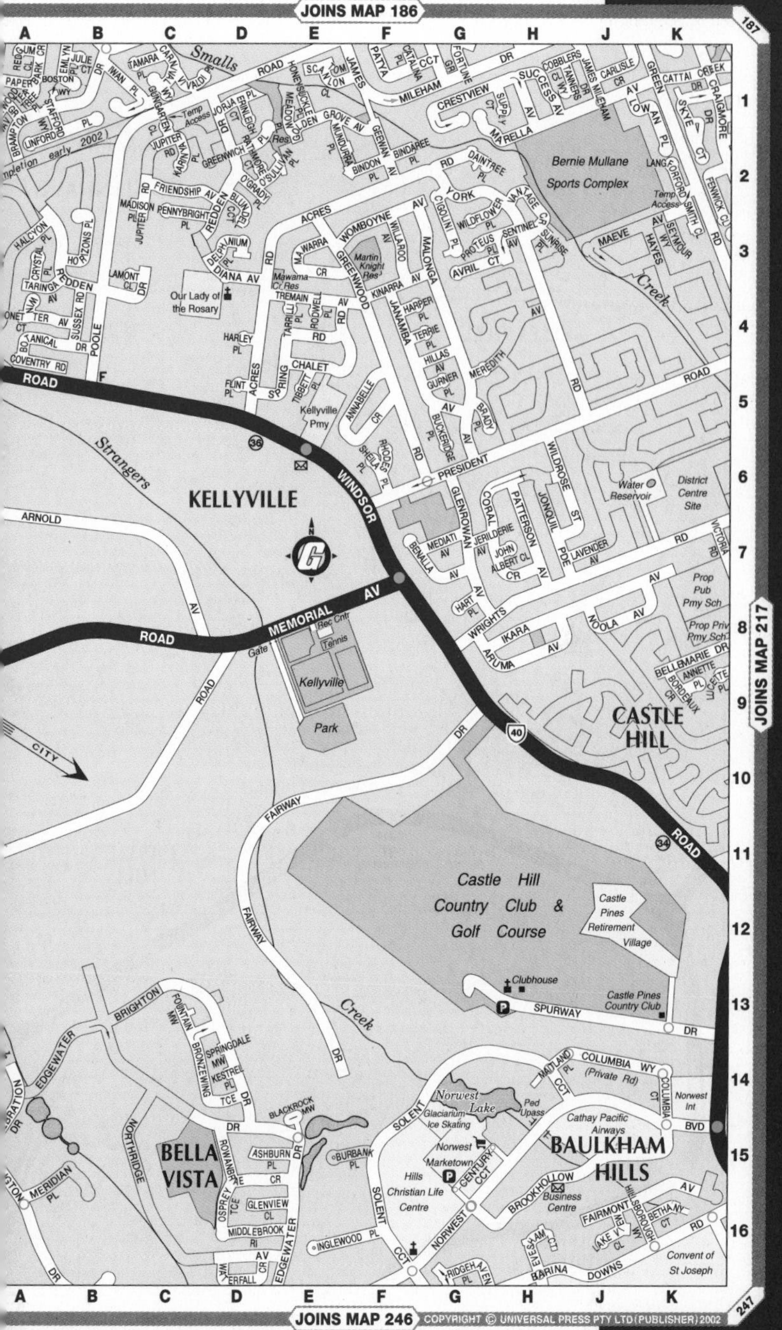

JOINS MAP 217

JOINS MAP 246

MAP 217

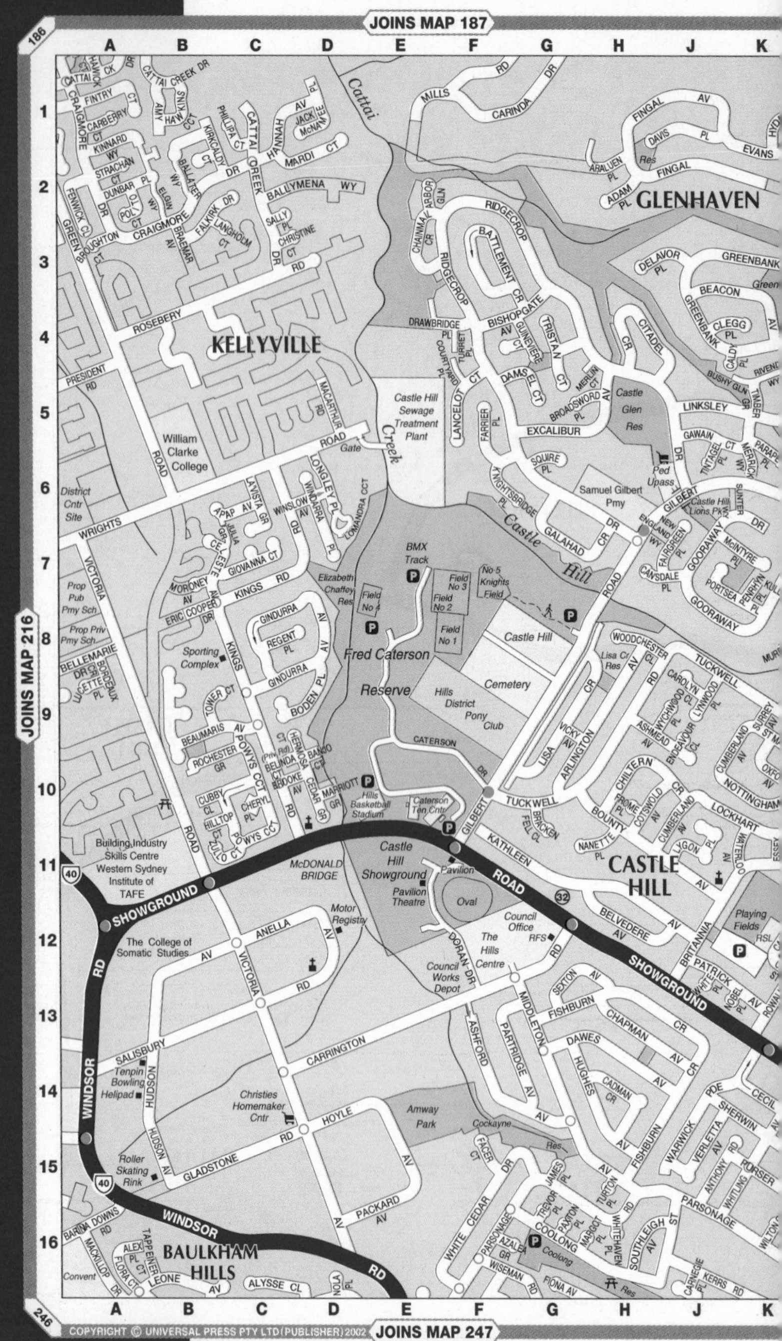
JOINS MAP 187
JOINS MAP 216
JOINS MAP 247
186
246
A B C D E F G H J K
1 2 3 4 5 6 7 8 9 10 11 12 13 14 15 16
KELLYVILLE
GLENHAVEN
CASTLE HILL
BAULKHAM HILLS
Cattai Creek
Castle Hill
William Clarke College
Castle Hill Sewage Treatment Plant
Castle Glen Res
Samuel Gilbert Pmy
Ped Upass
Castle Hill Lions Pk
District Cntr Site
Prop Pub Pmy Sch
Prop Priv Pmy Sch
Sporting Complex
Elizabeth Chaffey Res
BMX Track
Field No 1
Field No 2
Field No 3
Field No 4
No 5 Knights Field
Fred Caterson Reserve
Castle Hill Cemetery
Hills District Pony Club
Lisa Cr Res
Hills Basketball Stadium
Caterson Ten Cntr
Castle Hill Showground
Pavilion
Pavilion Theatre
Oval
Council Office
RFS
The Hills Centre
Council Works Depot
Building Industry Skills Centre Western Sydney Institute of TAFE
McDONALD BRIDGE
Motor Registry
The College of Somatic Studies
Tenpin Bowling
Helipad
Christies Homemaker Cntr
Amway Park
Cockayne Res
Roller Skating Rink
Playing Fields
RSL
Convent
Coolong Res
40
32
SHOWGROUND ROAD
WINDSOR RD
VICTORIA ROAD
GILBERT ROAD
OLD NORTHERN ROAD
WRIGHTS ROAD
KINGS RD
CARRINGTON RD
GLADSTONE RD
HOYLE AV
PACKARD AV
ANELLA AV
SALISBURY RD
HUDSON AV
CATERSON DR
TUCKWELL RD
KATHLEEN AV
BELVEDERE AV
MIDDLETON AV
FISHBURN CR
CHAPMAN AV
PARSONAGE RD
WHITE CEDAR DR
COOLONG RD
ROSEBERY RD
CRAIGMORE DR
PRESIDENT RD
GREEN RD
RIDGECROP DR
BATTLEMENT CR
BISHOPGATE AV
EXCALIBUR AV
KNIGHTSBRIDGE PL
GALAHAD CR
FINGAL AV
CARINDA DR
MILLS RD
GOORAWAY DR
LINKSLEY AV
ARLINGTON AV
LISA CR
VICKY AV
CHILTERN CR
NOTTINGHAM ST
LOCKHART AV
BRITANNIA RD
PATRICK AV
CECIL AV
SHERWIN AV
BARINA DOWNS RD
ALYSSE CL
LEONE AV
WISEMAN RD
KERRS RD

JOINS MAP 188

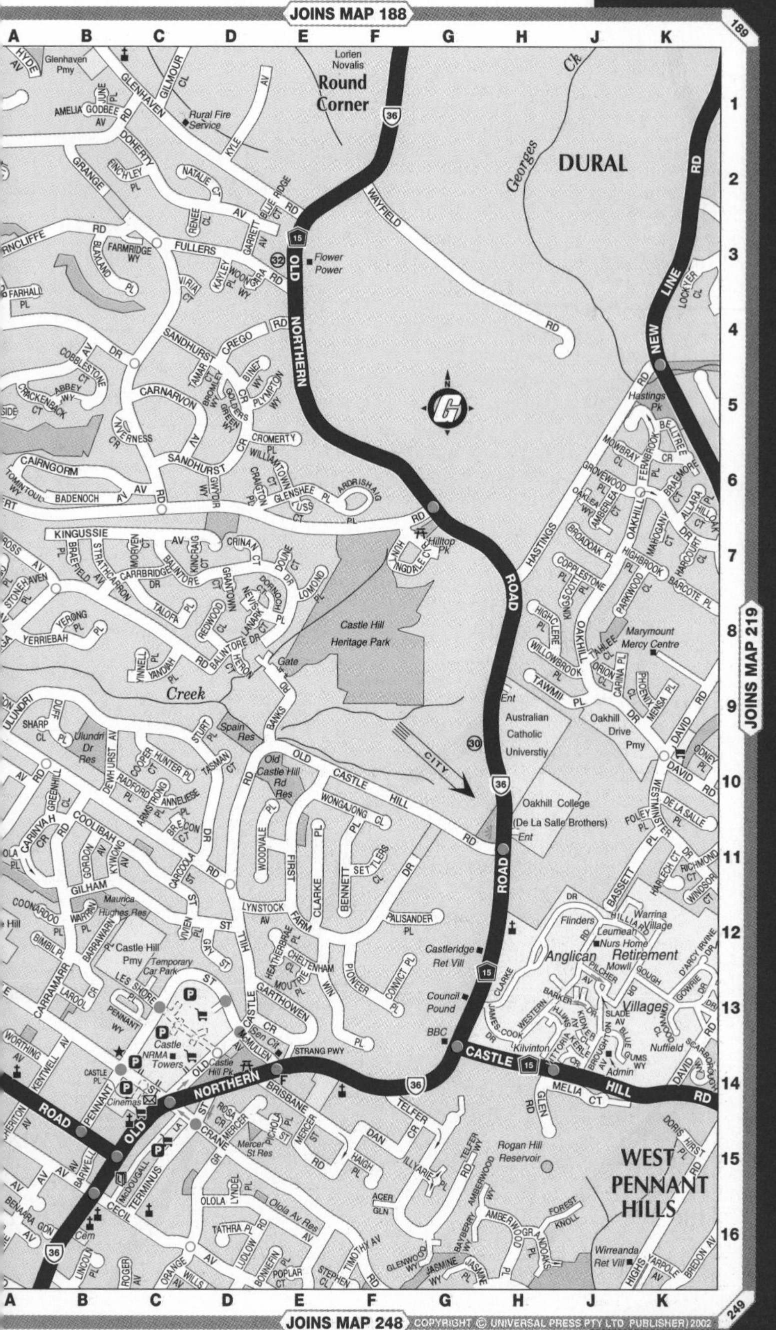

JOINS MAP 219

JOINS MAP 248

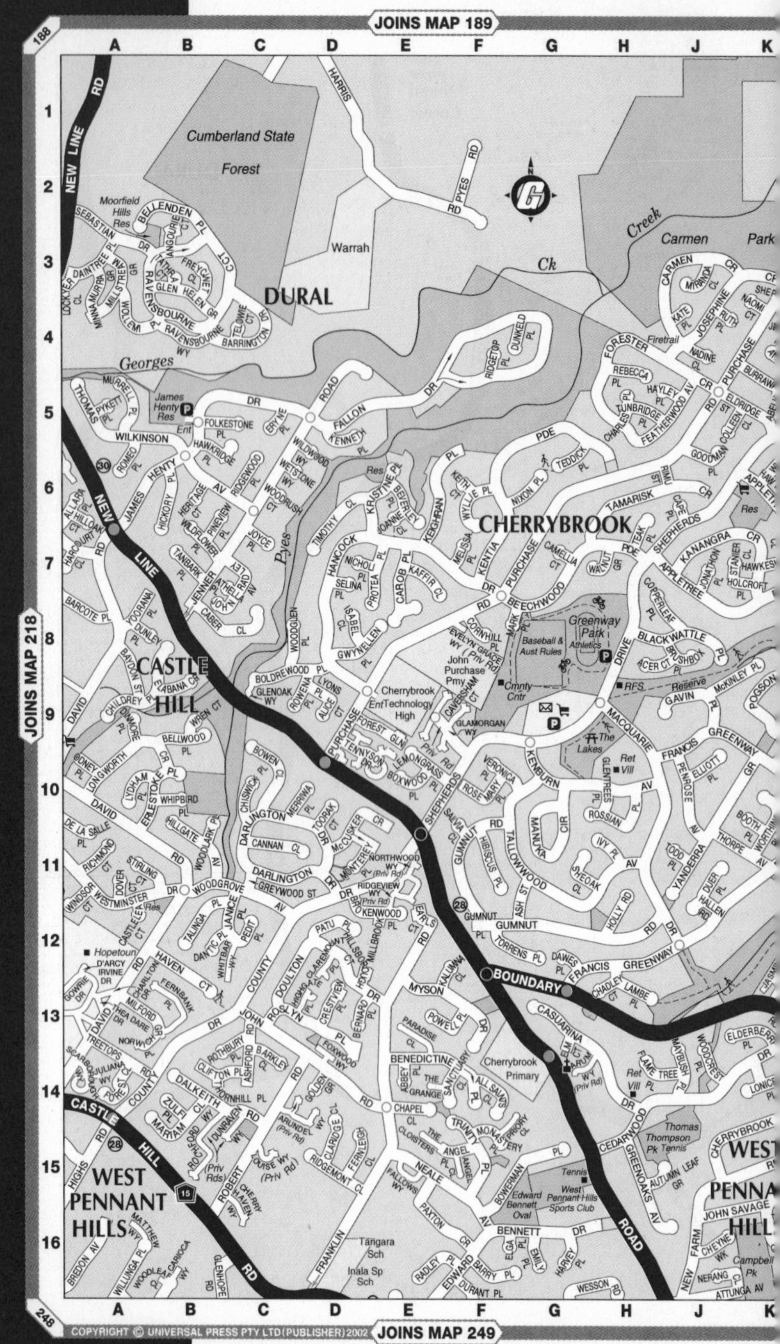
JOINS MAP 189
JOINS MAP 218
JOINS MAP 249
188
248
A B C D E F G H J K
1 2 3 4 5 6 7 8 9 10 11 12 13 14 15 16
NEW LINE RD
Cumberland State Forest
HARRIS
PYES RD
Warrah
DURAL
Moorfield Hills Res
BELLENDEN PL
SEBASTIAN DR
DAINTREE
LOCKYER CL
MINNAMURRA
MILLSTREET
WOLLEMI
RAVENSBOURNE
RAVENSBOURNE WY
GLEN HELEN GR
FREYCINET CL
LANGOURIE CT
TELOWIE CT
BARRINGTON DR
Georges
Creek
Ck
Carmen Park
CARMEN CR
MIRANDA CL
KATE PL
JOSEPHINE
RUTH PL
NAOMI CT
FORESTER CR
Firetrail
NADINE CL
PURCHASE RD
REBECCA PL
HAYLEY PL
TUNBRIDGE PL
CHARLES PL
FEATHERWOOD AV
ELDRIDGE ST
COLLEEN CL
GOODMAN PL
MURRELL PL
THOMAS
PYKETT PL
James Henty Res
Ent
FOLKESTONE PL
ERYNE PL
ROAD
FALLON DR
KENNETH PL
RIDGETOP PL
DUNKELD PL
WILKINSON
HAWKRIDGE PL
ROMEO PL
HENTY AV
WILDWOOD WY
WETSTONE WY
RIDGEWOOD PL
WOODRUSH CT
Res
KRISTINE PL
BEVERLEY CL
JOANNE CL
KEIGHRAN
KEITH CT
WYLLIE PL
PDE
TEDDICK PL
NIXON PL
TAMARISK
RIMU ST
SHEPHERDS
CAPE PL
CHERRYBROOK
ALLARA
HILLOAK CT
HARCOURT RD
NEW LINE
JAMES
HICKORY PL
HERITAGE CT
PINEVIEW PL
WILDFLOWER
TANBARK CL
JENNER
ATHELL AV
JOHN
LEY
JOYCE PL
TIMOTHY CL
Pyes
HANCOCK
NICHOLI PL
SELINA PL
PROTEA PL
CAROB PL
KAFFIR CL
MELISSA PL
KENTIA
PURCHASE
CAMELLIA CT
WALNUT GR
TEAK PL
KANANGRA CR
JONATHON
STANIER CL
HAWKESWORTH
HOLCROFT PL
APPLETREE
COPPERLEAF PL
BARCOTE PL
YOORANA
DUNLEY
CABER CL
WOODGLEN PL
ISABEL PL
GWYNELLEN
DR
RD
BEECHWOOD
CORNHILL PL
EVELYN GRACE WY (Priv Rd)
MARK
Greenway Park
Baseball & Aust Rules
Athletics
DRIVE
BLACKWATTLE
BRUSHBOX PL
ACER CT
John Purchase Pmy
CAVERSHAM CT
Cmnty Cntr
RFS
Reserve
GAVIN PL
McKINLEY PL
POGSON
BAYDON ST
CASTLE HILL
CABANA CR
CHILDREY PL
DINMORE
WREN CT
DAVID
BOLDREWOOD PL
GLENOAK WY
ROWENA PL
LYONS PL
ALICE CT
Cherrybrook Technology High
PURCHASE
FOREST GLN
TENNYSON DR
LEMONGRASS
BOXWOOD PL
GLAMORGAN WY
Priv Rd
MACQUARIE
The Lakes
Ret Vill
KENBURN
FRANCIS
GREENWAY
PENROSE
ELLIOTT PL
BELLWOOD PL
ODNEY PL
LONGWORTH
LYDHAM PL
ERLESTOKE PL
WHIPBIRD PL
BOWEN CL
CHISWICK PL
MERRIWA
DARLINGTON
TOORAK CT
McCUSKER CR
SHEPHERDS
SALVIA CL
VERONICA PL
ROSEMARY PL
GLENTREES
ROSSIAN
DE LA SALLE PL
RICHMOND
STIRLING
HILLGATE PL
WOODLARK PL
CANNAN CL
NORTHWOOD WY (Priv Rd)
MONTEREY
GUMNUT
HIBISCUS PL
TALLOWWOOD
MANUKA CIR
IVY PL
SHEOAK CL
BOOTH PL
THORPE AV
TODD PL
YANDERRA
DUER PL
HALLEN RD
WINDSOR CT
DOVER CT
WESTMINSTER
CASTLELEA CT
Res
WOODGROVE AV
DARLINGTON
GREYWOOD ST
RIDGEVIEW WY (Priv Rd)
KENWOOD PL
EARLS CT
ASH ST
HOLLY RD
TALINGA PL
JANICE PL
DANTIC PL
WHITBAR WY
PEDIT PL
PATU PL
CLAREMOUNT CT
HILLSBOROUGH
MILLBROOK PL
TORRENS PL
DAWES PL
FRANCIS GREENWAY
Hopetoun
D'ARCY IRVINE DR
HAVEN CT
FERNBANK PL
COUNTY DR
DOULTON
CRESTVIEW PL
BERNARD PL
MYSON DR
KALUMNA CL
POWELL PL
BOUNDARY RD
CHADLEY CT
LAMBE PL
CASUARINA
GOWRIE DR
CHARLTON
MILFORD GR
THEA DARE DR
NORWICH
JOHN
ROSLYN
FOXWOOD WY
PARADISE CL
BENEDICTINE PL
ELM CT
ARUM WY (Priv Rd)
MAYBUSH PL
WOODCREST
ELDERBERRY PL
TREETOPS
SCARBOROUGH WY
JULIANA PL
FOREST CL
ROTHBURY PL
CLIFTON PL
ASHFORD RD
BARKLEY CL
GOLDEN GR
ABBEY PL
THE GRANGE
SANCTUARY
ALL SAINTS CL
Cherrybrook Primary
FLAME TREE PL
Ret Vill
LONICERA
DALKEITH
THORNHILL PL
ZULFI PL
MARIAM CL
ROCHFORD
DUNRAVEN WY
CASTLE HILL RD
ARUNDEL WY (Priv Rd)
CLARIDGE CL
CHAPEL CL
CLOISTERS
THE ANGEL
TRINITY PL
MONASTERY
PRIORY CL
CEDARWOOD DR
GREENOAKS AV
Thomas Thompson Pk
Tennis
AUTUMN LEAF GR
CHERRYBROOK
WEST
(Priv Rds)
OUISE WY (Priv Rd)
RIDGEMONT CL
FERNLEIGH CL
NEALE AV
FALLOWS WY
BOWERMAN
Tennis
West Pennant Hills Sports Club
Edward Bennett Oval
PENNANT HILLS
JOHN SAVAGE
HIGHS
WEST PENNANT HILLS
ROBERT
CHERRY HAVEN WY
MATTHEW WY
PAXTON
BENNETT DR
BREDON AV
WILLUNGA PL
WOODLEA
CARIOCA WY
GLENHOPE RD
FRANKLIN
Tangara Sch
Inala Sp Sch
RADLEY PL
EDWARD
BARRY PL
DURANT PL
ELGA PL
EMILY PL
HARVEY PL
WESSON RD
ROAD
NEW FARM RD
CHEYNE WK
NERANG CL
ATTUNGA AV
Campbell Pk
28
29
30
15

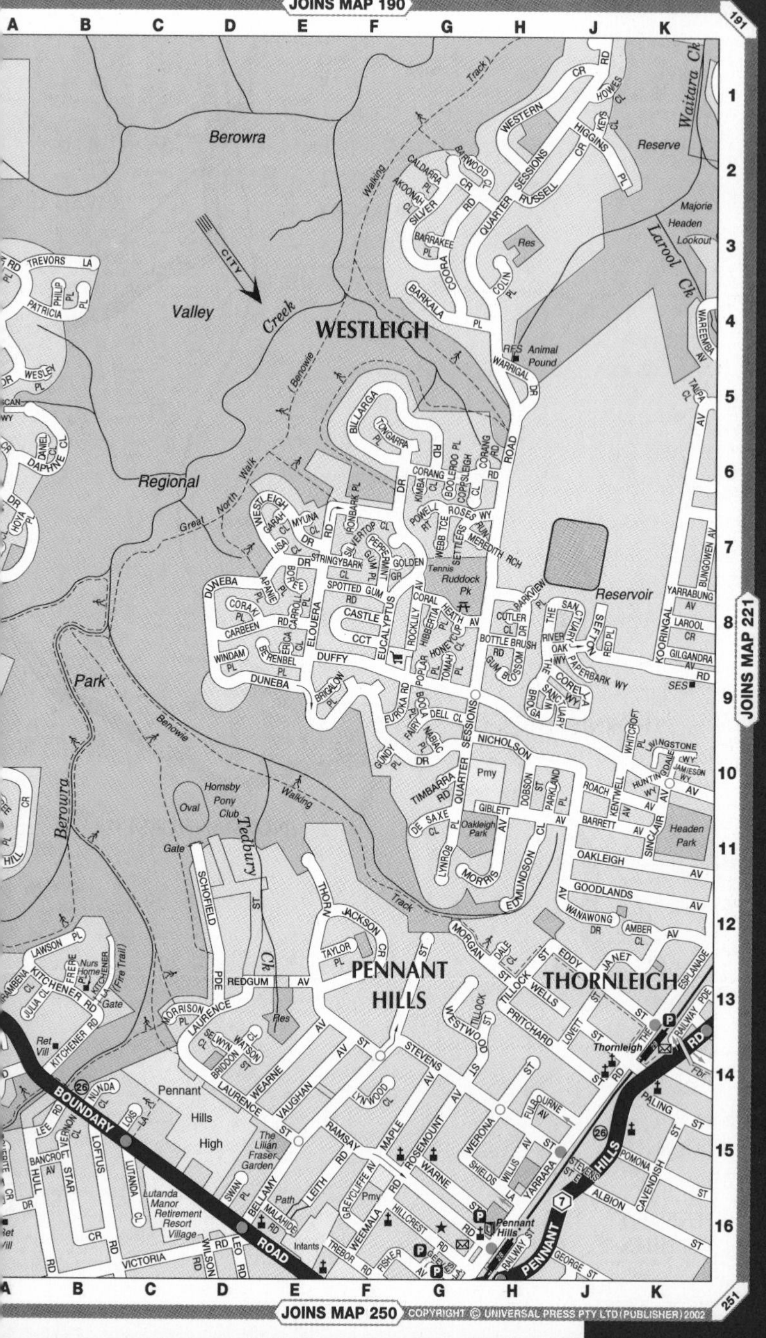
JOINS MAP 190
JOINS MAP 221
JOINS MAP 250
191
251
A B C D E F G H J K
1 2 3 4 5 6 7 8 9 10 11 12 13 14 15 16
WESTLEIGH
PENNANT HILLS
THORNLEIGH
Berowra
Valley
Regional
Park
Creek
Berowra
Great North Walk
Benowie Walking Track
Walking Track
Waitara Ck
Reserve
Majorie Headen Lookout
Larool Ck
Res
RFS
Animal Pound
Reservoir
Tennis
Ruddock Pk
Hornsby Pony Club
Oval
Gate
Tedbury Ck
Pmy
Oakleigh Park
Headen Park
SES
Nurs Home
Ret Vill
(Fire Trail)
Pennant Hills High
The Lilian Fraser Garden
Lutanda Manor Retirement Resort Village
Infants
Path
Thornleigh
Pennant Hills
Fbr
BOUNDARY ROAD
PENNANT HILLS RD
QUARTER SESSIONS ROAD
TREVORS LA
PATRICIA
PHILIP PL
WESLEY PL
DANIEL CL
DAPHNE CL
HOYA
WESTERN CR
HOWES CL
KEYS CL
HIGGINS PL
SESSIONS
RUSSELL
BARWOOD CL
CALDARRA PL
AKOONAH CL
SILVER
BARRAKEE PL
COORA RD
COLIN PL
BARKALA PL
WARRIGAL DR
WAREEMBA AV
TAUPA CL
BILLARGA
TONGARRA PL
CORANG RD
BOOLEROO PL
COPPSLEIGH CL
KIMBA CL
WESTLEIGH DR
GARAH
MYUNA CL
LISA CL
IRONBARK PL
SILVERTOP CL
PEPPERMINT
GUM PL
GOLDEN GR
POWELL RT
WEBB TCE
SETTLERS
ROSES WY
MEREDITH RCH
STRINGYBARK CL
SPOTTED GUM RD
CASTLE CCT
EUCALYPTUS
CORAL HEATH AV
DUNEBA
APANIE PL
BORONIA
CORAKI PL
CARBEEN RD
CARROLL CL
ELOUERA
ERICA CL
WINDAM PL
BEBRENBEL PL
DUFFY
BRIGALOW PL
ROCKLILY
HIBBERTIA PL
HONEYCUP CL
POPLAR PL
TOMAH PL
EUROKA RD
BOOLA
DELL CL
FAIRY PL
MABIAC PL
GUNDY PL
CUTLER CL
BOTTLE BRUSH RD
GUM BLOSSOM DR
PARKVIEW PL
THE SANCTUARY
RIVER OAK WY
PAPERBARK WY
COREL LA
BROLGA
SEFTON
RED PL
KOORINGAL
YARRABUNG AV
LAROOL CR
GILGANDRA AV
BUNGOWEN AV
NICHOLSON
TIMBARRA RD
DE SAXE CL
GIBLETT AV
LYNROB PL
MORRIS
EDMUNDSON CL
DOBSON ST
PARKLAND PL
WHITCROFT PL
WINGSTONE
HUNTINGDALE WY
JAMIESON WY
ROACH AV
KENTWELL AV
BARRETT AV
SINCLAIR AV
OAKLEIGH AV
GOODLANDS AV
WANAWONG DR
AMBER CL
SCHOFIELD PDE
THORN
JACKSON CR
TAYLOR PL
MORGAN ST
DALE CL
EDDY ST
JANET
ESPLANADE
TILLOCK
WELLS
PRITCHARD
WESTWOOD
LOVETT ST
RAILWAY PDE
REDGUM AV
LAWSON PL
FRERE PL
KITCHENER RD
JULIA CL
MORRISON PL
LAURENCE
SELWYN CL
WATSON CL
BRIDDON ST
WEARNE AV
VAUGHAN AV
STEVENS ST
LYNWOOD CL
MAPLE AV
ROSEMOUNT AV
WERONA AV
FULBOURNE AV
NUNDA CL
LOIS LA
LEE RD
VERNON CL
BANCROFT AV
HULL
STAR
LOFTUS
LUTANDA CL
SWAN PL
BELLAMY
MALAHIDE RD
LEITH
RAMSAY RD
GREYCLIFFE AV
WEEMALA
HILLCREST RD
WARNE
SHIELDS LA
WILLIS
YARRARA
PALING ST
POMONA
CAVENDISH
ALBION
GEORGE ST
TREBOR RD
FISHER AV
VICTORIA
WILSON RD
LEO RD
COPYRIGHT © UNIVERSAL PRESS PTY LTD (PUBLISHER) 2002

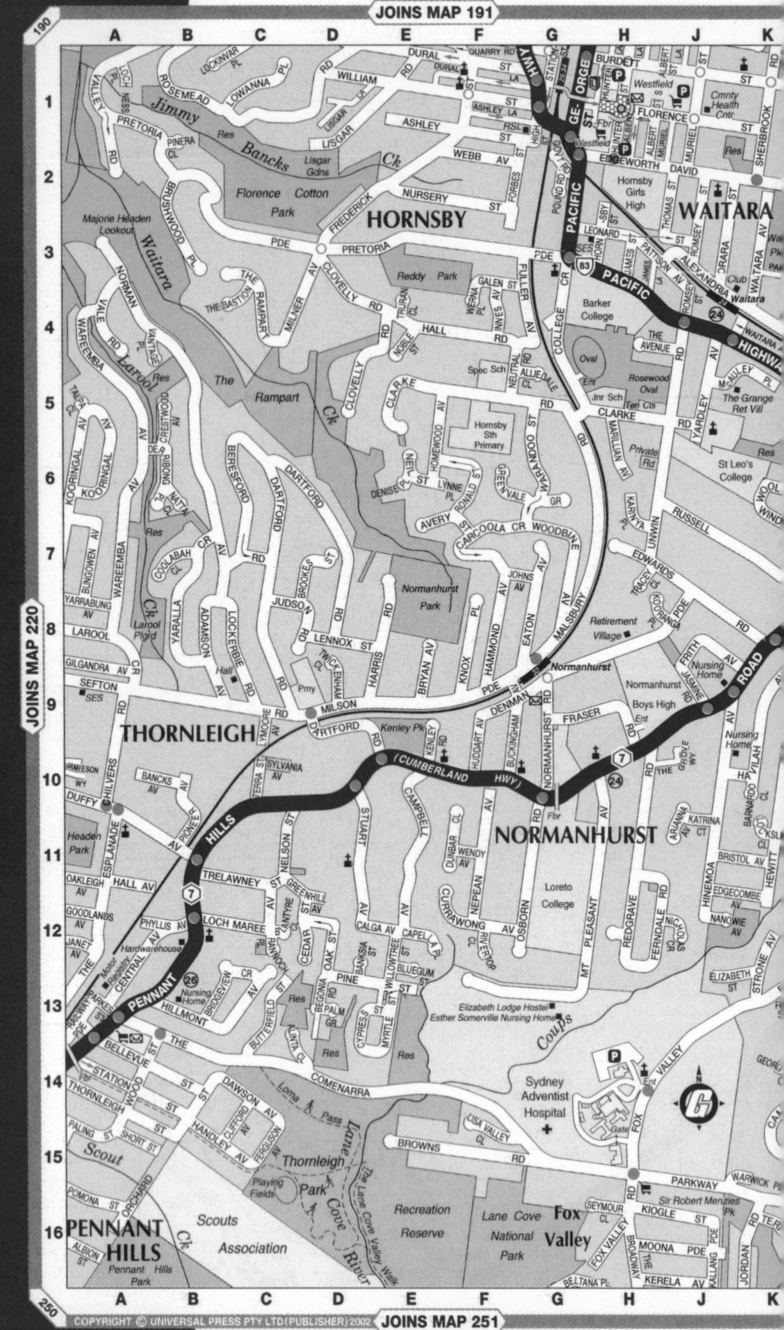

JOINS MAP 191
JOINS MAP 220
JOINS MAP 251
HORNSBY
WAITARA
THORNLEIGH
NORMANHURST
PENNANT HILLS
Fox Valley
Florence Cotton Park
Lisgar Gdns
Reddy Park
Barker College
Hornsby Girls High
Hornsby Sth Primary
Normanhurst Park
Normanhurst Boys High
Loreto College
Sydney Adventist Hospital
St Leo's College
The Grange Ret Vill
Majorie Headen Lookout
Headen Park
Larool Plgrd
Kenley Pk
Thornleigh Park
Recreation Reserve
Lane Cove National Park
Scouts Association
Pennant Hills Park
Sir Robert Menzies Pk
Elizabeth Lodge Hostel
Esther Somerville Nursing Home
Retirement Village
Jimmy Bancks Ck
Waitara
Larool Ck
The Rampart
Coups
Lane Cove River
The Lane Cove Valley Walk
Lorna Pass
PACIFIC HWY
PENNANT HILLS ROAD
(CUMBERLAND HWY)

JOINS MAP 192
JOINS MAP 223
JOINS MAP 252
193
253
A B C D E F G H J K
1 2 3 4 5 6 7 8 9 10 11 12 13 14 15 16
NORTH WAHROONGA
WAHROONGA
WARRAWEE
TURRAMURRA
Pearces Corner
Hornsby & Ku-ring-gai Hospital
Waitara Pmy
Fraser Park
Cliff Reserve
Caritas Christi Conf Cntr
St Edmunds
Wahroonga Pmy
Patrician Bros Training College
The Clive Evatt Res
Abbotsleigh Junior Campus
Abbotsleigh Senior Campus
Wahroonga Park Footbr
Wahroonga
Prouille Convent
Sisters of Mary Convent
Knox Gram Prep
Sisters of St Dominic Convent
Gillespie Field Pavilion
Sanity Res
Knox Grammar
The Glade Res
Ten Cts
Warrawee
Turramurra Memorial Pk
Turramurra Oval
Karuah Oval
William Lewis Park
Browns Field
Mitchell Cr Oval
Twin Creeks Reserve
Cameron Pk
Turramurra
The Lookout
Ret Vill & Nursing Home
Sheldon Forest
Temple
Pmy
Res
FREEWAY
NEWCASTLE
SYDNEY
PACIFIC
HIGHWAY
CITY
Spring Gully
Carrington Pk
Ck

MAP 223

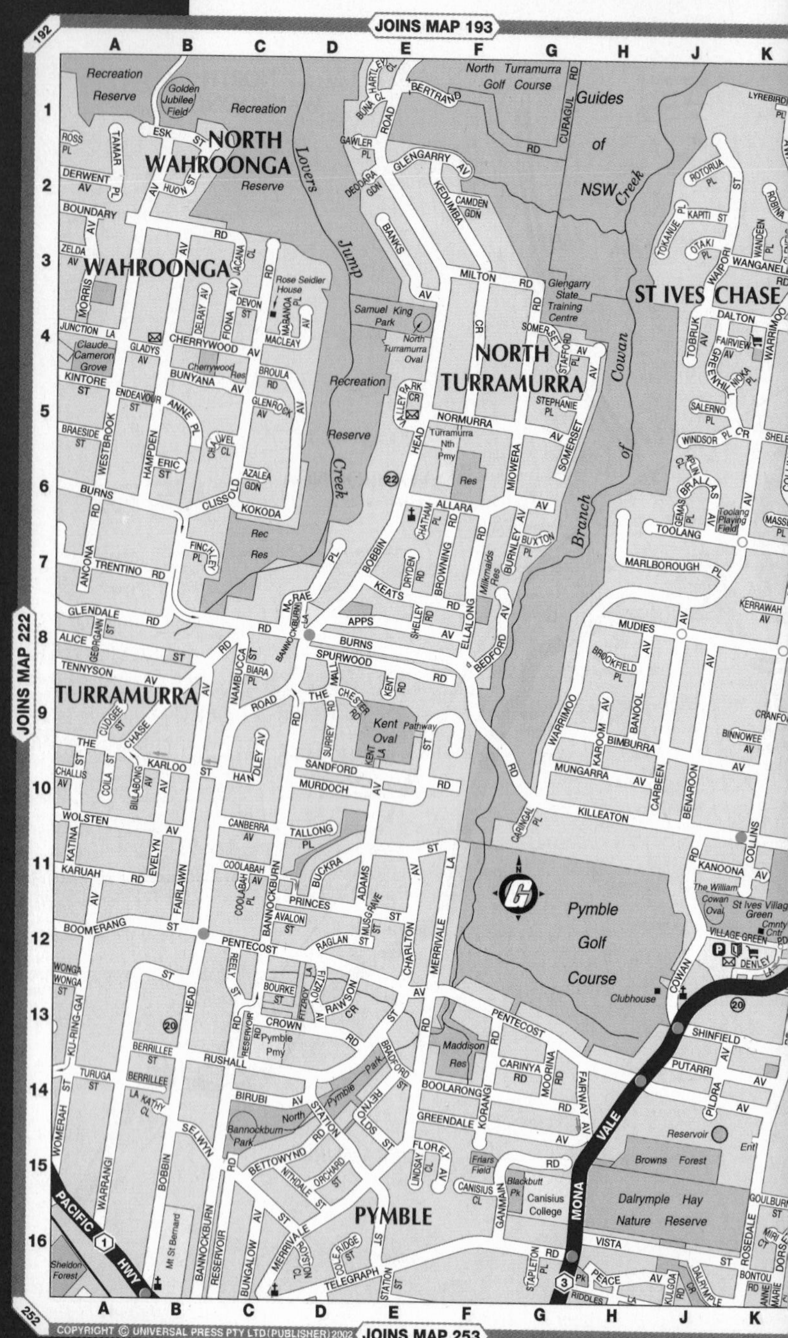

JOINS MAP 193
JOINS MAP 222
JOINS MAP 253
192
252
NORTH WAHROONGA
WAHROONGA
NORTH TURRAMURRA
ST IVES CHASE
TURRAMURRA
PYMBLE
Recreation Reserve
Golden Jubilee Field
North Turramurra Golf Course
Guides of NSW
Rose Seidler House
Samuel King Park
North Turramurra Oval
Glengarry State Training Centre
Claude Cameron Grove
Cherrywood Res
Turramurra Nth Pmy
Rec Res
Milkmaids Res
Kent Oval
Pymble Golf Course
Clubhouse
The William Cowan Oval
St Ives Village Green
Pymble Pmy
Maddison Res
North Bannockburn Park
Pymble Park
Friars Field
Blackbutt Pk
Canisius College
Browns Forest
Dalrymple Hay Nature Reserve
Reservoir
Sheldon Forest
Mt St Bernard
Toolang Playing Field
PACIFIC HWY
MONA VALE RD
COPYRIGHT © UNIVERSAL PRESS PTY LTD (PUBLISHER) 2002

JOINS MAP 194

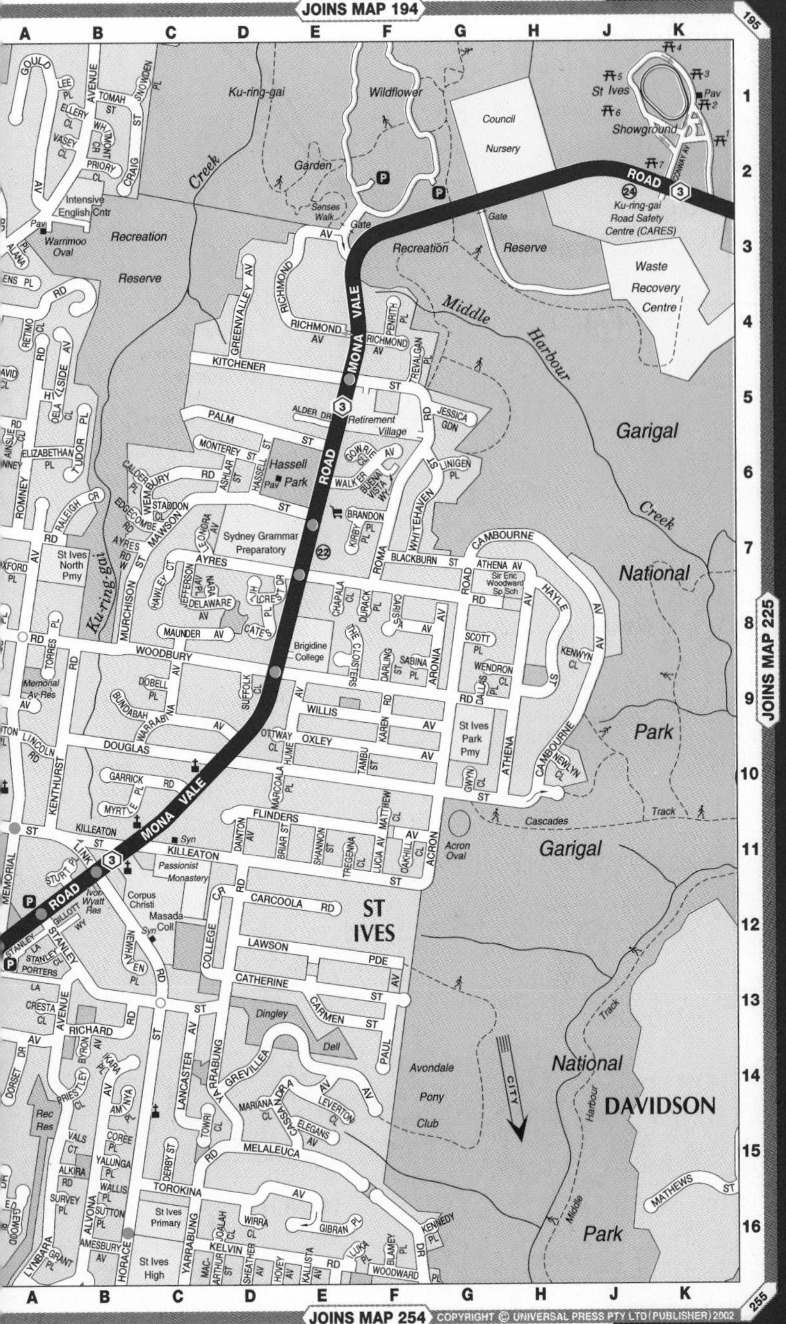

JOINS MAP 225

JOINS MAP 254

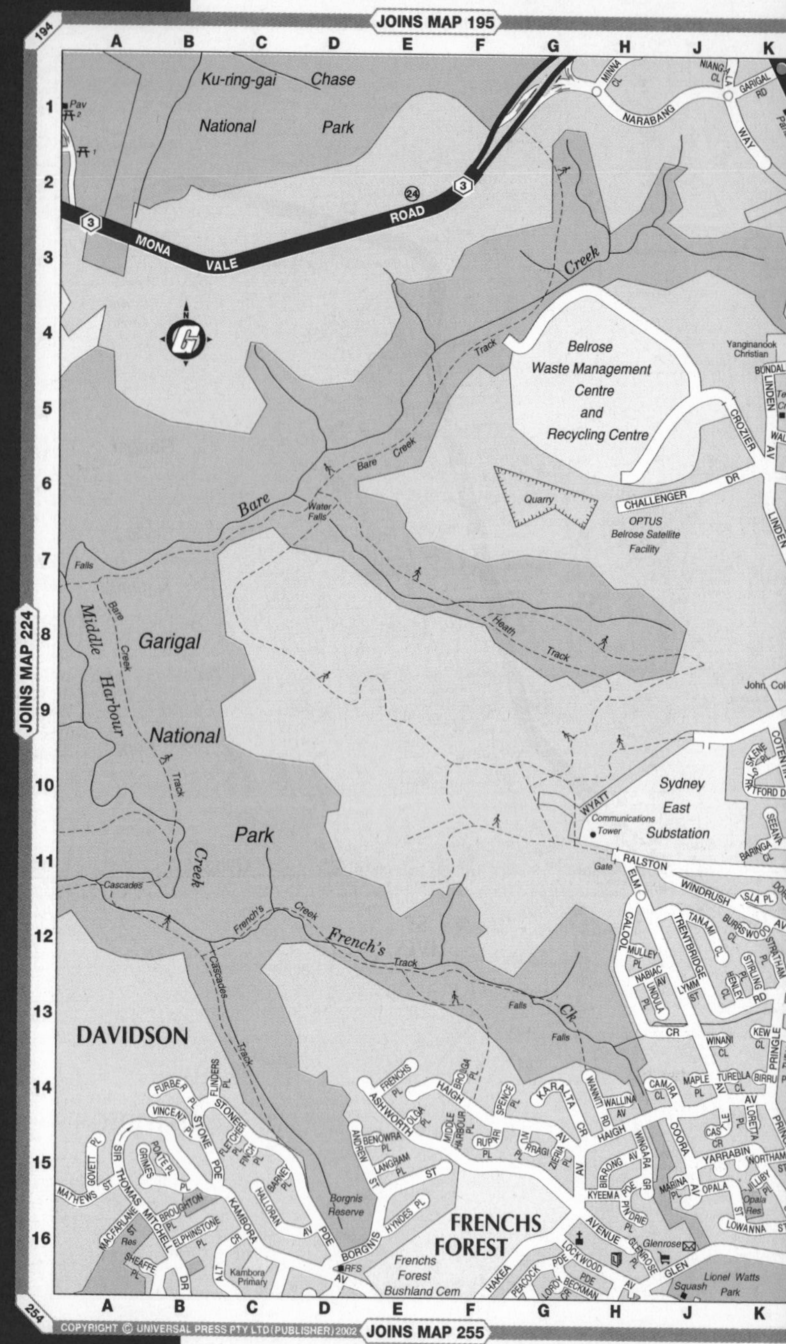

JOINS MAP 195
JOINS MAP 224
JOINS MAP 255
194
254
Ku-ring-gai Chase National Park
MONA VALE ROAD
Garigal National Park
Belrose Waste Management Centre and Recycling Centre
Quarry
CHALLENGER DR
OPTUS Belrose Satellite Facility
Sydney East Substation
Communications Tower
Gate
RALSTON
WYATT
Bare Creek
Middle Harbour
Middle Harbour Creek
Heath Track
French's Creek
French's Ck
Cascades
Cascades Track
Water Falls
Falls
Track
DAVIDSON
FRENCHS FOREST
Frenchs Forest Bushland Cem
Borgnis Reserve
Kambora Primary
Lionel Watts Park
Squash
Glenrose
RFS
Yanginanook Christian
John Cole
MINNA CL
NIANGALA CL
GARIGAL RD
NARABANG WAY
CROZIER
LINDEN AV
BUNDALLA
WINDRUSH AV
ELM
CALOOL
TRENTBRIDGE
TANAMI CL
BURRSWOOD CL
STRATHAM PL
STIRLING PL
HENLEY CL
LYMM ST
MULLEY PL
NABIAC AV
UNDULLA
WINANI CL
KEW CL
PRINGLE
MAPLE PL
TURELLA CL
CAMIRA CL
COORA
CASTLE CR
LORETA PL
YARRABIN
NORTHAM
OPALA
JILLIBY PL
Opala Res
LOWANNA ST
MARINA PL
WINGARA GR
HAIGH AV
BIRRONG AV
KYEEMA PDE
PINDRIE PL
AVENUE
GLENROSE PL
GLEN ST
LOCKWOOD
BECKMAN PDE
PEACOCK
HAKEA
WANNITI RD
WALLINA AV
KARALTA CR
ZIERIA PL
SPENCE PL
RUPARI PL
BROLGA PL
MIDDLE HARBOUR PL
OLGA PL
ASHWORTH
FRENCHS PL
ANDREW ST
BENOWRA PL
LANGHAM PL
HYNDES PL
BORGNIS AV
PDE
FURBER PL
VINCENT PL
FLINDERS PL
STONE PDE
STONECHEST
FLETCHER PL
FINCH PL
BARNET PL
HALLORAN AV
KAMBORA CR
ALT
SIR THOMAS MITCHELL DR
GOVETT PL
MATHEWS ST
POATE PL
GRIMES
BROUGHTON PL
ELPHINSTONE PL
MACFARLANE ST
SHEAFFE PL
Res
SKENE PL
COTENTIN
SEEANA
BARINGA CL
Pav

JOINS MAP 196
JOINS MAP 227
JOINS MAP 256
197
257
Garigal National Park
BELROSE
OXFORD FALLS
Warringah Radio Control Society
Recreation Reserve
OPTUS Oxford Falls Earth Station
Telstra Satellite Earth Station
Perentie Park
Belrose Country Club
Retirement Village
Wakehurst Rugby Club Field
Rec Res
Resvr
RFS
Glenaeon Retirement Village
Wesley Gdns Retirement Centre
Belrose Pmy
Hews Res
Wakehurst Pmy
Treacy Education Centre
FOREST WAY
MADANG ROAD
HILVERSUM CR
BUSH TR
MORGAN RD
OXFORD FALLS RD
PERENTIE RD
DAWES RD
WEARDEN RD
CORYMBIA CCT
SPICER RD
DREADNOUGHT RD
Snake Ck
Oxford Ck
CITY

MAP 227

JOINS MAP 197

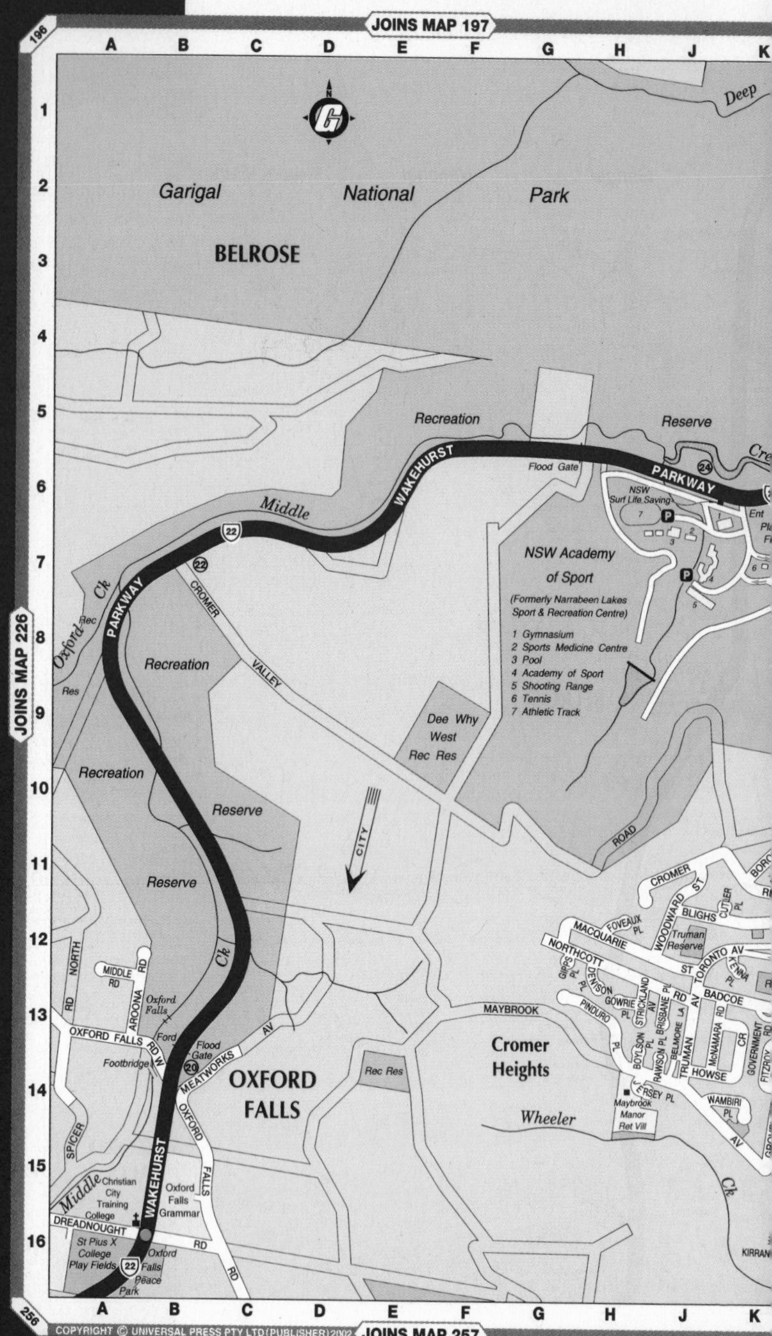

JOINS MAP 257

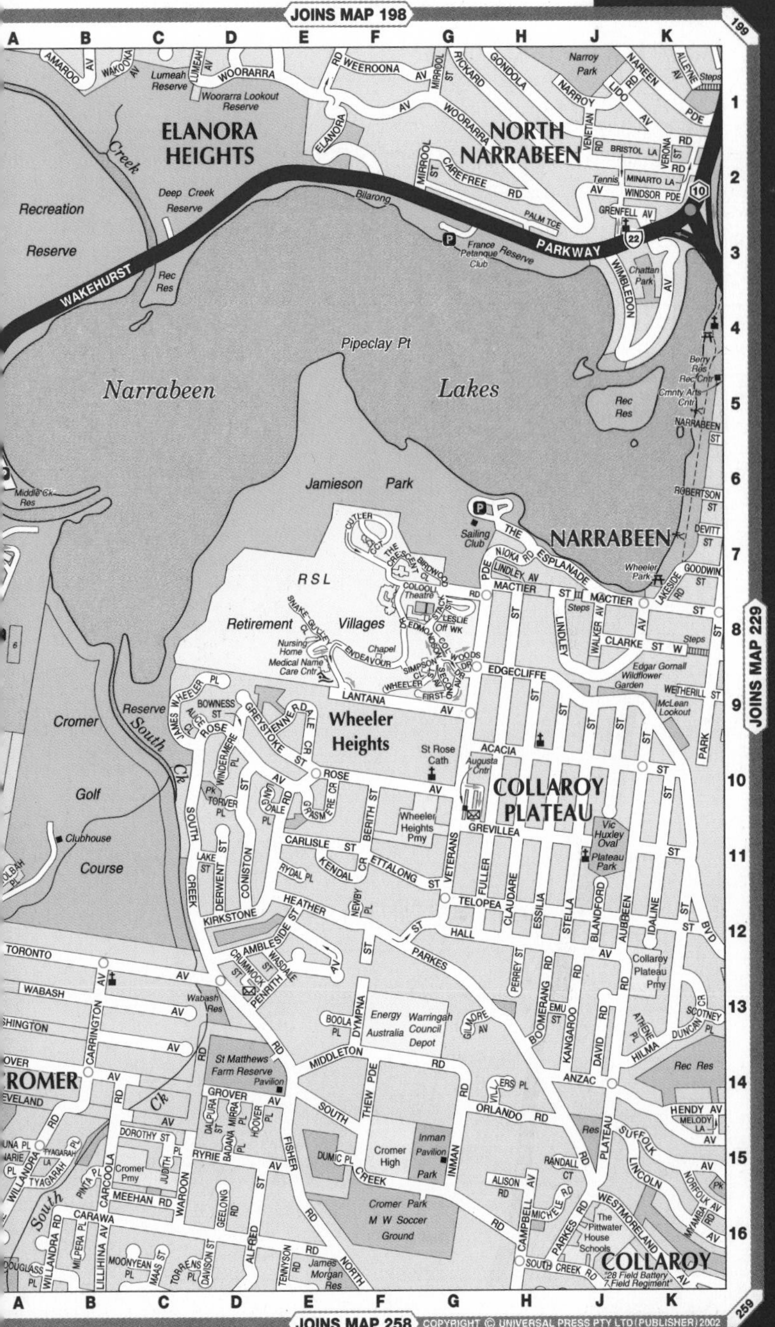
JOINS MAP 198
JOINS MAP 229
JOINS MAP 258
199
259
A B C D E F G H J K
1 2 3 4 5 6 7 8 9 10 11 12 13 14 15 16
ELANORA HEIGHTS
NORTH NARRABEEN
NARRABEEN
Wheeler Heights
COLLAROY PLATEAU
CROMER
COLLAROY
Narrabeen
Lakes
Pipeclay Pt
Jamieson Park
RSL Retirement Villages
Recreation Reserve
Cromer Golf Course
Clubhouse
Deep Creek Reserve
Lumeah Reserve
Woorarra Lookout Reserve
Rec Res
Narroy Park
Chattan Park
France Petanque Club
Reserve
Sailing Club
Middle Ck Res
Berry Res
Rec Cntr
Cmnty Arts Cntr
Wheeler Park
Edgar Gornall Wildflower Garden
McLean Lookout
Steps
St Rose Cath
Augusta Cntr
Wheeler Heights Pmy
Vic Huxley Oval
Plateau Park
Collaroy Plateau Pmy
Energy Australia
Warringah Council Depot
St Matthews Farm Reserve
Pavilion
Wabash Res
Cromer Pmy
Cromer High
Inman Pavilion Park
Cromer Park M W Soccer Ground
James Morgan Res
The Pittwater House Schools
"28 Field Battery 7 Field Regiment"
Nursing Home
Medical Name Care Cntr
Chapel
Colooli Theatre
Tennis
WAKEHURST PARKWAY
Bilarong
South Ck
Creek
Ck
AMAROO AV
WAKOOKA AV
LUMEAH AV
WOORARRA AV
WEEROONA AV
ELANORA RD
MIRROOL ST
RICKARD RD
GONDOLA RD
NARROY RD
LIDO AV
NAREEN PDE
ALLEYNE AV
VENETIAN RD
BRISTOL LA
VERONA ST
MINARTO LA
WINDSOR PDE
GRENFELL AV
PALM TCE
CAREFREE RD
WIMBLEDON AV
NARRABEEN ST
ROBERTSON ST
DEVITT ST
GOODWIN ST
LAKESIDE RD
THE ESPLANADE
NIOKA RD
LINDLEY AV
MACTIER ST
PDE
CUTLER CCT
THE CRESCENT
BIRDWOOD CL
SNAKE GULLY CL
EDMONDSON
LESLIE
ENDEAVOUR
SIMPSON
WHEELER
WOODS
FIRST
SECOND
LANTANA AV
EDGECLIFFE
CLARKE ST
WALKER AV
WETHERILL ST
PARK
JAMES WHEELER PL
BOWNESS ST
ALICE CL
ROSE AV
GREYSTOKE ST
ENNERDALE CR
WINDERMERE PL
TORVER PL
LANGDALE RD
GRASMERE CR
BERITH ST
ACACIA
GREVILLEA
CARLISLE ST
KENDAL CR
ETTALONG ST
RYDAL PL
VETERANS
FULLER
CLAUDARE
ESSILIA
STELLA
BLANDFORD
AUBREEN
IDALINE
TELOPEA
HALL
LAKE ST
DERWENT ST
CONISTON
SOUTH CREEK RD
KIRKSTONE
HEATHER
NEWBY PL
AMBLESIDE ST
WASDALE
CRUMMOCK ST
PENRITH
PARKES ST
TORONTO AV
WABASH AV
CARRINGTON AV
MIDDLETON RD
BOOLA PL
DYMPNA
GILMORE AV
PERREY ST
BOOMERANG RD
EMU ST
KANGAROO
DAVID RD
ATHENE PL
HILMA
DUNCAN
SCOTNEY PL
ANZAC
Rec Res
VILLIERS PL
ORLANDO RD
HENDY AV
MELODY LA
Res
PLATEAU RD
SUFFOLK AV
LINCOLN
NORFOLK AV
MYAMBA RD
WESTMORELAND AV
RANDALL CT
MICHELE RD
ALISON RD
CAMPBELL AV
PARKES RD
SOUTH CREEK RD
THEW PDE
INMAN
GROVER AV
DALPURA
BADANA
MIRRA PL
HOOVER
RYRIE AV
FISHER RD
DUMIC PL
CREEK RD
DOROTHY ST
JUDITH PL
WAROON
GEELONG RD
ST
ALFRED
TENNYSON RD
NORTH
MEEHAN RD
CARCOOLA
PINTA PL
CARAWA
WILLANDRA RD
TYAGARAH
MILPERA PL
LILLIHINA AV
MOONYEAN PL
MAAS ST
TORRENS PL
DAVISON ST
DOUGLASS PL
CLEVELAND
10
22

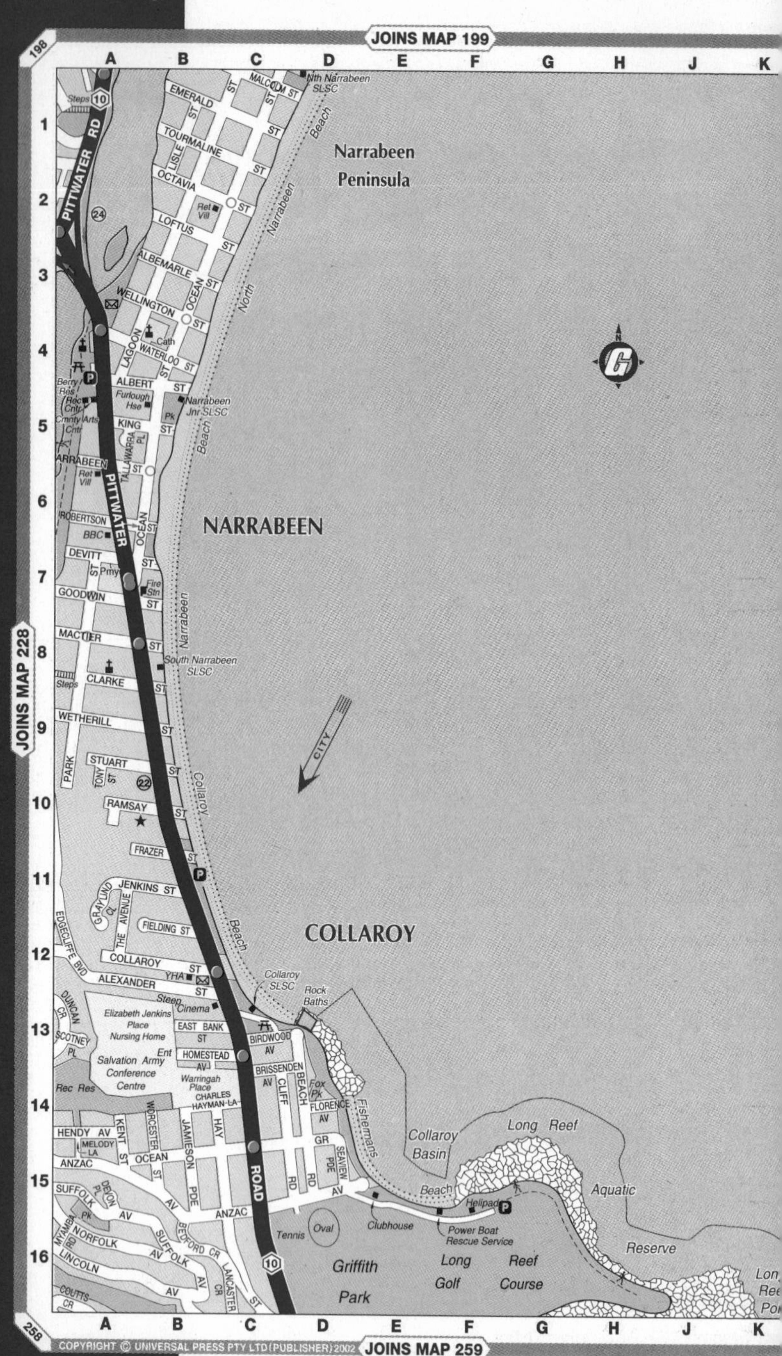
JOINS MAP 199
JOINS MAP 228
JOINS MAP 259
198
258
Narrabeen Peninsula
NARRABEEN
COLLAROY
Nth Narrabeen SLSC
North Narrabeen Beach
Narrabeen Jnr SLSC
South Narrabeen SLSC
Collaroy Beach
Collaroy SLSC
Rock Baths
Fishermans Beach
Collaroy Basin
Long Reef Aquatic Reserve
Helipad
Clubhouse
Power Boat Rescue Service
Long Reef Golf Course
Griffith Park
Tennis
Oval
PITTWATER RD
PITTWATER ROAD
EMERALD ST
MALCOLM ST
TOURMALINE ST
LISLE ST
OCTAVIA ST
LOFTUS ST
ALBEMARLE ST
OCEAN ST
WELLINGTON ST
LAGOON ST
WATERLOO ST
ALBERT ST
KING ST
TALLAWARRA PL
NARRABEEN
ROBERTSON
DEVITT ST
GOODWIN ST
MACTIER ST
CLARKE ST
WETHERILL ST
STUART ST
TONY ST
PARK
RAMSAY ST
FRAZER ST
JENKINS ST
GRAYLIND CL
THE AVENUE
FIELDING ST
EDGECLIFFE BVD
COLLAROY ST
ALEXANDER ST
DUNCAN CR
SCOTNEY PL
EAST BANK ST
HOMESTEAD AV
BIRDWOOD AV
BRISSENDEN AV
CLIFF
BEACH
FLORENCE AV
GR
PDE
SEAVIEW AV
RD
HENDY AV
MELODY LA
KENT ST
WORCESTER ST
JAMIESON PDE
HAY
OCEAN
ANZAC AV
SUFFOLK AV
DEVON PL
NORFOLK AV
MYAMBA RD
LINCOLN
COUTTS CR
BEDFORD CR
LANCASTER
CITY
Ret Vill
Cath
Berry Res
Rec Cntr
Cmnty Arts Cntr
Furlough Hse
Pk
BBC
Pmy
Fire Stn
Steps
Steep
Cinema
YHA
Elizabeth Jenkins Place Nursing Home
Ent
Salvation Army Conference Centre
Warringah Place
CHARLES HAYMAN LA
Rec Res
Fox Pk
Long Reef Pt
10
22
24
A B C D E F G H J K
1 2 3 4 5 6 7 8 9 10 11 12 13 14 15 16

JOINS MAP 200

A B C D E F G H J K

1 2 3 4 5 6 7 8 9 10 11 12 13 14 15 16

TASMAN

SEA

A B C D E F G H J K

JOINS MAP 260

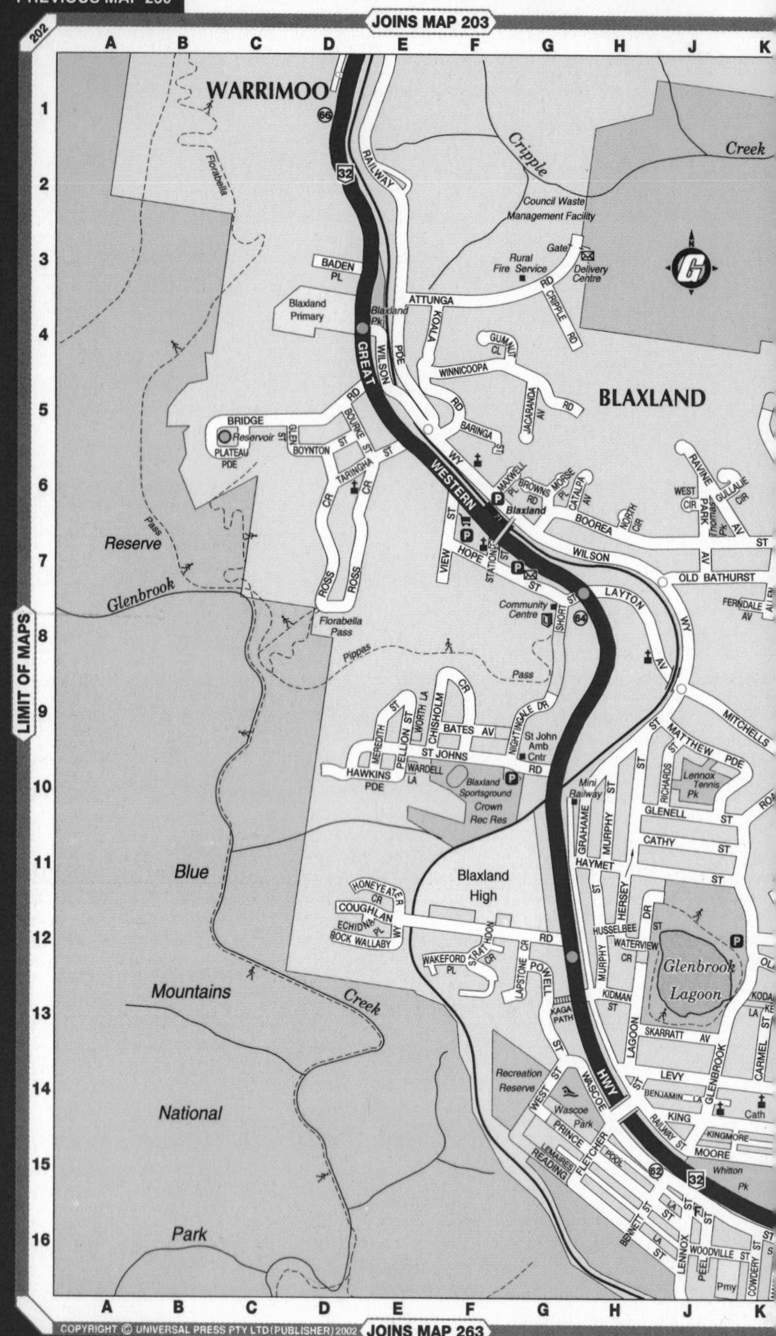

JOINS MAP 203
202
LIMIT OF MAPS
JOINS MAP 263
WARRIMOO
BLAXLAND
Blaxland Primary
Blaxland Pk
Reservoir
Council Waste Management Facility
Rural Fire Service
Delivery Centre
Gate
Cripple
Creek
Florabella
Florabella Pass
Pippas
Pass
Reserve
Glenbrook
Blue
Mountains
National
Park
Creek
GREAT
WESTERN
HWY
Blaxland
Community Centre
St John Amb Cntr
Blaxland Sportsground
Crown Rec Res
Blaxland High
Mini Railway
Lennox Tennis Pk
Glenbrook Lagoon
Recreation Reserve
Wascoe Park
Whitton Pk
Cath
Pmy
BADEN PL
ATTUNGA
CRIPPLE RD
KOALA
RAILWAY
WILSON
PDE
GUMNUT CL
WINNICOOPA
JACARANDA AV
RD
BRIDGE RD
PLATEAU PDE
GLEN ST
BOURKE ST
BOYNTON ST
TARINGHA ST
CR
ROSS
BARINGA ST
WY
MAXWELL PL
BROWNS RD
MORSE PL
CATALPA AV
BOOREA
NORTH CIR
RAVINE
WEST CIR
PARK
Thomas Pk
GULLALIE CIR
AV
ST
WILSON
OLD BATHURST
LAYTON
WY
FERNDALE AV
VIEW ST
HOPE ST
STATION
SHORT ST
MITCHELLS
MATTHEW PDE
RICHARDS ST
CHISHOLM CR
WORTH LA
PELLION ST
MEREDITH ST
BATES AV
NIGHTINGALE DR
ST JOHNS RD
HAWKINS PDE
WARDELL LA
GRAHAME
MURPHY
ST
GLENELL ST
CATHY ST
HAYMET ST
HERSEY
HONEYEATER CR
COUGHLAN
ECHIDNA PL
ROCK WALLABY WY
RD
STRATHDON CR
WAKEFORD PL
LAPSTONE CR
POWELL
HUSSELBEE ST
WATERVIEW CR
DR
KIDMAN ST
KAGA PATH
LAGOON
SKARRATT AV
LEVY
GLENBROOK
CARMEL
WEST ST
WASCOE
BENJAMIN LA
KING
RAILWAY ST
KINGMORE
MOORE
PRINCE
FLETCHER
POOL
LEMAIRES
READING
BENNETT ST
LA
ST
LENNOX
PEEL
WOODVILLE ST
COWDERY
32
66
64
62
A B C D E F G H J K
1 2 3 4 5 6 7 8 9 10 11 12 13 14 15 16

JOINS MAP 204

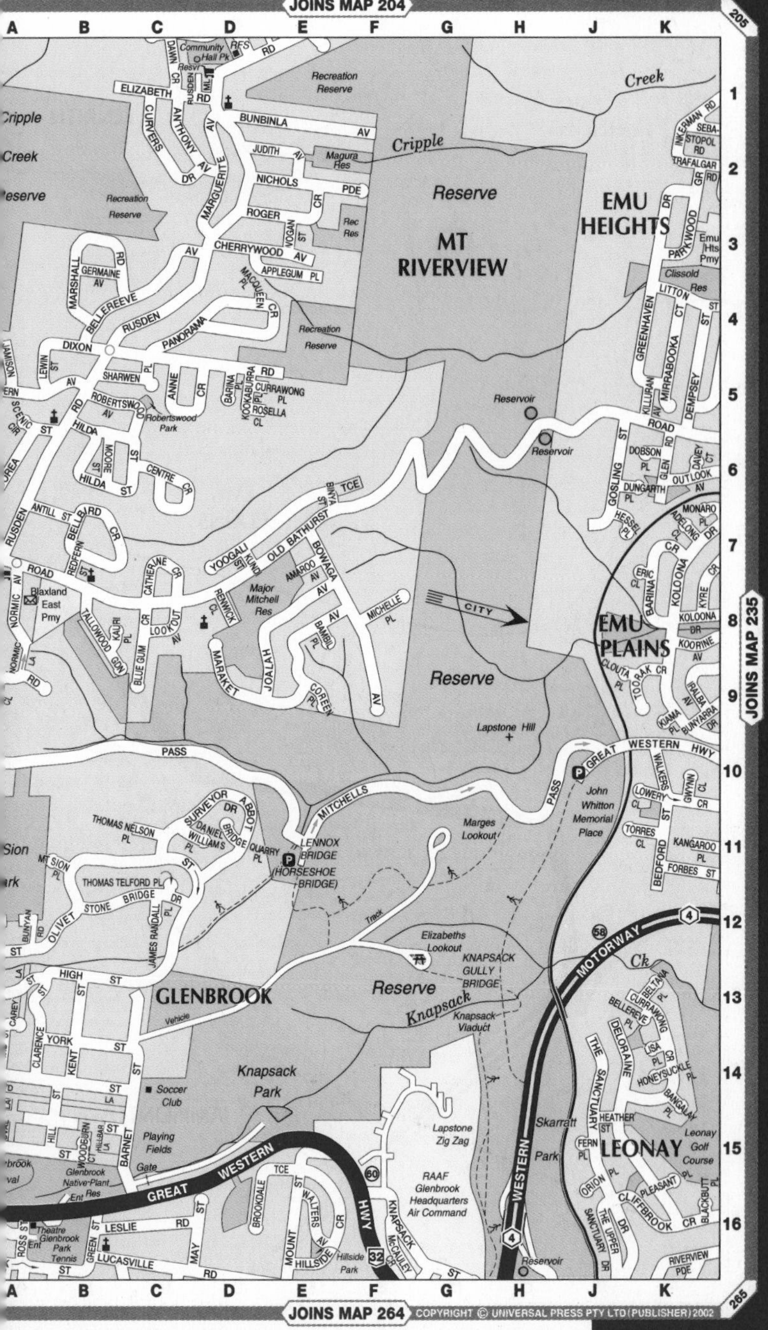

JOINS MAP 235

JOINS MAP 264
265

JOINS MAP 205

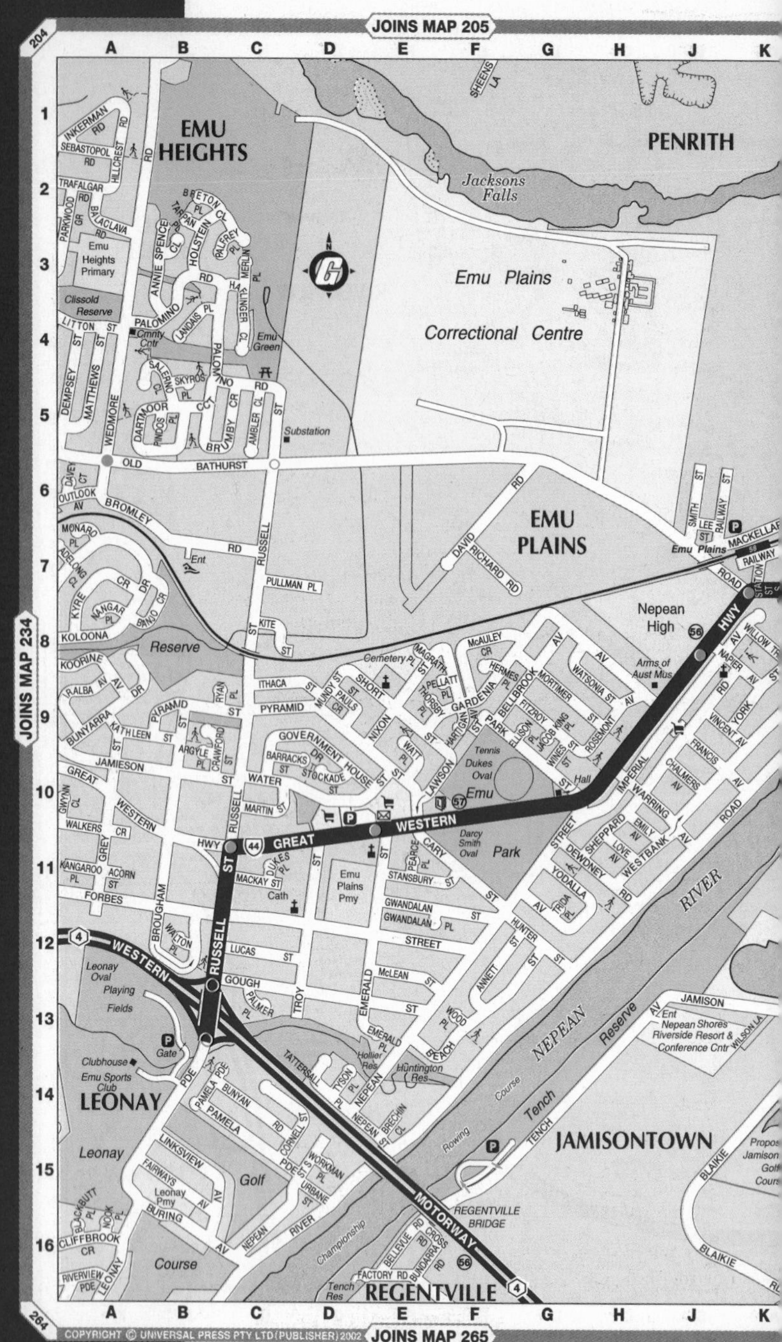

JOINS MAP 234

JOINS MAP 265

JOINS MAP 206

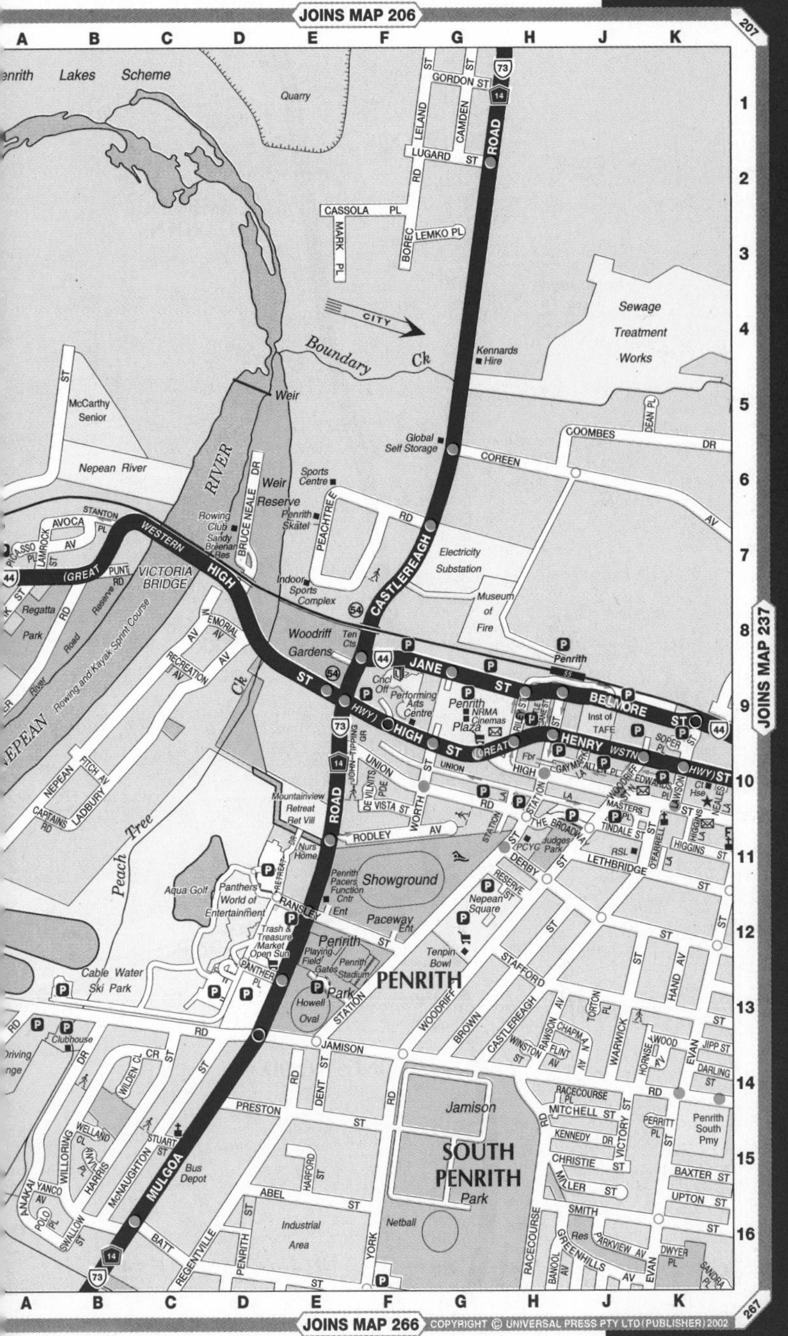

JOINS MAP 237

JOINS MAP 266

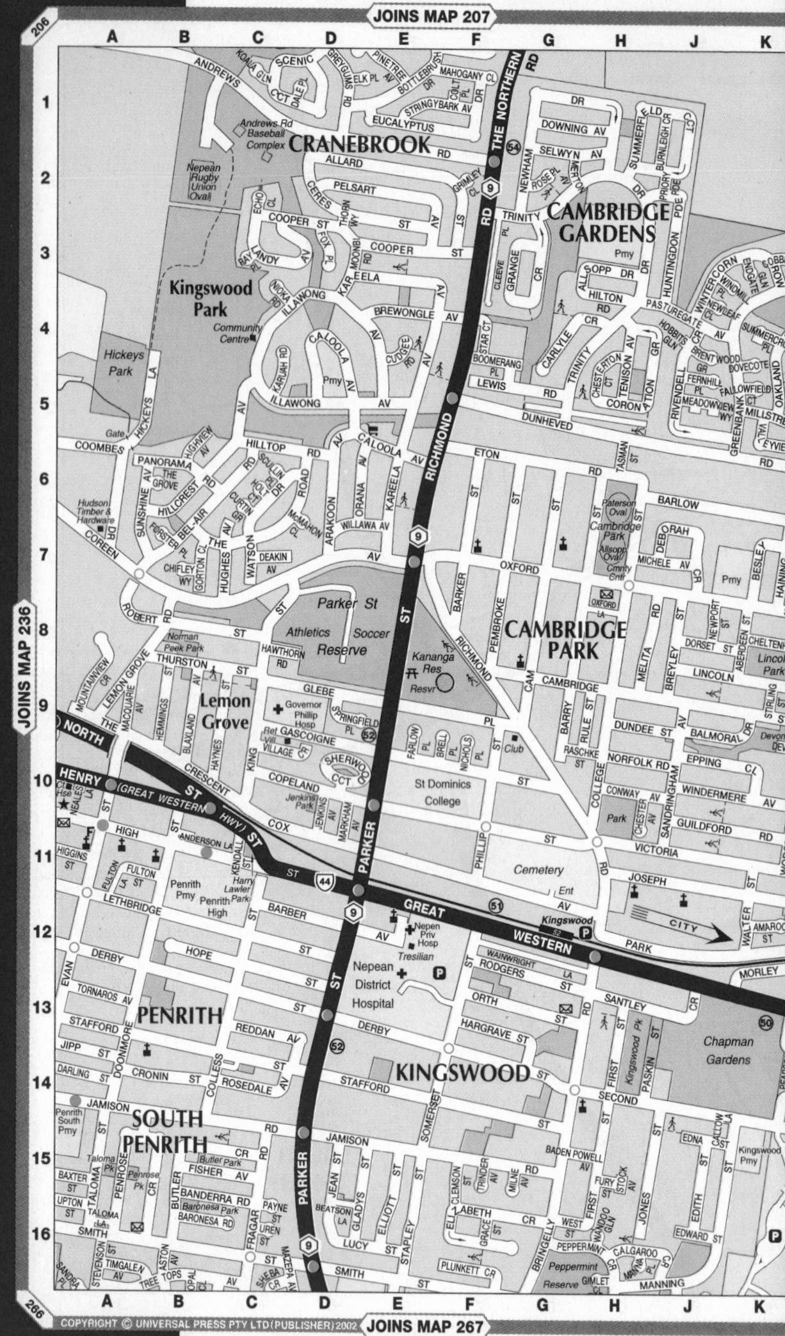
JOINS MAP 207
JOINS MAP 236
JOINS MAP 267
206
266
CRANEBROOK
CAMBRIDGE GARDENS
Kingswood Park
CAMBRIDGE PARK
Lemon Grove
PENRITH
KINGSWOOD
SOUTH PENRITH
THE NORTHERN RD
RICHMOND RD
PARKER ST
GREAT WESTERN HWY
Nepean Rugby Union Oval
Andrews Rd Baseball Complex
Hickeys Park
Parker St Athletics Soccer Reserve
Kananga Res
Governor Phillip Hosp
St Dominics College
Cemetery
Nepean District Hospital
Chapman Gardens
Peppermint Reserve
Paterson Oval
Cambridge Park
Allsopp Oval
Penrith Pmy
Penrith High
Kingswood Pmy
Penrith South Pmy

JOINS MAP 208

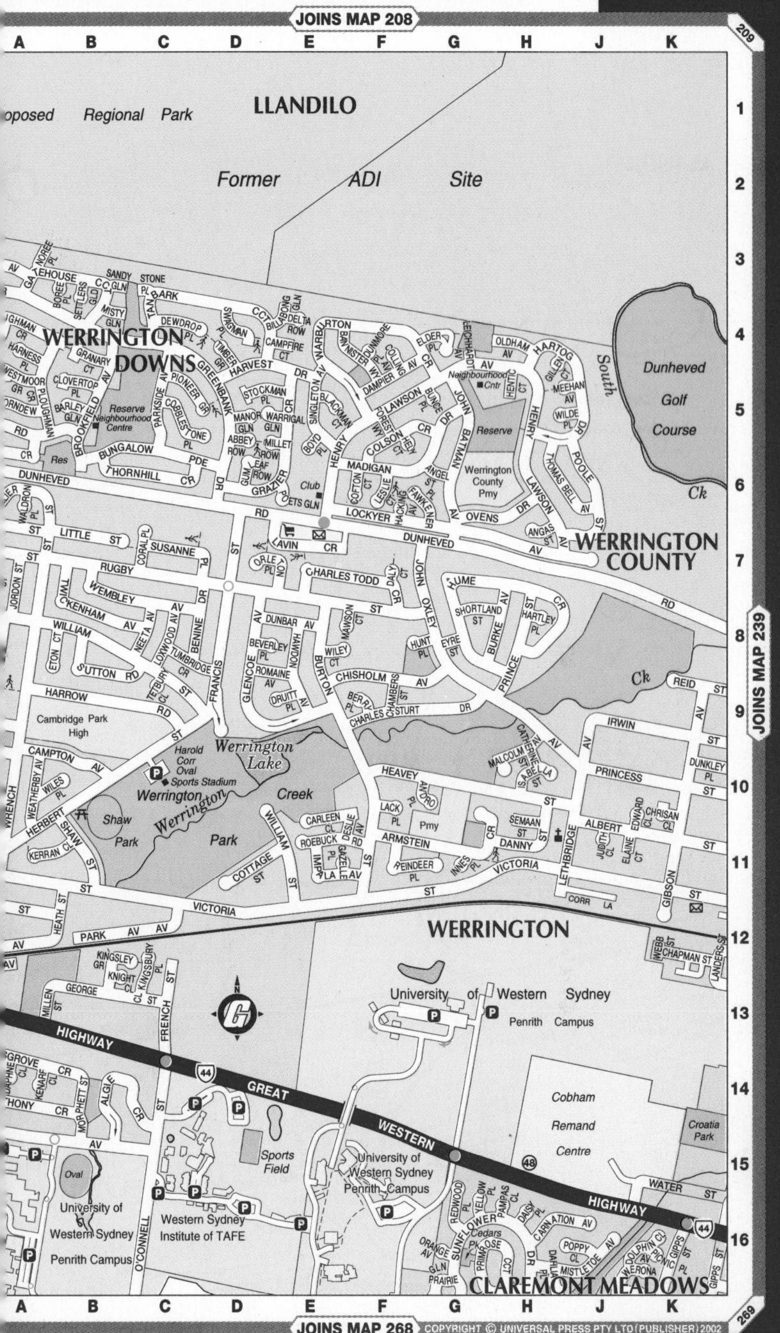

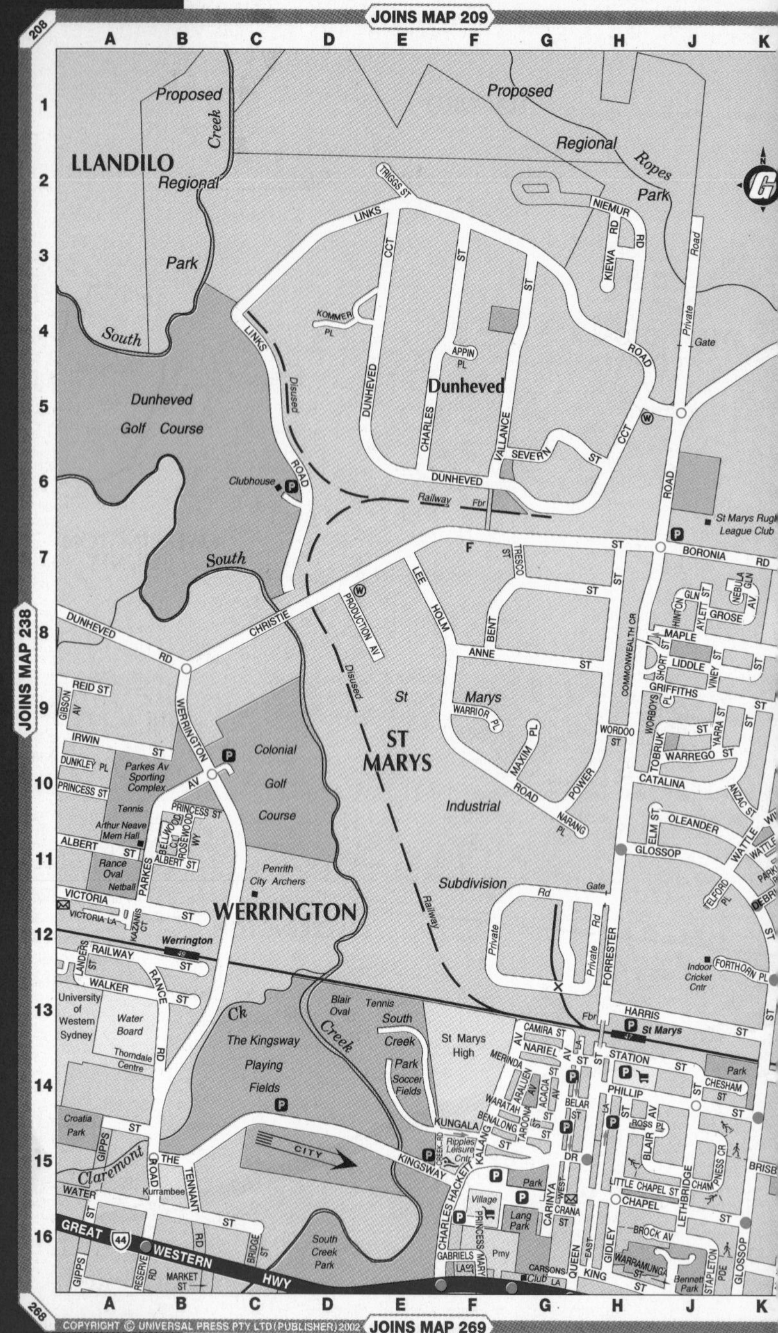
JOINS MAP 209
JOINS MAP 238
JOINS MAP 269
208
268
LLANDILO
Proposed Regional Park
Proposed Regional Ropes Park
South Creek
Dunheved Golf Course
Clubhouse
Dunheved
St Marys Industrial Subdivision
ST MARYS
Colonial Golf Course
Penrith City Archers
WERRINGTON
Parkes Av Sporting Complex
Arthur Neave Mem Hall
Rance Oval
University of Western Sydney
Water Board
Thorndale Centre
Croatia Park
Kurrambee
The Kingsway Playing Fields
Blair Oval
South Creek Park
Soccer Fields
St Marys High
Ripples Leisure Cntr
Village
Lang Park
South Creek Park
St Marys Rugby League Club
Indoor Cricket Cntr
Bennett Park
Werrington
St Marys
GREAT WESTERN HWY
CHRISTIE ST
DUNHEVED RD
LINKS RD
DUNHEVED CCT
FORRESTER RD
BORONIA RD
WERRINGTON RD
KINGSWAY
GLOSSOP ST
QUEEN ST
CHAPEL ST
STATION ST
HARRIS ST

JOINS MAP 210

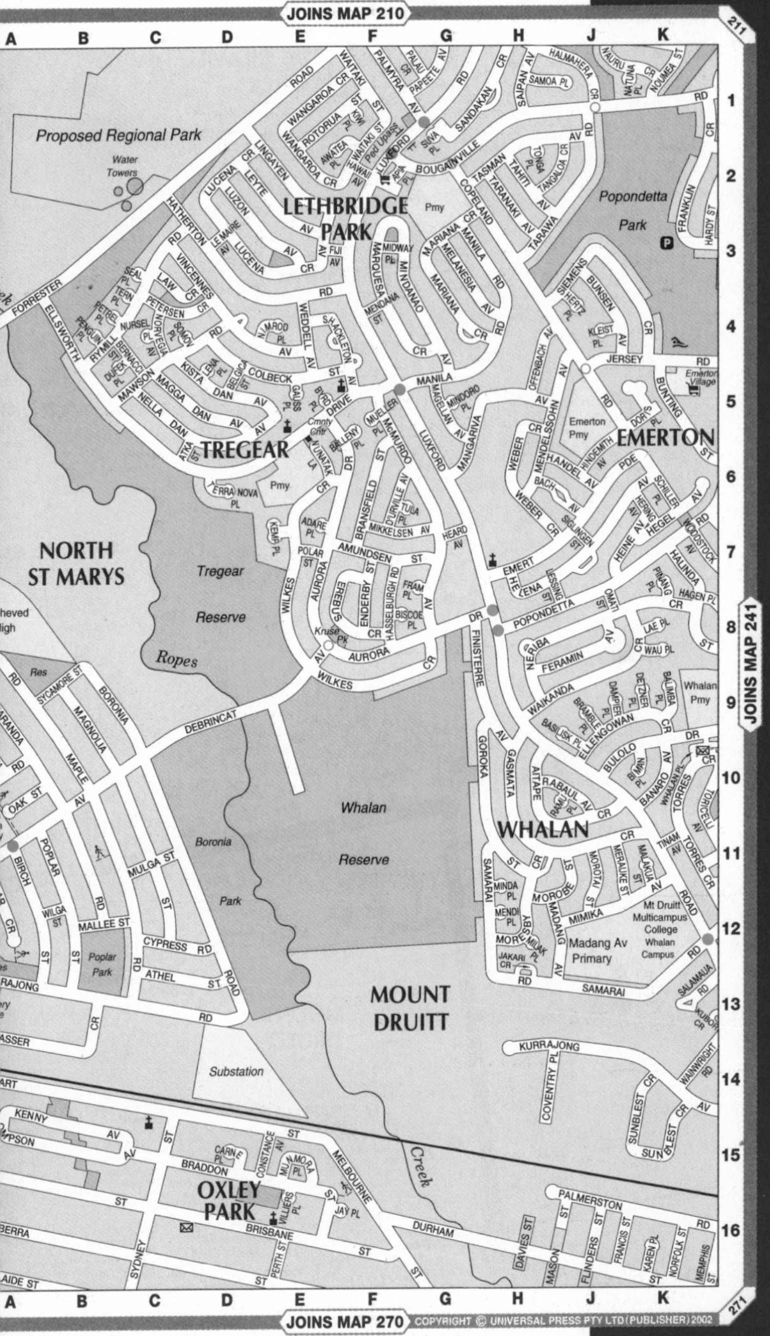

JOINS MAP 241

JOINS MAP 270

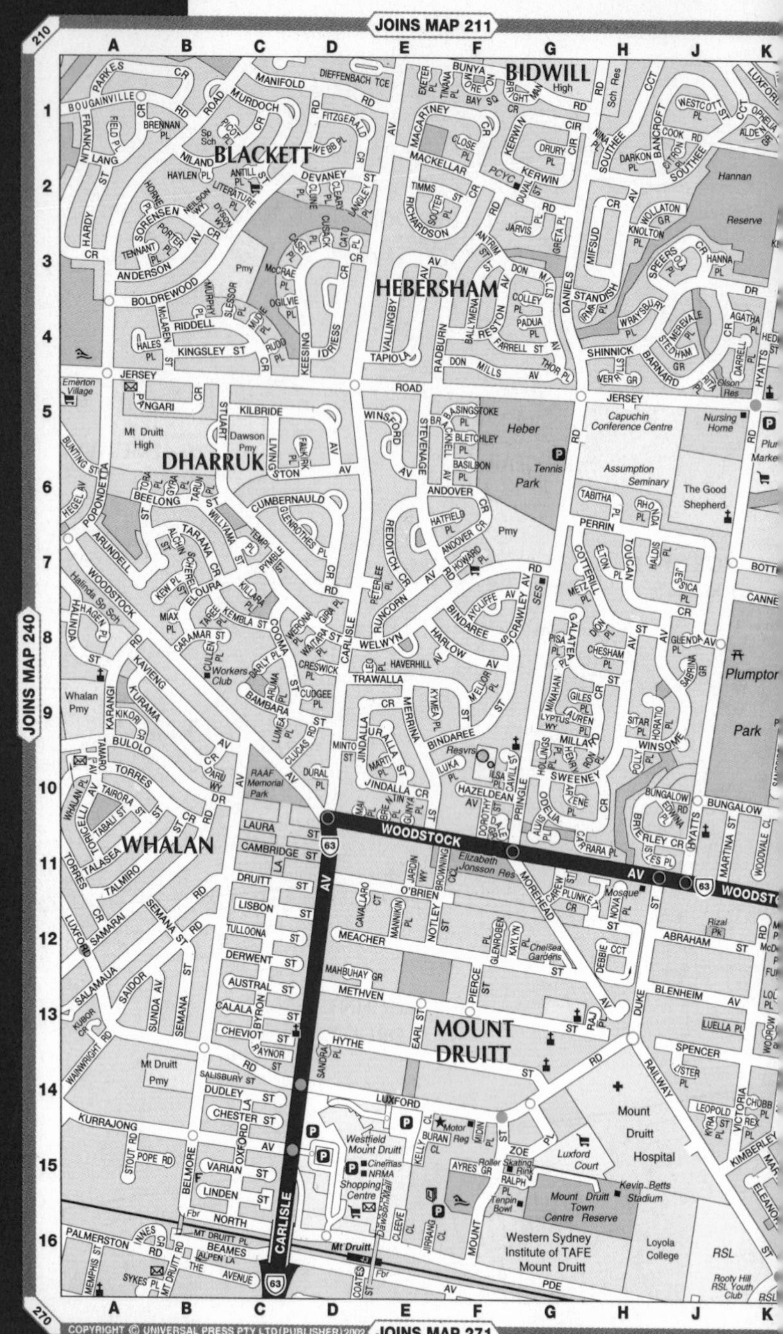
JOINS MAP 211
210
A
B
C
D
E
F
G
H
J
K
BIDWILL
BLACKETT
HEBERSHAM
DHARRUK
WHALAN
MOUNT DRUITT
JOINS MAP 240
JERSEY ROAD
WOODSTOCK AV
CARLISLE AV
LUXFORD RD
KURRAJONG
PALMERSTON RD
MT DRUITT RD
NORTH
BEAMES
PDE
RAILWAY
DUKE ST
HYATTS RD
Hannan Reserve
Heber Park
Tennis
Capuchin Conference Centre
Assumption Seminary
The Good Shepherd
Nursing Home
Plumpton Park
Mt Druitt High
Emerton Village
Dawson Pmy
Whalan Pmy
Halinda Sp Sch
Workers Club
RAAF Memorial Park
Elizabeth Jonsson Res
Mosque
Rizal Pk
Chelsea Gardens
Mt Druitt Pmy
Westfield Mount Druitt Shopping Centre
Cinemas
NRMA
Dawson Mall
Motor Reg
Roller Skating Rink
Tenpin Bowl
Luxford Court
Mount Druitt Hospital
Kevin Betts Stadium
Mount Druitt Town Centre Reserve
Western Sydney Institute of TAFE Mount Druitt
Loyola College
RSL
Rooty Hill RSL Youth Club
Mt Druitt
Fbr
63
270
JOINS MAP 271

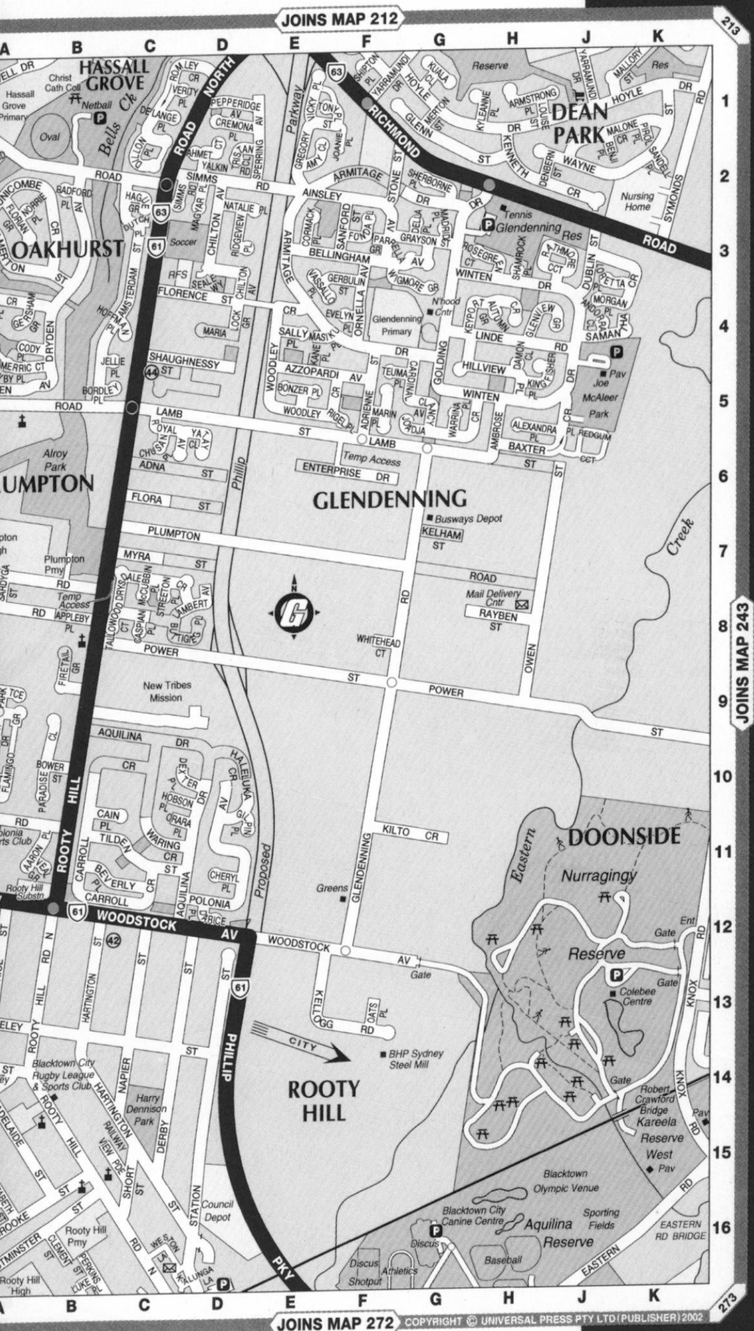
JOINS MAP 212
213
A B C D E F G H J K
1 2 3 4 5 6 7 8 9 10 11 12 13 14 15 16
HASSALL GROVE
Christ Cath Coll
Hassall Grove Primary
Netball
Oval
Bells Ck
OAKHURST
DEAN PARK
Reserve
Res
Nursing Home
Tennis
Glendenning Res
N'hood Cntr
Glendenning Primary
Soccer
RFS
Pav
Joe McAleer Park
Alroy Park
PLUMPTON
Plumpton Pmy
Temp Access
Temp Access
GLENDENNING
Busways Depot
Mail Delivery Cntr
New Tribes Mission
Creek
DOONSIDE
Nurragingy
Reserve
Colebee Centre
Gate
Ent
Eastern
Greens
BHP Sydney Steel Mill
CITY
ROOTY HILL
Rooty Hill Substn
Blacktown City Rugby League & Sports Club
Harry Dennison Park
Council Depot
Rooty Hill Pmy
Rooty Hill High
Robert Crawford Bridge
Kareela Reserve West
Pav
Blacktown Olympic Venue
Blacktown City Canine Centre
Aquilina Reserve
Sporting Fields
Baseball
Discus
Discus Shotput
Athletics
EASTERN RD BRIDGE
RICHMOND ROAD
ROAD NORTH
ARMITAGE
AINSLEY
BELLINGHAM
WINTEN
LINDE
HILLVIEW
AZZOPARDI AV
LAMB ST
ENTERPRISE DR
BAXTER ST
PLUMPTON ROAD
POWER ST
WOODSTOCK AV
ROOTY HILL RD N
GLENDENNING RD
PHILLIP PKY
KNOX RD
EASTERN RD
Proposed
HOYLE DR
WAYNE
SIMMS RD
FLORENCE ST
SHAUGHNESSY ST
ADNA ST
FLORA ST
MYRA ST
AQUILINA DR
KILTO CR
RAYBEN ST
OWEN
KELHAM ST
WHITEHEAD CT
KELLOGG RD
OATS PL
HARTINGTON
NAPIER
DERBY
STATION
SHORT
63 61 44 42
JOINS MAP 243
273
JOINS MAP 272

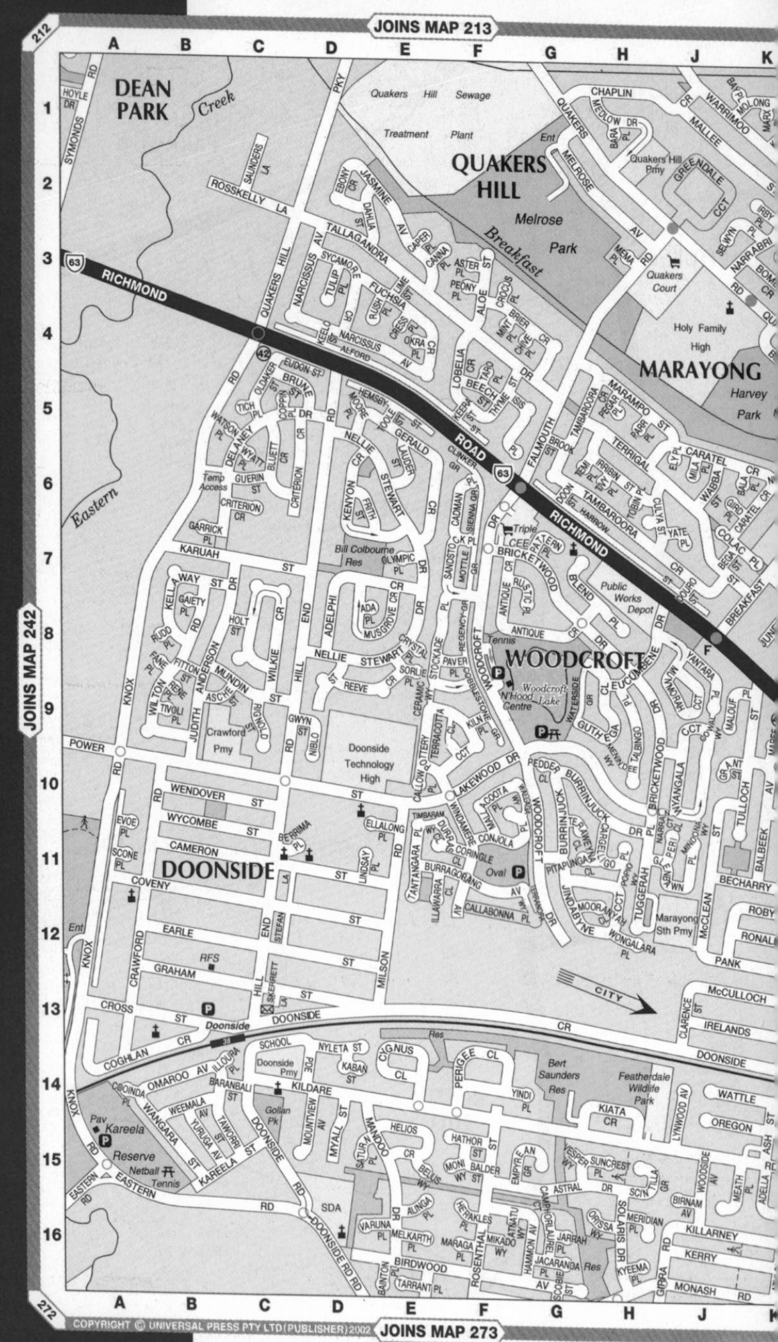
JOINS MAP 213
JOINS MAP 242
JOINS MAP 273
212
272
DEAN PARK
QUAKERS HILL
MARAYONG
WOODCROFT
DOONSIDE
Quakers Hill Sewage Treatment Plant
Melrose Park
Quakers Court
Holy Family High
Harvey Park
Bill Colbourne Res
Public Works Depot
Woodcroft Lake
N'Hood Centre
Crawford Pmy
Doonside Technology High
Oval
Marayong Sth Pmy
Doonside Pmy
Gollan Pk
Bert Saunders Res
Featherdale Wildlife Park
Kareela Reserve
RICHMOND ROAD
DOONSIDE CR
CITY

JOINS MAP 214

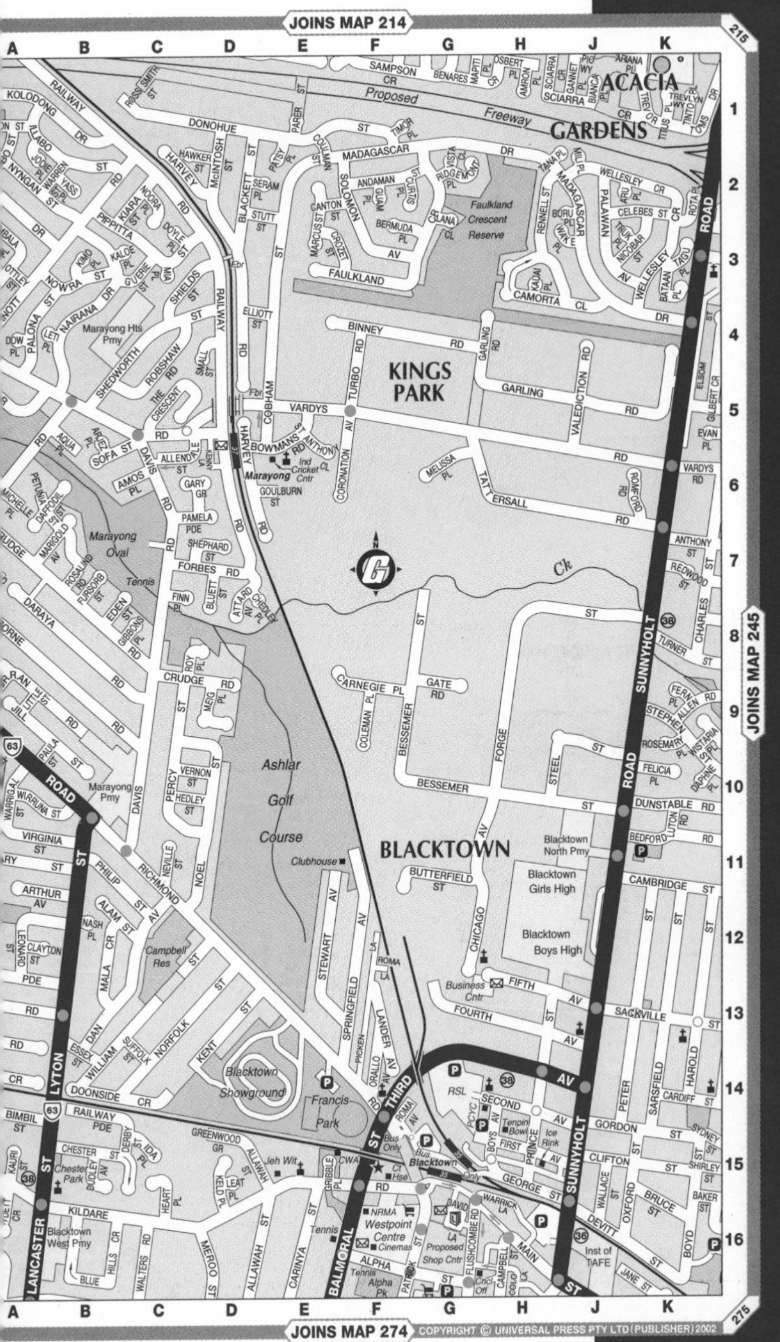

JOINS MAP 245

JOINS MAP 274

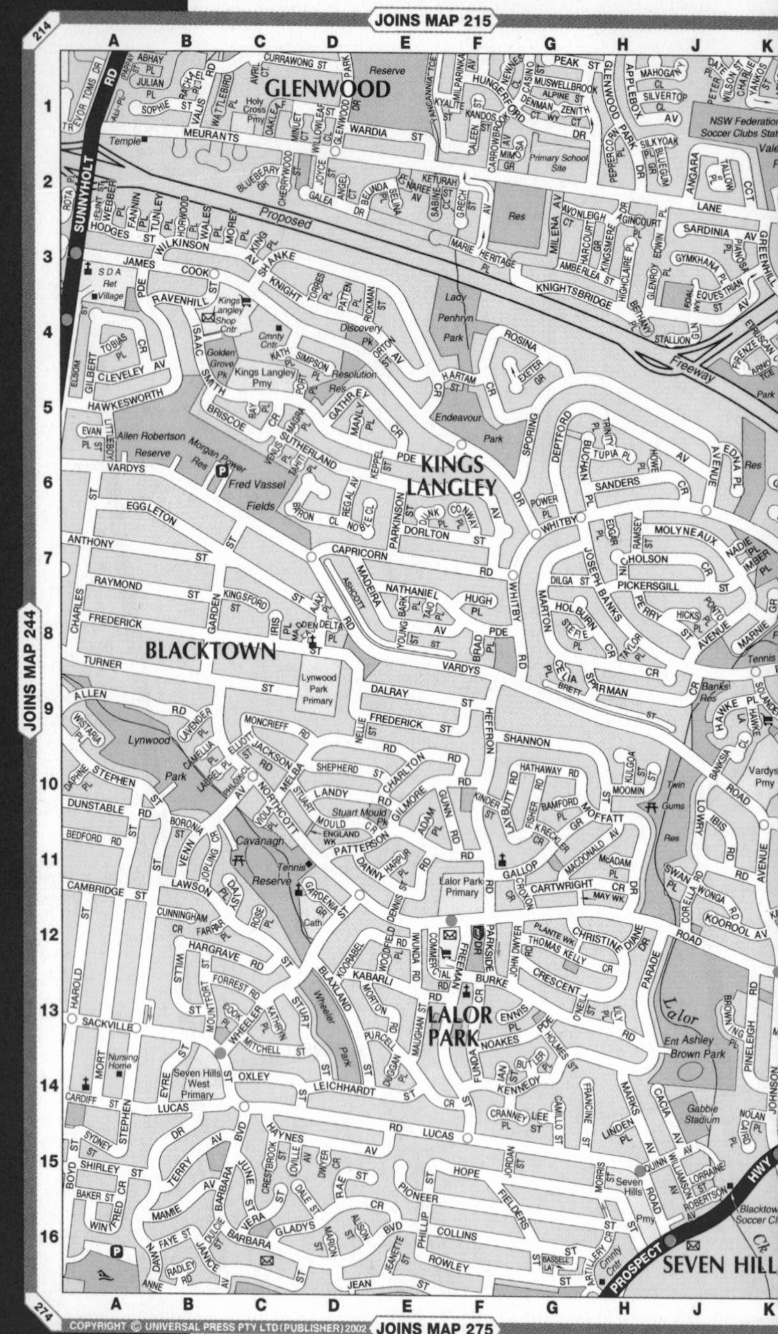
JOINS MAP 215
JOINS MAP 244
JOINS MAP 275
214
274
GLENWOOD
KINGS LANGLEY
BLACKTOWN
LALOR PARK
SEVEN HILL
SUNNYHOLT RD
Proposed
Freeway
MEURANTS
WARDIA ST
HUNGERFORD
GLENWOOD PARK DR
WILKINSON
JAMES
COOK ST
RAVENHILL
KNIGHTSBRIDGE
HAWKESWORTH
VARDYS RD
EGGLETON ST
ANTHONY ST
RAYMOND ST
FREDERICK ST
TURNER ST
CAPRICORN RD
WHITBY RD
SPORING AV
DEPTFORD AV
JOSEPH BANKS DR
ALLEN RD
DALRAY ST
HEFFRON RD
SHANNON RD
MOONMIN
STEPHEN ST
DUNSTABLE RD
BEDFORD RD
CAMBRIDGE ST
LAWSON PL
CUNNINGHAM CR
HARGRAVE RD
SACKVILLE
LUCAS RD
LEICHHARDT ST
OXLEY
KENNEDY
CHRISTINE CR
PARADE
MARKS AV
SEVEN HILLS RD
HAYNES AV
PIONEER CR
COLLINS
ROWLEY
JEAN ST
PROSPECT HWY
Temple
S D A Ret Village
Kings Langley Shop Cntr
Golden Grove Pk
Kings Langley Pmy
Cmnty Cntr
Resolution Res
Discovery Pk
Lady Penhryn Park
Endeavour Park
Allen Robertson Reserve
Morgan Power Res
Fred Vassel Fields
Holy Cross Pmy
Reserve
Primary School Site
Res
NSW Federation Soccer Clubs Stat
Lynwood Park Primary
Lynwood Park
Stuart Mould Pk
Cavanagh Reserve
Tennis
Cath
Lalor Park Primary
Wheeler Park
Seven Hills West Primary
Nursing Home
Twin Gums Res
Banks Res
Vardys Pmy
Lalor
Ent Ashley Brown Park
Gabbie Stadium
Seven Hills Pmy
Blacktown Soccer Cl
Cmnty Cntr
COPYRIGHT © UNIVERSAL PRESS PTY LTD (PUBLISHER) 2002

JOINS MAP 216
JOINS MAP 247
JOINS MAP 276
217
277
A B C D E F G H J K
1 2 3 4 5 6 7 8 9 10 11 12 13 14 15 16
BELLA VISTA
BAULKHAM HILLS
WINSTON HILLS
Convent of St Joseph
Hardware-house
Parklea Reservoir
Proposed Bella Vista Farm Park
Prop Ten Cts
Bella Vista Oval
Village Green
Prop Village Centre
Proposed Pk
The Charles McLaughlin Rec Res
Crestwood Res
Crestwood Pmy
Tennis
Field 3
Skate Bowl
Temp Acc
Clarke Res
Matthew Pearce Pmy
William Joyce Res
Michael Simpson Res
Col Sutton Park
Melody Gdn
Chopin Res
Nursing Home
Sierra Pl Res
Golf Driving Range
PYE'S CROSSING
Model Farms High
Toongabbie
CITY
Creek
Troubador Park
Proposed Freeway
OLD WINDSOR RD
WINDSOR
NORWEST DR
ABBOTT ROAD
M2 MOTORWAY
SEVEN HILLS RD
SEVEN HILLS WY
BAULKHAM HILLS RD
CHAPEL LANE
CRESTWOOD DR
BARINA DOWNS RD
MERINDAH RD
HILDA RD
PLOVER GLN (Priv Rd)
COPYRIGHT © UNIVERSAL PRESS PTY LTD (PUBLISHER) 2002

JOINS MAP 217

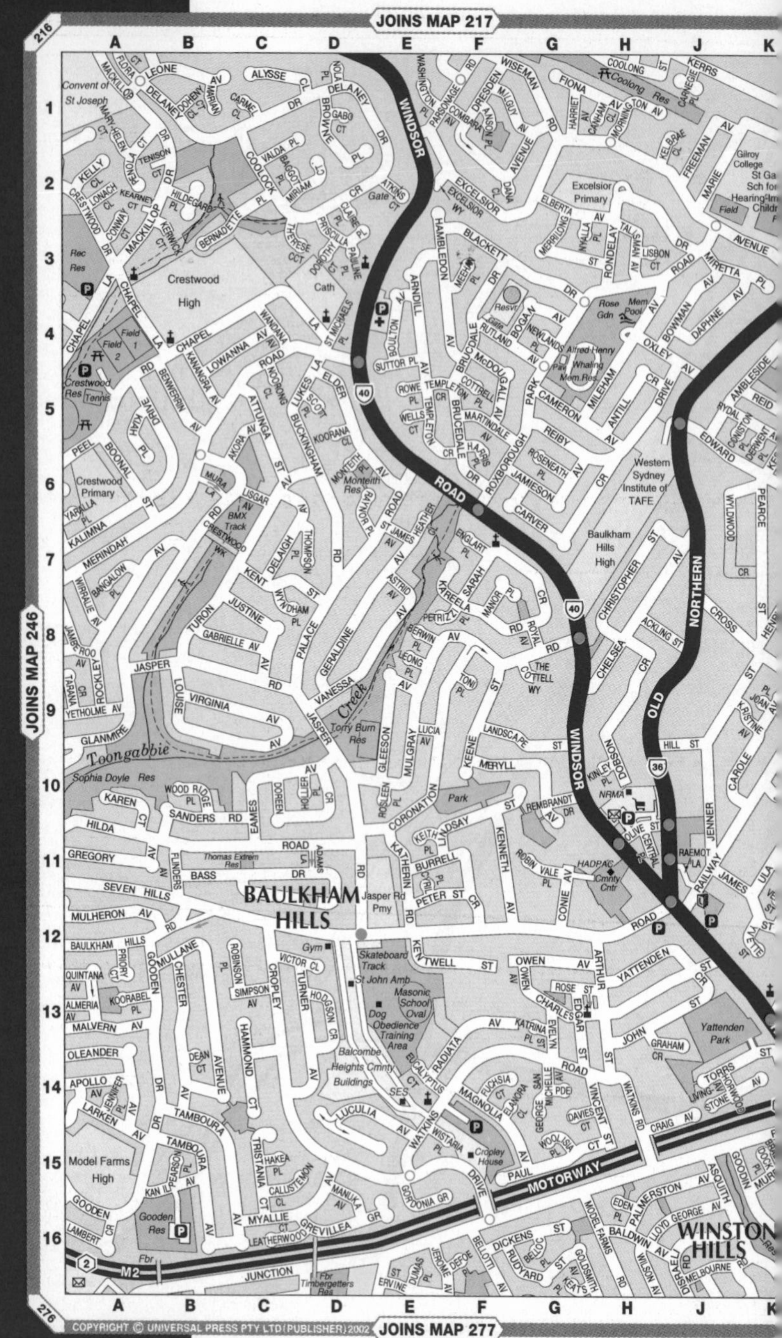

JOINS MAP 246

JOINS MAP 277

JOINS MAP 218

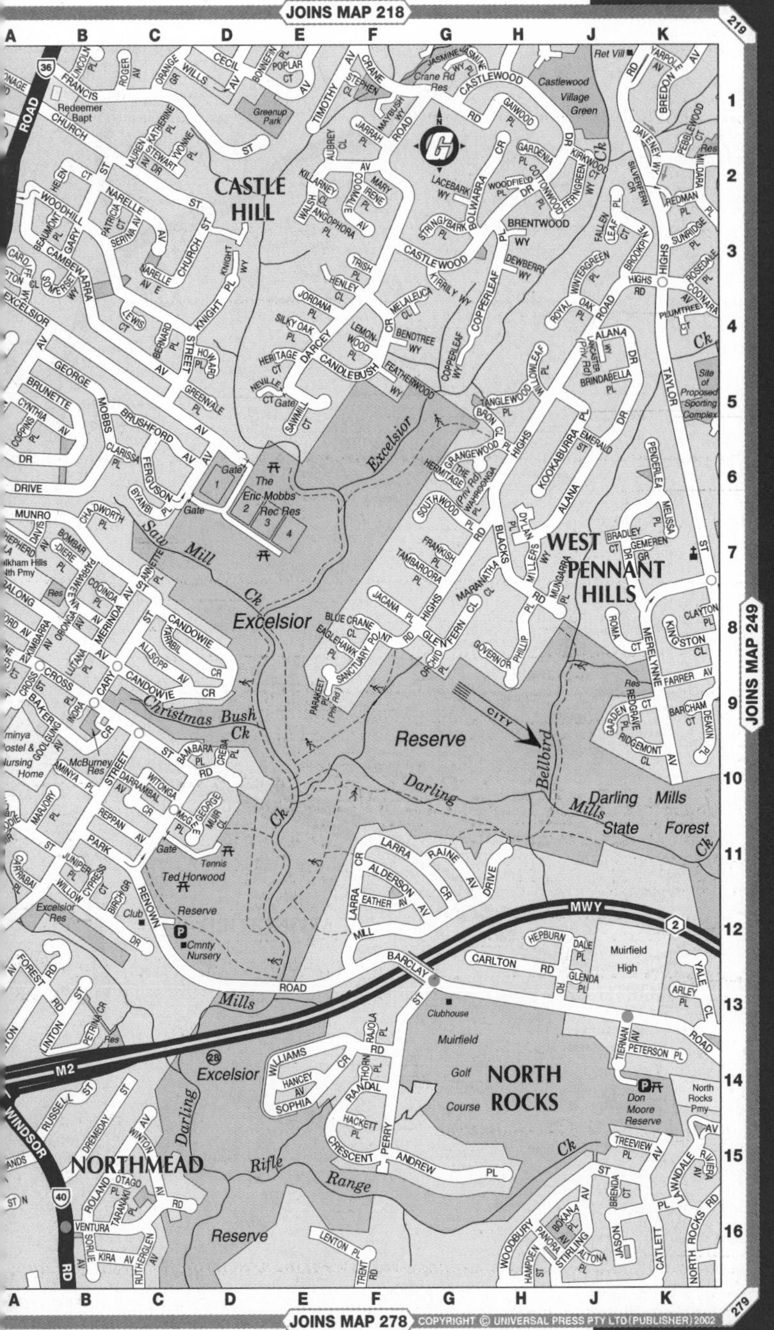

JOINS MAP 249

JOINS MAP 278

279

MAP 249

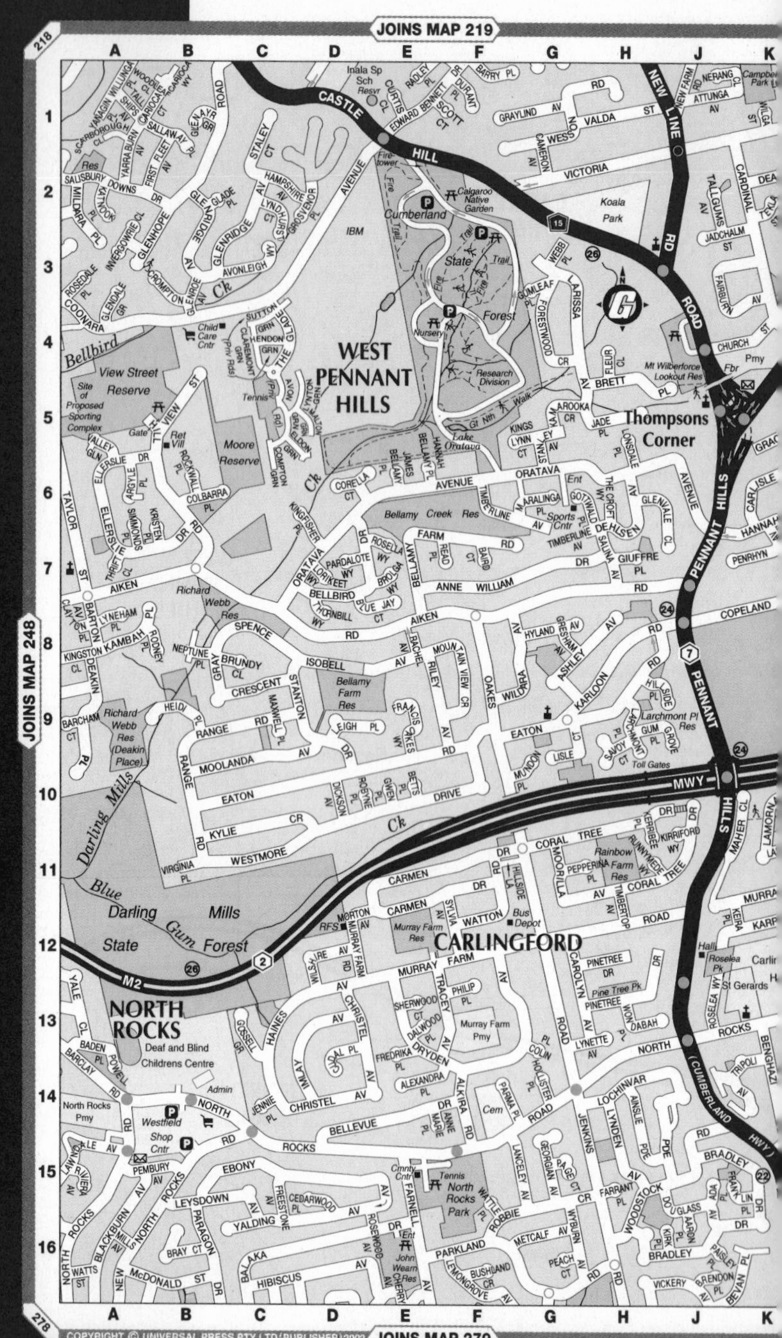

JOINS MAP 219
JOINS MAP 248
JOINS MAP 279
218
278
A B C D E F G H J K
1 2 3 4 5 6 7 8 9 10 11 12 13 14 15 16
WEST PENNANT HILLS
Thompsons Corner
CARLINGFORD
NORTH ROCKS
Cumberland State Forest
Koala Park
IBM
Calgaroo Native Garden
Research Division
Nursery
Lake Oratava
View Street Reserve
Site of Proposed Sporting Complex
Moore Reserve
Bellamy Creek Res
Richard Webb Res
Bellamy Farm Res
Richard Webb Res (Deakin Place)
Larchmont Pl Res
Rainbow Farm Res
Murray Farm Res
Murray Farm Pmy
Pine Tree Pk
Darling Mills Ck
Blue Gum Forest
Darling Mills State Forest
Deaf and Blind Childrens Centre
Westfield Shop Cntr
North Rocks Pmy
North Rocks Park
John Wearn Res
Mt Wilberforce Lookout Res
Roselea Pk
St Gerards
Bus Depot
Toll Gates
Sports Cntr
Child Care Cntr
Inala Sp Sch Resvr
CASTLE HILL
NEW LINE RD
PENNANT HILLS ROAD
(CUMBERLAND HWY)
M2
MWY
NORTH ROCKS RD
OAKES
ORATAVA AVENUE
AIKEN RD
VICTORIA
CHURCH
COPELAND
MURRAY FARM
NORTH

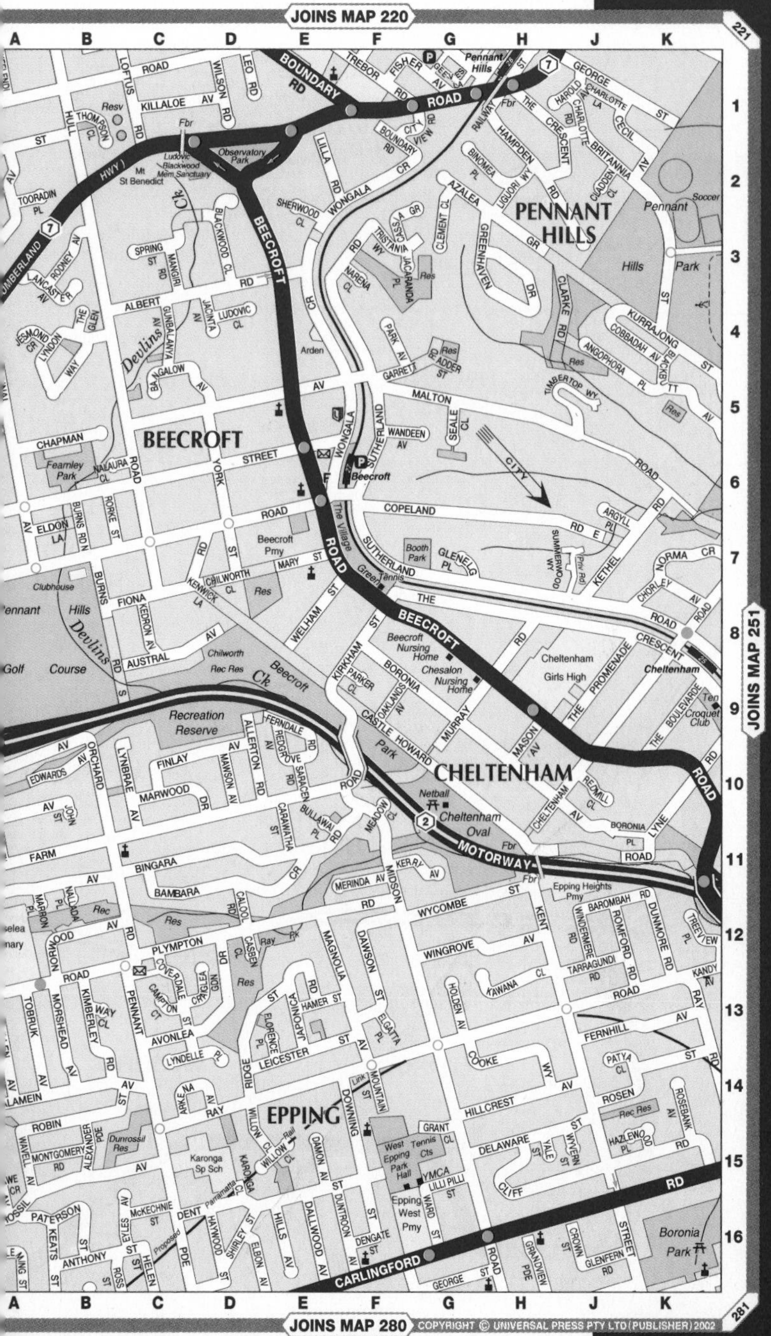
JOINS MAP 220
221
A B C D E F G H J K
1 2 3 4 5 6 7 8 9 10 11 12 13 14 15 16
JOINS MAP 251
JOINS MAP 280
281
BEECROFT
PENNANT HILLS
CHELTENHAM
EPPING
Pennant Hills
Beecroft
Cheltenham
BOUNDARY RD
ROAD
BEECROFT ROAD
BEECROFT
HWY
CUMBERLAND
MOTORWAY
CARLINGFORD RD
LOFTUS ROAD
KILLALOE AV
WILSON RD
LEO RD
TREBOR RD
FISHER AV
GEORGE ST
HAROLD RD
CHARLOTTE LA
CECIL AV
BRITANNIA
THE CRESCENT
HAMPDEN RD
BINOMEA PL
LIGUORI WY
AZALEA GR
CLEMENT CL
GREENHAVEN DR
CLARKE RD
KURRAJONG ST
COBBADAH AV
ANGOPHORA PL
TIMBERTOP WY
HULL
THOMPSON CL
Resv
Fbr
Ludovic Blackwood Mem Sanctuary
Observatory Park
Mt St Benedict
TOORADIN PL
RODNEY AV
LANCASTER AV
SPRING ST
MANGIRI RD
BLACKWOOD CL
SHERWOOD CL
WONGALA CR
LILLA RD
CITY VIEW RD
BOUNDARY RD
TRISTANIA WY
CASSIA GR
JACARANDA PL
NARENA CL
Res
ALBERT RD
JACINTA AV
LUDOVIC CL
GUNBALANYA AV
JESMOND CR
LYNDON WAY
THE GLEN
Devlins
Ck
BANGALOW AV
Arden
PARK AV
GARRETT RD
ADDER ST
MALTON AV
WONGALA
SUTHERLAND
WANDEEN AV
SEALE CL
CITY
CHAPMAN
Fearnley Park
NALAURA CL
STREET
ROAD
YORK
ELDON LA
BURNS RD N
RORKE ST
COPELAND RD
ARGYLL PL
KETHEL RD
NORMA CR
SUMMERWOOD WY
Beecroft Pmy
MARY ST
CHILWORTH CL
KENWICK LA
Booth Park
GLENELG PL
SUTHERLAND
The Village Green
Tennis
Clubhouse
Pennant Hills Golf Course
FIONA
KEDRON AV
AUSTRAL AV
Chilworth Rec Res
Beecroft Ck
WELHAM ST
THE CRESCENT
CHORLEY AV
ROAD
Beecroft Nursing Home
Chesalon Nursing Home
KIRKHAM ST
PARKER CL
BORONIA
OAKLANDS AV
CASTLE HOWARD ROAD
Park
MURRAY
Cheltenham Girls High
THE PROMENADE
THE BOULEVARDE
Ten Croquet Club
MASON AV
Recreation Reserve
ORCHARD
LYNBRAE AV
EDWARDS
FINLAY AV
MAWSON AV
ALLERTON RD
FERNDALE RD
REDGROVE AV
SARACEN RD
MARWOOD DR
CARAWATHA ST
BULLAWAI PL
MEADOW CL
Netball
Cheltenham Oval
CHELTENHAM AV
REDMILL CL
BORONIA PL
LYNE
ROAD
FARM
BINGARA CR
BAMBARA
CALOOL RD
MERINDA AV
KERRY AV
MIDSON RD
WYCOMBE ST
Epping Heights Pmy
KENT
BAROMBAH RD
WINDERMERE
ROMFORD RD
DUNMORE RD
TREVIEW PL
MARRON
NALLADA
Rec
Res
PLYMPTON RD
CASSEN CL
Ray Pk
MAGNOLIA
DAWSON ST
WINGROVE AV
TARRAGUNDI RD
KANDY AV
NORWOOD
ROAD
TOBRUK
MORSHEAD
KIMBERLEY RD
WAY CL
PENNANT
COVERDALE
CAMPTON CT
CRAIGLEA GDN
JAPONICA
HAMER ST
FLORENCE PL
ELGATTA PL
HOLDEN AV
KAWANA CL
RAY
FERNHILL AV
AVONLEA
LYNDELLE PL
RIDGE
LEICESTER ST
MOUNTAIN ST
COOKE WY
PATYA CL
ALAMEIN
ARKENA AV
DOWNING
Link
ROSEN
Rec Res
ROSEBANK AV
HILLCREST AV
ROBIN
WAVELL AV
MONTGOMERY RD
ALEXANDER PDE
Dunrossil Res
WILLOW CL
Rail
DAMON AV
GRANT CL
West Epping Park Hall
Tennis Cts
DELAWARE ST
YALE ST
WYVERN ST
HAZLEWOOD PL
RD
Karonga Sp Sch
KARONGA
YMCA
LILLI PILLI ST
CLIFF
PATERSON
KEATS ST
EYLES AV
McKECHNIE ST
DENT
Parramatta
Proposed
HAYWOOD
SHIRLEY
HILLS AV
DALLWOOD AV
DUNTROON AV
DENGATE ST
WARD ST
Epping West Pmy
ANTHONY
HELEN ST
ROSS ST
ELBON AV
GEORGE ST
ROAD
GRANDVIEW PDE
CROWN ST
GLENFERN RD
STREET
Boronia Park
COPYRIGHT © UNIVERSAL PRESS PTY LTD (PUBLISHER) 2002

JOINS MAP 221

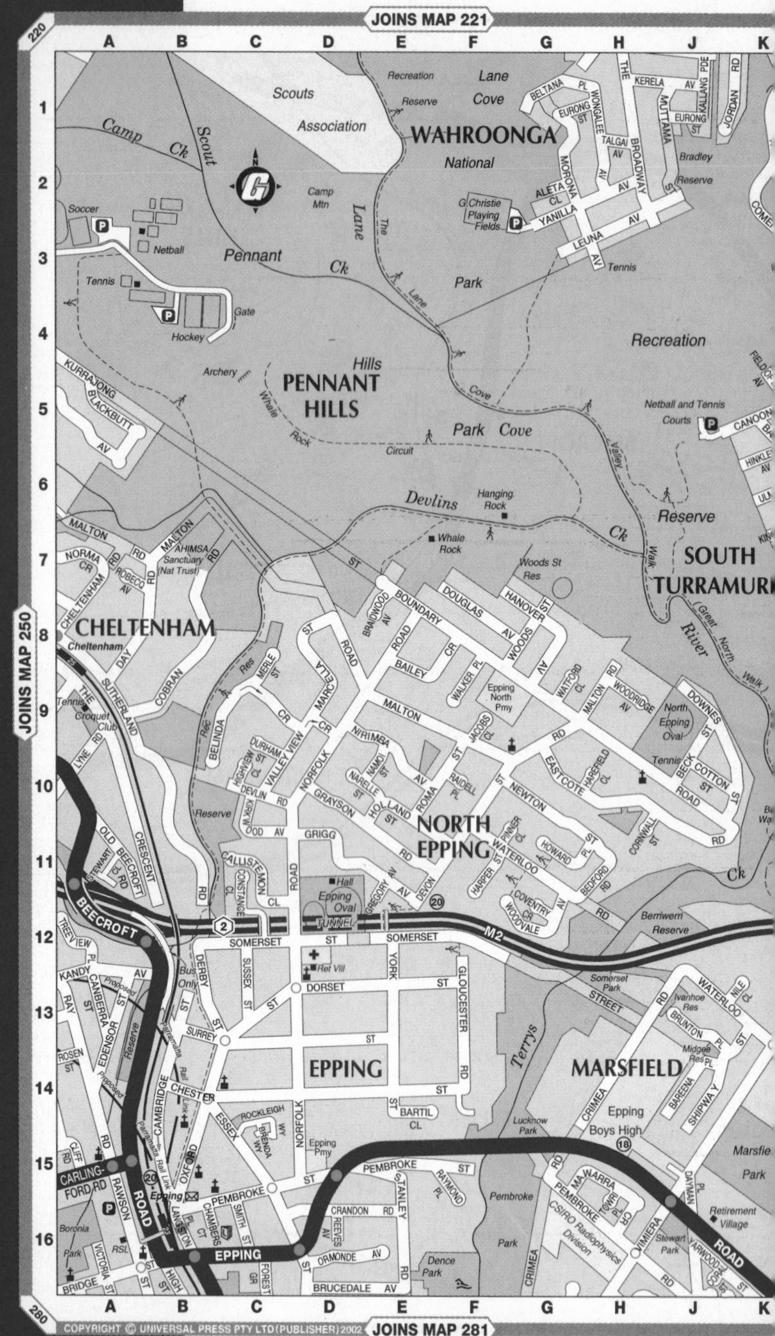

JOINS MAP 281

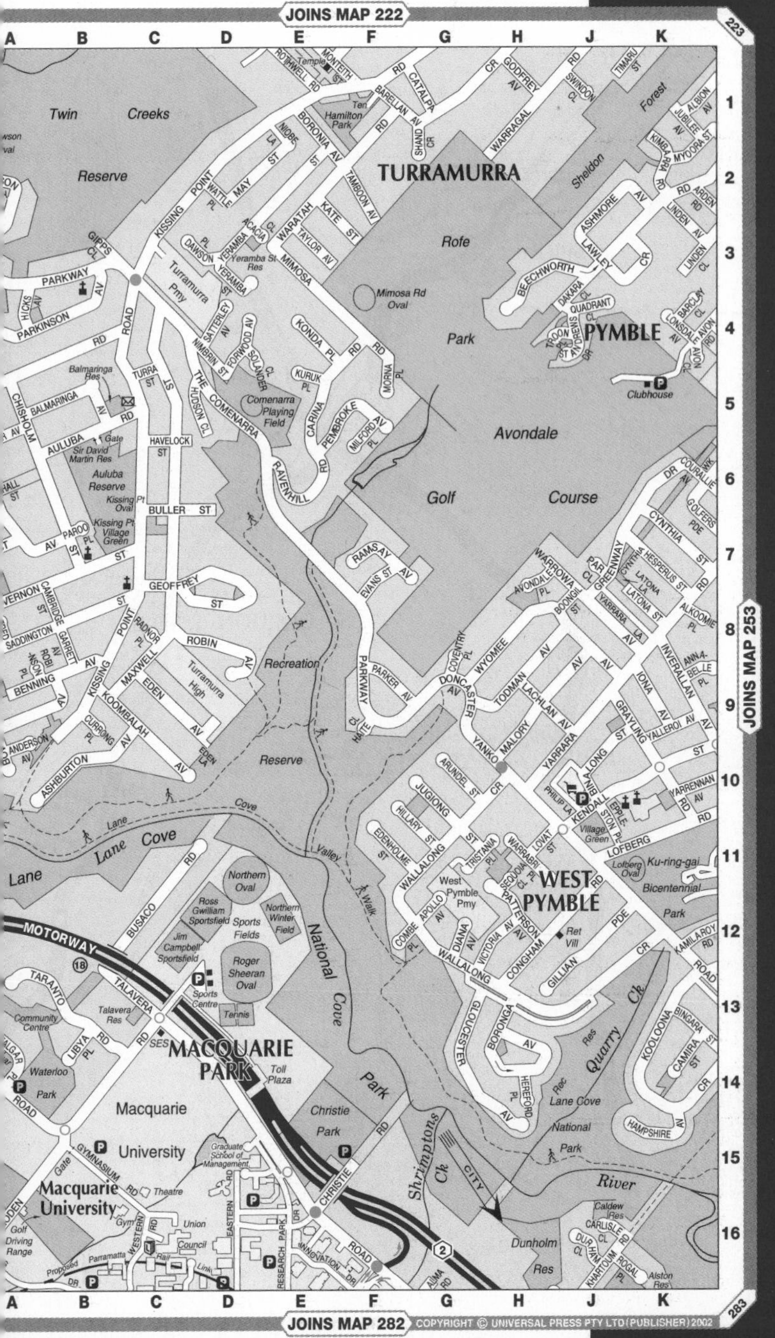
JOINS MAP 222
JOINS MAP 253
JOINS MAP 282
223
283
A
B
C
D
E
F
G
H
J
K
1
2
3
4
5
6
7
8
9
10
11
12
13
14
15
16
TURRAMURRA
PYMBLE
WEST PYMBLE
MACQUARIE PARK
Twin Creeks Reserve
Rofe Park
Avondale Golf Course
Sheldon Forest
Clubhouse
Ten Hamilton Park
Temple
Mimosa Rd Oval
Comenarra Playing Field
Balmaringa Res
Sir David Martin Res
Auluba Reserve
Kissing Pt Oval
Kissing Pt Village Green
Turramurra Pmy
Turramurra High
Yeramba St Res
Recreation Reserve
Lane Cove
Lane Cove Valley Walk
Lane Cove National Park
Lane Cove River
Northern Oval
Ross Gwilliam Sportsfield
Sports Fields
Northern Winter Field
Jim Campbell Sportsfield
Roger Sheeran Oval
Sports Centre
Tennis
Talavera Res
Community Centre
Waterloo Park
SES
Toll Plaza
Christie Park
Macquarie University
Graduate School of Management
Theatre
Gym
Union
Council
Golf Driving Range
Proposed Parramatta Rail Link
West Pymble Pmy
Ret Vill
Village Green
Lofberg Oval
Ku-ring-gai Bicentennial Park
Quarry Ck
Shrimptons Ck
Res
Dunholm Res
Caldew Res
Alston Res
MOTORWAY
18
2
CITY
PARKWAY
PARKINSON RD
HICKS AV
GIPPS CL
KISSING POINT RD
WATTLE PL
MAY ST
NIOBE LA
BORONIA AV
WARATAH ST
KATE ST
TAYLOR AV
TAMBOON AV
MIMOSA RD
ACACIA CL
YERAMBA PL
DAWSON PL
BARELLAN AV
CATALPA CR
SHAND CR
GODFREY AV
WARRAGAL RD
SWINDON CL
TIMARU ST
ALBION AV
JUBILEE AV
MYOORA ST
KIMBARRA RD
ARDEN RD
LINDEN AV
LINDEN CL
ASHMORE AV
LAWLEY CR
BEECHWORTH RD
DAKARA CL
QUADRANT
TROON PL
ST ANDREWS DR
BARCLAY CL
LONSDALE AV
AVON RD
ROTHWELL RD
MONTEITH ST
KONDA PL
KURUK PL
CARINA RD
PEMBROKE
MILFORD PL
MORNA PL
SATTERLEY AV
FORWOOD AV
SOLANDER CL
NIMBRIN ST
THE COMENARRA PKWY
HUDSON CL
RAVENHILL RD
TURRA ST
HAVELOCK ST
BULLER ST
GEOFFREY ST
CHISHOLM AV
BALMARINGA AV
AULUBA RD
PAROO PL
CAMBRIDGE ST
VERNON ST
SADDINGTON ST
GARRETT AV
BENNING AV
RADNOR PL
MAXWELL ST
ROBIN AV
EDEN AV
EDEN LA
KOOMBALAH AV
CURRONG PL
ASHBURTON AV
ANDERSON AV
RAMSAY AV
EVANS ST
PARKER AV
WAITE CL
DONCASTER AV
COVENTRY PL
WYOMEE AV
TODMAN AV
LACHLAN AV
MALORY AV
YANKO CR
YARRARA RD
ARUNDEL ST
JUGIONG ST
HILLARY ST
EDENHOLME ST
WALLALONG CR
TRISTANIA PL
WARRABRI
SEQUOIA CL
LOVAT ST
PATTERSON AV
APOLLO AV
COMBE PL
DIANA AV
VICTORIA AV
CONGHAM
GILLIAN PDE
WALLALONG
GLOUCESTER AV
BORONGA AV
HEREFORD PL
WARROWA AV
AVONDALE PL
BOONGIL ST
PAR CL
GREENWAY
CYNTHIA ST
HESPERUS ST
LATONA LA
LATONA ST
YARRARA LA
ALKOOMIE PL
INVERALLAN AV
ANNA-BELLE PL
IONA AV
GRAYLING ST
YALLEROI AV
YARRENNAN AV
BINALONG RD
KENDALL ST
PHILIP LA
EPPLESTON PL
LOFBERG RD
COURALLIE AV
GOLFERS PDE
KAMILAROY RD
KOOLOONA CR
BINGARA ST
CAMIRA ST
HAMPSHIRE AV
CARLISLE CL
DURHAM CL
KHARTOUM RD
ROGAL PL
BUSACO RD
TARANTO RD
TALAVERA RD
LIBYA PL
ALGAR
WATERLOO ROAD
GYMNASIUM RD
EASTERN RD
WESTERN RD
RESEARCH PARK DR
INNOVATION DR
CHRISTIE RD
EPPING ROAD
ALMA RD
COPYRIGHT © UNIVERSAL PRESS PTY LTD (PUBLISHER) 2002

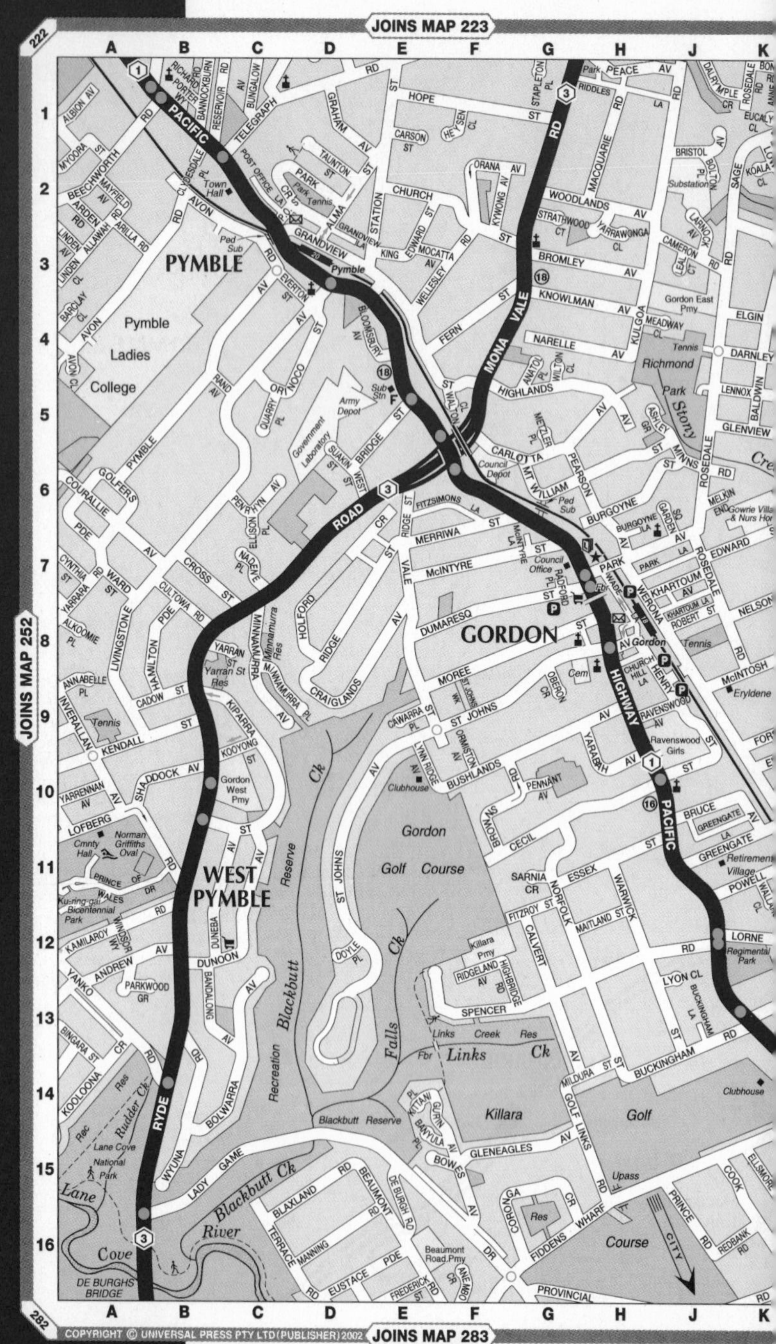
JOINS MAP 223
JOINS MAP 252
JOINS MAP 283
222
282
PYMBLE
Pymble Ladies College
GORDON
WEST PYMBLE
Gordon Golf Course
Killara Golf Course
Blackbutt Recreation Reserve
Lane Cove National Park
Lane Cove River
PACIFIC HIGHWAY
MONA VALE RD
RYDE ROAD
Army Depot
Government Laboratory
Town Hall
Council Depot
Council Office
Richmond Park
Gordon West Pmy
Norman Griffiths Oval
Ku-ring-gai Bicentennial Park
Links Creek Res
Beaumont Road Pmy
DE BURGHS BRIDGE
CITY

JOINS MAP 224

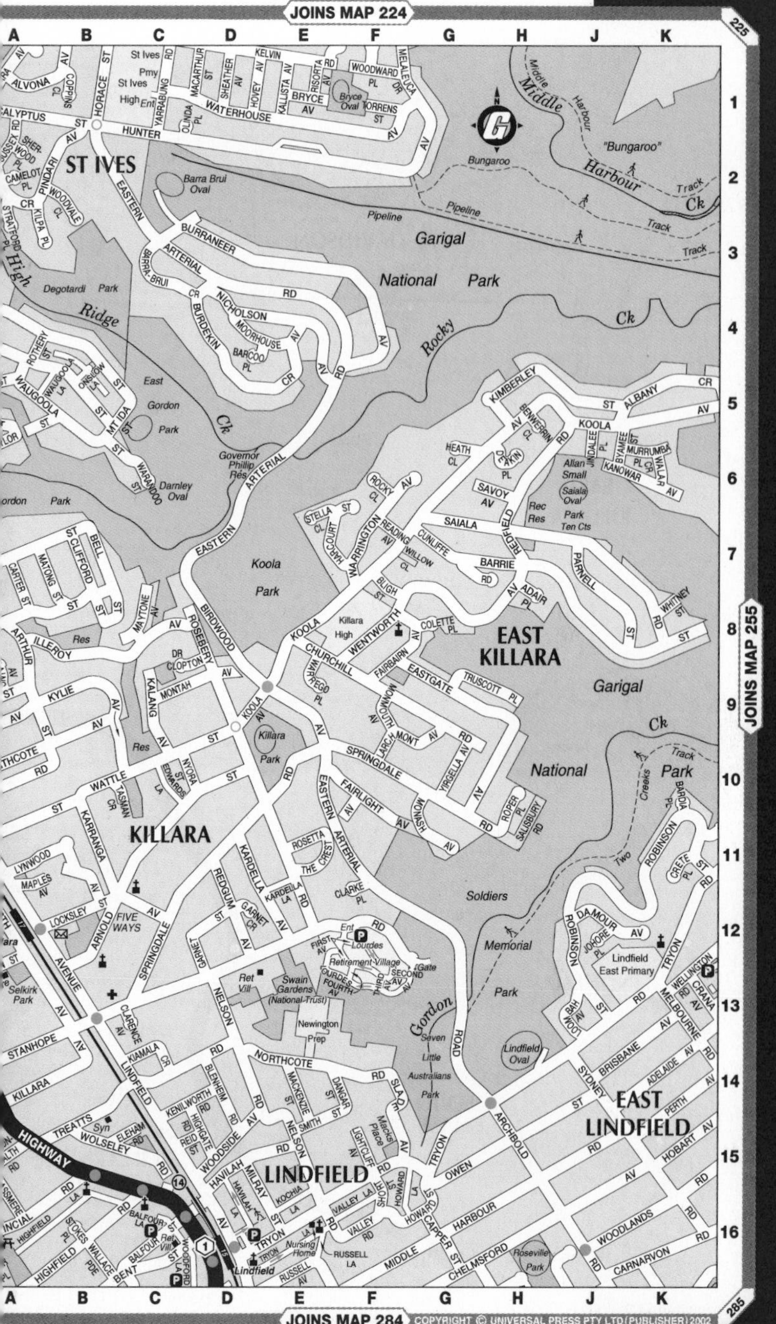

JOINS MAP 255

285

JOINS MAP 284

JOINS MAP 225

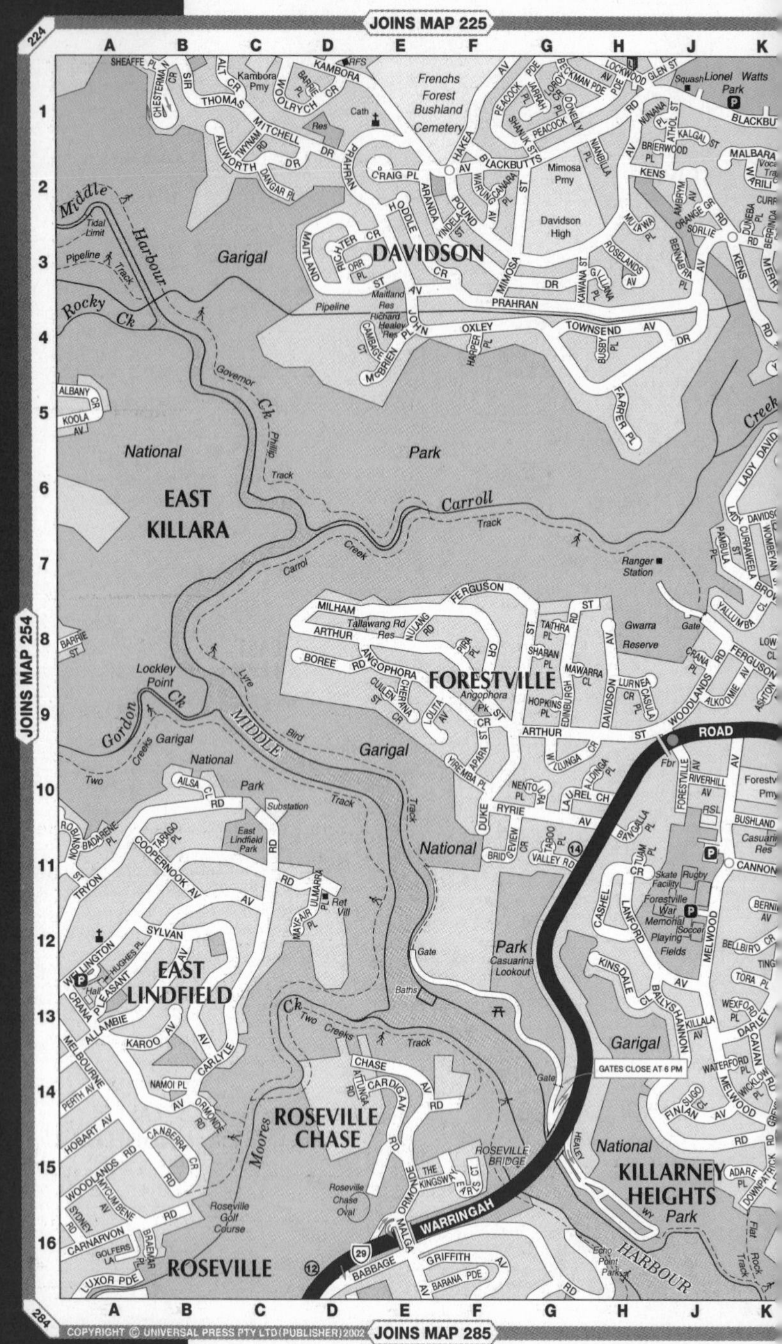

JOINS MAP 254

JOINS MAP 285

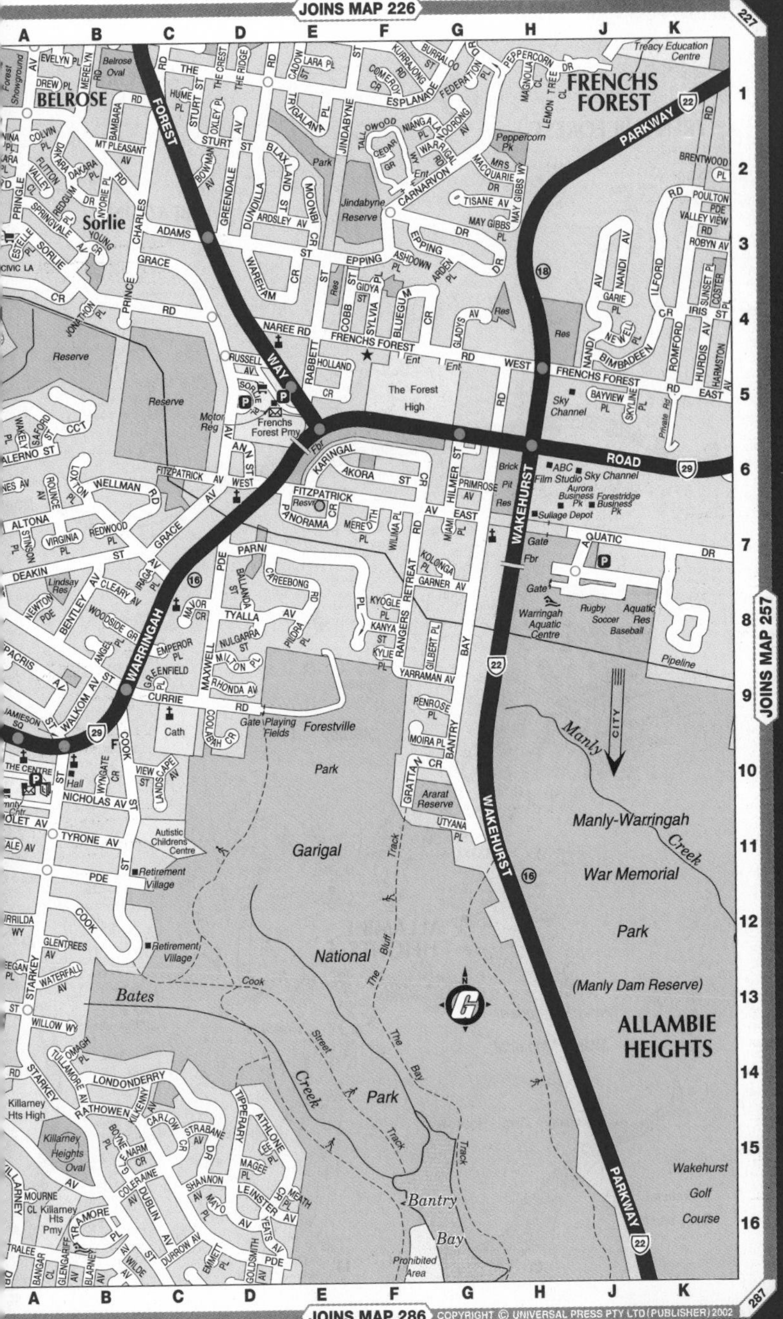
JOINS MAP 226
227
JOINS MAP 257
JOINS MAP 286
287
A B C D E F G H J K
1 2 3 4 5 6 7 8 9 10 11 12 13 14 15 16
BELROSE
Sorlie
FRENCHS FOREST
ALLAMBIE HEIGHTS
Forestville
Belrose Oval
Forest Showground
Tracey Education Centre
Peppercorn Pk
Jindabyne Reserve
Park
Reserve
Motor Reg
Frenchs Forest Pmy
The Forest High
Sky Channel
ABC Film Studio
Aurora Business Pk
Forestridge Business Pk
Sullage Depot
Brick Pit Res
Warringah Aquatic Centre
Rugby
Soccer
Baseball
Aquatic Res
Pipeline
Lindsay Res
Cath
Gate
Playing Fields
Forestville Park
Garigal National Park
Ararat Reserve
Autistic Childrens Centre
Retirement Village
THE CENTRE
Hall
Manly-Warringah War Memorial Park
(Manly Dam Reserve)
Manly Creek
CITY
Wakehurst Golf Course
Bates Creek
Cook Street Track
The Bluff Track
The Bay Track
Bantry Bay
Prohibited Area
Killarney Hts High
Killarney Heights Oval
Killarney Hts Pmy
FOREST WAY
WARRINGAH RD
FRENCHS FOREST RD WEST
FRENCHS FOREST RD EAST
WAKEHURST PARKWAY
ROAD
PARKWAY
AQUATIC DR
ADAMS ST
GRACE AV
EPPING DR
CARNARVON DR
ESPLANADE
CURRIE RD
NICHOLAS AV
TYRONE AV
STARKEY ST
LONDONDERRY DR
RATHOWEN
MAXWELL PDE
BANTRY BAY RD
RANGERS RETREAT RD
HILMER ST
FITZPATRICK AV WEST
FITZPATRICK AV EAST
KARINGAL CR
PANORAMA CR
COOK ST
PRINCE CHARLES RD
MT PLEASANT AV
DEAKIN ST
WALKOM AV
GRATTAN CR
YARRAMAN AV
18
16
22
29

JOINS MAP 227

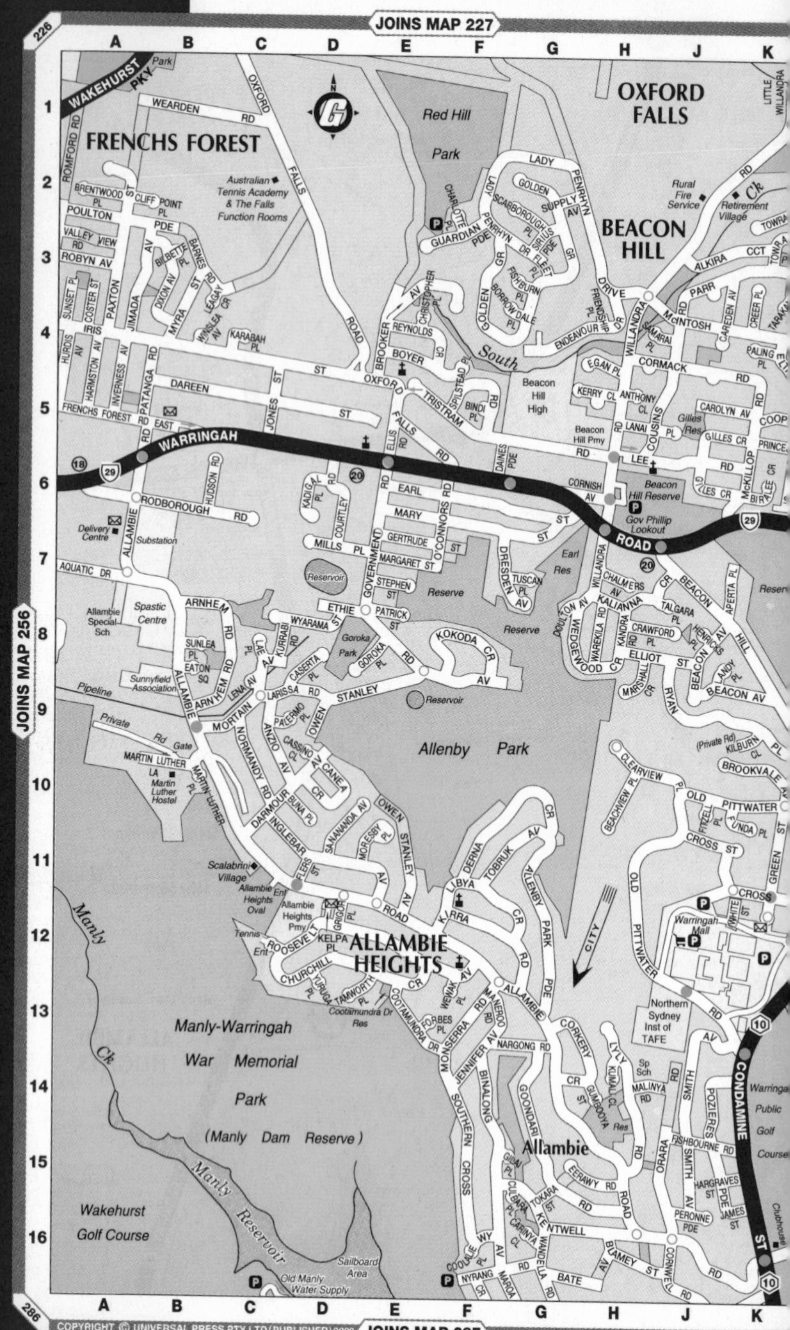

JOINS MAP 256

JOINS MAP 287

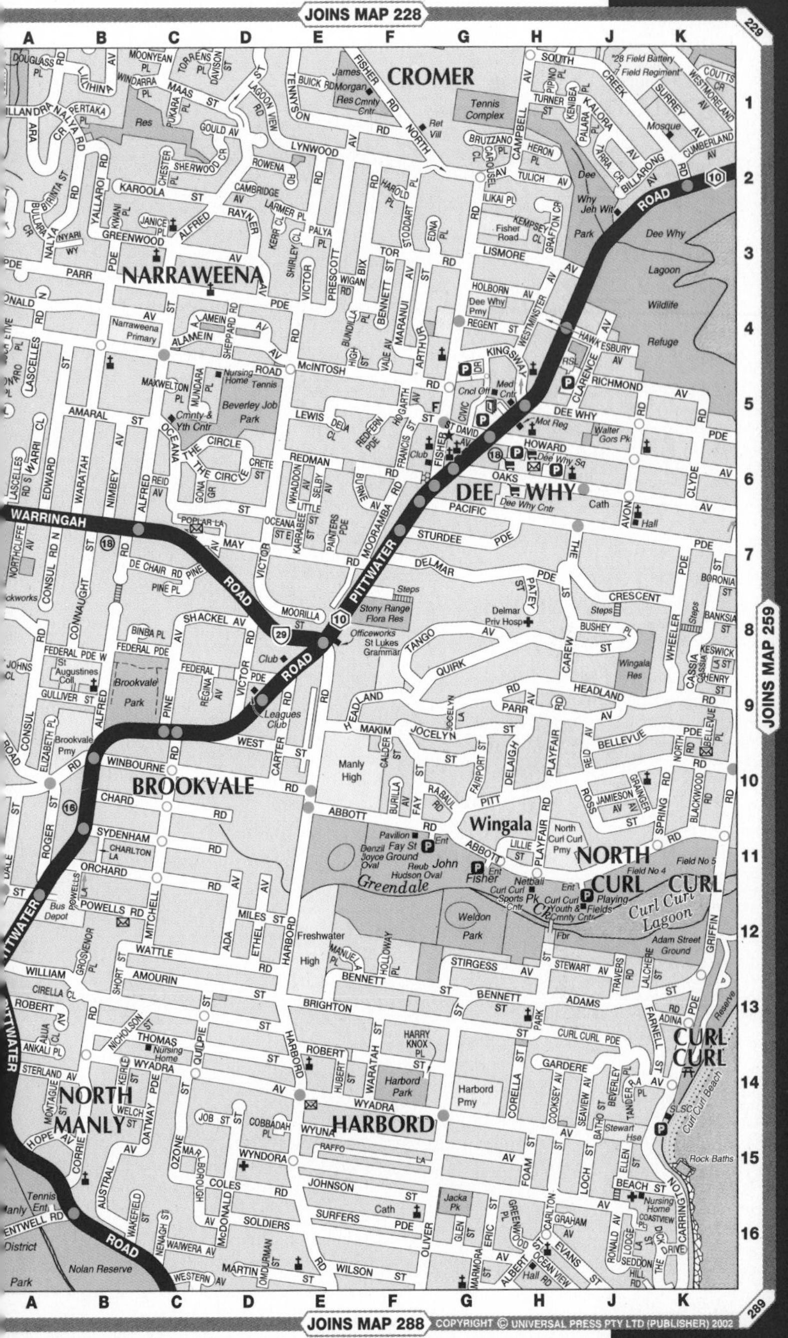
JOINS MAP 228
229
A
B
C
D
E
F
G
H
J
K
1
2
3
4
5
6
7
8
9
10
11
12
13
14
15
16
CROMER
NARRAWEENA
DEE WHY
BROOKVALE
Wingala
NORTH CURL CURL
CURL CURL
NORTH MANLY
HARBORD
JOINS MAP 259
Dee Why Lagoon Wildlife Refuge
Curl Curl Lagoon
Greendale Ck
Tennis Complex
James Morgan Res
Cmnty Cntr
Ret Vill
Mosque
"28 Field Battery 7 Field Regiment"
Dee Why Jeh Wit
Park
Fisher Road
Dee Why Pmy
Narraweena Primary
Nursing Home
Tennis
Beverley Job Park
Cmnty & Yth Cntr
Cncl Off
Med Cntr
Civic
RSL
Mot Reg
Walter Gors Pk
Dee Why Sq
Dee Why Cntr
Cath
Hall
Club
Stony Range Flora Res
Steps
Delmar Priv Hosp
Officeworks
St Lukes Grammar
Wingala Res
St Augustines Coll
Brookvale Park
Leagues Club
Brookvale Pmy
Manly High
Pavilion
Fay St
Denzil Joyce Ground Oval
Reub Hudson Oval
John Fisher
Ent
Netball
Curl Curl Sports Pk Cntr
Curl Curl Youth & Cmnty Cntr
Playing Fields
Field No 4
Field No 5
Weldon Park
Adam Street Ground
Freshwater High
Bus Depot
Charlton La
Harry Knox Pl
Harbord Park
Harbord Pmy
Stewart Hse
SLSC
Curl Curl Beach
Reserve
Rock Baths
Nursing Home
Coastview
Jacka Pk
Cath
Hall
Nolan Reserve
District Park
Manly Ent
WARRINGAH ROAD
PITTWATER ROAD
10
29
18
16
JOINS MAP 288
289

JOINS MAP 229

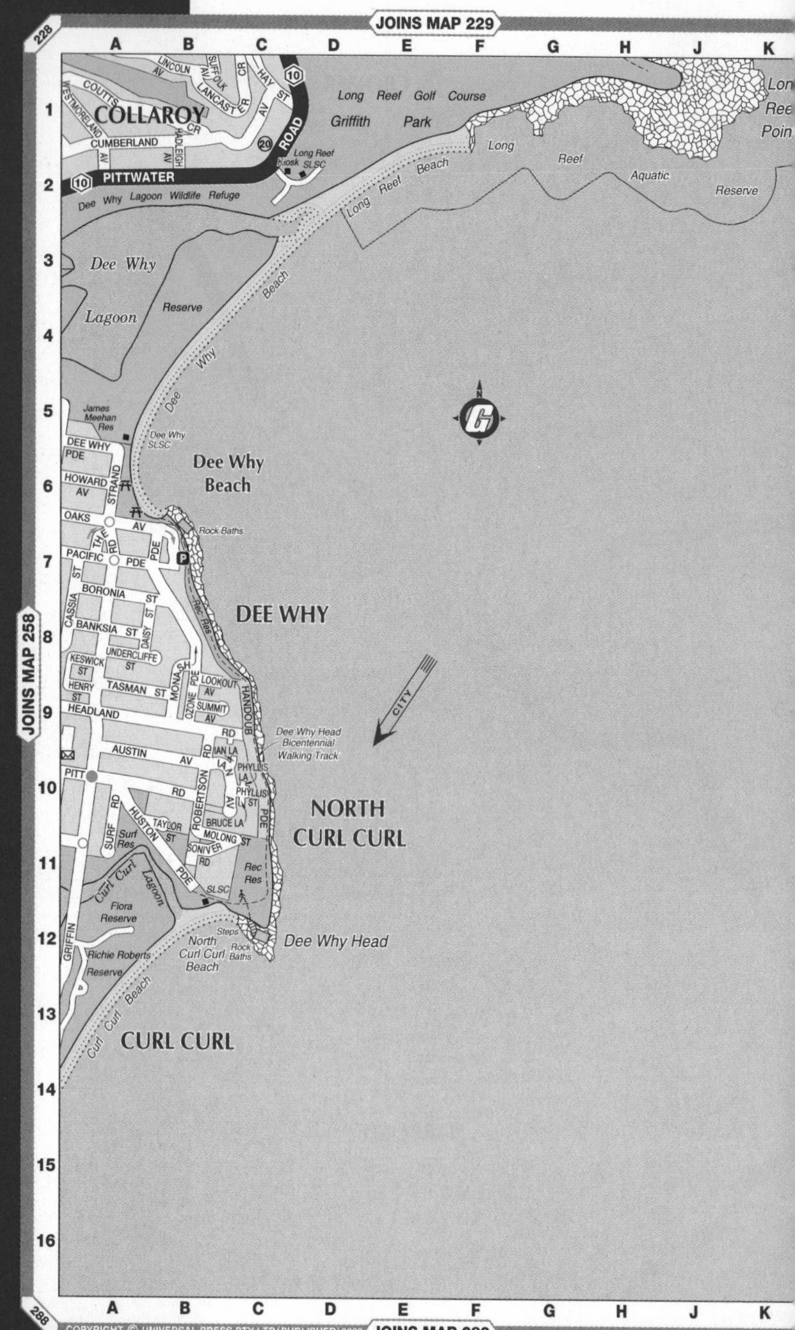

JOINS MAP 258

 JOINS MAP 289

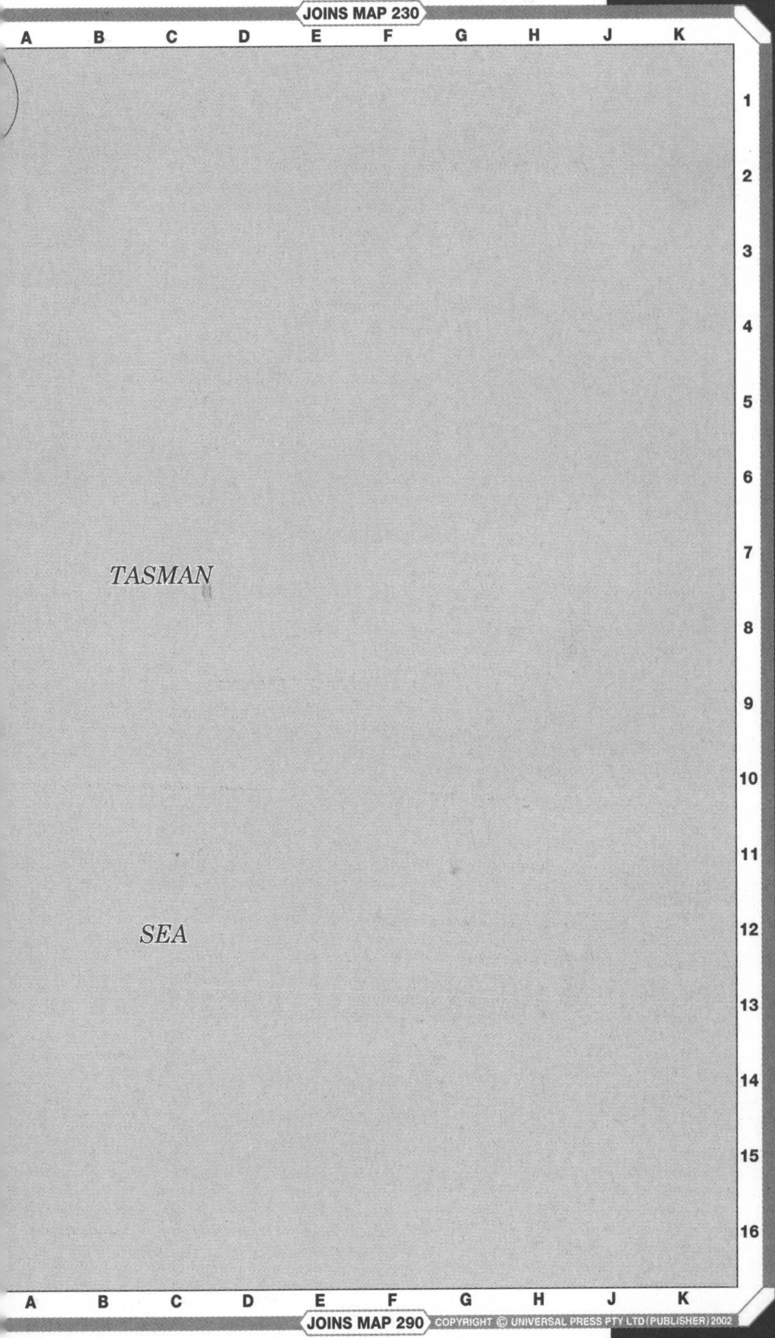

JOINS MAP 230

A B C D E F G H J K

1 2 3 4 5 6 7 8 9 10 11 12 13 14 15 16

TASMAN

SEA

A B C D E F G H J K

JOINS MAP 290

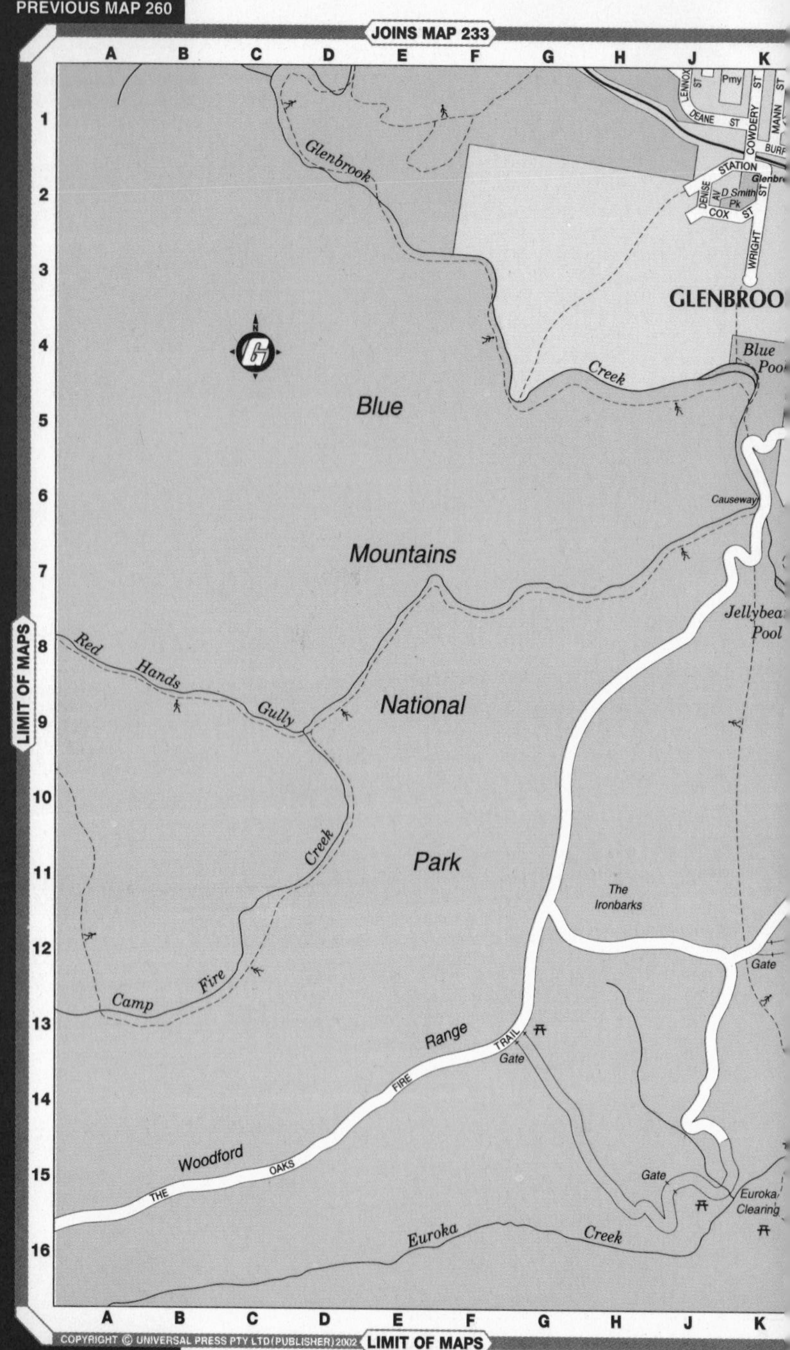

LIMIT OF MAPS

JOINS MAP 234

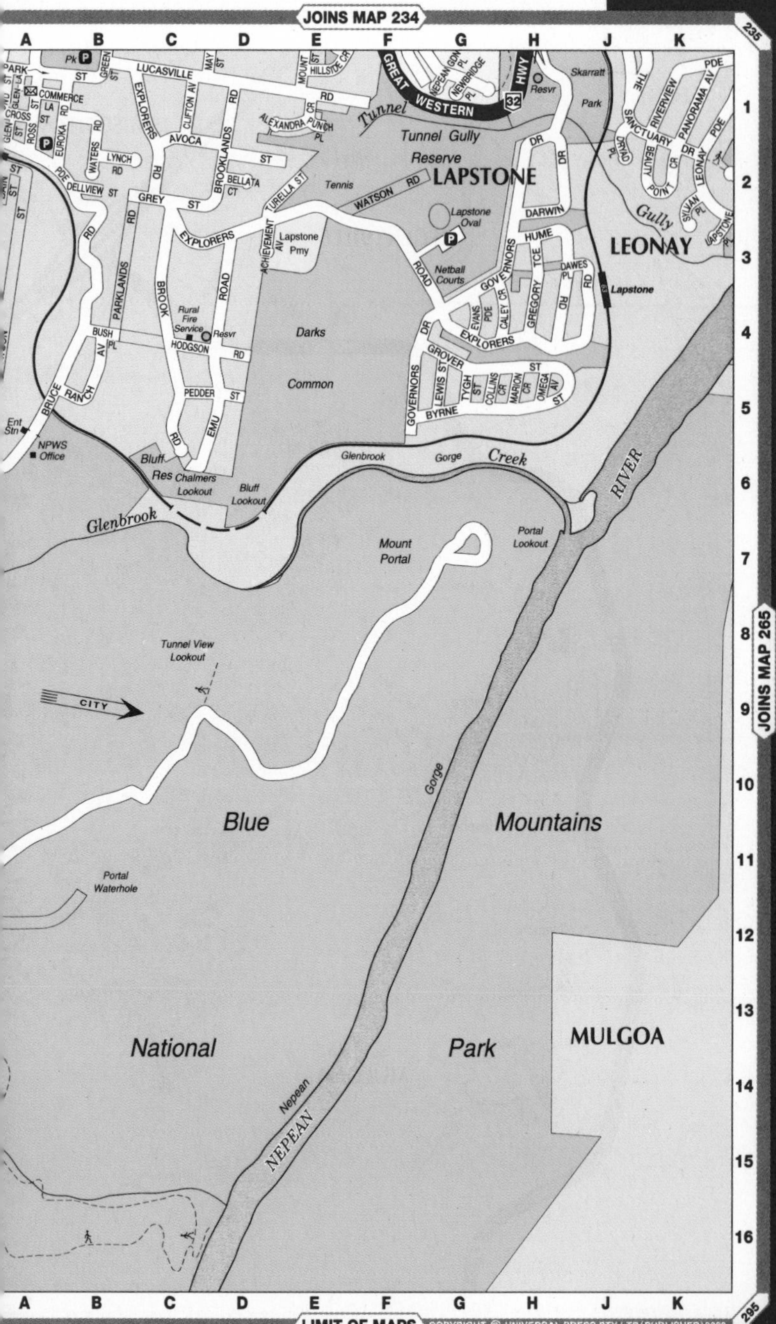

JOINS MAP 265

LIMIT OF MAPS

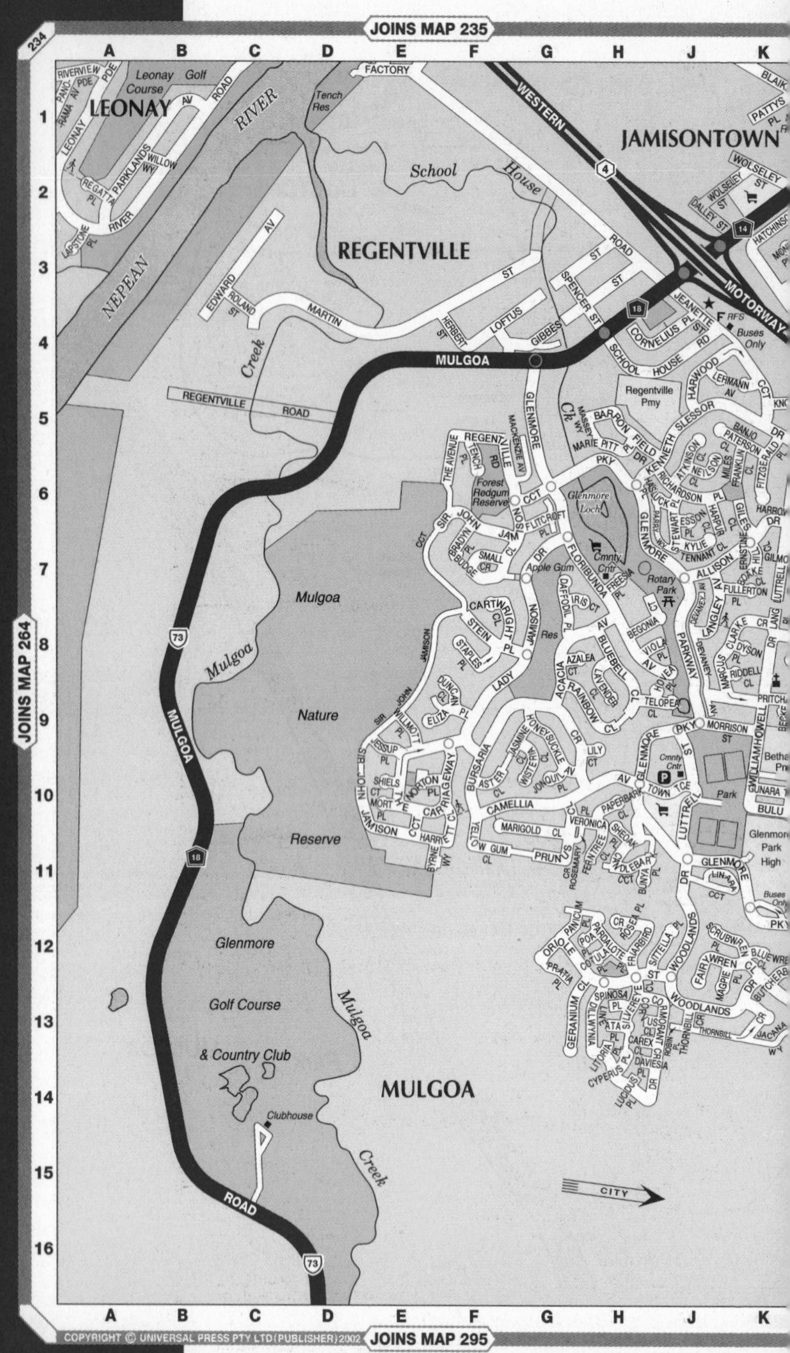
JOINS MAP 235
234
JOINS MAP 264
JOINS MAP 295
LEONAY
Leonay Golf Course
NEPEAN RIVER
Tench Res
REGENTVILLE
JAMISONTOWN
WESTERN MOTORWAY
School House Creek
MULGOA
REGENTVILLE ROAD
Mulgoa Nature Reserve
Glenmore Golf Course & Country Club
Clubhouse
Mulgoa Creek
Glenmore Loch
Regentville Pmy
Forest Redgum Reserve
Rotary Park
Glenmore Park High
MULGOA ROAD
GLENMORE PKY
CITY
COPYRIGHT © UNIVERSAL PRESS PTY LTD (PUBLISHER) 2002

JOINS MAP 236

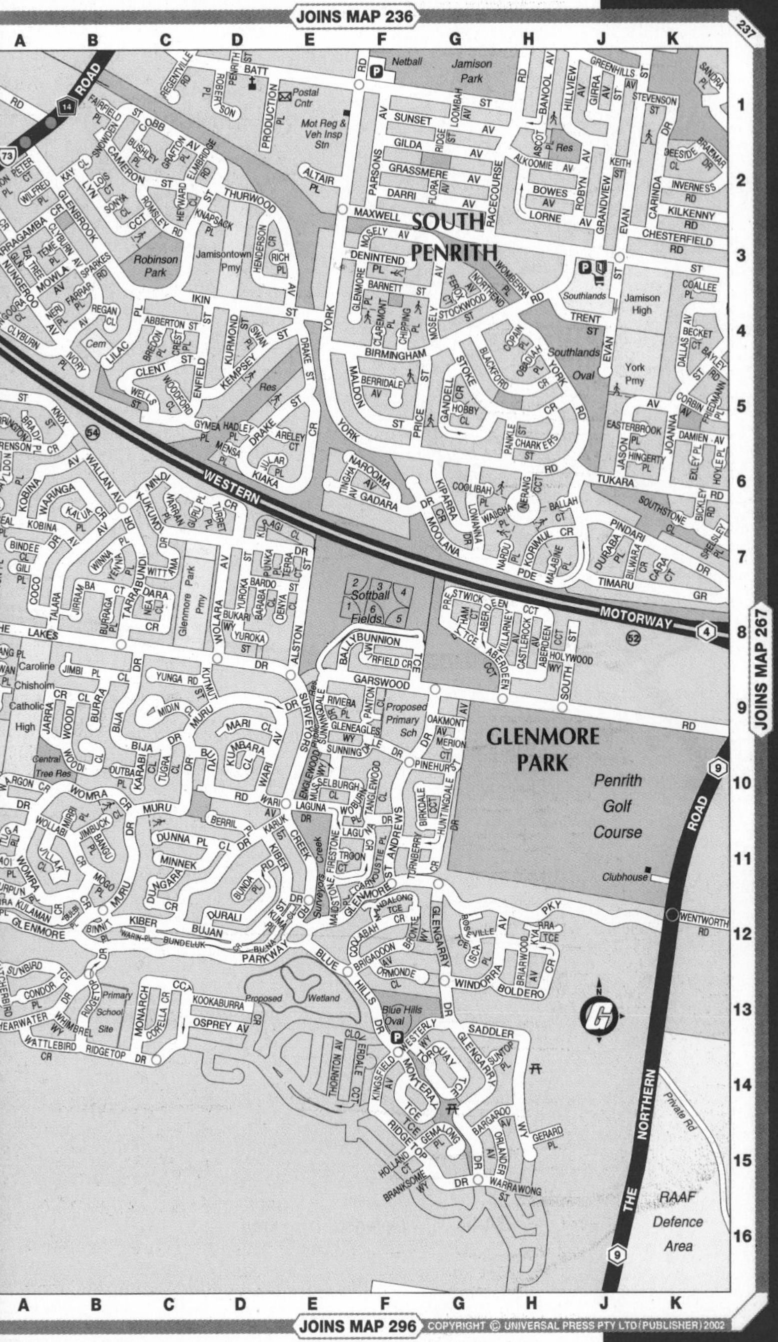

JOINS MAP 267

JOINS MAP 296

JOINS MAP 237

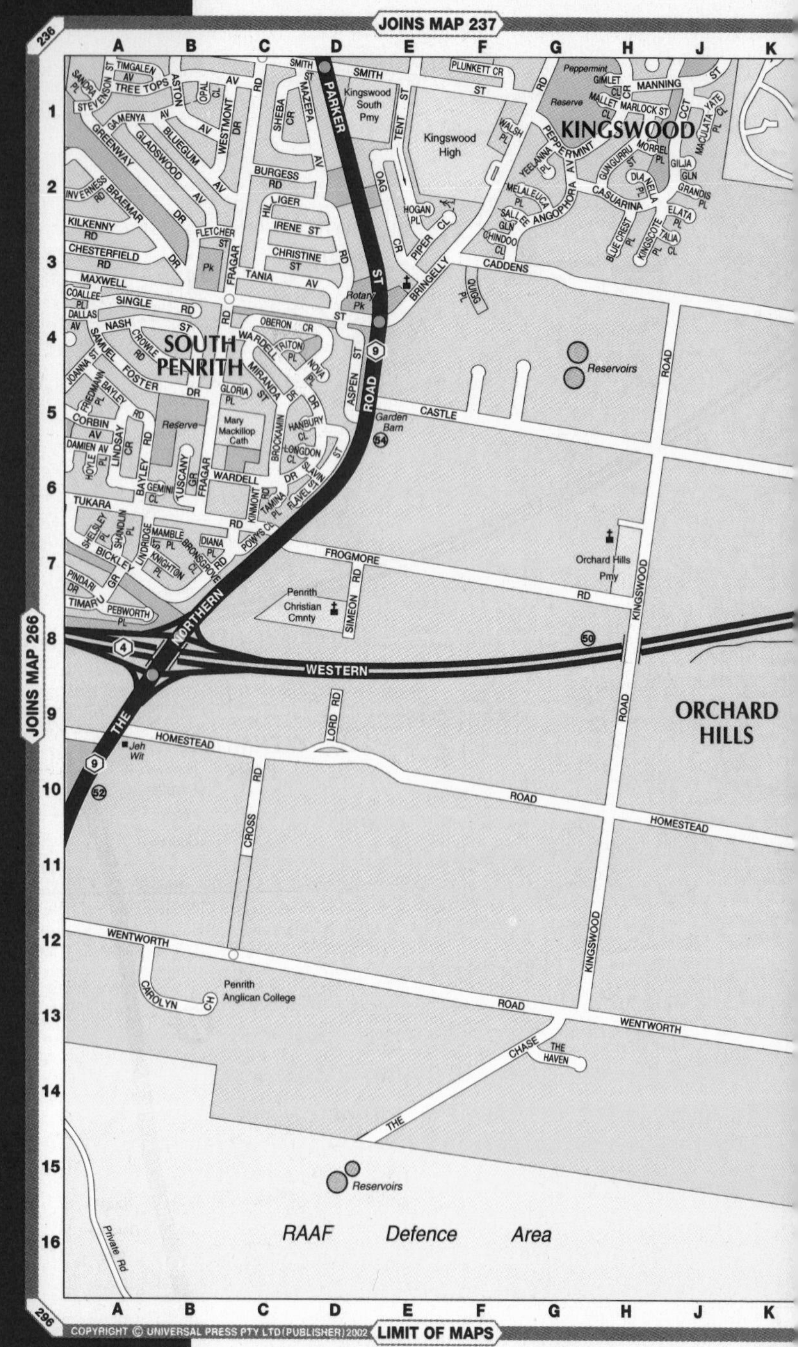

JOINS MAP 266

LIMIT OF MAPS

JOINS MAP 238

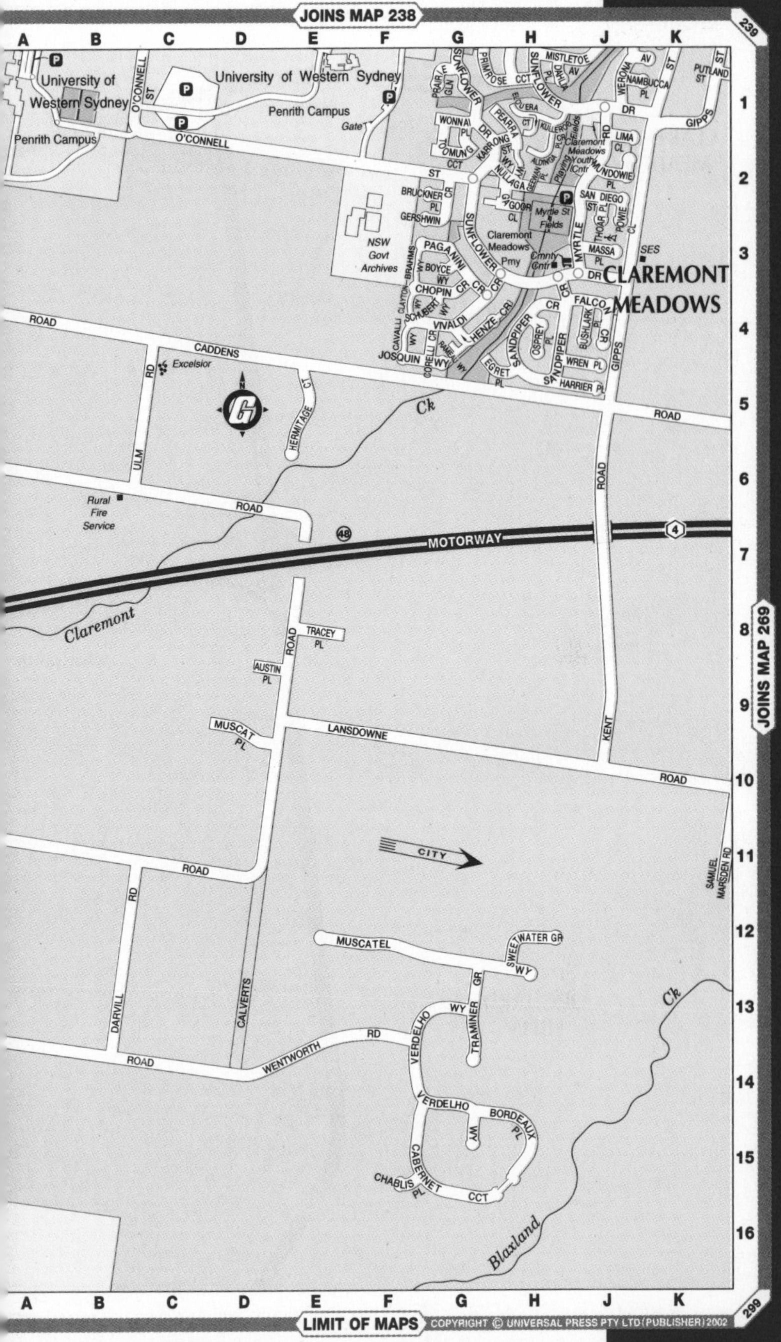

JOINS MAP 269

LIMIT OF MAPS

MAP 269

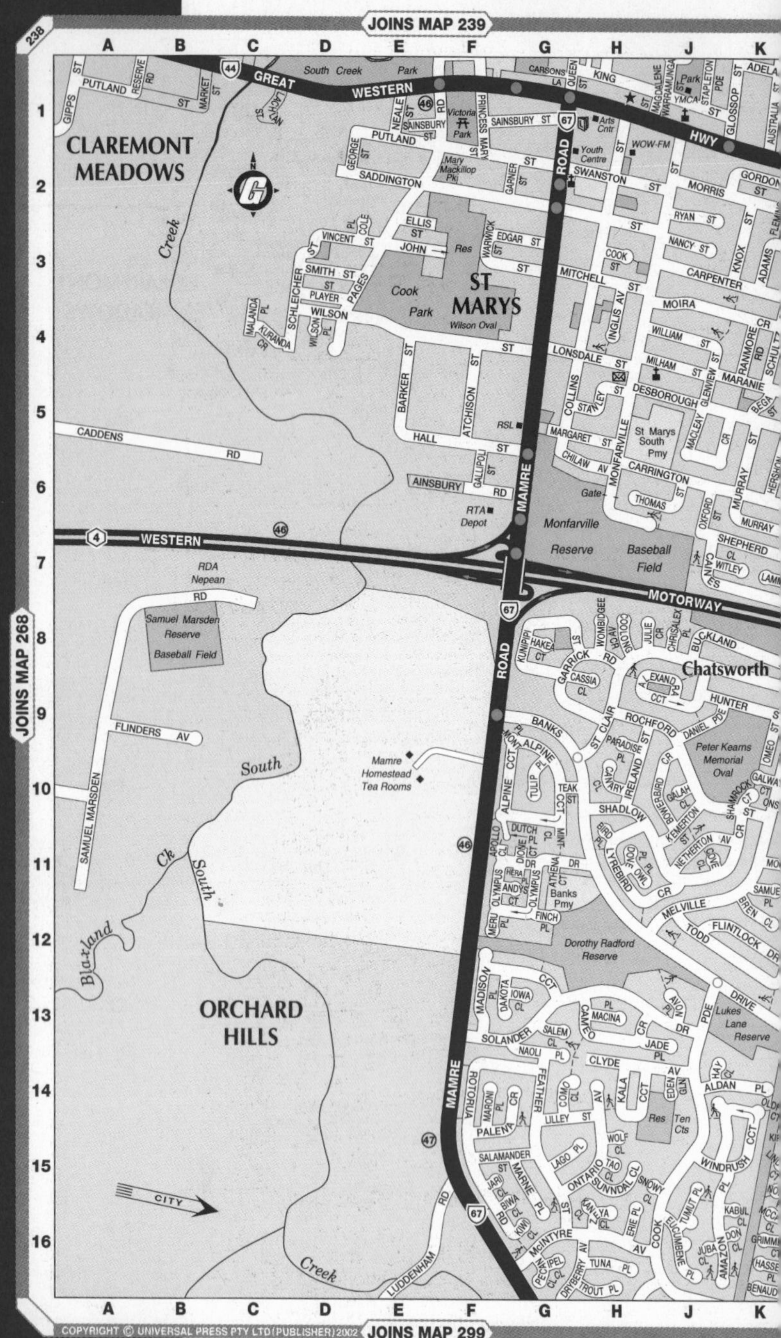
JOINS MAP 239
JOINS MAP 268
JOINS MAP 299
238
A B C D E F G H J K
1 2 3 4 5 6 7 8 9 10 11 12 13 14 15 16
CLAREMONT MEADOWS
ST MARYS
Chatsworth
ORCHARD HILLS
GREAT WESTERN HWY
WESTERN MOTORWAY
MAMRE ROAD
South Creek Park
Victoria Park
Mary Mackillop Pk
Cook Park
Wilson Oval
Res
Arts Cntr
Youth Centre
WOW-FM
YMCA
Park
RSL
RTA Depot
St Marys South Pmy
Monfarville Reserve
Baseball Field
Gate
RDA Nepean
Samuel Marsden Reserve
Baseball Field
Mamre Homestead Tea Rooms
Peter Kearns Memorial Oval
Banks Pmy
Dorothy Radford Reserve
Lukes Lane Reserve
Res
Ten Cts
South Creek
Blaxland Ck
South Creek
CITY
PUTLAND ST
RESERVE RD
MARKET ST
GIPPS ST
LACHLAN ST
NEALE ST
SAINSBURY ST
PRINCESS MARY ST
CARSONS LA
QUEEN ST
KING ST
MAGDALENE ST
WARRAMUNGA ST
STAPLETON PDE
GLOSSOP ST
ADELA
AUSTRALIA ST
PUTLAND ST
GEORGE ST
SADDINGTON ST
GARNER ST
SWANSTON ST
MORRIS ST
GORDON ST
RYAN ST
NANCY ST
KNOX ST
ADAMS
FLEMING
ELLIS ST
COLE PL
VINCENT ST
JOHN ST
EDGAR ST
WARWICK ST
SMITH ST
PLAYER ST
WILSON ST
PAGES
SCHLEICHER ST
MALANDA PL
KURANDA CR
WILSON PL
COOK ST
MITCHELL ST
INGLIS AV
CARPENTER ST
MOIRA
WILLIAM ST
RANMORE RD
SCHULTZ
LONSDALE ST
MILHAM ST
MARANIE
BARKER ST
ATCHISON ST
COLLINS ST
STANLEY ST
DESBOROUGH
GLENVIEW ST
BEGA ST
CADDENS RD
HALL ST
MARGARET ST
MONFARVILLE ST
MACLEAY CR
CHILAW AV
CARRINGTON
MURRAY ST
HERSHON
AINSBURY RD
GALLIPOLI ST
THOMAS
OXFORD ST
MURRAY
SHEPHERD
WITLEY CL
CAINES
KUNIPPI PL
HAKEA CT
WOMBIDGEE AV
COOLONG CR
JULIE CR
CHRISALEX PL
BUCKLAND
GARRICK RD
CASSIA CL
ALEXANDRA CCT
HUNTER
SAMUEL MARSDEN RD
FLINDERS AV
BANKS
ST CLAIR
ROCHFORD
DANIEL PDE
MONT ALPINE PL
ALPINE CCT
PARADISE PL
IRELAND ST
TULIP PL
TEAK CCT
CANARY CL
BOWERBIRD CR
GALAH CL
SHAMROCK CT
GALWAY
SHADLOW
KEMERTON ST
NETHERTON AV
DUTCH PL
MINT CL
APOLLO CL
DIONE CT
DR
BIRD PL
LYREBIRD
DOVE PL
OWL PL
COVE CL
HERA PL
ANDYS CT
OLYMPUS
ATHENA CT
CR
MELVILLE
SAMUEL PL
BREN CL
MERU PL
FINCH PL
TODD
FLINTLOCK DR
MADISON
DAKOTA CT
IOWA CL
CCT
MACINA PL
AVON PL
CAMEO
JADE PL
DR
DRIVE
PDE
SOLANDER
SALEM CL
NAOLI PL
CLYDE AV
EDEN GLN
HAY CL
ALDAN PL
ROTORUA
MARONI PL
CR
FEATHER ST
COMO CL
AV
KALA CCT
LILLEY ST
PALENA
WINDRUSH CCT
SALAMANDER ST
JARI CL
BIWA CL
MARNE PL
LAGO PL
WOLF CL
ONTARIO CL
TAO CL
SUNNDAL CL
SNOWY CL
TUMUT PL
KABUL CL
KIWI CL
RD
ST
YANA CL
ERIE PL
COOK
EUCUMBENE PL
DON CL
JUBA CL
AMAZON CL
McINTYRE AV
PECAN PL
PEL CL
DRYBERRY AV
TUNA PL
TROUT PL
LUDDENHAM RD
GRIMM
HASSE PL
BENAUD
44 46 4 67 47

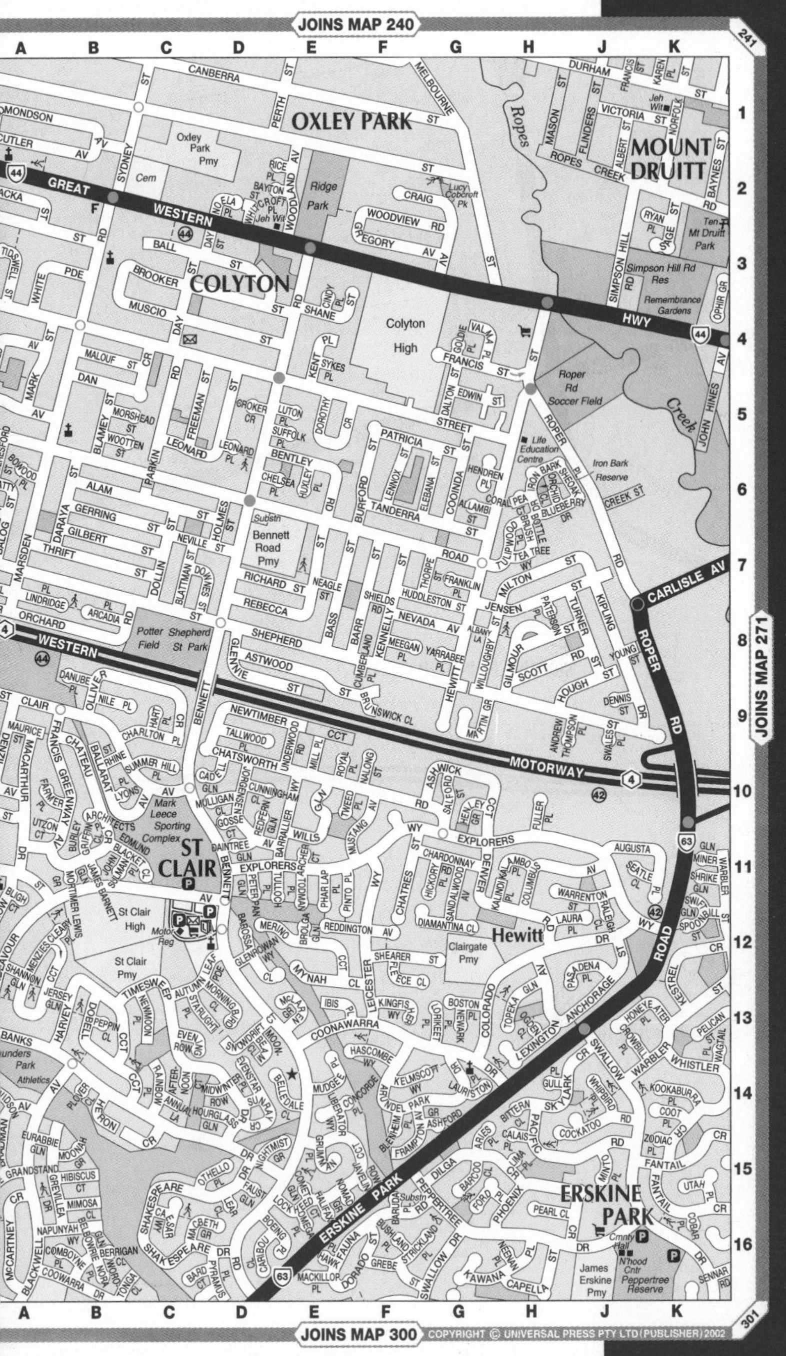
JOINS MAP 240
241
A B C D E F G H J K
1 2 3 4 5 6 7 8 9 10 11 12 13 14 15 16
OXLEY PARK
MOUNT DRUITT
COLYTON
ST CLAIR
Hewitt
ERSKINE PARK
CANBERRA ST
PERTH ST
MELBOURNE ST
DURHAM ST
VICTORIA ST
MASON ST
FLINDERS ST
ALBERT ST
NORFOLK ST
FRANCIS ST
KAREN PL
ROPES CREEK
Ropes
MONDSON
CUTLER AV
SYDNEY ST
Oxley Park Pmy
Cem
RICE PL
BAYTON PL
WHITCROFT PL
Jeh Wit
WOODLAND AV
Ridge Park
Lucy Cobcroft Pk
CRAIG
WOODVIEW RD
GREGORY AV
GREAT WESTERN HWY
44
BALL
BROOKER
MUSCIO
WHITE
PDE
SIMPSON HILL RD
RYAN PL
SAGE
BAYNES ST
Ten Mt Druitt Park
Simpson Hill Rd Res
Remembrance Gardens
OPHIR GR
SHANE
CINDY PL
Colyton High
VALMA PL
GOLDIE
FRANCIS ST
ROPER RD
Roper Rd Soccer Field
JOHN HINES AV
Creek
MALOUF ST
DAN
MARK
KENT
SYKES PL
DALTON
EDWIN ST
MORSHEAD ST
WOOTTEN ST
BLAMEY
FREEMAN
PARKIN
CROKER CR
LUTON
SUFFOLK
LEONARD PL
DOROTHY CR
PATRICIA
STREET
Life Education Centre
Iron Bark Reserve
IRON BARK
SHEOAK PL
ORCHID CL
BLUEBERRY DR
CREEK ST
HENDREN PL
CORAL PEA
BENTLEY
CHELSEA PL
HUXLEY PL
LENNOX
ELEBANA
COOINDA
ALLAMBI ST
BOWOOD
ALAM
GERRING ST
GILBERT ST
THRIFT ST
DARAYA
MARSDEN
BALOG
HOLMES
NEVILLE ST
Substn
Bennett Road Pmy
TANDERRA
BURFORD
ROAD
TULIPWOOD
BOTTLEBRUSH
TEA TREE WY
MILTON
DOLLIN
BLATTMAN ST
DOWNES ST
RICHARD ST
NEAGLE ST
SHIELDS RD
HUDDLESTON ST
THORPE
FRANKLIN PL
PATERSON
TURNER
KIPLING
CARLISLE AV
LINDRIDGE
ARCADIA
ORCHARD
REBECCA
BASS
BARR
NEVADA AV
JENSEN
ALBANY LA
WILLOUGHBY
Potter Field
Shepherd St Park
SHEPHERD
WESTERN
KENNELLY
MEEGAN PL
YARRABEE PL
GILMOUR
SCOTT
YOUNG ST
GLENNIE
ASTWOOD
CUMBERLAND
HEWITT
HOUGH
DENNIS ST
DANUBE PL
OLLIVER
NILE PL
ST CLAIR
BRUNSWICK CL
MARTIN GR
ANDREW THOMPSON PL
SWALES PL
MAURICE ST
FRANCIS GREENWAY
CHATEAU
BALLARAT
RHINE PL
HART PL
CHARLTON PL
BENNETT
NEWTIMBER
TALLWOOD
UNDERWOOD RD
MILL PL
CCT
ROYAL PL
NALONG
CHATSWORTH
MOTORWAY
4
SUMMER HILL PL
LYONS
MACARTHUR
FARMER
CADELL
GLN
JORGENSEN
CUNNINGHAM
ASHWICK
SALFORD
HENLEY GR
CCT
42
FULLER PL
Mark Leece Sporting Complex
MULLIGAN
GOSSE
REDFERN
BARRALLIER
TWEED PL
MUSTANG AV
RD
WY
EXPLORERS
UTZON
BURLEY
GRIFFIN
ARCHITECTS
EDMUND BLACKET
JOHN SULMAN
DAINTREE
WILLS
CHARDONNAY
DENVER
AUGUSTA
SEATTLE CL
JAMES BARNETT
MORTIMER LEWIS
PETER PAN
TULLOCH
ARCHER
PHAR LAP
PINTO PL
CHATRES
HICKORY
SANDALWOOD
KALINDI
AMBO PL
COLUMBUS
WARRENTON
RALEIGH
GLN
MINER
WARBLER
SHRIKE
SWIFT
SPOONBILL
BLIGH CT
St Clair High
Motor Reg
BAROSSA
MERINO
BROLGA
REDDINGTON AV
DIAMANTINA CL
Clairgate Pmy
LAURA PL
ROAD
CR
MENZIES
CLEARY
SHANNON GLN
JERSEY GLN
HARVEY
DOBELL
PEPPIN CL
St Clair Pmy
TIMESWEEP
NEWMOON
AUTUMN LEAF
MORNING BIRD
STARLIGHT
GLENROWAN WY
MYNAH
SHEARER ST
FLEECE CL
LEICESTER
TOPEKA
PASADENA PL
ANCHORAGE
KESTREL
BANKS
Saunders Park Athletics
EVENING ROW
SNOWDRIFT
MOONBEAM
McLAREN GR
IBIS
KINGFISHER WY
BOSTON
NEWARK
COLORADO
LORIKEET
LEXINGTON
HONEYEATER
CROWBILL
PELICAN
WAGTAIL
WHISTLER
RAINBOW
AFTERNOON
MIDWINTER
ANNUAL
HOURGLASS
EVENSTAR
SUNRAY
BELLEDALE
COONAWARRA
HASCOMBE WY
MUDGEE
CONCORDE
KELMSCOTT WY
LAURISTON
SWALLOW
WHIPBIRD
KOOKABURRA
COOT PL
SKYLARK
GULL
BITTERN
CALAIS
PACIFIC
COCKATOO
ZODIAC PL
PLOVER
HERON
EURABBIE GLN
MOONAH
NIGHTMIST
LIBERATOR
ARUNDEL PARK
BLENHEIM
FRAMPTON AV
ASHFORD
ARIES PL
LIMA
MINTO
FANTAIL
UTAH PL
GRANDSTAND
HIBISCUS CT
GREVILLEA
MIMOSA CL
OTHELLO
SHAKESPEARE
FAUST GLN
GRUMMAN
JAVELIN
NOMAD
COMET
LOCKHEED
HALIFAX
ERSKINE PARK RD
DILGA
PEPPERTREE
BARCOO
FORD
PHOENIX
PEARL CL
Cmnty Hall
N'hood Cntr
Peppertree Reserve
James Erskine Pmy
McCARTNEY
BLACKWELL
NAPUNYAH WY
COMBOYNE PL
BELBOWRIE
BERRIGAN CL
NORA
TONGA
COOWARRA
MACBETH GR
CAESAR
BARD CL
PYRAMUS
BOEING
CARIBOU
FAUNA
HAWK
BARUDA
BUSHLAND
STRICKLAND
SWALLOW DR
NEENAN
KAWANA
CAPELLA
GREBE
MACKILLOP
DORADO
63
SENNAR RD
COBAR
JOINS MAP 271
JOINS MAP 300
301

JOINS MAP 241

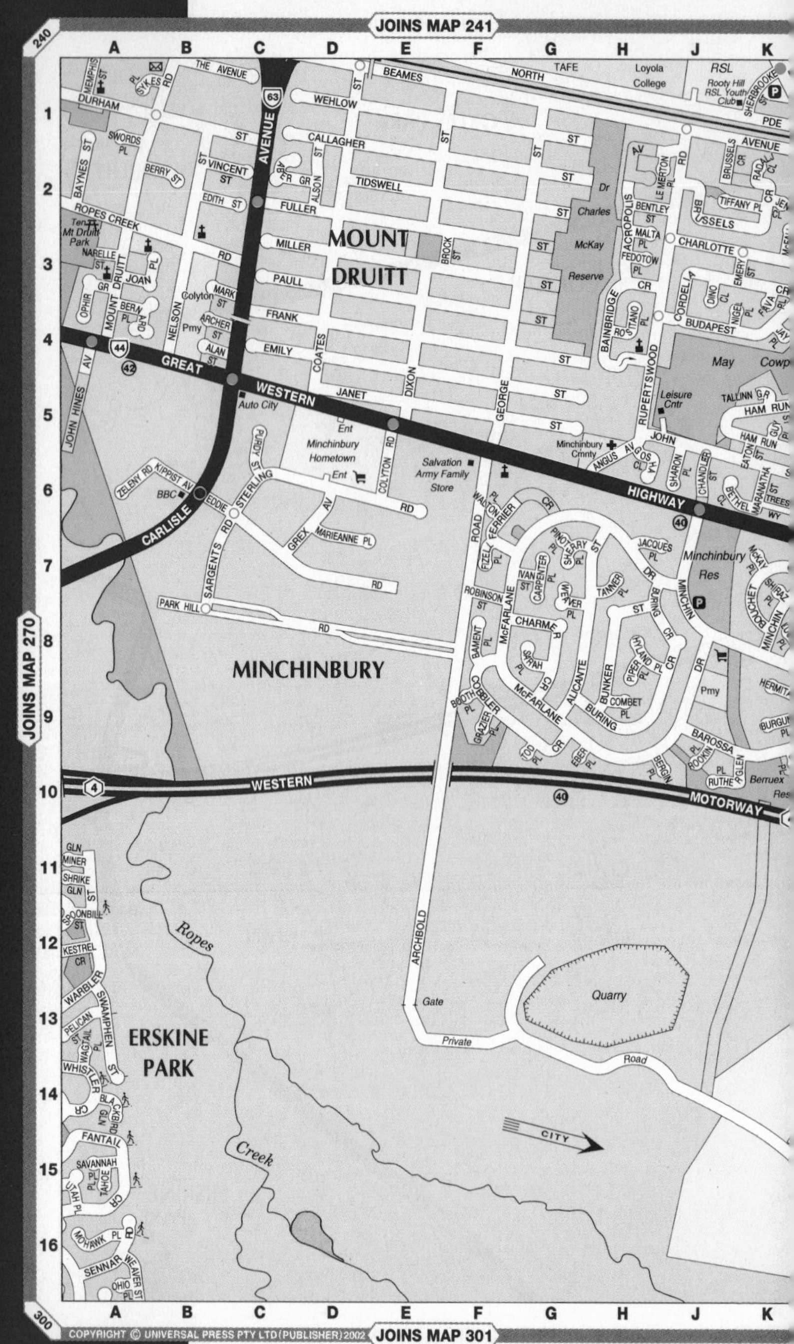

JOINS MAP 270

JOINS MAP 301

JOINS MAP 242

JOINS MAP 273

JOINS MAP 302

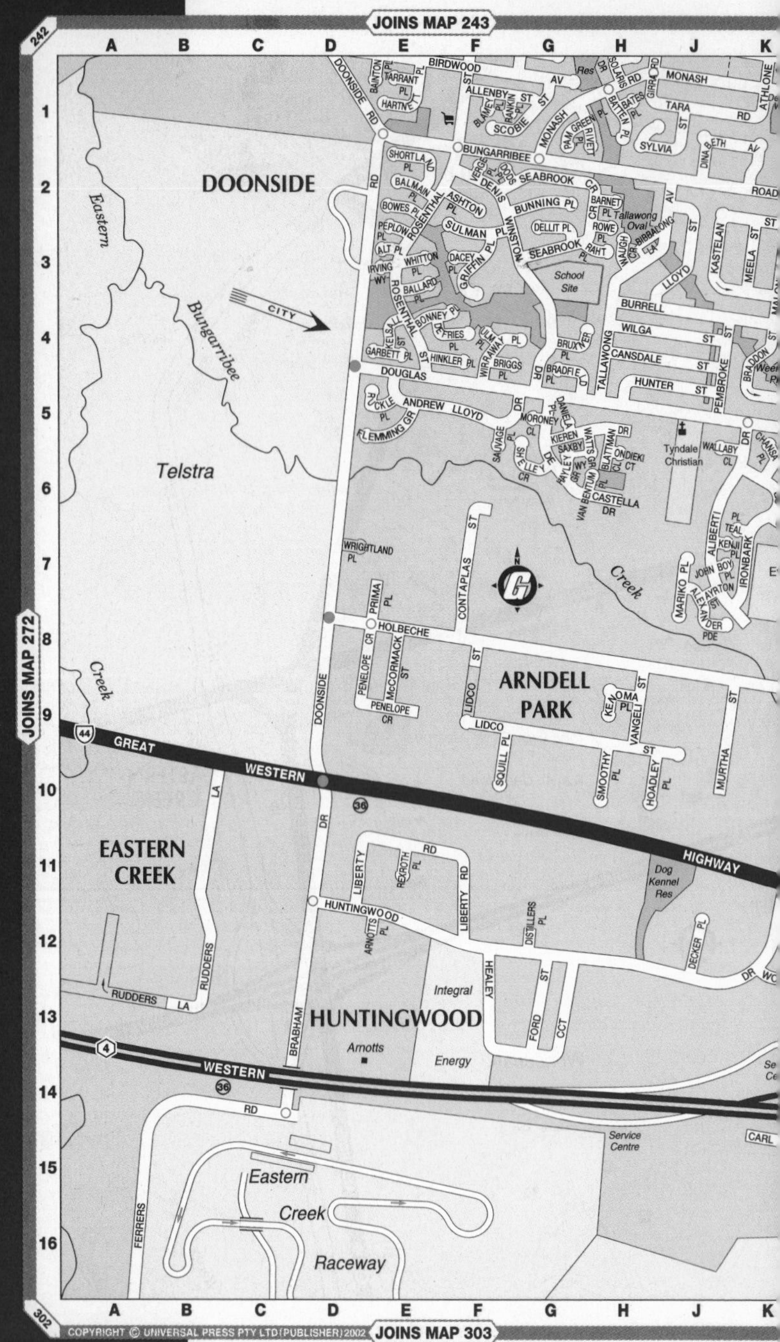
JOINS MAP 243
JOINS MAP 272
JOINS MAP 303
242
302
A B C D E F G H J K
1 2 3 4 5 6 7 8 9 10 11 12 13 14 15 16
DOONSIDE
Eastern
Bungarribee
Creek
Telstra
CITY
ARNDELL
PARK
EASTERN
CREEK
HUNTINGWOOD
Integral
Energy
Arnotts
GREAT
WESTERN
HIGHWAY
WESTERN
Dog
Kennel
Res
Service
Centre
Eastern
Creek
Raceway
School
Site
Tallawong
Oval
Tyndale
Christian
DOONSIDE RD
BIRDWOOD
ALLENBY ST
MONASH
BUNGARRIBEE
SEABROOK
ROSENTHAL
WINSTON
BUNNING PL
SULMAN PL
DOUGLAS
ANDREW LLOYD
CASTELLA DR
BURRELL
WILGA
CANSDALE
HUNTER ST
TALLAWONG
PEMBROKE
LLOYD
KASTELAN
MEELA ST
TARA
SYLVIA
HOLBECHE
CONTAPLAS ST
WRIGHTLAND PL
PRIMA PL
PENELOPE CR
McCORMACK ST
LIDCO
SQUILL PL
SMOOTHY PL
HOADLEY PL
VANGELI ST
MURTHA
LIBERTY RD
REXROTH PL
HUNTINGWOOD
ARNOTTS PL
DISTILLERS PL
HEALEY
FORD ST
CCT
DECKER PL
BRABHAM
RUDDERS LA
FERRERS
RD
CARL
44
4
36

JOINS MAP 244
JOINS MAP 275
JOINS MAP 304
245
305
A B C D E F G H J K
1 2 3 4 5 6 7 8 9 10 11 12 13 14 15 16
BLACKTOWN
PROSPECT
LANCASTER ST
NEWTON
PAUL ST
HIGHLANDS CR
NEWMAN ST
NERADA ST
MEROO ST
ALLAWAH
KIRKMAN RD
CARINYA ST
BALMORAL ST
BUNGARRIBEE
BELLEVISTA
MAUREEN PL
DELL ST
RUTHERFORD
LEICESTER SQ
HILLTOP AV
WENT
HILLSIDE PDE
DAGMAR ST
ALTONA PL
VINCENT ST
PROSPECT ST
COOPER ST
MAXWELL ST
MATTHEW CR
Brewongle Parkway
Res
BELLEVUE ST
WALTERS RD
ANNE ST
JOHN ST
CASTLE ST
VEZEY PL
GIBSON PL
POLLACK ST
SPARKLE AV
STARR PL
ROAD
CRAIG ST
ST PAULS PL
TEAGAN PL
Priv Rd
BURKE ST
Brewongle Walkway
ARCHER ST
BARNES LA
WESTERN CR
SELBY PL
Walters Rd Pmy
CEDAR PL
FLAME PL
SPRUCE ST
Ret Vill
BRISTOL CCT
St Dominics Home for the Elderly
HIGHVIEW ST
APEX ST
SAVERY CR
HAVENWOOD PL
SUNVILLE CT
HIGHPOINT DR
QUAIL RD
SPOONBILL AV
JABIRU PL
Substation
Ent
Tennis
Blacktown Workers Club
Harold Laybutt Sporting Complex
PENNY PL
GREAT WESTERN HIGHWAY
HONEMAN CL
BOILER CL
RESERVOIR RD
Nursing Home
Nagle Girls High
St Michaels
ROAD
NICHOLAS ST
ELA ST
NORA AV
THERESA ST
MARIA PL
DORA ST
JOSEPH ST
JULIE ST
TARONGA ST
JONG CR
KURRAJONG
ASHGROVE CR
HEAPY ST
ORWELL ST
HUNTLEY DR
FARMINGDALE
STERLING PL
GARDENSET DR
GR ANDREW
FRIEND PL
CLARE ST
OUTLOOK ST
ZINNIA WY
WIRILDA WY
INDIGO WY
SUNNINGDALE
MEADOWLANDS
THE PALMS
GREENWOOD
THISTLE WY
HELIOTROPE
DEODAR WY
CATALPA WY
ABELIA WY
ROYENA WY
PRIVET WY
JUNIPER WY
AZALEA ST
PAVONIA WY
BOOREEA ST
PATRICK ST
TURVEY ST
SWINSON ST
BENAUD ST
Blacktown South Pmy
VALDA ST
VALENTINE ST
MARANA ST
VALETTA CT
FLUSHCOMBE ROAD
STANLEY ST
MOREN ST
BRIDGE VIEW ST
STELLA PL
Pat Zikan Res
Gleesons Trees Res
PATRICIA ST
Tennis
Alpha Pk
ALPHA
Motor Reg
Cncl Off
Workers Club
Substation
ASHWELL RD
BOWRAL RD
CAMPBELL ST
COLO LA
KELSO LA
Inst of TAFE
Special School
Patrician Brothers College
MARION ST
HEREWARD
ROBINA ST
RUSSELL ST
QUEENSWAY
MONROE ST
WEST ST
SUTTON ST
NEWHAVEN AV
DUCKMALLOIS
MURRAY PL
FULLAM
SURREY ST
DORSET ST
CUMBERLAND ST
NORTHUMBERLAND
GLAMORGAN ST
Northumberland Park
RUTLAND ST
LAKER ST
MALCOLM ST
JONES ST
FINLAY ST
LEES CR
BETTY ST
MERLIN ST
MULGI ST
MAUD ST
GARETH ST
KAY ST
JUNE ST
GREEN ST
BERG ST
LANCELOT
OFT PL
TENBY ST
FILEY ST
WYE ST
ROA PL
WINTER PL
WITNEY ST
GORSE ST
SKYE PL
HEATH ST
DAX PL
OULTON
DAY PL
Temp Access
UPWEY ST
COWLEY CR
PIER ST
MYRTLE ST
RYDAL ST
ROATH PL
OAKTREE GR
FORRESTWOOD PL
Reserve
OLLIER CR
SLADE PL
SARRE PL
SHAW PL
SPA PL
NORMAN ST
ASHBY ST
TYNE PL
BRAE ST
ORDE PL
DESLEY CR
Res
Inst of TAFE
JANE ST
DEVITT ST
GRIFFITHS ST
MAIN ST
YAMBA ST
BLACKTOWN RD
GRAFTON ST
KEMPSEY ST
MARCEL CR
Ent
Blacktown District Hospital
LISMORE ST
PANORAMA PDE
Captain Cook Res
CRAIGLEA
PALMER ST
CALDWELL PL
ROSS ST
BRICKFIELD PL
SINCLAIR AV
MARTINS CR
Mitchell Res
TRESS ST
YALE PL
LOCK AV
Mitchell High
KEYWORTH DR
BEDIVERE ST
BALIN PL
TEMPLAR
HERRICK ST
HADRIAN AV
PENDANT ST
PELLEAS ST
William Lawson Park
ELTHAM ST
JEM PL
FOSS ST
LORNE ST
DINTON ST
GROVE ST
DANBY ST
GULL PL
CLEY PL
KISDON CR
CORY PL
HILDA ST
LYTE PL
HARROD ST
CCT
CHAPEL ST
HEBER PL
DEE PL
HAMPTON
PROSPECT HWY
Dog Pound
AUGUSTA ST
ALEXANDRA ST
MOTORWAY
Blacktown Ck
YALLOCK PL
RESERVOIR RD
CRICKETERS ARMS RD
Ent
Drive-in Theatre
FLORENCE ST
MANNING ST
WATCH HOUSE RD
63 36 34 4 32 44

JOINS MAP 245

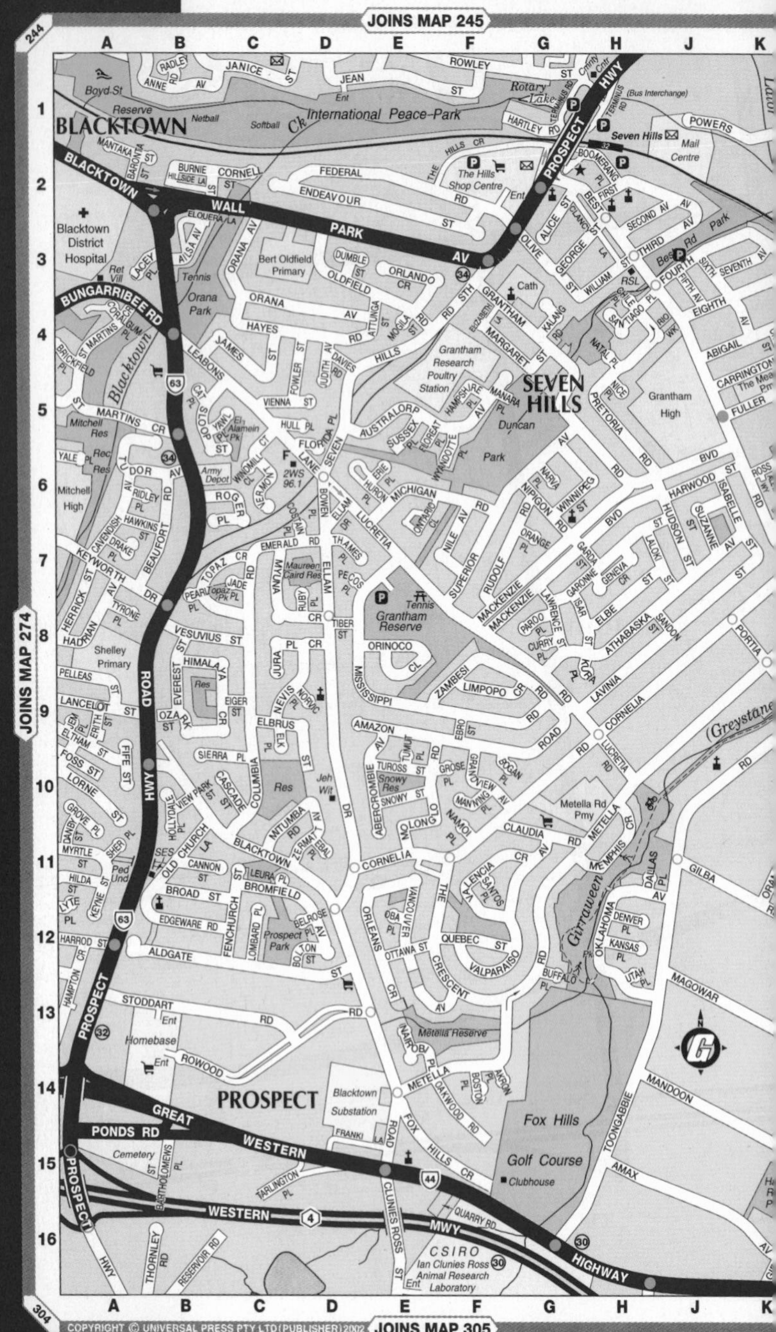

JOINS MAP 305

JOINS MAP 274

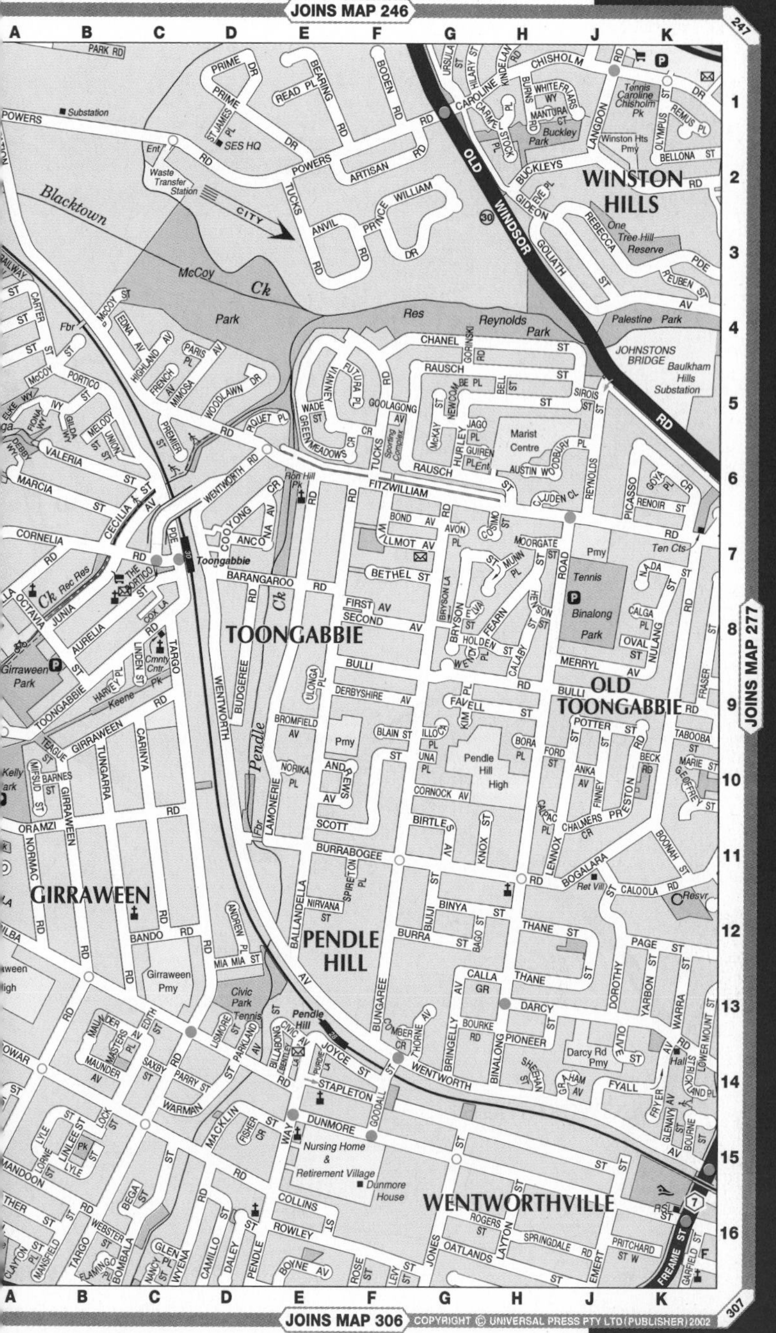
JOINS MAP 246
JOINS MAP 277
JOINS MAP 306
247
307
A B C D E F G H J K
1 2 3 4 5 6 7 8 9 10 11 12 13 14 15 16
WINSTON HILLS
TOONGABBIE
OLD TOONGABBIE
GIRRAWEEN
PENDLE HILL
WENTWORTHVILLE
OLD WINDSOR RD
POWERS RD
Blacktown
McCoy Ck
Park
Res
Reynolds Park
Palestine Park
JOHNSTONS BRIDGE
Baulkham Hills Substation
One Tree Hill Reserve
Tennis Caroline Chisholm Pk
Buckley Park
Winston Hts Pmy
Marist Centre
Binalong Park
Pendle Hill High
Girraween Park
Girraween Pmy
Civic Park
Nursing Home & Retirement Village
Dunmore House
Darcy Rd Pmy
SES HQ
Waste Transfer Station
Substation
Toongabbie
Pendle Hill
COPYRIGHT © UNIVERSAL PRESS PTY LTD (PUBLISHER) 2002

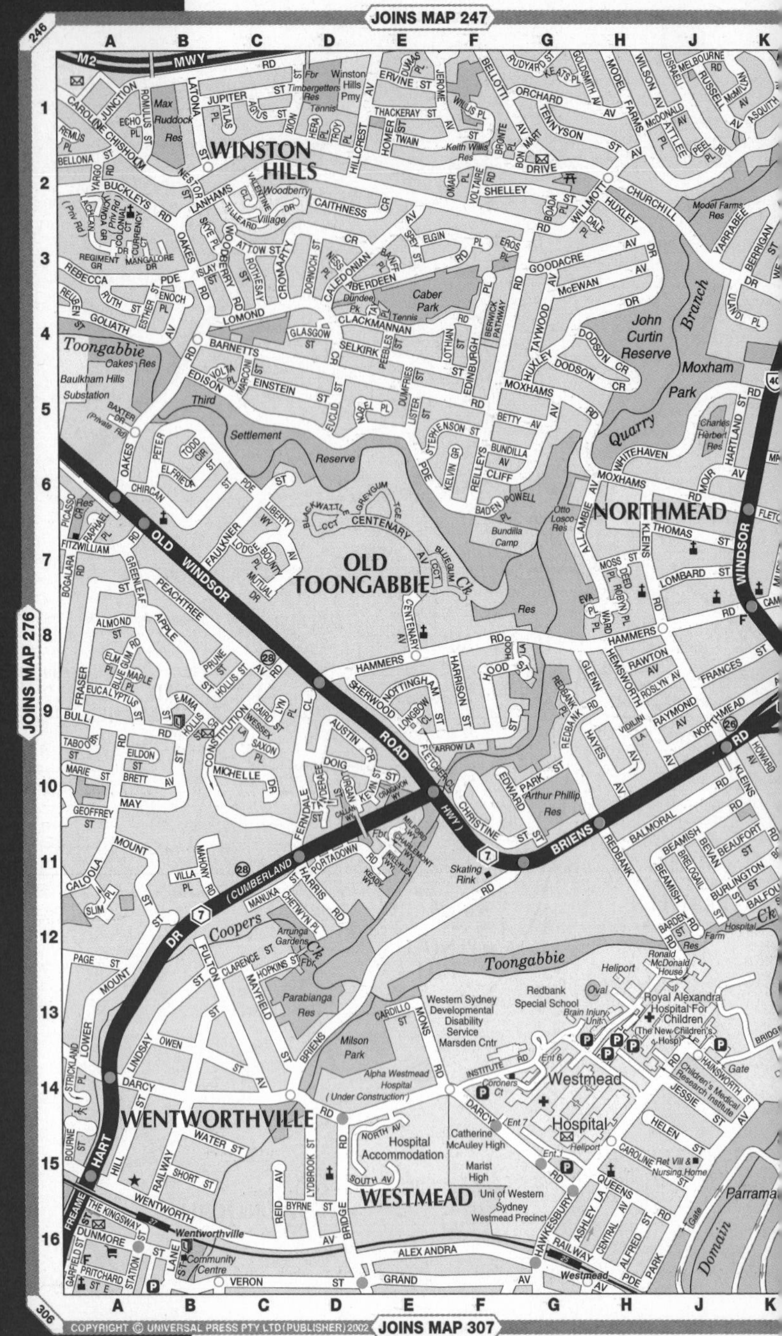
JOINS MAP 247
JOINS MAP 276
JOINS MAP 307
WINSTON HILLS
OLD TOONGABBIE
NORTHMEAD
WENTWORTHVILLE
WESTMEAD
Westmead Hospital
Royal Alexandra Hospital For Children (The New Children's Hosp)
John Curtin Reserve
Moxham Park
Caber Park
Third Settlement Reserve
Toongabbie Oakes Res
Arthur Phillip Res
Milson Park
Parabianga Res
Redbank Special School
Western Sydney Developmental Disability Service Marsden Cntr
Uni of Western Sydney Westmead Precinct
Catherine McAuley High
Marist High
Hospital Accommodation
OLD WINDSOR ROAD
CUMBERLAND HWY
BRIENS RD
HART DR
NORTHMEAD RD
WINDSOR RD
M2 MWY

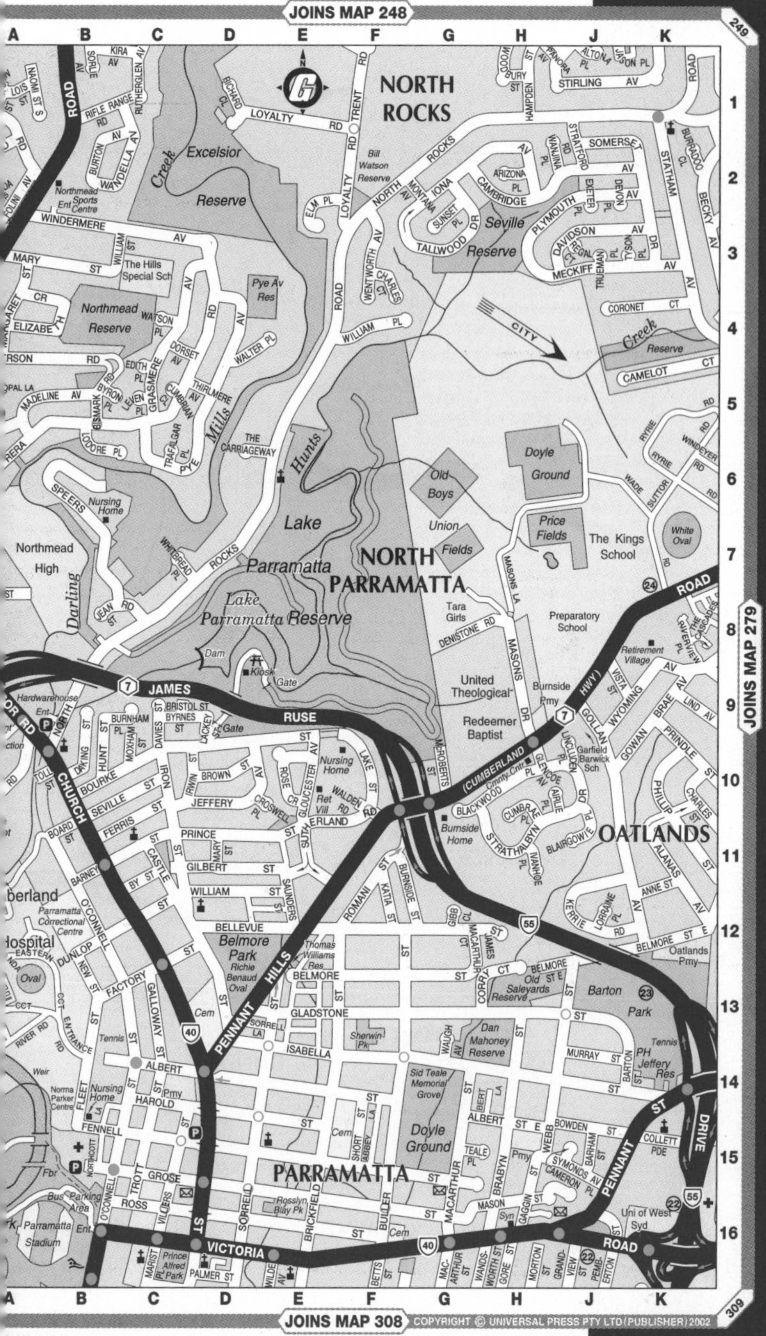
JOINS MAP 248
JOINS MAP 279
JOINS MAP 308
249
309
NORTH ROCKS
NORTH PARRAMATTA
PARRAMATTA
OATLANDS
Excelsior Reserve
Northmead Reserve
Northmead Sports Centre
The Hills Special Sch
Pye Av Res
Bill Watson Reserve
Seville Reserve
Creek Reserve
Nursing Home
Northmead High
Lake Parramatta
Lake Parramatta Reserve
Dam
Kiosk
Gate
Old Boys Union Fields
Doyle Ground
Price Fields
The Kings School
White Oval
Tara Girls
Preparatory School
Retirement Village
United Theological
Burnside Pmy
Redeemer Baptist
Garfield Barwick Sch
Burnside Home
Ret Vill
Cmnty Cntr
Hardwarehouse
Parramatta Correctional Centre
Hospital
Oval
Belmore Park
Richie Benaud Oval
Thomas Williams Res
Cem
Tennis
Weir
Norma Parker Centre
Nursing Home
Sherwin Pk
Sid Teale Memorial Grove
Doyle Ground
Dan Mahoney Reserve
Old Saleyards Reserve
Barton Park
Oatlands Pmy
PH Jeffery Res
Rosslyn Blay Pk
Bus Parking Area
Parramatta Stadium
Prince Alfred Park
Uni of West Syd
JAMES RUSE DR
CUMBERLAND HWY
CHURCH ST
PENNANT HILLS RD
VICTORIA RD
NORTH ROCKS RD
PENNANT ST
DRIVE
CITY
7
24
23
22
55
40
A B C D E F G H J K
1 2 3 4 5 6 7 8 9 10 11 12 13 14 15 16

JOINS MAP 249

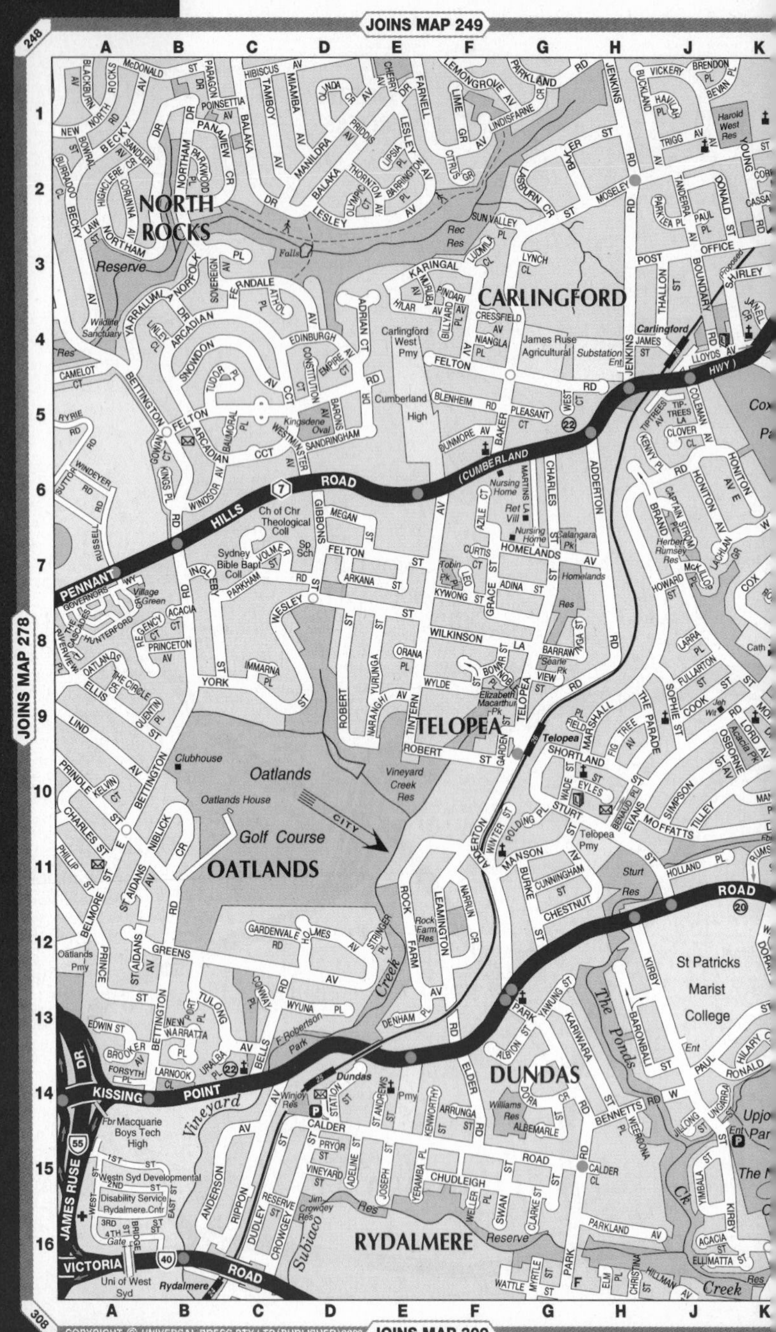

JOINS MAP 278

JOINS MAP 309

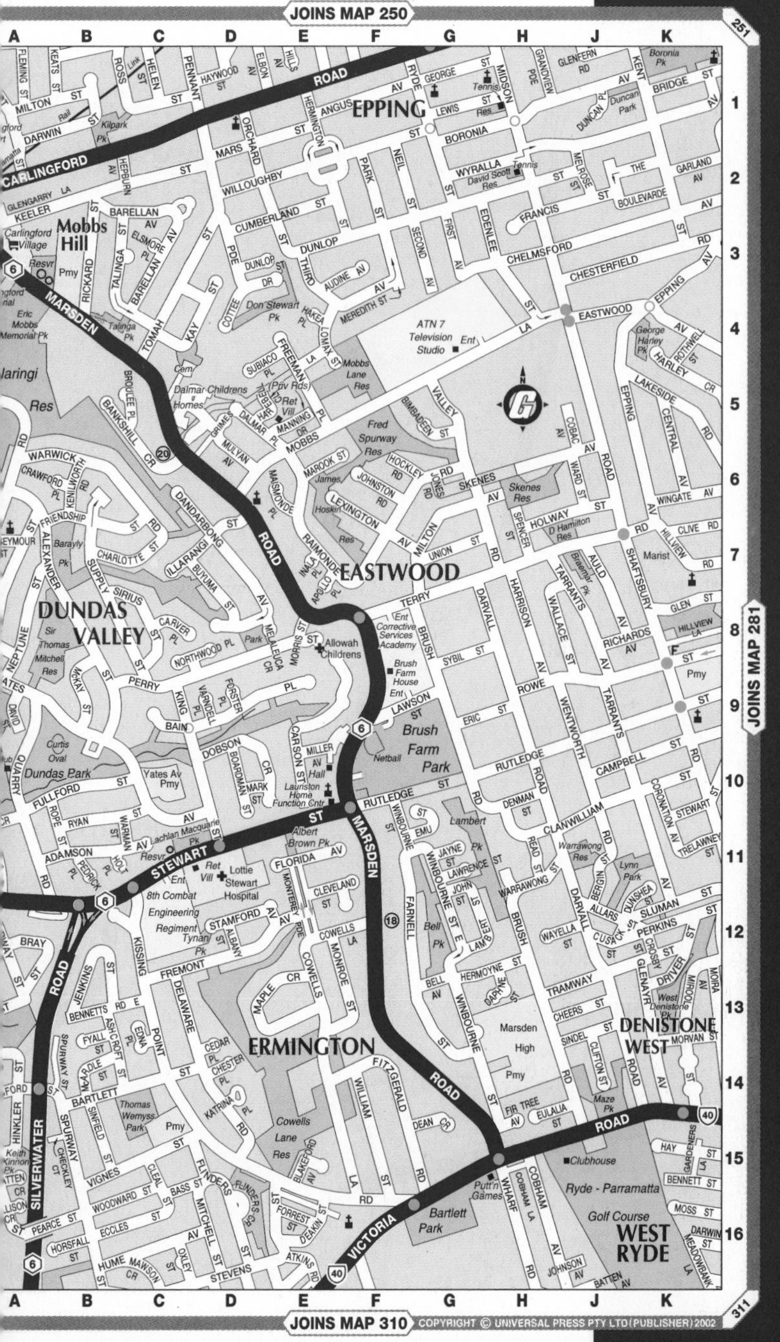
JOINS MAP 250
JOINS MAP 281
JOINS MAP 310
251
311
A B C D E F G H J K
1 2 3 4 5 6 7 8 9 10 11 12 13 14 15 16
EPPING
Mobbs Hill
EASTWOOD
DUNDAS VALLEY
ERMINGTON
DENISTONE WEST
WEST RYDE
CARLINGFORD ROAD
MARSDEN ROAD
STEWART ST
SILVERWATER ROAD
VICTORIA ROAD
ATN 7 Television Studio
Fred Spurway Res
Don Stewart Pk
Mobbs Lane Res
Skenes Res
Brush Farm Park
Corrective Services Academy
Brush Farm House
Allowah Childrens
Lambert Pk
Bell Pk
Marsden High
Lottie Stewart Hospital
8th Combat Engineering Regiment
Cowells Lane Res
Thomas Wemyss Park
Bartlett Park
Ryde - Parramatta Golf Course
Clubhouse
Putt'n Games
Dundas Park
Curtis Oval
Sir Thomas Mitchell Res
Carlingford Village
Eric Mobbs Memorial Pk
Dalmar Childrens Homes
Kilpark Pk
Boronia Pk
Duncan Park
David Scott Res
George Harley Pk
Marist
Warrawong Res
Lynn Park
West Denistone Pk
Maze Pk
Albert Brown Pk
Lachlan Macquarie Resvr
Tynan Pk
Lauriston Home Function Cntr
Braemar Pk
D Hamilton Res
Barayly Pk
Yates Av Pmy
Netball
Keith Kinnon Pk

JOINS MAP 251
JOINS MAP 280
JOINS MAP 311
250
310
A B C D E F G H J K
1 2 3 4 5 6 7 8 9 10 11 12 13 14 15 16
EPPING
MARSFIELD
EASTWOOD
DENISTONE
DENISTONE EAST
DENISTONE WEST
WEST RYDE
BLAXLAND ROAD
VICTORIA ROAD
Forest Park
Dence Park
Pembroke Park
TG Millner Sportsground
Edna Hunt Sanctuary
Somerville Park
Forrester Pk
Wood St Res
Terrys Ck
Eastwood Hts Pmy
Rotary Pk
Irene Pk
Lynelle Pk
St Anthonys Pmy
Town Hall
Curzon Hall
Nunook Res
Gwendale Park
Moore Pk
Jupp Res
Jim Walsh Park
Granny Smith Mem.Pk
Ten Cts
Croquet
Eastwood Park
St Kevins Pmy
Eastwood
Glen Res
Proposed
Marjorie Pk
Donovan Pk
Watts Pk
Acacia Pk
Denistone East Pmy
Colvin Pk
Kings Pk
Valerie Pk
Ryde Hospital
St Thereses Primary
Denistone Park
Symonds Res
Denistone
Darvall Park
Bimbi Res
Resvrs
Carara Res
Nursing Home
Lions Pk
Model Steam Trains
Hall
West Ryde
Leagues Club
Anzac Pk
Reservoir
Pumping Station
Northern Institute of TAFE Ryde College
Ped Tunnel
Private Rd
BRIDGE ST
VICTORIA ST
RAWSON ST
HIGH ST
WYRALLA AV
WILLIAM ST
GARLAND AV
WARRINGTON AV
CHELMSFORD AV
CHESTERFIELD RD
HILLSIDE CR
EPPING AV
YARAAN AV
FOREST GR
ESSEX ST
BRUCEDALE AV
STANLEY RD
MAIDA RD
KNOX ST
ROSE ST
BRIGG RD
BULKIRA RD
BRIGADOON CT
ALBUERA RD
ABUKLEA RD
MURIEL AV
WINIFRED AV
DONALD AV
DUIGNAN CL
WOOD ST
VIMIERA RD
ANEMBO PL
CRIMEA RD
MENZIES LA
RUGBY RD
YANGALLA ST
PEMBROKE ST
OSLO ST
AGINCOURT RD
COOINDA CL
KARALEE CL
KARINGAL CL
PLUNKETT ST
LANCASTER DR
THELMA ST
GUNYAH ST
CULLODEN RD
ENGEL AV
TORRINGTON DR
BALACLAVA RD
RAYMOND RD
LINCOLN ST
DESMOND ST
DEBORAH PL
ERINA ST
BELLAMY AV
CORUNNA RD
IRENE CR
LONGVIEW ST
NORTH RD
YAMBA CL
SUMMIT CL
DIANE ST
VALERIE ST
PEARL AV
DAVIS ST
COCOS AV
EASTWOOD AV
HARLEY CR
LAKESIDE AV
RAILWAY AV
DOOMBEN AV
BALL AV
VANIMO PL
CASSIA PL
BERTRAM ST
GWEN DALE CR
JUPP PL
MUNRO ST
HUNTS LA
BLIGH LA
MILHAM AV
THRELFALL ST
GLENDOWER AV
CULGOA AV
WILGA PL
VIMIERA RD
BALACLAVA RD
LANDSDOWNE ST
GORDON ST
ALEXANDRIA AV
GRAHAM AV
OAKES AV
ROKEVA ST
FONTI ST
SUSAN PL
STAR ST
O'KEEFE CR
KINGSFORD AV
WINGATE AV
CLIVE RD
NORMA AV
ALISON RD
EDGAR ST
DAFFODIL ST
FIG PL
ASTER ST
MAY ST
MAY LA
ETHEL ST
ETHEL LA
ROWE ST
ROWE LA
WELBY ST
WISHART ST
GROVE LA
WALSH ST
SHEEHAN ST
WOORANG ST
LILAC PL
ORANGE ST
GROVE ST
FERRABETTA AV
DONOVAN ST
VERA ST
HILLVIEW RD
GLEN ST
NRMA
PROGRESS LA
COOLGUN LA
WEST PDE
RAILWAY PDE
EAST PDE
HILLVIEW LA
THE AVENUE
TRELAWNEY ST
FIRST AV
LOVELL RD
PICKFORD AV
SPRING ST
DAWES CR
WARATAH ST
ACACIA ST
BANKSIA ST
TALLWOOD AV
RUTLEDGE ST
SECOND AV
DENISTONE RD
RYEDALE RD
DALTON AV
HOLLIS AV
RUSSELL ST
BRABYN ST
BORONIA LA
HENDERSON ST
SALTER CR
COLVIN CR
WATTS RD
RONALD AV
CLANALPINE ST
THIRD AV
YOUNG PDE
FOURTH AV
KARNAK ST
HEARD ST
ROCCA ST
SHAFTSBURY RD
STEWART ST
HOPETOUN AV
KINGS RD
GALLARD ST
MAYCOCK ST
RICHMOND ST
MACQUARIE PL
MASON ST
JACKSON CR
CECIL ST
FIFTH AV
SIXTH AV
FLORENCE AV
TRELAWNEY ST
BUENA VISTA AV
BELLEVUE AV
CHATHAM RD
WINTHINGTON PKY
INKERMAN RD
TERRY RD
PENNANT AV
BIRDWOOD ST
HAIG AV
SLUMAN ST
PERKINS ST
GENNER ST
MIROOL ST
BEAUMONT AV
BURMAH RD
KINGSON CR
BURNETT WK
GORDON CR
ELSTON AV
STRATFORD AV
ENID ST
BEATTIE AV
RICKARD AV
HEATH ST
RESERVOIR LA
SIMLA AV
ANTHONY RD
MIRIAM RD
MARLOW AV
MARLOW LA
COMMISSIONERS RD
VIVYAN CL
BELTANA ST
LUND ST
BENSON LA
MIMOS ST
MORVAN ST
MOIRA AV
BIGLAND AV
PARK AV
RESERVE ST
GOODWIN ST
ORCHARD ST
MAHON ST
MONDIAL PL
BENSON ST
MURRAY ST
BENCOOLEN AV
HALL ST
FERNVALE AV
BETTS ST
FORSTER LA
DICKSON AV
DICKSON LA
MARKET ST
GRAF AV
WATTLE ST
ANZAC RD
PARKES ST
MOUNT ST
HERBERT ST
WATTLE LA
CLARKE LA
MELVILLE ST
HAY ST
GARDENERS LA
BENNETT ST
RIVERVIEW ST
ENDEAVOUR ST
GAZA RD
GAZA LA
MAXIM ST
MAXIM LA
MOSS ST
STATION ST
MONS ST
FALCONER ST
SAMUEL ST
HINKLER AV
COLSTON ST
DARWIN ST
ANNIE LA
ADELAIDE ST
GRAND AV
FEDERAL RD
REX ST
DUNMORE RD
HUGHES ST
HERMITAGE RD
THE NOOK
NOOK LA
LINTON ST
LINTON LA
GRIFFITHS AV
GRIFFITHS LA
FORSYTH ST
BOWDEN ST
SHEPHERD ST
MEADOWBANK LA
HUXLEY ST
18
16
21
20
19
40

JOINS MAP 252

JOINS MAP 312

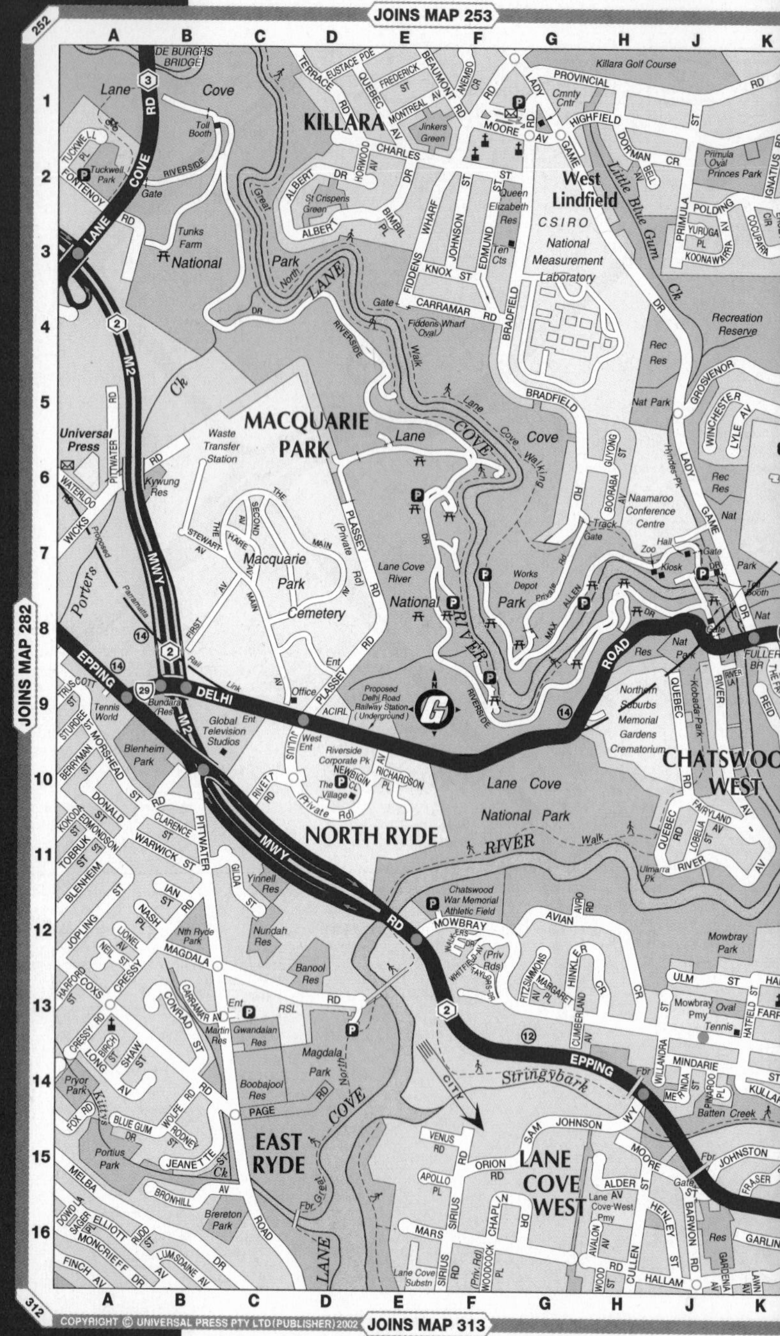
JOINS MAP 253
252
A B C D E F G H J K
1 2 3 4 5 6 7 8 9 10 11 12 13 14 15 16
JOINS MAP 282
KILLARA
West Lindfield
CSIRO
National Measurement Laboratory
Killara Golf Course
MACQUARIE PARK
Macquarie Park Cemetery
Waste Transfer Station
Universal Press
Lane Cove River National Park
Lane Cove National Park
Northern Suburbs Memorial Gardens Crematorium
CHATSWOOD WEST
Global Television Studios
Riverside Corporate Pk
Proposed Delhi Road Railway Station (Underground)
NORTH RYDE
Blenheim Park
Tennis World
Chatswood War Memorial Athletic Field
Nth Ryde Park
Magdala Park
EAST RYDE
Portius Park
Pryor Park
Brereton Park
LANE COVE WEST
Mowbray Park
Mowbray Oval
Recreation Reserve
Naamaroo Conference Centre
Tunks Farm
Lane Cove Rd
M2
EPPING RD
DELHI RD
MWY
PITTWATER RD
LADY GAME DR
Stringybark Ck
Little Blue Gum Ck
Porters Ck
Kittys Ck
Batten Creek
312
COPYRIGHT © UNIVERSAL PRESS PTY LTD (PUBLISHER) 2002
JOINS MAP 313

JOINS MAP 254

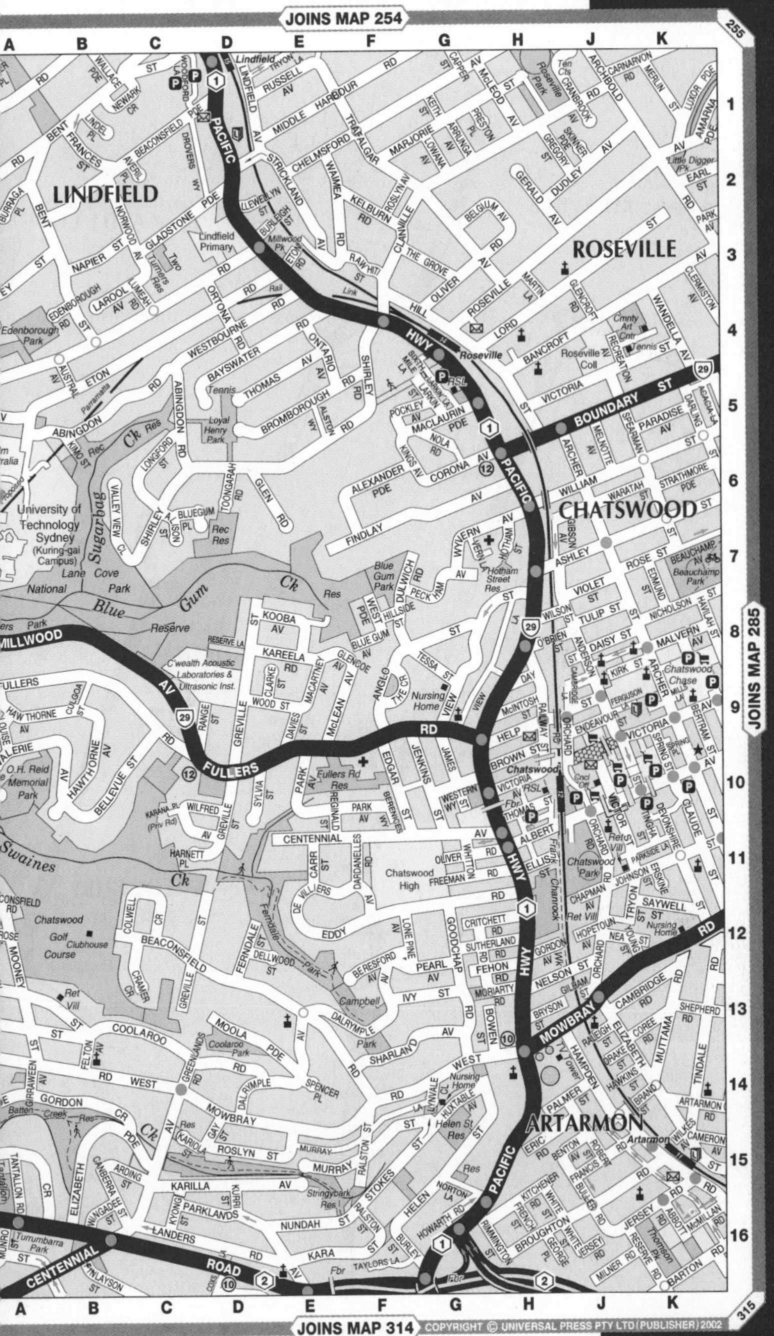

JOINS MAP 285

JOINS MAP 314

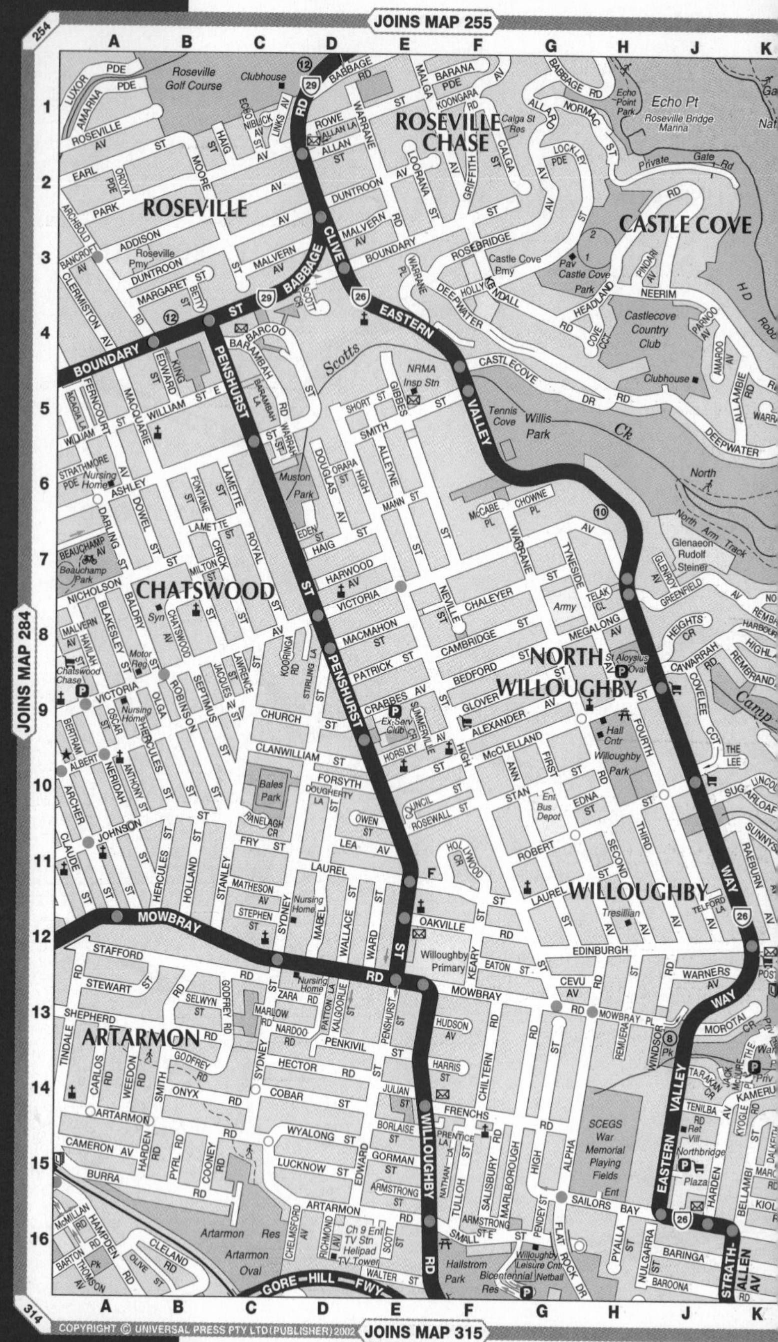
JOINS MAP 255
JOINS MAP 284
JOINS MAP 315
254
314
ROSEVILLE
ROSEVILLE CHASE
CASTLE COVE
CHATSWOOD
NORTH WILLOUGHBY
WILLOUGHBY
ARTARMON
Roseville Golf Course
Echo Pt
Roseville Bridge Marina
Echo Point Park
Castle Cove Pmy
Castle Cove Park
Castlecove Country Club
Roseville Pmy
Willis Park
Tennis Cove
NRMA Insp Stn
Muston Park
Beauchamp Park
Bales Park
Glenaeon Rudolf Steiner
St Aloysius Oval
Willoughby Park
Ent Bus Depot
Tresillian
Willoughby Primary
SCEGS War Memorial Playing Fields
Northbridge Plaza
Artarmon Res
Artarmon Oval
Hallstrom Park
Willoughby Leisure Cntr
Bicentennial Res
Netball
Ch 9 Ent TV Stn Helipad TV Tower
North Arm Track
Scotts Ck
PENSHURST ST
BOUNDARY ST
EASTERN VALLEY WAY
MOWBRAY RD
WILLOUGHBY RD
GORE HILL FWY
CLIVE ST
BABBAGE RD
VICTORIA AV
STRATHALLEN AV
COPYRIGHT © UNIVERSAL PRESS PTY LTD (PUBLISHER) 2002

JOINS MAP 256

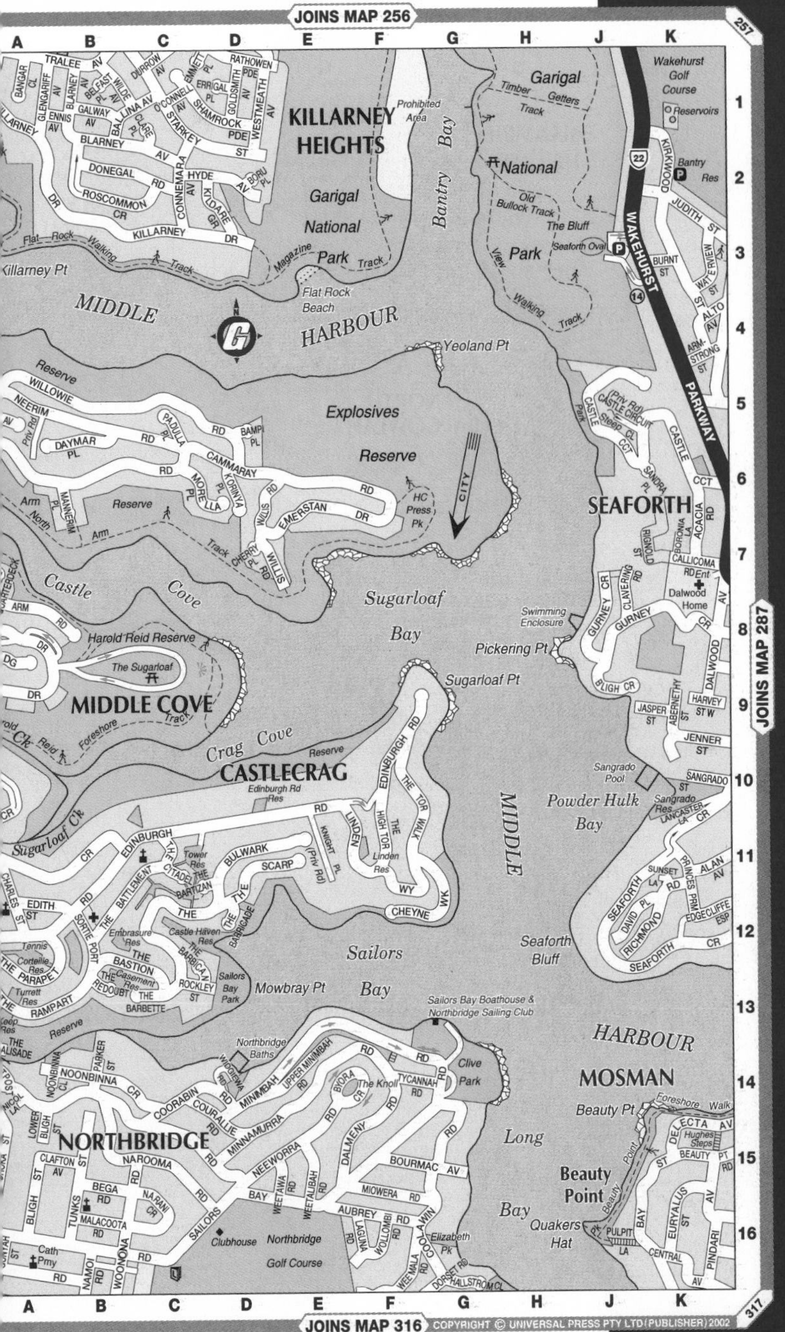

JOINS MAP 287

JOINS MAP 316

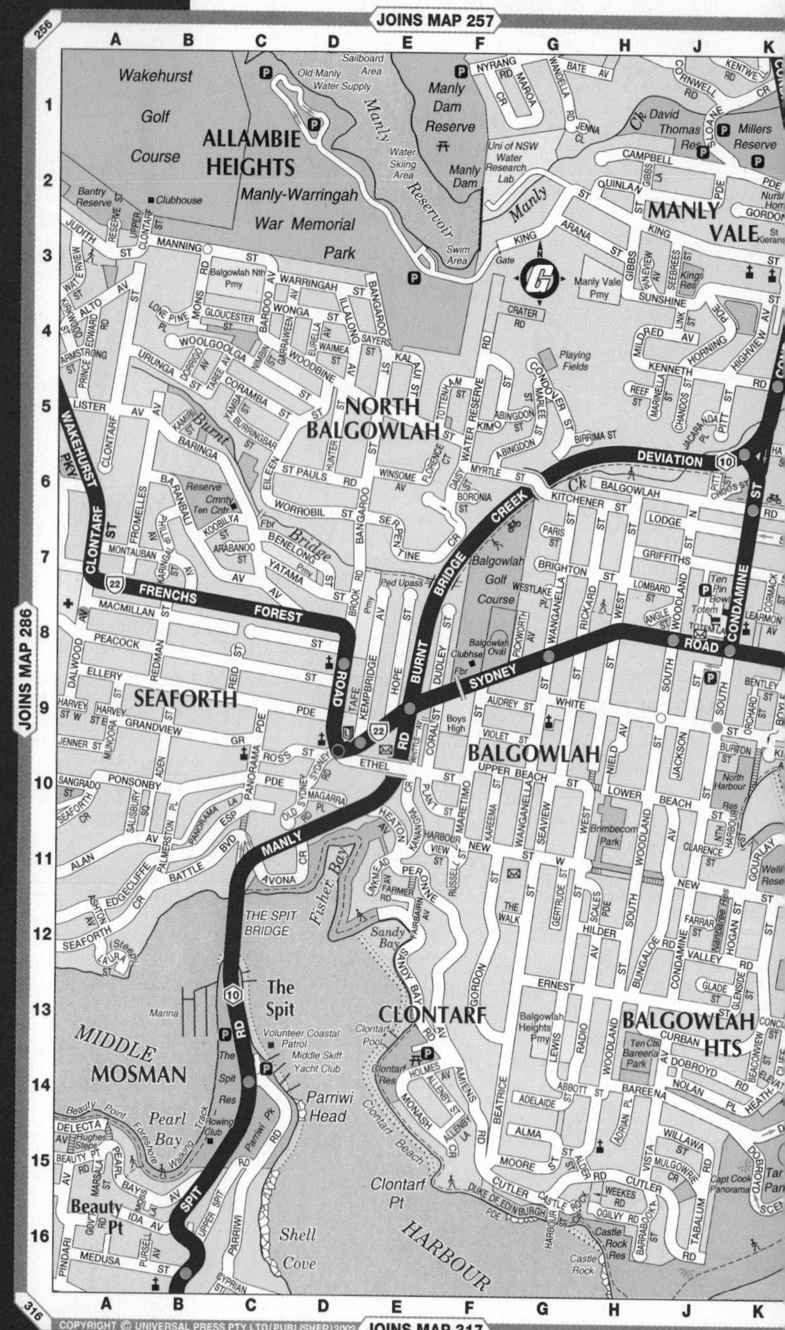
JOINS MAP 257
JOINS MAP 286
JOINS MAP 317
256
316
A B C D E F G H J K
1 2 3 4 5 6 7 8 9 10 11 12 13 14 15 16
Wakehurst Golf Course
ALLAMBIE HEIGHTS
Manly-Warringah War Memorial Park
Old Manly Water Supply
Sailboard Area
Manly Reservoir
Water Skiing Area
Manly Dam Reserve
Manly Dam
Swim Area
Uni of NSW Water Research Lab
David Thomas Res
Millers Reserve
MANLY VALE
Manly Vale Pmy
Kings Res
Bantry Reserve
Clubhouse
Balgowlah Nth Pmy
Playing Fields
NORTH BALGOWLAH
Reserve
Cmnty Ten Cntr
Burnt Bridge
WAKEHURST PKY
CLONTARF ST
FRENCHS FOREST ROAD
BURNT BRIDGE CREEK
DEVIATION
SYDNEY ROAD
CONDAMINE ST
MANLY RD
SPIT RD
Balgowlah Golf Course
Balgowlah Oval
Ped Upass
Ten Pin Bowl
SEAFORTH
Boys High
BALGOWLAH
North Harbour Res
Brimbecom Park
THE WALK
THE SPIT BRIDGE
Fisher Bay
Sandy Bay
The Spit
Volunteer Coastal Patrol
Middle Skiff Yacht Club
Marina
MIDDLE MOSMAN
The Spit Res
Rowing Club
Pearl Bay
Beauty Point Foreshore Walking Track
Hughes Steps
Beauty Pt
Parriwi Head
CLONTARF
Clontarf Pool
Clontarf Res
Clontarf Beach
Clontarf Pt
Shell Cove
HARBOUR
Balgowlah Heights Pmy
BALGOWLAH HTS
Ten Cts Bareena Park
Castle Rock Res
Castle Rock
Capt Cook Panorama

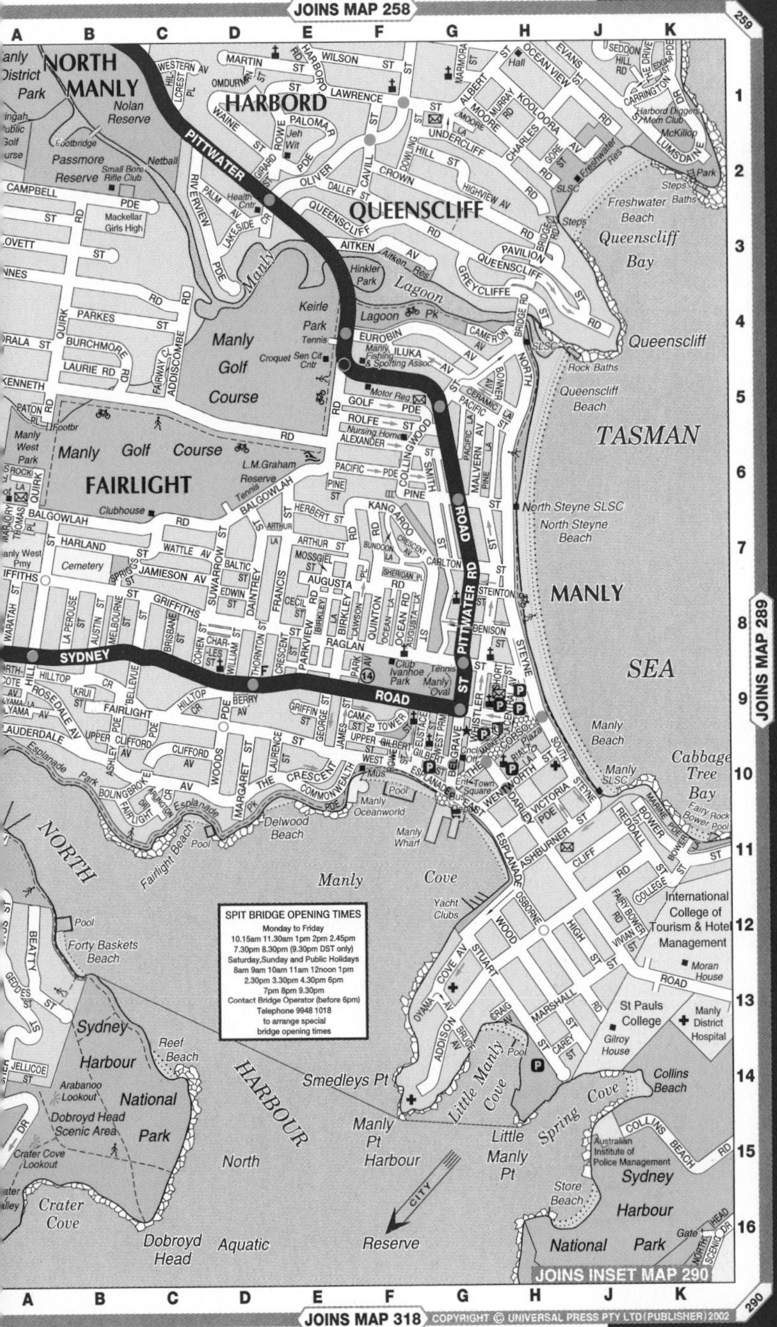
JOINS MAP 258
259
JOINS MAP 289
JOINS MAP 318
JOINS INSET MAP 290
290
NORTH MANLY
HARBORD
QUEENSCLIFF
FAIRLIGHT
MANLY
TASMAN
SEA
Manly Golf Course
Manly Lagoon
Queenscliff Bay
Freshwater Beach
Queenscliff Beach
North Steyne Beach
Manly Beach
Cabbage Tree Bay
Manly Cove
Little Manly Cove
Spring Cove
Sydney Harbour National Park
NORTH HARBOUR
North Harbour Aquatic Reserve
Manly Pt Harbour
Dobroyd Head
Crater Cove
Forty Baskets Beach
Delwood Beach
Fairlight Beach
Collins Beach
Store Beach
Smedleys Pt
Little Manly Pt
Manly Wharf
Manly Oceanworld
Manly Oval
St Pauls College
Manly District Hospital
International College of Tourism & Hotel Management
Australian Institute of Police Management
PITTWATER RD
SYDNEY ROAD
SPIT BRIDGE OPENING TIMES
Monday to Friday
10.15am 11.30am 1pm 2pm 2.45pm
7.30pm 8.30pm (9.30pm DST only)
Saturday,Sunday and Public Holidays
8am 9am 10am 11am 12noon 1pm
2.30pm 3.30pm 4.30pm 6pm
7pm 8pm 9.30pm
Contact Bridge Operator (before 6pm)
Telephone 9948 1018
to arrange special
bridge opening times
CITY
A B C D E F G H J K
1 2 3 4 5 6 7 8 9 10 11 12 13 14 15 16

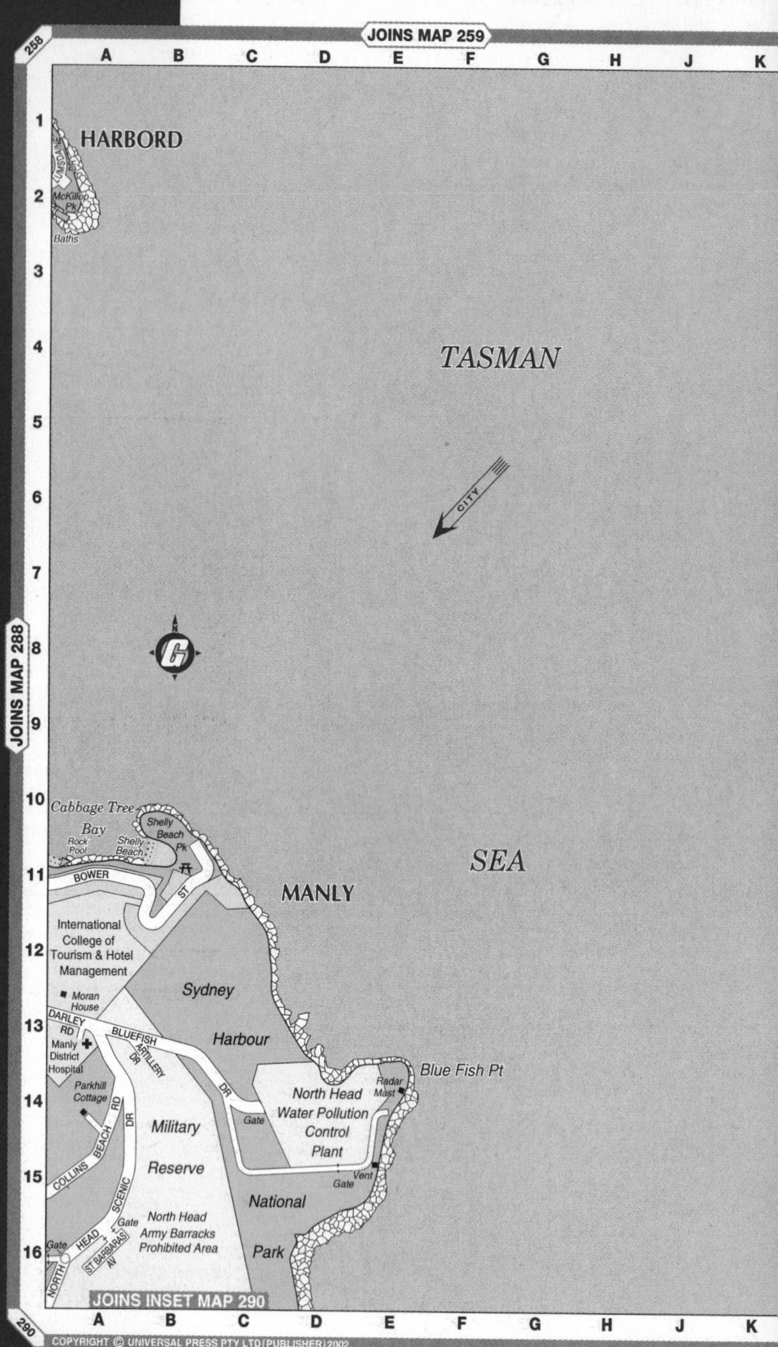
JOINS MAP 259
258
A B C D E F G H J K
1 2 3 4 5 6 7 8 9 10 11 12 13 14 15 16
HARBORD
LUMSDAINE DR
McKillop Pk
Baths
TASMAN
CITY
JOINS MAP 288
Cabbage Tree Bay
Rock Pool
Shelly Beach
Shelly Beach Pk
SEA
BOWER
ST
MANLY
International College of Tourism & Hotel Management
Sydney
Moran House
DARLEY RD
BLUEFISH
Harbour
Manly District Hospital
ARTILLERY DR
Blue Fish Pt
Parkhill Cottage
Radar Mast
North Head Water Pollution Control Plant
Gate
BEACH RD
DR
Military
Reserve
COLLINS
SCENIC
Vent
Gate
National
North Head Army Barracks Prohibited Area
Gate
Gate
HEAD
NORTH
ST BARBARAS AV
Park
JOINS INSET MAP 290
290

JOINS MAP 260

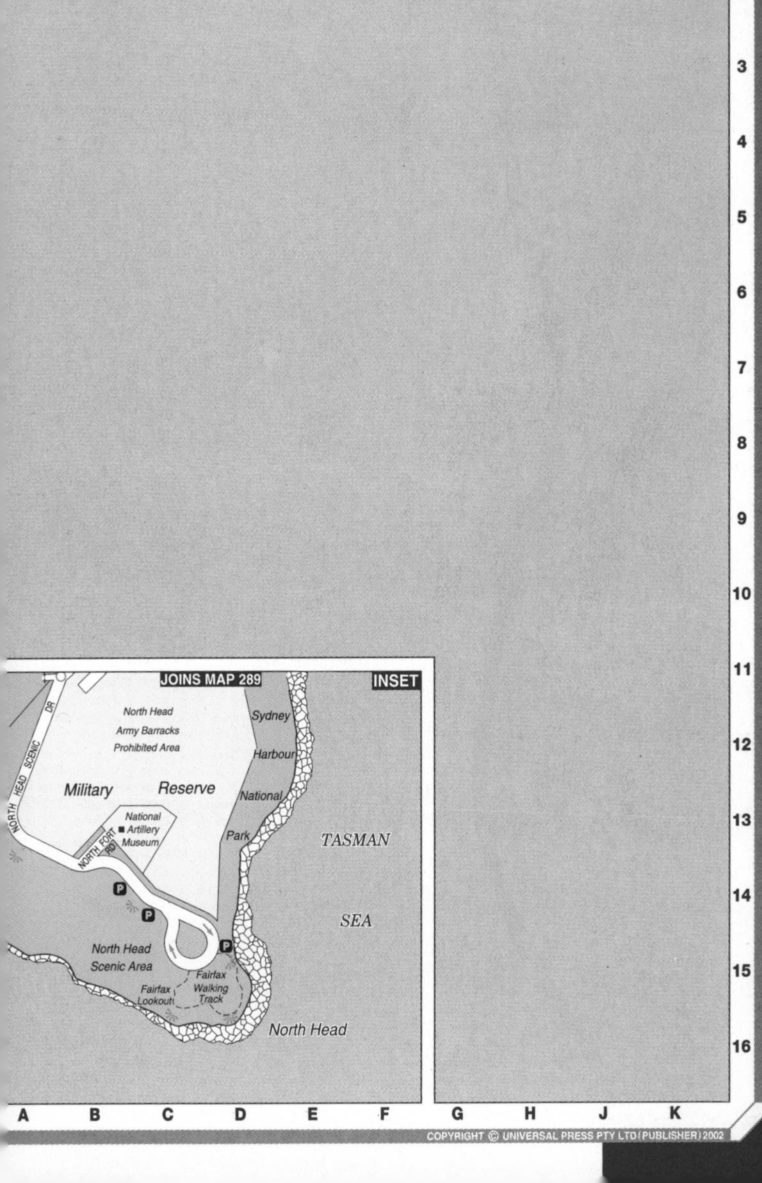

JOINS MAP 265
264

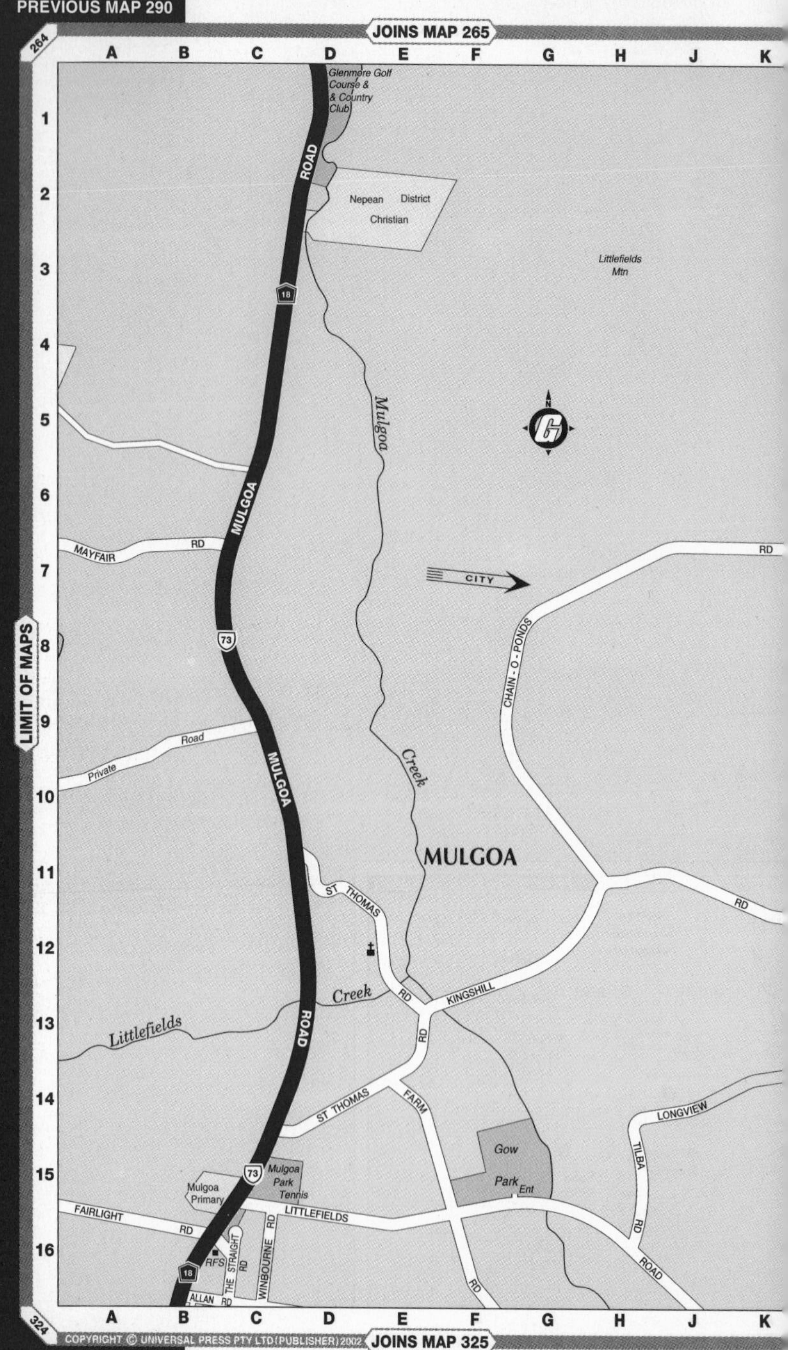

324
JOINS MAP 325

JOINS MAP 266

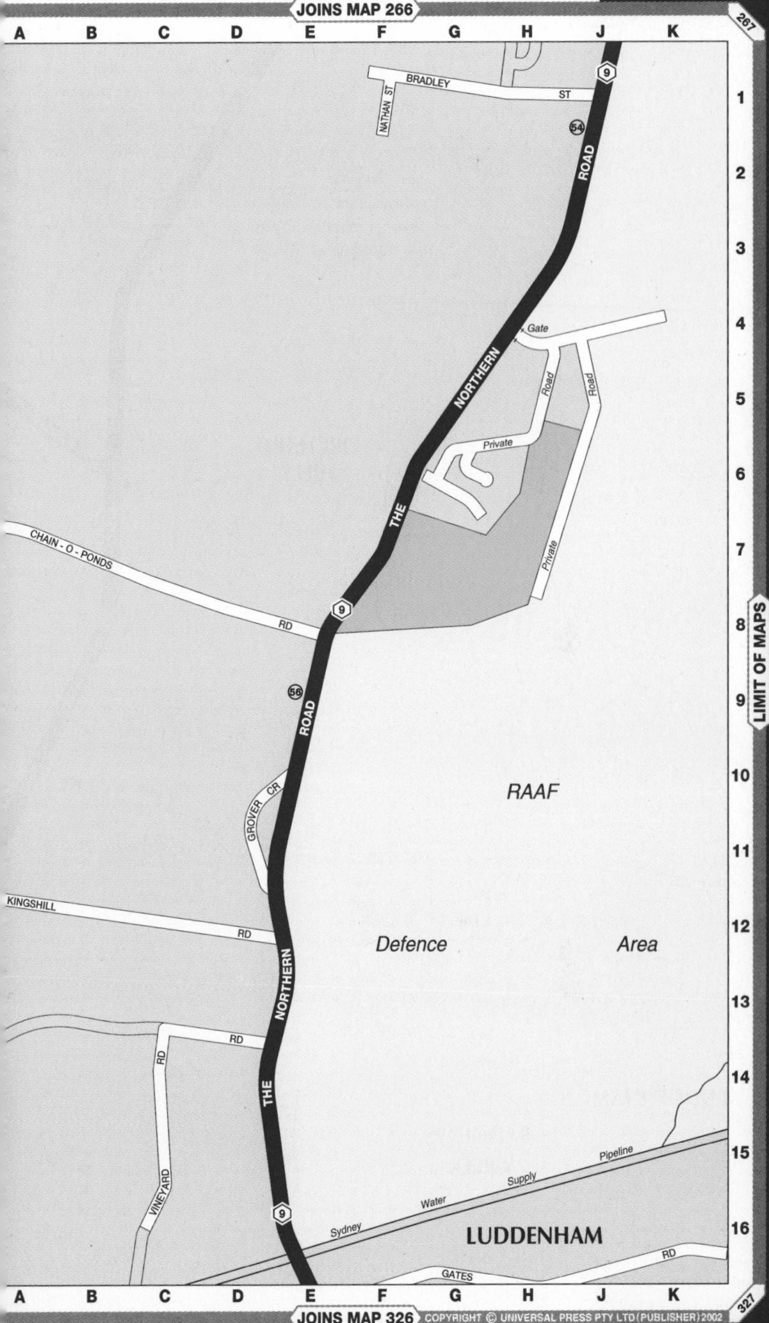

JOINS MAP 326

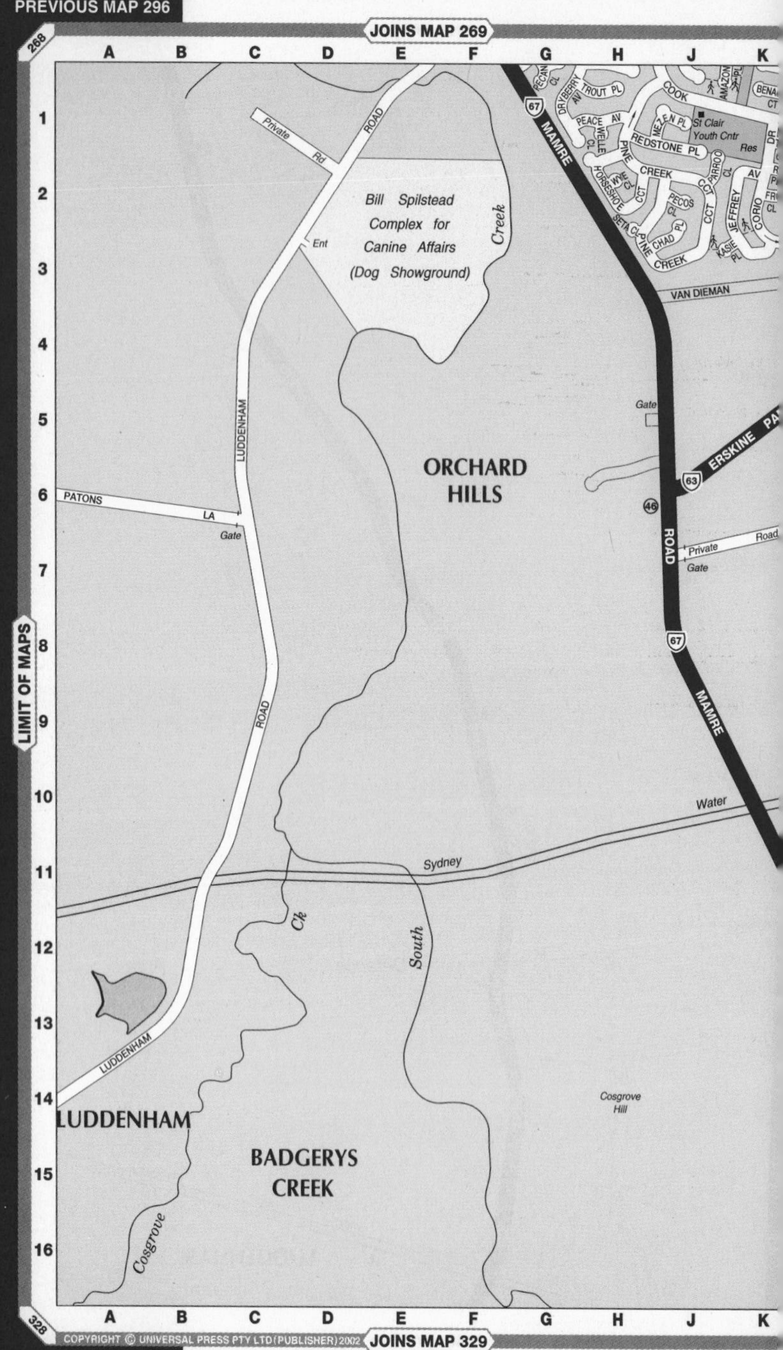
JOINS MAP 269
268
A B C D E F G H J K
1 2 3 4 5 6 7 8 9 10 11 12 13 14 15 16
LIMIT OF MAPS
Private Rd
ROAD
Bill Spilstead
Complex for
Canine Affairs
(Dog Showground)
Ent
Creek
MAMRE
67
PECAN CL
DRYBERRY AV
TROUT PL
COOK
AMAZON
PEACE AV
WELLE CL
MEZEN PL
St Clair
Youth Cntr
Res
REDSTONE PL
PINE
HORSESHOE
WYE CL
CREEK
CCT
PARROO
CL
PECOS CL
JEFFREY
CORIO
SETA CL
CHAD PL
KASIE PL
VAN DIEMAN
ORCHARD
HILLS
LUDDENHAM
PATONS
LA
Gate
ERSKINE
63
46
ROAD
Private
Road
Water
Sydney
Ck
South
Cosgrove
Hill
LUDDENHAM
BADGERYS
CREEK
Cosgrove
328
JOINS MAP 329

JOINS MAP 270

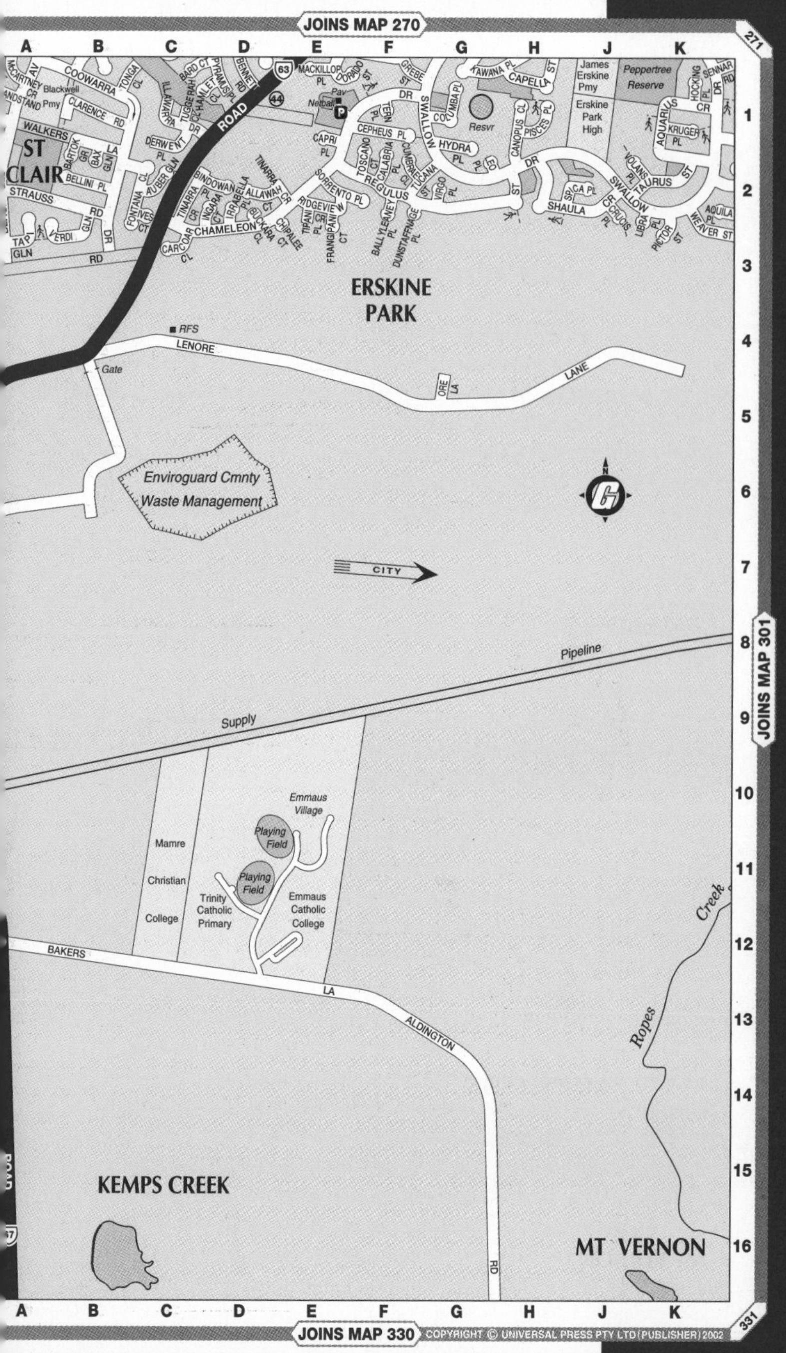

JOINS MAP 301

JOINS MAP 330

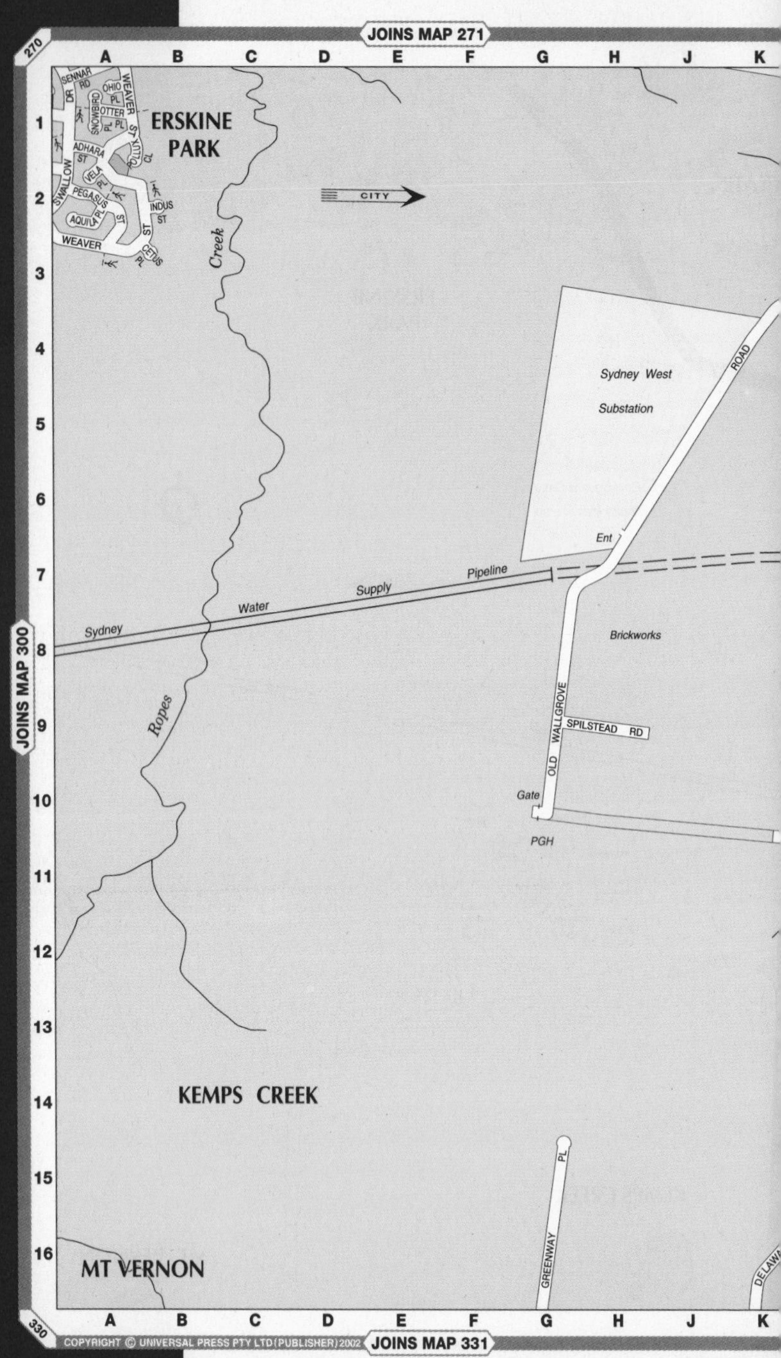
JOINS MAP 271
270
A B C D E F G H J K
ERSKINE
PARK
SENNAR
RD
DR
OHIO
PL
WEAVER
SNOWBIRD
OTTER
PL
PL
ADHARA
ST
CL
SWALLOW
VELA
PL
PEGASUS
INDUS
ST
AQUILA
PL
ST
ST
WEAVER
CETUS
PL
CITY
Creek
Sydney West
Substation
ROAD
Ent
Pipeline
Supply
Water
Sydney
Brickworks
Ropes
OLD WALLGROVE
SPILSTEAD RD
Gate
PGH
KEMPS CREEK
PL
GREENWAY
MT VERNON
JOINS MAP 300
1
2
3
4
5
6
7
8
9
10
11
12
13
14
15
16
330

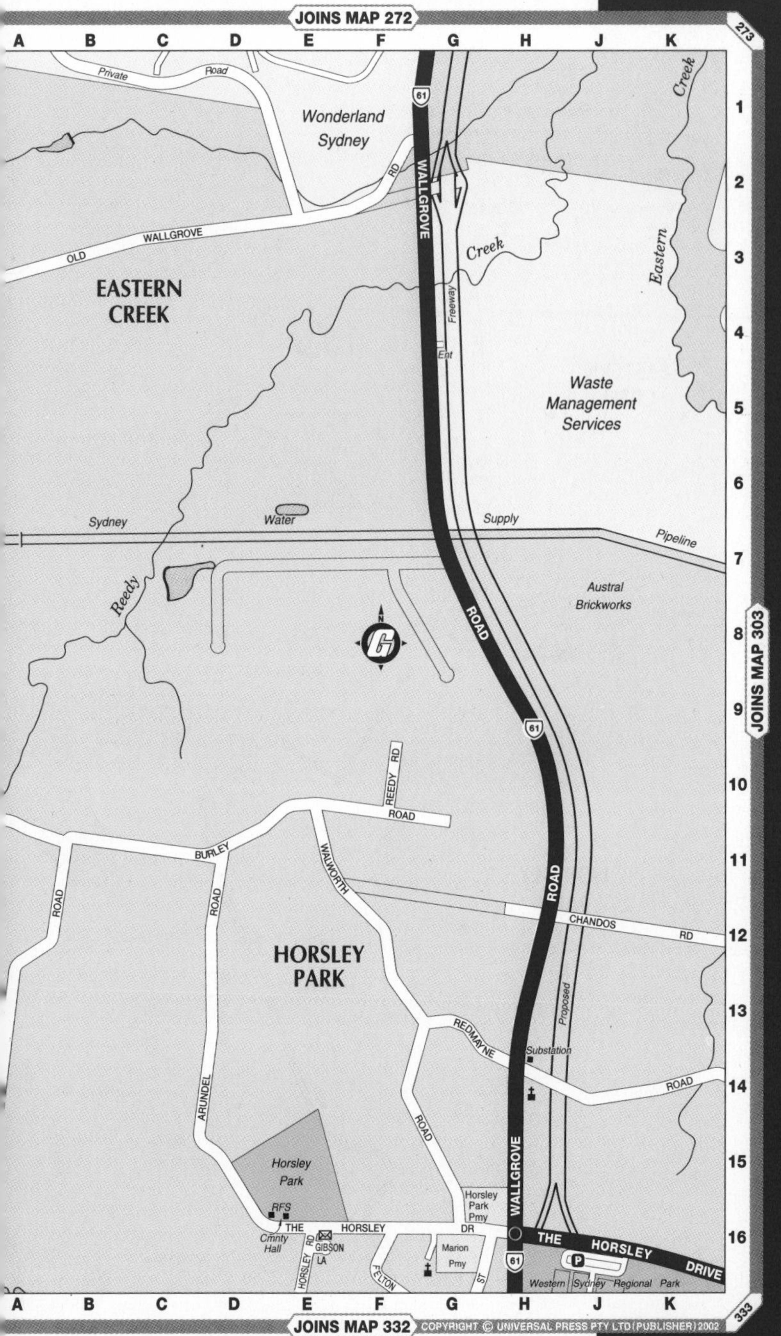
JOINS MAP 272
273
A
B
C
D
E
F
G
H
J
K
Private
Road
Wonderland
Sydney
61
RD
WALLGROVE
OLD
WALLGROVE
Creek
Eastern
Creek
EASTERN
CREEK
Freeway
Ent
Waste
Management
Services
Sydney
Water
Supply
Pipeline
Reedy
Austral
Brickworks
ROAD
JOINS MAP 303
REEDY RD
ROAD
BURLEY
WALWORTH
ROAD
ROAD
ROAD
CHANDOS
RD
HORSLEY
PARK
REDMAYNE
Proposed
Substation
ROAD
ARUNDEL
ROAD
Horsley
Park
WALLGROVE
RFS
Horsley
Park
Pmy
THE
HORSLEY
DR
THE
HORSLEY
DRIVE
Cmnty
Hall
RD
HORSLEY
GIBSON
LA
FELTON
Marion
Pmy
ST
Western
Sydney
Regional
Park
1
2
3
4
5
6
7
8
9
10
11
12
13
14
15
16
JOINS MAP 332
333

MAP 303

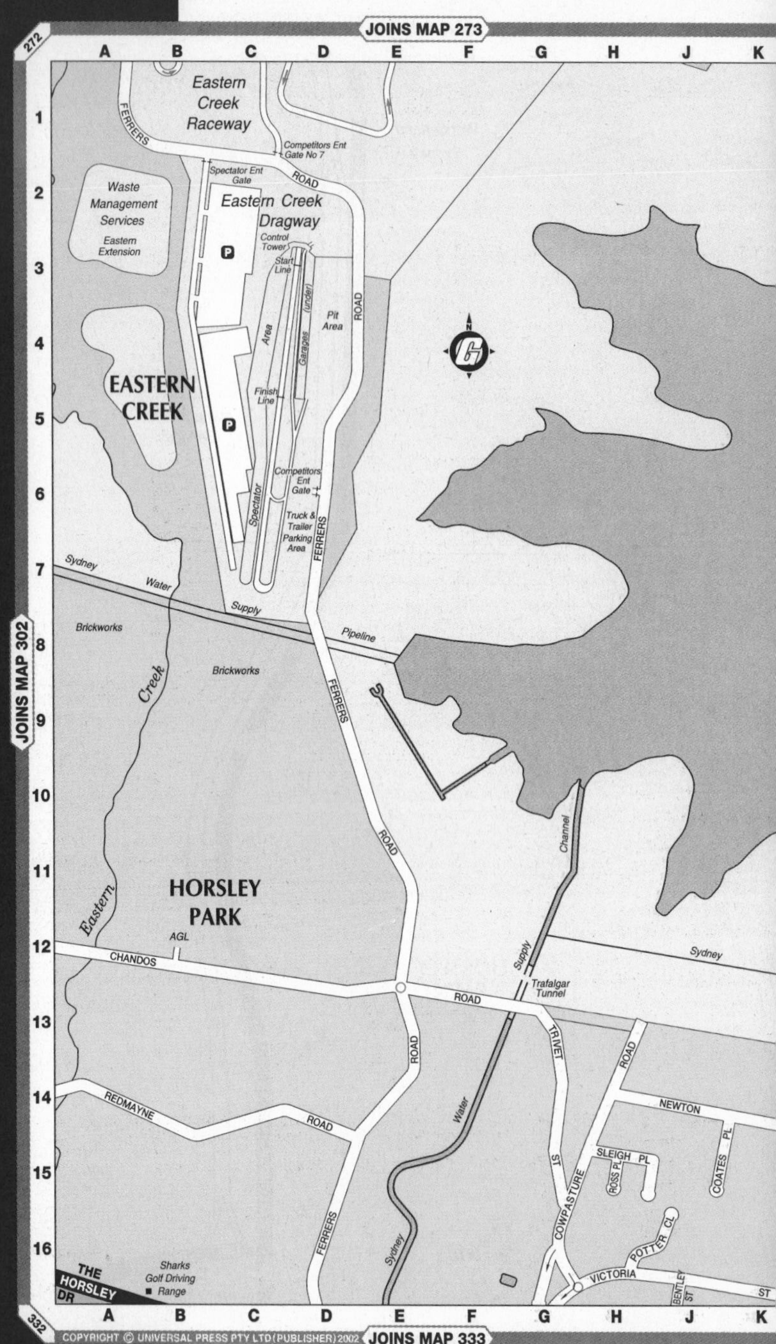

JOINS MAP 273
272
A B C D E F G H J K
1 2 3 4 5 6 7 8 9 10 11 12 13 14 15 16
Eastern Creek Raceway
FERRERS
Competitors Ent Gate No 7
Spectator Ent Gate
ROAD
Waste Management Services
Eastern Extension
Eastern Creek Dragway
Control Tower
Start Line
P
Area
Garages (under)
Pit Area
ROAD
EASTERN CREEK
Finish Line
P
Competitors Ent Gate
Spectator
Truck & Trailer Parking Area
FERRERS
Sydney
Water
Supply
Pipeline
Brickworks
Creek
Brickworks
JOINS MAP 302
FERRERS
ROAD
Channel
HORSLEY PARK
Eastern
AGL
CHANDOS
Supply
Trafalgar Tunnel
Sydney
ROAD
ROAD
TRIVET
ROAD
NEWTON
REDMAYNE
ROAD
Water
SLEIGH PL
PL
ST
ROSS PL
COATES
COWPASTURE
FERRERS
Sydney
POTTER CL
THE HORSLEY DR
Sharks Golf Driving Range
VICTORIA
BENTLEY ST
ST
332
JOINS MAP 333

JOINS MAP 274

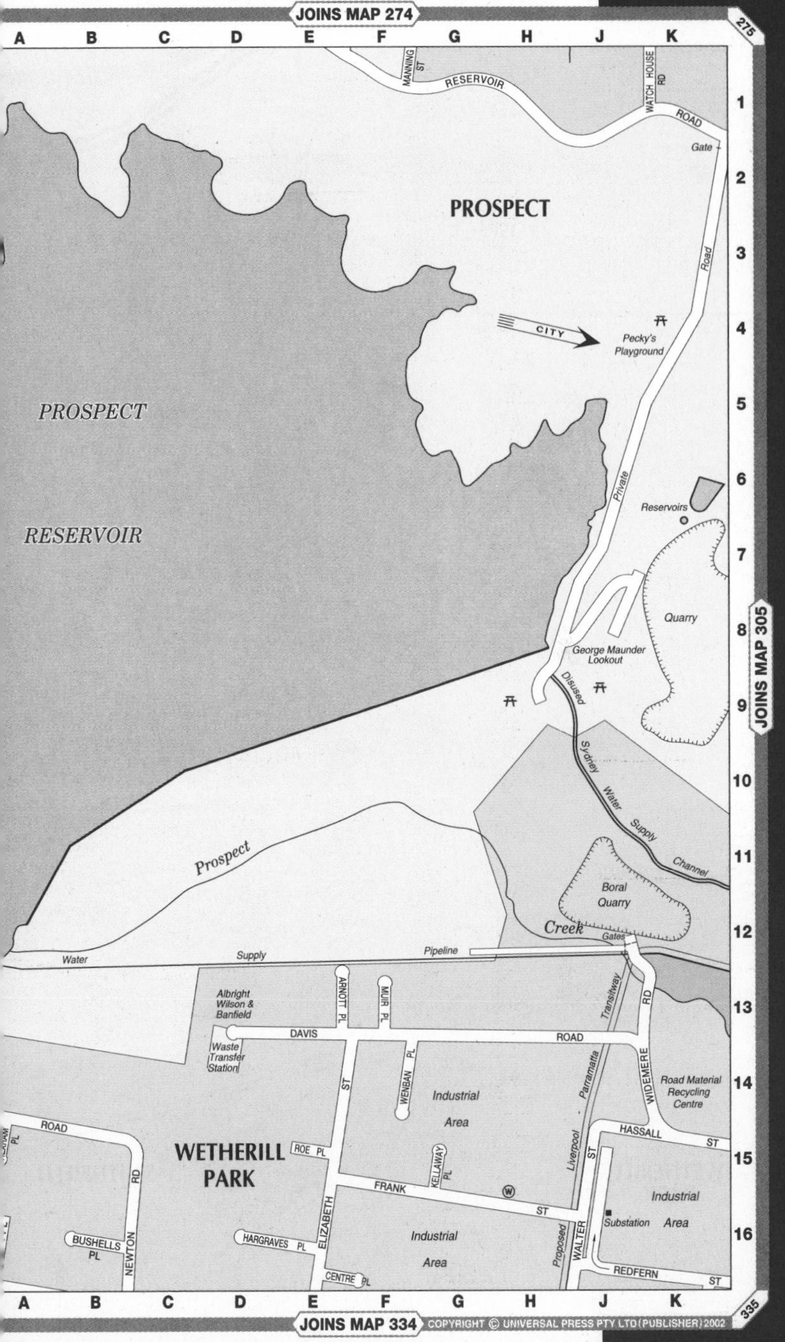

JOINS MAP 305

JOINS MAP 334

MAP 305

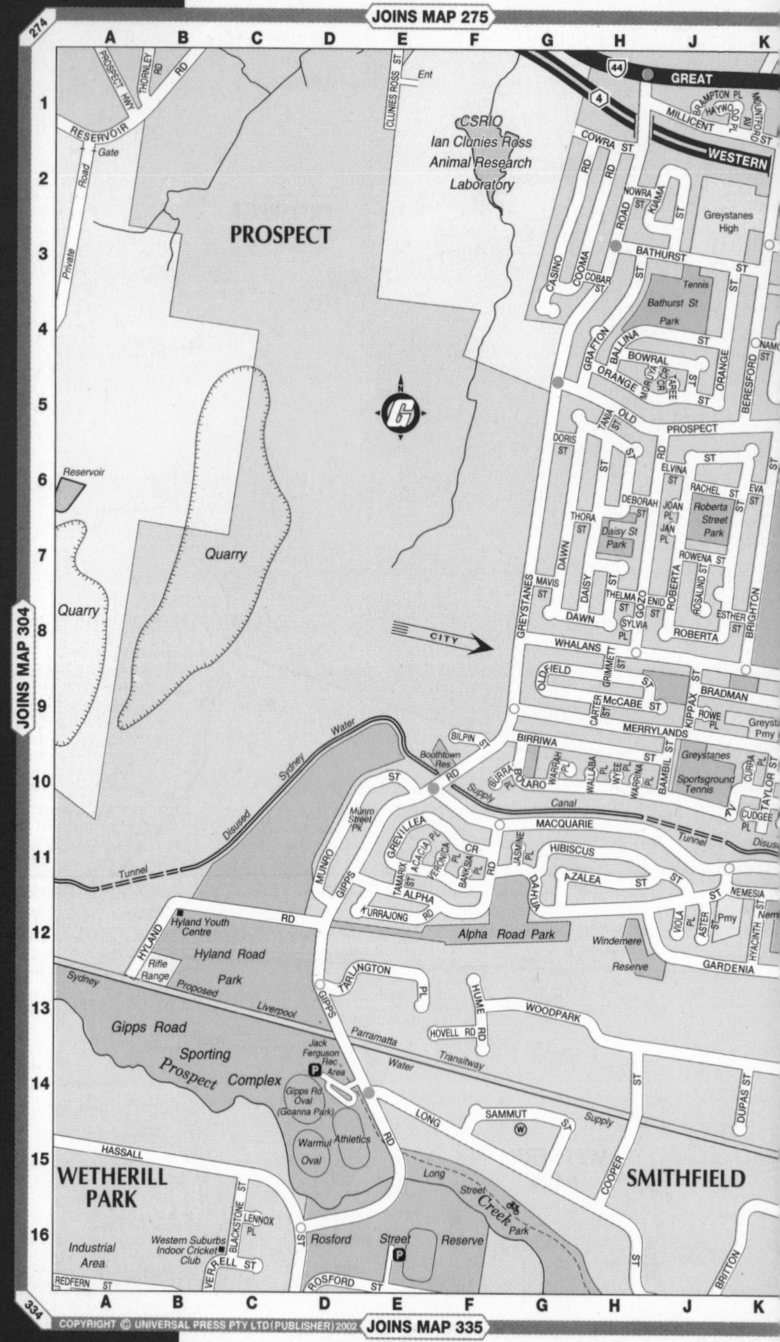

JOINS MAP 275
JOINS MAP 304
JOINS MAP 335
274
334
PROSPECT
CSRIO
Ian Clunies Ross
Animal Research
Laboratory
Quarry
Reservoir
PROSPECT HWY
THORNLEY RD
RESERVOIR RD
Private Road
Gate
CLUNIES ROSS ST
Ent
GREAT WESTERN
COWRA ST
MILLICENT ST
BRAMPTON PL
NOWRA ST
KIAMA ST
Greystanes High
BATHURST ST
CASINO
COOMA RD
COBAR ST
Bathurst St Park
Tennis
GRAFTON
BALLINA
BOWRAL ST
ORANGE ST
BERESFORD
OLD PROSPECT RD
TANIA ST
DORIS ST
ELVINA ST
RACHEL ST
EVA ST
DEBORAH ST
JOAN PL
JAN PL
Roberta Street Park
THORA ST
Daisy St Park
ROWENA ST
DAWN
DAISY
MAVIS ST
THELMA ST
GOZO
ENID ST
ROBERTA
ROSALIND ST
ESTHER ST
BRIGHTON
SYLVIA PL
GREYSTANES
CITY
WHALANS
OLDFIELD
GRIMMETT ST
BRADMAN
McCABE ST
CARTER ST
KIPPAX
ROWE PL
MERRYLANDS
BILPIN ST
BIRRIWA
Boothtown Res
Sydney Water
Disused
Tunnel
Supply Canal
Greystanes Sportsground
Tennis
BAMBIL ST
WALLABA
WYEE PL
WARRINA PL
CURRA PL
TAYLOR ST
CUDGEE PL
MUNRO ST
Munro Street Pk
MACQUARIE
GREVILLEA
ACACIA PL
VERONICA PL
BANKSIA PL
TAMARIX ST
JASMINE PL
HIBISCUS
AZALEA ST
DAHLIA
GIPPS
ALPHA RD
KURRAJONG
NEMESIA ST
VIOLA PL
ASTER ST
Pmy
HYACINTH ST
HYLAND RD
Hyland Youth Centre
Hyland Road Park
Rifle Range
Alpha Road Park
Windemere Reserve
GARDENIA
Sydney Proposed Liverpool Parramatta Transitway
TARLINGTON PL
HUME RD
WOODPARK
HOVELL RD
Gipps Road Sporting Complex
Prospect Water Supply
Jack Ferguson Rec Area
Gipps Rd Oval (Goanna Park)
Warmul Oval
Athletics
LONG ST
SAMMUT ST
DUPAS ST
COOPER ST
HASSALL
WETHERILL PARK
SMITHFIELD
Long Street Creek Park
BLACKSTONE ST
LENNOX PL
Western Suburbs Indoor Cricket Club
Industrial Area
VERRELL ST
Rosford Street Reserve
ROSFORD ST
REDFERN ST
BRITTON

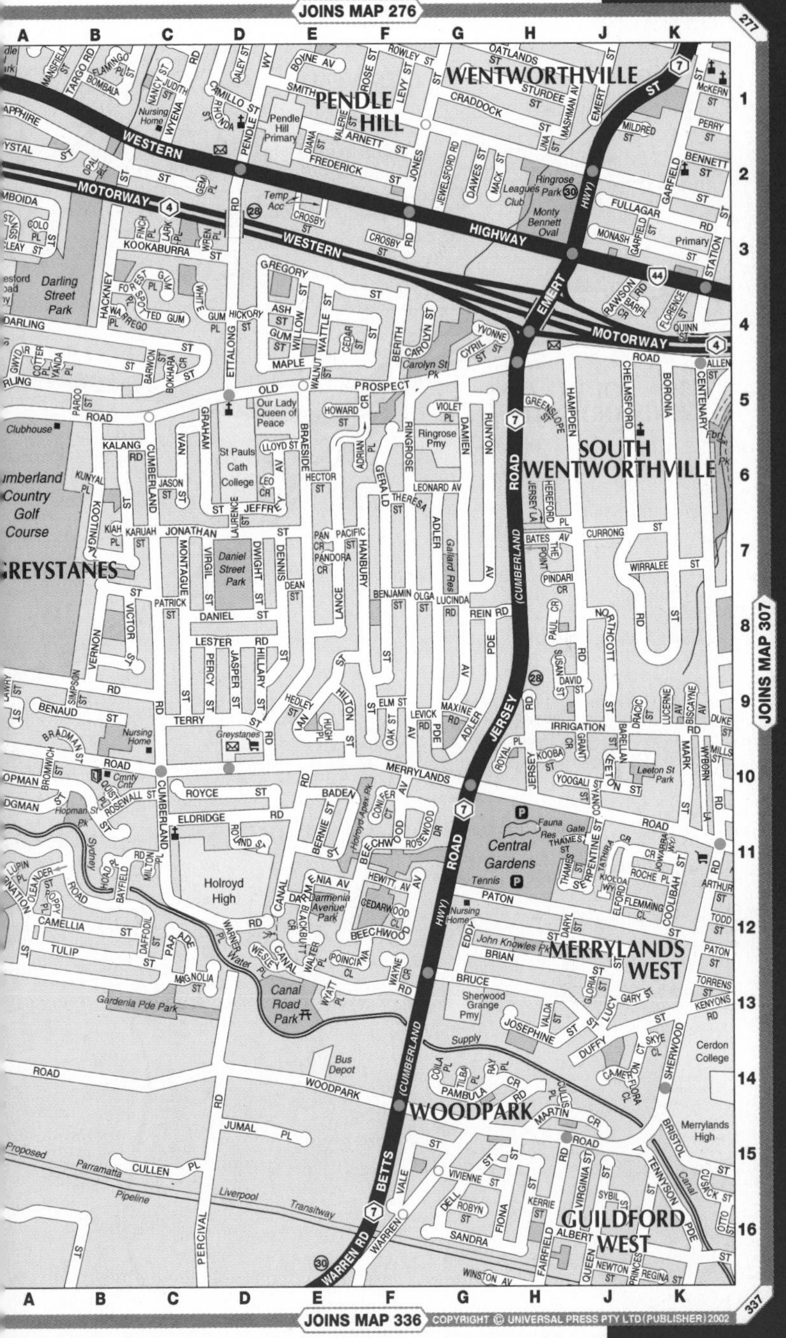
JOINS MAP 276
277
A B C D E F G H J K
1 2 3 4 5 6 7 8 9 10 11 12 13 14 15 16
WENTWORTHVILLE
PENDLE HILL
SOUTH WENTWORTHVILLE
GREYSTANES
MERRYLANDS WEST
WOODPARK
GUILDFORD WEST
WESTERN HIGHWAY
WESTERN MOTORWAY
CUMBERLAND HWY
JERSEY ROAD
OLD PROSPECT ROAD
MERRYLANDS ROAD
WOODPARK ROAD
BETTS RD
WARREN RD
Darling Street Park
Cumberland Country Golf Course
Pendle Hill Primary
Ringrose Park
Leagues Club
Monty Bennett Oval
Our Lady Queen of Peace
St Pauls Cath College
Ringrose Pmy
Carolyn St Pk
Daniel Street Park
Galliard Res
Leeton St Park
Central Gardens
Fauna Res
Tennis
Holroyd High
Holroyd Apex Pk
Darmenia Avenue Park
Canal Road Park
Hopman St Pk
Gardenia Pde Park
John Knowles Pk
Sherwood Grange Pmy
Bus Depot
Cerdon College
Merrylands High
Nursing Home
Proposed Parramatta Liverpool Transitway
Pipeline
Supply
Canal
JOINS MAP 307
JOINS MAP 336
337

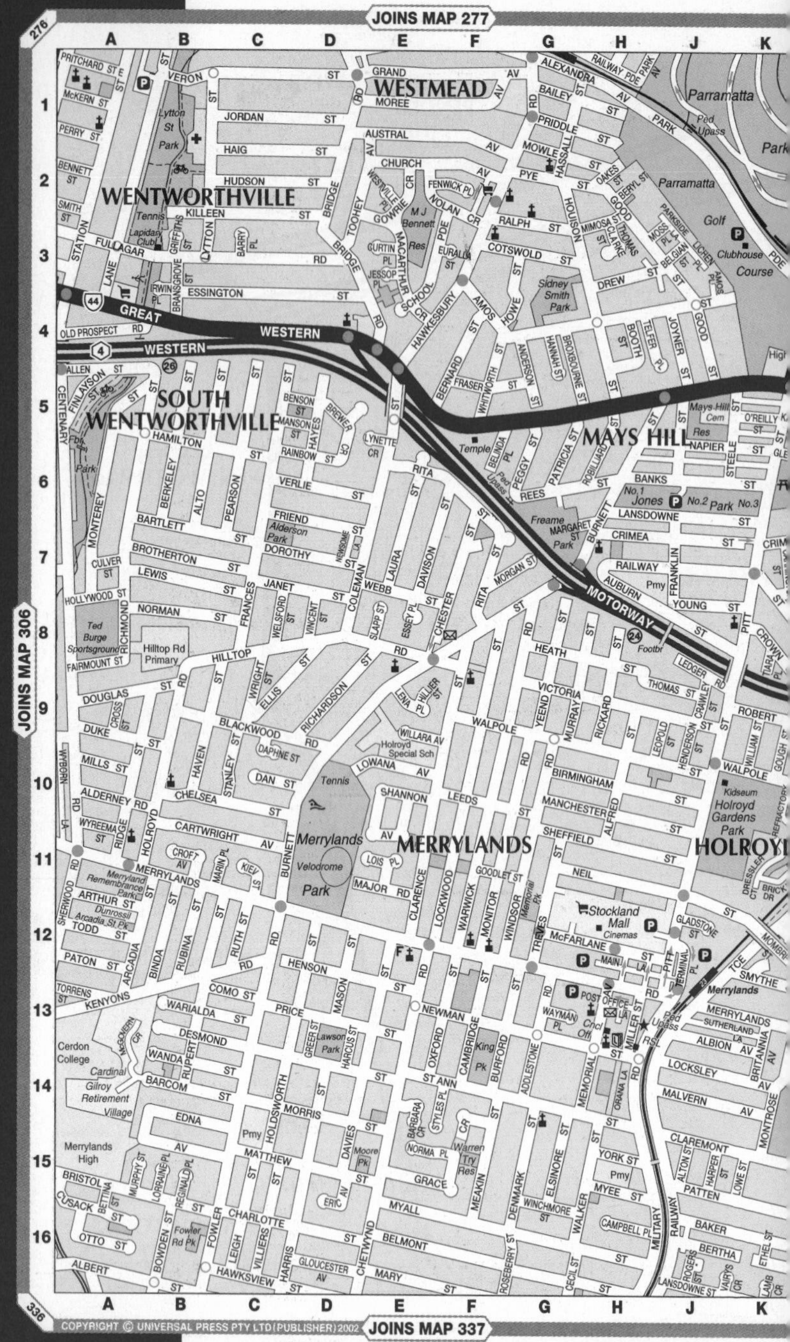
JOINS MAP 277
JOINS MAP 306
JOINS MAP 337
276
336
WESTMEAD
WENTWORTHVILLE
SOUTH WENTWORTHVILLE
MAYS HILL
MERRYLANDS
HOLROYD
Parramatta Park
Parramatta Golf Course
Clubhouse
Lytton St Park
M J Bennett Res
Sidney Smith Park
Mays Hill Cem Res
Jones Park
Freame Margaret Park
Alderson Park
Ted Burge Sportsground
Hilltop Rd Primary
Holroyd Special Sch
Merrylands Velodrome Park
Kidseum
Holroyd Gardens Park
Merryland Remembrance Park
Dunrossil Arcadia St Pk
Stockland Mall
Cinemas
Memorial Pk
Lawson Park
King Pk
Warren Try Res
Moore Pk
Fowler Rd Pk
Cerdon College
Cardinal Gilroy Retirement Village
Merrylands High
Merrylands
GREAT WESTERN
WESTERN
MOTORWAY
Temple
Footbr
Ped Upass

JOINS MAP 278

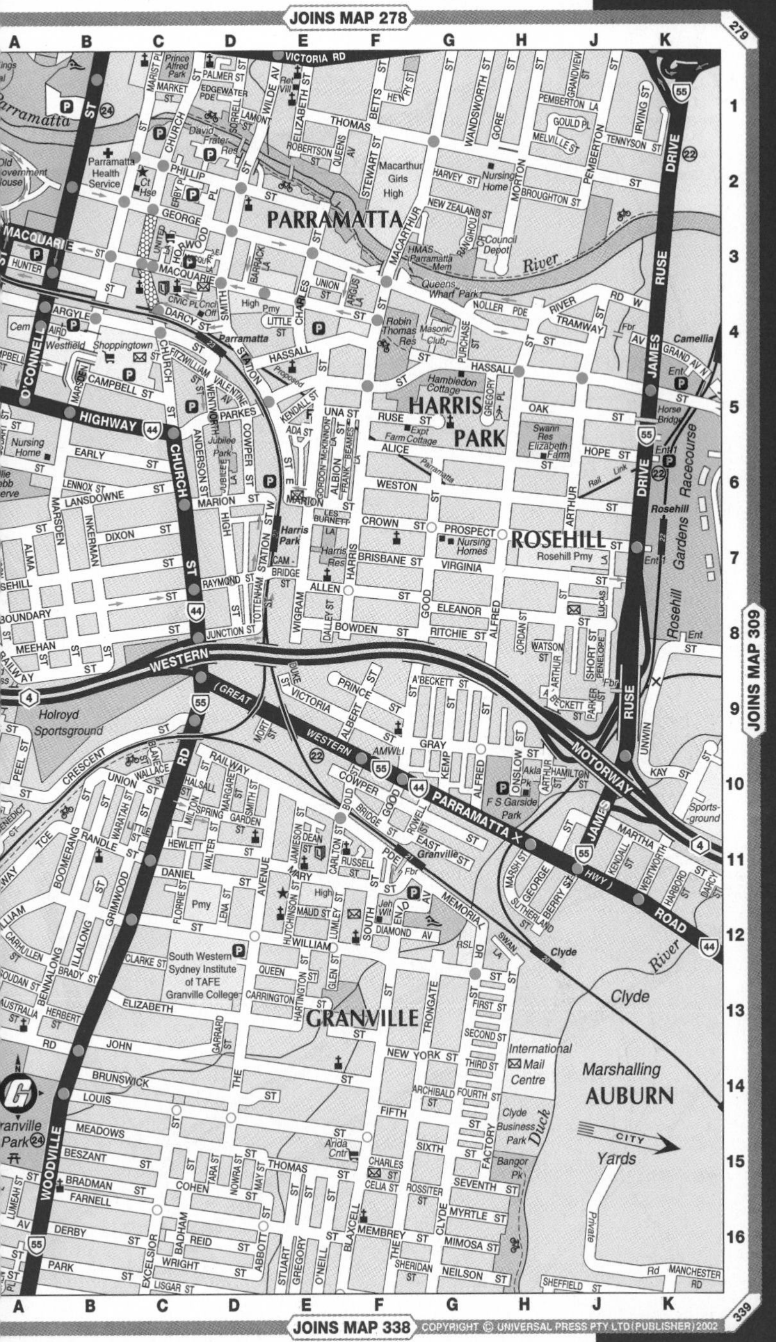

JOINS MAP 309

JOINS MAP 338

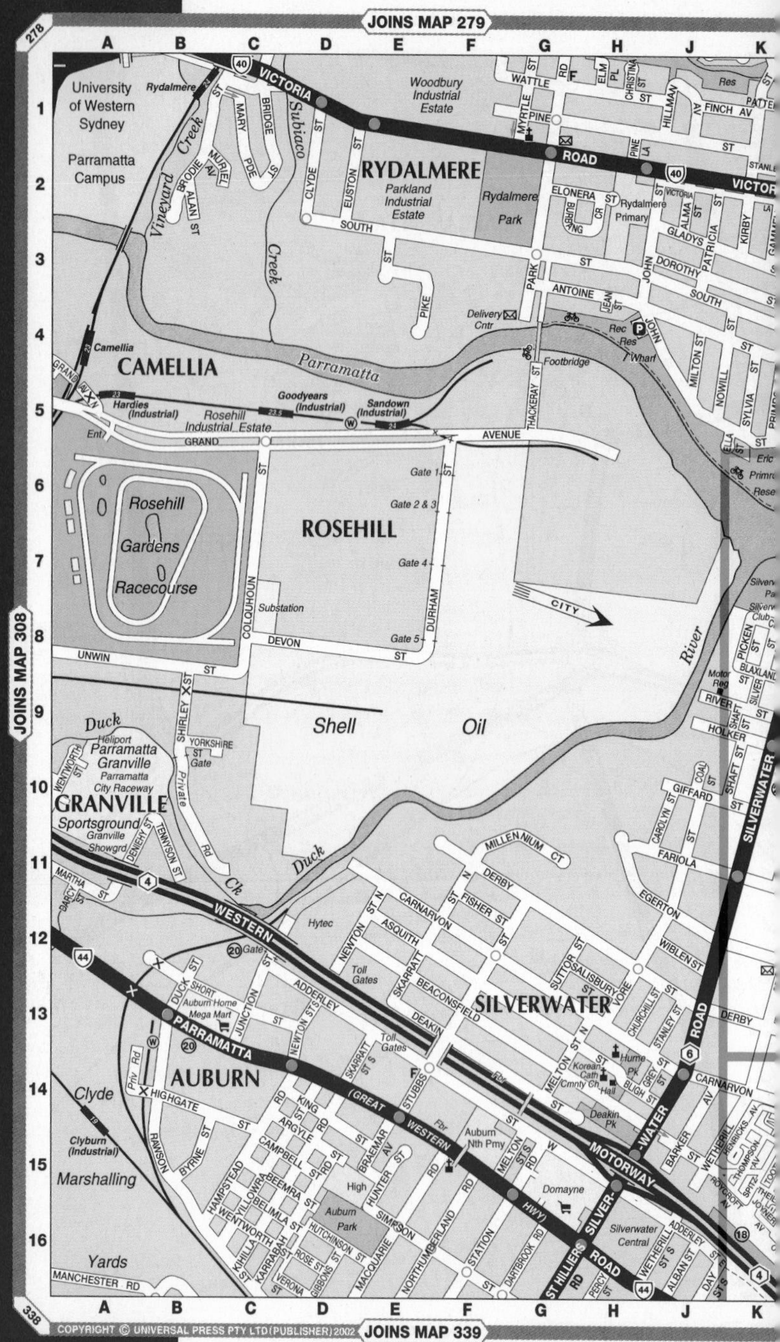
JOINS MAP 279
JOINS MAP 308
JOINS MAP 339
RYDALMERE
CAMELLIA
ROSEHILL
GRANVILLE
SILVERWATER
AUBURN
University of Western Sydney
Parramatta Campus
Woodbury Industrial Estate
Parkland Industrial Estate
Rydalmere Park
Rosehill Gardens Racecourse
Rosehill Industrial Estate
Shell
Oil
Parramatta River
Duck Creek
Vineyard Creek
Subiaco Creek
VICTORIA ROAD
GRAND AVENUE
PARRAMATTA (GREAT WESTERN HWY)
WESTERN MOTORWAY
SILVERWATER ROAD
Parramatta Granville Heliport
Parramatta City Raceway
Granville Sportsground
Granville Showgrd
Clyde Marshalling Yards
Clyburn (Industrial)
Auburn Park
Domayne
Silverwater Central
Deakin Pk
Hume Pk
Auburn Home Mega Mart
Auburn Nth Pmy
Rydalmere Primary
Footbridge
Substation
Hytec
Toll Gates
CITY

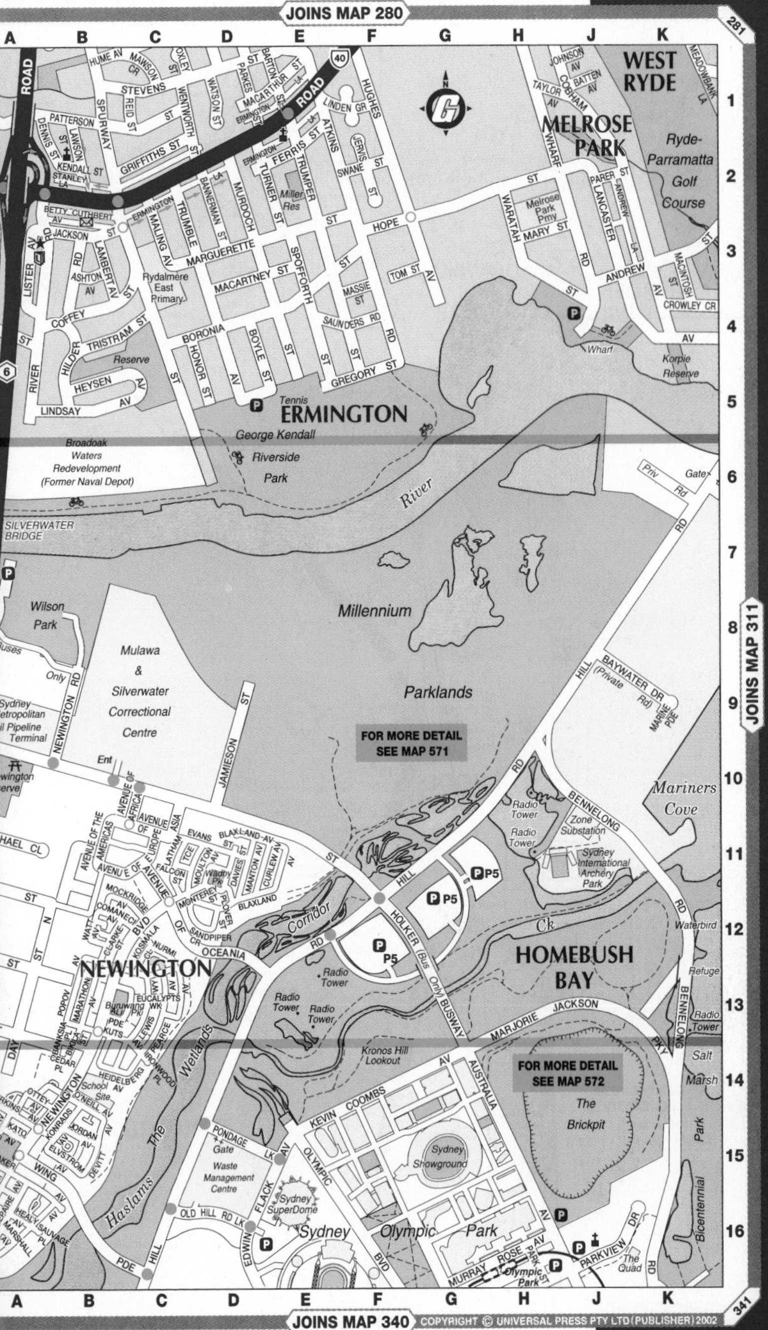

JOINS MAP 280
281
A B C D E F G H J K
1 2 3 4 5 6 7 8 9 10 11 12 13 14 15 16
WEST RYDE
MELROSE PARK
Ryde-Parramatta Golf Course
ERMINGTON
George Kendall Riverside Park
Broadoak Waters Redevelopment (Former Naval Depot)
SILVERWATER BRIDGE
River
Wilson Park
Mulawa & Silverwater Correctional Centre
Millennium Parklands
FOR MORE DETAIL SEE MAP 571
Sydney Metropolitan Oil Pipeline Terminal
Mariners Cove
Sydney International Archery Park
Zone Substation
Radio Tower
HOMEBUSH BAY
NEWINGTON
Corridor
The Wetlands
Haslams Ck
Kronos Hill Lookout
FOR MORE DETAIL SEE MAP 572
The Brickpit
Sydney Showground
Sydney SuperDome
Sydney Olympic Park
Waste Management Centre
Bicentennial Park
Salt Marsh
Waterbird Refuge
Wharf
Korpie Reserve
Rydalmere East Primary
Reserve
Melrose Park Prmy
Miller Res
Tennis
The Quad
ROAD
HOPE ST
HILL RD
JAMIESON ST
NEWINGTON RD
HOLKER (Bus Only) BUSWAY
MARJORIE JACKSON PKY
BENNELONG RD
KEVIN COOMBS AV
AUSTRALIA AV
OLYMPIC BVD
BAYWATER DR (Private Rd)
P5
JOINS MAP 311
JOINS MAP 340
341

JOINS MAP 281

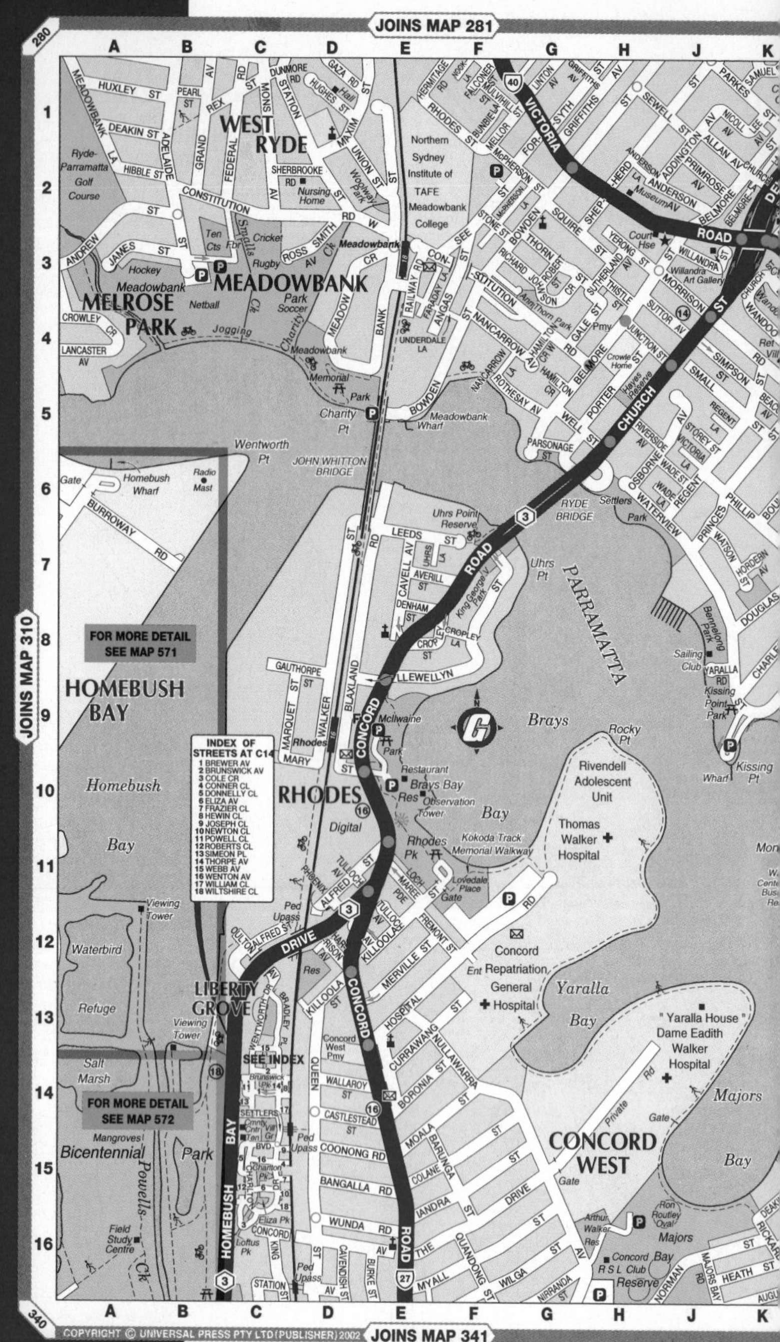

JOINS MAP 310

JOINS MAP 341

JOINS MAP 282

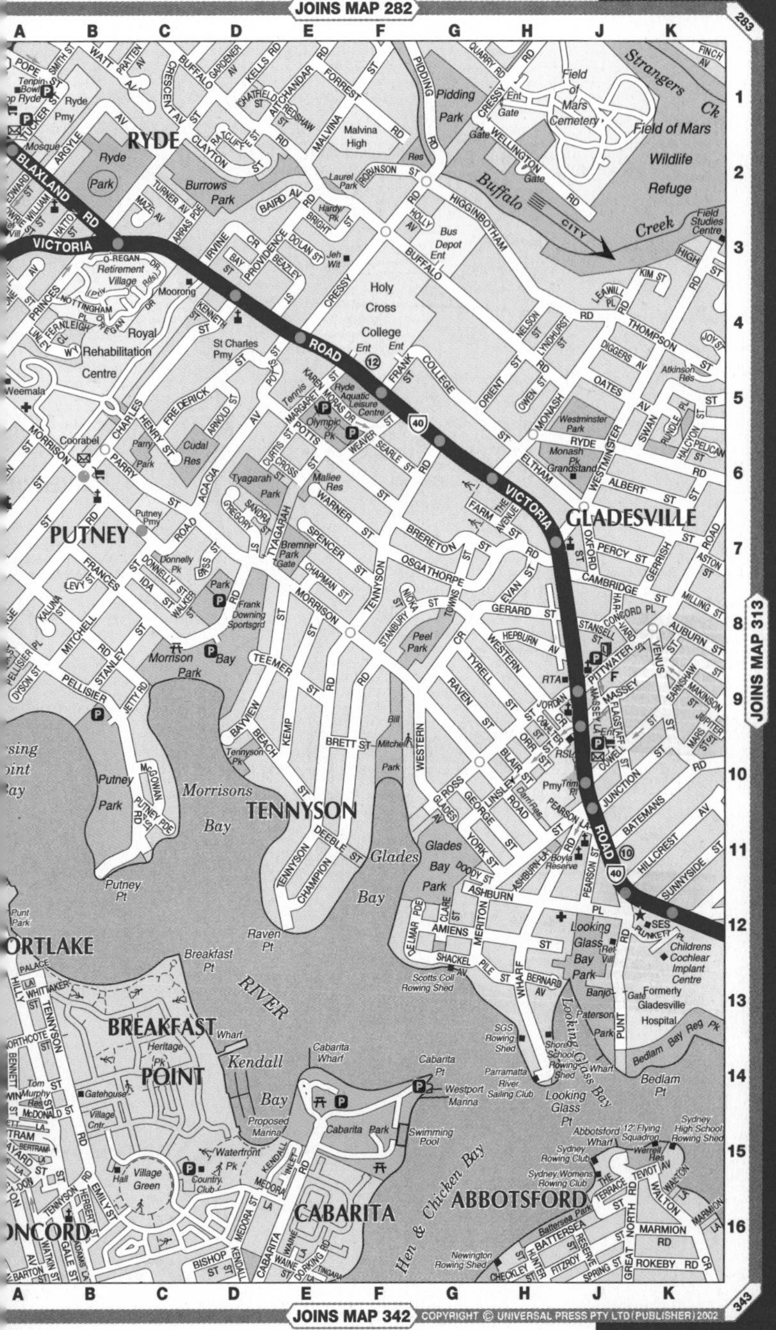

JOINS MAP 313

JOINS MAP 342

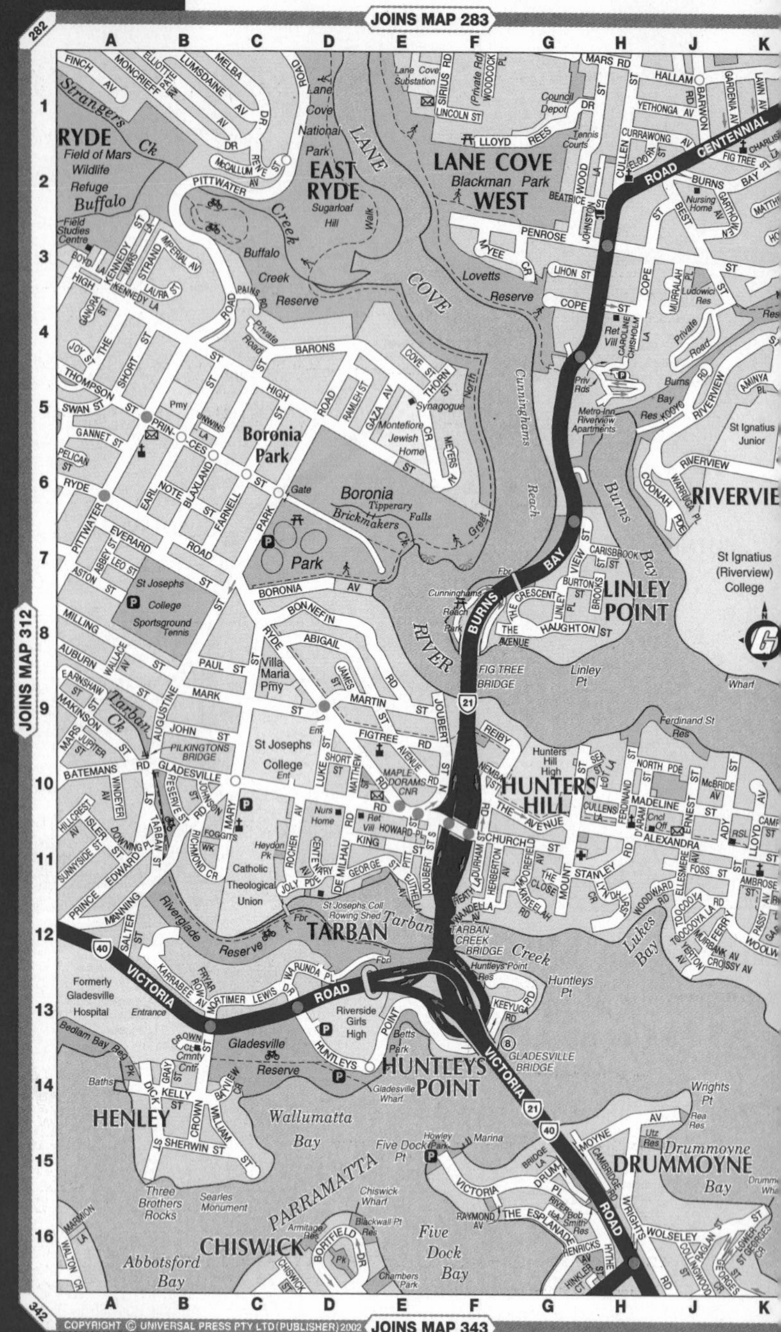
JOINS MAP 283
JOINS MAP 312
JOINS MAP 343
282
342
RYDE
EAST RYDE
LANE COVE WEST
Boronia Park
RIVERVIEW
LINLEY POINT
HUNTERS HILL
TARBAN
HUNTLEYS POINT
HENLEY
DRUMMOYNE
CHISWICK
Field of Mars Wildlife Refuge
Lane Cove National Park
Sugarloaf Hill
Buffalo Creek Reserve
Blackman Park
Lovetts Reserve
St Ignatius Junior
St Ignatius (Riverview) College
St Josephs College
Villa Maria Pmy
Catholic Theological Union
Riverglade Reserve
Formerly Gladesville Hospital
Riverside Girls High
Gladesville Reserve
FIG TREE BRIDGE
TARBAN CREEK BRIDGE
GLADESVILLE BRIDGE
Wallumatta Bay
PARRAMATTA
Five Dock Bay
Abbotsford Bay
Drummoyne Bay
Lukes Bay
VICTORIA ROAD
BURNS BAY ROAD
CENTENNIAL ROAD
LANE COVE RIVER
COPYRIGHT © UNIVERSAL PRESS PTY LTD (PUBLISHER) 2002

JOINS MAP 284

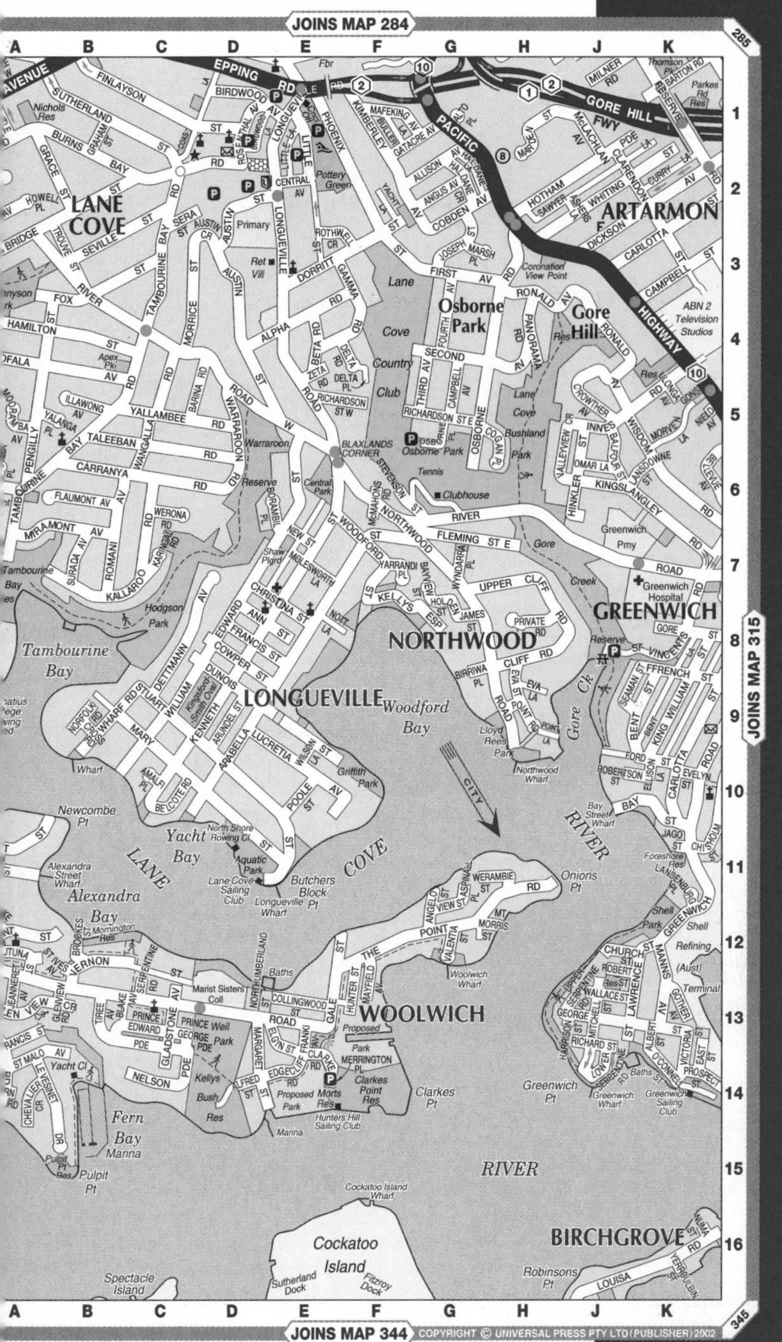

JOINS MAP 315

JOINS MAP 344

JOINS MAP 285
JOINS MAP 314
JOINS MAP 345
284
344
A B C D E F G H J K
1 2 3 4 5 6 7 8 9 10 11 12 13 14 15 16
ARTARMON
NAREMBURN
ST LEONARDS
CROWS NEST
Gore Hill
GREENWICH
WOLLSTONECRAFT
NORTH SYDNEY
WAVERTON
LAVENDER BAY
McMAHONS POINT
MILSONS POINT
BIRCHGROVE
FOR MORE DETAIL SEE MAP 5
Royal North Shore Hospital
Institute of TAFE (Nth Sydney College)
ABN 2 Television Studios
Gore Hill Cemetery
Artarmon Oval
Flat Rock Gully
SUSPENSION BRIDGE
Naremburn Park
Talus Reserve
St Thomas Rest Park
North Sydney Oval
St Leonards Park
Smoothey Park
Berry Island Reserve
Balls Head Bay
Balls Head Reserve
Gore Cove
Shell Refining (Aust) Cove Wharf Terminal
Manns Pt
Berrys Bay
Lavender Bay
HMAS Waterhen
Naval Wharves
Old Quarantine Depot
Graythwaite Nursing Home
SCEGS (Shore)
Yurulbin Pt
PACIFIC HWY
WARRINGAH FWY
MILLER ST
FALCON ST
WILLOUGHBY ROAD
GORE HILL FWY
CITY

JOINS MAP 286

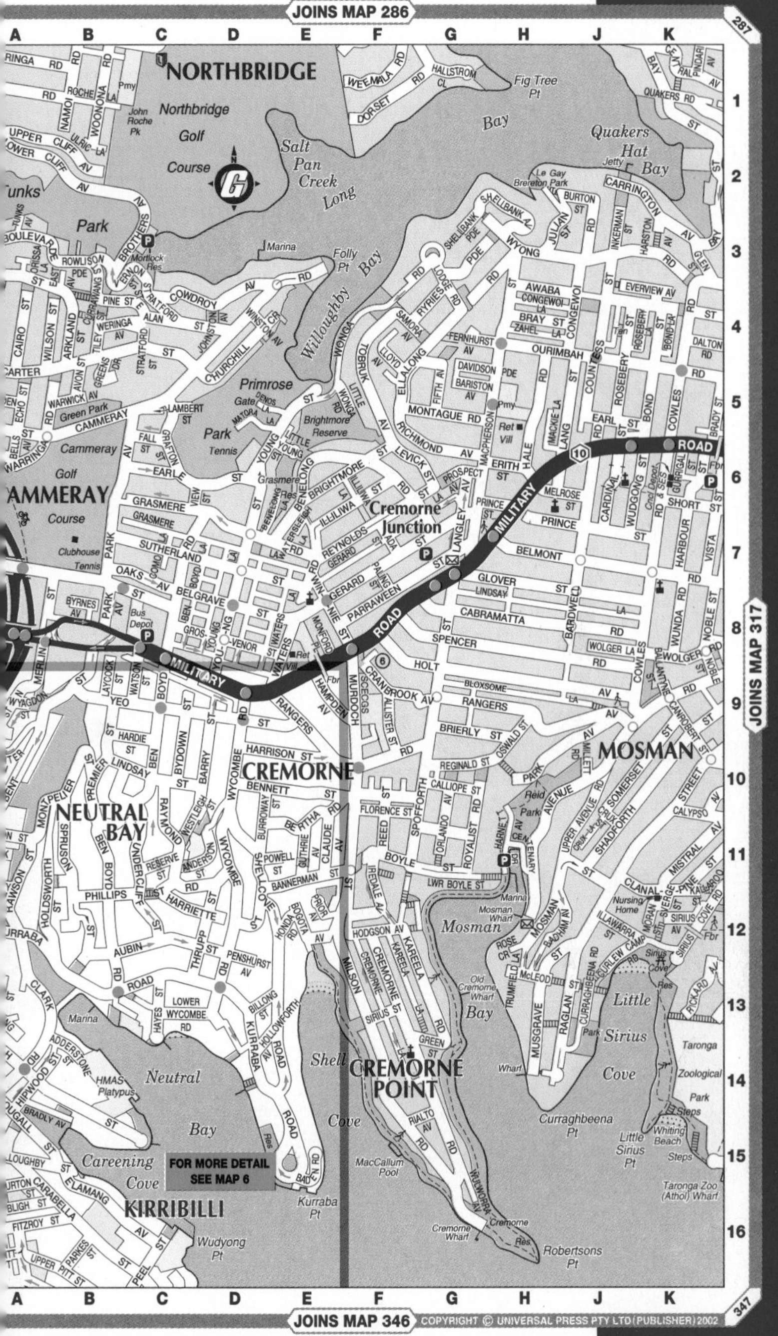

JOINS MAP 317

JOINS MAP 346

JOINS MAP 287

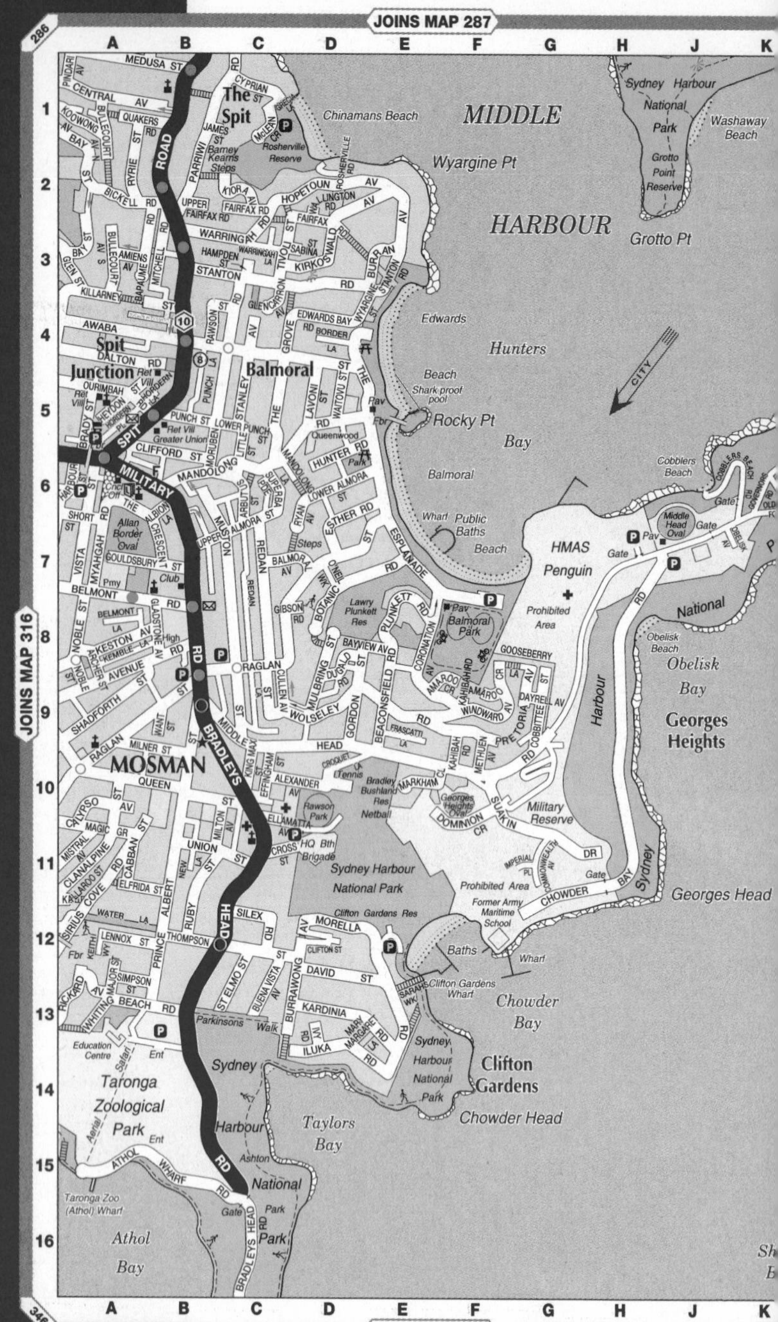

JOINS MAP 316

JOINS MAP 347

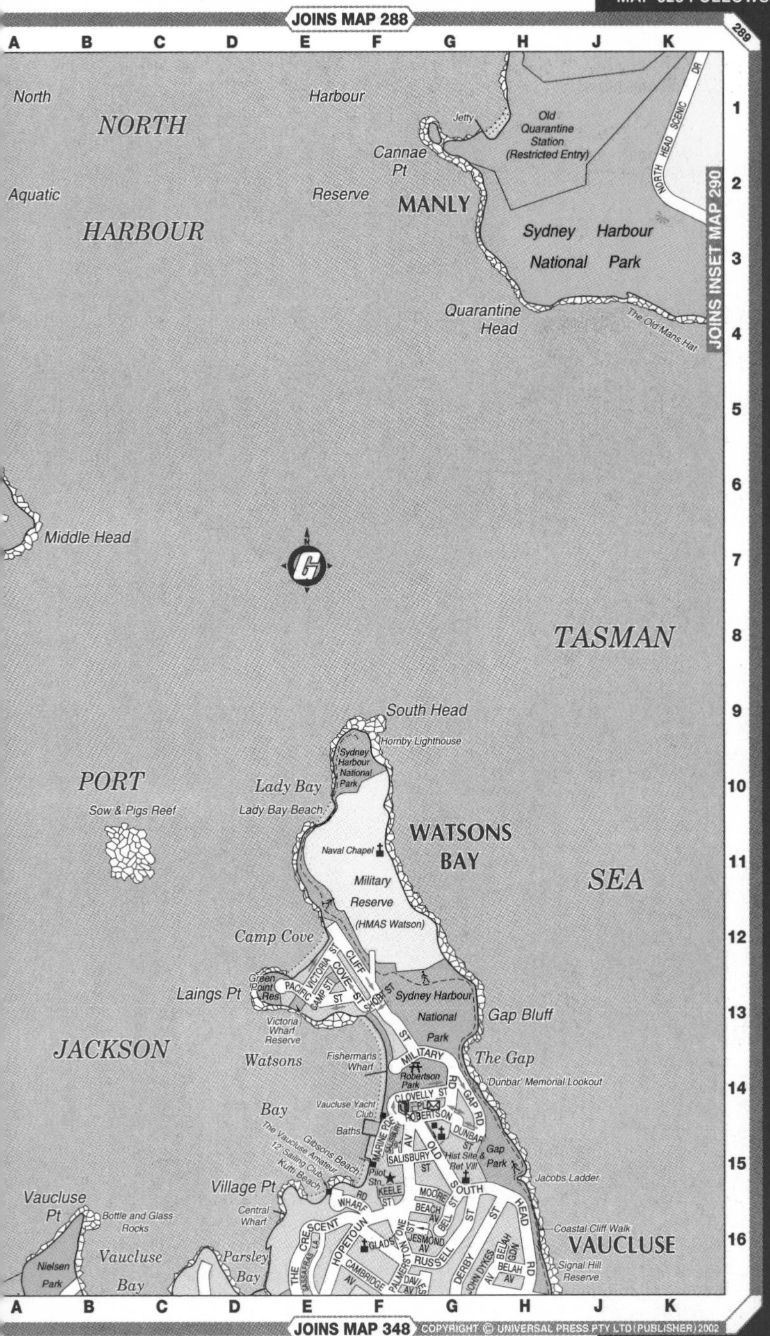
JOINS MAP 288
JOINS INSET MAP 290
JOINS MAP 348
North Harbour Aquatic Reserve
NORTH HARBOUR
Cannae Pt
MANLY
Jetty
Old Quarantine Station (Restricted Entry)
NORTH HEAD SCENIC DR
Sydney Harbour National Park
Quarantine Head
The Old Mans Hat
Middle Head
TASMAN SEA
South Head
Hornby Lighthouse
Sydney Harbour National Park
PORT JACKSON
Sow & Pigs Reef
Lady Bay
Lady Bay Beach
WATSONS BAY
Naval Chapel
Military Reserve (HMAS Watson)
Camp Cove
Laings Pt
Green Point Res
Victoria Wharf Reserve
Gap Bluff
The Gap
'Dunbar' Memorial Lookout
Fishermans Wharf
Robertson Park
Watsons Bay
Vaucluse Yacht Club
Baths
The Vaucluse Amateur 12' Sailing Club
Gibsons Beach
Kutti Beach
Pilot Stn
Hist Site & Ret Vill
Gap Park
Jacobs Ladder
Village Pt
Central Wharf
Coastal Cliff Walk
VAUCLUSE
Signal Hill Reserve
Vaucluse Pt
Bottle and Glass Rocks
Nielsen Park
Vaucluse Bay
Parsley Bay
PACIFIC ST
VICTORIA ST
CAMP ST
COVE ST
CLIFF ST
SHORT ST
MILITARY RD
GAP RD
CLOVELLY ST
ROBERTSON PL
DUNBAR ST
MARINE PDE
SALISBURY AV
OLD SOUTH HEAD RD
WHARF RD
KEELE ST
MOORE ST
BEACH AV
BELL ST
THE CRESCENT
SASSAFRAS LA
HOPETOUN AV
GLADSTONE ST
JESMOND AV
RUSSELL ST
CAMBRIDGE AV
PALMERSTON AV
DAVIES AV
DERBY ST
JOHN DYKES AV
BELAH GDN
BELAH AV

LIMIT OF MAPS

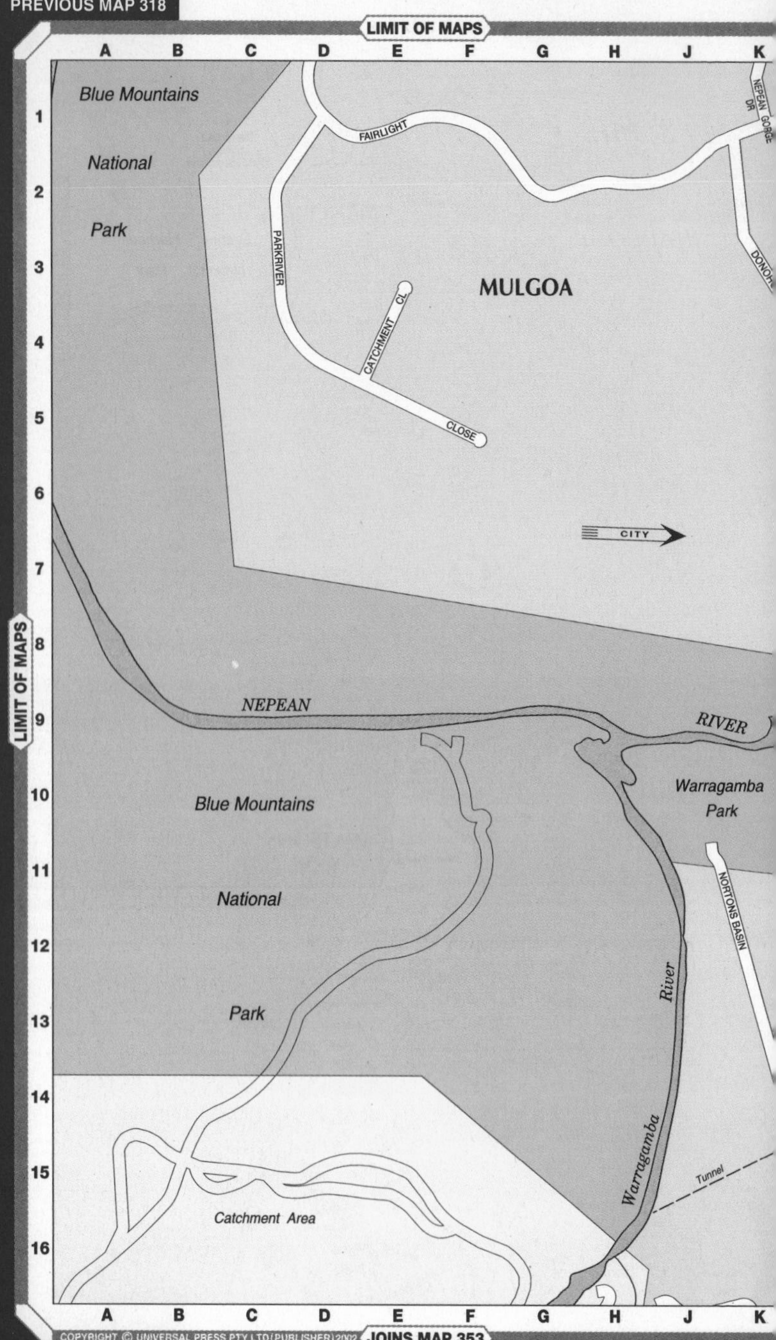

LIMIT OF MAPS

JOINS MAP 353

LIMIT OF MAPS

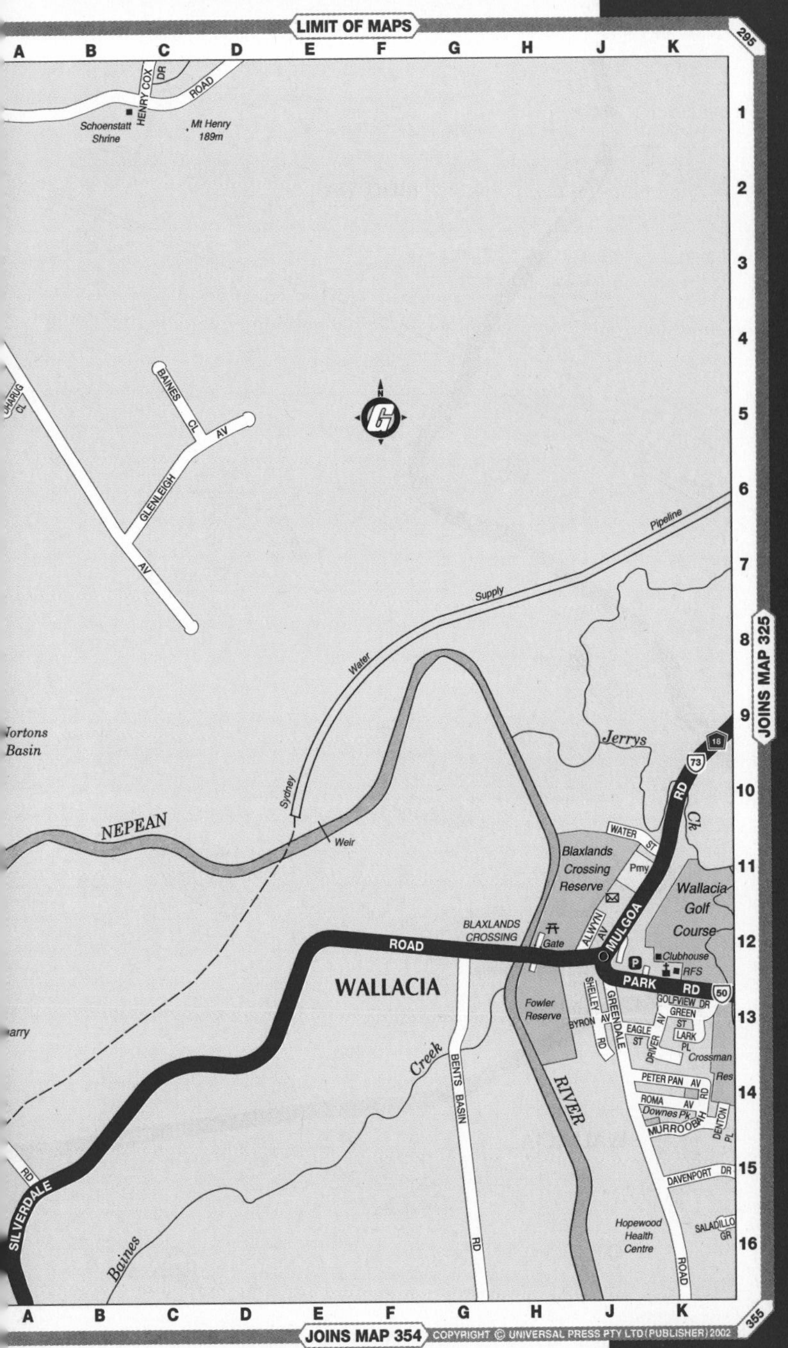

JOINS MAP 325

JOINS MAP 354

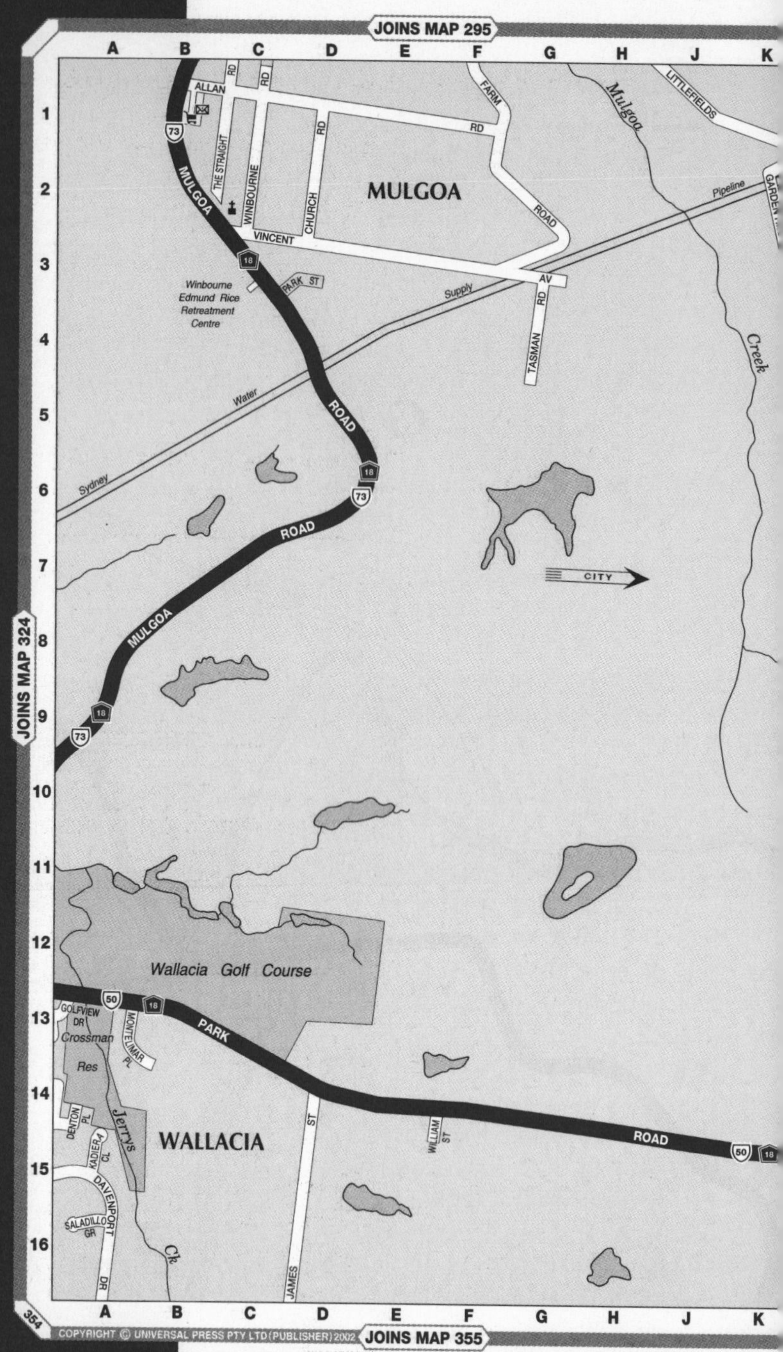
JOINS MAP 295
A B C D E F G H J K
1 2 3 4 5 6 7 8 9 10 11 12 13 14 15 16
ALLAN
RD
THE STRAIGHT
WINBOURNE
CHURCH
FARM
RD
ROAD
MULGOA
VINCENT
PARK ST
AV
TASMAN
Winbourne
Edmund Rice
Retreatment
Centre
MULGOA
ROAD
Mulgoa
Creek
LITTLEFIELDS
GARDEN
Pipeline
Supply
Water
Sydney
ROAD
MULGOA
CITY
JOINS MAP 324
Wallacia Golf Course
GOLFVIEW DR
Crossman
Res
MONTELIMAR PL
PARK
ROAD
DENTON PL
KADIERA CL
Jerrys
WALLACIA
DAVENPORT DR
SALADILLO GR
Ck
JAMES ST
WILLIAM ST
73
18
50
354
JOINS MAP 355

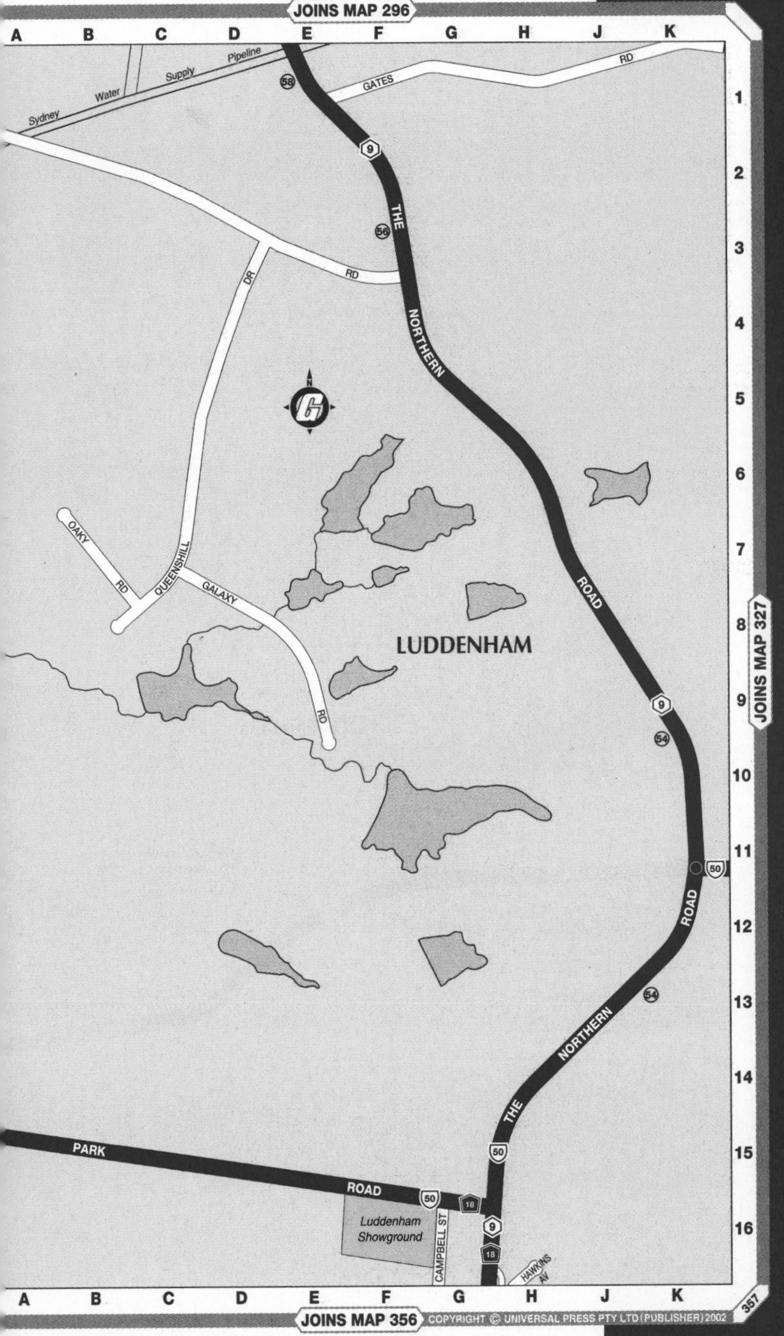
JOINS MAP 296
A B C D E F G H J K
1 2 3 4 5 6 7 8 9 10 11 12 13 14 15 16
Sydney Water Supply Pipeline
GATES RD
RD
THE NORTHERN ROAD
DR
QUEENSHILL
OAKY RD
GALAXY RD
LUDDENHAM
PARK ROAD
Luddenham Showground
CAMPBELL ST
HAWKINS AV
JOINS MAP 327
JOINS MAP 356

MAP 327

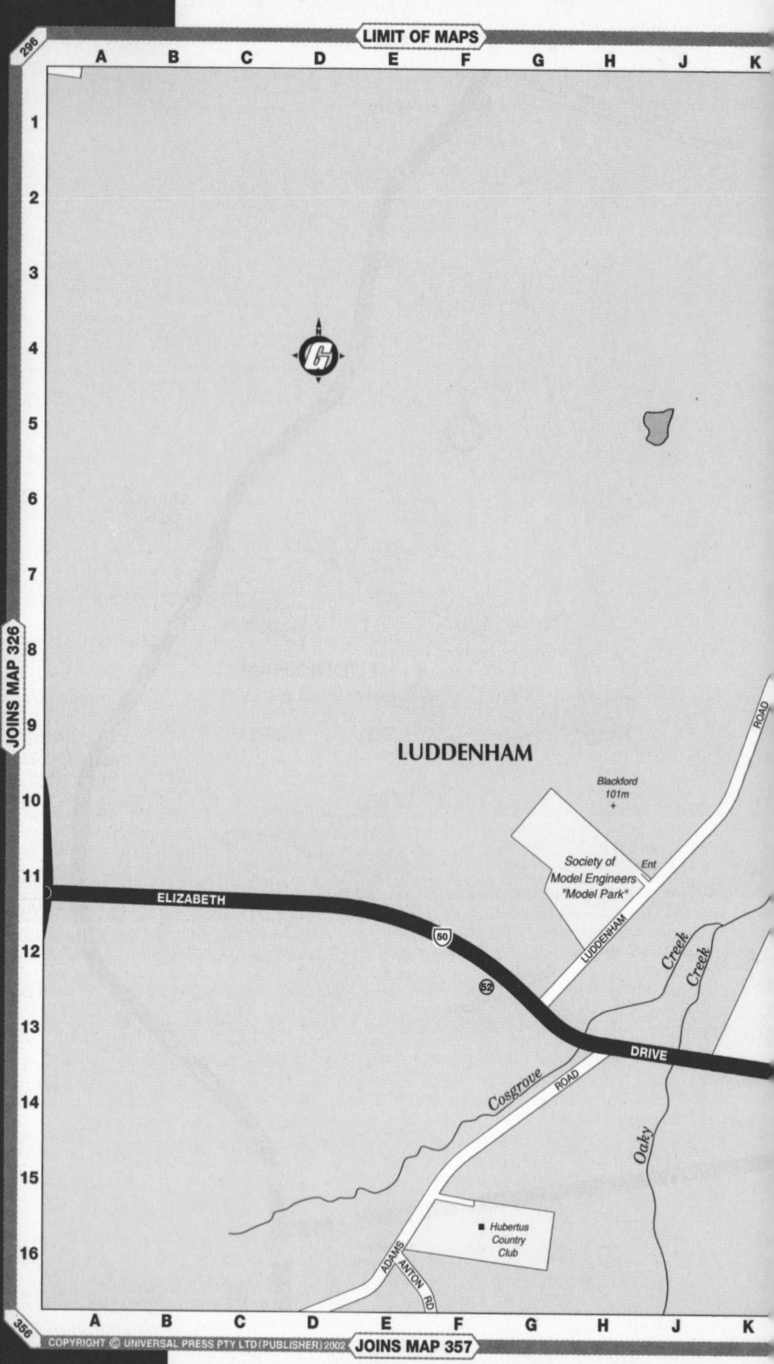

LIMIT OF MAPS
296
A
B
C
D
E
F
G
H
J
K
1
2
3
4
5
6
7
8
9
10
11
12
13
14
15
16
JOINS MAP 326
LUDDENHAM
Blackford
101m
Society of
Model Engineers
"Model Park"
Ent
LUDDENHAM
ROAD
ELIZABETH
DRIVE
50
52
Creek
Creek
Cosgrove
ROAD
Oaky
Hubertus
Country
Club
ADAMS
ANTON
RD
356
JOINS MAP 357

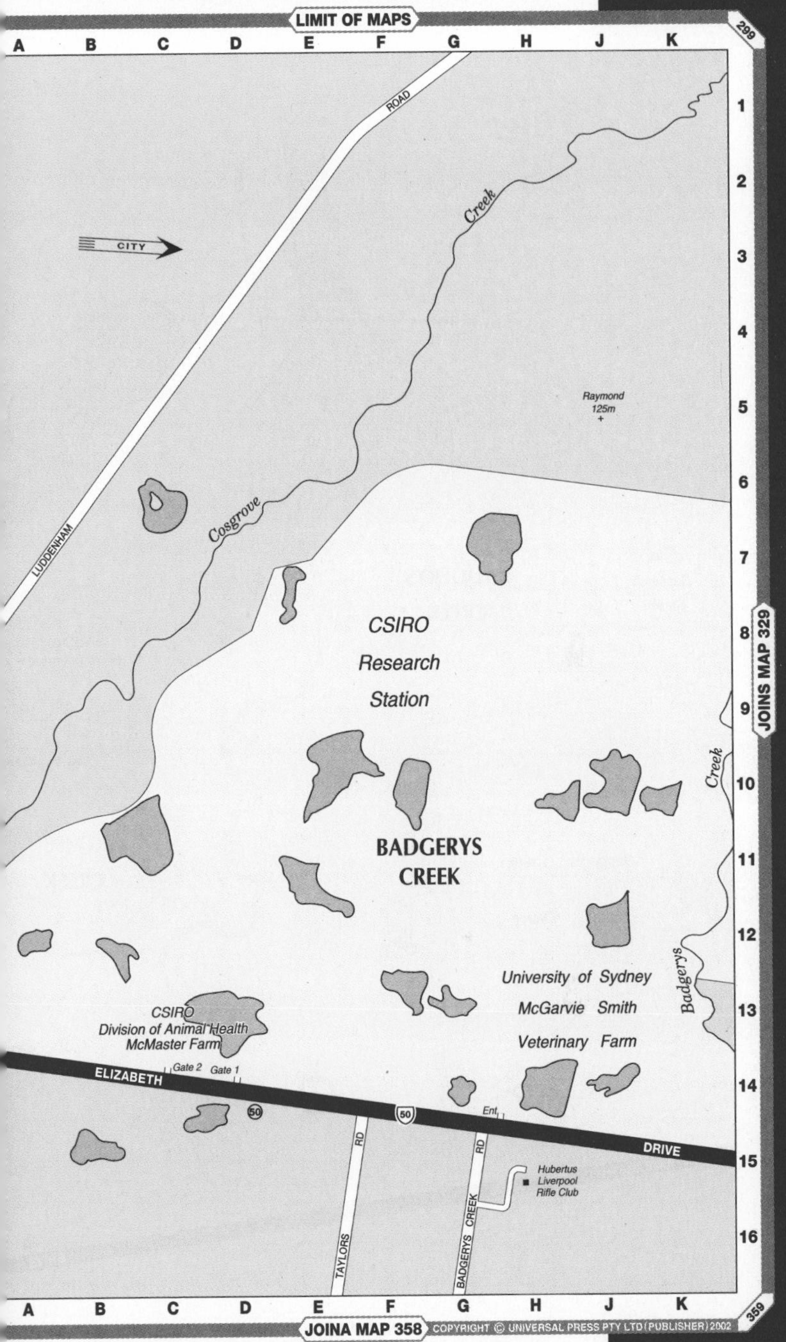
LIMIT OF MAPS
299
A
B
C
D
E
F
G
H
J
K
1
2
3
4
5
6
7
8
9
10
11
12
13
14
15
16
ROAD
LUDDENHAM
CITY
Creek
Cosgrove
Raymond
125m
CSIRO
Research
Station
JOINS MAP 329
Creek
BADGERYS
CREEK
Badgerys
University of Sydney
McGarvie Smith
Veterinary Farm
CSIRO
Division of Animal Health
McMaster Farm
Gate 2
Gate 1
ELIZABETH
50
50
Ent
DRIVE
RD
RD
Hubertus
Liverpool
Rifle Club
TAYLORS
BADGERYS CREEK
A
B
C
D
E
F
G
H
J
K
JOINA MAP 358
359

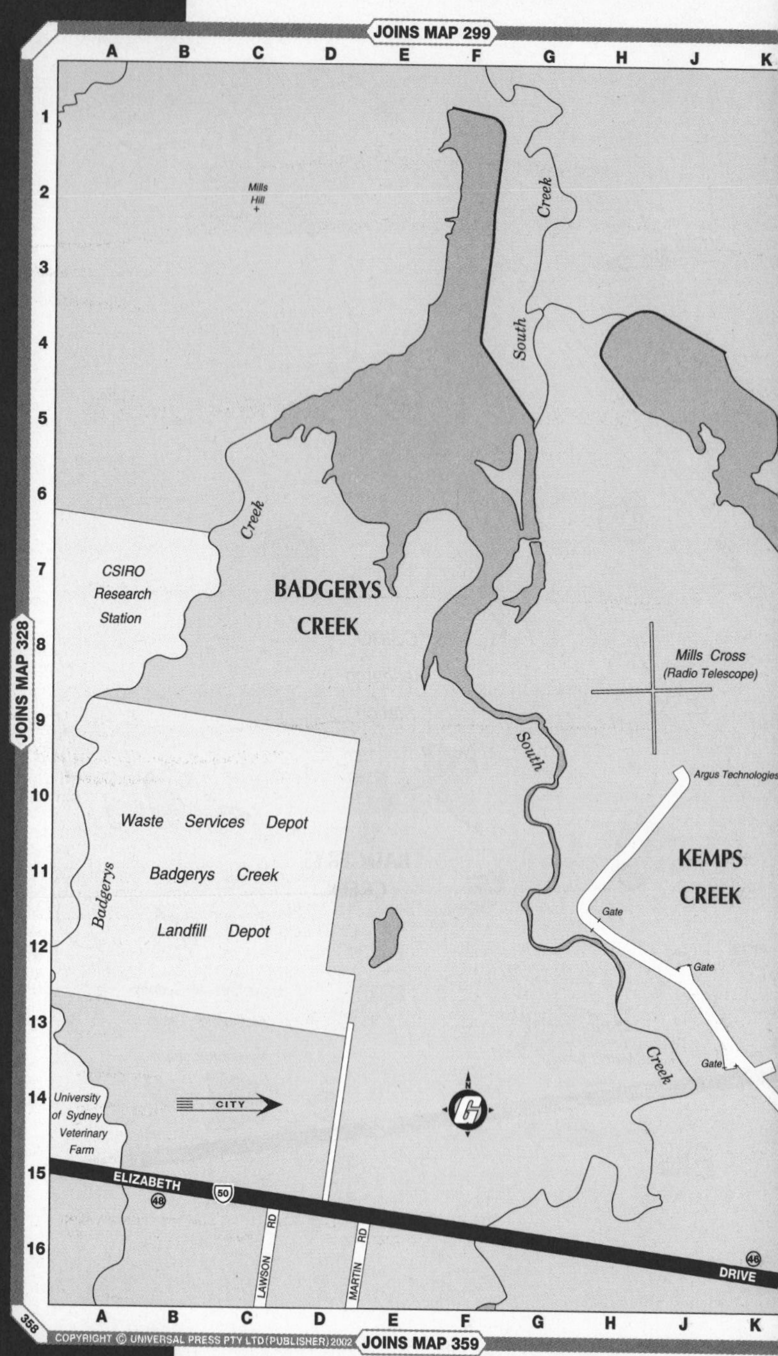
JOINS MAP 299
A
B
C
D
E
F
G
H
J
K
1
2
3
4
5
6
7
8
9
10
11
12
13
14
15
16
JOINS MAP 328
Mills Hill
South Creek
Creek
CSIRO Research Station
BADGERYS CREEK
Mills Cross (Radio Telescope)
South
Argus Technologies
Waste Services Depot
Badgerys Creek
Landfill Depot
KEMPS CREEK
Badgerys
Gate
Gate
Creek
Gate
University of Sydney Veterinary Farm
CITY
ELIZABETH
50
48
LAWSON RD
MARTIN RD
46
DRIVE
JOINS MAP 359

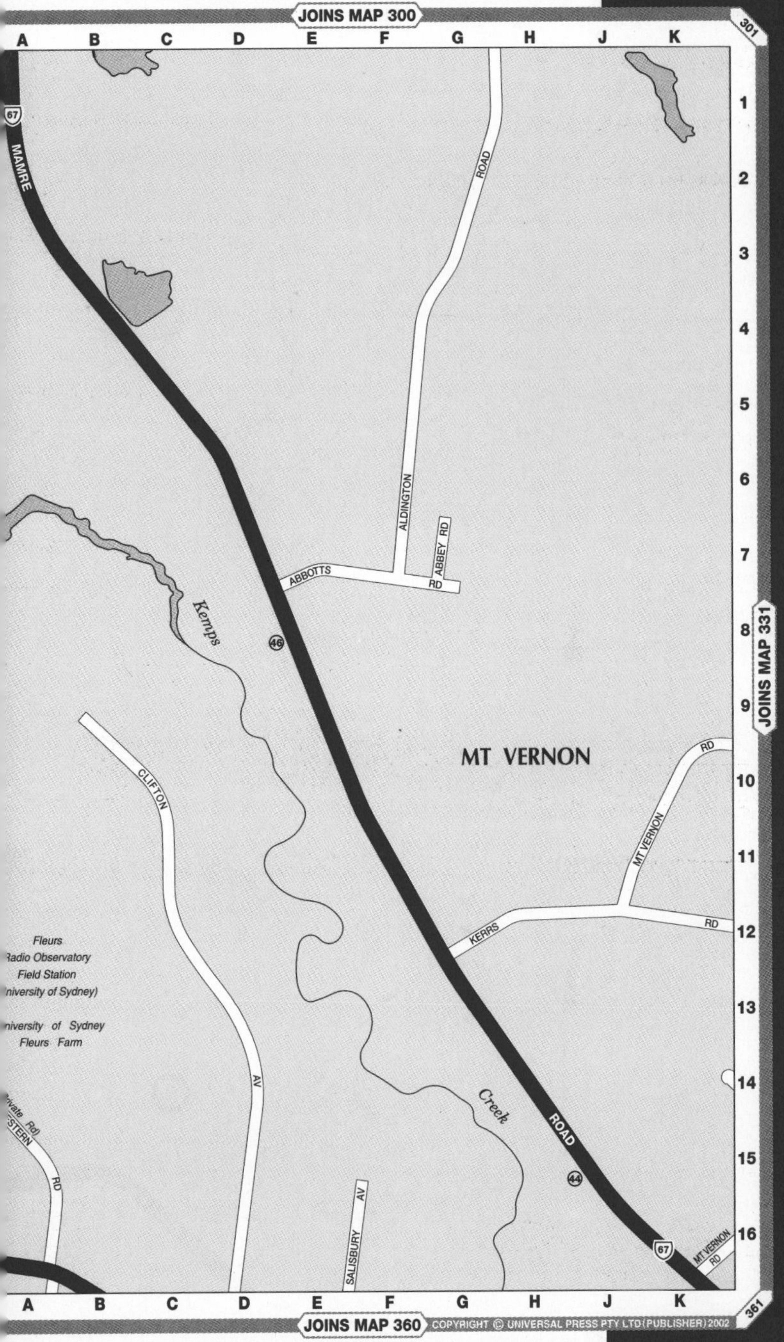
JOINS MAP 300
301
A B C D E F G H J K
1 2 3 4 5 6 7 8 9 10 11 12 13 14 15 16
67
MAMRE
ROAD
ALDINGTON
ABBEY RD
ABBOTTS
RD
Kemps
46
JOINS MAP 331
MT VERNON
RD
MT VERNON
CLIFTON
KERRS
RD
Fleurs
Radio Observatory
Field Station
(University of Sydney)
University of Sydney
Fleurs Farm
AV
Creek
ROAD
44
(Private Rd)
WESTERN
RD
SALISBURY
AV
67
MT VERNON
RD
A B C D E F G H J K
JOINS MAP 360
361

MAP 331

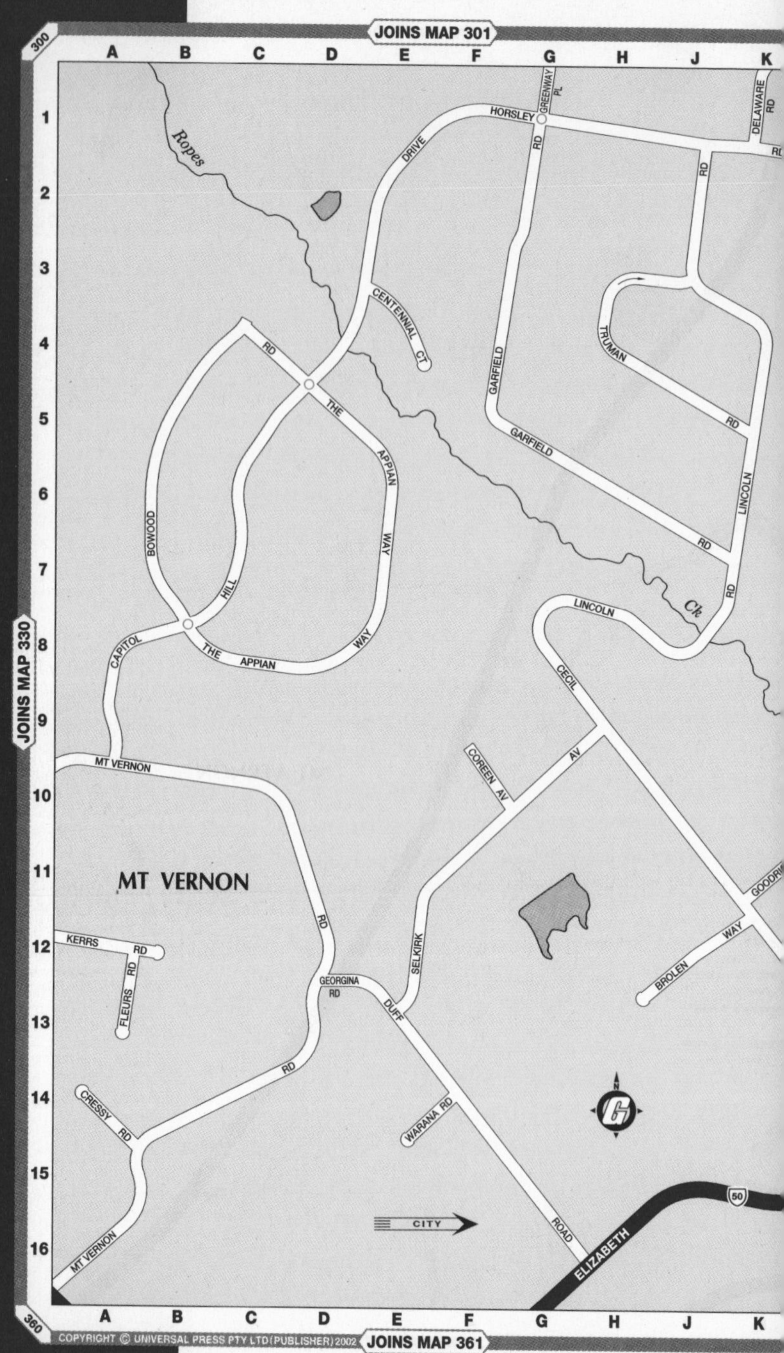
JOINS MAP 301
JOINS MAP 330
JOINS MAP 361
300
360
A B C D E F G H J K
1 2 3 4 5 6 7 8 9 10 11 12 13 14 15 16
Ropes
Ck
HORSLEY
GREENWAY PL
DELAWARE RD
DRIVE
RD
CENTENNIAL CT
TRUMAN RD
GARFIELD RD
GARFIELD
LINCOLN RD
LINCOLN
THE APPIAN WAY
HILL RD
BOWOOD
CAPITOL
MT VERNON
MT VERNON RD
CECIL AV
COREEN AV
SELKIRK
GOODRICH
BROLEN WAY
KERRS RD
FLEURS RD
GEORGINA RD
DUFF ROAD
WARANA RD
CRESSY RD
MT VERNON
CITY
ELIZABETH
50

JOINS MAP 302

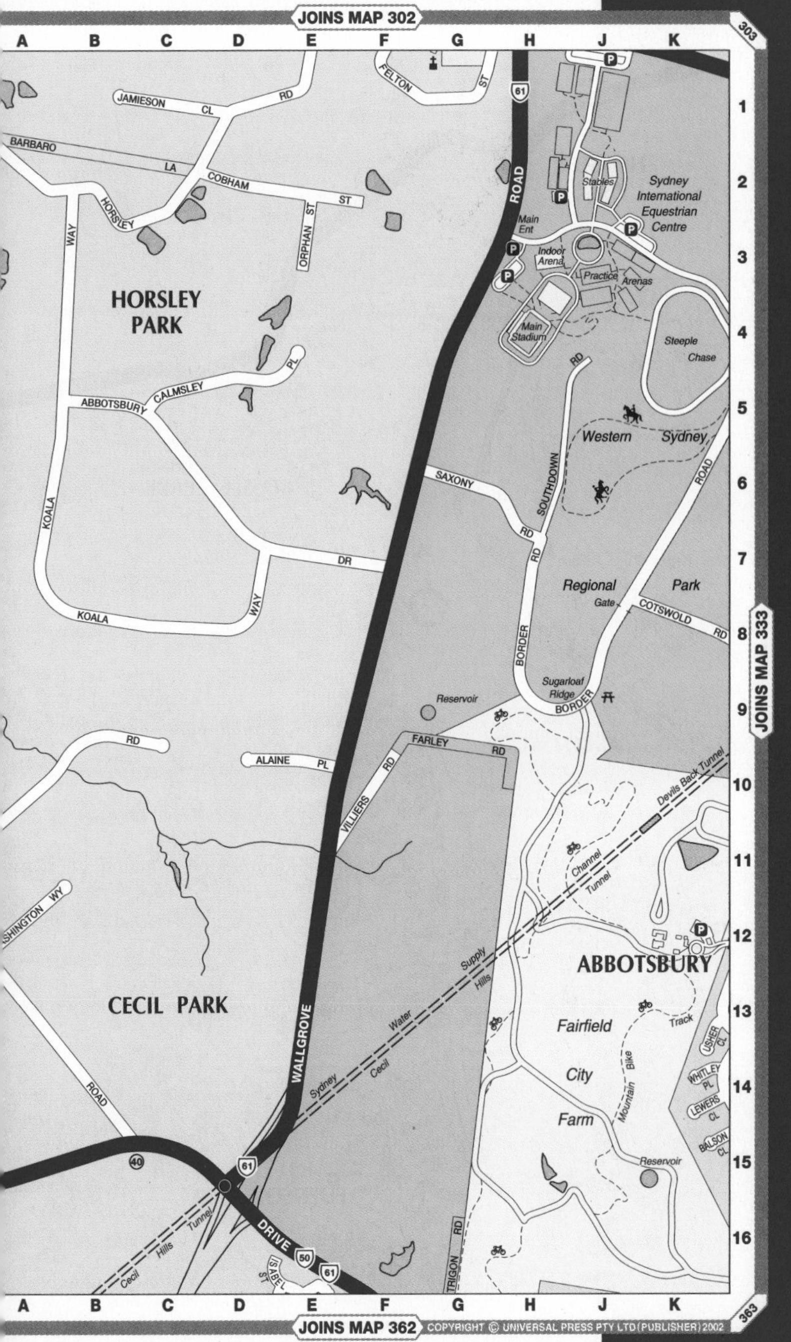

JOINS MAP 362

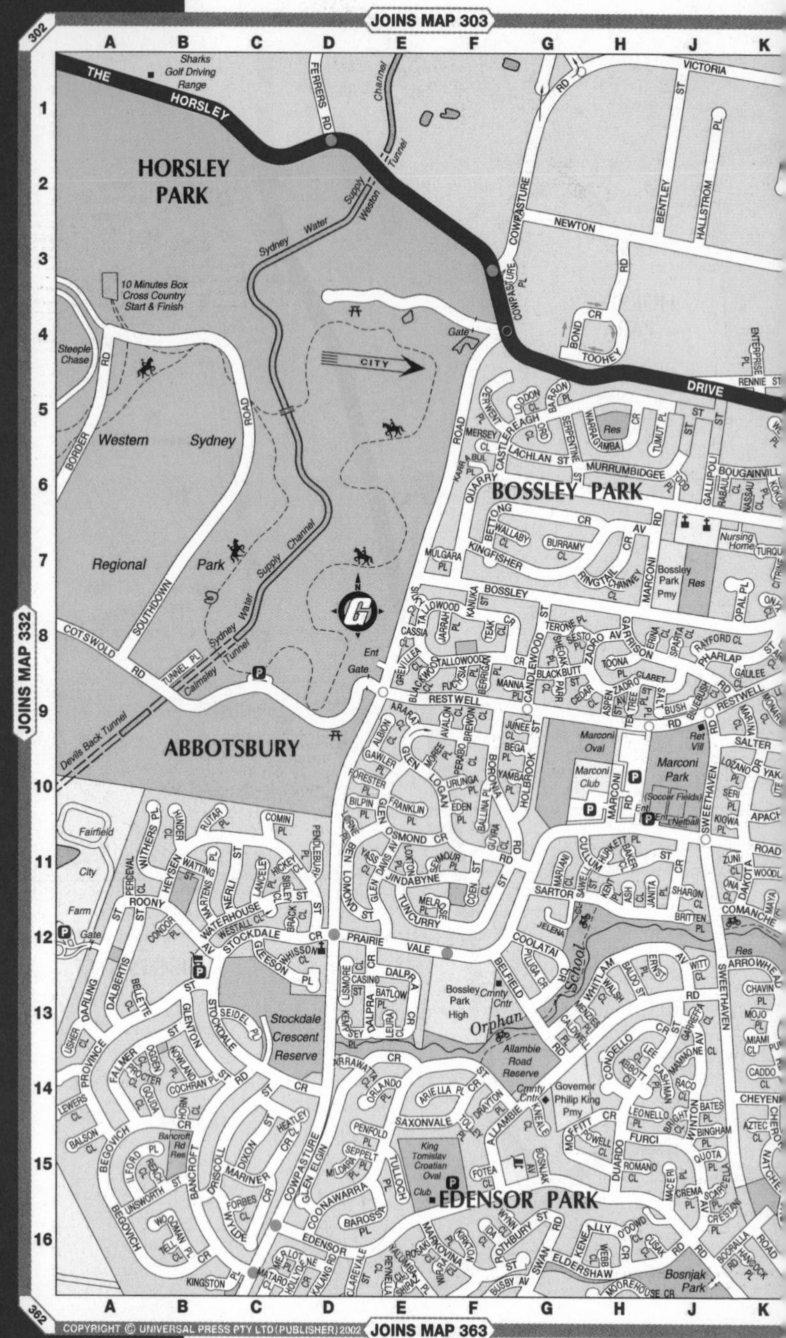
JOINS MAP 303
JOINS MAP 332
JOINS MAP 363
302
362
A B C D E F G H J K
1 2 3 4 5 6 7 8 9 10 11 12 13 14 15 16
THE HORSLEY DRIVE
Sharks Golf Driving Range
HORSLEY PARK
BOSSLEY PARK
ABBOTSBURY
EDENSOR PARK
Western Sydney Regional Park
10 Minutes Box Cross Country Start & Finish
Steeple Chase
Sydney Water Supply Channel
Weston Tunnel
Calmsley Tunnel
Devils Back Tunnel
CITY
Gate
Ent Gate
Fairfield City Farm
Stockdale Crescent Reserve
Bossley Park High
Allambie Road Reserve
Governor Philip King Pmy
King Tomislav Croatian Oval
Club
Marconi Oval
Marconi Club
Marconi Park
(Soccer Fields)
Netball
Ret Vill
Bossley Park Pmy
Nursing Home
Res
Bancroft Rd Res
Bosnjak Park
Orphan School
Cmnty Cntr
COPYRIGHT © UNIVERSAL PRESS PTY LTD (PUBLISHER) 2002

JOINS MAP 304

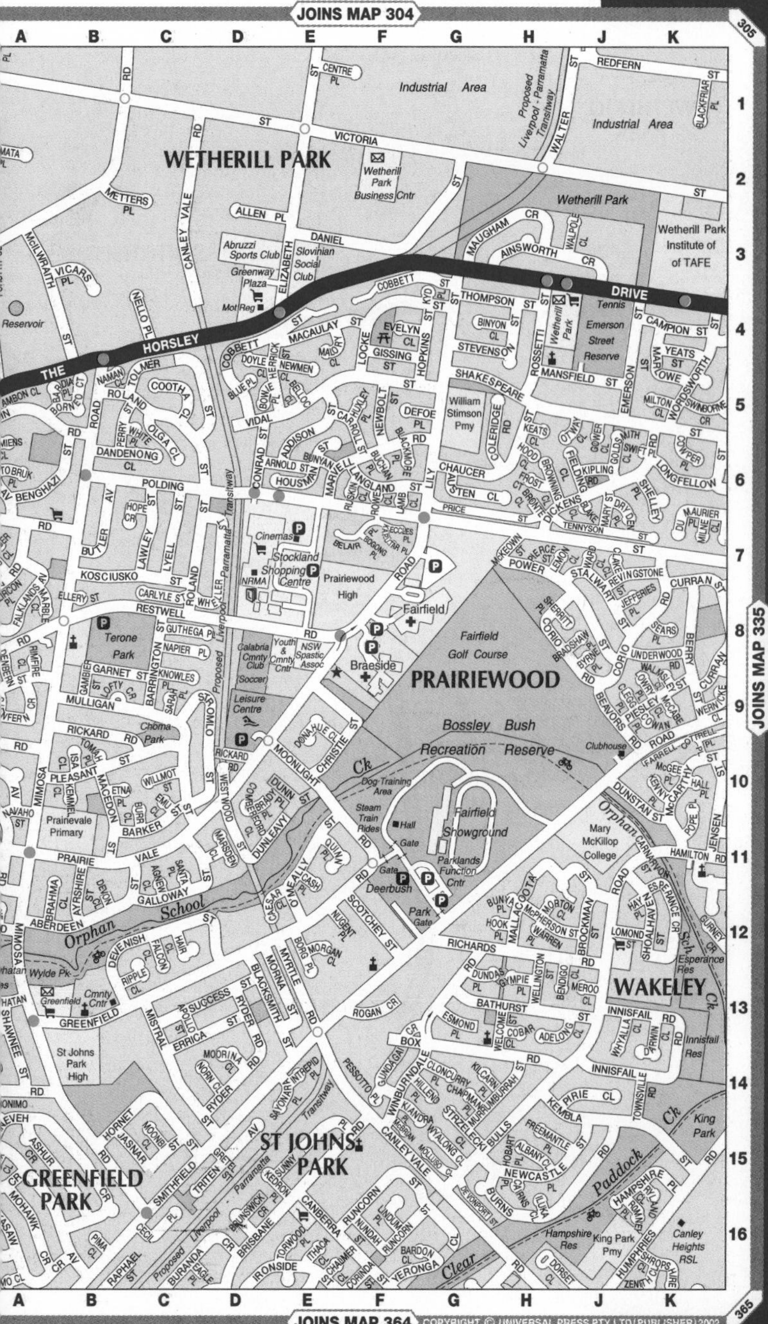

JOINS MAP 364

JOINS MAP 305
JOINS MAP 334
JOINS MAP 365
304
364
A
B
C
D
E
F
G
H
J
K
1
2
3
4
5
6
7
8
9
10
11
12
13
14
15
16
WETHERILL PARK
SMITHFIELD
FAIRFIELD WEST
CANLEY HEIGHTS
CANLEY VALE
Vehicle Inspection Station
Wetherill Park Inst of TAFE
Victoria St Pk
Smithfield Cemetery
Queens Square
Prospect
Long
Smithfield Primary
RSL
Footbridge
Thorley Park
Gipps Park
Charles Park
Smithfield West Pmy
Mosque
Cmnty Hall
Brenan Park
Baseball
Tennis
Prospect View Park
Motor Reg
Westfields Sports High
Primary
Avery Park
Fairvale High
Orphan School
King Park
Goodacre Reserve
Brian Wunsch Centre
Council Office
Netball
Endeavour Sports Reserve
No.1
No.2
No.3
No.4
No.5
Creek
Rosford Street
Reserve
REDFERN
BLACKFRIAR PL
VERRELL ST
ROSFORD
EYRE
RADNOR
RHONDDA
LONG
BRITTON ST
CHIFLEY
GALTON
VICTORIA
HINKLER
CLARENCE ST
MEGAN AV
SHAMROCK
DONEGAL AV
KILKENNY AV
GALWAY PL
KINGSFORD ST
HART ST
MOIR
HASSALL
SHARLAND
HELEN
VONN AV
WETHERILL ST
HAYWOOD CL
GRAY PL
THE HORSLEY DRIVE
BRONSDON ST
NEVILLE
CASANDA
GRADY GDNS
CANARA PL
CARTELA CR
ROWLEY ST
JANE
BRENAN
LINDSAY AV
JANICE AV
JUSTIN
O'CONNELL
MARKET
CAHILL ST
BRAESIDE AV
BEAUMONT
CHAMBERLAIN DR
BROWN
CHARLES
DUBLIN
IBSEN PL
WORDSWORTH
SWINBORNE
GOGOL PL
HOMER PL
LODGE PL
CRANE PL
SHAKESPEARE ST
LONGFELLOW
PLATO PL
THACKERAY CL
DU MAURIER PL
MILNE CL
WYATT CL
GEMOORE
DUNKLEY ST
GIPPS
ROSE ST
BENELONG AV
CRAIG ST
BOURKE
OXFORD
CLANCY ST
BRENAN
FARGOS
GREEN
MORRIS
CUMBERLAND
SMITHFIELD
GUMTREE WY
ALEXANDER
ROSEMONT AV
JENNIFER PL
LEAH CL
JESSIE
RESERVE
SLENDER AV
BOULEVARDE
ROSSITER
MURRAY
POLDING
NESBITT
CURRAN
WEBBER PL
KAVENAGH CL
WATTS PL
GARMENT
KING
BRAMLEY
BRAELYN
CORRYONG ST
ISIS ST
WAVERLEY ST
TELFORD
BRENTWOOD
ROAD
CLAYTON
BEST PL
WERNICKE
SMITHFIELD
COTTRELL
BUCKLEY
AKFORD PL
TULIP GR
LAVENDER
JORDAN
REED
DAMPIER
EDEL
MAGELLAN
PDE
QUIROS
MUSGRAVE
AINSLIE
BANDA PL
KIMBERLEY CR
EACHAM
FROME
TYRELL
BODALLA
KARABAR
KIHILLA
BEEMERA
MONTAGUE
NILE
ANN
STANBRO
McCARTHY
SADLIER
TAMAR PL
PERA PL
LEICHHARDT AV
DE WITT
SIRIUS ST
NORFOLK
DIEMAN
BRYANT
VANCOUVER
SELWYN
HAMERSLEY
CAMBEWARRA RD
ATHERTON
SABA ST
GIRRA ST
STACEY
PERCY
LIGAR
EVANS
STATION
CAMDEN
JENSEN
DALTON PL
HARTOG AV
JANSZ PL
BAUDIN
TASMAN
POOL PL
FLINDERS ST
MACDONNELL AV
WARRUMBUNGLE
LAWFORD ST
NOELENE
THROSBY
STELLA
DAWSON
STANLEY
LINDA
HAMILTON
CURREY PL
BOOTH
SULLIVAN
DALZIEL
HIRST
GURNEY
DWYER CL
DALEY
LYNESTA AV
LENTON AV
SAVERY PL
WRIGHT
KENDALL
PATERSON
HARPUR
CORONA
JULIUS ST
ROYLSTON
GREENVALE
SHAW PL
PALMERSTON RD
NEW CAMBRIDGE ST
CANOBOLAS
GARDINER
NANGAR CR
RAWSON
GARRAN
ADINA CL
ORAN PL
NATALIE
CAMBRIDGE CR
JAFFA
TRIPOLI
MELLICK
SCARFE
ZARLEE ST
THORNEY
BEALE
HAMBLY
GREGORY
CHADWICK
HAWKESBURY
GOODACRE
ROBBINS
NEPEAN
LOMBARD
ROSINA
MADELINE
MARGARET
MAUD
ELIZA
EUSTACE
RICHARD
HUBER
KALORA AV
WENDEN
WOLSELEY
PARKER ST
KAMBALA
BARAGOOLA
BARBARA PL
HUMPHRIES RD
AMELIA CR
KAROON AV
ROSEDALE
FOXLOW
HARDEN
AVOCA
TENELLA
WYHARBOROUGH
EDWARD PL
HOLMAN
BEELAR
STROKER
ANDREW AV
CHELSEA
ABEL
OAKLEA PL
PARKLEA
GLENLEA
AVONLEA
KINGSLEA PL
CAMBRIDGE (CUMBERLAND HWY) ST
INGSLEA PL
FERNLEA PL
FERNGROVE
CARRE AV
CLAREMONT AV
SWAGER PL
PAUL CR
SALISBURY
CLARENCE
DUKE
GLADSTONE
CHATHAM
PITT
THE
MALABAR
DELAMERE
CARDWELL
AVENEL ST
Herit
Fairv Pr

JOINS MAP 306

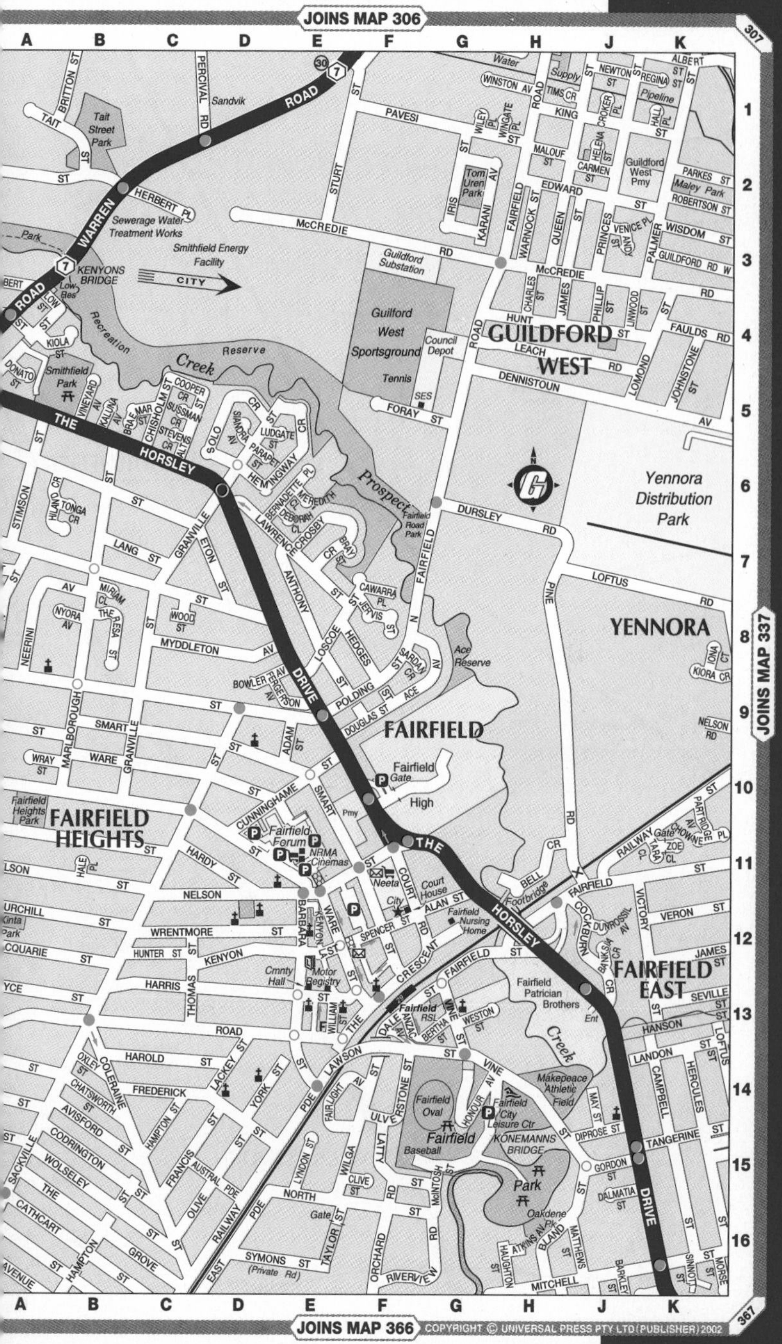

JOINS MAP 337

JOINS MAP 366

MAP 337

JOINS MAP 307

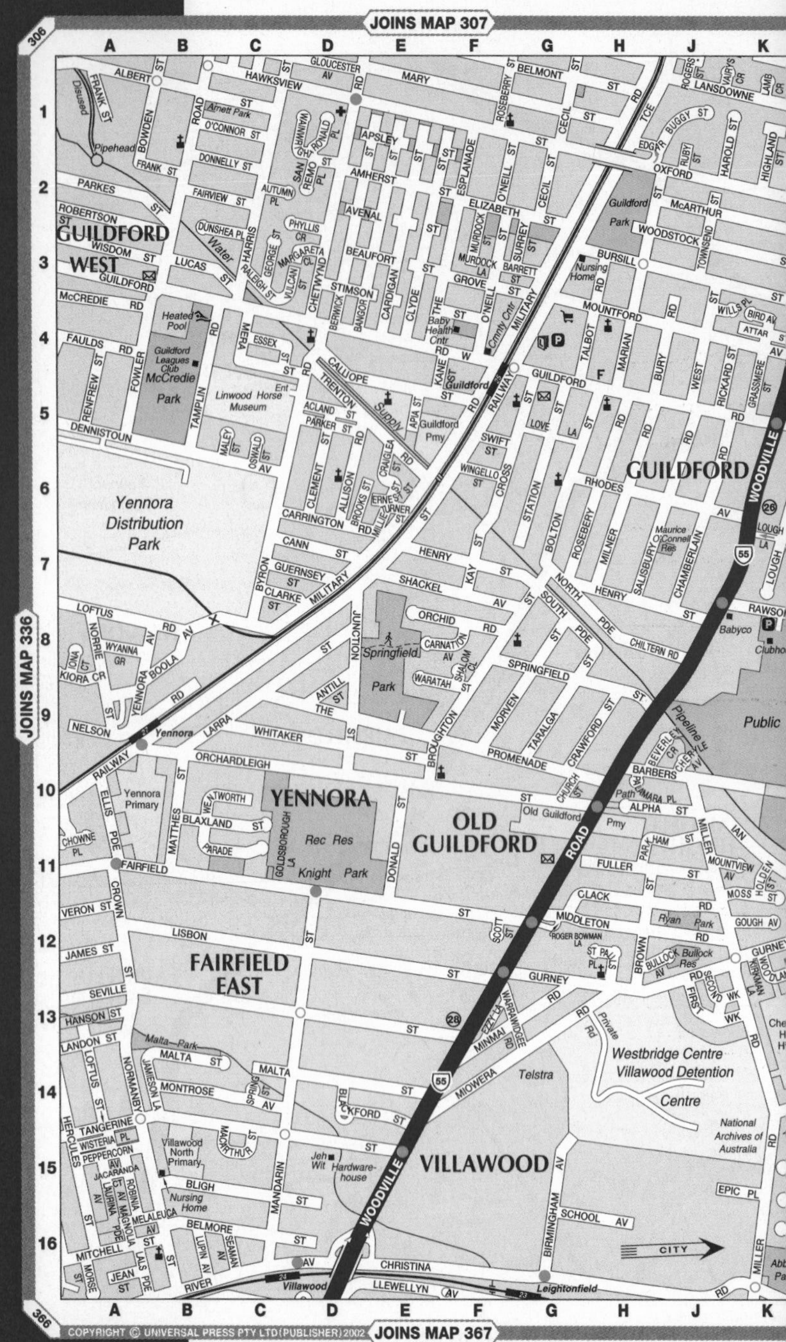

JOINS MAP 336

JOINS MAP 367

JOINS MAP 308

JOINS MAP 368

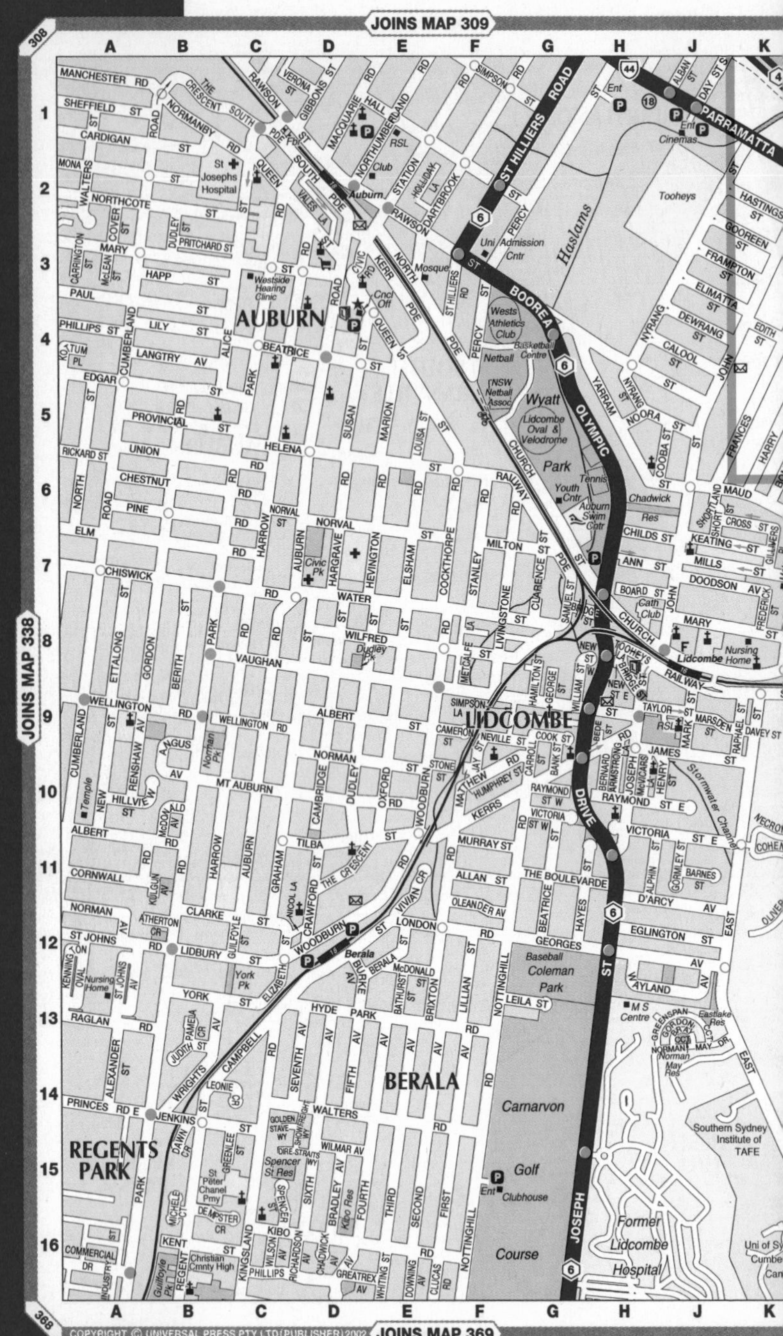
JOINS MAP 309
JOINS MAP 338
JOINS MAP 369
308
368
AUBURN
LIDCOMBE
BERALA
REGENTS PARK
Auburn
Lidcombe
Berala
St Josephs Hospital
Westside Hearing Clinic
Cncl Off
RSL
Club
Mosque
Uni Admission Cntr
Haslams
Tooheys
Cinemas
Wests Athletics Club
Basketball Centre
Netball
NSW Netball Assoc
Wyatt Park
Lidcombe Oval & Velodrome
Youth Cntr
Tennis
Auburn Swim Cntr
Chadwick Res
Civic Pk
Dudley Pk
Norman Pk
Cath Club
Nursing Home
Temple
York Pk
Baseball Coleman Park
Carnarvon Golf Course
Clubhouse
M S Centre
Eastlake Res
Norman May Res
Southern Sydney Institute of TAFE
Former Lidcombe Hospital
Stormwater Channel
Spencer St Res
Kibo Res
St Peter Chanel Pmy
Christian Cmnty High
Guilfoyle Pk
ST HILLIERS ROAD
PARRAMATTA
BOOREA
OLYMPIC DRIVE
JOSEPH ST

JOINS MAP 310

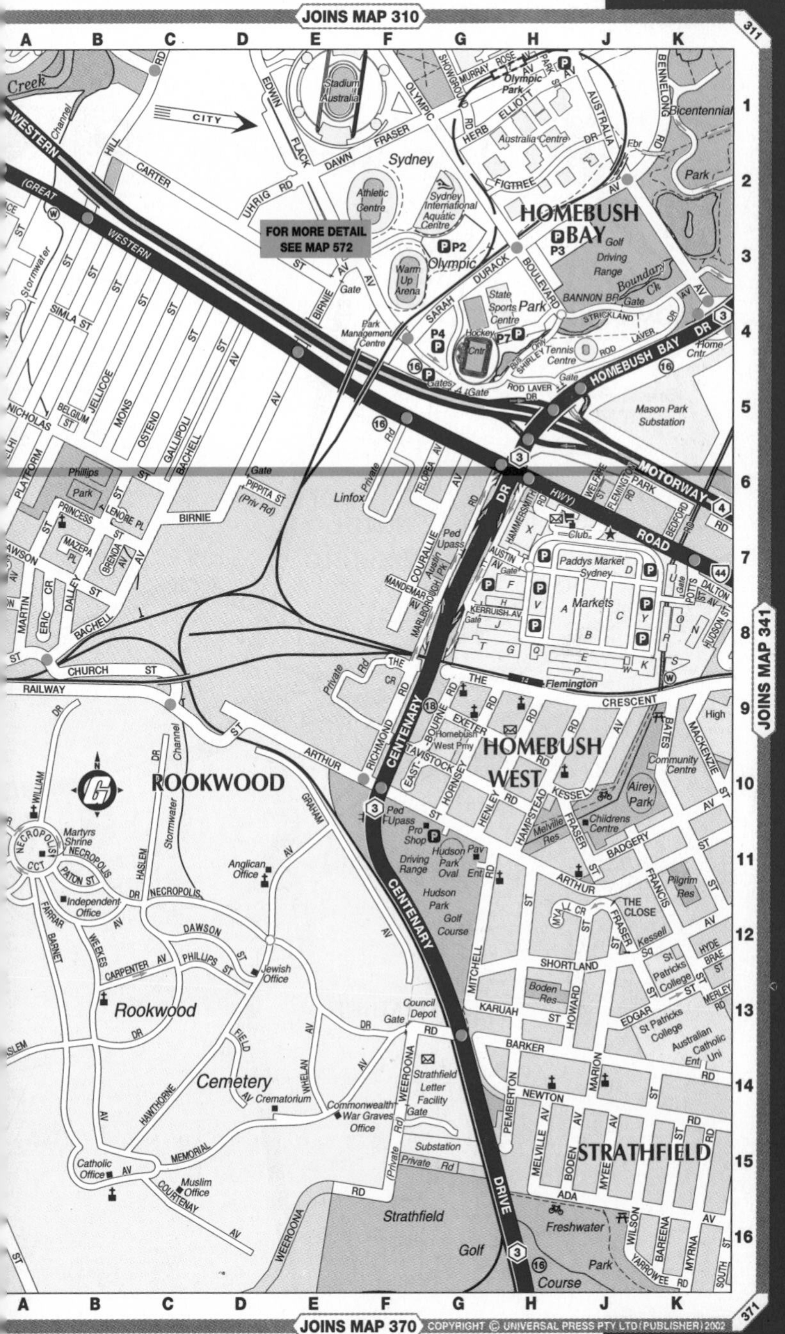

JOINS MAP 341

JOINS MAP 370

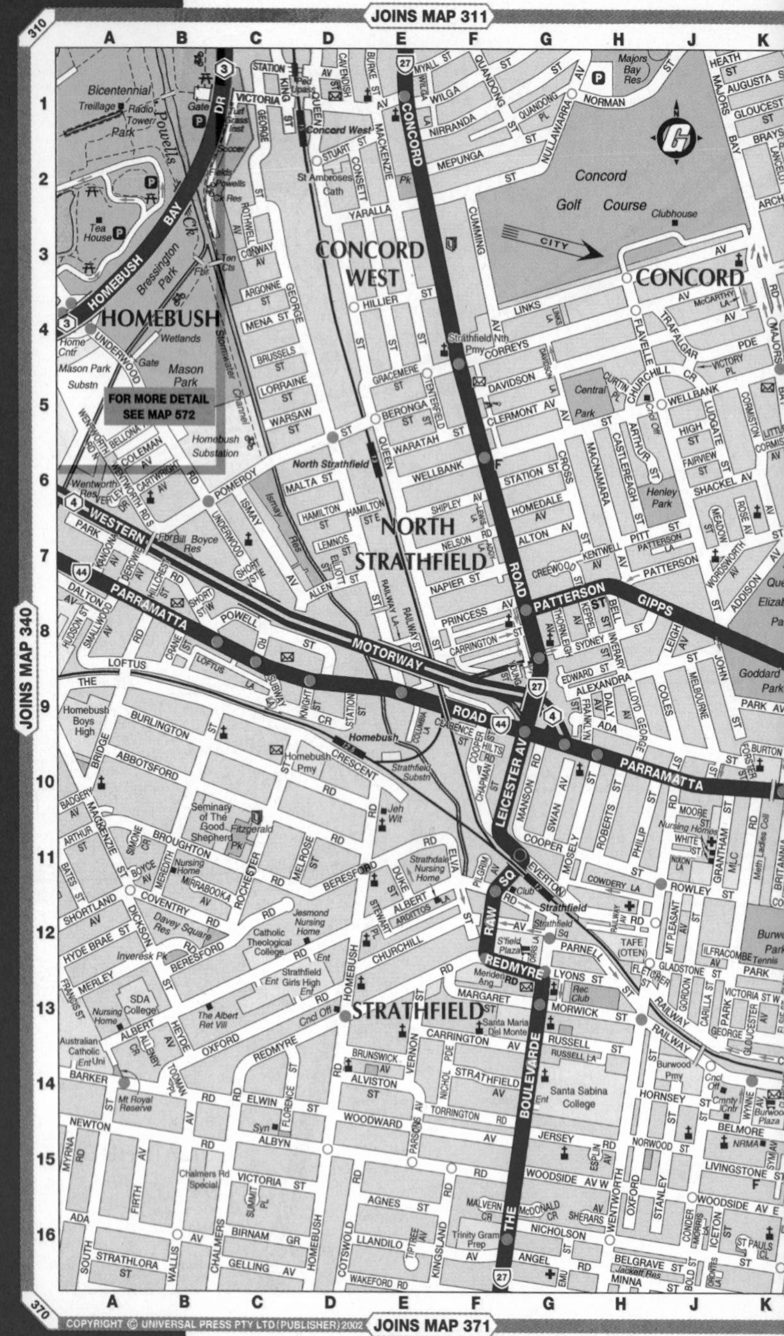
JOINS MAP 311
JOINS MAP 340
JOINS MAP 371
CONCORD WEST
CONCORD
HOMEBUSH
NORTH STRATHFIELD
STRATHFIELD
Concord Golf Course
Bicentennial Park
Mason Park
FOR MORE DETAIL SEE MAP 572
PARRAMATTA RD
WESTERN MOTORWAY
CONCORD RD
THE BOULEVARDE
HOMEBUSH BAY DR

JOINS MAP 312

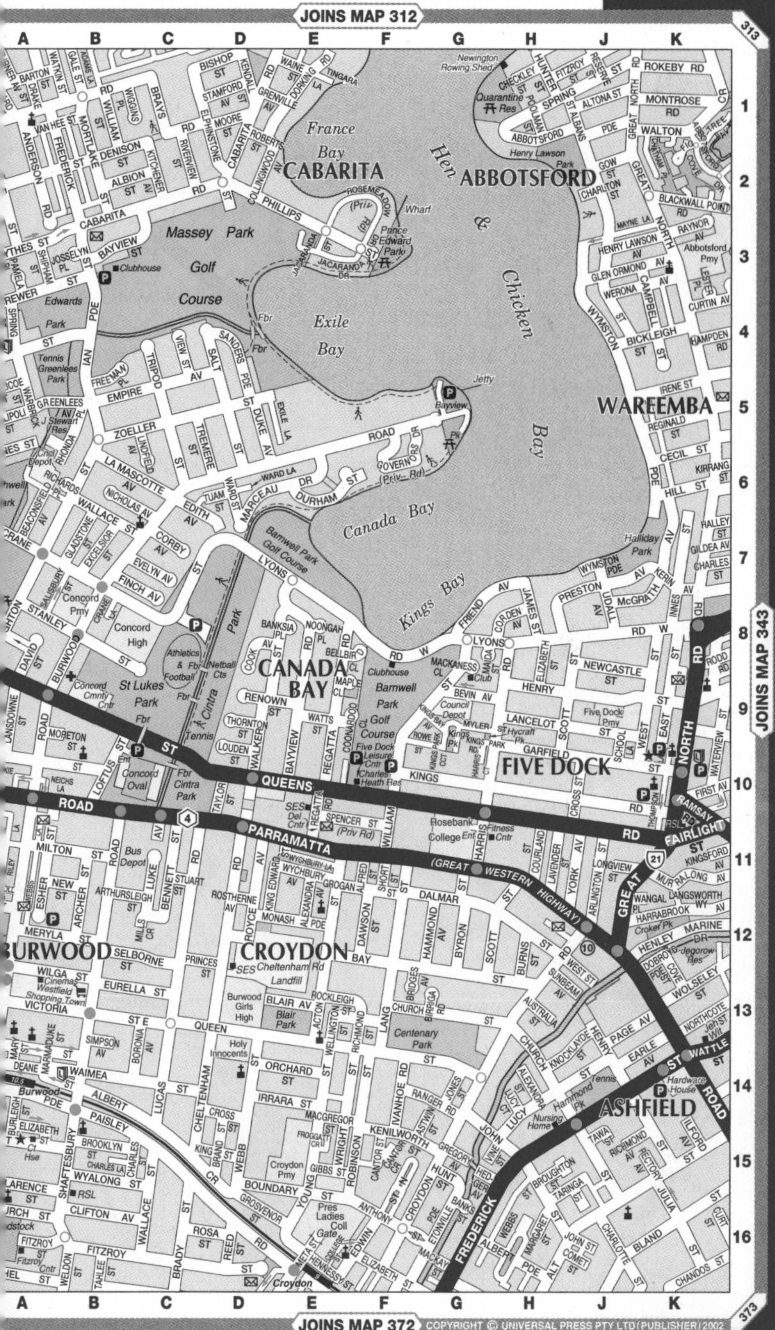

JOINS MAP 372

JOINS MAP 313

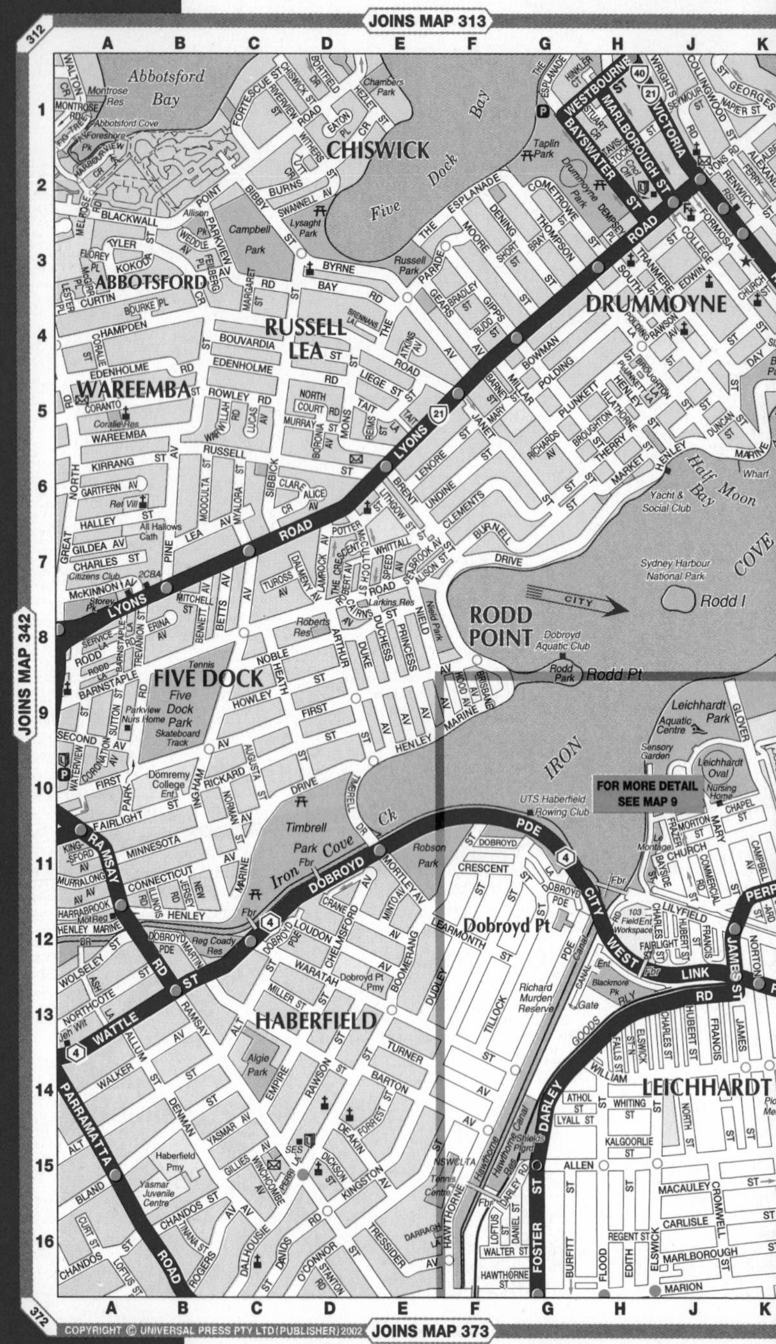

JOINS MAP 373

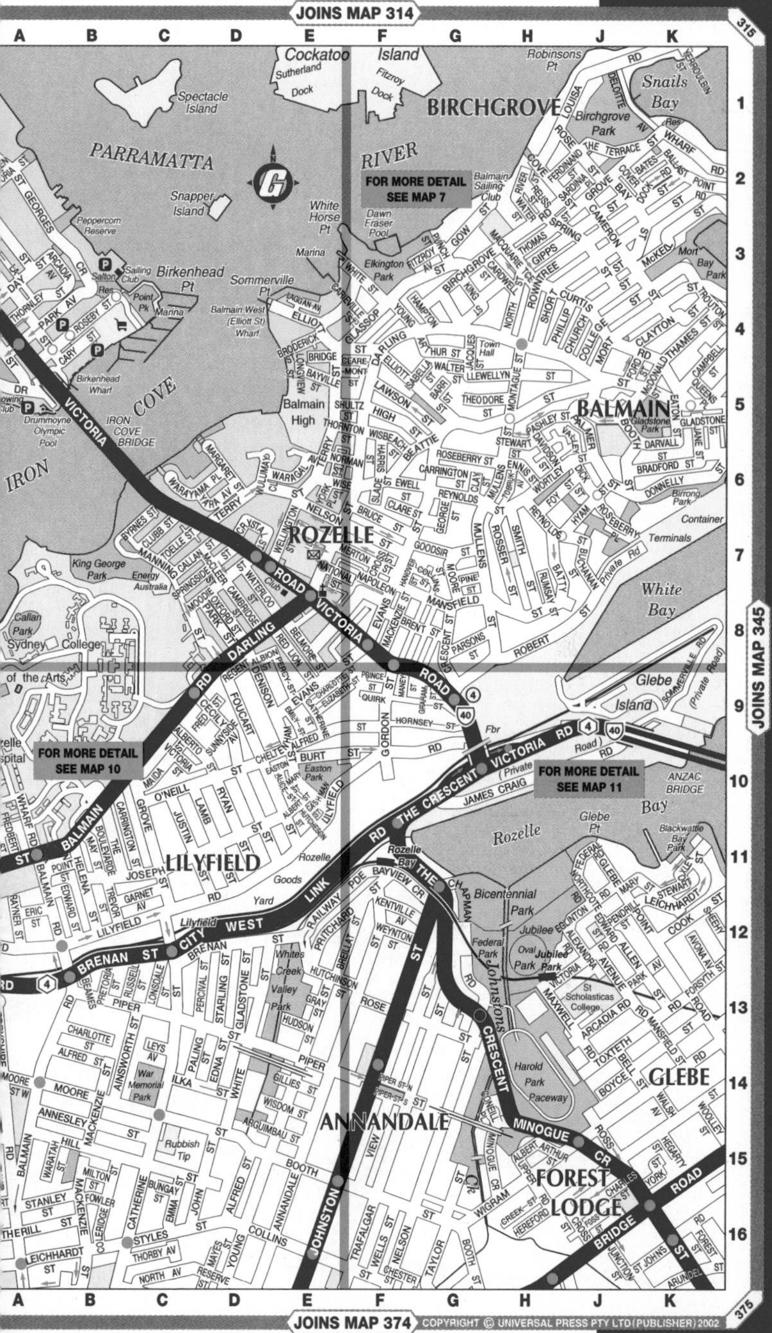
JOINS MAP 314
315
A B C D E F G H J K
1 2 3 4 5 6 7 8 9 10 11 12 13 14 15 16
Cockatoo Island
Sutherland Dock
Fitzroy Dock
Spectacle Island
BIRCHGROVE
Birchgrove Park
Snails Bay
Robinsons Pt
PARRAMATTA
RIVER
FOR MORE DETAIL SEE MAP 7
Balmain Sailing Club
Snapper Island
White Horse Pt
Dawn Fraser Pool
Peppercorn Reserve
Marina
Elkington Park
Salton Sailing Club
Birkenhead Pt
Sommerville Pt
Point Pk
Balmain West (Elliott St) Wharf
Birkenhead Wharf
Mort Bay Park
IRON COVE
Drummoyne Olympic Pool
IRON COVE BRIDGE
Balmain High
Town Hall
BALMAIN
Gladstone Park
Birrong Park
Container Terminals
White Bay
VICTORIA ROAD
ROZELLE
King George Park
Energy Australia
Callan Park
Sydney College of the Arts
DARLING RD
JOINS MAP 345
Glebe Island
FOR MORE DETAIL SEE MAP 10
FOR MORE DETAIL SEE MAP 11
Easton Park
THE CRESCENT
ANZAC BRIDGE
Rozelle Bay
Glebe Pt
Blackwattle Bay Park
LILYFIELD
Rozelle Goods Yard
CITY WEST LINK
BRENAN ST
Bicentennial Park
Jubilee Park
Federal Park
Jubilee Oval
St Scholasticas College
Whites Creek Valley Park
War Memorial Park
Rubbish Tip
Harold Park Paceway
GLEBE
ANNANDALE
MINOGUE CR
FOREST LODGE
BRIDGE ROAD
JOHNSTON ST
JOINS MAP 374
375

JOINS MAP 315

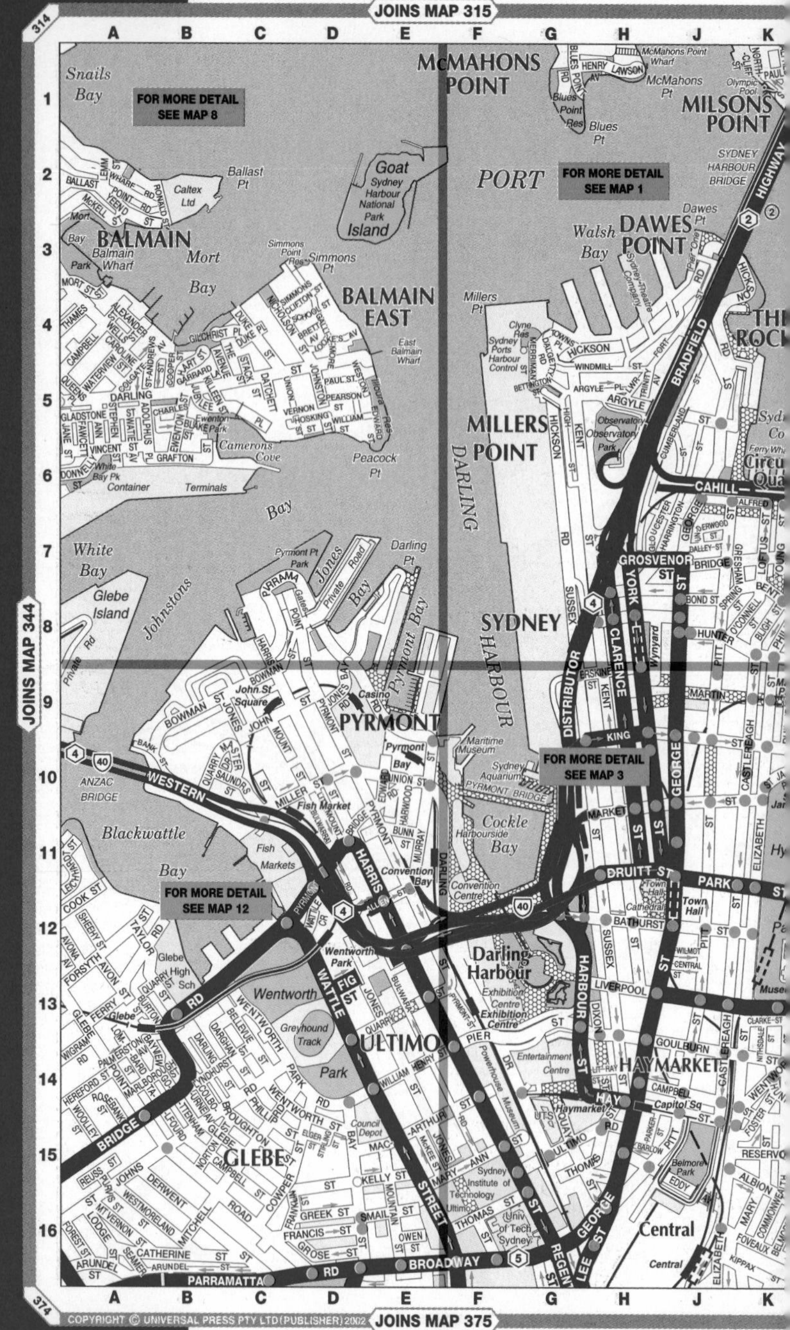

JOINS MAP 375

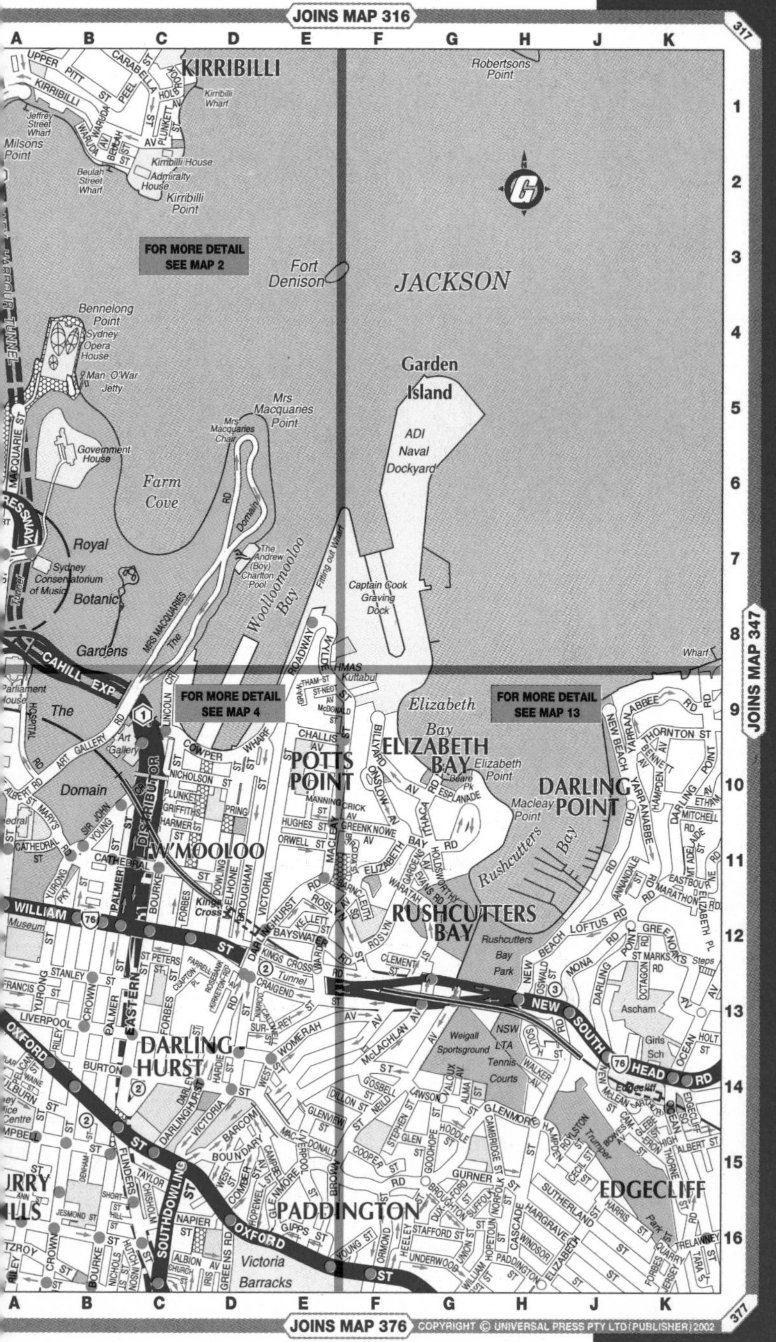
JOINS MAP 316
JOINS MAP 347
JOINS MAP 376
KIRRIBILLI
Robertsons Point
Kirribilli Wharf
Jeffrey Street Wharf
Milsons Point
Beulah Street Wharf
Kirribilli House
Admiralty House
Kirribilli Point
FOR MORE DETAIL SEE MAP 2
Fort Denison
JACKSON
Bennelong Point
Sydney Opera House
Man O'War Jetty
Garden Island
ADI Naval Dockyard
Mrs Macquaries Point
Mrs Macquaries Chair
Government House
Farm Cove
Royal
Sydney Conservatorium of Music
Botanic
Gardens
The Andrew (Boy) Charlton Pool
Woolloomooloo Bay
Fitting out Wharf
Captain Cook Graving Dock
Wharf
HMAS Kuttabul
FOR MORE DETAIL SEE MAP 4
FOR MORE DETAIL SEE MAP 13
Elizabeth Bay
ELIZABETH BAY
Elizabeth Point
POTTS POINT
Art Gallery
The Domain
W'MOOLOO
Kings Cross
Macleay Point
DARLING POINT
Rushcutters Bay
RUSHCUTTERS BAY
Rushcutters Bay Park
Museum
DARLING-HURST
Weigall Sportsground
NSW LTA Tennis Courts
Ascham
Girls Sch
Trumper Park
EDGECLIFF
PADDINGTON
Victoria Barracks
Parliament House
SURRY HILLS

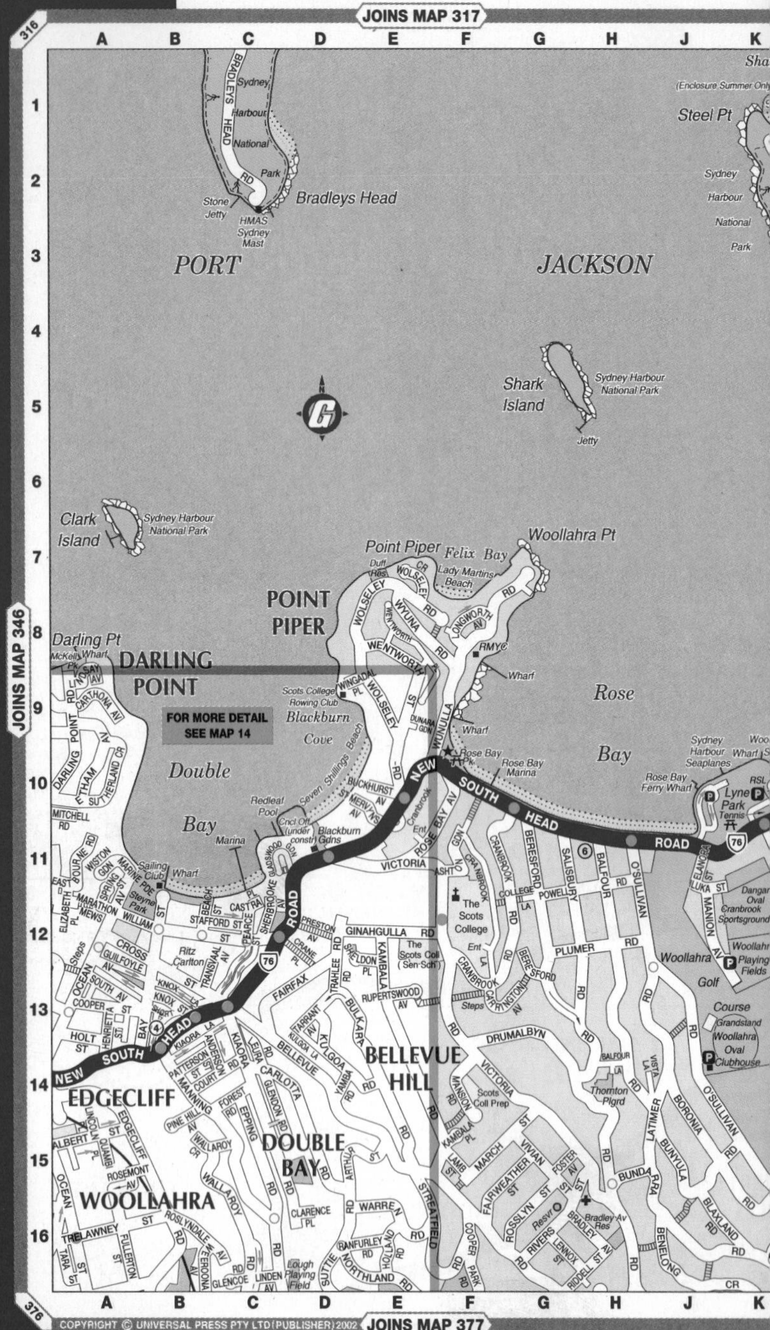
JOINS MAP 317
JOINS MAP 346
JOINS MAP 377
316
376
PORT
JACKSON
Bradleys Head
Sydney Harbour National Park
Stone Jetty
HMAS Sydney Mast
Steel Pt
Shark Island
Jetty
Clark Island
Woollahra Pt
Point Piper
Felix Bay
Lady Martins Beach
POINT PIPER
Darling Pt
DARLING POINT
FOR MORE DETAIL SEE MAP 14
Blackburn Cove
Double Bay
Rose Bay
Rose Bay Marina
Rose Bay Ferry Wharf
NEW SOUTH HEAD ROAD
The Scots College
Woollahra Golf Course
BELLEVUE HILL
EDGECLIFF
DOUBLE BAY
WOOLLAHRA
Thornton Plgrd
Bradley Av Res

JOINS MAP 318

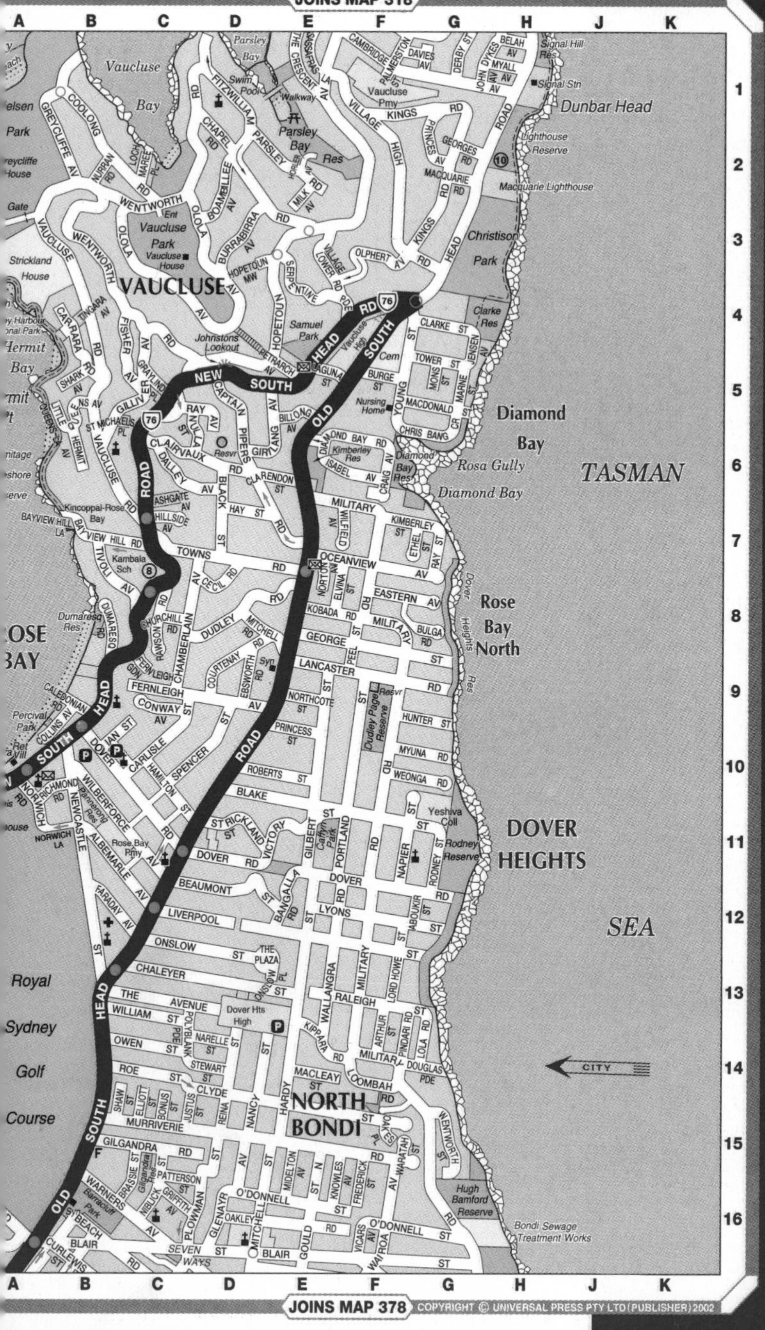

JOINS MAP 378

JOINS MAP 323

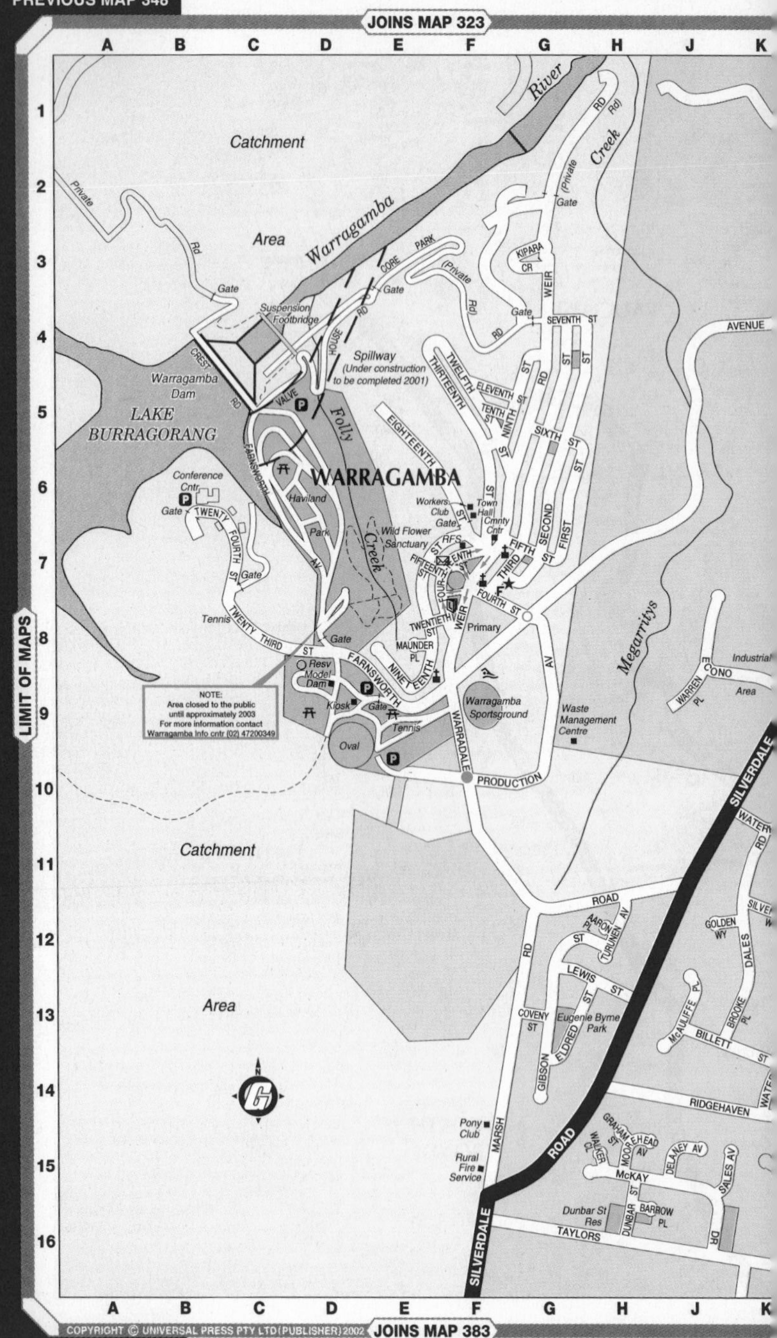

JOINS MAP 383

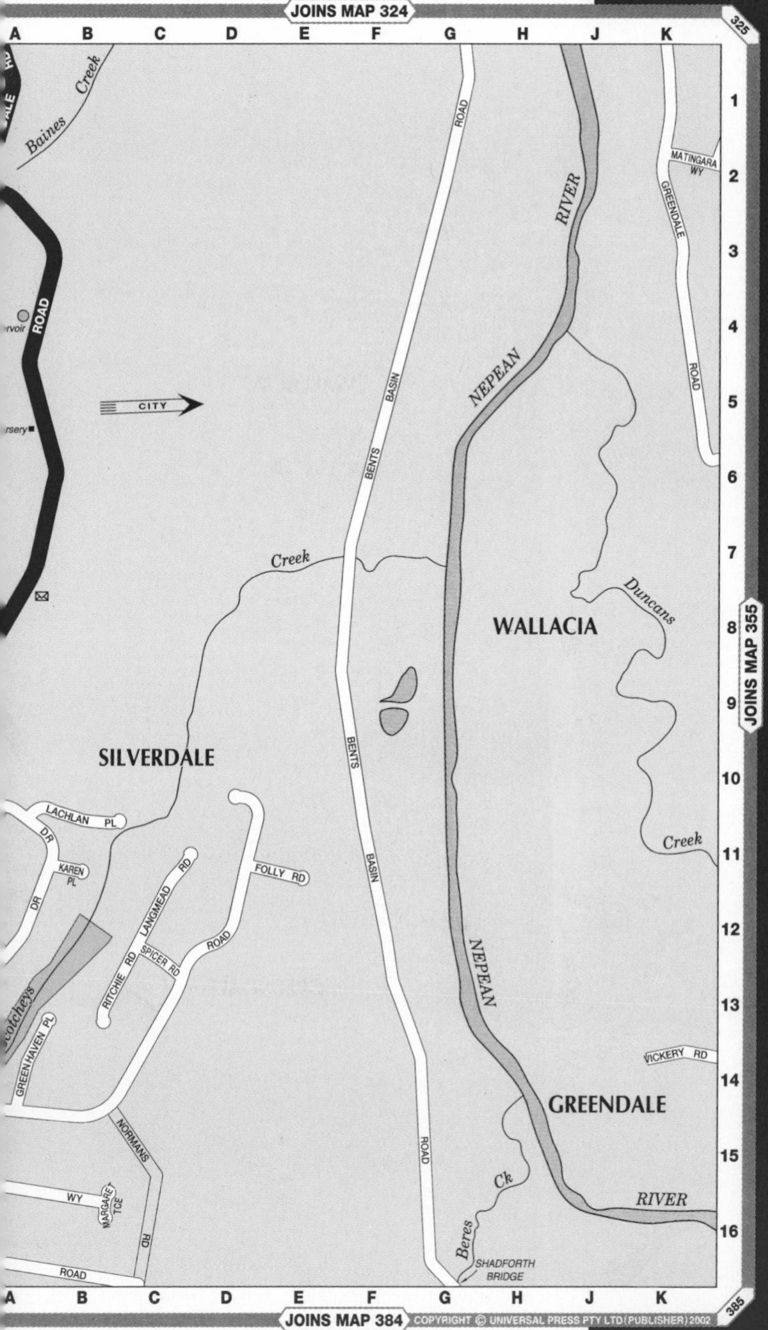
JOINS MAP 324
325
A B C D E F G H J K
1 2 3 4 5 6 7 8 9 10 11 12 13 14 15 16
Baines Creek
ROAD
CITY
BENTS BASIN ROAD
NEPEAN RIVER
MATINGARA WY
GREENDALE ROAD
Creek
Duncans
WALLACIA
SILVERDALE
LACHLAN PL
DR
KAREN PL
FOLLY RD
LANGMEAD RD
SPICER RD
RITCHIE RD
ROAD
GREEN HAVEN PL
NORMANS RD
WY
MARGARET TCE
ROAD
VICKERY RD
GREENDALE
Ck
Beres
SHADFORTH BRIDGE
RIVER
Creek
JOINS MAP 355
JOINS MAP 384
385

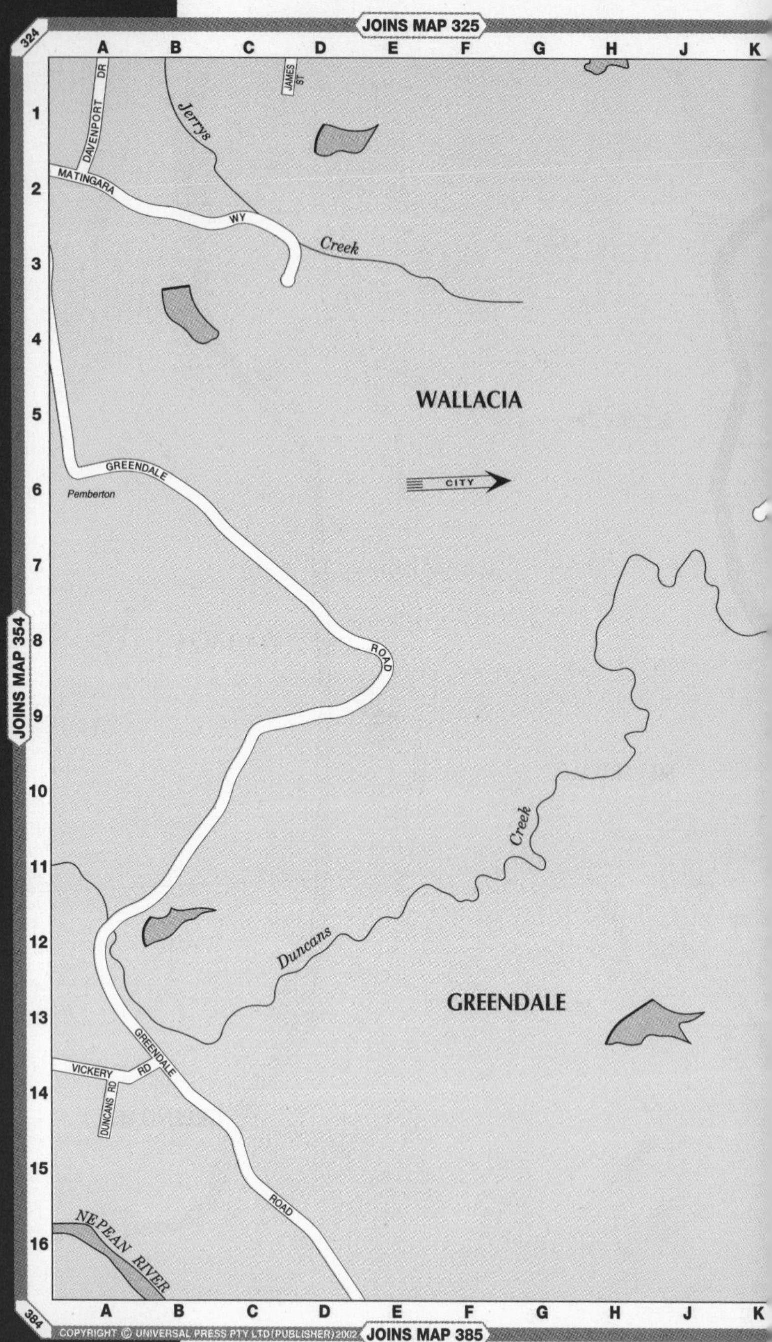
JOINS MAP 325
324
A B C D E F G H J K
1 2 3 4 5 6 7 8 9 10 11 12 13 14 15 16
JAMES ST
DAVENPORT DR
Jerrys
MATINGARA
WY
Creek
WALLACIA
GREENDALE
Pemberton
CITY
ROAD
JOINS MAP 354
Creek
Duncans
GREENDALE
GREENDALE
VICKERY
RD
DUNCANS RD
ROAD
NEPEAN RIVER
384
JOINS MAP 385

JOINS MAP 326

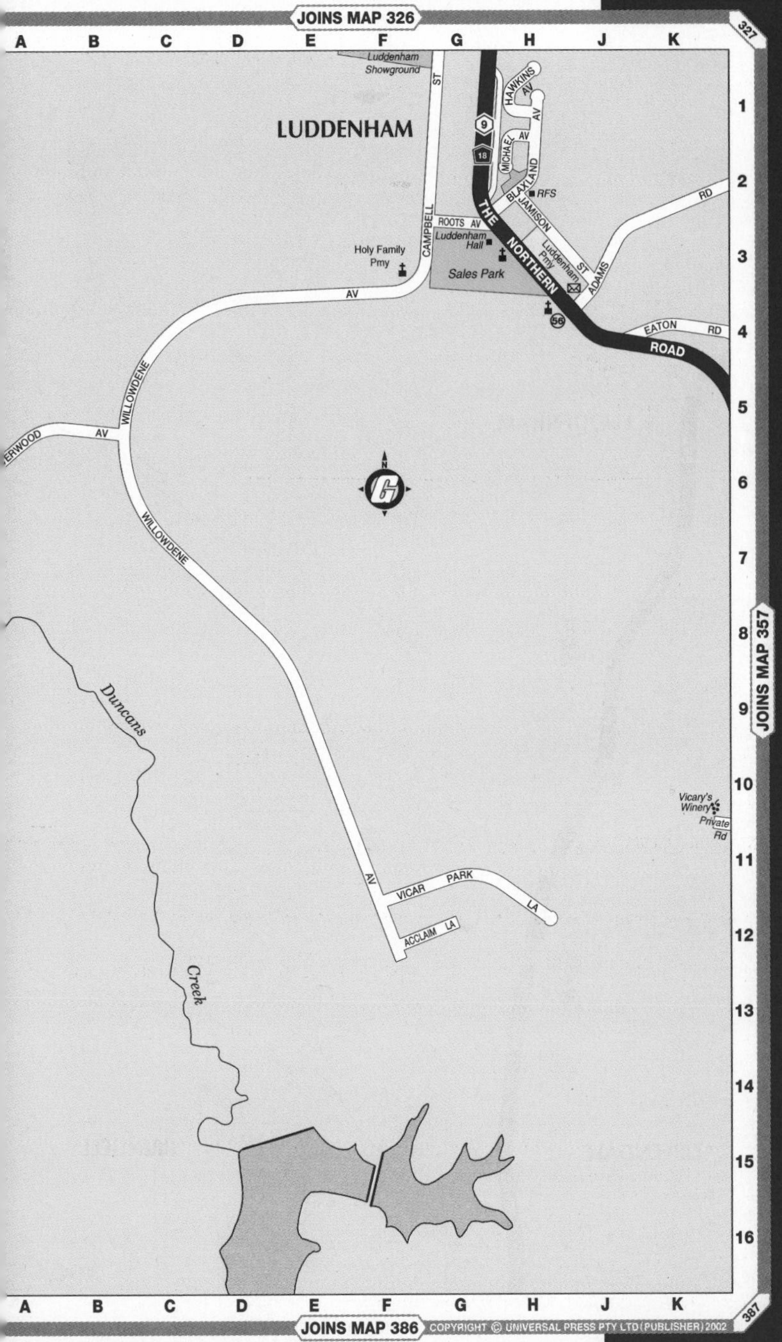

JOINS MAP 357

JOINS MAP 386

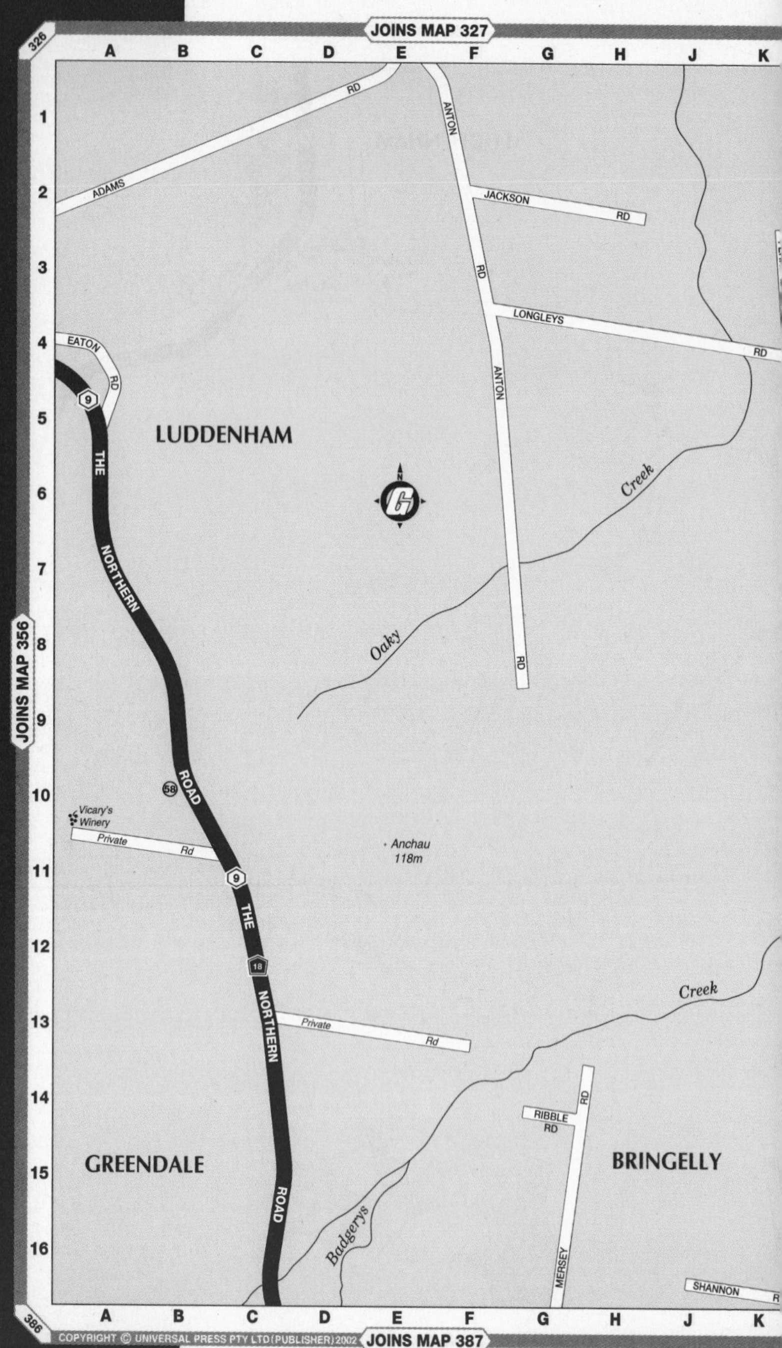
JOINS MAP 327
326
A
B
C
D
E
F
G
H
J
K
1
2
3
4
5
6
7
8
9
10
11
12
13
14
15
16
JOINS MAP 356
ADAMS
RD
ANTON
RD
JACKSON
RD
LONGLEYS
RD
ANTON
RD
EATON
RD
9
LUDDENHAM
THE
NORTHERN
ROAD
Creek
Oaky
58
Vicary's
Winery
Private
Rd
Anchau
118m
9
THE
18
NORTHERN
ROAD
Private
Rd
Creek
RIBBLE
RD
RD
GREENDALE
BRINGELLY
Badgerys
MERSEY
SHANNON
386
JOINS MAP 387

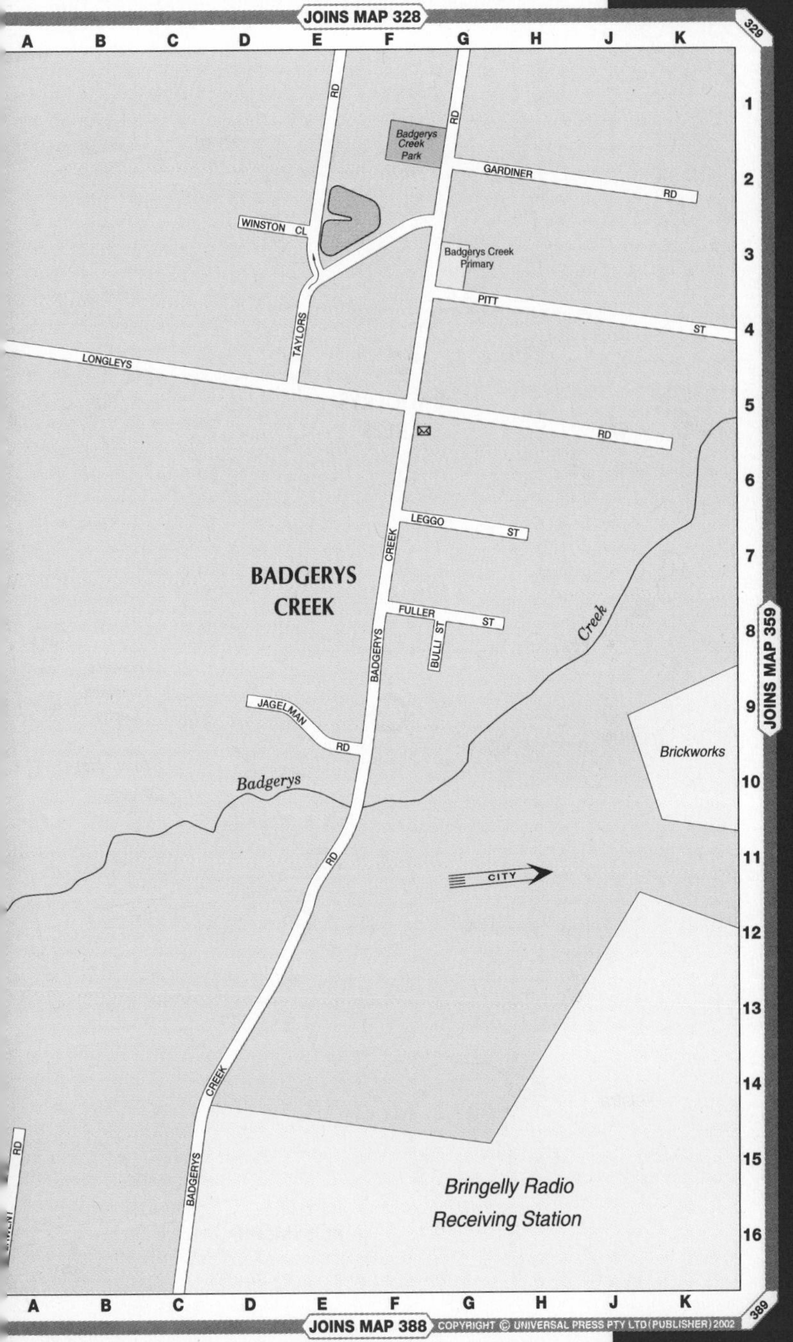
JOINS MAP 328
329
A B C D E F G H J K
1 2 3 4 5 6 7 8 9 10 11 12 13 14 15 16
RD
RD
Badgerys Creek Park
GARDINER RD
WINSTON CL
Badgerys Creek Primary
PITT ST
TAYLORS RD
LONGLEYS RD
LEGGO ST
BADGERYS CREEK
FULLER ST
BULLI ST
BADGERYS CREEK RD
JAGELMAN RD
Badgerys Creek
Brickworks
CITY
Bringelly Radio Receiving Station
RD
JOINS MAP 359
JOINS MAP 388
389

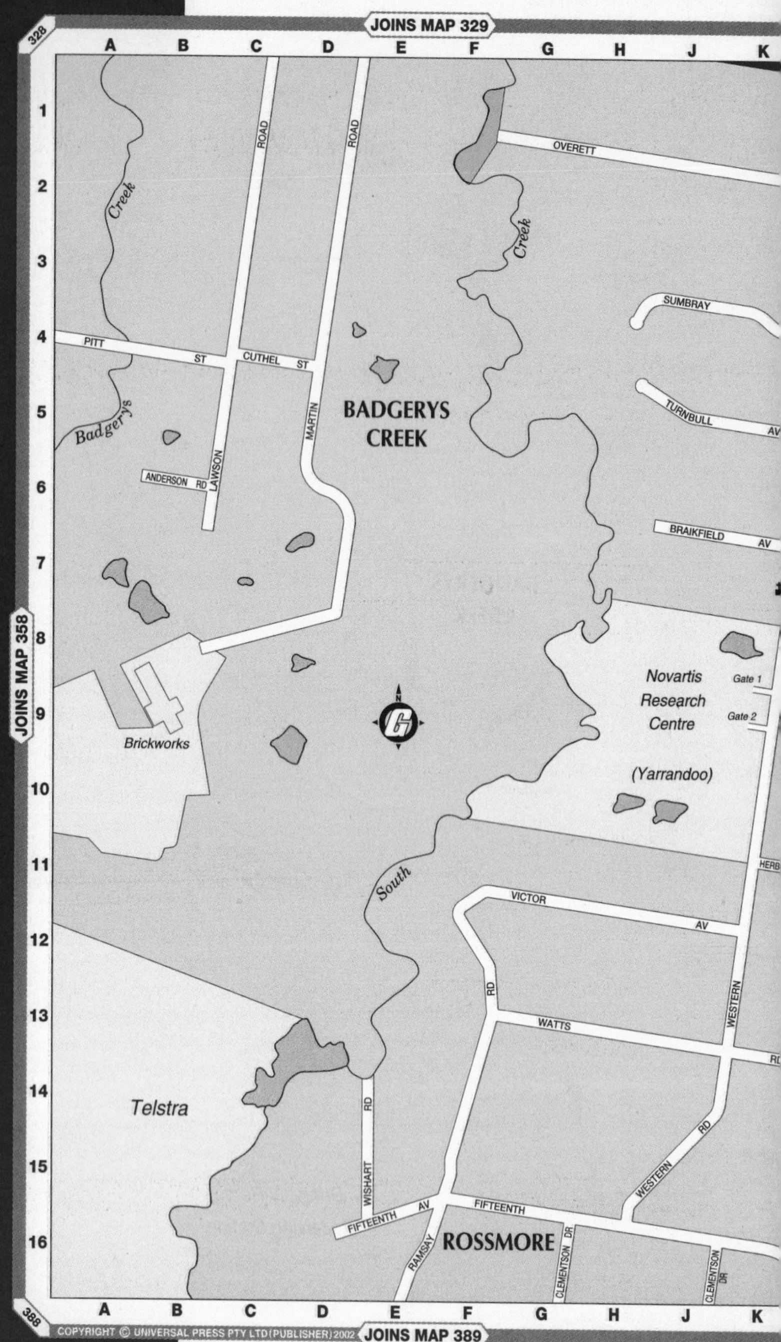
JOINS MAP 329
328
A B C D E F G H J K
1 2 3 4 5 6 7 8 9 10 11 12 13 14 15 16
JOINS MAP 358
OVERETT
ROAD
ROAD
Creek
Creek
SUMBRAY
PITT
ST
CUTHEL
ST
BADGERYS
CREEK
MARTIN
Badgerys
TURNBULL
AV
ANDERSON RD
LAWSON
BRAIKFIELD
AV
Novartis
Research
Centre
Gate 1
Gate 2
Brickworks
(Yarrandoo)
HERB
South
VICTOR
AV
RD
WESTERN
WATTS
RD
Telstra
RD
WISHART
RD
WESTERN
FIFTEENTH
AV
FIFTEENTH
RAMSAY
ROSSMORE
CLEMENTSON DR
CLEMENTSON DR
388
JOINS MAP 389

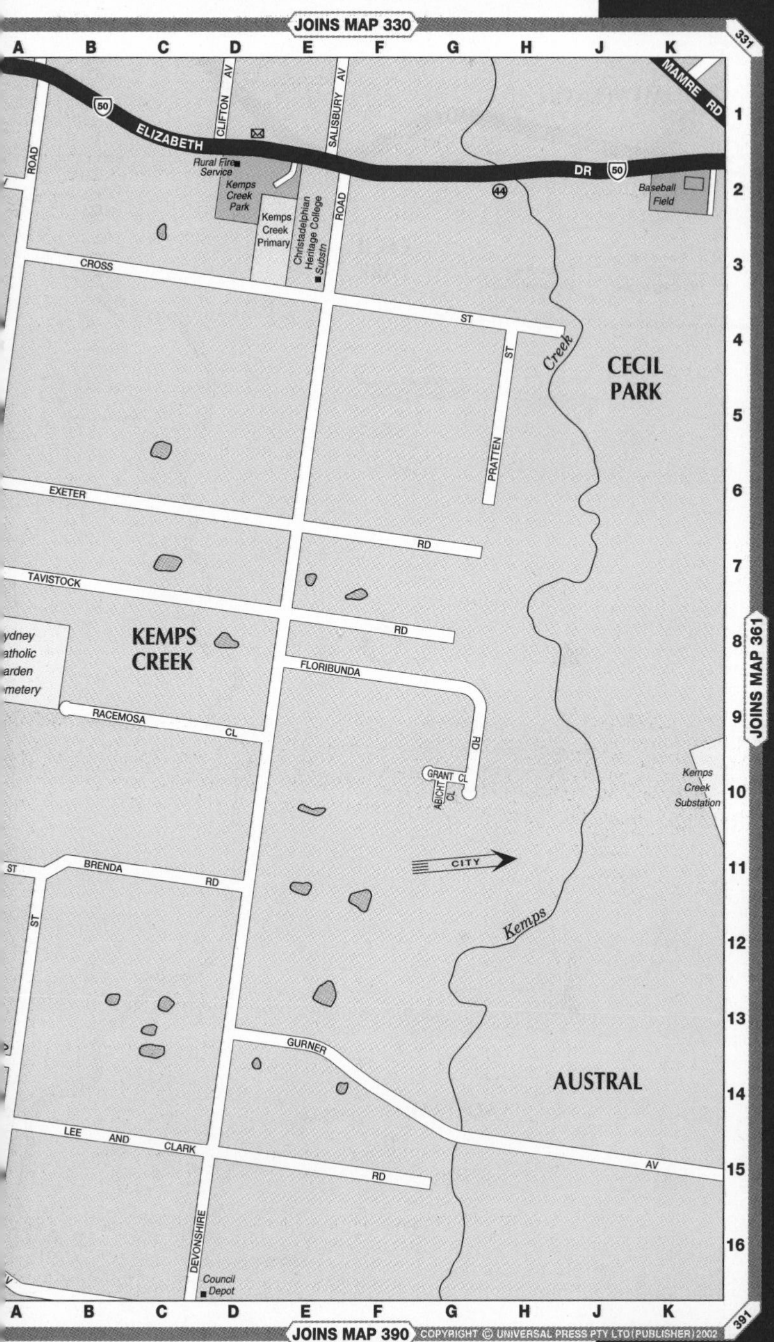
JOINS MAP 330
331
A B C D E F G H J K
1 2 3 4 5 6 7 8 9 10 11 12 13 14 15 16
50
ELIZABETH
DR
CLIFTON AV
SALISBURY AV
MAMRE RD
ROAD
Rural Fire Service
Kemps Creek Park
Kemps Creek Primary
Christadelphian Heritage College
Substn
ROAD
44
Baseball Field
CROSS
ST
ST
PRATTEN
Creek
CECIL PARK
EXETER
RD
TAVISTOCK
RD
KEMPS CREEK
ydney atholic arden metery
FLORIBUNDA
RACEMOSA
CL
RD
GRANT CL
ABICHT CL
Kemps Creek Substation
JOINS MAP 361
CITY
ST
BRENDA
RD
ST
Kemps
GURNER
AUSTRAL
LEE AND CLARK
RD
AV
DEVONSHIRE
Council Depot
JOINS MAP 390
391

JOINS MAP 331

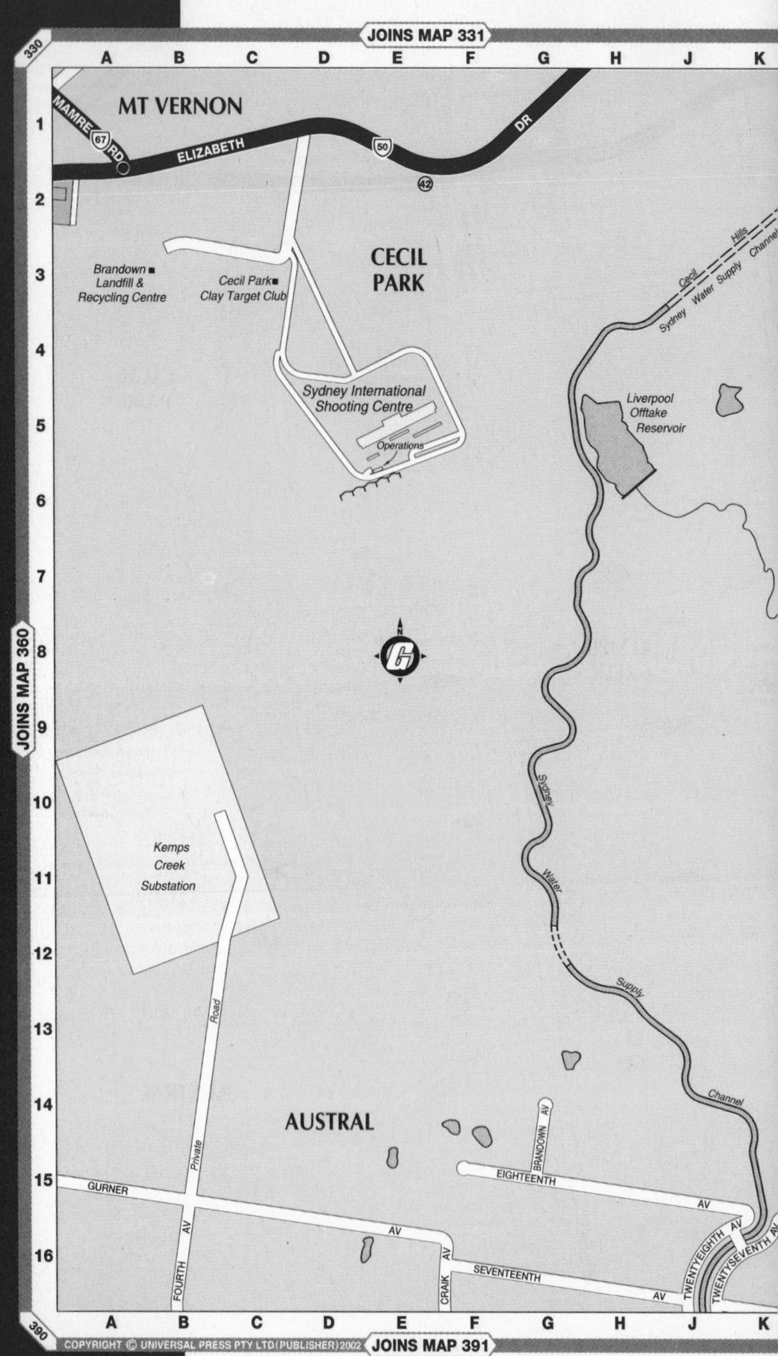

JOINS MAP 360

JOINS MAP 391

JOINS MAP 332

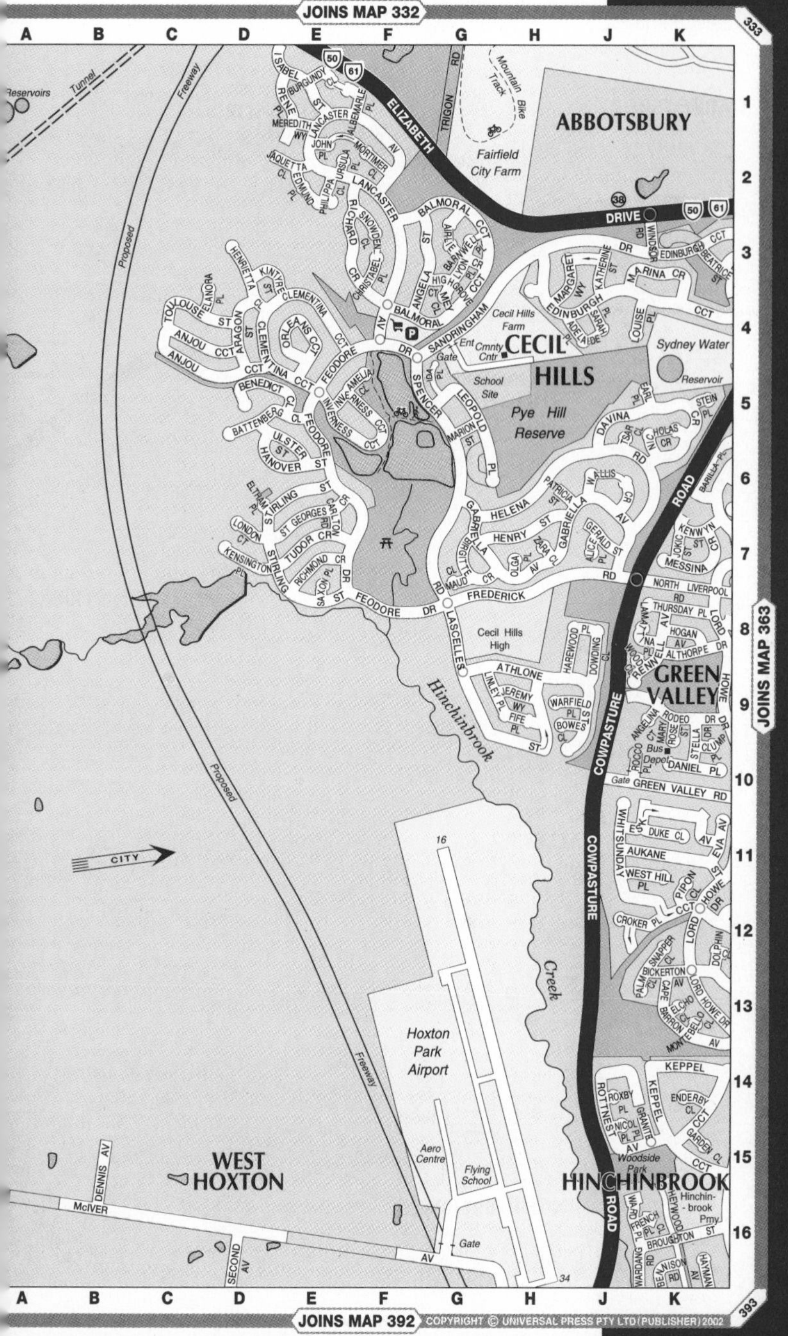

JOINS MAP 392

JOINS MAP 333

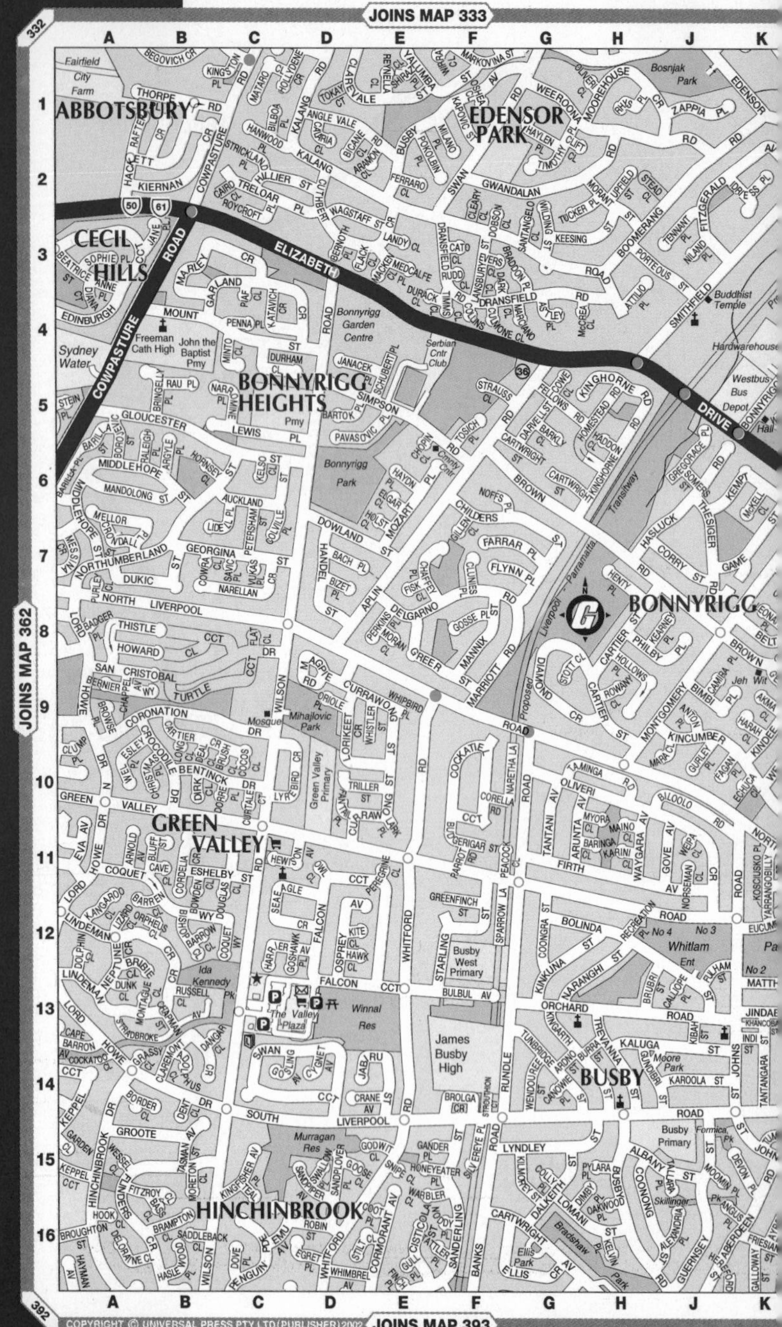

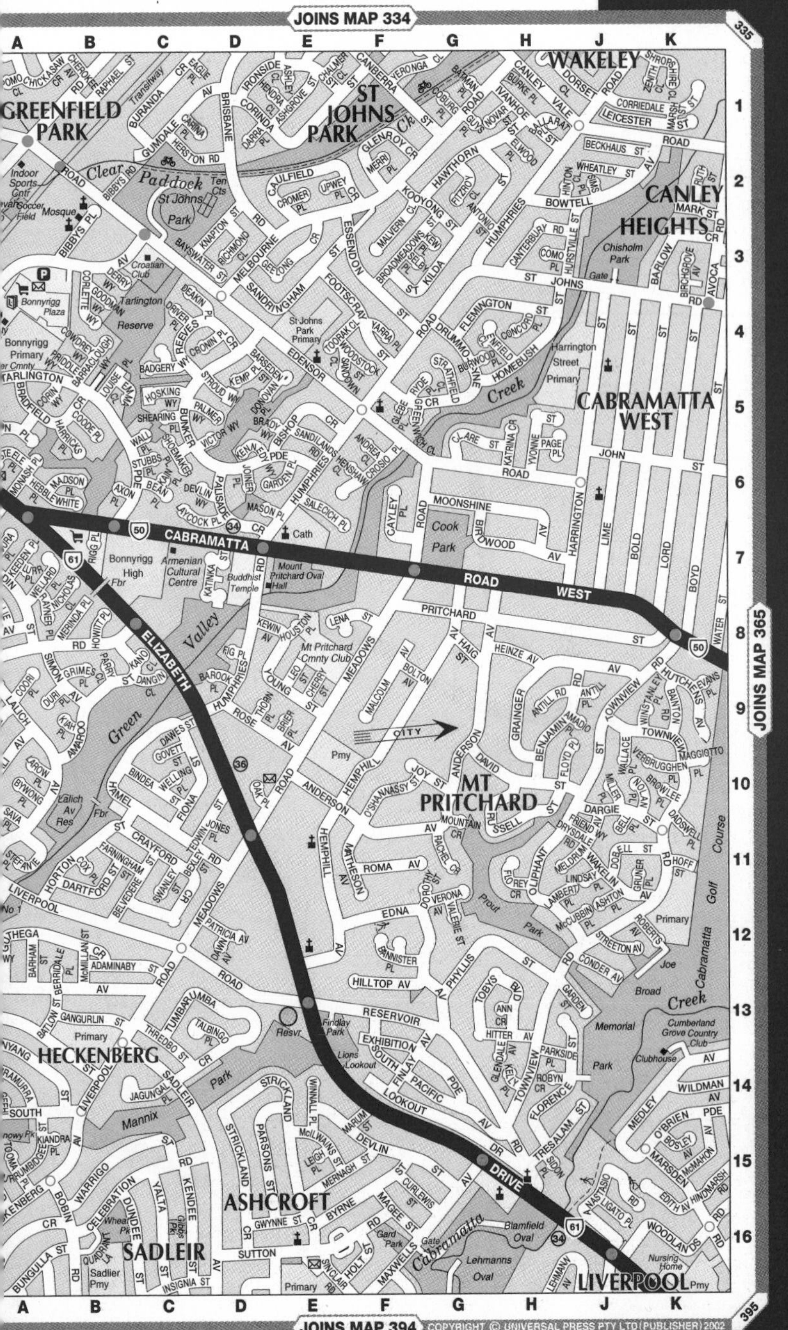
JOINS MAP 334
JOINS MAP 365
JOINS MAP 394
335
395
GREENFIELD PARK
ST JOHNS PARK
WAKELEY
CANLEY HEIGHTS
CABRAMATTA WEST
MT PRITCHARD
HECKENBERG
ASHCROFT
SADLEIR
LIVERPOOL
CABRAMATTA ROAD WEST
ELIZABETH DRIVE
St Johns Park
Bonnyrigg Plaza
Tarlington Reserve
Cook Park
Prout Park
Memorial Park
Mannix Park
Lehmanns Oval
Blamfield Oval
Cumberland Grove Country Club
Chisholm Park
Cabramatta Golf Course
Green Valley
Clear Paddock Ck
Cabramatta Creek

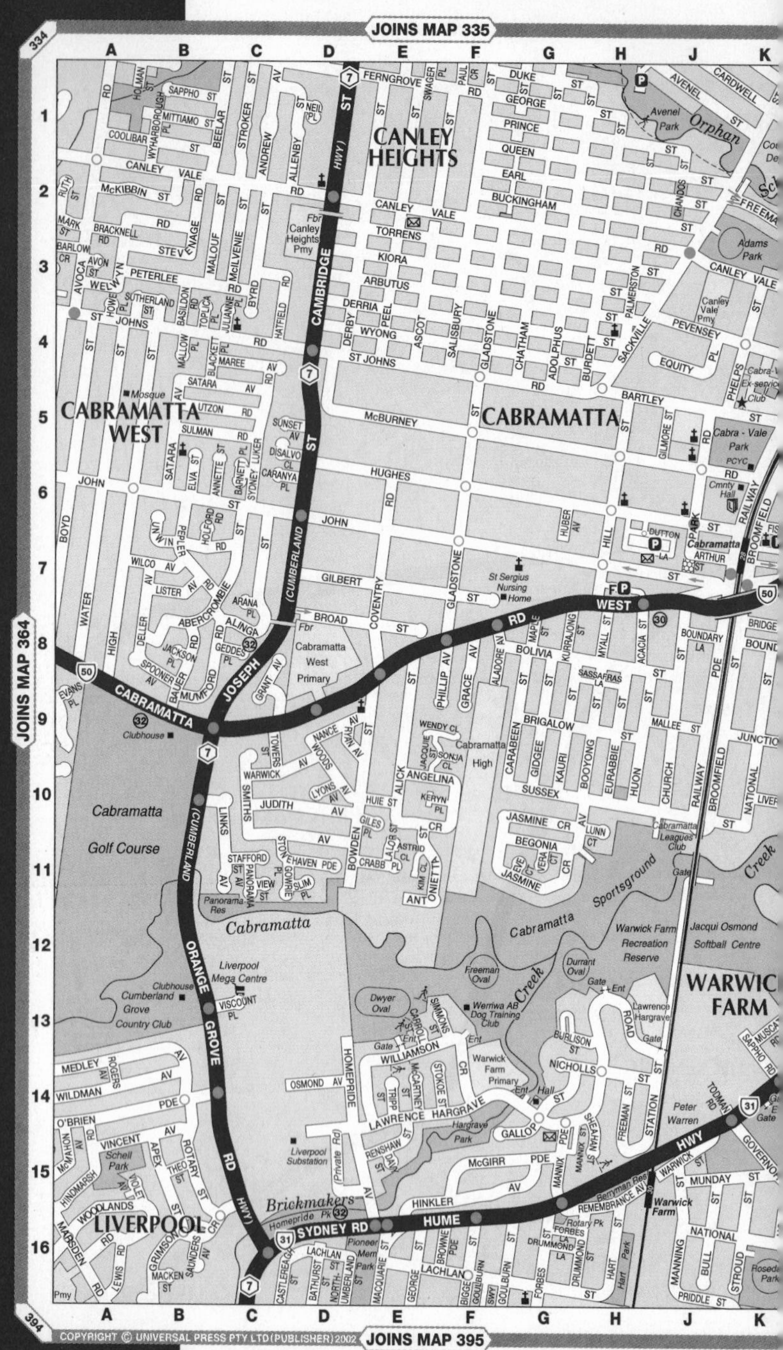
JOINS MAP 335
JOINS MAP 364
JOINS MAP 395
334
394
CANLEY HEIGHTS
CABRAMATTA WEST
CABRAMATTA
WARWICK FARM
LIVERPOOL
Cabramatta Golf Course
Cumberland Grove Country Club
Liverpool Mega Centre
Cabramatta Sportsground
Warwick Farm Recreation Reserve
Jacqui Osmond Softball Centre
Cabramatta West Primary
Cabramatta High
Warwick Farm Primary
Freeman Oval
Durrant Oval
Dwyer Oval
Adams Park
Cabra - Vale Park
Avenel Park
Schell Park
Hargrave Park
Peter Warren
Liverpool Substation
Werriwa AB Dog Training Club
St Sergius Nursing Home
Cabramatta Leagues Club
Cabramatta Creek
Orphan Creek
CUMBERLAND HWY
CABRAMATTA RD
WEST RD
HUME HWY
SYDNEY RD
ORANGE GROVE RD
CAMBRIDGE ST
JOSEPH ST

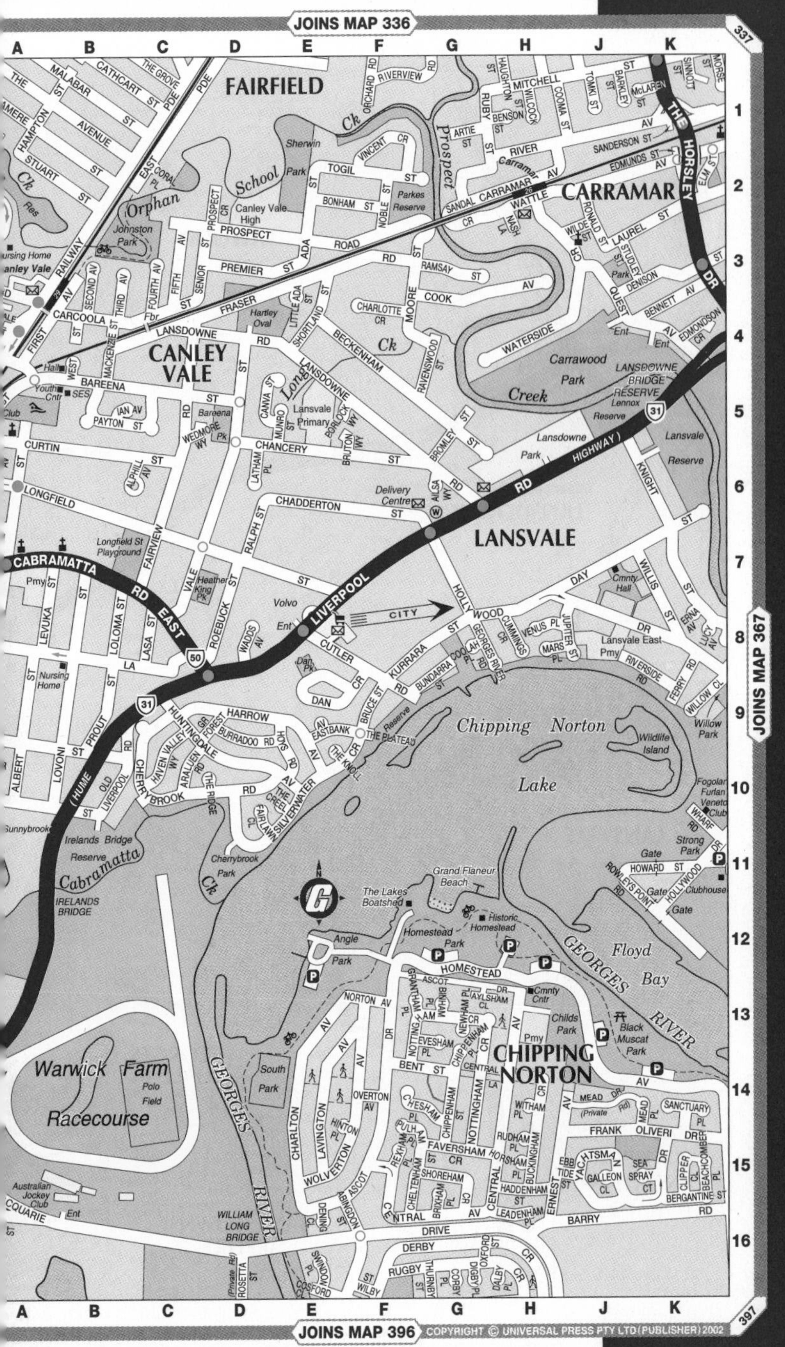
JOINS MAP 336
JOINS MAP 367
JOINS MAP 396
337
397
FAIRFIELD
CARRAMAR
CANLEY VALE
LANSVALE
CHIPPING NORTON
Chipping Norton
Lake
Carrawood Park
Prospect Creek
Long Ck
School Ck
Orphan Ck
Sherwin Park
Parkes Reserve
Canley Vale High
Johnston Park
Hartley Oval
Lansvale Primary
Delivery Centre
Longfield St Playground
Heather King Pk
Bareena Pk
Dan Pk
Lansdowne Park
Lansvale Reserve
LANSDOWNE BRIDGE RESERVE
Lennox Reserve
Lansvale East Pmy
Cmnty Hall
Wildlife Island
Willow Park
Fogolar Furlan Veneto Club
Strong Park
Clubhouse
Grand Flaneur Beach
The Lakes Boatshed
Historic Homestead
Homestead Park
Angle Park
Floyd Bay
GEORGES RIVER
Black Muscat Park
Childs Park
Cmnty Cntr
South Park
Ireland Bridge Reserve
IRELANDS BRIDGE
Cabramatta Ck
Cherrybrook Park
Warwick Farm
Polo Field
Racecourse
Australian Jockey Club
WILLIAM LONG BRIDGE
Nursing Home
Youth Cntr
SES
Club
Hall
Volvo
CITY
LIVERPOOL RD
HUME HIGHWAY
CABRAMATTA RD EAST
THE HORSLEY DR
COPYRIGHT © UNIVERSAL PRESS PTY LTD (PUBLISHER) 2002

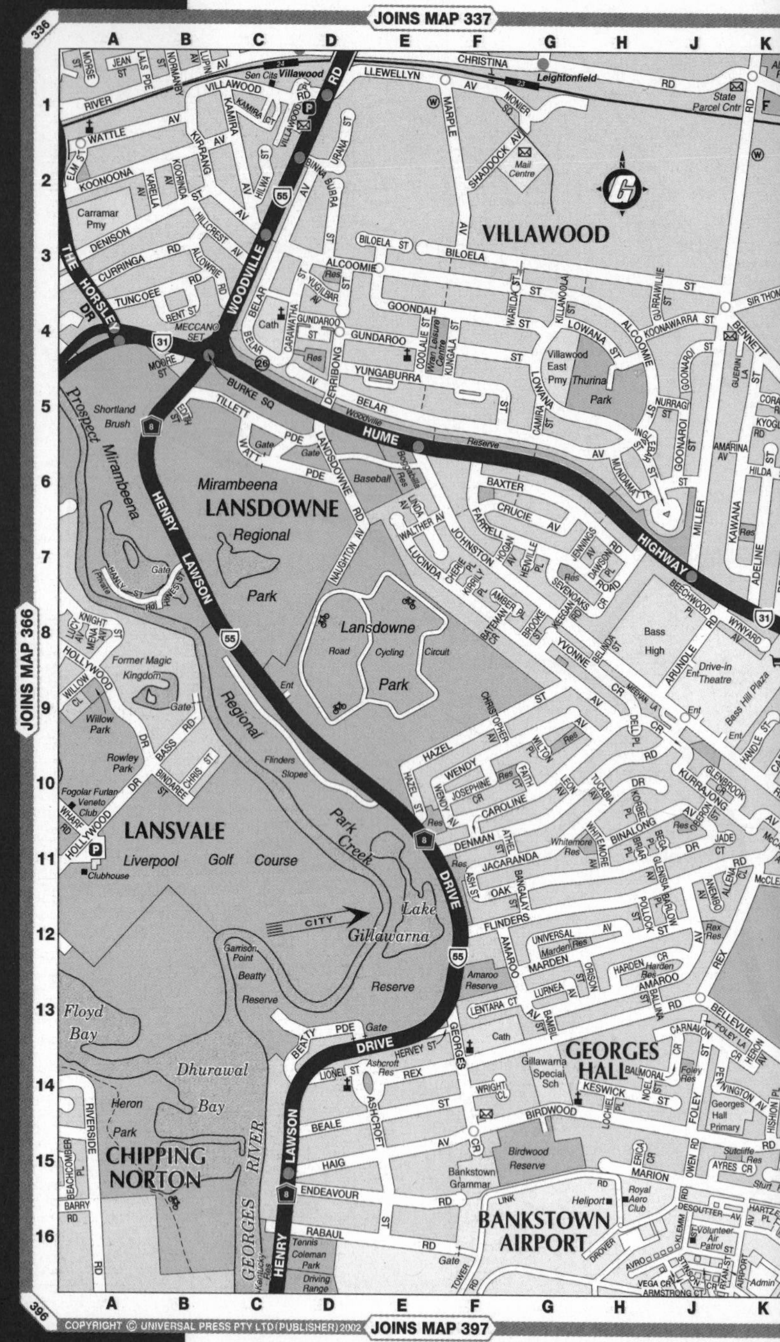
JOINS MAP 337
JOINS MAP 366
JOINS MAP 397
336
396
A B C D E F G H J K
1 2 3 4 5 6 7 8 9 10 11 12 13 14 15 16
VILLAWOOD
LANSDOWNE
LANSVALE
GEORGES HALL
CHIPPING NORTON
BANKSTOWN AIRPORT
Villawood
Leightonfield
Sen Cits
State Parcel Cntr
Mail Centre
CHRISTINA RD
LLEWELLYN AV
VILLAWOOD RD
WOODVILLE RD
THE HORSLEY DR
HUME HIGHWAY
HENRY LAWSON DRIVE
RIVER AV
WATTLE AV
KOONOONA AV
DENISON RD
CURRINGA RD
TUNCOEE RD
BILOELA ST
ALCOOMIE ST
GOONDAH ST
GUNDAROO ST
YUNGABURRA ST
BELAR AV
BURKE SQ
TILLETT PDE
WATT PDE
LANSDOWNE RD
MARPLE AV
SHADDOCK AV
MONIER SQ
BAXTER RD
CRUCIE AV
FARRELL
JOHNSTON
LUCINDA
YVONNE CR
HAZEL ST
WENDY AV
CAROLINE
DENMAN
JACARANDA
OAK ST
FLINDERS ST
MARDEN
AMAROO
BELLEVUE
REX RD
BIRDWOOD AV
HAIG AV
BEALE ST
ENDEAVOUR RD
RABAUL RD
MARION
KESWICK ST
BALMORAL
FOLEY
MILLER
GOONAROI
BEECHWOOD PL
ARUNDLE RD
Villawood East Pmy
Thurina Park
Wran Leisure Centre
Carramar Pmy
Shortland Brush
Prospect
Mirambeena Regional Park
Lansdowne Road Cycling Circuit Park
Former Magic Kingdom
Willow Park
Rowley Park
Fogolar Furlan Veneto Club
Liverpool Golf Course
Clubhouse
Flinders Slopes
Park Creek
Lake Gillawarna
Garrison Point
Beatty Reserve
Floyd Bay
Dhurawal Bay
Heron Park
GEORGES RIVER
Tennis Coleman Park
Driving Range
Amaroo Reserve
Gillawarna Special Sch
Birdwood Reserve
Bankstown Grammar
Georges Hall Primary
Bass High
Drive-in Theatre
Bass Hill Plaza
Royal Aero Club
Heliport
Volunteer Air Patrol
CITY

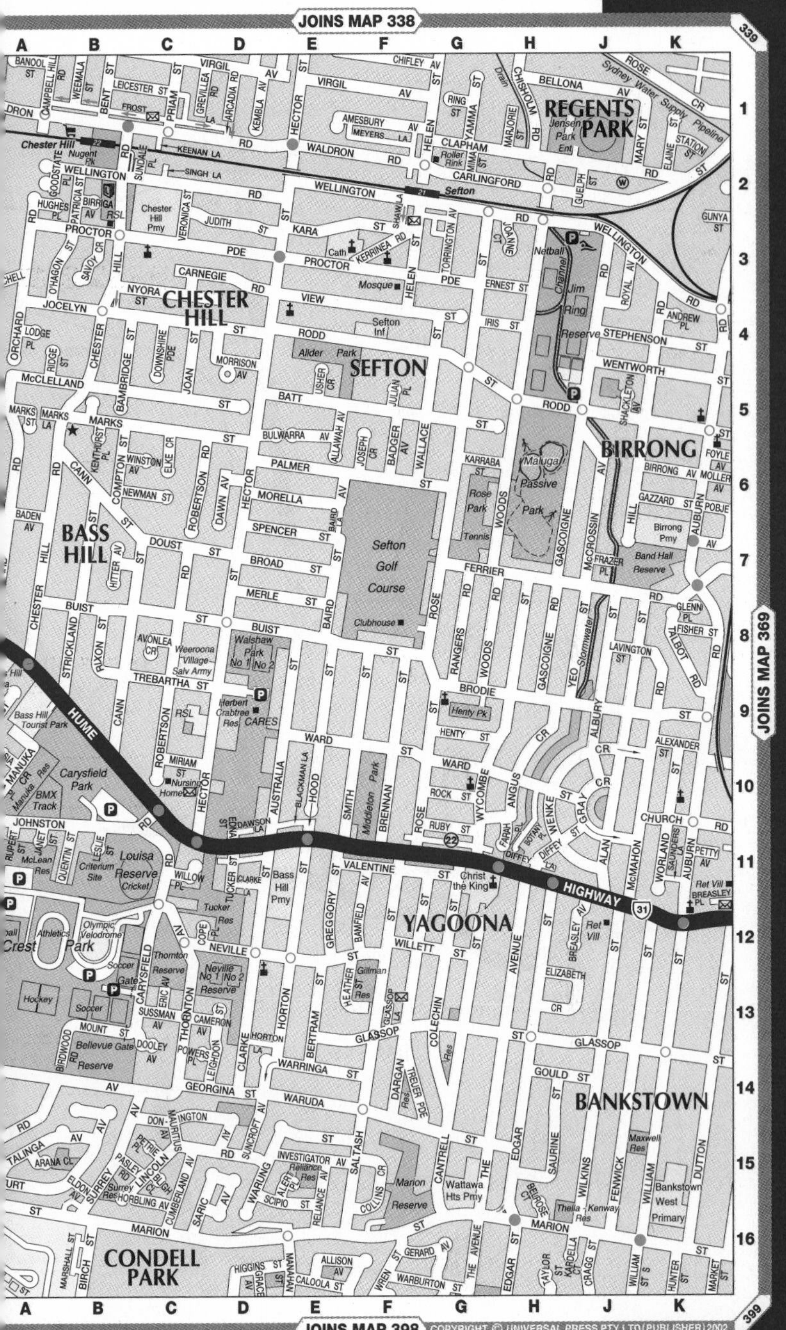
JOINS MAP 338
339
A B C D E F G H J K
1 2 3 4 5 6 7 8 9 10 11 12 13 14 15 16
REGENTS PARK
CHESTER HILL
SEFTON
BIRRONG
BASS HILL
YAGOONA
BANKSTOWN
CONDELL PARK
Chester Hill
Sefton
Jensen Park
Jim Ring Reserve
Allder Park
Maluga Passive Park
Rose Park
Sefton Golf Course
Birrong Pmy
Band Hall Reserve
Walshaw Park No 1 No 2
Weeroona Village Salv Army
Bass Hill Tourist Park
Carysfield Park
Louisa Reserve
Crest Park
Olympic Velodrome
Thornton Reserve
Neville No 1 No 2 Reserve
Bellevue Gate Reserve
Middleton Park
Henty Pk
Christ the King
Marion Reserve
Wattawa Hts Pmy
Thelma - Kenway Res
Bankstown West Primary
Maxwell Res
Gillman St Res
HUME HIGHWAY
31
22
WALDRON RD
WELLINGTON RD
PROCTOR PDE
CARNEGIE RD
JOCELYN ST
McCLELLAND ST
MARKS ST
RODD ST
BATT ST
PALMER ST
MORELLA ST
SPENCER ST
BROAD ST
MERLE ST
BUIST ST
TREBARTHA ST
DOUST ST
FERRIER RD
WARD ST
VALENTINE ST
NEVILLE ST
GLASSOP ST
GEORGINA ST
MARION ST
CHURCH RD
HECTOR ST
HELEN ST
CHESTER HILL RD
JOINS MAP 369
JOINS MAP 398
399

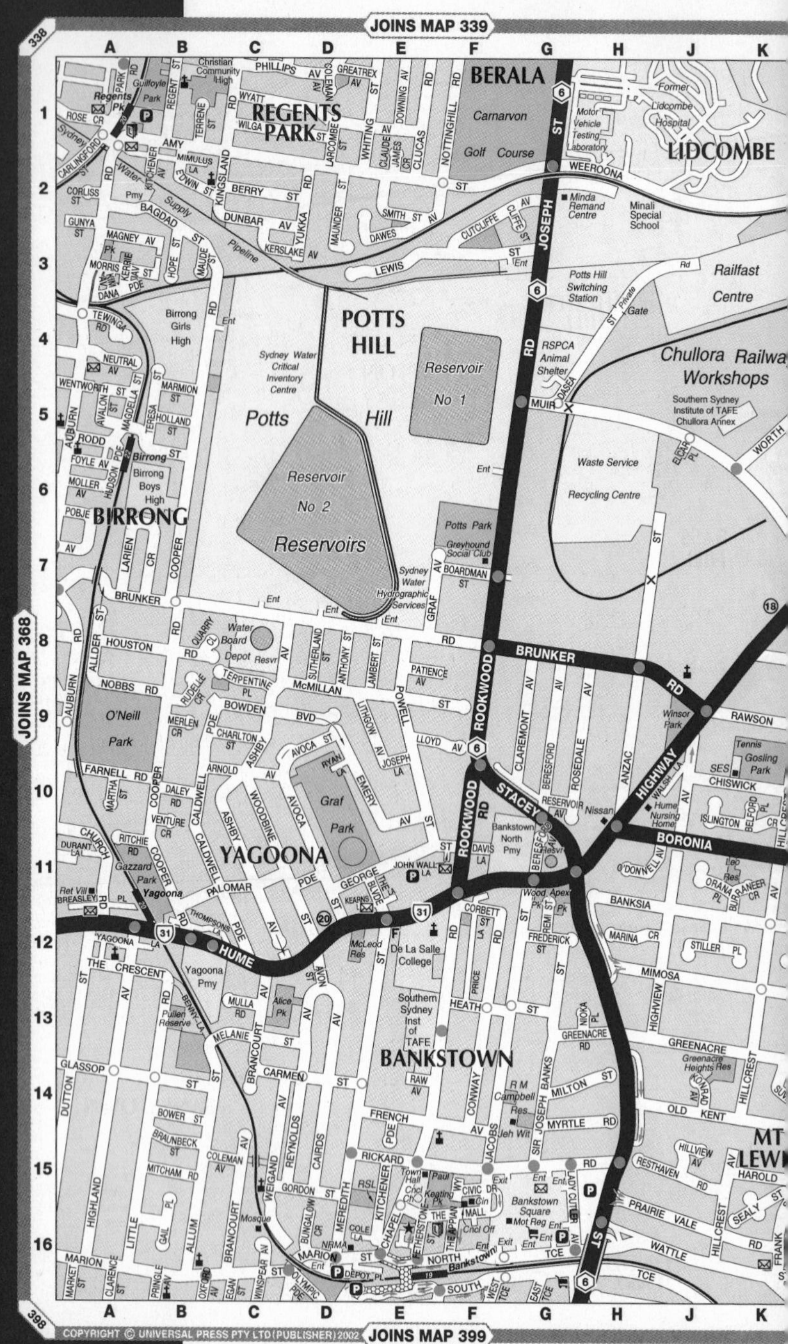

JOINS MAP 339
338
A B C D E F G H J K
BERALA
REGENTS PARK
LIDCOMBE
Carnarvon Golf Course
Former Lidcombe Hospital
Motor Vehicle Testing Laboratory
Minda Remand Centre
Minali Special School
POTTS HILL
Potts Hill Switching Station
Railfast Centre
Chullora Railway Workshops
Southern Sydney Institute of TAFE Chullora Annex
RSPCA Animal Shelter
Reservoir No 1
Reservoir No 2
Reservoirs
Sydney Water Critical Inventory Centre
Waste Service Recycling Centre
Birrong Girls High
Birrong Boys High
BIRRONG
Potts Park
Greyhound Social Club
Sydney Water Hydrographic Services
Water Board Depot
O'Neill Park
Graf Park
YAGOONA
Gazzard Park
Yagoona Pmy
Winsor Park
Gosling Park
Bankstown North Pmy
De La Salle College
Southern Sydney Inst of TAFE
BANKSTOWN
Alice Pk
Pullen Reserve
R M Campbell Res
Greenacre Heights Res
Bankstown Square
Town Hall
Paul Keating Pk
Mosque
MT LEWIS
JOINS MAP 368
398
JOINS MAP 399

JOINS MAP 340

JOINS MAP 371

JOINS MAP 400

JOINS MAP 341

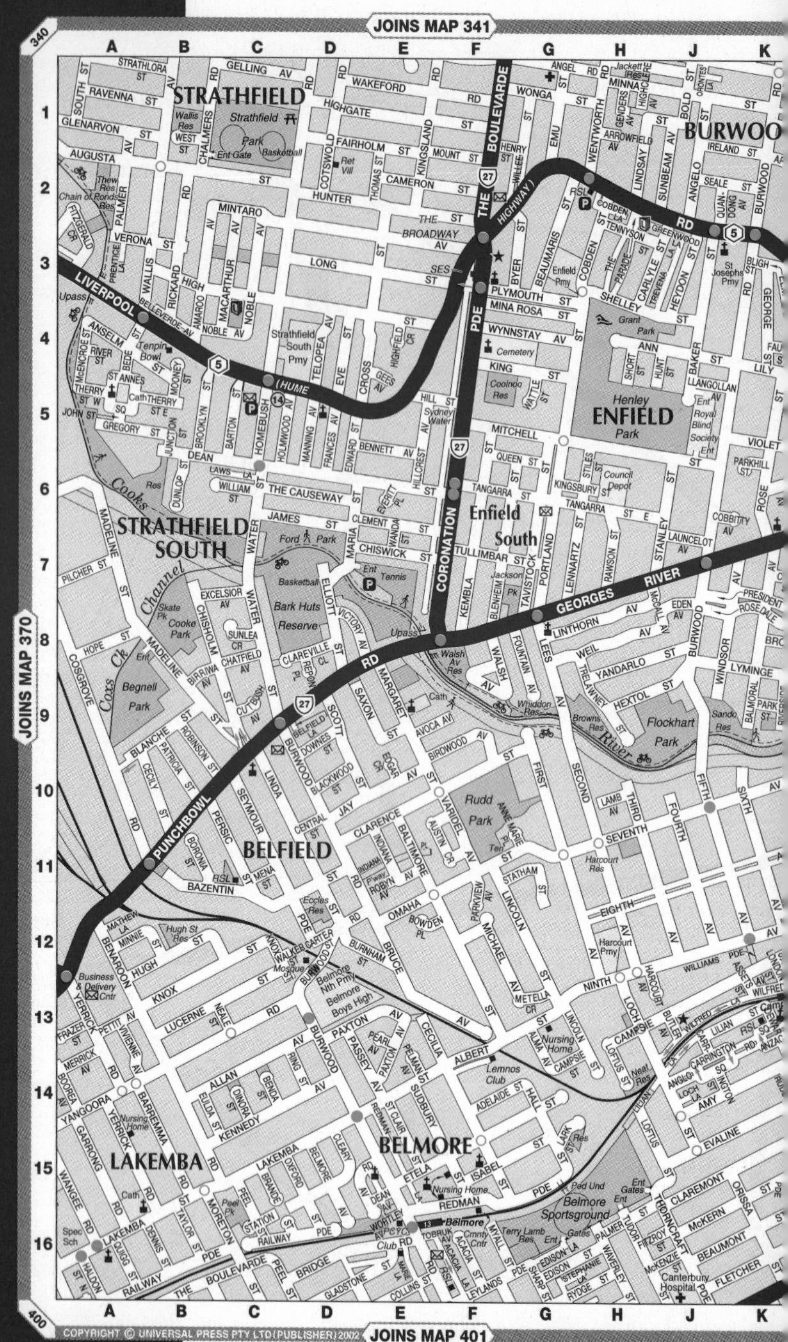

JOINS MAP 370

JOINS MAP 401

JOINS MAP 342
JOINS MAP 373
JOINS MAP 402
343
403
CROYDON
ASHFIELD
CROYDON PARK
ASHBURY
CANTERBURY
CAMPSIE
HURLSTONE PARK
EARLWOOD
LIVERPOOL
(HUME HIGHWAY)
FREDERICK
MILTON ST
BRIGHTON AV
CANTERBURY RD
BEAMISH ST
De La Salle Coll
Bethlehem Coll
Ashfield
Ashfield Pmy & High
Pratten Park
W H Wagener Oval
Peace Pk
Viewing Tower
Ashbury Pmy
Cardinal Freeman Village
Trinity Grammar
Yeo Park
NSW Private Hospital
Picken Oval
Croydon Park
Special Sch
Cooks River
Lees Park
Canterbury Park Racecourse
Canterbury Park
Campbell Oval
Blick Oval
Boys High
Girls High
Little Tasker Park
Tasker Park
Ice Rink
Sugar Works
Sutton Reserve
Ewen Park
Euston Pk
Clover Lea Nursing Home
Keith Smith Park
Senior Cits
Pat O'Connor Res
Simpson Res
Heynes Res
COPYRIGHT © UNIVERSAL PRESS PTY LTD (PUBLISHER) 2002

MAP 373

JOINS MAP 343

342
JOINS MAP 372
402

JOINS MAP 403

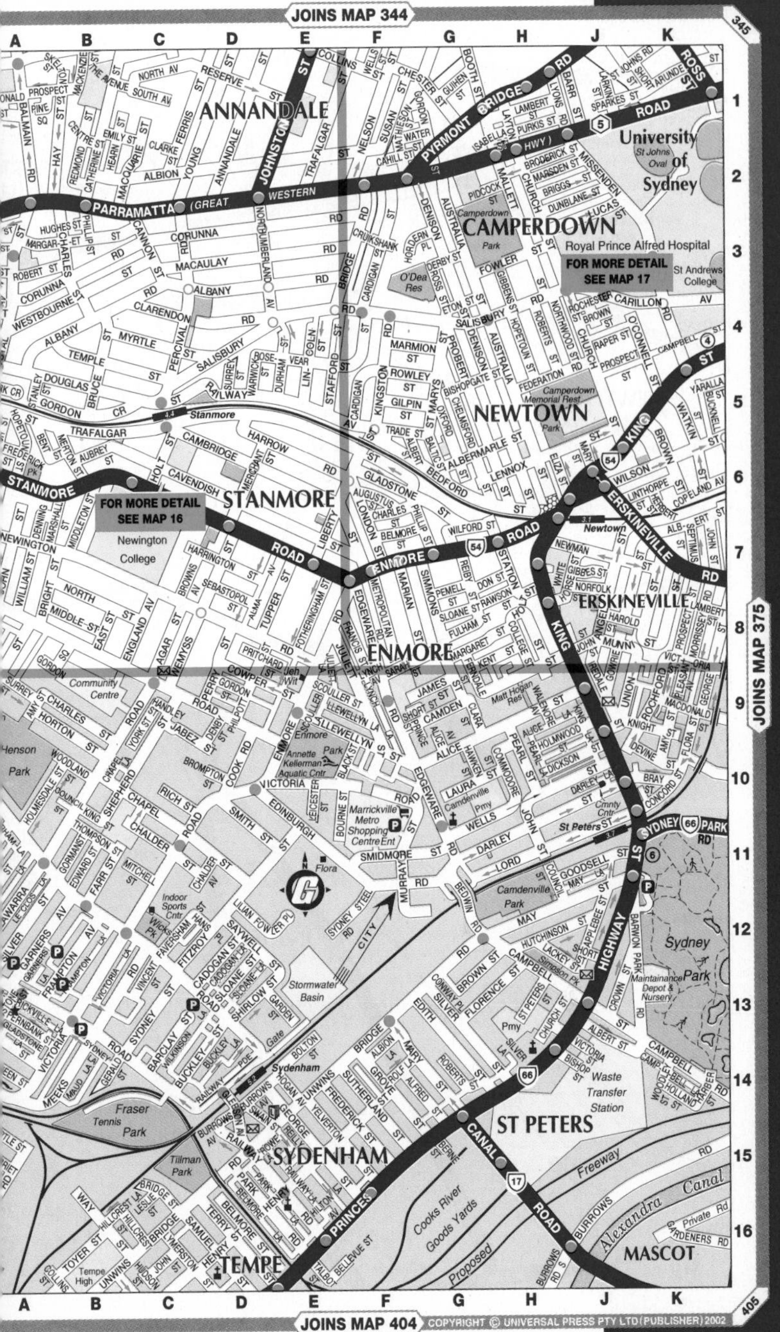
JOINS MAP 344
345
A B C D E F G H J K
1 2 3 4 5 6 7 8 9 10 11 12 13 14 15 16
ANNANDALE
University of Sydney
St Johns Oval
CAMPERDOWN
Camperdown Park
Royal Prince Alfred Hospital
FOR MORE DETAIL SEE MAP 17
St Andrews College
O'Dea Res
NEWTOWN
Camperdown Memorial Rest Park
Stanmore
STANMORE
FOR MORE DETAIL SEE MAP 16
Newington College
Newtown
ERSKINEVILLE
ENMORE
Community Centre
Henson Park
Matt Hogan Res
Enmore Park
Annette Kellerman Aquatic Cntr
Marrickville Metro Shopping Centre Ent
Camdenville Pmy
Cmnty Cntr
St Peters
Indoor Sports Cntr
Wicks Pk
Camdenville Park
Sydney Park
Maintainance Depot & Nursery
Stormwater Basin
Gate
Sydenham
Fraser Tennis Park
Tillman Park
SYDENHAM
ST PETERS
Waste Transfer Station
Cooks River Goods Yards
Alexandra Canal
Freeway
Proposed
MASCOT
TEMPE
Tempe High
PARRAMATTA (GREAT WESTERN HWY) ROAD
PYRMONT BRIDGE RD
STANMORE ROAD
ENMORE ROAD
KING ST
PRINCES HIGHWAY
CANAL ROAD
SYDNEY PARK RD
CITY
JOINS MAP 375
JOINS MAP 404
405

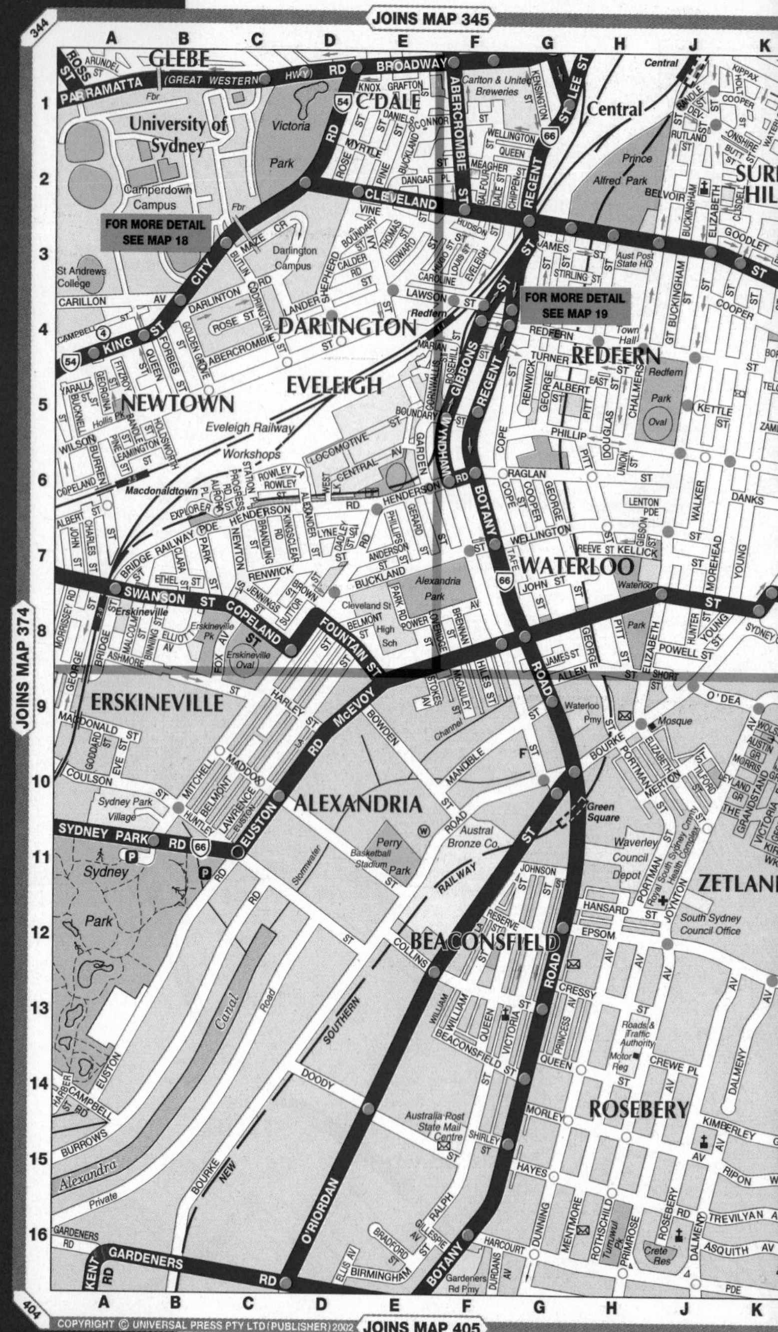
JOINS MAP 345
JOINS MAP 374
JOINS MAP 405
344
404
A B C D E F G H J K
1 2 3 4 5 6 7 8 9 10 11 12 13 14 15 16
GLEBE
C'DALE
Central
SURRY HILLS
DARLINGTON
EVELEIGH
NEWTOWN
REDFERN
WATERLOO
ERSKINEVILLE
ALEXANDRIA
ZETLAND
BEACONSFIELD
ROSEBERY
University of Sydney
Camperdown Campus
St Andrews College
Darlington Campus
Victoria Park
Prince Alfred Park
Carlton & United Breweries
Aust Post State HQ
Redfern Park Oval
Eveleigh Railway Workshops
Macdonaldtown
Erskineville
Erskineville Pk
Erskineville Oval
Alexandria Park
Cleveland St High Sch
Waterloo Park
Waterloo Pmy
Mosque
Green Square
Austral Bronze Co
Perry Park
Basketball Stadium
Waverley Council Depot
Royal South Sydney Cmty Health Complex
South Sydney Council Office
Sydney Park
Sydney Park Village
Roads & Traffic Authority
Motor Reg
Australia Post State Mail Centre
Crete Res
Turruwul Pk
Gardeners Rd Pmy
Alexandra Canal
FOR MORE DETAIL SEE MAP 18
FOR MORE DETAIL SEE MAP 19
PARRAMATTA RD (GREAT WESTERN HWY)
BROADWAY
CITY RD
KING ST
CLEVELAND ST
ABERCROMBIE ST
REGENT ST
LEE ST
GIBBONS ST
BOTANY RD
WYNDHAM
SWANSON ST
COPELAND ST
FOUNTAIN ST
McEVOY ST
EUSTON RD
SYDNEY PARK RD
O'RIORDAN ST
GARDENERS RD
KENT RD
BOURKE RD
SOUTHERN
RAILWAY
ELIZABETH ST
GOODLET ST
PHILLIP ST
RAGLAN ST
WELLINGTON ST
JOHN ST
POWELL ST
ALLEN ST
O'DEA AV
JOYNTON AV
EPSOM RD
HANSARD ST
MORLEY
KIMBERLEY GR
RIPON WY
TREVILYAN AV
ASQUITH AV
DALMENY AV
ROSEBERY
HARCOURT
BIRMINGHAM
COPYRIGHT © UNIVERSAL PRESS PTY LTD (PUBLISHER) 2002

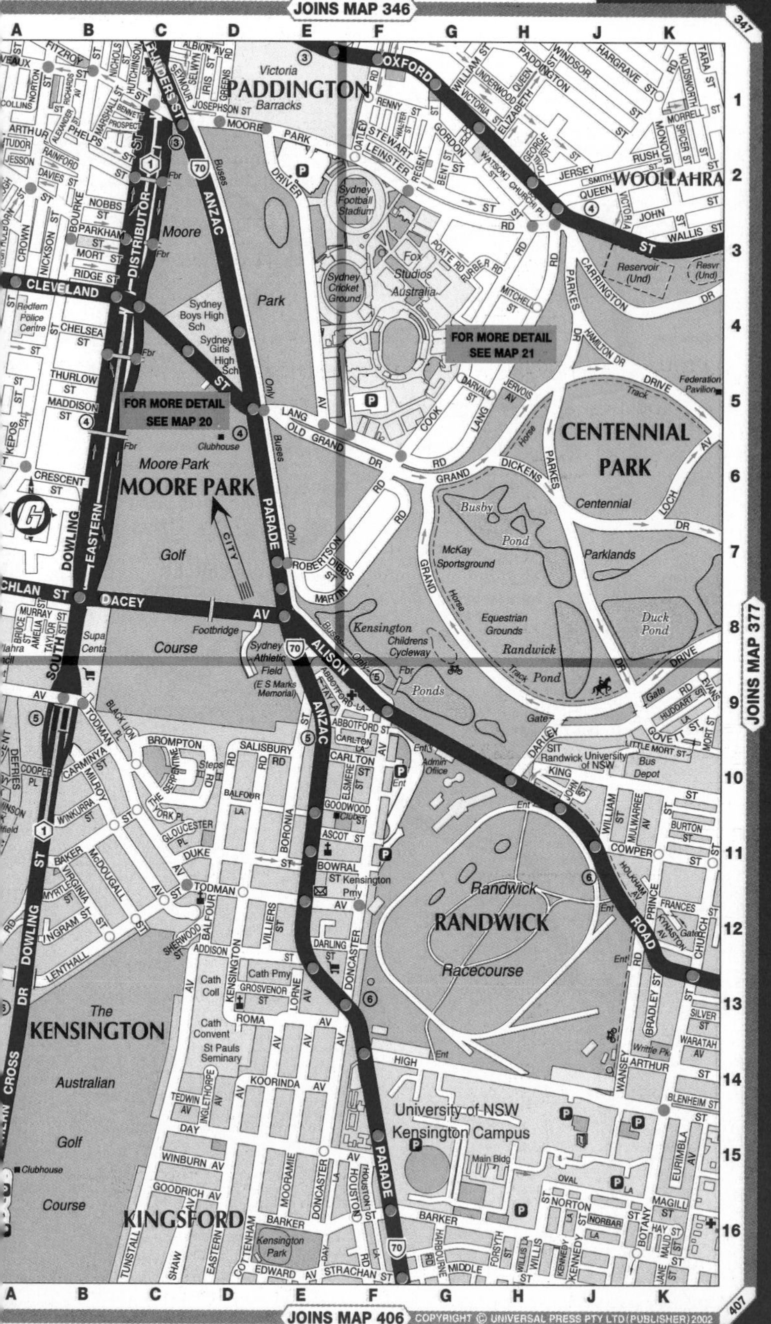
JOINS MAP 346
347
A B C D E F G H J K
1 2 3 4 5 6 7 8 9 10 11 12 13 14 15 16
PADDINGTON
Victoria
Barracks
WOOLLAHRA
OXFORD
ST
MOORE
PARK
RD
DRIVER
AV
Sydney Football Stadium
Sydney Cricket Ground
Fox Studios Australia
FOR MORE DETAIL SEE MAP 21
FOR MORE DETAIL SEE MAP 20
CLEVELAND
ST
DISTRIBUTOR
ANZAC
PARADE
Moore
Park
Sydney Boys High Sch
Sydney Girls High Sch
Clubhouse
Moore Park
MOORE PARK
Golf
Course
CITY
DACEY
AV
Footbridge
Sydney Athletic Field
(E S Marks Memorial)
ALISON
ROAD
LANG
OLD
GRAND
DR
CENTENNIAL
PARK
Centennial
Parklands
Busby Pond
McKay Sportsground
Equestrian Grounds
Randwick
Pond
Duck Pond
Kensington Childrens Cycleway
Ponds
Federation Pavilion
Reservoir (Und)
Resvr (Und)
CARRINGTON
PARKES
DICKENS
LOCH
DRIVE
Randwick
RANDWICK
Racecourse
SIT Randwick
University of NSW
Bus Depot
Admin Office
University of NSW
Kensington Campus
Main Bldg
The
KENSINGTON
Australian
Golf
Course
Clubhouse
KINGSFORD
Kensington Park
Cath Coll
Cath Pmy
Cath Convent
St Pauls Seminary
Kensington Pmy
DOWLING
SOUTH
EASTERN
HIGH
BARKER
STRACHAN
EDWARD
JOINS MAP 377
JOINS MAP 406
407

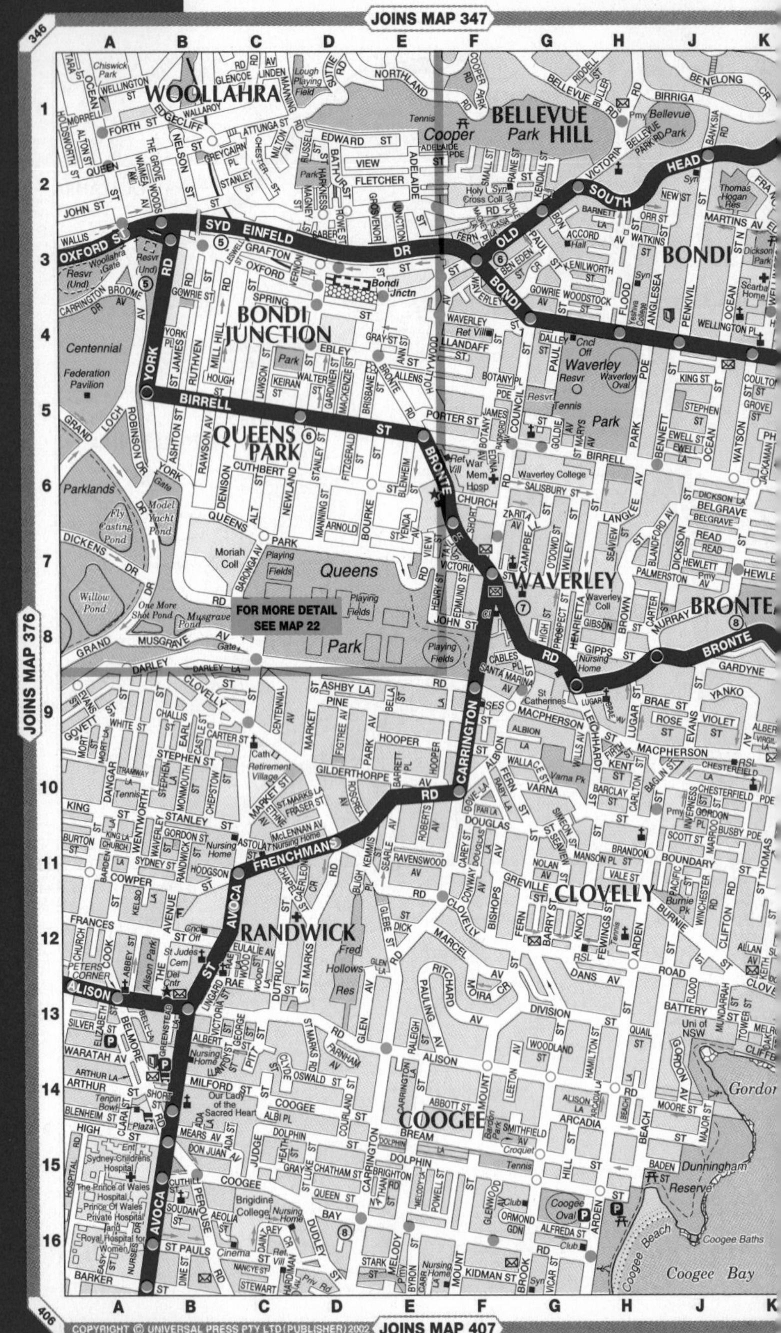
JOINS MAP 347
JOINS MAP 376
JOINS MAP 407
346
406
WOOLLAHRA
BELLEVUE HILL
BONDI JUNCTION
Bondi Jnctn
QUEENS PARK
BONDI
WAVERLEY
BRONTE
CLOVELLY
RANDWICK
COOGEE
Centennial
Federation Pavilion
Parklands
Queens Park
Moriah Coll
Waverley Park
Waverley College
Cooper Park
Fred Hollows Res
Brigidine College
Sydney Children's Hospital
The Prince of Wales Hospital
Prince Of Wales Private Hospital
Royal Hospital for Women
Uni of NSW
Gordon
Dunningham Reserve
Coogee Beach
Coogee Baths
Coogee Bay
Coogee Oval
FOR MORE DETAIL SEE MAP 22
OXFORD ST
SYD EINFELD DR
OLD SOUTH HEAD RD
BONDI RD
YORK RD
BIRRELL ST
BRONTE RD
CARRINGTON RD
FRENCHMANS RD
AVOCA ST
ALISON RD
BRONTE RD

JOINS MAP 348

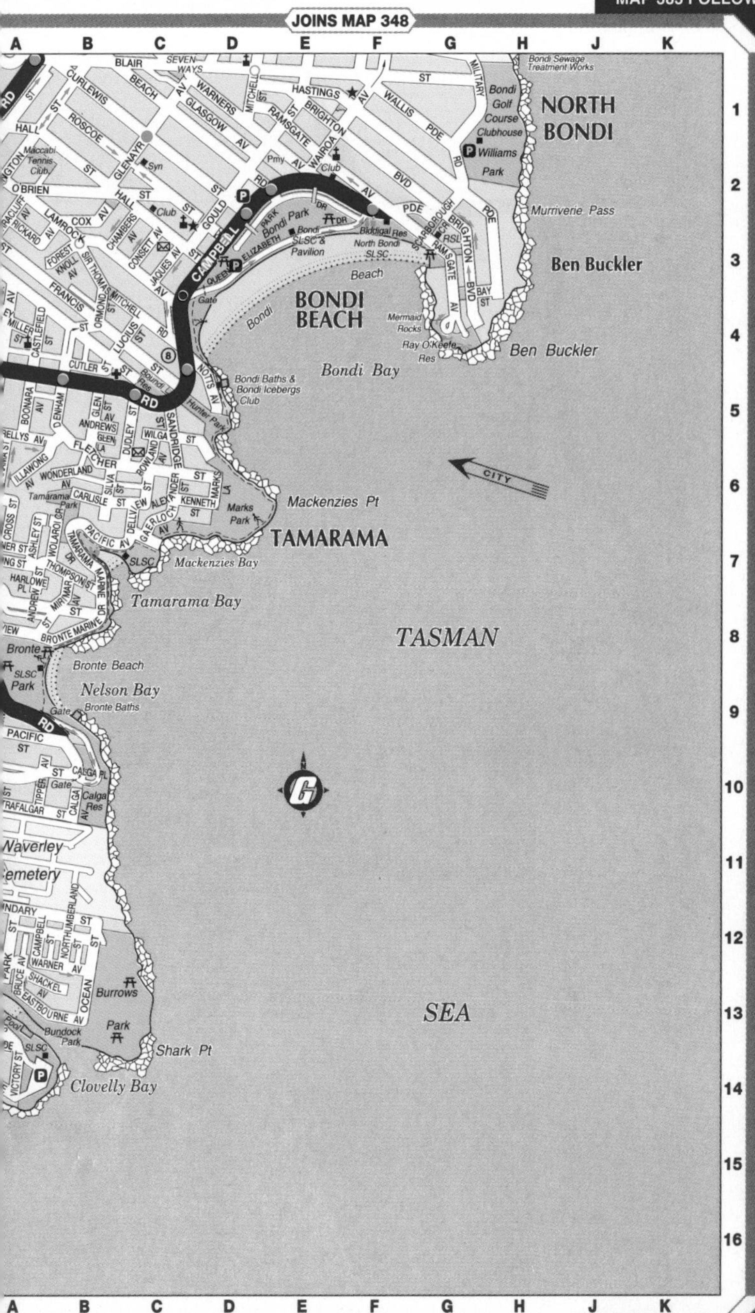

JOINS MAP 408

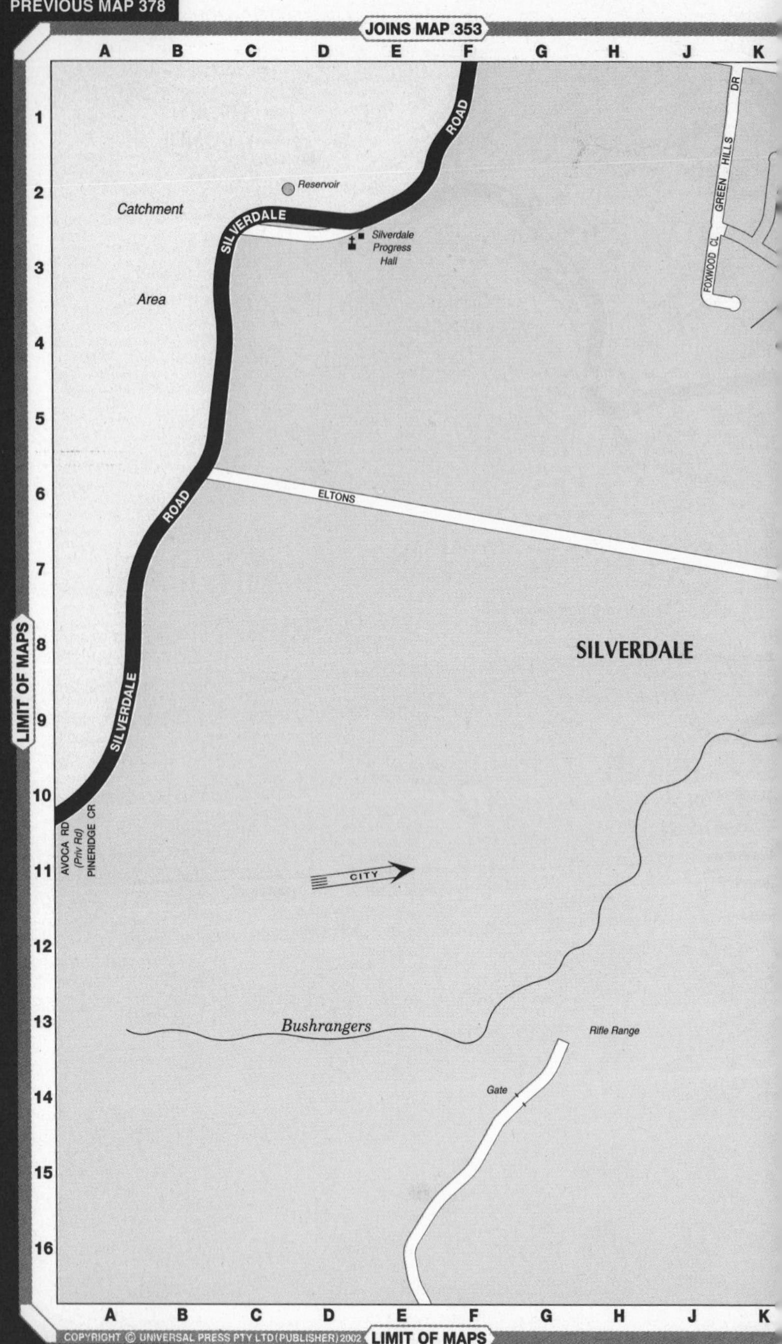
JOINS MAP 353
A B C D E F G H J K
1 2 3 4 5 6 7 8 9 10 11 12 13 14 15 16
SILVERDALE ROAD
Reservoir
Catchment
Area
Silverdale
Progress
Hall
GREEN HILLS DR
FOXWOOD CL
ELTONS
SILVERDALE
AVOCA RD
(Priv Rd)
PINERIDGE CR
CITY
Bushrangers
Rifle Range
Gate
LIMIT OF MAPS

JOINS MAP 354

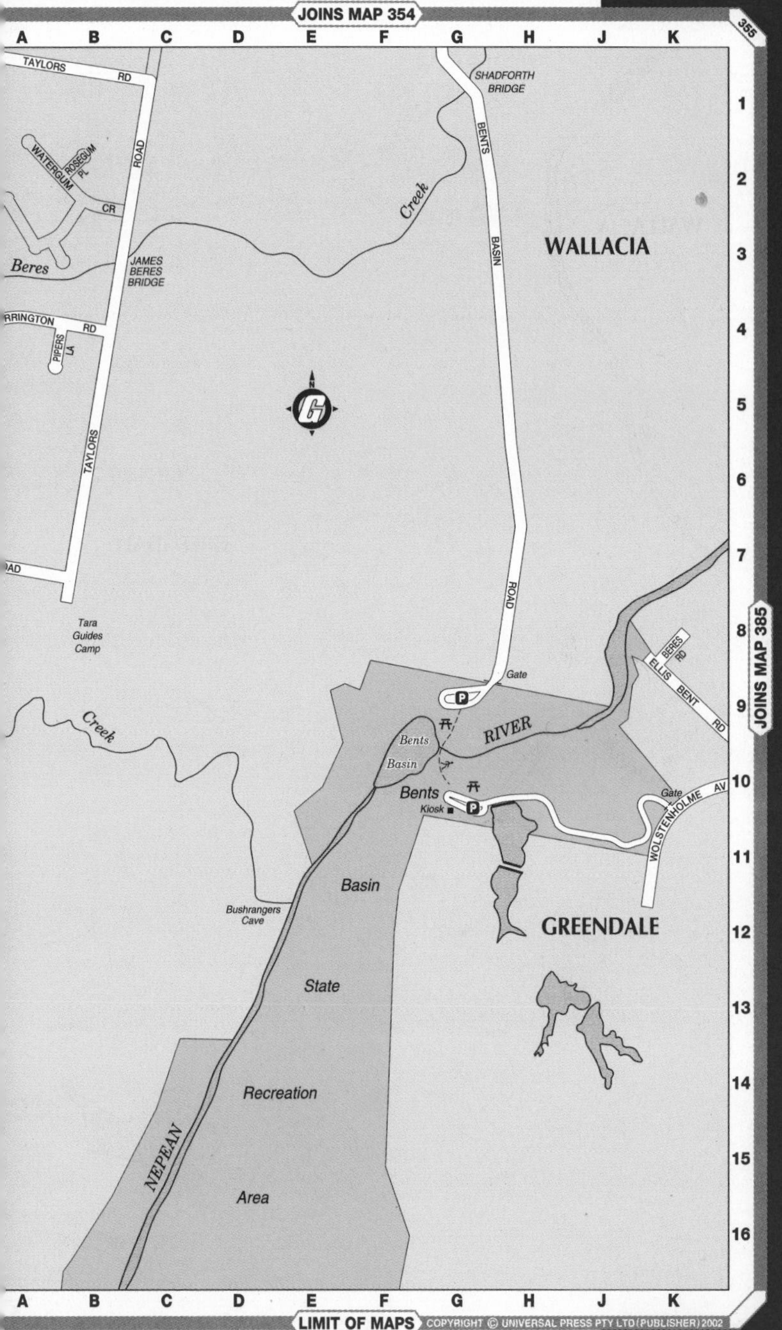

JOINS MAP 385

LIMIT OF MAPS

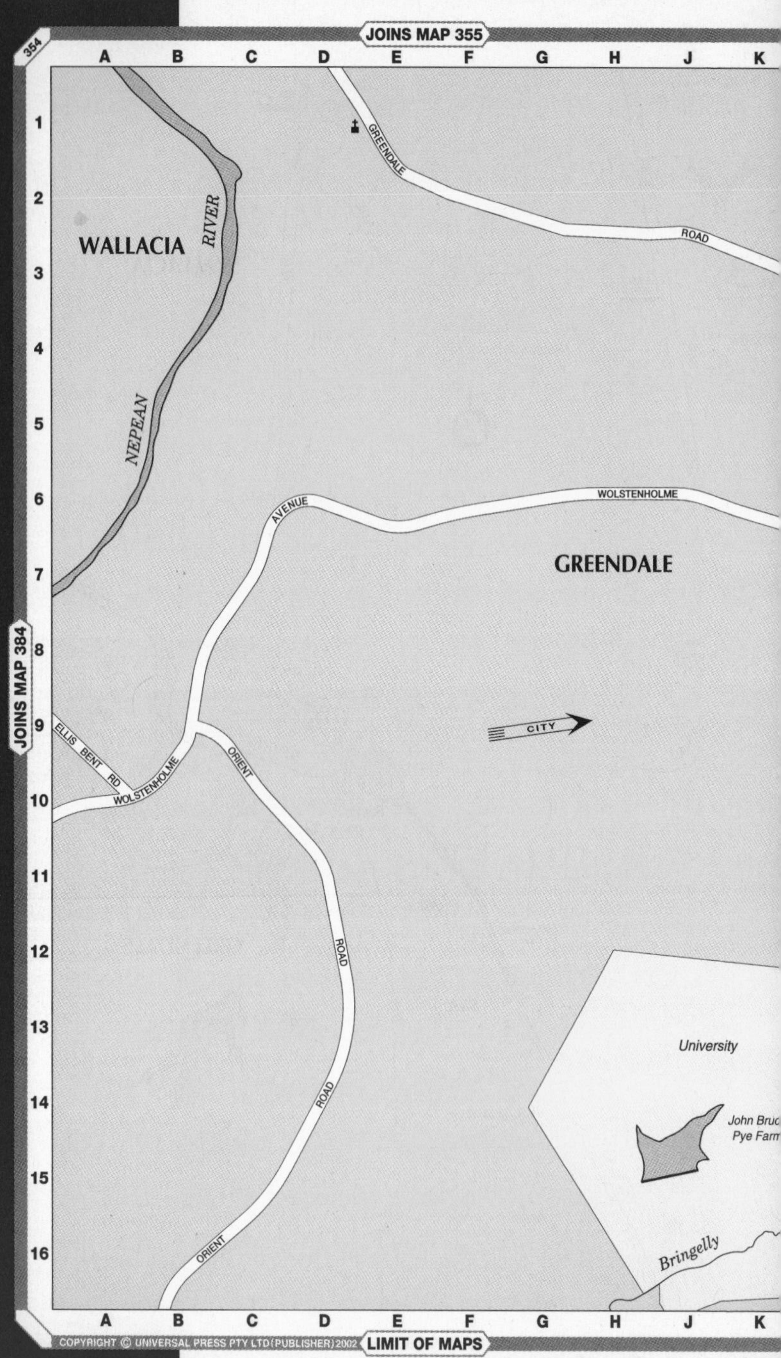

JOINS MAP 355
354
A
B
C
D
E
F
G
H
J
K
1
2
3
4
5
6
7
8
9
10
11
12
13
14
15
16
WALLACIA
NEPEAN
RIVER
GREENDALE
ROAD
AVENUE
WOLSTENHOLME
GREENDALE
CITY
ELLIS BENT RD
WOLSTENHOLME
ORIENT
ROAD
ROAD
ORIENT
University
John Bruc
Pye Farm
Bringelly
JOINS MAP 384
LIMIT OF MAPS

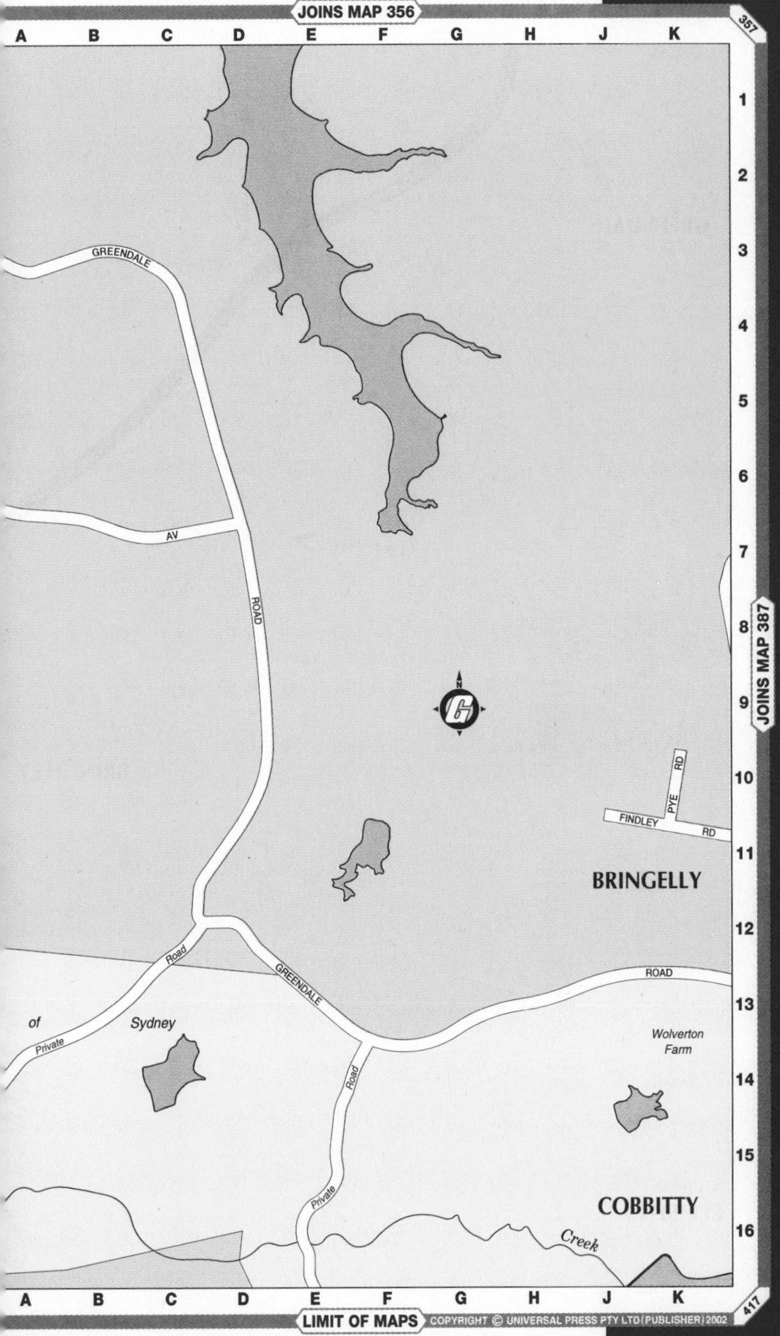
JOINS MAP 356
357
A
B
C
D
E
F
G
H
J
K
1
2
3
4
5
6
7
8
9
10
11
12
13
14
15
16
GREENDALE
AV
ROAD
PYE
RD
FINDLEY
RD
BRINGELLY
Road
GREENDALE
ROAD
of
Sydney
Private
Wolverton
Farm
Road
Private
COBBITTY
Creek
JOINS MAP 387
LIMIT OF MAPS
417

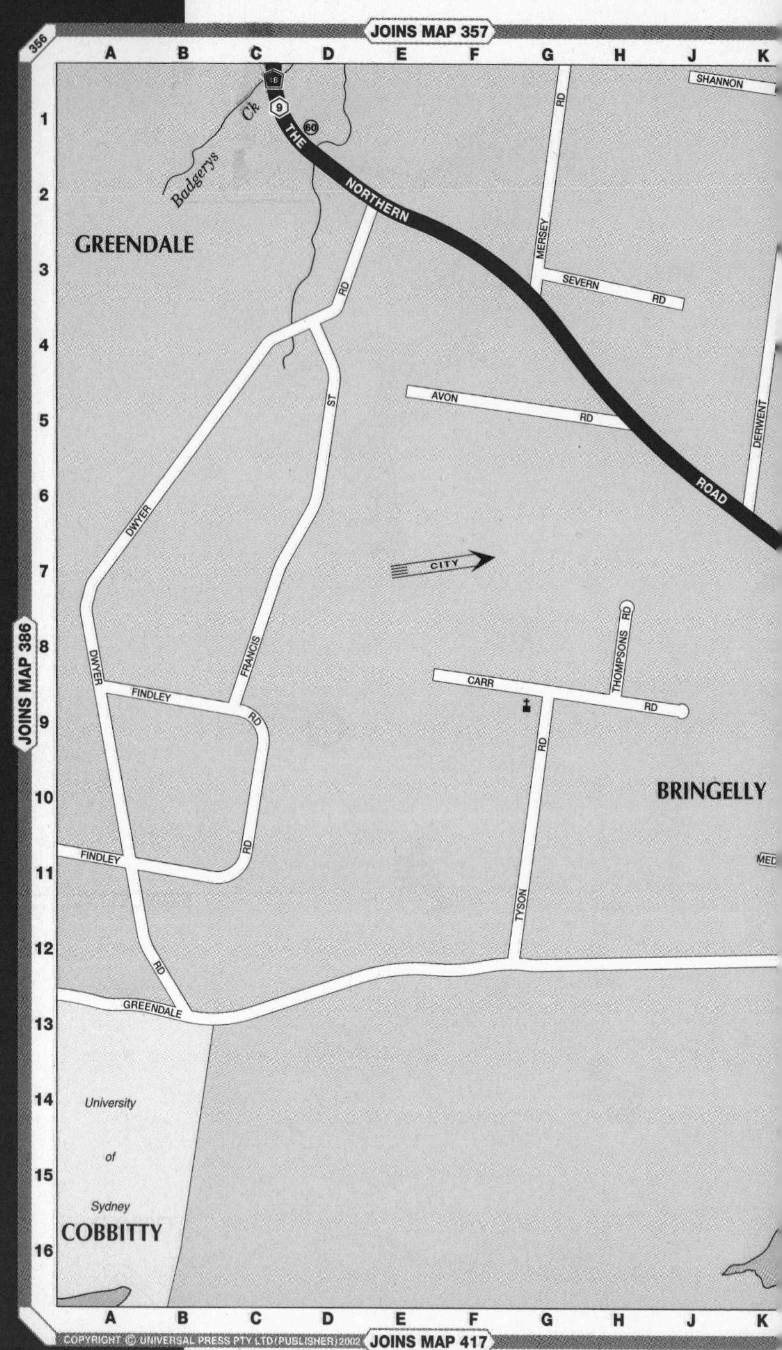
JOINS MAP 357
356
A B C D E F G H J K
1 2 3 4 5 6 7 8 9 10 11 12 13 14 15 16
JOINS MAP 386
18
9
60
Badgerys Ck
THE NORTHERN ROAD
SHANNON
MERSEY RD
SEVERN RD
GREENDALE
RD
AVON RD
DERWENT
ST
DWYER
CITY
THOMPSONS RD
FRANCIS
DWYER
FINDLEY
CARR RD
RD
RD
BRINGELLY
FINDLEY
RD
MED
TYSON
RD
GREENDALE
University of Sydney
COBBITTY
JOINS MAP 417

JOINS MAP 358

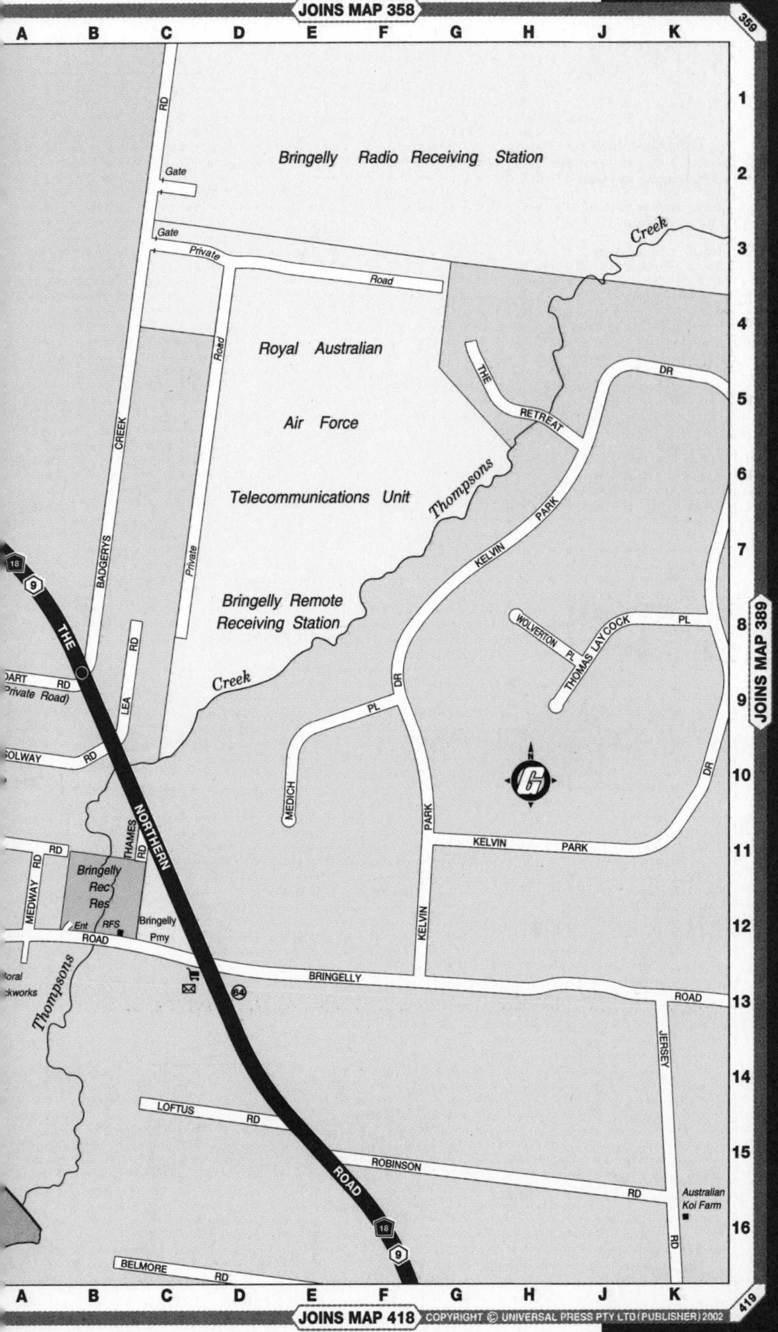

JOINS MAP 418

419

JOINS MAP 359

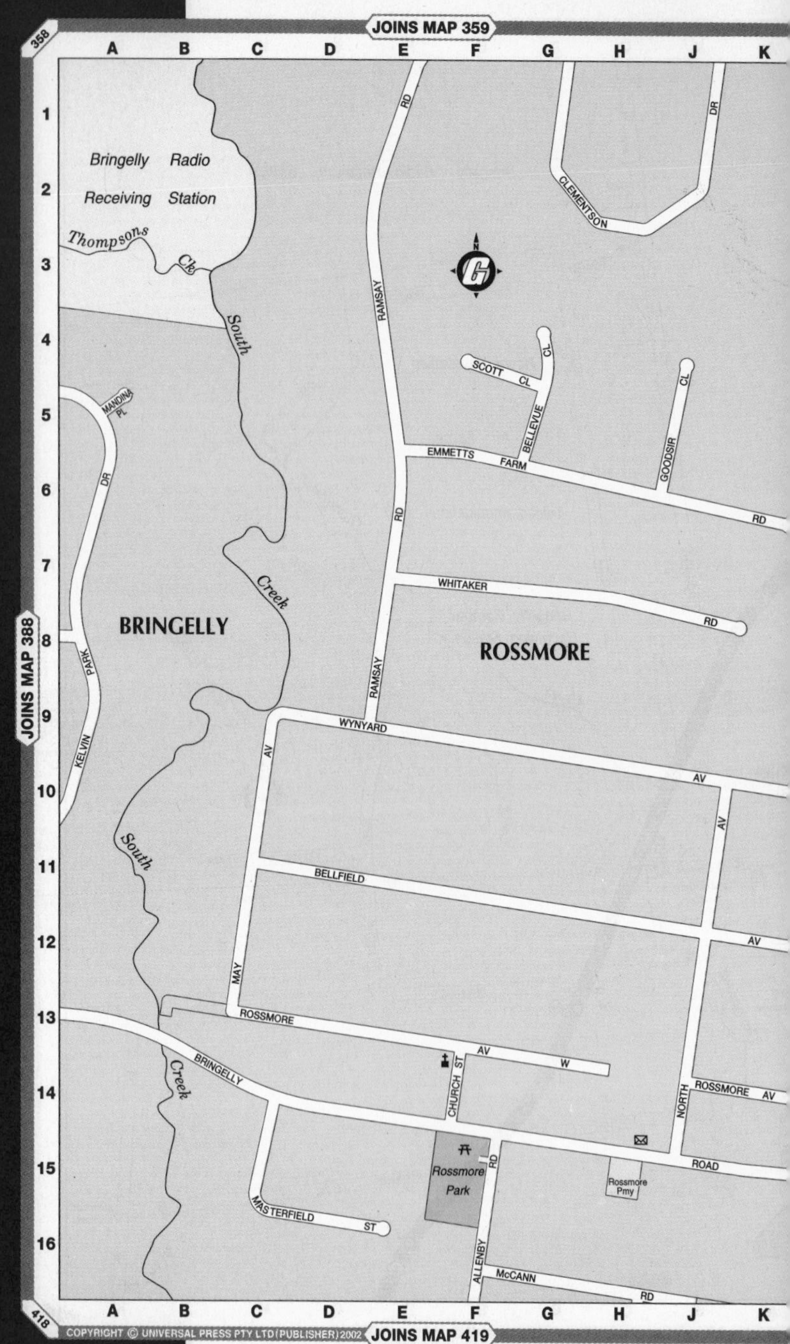

JOINS MAP 388

JOINS MAP 419

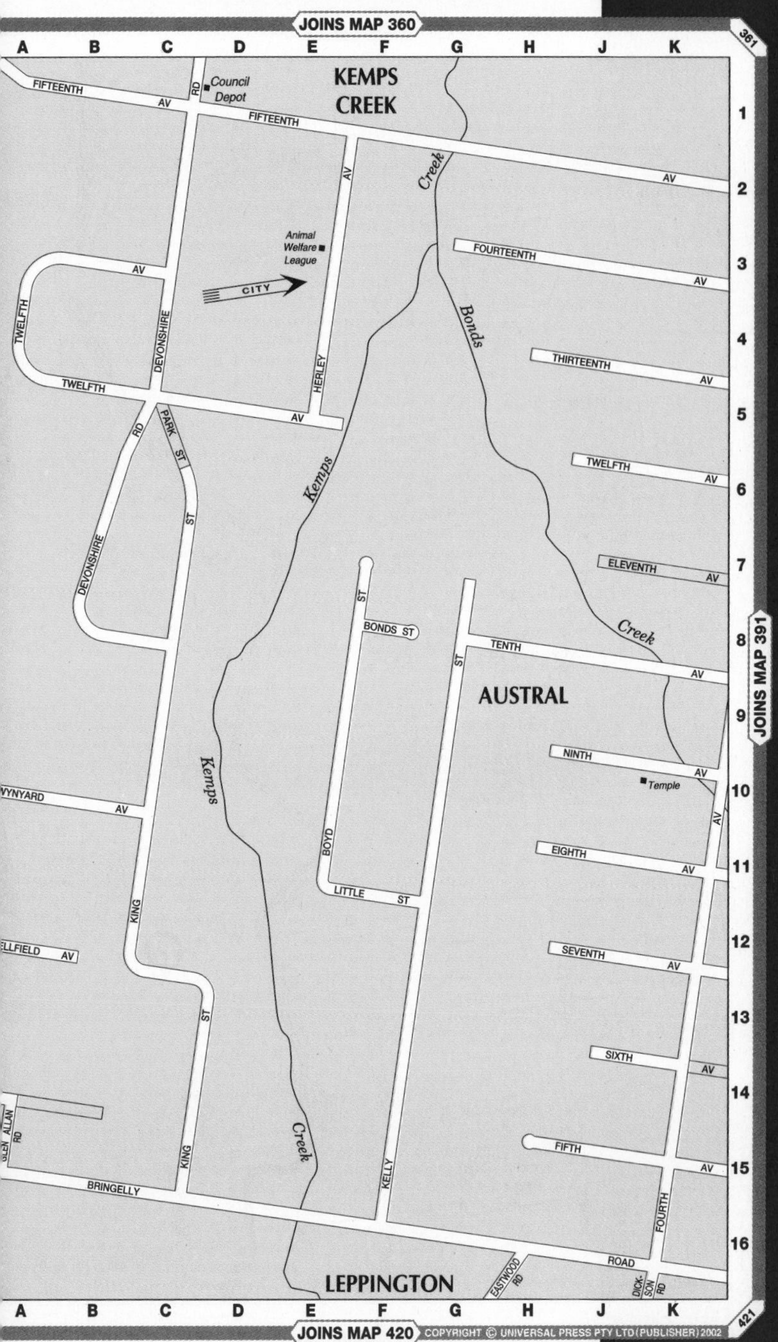
JOINS MAP 360
361
A B C D E F G H J K
KEMPS CREEK
Council Depot
FIFTEENTH AV
FIFTEENTH AV
RD
Animal Welfare League
CITY
Creek
Bonds
FOURTEENTH AV
THIRTEENTH AV
TWELFTH AV
ELEVENTH AV
TWELFTH
TWELFTH AV
DEVONSHIRE
HERLEY AV
PARK ST
RD
DEVONSHIRE
Kemps
ST
BONDS ST
TENTH AV
Creek
AUSTRAL
NINTH AV
Temple
WYNYARD AV
Kemps
BOYD
LITTLE ST
EIGHTH AV
KING
ELLFIELD AV
SEVENTH AV
ST
SIXTH AV
GLEN ALLAN RD
Creek
KING
FIFTH AV
BRINGELLY
KELLY
FOURTH
ROAD
EASTWOOD RD
DICK-SON RD
LEPPINGTON
1 2 3 4 5 6 7 8 9 10 11 12 13 14 15 16
JOINS MAP 391
JOINS MAP 420
421

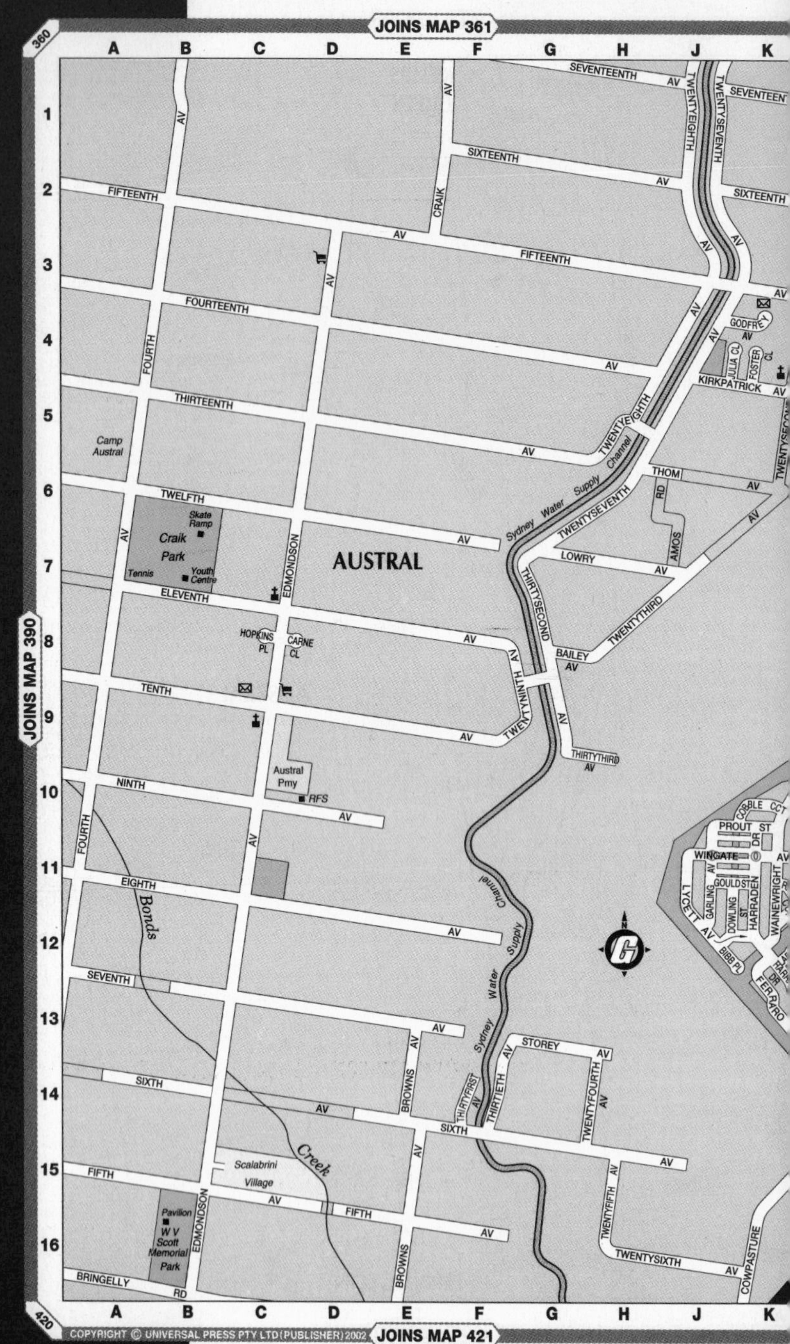
JOINS MAP 361
JOINS MAP 390
JOINS MAP 421
360
420
AUSTRAL
SEVENTEENTH AV
SIXTEENTH AV
FIFTEENTH AV
FOURTEENTH AV
THIRTEENTH AV
TWELFTH AV
ELEVENTH AV
TENTH AV
NINTH AV
EIGHTH AV
SEVENTH AV
SIXTH AV
FIFTH AV
BRINGELLY RD
FOURTH AV
CRAIK AV
EDMONDSON AV
BROWNS AV
TWENTYEIGHTH AV
TWENTYSEVENTH AV
TWENTYNINTH AV
THIRTYSECOND AV
THIRTYTHIRD AV
TWENTYTHIRD AV
THIRTYFIRST AV
THIRTIETH AV
TWENTYFOURTH AV
TWENTYFIFTH AV
TWENTYSIXTH AV
COWPASTURE
GODFREY AV
JULIA CL
FOSTER CL
KIRKPATRICK AV
THOM AV
AMOS RD
LOWRY AV
BAILEY AV
STOREY AV
HOPKINS PL
CARNE CL
PROUT ST
COBBLE CCT
WINGATE
LYCETT AV
GARLING AV
GOULD ST
DOWLING ST
HARRADEN DR
WAINEWRIGHT AV
BIBB PL
FERRARO
Sydney Water Supply Channel
Bonds Creek
Camp Austral
Craik Park
Skate Ramp
Tennis
Youth Centre
Austral Pmy
RFS
Scalabrini Village
Pavilion
W V Scott Memorial Park
A B C D E F G H J K
1 2 3 4 5 6 7 8 9 10 11 12 13 14 15 16

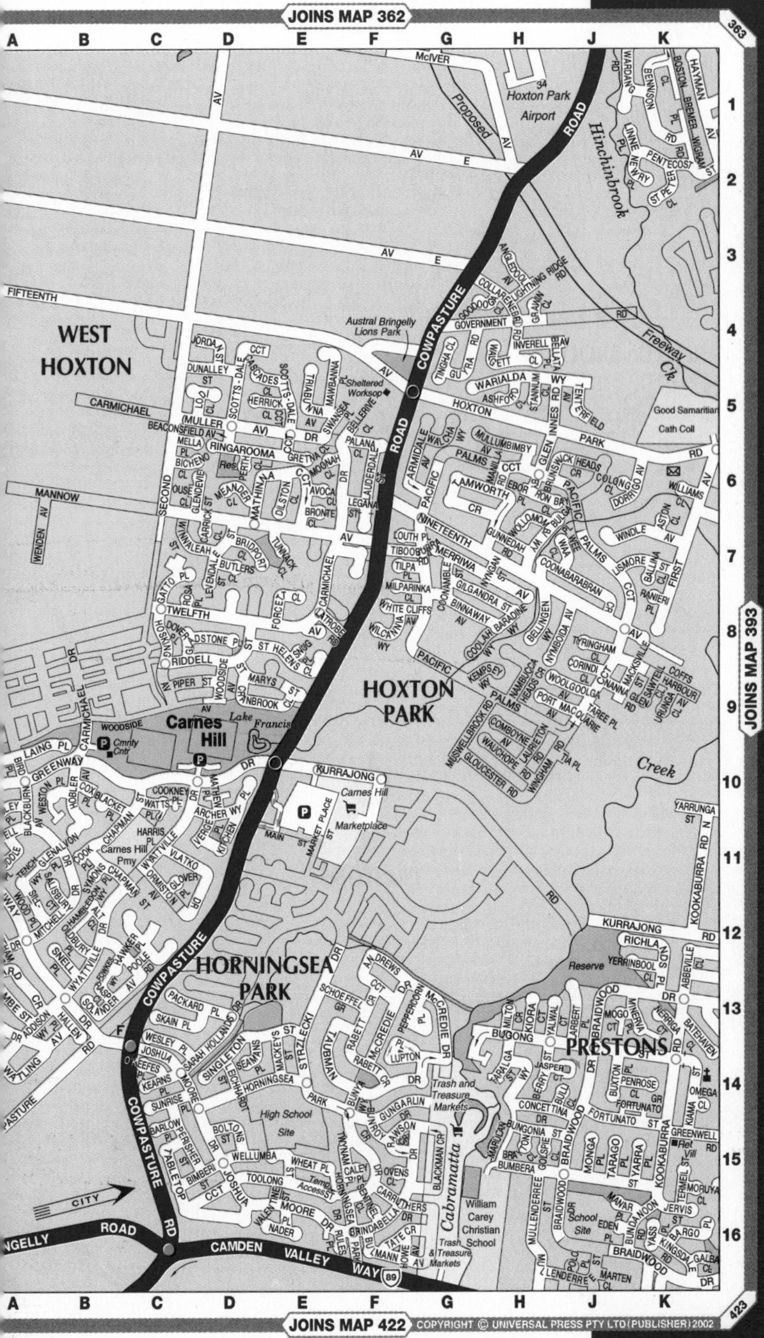
JOINS MAP 362
JOINS MAP 393
JOINS MAP 422
363
423
WEST HOXTON
HOXTON PARK
HORNINGSEA PARK
PRESTONS
Carnes Hill
Hoxton Park Airport
Hinchinbrook
Austral Bringelly Lions Park
Sheltered Worksop
Good Samaritan Cath Coll
Lake Francis
Carnes Hill Marketplace
Carnes Hill Pmy
High School Site
Trash and Treasure Markets
William Carey Christian School
Cabramatta
Creek
Reserve
COWPASTURE ROAD
CAMDEN VALLEY WAY
HOXTON PARK RD
KURRAJONG RD
FIFTEENTH AV
CITY

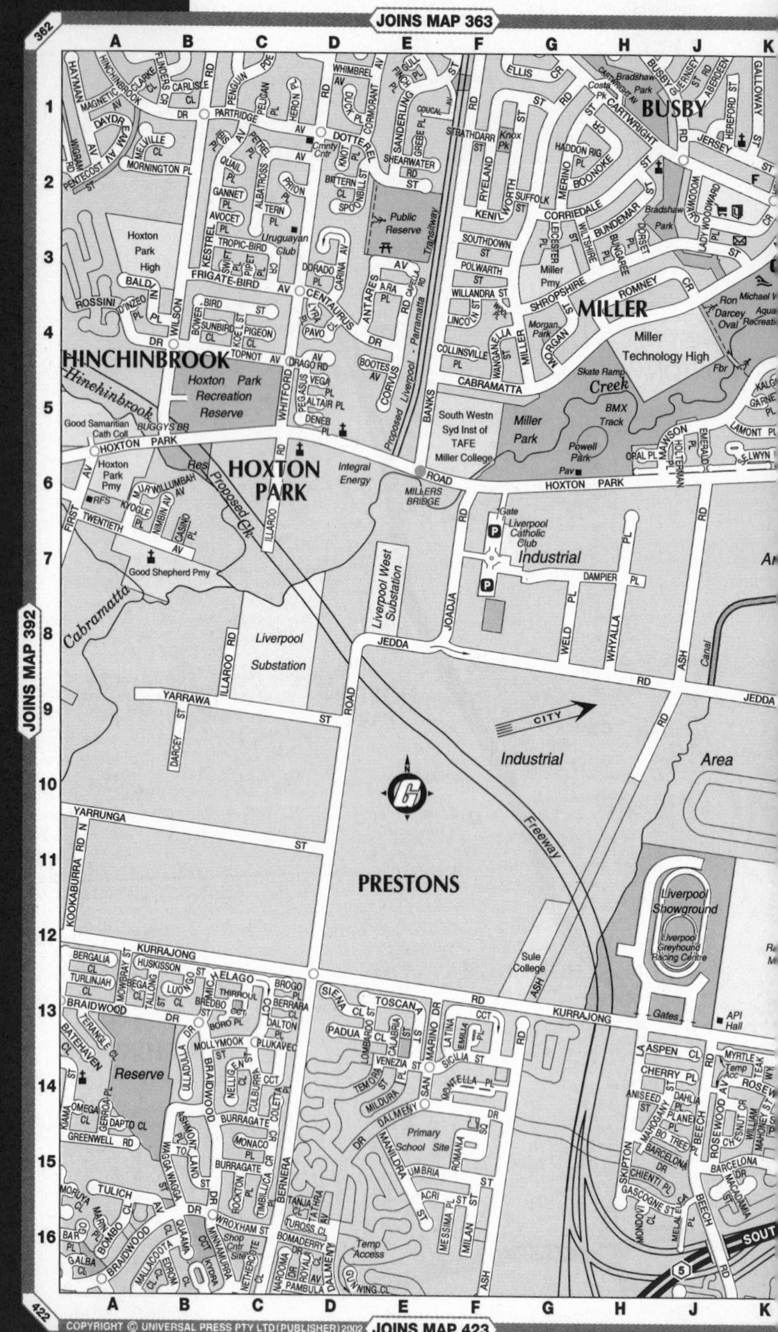
JOINS MAP 363
JOINS MAP 392
JOINS MAP 423
362
422
HINCHINBROOK
HOXTON PARK
MILLER
BUSBY
PRESTONS
Hoxton Park High
Hoxton Park Recreation Reserve
Good Samaritan Cath Coll
Hoxton Park Pmy
Good Shepherd Pmy
Uruguayan Club
Public Reserve
Integral Energy
Liverpool Substation
Liverpool West Substation
South Westn Syd Inst of TAFE Miller College
Miller Park
Miller Technology High
Miller Pmy
Morgan Park
Knox Pk
Bradshaw Park
Ron Darcey Oval
Skate Ramp
BMX Track
Powell Park
Liverpool Catholic Club
Industrial
Industrial Area
Liverpool Showground
Liverpool Greyhound Racing Centre
Sule College
API Hall
Reserve
Primary School Site
Freeway
Canal
Cabramatta Creek
Hinchinbrook
Proposed Liverpool - Parramatta Transitway
HOXTON PARK ROAD
KURRAJONG RD
JEDDA RD
CITY

JOINS MAP 364

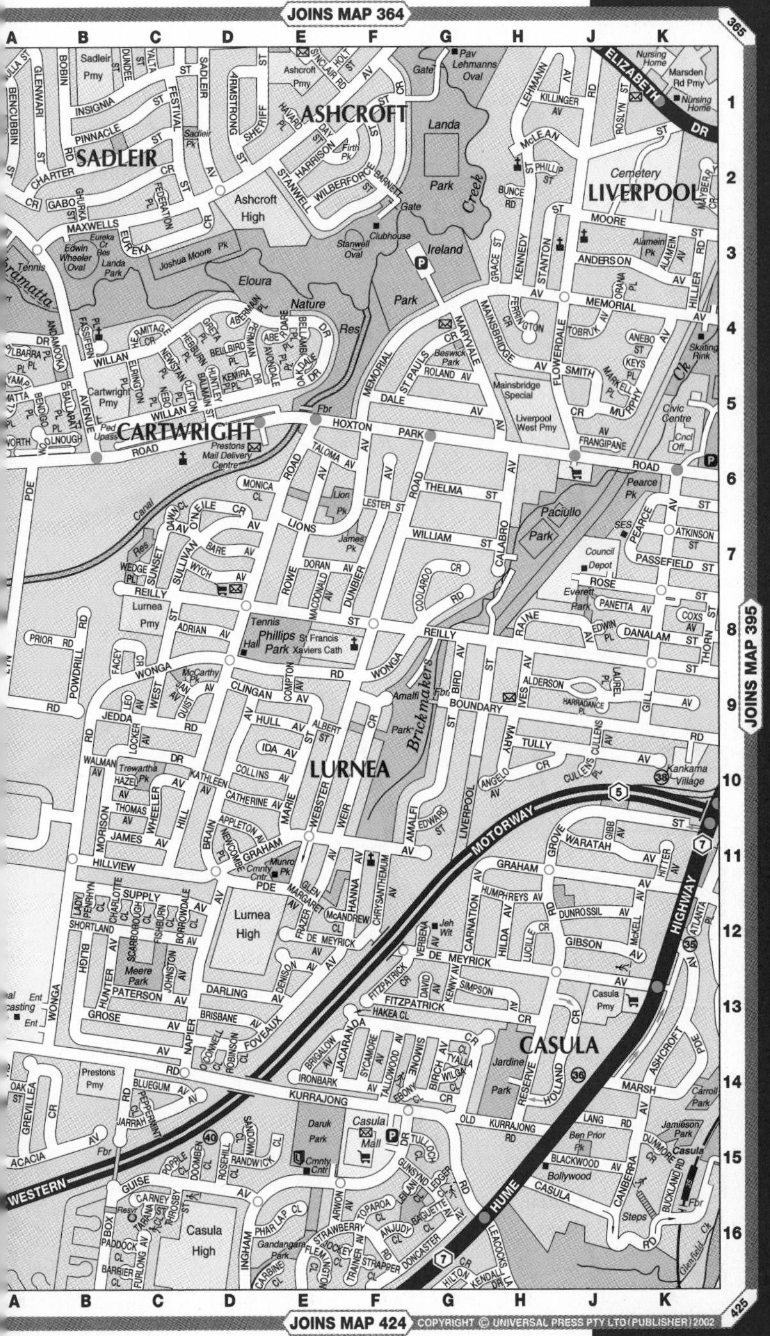

JOINS MAP 395

JOINS MAP 424

JOINS MAP 365

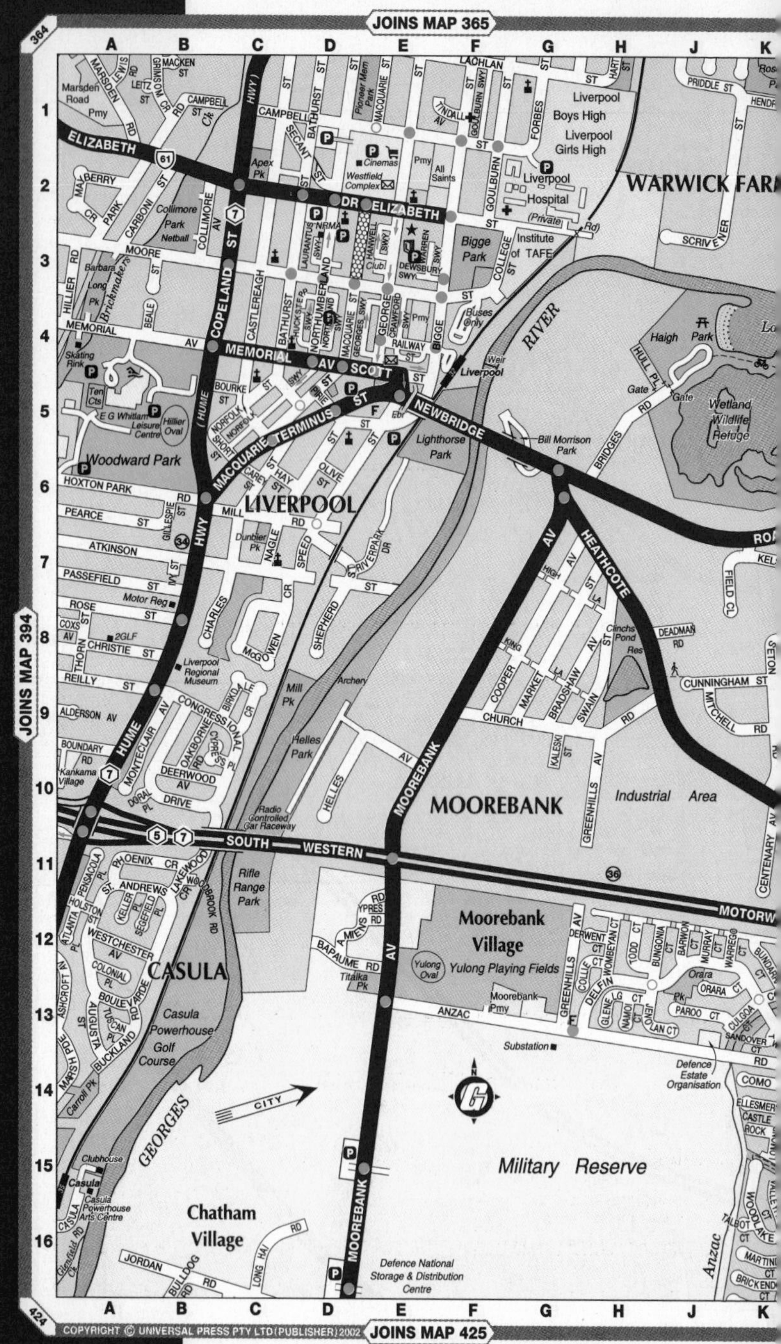

JOINS MAP 425

JOINS MAP 394

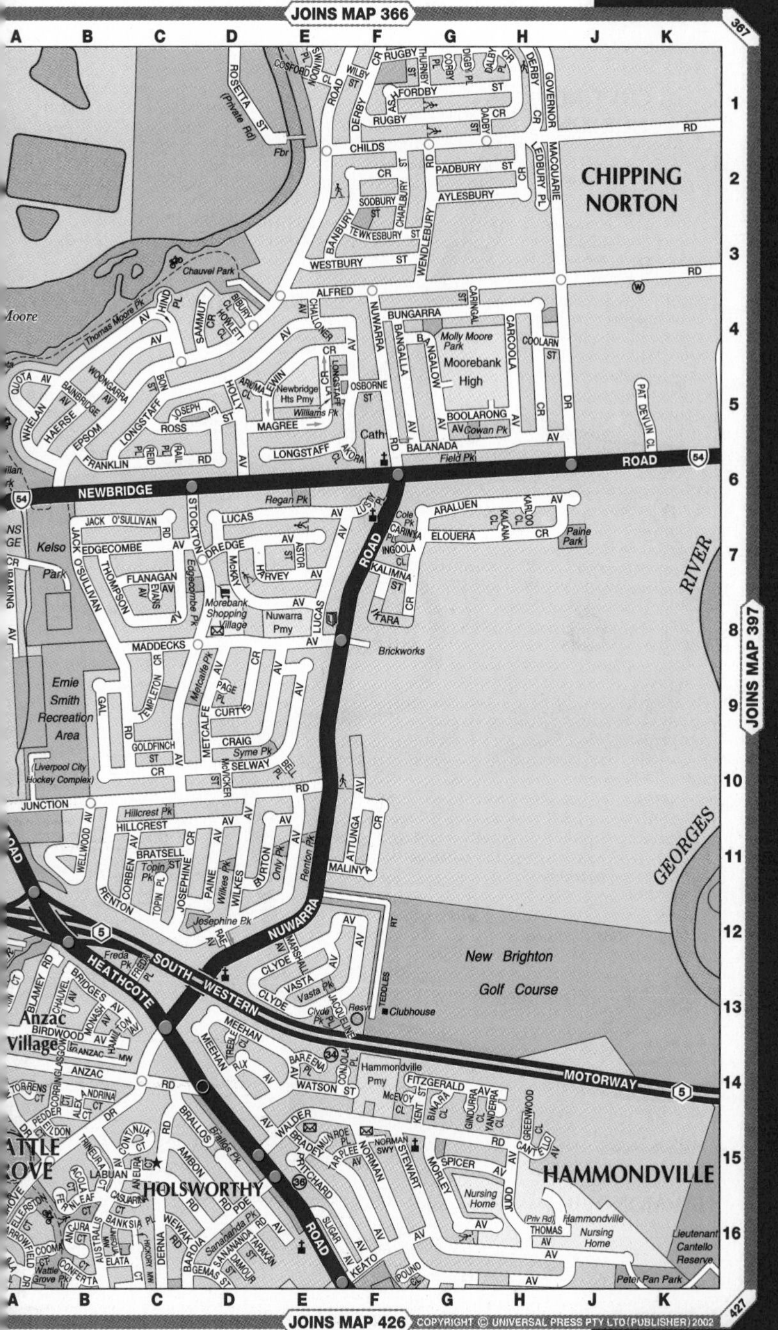
JOINS MAP 366
367
A B C D E F G H J K
1 2 3 4 5 6 7 8 9 10 11 12 13 14 15 16
CHIPPING NORTON
HAMMONDVILLE
HOLSWORTHY
Anzac Village
New Brighton Golf Course
Clubhouse
Moorebank High
Molly Moore Park
Newbridge Hts Pmy
Williams Pk
Cath
Field Pk
Cowan Pk
Regan Pk
Cole Pk
Paine Park
Kelso Park
Morebank Shopping Village
Nuwarra Pmy
Brickworks
Ernie Smith Recreation Area
(Liverpool City Hockey Complex)
Syme Pk
Hillcrest Pk
Topin Pk
Wilkes Pk
Only Pk
Renton Pk
Josephine Pk
Freda Pk
Vasta Pk
Clyde Pk
Resvr
Hammondville Pmy
Nursing Home
Hammondville Nursing Home
(Priv Rd)
Lieutenant Cantello Reserve
Peter Pan Park
Wattle Grove Pk
Chauvel Park
Thomas Moore Pk
ROSETTA ST (Private Rd)
Fbr
CHILDS RD
NEWBRIDGE ROAD
NUWARRA ROAD
HEATHCOTE ROAD
SOUTH-WESTERN MOTORWAY
GEORGES RIVER
JUNCTION RD
MADDECKS AV
ALFRED RD
WESTBURY ST
PADBURY ST
AYLESBURY
MACQUARIE DR
GOVERNOR
BOOLARONG AV
BALANADA AV
LONGSTAFF AV
FRANKLIN RD
ANZAC RD
MEEHAN
WATSON ST
FITZGERALD AV
WALDER RD
PRITCHARD
NORMAN AV
STEWART
MORLEY
SPICER
JUDD AV
THOMAS AV
PAT DEVLIN CL
ARALUEN AV
ELOUERA CR
HILLCREST AV
BRATSELL
RENTON
JOSEPHINE CR
PAINE AV
WILKES AV
BURTON
ATTUNGA
MALINYA
SELWAY
CRAIG
GOLDFINCH ST
METCALFE
CURTIS
TEMPLETON CR
THOMPSON
JACK O'SULLIVAN RD
EDGECOMBE AV
FLANAGAN AV
LUCAS AV
DREDGE AV
STOCKTON AV
HARVEY AV
ASTOR ST
54
5
34
36

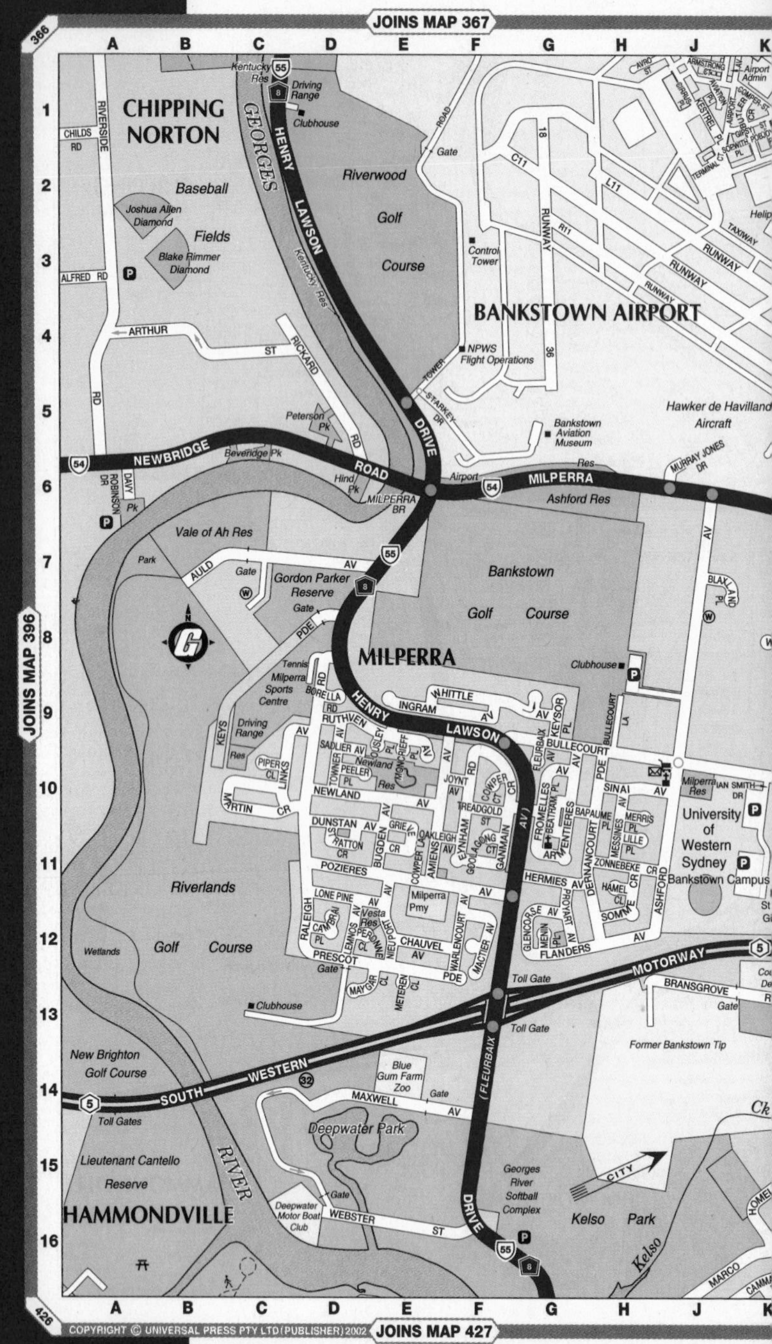
JOINS MAP 367
JOINS MAP 396
JOINS MAP 427
366
426
A B C D E F G H J K
1 2 3 4 5 6 7 8 9 10 11 12 13 14 15 16
CHIPPING NORTON
Baseball Fields
Joshua Allen Diamond
Blake Rimmer Diamond
CHILDS RD
RIVERSIDE RD
ALFRED RD
ARTHUR ST
RICKARD RD
GEORGES
HENRY LAWSON DRIVE
Kentucky Res
Driving Range
Clubhouse
Riverwood Golf Course
Gate
ROAD
Control Tower
BANKSTOWN AIRPORT
C11
L11
R11
18
36
RUNWAY
TAXIWAY
AVRO ST
ARMSTRONG
AVIATION
KESTREL PL
AIRPORT
TERMINAL CT
SOPWITH PL
Airport Admin
NPWS Flight Operations
TOWER
STARKEY DR
Bankstown Aviation Museum
Hawker de Havilland Aircraft
Peterson Pk
NEWBRIDGE ROAD
Beveridge Pk
Hind Pk
MILPERRA BR
Airport
MILPERRA
Res
Ashford Res
MURRAY JONES DR
ROBINSON DR
DAVY Pk
Vale of Ah Res
Park
AULD AV
Gate
Gordon Parker Reserve
PDE
Bankstown Golf Course
BLAXLAND PL
MILPERRA
Clubhouse
Tennis
Milperra Sports Centre
Driving Range
KEYS
BORELLA RD
INGRAM
WHITTLE
KEYSOR PL
LAWSON
RUTHVEN AV
SADLIER AV
Newland Res
PIPER CL
LINKS
MARTIN CR
NEWLAND AV
JOYNT AV
COWPER CT
TREADGOLD ST
BULLECOURT
BULLECOURT LA
FROMELLES AV
FLEURBAIX AV
BEATRAM PL
MENTIERES
BAPAUME PL
SINAI AV
MERRIS PL
LILLE PL
MESSINES
Milperra Res
IAN SMITH DR
University of Western Sydney Bankstown Campus
DUNSTAN AV
STRATTON CR
BUGDEN AV
GRIEVE CR
OAKLEIGH AV
EYNHAM
GOOLAGONG CT
GANMAIN
DERNANCOURT
ZONNEBEKE CR
POZIERES
AMIENS
HERMIES AV
HAMEL CL
SOMME
ASHFORD
Riverlands Golf Course
LONE PINE AV
Milperra Pmy
RALEIGH
CAMBRAI PL
Vesta Res
LEMNOS
PERONNE
NIEUPORT
WARLENCOURT
MACTIER AV
GLENCORSE AV
MENIN
PROYART AV
FLANDERS
CHAUVEL AV
PRESCOT PDE
Gate
MAYGAR CL
METEREN CL
Toll Gate
MOTORWAY
BRANSGROVE
Gate
Clubhouse
Wetlands
Former Bankstown Tip
New Brighton Golf Course
SOUTH WESTERN
Blue Gum Farm Zoo
MAXWELL AV
(FLEURBAIX)
Toll Gates
Deepwater Park
Lieutenant Cantello Reserve
RIVER
HAMMONDVILLE
Deepwater Motor Boat Club
WEBSTER ST
DRIVE
Georges River Softball Complex
Kelso Park
Kelso
CITY
MARCO
5
8
32
54
55
COPYRIGHT © UNIVERSAL PRESS PTY LTD (PUBLISHER) 2002

JOINS MAP 368

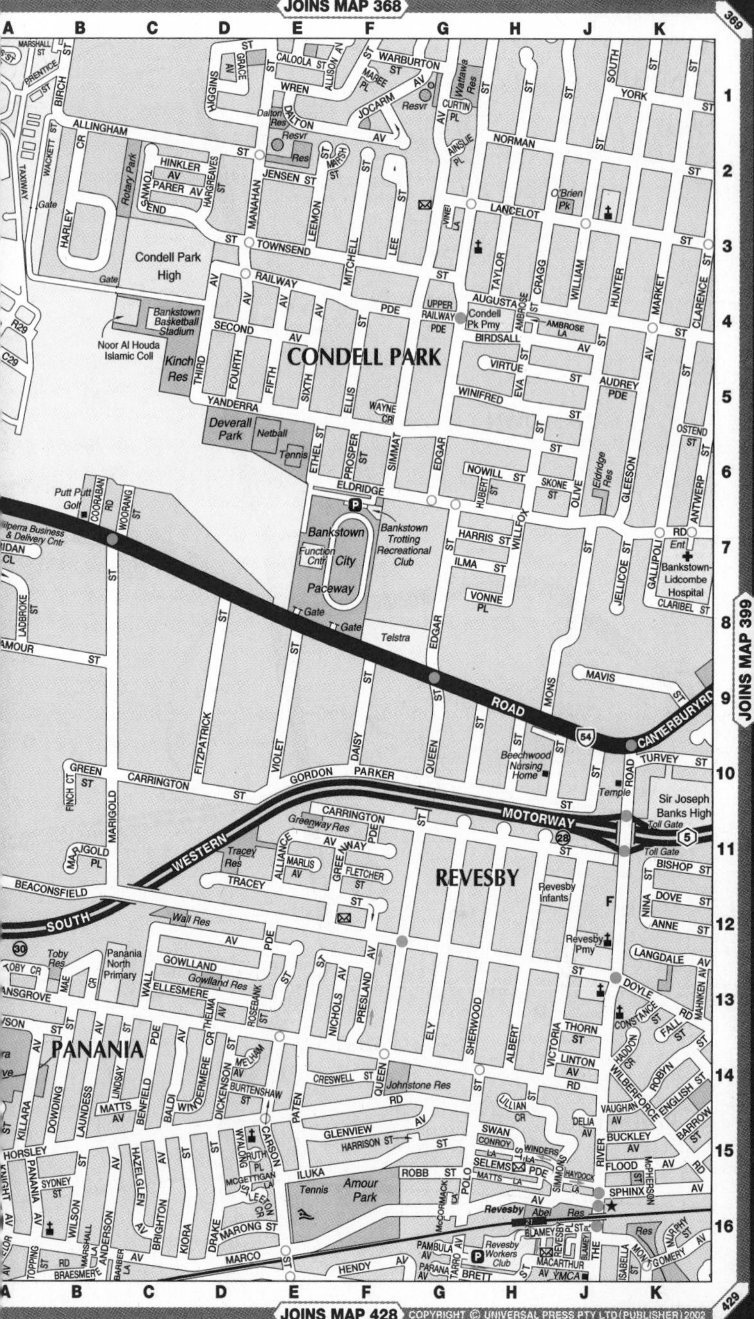

JOINS MAP 428

JOINS MAP 399

JOINS MAP 369
368
A B C D E F G H J K
1 2 3 4 5 6 7 8 9 10 11 12 13 14 15 16
CONDELL PARK
BANKSTOWN
PADSTOW
REVESBY
MARION ST
YORK ST
MARKET ST
BRANDON AV
CAMBRIDGE ST
NORMAN ST
EGAN ST
WINSPEAR AV
GREENWOOD AV
OLYMPIC PDE
DALE PDE
DEPOT PL
Bankstown
SOUTH TCE
Tenpin Bowl
STEWART LA
GREENFIELD PDE
Club
MONA ST
SWEETHAVEN RD
KOPEZ LA
RAYMOND ST
WEST TCE
EAST TCE
CROSS ST
STANLEY ST
McDONALD LA
Girls High
Bankstown Primary
St Brendans Cath
CHELMSFORD AV
Bankstown Memorial Park
Bankstown Oval
ROSS ST
VIMY ST
RESTWELL ST
LEONARD ST
PERCY ST
Stevens Res
CHERTSEY AV
LANCELOT ST
MACAULEY AV
CLARENCE ST
PRINGLE AV
OXFORD AV
KOONYA AV
OGMORE CT
DUDLEY AV
DELLWOOD ST
MARSHALL ST
MEGAN AV
WHITE AV
JUNE ST
DE WITT ST
DE WITT LA
NOUMEA AV
AUGUSTA ST
GALLIPOLI ST
SHENTON AV
SUNSET AV
TUMUT CL
Bankstown City Sports Complex
Ent
HIGH ST
OSTEND ST
ANTWERP ST
EDWARD ST
HIXSON ST
ARCHER CR
Ruse Park
Football Centre
GARTMORE AV
SEDDON ST
ARKLEY ST
ADEPT LA
TOPAZ PL
B'town Senior College
IRVINE ST
HOSKINS AV
ARTHUR ST
HERBERT ST
ELDRIDGE RD
Bankstown-Lidcombe Hosp
ARTEGALL ST
NORTHAM AV
CALIDORE ST
CLARIBEL ST
CHAPEL RD
Christies Homemaker Centre
CLEMENTS AV
COTTAM AV
EXCELLER AV
WARREN AV
FORT AV
ROAD
Bob Jane T-Mart
SES
CANTERBURY
54
Flood Res
Caroline Chisholm Special Sch
GIBSON ST
NELSON AV
GOW ST
LACHLAN ST
NAPOLI ST
REIBA CR
SNOWSILL AV
STILES AV
ATKINSON AV
TURVEY ST
WORDIE PL
CITY
Sir Joseph Banks High
WOLYROI CR
SOUTH WESTERN MOTORWAY
5
BRYANT ST
LAUREL CR
LOUIE ST
BISHOP ST
DRAVET ST
DOVE ST
MACKINNON AV
ANNE ST
RONALD ST
GWANDALAN RD
HALCYON AV
BEAMISH ST
LIBERA AV
MORO AV
NEWEY AV
Padstow North Primary
ENTERPRISE AV
FACTORY CT
STUART ST
ARAB RD
Clubhouse
Stuart St Reserve
LANGDALE AV
ARCHIBALD ST
MAHNKEN AV
MACKENZIE ST
CAROTANA ST
LESTER RD
Playford Park
Southern Sydney Institute of TAFE Padstow College
DOYLE RD
BLACKALL ST
CAHORS RD
ROBYN ST
PIVETTA ST
ENGLISH ST
Res
BARROW ST
WILBERFORCE RD
RHONDA ST
RAINE RD
CAIRO ST
SPHINX AV
PYRAMID AV
SHEARER LA
VANNAN AV
WATSON RD
Steps
DAVIES RD
FAIRFORD RD
JAYELEM CR
McEVOY ST
KURANDA AV
IBERIA ST
STEPHANIE ST
JEANETTE ST
NIGEL PL
Padstow Park
ALICE ST
HENDRICH AV
CORY AV
Little Res
MEMORIAL DR
BANKS ST
19
RSL
Padstow
STEPHENS RD
SHOULTS LA
CRUSADE AV
HOWARD RD
GLOUCESTER AV
SEGERS AV
PADSTOW PDE
Pmy
MAL AV
PARR AV
PARKER LA
RYAN RD
LOCK AV
MONTGOMERY AV
WYREEMA AV
TONY CR
McGIRR ST
CORAL AV
BADDELEY ST
SPRING ST
DOYLE RD
MEAGER AV
TREVONE ST
TRURO PDE
BRIDGE ST
STACEY ST
6
SOUTH ST
CARNATION AV
GRIFFITHS AV
GARDENIA AV
SALVIA AV
VERBENA AV
PETUNIA AV
DAPHNE AV
ASTER AV
MARCELLA LA
MARCELLA ST
JAMES ST
LAVENDER AV
SALADINE AV
COLUMBINE AV
PRATTEN LA
LANCASTER AV
MAWSON ST
GOWRIE AV
Salmon Res
Dorothy Park
SCOTT ST
GILLIAN PL
Arthur Pk
WARWICK ST
MICHAELS CR
BOXLEY CR
LANCASTER CR
NEVADA ST
SUNNY CR
WYLENA PL
VIOLA
PUNCHBOWL RD
Infants
HOMEDALE RD
JOHN ST
MOXON RD
CANTERBURY
WEYLAND ST
VERNON ST
BRAMHALL AV
SEPTIMUS AV
CARLTON
JOYCE
CRAIG ST
Craig St Res
WIGGS
Hardwarehouse
SHORT ST
Bankstown Substation
Salt Pan Ck
Baseball
McLaughlin Oval
IRIS
Fbr
Ped Upass
26
Salt Pan Reserve
Sports Field
Riverwood Pmy
Riverwood Park
WILLIAM
HENRY RD
LILLIAN
WEBB
BASIL ST
WEEMALA
SHENSTONE RD
JOINS MAP 398
JOINS MAP 429
428

JOINS MAP 370

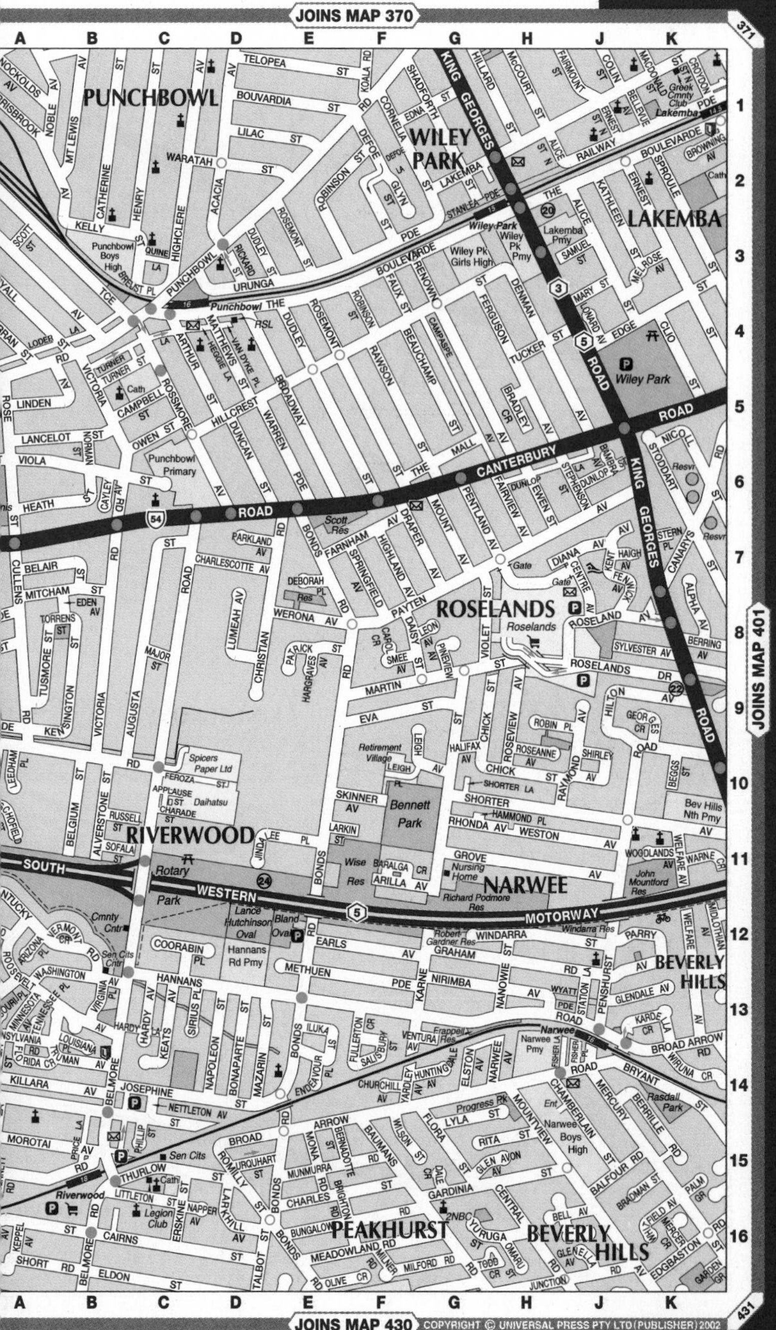

JOINS MAP 401

JOINS MAP 430

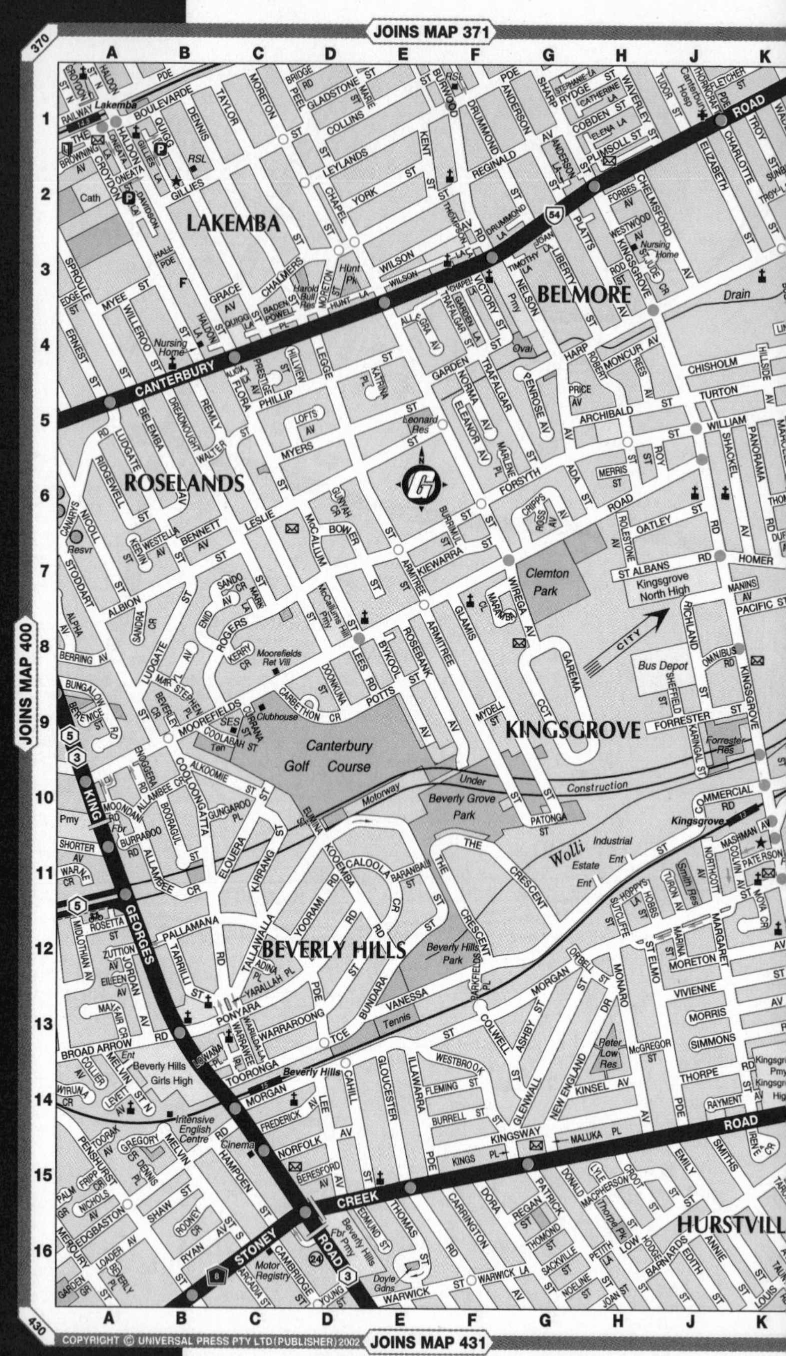
JOINS MAP 371
JOINS MAP 400
JOINS MAP 431
370
430
LAKEMBA
BELMORE
ROSELANDS
KINGSGROVE
BEVERLY HILLS
HURSTVILL
CANTERBURY
ROAD
KING
GEORGES
STONEY
CREEK
Lakemba
Kingsgrove
Beverly Hills
Canterbury Golf Course
Clubhouse
Clemton Park
Beverly Grove Park
Beverly Hills Park
Kingsgrove North High
Beverly Hills Girls High
Intensive English Centre
Moorefields Ret Vill
Bus Depot
Wolli
Industrial Estate
Motorway
Under Construction
Canterbury Hosp
Nursing Home
Hunt Pk
Harold Bull Res
Leonard Res
Forrester Res
Smith Res
Peter Low Res
Thorne Pk
Doyle Gdns
Motor Registry
Cinema
Tennis
Oval
Drain
Resvr
CITY
COPYRIGHT © UNIVERSAL PRESS PTY LTD (PUBLISHER) 2002

JOINS MAP 372

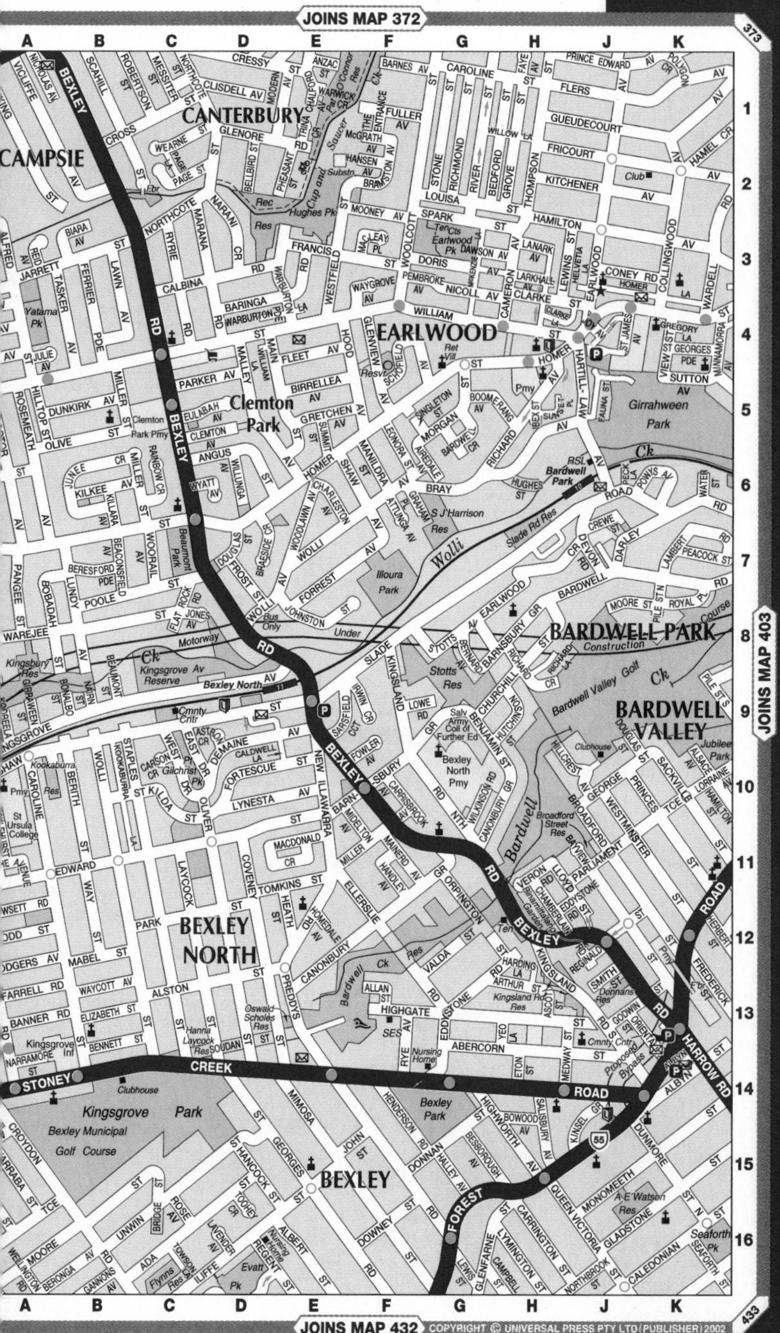

JOINS MAP 403

JOINS MAP 432
433

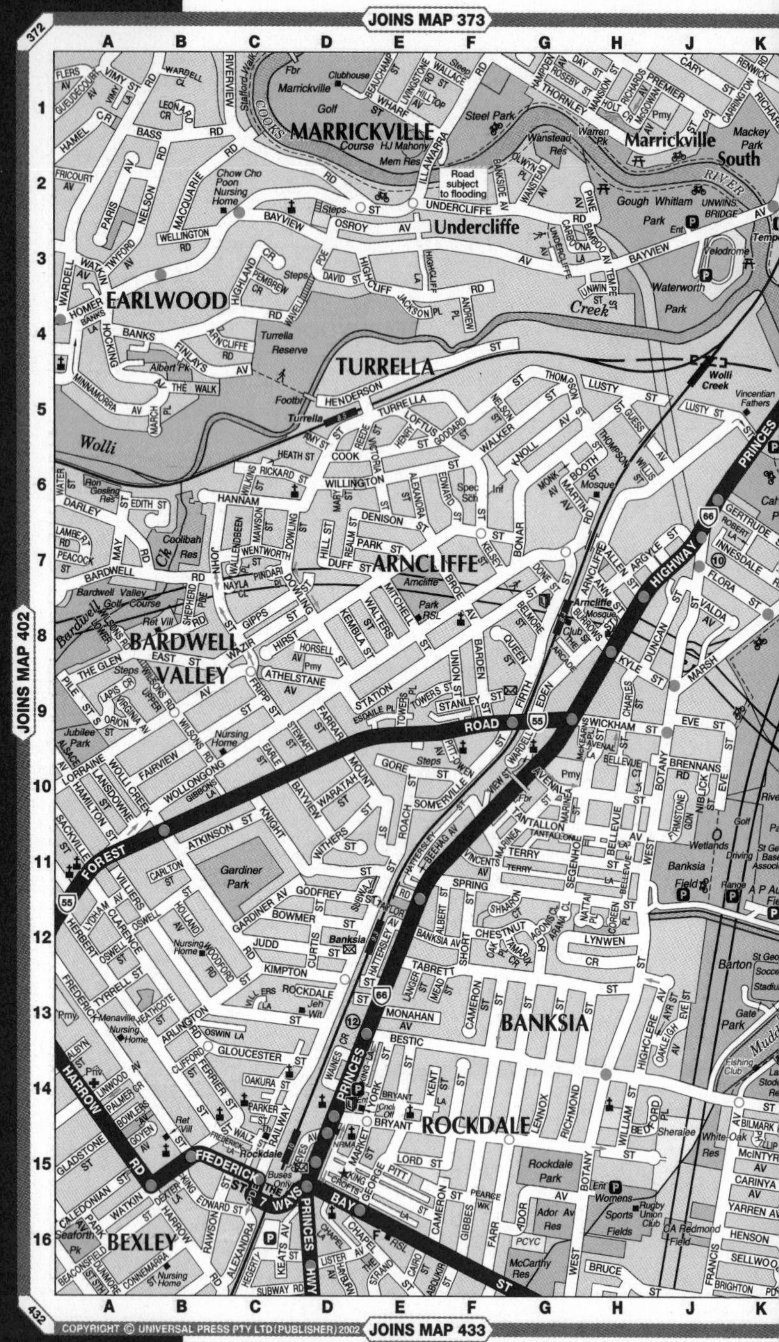
JOINS MAP 373
JOINS MAP 402
JOINS MAP 433
372
432
A B C D E F G H J K
1 2 3 4 5 6 7 8 9 10 11 12 13 14 15 16
MARRICKVILLE
Marrickville Golf Course
Clubhouse
HJ Mahony Mem Res
COOKS RIVER
Steel Park
Wanstead Res
Warren Pk
Marrickville South
Mackey Park
Gough Whitlam Park
UNWINS BRIDGE
Velodrome
Waterworth Park
Road subject to flooding
Undercliffe
EARLWOOD
Chow Cho Poon Nursing Home
Turrella Reserve
Albert Pk
TURRELLA
Wolli Creek
Wolli
Turrella
Footbr
Vincentian Fathers
Ron Gosling Res
Coolibah Res
Spec Sch
Mosque
ARNCLIFFE
Arncliffe
Arncliffe Park
RSL
Bardwell Valley Golf Course
Ret Vill
BARDWELL VALLEY
Jubilee Park
Nursing Home
Gardiner Park
Banksia
Banksia Field
Wetlands
Golf Driving Range
Barton Park
Gate Park
Fishing Club
BANKSIA
ROCKDALE
Rockdale Park
Ador Av Res
McCarthy Res
PCYC
Womens Sports Fields
Rugby Union Club
CA Redmond Field
Sheralee
White Oak Res
BEXLEY
Seaforth Pk
7 WAYS
Buses Only
Menaville Nursing Home
Jeh Wit
NRMA
PRINCES HWY
PRINCES HIGHWAY
FOREST ROAD
HARROW RD
FREDERICK ST
BAY ST
WOLLONGONG RD
BAYVIEW AV
UNDERCLIFFE ST
BARDWELL RD
STATION ST
ROCKDALE ST
BESTIC ST
WEST BOTANY ST

JOINS MAP 374

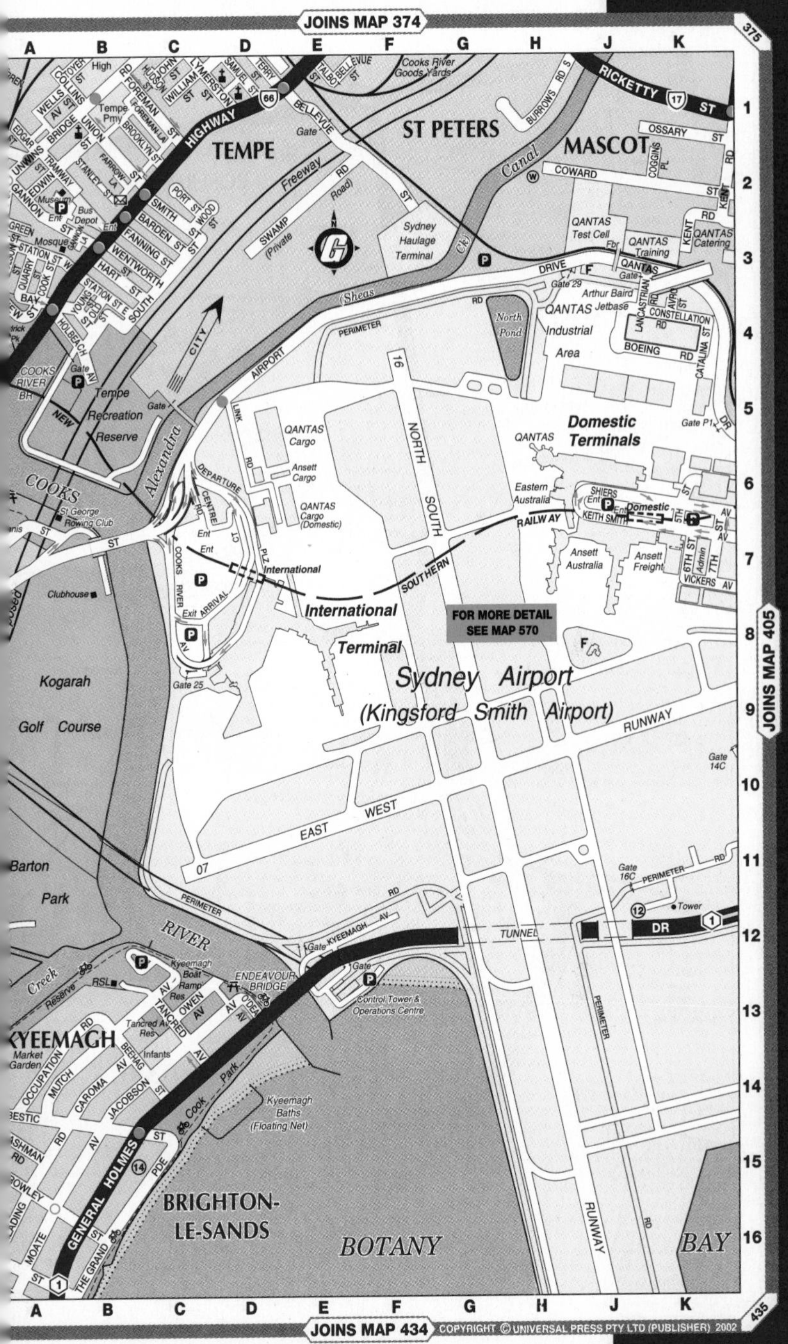

JOINS MAP 405

JOINS MAP 434

JOINS MAP 375

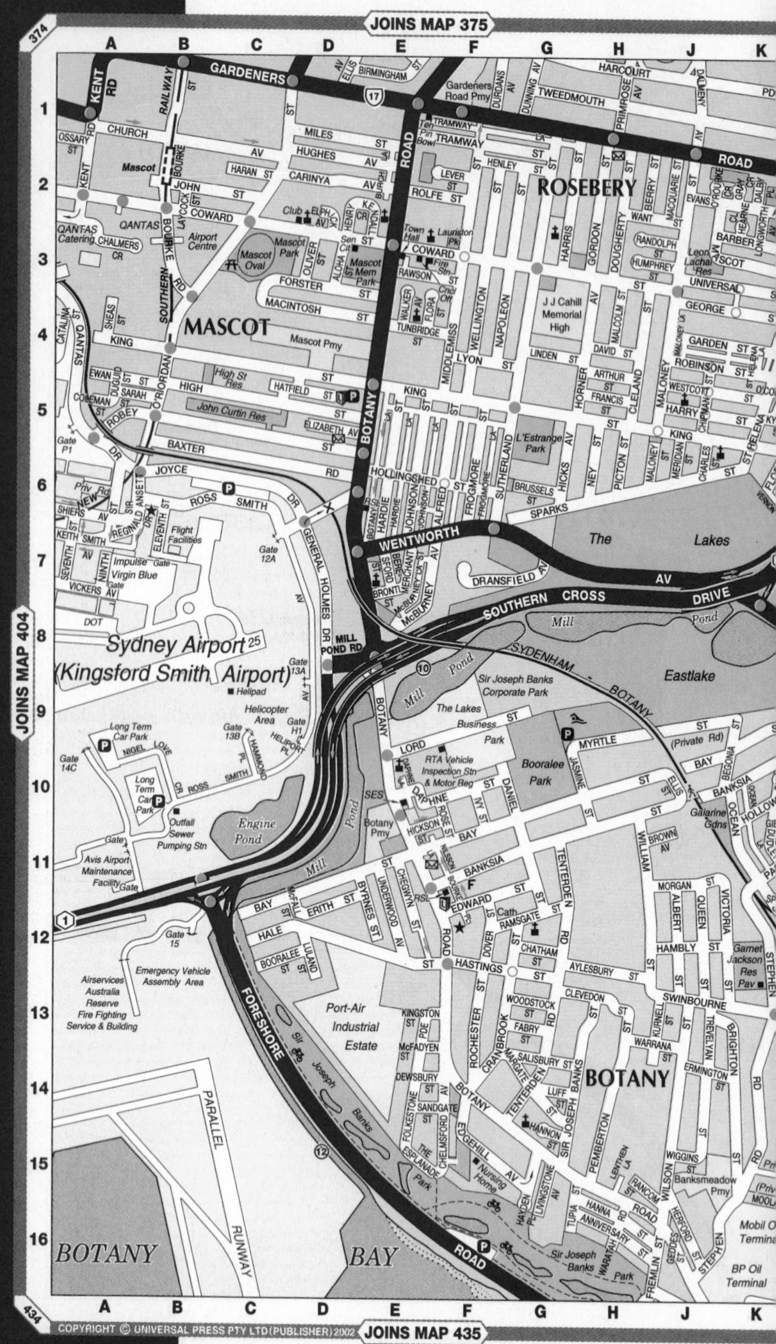

JOINS MAP 404

JOINS MAP 435

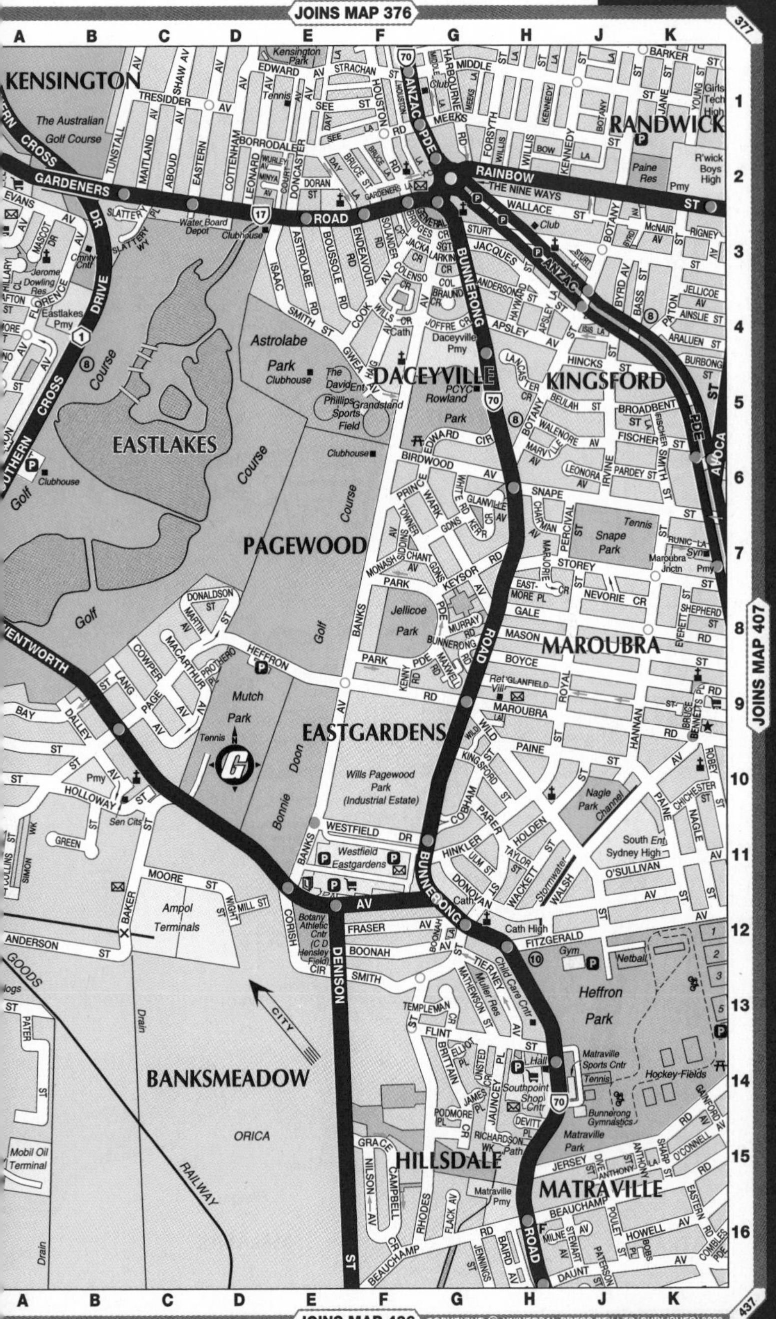
JOINS MAP 376
377
A B C D E F G H J K
1 2 3 4 5 6 7 8 9 10 11 12 13 14 15 16
KENSINGTON
RANDWICK
The Australian Golf Course
SOUTHERN CROSS DR
GARDENERS ROAD
RAINBOW ST
THE NINE WAYS
ANZAC PDE
BUNNERONG ROAD
DACEYVILLE
KINGSFORD
EASTLAKES
Astrolabe Park
The David Phillips Sports Field
Daceyville Pmy
Rowland Park
PAGEWOOD
Snape Park
MAROUBRA
Jellicoe Park
Mutch Park
EASTGARDENS
Wills Pagewood Park (Industrial Estate)
Bonnie Doon Golf Course
WENTWORTH AV
Westfield Eastgardens
Nagle Park
South Sydney High
Ampol Terminals
DENISON ST
Heffron Park
Matraville Sports Cntr
Hockey Fields
Bunnerong Gymnastics
Southpoint Shop Cntr
BANKSMEADOW
ORICA
Mobil Oil Terminal
HILLSDALE
MATRAVILLE
Matraville Park
Matraville Pmy
RAILWAY
JOINS MAP 407
437
JOINS MAP 436

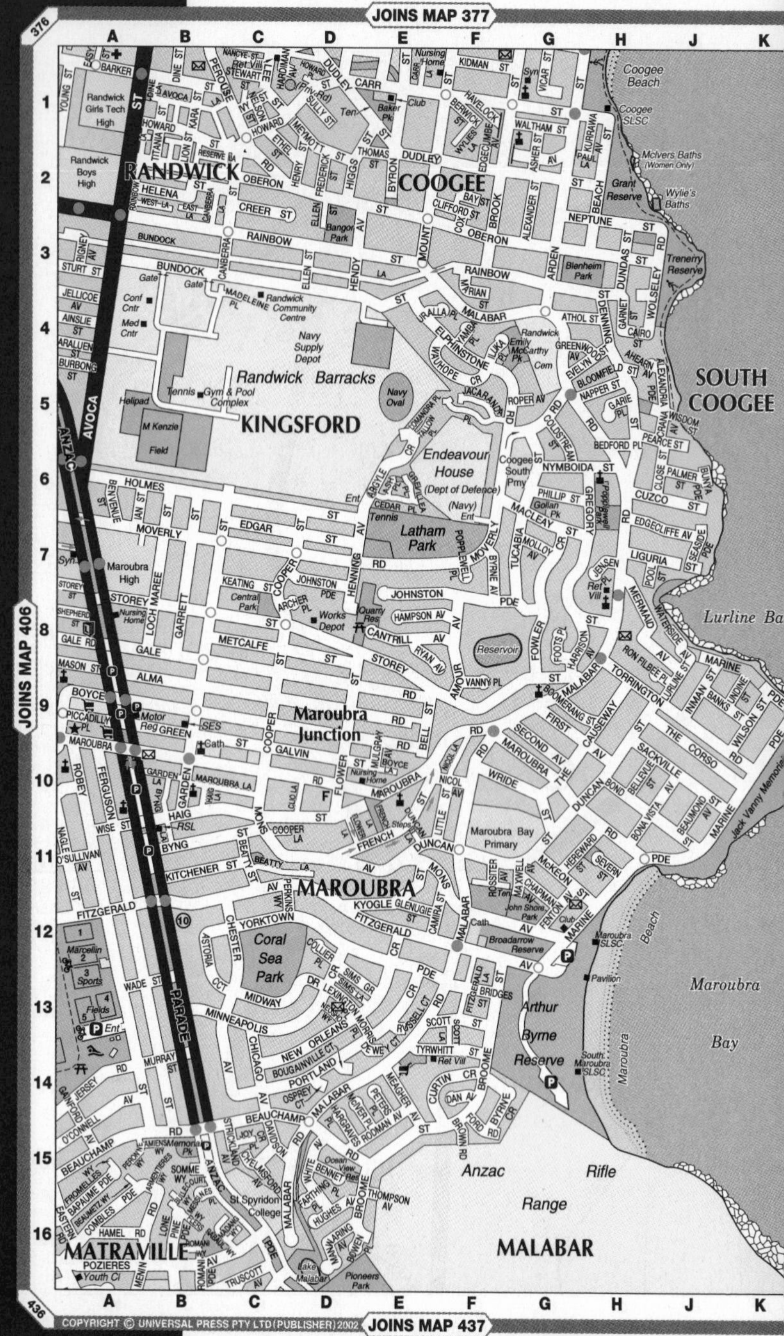
JOINS MAP 377
JOINS MAP 406
JOINS MAP 437
376
436
A B C D E F G H J K
1 2 3 4 5 6 7 8 9 10 11 12 13 14 15 16
RANDWICK
COOGEE
KINGSFORD
SOUTH COOGEE
MAROUBRA
Maroubra Junction
MATRAVILLE
MALABAR
Randwick Girls Tech High
Randwick Boys High
Randwick Barracks
Navy Supply Depot
Randwick Community Centre
Navy Oval
Tennis Gym & Pool Complex
Helipad
M Kenzie Field
Conf Cntr
Med Cntr
Endeavour House
(Dept of Defence)
(Navy)
Latham Park
Coogee South Pmy
Gollan Pk
Poppelwell Park
Randwick Emily McCarthy Pk
Cem
Coogee Beach
Coogee SLSC
McIvers Baths
(Women Only)
Grant Reserve
Wylie's Baths
Trenerry Reserve
Blenheim Park
Bangor Park
Baker Pk
Lurline Ba
Maroubra High
Central Park
Works Depot
Quarry Res
Reservoir
Maroubra Bay Primary
Coral Sea Park
Marcellin
Sports
Fields
Broadarrow Reserve
Arthur Byrne Reserve
Maroubra Beach
Maroubra SLSC
Pavilion
South Maroubra SLSC
Maroubra Bay
Anzac Rifle Range
St Spyridon College
Ocean View Res
Lake Malabar
Pioneers Park
Jack Vanny Memorial
AVOCA ST
ANZAC PARADE
DUDLEY ST
CARR ST
OBERON ST
RAINBOW ST
BUNDOCK ST
HOLMES ST
MOVERLY RD
STOREY ST
GALE RD
ALMA ST
MAROUBRA RD
FITZGERALD AV
BEAUCHAMP RD
MALABAR RD
MARINE PDE
HENNING AV
COOPER ST
BOYCE RD
PICCADILLY PL
MEDDLE RD
HAIG ST
BYNG ST
KITCHENER ST
WISE ST
O'SULLIVAN AV
NAGLE AV
FERGUSON ST
ROBEY ST
WADE ST
MURRAY ST
JERSEY RD
GANNON RD
O'CONNELL AV
MINNEAPOLIS CR
NEW ORLEANS CR
CHICAGO AV
MIDWAY DR
YORKTOWN PDE
CHESTER AV
ASTORIA CCT
BOUGAINVILLE CT
PORTLAND ST
OSPREY CT
BROOME ST
CURTIN CR
DAN AV
BYRNE CR
FORD RD
BROWN RD
HAMEL RD
POZIERES AV
Youth Cl
MENIN RD
ROMANI RD
TRUSCOTT AV
MAROUBRA BAY
TORRINGTON RD
THE CORSO
SACKVILLE ST
DUNCAN ST
WRIDE ST
MCKEON ST
HEREWARD ST
SEVERN ST
NAPPER ST
BLOOMFIELD ST
BEDFORD PL
NYMBOIDA ST
CUZCO ST
EDGECLIFFE AV
LIGURIA ST
WATERSIDE AV
MARINE PDE
INMAN ST
WILSON ST
BELLEVUE ST
BEAUMOND AV
BONA VISTA AV
MCKEON ST
CHAPMAN AV
ROSSITER AV
MAXWELL AV
JOHNSTON PDE
HAMPSON AV
CANTRILL AV
RYAN AV
VANNY PL
FOWLER CR
HARRISON ST
MACLEAY ST
MOLLOY AV
TUCABIA ST
GREGORY ST
BOOMERANG ST
FIRST AV
SECOND AV
MAROUBRA RD
CAUSEWAY
COPYRIGHT © UNIVERSAL PRESS PTY LTD (PUBLISHER) 2002

JOINS MAP 378

JOINS MAP 438

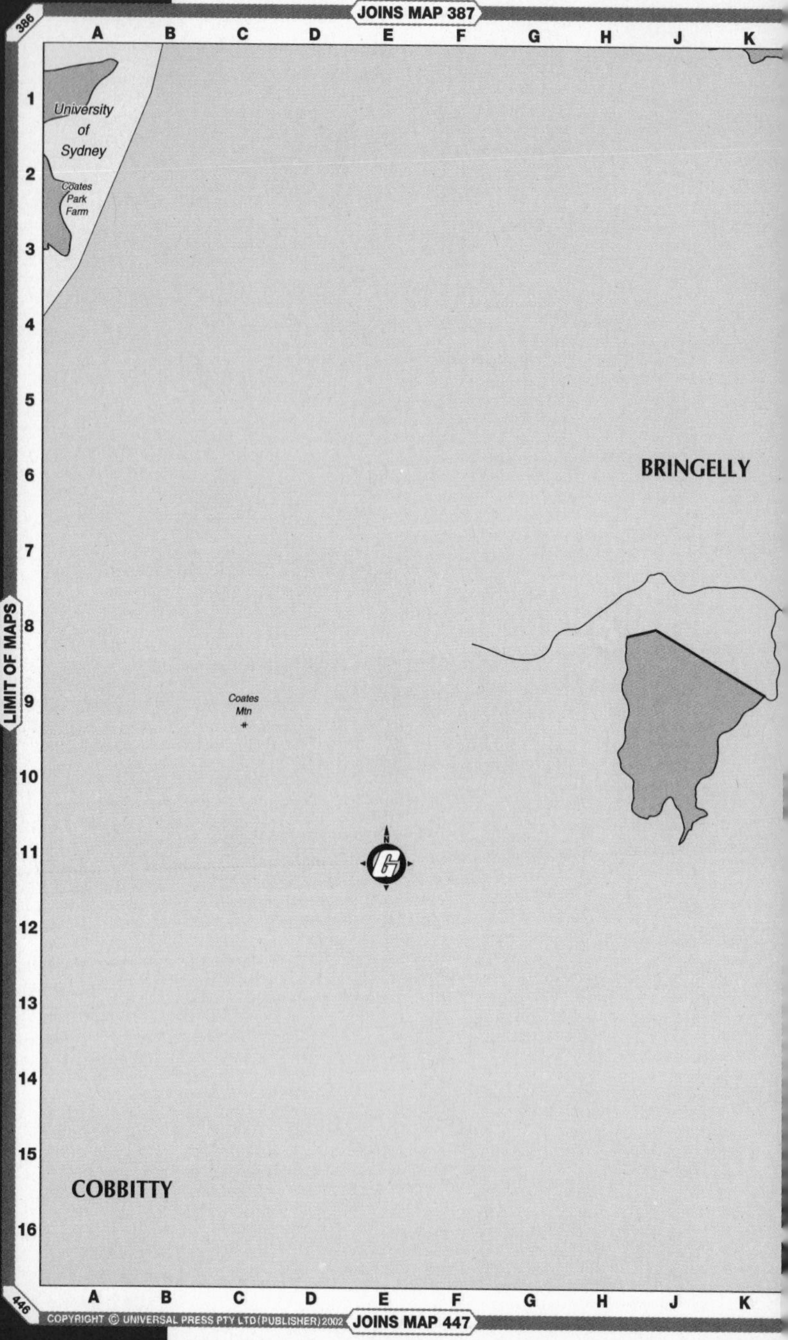

MAP 417
PREVIOUS MAP 408

JOINS MAP 387

386

A B C D E F G H J K

1 2 3 4 5 6 7 8 9 10 11 12 13 14 15 16

University of Sydney

Coates Park Farm

BRINGELLY

LIMIT OF MAPS

Coates Mtn

COBBITTY

A B C D E F G H J K

446

JOINS MAP 447

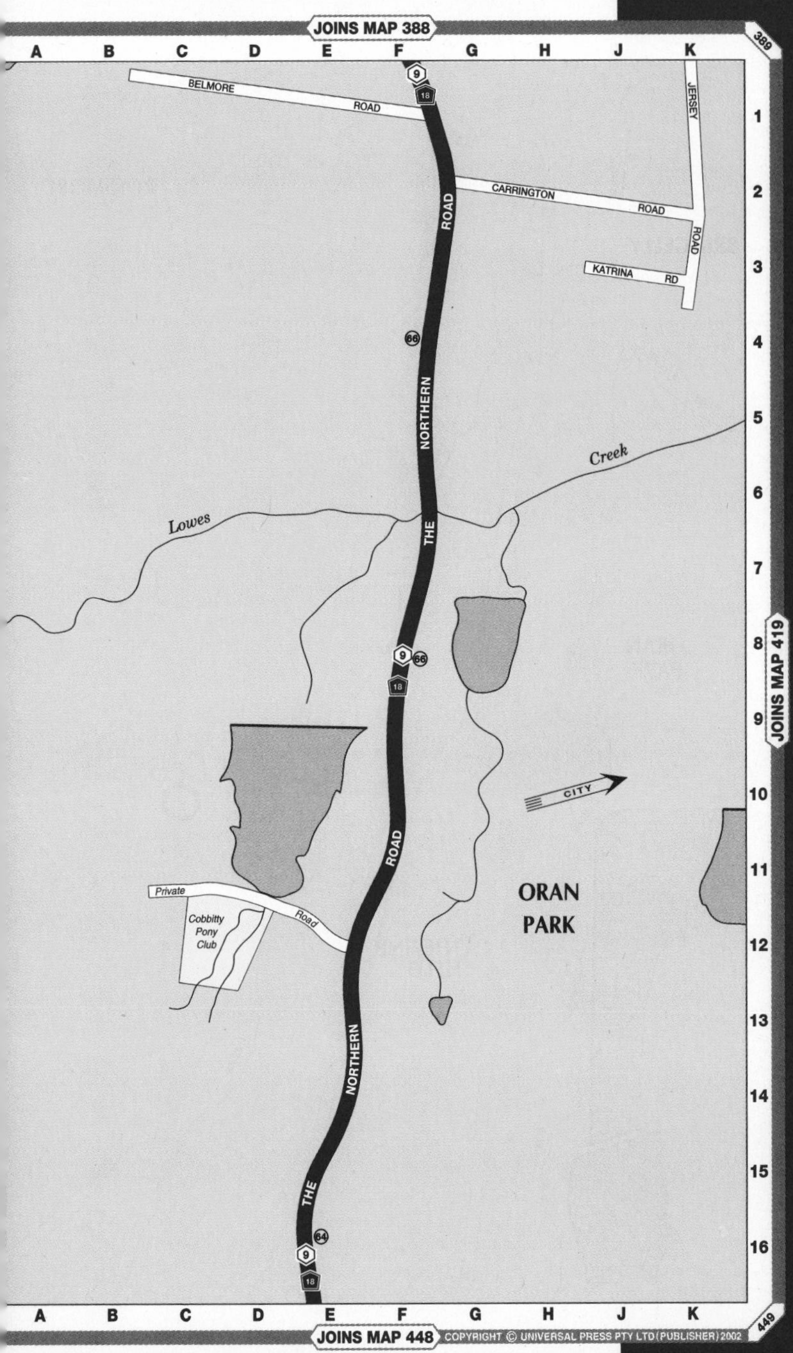
JOINS MAP 388
389
A B C D E F G H J K
1 2 3 4 5 6 7 8 9 10 11 12 13 14 15 16
BELMORE
ROAD
JERSEY
ROAD
CARRINGTON
ROAD
KATRINA
RD
THE NORTHERN ROAD
9
18
66
64
Creek
Lowes
CITY
ORAN
PARK
Private
Road
Cobbitty
Pony
Club
JOINS MAP 419
JOINS MAP 448
449

MAP 419

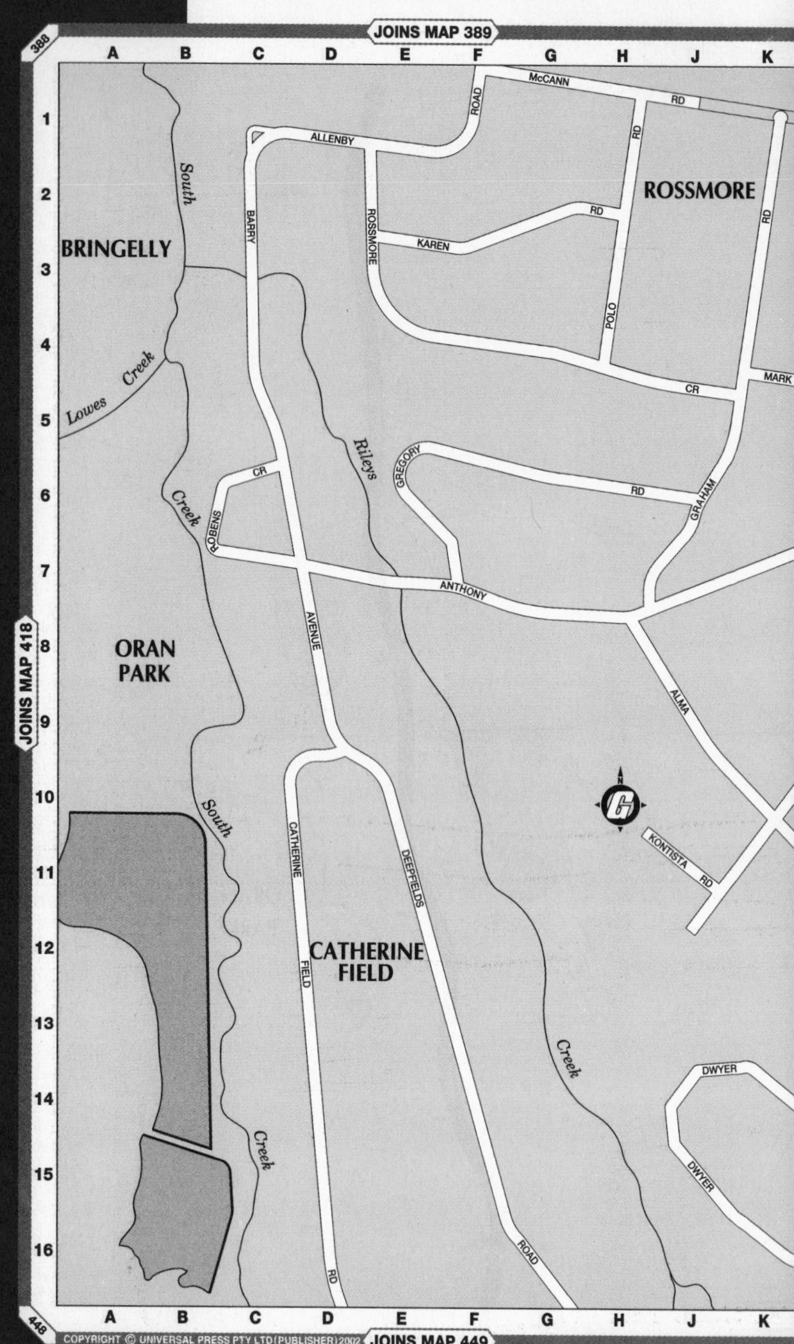

JOINS MAP 389
388
A
B
C
D
E
F
G
H
J
K
1
2
3
4
5
6
7
8
9
10
11
12
13
14
15
16
McCANN
RD
ROAD
ALLENBY
RD
ROSSMORE
RD
BRINGELLY
South
BARRY
ROSSMORE
KAREN
RD
POLO
RD
Lowes
Creek
MARK
CR
Rileys
GREGORY
CR
RD
Creek
ROBENS
GRAHAM
ANTHONY
JOINS MAP 418
ORAN
PARK
AVENUE
ALMA
South
CATHERINE
DEEPFIELDS
KONTISTA
RD
CATHERINE
FIELD
FIELD
Creek
DWYER
Creek
DWYER
ROAD
RD
448
JOINS MAP 449

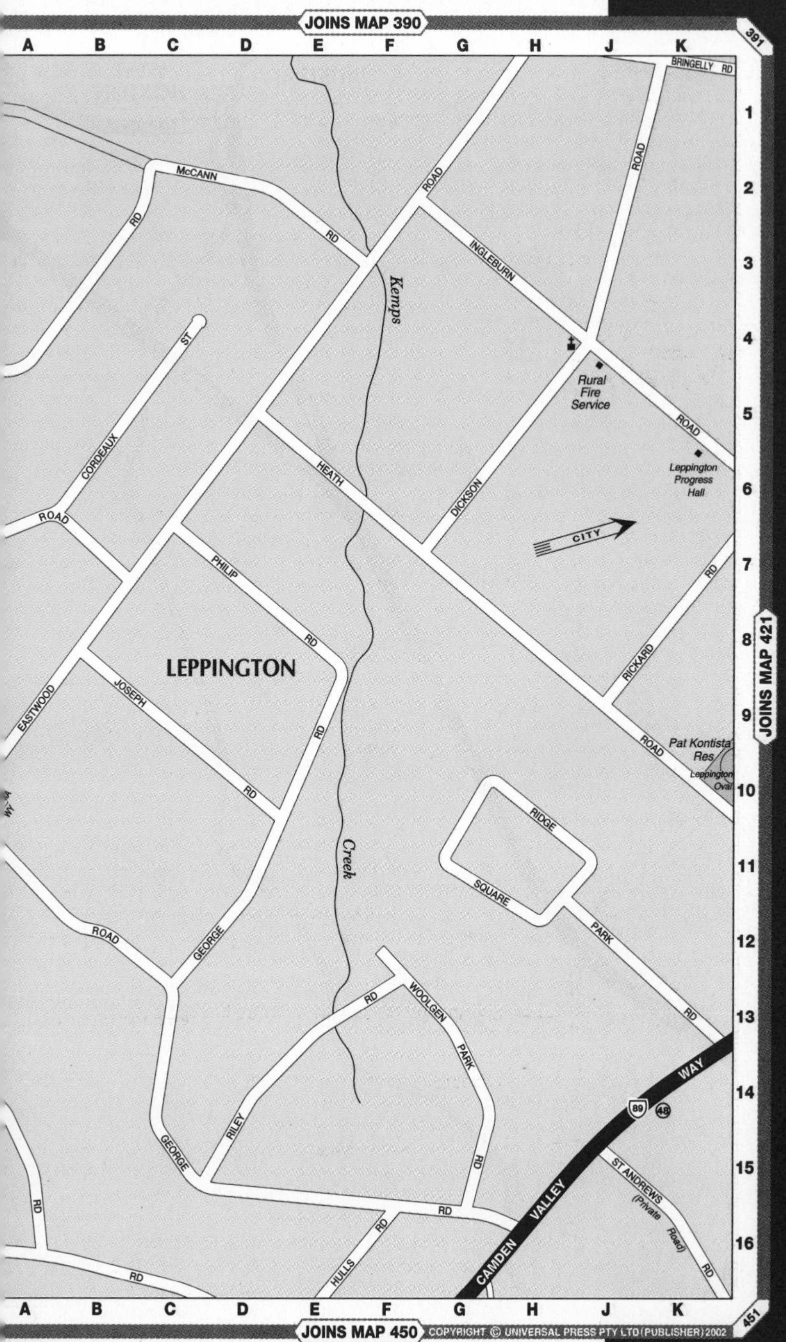
JOINS MAP 390
391
A B C D E F G H J K
1 2 3 4 5 6 7 8 9 10 11 12 13 14 15 16
BRINGELLY RD
McCANN
RD
RD
ROAD
INGLEBURN
ROAD
Kemps
Creek
ST
CORDEAUX
ROAD
Rural
Fire
Service
ROAD
Leppington
Progress
Hall
HEATH
DICKSON
CITY
RD
PHILIP
RD
RICKARD
LEPPINGTON
JOSEPH
EASTWOOD
RD
ROAD
Pat Kontista
Res
Leppington
Oval
RD
RIDGE
SQUARE
PARK
ROAD
GEORGE
RD
RD
WOOLGEN
PARK
WAY
89
48
RILEY
GEORGE
RD
ST ANDREWS
(Private
Road)
RD
VALLEY
CAMDEN
RD
RD
RD
HULLS
RD
JOINS MAP 421
JOINS MAP 450
451

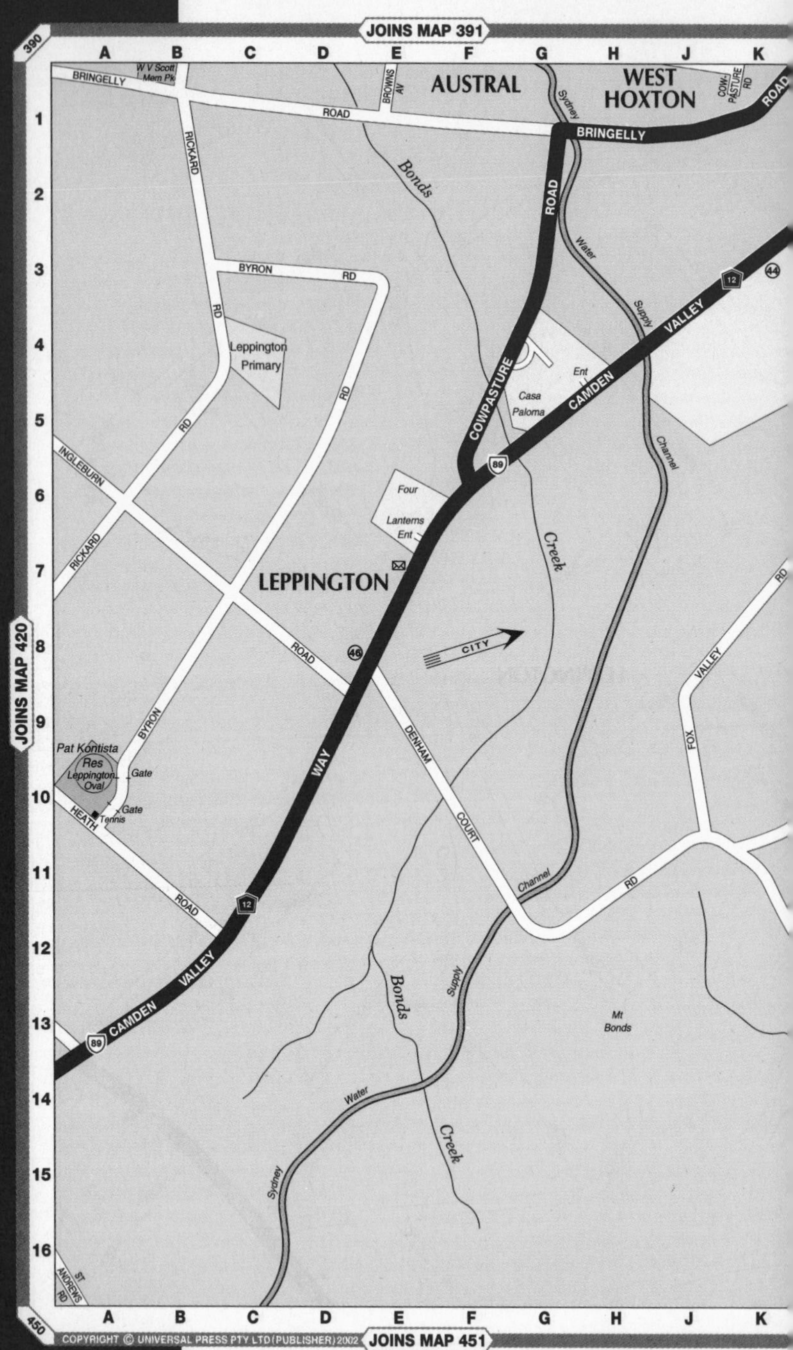
JOINS MAP 391
390
A B C D E F G H J K
1 2 3 4 5 6 7 8 9 10 11 12 13 14 15 16
W V Scott Mem Pk
BRINGELLY
ROAD
BROWNS AV
AUSTRAL
WEST HOXTON
COW-PASTURE RD
ROAD
Sydney
BRINGELLY
RICKARD
Bonds
ROAD
Water
BYRON
RD
RD
Supply
44
12
VALLEY
Leppington Primary
COWPASTURE
Ent
CAMDEN
Casa Paloma
RD
RD
89
Channel
INGLEBURN
Four Lanterns Ent
Creek
RICKARD
LEPPINGTON
RD
ROAD
46
CITY
VALLEY
JOINS MAP 420
BYRON
DENHAM
FOX
Pat Kontista Res
Leppington Oval
Gate
Gate
Tennis
HEATH
WAY
COURT
Channel
RD
ROAD
12
VALLEY
Bonds
Supply
CAMDEN
Mt Bonds
89
Water
Creek
Sydney
ST ANDREWS RD
450
JOINS MAP 451

JOINS MAP 392

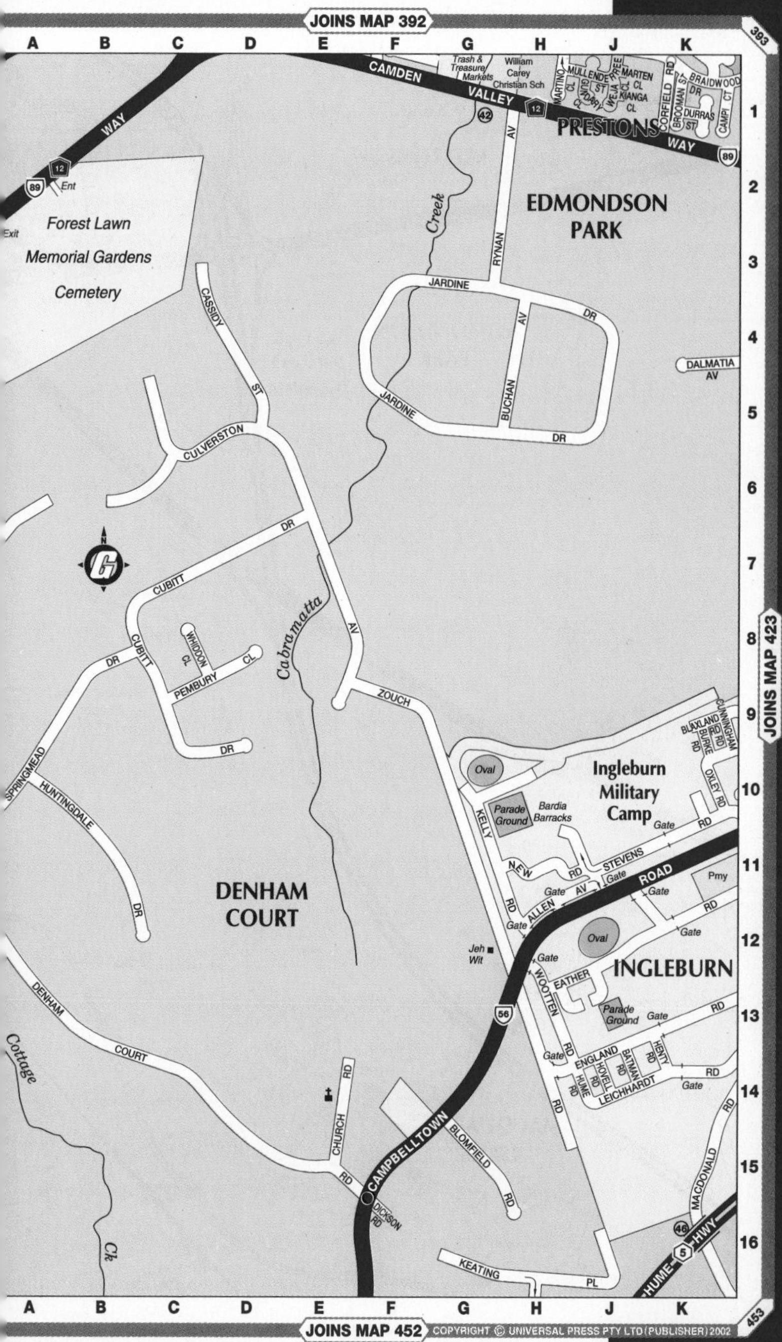

JOINS MAP 452

JOINS MAP 393

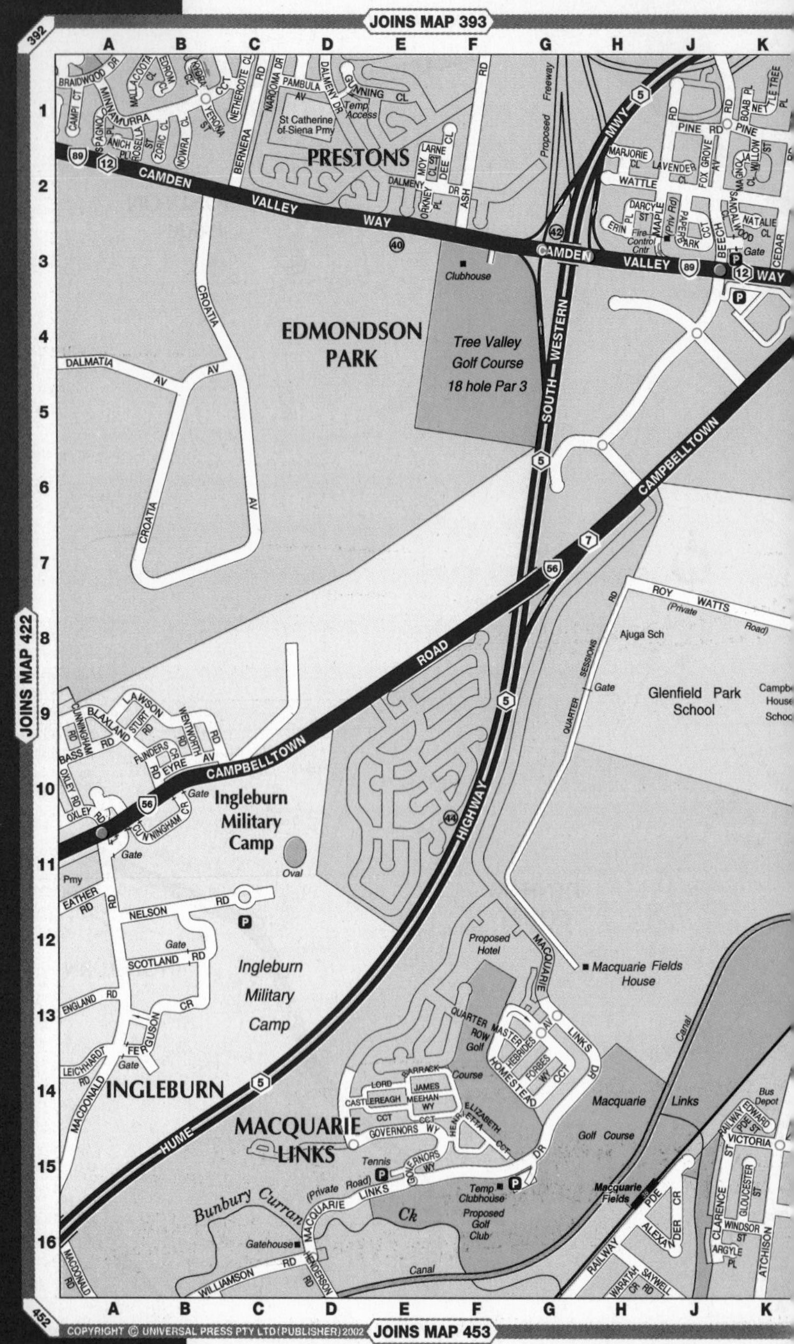

JOINS MAP 422

JOINS MAP 453

JOINS MAP 394

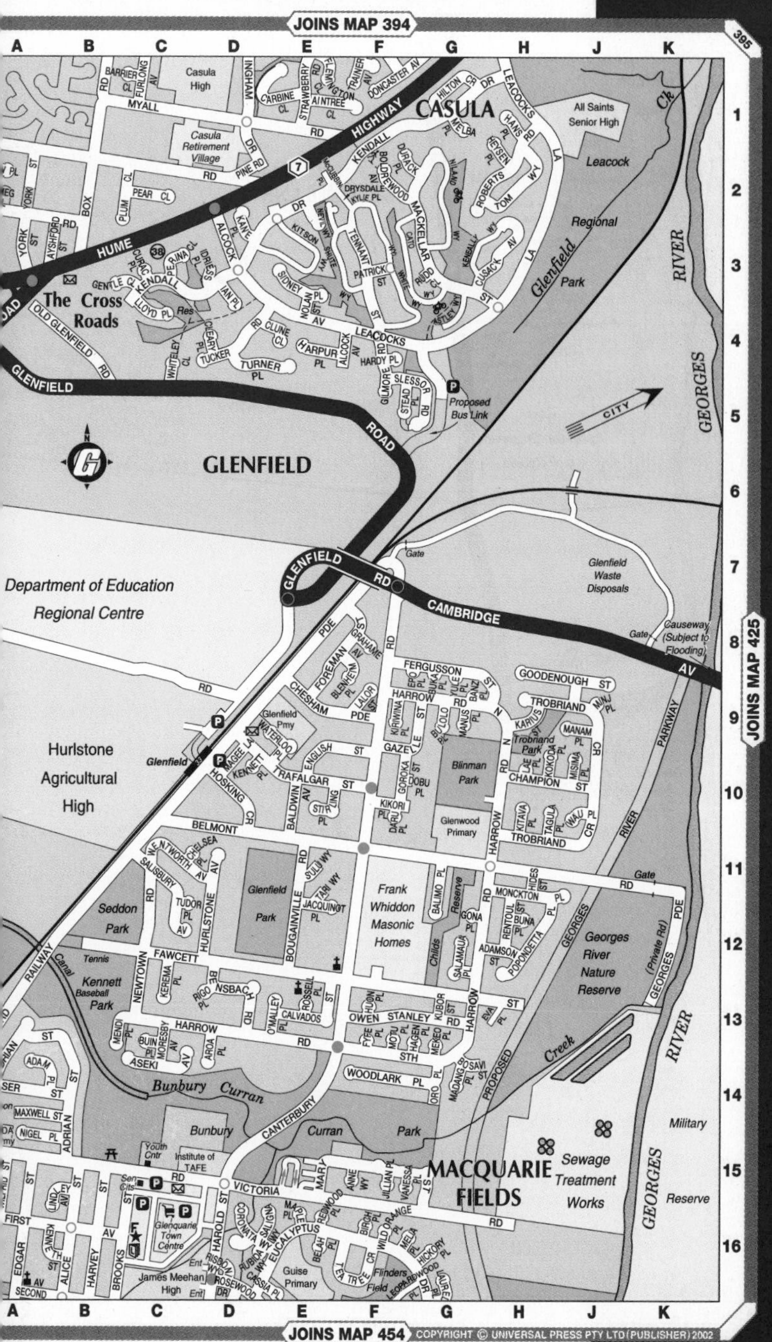

JOINS MAP 425

JOINS MAP 454

JOINS MAP 395

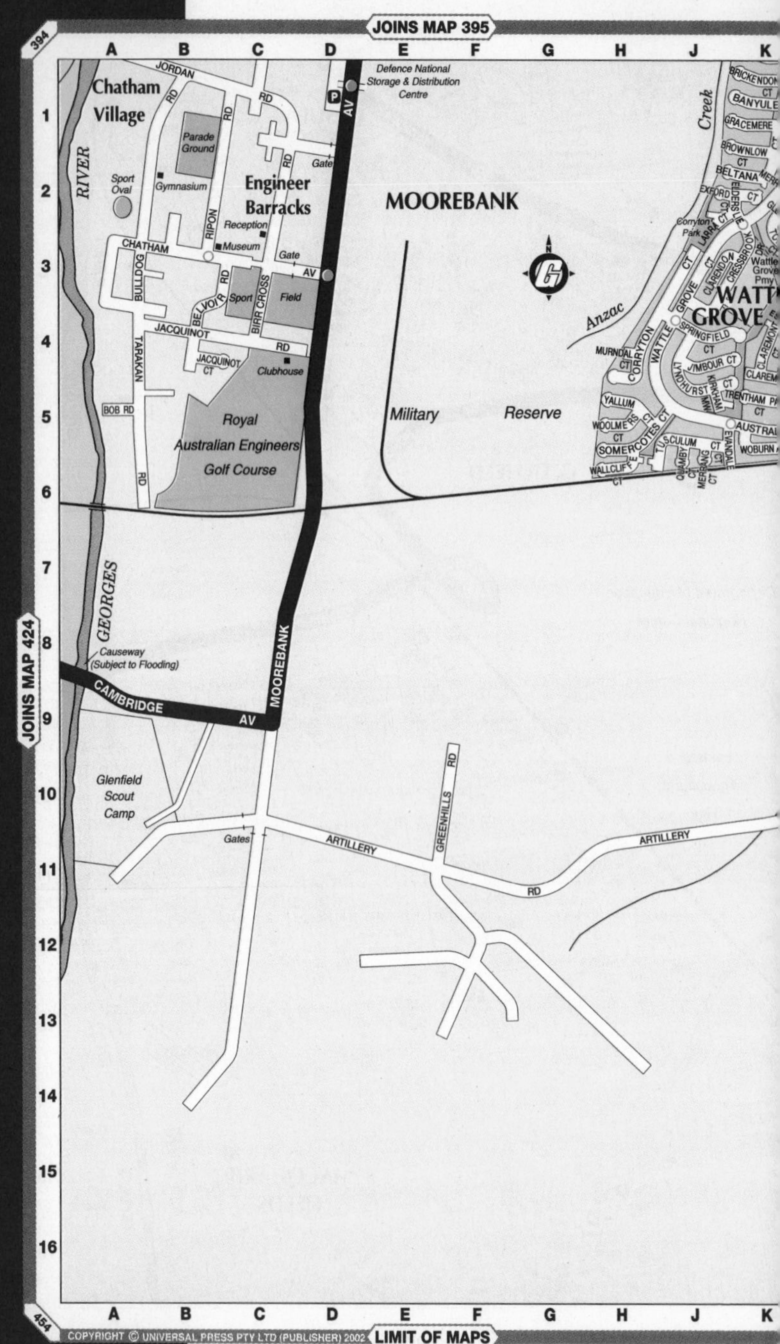

JOINS MAP 424

LIMIT OF MAPS

JOINS MAP 396

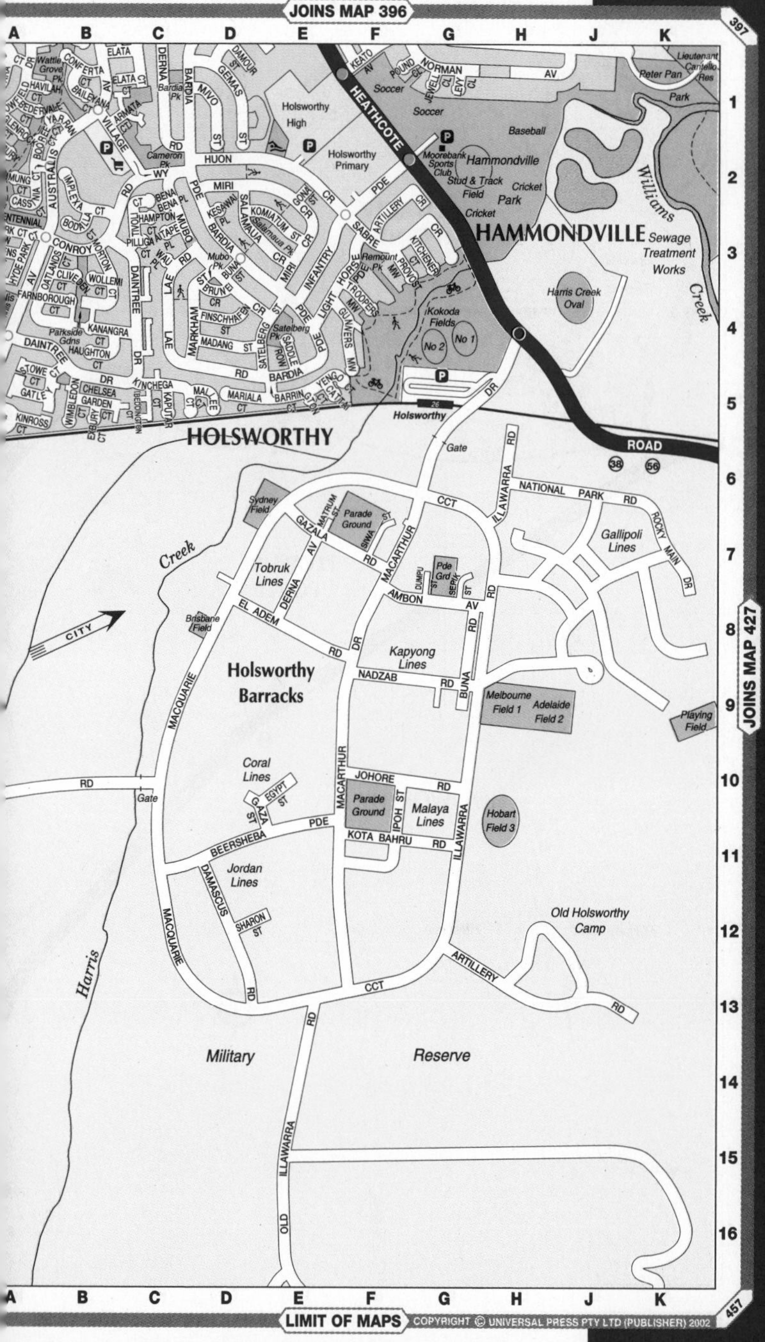

397

JOINS MAP 427

LIMIT OF MAPS

457

JOINS MAP 397

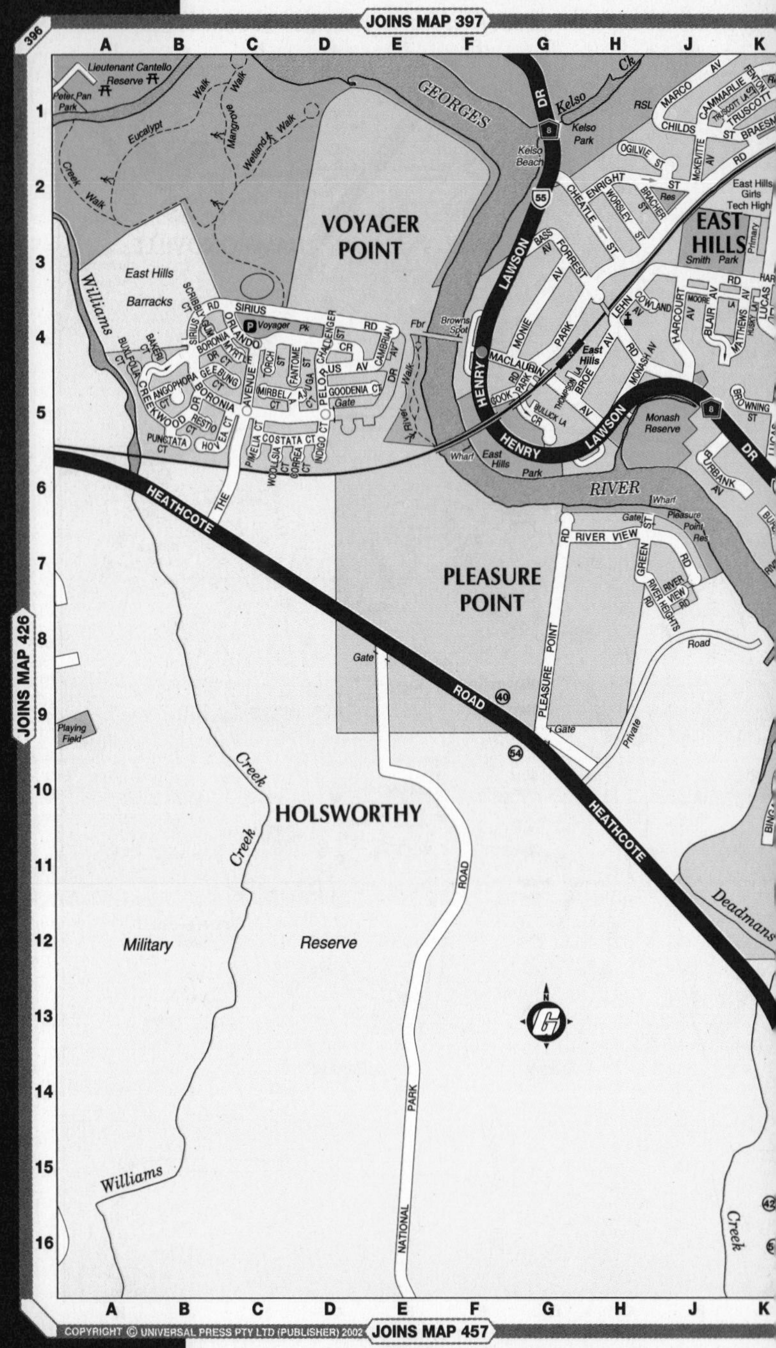

A B C D E F G H J K

1 2 3 4 5 6 7 8 9 10 11 12 13 14 15 16

396

JOINS MAP 426

JOINS MAP 457

JOINS MAP 398

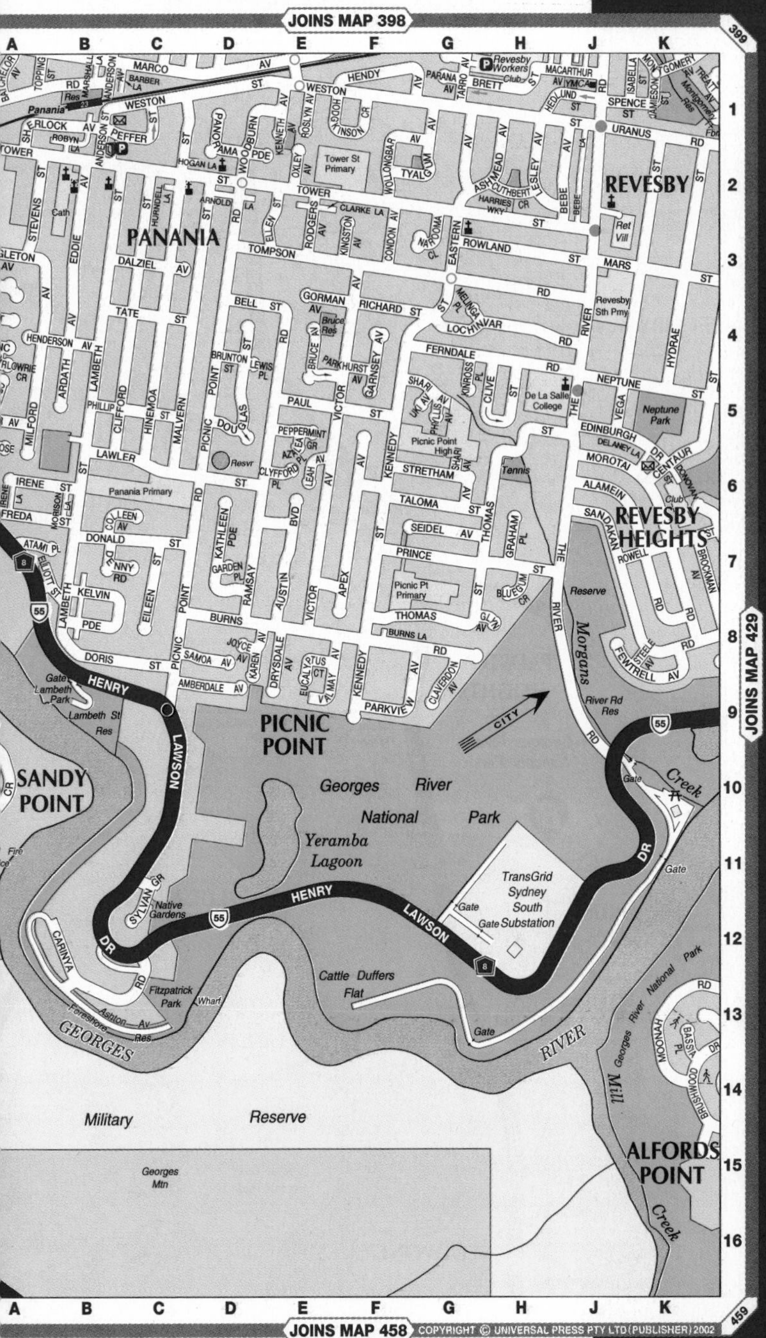

JOINS MAP 429

JOINS MAP 458

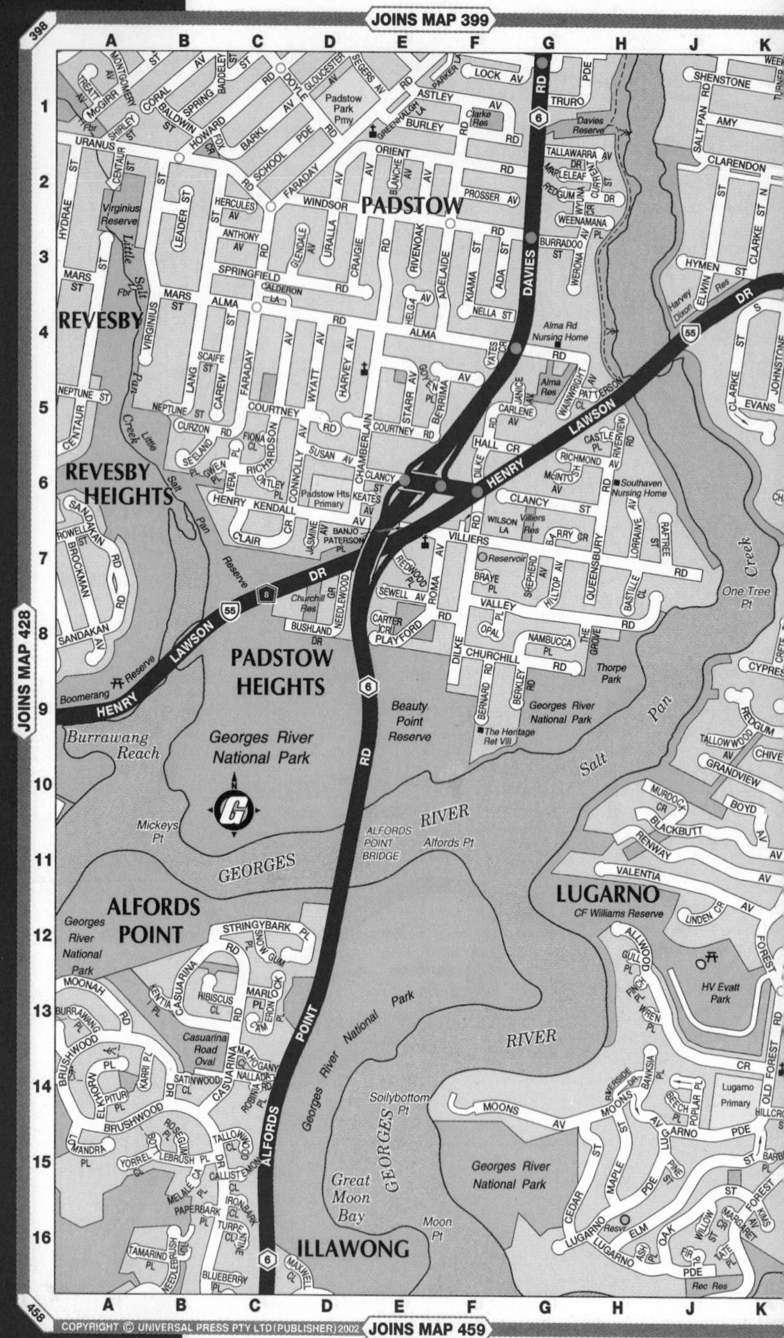

JOINS MAP 399
JOINS MAP 428
JOINS MAP 459
398
458
A B C D E F G H J K
1 2 3 4 5 6 7 8 9 10 11 12 13 14 15 16
PADSTOW
REVESBY
REVESBY HEIGHTS
PADSTOW HEIGHTS
ALFORDS POINT
LUGARNO
ILLAWONG
Padstow Park Pmy
Clarke Res
Davies Reserve
Virginius Reserve
Little Salt Pan Creek
Alma Rd Nursing Home
Alma Res
Southaven Nursing Home
Padstow Hts Primary
Villiers Res
Reservoir
Churchill Res
Thorpe Park
Harvey Dixon Res
One Tree Pt
Salt Pan Creek
Boomerang Reserve
Burrawang Reach
Georges River National Park
Beauty Point Reserve
The Heritage Ret Vill
Mickeys Pt
ALFORDS POINT BRIDGE
Alfords Pt
GEORGES RIVER
CF Williams Reserve
HV Evatt Park
Lugarno Primary
Casuarina Road Oval
Soilybottom Pt
Great Moon Bay
Moon Pt
Rec Res
HENRY LAWSON DR
DAVIES RD
ALFORDS POINT RD
COPYRIGHT © UNIVERSAL PRESS PTY LTD (PUBLISHER) 2002

JOINS MAP 400

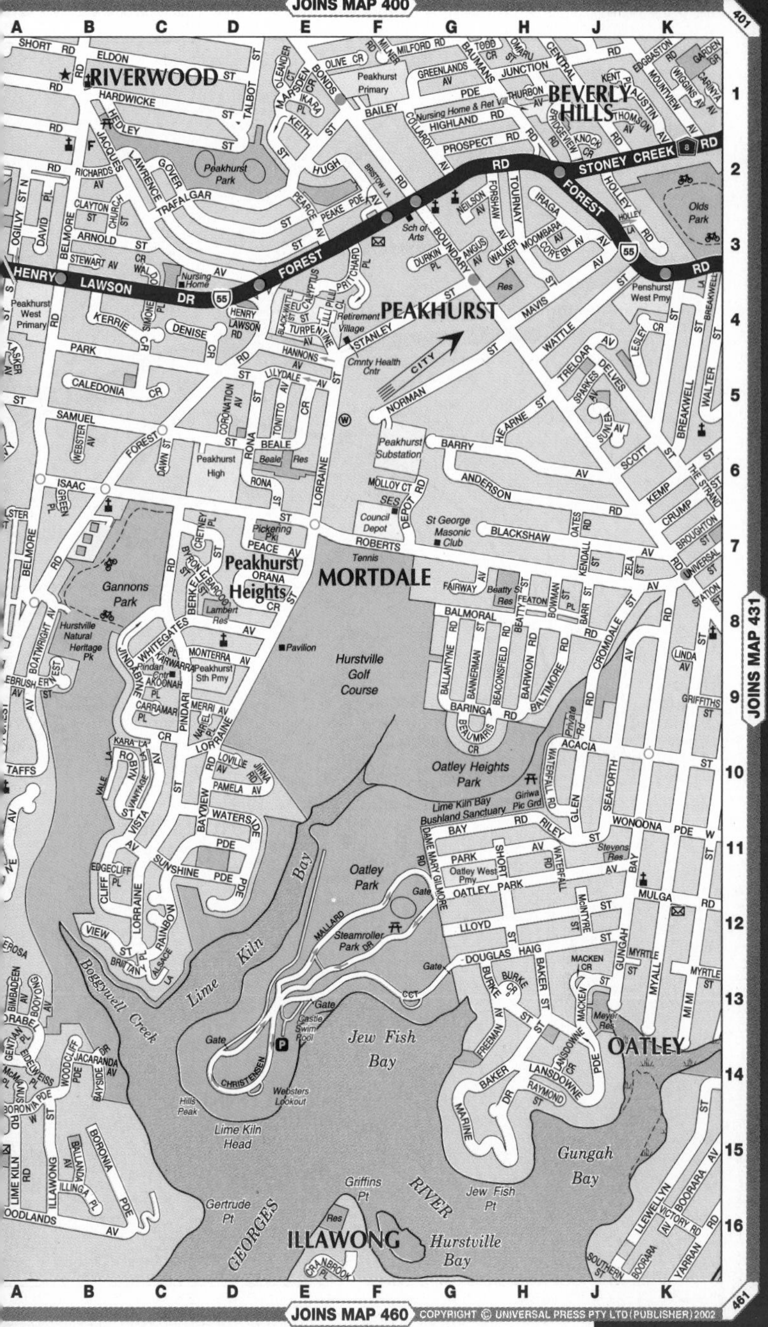

JOINS MAP 431

JOINS MAP 460

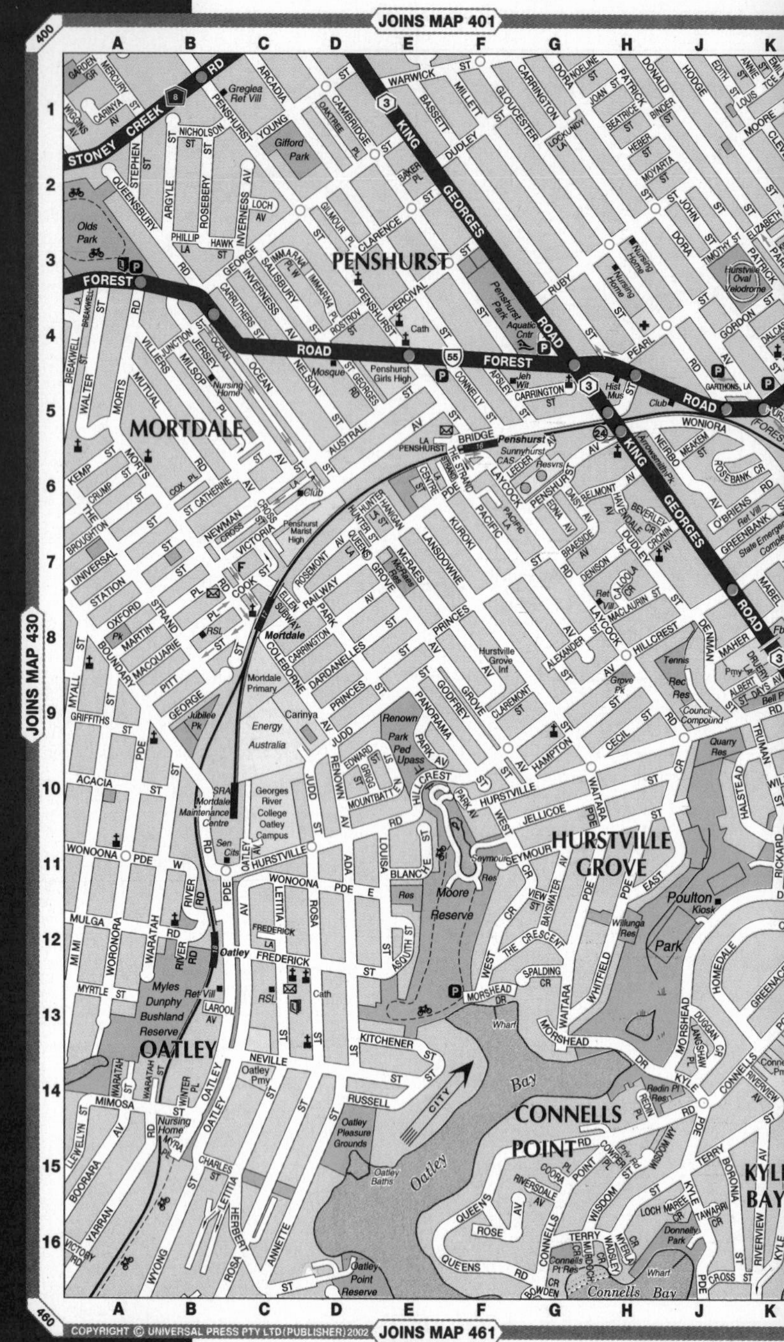
JOINS MAP 401
JOINS MAP 430
JOINS MAP 461
400
460
A B C D E F G H J K
1 2 3 4 5 6 7 8 9 10 11 12 13 14 15 16
PENSHURST
MORTDALE
HURSTVILLE GROVE
OATLEY
CONNELLS POINT
KYLE BAY
STONEY CREEK RD
FOREST ROAD
KING GEORGES ROAD
Gifford Park
Olds Park
Penshurst Park
Hurstville Oval Velodrome
Greglea Ref Vill
Penshurst Girls High
Penshurst Marist High
Mosque
Penshurst
Mortdale
Oatley
Mortdale Primary
Carinya
Energy Australia
SRA Mortdale Maintenance Centre
Georges River College Oatley Campus
Jubilee Pk
Renown Park Ped Upass
Moore Reserve
Hurstville Grove Inf
Grove Pk
Tennis Rec Res
Council Compound
Quarry Res
Poulton Kiosk
Poulton Park
Willunga Res
Myles Dunphy Bushland Reserve
Oatley Pleasure Grounds
Oatley Baths
Oatley Bay
Oatley Point Reserve
Connells Bay
Connells Pt Res
Donnelly Park
Redin Pl Res
Sunnyhurst CAS
Hist Mus
Nursing Home
Aquatic Cntr
CITY

JOINS MAP 402

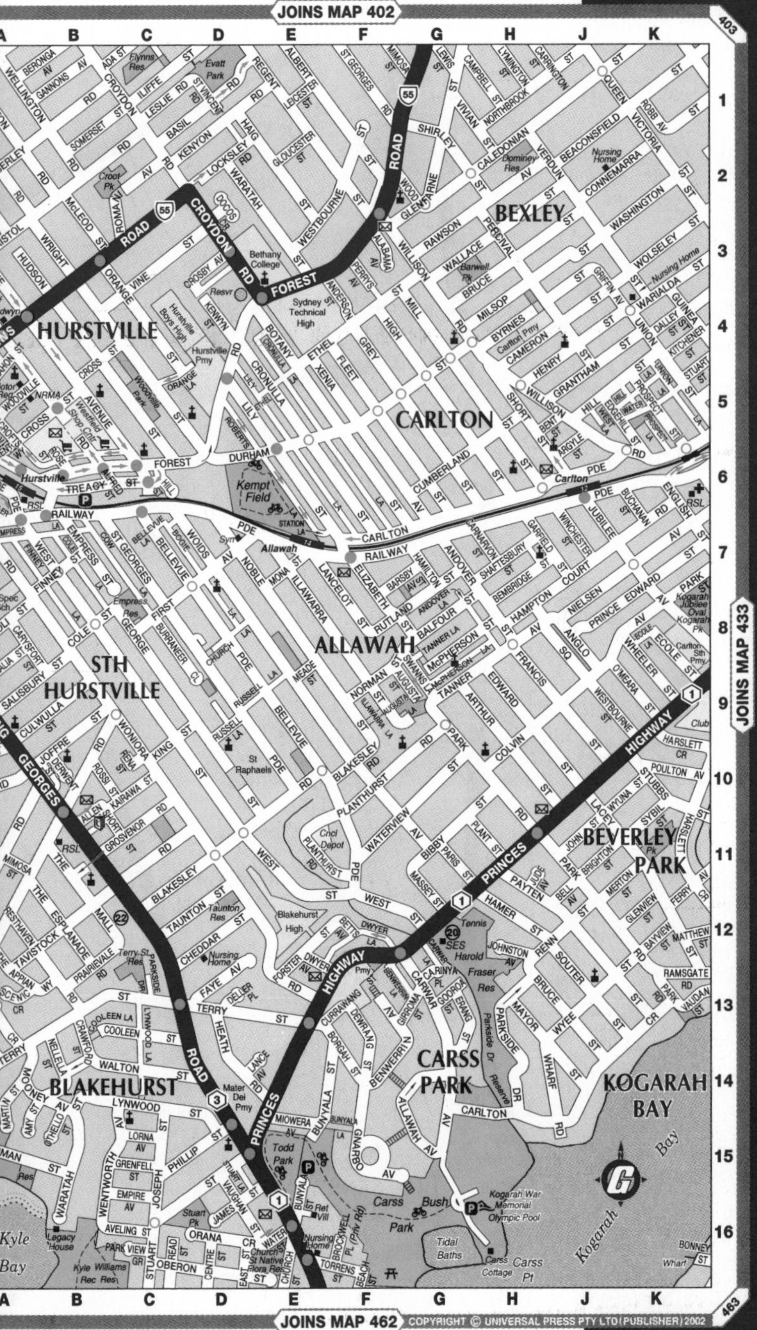

JOINS MAP 433
JOINS MAP 462

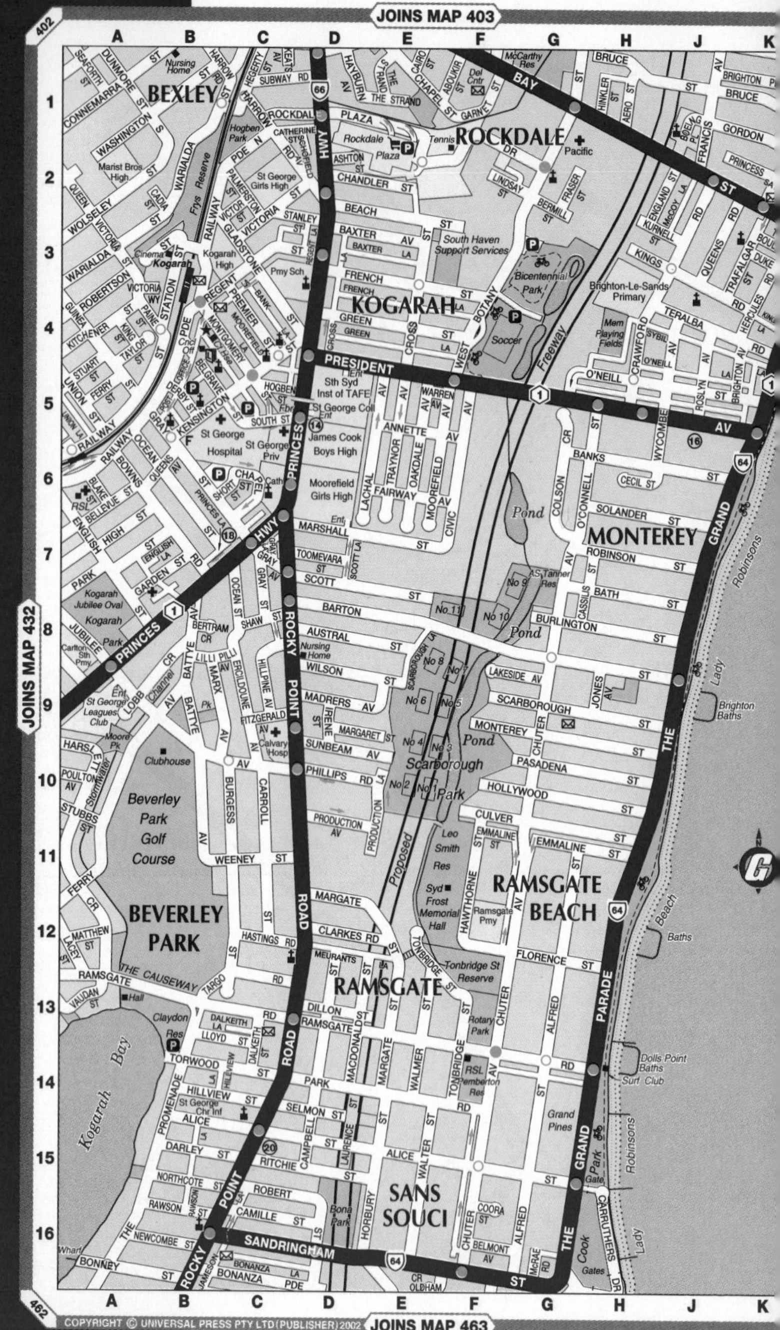
JOINS MAP 403
JOINS MAP 432
JOINS MAP 463
402
462
BEXLEY
ROCKDALE
KOGARAH
MONTEREY
BEVERLEY PARK
RAMSGATE
RAMSGATE BEACH
SANS SOUCI
Beverley Park Golf Course
Kogarah Bay
Scarborough Park
Bicentennial Park
Rockdale Plaza
St George Hospital
St George Girls High
Kogarah High
James Cook Boys High
Moorefield Girls High
Sth Syd Inst of TAFE
St George Coll
Brighton-Le-Sands Primary
Marist Bros High
Kogarah Jubilee Oval
St George Leagues Club
Calvary Hosp
Leo Smith Res
Syd Frost Memorial Hall
Ramsgate Pmy
Tonbridge St Reserve
Rotary Park
RSL Pemberton Res
Grand Pines
Cook Park
Brighton Baths
Dolls Point Baths
Surf Club
Claydon Res
Bona Park
South Haven Support Services
Frys Reserve
Hogben Park
Princes Hwy
Rocky Point Road
The Grand Parade
President Av
Bay St
Proposed Freeway
Lady Robinsons Beach

JOINS MAP 404

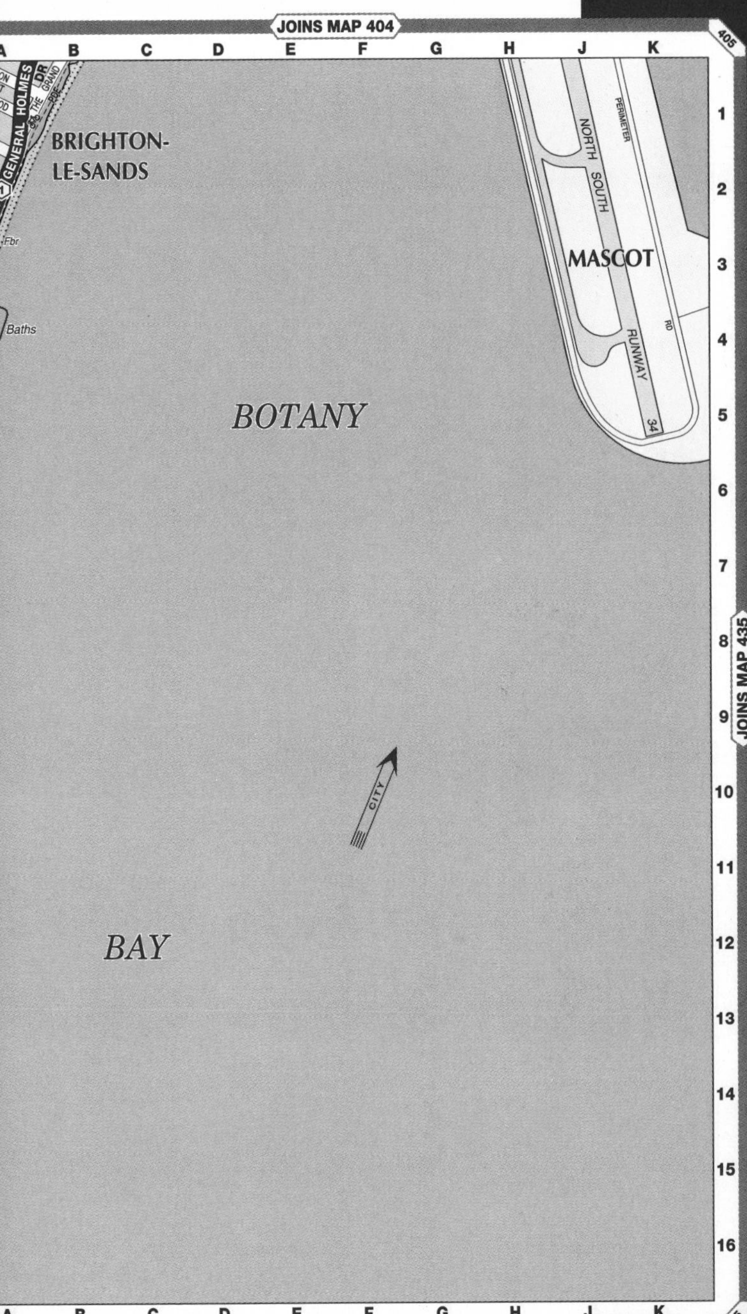

JOINS MAP 435

JOINS MAP 464

MAP 435

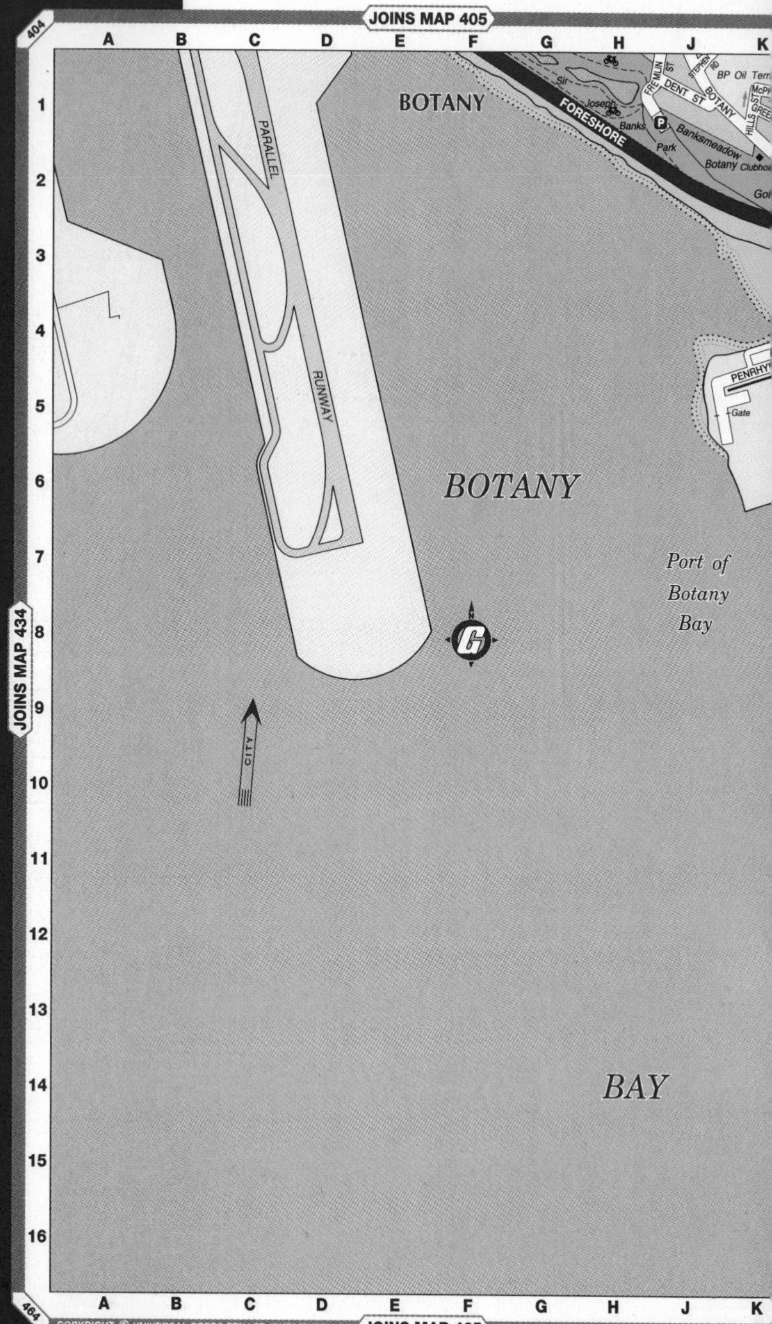

JOINS MAP 405
404
A
B
C
D
E
F
G
H
J
K
1
2
3
4
5
6
7
8
9
10
11
12
13
14
15
16
JOINS MAP 434
BOTANY
FORESHORE
Sir
Joseph
Banks
Park
FREMLIN ST
DENT ST
STEPHEN RD
BOTANY
BP Oil Term
Banksmeadow
Botany Clubho
PARALLEL
RUNWAY
PENRHYN
Gate
BOTANY
Port of
Botany
Bay
CITY
BAY
464
JOINS MAP 465

JOINS MAP 406

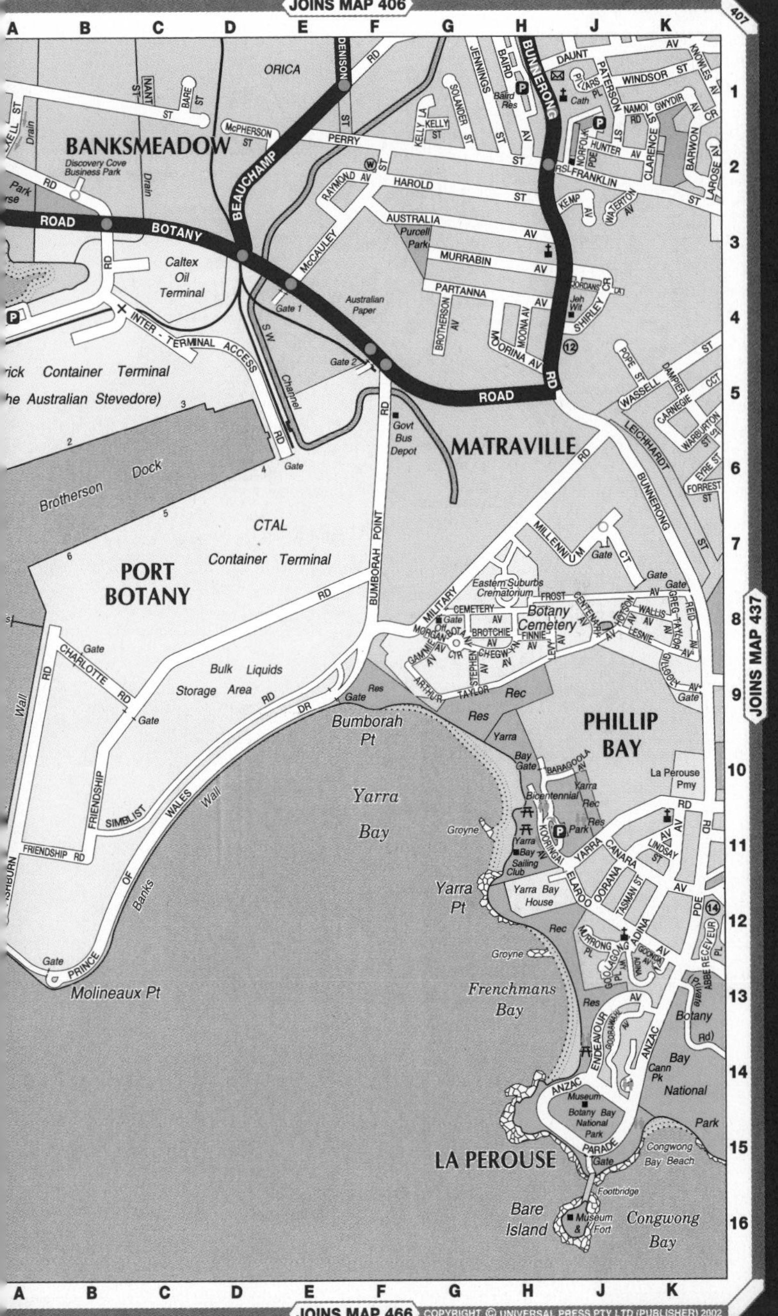

JOINS MAP 466

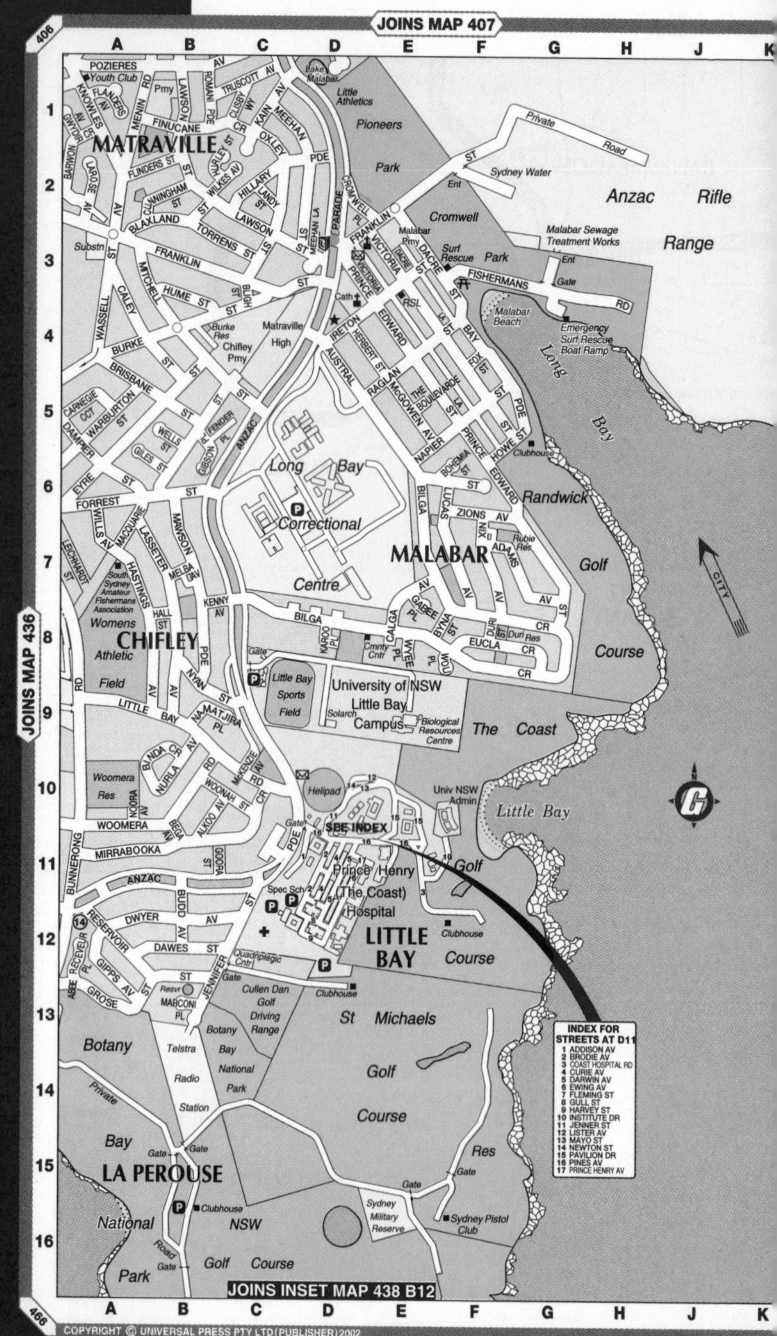
JOINS MAP 407
JOINS MAP 436
JOINS INSET MAP 438 B12
406
466
MATRAVILLE
CHIFLEY
MALABAR
LITTLE BAY
LA PEROUSE
Pioneers Park
Cromwell Park
Anzac Rifle Range
Malabar Sewage Treatment Works
Sydney Water
Long Bay
Long Bay Correctional Centre
Randwick Golf Course
Matraville High
University of NSW Little Bay Campus
Biological Resources Centre
The Coast
Little Bay
Prince Henry (The Coast) Hospital
Little Bay Golf Course
St Michaels Golf Course
Botany Bay National Park
Telstra Radio Station
Cullen Dan Golf Driving Range
NSW Golf Course
Sydney Military Reserve
Sydney Pistol Club
Womens Athletic Field
Woomera Res
Little Bay Sports Field
South Sydney Amateur Fishermans Association
Helipad
Univ NSW Admin
SEE INDEX
CITY
INDEX FOR STREETS AT D11
1 ADDISON AV
2 BRODIE AV
3 COAST HOSPITAL RD
4 CURIE AV
5 DARWIN AV
6 EWING AV
7 FLEMING ST
8 GULL ST
9 HARVEY ST
10 INSTITUTE DR
11 JENNER ST
12 LISTER AV
13 MAYO ST
14 NEWTON ST
15 PAVILION DR
16 PINES AV
17 PRINCE HENRY AV

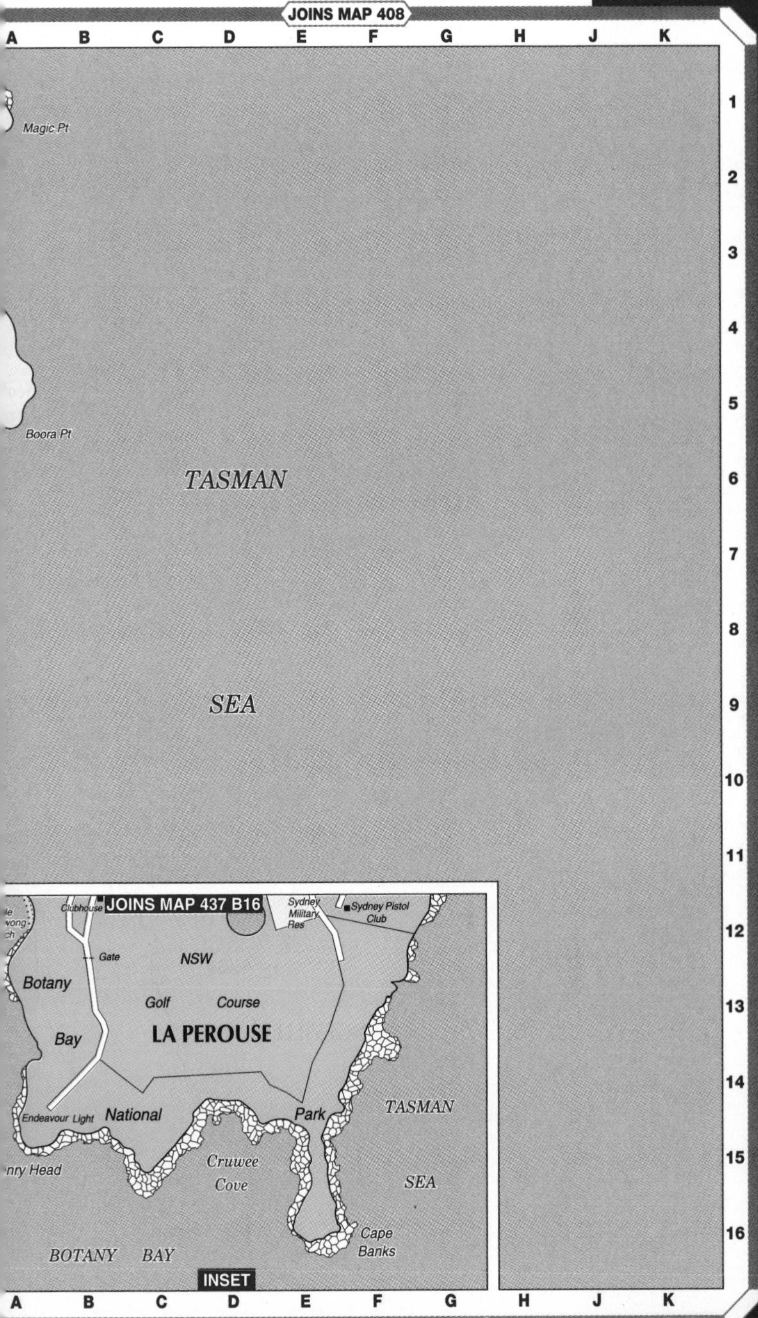

JOINS MAP 408

A B C D E F G H J K

Magic Pt

Boora Pt

TASMAN

SEA

JOINS MAP 437 B16

Clubhouse
Sydney Military Res
Sydney Pistol Club
Gate
NSW
Botany
Golf
Course
Bay
LA PEROUSE
Endeavour Light
National
Park
TASMAN
nry Head
Cruwee Cove
SEA
Cape Banks
BOTANY BAY

INSET

A B C D E F G H J K

MAP 443
PREVIOUS MAP 438

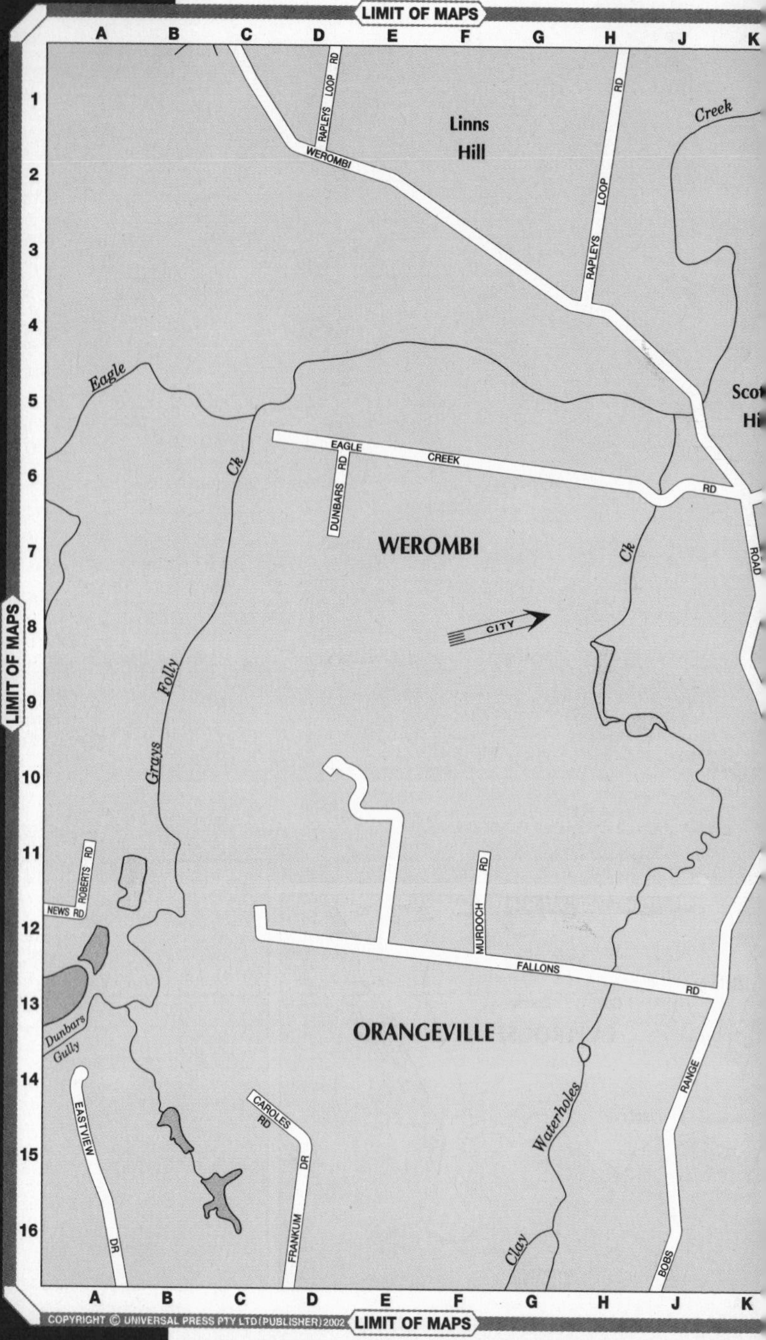

LIMIT OF MAPS

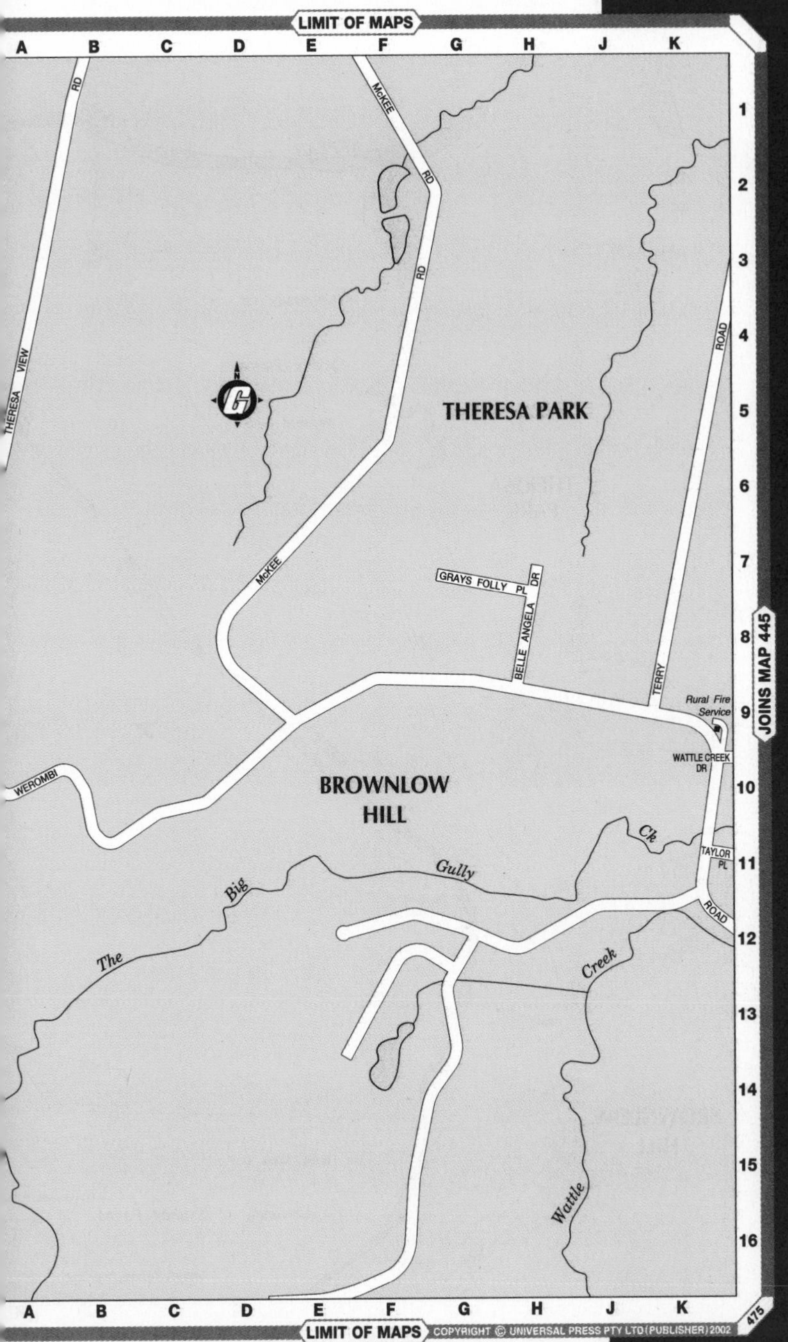
LIMIT OF MAPS
A
B
C
D
E
F
G
H
J
K
1
2
3
4
5
6
7
8
9
10
11
12
13
14
15
16
THERESA VIEW RD
McKEE RD
McKEE RD
THERESA PARK
GRAYS FOLLY PL
BELLE ANGELA DR
TERRY ROAD
Rural Fire Service
WATTLE CREEK DR
TAYLOR PL
ROAD
WEROMBI
BROWNLOW HILL
Ck
Gully
Big
The
Creek
Wattle
JOINS MAP 445
LIMIT OF MAPS

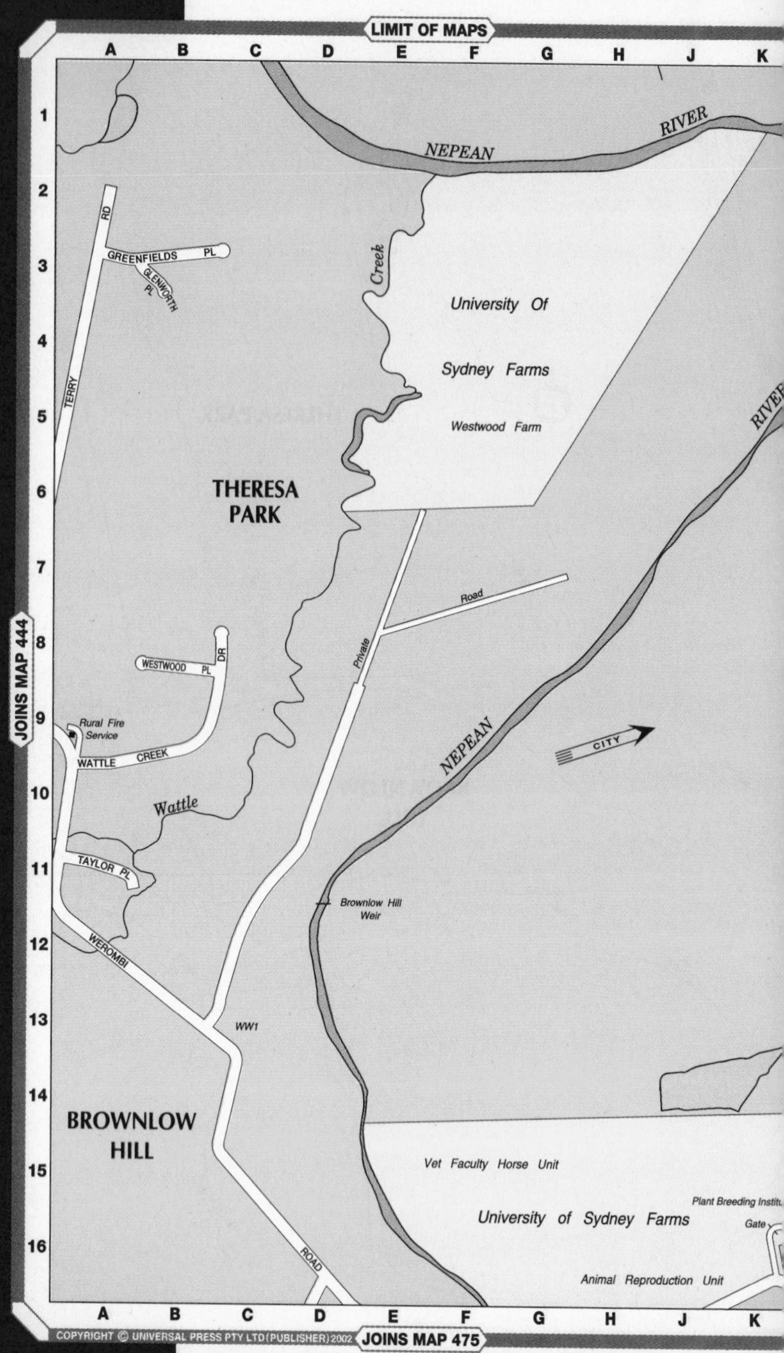

JOINS MAP 475

LIMIT OF MAPS

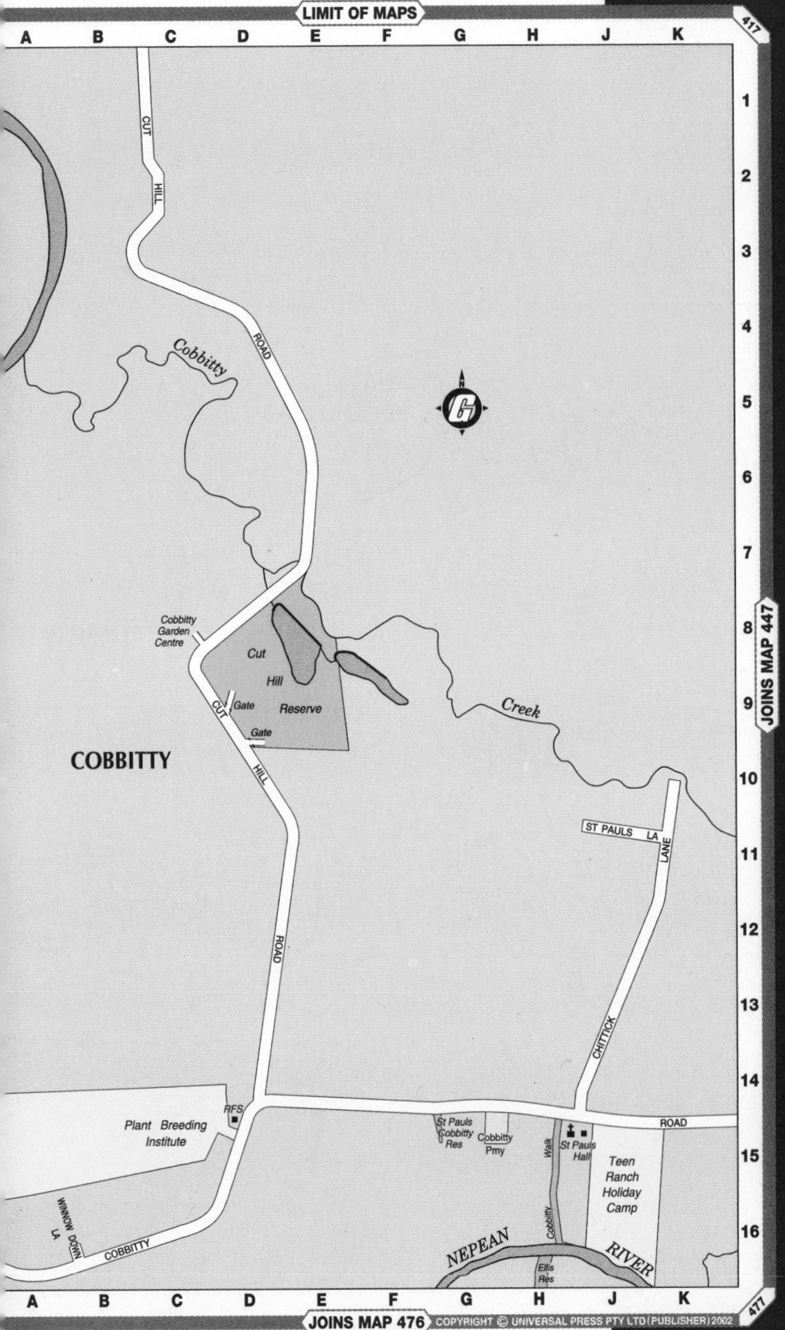

JOINS MAP 447

JOINS MAP 476

MAP 447

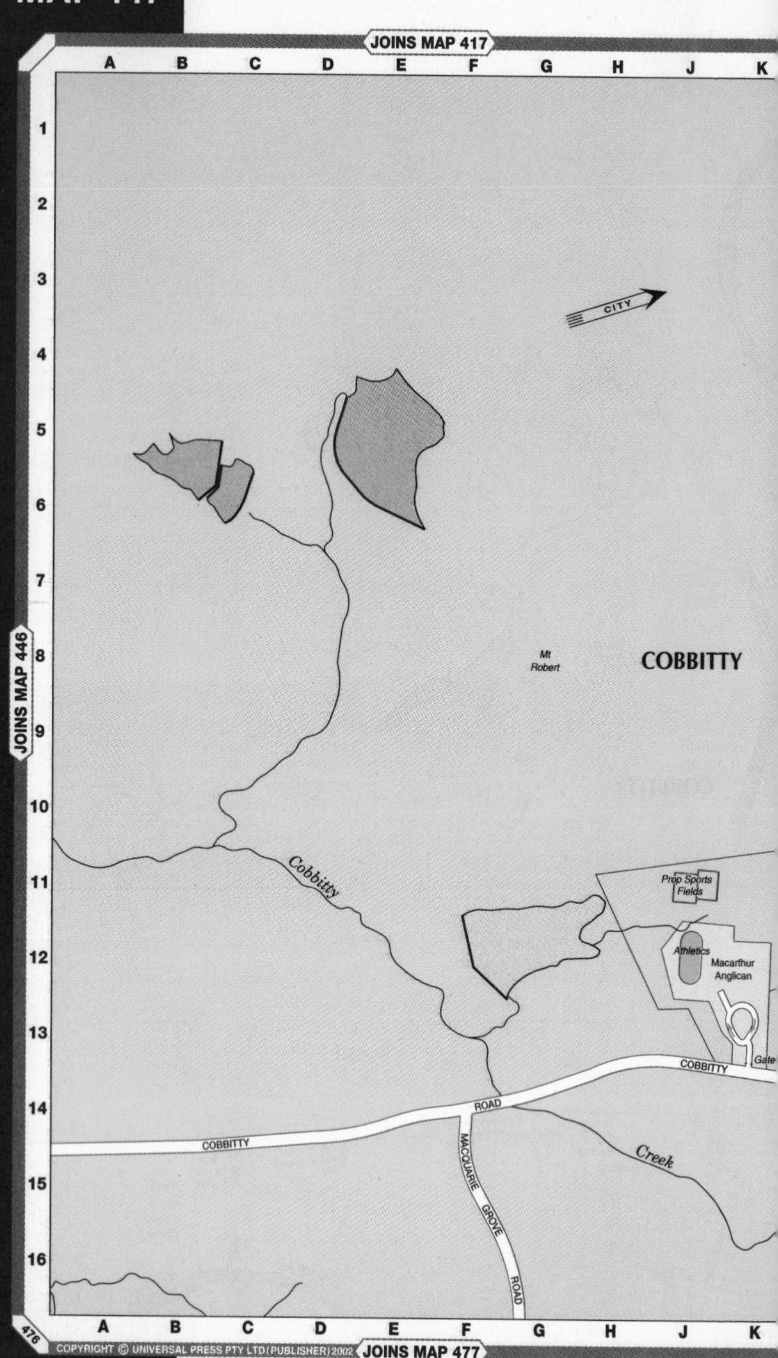
JOINS MAP 417
A
B
C
D
E
F
G
H
J
K
1
2
3
4
5
6
7
8
9
10
11
12
13
14
15
16
CITY
Mt
Robert
COBBITTY
JOINS MAP 446
Cobbitty
Prep Sports
Fields
Athletics
Macarthur
Anglican
Gate
COBBITTY
ROAD
COBBITTY
MACQUARIE
GROVE
ROAD
Creek
JOINS MAP 477
476

JOINS MAP 418

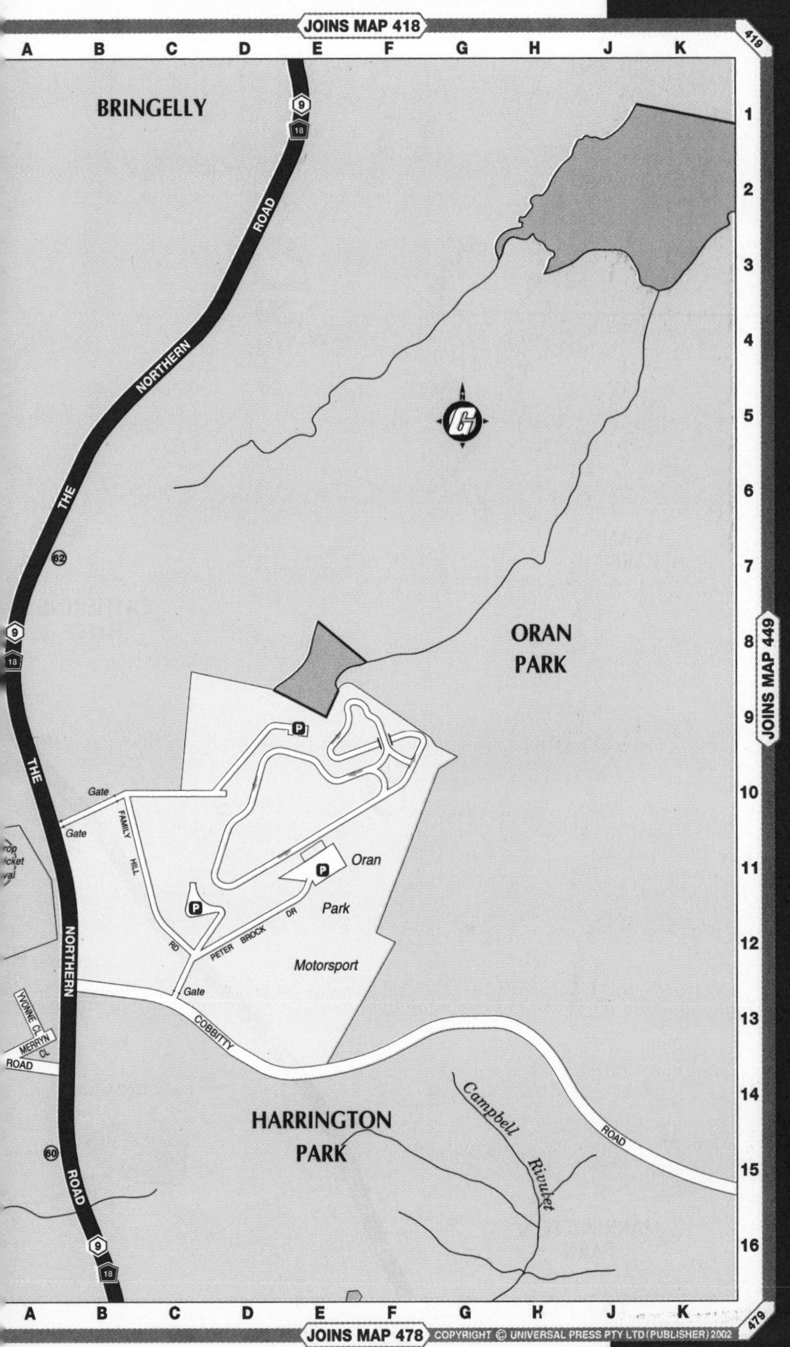

JOINS MAP 449

JOINS MAP 478

JOINS MAP 419

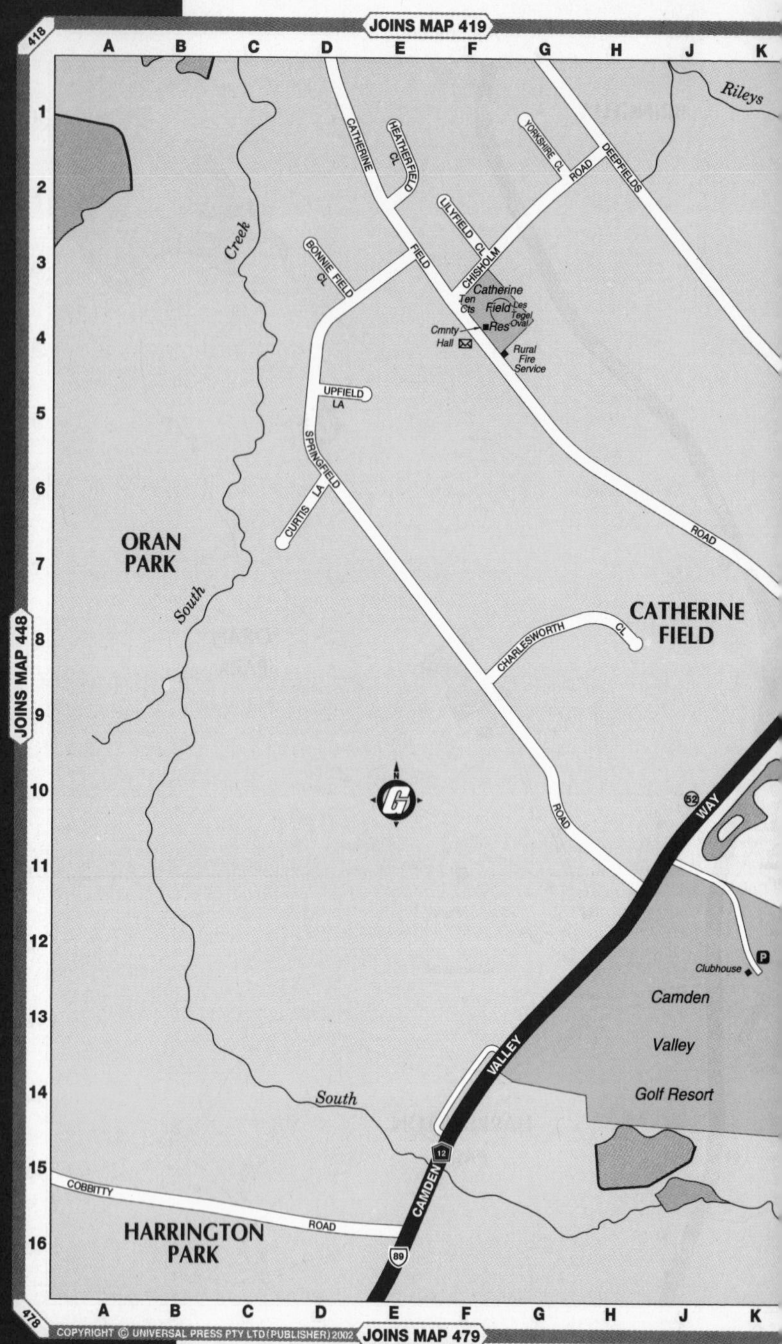

JOINS MAP 448

JOINS MAP 479

JOINS MAP 420

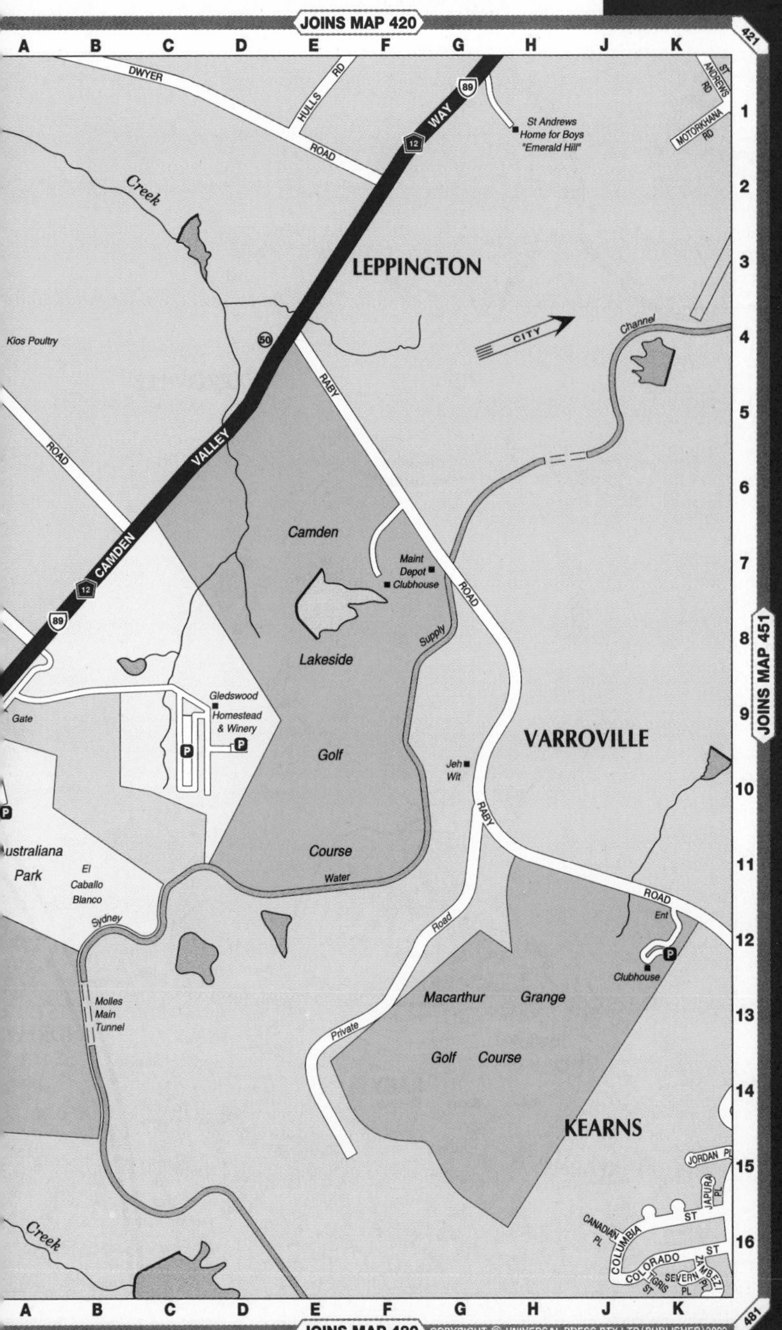

JOINS MAP 451

JOINS MAP 480

JOINS MAP 421

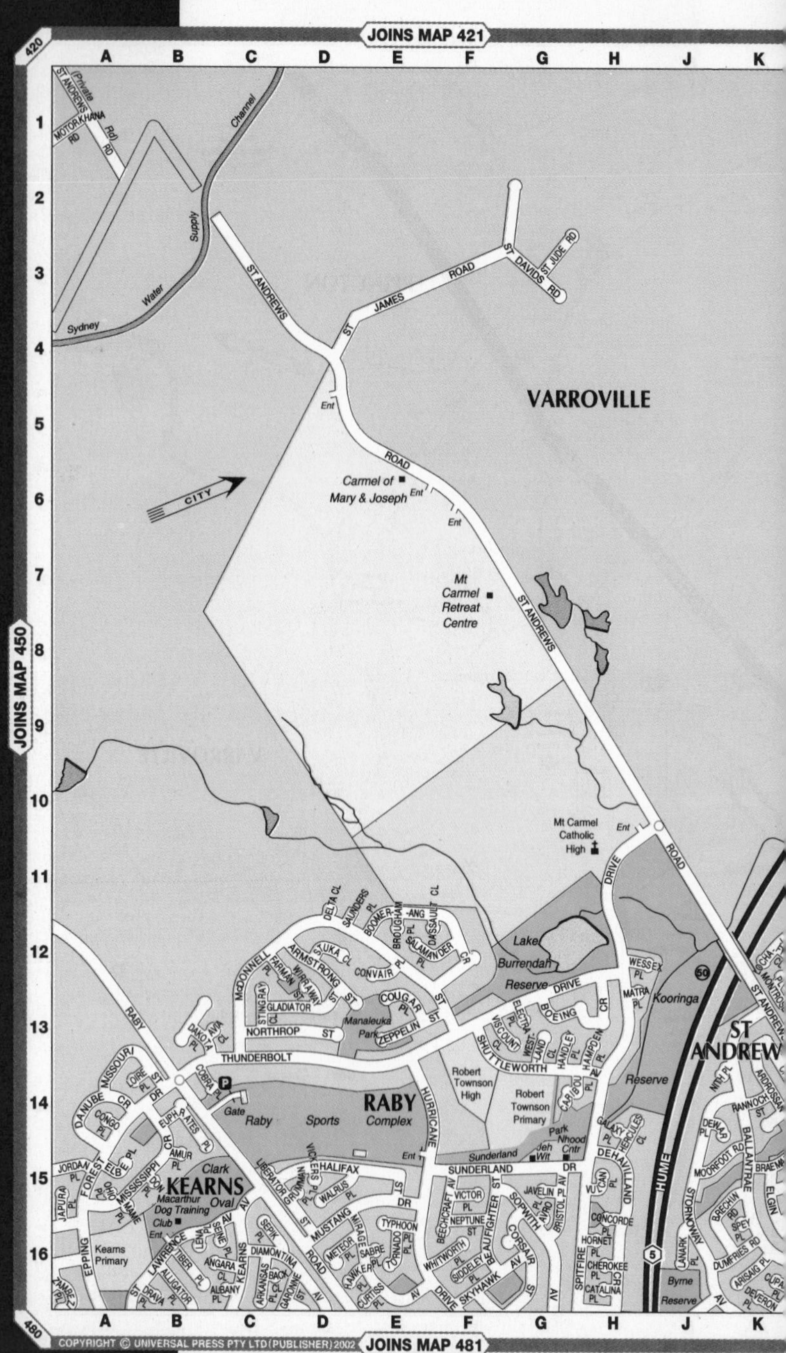

JOINS MAP 450

JOINS MAP 481

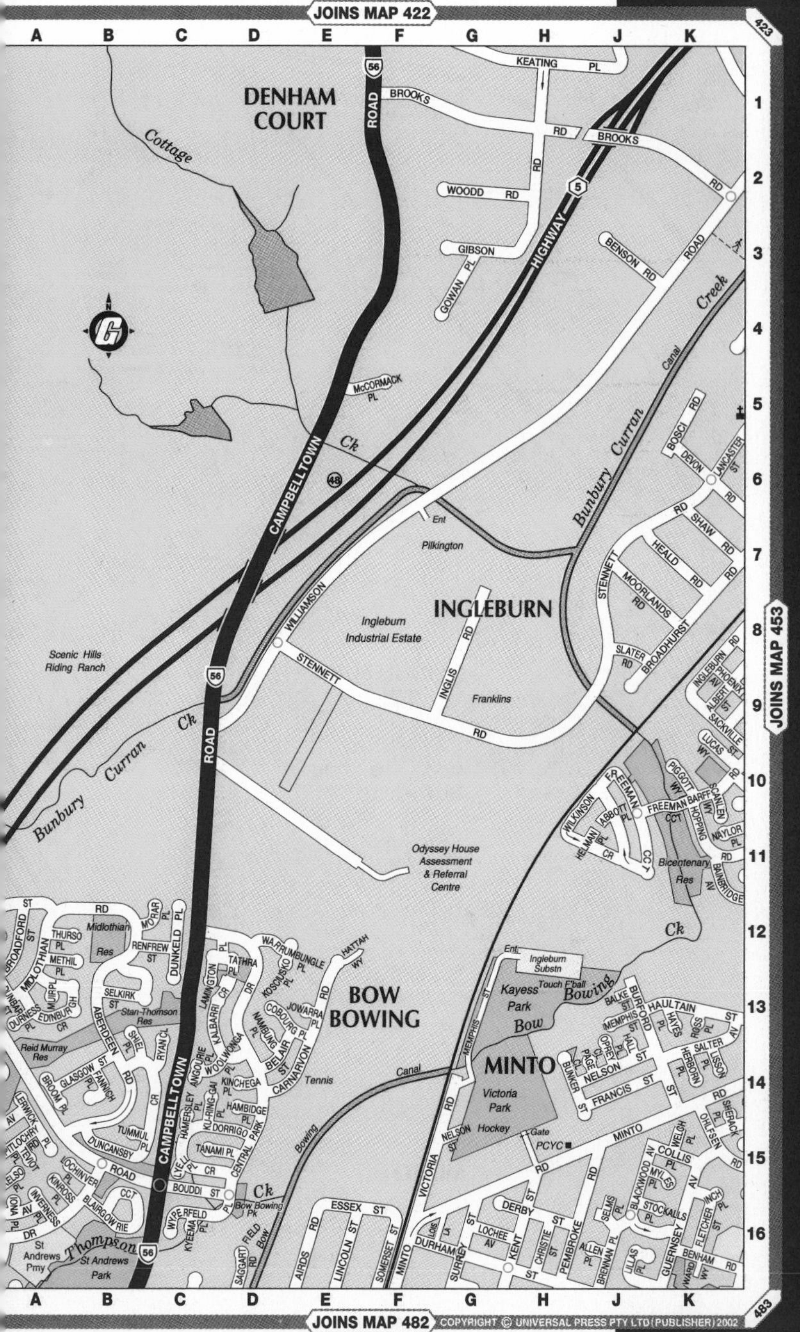
JOINS MAP 422
JOINS MAP 453
JOINS MAP 482
423
483
A B C D E F G H J K
1 2 3 4 5 6 7 8 9 10 11 12 13 14 15 16
DENHAM COURT
INGLEBURN
BOW BOWING
MINTO
Cottage
Ck
Bunbury Curran Ck
Bunbury Curran Creek Canal
Bow Bowing Canal
Bow Bowing Ck
Thompson Ck
CAMPBELLTOWN ROAD
HIGHWAY
KEATING PL
BROOKS RD
WOODD RD
GIBSON
GOWAN PL
BENSON RD
McCORMACK PL
WILLIAMSON
STENNETT RD
INGLIS RD
Ent
Pilkington
Ingleburn Industrial Estate
Franklins
Scenic Hills Riding Ranch
Odyssey House Assessment & Referral Centre
BOSCI RD
DEVON
LANCASTER ST
SHAW RD
HEALD RD
MOORLANDS RD
BROADHURST
SLATER RD
INGLEBURN RD
PHOENIX
ALBERT ST
SACKVILLE
LUCAS ST
PIGGOTT WY
FREEMAN CCT
WILKINSON
ABBOTT
HELMAN PL
BARFF
SCANLEN
HOPPING
NAYLOR PL
BAINBRIDGE AV
Bicentenary Res
Midlothian Res
BROADFORD ST
MIDLOTHIAN
THURSO PL
METHIL PL
RENFREW ST
MORAR PL
DUNKELD PL
SELKIRK ST
ABERDEEN
EDINBURGH CR
DURNESS PL
Stan Thomson Res
Reid Murray Res
GLASGOW ST
FANNICH
BROOM PL
SHIEL PL
RYAN CL
TUMMUL PL
DUNCANSBY
LOCHINVER
KINROSS
INVERNESS
BLAIRGOWRIE
IONA PL
ROAD
CCT
BOUDDI ST
WARRUMBUNGLE PL
HATTAH WY
TATHRA PL
LAMINGTON CR
KALBARRI CR
KOSCIUSKO PL
COBOURG PL
JOWARRA PL
NAMBUNG
BELAIR ST
CARNARVON
WOOLWONGA
ANGOURIE
KINCHEGA PL
HAMERSLEY PL
KU-RING-GAI
HAMBIDGE PL
DORRIGO PL
TANAMI PL
CENTRAL PARK
LYELL
WYPERFELD
KYEEMA PL
Bow Bowing Pk
St Andrews Pmy
St Andrews Park
SAGGART FIELD RD
Tennis
ESSEX ST
AIRDS RD
LINCOLN ST
SOMERSET ST
MINTO
Ingleburn Substn
Kayess Park
Touch F'ball
MEMPHIS ST
Victoria Park
Hockey
Gate
PCYC
NELSON ST
VICTORIA RD
BALKE ST
BURFORD ST
HAULTAIN ST
HAYES
ROSS PL
HALL ST
ORFEY PL
PAGE ST
BUNKER ST
NELSON ST
FRANCIS ST
SALTER
HERBORN PL
LISSON AV
MINTO RD
OHLFSEN
SHERACK
COLLIS PL
WELCH
BLACKWOOD AV
MYLES PL
STOCKALLS PL
SELMS PL
INCH
FLETCHER ST
GUERNSEY AV
BENHAM RD
WARD WY
LILLAS PL
BRENNAN PL
ALLEN PL
PEMBROKE RD
DERBY ST
CHRISTIE ST
KENT ST
LOCHEE AV
SURREY ST
DURHAM
LOIS LA
COPYRIGHT © UNIVERSAL PRESS PTY LTD (PUBLISHER) 2002

MAP 453

JOINS MAP 423

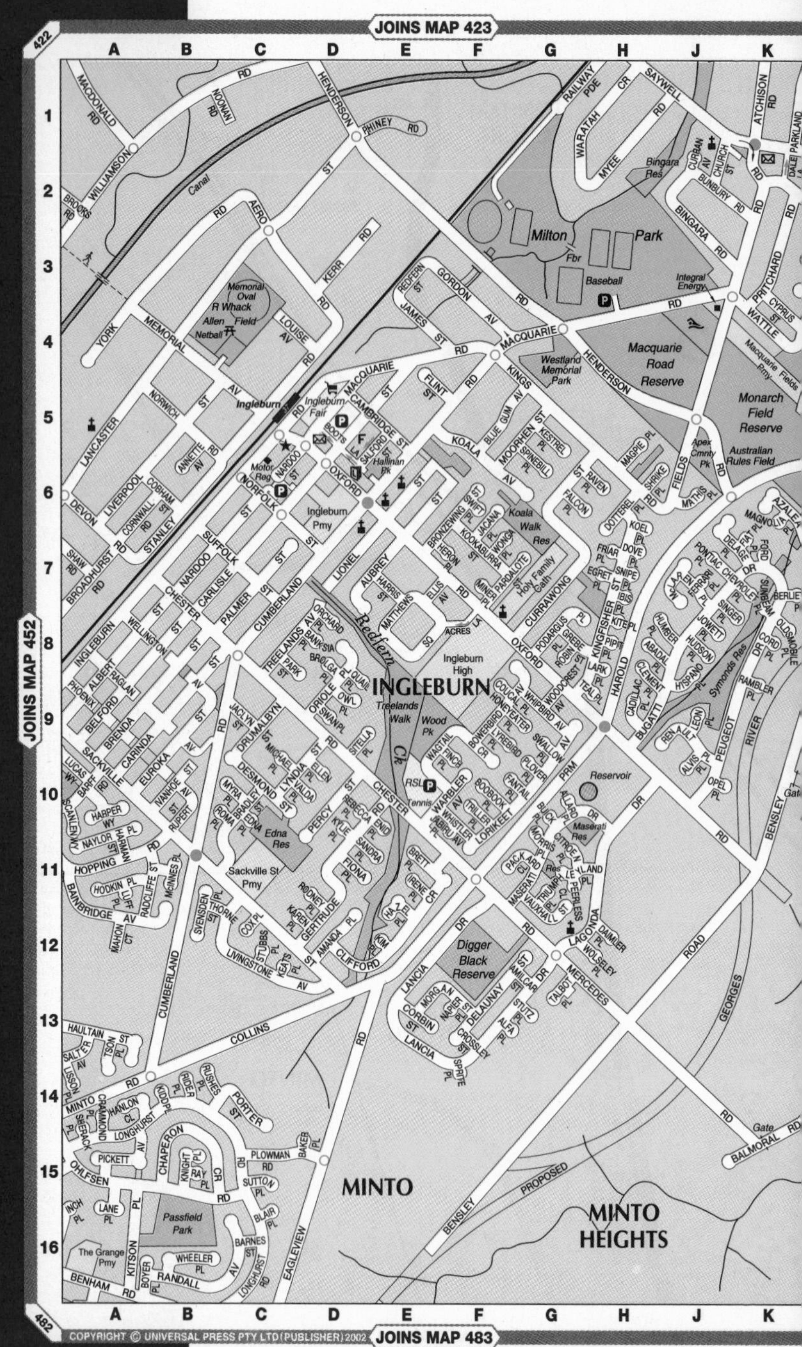

JOINS MAP 452
JOINS MAP 483

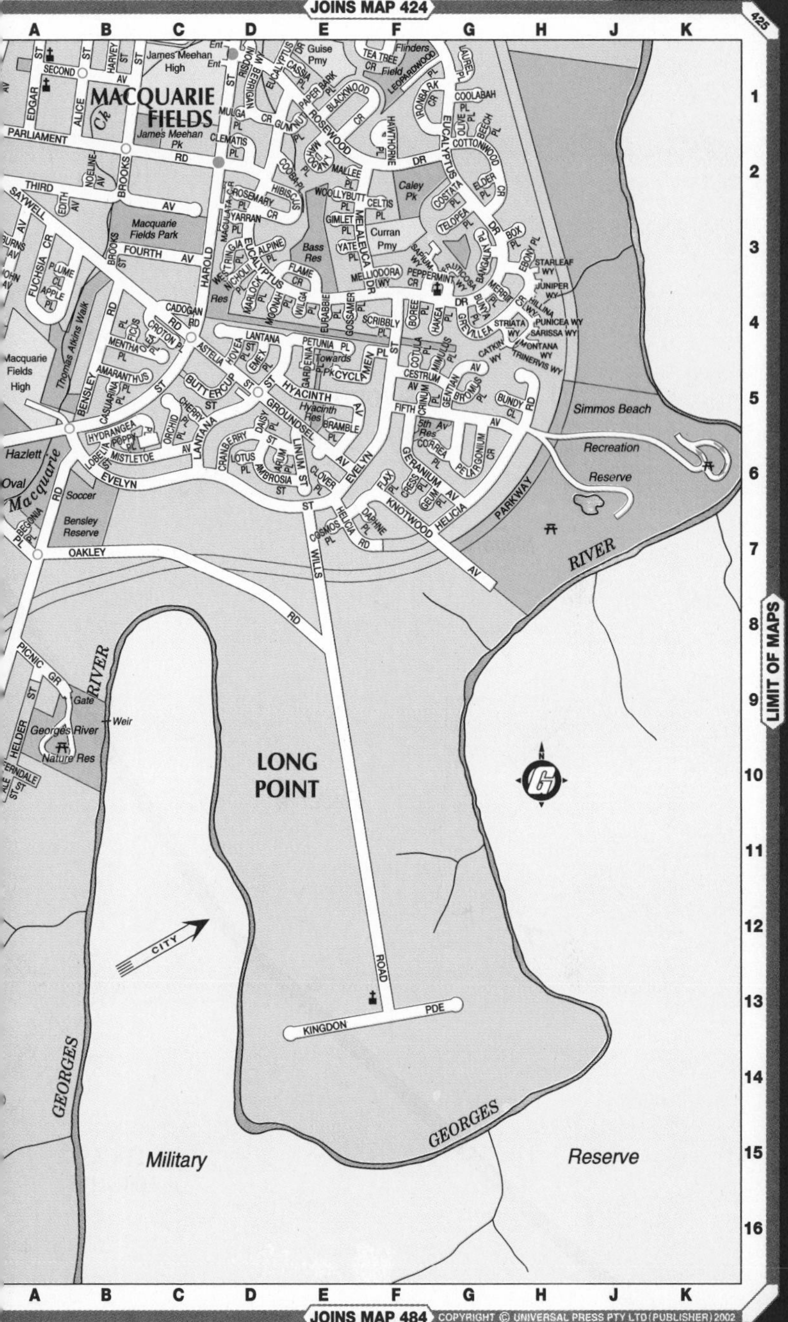
JOINS MAP 424
425
MACQUARIE FIELDS
James Meehan High
James Meehan Pk
Guise Pmy
Flinders Field
Caley Pk
Curran Pmy
Bass Res
Macquarie Fields Park
Macquarie Fields High
Thomas Atkins Walk
Hyacinth Res
5th Av Res
Towards Pk
Hazlett Oval
Soccer
Bensley Reserve
Macquarie
Simmos Beach
Recreation
Reserve
RIVER
PARKWAY
OAKLEY RD
WILLS ROAD
KINGDON PDE
LONG POINT
CITY
Georges River Nature Res
Weir
Gate
PICNIC GR
HELDER ST
GEORGES
Military
Reserve
LIMIT OF MAPS
JOINS MAP 484
COPYRIGHT © UNIVERSAL PRESS PTY LTD (PUBLISHER) 2002

JOINS MAP 427

426

A B C D E F G H J K

1 2 3 4 5 6 7 8 9 10 11 12 13 14 15 16

LIMIT OF MAPS

Williams Creek

NATIONAL PARK ROAD

Mt Deadmans

Creek

HOLSWORTHY

Military

Reserve

Deadmans

CITY

46

47

HEATHCOTE ROAD

Creek

Bardens

Mill

LUCAS HEIGHTS

Creek

A B C D E F G H J K

JOINS MAP 487

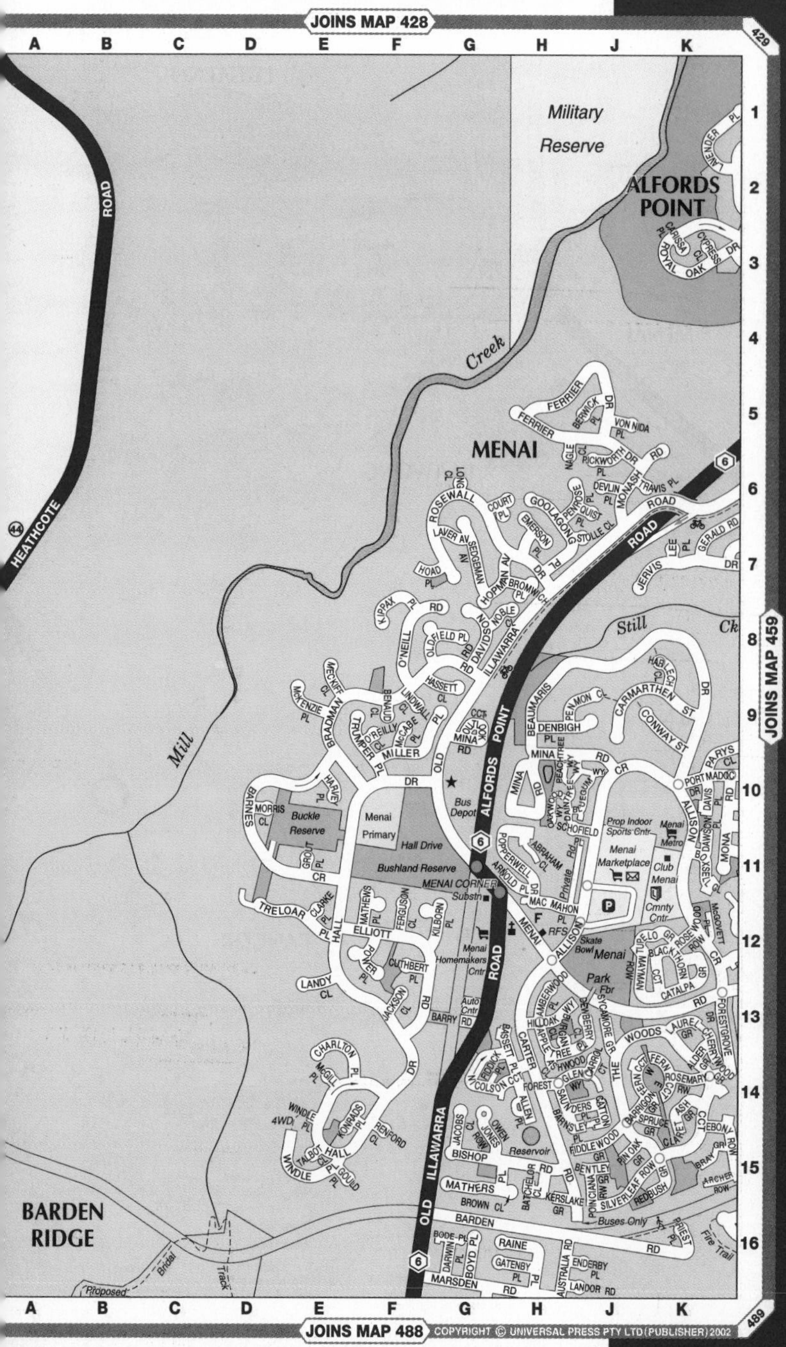
JOINS MAP 428
429
Military Reserve
ALFORDS POINT
MENAI
Creek
Mill
Still Ck
HEATHCOTE ROAD
ALFORDS POINT ROAD
OLD ILLAWARRA ROAD
Buckle Reserve
Menai Primary
Hall Drive
Bushland Reserve
MENAI CORNER
Bus Depot
Prop Indoor Sports Cntr
Menai Marketplace
Club Menai
Menai Metro
Cmnty Cntr
Menai Park
Skate Bowl
Menai Homemakers Cntr
Auto Cntr
Reservoir
Buses Only
Fire Trail
BARDEN RIDGE
Bridal Track
Proposed
JOINS MAP 459
JOINS MAP 488
489

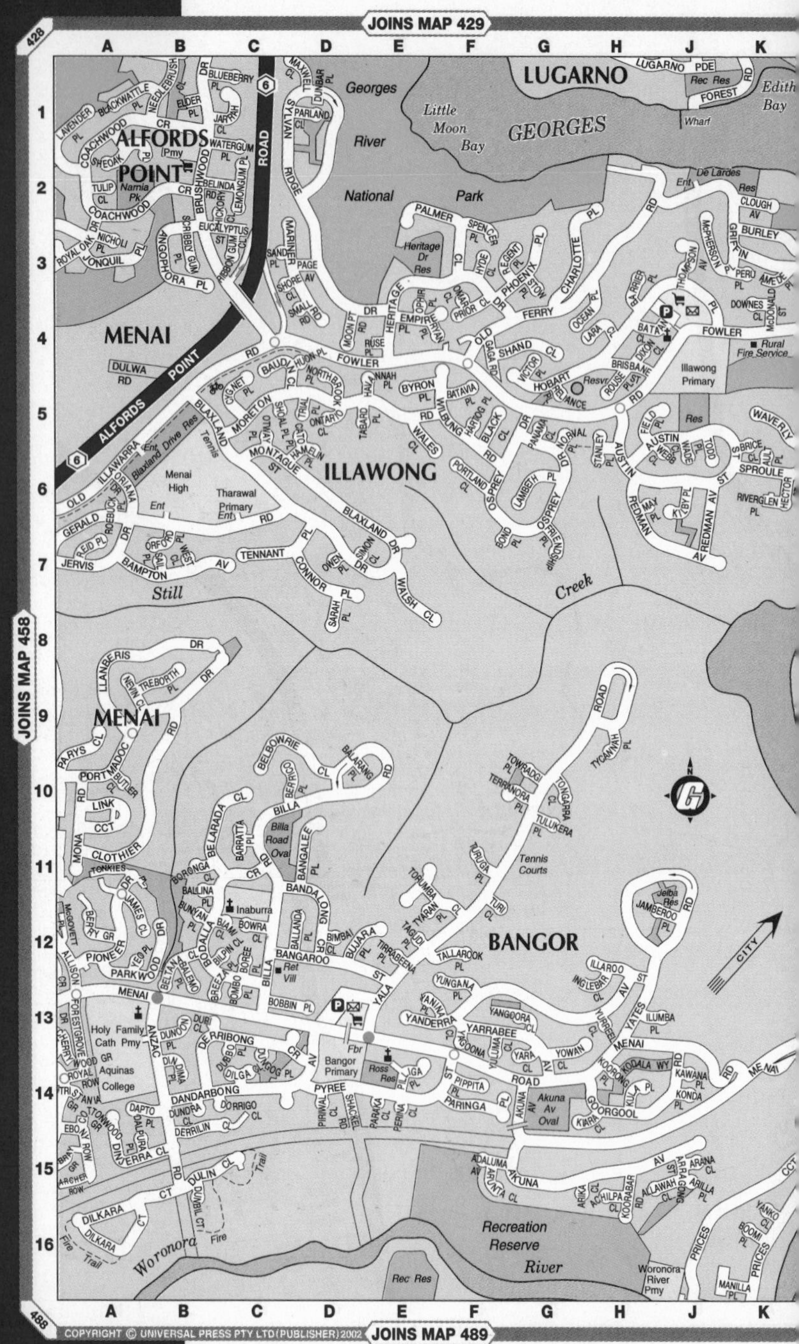

JOINS MAP 429
JOINS MAP 458
JOINS MAP 489
428
488
A B C D E F G H J K
1 2 3 4 5 6 7 8 9 10 11 12 13 14 15 16
LUGARNO
ALFORDS POINT
MENAI
ILLAWONG
BANGOR
Georges River
National Park
Little Moon Bay
GEORGES
Edith Bay
Still Creek
Woronora River
Recreation Reserve
Rec Res
Wharf
Menai High
Tharawal Primary
Illawong Primary
Bangor Primary
Holy Family Cath Pmy
Aquinas College
Woronora River Pmy
Billa Road Oval
Akuna Av Oval
Tennis Courts
Rural Fire Service
Heritage Dr Res
Blaxland Drive Res
Jelba Res
Ross Res
Narnia Pk
Inaburra
Ret Vill
Resvr
CITY
ALFORDS POINT ROAD
FOWLER RD
HOBART RD
BLAXLAND DR
MENAI RD
OLD ILLAWARRA RD
LUGARNO PDE
FOREST RD
De Lardes Res
FERRY RD
AUSTIN AV
REDMAN AV
WAVERLY
SPROULE ST
BAMPTON AV
JERVIS
TENNANT
CONNOR PL
WALSH CL
LLANBERIS DR
TREBORTH PL
PARYS CL
PORTMADOC
LINK CCT
CLOTHIER
MONA RD
PIONEER
PARKWOOD DR
ANZAC RD
DERRIBONG CR
DANDARBONG
PYREE ST
YALA RD
BANGAROO ST
BILLA RD
BANDALONG CR
TIRRABEENA
TALLAROOK PL
ILLAROO
YATES AV
KOODALA WY
PRICES
DILKARA CT
DULIN CT
Fire Trail
COPYRIGHT © UNIVERSAL PRESS PTY LTD (PUBLISHER) 2002

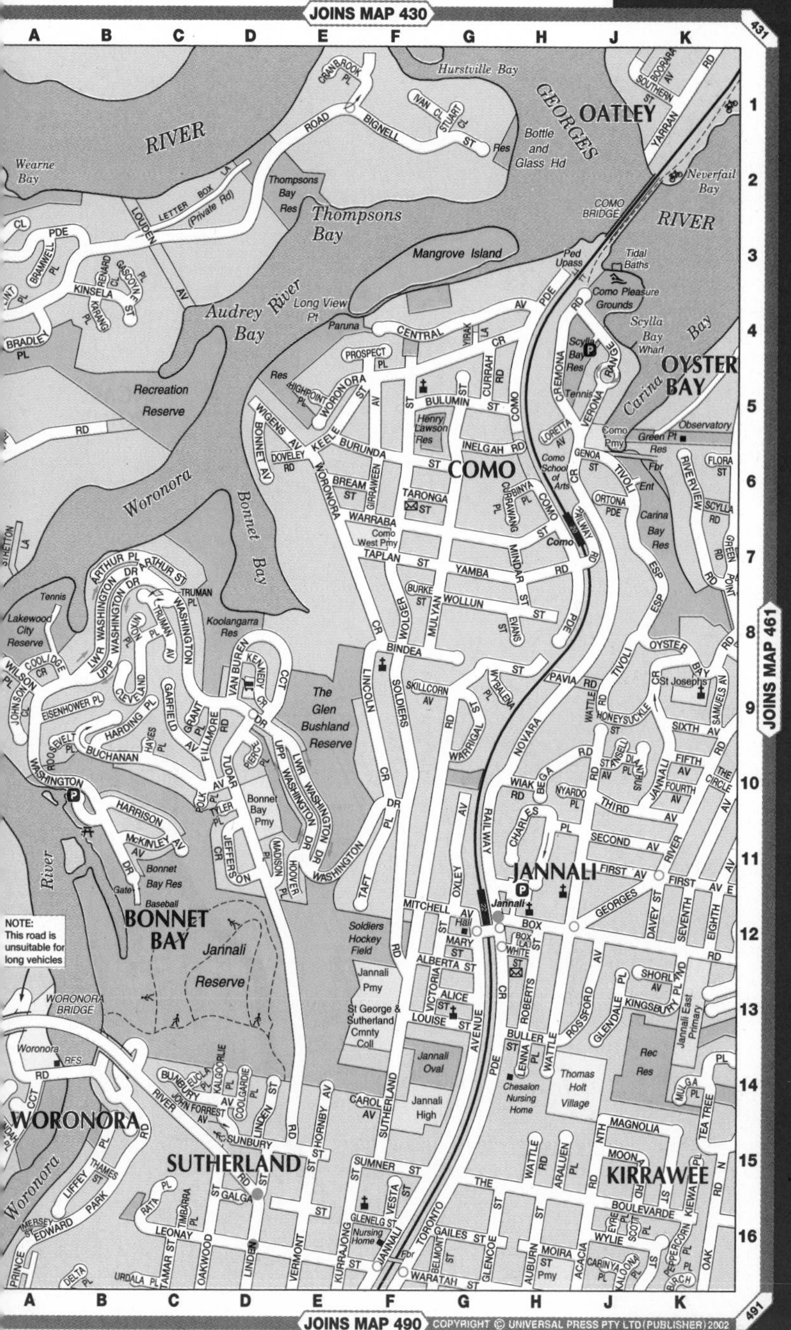
JOINS MAP 430
JOINS MAP 461
JOINS MAP 490
431
491
A
B
C
D
E
F
G
H
J
K
1
2
3
4
5
6
7
8
9
10
11
12
13
14
15
16
GEORGES
RIVER
OATLEY
COMO
JANNALI
BONNET BAY
WORONORA
SUTHERLAND
KIRRAWEE
OYSTER BAY
Hurstville Bay
Wearne Bay
Thompsons Bay
Thompsons Bay Res
Mangrove Island
Audrey Bay
Long View Pt
Paruna
Bottle and Glass Hd
Neverfail Bay
COMO BRIDGE
Ped Upass
Tidal Baths
Como Pleasure Grounds
Scylla Bay Wharf
Carina Bay
Observatory
Green Pt Res
Carina Bay Res
Recreation Reserve
Woronora
Bonnet Bay
Koolangarra Res
Lakewood City Reserve
Tennis
The Glen Bushland Reserve
Bonnet Bay Pmy
Bonnet Bay Res
Gate
Baseball
Jannali Reserve
NOTE: This road is unsuitable for long vehicles
WORONORA BRIDGE
Woronora RFS
Soldiers Hockey Field
Jannali Pmy
St George & Sutherland Cmnty Coll
Jannali Oval
Jannali High
Henry Lawson Res
Como West Pmy
Como School of Arts
Como Pmy
Scylla Bay Res
Jannali East Primary
Rec Res
Thomas Holt Village
Chesalon Nursing Home
Glenelg St Nursing Home
St Josephs
Hall
Fbr
Ent
Res
BIGNELL ST
CRANBROOK PL
IVAN CL
STUART CL
LETTER BOX LA (Private Rd)
LOUDEN AV
BRAMWELL PL
RENARD CL
GASCOYNE PL
KINSELA ST
KARANG PL
BRADLEY PL
CENTRAL AV
PROSPECT PL
HIGHPOINT PL
WORONORA AV
WIGENS AV
BONNET AV
DOVELEY RD
KEELE ST
BURUNDA ST
BREAM ST
GIRRAWEEN ST
TARONGA ST
WARRABA ST
TAPLAN ST
YAMBA RD
BURKE ST
WOLLUN ST
MULYAN AV
WOLGER RD
BINDEA ST
LINCOLN CR
SOLDIERS RD
SKILLCORN AV
WARRIGAL ST
WYBALENA PL
YIRAK LA
CURRAH RD
BULUMIN ST
INELGAH RD
COMO PDE
BINYA PL
CURRAWANG PL
MINDAR ST
EVANS ST
RAILWAY RD
CREMONA RD
VERONA RANGE
LORETTA AV
GENOA ST
TIVOLI ESP
ORTONA PDE
RIVERVIEW RD
FLORA ST
SCYLLA RD
GREEN POINT RD
OYSTER BAY RD
PAVIA RD
NOVARA CR
WATTLE RD
HONEYSUCKLE ST
SIXTH AV
FIFTH AV
FOURTH AV
THE CIRCLE
THIRD AV
SECOND AV
FIRST AV
SEVENTH AV
EIGHTH AV
DAVEY ST
SAMUELS AV
STANSELL AV
DIANTHUS PL
JANNALI AV
BEGA RD
NYARDO PL
WIAK RD
CHARLES PL
GEORGES RIVER RD
BOX RD
BOX LA
WHITE ST
ROBERTS AV
ROSSFORD AV
GLENDALE AV
SHORL AV
KINGSBURY PL
MULGA PL
TEA TREE PL
BULLER ST
LENNA PL
MAGNOLIA AV
MOONA RD
ARALUEN PL
THE BOULEVARDE
KIEWA ST
WYLIE ST
SCOTT PL
EYRE PL
PEPPERCORN PL
BIRCH PL
OAK RD
MOIRA ST
ACACIA RD
CARINYA PL
KALOONA ST
AUBURN ST
GAILES ST
BELMONT ST
GLENCOE ST
TORONTO PDE
WARATAH ST
ARTHUR PL
ARTHUR ST
TRUMAN PL
WASHINGTON DR
LWR WASHINGTON DR
UPP WASHINGTON DR
DIXON PL
TRUMAN AV
CLEVELAND AV
GARFIELD AV
GRANT PL
FILLMORE RD
VAN BUREN CR
KENNEDY CR
CCT
EISENHOWER PL
HARDING PL
HAYES PL
ROOSEVELT PL
BUCHANAN AV
COOLIDGE CR
WILSON PL
JOHNSON PL
POLK PL
TYLER CR
TUDAR AV
PIERCE PL
MADISON PL
JEFFERSON CR
HOOVER PL
HARRISON ST
McKINLEY AV
TAFT PL
MITCHELL AV
OXLEY AV
MARY ST
ALBERTA ST
VICTORIA AV
ALICE ST
LOUISE ST
AVENUE PDE
CAROL AV
SUTHERLAND RD
HORNBY AV
SUMNER ST
VESTA ST
GLENELG ST
KURRAJONG ST
JANNALI AV
VERMONT ST
LINDEN ST
OAKWOOD RD
TAMAR ST
URDALA PL
DELTA PL
PRINCE EDWARD PARK RD
MERSEY
LIFFEY PL
THAMES ST
RATA PL
TIMBARRA PL
GALGA ST
LEONAY ST
SUNBURY ST
BUNBURY AV
EUCLA PL
KALGOORLIE PL
COOLGARDIE PL
JOHN FORREST AV
RIVER RD
STRETTON LA
Jannali
Como

JOINS MAP 431

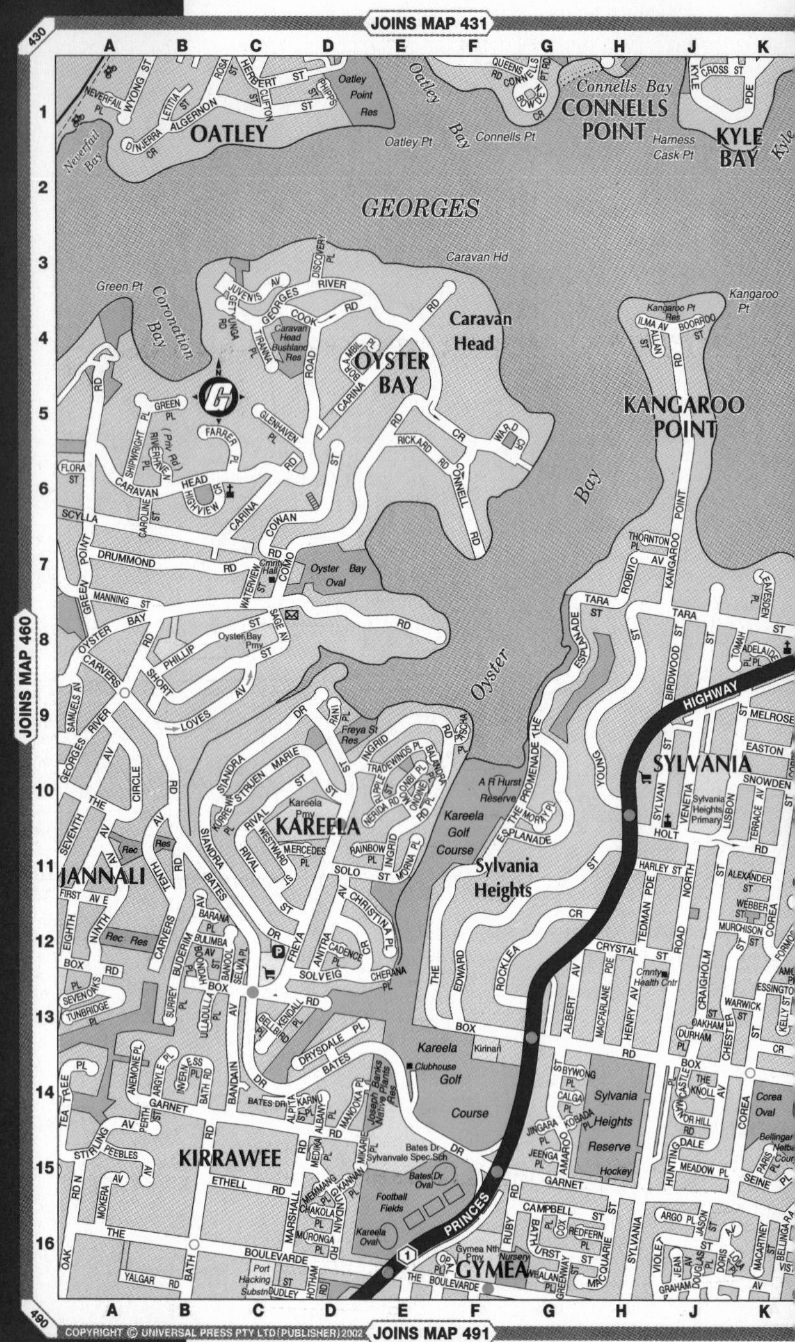

JOINS MAP 491

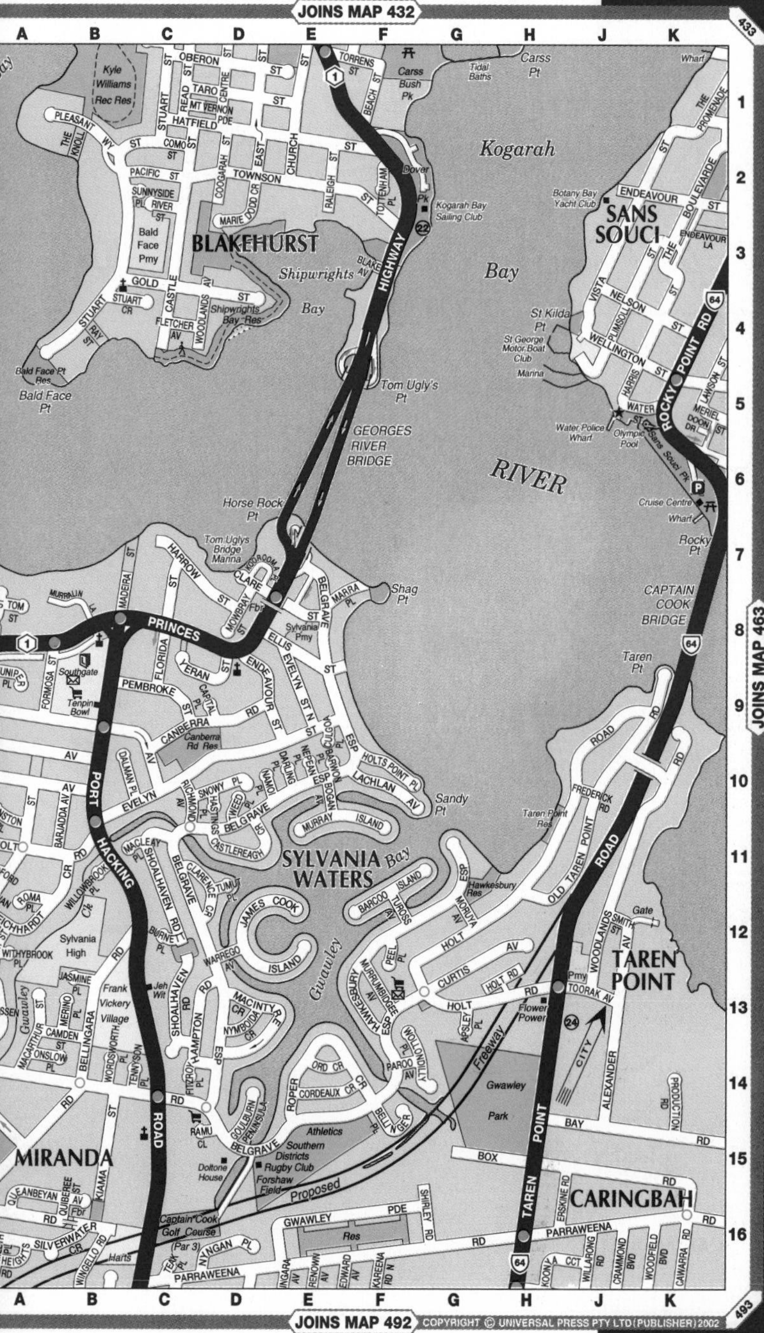
JOINS MAP 432
JOINS MAP 463
JOINS MAP 492
433
493
A
B
C
D
E
F
G
H
J
K
1
2
3
4
5
6
7
8
9
10
11
12
13
14
15
16
BLAKEHURST
SANS SOUCI
SYLVANIA WATERS
TAREN POINT
MIRANDA
CARINGBAH
Kogarah
Bay
RIVER
Shipwrights Bay
GEORGES RIVER BRIDGE
CAPTAIN COOK BRIDGE
Kyle Williams Rec Res
Bald Face Pmy
Bald Face Pt Res
Bald Face Pt
Carss Bush Pk
Carss Pt
Tidal Baths
Dover Pk
Kogarah Bay Sailing Club
Botany Bay Yacht Club
Shipwrights Bay Res
St Kilda Pt
St George Motor Boat Club
Marina
Tom Ugly's Pt
Water Police Wharf
Olympic Pool
Sans Souci Pk
Cruise Centre
Wharf
Rocky Pt
Horse Rock Pt
Tom Uglys Bridge Marina
Shag Pt
Taren Pt
Sylvania Pmy
Southgate
Tenpin Bowl
Canberra Rd Res
Sandy Pt
Taren Point Res
Hawkesbury Res
Gwawley Bay
Gwawley
Sylvania High
Frank Vickery Village
Jeh Wit
Flower Power
Gwawley Park
Athletics
Southern Districts Rugby Club
Forshaw Field
Doltone House
Captain Cook Golf Course (Par 3)
Res
Gate
Freeway
Proposed
CITY
HIGHWAY
PRINCES
PORT HACKING ROAD
ROCKY POINT RD
TAREN POINT ROAD
OLD TAREN POINT RD
GRAND PARADE
COPYRIGHT © UNIVERSAL PRESS PTY LTD (PUBLISHER) 2002

JOINS MAP 433

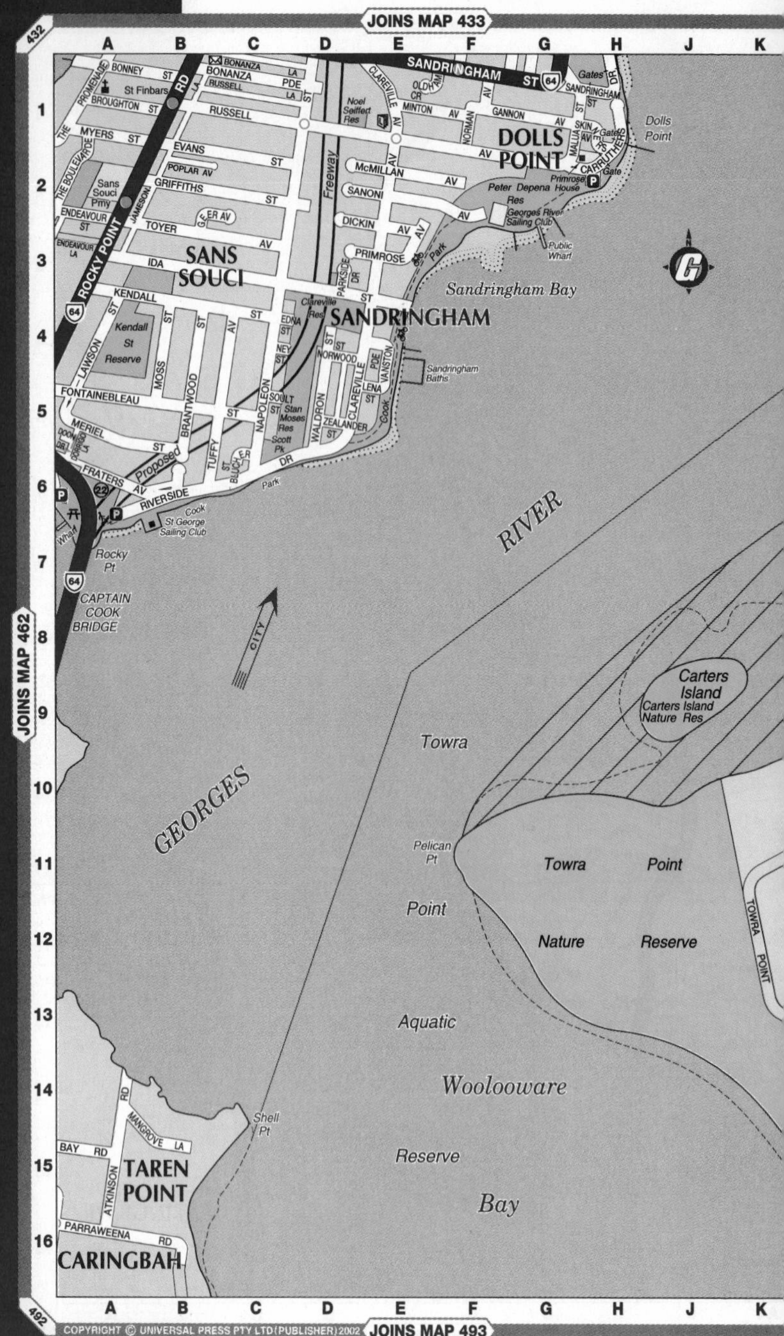

JOINS MAP 493

JOINS MAP 434

JOINS MAP 465

JOINS MAP 494

JOINS MAP 435

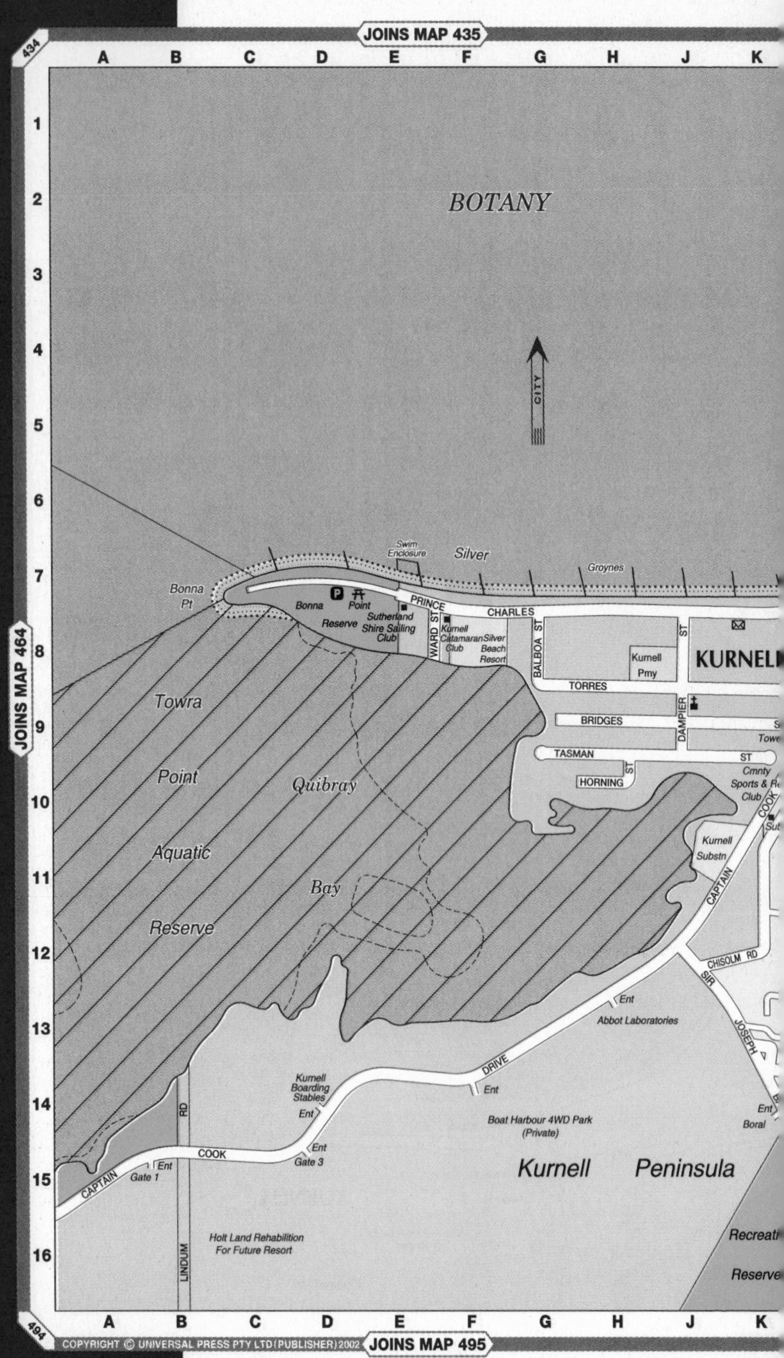

JOINS MAP 464

JOINS MAP 495

JOINS MAP 436

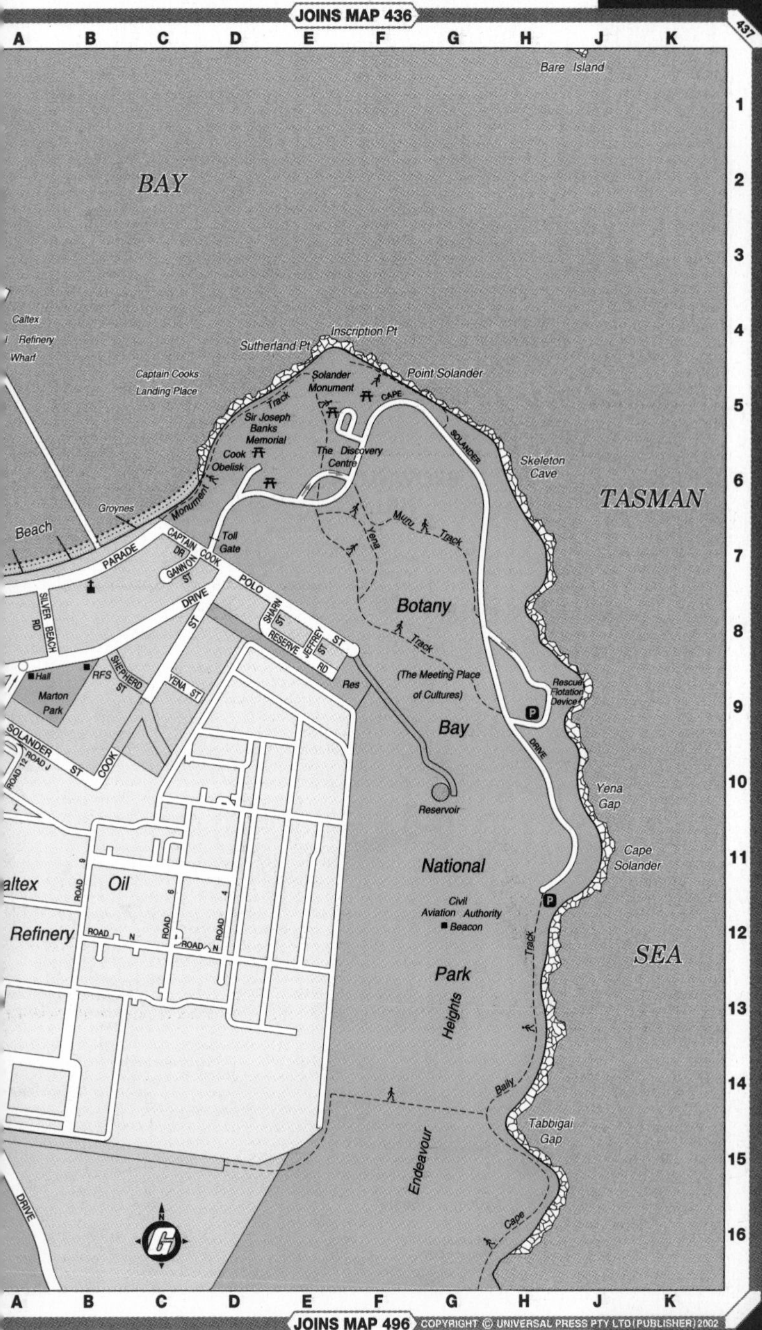

JOINS MAP 496

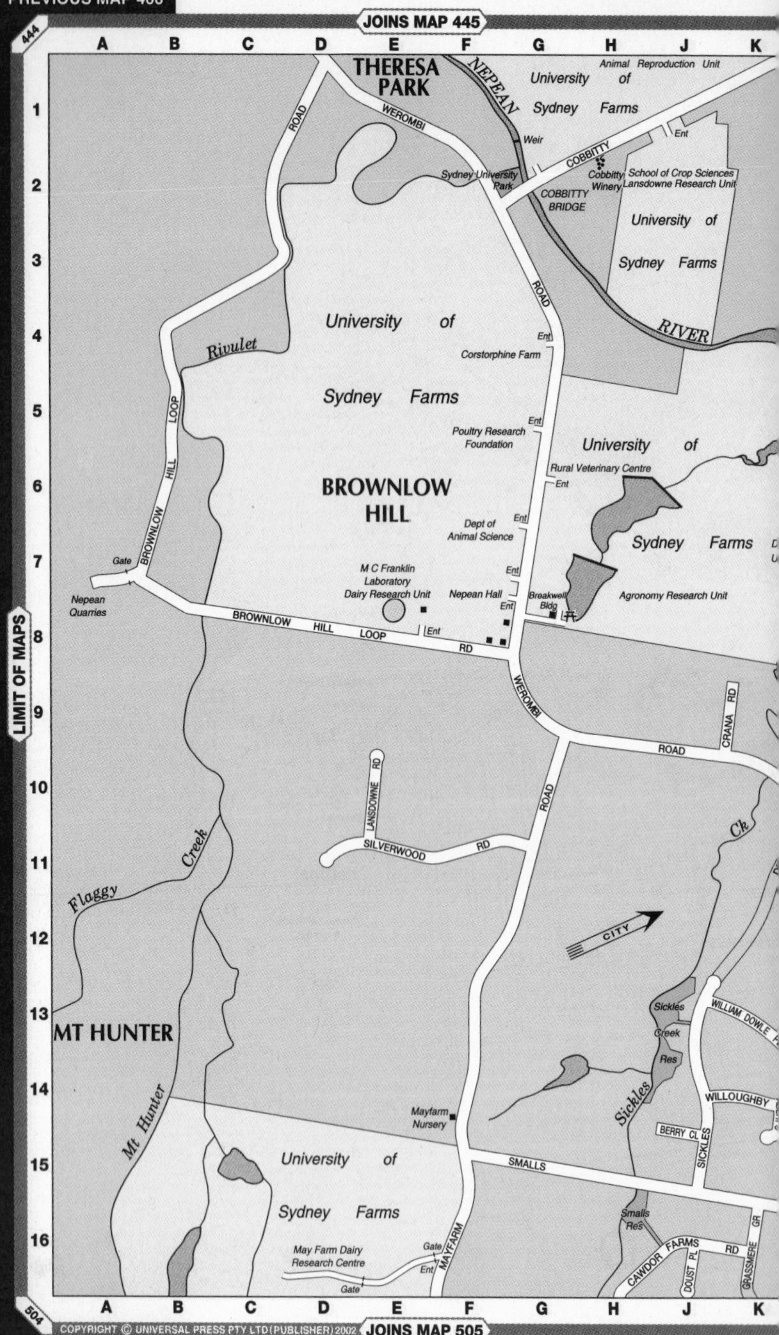
JOINS MAP 445
JOINS MAP 505
LIMIT OF MAPS
444
504
THERESA PARK
NEPEAN
RIVER
Animal Reproduction Unit
University of Sydney Farms
WEROMBI
ROAD
Weir
COBBITTY
Ent
Sydney University Park
Cobbitty Winery
School of Crop Sciences Lansdowne Research Unit
COBBITTY BRIDGE
University of Sydney Farms
Rivulet
Corstorphine Farm
Poultry Research Foundation
Rural Veterinary Centre
BROWNLOW HILL
Dept of Animal Science
Sydney Farms
BROWNLOW HILL LOOP
Gate
Nepean Quarries
M C Franklin Laboratory Dairy Research Unit
Nepean Hall
Breakwell Bldg
Agronomy Research Unit
BROWNLOW HILL LOOP RD
CRANA RD
LANSDOWNE RD
SILVERWOOD RD
Flaggy Creek
Ck
CITY
MT HUNTER
Sickles Creek Res
WILLIAM DOWLE
WILLOUGHBY
Mt Hunter
Mayfarm Nursery
BERRY CL
SICKLES
Sickles
SMALLS
University of Sydney Farms
Smalls Res
May Farm Dairy Research Centre
MAYFARM
CAWDOR FARMS RD
DOUST PL
GRASSMERE GR

JOINS MAP 446

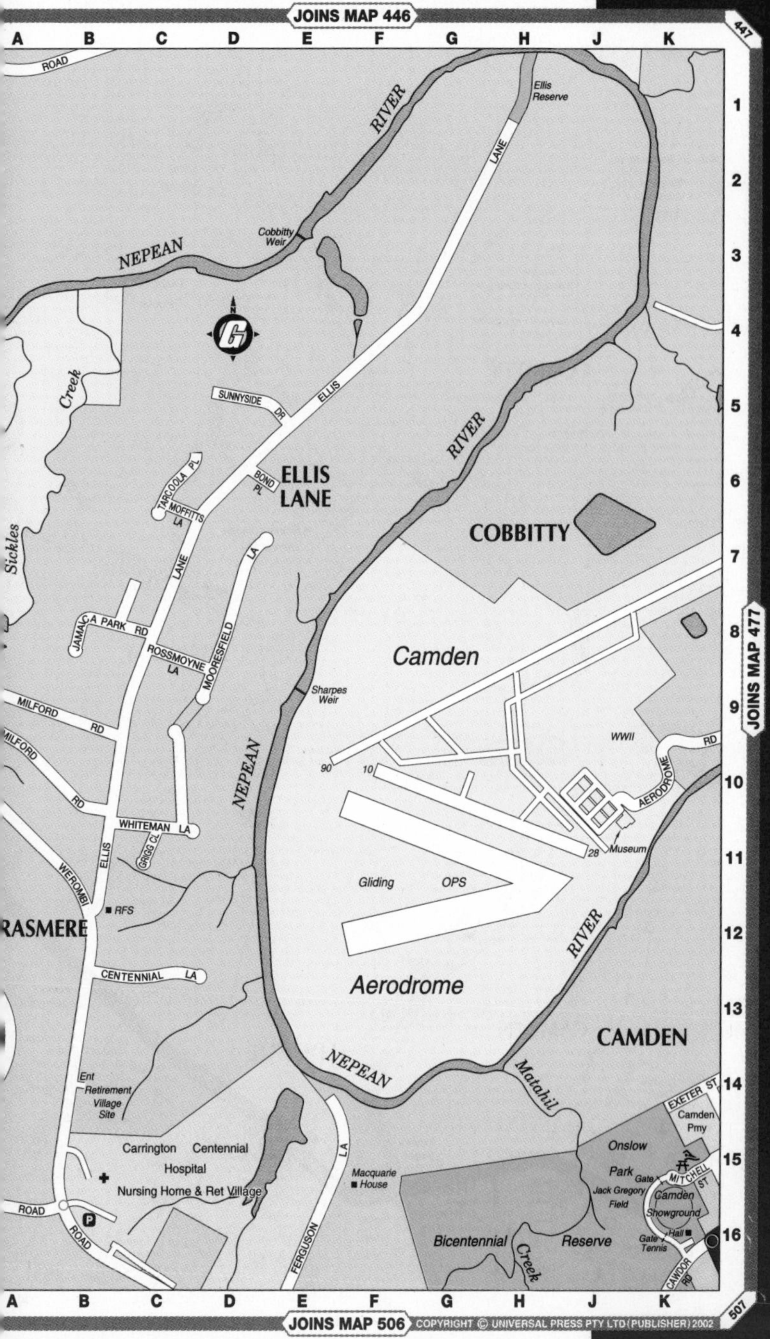

JOINS MAP 477

447

507

JOINS MAP 506

JOINS MAP 447

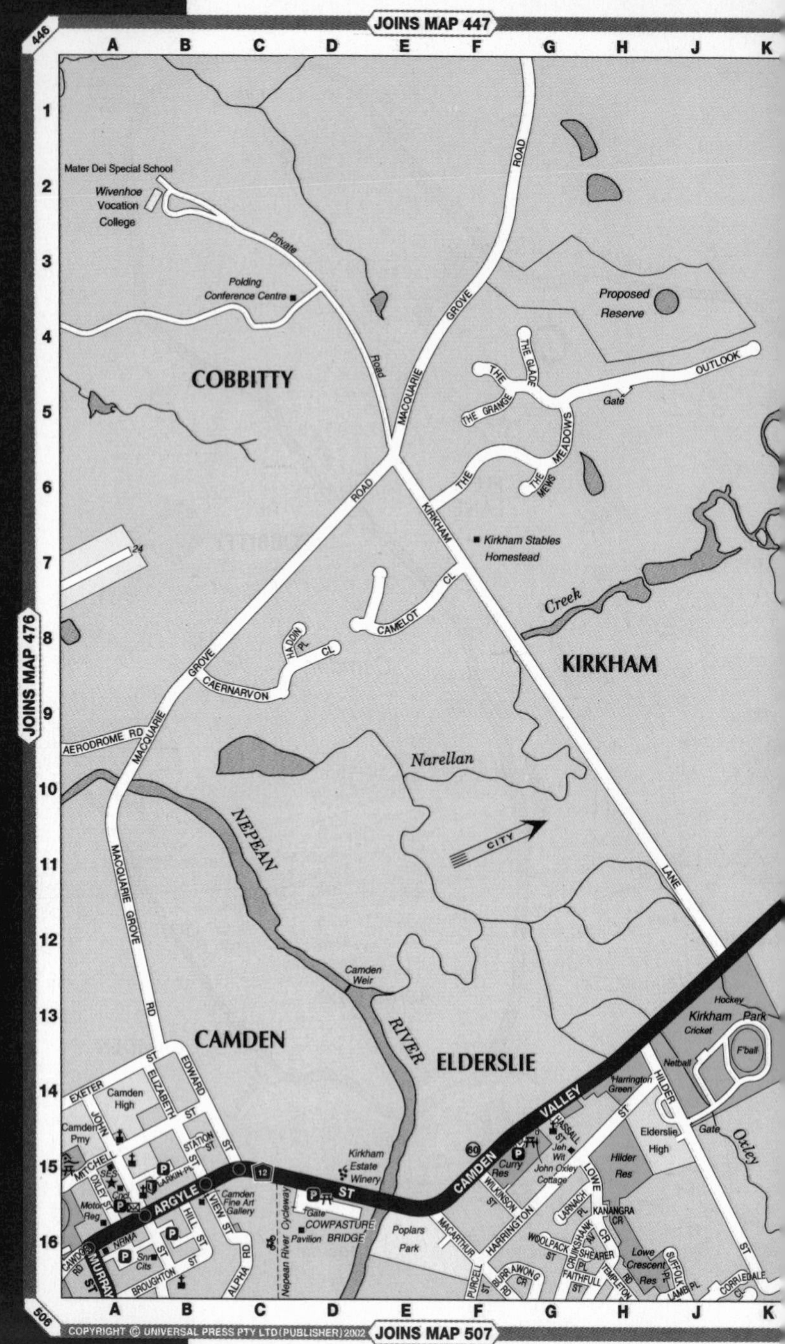

JOINS MAP 507
JOINS MAP 476

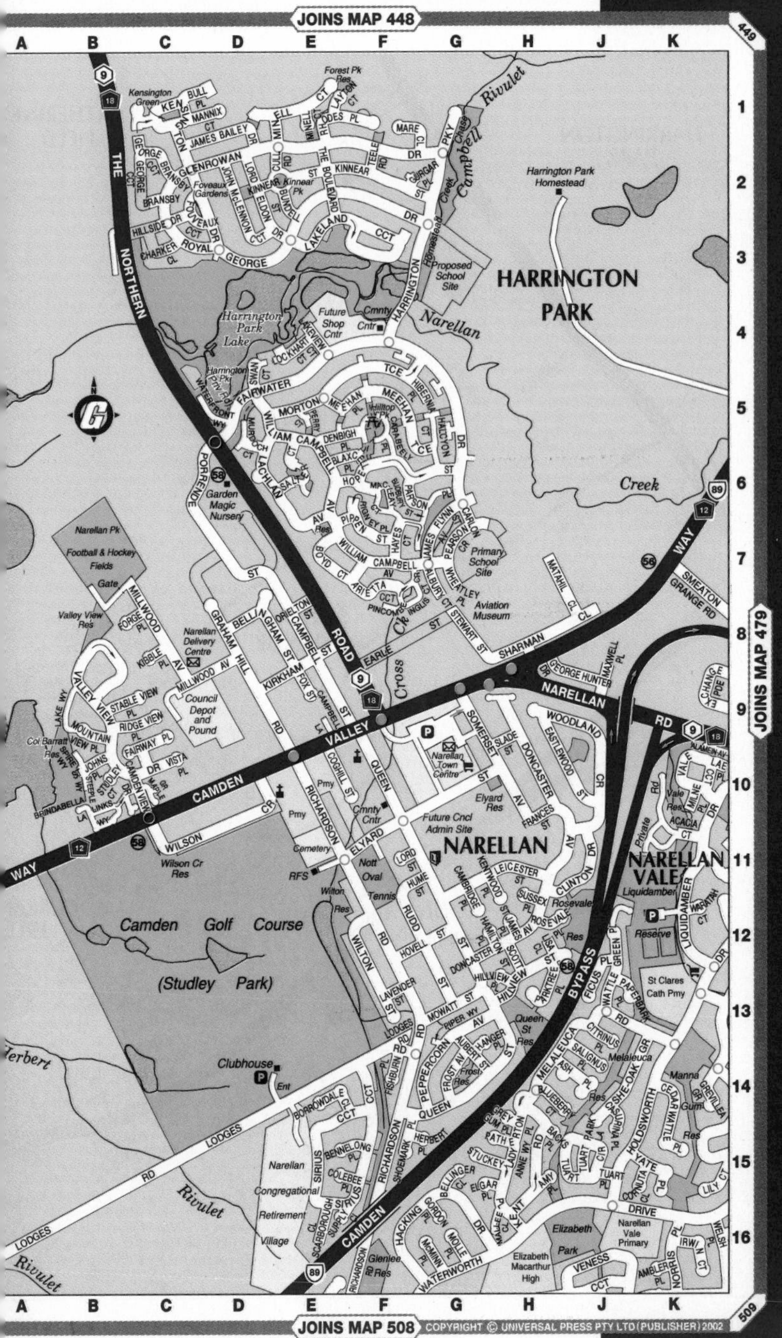
JOINS MAP 448
449
JOINS MAP 479
JOINS MAP 508
509
HARRINGTON PARK
NARELLAN
NARELLAN VALE
Camden Golf Course
(Studley Park)
Harrington Park Homestead
Proposed School Site
Future Shop Cntr
Cmnty Cntr
Harrington Park Lake
Garden Magic Nursery
Narellan Pk Football & Hockey Fields
Narellan Delivery Centre
Council Depot and Pound
Narellan Town Centre
Future Cncl Admin Site
Primary School Site
Aviation Museum
Cemetery
Nott Oval
Tennis
Clubhouse
Narellan Congregational Retirement Village
St Clares Cath Pmy
Narellan Vale Primary
Elizabeth Park
Elizabeth Macarthur High
Liquidamber Reserve
THE NORTHERN ROAD
CAMDEN VALLEY WAY
NARELLAN RD
CAMDEN BYPASS
LODGES RD
Rivulet
Campbell Creek
Narellan Creek
Cross Ck
Herbert Rivulet

JOINS MAP 449

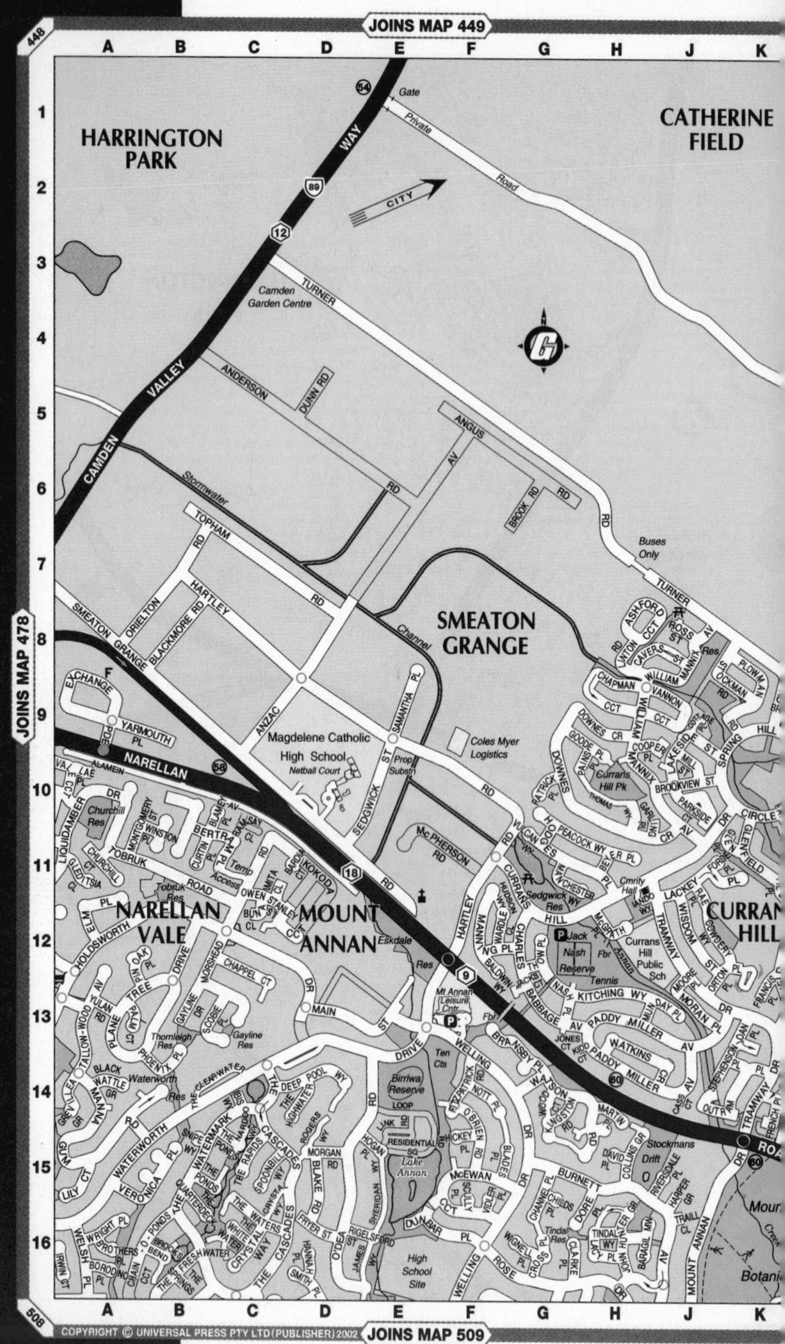

JOINS MAP 478

JOINS MAP 509

JOINS MAP 450

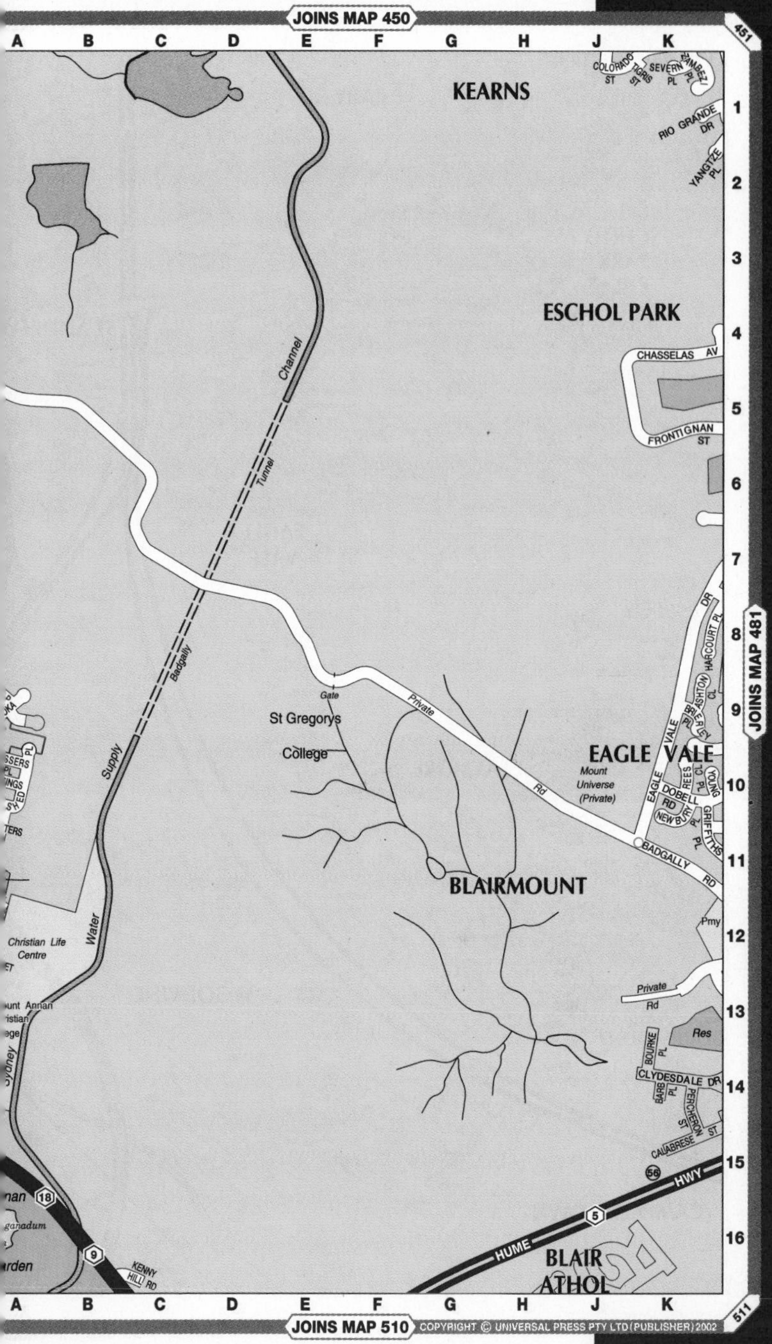

JOINS MAP 481

JOINS MAP 510

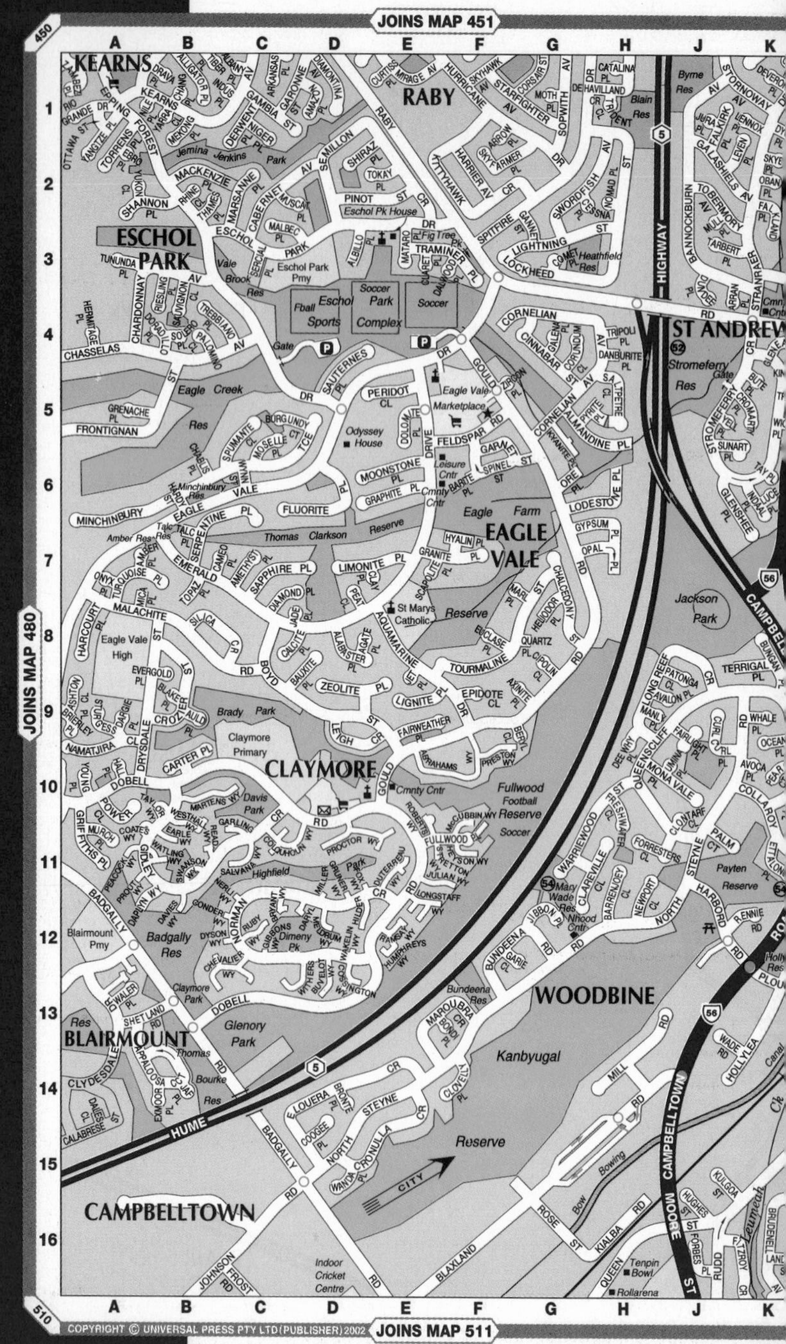
JOINS MAP 451
JOINS MAP 480
JOINS MAP 511
450
510
A B C D E F G H J K
1 2 3 4 5 6 7 8 9 10 11 12 13 14 15 16
KEARNS
RABY
ESCHOL PARK
ST ANDREWS
EAGLE VALE
CLAYMORE
WOODBINE
BLAIRMOUNT
CAMPBELLTOWN
Eschol Sports Complex
Eschol Park Pmy
Eschol Pk House
Eagle Vale Marketplace
Odyssey House
Leisure Cntr
Cmnty Cntr
Eagle Farm
Thomas Clarkson Reserve
Eagle Creek Res
Eagle Vale High
St Marys Catholic
Brady Park
Claymore Primary
Davis Park
Highfield Park
Badgally Res
Blairmount Pmy
Claymore Park
Glenory Park
Thomas Bourke Res
Fullwood Football Reserve
Mary Wade Res
Bundeena Res
Kanbyugal Reserve
Jackson Park
Payten Reserve
Indoor Cricket Centre
Tenpin Bowl
Rollarena
HUME HIGHWAY
CAMPBELLTOWN RD
MOORE ST
EAGLE VALE DR
GOULD RD
BADGALLY RD
RABY RD
ESCHOL PARK DR
COPYRIGHT © UNIVERSAL PRESS PTY LTD (PUBLISHER) 2002

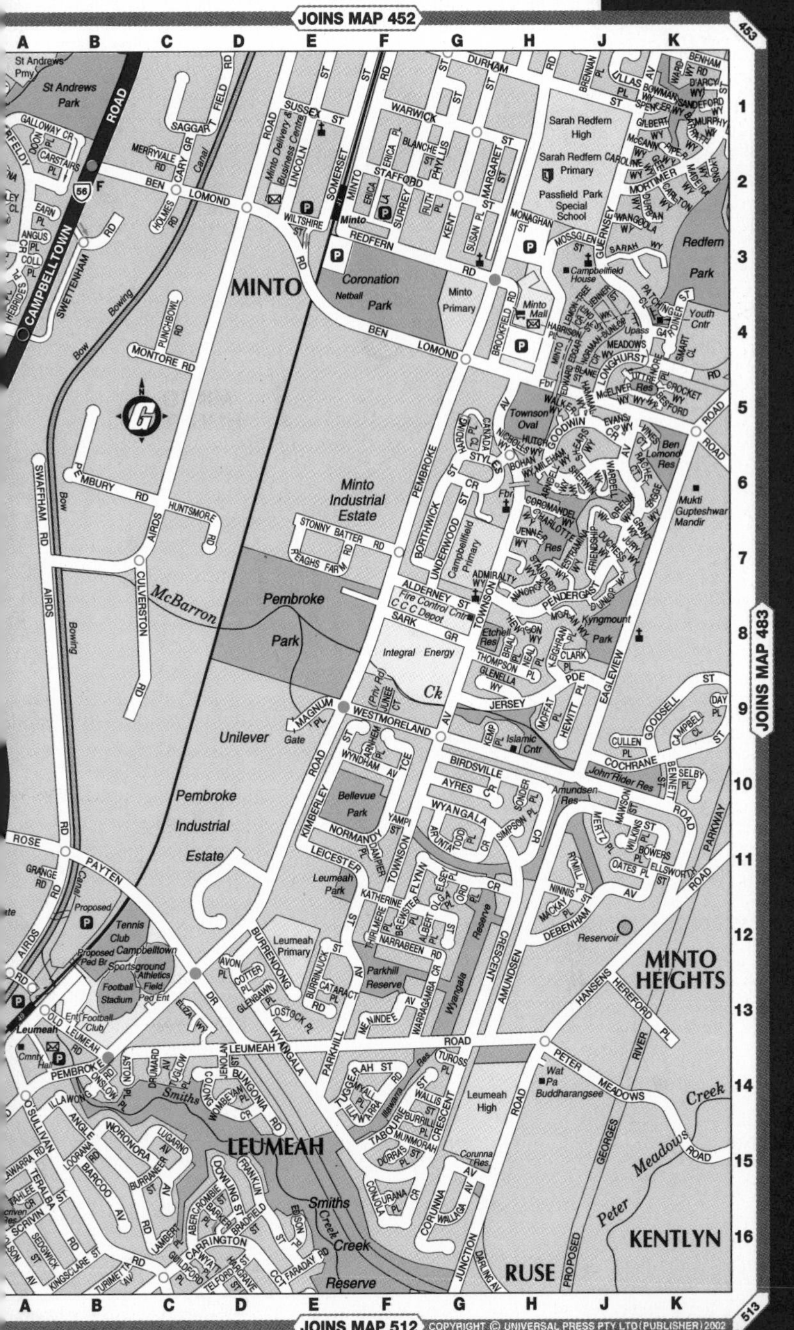
JOINS MAP 452
A
B
C
D
E
F
G
H
J
K
453
St Andrews Pmy
St Andrews Park
CAMPBELLTOWN ROAD
SAGGAR
FIELD
MERRYVALE RD
CARY GR
Canal
SUSSEX ST
Minto Delivery & Business Centre
LINCOLN
SOMERSET
MINTO
WARWICK
BLANCHE
ERICA
STAFFORD
SURREY
PHYLLIS
MARGARET
DURHAM
BRENNAN PL
Sarah Redfern High
Sarah Redfern Primary
Passfield Park Special School
CAROLINE WY
MORTIMER
CARLTON
WANGOOLA
SARAH
Redfern Park
BEN LOMOND
WILTSHIRE ST
Minto
REDFERN
MONAGHAN ST
MOSSGLEN ST
GUERNSEY
Campbellfield House
SWETTENHAM
Bowing
Bow
MINTO
Coronation Park
Netball
Minto Primary
BROOKFIELD RD
Minto Mall
PATCHING CL
POINER ST
Youth Cntr
Upass
SMART CL
PUNCHBOWL RD
MONTORE RD
BEN LOMOND
HARRISON
MEADOWS
LONGHURST
Fbr
WALKER WY
McELIVER WY
CROCKET WY
RESFORD
Townson Oval
GODWIN
EVANS CR
Ben Lomond Res
HARDING
CANADA
NICHOLLS WY
HUTCH WY
STYLES
BOHAN WY
MILEHAM
SHERWIN
WARDELL
VINES CT
ROAD
Mukti Gupteshwar Mandir
SWAFFHAM RD
PEMBURY RD
HUNTSMORE RD
AIRDS
Minto Industrial Estate
PEMBROKE
BORTHWICK
UNDERWOOD ST
CR
COROMANDEL WY
CHARLOTTE
STONNY BATTER RD
REAGHS FARM RD
Campbellfield Primary
JENNER WY
Res
ESTRAMINA
FRIENDSHIP
DUCHESS
JURY
GRANT
CULVERSTON
McBarron
Pembroke Park
ALDERNEY ST
Fire Control Cntr
C C C Depot
SARK GR
ADMIRALTY
TOWNSON
PENDERGAST
D'UNLOP
MORGAN WY
Kyngmount Park
Etchell Res
BRIAL PL
NEAL PL
HEWSON WY
KEIGHRAN
CLARK PL
EAGLEVIEW
Integral Energy
THOMPSON PL
GLENELLA WY
PDE
Ck
JUNEE CT
MAGNUM PL
Gate
WESTMORELAND AV
JERSEY
MOFFAT PL
HEWITT PL
KEMP PL
Islamic Cntr
GOODSELL
DAY PL
CAMPBELL CL
CULLEN PL
COCHRANE
John Rider Res
BENNETT ST
SELBY PL
Unilever
ARNHEM
WYNDHAM AV
TCE
BIRDSVILLE
AYRES
SONDER PL
Amundsen Res
Pembroke Industrial Estate
ROAD
KIMBERLEY
Bellevue Park
YAMPI ST
WYANGALA
ARUNTA
TODD PL
SIMPSON PL
MERTZ PL
MAWSON ST
WILKINS ST
BOWERS
OATES PL
ELLSWORTH
ROAD
PARKWAY
ROSE
RD
PAYTEN
NORMANDY
DAMPIER
LEICESTER
Leumeah Park
KATHERINE
FLYNN
ELSIE PL
OLGA PL
ORD PL
CR
RYMILL PL
NINNIS PL
MACKAY PL
DEBENHAM
AV
GRANGE RD
Canal
Proposed
Tennis Club
Proposed Ped Br
Campbelltown Sportsground
Athletics Field
Football Stadium
Ped Ent
BURRENDONG
Leumeah Primary
THIRLMERE
BREWSTER
ALBERT
NARRABEEN RD
Parkhill Reserve
Reserve
CRESCENT
AMUNDSEN
Reservoir
MINTO HEIGHTS
AIRDS
AVON PL
COTTER PL
GLENBAWN PL
LOSTOCK PL
BURRINJUCK
CATARACT
RD
WARRAGAMBA CR
Wyangala
HANSENS
HEREFORD PL
RIVER
Leumeah
Ent
Football Club
OLD LEUMEAH RD
Cmnty Hall
ELIZA WY
LEUMEAH
ROAD
PARKHILL
MENINDEE
PEMBROKE RD
ONSLOW
ASTON
DRUMARD AV
UGLOW PL
JENOLAN ST
BUNGONIA
TUGGERAH ST
MYALL PL
ILLAWARRA
TUROSS PL
WALLIS ST
Leumeah High
ROAD
Wat Pa Buddharangsee
PETER MEADOWS
Creek
O'SULLIVAN
ILLAWONG
ANGLE
Smiths
COLONGO
WOMBEYAN CR
RD
TABOURIE
BURRILL PL
MUNMORAH
DURRAS ST
GEORGES
WORONORA
LUGARNO AV
LEUMEAH
Corunna Res
Meadows
ROAD
ILLAWARRA RD
TERALBA
LOORANA RD
BARCOO
BURRANEER
AV
FRANKLIN
Smiths Creek
COOLONGA
CURANA PL
CORUNNA
WALLAGA
AV
Peter
SCRIVIN ST
SEDGWICK ST
KINGSCLARE
RD
LAMBERT
ABERCROMBIE
DOWLING ST
BARKER
BRADFIELD
EDISON
Creek
CARRINGTON
TURIMETTA AV
GUILDFORD
WYATT
HARGRAVE
TELFORD
FARADAY RD
CCT
Reserve
JUNCTION
DARLING AV
RUSE
PROPOSED
KENTLYN
JOINS MAP 483
1
2
3
4
5
6
7
8
9
10
11
12
13
14
15
16
JOINS MAP 512
513

JOINS MAP 453

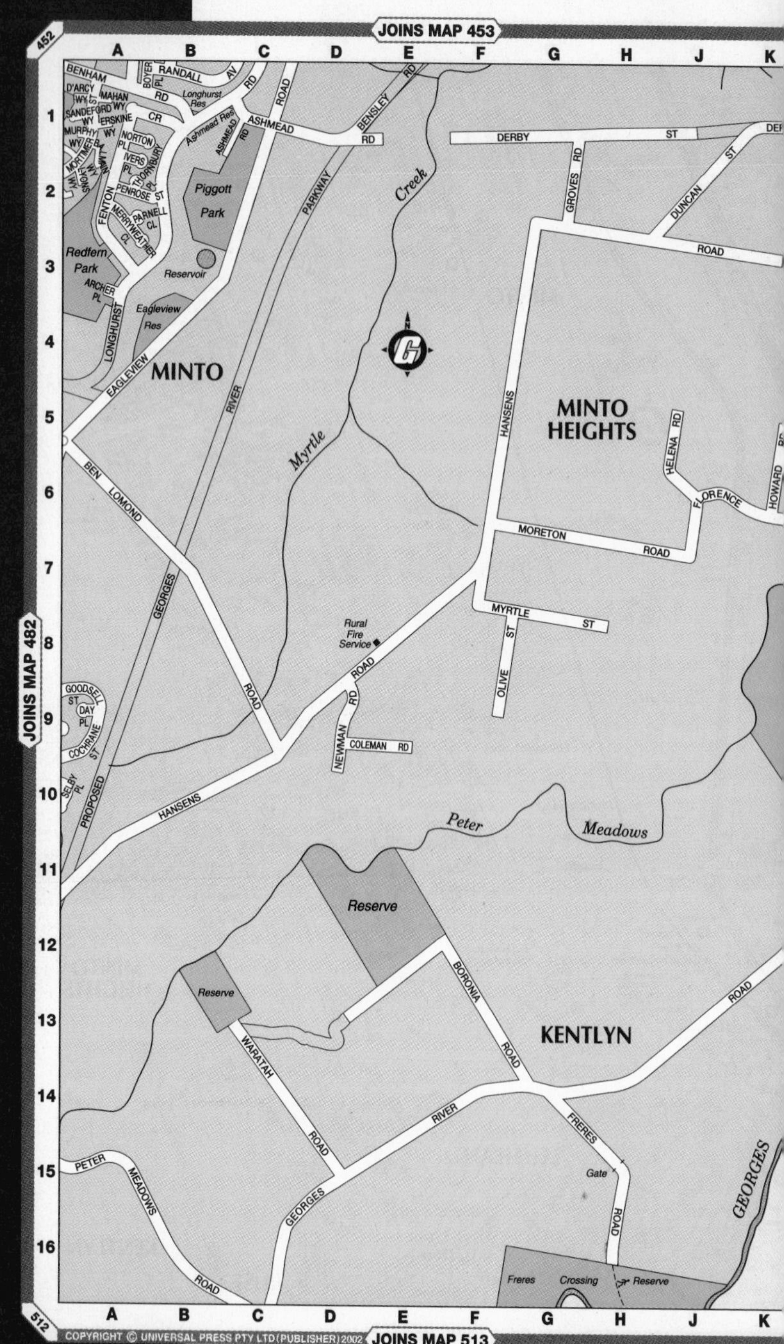

JOINS MAP 482

JOINS MAP 513

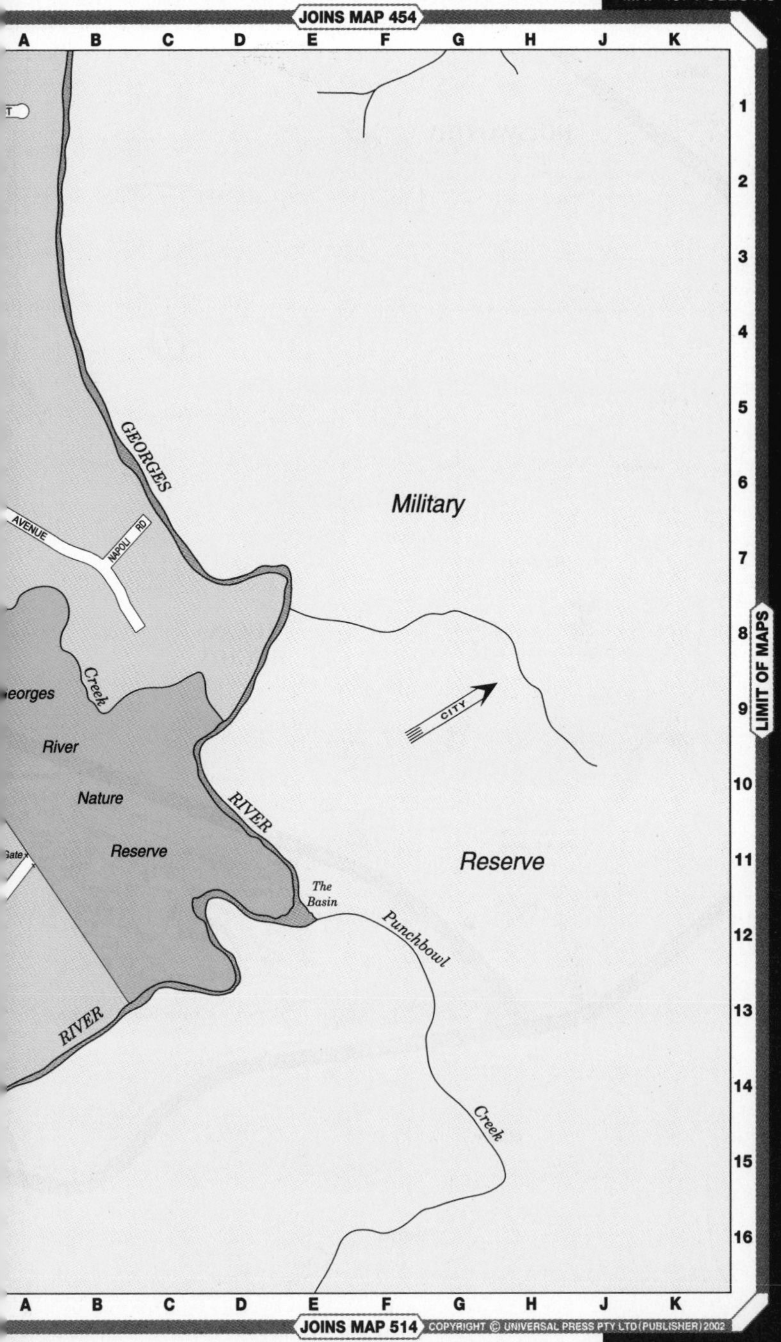
JOINS MAP 454
A B C D E F G H J K
1 2 3 4 5 6 7 8 9 10 11 12 13 14 15 16
GEORGES
Military
AVENUE
NAPOLI RD
Creek
eorges
River
Nature
Reserve
RIVER
CITY
Reserve
The Basin
Punchbowl
Creek
RIVER
Gate
LIMIT OF MAPS
JOINS MAP 514

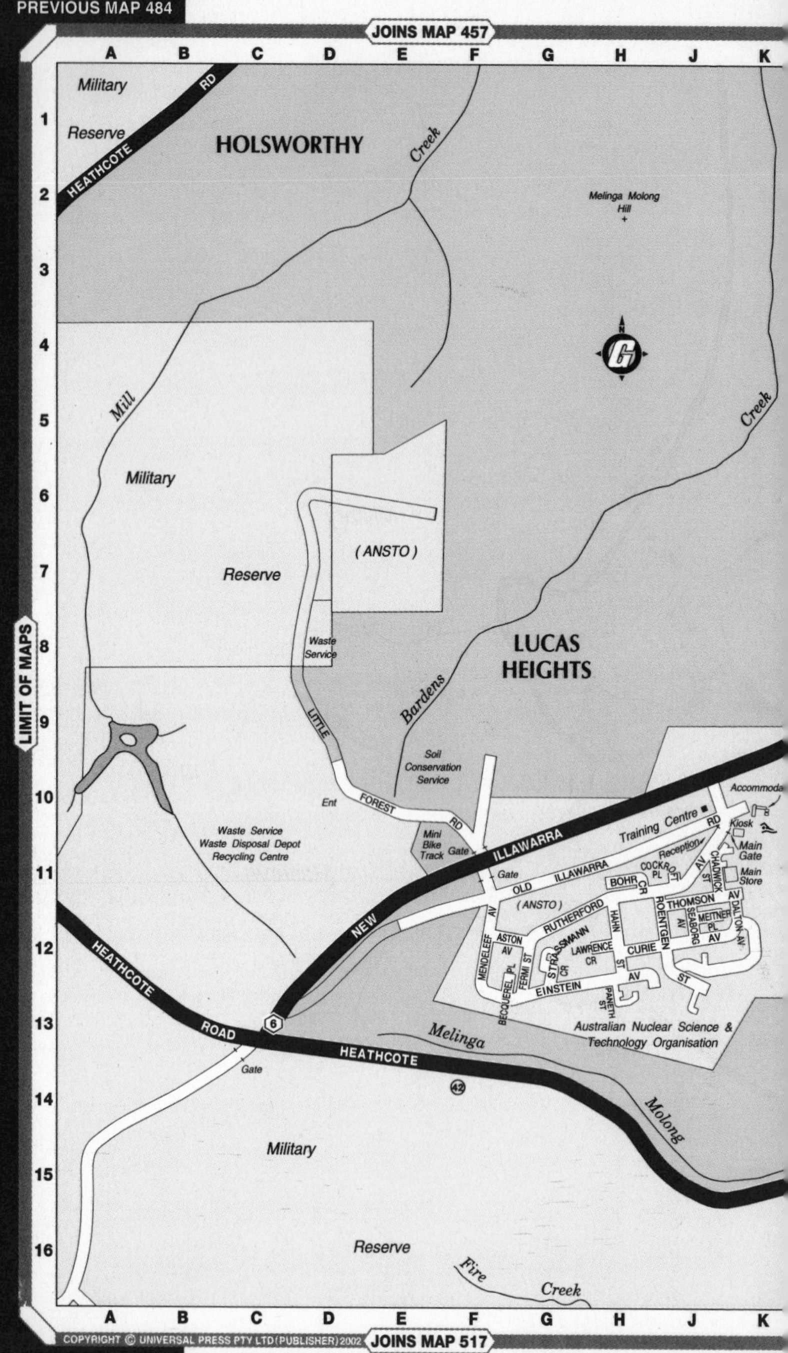

JOINS MAP 457
A
B
C
D
E
F
G
H
J
K
1
2
3
4
5
6
7
8
9
10
11
12
13
14
15
16
LIMIT OF MAPS
Military
Reserve
HEATHCOTE
RD
HOLSWORTHY
Creek
Melinga Molong
Hill
Mill
Military
Reserve
(ANSTO)
Creek
Waste
Service
LUCAS
HEIGHTS
Bardens
LITTLE
FOREST
RD
Ent
Soil
Conservation
Service
Waste Service
Waste Disposal Depot
Recycling Centre
Mini
Bike
Track
Gate
ILLAWARRA
NEW
Training Centre
Accommoda
RD
Kiosk
Main
Gate
Reception
Main
Store
Gate
OLD
ILLAWARRA
COCKROFT
PL
BOHR
CR
AV
ST
CHADWICK
(ANSTO)
RUTHERFORD
HAHN
ROENTGEN
THOMSON
AV
SEABORG
MEITNER
PL
DALTON
AV
AV
MENDELEEF
ASTON
AV
STRASSMANN
CR
LAWRENCE
CR
CURIE
ST
AV
ST
AV
BECQUEREL
PL
FERMI ST
EINSTEIN
PANETH
ST
Australian Nuclear Science &
Technology Organisation
HEATHCOTE
ROAD
6
HEATHCOTE
Melinga
42
Gate
Molong
Military
Reserve
Fire
Creek
A
B
C
D
E
F
G
H
J
K
COPYRIGHT © UNIVERSAL PRESS PTY LTD (PUBLISHER) 2002
JOINS MAP 517

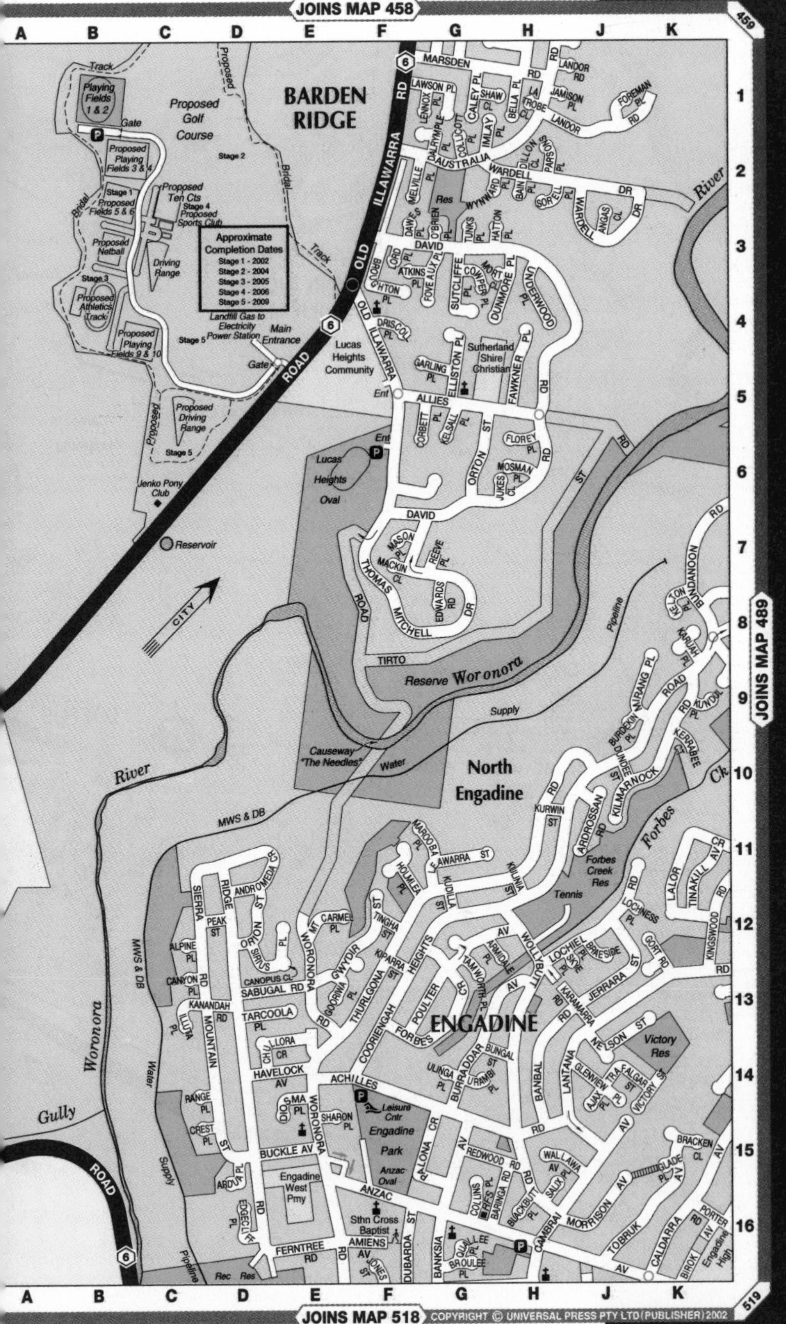
JOINS MAP 458
459
A B C D E F G H J K
1 2 3 4 5 6 7 8 9 10 11 12 13 14 15 16
BARDEN RIDGE
Proposed Golf Course
Playing Fields 1 & 2
Track
Gate
Proposed Playing Fields 3 & 4
Stage 1 Proposed Fields 5 & 6
Proposed Ten Cts
Stage 4 Proposed Sports Club
Proposed Netball
Driving Range
Stage 3
Proposed Athletics Track
Proposed Playing Fields 9 & 10
Stage 2
Stage 5
Bridal
Proposed
Approximate Completion Dates
Stage 1 - 2002
Stage 2 - 2004
Stage 3 - 2005
Stage 4 - 2006
Stage 5 - 2009
Landfill Gas to Electricity Power Station
Main Entrance
Proposed Driving Range
Jenko Pony Club
Reservoir
CITY
OLD ILLAWARRA RD
ROAD
Lucas Heights Community
Lucas Heights Oval
Sutherland Shire Christian
MARSDEN
LAWSON PL
LENNOX PL
DALRYMPLE
COLLICOTT PL
CALEY PL
SHAW CL
IMLAY PL
BELLA PL
LA TROBE CL
JAMISON PL
LANDOR RD
FOREMAN PL
AUSTRALIA
WARDELL DR
DILLON CL
PARSONS PL
WYNYARD PL
BAIN PL
SORELL PL
ANGAS CL
River
MELVILLE
Res
DAWES PL
O'BRIEN PL
TUNKS PL
HATTON PL
DAVID
LORD PL
BROUGHTON PL
ATKINS PL
FOVEAUX PL
SUTCLIFFE PL
COWPER PL
MORT CL
DUNMORE PL
UNDERWOOD PL
DRISCOLL PL
GARLING PL
ELLISTON PL
FAWKNER PL
ALLIES
Ent
CORBETT PL
KELSALL PL
ORTON ST
FLOREY PL
MOSMAN PL
JUKES CL
RD
ST
DAVID
MASON PL
MACKIN CL
REEVE PL
EDWARDS RD
THOMAS MITCHELL DR
ROAD
TIRTO
Reserve Woronora
Pipeline
Supply
Causeway "The Needles"
Water
North Engadine
River
MWS & DB
Woronora
Gully
BUNDANOON RD
KELTON PL
KARUAH
MIRANG PL
ROAD
KUNDUL PL
BURDEKIN PL
DUNDEE ST
KERRABEE CT
KILMARNOCK
Ck
KURWIN ST
ARDROSSAN RD
Forbes
Forbes Creek Res
Tennis
MAROOBA PL
LE AWARRA ST
HOLMLEA PL
KUDILLA ST
KIULINIA ST
LALOR
TINAKILL AV
CR
LOCHNESS PL
GORT RD
KINGSWOOD RD
SIERRA
RIDGE
ANDROMEDA CR
ORION ST
PEAK ST
ALPINE PL
SIRIUS PL
CANYON PL
CANOPUS CL
SABUGAL RD
KANANDAH RD
ILLUKA PL
MOUNTAIN
TARCOOLA PL
CHULLORA CR
HAVELOCK AV
RANGE PL
CREST PL
MT CARMEL PL
TINGHA ST
WORONORA
GWYDIR
KIPARRA
GOORIWA
THURLGONA
HEIGHTS
COORIENGAH
POULTER CR
FORBES
ARMIDALE PL
TAMWORTH PL
WOLLYBUTT
LOCHIEL PL
SKYE PL
BRAESIDE
JERRARA ST
KARAMARRA RD
NELSON ST
Victory Res
ENGADINE
BUNGAL ST
BURRADDAR
URAMBI PL
ULINGA PL
BANBAL
LANTANA
GLENVIEW
TRAFALGAR ST
AJAX PL
VICTORY ST
ACHILLES
DIOSMA PL
SHARON PL
Leisure Cntr
Engadine Park
Anzac Oval
PALONA CR
AV
REDWOOD RD
WALLAWA AV
SALIX PL
BRACKEN CL
GLADE AV
BUCKLE AV
ARDUA PL
Engadine West Pmy
ANZAC
COLLINS PL
REFS PL
BARINGA RD
BLACKBUTT PL
CAMBRAI
MORRISON AV
TOBRUK
CALDARRA
PORTER
BIROK AV
Engadine High
EDGECLIFF PL
RD
Sthn Cross Baptist
AMIENS AV
FERNTREE RD
DUBARDA ST
BANKSIA
QUAILEE PL
BROULEE
JONES ST
Rec Res
Pipeline
Supply
Water
JOINS MAP 489
JOINS MAP 518
519

JOINS MAP 459

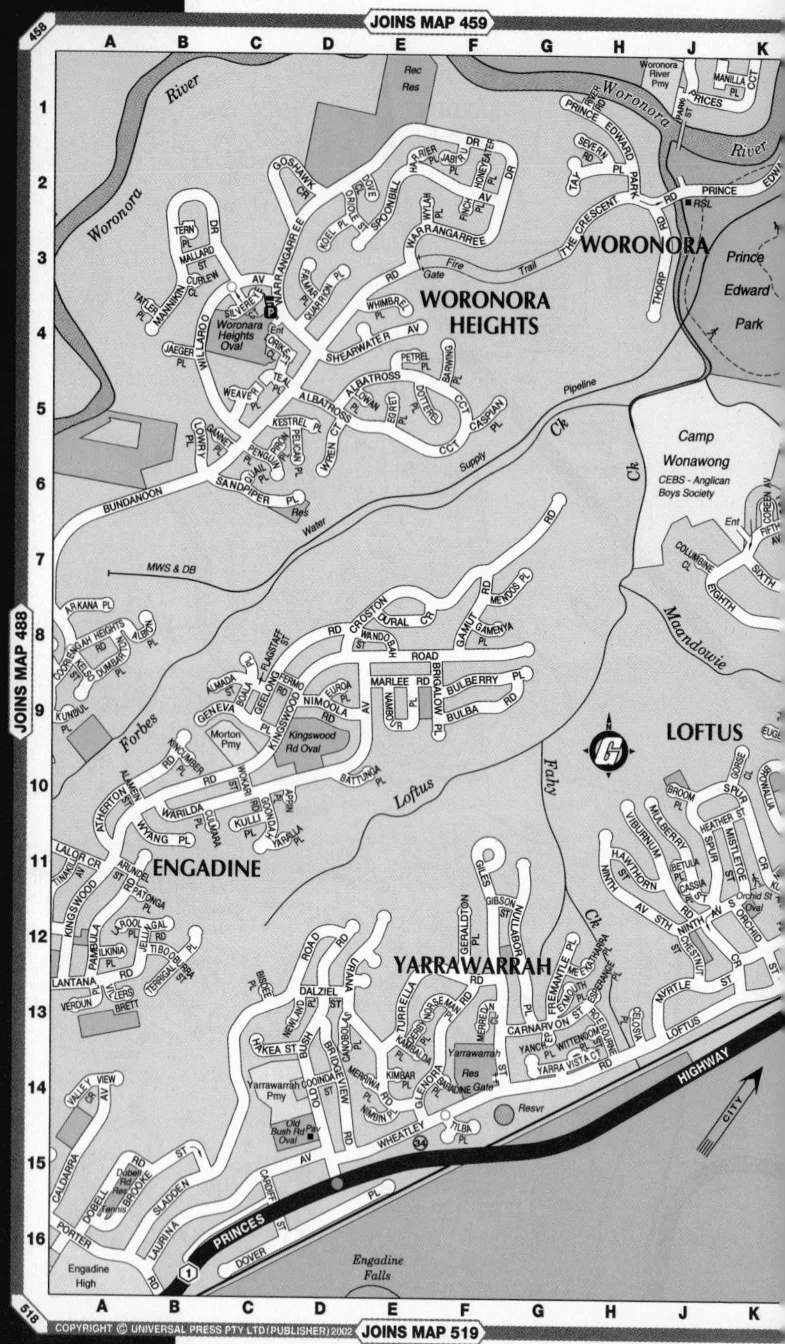

JOINS MAP 519

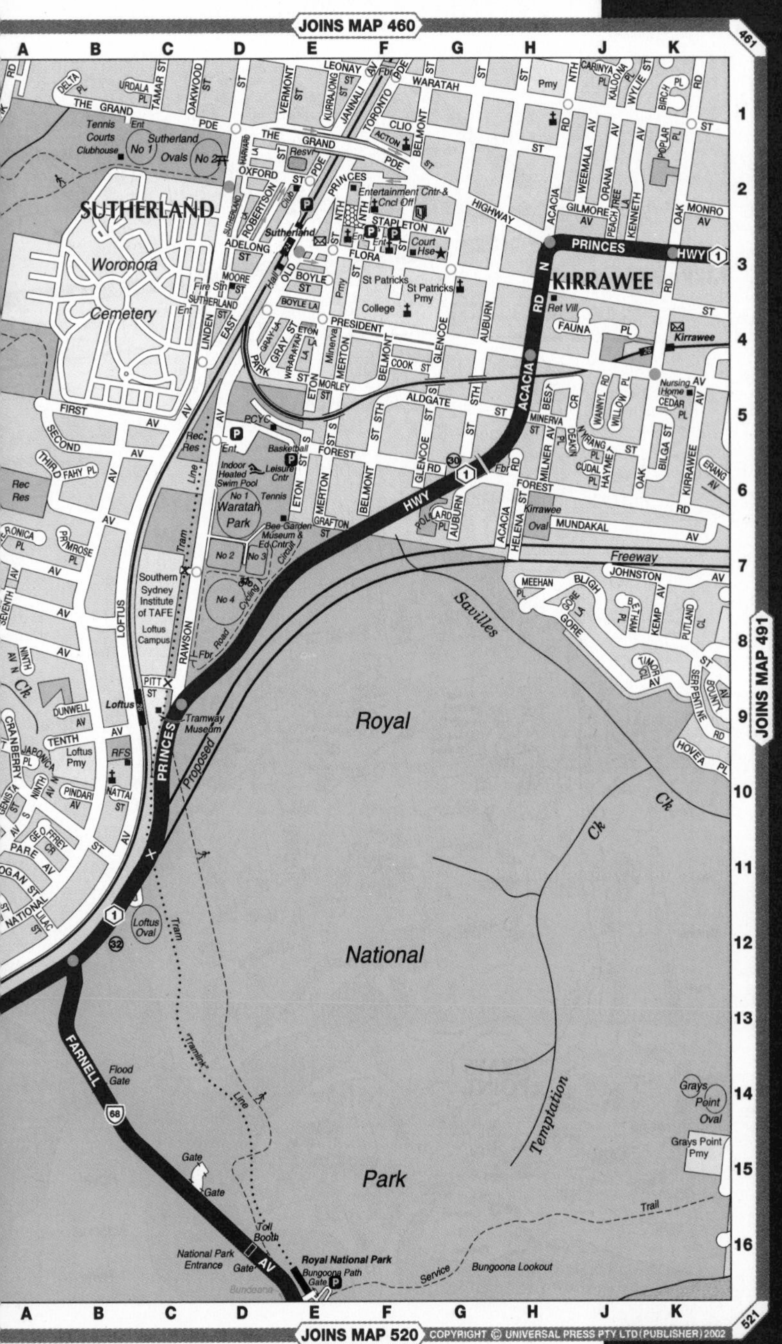

JOINS MAP 460
JOINS MAP 491
JOINS MAP 520
461
521
SUTHERLAND
KIRRAWEE
Woronora
Cemetery
Royal
National
Park
Sutherland Ovals
Tennis Courts
Clubhouse
Waratah Park
Southern Sydney Institute of TAFE
Loftus Campus
Tramway Museum
Loftus Oval
Loftus Pmy
Kirrawee Oval
Grays Point Oval
Grays Point Pmy
Entertainment Cntr & Cncl Off
Court Hse
St Patricks College
St Patricks Pmy
Indoor Heated Swim Pool
Leisure Cntr
Bee Garden Museum & Ed Cntr
PRINCES HWY
FARNELL AV
Freeway
Savilles
Temptation
Ck
Flood Gate
National Park Entrance
Toll Booth
Royal National Park
Bungoona Path Gate
Bungoona Lookout
Service
Trail
"Tramlink" Line
Proposed

MAP 491

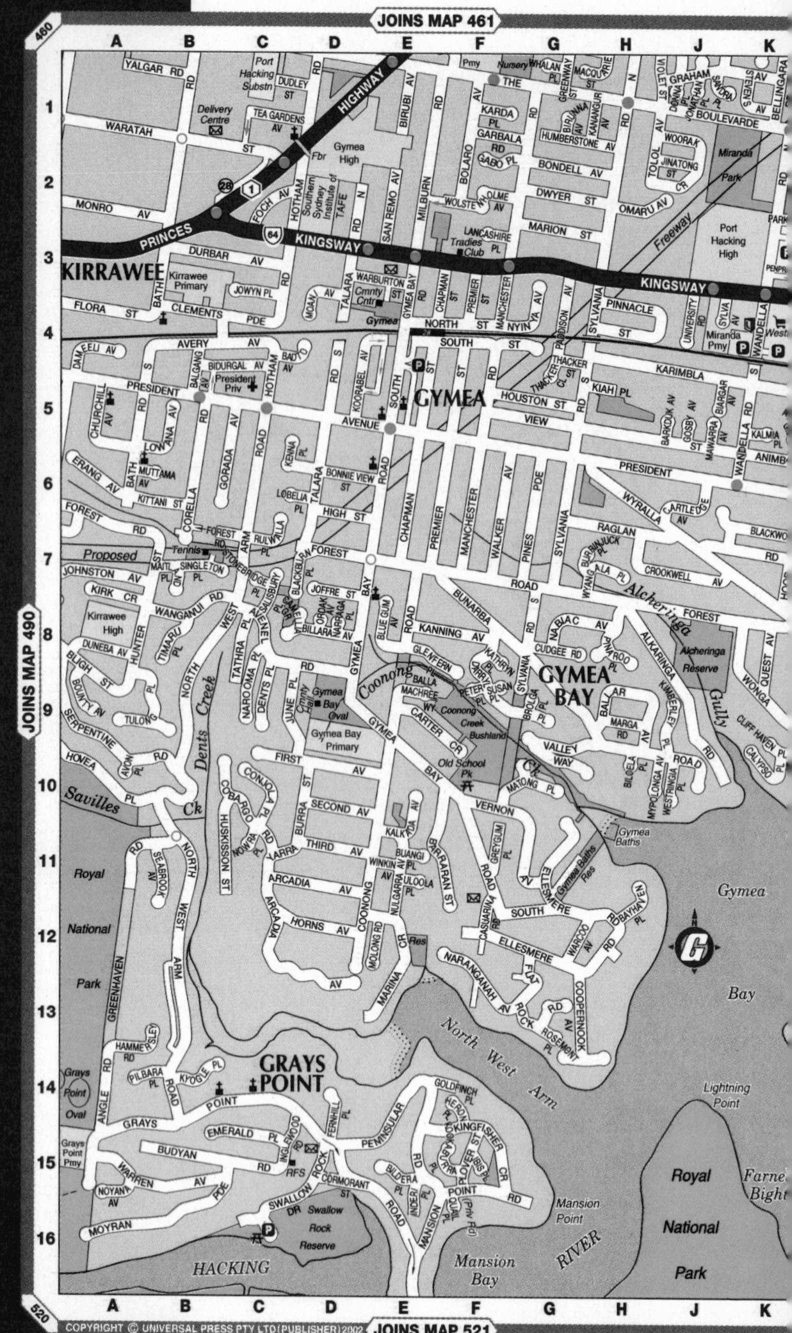

JOINS MAP 461
JOINS MAP 490
JOINS MAP 521
460
520
KIRRAWEE
GYMEA
GYMEA BAY
GRAYS POINT
PRINCES HIGHWAY
KINGSWAY
Freeway
Royal National Park
Gymea Bay
North West Arm
HACKING RIVER
Mansion Bay
Mansion Point
Lightning Point
Farnell Bight
Savilles Ck
Dents Creek
Coonong Ck
Alcheringa Gully
Port Hacking Substn
Delivery Centre
Gymea High
Southern Sydney Institute of TAFE
Tradies Club
Kirrawee Primary
Cmnty Cntr
President Priv
Port Hacking High
Miranda Park
Kirrawee High
Gymea Bay Oval
Gymea Bay Primary
Coonong Creek Bushland
Old School Pk
Alcheringa Reserve
Gymea Baths
Gymea Baths Res
Grays Point Oval
Grays Point Pmy
Swallow Rock Reserve
Miranda Pmy
RFS

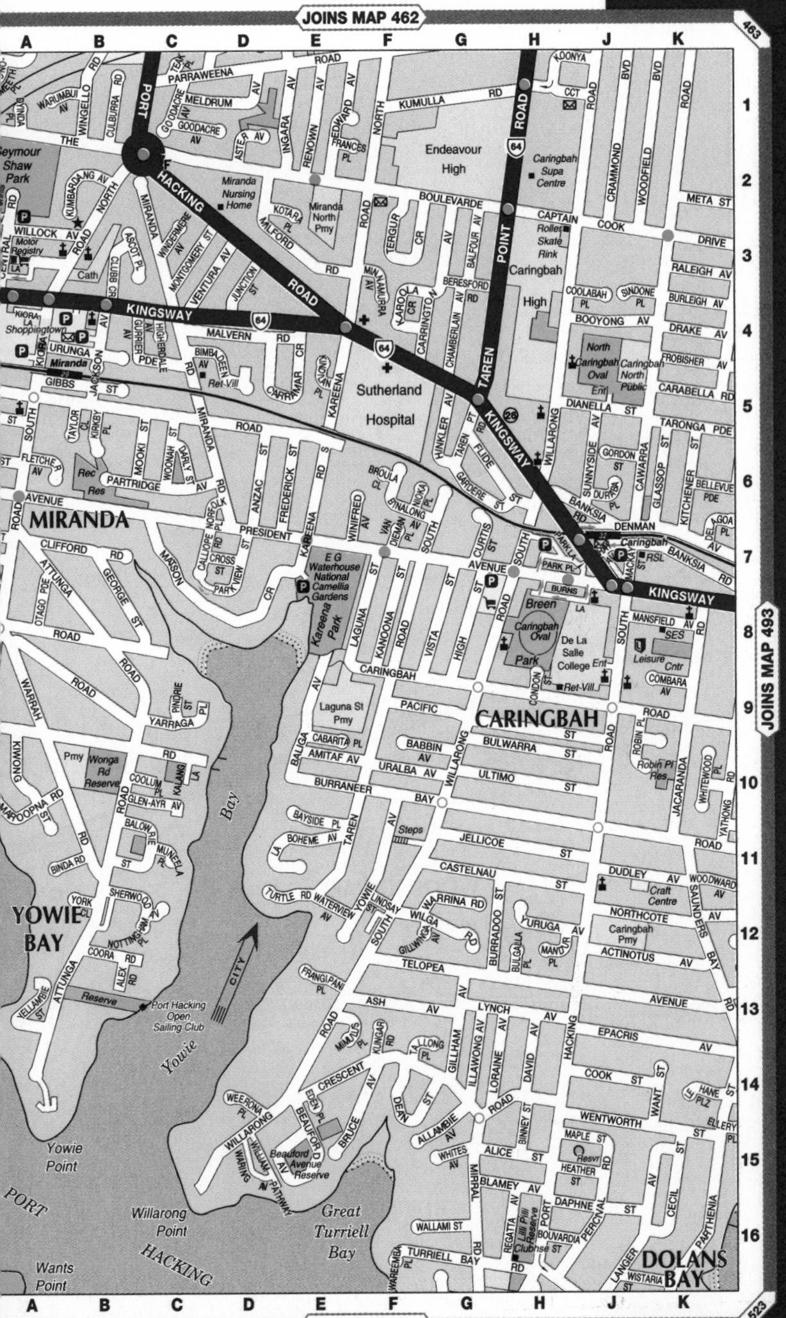
JOINS MAP 462
JOINS MAP 493
JOINS MAP 522
463
523
MIRANDA
CARINGBAH
YOWIE BAY
DOLANS BAY
Endeavour High
Sutherland Hospital
Caringbah High
E G Waterhouse National Camellia Gardens
Kareena Park
Breen Park
Caringbah Oval
De La Salle College
Seymour Shaw Park
Miranda Nursing Home
Laguna St Pmy
Caringbah Pmy
Yowie Point
Willarong Point
Wants Point
Great Turriell Bay
Port Hacking Open Sailing Club
KINGSWAY
TAREN POINT ROAD
PORT HACKING ROAD
Yowie Bay
PORT HACKING

MAP 493

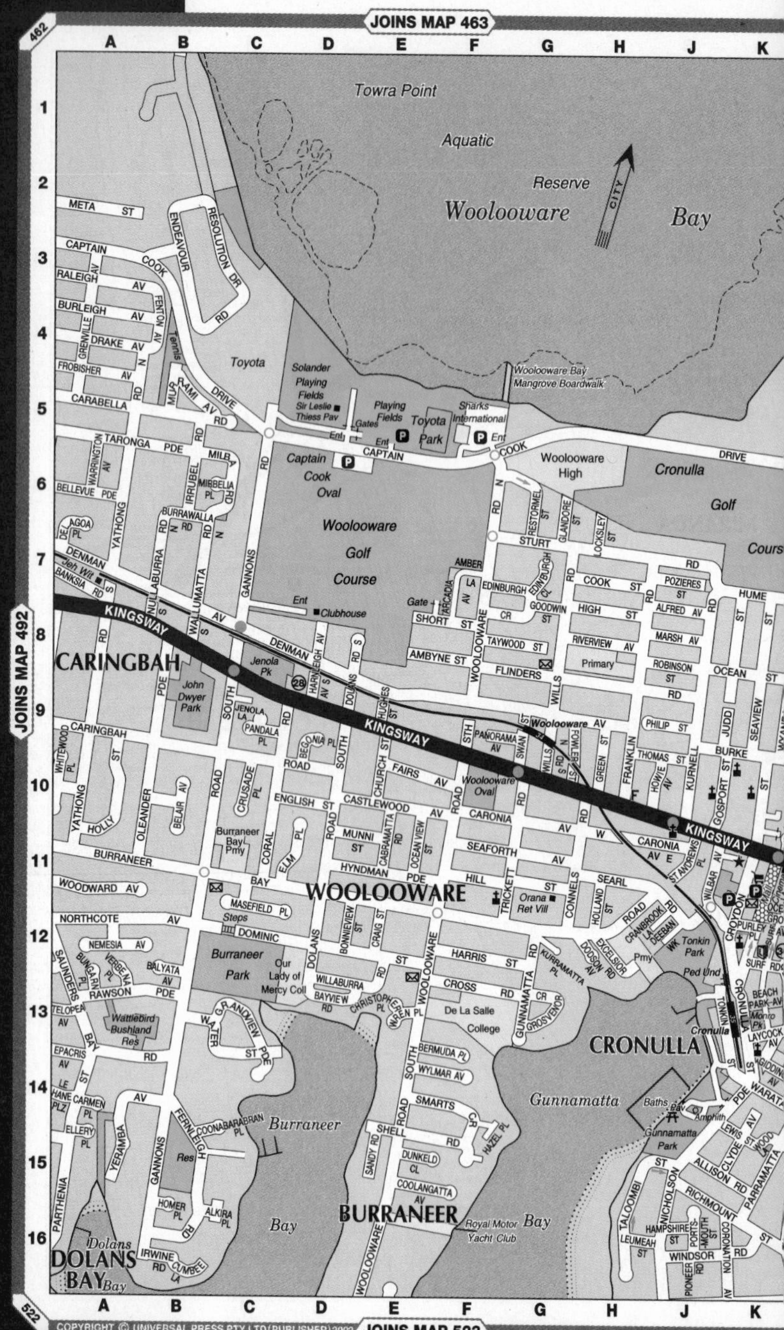

JOINS MAP 463
JOINS MAP 492
JOINS MAP 523
462
522
Towra Point
Aquatic
Reserve
Woolooware
Bay
CITY
Woolooware Bay Mangrove Boardwalk
Solander Playing Fields
Sir Leslie Thiess Pav
Playing Fields
Toyota Park
Sharks International
Toyota
Captain Cook Oval
Woolooware Golf Course
Clubhouse
Woolooware High
Cronulla Golf Course
KINGSWAY
CARINGBAH
John Dwyer Park
Jenola Pk
Woolooware Oval
Primary
Burraneer Bay Pmy
WOOLOOWARE
Orana Ret Vill
Burraneer Park
Our Lady of Mercy Coll
De La Salle College
Wattlebird Bushland Res
Res
Tonkin Park
Ped Und
Cronulla
CRONULLA
Monro Pk
Gunnamatta
Baths
Pav
Amphith
Gunnamatta Park
Burraneer
Bay
BURRANEER
Royal Motor Yacht Club
Dolans
DOLANS BAY
Bay
META ST
CAPTAIN COOK DRIVE
RALEIGH AV
BURLEIGH AV
DRAKE AV
FROBISHER AV
CARABELLA RD
TARONGA PDE
BELLEVUE PDE
DENMAN AV
BANKSIA RD
ENDEAVOUR RD
RESOLUTION DR
FENTON AV
GRENVILLE AV
MUNRAMI AV
WARRINGTON AV
MILBA RD
MIBBELIA PL
IRRUBEL RD
BURRAWALLA RD
YATHONG RD
NULLABURRA RD
WALLUMATTA RD
GANNONS RD
DE AGOA PL
CARINGBAH RD
WHITEWOOD PL
HOLLY ST
OLEANDER RD
BELAIR AV
CRUSADE PL
SOUTH RD
JENOLA LA
PANDALA PL
BEGONIA PL
HARNLEIGH AV
DOLANS RD
HUGHES ST
CHURCH ST
FAIRS AV
ENGLISH ST
CASTLEWOOD AV
MUNNI ST
CABRAMATTA RD
OCEAN VIEW ST
CORAL RD
ELM PL
BURRANEER BAY RD
HYNDMAN PDE
WOODWARD AV
MASEFIELD PL
Steps
DOMINIC ST
NORTHCOTE AV
NEMESIA AV
BUNGARN PL
VERBENA PL
BALYATA AV
SAUNDERS BAY RD
RAWSON PDE
TELOPEA AV
EPACRIS AV
CARMEN PL
ELLERY PL
YERAMBA
PARTHENIA
FERNLEIGH RD
COONABARABRAN PL
HOMER PL
ALKIRA PL
IRWINE RD
CUMBEE LA
WILLABURRA RD
BAYVIEW RD
CHRISTOPHER PL
WAREN PL
GRANDVIEW PDE
WATER ST
WOOLOOWARE RD
HARRIS ST
CROSS RD
HILL ST
SEAFORTH AV
CARONIA AV
TRICKETT RD
CONNELS RD
HOLLAND ST
SEARL RD
KURRAMATTA PL
GUNNAMATTA RD
GROSVENOR CR
DODSON AV
EXCELSIOR RD
CRANBROOK LA
DEEBAN WK
BERMUDA PL
WYLMAR AV
SMARTS CR
SHELL RD
SANDY RD
DUNKELD CL
COOLANGATTA AV
HAZEL PL
AMBER LA
ARCADIA AV
EDINBURGH CR
EDINBURGH CL
GOODWIN ST
SHORT ST
TAYWOOD ST
AMBYNE ST
FLINDERS
WILLS
PANORAMA AV
SWAN ST
RESTORMEL ST
GLANDORE ST
LOCKSLEY ST
STURT RD
COOK ST
HIGH ST
RIVERVIEW AV
POZIERES ST
ALFRED AV
MARSH AV
ROBINSON ST
PHILIP ST
THOMAS ST
HOWIE AV
FRANKLIN
GREEN ST
FOWLER ST
KURNELL
GOSPORT ST
JUDD
SEAVIEW
HUME ST
OCEAN ST
BURKE
ST ANDREWS PL
WILBAR AV
CROYDON
PURLEY PL
SURF
BEACH PARK AV
LAYCOCK AV
GIDDINGS AV
WARATAH
TONKIN ST
CRONULLA ST
LEWIS
CLYDE AV
ALLISON RD
RICHMOUNT ST
PARRAMATTA
WOOD LA
TALOOMBI ST
NICHOLSON
HAMPSHIRE ST
PORTSMOUTH ST
CORONATION AV
LEUMEAH ST
WINDSOR RD
PIONEER RD
Mall

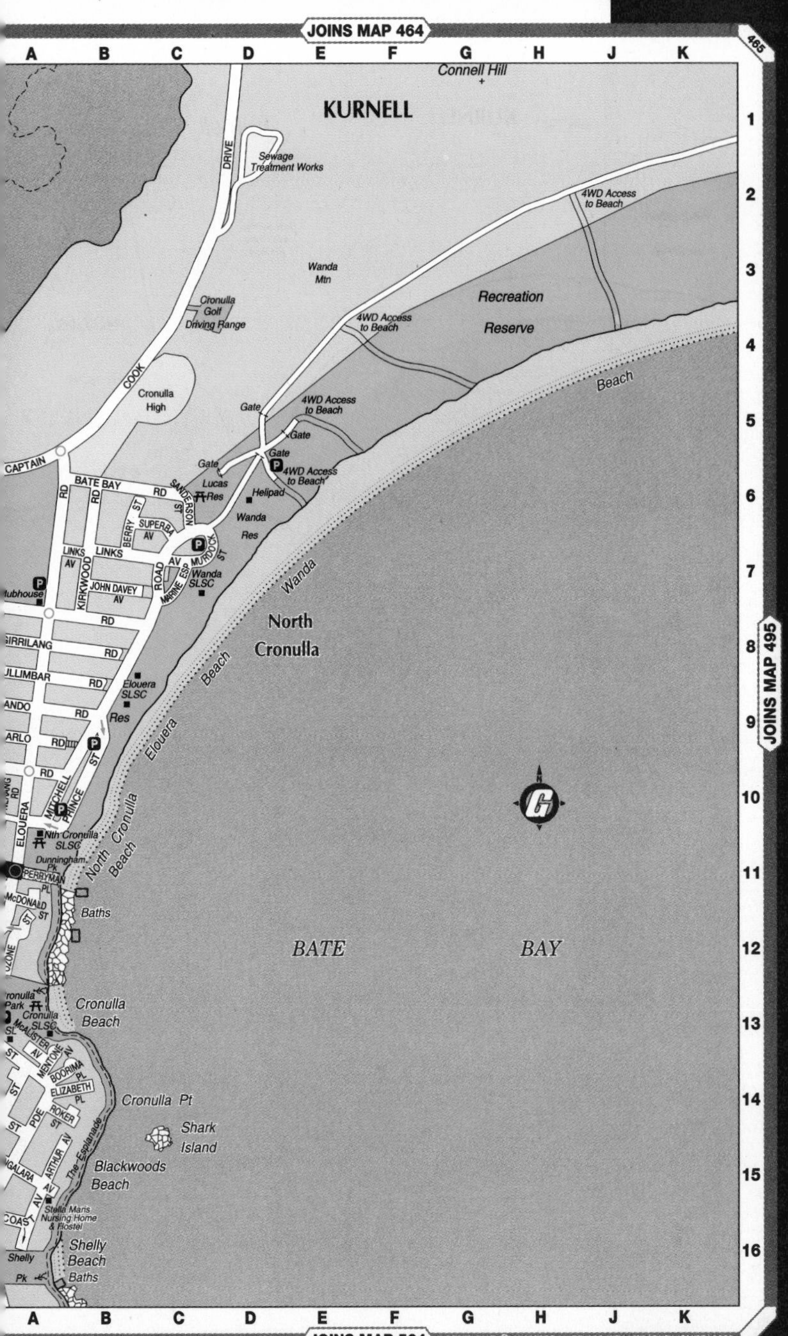
JOINS MAP 464
A B C D E F G H J K
465
Connell Hill
KURNELL
DRIVE
Sewage
Treatment Works
4WD Access
to Beach
Wanda
Mtn
Cronulla
Golf
Driving Range
Recreation
Reserve
4WD Access
to Beach
COOK
Cronulla
High
Beach
Gate
4WD Access
to Beach
Gate
Gate
Gate
4WD Access
to Beach
CAPTAIN
BATE BAY
RD
SANDERSON
Lucas
Res
Helipad
Wanda
Res
BERRY ST
SUPERBA AV
MURDOCK ST
LINKS AV
LINKS
KIRKWOOD RD
ROAD
MARINE ESP
Wanda
SLSC
JOHN DAVEY AV
Wanda
North
Cronulla
GIRRILANG RD
ULLIMBAR RD
Elouera
SLSC
ANDO RD
Res
ARLO RD
Elouera
Beach
MITCHELL
PRINCE ST
ELOUERA
Nth Cronulla
SLSC
Dunningham
Pk
North Cronulla
Beach
PERRYMAN PL
McDONALD ST
Baths
BATE
BAY
OZONE
Cronulla
Park
Cronulla
Beach
Cronulla
SLSC
McALISTER AV
MENTONE AV
BOORIMA PL
ELIZABETH PL
Cronulla Pt
ROKER ST
PDE
Shark
Island
ARTHUR AV
The Esplanade
Blackwoods
Beach
Stella Maris
Nursing Home
& Hostel
Shelly
Beach
Baths
Shelly
Pk
1 2 3 4 5 6 7 8 9 10 11 12 13 14 15 16
JOINS MAP 495
A B C D E F G H J K

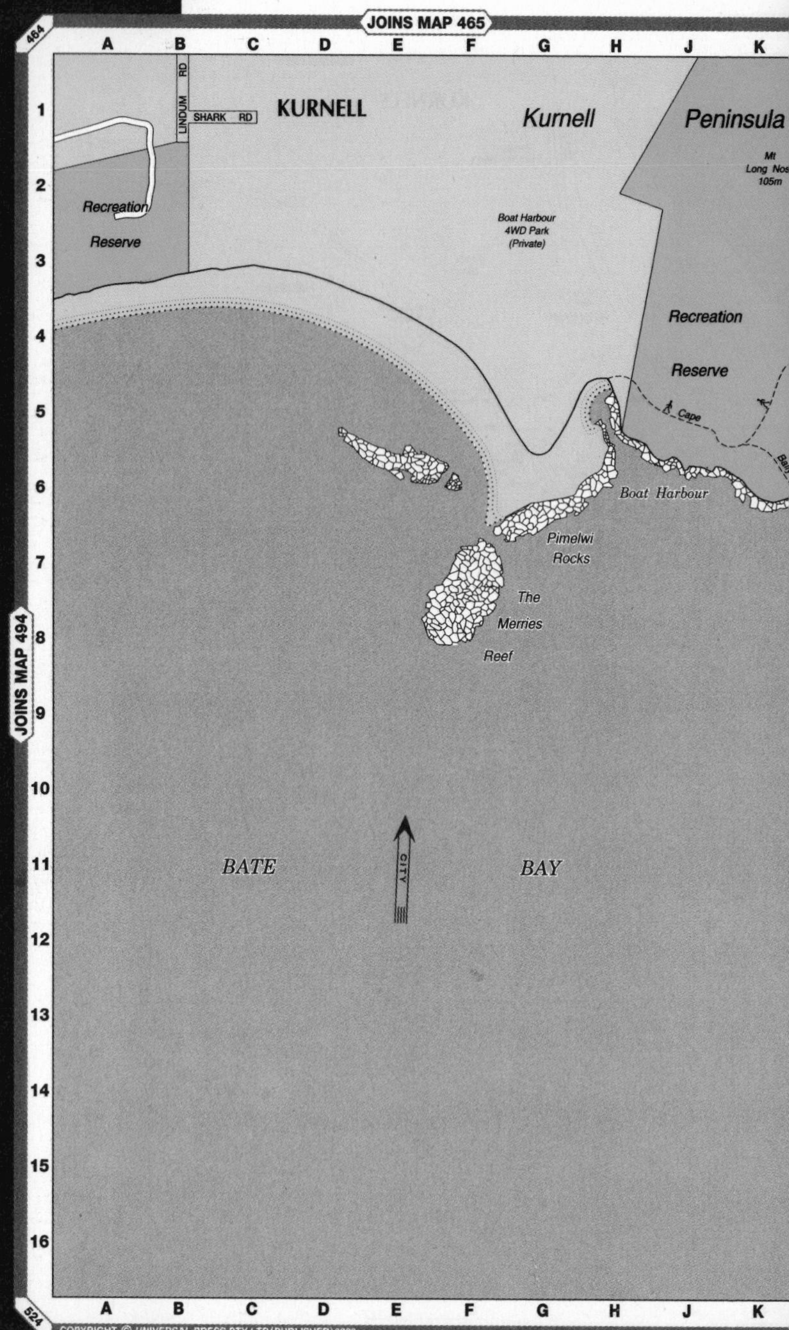
JOINS MAP 465
464
A
B
C
D
E
F
G
H
J
K
1
2
3
4
5
6
7
8
9
10
11
12
13
14
15
16
LINDUM RD
SHARK RD
KURNELL
Kurnell
Peninsula
Mt
Long Nos
105m
Recreation
Reserve
Boat Harbour
4WD Park
(Private)
Recreation
Reserve
Cape
Boat Harbour
Pimelwi
Rocks
The
Merries
Reef
JOINS MAP 494
BATE
CITY
BAY
524

JOINS MAP 466

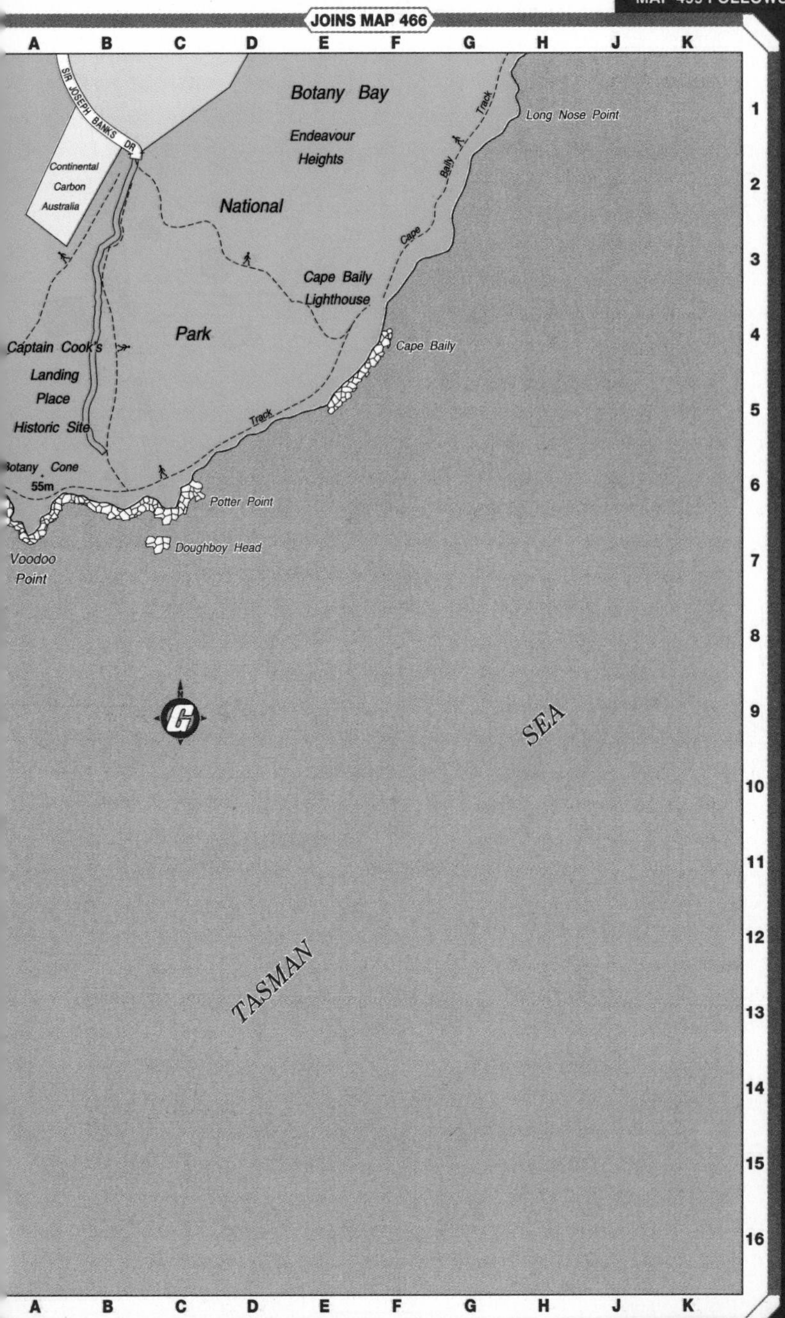

LIMIT OF MAPS
A B C D E F G H J K
1 2 3 4 5 6 7 8 9 10 11 12 13 14 15 16
STEVEYS FOREST RD
BURRAGORANG ROAD
Club
Sid Sharpe Oval
LIMIT OF MAPS

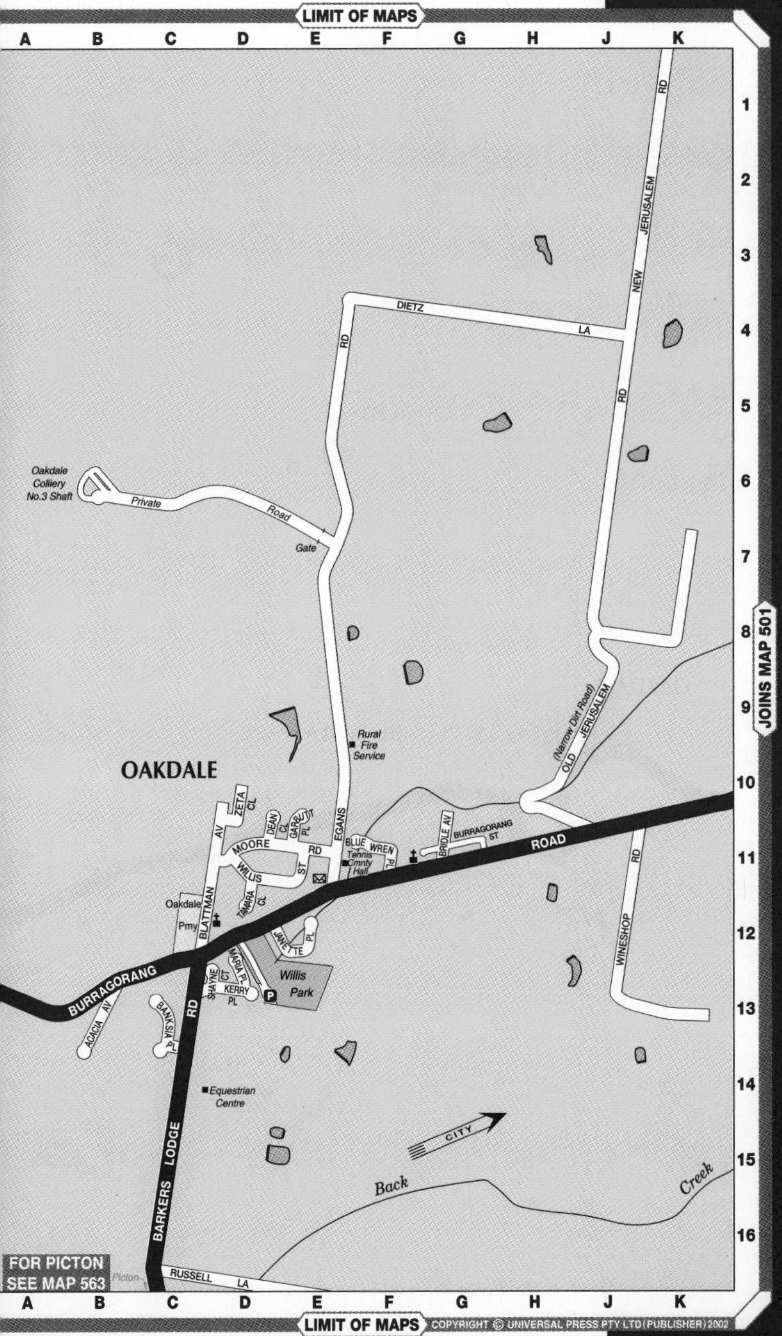

FOR PICTON SEE MAP 563

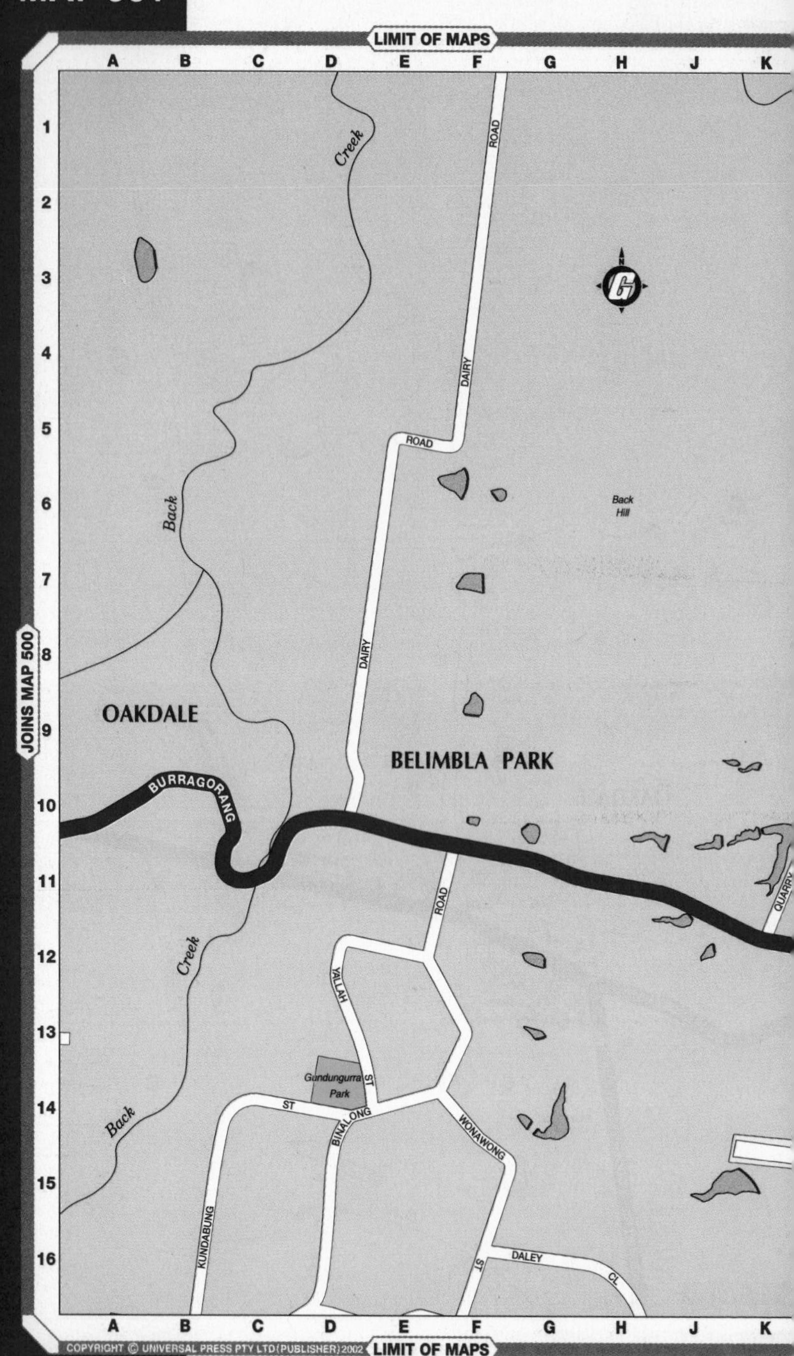
LIMIT OF MAPS
A
B
C
D
E
F
G
H
J
K
1
2
3
4
5
6
7
8
9
10
11
12
13
14
15
16
JOINS MAP 500
Creek
ROAD
DAIRY
ROAD
Back
Back
Hill
DAIRY
OAKDALE
BELIMBLA PARK
BURRAGORANG
ROAD
QUARRY
Creek
YALLAH
ST
Gundungurra
Park
ST
BINALONG
WONAWONG
Back
KUNDABUNG
ST
DALEY
CL
LIMIT OF MAPS

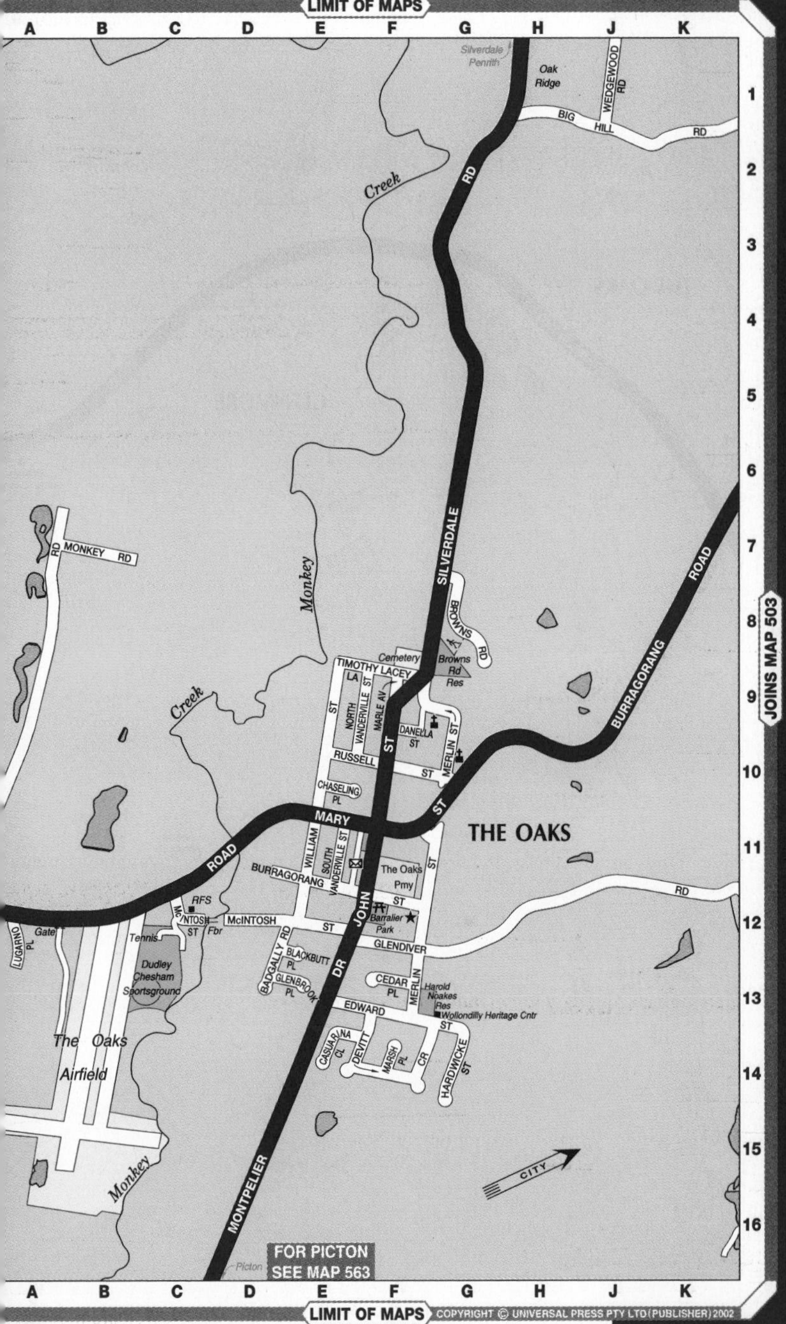
LIMIT OF MAPS
A B C D E F G H J K
1 2 3 4 5 6 7 8 9 10 11 12 13 14 15 16
Silverdale Penrith
Oak Ridge
WEDGEWOOD RD
BIG HILL RD
RD
Creek
SILVERDALE
Monkey
Creek
MONKEY RD
RD
BROWNS RD
Cemetery
Browns Rd Res
TIMOTHY LACEY
LA
ST
NORTH VANDERVILLE ST
MARLE AV
DANELLA ST
MERLIN ST
RUSSELL ST
CHASELING PL
MARY ST
BURRAGORANG ROAD
THE OAKS
ROAD
WILLIAM ST
SOUTH VANDERVILLE ST
The Oaks Pmy
ST
BURRAGORANG
RD
RFS
McINTOSH ST
McINTOSH ST
Fbr
Barralier Park
JOHN DR
GLENDIVER
BADGALLY RD
BLACKBUTT PL
GLENBROOK PL
CEDAR PL
MERLIN
Harold Noakes Res
Wollondilly Heritage Cntr
EDWARD ST
CASUARINA CL
DEVITT
MARSH PL
CR
HARDWICKE ST
LUGARNO PL
Gate
Tennis
Dudley Chesham Sportsground
The Oaks Airfield
CITY
Monkey
MONTPELIER
Picton
FOR PICTON SEE MAP 563
JOINS MAP 503
LIMIT OF MAPS

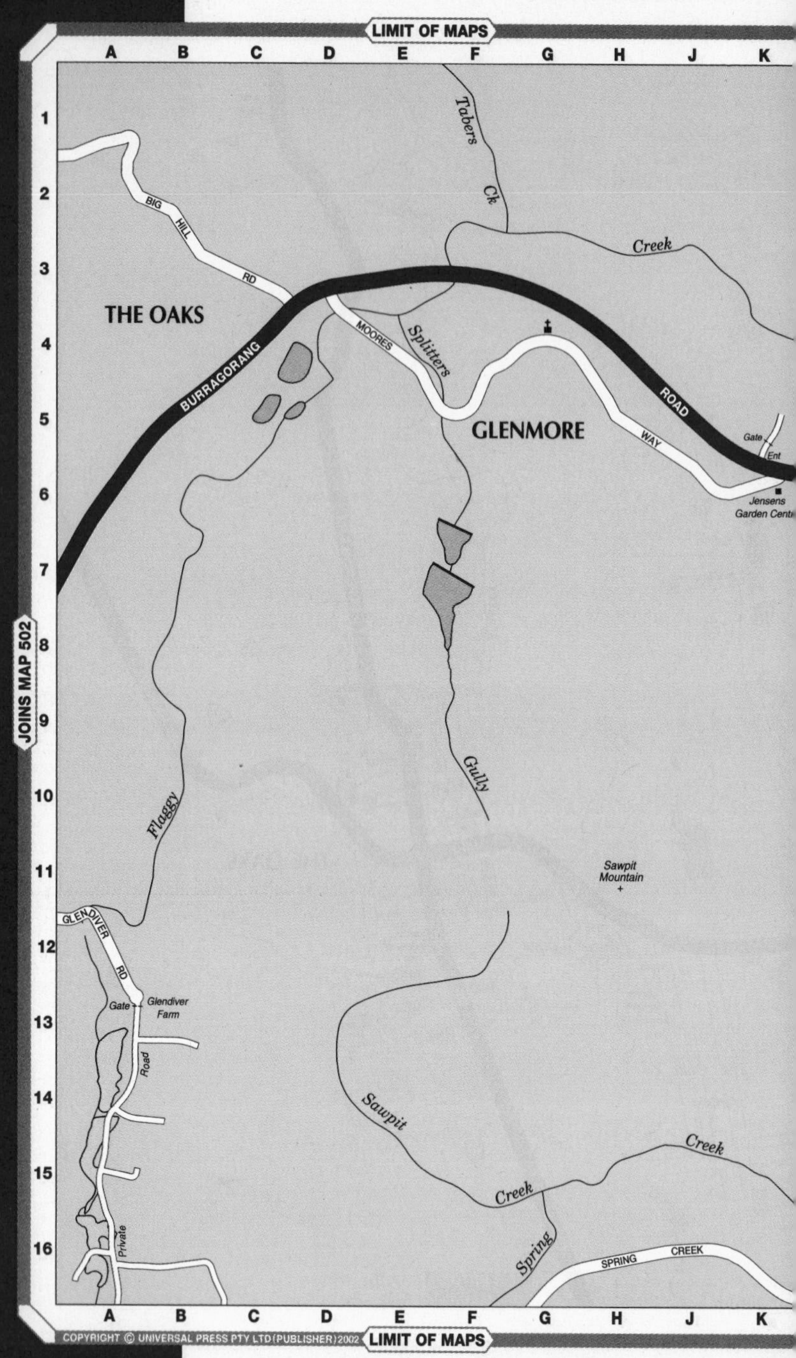
LIMIT OF MAPS
A
B
C
D
E
F
G
H
J
K
1
2
3
4
5
6
7
8
9
10
11
12
13
14
15
16
JOINS MAP 502
Tabers
Ck
Creek
BIG
HILL
RD
THE OAKS
BURRAGORANG
ROAD
MOORES
WAY
Splitters
GLENMORE
Gate
Ent
Jensens
Garden Centre
Gully
Flaggy
Sawpit
Mountain
GLENDIVER
RD
Gate
Glendiver
Farm
Road
Private
Sawpit
Creek
Creek
Spring
SPRING
CREEK
LIMIT OF MAPS

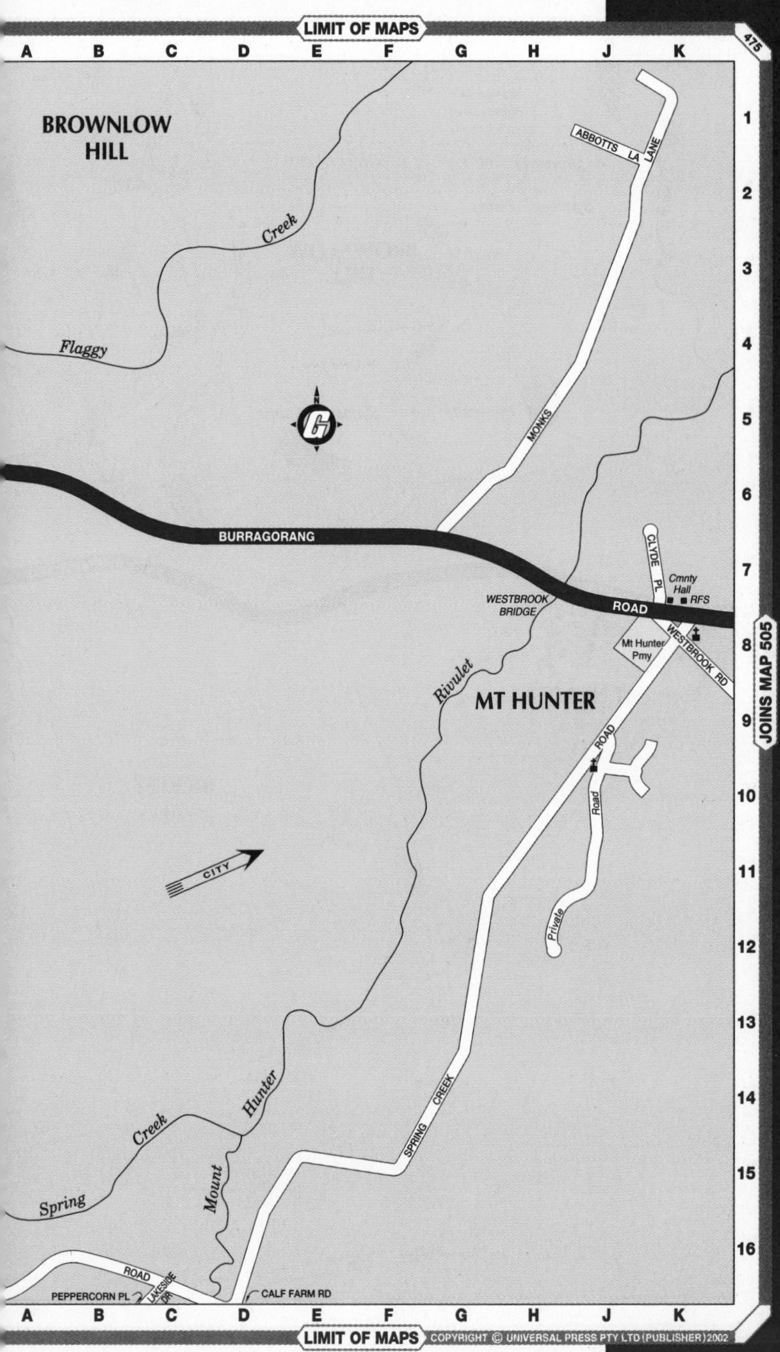
LIMIT OF MAPS
475
A
B
C
D
E
F
G
H
J
K
1
2
3
4
5
6
7
8
9
10
11
12
13
14
15
16
BROWNLOW HILL
ABBOTTS LA
LANE
Creek
Flaggy
MONKS
BURRAGORANG
ROAD
WESTBROOK BRIDGE
CLYDE PL
Cmnty Hall
RFS
Mt Hunter Pmy
WESTBROOK RD
Rivulet
MT HUNTER
ROAD
Road
Private
CITY
SPRING CREEK
Hunter
Creek
Mount
Spring
ROAD
LAKESIDE DR
PEPPERCORN PL
CALF FARM RD
JOINS MAP 505
LIMIT OF MAPS

MAP 505

JOINS MAP 475

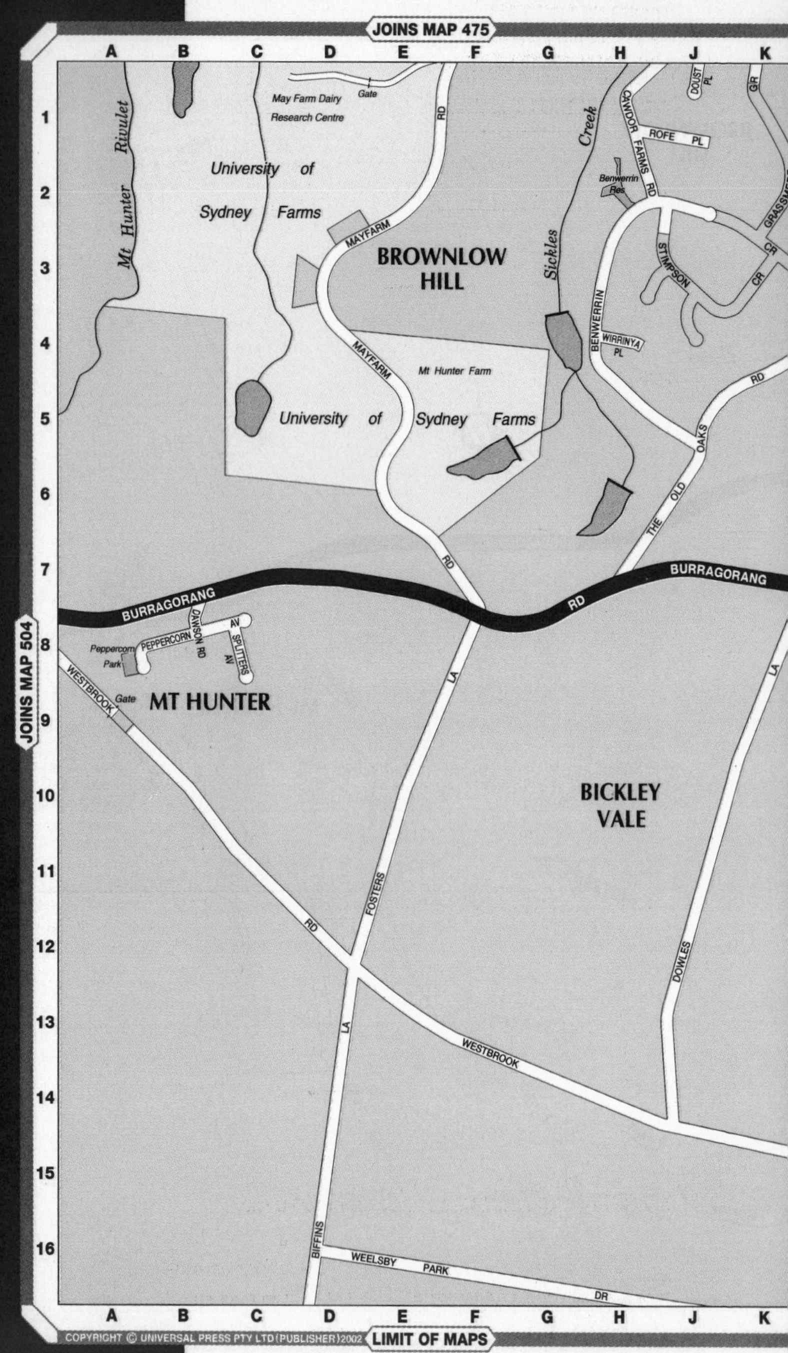

JOINS MAP 504

LIMIT OF MAPS

JOINS MAP 476

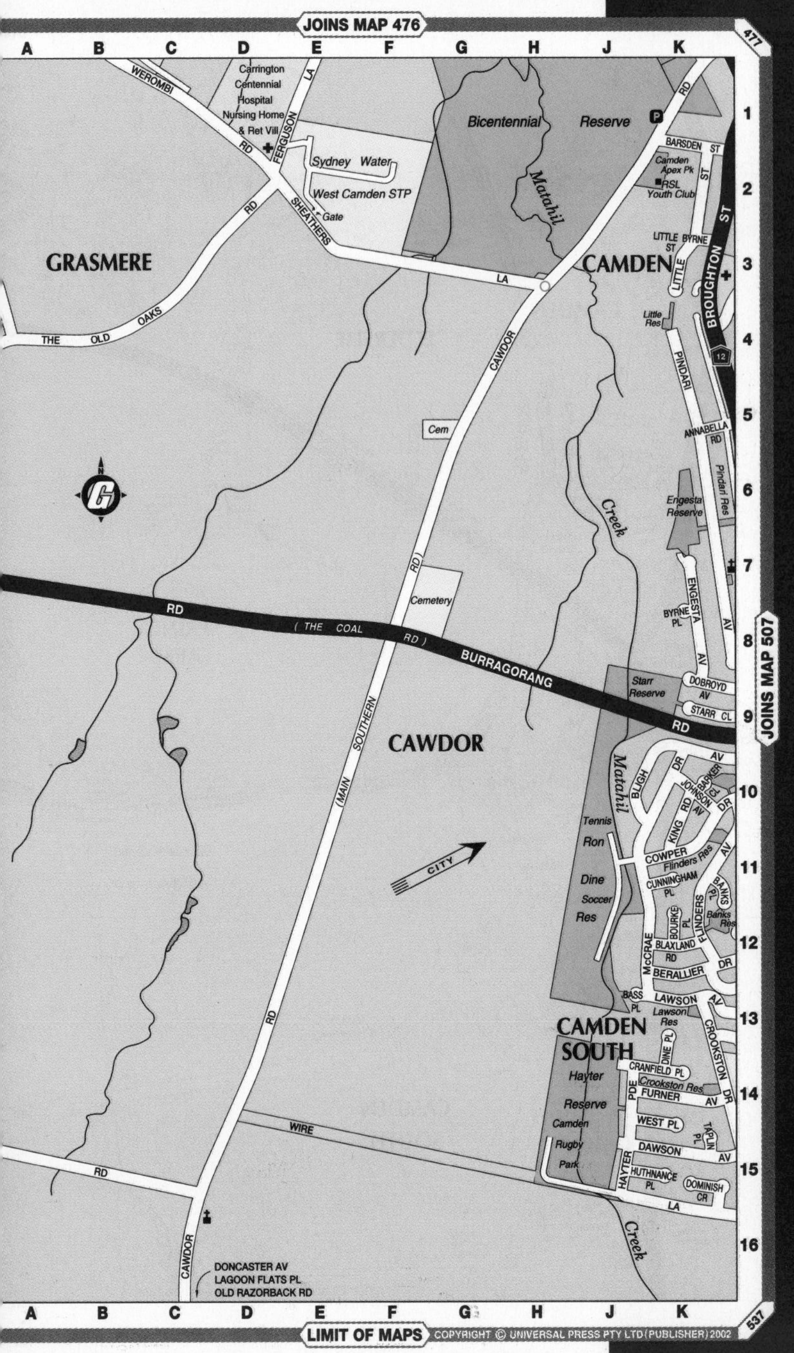

JOINS MAP 507

LIMIT OF MAPS

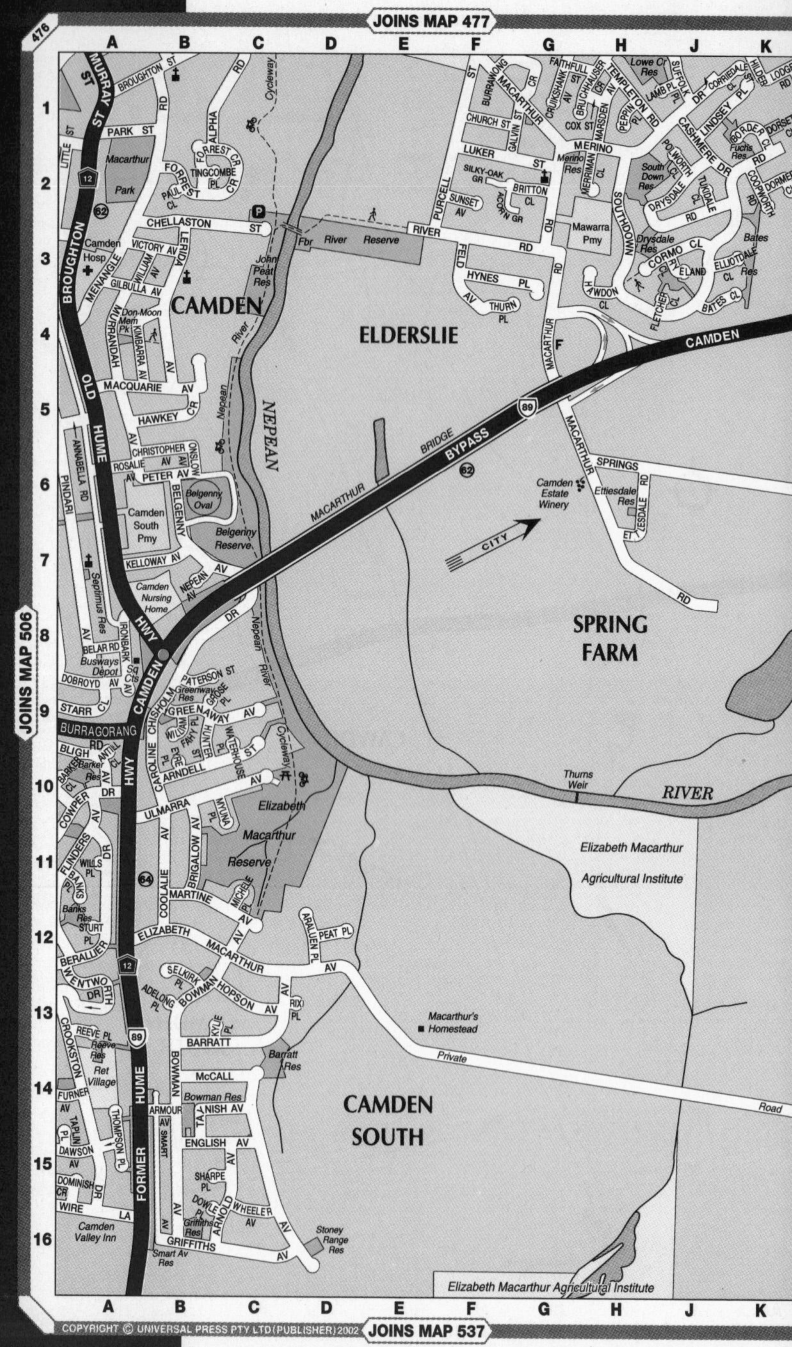
JOINS MAP 477
476
JOINS MAP 506
JOINS MAP 537
CAMDEN
ELDERSLIE
SPRING FARM
CAMDEN SOUTH
NEPEAN
RIVER
MACARTHUR BRIDGE BYPASS
CAMDEN
CITY
Camden Estate Winery
Thurns Weir
Elizabeth Macarthur Agricultural Institute
Macarthur's Homestead
Private Road
Elizabeth Macarthur Reserve
Belgenny Oval
Belgenny Reserve
Camden South Pmy
Camden Nursing Home
Macarthur Park
Camden Hosp
Don-Moon Mem Pk
River Reserve
John Peat Res
Mawarra Pmy
Camden Valley Inn
Ret Village
Busways Depot
OLD HUME HWY
CAMDEN HWY
FORMER HUME HWY
BROUGHTON ST
MURRAY ST
BURRAGORANG RD
MACARTHUR RD
ELIZABETH MACARTHUR AV
RIVER RD
CHELLASTON ST
MERINO ST
LUKER ST
SPRINGS RD

JOINS MAP 478

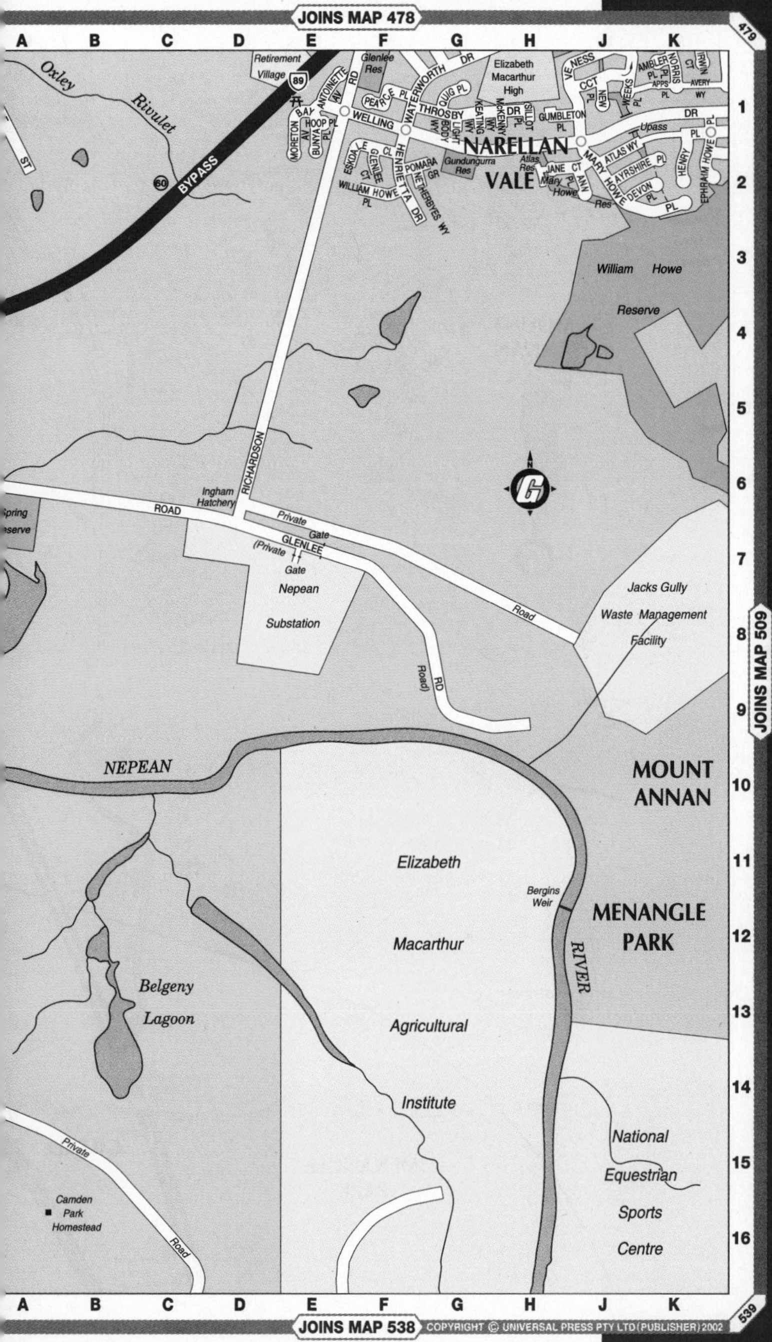

JOINS MAP 509

479

539

JOINS MAP 538

JOINS MAP 479

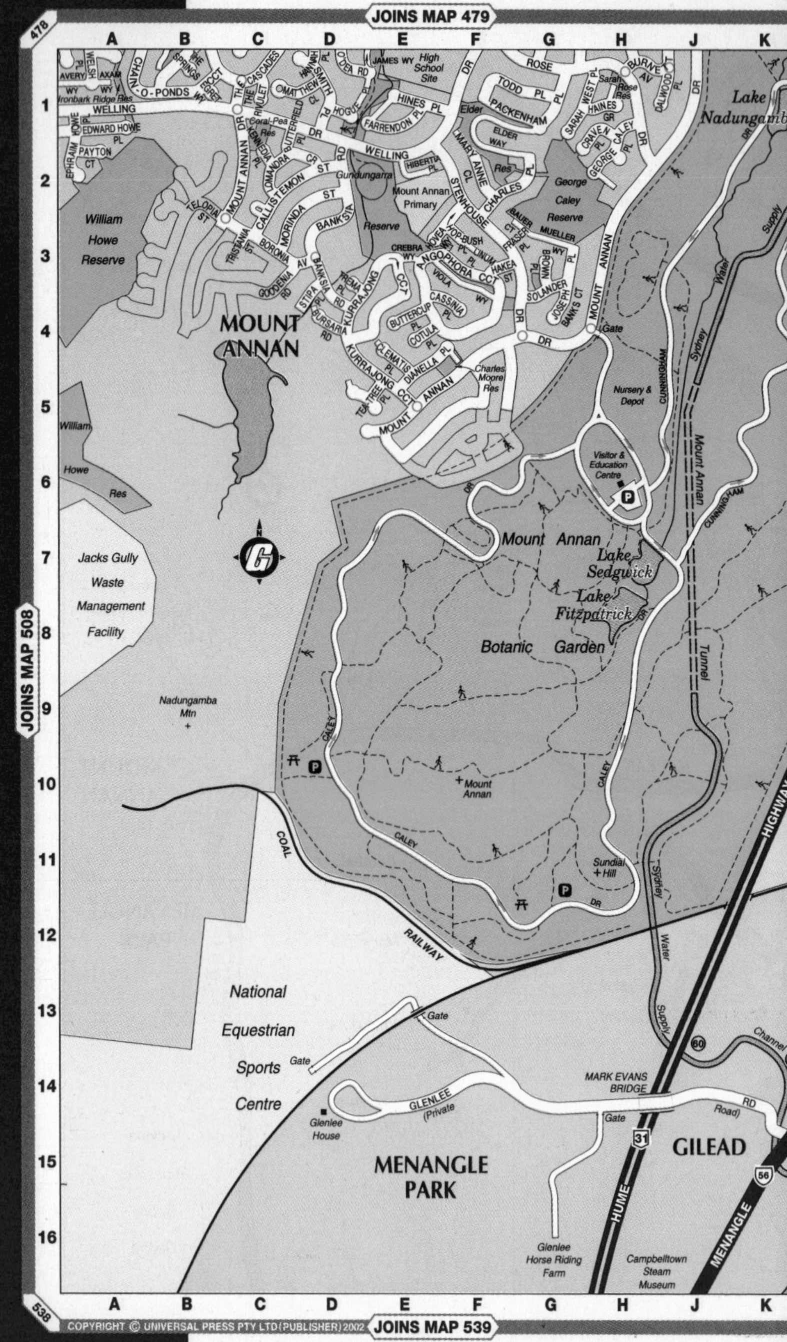

JOINS MAP 508

JOINS MAP 539

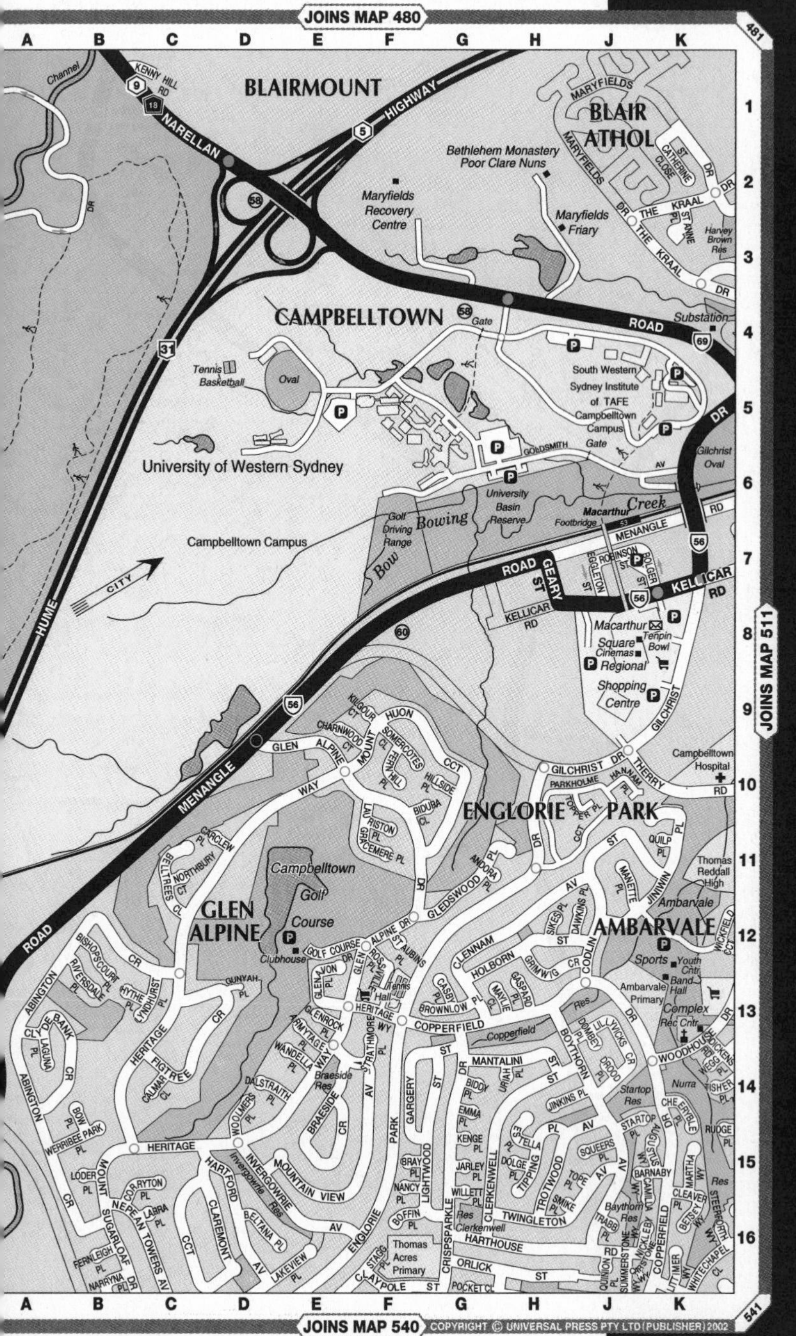
JOINS MAP 480
481
A B C D E F G H J K
BLAIRMOUNT
BLAIR ATHOL
CAMPBELLTOWN
ENGLORIE PARK
GLEN ALPINE
AMBARVALE
Channel
KENNY HILL RD
NARELLAN
HIGHWAY
HUME
ROAD
MENANGLE
ROAD
Bethlehem Monastery
Poor Clare Nuns
Maryfields Recovery Centre
Maryfields Friary
MARYFIELDS
ST CATHERINE CLOSE
THE KRAAL
ST ANNE
Harvey Brown Res
Substation
Gate
Tennis Basketball
Oval
South Western Sydney Institute of TAFE Campbelltown Campus
GOLDSMITH AV
Gilchrist Oval
University of Western Sydney
University Basin Reserve
Golf Driving Range
Bow Bowing Creek
Macarthur Footbridge
Campbelltown Campus
CITY
KELLICAR RD
GEARY ST
EGGLETON ST
ROBINSON ST
BOLGER ST
Macarthur Square Regional Shopping Centre
Cinemas
Tenpin Bowl
GILCHRIST DR
THERRY RD
Campbelltown Hospital
PARKHOLME
HANNAM
TOPPER PL
QUILP PL
Thomas Reddall High
Ambarvale Sports
Youth Cntr
Band Hall
Ambarvale Primary
Complex Rec Cntr
KILLGOUR CT
CHARNWOOD CT
HUON
SOMERCOTES
FERN HILL PL
HILLSIDE
CCT
BIDURA CL
LAURISTON PL
GRACEMERE PL
GLEN ALPINE WAY
MOUNT
ANDORA PL
GLEDSWOOD
CARCLEW PL
NORTHBURY CT
BELLTREES CL
Campbelltown Golf Course
Clubhouse
GOLF COURSE DR
ALPINE DR
ST AUBINS
BISHOPSCOURT
RIVERSDALE
HYTHE PL
LYNDHURST PL
GUNYAH PL
ABINGTON
CLYDE BANK
LAGUNA PL
HERITAGE
FIGTREE
CALMAR CL
DALSTRAITH
WOOLMERS
GLENAVON PL
GLENROCK PL
ARMYTAGE
WANDELLA WAY
Braeside Res
BRAESIDE
STRATHMORE
Tennis
Hall
COPPERFIELD
Copperfield
GLENNAM
HOLBORN
GRIMWIG CR
CODLIN
CASBY PL
BROWNLOW
MAYLIE CL
GASPARD PL
SIKES PL
DAWKINS PL
MANETTE PL
JINIWIN
WICKFIELD CCT
MANTALINI
URIAH PL
BIDDY PL
EMMA PL
KENGE PL
JARLEY PL
WILLETT PL
BOFFIN PL
NANCY PL
BRAY PL
LIGHTWOOD
GARGERY
PARK
ENGLORIE
CLERKENWELL
Res Clerkenwell
ESTELLA PL
DOLGE PL
TIPPING
TROTWOOD
JINKINS PL
SQUEERS PL
TOPE PL
SMIKE PL
TWINGLETON
HARTHOUSE
ORLICK ST
BOYTHORN
DOMBEY
LILLYVICKS CR
DROOD PL
Startop Res
STARTOP PL
BARNABY
CAMILLA
NICKLEBY
SUMMERSTONE
COPPERFIELD
QUINION PL
TRABB
Baythorn Res
CHEERYBLE
WOODHOUSE
DICKENS
WEGG
TISHER PL
Nurra
RUDGE PL
MARTHA
CLEAVER PL
BETSEY WY
STEERFORTH WY
LITTIMER
WHITECHAPEL CL
Res
HERITAGE
MOUNT SUGARLOAF
WERRIBEE PARK PL
BOW PL
LODER PL
CORRYTON PL
NEPEAN TOWERS AV
LABRA PL
HARTFORD
CLAREMONT
INVERGOWRIE
Invergowrie Res
MOUNTAIN VIEW AV
BELTANA PL
LAKEVIEW PL
FERNLEIGH PL
NARRYNA DR
CCT
Thomas Acres Primary
STAGG PL
CLAYPOLE ST
CRISPSPARKLE
POCKET CL
1 2 3 4 5 6 7 8 9 10 11 12 13 14 15 16
JOINS MAP 511
JOINS MAP 540
541

JOINS MAP 481

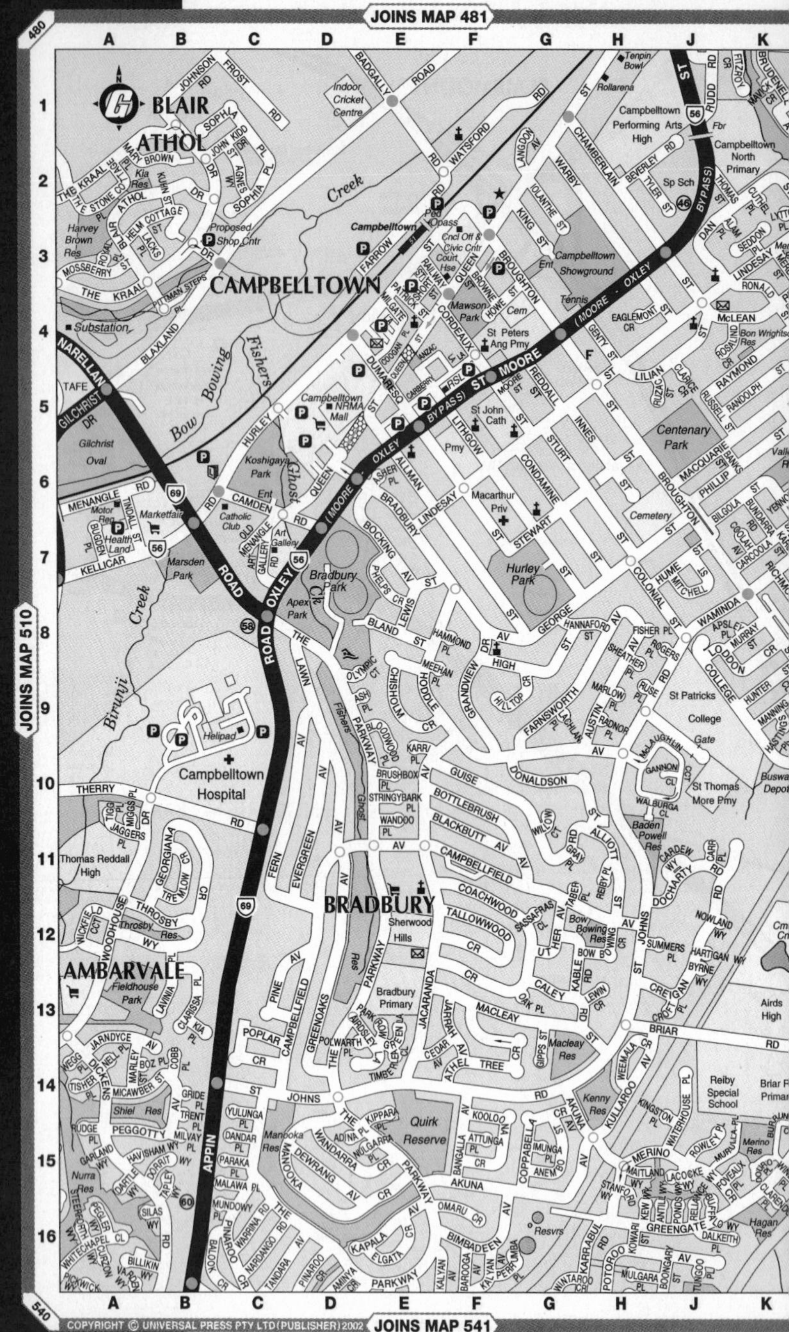

JOINS MAP 541

JOINS MAP 482

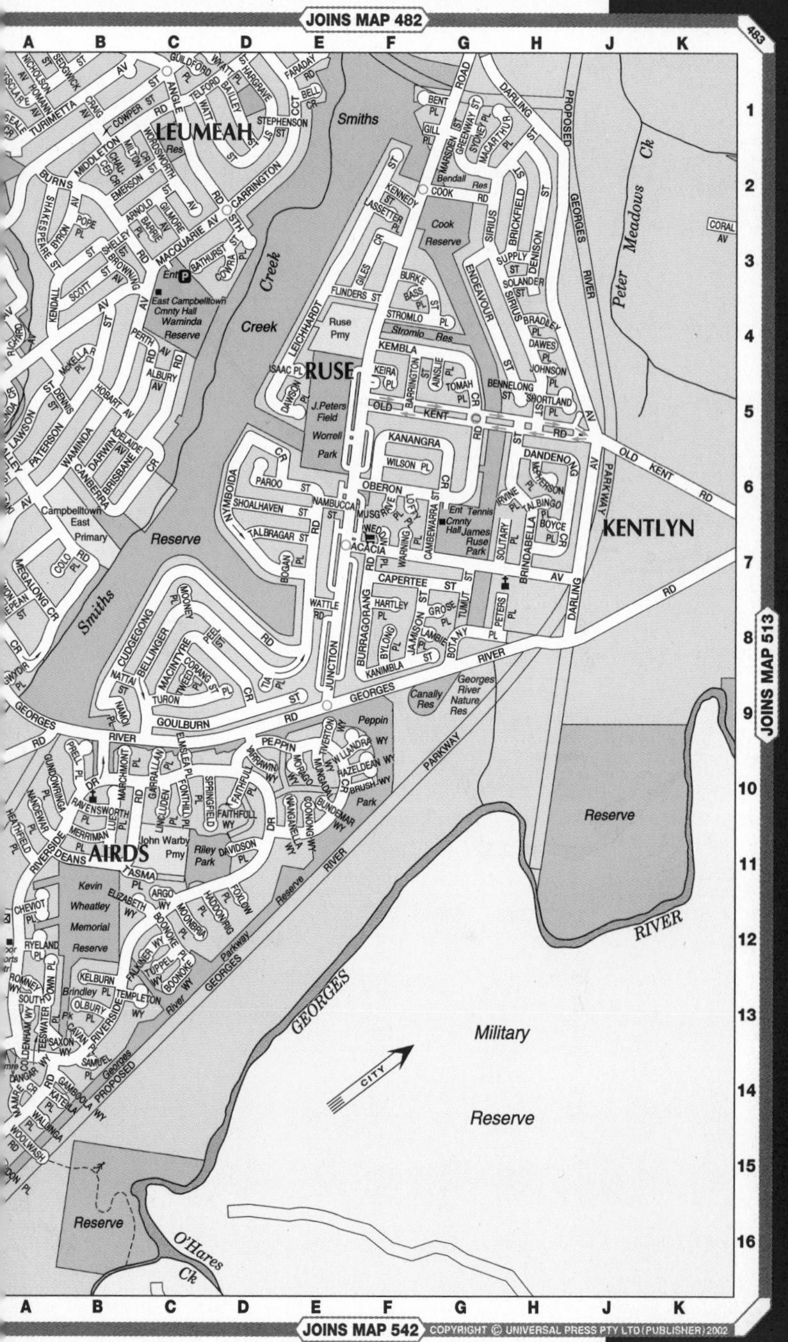

JOINS MAP 513

JOINS MAP 542

JOINS MAP 483

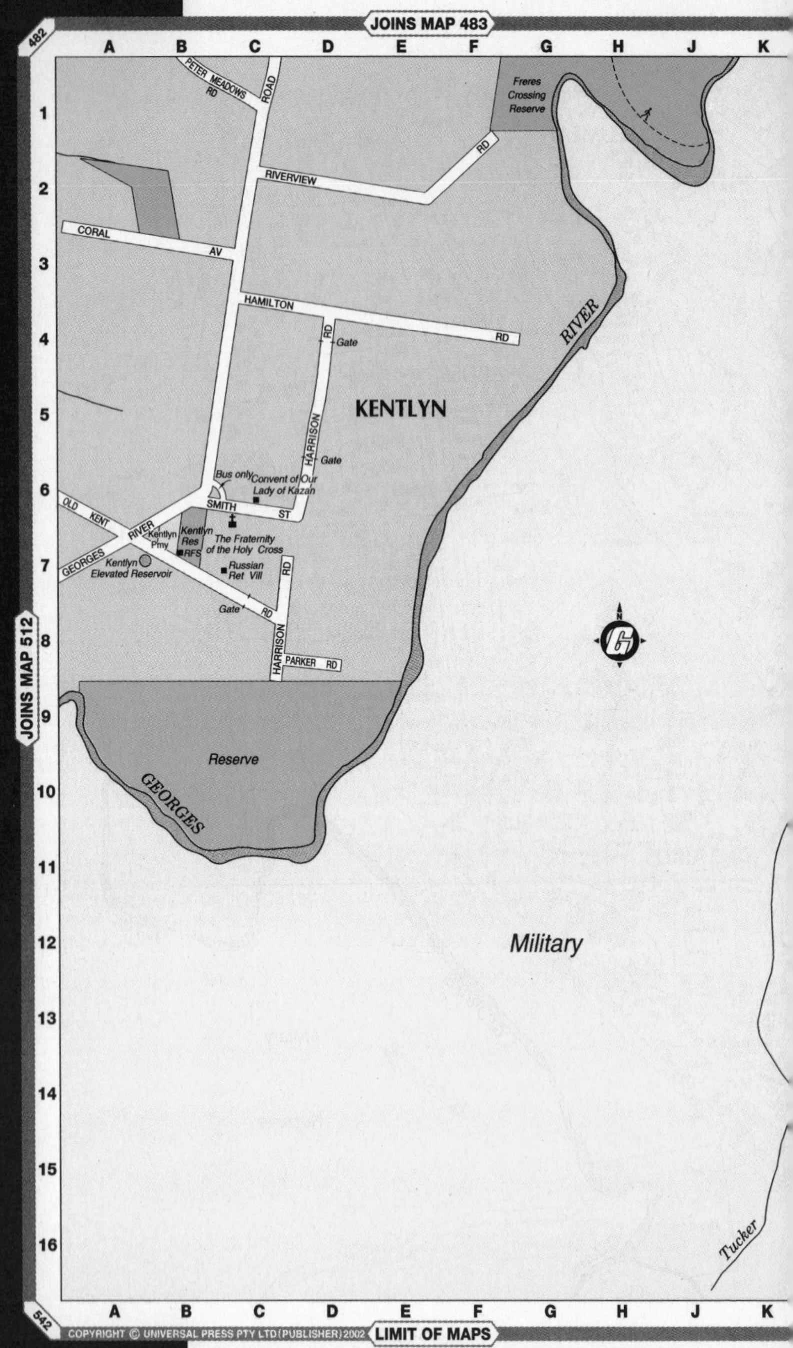

JOINS MAP 512

LIMIT OF MAPS

JOINS MAP 484

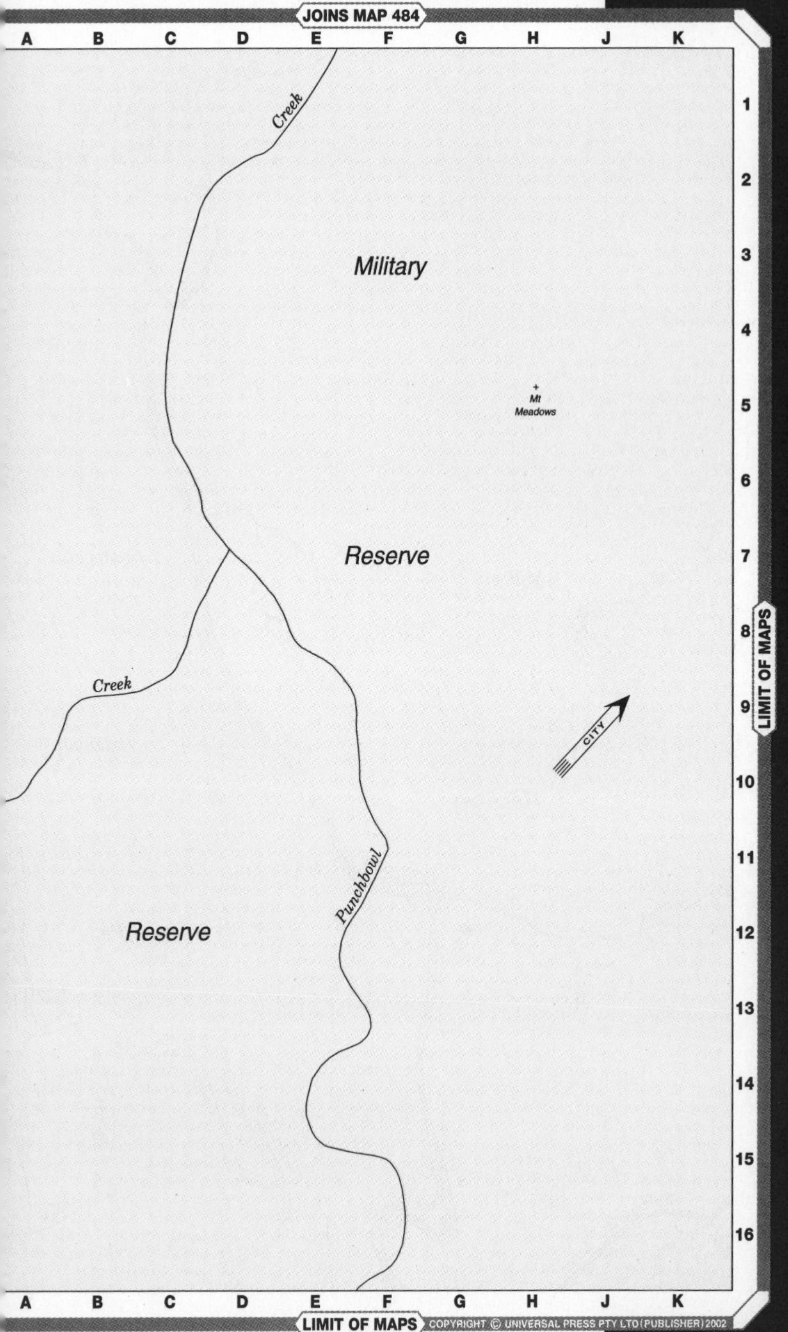

LIMIT OF MAPS

JOINS MAP 487

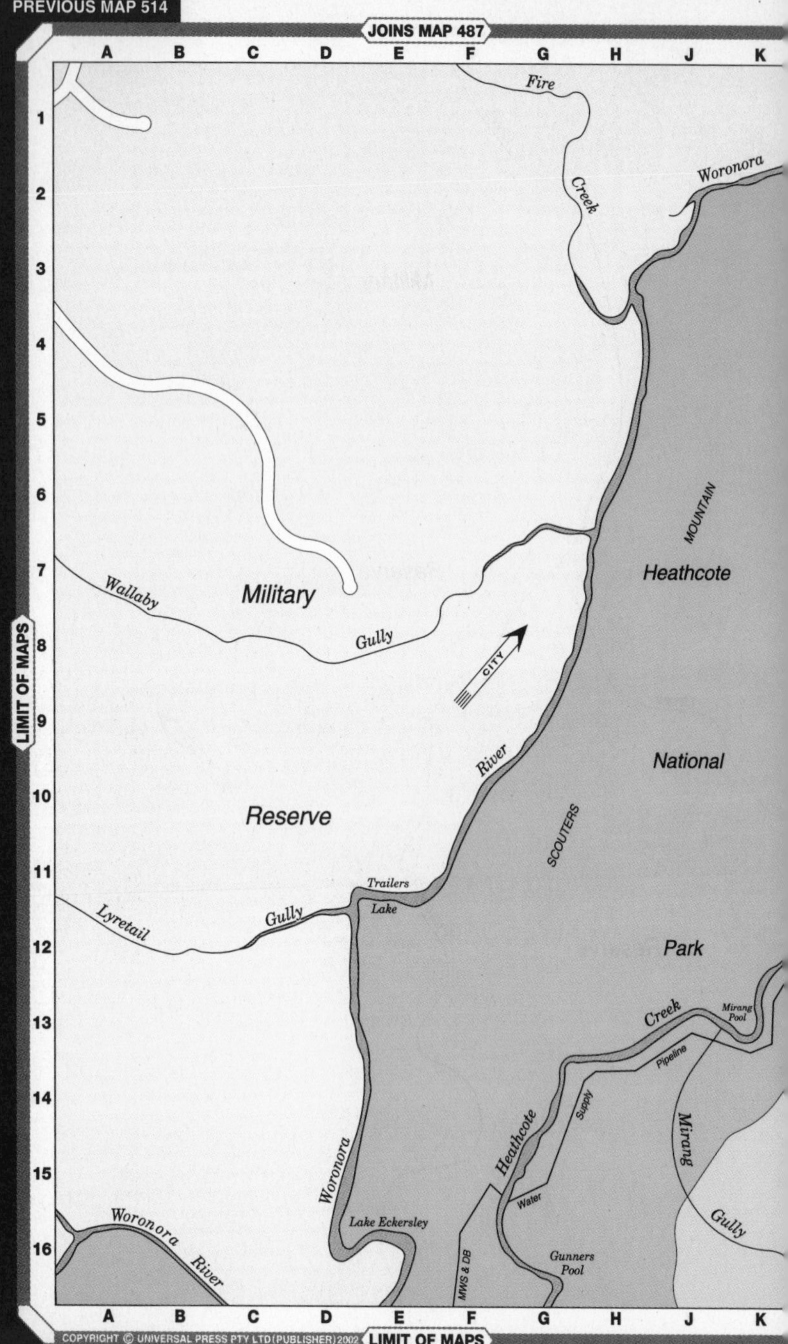

LIMIT OF MAPS

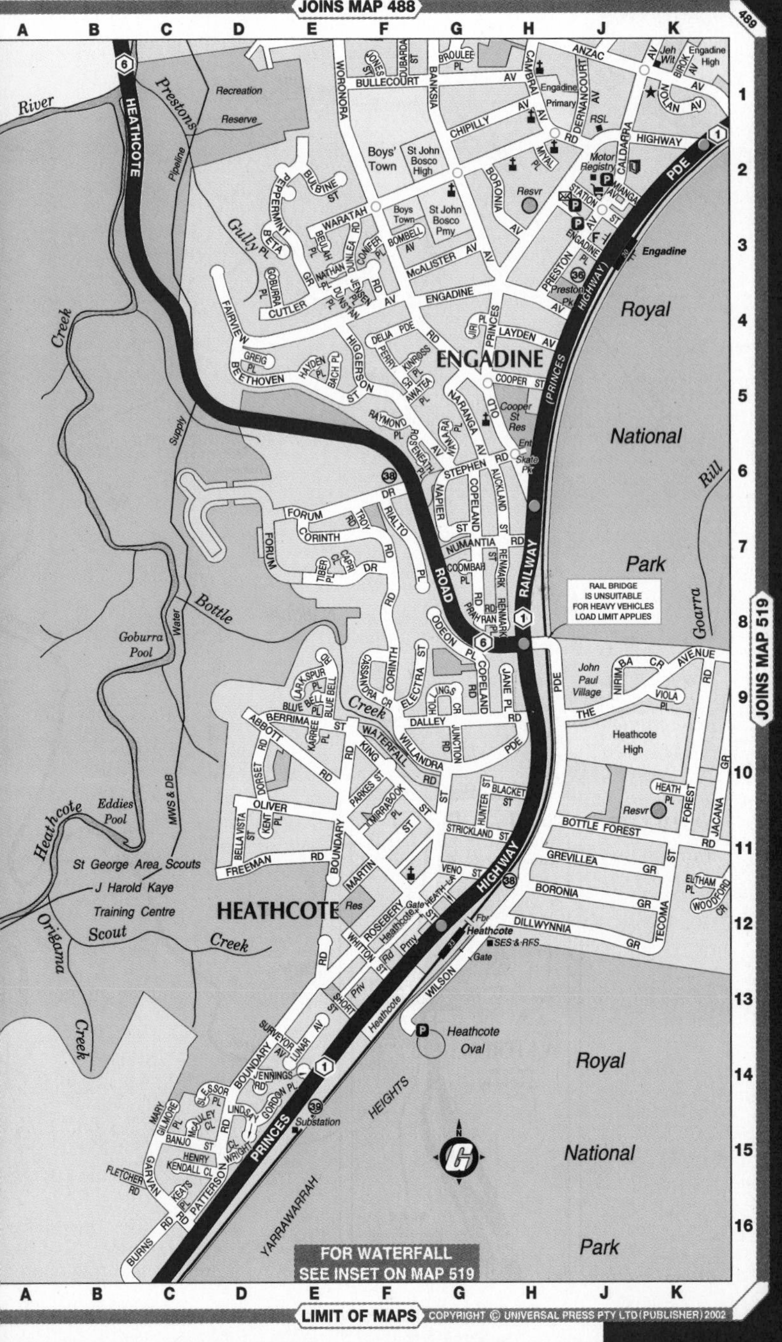

JOINS MAP 488
489
JOINS MAP 519
LIMIT OF MAPS
COPYRIGHT © UNIVERSAL PRESS PTY LTD (PUBLISHER) 2002
A B C D E F G H J K
1 2 3 4 5 6 7 8 9 10 11 12 13 14 15 16
ENGADINE
HEATHCOTE
Royal
National
Park
Royal
National
Park
HEATHCOTE ROAD
PRINCES HIGHWAY
(PRINCES HIGHWAY)
RAILWAY
PDE
HIGHWAY
RAIL BRIDGE
IS UNSUITABLE
FOR HEAVY VEHICLES
LOAD LIMIT APPLIES
FOR WATERFALL
SEE INSET ON MAP 519
Prestons
Recreation
Reserve
River
Pipeline
Supply
Water
MWS & DB
Gully
Creek
Bottle
Goburra
Pool
Eddies
Pool
Heathcote
Creek
Origama
Creek
St George Area Scouts
J Harold Kaye
Training Centre
Scout
Creek
Rill
Goarra
Boys' Town
St John Bosco High
Boys Town
St John Bosco Pmy
Engadine Primary
Engadine High
Jeh Wit
RSL
Motor Registry
Resvr
Engadine
Preston Pk
Cooper St Res
Ent
Skate Pk
John Paul Village
Heathcote High
Resvr
Res
Heathcote
Fbr
SES & RFS
Gate
Substation
Heathcote Oval
HEIGHTS
YARRAWARRAH
ANZAC
BULLECOURT
WORONORA
JONES
DUBARDA
BROULEE PL
BANKSIA
CAMBRAI
DERNANCOURT
BIROK
NOLAN
CHIPILLY
CALDARRA
HIGHWAY
MYAL
BORONIA
STATION
MIANGA
PEPPERMINT
BULBINE
WARATAH
BEULAH
DUNLEA
CONIFER
BOMBELL
McALISTER
BETA
GOBURRA
NATHAN
JENSEN
DUNSTAN
CUTLER
ENGADINE
FAIRVIEW
PRINCES
JIRI
LAYDEN
DELIA
PERRY
KINROSS
AWATEA
HIGGERSON
GREIG
HAYDEN
BACH
BEETHOVEN
COOPER
NARANGA
OLD
RAYMOND
ROSENEATH
NAMARA
STEPHEN
FORUM
CORINTH
TROY
RIALTO
NAPIER
COPELAND
AUCKLAND
NUMANTIA
COOMBAR
RENMARK
TIBER
CAPRI
PRAH
RAN
ODEON
CASSANDRA
ELECTRA
HOLLINGS
JANE
LARKSPUR
BLUE BELL
BERRIMA
ABBOTT
KARREE
WATERFALL
KING
WILLANDRA
DALLEY
JUNCTION
DORSET
PARKES
MIRRABOOK
BLACKET
HUNTER
STRICKLAND
OLIVER
KENT
BELLA VISTA
BOUNDARY
FREEMAN
MARTIN
VENO
HEATH LA
ROSEBERY
WHITTON
SHORT
Priv
Pmy
Heathcote
WILSON
SURVEYOR
LUNAR
JENNINGS
GORDON
SLESSOR
MARY GILMORE
McAULEY
LINDSAY
BANJO
HENRY KENDALL
WRIGHT
PATTERSON
FLETCHER
GARVAN
KEATS
BURNS
NIRIMBA
AVENUE
VIOLA
THE
HEATH
FOREST
JACANA
BOTTLE FOREST
GREVILLEA
BORONIA
DILLWYNNIA
TECOMA
ELTHAM
WOODFORD

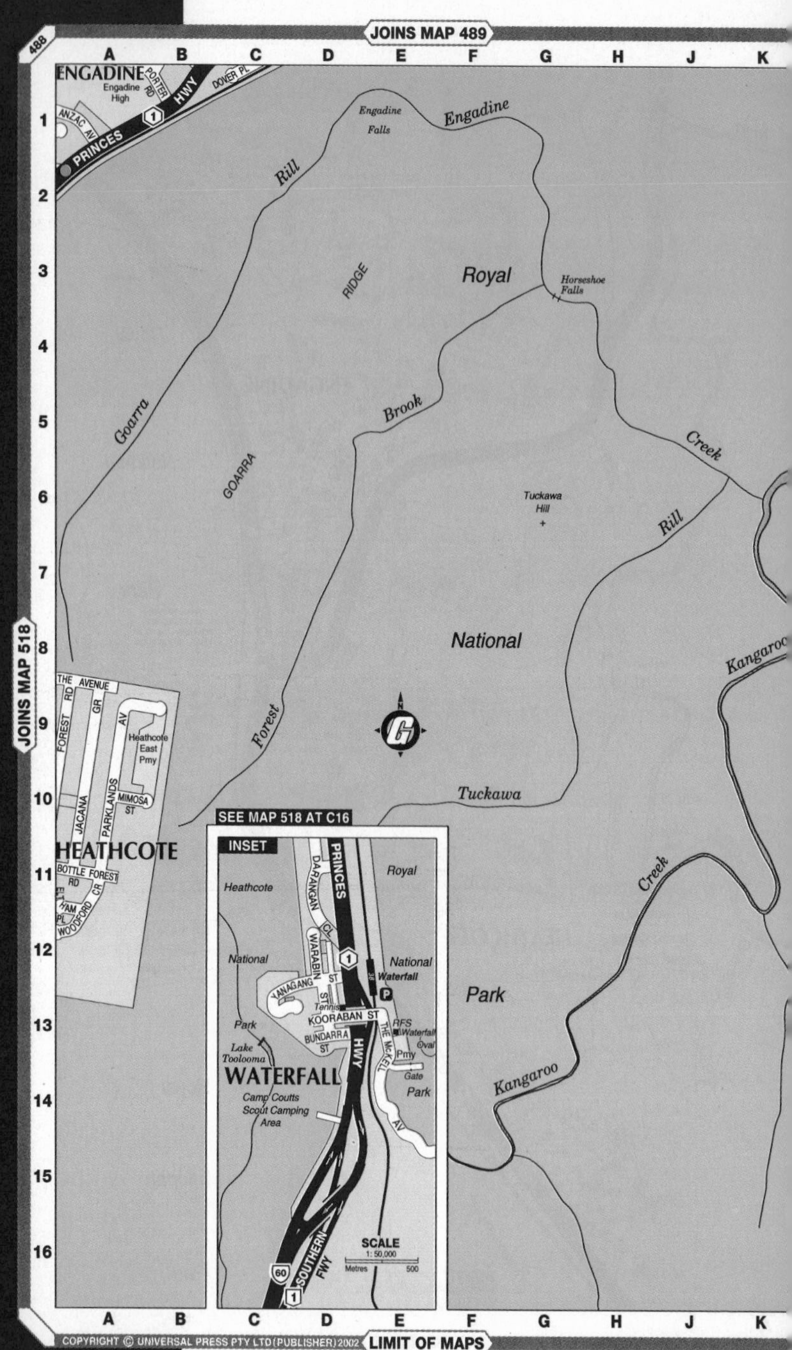

LIMIT OF MAPS

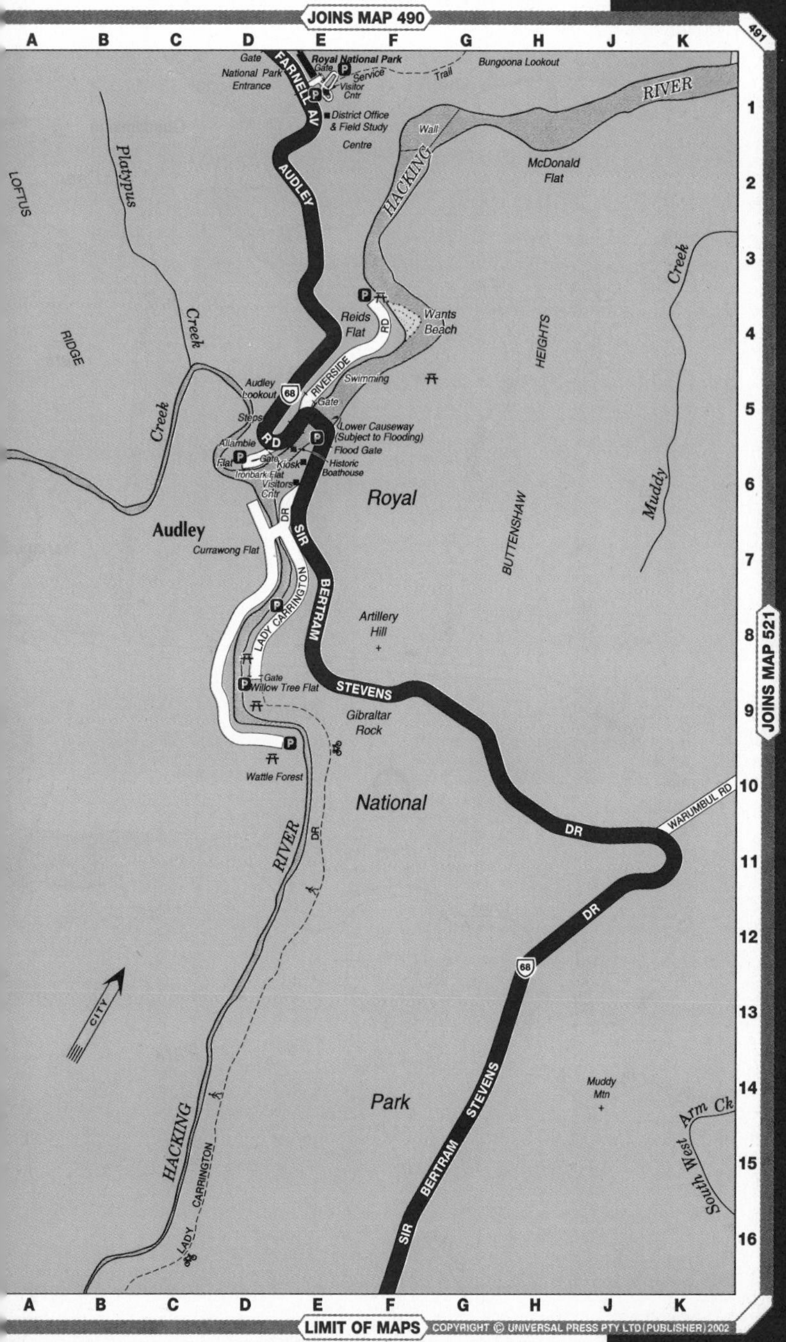
JOINS MAP 490
A B C D E F G H J K
491
1 2 3 4 5 6 7 8 9 10 11 12 13 14 15 16
Gate
National Park Entrance
FARNELL AV
Royal National Park
Gate
Service
Visitor Cntr
Trail
Bungoona Lookout
District Office & Field Study Centre
RIVER
Wall
HACKING
McDonald Flat
LOFTUS
Platypus
AUDLEY
Creek
Reids Flat
RD
Wants Beach
RIVERSIDE
HEIGHTS
RIDGE
Creek
Swimming
Audley Lookout
68
Gate
Steps
RD
Lower Causeway (Subject to Flooding)
Flood Gate
Allambie Flat
Gate
Kiosk
Historic Boathouse
Ironbark Flat
Visitors Cntr
Royal
BUTTENSHAW
Muddy
DR
SIR
Audley
Currawong Flat
LADY CARRINGTON
BERTRAM
Artillery Hill
JOINS MAP 521
Gate
Willow Tree Flat
STEVENS
Gibraltar Rock
Wattle Forest
National
WARUMBUL RD
RIVER
DR
DR
DR
68
CITY
Muddy Mtn
Park
STEVENS
HACKING
South West Arm Ck
CARRINGTON
BERTRAM
SIR
LADY
LIMIT OF MAPS

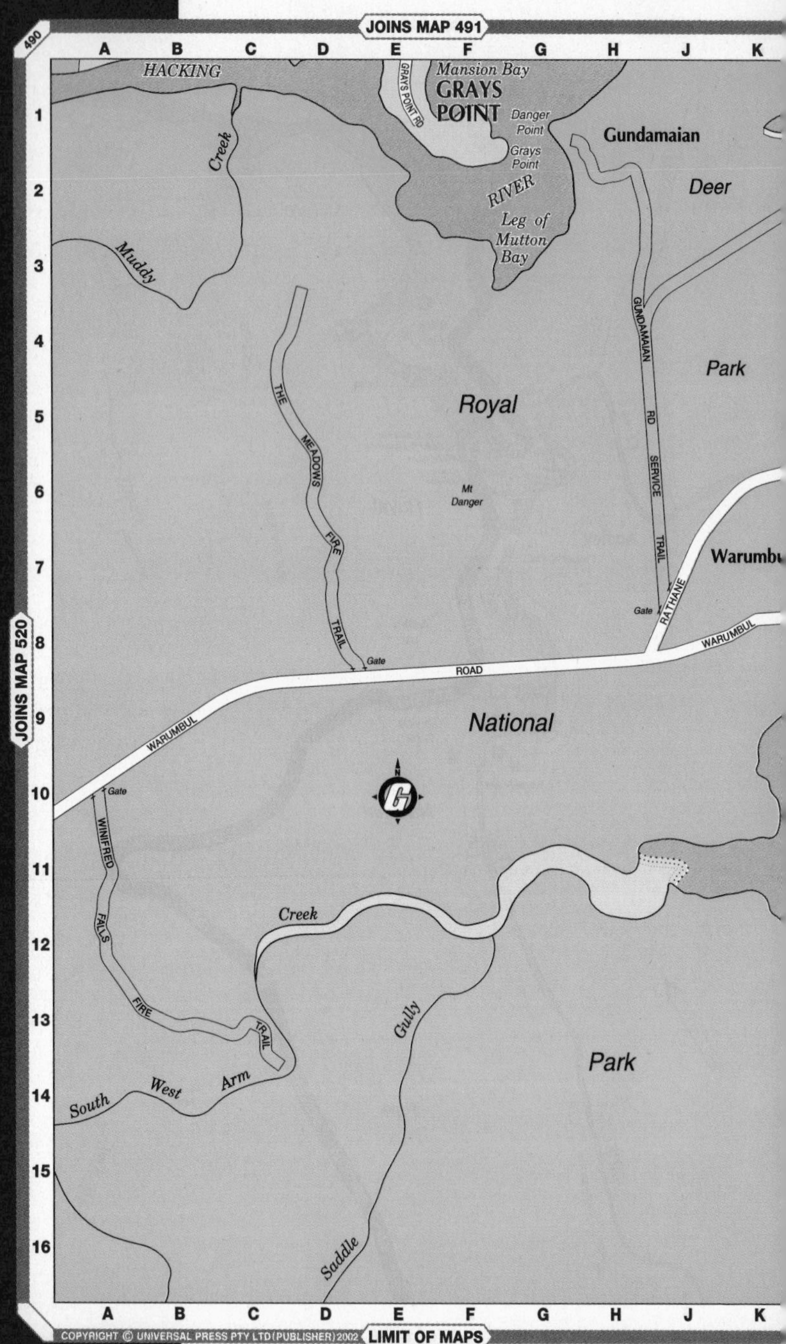
JOINS MAP 491
490
JOINS MAP 520
A B C D E F G H J K
1 2 3 4 5 6 7 8 9 10 11 12 13 14 15 16
HACKING
Mansion Bay
GRAYS POINT
GRAYS POINT RD
Danger Point
Grays Point
RIVER
Leg of Mutton Bay
Creek
Muddy
Gundamaian
Deer
Park
Royal
National
Park
THE MEADOWS FIRE TRAIL
Gate
Mt Danger
GUNDAMAIAN RD SERVICE TRAIL
Gate
RATHANE
Warumbu
WARUMBUL
ROAD
WARUMBUL
Gate
WINIFRED FALLS FIRE TRAIL
Creek
Gully
Saddle
South West Arm
LIMIT OF MAPS

JOINS MAP 492

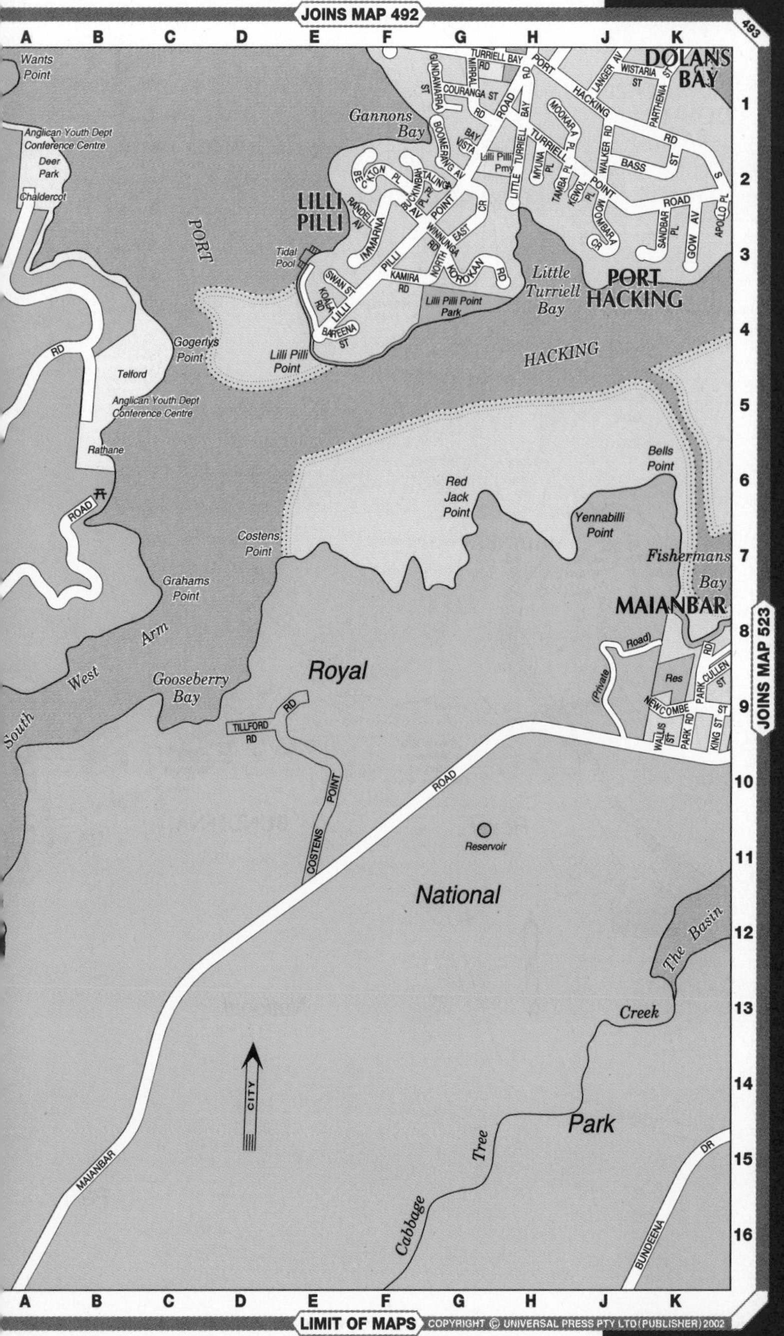

JOINS MAP 523

LIMIT OF MAPS

JOINS MAP 493

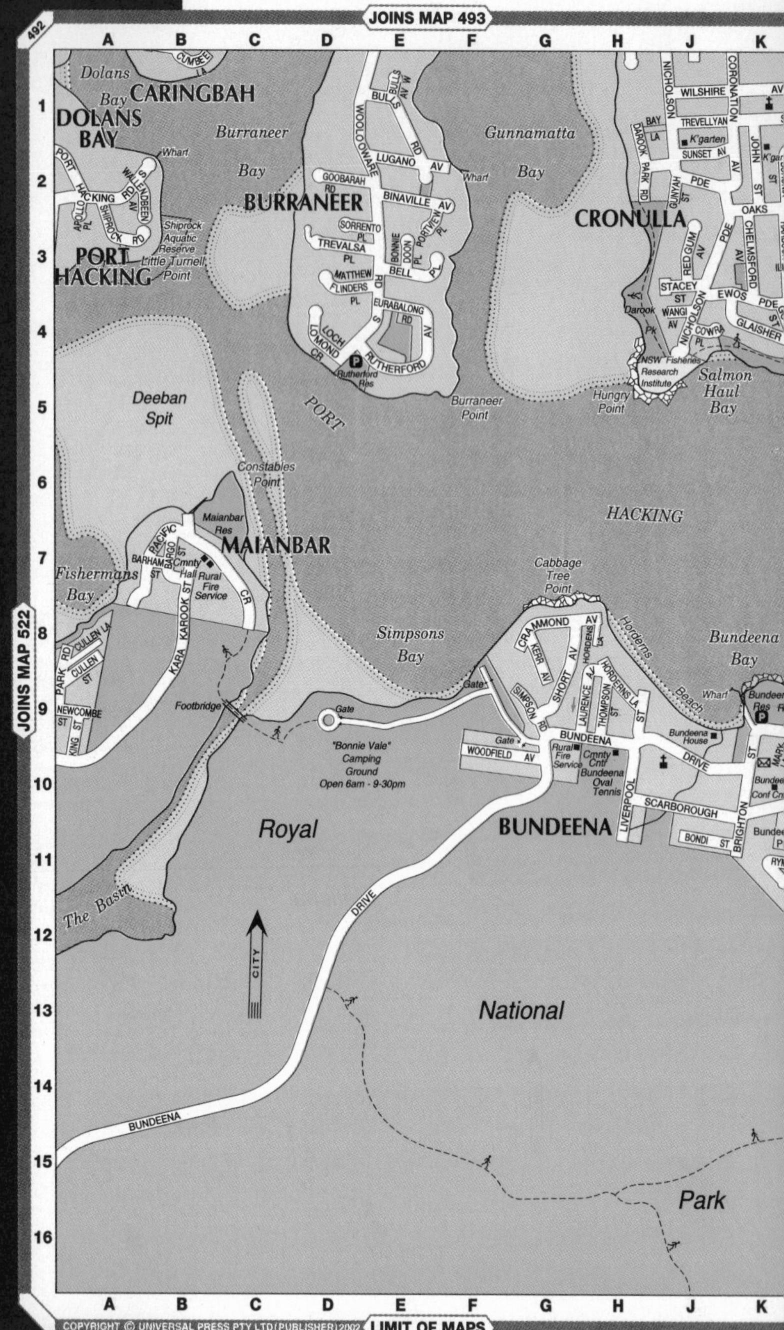

JOINS MAP 522

LIMIT OF MAPS

JOINS MAP 494

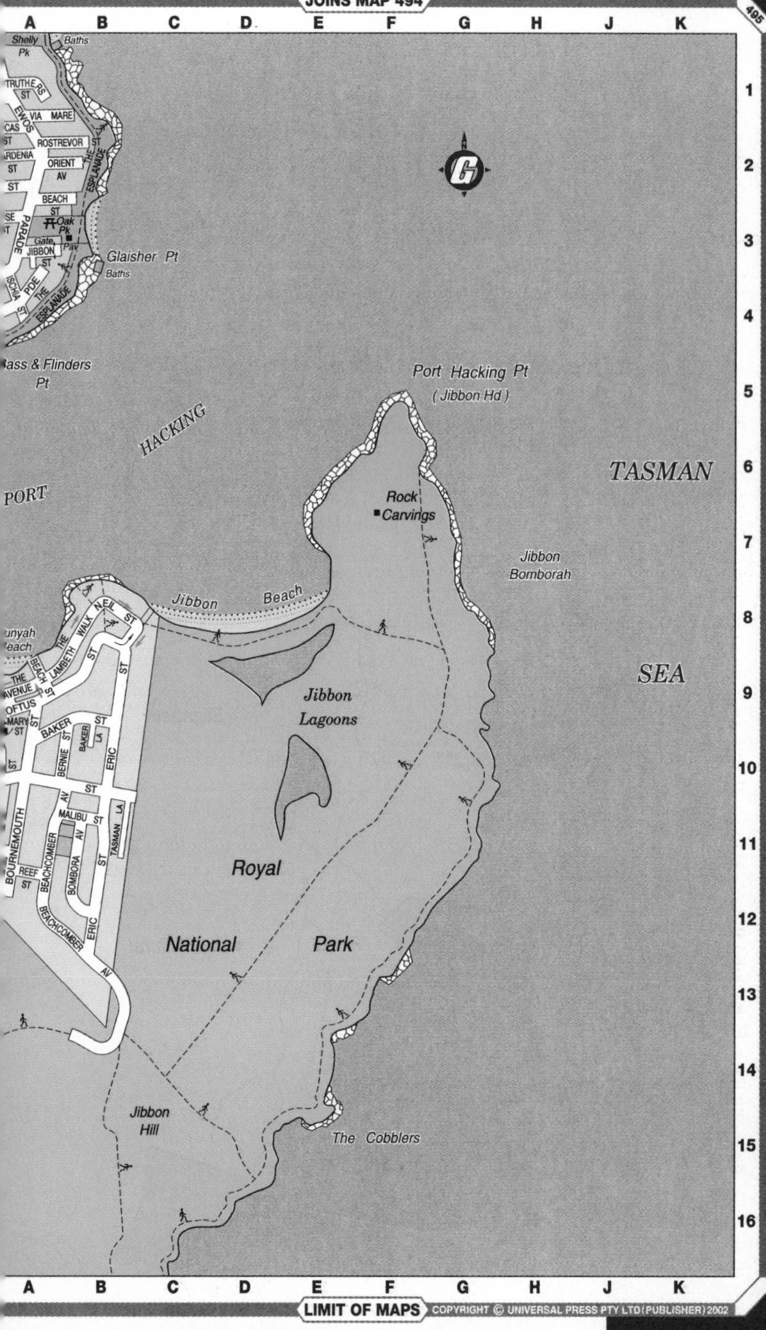

LIMIT OF MAPS

JOINS MAP 507
506

A B C D E F G H J K

LIMIT OF MAPS
FOR PICTON SEE MAP 563

1 2 3 4 5 6 7 8 9 10 11 12 13 14 15 16

A B C D E F G H J K

LIMIT OF MAPS

JOINS MAP 508

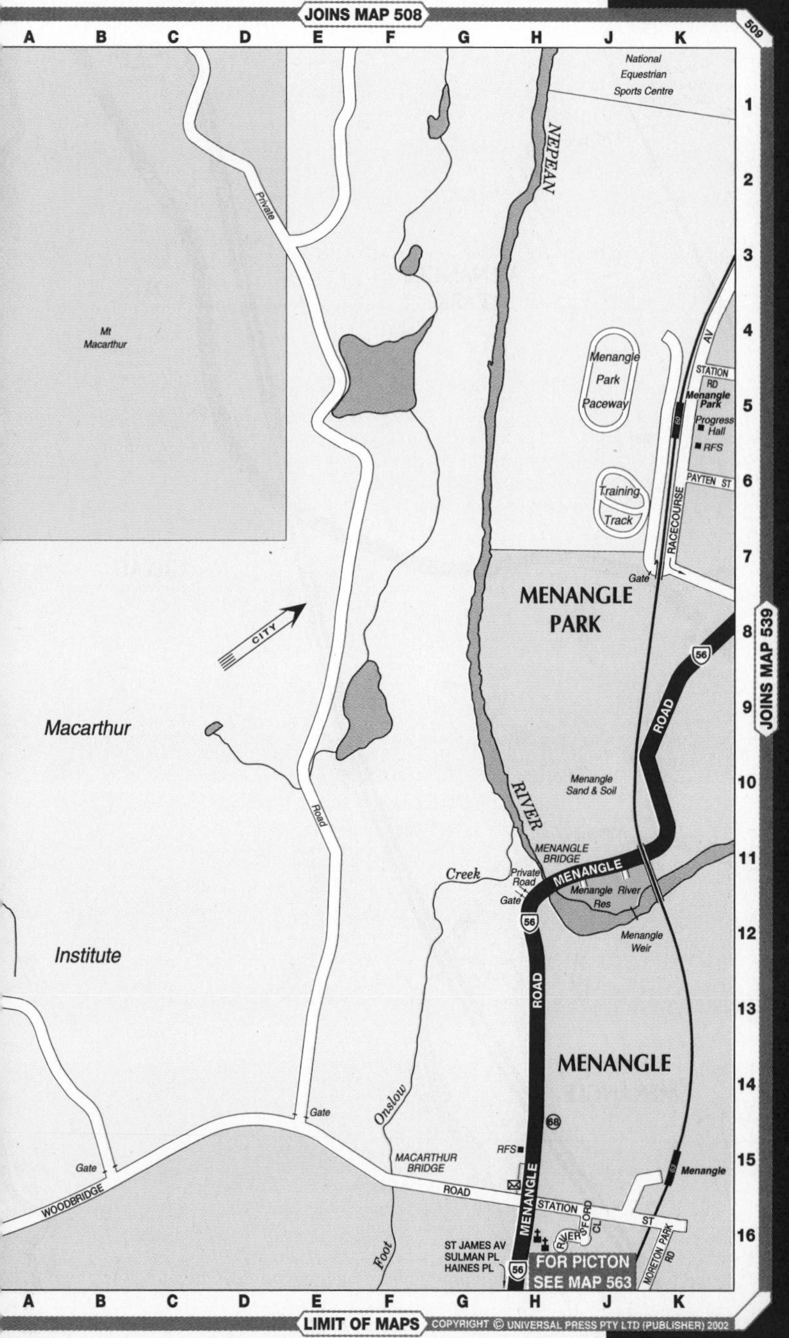

JOINS MAP 539

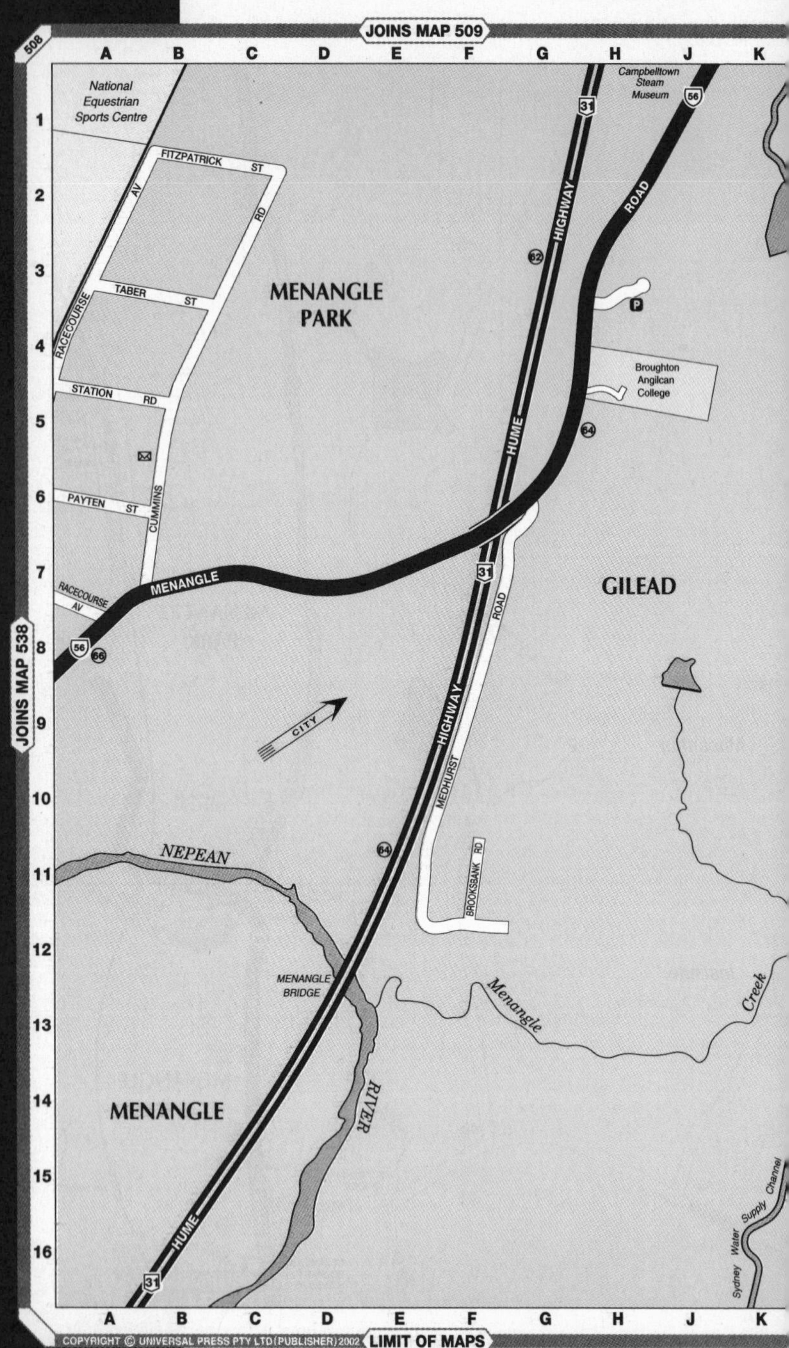
JOINS MAP 509
508
A B C D E F G H J K
1 2 3 4 5 6 7 8 9 10 11 12 13 14 15 16
National Equestrian Sports Centre
Campbelltown Steam Museum
FITZPATRICK ST
AV
RD
TABER ST
RACECOURSE
MENANGLE PARK
HIGHWAY
ROAD
31
56
62
Broughton Angilcan College
64
STATION RD
PAYTEN ST
CUMMINS
HUME
MENANGLE
RACECOURSE AV
66
GILEAD
ROAD
JOINS MAP 538
CITY
MEDHURST
BROOKSBANK RD
NEPEAN
MENANGLE BRIDGE
Menangle
Creek
RIVER
MENANGLE
Sydney Water Supply Channel
LIMIT OF MAPS

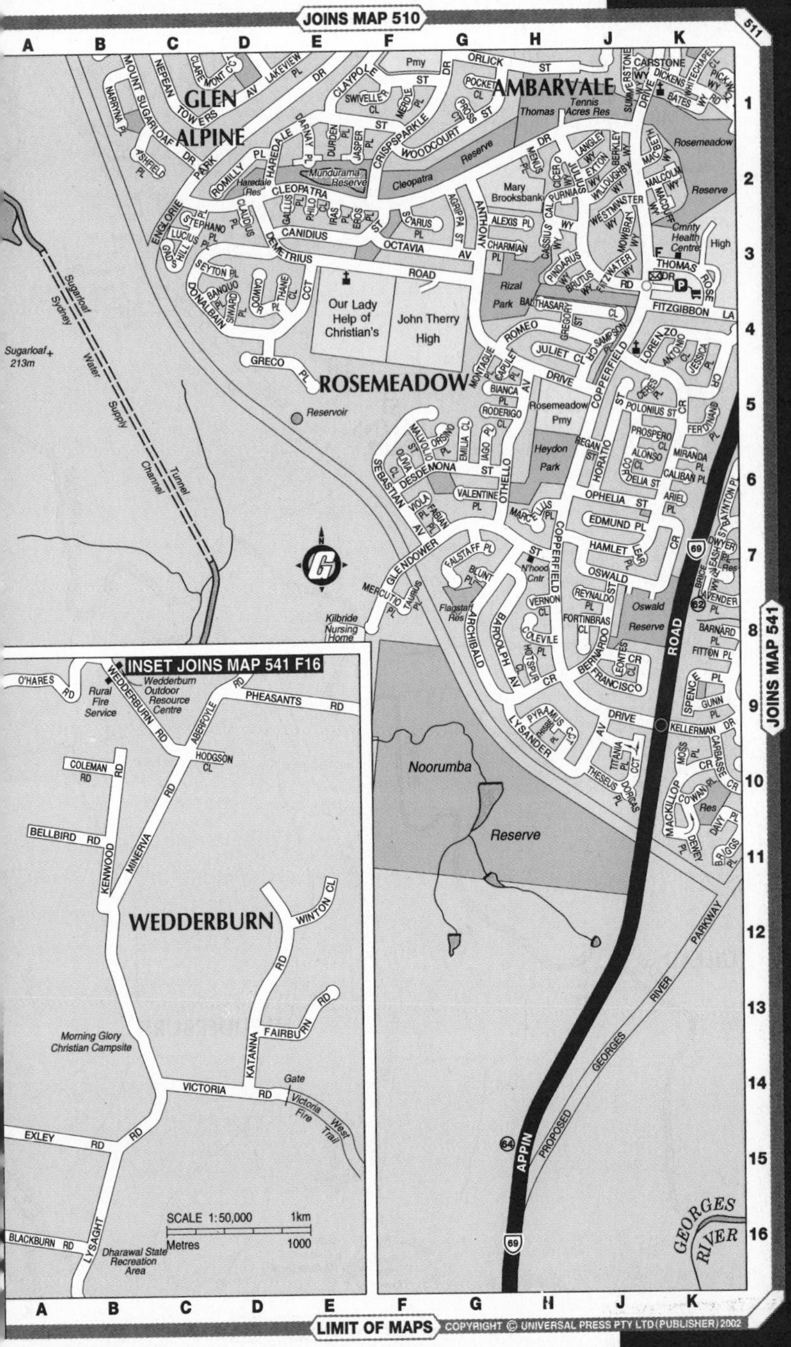

JOINS MAP 510
511
JOINS MAP 541
INSET JOINS MAP 541 F16
LIMIT OF MAPS
GLEN ALPINE
AMBARVALE
ROSEMEADOW
WEDDERBURN
Our Lady Help of Christian's
John Therry High
Sugarloaf 213m
Sydney Water Supply Channel
Sugarloaf Tunnel
Reservoir
Noorumba Reserve
Mary Brooksbank
Rizal Park
Heydon Park
Rosemeadow Pmy
Rosemeadow Reserve
Cleopatra Reserve
Mundurama Reserve
Haredale Res
Thomas Acres Res
Tennis
Oswald Reserve
Flagstaff Res
N'hood Cntr
Cmnty Health Centre
High
Kilbride Nursing Home
Wedderburn Outdoor Resource Centre
Rural Fire Service
Morning Glory Christian Campsite
Dharawal State Recreation Area
Victoria West Fire Trail
Gate
APPIN ROAD
PROPOSED GEORGES RIVER PARKWAY
GEORGES RIVER
SCALE 1:50,000
1km
Metres
1000

JOINS MAP 511

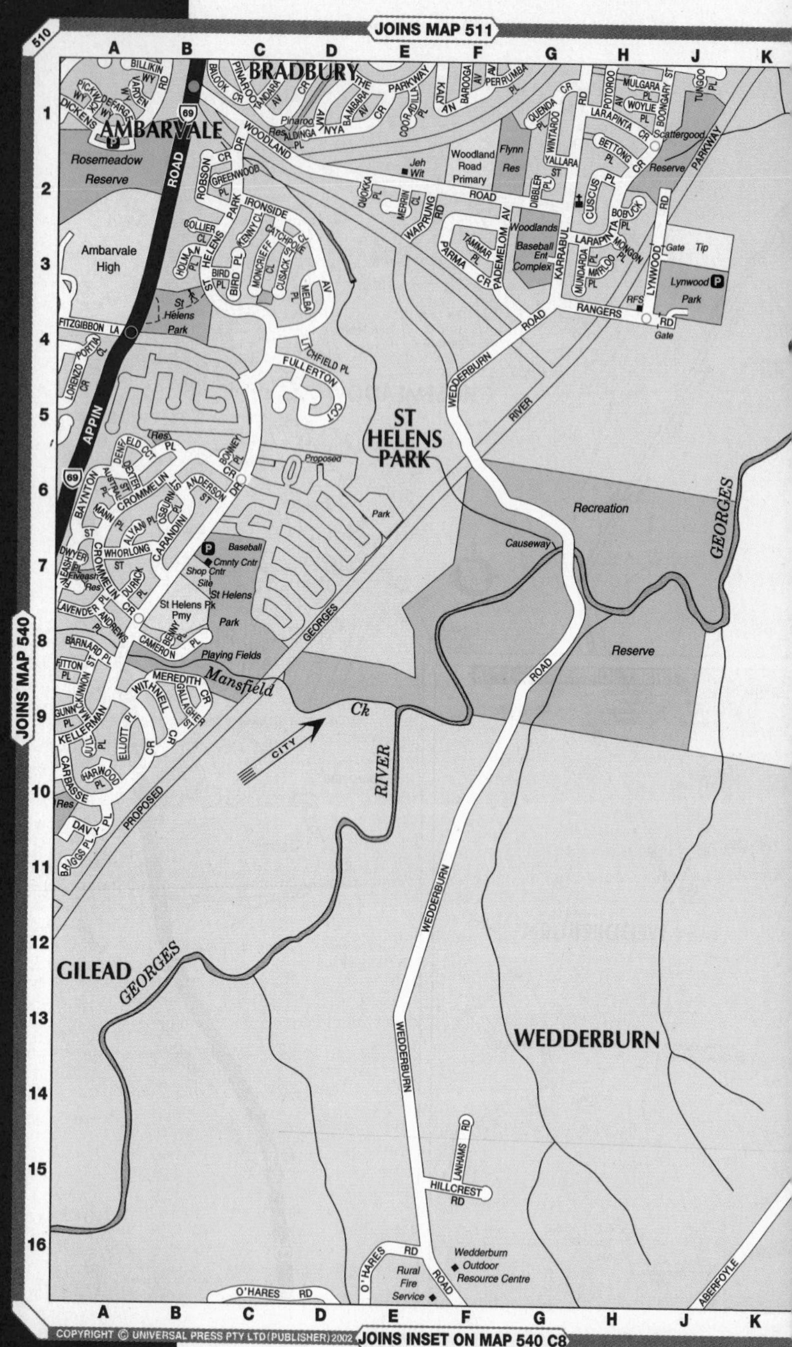

JOINS MAP 540

JOINS INSET ON MAP 540 C8

JOINS MAP 512

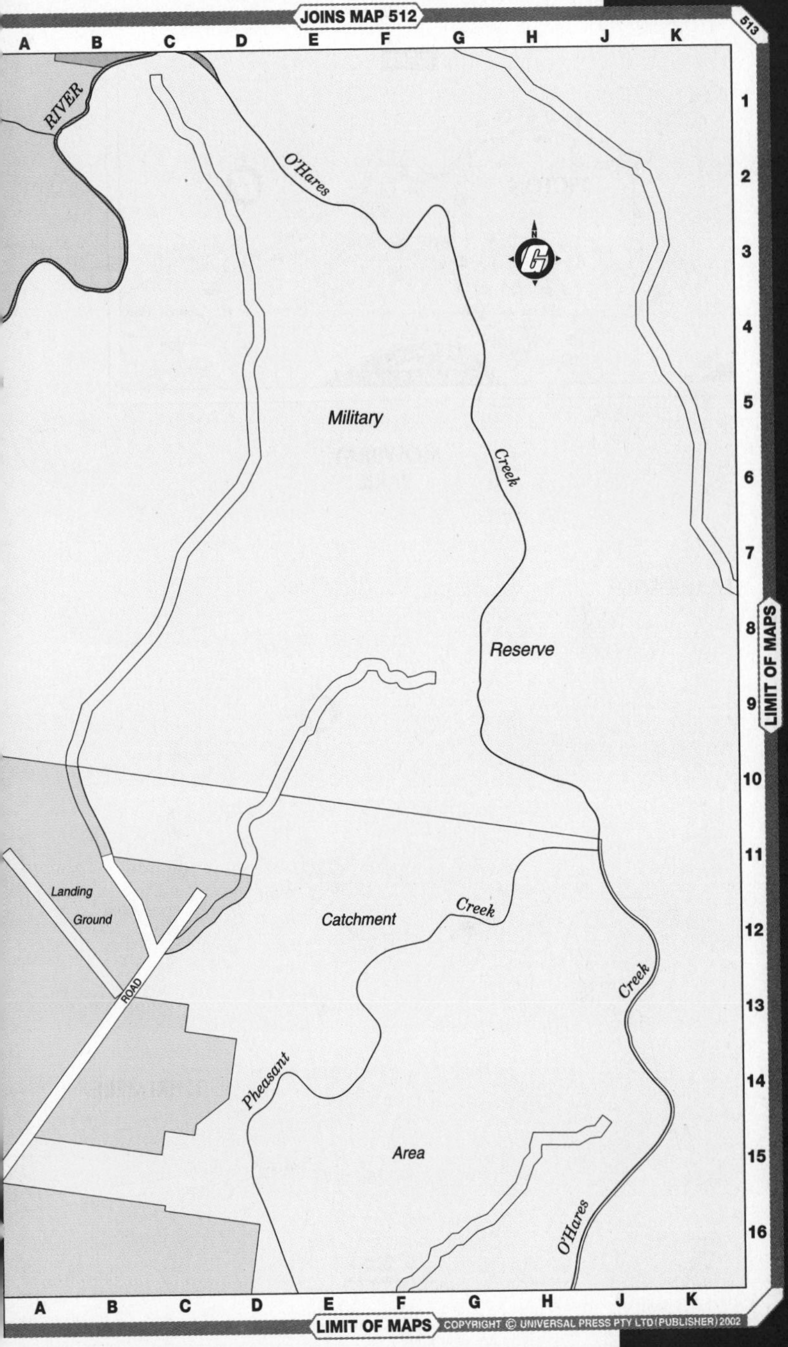

LIMIT OF MAPS

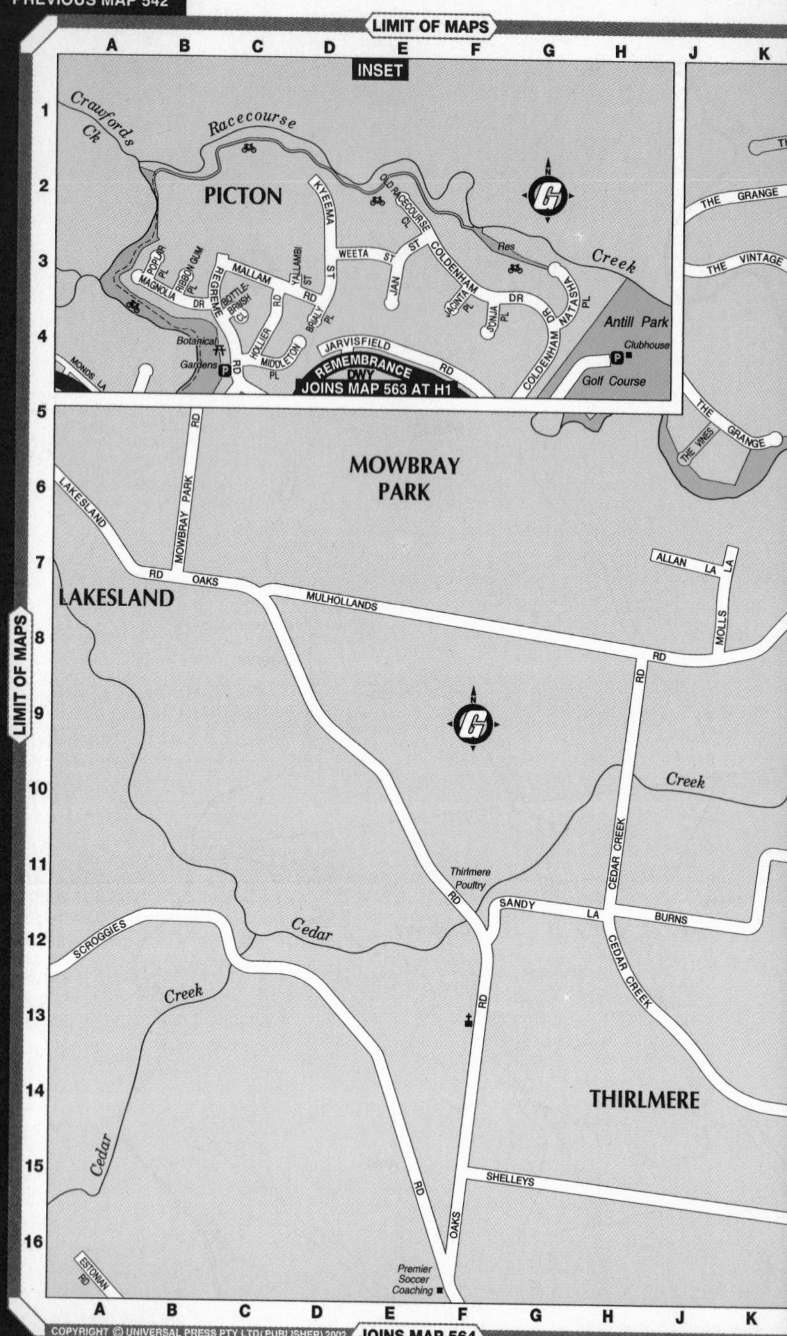

JOINS MAP 564

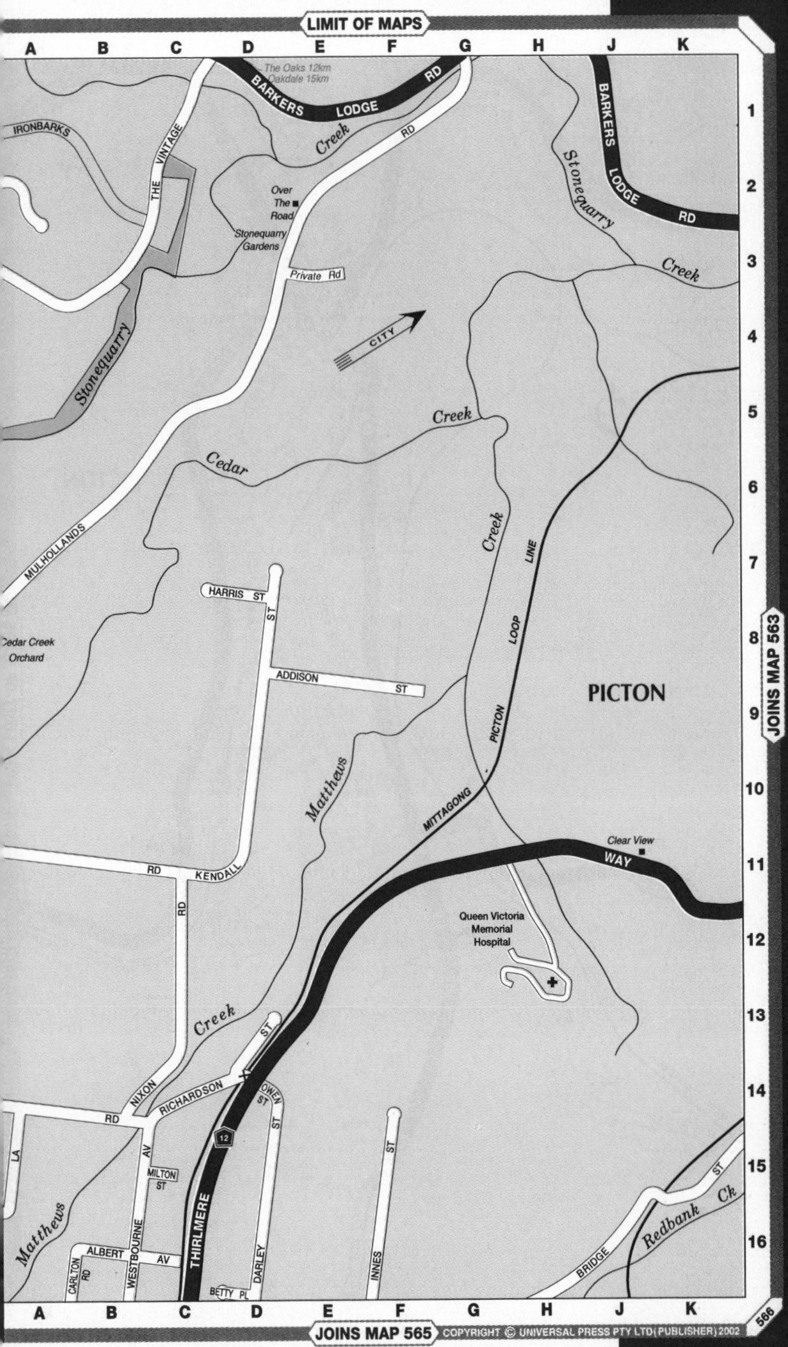

JOINS MAP 563

JOINS MAP 565

566

MAP 563

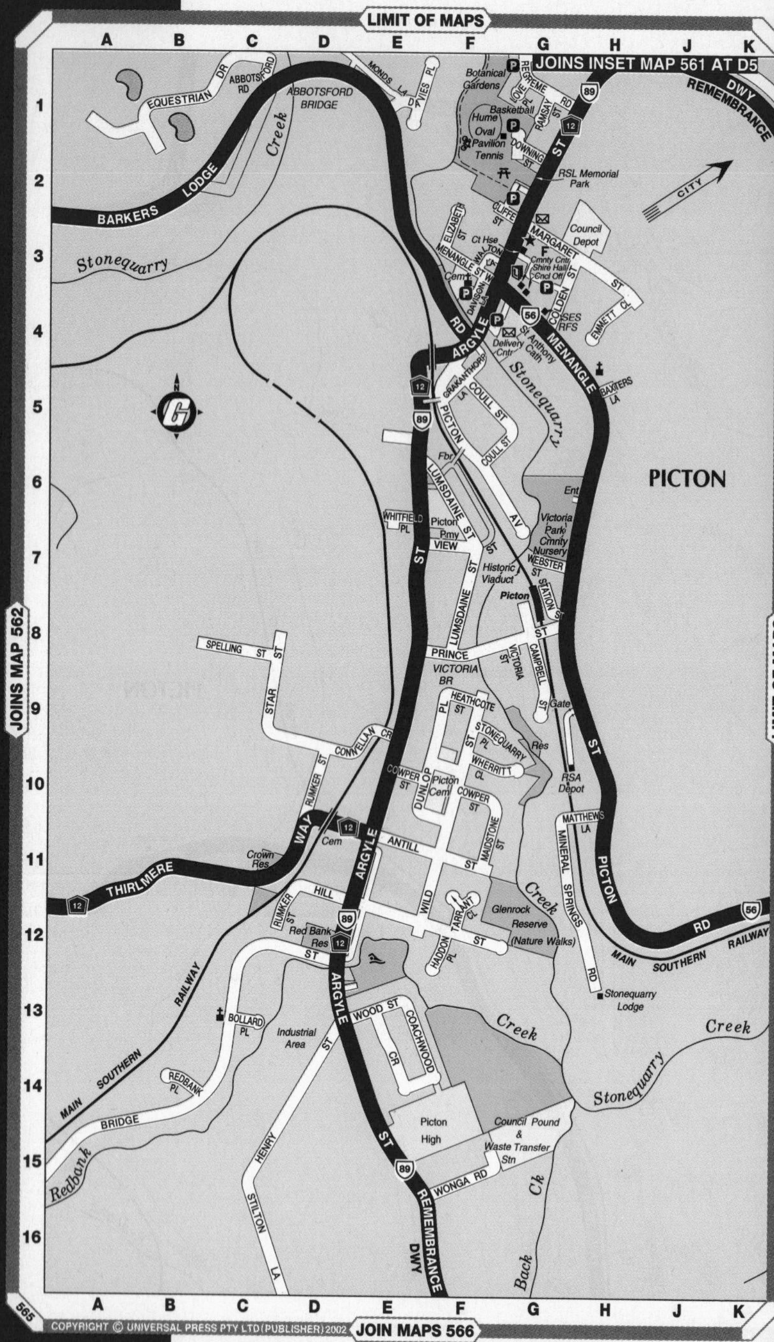

LIMIT OF MAPS
JOINS INSET MAP 561 AT D5
JOINS MAP 562
LIMIT OF MAPS
JOIN MAPS 566
565
PICTON
BARKERS LODGE
EQUESTRIAN DR
ABBOTSFORD RD
ABBOTSFORD BRIDGE
Stonequarry Creek
MONDS LA
DAVIES PL
Botanical Gardens
Hume Oval
Basketball
Pavilion
Tennis
REGREME RD
LOVE PL
RAMSAY ST
DOWNING ST
RSL Memorial Park
CLIFFE ST
ELIZABETH ST
Council Depot
MARGARET ST
Ct Hse
Cmnty Cntr
Shire Hall
Cncl Off
MENANGLE ST W
WALTON LA
DAVISON LA
GOLDEN ST
SES RFS
EMMETT CL
ARGYLE ST
MENANGLE RD
REMEMBRANCE DWY
CITY
Delivery Cntr
St Anthony Cath
BAXTERS LA
CRAWTHORP LA
COULL ST
PICTON AV
LUMSDAINE ST
WHITFIELD PL
Picton Pmy
VIEW ST
Ent
Victoria Park
Cmnty Nursery
WEBSTER ST
Historic Viaduct
Picton
STATION ST
SPELLING ST
STAR ST
PRINCE ST
VICTORIA BR
VICTORIA ST
CAMPBELL ST
HEATHCOTE PL
Gate
STONEQUARRY PL
Res
WHERRITT CL
RSA Depot
CONVELLAN CR
RUMKER ST
COWPER ST
DUNLOP ST
Picton Cem
MATTHEWS LA
MINERAL SPRINGS RD
MAIDSTONE ST
ANTILL ST
Cem
Crown Res
THIRLMERE WAY
HILL ST
WILD ST
TARRANT CL
Glenrock Reserve (Nature Walks)
Creek
PICTON RD
MAIN SOUTHERN RAILWAY
Red Bank Res
HADDON PL
Stonequarry Lodge
BOLLARD PL
Industrial Area
WOOD ST
COACHWOOD CR
REDBANK PL
BRIDGE ST
HENRY ST
Picton High
Council Pound & Waste Transfer Stn
Redbank
WONGA RD
Back Ck
STILTON LA

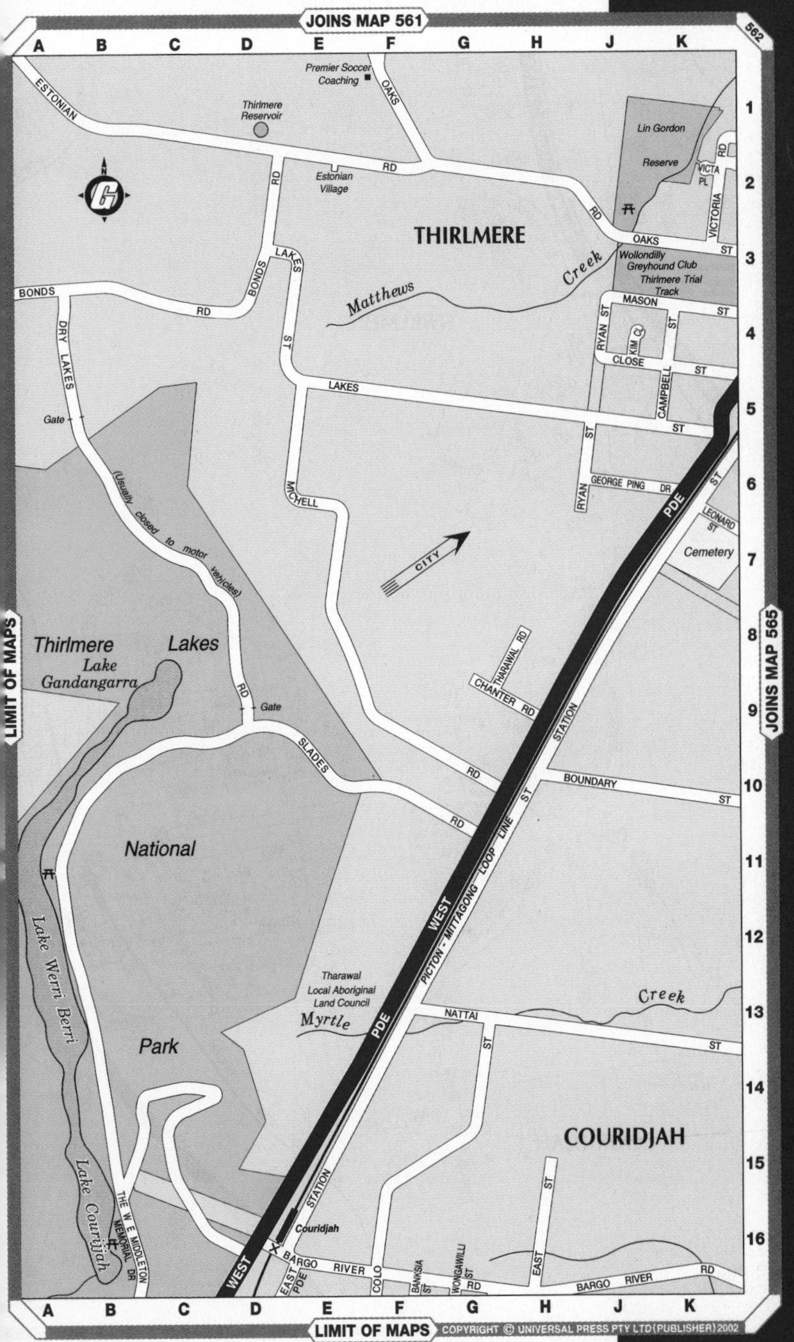
JOINS MAP 561
562
A B C D E F G H J K
1 2 3 4 5 6 7 8 9 10 11 12 13 14 15 16
THIRLMERE
COURIDJAH
Premier Soccer Coaching
Thirlmere Reservoir
Estonian Village
ESTONIAN RD
OAKS RD
OAKS ST
Lin Gordon Reserve
VICTA PL
VICTORIA RD
Wollondilly Greyhound Club
Thirlmere Trial Track
Matthews Creek
BONDS RD
LAKES ST
MASON ST
RYAN ST
KIM CL
CLOSE ST
CAMPBELL ST
LAKES ST
DRY LAKES RD
Gate
MITCHELL RD
GEORGE PING DR
LEONARD ST
Cemetery
CITY
(Usually closed to motor vehicles)
Thirlmere Lakes
Lake Gandangarra
THARAWAL RD
CHANTER RD
STATION ST
SLADES RD
BOUNDARY ST
National Park
WEST PDE
PICTON - MITTAGONG LOOP LINE
Tharawal Local Aboriginal Land Council
Myrtle Creek
NATTAI ST
Lake Werri Berri
Lake Courijjah
THE W E MIDDLETON MEMORIAL DR
Couridjah
BARGO RIVER RD
EAST PDE
COLO
BANKSIA ST
WONGAWILLI ST
EAST ST
LIMIT OF MAPS
JOINS MAP 565

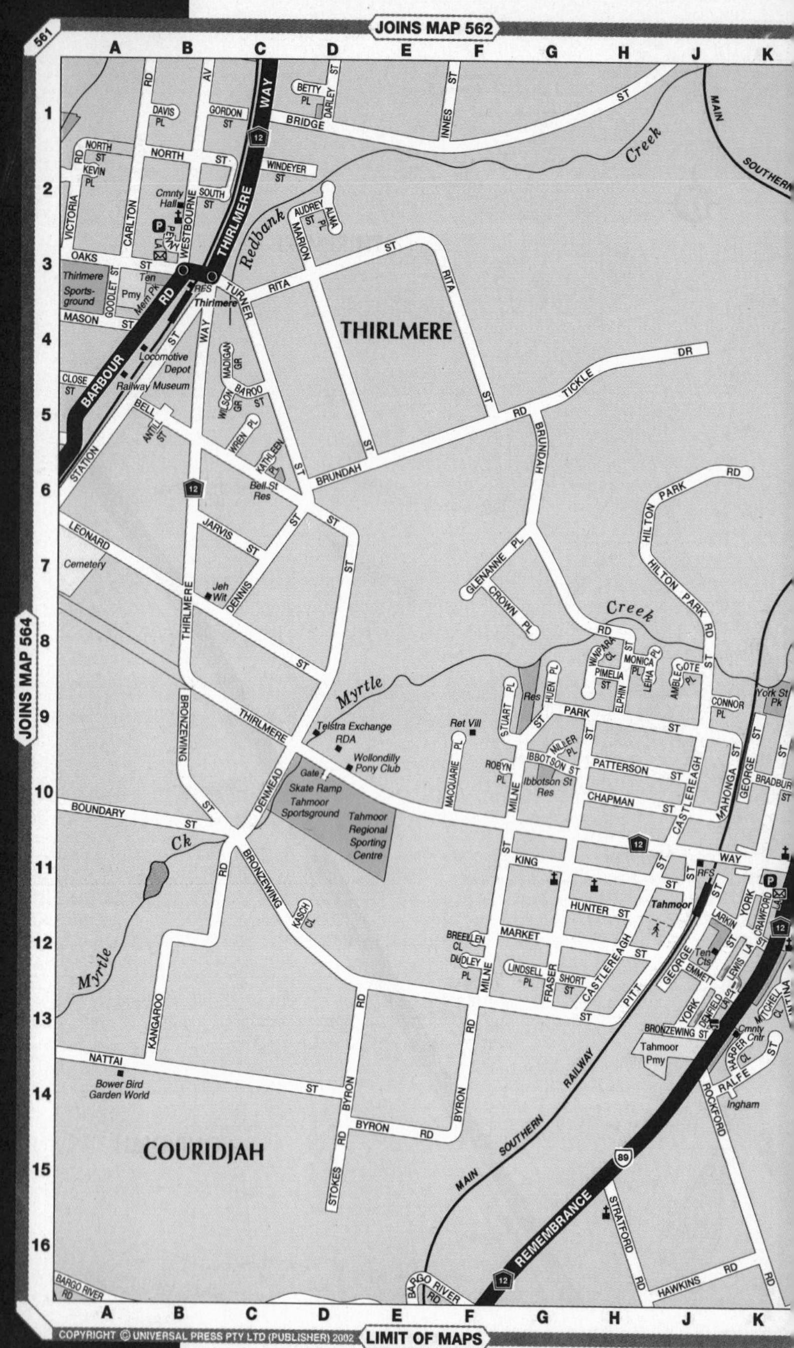
JOINS MAP 562
561
A B C D E F G H J K
1 2 3 4 5 6 7 8 9 10 11 12 13 14 15 16
THIRLMERE
COURIDJAH
THIRLMERE WAY
BARBOUR RD
BRIDGE ST
BETTY PL
DARLEY ST
INNES ST
DAVIS PL
GORDON ST
NORTH ST
KEVIN PL
VICTORIA RD
WINDEYER ST
Cmnty Hall
SOUTH ST
CARLTON
WESTBOURNE AV
PENNY LA
OAKS ST
Thirlmere Sports-ground
GOODLET ST
Ten
Mem PK
Pmy
MASON ST
RES
Thirlmere
TURNER
RITA ST
Redbank
Creek
AUDREY ST
ALMA PL
MARION
Locomotive Depot
Railway Museum
CLOSE ST
MADIGAN GR
BAROO ST
WILSON GR
WREN PL
BELL
ANTILL ST
STATION ST
KATHLEEN PL
Bell St Res
BRUNDAH RD
TICKLE DR
LEONARD
Cemetery
JARVIS ST
DENNIS
Jeh Wit
GLENANNE PL
CROWN PL
HILTON PARK RD
Myrtle
Telstra Exchange
RDA
Wollondilly Pony Club
Gate
Skate Ramp
Tahmoor Sportsground
Tahmoor Regional Sporting Centre
DENMEAD
BRONZEWING ST
BOUNDARY ST
Ck
Ret Vill
MACQUARIE PL
STUART PL
Res
HUEN PL
WINPARA CL
PIMELIA ST
ELPHIN ST
MONICA PL
LEIHA PL
AMBLECOTE PL
CONNOR PL
York St PK
PARK ST
MILLER PL
IBBOTSON ST
Ibbotson St Res
ROBYN PL
MILNE ST
PATTERSON ST
CHAPMAN ST
CASTLEREAGH
MAHONGA
GEORGE ST
BRADBURY ST
KING ST
WAY
RFS
HUNTER ST
Tahmoor
MARKET
BREELLEN CL
DUDLEY PL
LINDSELL PL
FRASER
SHORT ST
PITT ST
KASCH CL
LARKIN
YORK
CRAWFORD
Ten Cts
EMMETT
LEWIS LA
DENFIELD LA
MITCHELL CL
Cmnty Cntr
BRONZEWING ST
Tahmoor Pmy
HARPER CL
RALFE ST
Ingham
ROCKFORD
KANGAROO
NATTAI ST
Bower Bird Garden World
BYRON RD
STOKES RD
MAIN SOUTHERN RAILWAY
REMEMBRANCE
STRATFORD RD
HAWKINS RD
BARGO RIVER RD
JOINS MAP 564
LIMIT OF MAPS

JOINS MAP 563

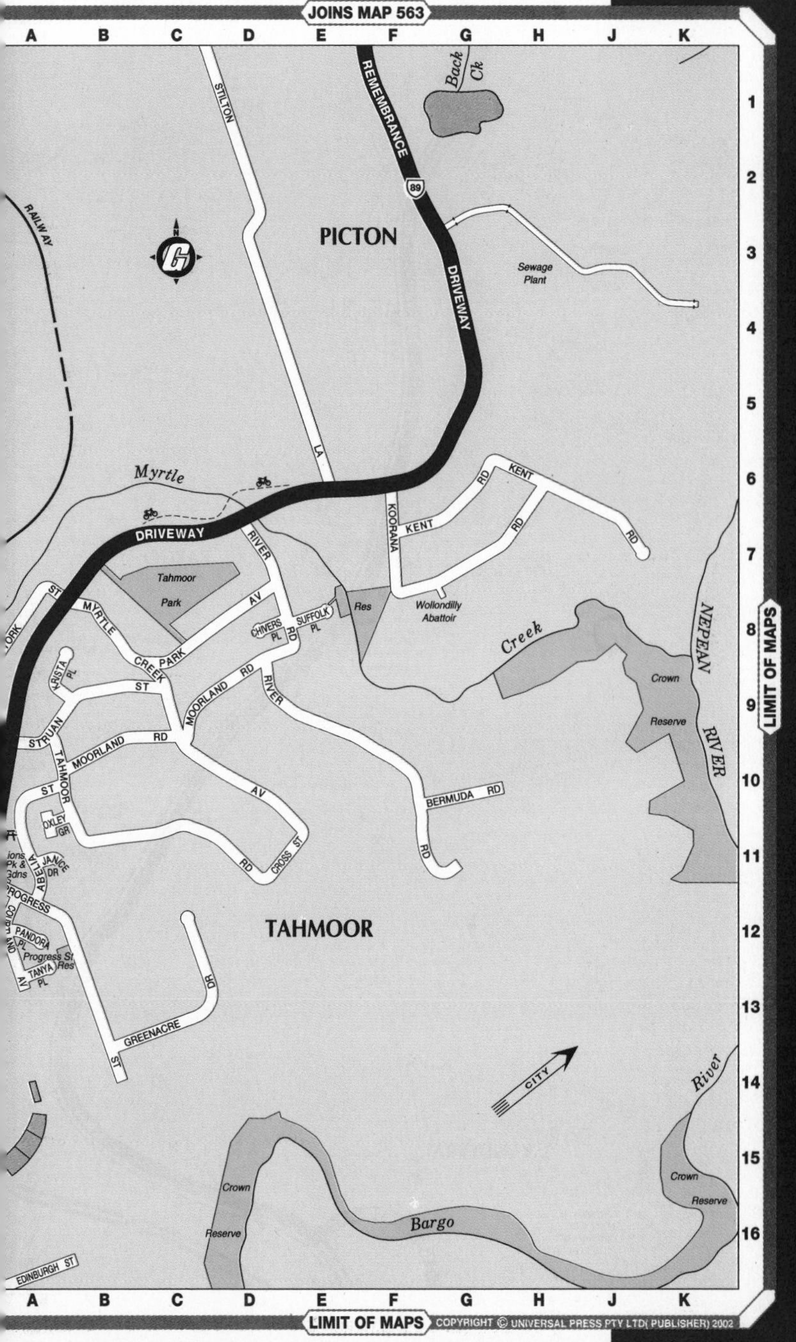

LIMIT OF MAPS

LIMIT OF MAPS

BARGO

SCALE 1:27 500
Metres 500 1000 1km

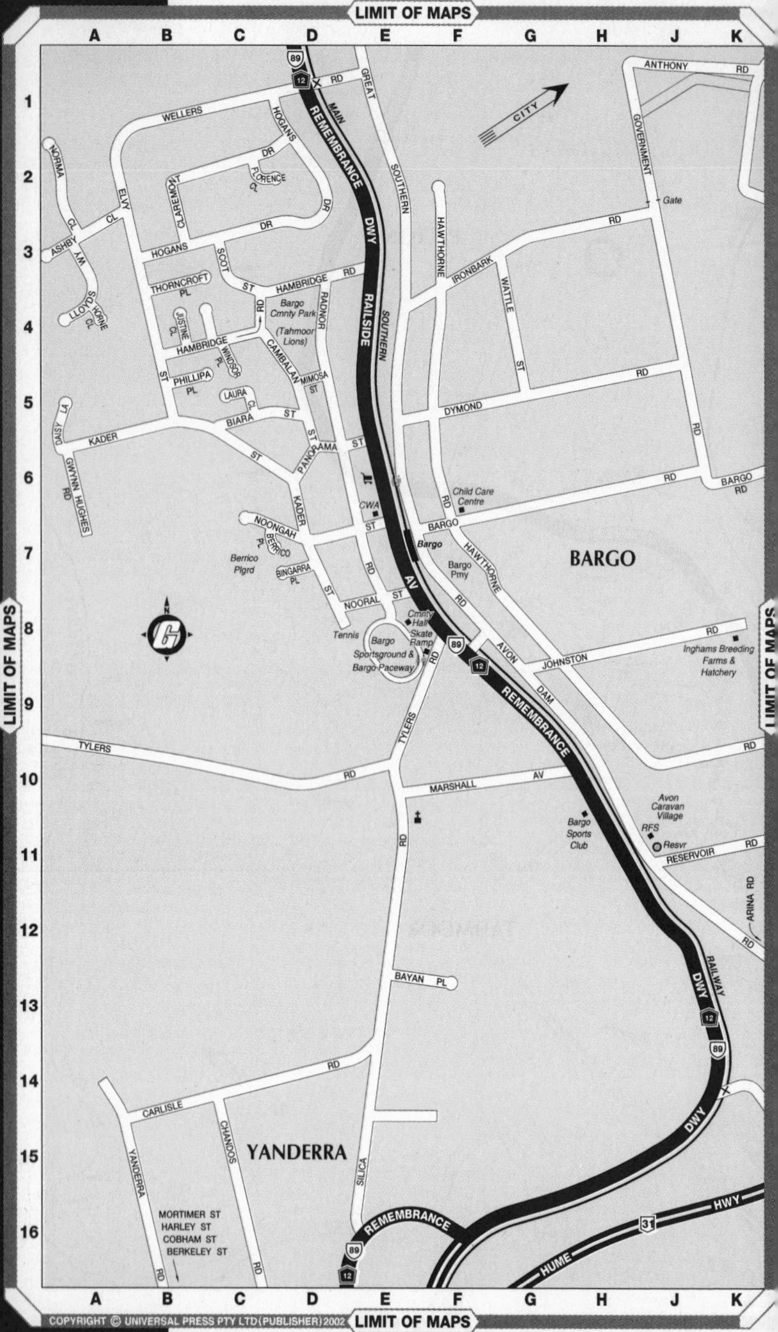

LIMIT OF MAPS

A B C D E F G H J K

BARGO
YANDERRA
CITY
ANTHONY RD
GOVERNMENT RD
Gate
WELLERS RD
HOGANS DR
FLORENCE CL
CLAREMONT DR
NORMA CL
ELVY CL
ASHBY WY
LLOYDS CL
HORNE CL
THORNCROFT PL
SCOTT ST
HAMBRIDGE RD
Bargo Cmnty Park (Tahmoor Lions)
JUSTINE CL
WINDSOR PL
PHILLIPA PL
LAURA CL
CAMBALAN
MIMOSA ST
RADNOR
BIARA ST
DAISY LA
KADER ST
GWYNN HUGHES RD
PANORAMA ST
NOONGAH ST
BERRICO PL
Berrico Plgrd
BINGARRA PL
NOORAL ST
Tennis
Bargo Sportsground & Bargo Paceway
Cmnty Hall
Skate Ramp
CWA
MAIN SOUTHERN RD
GREAT SOUTHERN RD
REMEMBRANCE DWY
RAILSIDE AV
HAWTHORNE RD
IRONBARK RD
WATTLE ST
DYMOND RD
Child Care Centre
BARGO RD
Bargo
Bargo Pmy
AVON DAM RD
JOHNSTON RD
Inghams Breeding Farms & Hatchery
TYLERS RD
MARSHALL AV
Bargo Sports Club
Avon Caravan Village
RFS
Resvr
RESERVOIR RD
ARINA RD
RAILWAY
BAYAN PL
CARLISLE RD
CHANDOS RD
YANDERRA RD
SILICA
MORTIMER ST
HARLEY ST
COBHAM ST
BERKELEY ST
HUME HWY
89 12 31

1 2 3 4 5 6 7 8 9 10 11 12 13 14 15 16

LIMIT OF MAPS

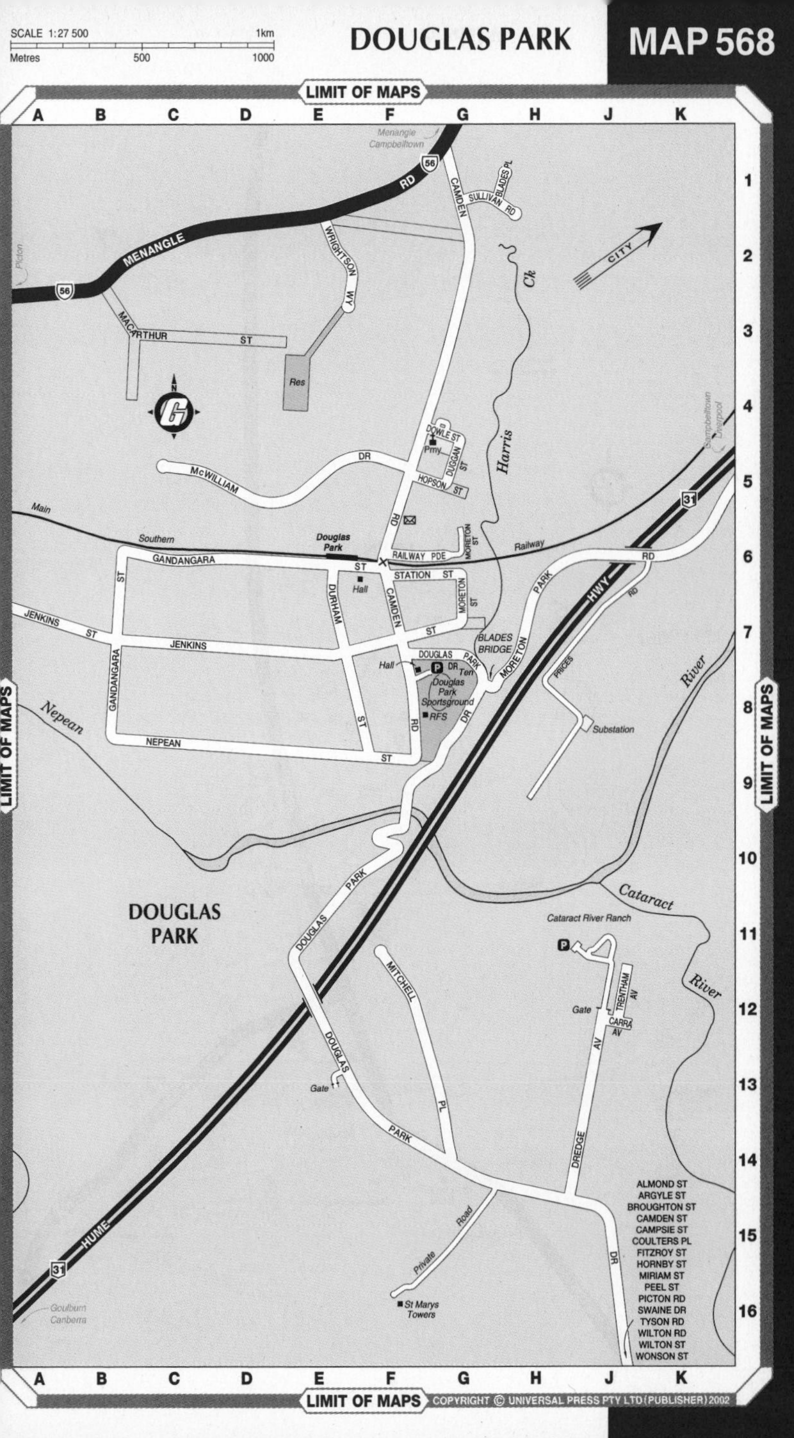
LIMIT OF MAPS
A B C D E F G H J K
1 2 3 4 5 6 7 8 9 10 11 12 13 14 15 16
Menangle Campbelltown
56
MENANGLE RD
CAMDEN
SULLIVAN RD
BLADES PL
WRIGHTSON WY
Picton
CITY
Ck
MACARTHUR ST
Res
DOWLE ST
Prmy
DUGGAN ST
HOPSON ST
McWILLIAM DR
Harris
Campbelltown Liverpool
31
Main
Southern
Douglas Park
Railway
RAILWAY PDE
MORETON ST
GANDANGARA ST
STATION ST
Hall
DURHAM
CAMDEN
RD
MORETON ST
PARK
RD
HWY
JENKINS ST
JENKINS
ST
BLADES BRIDGE
MORETON
DOUGLAS PARK DR
Hall
Ten
Douglas Park Sportsground
RFS
PRICES
River
GANDANGARA
Nepean
ST
RD
DR
Substation
NEPEAN ST
LIMIT OF MAPS
DOUGLAS PARK
Cataract
Cataract River Ranch
MITCHELL
TRENTHAM AV
Gate
CARRA AV
River
DOUGLAS
Gate
PL
AV
PARK
DREDGE
HUME
Private Road
DR
St Marys Towers
Goulburn Canberra
ALMOND ST
ARGYLE ST
BROUGHTON ST
CAMDEN ST
CAMPSIE ST
COULTERS PL
FITZROY ST
HORNBY ST
MIRIAM ST
PEEL ST
PICTON RD
SWAINE DR
TYSON RD
WILTON RD
WILTON ST
WONSON ST

APPIN

SCALE 1:27 500

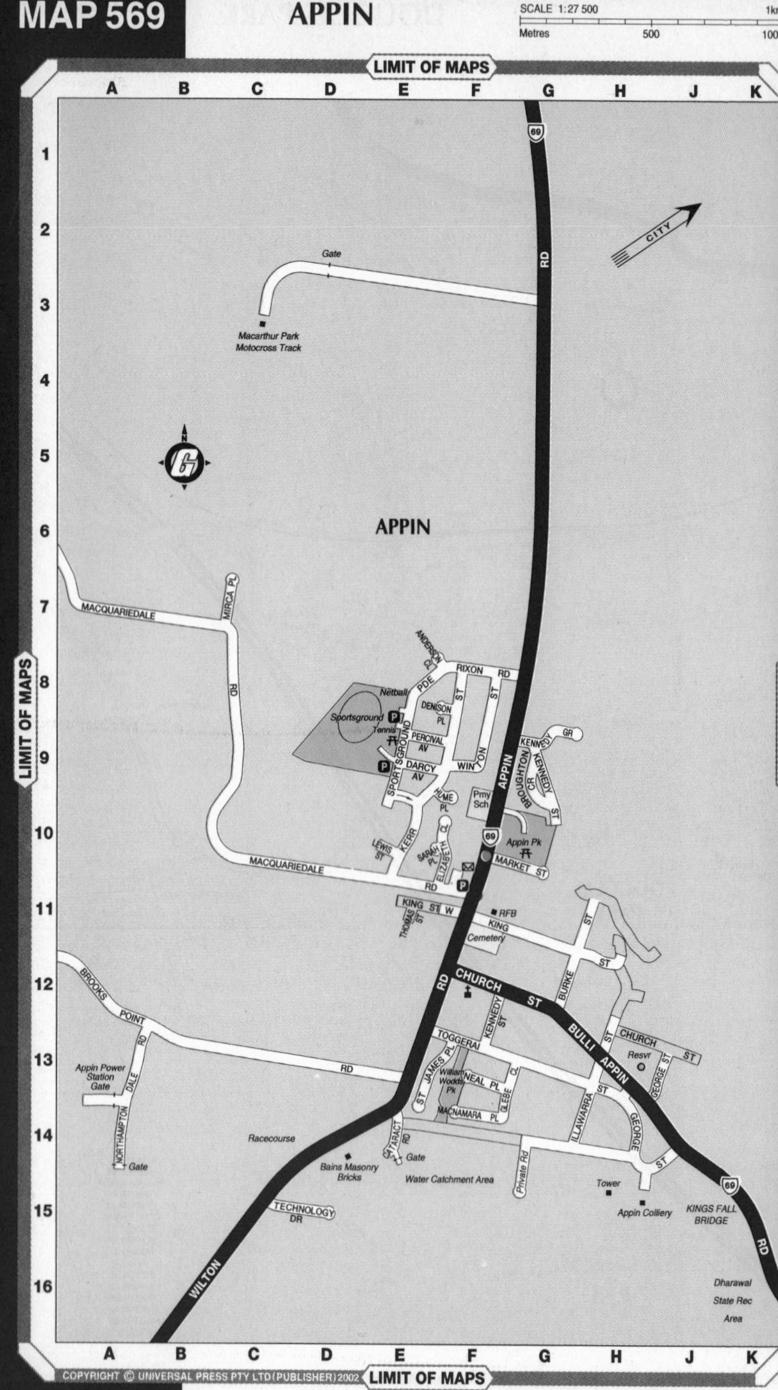

Domestic Terminal
SCALE 1:12,500
Metres
250
FOR LOCATION SEE MAP 404
QANTAS
Eastern Australia
Drop off & Pick up
SHIERS
Taxi
Ent 2
Ent 1
Domestic
Ent 3
KEITH SMITH
Drop off & Pick up
Bus/Coach
ST
5TH
AV
Australian Air Express
Private Rd
Right Lane ANSETT dep QANTAS dep (Upper level)
Left Lane ANSETT arr QANTAS arr (Lower level)
NINTH
SIR REGINALD
ANSETT
DR
ROSS
SMITH
AV
ST
ELEVENTH
Flight Facilities
Corporate Aviation
Gate
Virgin Blue
Ansett Australia
Ansett Freight
Admin
6TH
SEVENTH
VICKERS
AV
Gate
NINTH
DOT
Kingsford Smith Airport
F
EAST WEST RUNWAY
QANTAS
Gate P1
DR
ROBEY
O'RIORDON
ST
John Curtin Res
ST
BAXTER
RD
JOYCE
DR
ST

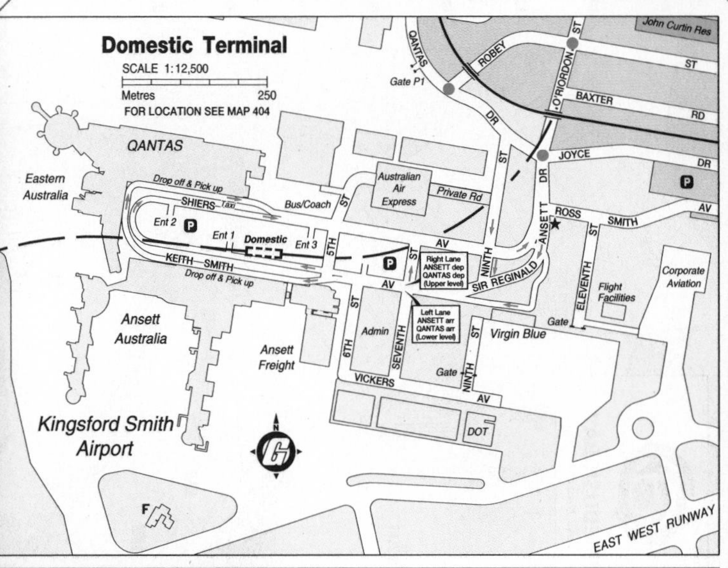

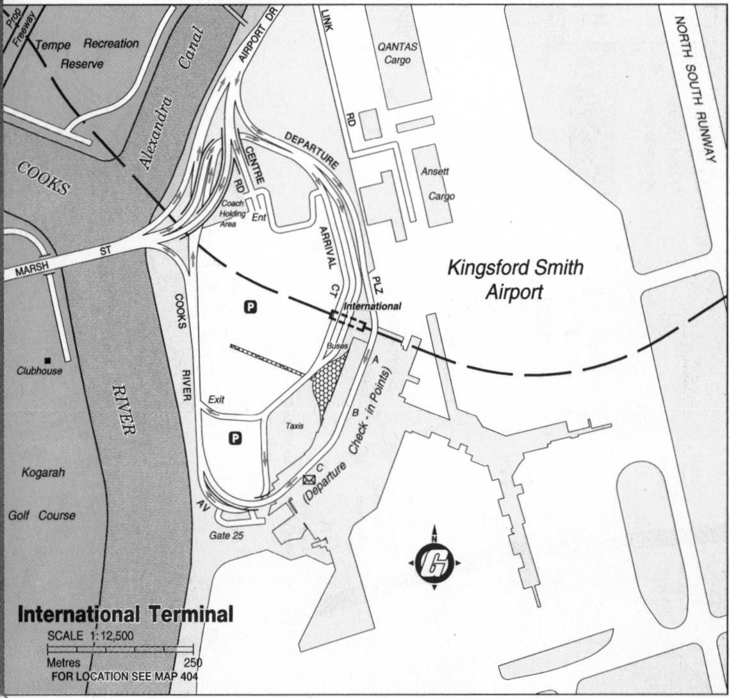

Prop Freeway
Tempe Recreation Reserve
Alexandra Canal
AIRPORT DR
LINK
RD
QANTAS Cargo
DEPARTURE
CENTRE
RD
Coach Holding Area
Ent
Ansett Cargo
NORTH SOUTH RUNWAY
COOKS
MARSH ST
ARRIVAL CT
PLZ
International
Kingsford Smith Airport
COOKS RIVER
Buses
A
B
C
(Departure Check - in Points)
Exit
Taxis
Clubhouse
RIVER
Kogarah Golf Course
AV
Gate 25
International Terminal
SCALE 1:12,500
Metres
250
FOR LOCATION SEE MAP 404

JOINS MAP 310

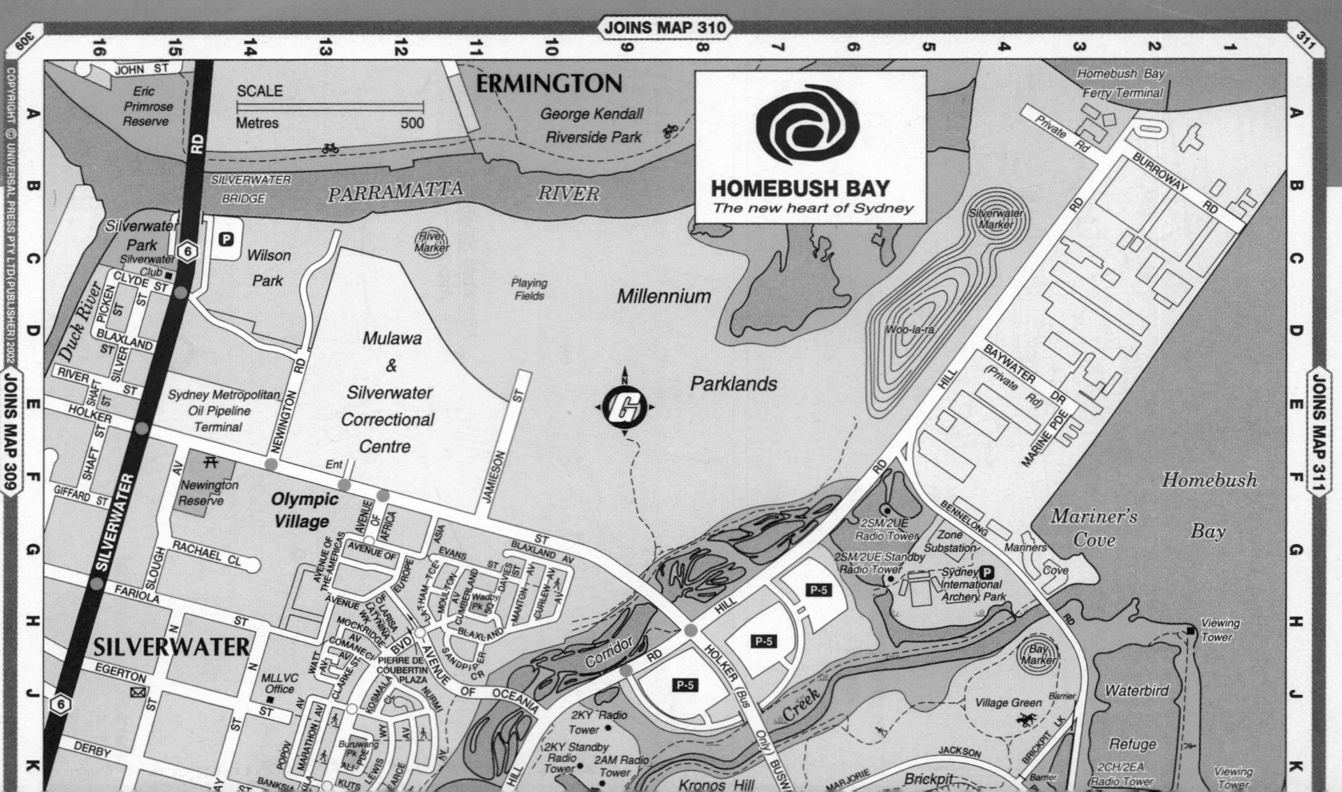

JOINS MAP 309